This book belongs to:

____

Webster's Thesaurus *for* Students

NEW EDITION

Created in Cooperation with the Editors of
MERRIAM-WEBSTER

A Division of Merriam-Webster, Incorporated
Springfield, Massachusetts

Federal Street Press is a trademark of Federal Street Press,
a division of Merriam-Webster, Incorporated.

This 2007 edition published by
Federal Street Press
A Division of Merriam-Webster, Incorporated
P.O. Box 281
Springfield, MA 01102

Federal Street Press books are available for bulk purchase for sales promotion and premium use. For details write the manager of special sales, Federal Street Press, P.O. Box 281, Springfield, MA 01102

ISBN 13 978-1-59695-023-8

Printed in the United States of America

08 09 10 11 5

Preface

This thesaurus is a guide for the understanding and selection of synonyms, near synonyms, and antonyms. This new edition provides more entries and offers greater ease of use than previous editions. It is a portable reference for students who need to find the "right" word to express themselves in speech and writing. As with any thesaurus, it should be used in conjunction with a dictionary.

While this thesaurus is concise, it shares many details of presentation with more comprehensive thesauruses. In addition to lists of synonyms, it includes lists of related words, (near synonyms) and antonyms at most entries to provide users with additional assistance. It provides at each main entry a statement of meaning shared by the listed synonyms, and it includes an entry at its own alphabetical place for every synonym that appears at a main entry.

Conciseness of presentation necessarily requires special treatment of entries, and this book has a number of special features uniquely its own. Users need to be familiar with the following major features of this thesaurus.

Entry Order: The body of the book consists of main and secondary entries introduced by alphabetically ordered boldface headwords.

Homographs: Words spelled the same but having different meanings are given separate entries and are identified with an italic part-of-speech label, as at **fair** *adj* and **fair** *n*.

Headwords: that are synonyms and alphabetically close to each other are sometimes listed together, as **finicky**, **finicking**, **finical**.

Headwords ordinarily conform to normal dictionary practice: nouns are styled as singulars; verbs as infinitives. Special situations, such as plural usage, are signaled by the use of boldface, as at the entry **wage**, **wages**, or at sense **2** of **game**, where **games** is shown as the alternate form of the headword synonymous with **athletics**.

Main Entry and Its Basic Elements: Each main entry consists of a headword followed by a part-of-speech label when needed, a sense number when needed, a meaning core, and a list of synonyms. Lists of related words (near synonyms) and antonyms follow the synonym list.

The **meaning core** is marked by a small symbol bullet (•) and indicates the area of meaning shared by the synonyms.

Two or more meanings (or senses) of a headword are separated and numbered with a boldface numeral (as **1**).

The italic abbreviation ***syn*** introduces a synonym list; the italic abbreviation ***rel*** introduces a list of related words (near synonyms); the italic abbreviation ***ant*** introduces a list of antonyms. More information about ***rel*** and ***ant*** lists is provided in the section on **Main and Secondary Entries: Elements Common to Both**, which appears below.

Secondary Entry and Its Basic Elements: A secondary entry consists of a boldface headword followed by a part-of-speech label when needed, a sense number when needed, and a list of synonyms. The first synonym in the list appears in small capitals and serves as a cross-reference to the main entry at which the meaning core appears. Lists of related words and antonyms may be included as well.

Main and Secondary Entries: Lists of related words and antonyms may appear at both main entries and secondary entries.

The italic abbreviation ***rel*** introduces a list of related words. The related words—words that are almost but not quite synonymous with the headword—are included in the entry after the synonym list. A ***rel*** list is often composed of words separated into subgroups that each share a common likeness or relation with the headword and its synonyms. Subgroups within ***rel*** lists are separated by semicolons (see also the section on **Punctuation**, below).

Related words are chosen because they are distinctly related to the headword, and the list of related words will be slightly different at the entries for each word in the synonym list. Therefore, the user should check the list of related words at the entries for each synonym in the list for the most complete listing of related words.

The italic abbreviation ***ant*** introduces an antonym or list of antonyms. Within ***ant*** lists, commas are used between words that are synonyms of one another; semicolons are used to separate words that do not have such a relationship (see also the section on **Punctuation**, below).

In lists of antonyms, italic notations in parentheses indicate the limited use or application in which the word serves as an antonym to the headword (see the section on ***Punctuation***, below).

At some entries users are directed to another entry at which the appropriate ***rel*** or ***ant*** list can be found, as at **mistreat**, where the user is directed to the entry for **ill-treat** to find related words, or at **hefty**, where the user is directed to the entry for **heavy** to find antonyms. When the user is being directed to a multisense entry, the cross-reference includes the number of the sense that includes the relevant ***syn*** and/or ***rel*** list, as **resort** *n*, where users are directed to sense **2** at the entry for **resource**.

Punctuation: A comma links items (as synonyms or members of a single group or subgroup of related words or antonyms) that are alike in their relation to the headword. A semicolon signals a break in the continuity and is used in ***rel*** and ***ant*** lists to separate subgroups of words which differ in their relation to the headword, as in the ***rel*** list at **fabulous** and the ***ant*** list at **facile**.

Parentheses enclose a particle or particles usually associated with a word. They may accompany a headword, as **rely** (*on or upon*), or a word in a list, as **fail** (*in*) in the ***ant*** list at **fulfill** and **fall short** (*of*) at another ***ant*** list in the same entry.

Parentheses also enclose material indicating a typical or, occasionally, a sole object of reference, as in the meaning core at **money** or the ***ant*** list at **gaudy**, where the antonym **quiet** carries the parenthetical note (in taste or style).

English and the Thesaurus

A Brief Look at the English Language

The English language is peculiarly rich in synonyms, which is not surprising considering its history. Over its history of more than a thousand years the language of England has woven together strands of the Celtic language, of earlier Roman words and later church Latin, and then of the Germanic tongues of the early invaders from the European continent.

Because English has so many words derived from Latin and from Greek by way of Latin, the casual observer might guess that English would be—like French, Spanish, and Italian—a Romance language derived from the Latin spoken by the ancient Romans. But although the Romans made a few visits to Britain in the first century A.D., long before the English were there (before there even was an England), English is not a Romance language. English is actually a member of the Germanic group, and thus a sister of such modern languages as Swedish, Dutch, and German.

We often speak of English as having its beginnings with the conquest and settlement of a large part of the island of Britain by Germanic tribes from the European continent in the fifth century, although the earliest written documents of the language belong to the seventh century. Of course these Germanic peoples did not suddenly begin to speak a new language the moment they arrived in England. They spoke the closely related Germanic languages of their continental homelands. And it was from these languages that the English language developed. In fact, the words *English* and *England* are derived from the name of one of these early Germanic peoples, the Angles.

From its beginnings English has been gradually changing and evolving, as language tends to do. To get a sense of how far evolution has taken us from the early tongue, we need only glance at a sample of Old English. Here is the beginning of the Lord's Prayer:

Fæder ūre, þu þe eart on heofonum: si þin nama gehālgod.
Tōbecume þin rīce. Geweorþe þin willa on eorþan swāswā on heofonum.

There is a certain continuity between the vocabularies of Old English and Modern English. Of the thousand most common Modern English words, four-fifths are of Old English origin. Think of such words as *asleep* and *awake* or *alive* and *dead*, words relating to the body, *blood, flesh, arm, leg, bone, tooth*—even words for the daily activities of farming, *acre, barn, plow, till,* or for after the harvest, *drink, eat, meal.*

Of the foreign languages affecting the Old English vocabulary, the most influential was Latin. Church terms especially, like *priest, vicar,* and *mass,* were borrowed from Latin, the language of the church. But words belonging to aspects of life other than the strictly religious, like *cap, inch, kiln, school,* and *noon,* also entered Old English from Latin. The Scandinavians, too, influenced the language of England during the Old English period. From the eighth century on, Vikings from Scandinavia raided and eventually settled in England, especially in the north and the east. In a few instances the influence of a Scandinavian word gave an English word a new meaning. Thus our *dream,* which meant "joy" in Old English, probably took on the now familiar sense "a series of thoughts, images, or emotions occurring during sleep" because its Scandinavian relative *draumr* had that meaning. A considerable number of common words, like *cross, fellow, ball,* and *raise,* also became naturalized as a result of the Viking incursions over the years. The initial consonants *sk-* often reveal the Scandinavian ancestry of words like *sky, skin,* and *skirt,* the last of which has persisted side by side with its native English relative *shirt.*

Additional foreign influence on English came about principally as a result of the Norman Conquest of 1066, which brought England under the rule of French speakers. The English language, though it did not die, was for a long time of only secondary importance in political, social, and cultural matters. French became the language of the upper classes in England. The lower classes continued to speak English, but many French words were borrowed into English. To this circumstance we owe, for example, a number of distinctions between the words used for animals in the pasture and the words for those animals prepared to be eaten. Living animals were under the care of English-speaking peasants; cooked, the animals were served to the French-speaking nobility. *Swine* in the sty became *pork* at the table, *cow* and *calf* became *beef* and *veal.* This Anglo-French also had an influence on the words used in the courts, such as *indict, jury,* and *verdict.*

English eventually reestablished itself as the major language of England, but the language did not lose its habit of borrowing. English still derives much of its learned vocabulary from Latin and Greek. We have also borrowed words from nearly all of the languages in Europe. From Modern French we have such words as *bikini, cliché,* and *discotheque;* from Dutch, *easel, gin,* and *yacht;* from German, *delicatessen, pretzel,* and *swindler;* from Swedish, *ombudsman* and *smorgasbord.* From Italian we have taken *carnival, fiasco,* and *pizza,* as well as many terms from music (including *piano*).

From the period of the Renaissance voyages of discovery through the days when the sun never set upon the British Empire and up to the present, a steady stream of new words has flowed into the language to match the new objects and experiences English speakers have encountered all over the globe. English has drawn words from India (*bandanna*), China (*gung ho*), and Japan (*tycoon*). Arabic has been a prolific source of words over the centuries, giving us *hazard, lute, magazine,* and a host of words beginning with the letter *a,* from *algebra* to *azimuth.*

How Meaning Has Developed

Whether borrowed or created, a word generally begins its life in English with one meaning. Yet no living language is static, and in time words develop new meanings and lose old ones. A word used in a specific sense may be extended, or generalized, to cover a host of similar senses. Our word *virtue* is derived from the Latin *virtus*, which originally meant "manliness." But we apply the term to any excellent quality possessed by man, woman, or beast; even inanimate objects have their *virtues*. In Latin, *decimare* meant "to select and kill a tenth part of" and described the Roman way of dealing with mutinous troops. Its English descendant, *decimate*, now simply means "to destroy a large part of."

The development of meaning can easily be followed in this example. Today when we think of the word *fast* we probably think of the sense involving great speed. But the word's oldest meaning is quite different: "firmly placed" or "immovable," as in "tent pegs set fast in the ground" and "a fast and impassable barrier." It is easy to see how this sense developed expanded uses, such as "a door that is stuck fast and won't open." We see something of this sense in the expression "fast asleep."

In time, users added senses, some of which are common today, from being "unable to leave something, as one's bed" to being "stable and unchangeable," which we find in such uses as "hard and fast rules" or "clothes that are colorfast." Then came the sense of being "steadfast" or "firmly or totally loyal," as in "they were fast friends."

The sense that is most common today, "quick, speedy," came later. It probably developed from an obsolete sense of the adverb meaning "near at hand," which may have led to another meaning "soon." From this obsolete sense of "soon" it is just a short step, in terms of language development, to the sense meaning "quick."

In addition to what could be thought of as a horizontal dimension of change—the extension or contraction of meaning—words also may rise and fall along a vertical scale of value. Perfectly unobjectionable words are sometimes used disparagingly or sarcastically. If we say, "You're a fine one to talk," we are using *fine* in a sense quite different from its usual meaning. If a word is used often enough in negative contexts, the negative coloring may eventually become an integral part of the meaning of the word. A *villain* was once a peasant. His social standing was not high, perhaps, but he was certainly not necessarily a scoundrel. *Scavenger* originally designated the collector of a particular kind of tax in late medieval England. *Puny* meant no more than "younger" when it first passed from French into English and its spelling was transformed. Only later did it acquire the derogatory meaning more familiar to us now.

The opposite process seems to take place somewhat less frequently, but change of meaning to a more positive sense does occasionally occur. In the fourteenth century nice, for example, meant "foolish." Its present meaning, of course, is quite different, and the attitude it conveys seems to have undergone a complete reversal from contempt to approval.

What Qualifies as a Synonym?

It is not surprising that with so much to work with, users of English have long been interested in synonyms as an element both in accuracy and in elegance in their expression. Synonyms relieve monotony and enhance expressiveness.

Earlier writers were clear on the meaning of *synonym*. They viewed synonyms as words meaning the same thing. Unfortunately, during the last century or so this simple, clear-cut meaning has become blurred. To many publishers of thesauruses the term has come to mean little more than words that are somewhat similar in meaning. But this loose definition is unsuitable for many people, since it deprives them of the guidance needed for finding the precise word in a particular context.

This thesaurus takes a different approach to describing the nature of a synonym. Groups of synonyms are organized around a segment of meaning that two or more words have in common. In order to create these groups, one has to analyze each word carefully, ignoring nonessential aspects such as connotations and implications and try to isolate the basic meaning, which we call an *elementary meaning*.

When we look at the synonymous relationship of words in terms of elementary meanings, the process of choosing synonyms is simpler and more exact. For example, it is easy to see that no term more restricted in definition than another word can be its synonym. For example, *station wagon* and *minivan* cannot be synonyms of *automobile*, nor can *biceps* be a synonym of *muscle*. Even though a very definite relationship exists between the members, *station wagon* and *minivan* are types of automobile and *biceps* is a type of muscle. So these words are narrower in their range of application. On the other hand, a word more broadly defined than another word in the dictionary may be considered a synonym of the other word so long as the two words share one or more elementary meanings. In order to pin down the area of shared meaning for you, each main entry in this work contains after its synonym list a *meaning core* which states the elementary meaning shared by all the words in that particular synonym group.

What is an Antonym?

Like the word *synonym, antonym* has been used by some writers with a great deal of vagueness and often applied loosely to words which show no real oppositeness when compared one to another. As in the case of synonyms, the relation needs to be seen as one between segments of meaning that can be isolated, rather than between words or dictionary senses of words. As is the case with synonyms, antonyms need to have one or more elementary meanings precisely opposite to or negating the same area of meaning of another word. This definition excludes from consideration as antonyms several classes of words that are sometimes treated as antonyms but that actually contain words which neither directly oppose nor directly negate the words with which they are said to be antonymous.

For example, some terms have such a relationship to each other that one can scarcely be used without suggesting the other (as *husband* and *wife, father* and *son, buyer* and *seller*), yet there is no real opposition or real negation between such pairs. These are merely *relative terms*—their relation is reciprocal or correlative rather than antonymous.

Complementary terms in a similar way are usually paired and have a reciprocal relationship to the point that one seems incomplete without the other (as in such pairs as *question* and *answer, seek* and *find*). This relation which involves no negation is better seen as sequential than antonymous.

And contrastive terms differ sharply from their "opposites" only in some parts of their meaning. They neither oppose nor negate fully, since they are significantly different in range of meaning and applicability, in emphasis, and in the suggestions they convey. An example is *destitute* (a strong word carrying suggestions of misery and distress) which is contrastive rather than antonymous with respect to *rich* (a rather neutral and matter-of-fact term), while *poor* (another neutral and matter-of-fact term) is the appropriate antonym of rich. Basically, contrastive words are only opposed incidentally; they do not meet head on.

What then is considered an antonym? True antonyms can be classified in three ways:

Opposites without intermediates: What is *perfect* can be in no way *imperfect;* you cannot at the same time *accept* and *reject* or *agree* and *disagree*.

Opposites with intermediates: Such words make up the extremes in a range of difference and are so completely opposed that the language allows no wider difference. Thus, a scale of excellence might include *superiority, adequacy, mediocrity*, and *inferiority*, but only *superiority* and *inferiority* are so totally opposed that each exactly negates what its opposite affirms.

Reverse opposites: These are words that are opposed in such a way that each means the undoing or nullification of what the other affirms. Such reverse opposites exactly oppose and fully negate the special features of their opposites. Thus, *disprove* so perfectly opposes and so clearly negates the implications of *prove* that it fits the concept of antonym, as does *unkind* with respect to *kind*.

In this book, antonyms, when they fit one of these criteria, are listed after the synonym to which they apply.

Webster's Thesaurus *for* Students

NEW EDITION

A

abaft • toward or at the stern (of a vessel) *syn* aft, astern *rel* after, rear, back, posterior, hind, hinder *ant* afore

abandon *vb* **1** • to quit absolutely *syn* desert, forsake *rel* discard, cast, scrap, junk; reject, repudiate, decline *ant* reclaim **2** *syn* RELINQUISH, surrender, yield, resign, leave *ant* cherish (*hopes, opinions*); restrain (*oneself*)

abandon *n, syn* UNCONSTRAINT, spontaneity *rel* license, freedom, liberty; relaxation, laxity, laxness, looseness *ant* self-restraint

abandoned • utterly depraved *syn* reprobate, profligate, dissolute *rel* depraved, debauched, perverted, debased; degenerate, corrupt, vicious; wanton, lewd, lascivious, libidinous, lecherous, licentious *ant* redeemed, regenerate

abase • to lower in one's own estimation or in that of others *syn* demean, debase, degrade, humble, humiliate *rel* cringe, truckle, cower, fawn, toady; grovel, wallow; abash, discomfit, disconcert, embarrass; mortify *ant* exalt; extol (*especially oneself*)

abash *syn* EMBARRASS, discomfit, disconcert, faze, rattle *rel* fluster, flurry, discompose, perturb, disturb, agitate; chagrin, mortify; confound, dumbfound, nonplus, puzzle *ant* embolden; reassure

abate **1** *syn* ABOLISH, extinguish, annihilate *rel* end, terminate, close; annul, void, abrogate; cancel, obliterate, erase; nullify, invalidate *ant* perpetuate **2** *syn* DECREASE, reduce, diminish, lessen *rel* retard, slow, slacken, delay; moderate, temper; mitigate, lighten, alleviate; relieve *ant* augment; accelerate (*pace, speed*); intensify (*hopes, fears, a fever*) **3** • to die down in force or intensity *syn* subside, wane, ebb *rel* dwindle, diminish, decrease *ant* rise; revive

abatement *syn* DEDUCTION, rebate, discount *ant* addition

abbey *syn* CLOISTER, convent, nunnery, monastery, priory

abbreviate *syn* SHORTEN, abridge, curtail *rel* reduce, decrease, lessen; contract, compress, shrink, condense; attenuate, extenuate, thin *ant* elongate, lengthen

abdicate • to give up formally or definitely a position of trust, honor, or glory *syn* renounce, resign *rel* relinquish, surrender, abandon, leave *ant* assume; usurp

abdomen • the part of the body between the chest and the pelvis *syn* belly, stomach, paunch, gut

abduct • to carry off (a person) surreptitiously for an illegal purpose *syn* kidnap *rel* seduce, entice, lure, inveigle

aberrant *syn* ABNORMAL, atypical *rel* divergent, different, disparate; irregular, anomalous, unnatural; exceptional; singular, peculiar, odd, strange, eccentric *ant* true (*to a type*)

aberration **1** *syn* DEVIATION, deflection *rel* abnormality, aberrancy; error, blunder, mistake, slip, lapse; fault, failing; anomaly *ant* conformity; regularity **2** • mental disorder *syn* derangement, alienation *rel* insanity, lunacy, dementia; delusion, hallucination, illusion; mania, delirium, hysteria, frenzy *ant* soundness (*of mind*)

abet *syn* INCITE, foment, instigate *rel* aid, assist, help; back, support, uphold; cooperate, concur; forward, further, promote, advance *ant* deter (*with a personal subject*)

abettor *syn* CONFEDERATE, accessory, accomplice, conspirator

abeyant *syn* LATENT, dormant, quiescent, potential *rel* deferred, suspended, postponed, stayed, intermitted; suppressed, repressed *ant* operative; active; revived

abhor *syn* HATE, abominate, loathe, detest *rel* despise, contemn, scorn; shun, avoid, eschew *ant* admire

abhorrence • a feeling of extreme disgust or dislike *syn* detestation, loathing, abomination, hatred, hate *rel* distaste, repugnance, repellency; horror, dismay *ant* admiration; enjoyment

abhorrent **1** *syn* HATEFUL, abominable, detestable, odious *rel* contemptible, despicable, scurvy; execrable, damnable *ant* admirable; enjoyable **2** *syn* REPUGNANT, repellent, obnoxious, distasteful, invidious *rel* antipathetic; uncongenial, unsympathetic; foreign, alien *ant* congenial

abide **1** *syn* STAY, wait, remain, tarry, linger *rel* dwell, reside, live, sojourn, lodge; stick, cleave, cling, adhere *ant* depart **2** *syn* CON-

TINUE, endure, last, persist *rel* stay, remain, linger; subsist, exist, live *ant* pass **3** *syn* BEAR, endure, suffer, tolerate, stand, brook *rel* submit, yield, bow, defer; acquiesce, accede, consent, assent; accept, receive, take

ability • physical, mental, or legal power to perform *syn* capacity, capability *rel* power, strength, might, force, energy; proficiency, skill, adeptness; aptitude, talent, genius, faculty, gift; competence, qualification *ant* inability, incapacity

abject *syn* MEAN, ignoble, sordid *rel* servile, slavish, menial, subservient; miserable, wretched; cringing, truckling, cowering; groveling; abased, demeaned, humbled, humiliated *ant* exalted (*in rank, state, condition, mood, behavior*); imperious (*in manner, speech, attitude*)

abjure • to abandon irrevocably and, usu., with solemnity or publicity *syn* renounce, forswear, recant, retract *rel* forgo, forbear, eschew; abstain, refrain; reject, repudiate, spurn, decline; abandon, relinquish *ant* pledge (*allegiance, a vow*); elect (*a way of life, a means to an end, an end*)

able • having marked power or fitness for work *syn* capable, competent, qualified *rel* skilled, skillful, proficient, expert; efficient, effective; clever, brilliant, intelligent, smart *ant* inept; unable

abnegate *syn* FORGO, sacrifice, eschew, forbear *rel* renounce, abdicate; surrender, abandon, relinquish, waive; abstain, refrain *ant* indulge (in)

abnegation *syn* RENUNCIATION, self-abnegation, self-denial *rel* forgoing, forbearance, eschewal; abstinence, abstemiousness, continence, temperance; restraining, curbing, bridling *ant* indulgence, self-indulgence

abnormal • deviating markedly from the rule or standard of its kind *syn* atypical, aberrant *rel* irregular, unnatural, anomalous; unusual, unwonted, uncustomary, unaccustomed; monstrous, prodigious *ant* normal

abode *syn* HABITATION, dwelling, residence, domicile, home, house

abolish • to make nonexistent *syn* annihilate, extinguish, abate *rel* extirpate, eradicate, wipe, exterminate; obliterate, efface, blot out, expunge, erase; negate, nullify, annul, abrogate *ant* establish

abominable *syn* HATEFUL, detestable, odious, abhorrent *rel* execrable, damnable, accursed, cursed; scurvy, despicable, contemptible, sorry; loathsome, repulsive, revolting, repugnant, offensive; horrid, horrible *ant* laudable; enjoyable, delightful

abominate *syn* HATE, loathe, detest, abhor *rel* despise, contemn, scorn, disdain; execrate, objurgate, curse, damn *ant* esteem; enjoy

abomination **1** *syn* ABHORRENCE, detestation, loathing, hatred, hate *rel* scorn, despite, contempt, disdain; execration, objurgation *ant* esteem; enjoyment **2** • a person or thing from which one shrinks with intense dislike *syn* anathema, bugbear, bête noire *rel* plague, pest, annoyance; aversion, antipathy *ant* joy

aboriginal *syn* NATIVE, indigenous, autochthonous *rel* primitive, primordial, primeval, pristine; savage, barbaric, barbarian, barbarous

abortive *syn* FUTILE, fruitless, vain, bootless *rel* immature, unmatured, unripe; unformed, formless; ineffectual, ineffective, inefficacious; unfortunate, unlucky *ant* consummated

abound *syn* TEEM, overflow, swarm *rel* predominate, preponderate *ant* fail, fall short

about • in reference to *syn* concerning, regarding, respecting

above • at a higher level *syn* over *ant* below

aboveboard *syn* STRAIGHFORWARD, forthright *rel* open, frank, candid; honest, upright, scrupulous; fair, impartial, just; ingenuous, unsophisticated, artless, natural *ant* underhand, underhanded

abracadabra *syn* GIBBERISH, hocus-pocus, mummery *rel* magic, sorcery, thaumaturgy; amulet, charm, fetish

abrade • to affect a surface by rubbing, scraping, or wearing away *syn* excoriate, chafe, fret, gall *rel* scrape, scratch, grate, grind, rasp; injure, damage, impair, mar; irritate, exasperate

abridge *syn* SHORTEN, curtail, abbreviate, retrench *rel* condense, contract, compress, shrink; cut, slash; limit, restrict; reduce, diminish, decrease *ant* expand; extend

abridgment • a condensation of a larger work *syn* abstract, epitome, brief, synopsis, conspectus *rel* digest, précis, compendium, sketch, syllabus *ant* expansion

abrogate **1** *syn* ANNUL, vacate, quash, void

rel abolish, extinguish, abate *ant* institute (*by enacting, decreeing*) **2** *syn* NULLIFY, annul, negate, invalidate *rel* abolish, annihilate, extinguish; destroy, demolish; ruin, wreck; cancel, obliterate, blot out, erase *ant* establish, fix (*a right, a character, a quality, a custom*)

abrupt **1** *syn* STEEP, precipitous, sheer *rel* perpendicular, vertical, plumb *ant* sloping **2** *syn* PRECIPITATE, sudden, headlong, impetuous, hasty *rel* quick, speedy, fast; hurried, hastened; unceremonious; curt, brusque, bluff *ant* deliberate, leisurely

abscess • a localized swollen area of infection containing pus *syn* boil, furuncle, carbuncle, pimple, pustule

abscond *syn* ESCAPE, decamp, flee, fly *rel* depart, leave, quit, go *ant* give (*oneself*) up

absence *syn* LACK, want, dearth, defect, privation *rel* need, necessity, exigency; deficiency; destitution; void, vacuum, *ant* presence

absent *syn* ABSTRACTED, preoccupied, absentminded, distraught *rel* engrossed, absorbed, intent, rapt; heedless, inadvertent; careless; oblivious, unmindful, forgetful *ant* attentive

absentminded *syn* ABSTRACTED, absent, preoccupied, distraught *rel* inattentive, thoughtless, inconsiderate; heedless, inadvertent careless; unobserving, unseeing, unperceiving, unnoticing *ant* wide-awake

absolute **1** *syn* PURE, simple, sheer *rel* perfect, whole, entire; real, true; abstract, ideal; consummate, finished *ant* mixed, qualified **2** • exercising power or authority without external restraint *syn* autocratic, arbitrary, despotic, tyrannical, tyrannous *rel* totalitarian, authoritarian; dictatorial, magisterial; domineering, imperious, masterful *ant* restrained; limited **3** *syn* ULTIMATE, categorical *rel* ideal, transcendent, transcendental, abstract; independent, autonomous, free, sovereign; infinite, eternal, boundless *ant* conditioned

absolution *syn* PARDON, amnesty *rel* forgiveness, remission *ant* condemnation

absolve *syn* EXCULPATE, exonerate, acquit, vindicate *rel* pardon, forgive, remit, excuse; release, free, discharge *ant* hold (*to a promise, an obligation*); charge (*with a sin, the blame, the responsibility*)

absorb **1** • to take (something) in so as to become imbued with it or to make it a part of one's being *syn* imbibe, assimilate *rel* soak, saturate, impregnate; receive, take; incorporate, embody, identify *ant* exude, give out **2** *syn* MONOPOLIZE, engross, consume *rel* fix, fasten; rivet, secure; immerse, submerge *ant* dissipate (*time, attention, energies*)

absorbed *syn* INTENT, engrossed, rapt *rel* immersed; riveted; fixed, fastened *ant* distracted

absorbing *syn* INTERESTING, engrossing, intriguing *ant* irksome

abstain *syn* REFRAIN, forbear *rel* forgo, eschew, abnegate; decline, refuse, spurn, reject; desist, stop *ant* indulge

abstemiousness *syn* TEMPERANCE, abstinence, sobriety, continence *rel* self-denial, self-abnegation, renunciation; asceticism, austerity *ant* gluttony

abstinence *syn* TEMPERANCE, continence, abstemiousness, sobriety *rel* forbearance, refrainment; forgoing, eschewal, abnegation; renunciation, self-denial, self-abnegation *ant* self-indulgence

abstract *adj* • having conceptual rather than concrete existence *syn* ideal, transcendent, transcendental *rel* universal, general, generic; ultimate, absolute, categorical *ant* concrete

abstract *n, syn* ABRIDGMENT, brief, synopsis, epitome, conspectus *rel* sketch, précis, aperçu, compendium, digest *ant* amplification

abstract *vb, syn* DETACH, disengage *rel* separate, part, divorce, divide; purloin, filch, steal *ant* insert, introduce

abstracted • inattentive to what presently claims or demands consideration *syn* preoccupied, absent, absentminded, distraught *rel* intent, engrossed; oblivious, unmindful, forgetful; ignoring, overlooking, disregarding *ant* alert

abstruse *syn* RECONDITE, occult, esoteric *rel* complex, complicated, intricate, knotty; abstract, ideal; enigmatic, cryptic, dark, obscure *ant* obvious, plain

absurd *syn* FOOLISH, silly, preposterous *rel* ludicrous, ridiculous, laughable, droll, funny, comic; irrational, unreasonable; asinine, silly, fatuous, simple *ant* rational, sensible

abundant *syn* PLENTIFUL, copious, ample, plenteous *rel* abounding, teeming, overflowing; profuse, lavish, luxuriant, lush, exuberant *ant* scarce

abuse *vb* • to use or treat a person or thing improperly or wrongfully *syn* misuse, mistreat, maltreat, ill-treat, outrage *rel* hurt, injure, harm, damage, impair, mar, spoil; wrong, persecute, oppress; pervert, corrupt, debase, debauch, vitiate *ant* respect, honor

abuse *n* • vehemently expressed condemnation or disapproval *syn* vituperation, invective, obloquy, scurrility, billingsgate *rel* aspersion, reflection, stricture, animadversion; reviling, railing, rating, berating, scold; vilification, malignment *ant* adulation

abusive • coarse, insulting, and contemptuous in character or utterance *syn* opprobrious, vituperative, contumelious, scurrilous *rel* insulting, affronting, offending, outraging; aspersing, maligning, vilifying *ant* complementary; respectful

abutment *syn* BUTTRESS, pier

abutting *syn* ADJACENT, contiguous, adjoining, tangent, conterminous, juxtaposed *rel* close, near, nigh, nearby; joining, connecting; nearest, next; impinging

abysm *syn* GULF, chasm, abyss

abysmal *syn* DEEP, profound *rel* illimitable, infinite

abyss *syn* GULF, chasm, abysm

academic **1** *syn* PEDANTIC, scholastic, bookish *rel* dry, arid; erudite, scholarly, learned **2** *syn* THEORETICAL, speculative

accede *syn* ASSENT, acquiesce, consent, agree, subscribe *rel* concur, cooperate; yield, submit, defer, relent; allow, permit, let *ant* demur

accelerate *syn* SPEED, quicken, hurry, hasten, precipitate *rel* forward, further, advance, promote; drive, impel, move *ant* decelerate; retard

accent **1** *syn* EMPHASIS, stress, accentuation *rel* beat, pulse, throb, pulsation; rhythm, cadence, meter **2** *syn* INFLECTION, intonation *rel* pronunciation, enunciation, articulation

accentuation *syn* EMPHASIS, accent, stress *rel* rhythm, cadence, meter; pronunciation, enunciation, articulation *ant* inaccentuation

accept *syn* RECEIVE, admit, take *rel* adopt, embrace, espouse; acquiesce, assent, agree, subscribe *ant* reject

acceptance • the act or fact of accepting or the state of being accepted *syn* acceptation

acceptation **1** *syn* MEANING, sense, signification, significance, import **2** *syn* ACCEPTANCE

access **1** *syn* ENTRANCE, ingress, entrée, entry *rel* approaching, approach, nearing; admittance, admission; way, route, passage; door, portal, gate, gateway *ant* outlet **2** *syn* FIT, accession, attack, paroxysm, spasm, convulsion *rel* onset, onslaught, assault; seizure, clutch, taking; twinge, pain, stitch, pang, throe

accession **1** *syn* ADDITION, accretion, increment *ant* discard **2** *syn* FIT, access, attack, paroxysm, spasm, convulsion *rel* see ACCESS 2

accessory *n* **1** *syn* APPENDAGE, appurtenance, adjunct *rel* concomitant, accompaniment; addition, accretion, increment **2** *syn* CONFEDERATE, accomplice, abettor, conspirator *ant* principal

accessory *adj*, *syn* AUXILIARY, contributory, subsidiary, adjuvant, ancillary, subservient *rel* secondary, collateral, tributary, subordinate; concomitant, concurrent, coincident; incidental, adventitious, accidental *ant* constituent, integral; principal (*in law*)

accident **1** *syn* QUALITY, character, attribute, property *rel* mark; sign, note, badge, token, symptom; characteristic, peculiarity *ant* substance (*in philosophy*) **2** *syn* CHANCE, hazard, luck, fortune, hap *rel* contingency, fortuity, adventitiousness *ant* design, intent **3** • chance or a chance event bringing injury or loss *syn* casualty, mishap *rel* disaster, catastrophe; mischance, misfortune, mishap

accidental • not amenable to planning or prediction *syn* casual, fortuitous, contingent, incidental *rel* haphazard, random, hit-or-miss, chance; unintended, undesigned, unpurposed; contingent, dependent, conditional *ant* planned; essential

acclaim *vb*, *syn* PRAISE, extol, laud, eulogize *rel* applaud, cheer, root; exalt, magnify; glorify, honor *ant* vituperate

acclaim *n*, *syn* APPLAUSE, acclamation, plaudits *rel* homage, honor, reverence; renown, glory, éclat, fame; cheer *ant* vituperation

acclamation *syn* APPLAUSE, acclaim, plaudits *rel*, *ant* see ACCLAIM

acclimate *syn* HARDEN, acclimatize, season *rel* accustom, habituate; adapt, adjust, conform

acclimatize *syn* HARDEN, acclimate, season *rel* see ACCLIMATE

accommodate 1 *syn* ADAPT, adjust, conform, reconcile *rel* yield, submit, bow, defer; modify, change, alter, vary; temper, moderate, qualify *ant* constrain **2** *syn* OBLIGE, favor *rel* help, aid, assist; gratify, gladden, please; indulge, humor *ant* incommode **3** *syn* CONTAIN, hold *rel* lodge, house, board, shelter, harbor, entertain; take (in), receive, admit

accompaniment • something attendant upon or found in association with another thing. *syn* concomitant

accompany • to go or be together with *syn* attend, conduct, escort, convoy, chaperon *rel* associate, link, combine, join; guide, lead, pilot

accomplice *syn* CONFEDERATE, accessory, abettor, conspirator

accomplish *syn* PERFORM, achieve, effect, fulfill, discharge, execute *rel* complete, finish, conclude, close; consummate; implement, enforce *ant* undo

accomplished *syn* CONSUMMATE, finished *rel* proficient, skillful, skilled, adept, expert, masterly; versatile, many-sided, all-around

accomplishment *syn* ACQUIREMENT, attainment, acquisition *rel* art, skill, craft; proficiency, adeptness, expertness

accord *vb* **1** *syn* AGREE, harmonize, correspond, tally, conform, square, jibe *rel* concur, coincide, agree; blend, fuse, merge, coalesce, mix; cohere, adhere, stick *ant* conflict **2** *syn* GRANT, vouchsafe, concede, award *rel* deign, condescend, stoop; bestow, present, confer, give *ant* withhold

accord *n* **1** *syn* HARMONY, concord, consonance *rel* agreement, acquiescence, consent; union, solidarity, unity; sympathy, affinity, attraction *ant* dissension, strife; antagonism **2** *syn* AGREEMENT, understanding *rel* pact, compact, treaty, entente, concordat, contract

accordingly *syn* THEREFORE, so, consequently, hence, then

accost *syn* ADDRESS, greet, hail, salute *rel* speak, talk, converse; affront, offend, insult

account *n* **1** *syn* USE, service, advantage, profit, avail *rel* benefit; usefulness, utility; worth, value **2** • a statement of actual events or conditions or of purported occurrences or conditions *syn* report, chronicle, version, story

account *vb* **1** *syn* CONSIDER, deem, regard, reckon *rel* regard, esteem; rate, appraise, evaluate, assess, estimate **2** *syn* EXPLAIN, justify, rationalize *rel* answer; expound, elucidate, interpret

accountable *syn* RESPONSIBLE, answerable, amenable, liable *rel* unaccountable

accouter *syn* FURNISH, equip, arm, outfit, appoint *rel* array, attire, clothe, dress; deck, adorn, embellish, decorate

accredit 1 *syn* APPROVE, certify, endorse, sanction *rel* recommend, commend; vouch, attest **2** *syn* AUTHORIZE, commission, license **3** *syn* ASCRIBE, credit, charge, assign, attribute, impute *rel* attach, fasten; connect, link, associate, join

accretion *syn* ADDITION, increment, accession *rel* adjunct, appendage; adhesion, cohesion; increase, augmentation, enlargement

accumulate • to bring together so as to make a store or great quantity *syn* amass, hoard *rel* gather, collect; heap, pile, stack *ant* dissipate

accumulative *syn* CUMULATIVE, summative, additive *rel* aggregative, conglomerative; multiplicative, augmentative

accurate *syn* CORRECT, exact, precise, nice, right *rel* true, veracious, truthful; impeccable, errorless, flawless, faultless; punctilious, meticulous, careful *ant* inaccurate

accursed *syn* EXECRABLE, damnable, cursed *rel* abominable, odious, hateful, abhorrent, detestable; revolting, repulsive, loathsome, offensive, repugnant *ant* blessed

accuse • to declare a person guilty of a fault or offense *syn* charge, incriminate, indict, impeach, arraign *rel* denounce, blame, reprobate, censure, criticize *ant* exculpate

accustom *syn* HABITUATE, addict, inure *rel* adapt, accommodate, adjust; harden, season, acclimatize *ant* disaccustom

accustomed *syn* USUAL, wonted, customary, habitual *rel* natural, normal, regular, typical; common, ordinary, familiar *ant* unaccustomed

acerbity *syn* ACRIMONY, asperity *rel* sour-ness, acidity, tartness; crabbedness, surliness, dourness, saturninity, sullenness; bitterness, acridity; harshness, roughness *ant* mellowness

ache *syn* PAIN, pang, throe, twinge, stitch *rel* distress, suffering, agony, misery; anguish, heartache, heartbreak, sorrow; hurt, injury; torment, torture, rack

achieve **1** *syn* PERFORM, accomplish, effect, fulfill, execute, discharge *rel* complete, finish, conclude, close; surmount, overcome, conquer *ant* fail **2** *syn* REACH, attain, gain, compass *rel* win, secure, obtain, acquire, get; realize, actualize; come, arrive *ant* miss (*getting or attaining*)

achievement *syn* FEAT, exploit *rel* deed, act, action; victory, conquest, triumph; consummation, accomplishment *ant* failure

achromatic *syn* COLORLESS, uncolored *rel* neutral, negative *ant* chromatic

acid *syn* SOUR, acidulous, tart, dry *rel* acrid, bitter; sharp *ant* bland; sweet; alkaline

acidulous *syn* SOUR, acid, tart, dry *rel* sharp; pungent, piquant; biting, cutting, incisive *ant* saccharine

acknowledge **1** • to disclose something against one's will or inclination *syn* admit, own, avow, confess *rel* disclose, divulge, reveal; grant, concede, allow; publish, declare, proclaim *ant* deny **2** • to take cognizance of in some way, usually in a way dictated by custom or convention and implying acceptance or assent *syn* recognize *rel* accept, receive; notice, note, remark; respond, reply, answer *ant* ignore

acme *syn* SUMMIT, apex, zenith, culmination, climax, peak, apogee, pinnacle, meridian

acoustic, acoustical *syn* AUDITORY

acquaint *syn* INFORM, apprise, advise, notify *rel* tell, reveal, disclose, divulge; teach, instruct, educate, school; accustom, habituate

acquaintance *syn* FRIEND, intimate, confidant *rel* associate, companion, comrade, crony

acquiesce *syn* ASSENT, consent, agree, accede, subscribe *rel* accept, receive; conform, adapt, adject, accommodate, reconcile (*oneself*); yield, submit, bow; concur, coincide *ant* object

acquiescence *syn* compliance, resignation *rel* deference, obeisance, honor; submissiveness *ant* rebelliousness, rebellion

acquiescent *syn* COMPLIANT, resigned *rel* submissive, tame; yielding, submitting, deferring, bowing, relenting *ant* rebellious

acquire *syn* GET, obtain, gain, win, secure, procure *rel* attain, achieve, compass, reach; annex, add, superadd; buy, purchase; take, seize, snatch, grab *ant* forfeit

acquirement • a power or skill that is the fruit of exertion or effort *syn* acquisition, attainment, accomplishment *rel* achievement, feat; addition, accretion

acquisition *syn* ACQUIREMENT, attainment, accomplishment *rel* addition, accession, accretion, increment; possessions, belongings, means, assets; gift, genius, talent, aptitude; art, skill, cunning

acquisitive *syn* COVETOUS, grasping, avaricious, greedy *rel* avid, eager, keen, athirst; possessing, possessive, owning, enjoying *ant* sacrificing, abnegating

acquit **1** *syn* EXCULPATE, absolve, exonerate, vindicate *rel* discharge, free, release, liberate; excuse, pardon, forgive, remit *ant* convict **2** *syn* BEHAVE, quit, conduct, demean, deport, comport *rel* act, behave, work, operate, react

acrid **1** *syn* BITTER *rel* pungent, piquant; biting, incisive; offensive, repugnant, loathsome *ant* savory **2** *syn* CAUSTIC, mordant, scathing *rel* sharp, keen; surly, crabbed, morose, sullen; malevolent, malign, spiteful, malicious; virulent, venomous, poisonous *ant* benign, kindly

acrimonious *syn* ANGRY, irate, indignant, wrathful, wroth, mad *rel* testy, splenetic, choleric, irascible, cranky, cross; rancorous, hostile, antagonistic; quarrelsome, contentious, belligerent *ant* irenic, peaceable

acrimony • temper or language marked by irritation or some degree of anger or resentment *syn* acerbity, asperity *rel* bitterness; ill will, malignity, malignancy, spite, spleen, malice, malevolence; rancor, animus, animosity, antipathy, enmity *ant* suavity

across • so as to intersect the length of something *syn* crosswise, crossways, athwart

act *n, syn* ACTION, deed *rel* performance, accomplishment, achievement; feat, exploit

act *vb* **1** • to perform esp. in an indicated way *syn* behave, work, operate, function, react **2** • to assume the appearance or role of another person or character *syn* play, impersonate

acting *syn* TEMPORARY, ad interim, provisional

action **1** • something done or effected *syn* act, deed *rel* process, proceeding, procedure; performance, execution, fulfillment; activity, operation, work, behavior, reaction **2** *syn* SUIT, cause, case, lawsuit **3** *syn* BATTLE, engagement *rel* combat, conflict, fight, fray, affray, contest; encounter, skirmish, brush

activate *syn* VITALIZE, energize *rel* animate, vivify, quicken, enliven; stir, rouse, arouse, rally, awaken *ant* arrest

active • at work or in effective action *syn* operative, dynamic, live *rel* agile, nimble, brisk; alert, wide-awake, watchful; busy, industrious, assiduous, diligent; energetic, strenuous, vigorous *ant* inactive

actor • one who, for the entertainment or edification of an audience, takes part in an exhibition simulating happenings in real life *syn* player, performer, mummer, mime, mimic, thespian, impersonator, trouper

actual *syn* REAL, true *rel* material, physical, phenomenal, objective; particular *ant* ideal; imaginary

actuality *syn* EXISTENCE, being *rel* realization, actualization, materialization, externalization, incarnation; attainment, achievement *ant* potentiality, possibility

actualize *syn* REALIZE, embody, incarnate, externalize, objectify, materialize, hypostatize, reify

actuate **1** *syn* MOVE, drive, impel *rel* stimulate, provoke, excite, galvanize, quicken; stir, rouse, arouse; energize, activate, vitalize **2** *syn* ACTIVATE, motivate *rel* influence, affect, sway; incline, dispose, predispose; induce, prevail *ant* deter

acumen *syn* DISCERNMENT, penetration, insight, perception, discrimination *rel* shrewdness, sagacity, perspicacity, astuteness; sharpness, keenness, acuteness *ant* obtuseness

acute **1** *syn* SHARP, keen *rel* incisive, trenchant, cutting; penetrating, piercing *ant* obtuse **2** • of uncertain outcome *syn* critical, crucial *rel* culminating, climactic; dangerous, hazardous, precarious, perilous; menacing, threatening; intensified, aggravated

adage *syn* SAYING, saw, proverb, maxim, motto, epigram, aphorism, apothegm

adamant, adamantine *syn* INFLEXIBLE, obdurate, inexorable *rel* unyielding, unsubmitting; immovable, immobile; grim, implacable, unrelenting *ant* yielding

adapt **1** • to bring into correspondence *syn* adjust, accommodate, conform, reconcile *rel* temper, qualify, moderate; acclimatize, acclimate, harden *ant* unfit **2** *syn* EDIT, rewrite, revise, redact, compile *rel* fit, prepare, condition, qualify

adaptable *syn* PLASTIC, pliant, ductile, pliable, malleable *rel* tractable, amenable, obedient; supple, flexible, resilient, elastic *ant* inadaptable, unadaptable

add **1** • to find or represent the amount reached by putting together arithmetically a series of numbers of quantities *syn* sum, total, tot, cast, figure, foot **2** • to bring in or join on something more so as to form a larger or more inclusive whole *syn* append, annex, subjoin, superadd *rel* fasten, attach, affix; augment, enlarge, increase *ant* subtract, deduct

addendum *syn* APPENDIX, supplement

addict *vb, syn* HABITUATE, accustom, inure *rel* incline, dispose, predispose, bias; devote, apply, address, direct *ant* wean

addict *n* • a person who by habit and strong inclination indulges in something or the pursuit of something *syn* votary, devotee, habitué

addition • a thing that serves to increase another in size, amount or content *syn* accretion, increment, accession

additive *syn* CUMULATIVE, summative, accumulative *rel* aggregative, conglomerative, agglomerative; constituent, component, elemental

addle *syn* CONFUSE, muddle, fuddle, befuddle *rel* confound, dumbfound, nonplus, bewilder, puzzle; amaze, flabbergast, astound, surprise; fluster, flurry, agitate, upset, discompose *ant* refresh (*mentally*)

address *vb* **1** *syn* DIRECT, devote, apply *rel* bend; appeal, pray, sue, plead; aim, point, level **2** • to speak to or less often to write or make a sign to a person in recognition or in order to obtain recognition *syn* accost, greet, salute, hail *rel* speak, talk, converse; court, woo

address *n* **1** *syn* TACT, savoir faire, poise *rel* dexterity, facility, ease, readiness; adroitness, cleverness; graciousness, affability; suavity, urbanity, diplomacy *ant* maladroitness, gaucherie **2** *syn* SPEECH, oration, harangue, lecture, talk, sermon, homily

adduce • to bring forward by way of explanation, proof, illustration, or demonstration *syn* advance, allege, cite *rel* exemplify, illustrate; remark, comment, commentate, animadvert

adept *n, syn* EXPERT, wizard, artiste, artist, virtuoso *ant* bungler

adept *adj, syn* PROFICIENT, skilled, skillful, expert, masterly *rel* conversant, versed; efficient, effective; dexterous, adroit, deft; competent, able, capable, qualified *ant* inadept, inept; bungling

adequate *syn* SUFFICIENT, enough, competent

adhere *syn* STICK, cohere, cling, cleave *rel* fasten, attach, affix; unite, link, combine, join

adherence • a physical adhering *syn* adhesion *ant* inadherence, nonadherence

adherent *syn* FOLLOWER, disciple, partisan, satellite, henchman, sectary *rel* supporter, upholder, backer, champion *ant* renegade

adhesion *syn* ADHERENCE *ant* nonadhesion, inadhesion

ad interim *syn* TEMPORARY, provisional, acting *ant* permanent

adjacent • in close proximity *syn* adjoining, contiguous, abutting, tangent, conterminous, juxtaposed *rel* nearest, next; successive, consecutive; joining, connecting *ant* nonadjacent

adjoining *syn* ADJACENT, contiguous, abutting, tangent, conterminous, juxtaposed *rel* joined, connected; attached *ant* detached, disjoined

adjudge *syn* JUDGE, adjudicate, arbitrate *rel* rule, decide, determine, settle; award, accord, grant; allot, assign

adjudicate *syn* JUDGE, adjudge, arbitrate *rel* determine, settle, rule, decide

adjunct *syn* APPENDAGE, appurtenance, accessory *rel* addition, accretion; appanage, right; attachment, affix, fixture

adjure *syn* BEG, entreat, beseech, implore, importune, supplicate *rel* pray, plead, appeal; request, ask; bid, enjoin, charge, command

adjust **1** • to set right or to rights *syn* regulate, fix *rel* rectify, correct; trim, steady, stabilize, balance; order, arrange; align, line, line up, range *ant* derange **2** *syn* ADAPT, accommodate, conform, reconcile *rel* harmonize, attune; correspond, conform, accord, square, agree

adjuvant *syn* AUXILIARY, contributory, ancillary, accessory, subsidiary, subservient *rel* aiding, helping, assisting; supporting, upholding, backing; effective, efficient, efficacious, effectual *ant* counteractive

administer • to act on the behalf of another in or as if in the capacity of a steward *syn* dispense

admiration **1** *syn* WONDER, wonderment, amazement *rel* astonishment, surprise; awe, fear, reverence; rapture, transport, ecstasy **2** *syn* REGARD, esteem, respect *rel* appreciation; liking, loving, enjoying; adoration, veneration, reverence, worship *ant* abhorrence

admire *syn* REGARD, esteem, respect *rel* appreciate, value, prize, cherish; revere, reverence, venerate, adore, worship *ant* abhor

admission *syn* ADMITTANCE

admit **1** *syn* RECEIVE, accept, take *rel* allow, permit, suffer, let; harbor, entertain, shelter, lodge, house *ant* eject, expel **2** *syn* ACKNOWLEDGE, own, confess, avow *rel* concede, grant, allow; assent, acquiesce, agree, subscribe; divulge, disclose, reveal *ant* gainsay; disdain **3** *syn* ENTER, introduce *rel* induct, initiate, install; introduce, insert, interject, interpose *ant* exclude

admittance • permitted entrance *syn* admission

admixture **1** *syn* MIXTURE, composite, blend, compound, amalgam **2** • an added ingredient that destroys the purity or genuineness of a substance *syn* alloy, adulterant *rel* addition, accretion; touch, suggestion, streak, dash, spice, tinge, smack, shade; infusion, suffusion, leaven

admonish *syn* REPROVE, chide, reproach, rebuke, reprimand *rel* warn, forewarn, caution; counsel, advise; criticize, reprehend, reprobate *ant* commend

ado *syn* STIR, fuss, pother, flurry, bustle *rel* trouble, pains, exertion, effort

adolescence *syn* YOUTH, puberty, pubescence *ant* senescence

adopt • to make one's own what in some fashion one owes to another *syn* embrace, espouse *rel* appropriate, arrogate, usurp; assume, affect *ant* repudiate; discard

adoration *syn* REVERENCE, worship, veneration *rel* honor, homage, obeisance; praise, laud, extolling *ant* blasphemy

adore **1** *syn* REVERE, worship, venerate, reverence *rel* laud, praise, extol; exalt, magnify *ant* blaspheme **2** • to love or admire excessively *syn* worship, idolize *rel* love, dote, like; admire, esteem *ant* detest

adorn • to add something unessential in order to enhance the appearance *syn* decorate, ornament, embellish, beautify, deck, bedeck, garnish *rel* enhance, heighten, intensify *ant* disfigure

adroit **1** *syn* DEXTEROUS, deft, handy *rel* agile, nimble; expert, masterly, adept, skillful, skilled, proficient; effortless, smooth, facile, easy *ant* maladroit **2** *syn* CLEVER, cunning, ingenious *rel* shrewd, astute, perspicacious; intelligent, quick-witted, smart; artful, crafty, sly *ant* stolid

adulation *syn* COMPLIMENT, flattery *rel* praise, laud; applause, acclaim; fulsomeness, unctuousness *ant* abuse

adult *syn* MATURE, grown-up, matured, ripe, mellow *rel* developed, ripened, aged *ant* juvenile; puerile

adulterant *syn* ADMIXTURE, alloy

adulterate • to alter fraudulently esp. for profit *syn* sophisticate, load, weight, doctor *rel* debase, vitiate, corrupt; pollute, defile, taint, contaminate *ant* refine

adumbrate *syn* SUGGEST, shadow *rel* symbolize, typify, emblematize; signify, denote, mean

adumbration *syn* SHADE, shadow, umbra, penumbra, umbrage *rel* symbol, type, emblem; sign, token, symptom, note; hint, suggestion, intimation *ant* revelation

advance *vb* **1** • to move or put ahead *syn* promote, forward, further *rel* help, aid, assist; hasten, accelerate, quicken, speed; elevate, raise, lift *ant* retard; check **2** • to move forward in space, in time, or in approach to a material or ideal objective *syn* progress *rel* develop, mature; intensify, heighten *ant* recede **3** *syn* ADDUCE, allege, cite *rel* offer, present, proffer; propose; broach, express, air

advance *n* **1** • movement forward in space, in time, or in approach to a material or ideal objective *syn* progress *rel* development, evolution; improvement, betterment *ant* recession, retrogression **2** *syn* OVERTURE, approach, tender, bid *rel* proposal, proposition; offer, proffer

advanced **1** *syn* PREMATURE, forward, precocious, untimely *ant* backward **2** *syn* LIBERAL, radical, progressive *rel* daring, venturesome, adventurous *ant* conservative

advancement • the act of raising a person in grade, rank, or dignity, or the honor that comes to one who is so raised *syn* preferment, promotion, elevation *ant* degradation; reduction (*in rank or status*)

advantage **1** • a factor or set of factors in a competition or rivalry giving one person or side a position of superiority over the other *syn* handicap, allowance, odds, edge *rel* preeminence, superlativeness; supremacy, ascendancy *ant* disadvantage; handicap **2** *syn* USE, service, account, profit, avail *rel* improvement, betterment; enhancement, heightening; benefit *ant* detriment

advantageous *syn* BENEFICIAL, profitable *rel* expedient, advisable; useful, utilitarian *ant* disadvantageous

advent *syn* ARRIVAL *rel* coming, arriving; approaching, nearing; appearing, emerging *ant* leaving, passing

adventure • an undertaking, an exploit, or an experience involving hazards and requiring boldness *syn* enterprise, quest *rel* exploit, feat, achievement; hazard, peril, risk, danger

adventurous • courting danger or exposing oneself to danger in a greater degree than is required for courage *syn* venturesome, daring, daredevil, rash, reckless, foolhardy *rel* audacious, bold, intrepid, doughty, brave; aspiring, panting; ambitious, emulous *ant* unadventurous; cautious

adversary *syn* OPPONENT, antagonist *rel* assailant, attacker, assaulter; enemy, foe; competitor, rival *ant* ally

adverse • so opposed as to cause interference, often harmful or fatal interference *syn* antagonistic, counter, counteractive *rel* harmful, hurtful, injurious; hindering, impeding, obstructing; detrimental, deleterious, pernicious; fatal, deadly *ant* propitious

adversity *syn* MISFORTUNE, mischance, mishap *rel* trial, tribulation, affliction; distress, misery, suffering; poverty, privation, indigence, destitution *ant* prosperity

advert *syn* REFER, allude *rel* remark, notice, note, observe

advertise *syn* DECLARE, publish, announce, proclaim, broadcast, promulgate *rel* report, recount, relate; communicate, impart

advertisement *syn* DECLARATION, publication, announcement, broadcasting, proclamation, promulgation *rel* publicity, ballyhoo, promotion, propaganda

advice **1** • a recommendation as to a decision or a course of conduct *syn* counsel *rel* admonition; warning, forewarning, cautioning; instruction, teaching **2** *syn* NEWS, intelligence, tidings

advisable *syn* EXPEDIENT, politic *rel* prudent, wise, sensible; beneficial, advantageous, profitable; practical, practicable *ant* inadvisable

advise **1** • to make a recommendation as to a decision or a course of conduct *syn* counsel *rel* admonish, reprove; warn, forewarn, caution; induce, persuade **2** *syn* CONFER, consult, commune, parley, treat, negotiate *rel* discuss, debate, argue; converse, talk, speak; deliberate, think **3** *syn* INFORM, notify, apprise, acquaint *rel* tell, disclose, reveal; communicate (with), impart (to)

advised *syn* DELIBERATE, considered, premeditated, designed, studied

advocate *n, syn* LAWYER, counselor, barrister, counsel, attorney, solicitor

advocate *vb, syn* SUPPORT, uphold, champion, back *rel* defend, justify, vindicate, maintain; espouse, adopt; promote, forward, advance *ant* impugn

aeon *syn* PERIOD, age, era, epoch

aerial *syn* AIRY, ethereal *rel* immaterial, incorporeal; impalpable, imperceptible, imponderable

aesthete • a person conspicuous for his enjoyment and appreciation of the beautiful, the exquisite, or the choice *syn* dilettante, connoisseur

affable *syn* GRACIOUS, cordial, genial, sociable *rel* courteous, polite, civil; open, candid, frank; amiable, obliging, complaisant; talkative, loquacious; suave, urbane *ant* reserved

affair **1** • something done or dealth with *syn* business, concern, matter, thing **2** *syn* AMOUR, intrigue, liaison

affect *syn* ASSUME, simulate, pretend, feign, counterfeit, sham

affect • to produce or to have an effect upon a person or upon a thing capable of a reaction *syn* influence, touch, impress, strike, sway *rel* move, actuate, drive, impel; pierce, penetrate; thrill, electrify

affectation *syn* POSE, air, mannerism *rel* pretense, pretension; pretentiousness, ostentation *ant* artlessness

affecting *syn* MOVING, touching, pathetic, poignant, impressive *rel* stirring, rousing, rallying; distressing, troubling; pitiful, piteous, pitiable

affection **1** *syn* FEELING, emotion, passion, sentiment *rel* propensity, leaning, penchant; predilection, bias; inclination, disposition *ant* antipathy **2** *syn* ATTACHMENT, love *rel* devotion, piety, fidelity; liking, doting, enjoying; tenderness, warmth, sympathy *ant* coldness **3** *syn* DISEASE, disorder, condition, ailment, malady, complaint, distemper, syndrome *rel* attack, access, paroxysm, fit; disorder, derangement

affectionate *syn* LOVING, devoted, fond, doting *rel* ardent, fervent, passionate, impassioned; tender, sympathetic, warm *ant* cold; undemonstrative

affiliated *syn* RELATED, allied, kindred, cognate *rel* dependent, subordinate *ant* unaffiliated

affinity **1** *syn* ATTRACTION, sympathy **2** *syn* LIKENESS, resemblance, similarity, similitude, analogy *rel* agreement, conformity, correspondence, accord

affirm *syn* ASSERT, profess, aver, avow, protest, avouch, declare, warrant, predicate *rel* attest, certify, couch, witness; state, relate *ant* deny

affix *syn* FASTEN, attach, fix *rel* append, add, subjoin, annex; stick, adhere *ant* detach

afflatus *syn* INSPIRATION, fury, frenzy

afflict • to inflict upon a person something which he finds hard to endure *syn* try, torment, torture, rack *rel* worry, annoy, harass, harry, plague, pester; vex, bother, irk, annoy; distress, trouble, ail *ant* comfort

affliction *syn* TRIAL, visitation, tribulation, cross *rel* adversity, misfortune, mischance, mishap; distress, suffering, misery, agony; anguish, sorrow, grief, woe, heartbreak *ant* solace, consolation

affluent *syn* RICH, wealthy, opulent *rel* possessing, owning, holding, having, enjoying; acquisitive, covetous *ant* impecunious; straitened

afford *syn* GIVE, confer, bestow, present, donate *rel* offer, proffer; furnish; grant, accord *ant* deny (*something one wants*)

affray *n, syn* CONTEST, fray, fight, combat, conflict *rel* brawl, row, fracas, melee, rumpus; encounter, skirmish, brush; dispute, argument, controversy

affray *vb, syn* FRIGHTEN, fright, affright, scare, alarm, terrify, terrorize, startle *rel, ant* see AFFRIGHT

affright *syn* FRIGHTEN, fright, affray, scare, alarm, terrify, terrorize, startle *rel* daunt, horrify, appall, dismay; cow, intimidate, bulldoze; confound, bewilder, puzzle *ant* nerve, embolden

affront *vb, syn* OFFEND, outrage, insult *rel* slight, ignore, neglect; nettle, peeve, provoke, irritate *ant* gratify (*by an attention*)

affront *n* • a speech or an action having for its intention or effect the dishonoring of something or someone *syn* insult, indignity *rel* slighting, ignoring, overlooking, neglecting; offending, outraging; impudence, brazenness, shamelessness *ant* gratification

afraid *syn* FEARFUL, apprehensive *rel* alarmed, scared, frightened; timorous, timid *ant* unafraid; sanguine

aft *syn* ABAFT, astern *rel* after, behind; rear, back, posterior, hind *ant* fore

after *prep, adj, adv* • following upon, especially in place or in time *syn* behind *rel* abaft, aft, astern *ant* before

after *adj, syn* POSTERIOR, hinder, hind, rear, back

aftereffect, aftermath *syn* EFFECT, result, consequence, upshot, sequel, issue, outcome, event

age *n* **1** • the period in one's life when one is old in years and declining in body or mind or both *syn* senility, senescence, dotage *ant* youth **2** *syn* PERIOD, era, epoch, aeon

age *vb, syn* MATURE, ripen, develop

aged • far advanced in years *syn* old, elderly, superannuated *rel* infirm, feeble, decrepit, weak *ant* youthful

agency *syn* MEAN, agent, instrumentality, instrument, medium, vehicle, channel, organ *rel* cause, determinant, antecedent; operation, action, working; activity; machinery, apparatus, gear, equipment

agenda *syn* PROGRAM, schedule, timetable

agent **1** *syn* MEAN, instrument, agency, instrumentality, medium, vehicle, organ, channel *rel* actor, operator, worker; activator, energizer; performer, executor, executive *ant* patient **2** • one who performs the duties of or transacts business for another *syn* factor, attorney, deputy, proxy *ant* principal

agglomerate, agglomeration *syn* AGGREGATE, conglomerate, conglomeration, aggregation *rel* combination, association; accumulation; heap, pile, mass

aggrandize *syn* EXALT, magnify *rel* heighten, enhance, aggravate, intensify; elevate, raise, lift, boost *ant* belittle

aggravate **1** *syn* INTENSIFY, heighten, enhance *rel* magnify, aggrandize, exalt; augment, increase, multiply, enlarge *ant* alleviate **2** *syn* IRRITATE, exasperate, provoke, rile, peeve, nettle *rel* perturb, upset, disturb, discompose; vex, irk, annoy; anger, incense, infuriate *ant* appease

aggregate **1** *syn* SUM, total, whole, number, amount, quantity *ant* individual; particular **2** • a mass formed by parts or particles that are not merged into each other *syn* aggregation, conglomerate, conglomeration, agglomerate, agglomeration *rel* union, unity, integrity; unification, consolidation; complex, system, organism, network *ant* constituent

aggregation *syn* AGGREGATE, conglomerate, conglomeration, agglomerate, agglomeration *rel, ant* see AGGREGATE 2

aggression *syn* ATTACK, offense, offensive *rel* invasion, incursion, raid, inroad *ant* resistance

aggressive **1** *syn* attacking, offensive *rel* invading, encroaching, trespassing *ant* resisting; repelling **2** • conspicuously or obtrusively active or energetic *syn* militant, assertive, self-assertive, pushing, pushy *rel* energetic, strenuous, vigorous; masterful, domineering, imperious; fighting, combating, combative

aggrieve *syn* WRONG, oppress, persecute *rel* afflict, try, torment; harass, harry, plague, annoy, worry; injure, hurt, harm *ant* rejoice

agile • acting or moving with quickness and alacrity *syn* nimble, brisk, spry *rel* dexterous, adroit, deft; quick, fleet, speedy, fast; limber, lithesome, supple; lively, sprightly *ant* torpid

agitate **1** *syn* SHAKE, rock, convulse *rel* stir, rouse, arouse; move, actuate, drive, impel *ant* quiet, lull, still **2** *syn* DISCOMPOSE, perturb, upset, fluster, flurry, disturb, disquiet *rel* irritate, provoke, rile, exasperate, peeve; worry, harass, plague; annoy, vex, irk, bother *ant* calm, tranquilize **3** *syn* DISCUSS, argue, dispute, debate *rel* controvert, disprove; assail, attack; consider; air, ventilate, broach, express

agitation *syn* COMMOTION, tumult, turmoil, turbulence, confusion, convulsion, upheaval *rel* motion, movement; stir, bustle, ado; disturbance, perturbation, disquiet *ant* tranquillity

agnostic *syn* ATHEIST, deist, freethinker, unbeliever, infidel

agog *syn* EAGER, keen, anxious, avid, athirst *rel* excited, galvanized, stimulated; roused, aroused, stirred; impatient, restive *ant* aloof

agonize *syn* WRITHE, squirm *rel* suffer, endure, bear; torment, rack, torture, afflict

agonizing *syn* EXCRUCIATING, racking *rel* torturing, tormenting, racking; intense, vehement, fierce, exquisite, violent

agony *syn* DISTRESS, suffering, passion, misery, dolor *rel* pang, throe, ache, pain, twinge; trial, tribulation, affliction, visitation

agrarian *syn* agricultural

agree **1** *syn* ASSENT, accede, consent, acquiesce, subscribe *rel* grant, concede, allow; accept, receive; admit, acknowledge *ant* protest (*against*); differ (*with*) **2** • to come into or to be in harmony regarding a matter of opinion or a policy *syn* concur, coincide *rel* unite, cooperate *ant* differ; disagree **3** • to exist or go together without conflict or incongruity *syn* square, conform, accord, harmonize, correspond, tally, jibe *ant* differ (*from*)

agreeable *syn* PLEASANT, grateful, pleasing, gratifying, welcome *rel* comfortable, easy, restful; delightful, delectable; attractive, charming, alluring *ant* disagreeable

agreement • a reconciliation of differences as to what should be done or not done *syn* accord, understanding *rel* pact, entente, concordat, convention, cartel, contract

agriculture • the science or the business of raising useful plants and animals *syn* farming, husbandry

ahead *syn* BEFORE, forward *ant* behind

aid *vb, syn* HELP, assist *rel* support, uphold, back; relieve, lighten, alleviate, mitigate; abet, incite *ant* injure

aid *n* **1** *syn* help, assistance *rel* relief, assuagement, alleviation, mitigation; remedy, cure, medicine; support, backing *ant* impediment **2** *syn* ASSISTANT, helper, coadjutor, aide, aide-de-camp

aide *syn* ASSISTANT, aide-de-camp, coadjutor, helper, aid

aide-de-camp *syn* ASSISTANT, aide, aid

ail *syn* TROUBLE, distress *rel* afflict, try; annoy, vex, irk, bother

ailment *syn* DISEASE, disorder, condition, affection, malady, complaint, distemper, syndrome

aim *vb* **1** *syn* DIRECT, point, level, train, lay *rel* bend, curve, twist **2** • to have as a controlling desire something beyond one's present power of attainment *syn* aspire, pant *rel* intend, purpose, propose, design; attempt, essay, endeavor, try

aim *n, syn* INTENTION, end, goal, objective, purpose, object, intent, design *rel* aspiration, ambition; effort, exertion, pains, trouble

air *n* **1** *syn* POSE, affectation, mannerism *rel* mien, bearing, port, presence; ostentation, pretentiousness, show; art, artifice, craft **2** *syn* MELODY, air, tune

air *vb, syn* EXPRESS, ventilate, vent, utter, voice, broach *rel* reveal, disclose, divulge, tell, discover; publish, proclaim, broadcast, declare

airport • a place where airplanes take off and land *syn* airdrome, airfield, airstrip, landing strip, flying field, landing field

airy • as light and insubstantial as air *syn* aerial, ethereal *rel* tenuous, rare, thin; delicate, dainty, exquisite, choice; light, volatile, frivolous *ant* substantial

aisle *syn* PASSAGE, passageway, ambulatory, corridor, gallery, hall, hallway, cloister, arcade

akin *syn* LIKE, alike, similar, analogous, comparable, parallel, uniform, identical *rel* related, kindred, cognate, allied; corresponding, agreeing, harmonizing, according, conforming *ant* alien

alacrity *syn* CELERITY, legerity *rel* eagerness, avidity, anxiety; quickness, promptness, readiness; agility, nimbleness, briskness; expedition, dispatch, haste *ant* languor

alarm *n* **1** • a signal that serves as a call to action or to be on guard especially in a time of imminent danger *syn* tocsin, alert **2** *syn* FEAR, fright, panic, terror, horror, dismay, dread, consternation, trepidation *rel* frightening, scaring, startling; agitation, perturbation, upset *ant* assurance; composure

alarm *vb, syn* FRIGHTEN, fright, scare, startle, terrify, affright, terrorize, affray *rel* appall, daunt, horrify, dismay; surprise, astound, amaze, astonish *ant* assure; relieve

albeit *syn* THOUGH, although

alchemy *syn* MAGIC, thaumaturgy, wizardry, sorcery, witchery, witchcraft

alcoholic *syn* DRUNKARD, inebriate, dipsomaniac, sot, soak, toper, tosspot, tippler

alert *adj* **1** *syn* WATCHFUL, wide-awake, vigilant *rel* agile, nimble, brisk; wary, circumspect, cautious **2** *syn* INTELLIGENT, clever, smart, bright, quick-witted, brilliant, knowing *rel* sharp, keen, acute; quick, ready, prompt, apt; shrewd, perspicacious

alert *n, syn* ALARM, tocsin

alias *syn* PSEUDONYM, nom de guerre, incognito, nom de plume, pen name

alibi *syn* APOLOGY, excuse, pretext, plea, apologia *rel* explanation, justification, rationalization

alien *adj, syn* EXTRINSIC, foreign, extraneous *rel* external, exterior, outside; adventitious, incidental, accidental; repugnant, repellent, abhorrent; incompatible, incongruous, inconsonant *ant* akin; assimilable

alien *n, syn* STRANGER, foreigner, outlander, outsider, immigrant, émigré *ant* citizen

alienate **1** *syn* TRANSFER, convey, deed **2** *syn* ESTRANGE, disaffect, wean *rel* convert, proselyte, proselytize; separate, part, sever, sunder, divorce *ant* unite; reunite

alienation **1** *syn* ABERRATION, derangement *rel* insanity, lunacy, mania, dementia; imbecility, idiocy, moronity **2** *syn* SOLITUDE, isolation, seclusion

alight **1** *syn* DESCEND, dismount **2** • to come to rest after or as if after a flight, a descent, or a fall *syn* light, land, perch, roost

align *syn* LINE, line up, range, array *rel* order, arrange, marshal; regulate, fix, adjust

alike *syn* LIKE, similar, analogous, comparable, akin, parallel, uniform, identical *rel* same, selfsame, equivalent, identical *ant* different

aliment *syn* FOOD, pabulum, nutriment, nourishment, sustenance, pap

alive **1** *syn* LIVING, animated, animate, vital *rel* active, dynamic, live, operative; lively, vivacious, sprightly; being, existing *ant* dead, defunct **2** *syn* AWARE, awake, sensible, cognizant, conscious *rel* alert, wide-awake, vigilant, watchful; intelligent, knowing, quick-witted *ant* blind (*to*); anesthetic (*to*)

alkaline • being a compound that reacts with an acid to form a salt *syn* basic

all **1** *syn* WHOLE, entire, total, gross *rel* complete, plenary, full **2** • including the entire membership of a group with no exceptions *syn* every, each *ant* no

all-round *syn* VERSATILE, many-sided *rel* complete, full; apt, ready, quick

allay *syn* RELIEVE, alleviate, lighten, assuage, mitigate *rel* abate, lessen, decrease, diminish; mollify, pacify, appease; moderate, temper *ant* intensify

allege *syn* ADDUCE, cite, advance *rel* affirm, assert, declare, profess, avouch, avow; recite, recount, rehearse, state, relate *ant* contravene; (*in law*) traverse

allegiance *syn* FIDELITY, fealty, loyalty, devotion, piety *rel* faithfulness, steadfastness, constancy, staunchness; obeisance, deference, homage, honor; obedience; obligation, duty *ant* treachery; treason

allegory **1** • a concrete representation in art of something that is abstract or for some other reason not directly representable *syn* symbolism **2** • a literary form that typically tells a story for the sake of presenting a truth or of enforcing a moral *syn* parable, myth, fable

alleviate *syn* RELIEVE, lighten, assuage, mitigate, allay *rel* moderate, temper; lessen, reduce, diminish, decrease; remedy, cure *ant* aggravate

alliance • a chiefly political combination for a common object *syn* league, coalition, fusion, confederacy, confederation, federation

allied *syn* RELATED, cognate, kindred, affiliated *rel* akin, parallel, similar, like; linked, associated, united, connected; cooperating, uniting, conjoining *ant* unallied

allocate *syn* ALLOT, assign, apportion *rel* distribute, dispense, divide, deal, dole; grant, accord, award

allot • to give as one's share, portion, role, or place *syn* assign, apportion, allocate *rel* divide, dispense, distribute, deal, dole; give, bestow

allow 1 *syn* LET, permit, suffer, leave *rel* tolerate, endure, stand, brook, bear; accede, acquiesce, assent; yield, submit, defer *ant* inhibit **2** *syn* GRANT, concede *rel* admit, acknowledge, confess; acquiesce, accede, assent *ant* disallow

allowance 1 *syn* RATION, dole, pittance *rel* allotment, apportionment, assignment; share; grant, appropriation, subsidy **2** • a change made by way of compromise or adjustment *syn* concession *rel* adjustment, accommodation, adaptation; modification, variation **3** *syn* ADVANTAGE, handicap, odds, edge

alloy *syn* ADMIXTURE, adulterant

allude *syn* REFER, advert *rel* suggest, imply, hint, intimate

allure *syn* ATTRACT, captivate, charm, fascinate, enchant, bewitch *rel* lure, entice, seduce; invite, solicit, woo, court; beguile, delude, deceive *ant* repel

alluring *syn* ATTRACTIVE, charming, fascinating, bewitching, enchanting, captivating *rel* lovely, fair, beautiful, pretty, bonny; seductive, enticing, tempting, luring; beguiling, delusive *ant* repulsive

ally *syn* PARTNER, colleague, copartner, confederate *rel* associate, comrade, companion, supporter, upholder, backer; cooperator *ant* adversary

almost *syn* NEARLY, approximately, well-nigh

alms *syn* DONATION, benefaction, contribution *rel* charity, philanthropy; dole, pittance, allowance, ration

alone *adj* **1** • isolated from others *syn* solitary, lonely, lonesome, lone, lorn, forlorn, desolate *rel* single, sole, lone, unique; deserted, abandoned, forsaken; isolated, secluded *ant* accompanied **2** *syn* ONLY

alone *adv, syn* ONLY

aloof *syn* INDIFFERENT, detached, uninterested, disinterested, unconcerned, incurious *rel* disdainful, haughty, arrogant, proud; cool, cold; reserved, reticent, silent *ant* familiar, close

alp *syn* MOUNTAIN, peak, mount

also *syn* too, likewise, besides, moreover, furthermore

alter 1 *syn* CHANGE, vary, modify *rel* adjust, accommodate, adapt; qualify, temper, moderate; transform, metamorphose, convert *ant* fix **2** *syn* STERILIZE, castrate, spay, emasculate, mutilate, geld

alteration *syn* CHANGE, variation, modification *rel* adjustment, adaptation, accommodation; transformation, metamorphosis, conversion *ant* fixation; fixity

altercate *vb, syn* QUARREL, wrangle, squabble, bicker, spat, tiff *rel* fight, contend, battle, war; dispute, debate, agitate, discuss *ant* concur

altercation *syn* QUARREL, wrangle, squabble, bickering, spat, tiff *rel* fight, conflict, combat, contest; discord, dissension, contention, difference, variance, strife; controversy, dispute, argument *ant* concurrence; accord

alternate *adj, syn* INTERMITTENT, recurrent, periodic *rel* alternating, rotating; reciprocal, corresponding, complementary *ant* consecutive

alternate *vb, syn* ROTATE *rel* recur, return, revert; oscillate, fluctuate, sway, waver, swing

alternate *n, syn* SUBSTITUTE, supply, understudy, double, stand-in, pinch hitter, locum tenens

alternation *syn* CHANGE, vicissitude, mutation, permutation *rel* rotation; oscillation, fluctuation, wavering; turning, revolving, rotating, wheeling; recurrence, return, reversion

alternative *syn* CHOICE, option, preference, selection, election

although *syn* THOUGH, albeit

altitude *syn* HEIGHT, elevation *rel* highness, tallness, loftiness; summit, peak, apex

altruistic *syn* CHARITABLE, benevolent, humanitarian, philanthropic, eleemosynary *rel* self-abnegating, self-denying; generous, bountiful, bounteous, openhanded, liberal *ant* egoistic

amalgam *syn* MIXTURE, admixture, compound, blend, composite

amalgamate *syn* MIX, blend, commingle, merge, coalesce, fuse, mingle *rel* combine,

unite, link, associate, join; consolidate, unify, compact
amalgamation *syn* CONSOLIDATION, merger
amass *syn* ACCUMULATE, hoard *rel* collect, gather, assemble; heap, pile, mass, stack *ant* distribute
amateur • a person who follows a pursuit without attaining proficiency or a professional status *syn* dilettante, dabbler, tyro *rel* novice, apprentice, probationer *ant* professional; expert
amative *syn* EROTIC, amorous, amatory
amatory *syn* EROTIC, aphrodisiac, amative, amorous
amaze *syn* SURPRISE, astound, flabbergast, astonish *rel* dumbfound, bewilder, confound, nonplus, puzzle; impress, touch, strike, affect
amazement *syn* WONDER, wonderment, admiration
amazon *syn* VIRAGO, termagant
ambassador • a diplomatic agent serving his or her sovereign or government in a foreign country *syn* legate, nuncio, minister, envoy, internuncio, chargé d'affaires
ambiguity • expression or, more often, an expression, capable of more than one interpretation *syn* equivocation, tergiversation, double entendre *ant* lucidity; explicitness
ambiguous *syn* OBSCURE, equivocal, cryptic, enigmatic, vague, dark *rel* dubious, doubtful, questionable *ant* explicit
ambition • strong desire for advancement *syn* aspiration, pretension *rel* urge, lust, desire; eagerness, avidity, keenness, anxiety; spur, goad, incentive, motive
ambitious **1** • extremely desirous of something that will give one power, fame, success, or riches *syn* emulous *rel* eager, avid, anxious, keen; aspiring, panting, aiming; daring, venturesome, adventurous *ant* unambitious **2** • straining or exceeding the capacity of their authors or executants *syn* pretentious, utopian *rel* audacious, bold, brave; daring, adventurous; ostentatious, showy *ant* modest
amble *syn* SAUNTER, stroll *rel* loiter, dawdle, delay; meander, ramble, roam, wander
ambulant *syn* ITINERANT, ambulatory, peripatetic, nomadic, vagrant *ant* bedridden
ambulatory *adj, syn* ITINERANT, ambulant, peripatetic, nomadic, vagrant
ambulatory *n, syn* PASSAGE, passageway, aisle, gallery, cloister, arcade, hall, hallway, corridor
ambuscade *syn* AMBUSH
ambush *vb, syn* SURPRISE, waylay *rel* attack, assault, assail; trap, entrap, snare, ensnare, capture, catch
ambush *n* • a device to entrap an enemy by lying in wait under cover for an opportune moment to make a surprise attack *syn* ambuscade *rel* trap, snare, lure; attack, onset, onslaught, assault
ameliorate *syn* IMPROVE, better, help *rel* amend, remedy, reform, rectify, correct; mitigate, alleviate, relieve, lighten *ant* worsen; deteriorate
amenable **1** *syn* RESPONSIBLE, answerable, liable, accountable *rel* open, subject, liable; subordinate, dependent *ant* independent (*of*); autonomous **2** *syn* OBEDIENT, tractable, docile, biddable *rel* pliant, adaptable, pliable, plastic; responsive, tender; sensitive, open, liable; submissive, tame, subdued *ant* recalcitrant, refractory
amend *syn* CORRECT, reform, rectify, revise, emend, remedy, redress *rel* improve, better, ameliorate; mend, repair; elevate, raise, lift *ant* debase; impair
amends *syn* REPARATION, redress, indemnity, restitution *rel* compensation, recompense, payment; atonement, expiation
amenity **1** • something that gives refined or exquisite pleasure or is exceedingly pleasing to the mind or senses *syn* luxury *rel* pleasure, delight, joy, enjoyment; ease, comfort, relaxation, rest; mildness, softness, blandness, lenity, leniency, gentleness *ant* rigor **2** *syn* COURTESY, attention, gallantry *rel* civility, politeness, courteousness; graciousness, affability, cordiality, geniality, sociability; form, convention, convenance; ceremony, formality, form *ant* acerbity, asperity; rudeness
amerce *syn* PENALIZE, fine, mulct
amercement *syn* FINE
amiable • having or manifesting the desire or disposition to please *syn* good-natured, obliging, complaisant *rel* gracious, cordial, affable, genial; warmhearted, warm, responsive, tender; kindly, kind, benignant, benign *ant* unamiable; surly
amicable • marked by or exhibiting goodwill or absence of antagonism *syn* neighborly, friendly *rel* peaceful, pacific, peace-

able; harmonious, concordant, accordant; social, gregarious, cooperative, hospitable *ant* antagonistic

amiss • otherwise than intended *syn* astray *rel* wrong, wrongly, bad, badly *ant* aright, right

amity *syn* FRIENDSHIP, comity, goodwill *rel* harmony, concord, accord; amicableness, neighborliness, friendliness *ant* enmity

amnesty *syn* PARDON, absolution

among *syn* BETWEEN

amorous *syn* EROTIC, amative, amatory *rel* passionate, fervid, ardent, impassioned; enamored, infatuated; lustful, lascivious, licentious *ant* frigid

amount *syn* SUM, total, quantity, number, aggregate, whole

amour • an instance of illicit sexual relationship *syn* liaison, intrigue, affair

amour propre *syn* CONCEIT, self-esteem, self-love, egoism, egotism *rel* pride, vanity, vainglory; complacency, self-complacency, smugness, self-satisfaction

ample **1** *syn* SPACIOUS, capacious, commodious *rel* expanded, distended, swelled, swollen, inflated; large, big, great *ant* meager; circumscribed **2** *syn* PLENTIFUL, abundant, plenteous, copious *rel* liberal, generous, handsome, bountiful, bounteous; profuse, lavish, prodigal *ant* scant, meager

amplify *syn* EXPAND, swell, distend, dilate, inflate *rel* develop, mature; enlarge, augment, increase *ant* abridge, condense

amplitude *syn* EXPANSE, spread, stretch *rel* largeness, bigness, greatness; spaciousness, commodiousness, capaciousness; magnitude, extent, size; bulk, mass, volume *ant* straitness; limitation

amulet *syn* FETISH, charm, talisman

amuse • to cause or enable one to pass one's time in pleasant or agreeable activity *syn* divert, entertain, recreate *rel* engross, absorb; beguile, while, wile; enliven, quicken, animate; thrill, electrify *ant* bore

amusement • an agreeable activity or its effect *syn* diversion, entertainment, recreation *rel* engrossment, absorption; play, sport, fun, jest; disporting, frolicking, rollicking, romping; jollity, mirth *ant* boredom

anagogic *syn* MYSTICAL, mystic, cabalistic *rel* allegorical, symbolical; occult, esoteric, recondite

analgesic *syn* ANODYNE, anesthetic *ant* irritant

analogous *syn* LIKE, alike, similar, comparable, akin, parallel, uniform, identical *rel* corresponding, convertible, reciprocal; kindred, related, allied, cognate

analogue *syn* PARALLEL, counterpart, correlate

analogy **1** *syn* LIKENESS, similitude, resemblance, similarity, affinity **2** • a comparison between things essentially or generically different but strikingly alike in one or more pertinent aspects *syn* simile, metaphor

analysis • separation of a whole into its fundamental elements or constituent parts *syn* resolution, dissection, breakdown *rel* separation, division; disintegration, decomposition *ant* synthesis

analytical *syn* LOGICAL, subtle *rel* acute, keen, sharp; profound, deep; penetrating, piercing; organizing, ordering, marshaling *ant* creative, inventive, constructive

analyze • to divide a complex whole or unit into its component parts or constituent elements *syn* resolve, dissect, break down *rel* separate, divide, part; classify, pigeonhole, assort *ant* compose, compound; construct

anarchy • absence, suspension, breakdown, or widespread defiance of government, law, and order *syn* chaos, lawlessness *ant* order; discipline

anathema **1** *syn* ABOMINATION, bête noire, bugbear **2** *syn* CURSE, malediction, imprecation *rel* denunciation, condemnation, reprobation, censure, criticism

anathematize *syn* EXECRATE, curse, damn, objurgate *rel* denounce, condemn, censure, reprobate, criticize; proscribe, sentence

anatomy *syn* STRUCTURE, skeleton, framework

ancestor • a person from whom one is descended *syn* progenitor, forefather, forebear *ant* descendant

ancestry • one's progenitors or their character or quality as a whole *syn* lineage, pedigree *ant* descendants; posterity

anchor *syn* SECURE, rivet *rel* fasten, attach, fix, affix

anchorite *syn* RECLUSE, hermit, eremite, cenobite *rel* ascetic, mystic; religious, monk, friar

ancient *syn* OLD, venerable, antediluvian,

antique, antiquated, archaic, obsolete *rel* primeval, pristine, primal, primordial *ant* modern

ancillary *syn* AUXILIARY, contributory, subsidiary, adjuvant, subservient, accessory *rel* assisting, aiding, helping; secondary, subordinate; supplementary, complementary

androgynous *syn* BISEXUAL, hermaphroditic, hermaphrodite, epicene

anecdote *syn* STORY, tale, yarn, narrative *rel* incident, episode, event, occurrence; narration, relation, recital

anemic *syn* PALE, bloodless *ant* full-blooded; florid

anesthetic *adj, syn* INSENSIBLE, insensitive, impassible *rel* dull, obtuse; impassive, apathetic, stolid; impervious, impermeable, impenetrable, impassable *ant* alive

anesthetic *n, syn* ANODYNE, analgesic *ant* stimulant

angel *syn* SPONSOR, backer, patron, surety, guarantor

anger *n* • emotional excitement induced by intense displeasure *syn* ire, rage, fury, indignation, wrath *rel* acrimony, asperity; exasperation, irritation, provocation *ant* pleasure, gratification; forbearance

anger *vb* • to make angry *syn* incense, enrage, infuriate, madden *rel* offend, outrage, affront; exasperate, provoke, irritate, nettle, rile; vex, annoy, irk *ant* please, gratify; pacify

angle **1** *syn* POINT OF VIEW, viewpoint, standpoint, slant *rel* attitude, position, stand **2** *syn* PHASE, aspect, facet, side *rel* item, detail, particular

angry • feeling or showing strong displeasure or bad temper *syn* irate, indignant, wrathful, wroth, acrimonious, mad *rel* impassioned, passionate; angered, incensed, enraged, infuriated, maddened

anguish *syn* SORROW, woe, heartache, heartbreak, grief, regret *rel* distress, suffering, dolor, misery, agony; worry, anxiety, care; pain, pang, throe, ache; torture, torment, affliction *ant* relief

angular *syn* LEAN, gaunt, rawboned, lank, lanky, spare, scrawny, skinny *rel* thin, slender, slim; awkward, clumsy; cadaverous, haggard *ant* rotund

animadversion • a remark or statement that is an adverse criticism *syn* stricture, aspersion, reflection *rel* criticism, reprehension, censure; observation, comment, remark; captiousness, faultfinding, caviling, carping, censoriousness *ant* commendation

animadvert *syn* REMARK, comment, commentate *rel* criticize, reprehend, censure, reprobate; deprecate, disapprove; depreciate, disparage, decry

animal *syn* CARNAL, fleshly, sensual *rel* physical, corporeal, bodily; bestial, brutal *ant* rational

animalism *syn* ANIMALITY *rel* sensualism, voluptuousness; lustfulness, lasciviousness, lecherousness

animality • the animal aspect or quality of human beings or human nature *syn* animalism *rel* virility, maleness, masculinity

animate *adj, syn* LIVING, alive, animated, vital *rel* physical, corporeal, bodily; animal, carnal, fleshly *ant* inanimate

animate *vb* **1** *syn* QUICKEN, vivify, enliven *rel* vitalize, activate, energize **2** *syn* INFORM, inspire, fire *rel* motivate, actuate, activate; move, drive, impel, actuate; stir, rouse, arouse *ant* inhibit

animated **1** *syn* LIVING, alive, animate, vital *rel* active, live, dynamic; vitalized, energized, activated *ant* inert **2** *syn* LIVELY, vivacious, sprightly, gay *rel* buoyant, volatile, effervescent; agile, brisk, spry, nimble; spirited, high-spirited *ant* depressed, dejected

animosity *syn* ENMITY, animus, rancor, hostility, antipathy, antagonism *rel* hatred, hate, detestation, abhorrence; vindictiveness, revengefulness, vengefulness; malice, ill will, malevolence, spite *ant* goodwill

animus *syn* ENMITY, animosity, rancor, hostility, antipathy, antagonism *rel* ill will, spite, spleen, grudge, malice; prejudice, bias *ant* favor

annals *syn* HISTORY, chronicle

annex *vb, syn* ADD, append, subjoin, superadd *rel* join, unite, connect, link, associate; attach, affix, fasten

annex *n* • an addition to a main (and, often, the original) building *syn* extension, wing, ell *rel* addition, increment, accretion

annihilate *syn* ABOLISH, extinguish, abate *rel* obliterate, efface, expunge, blot out, cancel, erase; extirpate, exterminate, eradicate, wipe

annotate • to add or append comment *syn* gloss *rel* elucidate, interpret, construe, explain, expound; comment, commentate, remark

annotation • added or appended comment intended to be helpful in interpreting a passage or text *syn* gloss *rel* commentary, comment, observation, note, remark

announce *syn* DECLARE, publish, proclaim, promulgate, advertise, broadcast *rel* disclose, reveal, divulge, tell; communicate, impart

announcement *syn* DECLARATION, publication, proclamation, promulgation, advertisement, broadcasting

annoy **1** • to disturb and nervously upset a person *syn* vex, irk, bother *rel* irritate, nettle, aggravate, exasperate, rile; perturb, disturb, upset, agitate, discompose *ant* soothe **2** *syn* WORRY, pester, plague, tantalize, tease, harass, harry *rel* fret, chafe, abrade; badger, hector, heckle, chivy, bait; trouble, inconvenience

annul **1** *syn* NULLIFY, negate, invalidate, abrogate *rel* neutralize, negative, counteract; cancel, efface, obliterate, blot out, erase; annihilate, abolish, extinguish **2** • to deprive of legal validity, force, or authority *syn* abrogate, void, vacate, quash

anodyne **1** • something used to relieve or prevent pain *syn* analgesic, anesthetic **2** • something used to dull or deaden one's senses or one's sensibility *syn* opiate, narcotic, nepenthe *ant* stimulant; irritant

anoint *syn* OIL, cream, grease, lubricate

anomalous *syn* IRREGULAR, unnatural *rel* abnormal, aberrant, atypical; monstrous, prodigious; singular, unique, peculiar, strange

anomaly *syn* PARADOX, antinomy

answer *n* • something spoken or written by way of return to a question or demand *syn* reply, response, rejoinder, retort *rel* defense, vindication, justification refutation, rebuttal

answer *vb* **1** • to say, write, or do something in response *syn* respond, reply, rejoin, retort *rel* acknowledge, recognize; disprove, refute, rebut; defend, justify, vindicate, maintain **2** *syn* SATISFY, meet, fulfill

answerable *syn* RESPONSIBLE, accountable, amenable, liable *rel* obliged, constrained, compelled; subject, subordinate

antagonism *syn* ENMITY, antipathy, hostility, animosity, rancor, animus *rel* opposition, resistance, withstanding, contesting, fighting, combating, conflict; strife, difference, variance, dissension, contention, discord *ant* accord; comity

antagonist *syn* OPPONENT, adversary *rel* foe, enemy; rival, competitor; assailant, attacker *ant* supporter

antagonistic *syn* ADVERSE, counteractive, counter *rel* opposing, resisting, withstanding, contesting, fighting, combating, conflicting; incompatible, discordant, inconsonant; hostile; antipathetic, averse *ant* favoring, favorable

antagonize *syn* RESIST, withstand, contest, oppose, fight, combat, conflict *rel* attack, assail, assault; offend, outrage, affront, insult; incite, foment, instigate *ant* conciliate

ante *syn* BET, stake, pot, wager

antecedent *n, syn* CAUSE, determinant, reason, occasion *rel* precursor, forerunner; progenitor, forebear, ancestor *ant* consequence

antecedent *adj, syn* PRECEDING, precedent, foregoing, previous, prior, former, anterior *ant* subsequent; consequent

antediluvian *syn* OLD, ancient, antiquated, obsolete, antique, venerable, archaic *rel* primordial, primeval, primal, pristine, primary; early

anterior *syn* PRECEDING, precedent, previous, prior, foregoing, antecedent, former *ant* posterior

anthropoid • resembling man *syn* anthropomorphic, anthropomorphous

anthropomorphic, anthropomorphous *syn* ANTHROPOID

antic *n, syn* PRANK, monkeyshine, caper, dido *rel* trick, wile, artifice; caprice, freak, vagary, whim; gambol, frolic, romp

antic *adj, syn* FANTASTIC, grotesque, bizarre *rel* preposterous, absurd, foolish; ludicrous, ridiculous, comic, comical, farcical, laughable

anticipate **1** *syn* PREVENT, forestall *rel* introduce, enter; foretell, forecast, presage; frustrate, thwart, balk *ant* consummate **2** *syn* FORESEE, apprehend, foreknow, divine *rel* foretell, forecast, prognosticate; foretaste; await, expect

anticipation *syn* PROSPECT, foretaste, outlook *rel* foreseeing, foreknowing; presentiment, foreboding, apprehension; forecast, prophecy, prediction, presage; conceiving, envisioning, imagining *ant* retrospect

antidote *syn* CORRECTIVE, check, control *rel* counteractive, neutralizer; nullifier, negator, annuller; remedy, medicine, physic

antinomy *syn* PARADOX, anomaly *rel* opposite, contradictory, contrary, antithesis; contradiction, denial; conflict, variance, discord

antipathetic • arousing marked aversion or dislike *syn* unsympathetic *rel* repellent, repugnant, distasteful, abhorrent, obnoxious; offensive, loathsome, repulsive, revolting *ant* congenial

antipathy **1** *syn* ENMITY, antagonism, hostility, animosity, rancor, animus *rel* repugnance, abhorrence, repellency, distaste; avoidance, evasion, eschewal, escape *ant* taste (*for*); affection (*for*) **2** • the state of mind created by what is antipathetic *syn* aversion *rel, ant* see ANTIPATHY 1

antipodal, antipodean *syn* OPPOSITE, antithetical, contrary, contradictory, antonymous

antipode *syn* OPPOSITE, antithesis, contrary, opposite, contradictory, antonym *rel* converse, counter, reverse

antiquated *syn* OLD, archaic, obsolete, antediluvian, antique, ancient, venerable *rel* superannuated, aged *ant* modernistic; modish

antique *syn* OLD, ancient, venerable, antiquated, antediluvian, obsolete, archaic *ant* modern; current

antisocial *syn* UNSOCIAL, asocial, nonsocial *rel* anarchic, anarchistic, anarchist; misanthropic, pessimistic, cynical *ant* social

antithesis **1** *syn* COMPARISON, contrast, parallel, collation **2** *syn* OPPOSITE, antipode, contradictory, contrary, antonym *rel* converse, counter, reverse

antithetical *syn* OPPOSITE, contrary, contradictory, antonymous, antipodal, antipodean

antonym *syn* OPPOSITE, contradictory, contrary, antithesis, antipode *rel* converse, counter, reverse

antonymous *syn* OPPOSITE, contradictory, contrary, antithetical, antipodal, antipodean

anxiety *syn* CARE, worry, concern, solicitude *rel* distress, suffering, misery; fear, dread, alarm, panic; apprehension, foreboding, misgiving; doubt, uncertainty, mistrust *ant* security

anxious **1** *syn* WORRIED, concerned, solicitous *rel* fearful, apprehensive, afraid; uneasy, jittery, impatient; perturbed, agitated, upset *ant* composed **2** *syn* EAGER, keen, agog, avid *rel* desiring, desirous, wishing, wishful, craving; yearning, longing, pining *ant* loath

apartment *syn* ROOM, chamber

apathetic *syn* IMPASSIVE, phlegmatic, stolid, stoic *rel* insensitive, impassible, insensible, anesthetic; callous, hardened; unaffected, untouched, unimpressed; listless, spiritless, languid *ant* alert; aghast

apathy *syn* IMPASSIVITY, impassiveness, phlegm, stolidity, stoicism *rel* inertness, inactivity, passiveness, supineness; indifference, unconcern, aloofness, detachment; lethargy, torpidity, torpor *ant* zeal; enthusiasm

ape *syn* COPY, imitate, mimic, mock *rel* caricature, burlesque; emulate, rival

aperçu *syn* COMPENDIUM, sketch, précis, survey, digest, pandect, syllabus *rel* epitome, brief, abstract, abridgment

aperitif *syn* APPETIZER

aperture • an opening allowing passage through or in and out *syn* interstice, orifice *rel* perforation, puncture, bore, prick; hole, hollow, cavity; slit, slash, cut

apex *syn* SUMMIT, peak, culmination, pinnacle, climax, acme, meridian, zenith, apogee

aphorism *syn* SAYING, apothegm, epigram, saw, maxim, adage, proverb, motto

aphrodisiac *syn* EROTIC, amatory, amorous *ant* anaphrodisiac

apiece *syn* EACH, severally, individually, respectively

aplomb *syn* CONFIDENCE, assurance, self-assurance, self-possession, self-confidence *rel* coolness, collectedness, nonchalance, imperturbability; equanimity, composure, sangfroid; poise, savoir faire, tact *ant* shyness

apocalypse *syn* REVELATION, vision, prophecy

apocryphal *syn* FICTITIOUS, mythical, legendary, fabulous *rel* questionable, dubious, doubtful

apogee *syn* SUMMIT, climax, peak, culmination, apex, acme, meridian, zenith, pinnacle *ant* perigee

apologia *syn* APOLOGY, excuse, plea, alibi, pretext *rel* defense, justification, vindication; interpretation, elucidation, explanation

apology • the reason or reasons offered in explanation or defense of something (as an act, a policy, or a view) *syn* apologia, excuse, plea, pretext, alibi *rel* defense, justification, vindication; extenuation, palliation, glozing, whitewashing; amends, reparation

apostasy *syn* DEFECTION, desertion

apostate *syn* RENEGADE, turncoat, recreant, backslider *rel* deserter, forsaker, abandoner; heretic, schismatic, dissenter, nonconformist

apothecary *syn* DRUGGIST, pharmacist, chemist

apothegm *syn* SAYING, aphorism, epigram, saw, maxim, adage, proverb, motto

apotheosis *syn* PARAGON, nonpareil, nonesuch

appall *syn* DISMAY, horrify, daunt *rel* terrify, affright, frighten; confound, dumbfound, bewilder, puzzle *ant* nerve, embolden

appalling *syn* FEARFUL, dreadful, terrible, horrible, frightful, shocking, awful, terrific, horrific *rel* dismaying, horrifying, daunting; bewildering, dumbfounding, confounding *ant* reassuring

appanage *syn* RIGHT, prerogative, privilege, perquisite, birthright

apparatus **1** *syn* EQUIPMENT, gear, tackle, outfit, paraphernalia, machinery, matériel *rel* tool, implement, utensil, instrument; network, system, scheme **2** *syn* MACHINE, mechanism, machinery, engine, motor *rel* device, contrivance, contraption, gadget

apparel *vb, syn* CLOTHE, attire, dress, array, robe *rel* outfit, accouter, appoint, equip, furnish *ant* divest

apparel *n, syn* CLOTHES, clothing, dress, attire, raiment

apparent **1** *syn* EVIDENT, manifest, patent, distinct, obvious, palpable, plain, clear *rel* discernible, noticeable; perceptible, ponderable, tangible, appreciable *ant* unintelligible **2** • not actually being what appearance indicates *syn* illusory, seeming, ostensible *rel* false, wrong; deceptive, delusory, delusive, misleading; specious, credible, plausible *ant* real

apparition • a visible but immaterial appearance of a person or thing, esp. a likeness of a dead person or of a person or thing that is not physically present *syn* phantasm, phantom, wraith, ghost, spirit, specter, shade, revenant *rel* illusion, delusion, hallucination

appeal *n, syn* PRAYER, plea, petition, suit *rel* entreating, entreaty, beseeching, supplicating, supplication, imploring; soliciting, solicitation, requesting, request, asking

appeal *vb, syn* PRAY, plead, sue, petition *rel* implore, beg, beseech, entreat, supplicate; solicit, request, ask

appear **1** • to come out into view *syn* loom, emerge *rel* come, arrive; issue, emanate, rise, arise, spring *ant* disappear; vanish **2** *syn* SEEM, look

appearance • the outward show presented by a person or thing *syn* look, aspect, semblance

appease *syn* PACIFY, placate, mollify, propitiate, conciliate *rel* assuage, alleviate, mitigate, lighten, relieve; palliate, extenuate; satisfy, content *ant* exasperate, aggravate

appellation *syn* NAME, title, designation, denomination, style

append *syn* ADD, subjoin, annex, superadd *rel* affix, attach, fasten

appendage • something regarded as additional and at the same time as subsidiary to another object *syn* appurtenance, accessory, adjunct

appendix • additional matter subjoined to a book *syn* addendum, supplement

apperception *syn* RECOGNITION, assimilation, identification

appertain *syn* BEAR, pertain, belong, relate, apply

appetite *syn* DESIRE, lust, passion, urge *rel* hungering, hunger, thirsting, thirst, yearning, longing; craving, wishing, coveting impulse, spring, motive; cupidity, greed

appetizer *syn* hors d'oeuvre, aperitif

appetizing *syn* PALATABLE, relishing, tasty, toothsome, flavorsome, savory, sapid *ant* nauseating

applaud **1** • to demonstrate one's feeling, esp. one's approbation or joy, audibly and enthusiastically *syn* cheer, root *rel* acclaim, extol, praise *ant* hiss; boo **2** *syn* COMMEND, compliment, recommend *rel* praise, eulogize, laud; approve, endorse, sanction *ant* disparage; criticize

applause • public expression of approbation *syn* acclamation, acclaim, plaudits *rel* cheering, cheers, rooting *ant* hisses; boos

appliance *syn* IMPLEMENT, tool, instrument, utensil *rel* accessory, adjunct; device, contrivance, gadget

applicable *syn* RELEVANT, pertinent, apposite, apropos, germane, material *rel* fit, suitable, appropriate, apt, felicitous, happy, meet, fitting, proper *ant* inapplicable

applicant *syn* CANDIDATE, aspirant

application *syn* ATTENTION, concentration, study *rel* intentness, engrossment, absorption; toil, grind, drudgery, work; sedulousness, assiduousness, industriousness, industry, diligence *ant* indolence

appliqué *syn* OVERLAY, superpose, superimpose *rel* ornament, adorn, decorate; affix, attach, fasten

apply **1** *syn* USE, employ, utilize, avail **2** *syn* DIRECT, devote, address *rel* attend, mind, tend; addict, accustom, habituate; toil, labor, work, grind **3** *syn* RESORT, go, turn, refer *rel* appeal, petition; beg, beseech, implore, supplicate **4** *syn* BEAR, relate, pertain, appertain

appoint **1** *syn* DESIGNATE, name, nominate, elect *rel* choose, select, pick, single; commission, authorize, accredit **2** *syn* FURNISH, equip, accouter, outfit, arm *rel* garnish, beautify, embellish, bedeck, deck, adorn; array, clothe

appointment *syn* ENGAGEMENT, rendezvous, tryst, assignation, date

apportion **1** *syn* ALLOT, allocate, assign *rel* distribute, divide, dispense, deal, dole; share, participate, partake **2** • to divide something carefully and distribute it among a number *syn* portion, parcel, ration, prorate *rel* grant, accord, award; give, bestow; separate, divide, part

apposite *syn* RELEVANT, pertinent, germane, apropos, applicable, material *rel* felicitous, happy, apt, appropriate, suitable, fit, fitting; pat, timely, opportune, seasonable *ant* inapposite, inapt

appraise *syn* ESTIMATE, value, evaluate, assay, rate, assess *rel* judge, adjudge; determine, ascertain, discover; inspect, examine, scrutinize, audit

appreciable *syn* PERCEPTIBLE, sensible, ponderable, palpable, tangible *rel* apparent, evident; discernible, noticeable *ant* inappreciable

appreciate **1** *syn* UNDERSTAND, comprehend *rel* appraise, value, rate, estimate, evaluate; judge, adjudge; apprehend, comprehend *ant* depreciate **2** • to hold in high estimation *syn* value, prize, treasure, cherish *rel* admire, esteem, respect, regard; enjoy, like, relish *ant* despise

apprehend **1** *syn* ARREST, detain, attach *rel* seize, take; capture, catch **2** • to lay hold of something with the mind so as to know it *syn* comprehend *rel* understand, appreciate; grasp, take; perceive, observe, notice, note, see **3** *syn* FORESEE, divine, anticipate, foreknow *rel* fear, dread forecast, predict, forebode, foretell

apprehension **1** *syn* ARREST, detention, attachment *rel* seizing, seizure, taking; capturing, capture, catching **2** • something that is known *syn* comprehension *rel* understanding, appreciation; perceiving, perception, observing, observation, noticing, notice, noting **3** • fear (or an instance of it) that something is going wrong or will go wrong *syn* foreboding, misgiving, presentiment *rel* fear, dread, alarm, panic; worry, anxiety, care *ant* confidence

apprehensive *syn* FEARFUL, afraid *rel* anxious, worried, solicitous; nervous, uneasy, jittery *ant* confident

apprentice *syn* NOVICE, novitiate, probationer, postulant, neophyte *rel* beginner, starter; tyro, amateur

apprise *syn* INFORM, advise, notify, acquaint *rel* tell, reveal, disclose, divulge, discover, betray; publish, proclaim, declare, announce

approach *vb* **1** • to come or draw close (to) *syn* near, approximate *rel* accost, address; begin, commence, initiate; consult, confer, advise, negotiate **2** *syn* MATCH, touch, equal, rival

approach *n, syn* OVERTURE, advance, tender, bid *rel* attempt, endeavor, essay, try *ant* repulse

approbation • warmly commending acceptance or agreement *syn* approval *rel* admiration, esteem, respect, regard; applause, acclaim, acclamation, plaudits *ant* disapprobation

appropriate *vb, syn* ARROGATE, preempt,

confiscate, usurp *rel* take, seize, grab; annex, add

appropriate *adj, syn* FIT, fitting, proper, suitable, apt, meet, happy, felicitous *rel* apposite, pertinent, germane, relevant; pat, timely, seasonable, opportune *ant* inappropriate

appropriation • money or property given or set apart by an authorized body for a predetermined use by others *syn* grant, subvention, subsidy

approval *syn* APPROBATION *rel* commending, commendation, applauding, applause, compliment; endorsing, endorsement, sanction *ant* disapproval

approve • to have or to express a favorable opinion of *syn* endorse, sanction, accredit, certify *rel* commend, applaud, compliment; ratify, confirm *ant* disapprove

approximate *syn* APPROACH, near

approximately *syn* NEARLY, almost, well-nigh *ant* precisely, exactly

appurtenance *syn* APPENDAGE, accessory, adjunct *rel* furnishing, furniture, equipment, appointment

apropos *syn* RELEVANT, apposite, pertinent, germane, applicable, material *rel* pat, timely, opportune, seasonable; appropriate, fitting, fit, suitable, apt, proper, meet, happy *ant* unapropos

apt **1** *syn* FIT, happy, felicitous, appropriate, fitting, suitable, meet, proper *rel* apposite, pertinent, relevant, apropos; pat, timely, opportune, seasonable; telling, convincing, compelling, valid; right, nice, precise, exact, correct *ant* inapt, inept **2** *syn* likely, liable *rel* inclined, disposed, predisposed; prone **3** *syn* QUICK, prompt, ready *rel* clever, smart, bright, intelligent, quick-witted, alert; gifted, talented

aptitude *syn* GIFT, bent, turn, talent, faculty, knack, genius *rel* taste, gusto, zest; propensity, leaning, penchant, flair *ant* inaptitude

aqueduct *syn* CHANNEL, canal, conduit, duct

arbiter *syn* JUDGE, arbitrator, umpire, referee

arbitrary *syn* ABSOLUTE, autocratic, despotic, tyrannical, tyrannous *rel* dictatorial, authoritarian, magisterial, oracular; domineering, masterful, imperious, peremptory, imperative *ant* legitimate

arbitrate *syn* JUDGE, adjudicate, adjudge *rel* mediate, intervene, interpose; decide, determine, settle; conciliate, placate, appease, pacify

arbitrator *syn* JUDGE, referee, arbiter, umpire

arc *syn* CURVE, arch, bow

arcade *syn* PASSAGE, gallery, cloister, ambulatory, passageway, corridor, hall, hallway, aisle

arcane *syn* MYSTERIOUS, inscrutable *rel* occult, esoteric, recondite; cabalistic, anagogic, mystic, mystical

arch *n, syn* CURVE, bow, arc

arch *adj, syn* SAUCY, pert *rel* roguish, waggish, impish, mischievous, playful; mocking, deriding, derisive, twitting

archaic *syn* OLD, obsolete, antiquated, antique, ancient, antediluvian, venerable *ant* up-to-date

architect *syn* ARTIST, artificer, artisan

archive *syn* DOCUMENT, record, monument

arctic *syn* COLD, frigid, freezing, frosty, icy, gelid, glacial, chilly, cool *ant* torrid

ardent *syn* IMPASSIONED, passionate, fervid, perfervid, fervent *rel* intense, fierce; enthusiastic, zealous; eager, avid, keen; glowing, flaming, blazing *ant* cool

ardor *syn* PASSION, fervor, enthusiasm, zeal *rel* excitement, stimulation, quickening, galvanizing; eagerness, avidity; zest, gusto *ant* coolness; indifference

arduous *syn* HARD, difficult *rel* laborious, toilsome; exhausting, wearying, wearisome, tiring, fatiguing; onerous, exacting, oppressive *ant* light, facile

area **1** • a distinguishable extent of surface and esp. of the earth's surface *syn* tract, region, zone, belt *rel* locality, district; expanse, stretch **2** *syn* SIZE, extent, dimensions, magnitude, volume

argot *syn* DIALECT, cant, jargon, slang, lingo, vernacular, patois

argue **1** *syn* DISCUSS, debate, dispute, agitate *rel* prove, demonstrate; disprove, refute, rebut, controvert; expostulate, protest, object, remonstrate **2** *syn* INDICATE, bespeak, prove, attest, betoken *rel* show, manifest, evidence, demonstrate, evince; imply, suggest, intimate

argument **1** *syn* REASON, proof, ground *rel* proving, demonstrating, demonstration; disproving, disproof, refuting, refutation, rebutting, rebuttal **2** • a vigorous and often heated discussion of a moot question *syn* dispute, controversy *rel* argumentation, disputation, debate; controverting, refuting, rebutting; contention, dissension, discord **3** *syn* SUBJECT, theme, matter, subject matter, topic, text, motive, motif, leitmotiv

argumentation • the act or art of argument or an exercise of one's powers of argument *syn* disputation, debate, forensic, dialectic *rel* argument, dispute, controversy

arid *syn* DRY *rel* barren, infertile, sterile, unfruitful; bare, bald, barren; desiccated, dehydrated, parched *ant* moist; verdant

arise **1** *syn* RISE, ascend, mount, soar, levitate, surge, tower, rocket *rel* lift, raise, elevate, rear *ant* recline; slump **2** *syn* SPRING, rise, originate, derive, flow, issue, emanate, proceed, stem *rel* emerge, appear, loom; begin, commence, start; ensue, succeed, follow

aristocracy **1** *syn* OLIGARCHY, plutocracy **2** • a body of persons who constitute a socially superior caste *syn* nobility, gentry, county, elite, society *ant* people, proletariat

aristocrat *syn* GENTLEMAN, patrician *ant* commoner

arm *syn* FURNISH, accouter, outfit, equip, appoint *ant* disarm

armistice *syn* TRUCE, cease-fire, peace

army *syn* MULTITUDE, host, legion *rel* throng, press, crush, crowd, mob, rout, horde

aroma *syn* SMELL, odor, scent *rel* fragrance, perfume, redolence, incense, bouquet; savor, taste *ant* stink, stench

aromatic *syn* ODOROUS, balmy, redolent, fragrant *rel* spicy, pungent, piquant; savory, palatable *ant* acrid (*of odors*)

arouse *syn* STIR, rouse, awaken, waken, rally *rel* stimulate, quicken, galvanize, excite, provoke; electrify, thrill; kindle, fire, light; move, drive, impel *ant* quiet, calm

arraign *syn* ACCUSE, charge, impeach, indict, incriminate *rel* summon, cite; try, test

arrange **1** *syn* ORDER, marshal, organize, systematize, methodize *rel* dispose; line, line up, range, array, align; assort, classify, pigeonhole, sort *ant* derange, disarrange **2** *syn* NEGOTIATE, concert *rel* plan, design, scheme, project

arrant *syn* OUTRIGHT, out-and-out, unmitigated

array *vb* **1** *syn* LINE, line up, range, align *rel* marshal, arrange, order *ant* disarray **2** *syn* CLOTHE, apparel, attire, robe, dress

array *n, syn* DISPLAY, parade, pomp *rel* showing, show, exhibiting, exhibition, exposing, exposition; arranging, arrangement, marshaling; disposition

arrear *syn* DEBT, indebtedness, debit, obligation, liability

arrest *vb* **1** • to stop in midcourse *syn* check, interrupt *rel* interpose, intervene, interfere; delay, detain, retard; frustrate, thwart, balk *ant* activate; quicken **2** • to seize and hold under restraint or in custody by authority of the law *syn* apprehend, attach, detain *rel* seize, take; catch, capture; imprison, incarcerate, jail

arrest *n* • seizing and holding under restraint or in custody by authority of the law *syn* apprehension, detention, attachment *rel* seizing, seizure, taking; capturing, capture, catching

arresting *syn* NOTICEABLE, striking, remarkable, outstanding, salient, signal, prominent, conspicuous *rel* impressive, moving, touching, affecting, poignant; fascinating, attractive, enchanting

arrival • the reaching of a destination *syn* advent *rel* coming; appearing, appearance, emerging, emergence *ant* departure

arrive *syn* COME *ant* depart

arrogant *syn* PROUD, haughty, lordly, insolent, overbearing, supercilious, disdainful *rel* imperious, domineering, masterful, peremptory, imperative; pretentious, ostentatious, showy *ant* meek; unassuming

arrogate • to seize or take over in a high-handed manner *syn* usurp, preempt, appropriate, confiscate *rel* seize, take, grab *ant* renounce; yield

art **1** • the faculty of performing or executing expertly what is planned or devised *syn* skill, cunning, artifice, craft **2** *syn* TRADE, craft, handicraft, profession

artery *syn* WAY, route, course, passage, pass

artful *syn* SLY, wily, guileful, crafty, cunning, tricky, foxy, insidious *rel* adroit, dexterous; politic, diplomatic, smooth, suave *ant* artless

article **1** *syn* PARAGRAPH, clause, plank, count, verse **2** *syn* THING, object *rel* item, detail, particular **3** *syn* ESSAY, paper, theme, composition

articled *syn* BOUND, indentured, bond

articulate *adj* **1** *syn* VOCAL, oral *rel* distinct, clear, evident; uttered, voiced *ant* inarticulate, dumb **2** *syn* VOCAL, fluent, eloquent, voluble, glib *rel* expressing, voicing, uttering, venting; expressive, meaningful, significant; voluble, glib, talkative *ant* inarticulate, dumb

articulate *vb* **1** *syn* INTEGRATE, concatenate *rel* unite, join, connect, link, relate; organize, systematize, methodize, order **2** • to form speech sounds *syn* pronounce, enunciate

articulation **1** *syn* INTEGRATION, concatenation *rel* organization, systematizing, methodizing; system, organism, economy, scheme, complex **2** *syn* JOINT, suture

artifact *syn* WORK, product, production, opus

artifice **1** *syn* ART, cunning, craft, skill *rel* ingeniousness, ingenuity, cleverness, adroitness; adeptness, proficiency, expertness **2** *syn* TRICK, ruse, wile, stratagem, maneuver, gambit, ploy, feint *rel* deception, chicanery, chicane, trickery; deceit, guile, duplicity, dissimulation

artificer *syn* ARTIST, artisan, architect *rel* craftsman, handicraftsman, mechanic, workman, worker

artificial • not brought into being by nature but by human art or effort or by some process of manufacture *syn* factitious, synthetic, ersatz *rel* fabricated, manufactured, fashioned; simulated, feigned, counterfeited, counterfeit *ant* natural

artisan **1** *syn* ARTIST, artificer, architect **2** *syn* WORKER, mechanic, workman, workingman, operative, craftsman, handicraftsman, hand, laborer, roustabout

artist **1** • one who makes something beautiful or useful or both *syn* artificer, artisan, architect *rel* craftsman, workman, worker; creator, maker; writer, composer, author **2** *syn* EXPERT, artiste, virtuoso, adept, wizard

artiste *syn* EXPERT, artist, virtuoso, adept, wizard

artless *syn* NATURAL, simple, ingenuous, naïve, unsophisticated, unaffected *rel* spontaneous, impulsive; candid, open, plain, frank; straightforward, aboveboard, forthright *ant* artful; affected

as *syn* BECAUSE, since, for, inasmuch as

ascend **1** *syn* RISE, arise, mount, soar, tower, rocket, levitate, surge *rel* elevate, raise, rear, lift; advance, progress *ant* descend **2** • to move upward to or toward a summit *syn* mount, climb, scale *ant* descend

ascendancy *syn* SUPREMACY *rel* dominance, predominance; command, sway, dominion, control, power, authority; sovereignty

ascension • the act of moving upward or the movement upward *syn* ascent

ascent *syn* ASCENSION

ascertain *syn* DISCOVER, determine, unearth, learn *rel* inquire, query, interrogate, ask; study, contemplate, weigh, consider; observe, survey, see

ascetic *syn* SEVERE, austere, stern *rel* disciplined, trained, schooled; self-denying, self-abnegating; abstaining, abstinent, forbearing; abstemious *ant* luxurious, voluptuous, sensuous

ascribe • to lay something (creditable, discreditable, or neutral) to the account of a person or thing *syn* attribute, impute, assign, refer, credit, accredit, charge *rel* attach, fasten, affix; conjecture, surmise, guess; allege, advance, adduce, cite

ash • the remains of combustible material after it has been destroyed by fire *syn* cinders, clinkers, embers

ashamed • acutely or manifestly conscious of embarrassment and humiliation *syn* mortified, chagrined *rel* embarrassed, discomfited, abashed; humiliated, humbled, abased; abject, mean; contrite, penitent, repentant *ant* proud

ashen *syn* PALE, ashy, livid, pallid, wan *rel* ghastly, grim, macabre; blanched, bleached, decolorized, whitened

ashy *syn* PALE, ashen, livid, pallid, wan *rel* see ASHEN

asinine *syn* SIMPLE, fatuous, silly, foolish *rel* stupid, crass, dumb, dense, dull, slow; puerile, youthful; irrational, unreasonable *ant* sensible, judicious

ask **1** • to address a person in an attempt to elicit information *syn* question, interrogate, query, inquire, catechize, quiz, examine **2** • to seek to obtain by making one's wants or desires known *syn* request, solicit *rel* appeal, petition, plead, pray, sue; address, accost

askance *syn* AWRY, askew *rel* mistrustfully, distrustfully; enviously, jealously *ant* straightforwardly, directly

askew *syn* AWRY, askance *rel* crookedly, obliquely *ant* straight

asocial *syn* UNSOCIAL, antisocial, nonsocial *ant* social

aspect **1** *syn* APPEARANCE, look, semblance *rel* face, countenance, visage; bearing, mien, port, presence **2** *syn* PHASE, side, facet, angle *rel* slant, point of view, viewpoint, standpoint

asperity *syn* ACRIMONY, acerbity *rel* sharpness, keenness; causticity, mordancy; snappishness, waspishness, irritability *ant* amenity

asperse *syn* MALIGN, vilify, traduce, calumniate, slander, defame, libel *rel* disparage, depreciate, derogate, detract, decry; revile, vituperate, scold; defile

aspersion *syn* ANIMADVERSION, reflection, stricture *rel* libel, lampoon, pasquinade, squib, skit; abuse, vituperation, invective, obloquy; detraction, backbiting, calumny, slander, scandal

asphyxiate *syn* SUFFOCATE, stifle, smother, choke, strangle, throttle

aspirant *syn* CANDIDATE, applicant, nominee

aspiration *syn* AMBITION, pretension *rel* aim, goal, objective, intention; desire, passion, lust

aspire *syn* AIM, pant *rel* crave, covet, desire; long, yearn, hunger, thirst, pine

assail *syn* ATTACK, bombard, assault, storm *rel* beset, infest; belabor, pummel, buffet, pound, beat

assassin • one who can be hired to murder *syn* cutthroat, gunman, bravo *rel* murderer, slayer, killer

assassinate *syn* KILL, murder, slay, dispatch, execute

assault *n, syn* ATTACK, onslaught, onset *rel* assailing, bombarding, bombardment, storming, storm; invasion, incursion, raid

assault *vb, syn* ATTACK, storm, bombard, assail *rel* smite, slug, strike; beat, pound, buffet, pummel

assay *syn* ESTIMATE, assess, evaluate, appraise, value, rate *rel* analyze, resolve; calculate, compute, reckon; prove, test, try, demonstrate

assemblage *syn* GATHERING, assembly, collection, congregation *rel* aggregate, aggregation; crowd, throng, horde, crush, press

assemble *syn* GATHER, congregate, collect *rel* convene, convoke, muster, summon; combine, associate, unite, join *ant* disperse

assembly *syn* GATHERING, assemblage, congregation, collection *rel* company, party, troop, band; crowd, throng, crush, press

assent • concurrence with what someone else has stated or proposed *syn* consent, accede, acquiesce, agree, subscribe *rel* accept, receive; adopt, embrace, espouse; believe, credit *ant* dissent

assert **1** • to state positively usu. either in anticipation of denial or objection or in the face of it *syn* declare, profess, affirm, aver, protest, avouch, avow, predicate, warrant *rel* allege, advance, cite, adduce *ant* deny; controvert **2** *syn* MAINTAIN, vindicate, justify, defend *rel* proclaim, declare, publish, advertise; express, voice, utter

assertive *syn* AGGRESSIVE, self-assertive, pushing, pushy, militant *rel* positive, affirmative; blatant, clamorous, vociferous; cocksure, certain, sure, positive; confident, assured, sanguine, presumptuous *ant* retiring; acquiescent

assess *syn* ESTIMATE, assay, appraise, value, evaluate, rate *rel* calculate, compute, reckon

asset **1 assets** *pl syn* POSSESSIONS, resources, means, effects, belongings *ant* liabilities **2** *syn* CREDIT *ant* handicap

assiduous *syn* BUSY, sedulous, diligent, industrious *rel* indefatigable, tireless, untiring, unwearied *ant* desultory

assign **1** *syn* ALLOT, allocate, apportion *rel* fix, set, establish, settle; distribute, deal, dole, dispense **2** *syn* ASCRIBE, refer, attribute, impute, credit, accredit, charge *rel* attach, fasten, affix; relate, link, associate, join; pigeonhole, classify, assort **3** *syn* PRESCRIBE, define *rel* determine, settle, decide; consign, relegate, commit, entrust

assignation *syn* ENGAGEMENT, rendezvous, tryst, date, appointment

assignment *syn* TASK, duty, job, stint, chore

assimilate **1** *syn* IDENTIFY, incorporate, embody *rel* change, alter, modify, vary; transform, metamorphose, transmute; blend, fuse, merge, commingle, mix **2** *syn* ABSORB, imbibe *rel* engross, absorb, monopolize; adopt, embrace, espouse; infuse, imbue, ingrain, suffuse, inoculate, leaven

assimilation *syn* RECOGNITION, apperception, identification

assist *syn* HELP, aid *rel* support, uphold,

back, champion; profit, avail, benefit; attend, accompany, escort; cooperate, concur, unite *ant* hamper; impede

assistance *syn* HELP, aid *rel* service, advantage, profit, avail, use; supporting, upholding, backing; subsidy, grant, subvention, appropriation; cooperation, concurrence *ant* impediment; obstruction

assistant • a person who takes over part of the duties of another, esp. in a subordinate capacity *syn* helper, coadjutor, aid, aide, aide-de-camp

associate *vb, syn* JOIN, connect, relate, link, conjoin, combine, unite *rel* merge, mingle, mix, blend, amalgamate, coalesce; organize

associate *n* • mean a person frequently found in the company of another *syn* companion, comrade, crony *rel* partner, colleague, ally, confederate; accomplice, abettor, accessory, confederate; assistant, helper, coadjutor, aide

association • a body of persons who unite in the pursuit of a common aim or object *syn* society, club, order

assort • to arrange in systematic order or according to some definite method of arrangement or distribution *syn* sort, classify, pigeonhole *rel* arrange, methodize, systematize, order

assorted *syn* MISCELLANEOUS, heterogeneous, motley, promiscuous *rel* diverse, different, various, disparate, divergent; selected, picked, chosen, preferred; mixed, mingled *ant* jumbled

assuage *syn* RELIEVE, alleviate, mitigate, lighten, allay *rel* temper, moderate; comfort, solace, console; mollify, placate, appease, pacify *ant* exacerbate; intensify

assume **1** • to put on a false or deceptive appearance *syn* affect, pretend, simulate, feign, counterfeit, sham *rel* dissemble, disguise, cloak, mask, camouflage **2** *syn* PRESUPPOSE, postulate, presume, premise, posit *rel* conjecture, surmise; grant, concede, allow; assert, affirm, aver, predicate, profess

assumption • something that is taken for granted or advanced as fact *syn* presupposition, postulate, posit, presumption, premise *rel* hypothesis, theory; principle, fundamental, axiom, theorem; conjecture, surmise

assurance **1** *syn* CERTAINTY, certitude, conviction *rel* belief, faith, credence, credit; trust, confidence, reliance, dependence; positiveness, sureness, cocksureness *ant* mistrust; dubiousness **2** *syn* CONFIDENCE, self-assurance, self-confidence, self-possession, aplomb *rel* sangfroid, composure, equanimity; sureness, sanguineness; mettle, resolution, spirit, courage, tenacity; effrontery, temerity, nerve *ant* diffidence; alarm

assure *syn* ENSURE, insure, secure *ant* alarm

assured *syn* CONFIDENT, sanguine, sure, presumptuous *rel* fearless, unapprehensive, unafraid; cool, composed, unruffled, imperturbable, unflappable, collected *ant* abashed; timorous

astern *syn* ABAFT, aft *rel* after, hind, rear, back *ant* ahead

astonish *syn* SURPRISE, astound, amaze, flabbergast *rel* nonplus, dumbfound, bewilder, confound, puzzle; impress, strike, touch, affect

astound *syn* SURPRISE, astonish, amaze, flabbergast *rel* dumbfound, confound, nonplus, bewilder, puzzle; startle, affright, alarm, terrify, frighten

astral *syn* STARRY, stellar, sidereal

astray *syn* AMISS

astute *syn* SHREWD, perspicacious, sagacious *rel* sharp, keen, acute; discreet, prudent, foresighted; knowing, intelligent, clever, smart; wily, crafty, cunning, sly *ant* gullible

asylum *syn* SHELTER, refuge, retreat, sanctuary, cover

atavism *syn* REVERSION, throwback

atavistic *syn* REVERSIONARY

atheist • a person who rejects some or all of the essential doctrines of religion and particularly the existence of God *syn* agnostic, deist, freethinker, unbeliever, infidel *ant* theist

athirst *syn* EAGER, avid, keen, anxious, agog *rel* thirsting, hungering, pining, yearning, longing; craving, coveting, covetous, desiring, desirous

athletic *syn* MUSCULAR, husky, sinewy, brawny, burly *rel* strong, stalwart, sturdy; lusty, vigorous, strenuous, energetic

athletics • physical activities engaged in for exercise or play *syn* sports, games

athwart *syn* ACROSS, crosswise, crossways

atmosphere • an intangible and usually

unanalyzable quality or aggregate of qualities which gives something an individual and distinctly recognizable character *syn* feeling, feel, aura *rel* quality, character, property; peculiarity, individuality, characteristic; impression, impress

atom *syn* PARTICLE, bit, mite, smidgen, jot, tittle, iota, whit *rel* smack, spice, dash, suspicion, soupçon, touch, suggestion, tincture, tinge, shade

atone *syn* EXPIATE *rel* compensate, pay; propitiate, conciliate, appease, pacify

atonement *syn* EXPIATION *rel* compensating, compensation, offsetting; conciliation, propitiation, appeasement; reparation, amends

atrabilious *syn* MELANCHOLIC, hypochondriac, melancholy *rel* morose, glum, saturnine, crabbed, sullen; despondent, hopeless, forlorn; depressed, dejected, gloomy, sad *ant* blithe

atrocious *syn* OUTRAGEOUS, heinous, monstrous *rel* flagrant, gross, rank, glaring; nefarious, flagitious, infamous, iniquitous, vicious; barbaric, savage, barbarous, barbarian *ant* humane; noble, moral

attach **1** *syn* ARREST, apprehend, detain *rel* seize, take, grab; capture, catch **2** *syn* FASTEN, affix, fix *rel* join, link, unite, connect; annex, add, append; tie, bind *ant* detach

attachment **1** *syn* ARREST, apprehension, detention **2** • the feeling which animates a person who is genuinely fond of someone or something *syn* affection, love *rel* fondness, devotedness; devotion, piety, fealty, fidelity, allegiance *ant* aversion

attack *vb* • to make an onslaught upon *syn* assail, assault, bombard, storm *rel* fight, contend, battle, war; beset, overrun, infest; surprise, waylay, ambush

attack *n* **1** • an attempt made on another or on others to injure, destroy, or defame *syn* assault, onslaught, onset *rel* action, battle; striking, hitting, smiting, slugging; criticism, condemnation, denouncing, denunciation **2** • action in a struggle for supremacy which must be met with defense or by means of defenses *syn* aggression, offense, offensive **3** *syn* FIT, access, accession, paroxysm, spasm, convulsion

attacking • initiating hostile action in a struggle for supremacy *syn* aggressive, offensive

attain *syn* REACH, compass, gain, achieve *rel* come, arrive; win, acquire, secure, obtain, get; accomplish, effect

attainment *syn* ACQUIREMENT, accomplishment, acquisition

attaint *syn* CONTAMINATE, taint, pollute, defile

attempt *vb* • to make an effort to do something that may or may not be successful *syn* try, endeavor, essay, strive, struggle *rel* begin, commence, start, initiate, inaugurate *ant* succeed

attempt *n* • an effort made to do or accomplish something *syn* endeavor, essay, try, striving, struggle *rel* trial, test; beginning, commencement, starting, start, initiation

attend **1** *syn* TEND, mind, watch *rel* nurse, foster, nurture, cherish; supervise, oversee **2** *syn* ACCOMPANY, escort, chaperon, convoy

attention **1** • the direct focusing of the mind esp. on something to be learned, worked out, or dealt with *syn* study, concentration, application *rel* diligence, assiduity, sedulousness, industriousness *ant* inattention **2** *syn* COURTESY, gallantry, amenity *rel* courting, court, wooing; deference, homage, honor, reverence; solicitude, care

attentive *syn* THOUGHTFUL, considerate *rel* courteous, polite, gallant, chivalrous, civil; solicitous, concerned, careful *ant* inattentive; neglectful

attenuate *syn* THIN, rarefy, dilute, extenuate *rel* weaken, sap; reduce, lessen, decrease; dissipate, scatter; contract, shrink, constrict, deflate *ant* enlarge; dilate; enrich

attest **1** *syn* CERTIFY, witness, vouch *rel* confirm, corroborate, substantiate, verify **2** *syn* INDICATE, argue, prove, bespeak, betoken *rel* demonstrate, test, prove; confirm, authenticate, substantiate *ant* belie

attire *vb, syn* CLOTHE, apparel, array, dress, robe *rel* accouter, appoint, equip, outfit, arm, furnish *ant* divest

attire *n, syn* CLOTHES, clothing, apparel, raiment, dress

attitude **1** *syn* POSTURE, pose *rel* mien, bearing, port, presence, demeanor **2** *syn* POSITION, stand *rel* point of view, angle, slant, viewpoint, standpoint; bias, prepossession, prejudice, predilection

attorney **1** *syn* AGENT, deputy, proxy, factor *rel* substitute, supply, alternate **2** *syn*

LAWYER, solicitor, counselor, barrister, counsel, advocate

attract • to draw another by exerting an irresistible or compelling influence *syn* allure, charm, fascinate, bewitch, enchant, captivate *rel* invite, solicit, court; entice, lure, tempt, seduce; catch, capture *ant* repel

attraction • the relationship between persons or things that are involuntarily or naturally drawn together *syn* affinity, sympathy

attractive • drawing another by exerting a compelling influence *syn* alluring, charming, fascinating, bewitching, enchanting, captivating *rel* lovely, fair, beautiful, bonny, pretty, comely; luring, enticing, tempting, seductive *ant* repellent; forbidding

attribute *n* **1** *syn* QUALITY, property, character, accident **2** *syn* SYMBOL, emblem, type *rel* sign, mark, token, badge, note; character, symbol, sign

attribute *vb, syn* ASCRIBE, impute, assign, credit, accredit, refer, charge *rel* fasten, attach, fix; predicate, assert; blame, criticize; accuse, charge

attrition *syn* PENITENCE, contrition, repentance, remorse, compunction *rel* regret, sorrow, grief, anguish

attune *syn* HARMONIZE, tune *rel* adapt, adjust, accommodate, reconcile, conform; accord, agree, harmonize; temper, moderate; balance, counterbalance, compensate

atypical *syn* ABNORMAL, aberrant *rel* irregular, anomalous, unnatural; divergent, different; deviating, departing; exceptional *ant* typical; representative

audacious *syn* BRAVE, courageous, unafraid, fearless, intrepid, valiant, valorous, dauntless, undaunted, doughty, bold *rel* daring, daredevil, reckless, venturesome, adventurous, rash, foolhardy; brazen, brash, shameless *ant* circumspect

audacity *syn* TEMERITY, hardihood, effrontery, nerve, cheek, gall *rel* intrepidity, boldness, courageousness, bravery; daring, daredeviltry, recklessness, rashness, foolhardiness, adventurousness; courage, mettle, spirit; brazenness, brass, shamelessness *ant* circumspection

audience **1** *syn* HEARING, audition **2** *syn* FOLLOWING, public, clientele *rel* devotees, votaries

audit *n, syn* SCRUTINY, examination, inspection, scrutiny, scanning *rel* check, corrective, control; investigation, probe, inquiry

audit *vb, syn* SCRUTINIZE, examine, inspect, scan

audition *syn* HEARING, audience

auditory • of or relating to the hearing of sounds *syn* acoustic, acoustical

augment *syn* INCREASE, enlarge, multiply *rel* intensify, aggravate, enhance, heighten; swell, expand, amplify, dilate *ant* abate

augur *syn* FORETELL, prognosticate, presage, portend, forebode, prophesy, forecast, predict *rel* betoken, indicate, bespeak, argue; apprehend, anticipate, divine, foreknow, foresee

augury *syn* FORETOKEN, omen, portent, presage, prognostic *rel* sign, symptom, token, note, badge, mark; precursor, forerunner, harbinger, herald

august *syn* GRAND, majestic, imposing, stately, noble, grandiose, magnificent *rel* impressive, moving; splendid, sublime, superb; awful, fearful *ant* unimpressive; unimposing

aura *syn* ATMOSPHERE, feeling, feel

aureate *syn* RHETORICAL, euphuistic, flowery, grandiloquent, magniloquent, bombastic *rel* ornate, florid, flamboyant, rococo, baroque *ant* austere (*in style*)

auspicious *syn* FAVORABLE, propitious, benign *rel* lucky, fortunate, happy, providential; hopeful, roseate; indicating, indicative, betokening *ant* inauspicious; ill-omened

austere *syn* SEVERE, stern, ascetic *rel* bald, bare; unembellished, unadorned, unornamented, undecorated; dispassionate, fair; rigorous, strict, rigid; grave, somber, serious, sober, earnest *ant* luscious (*of fruits*); warm, ardent (*of persons, feelings*); exuberant (*of style, quality*)

autarchic *syn* FREE, autarkic, autonomous, independent, sovereign

autarchy *syn* FREEDOM, autarky, autonomy, independence, sovereignty

autarkic *syn* FREE, autarchic, autonomous, independent, sovereign

autarky *syn* FREEDOM, autarchy, autonomy, independence, sovereignty

authentic • being exactly as appears or is claimed *syn* genuine, veritable, bona fide *rel* authoritarian, oracular, dictatorial; reliable, trustworthy, dependable; correct, right, exact; true, real, actual *ant* spurious

authenticate *syn* CONFIRM, validate, verify, substantiate, corroborate *rel* certify, accredit, endorse, approve; prove, try, test, demonstrate; avouch, warrant, assert *ant* impugn

author *syn* MAKER, creator

authoritarian *syn* DICTATORIAL, dogmatic, magisterial, doctrinaire, oracular *rel* despotic, autocratic, arbitrary, tyrannical, tyrannous, absolute; domineering, imperious, masterful *ant* liberal, libertarian; anarchistic, anarchic

authority **1** *syn* POWER, jurisdiction, command, control, dominion, sway *rel* ascendancy, supremacy; government, ruling, rule **2** *syn* INFLUENCE, weight, credit, prestige *rel* exemplar, ideal, standard, pattern, model, example; expert, adept, artist; connoisseur, aesthete

authorize • to invest with power or the right to act *syn* commission, accredit, license *rel* empower, enable; permit, allow, let

autobiography *syn* BIOGRAPHY, memoir, life, confessions

autochthonous *syn* NATIVE, indigenous, aboriginal, endemic *ant* naturalized

autocratic *syn* ABSOLUTE, arbitrary, despotic, tyrannical, tyrannous *rel* dictatorial, magisterial; authoritarian, totalitarian; masterful, domineering, imperious; overbearing, arrogant, proud

automatic *syn* SPONTANEOUS, mechanical, instinctive, impulsive *rel* trained, disciplined, schooled, instructed; prompt, quick, ready

autonomous *syn* FREE, independent, sovereign, autarchic, autarkic

autonomy *syn* FREEDOM, independence, sovereignty, autarchy, autarky

auxiliary • supplying aid or support *syn* subsidiary, accessory, contributory, subservient, ancillary, adjuvant *rel* subordinate, secondary, tributary; supporting, upholding, backing; helping, aiding, assisting; supplementary, complementary

avail *vb* **1** *syn* BENEFIT, profit *rel* meet, answer, satisfy, fulfill; help, aid **2** *syn* USE, utilize, employ, apply

avail *n, syn* USE, service, account, advantage, profit

avarice *syn* CUPIDITY, greed, rapacity *rel* avariciousness, covetousness, acquisitiveness; stinginess, niggardliness, miserliness, parsimoniousness *ant* prodigality

avaricious *syn* COVETOUS, acquisitive, grasping, greedy *rel* miserly, close, closefisted, parsimonious, stingy *ant* generous

avenge • to inflict punishment by way of repayment for *syn* revenge *rel* requite, recompense, compensate, pay; vindicate, defend, justify, maintain; punish, chasten, chastise

aver *syn* ASSERT, declare, avouch, avow, profess, affirm, protest *rel* maintain, defend, justify *ant* deny

average *n* • something (as a number, quantity, or condition) that represents a middle point between extremes *syn* mean, median, norm, par *ant* maximum; minimum

average *adj, syn* MEDIUM, middling, indifferent, fair, moderate, mediocre, second-rate *rel* common, ordinary, familiar; usual, customary *ant* exceptional; extraordinary

averse *syn* DISINCLINED, indisposed, loath, reluctant, hesitant *rel* recoiling, shrinking, flinching, quailing; uncongenial, unsympathetic, inconsonant; balky, contrary, perverse *ant* avid (*of* or *for*); athirst (*for*)

aversion **1** *syn* DISLIKE, distaste, disfavor *rel* antipathy, hostility, antagonism, enmity; horror, dread, fear *ant* predilection **2** *syn* ANTIPATHY *rel* repugnance, repellency, abhorrence, distaste, distastefulness; horror, dread, fear *ant* attachment, predilection

avert **1** *syn* TURN, deflect, sheer, divert *rel* bend, twist, curve; shift, remove, transfer, move **2** *syn* PREVENT, ward, obviate, preclude *rel* escape, avoid, shun, eschew, evade, elude; forestall, anticipate, prevent; frustrate, balk, thwart, foil

avid *syn* EAGER, keen, anxious, agog, athirst *rel* desiring, desirous, craving, coveting, covetous; longing, yearning, pining, hankering, hungering, thirsting *ant* indifferent; averse

avoid *syn* ESCAPE, shun, eschew, evade, elude *rel* avert, ward, prevent, obviate; forestall, anticipate, prevent; flee, fly, escape *ant* face; meet

avouch *syn* ASSERT, aver, affirm, avow, profess, declare, protest, warrant, predicate *rel* confirm, corroborate

avow **1** *syn* ASSERT, affirm, profess, declare, aver, avouch, warrant, protest, predicate *rel* maintain, defend, vindicate **2** *syn* ACKNOWLEDGE, own, confess, admit *rel* proclaim, declare, publish, announce; reveal, discover, disclose, divulge, tell *ant* disavow

await *syn* EXPECT, hope, look *rel* wait, abide, stay *ant* despair

awake *syn* AWARE, alive, cognizant, conscious, sensible *rel* alert, vigilant, watchful; roused, aroused, stirred up, awakened

awaken *syn* STIR, waken, rouse, arouse, rally *rel* excite, galvanize, quicken, stimulate, provoke; kindle, fire, light; elicit, evoke, educe *ant* subdue

award *vb, syn* GRANT, accord, vouchsafe, concede *rel* bestow, confer, present, give; assign, allot, apportion, allocate; adjudicate, adjudge, judge, arbitrate

award *n, syn* PREMIUM, prize, reward, guerdon, meed, bonus, bounty

aware • having knowledge of something *syn* cognizant, conscious, sensible, alive, awake *rel* sure, certain, positive; informed, acquainted, apprised *ant* unaware

awe *syn* REVERENCE, fear *rel* respect, esteem, regard; wonder, wonderment, admiration, amazement

awful *syn* FEARFUL, dreadful, frightful, terrible, horrible, shocking, appalling, terrific, horrific *rel* impressive, moving; solemn, serious, grave; imposing, august, majestic; sublime, superb, splendid; ominous, portentous

awkward • not marked by ease (as of performance, movement, or social conduct) *syn* clumsy, maladroit, inept, gauche *rel* stiff, wooden, rigid; embarrassing, discomfiting, disconcerting *ant* handy, deft; graceful

awry • deviating from a straight line or direction *syn* askew, askance

axiom *syn* PRINCIPLE, fundamental, law, theorem

B

babble *syn* CHAT, gabble, jabber, prattle, chatter, patter, prate, gibber, gab *rel* gossip, blab, tattle; converse, talk, speak

babel *syn* DIN, hubbub, clamor, racket, uproar, hullabaloo, pandemonium *rel* clamorousness, clamor, vociferousness; confusion, disorder

baby *syn* INDULGE, mollycoddle, humor, pamper, spoil

back *n, syn* SPINE, backbone, vertebrae, chine

back *adj, syn* POSTERIOR, rear, hind, hinder, after *ant* front

back *vb* **1** *syn* SUPPORT, uphold, champion, advocate *rel* assist, aid, help; favor, accommodate, oblige; abet, incite **2** *syn* RECEDE, retrograde, retreat, retract

backbiting *syn* DETRACTION, slander, scandal, calumny *rel* aspersion, animadversion, reflection, stricture; abuse, invective, obloquy, vituperation; vilifying, vilification, defaming, defamation *ant* vindication

backbone **1** *syn* SPINE, back, vertebrae, chine **2** *syn* FORTITUDE, grit, guts, sand, pluck *rel* courage, resolution, tenacity, mettle, spirit; courageousness, intrepidity, dauntlessness, valiancy; nerve, temerity, hardihood *ant* spinelessness

backdrop *syn* BACKGROUND, setting, milieu, mise-en-scène, environment

backer *syn* SPONSOR, surety, guarantor, patron, angel

background • the place, time, and circumstances in which something occurs *syn* setting, environment, milieu, mise-en-scène, backdrop

backslide *syn* LAPSE, relapse *rel* revert, return; deteriorate, degenerate, decline; recede, retreat, retrograde

backslider *syn* RENEGADE, apostate, recreant, turncoat

backsliding *syn* LAPSE, relapse *rel* retrogressiveness, retrogression, retrogradation; abandoning, deserting, forsaking

backward • not moving or going ahead *syn* retrograde, retrogressive, regressive *rel* laggard, dilatory, slow; stupid, dull, dense; lethargic, sluggish; abnormal, atypical *ant* advanced

bad **1** • deviating from the dictates of moral law *syn* evil, ill, wicked, naughty *rel* iniquitous, vicious, villainous; base, low, vile; immoral, unmoral, amoral *ant* good **2** • not measuring up to a standard of what is satisfactory *syn* poor, wrong *ant* good

badge *syn* SIGN, token, mark, note, symptom

badger *syn* BAIT, hound, chivy, hector, ride, heckle *rel* annoy, vex, bother, irk; harass, harry, worry, pester, plague, tease

badinage • animated back-and-forth exchange of remarks *syn* persiflage, raillery *rel* bantering, banter, chaffing, kidding, joshing, jollying; fun, game, jest, sport

badlands *syn* WASTE, desert, wilderness

baffle *syn* FRUSTRATE, balk, circumvent, outwit, foil, thwart *rel* puzzle, mystify, confound, dumbfound; discomfit, rattle, faze, embarrass, disconcert; confuse, addle, muddle; hamper, fetter, hog-tie; hinder, impede, obstruct, block

bag *n* • a container made of a flexible material and open or opening at the top *syn* sack, pouch

bag *vb, syn* CATCH, capture, trap, snare, entrap, ensnare

bail *n, syn* GUARANTEE, bond, surety, security, guaranty

bail *vb, syn* DIP, ladle, scoop, spoon, dish

bailiwick *syn* FIELD, province, domain, territory, sphere

bait *vb* • to persist in tormenting or harassing another *syn* badger, heckle, hector, chivy, hound, ride *rel* worry, annoy, harass, harry; torment, rack, torture, try, afflict

bait *n, syn* LURE, snare, trap, decoy *rel* allurement, attraction; enticement, temptation

bake *syn* DRY, parch, desiccate, dehydrate

balance *n* **1** • the stability or efficiency resulting from the equalization or exact adjustment of opposing forces *syn* equilibrium, equipoise, poise, tension **2** *syn* SYMMETRY, proportion, harmony **3** *syn* REMAINDER, rest, residue, residuum, leavings, remnant, remains

balance *vb* **1** *syn* COMPENSATE, counterpoise, counterbalance, countervail, offset *rel* attune, harmonize, tune; correspond, accord, square, agree **2** *syn* STABILIZE, poise, ballast, trim, steady *rel* settle, set; waver, sway, oscillate, fluctuate

bald *syn* BARE, barren, naked, nude *rel* austere, severe; unembellished, unadorned, unornamented; colorless, uncolored

balderdash *syn* NONSENSE, twaddle, drivel, bunk, poppycock, gobbledygook, trash, rot, bull

bale *syn* BUNDLE, package, pack, parcel, bunch, packet

baleful *syn* SINISTER, maleficent, malefic, malign *rel* threatening, menacing; ominous, portentous, fateful; hellish, infernal; diabolical, fiendish, devilish *ant* beneficent

balk **1** *syn* FRUSTRATE, thwart, foil, baffle, circumvent, outwit *rel* defeat, beat, lick, conquer, overcome; block, obstruct, impede, hinder; prevent, forestall *ant* forward **2** *syn* DEMUR, jib, shy, boggle, stickle, scruple, strain, stick *rel* hesitate, falter, waver; refuse, decline; shrink, flinch, quail, recoil

balky *syn* CONTRARY, restive, perverse, froward, wayward *rel* hesitant, reluctant, averse, loath, disinclined, indisposed; obstinate, stubborn, mulish; refractory, recalcitrant, unruly

ballast *syn* STABILIZE, steady, balance, trim, poise

ballot *syn* SUFFRAGE, vote, franchise

ballyhoo *syn* PUBLICITY, promotion, propaganda *rel* advertisement, broadcasting

balmy **1** *syn* ODOROUS, aromatic, fragrant, redolent *rel* refreshing, restoring, rejuvenating; pleasing, grateful, welcome, pleasant *ant* rank, noisome **2** *syn* SOFT, gentle, smooth, bland, mild, lenient *rel* agreeable, pleasant, gratifying, grateful; gladdening, delighting, rejoicing, regaling; assuaging, allaying, lightening, relieving; salubrious, salutary, healthful

bamboozle *syn* DUPE, trick, hoodwink, gull, hoax, befool *rel* delude, deceive, beguile, mislead; outwit, circumvent, frustrate; defraud, cozen, overreach, cheat, swindle

ban *syn* FORBID, prohibit, interdict, inhibit, enjoin *rel* bar, block, hinder; prevent, preclude; exclude, debar, rule out

banal *syn* INSIPID, flat, jejune, inane, vapid, wishy-washy *rel* trite, hackneyed; simple, fatuous, silly, asinine; commonplace, platitudinous, bromidic *ant* original; recherché

band **1** *syn* BOND, tie *rel* connection, link, joining; joint, articulation, suture **2** *syn* STRIP, stripe, ribbon, fillet **3** *syn* COMPANY, troop, troupe, party *rel* coterie, clique, set, circle; horde, mob, crowd; society, club, association, order

bandy *syn* EXCHANGE, interchange

bane *syn* POISON, venom, virus, toxin

baneful *syn* PERNICIOUS, noxious, deleterious, detrimental *rel* harmful, injurious, mischievous, hurtful; malign, sinister, baleful; poisonous, venomous, toxic *ant* beneficial

banish • to remove by authority or force from a country, state, or sovereignty *syn* exile, expatriate, ostracize, deport, transport, extradite *rel* eject, expel, oust; exclude, debar, eliminate, shut out

bank *n* **1** *syn* SHOAL, bar, reef **2** *syn* SHORE, strand, coast, beach, foreshore, littoral **3** *syn* HEAP, mass, pile, stack, shock, cock *rel* aggregate, aggregation, conglomerate, conglomeration; assemblage, assembly, collection, gathering

bank *vb, syn* HEAP, mass, pile, stack, shock, cock *rel* collect, assemble, gather

bank *vb, syn* RELY, count, reckon, trust, depend

bankrupt *syn* DEPLETE, impoverish, exhaust, drain *rel* denude, strip, bare; sap, cripple, disable, undermine, weaken

banner *syn* FLAG, standard, ensign, color, streamer, pennant, pendant, pennon, jack

banquet *syn* DINNER, feast

banter • to make fun of good-naturedly *syn* chaff, kid, rag, rib, josh, jolly *rel* twit, rally, deride, ridicule

baptize • to administer the rite of baptism *syn* christen

bar *n* **1** • something which hinders or obstructs *syn* barrier, barricade **2** *syn* OBSTACLE, obstruction, impediment, snag *rel* hindrance, block, dam; difficulty, hardship, vicissitude *ant* advantage **3** *syn* SHOAL, bank, reef

bar *vb, syn* HINDER, obstruct, block, dam, impede *rel* shut out, debar, exclude; prevent, preclude, obviate; forbid, prohibit, interdict; close, shut *ant* admit; open

barbarian • of, relating to, or characteristic of people that are not fully civilized *syn* barbaric, barbarous, savage *ant* civilized

barbaric *syn* BARBARIAN, savage, barbarous *rel* showy, ostentatious; florid, ornate, flamboyant; gaudy, garish, flashy, meretricious *ant* restrained; refined; subdued

barbarism • a word or expression which offends against standards of correctness *syn* corruption, impropriety, solecism, vernacularism, vulgarism

barbarous **1** *syn* BARBARIAN, savage, barbaric *rel* rough, harsh; untutored, untaught, uneducated, illiterate, ignorant; rude, rough, crude *ant* civilized; humane **2** *syn* FIERCE, savage, inhuman, ferocious, cruel, fell, truculent *rel* pitiless, ruthless, uncompassionate; atrocious, monstrous, outrageous *ant* clement

bard *syn* POET, minstrel, troubadour, rhymer, rhymester, versifier, poetaster

bare *adj* **1** • lacking naturally or conventionally appropriate covering or clothing *syn* naked, nude, bald, barren *rel* stripped, divested, denuded; unclothed, undressed, unrobed *ant* covered **2** *syn* MERE, very

bare *vb, syn* STRIP, denude, divest, dismantle *ant* cover

barefaced *syn* SHAMELESS, brazen, brash, impudent *rel* open, plain, frank, candid; indecent, unseemly, indecorous *ant* furtive

bargain *syn* CONTRACT, compact, pact

bark *vb* • to make the sound of or a sound suggestive of a dog *syn* bay, howl, growl, snarl, yelp, yap *rel* bellow, vociferate, bawl, roar; yell, shout, scream, shriek

bark *n, syn* SKIN, rind, peel, hide, pelt

baroque *syn* ORNATE, florid, rococo, flamboyant

barren **1** *syn* STERILE, unfruitful, infertile, impotent *ant* fecund **2** *syn* BARE, bald, naked, nude *rel* arid, dry; desolate, forlorn, alone; impoverished, exhausted, depleted; austere, severe, stern

barricade *syn* BAR, barrier

barrier *syn* BAR, barricade

barrister *syn* LAWYER, counselor, counsel, advocate, attorney, solicitor

basal **1** *syn* FUNDAMENTAL, basic, underlying, radical **2** *syn* ELEMENTARY, beginning, elemental, rudimentary

base *n* • something on which another thing is reared or built or by which it is supported or fixed in place *syn* basis, foundation, ground, groundwork *ant* top

base *vb* • to supply or to serve as a basis *syn* found, ground, bottom, stay, rest *rel* support, sustain; set, establish, fix, settle

base *adj* • deserving of contempt because of the absence of higher values *syn* low, vile *rel* mean, ignoble, abject, sordid; bad, evil, ill, wicked; ignominious, infamous, disgraceful *ant* noble

baseless • not justified or justifiable in any way *syn* groundless, unfounded, unwarranted *rel* false, wrong; unsupported, unsustained

bashful *syn* SHY, diffident, modest, coy *rel*

shrinking, recoiling; timorous, timid; embarrassed, abashed *ant* forward; brazen

basic 1 *syn* FUNDAMENTAL, basal, underlying, radical *rel* principal, capital, chief, main; primordial, primary *ant* top; peak **2** *syn* ALKALINE *syn* ELEMENTAL, elementary, essential, fundamental, primitive, underlying

basis *syn* BASE, foundation, ground, groundwork *rel* principle, fundamental, axiom, law, theorem; premise, postulate, presupposition, presumption, assumption

baste *syn* BEAT, pummel, thrash, buffet, pound, belabor *rel* chastise, castigate, punish, discipline

bastion *syn* BULWARK, breastwork, parapet, rampart

bathos *syn* PATHOS, poignancy *rel* mawkishness, maudlinism, soppiness, mushiness

batter *syn* MAIM, mangle, mutilate, cripple *rel* beat, pound, pummel, thrash, buffet, belabor, baste

battle *n* • a hostile meeting between opposing military forces *syn* engagement, action *rel* encounter, skirmish, brush; attack, assault, onslaught, onset; combat, conflict, fight, contest

battle *vb, syn* CONTEND, war, fight *rel* combat, oppose, resist, withstand, fight; attack, assail, assault, bombard; kick, protest, object

bawl *vb* **1** *syn* ROAR, bellow, bluster, vociferate, clamor, howl, ululate *rel* yell, shout, scream, shriek; bay, bark, growl, yelp; cry, wail **2** *syn* SCOLD, rate, berate, tongue-lash, upbraid, chew out, wig, rail, revile, vituperate *rel* reprimand, rebuke, reproach, reprove, chide; censure, denounce, condemn, reprehend, reprobate, criticize

bawl *n, syn* ROAR, bellow, bluster, vociferation, ululation

bay *syn* BARK, howl, growl, snarl, yelp, yap *rel* bellow, vociferate, clamor, roar; yell, holler, shout

be • to have actuality or reality *syn* exist, live, subsist

beach *syn* SHORE, strand, coast, foreshore, bank, littoral

beak *syn* BILL, neb, nib

beam *syn* RAY *rel* flash, gleam, glint, scintillation, coruscation

beaming *syn* BRIGHT, radiant, refulgent, effulgent, brilliant, luminous, lustrous, lambent, lucent, incandescent *rel* flashing, gleaming, glittering, glistening, glinting, sparkling, coruscating, scintillating; glowing, flaming

bear 1 *syn* CARRY, convey, transport, transmit *rel* move, remove, shift, transfer; hold, contain **2** • to bring forth as products *syn* produce, yield, turn out *rel* reproduce, propagate, breed, generate **3** • to sustain something trying or painful *syn* suffer, endure, abide, tolerate, stand, brook *rel* accept, receive; afflict, try, torment, torture **4** *syn* PRESS, bear down, squeeze, crowd, jam *rel* weigh, oppress, depress; burden, encumber, load, saddle **5** • to have a connection especially logically *syn* relate, pertain, appertain, belong, apply *rel* concern, affect; touch, influence, affect; weigh

beard *syn* FACE, brave, challenge, dare, defy *rel* confront, meet, encounter

bear down *syn* PRESS, bear, squeeze, crowd, jam

bearing • the way in which or the quality by which a person outwardly manifests personality *syn* deportment, demeanor, mien, port, presence *rel* posture, attitude, pose; behavior, conduct; attitude, stand, position; poise, address, tact

beastly *syn* BRUTAL, bestial, brute, brutish, feral *rel* abominable, detestable, hateful; loathsome, repulsive, revolting, offensive; disgusting, sickening, nauseating

beat *vb* **1** • to strike repeatedly *syn* pound, pummel, thrash, buffet, baste, belabor *rel* slug, clout, swat, punch, strike, hit, smite, slap, box, cuff **2** *syn* CONQUER, defeat, lick, vanquish, subdue, subjugate, reduce, overcome, surmount, overthrow, rout *rel* surpass, excel, outstrip, exceed; confound, nonplus, puzzle **3** *syn* PULSATE, throb, pulse, palpitate *rel* quiver, quaver, quake, shake; vibrate, oscillate, fluctuate, pendulate, swing

beat *n, syn* PULSATION, pulse, throb, palpitation *rel* accent, accentuation, stress, emphasis; rhythm, cadence

beatitude *syn* HAPPINESS, blessedness, bliss, felicity *rel* rapture, ecstasy, transport; joy, fruition, enjoyment, pleasure *ant* despair; dolor

beau *syn* FOP, exquisite, dandy, coxcomb, dude, buck

beau ideal *syn* MODEL, ideal, exemplar, pattern, example, mirror, standard

beauteous *syn* BEAUTIFUL, pulchritudinous, fair, good-looking, handsome, pretty, comely, bonny, lovely *rel* alluring, attractive, fascinating, charming

beautiful • very pleasing or delightful to look at *syn* lovely, handsome, pretty, bonny, comely, fair, beauteous, pulchritudinous, good-looking *rel* splendid, resplendent, glorious, sublime, superb; exquisite, elegant, choice *ant* ugly

beautify *syn* ADORN, embellish, deck, bedeck, ornament, decorate, garnish *rel* enhance, heighten, intensify *ant* uglify

because • for the reason that *syn* for, since, as, inasmuch as

becloud *syn* OBSCURE, cloud, eclipse, fog, befog, dim, bedim, darken, obfuscate *rel* confuse, muddle, addle, befuddle; puzzle, perplex, distract

bedeck *syn* ADORN, deck, garnish, embellish, beautify, decorate, ornament

bedim *syn* OBSCURE, dim, eclipse, cloud, becloud, fog, befog, obfuscate, darken *rel* cloak, mask, disguise; conceal, hide, screen

beetle *syn* BULGE, overhang, jut, project, protrude, stick out *rel* menace, threaten

befall *syn* HAPPEN, betide, occur, chance, transpire

befog *syn* OBSCURE, fog, cloud, becloud, eclipse, darken, dim, bedim, obfuscate *rel* puzzle, perplex, distract, bewilder, dumbfound; confuse, muddle, addle

befool *syn* DUPE, trick, hoax, hoodwink, gull, bamboozle *rel* cheat, cozen, overreach; deceive, delude, beguile, mislead; blandish, cajole, wheedle, coax

before • in advance, especially in place or in time *syn* ahead, forward *ant* after

beforehand *syn* EARLY, betimes, soon *ant* behindhand

befoul *syn* SOIL, foul, dirty, sully, smirch, besmirch, grime, begrime, tarnish *rel* spot, spatter, sprinkle

befuddle *syn* CONFUSE, fuddle, addle, muddle *rel* bewilder, distract, confound, perplex, puzzle; intoxicate, inebriate *ant* clarify, clear

beg • to ask or request urgently *syn* entreat, beseech, implore, supplicate, adjure, importune *rel* solicit, request, ask; plead, pray, petition, sue; demand, exact

beget *syn* GENERATE, get, sire, procreate, engender, breed, propagate, reproduce *rel* bear, produce, yield

beggarly *syn* CONTEMPTIBLE, cheap, scurvy, shabby, sorry, despicable, pitiable *rel* paltry, measly, petty, trifling; mean, abject, sordid

begin • to take the first step in a course, process, or operation *syn* commence, start, initiate, inaugurate *rel* found, institute, establish, organize; introduce, admit, enter; originate, derive, spring, arise, rise *ant* end

beginning *n* • the first part or stage of a process or development *syn* genesis, rise, initiation *rel* origin, source, inception, root; rise, derivation, emanation; emergence, appearance

beginning *adj, syn* ELEMENTARY, basal, elemental, rudimentary

begrime *syn* SOIL, grime, smirch, besmirch, dirty, sully, foul, befoul, tarnish *rel* spot, spatter, sprinkle

begrudge *syn* COVET, envy, grudge

beguile **1** *syn* DECEIVE, delude, mislead, betray, double-cross *rel* dupe, gull, befool, trick, hoax, hoodwink, bamboozle; cajole, wheedle, blandish, coax; cheat, cozen; lure, entice, seduce **2** *syn* WHILE, wile, beguile, fleet *rel* divert, amuse, entertain; comfort, solace; speed, hasten, hurry

behave **1** • to act or to cause oneself to do something in a certain way *syn* conduct, comport, demean, deport, acquit, quit *rel* bear, carry; manage, control, direct *ant* misbehave **2** *syn* ACT, react, operate, work, function

behavior • one's actions in general or on a particular occasion *syn* conduct, deportment *rel* demeanor, mien, bearing; action, act, deed

behest *syn* COMMAND, bidding, dictate, injunction, order, mandate *rel* precept, rule, law; request, solicitation

behind *syn* AFTER *ant* ahead

behindhand *syn* TARDY, late, overdue *rel* dilatory, laggard, slow; delayed, retarded, detained *ant* beforehand

behold *syn* SEE, view, survey, observe, descry, espy, notice, perceive, discern, remark, note, contemplate *rel* watch, look, see; regard, consider

beholder *syn* SPECTATOR, onlooker, looker-on, observer, witness, eyewitness, bystander, kibitzer

being **1** *syn* EXISTENCE, actuality *rel* personality, individuality, character, disposition *ant* becoming; nonbeing **2** *syn* ENTITY, creature, individual, person *rel* thing, object, article; idea, concept, thought

belabor *syn* BEAT, pound, pummel, thrash, buffet, baste *rel* strike, hit, smite, slug, clout, swat, punch, box, cuff, slap

belch • to eject (gas) from the stomach by way of the mouth or matter from a containing cavity by way of an opening *syn* burp, vomit, disgorge, regurgitate, spew, throw up *rel* eject, expel

beleaguer *syn* BESIEGE, invest, blockade *rel* surround, environ, encircle, encompass, hem, gird; enclose, envelop; harass, pester, worry, annoy

belie *syn* MISREPRESENT, falsify, garble *rel* contradict, contravene, negative, deny; controvert, disprove *ant* attest

belief 1 • the act of one who assents intellectually to something proposed or offered for acceptance as true or the state of mind of one who so assents *syn* faith, credence, credit *rel* certitude, assurance, certainty, conviction; assenting, assent, acquiescing, acquiescence *ant* unbelief, disbelief **2** *syn* OPINION, conviction, persuasion, view, sentiment *rel* doctrine, dogma, tenet; principle, fundamental; conclusion, judgment

believable *syn* PLAUSIBLE, credible, colorable, specious *rel* probable, possible, likely *ant* unbelievable

belittle *syn* DECRY, depreciate, disparage, derogate, detract, minimize *rel* underestimate, undervalue, underrate; diminish, reduce, lessen, decrease *ant* aggrandize, magnify

bellicose *syn* BELLIGERENT, pugnacious, combative, contentious, quarrelsome *rel* militant, aggressive, assertive; antagonizing, antagonistic, combating, combative; fighting, warring, battling, contending; rebellious, factious, seditious, mutinous, insubordinate *ant* pacific; amicable

belligerent • having or taking an aggressive or fighting attitude *syn* bellicose, pugnacious, combative, quarrelsome, contentious *rel* hostile, antagonistic; fighting, warring, battling, contending; warlike, martial *ant* friendly

bellow *vb, syn* ROAR, bluster, bawl, vociferate, clamor, howl, ululate *rel* yell, shout, scream, shriek; bay, bark, yelp; cry, wail, keen

bellow *n, syn* ROAR, bluster, bawl, vociferation, ululation

belly *syn* ABDOMEN, stomach, paunch, gut

belong *syn* BEAR, pertain, appertain, relate, apply

belongings *syn* POSSESSIONS, effects, means, resources, assets

below • in a lower position relative to some other object or place *syn* under, beneath, underneath *ant* above

belt *syn* AREA, zone, tract, region

bemoan *syn* DEPLORE, bewail, lament *rel* grieve, mourn, sorrow *ant* exult

bemuse *syn* DAZE, stun, stupefy, benumb, paralyze, petrify *rel* confuse, muddle, addle, fuddle, befuddle

bend *syn* CURVE, twist *rel* contort, deform; deflect, divert, turn *ant* straighten

beneath *syn* BELOW, underneath, under *ant* above, over

benefaction *syn* DONATION, contribution, alms *rel* gift, present, largess, boon; endowment; grant, subvention, appropriation; charity, philanthropy

beneficial • bringing good or gain *syn* advantageous, profitable *rel* salutary, healthful, wholesome; favorable, benign, propitious *ant* harmful; detrimental

benefit • to do good or to be of advantage to someone *syn* profit, avail *rel* better, improve, ameliorate; help, assist, aid *ant* harm

benevolent *syn* CHARITABLE, philanthropic, eleemosynary, humanitarian, humane, altruistic *rel* benign, benignant, kindly, kind; generous, liberal, bountiful, bounteous, openhanded; obliging, complaisant, amiable *ant* malevolent

benign 1 *syn* KIND, benignant, kindly *rel* gracious, genial, cordial, affable; sympathetic, tender, compassionate; suave, urbane, bland *ant* malign **2** *syn* FAVORABLE, auspicious, propitious *rel* fortunate, happy, providential, lucky; gentle, mild, soft; benevolent, humane, charitable; merciful, clement, forbearing *ant* malign

benignant *syn* KIND, benign, kindly *rel* benevolent, humane, charitable, humanitarian, philanthropic, eleemosynary; gracious, affable; compassionate, tender, sympathetic *ant* malignant

bent *syn* GIFT, turn, talent, aptitude, knack, faculty, genius *rel* propensity, penchant, leaning, proclivity, flair; predilection, bias, prepossession, prejudice, partiality; capacity, ability, capability

benumb *syn* DAZE, stun, bemuse, stupefy, paralyze, petrify *rel* chill, freeze; congeal, coagulate; dumbfound, confound, nonplus, bewilder, puzzle

bequeath *syn* WILL, devise, leave, legate *rel* give, present, bestow; distribute, dispense

berate *syn* SCOLD, rate, tongue-lash, upbraid, jaw, bawl, chew out, wig, rail, revile, vituperate *rel* censure, denounce, condemn, reprehend, reprobate, criticize; rebuke, reprimand, reproach, reprove, chide

berth 1 *syn* ROOM, play, elbowroom, leeway, margin, clearance **2** *syn* WHARF, dock, pier, quay, slip, jetty, levee

beseech *syn* BEG, entreat, implore, supplicate, importune, adjure *rel* pray, petition, sue, plead, appeal

beset *syn* INFEST, overrun *rel* worry, annoy, harass, harry, pester, plague; assail, attack, assault

besides *syn* ALSO, moreover, furthermore, too, likewise

besiege • to surround an enemy in a fortified or strong position so as to prevent ingress or egress *syn* beleaguer, invest, blockade *rel* enclose, envelop, pen; surround, environ, encircle, encompass, hem; beset, infest; assail, attack, assault

besmirch *syn* SOIL, smirch, dirty, sully, foul, befoul, grime, begrime, tarnish *rel* spot, spatter, sprinkle *ant* cleanse

besotted *syn* FOND, infatuated, insensate *rel* fatuous, asinine, foolish, silly, simple; drunk, drunken, intoxicated, inebriated; stupid, slow, dull, dense, crass

bespangle *syn* SPOT, spangle, spatter, sprinkle, mottle, fleck, stipple, marble, speckle *rel* illuminate, illumine, lighten, light; glow, blaze, flame; flash, gleam, sparkle, scintillate, twinkle

bespangled *syn* SPOTTED, spangled, spattered, sprinkled, mottled, flecked, stippled, marbled, speckled *rel* bright, brilliant, radiant, luminous; illuminated, illumined, lighted

bespeak *syn* INDICATE, betoken, attest, argue, prove *rel* manifest, evidence, show, evince, demonstrate; imply, hint, suggest

bestial *syn* BRUTAL, brutish, brute, feral, beastly *rel* debased, depraved, corrupted, corrupt; degenerate, vicious; degraded; sensual, fleshly, carnal

bestow *syn* GIVE, confer, present, donate, afford *rel* distribute, dispense, divide; grant, award

bet • something (as money) staked on a winner-take-all basis on the outcome of an uncertainty *syn* wager, stake, pot, ante

bête noire *syn* ABOMINATION, bugbear, anathema

bethink *syn* REMEMBER, recollect, remind, recall, reminisce, mind

betide *syn* HAPPEN, befall, chance, occur, transpire

betimes *syn* EARLY, soon, beforehand *ant* unseasonably, inopportunely

betoken *syn* INDICATE, bespeak, attest, argue, prove *rel* presage, augur, portend, forebode, foretell; import, signify, denote, mean; evidence, manifest, show, evince, demonstrate

betray 1 *syn* DECEIVE, mislead, delude, beguile, double-cross *rel* trap, entrap, snare, ensnare, catch; dupe, trick, befool, hoodwink, gull **2** *syn* REVEAL, discover, disclose, divulge, tell *rel* manifest, evidence, evince, show, demonstrate; attest, betoken, bespeak, argue, indicate

better *adj* • more worthy or more pleasing than another or others *syn* superior, preferable *rel* choice, delicate, dainty; selected, culled, picked, preferred

better *vb, syn* IMPROVE, ameliorate, help *rel* correct, amend, reform, rectify, remedy, redress; enhance, intensify *ant* worsen

between • in common to (as in position, in a distribution, or in participation) *syn* among

bewail *syn* DEPLORE, lament, bemoan *rel* sorrow, grieve, mourn; wail, weep, cry *ant* rejoice

bewilder *syn* PUZZLE, mystify, perplex, distract, confound, nonplus, dumbfound *rel* confuse, addle, fuddle, muddle; fluster, flurry, perturb, agitate, upset, discompose; baffle, foil, frustrate

bewitch *syn* ATTRACT, enchant, captivate, fascinate, charm, allure *rel* thrill, electrify; delight, please; infatuate, enamor

bewitching *syn* ATTRACTIVE, enchanting, captivating, fascinating, charming, alluring

beyond *syn* FARTHER further

bias *n, syn* PREDILECTION, prejudice, prepossession, partiality *rel* slant, standpoint, point of view, viewpoint, angle; leaning, propensity; inclining, inclination, predisposition, disposition

bias *vb, syn* INCLINE, dispose, predispose *rel* sway, influence, affect, impress

bicker *syn* QUARREL, squabble, spat, tiff, wrangle, altercate *rel* contend, fight, battle, war

bickering *syn* QUARREL, spat, tiff, squabble, wrangle, altercation *rel* discord, contention, dissension, strife, conflict

bid *vb* **1** *syn* COMMAND, order, enjoin, direct, instruct, charge *rel* summon, summons, call, cite *ant* forbid **2** *syn* INVITE, solicit, court, woo *rel* ask, request

bid *n, syn* OVERTURE, tender, advance, approach *rel* offering, offer, proffering, proffer; proposal, proposition; inviting, invitation, soliciting, solicitation

biddable *syn* OBEDIENT, docile, amenable, tractable *rel* compliant, acquiescent; obliging, complaisant, good-natured, amiable; submissive, tame *ant* willful

bidding *syn* COMMAND, behest, order, injunction, mandate, dictate *rel* direction, instruction; summoning, summons, calling, call, citing, citation

big *syn* LARGE, great *rel* grand, magnificent, imposing, grandiose, majestic, august; huge, immense, enormous, gigantic, colossal *ant* little

bigot *syn* ENTHUSIAST, fanatic, zealot

bigoted *syn* ILLIBERAL, narrow-minded, narrow, intolerant, hidebound

bill • the jaws of a bird together with their horny covering *syn* beak, neb, nib

billingsgate *syn* ABUSE, scurrility, vituperation, invective, obloquy

bind *syn* TIE *rel* fasten, attach; join, link, unite, connect *ant* loose; unbind

biography • an account of the events and circumstances of a person's life *syn* life, memoir, autobiography, confessions

biologic *syn* DRUG, simple, medicinal, pharmaceutical

biotope *syn* HABITAT, range, station

birthright **1** *syn* RIGHT, appanage, prerogative, privilege, perquisite **2** *syn* HERITAGE, patrimony, inheritance

bisexual • combining male and female qualities *syn* hermaphroditic, hermaphrodite, androgynous, epicene

bit *syn* PARTICLE, mite, smidgen, whit, atom, iota, jot, tittle *rel* piece, fragment, detail, fraction, part, portion

bite • to attack with or as if with the teeth *syn* gnaw, champ, gnash *rel* eat, consume, devour

biting *syn* INCISIVE, cutting, crisp, trenchant, clear-cut *rel* caustic, mordant, acrid; pungent, poignant, piquant, racy

bitter • having or being an unusually unpleasant flavor or odor *syn* acrid *rel* sour, acid, acidulous, tart; pungent, piquant *ant* delicious

bizarre *syn* FANTASTIC, grotesque, antic *rel* outlandish, erratic, eccentric, strange, singular, odd, queer, curious; extravagant, extreme, excessive *ant* chaste; subdued

blab *syn* GOSSIP, tattle *rel* babble, gabble, chatter, prate, chat; divulge, disclose, betray, reveal

blackball *syn* EXCLUDE, debar, shut out, eliminate, rule out, disbar, suspend

blackguard *syn* VILLAIN, scoundrel, knave, rascal, rogue, scamp, rapscallion, miscreant

blame *vb, syn* CRITICIZE, reprehend, reprobate, condemn, denounce, censure *rel* accuse, charge, indict, impeach; impute, attribute; ascribe; implicate, involve

blame *n* • responsibility for misdeed or delinquency *syn* culpability, guilt, fault *rel* responsibility, accountability, answerability; censure, condemnation, denunciation, reprehension

blameworthy • deserving reproach and punishment for a wrong, sinful, or criminal act, practice, or condition *syn* guilty, culpable *ant* blameless

blanch *syn* WHITEN, bleach, decolorize, etiolate

bland **1** *syn* SUAVE, smooth, urbane, diplomatic, politic *rel* benign, benignant, kind, kindly; amiable, complaisant, obliging, good-natured; slick, unctuous, fulsome *ant* brusque **2** *syn* SOFT, mild, gentle, smooth, balmy, lenient *rel* neutral, indifferent; temperate, moderate; insipid, flat, vapid, wishy-washy *ant* pungent, piquant; savory, tasty, palatable

blandish *syn* COAX, wheedle, cajole *rel* allure, charm, bewitch, captivate, attract; lure, entice, seduce; beguile, delude, deceive

blank *syn* EMPTY, void, vacant, vacuous *rel* bare, barren; clean

blasé *syn* SOPHISTICATED, worldly-wise, worldly, disillusioned *rel* indifferent, unconcerned, incurious; nonchalant, imperturbable, unruffled, cool

blasphemous *syn* IMPIOUS, profane, sacrilegious *rel* cursing, damning, execrating, anathematizing, objurgating; irreligious, ungodly, godless *ant* reverent

blasphemy **1** • impious or irreverent speech *syn* profanity, swearing, cursing *rel* insult, affront, indignity; scurrility, vituperation, abuse *ant* adoration **2** *syn* PROFANATION, desecration, sacrilege *rel* debasement, corruption, perversion; misrepresentation, falsehood, untruth, lie

blast *n* • severe, sudden, or surprising ruin or injury *syn* blight, nip *rel* destruction; extermination, extirpation, wiping out; ruin, wreck

blast *vb* • to ruin or to injure severely, suddenly, or surprisingly *syn* blight, nip *rel* destroy; ruin, wreck; exterminate, extirpate, wipe; injure, damage, spoil

blatant *syn* VOCIFEROUS, clamorous, strident, boisterous, obstreperous *rel* assertive, self-assertive, pushing, aggressive, militant; vocal, articulate, voluble, glib; vulgar, coarse, gross *ant* decorous; reserved

blaze *n* • brightly burning light or fire *syn* flare, flame, glare, glow *rel* firing, fire, kindling, igniting, ignition; effulgence, refulgence, radiance, brilliance, brilliancy

blaze *vb* • to burn or appear to burn brightly *syn* flame, flare, glare, glow *rel* illuminate, illumine, light; burn; flash, gleam, glance

bleach *syn* WHITEN, etiolate, decolorize, blanch *ant* dye

bleak *syn* DISMAL, cheerless, dispiriting, dreary, desolate *rel* cold, chilly, frigid, freezing; barren, bare, bald; stripped, denuded

blemish • an imperfection (as a spot or crack) *syn* defect, flaw *rel* blot, stain, stigma; tainting, taint, pollution, defilement; fault, failing, frailty; lack, want, privation *ant* immaculateness

blench *syn* RECOIL, quail, shrink, flinch, wince *rel* evade, elude, avoid, shun, eschew, escape; tremble, quiver, shudder, quake, shake

blend *vb, syn* MIX, fuse, merge, coalesce, mingle, commingle, amalgamate *rel* combine, unite, conjoin, join; integrate; consolidate, unify, compact *ant* resolve

blend *n, syn* MIXTURE, admixture, compound, composite, amalgam

blessed *syn* HOLY, sacred, divine, spiritual, religious *ant* accursed

blessedness *syn* HAPPINESS, beatitude, bliss, felicity *rel* enjoyment, fruition, joy, pleasure *ant* misery, dolor

blight *n, syn* BLAST, nip *rel* injury, damage, hurt, harm; frustration, thwarting

blight *vb, syn* BLAST, nip *rel* injure, damage, hurt, harm, spoil; maim, cripple, batter; frustrate, thwart

blind *adj* • lacking or deficient in the power to see or to discriminate objects *syn* sightless, purblind

blind *n* • a device that serves as a screen for a window *syn* shade, shutter

blink *syn* WINK *rel* ignore, disregard, overlook, slight, neglect; evade, elude, avoid, shun, escape

bliss *syn* HAPPINESS, beatitude, blessedness, felicity *rel* enjoyment, joy, delectation, fruition, pleasure; rapture, ecstasy, transport *ant* anguish; bale

blithe *syn* MERRY, jocund, jovial, jolly *rel* gay, lively, animated, vivacious, sprightly; joyful, joyous, lighthearted, glad, happy, cheerful; buoyant, effervescent, volatile *ant* morose; atrabilious

bloc *syn* COMBINATION, party, faction, ring, combine

block *syn* HINDER, obstruct, bar, dam, impede *rel* check, arrest, interrupt; hamper, clog, trammel; prohibit, forbid, inhibit; frustrate, thwart, foil; prevent, forestall

blockade *n* • the isolation of an enemy area by a belligerent force to prevent the passage of persons or supplies *syn* siege

blockade *vb, syn* BESIEGE, beleaguer, invest *rel* close, shut; block, impede, obstruct, hinder; enclose; surround, environ, encircle

bloodless *syn* PALE, anemic *rel* colorless, uncolored; wishy-washy, vapid, inane, insipid *ant* sanguine; plethoric

bloody • affected by or involving the shedding of blood *syn* sanguinary, sanguine, sanguineous, gory

bloom *n, syn* BLOSSOM,flower, blow

bloom *vb, syn* BLOSSOM, flower, blow *rel* flourish, thrive, succeed

blossom *n* • the period or state of florescence of a seed plant *syn* flower, bloom, blow

blossom *vb* • to become florescent *syn* bloom, flower, blow

blot *syn* STIGMA, brand, stain *rel* taint, defilement, pollution; blemish, flaw, defect; shame, disgrace, ignominy, obloquy

blot out *syn* ERASE, delete, obliterate, expunge, cancel, efface *rel* abolish, annihilate, extinguish; wipe, exterminate, extirpate

blow *vb, syn* BLOSSOM, bloom, flower *rel* expand, swell; enlarge, augment, increase

blow *n, syn* BLOSSOM, bloom, flower

blowsy *syn* SLATTERNLY, frowzy, dowdy *rel* flashy, tawdry, gaudy, garish; slovenly, sloppy, disheveled, unkempt, slipshod; florid, flamboyant, ornate; vulgar, coarse *ant* smart, spruce; dainty

blubber *syn* CRY, weep, wail, keen, whimper

bluejacket *syn* MARINER, sailor, seaman, tar, gob

blueprint *n, syn* SKETCH, draft, tracing, plot, diagram, delineation, outline

blueprint *vb, syn* SKETCH, draft, trace, plot, diagram, delineate, outline

blues *syn* SADNESS, dejection, depression, melancholy, gloom, dumps

bluff • abrupt and unceremonious in speech or manner *syn* blunt, brusque, curt, crusty, gruff *rel* hearty, sincere; plain, open, frank, candid; abrupt, precipitate *ant* suave, smooth

blunder *vb, syn* STUMBLE, lurch, flounder, trip, lumber, galumph, lollop, bumble *rel* stagger, reel, totter; wallow, welter

blunder *n, syn* ERROR, mistake, bull, howler, boner, slip, lapse, faux pas *rel* fault, failing, frailty, vice; anachronism, solecism; aberration, deviation; transgression, violation, breach

blunt **1** *syn* DULL, obtuse *ant* keen, sharp **2** *syn* BLUFF, brusque, curt, gruff, crusty *rel* plain, candid, frank; rude, discourteous, ungracious, uncivil, impolite; forthright, downright *ant* tactful; subtle

blurb *syn* CRITICISM, puff, review, critique

blush *vb* • to turn or grow red in the face *syn* flush *rel* color, tint, tinge

blush *n* • reddening of the face *syn* flush *rel* color, tint, tinge, hue

bluster *vb, syn* ROAR, bellow, bawl, vociferate, clamor, howl, ululate *rel* boast, brag, vaunt, crow; threaten, menace

bluster *n, syn* ROAR, bellow, bawl, vociferation, ululation *rel* boast, brag, vaunt, crow; threaten, menace

board *syn* HARBOR, house, lodge, shelter, entertain *rel* feed, nourish

boast • to give vent in speech to one's pride in oneself or something intimately connected with oneself *syn* brag, vaunt, crow, gasconade *rel* flaunt, parade, show; pride, plume, pique, preen; exalt, magnify, aggrandize *ant* depreciate (*oneself, one's accomplishments*)

boat • a floating structure designed to carry persons or goods over water *syn* vessel, ship, craft

bodily • of or relating to the human body *syn* physical, corporeal, corporal, somatic *rel* carnal, fleshly, animal, sensual

body • the dead physical substance of a human being or animal *syn* corpse, carcass, cadaver

boggle *syn* DEMUR, stickle, stick, strain, scruple, balk, jib, shy *rel* object, protest, kick, remonstrate, expostulate; recoil, shrink, flinch, wince, blench, quail *ant* subscribe (*to*)

bogus *syn* COUNTERFEIT, spurious, fake, sham, pseudo, pinchbeck, phony *rel* fraudulent, deceitful, deceptive; duping, hoaxing, gulling, hoodwinking

boil *n, syn* ABSCESS, furuncle, carbuncle, pimple, pustule

boil *vb* • to prepare (as food) in a liquid heated to the point where it emits considerable steam *syn* seethe, simmer, parboil, stew

boisterous *syn* VOCIFEROUS, obstreperous, clamorous, blatant, strident *rel* sporting, disporting, rollicking, frolicking, gamboling; unruly, ungovernable; indecorous, unseemly

bold *syn* BRAVE, courageous, unafraid, fearless, intrepid, valiant, valorous, dauntless, undaunted, doughty, audacious *rel* daring, reckless, venturesome, adventurous, daredevil, rash, foolhardy; mettlesome, spirited; fearless, unapprehensive, unafraid *ant* cowardly

bolster *syn* SUPPORT, prop, sustain, buttress, brace *rel* strengthen, reinforce, fortify; uphold, champion

bombard *syn* ATTACK, assail, storm, assault

bombast • speech or writing characterized by high-flown pomposity or pretentiousness of language disproportionate to the thought or subject matter *syn* rhapsody, rant, fustian, rodomontade *rel* grandiloquence, magniloquence, rhetoric; inflatedness, turgidity, tumidity, flatulence

bombastic *syn* RHETORICAL, grandiloquent, magniloquent, aureate, flowery, euphuistic *rel* inflated, turgid, tumid; verbose, diffuse, wordy; eloquent, voluble, fluent, articulate, vocal

bona fide *syn* AUTHENTIC, genuine, veritable *rel* true, real, actual; reliable, dependable, trustworthy; pure, absolute, simple, sheer *ant* counterfeit, bogus

bond *adj, syn* BOUND, indentured, articled *ant* free

bond *n* **1** • something which serves to bind or bring two or more things firmly together *syn* band, tie **2** *syn* GUARANTEE, surety, security, bail, guaranty

bondage *syn* SERVITUDE, slavery

boner *syn* ERROR, blunder, mistake, howler, bull, slip, lapse, faux pas

bonny *syn* BEAUTIFUL, comely, pretty, good-looking, fair, lovely, handsome, beauteous, pulchritudinous *rel* pleasing, agreeable, pleasant; attractive, charming, captivating *ant* homely

bonus *syn* PREMIUM, bounty, reward, guerdon, award, prize, meed

bon vivant *syn* EPICURE, gastronome, gourmet, gourmand, glutton *ant* ascetic

bookish *syn* PEDANTIC, academic, scholastic

boon *syn* GIFT, favor, present, gratuity, largess *rel* benefaction, donation, contribution *ant* calamity

boor • an uncouth ungainly person *syn* churl, lout, clown, clodhopper, bumpkin, hick, yokel, rube *ant* gentleman

boorish • uncouth in manners, or appearance *syn* loutish, clownish, churlish *rel* awkward, clumsy, maladroit, inept; rude, discourteous, ungracious, uncivil, impolite, ill-mannered *ant* gentlemanly

boost *syn* LIFT, raise, elevate, hoist, rear, heave *rel* exalt, aggrandize; heighten, enhance, intensify; mount, soar, levitate, surge, ascend, rise

bootleg *syn* SMUGGLED, contraband

bootless *syn* FUTILE, fruitless, vain, abortive *rel* idle, empty, hollow, nugatory, vain, otiose

bootlicker *syn* PARASITE, sycophant, toady, lickspittle, hanger-on, favorite, leech, sponge, sponger

booty *syn* SPOIL, loot, plunder, prize, swag

border • the line or relatively narrow space which marks the limit or outermost bound of something *syn* margin, verge, edge, rim, brim, brink *rel* limit, bound, confine, end

bore *syn* PERFORATE, drill, puncture, punch, prick *rel* penetrate, pierce, enter

boredom *syn* TEDIUM, ennui, doldrums *rel* amusement

boring *syn* IRKSOME, tiresome, wearisome, tedious *rel* dull, humdrum, monotonous, dreary, stodgy, pedestrian

botch • to handle or treat awkwardly or unskillfully *syn* bungle, fumble, muff, cobble *rel* patch, mend, repair; treat, handle; mutilate; wreck, ruin

bother *syn* ANNOY, vex, irk *rel* worry, harass, harry, pester, tease, tantalize; interfere, meddle, tamper; puzzle, perplex, distract; trouble, inconvenience, incommode, discommode *ant* comfort

bottom *syn* BASE, found, ground, stay, rest *rel* support, sustain; set, fix, establish

bough *syn* SHOOT, branch, limb

bounce *syn* DISMISS, drop, sack, fire, discharge, cashier

bound *n, syn* LIMIT, confine, end, term *rel* border, verge, edge

bound *adj* • obliged to serve a master or in a clearly defined capacity for a certain number of years by the terms of a contract or mutual agreement *syn* bond, indentured, articled

bound *n, syn* JUMP, leap, spring, vault *rel* advance, progress; haste, hurry, speed, expedition

bound *vb* **1** *syn* JUMP, leap, spring, vault *rel* advance, progress; speed, precipitate, hasten, hurry **2** *syn* SKIP, ricochet, hop, curve, lope, lollop *rel* dart, skim, skud, fly; rebound, recoil, resile

bounder *syn* CAD, rotter

boundless *syn* INFINITE, uncircumscribed, illimitable, eternal, sempiternal *rel* vast, immense, enormous, huge; monstrous, prodigious, tremendous, stupendous

bountiful, bounteous *syn* LIBERAL, generous, openhanded, munificent, handsome *rel* charitable, philanthropic, benevolent; prodigal, lavish, profuse *ant* niggardly

bounty *syn* PREMIUM, award, reward, meed, guerdon, prize, bonus *rel* gratuity, largess, gift, boon; grant, subvention, subsidy, appropriation

bouquet *syn* FRAGRANCE, perfume, redolence, incense *rel* odor, aroma, smell, scent

bout *syn* SPELL, stint, turn, trick, tour, shift, go

bow *vb, syn* YIELD, defer, submit, capitulate, succumb, relent, cave

bow *n, syn* CURVE, arc, arch

bow *vb, syn* FLEX, crook, buckle *rel* bend, curve, twist

box *syn* STRIKE, hit, smite, punch, slug, slog, swat, clout, slap, cuff

boyish *syn* YOUTHFUL, juvenile, puerile, maiden, virgin, virginal

brace *n, syn* COUPLE, pair, yoke

brace *vb, syn* SUPPORT, sustain, buttress, prop, bolster *rel* strengthen, reinforce, fortify, energize, invigorate

brag *syn* BOAST, vaunt, crow, gasconade *rel* plume, pique, pride, preen; flaunt, parade *ant* apologize

braid *syn* WEAVE, plait, knit, crochet, tat

brain *syn* MIND, intellect, intelligence, wit, psyche, soul

branch *syn* SHOOT, limb, bough

brand *n* **1** *syn* MARK, stamp, label, tag, ticket *rel* impression, impress, imprint, print **2** *syn* STIGMA, blot, stain *rel* sear, scorch, burn; tainting, taint, defilement; blemish, defect, flaw

brand *vb, syn* MARK, stamp, label, tag, ticket

brandish *syn* SWING, flourish, shake, wave, thrash *rel* wield, swing, handle, manipulate, ply; flaunt, parade, display, exhibit, show

brash *syn* SHAMELESS, brazen, barefaced, impudent *rel* bold, audacious, brave; rash, reckless, adventurous; impetuous, headlong, abrupt, precipitate; intrusive, officious, impertinent *ant* wary

brave *adj* • having or showing no fear when faced with something dangerous, difficult, or unknown *syn* courageous, unafraid, fearless, intrepid, valiant, valorous, dauntless, undaunted, doughty, bold, audacious *rel* daring, venturesome, daredevil, adventurous; heroic, gallant; plucky, gritty *ant* craven

brave *vb, syn* FACE, dare, defy, beard, challenge *rel* confront, meet, encounter; oppose, combat, resist, fight

bravo *syn* ASSASSIN, cutthroat, gunman

brawl • a noisy fight or quarrel *syn* broil, fracas, melee, row, rumpus, scrap *rel* conflict, fight, fray, affray, contest; contention, dissension, strife, discord; wrangle, altercation, quarrel, squabble; uproar, racket, din, hubbub, clamor

brawny *syn* MUSCULAR, burly, husky, sinewy, athletic *rel* stalwart, strong, sturdy, stout, tough; fleshy *ant* scrawny

brazen *syn* SHAMELESS, brash, impudent *rel* callous, hardened, indurated; insolent, arrogant, proud; rash, reckless, adventurous; bold, audacious, brave *ant* bashful

breach **1** • the act or the offense of failing to keep the law or to do what the law, duty, or obligation requires *syn* infraction, violation, transgression, trespass, infringement, contravention *ant* observance **2** • a pulling apart in relations or in connections *syn* break, split, schism, rent, rupture, rift *rel* division, severance, separation; dissension, discord, difference, variance, strife; estrangement, alienation

bread, bread and butter *syn* LIVING, sustenance, livelihood, subsistence, maintenance, support, keep

break *vb* • to come apart or cause to come apart *syn* crack, burst, bust, snap, shatter, shiver *rel* disintegrate, crumble, decay; detach, disengage; demolish, destroy *ant* cleave (*together*); keep (*of laws*)

break *n* **1** • a lapse in continuity *syn* gap, interruption, interval, interim, hiatus, lacuna *rel* division, separation, severance; falling, sinking, dropping; respite, lull, intermission, recess, pause **2** *syn* BREACH, split, schism, rent, rupture, rift *rel* see BREACH 2 **3** *syn* OPPORTUNITY, chance, occasion, time

break down *syn* ANALYZE, resolve, dissect

breakdown *syn* ANALYSIS, resolution, dissection

breastwork *syn* BULWARK, bastion, parapet, rampart

breed *vb, syn* GENERATE, engender, propagate, reproduce, procreate, beget, sire, get

breed *n, syn* VARIETY, subspecies, race, cultivar, strain, clone, stock

breeding *syn* CULTURE, cultivation, refinement *rel* tact, address, poise, savoir faire;

courtesy, amenity, gallantry; grace, dignity, elegance *ant* vulgarity

breeze *syn* WIND, gale, hurricane, zephyr

bridle **1** *syn* RESTRAIN, check, curb, inhibit *rel* repress, suppress; govern, rule; control, direct, manage, conduct *ant* vent **2** *syn* STRUT, bristle, swagger *rel* plume, preen, pique, pride

brief *adj* • not long *syn* short *rel* transient, fleeting, passing, momentary, short-lived; concise, terse, succinct, laconic, pithy; compacted, compact, concentrated; shortened, abbreviated, abridged, curtailed *ant* prolonged, protracted

brief *n, syn* ABRIDGMENT, abstract, epitome, synopsis, conspectus

bright **1** • actually or seemingly shining or glowing with light *syn* brilliant, radiant, luminous, lustrous, effulgent, refulgent, beaming, lambent, lucent, incandescent *rel* illuminated, illumined, lighted, lightened, enlightened; flashing, gleaming, glistening, sparkling; glowing, flaming *ant* dull; dim **2** *syn* INTELLIGENT, smart, quick-witted, brilliant, clever, knowing, alert *rel* sharp, keen, acute; quick, ready, prompt, apt; precocious, advanced *ant* dense, dull

brilliant **1** *syn* BRIGHT, radiant, luminous, effulgent, lustrous, refulgent, beaming, lambent, lucent, incandescent *rel* flashing, scintillating, sparkling, gleaming, glittering, coruscating; blazing, flaming, flaring, glowing *ant* subdued (*of light, color*) **2** *syn* INTELLIGENT, clever, bright, smart, alert, quick-witted, knowing *rel* erudite, learned, scholarly; sage, sapient, wise *ant* crass

brim *syn* BORDER, rim, edge, brink, verge, margin

bring • to convey from one place to another *syn* take, fetch *rel* bear, carry, convey; obtain, procure, get *ant* withdraw, remove

brink *syn* BORDER, rim, brim, verge, edge, margin *rel* limit, bound, end, confine; shore, strand, coast

brisk *syn* AGILE, nimble, spry *rel* fast, quick, rapid, fleet, swift, speedy; ready, prompt, quick; dynamic, live, active *ant* sluggish

bristle *syn* STRUT, bridle, swagger *rel* preen, plume, pride, pique; evince, manifest, show, evidence; flaunt, parade, display, exhibit

brittle *syn* FRAGILE, crisp, frangible, short, friable *rel* hardened, indurated *ant* supple

broach *syn* EXPRESS, voice, utter, vent, air, ventilate *rel* reveal, disclose, divulge; introduce, interject, interpose

broad • having horizontal extent *syn* wide, deep *rel* extended, extensive; spacious, capacious, commodious, ample; vast, immense, huge; expanded, dilated *ant* narrow

broadcast **1** *syn* STREW, straw, scatter, sow *rel* spread, circulate, disseminate, propagate **2** *syn* DECLARE, promulgate, publish, advertise, announce, proclaim

broadcasting *syn* DECLARATION, promulgation, publication, advertisement, announcement, proclamation

Brobdingnagian *syn* HUGE, vast, immense, enormous, elephantine, mammoth, giant, gigantic, gigantean, colossal, gargantuan, Herculean, cyclopean, titanic *ant* lilliputian

broil *syn* BRAWL, fracas, melee, row, rumpus, scrap *rel* fray, affray, fight, conflict, combat, contest; altercation, wrangle, quarrel; contention, strife, dissension, conflict, discord

bromide *syn* COMMONPLACE, cliché, platitude, truism

brook *syn* BEAR, stand, abide, tolerate, suffer, endure

browbeat *syn* INTIMIDATE, bulldoze, bully, cow *rel* terrorize, terrify, frighten, scare

bruise *vb, syn* CRUSH, mash, smash, squash, macerate *rel* batter, mangle, maim; press, squeeze

bruise *n, syn* WOUND, contusion, trauma, traumatism, lesion

brush *vb* • to touch lightly in passing *syn* graze, glance, shave, skim *rel* touch, contact; scatter, disperse, dispel; slide, slip, glide

brush *n, syn* ENCOUNTER, skirmish *rel* contest, conflict, combat, fight, fray; engagement, action, battle; attack, assault, onset, onslaught

brusque *syn* BLUFF, curt, blunt, gruff, crusty *rel* ungracious, rude, impolite, uncivil, discourteous; rough, harsh *ant* unctuous; bland

brutal • characteristic of an animal in nature, action, or instinct *syn* brute, brutish, bestial, beastly, feral *rel* sensual, animal, fleshly, carnal; coarse, gross, vulgar; stupid, dull, dense, crass; barbarous, savage, barbarian

brute *syn* BRUTAL, brutish, bestial, beastly, feral *rel* inanimate, lifeless, dead; inert, supine, inactive; impotent, powerless

brutish *syn* BRUTAL, brute, bestial, beastly, feral *rel* dull, dense, crass, stupid; sluggish, comatose, lethargic; stolid, impassive, apathetic

buccaneer *syn* PIRATE, freebooter, privateer, corsair

buck *syn* FOP, dude, dandy, beau, coxcomb, exquisite

buckle *syn* FLEX, crook, bow *rel* break, crack, snap, burst; bend, twist, curve

bucolic *syn* RURAL, pastoral, rustic *rel* boorish, loutish, clownish, churlish; natural, simple, naïve, ingenuous *ant* urbane

buffet *syn* BEAT, baste, pummel, pound, belabor, thrash *rel* strike, smite, hit, slap, slug; batter

bugbear *syn* ABOMINATION, bête noire, anathema

build *vb* • to form or fashion a structure or something comparable to a structure *syn* construct, erect, frame, raise, rear *rel* fabricate, fashion, manufacture, make; produce, turn out, yield, bear *ant* unbuild, destroy

build *n, syn* PHYSIQUE, habit, constitution *rel* form, figure, shape, conformation, configuration; structure, framework; contour, outline; style, fashion

building • a construction (as of wood, brick, or stone) intended to house a family, a business, or an institution *syn* edifice, structure, pile

bulge *vb* • to extend outward beyond the usual and normal line *syn* jut, stick out, protrude, project, overhang, beetle *rel* swell, distend, dilate, expand

bulge *n, syn* PROJECTION, protuberance, protrusion

bulk • a body of usually material substance that constitutes a thing or unit *syn* mass, volume *rel* form, figure, shape

bulky *syn* MASSIVE, massy, monumental, substantial *rel* huge, gigantic, colossal, mammoth, elephantine, enormous; corpulent, obese, portly, fleshy; burly, husky, muscular

bull **1** *syn* ERROR, blunder, howler, boner, mistake, slip, lapse, faux pas **2** *syn* NONSENSE, twaddle, drivel, bunk, balderdash, poppycock, gobbledygook, trash, rot

bulldoze *syn* INTIMIDATE, bully, browbeat, cow *rel* threaten, menace; terrorize, terrify, frighten; worry, harass, harry

bullheaded *syn* OBSTINATE, pigheaded, stiff-necked, stubborn, mulish, dogged, pertinacious

bully *syn* INTIMIDATE, bulldoze, browbeat, cow *rel* torment, rack, torture, afflict; threaten, menace; terrorize, terrify, frighten, scare *ant* coax

bulwark • an aboveground defensive structure that forms part of a fortification *syn* breastwork, rampart, parapet, bastion *rel* stronghold, fortress, fort, citadel

bum *syn* VAGABOND, vagrant, tramp, hobo, truant

bumble *syn* STUMBLE, trip, blunder, lurch, flounder, lumber, galumph, lollop

bump • to come or cause to come into violent contact or close or direct opposition *syn* clash, collide, conflict *rel* hit, strike, smite; impinge, jolt, jar, impact

bumpkin *syn* BOOR, hick, yokel, rube, clodhopper, clown, lout, churl

bunch **1** *syn* GROUP, cluster, parcel, lot *rel* see BUNCH 2 **2** *syn* BUNDLE, bale, parcel, pack, package, packet *rel* collection, assemblage, gathering; quantity, number, aggregate, sum

bundle • things done up for storage, sale, or carriage *syn* bunch, bale, parcel, pack, package, packet *rel* collection, assemblage, gathering; bag, sack

bungle *syn* BOTCH, fumble, muff, cobble *rel* confuse, muddle, addle, befuddle; confuse, confound, mistake; disorder, disarrange, disorganize, derange; entangle, enmesh

bunk *syn* NONSENSE, twaddle, drivel, balderdash, poppycock, gobbledygook, trash, rot, bull

buoyant *syn* ELASTIC, volatile, expansive, resilient, effervescent *rel* spirited, high-spirited, mettlesome, gingery; lively, vivacious, animated, sprightly; jocund, blithe, merry; optimistic, hopeful *ant* depressed, dejected

burden *n, syn* LOAD, cargo, freight, lading

burden *vb* • to lay a heavy load upon or to lie like a heavy load upon a person or thing *syn* encumber, cumber, weigh, weight, load, lade, tax, charge, saddle *rel* oppress, depress, weigh; crush, mash

burden *n, syn* SUBSTANCE, purport, gist, core, pith *rel* subject, matter, subject matter, theme, text, topic

burdensome *syn* ONEROUS, oppressive, exacting *rel* heavy, ponderous, cumbersome, cumbrous, weighty; irksome, wearisome; fatiguing, exhausting, fagging, tiring; arduous, hard, difficult *ant* light

burglar *syn* THIEF, robber, larcener, larcenist *rel* stealer, pilferer, filcher, purloiner; plunderer, looter, rifler

burglarize *syn* ROB, plunder, rifle, loot *rel* steal, pilfer, filch, purloin, lift, pinch, snitch, cop, swipe; sack, pillage, ravage, despoil

burglary *syn* THEFT, larceny, robbery

burlesque *n, syn* CARICATURE, parody, travesty *rel* mimicry, mockery, imitation; fun, jest, sport, game; satire, sarcasm, humor, wit; derision, ridicule

burlesque *vb, syn* CARICATURE, parody, travesty *rel* mimic, ape, mock, imitate, copy; ridicule, deride

burly *syn* MUSCULAR, husky, brawny, athletic, sinewy *rel* corpulent, fleshy, portly; bulky, substantial, massive; vigorous, lusty; powerful, forceful, potent *ant* lanky, lank

burn • to injure by exposure to fire or intense heat *syn* scorch, char, sear, singe *rel* kindle, fire, ignite, light; blaze, flame, glow

burp *syn* BELCH, vomit, disgorge, regurgitate, spew, throw up

burst *syn* BREAK, crack, bust, snap, shatter, shiver *rel* distend, swell, expand; push, shove, thrust, propel

bury *syn* HIDE, secrete, cache, conceal, screen, ensconce

business 1 *syn* WORK, occupation, pursuit, calling, employment *rel* trade, craft, handicraft, art, profession **2** *syn* AFFAIR, concern, matter, thing *rel* function, office, duty, province; task, job, assignment, chore, stint **3** • one of the forms or branches of human endeavor which have for their objective the supplying of commodities *syn* commerce, trade, industry, traffic

bust *syn* BREAK, crack, burst, snap, shatter, shiver *rel* see BURST

bustle *syn* STIR, flurry, ado, fuss, pother *rel* business, commerce, trade, industry, traffic; movement, motion; hubbub, clamor, racket, babel, din

busy • actively engaged or occupied in work or in accomplishing a purpose or intention *syn* industrious, diligent, assiduous, sedulous *rel* engrossed, absorbed, intent; working, toiling, laboring, travailing *ant* idle; unoccupied

butchery *syn* MASSACRE, slaughter, carnage, pogrom *rel* murdering, murder, slaying, killing

butt in *syn* INTRUDE, obtrude, interlope *rel* interfere, meddle, intermeddle; interpose, intervene, interfere, mediate, intercede

buttress *n* • auxiliary structures designed to serve as a prop, shore, or support for a wall (as of a building) *syn* pier, abutment

buttress *vb, syn* SUPPORT, sustain, prop, bolster, brace *rel* uphold, back, champion; strengthen, reinforce, fortify; defend, protect, shield, guard

buy • to acquire something for money or an equivalent *syn* purchase *rel* obtain, acquire, procure, get; pay, compensate, remunerate

by • using as a means of approach or action *syn* through, with

bystander *syn* SPECTATOR, onlooker, looker-on, witness, eyewitness, observer, beholder

byword *syn* CATCHWORD, shibboleth, slogan *rel* proverb, saying, saw, motto; abuse, invective; legend, caption, inscription

C

cabal *syn* PLOT, intrigue, conspiracy, machination

cabalistic *syn* MYSTICAL, anagogic, mystic *rel* occult, esoteric, recondite, abstruse; cryptic, enigmatic, obscure; arcane, mysterious

cache *syn* HIDE, secrete, bury, conceal, ensconce, screen

cad • one who shows himself to be no gentleman *syn* bounder, rotter

cadaver *syn* BODY, corpse, carcass

cadaverous *syn* HAGGARD, wasted, pinched, worn, careworn *rel* gaunt, skinny, scrawny, angular, rawboned, lank, lanky, lean, spare *ant* plump, stout

cadence *syn* RHYTHM, meter *rel* accentuation, accent, stress, emphasis; beat, pulse, throb, pulsation

cage *syn* ENCLOSE, envelop, fence, pen, coop, corral, wall *rel* confine, circumscribe, limit; imprison, incarcerate, jail; surround, environ, encompass, hem

cajole *syn* COAX, wheedle, blandish *rel* entice, inveigle, seduce, decoy, lure; beguile, delude, deceive; tease, tantalize, worry

cake *syn* HARDEN, solidify, indurate, petrify *rel* compact, consolidate; contract, compress, condense, shrink

calamitous *syn* UNLUCKY, disastrous, ill-starred, ill-fated, unfortunate, luckless, hapless

calamity *syn* DISASTER, catastrophe, cataclysm *rel* accident, casualty, mishap; misfortune, mischance, adversity, mishap; tribulation, visitation, affliction, trial, cross; ruin, wreck *ant* boon

calculate • to determine something (as cost, speed, or quantity) by mathematical processes *syn* compute, estimate, reckon *rel* weigh, study, consider; ponder, ruminate; determine, ascertain, discover

calculating *syn* CAUTIOUS, circumspect, wary, chary *rel* deliberate, designed, considered, studied, premeditated; designing, scheming, plotting; wily, guileful, crafty, artful, cunning, sly *ant* reckless, rash

calculation *syn* CAUTION, circumspection, wariness, chariness *rel* prudence, forethought, foresight, providence, discretion; care, concern, solicitude; astuteness, perspicacity, sagacity, shrewdness *ant* recklessness, rashness

caliber *syn* QUALITY, stature *rel* capability, capacity, ability; force, power

call *vb, syn* SUMMON, summons, cite, convoke, convene, muster *rel* assemble, gather, collect; invite, bid

call *n, syn* VISIT, visitation

caller *syn* VISITOR, visitant, guest

calling *syn* WORK, occupation, pursuit, business, employment *rel* profession, trade, craft, art, handicraft

callous *syn* HARDENED, indurated *rel* tough, tenacious, stout, strong; firm, solid, hard; inflexible, adamant, obdurate, inexorable; insensitive, impassible, insensible, anesthetic *ant* tender

callow *syn* RUDE, green, crude, raw, rough, uncouth *rel* puerile, boyish, juvenile, youthful; naïve, ingenuous, simple, unsophisticated, artless, natural; adolescent, pubescent *ant* full-fledged, grown-up

calm *adj* • quiet and free from all that disturbs or excites *syn* tranquil, serene, placid, peaceful, halcyon *rel* still, quiet, stilly, noiseless; pacific, peaceable; impassive, stoic; unruffled, composed, collected, imperturbable, unflappable, cool *ant* stormy; agitated

calm *vb* • to relieve or to bring to an end whatever distresses, agitates, or disturbs *syn* compose, quiet, quieten, still, lull, soothe, settle, tranquilize *rel* allay, assuage, mitigate, alleviate, relieve; mollify, placate, appease, pacify *ant* agitate, arouse

calumniate *syn* MALIGN, defame, slander, asperse, traduce, vilify, libel *rel* revile, vituperate, scold; decry, derogate, detract, belittle, disparage *ant* eulogize; vindicate

calumny *syn* DETRACTION, slander, backbiting, scandal *rel* aspersion, reflection, animadversion, stricture; defaming, defamation, maligning, traducing, vilifying, vilification, libeling, libel *ant* eulogy; vindication

camouflage *syn* DISGUISE, cloak, mask, dissemble

canal *syn* CHANNEL, conduit, duct, aqueduct

cancel *syn* ERASE, efface, obliterate, expunge, delete, blot out *rel* invalidate, annul, nullify; void, abrogate; deface, disfigure; neutralize, counteract, negative

candid *syn* FRANK, open, plain *rel* truthful, veracious; fair, dispassionate, impartial, unbiased, just; sincere; honest, scrupulous, upright *ant* evasive

candidate • one who seeks an office, honor, position, or award *syn* aspirant, nominee, applicant

canon *syn* LAW, precept, regulation, rule, statute, ordinance *rel* principle, fundamental, axiom; criterion, standard, yardstick, touchstone, gauge

cant **1** *syn* DIALECT, jargon, argot, lingo, vernacular, slang, patois *rel* phraseology, vocabulary, diction, language; idiom, speech **2** *syn* HYPOCRISY, sanctimony, pharisaism

canting *syn* HYPOCRITICAL, sanctimonious, pharisaical

capability *syn* ABILITY, capacity *rel* competence, qualification, qualifications; proficiency, adeptness, expertness, skillfulness; art, skill, cunning *ant* incapability, incompetence

capable *syn* ABLE, competent, qualified *rel* efficient, effective, effectual, efficacious *ant* incapable

capacious *syn* SPACIOUS, commodious, ample *rel* broad, wide; extended, extensive; expanded, expansive *ant* exiguous

capacity *syn* ABILITY, capability *rel* amplitude, expanse, spread; extent, magnitude, size, volume; aptitude, gift, faculty, talent, bent, turn, knack *ant* incapacity

caper *syn* PRANK, monkeyshine, antic, dido *rel* gamboling, gambol, rollicking, rollick, romping, romp, frolicking, frolic; skipping, skip, hopping, hop, bounding, bound

capital *syn* CHIEF, principal, main, leading, foremost *rel* primary, primordial, primal; fundamental, basic, radical, underlying; cardinal, vital, essential

capitulate *syn* YIELD, submit, succumb, relent, defer, bow, cave *rel* surrender, abandon, waive, cede, relinquish

capitulation *syn* SURRENDER, submission *rel* yielding, relenting, succumbing, caving in; truce, cease-fire, armistice, peace

caprice • an arbitrary notion that usually lacks a logical basis and therefore may be unsound, impractical, or even irrational *syn* freak, fancy, whim, whimsy, conceit, vagary, crotchet *rel* humor, mood, temper, vein; notion, idea; impulse, motive; irrationality, unreasonableness; perverseness, contrariness

capricious *syn* INCONSTANT, mercurial, unstable, fickle *rel* changeable, changeful, protean, variable; moody, humorsome; volatile, effervescent *ant* steadfast

capsize *syn* OVERTURN, upset, overthrow, subvert

caption *syn* INSCRIPTION, legend

captious *syn* CRITICAL, caviling, carping, hypercritical, faultfinding, censorious *rel* contrary, perverse; exacting, demanding; peevish, petulant, snappish, irritable; testy, choleric, irascible *ant* appreciative

captivate *syn* ATTRACT, fascinate, bewitch, enchant, charm, allure *rel* delight, please, gratify; win, gain, get *ant* repulse

captivating *syn* ATTRACTIVE, fascinating, bewitching, enchanting, charming, alluring *rel* pleasing, pleasant, agreeable, grateful; delightful, delectable; lovely, bonny, fair, beautiful *ant* repulsive

captive *syn* PRISONER

capture *syn* CATCH, trap, snare, entrap, ensnare, bag *rel* seize, take, grasp, clutch, snatch; arrest, apprehend

carbon copy *syn* REPRODUCTION, copy, duplicate, transcript, facsimile, replica

carbuncle *syn* ABSCESS, boil, furuncle, pimple, pustule

carcass *syn* BODY, corpse, cadaver

cardinal *syn* ESSENTIAL, vital, fundamental *rel* requisite, necessary, indispensable, needful; radical, fundamental, basic; capital, principal, chief, main, leading; important, significant, momentous *ant* negligible

care • a troubled or engrossed state of mind or the thing that causes this *syn* concern, solicitude, anxiety, worry *rel* trouble, pains, effort, exertion; disquieting, disquiet, perturbing, perturbation, discomposing, discomposure; vigilance, watchfulness, alertness

careful • marked by close attention to details or care in execution or performance *syn* meticulous, scrupulous, punctilious, punctual *rel* cautious, circumspect, wary; provident, foresighted, prudent; accurate, precise, nice, exact, correct; studied, deliberate *ant* careless

careless • showing lack of concern or attention *syn* heedless, thoughtless, inadvertent *rel* negligent, neglectful, lax, slack, remiss; casual, desultory, haphazard, random, hit-or-miss, happy-go-lucky *ant* careful

caress • to show affection or love by touching or handling *syn* fondle, pet, cosset, cuddle, dandle *rel* trifle, toy, dally, flirt, coquet; cherish, nurse

careworn *syn* HAGGARD, worn, pinched, wasted, cadaverous *rel* troubled, distressed; lean, gaunt, scrawny, skinny; exhausted, fagged, jaded, tuckered *ant* carefree

cargo *syn* LOAD, burden, freight, lading

caricature *n* • a grotesque or bizarre imitation of something *syn* burlesque, parody, travesty *rel* satire, humor, sarcasm, wit; grotesqueness, fantasticality, bizarreness; lampoon, libel, skit, squib, pasquinade

caricature *vb* • to make a grotesque or bizarre imitation of something *syn* burlesque, parody, travesty *rel* mimic, mock, ape, imitate, copy; distort, deform; simulate, counterfeit, assume; ridicule, deride

carnage *syn* MASSACRE, slaughter, butchery, pogrom

carnal • characterized by physical rather than intellectual or spiritual orientation *syn* fleshly, sensual, animal *rel* physical, bodily, corporeal, corporal, somatic; sensuous; gross, coarse, vulgar, obscene; earthly, earthy, worldly, mundane; lustful, lewd, wanton, lascivious, licentious *ant* spiritual; intellectual

carol *syn* SING, toll, descant, warble, trill, hymn, chant, intone

carping *syn* CRITICAL, caviling, faultfinding, captious, hypercritical, censorious *rel* blaming, reprehending, reprobating, criticizing; upbraiding, jawing, railing; depreciating, depreciative, disparaging, decrying *ant* fulsome

carry • to be the agent or the means whereby something or someone is moved from one place to another *syn* bear, convey, transport, transmit *rel* take, bring, fetch; move, remove, shift, transfer; drive, ride

cartel **1** *syn* CONTRACT, compact, pact, convention, bargain, concordat, treaty, entente **2** *syn* MONOPOLY, pool, syndicate, corner, trust *rel* combine, combination; consolidation, merger, amalgamation

carve **1** *syn* CUT, slit, hew, chop, slash *rel* shape, fashion, form, make; separate, divide, part **2** • to cut an outline or a shape out of or into some substance *syn* incise, engrave, etch, chisel, sculpture, sculpt, sculp *rel* shape, fashion, form, make; produce, turn out

case **1** *syn* INSTANCE, illustration, example, specimen, sample *rel* occurrence, event, incident, episode, circumstance; situation, condition, state **2** *syn* SUIT, cause, action, lawsuit

casement *syn* WINDOW, dormer, oriel

cash *syn* MONEY, currency, legal tender, specie, coin, coinage

cashier *syn* DISMISS, discharge, drop, fire, sack, bounce *rel* eject, expel, oust; eliminate, disbar, exclude, suspend

cast **1** *syn* THROW, fling, hurl, pitch, toss, sling *rel* direct, aim, point, level, train, lay; scatter, disperse **2** *syn* DISCARD, shed, molt, slough, scrap, junk *rel* relinquish, abandon, yield, surrender, leave; repudiate, reject, decline; dismiss, drop **3** *syn* ADD, figure, foot, sum, total, tot *rel* compute, calculate, reckon

castaway *syn* OUTCAST, derelict, reprobate, pariah, untouchable

castigate *syn* PUNISH, chastise, chasten, discipline, correct *rel* beat, baste, thrash, pummel, belabor; berate, tongue-lash, rate, upbraid, wig, rail, scold; penalize, fine, amerce, mulct

castrate *syn* STERILIZE, spay, emasculate, alter, mutilate, geld

casual **1** *syn* ACCIDENTAL, incidental, contingent, fortuitous *rel* unpremeditated, extemporaneous; indifferent, unconcerned, incurious; negligent, slack, lax, remiss; inadvertent, careless, heedless **2** *syn* RANDOM, desultory, haphazard, chancy, hit-or-miss, happy-go-lucky *rel* offhand, impromptu, improvised, extemporaneous, extempore; spontaneous, impulsive; unmethodical, unsystematic *ant* deliberate

casualty *syn* ACCIDENT, mishap *rel* disaster, calamity, catastrophe, cataclysm; misfortune, mischance, mishap

casuistical *syn* FALLACIOUS, sophistical *rel* plausible, specious; tortuous, winding; oblique, devious, crooked; misleading, delusive, deceptive, delusory

casuistry *syn* FALLACY, sophistry, sophism

cataclysm *syn* DISASTER, catastrophe,

calamity *rel* convulsing, convulsion, rocking, shaking, agitation; revolution, rebellion; misfortune, mischance, mishap

catalog *n, syn* LIST, inventory, table, schedule, register, roll, roster

catalog *vb, syn* RECORD, register, list, enroll *rel* enumerate, number, count; enter, admit

cataract *syn* FLOOD, deluge, inundation, torrent, spate

catastrophe *syn* DISASTER, calamity, cataclysm *rel* trial, tribulation, visitation; defeating, defeat, overthrowing, overthrow, routing, rout

catch 1 • to come to possess or control by or as if by seizing *syn* capture, trap, snare, entrap, ensnare, bag *rel* seize, take, grasp, grab, clutch, snatch; apprehend, arrest *ant* miss **2** *syn* INCUR, contract

catching *syn* INFECTIOUS, contagious, communicable

catchword • a phrase that catches the eye or the ear and is repeated so often that it becomes a formula *syn* byword, shibboleth, slogan *rel* caption, legend, inscription; phrase, expression, idiom; commonplace, platitude, truism, bromide, cliché

catechize *syn* ASK, interrogate, quiz, examine, question, query, inquire

categorical 1 *syn* ULTIMATE, absolute **2** *syn* EXPLICIT, express, definite, specific *rel* positive, certain, sure; forthright, downright

category *syn* CLASS, *rel* genus, species, denomination, genre; division, section, part; classification

cater • to furnish with what satisfies the appetite or desires *syn* purvey, pander *rel* furnish, equip, appoint, accouter; pamper, indulge, humor; satisfy, content

catholic *syn* UNIVERSAL, cosmic, ecumenical, cosmopolitan *rel* whole, entire, total; all-around, many-sided, versatile; prevalent, prevailing, current *ant* parochial; provincial

catnap *syn* SLEEP, nap, snooze, slumber, drowse, doze

cause • that (as a person, fact, or condition) which is responsible for an effect *syn* determinant, antecedent, reason, occasion *rel* motive, spring, incentive, inducement, spur, goad, impulse; motivation, activation, actuation; agent, agency; origin, root, source, prime mover **2** *syn* SUIT, lawsuit, action, cause, case

caustic • stingingly incisive *syn* mordant, acrid, scathing *rel* biting, cutting, incisive, trenchant; bitter; sharp, keen, acute; sarcastic, satiric, ironic *ant* genial

caution *n* • careful prudence esp. in reducing or avoiding risk or danger *syn* circumspection, wariness, chariness, calculation *rel* watchfulness, vigilance, alertness; prudence, providence, foresight, forethought, discretion *ant* temerity; adventurousness

caution *vb, syn* WARN, forewarn *rel* admonish, reprove; counsel, advise

cautious • prudently watchful and discreet in the face of danger or risk *syn* circumspect, wary, chary, calculating *rel* watchful, vigilant, alert; prudent, provident, foresighted, forethoughtful, discreet; heedful, careful *ant* adventurous, temerarious

cavalcade *syn* PROCESSION, parade, cortege, motorcade *rel* succession, progression, chain, train; array, display

cave *syn* YIELD, succumb, submit, capitulate, relent, defer, bow

caviling *syn* CRITICAL, captious, faultfinding, censorious, carping, hypercritical *rel* exacting, demanding; contrary, perverse; objecting, protesting, expostulating, kicking

cavity *syn* HOLE, hollow, pocket, void, vacuum

cease *syn* STOP, quit, discontinue, desist *rel* end, terminate, close, conclude, finish; stay, suspend, intermit, defer

cease-fire *syn* TRUCE, armistice, peace

cede *syn* RELINQUISH, surrender, abandon, waive, resign, yield, leave *rel* grant, concede, award, accord, vouchsafe

celebrate *syn* KEEP, commemorate, solemnize, observe

celebrated *syn* FAMOUS, renowned, famed, eminent, illustrious *rel* prominent, conspicuous, outstanding, signal, noticeable *ant* obscure

celebrity *syn* FAME, renown, glory, honor, éclat, reputation, repute, notoriety *rel* prominence, conspicuousness *ant* obscurity

celerity • quickness in movement or action *syn* alacrity, legerity *rel* expedition, dispatch, speed, hurry, haste; quickness, rapidity, swiftness, fleetness; velocity, speed; agility, briskness, nimbleness *ant* leisureliness

celestial • of, relating to, or fit for heaven or the heavens *syn* heavenly, empyrean, empyreal *rel* ethereal, aerial, airy; divine, spiritual, holy *ant* terrestrial

celibate *syn* UNMARRIED, single, virgin, maiden

cenobite *syn* RECLUSE, eremite, hermit, anchorite *rel* monk, friar, religious, nun

censorious *syn* CRITICAL, faultfinding, hypercritical, captious, carping, caviling *rel* reproaching, reproachful, chiding; condemning, condemnatory, denouncing, denunciatory, reprehending *ant* eulogistic

censure *syn* CRITICIZE, reprehend, blame, condemn, denounce, reprobate *rel* reprimand, rebuke, reproach, reprove; upbraid, berate, tongue-lash, scold *ant* commend

center *n* • the point, spot, or portion of a thing which is comparable to a point around which a circle is described *syn* middle, midst, core, hub, focus, nucleus, heart

center *vb* • to draw to or fix upon a center *syn* focus, centralize, concentrate *rel* depend, hinge, hang, turn; rest, base, ground

central • dominant or most important *syn* focal, pivotal *rel* dominant, paramount, predominant, preponderant; outstanding, salient, signal, noticeable; important, significant

centralize *syn* CENTER, focus, concentrate *rel* gather, collect, assemble; accumulate, amass; compact, consolidate, unify

cerebral *syn* MENTAL, intellectual, psychic, intelligent

ceremonial *adj* • characterized or marked by attention to the forms, procedures, and details prescribed as right, proper, or requisite *syn* ceremonious, formal, conventional, solemn *rel* liturgical, ritualistic

ceremonial *n, syn* FORM, ceremony, ritual, rite, liturgy, formality

ceremonious *syn* CEREMONIAL, formal, solemn, conventional *rel* impressive, moving; decorous, seemly, proper; stately, imposing, majestic, grandiose, grand *ant* unceremonious, informal

ceremony *syn* FORM, ceremonial, ritual, liturgy, rite, formality

certain **1** *syn* SURE, positive, cocksure *rel* confident, assured, sanguine *ant* uncertain **2** • bound to follow in obedience to the laws of nature or of thought *syn* inevitable, necessary *ant* probable; supposed

certainty • a state of mind in which one is free from doubt *syn* certitude, assurance, conviction *rel* belief, faith, credence; proof, demonstration *ant* uncertainty

certify **1** • to testify to the truth or genuineness of something *syn* attest, witness, vouch *rel* avouch, avow, aver, assert, profess **2** *syn* APPROVE, endorse, accredit, sanction *rel* vouch; authorize, commission, license

certitude *syn* CERTAINTY, assurance, conviction *rel* belief, faith, credence, credit; sureness, positiveness, cocksureness *ant* doubt

chafe *syn* ABRADE, excoriate, fret, gall *rel* injure, hurt, damage, impair; flay, skin, peel; abuse, maltreat, outrage; irritate, exasperate

chaff *syn* BANTER, kid, rag, jolly, rib, josh *rel* tease, tantalize, worry; ridicule, deride, twit, taunt

chagrined *syn* ASHAMED, mortified *rel* discomfited, abashed, embarrassed, disconcerted; humiliated; discomposed, perturbed, upset

chain *syn* SUCCESSION, series, train, string, sequence, progression

challenge *syn* FACE, brave, dare, defy, beard *rel* question, ask; dispute, discuss; claim; demand, require; invite, solicit

chamber *syn* ROOM, apartment

champ *syn* BITE, gnaw, gnash *rel* crush, smash, mash, macerate

champion *n, syn* VICTOR, vanquisher, winner, conqueror

champion *vb, syn* SUPPORT, back, advocate, uphold *rel* contend, fight, battle; espouse, adopt; defend, justify, vindicate, maintain; aid, assist, help *ant* combat

chance *n* **1** • something that happens without an apparent or determinable cause or as a result of unpredictable forces *syn* accident, fortune, luck, hap, hazard *rel* contingency, emergency, pass, juncture, exigency *ant* law, principle **2** *syn* OPPORTUNITY, occasion, break, time *rel* possibility, likelihood, probability; prospect, outlook, foretaste, anticipation

chance *vb* **1** *syn* HAPPEN, befall, betide, occur, transpire **2** *syn* VENTURE, hazard, risk, jeopardize, endanger, imperil *rel* dare, beard, face; meet, encounter, confront

chance *adj, syn* RANDOM, haphazard,

chancy, casual, desultory, hit-or-miss, happy-go-lucky

chancy *syn* RANDOM, haphazard, chance, hit-or-miss, happy-go-lucky, casual, desultory

change *vb* • to make or become different *syn* alter, vary, modify *rel* transform, metamorphose, transmute, convert, transmogrify; exchange, interchange; fluctuate, oscillate, swing

change *n* **1** • a making different *syn* alteration, variation, modification *rel* variety, diversity; divergence, deviation, aberration *ant* uniformity; monotony **2** • a result of a making different *syn* mutation, permutation, vicissitude, alternation *rel* metamorphosis, transformation, conversion, transmutation, transmogrification; substitute, surrogate, shift

changeable • having or showing a marked capacity for changes or a marked tendency to alter under slight provocation *syn* changeful, variable, mutable, protean *rel* unstable, inconstant, mercurial, capricious, fickle; mobile, movable *ant* stable; unchangeable

changeful *syn* CHANGEABLE, variable, protean, mutable *rel* fluid, liquid; active, dynamic, live; progressing, advancing; declining, deteriorating, degenerating *ant* changeless; stereotyped

channel **1** *syn* STRAIT, passage, narrows, sound **2** • something through which a fluid (as water) is led or flows *syn* canal, conduit, duct, aqueduct *rel* passage, pass, way **3** *syn* MEAN, vehicle, instrument, instrumentality, organ, agency, agent, medium

chant *syn* SING, troll, carol, descant, warble, trill, hymn, intone

chaos **1** *syn* CONFUSION, disorder, disarray, jumble, clutter, snarl, muddle *ant* system **2** *syn* ANARCHY, lawlessness

chaperon *syn* ACCOMPANY, attend, escort, convoy, conduct *rel* protect, shield, guard, safeguard, defend

char *syn* BURN, scorch, sear, singe

character **1** • an arbitrary or conventional device that is used in writing and in printing, but is neither a word nor a phrase nor a picture *syn* symbol, sign, mark **2** *syn* QUALITY, property, attribute, accident *rel* characteristic, peculiarity, distinctiveness, distinction, individuality **3** *syn* DISPOSITION, individuality, personality, complexion, temperament, temper *rel* mind, intellect, soul, intelligence; soul, spirit; courage, mettle, spirit, resolution **4** *syn* TYPE, nature, description, kind, ilk, sort, stripe, kidney **5** *syn* CREDENTIAL, reference, recommendation, testimonial

characteristic *adj* • being or revealing a quality specific or identifying to an individual or group *syn* individual, peculiar, distinctive *rel* special, especial, specific, particular; typical, natural, normal, regular

characteristic *n* • something that marks or sets apart a person or thing *syn* trait, feature *rel* quality, property, character; peculiarity, individuality

characterize • to be a peculiar or significant quality or feature of something *syn* distinguish, mark, qualify *rel* distinguish, differentiate, demarcate; individualize, peculiarize

charge *vb* **1** *syn* BURDEN, encumber, cumber, weigh, weight, load, lade, tax, saddle **2** *syn* COMMAND, direct, instruct, bid, enjoin, order *rel* request, solicit, ask; adjure, beg **3** *syn* ACCUSE, incriminate, indict, impeach, arraign *rel* denounce, blame, censure, condemn, criticize *ant* absolve **4** *syn* ASCRIBE, attribute, impute, assign, refer, credit, accredit *rel* fasten, attach, fix, affix; join, connect, link **5** *syn* RUSH, dash, tear, shoot *rel* impel, drive, move; fly, dart, scud

charge *n, syn* PRICE, cost, expense

chargé d'affaires *syn* AMBASSADOR, legate, nuncio, minister, envoy, internuncio

chariness *syn* CAUTION, circumspection, wariness, calculation *rel* prudence, providence, discretion, foresight, forethought

charitable • having or showing interest in or being concerned with the welfare of others *syn* benevolent, humane, humanitarian, philanthropic, eleemosynary, altruistic *rel* generous, liberal, bountiful, bounteous, openhanded, munificent; merciful, forbearing, lenient, clement, tolerant; tender, compassionate, warmhearted, sympathetic *ant* uncharitable

charity **1** *syn* MERCY, clemency, grace, lenity *rel* love, affection, attachment; benevolence, humaneness, altruism; benignity, benignancy, kindness, kindliness; generousness, generosity, liberalness, liberality, bountifulness, bounty, openhandedness; goodwill, amity, friendship *ant* malice, ill will **2** • love for one's fellowmen and a disposition to help those who are in need *syn* philanthropy

charlatan *syn* IMPOSTOR, mountebank, quack, faker *rel* humbug, fraud, cheat, fake pretender, feigner, counterfeiter

charm *n, syn* FETISH, talisman, amulet

charm *vb, syn* ATTRACT, fascinate, allure, captivate, enchant, bewitch *rel* delight, rejoice, please, gratify *ant* disgust

charming *syn* ATTRACTIVE, fascinating, alluring, captivating, enchanting, bewitching *rel* delightful, delectable, delicious; pleasing, agreeable, grateful, pleasant *ant* forbidding

chart *n* • a stylized or symbolic depiction of something incapable of direct verbal or pictorial representation *syn* map, graph *rel* plan, plot, scheme, design, project

chart *vb* • to make a representation of something with a chart *syn* map, graph *rel* see CHART *n*

charter *syn* HIRE, let, lease, rent

chary *syn* CAUTIOUS, circumspect, wary, calculating *rel* prudent, discreet, provident; sparing, economical, frugal, thrifty; reluctant, hesitant, loath, disinclined

chase *syn* FOLLOW, pursue, trail, tag, tail

chasm *syn* GULF, abyss, abysm

chaste • free from all taint of what is lewd or salacious *syn* pure, modest, decent *rel* virtuous, moral, righteous, ethical; faithful, true, constant, loyal; austere, severe *ant* lewd, wanton, immoral; bizarre (*of style, effect*)

chasten *syn* PUNISH, discipline, correct, chastise, castigate *rel* humble, humiliate, abase; afflict; test, try, prove *ant* pamper, mollycoddle

chastise *syn* PUNISH, discipline, correct, castigate, chasten *rel* beat, thrash, pummel, baste, belabor

chat • to emit a loose and ready flow of inconsequential talk *syn* gab, chatter, patter, prate, prattle, babble, gabble, jabber, gibber *rel* converse, talk, speak; gossip

chatter *syn* CHAT, gab, patter, prate, babble, gabble, jabber, gibber *rel* see CHAT

cheap *syn* CONTEMPTIBLE, beggarly, shabby, pitiable, sorry, despicable, scurvy *rel* mean, ignoble, sordid, abject; paltry, petty, measly, trifling; meretricious, tawdry, gaudy; low, base, vile; poor, bad, wrong *ant* noble

cheat *n, syn* IMPOSTURE, fraud, fake, deceit, deception, counterfeit, sham, humbug *rel* hoaxing, hoax, bamboozling, bamboozlement; deception, trickery, chicanery, chicane; charlatan, quack, mountebank, faker, impostor; swindler, defrauder, cozener

cheat *vb* • to obtain something and esp. money or valuables from or an advantage over another by dishonesty and trickery *syn* cozen, defraud, swindle, overreach *rel* dupe, gull, hoax, hoodwink, bamboozle, trick, befool; deceive, delude, beguile, double-cross, mislead

check *n, syn* CORRECTIVE, control, antidote *rel* oversight, supervision, surveillance

check *vb* **1** *syn* ARREST, interrupt *rel* stay, suspend; stop, cease, discontinue, desist; repress, suppress; frustrate, thwart, foil, circumvent **2** *syn* RESTRAIN, bridle, curb, inhibit *rel* hinder, impede, obstruct, block; prevent, preclude, obviate; baffle, balk, frustrate; control, manage, conduct *ant* accelerate (*of speed*); advance (*of movements, plans, hopes*); release (*of feelings, energies*)

checked, checkered *syn* VARIEGATED, parti-colored, motley, pied, piebald, skewbald, dappled, freaked

cheek *syn* TEMERITY, nerve, effrontery, hardihood, gall, audacity *rel* boldness, intrepidity; impudence, brazenness, shamelessness, brashness *ant* diffidence

cheep *vb, syn* CHIRP, chirrup, peep, tweet, twitter, chitter

cheep *n, syn* CHIRP, chirrup, peep, tweet, twitter, chitter

cheer **1** *syn* ENCOURAGE, inspirit, hearten, embolden, nerve, steel *rel* comfort, console, solace; gladden, gratify, please; stimulate, excite, quicken, provoke *ant* deject; dismay **2** *syn* APPLAUD, root *rel* acclaim, laud, praise

cheerful *syn* GLAD, lighthearted, joyful, joyous, happy *rel* jolly, jovial, merry, blithe, jocund; mirthful, gleeful; gay, vivacious, lively, animated *ant* glum, gloomy

cheerless *syn* DISMAL, dreary, dispiriting, bleak, desolate *rel* discouraging, disheartening, dejecting *ant* cheerful

cheeseparing *syn* STINGY, close, closefisted, tight, tightfisted, niggardly, penny-pinching, parsimonious, penurious, miserly

chemist *syn* DRUGGIST, apothecary, pharmacist

cherish **1** *syn* APPRECIATE, prize, treasure, value *rel* love, enjoy, like; esteem, respect, regard; revere, venerate, reverence; protect, defend, shield, safeguard, guard *ant* neglect **2** *syn* NURSE, foster, nurture, cultivate *rel* preserve, conserve, save; harbor, shelter, entertain *ant* abandon

chew out *syn* SCOLD, upbraid, rate, berate, tongue-lash, jaw, bawl, wig, rail, revile, vituperate

chic *syn* STYLISH, smart, fashionable, modish, dashing

chicane, chicanery *syn* DECEPTION, trickery, double-dealing, fraud *rel* artifice, stratagem, maneuver, ruse, feint, trick, wile, gambit, ploy; intrigue, machination, plot; underhandedness, furtiveness, surreptitiousness

chide *syn* REPROVE, reproach, rebuke, reprimand, admonish *rel* criticize, reprehend, censure, blame, condemn, denounce; scold, upbraid, rate, berate *ant* commend

chief *n* • the person in whom resides authority or ruling power *syn* chieftain, head, headman, leader, master *rel* governor, ruler

chief *adj* • first in importance or in standing *syn* principal, main, leading, foremost, capital *rel* dominant, paramount, sovereign, predominant, preponderant, preponderating; primary, prime; supreme, preeminent *ant* subordinate

chiefly *syn* LARGELY, greatly, mostly, mainly, principally, generally

chieftain *syn* CHIEF, head, leader, master

childish *syn* CHILDLIKE *rel* puerile, boyish, youthful; simple, foolish, silly, fatuous, asinine *ant* mature, grown-up

childlike • having or showing the manner, spirit, or disposition of a child *syn* childish *rel* naïve, unsophisticated, ingenuous, artless, natural; docile, obedient, tractable, biddable

chilly *syn* COLD, cool, frigid, freezing, frosty, gelid, icy, glacial, arctic *ant* balmy

chimerical *syn* IMAGINARY, fantastic, fanciful, visionary, quixotic *rel* utopian, ambitious, pretentious; illusory, apparent; delusive, delusory, misleading, deceptive; fabulous, mythical, fictitious; preposterous, absurd, foolish *ant* feasible

chine *syn* SPINE, backbone, back, vertebrae

chink *syn* CRACK, cleft, fissure, crevasse, crevice, cranny *rel* break, gap, interruption; split, rift, breach

chirp *vb* • to make a short, sharp, and usu. repetitive sound *syn* chirrup, cheep, peep, tweet, twitter, chitter

chirp *n* • the little sounds characteristic of small animals or sounds that suggest such small animal sounds *syn* chirrup, cheep, peep, tweet, twitter, chitter

chirrup *vb, syn* CHIRP, cheep, peep, tweet, twitter, chitter

chirrup *n, syn* CHIRP, cheep, peep, tweet, twitter, chitter

chisel *syn* CARVE, sculpture, sculpt, sculp, incise, engrave, etch *rel* cut, chop; produce, turn out; shape, fashion, form, make

chitter *vb, syn* CHIRP, chirrup, cheep, peep, tweet, twitter

chitter *n, syn* CHIRP, chirrup, cheep, peep, tweet, twitter

chivalrous *syn* CIVIL, gallant, courtly, courteous, polite *rel* spirited, mettlesome, high-spirited *ant* churlish

chivy *syn* BAIT, badger, heckle, hector, hound, ride *rel* worry, annoy, harry, harass, tease; chase, pursue, trail, follow; torment, try, afflict

choice *n* • the act or opportunity of choosing or the thing chosen *syn* option, alternative, preference, selection, election

choice *adj* • having qualities that appeal to a fine or highly refined taste *syn* exquisite, elegant, recherché, rare, dainty, delicate *rel* preeminent, surpassing, peerless, incomparable, supreme, superlative; picked, selected, culled, chosen *ant* indifferent, medium

choke *syn* SUFFOCATE, asphyxiate, stifle, smother, strangle, throttle

choleric *syn* IRASCIBLE, splenetic, testy, touchy, cranky, cross *rel* irritable, fractious, huffy, querulous, petulant, peevish; angry, acrimonious, wrathful, wroth, indignant, mad, irate; fiery, peppery, spunky, spirited; captious, carping, faultfinding, critical *ant* placid; imperturbable

choose • to fix upon one of a number of things as the one to be taken, accepted, or adopted *syn* select, elect, opt, pick, cull, prefer, single *rel* adopt, espouse, embrace; desire, wish, crave *ant* reject; eschew

chop *syn* CUT, hew, slit, slash, carve *rel* split, cleave, rive, tear

chore *syn* TASK, duty, assignment, job, stint *rel* work, occupation, employment, business

christen *syn* BAPTIZE

chronic *syn* INVETERATE, confirmed, deep-seated, deep-rooted *rel* established, fixed, settled, set; hardened, indurated, callous *ant* acute (*of illness*)

chronicle **1** *syn* HISTORY, annals **2** *syn* ACCOUNT, story, report, version *rel* narration, recital, recountal

chthonic, chthonian *syn* INFERNAL, Hadean, stygian, hellish, Tartarean

chubby *syn* FLESHY, rotund, plump, fat, stout, portly, corpulent, obese *rel* chunky, stubby, dumpy, squat, stocky *ant* slim

chummy *syn* FAMILIAR, intimate, close, thick, confidential

chunky *syn* STOCKY, thickset, thick, stubby, squat, dumpy *rel* rotund, chubby, fleshy

church *syn* RELIGION, denomination, sect, communion, creed, faith, cult, persuasion

churl *syn* BOOR, lout, clown, clodhopper, bumpkin, hick, yokel, rube *rel* gentleman, aristocrat

churlish *syn* BOORISH, loutish, clownish *rel* ungracious, ill-mannered, discourteous, rude, uncivil, impolite; curt, blunt, brusque, gruff, crusty, bluff; surly, dour, sullen *ant* courtly

cinders *syn* ASH, clinkers, embers

circadian *syn* DAILY, diurnal, quotidian

circle *n, syn* SET, coterie, clique *rel* friends, acquaintances, intimates; associates, companions, comrades

circle *vb* **1** *syn* SURROUND, environ, encircle, encompass, compass, hem, gird, girdle, ring *rel* enclose, envelop; circumscribe, restrict, limit **2** *syn* TURN, revolve, rotate, gyrate, wheel, spin, twirl, whirl, eddy, swirl, pirouette

circuit *syn* CIRCUMFERENCE, compass, perimeter, periphery *rel* route, course, way; tour, journey

circuitous *syn* INDIRECT, roundabout *rel* winding, serpentine, sinuous, tortuous, flexuous *ant* straight

circulate *syn* SPREAD, disseminate, diffuse, propagate, radiate *rel* revolve, rotate, turn; interchange, exchange

circumference • a continuous line enclosing an area or space *syn* perimeter, periphery, circuit, compass *rel* outline, contour

circumlocution *syn* VERBIAGE, periphrasis, pleonasm, redundancy, tautology *rel* prolixity, diffuseness, wordiness, verbosity

circumscribe *syn* LIMIT, confine, restrict *rel* restrain, inhibit, curb, check; hamper, trammel, fetter *ant* expand, dilate

circumspect *syn* CAUTIOUS, wary, calculating, chary *rel* careful, punctilious, punctual, meticulous, scrupulous; vigilant, watchful, alert *ant* audacious

circumspection *syn* CAUTION, wariness, calculation, chariness *rel* carefulness, care, punctiliousness, punctuality, meticulosity, scrupulousness; discretion, forethought, foresight, providence, prudence *ant* audacity

circumstance *syn* OCCURRENCE, event, incident, episode *rel* item, detail, particular; factor, constituent, component, element

circumstantial • dealing with a matter fully and usu. point by point *syn* minute, particular, particularized, detailed, itemized *rel* precise, nice, exact, accurate, correct; full, complete, replete *ant* abridged; summary

circumvent *syn* FRUSTRATE, outwit, baffle, balk, thwart, foil *rel* forestall, anticipate, prevent; evade, escape, elude, avoid; trick, befool, hoodwink, dupe *ant* conform (to *laws, orders*); cooperate (with *persons*)

citadel *syn* FORT, stronghold, fortress, fastness

citation *syn* ENCOMIUM, eulogy, tribute, panegyric *rel* commendation, recommendation, complimenting, compliment; award, guerdon, reward, premium

cite **1** *syn* SUMMON, summons, call, convoke, convene, muster *rel* bid, invite; arrest, detain, apprehend; praise, extol, eulogize, laud, acclaim; award, accord, grant **2** *syn* QUOTE, repeat **3** *syn* ADDUCE, advance, allege *rel* enumerate, tell, count, number; recount, recite, narrate, rehearse, relate

citizen **1** *syn* INHABITANT, resident, denizen **2** • a person who is regarded as a member of a sovereign state, entitled to its protection, and subject to its laws *syn* subject, national *ant* alien

civil • observant of the forms required by good breeding *syn* polite, courteous, courtly, gallant, chivalrous *rel* complaisant, obliging, amiable; gracious, affable, cordial; politic, diplomatic, bland, urbane, suave *ant* uncivil, rude

claim *vb, syn* DEMAND, exact, require *rel* maintain, assert, defend, vindicate, justify; allege, adduce, advance *ant* disclaim; renounce

claim *n* • an actual or alleged right to demand something as one's possession, quality, power, or prerogative *syn* title, pretension, pretense *rel* assertion, affirmation, protestation, declaration right, prerogative, birthright, privilege

clamor *n, syn* DIN, uproar, pandemonium, hullabaloo, babel, hubbub, racket

clamor *vb, syn* ROAR, bellow, bluster, bawl, vociferate, howl, ululate *rel* shout, yell, scream, shriek, screech, holler; agitate, dispute, debate, discuss; demand, claim

clamorous *syn* VOCIFEROUS, blatant, strident, boisterous, obstreperous *rel* importuning, importunate, begging, imploring, adjuring; vocal, articulate, voluble, eloquent; protesting, expostulating, remonstrating *ant* taciturn

clandestine *syn* SECRET, covert, surreptitious, furtive, underhand, underhanded, stealthy *rel* concealed, hidden; sly, artful, foxy; illicit, illegitimate *ant* open

clash *vb, syn* BUMP, collide, conflict *rel* contend, fight, battle, war; compete, vie, rival; resist, combat, withstand, oppose; disagree, differ *ant* blend

clash *n, syn* IMPACT, collision, impingement, shock, concussion, percussion, jar, jolt *rel* conflict, strife, discord; noise, sound; incompatibility, incongruousness, discordance

class *n* • a group including all individuals with a common characteristic *syn* category *rel* genus, species, denomination, genre; division, section, part; classification; grade, rank, gradation, rating

class *vb* • to order a number of things according to a scale or to place a thing in its due order *syn* grade, rank, rate, graduate, gradate *rel* divide, separate, part; assign, allot; distribute

classify *syn* ASSORT, pigeonhole, sort *rel* order, arrange, systematize, methodize, marshal

clause *syn* PARAGRAPH, verse, article, plank, count

clean • to remove whatever soils, stains, or contaminates *syn* cleanse *ant* soil

cleanse *syn* CLEAN *rel* sterilize, disinfect, sanitize *ant* defile, besmirch

clear *adj* **1** • having the property of being literally or figuratively seen through *syn* transparent, translucent, lucid, pellucid, diaphanous, limpid *rel* bright, luminous; liquid; pure, sheer *ant* turbid; confused **2** • quickly and easily understood *syn* perspicuous, lucid *rel* express, explicit, definite; graphic, vivid; clear-cut, incisive, trenchant *ant* unintelligible; abstruse **3** *syn* EVIDENT, manifest, obvious, distinct, apparent, patent, palpable, plain

clear *vb, syn* RID, unburden, disabuse, purge *rel* free, release, liberate, deliver; clean, cleanse; eliminate, rule out, exclude

clearance *syn* ROOM, berth, play, elbowroom, leeway, margin

clear-cut *syn* INCISIVE, trenchant, cutting, biting, crisp *rel* distinct, plain, clear, manifest, evident; definite, explicit, express; precise, exact, nice, correct

cleave *vb, syn* STICK, cling, adhere, cohere *rel* fasten, attach, fix, affix; unite, join, associate, link, combine, conjoin *ant* part

cleave *vb, syn* TEAR, split, rive, rend, rip *rel* separate, divide, sever, sunder, part, divorce; cut, hew, chop, slit

cleft *syn* CRACK, fissure, crevasse, crevice, cranny, chink *rel* split, rift, breach; gap, break, interruption

clemency **1** *syn* MERCY, lenity, charity, grace *rel* compassion, pity, commiseration, sympathy, ruth; gentleness, mildness; fairness, equitableness, justness *ant* harshness **2** *syn* FORBEARANCE, mercifulness, leniency, indulgence, tolerance *rel, ant* see CLEMENCY 1

clement *syn* FORBEARING, merciful, lenient, indulgent, tolerant *rel* compassionate, tender, sympathetic; benign, benignant, kindly, kind; humane, benevolent, charitable *ant* harsh; barbarous

clemently *syn* FORBEARINGLY, tolerantly, mercifully, leniently, indulgently

clever **1** *syn* INTELLIGENT, quick-witted, brilliant, bright, smart, alert, knowing *rel* quick, apt, ready, prompt; versatile, all-around, many-sided; capable, competent, able; sharp, keen, acute *ant* dull **2** • having or showing a high degree of practical intelligence or skill in contrivance *syn* adroit, cunning, ingenious *rel* dexterous, deft, handy; nimble, agile; proficient, skillful, skilled, adept, expert, masterly

cliché *syn* COMMONPLACE, platitude, truism, bromide

clientele *syn* FOLLOWING, public, audience

climax *syn* SUMMIT, culmination, peak, apex, acme, zenith, apogee, pinnacle, meridian

climb *syn* ASCEND, mount, scale *ant* descend

cling *syn* STICK, cleave, adhere, cohere *rel* depend, RELY, trust, count, bank, reckon; attach, affix, fasten; hang, dangle, suspend

clinkers *syn* ASH, cinders, embers

clip *syn* SHEAR, poll, trim, prune, lop, snip, crop *rel* cut, chop, slash, slit; curtail, shorten; sever, separate

clique *syn* SET, circle, coterie *rel* party, faction, bloc, ring, combine, combination

cloak *syn* DISGUISE, mask, dissemble, camouflage *rel* conceal, hide, screen *ant* uncloak

clodhopper *syn* BOOR, bumpkin, hick, yokel, rube, lout, clown, churl

clog *syn* HAMPER, fetter, hog-tie, shackle, manacle, trammel *rel* impede, obstruct, hinder, block; balk, baffle, frustrate; check, curb, restrain *ant* expedite, facilitate

cloister **1** • a place of retirement from the world for members of a religious community *syn* convent, monastery, nunnery, abbey, priory **2** *syn* PASSAGE, arcade, passageway, ambulatory, gallery, corridor, aisle, hall, hallway

clone *syn* VARIETY, subspecies, race, breed, cultivar, strain, stock

close *vb* **1** • to stop or fill in an opening by means of a closure *syn* shut *rel* exclude, debar; block, bar, dam, hinder *ant* open **2** • to bring or come to a limit or a natural or appropriate stopping point *syn* end, conclude, finish, complete, terminate *rel* stop, cease, quit, desist

close *adj* **1** • not far (as in place, time, or relationship) from the point, position, or relation that is indicated or understood *syn* near, nigh, nearby *rel* adjoining, adjacent, contiguous, abutting; related, kindred *ant* remote, remotely **2** • having constituent parts that are massed tightly together *syn* dense, compact, thick *rel* compressed, condensed, constricted; concentrated, compacted *ant* open **3** *syn* SILENT, close-lipped, closemouthed, tight-lipped, secretive, reserved, taciturn, reticent, uncommunicative *ant* open, frank **4** *syn* FAMILIAR, intimate, confidential, chummy, thick *ant* aloof **5** *syn* STINGY, closefisted, tight, tightfisted, niggardly, parsimonious, penurious, cheeseparing, penny-pinching *rel* sparing, economical, frugal, thrifty *ant* liberal

closefisted *syn* STINGY, close, tight, tightfisted, niggardly, parsimonious, penurious, miserly, cheeseparing, penny-pinching *rel, ant* see CLOSE *adj* 5

close-lipped *syn* SILENT, close, closemouthed, uncommunicative, taciturn, reserved, reticent, secretive, tight-lipped *ant* see CLOSE *adj* 3

closemouthed *syn* SILENT, close, close-lipped, tight-lipped, reticent, reserved, uncommunicative, taciturn, secretive *ant* see CLOSE *adj* 3

clot *syn* COAGULATE, congeal, curdle, set, jelly, jell

clothe • to cover with or as if with garments *syn* attire, dress, apparel, array, robe *ant* unclothe

clothes • a person's garments considered collectively *syn* clothing, dress, attire, apparel, raiment

clothing *syn* CLOTHES, dress, attire, apparel, raiment

cloud *syn* OBSCURE, dim, bedim, darken, eclipse, becloud, fog, befog, obfuscate *rel* confuse, muddle, addle, befuddle; puzzle, perplex, distract

clout *syn* STRIKE, hit, smite, punch, slug, slog, swat, slap, cuff, box *rel* beat, pummel, thrash, baste, belabor

clown *syn* BOOR, clodhopper, lout, bumpkin, hick, yokel, rube, churl *rel* simpleton, natural, fool

clownish *syn* BOORISH, loutish, churlish *rel* awkward, clumsy, gauche; rude, rough, raw, green, uncouth *ant* urbane

cloy *syn* SATIATE, sate, surfeit, pall, glut, gorge *rel* whet

club *syn* ASSOCIATION, society, order

clumsy *syn* AWKWARD, gauche, maladroit, inept *rel* rude, rough, green, callow, uncouth; loutish, clownish, boorish; stiff, wooden, tense, rigid *ant* dexterous, adroit; facile

cluster *syn* GROUP, bunch, parcel, lot *rel*

collection, assemblage; aggregate, number, quantity, sum

clutch *vb, syn* TAKE, grasp, grab, seize, snatch *rel* capture, catch; hold, have, possess, own

clutch *n, syn* HOLD, grip, grasp *rel* seizing, grabbing, taking

clutter *syn* CONFUSION, disorder, disarray, jumble, chaos, muddle, snarl

coadjutor *syn* ASSISTANT, helper, aid, aide, aide-de-camp

coagulate • to alter by chemical reaction from a liquid to a more or less firm jelly *syn* congeal, set, curdle, clot, jelly, jell *rel* solidify, harden; cohere, stick; coalesce, fuse, blend, mix; concentrate, consolidate, compact

coalesce *syn* MIX, merge, fuse, blend, mingle, commingle, amalgamate *rel* compact, consolidate, concentrate, unify; contract, condense, compress; cohere, adhere, stick, cleave, cling; mass, heap

coalition *syn* ALLIANCE, fusion, confederacy, confederation, federation, league

coarse • offensive to good taste or morals *syn* vulgar, gross, obscene, ribald *rel* rough, crude, rude, raw, green, callow, uncouth; rank, rampant; boorish, loutish, clownish *ant* fine; refined

coast *n, syn* SHORE, strand, beach, bank, foreshore, littoral

coast *vb, syn* SLIDE, toboggan, glide, slip, skid, glissade, slither

coax • to use ingratiating art in persuading or attempting to persuade *syn* cajole, wheedle, blandish *rel* induce, persuade, prevail, get; tease, pester, worry; inveigle, entice, tempt, lure *ant* bully

cobble *syn* BOTCH, bungle, fumble, muff *rel* patch, mend, repair; fabricate, forge, manufacture, make; impair, mar, spoil, injure

cock *vb, syn* HEAP, stack, shock, pile, mass, bank *rel* gather, collect, assemble

cock *n, syn* HEAP, stack, shock, pile, mass, bank

cocksure *syn* SURE, positive, certain *rel* confident, assured, sanguine, presumptuous; pretentious, showy; decided, decisive *ant* dubious, doubtful

coerce *syn* FORCE, compel, constrain, oblige *rel* intimidate, bulldoze, bully, browbeat, cow; threaten, menace; drive, impel, move; terrorize, frighten

coercion *syn* FORCE, compulsion, violence, duress, constraint, restraint *rel* power, might, puissance, strength; intimidation, bulldozing, bullying, browbeating; threatening, threat, menacing, menace

coetaneous *syn* CONTEMPORARY, coeval, contemporaneous, synchronous, simultaneous, coincident, concomitant, concurrent

coeval *syn* CONTEMPORARY, coetaneous, synchronous, concurrent, simultaneous, coincident, concomitant, contemporaneous

cogent *syn* VALID, convincing, compelling, telling, sound *rel* forceful, forcible, potent, powerful, puissant; compelling, constraining; inducing, persuading, persuasive; proving, demonstrating; effective, effectual

cogitate *syn* THINK, reflect, deliberate, reason, speculate *rel* ponder, ruminate, meditate, muse; consider, excogitate, weigh, contemplate, study; think, conceive, imagine, envisage, envision

cognate *syn* RELATED, allied, kindred, affiliated *rel* akin, alike, identical, similar, like; common, generic, general, universal

cognizant *syn* AWARE, conscious, sensible, alive, awake *rel* conversant, versed; informed, acquainted, apprised *ant* ignorant

cohere *syn* STICK, adhere, cleave, cling *rel* coalesce, fuse, merge, blend, mix; fasten, attach, affix; join, combine, unite, connect, associate

coherence • the quality or character of a whole all of whose parts cohere or stick together *syn* cohesion *rel* unity, integrity, solidarity, union; clearness, perspicuousness, lucidity *ant* incoherence

cohesion *syn* COHERENCE *rel* unification, consolidation, concentration, compacting; coalescence, fusing, fusion, blending, blend, merging

coil *syn* WIND, curl, twist, twine, wreathe, entwine *rel* turn, revolve, rotate, circle

coin *syn* MONEY, coinage, currency, specie, legal tender, cash

coinage *syn* MONEY, coin, currency, cash, specie, legal tender

coincide *syn* AGREE, concur *rel* accord, correspond, jibe, harmonize, tally; match, equal *ant* differ

coincident *syn* CONTEMPORARY, synchronous, simultaneous, concurrent, concomitant, coeval, coetaneous, contemporaneous

cold • having a temperature below that which is normal or comfortable *syn* cool, chilly, frigid, freezing, frosty, gelid, icy, glacial, arctic *ant* hot

collate *syn* COMPARE, contrast

collateral *syn* SUBORDINATE, secondary, dependent, subject, tributary *rel* related, allied, kindred, cognate; correlative, complementary, corresponding, reciprocal

collation *syn* COMPARISON, parallel, contrast, antithesis *rel* corroboration, verification, confirmation, authentication; emending, emendation, revising, revision, correcting, correction

colleague *syn* PARTNER, copartner, ally, confederate *rel* associate, companion, comrade

collect *syn* GATHER, assemble, congregate *rel* mass, heap, pile; accumulate, amass, hoard; consolidate, concentrate, compact *ant* disperse; distribute

collected *syn* COOL, composed, unruffled, imperturbable, unflappable, nonchalant *rel* calm, placid, tranquil, serene; quiet, still; assured, confident, sure, sanguine; complacent, smug, self-satisfied *ant* distracted, distraught

collection *syn* GATHERING, assemblage, assembly, congregation *rel* heap, pile, mass, stack; accumulation, hording, hoard

collide *syn* BUMP, clash, conflict *rel* hit, strike; impinge, impact; dash, charge, rush

collision *syn* IMPACT, impingement, clash, shock, concussion, percussion, jar, jolt *rel* striking, hitting; wrecking, wreck, ruining, ruin, dilapidation; demolishment, destruction

color 1 • a property or attribute of a visible thing recognizable only when rays of light fall upon it and serving to distinguish things otherwise visually identical (as shape or size) *syn* hue, shade, tint, tinge, tone **2** *usu pl* **colors** *syn* FLAG, ensign, standard, banner, streamer, pennant, pendant, pennon, jack

colorable *syn* PLAUSIBLE, credible, believable, specious *rel* convincing, compelling, telling, cogent, sound, valid

colorless • without color *syn* uncolored, achromatic *rel* pale, pallid, ashen, wan; whitened, blanched, bleached, decolorized *ant* colorful

colossal *syn* HUGE, vast, immense, enormous, elephantine, mammoth, giant, gigantic, gigantean, gargantuan, Herculean, cyclopean, titanic, Brobdingnagian *rel* monumental, stupendous, tremendous, prodigious, monstrous

column *syn* PILLAR, pilaster

comatose *syn* LETHARGIC, torpid, sluggish *rel* languid, languorous, listless, languishing; phlegmatic, impassive; insensible, anesthetic, impassible; inert, passive, supine, inactive *ant* awake

comb *syn* SEEK, search, scour, hunt, ferret out, ransack, rummage *rel* scrutinize, inspect, examine; investigate, probe

combat *vb, syn* RESIST, withstand, contest, oppose, fight, conflict, antagonize *rel* fight, contend, battle, war; attack, assail, assault, bombard, storm *ant* champion; defend

combat *n, syn* CONTEST, conflict, fight, affray, fray *rel* battle, engagement, action; encounter, skirmish, brush; controversy, dispute, argument; contention, strife, conflict, discord

combative *syn* BELLIGERENT, bellicose, pugnacious, quarrelsome, contentious *rel* aggressive, militant; strenuous, energetic, vigorous; virile, manly, manful *ant* pacifistic

combination • a union, either of individuals or of organized interests, for mutual support in obtaining common political or private ends *syn* combine, party, bloc, faction, ring *rel* monopoly, corner, pool, cartel, syndicate, trust

combine *vb* **1** *syn* JOIN, unite, associate, link, conjoin, connect, relate *rel* mix, mingle, commingle, blend, fuse, amalgamate; consolidate, unify, compact *ant* separate **2** *syn* UNITE, cooperate, concur, conjoin *rel* coalesce, merge, mix; coincide, agree, concur

combine *n, syn* COMBINATION, party, bloc, faction, ring *rel* see COMBINATION

combustible • showing a tendency to catch or be set on fire *syn* inflammable, flammable, incendiary, inflammatory *rel* burnable; kindling, firing, igniting

come • to get to one point from another more or less distant in space, time, relation, or development *syn* arrive *rel* approach, near; rise, arise, spring, proceed, emanate, issue, stem *ant* go

comely *syn* BEAUTIFUL, fair, pretty, bonny, handsome, lovely, good-looking, beauteous, pulchritudinous *ant* homely

comestibles *syn* FOOD, provisions, viands, victuals, feed, provender, fodder, forage

comfort *n, syn* REST, ease, repose, relaxation, leisure *rel* contentedness, content, satisfaction; enjoyment, joy, fruition, pleasure; relief, assuagement, alleviation *ant* discomfort

comfort *vb* • to give or offer a person help or assistance in relieving his suffering or sorrow *syn* console, solace *rel* delight, gladden, rejoice, please; relieve, assuage, mitigate, alleviate; refresh, restore, renew *ant* afflict; bother

comfortable • enjoying or providing condition or circumstances which make for one's contentment and security *syn* cozy, snug, easy, restful *rel* comforting, consoling, solacing; content, contented, satisfied; grateful, welcome, agreeable, gratifying, pleasant *ant* uncomfortable; miserable

comic *syn* LAUGHABLE, comical, farcical, funny, droll, risible, ludicrous, ridiculous *rel* diverting, amusing, entertaining; witty, humorous, facetious; grotesque, antic, fantastic *ant* tragic

comical *syn* LAUGHABLE, comic, farcical, ludicrous, ridiculous, risible, droll, funny *rel* absurd, silly, foolish; jocular, jocose, humorous, witty; waggish, impish, roguish, sportive, playful; deriding, derisive, ridiculing, mocking *ant* pathetic

comity *syn* FRIENDSHIP, amity, goodwill *rel* association, society; companionship, comradeship; concord, accord, harmony

command *vb* • to issue orders to someone to give, get, or do something *syn* order, bid, enjoin, direct, instruct, charge *rel* control, manage, conduct, direct; exact, demand, require; force, compel, coerce, constrain, oblige *ant* comply, obey

command *n* **1** • a direction that must or should be obeyed *syn* order, injunction, bidding, behest, mandate, dictate *rel* direction, instruction, charging, charge; precept, ordinance, law, statute, canon, rule **2** *syn* POWER, control, authority, jurisdiction, sway, dominion *rel* ascendancy, supremacy; sovereignty

commemorate *syn* KEEP, celebrate, observe, solemnize

commence *syn* BEGIN, start, initiate, inaugurate *rel* institute, found, organize, establish

commend • to voice or otherwise manifest to others one's warm approval *syn* recommend, applaud, compliment *rel* praise, laud, extol, eulogize, acclaim *ant* censure; admonish

commensurable *syn* PROPORTIONAL, commensurate, proportionate *rel* equivalent, equal, identical, tantamount, same; reciprocal, corresponding *ant* incommensurable

commensurate *syn* PROPORTIONAL, commensurable, proportionate *rel* corresponding, correspondent, according, accordant, squaring, conforming; balancing, counterbalancing, compensating, offsetting *ant* incommensurate

comment *n, syn* REMARK, commentary, observation, note, obiter dictum *rel* interpreting, interpretation, elucidation, explication, expounding, exposition, explaining, explanation; annotation, gloss

comment *vb, syn* REMARK, commentate, animadvert *rel* interpret, elucidate, expound, explain, construe, explicate; annotate, gloss; criticize; illustrate, exemplify

commentary *syn* REMARK, comment, observation, note, obiter dictum *rel* see COMMENT *n*

commentate *syn* REMARK, comment, animadvert *rel* see COMMENT *vb*

commerce **1** *syn* BUSINESS, trade, industry, traffic **2** *syn* INTERCOURSE, traffic, dealings, communication, communion, conversation, converse, correspondence

commercial • of, relating to, or dealing with the supplying of commodities *syn* mercantile

commingle *syn* MIX, mingle, blend, merge, coalesce, fuse, amalgamate *rel* combine, unite, conjoin, associate, join; integrate

commiseration *syn* SYMPATHY, compassion, pity, condolence, ruth, empathy *rel* compassionateness, tenderness, warmheartedness; mercifulness, clemency; lamenting, lamentation, bewailing, bemoaning; pitifulness, piteousness, pitiableness *ant* ruthlessness, pitilessness

commission *syn* AUTHORIZE, accredit, license *rel* appoint, designate, name, nominate; empower, enable; instruct, enjoin, charge, bid, order, command

commit **1** • to assign to a person or place

for some definite end or purpose (as custody or safekeeping) *syn* entrust, confide, consign, relegate *rel* transfer, shift, remove, move; assign, allot **2** • to be responsible for or to be guilty of some offense or mistake *syn* perpetrate *rel* offend, sin, scandalize; transgress, trespass, violate, contravene

commodious *syn* SPACIOUS, capacious, ample *rel* comfortable; large, big, great; broad, wide, deep

common **1** *syn* UNIVERSAL, general, generic *rel* shared, partaken, participated; joined, joint, united, conjoined, connected, associated; merged, blended, amalgamated *ant* individual **2** *syn* RECIPROCAL, mutual *rel, ant* see COMMON 1 **3** • generally met with and not in any way special, strange, or unusual *syn* ordinary, familiar, popular, vulgar *rel* prevalent, prevailing, rife, current; usual, customary; plentiful, abundant, ample *ant* uncommon; exceptional

commonplace • an idea or expression lacking in originality or freshness *syn* platitude, truism, bromide, cliché *rel* expression, phrase, idiom, locution; banality, jejuneness, inanity, wishy-washiness; triteness, threadbareness

common sense *syn* see SENSE 2

commotion • great physical, mental, or emotional excitement *syn* agitation, tumult, turmoil, turbulence, confusion, convulsion, upheaval *rel* hubbub, racket, din, uproar, pandemonium; motion, movement; stir, bustle, flurry, ado

commune *syn* CONFER, consult, advise, parley, treat, negotiate *rel* converse, talk, speak; discuss, debate, argue

communicable *syn* INFECTIOUS, contagious, catching

communicate • to convey or transfer something (as information, feelings, or qualities) neither tangible nor concrete *syn* impart *rel* acquaint, apprise, inform, advise, notify; tell, disclose, reveal, divulge, discover; convey, transfer

communication *syn* INTERCOURSE, commerce, traffic, dealings, conversation, converse, correspondence, communion *rel* exchanging, exchange, interchanging, interchange; conversing, talking; news, tidings, advice, intelligence

communion **1** *syn* INTERCOURSE, commerce, traffic, converse, dealings, communication, conversation, correspondence *rel* empathy, sympathy; mysticism; contemplation; ecstasy, rapture, transport **2** *syn* RELIGION, denomination, faith, church, creed, sect, cult, persuasion

compact *adj, syn* CLOSE, dense, thick *rel* compressed, condensed, contracted; concentrated, consolidated, compacted; solid, firm, hard; tight

compact *vb* • to bring or gather together the parts, particles, elements, or units of a thing so as to form a close mass or an integral whole *syn* consolidate, unify, concentrate *rel* compress, condense, contract; bind, tie; unite, combine, join; knit, weave

compact *n, syn* CONTRACT, pact, entente, convention, concordat, treat, cartel, bargain

companion *syn* ASSOCIATE, comrade, crony *rel* friend, confidant, intimate, acquaintance; partner, colleague; attendant, escort, chaperon

companionable *syn* SOCIAL, cooperative, convivial, gregarious, hospitable *rel* friendly, neighborly, amicable; amiable, obliging, complaisant, good-natured; sociable, affable, gracious, cordial

company • a group of persons who are associated in a joint endeavor or who are assembled for a common end *syn* party, band, troop, troupe *rel* set, circle, coterie, clique; association, society, club, order; crowd, throng, mob, horde

comparable *syn* LIKE, alike, similar, analogous, akin, parallel, uniform, identical *ant* disparate

compare • to set two or more things side by side in order to show likenesses and differences *syn* contrast, collate *rel* match, equal, approach, touch, rival

comparison • a setting of things side by side so as to discover or exhibit their likenesses and differences *syn* contrast, antithesis, collation, parallel *rel* likeness, similarity, resemblance, analogy, similitude, affinity; parallel, counterpart, analogue, correlate

compass *vb* **1** *syn* SURROUND, environ, encircle, circle, encompass, hem, gird, girdle, ring *rel* enclose, envelop; confine, circumscribe, restrict, limit **2** *syn* REACH, gain, attain, achieve *rel* effect, fulfill, accomplish, perform; complete, finish, close

compass *n* **1** *syn* CIRCUMFERENCE, perimeter, periphery, circuit *rel* area, extent, magnitude, size; field, sphere, domain **2** *syn* RANGE, gamut, reach, radius, sweep, scope, orbit, horizon, ken, purview *rel* circumscription, limitation, restriction; limits, bounds, confines

compassion *syn* SYMPATHY, pity, commiseration, ruth, empathy, condolence *rel* tenderness, compassionateness, responsiveness, warmheartedness; mercy, charity, grace, lenity, clemency

compassionate *syn* TENDER, sympathetic, warmhearted, warm, responsive *rel* pitiful, piteous; merciful, forbearing, clement, lenient; humane, benevolent, charitable

compatible *syn* CONSONANT, congruous, consistent, congenial, sympathetic *rel* suitable, appropriate, proper, meet, fitting, fit; harmonizing, corresponding, correspondent, according, accordant; harmonious *ant* incompatible

compel *syn* FORCE, coerce, constrain, oblige *rel* impel, drive, move; command, order, enjoin

compelling *syn* VALID, telling, convincing, cogent, sound

compendious *syn* CONCISE, summary, pithy, succinct, terse, laconic *rel* compact, close; condensed, contracted; abridged, abbreviated, shortened

compendium • a condensed treatment of a subject *syn* syllabus, digest, pandect, survey, sketch, précis, aperçu *rel* conspectus, epitome, brief, abstract, abridgement

compensate **1** • to make up for or to undo the effects of *syn* countervail, balance, offset, counterbalance, counterpoise *rel* counteract, neutralize, negative; nullify, negate, annul, abrogate, invalidate; complement, supplement; correspond, square, tally, jibe, agree **2** *syn* PAY, remunerate, recompense, repay, reimburse, satisfy, indemnify

compete **1** • to strive to gain the mastery or upper hand *syn* contend, contest *rel* battle, fight; rival, vie; oppose, combat, withstand, resist **2** *syn* RIVAL, vie, emulate *rel* contend, fight; match, rival, approach, equal, touch

competent **1** *syn* ABLE, capable, qualified *rel* proficient, skillful, skilled, adept, expert, masterly; efficient, effective *ant* incompetent **2** *syn* sufficient, enough, adequate

compile *syn* EDIT, revise, redact, rewrite, adapt

complacent • feeling or showing an often excessive or unjustified satisfaction in one's possessions, attainments, accomplishments, or virtues *syn* self-complacent, self-satisfied, smug, priggish *rel* self-assured, self-confident, self-possessed, assured, confident; conceited, egotistic, egoistic; proud, vain, vainglorious

complaint *syn* DISEASE, ailment, disorder, condition, affection, malady, distemper, syndrome

complaisant *syn* AMIABLE, obliging, good-natured *rel* affable, genial, cordial, gracious; courteous, courtly, gallant, polite, civil; suave, urbane, politic, diplomatic, smooth, bland; agreeable, pleasant, pleasing *ant* contrary, perverse

complement *n* • something that makes up for a want or deficiency in another thing *syn* supplement *rel* counterpart, correlate, parallel

complement *vb* • to supply what is needed to make up for a want or deficiency *syn* supplement *rel* complete, finish, close

complementary, complemental *syn* RECIPROCAL, correlative, corresponding, convertible *rel* complementing, supplementing; completing, finishing; related, associated

complete *adj, syn* FULL, plenary, replete *rel* entire, whole, total, all; perfect, intact, whole, entire *ant* incomplete

complete *vb, syn* CLOSE, finish, conclude, end, terminate *rel* effect, fulfill, achieve, execute, accomplish, perform, discharge

complex *adj* • having parts or elements that are more or less confusingly interrelated *syn* complicated, intricate, involved, knotty *rel* mixed, mingled, blended, merged, fused, amalgamated; composite, compound *ant* simple

complex *n, syn* SYSTEM, network, organism, scheme *ant* component

complexion *syn* DISPOSITION, temperament, temper, character, personality, individuality *rel* humor; mood, vein, temper; nature, kind, type, sort

compliance • passive or weak agreement to what is asked or demanded *syn* acquiescence, resignation *rel* obedience, docility, amenableness, tractableness; submitting, submission, yielding, deferring, deference *ant* forwardness

compliant • manifesting acceptance (as of another's will or something disagreeable) *syn* acquiescent, resigned *rel* obedient, amenable, tractable, docile; submissive, tame, subdued; accommodating, conforming, adapting, adaptable *ant* forward

complicated *syn* COMPLEX, intricate, involved, knotty *rel* difficult, arduous, hard; abstruse, recondite; perplexing, puzzling, mystifying *ant* simple

compliment *n* • praise addressed directly to a person *syn* flattery, adulation *rel* encomium, tribute, panegyric, eulogy; praise, lauding, laudation, extolling, extollation *ant* taunt

compliment *vb, syn* COMMEND, applaud, recommend *rel* praise, laud, extol, eulogize, acclaim

comply *syn* OBEY, mind *rel* accede, consent, agree, acquiesce, assent; yield, submit, defer, bow *ant* command, enjoin

component *syn* ELEMENT, constituent, ingredient, factor *rel* member, part, detail, portion, piece; item, particular *ant* composite; complex

comport *syn* BEHAVE, acquit, quit, demean, conduct, deport

compose *syn* CALM, quiet, quieten, still, lull, soothe, settle, tranquilize *rel* pacify, mollify, propitiate, conciliate; moderate, temper *ant* discompose

composed *syn* COOL, collected, unruffled, imperturbable, unflappable, nonchalant *rel* quiet, still; serene, placid, tranquil, calm; sedate, staid, serious; repressed, suppressed *ant* discomposed; anxious

composite *syn* MIXTURE, admixture, blend, compound, amalgam *rel* combining, combination, uniting, union

composition *syn* ESSAY, theme, paper, article

composure *syn* EQUANIMITY, sangfroid, phlegm *rel* coolness, collectedness, imperturbability, nonchalance; self-possession, aplomb, confidence; placidity, serenity, calmness *ant* discomposure, perturbation

compound *syn* MIXTURE, amalgam, composite, admixture, blend *rel* combining, combination, uniting, union; coalescence, fusing, fusion, merging, merger *ant* element

comprehend **1** *syn* UNDERSTAND, appreciate *rel* seize, grasp, take; conceive, envisage, envision, think **2** *syn* APPREHEND *rel* see COMPREHEND 1 **3** *syn* INCLUDE, embrace, involve, imply, subsume *rel* contain, hold; classify, pigeonhole, assort

comprehension *syn* APPREHENSION, *rel* understanding, appreciating, appreciation; knowledge, science, learning, erudition

compress *syn* CONTRACT, constrict, deflate, condense, shrink *rel* compact, concentrate, consolidate; bind, tie *ant* stretch; spread

compulsion *syn* FORCE, coercion, constraint, duress, violence, restraint *rel* impelling, impulsion, driving, drive; pressure, stress; necessity, exigency, need

compunction **1** *syn* PENITENCE, remorse, repentance, contrition, attrition *rel* regret, sorrow; conscientiousness, scrupulousness, scrupulosity **2** *syn* QUALM, scruple, demur *rel* hesitation, hesitancy; reluctance, disinclination

compute *syn* CALCULATE, reckon, estimate *rel* count, enumerate, number; sum, total, tot, figure, cast, add

comrade *syn* ASSOCIATE, companion, crony *rel* friend, intimate, confidant; colleague, partner, confederate, ally

conation *syn* WILL, volition *rel* effort, exertion; action, act; choice, selection, option

concatenate *syn* INTEGRATE, articulate *rel* link, connect, relate, unite, combine, join, associate; fuse, blend, merge, coalesce, mix; organize, systematize, order

concatenation *syn* INTEGRATION, articulation *rel* sequence, succession, chain, train

conceal *syn* HIDE, screen, secrete, bury, cache, ensconce *rel* cloak, mask, disguise, dissemble, camouflage *ant* reveal

concede **1** *syn* GRANT, allow *rel* admit, acknowledge; waive, cede, relinquish *ant* dispute **2** *syn* GRANT, vouchsafe, accord, award *rel* yield, submit; surrender, resign, cede, relinquish *ant* deny (*something to somebody*)

conceit **1** • an attitude of regarding oneself with favor *syn* egotism, egoism, self-esteem, self-love, amour propre *rel* pride, vanity, vainglory; arrogance, superciliousness, insolence; complacency, smugness, priggishness *ant* humility **2** *syn* CAPRICE, freak, fancy, whim, whimsy, vagary, crotchet

conceive *syn* THINK, imagine, fancy, realize, envisage, envision *rel* consider, excogitate; speculate, cogitate, think; ponder, ruminate, meditate

concentrate **1** *syn* CENTER, focus, centralize *rel* fix, set, settle, establish; muster, convoke, convene, summon **2** *syn* COMPACT, consolidate, unify *rel* gather, collect, assemble; mass, heap, pile; fix, fasten, attach; engross, monopolize, absorb *ant* dissipate

concentration *syn* ATTENTION, application, study *rel* intentness, raptness, engrossment, absorption *ant* distraction

concept *syn* IDEA, conception, notion, thought, impression

conception *syn* IDEA, concept, thought, notion, impression *rel* opinion, view, belief, conviction, persuasion, sentiment; theory, hypothesis

concern **1** *syn* AFFAIR, business, matter, thing **2** *syn* CARE, solicitude, anxiety, worry *rel* thoughtfulness, considerateness, consideration, attentiveness, attention *ant* unconcern

concerned *syn* WORRIED, solicitous, anxious *rel* engrossed, absorbed, intent; impressed, affected, influenced, touched; troubled, distressed *ant* unconcerned

concerning *syn* ABOUT, regarding, respecting

concert *syn* NEGOTIATE, arrange *rel* discuss, debate, argue; concur, cooperate, unite, conjoin, combine

concession *syn* ALLOWANCE *rel* favor, boon, gift; indulgence, leniency, tolerance, forbearance

conciliate *syn* PACIFY, appease, placate, propitiate, mollify *rel* arbitrate, adjudicate, judge; mediate, intervene, interpose; persuade, prevail, induce; calm, tranquilize; adjust, accommodate, reconcile, adapt *ant* antagonize

concise • presented with or given to brevity of expression *syn* terse, succinct, laconic, summary, pithy, compendious *rel* condensed, compressed; compacted, concentrated; abridged, abbreviated, shortened; brief, short *ant* redundant

conclude **1** *syn* CLOSE, finish, terminate, end, complete *ant* open **2** *syn* INFER, judge, gather, deduce *rel* reason, speculate, think; conjecture, surmise, guess

concluding *syn* LAST, final, terminal, latest, ultimate *rel* closing, terminating, ending, finishing, completing *ant* opening

conclusion *syn* INFERENCE, judgment, deduction

conclusive • having or manifesting qualities that bring something to a finish or end *syn* decisive, determinative, definitive *rel* convincing, compelling, telling, cogent, valid; certain, inevitable, necessary *ant* inconclusive

concoct *syn* CONTRIVE, devise, invent, frame *rel* make, fabricate, fashion, manufacture; create, discover, invent; conceive, envisage, envision, think

concomitant *adj, syn* CONTEMPORARY, coincident, concurrent, synchronous, simultaneous, contemporaneous, coeval, coetaneous *rel* attending, attendant, accompanying; associated, connected, related, linked

concomitant *n, syn* ACCOMPANIMENT

concord *syn* HARMONY, consonance, accord *rel* agreement, concurrence, coincidence; peacefulness, peace, tranquillity, serenity, placidity, calmness; amity, comity, goodwill, friendship *ant* discord

concordat *syn* CONTRACT, compact, pact, treaty, entente, convention, cartel, bargain

concourse *syn* JUNCTION, confluence

concur **1** *syn* UNITE, conjoin, combine, cooperate *rel* accord, harmonize, agree, jibe **2** *syn* AGREE, coincide *rel* consent, assent, accede, acquiesce, agree *ant* contend; altercate

concurrent *syn* CONTEMPORARY, coincident, simultaneous, synchronous, concomitant, contemporaneous, coeval, coetaneous

concussion *syn* IMPACT, shock, percussion, impingement, collision, clash, jar, jolt *rel* beating, pounding, buffeting ; striking, smiting, swatting, slapping

condemn **1** *syn* CRITICIZE, denounce, censure, blame, reprobate, reprehend *rel* judge, adjudge; decry, belittle, depreciate, disparage; disapprove, deprecate **2** *syn* SENTENCE, doom, damn, proscribe

condense *syn* CONTRACT, shrink, compress, constrict, deflate *rel* abridge, abbreviate, shorten, curtail; reduce, diminish, decrease; compact, concentrate, consolidate *ant* amplify

condescend *syn* STOOP, deign *rel* favor,

accommodate, oblige; vouchsafe, concede, grant *ant* presume

condign *syn* DUE, rightful *rel* just, equitable, fair; merited, deserved

condition *n* **1** • something that limits or qualifies an agreement or offer *syn* stipulation, terms, provision, proviso, reservation, strings *rel* prerequisite, requisite, requirement **2** *syn* STATE, situation, mode, posture, status *rel* circumstance, occurrence, event; occasion, antecedent, cause; phase, aspect, side, facet, angle **3** *syn* DISEASE, disorder, affection, ailment, malady, complaint, distemper, syndrome

condition *vb, syn* PREPARE, fit, qualify, ready

conditional *syn* DEPENDENT, contingent, relative *rel* problematic, questionable, doubtful; provisional, tentative; subject, prone, liable, open; accidental, fortuitous, incidental *ant* unconditional

condolence *syn* SYMPATHY, pity, commiseration, compassion, ruth, empathy *rel* consoling, consolation, solacing, solace, comforting

condone *syn* EXCUSE, forgive, pardon, remit *rel* disregard, overlook, forget, ignore, neglect; exculpate, absolve, acquit

conduct *n, syn* BEHAVIOR, deportment *rel* act, deed, action; demeanor, mien, deportment, bearing

conduct *vb* **1** *syn* ACCOMPANY, escort, convoy, attend, chaperon *rel* guide, lead; convey, transmit, carry **2** • to use one's skill, authority, or other powers in order to lead, guide, command, or dominate persons or things *syn* manage, control, direct *rel* supervise, oversee; govern, rule; engineer, pilot, steer, lead, guide; operate, work, function **3** *syn* BEHAVE, demean, deport, comport, acquit, quit

conduit *syn* CHANNEL, canal, duct, aqueduct

confederacy, confederation *syn* ALLIANCE, federation, coalition, fusion, league

confederate **1** *syn* PARTNER, copartner, colleague, ally *rel, ant* see ALLY **2** • one associated with another or others in a wrong or unlawful act *syn* conspirator, accessory, abettor, accomplice

confer **1** *syn* GIVE, bestow, present, donate, afford *rel* accord, award, vouchsafe, grant **2** • to carry on a conversation or discussion esp. in order to reach a decision or settlement *syn* commune, consult, advise, parley, treat, negotiate *rel* converse, talk, speak; discuss, debate, argue

confess *syn* ACKNOWLEDGE, avow, admit, own *rel* grant, concede, allow; disclose, divulge, reveal, discover; declare, proclaim, publish *ant* renounce (*one's beliefs, principles*)

confessions *syn* BIOGRAPHY, life, memoir, autobiography

confidant *syn* FRIEND, intimate, acquaintance *rel* comrade, crony, companion, associate

confide *syn* COMMIT, entrust, consign, relegate *rel* bestow, present, give; grant, vouchsafe, accord, award

confidence **1** *syn* TRUST, reliance, dependence, faith *rel* certitude, assurance, conviction, certainty; credence, credit, belief, faith *ant* doubt; apprehension **2** • a feeling or showing of adequacy or reliance on oneself and one's powers *syn* self-confidence, assurance, self-assurance, self-possession, aplomb *rel* courage, resolution, mettle, spirit, tenacity *ant* diffidence

confident • not inhibited by doubts, fears, or a sense of inferiority *syn* assured, sanguine, sure, presumptuous *rel* courageous, intrepid, brave, bold, dauntless, undaunted, valiant, fearless, unafraid; positive, certain, sure *ant* apprehensive; diffident

confidential *syn* FAMILIAR, close, intimate, chummy, thick *rel* secret; trusty, tried, trustworthy, reliable

configuration *syn* FORM, conformation, figure, shape *rel* outline, contour, silhouette, profile, skyline

confine *vb, syn* LIMIT, circumscribe, restrict *rel* bind, tie; restrain, curb, inhibit, check; hamper, trammel, fetter, shackle, hog-tie, manacle; imprison, incarcerate, immure, intern, jail

confine *n, syn* LIMIT, bound, end, term *rel* verge, edge, border; circumference, periphery, compass

confirm **1** *syn* RATIFY *rel* assent, consent, acquiesce accede, subscribe; validate; sanction, approve, endorse **2** • to attest to the truth, genuineness, accuracy, or validity of something *syn* corroborate, substantiate, verify, authenticate, validate *rel* support, uphold, back; vouch, attest, certify *ant* deny; contradict

confirmed *syn* INVETERATE, chronic, deep-seated, deep-rooted *rel* established, fixed, set, settled; hardened, indurated, callous

confiscate *syn* ARROGATE, appropriate, usurp, preempt *rel* seize, take, grab; condemn, proscribe, sentence

conflagration *syn* FIRE, holocaust

conflict *n* **1** *syn* CONTEST, combat, fight, affray, fray *rel* engagement, battle, action; encounter, skirmish, brush; controversy, dispute, argument **2** *syn* DISCORD, strife, contention, dissension, difference, variance *rel* clash, collision, impingement, impact; antagonism, hostility, enmity; incompatibility, incongruousness, inconsistency, inconsonance, discordance *ant* harmony

conflict *vb* **1** *syn* RESIST, withstand, contest, oppose, fight, combat, antagonize **2** *syn* BUMP, clash, collide *rel* contend, fight; differ, vary, disagree *ant* accord

confluence *syn* JUNCTION, concourse

conform **1** *syn* ADAPT, adjust, accommodate, reconcile *rel* harmonize, tune, attune; assent, accede, acquiesce; accept, receive **2** *syn* AGREE, accord, harmonize, correspond, square, tally, jibe *ant* diverge

conformation *syn* FORM, configuration, shape, figure *rel* structure, anatomy, framework, skeleton

confound **1** *syn* PUZZLE, dumbfound, nonplus, bewilder, mystify, perplex, distract *rel* flabbergast, amaze, astound, astonish, surprise; discomfit, faze, rattle, abash, embarrass, disconcert **2** *syn* MISTAKE, confuse *rel* muddle, addle, confuse; mix, mingle *ant* distinguish, discriminate

confront *syn* MEET, face, encounter *rel* defy, beard, challenge, brave, dare; oppose, withstand, resist *ant* recoil

confuse **1** • to make unclear in mind or purpose *syn* muddle, addle, fuddle, befuddle *rel* confound, bewilder, mystify, perplex, puzzle; discomfit, disconcert, faze, rattle, embarrass; fluster, flurry, discompose *ant* enlighten **2** *syn* MISTAKE, confound *ant* differentiate

confusion **1** • a condition in which things are not in their normal or proper places or relationships *syn* disorder, chaos, disarray, jumble, clutter, snarl, muddle *rel* derangement, disarrangement, disorganization, disturbance; din, babel, pandemonium, hullabaloo; anarchy, lawlessness **2** *syn* COMMOTION, agitation, tumult, turmoil, turbulence, convulsion, upheaval *rel* disorder, disorganization, disturbance; perturbation, agitation, disquiet, upset, discomposure; discomfiture, embarrassment

confute *syn* DISPROVE, controvert, refute, rebut

congeal *syn* COAGULATE, set, curdle, clot, jelly, jell *rel* solidify, harden; compact, concentrate, consolidate; cool, chill, freeze

congenial *syn* CONSONANT, consistent, compatible, congruous, sympathetic *rel* companionable, cooperative, social; sociable, genial, cordial, gracious, affable; pleasing, pleasant, agreeable *ant* uncongenial; antipathetic (*of persons*); abhorrent (*of tasks, duties*)

congenital *syn* INNATE, inborn, hereditary, inherited, inbred *rel* inherent, constitutional, ingrained; native

conglomerate, conglomeration *syn* AGGREGATE, agglomerate, agglomeration, aggregation *rel* mass, heap, pile, stack; accumulation, amassment, hoarding, hoard

congratulate *syn* FELICITATE

congregate *syn* GATHER, assemble, collect *rel* swarm, teem *ant* disperse

congregation *syn* GATHERING, assembly, assemblage, collection *rel* audience, following, public; crowd, throng, press, crush

congruous *syn* CONSONANT, compatible, congenial, sympathetic, consistent *rel* harmonizing, harmonious, according, accordant, corresponding, correspondent, agreeing, agreeable; seemly, proper , decorous; meet, appropriate, fitting fit *ant* incongruous

conjectural *syn* SUPPOSED, hypothetical, supposititious, reputed, putative, purported *rel* presumed, assumed, postulated ; theoretical, speculative; alleged

conjecture *vb* • to draw an inference from slight evidence *syn* surmise, guess *rel* infer, gather, conclude, judge, deduce; speculate, reason; imagine, fancy, conceive, think

conjecture *n* • an inference based on slight evidence *syn* surmise, guess *rel* theory, hypothesis; opinion, view, belief, sentiment; inference, deduction, conclusion, judgment *ant* fact

conjoin 1 *syn* JOIN, combine, unite, connect, link, associate, relate **2** *syn* UNITE, combine, concur, cooperate

conjugal *syn* MATRIMONIAL, marital, connubial, nuptial, hymeneal *ant* single

connect *syn* JOIN, link, associate, relate, unite, conjoin, combine *rel* attach, fasten, affix; articulate, concatenate, integrate *ant* disconnect

connoisseur *syn* AESTHETE, dilettante *rel* epicure, gourmet, bon vivant; expert, adept

connubial *syn* MATRIMONIAL, conjugal, marital, nuptial, hymeneal

conquer • to get the better of or to bring into subjection by force or strategy *syn* defeat, vanquish, overcome, surmount, subdue, subjugate, reduce, overthrow, rout, beat, lick *rel* frustrate, thwart, foil, circumvent, outwit, baffle, balk

conqueror *syn* VICTOR, vanquisher, winner, champion

conquest *syn* VICTORY, triumph *rel* subjugation, subdual, defeating, defeat, overthrowing, overthrow, routing, rout

conscientious *syn* UPRIGHT, scrupulous, honorable, honest, just *rel* righteous, virtuous, ethical, moral; strict, rigid; particular, fastidious, finicky, nice; meticulous, punctilious, careful *ant* unconscientious, unscrupulous

conscious *syn* AWARE, sensible, cognizant, alive, awake *rel* attending, attentive, minding, mindful, watching; watchful, alert, vigilant; perceiving, noticing, noting, remarking, observing *ant* unconscious

consecrate *syn* DEVOTE, hallow, dedicate

consecutive • following one after the other in order *syn* successive, sequent, sequential, serial *rel* following, succeeding, ensuing; continuous, continual, incessant; coherent; logical *ant* inconsecutive

consent *syn* ASSENT, accede, acquiesce, agree, subscribe *rel* yield, submit, defer, relent; permit, allow, let; approve, sanction; concur *ant* dissent

consequence 1 *syn* EFFECT, result, upshot, aftereffect, aftermath, sequel, issue, outcome, event *ant* antecedent **2** *syn* IMPORTANCE, moment, weight, significance, import *rel* necessity, need, exigency; worth, value; renown, honor, reputation, repute, fame; eminence, illustriousness

consequently *syn* THEREFORE, hence, then, accordingly, so

conserve *syn* SAVE, preserve *rel* protect, shield, safeguard, guard, defend *ant* waste, squander

consider 1 • to give serious thought to *syn* study, contemplate, weigh, excogitate *rel* ponder, meditate, ruminate, muse; reflect, cogitate, think, reason, speculate; inspect, examine, scrutinize, scan **2** • to come to view, judge, or classify *syn* regard, account, reckon, deem *rel* think, conceive, imagine, fancy; judge, gather, infer, conclude

considerate *syn* THOUGHTFUL, attentive *rel* kindly, kind; tender, sympathetic, warmhearted, compassionate; obliging, complaisant, amiable *ant* inconsiderate

considered *syn* DELIBERATE, premeditated, advised, designed, studied *rel* intentional, voluntary, willful; planned, projected, schemed *ant* unconsidered

consign *syn* COMMIT, entrust, confide, relegate *rel* transfer, move, remove, shift; assign, allocate, allot; resign, surrender, yield, relinquish

consistent *syn* CONSONANT, congruous, compatible, congenial, sympathetic *rel* conforming, conformable, tallying, jibing, squaring; matching, equaling; identical, alike, similar, like *ant* inconsistent

console *syn* COMFORT, solace *rel* assuage, alleviate, mitigate, relieve, allay; calm, tranquilize; satisfy, content

consolidate *syn* COMPACT, unify, concentrate *rel* integrate, articulate, concatenate; amalgamate, merge, fuse, blend, mix; condense, compress, contract; weave, knit

consolidation • a union of two or more business corporations *syn* merger, amalgamation *ant* dissolution

consonance *syn* HARMONY, concord, accord *rel* agreement, conformity, correspondence; concurrence, coincidence; compatibility, congruity *ant* dissonance (*in music*); discord

consonant • conforming (as to a pattern, standard, or relationship) without discord or difficulty *syn* consistent, compatible, congruous, congenial, sympathetic *rel* conforming, conformable, harmonizing, harmonious, agreeing, agreeable, according, accordant; concurring, concurrent, co-

inciding, coincident *ant* inconstant; dissonant (*in music*)
conspectus *syn* ABRIDGMENT, synopsis, epitome, abstract, brief *rel* compendium, syllabus, digest, survey, sketch, précis, aperçu
conspicuous *syn* NOTICEABLE, prominent, salient, signal, remarkable, striking, arresting, outstanding *rel* patent, manifest, evident, distinct, obvious; eminent, celebrated, illustrious, famous *ant* inconspicuous
conspiracy *syn* PLOT, cabal, intrigue, machination *rel* sedition, treason; treacherousness, treachery, perfidiousness, perfidy, disloyalty, faithlessness, falseness, falsity
conspirator *syn* CONFEDERATE, accessory, accomplice, abettor
constant **1** *syn* FAITHFUL, true, loyal, staunch, steadfast, resolute *rel* abiding, enduring, persisting, persistent, lasting; dependable, trustworthy, reliable, trusty, tried *ant* inconstant, fickle **2** *syn* STEADY, uniform, even, equable *rel* established, settled, set, fixed; invariable, immutable, unchangeable; regular, normal, typical, natural *ant* variable **3** *syn* CONTINUAL, incessant, unremitting, continuous, perpetual, perennial *rel* persisting, persistent, persevering; pertinacious, dogged, obstinate, stubborn; chronic, confirmed, inveterate *ant* fitful
consternation *syn* FEAR, panic, terror, alarm, fright, dread, dismay, horror, trepidation *rel* confusion, muddlement, muddle; bewilderment, distraction, perplexity agitation, perturbation
constituent *syn* ELEMENT, component, ingredient, factor *rel* part, portion, piece, detail, member; item, particular *ant* whole, aggregate
constitution *syn* PHYSIQUE, build, habit *rel* temperament, temper, personality, disposition; organism, system; structure, framework, anatomy
constitutional *syn* INHERENT, intrinsic, essential, ingrained *rel* congenital, innate, inborn; native; natural, normal, regular; characteristic, individual, peculiar
constrain *syn* FORCE, oblige, coerce, compel *rel* impel, drive, move, actuate; require, exact, demand
constraint *syn* FORCE, compulsion, coercion, duress, restraint, violence *rel* suppression, repression; impelling, impulsion, driving, drive; goad, spur, motive, spring; obligation, duty
constrict *syn* CONTRACT, compress, shrink, condense, deflate *rel* tie, bind; restrict, confine, circumscribe, limit; restrain, curb
construct *syn* BUILD, erect, frame, raise, rear *rel* fabricate, manufacture, fashion, make; produce, turn out, yield, bear *ant* demolish; analyze
constructive *syn* IMPLICIT, virtual *rel* inferential, ratiocinative; implied, involved *ant* manifest
construe *syn* EXPLAIN, explicate, elucidate, interpret, expound *rel* analyze, resolve, break down, dissect; understand, comprehend, appreciate
consult *syn* CONFER, advise, parley, commune, treat, negotiate *rel* discuss, debate; deliberate, cogitate, think; counsel, advise
consume **1** *syn* WASTE, squander, dissipate, fritter *rel* exhaust, deplete, drain; dispel, disperse, scatter **2** *syn* EAT, swallow, ingest, devour **3** *syn* MONOPOLIZE, engross, absorb
consummate • brought to completion or perfection *syn* finished, accomplished *rel* perfect, whole, entire, intact; complete, full; flawless, impeccable, faultless; supreme, superlative, transcendent, peerless, surpassing *ant* crude
contact • the state of coming into direct connection or close association *syn* touch *rel* impingement, impact; connection, association, relation; union, unity; closeness, nearness
contagious *syn* INFECTIOUS, communicable, catching *rel* toxic, pestilential, pestilent, virulent, mephitic, miasmic, poisonous
contain • to have or be capable of having within *syn* hold, accommodate *rel* receive, admit, take; harbor, shelter, lodge, house
contaminate • to debase by making impure or unclean *syn* taint, attaint, pollute, defile *rel* debase, vitiate, corrupt, deprave; impair, spoil, injure, harm
contemn *syn* DESPISE, disdain, scorn, scout

rel repudiate, reject, decline; slight, neglect, disregard; flout, scoff, jeer

contemplate 1 *syn* CONSIDER, study, weigh, excogitate *rel* ponder, meditate, muse, ruminate; reflect, cogitate, speculate, think 2 *syn* SEE, observe, survey, notice, remark, note, perceive, discern, view, behold, decry, espy *rel* scrutinize, inspect, examine, scan

contemplative *syn* THOUGHTFUL, meditative, reflective, speculative, pensive *rel* intent, rapt, engrossed, absorbed; musing, ruminating, pondering; reflecting, cogitating, reasoning, thinking

contemporaneous *syn* CONTEMPORARY, coeval, coetaneous, synchronous, simultaneous, coincident, concomitant, concurrent

contemporary • existing, living, or occurring at the same time *syn* contemporaneous, coeval, coetaneous, synchronous, simultaneous, coincident, concomitant, concurrent *rel* living, existing, subsisting

contempt *syn* DESPITE, disdain, scorn *rel* abhorrence, detestation, loathing, hatred, hate; aversion, antipathy; repugnance, distaste *ant* respect

contemptible • arousing or deserving scorn or disdain *syn* despicable, pitiable, sorry, scurvy, cheap, beggarly, shabby *rel* detestable, abominable, abhorrent, odious, hateful; vile, low, base; abject, mean, sordid, ignoble *ant* admirable, estimable; formidable

contend 1 • to strive in opposition to someone or something *syn* fight, battle, war *rel* quarrel, wrangle, altercate, squabble; resist, combat, withstand, oppose, fight; compete, vie, rival 2 *syn* COMPETE, contest *rel* battle, war; oppose, resist, withstand, combat, fight

content, contented *adj, syn* SATISFIED, *rel* gratified, pleased; sated, satiated, cloyed, surfeited; replete, full

content *vb, syn* SATISFY *rel* gratify, please; sate, satiate, surfeit, cloy

contention *syn* DISCORD, dissension, difference, variance, strife, conflict *rel* quarrel, wrangle, altercation, squabble; controversy, dispute, argument; contending, fighting, warring

contentious *syn* BELLIGERENT, quarrelsome, bellicose, pugnacious, combative *rel* contrary, perverse, froward; captious, faultfinding, caviling, carping, critical; aggressive, militant *ant* peaceable

conterminous *syn* ADJACENT, contiguous, abutting, adjoining, tangent, juxtaposed

contest *vb* 1 *syn* COMPETE, contend *rel* struggle, strive, endeavor, attempt; fight, battle, contend 2 *syn* RESIST, withstand, oppose, fight, combat, conflict, antagonize

contest *n* • a battle between opposing forces for supremacy, for power, or for possessions *syn* conflict, combat, fight, affray, fray *rel* encounter, skirmish, brush; competition, emulation, rivalry; battle, engagement, action

contiguous *syn* ADJACENT, adjoining, abutting, conterminous, tangent, juxtaposed *rel* nearest, next; close, near, nigh, nearby

continence *syn* TEMPERANCE, abstemiousness, sobriety, abstinence *rel* chasteness, chastity, purity; moderateness, moderation, temperateness *ant* incontinence

continent *syn* SOBER, temperate, unimpassioned *rel* restrained, bridled, curbed, inhibited; decent, chaste, pure; self-denying, self-abnegating *ant* incontinent

contingency *syn* JUNCTURE, emergency, exigency, pinch, pass, strait, crisis *rel* chance, break, opportunity, occasion, time

contingent 1 *syn* ACCIDENTAL, fortuitous, casual, incidental *rel* possible, probable, likely; unforeseen, unforeseeable, unanticipated 2 *syn* DEPENDENT, conditional, relative *rel* subject, liable, open, exposed

continual • characterized by continued occurrence or recurrence over a relatively long period of time *syn* continuous, constant, incessant, unremitting, perpetual, perennial *rel* unceasing, endless, interminable, everlasting; eternal, infinite; lasting, permanent, perdurable *ant* intermittent

continuance *syn* CONTINUATION, continuity *rel* endurance, persistence, lasting; perseverance, persistence; remaining, staying, tarrying

continuation • the quality, the act, or the state of continuing or of being continued *syn* continuance, continuity *rel* extending, extension, prolonging, prolongation, protracting, protraction *ant* cessation

continue • to remain indefinitely in existence or in a given condition or course *syn* last, endure, abide, persist *rel* remain, stay; survive, outlive, outlast

continuity *syn* CONTINUATION, continuance *rel* succession, sequence, chain, train, progression

continuous *syn* CONTINUAL, constant, perpetual, perennial, incessant, unremitting *rel* connected, related, linked, joined; successive, consecutive, sequent, serial; steady, constant, uniform *ant* interrupted

contort *syn* DEFORM, distort, warp *rel* twist, bend, curve

contour *syn* OUTLINE, silhouette, skyline, profile *rel* configuration, shape, form, conformation, figure

contraband *syn* SMUGGLED, bootleg

contract *n* • an agreement reached after negotiation and ending in an exchange of promises between the parties concerned *syn* bargain, compact, pact, treaty, entente, convention, cartel, concordat

contract *vb* **1** *syn* PROMISE, pledge, covenant, engage, plight **2** *syn* INCUR, catch **3** • to decrease in bulk, volume, or content *syn* shrink, condense, compress, constrict, deflate *rel* dwindle, diminish, decrease, reduce *ant* expand

contradict *syn* DENY, gainsay, negative, contravene, traverse, impugn *rel* dispute, discuss; controvert, disprove, refute, confute; belie, falsify, garble, misrepresent *ant* corroborate

contradictory *n, syn* OPPOSITE, contrary, antithesis, antonym, antipode *rel* converse, reverse

contradictory *adj, syn* OPPOSITE, contrary, antithetical, antonymous, antipodal, antipodean, converse, counter, reverse *rel* negating, nullifying; counteractive, antagonistic, adverse

contraption *syn* DEVICE, gadget, contrivance *rel* appliance, tool, instrument, implement, utensil; machine, mechanism, apparatus; expedient, makeshift, resource

contrary *n, syn* OPPOSITE, antithesis, contradictory, antonym, antipode *rel* converse, reverse

contrary *adj* **1** *syn* OPPOSITE, antithetical, contradictory, antonymous, antipodal, antipodean, converse, counter, reverse *rel* divergent, disparate, different; counter, antagonistic, adverse; negating, nullifying **2** • given to opposing or resisting wishes, commands, conditions, or circumstances *syn* perverse, restive, balky, froward, wayward *rel* refractory, recalcitrant, intractable, headstrong, unruly; contumacious, rebellious, insubordinate *ant* good-natured, complaisant

contrast *n, syn* COMPARISON, collation, parallel, antithesis *rel* distinction, difference, divergence, divergency, dissimilarity, unlikeness; conflict, discord

contrast *vb, syn* COMPARE, collate

contravene *syn* DENY, contradict, traverse, impugn, negative *rel* oppose, combat, resist, fight; controvert, disprove; trespass, encroach, infringe *ant* uphold (*law, principle*); allege (*right, claim, privilege*)

contravention *syn* BREACH, trespass, transgression, violation, infringement, infraction *rel* offense, vice, sin, crime

contribution *syn* DONATION, benefaction, alms *rel* grant, subvention, subsidy, appropriation; gift, present, largess, boon

contributory *syn* AUXILIARY, ancillary, adjuvant, subservient, accessory *rel* concurring, cooperating; helping, helpful, aiding, assisting, assistant

contrition *syn* PENITENCE, attrition, repentance, compunction, remorse *rel* sorrow, grief, regret

contrivance *syn* DEVICE, gadget, contraption *rel* invention, creation, discovery; implement, tool, instrument, appliance, utensil; machine, mechanism, apparatus

contrive • to find a way of making or doing something or of achieving an end by the exercise of one's mind *syn* devise, invent, frame, concoct *rel* plan, scheme, project; manipulate, ply, swing , handle

control *vb, syn* CONDUCT, direct, manage *rel* govern, rule; regulate, adjust; guide, lead, pilot, engineer, steer; restrain, curb, check

control *n* **1** *syn* POWER, command, dominion, authority, jurisdiction, sway *rel* ascendancy, supremacy; might, puissance, power, force; management, direction **2** *syn* CORRECTIVE, check, antidote *rel* regulation, law, ordinance, rule, precept, statute, canon

controversy *syn* ARGUMENT, dispute *rel* contention, dissension, discord; disputation, argumentation, forensic, debate

controvert *syn* DISPROVE, rebut, refute, confute *rel* contravene, traverse, impugn, deny, gainsay; oppose, combat, fight, resist; dispute, debate, agitate, argue, discuss *ant* assert

contumacious *syn* INSUBORDINATE, rebellious, mutinous, seditious, factious *rel* contrary, perverse, froward; refractory, recalcitrant, intractable, ungovernable, unruly, headstrong *ant* obedient

contumelious *syn* ABUSIVE, opprobrious, vituperative, scurrilous *rel* insolent, overbearing, arrogant, disdainful, proud; humiliating, demeaning, debasing, abasing; flouting, scoffing, jeering, sneering *ant* obsequious

contusion *syn* WOUND, bruise, trauma, traumatism, lesion

conundrum *syn* MYSTERY, puzzle, riddle, enigma, problem

convalesce *syn* IMPROVE, recover, recuperate, gain *rel* progress, advance; strengthen, invigorate; cure, heal, remedy

convenance *syn* FORM, convention, usage

convene *syn* SUMMON, convoke, muster, summons, call, cite *rel* gather, congregate, assemble, collect *ant* adjourn

convent *syn* CLOISTER, nunnery, monastery, abbey, priory

convention **1** *syn* CONTRACT, entente, compact, pact, treaty, cartel, concordat, bargain *rel* agreement, accord, understanding **2** *syn* FORM, convenance, usage *rel* custom, practice, habit; canon, precept, rule, law; etiquette, propriety, decorum

conventional *syn* CEREMONIAL, formal, ceremonious, solemn *rel* decorous, proper, seemly, decent; correct, right, precise *ant* unconventional

conversant • familiar with something *syn* versed *rel* intimate, familiar; informed, acquainted; learned, erudite; adept, proficient, skilled, expert, skillful, masterly *ant* ignorant

conversation, converse *syn* INTERCOURSE, communion, communication, commerce, traffic, dealings, correspondence *rel* conversing, talking, talk, speaking, speech

converse *vb, syn* SPEAK, talk *rel* express, voice, broach, air, ventilate, vent, utter; chat, chatter, gabble; gossip, tattle; discourse, descant, expatiate, dilate

converse *n, syn* OPPOSITE, contrary, antithesis, contradictory, antipode, antonym, counter, reverse

conversion *syn* TRANSFORMATION, metamorphosis, transmutation, transmogrification, transfiguration

convert *vb, syn* TRANSFORM, metamorphose, transmute, transmogrify, transfigure *rel* manufacture, fabricate, forge, make; apply, utilize, employ, use

convert *n* • a person who has embraced another creed, opinion, or doctrine than the one he or she has previously accepted or adhered to *syn* proselyte *rel* neophyte, novice

convertible *syn* RECIPROCAL, corresponding, correlative, complementary, complemental *rel* interchangeable, exchangeable

convey **1** *syn* CARRY, transport, transmit, bear *rel* move, remove, shift, transfer; take, fetch, bring **2** *syn* TRANSFER, deed, alienate *rel* consign, commit, relegate

convict *syn* CRIMINAL, felon, malefactor, culprit, delinquent *rel* miscreant, blackguard, scoundrel, villain; offender, sinner

conviction **1** *syn* CERTAINTY, assurance, certitude *rel* faith, belief, credence, credit **2** *syn* OPINION, belief, persuasion, view, sentiment *rel* tenet, dogma, doctrine; judgment, conclusion

convincing *syn* VALID, compelling, telling, cogent, sound *rel* proving, demonstrating; persuading, persuasive, inducing; forceful, forcible, potent, powerful

convivial *syn* SOCIAL, companionable, gregarious, hospitable, cooperative *rel* sociable, genial, cordial, affable, gracious; gay, lively, vivacious; merry, jocund, jolly, jovial; hilarious, mirthful *ant* taciturn; staid

convoke *syn* SUMMON, convene, muster, summons, call, cite *rel* assemble, gather, congregate, collect; invite, bid *ant* prorogue, dissolve

convoy *syn* ACCOMPANY, escort, conduct, attend, chaperon *rel* protect, shield, guard, safeguard, defend; guide, lead, pilot

convulse *syn* SHAKE, rock, agitate *rel* discompose, disturb, disquiet, perturb

convulsion **1** *syn* FIT, spasm, paroxysm, attack, access, accession **2** *syn* COMMOTION, agitation, tumult, turmoil, turbulence, confusion, upheaval *rel* shaking, rocking; quaking, trembling, tottering; revolution, revolt, rebellion; cataclysm, disaster

convulsive *syn* FITFUL, spasmodic

cool **1** *syn* COLD, chilly, frigid, freezing, frosty, gelid, icy, glacial, arctic *ant* warm **2** • showing or seeming to show freedom from agitation or excitement *syn* composed, collected, unruffled, imperturbable, unflappable, nonchalant *rel* calm, tranquil, serene, placid; detached, aloof, indifferent; impassive, stoic, phlegmatic *ant* ardent; agitated

coop *syn* ENCLOSE, envelop, fence, pen, corral, cage, wall *rel* confine, circumscribe, limit, restrict; hinder, impede, obstruct, block, bar

cooperate *syn* UNITE, conjoin, combine *rel* coincide, agree, concur *ant* counteract

cooperative *syn* SOCIAL, companionable, gregarious, convivial, hospitable *rel* sociable, cordial, genial, affable, gracious; helping, helpful, aiding, assisting *ant* uncooperative

cop *syn* STEAL, filch, pinch, snitch, swipe, lift, pilfer, purloin

copartner *syn* PARTNER, colleague, ally, confederate *rel* associate, companion, comrade

copious *syn* PLENTIFUL, abundant, ample, plenteous *rel* profuse, lavish, exuberant, prodigal, luxuriant, lush *ant* meager

copy *n, syn* REPRODUCTION, duplicate, carbon, carbon copy, transcript, facsimile, replica *rel* counterpart, parallel; imprint, print, impression, impress; image, effigy *ant* original

copy *vb* • to make something like an already existing thing in form, appearance, or obvious or salient characteristics *syn* imitate, mimic, ape, mock *ant* originate

coquet *syn* TRIFLE, flirt, dally, toy

cordial *syn* GRACIOUS, genial, affable, sociable *rel* warm, warmhearted, responsive, sympathetic, tender; sincere, heartfelt, hearty, wholehearted

core **1** *syn* CENTER, middle, midst, hub, focus, nucleus, heart **2** *syn* SUBSTANCE, purport, gist, burden, pith *rel* import, significance, importance, consequence; center, heart, nucleus

corner *syn* MONOPOLY, pool, syndicate, trust, cartel

corporal *syn* BODILY, corporeal, physical, somatic *rel* fleshly, carnal, animal, sensual

corporeal **1** *syn* MATERIAL, physical, sensible, phenomenal, objective *rel* actual, real; tangible, palpable, ponderable, perceptible *ant* incorporeal **2** *syn* BODILY, physical, corporal, somatic *rel* see CORPORAL

corpse • *syn* BODY, carcass, cadaver *rel* remains, remainder

corpulent *syn* FLESHY, portly, fat, stout, obese, rotund, plump, chubby *rel* burly, husky, brawny, muscular; thickset, chunky, stubby, dumpy, stocky *ant* spare

corral *syn* ENCLOSE, envelop, fence, pen, coop, cage, wall

correct *vb* **1** • to set or make right something which is wrong *syn* rectify, emend, remedy, redress, amend, reform, revise *rel* improve, better, ameliorate; offset, compensate, countervail, counterbalance, balance; neutralize, counteract; adjust, regulate, fix; reprove, reprimand, admonish, chide **2** *syn* PUNISH, discipline, chastise, chasten, castigate

correct *adj* • conforming to standard, fact, or truth *syn* accurate, exact, precise, nice, right *rel* impeccable, faultless, flawless; punctilious, punctual, scrupulous, meticulous, careful *ant* incorrect

corrective *adj, syn* CURATIVE, remedial, restorative, sanative *rel* helping, aiding, assisting; salutary, hygienic, healthful

corrective *n* • something which serves to keep another thing in its desired place or condition *syn* control, check, antidote

correlate *syn* PARALLEL, analogue, counterpart

correlative *syn* RECIPROCAL, corresponding, complementary, complemental, convertible

correspond *syn* AGREE, square, accord, tally, jibe, harmonize, conform *rel* approach, touch, match, rival, equal

correspondence *syn* INTERCOURSE, communication, conversation, converse, communion, commerce, traffic, dealings

corresponding *syn* RECIPROCAL, correlative, complementary, complemental, convertible *rel* similar, analogous, like, parallel, comparable

corridor *syn* PASSAGE, passageway, hall, hallway, gallery, arcade, cloister, aisle, ambulatory

corroborate *syn* CONFIRM, substantiate, verify, authenticate, validate *rel* attest, vouch, certify; support, uphold, back *ant* contradict

corrupt *vb, syn* DEBASE, deprave, debauch, pervert *rel* degrade, debase, abase; ruin, wreck; pollute, defile, contaminate

corrupt *adj, syn* VICIOUS, iniquitous, nefarious, flagitious, infamous, villainous, degenerate *rel* crooked, devious, oblique; venal, mercenary; base, low, vile; pernicious, noxious, deleterious, detrimental, baneful; degraded, abased

corrupted *syn* DEBASED, corrupt, vitiated, depraved, debauched, perverted

corruption *syn* BARBARISM, impropriety, solecism, vulgarism, vernacular

corsair *syn* PIRATE, freebooter, buccaneer, privateer

cortege *syn* PROCESSION, cavalcade, parade, motorcade *rel* train, string, succession; followers, satellites, disciples, partisans, henchmen

coruscate *syn* FLASH, gleam, scintillate, glance, glint, sparkle, glitter, glisten, twinkle

cosmic *syn* UNIVERSAL, catholic, ecumenical, cosmopolitan

cosmopolitan *syn* UNIVERSAL, catholic, ecumenical, cosmic *rel* liberal, progressive; all-around, many-sided, versatile *ant* provincial; insular; parochial

cosset *syn* CARESS, fondle, pet, cuddle, dandle

cost *syn* PRICE, expense, charge

costly • having a high value or valuation, esp. in terms of money *syn* expensive, dear, valuable, precious, invaluable, priceless *rel* exorbitant, extravagant, excessive; sumptuous, luxurious, opulent *ant* cheap

coterie *syn* SET, circle, clique

couchant *syn* PRONE, recumbent, dormant, supine, prostrate

counsel *n* **1** *syn* ADVICE *rel* admonishing, admonition, chiding, reproaching, reproach; warning, forewarning, cautioning, caution; precept, rule, law **2** *syn* LAWYER, counselor, barrister, advocate, attorney, solicitor

counsel *vb, syn* ADVISE, *rel* admonish, chide, reprove; warn, forewarn, caution; remonstrate, expostulate, object; instruct, direct, command

counselor *syn* LAWYER, barrister, counsel, advocate, attorney, solicitor

count *vb* **1** • to ascertain the total of units in a collection by noting one after another *syn* tell, enumerate, number *rel* calculate, compute, reckon, estimate; add, sum, figure, total, tot, cast, foot **2** *syn* RELY, depend, bank, trust, reckon

count *n, syn* PARAGRAPH, verse, article, clause, plank

countenance *n, syn* FACE, visage, physiognomy, mug, puss

countenance *vb, syn* FAVOR, encourage *rel* approve, sanction, endorse; commend, applaud; support, uphold, champion, back

counter *adj, syn* ADVERSE, antagonistic, counteractive *rel* contrary, opposite, antithetical, antipodal, antipodean, antonymous, contradictory; hostile, inimical

counter *n, syn* OPPOSITE, contradictory, contrary, antithesis, antipode, antonym, converse, reverse

counteract *syn* NEUTRALIZE, negative *rel* correct, rectify; offset, counterbalance, countervail, counterpoise, balance, compensate *ant* cooperate

counteractive *syn* ADVERSE, counter, antagonistic *rel* countervailing, counterbalancing, counterpoising, compensating, offsetting, balancing; correcting; neutralizing

counterbalance *syn* COMPENSATE, offset, countervail, balance, counterpoise *rel* stabilize, steady, poise; correct

counterfeit *vb, syn* ASSUME, feign, sham, simulate, pretend, affect *rel* copy, imitate, mimic, ape; dissemble, disguise

counterfeit *adj* • being an imitation intended to mislead or deceive *syn* spurious, bogus, fake, sham, pseudo, pinchbeck, phony *rel* simulated, feigned, pretended; fraudulent; deceptive, misleading, delusive, delusory *ant* bona fide, genuine

counterfeit *n, syn* IMPOSTURE, fraud, sham, fake, cheat, humbug, deceit, deception *rel* reproduction, copy, facsimile

counterpart *syn* PARALLEL, correlate, analogue *rel* complement, supplement; duplicate, copy, facsimile, replica, reproduction

counterpoise *syn* COMPENSATE, balance, countervail, counterbalance, offset *rel* poise, stabilize, steady, balance, ballast, trim

countervail *syn* COMPENSATE, offset, balance, counterbalance, counterpoise *rel* correct; counteract, neutralize, negative; overcome, surmount, conquer; foil, thwart, frustrate

county *syn* ARISTOCRACY, gentry, elite, nobility, society

coup, coup d'etat *syn* REBELLION, revolution, uprising, revolt, insurrection, mutiny, putsch

couple • two things of the same kind *syn* pair, brace, yoke

courage • a quality of mind or temperament that enables one to stand fast in the face of opposition, danger, or hardship *syn* mettle, spirit, resolution, tenacity *rel* bravery, boldness, audacity, dauntlessness, intrepidity, doughtiness, fearlessness; valor, heroism, gallantry; fortitude, grit, pluck, guts, backbone, sand *ant* cowardice

courageous *syn* BRAVE, unafraid, fearless, intrepid, valiant, valorous, dauntless, undaunted, doughty, bold, audacious *rel* mettlesome, spirited, high-spirited, fiery; resolute, staunch, faithful; stout, tenacious, strong *ant* pusillanimous

course *syn* WAY, route, passage, pass, artery *rel* circuit, circumference; orbit, scope, range; drift, trend, tendency; procedure, process

court *syn* INVITE, woo, bid, solicit *rel* allure, attract, captivate, charm; toady, truckle, fawn, cringe

courteous *syn* CIVIL, polite, courtly, gallant, chivalrous *rel* gracious, affable, cordial; suave, urbane, politic, diplomatic; considerate, thoughtful, attentive; obliging, complaisant, amiable *ant* discourteous

courtesy • a manner or an act which promotes agreeable or pleasant social relations *syn* amenity, attention, gallantry *rel* graciousness, cordiality, affability, geniality; politeness, courteousness, courtliness, chivalrousness, chivalry, civility; considerateness, consideration, attentiveness, thoughtfulness *ant* discourtesy

courtly *syn* CIVIL, courteous, gallant, chivalrous, polite *rel* ceremonious, formal, conventional, ceremonial; elegant, dignified, graceful; finished, consummate *ant* churlish

covenant *syn* PROMISE, pledge, engage, plight, contract *rel* agree, concur, coincide; unite, combine, conjoin, cooperate

cover *vb* • to put or place or to be put or placed over or around *syn* overspread, envelop, wrap, shroud, veil *rel* hide, conceal, screen; close, shut; enclose, envelop; shield, protect, defend *ant* bare

cover *n, syn* SHELTER, retreat, refuge, asylum, sanctuary *rel* hiding, hiding place, concealment, screening, screen; safety, security *ant* exposure

covert *syn* SECRET, clandestine, surreptitious, underhand, underhanded, stealthy, furtive *rel* hidden, concealed, screened; disguised, dissembled, masked, cloaked, camouflaged *ant* overt

covet **1** • to desire selfishly to have something for one's own *syn* envy, grudge, begrudge **2** *syn* DESIRE, crave, wish, want *rel* yearn, long, pine, hanker, thirst, hunger; pant, aspire, aim *ant* renounce (*something desirable*)

covetous • having or manifesting a strong desire for esp. material possessions *syn* greedy, acquisitive, grasping, avaricious *rel* envious, jealous; desirous, lustful; avid, athirst, eager; rapacious, ravening, gluttonous, ravenous, voracious

cow *syn* INTIMIDATE, browbeat, bulldoze, bully *rel* frighten, terrorize, terrify; daunt, dismay, appall; abash, discomfit, rattle, faze, disconcert, embarrass

cower *syn* FAWN, cringe, truckle, toady *rel* shrink, quail, flinch, blench, wince, recoil

coxcomb *syn* FOP, dandy, beau, exquisite, dude, buck

coy *syn* SHY, bashful, diffident, modest *rel* nice, proper, seemly, decorous, decent; aloof, detached, indifferent; cautious, wary, chary *ant* pert

cozen *syn* CHEAT, defraud, swindle, overreach *rel* dupe, bamboozle, gull, trick, hoax, hoodwink, befool; delude, beguile, deceive, mislead

cozy *syn* COMFORTABLE, snug, easy, restful *rel* sheltering, harboring, housing, lodging; safe, secure; contenting, satisfying

crabbed *syn* SULLEN, surly, glum, morose, gloomy, sulky, saturnine, dour *rel* crusty, gruff, brusque, blunt, bluff; testy, choleric, cranky, cross, splenetic, irascible; snappish, huffy, irritable

crack *vb, syn* BREAK, burst, bust, snap, shatter, shiver *rel* split, rend, cleave, rive, tear

crack *n* **1** • an opening, break, or discontinuity made by or as if by splitting or rupture *syn* cleft, fissure, crevasse, crevice, cranny, chink *rel* split, rent, rift, breach **2** *syn* JOKE, wisecrack, witticism, jest, jape, quip, gag

craft **1** *syn* ART, skill, cunning, artifice *rel* adeptness, expertness, proficiency; ingeniousness, ingenuity, cleverness; competence, capability; efficiency **2** *syn* TRADE, handicraft, art, profession *rel* occupation, employment, pursuit, work **3** *syn* BOAT, ship, vessel

craftsman *syn* WORKER, handicraftsman, mechanic, artisan, workman, workingman, laborer, hand, operative, roustabout

crafty *syn* SLY, tricky, cunning, insidious, foxy, guileful, wily, artful *rel* adroit, clever, cunning; shrewd, astute; sharp, keen, acute

cram *syn* PACK, crowd, stuff, ram, tamp *rel* press, squeeze, jam; compress, contract; compact, consolidate; force, compel

cranky *syn* IRASCIBLE, cross, choleric, splenetic, testy, touchy *rel* irritable, fractious, peevish, petulant, snappish; contrary, perverse, froward; impatient, nervous, jittery

cranny *syn* CRACK, cleft, fissure, crevasse, crevice, chink *rel* hole, cavity, pocket, hollow; perforation, puncture, bore; interstice, aperture

crass *syn* STUPID, dense, slow, dull, dumb *rel* obtuse, dull; crude, raw, rude, rough, uncouth *ant* brilliant

crave *syn* DESIRE, covet, wish, want *rel* long, hanker, yearn, pine, hunger, thirst *ant* spurn

crawl *syn* CREEP

craze *syn* FASHION, vogue, fad, rage, style, mode, dernier cri, cry

crazy, crazed *syn* INSANE, mad, demented, lunatic, maniac, deranged, non compos mentis

cream *syn* OIL, grease, lubricate, anoint

create *syn* ESTABLISH, institute, organize *rel* make, form, fashion, shape, forge; design, plan, scheme; generate, engender

creator *syn* MAKER, author *rel* artist, architect, artificer; composer, writer, author

creature *syn* ENTITY, being, individual, person

credence *syn* BELIEF, credit, faith *rel* conviction, assurance, certitude, certainty; accepting, acceptance, admitting, admission, receiving, reception; assenting, assent, acquiescing, acquiescence; reliance, confidence, trust, faith

credential • something presented by one person to another in proof that he is what or who he claims to be *syn* testimonial, recommendation, character, reference *rel* certification, accreditation, endorsement, sanction

credible *syn* PLAUSIBLE, believable, colorable, specious *rel* probable, likely, possible; reasonable, rational; trustworthy, reliable, dependable *ant* incredible

credit *n* **1** *syn* BELIEF, faith, credence *rel* reliance, trust, confidence, faith; assurance, certitude, conviction, certainty **2** *syn* INFLUENCE, prestige, authority, weight *rel* reputation, repute, fame, renown; authority, power, sway *ant* discredit **3** • a person or thing that enhances another *syn* asset

credit *vb, syn* ASCRIBE, accredit, assign, attribute, impute, refer, charge

credulity • undue trust or confidence *syn* gullibility *rel* credence, credit, belief *ant* incredulity; skepticism

credulous • unduly trusting or confiding *syn* gullible *rel* assenting, acquiescing, acquiescent, agreeing, subscribing; believing, crediting *ant* incredulous; skeptical

creed *syn* RELIGION, faith, persuasion, denomination, sect, cult, communion, church

creep • to move slowly along a surface in a prone or crouching position *syn* crawl

crevasse *syn* CRACK, cleft, fissure, crevice, cranny, chink *rel* chasm, gulf; breach, split, rent, rift

crevice *syn* CRACK, cleft, fissure, crevasse, cranny, chink *rel* breach, split, rift, rent; break, gap

crime *syn* OFFENSE, vice, sin, scandal *rel* fault, failing, frailty, foible, vice

criminal • one who has committed a usu. serious offense esp. against the law *syn* felon, convict, malefactor, culprit, delinquent *rel* offender, sinner; transgressor, trespasser, violator

cringe *syn* FAWN, cower, truckle, toady *rel* recoil, quail, flinch, blench, wince; bow, cave, yield, submit, defer

cripple **1** *syn* MAIM, mutilate, batter, mangle *rel* injure, hurt **2** *syn* WEAKEN, disable, enfeeble, debilitate, undermine, sap *rel* damage, harm, impair, mar, injure

crisis *syn* JUNCTURE, exigency, emergency, pinch, pass, contingency, strait

crisp **1** *syn* FRAGILE, brittle, short, friable, frangible **2** *syn* INCISIVE, clear-cut, cutting, trenchant, biting *rel* terse, pithy, laconic, succinct, concise; piquing, stimulating, provoking, provocative

criterion *syn* STANDARD, touchstone, yardstick, gauge *rel* test, proof, trial, demonstration; principle, axiom, law; judging, judgment, adjudgment, adjudication

critical **1** • exhibiting the spirit of one who detects and points out faults or defects *syn* hypercritical, faultfinding, captious, caviling, carping, censorious *rel* judicious; wise; judicial; fastidious, finicky, particular, nice, fussy, squeamish; discriminating, discerning, penetrating; understanding, comprehending, appreciating *ant* uncritical **2** *syn* ACUTE, crucial *rel* decisive, determinative, conclusive; momentous, consequential, weighty, significant, important

criticism • a discourse presenting one's conclusions after examining a work of art and esp. of literature *syn* critique, review, blurb, puff

criticize • to find fault with someone or something openly, often publicly, and with varying degrees of severity *syn* reprehend, blame, censure, reprobate, condemn, denounce *rel* inspect, examine, scrutinize, scan; judge, adjudge; appraise, evaluate, assess, estimate

critique *syn* CRITICISM, review, blurb, puff

crochet *syn* WEAVE, knit, plait, braid, tat

crony *syn* ASSOCIATE, comrade, companion *rel* intimate, friend, confidant

crook *syn* FLEX, bow, buckle *rel* curve, bend, twist; contort, deform

crooked • not straight or straightforward *syn* devious, oblique *rel* awry, askew; twisted, bended, bent; distorted, contorted, deformed, warped; tortuous, winding; corrupt, nefarious, iniquitous, vicious; stealthy, furtive, underhand, secret *ant* straight

crop *syn* SHEAR, poll, clip, trim, prune, lop, snip *rel* cut, chop, hew, slash; detach, disengage

cross *n, syn* TRIAL, tribulation, affliction, visitation

cross *adj, syn* IRASCIBLE, cranky, testy, touchy, choleric, splenetic *rel* captious, carping, caviling, faultfinding, critical; irritable, fractious, peevish, petulant, snappish, waspish, querulous

crosswise, crossways *syn* ACROSS, athwart

crotchet *syn* CAPRICE, freak, fancy, whim, whimsy, conceit, vagary

crow *syn* BOAST, brag, vaunt, gasconade

crowd *vb* **1** *syn* PRESS, bear, bear down, squeeze, jam *rel* push, shove, thrust, propel; force, compel, constrain **2** *syn* PACK, cram, stuff, ram, tamp *rel* compress, contract; compact, consolidate, concentrate

crowd *n* • a more or less closely assembled multitude usually of persons *syn* throng, press, crush, mob, rout, horde *rel* multitude, army, host, legion

crucial *syn* ACUTE, critical *rel* threatening, menacing; trying, afflicting, torturing, torturous

crude *syn* RUDE, rough, uncouth, raw, callow, green *rel* primitive, primeval, primary; immature, unmatured; coarse, vulgar, gross *ant* consummate, finished

cruel *syn* FIERCE, inhuman, fell, truculent, ferocious, barbarous, savage *rel* atrocious, outrageous, monstrous, heinous; brutal, bestial; merciless, relentless, implacable, grim *ant* pitiful

cruise *syn* JOURNEY, voyage, tour, trip, jaunt, excursion, expedition, pilgrimage

crumble *syn* DECAY, disintegrate, decompose, rot, putrefy, spoil

crush *vb* **1** • to reduce or be reduced to a pulpy or broken mass *syn* mash, smash, bruise, squash, macerate *rel* press, squeeze, crowd, jam; batter, mangle, maim; beat, pound **2** • to bring to an end by destroying or defeating *syn* quell, extinguish, suppress, quench, quash *rel* destroy, demolish; ruin, wreck; annihilate, abolish; obliterate, blot out, efface, erase

crush *n, syn* CROWD, press, throng, horde, mob, rout *rel* multitude, army, legion, host

crusty *syn* BLUFF, brusque, gruff, blunt, curt *rel* snappish, waspish, irritable; choleric, splenetic, cranky, testy, irascible; crabbed, surly, saturnine, dour, sullen

cry *vb* • to show grief, pain, or distress by tears and usu. inarticulate utterances *syn* weep, wail, keen, whimper, blubber *rel* lament, bewail, bemoan, deplore; sob, moan, sigh, groan

cry *syn* FASHION, vogue, rage, style, mode, fad, craze, dernier cri

crying *syn* PRESSING, urgent, imperative, importunate, insistent, exigent, instant *rel* outstanding, conspicuous, noticeable; compelling, constraining

cryptic *syn* OBSCURE, enigmatic, dark, vague, ambiguous, equivocal *rel* puzzling, perplexing, mystifying; occult, esoteric, recondite; mysterious, arcane

cuddle *syn* CARESS, fondle, dandle, pet, cosset

cuff *syn* STRIKE, hit, smite, punch, slug, slog, swat, clout, slap, box

cull *syn* CHOOSE, pick, single, select, elect, opt, prefer

culmination *syn* SUMMIT, peak, climax, apex, acme, pinnacle, meridian, zenith, apogee

culpability *syn* BLAME, guilt, fault *rel* responsibility, accountability

culpable *syn* BLAMEWORTHY, guilty *rel* responsible, accountable, answerable, amenable, liable

culprit *syn* CRIMINAL, felon, convict, malefactor, delinquent *rel* prisoner; offender, sinner; scoundrel, blackguard, miscreant, rogue, rascal, villain

cult *syn* RELIGION, sect, denomination, communion, faith, creed, persuasion, church

cultivar *syn* VARIETY, subspecies, race, breed, strain, clone, stock

cultivate *syn* NURSE, nurture, foster, cherish *rel* develop, mature, ripen; raise, rear; educate, train, instruct, teach; improve, better, ameliorate

cultivation *syn* CULTURE, breeding, refinement

culture • enlightenment and excellence of taste acquired by intellectual and aesthetic training *syn* cultivation, breeding, refinement

cumber *syn* BURDEN, encumber, weigh, weight, load, lade, tax, charge, saddle *rel* see ENCUMBER

cumbersome, cumbrous *syn* HEAVY, ponderous, weighty, hefty *rel* burdensome, onerous; awkward, clumsy; irksome, wearisome, tiresome

cumulative • increasing or produced by the addition of like or assimilable things *syn* accumulative, additive, summative *rel* accumulated, amassed; multiplying, increasing, augmenting

cunning *adj* **1** *syn* CLEVER, ingenious, adroit *rel* skillful, skilled, adept, proficient, expert, masterly **2** *syn* SLY, crafty, tricky, artful, foxy, insidious, wily, guileful *rel* devious, oblique, crooked; sharp, acute, keen; shrewd, astute; knowing, smart, intelligent *ant* ingenuous

cunning *n* **1** *syn* ART, skill, craft, artifice *rel* dexterousness, dexterity, adroitness, deftness; proficiency, adeptness, expertness; ingeniousness, ingenuity, cleverness **2** *syn* DECEIT, guile, duplicity, dissimulation *rel* craftiness, insidiousness, wiliness, guilefulness, trickiness, trickery, artfulness, slyness; stratagem, ruse, maneuver, feint, trick, wile, gambit, ploy *ant* ingenuousness

cupidity • intense desire for wealth or possessions *syn* greed, rapacity, avarice *rel* covetousness, avariciousness, greediness, acquisitiveness; avidity, eagerness; lust, desire

curative • returning or tending to return to a state of normalcy or health *syn* sanative, restorative, remedial, corrective *rel* healing, curing, remedying

curb *syn* RESTRAIN, check, bridle, inhibit *rel* repress, suppress; shackle, manacle, fetter, hamper, hog-tie; thwart, foil, balk, frustrate *ant* spur

curdle *syn* COAGULATE, congeal, set, clot, jelly, jell

cure *n, syn* REMEDY, medicine, medicament, medication, specific, physic

cure *vb* • to rectify an unhealthy or undesirable condition especially by some specific treatment *syn* heal, remedy

curious **1** • interested in what is not one's

personal or proper concern *syn* inquisitive, prying, snoopy, nosy *rel* meddling, intermeddling, interfering, tampering; scrutinizing, inspecting, examining; intrusive, meddlesome, impertinent *ant* incurious; uninterested **2** *syn* STRANGE, singular, peculiar, unique, odd, queer, quaint, outlandish, eccentric, erratic

curl *syn* WIND, coil, twist, twine, wreathe, entwine *rel* curve, bend; flex, crook

currency *syn* MONEY, cash, legal tender, specie, coin, coinage

current *adj, syn* PREVAILING, prevalent, rife *rel* general, universal, common; popular, ordinary, familiar, common; usual, customary *ant* antique, antiquated; obsolete

current *n, syn* FLOW, stream, flood, tide, flux

curse *n* • a denunciation that conveys a wish or threat of evil *syn* imprecation, malediction, anathema *rel* execration, objurgation; profanity, blasphemy, swearing *ant* blessing

curse *vb, syn* EXECRATE, damn, anathematize, objurgate *rel* condemn, denounce, reprobate, criticize; blaspheme, swear *ant* bless

cursed *syn* EXECRABLE, accursed, damnable *rel, ant* see ACCURSED

cursing *syn* BLASPHEMY, profanity, swearing *rel* curse, imprecation, malediction, anathema; execration, objurgation

cursory *syn* SUPERFICIAL, shallow, uncritical *rel* hasty, speedy, quick, rapid, swift, fast; brief, short; casual, desultory, random, haphazard *ant* painstaking

curt *syn* BLUFF, brusque, blunt, crusty, gruff *rel* laconic, terse, summary, concise; brief, short; snappish, waspish, irritable; peremptory, imperious, masterful *ant* voluble

curtail *syn* SHORTEN, abbreviate, abridge, retrench *rel* reduce, decrease, lessen; cut, slash *ant* protract, prolong

curve *vb* • to swerve or cause to swerve from a straight line or course *syn* bend, twist *rel* deflect, divert, turn; swerve, veer, deviate

curve *n* • a line or something which follows a line that is neither straight nor angular but rounded *syn* arc, bow, arch *rel* circuit, compass, circumference

curvet *syn* SKIP, bound, hop, lope, lollop, ricochet

custom *syn* HABIT, usage, habitude, practice, use, wont *rel* convention, form, usage, convenance; rule, precept, canon, law

customary *syn* USUAL, wonted, accustomed, habitual *rel* regular, normal, typical, natural; prevailing, prevalent, current; familiar, ordinary, common; general, universal *ant* occasional

cut • to penetrate and divide something with a sharp-bladed tool or instrument *syn* hew, chop, carve, slit, slash *rel* split, cleave, rive, tear; sever, sunder, separate; curtail, shorten

cutthroat *syn* ASSASSIN, gunman, bravo

cutting *syn* INCISIVE, trenchant, clear-cut, biting, crisp *rel* sharp, keen, acute; piercing, penetrating, probing

cyclone *syn* TORNADO, twister *rel* whirlwind, whirly; hurricane, tropical storm, typhoon

cyclopean *syn* HUGE, vast, immense, enormous, elephantine, mammoth, giant, gigantic, gigantean, colossal, gargantuan, Herculean, titanic, Brobdingnagian

cynical • deeply and often contemptuously distrustful *syn* misanthropic, pessimistic *rel* sneering, girding, flouting, scoffing; captious, caviling, carping, censorious, critical; disbelieving, unbelieving

D

dabbler *syn* AMATEUR, tyro, dilettante

daily • of each or every day *syn* diurnal, quotidian, circadian

dainty **1** *syn* CHOICE, delicate, exquisite, elegant, recherché, rare *rel* petite, diminutive, little, small; pretty, bonny, fair, lovely, beautiful; delightful, delectable, delicious *ant* gross **2** *syn* NICE, fastidious, finicky, finicking, finical, particular, fussy, squeamish, persnickety, pernickety *rel* careful, meticulous, punctilious, scrupulous; discriminating, discerning

dally *syn* TRIFLE, flirt, coquet, toy *rel* play, sport, frolic, gambol; caress, fondle, pet

dam *syn* HINDER, bar, block, obstruct, impede *rel* clog, hamper, trammel, shackle, fetter, hog-tie; suppress, repress

damage *n, syn* INJURY, harm, hurt, mischief *rel* impairment, marring; ruining, dilapidation, wrecking; detriment, deleteriousness

damage *vb, syn* INJURE, harm, impair, mar, hurt, spoil *rel* ruin, dilapidate, wreck; deface, disfigure; abuse, misuse, mistreat, ill-treat, maltreat, outrage

damn **1** *syn* SENTENCE, doom, condemn, proscribe *rel* judge, adjudge; punish, castigate, discipline *ant* save (*from eternal punishment*) **2** *syn* EXECRATE, curse, anathematize, objurgate *rel* denounce, condemn, criticize; revile, vituperate, scold

damnable *syn* EXECRABLE, accursed, cursed *rel* atrocious, outrageous, monstrous, heinous; hateful, abominable, detestable, odious, abhorrent

damp *syn* WET, moist, dank, humid

dandle *syn* CARESS, cuddle, pet, cosset, fondle *rel* trifle, toy, dally; play, sport, disport; handle, swing

dandy *syn* FOP, beau, coxcomb, exquisite, dude, buck *ant* sloven

danger • the state of being exposed to injury, pain, or loss *syn* peril, jeopardy, hazard, risk *rel* threatening, threat, menacing, menace; precariousness; emergency, exigency, pass *ant* security

dangerous • attended by or involving the possibility of loss, evil, injury, or harm *syn* hazardous, precarious, perilous, risky *rel* unsafe, insecure; chancy, chance, haphazard, random, hit-or-miss *ant* safe, secure

dangle *syn* HANG, suspend, sling *rel* oscillate, sway, pendulate, fluctuate; swing, wave

dank *syn* WET, damp, humid, moist *rel* soaked, saturated, sopped, soppy, drenched

dappled *syn* VARIEGATED, parti-colored, motley, checkered, checked, pied, piebald, skewbald, freaked

dare *syn* FACE, brave, challenge, defy, beard *rel* venture, risk, chance, hazard

daredevil *syn* ADVENTUROUS, daring, rash, reckless, foolhardy, venturesome *rel* see DARING

daring *syn* ADVENTUROUS, rash, reckless, daredevil, foolhardy, venturesome *rel* bold, intrepid, audacious, brave

dark **1** • deficient in light *syn* dim, dusky, obscure, murky, gloomy *ant* light **2** *syn* OBSCURE, vague, enigmatic, cryptic, ambiguous, equivocal *rel* abstruse, occult, recondite, esoteric; mystical, mystic, anagogic, cabalistic; intricate, complicated, knotty, complex *ant* lucid

darken *syn* OBSCURE, dim, bedim, eclipse, cloud, becloud, fog, befog, obfuscate *ant* illuminate

dart *syn* FLY, scud, skim, float, shoot, sail *rel* speed, precipitate, hasten, hurry

dash *vb, syn* RUSH, tear, shoot, charge *rel* dart, fly, scud

dash *n* **1** *syn* VIGOR, vim, spirit, esprit, verve, punch, élan, drive *rel* force, energy, might, power; vehemence, intensity; impressiveness **2** *syn* TOUCH, suggestion, suspicion, soupçon, tincture, tinge, shade, smack, spice, vein, strain, streak

dashing *syn* STYLISH, smart, fashionable, modish, chic

date *syn* ENGAGEMENT, rendezvous, tryst, appointment, assignation

daunt *syn* DISMAY, appall, horrify *rel* cow, intimidate, browbeat; discomfit, disconcert, faze, embarrass; foil, thwart, baffle, frustrate; frighten, alarm, scare, terrify

dauntless *syn* BRAVE, courageous, unafraid, fearless, intrepid, valiant, valorous, undaunted, doughty, bold, audacious *rel* indomitable, unconquerable, invincible; heroic, gallant *ant* poltroon

dawdle *syn* DELAY, procrastinate, loiter, lag *rel* linger, tarry, wait, stay; trifle, toy, dally; play, sport, disport

daydream *syn* FANCY, dream, fantasy, phantasy, phantasm, vision, nightmare *rel* imagining, imagination, conceiving, conception, fancying; illusion, delusion, hallucination

daze • to dull or deaden the powers of the mind through some disturbing experience or influence *syn* stun, bemuse, stupefy, benumb, paralyze, petrify *rel* confound, bewilder, mystify, puzzle; confuse, muddle, befuddle; dazzle, dizzy

dazzled *syn* GIDDY, dizzy, vertiginous, swimming *rel* confused, addled, befuddled, muddled; confounded, bewildered, puzzled, perplexed

dead • devoid of life *syn* defunct, deceased, departed, late, lifeless, inanimate *ant* alive

deadlock *syn* DRAW, tie, stalemate, standoff *rel* situation, condition, state, posture; predicament, plight, dilemma, quandary

deadly • causing or causative of death *syn* mortal, fatal, lethal *rel* destroying, destructive; malignant, malign; baneful, pernicious; toxic, virulent, poisonous, pestilential, pestilant; ruinous

deal 1 *syn* DISTRIBUTE, divide, dispense, dole *rel* apportion, allot, assign, allocate; share, participate, partake **2** *syn* TREAT, handle *rel* manage, control, conduct, direct; rid, clear, unburden

dealings *syn* INTERCOURSE, commerce, traffic, communication, communion, conversation, converse, correspondence

dear *syn* COSTLY, expensive, precious, valuable, invaluable, priceless *rel* exorbitant, excessive, extravagant, inordinate *ant* cheap

dearth *syn* LACK, want, absence, defect, privation *rel* scarcity, infrequency, rareness, uncommonness; scantiness, meagerness, scantness *ant* excess

death • the end or the ending of life *syn* decease, demise, passing *ant* life

deathless *syn* IMMORTAL, undying, unfading *rel* everlasting, endless; eternal, infinite; enduring, abiding, persisting

debar *syn* EXCLUDE, blackball, disbar, suspend, shut out, eliminate, rule out *rel* preclude, obviate, prevent; forbid, prohibit, ban, interdict

debase 1 • to cause a person or thing to become impaired and lowered in quality or character *syn* vitiate, deprave, corrupt, debauch, pervert *rel* defile, pollute, taint, contaminate; adulterate, sophisticate, load, weight, doctor; impair, spoil, mar, damage, harm, injure *ant* elevate (*taste, character*); amend (*morals, way of life*) **2** *syn* ABASE, degrade, demean, humble, humiliate *rel* weaken, undermine, sap, enfeeble, debilitate, cripple, disable

debased • being lowered in quality or character *syn* vitiated, depraved, corrupted, debauched, perverted *rel* deteriorated, degenerated, degenerate, decadent

debate *n, syn* ARGUMENTATION, disputation, forensic, dialectic *rel* controversy, argument, dispute; contention, dissension, discord

debate *vb, syn* DISCUSS, dispute, argue, agitate *rel* contend, fight, battle, war; wrangle, altercate, quarrel; controvert, refute, confute, rebut, disprove; prove, demonstrate

debauch *syn* DEBASE, corrupt, deprave, pervert, vitiate *rel* injure, harm, damage, spoil, mar; seduce, inveigle, decoy, tempt, lure; pollute, defile, taint, contaminate

debauched *syn* DEBASED, corrupted, depraved, perverted, vitiated *rel* dissolute, reprobate, abandoned, profligate; licentious, libertine, lascivious, libidinous, lecherous, lewd, wanton

debilitate *syn* WEAKEN, enfeeble, undermine, sap, cripple, disable *rel* impair, injure, damage, harm, hurt, mar, spoil *ant* invigorate

debit *syn* DEBT, indebtedness, liability, obligation, arrear *ant* credit

debris *syn* REFUSE, waste, rubbish, trash, garbage, offal

debt • something, and esp. a sum of money, that is owed *syn* indebtedness, obligation, liability, debit, arrear

decadence *syn* DETERIORATION, decline, declension, degeneration, devolution *rel* retrogressiveness, retrogression, regressiveness, regression, regress, retrograding, retrogradation *ant* rise; flourishing

decamp *syn* ESCAPE, flee, fly, abscond *rel* depart, quit, leave, go; elude, evade, escape, shun, avoid

decay • to undergo or to cause to undergo destructive changes *syn* decompose, rot, putrefy, spoil, disintegrate, crumble *rel* weaken, undermine, sap, debilitate, enfeeble; taint, contaminate, defile, pollute; dilapidate, ruin, wreck

decease *syn* DEATH, demise, passing

deceased *syn* DEAD, departed, late, defunct, lifeless, inanimate

deceit 1 • the act or practice of imposing upon the credulity of others by dishonesty, fraud, or trickery *syn* duplicity, dissimulation, cunning, guile *rel* deception, fraud, trickery, double-dealing, chicane, chicanery; craft, artifice; cheating, cozening, defrauding, overreaching **2** *syn* IMPOSTURE, cheat, fraud, sham, fake, deception, counterfeit, humbug *rel* ruse, wile, trick, feint, stratagem, maneuver, artifice, gambit, ploy

deceitful *syn* DISHONEST, mendacious, lying, untruthful *rel* crafty, tricky, wily, guileful, foxy, insidious, cunning, sly, artful; underhand, underhanded, stealthy, furtive, clandestine, secret; crooked, devious, oblique; delusory, deceptive, delusive, misleading *ant* trustworthy

deceive • to lead astray or into evil or to frustrate by underhandedness or craft *syn* mislead, delude, beguile, betray, double-cross *rel* cheat, cozen, defraud, overreach; outwit, circumvent; dupe, gull, befool, trick, hoax, hoodwink, bamboozle *ant* undeceive; enlighten

decency *syn* DECORUM, propriety, dignity, etiquette *rel* seemliness, decorousness; fitness, suitability, fittingness, appropriateness

decent **1** *syn* DECOROUS, seemly, proper, nice *rel* fitting, fit, appropriate, suitable, meet; conventional, formal, ceremonious, ceremonial **2** *syn* CHASTE, modest, pure *rel* virtuous, moral, ethical, noble; pleasing, grateful, welcome, agreeable, pleasant *ant* indecent; obscene

deception **1** • the act or practice of deliberately deceiving *syn* fraud, double-dealing, trickery, chicane, chicanery *rel* deceit, duplicity, dissimulation, cunning, guile; cheating, cozening, defrauding, overreaching; duping, gulling, hoaxing, hoodwinking, bamboozling, befooling **2** *syn* IMPOSTURE, cheat, fraud, sham, fake, humbug, counterfeit, deceit *rel* illusion, delusion, hallucination, mirage

deceptive *syn* MISLEADING, delusory, delusive *rel* specious, plausible, colorable; false, wrong

decide • to come or to cause to come to a conclusion *syn* determine, settle, rule, resolve *rel* conclude, judge, gather; judge, adjudge, adjudicate

decided • free from any doubt, wavering, or ambiguity *syn* decisive, determined, resolved *rel* definite, definitive; positive, cocksure, certain, sure; categorical, explicit, express

decipher *syn* SOLVE, resolve, unfold, unravel *rel* interpret, construe, elucidate; translate, paraphrase

decisive **1** *syn* CONCLUSIVE, determinative, definitive *rel* critical, crucial, acute; momentous, significant, consequential, important *ant* indecisive **2** *syn* DECIDED, determined, resolved *rel* peremptory, imperative, masterful, imperious; certain, sure, positive, cocksure; resolute, steadfast *ant* irresolute

deck *syn* ADORN, bedeck, decorate, ornament, garnish, embellish, beautify *rel* array, apparel, attire, dress, clothe

declaration • the act of making known openly or publicly *syn* announcement, publication, advertisement, proclamation, promulgation, broadcasting

declare **1** • to make known explicitly or plainly *syn* announce, publish, advertise, proclaim, promulgate, broadcast *rel* inform, apprise, acquaint, advise, notify; impart, communicate; reveal, disclose, discover, divulge **2** *syn* ASSERT, profess, affirm, aver, avouch, avow, protest, predicate, warrant *rel* express, voice, utter, vent, broach, air, ventilate

declass *syn* DEGRADE, demote, reduce, disrate

declension *syn* DETERIORATION, decline, decadence, degeneration, devolution *rel* decaying, decay, disintegration, crumbling; retrogressiveness, retrogression, regressiveness, regression

decline *vb,* • to turn away by not accepting, receiving, or considering *syn* refuse, reject, repudiate, spurn *rel* demur, balk, shy, boggle, jib, stick, stickle, scruple *ant* accept

decline *n, syn* DETERIORATION, declension, decadence, degeneration, devolution

decolorize *syn* WHITEN, blanch, bleach, etiolate

decompose *syn* DECAY, rot, putrefy, spoil, disintegrate, crumble *rel* deliquesce, liquefy, melt

decorate *syn* ADORN, ornament, embellish, beautify, deck, bedeck, garnish *rel* enhance, heighten, intensify

decorous • conforming to an accepted standard of what is right or fitting or is regarded as good form *syn* decent, seemly, proper, nice *rel* formal, conventional, ceremonious, ceremonial; dignified, elegant *ant* indecorous; blatant

decorticate *syn* SKIN, peel, pare, flay

decorum • the quality or character of rightness, fitness, or honorableness in behavior or conduct *syn* decency, propriety, dignity, etiquette *rel* formality, conventionality, ceremoniousness; form, convention, convenance, usage *ant* indecorum; license

decoy *n, syn* LURE, bait, snare, trap

decoy *vb, syn* LURE, entice, inveigle, tempt, seduce *rel* snare, ensnare, trap, entrap, capture, catch, bag; beguile, delude, deceive, mislead

decrease • to make or grow less esp. gradually *syn* lessen, diminish, reduce, abate, dwindle *rel* curtail, shorten, retrench, abridge, abbreviate; contract, shrink *ant* increase

decree *syn* DICTATE, prescribe, ordain, impose *rel* command, order, enjoin, charge, direct; constrain, oblige, compel, force

decrepit *syn* WEAK, infirm, feeble, frail, fragile *rel* worn, wasted, haggard; aged, superannuated, old; tottering, quavering, shaking *ant* sturdy

decry • to indicate one's low opinion of something *syn* deprecate, disparage, derogate, detract, belittle, minimize *rel* disapprove; criticize, denounce, reprehend, censure, reprobate, condemn *ant* extol

dedicate *syn* DEVOTE, consecrate, hallow *rel* direct, address, apply

deduce *syn* INFER, gather, conclude, judge *rel* reason, cogitate, think, speculate

deduct • to take away one quantity from another *syn* subtract *ant* add

deduction **1** • an amount subtracted from a gross sum *syn* abatement, rebate, discount **2** *syn* INFERENCE, conclusion, judgment

deed *n, syn* ACTION, act *rel* exploit, feat, achievement

deed *vb, syn* TRANSFER, convey, alienate

deem *syn* CONSIDER, regard, account, reckon *rel* conclude, gather, infer

deep **1** • having great extension downward or inward *syn* profound, abysmal **2** *syn* BROAD, wide

deep-rooted *syn* INVETERATE, deep-seated, chronic, confirmed *rel* established, fixed, set, settled

deep-seated *syn* INVETERATE, chronic, deep-rooted, confirmed *rel* ingrained, constitutional, inherent; profound, deep

deface • to mar the appearance of *syn* disfigure *rel* injure, damage, mar; deform, distort, contort; mutilate, batter, mangle, maim

defame *syn* MALIGN, vilify, calumniate, traduce, asperse, slander, libel *rel* vituperate, revile; decry, disparage, detract, derogate

default *syn* FAILURE, neglect, miscarriage, dereliction *rel* absence, lack, want, privation; imperfection, deficiency, shortcoming, fault

defeat *syn* CONQUER, beat, vanquish, lick, subdue, subjugate, reduce, overcome, surmount, overthrow, rout *rel* frustrate, thwart, foil, baffle, balk, circumvent, outwit

defect **1** *syn* LACK, want, dearth, absence, privation *rel* deficiency, defectiveness; need, necessity, exigency **2** *syn* BLEMISH, flaw *rel* fault, failing, frailty, foible

defection • conscious abandonment of allegiance or duty *syn* desertion, apostasy *rel* disaffection, alienation, estrangement; abandonment, forsaking

defective *syn* DEFICIENT *rel* impaired, damaged, injured, marred; vitiated, corrupted, debased; deranged, disordered *ant* intact

defend **1** • to keep secure from danger or against attack *syn* protect, shield, guard, safeguard *rel* ward, avert, prevent; oppose, resist, withstand; fight, battle, war, contend *ant* combat; attack **2** *syn* MAINTAIN, assert, vindicate *rel* voice, vent, utter, express, air; explain, account, rationalize; support, champion, uphold, back

defer *vb* • to a delay an action, activity, or proceeding *syn* postpone, intermit, suspend, stay *rel* delay, retard, slow

defer *vb, syn* YIELD, bow, submit, cave, capitulate, succumb, relent *rel* accede, acquiesce, assent, agree; conform, accommodate, adapt, adjust; truckle, fawn, cringe

deference *syn* HONOR, reverence, homage, obeisance *rel* veneration, worship, adoration; respect, esteem, admiration, regard *ant* disrespect

deficiency *syn* IMPERFECTION, shortcoming, fault *rel* lack, want, dearth, defect; flaw, blemish; failure, neglect, default, miscarriage, dereliction *ant* excess

deficient • showing lack of something necessary *syn* defective *rel* meager, scanty, scant, sparse, exiguous; scarce, rare, infrequent, uncommon *ant* sufficient, adequate; excessive

defile *syn* CONTAMINATE, pollute, taint, attaint *rel* debase, vitiate, deprave, corrupt, pervert, debauch; profane, desecrate *ant* cleanse; purify

define *syn* PRESCRIBE, assign *rel* limit, circumscribe; fix, set, establish

definite *syn* EXPLICIT, express, specific, categorical *rel* clear, plain, distinct; full, complete; downright, forthright; precise, exact; clear-cut, incisive *ant* indefinite; equivocal

definitive *syn* CONCLUSIVE, determinative, decisive *rel* settling, deciding, determining; final, concluding, last, terminal, ultimate *ant* tentative, provisional

deflate *syn* CONTRACT, compress, shrink, condense, constrict *rel* reduce, decrease, lessen; exhaust, deplete, drain; puncture, prick, perforate; attenuate, extenuate *ant* inflate

deflect *syn* TURN, divert, avert, sheer *rel* deviate, depart, diverge, swerve, veer, digress; bend, curve, twist

deflection *syn* DEVIATION, aberration, divergence *rel* bending, curving, twisting; swerving, swerve, veering, veer, departing, departure

deform • to mar or spoil by or as if by twisting *syn* distort, contort, warp *rel* maim, cripple, mutilate, mangle, batter; disfigure, deface; injure, mar, damage, impair

defraud *syn* CHEAT, swindle, overreach, cozen *rel* trick, bamboozle, hoax, gull, dupe, befool; outwit, circumvent, foil

deft *syn* DEXTEROUS, adroit, handy *rel* nimble, agile, brisk; quick, ready, apt, prompt; skillful, skilled, adept, proficient; sure, assured, confident *ant* awkward

defunct *syn* DEAD, deceased, departed, late, lifeless, inanimate *ant* alive; live

defy *syn* FACE, brave, challenge, dare, beard *rel* mock, deride, ridicule; flout, scoff; withstand, resist, oppose, fight; confront, encounter, meet *ant* recoil

degenerate *syn* VICIOUS, corrupt, infamous, villainous, iniquitous, nefarious, flagitious *rel* degraded, demeaned; debased, depraved, debauched, perverted; dissolute, abandoned, reprobate, profligate

degeneration *syn* DETERIORATION, devolution, decadence, decline, declension *rel* retrogressiveness, retrogression, regressiveness, regression; debasement, degradation

degrade **1** • to lower in station, rank, or grade *syn* demote, reduce, declass, disrate *rel* humble, humiliate, abase, debase; disbar, rule out, exclude *ant* elevate **2** *syn* ABASE, debase, demean, humble, humiliate *rel* deprave, debauch, pervert, corrupt, vitiate *ant* uplift

dehydrate *syn* DRY, desiccate, parch, bake

deign *syn* STOOP, condescend *rel* vouchsafe, accord, concede, grant, award

deject *syn* DISCOURAGE, dishearten, dispirit *rel* depress, weigh, oppress; distress, trouble *ant* exhilarate; cheer

dejected *syn* DOWNCAST, depressed, dispirited, disconsolate, woebegone *rel* weighed down, oppressed; despondent, forlorn, hopeless; morose, glum, gloomy, sullen

dejection *syn* SADNESS, depression, melancholy, melancholia, gloom, blues, dumps *rel* despondency, hopelessness, forlornness, despair, desperation *ant* exhilaration

delay **1** • to cause to be late or behind in movement or progress *syn* retard, slow, slacken, detain *rel* impede, obstruct, hinder, block; defer, postpone, stay, suspend, intermit *ant* expedite; hasten **2** • to move or act slowly so that progress is hindered or work remains undone or unfinished *syn* procrastinate, lag, loiter, dawdle *rel* linger, tarry, wait, stay; hesitate, falter, vacillate, waver *ant* hasten, hurry

delectable *syn* DELIGHTFUL, delicious, luscious *rel* gratifying, grateful, agreeable, pleasing, welcome, pleasant; exquisite, rare, delicate, dainty, choice; palatable, savory, sapid, toothsome

delectation *syn* PLEASURE, enjoyment, delight, joy, fruition *rel* amusement, diversion, entertainment; gratifying, gratification, regaling, regalement

delegate • a person who stands in place of another or others *syn* deputy, representative

delete *syn* ERASE, cancel, efface, obliterate, blot out, expunge *rel* eliminate, exclude, rule out; omit, neglect

deleterious *syn* PERNICIOUS, detrimental, baneful, noxious *rel* injuring, injurious, harming, harmful, hurting, hurtful; destroying, destructive; ruining, ruinous *ant* salutary

deliberate *adj* **1** *syn* VOLUNTARY, willful, intentional, willing *rel* purposed, intended; conscious, cognizant, aware; mortal, deadly *ant* impulsive **2** • arrived at after due thought *syn* considered, advised, premeditated, designed, studied *rel* planned, schemed, projected; calculated; careful, meticulous, scrupulous *ant* casual **3** *syn* SLOW, leisurely, dilatory, laggard *rel* cautious, circumspect, wary, chary, calculating; cool, collected, composed, imperturbable *ant* precipitate, abrupt

deliberate *vb, syn* THINK, reflect, cogitate, reason, speculate *rel* ponder, meditate, ruminate, muse

delicate *syn* CHOICE, exquisite, dainty, rare, recherché, elegant *rel* delectable, delightful, delicious; soft, gentle, mild, lenient, balmy; ethereal, airy, aerial *ant* gross

delicious *syn* DELIGHTFUL, delectable, luscious *rel* palatable, sapid, savory, toothsome, appetizing; delicate, dainty, exquisite, choice, rare

delight *n, syn* PLEASURE, delectation, enjoyment, joy, fruition *rel* glee, mirth, jollity, hilarity; rapture, transport, ecstasy; satisfaction, contentment *ant* disappointment; discontent

delight *vb, syn* PLEASE, gratify, rejoice, gladden, tickle, regale *rel* satisfy, content; divert, amuse, entertain; charm, enchant, fascinate, allure, attract *ant* distress; bore

delightful • highly pleasing to the senses or to aesthetic taste *syn* delicious, delectable, luscious *rel* enchanting, charming, fascinating, alluring, attractive; lovely, fair, beautiful; ineffable *ant* distressing; boring; horrid

delineate **1** *syn* SKETCH, trace, outline, diagram, draft, plot, blueprint *rel* describe, relate; design, plan **2** *syn* REPRESENT, depict, portray, picture, limn

delineation *syn* SKETCH, tracing, outline, sketch, diagram, plot, blueprint *rel* map, chart, graph; design, plan

delinquent *syn* CRIMINAL, felon, convict, malefactor, culprit

deliquesce *syn* LIQUEFY, melt, fuse, thaw *rel* decay, decompose, disintegrate

delirious *syn* FURIOUS, frantic, frenzied, wild, frenetic, rabid *rel* excited, stimulated; enthusiastic, fanatic; ecstatic, rapturous, transported

delirium *syn* MANIA, frenzy, hysteria

deliver *syn* RESCUE, redeem, save, ransom, reclaim

delude *syn* DECEIVE, beguile, mislead, betray, double-cross *rel* dupe, gull, hoodwink, befool, bamboozle, hoax, trick; cheat, cozen, overreach *ant* enlighten

deluge *syn* FLOOD, inundation, torrent, spate, cataract *rel* flow, stream, current, flux, tide

delusion • something which is believed to be or is accepted as being true or real but which is actually false or unreal *syn* illusion, hallucination, mirage *rel* deception, trickery, chicane, chicanery; imposture, counterfeit, cheat, fraud, sham, fake, humbug, deceit; fantasy, vision, dream, daydream, fancy

delusive, delusory *syn* MISLEADING, deceptive *rel* fantastic, chimerical, visionary, imaginary, fanciful, quixotic; fallacious, sophistical, casuistical; illusory, seeming, ostensible, apparent

delve *syn* DIG, spade, grub, excavate

demand • to ask or call for something as due or as necessary or as strongly desired *syn* claim, require, exact *rel* request, ask, solicit; order, command, charge, enjoin, direct, bid; call, summon, summons, cite

demarcate *syn* DISTINGUISH, differentiate, discriminate *rel* limit, restrict, circumscribe, confine; define, assign, prescribe

demean *vb, syn* BEHAVE, deport, comport, conduct, acquit, quit *rel* carry, bear (*as reflexive verbs*)

demean *vb, syn* ABASE, degrade, debase, humble, humiliate

demeanor *syn* BEARING, deportment, mien, port, presence *rel* behavior, conduct; posture, attitude, pose; air, mannerism, affectation

demented *syn* INSANE, mad, crazy, crazed, deranged, lunatic, maniac, non compos mentis *rel* irrational, unreasonable; delirious, hysterical, frenzied *ant* rational

dementia *syn* INSANITY, lunacy, mania, psychosis *rel* delirium, hysteria, frenzy

demise *syn* DEATH, decease, passing

demolish *syn* DESTROY, raze *rel* wreck, ruin, dilapidate; devastate, ravage, waste, sack *ant* construct

demoniac, demonic *syn* FIENDISH, diabolic, diabolical, devilish *rel* hellish, infernal; crazed, crazy, maniac, insane; inspired, fired

demonstrate **1** *syn* SHOW, manifest, evince, evidence *rel* reveal, disclose, discover, betray; display, exhibit, parade, flaunt, expose, show **2** *syn* PROVE, try, test *rel* argue, debate; substantiate, verify, authenticate, confirm, corroborate, validate

demonstration *syn* PROOF, trial, test *rel*

substantiation, confirming, confirmation, corroboration, verification

demote *syn* DEGRADE, reduce, declass, disrate *ant* promote (*in rank, grade*)

demur *vb* • to hesitate or show reluctance because of difficulties in the way *syn* scruple, balk, jib, shy, boggle, stick, stickle, strain *rel* hesitate, falter, vacillate, waver; oppose, resist, combat, fight; object, remonstrate; disapprove, deprecate *ant* accede

demur *n, syn* QUALM, compunction, scruple *rel* hesitation, hesitancy; reluctance, loathness, aversion, disinclination; objection, remonstrance

denizen *syn* INHABITANT, resident, citizen

denomination **1** *syn* NAME, designation, appellation, title, style **2** *syn* RELIGION, sect, communion, faith, creed, cult, persuasion, church

denote *syn* MEAN, signify, import *rel* betoken, bespeak, indicate, attest, argue, prove; intend, mean; suggest, imply, hint, intimate, insinuate

denounce *syn* CRITICIZE, condemn, censure, reprobate, reprehend, blame *rel* accuse, charge, arraign, impeach, incriminate, indict; decry, disparage, depreciate; revile, vituperate, scold *ant* eulogize

dense **1** *syn* CLOSE, compact, thick *rel* consolidated, concentrated, compacted; compressed, condensed; massed, heaped, piled, stacked *ant* sparse (*of population, forests*); tenuous (*of clouds, air, masses*) **2** *syn* STUPID, crass, slow, dull, dumb *rel* obtuse; stolid, phlegmatic, impassive *ant* subtle; bright

denude *syn* STRIP, bare, divest, dismantle *ant* clothe

deny • to refuse to accept as true or valid *syn* gainsay, contradict, negative, traverse, impugn, contravene *rel* decline, refuse, reject, repudiate; controvert, refute, rebut, confute, disprove *ant* confirm; concede

depart **1** *syn* GO, leave, withdraw, retire, quit *ant* arrive; remain, abide **2** *syn* SWERVE, digress, deviate, diverge, veer *rel* forsake, abandon, desert; reject, repudiate, decline; discard, cast

departed *syn* DEAD, deceased, late, defunct, lifeless, inanimate

depend **1** • (on *or* upon) *syn* RELY, trust, count, reckon, bank *rel* lean, incline **2** • to rest or to be contingent upon something uncertain, variable, or indeterminable *syn* hinge, hang, turn

dependable *syn* RELIABLE, trustworthy, trusty, tried *rel* sure, assured, confident; responsible; staunch, steadfast, constant, faithful

dependence *syn* TRUST, reliance, confidence, faith

dependent **1** • determined or conditioned by another *syn* contingent, conditional, relative *rel* subject, liable, open, exposed, susceptible *ant* absolute; infinite; original **2** *syn* SUBORDINATE, subject, tributary, secondary, collateral *rel* relying, depending, trusting, reckoning, counting; subsidiary, subservient, auxiliary; abased, humbled, debased *ant* independent

depict *syn* REPRESENT, portray, delineate, picture, limn *rel* describe, narrate, relate; sketch, draft, outline, trace

deplete • to bring to a low estate by depriving of something essential *syn* drain, exhaust, impoverish, bankrupt *rel* undermine, sap, debilitate, weaken, enfeeble, cripple, disable; reduce, diminish, decrease, lessen

deplore • to manifest grief or sorrow for something *syn* lament, bewail, bemoan *rel* deprecate, disapprove; grieve, mourn, sorrow; weep, wail, cry

deport **1** *syn* BEHAVE, demean, comport, conduct, acquit, quit *rel* see DEMEAN **2** *syn* BANISH, transport, exile, expatriate, ostracize, extradite

deportment **1** *syn* BEHAVIOR, conduct *rel* see BEHAVIOR **2** *syn* BEARING, demeanor, mien, port, presence *rel* form, formality, ceremony, ceremonial, ritual; culture, cultivation, breeding, refinement; dignity, grace, elegance

deposit • matter which settles to the bottom of a liquid *syn* precipitate, sediment, dregs, lees, grounds

deprave *syn* DEBASE, vitiate, corrupt, debauch, pervert *rel* defile, pollute, taint, contaminate; injure, impair, damage, spoil

depraved *syn* DEBASED, vitiated, corrupted, debauched, perverted *rel* dissolute, abandoned, reprobate, profligate; degenerate, infamous, villainous, vicious; degraded

deprecate *syn* DISAPPROVE *rel* deplore,

lament, bewail, bemoan; reprobate, reprehend, condemn, criticize *ant* endorse
depreciate *syn* DECRY, disparage, derogate, detract, belittle, minimize *rel* underestimate, undervalue, underrate; asperse, malign *ant* appreciate
depreciative, depreciatory *syn* DEROGATORY, disparaging, slighting, pejorative *rel* decrying, belittling, minimizing; aspersing, maligning; underrating, underestimating, undervaluing
depress • to lower in spirit or mood *syn* weigh, oppress *rel* distress, trouble, ail; afflict, try, torment; tire, weary, fatigue, exhaust, fag, jade, tucker *ant* elate; cheer
depressed *syn* DOWNCAST, dejected, dispirited, disconsolate, woebegone *rel* gloomy, glum, morose, sullen; discouraged, disheartened; melancholy, lugubrious
depression *syn* SADNESS, dejection, gloom, blues, dumps, melancholy, melancholia *rel* despondency, forlornness, hopelessness, despair, desperation; doldrums, boredom, ennui, tedium *ant* buoyancy
deputy **1** *syn* AGENT, attorney, factor, proxy *rel* substitute, surrogate **2** *syn* DELEGATE, representative
deracinate *syn* EXTERMINATE, uproot, eradicate, extirpate, wipe *rel* abolish, extinguish, annihilate, abate; destroy, demolish
derange *syn* DISORDER, disarrange, unsettle, disturb, disorganize *rel* upset, discompose, perturb; discommode, incommode, inconvenience *ant* arrange; adjust
deranged *syn* INSANE, demented, non compos mentis, crazed, crazy, mad, lunatic, maniac
derangement *syn* ABERRATION, aliena tion
derelict *syn* OUTCAST, castaway, reprobate, pariah, untouchable *rel* vagabond, vagrant, tramp, hobo
dereliction *syn* FAILURE, neglect, default, miscarriage *rel* abuse, misuse, outrage
deride *syn* RIDICULE, mock, taunt, twit, rally *rel* scoff, jeer, gibe, flout, sneer, gird, fleer; chaff, banter, kid, rag, jolly, rib
derive *syn* SPRING, originate, arise, rise, emanate, issue, stem, flow, proceed
dernier cri *syn* FASHION, style, mode, vogue, fad, rage, craze, cry
derogate *syn* DECRY, disparage, detract, belittle, minimize, depreciate *rel* reduce, lessen, decrease, diminish
derogatory • designed or tending to belittle *syn* depreciatory, depreciative, disparaging, slighting, pejorative *rel* belittling, minimizing, decrying; aspersing, maligning
descant **1** *syn* SING, troll, carol, warble, trill, hymn, chant, intone **2** *syn* DISCOURSE, expatiate, dilate
descend • to get or come down from a height *syn* dismount, alight *ant* ascend, climb
descendant *syn* OFFSPRING, young, progeny, issue, posterity
describe *syn* RELATE, narrate, state, report, rehearse, recite, recount *rel* delineate, sketch, outline
description *syn* TYPE, kind, sort, character, nature, stripe, kidney, ilk
descry *syn* SEE, espy, behold, observe, notice, remark, note, perceive, discern, view, survey, contemplate
desecration *syn* PROFANATION, sacrilege, blasphemy *rel* defilement, pollution
desert *n, syn* WASTE, badlands, wilderness
desert *n, syn* DUE, merit *rel* meed, guerdon; punishment, chastisement, chastening, disciplining, discipline
desert *vb, syn* ABANDON, forsake *rel* leave, quit, depart *ant* stick to, cleave to
desertion *syn* DEFECTION, apostasy *rel* perfidiousness, perfidy, treacherousness, treachery, disloyalty, faithlessness
deserve • to be or become worthy of *syn* merit, earn, rate *rel* gain, win, get; evaluate, value, estimate; claim, demand
desiccate *syn* DRY, dehydrate, parch, bake
design *vb* **1** *syn* INTEND, mean, propose, purpose *rel* aim, aspire **2** *syn* PLAN, plot, scheme, project *rel* sketch, outline, diagram, delineate, blueprint, draft; invent, create
design *n* **1** *syn* PLAN, plot, scheme, project *rel* delineation, sketch, draft, outline, tracing, diagram; conception, idea **2** *syn* INTENTION, intent, purpose, aim, end, object, objective, goal *rel* will, volition, conation; deliberation, reflection, thinking, thought; intrigue, machination *ant* accident **3** *syn* FIGURE, pattern, motif, device
designate • to declare a person one's choice *syn* name, nominate, elect, appoint *rel* choose, select, single, opt, pick

designation *syn* NAME, denomination, appellation, title, style *rel* identification, recognition; classification, pigeonholing, pigeonhole

designed *syn* DELIBERATE, premeditated, considered, advised, studied *rel* intentional, voluntary, willful, deliberate, willing; purposed, intended; resolved, determined, decided *ant* accidental

desire *vb* • to have a longing for something *syn* wish, want, crave, covet *rel* long, yearn, hanker, pine, hunger, thirst; aspire, pant, aim

desire *n* • a longing for something that promises enjoyment or satisfaction *syn* appetite, lust, passion, urge *rel* longing, yearning, hankering, pining, hungering, hunger, thirsting, thirst; cupidity, greed, avarice, rapacity *ant* distaste

desist *syn* STOP, discontinue, cease, quit *rel* refrain, abstain, forbear; relinquish, yield, abandon, resign *ant* persist

desolate **1** *syn* ALONE, forlorn, lorn, lonesome, lone, solitary, lonely *rel* deserted, forsaken, abandoned; miserable, wretched **2** *syn* DISMAL, dreary, cheerless, dispiriting, bleak *rel* bare, barren, bald; destitute, poverty-stricken, poor

despair *syn* DESPONDENCY, hopelessness, desperation, forlornness *rel* dejection, melancholy, sadness, gloom, depression *ant* hope; optimism; beatitude

despairing *syn* DESPONDENT, hopeless, desperate, forlorn *rel* melancholy, melancholic, atrabilious; pessimistic, misanthropic, cynical; depressed, weighed down *ant* hopeful

desperate *syn* DESPONDENT, hopeless, despairing, forlorn *rel* reckless, rash, foolhardy, venturesome; precipitate, headlong; thwarted, foiled, frustrated, outwitted, circumvented, baffled, balked

desperation *syn* DESPONDENCY, hopelessness, despair, forlornness *rel* fury, frenzy; grit, pluck, guts, sand, fortitude; recklessness, rashness, foolhardiness; temerity, audacity

despicable *syn* CONTEMPTIBLE, pitiable, sorry, scurvy, cheap, beggarly, shabby *rel* base, low, vile; ignominious, infamous, disgraceful; ignoble, mean, abject, sordid *ant* praiseworthy, laudable

despise • to regard as beneath one's notice and as unworthy of attention or interest *syn* contemn, scorn, disdain, scout *rel* abominate, loathe, abhor, detest, hate; spurn, repduiate *ant* appreciate

despite *n* **1** *syn* MALICE, spite, ill will, malevolence, spleen, grudge, malignity, malignancy *rel* contempt, scorn, disdain; abhorrence, loathing, detestation, abomination, hatred, hate *ant* appreciation; regard **2** • the feeling or attitude of despising *syn* contempt, scorn, disdain

despite *prep, syn* NOTWITHSTANDING, in spite of

despoil *syn* RAVAGE, devastate, waste, sack, pillage, spoliate *rel* plunder, rob, rifle, loot; strip, bare, denude

despondency • the state or feeling of having lost hope *syn* despair, desperation, hopelessness, forlornness *rel* dejection, depression, melancholy, melancholia, sadness, blues, dumps *ant* lightheartedness

despondent • having lost all or nearly all hope *syn* despairing, desperate, hopeless, forlorn *rel* grieving, mourning, sorrowing; depressed, dejected, melancholy, sad *ant* lighthearted

despotic *syn* ABSOLUTE, tyrannical, tyrannous, arbitrary, autocratic *rel* domineering, imperious, masterful, imperative; dictatorial, authoritarian, magisterial

destiny *syn* FATE, lot, doom, portion *rel* end, termination, terminus, ending; goal, objective

destitute **1** *syn* DEVOID, void *rel* lacking, wanting; empty; barren, bare; depleted, drained, exhausted, bankrupted, bankrupt **2** *syn* POOR, indigent, needy, penniless, impecunious, poverty-stricken, necessitous *ant* opulent

destitution *syn* POVERTY, want, indigence, penury, privation *rel* need, necessity, exigency; lack, absence, want, privation, dearth; adversity, misfortune; strait *ant* opulence

destroy • to bring to ruin *syn* demolish, raze *rel* ruin, wreck, dilapidate; abolish, extinguish, annihilate; ravage, devastate, sack

destruction *syn* RUIN, havoc, devastation *rel* demolishing, demolition, razing; annihilation, extinction

desultory *syn* RANDOM, casual, hit or miss, haphazard, happy-go-lucky, chance, chancy *rel* fitful, spasmodic; unsystematic, unmethodical, disorderly; capricious, mercurial; inconstant, fickle *ant* assiduous; methodical

detach • to remove one thing from another with which it is in union or association *syn* disengage, abstract *rel* separate, part, sever, sunder, divorce; disjoin, disconnect, disunite *ant* attach, affix

detached *syn* INDIFFERENT, aloof, uninterested, disinterested, unconcerned, incurious *rel* impartial, dispassionate, objective, unbiased, fair; altruistic *ant* interested; selfish

detail **1** *syn* ITEM, particular **2** *syn* PART, portion, piece, parcel, member, division, segment, sector, fraction, fragment

detailed *syn* CIRCUMSTANTIAL, itemized, particularized, minute, particular *rel* full, complete, replete; copious, abundant; exhausting, exhaustive

detain **1** *syn* ARREST, apprehend, attach *rel* catch, capture; seize, take; imprison, incarcerate, intern, jail **2** *syn* KEEP, withhold, hold, hold back, keep back, keep out, retain, reserve **3** *syn* DELAY, retard, slow, slacken *rel* curb, check, restrain, inhibit; arrest, interrupt; defer, suspend, stay

detention *syn* ARREST, apprehension, attachment *rel* imprisonment, internment, incarceration

deter *syn* DISSUADE, discourage, divert *rel* prevent; hinder, impede, obstruct, block; debar, shut out, exclude; frighten, scare; restrain, inhibit *ant* abet; actuate, motivate

deterioration • a falling from a higher to a lower level in quality, character, or vitality *syn* degeneration, devolution, decadence, decline, declension *rel* impairment, spoiling; decaying, decay, decomposition, disintegration, rotting, crumbling; debasement, degradation *ant* improvement, amelioration

determinant *syn* CAUSE, antecedent, reason, occasion *rel* factor, element; influence, weight, authority

determinative *syn* CONCLUSIVE, decisive, definitive *rel* determining, deciding, settling; influencing, affecting; shaping, fashioning, forming, formative

determine **1** *syn* DECIDE, settle, rule, resolve *rel* fix, set, establish; dispose, predispose, incline, bias; drive, impel, move, actuate; induce, persuade **2** *syn* DISCOVER, ascertain, unearth, learn

determined *syn* DECIDED, decisive, resolved

detest *syn* HATE, abhor, abominate, loathe *rel* despise, contemn, scorn, disdain; spurn, repudiate, reject *ant* adore

detestable *syn* HATEFUL, odious, abominable, abhorrent *rel* contemptible, despicable, sorry, scurvy; atrocious, outrageous, monstrous, heinous; execrable, damnable, accursed

detestation *syn* ABHORRENCE, hate, hatred, abomination, loathing *rel* antipathy, aversion; despite, contempt, scorn, disdain

detract *syn* DECRY, belittle, minimize, disparage, derogate, depreciate *rel* asperse, malign, traduce, defame, vilify, calumniate, slander, libel; reduce, lessen, diminish, decrease

detraction • the expression of damaging or malicious opinions *syn* backbiting, calumny, slander, scandal *rel* injury, damage, harm, hurt; injustice, injury, wrong; defaming, defamation, aspersion, maligning, traducing, slandering, calumniation, vilification, libeling, libel

detriment *syn* DISADVANTAGE, handicap, drawback *rel* damage, injury, harm, hurt; impairment, spoiling, marring *ant* advantage, benefit

detrimental *syn* PERNICIOUS, deleterious, noxious, baneful *rel* harming, harmful, hurting, hurtful, injuring, injurious, damaging, impairing *ant* beneficial

devastate *syn* RAVAGE, waste, sack, pillage, despoil, spoliate *rel* destroy, demolish, raze; ruin, wreck; plunder, loot, rob, rifle

devastation *syn* RUIN, havoc, destruction *rel* demolishment, razing; ravaging, sacking, pillaging, despoliation

develop **1** *syn* UNFOLD, evolve, elaborate, perfect *rel* actualize, realize, materialize; attain, achieve, compass, reach **2** *syn* MATURE, ripen, age *rel* advance, progress; expand, dilate

development • advance from a lower to a higher form *syn* evolution

deviate *syn* SWERVE, digress, diverge, veer, depart *rel* deflect, turn, divert, avert, sheer; stray, wander, rove

deviation • departure from a straight course or procedure or from a norm or standard *syn* aberration, divergence, deflection

device **1** • something usu. of a mechanical

character that performs a function or effects a desired end *syn* contrivance, gadget, contraption *rel* instrument, tool, implement, appliance, utensil; apparatus, machine, mechanism; expedient, resource, shift, makeshift, resort; invention, creation; artifice, ruse, trick, gambit, ploy **2** *syn* FIGURE, design, motif, pattern *rel* symbol, emblem, attribute, type

devilish *syn* FIENDISH, diabolical, diabolic, demoniac, demonic *rel* infernal, hellish; nefarious, iniquitous, villainous, vicious *ant* angelic

devious *syn* CROOKED, oblique *rel* deviating, diverging, digressing; aberrant, abnormal; tricky, crafty, artful, cunning, foxy, insidious, sly *ant* straightforward

devise 1 *syn* CONTRIVE, invent, frame, concoct *rel* create, discover, invent; fashion, forge, fabricate, shape, form, make; design, plan, scheme, plot **2** *syn* WILL, bequeath, leave, legate

devoid • showing a want or lack *syn* void, destitute *rel* barren, bare; lacking, wanting; empty

devolution *syn* DETERIORATION, decadence, decline, declension, degeneration *rel* retrogressiveness, retrogression, regressiveness, regression; receding, recession, retrograding, retrogradation *ant* evolution

devote 1 • to set apart for a particular and often a better or higher use or end *syn* dedicate, consecrate, hallow *rel* commit, consign, confide, entrust; assign, allot; sentence, doom **2** *syn* DIRECT, apply, address *rel* endeavor, strive, struggle, try, attempt

devoted *syn* LOVING, affectionate, fond, doting *rel* faithful, loyal, true, constant; attentive, considerate, thoughtful

devotee *syn* ADDICT, votary, habitué *rel* enthusiast, zealot, fanatic

devotion *syn* FIDELITY, loyalty, fealty, piety, allegiance *rel* fervor, ardor, zeal, enthusiasm, passion; love, affection, attachment; dedication, consecration

devour *syn* EAT, swallow, ingest, consume *rel* waste, squander, dissipate; destroy, demolish; wreck, ruin

devout • showing fervor and reverence in the practice of religion *syn* pious, religious, pietistic, sanctimonious *rel* fervent, fervid, ardent, impassioned; worshiping, adoring, venerating

dexterity *syn* READINESS, facility, ease *rel* dexterousness, adroitness, deftness; expertness, adeptness, skillfulness, proficiency *ant* clumsiness

dexterous • ready and skilled in physical movements *syn* adroit, deft, handy *rel* nimble, agile; skilled, skillful, expert, masterly, adept, proficient; easy, effortless, smooth, facile *ant* clumsy

diabolical, diabolic *syn* FIENDISH, demonic, devilish, demoniac *rel, ant* see DEVILISH

diagram *n, syn* SKETCH, outline, draft, tracing, delineation, plot, blueprint *rel* design, plan, plot, scheme

diagram *vb, syn* SKETCH, outline, plot, blueprint, draft, trace, delineate *rel* design, plan, plot, scheme

dialect 1 • a form of language that is not recognized as standard *syn* vernacular, patois, lingo, jargon, cant, argot, slang **2** *syn* LANGUAGE, tongue, speech, idiom

dialectic *syn* ARGUMENTATION, disputation, debate, forensic

diaphanous *syn* CLEAR, limpid, pellucid, transparent, translucent, lucid

diatribe *syn* TIRADE, jeremiad, philippic *rel* invective, vituperation, obloquy, abuse

dictate *vb* • to lay down expressly something to be followed, observed, obeyed, or accepted *syn* prescribe, ordain, decree, impose *rel* direct, control, manage; guide, lead; govern, rule; tell, utter, say

dictate *n, syn* COMMAND, behest, bidding, injunction, order, mandate *rel* law, rule, precept, canon, ordinance, statute, regulation

dictatorial • imposing one's will or opinions on others *syn* magisterial, authoritarian, dogmatic, doctrinaire, oracular *rel* masterful, domineering, imperative, imperious, peremptory; despotic, tyrannical, arbitrary, autocratic, absolute

diction *syn* LANGUAGE, vocabulary, phraseology, phrasing, style *rel* speech, tongue, idiom; enunciation, pronunciation, articulation

dido *syn* PRANK, caper, antic, monkeyshine

differ • to be unlike or out of harmony *syn* vary, disagree, dissent *rel* diverge, deviate, depart *ant* agree

difference 1 *syn* DISSIMILARITY, unlikeness, divergence, divergency, distinction *rel* discrepancy, inconsistency, inconsonance, discordance; variation, modification; disparity, diversity *ant* resemblance **2** *syn* DISCORD, strife, conflict, contention, dissension, variance

different • unlike in kind or character *syn* diverse, divergent, disparate, various *rel* distinct, separate, several; single, particular; sundry, divers, many *ant* identical, alike, same

differentiate *syn* DISTINGUISH, discriminate, demarcate *rel* separate, divide, part; detach, disengage *ant* confuse

difficult *syn* HARD, arduous *rel* perplexing, puzzling, mystifying; intricate, involved, complicated, complex, knotty; obscure, enigmatic, cryptic; exacting, onerous, burdensome *ant* simple

difficulty • something which demands effort and endurance if it is to be overcome or one's end achieved *syn* hardship, rigor, vicissitude *rel* obstacle, impediment, snag, obstruction; predicament, dilemma, quandary, plight, scrape, fix, jam, pickle; pinch, strait, emergency, exigency, pass

diffident *syn* SHY, modest, bashful, coy *rel* shrinking, flinching, blenching; hesitant, reluctant, disinclined; timorous, timid *ant* confident

diffuse *adj, syn* WORDY, prolix, redundant, verbose *rel* profuse, lavish, exuberant; desultory, casual, random; copious; loose, relaxed, slack, lax *ant* succinct

diffuse *vb, syn* SPREAD, circulate, disseminate, propagate, radiate *rel* disperse, dissipate, scatter; extend; expand *ant* concentrate

dig • to loosen and turn over or remove (as soil) with or as if with a spade *syn* delve, spade, grub, excavate *rel* pierce, penetrate, probe, enter

digest *syn* COMPENDIUM, syllabus, pandect, survey, sketch, précis, aperçu *rel* collection, assemblage, gathering; abridgment, conspectus, abstract, brief, synopsis, epitome

digit *syn* NUMBER, numeral, figure, integer

dignify • to enhance the status of or raise in human estimation *syn* ennoble, honor, glorify *rel* elevate, raise, lift; exalt, magnify, aggrandize; heighten, enhance, intensify

dignity **1** *syn* DECORUM, decency, propriety, etiquette *rel* excellence, virtue, merit, perfection; nobleness, nobility, morality, ethicalness, ethics **2** *syn* ELEGANCE, grace *rel* worth, value; beautifulness, beauty, loveliness, comeliness; grandness, grandeur, magnificence, stateliness, majesty, augustness

digress *syn* SWERVE, deviate, diverge, depart, veer *rel* wander, stray

digression • a departure from a subject or theme *syn* episode, excursus, divagation

dilapidate *syn* RUIN, wreck *rel* decay, disintegrate, crumble, decompose; neglect, ignore, disregard, forget, slight, overlook

dilapidated *syn* SHABBY, dingy, faded, seedy, threadbare *rel* damaged, injured, impaired, marred; ruined, wrecked

dilate **1** *syn* DISCOURSE, expatiate, descant *rel* relate, recount, rehearse, recite, narrate, describe; expound, explain; discuss, argue **2** *syn* EXPAND, distend, swell, amplify, inflate *rel* enlarge, increase, augment; extend, protract, prolong, lengthen; widen, broaden *ant* constrict; circumscribe; attenuate

dilatory *syn* SLOW, laggard, deliberate, leisurely *rel* procrastinating, delaying, dawdling; negligent, neglectful, lax, slack, remiss *ant* diligent

dilemma *syn* PREDICAMENT, quandary, plight, scrape, fix, jam, pickle *rel* perplexity, bewilderment, mystification; difficulty, vicissitude

dilettante **1** *syn* AMATEUR, dabbler, tyro **2** *syn* AESTHETE, connoisseur

diligent *syn* BUSY, assiduous, sedulous, industrious *rel* persevering, persisting, persistent; indefatigable, tireless, untiring, unwearied, unflagging *ant* dilatory

dilute *syn* THIN, attenuate, rarefy *rel* temper, moderate, qualify; weaken, enfeeble; liquefy, deliquesce; adulterate, sophisticate *ant* condense; concentrate

dim *adj, syn* DARK, dusky, obscure, murky, gloomy *ant* bright; distinct

dim *vb, syn* OBSCURE, bedim, darken, eclipse, cloud, becloud, fog, befog, obfuscate *rel* screen, conceal, hide; cloak, mask, camouflage, disguise *ant* illustrate

dimensions *syn* SIZE, extent, area, magnitude, volume

diminish *syn* DECREASE, reduce, lessen, abate, dwindle *rel* wane, ebb, subside; moderate, temper; lighten, alleviate, mitigate; attenuate, extenuate

diminutive *syn* SMALL, little, wee, tiny, minute, miniature

din *n* • a disturbing or confusing welter of sounds *syn* uproar, pandemonium, hullabaloo, babel, hubbub, clamor, racket *rel* clamorousness, stridency, boisterousness, blatancy; clash, percussion *ant* quiet

dingy *syn* SHABBY, dilapidated, faded, seedy, threadbare *rel* soiled, grimed, sullied, smirched, tarnished; dull; dusky, murky, gloomy, dark

dinner • a usu. elaborate meal served to guests or to a group often to mark an occasion or honor an individual *syn* banquet, feast

dip 1 • to plunge a person or thing into or as if into liquid *syn* immerse, submerge, duck, souse, dunk **2** • to remove a liquid or a loose or soft substance from a container by means of an implement shaped to hold liquid *syn* bail, scoop, ladle, spoon, dish

diplomatic *syn* SUAVE, politic, smooth, bland, urbane *rel* astute, shrewd; courteous, courtly, polite, civil; artful, wily, guileful, crafty; tactful, poised

dipsomaniac *syn* DRUNKARD, alcoholic, inebriate, sot, soak, toper, tosspot, tippler

direct *vb* **1** • to turn or bend one's attention or efforts toward a certain object or objective *syn* address, devote, apply *rel* bend; set, fix, settle; endeavor, strive, try, attempt **2** • to turn something toward its appointed or intended mark or goal *syn* aim, point, level, train, lay *rel* steer, pilot, guide, lead, engineer *ant* misdirect **3** *syn* CONDUCT, manage, control *rel* govern, rule **4** *syn* COMMAND, order, bid, enjoin, instruct, charge *rel* prescribe, assign, define

direct *adj* • marked by the absence of interruption (as between the cause and the effect, the source and the issue, or the beginning and the end) *syn* immediate

directly *syn* PRESENTLY, shortly, soon

dirty *adj* • conspicuously unclean or impure *syn* filthy, foul, nasty, squalid *ant* clean

dirty *vb, syn* SOIL, sully, tarnish, foul, befoul, smirch, besmirch, grime, begrime *rel* pollute, defile, contaminate; spot, spatter

disable *syn* WEAKEN, cripple, undermine, enfeeble, debilitate, sap *rel* injure, damage, harm, hurt, impair, mar, spoil; maim, mutilate, mangle, batter; ruin, wreck *ant* rehabilitate

disabuse *syn* RID, clear, unburden, purge *rel* free, liberate, release; enlighten, illuminate

disadvantage • something which interferes with the success or well-being of a person or thing *syn* detriment, handicap, drawback *rel* obstacle, impediment, bar; barrier; hindrance, blocking *ant* advantage

disaffect *syn* ESTRANGE, alienate, wean *rel* upset, agitate, discompose, disquiet, disturb; sever, sunder, divorce, separate *ant* win over

disagree *syn* DIFFER, vary, dissent *rel* object, protest; demur, balk, jib; disapprove, deprecate; conflict, clash *ant* agree

disallow *syn* DISCLAIM, disavow, repudiate, disown *rel* reject, refuse, spurn, decline; deny, gainsay, traverse; debar, shut out, exclude *ant* allow

disappear *syn* VANISH, evanesce, evaporate, fade *rel* depart, leave, go *ant* appear

disapprove • to feel or to express an objection to or condemnation of *syn* deprecate *rel* reprehend, reprobate, censure, criticize; decry, disparage *ant* approve

disarrange *syn* DISORDER, derange, disorganize, unsettle, disturb *rel* misplace, mislay; displace, replace; upset, overturn *ant* arrange

disarray *syn* CONFUSION, disorder, chaos, jumble, clutter, snarl, muddle

disaster • an event bringing great damage, loss, or destruction *syn* calamity, catastrophe, cataclysm *rel* mishap, accident, casualty; adversity, misfortune, mischance

disastrous *syn* UNLUCKY, ill-starred, ill-fated, unfortunate, calamitous, luckless, hapless *rel* malign, sinister, baleful; unpropitious, inauspicious, ominous, portentous, fateful

disavow *syn* DISCLAIM, repudiate, disown, disallow *rel* deny, gainsay, traverse; disapprove, deprecate; reject, refuse, decline *ant* avow

disbar *syn* EXCLUDE, shut out, eliminate, rule out, suspend, debar, blackball

disbelief *syn* UNBELIEF, incredulity *rel* atheism, deism; rejection, repudiation, spurning *ant* belief

disburse *syn* SPEND, expend *rel* distribute, dispense; apportion, allot, allocate; pay

discard • to get rid of *syn* cast, shed, molt, slough, scrap, junk *rel* abandon, forsake, desert; reject, repudiate, spurn; dismiss, eject, oust

discern *syn* SEE, perceive, descry, observe, notice, remark, note, espy, behold, view, survey, contemplate *rel* discover, ascertain; divine, apprehend, anticipate, foresee; pierce, penetrate, probe

discernment • a power to see what is not evident to the average mind *syn* discrimination, perception, penetration, insight, acumen *rel* intuition, understanding, reason; perspicaciousness, perspicacity, sagaciousness, sagacity, shrewdness, astuteness

discharge **1** *syn* FREE, release, liberate, emancipate, manumit *rel* eject, expel, oust; eliminate, exclude; deliver, enfranchise **2** *syn* DISMISS, cashier, drop, sack, fire, bounce *rel* displace, supplant, supersede, replace **3** *syn* PERFORM, execute, accomplish, achieve, effect, fulfill *rel* finish, complete, close, end, terminate

disciple *syn* FOLLOWER, adherent, henchman, satellite, sectary, partisan *rel* votary, devotee; enthusiast, zealot, fanatic

discipline *n, syn* MORALE, esprit de corps *rel* self-control, self-command; self-confidence, self-possession; nerving, steeling *ant* anarchy, lawlessness

discipline *vb* **1** *syn* TEACH, train, educate, instruct, school *rel* lead, guide; control, manage, direct, conduct; drill, exercise, practice **2** *syn* PUNISH, chastise, castigate, chasten, correct *rel* subdue, overcome, reduce, subjugate; restrain, curb, bridle, check, inhibit

disclaim • to refuse to admit, accept, or approve *syn* disavow, repudiate, disown, disallow *rel* deny, gainsay, traverse, contradict; reject, refuse, spurn; deprecate, disapprove; belittle, minimize, disparage, decry *ant* claim

disclose *syn* REVEAL, divulge, tell, discover, betray *rel* confess, admit, own, acknowledge, avow; declare, proclaim, announce, publish, broadcast, advertise

discomfit *syn* EMBARRASS, disconcert, faze, abash, rattle *rel* annoy, vex, irk, bother; perturb, discompose, agitate, upset, disturb; check, arrest, interrupt

discommode *syn* INCONVENIENCE, incommode, trouble *rel* disturb, perturb, upset, fluster, flurry, discompose; vex, irk, bother, annoy

discompose • to excite one so as to destroy one's capacity for clear or collected thought or prompt action *syn* disquiet, disturb, perturb, agitate, upset, fluster, flurry *rel* discomfit, disconcert, rattle, faze, embarrass; vex, irk, bother, annoy; worry, harass, plague, pester

disconcert *syn* EMBARRASS, rattle, faze, discomfit, abash *rel* bewilder, nonplus, perplex, puzzle; discompose, fluster, flurry, disturb, perturb

disconsolate *syn* DOWNCAST, woebegone, dejected, depressed, dispirited *rel* inconsolable, comfortless; sorrowful, woeful; melancholy, doleful

discontinue *syn* STOP, desist, cease, quit *rel* suspend, intermit, stay, defer; arrest, check, interrupt *ant* continue

discord • a state or condition marked by disagreement and lack of harmony *syn* strife, conflict, contention, dissension, difference, variance *rel* incompatibility, incongruity, inconsonance, inconsistency, uncongeniality, discrepancy; antagonism, hostility, enmity, rancor, animosity, antipathy

discordant *syn* INCONSONANT, incongruous, uncongenial, unsympathetic, incompatible, inconsistent, discrepant

discount *syn* DEDUCTION, rebate, abatement

discourage **1** • to weaken the stamina, interest, or zeal of *syn* dishearten, dispirit, deject *rel* depress, weigh; try, afflict; vex, bother, irk *ant* encourage **2** *syn* DISSUADE, deter, divert *rel* restrain, inhibit; prevent; frighten, scare

discourse *n* • a systematic, serious, and often learned exposition of a subject or topic *syn* treatise, disquisition, dissertation, thesis, monograph *rel* paper, article, essay; speech, lecture, talk, sermon

discourse *vb* • to talk or sometimes write esp. formally and at length upon a subject *syn* expatiate, dilate, descant *rel* discuss, argue, dispute; converse, talk, speak; lecture, harangue, orate, sermonize

discourteous *syn* RUDE, impolite, uncivil, ungracious, ill-mannered *rel* brusque, curt, crusty, gruff, blunt, bluff; boorish, churlish *ant* courteous

discover **1** *syn* REVEAL, disclose, divulge, tell, betray *rel* impart, communicate; declare, announce, publish, advertise, proclaim **2** • to find out something not previously known *syn* ascertain, determine, unearth, learn *rel* discern, observe, perceive, espy

discreet *syn* PRUDENT, forethoughtful, foresighted, provident *rel* cautious, circumspect, wary; politic, diplomatic, suave *ant* indiscreet

discrepant *syn* INCONSONANT, inconsistent, discordant, incompatible, incongruous, uncongenial, unsympathetic *rel* divergent, disparate, different, diverse *ant* identical (*as accounts, explanations*)

discrete *syn* DISTINCT, separate, several *rel* individual, distinctive, peculiar

discretion *syn* PRUDENCE, forethought, foresight, providence *rel* caution, circumspection, wariness; judgment, sense, wisdom, gumption *ant* indiscretion

discriminate *syn* DISTINGUISH, differentiate, demarcate *rel* compare, contrast, collate, separate, divide, part; detach, disengage *ant* confound

discrimination *syn* DISCERNMENT, penetration, insight, perception, acumen *rel* wisdom, judgment, sense; subtlety, logicalness, logic

discuss • to exchange views about something in order to arrive at the truth or to convince others *syn* argue, debate, dispute, agitate *rel* explain, expound, interpret, elucidate, explicate; discourse, expatiate, dilate, descant

disdain *n, syn* DESPITE, scorn, contempt *rel* aversion, antipathy; insolence, superciliousness, arrogance

disdain *vb, syn* DESPISE, scorn, scout, contemn *rel* spurn, repudiate, reject *ant* favor; admit

disdainful *syn* PROUD, supercilious, overbearing, insolent, arrogant, lordly, haughty *rel* spurning, repudiating, rejecting; scorning, despising, contemning, scouting; averse, antipathetic, unsympathetic

disease • an impairment of the normal state of the living body that interferes with normal bodily functions *syn* disorder, condition, affection, ailment, malady, complaint, distemper, syndrome

diseased *syn* UNWHOLESOME, morbid, sickly, pathological

disembarrass *syn* EXTRICATE, disencumber, disentangle, untangle *rel* release, free, liberate; relieve; disengage, detach

disencumber *syn* EXTRICATE, disembarrass, disentangle, untangle *rel* relieve, alleviate, lighten; disengage, detach; liberate, release, free

disengage *syn* DETACH, abstract *rel* disembarrass, disencumber, disentangle, untangle, extricate; release, liberate, free; disconnect, disjoin, dissociate, disunite *ant* engage

disentangle *syn* EXTRICATE, untangle, disembarrass, disencumber *rel* disengage, detach; separate, part, sever, sunder; free, release, liberate *ant* entangle

disfavor *syn* DISLIKE, distaste, aversion *rel* disapproval, deprecation; distrust, mistrust

disfigure *syn* DEFACE, *rel* mangle, batter, maim, mutilate; deform, distort, contort, warp; injure, damage, mar, impair *ant* adorn

disgorge *syn* BELCH, burp, vomit, regurgitate, spew, throw up

disgrace • the state of suffering loss of esteem and of enduring reproach *syn* dishonor, disrepute, shame, infamy, ignominy, opprobrium, obloquy, odium *rel* degradation, debasement, abasement, humbling, humiliation; stigma, brand, blot, stain *ant* respect, esteem

disguise • to alter so as to hide the true appearance or character of *syn* cloak, mask, dissemble, camouflage *rel* conceal, hide; misrepresent, belie, falsify, garble; assume, pretend, feign, counterfeit, sham, simulate, affect

disgust • to arouse an extreme distaste in *syn* sicken, nauseate *rel* revolt, repulse, offend *ant* charm

dish *syn* DIP, ladle, spoon, bail, scoop

dishearten *syn* DISCOURAGE, dispirit, deject *rel* depress, weigh; despair, despond *ant* hearten

disheveled *syn* SLIPSHOD, unkempt, sloppy, slovenly *rel* negligent, neglectful, lax, slack, remiss; slatternly, blowsy, frowzy, dowdy

dishonest • unworthy of trust or belief *syn* DECEITFUL, mendacious, lying, untruthful *rel* crooked, devious, oblique; false, faithless, perfidious; cheating, cozening, defrauding, swindling *ant* honest

dishonor *syn* DISGRACE, disrepute, shame, infamy, ignominy, opprobrium, obloquy, odium *rel* humiliation, humbling, debasement, degradation, abasement; stigma, brand, blot, stain *ant* honor

disillusioned *syn* SOPHISTICATED, worldly-wise, worldly, blasé *rel* undeceived; disenchanted

disinclined • lacking the will or the desire to do something *syn* indisposed, hesitant, reluctant, loath, averse *rel* antipathetic, unsympathetic; opposing, resisting; balking, shying, boggling, sticking, stickling; objecting, protesting

disinfect *syn* STERILIZE, sanitize, fumigate *ant* infect

disintegrate *syn* DECAY, crumble, decompose, rot, putrefy, spoil *rel* deliquesce; scatter, disperse, dissipate; break down, resolve, analyze, dissect *ant* integrate

disinterested *syn* INDIFFERENT, uninterested, detached, aloof, unconcerned, incurious *rel* dispassionate, unbiased, impartial, fair, just; neutral, negative *ant* interested; prejudiced, biased

dislike • a feeling of aversion or disapproval *syn* distaste, aversion, disfavor *rel* hate, hatred, detestation; disapproval, deprecation *ant* liking

disloyal *syn* FAITHLESS, false, perfidious, traitorous, treacherous *rel* disaffected, estranged, alienated; inconstant, fickle, unstable *ant* loyal

dismal • devoid of all that makes for cheer or comfort *syn* dreary, cheerless, dispiriting, bleak, desolate *rel* murky, gloomy, dark; forlorn, hopeless; barren, bare

dismantle *syn* STRIP, divest, denude, bare

dismay *vb* • to unnerve and check by arousing fear, apprehension, or aversion *syn* appall, horrify, daunt *rel* perplex, confound, bewilder, nonplus, dumbfound, mystify, puzzle; disconcert, rattle, faze, abash, discomfit, embarrass; alarm, frighten, terrify *ant* cheer

dismay *n, syn* FEAR, alarm, consternation, panic, dread, fright, terror, horror, trepidation *rel* perturbing, perturbation, agitation, disquieting, disquietude, discomposing, discomposure, upsetting, upset; apprehension, foreboding

dismiss **1** • to let go from one's employ or service *syn* discharge, cashier, drop, sack, fire, bounce **2** *syn* EJECT, oust, expel, evict *rel* discard, cast, shed, slough; spurn, repudiate, reject, refuse; scorn, scout

dismount *syn* DESCEND, alight *rel* mount

disorder *vb* • to undo the fixed or proper order of something *syn* derange, disarrange, disorganize, unsettle, disturb *rel* order

disorder *n* **1** *syn* CONFUSION, disarray, clutter, jumble, chaos, snarl, muddle *rel* derangement, disarrangement, disorganization, disturbance, unsettlement; anarchy, chaos, lawlessness *ant* order **2** *syn* DISEASE, condition, affection, ailment, malady, complaint, distemper, syndrome

disorganize *syn* DISORDER, disturb, unsettle, derange, disarrange *rel* organize

disown *syn* DISCLAIM, disavow, repudiate, disallow *rel* reject, spurn, refuse, decline *ant* own

disparage *syn* DECRY, depreciate, derogate, detract, belittle, minimize *rel* asperse, malign, traduce, defame, slander, libel; deprecate, disapprove *ant* applaud

disparaging *syn* DEROGATORY, depreciatory, depreciative, slighting, pejorative *rel* belittling, decrying, minimizing; underestimating, undervaluing, underrating

disparate *syn* DIFFERENT, diverse, divergent, various *rel* inconsonant, incompatible, incongruous, discrepant, discordant, inconsistent; distinct, separate *ant* comparable, analogous

dispassionate *syn* FAIR, unbiased, impartial, objective, uncolored, just, equitable *rel* disinterested, detached, aloof, indifferent; cool, collected, composed; candid, open, frank *ant* passionate; intemperate

dispatch *vb* **1** *syn* SEND, forward, transmit, remit, route, ship *rel* hasten, quicken, speed **2** *syn* KILL, slay, murder, assassinate, execute

dispatch *n* **1** *syn* HASTE, speed, expedition, hurry *rel* celerity, alacrity, legerity; quickness, fleetness, swiftness, rapidity; diligence *ant* delay **2** *syn* LETTER, message, note, epistle, report, memorandum, missive

dispel *syn* SCATTER, dissipate, disperse *rel* expel, eject, oust, dismiss; disintegrate, crumble, decay

dispense *syn* DISTRIBUTE, divide, deal, dole *rel* allot, assign, apportion, allocate; portion, parcel, ration, prorate **2** *syn* ADMINISTER

disperse *syn* SCATTER, dissipate, dispel *rel* separate, part, divide; dismiss, discharge *ant* assemble, congregate; collect

dispirit *syn* DISCOURAGE, dishearten, deject *rel* depress, weigh *ant* inspirit

dispirited *syn* DOWNCAST, depressed, dejected, disconsolate, woebegone *rel* sad, melancholy; gloomy, glum, morose, sullen;

discouraged, disheartened *ant* high-spirited

dispiriting *syn* DISMAL, dreary, cheerless, bleak, desolate *rel* disheartening, discouraging, dejecting; depressing, oppressing, oppressive *ant* inspiriting

displace *syn* REPLACE, supplant, supersede *rel* transpose, reverse, invert; shift, remove, transfer, move; derange, disarrange, disorder; eject, oust, expel, dismiss

display *vb, syn* SHOW, exhibit, expose, parade, flaunt *rel* manifest, evidence, evince, demonstrate; reveal, disclose, discover

display *n* • a striking or spectacular show or exhibition for the sake of effect *syn* parade, array, pomp *rel* ostentatiousness, ostentation, pretentiousness, pretension, showiness, show

disport *n, syn* PLAY, sport, frolic, rollick, romp, gambol *rel* recreation, diversion, amusement, entertainment; merriment, jollity

disport *vb, syn* PLAY, sport, frolic, rollick, romp, gambol *rel* divert, amuse, recreate, entertain

disposal • the act or the power of disposing of something *syn* disposition *rel* destroying, destruction, demolishing, demolition

dispose *syn* INCLINE, predispose, bias *rel* influence, affect, sway

disposition **1** *syn* DISPOSAL *rel* administering, administration, dispensing, dispensation; management, direction, controlling, control, conducting, conduct; arrangement, ordering **2** • the prevailing and dominant quality or qualities which distinguish or identify a person or group *syn* temperament, temper, complexion, character, personality, individuality

disprove • to show by presenting evidence that something is not true *syn* refute, confute, rebut, controvert *rel* negative, traverse, impugn, contravene *ant* prove, demonstrate

disputation *syn* ARGUMENTATION, debate, forensic, dialectic *rel* argument, dispute, controversy

dispute *vb, syn* DISCUSS, argue, debate, agitate *ant* concede

dispute *n, syn* ARGUMENT, controversy *rel* argumentation, disputation, debate, forensic, dialectic; contention, dissension, strife, discord, conflict

disquiet *syn* DISCOMPOSE, disturb, agitate, perturb, upset, fluster, flurry *rel* annoy, vex, irk, bother; worry, harass, harry; trouble, distress *ant* tranquilize, soothe

disquisition *syn* DISCOURSE, dissertation, thesis, treatise, monograph *rel* paper, essay, article; inquiry, investigation

disrate *syn* DEGRADE, demote, reduce, declass

disregard *syn* NEGLECT, ignore, overlook, slight, forget, omit

disrepute *syn* DISGRACE, dishonor, shame, infamy, ignominy, opprobrium, obloquy, odium *rel* repute

dissect *syn* ANALYZE, break down, resolve *rel* scrutinize, examine, inspect; pierce, penetrate, probe

dissection *syn* ANALYSIS, breakdown, resolution

dissemble *syn* DISGUISE, mask, cloak, camouflage *rel* simulate, feign, counterfeit, sham, pretend, assume, affect *ant* betray

disseminate *syn* SPREAD, circulate, diffuse, propagate, radiate *rel* scatter, disperse; distribute, dispense, divide; share, participate

dissension *syn* DISCORD, difference, variance, strife, conflict, contention *rel* altercation, wrangle, quarrel, bickering; argument, dispute, controversy *ant* accord; comity

dissent *syn* DIFFER, vary, disagree *rel* object, protest; demur, balk, boggle, shy, stickle *ant* concur; assent; consent

dissenter *syn* HERETIC, nonconformist, sectarian, sectary, schismatic

dissertation *syn* DISCOURSE, disquisition, thesis, treatise, monograph *rel* exposition; argumentation, disputation; article, paper, essay

dissimilarity • lack of agreement or correspondence or an instance of this *syn* unlikeness, difference, divergence, divergency, distinction *rel* diversity, disparity ; discrepancy, discordance, inconsonance *ant* similarity

dissimulation *syn* DECEIT, duplicity, cunning, guile *rel* dissembling, cloaking, masking, disguising, camouflaging; hiding, concealing, secreting; pretending, pretense, feigning, shamming; hypocrisy, pharisaism, sanctimony

dissipate **1** *syn* SCATTER, dispel, disperse *rel* disintegrate, crumble; separate, part, divide; deliquesce, melt *ant* accumulate; absorb; concentrate **2** *syn* WASTE, squander, fritter, consume *rel* spend, expend, disburse; scatter, disperse; vanish, evanesce, disappear, evaporate

dissolute *syn* ABANDONED, profligate, reprobate *rel* licentious, libertine, wanton, lewd; inebriated, intoxicated, drunken, drunk; debauched, depraved, corrupt, debased, perverted

dissuade • to turn one aside from a purpose, a project, or a plan *syn* deter, discourage, divert *rel* advise, counsel; urge, exhort, prick *ant* persuade

distant • not close in space, time, or relationship *syn* far, faraway, far-off, remote, removed

distaste *syn* DISLIKE, aversion, disfavor *rel* repugnance, repulsion, abhorrence; antipathy, hostility, enmity *ant* taste

distasteful *syn* REPUGNANT, obnoxious, repellent, abhorrent, invidious *rel* hateful, odious, detestable, abominable; offensive, loathsome, repulsive, repugnant, revolting *ant* agreeable; palatable

distemper *syn* DISEASE, complaint, syndrome, malady, ailment, disorder, condition, affection

distend *syn* EXPAND, swell, dilate, inflate, amplify *rel* enlarge, increase, augment; extend, lengthen *ant* constrict

distinct **1** • capable of being distinguished as differing *syn* separate, several, discrete *rel* individual, distinctive, peculiar; single, sole, separate, particular; special, especial; different, diverse, disparate, divergent **2** *syn* EVIDENT, manifest, patent, obvious, apparent, palpable, plain, clear *rel* defined, prescribed; explicit, definite, express, specific, categorical; perspicuous, clear, lucid; clear-cut, incisive, trenchant *ant* indistinct; nebulous

distinction *syn* DISSIMILARITY, difference, divergence, divergency, unlikeness *rel* resemblance

distinctive *syn* CHARACTERISTIC, peculiar, individual *rel* special, particular, specific, especial; unique, separate, single; distinct, several, discrete *ant* typical

distinguish **1** • to recognize the differences between *syn* differentiate, discriminate, demarcate *rel* separate, part, divide; detach, disengage *ant* confound **2** *syn* CHARACTERIZE, mark, qualify *rel* individualize, peculiarize

distort *syn* DEFORM, contort, warp *rel* twist, bend, curve; disfigure, deface; injure, damage, mar, impair; misinterpret, misconstrue

distract *syn* PUZZLE, bewilder, nonplus, confound, dumbfound, mystify, perplex *rel* confuse, muddle, addle, fuddle, befuddle; baffle, balk, frustrate; agitate, upset, fluster, flurry, perturb, discompose *ant* collect (*one's thoughts, one's powers*)

distraught *syn* ABSTRACTED, absent-minded, absent, preoccupied *rel* distracted, bewildered, nonplused; muddled, addled, confused; agitated, perturbed, discomposed, flustered *ant* collected

distress *n* • the state of being in great trouble or in mental or physical anguish *syn* suffering, misery, agony, dolor, passion *rel* affliction, trial, tribulation; sorrow, grief, anguish, woe, heartbreak; strait, pass, pinch, exigency; hardship, difficulty, rigor, vicissitude; pain, pang, ache

distress *vb, syn* TROUBLE, ail *rel* afflict, try, torment, torture, rack; worry, annoy, harass, harry, plague, pester; depress, oppress, weigh

distribute • to give out, usu. in shares, to each member of a group *syn* dispense, divide, deal, dole *rel* apportion, allot, allocate, assign; ration, portion, parcel, prorate, administer, *ant* collect; amass

district *syn* LOCALITY, vicinity, neighborhood *rel* area, tract, region, zone, belt; section, sector, division, parcel; field, province, territory, sphere

distrust *vb* • to lack trust or confidence in *syn* mistrust, doubt, misdoubt, suspect

distrust *n* • a lack of trust or confidence *syn* mistrust *rel* doubt, uncertainty, dubiety, dubiosity, suspicion; apprehension, foreboding, misgiving, presentiment

disturb **1** *syn* DISORDER, unsettle, derange, disarrange, disorganize *rel* displace, replace; shift, remove, move; arrest, interrupt, check; meddle, intermeddle, interfere, tamper **2** *syn* DISCOMPOSE, perturb, upset, disquiet, agitate, fluster, flurry *rel* frighten, alarm, terrify, scare; perplex, puzzle, bewilder, distract; discomfit, rattle, faze, disconcert; discommode, incommode, trouble, inconvenience

dither *syn* SHAKE, tremble, quake, quiver,

shiver, quaver, wobble, teeter, shimmy, shudder, totter

diurnal *syn* DAILY, quotidian

divagation *syn* DIGRESSION, episode, excursus

dive *syn* PLUNGE, pitch *rel* leap, jump, spring, bound; move, drive, impel; push, propel

diverge *syn* SWERVE, veer, deviate, depart, digress *rel* differ, disagree, vary; divide, part, separate *ant* converge; conform

divergence 1 *syn* DEVIATION, deflection, aberration *rel* division, separation, parting; differing, disagreeing, varying *ant* convergence **2** *syn* DISSIMILARITY, divergency, difference, unlikeness, distinction *rel* diversity, variety *ant* conformity, correspondence

divergency *syn* DISSIMILARITY, divergence, difference, unlikeness, distinction *rel, ant* see DIVERGENCE 2

divergent *syn* DIFFERENT, diverse, disparate, various *rel* opposite, contradictory, contrary, antithetical *ant* convergent

divers *syn* MANY, several, sundry, various, numerous, multifarious

diverse *syn* DIFFERENT, divergent, disparate, various *rel* contrasted, contrasting; contrary, opposite, contradictory; distinct, separate *ant* identical, selfsame

diversion *syn* AMUSEMENT, recreation, entertainment *rel* play, sport, disport; levity, frivolity

diversity *syn* VARIETY *rel* divergence, divergency, difference, dissimilarity, unlikeness, distinction; multifariousness *ant* uniformity; identity

divert 1 *syn* TURN, deflect, avert, sheer *rel* bend, curve, twist; deviate, digress, diverge, swerve, veer; change, alter, modify **2** *syn* AMUSE, entertain, recreate *rel* beguile, while, wile, fleet; regale, delight, gladden, tickle, please **3** *syn* DISSUADE, deter, discourage *rel* detach, disengage, abstract

divest *syn* STRIP, denude, bare, dismantle *ant* invest, vest (*in robes of office, with power or authority*); apparel, clothe

divide 1 *syn* SEPARATE, part, sever, sunder, divorce *rel* cleave, split, rend, rive, tear; cut, carve, chop *ant* unite **2** *syn* DISTRIBUTE, dispense, deal, dole *rel* apportion, portion, prorate, ration, parcel; share, participate, partake; allot, assign, allocate

divine *adj, syn* HOLY, sacred, spiritual, religious, blessed

divine *vb, syn* FORESEE, foreknow, apprehend, anticipate *rel* discern, perceive, descry; predict, prophesy, prognosticate, presage, foretell

division *syn* PART, section, segment, sector, portion, piece, detail, member, fraction, fragment, parcel

divorce *syn* SEPARATE, sever, sunder, part, divide *rel* alienate, estrange, wean, disaffect

divulge *syn* REVEAL, tell, disclose, betray, discover *rel* impart, communicate; announce, declare, publish, advertise, proclaim; blab, tattle, gossip

dizzy *syn* GIDDY, vertiginous, swimming, dazzled *rel* reeling, whirling; confounded, bewildered, puzzled

docile *syn* OBEDIENT, biddable, tractable, amenable *rel* compliant, acquiescent; pliant, pliable, adaptable; yielding, submitting, submissive *ant* indocile; unruly, ungovernable

dock *syn* WHARF, pier, quay, slip, berth, jetty, levee

doctor *syn* ADULTERATE, sophisticate, load, weight

doctrinaire *syn* DICTATORIAL, dogmatic, magisterial, oracular, authoritarian

doctrine • a principle accepted as valid and authoritative *syn* dogma, tenet *rel* teaching, instruction; principle, fundamental

document • something preserved and serving as evidence (as of an event, a situation, or the culture of the period) *syn* monument, record, archive *rel* evidence, testimony

dodge • to avoid or evade by some maneuver or shift *syn* parry, sidestep, duck, shirk, fence, malinger *rel* evade, avoid, elude, escape; slide, slip *ant* face

dogged *syn* OBSTINATE, pertinacious, mulish, stubborn, stiff-necked, pigheaded, bullheaded *rel* determined, resolved, decided; tenacious; persevering, persistent; resolute, steadfast *ant* faltering

dogma *syn* DOCTRINE, tenet *rel* belief, conviction, persuasion, view; principle, fundamental

dogmatic *syn* DICTATORIAL, magisterial, doctrinaire, oracular, authoritarian *rel* peremptory, masterful, imperative, imperious, domineering

doldrums *syn* TEDIUM, boredom, ennui *rel* dejection, depression, gloom, blues, dumps *ant* spirits, high spirits

dole *n, syn* RATION, allowance, pittance *rel* apportioning, apportionment, parceling, parcel, portioning, portion; sharing, share

dole *vb, syn* DISTRIBUTE, dispense, deal, divide *rel* apportion, ration, portion, parcel, prorate; bestow, confer, present, give

doleful *syn* MELANCHOLY, lugubrious, dolorous, plaintive, rueful *rel* mourning, mournful, sorrowing, sorrowful, grieving; piteous, pitiful *ant* cheerful, cheery

dolor *syn* DISTRESS, agony, suffering, passion, misery *rel* anguish, woe, sorrow, grief; tribulation, trial, affliction, cross, visitation *ant* beatitude, blessedness

dolorous *syn* MELANCHOLY, doleful, plaintive, lugubrious, rueful *rel, ant* see DOLEFUL

domain *syn* FIELD, sphere, province, territory, bailiwick *rel* area, region, zone; district, locality; jurisdiction, dominion

domicile *syn* HABITATION, dwelling, abode, residence, house, home

dominant • superior to all others in power, influence, position, or rank *syn* predominant, paramount, preponderant, preponderating, sovereign *rel* prevailing, prevalent; preeminent, supreme, transcendent, surpassing; outstanding, salient, signal; governing, ruling *ant* subordinate

domineering *syn* MASTERFUL, imperious, imperative, peremptory *rel* arrogant, overbearing, lordly, insolent; magisterial, dictatorial *ant* subservient

dominion *syn* POWER, control, command, sway, authority, jurisdiction *rel* ascendancy, supremacy; sovereignty

donate *syn* GIVE, present, bestow, confer, afford *rel* grant, accord, award

donation • a gift of money or its equivalent for a charitable, philanthropic, or humanitarian object *syn* benefaction, contribution, alms *rel* grant, subvention, appropriation, subsidy

doom *n, syn* FATE, destiny, lot, portion

doom *vb, syn* SENTENCE, damn, condemn, proscribe

door • an entrance to a place *syn* gate, portal, postern, doorway, gateway *rel* entrance, entry, entrée, ingress, access

doorway *syn* DOOR, portal, postern, gate, gateway

dormant 1 *syn* LATENT, quiescent, abeyant, potential *rel* inactive, inert, passive, idle *ant* active, live 2 *syn* PRONE, couchant, recumbent, supine, prostrate

dormer *syn* WINDOW, casement, oriel

dotage *syn* AGE, senility, senescence *ant* infancy

dote *syn* LIKE, love, relish, enjoy, fancy *ant* loathe

doting *syn* LOVING, fond, devoted, affectionate *rel* infatuated, enamored; fatuous, foolish, silly, asinine, simple

double *syn* SUBSTITUTE, understudy, stand-in, supply, locum tenens, alternate, pinch hitter

double-cross *syn* DECEIVE, delude, betray, beguile, mislead

double-dealing *syn* DECEPTION, chicanery, chicane, trickery, fraud *rel* duplicity, dissimulation, deceit, guile, cunning

double entendre *syn* AMBIGUITY, equivocation, tergiversation

doubt *n, syn* UNCERTAINTY, skepticism, suspicion, mistrust, dubiety, dubiosity *rel* dubiousness, doubtfulness, questionableness; incredulity, unbelief, disbelief *ant* certitude; confidence

doubt *vb, syn* DISTRUST, mistrust, misdoubt, suspect

doubtful • not affording assurance of the worth, soundness, success, or certainty of something or someone *syn* dubious, problematic, questionable *rel* distrusting, distrustful, mistrusting, mistrustful; fearful, apprehensive, afraid *ant* cocksure, positive

doughty *syn* BRAVE, courageous, unafraid, fearless, intrepid, valiant, valorous, dauntless, undaunted, bold, audacious *rel* venturesome, adventurous, daring

dour *syn* SULLEN, saturnine, glum, gloomy, morose, surly, sulky, crabbed *rel* severe, stern, austere; rigorous, strict, rigid; grim, implacable

dowdy *syn* SLATTERNLY, frowzy, blowsy *rel* slovenly, slipshod, unkempt, disheveled, sloppy *ant* smart (*in dress, appearance*)

dower • to furnish or provide with a gift *syn* endow, endue *rel* furnish, equip, outfit, appoint, accouter

downcast • very low in spirits *syn* dispirited, dejected, depressed, disconsolate, woebegone *rel* weighed down, oppressed; distressed, troubled; despondent, forlorn *ant* elated

downright *syn* FORTHRIGHT *rel* blunt, bluff, brusque, curt; candid, plain, open, frank; straightforward, aboveboard

doze *syn* SLEEP, drowse, snooze, slumber, nap, catnap

draft *n, syn* SKETCH, outline, diagram, delineation, tracing, plot, blueprint

draft *vb, syn* SKETCH, outline, diagram, delineate, trace, plot, blueprint

drag *syn* PULL, draw, haul, hale, tug, tow

drain *syn* DEPLETE, exhaust, impoverish, bankrupt *rel* sap, undermine, debilitate, weaken

dramatic • of, relating to, or suggestive of plays, or the performance of a play *syn* theatrical, dramaturgic, melodramatic, histrionic

dramaturgic *syn* DRAMATIC, theatrical, histrionic, melodramatic

draw *vb, syn* PULL, drag, tug, tow, haul, hale *rel* bring, fetch; attract, allure; lure, entice; extract, elicit, evoke, educe

draw *n* • an indecisive ending to a contest or competition *syn* tie, stalemate, deadlock, standoff

drawback *syn* DISADVANTAGE, detriment, handicap *rel* evil, ill; inconvenience, trouble; obstruction, hindrance

dread *syn* FEAR, horror, terror, fright, alarm, trepidation, panic, consternation, dismay *rel* apprehension, foreboding, misgiving, presentiment; timidity, timorousness

dreadful *syn* FEARFUL, horrible, horrific, appalling, awful, frightful, terrible, terrific, shocking

dream *syn* FANCY, fantasy, phantasy, phantasm, vision, daydream, nightmare *rel* delusion, illusion, hallucination

dreary **1** *syn* DISMAL, cheerless, dispiriting, bleak, desolate *rel* discouraging, disheartening; barren, bare; forlorn, hopeless **2** *syn* DULL, humdrum, monotonous, pedestrian, stodgy *rel* irksome, tiresome, wearisome, tedious, boring; fatiguing, exhausting, fagging, tiring

dregs *syn* DEPOSIT, sediment, precipitate, lees, grounds

drench *syn* SOAK, saturate, sop, steep, impregnate, waterlog *rel* permeate, pervade, penetrate, impenetrate

dress *vb, syn* CLOTHE, attire, apparel, array, robe *ant* undress

dress *n, syn* CLOTHES, clothing, attire, apparel, raiment

drift *syn* TENDENCY, trend, tenor *rel* flow, stream, current; movement, motion, progression, progress; intention, purpose, end, objective, goal, intent, aim

drill *vb* **1** *syn* PERFORATE, bore, punch, puncture, prick *rel* pierce, penetrate, enter, probe **2** *syn* PRACTICE, exercise *rel* train, discipline, teach, instruct, school; habituate, accustom

drill *n, syn* PRACTICE, exercise

drive *vb, syn* MOVE, impel, actuate *rel* push, shove, propel; compel, force, coerce; incite, instigate

drive *n* **1** *syn* RIDE **2** *syn* VIGOR, vim, spirit, dash, esprit, verve, punch, élan *rel* power, force, energy, strength, might; impetus, momentum, speed, velocity

drivel *syn* NONSENSE, twaddle, bunk, balderdash, poppycock, gobbledygook, trash, rot, bull *rel* gibberish, mummery, abracadabra

droll *syn* LAUGHABLE, risible, comic, comical, funny, ludicrous, ridiculous, farcical *rel* amusing, diverting, entertaining; absurd, preposterous; humorous, witty, facetious

droop • to become literally or figuratively limp through loss of vigor or freshness *syn* wilt, flag, sag *rel* sink, slump, subside, fall, drop; languish; wither, shrivel, wizen

drop **1** *syn* FALL, sink, slump, subside *rel* descend, dismount; lapse, relapse, backslide; slip, slide; expire, elapse *ant* mount **2** *syn* DISMISS, discharge, cashier, sack, fire, bounce

drowse *syn* SLEEP, doze, snooze, slumber, nap, catnap

drowsy *syn* SLEEPY, somnolent, slumberous *rel* comatose, lethargic, sluggish, torpid

drudgery *syn* WORK, toil, travail, labor, grind *rel* exertion, effort, pains, trouble

drug • a substance used by itself or in a mixture for the treatment or in the diagnosis of disease *syn* medicinal, pharmaceutical, biologic, simple *rel* medicine, medicament, medication, remedy, physic, specific, cure

druggist • one who deals in medicinal drugs *syn* pharmacist, apothecary, chemist

drunk • having the faculties impaired by alcohol *syn* drunken, intoxicated, inebriated, tipsy, tight *rel* fuddled, befuddled, confused; maudlin, soppy *ant* sober

drunkard • one who is habitually drunk *syn* inebriate, alcoholic, dipsomaniac, sot, soak, toper, tosspot, tippler *ant* teetotaler

drunken *syn* DRUNK, intoxicated, inebriated, tipsy, tight *rel, ant* see DRUNK

dry *adj* **1** • devoid of moisture *syn* arid *rel* barren, bare, bald; dehydrated, desiccated, dried, parched, baked; drained, depleted, exhausted, impoverished; sapped *ant* wet **2** *syn* SOUR, acid, acidulous, tart *ant* sweet (*wine*)

dry *vb* • to treat or to affect so as to deprive of moisture *syn* desiccate, dehydrate, bake, parch *rel* drain, deplete, exhaust; wither, shrivel, wizen *ant* moisten, wet

dubiety *syn* UNCERTAINTY, dubiosity, doubt, skepticism, suspicion, mistrust *rel* hesitation, hesitancy; wavering, vacillation, faltering *ant* decision

dubiosity *syn* UNCERTAINTY, dubiety, doubt, skepticism, suspicion, mistrust *rel* confusion, muddlement, addlement; wavering, vacillation, faltering, hesitation *ant* decidedness

dubious *syn* DOUBTFUL, questionable, problematic *rel* suspicious, skeptical, mistrustful, uncertain; hesitant, reluctant, disinclined *ant* cocksure; reliable; trustworthy

duck **1** *syn* DIP, immerse, submerge, souse, dunk **2** *syn* DODGE, parry, shirk, sidestep, fence, malinger *rel* avoid, elude, shun, evade, escape; avert, ward, prevent

duct *syn* CHANNEL, canal, conduit, aqueduct

ductile *syn* PLASTIC, pliable, pliant, malleable, adaptable *rel* tractable, amenable; responsive; yielding, submitting; fluid, liquid; flexible, elastic, resilient

dude *syn* FOP, dandy, beau, coxcomb, exquisite, buck

dudgeon *syn* OFFENSE, umbrage, huff, pique, resentment *rel* anger, indignation, wrath, rage, fury, ire; temper, humor, mood

due *adj* • being in accordance with what is just and appropriate *syn* rightful, condign *rel* appropriate, meet, suitable, fit, fitting, proper; right, good; just, fair, equitable

due *n* • what is justly owed to a person (sometimes a thing), esp. as a recompense or compensation *syn* desert, merit *rel* compensation, recompensing, recompense, repayment, satisfaction, payment; retribution, retaliation, reprisal, vengeance, revenge; reward, meed, guerdon

dulcet *syn* SWEET, engaging, winning, winsome *rel* soft, gentle, mild, balmy, lenient; serene, calm, tranquil; harmonious, consonant, accordant, concordant *ant* grating

dull **1** *syn* STUPID, slow, dumb, dense, crass *rel* lethargic, sluggish, comatose; phlegmatic, stolid, impassive, apathetic; backward; retarded *ant* clever, bright **2** • lacking sharpness of edge or point *syn* blunt, obtuse *ant* sharp; poignant (*sensation, feeling, reaction*) **3** • being so unvaried and uninteresting as to provoke boredom or tedium *syn* humdrum, dreary, monotonous, pedestrian, stodgy *rel* irksome, tiresome, wearisome, tedious, boring; prosy, prosaic, matter-of-fact *ant* lively

dumb **1** • lacking the power to speak *syn* mute, speechless, inarticulate **2** *syn* STUPID, dull, slow, dense, crass *rel ant* articulate

dumbfound *syn* PUZZLE, confound, nonplus, bewilder, distract, mystify, perplex *rel* astound, flabbergast, amaze, astonish, surprise; confuse, muddle, addle, fuddle; disconcert, rattle, faze, discomfit

dumps *syn* SADNESS, dejection, gloom, blues, depression, melancholy, melancholia *rel* despondency, forlornness, hopelessness, despair; doldrums, ennui, boredom, tedium

dumpy *syn* STOCKY, thickset, thick, chunky, stubby, squat

dunk *syn* DIP, immerse, souse, submerge, duck *rel* soak, saturate, sop

dupe • mean to delude by underhanded means or methods *syn* gull, befool, trick, hoax, hoodwink, bamboozle *rel* deceive, beguile, delude, mislead, double-cross, betray; cheat, cozen, defraud, overreach; outwit, baffle, circumvent

duplicate *syn* REPRODUCTION, facsimile, copy, carbon copy, transcript, replica *rel* counterpart, parallel, analogue

duplicity *syn* DECEIT, dissimulation, cunning, guile *rel* double-dealing, chicanery, chicane, trickery, deception, fraud; treacherousness, treachery, perfidiousness, perfidy, faithlessness

durable *syn* LASTING, perdurable, permanent, stable, perpetual *rel* enduring, abiding, persisting; strong, stout, tenacious

duress *syn* FORCE, constraint, coercion, compulsion, violence, restraint

dusky *syn* DARK, dim, obscure, murky, gloomy

duty **1** *syn* OBLIGATION *rel* responsibility, accountability, amenability, answerability, liability **2** *syn* FUNCTION, office, province *rel* concern, business, affair **3** *syn* TASK, assignment, job, stint, chore *rel* work, business, employment, occupation, calling; trade, craft, art, profession

dwarf • an individual and usu. a person of very small size *syn* pygmy, midget, manikin, homunculus, runt

dwell *syn* RESIDE, live, lodge, sojourn, stay, put up, stop

dwelling *syn* HABITATION, abode, residence, domicile, home, house

dwindle *syn* DECREASE, diminish, lessen, reduce, *rel* wane, ebb, abate, subside; attenuate, extenuate, thin; moderate; disappear

dynamic *syn* ACTIVE, live, operative *rel* potent, forceful, forcible, powerful; intense, vehement, fierce, exquisite, violent; vitalizing, energizing, activating

E

each *adj, syn* ALL, every

each *adv* • by, for, or to every one of the many *syn* apiece, severally, individually, respectively

eager • moved by a strong and urgent desire or interest *syn* avid, keen, anxious, agog, athirst *rel* desiring, coveting, craving; longing, yearning, hungering, thirsting; impatient, restless, restive *ant* listless

early • at or nearly at the beginning of a specified or implied period of time *syn* soon, beforehand, betimes *ant* late

earn *syn* DESERVE, merit, rate *rel* gain, win, get

earnest *adj, syn* SERIOUS, solemn, grave, somber, sober, sedate, staid *rel* zealous, enthusiastic, passionate; diligent, busy, industrious, assiduous, sedulous; sincere, wholehearted, whole-souled *ant* frivolous

earnest *n, syn* PLEDGE, token, pawn, hostage

earsplitting *syn* LOUD, stentorian, hoarse, raucous, strident, stertorous

earth • the entire area or extent of space in which human beings think of themselves as living and acting *syn* world, globe, planet *rel* universe, cosmos, macrocosm

earthly • of, belonging to, or characteristic of the earth or life on earth *syn* terrestrial, earthy, mundane, worldly, sublunary *rel* temporal, profane, secular; material, physical, corporeal

earthy *syn* EARTHLY, mundane, worldly, terrestrial, sublunary *rel* material, physical, corporeal; fleshly, carnal, sensual; gross, coarse

ease **1** *syn* REST, comfort, relaxation, repose, leisure *rel* inactivity, idleness, inertness, passiveness, supineness; tranquillity, serenity, placidity, calmness, peacefulness **2** *syn* READINESS, facility, dexterity *rel* effortlessness, smoothness, easiness; grace, elegance; expertness, adeptness, skillfulness, proficiency; deftness, adroitness *ant* effort

easy **1** *syn* COMFORTABLE, restful, cozy, snug *rel* soft, lenient, gentle; commodious, spacious; calm, tranquil, serene, placid; unconstrained, spontaneous *ant* disquieting, disquieted **2** • causing or involving little or no difficulty *syn* facile, simple, light, effortless, smooth *ant* hard

eat • to take food into the stomach through the mouth *syn* swallow, ingest, devour, consume *rel* bite, champ, gnaw

ebb *syn* ABATE, subside, wane *rel* dwindle, diminish, decrease, lessen; recede, retrograde, retreat *ant* flow

eccentric *syn* STRANGE, erratic, odd, queer, peculiar, singular, unique, quaint, outlandish, curious *rel* abnormal, atypical, aberrant; irregular, anomalous, unnatural; exceptional, exceptionable; fantastic, bizarre, grotesque

eccentricity • an act, a practice, or a characteristic that impresses the observer as strange or singular *syn* idiosyncrasy *rel* deviation, aberration, divergence; peculiarity, oddity, queerness, singularity; freak, conceit, vagary, crotchet, caprice, fancy, whim, whimsy

echelon *syn* LINE, row, rank, file, tier

éclat *syn* FAME, renown, glory, celebrity, notoriety, repute, reputation, honor *rel* prominence, conspicuousness, remarkableness, noticeableness; illustriousness, luster, eminence

eclipse *syn* OBSCURE, dim, bedim, darken, cloud, becloud, fog, befog, obfuscate *rel* hide, conceal, screen; cloak, mask, camouflage

economical *syn* SPARING, frugal, thrifty *rel* prudent, provident; close, cheeseparing, parsimonious, penurious, stingy *ant* extravagant

ecstasy • a feeling or a state of intense, sometimes excessive or extreme, mental and emotional exaltation *syn* rapture, transport *rel* bliss, beatitude, blessedness, felicity, happiness; joy, delectation, delight, pleasure; inspiration, fury, frenzy, afflatus

ecumenical *syn* UNIVERSAL, cosmic, catholic, cosmopolitan *ant* provincial; diocesan

eddy *n* • a swirling mass esp. of water *syn* whirlpool, maelstrom, vortex

eddy *vb, syn* TURN, rotate, gyrate, circle, spin, whirl, revolve, twirl, wheel, swirl, pirouette

edge **1** *syn* BORDER, verge, rim, brink, margin, brim *rel* limit, end, bound, confine; circumference, periphery, compass **2** *syn* ADVANTAGE, odds, handicap, allowance

edifice *syn* BUILDING, structure, pile

edit • to prepare material for publication *syn* compile, revise, redact, rewrite, adapt *rel* make, fabricate, fashion, form

edition • the total number of copies of the same work printed during a stretch of time *syn* impression, reprinting, printing, reissue

educate *syn* TEACH, train, discipline, school, instruct

educe • to bring or draw out what is hidden, latent, or reserved *syn* evoke, elicit, extract, extort *rel* draw, drag, pull; produce, bear, yield, turn out; summon, call

eerie *syn* WEIRD, uncanny *rel* fantastic, bizarre, grotesque; mysterious, inscrutable, arcane; fearful, awful, dreadful, horrific; strange, odd, queer, curious, peculiar

efface *syn* ERASE, obliterate, expunge, blot out, delete, cancel *rel* remove, move, shift; eradicate, extirpate, wipe out; eliminate, exclude, rule out

effect *n* **1** • a condition, situation, or occurrence, ascribable to a cause *syn* result, consequence, upshot, aftereffect, aftermath, sequel, issue, outcome, event *ant* cause **2** *pl* **effects** *syn* POSSESSIONS, belongings, means, resources, assets

effect *vb, syn* PERFORM, accomplish, achieve, execute, discharge, fulfill *rel* reach, attain, achieve, compass, gain; finish, complete, conclude, end, terminate, close; implement, enforce; realize, actualize

effective • producing or capable of producing a result *syn* effectual, efficient, efficacious *rel* forceful, forcible, potent, powerful; producing, productive, bearing; telling, cogent, convincing, compelling; operative, active, dynamic *ant* ineffective; futile

effectual *syn* EFFECTIVE, efficacious, efficient *rel* effecting, accomplishing, achieving, fulfilling; operative, dynamic, active; decisive, determinative, conclusive *ant* ineffectual; fruitless

effervescent *syn* ELASTIC, volatile, buoyant, expansive, resilient *rel* lively, vivacious, sprightly, gay, animated; hilarious, jolly, gleeful, mirthful *ant* subdued

efficacious *syn* EFFECTIVE, effectual, efficient *rel* potent, powerful, puissant; cogent, telling, sound, convincing, compelling *ant* inefficacious; powerless

efficient *syn* EFFECTIVE, effectual, efficacious *rel* competent, qualified, able, capable; expert, skillful, skilled, proficient, adept, masterly *ant* inefficient

effort • the active use or expenditure of physical or mental power to produce a desired result *syn* exertion, pains, trouble *rel* work, labor, toil, travail; energy, force, power, might, puissance; endeavor, essay *ant* ease

effortless *syn* EASY, smooth, facile, simple, light *rel* proficient, skilled, skillful, expert, adept, masterly *ant* painstaking

effrontery *syn* TEMERITY, audacity, hardihood, nerve, cheek, gall *rel* impudence, brazenness, brashness; impertinence, intrusiveness, officiousness

effulgent *syn* BRIGHT, radiant, luminous, brilliant, lustrous, refulgent, beaming, lambent, lucent, incandescent *rel* flaming, blazing, glowing, flaring; flashing, gleaming; resplendent, splendid, glorious

egg *syn* URGE, exhort, goad, spur, prod, prick, sic *rel* stimulate, excite, provoke, pique; incite, instigate; rally, arouse, rouse, stir

egoism *syn* CONCEIT, egotism, amour propre, self-love, self-esteem *rel* self-confidence, self-assurance, self-possession; self-satisfaction, self-complacency, complacency, smugness, priggishness *ant* altruism

egotism *syn* CONCEIT, egoism, self-love, amour propre, self-esteem *rel* vanity, vainglory, pride; boasting, boastfulness, vaunting, vauntfulness, gasconading; pluming, piquing, priding, preening *ant* modesty

eject • to force or thrust something or someone out *syn* expel, oust, evict, dismiss *rel* exclude, eliminate, shut out, rule out, debar, disbar; dismiss, discharge, cashier, fire, sack; discard, cast, shed; reject, repudiate, spurn *ant* admit

elaborate *syn* UNFOLD, evolve, develop, perfect *rel* expand, amplify, dilate; enlarge, augment, increase; heighten, enhance

élan *syn* VIGOR, vim, spirit, dash, esprit, verve, punch, drive

elapse *syn* PASS, pass away, expire *rel* slip, slide, glide; end, terminate

elastic **1** • able to endure strain without being permanently affected or injured *syn* resilient, springy, flexible, supple *rel* pliable, pliant, ductile; plastic, malleable; limber, lithe, supple *ant* rigid **2** • able to recover quickly from depression and maintain high spirits *syn* expansive, resilient, buoyant, volatile, effervescent *rel* spirited, high-spirited, mettlesome; lively, vivacious, sprightly, animated, gay *ant* depressed

elbowroom *syn* ROOM, berth, play, leeway, margin, clearance

elderly *syn* AGED, old, superannuated *ant* youthful

elect *adj*, *syn* SELECT, picked, exclusive *rel* choice, exquisite, rare; selected, preferred, chosen, singled out; redeemed, saved, delivered *ant* reprobate (*in theology*)

elect *vb* **1** *syn* CHOOSE, select, pick, prefer, single, opt, cull *rel* decide, determine, settle, resolve; conclude, judge; receive, accept, admit, take *ant* abjure **2** *syn* DESIGNATE, name, nominate, appoint

election *syn* CHOICE, selection, option, preference, alternative *rel* deciding, decision, determining, determination, settling, settlement

electrify *syn* THRILL, enthuse *rel* galvanize, excite, stimulate, quicken, provoke; stir, rouse, arouse, rally

eleemosynary *syn* CHARITABLE, benevolent, humane, humanitarian, philanthropic, altruistic

elegance • impressive beauty of form, appearance, or behavior *syn* grace, dignity *rel* beautifulness, beauty, handsomeness, comeliness; fastidiousness, niceness, nicety, daintiness; perfection, excellence; taste

elegant *syn* CHOICE, exquisite, recherché, rare, dainty, delicate *rel* majestic, stately, noble, august, grand; beautiful, handsome; fastidious, nice; consummate, finished; sumptuous, luxurious, opulent

element • one of the parts of a compound or complex whole *syn* component, constituent, ingredient, factor *rel* principle, fundamental; part, portion, member; item, detail, particular *ant* compound (*in science*); composite

elemental **1** • of, relating to, or being an ultimate or irreducible element *syn* basic, elementatry, essential, fundamental, primitive, underlying **2** *syn* ELEMENTARY, basal, beginning, rudimentary

elementary **1** • of, relating to, or dealing with the simplest principles *syn* basal, beginning, elemental, rudimentary **2** *syn* ELEMENTAL, basic, essential, fundamental, primitive, underlying

elephantine *syn* HUGE, vast, immense, enormous, mammoth, giant, gigantic, gigantean, colossal, gargantuan, Herculean, cyclopean, titanic, Brobdingnagian

elevate *syn* LIFT, raise, rear, hoist, heave, boost *rel* exalt, aggrandize, magnify; heighten, enhance; rise, mount, ascend, tower, soar, rocket *ant* lower

elevation **1** *syn* HEIGHT, altitude *rel* ascension, ascent **2** *syn* ADVANCEMENT, promotion, preferment *rel* exaltation, aggrandizement *ant* degradation

elicit *syn* EDUCE, evoke, extract, extort *rel* draw, drag, pull; bring, fetch

eliminate *syn* EXCLUDE, rule out, debar, blackball, disbar, suspend, shut out *rel* eject, oust, dismiss, expel, evict; eradicate, extirpate, exterminate, uproot, wipe; expunge, erase, delete, efface

elite *syn* ARISTOCRACY, society, nobility, gentry, county *ant* rabble

ell *syn* ANNEX, wing, extension

elongate *syn* EXTEND, lengthen, prolong, protract *ant* abbreviate, shorten

eloquent **1** *syn* VOCAL, articulate, voluble, fluent, glib *rel* impassioned, passionate, fervid, perfervid, ardent, fervent; expressing, voicing, venting, uttering; forceful, forcible, potent, powerful **2** *syn* EXPRESSIVE, significant, meaningful, pregnant, sententious *rel* revealing, disclosing, telling, betraying; impressive, moving, poignant, touching, affecting

elucidate *syn* EXPLAIN, interpret, construe, expound, explicate *rel* illustrate, exemplify; demonstrate, prove

elude *syn* ESCAPE, evade, avoid, shun, eschew *rel* thwart, foil, outwit, circumvent, baffle; flee, fly, escape

emanate *syn* SPRING, issue, proceed, rise, arise, originate, derive, flow, stem *rel* emerge, loom, appear; begin, commence, start, initiate

emancipate *syn* FREE, manumit, liberate, release, discharge *rel* deliver, enfranchise

emasculate **1** *syn* STERILIZE, castrate, spay, alter, mutilate, geld **2** *syn* UNNERVE, enervate, unman *rel* weaken, enfeeble, debilitate, sap, undermine

embarrass • to distress by confusing or confounding *syn* discomfit, abash, disconcert, rattle, faze *rel* discompose, disturb, perturb, fluster, flurry; bewilder, nonplus, perplex; trouble, distress; vex, annoy, bother, irk; impede, obstruct, block, hinder; hamper, fetter, shackle, hog-tie *ant* relieve; facilitate

embellish *syn* ADORN, beautify, deck, bedeck, garnish, decorate, ornament *rel* enhance, heighten, intensify; apparel, array

embers *syn* ASH, cinders, clinkers

emblem *syn* SYMBOL, attribute, type *rel* device, motif, design, figure, pattern; sign, mark, token, badge

embody **1** *syn* REALIZE, incarnate, materialize, externalize, objectify, actualize, hypostatize, reify *rel* invest, clothe; illustrate, exemplify; manifest, demonstrate, evidence, evince, show *ant* disembody **2** *syn* IDENTIFY, incorporate, assimilate *rel* add, annex, superadd, append; introduce, insert, interpolate, interject; comprehend, include, embrace, involve, imply

embolden *syn* ENCOURAGE, inspirit, hearten, cheer, nerve, steel *rel* strengthen, fortify; venture, chance, hazard *ant* abash

embrace **1** *syn* ADOPT, espouse *rel* accept, receive; seize, grasp, take *ant* spurn **2** *syn* INCLUDE, comprehend, involve, imply, subsume *rel* contain, hold, accommodate; embody, incorporate

emend *syn* CORRECT, rectify, revise, amend, remedy, redress, reform *rel* mend, repair; improve, better, ameliorate *ant* corrupt (*a text, passage*)

emerge *syn* APPEAR, loom *rel* issue, emanate, spring, flow, arise, rise, proceed, stem, derive, originate

emergency *syn* JUNCTURE, exigency, contingency, crisis, pass, pinch, strait *rel* situation, condition, posture, state; difficulty, vicissitude

emigrant • a person who leaves one country in order to settle in another *syn* immigrant, migrant *rel* foreigner, alien, emigré, exile, expatriate, fugitive, refugee

emigrate *syn* MIGRATE immigrate

émigré *syn* STRANGER, immigrant, alien, foreigner, outlander, outsider

eminent *syn* FAMOUS, illustrious, renowned, celebrated, famed *rel* signal, outstanding, prominent, remarkable, conspicuous, noticeable

emolument *syn* WAGE, stipend, salary, fee, pay, hire *rel* compensation, remuneration, recompensing, recompense; reward, meed, guerdon

emotion *syn* FEELING, affection, passion, sentiment

empathy *syn* SYMPATHY, pity, compassion, commiseration, ruth, condolence *rel* imagination, fancy, fantasy; appreciation, understanding, comprehension

emphasis • exerted force or special stress

that gives impressiveness or importance to something *syn* stress, accent, accentuation

employ *syn* USE, utilize, apply, avail *rel* practice, exercise, drill; engross, absorb, monopolize; choose, select, pick

employment *syn* WORK, occupation, business, calling, pursuit *rel* trade, craft, handicraft, art, profession

empower *syn* ENABLE *rel* authorize, commission, accredit, license; train, instruct, discipline, teach; endow, endue

empty 1 • lacking the contents that could or should be present *syn* vacant, blank, void, vacuous *rel* devoid, destitute, void; bare, barren; exhausted, drained, depleted *ant* full **2** *syn* VAIN, idle, hollow, nugatory, otiose *rel* inane, insipid, vapid, flat, jejune, banal; trifling, trivial, paltry, petty; fruitless, futile, bootless

empyrean, empyreal *syn* CELESTIAL, heavenly

emulate *syn* RIVAL, compete, vie *rel* imitate, copy, ape; match, equal, approach, touch

emulous *syn* AMBITIOUS *rel* aspiring, aiming, panting; eager, avid, keen, anxious, athirst, agog

enable • to render able often by giving power, strength, or means to *syn* empower *rel* permit, allow, let

enamored • possessed by a strong or unreasoning love or admiration *syn* infatuated *rel* bewitched, captivated, fascinated; fond, devoted, doting, loving

enchant *syn* ATTRACT, charm, captivate, allure, fascinate, bewitch *rel* delight, rejoice, gladden, gratify, please *ant* disenchant

enchanting *syn* ATTRACTIVE, charming, captivating, alluring, fascinating, bewitching, *rel* delightful, delectable; pleasant, pleasing, grateful, gratifying

encircle *syn* SURROUND, environ, circle, encompass, compass, hem, gird, girdle, ring *rel* enclose, envelop; circumscribe, confine, limit

enclose • to shut in or confine by or as if by barriers *syn* envelop, fence, pen, coop, corral, cage, wall *rel* confine, circumscribe, limit, restrict; environ, surround, encircle, circle, encompass, compass, hem

encomium • a more or less formal and public expression of praise *syn* eulogy, panegyric, tribute, citation *rel* lauding, laudation, extolling, extollation, praising, praise; plaudits, applause, acclaim, acclamation; commending, commendation, complimenting, compliment

encompass *syn* SURROUND, environ, encircle, circle, compass, hem, gird, girdle, ring *rel* envelop, enclose, wall; circumscribe, confine

encounter *vb, syn* MEET, face, confront *rel* collide, conflict, clash, bump; brave, beard, defy, challenge

encounter *n* • a sudden, hostile, and usu. brief confrontation or dispute between factions or persons *syn* skirmish, brush *rel* battle, engagement; contest, combat, conflict, fight, fray; clash, collision, impact, impingement

encourage 1 • to fill with courage or strength of purpose esp. in preparation for a hard task *syn* inspirit, hearten, embolden, cheer, nerve, steel *rel* stimulate, excite, provoke, quicken, pique, galvanize; strengthen, fortify, energize, invigorate; rally, stir *ant* discourage **2** *syn* FAVOR, countenance *rel* sanction, endorse, approve; incite, instigate, abet; induce, prevail *ant* discourage

encroach *syn* TRESPASS, entrench, infringe, invade *rel* enter, penetrate, pierce, probe; intrude, butt in, obtrude, interlope; interfere, intervene, interpose

encumber *syn* BURDEN, cumber, weigh, weight, load, lade, tax, charge, saddle *rel* discommode, incommode, inconvenience; clog, fetter, hamper; impede, obstruct, block, hinder

end *n* **1** *syn* LIMIT, bound, term, confine *rel* extreme, extremity **2** • the point at which something ceases *syn* termination, ending, terminus *rel* closing, close, concluding, conclusion, finishing, finish, completion; culmination, climax; term, bound, limit *ant* beginning **3** *syn* INTENTION, objective, goal, aim, object, intent, purpose, design *rel* destiny, fate, lot, doom, portion; function, office, duty

end *vb, syn* CLOSE, conclude, terminate, finish, complete *ant* begin

endanger *syn* VENTURE, hazard, risk, chance, jeopardize, imperil *rel* encounter, confront, meet, face; dare, brave; incur, contract, catch

endeavor *vb, syn* ATTEMPT, try, essay,

strive, struggle *rel* apply, devote, direct, address; determine, resolve, decide

endeavor *n, syn* ATTEMPT, essay, striving, struggle, try *rel* toil, labor, travail, work; effort, exertion, pains, trouble

endemic *syn* NATIVE, indigenous, autochthonous, aboriginal *ant* exotic; pandemic

ending *syn* END, terminus, termination

endless *syn* EVERLASTING, interminable, unceasing *rel* lasting, perdurable, perpetual, permanent; eternal, illimitable, boundless, infinite; immortal, deathless, undying

endorse *syn* APPROVE, sanction, accredit, certify *rel* vouch, attest, witness; commend, recommend; support, uphold, champion, back, advocate

endow *syn* DOWER, endue *rel* bestow, confer, give; grant, award, accord; empower, enable; furnish, equip

endue *syn* DOWER, endow *rel* clothe, invest, vest; furnish, equip, outfit, accouter; bestow, confer, give

endure **1** *syn* CONTINUE, last, abide, persist *rel* survive, outlast, outlive; stay, remain, wait, linger, tarry *ant* perish **2** *syn* BEAR, abide, tolerate, suffer, stand, brook *rel* accept, receive, take; submit, yield

enemy • an individual or a group that is hostile toward another *syn* foe *rel* opponent, adversary, antagonist; rival, competitor

energetic *syn* VIGOROUS, strenuous, lusty, nervous *rel* forceful, forcible, powerful, potent; active, dynamic, live; busy, industrious, diligent; strong, stout, sturdy, stalwart, tough, tenacious *ant* lethargic

energize **1** *syn* VITALIZE, activate *rel* stimulate, quicken, galvanize, excite, provoke; stir, arouse, rouse, rally **2** *syn* STRENGTHEN, invigorate, fortify, reinforce *rel* empower, enable; stir, rally, rouse, arouse

energy *syn* POWER, force, strength, might, puissance *rel* dynamism, activity, operativeness, operation; momentum, impetus, speed, velocity, headway *ant* inertia

enervate *syn* UNNERVE, emasculate, unman *rel* weaken, enfeeble, debilitate, undermine, sap, disable; abase, demean, debase, degrade; exhaust, jade, fatigue, tire, weary *ant* harden, inure

enervated *syn* LANGUID, languishing, languorous, lackadaisical, spiritless, listless *rel* decadent, degenerated, deteriorated; enfeebled, debilitated, weakened

enfeeble *syn* WEAKEN, debilitate, sap, undermine, cripple, disable *rel* impair, mar, harm, injure; enervate, emasculate, unnerve, unman *ant* fortify

enforce • to put something into effect or operation *syn* implement *rel* execute, fulfill, discharge, perform; compel, constrain, oblige, force *ant* relax (*discipline, rules, demands*)

engage *syn* PROMISE, pledge, plight, covenant, contract *rel* bind, tie; agree, accede, acquiesce, assent, consent, subscribe

engagement **1** • a promise to be in an agreed place at a specified time, usu. for a particular purpose *syn* appointment, rendezvous, tryst, assignation, date **2** *syn* BATTLE, action *rel* encounter, skirmish, brush; contest, conflict, combat, fight

engaging *syn* SWEET, winning, winsome, dulcet *rel* alluring, attractive, enchanting, charming, captivating; interesting, intriguing *ant* loathsome

engender *syn* GENERATE, breed, beget, get, sire, procreate, propagate, reproduce *rel* produce, bear, yield; provoke, excite, stimulate, quicken; rouse, arouse, stir

engine *syn* MACHINE, mechanism, machinery, apparatus, motor

engineer *syn* GUIDE, pilot, lead, steer *rel* manage, direct, conduct, control

engrave *syn* CARVE, incise, etch, sculpture, sculpt, sculp, chisel *rel* delineate, depict, limn, portray; imprint, impress, print

engross *syn* MONOPOLIZE, absorb, consume *rel* utilize, employ, use, apply; control, manage

engrossed *syn* INTENT, absorbed, rapt *rel* monopolized, consumed; fixed, set, settled; busy, industrious, diligent, sedulous, assiduous

engrossing *syn* INTERESTING, absorbing, intriguing *rel* monopolizing, consuming; controlling, managing, directing; transporting, ravishing, enrapturing, entrancing *ant* irksome

enhance *syn* INTENSIFY, heighten, aggravate *rel* lift, elevate, raise; exalt, magnify, aggrandize; augment, increase; adorn, embellish, beautify

enigma *syn* MYSTERY, riddle, puzzle, conundrum, problem

enigmatic *syn* OBSCURE, cryptic, dark,

vague, ambiguous, equivocal *rel* puzzling, perplexing, mystifying, bewildering; abstruse, occult, esoteric, recondite; dubious, problematic, doubtful *ant* explicit

enjoin **1** *syn* COMMAND, direct, order, bid, instruct, charge *rel* advise, counsel; admonish, reprove; warn, forewarn, caution **2** *syn* FORBID, interdict, prohibit, inhibit, ban *rel* debar, shut out, rule out; bar, hinder, impede

enjoy **1** *syn* LIKE, love, relish, fancy, dote *rel* delight, rejoice, gratify, gladden, regale, tickle, please *ant* loathe, abhor, abominate **2** *syn* HAVE, possess, own, hold

enjoyment *syn* PLEASURE, delight, joy, delectation, fruition *rel* delighting, rejoicing, gratifying, regaling, gladdening, pleasing; happiness, felicity, bliss, beatitude; zest, relish, gusto, taste *ant* abhorrence

enlarge *syn* INCREASE, augment, multiply *rel* extend, lengthen, elongate, prolong, protract; amplify, expand, distend, dilate, inflate; magnify, aggrandize

enlighten *syn* ILLUMINATE, illustrate, illume, light, lighten *rel* educate, instruct, train, teach, school; inform, apprise, acquaint, advise *ant* confuse, muddle

enliven *syn* QUICKEN, animate, vivify *rel* refresh, renew, restore, rejuvenate; stimulate, excite, galvanize, provoke; entertain, recreate, divert, amuse; inspire, fire, inform *ant* deaden; subdue

enmesh *syn* ENTANGLE, involve *rel* ensnare, entrap, snare, trap, capture, catch; hamper, clog, hog-tie, fetter

enmity • deep-seated dislike or ill will or a manifestation of such a feeling *syn* hostility, antipathy, antagonism, animosity, rancor, animus *rel* hate, hatred, detestation, abhorrence, loathing; aversion, antipathy; malignity, malignancy, ill will, malevolence, malice *ant* amity

ennoble *syn* DIGNIFY, honor, glorify *rel* exalt, magnify; elevate, raise, lift; heighten, enhance, intensify

ennui *syn* TEDIUM, doldrums, boredom *rel* depression, dejection, dumps, blues, melancholy, sadness; listlessness, languidness, languorousness, languor, spiritlessness; satiation, satiety, surfeiting, surfeit, cloying

enormous *syn* HUGE, vast, immense, elephantine, mammoth, giant, gigantic, gigantean, colossal, gargantuan, Herculean, cyclopean, titanic, Brobdingnagian *rel* prodigious, stupendous, tremendous, monstrous, monumental; inordinate, exorbitant, excessive, extravagant

enough *syn* SUFFICIENT, adequate, competent

enrage *syn* ANGER, infuriate, madden, incense *rel* exasperate, provoke, aggravate, rile, irritate *ant* placate

enrapture *syn* TRANSPORT, ravish, entrance *rel* rejoice, delight, gladden, please, gratify; charm, enchant, captivate, fascinate, attract

enroll *syn* RECORD, register, list, catalog *rel* enter; insert

ensconce *syn* HIDE, screen, secrete, conceal, cache, bury *rel* shield, guard, safeguard, protect, defend; shelter, lodge, harbor

ensign *syn* FLAG, standard, banner, color, streamer, pennant, pendant, pennon, jack

ensnare *syn* CATCH, snare, entrap, trap, bag, capture *rel* lure, entice, inveigle, decoy

ensue *syn* FOLLOW, succeed, supervene *rel* issue, emanate, proceed, stem, spring, derive, originate, rise, arise; pursue, chase

ensure • to make a person or thing certain or sure *syn* insure, assure, secure

entangle • to catch or hold as if in a net from which it is difficult to escape *syn* involve, enmesh *rel* hamper, trammel, fetter, clog, hog-tie; embarrass, discomfit; ensnare, snare, entrap, trap, capture, catch *ant* disentangle

entente *syn* CONTRACT, treaty, pact, compact, concordat, convention, cartel, bargain

enter **1** • to make way into something so as to reach or pass through the interior *syn* penetrate, pierce, probe *rel* invade, entrench, trespass, encroach; intrude, butt in; begin, commence, start *ant* issue from **2** • to cause or permit to go in or get in *syn* introduce, admit *rel* insert, interpolate, intercalate, insinuate, introduce

enterprise *syn* ADVENTURE, quest *rel* exploit, feat, achievement; struggle, striving, endeavor, essay, attempt

entertain **1** *syn* HARBOR, shelter, lodge, house, board *rel* receive, admit; cultivate, cherish, foster, nurse; feed, nourish **2** *syn*

AMUSE, divert, recreate *rel* please, delight, gratify, rejoice, gladden, regale; beguile, while, wile

entertainment *syn* AMUSEMENT, diversion, recreation *rel* dinner, banquet, feast; play, sport, disport

enthuse *syn* THRILL, electrify

enthusiasm *syn* PASSION, fervor, ardor, zeal *ant* apathy

enthusiast • a person who manifests excessive ardor, fervor, or devotion in an attachment to some cause, idea, party, or church *syn* fanatic, zealot, bigot *rel* devotee, votary, addict

entice *syn* LURE, inveigle, decoy, tempt, seduce *rel* snare, ensnare, trap, entrap, catch; cajole, blandish, coax, wheedle *ant* scare

entire **1** *syn* WHOLE, total, all, gross *rel* complete, full, plenary *ant* partial **2** *syn* PERFECT, whole, intact *rel* integrated, concatenated; unified, consolidated, compacted *ant* impaired

entity • one that has real and independent existence *syn* being, creature, individual, person

entrance *n* • the act or fact of going in or coming in *syn* entry, entrée, ingress, access *ant* exit

entrance *vb, syn* TRANSPORT, ravish, enrapture *rel* delight, gladden, rejoice, please; enchant, captivate, bewitch, charm, attract

entrap *syn* CATCH, trap, snare, ensnare, bag, capture *rel* seize, take, clutch; lure, inveigle, decoy, entice

entreat *syn* BEG, beseech, implore, supplicate, importune, adjure *rel* ask, request, solicit; pray, appeal, plead, petition, sue

entrée *syn* ENTRANCE, entry, ingress, access *rel* admission, admittance

entrench *syn* TRESPASS, encroach, infringe, invade *rel* monopolize, engross, consume, absorb; interpose, interfere, intervene

entrust *syn* COMMIT, confide, consign, relegate *rel* allot, assign, allocate; rely, trust, depend, count, bank, reckon

entry *syn* ENTRANCE, entrée, ingress, access *rel* door, doorway, gate, gateway, portal, postern

entwine *syn* WIND, coil, curl, twist, twine, wreathe *rel* curve, bend; interweave, weave; entangle, enmesh

enumerate *syn* COUNT, tell, number *rel* compute, calculate, reckon; add, sum, total, figure; rehearse, recount, recite, relate

enunciate *syn* ARTICULATE, pronounce

envelop **1** *syn* COVER, overspread, wrap, shroud, veil *rel* surround, environ, encompass; cloak, mask, disguise **2** *syn* ENCLOSE, fence, pen, coop, corral, cage, wall *rel* confine, circumscribe; protect, shield, guard

envious • maliciously grudging another's advantages *syn* jealous *rel* covetous, grasping, greedy; grudging, coveting, envying; malign, malignant, spiteful, malicious, malevolent

environ *syn* SURROUND, encircle, circle, encompass, compass, hem, gird, girdle, ring *rel* enclose, envelop, fence; circumscribe, confine

environment *syn* BACKGROUND, setting, milieu, backdrop, mise-en-scène

envisage, envision *syn* THINK, conceive, imagine, realize, fancy *rel* view, behold, survey, contemplate, see; objectify, externalize, materialize, realize

envoy *syn* AMBASSADOR, legate, minister, nuncio, internuncio, chargé d'affaires

envy *syn* COVET, grudge, begrudge *rel* long, pine, hanker, yearn

ephemeral *syn* TRANSIENT, transitory, passing, fugitive, fleeting, evanescent, momentary, short-lived *rel* brief, short

epicene *syn* BISEXUAL, hermaphroditic, hermaphrodite, androgynous

epicure • one who takes great pleasure in eating and drinking *syn* gourmet, gourmand, glutton, bon vivant, gastronome *rel* connoisseur, aesthete, dilettante

epicurean *syn* SENSUOUS, sybaritic, luxurious, sensual, voluptuous *rel* fastidious, dainty, nice, particular *ant* gross

epigram *syn* SAYING, aphorism, apothegm, saw, maxim, adage, proverb, motto

episode **1** *syn* DIGRESSION, divagation, excursus *rel* deviation, divergence, deflection; departing, departure **2** *syn* OCCURRENCE, incident, event, circumstance

epistle *syn* LETTER, missive, note, message, dispatch, report, memorandum

epitome *syn* ABRIDGMENT, conspectus, synopsis, abstract, brief *rel* précis, aperçu, sketch, digest, compendium

epoch *syn* PERIOD, era, age, aeon

equable *syn* STEADY, even, constant, uniform *rel* regular, orderly, methodical, systematic; invariable, immutable, unchangeable; same, equal, equivalent *ant* variable, changeable

equal *adj, syn* SAME, equivalent, very, identical, identic, tantamount *rel* equable, even, uniform; like, alike; proportionate, commensurate, proportional *ant* unequal

equal *vb, syn* MATCH, rival, approach, touch *rel* compare; square, accord, tally, correspond, agree

equanimity • the characteristic quality of one who is self-possessed or not easily disturbed or perturbed *syn* composure, sangfroid, phlegm *rel* poise, equipose, balance, equilibrium; self-possession, self-assurance, aplomb, confidence; tranquillity, serenity, placidity, calmness

equilibrium *syn* BALANCE, equipoise, poise, tension *rel* stableness, stability; stabilization, steadying; counterbalancing, counterbalance, counterpoising, counterpoise

equip *syn* FURNISH, outfit, appoint, accouter, arm

equipment • items needed for the performance of a task or useful in effecting a given end *syn* apparatus, machinery, paraphernalia, outfit, tackle, gear, matériel

equipoise *syn* BALANCE, equilibrium, poise, tension

equitable *syn* FAIR, just, impartial, unbiased, dispassionate, uncolored, objective *rel* proportional, proportionate, commensurate, commensurable; equal, equivalent, same, identical *ant* inequitable, unfair

equity *syn* JUSTICE

equivalent *syn* SAME, equal, identical, identic, selfsame, very, tantamount *rel* like, alike, comparable, parallel, uniform, similar; proportionate, commensurate, proportional; reciprocal, corresponding, convertible *ant* different

equivocal *syn* OBSCURE, ambiguous, dark, vague, enigmatic, cryptic *rel* dubious, questionable, doubtful *ant* unequivocal

equivocate *syn* LIE, prevaricate, palter, fib *rel* deceive, mislead, delude; evade, elude, escape

equivocation *syn* AMBIGUITY, tergiversation, double entendre *rel* prevarication, lying, lie, paltering, fibbing, fib; duplicity, dissimulation, deceit

era *syn* PERIOD, age, epoch, aeon

eradicate *syn* EXTERMINATE, uproot, deracinate, extirpate, wipe *rel* abolish, annihilate, extinguish, abate; destroy, demolish, raze; obliterate, efface, erase, blot out

erase • to strike, rub, or scrape out something so that it no longer has effect or existence *syn* expunge, cancel, efface, obliterate, blot out, delete *rel* annul, nullify, negate; abolish, extinguish

erect *syn* BUILD, construct, frame, raise, rear *rel* fabricate, fashion, form, make; lift, raise, elevate *ant* raze

eremite *syn* RECLUSE, hermit, anchorite, cenobite

erotic • of, devoted to, affected by, or tending to arouse sexual love or desire *syn* amatory, amorous, amative, aphrodisiac *rel* passionate, impassioned, fervid, perfervid, ardent, fervent; carnal, fleshly, sensual

erratic *syn* STRANGE, eccentric, odd, queer, singular, peculiar, unique, quaint, outlandish, curious *rel* aberrant, abnormal, atypical; irregular, unnatural, anomalous; capricious, fickle, mercurial, inconstant

error • something (as an act, statement, or belief) that departs from what is or is generally held to be acceptable *syn* mistake, blunder, slip, lapse, faux pas, bull, howler, boner

errorless *syn* IMPECCABLE, flawless, faultless *rel* correct, accurate, exact, precise, right, nice

ersatz *syn* ARTIFICIAL, synthetic, factitious

erudite *syn* LEARNED, scholarly

erudition *syn* KNOWLEDGE, learning, scholarship, science, information, lore

escape **1** • to run away esp. from something that limits one's freedom or threatens one's well-being *syn* flee, fly, decamp, abscond **2** • to get away or keep away from what one does not wish to incur, endure, or encounter *syn* avoid, evade, elude, shun, eschew

eschew **1** *syn* ESCAPE, shun, elude, avoid, evade *ant* choose **2** *syn* FORGO, forbear, abnegate, sacrifice *rel* abstain, refrain

escort *syn* ACCOMPANY, conduct, convoy, chaperon, attend *rel* protect, shield, guard, safeguard, defend; lead, guide, pilot, steer

esoteric *syn* RECONDITE, occult, abstruse

rel mystic, mystical, anagogic, cabalistic; arcane, mysterious

especial *syn* SPECIAL, specific, particular, individual *rel* preeminent, surpassing, supreme; paramount, dominant, predominant, preponderant, sovereign; exceptional

espousal *syn* MARRIAGE, matrimony, nuptial, wedding, wedlock

espouse *syn* ADOPT, embrace *rel* support, uphold, advocate, champion, back

esprit *syn* VIGOR, vim, spirit, dash, verve, punch, élan, drive *rel* wit, brain, intelligence, mind; courage, mettle, tenacity; ardor, fervor, passion, enthusiasm

esprit de corps *syn* MORALE, discipline

espy *syn* SEE, descry, behold, perceive, discern, notice, remark, note, observe, survey, view, contemplate

essay *vb, syn* ATTEMPT, endeavor, strive, struggle, try *rel* work, labor, toil, travail

essay *n* **1** *syn* ATTEMPT, endeavor, striving, struggle, try *rel* effort, exertion, trouble, pains; toil, labor, work, travail **2** • a relatively brief discourse written for others' reading or consideration *syn* article, paper, theme, composition

essential **1** *syn* INHERENT, intrinsic, constitutional, ingrained *rel* innate, inborn, inbred, congenital; inner, inward; elemental, elementary; characteristic, individual, peculiar, distinctive *ant* accidental **2** • so important as to be indispensable *syn* fundamental, vital, cardinal *rel* basic, basal, underlying; principal, foremost, capital, chief, main, leading; prime, primary, primal **3** *syn* NEEDFUL, indispensable, requisite, necessary *rel* required, needed, wanted *ant* nonessential **4** *syn* ELEMENTAL, basic, elementary, fundamental, primitive, underlying

establish **1** *syn* SET, settle, fix *rel* implant, inculcate, instill; secure, rivet, anchor, moor *ant* uproot; abrogate **2** *syn* FOUND, institute, organize, create *rel* start, inaugurate, begin, commence, initiate *ant* abolish

esteem *n, syn* REGARD, respect, admiration *rel* honor, homage, reverence, deference, obeisance; veneration, reverence, worship, adoration *ant* abomination; contempt

esteem *vb, syn* REGARD, respect, admire *rel* prize, value, appreciate, treasure, cherish; revere, reverence, venerate *ant* abominate

estimate *vb* **1** • to judge a thing with respect to its worth *syn* appraise, evaluate, value, rate, assess, assay *rel* judge, adjudge, adjudicate; determine, discover, ascertain; settle, decide **2** *syn* CALCULATE, reckon, compute *rel* figure, cast, sum, add; count, enumerate; conjecture, surmise, guess

estimate *n, syn* ESTIMATION *rel* valuation, evaluation, appraisal, assessment; cost, expense, price

estimation • the act of valuing or appraising *syn* estimate *rel* esteem, regard, respect; opinion, view; conjecture, guess, surmise

estrange • to cause one to break a bond or tie of affection or loyalty *syn* alienate, disaffect, wean *rel* separate, part, divide, sunder, sever, divorce *ant* reconcile

etch *syn* CARVE, incise, engrave, chisel, sculpture, sculpt, sculp

eternal *syn* INFINITE, sempiternal, boundless, illimitable, uncircumscribed *rel* everlasting, endless, unceasing, interminable; lasting, perdurable, perpetual, permanent; immortal, deathless, undying *ant* mortal

ethereal *syn* AIRY, aerial *rel* celestial, heavenly, empyrean, empyreal; tenuous, rare, thin *ant* substantial

ethical *syn* MORAL, righteous, virtuous, noble *ant* unethical

etiolate *syn* WHITEN, decolorize, blanch, bleach

etiquette *syn* DECORUM, propriety, decency, dignity *rel* deportment, demeanor, mien, bearing

eulogize *syn* PRAISE, extol, acclaim, laud *rel* exalt, magnify, aggrandize; commend, applaud, compliment *ant* calumniate, vilify

eulogy *syn* ENCOMIUM, panegyric, tribute, citation *rel* compliment, flattery, adulation; lauding, laudation, extolling, extollation, praising, praise *ant* calumny; tirade

euphuistic *syn* RHETORICAL, flowery, aureate, grandiloquent, magniloquent, bombastic

evade *syn* ESCAPE, elude, avoid, shun, eschew *rel* flee, fly; thwart, foil, circumvent, outwit

evaluate *syn* ESTIMATE, appraise, value, rate, assess, assay *rel* judge, adjudge; criticize

evanesce *syn* VANISH, evaporate, disappear, fade *rel* escape, flee, fly; scatter, dissipate, dispel, disperse; squander, dissipate, consume, waste

evanescent *syn* TRANSIENT, ephemeral, passing, fugitive, fleeting, transitory, momentary, short-lived

evaporate *syn* VANISH, evanesce, disappear, fade *rel* escape, decamp, flee, fly; dissipate, dispel

even **1** *syn* LEVEL, smooth, flat, plane, plain, flush *ant* uneven **2** *syn* STEADY, uniform, equable, constant *rel* same, equal, identical; continuous, constant, incessant, continual

event **1** *syn* OCCURRENCE, incident, episode, circumstance *rel* action, act, deed; exploit, feat, achievement; chance, accident, fortune; happening, befalling, transpiring **2** *syn* EFFECT, result, consequence, upshot, aftereffect, aftermath, sequel, issue, outcome

eventual *syn* LAST, ultimate, concluding, terminal, final, latest *rel* ensuing, succeeding; terminating, closing, ending

everlasting • continuing on and on without end *syn* endless, interminable, unceasing *rel* eternal, boundless, infinite; lasting, perdurable, perpetual; immortal, deathless, undying *ant* transitory

every *syn* ALL, each

evict *syn* EJECT, oust, expel, dismiss *rel* exclude, eliminate, shut out; reject, repudiate, spurn; fire, cashier, discharge

evidence *syn* SHOW, evince, manifest, demonstrate *rel* reveal, disclose, betray, divulge; display, exhibit, expose; prove, indicate, betoken, attest, bespeak

evident • readily perceived or apprehended *syn* manifest, patent, distinct, obvious, apparent, palpable, plain, clear *rel* perceptible, sensible, tangible, appreciable, ponderable; conspicuous, prominent, noticeable

evil *adj, syn* BAD, ill, wicked, naughty *rel* base, low, vile; iniquitous, nefarious, flagitious, vicious, villainous, infamous; pernicious, baneful; execrable, damnable *ant* exemplary; salutary

evil *n* • whatever is harmful or disastrous to morals or well-being *syn* ill *ant* good

evince *syn* SHOW, manifest, evidence, demonstrate *rel* betoken, indicate, attest, prove, argue, bespeak; display, exhibit, expose disclose, reveal, discover, betray

evoke *syn* EDUCE, elicit, extract, extort *rel* provoke, excite, stimulate; arouse, rouse, rally, awaken, waken, stir

evolution *syn* DEVELOPMENT

evolve *syn* UNFOLD, develop, elaborate, perfect *rel* progress, advance; mature, ripen

exact *vb, syn* DEMAND, require, claim *rel* ask, request, solicit; compel, force, constrain, coerce, oblige

exact *adj, syn* CORRECT, accurate, right, precise, nice *rel* careful, meticulous, scrupulous, punctilious; agreeing, squaring, tallying, jibing, conforming

exacting *syn* ONEROUS, burdensome, oppressive *rel* severe, stern; rigid, rigorous, strict, stringent; arduous, difficult, hard *ant* easy; lenient

exaggeration • an overstepping of the bounds of truth, especially in describing the goodness or badness or the greatness or the smallness of something *syn* overstatement, hyperbole *rel* misrepresentation, untruth; fallacy, sophistry

exalt • to increase in importance or in prestige *syn* magnify, aggrandize *rel* elevate, raise, lift; heighten, enhance, intensify; extol, laud, praise *ant* abase

examination *syn* SCRUTINY, inspection, scanning, audit *rel* questioning, interrogation, inquiry, catechism, quizzing, quiz

examine **1** *syn* SCRUTINIZE, inspect, scan, audit *rel* analyze, dissect, resolve; contemplate, observe, survey, view, notice, note **2** *syn* ASK, question, interrogate, quiz, catechize, query, inquire *rel* penetrate, probe; test, try

example **1** *syn* INSTANCE, sample, specimen, case, illustration **2** *syn* MODEL, exemplar, pattern, ideal, standard, beau ideal, mirror *rel* paragon, apotheosis

exasperate *syn* IRRITATE, provoke, nettle, aggravate, rile, peeve *rel* vex, annoy, irk, bother; anger, incense, enrage, madden, infuriate *ant* mollify

excavate *syn* DIG, delve, spade, grub

exceed • to go or to be beyond a stated or implied limit, measure, or degree *syn* surpass, transcend, excel, outdo, outstrip

excel *syn* EXCEED, surpass, transcend, outdo, outstrip

excellence • the quality of especial worth or value *syn* merit, virtue, perfection *rel* value, worth; property, quality, character *ant* fault

exceptionable *syn* OBJECTIONABLE, unacceptable, undesirable, unwanted, unwelcome *rel* offensive, repugnant, loathsome, repulsive, revolting; repellent, distasteful, obnoxious, invidious, repugnant *ant* unexceptionable; exemplary

exceptional • being out of the ordinary *syn* extraordinary, phenomenal, unusual, unwonted *rel* outstanding, remarkable, noticeable, conspicuous, prominent, salient, signal; rare, infrequent, uncommon, scarce; singular, unique, strange; anomalous, irregular *ant* common; average

excerpt *syn* EXTRACT

excess • whatever exceeds a limit, measure, bound, or usual degree *syn* superfluity, surplus, surplusage, overplus *rel* lavishness, prodigality, profuseness, profusion, luxuriance, exuberance; inordinateness, immoderation, extravagance *ant* deficiency; dearth, paucity

excessive • going beyond a normal or acceptable limit *syn* immoderate, inordinate, extravagant, exorbitant, extreme *rel* superfluous, surplus, supernumerary, extra, spare; intense, vehement, fierce, exquisite, violent; redundant *ant* deficient

exchange • to give and receive reciprocally *syn* interchange, bandy

excitant *syn* STIMULUS, stimulant, incitement, impetus

excite *syn* PROVOKE, stimulate, pique, quicken, galvanize *rel* stir, rouse, arouse, rally, waken, awaken; agitate, disturb, perturb, discompose, disquiet; animate, inspire, fire *ant* soothe, quiet; allay (*fears, anxiety*)

exclude • to prevent the participation, consideration, or inclusion of *syn* debar, blackball, eliminate, rule out, shut out, disbar, suspend *rel* hinder, bar, block; preclude, obviate, ward, prevent; banish, exile, ostracize, deport *ant* admit; include

exclusive *syn* SELECT, elect, picked *rel* excluding, eliminating, debarring, shutting out, ruling out; aristocratic, patrician *ant* inclusive

excogitate *syn* CONSIDER, weigh, study, contemplate *rel* ponder, meditate, ruminate, muse; cogitate, reflect, deliberate, speculate, think

excoriate *syn* ABRADE, chafe, fret, gall *rel* strip, divest, denude, bare; flay, skin; torture, torment, rack; tongue-lash, revile, berate, scold

excruciating • intensely or unbearably painful *syn* agonizing, racking *rel* torturing, tormenting; intense, vehement, fierce, exquisite, violent

exculpate • to free from alleged fault or guilt *syn* absolve, exonerate, acquit, vindicate *rel* justify, explain, rationalize; excuse, condone, pardon, forgive, remit *ant* inculpate; accuse

excursion *syn* JOURNEY, trip, jaunt, tour, cruise, voyage, expedition, pilgrimage *rel* ride, drive

excursus *syn* DIGRESSION, divagation, episode

excuse *vb* • to exact neither punishment nor redress for or from *syn* condone, pardon, forgive, remit *rel* justify, explain, account, rationalize; acquit, vindicate, exculpate, absolve, exonerate; palliate, extenuate, gloss, whitewash *ant* punish

excuse *n, syn* APOLOGY, plea, pretext, apologia, alibi *rel* explanation, justification, rationalization; palliation, extenuation, whitewashing, glossing

execrable • so odious as to be utterly detestable *syn* damnable, accursed, cursed *rel* outrageous, atrocious, heinous, monstrous; base, low, vile; loathsome, revolting, repulsive, offensive, repugnant

execrate • to denounce violently *syn* curse, damn, anathematize, objurgate *rel* denounce, condemn, reprobate, censure, reprehend; revile, berate, rate

execute **1** *syn* PERFORM, effect, fulfill, discharge, accomplish, achieve *rel* complete, finish, conclude, close; realize, actualize, externalize, objectify **2** *syn* KILL, dispatch, slay, murder, assassinate

exemplar *syn* MODEL, pattern, ideal, beau ideal, example, mirror, standard *rel* apotheosis, paragon, nonpareil, nonesuch; type, symbol

exemplify • to use examples or show instances of in order to clarify *syn* illustrate

exemption • freeing or the state of being free or freed from a charge or obligation to which others are subject *syn* immunity

exercise *n* • repeated activity or exertion *syn* practice, drill *rel* action, act, deed; using, use, employment, utilization, application; operation, functioning, behavior

exercise *vb, syn* PRACTICE, drill *rel* use,

employ, utilize; display, exhibit, show; wield, ply, manipulate, handle

exertion *syn* EFFORT, pains, trouble *rel* labor, toil, travail, work, grind, drudgery; struggle, striving, endeavor

exhaust **1** *syn* DEPLETE, drain, impoverish, bankrupt *rel* sap, undermine, weaken; consume, absorb, engross, monopolize; dissipate, disperse, dispel, scatter **2** *syn* TIRE, fatigue, jade, weary, fag, tucker *rel* unnerve, enervate, emasculate; disable, cripple, debilitate, enfeeble

exhibit *vb, syn* SHOW, display, expose, parade, flaunt *rel* reveal, disclose, discover, divulge; manifest, evidence, evince, demonstrate

exhibit *n, syn* EXHIBITION, show, exposition, fair

exhibition • a public display of objects of interest *syn* show, exhibit, exposition, fair

exhort *syn* URGE, egg, goad, spur, prod, prick, sic *rel* plead, appeal; entreat, implore, beseech, beg; stimulate, excite, provoke; advise, counsel

exigency **1** *syn* JUNCTURE, pass, emergency, pinch, strait, crisis, contingency *rel* difficulty, vicissitude, rigor, hardship; predicament, plight, fix, quandary, dilemma, jam, pickle, scrape **2** *syn* NEED, necessity *rel* demanding, demand, requirement, exacting, exaction, claiming, claim; compulsion, coercion, constraint, duress

exigent *syn* PRESSING, urgent, imperative, crying, importunate, insistent, instant *rel* critical, crucial, acute; threatening, menacing; compelling, constraining

exiguous *syn* MEAGER, scant, scanty, skimpy, scrimpy, spare, sparse *rel* diminutive, tiny, small, little; tenuous, slender, slight, thin; limited, restricted, confined *ant* capacious, ample

exile *syn* BANISH, expatriate, ostracize, deport, transport, extradite *rel* proscribe, condemn; expel, eject, oust

exist *syn* BE, live, subsist

existence • the state or fact of having independent reality *syn* being, actuality *rel* state, condition, situation, status; subsisting, subsistence, living, life *ant* nonexistence

exonerate *syn* EXCULPATE, acquit, vindicate, absolve *rel* relieve, lighten, alleviate; excuse, remit *ant* charge

exorbitant *syn* EXCESSIVE, inordinate, extravagant, immoderate, extreme *rel* onerous, burdensome, oppressive, exacting; greedy, grasping, covetous; extorting, extortionate *ant* just

exordium *syn* INTRODUCTION, preamble, preface, foreword, prologue, prelude

expand • to increase or become increased in size, bulk, or volume *syn* amplify, swell, distend, inflate, dilate *rel* enlarge, increase, augment; extend, protract, prolong *ant* contract; abridge; circumscribe

expanse • a significantly large area or range *syn* amplitude, spread, stretch *rel* range, reach, scope, compass, sweep, orbit; domain, territory, sphere, field

expansive *syn* ELASTIC, resilient, buoyant, volatile, effervescent *rel* exuberant, luxuriant, lavish, prodigal; generous, liberal, bountiful, bounteous, open-handed; exalted, magnified, aggrandized *ant* tense; reserved

expatiate *syn* DISCOURSE, descant, dilate *rel* speak, talk, converse; expand, amplify; discuss, argue, dispute; expound, explain; relate, narrate, recount, recite, rehearse

expatriate *syn* BANISH, exile, ostracize, deport, transport, extradite *ant* repatriate

expect • to anticipate in the mind *syn* hope, look, await *rel* foresee, foreknow, anticipate, apprehend, divine *ant* despair of

expedient *adj* • dictated by practical wisdom or by motives of prudence *syn* politic, advisable *rel* advantageous, beneficial, profitable; useful, utilitarian; seasonable, opportune, timely, well-timed; feasible, practicable, possible *ant* inexpedient

expedient *n, syn* RESOURCE, resort, shift, makeshift, stopgap, substitute, surrogate *rel* device, contrivance, contraption; mean, agency, instrument, instrumentality, medium

expedition **1** *syn* HASTE, dispatch, speed, hurry *rel* celerity, legerity, alacrity; agility, nimbleness, briskness *ant* procrastination **2** *syn* JOURNEY, voyage, tour, trip, jaunt, excursion, cruise, pilgrimage

expeditious *syn* FAST, speedy, swift, rapid, fleet, quick, hasty *rel* efficient, effective, efficacious, effectual; brisk, agile, nimble; quick, ready, prompt *ant* sluggish

expel *syn* EJECT, oust, dismiss, evict *rel* banish, exile, ostracize; discharge, cashier, fire; discard, cast out; exclude, shut out, eliminate *ant* admit

expend *syn* SPEND, disburse *rel* pay, repay, compensate, reimburse, remunerate; distribute, dispense

expense *syn* PRICE, cost, charge

expensive *syn* COSTLY, dear, valuable, precious, invaluable, priceless *rel* exorbitant, extravagant, excessive, immoderate *ant* inexpensive

experience • to pass through the process of actually coming to know or to feel *syn* undergo, sustain, suffer *rel* see, perceive, behold, view, survey

expert *adj, syn* PROFICIENT, adept, skilled, skillful, masterly *rel* practiced, drilled; trained, schooled; dexterous, deft, adroit *ant* amateurish

expert *n* • one who shows mastery in a subject, an art, or a profession or who reveals extraordinary skill in execution, performance, or technique *syn* adept, artist, artiste, virtuoso, wizard *ant* amateur

expiate • to make amends or give satisfaction for wrong done *syn* atone *rel* redress, remedy, rectify, correct, amend; redeem, deliver, save

expiation • the making of amends or the giving of satisfaction for wrongs done *syn* atonement *rel* penitence, repentance, contrition; trial, tribulation, cross, visitation

expire *syn* PASS, pass away, elapse *rel* end, terminate, close; cease, discontinue, stop

explain **1** • to make the meaning of something understood or more comprehensible *syn* expound, explicate, elucidate, interpret, construe *rel* analyze, resolve, dissect, break down; discuss, argue, dispute; exemplify, illustrate **2** • to give the reason for or cause of *syn* account, justify, rationalize *rel* excuse, condone; exculpate, exonerate, acquit, absolve

explicate *syn* EXPLAIN, expound, elucidate, interpret, construe

explicit • characterized by full precise expression and meaning that is perfectly clear *syn* express, specific, definite, categorical *rel* precise, exact, accurate; clear, lucid, perspicuous *ant* ambiguous

exploit *syn* FEAT, achievement *rel* act, deed, action; adventure, enterprise, quest

expose *syn* SHOW, display, exhibit, parade, flaunt *rel* reveal, disclose, discover, divulge; demonstrate, evince, manifest, evidence; air, ventilate, vent, voice, utter, express; publish, advertise, proclaim, broadcast, declare

exposé *syn* EXPOSITION, exposure

exposed *syn* LIABLE, open, subject, prone, susceptible, sensitive *rel* threatened, menaced

exposition **1** *syn* EXHIBITION, fair, exhibit, show **2** • a setting forth or laying open of a thing or things hitherto not known or fully understood *syn* exposure, exposé

expostulate *syn* OBJECT, remonstrate, protest, kick *rel* oppose, resist, combat, fight; argue, debate, dispute, discuss

exposure *syn* EXPOSITION, exposé *ant* cover; covering

expound *syn* EXPLAIN, explicate, elucidate, interpret, construe *rel* dissect, break down, analyze, resolve; illustrate, exemplify

express *adj, syn* EXPLICIT, definite, specific, categorical *rel* expressed, voiced, uttered; lucid, clear, perspicuous; distinct, plain, evident; precise, exact, accurate

express *vb* • to let out what one feels or thinks *syn* vent, utter, voice, broach, air, ventilate *rel* speak, talk; pronounce, articulate, enunciate; reveal, disclose, divulge, tell; declare, proclaim, announce *ant* imply

expression *syn* PHRASE, locution, idiom

expressive • clearly conveying or manifesting a thought, idea, or feeling or a combination of these *syn* eloquent, significant, meaningful, pregnant, sententious *rel* revealing, revelatory, disclosing, divulging; graphic, vivid, picturesque, pictorial; suggesting, suggestive, adumbrating, shadowing

expunge *syn* ERASE, cancel, efface, obliterate, blot out, delete *rel* wipe, eradicate, extirpate, exterminate

exquisite *adj* **1** *syn* CHOICE, recherché, rare, dainty, delicate, elegant *rel* precious, valuable, priceless, costly; consummate, finished; flawless, impeccable, faultless; perfect, intact, whole, entire **2** *syn* INTENSE, vehement, fierce, violent *rel* consummate; perfect; supreme, superlative; heightened, aggravated, intensified, enhanced; exalted, magnified

exquisite *n, syn* FOP, coxcomb, beau, dandy, dude, buck

extemporaneous • composed, devised, or done at the moment rather than beforehand *syn* extempore, extemporary, improvised, impromptu, offhand, unpremeditated *rel* spontaneous, impulsive; ready, prompt, apt, quick

extemporary, extempore *syn* EXTEMPORANEOUS, improvised, impromptu, offhand, unpremeditated

extend • to make or become longer *syn* lengthen, elongate, prolong, protract *rel* increase, enlarge, augment; expand, amplify, distend, dilate *ant* abridge, shorten

extension *syn* ANNEX, wing, ell

extent *syn* SIZE, dimensions, area, magnitude, volume *rel* range, scope, compass, sweep, reach, radius; stretch, spread, amplitude, expanse

extenuate *syn* THIN, attenuate, dilute, rarefy *rel* diminish, lessen, reduce, decrease; weaken, enfeeble, debilitate; moderate, temper, qualify *ant* intensify **2** *syn* PALLIATE, gloze, gloss, whitewash, whiten *rel* condone, excuse; rationalize, explain, justify

exterior *syn* OUTER, external, outward, outside *rel* extrinsic, extraneous, foreign, alien *ant* interior

exterminate • to destroy utterly *syn* extirpate, eradicate, uproot, deracinate, wipe *rel* abolish, extinguish, annihilate, abate; obliterate, efface, expunge, blot out, erase; destroy, demolish, raze

external *syn* OUTER, exterior, outward, outside *rel* extrinsic, extraneous, foreign, alien *ant* internal

externalize *syn* REALIZE, materialize, actualize, embody, incarnate, objectify, hypostatize, reify

extinguish 1 *syn* CRUSH, quell, suppress, quench, quash *rel* obliterate, expunge, efface, delete; destroy; ruin, wreck *ant* inflame **2** *syn* ABOLISH, annihilate, abate *rel* extirpate, exterminate, eradicate, uproot, wipe; obliterate, efface, blot out, expunge, erase; suppress, repress

extirpate *syn* EXTERMINATE, eradicate, uproot, deracinate, wipe *rel* extinguish, abolish, annihilate; obliterate, efface, expunge, erase, blot out; destroy, demolish, raze

extol *syn* PRAISE, laud, eulogize, acclaim *rel* applaud, commend, compliment; exalt, magnify, aggrandize *ant* decry; abase (*oneself*)

extort *syn* EDUCE, extract, elicit, evoke *rel* draw, drag, pull; compel, force, constrain, oblige, coerce; exact, demand, require

extra *syn* SUPERFLUOUS, supernumerary, spare, surplus

extract *vb, syn* EDUCE, extort, elicit, evoke *rel* draw, pull, drag; demand, require, exact; obtain, procure, gain, win, acquire, get

extract *n* • a passage transcribed or quoted from a book or document *syn* excerpt

extradite *syn* BANISH, deport, transport, expatriate, exile, ostracize *rel* surrender, relinquish, yield, resign

extraneous *syn* EXTRINSIC, foreign, alien *rel* external, exterior, outside, outer, outward; adventitious, accidental, incidental *ant* relevant

extraordinary *syn* EXCEPTIONAL, phenomenal, unusual, unwonted *rel* amazing, stupendous, terrific, wonderful

extravagant *syn* EXCESSIVE, inordinate, immoderate, exorbitant, extreme *rel* preposterous, absurd, foolish, silly; profuse, prodigal, lavish, exuberant *ant* restrained

extreme *adj, syn* EXCESSIVE, exorbitant, inordinate, immoderate, extravagant

extreme *n* • the utmost limit or degree of something *syn* extremity

extremity *syn* EXTREME

extricate • to free or release from what binds or holds back *syn* disentangle, untangle, disencumber, disembarrass *rel* disengage, detach, abstract; liberate, release, free; rescue, deliver

extrinsic • external to a thing, its essential nature, or its original character *syn* extraneous, foreign, alien *rel* external, outer, outside, exterior, outward; acquired, gained *ant* intrinsic

exuberant *syn* PROFUSE, lavish, prodigal, luxuriant, lush *rel* prolific, fertile, fruitful, fecund; vigorous, lusty, energetic, nervous; rampant, rank; copious, plentiful *ant* austere; sterile

eyewitness *syn* SPECTATOR, witness, onlooker, looker-on, observer, beholder, bystander, kibitzer

F

fable **1** *syn* FICTION, fabrication, figment **2** *syn* ALLEGORY, myth, parable

fabricate *syn* MAKE, fashion, forge, form, shape, manufacture *rel* invent, create; produce, turn out; devise, contrive

fabrication *syn* FICTION, figment, fable *rel* invention, creation; art, craft, handicraft, trade; work, product, production, opus, artifact

fabulous *syn* FICTITIOUS, mythical, legendary, apocryphal *rel* astonishing, amazing, astounding, surprising; extravagant, inordinate, excessive; monstrous, prodigious, stupendous

face *n* • the front part of a human or, sometimes, animal head including the mouth, nose, eyes, forehead, and cheeks *syn* countenance, visage, physiognomy, mug, puss

face *vb* **1** *syn* MEET, encounter, confront *rel* look, watch, see; gaze, stare, glare; await, look, expect **2** • to confront with courage or boldness *syn* brave, challenge, dare, defy, beard *rel* confront, encounter, meet; oppose, withstand, resist; contend, fight *ant* avoid

facet *syn* PHASE, aspect, side, angle

facetious *syn* WITTY, humorous, jocose, jocular *rel* joking, jesting, quipping, wisecracking; jolly, jovial, jocund, merry, blithe; comical, comic, droll, funny, ludicrous, laughable *ant* lugubrious

facile *syn* EASY, smooth, light, simple, effortless *rel* adroit, deft, dexterous; fluent, voluble, glib, vocal; superficial, shallow, uncritical, cursory *ant* arduous; constrained, clumsy

facility *syn* READINESS, ease, dexterity *rel* spontaneity, unconstraint, abandon; address, poise, tact; lightness, effortlessness, smoothness

facsimile *syn* REPRODUCTION, copy, carbon copy, duplicate, replica, transcript

faction *syn* COMBINATION, bloc, party, combine, ring *rel* clique, set, coterie, circle

factious *syn* INSUBORDINATE, contumacious, seditious, mutinous, rebellious *rel* contending, fighting, warring; contentious, quarrelsome, belligerent; disaffected, estranged, alienated *ant* cooperative

factitious *syn* ARTIFICIAL, synthetic, ersatz *rel* manufactured, fabricated; forced, compelled, constrained; simulated, feigned, counterfeited, shammed, pretended, affected, assumed *ant* bona fide, veritable

factor **1** *syn* AGENT, attorney, deputy, proxy **2** *syn* ELEMENT, constituent, component, ingredient *rel* determinant, cause, antecedent; influence; agency, agent, instrument, instrumentality, mean

faculty **1** *syn* POWER, function **2** *syn* GIFT, aptitude, knack, bent, turn, genius, talent *rel* ability, capacity, capability; property, quality; penchant, flair, propensity, proclivity, leaning; predilection

fad *syn* FASHION, vogue, style, rage, craze, mode, dernier cri, cry *rel* fancy, whim, whimsy, caprice, conceit, vagary

fade *syn* VANISH, evanesce, evaporate, disappear *rel* deliquesce, melt, liquefy; thin, rarefy, attenuate; reduce, lessen, decrease

faded *syn* SHABBY, dilapidated, dingy, seedy, threadbare *rel* worn, wasted, haggard; dim, murky, gloomy, dark; colorless, achromatic; pale, pallid, ashen, wan

fag *syn* TIRE, exhaust, jade, fatigue, weary, tucker

failing *syn* FAULT, frailty, foible, vice *rel* blemish, flaw, defect; weakness, infirmity *ant* perfection

failure • an omission on the part of someone or something of what is expected or required *syn* neglect, default, miscarriage, dereliction *rel* fault, failing; shortcoming, deficiency, imperfection; lack, want, absence, privation, dearth; negligence, laxness, slackness, remissness; indifference, unconcernedness, unconcern

faineant *syn* LAZY, indolent, slothful *rel* supine, passive, inactive, inert, idle; apathetic, impassive, phlegmatic; lethargic, sluggish; languorous, lackadaisical, languid

fair *adj* **1** *syn* BEAUTIFUL, comely, lovely, pretty, bonny, handsome, beauteous, pulchritudinous, good-looking *rel* delicate, dainty, exquisite, choice; charming, attractive, enchanting; pure, chaste *ant* foul; ill-favored **2** • characterized by honesty, justice, and freedom from improper influence *syn* just, equitable, impartial, unbiased, dispassionate, uncolored, objective *rel* disinterested, detached, indifferent; reasonable, rational *ant* unfair **3** *syn* MEDIUM, average, middling, mediocre, second-rate, moderate, indifferent *rel* ordinary, common

fair *n, syn* EXHIBITION, exposition, show, exhibit

faith 1 *syn* BELIEF, credence, credit *rel* assurance, conviction, certainty, certitude; assenting, assent, acquiescence, agreement *ant* doubt **2** *syn* TRUST, dependence, reliance, confidence *rel* assurance, certitude, certainty **3** *syn* RELIGION, creed, persuasion, church, denomination, sect, cult, communion *rel* tenets, dogmas, doctrines

faithful • firm in adherence to whatever one is bound to by duty or promise *syn* loyal, true, constant, staunch, steadfast, resolute *rel* devoted, loving, affectionate; tried, trustworthy, reliable, dependable *ant* faithless

faithless • not true to allegiance or duty *syn* false, disloyal, traitorous, treacherous, perfidious *rel* inconstant, unstable, fickle, capricious; wavering, fluctuating; changeable, changeful *ant* faithful

fake *n, syn* IMPOSTURE, sham, humbug, counterfeit, cheat, fraud, deceit, deception

fake *adj, syn* COUNTERFEIT, spurious, bogus, sham, pseudo, pinchbeck, phony *rel* fabricated, forged; framed, invented, concocted, contrived

faker *syn* IMPOSTOR, mountebank, charlatan, quack *rel* defrauder, cheater, cheat, swindler, cozener

fall • to go or to let go downward freely *syn* drop, sink, slump, subside *rel* descend, dismount, alight; droop, sag, flag, wilt; ebb, abate, wane; recede *ant* rise

fallacious • contrary to or devoid of logic *syn* sophistical, casuistical *rel* irrational, unreasonable; misleading, deceptive, delusive, delusory; equivocal, ambiguous, obscure *ant* sound, valid

fallacy • unsound and misleading reasoning or line of argument *syn* sophism, sophistry, casuistry

false 1 • not in conformity with what is true or right *syn* wrong *rel* misleading, deceptive, delusive, delusory; fallacious, sophistical; mendacious, deceitful, dishonest, untruthful; factitious, artificial *ant* true **2** *syn* FAITHLESS, perfidious, disloyal, traitorous, treacherous *rel* recreant, apostate, renegade, backsliding; inconstant, unstable; crooked, devious *ant* true

falsehood *syn* LIE, untruth, fib, misrepresentation, story *ant* truth

falsify *syn* MISREPRESENT, belie, garble *rel* change, alter, modify, vary; distort, contort, warp, deform; pervert, corrupt, debase; contradict, contravene, traverse, deny

falter *syn* HESITATE, waver, vacillate *rel* flinch, blench, recoil, quail, shrink; fluctuate, oscillate, swing; shake, tremble, quake, shudder

fame • the state of being widely known for one's deeds *syn* renown, honor, glory, celebrity, reputation, repute, notoriety, éclat *rel* acclaim, acclamation, applause; recognizing, recognition, acknowledgment; eminence, illustriousness *ant* infamy; obscurity

famed *syn* FAMOUS, renowned, celebrated, eminent, illustrious *ant* obscure

familiar 1 • near to one another because of frequent association or shared interests *syn* intimate, close, confidential, chummy, thick *rel* friendly, neighborly, amicable; sociable, cordial, genial, affable, gracious; easy, comfortable, cozy, snug; intrusive, obtrusive, officious, impertinent *ant* aloof **2** *syn* COMMON, ordinary, popular, vulgar *rel* usual, wonted, accustomed, customary, habitual *ant* unfamiliar; strange

famous • widely known and honored for achievement *syn* famed, renowned, celebrated, eminent, illustrious *ant* obscure

fanatic *syn* ENTHUSIAST, bigot, zealot

fanciful *syn* IMAGINARY, visionary, fantastic, chimerical, quixotic *rel* fictitious, fabulous, mythical, apocryphal, legendary; bizarre, grotesque, fantastic; preposterous, absurd, foolish; false, wrong *ant* realistic

fancy *n* **1** *syn* CAPRICE, freak, whim, whimsy, conceit, vagary, crotchet **2** *syn* IMAGINATION, fantasy *ant* experience **3** • a vivid idea or image present in the mind but having no concrete or objective reality *syn* fantasy, phantasy, phantasm, vision, dream, daydream, nightmare *rel* figment, fabrication, fable, fiction; notion, conception, idea, concept *ant* reality

fancy *vb* **1** *syn* LIKE, dote, love, enjoy, relish *rel* approve, endorse, sanction **2** *syn*

THINK, imagine, conceive, envisage, envision, realize *rel* conjecture, surmise, guess

fantastic 1 *syn* IMAGINARY, chimerical, visionary, fanciful, quixotic *rel* extravagant, extreme, excessive; incredible, unbelievable, implausible; preposterous, absurd, foolish; irrational, unreasonable; delusory, delusive, deceptive, misleading **2** • conceived or made without reference to reality *syn* bizarre, grotesque, antic *rel* imagined, fancied, conceived; externalized, objectified, realized; ingenious, adroit, clever; eccentric, erratic, singular, strange, odd, queer

fantasy 1 *syn* IMAGINATION, fancy *rel* imagining, fancying, conceiving, envisioning; externalizing, objectifying, realizing **2** *syn* FANCY, phantasy, phantasm, vision, dream, daydream, nightmare *rel* delusion, illusion, hallucination; vagary, caprice, whimsy, whim, freak, fancy; grotesquerie, bizarrerie

far, faraway,, far-off *syn* DISTANT, remote, removed *ant* near, nigh, nearly

farcical *syn* LAUGHABLE, comical, comic, ludicrous, ridiculous, risible, droll, funny

farfetched *syn* FORCED, labored, strained *rel* fantastic, grotesque, bizarre; eccentric, erratic, strange, queer

farming *syn* AGRICULTURE, husbandry

farther • at or to a greater distance or more avanced point *syn* further, beyond

fascinate *syn* ATTRACT, charm, bewitch, enchant, captivate, allure *rel* influence, impress, affect, sway, strike, touch; delight, rejoice, gladden, please

fascinating *syn* ATTRACTIVE, charming, bewitching, enchanting, captivating, alluring *rel* delightful, delectable; luring, enticing, seducing, seductive, tempting

fashion *n* **1** *syn* METHOD, manner, way, mode, system *rel* practice, habit, custom, usage, wont **2** • the prevailing or accepted custom *syn* style, mode, vogue, fad, rage, craze, dernier cri, cry *rel* trend, drift, tendency; convention, form, usage

fashion *vb, syn* MAKE, form, shape, fabricate, manufacture, forge *rel* devise, contrive; design, plan, plot; produce, turn out

fashionable *syn* STYLISH, modish, smart, chic, dashing *ant* unfashionable; old-fashioned

fast • moving, proceeding, or acting with great celerity *syn* rapid, swift, fleet, quick, speedy, hasty, expeditious *ant* slow

fasten • to cause one thing to hold to another *syn* fix, attach, affix *rel* secure, rivet, moor, anchor; join, connect, link, unite; adhere, cleave, cling, stick, cohere; bind, tie *ant* unfasten; loosen, loose

fastidious *syn* NICE, finicky, finicking, finical, particular, fussy, dainty, squeamish, persnickety, pernickety *rel* exacting, demanding; critical, hypercritical, captious; careful, meticulous, punctilious, scrupulous

fastness *syn* FORT, stronghold, fortress, citadel

fat *syn* FLESHY, stout, portly, plump, corpulent, obese, rotund, chubby *ant* lean

fatal *syn* DEADLY, mortal, lethal *rel* killing, slaying; destroying, destructive; baneful, pernicious

fate • whatever is destined or inevitably decreed for one *syn* destiny, lot, portion, doom *rel* issue, outcome, upshot, consequence, result, effect; end, ending, termination

fateful *syn* OMINOUS, portentous, inauspicious, unpropitious *rel* momentous, significant, important; decisive, determinative, conclusive; crucial, critical, acute

fathom • to measure depth typically with a weighted line *syn* sound, plumb

fatigue *syn* TIRE, exhaust, jade, weary, fag, tucker *rel* deplete, drain; debilitate, disable, weaken *ant* rest

fatuous *syn* SIMPLE, asinine, silly, foolish *rel* idiotic, imbecile, moronic; fond, infatuated, besotted, insensate *ant* sensible

fault 1 *syn* IMPERFECTION, deficiency, shortcoming *rel* flaw, defect, blemish; weakness, infirmity *ant* excellence **2** • an imperfection in character or an ingrained moral weakness *syn* failing, frailty, foible, vice *rel* weakness, infirmity; flaw, defect, blemish *ant* merit **3** *syn* BLAME, culpability, guilt *rel* responsibility, answerability, accountability; sin, offense, crime

faultfinding *syn* CRITICAL, captious, caviling, carping, censorious, hypercritical *rel* exacting, demanding, requiring; fussy, particular, finicky, pernickety, nice

faultless *syn* IMPECCABLE, flawless, errorless *rel* correct, right, nice, accurate, exact, precise; perfect, intact, entire, whole *ant* faulty

faux pas *syn* ERROR, blunder, slip, mistake, lapse, bull, howler, boner

favor *n, syn* GIFT, boon, largess, present, gratuity *rel* token, pledge, earnest; concession, allowance; honor, homage, deference; benefaction, donation, contribution

favor *vb* **1** • to give the support of one's approval to *syn* countenance, encourage *rel* approve, endorse; support, uphold, back *ant* disapprove **2** *syn* OBLIGE, accommodate *rel* help, aid, assist; indulge, pamper, humor; benefit, profit

favorable • being of good omen or presaging a happy or successful outcome *syn* benign, auspicious, propitious *rel* advantageous, beneficial, profitable; salutary, wholesome, healthful; benignant, kindly, kind *ant* unfavorable; antagonistic

favorite *syn* PARASITE, sycophant, toady, lickspittle, bootlicker, hanger-on, leech, sponge, sponger

fawn • to behave abjectly before a superior *syn* toady, truckle, cringe, cower *rel* blandish, cajole, wheedle, coax; defer, bow, cave, yield, submit; court, woo, invite *ant* domineer

faze *syn* EMBARRASS, disconcert, discomfit, rattle, abash *rel* nonplus, confound, dumbfound, perplex, mystify, puzzle; confuse, muddle; fluster, flurry, perturb, discompose

fealty *syn* FIDELITY, loyalty, devotion, allegiance, piety *rel* faithfulness, faith, trueness, truth, constancy, staunchness, steadfastness; obligation, duty *ant* perfidy

fear **1** • agitation or dismay which overcomes one in the anticipation or in the presence of danger *syn* dread, fright, alarm, dismay, consternation, panic, terror, horror, trepidation *rel* apprehension, foreboding, misgiving, presentiment; anxiety, worry, concern, care *ant* fearlessness **2** *syn* REVERENCE, awe *rel* veneration, worship, adoration; admiration, wonder, amazement; respect, esteem, regard *ant* contempt

fearful **1** • inspired or moved by fear *syn* apprehensive, afraid *rel* timid, timorous; anxious, worried, concerned, care; hesitant, reluctant, disinclined *ant* fearless; intrepid **2** • causing fear *syn* awful, dreadful, frightful, terrible, terrific, horrible, horrific, shocking, appalling *rel* frightening, terrifying, alarming; ghastly, gruesome, grisly, grim, macabre, lurid; sinister, baleful, malign; sublime, splendid

fearless *syn* BRAVE, unafraid, dauntless, undaunted, bold, intrepid, audacious, courageous, valiant, valorous, doughty *rel* daring, venturesome, adventurous; heroic, gallant; plucky, gritty *ant* fearful

feasible *syn* POSSIBLE, practicable *rel* practical, practicable; advisable, expedient, politic; advantageous, beneficial, profitable; suitable, appropriate, fitting, fit *ant* unfeasible, infeasible; chimerical

feast *syn* DINNER, banquet

feat • a remarkable deed or performance *syn* exploit, achievement *rel* deed, act, action; triumph, conquest, victory; enterprise, adventure, quest

feature *syn* CHARACTERISTIC, trait *rel* detail, particular, item; speciality, particularity; quality, character, property

fecund *syn* FERTILE, fruitful, prolific *rel* bearing, producing, yielding; breeding, propagating, reproducing, generating *ant* barren

fecundity *syn* FERTILITY, fruitfulness, prolificacy *rel* producing, productiveness; profuseness, profusion, luxuriance, lavishness, prodigality, lushness, exuberance *ant* barrenness

federation *syn* ALLIANCE, confederacy, confederation, coalition, fusion

fee *syn* WAGE, stipend, emolument, salary, wages, pay, hire *rel* remuneration, compensation; charge, price, cost, expense

feeble *syn* WEAK, infirm, decrepit, frail, fragile *rel* unnerved, enervated, emasculated, unmanned; debilitated, weakened, enfeebled, disabled, crippled; powerless, impotent *ant* robust

feed *vb* • to provide the food that one needs or desires *syn* nourish, pasture, graze *rel* nurse, nurture, foster, cherish; support, sustain, maintain *ant* starve

feed *n, syn* FOOD, fodder, forage, provender, victuals, viands, provisions, comestibles

feel *vb, syn* TOUCH, palpate, handle, paw *rel* apprehend, comprehend; perceive, observe, notice, see

feel *n, syn* ATMOSPHERE, feeling, aura *rel* see FEELING 3

feeling **1** *syn* SENSATION, sensibility, sense *rel* reacting, reaction, behaving, behavior; responsiveness; sensitiveness, susceptibility **2** • subjective response or reaction *syn* affection, emotion, sentiment, passion *rel* impressing, impression, touching, affecting, affection; mood, humor, temper, vein **3** *syn* ATMOSPHERE, feel, aura *rel* impression, impress, imprint; peculiarity, individuality, characteristic; quality, property, character, attribute

feign *syn* ASSUME, simulate, counterfeit, sham, pretend, affect *rel* fabricate, manufacture, forge, make; dissemble, disguise, cloak, mask, camouflage

feint *syn* TRICK, artifice, wile, ruse, gambit, ploy, stratagem, maneuver *rel* pretense, pretension, make-believe; hoaxing, hoax, hoodwinking, befooling, dupe; resort, expedient, shift

felicitate • to express one's pleasure in the joy, success, elevation, or prospects of another *syn* congratulate

felicitous *syn* FIT, happy, apt, fitting, appropriate, suitable, meet, proper *rel* telling, convincing, valid; pat, timely, opportune, seasonable, well-timed; apposite, pertinent, relevant *ant* infelicitous; inept, maladroit

felicity *syn* HAPPINESS, bliss, beatitude, blessedness *rel* rapture, transport, ecstasy; joy, delight, delectation, pleasure, fruition *ant* misery

fell *syn* FIERCE, cruel, inhuman, savage, barbarous, ferocious, truculent *rel* baleful, malign, malefic, maleficent, sinister; pitiless, ruthless; relentless, unrelenting, merciless, grim, implacable

felon *syn* CRIMINAL, convict, malefactor, culprit, delinquent

female *n* • a person and esp. an adult who belongs to the sex that is the counterpart of the male sex *syn* woman, lady

female *adj* • of, characteristic of, or like a female esp. of the human species *syn* feminine, womanly, womanlike, womanish, ladylike *ant* male

feminine *syn* FEMALE, womanly, womanish, ladylike, womanlike *ant* masculine

fence 1 *syn* ENCLOSE, envelop, pen, coop, corral, cage, wall *rel* confine, circumscribe, limit; surround, gird, environ **2** *syn* DODGE, parry, sidestep, duck, shirk, malinger *rel* evade, avoid, shun, elude, escape; maneuver, feint; baffle, foil, outwit, frustrate

feral *syn* BRUTAL, brute, brutish, bestial, beastly *rel* fierce, ferocious

ferocious *syn* FIERCE, truculent, barbarous, savage, inhuman, cruel, fell *rel* infuriated, maddened, enraged; rapacious, voracious, ravening, ravenous; relentless, implacable, merciless, grim

ferret out *syn* SEEK, search, scour, hunt, comb, ransack, rummage *rel* extract, elicit, educe; penetrate, pierce, probe, enter

fertile • marked by abundant productivity *syn* fecund, fruitful, prolific *rel* producing, bearing, yielding; inventing, inventive, creating, creative; quickening, stimulating, provoking, exciting, galvanizing *ant* infertile, sterile

fertility • the quality or state of being fertile *syn* fruitfulness, fecundity, prolificacy *ant* infertility, sterility

fervent *syn* IMPASSIONED, ardent, fervid, perfervid, passionate *rel* devout, pious, religious; warm, warmhearted, tender, responsive; sincere, wholehearted, heartfelt, hearty, whole-souled, unfeigned; intense, vehement, fierce, exquisite, violent

fervid *syn* IMPASSIONED, fervent, ardent, perfervid, passionate *rel* intense, vehement, fierce, exquisite, violent; earnest, serious, solemn; sincere, heartfelt, hearty, wholehearted, whole-souled

fervor *syn* PASSION, ardor, enthusiasm, zeal *rel* devoutness, piousness, piety; earnestness, seriousness, solemnity; sincerity, heartiness, wholeheartedness

fetch *syn* BRING, take *rel* get, obtain, procure; transfer, shift, move, remove; convey, transport, transmit, carry, bear

fetid *syn* MALODOROUS, noisome, stinking, putrid, rank, rancid, fusty, musty *rel* foul, nasty, dirty; offensive, loathsome, repulsive, repugnant, revolting *ant* fragrant

fetish • an object believed to be endowed with the virtue of averting evil or of bringing good fortune *syn* talisman, charm, amulet

fetter *syn* HAMPER, shackle, trammel, clog, manacle, hog-tie *rel* hinder, impede, obstruct, block, bar, dam; restrain, curb, check; baffle, balk, thwart, foil, frustrate; bind, tie

fib *n, syn* LIE, untruth, falsehood, misrepresentation, story

fib *vb, syn* LIE, equivocate, palter, prevaricate

fickle *syn* INCONSTANT, unstable, capricious, mercurial *rel* changeable, changeful, variable, protean; fitful, spasmodic; light, light-minded, frivolous, flighty, volatile *ant* constant, true

fiction • a story, account, explanation, or conception which is an invention of the human mind *syn* figment, fabrication, fable *rel* narrative, story, tale, anecdote, yarn

fictitious • having the character of something invented or imagined as opposed to something true or genuine *syn* fabulous, legendary, mythical, apocryphal *rel* invented, created; imaginary, fanciful, fantastic; fabricated, fashioned *ant* historical

fidelity • faithfulness to something to which one is bound by a pledge or duty *syn* allegiance, fealty, loyalty, devotion, piety *rel* faithfulness, constancy, staunchness, steadfastness *ant* faithlessness; perfidy

fidgety *syn* IMPATIENT, restless, restive, uneasy, jumpy, jittery, nervous, unquiet

field • a limited area of knowledge or endeavor to which pursuits, activities, and interests are confined *syn* domain, province, sphere, territory, bailiwick *rel* limits, bounds, confines; extent, area, size, magnitude

fiendish • having or manifesting qualities associated with devils, demons, and fiends *syn* devilish, diabolical, diabolic, demoniac, demonic *rel* hellish, infernal; malign, malefic, maleficent, baleful, sinister; malignant, malevolent, malicious

fierce **1** • displaying fury or malignity in looks or actions *syn* truculent, ferocious, barbarous, savage, inhuman, cruel, fell *rel* menacing, threatening; infuriated, maddened, enraged; ravening, ravenous, rapacious, voracious; fearful, terrible, horrible, horrific *ant* tame; mild **2** *syn* INTENSE, vehement, exquisite, violent *rel* extreme, excessive, inordinate; penetrating, piercing; supreme, superlative, transcendent

fiery *syn* SPIRITED, high-spirited, peppery, gingery, mettlesome, spunky *rel* impetuous, precipitate, headlong; passionate, perfervid, ardent, impassioned, fervid; vehement, intense, fierce, violent

fight *vb* **1** *syn* CONTEND, battle, war *rel* struggle, strive, attempt; dispute, debate, discuss; wrangle, squabble, quarrel, altercate **2** *syn* RESIST, withstand, contest, oppose, combat, conflict, antagonize

fight *n, syn* CONTEST, combat, fray, affray, conflict *rel* struggle, striving; strife, contention, conflict, dissension, discord, difference, variance

figment *syn* FICTION, fabrication, fable *rel* fancy, fantasy, dream, daydream, nightmare; invention, creation

figure *n* **1** *syn* NUMBER, numeral, digit, integer *rel* symbol, character **2** *syn* FORM, shape, configuration, conformation *rel* outline, contour, profile, silhouette; character, symbol, sign, mark **3** • a unit in a decorative composition (as in fabric) *syn* pattern, design, motif, device

figure *vb, syn* ADD, cast, sum, total, tot, foot *rel* compute, calculate, reckon, estimate; count, enumerate, number

filch *syn* STEAL, purloin, lift, pilfer, pinch, snitch, swipe, cop *rel* snatch, grab, take, seize, grasp; rob, plunder, loot, rifle

file *syn* LINE, row, rank, echelon, tier

fillet *syn* STRIP, band, ribbon, stripe

filthy *syn* DIRTY, foul, squalid, nasty *rel* slovenly, unkempt, disheveled, sloppy, slipshod; offensive, loathsome, repulsive, revolting *ant* neat, spick-and-span

final *syn* LAST, terminal, concluding, latest, ultimate, eventual *rel* closing, ending, terminating; decisive, determinative, conclusive, definitive

financial • of or relating to the possession, making, borrowing, lending, or expenditure of money *syn* monetary, pecuniary, fiscal

fine *n* • a pecuniary penalty exacted by an authority *syn* amercement

fine *vb, syn* PENALIZE, amerce, mulct

finicky, finicking, finical *syn* NICE, particular, fussy, fastidious, dainty, squeamish, persnickety, pernickety *rel* exacting, demanding; captious, carping, hypercritical, critical; meticulous, punctilious, careful; conscientious, scrupulous, upright

finish *syn* CLOSE, complete, conclude, end, terminate *rel* achieve, accomplish, effect, fulfill, perform

finished *syn* CONSUMMATE, accomplished *rel* perfect, entire, intact, whole; refined, cultivated, cultured; suave, urbane, smooth; elegant, exquisite, choice *ant* crude

fire *n* • a destructive burning *syn* conflagration, holocaust *rel* blaze, glare, flame, flare; burning, charring, scorching

fire *vb* **1** *syn* LIGHT, kindle, ignite *rel* burn, scorch, char; blaze, flame, flare, glare, glow; illuminate, lighten **2** *syn* INFORM, animate, inspire *rel* excite, provoke, stimulate, galvanize; thrill, electrify; stir, rouse, arouse; enliven, quicken, vivify *ant* daunt **3** *syn* DISMISS, discharge, cashier, drop, sack, bounce *rel* eject, oust, expel; discard

firm • having a texture or consistency that resists deformation by external force *syn* hard, solid *rel* compact, close, dense, thick; tough, tenacious, strong; stiff, rigid, inflexible *ant* loose, flabby

fiscal *syn* FINANCIAL, monetary, pecuniary

fish • to attempt to catch fish *syn* angle

fissure *syn* CRACK, cleft, crevasse, crevice, cranny, chink *rel* break, gap; breach, split, rent, rupture, rift

fit *n* • an episode of bodily or mental disorder or excess *syn* attack, access, accession, paroxysm, spasm, convulsion

fit *adj* • right with respect to some end, need, use, or circumstances *syn* suitable, meet, proper, appropriate, fitting, apt, happy, felicitous *rel* adapted, adaptable, adjusted, adjustable, conformed, conformable; qualified, capable, able, competent *ant* unfit

fit *vb, syn* PREPARE, qualify, condition, ready *rel* endow, endue; furnish, provide, supply

fitful • lacking steadiness or regularity in course, movement, or succession *syn* spasmodic, convulsive *rel* intermittent, periodic, recurrent; desultory, hit-or-miss, random, haphazard *ant* constant

fitting *syn* FIT, appropriate, proper, meet, suitable, apt, happy, felicitous *rel* relevant, pertinent, germane, apposite, apropos; seemly, decorous, decent, proper; congruous, consonant; harmonious, concordant, accordant *ant* unfitting

fix *vb* **1** *syn* SET, settle, establish *rel* stabilize, steady; determine, decide, rule, settle; prescribe, define *ant* alter; abrogate (*a custom, rule, law*) **2** *syn* FASTEN, attach, affix *rel* implant, instill, inculcate; secure, rivet, anchor, moor **3** *syn* ADJUST, regulate *rel* repair, mend, patch, rebuild; correct, rectify, revise, amend, emend

fix *n, syn* PREDICAMENT, plight, dilemma, quandary, scrape, jam, pickle

flabbergast *syn* SURPRISE, amaze, astound, astonish *rel* dumbfound, confound, bewilder, nonplus, perplex, puzzle; disconcert, rattle, faze, discomfit, embarrass

flabby *syn* LIMP, flaccid, floppy, flimsy, sleazy *rel* loose, relaxed, slack, lax; soft; yielding, caving in; powerless, impotent; spiritless, listless, enervated, languid *ant* firm

flaccid *syn* LIMP, flabby, floppy, flimsy, sleazy *rel* slack, relaxed, lax, loose; unnerved, enervated, emasculated, unnerved; weakened, debilitated, enfeebled, sapped *ant* resilient

flag *n* • a piece of fabric that is used as a symbol (as of a nation) or as a signaling device *syn* ensign, standard, banner, color, streamer, pennant, pendant, pennon, jack

flag *vb, syn* DROOP, wilt, sag *rel* fall, subside, slump, sink, drop; ebb, wane, abate

flagitious *syn* VICIOUS, nefarious, infamous, iniquitous, villainous, corrupt, degenerate *rel* scandalous, criminal, sinful; shameful, disgraceful; flagrant, gross, glaring

flagrant • bad or objectionable *syn* glaring, gross, rank *rel* heinous, outrageous, atrocious, monstrous; nefarious, flagitious, infamous, vicious

flair *syn* LEANING, proclivity, propensity, penchant

flamboyant *syn* ORNATE, florid, rococo, baroque *rel* luxuriant, exuberant, profuse; resplendent, gorgeous, glorious, splendid; dashing, stylish; ostentatious, showy, pretentious; flashy, gaudy

flame *n, syn* BLAZE, flare, glare, glow *rel* effulgence, radiance, brilliance, brilliancy, refulgence, luminosity, brightness; ardor, fervor, passion; flashing, coruscation, gleaming, scintillation

flame *vb, syn* BLAZE, flare, glare, glow *rel* flash, gleam, glance, glint, coruscate; burn; fire, ignite, kindle, light

flammable *syn* COMBUSTIBLE, inflammable, incendiary, inflammatory

flare *vb, syn* BLAZE, glare, flame, glow *rel* dart, shoot, fly; flutter, flicker, flit; rise, arise, spring; flash, glance, glint, coruscate, scintillate; kindle, light, fire *ant* gutter out

flare *n, syn* BLAZE, glare, flame, glow *rel* rising, rise, surging, surge, towering; darting, dart, shooting; flashing, flash, coruscation, scintillation

flash *vb* • to shoot forth light (as in rays or sparks) *syn* gleam, glance, glint, sparkle, glitter, glisten, scintillate, coruscate, twinkle *rel* shoot, dart, fly; rise, surge, tower, rocket; blaze, flame, flare, glare, glow

flash *n, syn* INSTANT, second, moment, minute, jiffy, twinkling, split second

flashy *syn* GAUDY, garish, tawdry, meretricious *rel* showy, pretentious, ostentatious; flamboyant, ornate, florid; glittering, flashing, sparkling

flat **1** *syn* LEVEL, plane, plain, even, smooth, flush **2** *syn* INSIPID, vapid, jejune, banal, wishy-washy, inane

flattery *syn* COMPLIMENT, adulation *rel* blandishment, cajolery; fawning, toadying, truckling; eulogy, panegyric, encomium; homage, obeisance, deference, honor

flatulent *syn* INFLATED, tumid, turgid *rel* empty, hollow, vain; superficial, shallow; bombastic, grandiloquent, magniloquent, rhetorical

flaunt *syn* SHOW, parade, expose, display, exhibit *rel* boast, brag, vaunt, gasconade; reveal, disclose, discover, divulge; advertise, publish, broadcast, proclaim, declare

flavor *syn* TASTE, savor, tang, relish, smack

flavorsome *syn* PALATABLE, toothsome, tasty, savory, sapid, relishing, appetizing

flaw *syn* BLEMISH, defect *rel* cleaving, cleavage, riving, splitting, split, rending, rent, ripping, rip, tearing, tear

flawless *syn* IMPECCABLE, faultless, errorless *rel* intact, entire, whole, perfect; correct, accurate, precise, right, nice, exact

flay *syn* SKIN, decorticate, peel, pare *rel* abrade, excoriate, chafe; rack, torture, torment, afflict; chastise, castigate, punish

fleck *syn* SPOT, spatter, sprinkle, mottle, stipple, marble, speckle, spangle, bespangle

flecked *syn* SPOTTED, spattered, sprinkled, mottled, stippled, marbled, speckled, spangled, bespangled *rel* dappled, freaked, variegated

flee *syn* ESCAPE, fly, decamp, abscond *rel* evade, elude, avoid, escape

fleer *syn* SCOFF, jeer, gibe, gird, sneer, flout *rel* deride, mock, ridicule; grin, smile, smirk

fleet *vb, syn* WHILE, wile, beguile *rel* speed, hasten, hurry, quicken, accelerate

fleet *adj, syn* FAST, swift, rapid, quick, speedy, hasty, expeditious *rel* agile, brisk, nimble, spry; darting, skimming, scudding, flying

fleeting *syn* TRANSIENT, evanescent, fugitive, passing, transitory, ephemeral, momentary, short-lived *ant* lasting

fleshly *syn* CARNAL, sensual, animal *rel* physical, bodily, corporeal, corporal, somatic; sensuous, sensual, voluptuous, luxurious, sybaritic, epicurean

fleshy • thick and heavy in body because of superfluous fat *syn* fat, stout, portly, plump, rotund, chubby, corpulent, obese *rel* muscular, brawny, burly, husky *ant* skinny, scrawny

flex • to bend *syn* crook, bow, buckle *rel* bend, curve, twist *ant* extend

flexible *syn* ELASTIC, supple, resilient, springy *rel* pliable, pliant, malleable, ductile, plastic; tractable, obedient; limber, lithe, supple *ant* inflexible

flexuous *syn* WINDING, sinuous, serpentine, tortuous

flicker *syn* FLIT, flutter, flitter, hover *rel* waver, vibrate, oscillate, fluctuate, swing; flare, flame, glare, blaze; flash, gleam, glance, glint, coruscate; quiver, quaver, tremble, shake

flightiness *syn* LIGHTNESS, light-mindedness, volatility, levity, frivolity, flippancy *rel* capriciousness, unstableness, instability, fickleness, mercurialness, mercuriality, inconstancy; effervescence, buoyancy, elasticity; liveliness, gaiety, sprightliness *ant* steadiness; steadfastness

flimsy *syn* LIMP, sleazy, floppy, flaccid, flabby *rel* thin, slight, tenuous; loose, slack; weak, feeble

flinch *syn* RECOIL, shrink, wince, blench, quail *rel* falter, hesitate, vacillate; evade, elude, shun, eschew, avoid, escape; withdraw, retire, go; retreat, recede

fling *syn* THROW, hurl, sling, toss, cast, pitch *rel* thrust, shove, propel, push; impel, drive, move

flippancy *syn* LIGHTNESS, levity, light-mindedness, frivolity, volatility, flightiness *rel* sauciness, pertness, archness; impishness, waggishness, roguishness, mischievousness, playfulness *ant* seriousness

flirt *syn* TRIFLE, coquet, dally, toy *rel* play, sport, disport; caress, fondle, pet

flit • to move or fly briskly, irregularly, and

usu. intermittently *syn* flutter, flitter, flicker, hover *rel* fly, dart, skim, float, scud

flitter *syn* FLIT, flutter, flicker, hover *rel* fly, dart, skim; quiver, quaver, teeter, shake

float *syn* FLY, skim, sail, dart, scud, shoot *rel* glide, slide, slip; flit, hover, flitter

flood 1 *syn* FLOW, stream, current, tide, flux *rel* excess, superfluity, surplus; incursion, invasion **2** • a great or overwhelming flow of or as if of water *syn* deluge, inundation, torrent, spate, cataract *rel* flow, stream, tide, current

floppy *syn* LIMP, flabby, flaccid, flimsy, sleazy *rel* loose, relaxed, lax, slack

florid *syn* ORNATE, flamboyant, rococo, baroque *rel* aureate, flowery, euphuistic, grandiloquent, magniloquent, rhetorical, bombastic; sumptuous, luxurious, opulent; showy, ostentatious, pretentious *ant* chaste (*in style, decoration*)

flounder *syn* STUMBLE, trip, blunder, lurch, lumber, galumph, lollop, bumble *rel* struggle, strive, attempt; toil, travail, labor; wallow, welter

flourish 1 *syn* SUCCEED, prosper, thrive *rel* bloom, flower, blossom, blow; increase, augment, multiply; expand, amplify *ant* languish **2** *syn* SWING, brandish, shake, wave, thrash *rel* wield, manipulate, ply, handle; flaunt, display, exhibit, show

flout *syn* SCOFF, jeer, gibe, fleer, gird, sneer *rel* scout, scorn, despise, contemn, disdain; spurn, repudiate, decline; deride, ridicule, mock *ant* revere

flow *vb, syn* SPRING, issue, emanate, proceed, stem, derive, arise, rise, originate *rel* emerge, appear, loom; start, begin, commence

flow *n* • something suggestive of running water *syn* stream, current, flood, tide, flux *rel* succession, progression, series, sequence; continuity, continuation, continuance

flower *n, syn* BLOSSOM, bloom, blow

flower *vb, syn* BLOSSOM, bloom, blow *rel* flourish, prosper, succeed

flowery *syn* RHETORICAL, aureate, grandiloquent, magniloquent, euphuistic, bombastic *rel* florid, ornate, flamboyant; inflated, tumid, turgid; wordy, verbose, redundant, prolix, diffuse

fluctuate *syn* SWING, oscillate, sway, vibrate, pendulate, waver, undulate *rel* alternate, rotate; waver, vacillate, hesitate

fluent *syn* VOCAL, eloquent, voluble, glib, articulate *rel* facile, effortless, smooth, easy; quick, prompt, ready, apt

fluid *syn* LIQUID *rel* liquefied, melted, fused, deliquesced, deliquescent

flurry *n, syn* STIR, bustle, fuss, ado, pother *rel* perturbation, agitation, disturbance, discomposure; haste, hurry

flurry *vb, syn* DISCOMPOSE, fluster, agitate, perturb, disturb, disquiet *rel* bewilder, distract, perplex, puzzle; quicken, excite, galvanize, stimulate, provoke

flush *n, syn* BLUSH *rel* color, tinge, tint

flush *vb, syn* BLUSH *rel* color, tinge, tint; surge, rise; betray, divulge, disclose, reveal

flush *adj, syn* LEVEL, even, flat, plane, plain, smooth

fluster *syn* DISCOMPOSE, upset, agitate, perturb, flurry, disturb, disquiet *rel* bewilder, distract, confound, nonplus, mystify, perplex, puzzle; rattle, faze, disconcert, discomfit, embarrass; confuse, muddle, addle, fuddle

flutter *syn* FLIT, flitter, flicker, hover *rel* shake, tremble, quiver, quaver, wobble; beat, throb, pulsate, palpitate; fluctuate, vibrate, oscillate, swing

flux *syn* FLOW, current, tide, stream, flood *rel* swinging, swing, fluctuation, oscillation, wavering, swaying, sway; shifting, moving; motion, movement, stir

fly 1 • to pass lightly or quickly over or above a surface *syn* dart, float, skim, scud, shoot, sail *rel* flit, flutter, flitter, flicker, hover; soar, mount, rise, arise, ascend; glide, slide, slip **2** *syn* ESCAPE, flee, decamp, abscond

flying field *syn* AIRPORT, airdrome, airfield, airstrip, landing strip, landing field

foam • a mass of bubbles gathering in or on the surface of a liquid or something as insubstantial as such a mass *syn* froth, spume, scum, lather, suds, yeast

focal *syn* CENTRAL, pivotal *rel* significant, important, momentous; salient, signal, striking, arresting, outstanding, noticeable

focus *n, syn* CENTER, heart, nucleus, core, middle, midst, hub

focus *vb, syn* CENTER, centralize, concentrate *rel* fix, set, settle, establish

fodder *syn* FOOD, forage, feed, provender, provisions, comestibles, victuals, viands

foe *syn* ENEMY *rel* antagonist, opponent,

adversary; assailant, attacker; rival, competitor *ant* friend

fog *n, syn* HAZE, smog, mist

fog *vb, syn* OBSCURE, dim, bedim, darken, eclipse, cloud, becloud, befog, obfuscate *rel* puzzle, perplex, mystify, bewilder, distract; confuse, muddle, addle

foible *syn* FAULT, failing, frailty, vice *rel* weakness, infirmity; defect, flaw, blemish; aberration, deviation

foil *syn* FRUSTRATE, thwart, circumvent, balk, baffle, outwit *rel* discomfit, embarrass, disconcert, faze, rattle; curb, check, restrain, inhibit

follow **1** • to come after in time *syn* succeed, ensue, supervene **2** • to go after or on the trail of *syn* pursue, chase, trail, tag, tail *rel* attend, accompany, convoy; copy, imitate, ape; practice, exercise *ant* precede; forsake (*a teacher or teachings*)

follower • one who attaches himself to another *syn* adherent, disciple, sectary, partisan, henchman, satellite *rel* devotee, votary, addict, habitué; parasite, sycophant, toady *ant* leader

following • the body of persons who attach themselves to another esp. as disciples, patrons, or admirers *syn* clientele, public, audience

foment *syn* INCITE, abet, instigate *rel* goad, spur; stimulate, quicken, excite, galvanize, provoke; nurture, nurse, foster, cultivate *ant* quell

fond **1** • made blindly or stupidly foolish *syn* infatuated, besotted, insensate *rel* foolish, silly, fatuous, asinine, simple; stupid, dumb **2** *syn* LOVING, devoted, affectionate, doting *rel* enamored, infatuated; tender, sympathetic, warm, responsive; ardent, passionate, impassioned

fondle *syn* CARESS, pet, cosset, cuddle, dandle

food **1** • things that are edible for human beings or animals *syn* feed, victuals, viands, provisions, comestibles, provender, fodder, forage **2** • material which feeds and supports the mind or the spirit *syn* aliment, pabulum, nutriment, nourishment, sustenance, pap

fool • one regarded as lacking sense or good judgment *syn* idiot, imbecile, moron, simpleton, natural

foolhardy *syn* ADVENTUROUS, daring, daredevil, rash, reckless, venturesome *rel* bold, audacious, brave; headlong, precipitate, impetuous *ant* wary

foolish **1** *syn* SIMPLE, silly, fatuous, asinine *rel* idiotic, imbecilic, moronic **2** • felt to be ridiculous because not exhibiting good sense *syn* silly, absurd, preposterous *rel* ridiculous, ludicrous, laughable *ant* sensible

foot *syn* ADD, figure, cast, sum, total, tot

fop • a man who is conspicuously fashionable or elegant in dress or manners *syn* dandy, beau, coxcomb, exquisite, dude, buck

for *syn* BECAUSE, since, as, inasmuch as

forage *syn* FOOD, fodder, provender, feed, provisions, comestibles, victuals, viands

forbear **1** *syn* FORGO, abnegate, eschew, sacrifice *rel* restrain, curb, bridle, inhibit; avoid, escape, evade, shun; desist, cease, stop **2** *syn* REFRAIN, abstain *rel* suffer, tolerate, endure, bear

forbearance **1** *syn* PATIENCE, long-suffering, longanimity, resignation *rel, ant* see FORBEARANCE 2 **2** • a disinclination to be severe or rigorous *syn* tolerance, clemency, mercifulness, leniency, indulgence *rel* patience, long-suffering, longanimity; mercy, lenity, grace, charity *ant* vindictiveness; anger

forbearing • disinclined by nature, disposition, or circumstances to be severe or rigorous *syn* tolerant, clement, merciful, lenient, indulgent *rel* gentle, mild, soft; patient, long-suffering, longanimous *ant* unrelenting

forbearingly • in a forbearing manner *syn* tolerantly, clemently, mercifully, leniently, indulgently

forbid • to debar one from using, doing, or entering or something from being used, done, or entered *syn* prohibit, enjoin, interdict, inhibit, ban *rel* debar, rule out, exclude; preclude, obviate, prevent; prevent, forestall *ant* permit; bid

force *n* **1** *syn* POWER, energy, strength, might, puissance *rel* stress, strain, pressure, tension; speed, velocity, momentum, impetus, headway **2** • the exercise of power in order to impose one's will on a person or to have one's will with a thing *syn* violence, compulsion, coercion, duress, constraint, restraint *rel* intensity, vehemence, fierceness; effort, exertion, pains, trouble

force *vb* • to cause a person or thing to yield to pressure *syn* compel, coerce, constrain, oblige *rel* impel, drive, move; command, order, enjoin; exact, demand, require

forced • produced or kept up through effort *syn* labored, strained, farfetched *rel* compelled, coerced, constrained; factitious, artificial; fatiguing, exhausting, tiring

forceful *syn* POWERFUL, potent, forcible, puissant *rel* compelling, constraining; virile, manful; cogent, telling, convincing, compelling, valid; effective, efficient *ant* feeble

forcible *syn* POWERFUL, forceful, potent, puissant *rel* vehement, intense, violent; energetic, strenuous, vigorous; aggressive, militant, assertive, self-assertive; coercing, coercive

forebear *syn* ANCESTOR, forefather, progenitor

forebode *syn* FORETELL, portend, presage, augur, prognosticate, predict, forecast, prophesy *rel* betoken, bespeak, indicate; import, signify, mean; fear, dread

foreboding *syn* APPREHENSION, misgiving, presentiment *rel* foretoken, presage, omen, portent, augury, prognostic; forewarning, warning

forecast *syn* FORETELL, predict, prophesy, prognosticate, augur, presage, portend, forebode *rel* foresee, foreknow, anticipate, apprehend, divine; surmise, conjecture, guess; infer, gather, conclude

forefather *syn* ANCESTOR, forebear, progenitor

foregoing *syn* PRECEDING, antecedent, precedent, previous, prior, former, anterior *ant* following

foreign *syn* EXTRINSIC, alien, extraneous *rel* external, outside, outer; inconsonant, inconsistent, incongruous, incompatible; repugnant, repellent, obnoxious, distasteful; adventitious, accidental *ant* germane

foreigner *syn* STRANGER, alien, outlander, outsider, immigrant, émigré

foreknow *syn* FORESEE, divine, anticipate, apprehend *rel* foretell, predict, forecast, prophesy, prognosticate; infer, gather, conclude

foremost *syn* CHIEF, leading, principal, main, capital

forensic *syn* ARGUMENTATION, debate, disputation, dialectic

forerunner • one that goes before or in some way announces the coming of another *syn* precursor, harbinger, herald *rel* anticipator; announcer, announcement, advertiser, advertisement; portent, prognostic, omen, foretoken, presage, augury; forewarning, warning

foresee • to know or expect in advance that something will happen or come into existence or be made manifest *syn* foreknow, divine, apprehend, anticipate *rel* forecast, predict, foretell, prophesy, prognosticate; perceive, discern, descry, espy, see

foreshore *syn* SHORE, beach, strand, coast, littoral

foresight *syn* PRUDENCE, forethought, providence, discretion *rel* sagacity, perspicacity, shrewdness, astuteness; acumen, clairvoyance, discernment, perception *ant* hindsight

foresighted *syn* PRUDENT, forethoughtful, provident, discreet *rel* sagacious, perspicacious, shrewd, astute; intelligent, alert, quick-witted, brilliant, knowing; wise, judicious, sage, sapient *ant* hindsighted

forestall *syn* PREVENT, anticipate *rel* ward, avert, prevent, preclude, obviate; frustrate, thwart, foil, circumvent

foretaste *syn* PROSPECT, anticipation, outlook *rel* realization, actualization; token, earnest, pledge; presentiment, foreboding, apprehension

foretell • to tell something before it happens through special knowledge or occult power *syn* predict, forecast, prophesy, prognosticate, augur, presage, portend, forebode *rel* divine, foreknow, foresee, anticipate, apprehend; announce, declare, proclaim; reveal, divulge, disclose, discover; forewarn, warn

forethought *syn* PRUDENCE, foresight, providence, discretion *rel* premeditatedness, premeditation, deliberateness, deliberation; wisdom, judgment, sense, gumption

forethoughtful *syn* PRUDENT, foresighted, provident, discreet *rel* cautious, circumspect, wary, calculating; deliberate, premeditated, considered, advised, studied

foretoken • something that serves as a sign of future happenings *syn* presage, prognostic, omen, augury, portent *rel* sign, symptom, token, mark, badge, note; forerunner, harbinger, precursor, herald

forewarn *syn* WARN, caution *rel* notify, advise, apprise, inform; admonish, reprove; advise, counsel

foreword *syn* INTRODUCTION, preface, exordium, prologue, prelude, preamble

forge *syn* MAKE, fabricate, fashion, manufacture, form, shape *rel* beat, pound; produce, turn out, bear; counterfeit, simulate; copy, imitate

forget *syn* NEGLECT, overlook, ignore, disregard, omit, slight *ant* remember

forgetful • losing or letting go from one's mind something once known or learned *syn* oblivious, unmindful *rel* remiss, negligent, neglectful, lax, slack; heedless, thoughtless, careless

forgive *syn* EXCUSE, pardon, remit, condone *rel* absolve, exculpate, acquit, exonerate, vindicate

forgo • to deny oneself something for the sake of an end *syn* forbear, abnegate, eschew, sacrifice *rel* waive, relinquish, surrender, abandon; renounce, resign, abdicate

forlorn **1** *syn* ALONE, lorn, lone, desolate, lonesome, lonely, solitary *rel* separated, parted, divorced, severed, sundered; forsaken, deserted, abandoned; wretched, miserable; depressed, weighed down, oppressed **2** *syn* DESPONDENT, hopeless, despairing, desperate *rel* pessimistic, cynical; futile, vain, fruitless

forlornness *syn* DESPONDENCY, hopelessness, despair, desperation *rel* dejection, depression, gloom, melancholy, blues, dumps, sadness

form *n* **1** • outward appearance of something as distinguished from the substance of which it is made *syn* figure, shape, conformation, configuration *rel* contour, outline, profile, silhouette; structure, anatomy, framework, skeleton; organism, system, economy, scheme **2** • conduct regulated by an external control (as custom or a formal protocol of procedure) *syn* formality, ceremony, ceremonial, rite, ritual, liturgy *rel* proceeding, procedure, process; practice, usage, custom, habit; rule, regulation, precept, law, canon; method, mode; decorum, propriety, etiquette **3** • a fixed or accepted way of doing or sometimes of expressing something *syn* usage, convention, convenance

form *vb, syn* MAKE, shape, fashion, fabricate, manufacture, forge *rel* devise, contrive; invent, create; produce, turn out, bear; design, project, scheme, plan, plot; organize, found, establish

formal *syn* CEREMONIAL, conventional, ceremonious, solemn *rel* systematic, methodical, orderly, regular; decorous, proper, seemly *ant* informal

formality *syn* FORM, ceremony, ceremonial, rite, liturgy, ritual *rel* convention, convenance, usage, form; practice, custom, habit, use, wont

former *syn* PRECEDING, prior, previous, antecedent, precedent, foregoing, anterior *ant* latter

formless • having no definite or recognizable form *syn* unformed, shapeless *rel* fluid, liquid; rough, raw, crude, rude

forsake *syn* ABANDON, desert *rel* repudiate, spurn, reject, decline; abdicate, renounce, resign; quit, leave, go *ant* return to; revert to

forswear **1** *syn* ABJURE, renounce, recant, retract *rel* abandon, desert, forsake; repudiate, spurn, reject, decline; deny, contravene, traverse, gainsay **2** *syn* PERJURE

fort • a structure or place offering resistance to a hostile force *syn* fortress, citadel, stronghold, fastness

forth *syn* ONWARD, forward

forthright *syn* STRAIGHTFORWARD, aboveboard *rel* honest, upright, conscientious, just, honorable *ant* furtive

fortify *syn* STRENGTHEN, invigorate, energize, reinforce *rel* rally, stir, arouse, rouse; stimulate, quicken, provoke; renew, restore, refresh *ant* enfeeble

fortitude • a quality of character combining courage and staying power *syn* grit, backbone, pluck, guts, sand *rel* courage, mettle, spirit, resolution, tenacity; bravery, courageousness, intrepidity, dauntlessness, valorousness *ant* pusillanimity

fortress *syn* FORT, citadel, stronghold, fastness

fortuitous *syn* ACCIDENTAL, contingent, casual, incidental *rel* random, haphazard, chance, chancy, hit-or-miss

fortunate *syn* LUCKY, providential, happy *rel* auspicious, propitious, favorable, benign; advantageous, beneficial, profitable; felicitous, happy, fit *ant* unfortunate; disastrous

fortune *syn* CHANCE, accident, luck, hap,

hazard *rel* fate, destiny, lot, portion, doom; opportunity, occasion, break, time

forward *adj, syn* PREMATURE, advanced, untimely, precocious *ant* backward

forward *adv* **1** *syn* BEFORE, ahead *ant* backward **2** *syn* ONWARD, forth *ant* backward

forward *vb* **1** *syn* ADVANCE, promote, further *rel* speed, accelerate, quicken, hasten; help, aid, assist; support, uphold, back, champion *ant* hinder; balk **2** *syn* SEND, dispatch, transmit, remit, route, ship

foster *syn* NURSE, nurture, cherish, cultivate *rel* support, uphold, back, champion; harbor, shelter, entertain, lodge, house; promote, further, forward, advance; favor, accommodate, oblige

foul *adj, syn* DIRTY, filthy, nasty, squalid *rel* putrid, stinking, fetid, noisome, malodorous; offensive, revolting, repulsive, loathsome; obscene, gross, vulgar, coarse *ant* fair; undefiled

foul *vb, syn* SOIL, dirty, sully, tarnish, befoul, smirch, besmirch, grime, begrime *rel* pollute, defile, contaminate; profane, desecrate

found **1** *syn* BASE, ground, bottom, stay, rest *rel* set, fix, settle, establish; sustain, support; build, erect, raise, rear **2** • to set going or to bring into existence *syn* establish, institute, organize, create *rel* begin, commence, start, initiate, inaugurate; form, fashion, make

foundation *syn* BASE, basis, ground, groundwork *ant* superstructure

foxy *syn* SLY, insidious, wily, guileful, tricky, crafty, cunning, artful *rel* devious, crooked, oblique; deceitful, dishonest

fracas *syn* BRAWL, broil, melee, row, rumpus, scrap *rel* fray, affray, fight, conflict, combat, contest; altercation, wrangle, quarrel, squabble; contention, dissension, strife, discord

fraction *syn* PART, fragment, piece, portion, section, segment, sector, detail, member, division, parcel

fractious *syn* IRRITABLE, peevish, snappish, waspish, petulant, pettish, huffy, fretful, querulous *rel* unruly, refractory, recalcitrant, ungovernable, intractable, willful; perverse, contrary, froward, restive, wayward

fragile **1** • easily broken *syn* frangible, brittle, crisp, short, friable *ant* tough **2** *syn* WEAK, frail, feeble, decrepit, infirm *rel* impotent, powerless; delicate, dainty, choice; evanescent, ephemeral, transient, transitory *ant* durable

fragment *syn* PART, fraction, piece, portion, section, segment, sector, division, detail, member, parcel *rel* remnant, remainder

fragrance • a sweet or pleasant odor *syn* perfume, incense, redolence, bouquet *rel* smell, scent, odor, aroma *ant* stench, stink

fragrant *syn* ODOROUS, aromatic, redolent, balmy *rel* delicious, delectable, delightful *ant* fetid

frail *syn* WEAK, fragile, feeble, infirm, decrepit *rel* slight, slender, tenuous, thin, slim; puny, petty; flimsy, sleazy, limp; powerless, impotent *ant* robust

frailty *syn* FAULT, failing, foible, vice *rel* defect, flaw, blemish; infirmity, fragility, feebleness, weakness

frame **1** *syn* BUILD, construct, erect, raise, rear *rel* fabricate, manufacture, fashion, make **2** *syn* CONTRIVE, devise, invent, concoct *rel* plan, scheme, project; conceive, envisage, think

framework *syn* STRUCTURE, skeleton, anatomy

franchise *syn* SUFFRAGE, vote, ballot

frangible *syn* FRAGILE, brittle, crisp, short, friable

frank • marked by free, forthright, and sincere expression *syn* candid, open, plain *rel* ingenuous, naïve, unsophisticated, simple, natural; forthright, downright; straightforward, aboveboard *ant* reticent

frantic *syn* FURIOUS, frenzied, wild, frenetic, delirious, rabid *rel* crazy, crazed, mad, insane; hysterical; irrational, unreasonable

fraud **1** *syn* DECEPTION, trickery, chicanery, chicane, double-dealing *rel* duplicity, deceit, guile, dissimulation; defrauding, swindling, cheating, cozening, overreaching **2** *syn* IMPOSTURE, cheat, sham, fake, humbug, deceit, deception, counterfeit *rel* hoaxing, hoax, bamboozling, bamboozlement, hoodwinking, duping, dupery; trick, ruse, stratagem, maneuver, gambit, ploy, wile, artifice

fray *syn* CONTEST, affray, fight, conflict, combat *rel* fracas, broil, brawl, melee; altercation, wrangle, quarrel; contention, strife, dissension, discord

freak *syn* CAPRICE, fancy, whim, whimsy,

conceit, vagary, crotchet *rel* notion, idea; fancy, fantasy, dream, daydream

freaked *syn* VARIEGATED, parti-colored, motley, checkered, checked, pied, piebald, skewbald, dappled *rel* spotted, flecked, speckled, spattered, sprinkled

free *adj* • not subject to the rule or control of another *syn* independent, sovereign, autonomous, autarchic, autarkic *rel* liberated, emancipated, delivered, freed, released, enfranchised *ant* bond

free *vb* • to relieve from constraint or restraint *syn* release, liberate, emancipate, manumit, discharge *rel* deliver, enfranchise

freebooter *syn* PIRATE, buccaneer, privateer, corsair

freedom **1** • the state or condition of not being subject to external rule or control *syn* independence, autonomy, sovereignty, autarchy, autarky *rel* liberation, emancipation, release, delivery, enfranchisement, manumission; liberty, license *ant* bondage **2** • the power or condition of acting without compulsion *syn* liberty, license *rel* exemption, immunity; scope, range, compass, sweep *ant* necessity

freethinker *syn* ATHEIST, unbeliever, agnostic, deist, infidel

freezing *syn* COLD, frigid, frosty, gelid, icy, glacial, arctic, chilly, cool

freight *syn* LOAD, cargo, burden, lading

frenetic *syn* FURIOUS, frantic, frenzied, wild, delirious, rabid *rel* demented, insane, mad; irrational, unreasonable; provoked, excited, stimulated

frenzied *syn* FURIOUS, frantic, wild, frenetic, delirious, rabid *rel* demented, deranged, insane, crazed, mad; distracted, bewildered

frenzy **1** *syn* MANIA, delirium, hysteria **2** *syn* INSPIRATION, fury, afflatus *rel* ecstasy, rapture, transport

frequently *syn* OFTEN, oft, oftentimes *ant* rarely, seldom

fresh *syn* NEW, novel, new-fashioned, newfangled, modern, modernistic, original *rel* gleaming, glistening, sparkling; virginal, youthful; raw, green, crude, uncouth, rude; naïve, unsophisticated, artless, natural *ant* stale

fret *syn* ABRADE, excoriate, chafe, gall *rel* eat, devour, consume; worry, harass

fretful *syn* IRRITABLE, peevish, petulant, querulous, fractious, snappish, waspish, pettish, huffy *rel* cross, cranky, touchy, choleric, irascible; captious, carping, caviling, faultfinding, critical; contrary, perverse

friable *syn* FRAGILE, short, frangible, crisp, brittle *rel* crumbling, crumbly, disintegrating

friar *syn* RELIGIOUS, monk, nun

friend • a person, esp. not related by blood, with whom one is on good and usu. familiar terms *syn* acquaintance, intimate, confidant *rel* comrade, companion, crony, associate; ally, colleague, partner *ant* foe

friendly *syn* AMICABLE, neighborly *rel* familiar, intimate, close; loving, affectionate, devoted; loyal, true, steadfast, faithful *ant* unfriendly; belligerent

friendship • the relation existing between persons, communities, states, or peoples that are in accord and in sympathy with each other *syn* amity, comity, goodwill *rel* sympathy, affinity, attraction; empathy; accord, concord, consonance, harmony; alliance, league, coalition, fusion, federation *ant* animosity

fright *n, syn* FEAR, alarm, consternation, panic, dread, dismay, terror, horror, trepidation *rel* scaring, scare, startling, affrighting, frightening

fright *vb, syn* FRIGHTEN, scare, alarm, terrify, terrorize, startle, affray, affright *rel* see FRIGHTEN

frighten • to strike or to fill with fear or dread *syn* fright, scare, alarm, terrify, terrorize, startle, affray, affright *rel* appall, horrify, dismay, daunt; intimidate, cow, browbeat, bulldoze; agitate, perturb, upset, disquiet, discompose

frightful *syn* FEARFUL, dreadful, awful, terrible, terrific, horrible, horrific, shocking, appalling *rel* ghastly, grisly, gruesome, macabre, grim, lurid; sinister, baleful, malign

frigid *syn* COLD, freezing, gelid, icy, glacial, arctic, cool, chilly, frosty *ant* torrid (*temperature*); amorous (*persons*)

fritter *syn* WASTE, squander, dissipate, consume *rel* disperse, scatter; dispense, distribute; disburse, spend, expend

frivolity *syn* LIGHTNESS, levity, flippancy, light-mindedness, volatility, flightiness *rel* trifling, flirting, dallying, coquetting, toying; play, sport, fun, jest, game; gaiety, liveliness, vivaciousness, sprightliness *ant* seriousness, staidness

frolic *vb, syn* PLAY, sport, disport, rollick, romp, gambol

frolic *n, syn* PLAY, sport, disport, rollick, romp, gambol *rel* fun, jest, game, play, sport; caper, prank, antic, monkeyshine, dido; levity, lightness, frivolity

frolicsome *syn* PLAYFUL, sportive, roguish, waggish, impish, mischievous *rel* merry, blithe, jocund, jovial, jolly; mirthful, gleeful, hilarious; lively, vivacious, sprightly, gay

frosty *syn* COLD, chilly, cool, frigid, freezing, gelid, icy, glacial, arctic

froth *syn* FOAM, spume, scum, lather, suds, yeast *rel* lightness, levity, frivolity, flippancy

froward *syn* CONTRARY, perverse, balky, restive, wayward *rel* obstinate, stubborn, mulish, pigheaded, stiff-necked; willful, headstrong, refractory, unruly, ungovernable, intractable, recalcitrant; contumacious, insubordinate, rebellious *ant* compliant

frown • to put on a dark or malignant countenance or aspect *syn* scowl, glower, lower, gloom *ant* smile

frowzy *syn* SLATTERNLY, blowsy, dowdy *rel* slovenly, unkempt, disheveled, sloppy, slipshod; squalid, dirty, filthy; negligent, neglectful, lax, slack, remiss *ant* trim; smart

frugal *syn* SPARING, thrifty, economical *rel* careful, meticulous; provident, prudent, discreet; saving, preserving, conserving; parsimonious, cheeseparing, penny-pinching, stingy *ant* wasteful

fruitful *syn* FERTILE, fecund, prolific *rel* reproducing, reproductive, propagating, breeding; bearing, producing, productive, yielding; teeming, abounding; luxuriant, lush, exuberant, profuse *ant* unfruitful; fruitless

fruitfulness *syn* FERTILITY, prolificacy, fecundity

fruition *syn* PLEASURE, enjoyment, delectation, delight, joy *rel* realization, actualization, materialization; fulfillment, accomplishment; attainment, achievement; possession, enjoyment

fruitless *syn* FUTILE, vain, bootless, abortive *rel* unfruitful, barren, infertile, sterile; vain, idle, otiose, nugatory, empty, hollow; frustrated, thwarted, foiled *ant* fruitful

frustrate • to come between a person and his or her aim or desire or to defeat another's plan *syn* thwart, foil, baffle, balk, circumvent, outwit *rel* negative, counteract, neutralize; defeat, beat, overcome, conquer; forbid, prohibit, inhibit; prevent, preclude, obviate; hinder, impede, obstruct, block, bar *ant* fulfill

fuddle *syn* CONFUSE, muddle, addle *rel, ant* see BEFUDDLE

fugitive *syn* TRANSIENT, evanescent, transitory, fleeting, passing, ephemeral, momentary, short-lived

fulfill **1** *syn* PERFORM, effect, achieve, accomplish, execute, discharge *rel* enforce, implement; compass, attain, reach, gain; realize, actualize; finish, complete, close *ant* frustrate; fail (in) **2** *syn* SATISFY, meet, answer *rel* equal, approach, match, touch, rival *ant* fall short (of)

full • containing all that is wanted or needed or possible *syn* complete, plenary, replete *rel* including, inclusive, comprehending, comprehensive; teeming, abounding; glutted, cloyed, gorged, surfeited, sated *ant* empty

fulsome • too obviously extravagant or ingratiating to be accepted as genuine or sincere *syn* oily, unctuous, oleaginous, slick, soapy *rel* lavish, profuse, exuberant; excessive, extravagant; cloying, satiating, sating; bombastic, grandiloquent, magniloquent, rhetorical

fumble *syn* BOTCH, bungle, muff, cobble *rel* blunder, flounder, stumble

fumigate *syn* STERILIZE, disinfect, sanitize

fun • action or speech that is intended to amuse or arouse laughter *syn* jest, sport, game, play *rel* amusement, diversion, recreation, entertainment; merriment, jocundity, blitheness, joviality; mirth, glee, hilarity, jollity

function *n* **1** • acts or operations expected of a person or thing *syn* office, duty, province *rel* end, goal, object, objective, purpose, intention; business, concern, affair; task, job **2** *syn* POWER, faculty *rel* ability, capacity, capability; action, behavior, operation

function *vb, syn* ACT, operate, work, behave, react

fundamental *adj* **1** • forming or affecting

the groundwork, roots, or lowest part of something *syn* basic, basal, underlying, radical *rel* primary, primal, primordial, prime; elementary, elemental **2** *syn* ESSENTIAL, vital, cardinal *rel* requisite, needful, necessary, indispensable; paramount, dominant; principal, capital, foremost, chief **3** *syn* ELEMENTAL, basic, elementary, essential, primitive, underlying

fundamental *n, syn* PRINCIPLE, axiom, law, theorem *rel* element, constituent, component, factor; ground, basis, foundation, base, groundwork

funny *syn* LAUGHABLE, risible, ludicrous, ridiculous, comic, comical, farcical, droll *rel* humorous, witty, jocose, jocular, facetious; amusing, diverting, entertaining; grotesque, bizarre, fantastic, antic

furious • marked by uncontrollable excitement esp. under the stress of a powerful emotion *syn* frantic, frenzied, wild, frenetic, delirious, rabid *rel* excited, stimulated, provoked; infuriated, enraged, maddened; violent, fierce, vehement, intense

furnish **1** *syn* PROVIDE, supply *rel* get, obtain, procure, acquire, secure; prepare, fit, ready, qualify, condition *ant* strip **2** • to supply one with what is needed (as for daily living or a particular activity) *syn* equip, outfit, appoint, accouter, arm *rel* endue, endow, dower; array, apparel, clothe

further *adv , syn* FARTHER, beyond

further *vb, syn* ADVANCE, forward, promote *rel* help, aid, assist; back, champion, support, uphold; propagate, generate, engender; accelerate, speed, hasten, quicken *ant* hinder; retard

furthermore *syn* ALSO, moreover, besides, likewise, too

furtive *syn* SECRET, stealthy, clandestine, surreptitious, underhand, underhanded, covert *rel* sly, cunning, crafty, wily, guileful, artful; cautious, calculating, wary, circumspect; disguised, cloaked, masked *ant* forthright; brazen

furuncle *syn* ABSCESS, boil, carbuncle, pimple, pustule

fury **1** *syn* ANGER, rage, ire, wrath, indignation *rel* passion; exasperation, irritation, aggravation; acrimony, asperity, acerbity **2** *syn* INSPIRATION, frenzy, afflatus

fuse **1** *syn* LIQUEFY, melt, deliquesce, thaw **2** *syn* MIX, amalgamate, merge, coalesce, blend, mingle, commingle *rel* consolidate, unify, compact; unite, combine, conjoin

fusion *syn* ALLIANCE, coalition, league, federation, confederation, confederacy

fuss *syn* STIR, pother, ado, flurry, bustle *rel* agitation, perturbation, disturbance, flustering, fluster; haste, hurry, speed

fussy *syn* NICE, finicky, finicking, finical, particular, persnickety, pernickety, dainty, fastidious, squeamish *rel* exacting, demanding, requiring ; querulous, fretful, irritable

fustian *syn* BOMBAST, rant, rodomontade, rhapsody

fusty *syn* MALODOROUS, musty, rancid, putrid, fetid, stinking, noisome, rank *rel* dirty, squalid, nasty, filthy, foul; slovenly, unkempt, disheveled, sloppy, slipshod

futile • barren of result *syn* vain, fruitless, bootless, abortive *rel* vain, idle, otiose, nugatory; ineffective, ineffectual, inefficacious

G

gab *syn* CHAT, chatter, patter, prate, prattle, babble, gabble, jabber, gibber

gabble *syn* CHAT, babble, gab, chatter, patter, prate, prattle, jabber, gibber

gad *syn* WANDER, stray, roam, ramble, rove, range, prowl, gallivant, traipse, meander

gadget *syn* DEVICE, contraption, contrivance

gag *syn* JOKE, jest, jape, quip, witticism, wisecrack, crack

gain **1** *syn* GET, win, obtain, procure, secure, acquire *rel* achieve, accomplish, effect, perform; endeavor, strive, struggle, attempt, try *ant* forfeit; lose **2** *syn* REACH, compass, achieve, attain *rel, ant* see GAIN 1 **3** *syn* IMPROVE, recover, recuperate, convalesce *rel* progress, advance; cure, heal, remedy; strengthen, invigorate

gainful *syn* PAYING, remunerative, lucrative, profitable *rel* productive, yielding, bearing

gainsay *syn* DENY, contradict, impugn, contravene, negative, traverse *rel* controvert, refute, confute, disprove; oppose, combat, resist, withstand, fight *ant* admit

gall *n, syn* TEMERITY, effrontery, nerve, cheek, hardihood, audacity

gall *vb, syn* ABRADE, chafe, excoriate, fret *rel* injure, hurt, harm, damage; worry, harass

gallant *syn* CIVIL, courtly, chivalrous, courteous, polite *rel* attentive, considerate, thoughtful; spirited, mettlesome, high-spirited; urbane, suave

gallantry **1** *syn* HEROISM, valor, prowess *rel* bravery, intrepidity, valorousness, dauntlessness; courage, mettle, spirit, resolution *ant* dastardliness **2** *syn* COURTESY, attention, amenity *rel* chivalrousness, chivalry, courtliness; deference, homage, honor; suavity, urbanity; address, poise, tact, savoir faire

gallery *syn* PASSAGE, passageway, corridor, arcade, cloister, ambulatory, aisle, hall, hallway

gallivant *syn* WANDER, stray, roam, ramble, rove, range, prowl, gad, traipse, meander

galumph *syn* STUMBLE, trip, blunder, lurch, flounder, lumber, lollop, bumble

galvanize *syn* PROVOKE, excite, stimulate, quicken, pique *rel* rouse, arouse, rally, stir, awaken, waken; electrify, thrill, enthuse; kindle, fire, light

gambit *syn* TRICK, ruse, stratagem, maneuver, ploy, artifice, wile, feint

gambol *n, syn* PLAY, frolic, disport, sport, rollick, romp

gambol *vb, syn* PLAY, frolic, disport, sport, rollick, romp

game **1** *syn* FUN, sport, play, jest *rel* diversion, amusement, recreation, entertainment **2** *pl* **games** *syn* ATHLETICS, sports *rel* contest, conflict

gamut *syn* RANGE, reach, radius, compass, sweep, scope, orbit, horizon, ken, purview

gap *syn* BREAK, interruption, interval, interim, hiatus, lacuna *rel* breach, split, rent, rift; hole, hollow, cavity; division, separation; pass, passage, way

gape *syn* GAZE, stare, glare, gloat, peer *rel* regard, admire; look, watch, see

garbage *syn* REFUSE, waste, offal, rubbish, trash, debris

garble *syn* MISREPRESENT, falsify, belie *rel* distort, contort, warp, deform; misinterpret, misconstrue

gargantuan *syn* HUGE, vast, immense, enormous, elephantine, mammoth, giant, gigantic, gigantean, colossal, Herculean, cyclopean, titanic, Brobdingnagian

garish *syn* GAUDY, tawdry, flashy, meretricious *rel* resplendent, gorgeous, splendid; showy, ostentatious, pretentious *ant* somber

garner *syn* REAP, glean, gather, harvest *rel* amass, accumulate

garnish *syn* ADORN, embellish, beautify, deck, bedeck, decorate, ornament *rel* enhance, heighten, intensify

garrulity, garrulousness *syn* TALKATIVENESS, loquacity, volubility, glibness *rel* verbiage; prolixity, verboseness, diffuseness, wordiness; chattering, prating, babbling, jabbering

garrulous *syn* TALKATIVE, loquacious, voluble, glib *rel* fluent, vocal, articulate, eloquent *ant* taciturn

gasconade *syn* BOAST, vaunt, brag, crow

gastronome *syn* EPICURE, gourmet, gourmand, bon vivant, glutton

gate *syn* DOOR, portal, gateway, postern, doorway

gateway *syn* DOOR, gate, portal, postern, doorway

gather **1** • to come or bring together *syn* collect, assemble, congregate *rel* accumulate, amass, hoard; heap, pile, stack, mass **2** *syn* REAP, glean, garner, harvest *rel* see GATHER 1 **3** *syn* INFER, deduce, conclude, judge

gathering • a number of individuals come or brought together *syn* collection, assemblage, assembly, congregation *rel* crowd, throng, press, horde, mob, rout, crush; accumulation

gauche *syn* AWKWARD, maladroit, clumsy, inept

gaudy • vulgar or cheap in its showiness *syn* tawdry, garish, flashy, meretricious *rel* showy, pretentious, ostentatious; vulgar, coarse, gross; resplendent, gorgeous, splendid *ant* quiet (*in taste or style*)

gauge *syn* STANDARD, criterion, yardstick, touchstone

gaunt *syn* LEAN, rawboned, angular, lank, lanky, spare, scrawny, skinny *rel* cadaverous, wasted, haggard, worn; thin, slim, slender, slight

gay *syn* LIVELY, vivacious, sprightly, animated *rel* merry, blithe, jocund, jovial, jolly; playful, frolicsome, sportive *ant* grave, sober

gaze • to look at long and attentively *syn* gape, stare, glare, peer, gloat *rel* watch, look, see; observe, survey, contemplate; regard, admire

gear *syn* EQUIPMENT, tackle, paraphernalia, outfit, apparatus, machinery *rel* appurtenances, accessories, adjuncts, appendages; possessions, belongings, effects, means

geld *syn* STERILIZE, castrate, spay, emasculate, alter, mutilate

gelid *syn* COLD, icy, frigid, freezing, frosty, glacial, arctic, cool, chilly

general *syn* UNIVERSAL, generic, common *rel* regular, typical, normal, natural

generally *syn* LARGELY, mostly, chiefly, mainly, principally, greatly

generate • to give life or origin to or to bring into existence by or as if by natural processes *syn* engender, breed, beget, get, sire, procreate, propagate, reproduce *rel* bear, produce, yield; teem, abound

generic *syn* UNIVERSAL, general, common *rel* typical, regular, normal; specific, special

generous *syn* LIBERAL, bountiful, bounteous, openhanded, munificent, handsome *rel* lavish, prodigal, profuse, exuberant; benevolent, philanthropic, eleemosynary, charitable, altruistic *ant* stingy

genesis *syn* BEGINNING, rise, initiation *rel* origin, source, root, inception, provenance, provenience; derivation, origination; commencement, start

genial *syn* GRACIOUS, sociable, affable, cordial *rel* kind, kindly, benign, benignant; friendly, neighborly, amicable; jocund, jovial, jolly, blithe, merry; cheerful, happy, glad *ant* saturnine; caustic

genius *syn* GIFT, talent, faculty, aptitude, knack, bent, turn *rel* ability, capacity, capability; originality; inspiration, afflatus

gentle *syn* SOFT, mild, smooth, lenient, bland, balmy *rel* moderate, temperate; pleasant, agreeable, grateful, pleasing, welcome; calm, tranquil, serene, placid, peaceful, halcyon *ant* rough, harsh

gentleman • a person of good or noble birth *syn* patrician, aristocrat *ant* boor

gentry *syn* ARISTOCRACY, county, nobility, elite, society

genuine *syn* AUTHENTIC, bona fide, veritable *rel* true, real, actual; unadulterated, unsophisticated; pure, sheer, absolute; sincere, unfeigned *ant* counterfeit; fraudulent

germane *syn* RELEVANT, pertinent, material, apposite, applicable, apropos *rel* appropriate, fitting, apt, happy, felicitous, fit; akin, analogous, comparable, parallel, like; related, allied, cognate, kindred *ant* foreign

gesticulation *syn* GESTURE

gesture • an expressive movement of the body or the use of such a movement *syn* gesticulation

get **1** • to come into possession of *syn* obtain, procure, secure, acquire, gain, win *rel* fetch, bring; extract, elicit, extort, educe, evoke; receive, accept; seize, take, grasp, grab, clutch; effect, accomplish, achieve; incur, contract, catch **2** *syn* GENERATE, beget, procreate, sire, engender, breed, propagate, reproduce *rel* see BEGET **3** *syn* INDUCE, persuade, prevail *rel* move, actuate, drive, impel; incite, instigate, abet

ghastly • horrifying and repellent in appearance or aspect *syn* grisly, gruesome, macabre, grim, lurid *rel* deathly, deadly; frightful, horrible, horrific, dreadful, fearful, appalling; repellent, repugnant; repulsive, revolting, loathsome, offensive

ghost *syn* APPARITION, spirit, specter, shade, phantasm, phantom, wraith, revenant

giant *syn* HUGE, vast, immense, enormous, elephantine, mammoth, gigantic, gigantean, colossal, gargantuan, Herculean, cyclopean, titanic, Brobdingnagian

gibber *syn* CHAT, prate, chatter, gab, patter, prattle, babble, gabble, jabber

gibberish • speech or actions that are esoteric in nature and suggest the magical, strange, or unknown *syn* mummery, hocus-pocus, abracadabra

gibe *syn* SCOFF, jeer, sneer, flout, gird, fleer *rel* ridicule, deride, mock, taunt, twit, rally

giddy • affected by a sensation of being whirled about or around *syn* dizzy, vertiginous, swimming, dazzled *rel* whirling, reeling; confusing, addling, fuddling, muddling; bewildering, distracting, mystifying; frivolous, flighty

gift 1 • something, often of value but not necessarily material, given freely to another for his benefit or pleasure *syn* present, gratuity, favor, boon, largess *rel* donation, benefaction, contribution, alms **2** • a special ability or a capacity for a definite kind of activity or achievement *syn* faculty, aptitude, genius, talent, knack, bent, turn *rel* endowment, dowry; power, faculty, function; acquirement, attainment, accomplishment, acquisition

gigantic, gigantean *syn* HUGE, vast, immense, enormous, elephantine, mammoth, giant, colossal, gargantuan, Herculean, cyclopean, titanic, Brobdingnagian *rel* prodigious, stupendous, tremendous, monstrous, monumental

gingery *syn* SPIRITED, fiery, peppery, high-spirited, mettlesome, spunky

gird *vb, syn* SURROUND, environ, encircle, circle, encompass, compass, hem, girdle, ring *rel* enclose, envelop, wall; confine, circumscribe, limit

gird *vb, syn* SCOFF, sneer, flout, jeer, gibe, fleer *rel* deride, mock, taunt, twit, rally, ridicule

girdle *syn* SURROUND, environ, encircle, circle, encompass, compass, hem, gird, ring *rel* see GIRD (to surround)

gist *syn* SUBSTANCE, purport, burden, core, pith *rel* center, heart, nucleus; import, significance; theme, topic, subject

give • to convey something or make something over or available to another *syn* present, donate, bestow, confer, afford *rel* award, accord, vouchsafe, grant, concede; assign, allot, apportion, allocate; distribute, dispense, deal, dole

glacial *syn* COLD, arctic, icy, gelid, frigid, freezing, frosty, cool, chilly

glad • characterized by or expressing the mood of one who is pleased or delighted *syn* happy, cheerful, lighthearted, joyful, joyous *rel* pleased, delighted, gratified, tickled, rejoiced; blithe, jocund, merry, jolly, jovial; gleeful, mirthful, hilarious *ant* sad

gladden *syn* PLEASE, delight, rejoice, gratify, tickle, regale *rel* comfort, console, solace; enliven, animate, quicken, vivify *ant* sadden

glance *vb* **1** *syn* BRUSH, graze, shave, skim *rel* slide, slip, glide; touch, contact; dart, fly **2** *syn* FLASH, glint, gleam, sparkle, glitter, glisten, scintillate, coruscate, twinkle

glance *n, syn* LOOK, glimpse, peep, peek, sight, view

glare *vb* **1** *syn* BLAZE, glow, flare, flame *rel* flash, gleam, glitter, glisten, scintillate, coruscate, sparkle **2** *syn* GAZE, stare, peer, gloat, gape *rel* glower, lower, scowl, frown

glare *n, syn* BLAZE, flare, glow, flame *rel* effulgence, refulgence, radiance, brilliance; glittering, glitter, sparkling, sparkle, flashing, flash

glaring *syn* FLAGRANT, gross, rank *rel* noticeable, conspicuous, outstanding; obtrusive, impertinent; extreme, excessive, inordinate

glaze *syn* LUSTER, gloss, sheen

gleam *syn* FLASH, glance, glint, sparkle, glitter, glisten, scintillate, coruscate, twinkle

glean *syn* REAP, gather, garner, harvest *rel* pick, choose; strip, divest

glee *syn* MIRTH, jollity, hilarity *rel* delight, joy, pleasure, enjoyment, delectation; merriment, jocundity, blitheness, joviality; gladness, happiness, cheerfulness, joyfulness, joyousness *ant* gloom

glib 1 *syn* VOCAL, fluent, voluble, articulate, eloquent *rel* garrulous, loquacious, voluble, talkative; facile, smooth, effortless, easy **2** *syn* TALKATIVE, loquacious, garrulous, voluble

glibness *syn* TALKATIVENESS, loquacity, garrulity, volubility

glide *syn* SLIDE, slip, skid, glissade, slither, coast, toboggan *rel* float, fly, skim, scud, sail, shoot

glimpse *syn* LOOK, glance, peep, peek, sight, view

glint *syn* FLASH, glance, gleam, sparkle, glitter, glisten, scintillate, coruscate, twinkle

glissade *syn* SLIDE, glide, slip, skid, slither, coast, toboggan

glisten *syn* FLASH, sparkle, glitter, gleam, glance, glint, scintillate, coruscate, twinkle

glitter *syn* FLASH, glisten, sparkle, gleam, glance, glint, scintillate, coruscate, twinkle

gloat *syn* GAZE, gape, stare, glare, peer
globe *syn* EARTH, world, planet
gloom *vb, syn* FROWN, lower, glower, scowl
gloom *n, syn* SADNESS, dejection, depression, melancholy, melancholia, blues, dumps *rel* despondency, forlornness, hopelessness, despair, desperation *ant* glee
gloomy **1** *syn* DARK, murky, obscure, dim, dusky *ant* brilliant **2** *syn* SULLEN, glum, morose, saturnine, dour, surly, sulky, crabbed *rel* depressed, weighed down, oppressed *ant* cheerful
glorify *syn* DIGNIFY, ennoble, honor *rel* extol, laud, acclaim, praise; exalt, magnify
glorious *syn* SPLENDID, resplendent, sublime, superb, gorgeous *rel* radiant, brilliant, effulgent, lustrous, bright; transcendent, superlative, surpassing, peerless, supreme; illustrious, renowned, eminent, famous *ant* inglorious
glory *syn* FAME, renown, honor, celebrity, éclat, reputation, repute, notoriety *ant* ignominy, shame
gloss *n, syn* LUSTER, sheen, glaze *rel* sleekness, slickness, glossiness
gloss *vb, syn* PALLIATE, gloze, extenuate, whitewash, whiten *rel* disguise, cloak, mask, dissemble, camouflage; rationalize, account, justify, explain
gloss *n, syn* ANNOTATION *rel* commentary, comment, note, remark, observation
gloss *vb, syn* ANNOTATE *rel* interpret, construe, explain, elucidate, expound, explicate
glossy *syn* SLEEK, slick, velvety, silken, silky, satiny *rel* lustrous, bright, brilliant, lucent, lambent
glow *vb, syn* BLAZE, flame, flare, glare *rel* burn; kindle, ignite, light; illuminate, lighten, illumine
glow *n, syn* BLAZE, flame, flare, glare *rel* brightness, brilliance, radiance, effulgence, luminosity, incandescence; fervor, ardor, passion
glower *syn* FROWN, lower, scowl, gloom *rel* glare, stare, gaze; watch, look, see
gloze *syn* PALLIATE, gloss, whitewash, extenuate, whiten *rel* condone, excuse; justify, rationalize, explain, account; dissemble, cloak, mask, disguise, camouflage
glum *syn* SULLEN, gloomy, morose, saturnine, dour, surly, sulky, crabbed *rel* silent, taciturn, close-lipped, tight-lipped; depressed, weighed down, oppressed; scowling, frowning, lowering, glowering, glooming *ant* cheerful
glut *syn* SATIATE, gorge, surfeit, sate, cloy, pall
glutton *syn* EPICURE, gourmand, gastronome, bon vivant, gourmet
gluttonous *syn* VORACIOUS, ravenous, ravening, rapacious *rel* greedy, covetous, grasping *ant* abstemious
gnash *syn* BITE, gnaw, champ *rel* grind, grate, rasp, scrape; strike, smite
gnaw *syn* BITE, champ, gnash *rel* fret, abrade; worry, annoy
go *vb* **1** • to move out of or away from where one is *syn* leave, depart, quit, withdraw, retire *rel* escape, decamp, abscond, flee, fly *ant* come **2** *syn* RESORT, refer, apply, turn
go *n, syn* SPELL, shift, tour, trick, turn, stint, bout
goad *n, syn* MOTIVE, spur, incentive, inducement, spring, impulse *rel* impelling, impulsion, driving, drive; urge, lust, passion, desire *ant* curb
goad *vb, syn* URGE, egg, exhort, spur, prod, prick, sic *rel* drive, impel, move; coerce, compel, constrain, force; incite, instigate; worry, harass
goal *syn* INTENTION, objective, object, end, aim, intent, purpose, design *rel* limit, bound, confine, end, term; aspiration, ambition
gob *syn* MARINER, sailor, seaman, tar, bluejacket
gobbledygook *syn* NONSENSE, twaddle, drivel, bunk, balderdash, poppycock, trash, rot, bull
godless *syn* IRRELIGIOUS, ungodly, unreligious, nonreligious *rel* atheistic, agnostic, infidel
good • in accordance with one's standard of what is satisfactory *syn* right *ant* bad; poor
good-looking *syn* BEAUTIFUL, comely, pretty, bonny, fair, beauteous, pulchritudinous, handsome, lovely *rel* attractive, alluring, charming; pleasing, pleasant, agreeable
good-natured *syn* AMIABLE, obliging, complaisant *rel* compliant, acquiescent; kindly, kind; altruistic, benevolent, charitable *ant* contrary
goodness • moral excellence *syn* virtue, rectitude, morality *rel* righteousness, no-

bility, virtuousness; honesty, integrity, probity, honor *ant* badness, evil

good sense *syn* SENSE

goodwill *syn* FRIENDSHIP, amity, comity *ant* animosity

gorge *syn* SATIATE, surfeit, sate, glut, cloy, pall

gorgeous *syn* SPLENDID, resplendent, glorious, sublime, superb *rel* luxurious, sumptuous, opulent; showy, ostentatious, pretentious

gory *syn* BLOODY, sanguinary, sanguine, sanguineous

gossip *n, syn* REPORT, rumor, hearsay *rel* talk, conversation; tattling, blabbing

gossip *vb* • to disclose something, often of questionable veracity, that is better kept to oneself *syn* blab, tattle

gourmand *syn* EPICURE, glutton, gastronome, bon vivant, gourmet

gourmet *syn* EPICURE, bon vivant, gastronome, gourmand, glutton

govern • to exercise sovereign authority *syn* rule *rel* conduct, direct, control, manage; restrain, curb, inhibit

grab *syn* TAKE, grasp, clutch, seize, snatch *rel* catch, capture

grace **1** *syn* MERCY, clemency, lenity, charity *rel* kindliness, kindness, benignity, benignancy; tenderness, compassionateness, responsiveness; indulgence, forbearance, leniency **2** *syn* ELEGANCE, dignity *rel* loveliness, beautifulness, beauty, fairness, comeliness; suppleness, litheness, lithesomeness, lissomeness; attractiveness, alluringness, allurement, charmingness, charm

gracious • marked by kindly courtesy *syn* cordial, affable, genial, sociable *rel* obliging, complaisant, amiable; benignant, benign, kindly, kind; courteous, courtly, chivalrous, civil *ant* ungracious

gradate *syn* CLASS, grade, rank, rate, graduate *rel* order, arrange; divide, separate; classify, assort, sort; differentiate, discriminate, demarcate, distinguish

gradation • difference or variation between two things that are nearly alike *syn* shade, nuance *rel* difference, divergence, distinction, dissimilarity; variation, modification, change

grade *syn* CLASS, rank, rate, graduate, gradate *rel* order, arrange; divide, separate; assort, sort, classify

graduate *syn* CLASS, grade, rank, rate, gradate *rel* order, arrange; divide, separate; distinguish, differentiate, demarcate, discriminate

grand • large, handsome, dignified, and impressive *syn* magnificent, imposing, stately, majestic, august, noble, grandiose *rel* sumptuous, luxurious, opulent; sublime, superb, splendid, gorgeous; monumental, tremendous, stupendous, prodigious, monstrous

grandiloquent *syn* RHETORICAL, magniloquent, aureate, flowery, euphuistic, bombastic *rel* grandiose, imposing, grand; inflated, turgid, tumid

grandiose *syn* GRAND, imposing, stately, august, magnificent, majestic, noble *rel* ostentatious, pretentious, showy; grandiloquent, magniloquent, rhetorical

grant *vb* **1** • to give as a favor or as a right *syn* concede, vouchsafe, accord, award *rel* bestow, confer, give, present, donate; allot, assign, apportion, allocate; cede, yield, surrender, relinquish **2** • to admit something in question, esp. a contention of one's opponent in an argument *syn* concede, allow *rel* admit, acknowledge; agree, concur, coincide

grant *n, syn* APPROPRIATION, subvention, subsidy *rel* donation, benefaction, contribution

graph *n, syn* CHART, map *rel* plot, scheme, design, plan; diagram, outline, sketch

graph *vb, syn* CHART, map *rel* see GRAPH *n*

graphic • giving a clear visual impression esp. in words *syn* vivid, picturesque, pictorial *rel* lucid, perspicuous, clear; clear-cut, incisive; telling, convincing, compelling, cogent, valid

grapple *syn* WRESTLE, tussle, scuffle *rel* battle, fight, contend; vie, compete, rival; oppose, combat, resist

grasp *vb, syn* TAKE, clutch, grab, seize, snatch *rel* catch, capture; apprehend, arrest; comprehend

grasp *n, syn* HOLD, grip, clutch *rel* control, power, sway; comprehension, understanding, appreciation

grasping *syn* COVETOUS, greedy, avaricious, acquisitive *rel* rapacious, ravening, ravenous, voracious; extorting, extortionate

grate *syn* SCRAPE, scratch, rasp, grind *rel*

abrade, chafe, gall; harass, annoy, harry, worry; offend, outrage; exasperate, irritate

grateful **1** • feeling or expressing gratitude *syn* thankful *rel* appreciating, appreciative, valuing, prizing, cherishing; gratified, pleased, delighted; satisfied, contented *ant* ungrateful **2** *syn* PLEASANT, agreeable, gratifying, pleasing, welcome *rel* comforting, consoling, solacing; refreshing, restoring, restorative, renewing, rejuvenating; delicious, delightful, delectable *ant* obnoxious

gratify *syn* PLEASE, delight, rejoice, gladden, tickle, regale *rel* content, satisfy; indulge, humor, pamper *ant* anger; offend, affront; disappoint

gratifying *syn* PLEASANT, grateful, agreeable, pleasing, welcome *rel* satisfying, contenting; delighting, rejoicing, gladdening, regaling

gratuitous *syn* SUPEREROGATORY, uncalled-for, wanton *rel* voluntary, willing; unrecompensed, unremunerated; unprovoked, unexcited; unjustified, unwarranted

gratuity *syn* GIFT, largess, boon, favor, present

grave *syn* SERIOUS, solemn, somber, sedate, sober, earnest, staid *rel* austere, stern, ascetic, severe; saturnine, dour, sullen *ant* gay

graze *vb, syn* FEED, pasture, nourish

graze *vb, syn* BRUSH, glance, shave, skim *rel* touch, contact; injure, hurt, harm; deface, disfigure; wound, bruise, contuse

grease *syn* OIL, lubricate, anoint, cream

great *syn* LARGE, big *rel* enormous, immense, huge, mammoth; tremendous, prodigious, stupendous, monumental, monstrous; eminent, illustrious, renowned, famous; supreme, superlative, surpassing, transcendent *ant* little

greatly *syn* LARGELY, mostly, chiefly, mainly, principally, generally

greed *syn* CUPIDITY, rapacity, avarice *rel* greediness, covetousness, avariciousness, acquisitiveness; voraciousness, ravenousness, rapaciousness, gluttonousness, gluttony

greedy *syn* COVETOUS, acquisitive, grasping, avaricious *rel* rapacious, ravening, ravenous, voracious, gluttonous; stingy, parsimonious, miserly, close, closefisted

green *syn* RUDE, callow, raw, crude, rough, uncouth *ant* experienced; seasoned

greet *syn* ADDRESS, salute, hail, accost

greeting • the ceremonial words or acts of one who meets, welcomes, or formally addresses another *syn* salutation, salute

gregarious *syn* SOCIAL, cooperative, convivial, companionable, hospitable

grief *syn* SORROW, anguish, woe, heartache, heartbreak, regret *rel* mourning, grieving, sorrowing; lamenting, lamentation, bewailing, bemoaning, deploring

grievance *syn* INJUSTICE, wrong, injury *rel* hardship, rigor, difficulty; trial, tribulation, affliction, cross

grieve • to feel or express sorrow or grief *syn* mourn, sorrow *rel* suffer, bear, endure; lament, bemoan, bewail, deplore; cry, weep, wail, keen *ant* rejoice

grim **1** • being extremely obdurate or firm in action or purpose *syn* implacable, relentless, unrelenting, merciless *rel* inexorable, obdurate, adamant, inflexible; inevitable, certain; fierce, ferocious, cruel, fell; malignant, malevolent, malicious *ant* lenient **2** *syn* GHASTLY, grisly, gruesome, macabre, lurid *rel* fierce, truculent, savage; repellent, repugnant; repulsive, revolting, loathsome, offensive

grime *syn* SOIL, dirty, sully, tarnish, foul, befoul, smirch, besmirch, begrime *rel* pollute, defile, contaminate

grin *vb, syn* SMILE, smirk, simper

grin *n, syn* SMILE, smirk, simper

grind *vb, syn* SCRAPE, scratch, grate, rasp *rel* abrade; sharpen; press, bear, squeeze; gnash, gnaw, bite

grind *n, syn* WORK, drudgery, toil, travail, labor *rel* pains, trouble, exertion, effort

grip *syn* HOLD, grasp, clutch *rel* tenaciousness, toughness, stoutness; power, force; duress, coercion, restraint, constraint, force

grisly *syn* GHASTLY, gruesome, macabre, grim, lurid *rel* horrific, horrible, horrendous, horrid; uncanny, eerie, weird

grit *syn* FORTITUDE, pluck, backbone, guts, sand *rel* courage, resolution, tenacity, mettle, spirit *ant* faintheartedness

groan *vb, syn* SIGH, moan, sob *rel* wail, weep, cry; lament, bemoan, bewail, deplore

groan *n, syn* SIGH, moan, sob

gross **1** *syn* WHOLE, total, entire, all *ant* net **2** *syn* COARSE, vulgar, obscene, ribald *rel* fleshly, carnal, sensual, animal; material, physical, corporeal; loathsome, offensive, revolting, repulsive *ant* delicate, dainty; ethereal **3** *syn* FLAGRANT, glaring, rank *rel* extreme, excessive, inordinate, immoderate, exorbitant; outrageous, atrocious, monstrous, heinous *ant* petty

grotesque *syn* FANTASTIC, bizarre, antic *rel* baroque, rococo, flamboyant, ornate; weird, eerie, uncanny; extravagant, extreme, excessive; preposterous, absurd, foolish; ludicrous, ridiculous, comical, comic, droll, laughable

ground *n* **1** *syn* BASE, basis, foundation, groundwork *rel* background, backdrop **2** *syn* REASON, argument, proof *rel* evidence, testimony; determinant, cause, antecedent; demonstration, proof, trial, test **3** *pl* **grounds** *syn* DEPOSIT, precipitate, sediment, dregs, lees

ground *vb, syn* BASE, found, bottom, stay, rest *rel* establish, fix, settle, set; implant; sustain, support, buttress

groundless *syn* BASELESS, unfounded, unwarranted *rel* unsupported, unsustained

groundwork *syn* BASE, foundation, basis, ground *ant* superstructure

group • a collection or assemblage of persons or things *syn* cluster, bunch, parcel, lot *rel* company, party, band, troop, troupe; set, circle, coterie, clique; crowd, mob, horde

grovel *syn* WALLOW, welter *rel* fawn, cringe, cower, toady, truckle; crawl, creep; abase, demean, humble

growl *syn* BARK, bay, howl, snarl, yelp, yap *rel* threaten, menace; irritate

grown-up *syn* MATURE, adult, matured, ripe, mellow *ant* childish; callow

grub *syn* DIG, delve, spade, excavate

grudge *vb, syn* COVET, begrudge, envy *rel* deny; refuse, decline

grudge *n, syn* MALICE, ill will, malevolence, spite, despite, malignity, malignancy, spleen *rel* animus, antipathy, animosity, rancor, enmity; hate, hatred; grievance, injustice, injury

gruesome *syn* GHASTLY, macabre, grisly, grim, lurid *rel* daunting, appalling, horrifying; horrendous, horrific, horrible; baleful, sinister

gruff *syn* BLUFF, crusty, brusque, blunt, curt *rel* surly, morose, sullen, saturnine, crabbed, dour; churlish, boorish; truculent, fierce

guarantee • an assurance for the fulfillment of a condition or a person who provides such assurance *syn* guaranty, surety, security, bond, bail *rel* pledge, earnest, token; guarantor, surety , sponsor

guarantor *syn* SPONSOR, surety, patron, backer, angel *rel* guarantee

guaranty *syn* GUARANTEE, surety, security, bond, bail *rel* pledge, earnest, token; contract, bargain

guard *syn* DEFEND, shield, protect, safeguard *rel* watch, attend, tend, mind; convoy, escort, chaperon, conduct, accompany

guerdon *syn* PREMIUM, reward, meed, bounty, award, prize, bonus

guess *vb, syn* CONJECTURE, surmise *rel* speculate, think, reason; imagine, fancy; gather, infer, deduce; estimate, reckon, calculate

guess *n, syn* CONJECTURE, surmise *rel* hypothesis, theory; belief, opinion, view *ant* certainty

guest *syn* VISITOR, caller, visitant

guide • to put or lead on a course or into the way to be followed *syn* lead, steer, pilot, engineer *rel* conduct, convoy, escort, chaperon, accompany; direct, manage, control, conduct *ant* misguide

guile *syn* DECEIT, duplicity, dissimulation, cunning *rel* trickery, double-dealing, chicanery, chicane, deception; craft, artifice, art *ant* ingenuousness; candor

guileful *syn* SLY, cunning, crafty, tricky, foxy, insidious, wily, artful

guilt *syn* BLAME, culpability, fault *rel* sin, crime, offense; responsibility, answerability, liability *ant* innocence; guiltlessness

guilty *syn* BLAMEWORTHY, culpable *rel* responsible, answerable, accountable; indicted, impeached, incriminated, accused *ant* innocent

gulf • a hollow place of vast width and depth *syn* chasm, abysm, abyss

gull *syn* DUPE, befool, trick, hoax, hoodwink, bamboozle *rel* delude, beguile, deceive, mislead, double-cross, betray

gullibility *syn* CREDULITY *ant* astuteness

gullible *syn* CREDULOUS *rel* duped, befooled, hoaxed, hoodwinked; deluded, beguiled, deceived, misled; impressionable, susceptible, sentient *ant* astute

gumption *syn* SENSE, common sense, good sense, judgment, wisdom *rel* sagaciousness, sagacity, shrewdness, perspicaciousness, perspicacity, astuteness

gunman *syn* ASSASSIN, cutthroat, bravo

gush *syn* POUR, stream, sluice *rel* flow, stream, flood; spring, issue, emanate

gusto *syn* TASTE, relish, zest, palate *rel* enjoyment, delight, delectation, pleasure; enthusiasm, fervor, ardor, passion, zeal

gut 1 *syn* ABDOMEN, belly, stomach, paunch **2** *pl* **guts** *syn* FORTITUDE, grit, pluck, backbone, sand *rel* tenacity, resolution, mettle, spirit, courage

gyrate *syn* TURN, rotate, revolve, spin, whirl, wheel, circle, twirl, eddy, swirl, pirouette

H

habit 1 • a mode of behaving or doing that has become fixed by constant repetition *syn* habitude, practice, usage, custom, use, wont *rel* instinct; convention, convenance, usage, form **2** *syn* PHYSIQUE, build, constitution *rel* body, carcass; structure, anatomy, framework; figure, form, shape; outline, contour

habitat • the place in which a particular kind of organism lives or grows *syn* biotope, range, station

habitation • the place where one lives *syn* dwelling, abode, residence, domicile, home, house

habitual *syn* USUAL, customary, wonted, accustomed *rel* habituated, addicted; practiced, drilled; confirmed, inveterate, chronic, deep-seated, deep-rooted *ant* occasional

habituate • to make used to something *syn* accustom, addict, inure *rel* train, discipline, school, teach; harden, season, acclimatize, acclimate; practice, exercise, drill

habitude *syn* HABIT, practice, usage, custom, use, wont *rel* attitude, stand, position; state, condition, situation

habitué *syn* ADDICT, votary, devotee

hack *syn* MERCENARY, hireling, venal *rel* toiling, drudging, grinding, laboring; hired, employed; mean, abject, sordid

hackneyed *syn* TRITE, stereotyped, threadbare, shopworn *rel* antiquated, archaic, obsolete, antediluvian, old; worn, wasted, haggard; attenuated, diluted, thin

Hadean *syn* INFERNAL, chthonian, Tartarean, stygian, hellish, chthonic

haggard • thin and drawn by or as if by worry, fatigue, hunger, or illness *syn* worn, careworn, pinched, wasted, cadaverous *rel* gaunt, scrawny, skinny, lean; fatigued, exhausted, wearied, fagged, jaded, tired; wan, pallid, ashen, pale

hail *syn* ADDRESS, salute, greet, accost

halcyon *syn* CALM, serene, placid, tranquil, peaceful

hale *adj, syn* HEALTHY, robust, sound, wholesome, well *rel* lusty, vigorous; sturdy, stalwart, strong, stout; spry, agile *ant* infirm

hale *vb, syn* PULL, haul, draw, drag, tug, tow

hall, hallway *syn* PASSAGE, passageway, corridor, gallery, arcade, cloister, aisle, ambulatory

hallow *syn* DEVOTE, consecrate, dedicate

hallucination *syn* DELUSION, mirage, illusion *rel* apparition, phantasm, phantom, wraith; fantasy, fancy, vision, dream, nightmare

hamper • to hinder or impede in moving, progressing, or acting freely *syn* trammel, clog, fetter, shackle, manacle, hog-tie *rel* hinder, impede, obstruct, block, bar; embarrass, discomfit; baffle, balk, thwart, foil, frustrate *ant* assist (*persons*); expedite (*work, projects*)

hand *syn* WORKER, operative, workman, workingman, laborer, craftsman, handicraftsman, mechanic, artisan, roustabout

handicap 1 *syn* ADVANTAGE, allowance, odds, edge **2** *syn* DISADVANTAGE, detriment, drawback *rel* burden, encumbrance, load; disability, inability; impediment, obstacle *ant* asset, advantage

handicraft *syn* TRADE, craft, art, profession

handicraftsman *syn* WORKER, craftsman, workman, artisan, mechanic, workingman, laborer, operative, hand, roustabout

handle 1 • to deal with or manage usu. with dexterity or efficiency *syn* manipulate, wield, swing, ply *rel* swing, flourish, brandish, shake, wave; direct, aim, point, level, train, lay **2** *syn* TREAT, deal *rel* manage, control, conduct, direct **3** *syn* TOUCH, feel, palpate, paw *rel* inspect, examine, scrutinize; try, test, prove

handsome **1** *syn* LIBERAL, generous, bountiful, bounteous, openhanded, munificent *rel* lavish, prodigal, profuse **2** *syn* BEAUTIFUL, pulchritudinous, beauteous, comely, good-looking, lovely, pretty, bonny, fair *rel* majestic, stately, august, noble, grand; elegant, exquisite, choice; smart, modish, fashionable, stylish

handy *syn* DEXTEROUS, deft, adroit *rel* adept, skillful, skilled, proficient; able, capable, competent

hang **1** • to place or be placed so as to be supported at one point or side usu. at the top *syn* suspend, sling, dangle *rel* stick, adhere, cling; hover, flit **2** *syn* DEPEND, hinge, turn

hanger-on *syn* PARASITE, sycophant, leech, sponge, sponger, favorite, toady, lickspittle, bootlicker

hanker *syn* LONG, yearn, pine, hunger, thirst *rel* crave, desire, covet, wish, want; aspire, pant, aim

hap *syn* CHANCE, fortune, luck, accident, hazard *rel* fate, destiny, lot, portion

haphazard *syn* RANDOM, chance, chancy, casual, desultory, hit-or-miss, happy-go-lucky *rel* accidental, fortuitous, casual

hapless *syn* UNLUCKY, disastrous, ill-starred, ill-fated, unfortunate, calamitous, luckless *rel* unhappy, infelicitous, unfit; miserable, wretched

happen • to come to pass or to come about *syn* chance, occur, befall, betide, transpire

happiness • a state of well-being or pleasurable satisfaction *syn* felicity, beatitude, blessedness, bliss *rel* contentedness, content, satisfiedness, satisfaction; pleasure, enjoyment, delight, delectation, joy, fruition *ant* unhappiness

happy **1** *syn* LUCKY, fortunate, providential *rel* accidental, incidental, fortuitous, casual; favorable, auspicious, propitious, benign; opportune, timely, seasonable *ant* unhappy **2** *syn* FIT, felicitous, apt, appropriate, fitting, suitable, meet, proper *rel* effective, efficacious, efficient, effectual; telling, cogent, convincing, valid; pat, seasonable, well-timed; right, correct, nice *ant* unhappy **3** *syn* GLAD, cheerful, lighthearted, joyful, joyous *rel* contented, satisfied; gratified, delighted, pleased, gladdened, rejoiced *ant* unhappy; disconsolate

happy-go-lucky *syn* RANDOM, haphazard, hit-or-miss, chance, chancy, casual, desultory

harangue *syn* SPEECH, oration, address, lecture, talk, sermon, homily *rel* rant, rodomontade, bombast

harass *syn* WORRY, harry, annoy, plague, pester, tease, tantalize *rel* bait, badger, hound, ride, hector, chivy, heckle; vex, irk, bother, annoy

harbinger *syn* FORERUNNER, precursor, herald

harbor *n* • a place where seacraft may ride secure *syn* haven, port

harbor *vb* • to provide with shelter or refuge *syn* shelter, entertain, lodge, house, board *rel* foster, cherish, nurture, nurse; hide, conceal, secrete; protect, shield, defend

hard **1** *syn* FIRM, solid *rel* compact, dense, close; consolidated, compacted, concentrated; hardened, indurated, callous *ant* soft **2** • demanding great toil or effort *syn* difficult, arduous *rel* onerous, burdensome, oppressive, exacting; intricate, knotty, complicated, involved, complex; exhausting, fatiguing, wearying, tiring *ant* easy

harden **1** • to make or to become physically hard or solid *syn* solidify, indurate, petrify, cake *rel* compact, consolidate, concentrate; compress, condense, contract *ant* soften **2** • to make proof against hardship, strain, or exposure *syn* season, acclimatize, acclimate *rel* habituate, accustom, inure; adapt, adjust, accommodate *ant* soften

hardened • grown or become hard *syn* indurated, callous *rel* consolidated, compacted, concentrated *ant* softened.

hardihood *syn* TEMERITY, audacity, effrontery, nerve, cheek, gall *rel* boldness, intrepidity; brazenness, impudence, brashness; guts, sand, grit, pluck, fortitude

hardship *syn* DIFFICULTY, rigor, vicissitude *rel* adversity, misfortune, mischance; peril, danger, jeopardy, hazard; trial, tribulation, affliction; toil, travail, drudgery, work

harm *n, syn* INJURY, damage, hurt, mischief *rel* detrimentalness, detriment, deleteriousness, perniciousness, noxiousness; misfortune, mischance, mishap; impairing, impairment, marring *ant* benefit

harm *vb, syn* INJURE, impair, hurt, damage, mar, spoil *rel* abuse, maltreat, mistreat, misuse; ruin, dilapidate; discommode, incommode, inconvenience; sap, undermine, weaken *ant* benefit

harmless • not having hurtful or injurious qualities *syn* innocuous, innocent, inoffensive, unoffending *ant* harmful

harmonize 1 *syn* AGREE, accord, correspond, square, conform, tally, jibe *rel* reconcile, adjust, adapt, accommodate; match, equal, approach, touch, rival *ant* clash; conflict **2** • to bring into consonance or accord *syn* tune, attune *rel* adjust, reconcile, adapt

harmony 1 • the effect produced when different things come together without clashing or disagreement *syn* consonance, accord, concord *rel* integration, articulation, concatenation; congruousness, congruity, consonance, compatibility; concurrence, agreement *ant* conflict **2** *syn* SYMMETRY, proportion, balance *rel* grace, elegance, dignity; unity, integrity

harry *syn* WORRY, harass, annoy, plague, pester, tease, tantalize *rel* torment, torture, rack, afflict, try; trouble, distress; bait, badger, hound, ride, hector; fret, gall, chafe, abrade

harsh *syn* ROUGH, rugged, scabrous, uneven *rel* repellent, repugnant, distasteful, abhorrent, obnoxious; coarse, gross; strident, vociferous, blatant; rigorous, strict, stringent, rigid *ant* pleasant; mild

harvest *syn* REAP, glean, gather, garner *rel* collect, assemble; accumulate, amass, hoard

haste • rapidity of motion or action *syn* hurry, speed, expedition, dispatch *rel* celerity, alacrity, legerity; rapidity, swiftness, quickness, expeditiousness; readiness, promptness; agility, briskness *ant* deliberation

hasten *syn* SPEED, accelerate, quicken, hurry, precipitate *ant* delay

hasty 1 *syn* FAST, speedy, quick, expeditious, rapid, swift, fleet *rel* agile, brisk, nimble; hurried, quickened **2** *syn* PRECIPITATE, headlong, abrupt, impetuous, sudden

hate *n, syn* ABHORRENCE, hatred, detestation, abomination, loathing *rel* antipathy, aversion; animosity, rancor, hostility, enmity; despite, contempt, scorn, disdain *ant* love

hate *vb* • to feel extreme enmity or dislike *syn* detest, abhor, abominate, loathe *rel* despise, contemn, scorn, disdain; disapprove, deprecate *ant* love

hateful • deserving of or arousing hate *syn* odious, abhorrent, detestable, abominable *rel* antipathetic, unsympathetic, averse; repellent, repugnant, obnoxious, distasteful *ant* lovable; sympathetic

hatred *syn* ABHORRENCE, hate, detestation, abomination, loathing *rel* animosity, enmity, hostility, rancor; aversion, antipathy; malevolence, malignity, malignancy, ill will, despite, malice; envy, jealousy

haughty *syn* PROUD, arrogant, insolent, lordly, overbearing, supercilious, disdainful *rel* aloof, detached, indifferent; vain, vainglorious, proud; contemptuous, scornful *ant* lowly

haul *syn* PULL, hale, draw, drag, tug, tow *rel* move, remove, shift; lift, raise, hoist, heave, boost, elevate; convey, transport, carry

have • to keep, control, or experience as one's own *syn* hold, own, possess, enjoy

haven *syn* HARBOR, port *rel* asylum, refuge, retreat, shelter, cover

havoc *syn* RUIN, devastation, destruction *rel* calamity, cataclysm, catastrophe, disaster; ravaging, pillaging, despoiling

hazard *n* **1** *syn* CHANCE, accident, fortune, luck, hap **2** *syn* DANGER, jeopardy, peril, risk *rel* possibility, probability, likelihood; contingency, exigency, emergency, juncture

hazard *vb, syn* VENTURE, risk, chance, jeopardize, endanger, imperil *rel* dare, beard, face; confront, encounter, meet; expose, open, subject

hazardous *syn* DANGEROUS, precarious, risky, perilous *rel* venturesome, adventurous; chancy, chance, haphazard, happy-go-lucky, random

haze • an atmospheric condition that is characterized by the presence of fine particulate material in the air and that deprives the air of its transparency *syn* mist, fog, smog

head, headman *syn* CHIEF, leader, chieftain, master

headlong *syn* PRECIPITATE, impetuous, abrupt, hasty, sudden *rel* rash, reckless, daring, daredevil, foolhardy, adventurous

headstrong *syn* UNRULY, ungovernable, intractable, refractory, recalcitrant, willful *rel* perverse, contrary, froward, wayward; stubborn, obstinate, pigheaded, stiff-necked

headway *syn* SPEED, pace, velocity, momentum, impetus *rel* advance, progress; motion, movement

heal *syn* CURE, remedy

healthful • conducive or beneficial to the health or soundness of body or mind *syn* healthy, wholesome, salubrious, salutary, hygienic, sanitary *rel* beneficial, advantageous, profitable; remedying, remedial, correcting, corrective; helping, helpful, aiding

healthy **1** *syn* HEALTHFUL, wholesome, salubrious, salutary, hygienic, sanitary *rel* see HEALTHFUL **2** • having or manifesting health of mind or body or indicative of such health *syn* sound, wholesome, robust, hale, well *rel* vigorous, lusty, energetic; strong, sturdy, stalwart, tough, tenacious *ant* unhealthy

heap *n* • a quantity of things brought together into a more or less compact group *syn* pile, stack, shock, cock, mass, bank *rel* aggregate, aggregation, conglomerate, conglomeration; collection, assemblage

heap *vb* • to bring a number of things together into a more or less compact group or collection *syn* pile, stack, shock, cock, mass, bank *rel* accumulate, amass, hoard; collect, assemble, gather

hearing • an opportunity to be heard *syn* audience, audition

hearsay *syn* REPORT, rumor, gossip

heart *syn* CENTER, middle, core, hub, nucleus, midst, focus

heartache, heartbreak *syn* SORROW, grief, anguish, woe, regret

hearten *syn* ENCOURAGE, inspirit, embolden, cheer, nerve, steel *rel* strengthen, fortify, invigorate, energize; rally, arouse, rouse, stir *ant* dishearten

heartfelt *syn* SINCERE, hearty, unfeigned, wholehearted, whole-souled *rel* genuine, veritable, authentic, bona fide; profound, deep

hearty *syn* SINCERE, heartfelt, unfeigned, wholehearted, whole-souled *rel* warm, warmhearted, responsive, tender; deep, profound; exuberant, profuse *ant* hollow

heave *syn* LIFT, raise, hoist, elevate, boost, rear

heavenly *syn* CELESTIAL, empyrean, empyreal

heavy • having great weight *syn* weighty, ponderous, cumbrous, cumbersome, hefty *rel* solid, hard, firm; oppressing, oppressive, weighing down, depressing *ant* light

heckle *syn* BAIT, badger, hector, chivy, hound, ride *rel* plague, pester, harass, harry, worry, annoy; disconcert, rattle, faze, discomfit, embarrass; rack, torment, afflict

hector *syn* BAIT, badger, chivy, heckle, hound, ride *rel* tease, tantalize, plague, pester, worry; bother, vex, irk, annoy; fret, chafe, gall, abrade

heedless *syn* CARELESS, thoughtless, inadvertent *rel* forgetful, oblivious, unmindful; abstracted, absent, absentminded, distraught; frivolous, light-minded, flippant, volatile; remiss, lax, slack, negligent, neglectful *ant* heedful

hefty *syn* HEAVY, weighty, ponderous, cumbrous, cumbersome *rel, ant* see HEAVY

height • the distance a thing rises above the level on which it stands *syn* altitude, elevation

heighten *syn* INTENSIFY, enhance, aggravate *rel* exalt, magnify, aggrandize; elevate, lift, raise; improve, better

heinous *syn* OUTRAGEOUS, atrocious, monstrous *rel* flagrant, glaring, gross, rank; nefarious, flagitious, infamous, vicious *ant* venial

hellish *syn* INFERNAL, chthonian, chthonic, Hadean, Tartarean, stygian *rel* devilish, diabolical, fiendish, demoniac

help *vb* **1** • to give assistance or support *syn* aid, assist *rel* support, uphold, back, champion; benefit, profit, avail; forward, further, promote, advance *ant* hinder **2** *syn* IMPROVE, better, ameliorate *rel* palliate, gloss, extenuate, whitewash, whiten; alleviate, relieve, mitigate

help *n* • an act or instance of giving what will benefit or assist *syn* aid, assistance *rel* cooperation, uniting, union; supporting, support, backing

helper *syn* ASSISTANT, coadjutor, aid, aide, aide-de-camp

hem *syn* SURROUND, environ, encircle, circle, encompass, compass, gird, girdle, ring *rel* enclose, envelop, wall, cage, fence; confine, circumscribe, restrict, limit

hence *syn* THEREFORE, consequently, then, accordingly, so

henchman *syn* FOLLOWER, adherent, disciple, partisan, satellite, sectary

herald *syn* FORERUNNER, harbinger, precursor

Herculean *syn* HUGE, vast, immense, enormous, elephantine, mammoth, giant, gigantic, gigantean, colossal, gargantuan, cyclopean, titanic, Brobdingnagian

hereditary *syn* INNATE, congenital, inborn, inherited, inbred *rel* transmitted, conveyed; inherent, constitutional, intrinsic, ingrained

heretic • one who is not orthodox in his beliefs *syn* schismatic, sectarian, sectary, dissenter, nonconformist *rel* freethinker, deist, unbeliever, atheist; renegade, apostate

heretical *syn* HETERODOX

heritage • something which one receives or is entitled to receive by succession *syn* inheritance, patrimony, birthright

hermaphroditic, hermaphrodite *syn* BISEXUAL, androgynous, epicene

hermit *syn* RECLUSE, eremite, anchorite, cenobite

heroism • conspicuous courage or bravery *syn* valor, prowess, gallantry *rel* bravery, intrepidity, dauntlessness, doughtiness; courage, tenacity, resolution, mettle, spirit; fortitude, pluck, grit, guts, sand

hesitancy *syn* HESITATION *rel* reluctance, averseness, indisposedness, indisposition; faltering, wavering, vacillation

hesitant *syn* DISINCLINED, reluctant, loath, averse, indisposed *rel* fearful, afraid, apprehensive; diffident, shy, bashful; recoiling, flinching, blenching, shrinking

hesitate • to show irresolution or uncertainty *syn* waver, vacillate, falter *rel* balk, boggle, stick, stickle, scruple, demur, shy; fluctuate, oscillate, swing

hesitation • an act or action of hesitating *syn* hesitancy *rel* uncertainty, doubt, dubiety, dubiosity, mistrust; procrastination, delaying, delay, dawdling

heterodox • not in conformity with orthodox beliefs or teachings *syn* heretical *ant* orthodox

heterogeneous *syn* MISCELLANEOUS, motley, promiscuous, assorted *rel* diverse, disparate, various, divergent, different; mixed, mingled, commingled; multifarious, divers, many *ant* homogeneous

hew *syn* CUT, chop, carve, slit, slash *rel* cleave, rive, split, tear

hiatus *syn* BREAK, gap, interruption, interval, interim, lacuna

hick *syn* BOOR, bumpkin, yokel, rube, clodhopper, clown, lout, churl

hide *vb* • to withdraw or to withhold from sight or observation *syn* conceal, screen, secrete, cache, bury, ensconce *rel* cloak, mask, disguise, dissemble, camouflage; suppress, repress

hide *n, syn* SKIN, pelt, rind, bark, peel

hidebound *syn* ILLIBERAL, narrow-minded, narrow, intolerant, bigoted *rel* restricted, circumscribed, limited

hideous *syn* UGLY, ill-favored, unsightly *rel* revolting, repulsive, offensive, loathsome; repellent, obnoxious, abhorrent, distasteful, repugnant; homely, plain *ant* fair

high • having a relatively great upward extension *syn* tall, lofty *rel* elevated, lifted, raised, reared; deep, profound, abysmal; heightened, enhanced, intensified; increased, augmented *ant* low

high-spirited *syn* SPIRITED, mettlesome, spunky, fiery, peppery, gingery *rel* gallant, chivalrous, courtly, courteous, civil; audacious, bold, brave, intrepid

hilarity *syn* MIRTH, jollity, glee *rel* merriment, blitheness, jocundity; cheerfulness, gladness, joyfulness, joyousness, lightheartedness; fun, play, sport, jest, game

hind *syn* POSTERIOR, hinder, rear, after, back *ant* fore, front

hinder *vb* • to put obstacles in the way *syn* impede, obstruct, block, bar, dam *rel* arrest, check, interrupt; hamper, fetter, clog, trammel, shackle, manacle, hog-tie; restrain, inhibit, curb, check; baffle, balk, frustrate *ant* further

hinder *adj, syn* POSTERIOR, hind, rear, after, back *ant* front, fore

hinge *syn* DEPEND, hang, turn *rel* swing, fluctuate, undulate

hint *syn* SUGGEST, intimate, insinuate, imply *rel* allude, advert, refer

hire *n, syn* WAGE, wages, pay, salary, stipend, fee, emolument

hire *vb* • to take or engage something or grant the use of something for a stipulated price or rate *syn* let, lease, rent, charter *rel* secure, obtain, get, procure; engage, contract, promise

hireling *syn* MERCENARY, venal, hack *rel* servile, menial, subservient; mean, abject, sordid

history • a chronological record of events *syn* chronicle, annals

histrionic *syn* DRAMATIC, theatrical, dramaturgic, melodramatic *rel* acting, playing, impersonating

hit *syn* STRIKE, smite, punch, slug, slog, swat, clout, slap, cuff, box *rel* beat, buffet, pound, pummel, thrash

hit-or-miss *syn* RANDOM, haphazard, happy-go-lucky, desultory, casual, chance, chancy

hoard *syn* ACCUMULATE, amass *rel* collect, assemble, gather; pile, heap, stack, mass

hoarse *syn* LOUD, raucous, strident, stentorian, earsplitting, stertorous *rel* harsh, rough; gruff, crusty, bluff

hoax *syn* DUPE, hoodwink, bamboozle, gull, befool, trick *rel* delude, mislead, deceive; cheat, cozen, overreach, defraud

hobo *syn* VAGABOND, tramp, vagrant, truant, bum

hocus-pocus *syn* GIBBERISH, mummery, abracadabra

hog-tie *syn* HAMPER, trammel, clog, fetter, shackle, manacle *rel* impede, hinder, obstruct, block, bar, dam; curb, check, restrain; tie, bind

hoist *syn* LIFT, raise, elevate, boost, heave, rear *rel* rise, arise, ascend, mount, levitate

hold *vb* **1** *syn* KEEP, hold back, withhold, reserve, detain, retain, keep back, keep out *rel* restrain, inhibit, curb, check; preserve, conserve, save **2** *syn* CONTAIN, accommodate *rel* carry, bear, convey; receive, admit, take; house, lodge, harbor, shelter; include, comprehend **3** *syn* HAVE, own, possess, enjoy *rel* control, direct, manage, conduct

hold *n* • the act or manner of grasping or holding *syn* grip, grasp, clutch *rel* possession, ownership; control, command, power, authority

hold back *syn* KEEP, hold, withhold, reserve, detain, retain, keep back, keep out

hole • a space within the substance of a body or mass *syn* hollow, cavity, pocket, void, vacuum *rel* aperture, orifice, interstice; perforation, puncture, bore, prick; slit, slash, cut

holiness • a state of spiritual soundness and unimpaired virtue *syn* sanctity *rel* sacredness, divineness, divinity, spirituality, blessedness, religiousness; devoutness, devotion, piousness, piety; goodness, virtue, rectitude

holler *vb, syn* SHOUT, yell, shriek, scream, screech, squeal, whoop *rel* vociferate, clamor, bellow, roar

holler *n, syn* SHOUT, yell, shriek, scream, screech, squeal, whoop *rel* bellow, roar, vociferation, bawl

hollow *adj, syn* VAIN, empty, nugatory, otiose, idle *rel* see EMPTY *adj* 2

hollow *n, syn* HOLE, cavity, pocket, void, vacuum *rel* excavation, digging; gulf, chasm, abyss; orifice, aperture

holocaust *syn* FIRE, conflagration

holy • dedicated to the service of or set apart by religion *syn* sacred, divine, spiritual, religious, blessed *rel* hallowed, consecrated, dedicated; adored, worshiped, venerated, reverenced, revered; devout, pious, religious *ant* unholy

homage *syn* HONOR, reverence, deference, obeisance *rel* worship, adoration, veneration, reverence; fealty, fidelity, devotion, loyalty, allegiance; tribute, panegyric, eulogy, encomium

home *syn* HABITATION, house, dwelling, abode, residence, domicile

homely *syn* PLAIN, simple, unpretentious *rel* familiar, intimate, close; usual, wonted, customary, habitual; ill-favored, ugly *ant* comely, bonny

homily *syn* SPEECH, sermon, talk, address, oration, harangue, lecture

homunculus *syn* DWARF, manikin, midget, pygmy, runt

honest *syn* UPRIGHT, just, conscientious, scrupulous, honorable *rel* truthful, veracious; candid, open, plain, frank; straightforward, aboveboard, forthright; fair, equitable, dispassionate, objective *ant* dishonest

honesty • uprightness as evidenced in character and actions *syn* honor, integrity, probity *rel* veracity, truth, verity; uprightness, justness, conscientiousness, scrupulousness; candidness, candor, openness, plainness, frankness; reliability, trustworthiness, dependability; rectitude, virtue, goodness *ant* dishonesty

honor *n* **1** *syn* FAME, glory, renown, celebrity, éclat, reputation, repute, notoriety *rel* esteem, respect, regard, admiration; reverence, veneration, worship, adoration; prestige, credit, authority, influence, weight *ant* dishonor **2** • respect or esteem shown one as his or her due or claimed by one as a right *syn* homage, reverence, deference, obeisance *rel* recognition, acknowledgment; adulation, compliment; tribute, panegyric, eulogy, encomium **3** *syn* HONESTY, integrity, probity *rel* uprightness, justness, honorableness, scrupulousness, conscientiousness; truth, veracity; straightforwardness, forthrightness; rectitude, virtue, goodness

honor *vb, syn* DIGNIFY, ennoble, glorify *rel* exalt, magnify, aggrandize; extol, laud, acclaim, praise; reverence, revere, venerate

honorable *syn* UPRIGHT, just, scrupulous, conscientious, honest *rel* trustworthy, reliable, dependable; noble, virtuous, righteous, moral, ethical *ant* dishonorable

hoodwink *syn* DUPE, hoax, trick, gull, befool, bamboozle *rel* delude, deceive, mislead; cozen, cheat, overreach; confuse, muddle, fuddle, befuddle; baffle, outwit, circumvent, frustrate

hop *syn* SKIP, bound, curvet, lope, lollop, ricochet

hope *syn* EXPECT, look, await *rel* aspire, aim, pant; yearn, long, hunger, thirst, pine; rely, trust, depend, count, bank, reckon; anticipate, foresee, foreknow, divine *ant* despair (*of*); despond

hopeful • having or showing confidence that the end or outcome will be favorable *syn* optimistic, roseate, rose-colored *rel* expecting, hoping, awaiting; anticipating, foreseeing, divining; sanguine, sure, confident, assured *ant* hopeless, despairing

hopeless *syn* DESPONDENT, despairing, desperate, forlorn *rel* dejected, depressed, melancholy, sad; gloomy, glum, morose, sullen; acquiescent, compliant *ant* hopeful

hopelessness *syn* DESPONDENCY, despair, desperation, forlornness *rel* dejection, depression, melancholy, gloom, sadness *ant* hopefulness

horde *syn* CROWD, mob, throng, crush, press, rout

horizon *syn* RANGE, gamut, reach, radius, compass, sweep, scope, orbit, ken, purview *rel* limit, bound, confine, term, end; spread, stretch, amplitude, expanse

horrendous *syn* HORRIBLE, horrific, horrid

horrible 1 • inspiring horror or abhorrence *syn* horrid, horrific, horrendous *rel* abhorrent, abominable, detestable, hateful; repugnant, repellent, obnoxious; offensive, repulsive, revolting, loathsome *ant* fascinating **2** *syn* FEARFUL, horrific, shocking, appalling, awful, dreadful, frightful, terrible, terrific *rel, ant* see HORRIBLE 1

horrid *syn* HORRIBLE, horrific, horrendous *rel* distasteful, repellent, repugnant, obnoxious; loathsome, offensive, revolting, repulsive *ant* delightful

horrific 1 *syn* HORRIBLE, horrid, horrendous *rel* horrifying, appalling, dismaying, daunting; terrorizing, terrifying, frightening, alarming **2** *syn* FEARFUL, horrible, terrible, terrific, shocking, appalling, awful, dreadful, frightful *rel* see HORRIFIC 1

horrify *syn* DISMAY, daunt, appall *rel* agitate, upset, perturb, discompose; offend, outrage

horror *syn* FEAR, terror, dread, fright, alarm, dismay, consternation, panic, trepidation *rel* aversion, antipathy; repugnance, abhorrence, repellency, repulsion, distastefulness, distaste; recoiling, recoil, flinching, shrinking, blenching *ant* fascination

hors d'oeuvre *syn* APPETIZER, aperitif

horse sense *syn* SENSE, common sense, good sense, gumption, judgment, wisdom

hospitable *syn* SOCIAL, gregarious, convivial, cooperative, companionable *rel* sociable, gracious, cordial, genial, affable; generous, liberal, bountiful, bounteous, openhanded; friendly, neighborly, amicable *ant* inhospitable

host *syn* MULTITUDE, army, legion

hostage *syn* PLEDGE, pawn, earnest, token *rel* surety, security, guarantee, guaranty

hostility *syn* ENMITY, animosity, antagonism, antipathy, rancor, animus *rel* hatred, hate; ill will, malevolence, malignity, malignancy, malice; aggression, attack; opposing, opposition, combating, resisting, resistance

hound *syn* BAIT, ride, hector, badger, heckle, chivy *rel* harry, harass, worry, annoy; torment, torture, try, afflict; persecute, oppress, wrong

house *n, syn* HABITATION, home, dwelling, abode, residence, domicile

house *vb, syn* HARBOR, lodge, board, shelter, entertain *rel* accommodate, hold, contain

hover *syn* FLIT, flutter, flitter, flicker *rel* hang, suspend; poise, balance, stabilize; float, fly, skim, sail

howl **1** *syn* BARK, bay, growl, snarl, yelp, yap **2** *syn* ROAR, bellow, bluster, bawl, vociferate, clamor, ululate *rel* wail, blubber, cry; lament, bewail, deplore

howler *syn* ERROR, boner, mistake, blunder, slip, lapse, faux pas, bull

hub *syn* CENTER, core, middle, nucleus, heart, focus, midst

hubbub *syn* DIN, uproar, pandemonium, hullabaloo, babel, clamor, racket

hue *syn* COLOR, shade, tint, tinge, tone

huff *syn* OFFENSE, dudgeon, pique, resentment, umbrage *rel* petulance, huffiness, irritability, fractiousness; anger, indignation, rage, wrath

huffy *syn* IRRITABLE, petulant, pettish, fractious, peevish, snappish, waspish, fretful, querulous *rel* angry, mad, indignant, irate

huge • exceedingly or excessively large *syn* vast, immense, enormous, elephantine, mammoth, giant, gigantic, gigantean, colossal, gargantuan, Herculean, cyclopean, titanic, Brobdingnagian *rel* stupendous, tremendous, prodigious, monumental, monstrous; big, great, large

hullabaloo *syn* DIN, uproar, pandemonium, babel, hubbub, clamor, racket

humane *syn* CHARITABLE, humanitarian, benevolent, philanthropic, eleemosynary, altruistic *rel* compassionate, tender, warmhearted; gentle, lenient, mild, soft; clement, merciful, tolerant, forbearing; kindly, kind, benign, benignant *ant* barbarous, inhuman; atrocious

humanitarian *syn* CHARITABLE, humane, benevolent, philanthropic, eleemosynary, altruistic

humble *adj* • lacking all signs of pride, aggressiveness, or self-assertiveness *syn* meek, modest, lowly *rel* submissive, subdued, tame; resigned, acquiescent, compliant

humble *vb, syn* ABASE, humiliate, demean, debase, degrade *rel* abash, discomfit, embarrass; chagrin, mortify

humbug *syn* IMPOSTURE, fake, sham, cheat, fraud, deceit, deception, counterfeit *rel* pretense, pretension, make-believe; impostor, faker, charlatan, mountebank; hocus-pocus, mummery, gibberish, abracadabra

humdrum *syn* DULL, dreary, monotonous, pedestrian, stodgy *rel* irksome, tiresome, wearisome, tedious, boring

humid *syn* WET, moist, damp, dank

humiliate *syn* ABASE, humble, degrade, debase, demean *rel* mortify, chagrin; confound, bewilder, nonplus, puzzle; embarrass, discomfit, abash, disconcert, faze, rattle

humor *n* **1** *syn* MOOD, temper, vein *rel* caprice, freak, fancy, whim, whimsy, conceit, vagary, crotchet; attitude, position, stand **2** *syn* WIT, irony, satire, sarcasm, repartee

humor *vb, syn* INDULGE, pamper, spoil, baby, mollycoddle *rel* gratify, delight, please, rejoice, gladden, tickle; content, satisfy

humorous *syn* WITTY, facetious, jocular, jocose *rel* droll, comic, comical, farcical, funny, laughable; amusing, diverting, entertaining

hunger *syn* LONG, yearn, hanker, pine, thirst *rel* crave, desire, covet, wish, want

hunt *syn* SEEK, search, ransack, rummage, scour, comb, ferret out *rel* pursue, chase, follow, trail

hurl *syn* THROW, fling, cast, pitch, toss, sling

hurricane • a violent rotating storm originating in the tropics and often moving into temperate latitudes *syn* tropical storm, typhoon *rel* whirlwind, whirly; cyclone, tornado, twister

hurry *vb, syn* SPEED, quicken, precipitate, hasten *rel* impel, drive, move *ant* delay

hurry *n, syn* HASTE, speed, dispatch, expedition *rel* swiftness, rapidity, expeditiousness, quickness, speediness; celerity, alacrity, legerity; flurry, stir, bustle, pother, ado

hurt *vb, syn* INJURE, harm, damage, impair, mar, spoil *rel* afflict, torture, torment; trouble, distress; wrong, oppress, persecute, aggrieve

hurt *n, syn* INJURY, harm, damage, mischief *rel* pain, ache, pang, throe, twinge, stitch; injustice, wrong, grievance

husbandry *syn* AGRICULTURE, farming

husky *syn* MUSCULAR, brawny, sinewy, athletic, burly *rel* stalwart, stout, strong, sturdy, tough; powerful, puissant, potent, forceful

hygienic *syn* HEALTHFUL, sanitary, healthy, wholesome, salubrious, salutary

hymeneal *syn* MATRIMONIAL, nuptial, marital, connubial, conjugal

hymn *syn* SING, troll, carol, descant, warble, trill, chant, intone *rel* extol, laud, acclaim, praise

hyperbole *syn* EXAGGERATION, overstatement

hypercritical *syn* CRITICAL, captious, caviling, carping, censorious, faultfinding *rel* finicky, fastidious, fussy, pernickety, squeamish, particular, nice

hypochondriac *syn* MELANCHOLIC, melancholy, atrabilious

hypocrisy • the pretense or affectation of having virtues, principles, or beliefs that one does not actually have *syn* sanctimony, pharisaism, cant *rel* dissimulation, duplicity, guile, deceit; pretense, pretension, make-believe

hypocritical • characterized by hypocrisy *syn* sanctimonious, pharisaical, canting *rel* unctuous, oily, slick, fulsome; feigned, affected, assumed, simulated, shammed, counterfeited, pretended

hypostatize *syn* REALIZE, reify, externalize, materialize, incarnate, actualize, embody, objectify

hypothetical *syn* SUPPOSED, conjectural, supposititious, reputed, putative, purported *rel* theoretical, speculative, academic; doubtful, dubious, problematic, questionable

hysteria *syn* MANIA, delirium, frenzy

I

icon *syn* IMAGE, portrait, effigy, statue, photograph, mask

iconoclast *syn* REBEL, insurgent

icy *syn* COLD, glacial, arctic, gelid, frigid, freezing, frosty, cool, chilly *ant* fiery

idea • what exists in the mind as a representation as of something comprehended or as a formulation as of a plan *syn* concept, conception, thought, notion, impression *rel* opinion, view, belief, conviction, sentiment; hypothesis, theory, law

ideal *adj, syn* ABSTRACT, transcendent, transcendental *rel* utopian; surpassing, peerless, supreme *ant* actual

ideal *n, syn* MODEL, pattern, exemplar, example, standard, beau ideal, mirror *rel* truth, verity; perfection, excellence

identical **1** *also* **identic** *syn* SAME, selfsame, very, equivalent, equal, tantamount *rel* corresponding, correlative, convertible, reciprocal *ant* diverse **2** *syn* LIKE, alike, similar, analogous, comparable, akin, parallel, uniform *rel* matching, equaling; agreeing, squaring, tallying, jibing, corresponding *ant* different

identification *syn* RECOGNITION, apperception, assimilation *rel* perception, discernment, discrimination; image, percept, sense-datum, sensum, sensation

identify • to bring (one or more things) into union with another thing *syn* incorporate, embody, assimilate *rel* fuse, blend, merge, mix; mistake, confuse, confound

idiom **1** *syn* LANGUAGE, dialect, speech, tongue *rel* jargon, patois, cant, argot **2** *syn* PHRASE, expression, locution

idiosyncrasy *syn* ECCENTRICITY *rel* peculiarity, individuality, distinctiveness, distinction, characteristicness, characteristic; manner, way, method, mode; mannerism, affectation, pose

idiot *syn* FOOL, imbecile, moron, simpleton, natural

idle *adj* **1** *syn* VAIN, nugatory, otiose, empty, hollow *rel* fruitless, bootless, futile; ineffective, ineffectual, inefficacious; trivial, paltry, petty, trifling **2** *syn* INACTIVE, inert, passive, supine *rel* indolent, faineant, lazy, slothful; dawdling, lagging, procrastinating *ant* busy

idle *vb* • to spend time not in work but in idleness *syn* loaf, lounge, loll, laze *rel* rest, relax, repose; saunter, stroll, amble

idolize *syn* ADORE, worship *rel* dote, love, like; venerate, revere, reverence

ignite *syn* LIGHT, kindle, fire *ant* stifle; extinguish

ignoble *syn* MEAN, sordid, abject *rel* base, low, vile; churlish, boorish, loutish; petty, puny, paltry, measly, trivial; abased, debased, degraded *ant* noble; magnanimous

ignominy *syn* DISGRACE, infamy, shame, opprobrium, dishonor, disrepute, obloquy, odium *rel* humiliation, degradation, abasement; contempt, scorn, disdain, despite; mortification, chagrin

ignorant • lacking knowledge or education *syn* illiterate, unlettered, uneducated, untaught, untutored, unlearned *rel* rude, crude, raw, callow, green, uncouth; simple, ingenuous, unsophisticated, naïve *ant* cognizant (*of something*); conversant; informed

ignore *syn* NEGLECT, disregard, overlook, slight, omit, forget *rel* blink, wink; evade, elude, escape, avoid, shun, eschew *ant* heed (*a warning, a sign, a symptom*); acknowledge

ilk *syn* TYPE, kind, sort, nature, description, character, stripe, kidney

ill *adj, syn* BAD, evil, wicked, naughty *rel* see EVIL *ant* good

ill *n, syn* EVIL *ant* good

illegal *syn* UNLAWFUL, illegitimate, illicit *ant* legal

illegitimate *syn* UNLAWFUL, illegal, illicit *ant* legitimate

ill-fated *syn* UNLUCKY, ill-starred, disastrous, unfortunate, calamitous, luckless, hapless *rel* ominous, portentous, fateful; malefic, malign, baleful, sinister

ill-favored *syn* UGLY, hideous, unsightly *rel* plain, homely *ant* well-favored; fair

illiberal • unwilling or unable to understand the point of view of others *syn* narrow-minded, narrow, intolerant, bigoted, hidebound *ant* liberal

illicit *syn* UNLAWFUL, illegal, illegitimate *ant* licit

illimitable *syn* INFINITE, boundless, uncircumscribed, eternal, sempiternal *rel* endless, everlasting, interminable

illiterate *syn* IGNORANT, unlettered, uneducated, untaught, untutored, unlearned *ant* literate

ill-mannered *syn* RUDE, uncivil, ungracious, impolite, discourteous *rel* boorish, loutish, churlish *ant* well-bred

ill-starred *syn* UNLUCKY, ill-fated, disastrous, unfortunate, calamitous, luckless, hapless *rel* malefic, malign, baleful, sinister; ominous, portentous, fateful

ill-treat *syn* ABUSE, maltreat, mistreat, misuse, outrage *rel* wrong, oppress, persecute, aggrieve; injure, harm, hurt

illuminate, illumine • to fill with or to throw light upon *syn* light, lighten, enlighten, illustrate *rel* fire, kindle; elucidate, explain; exemplify *ant* darken, obscure

illusion *syn* DELUSION, mirage, hallucination *rel* imagination, fancy, fantasy; sensation, percept, sense-datum, sensum, image

illusory *syn* APPARENT, seeming, ostensible *rel* chimerical, fanciful, visionary, imaginary, fantastic; delusory, delusive, misleading, deceptive *ant* factual; matter-of-fact

illustrate **1** *syn* ILLUMINATE, enlighten, illumine, light, lighten *rel* adorn, embellish; expose, exhibit, display, show; reveal, disclose, discover *ant* dim **2** *syn* EXEMPLIFY *rel* elucidate, interpret, explain, expound; vivify, enliven; demonstrate, manifest, show

illustration *syn* INSTANCE, example, case, sample, specimen

illustrious *syn* FAMOUS, eminent, renowned, celebrated, famed *rel* glorious, splendid, resplendent, sublime; outstanding, signal, striking, conspicuous *ant* infamous

ill will *syn* MALICE, malevolence, malignity, malignancy, spite, despite, spleen, grudge *rel* animosity, antipathy, rancor, animus, hostility, enmity; hate, hatred *ant* goodwill; charity

image **1** • a lifelike representation esp. of a living being *syn* effigy, statue, icon, portrait, photograph, mask *rel* reproduction, copy, duplicate, facsimile, replica; form, figure, shape **2** *syn* SENSATION, percept, sense-datum, sensum *rel* idea, concept, impression, conception, notion; fabrication, figment; phantasy, fancy, fantasy

imaginary • unreal or unbelievable or conceiving such unreal or unbelievable things *syn* fanciful, visionary, fantastic, chimerical, quixotic *rel* fictitious, fabulous, mythical, legendary, apocryphal; ideal, transcendent, transcendental, abstract;

utopian; delusory, delusive, misleading; illusory, seeming, apparent *ant* real, actual

imagination • the power or function of the mind by which mental images of things are formed or the exercise of that power *syn* fancy, fantasy *rel* invention, creation; conceiving, conception, realizing, realization

imagine *syn* THINK, conceive, fancy, realize, envisage, envision *rel* invent, create; fabricate, form, fashion, shape, make; conjecture, surmise, guess

imbecile *syn* FOOL, idiot, moron, simpleton, natural

imbibe *syn* ABSORB, assimilate *rel* receive, take, admit, accept; soak, saturate, steep, impregnate; permeate, pervade, penetrate, impenetrate; acquire, obtain, get *ant* ooze, exude

imbue *syn* INFUSE, inoculate, leaven, ingrain, suffuse *rel* inform, inspire, fire, animate; impregnate, saturate, permeate, pervade

imitate *syn* COPY, mimic, ape, mock *rel* impersonate; simulate, feign, counterfeit; caricature, burlesque, parody, travesty

immaterial • not composed of matter *syn* spiritual, incorporeal *ant* material

immature • not fully developed *syn* unmatured, unripe, unmellow *rel* crude, callow, green, rude; premature, precocious, untimely; childish, childlike *ant* mature

immediate *syn* DIRECT *rel* nearest, next; intuitive, instinctive *ant* mediate (*knowledge, relation, operation*); distant (*relatives*)

immense *syn* HUGE, vast, enormous, elephantine, mammoth, giant, gigantic, gigantean, colossal, gargantuan, Herculean, cyclopean, titanic, Brobdingnagian *rel* tremendous, prodigious, stupendous, monstrous; large, big, great

immerse *syn* DIP, submerge, duck, souse, dunk *rel* drench, soak, saturate, sop, impregnate; infuse, imbue, ingrain; engross, absorb

immigrant **1** *syn* STRANGER, alien, foreigner, outlander, outsider, émigré **2** *syn* EMIGRANT, migrant

immigrate *syn* MIGRATE, emigrate

imminent *syn* IMPENDING *rel* threatening, menacing; likely, probable, possible; inevitable, ineluctable, inescapable, unescapable, unavoidable; expected, awaited

immobile *syn* IMMOVABLE, immotive *ant* mobile

immoderate *syn* EXCESSIVE, inordinate, exorbitant, extreme, extravagant *rel* profuse, lavish, prodigal, exuberant; teeming, overflowing *ant* moderate

immortal • not subject to death or decay *syn* deathless, undying, unfading *rel* everlasting, endless *ant* mortal

immotive *syn* IMMOVABLE, immobile

immovable • incapable of moving or being moved *syn* immobile, immotive *ant* movable

immunity *syn* EXEMPTION *ant* susceptibility

immure *syn* IMPRISON, incarcerate, jail, intern *rel* confine, circumscribe, limit, restrict

impact • a forcible or enforced contact between two or more things *syn* impingement, collision, clash, shock, concussion, percussion, jar, jolt *rel* hitting, hit, striking, stroke, smiting, slapping, slap; beating, pounding, buffeting

impair *syn* INJURE, damage, mar, harm, hurt, spoil *rel* weaken, enfeeble, debilitate, sap, undermine, disable, cripple; deface, disfigure; deform, distort, contort, warp *ant* improve, amend; repair

impalpable *syn* IMPERCEPTIBLE, insensible, intangible, inappreciable, imponderable *rel* tenuous, rare, slight, thin; attenuated, extenuated, rarefied *ant* palpable

impart *syn* COMMUNICATE *rel* share, participate, partake; distribute, dispense, divide; convey, transfer; instill, inculcate, implant; imbue, inoculate, leaven, infuse

impartial *syn* FAIR, equitable, unbiased, objective, just, dispassionate, uncolored *rel* disinterested, detached, aloof, indifferent *ant* partial

impassable • not allowing passage *syn* impenetrable, impervious, impermeable *ant* passable

impassible *syn* INSENSIBLE, insensitive, anesthetic

impassioned • actuated by or showing intense feeling *syn* passionate, ardent, fervent, fervid, perfervid *rel* vehement, intense, fierce, violent; deep, profound; sentimental, romantic, maudlin *ant* unimpassioned

impassive • unresponsive to what might normally excite interest or emotion *syn* stoic, phlegmatic, apathetic, stolid *rel* cool, composed, collected, imperturbable; reserved, taciturn, silent, reticent; callous, hardened, indurated; insensible, insensitive *ant* responsive

impassivity, impassiveness • unresponsiveness to something that might normally excite interest or emotion *syn* apathy, stolidity, phlegm, stoicism

impatient • manifesting signs of unrest or an inability to keep still or quiet *syn* nervous, unquiet, restless, restive, uneasy, fidgety, jumpy, jittery *rel* fretful, querulous, irritable, snappish, waspish; eager, anxious, avid, keen; impetuous, precipitate, headlong, hasty, sudden, abrupt *ant* patient

impeach *syn* ACCUSE, indict, incriminate, charge, arraign *rel* condemn, denounce, blame, censure; try, test, prove

impeccable • absolutely correct and beyond criticism *syn* faultless, flawless, errorless *rel* inerrant, unerring, infallible; correct, accurate, precise, right, nice; perfect, entire, whole, intact

impecunious *syn* POOR, indigent, needy, destitute, penniless, poverty-stricken, necessitous *ant* flush

impede *syn* HINDER, obstruct, block, bar, dam *rel* clog, hamper, fetter, trammel, shackle, manacle, hog-tie; embarrass, discomfit, disconcert, rattle, faze; thwart, baffle, balk, frustrate *ant* assist; promote

impediment *syn* OBSTACLE, obstruction, bar, snag *rel* difficulty, hardship, rigor, vicissitude; barrier, bar; handicap *ant* aid, assistance; advantage

impel *syn* MOVE, drive, actuate *rel* compel, constrain, force; provoke, excite, stimulate; incite, instigate, foment; goad, spur *ant* restrain

impending • likely to occur soon or without further warning *syn* imminent *rel* close, near, nigh; approaching, nearing; likely, probable; threatening, menacing

impenetrable *syn* IMPASSABLE, impervious, impermeable *rel* close, dense, compact, thick; solid, hard, firm; compacted, concentrated, consolidated; callous, hardened, indurated; obdurate, adamant, inflexible *ant* penetrable

impenetrate *syn* PERMEATE, interpenetrate, penetrate, pervade, impregnate, saturate *rel* enter, pierce, probe; invade, entrench trespass; drench, soak

imperative **1** *syn* MASTERFUL, peremptory, imperious, domineering *rel* commanding, ordering, bidding; magisterial, dictatorial, dogmatic, oracular; arbitrary, autocratic, despotic, absolute **2** *syn* PRESSING, urgent, crying, importunate, insistent, exigent, instant *rel* compelling, constraining; critical, crucial, acute

imperceptible • incapable of being apprehended by the senses or intellect *syn* insensible, impalpable, intangible, inappreciable, imponderable *ant* perceptible

imperfection • an instance of failure to reach a standard of excellence or perfection *syn* deficiency, shortcoming, fault *rel* failure, neglect, dereliction; failing, frailty, foible; blemish, flaw, defect; weakness, infirmity *ant* perfection

imperial *syn* KINGLY, regal, royal, queenly, princely *rel* majestic, august, stately, noble, grand; sovereign, dominant

imperil *syn* VENTURE, hazard, risk, chance, jeopardize, endanger *rel* dare, brave; encounter, confront, meet, face; threaten, menace

imperious *syn* MASTERFUL, domineering, peremptory, imperative *rel* dictatorial, authoritarian, magisterial; despotic, tyrannical, arbitrary, autocratic, absolute; lordly, overbearing *ant* abject

impermeable *syn* IMPASSABLE, impervious, impenetrable *rel* solid, hard, firm; tight

impersonate *syn* ACT, play *rel* imitate, mimic, ape, copy; simulate, counterfeit, feign; caricature, burlesque

impersonator *syn* ACTOR, player, mummer, mime, mimic, performer, thespian, trouper

impertinent • given to thrusting oneself into the affairs of others *syn* officious, meddlesome, intrusive, obtrusive *rel* interfering, meddling; arrogant, insolent; brazen, impudent, brash, barefaced, shameless; offensive, repugnant

imperturbable *syn* COOL, composed, collected, unruffled, unflappable, nonchalant *rel* immobile, immovable; serene, calm, tranquil, placid; complacent, self-satisfied, smug *ant* choleric, touchy

impervious *syn* IMPASSABLE, impenetrable, impermeable *rel* resisting, resistant, withstanding, opposing, combating, fighting; hardened, indurated, callous; obdurate, adamant, adamantine, inflexible

impetuous *syn* PRECIPITATE, headlong, abrupt, hasty, sudden *rel* impulsive, spontaneous; vehement, intense, violent; forceful, forcible, powerful; violent; impatient, restive; impassioned, passionate, fervid, ardent

impetus **1** *syn* SPEED, momentum, velocity, pace *rel* energy, force, power; impelling, impulsion, driving, moving **2** *syn* STIMULUS, excitant, incitement, stimulant *rel* incentive, impulse, spur, goad, motive, spring

impingement *syn* IMPACT, collision, clash, shock, concussion, percussion, jar, jolt *rel* hitting, hit, striking, stroke, smiting; encroachment, entrenchment; impression, impress, imprint, stamp, print

impious • lacking in reverence for what is sacred or divine *syn* profane, blasphemous, sacrilegious *rel* nefarious, iniquitous, flagitious; irreligious, ungodly, godless *ant* pious; reverent

impish *syn* PLAYFUL, roguish, waggish, mischievous, frolicsome, sportive *rel* saucy, pert, arch; naughty, bad; sly, cunning, tricky

implacable *syn* GRIM, relentless, unrelenting, merciless *rel* inflexible, inexorable, obdurate, adamant; pitiless, ruthless, compassionless

implant • to introduce into the mind *syn* inculcate, instill *rel* infuse, imbue, inoculate, ingrain, leaven; impregnate, saturate, impenetrate, penetrate, permeate, pervade

implement *n* • a relatively simple device for performing work *syn* tool, instrument, appliance, utensil *rel* machine, mechanism, apparatus; contrivance, device, contraption, gadget

implement *vb, syn* ENFORCE *rel* effect, fulfill, execute, achieve, accomplish, perform; realize, actualize, materialize

implicate *syn* INVOLVE *rel* concern, affect; incriminate, accuse

implication • something hinted at but not explicitly stated *syn* inference *rel* hinting, hint, suggestion, intimation; insinuation, innuendo

implicit • understood though not directly stated *syn* virtual, constructive *rel* implied, suggested, intimated, hinted; inferred, deduced, gathered *ant* explicit

implore *syn* BEG, entreat, beseech, supplicate, importune, adjure *rel* pray, plead, sue, appeal, petition; ask, request, solicit

imply **1** *syn* INCLUDE, involve, comprehend, embrace, subsume *rel* import, mean, signify, denote; contain, hold; convey, carry, bear **2** *syn* SUGGEST, hint, intimate, insinuate *rel* connote, denote; presuppose, presume, assume, postulate; betoken, bespeak, indicate, attest, argue, prove *ant* express

impolite *syn* RUDE, uncivil, discourteous, ill-mannered, ungracious *rel* churlish, boorish, loutish; curt, gruff, brusque, blunt, bluff *ant* polite

imponderable *syn* IMPERCEPTIBLE, impalpable, inappreciable, insensible, intangible *ant* ponderable, appreciable

import *vb, syn* MEAN, denote, signify *rel* connote; involve, imply, include, comprehend; suggest, intimate, hint; intend

import *n* **1** *syn* MEANING, significance, sense, acceptation, signification *rel* denotation, connotation; interpreting, interpretation, construing, construction; drift, tenor; implication **2** *syn* IMPORTANCE, significance, consequence, moment, weight *rel* worth, value; purpose, intent, design, object, objective, intention; emphasis, stress

importance • the quality or state of being of notable worth or influence *syn* consequence, moment, weight, significance, import *rel* prominence, conspicuousness, saliency; eminence, illustriousness; seriousness, gravity; magnitude, size, extent *ant* unimportance

importunate *syn* PRESSING, urgent, imperative, crying, insistent, exigent, instant *rel* demanding, claiming, requiring; persistent, persevering; pertinacious, dogged, obstinate

importune *syn* BEG, entreat, beseech, implore, supplicate, adjure *rel* tease, pester, plague, harry, worry; hound, hector, badger; plead, appeal, sue

impose *syn* DICTATE, prescribe, ordain, decree *rel* order, enjoin, command, charge; exact, demand, require; constrain, oblige, compel, force

imposing *syn* GRAND, stately, majestic, august, noble, magnificent, grandiose *rel* showy, pretentious, ostentatious; impressive, moving; regal, imperial; monumental, stupendous, prodigious *ant* unimposing

impostor • a person who fraudulently pretends to be someone or something else *syn* faker, quack, mountebank, charlatan *rel* cheat, fraud, fake, humbug, imposture; deceiver, beguiler, misleader

imposture • a thing made to seem other than it is *syn* cheat, fraud, sham, fake, humbug, deceit, deception, counterfeit *rel* trick, ruse, feint, artifice, wile, stratagem, maneuver, gambit, ploy

impotent **1** *syn* POWERLESS *rel* ineffective, ineffectual, inefficacious, inefficient; incapable, incompetent; disabled, crippled, debilitated, enfeebled *ant* potent **2** *syn* STERILE, barren, unfruitful, infertile *ant* virile

impoverish *syn* DEPLETE, bankrupt, exhaust, drain *ant* enrich

imprecation *syn* CURSE, malediction, anathema *rel* execration, damning, objurgation; blasphemy, profanity, swearing *ant* prayer

impregnable *syn* INVINCIBLE, inexpugnable, unassailable, invulnerable, unconquerable, indomitable *rel* secure, safe; protected, shielded, guarded, safeguarded, defended

impregnate **1** *syn* PERMEATE, saturate, pervade, penetrate, impenetrate, interpenetrate *rel* imbue, inoculate, ingrain, infuse, suffuse, leaven; enter, pierce, probe **2** *syn* SOAK, saturate, drench, steep, sop, waterlog *rel* immerse, submerge, dip, souse

impress *vb, syn* AFFECT, touch, strike, influence, sway *rel* move, actuate; thrill, electrify, enthuse; provoke, excite, stimulate, galvanize, pique

impress *n, syn* IMPRESSION, imprint, print, stamp *rel* see IMPRESSION 1

impressible *syn* SENTIENT, sensitive, impressionable, responsive, susceptible *rel* subject, exposed, open, liable, prone; predisposed, disposed, inclined

impression **1** • the perceptible trace or traces left by pressure *syn* impress, imprint, print, stamp *rel* trace, vestige, track; mark, token, sign; stigma, brand, blot, stain **2** *syn* IDEA, notion, thought, concept, conception *rel* image, percept, sensedatum, sensum, sensation; sentiment, opinion, view **3** *syn* EDITION, reprinting, printing, reissue

impressionable *syn* SENTIENT, sensitive, impressible, responsive, susceptible *rel* affectable, influenceable; open, liable, subject, exposed, prone; predisposed, disposed, inclined

impressive *syn* MOVING, affecting, poignant, touching, pathetic *rel* imposing, majestic, august, noble, magnificent, grandiose, grand; sublime, superb, glorious, splendid; striking, arresting, remarkable, noticeable *ant* unimpressive

imprint *syn* IMPRESSION, print, impress, stamp

imprison • to confine closely so that escape is impossible or unlikely *syn* incarcerate, jail, immure, intern *rel* confine, circumscribe, restrict, limit; restrain, curb, check

impromptu *syn* EXTEMPORANEOUS, unpremeditated, offhand, improvised, extempore, extemporary *rel* spontaneous, impulsive; ready, prompt, quick, apt

improper **1** *syn* UNFIT, inappropriate, unfitting, unsuitable, inapt, unhappy, infelicitous *rel* wrong, bad, poor; amiss, astray; incongruous, inconsonant *ant* proper **2** *syn* INDECOROUS, indecent, unseemly, unbecoming, indelicate *rel* unconventional, unceremonious, informal; shameless, brazen, impudent, brash, barefaced; obscene, ribald, coarse, vulgar, gross *ant* proper

impropriety *syn* BARBARISM, corruption, solecism, vulgarism, vernacular

improve **1** • to make more acceptable or bring nearer to some standard *syn* better, help, ameliorate *rel* benefit, profit; amend, correct, rectify, reform, revise; enhance, heighten *ant* impair; worsen **2** • to grow or become better (as in health or well-being) *syn* recover, recuperate, convalesce, gain

improvised *syn* EXTEMPORANEOUS, unpremeditated, impromptu, offhand, extempore, extemporary *rel* see IMPROMPTU

impudent *syn* SHAMELESS, brazen, barefaced, brash *rel* impertinent, intrusive, obtrusive, officious, meddlesome; rude, impolite, discourteous, uncivil, ungracious *ant* respectful

impugn *syn* DENY, gainsay, contradict, negative, traverse, contravene *rel* attack, assail; refute, rebut, confute, controvert, disprove *ant* authenticate; advocate

impulse *syn* MOTIVE, spring, incentive, inducement, spur, goad *rel* impetus, stimulus, incitement, stimulant, excitant; urge, passion, lust, desire, appetite; moving, movement, driving, drive, impelling, impulsion, actuation

impulsive *syn* SPONTANEOUS, instinctive, automatic, mechanical *rel* impetuous, precipitate, headlong, abrupt, sudden, hasty *ant* deliberate

impute *syn* ASCRIBE, attribute, assign, refer, credit, accredit, charge *rel* attach, fasten, affix; accuse, indict; allege, advance, adduce; intimate, insinuate, hint, suggest

inactive • not engaged in work or activity *syn* idle, inert, passive, supine *rel* latent, quiescent, dormant, abeyant, potential; torpid, comatose, sluggish, lethargic *ant* active, live

inadvertent *syn* CARELESS, heedless, thoughtless

inane *syn* INSIPID, banal, wishy-washy, jejune, vapid, flat *rel* foolish, silly, fatuous, asinine, simple; vain, idle, empty, hollow, nugatory; vacuous, blank, empty

inanimate *syn* DEAD, lifeless, defunct, deceased, departed, late *rel* inert, inactive *ant* animate

inappreciable *syn* IMPERCEPTIBLE, imponderable, impalpable, insensible, intangible *ant* appreciable, ponderable

inappropriate *syn* UNFIT, unfitting, inapt, improper, unsuitable, unhappy, infelicitous *rel* unbecoming, unseemly, indecorous; incongruous, discordant, inconsonant *ant* appropriate

inapt *syn* UNFIT, unhappy, infelicitous, inappropriate, unfitting, unsuitable, improper *rel* inept, maladroit, gauche, awkward, clumsy; banal, flat, jejune, insipid *ant* apt

inarticulate *syn* DUMB, speechless, mute *rel* silent, taciturn, reserved *ant* articulate

inasmuch as *syn* BECAUSE, since, for, as

inaugurate **1** *syn* INITIATE, install, induct, invest *rel* introduce, admit, enter **2** *syn* BEGIN, start, commence *rel* found, establish, institute, organize

inauspicious *syn* OMINOUS, unpropitious, portentous, fateful *rel* threatening, menacing; sinister, malign, malefic, maleficent, baleful *ant* auspicious

inborn *syn* INNATE, congenital, hereditary, inherited, inbred *rel* inherent, intrinsic, constitutional, essential; natural, normal, regular, typical; native, indigenous *ant* acquired

inbred *syn* INNATE, inborn, congenital, hereditary, inherited *rel* ingrained, inherent, constitutional, intrinsic; deep-rooted, deep-seated, inveterate, confirmed, chronic

incapable • mentally or physically unfit, or untrained to do a given kind of work *syn* incompetent, unqualified *rel* inefficient, ineffective; disabled, crippled, debilitated *ant* capable

incarcerate *syn* IMPRISON, jail, immure, intern *rel* confine, circumscribe, restrict, limit

incarnate *syn* REALIZE, embody, hypostatize, materialize, externalize, objectify, actualize, reify

incendiary *syn* COMBUSTIBLE, inflammable, flammable, inflammatory

incense *n, syn* FRAGRANCE, redolence, perfume, bouquet *rel* odor, aroma, smell

incense *vb, syn* ANGER, enrage, infuriate, madden *rel* exasperate, irritate, rile, provoke, nettle, aggravate; offend, outrage, affront, insult *ant* placate

incentive *syn* MOTIVE, inducement, spring, spur, goad, impulse *rel* stimulus, incitement, stimulant, excitant, impetus; provoking, provocation, excitement, stimulation; reason, cause, determinant

inception *syn* ORIGIN, source, root, provenance, provenience *rel* beginning, commencement, starting, start, initiation, inauguration; rising, rise, origination, derivation *ant* termination

incessant *syn* CONTINUAL, continuous, constant, unremitting, perpetual, perennial *rel* unceasing, interminable, endless, everlasting; steady, constant; vexing, irking, annoying, bothering *ant* intermittent

incident *syn* OCCURRENCE, episode, event, circumstance

incidental *syn* ACCIDENTAL, casual, fortuitous, contingent *rel* subordinate, secondary, collateral; associated, related, linked, connected *ant* essential

incise *syn* CARVE, engrave, etch, chisel, sculpture, sculpt, sculp *rel* imprint, print, stamp, impress; depict, delineate, limn, represent

incisive • having, manifesting, or suggesting a keen alertness of mind *syn* trenchant, clear-cut, cutting, biting, crisp *rel* terse, succinct, laconic, concise; poignant, pungent, piquant

incite • to spur to action *syn* instigate, abet, foment *rel* stimulate, excite, provoke, pique, galvanize; arouse, rouse, stir *ant* restrain

incitement *syn* STIMULUS, stimulant, excitant, impetus *rel* spur, goad, incentive, inducement, impulse, motive, spring; provoking, provocation, excitement, stimulation, piquing; motivation, activation, actuation *ant* restraint; inhibition

incline **1** *syn* SLANT, lean, slope *rel* bend, curve; swerve, veer, deviate; deflect, turn **2** • to influence one to have or to take an attitude toward something *syn* bias, dispose, predispose *rel* influence, affect, sway; move, drive, impel *ant* disincline, indispose

include • to contain within as part of the whole *syn* comprehend, embrace, involve, imply, subsume *rel* contain, hold, accommodate *ant* exclude

incognito *syn* PSEUDONYM, alias, nom de guerre, pen name, nom de plume

incommode *syn* INCONVENIENCE, discommode, trouble *rel* hinder, impede, obstruct, block; disturb, discompose; bother, irk, vex, annoy *ant* accommodate

incomparable *syn* SUPREME, peerless, superlative, transcendent, surpassing, preeminent *rel* unrivaled, unmatched, unapproached, unequaled

incompatible *syn* INCONSONANT, incongruous, inconsistent, discordant, discrepant, uncongenial, unsympathetic *rel* antagonistic, counter, adverse; antipathetic, averse; contrary, contradictory, antithetical, antipodal, antipodean, opposite; irreconcilable, unconformable, unadaptable *ant* compatible

incompetent *syn* INCAPABLE, unqualified *rel* inefficient, ineffective *ant* competent

incongruous *syn* INCONSONANT, uncongenial, incompatible, inconsistent, discordant, discrepant, unsympathetic *rel* alien, foreign, extraneous; grotesque, bizarre, fantastic *ant* congruous

inconsistent *syn* INCONSONANT, incompatible, incongruous, uncongenial, unsympathetic, discordant, discrepant *rel* divergent, disparate, diverse, different; irreconcilable *ant* consistent

inconsonant • not in agreement with or not agreeable to *syn* inconsistent, incompatible, incongruous, uncongenial, unsympathetic, discordant, discrepant *ant* consonant

inconstant • lacking firmness or steadiness (as in purpose or devotion) *syn* fickle, capricious, mercurial, unstable *rel* changeable, changeful, variable, protean, mutable; faithless, disloyal, false, treacherous, traitorous, perfidious; volatile, frivolous, light, light-minded *ant* constant

inconvenience • to subject to disturbance or discomfort *syn* incommode, discommode, trouble *rel* disturb, discompose; interfere, intermeddle, meddle

incorporate *syn* IDENTIFY, embody, assimilate *rel* merge, blend, fuse, coalesce, mix; unite, combine, conjoin; consolidate, unify, compact

incorporeal *syn* IMMATERIAL, spiritual *ant* corporeal

increase • to make or become greater *syn* enlarge, augment, multiply *rel* intensify, aggravate, heighten, enhance; expand, swell, amplify, dilate, distend, inflate; extend, lengthen, elongate, prolong, protract *ant* decrease

incredulity *syn* UNBELIEF, disbelief *rel* doubt, dubiety, dubiosity, skepticism, uncertainty *ant* credulity

increment *syn* ADDITION, accretion, accession

incriminate *syn* ACCUSE, impeach, indict, charge, arraign *rel* involve, implicate

inculcate *syn* IMPLANT, instill *rel* infuse, inoculate, imbue, leaven; teach, instruct, educate; impart, communicate

incur • to bring upon oneself something usu. unpleasant or injurious *syn* contract, catch *rel* get, obtain, acquire

incurious *syn* INDIFFERENT, unconcerned, aloof, detached, uninterested, disinterested *rel* abstracted, preoccupied, absent, absentminded, distraught *ant* curious, inquisitive

incursion *syn* INVASION, raid, inroad

indebtedness *syn* DEBT, debit, obligation, liability, arrear

indecent *syn* INDECOROUS, unseemly, indelicate, improper, unbecoming *rel* obscene, ribald, coarse, gross, vulgar; lewd, lascivious, licentious; immoral; offensive, revolting, repulsive, repugnant, loathsome *ant* decent

indecorous • not conforming to what is accepted as right, fitting, or in good taste *syn* improper, unseemly, indecent, unbecoming, indelicate *rel* unfitting, inappropriate, unsuitable, unfit; incongruous, inconsonant; rude, ill-mannered, uncivil, discourteous, impolite; coarse, vulgar, gross *ant* decorous

indefatigable • capable of prolonged and arduous effort *syn* tireless, weariless, untiring, unwearying, unwearied, unflagging *rel* diligent, assiduous, sedulous, industrious, busy; dogged, pertinacious, obstinate; energetic, strenuous, vigorous

indefinable *syn* UNUTTERABLE, inexpressible, unspeakable, ineffable, indescribable

indelicate *syn* INDECOROUS, indecent, unseemly, improper, unbecoming *rel* coarse, gross, vulgar, obscene; rude, rough, crude, callow, uncouth; lewd, wanton, licentious *ant* delicate, refined

indemnify *syn* PAY, reimburse, recompense, compensate, remunerate, repay, satisfy

indemnity *syn* REPARATION, redress, amends, restitution

indentured *syn* BOUND, articled, bond

independence *syn* FREEDOM, autonomy, sovereignty, autarchy, autarky *rel* liberty, license *ant* dependence

independent *syn* FREE, autonomous, sovereign, autarchic, autarkic *rel* alone, solitary; self-governed, self-ruled *ant* dependent

indescribable *syn* UNUTTERABLE, inexpressible, ineffable, unspeakable, indefinable

indicate • to give evidence of or to serve as ground for a valid or reasonable inference *syn* betoken, attest, bespeak, argue, prove *rel* intimate, hint, suggest; evince, evidence, demonstrate, manifest, show; import, signify, denote, mean

indict *syn* ACCUSE, incriminate, impeach, charge, arraign *rel* blame, denounce, condemn

indifferent **1** • not showing or feeling interest *syn* unconcerned, incurious, aloof, detached, uninterested, disinterested *rel* impartial, unbiased, dispassionate, fair; apathetic, impassive, phlegmatic; cool, nonchalant *ant* avid **2** *syn* MEDIUM, average, moderate, middling, fair, mediocre, second-rate *rel* ordinary, common *ant* choice **3** *syn* NEUTRAL

indigence *syn* POVERTY, penury, want, destitution, privation *rel* strait, exigency, emergency, pass *ant* affluence, opulence

indigenous *syn* NATIVE, autochthonous, endemic, aboriginal *ant* naturalized; exotic

indigent *syn* POOR, needy, destitute, penniless, impecunious, poverty-stricken, necessitous *ant* opulent

indignant *syn* ANGRY, irate, wrathful, wroth, acrimonious, mad *rel* incensed, infuriated, enraged, angered, maddened; exasperated, riled, provoked, nettled; roused, aroused, stirred

indignation *syn* ANGER, wrath, ire, rage, fury *rel* resentment, dudgeon, offense; passion

indignity *syn* AFFRONT, insult *rel* injury, wrong, injustice, grievance; offending, offense, outraging, outrage

indirect • deviating from a direct line or straightforward course *syn* circuitous, roundabout *rel* devious, oblique, crooked; winding, sinuous, tortuous *ant* direct; forthright, straightforward

indiscriminate • including all or nearly all within the range of choice, operation, or effectiveness *syn* wholesale, sweeping *rel* promiscuous, motley, heterogeneous, assorted, miscellaneous; uncritical, superficial, shallow *ant* selective; discriminating

indispensable *syn* NEEDFUL, essential, necessary, requisite *rel* vital, cardinal, fundamental, *ant* dispensable

indisposed *syn* DISINCLINED, loath, averse, hesitant, reluctant *rel* inimical, hostile, antagonistic, antipathetic *ant* disposed

individual *adj* **1** *syn* SPECIAL, particular, specific, especial *rel* single, sole, separate *ant* general **2** *syn* CHARACTERISTIC, peculiar, distinctive *rel* unique, singular, strange; distinct, separate, several *ant* common

individual *n, syn* ENTITY, being, creature, person *rel* aggregate

individuality *syn* DISPOSITION, personality, temperament, temper, complexion, character

individually *syn* EACH, apiece, severally, respectively

indolent *syn* LAZY, faineant, slothful *rel*

lethargic, sluggish, comatose; inactive, inert, idle, passive, supine; languid, languorous, lackadaisical, listless *ant* industrious

indomitable *syn* INVINCIBLE, unconquerable, impregnable, inexpugnable, unassailable, invulnerable *rel* stubborn, dogged, pertinacious, obstinate; resolute, staunch, steadfast, faithful; undaunted, dauntless, intrepid, doughty, brave

induce • to move another to do or agree to something *syn* persuade, prevail, get *rel* incite, instigate, abet; move, actuate, drive, impel; motivate, activate

inducement *syn* MOTIVE, incentive, spur, goad, spring, impulse *rel* temptation, enticement, seduction, luring, lure; stimulus, incitement, impetus, stimulant, excitant

induct *syn* INITIATE, inaugurate, install, invest

indulge • to show undue favor to a person's desires and feelings *syn* pamper, humor, spoil, baby, mollycoddle *rel* favor, accommodate, oblige; gratify, please, regale, delight *ant* discipline (*others*); abstain (*with reference to oneself, one's appetite*)

indulgence *syn* FORBEARANCE, tolerance, clemency, mercifulness, leniency *rel* mercy, charity, lenity, grace; kindness, benignancy, benignity, benignness, kindliness; mildness, gentleness *ant* strictness

indulgent *syn* FORBEARING, lenient, tolerant, clement, merciful *rel* humoring, pampering; forgiving, pardoning, condoning, excusing; benignant, benign, kind, kindly; mild, gentle, soft *ant* strict

indulgently *syn* FORBEARINGLY, tolerantly, clemently, mercifully, leniently

indurate *syn* HARDEN, solidify, petrify, cake *rel* season; fix, establish, set

indurated *syn* HARDENED, callous *rel* rigid, stiff, inflexible; obdurate, adamant, adamantine, inexorable, inflexible *ant* pliable

industrious *syn* BUSY, diligent, assiduous, sedulous *rel* active, operative, live, dynamic; persevering, persisting, persistent; indefatigable, tireless, untiring, unflagging, unwearied *ant* slothful, indolent

industry *syn* BUSINESS, trade, commerce, traffic

inebriate *syn* DRUNKARD, alcoholic, dipsomaniac, sot, soak, toper, tosspot, tippler *ant* teetotaler

inebriated *syn* DRUNK, drunken, intoxicated, tipsy, tight

ineffable *syn* UNUTTERABLE, inexpressible, unspeakable, indescribable, indefinable *rel* celestial, heavenly, empyrean, empyreal; ethereal; spiritual, divine, holy, sacred; transcendent, transcendental, ideal, abstract

ineffective • not producing or incapable of producing an intended result *syn* ineffectual, inefficient, inefficacious *rel* futile, vain, fruitless, bootless, abortive; nugatory, otiose, idle, empty, hollow; sterile, barren, unfruitful, infertile *ant* effective

ineffectual *syn* INEFFECTIVE, inefficacious, inefficient *rel* see INEFFECTIVE *ant* effectual

inefficacious *syn* INEFFECTIVE, ineffectual, inefficient *rel* inactive, inert, idle; futile, vain, fruitless, bootless, abortive; powerless, impotent *ant* efficacious

inefficient *syn* INEFFECTIVE, ineffectual, inefficacious *rel* incompetent, unqualified, incapable; infirm, decrepit, feeble, weak; indolent, slothful, faineant, lazy; remiss, lax, slack, negligent, neglectful *ant* efficient

ineluctable *syn* INEVITABLE, inescapable, unescapable, unavoidable *rel* certain, necessary

inept *syn* AWKWARD, clumsy, maladroit, gauche *rel* inapt, unfit, unsuitable, inappropriate; impertinent, intrusive, obtrusive; vain, nugatory, idle, empty, hollow, otiose; fatuous, asinine, foolish, silly *ant* apt; adept; able

inerrable *syn* INFALLIBLE, inerrant, unerring

inerrant *syn* INFALLIBLE, unerring *rel* impeccable, flawless, faultless; accurate, exact, correct, precise; reliable, dependable, trustworthy; inevitable, certain

inert *syn* INACTIVE, passive, idle, supine *rel* lifeless, inanimate, dead; impotent, powerless; apathetic, impassive, phlegmatic, stolid *ant* dynamic; animated

inescapable *syn* INEVITABLE, ineluctable, unescapable, unavoidable *rel* certain, necessary; inexorable, inflexible *ant* escapable

inevitable 1 • incapable of being avoided or escaped *syn* ineluctable, inescapable, unescapable, unavoidable *rel* certain, necessary; determined, settled, decided; inexorable, inflexible *ant* evitable **2** *syn* CERTAIN, necessary *rel* infallible, inerrant, unerring; perfect, entire, whole; definitive, determinative, decisive, conclusive

inexorable *syn* INFLEXIBLE, obdurate, adamant, adamantine *rel* rigid, rigorous, strict; resolute, steadfast, faithful; immovable, immobile; implacable, unrelenting, relentless, merciless, grim *ant* exorable

inexpressible *syn* UNUTTERABLE, ineffable, unspeakable, indescribable, indefinable *rel* tenuous, rare; infinite, boundless, illimitable *ant* expressible

inexpugnable *syn* INVINCIBLE, unassailable, impregnable, unconquerable, invulnerable, indomitable *rel* uncombatable, irresistible, unopposable *ant* expugnable

infallible • incapable of making mistakes or errors *syn* inerrable, inerrant, unerring *rel* certain, inevitable, necessary; impeccable, flawless, faultless *ant* fallible

infamous *syn* VICIOUS, nefarious, flagitious, iniquitous, villainous, corrupt, degenerate *rel* ignominious, disgraceful, disreputable, shameful *ant* illustrious

infamy *syn* DISGRACE, ignominy, shame, dishonor, disrepute, opprobrium, obloquy, odium *rel* notoriety; degradation, humiliation, debasement, abasement

infancy • the state or period of being under the age established by law for the attainment of full civil rights *syn* minority, nonage

infatuated **1** *syn* FOND, besotted, insensate *rel* deluded, deceived, beguiled, misled; duped, gulled, befooled; foolish, silly, fatuous, asinine **2** *syn* ENAMORED

infectious **1** • transmissible by infection *syn* contagious, communicable, catching *rel* toxic, mephitic, pestilent, pestilential, virulent, poisonous **2** • capable of infecting or tending to infect *syn* infective

infective *syn* INFECTIOUS *rel* contaminating, tainting, polluting, defiling; corrupting, vitiating; poisonous, virulent, toxic, mephitic

infelicitous *syn* UNFIT, unhappy, inapt, inappropriate, unfitting, unsuitable, improper *rel* unbecoming, unseemly, indecorous, improper, indelicate, indecent; inept, maladroit, gauche, awkward *ant* felicitous

infer • to arrive at by reasoning from evidence or from premises *syn* deduce, conclude, judge, gather *rel* reason, speculate, think; surmise, conjecture, guess

inference **1** • the deriving of a conclusion by reasoning *syn* deduction, conclusion, judgment **2** • the process of arriving at conclusions from data or premises *syn* ratiocination *rel* deduction, conclusion, judgment; reasoning, thinking, speculation, cogitation; surmise, conjecture **3** *syn* IMPLICATION

inferential • deduced or deducible by reasoning *syn* ratiocinative *rel* hypothetical, putative, purported, conjectural, supposititious, supposed; theoretical, speculative, academic; implicit, constructive, virtual

inferior • one who is lower than another esp. in station or rank *syn* underling, subordinate *rel* dependent, subject *ant* superior

infernal • of or relating to a nether world of the dead *syn* chthonian, chthonic, hellish, Hadean, Tartarean, stygian *rel* fiendish, devilish, diabolical, demoniac; damnable, accursed, cursed, execrable; nefarious, flagitious, iniquitous, villainous, vicious *ant* supernal

infertile *syn* STERILE, barren, impotent, unfruitful *rel* dry, arid; impoverished, exhausted, drained, depleted *ant* fertile

infest • to spread or swarm over in a troublesome manner *syn* overrun, beset *rel* teem, swarm, abound; harass, harry, pester, plague, worry, annoy *ant* disinfest

infidel *syn* ATHEIST, unbeliever, freethinker, agnostic, deist

infinite • being without known limits *syn* eternal, sempiternal, boundless, illimitable, uncircumscribed *ant* finite

infirm *syn* WEAK, feeble, decrepit, frail, fragile *rel* debilitated, disabled, crippled *ant* hale

inflammable *syn* COMBUSTIBLE, flammable, incendiary, inflammatory *rel* igniting, kindling, firing, lighting; flaring, blazing; infuriating, enraging, incensing *ant* extinguishable

inflammatory *syn* COMBUSTIBLE, inflammable, flammable, incendiary *rel* inciting, instigating; stimulating, exciting; sensitive, susceptible

inflate *syn* EXPAND, distend, swell, amplify, dilate *rel* enlarge, increase, augment; magnify, aggrandize, exalt *ant* deflate

inflated • swollen with or as if with something insubstantial *syn* flatulent, tumid, turgid *rel* bombastic, grandiloquent, magniloquent, aureate, flowery, rhetorical; pretentious, ostentatious, showy; rhapsodical, ranting, fustian; wordy, verbose, prolix, diffuse *ant* pithy

inflection • a particular manner of employing the sounds of the voice in speech *syn* intonation, accent *rel* enunciation, pronunciation, articulation

inflexible 1 *syn* STIFF, rigid, tense, stark, wooden *rel* hard, solid, firm; rigorous, strict, stringent; tough, tenacious, stout, strong; immobile, immovable *ant* flexible **2** • unwilling to alter a predetermined course or purpose *syn* inexorable, obdurate, adamant, adamantine *rel* rigid, strict, rigorous, stringent; intractable, refractory, headstrong, unruly, ungovernable; implacable, relentless, unrelenting, grim; stubborn, obstinate, dogged, stiff-necked, mulish *ant* flexible

influence *n* • power exerted over the minds or behavior of others *syn* authority, prestige, weight, credit *rel* driving, drive, impelling, impulsion, actuation; power, control, dominion, sway, authority; ascendancy, supremacy; dominance

influence *vb, syn* AFFECT, sway, impress, touch, strike *rel* move, actuate, drive, impel; stimulate, provoke, excite; stir, arouse, rouse; incline, dispose, predispose, bias

inform 1 • to stimulate (as mental powers) to higher or more intense activity *syn* animate, inspire, fire *rel* infuse, inoculate, imbue, leaven; instill, implant, inculcate; enlighten, illuminate; fire, kindle; endue, endow, dower **2** • to make one aware of something *syn* acquaint, apprise, advise, notify *rel* communicate, impart; teach, instruct, school, discipline, educate, train; warn, forewarn, caution

information *syn* KNOWLEDGE, lore, learning, science, erudition, scholarship *rel* news, tidings, intelligence, advice

infraction *syn* BREACH, violation, transgression, infringement, trespass, contravention *rel* offense, sin, crime, vice, scandal; slip, lapse, faux pas, error *ant* observance

infrequent • not common or abundant *syn* uncommon, scarce, rare, occasional, sporadic *rel* exceptional; singular, unique, strange; irregular, anomalous, unnatural *ant* frequent

infringe *syn* TRESPASS, encroach, entrench, invade *rel* intrude, obtrude, butt in, interlope; violate, break, transgress

infringement *syn* BREACH, infraction, violation, trespass, transgression, contravention *rel* encroachment, invading, invasion, entrenchment; intruding, intrusion, obtruding, obtrusion

infuriate *syn* ANGER, enrage, incense, madden *rel* provoke, rile, exasperate, aggravate, irritate; outrage, insult, affront, offend

infuse • to introduce one thing into another so as to affect it throughout *syn* suffuse, imbue, ingrain, inoculate, leaven *rel* impregnate, saturate, impenetrate, permeate, pervade; inform, inspire, animate, fire; instill, inculcate, implant

ingeminate *syn* REPEAT, iterate, reiterate

ingenious *syn* CLEVER, cunning, adroit *rel* inventing, inventive, creating, creative, discovering; dexterous, handy, deft; skillful, adept, skilled, expert, proficient, masterly

ingenuous *syn* NATURAL, simple, naïve, unsophisticated, artless *rel* open, frank, candid, plain; transparent, clear; childlike, childish; straightforward, aboveboard; sincere, unfeigned *ant* disingenuous; cunning

ingest *syn* EAT, swallow, devour, consume *rel* introduce, insert; receive, take, accept

ingrain *syn* INFUSE, suffuse, imbue, inoculate, leaven *rel* impregnate, saturate, permeate, pervade, impenetrate, interpenetrate; instill, inculcate, implant; incorporate, embody

ingrained *syn* INHERENT, constitutional, essential, intrinsic *rel* confirmed, inveterate, deep-seated, deep-rooted, chronic; implanted; imbued, inoculated

ingredient *syn* ELEMENT, constituent, component, factor *rel* item, detail, particular

ingress *syn* ENTRANCE, entry, entrée, access *ant* egress

inhabitant • one that occupies a particular place regularly *syn* denizen, resident, citizen

inherent • being a part, element, or quality of a thing's inmost being *syn* ingrained, intrinsic, essential, constitutional *rel* innate, inborn, inbred, congenital; inner, inward, internal; natural, typical, normal, regular; integrated, integral *ant* adventitious

inheritance *syn* HERITAGE, patrimony, birthright

inherited *syn* INNATE, hereditary, inborn, inbred, congenital *rel* transmitted, conveyed; generated, engendered, bred

inhibit **1** *syn* FORBID, prohibit, interdict, ban, enjoin *rel* prevent, preclude, obviate, avert, ward; debar, rule out, exclude; hinder, impede, obstruct, block, bar *ant* allow **2** *syn* RESTRAIN, curb, check, bridle *rel* suppress, repress; prevent, forestall; arrest *ant* animate; activate

inhuman *syn* FIERCE, savage, barbarous, truculent, ferocious, cruel, fell *rel* pitiless, ruthless; malign, malignant, malicious; merciless, relentless, unrelenting, implacable, grim; fiendish, diabolical, devilish *ant* humane

iniquitous *syn* VICIOUS, nefarious, flagitious, villainous, infamous, corrupt, degenerate *rel* wicked, evil, ill, bad; atrocious, heinous, outrageous, monstrous; ungodly, godless, irreligious *ant* righteous

initial • marking a beginning or constituting a start *syn* original, primordial *rel* starting, beginning, commencing; primary, primal, primeval, pristine; elementary *ant* final

initiate **1** *syn* BEGIN, commence, start, inaugurate *rel* found, establish, organize, institute *ant* consummate **2** • to put through the formalities for becoming a member or an official *syn* induct, inaugurate, install, invest *rel* introduce, admit, enter

initiation *syn* BEGINNING, genesis, rise *rel* starting, start, commencing, commencement; introducing, introduction, entering, entrance

initiative *syn* MANDATE, referendum, plebiscite

injunction *syn* COMMAND, order, bidding, behest, mandate, dictate *rel* instruction, direction, charging, charge; warning; precept, rule, regulation, law, statute, ordinance, canon

injure • to deplete the soundness, strength, effectiveness, or perfection of something *syn* harm, hurt, damage, impair, mar, spoil *rel* deface, disfigure; deform, distort, contort; afflict, torture, torment; maim, cripple, mutilate, mangle, batter; abuse, ill-treat, maltreat, outrage, mistreat, misuse *ant* aid

injury **1** • the act or the result of inflicting something that causes loss or pain *syn* hurt, damage, harm, mischief *rel* distress, suffering, agony, misery; pain, pang; violation, transgression, trespass, infringement, breach; detriment; evil, ill **2** *syn* INJUSTICE, wrong, grievance *rel* see INJURY 1

injustice • an act that inflicts undeserved hurt *syn* injury, wrong, grievance *rel* damage, hurt, harm, mischief; infringement, trespass, transgression, violation, infraction, breach; unfairness, inequitableness

innate • not acquired after birth *syn* inborn, inbred, congenital, hereditary, inherited *rel* constitutional, inherent, intrinsic, essential, ingrained; instinctive, intuitive; natural, typical, regular, normal; native, indigenous *ant* acquired

inner • situated further in *syn* inward, inside, interior, internal, intestine *rel* central, middle, focal, nuclear; intimate, close, familiar; intrinsic, constitutional, essential, inherent; instinctive, intuitive; deep-seated, deep-rooted *ant* outer

innocent *syn* HARMLESS, innocuous, inoffensive, unoffending

innocuous *syn* HARMLESS, innocent, inoffensive, unoffending *ant* pernicious

innuendo *syn* INSINUATION *rel* hinting, hint, intimation, suggestion; implication, inference; allusion

inoculate *syn* INFUSE, imbue, ingrain, leaven, suffuse *rel* impregnate, saturate, impenetrate, interpenetrate, permeate, pervade; introduce, admit, enter; instill, inculcate, implant

inoffensive *syn* HARMLESS, innocuous, innocent, unoffending *ant* offensive

inordinate *syn* EXCESSIVE, immoderate, exorbitant, extreme, extravagant *rel* irrational, unreasonable; supererogatory, wanton, uncalled-for, gratuitous; superfluous, surplus, extra *ant* temperate

inquest *syn* INQUIRY, investigation, probe, inquisition, research *rel* examination, inspection, scrutiny, audit; questioning, interrogation, catechizing, examining

inquire *syn* ASK, query, question, interrogate, catechize, quiz, examine

inquiry • a search for truth, knowledge, or information *syn* inquisition, investigation, inquest, probe, research *rel* questioning, interrogation, catechizing; examination, inspection, scrutiny, audit

inquisition *syn* INQUIRY, inquest, probe, investigation, research *rel*

inquisitive *syn* CURIOUS, prying, snoopy, nosy *rel* impertinent, intrusive, meddlesome; interfering, meddling, intermeddling *ant* incurious

inroad *syn* INVASION, incursion, raid *rel* intrusion, butting in; encroachment, entrenchment, infringement, trespassing, trespass; entrance, entry, ingress

insane • afflicted by or manifesting unsoundness of mind or an inability to control one's rational processes *syn* mad, crazy, crazed, demented, deranged, lunatic, maniac, non compos mentis *rel* irrational, unreasonable; distracted, bewildered *ant* sane

insanity • a deranged state of mind or serious mental disorder *syn* lunacy, psychosis, mania, dementia *rel* alienation, derangement, aberration; frenzy, delirium, hysteria *ant* sanity

inscription • something written, printed, or engraved (as on a coin or a medal or under or over a picture) to indicate or describe the purpose or the nature of the thing *syn* legend, caption

inscrutable *syn* MYSTERIOUS, arcane *rel* profound, abysmal, deep; baffling, balking, thwarting, frustrating, foiling; hidden, concealed, secreted; enigmatic, cryptic, dark, obscure, vague; mystifying, perplexing, puzzling

insensate *syn* FOND, besotted, infatuated *rel* fatuous, asinine, foolish, silly; stupid, slow, dense, crass, dull, dumb; irrational, unreasonable

insensible 1 • unresponsive to stimuli or to external influences *syn* insensitive, impassible, anesthetic *rel* obtuse, dull, blunt; impassive, apathetic, phlegmatic, stolid, stoic; hardened, indurated, callous; engrossed, absorbed, intent, rapt *ant* sensible (*to or of something*) **2** *syn* IMPERCEPTIBLE, impalpable, intangible, inappreciable, imponderable *rel* tenuous, rare, slight, slender, thin; attenuated, extenuated, diluted, rarefied *ant* sensible, palpable

insensitive *syn* INSENSIBLE, impassible, anesthetic *rel* hardened, indurated, callous; indifferent, unconcerned, aloof, incurious; impassive, stoic, apathetic, phlegmatic, stolid *ant* sensitive

insert *syn* INTRODUCE, interpolate, intercalate, insinuate, interpose, interject *rel* intrude, obtrude, interlope; instill, inculcate, implant; enter, admit *ant* abstract; extract

inside *syn* INNER, interior, internal, intestine, inward *ant* outside

insidious *syn* SLY, cunning, crafty, tricky, foxy, wily, guileful, artful *rel* treacherous, perfidious; dangerous, perilous; furtive, stealthy, covert, underhand, underhanded

insight *syn* DISCERNMENT, penetration, acumen, discrimination, perception *rel* intuition, understanding, reason; comprehension, apprehension; appreciation, understanding; perspicaciousness, sagacity, shrewdness *ant* obtuseness

insinuate 1 *syn* INTRODUCE, insert, interject, interpolate, intercalate, interpose *rel* infuse, inoculate, imbue, leaven; instill, inculcate, implant **2** *syn* SUGGEST, intimate, hint, imply *rel* allude, advert, refer; impute, ascribe

insinuation • a subtle or covert hinting or suggestion *syn* innuendo *rel* hinting, hint, implying, implication, suggestion, intimation; animadversion, aspersion, reflection; imputation, ascription; allusion

insipid • devoid of qualities that make for spirit and character *syn* vapid, flat, jejune, banal, wishy-washy, inane *rel* thin, slight, tenuous, rare; weak, feeble; tame, subdued; bland, mild, soft *ant* sapid; zestful

insistent *syn* PRESSING, urgent, imperative, crying, importunate, exigent, instant *rel* persistent, persevering; pertinacious, dogged, obstinate; obtrusive, impertinent

insolent *syn* PROUD, arrogant, overbearing, supercilious, disdainful, haughty, lordly *rel* domineering, masterful, imperious, peremptory, imperative; pretentious, ostentatious, showy; dictatorial, magisterial; scornful, contemptuous *ant* deferential

inspect *syn* SCRUTINIZE, examine, scan, audit *rel* survey, view, observe, notice; probe, penetrate; inquire, interrogate, question, catechize, ask

inspection *syn* SCRUTINY, examination, scanning, audit *rel* investigation, probe, inquest, inquiry, inquisition, research; surveillance, oversight, supervision

inspiration • a divine or seemingly divine

imparting of knowledge or power *syn* afflatus, fury, frenzy *rel* enlightenment, illumination; ecstasy, rapture, transport; revelation, vision, apocalypse, prophecy

inspire *syn* INFORM, animate, fire *rel* enlighten, illuminate; quicken, stimulate, excite, galvanize, provoke; activate, energize, vitalize; endue, endow

inspirit *syn* ENCOURAGE, hearten, embolden, cheer, nerve, steel *rel* enliven, animate, quicken, vivify; stimulate, excite, galvanize *ant* dispirit

in spite of *syn* NOTWITHSTANDING, despite

install *syn* INITIATE, induct, inaugurate, invest

instance *n* • something that exhibits distinguishing characteristics in its category *syn* case, illustration, example, sample, specimen *rel* proof, reason, ground; evidence; particular, item, detail

instance *vb, syn* MENTION, name, specify *rel* exemplify, illustrate; cite, quote

instant *n* • an almost imperceptible point or stretch of time *syn* moment, minute, second, flash, jiffy, twinkling, split second

instant *adj, syn* PRESSING, urgent, imperative, crying, importunate, insistent, exigent *rel* immediate, direct; compelling, constraining, obliging

instigate *syn* INCITE, abet, foment *rel* activate, actuate, motivate; suggest, hint, insinuate; plan, plot, scheme

instill *syn* IMPLANT, inculcate *rel* infuse, inoculate, imbue, ingrain, leaven; impregnate, permeate, saturate, pervade, impenetrate, interpenetrate

instinctive **1** • prompted by natural instinct or propensity *syn* intuitive *rel* innate, inborn, congenital; constitutional, inherent, ingrained *ant* reasoned **2** *syn* SPONTANEOUS, impulsive, automatic, mechanical *rel* natural, normal, typical, regular; habitual, customary, wonted, accustomed, usual *ant* intentional

institute *syn* FOUND, establish, organize, create *rel* begin, commence, start, initiate, inaugurate; introduce *ant* abrogate

instruct **1** *syn* TEACH, train, educate, discipline, school *rel* impart, communicate; inform, acquaint, apprise; lead, guide, steer, pilot, engineer; practice, drill, exercise **2** *syn* COMMAND, direct, enjoin, bid, order, charge *rel* prescribe, assign, define

instrument **1** *syn* MEAN, instrumentality, agency, medium, agent, organ, vehicle, channel *rel* method, system, mode, way, manner, fashion; machinery, apparatus, tackle, gear, equipment, paraphernalia; device, contrivance, contraption **2** *syn* IMPLEMENT, tool, appliance, utensil **3** *syn* PAPER, document

instrumentality *syn* MEAN, agent, agency, instrument, medium, organ, vehicle, channel *rel* work, labor, toil; effort, exertion, trouble, pains; power, energy, force, might; action, deed, act

insubordinate • unwilling to submit to authority *syn* rebellious, mutinous, seditious, factious, contumacious *rel* recalcitrant, refractory, unruly, ungovernable, intractable

insular • having the narrow and limited outlook characteristic of geographic isolation *syn* provincial, parochial, local, small-town *rel* isolated, insulated, secluded; circumscribed, limited, restricted, confined; narrow, narrow-minded, illiberal; aloof, unconcerned, indifferent

insulate *syn* ISOLATE, segregate, seclude, sequester *rel* separate, part, sever, sunder; detach, disengage

insult *vb, syn* OFFEND, affront, outrage *rel* humiliate, humble, debase, degrade, abase; flout, scoff, jeer, gird, gibe, fleer, sneer; mock, taunt, deride, ridicule *ant* honor

insult *n, syn* AFFRONT, indignity *rel* abuse, vituperation, invective, obloquy; dishonor, shame, ignominy, opprobrium, disgrace; insolence, superciliousness, disdainfulness; contempt, despite, scorn, disdain

insure *syn* ENSURE, assure, secure *rel* protect, shield, guard, safeguard, defend; indemnify, compensate

insurgent *syn* REBEL, iconoclast

insurrection *syn* REBELLION, uprising, revolt, mutiny, revolution, putsch, coup

intact *syn* PERFECT, whole, entire *rel* flawless, faultless, impeccable; complete, replete, full; consummate, finished *ant* defective

intangible *syn* IMPERCEPTIBLE, impalpable, insensible, inappreciable, imponderable *rel* tenuous, rare, slight, slender, thin; ethereal, airy, aerial; eluding, elusive, evading, evasive *ant* tangible

integer *syn* NUMBER, numeral, figure, digit

integrate • to join together systematically *syn* articulate, concatenate *rel* unite, combine, conjoin; unify, consolidate, concentrate, compact; fuse, blend, merge, coalesce, mix; organize, systematize *ant* disintegrate

integration • the act or process of operating as a unit or whole *syn* articulation, concatenation *rel* unification, consolidation, concentration; integrity, union, unity, solidarity

integrity 1 *syn* UNITY, solidarity, union *rel* wholeness, entirety, perfection, intactness; consummateness; purity, simplicity, absoluteness **2** *syn* HONESTY, probity, honor *rel* uprightness, justness, conscientiousness, scrupulousness, scrupulosity; rectitude, virtue, goodness, morality; truth, veracity, verity *ant* duplicity

intellect *syn* MIND, soul, psyche, brain, intelligence, wit *rel* reason, understanding, intuition

intellectual *syn* MENTAL, psychic, cerebral, intelligent *ant* carnal

intelligence 1 *syn* MIND, brain, intellect, soul, psyche, wit *rel* sense, judgment, wisdom, gumption; discernment, penetration, insight, acumen; sagaciousness, sagacity, perspicaciousness, perspicacity, astuteness, shrewdness **2** *syn* NEWS, tidings, advice

intelligent 1 *syn* MENTAL, intellectual, cerebral, psychic **2** • mentally quick or keen *syn* clever, alert, quick-witted, bright, smart, knowing, brilliant *rel* sharp, keen, acute; shrewd, sagacious, perspicacious, astute; cunning, ingenious, adroit *ant* unintelligent

intend • to have in mind as a purpose or goal *syn* mean, design, propose, purpose *rel* aim, aspire; attempt, try, endeavor, strive, essay; plan, design, scheme, plot

intense • extreme in degree, power, or effect *syn* vehement, fierce, exquisite, violent *rel* intensified, enhanced, heightened, aggravated; accentuated, emphasized, stressed *ant* subdued

intensify • to increase markedly in degree or measure *syn* aggravate, heighten, enhance *rel* accentuate, emphasize, stress, accent; magnify, aggrandize, exalt *ant* temper; mitigate, allay; abate

intent *n, syn* INTENTION, purpose, design, aim, end, object, objective, goal *rel* will, volition, conation *ant* accident

intent *adj* • having one's mind or attention deeply fixed *syn* engrossed, absorbed, rapt *rel* attending, attentive, minding, watching; abstracted, preoccupied; concentrated; riveted *ant* distracted

intention • what one intends to accomplish or attain *syn* intent, purpose, design, aim, end, object, objective, goal *rel* plan, scheme, project; desiring, desire, wishing, wish

intentional *syn* VOLUNTARY, deliberate, willful, willing *rel* intended, meant, purposed, proposed; considered, premeditated, advised, studied, designed, deliberate *ant* instinctive

intercalate *syn* INTRODUCE, interpolate, insert, interpose, interject, insinuate

intercede *syn* INTERPOSE, mediate, intervene, interfere *rel* plead, petition, sue, pray

interchange *syn* EXCHANGE, bandy *rel* transpose, reverse

intercourse • connection or dealing between persons or groups *syn* commerce, traffic, dealings, communication, communion, conversation, converse, correspondence

interdict *syn* FORBID, ban, inhibit, enjoin, prohibit *rel* proscribe, sentence; debar, rule out, exclude; restrain, curb, check *ant* sanction

interesting • holding the attention for some time *syn* engrossing, absorbing, intriguing *rel* stimulating, exciting, provoking, quickening; stirring, rousing, awakening; thrilling, electrifying; amusing, diverting, entertaining; inspiring, animating *ant* boring

interfere 1 *syn* INTERPOSE, intervene, mediate, intercede *rel* impede, obstruct, block, hinder, bar **2** *syn* MEDDLE, intermeddle, tamper *rel* intrude, interlope, butt in, obtrude; incommode, discommode, inconvenience, trouble; thwart, foil, balk, baffle, frustrate

interim *syn* BREAK, gap, interruption, interval, hiatus, lacuna

interior *syn* INNER, inside, internal, inward, intestine *rel* intimate, familiar; spiritual; intrinsic, constitutional, inherent *ant* exterior

interject *syn* INTRODUCE, interpolate, interpose, insert, intercalate, insinuate *rel* throw, cast, toss; obtrude, intrude, interlope, butt in; comment, remark, animadvert

interlope *syn* INTRUDE, butt in, obtrude *rel* trespass, encroach, invade, entrench, infringe; interfere, interpose, intervene

intermeddle *syn* MEDDLE, interfere, tamper *rel* intrude, obtrude, butt in, interlope; entrench, encroach, trespass, invade

interminable *syn* EVERLASTING, unceasing, endless *rel* perpetual, lasting, perdurable, permanent; incessant, continual, continuous, constant; eternal, infinite

intermission *syn* PAUSE, recess, respite, lull *rel* interruption, interval, gap, break; ceasing, cessation, stopping, stop

intermit *syn* DEFER, suspend, stay, postpone *rel* interrupt, arrest, check; stop, discontinue; abate, reduce, lessen, decrease

intermittent • occurring or appearing in interrupted sequence *syn* recurrent, periodic, alternate *rel* interrupted, checked, arrested; fitful, spasmodic; sporadic, occasional, infrequent; discontinuing, discontinuous, stopping, quitting *ant* incessant, continual

intern *syn* IMPRISON, immure, incarcerate, jail *rel* confine, circumscribe, restrict, limit; restrain, curb, check; fetter, manacle, shackle, hamper

internal *syn* INNER, interior, intestine, inward, inside *rel* intrinsic, constitutional, inherent, essential *ant* external

internuncio *syn* AMBASSADOR, nuncio, legate, minister, envoy, chargé d'affaires

interpenetrate *syn* PERMEATE, impenetrate, penetrate, pervade, impregnate, saturate *rel* see IMPENETRATE

interpolate *syn* INTRODUCE, insert, intercalate, insinuate, interpose, interject *rel* enter, introduce, admit; intrude, interlope; add, superadd, annex, append

interpose **1** *syn* INTRODUCE, interject, insert, insinuate, interpolate, intercalate *rel* throw, toss, cast; intrude, obtrude; push, shove, thrust **2** • to come or go between *syn* interfere, intervene, mediate, intercede *rel* intrude, butt in, interlope; meddle, intermeddle; interrupt

interpret *syn* EXPLAIN, elucidate, construe, expound, explicate *rel* illustrate, exemplify; gloss, annotate; comment, commentate

interrogate *syn* ASK, question, catechize, quiz, examine, query, inquire

interrupt *syn* ARREST, check *rel* suspend, stay, intermit, defer, postpone; intrude, obtrude, interlope, butt in; interfere, interpose, intervene

interruption *syn* BREAK, gap, interval, interim, hiatus, lacuna *rel* pause, recess, respite, lull, intermission; breach, rupture, rent, split, rift

interstice *syn* APERTURE, orifice

interval *syn* BREAK, gap, interruption, interim, hiatus, lacuna *rel* period, epoch, age, era; pause, respite, lull, intermission, recess; distance, remoteness, removedness; aperture, interstice, orifice

intervene *syn* INTERPOSE, mediate, intercede, interfere *rel* separate, part, divide, sever; intrude, interlope, butt in, obtrude

intestine *syn* INNER, internal, interior, inside *ant* foreign

intimate *vb, syn* SUGGEST, imply, hint, insinuate *rel* indicate, betoken, attest, bespeak; allude, advert, refer

intimate *adj, syn* FAMILIAR, close, confidential, chummy, thick *rel* nearest, next; devoted, fond, affectionate, loving; secret, privy; friendly, neighborly, amicable; companionable, convivial, social, hospitable, cooperative

intimate *n, syn* FRIEND, confidant, acquaintance *rel* comrade, companion, crony, associate *ant* stranger, outsider

intimidate • to frighten into submission *syn* cow, bulldoze, bully, browbeat *rel* terrorize, terrify, frighten; hector, hound, ride, chivy, bait, badger; coerce, force, compel, constrain, oblige

intolerant *syn* ILLIBERAL, narrow-minded, narrow, bigoted, hidebound *rel* obdurate, inflexible; antipathetic, unsympathetic, averse *ant* tolerant

intonation *syn* INFLECTION, accent

intone *syn* SING, troll, carol, descant, warble, trill, hymn, chant

intoxicated *syn* DRUNK, drunken, inebriated, tipsy, tight *rel* fuddled, befuddled, confused, muddled; maudlin, sentimental

intractable *syn* UNRULY, ungovernable, refractory, recalcitrant, willful, headstrong *rel* obstreperous, boisterous, vociferous; contumacious, rebellious, factious, insubordinate; froward, perverse, contrary, wayward, balky *ant* tractable

intrepid *syn* BRAVE, courageous, unafraid, fearless, valiant, valorous, dauntless, undaunted, doughty, bold, audacious *rel* daring, venturesome, adventurous, daredevil; mettlesome, high-spirited, spirited, fiery; plucky, gritty

intricate *syn* COMPLEX, complicated, involved, knotty *rel* perplexing, puzzling, mystifying, bewildering; tortuous, winding; difficult, hard, arduous

intrigue **1** *syn* PLOT, conspiracy, machination, cabal *rel* scheme, design, plan; stratagem, maneuver, ruse, artifice, trick, feint, gambit, ploy **2** *syn* AMOUR, liaison, affair

intriguing *syn* INTERESTING, engrossing, absorbing *rel* provoking, provocative, piquing, exciting; mystifying, puzzling; luring, tempting, enticing, inveigling

intrinsic *syn* INHERENT, ingrained, constitutional, essential *rel* inner, inward, internal, interior, inside, intestine; innate, inborn, inbred, congenital; natural, normal, typical, regular *ant* extrinsic

introduce **1** *syn* ENTER, admit *rel* induct, install, inaugurate, initiate; instill, inculcate, implant; infuse, inoculate, imbue **2** • to put among or between others *syn* insert, insinuate, interpolate, intercalate, interpose, interject *ant* withdraw; abstract

introduction • something that serves as a preliminary or antecedent *syn* prologue, prelude, preface, foreword, exordium, preamble

introductory *syn* PRELIMINARY, preparatory, prefatory *ant* closing, concluding

intrude • to thrust or force in or upon without permission, welcome, or fitness *syn* obtrude, interlope, butt in *rel* trespass, invade, encroach, entrench, infringe; interject, interpose, insinuate, interpolate, intercalate, introduce; interfere, intervene; meddle, intermeddle, tamper *ant* stand off

intrusive *syn* IMPERTINENT, officious, meddlesome, obtrusive *rel* intruding, butting in, interloping, obtruding; inquisitive, prying, snoopy, nosy, curious; interfering, meddling, intermeddling *ant* retiring; unintrusive

intuition *syn* REASON, understanding *rel* intellect, soul, mind; insight, acumen, discernment *ant* ratiocination

intuitive *syn* INSTINCTIVE *rel* immediate, direct *ant* ratiocinative

inundation *syn* FLOOD, deluge, torrent, spate, cataract

inure *syn* HABITUATE, accustom, addict *rel* adapt, adjust, accommodate

invade *syn* TRESPASS, encroach, entrench, infringe *rel* intrude, obtrude, butt in, interlope; enter, penetrate, pierce, probe; permeate, pervade, impenetrate, interpenetrate

invalidate *syn* NULLIFY, negate, annul, abrogate *rel* negative, counteract, neutralize; void, vacate, quash, annul *ant* validate

invaluable *syn* COSTLY, priceless, precious, valuable, dear, expensive *ant* worthless

invasion • a hostile entrance into the territory of another *syn* incursion, raid, inroad *rel* aggression, attack, offense, offensive; trespass, violation, transgression, infringement, infraction, breach; intruding, intrusion, interloping, butting in, obtruding, obtrusion; encroachment, entrenchment

invective *syn* ABUSE, vituperation, obloquy, scurrility, billingsgate *rel* vilifying, vilification, maligning, calumniation, traducing; animadversion, stricture, aspersion, reflection

inveigle *syn* LURE, decoy, entice, tempt, seduce *rel* snare, ensnare, trap, entrap; beguile, mislead, delude, deceive, betray; cajole, wheedle, blandish, coax

invent *syn* CONTRIVE, devise, frame, concoct *rel* initiate, inaugurate, begin; institute, found, establish

inventory *syn* LIST, register, schedule, catalog, table, roll, roster

invert *syn* REVERSE, transpose *rel* upset, overturn, capsize; interchange, exchange; derange, disarrange

invest **1** *syn* INITIATE, induct, install, inaugurate *rel* endue, endow; consecrate, devote *ant* divest, strip unfrock **2** *syn* BESIEGE, beleaguer, blockade

investigation *syn* INQUIRY, probe, inquest, inquisition, research *rel* inspection, examination, scrutiny, audit; surveying, survey, observing, observation

inveterate • so firmly established that change is almost impossible *syn* confirmed, chronic, deep-seated, deep-rooted *rel* habituated, accustomed, addicted; habitual, customary, usual; hardened, indurated; settled, set, fixed, established; inbred, innate; persisting, persistent, enduring, abiding

invidious *syn* REPUGNANT, distasteful, obnoxious, repellent, abhorrent *rel* hateful, odious, abominable, detestable; offensive, loathsome, revolting, repulsive

invigorate *syn* STRENGTHEN, fortify, energize, reinforce *rel* renew, restore, refresh, rejuvenate; stir, rally, rouse; vitalize, activate *ant* debilitate

invincible • incapable of being conquered *syn* unconquerable, indomitable, impregnable, inexpugnable, unassailable, invulnerable *rel* dauntless, undaunted, intrepid

inviolable *syn* SACRED, inviolate, sacrosanct *rel* hallowed, consecrated, dedicated; holy, blessed, divine, religious; pure, chaste

inviolate *syn* SACRED, sacrosanct, inviolable *ant* violated

invite • to request the presence or participation of *syn* bid, solicit, court, woo *rel* ask, request; lure, tempt, entice, inveigle; excite, provoke, stimulate

involve **1** *syn* ENTANGLE, enmesh *rel* complicate; confuse, confound, mistake; perplex, mystify, nonplus, puzzle **2** *syn* INCLUDE, comprehend, embrace, imply, subsume *rel* import, mean, signify, denote; bespeak, attest, betoken, indicate, argue, prove **3** • to bring a person or thing into circumstances or a situation from which extrication is difficult *syn* implicate *rel* ensnare, entrap, snare, trap, catch; connect, link, associate, relate, join; embarrass; fetter, shackle, hamper

involved *syn* COMPLEX, intricate, complicated, knotty *rel* confused, muddled; perplexing, puzzling, bewildering, mystifying; difficult, hard, arduous

invulnerable *syn* INVINCIBLE, impregnable, inexpugnable, unassailable, unconquerable, indomitable *ant* vulnerable

inward *syn* INNER, interior, internal, inside, intestine *rel* inbred, innate, inborn; ingrained, inherent, intrinsic, constitutional; intimate, familiar; objective, sensible, material; heartfelt, unfeigned, sincere; impalpable, imperceptible *ant* outward

iota *syn* PARTICLE, jot, tittle, whit, bit, mite, smidgen, atom

irascible • easily aroused to anger *syn* choleric, splenetic, testy, touchy, cranky, cross *rel* irritable, fractious, snappish, waspish, huffy, querulous, petulant, peevish; impatient, restive, jumpy, jittery, nervous; crabbed, surly

irate *syn* ANGRY, wrathful, wroth, mad, indignant, acrimonious *rel* provoked, exasperated, nettled, irritated; incensed, infuriated, enraged

ire *syn* ANGER, rage, fury, indignation, wrath *rel* passion; temper, humor, mood

irenic *syn* PACIFIC, peaceable, peaceful, pacifist, pacifistic *rel* conciliating, conciliatory, placating, placatory, propitiating, propitiatory *ant* acrimonious

iridescent *syn* PRISMATIC, opalescent, opaline

irk *syn* ANNOY, vex, bother *rel* perturb, disturb, upset, discompose; discommode, incommode, trouble, inconvenience; fret, chafe, abrade

irksome • tending to cause boredom or tedium *syn* tiresome, wearisome, tedious, boring *rel* dull, stupid, slow; fatiguing, exhausting, fagging, tiring *ant* absorbing, engrossing

ironic *syn* SARCASTIC, satiric, sardonic *rel* biting, cutting, incisive, trenchant; caustic, mordant, scathing

irony *syn* WIT, satire, sarcasm, humor, repartee

irrational • not governed or guided by reason *syn* unreasonable *rel* absurd, preposterous, foolish, silly; fatuous, asinine, simple; crazy, demented, mad, insane *ant* rational

irregular • not conforming to rule, law, or custom *syn* anomalous, unnatural *rel* aberrant, abnormal, atypical; exceptional; singular, unique, strange, peculiar, odd, queer *ant* regular

irreligious • lacking religious emotions, doctrines, or practices *syn* unreligious, nonreligious, ungodly, godless *rel* impious, profane, blasphemous, sacrilegious; immoral, amoral, unmoral *ant* religious

irritable • easily exasperated *syn* fractious, peevish, snappish, waspish, petulant, pettish, huffy, fretful, querulous *rel* cranky, cross, testy, touchy, choleric, splenetic, irascible *ant* easygoing

irritate • to excite a feeling of anger or annoyance *syn* exasperate, nettle, provoke, aggravate, rile, peeve *rel* annoy, vex, irk, bother; incense, anger, madden, enrage, infuriate; offend, affront; fret, chafe, abrade

isolate • to set apart from others *syn* segregate, seclude, insulate, sequester *rel* detach, disengage, abstract; separate, part, sever, sunder

isolation *syn* SOLITUDE, alienation, seclusion *rel* loneliness, solitariness, loneness, desolateness, desolation

issue *n* **1** *syn* EFFECT, outcome, result, consequence, upshot, aftereffect, aftermath, sequel, event *rel* ending, end, termination, concluding, conclusion, closing **2** *syn* OFFSPRING, young, progeny, descendant, posterity

issue *vb, syn* SPRING, emanate, proceed, flow, derive, originate, arise, rise, stem *rel* emerge, appear, loom

item • one of the distinct parts of a whole *syn* detail, particular *rel* thing, object, article; constituent, component, element, factor

itemized *syn* CIRCUMSTANTIAL, detailed, particularized, minute, particular *ant* summarized

iterate *syn* REPEAT, reiterate, ingeminate

itinerant • traveling from place to place *syn* peripatetic, ambulatory, ambulant, nomadic, vagrant *rel* wandering, roving, rambling, straying, roaming, ranging; moving, shifting

J

jabber *syn* CHAT, chatter, gab, patter, prate, prattle, babble, gabble, gibber

jack *syn* FLAG, ensign, standard, banner, color, streamer, pennant, pendant, pennon

jade *syn* TIRE, exhaust, fatigue, weary, fag, tucker *rel* oppress, depress, weigh; enervate, unnerve, unman, emasculate; sate, satiate, surfeit, pall, cloy *ant* refresh

jail *syn* IMPRISON, incarcerate, immure, intern *rel* confine, circumscribe, restrict, limit; shackle, manacle, fetter

jam *vb, syn* PRESS, crowd, squeeze, bear, bear down *rel* crush, squash; pack, cram, stuff, ram, tamp

jam *n, syn* PREDICAMENT, plight, fix, dilemma, quandary, scrape, pickle *rel* difficulty, vicissitude; pinch, strait, exigency

jape *syn* JOKE, jest, quip, witticism, wisecrack, crack, gag

jar *syn* IMPACT, jolt, impingement, collision, clash, shock, concussion, percussion *rel* shaking, shake, quaking, quake; vibration, fluctuation, swaying, sway; agitation, disturbance, upsetting, upset

jargon *syn* DIALECT, vernacular, patois, lingo, cant, argot, slang *rel* idiom, speech, language; abracadabra, gibberish

jaunt *syn* JOURNEY, excursion, trip, tour, voyage, cruise, expedition, pilgrimage

jaw *syn* SCOLD, upbraid, rate, berate, tongue-lash, bawl, chew out, wig, rail, revile, vituperate *rel* censure, denounce, reprobate, reprehend, criticize, blame, condemn; reprove, reproach, chide, reprimand, rebuke

jealous *syn* ENVIOUS *rel* suspicious, mistrustful; doubtful, dubious; vigilant, watchful, alert; distrusting, mistrusting

jeer *syn* SCOFF, gibe, fleer, gird, sneer, flout *rel* deride, ridicule, mock, taunt, twit, rally

jejune *syn* INSIPID, vapid, flat, wishy-washy, inane, banal *rel* thin, slight, slim, tenuous; arid, dry; attenuated, extenuated, diluted, thinned; meager, skimpy, exiguous

jell, jelly *syn* COAGULATE, congeal, set, curdle, clot *rel* solidify, harden; cohere, stick; compact, consolidate

jeopardize *syn* VENTURE, hazard, risk, chance, endanger, imperil *rel* brave, dare; meet, encounter, confront, face

jeopardy *syn* DANGER, peril, hazard, risk *rel* threatening, threat, menacing, menace; exposure; liability, susceptibility, sensitiveness, openness; chance, accident, hap

jeremiad *syn* TIRADE, diatribe, philippic

jerk • to make a sudden sharp quick movement *syn* snap, twitch, yank *rel* pull, drag, toss, sling, fling, throw; wrench, wrest, wring

jest **1** *syn* JOKE, jape, quip, witticism, wisecrack, crack, gag *rel* badinage, persiflage, raillery; bantering, banter, chaffing, chaff, jollying, jolly; twitting, twit, ridiculing, ridicule, deriding, derision **2** *syn* FUN, sport, game, play *rel* diversion, entertainment, amusement; joviality, merriment

jetty *syn* WHARF, dock, pier, quay, slip, berth, levee

jib *syn* DEMUR, balk, shy, boggle, stickle, stick, strain, scruple

jibe *syn* AGREE, harmonize, accord, conform, square, tally, correspond

jiffy *syn* INSTANT, moment, minute, second, flash, twinkling, split second

jittery *syn* IMPATIENT, jumpy, nervous, unquiet, restless, restive, uneasy, fidgety *rel* unnerved, unmanned; perturbed, agitated, disquieted, upset, discomposed

job *syn* TASK, duty, assignment, stint, chore *rel* office, function, province; business, concern, affair, matter, thing

jocose *syn* WITTY, jocular, facetious, humorous *rel* waggish, sportive, playful, roguish; comic, comical, laughable, ludicrous, droll, funny; merry, jolly, jovial, jocund, blithe

jocular *syn* WITTY, jocose, humorous, facetious *rel* jovial, jolly, merry; playful, sportive; funny, droll, comic, comical, laughable, ludicrous, ridiculous

jocund *syn* MERRY, blithe, jolly, jovial *rel* joyful, joyous, cheerful, lighthearted, happy, glad; mirthful, hilarious, gleeful; sportive, playful, mischievous

jog *vb, syn* POKE, prod, nudge *rel* shake, agitate; push, shove

jog *n, syn* POKE, prod, nudge

join • to bring or come together into some manner of union *syn* conjoin, combine, unite, connect, link, associate, relate *rel* cooperate, concur; articulate, concatenate, integrate; attach, affix, fasten; knit, weave; tie, bind *ant* disjoin; part

joint • a place where two or more things are united *syn* articulation, suture

joke • something said or done to provoke laughter *syn* jest, jape, quip, witticism, wisecrack, crack, gag *rel* prank, caper, antic, monkeyshine, dido; trick, ruse, wile; travesty, parody, burlesque, caricature; raillery, badinage, persiflage; jocoseness, jocularity, facetiousness, wittiness, humorousness; wit, humor, repartee, sarcasm

jollity *syn* MIRTH, hilarity, glee *rel* merriment, joviality, jocundity, blitheness; sport, disport, play, frolic, rollick, gambol, romp; diversion, amusement, recreation, entertainment; fun, jest, game

jolly *adj, syn* MERRY, jovial, jocund, blithe *rel* bantering, chaffing, jollying, joshing; jocular, jocose, witty, humorous, facetious; sportive, playful, mischievous, roguish, waggish, frolicsome; gay, lively, vivacious, animated, sprightly

jolly *vb, syn* BANTER, chaff, kid, rag, rib, josh *rel* blandish, cajole; deride, ridicule, twit, rally, mock, taunt

jolt *syn* IMPACT, jar, shock, impingement, collision, clash, concussion, percussion *rel* shaking, shake, rocking, rock, convulsing, convulsion

josh *syn* BANTER, chaff, kid, rag, rib, jolly

jot *syn* PARTICLE, tittle, iota, bit, mite, smidgen, whit, atom

journal • a publication that appears at regular intervals *syn* periodical, newspaper, magazine, review, organ

journey • travel or a passage from one place to another *syn* voyage, tour, trip, jaunt, excursion, cruise, expedition, pilgrimage

jovial *syn* MERRY, jolly, jocund, blithe *rel* jocular, jocose, facetious, humorous, witty; genial, sociable, affable; good-natured, amiable; bantering, chaffing, jollying, joshing

joy *syn* PLEASURE, delight, enjoyment, delectation, fruition *rel* bliss, beatitude, happiness, felicity; ecstasy, rapture, transport *ant* sorrow; misery; abomination

joyful *syn* GLAD, joyous, cheerful, happy, lighthearted *rel* blithe, jocund, merry, jolly; buoyant, effervescent, expansive *ant* joyless

joyous *syn* GLAD, joyful, happy, cheerful, lighthearted *rel* blithe, jocund, merry; rapturous, ecstatic, transported *ant* lugubrious

judge *vb* **1** • to decide something in dispute or controversy upon its merits and upon evidence *syn* adjudge, adjudicate, arbitrate *rel* determine, decide, settle, rule **2** *syn* INFER, conclude, deduce, gather *rel* prove, demonstrate, try, test

judge *n* • a person who impartially decides unsettled questions or controversial issues *syn* arbiter, arbitrator, referee, umpire

judgment **1** *syn* INFERENCE, conclusion, deduction *rel* decision, determination, ruling; opinion, conviction, persuasion, view, belief **2** *syn* SENSE, wisdom, gumption *rel* intelligence, wit, brain, mind; sagaciousness, sagacity, perspicaciousness, perspicacity, shrewdness, astuteness; acumen, discernment, insight, penetration; prudence, discretion

judicious *syn* WISE, sage, sapient, prudent, sensible, sane *rel* rational, reasonable; just, fair, equitable, dispassionate, objective; sagacious, perspicacious, astute, shrewd; discreet, prudent *ant* injudicious; asinine

jumble *syn* CONFUSION, disorder, chaos, disarray, clutter, snarl, muddle

jump *vb* • to move suddenly through space by or as if by muscular action *syn* leap, spring, bound, vault

jump *n* • a sudden move through space *syn* leap, spring, bound, vault

jumpy *syn* IMPATIENT, jittery, nervous, restless, uneasy, fidgety, unquiet, restive *ant* steady

junction • the act, state, or place of meeting or uniting *syn* confluence, concourse

juncture • a critical or crucial time or state of affairs *syn* pass, exigency, emergency, contingency, pinch, strait, crisis *rel* state, posture, situation, condition, status; predicament, plight, quandary

junk *syn* DISCARD, scrap, cast, shed, molt, slough

jurisdiction *syn* POWER, authority, control, command, sway, dominion *rel* limits, bounds, confines; range, scope, compass, reach; circuit, periphery; province, office, function, duty; domain, territory, field, sphere, bailiwick

just **1** *syn* UPRIGHT, honorable, conscientious, scrupulous, honest *rel* strict, rigid; virtuous, righteous, moral, ethical, noble; reliable, dependable, tried, trustworthy **2** *syn* FAIR, equitable, impartial, unbiased, dispassionate, uncolored, objective *rel* detached, disinterested, aloof, indifferent; due, rightful, condign; rational, reasonable *ant* unjust

justice • awarding each what is rightly due *syn* equity

justify **1** *syn* MAINTAIN, vindicate, defend, assert *rel* prove, demonstrate; support, uphold, back **2** *syn* EXPLAIN, account, rationalize *rel* excuse, condone; exculpate, exonerate, absolve, acquit, vindicate; extenuate, gloze, gloss, whitewash, palliate **3** • to constitute sufficient grounds *syn* warrant *rel* allow, permit, let; sanction, approve; authorize

jut *syn* BULGE, stick out, protrude, project, overhang, beetle *rel* extend, lengthen, elongate; swell, distend, dilate, expand

juvenile *syn* YOUTHFUL, puerile, boyish, virgin, virginal, maiden *rel* immature, unmatured; callow, green, crude *ant* adult; senile

juxtaposed *syn* ADJACENT, adjoining, contiguous, abutting, tangent, conterminous *rel* close, near, nigh

K

keen *adj* **1** *syn* SHARP, acute *rel* piercing, penetrating, probing; pungent, poignant, piquant; cutting, biting, incisive, trenchant *ant* blunt **2** *syn* EAGER, avid, agog, athirst, anxious *rel* ardent, fervent, fervid, perfervid, impassioned; intense, vehement, fierce; fired

keen *vb, syn* CRY, wait, weep, whimper, blubber *rel* lament, bewail, bemoan; mourn, sorrow, grieve

keep *vb* **1** • to notice or honor a day, occasion, or deed *syn* observe, celebrate, solemnize, commemorate *rel* regard, respect *ant* break **2** • to hold in one's possession or under one's control *syn* keep back, keep out, retain, detain, withhold, reserve, hold back *rel* save, preserve, conserve; hold, have, enjoy, possess, own; control, direct, manage, conduct *ant* relinquish

keep *n, syn* LIVING, livelihood, subsistence, sustenance, maintenance, support, bread

keep back, keep out *syn* KEEP, retain, detain, withhold, reserve, hold, hold back

keepsake *syn* REMEMBRANCE, remembrancer, reminder, memorial, memento, token, souvenir

ken *syn* RANGE, gamut, reach, radius, compass, sweep, scope, orbit, horizon, purview *rel* field, sphere, province, domain; view, sight

kibitzer *syn* SPECTATOR, onlooker, looker-on, bystander, observer, beholder, witness, eyewitness

kick *syn* OBJECT, protest, remonstrate, expostulate *rel* oppose, combat, resist, withstand, fight; criticize, denounce, condemn; objurgate, execrate, curse, damn, anathematize

kid *syn* BANTER, chaff, rag, rib, josh, jolly *rel* tease, plague, pester, harry, worry

kidnap *syn* ABDUCT

kidney *syn* TYPE, kind, sort, nature, description, character, stripe, ilk

kill • to deprive of life *syn* slay, murder, assassinate, dispatch, execute

kind *n, syn* TYPE, sort, stripe, kidney, ilk, description, nature, character

kind *adj* • showing or having a gentle considerate nature *syn* kindly, benign, benignant *rel* benevolent, charitable, humane, altruistic, philanthropic, eleemosynary, humanitarian; sympathetic, warm, warmhearted, responsive, tender, compassionate; clement, lenient, indulgent, merciful, forbearing, tolerant; amiable, good-natured, complaisant, obliging *ant* unkind

kindle *syn* LIGHT, ignite, fire *rel* blaze, flame, flare, glow; provoke, excite, stimulate; arouse, rouse, stir; incite, foment, instigate *ant* smother, stifle

kindly *syn* KIND, benign, benignant *rel* gracious, cordial, genial, affable, sociable; amiable, good-natured, complaisant, obliging; friendly, neighborly, amicable; considerate, thoughtful, attentive *ant* unkindly; acrid (*of temper, attitudes, comments*)

kindred *syn* RELATED, cognate, allied, affiliated *ant* alien

kingly • of, relating to, or befitting one who occupies a throne *syn* regal, royal, queenly, imperial, princely

knack *syn* GIFT, bent, turn, faculty, aptitude, genius, talent *rel* ability, capacity, capability; aptness, readiness, quickness; facility, dexterity, ease *ant* ineptitude

knave *syn* VILLAIN, scoundrel, blackguard, rascal, rogue, scamp, rapscallion, miscreant

knit *syn* WEAVE, crochet, braid, plait, tat *rel* join, connect, link, unite

knock *vb, syn* TAP, rap, thump, thud *rel* strike, hit, smite; beat, pound, pummel

knock *n, syn* TAP, rap, thump, thud *rel* pounding, beating

knotty *syn* COMPLEX, intricate, involved, complicated

knowing *syn* INTELLIGENT, alert, bright, smart, clever, quick-witted, brilliant *rel* shrewd, astute, perspicacious, sagacious; watchful, vigilant; discerning, observing, observant, perceiving, perceptive

knowledge • what is or can be known by an individual or by mankind *syn* science, learning, erudition, scholarship, information, lore *ant* ignorance

L

label *n, syn* MARK, brand, stamp, tag, ticket

label *vb, syn* MARK, brand, stamp, tag, ticket

labor *syn* WORK, toil, travail, drudgery, grind *rel* effort, exertion, pains, trouble; endeavor, striving, struggle

labored *syn* FORCED, strained, farfetched *rel* heavy, ponderous, weighty; awkward, clumsy, maladroit, inept; stiff, wooden, rigid

laborer *syn* WORKER, working man, workman, craftsman, handicraftsman, mechanic, artisan, operative, hand, roustabout

lack *vb* • to be without something, esp. something essential or greatly needed *syn* want, need, require

lack *n* • the fact or state of being wanting or deficient *syn* want, dearth, absence, defect, privation *rel* need, necessity, exigency; deficiency; exhaustion, impoverishment, draining, depletion

lackadaisical *syn* LANGUID, listless, spiritless, enervated, languishing, languorous *rel* indifferent, unconcerned, incurious; indolent, slothful, faineant, lazy; inert, inactive, passive, supine, idle; sentimental, romantic; emasculated

laconic *syn* CONCISE, succinct, terse, summary, pithy, compendious *rel* curt, brusque, bluff; brief, short *ant* verbose

lacuna *syn* BREAK, gap, hiatus, interruption, interval, interim

lade *syn* BURDEN, load, encumber, cumber, weigh, weight, tax, charge, saddle *ant* unlade

lading *syn* LOAD, freight, cargo, burden

ladle *syn* DIP, scoop, spoon, dish, bail

lady *syn* FEMALE, woman

ladylike *syn* FEMALE, feminine, womanly,

womanlike, womanish *rel* dainty, fastidious, finicky, particular, nice; fashionable, modish, smart, chic, stylish; decorous, proper, seemly

lag *syn* DELAY, loiter, dawdle, procrastinate *rel* slow, slacken, retard; tarry, linger, wait, stay

laggard *syn* SLOW, dilatory, leisurely, deliberate *rel* dawdling, loitering, delaying, procrastinating; lethargic, sluggish, comatose; phlegmatic, apathetic, impassive *ant* prompt, quick

lambent *syn* BRIGHT, beaming, luminous, brilliant, radiant, lustrous, effulgent, refulgent, lucent, incandescent *rel* gleaming, glistening

lament *syn* DEPLORE, bewail, bemoan *rel* weep, keen, wail, cry; grieve, mourn, sorrow *ant* exult; rejoice

lampoon *syn* LIBEL, skit, squib, pas quinade

land *syn* ALIGHT, light, perch, roost *rel* arrive, come; reach, gain, achieve, attain; appear, emerge

landing field, landing strip *syn* AIRPORT, airdrome, airfield, airstrip, flying field

language 1 • a body or system of words and phrases used by a large community or by a people, a nation, or a group of nations *syn* dialect, tongue, speech, idiom *rel* vernacular, patois, lingo, jargon, cant, argot, slang **2** • oral or written expression or a quality of such expression that is dependent on the variety, or arrangement, or expressiveness of words *syn* vocabulary, phraseology, phrasing, diction, style

languid • lacking in vim or energy *syn* languishing, languorous, lackadaisical, listless, spiritless, enervated *rel* lethargic, sluggish, comatose, torpid; phlegmatic, apathetic, impassive; inert, inactive, supine *ant* vivacious; chipper

languishing *syn* LANGUID, languorous, lackadaisical, listless, spiritless, enervated *rel* weakened, enfeebled, debilitated; indolent, faineant, lazy; inert, inactive, supine; sentimental, romantic; pining, longing, yearning *ant* thriving, flourishing; unaffected

languor *syn* LETHARGY, lassitude, stupor, torpor, torpidity *rel* exhaustion, fatigue, weariness; ennui, doldrums, tedium; depression, blues, dumps *ant* alacrity

languorous *syn* LANGUID, languishing, lackadaisical, listless, spiritless, enervated *rel* leisurely, laggard, slow, dilatory; indolent, slothful, faineant, lazy; passive, inert, inactive, supine; relaxed, slack, lax, loose; pampered, indulged *ant* vigorous; strenuous (*of times, seasons*)

lank, lanky *syn* LEAN, gaunt, rawboned, spare, angular, scrawny, skinny *rel* thin, slim, slender, slight; attenuated, extenuated *ant* burly

lapse *n* **1** *syn* ERROR, slip, mistake, blunder, faux pas, bull, howler, boner *rel* offense, sin, vice, crime; fault, failing, frailty, foible; transgression, breach, violation, trespass **2** • a fall back into a state or condition from which one has been raised *syn* relapse, backsliding *rel* deterioration, decline, declension, decadence, degeneration, devolution; retrograding, retrogradation, receding, recession; retrogressiveness, retrogression, regressiveness, regression

lapse *vb* • to fall from a better or higher state into a lower or poorer one *syn* relapse, backslide *rel* revert, return; slip, slide; deteriorate, degenerate, decline; descend; recede, retrograde

larcener, larcenist *syn* THIEF, robber, burglar

larceny *syn* THEFT, robbery, burglary

large • above the average of its kind in magnitude *syn* big, great *rel* vast, immense, enormous, huge, mammoth, colossal, gigantic; tremendous, prodigious, monumental, stupendous, monstrous; inordinate, excessive, exorbitant, extreme, immoderate, extravagant *ant* small

largely • in a reasonably inclusive manner *syn* greatly, mostly, chiefly, mainly, principally, generally

largess *syn* GIFT, boon, present, gratuity, favor *rel* benefaction, donation, contribution; grant, subvention

lascivious *syn* LICENTIOUS, lewd, libertine, lustful, libidinous, lecherous, wanton *rel* immoral, unmoral, amoral; sensual, carnal, fleshly, animal; obscene, gross, coarse

lassitude *syn* LETHARGY, languor, stupor, torpor, torpidity *rel* exhaustion, weariness, fatigue; ennui, doldrums, tedium; dumps, blues, depression; impotence, powerlessness *ant* vigor

last *vb*, *syn* CONTINUE, endure, abide, persist *rel* survive, outlast, outlive; remain, stay *ant* fleet

last *adj* • following all others as in time, order, or importance *syn* latest, final, terminal, concluding, eventual, ultimate *ant* first

lasting • enduring so long as to seem fixed or established *syn* permanent, perdurable, durable, stable, perpetual *rel* enduring, abiding, persisting, persistent, continuing; everlasting, endless, unceasing; continual, continuous, incessant, unremitting, perennial; eternal, sempiternal *ant* fleeting

late 1 *syn* TARDY, behindhand, overdue *rel* delayed, retarded, detained *ant* early; punctual, prompt **2** *syn* DEAD, departed, deceased, defunct, lifeless, inanimate **3** *syn* MODERN, recent

latent • not now showing signs of activity or existence *syn* dormant, quiescent, potential, abeyant *rel* hidden, concealed; inactive, inert, idle; unripe, unmatured, immature *ant* patent

latest *syn* LAST, final, terminal, concluding, eventual, ultimate *ant* earliest

lather *syn* FOAM, suds, froth, spume, scum, yeast

laud *syn* PRAISE, extol, eulogize, acclaim *rel* magnify, aggrandize, exalt; worship, adore, venerate, revere, reverence; commend, applaud, compliment *ant* revile

laughable • provoking laughter or mirth *syn* risible, ludicrous, ridiculous, comic, comical, farcical, droll, funny *rel* amusing, diverting, entertaining; humorous, witty, facetious, jocular, jocose

lavish *syn* PROFUSE, prodigal, luxuriant, lush, exuberant *rel* liberal, bountiful, bounteous, openhanded, generous, munificent, handsome; sumptuous, opulent, luxurious; excessive, inordinate, extravagant *ant* sparing

law 1 • a principle governing action or procedure *syn* rule, regulation, precept, statute, ordinance, canon *rel* mandate, dictate, command **2** *syn* PRINCIPLE, axiom, fundamental, theorem *rel* necessity, exigency *ant* chance

lawful • being in accordance with law *syn* legal, legitimate, licit *rel* rightful, due, condign; allowed, allowable, permitted, permissible; justified, justifiable, warranted, warrantable *ant* unlawful

lawlessness *syn* ANARCHY, chaos *rel* discord, strife, dissension, contention, conflict, difference, variance; confusion, disorder *ant* discipline; order

lawsuit *syn* SUIT, action, cause, case

lawyer • a person authorized to practice law in the courts or to serve clients in the capacity of legal agent or adviser *syn* counselor, barrister, counsel, advocate, attorney, solicitor

lax 1 *syn* LOOSE, relaxed, slack *rel* limp, floppy, flabby, flaccid *ant* rigid **2** *syn* NEGLIGENT, remiss, neglectful *rel* careless, heedless, thoughtless; indifferent, unconcerned; forgetful, unmindful, oblivious *ant* strict, stringent

lay *vb, syn* DIRECT, aim, point, level, train

lay *adj, syn* PROFANE, secular, temporal

laze *syn* IDLE, loaf, lounge, loll *rel* relax, rest, repose

lazy • not easily aroused to activity *syn* indolent, slothful, faineant *rel* inert, idle, inactive, supine, passive; torpid, comatose, sluggish, lethargic; languid, languorous, lackadaisical, listless; slack, remiss, lax, negligent, neglectful

lead *syn* GUIDE, pilot, engineer, steer *rel* conduct, direct, manage, control; set, fix, establish; command, order; induce, persuade, prevail, get *ant* follow

leader *syn* CHIEF, head, chieftain, master *ant* follower

leading *syn* CHIEF, principal, main, foremost, capital *rel* governing, ruling; conducting, directing, managing, controlling; prominent, outstanding; eminent, famous; preeminent, supreme, superlative *ant* subordinate

league *syn* ALLIANCE, coalition, fusion, confederacy, confederation, federation

lean *vb, syn* SLANT, slope, incline *rel* bend, curve; turn, deflect, divert, sheer

lean *adj* • thin because of an absence of excess flesh *syn* spare, lank, lanky, gaunt, rawboned, angular, scrawny, skinny *rel* slender, slim, thin, slight; cadaverous, wasted, pinched, haggard *ant* fleshy

leaning • a strong instinct or liking for something *syn* propensity, proclivity, penchant, flair *rel* bias, predilection, partiality, prepossession, prejudice; inclining, inclination, predisposition; bent, turn, aptitude, faculty, gift *ant* distaste

leap *vb, syn* JUMP, spring, bound, vault *rel* rise, arise, mount, soar, ascend

leap *n, syn* JUMP, spring, bound, vault

learn *syn* DISCOVER, ascertain, determine, unearth

learned • possessing or manifesting unusually wide and deep knowledge *syn* scholarly, erudite *rel* cultivated, cultured; pedantic, academic, scholastic, bookish; recondite, abstruse, esoteric

learning *syn* KNOWLEDGE, erudition, scholarship, science, information, lore *rel* culture, cultivation, breeding, refinement; enlightenment

lease *syn* HIRE, let, charter, rent

leave *vb* **1** *syn* WILL, bequeath, devise, legate *rel* commit, entrust, confide, consign; assign, allot, apportion **2** *syn* RELINQUISH, resign, surrender, abandon, yield, cede, waive *rel* forsake, desert; forgo, forbear, sacrifice, abnegate, eschew; neglect, ignore, forget, omit; grant, concede, vouchsafe; relegate, commit, confide, entrust **3** *syn* GO, depart, quit, withdraw, retire *rel* escape, flee, fly, abscond, decamp **4** *syn* LET, allow, permit, suffer

leave *n, syn* PERMISSION, sufferance *rel* consenting, consent, assenting, assent; sanctioning, sanction, endorsement, approval; authorization

leaven *syn* INFUSE, imbue, inoculate, ingrain, suffuse *rel* temper, qualify, moderate; inform, animate, inspire; pervade, permeate, impregnate, saturate; vivify, enliven, quicken

leavings *syn* REMAINDER, remains, residue, residuum, rest, balance, remnant *rel* fragments, pieces, portions; discardings, discards, scrappings, scraps, junkings; junk

lecherous *syn* LICENTIOUS, libidinous, lascivious, lustful, lewd, wanton, libertine *rel* dissolute, abandoned, reprobate, profligate; degenerate, corrupt

lecture *syn* SPEECH, address, oration, harangue, talk, sermon, homily

leech *syn* PARASITE, sponge, sponger, sycophant, toady, lickspittle, bootlicker, hanger-on, favorite

lees *syn* DEPOSIT, precipitate, sediment, dregs, grounds *rel* refuse, waste

leeway *syn* ROOM, berth, play, elbowroom, margin, clearance

legal *syn* LAWFUL, legitimate, licit *ant* illegal

legal tender *syn* MONEY, cash, currency, specie, coin, coinage

legate *n, syn* AMBASSADOR, nuncio, internuncio, chargé d'affaires, minister, envoy

legate *vb, syn* WILL, bequeath, devise, leave

legend **1** *syn* MYTH, saga **2** *syn* INSCRIPTION, caption

legendary *syn* FICTITIOUS, mythical, apocryphal, fabulous

legerity *syn* CELERITY, alacrity *rel* nimbleness, agility, briskness, spryness; swiftness, fleetness, rapidity; dexterity, ease, readiness, facility; dispatch, expedition, speed *ant* deliberateness; sluggishness

legion *syn* MULTITUDE, host, army

legitimate *syn* LAWFUL, legal, licit *rel* justified, justifiable, warranted, warrantable; valid, sound, cogent; recognized, acknowledged; customary, usual; regular, normal, typical, natural *ant* illegitimate; arbitrary

leisure *syn* REST, relaxation, repose, ease, comfort *ant* toil

leisurely *syn* SLOW, deliberate, dilatory, laggard *rel* relaxed, slack, lax, loose; slackened, retarded, delayed; easy, comfortable, restful *ant* hurried; abrupt

leitmotiv *syn* SUBJECT, motive, motif, theme, matter, subject matter, argument, topic, text

lengthen *syn* EXTEND, elongate, prolong, protract *rel* increase, augment; expand, amplify, distend *ant* shorten

leniency *syn* FORBEARANCE, clemency, mercifulness, tolerance, indulgence *rel* lenity, mercy, charity, grace; kindliness, benignity, benignancy, kindness; compassionateness, tenderness

lenient **1** *syn* SOFT, gentle, smooth, mild, bland, balmy *rel* assuaging, alleviating, relieving; grateful, agreeable, welcome, gratifying, pleasing, pleasant *ant* caustic **2** *syn* FORBEARING, indulgent, merciful, clement, tolerant *rel* forgiving, excusing, condoning, pardoning; kindly, benign, benignant; compassionate, tender; indulging, pampering, humoring, spoiling, mollycoddling; lax *ant* stern; exacting

leniently *syn* FORBEARINGLY, tolerantly, clemently, mercifully, indulgently

lenity *syn* MERCY, clemency, charity, grace *rel* leniency, indulgence, clemency, mercifulness, forbearance, tolerance; benignity, benignancy, kindliness, kindness; compassionateness, compassion, tenderness;

benevolence, humaneness, charitableness; laxity *ant* severity

lesion *syn* WOUND, trauma, traumatism, bruise, contusion *rel* injury, hurt, damage

lessen *syn* DECREASE, diminish, reduce, abate, dwindle *rel* shorten, curtail, retrench, abridge, abbreviate; shrink, contract; lighten, mitigate, alleviate, relieve; thin, dilute, attenuate

let 1 *syn* HIRE, lease, rent, charter **2** • to neither forbid nor prevent *syn* allow, permit, suffer, leave *rel* sanction, endorse, approve, accredit, certify; authorize, license, commission

lethal *syn* DEADLY, fatal, mortal *rel* destroying, destructive; killing, slaying; pernicious, baneful, noxious; poisonous, virulent, venomous, toxic

lethargic • deficient in alertness or activity *syn* sluggish, torpid, comatose *rel* inert, idle, inactive, supine, passive; phlegmatic, stolid, impassive, apathetic; languid, languorous, lackadaisical, listless; slow, dilatory, laggard *ant* energetic, vigorous

lethargy • physical or mental inertness *syn* languor, lassitude, stupor, torpor, torpidity *rel* sluggishness, comatoseness; indolence, slothfulness, sloth, laziness; inertness, inertia, inactivity, idleness, passiveness, supineness; apathy, phlegm, impassivity *ant* vigor

letter • a direct or personal written or printed message addressed to a person or organization *syn* epistle, missive, note, message, dispatch, report, memorandum

levee *syn* WHARF, dock, pier, quay, slip, berth, jetty

level *vb, syn* DIRECT, point, train, aim, lay

level *adj* • having a surface without bends, curves, or irregularities *syn* flat, plane, plain, even, smooth, flush *rel* parallel, uniform, like, alike, akin, identical, similar; same, equivalent, equal

levitate *syn* RISE, arise, ascend, mount, soar, tower, rocket, surge *ant* gravitate, sink

levity *syn* LIGHTNESS, light-mindedness, frivolity, flippancy, volatility, flightiness *rel* foolishness, folly, silliness, absurdity; gaiety, liveliness, sprightliness, vivaciousness, vivacity *ant* gravity

lewd *syn* LICENTIOUS, lustful, lascivious, libidinous, lecherous, wanton, libertine *rel* immoral, unmoral, amoral; gross, coarse, obscene; indecent, indelicate, indecorous *ant* chaste

liability *syn* DEBT, indebtedness, obligation, debit, arrear *ant* asset (*or plural* assets)

liable 1 *syn* RESPONSIBLE, amenable, answerable, accountable *rel* obliged, constrained, compelled; bound, tied **2** • being by nature or through circumstances likely to experience something adverse *syn* open, exposed, subject, prone, susceptible, sensitive *ant* exempt, immune **3** *syn* APT, likely

liaison *syn* AMOUR, intrigue, affair

libel *n* • a public and often satirical presentation of the faults or weaknesses, esp. of an individual *syn* skit, squib, lampoon, pasquinade *rel* scurrility, invective, vituperation, abuse; burlesque, travesty, caricature

libel *vb, syn* MALIGN, defame, slander, traduce, asperse, vilify, calumniate *rel* revile, vituperate; decry, disparage, derogate, detract; caricature, travesty, burlesque

liberal 1 • giving or given freely and unstintingly *syn* generous, bountiful, bounteous, openhanded, munificent, handsome *rel* lavish, prodigal, profuse, exuberant; benevolent, philanthropic, eleemosynary, charitable *ant* close **2** • not bound by what is orthodox, established, or traditional *syn* progressive, advanced, radical *rel* tolerant, forbearing, indulgent, lenient *ant* authoritarian

liberate *syn* FREE, release, emancipate, manumit, discharge *rel* deliver, enfranchise; disengage, detach; extricate, disentangle, untangle, disencumber, disembarrass; rescue, redeem, ransom

libertine *syn* LICENTIOUS, lewd, wanton, lustful, lascivious, libidinous, lecherous *rel* debauched, corrupted, corrupt; abandoned, dissolute, profligate, reprobate; immoral, unmoral, amoral *ant* straitlaced

liberty *syn* FREEDOM, license *rel* independence, autonomy; exemption, immunity; liberation, emancipation, enfranchisement, delivery; scope, range, compass, sweep *ant* restraint

libidinous *syn* LICENTIOUS, lecherous, lustful, lascivious, lewd, wanton, libertine *rel* sensual, animal, carnal; immoral; gross, obscene, coarse; dissolute, abandoned, profligate, reprobate

license *n, syn* FREEDOM, liberty *rel* exemption, immunity; looseness, laxity, slackness, relaxedness, relaxation; privilege, prerogative, right *ant* decorum

license *vb, syn* AUTHORIZE, commission, accredit *rel* permit, let, allow, suffer; approve, endorse, sanction, certify; empower, enable *ant* ban

licentious • lacking moral restraint esp. in a disregarding of sexual restraints *syn* libertine, lewd, wanton, lustful, lascivious, libidinous, lecherous *rel* profligate, reprobate, dissolute, abandoned; debauched, depraved, corrupted, corrupt; lax, loose, relaxed; immoral, unmoral, amoral *ant* continent

licit *syn* LAWFUL, legitimate, legal *rel* permitted, allowed; sanctioned, approved; authorized, licensed; regulated *ant* illicit

lick *syn* CONQUER, beat, defeat, vanquish, subdue, subjugate, reduce, overcome, surmount, overthrow, rout

lickspittle *syn* PARASITE, sycophant, toady, bootlicker, hanger-on, leech, sponge, sponger, favorite

lie *vb* • to tell an untruth *syn* prevaricate, equivocate, palter, fib *rel* deceive, delude, mislead, beguile

lie *n* • a statement or declaration that is not true *syn* falsehood, untruth, fib, misrepresentation, story *rel* prevarication, equivocation, fibbing, fib; mendaciousness, mendacity, untruthfulness, dishonesty, deceitfulness *ant* truth

life *syn* BIOGRAPHY, memoir, autobiography, confessions

lifeless *syn* DEAD, inanimate, defunct, deceased, departed, late *rel* inert, inactive, passive; stiff, rigid, stark, wooden, inflexible; torpid *ant* living

lift **1** • to move from a lower to a higher place or position *syn* raise, rear, elevate, hoist, heave, boost *rel* rise, arise, ascend, levitate, mount, soar, tower, rocket, surge; exalt, magnify, aggrandize; heighten, enhance, intensify *ant* lower **2** *syn* STEAL, purloin, filch, pilfer, pinch, snitch, swipe, cop

light *vb* **1** • to cause something to start burning *syn* kindle, ignite, fire **2** *syn* ILLUMINATE, lighten, illumine, enlighten, illustrate

light *adj, syn* EASY, simple, facile, effortless, smooth *rel* slight; trivial, trifling, petty, puny *ant* heavy; arduous; burdensome

light *vb, syn* ALIGHT, land, perch, roost

lighten *vb, syn* ILLUMINATE, illumine, light, enlighten, illustrate *ant* darken

lighten *vb, syn* RELIEVE, alleviate, mitigate, assuage, allay *rel* lessen, reduce, diminish, decrease, abate; moderate, temper, qualify; attenuate, extenuate, thin, dilute

lighthearted *syn* GLAD, cheerful, happy, joyful, joyous *rel* buoyant, resilient, volatile, effervescent, expansive; blithe, jocund, merry, jolly; high-spirited, spirited; gay, sprightly, vivacious, lively *ant* despondent

light-mindedness *syn* LIGHTNESS, levity, frivolity, flippancy, volatility, flightiness

lightness • gaiety or indifference where seriousness and attention are called for *syn* light-mindedness, levity, frivolity, flippancy, volatility, flightiness *rel* buoyancy, resiliency, elasticity, effervescence, expansiveness; gaiety, liveliness, vivaciousness, vivacity; lightheartedness, cheerfulness *ant* seriousness

like *vb* • to feel attraction toward or take pleasure in *syn* love, enjoy, relish, fancy, dote *rel* prefer, choose, select, elect; admire, esteem, respect, regard; approve, endorse; appreciate, comprehend, understand *ant* dislike

like *adj* • the same or nearly the same (as in appearance, character, or quantity) *syn* alike, similar, analogous, comparable, akin, parallel, uniform, identical *rel* equivalent, equal, same, selfsame; cognate, allied, related *ant* unlike

likely **1** *syn* PROBABLE, possible *rel* credible, believable, colorable, plausible; reasonable, rational *ant* unlikely **2** *syn* APT, liable

likeness • agreement or correspondence in details *syn* similarity, resemblance, similitude, analogy, affinity *rel* equivalence, equality, sameness, identicalness, identity; agreement, conformity, correspondence; analogousness, comparableness, uniformity, parallelism *ant* unlikeness

likewise *syn* ALSO, too, besides, moreover, furthermore

limb *syn* SHOOT, bough, branch

limber *syn* SUPPLE, lithe, lithesome, lissome *rel* pliant, pliable, plastic; flexible, elastic, resilient, springy

limit *n* • a material or immaterial point beyond which something does not or cannot extend *syn* bound, confine, end, term *rel* limitation, restriction, circumscription, confinement; border, margin, verge, edge, rim, brim, brink

limit *vb* • to set bounds for *syn* restrict, circumscribe, confine *rel* define, prescribe, assign; restrain, curb, check *ant* widen

limn *syn* REPRESENT, depict, portray, delineate, picture

limp • deficient in firmness of texture, substance, or structure *syn* floppy, flaccid, flabby, flimsy, sleazy *rel* loose, slack, relaxed, lax; limber, supple

limpid *syn* CLEAR, transparent, translucent, lucid, pellucid, diaphanous *rel* pure, sheer; perspicuous *ant* turbid

line *n* • a series of things arranged in continuous or uniform order *syn* row, rank, file, echelon, tier *rel* succession, progression, series, sequence, chain

line *vb* • to arrange in a line or in lines *syn* line up, align, range, array *rel* marshal, arrange, order

lineage *syn* ANCESTRY, pedigree

line up *syn* LINE, align, range, array

linger *syn* STAY, tarry, wait, remain, abide *rel* delay, procrastinate, loiter, dawdle, lag

lingo *syn* DIALECT, vernacular, patois, jargon, cant, argot, slang

link *syn* JOIN, connect, relate, associate, conjoin, combine, unite *rel* concatenate, articulate, integrate; tie, bind *ant* sunder

liquefy • to convert or to become converted to a liquid state *syn* melt, deliquesce, fuse, thaw

lissome *syn* SUPPLE, lithesome, lithe, limber

list *n* • a series of items (as names) written down or printed as a memorandum or record *syn* table, catalog, schedule, register, roll, roster, inventory

list *vb, syn* RECORD, register, enroll, catalog

listless *syn* LANGUID, spiritless, languishing, languorous, lackadaisical, enervated *rel* apathetic, impassive, phlegmatic; heedless, thoughtless, careless; inert, inactive, passive, supine, idle *ant* eager

lithe, lithesome *syn* SUPPLE, lissome, limber *rel* slender, slim, slight, thin; lean, spare; pliant, pliable, plastic; nimble, agile, brisk, spry; graceful, elegant

little *syn* SMALL, diminutive, wee, tiny, minute, miniature *rel* petty, paltry, puny, trivial, trifling; slight, slim, slender, thin; meager, scanty, scrimpy, skimpy *ant* big

littoral *syn* SHORE, coast, beach, strand, bank, foreshore

liturgy *syn* FORM, ritual, rite, ceremony, ceremonial, formality

live *vb* **1** *syn* BE, exist, subsist *rel* endure, abide, persist, continue **2** *syn* RESIDE, dwell, sojourn, lodge, stay, put up, stop

live *adj, syn* ACTIVE, operative, dynamic *rel* vigorous, energetic, lusty, strenuous; powerful, potent, forcible, forceful; effective, efficacious, effectual, efficient *ant* inactive, inert; dormant; defunct

livelihood *syn* LIVING, subsistence, sustenance, maintenance, support, keep, bread *rel* trade, craft, handicraft, art, profession; wage, wages, salary, pay, stipend, fee, emolument

lively • keenly alive and spirited *syn* animated, vivacious, sprightly, gay *rel* agile, nimble, brisk, spry; buoyant, effervescent, volatile, expansive, resilient, elastic; merry, blithe, jocund, jolly; mirthful, gleeful, hilarious *ant* dull

livid *syn* PALE, ashen, ashy, pallid, wan *rel* ghastly, grisly, lurid; murky, gloomy, dusky, dark

living *adj* • having or showing life *syn* alive, animate, animated, vital *rel* existing, being, subsisting; active, live, operative, dynamic *ant* lifeless

living *n* • supplies or resources needed to live *syn* livelihood, subsistence, sustenance, maintenance, support, keep, bread, bread and butter

load *n* • something which is carried, conveyed, or transported from one place to another *syn* burden, freight, cargo, lading

load *vb* **1** *syn* BURDEN, encumber, cumber, weigh, weight, lade, tax, charge, saddle *rel* bear, convey, carry, transport *ant* unload **2** *syn* ADULTERATE, weight, sophisticate, doctor

loaf *syn* IDLE, lounge, loll, laze *rel* rest, repose, relax; saunter, stroll, amble

loath *syn* DISINCLINED, indisposed, averse, hesitant, reluctant *rel* adverse, averse; antipathetic, unsympathetic *ant* anxious

loathe *syn* HATE, abominate, detest, abhor *rel* despise, contemn, scorn, disdain; refuse, reject, spurn, repudiate, decline;

recoil, shrink, flinch, blench, quail *ant* dote on

loathing *syn* ABHORRENCE, detestation, abomination, hate, hatred *rel* aversion, antipathy; repugnance, repellency, distaste *ant* tolerance

loathsome *syn* OFFENSIVE, repulsive, repugnant, revolting *rel* abominable, abhorrent, detestable, odious, hateful; repellent, repugnant, distasteful, obnoxious, invidious *ant* engaging, inviting

local *syn* INSULAR, provincial, parochial, small-town *rel* narrow, narrow-minded; circumscribed, limited, restricted, confined *ant* cosmopolitan

locality • a more or less definitely circumscribed place or region *syn* district, vicinity, neighborhood *rel* region, area, zone, belt, tract; section, sector; territory, field, bailiwick, province, sphere, domain

location *syn* PLACE, position, situation, site, spot, station

locomotion *syn* MOTION, movement, move, stir

locum tenens *syn* SUBSTITUTE, supply, alternate, understudy, pinch hitter, double, stand-in

locution *syn* PHRASE, idiom, expression

lodge 1 *syn* HARBOR, house, board, shelter, entertain *rel* receive, take, accept, admit; accommodate, contain, hold **2** *syn* RESIDE, live, dwell, sojourn, stay, put up, stop

lofty *syn* HIGH, tall *rel* elevated, raised, lifted; exalted, magnified, aggrandized; imposing, stately, august, majestic, grand; sublime, glorious, superb, splendid

logical • having or showing skill in thinking or reasoning *syn* analytical, subtle *rel* cogent, valid, sound, telling, convincing, compelling; clear, lucid, perspicuous; rational, reasonable; inferential, ratiocinative *ant* illogical

logistic, logistical *syn* STRATEGIC, tactical

logistics *syn* STRATEGY, tactics

loiter *syn* DELAY, dawdle, lag, procrastinate *rel* tarry, linger, wait

loll *syn* IDLE, loaf, lounge, laze *rel* relax, rest, repose; lean, incline

lollop 1 *syn* SKIP, bound, hop, curvet, lope, ricochet **2** *syn* STUMBLE, trip, blunder, lurch, flounder, lumber, galumph, bumble

lone 1 *syn* ALONE, lonely, lonesome, forlorn, lorn, solitary, desolate **2** *syn* SINGLE, sole, unique, solitary, separate, particular

lonely *syn* ALONE, lonesome, lone, solitary, forlorn, lorn, desolate *rel* abandoned, deserted, forsaken; secluded, isolated

lonesome *syn* ALONE, lonely, lone, solitary, forlorn, lorn, desolate *rel* see LONELY

long • to have a strong desire for something *syn* yearn, hanker, pine, hunger, thirst *rel* crave, desire, wish, want, covet; pant, aspire, aim

longanimity *syn* PATIENCE, long-suffering, forbearance, resignation *rel* fortitude, sand, grit, pluck, backbone; endurance, toleration, tolerance; submissiveness

long-suffering *syn* PATIENCE, resignation, forbearance *rel* submissiveness, subduedness; meekness, humbleness, humility, lowliness; fortitude, grit; endurance, toleration

look *vb* **1** *syn* SEE, watch *rel* gaze, gape, stare, glare, peer; scrutinize, scan, inspect, examine **2** *syn* SEEM, appear *rel* indicate, betoken, bespeak; show, manifest, evidence, evince, demonstrate **3** *syn* EXPECT, hope, await *rel* foresee, foreknow, anticipate, divine

look *n* **1** • the directing of one's eyes in order to see *syn* sight, view, glance, glimpse, peep, peek *rel* gazing, gaze, staring, stare; scrutiny, inspection, examination **2** *syn* APPEARANCE, aspect, semblance *rel* bearing, demeanor, mien; posture, attitude, pose; face, countenance, visage, physiognomy

looker-on *syn* SPECTATOR, onlooker, beholder, observer, witness, eyewitness, bystander, kibitzer

loom *syn* APPEAR, emerge *ant* vanish

loose • not tightly bound, held, restrained, or stretched *syn* relaxed, slack, lax *rel* limp, flabby, flaccid, flimsy; free, independent; disengaged, detached; casual, desultory, hit-or-miss, happy-go-lucky, random, haphazard; negligent, remiss; careless, heedless, thoughtless *ant* tight; strict

loot *n, syn* SPOIL, booty, plunder, swag, prize

loot *vb, syn* ROB, plunder, rifle, burglarize *rel* sack, pillage, despoil, ravage, spoliate, devastate, waste; steal, pilfer, filch, purloin

lop *syn* SHEAR, poll, clip, trim, prune, snip,

crop *rel* cut, slash, chop, hew; shorten, curtail

lope *syn* SKIP, bound, hop, curvet, lollop, ricochet

loquacious *syn* TALKATIVE, garrulous, voluble, glib *rel* fluent, vocal, articulate, glib, eloquent, voluble; chatting, chatty, gabbing, gabby, chattering, prating, jabbering

loquacity, loquaciousness *syn* TALKATIVENESS, garrulity, volubility, glibness *rel* chattering, chatter, chatting, chat, gabbing, gab, prating, prate, jabbering, jabber; fluency, articulateness, volubleness; readiness, ease, facility

lordly *syn* PROUD, haughty, arrogant, overbearing, insolent, supercilious, disdainful *rel* pretentious, showy; dictatorial, magisterial, authoritarian; imperious, domineering, masterful

lore *syn* KNOWLEDGE, science, learning, erudition, scholarship, information

lorn *syn* ALONE, forlorn, lonely, lonesome, lone, solitary, desolate *rel* see FORLORN

lot **1** *syn* FATE, destiny, portion, doom *rel* fortune, luck, hap, chance, hazard **2** *syn* GROUP, cluster, bunch, parcel *rel* collection, assemblage; aggregate, aggregation, conglomeration, conglomerate

loud • marked by intensity or volume of sound *syn* stentorian, earsplitting, hoarse, raucous, strident, stertorous *ant* low-pitched, low

lounge *syn* IDLE, loaf, loll, laze *rel* incline, lean; relax, repose, rest

lout *syn* BOOR, churl, clown, clodhopper, bumpkin, hick, yokel, rube

loutish *syn* BOORISH, churlish, clownish *rel* clumsy, gauche, maladroit, inept, awkward; burly, brawny, husky, muscular; rude, rough, crude, raw, callow, green, uncouth

love *n, syn* ATTACHMENT, affection *rel* devotion, piety, fidelity, allegiance, loyalty; adoration, worship, idolatry; passion, fervor, ardor, enthusiasm, zeal *ant* hate

love *vb, syn* LIKE, enjoy, dote, relish, fancy *rel* adore, worship, idolize; cherish, treasure, value, prize, appreciate *ant* hate

lovely *syn* BEAUTIFUL, fair, comely, pretty, bonny , handsome, beauteous, pulchritudinous, good-looking *rel* alluring, enchanting, charming, attractive; delightful, delectable; exquisite, delicate, dainty, rare *ant* unlovely; plain

loving • feeling or expressing love *syn* affectionate, devoted, fond, doting *rel* amorous, amatory, erotic; enamored, infatuated; attentive, considerate, thoughtful; impassioned, passionate, ardent, fervent; true, constant, faithful *ant* unloving

low *syn* BASE, vile *rel* abject, ignoble, mean, sordid; coarse, vulgar, gross, obscene, ribald; crooked, devious, oblique

lower *syn* FROWN, glower, scowl, gloom *rel* glare, stare, peer

lowly *syn* HUMBLE, meek, modest *rel* submissive, subdued, tame; retiring, withdrawing; reverential, deferential, obeisant *ant* pompous

loyal *syn* FAITHFUL, true, constant, staunch, steadfast, resolute *ant* disloyal

loyalty *syn* FIDELITY, allegiance, fealty, devotion, piety *rel* trueness, truth, faithfulness, constancy, staunchness, steadfastness; attachment, affection, love *ant* disloyalty

lubricate *syn* OIL, grease, anoint, cream

lucent *syn* BRIGHT, brilliant, radiant, luminous, lustrous, effulgent, refulgent, beaming, lambent, incandescent *rel* glowing, blazing, flaming; splendid, resplendent, glorious

lucid **1** *syn* CLEAR, pellucid, transparent, translucent, diaphanous, limpid *rel* luminous, bright, brilliant, lucent **2** *syn* CLEAR, perspicuous *rel* distinct, plain, manifest, evident *ant* obscure, vague, dark

luck *syn* CHANCE, fortune, hap, accident, hazard *rel* break, chance, occasion, opportunity; lot, portion, destiny, fate

luckless *syn* UNLUCKY, disastrous, ill-starred, ill-fated, unfortunate, calamitous, hapless *rel* unhappy, infelicitous; miserable, wretched

lucky • meeting with unforeseen success *syn* fortunate, happy, providential *rel* favorable, benign, auspicious, propitious; advantageous, beneficial, profitable; felicitous, meet *ant* unlucky

lucrative *syn* PAYING, gainful, remunerative, profitable

ludicrous *syn* LAUGHABLE, risible, ridiculous, comic, comical, farcical, droll, funny *rel* absurd, preposterous, foolish, silly; grotesque, bizarre, antic, fantastic; amusing, diverting, entertaining

lugubrious *syn* MELANCHOLY, doleful, dolorous, rueful, plaintive *rel* depressing, oppressing, oppressive; sorrowful, woeful; gloomy, saturnine, dour, morose, glum, sullen *ant* joyous; facetious

lull *vb, syn* CALM, compose, quiet, quieten, still, soothe, settle, tranquilize *rel* pacify, placate, appease, mollify; moderate, qualify, temper; allay, assuage, alleviate, relieve *ant* agitate

lull *n, syn* PAUSE, recess, respite, intermission *rel* quiescence, abeyance; period, epoch, era; interval, interruption, break

lumber *syn* STUMBLE, trip, blunder, lurch, flounder, galumph, lollop, bumble

luminous *syn* BRIGHT, brilliant, radiant, lustrous, effulgent, lucent, refulgent, beaming, lambent, incandescent *rel* glowing, blazing, flaming; gleaming, glittering, flashing, scintillating; resplendent, glorious, splendid

lunacy *syn* INSANITY, psychosis, mania, dementia *rel* alienation, derangement, aberration; delirium, frenzy, hysteria

lunatic *syn* INSANE, mad, crazy, crazed, demented, deranged, maniac, non compos mentis

lurch *syn* STUMBLE, trip, blunder, flounder, lumber, galumph, lollop, bumble *rel* reel, stagger, totter; plunge, pitch, dive

lure *n* • something that leads an animal or a person into a place or situation from which escape is difficult *syn* bait, decoy, snare, trap

lure *vb* • to lead astray from one's true course *syn* entice, inveigle, decoy, tempt, seduce *rel* ensnare, snare, entrap, trap, capture, catch, bag; bewitch, fascinate, allure, captivate, attract; blandish, wheedle, cajole, coax *ant* revolt, repel

lurid *syn* GHASTLY, grisly, gruesome, macabre, grim *rel* livid, pale, pallid, wan, ashy, ashen; sinister, malign, baleful, malefic, maleficent

lurk • to behave so as to escape attention *syn* skulk, slink, sneak *rel* hide, conceal, secrete; ambush, waylay, surprise

luscious *syn* DELIGHTFUL, delicious, delectable *rel* sapid, flavorsome, toothsome, palatable, appetizing; grateful, gratifying, pleasing, pleasant *ant* austere; tasteless

lush *syn* PROFUSE, luxuriant, lavish, prodigal, exuberant *rel* abounding, abundant, teeming, swarming; sumptuous, opulent, luxurious

lust *syn* DESIRE, appetite, passion, urge *rel* cupidity, greed, avarice, rapacity; yearning, longing, hankering, thirsting, thirst, hungering, hunger; craving, coveting; gusto, zest, taste

luster • the quality or condition of shining by reflected light *syn* sheen, gloss, glaze *rel* iridescence, opalescence; brilliancy, radiance, luminosity, effulgence, refulgence

lustful *syn* LICENTIOUS, lascivious, libidinous, lecherous, wanton, lewd, libertine *rel* carnal, fleshly, sensual, animal; immoral, unmoral, amoral

lustrous *syn* BRIGHT, luminous, radiant, brilliant, effulgent, refulgent, beaming, lambent, lucent, incandescent *rel* glorious, resplendent, splendid; glowing, blazing, flaming

lusty *syn* VIGOROUS, energetic, strenuous, nervous *rel* robust, sound, healthy, hale; stout, sturdy, strong, stalwart; husky, brawny, muscular, sinewy, athletic *ant* effete

luxuriant *syn* PROFUSE, lush, exuberant, lavish, prodigal *rel* fruitful, fecund, fertile, prolific; rank, rampant; abounding, abundant, teeming

luxurious **1** *syn* SENSUOUS, voluptuous, sybaritic, epicurean, sensual *rel* self-indulging, self-indulgent, self-pampering; languorous, languishing *ant* ascetic **2** • ostentatiously rich or magnificent *syn* sumptuous, opulent *rel* ostentatious, pretentious, showy; magnificent, stately, imposing, majestic, grand; costly, expensive, valuable, precious

luxury *syn* AMENITY *rel* pleasure, joy, delight; agreeableness, gratification, gratefulness *ant* hardship

lying *syn* DISHONEST, mendacious, untruthful, deceitful *rel* false, wrong; deceptive, misleading, delusive, delusory *ant* truthtelling

M

macabre *syn* GHASTLY, gruesome, grisly, grim, lurid *rel* horrifying, daunting, appalling, dismaying; horrific, horrendous, horrible, horrid

macerate *syn* CRUSH, mash, smash, bruise, squash *rel* separate, part, divide; stew, seethe, simmer; soften

machination *syn* PLOT, intrigue, conspiracy, cabal *rel* trick, ruse, stratagem, maneuver, gambit, ploy, artifice, feint, wile

machine • a device or system by which energy can be converted into useful work *syn* mechanism, machinery, apparatus, engine, motor *rel* contrivance, device, contraption, gadget; implement, tool, instrument, utensil, appliance

machinery **1** *syn* EQUIPMENT, apparatus, paraphernalia, outfit, tackle, gear, matériel *rel* mean, instrument, instrumentality, agency, medium, vehicle, organ, channel, agent; machine, mechanism, engine, motor; device, contrivance, contraption, gadget; implement, tool, instrument, utensil, appliance **2** *syn* MACHINE, mechanism, apparatus, engine, motor

mad **1** *syn* INSANE, crazy, crazed, demented, deranged, lunatic, maniac, non compos mentis *rel* frenzied, hysterical, delirious; irrational, unreasonable **2** *syn* ANGRY, irate, wrathful, wroth, indignant, acrimonious *rel* maddened, incensed, infuriated, enraged; offended, outraged, affronted

madden *syn* ANGER, incense, enrage, infuriate *rel* vex, annoy, irk; exasperate, provoke, rile, aggravate, irritate

maelstrom *syn* EDDY, whirlpool, vortex

magazine *syn* JOURNAL, periodical, review, organ, newspaper

magic • the use of means (as charms or spells) believed to have supernatural power over natural forces *syn* sorcery, witchcraft, witchery, wizardry, alchemy, thaumaturgy

magisterial *syn* DICTATORIAL, authoritarian, dogmatic, doctrinaire, oracular *rel* masterful, domineering, imperious, imperative, peremptory; directing, controlling, conducting, managing

magnificent *syn* GRAND, imposing, stately, majestic, august, noble, grandiose *rel* splendid, resplendent, glorious, sublime, superb; opulent, sumptuous, luxurious; ostentatious, pretentious, showy *ant* modest

magnify *syn* EXALT, aggrandize *rel* extol, praise, laud, acclaim, eulogize; enlarge, increase, augment; expand, amplify, distend, swell, inflate, dilate *ant* minimize, belittle

magniloquent *syn* RHETORICAL, grandiloquent, aureate, flowery, euphuistic, bombastic *rel* turgid, tumid, inflated, flatulent; theatrical, histrionic, melodramatic, dramatic

magnitude *syn* SIZE, volume, extent, dimensions, area *rel* amplitude, expanse, stretch, spread; bulk, mass, volume

maiden **1** *syn* UNMARRIED, single, celibate, virgin **2** *syn* YOUTHFUL, juvenile, virgin, virginal, puerile, boyish *ant* experienced

maim • to injure so severely as to cause lasting damage *syn* cripple, mutilate, batter, mangle *rel* mar, spoil, damage, injure; deface, disfigure

main *syn* CHIEF, principal, leading, foremost, capital *rel* cardinal, vital, essential, fundamental; prime, primary, primal

mainly *syn* LARGELY, greatly, mostly, chiefly, principally, generally

maintain • to uphold as true, right, just, or reasonable *syn* assert, defend, vindicate, justify *rel* affirm, aver, protest, avow, declare, profess, avouch; contend, fight, battle, war; persist, persevere

maintenance *syn* LIVING, sustenance, support, livelihood, subsistence, keep, bread

majestic *syn* GRAND, stately, august, noble, magnificent, imposing, grandiose *rel* lofty, high; sublime, superb, glorious, splendid, resplendent; monumental, tremendous; exceptional

make • to bring something into being by forming, shaping, combining, or altering materials *syn* form, shape, fashion, fabricate, manufacture, forge *rel* produce, turn out, yield, bear; accomplish, achieve, effect, fulfill

make-believe *syn* PRETENSE, pretension

maker • one who brings something into being or existence *syn* creator, author

makeshift *syn* RESOURCE, shift, expedient, resort, stopgap, substitute, surrogate *rel* device, contrivance, contraption, gadget; mean, instrument, agency, instrumentality

maladroit *syn* AWKWARD, clumsy, gauche, inept *ant* adroit

malady *syn* DISEASE, ailment, disorder, condition, affection, complaint, distemper, syndrome

male • of, characteristic of, or like a male, esp. of the human species *syn* masculine, manly, manlike, mannish, manful, virile *ant* female

malediction *syn* CURSE, imprecation, anathema *ant* benediction

malefactor *syn* CRIMINAL, felon, convict, culprit, delinquent *rel* miscreant, scoundrel, villain, blackguard *ant* benefactor; well-doer

malefic, maleficent *syn* SINISTER, malign, baleful

malevolence *syn* MALICE, ill will, malignity, malignancy, spite, despite, spleen, grudge *rel* animosity, rancor, animus, antipathy, antagonism, enmity, hostility; hate, hatred, detestation, abhorrence, abomination *ant* benevolence

malevolent *syn* MALICIOUS, malignant, malign, spiteful *rel* sinister, baleful, malefic, maleficent *ant* benevolent

malice • the desire to see another experience pain, injury, or distress *syn* ill will, malevolence, spite, despite, malignity, malignancy, spleen, grudge *rel* maliciousness, spitefulness; venom, bane, poison; animosity, animus, rancor, antipathy, enmity *ant* charity

malicious • having, showing, or indicative of intense often vicious ill will *syn* malevolent, malignant, malign, spiteful *rel* poisonous, venomous, virulent, toxic; pernicious, noxious, baneful, deleterious, detrimental; envious, jealous; wanton, gratuitous, uncalled-for, supererogatory

malign *adj* **1** *syn* MALICIOUS, malignant, malevolent, spiteful *rel* inimical, hostile, rancorous, antipathetic, antagonistic; venomous, virulent, poisonous, toxic *ant* benign **2** *syn* SINISTER, baleful, malefic, maleficent *rel* threatening, menacing; baneful, noxious, pernicious, deleterious; disastrous, catastrophic, cataclysmic, calamitous *ant* benign

malign *vb* • to injure by speaking ill of *syn* traduce, asperse, vilify, calumniate, defame, slander, libel *rel* detract, decry, disparage, depreciate, derogate; vituperate, revile; defile, pollute, contaminate *ant* defend

malignancy *syn* MALICE, malignity, ill will, malevolence, spite, despite, spleen, grudge *ant* see MALIGNITY

malignant *syn* MALICIOUS, malign, malevolent, spiteful *rel* virulent, venomous, poisonous; envious, jealous; baneful, noxious, pernicious; diabolical, devilish, fiendish *ant* benignant

malignity *syn* MALICE, malignancy, ill will, malevolence, spite, despite, spleen, grudge *rel* rancor, animus, animosity, enmity, hostility; maliciousness, spitefulness; hatred, hate; vindictiveness, revengefulness, vengefulness *ant* benignity

malinger *syn* DODGE, parry, sidestep, duck, shirk, fence *rel* evade, avoid, elude, escape, shun

malleable *syn* PLASTIC, pliable, pliant, ductile, adaptable *rel* tractable, amenable *ant* refractory

malodorous • having an unpleasant smell *syn* stinking, fetid, noisome, putrid, rank, rancid, fusty, musty *ant* odorous

maltreat *syn* ABUSE, mistreat, ill-treat, misuse, outrage

mammoth *syn* HUGE, vast, immense, enormous, elephantine, giant, gigantic, gigantean, colossal, gargantuan, Herculean, cyclopean, titanic, Brobdingnagian *rel* monstrous, monumental, stupendous, tremendous, prodigious; ponderous, weighty, cumbrous, cumbersome, heavy

manacle *syn* HAMPER, trammel, clog, fetter, shackle, hog-tie *rel* hinder, impede, obstruct, bar, block; tie, bind; restrain, inhibit, curb, check

manage *syn* CONDUCT, control, direct *rel* govern, rule; guide, lead, steer, pilot, engineer; handle, manipulate, wield, swing, ply

mandate **1** *syn* COMMAND, dictate, order, injunction, bidding, behest *rel* charging, charge, direction, instruction; sanctioning, sanction, endorsement, approval **2** • an authorization to take a political action given to a representative *syn* initiative, referendum, plebiscite

maneuver *syn* TRICK, stratagem, ruse, gambit, ploy, artifice, wile, feint *rel* device, contrivance; expedient, resort, resource, shift, makeshift; intrigue, machination, plot

manful *syn* MALE, virile, mannish, manlike, manly, masculine *rel* sturdy, stout, tenacious, stalwart, tough, strong; resolute, steadfast, staunch; intrepid, bold, brave

mangle *syn* MAIM, batter, mutilate, cripple *rel* injure, damage, mar, impair; deface, disfigure; deform, contort, distort

mania **1** *syn* INSANITY, lunacy, psychosis, dementia *rel* alienation, derangement, aberration *ant* lucidity **2** • a state of mind in which there is loss of control over emotional, nervous, or mental processes *syn* delirium, frenzy, hysteria *rel* depression, dejection, melancholia, melancholy, sadness; ecstasy, transport; excitement, provocation

maniac *syn* INSANE, mad, crazy, crazed, demented, deranged, lunatic, non compos mentis *rel* irrational, unreasonable

manifest *adj, syn* EVIDENT, patent, distinct, obvious, apparent, palpable, plain, clear *rel* revealed, disclosed, divulged, told; shown, evidenced, evinced; conspicuous, noticeable, prominent *ant* latent; constructive

manifest *vb, syn* SHOW, evidence, evince, demonstrate *rel* exhibit, display, expose; express, vent, utter, voice; reveal, discover, disclose, divulge *ant* suggest

manikin *syn* DWARF, midget, pygmy, homunculus, runt *ant* giant

manipulate *syn* HANDLE, wield, swing, ply *rel* flourish, brandish, shake, wave, thrash

manlike *syn* MALE, mannish, manful, virile, manly, masculine

manly *syn* MALE, manlike, manful, virile, masculine, mannish *rel* mature, matured, grown-up, adult; sturdy, strong, stout, stalwart *ant* unmanly, womanly

manner *syn* METHOD, mode, way, fashion, system *rel* custom, usage, use, wont, practice, habit, habitude

mannerism *syn* POSE, air, affectation *rel* eccentricity, idiosyncrasy; peculiarity, singularity, oddness, queerness

mannish *syn* MALE, manlike, virile, masculine, manful, manly *ant* womanish

manufacture *syn* MAKE, fabricate, forge, form, shape, fashion *rel* produce, turn out, yield

manumit *syn* FREE, emancipate, enfranchise, deliver, discharge, release, liberate *ant* enslave

many • amounting to or being one at a large indefinite number *syn* several, sundry, various, divers, numerous, multifarious *ant* few

many-sided *syn* VERSATILE, all-around

map *syn* CHART, graph *rel* plan, plot, scheme, design; sketch, outline, diagram

mar *syn* INJURE, damage, hurt, harm, impair, spoil *rel* deface, disfigure; deform, contort, distort, warp; ruin, wreck

marble *syn* SPOT, spatter, sprinkle, mottle, fleck, stipple, speckle, spangle, bespangle

marbled *syn* SPOTTED, spattered, sprinkled, mottled, flecked, stippled, speckled, spangled, bespangled

margin **1** *syn* BORDER, verge, edge, rim, brim, brink *rel* bound, end, term, confine, limit; penumbra **2** *syn* ROOM, berth, play, elbowroom, leeway, clearance

marine • of or relating to the navigation of the sea *syn* maritime, nautical, naval

mariner • a person engaged in sailing or handling a ship *syn* sailor, seaman, tar, gob, bluejacket

marital *syn* MATRIMONIAL, conjugal, connubial, nuptial, hymeneal

maritime *syn* MARINE, nautical, naval

mark *n* **1** *syn* SIGN, symptom, note, token, badge *rel* stigma, brand, blot, stain; criterion, touchstone, gauge, yardstick, standard; trace, vestige, track; stamp, print, imprint, impress, impression **2** *syn* CHARACTER, symbol, sign *rel* device, contrivance **3** • a symbol or device used for identification or indication of ownership *syn* brand, stamp, label, tag, ticket

mark *vb* **1** • to affix, attach, or impress something which serves for identification *syn* brand, stamp, label, tag, ticket *rel* imprint, impress, print; recognize, identify **2** *syn* CHARACTERIZE, distinguish, qualify *rel* indicate, betoken, attest, bespeak, prove, argue; intimate, hint, suggest

marriage • acts by which a man and woman become husband and wife or the state of being husband and wife *syn* matrimony, wedlock, wedding, nuptial, espousal

marshal *syn* ORDER, arrange, organize, systematize, methodize *rel* array, range, align, line, line up

martial • of, relating to, or suited for war or a warrior *syn* warlike, military *rel* belligerent, bellicose, pugnacious, combative; aggressive, militant; spirited, high-spirited, mettlesome

marvel *syn* WONDER, prodigy, miracle, phenomenon *rel* astonishment, amazement, surprise; perplexity, mystification, puzzle

masculine *syn* MALE, virile, manful, manly, manlike, mannish *rel* vigorous, energetic, lusty, strenuous; robust, healthy, sound *ant* feminine

mash *syn* CRUSH, smash, bruise, squash, macerate *rel* pound, beat

mask *syn* DISGUISE, cloak, dissemble, camouflage *rel* conceal, hide, secrete, screen; protect, shield, defend, guard, safeguard

mass *n* **1** *syn* BULK, volume *rel* aggregate, aggregation, conglomerate, conglomeration; sum, amount, total, whole **2** *syn* HEAP, pile, stack, shock, cock, bank *rel* accumulation, hoarding, hoard, amassment

mass *vb, syn* HEAP, pile, stack, shock, cock, bank *rel* gather, collect, assemble, congregate; accumulate, amass, hoard; merge, blend, fuse, coalesce, mix; consolidate, compact, unify, concentrate

massacre • the act or an instance of killing a number of usu. helpless or unresisting human beings under circumstances of atrocity or cruelty *syn* slaughter, butchery, carnage, pogrom *rel* assassination, murdering, murder, slaying, killing

massive • impressively large or heavy *syn* massy, bulky, monumental, substantial *rel* heavy, weighty, ponderous; solid, hard, firm; immense, enormous, huge, gigantic, colossal

massy *syn* MASSIVE, bulky, monumental, substantial *rel* ponderous, hefty, cumbrous, cumbersome, weighty, heavy; large, big, great; solid, firm, hard

master *syn* CHIEF, chieftain, head, leader

masterful • tending to impose one's will on others *syn* domineering, imperious, peremptory, imperative *rel* magisterial, dictatorial, authoritarian, oracular, dogmatic, doctrinaire; arbitrary, absolute, despotic, tyrannical

masterly *syn* PROFICIENT, adept, skilled, skillful, expert *rel* dexterous, deft, adroit; preeminent, superlative, transcendent, supreme

match • to come up to or nearly up to the level or standard of *syn* rival, equal, approach, touch *rel* correspond, harmonize, agree, conform, square, accord

material *adj* **1** • of or belonging to actuality *syn* physical, corporeal, phenomenal, sensible, objective *rel* carnal, fleshly, sensual, animal; actual, true, real; tangible, perceptible, appreciable, palpable *ant* immaterial **2** *syn* RELEVANT, germane, pertinent, apposite, applicable, apropos *rel* important, significant, consequential, momentous; vital, cardinal, essential, fundamental *ant* immaterial

material *n, syn* MATTER, substance, stuff *rel* element, constituent, ingredient, component

materialize *syn* REALIZE, externalize, objectify, incarnate, embody, actualize, hypostatize, reify

matériel *syn* EQUIPMENT, apparatus, machinery, paraphernalia, outfit, tackle, gear

matrimonial • of, relating to, or characteristic of marriage *syn* marital, conjugal, connubial, nuptial, hymeneal

matrimony *syn* MARRIAGE, wedlock, wedding, nuptial, espousal

matter **1** • what goes into the makeup or forms the being of a thing whether physical or not *syn* substance, material, stuff **2** *syn* AFFAIR, business, concern, thing **3** *syn* SUBJECT, subject matter, argument, topic, text, theme, motive, motif, leitmotiv

matter-of-fact *syn* PROSAIC, prosy *rel* stolid, phlegmatic, impassive; arid, dry; downright, forthright

mature *adj* • having attained the normal peak of natural growth and development *syn* matured, ripe, mellow, adult, grown-up *ant* immature; childish

mature *vb* • to become fully developed or ripe *syn* develop, ripen, age *rel* harden, season, acclimatize, acclimate; habituate, accustom, inure, addict

matured *syn* MATURE, ripe, mellow, adult, grown-up *rel* completed, finished; deliberate, considered, advised, designed, studied, premeditated *ant* unmatured; premature

maudlin *syn* SENTIMENTAL, mawkish, romantic, soppy, mushy, slushy *rel* confused, muddled, fuddled, addled, befuddled; embarrassed, rattled, fazed, discomfited, disconcerted

mawkish *syn* SENTIMENTAL, maudlin, romantic, soppy, mushy, slushy *rel* flat, vapid, jejune, insipid, banal, inane

maxim *syn* SAYING, saw, adage, proverb, motto, epigram, aphorism, apothegm

meager • falling short of what is normal, necessary, or desirable *syn* scanty, scant, skimpy, scrimpy, exiguous, spare, sparse *rel* thin, slender, slim, slight, tenuous, rare; thinned, attenuated, extenuated, diluted; jejune, flat, insipid, inane; penurious, stingy, parsimonious *ant* ample; copious

mean *adj* • being below the normal standards of human decency and dignity *syn* ignoble, abject, sordid *rel* base, low, vile; contemptible, despicable, sorry, scurvy, cheap, beggarly, shabby, pitiable

mean *vb* **1** *syn* INTEND, design, propose, purpose *rel* wish, want, desire; aim, aspire, plan **2** • to convey (as an idea) to the mind *syn* denote, signify, import *rel* carry, convey, bear, transmit; connote; define, assign, prescribe; suggest, imply, intimate, hint

mean *n* **1** *syn* AVERAGE, median, norm, par **2** • one by which work is accomplished or an end effected *syn* instrument, instrumentality, agent, agency, medium, organ, vehicle, channel *rel* method, mode, manner, way, fashion, system; machinery, apparatus, equipment, paraphernalia **3** *pl* **means** *syn* POSSESSIONS, resources, assets, effects, belongings *rel* money, cash, currency; riches, wealthiness, affluence, opulence

mean *adj, syn* AVERAGE, median, par *ant* extreme

meander *syn* WANDER, stray, roam, ramble, rove, range, prowl, gad, gallivant, traipse

meaning • the idea that something conveys to the mind *syn* sense, acceptation, signification, significance, import *rel* suggestion, implication, intimation, hinting, hint; denotation, connotation

meaningful *syn* EXPRESSIVE, significant, pregnant, sententious, eloquent *rel* important, consequential, momentous, weighty *ant* meaningless

measly *syn* PETTY, paltry, trifling, trivial, puny, picayunish, picayune *rel* contemptible, despicable, sorry, scurvy, cheap, beggarly, shabby; stingy, parsimonious, penurious, miserly

mechanic *syn* WORKER, workman, workingman, artisan, operative, hand, laborer, craftsman, handicraftsman, roustabout

mechanical *syn* SPONTANEOUS, automatic, instinctive, impulsive *rel* stereotyped, hackneyed, trite; dull, slow, stupid, dense, crass, dumb

mechanism *syn* MACHINE, machinery, apparatus, engine, motor

meddle • to interest oneself in what is not one's concern *syn* interfere, intermeddle, tamper *rel* intrude, obtrude, interlope, butt in; interpose, intervene; discommode, incommode, trouble, inconvenience

meddlesome *syn* IMPERTINENT, intrusive, obtrusive, officious *rel* interfering, meddling, intermeddling, tampering; prying, snoopy, nosy, inquisitive, curious

median *n, syn* AVERAGE, mean, norm, par

median *adj, syn* AVERAGE, mean, par

mediate *syn* INTERPOSE, intercede, intervene, interfere *rel* arbitrate, judge, adjudge, adjudicate; conciliate, propitiate, pacify; reconcile, accommodate, adapt

medicament, medication *syn* REMEDY, medicine, cure, specific, physic

medicinal *syn* DRUG, pharmaceutical, biologic, simple

medicine *syn* REMEDY, cure, medicament, medication, specific, physic

mediocre *syn* MEDIUM, middling, second-rate, moderate, average, fair, indifferent *rel* poor, wrong, bad; common, ordinary, vulgar

meditate *syn* PONDER, muse, ruminate *rel* contemplate, consider, study, weigh; reflect, reason, speculate, deliberate, think, cogitate; examine, inspect, scrutinize

meditative *syn* THOUGHTFUL, contemplative, speculative, reflective, pensive *rel* pondering, musing, ruminating

medium *n, syn* MEAN, instrument, instrumentality, agent, agency, organ, vehicle, channel

medium *adj* • about midway between the extremes of a scale, measurement, or evaluation *syn* middling, mediocre, second-rate, moderate, average, fair, indifferent *rel* mean, median, average, par; common, ordinary, vulgar, popular

meed *syn* PREMIUM, guerdon, prize, award, reward, bounty, bonus *rel* recompensing, recompense, remuneration, satisfaction

meek *syn* HUMBLE, modest, lowly *rel* gentle, mild, soft; subdued, submissive, tame; compliant, acquiescent, resigned; forbearing, tolerant, lenient; patient, long-suffering *ant* arrogant

meet *vb* **1** • to come together face-to-face or as if face-to-face *syn* face, encounter, confront *rel* accost, greet, salute, address; collide, bump, clash; experience, undergo, sustain, suffer; wrestle, grapple, tussle; forestall, anticipate *ant* avoid **2** *syn* SATISFY, fulfill, answer *rel* equal, approach, match, touch; gratify, please; content *ant* disappoint

meet *adj, syn* FIT, suitable, proper, appropriate, fitting, apt, happy, felicitous *rel* adapted, adjusted, accommodated, conformed, reconciled; right, good; just, equitable, fair *ant* unmeet

melancholia *syn* SADNESS, melancholy, depression, dejection, gloom, blues, dumps

melancholic • gloomy or depressed, esp. as a manifestation of one's temperament or state of health *syn* melancholy, atrabilious, hypochondriac *rel* despondent, despairing, hopeless, forlorn, desperate; pessimistic, misanthropic, cynical, misogynic

melancholy *n, syn* SADNESS, melancholia, dejection, gloom, depression, blues, dumps *rel* miserableness, misery, wretchedness; despondency, despair, hopelessness, forlornness, desperation; tedium, boredom, ennui, doldrums *ant* exhilaration

melancholy *adj* **1** *syn* MELANCHOLIC, atrabilious, hypochondriac *rel* morose, gloomy, glum, sullen, dour, saturnine; depressed, oppressed, weighed down; despondent, despairing, hopeless, forlorn, desperate **2** • expressing or suggesting sorrow or mourning *syn* dolorous, doleful, lugubrious, rueful, plaintive *rel* pathetic, poignant, moving, touching; hopeless, forlorn, despairing, despondent; pensive, reflective, thoughtful; discomposing, disquieting, perturbing, disturbing

melee *syn* BRAWL, fracas, row, broil, rumpus, scrap *rel* altercation, quarrel, wrangle, squabble; confusion, disorder

mellow *syn* MATURE, ripe, matured, adult, grown-up *rel* tender, warm, sympathetic, responsive, warmhearted *ant* unmellow; green

melodramatic *syn* DRAMATIC, histrionic, theatrical, dramaturgic *rel* showy, pretentious, ostentatious; sentimental, romantic, maudlin, mawkish

melody • a rhythmic succession of single tones organized as an aesthetic whole *syn* air, tune

melt *syn* LIQUEFY, deliquesce, fuse, thaw

member *syn* PART, portion, piece, detail, division, section, segment, sector, fraction, fragment, parcel *rel* element, component, constituent; branch, limb, shoot, bough

memento *syn* REMEMBRANCE, remembrancer, reminder, memorial, token, keepsake, souvenir *rel* earnest, pledge; gift, present, favor

memoir *syn* BIOGRAPHY, life, autobiography, confessions

memorable *syn* NOTEWORTHY, notable *rel* remembered, recollected, recalled; salient, remarkable, noticeable, outstanding, striking, arresting; exceptional

memorandum *syn* LETTER, epistle, missive, note, message, dispatch, report

memorial *syn* REMEMBRANCE, remembrancer, reminder, memento, token, keepsake, souvenir *rel* monument, record; sign, mark

memory • the capacity for or the act of remembering, or the thing remembered *syn* remembrance, recollection, reminiscence, mind, souvenir *rel* intellect, soul, intelligence, brain, wit; remembering, minding, recalling, reminding; awareness, consciousness, cognizance *ant* oblivion

menace *syn* THREATEN *rel* alarm, terrify, scare, frighten; intimidate, cow; presage, portend, forebode, forecast, foretell

mend • to put into good order something that is injured, damaged, or defective *syn* repair, patch, rebuild *rel* improve, better, ameliorate, help; emend, remedy, redress, correct, rectify, reform; renew, restore, renovate, rejuvenate, refurbish; fix, adjust, regulate

mendacious *syn* DISHONEST, lying, untruthful, deceitful *rel* false, wrong; prevaricating, equivocating, paltering, fibbing *ant* veracious

menial *syn* SUBSERVIENT, servile, slavish, obsequious *rel* abject, mean, sordid, ignoble; base, low, vile; groveling, wallowing

mental • of or relating to the mind *syn* intellectual, psychic, intelligent, cerebral

mention • to refer to someone or something in a clear unmistakable manner *syn* name, instance, specify *rel* refer, allude, advert; cite, quote

mephitic *syn* POISONOUS, toxic, venomous, virulent, pestilent, pestilential, miasmic, miasmatic, miasmal *rel* offensive, loathsome, revolting, repulsive, repugnant; fetid, noisome, putrid, malodorous; noxious, pernicious, baneful

mercantile *syn* COMMERCIAL

mercenary • serving merely for pay or sordid advantage *syn* hireling, venal, hack *rel* abject, mean, sordid, ignoble; covetous, greedy, acquisitive, grasping, avaricious; debased, corrupt, corrupted, depraved

merciful *syn* FORBEARING, clement, tolerant, lenient, indulgent *rel* compassionate, tender; benignant, benign, kind, kindly; forgiving, pardoning, condoning *ant* merciless

mercifully *syn* FORBEARINGLY, tolerantly, clemently, leniently, indulgently

mercifulness *syn* FORBEARANCE, clemency, tolerance, leniency, indulgence *rel* mercy, lenity, charity, grace; compassion, commiseration, pity, ruth, sympathy

merciless *syn* GRIM, implacable, relentless, unrelenting *rel* pitiless, ruthless, compassionless; wanton, uncalled-for, gratuitous, supererogatory; cruel, fell, fierce; inexorable, obdurate, inflexible, adamant, adamantine *ant* merciful

mercurial *syn* INCONSTANT, fickle, capricious, unstable *rel* volatile, effervescent, buoyant, expansive, elastic, resilient; changeable, changeful, variable, protean, mutable; mobile, movable; clever, adroit, cunning, ingenious *ant* saturnine

mercy • a disposition to show compassion or kindness *syn* charity, grace, clemency, lenity *rel* compassion, ruth, pity, commiseration, sympathy; mercifulness, forbearance, tolerance, leniency, indulgence

mere • being as stated with nothing more added or extra *syn* bare, very

meretricious *syn* GAUDY, tawdry, garish, flashy *rel* showy, pretentious, ostentatious; vulgar, coarse, gross; deceptive, delusive, delusory, misleading

merge *syn* MIX, blend, fuse, coalesce, amalgamate, commingle, mingle *rel* consolidate, concentrate, compact, unify; unite, combine, conjoin; integrate, concatenate, articulate

merger *syn* CONSOLIDATION, amalgamation

meridian *syn* SUMMIT, culmination, zenith, apogee, peak, pinnacle, climax, apex, acme

merit *n* **1** *syn* DUE, desert *rel* meed, reward, guerdon; worth, value; gaining, gainings, winning, winnings **2** *syn* EXCELLENCE, virtue, perfection *ant* fault; defect

merit *vb, syn* DESERVE, earn, rate *rel* reward, award; requite, recompense, repay, pay

merry • showing high spirits or lightheartedness *syn* blithe, jocund, jovial, jolly *rel* gay, vivacious, lively, sprightly, animated; joyful, joyous, cheerful, glad, happy, lighthearted; mirthful, gleeful, hilarious

mesa *syn* MOUNTAIN, mount, peak, alp, volcano

message *syn* LETTER, missive, note, epistle, dispatch, report, memorandum

metamorphose *syn* TRANSFORM, transmute, convert, transmogrify, transfigure *rel* change, vary, alter, modify; develop, mature, age, ripen

metamorphosis *syn* TRANSFORMATION, transmutation, conversion, transmogrification, transfiguration *rel* change, mutation, alternation, permutation, vicissitude; variation, alteration, modification

metaphor *syn* ANALOGY, simile

metaphrase *syn* TRANSLATION, version, paraphrase

meter *syn* RHYTHM, cadence

method • the means taken or procedure followed in achieving an end *syn* mode, manner, way, fashion, system *rel* process, procedure, proceeding; classification; disposition, disposal

methodical *syn* ORDERLY, systematic, regular *rel* methodized, systematized, organized; careful, meticulous, scrupulous; logical, analytical *ant* unmethodical; desultory

methodize *syn* ORDER, systematize, organize, arrange, marshal *rel* regulate, adjust; set, settle, fix, establish

meticulous *syn* CAREFUL, scrupulous, punctilious, punctual *rel* fastidious, finicky, particular, fussy, pernickety, nice; accurate, exact, precise, correct

mettle *syn* COURAGE, spirit, resolution, tenacity *rel* fortitude, backbone, sand, grit, pluck, guts; nerve, hardihood, temerity, audacity; gallantry, valor, heroism

mettlesome *syn* SPIRITED, high-spirited, spunky, fiery, peppery, gingery *rel* courageous, bold, audacious, intrepid, brave; impassioned, passionate, ardent, fervent; restive, impatient, restless

miasmic, miasmatic, miasmal *syn* POISONOUS, toxic, venomous, virulent, pestilent, pestilential, mephitic *rel* contagious, infectious, catching; noxious, pernicious, baneful, deleterious

microscopic *syn* SMALL, minute, little, diminutive, miniature, petite, wee, tiny, teeny, weeny

middle *syn* CENTER, midst, core, hub, focus, nucleus, heart

middling *syn* MEDIUM, mediocre, second-rate, moderate, average, fair, indifferent

midget *syn* DWARF, manikin, pygmy, homunculus, runt

midst *syn* CENTER, middle, core, hub, focus, nucleus, heart

mien *syn* BEARING, demeanor, deportment, port, presence *rel* air, pose, affectation, mannerism; aspect, appearance, semblance, look

might *syn* POWER, strength, energy, force, puissance *rel* vigorousness, vigor, strenuousness, energeticness, lustiness; potency, powerfulness, forcibleness, forcefulness

migrant *syn* EMIGRANT, immigrant

migrate • to move from one country, place, or locality to another *syn* emigrate, immigrate

mild *syn* SOFT, gentle, smooth, lenient, bland, balmy *rel* forbearing, tolerant, clement, merciful, lenient, indulgent; delicate, dainty, exquisite, choice; temperate, moderate; calm, serene, tranquil, placid *ant* harsh; fierce

milieu *syn* BACKGROUND, environment, setting, mise-en-scène, backdrop

militant *syn* AGGRESSIVE, assertive, self-assertive, pushing, pushy *rel* bellicose, pugnacious, combative, contentious, belligerent; combating, opposing, antagonizing, antagonistic; fighting, warring, contending, battling

military *syn* MARTIAL, warlike

mime *syn* ACTOR, player, performer, mummer, mimic, thespian, impersonator, trouper

mimic *n, syn* ACTOR, player, performer, mummer, mime, thespian, impersonator, trouper

mimic *vb, syn* COPY, imitate, ape, mock *rel* play, impersonate, act; counterfeit, feign, simulate, sham, pretend, assume

mind *n* **1** *syn* MEMORY, remembrance, recollection, reminiscence, souvenir **2** • the element or complex of elements in an individual that feels, perceives, thinks, wills, and esp. reasons *syn* intellect, soul, psyche, brain, intelligence, wit *rel* power, function, faculty; reason, understanding, intuition; wisdom, judgment, sense, gumption

mind *vb* **1** *syn* REMEMBER, recollect, recall, remind, reminisce, bethink **2** *syn* OBEY, comply *rel* defer, yield, submit, bow; accede, assent, consent, agree, acquiesce **3** *syn* TEND, attend, watch

mingle *syn* MIX, commingle, blend, merge, coalesce, amalgamate, fuse *rel* join, combine, unite, conjoin, connect; consolidate, compact, unify, concentrate

miniature *syn* SMALL, minute, diminutive, little, wee, tiny, teeny, weeny

minimize *syn* DECRY, depreciate, belittle, disparage, derogate, detract *ant* magnify

minister *syn* AMBASSADOR, envoy, legate, nuncio, internuncio, chargé d'affaires

minority *syn* INFANCY, nonage *ant* majority

minstrel *syn* POET, bard, troubadour, versifier, rhymer, rhymester, poetaster

minute *n, syn* INSTANT, moment, second, flash, jiffy, twinkling, split second

minute *adj* **1** *syn* SMALL, little, diminutive, miniature, wee, tiny, teeny, weeny **2** *syn* CIRCUMSTANTIAL, particular, particularized, detailed, itemized *rel* meticulous, scrupulous, careful, punctilious; precise, accurate, exact, right, nice, correct

miracle *syn* WONDER, marvel, prodigy, phenomenon

miraculous *syn* SUPERNATURAL, supranatural, preternatural, superhuman

mirage *syn* DELUSION, hallucination, illusion

mirror *syn* MODEL, example, pattern, exemplar, ideal, standard, beau ideal

mirth • a mood or temper characterized by joy and high spirits and usu. manifested in laughter and merrymaking *syn* glee, jollity, hilarity *rel* cheerfulness, cheer, lightheartedness, joyfulness, gladness, happiness; joy, pleasure, delight; merriment, blitheness, jocundity, joviality

misanthropic *syn* CYNICAL, pessimistic *ant* philanthropic

miscarriage *syn* FAILURE, neglect, default, dereliction *rel* abuse, maltreatment, misuse

miscellaneous • consisting of diverse things or members *syn* assorted, heterogeneous, motley, promiscuous *rel* various, diverse, divergent, disparate, different; multifarious, divers, sundry, many

mischance *syn* MISFORTUNE, adversity, mishap *rel* accident, casualty; disaster, calamity, catastrophe, cataclysm

mischief *syn* INJURY, hurt, damage, harm *rel* perniciousness, detrimentalness, detriment, deleteriousness, noxiousness, banefulness, bane; evil, ill; impairment, marring, spoiling

mischievous *syn* PLAYFUL, roguish, waggish, impish, frolicsome, sportive *rel* annoying, bothering, bothersome, vexing, vexatious, irking, irksome; naughty, bad, evil, ill, wicked; tricky, foxy, insidious, artful, sly

miscreant *syn* VILLAIN, scoundrel, blackguard, knave, rascal, rogue, scamp, rapscallion *rel* criminal, malefactor, culprit, delinquent

misdoubt *syn* DISTRUST, mistrust, doubt, suspect

mise-en-scène *syn* BACKGROUND, setting, environment, milieu, backdrop

miserable • being in a pitiable state of distress or unhappiness (as from want or shame) *syn* wretched *rel* forlorn, hopeless, despairing, despondent; pitiable, piteous, pitiful; doleful, dolorous, melancholy *ant* comfortable

miserly *syn* STINGY, penurious, parsimonious, niggardly, tight, tightfisted, close, closefisted, cheeseparing, penny-pinching *rel* avaricious, greedy, covetous, grasping; mean, sordid, abject, ignoble

misery *syn* DISTRESS, suffering, agony, dolor, passion *rel* adversity, misfortune; affliction, visitation, trial, tribulation; melancholy, dejection, sadness, depression *ant* felicity, blessedness

misfortune • adverse fortune or an instance of this *syn* mischance, adversity, mishap *rel* disaster, calamity, catastrophe, cataclysm; accident, casualty; trial, tribulation, cross, affliction, visitation *ant* happiness; prosperity

misgiving *syn* APPREHENSION, foreboding, presentiment *rel* mistrust, distrust; suspicion, doubt, skepticism, uncertainty; fear, alarm, dread, fright

mishap **1** *syn* MISFORTUNE, mischance, adversity **2** *syn* ACCIDENT, casualty *rel* misfortune, mischance; disaster, calamity; chance, fortune, hap, hazard

mislay *syn* MISPLACE

mislead *syn* DECEIVE, delude, beguile, betray, double-cross *rel* entice, inveigle, lure, tempt, seduce; dupe, gull, hoodwink, hoax, bamboozle

misleading • having an appearance or character that leads one astray or into error *syn* deceptive, delusive, delusory *rel* fallacious, casuistical, sophistical; false, wrong; confounding, bewildering, distracting, perplexing, puzzling

misplace • to put in the wrong place *syn* mislay *rel* displace; derange, disarrange, disorder

misrepresent • to give a false or misleading representation of usu. with an intent to deceive *syn* falsify, belie, garble *rel* disguise, dissemble, cloak, mask, camouflage; simulate, counterfeit, feign; lie, prevaricate, equivocate, palter

misrepresentation *syn* LIE, falsehood, untruth, fib, story *rel* dishonesty, deceitfulness, mendaciousness, mendacity; sophistication, doctoring, loading, weighting, adulteration; sophistry, casuistry

missive *syn* LETTER, epistle, note, message, dispatch, report, memorandum

mist *syn* HAZE, fog, smog

mistake *vb* • to take one thing to be another *syn* confuse, confound *rel* addle, muddle *ant* recognize

mistake *n, syn* ERROR, slip, lapse, blunder, faux pas, bull, howler, boner *rel* confusion, confounding, mistaking; inadvertence; neglecting, neglect, omitting, omission, disregarding, slighting, slight

mistreat *syn* ABUSE, maltreat, ill-treat, misuse, outrage *rel* see ILL-TREAT

mistrust *n* **1** *syn* UNCERTAINTY, suspicion, skepticism, doubt, dubiety, dubiosity *rel* misgiving, presentiment, foreboding, apprehension *ant* trust; assurance **2** *syn* DISTRUST

mistrust *vb, syn* DISTRUST, doubt, suspect, misdoubt *rel* apprehend, anticipate, foresee; alarm, frighten, scare; appall, dismay

misuse *syn* ABUSE, mistreat, maltreat, ill-treat, outrage *rel* hurt, injure, harm, damage, impair, mar, spoil; pervert, debase, corrupt *ant* respect

mite *syn* PARTICLE, bit, smidgen, whit, atom, iota, jot, tittle

mitigate *syn* RELIEVE, allay, alleviate, lighten, assuage *rel* temper, moderate; abate, reduce, lessen, diminish, decrease; palliate, extenuate *ant* intensify

mix • to combine or be combined into a more or less uniform whole *syn* mingle, commingle, blend, merge, coalesce, amalgamate, fuse *rel* join, combine, unite, conjoin

mixture • a product formed by the combination of two or more things *syn* admixture, blend, compound, composite, amalgam *rel* joining, combining, uniting

moan *n, syn* SIGH, groan, sob *rel* crying, cry, wailing, wail; lamenting, lament, bemoaning, bewailing

moan *vb, syn* SIGH, groan, sob *rel* mourn, grieve, sorrow; bemoan, bewail, lament, deplore

mob *syn* CROWD, throng, press, crush, rout, horde *rel* multitude, army, host, legion

mobile *syn* MOVABLE, motive *rel* fluid, liquid; changeable, changeful, protean, variable; inconstant, unstable, mercurial, fickle, capricious *ant* immobile

mock **1** *syn* RIDICULE, taunt, deride, twit, rally *rel* flout, scoff, jeer, gird, gibe; caricature, parody, travesty, burlesque **2** *syn* COPY, imitate, mimic, ape *rel* counterfeit, feign, affect, simulate, assume

mode *n* **1** *syn* STATE, condition, situation, posture, status **2** *syn* METHOD, manner, way, fashion, system *rel* trend, drift, tendency, tenor; procedure, process

mode *n, syn* FASHION, style, vogue, fad, rage, craze, dernier cri, cry

model • someone or something set before one for guidance or imitation *syn* example, pattern, exemplar, ideal, standard, beau ideal, mirror *rel* criterion, touchstone, gauge, standard

moderate *adj* **1** • not excessive in degree, amount, or intensity *syn* temperate *rel* ordinary, common, familiar; gentle, mild, bland, soft; sparing, economical *ant* immoderate **2** *syn* MEDIUM, middling, mediocre, second-rate, average, fair, indifferent *rel* decent, decorous, proper; steady, even, equable, constant

moderate *vb* • to modify something so as to avoid an extreme or to keep within bounds *syn* qualify, temper *rel* abate, reduce, lessen, diminish, decrease; mitigate, alleviate, lighten, relieve; slow, slacken, delay

modern **1** • having taken place, existed, or developed in times close to the present *syn* recent, late **2** *syn* NEW, modernistic, novel, new-fashioned, newfangled, original, fresh *rel* contemporary, contemporaneous, coincident, concomitant, concurrent; prevailing, current, prevalent *ant* antique; ancient

modernistic *syn* NEW, new-fashioned, newfangled, novel, modern, original, fresh *ant* antiquated

modest **1** *syn* HUMBLE, meek, lowly *rel* retiring, withdrawing; moderate, temperate *ant* ambitious **2** *syn* SHY, bashful, diffident, coy *rel* reserved, reticent, silent; shrinking, recoiling; nice, seemly, proper, decorous **3** *syn* CHASTE, decent, pure *rel* moral, virtuous; decorous, proper, seemly *ant* immodest

modification *syn* CHANGE, alteration, variation *rel* transformation, metamorphosis, conversion, transmogrification; qualification, tempering

modify *syn* CHANGE, alter, vary *rel* temper, moderate, qualify; transform, convert, metamorphose, transmogrify

modish *syn* STYLISH, fashionable, smart, chic, dashing *ant* antiquated

moist *syn* WET, damp, humid, dank

mollify *syn* PACIFY, appease, placate, propitiate, conciliate *rel* relieve, allay, mitigate, lighten; moderate, temper, qualify; abate, lessen, reduce, decrease *ant* exasperate

mollycoddle *syn* INDULGE, humor, pamper, spoil, baby

molt *syn* DISCARD, cast, shed, slough, scrap, junk

moment **1** *syn* INSTANT, minute, second, flash, jiffy, twinkling, split second **2** *syn* IMPORTANCE, consequence, significance, import, weight *rel* value, worth; advantage, profit, avail, use

momentary *syn* TRANSIENT, transitory, passing, ephemeral, fugitive, fleeting, evanescent, short-lived *ant* agelong

momentum *syn* SPEED, impetus, velocity, pace, headway

monastery *syn* CLOISTER, convent, nunnery, abbey, priory

monetary *syn* FINANCIAL, pecuniary, fiscal

money • something (as pieces of stamped metal or paper certificates) customarily and legally used as a medium of exchange *syn* cash, currency, legal tender, specie, coin, coinage

monk *syn* RELIGIOUS, friar, nun *rel* recluse, hermit, eremite, anchorite, cenobite

monkeyshine *syn* PRANK, caper, antic, dido

monograph *syn* DISCOURSE, treatise, disquisition, dissertation, thesis *rel* article, paper, essay

monopolize • to take up completely *syn* engross, absorb, consume *rel* possess, own, have, hold; utilize, use, employ; control, manage, conduct

monopoly • exclusive possession or control *syn* corner, pool, syndicate, trust, cartel

monotonous *syn* DULL, dreary, pedestrian, humdrum, stodgy *rel* wearisome, boring, irksome, tedious, tiresome

monstrous **1** • extremely impressive *syn* prodigious, tremendous, stupendous, monumental *rel* enormous, immense, huge, vast, colossal, mammoth, gigantic **2** *syn* OUTRAGEOUS, heinous, atrocious *rel* flagrant, glaring, gross, rank; ominous, portentous, fateful; flagitious, nefarious, infamous

monument *syn* DOCUMENT, record, archive

monumental **1** *syn* MONSTROUS, prodigious, tremendous, stupendous *rel* colossal, gigantic, enormous, mammoth, huge; impressive, moving **2** *syn* MASSIVE, massy, bulky, substantial *rel* imposing, stately, majestic, august, magnificent, grand

mood • a state of mind in which an emotion or set of emotions gains ascendancy *syn* humor, temper, vein *rel* disposition, temperament, character, personality, individuality; soul, spirit; emotion, feeling, affection

moor *syn* SECURE, anchor, rivet *rel* tie, bind; attach, fasten, affix, fix; balance, steady, stabilize, trim

moral • conforming to a standard of what is right and good *syn* ethical, virtuous, righteous, noble *rel* right, good; upright, honest, just, honorable, scrupulous, conscientious; chaste, pure, modest, decent; ideal, abstract

morale • a sense of common purpose or dedication with respect to a group *syn* discipline, esprit de corps *rel* vigor, spirit, drive; self-confidence, self-possession, assurance, confidence; nerving, steeling

morality *syn* GOODNESS, virtue, rectitude *rel* integrity, probity, honor, honesty; excellence, perfection, merit

morally *syn* VIRTUALLY, practically

morbid *syn* UNWHOLESOME, sickly, diseased, pathological *rel* hypochondriac, atrabilious, melancholic; gloomy, morose, saturnine, sullen *ant* sound

mordant *syn* CAUSTIC, acrid, scathing *rel* incisive, trenchant, cutting, biting, clear-cut, crisp; pungent, poignant, piquant, racy, spicy, snappy; sharp, keen, acute

moreover *syn* ALSO, besides, furthermore, likewise, too

moron *syn* FOOL, imbecile, idiot, simpleton, natural

morose *syn* SULLEN, glum, gloomy, saturnine, dour, surly, sulky, crabbed *rel* splenetic, choleric, irascible, testy, cranky, cross; peevish, snappish, waspish, petulant, irritable; brusque, gruff

mortal *syn* DEADLY, fatal, lethal *rel* destructive; virulent, venomous, poisonous; implacable, unrelenting, relentless, grim *ant* venial (*especially of a sin*)

mortified *syn* ASHAMED, chagrined *rel* harassed, harried, worried, annoyed; humiliated, humbled, abased; abashed, embarrassed, discomfited

mostly *syn* LARGELY, greatly, chiefly, mainly, princially, generally

motif **1** *syn* FIGURE, device, design, pattern **2** *syn* SUBJECT, matter, subject matter, argument, topic, text, theme, motive, leitmotiv

motion • the act or an instance of moving *syn* movement, move, locomotion, stir *rel* impetus, momentum, speed, velocity, pace, headway

motivate *syn* ACTIVATE, actuate *rel* stimulate, quicken, provoke, excite; arouse, rouse, stir; inspire, animate, fire, inform

motive *n* **1** • a stimulus to action *syn* spring, impulse, incentive, inducement, spur, goad *rel* cause, determinant, antecedent, reason; desire, appetite, urge, passion, lust; feeling, emotion; purpose, intent, intention, aim, end **2** *syn* SUBJECT, matter, subject matter, argument, topic, text, theme, motif, leitmotiv

motive *adj, syn* MOVABLE, mobile *rel* active, operative, dynamic; moving, driving, impelling, impulsive

motley **1** *syn* VARIEGATED, parti-colored, checkered, checked, pied, piebald, skewbald, dappled, freaked **2** *syn* MISCELLANEOUS, heterogeneous, assorted, promiscuous *rel* different, diverse, divergent, disparate, various; discrepant, incompatible, uncongenial, incongruous, inconsonant

motor *syn* MACHINE, mechanism, machinery, apparatus, engine

motorcade *syn* PROCESSION, parade, cortege, cavalcade

mottle *syn* SPOT, spatter, sprinkle, fleck, stipple, marble, speckle, spangle, bespangle

mottled *syn* SPOTTED, spattered, sprinkled, flecked, stippled, marbled, speckled, spangled, bespangled

motto *syn* SAYING, proverb, adage, saw, maxim, epigram, aphorism, apothegm

mount *n, syn* MOUNTAIN, peak, alp, volcano, mesa

mount *vb* **1** *syn* RISE, ascend, soar, arise, tower, rocket, levitate, surge *ant* drop **2** *syn* ASCEND, climb, scale *ant* dismount

mountain • a relatively steep and high elevation of land *syn* mount, peak, alp, volcano, mesa *rel* height, altitude, elevation

mountebank *syn* IMPOSTOR, faker, charlatan, quack

mourn *syn* GRIEVE, sorrow *rel* lament, bewail, bemoan; weep, keen, wail, cry

movable • capable of moving or of being moved *syn* mobile, motive *rel* changeable, changeful, variable, mutable *ant* immovable; stationary

move *vb* **1** • to set or keep in motion *syn* actuate, drive, impel *rel* activate, motivate; provoke, excite, quicken, stimulate; induce, persuade, prevail, get **2** • to change or to cause to change from one place to another *syn* remove, shift, transfer *rel* displace, replace, supplant, supersede; convey, carry, bear, transport, transmit

move *n, syn* MOTION, movement, locomotion, stir *rel* change, alteration, variation, modification; transformation, metamorphosis, conversion, transmogrification

movement *syn* MOTION, move, locomotion, stir *rel* action, act, deed; change, alteration, variation, modification; activity, operativeness, operation, dynamism, liveness

moving • having the power to produce deep emotion *syn* impressive, poignant, affecting, touching, pathetic *rel* exciting, stimulating, quickening, provoking; thrilling, electrifying; stirring, arousing, rousing, awakening, rallying

muddle *vb, syn* CONFUSE, addle, fuddle, befuddle *rel* puzzle, perplex, mystify, bewilder, distract, nonplus, confound, dumbfound; faze, rattle, discomfit, embarrass; fluster, flurry, upset, agitate, discompose *ant* enlighten

muddle *n, syn* CONFUSION, disorder, chaos, disarray, jumble, clutter, snarl

muddy *syn* TURBID, roily *rel* murky, gloomy, obscure, dark; confused, muddled, addled; dirty, filthy, foul, nasty, squalid

muff *syn* BOTCH, bungle, fumble, cobble

mug *syn* FACE, countenance, visage, physiognomy, puss

mulct *syn* PENALIZE, fine, amerce *rel* exact, require, demand, claim

mulish *syn* OBSTINATE, dogged, stubborn, pertinacious, stiff-necked, pigheaded, bullheaded *rel* headstrong, intractable, recalcitrant, refractory, ungovernable, unruly; fixed, set

multifarious *syn* MANY, divers, numerous, various, several, sundry *rel* disparate, diverse, divergent, different; incongruous, incompatible, uncongenial, discrepant, discordant, inconsonant, inconsistent

multiply *syn* INCREASE, augment, enlarge *rel* propagate, reproduce, breed, generate; expand, spread, stretch

multitude • a very large number of individuals or things *syn* army, host, legion *rel* horde, throng, press, mob, crush, crowd

mummer *syn* ACTOR, performer, mime, mimic, player, thespian, impersonator, trouper

mummery *syn* GIBBERISH, hocus-pocus, abracadabra

mundane *syn* EARTHLY, worldly, earthy, terrestrial, sublunary *rel* fleshly, sensual, carnal, animal; secular, temporal, profane *ant* eternal

munificent *syn* LIBERAL, bountiful, bounteous, openhanded, generous, handsome *rel* benevolent, charitable, philanthropic, eleemosynary, altruistic; profuse, lavish, prodigal

murder *syn* KILL, slay, assassinate, dispatch, execute

murky *syn* DARK, obscure, gloomy, dim, dusky *rel* turbid, muddy, roily; lowering, glowering, glooming, gloomy; lurid, grim, ghastly

muscular • strong and powerful in build or action *syn* brawny, sinewy, athletic, burly, husky *rel* robust, healthy, hale, sound; strong, sturdy, stalwart, stout; vigorous, lusty

muse *syn* PONDER, meditate, ruminate *rel* consider, study, contemplate, weigh, excogitate; reflect, reason, think

mushy *syn* SENTIMENTAL, romantic, mawkish, maudlin, soppy, slushy

muster *syn* SUMMON, summons, call, cite, convoke, convene *rel* collect, congregate, assemble, gather; marshal, organize, arrange, order; align, line, line up, range, array

musty *syn* MALODOROUS, fusty, stinking, fetid, noisome, putrid, rank, rancid *rel* dirty, filthy, foul, nasty, squalid; sloppy, slipshod, unkempt, slovenly

mutable *syn* CHANGEABLE, changeful, variable, protean *rel* unstable, inconstant, fickle; fluctuating, wavering, swinging, swaying *ant* immutable

mutation *syn* CHANGE, permutation, vicissitude, alternation *rel* shifting, shift, moving, move, removing, remove; variation, modification, alteration

mute *syn* DUMB, speechless, inarticulate

mutilate **1** *syn* MAIM, cripple, batter, mangle *rel* injure, damage, hurt, spoil, mar; disfigure, deface **2** *syn* STERILIZE, castrate, spay, emasculate, alter, geld

mutinous *syn* INSUBORDINATE, rebellious, seditious, factious, contumacious *rel* recalcitrant, refractory, intractable, unruly, ungovernable; disaffected, alienated

mutiny *syn* REBELLION, revolution, uprising, revolt, insurrection, putsch, coup *rel* sedition, treason; traitorousness, treacherousness, perfidiousness, perfidy, faithlessness

mutual *syn* RECIPROCAL, common *rel* shared, participated, partaken; joined, joint, united, connected, related, associated

mysterious • being beyond one's power to discover, understand, or explain *syn* inscrutable, arcane *rel* occult, esoteric, recondite, abstruse; cryptic, enigmatic, ambiguous, equivocal, obscure; mystical, mystic, anagogical, cabalistic

mystery • something which baffles or perplexes *syn* problem, enigma, riddle, puzzle, conundrum

mystic *syn* MYSTICAL, anagogic, cabalistic *rel* occult, esoteric, recondite, abstruse; mysterious, inscrutable; visionary, quixotic, imaginary

mystical • having a spiritual meaning or reality that is neither apparent to the senses nor obvious to the intelligence *syn* mystic, anagogic, cabalistic *rel* profound, deep, abysmal; ultimate, absolute, categorical; spiritual, divine, sacred, holy; supernatural, supranatural, miraculous

mystify *syn* PUZZLE, bewilder, perplex, distract, nonplus, confound, dumbfound *rel* discomfit, faze, rattle, embarrass; discompose, disquiet, perturb, disturb, agitate, upset *ant* enlighten

myth **1** • a traditional story of ostensibly historical content whose origin has been lost *syn* legend, saga *rel* fiction, fable, fabrication, figment; invention, creation **2** *syn* ALLEGORY, parable, fable

mythical *syn* FICTITIOUS, fabulous, legendary, apocryphal *rel* imaginary, visionary, fanciful, fantastic; invented, created

N

naïve *syn* NATURAL, unsophisticated, artless, ingenuous, simple *rel* sincere, unfeigned; spontaneous, impulsive, instinctive; fresh, original, new

naked *syn* BARE, nude, bald, barren *rel* revealed, disclosed, discovered; evident, manifest, palpable, obvious; uncolored, colorless; pure, simple, sheer

name *n* • the word or combination of words by which something is called and by means of which it can be distinguished or identified *syn* designation, denomination, appellation, title, style

name *vb* **1** *syn* DESIGNATE, nominate, elect, appoint *rel* choose, select, prefer, opt; declare, announce, publish, advertise **2** *syn* MENTION, instance, specify *rel* refer, allude, advert; designate; identify, recognize; cite, quote

nap *syn* SLEEP, catnap, doze, drowse, snooze, slumber

narcotic *syn* ANODYNE, opiate, nepenthe

narrate *syn* RELATE, rehearse, recite, recount, describe, state, report *rel* tell, reveal, disclose, discover; discourse, expatiate, dilate, descant

narrative *syn* STORY, tale, anecdote, yarn *rel* chronicle, account, report, story, version; fiction, fabrication, figment, fable

narrow, narrow-minded *syn* ILLIBERAL, intolerant, bigoted, hidebound *rel* rigorous, rigid, strict, stringent; obdurate, inflexible, inexorable; provincial, parochial, local, small-town, insular *ant* broad, broad-minded

narrows *syn* STRAIT, sound, channel, passage

nasty *syn* DIRTY, filthy, squalid, foul *rel* coarse, gross, vulgar, obscene, ribald; tainted, contaminated, polluted, defiled; indelicate, indecent, unseemly, improper, indecorous

national *syn* CITIZEN, subject

native • belonging to a particular place by birth or origin *syn* indigenous, endemic, aboriginal, autochthonous *ant* alien, foreign

natural *adj* **1** *syn* REGULAR, normal, typical *rel* ordinary, common, familiar; usual, customary, habitual, accustomed, wonted *ant* unnatural; artificial; adventitious **2** • free from pretension or calculation *syn* simple, ingenuous, naïve, unsophisticated, artless, unaffected *rel* spontaneous, impulsive, instinctive; ingrained, constitutional, inherent

natural *n, syn* FOOL, idiot, imbecile, moron, simpleton

nature *syn* TYPE, kind, sort, stripe, kidney, ilk, description, character *rel* structure, anatomy, framework; disposition, temperament, personality; form, figure, shape, conformation

naughty *syn* BAD, evil, ill, wicked *rel* mischievous, roguish, impish, waggish; froward, balky, restive, wayward, contrary, perverse

nauseate *syn* DISGUST, sicken *rel* vomit, disgorge, belch; offend, outrage

nautical *syn* MARINE, maritime, naval

naval *syn* MARINE, nautical, maritime

near *adj & adv, syn* CLOSE, nigh, nearby *ant* far

near *vb, syn* APPROACH, approximate *rel* rival, match, touch, equal

nearby *syn* CLOSE, near, nigh *ant* far off

nearly • very close to *syn* almost, approximately, well-nigh

neat • manifesting care and orderliness *syn* tidy, trim, trig, snug, shipshape, spick-and-span *rel* clean, cleanly; fastidious, nice, dainty, finicky; exact, precise, correct, accurate *ant* filthy

neb *syn* BILL, beak, nib

necessary **1** *syn* NEEDFUL, requisite, indispensable, essential *rel* compelling, compulsory, obliging, obligatory, constraining; important, significant, momentous; cardinal, vital, fundamental **2** *syn* CERTAIN, inevitable *rel* unavoidable, unescapable, inescapable, ineluctable; infallible, inerrable, inerrant, unerring

necessitous *syn* POOR, indigent, needy, destitute, penniless, impecunious, poverty-stricken *rel* impoverished, drained, depleted, exhausted, bankrupt

necessity *syn* NEED, exigency *rel* compelling, compulsion, constraining, constraint, obliging, obligation, coercing, coercion; indispensableness, requisiteness, requisition, needfulness

need *n* • a pressing lack of something essential *syn* necessity, exigency *rel* stress, strain, pressure; lack, want, dearth, absence, defect, privation; poverty, indigence, penury, destitution

need *vb, syn* LACK, want, require *rel* demand, claim, exact; long, hanker, pine, yearn, hunger, thirst; crave, covet, desire, wish

needful • required for supply or relief *syn* necessary, requisite, indispensable, essential *rel* wanted, needed, required, lacked; vital, cardinal, fundamental

needy *syn* POOR, indigent, destitute, penniless, impecunious, poverty-stricken, necessitous *rel* see NECESSITOUS

nefarious *syn* VICIOUS, iniquitous, flagitious, infamous, corrupt, degenerate, villainous *rel* heinous, outrageous, atrocious, monstrous; flagrant, glaring, gross, rank

negate *syn* NULLIFY, annul, abrogate, invalidate *rel* negative, neutralize, counteract

negative 1 *syn* DENY, gainsay, traverse, contradict, impugn, contravene 2 *syn* NEUTRALIZE, counteract *rel* nullify, negate, annul, abrogate, invalidate

neglect *vb* • to pass over without giving due attention *syn* omit, disregard, ignore, overlook, slight, forget *ant* cherish

neglect *n* 1 *syn* FAILURE, default, miscarriage, dereliction *rel* omitting, omission, disregarding, disregard, ignoring, slighting, forgetting, overlooking; forgetfulness, obliviousness 2 *syn* NEGLIGENCE *rel* neglecting, omitting, omission, disregarding, disregard, ignoring, slighting, forgetting, overlooking

neglectful *syn* NEGLIGENT, lax, slack, remiss *rel* careless, heedless, thoughtless *ant* attentive

negligence • a failure to exercise proper or due care *syn* neglect *rel* laxness, slackness, remissness; indifference, unconcernedness, unconcern, incuriousness *ant* attention; solicitude

negligent • culpably careless or indicative of such carelessness *syn* neglectful, lax, slack, remiss *rel* careless, heedless, thoughtless, inadvertent; indifferent, unconcerned, incurious; slipshod, slovenly

negotiate 1 *syn* CONFER, parley, treat, commune, consult, advise 2 • to bring about by mutual agreement *syn* arrange, concert

neighborhood *syn* LOCALITY, district, vicinity

neighborly *syn* AMICABLE, friendly *rel* peaceful, peaceable, pacific; social, hospitable, gregarious, cooperative; cordial, sociable, gracious *ant* unneighborly; ill-disposed

neophyte *syn* NOVICE, novitiate, probationer, postulant, apprentice

nepenthe *syn* ANODYNE, opiate, narcotic

nerve *n, syn* TEMERITY, effrontery, audacity, hardihood, cheek, gall *rel* boldness, intrepidity; fortitude, grit, pluck, sand, guts; foolhardiness, recklessness

nerve *vb, syn* ENCOURAGE, inspirit, hearten, embolden, cheer, steel *rel* strengthen, invigorate, fortify, energize; rally, stir, rouse, arouse; renew, restore, refresh *ant* unnerve

nervous 1 *syn* VIGOROUS, lusty, energetic, strenuous *rel* forceful, forcible, potent, powerful; spirited, mettlesome; virile, manly 2 *syn* IMPATIENT, restless, restive, unquiet, uneasy, fidgety, jumpy, jittery *rel* excited, excitable, stimulated, provoked, provocative; inconstant, unstable, mercurial *ant* steady

nettle *syn* IRRITATE, provoke, exasperate, aggravate, rile, peeve *rel* annoy, irk, bother, vex; disturb, perturb, agitate, upset, discompose; fret, chafe, gall, abrade

network *syn* SYSTEM, scheme, complex, organism

neutral • lacking decisiveness or distinctiveness in character, quality, action, or effect *syn* indifferent

neutralize • to make inoperative or ineffective usu. by means of an opposite force, influence, or effect *syn* counteract, negative *rel* offset, countervail, counterbalance, counterpoise, compensate; defeat, overcome, subdue, conquer

new • having recently come into existence or use *syn* novel, new-fashioned, newfangled, modern, modernistic, original, fresh *ant* old

newfangled *syn* NEW, novel, new-fashioned, modernistic, modern, original, fresh

new-fashioned *syn* NEW, novel, newfangled, modernistic, modern, original, fresh

news • a report of events or conditions not

previously known *syn* tidings, intelligence, advice

newspaper *syn* JOURNAL, periodical, magazine, review, organ

nib *syn* BILL, beak, neb

nice 1 • having or displaying exacting standards *syn* dainty, fastidious, finicky, finicking, finical, particular, fussy, squeamish, persnickety, pernickety *rel* wise, judicious, sage, sapient; punctilious, meticulous, scrupulous, careful; discriminating, discerning, penetrating **2** *syn* CORRECT, precise, exact, accurate, right *rel* strict, rigid, rigorous, stringent; exquisite, delicate, rare, choice **3** *syn* DECOROUS, proper, seemly, decent *rel* fitting, fit, appropriate, suitable, meet

niggardly *syn* STINGY, parsimonious, penurious, miserly, close, closefisted, tight, tightfisted, cheeseparing, penny-pinching *rel* covetous, avaricious, grasping, greedy; sparing, economical, frugal, thrifty; mean, ignoble *ant* bountiful

nigh *syn* CLOSE, near, nearby *ant* far

night *syn* NIGHTLY, nocturnal

nightly • of, relating to, or associated with the night *syn* nocturnal, night *ant* daily

nightmare *syn* FANCY, dream, vision, fantasy, phantasy, phantasm, daydream *rel* delusion, hallucination, illusion; threatening, threat, menacing, menace

nimble *syn* AGILE, brisk, spry *rel* sprightly, lively, animated; alert, wide-awake, vigilant, watchful; supple, limber, lithe

nip *vb, syn* BLAST, blight *rel* check, arrest; squeeze, press; frustrate, thwart, balk

nip *n, syn* BLAST, blight *rel* arresting, checking; frigidity, freezing

nobility *syn* ARISTOCRACY, gentry, county, elite, society

noble 1 *syn* GRAND, stately, majestic, imposing, august, magnificent, grandiose *rel* glorious, splendid, resplendent, superb, sublime; illustrious, eminent, famous *ant* ignoble; cheap **2** *syn* MORAL, virtuous, righteous, ethical *rel* honorable, upright, just, honest *ant* base (*of actions*); atrocious (*of acts, deeds*)

nocturnal *syn* NIGHTLY *ant* diurnal

noise *syn* SOUND *rel* din, uproar, babel, hubbub, clamor, racket, pandemonium

noiseless *syn* STILL, silent, quiet, stilly *rel* calm, tranquil, serene, placid

noisome *syn* MALODOROUS, fetid, stinking, putrid, rank, rancid, fusty, musty *rel* foul, nasty, squalid, filthy, dirty; noxious, baneful, pernicious, deleterious; loathsome, offensive, revolting *ant* balmy

nomadic *syn* ITINERANT, peripatetic, ambulatory, ambulant, vagrant

nom de guerre, nom de plume *syn* PSEUDONYM, alias, pen name, incognito

nominate *syn* DESIGNATE, name, elect, appoint *rel* propose, intend, mean, purpose; present, tender, offer, proffer

nominee *syn* CANDIDATE, aspirant, applicant

nonage *syn* INFANCY, minority *ant* age

nonchalant *syn* COOL, unruffled, imperturbable, unflappable, composed, collected *rel* unconcerned, indifferent, aloof, detached; lighthearted, cheerful, glad; easy, effortless, light, smooth

non compos mentis *syn* INSANE, mad, crazy, crazed, demented, deranged, lunatic, maniac

nonconformist *syn* HERETIC, dissenter, sectary, sectarian, schismatic

nonesuch *syn* PARAGON, apotheosis, nonpareil

nonpareil *syn* PARAGON, apotheosis, nonesuch

nonplus *syn* PUZZLE, bewilder, distract, confound, dumbfound, mystify, perplex *rel* faze, rattle, embarrass, discomfit, disconcert; confuse, muddle; baffle, balk, frustrate

nonreligious *syn* IRRELIGIOUS, unreligious, ungodly, godless *rel* secular, profane, lay, temporal

nonsense • something said or proposed that seems senseless or absurd *syn* twaddle, drivel, bunk, balderdash, poppycock, gobbledygook, trash, rot, bull *rel* absurdity, preposterousness, silliness, foolishness; asininity, fatuousness

nonsocial *syn* UNSOCIAL, asocial, antisocial

norm *syn* AVERAGE, mean, median, par

normal *syn* REGULAR, typical, natural *rel* ordinary, common, familiar; usual, customary, habitual, wonted, accustomed *ant* abnormal

nosy *syn* CURIOUS, inquisitive, prying, snoopy *rel* meddlesome, impertinent, intrusive, obtrusive

notable *syn* NOTEWORTHY, memorable *rel* noticeable, remarkable, prominent, outstanding, extraordinary; eminent, celebrated, famous

note *vb, syn* SEE, remark, notice, perceive, discern, observe, contemplate, survey, view, behold, descry, espy

note *n* **1** *syn* SIGN, mark, token, badge, symptom *rel* indication, betokening, bespeaking, attesting; character, quality, property, attribute, accident **2** *syn* REMARK, observation, comment, commentary, obiter dictum *rel* annotation, gloss; remembering, reminding, reminder, recalling **3** *syn* LETTER, epistle, missive, message, dispatch, report, memorandum

noteworthy • having some quality that attracts one's attention *syn* notable, memorable *rel* noticeable, remarkable, prominent, conspicuous; patent, manifest, evident

notice *syn* SEE, remark, observe, note, perceive, discern, behold, descry, espy, view, survey, contemplate *rel* recognize, acknowledge; refer, advert, allude

noticeable • attracting notice or attention *syn* remarkable, prominent, outstanding, conspicuous, salient, signal, striking, arresting *rel* evident, manifest, obvious, palpable, patent

notify *syn* INFORM, apprise, advise, acquaint *rel* announce, declare, proclaim, publish, promulgate, broadcast; reveal, disclose, discover, divulge, tell

notion *syn* IDEA, concept, conception, thought, impression *rel* opinion, view, belief, conviction, persuasion, sentiment

notoriety *syn* FAME, reputation, repute, éclat, celebrity, renown, honor, glory *rel* publicity, ballyhoo, promotion, propaganda

notwithstanding • without being prevented or obstructed by *syn* in spite of, despite

nourish *syn* FEED, pasture, graze *rel* nurse, nurture, foster, cultivate

nourishment *syn* FOOD, nutriment, sustenance, aliment, pabulum, pap *rel* support, keep, maintenance, living

novel *syn* NEW, new-fashioned, newfangled, modern, modernistic, original, fresh *rel* strange, singular, unique, peculiar

novice • one who is just entering a field in which he or she has no previous experience *syn* novitiate, apprentice, probationer, postulant, neophyte *rel* beginner, starter, commencer; amateur, dilettante, dabbler, tyro

novitiate *syn* NOVICE, apprentice, probationer, postulant, neophyte

noxious *syn* PERNICIOUS, baneful, deleterious, detrimental *rel* injurious, hurtful, harmful; poisonous, virulent, venomous, toxic, pestilent, miasmatic; noisome, stinking, fetid, putrid, malodorous *ant* wholesome, sanitary

nuance *syn* GRADATION, shade *rel* distinction, difference, dissimilarity; touch, suggestion, suspicion, soupçon, dash, tinge; trace, vestige

nucleus *syn* CENTER, middle, midst, core, hub, focus, heart

nude *syn* BARE, naked, bald, barren *ant* clothed

nudge *vb, syn* POKE, prod, jog *rel* push, thrust, shove

nudge *n, syn* POKE, prod, jog

nugatory *syn* VAIN, otiose, idle, empty, hollow *rel* worthless, valueless; trifling, trivial, petty, paltry; ineffectual, ineffective, inefficacious; fruitless, bootless, futile, vain, abortive

nullify • to deprive of effective or continued existence *syn* negate, annul, abrogate, invalidate *rel* neutralize, negative, counteract; offset, countervail, counterbalance, compensate; limit, restrict, confine

number *n* **1** *syn* SUM, quantity, whole, total, aggregate, amount **2** • a character by which an arithmetical value is designated *syn* numeral, figure, digit, integer

number *vb, syn* COUNT, tell, enumerate *rel* calculate, compute, estimate, reckon

numeral *syn* NUMBER, figure, digit, integer

numerous *syn* MANY, several, sundry, various, divers, multifarious *rel* large, great, big; abundant, plentiful, plenteous

nun *syn* RELIGIOUS, monk, friar

nuncio *syn* AMBASSADOR, legate, internuncio, chargé d'affaires, minister, envoy

nunnery *syn* CLOISTER, monastery, convent, abbey, priory

nuptial *adj, syn* MATRIMONIAL, conjugal, connubial, hymeneal, marital

nuptial *n, syn* MARRIAGE, matrimony, wedlock, wedding, espousal

nurse • to promote the growth, development, or progress of *syn* nurture, foster, cherish, cultivate *rel* feed, nourish; promote, advance, further, forward; indulge, pamper, humor

nurture *syn* NURSE, foster, cherish, cultivate *rel* raise, rear; train, educate, school, discipline, teach; support, uphold, back

nutriment *syn* FOOD, nourishment, sustenance, aliment, pabulum, pap *rel* maintenance, support, keep, bread and butter, living

O

obdurate *syn* INFLEXIBLE, inexorable, adamant, adamantine *rel* hardened, indurated, callous; obstinate, stubborn, mulish, stiff-necked; immovable, immobile

obedient • submissive to the will of another *syn* docile, tractable, amenable, biddable *rel* compliant, acquiescent, resigned; submissive, subdued, tame; deferential, obeisant *ant* disobedient; contumacious

obeisance *syn* HONOR, deference, homage, reverence *rel* allegiance, fealty, loyalty, fidelity; respect, esteem, regard; veneration, reverence

obese *syn* FLESHY, corpulent, rotund, chubby, fat, stout, portly, plump *ant* scrawny

obey • to follow the wish, direction, or command of another *syn* comply, mind *rel* submit, yield, defer, bow, succumb; accede, acquiesce, subscribe, agree, assent *ant* command, order

obfuscate *syn* OBSCURE, dim, bedim, darken, eclipse, cloud, becloud, fog, befog *rel* confuse, muddle, befuddle, fuddle, addle; stupefy, bemuse, daze; perplex, mystify, bewilder, puzzle

obiter dictum *syn* REMARK, observation, comment, commentary, note

object *n* **1** *syn* THING, article *rel* affair, concern, matter; form, figure, shape, configuration **2** *syn* INTENTION, objective, goal, end, aim, design, purpose, intent *rel* motive, incentive, inducement

object *vb* • to oppose by arguing against *syn* protest, remonstrate, expostulate, kick *rel* demur, balk, scruple, jib, boggle, shy, stick, stickle; criticize, denounce, reprobate *ant* acquiesce

objectify *syn* REALIZE, externalize, materialize, incarnate, embody, actualize, hypostatize, reify

objectionable • arousing or likely to arouse objection *syn* exceptionable, unacceptable, undesirable, unwanted, unwelcome

objective *adj* **1** *syn* MATERIAL, physical, corporeal, phenomenal, sensible *rel* external, outside, outer, outward; tangible, palpable, perceptible *ant* subjective **2** *syn* FAIR, impartial, unbiased, dispassionate, uncolored, just, equitable *rel, ant* see OBJECTIVE 1

objective *n, syn* INTENTION, object, end, goal, aim, design, purpose, intent

objurgate *syn* EXECRATE, curse, damn, anathematize *rel* revile, vituperate, scold; condemn, denounce, reprobate, criticize

obligation **1** • something one is bound to do or forbear *syn* duty *rel* compulsion, constraint, restraint; responsibility, accountability, answerability **2** *syn* DEBT, indebtedness, liability, debit, arrear *rel* burden, load; promising, promise, engagement, pledging, pledge

oblige **1** *syn* FORCE, constrain, coerce, compel *rel* tie, bind **2** • to do a service or courtesy *syn* accommodate, favor *rel* gratify, please; benefit, profit, avail; help, aid, assist; support, uphold, back *ant* disoblige

obliging *syn* AMIABLE, good-natured, complaisant *rel* helping, helpful, aiding, assisting; accommodating, favoring; compliant, acquiescent; thoughtful, considerate *ant* disobliging; inconsiderate

oblique *syn* CROOKED, devious *rel* awry, askance, askew; indirect, circuitous, roundabout

obliterate *syn* ERASE, efface, cancel, expunge, blot out, delete *rel* abolish, annihilate, extinguish; destroy, raze; annul, abrogate, negate, invalidate, nullify

oblivious *syn* FORGETFUL, unmindful *rel* disregarding, ignoring, forgetting, neglecting, overlooking

obloquy **1** *syn* ABUSE, vituperation, invective, scurrility, billingsgate *rel* censuring, censure, condemning, condemnation, denouncing, denunciation, criticizing, criticism; calumny, detraction, backbiting, slander, scandal **2** *syn* DISGRACE, dishonor, disrepute, shame, infamy, ignominy, opprobrium, odium *rel* stigma, brand, blot, stain; humiliation, humbling, degradation

obnoxious *syn* REPUGNANT, distasteful, invidious, abhorrent, repellent *rel* hateful, odious, detestable, abominable; offensive, loathsome, repulsive, revolting *ant* grateful

obscene *syn* COARSE, gross, vulgar, ribald *rel* indecent, indelicate, indecorous; lewd, lascivious, wanton, licentious; foul, nasty, dirty *ant* decent

obscure *adj* **1** *syn* DARK, murky, gloomy, dim, dusky *rel* shady, shadowy, umbrageous **2** • not clearly understandable *syn* dark, vague, enigmatic, cryptic, ambiguous, equivocal *rel* abstruse, recondite, occult, esoteric; difficult, hard; complicated, intricate, involved, complex; mysterious, inscrutable *ant* distinct, obvious

obscure *vb* • to make dark, dim, or indistinct *syn* dim, bedim, darken, eclipse, cloud, becloud, fog, befog, obfuscate *rel* hide, conceal, screen; disguise, cloak, mask, camouflage; misrepresent, belie, falsify *ant* illuminate, illumine

obsequious *syn* SUBSERVIENT, servile, slavish, menial *rel* deferential, obeisant; compliant, acquiescent; sycophantic, parasitic, toadyish; cringing, fawning, truckling, cowering *ant* contumelious

observation *syn* REMARK, comment, commentary, note, obiter dictum *rel* opinion, view, belief; annotation, gloss; criticism, critique

observe **1** *syn* KEEP, celebrate, solemnize, commemorate *rel* respect, esteem, regard; revere, reverence, venerate *ant* violate **2** *syn* SEE, survey, view, contemplate, notice, remark, note, perceive, discern, behold, descry, espy *rel* scrutinize, examine, scan, inspect

observer *syn* SPECTATOR, beholder, looker-on, onlooker, witness, eyewitness, bystander, kibitzer

obsolete *syn* OLD, antiquated, archaic, antique, ancient, venerable, antediluvian *ant* current

obstacle • something that seriously hampers action or progress *syn* obstruction, impediment, bar, snag *rel* barrier; hindering, hindrance, blocking, block

obstinate • fixed and unyielding in course or purpose *syn* dogged, stubborn, pertinacious, mulish, stiff-necked, pigheaded, bullheaded *rel* headstrong, willful, recalcitrant, unruly; obdurate, inexorable, inflexible; resolute, steadfast, staunch *ant* pliant, pliable

obstreperous *syn* VOCIFEROUS, clamorous, blatant, strident, boisterous *rel* unruly, ungovernable, intractable, headstrong, refractory; uproarious, rackety

obstruct *syn* HINDER, impede, block, bar, dam *rel* prevent, preclude, obviate, avert; restrain, check, curb, inhibit

obstruction *syn* OBSTACLE, impediment, bar, snag *rel* hindering, hindrance, blocking, block; arresting, arrest, checking, check, interruption *ant* assistance

obtain *syn* GET, procure, secure, acquire, gain, win *rel* reach, achieve, attain; effect, fulfill, accomplish, perform

obtrude *syn* INTRUDE, interlope, butt in *rel* interpose, interfere, intervene, mediate

obtrusive *syn* IMPERTINENT, intrusive, meddlesome, officious *rel* inquisitive, curious, prying, snoopy, nosy; blatant, strident *ant* unobtrusive; shy

obtuse *syn* DULL, blunt *rel* insensitive, insensible, anesthetic, impassible; stolid, phlegmatic, impassive *ant* acute

obviate *syn* PREVENT, preclude, avert, ward *rel* evade, elude, avoid, escape; forestall, anticipate; interpose, interfere, intervene

obvious *syn* EVIDENT, manifest, patent, distinct, apparent, palpable, plain, clear *rel* prominent, conspicuous, salient, signal, striking, noticeable *ant* obscure; abstruse

occasion **1** *syn* OPPORTUNITY, chance, break, time *rel* juncture, pass; situation, posture, condition, state; moment, instant **2** *syn* CAUSE, determinant, antecedent, reason *rel* incident, occurrence, event; origin, source, inception

occasional *syn* INFREQUENT, uncommon, scarce, rare, sporadic *rel* casual, desultory, random; incidental, accidental *ant* customary

occult *syn* RECONDITE, esoteric, abstruse *rel* mysterious, inscrutable, arcane; mystic, cabalistic, mystical, anagogic

occupation *syn* WORK, employment, calling, pursuit, business

occur *syn* HAPPEN, chance, befall, betide,

transpire *rel* rise, arise, spring, emanate, issue, proceed; follow, succeed, ensue, supervene

occurrence • something that happens or takes place *syn* event, incident, episode, circumstance *rel* appearance, emergence; juncture, pass, exigency, emergency, contingency; posture, situation, condition, state

odd *syn* STRANGE, queer, quaint, singular, unique, peculiar, eccentric, erratic, outlandish, curious *rel* bizarre, grotesque, fantastic; anomalous, irregular, unnatural

odds *syn* ADVANTAGE, handicap, allowance, edge

odious *syn* HATEFUL, abhorrent, abominable, detestable *rel* repugnant, repellent, distasteful, obnoxious; offensive, loathsome, repulsive, revolting

odium *syn* DISGRACE, obloquy, opprobrium, ignominy, infamy, dishonor, disrepute, shame *rel* hate, hatred; antipathy, aversion; abhorrence, abomination, detestation, loathing

odor *syn* SMELL, scent, aroma *rel* fragrance, perfume, redolence, incense, bouquet

odorous • emitting and diffusing scent *syn* fragrant, redolent, aromatic, balmy *ant* malodorous; odorless

offal *syn* REFUSE, waste, rubbish, trash, debris, garbage

offend • to cause hurt feelings or deep resentment *syn* outrage, affront, insult *rel* annoy, vex, irk, bother; exasperate, nettle, irritate; pique, provoke, excite; chafe, fret, gall

offense **1** *syn* ATTACK, offensive, aggression *rel* assault, onslaught, onset **2** • an emotional response to a slight or indignity *syn* resentment, umbrage, pique, dudgeon, huff *rel* affront, insult, indignity; indignation, wrath, anger **3** • a transgression of law *syn* sin, vice, crime, scandal *rel* injustice, injury, wrong, grievance; breach, infraction, violation, transgression, trespass, infringement, contravention

offensive *adj* **1** *syn* ATTACKING, aggressive *rel* invasive, incursive; assaulting, assailing, attacking, bombarding, storming **2** • utterly distasteful or unpleasant to the senses or sensibilities *syn* loathsome, repulsive, repugnant, revolting *rel* repellent, abhorrent, distasteful, obnoxious, invidious; hateful, odious, abominable, detestable

offensive *n, syn* ATTACK, aggression, offense *rel* assault, onslaught, onset

offer • to put something before another for acceptance or consideration *syn* proffer, tender, present, prefer *rel* give, bestow, confer; adduce, advance; propose, design, purpose, intend

offhand *syn* EXTEMPORANEOUS, extempore, extemporary, improvised, impromptu, unpremeditated *rel* casual, desultory, random; abrupt, hasty, sudden, precipitate, impetuous; brusque, curt, blunt, bluff

office *syn* FUNCTION, duty, province *rel* work, business, calling; task, job, chore, stint

officious *syn* IMPERTINENT, meddlesome, intrusive, obtrusive *rel* meddling, interfering, intermeddling, tampering; annoying, vexing, irking, bothering; pushing, assertive, aggressive

offset *syn* COMPENSATE, countervail, balance, counterbalance, counterpoise *rel* neutralize, negative, counteract; nullify, negate; redeem, reclaim, save, rescue

offspring • those who follow in direct parental line *syn* young, progeny, issue, descendants, posterity

oft *syn* OFTEN, frequently, oftentimes

often • many times *syn* frequently, oft, oftentimes

oftentimes *syn* OFTEN, frequently, oft

oil • to smear, rub over, or lubricate with oil or an oily substance *syn* grease, lubricate, anoint, cream

oily *syn* FULSOME, unctuous, oleaginous, slick, soapy *rel* hypocritical, pharisaical, sanctimonious; bland, politic, diplomatic, smooth, suave

old **1** *syn* AGED, elderly, superannuated *rel* weak, feeble, infirm, decrepit *ant* young **2** • having come into existence or use in the more or less distant past *syn* ancient, venerable, antique, antiquated, antediluvian, archaic, obsolete *rel* primitive, primeval, pristine, primal *ant* new

oleaginous *syn* FULSOME, oily, unctuous, slick, soapy *rel*

oligarchy • government by, or a state governed by, the few *syn* aristocracy, plutocracy

omen *syn* FORETOKEN, augury, portent,

presage, prognostic *rel* sign, mark, token, badge, note, symptom; foreboding, apprehension, presentiment, misgiving

ominous • having a menacing or threatening aspect *syn* portentous, fateful, inauspicious, unpropitious *rel* sinister, baleful, malign, malefic, maleficent; threatening, menacing

omit *syn* NEGLECT, disregard, ignore, overlook, slight, forget *rel* cancel, delete, efface, erase; exclude, eliminate

omnipresent • present at all places at all times *syn* ubiquitous

onerous • imposing great hardship or strain *syn* burdensome, oppressive, exacting *rel* heavy, weighty, ponderous, cumbrous, cumbersome, hefty; arduous, hard, difficult

onlooker *syn* SPECTATOR, looker-on, observer, beholder, witness, eyewitness, bystander, kibitzer

only • being one or more of which there are no others *syn* alone *rel* solitary; single, sole, lone, unique

onset *syn* ATTACK, assault, onslaught *rel* aggression, offensive, offense; storming, bombarding, assailing; invasion, raid, incursion

onslaught *syn* ATTACK, assault, onset *rel* see ONSET

onward • toward or at a point lying ahead in space or time *syn* forward, forth

opalescent, opaline *syn* PRISMATIC, iridescent

open **1** *syn* LIABLE, exposed, subject, prone, susceptible, sensitive *ant* closed **2** *syn* FRANK, plain, candid *rel* straightforward, aboveboard, forthright; natural, simple, ingenuous, naïve, unsophisticated; fair, equitable, impartial *ant* close, close-mouthed, close-lipped; clandestine

openhanded *syn* LIBERAL, bountiful, bounteous, generous, munificent, handsome *ant* closefisted, tightfisted

operate *syn* ACT, behave, work, function, react

operative *adj, syn* ACTIVE, dynamic, live *rel* effective, effectual, efficacious, efficient; fertile, fecund, fruitful *ant* abeyant

operative *n, syn* WORKER, mechanic, artisan, hand, workman, workingman, laborer, craftsman, handicraftsman, roustabout

opiate *syn* ANODYNE, narcotic, nepenthe

opinion • a judgment one holds as true *syn* view, belief, conviction, persuasion, sentiment *rel* thought, notion, impression, idea, concept, conception; inference, deduction, conclusion, judgment; deciding, decision, determining, determination, settling, settlement

opponent • one who expresses or manifests opposition *syn* antagonist, adversary *rel* enemy, foe; rival, competitor, emulator

opportune *syn* SEASONABLE, timely, well-timed, pat *rel* happy, felicitous, appropriate, fitting, fit; propitious, auspicious, favorable; ready, prompt, quick, apt *ant* inopportune

opportunity • a state of affairs or a combination of circumstances favorable to some end *syn* occasion, chance, break, time *rel* juncture, pass, contingency, emergency; posture, situation, condition, state

oppose *syn* RESIST, contest, fight, combat, conflict, antagonize, withstand *rel* contend, fight, battle, war; attack, assail, assault, storm, bombard; defend, protect, shield, guard, safeguard

opposite *n* • something that is exactly opposed or contrary *syn* contradictory, contrary, antithesis, antipode, antonym, converse, counter, reverse

opposite *adj* • so far apart as to be or to seem irreconcilable *syn* contradictory, contrary, antithetical, antipodal, antipodean, antonymous *rel* reverse, converse; antagonistic, adverse, counter, counteractive

oppress **1** *syn* DEPRESS, weigh *rel* abuse, mistreat, maltreat, ill-treat, outrage; worry, annoy, harass, harry **2** *syn* WRONG, persecute, aggrieve *rel* afflict, torment, torture; overcome, subdue, subjugate, reduce, overthrow, conquer

oppressive *syn* ONEROUS, burdensome, exacting *rel* extorting, extortionate, extracting; compelling, compulsory, coercing, coercion, constraining, obliging, obligatory; despotic, tyrannical, absolute, arbitrary

opprobrious *syn* ABUSIVE, vituperative, contumelious, scurrilous *rel* reviling, vituperating, railing, berating; malicious, malevolent, malign, malignant; execrable, damnable, accursed

opprobrium *syn* DISGRACE, obloquy, odium, ignominy, infamy, shame, dishonor, disrepute *rel* abuse, invective, vituperation, obloquy, scurrility; censure, denunciation, condemnation, reprehension

opt *syn* CHOOSE, select, elect, pick, cull, prefer, single *rel* take, accept, receive; adopt, embrace, espouse

optimistic *syn* HOPEFUL, roseate, rose-colored *rel* confident, sanguine, assured; cheerful, lighthearted, joyous, glad *ant* pessimistic

option *syn* CHOICE, alternative, preference, selection, election *rel* right, prerogative, privilege

opulent **1** *syn* RICH, affluent, wealthy *rel* lavish, profuse, prodigal; showy, pretentious, ostentatious *ant* destitute; indigent **2** *syn* LUXURIOUS, sumptuous *rel* luxuriant, lush, exuberant, profuse; splendid, resplendent, gorgeous, superb

opus *syn* WORK, product, production, artifact

oracular *syn* DICTATORIAL, doctrinaire, dogmatic, authoritarian, magisterial *rel* positive, certain, sure, cocksure

oral *syn* VOCAL, articulate *ant* written

oration *syn* SPEECH, address, harangue, lecture, talk, sermon, homily

orbit *syn* RANGE, gamut, reach, radius, compass, sweep, scope, horizon, ken, purview

ordain *syn* DICTATE, prescribe, decree, impose *rel* order, command, enjoin, direct

order *n* **1** *syn* ASSOCIATION, society, club **2** *syn* COMMAND, injunction, bidding, behest, mandate, dictate *rel* instruction, direction, charging, charge

order *vb* **1** • to put persons or things into their proper places in relation to each other *syn* arrange, marshal, organize, systematize, methodize *rel* adjust, regulate; line, line up, align, range, array **2** *syn* COMMAND, bid, enjoin, direct, instruct, charge *rel* prohibit, forbid, interdict, inhibit, ban

orderly • following a set arrangement, design, or pattern *syn* methodical, systematic, regular *rel* tidy, neat, trim, spick-and-span; formal, conventional, ceremonious, ceremonial; peaceable, pacific, peaceful *ant* disorderly; chaotic

ordinance *syn* LAW, canon, precept, rule, regulation, statute

ordinary *syn* COMMON, familiar, popular, vulgar *rel* usual, customary, habitual, wonted, accustomed *ant* extraordinary

organ **1** *syn* MEAN, medium, vehicle, channel, instrument, instrumentality, agent, agency **2** *syn* JOURNAL, periodical, newspaper, magazine, review

organism *syn* SYSTEM, scheme, network, complex

organize **1** *syn* ORDER, systematize, methodize, arrange, marshal *rel* design, project, plan, scheme; form, fashion, shape, make *ant* disorganize **2** *syn* FOUND, institute, establish, create *rel* begin, commence, start, initiate, inaugurate; adjust, regulate

oriel *syn* WINDOW, casement, dormer

orifice *syn* APERTURE, interstice

origin • the point at which something begins its course or its existence *syn* source, inception, root, provenance, provenience, prime mover *rel* beginning, commencement, initiation, starting; derivation, origination, rising, rise; ancestry, lineage

original **1** *syn* INITIAL, primordial *rel* beginning, commencing, starting; primary, primal, pristine, primeval; basic, fundamental **2** *syn* NEW, fresh, novel, new-fashioned, newfangled, modern, modernistic *ant* dependent; banal; trite

originate *syn* SPRING, rise, derive, arise, flow, issue, emanate, proceed, stem *rel* begin, commence, start

ornament *syn* ADORN, decorate, embellish, beautify, deck, bedeck, garnish *rel* enhance, heighten, intensify

ornate • elaborately and often pretentiously decorated or designed *syn* rococo, baroque, flamboyant, florid *rel* adorned, decorated, ornamented, embellished; flowery, aureate; luxurious, sumptuous, opulent; showy, ostentatious *ant* chaste; austere

orotund *syn* RESONANT, sonorous, ringing, resounding, vibrant *rel* loud, stentorian, strident

oscillate *syn* SWING, sway, vibrate, fluctuate, pendulate, waver, undulate *rel* vacillate, hesitate, falter; shake, tremble, quiver, quaver

ostensible *syn* APPARENT, seeming, illusory *rel* specious, plausible, colorable; pretended, assumed, affected, simulated, feigned

ostentatious *syn* SHOWY, pretentious *rel* vainglorious, vain, proud; flaunting, parading, displaying; boasting, bragging, gasconading

ostracize *syn* BANISH, exile, expatriate, deport, transport, extradite
otiose *syn* VAIN, nugatory, idle, empty, hollow *rel* superfluous, supernumerary, surplus; futile, vain, fruitless, bootless
oust *syn* EJECT, expel, evict, dismiss *rel* exclude, eliminate, shut out, rule out, debar, disbar; discharge, fire, cashier, sack
out-and-out *syn* OUTRIGHT, unmitigated, arrant
outcast • one that is cast out or refused acceptance by society *syn* castaway, derelict, reprobate, pariah, untouchable *rel* vagabond, vagrant, tramp, hobo
outcome *syn* EFFECT, result, consequence, upshot, aftereffect, aftermath, sequel, issue, event *rel* fate, lot, portion, destiny; termination, end
outdo *syn* EXCEED, excel, outstrip, transcend, surpass
outer • being or located outside something *syn* outward, outside, external, exterior *rel* extrinsic, extraneous, foreign, alien *ant* inner
outfit *n, syn* EQUIPMENT, apparatus, paraphernalia, tackle, machinery, gear, matériel
outfit *vb, syn* FURNISH, equip, appoint, accouter, arm
outlander *syn* STRANGER, foreigner, alien, outsider, immigrant, émigré
outlandish *syn* STRANGE, singular, unique, peculiar, eccentric, erratic, odd, queer, quaint, curious *rel* bizarre, grotesque, fantastic, antic; alien, foreign, extraneous, extrinsic
outlast *syn* OUTLIVE, survive *rel* endure, persist, abide, continue; withstand, resist
outline *n* **1** • the line that bounds and gives form to something *syn* contour, profile, skyline, silhouette *rel* figure, form, shape, conformation, configuration **2** *syn* SKETCH, diagram, delineation, draft, tracing, plot, blueprint
outline *vb, syn* SKETCH, diagram, delineate, draft, trace, plot, blueprint
outlive • to remain in existence longer than *syn* outlast, survive *rel* endure, persist, abide, continue; surpass, exceed
outlook *syn* PROSPECT, anticipation, foretaste *rel* forecasting, forecast, predicting, prediction, prophesying, prophecy, presaging, presage; possibility, probability, likelihood
outrage **1** *syn* ABUSE, misuse, mistreat, maltreat, ill-treat *rel* wrong, persecute, oppress, aggrieve; corrupt, pervert, vitiate, deprave, debase **2** *syn* OFFEND, affront, insult *rel* vex, annoy, irk, bother; mortify, chagrin
outrageous • enormously or flagrantly bad or horrible *syn* monstrous, heinous, atrocious *rel* flagrant, glaring, gross, rank; excessive, inordinate, immoderate, extreme; flagitious, nefarious, iniquitous, vicious
outright • being exactly what is stated *syn* out-and-out, unmitigated, arrant
outside *syn* OUTER, outward, external, exterior *rel* extrinsic, extraneous, alien, foreign *ant* inside
outsider *syn* STRANGER, foreigner, alien, outlander, immigrant, émigré
outstanding *syn* NOTICEABLE, prominent, conspicuous, salient, signal, striking, arresting, remarkable *rel* exceptional *ant* commonplace
outstrip *syn* EXCEED, outdo, surpass, transcend, excel
outward *syn* OUTER, outside, external, exterior *rel* extraneous, extrinsic, alien, foreign *ant* inward
outwit *syn* FRUSTRATE, thwart, foil, baffle, balk, circumvent *rel* defeat, overcome, surmount, conquer; prevent, preclude, obviate, avert; overreach, cheat, defraud
over *syn* ABOVE *ant* beneath
overbearing *syn* PROUD, supercilious, disdainful, lordly, arrogant, haughty, insolent *rel* domineering, masterful, imperious; scorning, scornful, despising, despiteful, contemning; autocratic, despotic, tyrannical, absolute *ant* subservient
overcome *syn* CONQUER, surmount, overthrow, subjugate, rout, vanquish, defeat, beat, lick, subdue *rel* capture, catch; outstrip, outdo, exceed; suppress, repress
overdue *syn* TARDY, behindhand, late *rel* delayed, retarded, detained, slowed, slackened; deferred, postponed
overflow *syn* TEEM, swarm, abound
overhang *syn* BULGE, jut, stick out, protrude, project, beetle *rel* threaten, menace; suspend, hang, dangle
overlay • to lay or spread over or across *syn* superpose, superimpose, appliqué
overlook *syn* NEGLECT, slight, forget, ignore, disregard, omit

overplus *syn* EXCESS, superfluity, surplus, surplusage

overreach *syn* CHEAT, cozen, defraud, swindle

overrun *syn* INFEST, beset

oversight • the function or duty of watching or guarding for the sake of proper control or direction *syn* supervision, surveillance *rel* management, direction, controlling, control; inspection, scrutiny, examination

overspread *syn* COVER, envelop, wrap, shroud, veil *rel* hide, conceal, screen; cloak, mask, disguise, camouflage

overstatement *syn* EXAGGERATION, hyperbole *ant* understatement

overthrow **1** *syn* OVERTURN, subvert, upset, capsize *rel* throw, cast, fling, hurl, toss **2** *syn* CONQUER, rout, surmount, overcome, vanquish, defeat, beat, lick, subdue, subjugate, reduce

overture • an action taken to win the favor or approval of another person or party *syn* approach, advance, tender, bid *rel* proposal, proposition; offering, offer, proffering

overturn • to turn from an upright or proper position *syn* upset, capsize, overthrow, subvert *rel* invert, reverse, trans pose

own **1** *syn* HAVE, possess, hold, enjoy *rel* control, manage, direct, conduct; keep, retain **2** *syn* ACKNOWLEDGE, avow, admit, confess *rel* concede, grant, allow; reveal, disclose, divulge *ant* disown; repudiate

P

pabulum *syn* FOOD, aliment, nutriment, nourishment, sustenance, pap

pace *syn* SPEED, velocity, momentum, impetus, headway

pacific • affording or promoting peace *syn* peaceable, peaceful, irenic, pacifist, pacifistic *rel* calm, placid, serene, tranquil; conciliating, conciliatory, propitiating, propitiatory, appeasing, pacifying, pacificatory *ant* bellicose

pacifist, pacifistic *syn* PACIFIC, peaceable, peaceful, irenic

pacify • to ease the anger or disturbance of *syn* appease, placate, mollify, propitiate, conciliate *rel* assuage, alleviate, allay, mitigate, relieve; moderate, qualify, temper *ant* anger

pack *n, syn* BUNDLE, bunch, package, packet, bale, parcel

pack *vb* • to fill a limited space with more than is practicable or fitting *syn* crowd, cram, stuff, ram, tamp *rel* compact, consolidate; press, squeeze, jam; compress, constrict, contract

package *syn* BUNDLE, packet, bunch, bale, parcel, pack

packet *syn* BUNDLE, package, pack, bunch, bale, parcel

pact *syn* CONTRACT, compact, bargain, treaty, entente, convention, cartel, concordat

pain **1** • a bodily sensation that causes acute discomfort or suffering *syn* ache, pang, throe, twinge, stitch *rel* agony, distress, suffering, passion; anguish, sorrow, grief, heartbreak **2** *pl* **pains** *syn* EFFORT, exertion, trouble *rel* labor, toil, travail, work; industriousness, industry, diligence, sedulousness, assiduousness

pair *syn* COUPLE, brace, yoke

palatable • agreeable or pleasant to the taste *syn* appetizing, savory, sapid, tasty, toothsome, flavorsome, relishing *rel* delightful, delicious, delectable, luscious; piquant, pungent, spicy *ant* unpalatable; distasteful

palate *syn* TASTE, relish, gusto, zest

pale **1** • deficient in color or in intensity of color *syn* pallid, ashen, ashy, wan, livid *rel* ghastly, macabre; cadaverous, haggard, worn **2** • being weak and thin in substance or in vital qualities *syn* anemic, bloodless *rel* insipid, wishy-washy, inane, jejune; ineffective, ineffectual

pall *syn* SATIATE, cloy, surfeit, sate, glut, gorge

palliate • to give a speciously fine appearance to what is base, evil, or erroneous *syn* extenuate, gloze, gloss, whitewash, whiten *rel* mitigate, alleviate, lighten, relieve; condone, excuse; moderate, qualify, temper; cloak, mask, disguise, dissemble, camouflage

pallid *syn* PALE, ashen, ashy, wan, livid

palpable 1 *syn* PERCEPTIBLE, sensible, tangible, appreciable, ponderable *rel* apparent, ostensible, seeming; believable, credible, colorable, plausible *ant* insensible **2** *syn* EVIDENT, plain, clear, apparent, manifest, patent, obvious, distinct *rel* sure, certain, positive; noticeable, remarkable, striking, arresting *ant* impalpable

palpate *syn* TOUCH, feel, handle, paw

palpitate *syn* PULSATE, beat, throb, pulse *rel* vibrate, oscillate, fluctuate, swing, sway

palpitation *syn* PULSATION, beat, throb, pulse *rel* vibration, oscillation, fluctuation, swinging, swaying

palter *syn* LIE, prevaricate, equivocate, fib *rel* evade, elude, escape; trifle, dally

paltry *syn* PETTY, trifling, trivial, puny, measly, picayunish, picayune *rel* contemptible, despicable, sorry, scurvy, cheap, beggarly, shabby; abject, ignoble, mean; base, low, vile

pamper *syn* INDULGE, humor, spoil, baby, mollycoddle *rel* gratify, tickle, regale, please; fondle, pet, cosset, caress, dandle *ant* chasten

pandect *syn* COMPENDIUM, syllabus, digest, survey, sketch, précis, aperçu

pandemonium *syn* DIN, uproar, hullabaloo, babel, hubbub, clamor, racket

pander *syn* CATER, purvey *rel* truckle, toady, fawn, cringe; gratify, tickle, regale, please

panegyric *syn* ENCOMIUM, tribute, eulogy, citation *rel* commendation, applauding, applause, complimenting, compliment; acclaiming, acclaim, laudation, praising, praise, extolling, extollation

pang *syn* PAIN, ache, throe, twinge, stitch *rel* agony, distress, suffering; anguish, sorrow, grief, heartache, heartbreak; torturing, torture, tormenting, torment

panic *syn* FEAR, terror, horror, trepidation, consternation, dismay, alarm, fright, dread *rel* agitation, upsetting, upset, perturbation, disquieting, disquiet, discomposing, discomposure

pant *syn* AIM, aspire *rel* thirst, hunger, long, yearn, pine; crave, covet, desire, wish, want

pap *syn* FOOD, aliment, pabulum, nutriment, nourishment, sustenance

paper 1 • a written or printed statement that is of value as a source of information or proof of a right, contention, or claim *syn* instrument, document **2** *syn* ESSAY, article, theme, composition

par *n, syn* AVERAGE, norm, mean, median

par *adj, syn* AVERAGE, mean, median

parable *syn* ALLEGORY, myth, fable

parade *n* **1** *syn* DISPLAY, array, pomp *rel* showiness, ostentatiousness, ostentation, pretentiousness **2** *syn* PROCESSION, cavalcade, cortege, motorcade

parade *vb, syn* SHOW, flaunt, expose, display, exhibit *rel* reveal, disclose, divulge; declare, proclaim, publish, advertise; vaunt, boast, brag, gasconade

paradox • an expression or revelation of an inner or inherent contradiction *syn* antinomy, anomaly

paragon • a model of excellence or perfection *syn* apotheosis, nonpareil, nonesuch

paragraph • one of the several and individually distinct statements of a discourse or instrument, each of which deals with a particular point or item *syn* verse, article, clause, plank, count

parallel *adj, syn* LIKE, alike, similar, analogous, comparable, akin, uniform, identical *rel* same, equal, equivalent;

parallel *n* **1** *syn* COMPARISON, contrast, antithesis, collation *rel* likeness, similarity, resemblance, similitude **2** • one that corresponds to or closely resembles another *syn* counterpart, analogue, correlate

paralyze *syn* DAZE, stun, bemuse, stupefy, benumb, petrify *rel* dismay, daunt, appall, horrify; disable, cripple, weaken, enfeeble; astound, flabbergast, surprise; dumbfound, confound, nonplus, puzzle

paramount *syn* DOMINANT, preponderant, preponderating, predominant, sovereign *rel* supreme, surpassing, preeminent, superlative; capital, foremost, principal, main, leading, chief

parapet *syn* BULWARK, rampart, breastwork, bastion

paraphernalia *syn* EQUIPMENT, apparatus, machinery, outfit, tackle, gear, matériel

paraphrase *syn* TRANSLATION, metaphrase, version

parasite • a usu. obsequious flatterer or self-seeker *syn* sycophant, favorite, toady, lickspittle, bootlicker, hanger-on, leech, sponge, sponger *rel* fawner, cringer, truckler

parboil *syn* BOIL, seethe, simmer, stew

parcel *n* **1** *syn* PART, portion, piece, detail, member, division, section, segment, sector, fraction, fragment **2** *syn* BUNDLE, bunch, pack, package, packet, bale **3** *syn* GROUP, cluster, bunch, lot *rel* collection, assemblage; aggregate, aggregation, conglomerate, conglomeration

parcel *vb, syn* APPORTION, portion, ration, prorate *rel* allot, assign, allocate; grant, accord, award

parch *syn* DRY, desiccate, dehydrate, bake *rel* sear, scorch, char, burn; shrivel, wizen, wither

pardon *n* • a remission of penalty or punishment *syn* amnesty, absolution

pardon *vb, syn* EXCUSE, forgive, remit, condone *rel* free, release, liberate; acquit, absolve, exculpate *ant* punish

pardonable *syn* VENIAL

pare *syn* SKIN, peel, decorticate, flay

pariah *syn* OUTCAST, castaway, derelict, reprobate, untouchable

parley *syn* CONFER, treat, negotiate, commune, consult, advise *rel* discuss, debate, dispute, argue, agitate; converse, talk, speak

parochial *syn* INSULAR, provincial, local, small-town *rel* circumscribed, restricted, limited, confined; narrow, narrow-minded, illiberal, intolerant, hidebound, bigoted *ant* catholic

parody *n, syn* CARICATURE, travesty, burlesque *rel* skit, squib, lampoon, libel

parody *vb, syn* CARICATURE, travesty, burlesque

paroxysm *syn* FIT, spasm, convulsion, attack, access, accession

parry *syn* DODGE, shirk, sidestep, duck, fence, malinger *rel* ward, avert, prevent, preclude; forestall, anticipate; elude, evade, avoid, shun, escape

parsimonious *syn* STINGY, niggardly, penurious, close, closefisted, tight, tightfisted, miserly, cheeseparing, penny-pinching *rel* avaricious, covetous, grasping, greedy; sparing, frugal; mean, ignoble, sordid, abject *ant* prodigal

part *n* • something less than the whole *syn* portion, piece, detail, member, division, section, segment, sector, fraction, fragment, parcel *ant* whole

part *vb, syn* SEPARATE, divide, sever, sunder, divorce *rel* detach, disengage; apportion, allot, allocate, assign; tear, rend, cleave

partake *syn* SHARE, participate *rel* separate, part, divide; take, receive, accept; have, hold, own, possess, enjoy; get, obtain, procure, acquire

partiality *syn* PREDILECTION, prepossession, prejudice, bias *rel* approving, approval, endorsing, endorsement *ant* impartiality

participate *syn* SHARE, partake *rel* separate, divide, part; take, receive, accept; have, hold, own, possess, enjoy

particle • a tiny or insignificant amount, part, or piece *syn* bit, mite, smidgen, whit, atom, iota, jot, tittle

parti-colored *syn* VARIEGATED, motley, checkered, checked, pied, piebald, skewbald, dappled, freaked

particular *adj* **1** *syn* SINGLE, sole, separate, unique, lone, solitary *ant* general **2** *syn* SPECIAL, individual, specific, especial *ant* general, universal **3** *syn* CIRCUMSTANTIAL, particularized, detailed, itemized, minute *rel* scrupulous, meticulous, careful, punctilious **4** *syn* NICE, fussy, squeamish, dainty, fastidious, finicky, finicking, finical, persnickety, pernickety *rel* exacting, demanding, requiring; strict, rigid, rigorous

particular *n, syn* ITEM, detail *ant* universal; whole; aggregate

particularized *syn* CIRCUMSTANTIAL, particular, detailed, itemized, minute *rel* accurate, precise, exact, correct *ant* generalized

partisan *syn* FOLLOWER, adherent, disciple, sectary, henchman, satellite *rel* supporter, upholder, backer, champion; helper, aider, aid, assistant

partner • one associated in action with another *syn* copartner, colleague, ally, confederate *ant* rival

party **1** *syn* COMPANY, band, troop, troupe *rel* clique, set, coterie, circle; gathering, collection, assembly, assemblage, congregation **2** *syn* COMBINATION, combine, bloc, faction, ring

pasquinade *syn* LIBEL, lampoon, squib, skit

pass *vb* • move or come to a termination or end *syn* pass away, elapse, expire *rel* depart, leave, quit, go, withdraw; end, terminate, close

pass *n, syn* WAY, passage, route, course, artery

pass *n, syn* JUNCTURE, exigency, emergency, contingency, pinch, strait, crisis *rel* situation, condition, state, posture; plight, predicament, quandary

passage 1 *syn* WAY, pass, route, course, artery **2** • a typically long narrow way connecting parts of a building *syn* passageway, corridor, hall, hallway, gallery, arcade, cloister, aisle, ambulatory **3** *syn* STRAIT, sound, channel, narrows

passageway *syn* PASSAGE, corridor, hall, hallway, gallery, arcade, cloister, aisle, ambulatory

pass away *syn* PASS, elapse, expire

passing *n, syn* DEATH, decease, demise

passing *adj, syn* TRANSIENT, transitory, ephemeral, momentary, fugitive, fleeting, evanescent, short-lived

passion 1 *syn* DISTRESS, suffering, agony, dolor, misery *rel* trial, tribulation, cross, visitation, affliction **2** *syn* FEELING, emotion, affection, sentiment *rel* inspiration, frenzy; ecstasy, rapture, transport **3** *syn* DESIRE, lust, appetite, urge *rel* craving, coveting; longing, yearning, hungering, hunger, thirsting, thirst; panting, aspiring, aiming **4** • intense emotion compelling action *syn* fervor, ardor, enthusiasm, zeal *rel* ecstasy, rapture, transport; anger, rage, fury, wrath; eroticism, amorousness

passionate *syn* IMPASSIONED, ardent, fervent, fervid, perfervid *rel* intense, vehement, fierce, violent; impetuous, headlong, precipitate, abrupt; excited, quickened, stimulated

passive *syn* INACTIVE, inert, idle, supine *rel* impassive, phlegmatic, stolid, apathetic *ant* active

pastoral *syn* RURAL, rustic, bucolic

pasture *syn* FEED, graze, nourish

pat *syn* SEASONABLE, timely, well-timed, opportune *rel* apt, happy, felicitous, appropriate, fitting, fit; pertinent, apposite, apropos, applicable, relevant

patch *syn* MEND, repair, rebuild *rel* emend, remedy, redress, amend, correct; fix, adjust, regulate

patent *syn* EVIDENT, manifest, distinct, obvious, apparent, palpable, plain, clear *rel* noticeable, conspicuous, salient, prominent; flagrant, glaring, gross, rank *ant* latent

pathetic *syn* MOVING, poignant, affecting, touching, impressive *rel* pitiful, piteous, pitiable; plaintive, melancholy, doleful *ant* comical

pathological *syn* UNWHOLESOME, morbid, sickly, diseased

pathos • a quality that moves one to pity and sorrow *syn* poignancy, bathos

patience • the power or capacity to endure without complaint something difficult or disagreeable *syn* long-suffering, longanimity, forbearance, resignation *rel* perseverance, persistence; fortitude, backbone, pluck, grit, sand, guts; equanimity, composure *ant* impatience

patois *syn* DIALECT, vernacular, lingo, jargon, cant, argot, slang

patrician *syn* GENTLEMAN, aristocrat

patrimony *syn* HERITAGE, inheritance, birthright

patron *syn* SPONSOR, surety, guarantor, backer, angel *rel* supporter, upholder, champion; benefactor, contributor; protector, defender *ant* client; protégé

patter *syn* CHAT, chatter, prate, gab, prattle, babble, gabble, jabber, gibber

pattern 1 *syn* MODEL, exemplar, example, ideal, standard, beau ideal, mirror *rel* paragon, apotheosis **2** *syn* FIGURE, design, motif, device *rel* form, shape, conformation, configuration

paunch *syn* ABDOMEN, belly, stomach, gut

pause • a temporary cessation of activity or of an activity *syn* recess, respite, lull, intermission *rel* interruption, gap, interval, break, interim; stopping, stop, ceasing, cessation

paw *syn* TOUCH, feel, palpate, handle

pawn *syn* PLEDGE, hostage, earnest, token

pay *vb* • to give money or its equivalent in return for something *syn* compensate, remunerate, satisfy, reimburse, indemnify, repay, recompense

pay *n, syn* WAGE, wages, salary, stipend, fee, hire, emolument *rel* reparation, restitution, indemnity, redress, amends

paying • yielding a profit *syn* gainful, remunerative, lucrative, profitable

peace *syn* TRUCE, cease-fire, armistice

peaceable *syn* PACIFIC, peaceful, pacifist, pacifistic, irenic *rel* amicable, friendly, neighborly; amiable, complaisant; calm, placid, serene, tranquil *ant* contentious; acrimonious

peaceful **1** *syn* CALM, tranquil, serene, placid, halcyon *rel* soft, gentle, mild; still, stilly, quiet, silent, noiseless *ant* turbulent **2** *syn* PACIFIC, peaceable, pacifist, pacifistic, irenic *rel* composed, collected, unruffled, cool; equable, constant, steady

peak **1** *syn* MOUNTAIN, mount, alp, volcano, mesa **2** *syn* SUMMIT, pinnacle, climax, apex, acme, culmination, meridian, zenith, apogee

peculiar **1** *syn* CHARACTERISTIC, individual, distinctive *rel* special, especial, particular, specific; idiosyncratic, eccentric **2** *syn* STRANGE, eccentric, odd, queer, singular, unique, quaint, outlandish, curious *rel* bizarre, grotesque, fantastic; abnormal, atypical, aberrant; unusual, uncustomary

pecuniary *syn* FINANCIAL, monetary, fiscal

pedantic • too narrowly concerned with scholarly matters *syn* academic, scholastic, bookish *rel* learned, erudite; recondite, abstruse

pedestrian *syn* DULL, humdrum, dreary, monotonous, stodgy *rel* commonplace, platitudinous, truistic; banal, jejune, inane, wishy-washy, insipid; irksome, wearisome, tiresome, boring

pedigree *syn* ANCESTRY, lineage

peek *syn* LOOK, peep, glimpse, glance, sight, view

peel *vb, syn* SKIN, decorticate, pare, flay

peel *n, syn* SKIN, bark, rind, hide, pelt

peep *vb, syn* CHIRP, chirrup, cheep, tweet, twitter, chitter

peep *n, syn* CHIRP, chirrup, cheep, tweet, twitter, chitter

peep *n, syn* LOOK, glance, glimpse, peek, sight, view *rel* peering, peer, gazing, gaze, staring, stare

peer *syn* GAZE, gape, stare, glare, gloat *rel* peep, glance, glimpse, look

peerless *syn* SUPREME, surpassing, preeminent, superlative, transcendent, incomparable *rel* paramount, sovereign, dominant, predominant; unmatched, unrivaled, unequaled

peeve *syn* IRRITATE, exasperate, nettle, provoke, aggravate, rile *rel* vex, annoy, irk, bother; chafe, fret, gall, abrade

peevish *syn* IRRITABLE, fractious, snappish, waspish, petulant, pettish, huffy, fretful, querulous *rel* captious, carping, caviling, faultfinding, critical

pejorative *syn* DEROGATORY, depreciatory, depreciative, disparaging, slighting *rel* contemptuous, despiteful, scornful, disdainful; decrying, belittling, minimizing

pellucid *syn* CLEAR, transparent, translucent, lucid, diaphanous, limpid *rel* pure, sheer; bright, brilliant, luminous, radiant

pelt *syn* SKIN, hide, rind, bark, peel

pen *syn* ENCLOSE, envelop, fence, coop, corral, cage, wall *rel* confine, circumscribe, restrict, limit

penalize • to inflict a penalty on *syn* fine, amerce, mulct *rel* punish, discipline, correct, chasten

penchant *syn* LEANING, propensity, proclivity, flair *rel* bent, turn, talent, knack, gift; bias, prepossession, predilection, prejudice

pendant *syn* FLAG, ensign, standard, banner, color, streamer, pennant, pennon, jack

pendent *syn* SUSPENDED, pendulous

pendulate *syn* SWING, sway, oscillate, vibrate, fluctuate, waver, undulate

pendulous *syn* SUSPENDED, pendent

penetrate **1** *syn* ENTER, pierce, probe *rel* invade, entrench, encroach, trespass; perforate, puncture, bore, prick **2** *syn* PERMEATE, pervade, impenetrate, interpenetrate, impregnate, saturate *rel* insert, insinuate, interpolate, introduce; soak, saturate, drench, steep

penetration *syn* DISCERNMENT, insight, acumen, discrimination, perception *rel* sharpness, keenness, acuteness; shrewdness, astuteness, perspicaciousness, perspicacity, sagaciousness, sagacity

penitence • regret for sin or wrongdoing *syn* repentance, contrition, attrition, compunction, remorse *rel* regret, sorrow, anguish; humiliation, humbling, degradation, debasement; qualm, scruple

pen name *syn* PSEUDONYM, nom de plume, alias, nom de guerre, incognito

pennant *syn* FLAG, ensign, standard, banner, color, streamer, pendant, pennon, jack

penniless *syn* POOR, indigent, needy, destitute, impecunious, poverty-stricken, necessitous *rel* impoverished, bankrupt, drained; penurious

pennon *syn* FLAG, ensign, standard, banner, color, streamer, pennant, pendant, jack

penny-pinching *syn* STINGY, close, closefisted, tight, tightfisted, niggardly, parsimonious, penurious, miserly, cheeseparing

pensive *syn* THOUGHTFUL, reflective, speculative, contemplative, meditative *rel* solemn, somber, serious, earnest, sober, grave; musing, pondering, ruminating

penumbra *syn* SHADE, umbra, adumbration, umbrage, shadow

penurious *syn* STINGY, parsimonious, niggardly, close, closefisted, tight, tightfisted, miserly, cheeseparing, penny-pinching *rel* avaricious, grasping, greedy, covetous; mercenary, venal; mean, abject, sordid, ignoble

penury *syn* POVERTY, indigence, want, destitution, privation *rel* need, necessity, exigency; pinch, strait, pass, juncture *ant* luxury

peppery *syn* SPIRITED, fiery, gingery, high-spirited, mettlesome, spunky *rel* impetuous, headlong, precipitate, abrupt; pungent, piquant, spicy, snappy

perceive *syn* SEE, discern, note, remark, notice, observe, contemplate, behold, descry, espy, view, survey *rel* grasp, seize, take; apprehend, comprehend; enter, penetrate, pierce, probe

percept *syn* SENSATION, sense-datum, sensum, image *rel* idea, concept, notion; recognition, acknowledgment

perceptible • apprehensible as real or existent *syn* sensible, palpable, tangible, appreciable, ponderable *rel* clear, lucid, perspicuous; noticeable, conspicuous, signal; discerned, discernible, noted, notable, observed, observable *ant* imperceptible

perception *syn* DISCERNMENT, penetration, insight, acumen, discrimination *rel* appreciation, comprehension, understanding; sharpness, keenness, acuteness

perch *syn* ALIGHT, light, land, roost

percussion *syn* IMPACT, concussion, clash, shock, impingement, collision, jar, jolt *rel* striking, hitting, smiting; vibration, oscillation, fluctuation

perdurable *syn* LASTING, durable, permanent, stable, perpetual *rel* enduring, abiding, persisting, continuing; everlasting, endless, interminable *ant* fleeting

peremptory *syn* MASTERFUL, imperative, imperious, domineering *rel* decisive, decided; positive, certain, sure; dictatorial, dogmatic, oracular

perennial *syn* CONTINUAL, perpetual, incessant, unremitting, constant, continuous *rel* lasting, perdurable, stable; everlasting, unceasing

perfect *adj* • not lacking or faulty in any particular *syn* whole, entire, intact *rel* pure, absolute, simple, sheer; consummate, finished, accomplished; impeccable, flawless, faultless, errorless *ant* imperfect

perfect *vb, syn* UNFOLD, evolve, develop, elaborate *rel* complete, finish

perfection *syn* EXCELLENCE, virtue, merit *ant* failing

perfervid *syn* IMPASSIONED, fervid, passionate, ardent, fervent *rel* intense, vehement, fierce, violent; heightened, enhanced, intensified

perfidious *syn* FAITHLESS, false, disloyal, traitorous, treacherous *rel* mercenary, venal; disaffected, alienated, estranged; deceitful, dishonest; perjured, forsworn

perforate • to pierce through so as to leave a hole *syn* puncture, punch, prick, bore, drill *rel* enter, penetrate, pierce, probe

perform • to carry out or into effect *syn* execute, discharge, accomplish, achieve, effect, fulfill *rel* reach, gain, compass, attain; finish, complete, conclude

performer *syn* ACTOR, player, mummer, mime, mimic, thespian, impersonator, trouper

perfume *syn* FRAGRANCE, bouquet, redolence, incense *rel* odor, scent, aroma, smell

peril *syn* DANGER, jeopardy, hazard, risk *rel* menacing, menace, threatening, threat; exposure, subjection, openness, liability

perilous *syn* DANGEROUS, hazardous, risky, precarious *rel* desperate, forlorn, hopeless; chancy, chance, haphazard, random

perimeter *syn* CIRCUMFERENCE, periphery, circuit, compass

period • a division of time *syn* epoch, era, age, aeon

periodic *syn* INTERMITTENT, recurrent, alternate *rel* fitful, spasmodic, convulsive; sporadic, occasional, infrequent

periodical *syn* JOURNAL, magazine, newspaper, review, organ

peripatetic *syn* ITINERANT, ambulatory, ambulant, nomadic, vagrant

periphery *syn* CIRCUMFERENCE, perimeter, circuit, compass *rel* limit, confine, bound, end

periphrasis *syn* VERBIAGE, redundancy, tautology, pleonasm, circumlocution

perjure • to make a false swearer of oneself by violating one's oath to tell the truth *syn* forswear *rel* deceive, delude, mislead, beguile; lie, prevaricate

permanent *syn* LASTING, perdurable, durable, stable, perpetual *rel* perennial, constant, continuous, continual *ant* temporary; ad interim (*of persons*)

permeate • to pass or cause to pass through every part of a thing *syn* pervade, penetrate, impenetrate, interpenetrate, impregnate, saturate *rel* infuse, imbue, ingrain; drench, steep, soak, saturate; inform, animate, inspire, fire

permission • a sanctioning to act or do something that is granted by one in authority *syn* leave, sufferance *rel* authorization, commissioning, commission, licensing, license; letting, allowing; sanctioning, approval, endorsement *ant* prohibition

permit *syn* LET, allow, suffer, leave *rel* authorize, license, commission; sanction, endorse, approve *ant* prohibit, forbid

permutation *syn* CHANGE, mutation, vicissitude, alternation *rel* moving, move, shifting, shift, removing, remove; transformation, conversion, metamorphosis

pernicious • exceedingly harmful or destructive *syn* baneful, noxious, deleterious, detrimental *rel* baleful, malign, sinister, malefic, maleficent; poisonous, venomous, toxic, pestilent, miasmatic; injurious, hurtful, harmful, mischievous *ant* innocuous

pernickety *syn* NICE, persnickety, fastidious, finicky, finicking, finical, dainty, particular, fussy, squeamish *rel* exacting, demanding, requiring; annoyed, vexed, irked

perpendicular *syn* VERTICAL, plumb *rel* steep, abrupt, precipitous, sheer *ant* horizontal

perpetrate *syn* COMMIT *rel* accomplish, achieve, effect

perpetual **1** *syn* LASTING, permanent, perdurable, durable, stable *rel* everlasting, endless, unceasing, interminable; eternal, sempiternal, infinite **2** *syn* CONTINUAL, continuous, constant, incessant, unremitting, perennial *rel* enduring, persisting, abiding, continuing; set, settled, fixed, established *ant* transitory, transient

perplex *syn* PUZZLE, mystify, bewilder, distract, nonplus, confound, dumbfound *rel* disturb, perturb, upset, discompose; baffle, balk, thwart, frustrate; astound, amaze, astonish, surprise

perquisite *syn* RIGHT, prerogative, privilege, appanage, birthright

persecute *syn* WRONG, oppress, aggrieve *rel* worry, annoy, harass, harry; torture, torment, rack; bait, badger, hound, ride

persevere • to continue in a given course in the face of difficulty or opposition *syn* persist *rel* continue, abide, endure, last

persiflage *syn* BADINAGE, raillery *rel* bantering, banter, chaffing, chaff; ridiculing, ridicule, twitting, deriding, derision

persist **1** *syn* PERSEVERE *ant* desist **2** *syn* CONTINUE, last, endure, abide *ant* desist

persnickety *syn* NICE, pernickety, fastidious, finicky, finicking, finical, dainty, particular, fussy, squeamish *rel* exacting, demanding, requiring; annoyed, vexed, irked

person *syn* ENTITY, being, creature, individual

personality *syn* DISPOSITION, character, individuality, temperament, temper, complexion

perspicacious *syn* SHREWD, sagacious, astute *rel* sharp, keen, acute; penetrating, piercing, probing *ant* dull

perspicuous *syn* CLEAR, lucid *rel* manifest, evident, plain, distinct; explicit, express, specific, definite

persuade *syn* INDUCE, prevail, get *rel* influence, affect, touch, sway, impress; move, drive, impel, actuate *ant* dissuade

persuasion **1** *syn* OPINION, conviction, belief, view, sentiment *rel* predilection, prepossession, bias, partiality, prejudice; tenet, dogma, doctrine **2** *syn* RELIGION, denomination, sect, cult, communion, faith, creed, church

pert *syn* SAUCY, arch *rel* flippant, frivolous, volatile, light-minded; impertinent, intrusive; brash, impudent, shameless *ant* coy

pertain *syn* BEAR, relate, appertain, belong, apply *rel* connect, join, combine, associate

pertinacious *syn* OBSTINATE, stubborn, dogged, mulish, stiff-necked, pigheaded, bullheaded *rel* tenacious, tough, stout, sturdy, strong; persistent, persevering; resolute, steadfast, staunch; headstrong, willful, unruly

pertinent *syn* RELEVANT, germane, material, apposite, applicable, apropos *rel* fitting, apt, happy, felicitous, fit; pat, seasonable, opportune, timely, well-timed *ant* impertinent; foreign

perturb *syn* DISCOMPOSE, disturb, agitate, upset, disquiet, fluster, flurry *rel* annoy, vex, irk, bother; confuse, muddle, addle; confound, nonplus, distract, bewilder, dumbfound, puzzle

pervade *syn* PERMEATE, penetrate, impenetrate, interpenetrate, impregnate, saturate *rel* infuse, imbue, ingrain, leaven; inform, animate, inspire, fire

perverse *syn* CONTRARY, restive, balky, froward, wayward *rel* unruly, ungovernable, recalcitrant, refractory; obstinate, stubborn, mulish, pigheaded, stiff-necked; fractious, irritable, peevish

pervert *syn* DEBASE, deprave, corrupt, vitiate, debauch *rel* abuse, misuse, ill-treat, maltreat, mistreat, outrage; contort, distort, warp, deform

perverted *syn* DEBASED, corrupted, depraved, vitiated, debauched *rel* distorted, contorted, warped; abused, misused, outraged

pessimistic *syn* CYNICAL, misanthropic *rel* gloomy, morose, sullen; depressed, oppressed, weighed down *ant* optimistic

pester *syn* WORRY, plague, tease, tantalize, annoy, harass, harry *rel* bait, badger, hector, heckle, chivy; fret, gall, chafe; perturb, disturb, agitate, upset, discompose

pestilent, pestilential *syn* POISONOUS, venomous, virulent, toxic, mephitic, miasmic, miasmatic, miasmal *rel* infectious, contagious, catching; noxious, pernicious, baneful, deleterious

pet *syn* CARESS, fondle, cosset, cuddle, dandle *rel* indulge, humor, pamper, mollycoddle, baby

petite *syn* SMALL, little, diminutive, wee, tiny, teeny, weeny, minute, microscopic, miniature

petition *n, syn* PRAYER, suit, plea, appeal

petition *vb, syn* PRAY, sue, plead, appeal

petrify **1** *syn* HARDEN, solidify, indurate, cake *rel* deposit, precipitate; compact, consolidate **2** *syn* DAZE, stun, bemuse, stupefy, benumb, paralyze *rel* terrify, alarm, frighten, startle; appall, horrify, dismay

pettish *syn* IRRITABLE, fractious, peevish, petulant, snappish, waspish, huffy, fretful, querulous

petty • being often contemptibly insignificant or unimportant *syn* puny, trivial, trifling, paltry, measly, picayunish, picayune *rel* small, little, diminutive, minute *ant* important, momentous; gross

petulant *syn* IRRITABLE, fractious, peevish, pettish, snappish, waspish, huffy, fretful, querulous *rel* cross, cranky, touchy, testy, irascible; impatient, restive, fidgety

phantasm **1** *syn* APPARITION, phantom, wraith, ghost, spirit, specter, shade, revenant *rel* delusion, illusion, hallucination **2** *syn* FANCY, fantasy, phantasy, vision, dream, daydream, nightmare

phantasy *syn* FANCY, fantasy, phantasm, vision, dream, daydream, nightmare

phantom *syn* APPARITION, phantasm, wraith, ghost, spirit, specter, shade, revenant *rel* counterfeit, deception, imposture; delusion, illusion, hallucination

pharisaical *syn* HYPOCRITICAL, sanctimonious, canting

pharisaism *syn* HYPOCRISY, sanctimony, cant

pharmaceutical *syn* DRUG, medicinal, biologic, simple

pharmacist *syn* DRUGGIST, apothecary, chemist

phase • one of the possible ways of viewing or being presented to view *syn* aspect, side, facet, angle *rel* state, condition, situation, posture; appearance, look, semblance

phenomenal **1** *syn* MATERIAL, physical, corporeal, sensible, objective *rel* actual, real *ant* noumenal **2** *syn* EXCEPTIONAL, extraordinary, unusual, unwonted

phenomenon *syn* WONDER, marvel, prodigy, miracle *rel* abnormality; anomaly, paradox; singularity, peculiarity, uniqueness

philanthropic *syn* CHARITABLE, benevolent, humane, humanitarian, eleemosynary, altruistic *rel* liberal, munificent, bountiful, bounteous, openhanded, generous; lavish, profuse, prodigal *ant* misanthropic

philanthropy *syn* CHARITY *ant* misanthropy

philippic *syn* TIRADE, diatribe, jeremiad *rel* harangue, speech, address, oration; condemnation, denunciation

phlegm **1** *syn* IMPASSIVITY, impassiveness,

stolidity, apathy, stoicism *rel* insensibility, insensitiveness, impassibility, anesthesia **2** *syn* EQUANIMITY, composure, sangfroid *rel* imperturbability, nonchalance, coolness, collectedness; calmness, calm, tranquillity, serenity

phlegmatic *syn* IMPASSIVE, stolid, apathetic, stoic *rel* indifferent, unconcerned, incurious, aloof; cool, chilly, cold, frigid; sluggish, lethargic

phony *syn* COUNTERFEIT, spurious, bogus, fake, sham, pseudo, pinchbeck

phrase • a group of words which, taken together, express a notion and may be used as a part of a sentence *syn* idiom, expression, locution

phraseology, phrasing *syn* LANGUAGE, vocabulary, diction, style

physic *syn* REMEDY, cure, medicine, medicament, medication, specific

physical **1** *syn* BODILY, corporeal, corporal, somatic *rel* fleshly, carnal, sensual, animal **2** *syn* MATERIAL, corporeal, phenomenal, sensible, objective *rel* actual, real, true; elemental, elementary

physiognomy *syn* FACE, countenance, visage, mug, puss

physique • bodily makeup or type *syn* build, habit, constitution *rel* body; structure, framework, anatomy; system, organism

picayunish, picayune *syn* PETTY, trivial, trifling, puny, paltry, measly

pick *syn* CHOOSE, select, elect, opt, cull, prefer, single *rel* take, seize, grasp; determine, decide, settle

picked *syn* SELECT, elect, exclusive

pickle *syn* PREDICAMENT, plight, dilemma, quandary, scrape, fix, jam

pictorial *syn* GRAPHIC, vivid, picturesque

picture *syn* REPRESENT, depict, portray, delineate, limn *rel* describe, relate, narrate, recount; sketch, outline

picturesque *syn* GRAPHIC, vivid, pictorial *rel* charming, attractive, alluring; conspicuous, salient, striking, arresting

piece *syn* PART, portion, detail, member, division, section, segment, sector, fraction, fragment, parcel

pied, piebald *syn* VARIEGATED, parti-colored, motley, checkered, checked, skewbald, dappled, freaked

pier **1** *syn* BUTTRESS, abutment **2** *syn* WHARF, dock, quay, slip, berth, jetty, levee

pierce *syn* ENTER, penetrate, probe *rel* perforate, bore, drill, puncture; rend, tear, cleave, split, rive

pietistic *syn* DEVOUT, sanctimonious, pious, religious *rel* reverencing, reverential, venerating, adoring, worshiping; fervid, perfervid, ardent, fervent, impassioned; sentimental, maudlin, romantic

piety *syn* FIDELITY, devotion, allegiance, fealty, loyalty *rel* obedience, docility; fervor, ardor, zeal, enthusiasm, passion; holiness, sanctity *ant* impiety

pigeonhole *syn* ASSORT, sort, classify *rel* systematize, methodize, organize, arrange, order

pigheaded *syn* OBSTINATE, stubborn, mulish, stiff-necked, bullheaded, dogged, pertinacious *rel* headstrong, willful, recalcitrant, refractory; contrary, perverse, froward

pilaster *syn* PILLAR, column

pile *n* **1** *syn* HEAP, stack, mass, bank, shock, cock **2** *syn* BUILDING, edifice, structure

pile *vb, syn* HEAP, stack, mass, bank, shock, cock *rel* gather, collect, assemble, congregate; accumulate, amass, hoard

pilfer *syn* STEAL, filch, purloin, lift, pinch, snitch, swipe, cop *rel* seize, take, grasp, grab, snatch; catch, capture; rob, rifle, loot, plunder

pilgrimage *syn* JOURNEY, voyage, tour, trip, jaunt, excursion, cruise, expedition

pillage *syn* RAVAGE, devastate, waste, sack, despoil, spoliate *rel* plunder, loot, rob, rifle; invade, encroach, trespass; confiscate, arrogate, appropriate, usurp

pillar • a firm upright support for a superstructure *syn* column, pilaster

pilot *syn* GUIDE, steer, lead, engineer *rel* direct, manage, conduct, control; handle, manipulate

pimple *syn* ABSCESS, boil, furuncle, carbuncle, pustule

pinch *vb, syn* STEAL, pilfer, filch, purloin, lift, snitch, swipe, cop

pinch *n, syn* JUNCTURE, pass, exigency, emergency, contingency, strait, crisis *rel* difficulty, hardship, rigor, vicissitude

pinchbeck *syn* COUNTERFEIT, spurious, bogus, fake, sham, pseudo, phony

pinched *syn* HAGGARD, cadaverous, worn, careworn, wasted *rel* gaunt, scrawny, skinny, angular, rawboned, lean

pinch hitter *syn* SUBSTITUTE, supply, locum tenens, alternate, understudy, double, stand-in

pine *syn* LONG, yearn, hanker, hunger, thirst *rel* crave, covet, desire; languish, enervate

pinnacle *syn* SUMMIT, peak, apex, acme, climax, culmination, meridian, zenith, apogee

pious *syn* DEVOUT, religious, pietistic, sanctimonious *rel* holy, sacred, divine; worshiping, adoring, reverencing, venerating, revering; fervent, ardent, fervid, impassioned *ant* impious

piquant *syn* PUNGENT, poignant, racy, spicy, snappy *rel* incisive, trenchant, cutting, biting, clear-cut *ant* bland

pique *n, syn* OFFENSE, resentment, umbrage, dudgeon, huff *rel* annoyance, vexation, irking, irk; irritation, exasperation, provocation

pique *vb* **1** *syn* PROVOKE, excite, stimulate, quicken, galvanize *rel* stir, rouse, arouse; prick, punch; kindle, ignite **2** *syn* PRIDE, plume, preen

pirate • a robber on the high seas *syn* freebooter, buccaneer, privateer, corsair

pirouette *syn* TURN, revolve, rotate, gyrate, circle, spin, twirl, whirl, wheel, eddy, swirl

pitch **1** *syn* THROW, hurl, fling, cast, toss, sling *rel* heave, lift, raise, hoist; move, drive, impel **2** *syn* PLUNGE, dive *rel* fall, drop, sink; descend; jump, leap, spring

piteous *syn* PITIFUL, pitiable *rel* imploring, supplicating, entreating, beseeching; melancholy, doleful, dolorous, plaintive

pith *syn* SUBSTANCE, purport, gist, burden, core *rel* center, nucleus, heart, focus; spirit, soul

pithy *syn* CONCISE, summary, compendious, terse, succinct, laconic *rel* sententious, pregnant, meaningful, expressive; brief, short

pitiable **1** *syn* PITIFUL, piteous *rel* sad, depressed, dejected, melancholy; forlorn, hopeless, despairing, desperate, despondent **2** *syn* CONTEMPTIBLE, despicable, sorry, scurvy, cheap, beggarly, shabby *rel* miserable, wretched; deplorable, lamentable

pitiful • arousing or deserving pity *syn* piteous, pitiable *rel* touching, moving, pathetic, affecting; tender, compassionate, responsive, sympathetic *ant* cruel

pittance *syn* RATION, allowance, dole

pity *syn* SYMPATHY, compassion, commiseration, condolence, ruth, empathy *rel* sadness, melancholy, dejection, depression; pathos, poignancy; charity, mercy, clemency, lenity

pivotal *syn* CENTRAL, focal *rel* essential, cardinal, vital; important, significant, momentous; capital, principal, chief

placate *syn* PACIFY, appease, mollify, propitiate, conciliate *ant* enrage

place • the portion of space occupied by or chosen for something *syn* position, location, situation, site, spot, station *rel* locality, vicinity, district; region, tract, area, zone; field, territory, province

placid *syn* CALM, tranquil, serene, peaceful, halcyon *rel* imperturbable, nonchalant, cool, collected, composed; gentle, mild, lenient, smooth; steady, equable, even, constant *ant* choleric (*of persons*); ruffled (*of things*)

plague *syn* WORRY, pester, tease, tantalize, harry, harass, annoy *rel* gall, fret, chafe; bait, badger, hector, hound, ride; torment, afflict, try

plain **1** *syn* LEVEL, plane, flat, even, smooth, flush *ant* solid **2** *syn* EVIDENT, clear, distinct, obvious, manifest, patent, apparent, palpable *rel* clear, lucid, perspicuous; explicit, express, definite, specific, categorical *ant* abstruse **3** • free from all ostentation or superficial embellishment *syn* homely, simple, unpretentious *rel* ugly, ill-favored, unsightly, hideous; barren, bare, bald; unembellished, unadorned, undecorated, unornamented, ungarnished *ant* lovely **4** *syn* FRANK, candid, open *rel* forthright, straightforward, aboveboard; blunt, bluff; sincere, unfeigned

plaintive *syn* MELANCHOLY, dolorous, doleful, lugubrious, rueful *rel* pensive, reflective, meditative, thoughtful; lamenting, deploring; pitiful, piteous

plait *syn* WEAVE, knit, crochet, braid, tat

plan *n* • a method devised for making or doing something or achieving an end *syn* design, plot, scheme, project *rel* intention, intent, purpose; idea, conception, notion; chart, map, graph; diagram, outline, sketch

plan *vb* • to formulate a plan for arranging, realizing, or achieving something *syn* design, plot, scheme, project *rel* propose, purpose, intend; sketch, outline, diagram, delineate

plane *syn* LEVEL, plain, flat, even, smooth, flush *ant* solid

planet *syn* EARTH, world, globe

plank *syn* PARAGRAPH, verse, article, clause, count

plastic • susceptible of being modified in form or nature *syn* pliable, pliant, ductile, malleable, adaptable *rel* flexible, supple, elastic, resilient; tractable, amenable

platitude *syn* COMMONPLACE, truism, bromide, cliché *rel* banality, inanity, vapidity, insipidity; mawkishness, sentimentality

plaudits *syn* APPLAUSE, acclamation, acclaim *rel* cheering

plausible • appearing worthy of belief *syn* credible, believable, colorable, specious *rel* smooth, bland, politic, diplomatic, suave; likely, probable, possible; unctuous, fulsome, slick, oily

play *n* **1** • activity engaged in for amusement *syn* sport, disport, frolic, rollick, romp, gambol *rel* enjoyment, delectation, pleasure, delight; amusement, diversion, recreation, entertainment; athletics, sports, games *ant* work **2** *syn* FUN, jest, sport, game *ant* earnest **3** *syn* ROOM, berth, elbowroom, leeway, margin, clearance

play *vb* **1** • to engage in an activity for amusement or recreation *syn* sport, disport, frolic, rollick, romp, gambol *rel* divert, entertain, recreate, amuse; trifle, toy, dally **2** *syn* ACT, impersonate *rel* feign, simulate, counterfeit, assume

player *syn* ACTOR, performer, mummer, mime, mimic, thespian, impersonator, trouper

playful • given to or characterized by play, jests, or tricks *syn* frolicsome, sportive, roguish, waggish, impish, mischievous *rel* gay, sprightly, lively; merry, blithe, jocund, jolly, jovial; mirthful, gleeful, hilarious

plea **1** *syn* APOLOGY, apologia, excuse, pretext, alibi *rel* explanation, justification, rationalization; defense, vindication **2** *syn* PRAYER, suit, petition, appeal *rel* entreaty, supplication, imploring, beseeching, begging

plead *syn* PRAY, sue, petition, appeal *rel* entreat, implore, supplicate, beseech, beg; intercede, mediate, intervene, interpose

pleasant • highly acceptable to the mind or the senses *syn* pleasing, agreeable, grateful, gratifying, welcome *rel* charming, attractive, alluring; soft, gentle, mild, balmy, smooth *ant* unpleasant; distasteful; harsh

please • to give or be a source of pleasure to *syn* gratify, delight, rejoice, gladden, tickle, regale *rel* satisfy, content; beguile, while, wile *ant* displease; anger; vex

pleasing *syn* PLEASANT, agreeable, grateful, gratifying, welcome *rel* winning; charming, attractive, alluring, enchanting *ant* displeasing; repellent

pleasure • the agreeable emotion accompanying the expectation, acquisition, or possession of something good or greatly desired *syn* delight, joy, delectation, enjoyment, fruition *rel* happiness, felicity, bliss; amusement, diversion, recreation, entertainment *ant* displeasure; anger; vexation

plebiscite *syn* MANDATE, initiative, referendum

pledge *n* • something given or held as a sign of another's good faith or intentions *syn* earnest, token, pawn, hostage *rel* guarantee, guaranty, security, surety, bond, bail

pledge *vb, syn* PROMISE, engage, plight, covenant, contract *rel* bind, tie; commit, consign, confide, entrust *ant* abjure

plenary *syn* FULL, complete, replete *ant* limited

plenteous *syn* PLENTIFUL, ample, abundant, copious *rel, ant* see PLENTIFUL

plentiful • more than sufficient without being excessive *syn* plenteous, ample, abundant, copious *rel* fruitful, prolific; sumptuous, opulent, luxurious; profuse, lavish, prodigal *ant* scanty, scant

pleonasm *syn* VERBIAGE, redundancy, tautology, circumlocution, periphrasis

pliable *syn* PLASTIC, pliant, ductile, malleable, adaptable *rel* lithe, limber, supple; elastic, resilient, springy, flexible; compliant, acquiescent *ant* obstinate

pliant *syn* PLASTIC, pliable, ductile, malleable, adaptable *rel* see PLIABLE

plight *vb, syn* PROMISE, engage, pledge, covenant, contract

plight *n, syn* PREDICAMENT, dilemma, quandary, scrape, fix, jam, pickle *rel* situation, condition, state, posture; difficulty, rigor, hardship, vicissitude

plot *n* **1** *syn* PLAN, design, scheme, project

rel chart, map, graph **2** • a plan secretly devised to accomplish an evil or treacherous end *syn* intrigue, machination, conspiracy, cabal *rel* contrivance, device, contraption; maneuver, stratagem, trick, ruse, artifice **3** *syn* SKETCH, outline, diagram, delineation, draft, tracing, blueprint

plot *vb* **1** *syn* PLAN, design, scheme, project *rel* fashion, fabricate, forge, form, shape, make **2** *syn* SKETCH, outline, diagram, delineate, draft, trace, blueprint *rel* create, invent; chart, map, graph

ploy *syn* TRICK, ruse, stratagem, maneuver, gambit, artifice, wile, feint

pluck *syn* FORTITUDE, grit, backbone, guts, sand *rel* courage, spirit, mettle, resolution, tenacity; hardihood, audacity, temerity

plumb *vb, syn* FATHOM, sound

plumb *adj, syn* VERTICAL, perpendicular

plume *syn* PRIDE, pique, preen *rel* appreciate, value, prize

plump *syn* FLESHY, stout, portly, rotund, chubby, fat, corpulent, obese *ant* cadaverous

plunder *vb, syn* ROB, rifle, loot, burglarize *rel* despoil, spoliate, sack, pillage, ravage; strip, denude, bare

plunder *n, syn* SPOIL, booty, prize, loot, swag *rel* robbery, larceny, theft

plunge • to thrust or cast oneself or something into or as if into deep water *syn* dive, pitch *rel* submerge, immerse, dip; throw, cast, fling, hurl; push, thrust, shove, propel

plutocracy *syn* OLIGARCHY, aristocracy

ply *syn* HANDLE, manipulate, wield, swing *rel* exercise, practice, drill; operate, work, function; manage, direct, control, conduct

pocket *syn* HOLE, hollow, cavity, void, vacuum

poet • a writer of verse *syn* versifier, rhymer, rhymester, poetaster, bard, minstrel, troubadour *rel* maker, creator, author; writer, composer

poetaster *syn* POET, versifier, rhymer, rhymester, bard, minstrel, troubadour

pogrom *syn* MASSACRE, slaughter, butchery, carnage

poignancy *syn* PATHOS, bathos

poignant **1** *syn* PUNGENT, piquant, racy, spicy, snappy *rel* penetrating, piercing, probing; sharp, keen, acute; incisive, trenchant, cutting, biting, crisp *ant* dull **2** *syn* MOVING, touching, pathetic, impressive, affecting *rel* exciting, stimulating, provoking; disturbing, agitating, perturbing

point *syn* DIRECT, aim, level, train, lay *rel* bend; direct, address, devote; steer, pilot, engineer, guide

point of view • a position from which something is considered or evaluated *syn* viewpoint, standpoint, angle, slant *rel* position, stand, attitude

poise *vb, syn* STABILIZE, steady, balance, ballast, trim *rel* support, uphold, back

poise *n* **1** *syn* BALANCE, equilibrium, equipoise, tension *rel* suspending, suspension, hanging; equanimity, composure **2** *syn* TACT, address, savoir faire *rel* self-possession, aplomb, assurance, confidence; calmness, tranquillity, serenity; grace, dignity, elegance

poison • something that harms, interferes with, or destroys the activity, progress, or welfare of something else *syn* venom, virus, toxin, bane

poisonous • having the properties or effects of poison *syn* venomous, virulent, toxic, mephitic, pestilent, pestilential, miasmic, miasmatic, miasmal *rel* mortal, fatal, lethal, deadly; pernicious, baneful, noxious, deleterious, detrimental

poke *vb* • to thrust something into so as to stir up, urge on, or attract attention *syn* prod, nudge, jog *rel* push, shove, thrust; stir, arouse, rouse, awaken; provoke, excite, stimulate, galvanize, quicken

poke *n* • a quick thrust with or as if with the hand *syn* prod, nudge, jog

polite *syn* CIVIL, courteous, courtly, gallant, chivalrous *rel* suave, urbane, diplomatic, politic; thoughtful, considerate, attentive *ant* impolite

politic **1** *syn* EXPEDIENT, advisable *rel* practical, practicable; possible, feasible; shrewd, astute, perspicacious, sagacious **2** *syn* SUAVE, diplomatic, bland, smooth, urbane *rel* unctuous, slick, oily, fulsome; wise, prudent, judicious

politician • a person engaged in the art or science of government *syn* statesman, politico

politico *syn* POLITICIAN, statesman

poll *syn* SHEAR, clip, trim, prune, lop, snip, crop *rel* cut, slash; sever, separate

pollute *syn* CONTAMINATE, defile, taint, attaint *rel* debase, vitiate, corrupt, deprave, pervert; abuse, outrage, mistreat; profane, desecrate, blaspheme

pomp *syn* DISPLAY, parade, array *rel* ceremony, ceremonial, liturgy, ritual, formality, form; ostentatiousness, ostentation, showiness, show

ponder • to consider or examine attentively or deliberately *syn* meditate, muse, ruminate *rel* weigh, consider, contemplate; reflect, deliberate, speculate, think, cogitate

ponderable *syn* PERCEPTIBLE, appreciable, sensible, palpable, tangible *rel* important, significant, momentous, weighty, consequential

ponderous *syn* HEAVY, cumbrous, cumbersome, weighty, hefty *rel* massive, massy, bulky, substantial; clumsy, awkward, maladroit; onerous, burdensome, oppressive, exacting

pool *syn* MONOPOLY, corner, syndicate, trust, cartel

poor 1 • lacking money or material possessions *syn* indigent, needy, destitute, penniless, impecunious, poverty-stricken, necessitous *ant* rich **2** *syn* BAD, wrong *rel* deficient, defective; petty, puny, trivial, trifling, paltry; base, low, vile

poppycock *syn* NONSENSE, twaddle, drivel, bunk, balderdash, gobbledygook, trash, rot, bull

popular *syn* COMMON, ordinary, familiar, vulgar *rel* general, universal, generic, common; accepted, received, admitted; prevalent, prevailing, current *ant* unpopular; esoteric

port *n, syn* HARBOR, haven

port *n, syn* BEARING, presence, deportment, demeanor, mien

portal *syn* DOOR, gate, doorway, gateway, postern

portend *syn* FORETELL, presage, augur, prognosticate, predict, forecast, prophesy, forebode *rel* betoken, indicate, bespeak, attest; signify, import, mean, denote

portent *syn* FORETOKEN, presage, prognostic, omen, augury *rel* presentiment, foreboding, misgiving, apprehension; forewarning, warning, cautioning, caution

portentous *syn* OMINOUS, unpropitious, inauspicious, fateful *rel* threatening, menacing; prodigious, monstrous; prophesying, prophetic, presaging, foreboding, predicting, foretelling

portion *n* **1** *syn* PART, piece, detail, member, division, section, segment, sector, fraction, fragment, parcel *rel* quantity, amount, sum; apportionment, rationing, ration; allotment, assignment, allocation **2** *syn* FATE, destiny, lot, doom *rel* distribution, dispensation, division, dealing; fortune, hap, chance, luck

portion *vb, syn* APPORTION, parcel, ration, prorate *rel* allot, assign, allocate; distribute, dispense, divide, deal

portly *syn* FLESHY, stout, plump, rotund, chubby, fat, corpulent, obese *rel* burly, husky, brawny, muscular

portray *syn* REPRESENT, depict, delineate, picture, limn *rel* image, photograph; describe, relate, narrate; reproduce, copy, duplicate

pose *vb, syn* PROPOSE, propound *rel* ask, question, query; puzzle, confound; baffle, frustrate

pose *n* **1** • an adopted way of speaking or behaving *syn* air, affectation, mannerism **2** *syn* POSTURE, attitude

posit *vb, syn* PRESUPPOSE, presume, assume, postulate, premise

posit *n, syn* ASSUMPTION, presupposition, presumption, postulate, premise

position 1 • a firmly held point of view or way of regarding something *syn* stand, attitude *rel* point of view, viewpoint, standpoint, angle, slant **2** *syn* PLACE, location, situation, site, spot, station

positive *syn* SURE, certain, cocksure *rel* confident, assured, sanguine; dogmatic, doctrinaire, oracular, dictatorial *ant* doubtful

possess *syn* HAVE, own, enjoy, hold *rel* control, manage, direct, conduct; retain, keep, reserve, withhold

possessions • all the items that taken together constitute a person's or group's property or wealth *syn* belongings, effects, means, resources, assets

possible 1 • capable of being realized *syn* practicable, feasible *rel* practical; expedient, advisable **2** *syn* PROBABLE, likely *rel* credible, believable, colorable, plausible; potential, dormant, latent

posterior • situated at or toward the back *syn* rear, hind, hinder, after, back *ant* anterior

posterity *syn* OFFSPRING, young, progeny, issue, descendant *ant* ancestry

postern *syn* DOOR, gate, gateway, doorway, portal

postpone *syn* DEFER, suspend, stay, intermit *rel* delay, retard, slow, slacken

postulant *syn* NOVICE, novitiate, probationer, neophyte, apprentice

postulate *vb, syn* PRESUPPOSE, presume, assume, premise, posit *rel* affirm, aver, predicate, assert

postulate *n, syn* ASSUMPTION, presupposition, presumption, premise, posit *rel* principle, axiom, theorem, fundamental, law; theory, hypothesis

posture **1** • the position or bearing of the body *syn* attitude, pose *rel* bearing, deportment, mien **2** *syn* STATE, situation, condition, mode, status *rel* position, stand, attitude; readiness, quickness, promptness

pot *syn* BET, wager, stake, ante

potent *syn* POWERFUL, puissant, forceful, forcible *rel* vigorous, energetic, strenuous, lusty; effective, efficacious, effectual; strong, sturdy, tenacious *ant* impotent

potential *syn* LATENT, dormant, quiescent, abeyant *ant* active, actual

pother *syn* STIR, flurry, fuss, ado, bustle *rel* haste, hurry, speed, dispatch; agitation, upset, perturbation, disturbance

pouch *syn* BAG, sack

pound *syn* BEAT, pummel, buffet, baste, belabor, thrash *rel* strike, hit, smite, slug; batter, mutilate, maim

pour • to send forth or come forth abundantly *syn* stream, gush, sluice *rel* emerge, appear; flow, issue, proceed, spring

poverty • the state of one with insufficient resources *syn* indigence, penury, want, destitution, privation *rel* necessity, need, exigency; strait, pass, pinch, juncture *ant* riches

poverty-stricken *syn* POOR, indigent, needy, destitute, penniless, impecunious, necessitous

power **1** • the ability to exert effort *syn* force, energy, strength, might, puissance *rel* ability, capacity, capability; gift, genius, talent, faculty; qualification, competence *ant* impotence **2** • the ability of a living being to perform in a given way or a capacity for a particular kind of performance *syn* faculty, function **3** • the right to govern or rule or determine *syn* authority, jurisdiction, control, command, sway, dominion *rel* right, privilege, prerogative, birthright; management, direction; ascendancy, supremacy

powerful • having or manifesting power to effect great or striking results *syn* potent, puissant, forceful, forcible *rel* able, capable, competent; efficacious, effectual, effective, efficient; vigorous, energetic, strenuous *ant* powerless; inefficacious

powerless • unable to effect one's purpose, intention, or end *syn* impotent *rel* inert, inactive, passive, supine; feeble, weak, infirm, decrepit *ant* powerful; efficacious

practicable *syn* POSSIBLE, feasible *rel* operating, operable, working, workable, functioning *ant* impracticable

practically *syn* VIRTUALLY, morally

practice *vb* • to perform or cause one to perform an act or series of acts repeatedly in order to master or strengthen a skill or ability *syn* exercise, drill *rel* perform, execute, fulfill; follow, pursue; repeat, iterate

practice *n* **1** *syn* HABIT, habitude, usage, custom, use, wont *rel* procedure, process, proceeding; method, system, way, fashion, mode, manner **2** • repeated activity or exertion in order to develop or improve a strength or skill *syn* exercise, drill *rel* use, utility, usefulness; usage, form, convention, convenance; pursuit, calling, work *ant* theory; precept

praise • to express approval of or esteem for *syn* laud, acclaim, extol, eulogize *rel* commend, applaud, compliment; exalt, magnify, aggrandize *ant* blame

prank • a playful, often a mischievous, act or trick *syn* caper, antic, monkeyshine, dido *rel* frolic, gambol, rollick, sport, play; levity, lightness, frivolity; vagary, caprice, freak, fancy, whim, whimsy, conceit

prate *syn* CHAT, chatter, gab, patter, prattle, babble, gabble, jabber, gibber

prattle *syn* CHAT, chatter, patter, prate, gab, babble, gabble, jabber, gibber

pray • to request or make a request for in a humble, beseeching manner *syn* plead, petition, appeal, sue *rel* supplicate, entreat, beseech, implore, beg

prayer • an earnest and usu. a formal request for something *syn* suit, plea, petition, appeal *rel* supplication, entreaty, beseeching, imploring, begging; worship, adoration

preamble *syn* INTRODUCTION, prologue, prelude, preface, foreword, exordium

precarious *syn* DANGEROUS, hazardous, perilous, risky *rel* doubtful, dubious, questionable; distrustful, mistrustful; chance, chancy, haphazard, random

precedence *syn* PRIORITY *rel* leading, lead, guiding; guide; antecedence, foregoing

precedent *syn* PRECEDING, antecedent, foregoing, previous, prior, former, anterior

preceding • being before, esp. in time or in arrangement *syn* antecedent, precedent, foregoing, previous, prior, former, anterior *ant* following

precept *syn* LAW, rule, canon, regulation, statute, ordinance *rel* principle, fundamental, axiom; doctrine, tenet, dogma; injunction, behest, bidding, command *ant* practice; counsel

precious *syn* COSTLY, expensive, dear, valuable, invaluable, priceless *rel* choice, exquisite, recherché, rare; valued, prized, appreciated, cherished

precipitate *vb, syn* SPEED, accelerate, quicken, hasten, hurry *rel* drive, impel, move; force, compel, coerce, constrain

precipitate *n, syn* DEPOSIT, sediment, dregs, lees, grounds

precipitate *adj* • showing undue haste or unexpectedness *syn* headlong, abrupt, impetuous, hasty, sudden *rel* headstrong, willful, refractory *ant* deliberate

precipitous *syn* STEEP, abrupt, sheer *rel* soaring, towering, rocketing, ascending, rising

précis *syn* COMPENDIUM, sketch, aperçu, survey, syllabus, digest, pandect

precise *syn* CORRECT, exact, accurate, nice, right *rel* definite, express, explicit; strict, rigid, rigorous, stringent *ant* loose

preciseness *syn* PRECISION

precision • the quality or character of what is precise *syn* preciseness

preclude *syn* PREVENT, obviate, avert, ward *rel* hinder, obstruct, impede, block, bar; stop, discontinue, quit, cease; exclude, eliminate, shut out, debar

precocious *syn* PREMATURE, untimely, forward, advanced *rel* immature, unmatured, unripe *ant* backward

precursor *syn* FORERUNNER, harbinger, herald *rel* sign, mark, token, symptom; antecedent, determinant, cause, reason

predicament • a difficult, perplexing, or trying situation *syn* dilemma, quandary, plight, scrape, fix, jam, pickle *rel* state, situation, condition, posture; pass, pinch, strait, emergency, exigency, juncture

predicate *syn* ASSERT, affirm, declare, profess, aver, protest, avouch, avow, warrant

predict *syn* FORETELL, forecast, prophesy, prognosticate, augur, presage, portend, forebode *rel* foresee, foreknow, divine; warn, forewarn, caution; surmise, conjecture, guess

predilection • an attitude of mind that predisposes one to favor something *syn* partiality, prepossession, prejudice, bias *rel* leaning, propensity, proclivity, flair; bent, turn, knack, aptitude, gift *ant* aversion

predispose *syn* INCLINE, dispose, bias *rel* influence, sway, affect, touch, impress, strike

predominant *syn* DOMINANT, paramount, preponderant, preponderating, sovereign *rel* controlling, directing, conducting, managing; prevailing, prevalent; chief, principal, leading, main, foremost

preeminent *syn* SUPREME, surpassing, transcendent, superlative, peerless, incomparable *rel* dominant, predominant, paramount; excelling, excellent, outdoing, outstripping; consummate, finished

preempt *syn* ARROGATE, usurp, appropriate, confiscate *rel* take, seize, grasp, grab; exclude, eliminate, shut out, debar

preen *syn* PRIDE, plume, pique *rel* congratulate, felicitate

preface *syn* INTRODUCTION, prologue, prelude, foreword, exordium, preamble

prefatory *syn* PRELIMINARY, introductory, preparatory *rel* preparing, fitting, readying

prefer **1** *syn* CHOOSE, select, elect, opt, pick, cull, single *rel* accept, receive, admit, take; approve, endorse, sanction; favor, oblige, accommodate **2** *syn* OFFER, proffer, tender, present

preferable *syn* BETTER, superior

preference *syn* CHOICE, selection, election, option, alternative *rel* predilection, prepossession, partiality

preferment *syn* ADVANCEMENT, promotion, elevation *rel* advance, progress; rising, rise, ascending, ascent

pregnant *syn* EXPRESSIVE, meaningful, significant, eloquent, sententious *rel* weighty, momentous, consequential, significant, important

prejudice *syn* PREDILECTION, bias, partiality, prepossession *rel* predisposition, disposition, inclination; leaning, penchant

preliminary • serving to make ready the way for something that follows *syn* introductory, preparatory, prefatory *rel* primary, primal; elementary, elemental; basic, fundamental

prelude *syn* INTRODUCTION, prologue, preface, foreword, exordium, preamble

premature • unduly early in coming, happening, or developing *syn* untimely, forward, advanced, precocious *rel* immature, unmatured, unripe, unmellow; abortive, fruitless; precipitate, hasty, sudden, abrupt *ant* matured

premeditated *syn* DELIBERATE, considered, advised, designed, studied *rel* intended, purposed, meant; voluntary, intentional, willful *ant* unpremeditated; casual, accidental

premise *n, syn* ASSUMPTION, postulate, posit, presupposition, presumption *rel* ground, reason; proposition, proposal

premise *vb, syn* PRESUPPOSE, postulate, posit, presume, assume

premium • something that is offered or given for some service or attainment *syn* prize, award, reward, meed, guerdon, bounty, bonus *rel* gift, present, gratuity, favor; enhancement, intensification, heightening

preoccupied *syn* ABSTRACTED, absent, absentminded, distraught *rel* intent, engrossed, absorbed; forgetful, oblivious, unmindful

preparatory *syn* PRELIMINARY, introductory, prefatory *rel* fitting, preparing, qualifying, readying, conditioning

prepare • to make ready beforehand usu. for some purpose, use, or activity *syn* fit, qualify, condition, ready *rel* provide, supply, furnish; endow, endue, dower; equip, outfit; predispose, dispose, incline

preponderant, preponderating *syn* DOMINANT, predominant, paramount, sovereign *rel* supreme, preeminent, transcendent, surpassing; outstanding, salient, signal

prepossession *syn* PREDILECTION, partiality, prejudice, bias *rel* bent, turn, knack, aptitude, gift; leaning, penchant; predisposition, inclination

preposterous *syn* FOOLISH, absurd, silly *rel* irrational, unreasonable; bizarre, grotesque, fantastic

prerequisite *syn* REQUIREMENT, requisite *rel* necessity, need, exigency

prerogative *syn* RIGHT, privilege, perquisite, appanage, birthright *rel* immunity, exemption; claim, title; freedom, license, liberty

presage *n, syn* FORETOKEN, prognostic, omen, augury, portent *rel* sign, symptom, mark, token; forewarning, warning

presage *vb, syn* FORETELL, augur, portend, forebode, prognosticate, predict, forecast, prophesy *rel* indicate, betoken, bespeak; signify, import, denote, mean

prescribe **1** *syn* DICTATE, ordain, decree, impose *rel* order, command, enjoin, bid; exact, demand, require **2** • to fix arbitrarily or authoritatively for the sake of order or of a clear understanding *syn* assign, define *rel* set, settle, fix, establish; direct, enjoin, instruct, order, command

prescription *syn* RECEIPT, recipe

presence *syn* BEARING, deportment, demeanor, mien, port *rel* personality, individuality, disposition; aspect, appearance, look

present *n, syn* GIFT, gratuity, favor, boon, largess *rel* contribution, donation, benefaction; grant, subvention, appropriation

present *vb* **1** *syn* GIVE, bestow, confer, donate, afford *rel* grant, award, accord **2** *syn* OFFER, tender, proffer, prefer *rel* exhibit, display, parade, show; advance, adduce, allege, cite

presentiment *syn* APPREHENSION, misgiving, foreboding *rel* fear, dread, alarm, terror; foretaste, anticipation, prospect; disquieting, disquietude, discomposing, discomposure, disturbance, perturbation

presently • without undue time lapse *syn* shortly, soon, directly

preserve *syn* SAVE, conserve *rel* rescue, deliver, redeem, ransom; protect, guard, safeguard, defend

press *n, syn* CROWD, throng, crush, mob, rout, horde *rel* multitude, army, host, legion

press *vb* • to act upon through steady pushing or thrusting force exerted in contact *syn* bear, bear down, squeeze, crowd, jam *rel* push, thrust, propel, shove; drive, impel, move; pack, cram, stuff, ram

pressing • demanding or claiming esp. immediate attention *syn* urgent, imperative, crying, importunate, insistent, exigent, instant *rel* immediate, direct; demanding, claiming, requiring, exacting; compelling, constraining, forcing, obliging

pressure *syn* STRESS, strain, tension

prestige *syn* INFLUENCE, authority, weight, credit *rel* ascendancy, supremacy; power, sway, dominion; reputation, repute, honor, glory, fame

presume *syn* PRESUPPOSE, postulate, premise, posit, assume *rel* surmise, conjecture; deduce, infer, judge, gather, conclude

presumption *syn* ASSUMPTION, presupposition, postulate, premise, posit *rel* view, opinion, conviction, belief; conjecture, surmise

presumptuous *syn* CONFIDENT, assured, sanguine, sure *rel* self-confident, self-assured, self-possessed; presuming, assuming; positive, cocksure, certain, sure; arrogant, insolent, overbearing, proud

presuppose • to take something for granted or as true or existent esp. as a basis for action or reasoning *syn* presume, assume, postulate, premise, posit *rel* surmise, conjecture, guess; infer, deduce, gather, judge

presupposition *syn* ASSUMPTION, presumption, postulate, premise, posit *rel* surmise, conjecture, guess; inference, deduction, judgment; belief, conviction, opinion, view

pretend *syn* ASSUME, affect, simulate, feign, counterfeit, sham *rel* disguise, dissemble, cloak, mask, camouflage; deceive, delude, mislead, beguile

pretense **1** *syn* CLAIM, pretension, title *rel* plea, pretext, excuse, apology, apologia; right, birthright, privilege **2** • the offering of something false as real or true *syn* pretension, make-believe *rel* humbug, fake, sham, fraud, deceit, deception, imposture; affectation, pose, air, mannerism

pretension **1** *syn* CLAIM, title, pretense *rel* right, privilege, prerogative; assertion, affirmation, declaration, protestation **2** *syn* PRETENSE, make-believe *rel* hypocrisy, sanctimony, cant; dissimulation, duplicity, guile, deceit **3** *syn* AMBITION, aspiration *rel* hoping, hope, expectation; dream, vision, fancy

pretentious **1** *syn* SHOWY, ostentatious *rel* gaudy, garish, flashy; ornate, flamboyant, florid, baroque, rococo *ant* unpretentious **2** *syn* AMBITIOUS, utopian *rel* aiming, aspiring, panting; conspicuous, striking, arresting, noticeable

preternatural *syn* SUPERNATURAL, supranatural, miraculous, superhuman *rel* unnatural, anomalous, irregular; abnormal, atypical; outstanding, remarkable, salient, noticeable; exceptional

pretext *syn* APOLOGY, excuse, plea, alibi, apologia *rel* ruse, trick, maneuver, stratagem; deception; justification, vindication, defending, defense

pretty *syn* BEAUTIFUL, bonny, comely, fair, lovely, handsome, good-looking, beauteous, pulchritudinous *rel* charming, attractive, alluring; dainty, delicate, exquisite, choice

prevail *syn* INDUCE, persuade, get *rel* move, actuate, drive, impel; influence, affect, impress, sway

prevailing • general (as in circulation, acceptance, or use) in a given place or at a given time *syn* prevalent, rife, current *rel* dominant, predominant, preponderant; common, ordinary, familiar; general, universal

prevalent *syn* PREVAILING, rife, current *rel* common, ordinary, familiar; pervading, impregnating, saturating; usual, wonted, accustomed, customary

prevaricate *syn* LIE, equivocate, palter, fib *rel* evade, elude, escape; misrepresent, falsify, belie, garble

prevent **1** • to deal with beforehand *syn* anticipate, forestall *rel* frustrate, thwart, foil, baffle, balk; arrest, check, interrupt; avoid, shun, eschew, evade, escape **2** • to stop from advancing or occurring *syn* preclude, obviate, avert, ward *rel* hinder, impede, obstruct, block, bar, dam; debar, shut out, exclude; prohibit, forbid, interdict, inhibit *ant* permit

previous *syn* PRECEDING, foregoing, prior, antecedent, precedent, former, anterior *ant* subsequent; consequent

prey *syn* VICTIM, quarry *rel* spoil, booty, prize

price • the quantity of one thing that is exchanged or demanded in barter or sale for another *syn* charge, cost, expense

priceless *syn* COSTLY, invaluable, precious, expensive, dear, valuable *rel* cherished, treasured, prized, valued

prick 1 *syn* PERFORATE, punch, puncture, bore, drill *rel* enter, pierce, probe, penetrate; cut, slit, slash 2 *syn* URGE, egg, exhort, goad, spur, prod, sic *rel* stimulate, excite, pique, provoke; activate, actuate, motivate; compel, constrain, force

pride *n* • an attitude of inordinate self-esteem or superiority *syn* vanity, vainglory *rel* arrogance, haughtiness, superciliousness, disdainfulness, disdain, insolence; complacency, smugness, priggishness; self-esteem, self-love, egotism, egoism, conceit *ant* humility; shame

pride *vb* • to congratulate oneself because of something one is, has, or has done or achieved *syn* plume, pique, preen *rel* boast, brag, vaunt, crow, gasconade; congratulate, felicitate

priggish 1 *syn* COMPLACENT, smug, self-complacent, self-satisfied *rel* righteous, ethical, moral; conceited, egotistic, self-esteeming, self-loving 2 *syn* PRIM, prissy, prudish, puritanical, straitlaced, stuffy *rel* see PRIGGISH 1

prim • excessively concerned with what one regards as proper or right *syn* priggish, prissy, prudish, puritanical, straitlaced, stuffy *rel* precise, correct, nice; decorous, proper; stiff, rigid, wooden

primal *syn* PRIMARY, primordial, primitive, pristine, primeval, prime *rel* ultimate, absolute, categorical; original, fresh, new

primary • first in some respect (as order, character, or importance) *syn* primal, primordial, primitive, pristine, primeval, prime *rel* initiating, initial, beginning, commencing, starting; elemental, elementary; basic, fundamental, radical; chief, leading, principal

prime *syn* PRIMARY, primal, primordial, primitive, pristine, primeval *rel* chief, leading, principal, main; choice, exquisite, recherché

prime mover *syn* ORIGIN, source, provenance, provenience, inception, root

primeval *syn* PRIMARY, pristine, primitive, primordial, primal, prime *rel* aboriginal, native, indigenous, autochthonous; original, new

primitive 1 *syn* PRIMARY, primal, primordial, pristine, primeval, prime *rel* fundamental, basic, radical; elemental, elementary; aboriginal, native 2 *syn* ELEMENTAL, basic, elementary, essential, fundamental, underlying

primordial 1 *syn* PRIMARY, primeval, pristine, primitive, primal, prime 2 *syn* INITIAL, original

princely *syn* KINGLY, regal, royal, queenly, imperial *rel* luxurious, sumptuous, opulent; munificent, bountiful, bounteous, openhanded, liberal

principal *syn* CHIEF, main, leading, foremost, capital *rel* dominant, predominant, paramount; vital, cardinal, fundamental, essential; preeminent, supreme, superlative

principally *syn* LARGELY, mainly, chiefly, mostly, greatly, generally

principle • a comprehensive and fundamental rule, doctrine, or assumption *syn* axiom, fundamental, law, theorem *rel* basis, foundation, ground; law, rule, canon, precept; form, usage, convention

print *syn* IMPRESSION, impress, imprint, stamp *rel* mark, token, sign; trace, vestige

printing *syn* EDITION, impression, reprinting, reissue

prior *syn* PRECEDING, previous, foregoing, precedent, anterior, former, antecedent *rel* ahead, before, forward

priority • the act, the fact, or the right of preceding another *syn* precedence *rel* ordering, order, arrangement; ascendancy, supremacy; preeminence, transcendence

priory *syn* CLOISTER, monastery, nunnery, convent, abbey

prismatic • marked by or displaying a variety of colors *syn* iridescent, opalescent, opaline

prisoner • one who is deprived of liberty and kept under involuntary restraint *syn* captive

prissy *syn* PRIM, priggish, prudish, puritanical, straitlaced, stuffy *rel* womanish, effeminate, ladylike, female; finicky, fastidious, nice, squeamish; scrupulous, punctilious, meticulous, careful

pristine *syn* PRIMARY, primeval, primordial, primitive, primal, prime *rel* original, fresh, new

privateer *syn* PIRATE, freebooter, buccaneer, corsair

privation 1 *syn* LACK, want, dearth, absence, defect *rel* negation, nullification, annulling, abrogation 2 *syn* POVERTY, want, destitution, indigence, penury *rel* depletion, draining, exhaustion, impoverishment; need, necessity, exigency; pinch, strait

privilege *syn* RIGHT, prerogative, birthright, perquisite, appanage *rel* concession, allowance; favor, boon, gift; claim, title

prize *n, syn* PREMIUM, award, reward, meed, guerdon, bounty, bonus *rel* recompensing, recompense, compensation; winning, winnings *ant* forfeit

prize *vb, syn* APPRECIATE, value, treasure, cherish *rel* esteem, respect, admire, regard; estimate, evaluate, assess, assay, rate

prize *n, syn* SPOIL, booty, plunder, loot, swag

probable • almost sure to be or to become true or real *syn* possible, likely *rel* credible, believable, colorable, plausible; reasonable, rational *ant* certain; improbable

probationer *syn* NOVICE, novitiate, apprentice, postulant, neophyte

probe *n, syn* INQUIRY, investigation, inquisition, inquest, research

probe *vb, syn* ENTER, pierce, penetrate *rel* examine, inspect, scrutinize; prove, try, test

probity *syn* HONESTY, honor, integrity *rel* uprightness, justness, conscientiousness, scrupulousness; truth, veracity; rectitude, goodness, virtue

problem *syn* MYSTERY, enigma, fiddle, puzzle, conundrum *rel* perplexity, mystification, bewilderment, distraction; predicament, dilemma, plight, quandary *ant* solution

problematic *syn* DOUBTFUL, dubious, questionable *rel* ambiguous, equivocal, obscure, vague, cryptic, enigmatic; uncertain, suspicious, mistrustful

procedure *syn* PROCESS, proceeding *rel* ordering, order, arrangement; method, system, manner, way; conducting, conduct, management

proceed *syn* SPRING, issue, emanate, stem, flow, derive, arise, rise, originate *rel* follow, succeed, ensue; come, arrive

proceeding *syn* PROCESS, procedure *rel* action, act, deed; affair, business, concern; operation, functioning, working

process • the series of actions, operations, or motions involved in the accomplishment of an end *syn* procedure, proceeding *rel* progress, advance; conducting, conduct, management, controlling, control, direction; performance, execution, accomplishment, fulfillment

procession • a body (as of persons and vehicles) moving along in a usu. ceremonial order *syn* parade, cortege, cavalcade, motorcade *rel* succession, sequence, train; pomp, array, display

proclaim *syn* DECLARE, announce, publish, advertise, promulgate, broadcast *rel* reveal, disclose, discover, divulge, tell; voice, utter, vent, ventilate, express; inform, apprise

proclamation *syn* DECLARATION, announcement, publication, advertisement, promulgation, broadcasting

proclivity *syn* LEANING, propensity, penchant, flair *rel* knack, aptitude, gift, bent, turn; inclination, disposition, predisposition; predilection, prepossession, prejudice, bias

procrastinate *syn* DELAY, lag, dawdle, loiter *rel* defer, suspend, stay, postpone; protract, prolong, extend *ant* hasten, hurry

procreate *syn* GENERATE, engender, beget, get, sire, breed, propagate, reproduce

procure *syn* GET, obtain, secure, acquire, gain, win *rel* negotiate, arrange, concert; reach, compass, achieve, attain

prod *vb* **1** *syn* POKE, nudge, jog *rel* prick, punch, bore, perforate; goad, spur; pierce, penetrate **2** *syn* URGE, egg, exhort, goad, spur, prick, sic *rel* incite, instigate; stimulate, excite, pique, provoke

prod *n, syn* POKE, nudge, jog *rel* stimulus, stimulant, incitement, impetus

prodigal *adj, syn* PROFUSE, lavish, exuberant, luxuriant, lush *rel* extravagant, exorbitant, immoderate, excessive; abundant, plentiful, plenteous, ample, copious; supererogatory, uncalled-for, gratuitous *ant* parsimonious; frugal

prodigal *n, syn* SPENDTHRIFT, profligate, waster, wastrel *rel* spender, expender, disburser

prodigious *syn* MONSTROUS, tremendous, stupendous, monumental *rel* enormous, immense, huge, vast, gigantic, mammoth, colossal; amazing, astounding, flabbergasting

prodigy *syn* WONDER, marvel, miracle, phenomenon *rel* abnormality; monstrosity; anomaly, paradox

produce *vb, syn* BEAR, yield, turn out *rel* generate, breed, propagate; make, form, shape, fabricate, manufacture; create, invent

produce *n, syn* PRODUCT, production

product **1** *syn* WORK, production, opus, artifact *rel* forming, form, fabrication, manufacturing, manufacture; article, object, thing **2** • something produced by physical labor or intellectual effort *syn* production, produce

production **1** *syn* WORK, product, opus, artifact *rel* execution, fulfillment, performance; effort, exertion **2** *syn* PRODUCT, produce

profanation • a violation or a misuse of something normally held sacred *syn* desecration, sacrilege, blasphemy *rel* defilement, pollution, contamination; debasement, vitiation, corruption, perversion; violation, transgression, trespass, breach

profane **1** • not concerned with religion or religious purposes *syn* secular, lay, temporal *rel* worldly, mundane, earthly, terrestrial *ant* sacred **2** *syn* IMPIOUS, blasphemous, sacrilegious *rel* foul, filthy, dirty, nasty; ungodly, godless, irreligious; iniquitous, nefarious, villainous, vicious

profanity *syn* BLASPHEMY, cursing, swearing *rel* imprecation, curse, malediction; execration, objurgation, damning

profess *syn* ASSERT, declare, affirm, aver, protest, avouch, avow, predicate, warrant *rel* allege, adduce, advance

profession *syn* TRADE, art, handicraft, craft

proffer *syn* OFFER, tender, present, prefer *rel* propose, design, intend; confer, bestow, give

proficient • having great knowledge and experience in a trade or profession *syn* adept, skilled, skillful, expert, masterly *rel* efficient, effectual, effective; capable, able, competent, qualified; finished, accomplished, consummate; practiced, drilled, exercised

profile *syn* OUTLINE, contour, silhouette, skyline

profit *n, syn* USE, service, advantage, account, avail *rel* reward, award, meed, guerdon, premium; gaining, gain, winning

profit *vb, syn* BENEFIT, avail *rel* get, gain, win; advance, progress

profitable **1** *syn* BENEFICIAL, advantageous *rel* favorable, auspicious, propitious; expedient, advisable, politic *ant* unprofitable **2** *syn* PAYING, gainful, remunerative, lucrative *rel* fruitful; compensating, recompensing, repaying; valuable, precious, costly

profligate *adj, syn* ABANDONED, dissolute, reprobate *rel* debauched, corrupted, depraved, debased, perverted; degenerate, corrupt, vicious; loose, relaxed, slack, lax

profligate *n, syn* SPENDTHRIFT, prodigal, wastrel, waster *rel* debauchee, pervert, corrupter; libertine, lecher

profound *syn* DEEP, abysmal *rel* penetrating, probing, piercing; scrutinizing, inspecting, examining *ant* shallow

profuse • giving or given out in great abundance *syn* lavish, prodigal, luxuriant, lush, exuberant *rel* copious, abundant, plentiful; excessive, immoderate, extravagant; liberal, bountiful, bounteous, openhanded, munificent, generous *ant* spare, scanty, scant

progenitor *syn* ANCESTOR, forefather, forebear *ant* progeny

progeny *syn* OFFSPRING, young, issue, descendant, posterity *ant* progenitor

prognostic *syn* FORETOKEN, presage, omen, augury, portent *rel* indication, betokening, bespeaking; symptom, sign, mark, token

prognosticate *syn* FORETELL, predict, forecast, prophesy, augur, presage, portend, forebode *rel* indicate, betoken, bespeak; foresee, foreknow, apprehend, divine, anticipate

program • a formulated plan listing things to be done or to take place esp. in chronological order *syn* schedule, timetable, agenda

progress *n* **1** *syn* ADVANCE *rel* improvement, betterment; headway, impetus **2** • a movement forward (as in time or space) *syn* progression

progress *vb, syn* ADVANCE *rel* move, drive, impel; further, forward, promote, advance; develop, mature *ant* retrogress

progression **1** *syn* SUCCESSION, series, sequence, chain, train, string **2** *syn* PROGRESS

progressive *syn* LIBERAL, advanced, radical *ant* reactionary

prohibit *syn* FORBID, inhibit, enjoin, interdict, ban *rel* prevent, preclude, obviate;

debar, shut out, exclude; hinder, impede, obstruct; restrain, curb, check *ant* permit

project *n, syn* PLAN, scheme, design, plot *rel* sketch, delineation, draft, outline, diagram; device, contrivance

project *vb* **1** *syn* PLAN, scheme, design, plot *rel* propose, purpose, intend; sketch, outline, diagram, delineate **2** *syn* BULGE, jut, stick out, protrude, overhang, beetle *rel* extend, prolong, lengthen; swell, distend, expand

projection • an extension beyond the normal line or surface *syn* protrusion, protuberance, bulge

prolific *syn* FERTILE, fruitful, fecund *rel* teeming, swarming, abounding; generating, breeding, propagating, reproducing, reproductive *ant* barren, unfruitful

prolificacy *syn* FERTILITY, fruitfulness, fecundity *ant* barrenness, unfruitfulness

prolix *syn* WORDY, verbose, diffuse, redundant *rel* tedious, irksome, tiresome, wearisome; prolonged, protracted; pleonastic, circumlocutory, redundant, tautological

prologue *syn* INTRODUCTION, prelude, preface, foreword, exordium, preamble

prolong *syn* EXTEND, protract, lengthen, elongate *rel* continue, last, persist, endure; increase, augment, enlarge; expand, amplify *ant* curtail

prominent *syn* NOTICEABLE, remarkable, conspicuous, salient, outstanding, signal, striking, arresting *rel* chief, leading, main, principal; important, significant

promiscuous *syn* MISCELLANEOUS, heterogeneous, motley *rel* mixed, mingled, blended, merged; random, haphazard, desultory, casual; indiscriminate, wholesale, sweeping; licentious, lewd, wanton, lascivious

promise • to give one's word to do, bring about, or provide *syn* engage, pledge, plight, covenant, contract *rel* agree, consent, assent, accede; assure, ensure, insure

promote *syn* ADVANCE, forward, further *rel* help, aid, assist; speed, quicken, hasten, hurry *ant* impede

promotion **1** *syn* ADVANCEMENT, preferment, elevation *rel* progress, progression; exaltation, magnifying, aggrandizement *ant* demotion **2** *syn* PUBLICITY, ballyhoo, propaganda *rel* advertisement, promulgation, broadcasting

prompt *syn* QUICK, ready, apt *rel* alert, wide-awake, vigilant, watchful; expeditious, speedy, swift, fast; trained, disciplined; eager, keen, avid

promulgate *syn* DECLARE, proclaim, announce, publish, advertise, broadcast *rel* reveal, disclose, divulge, discover; profess, affirm, aver, avow, avouch, assert; communicate, impart

promulgation *syn* DECLARATION, proclamation, announcement, publication, advertisement, broadcasting

prone **1** *syn* LIABLE, subject, exposed, open, susceptible, sensitive *rel* inclined, predisposed, disposed; addicted, habituated, accustomed **2** • lying down *syn* supine, prostrate, recumbent, couchant, dormant *rel* flat, level; groveling, wallowing, weltering; *ant* erect

pronounce *syn* ARTICULATE, enunciate

proof **1** *syn* REASON, ground, argument *rel* demonstration, trial, test; corroboration, confirmation, substantiation, verification **2** • something that serves as evidence compelling the acceptance of a truth or fact *syn* demonstration, test, trial *ant* disproof

prop *syn* SUPPORT, sustain, bolster, buttress, brace *rel* uphold, back; hoist, heave, boost, lift

propaganda *syn* PUBLICITY, ballyhoo, promotion *rel* propagation, engendering, generating; spread, stretch, expanse; inculcation, instillment, implanting

propagate **1** *syn* GENERATE, engender, breed, beget, procreate, sire, reproduce *rel* increase, multiply, augment; continue, persist; extend, lengthen, prolong **2** *syn* SPREAD, circulate, disseminate, diffuse, radiate *rel* scatter, disperse, dissipate; distribute, dispense; teach, instruct, educate; communicate, impart; inculcate, instill, implant

propel *syn* PUSH, shove, thrust *rel* move, drive, impel; force, compel, constrain, oblige

propensity *syn* LEANING, proclivity, penchant, flair *rel* predilection, prejudice, bias, prepossession; gift, aptitude, bent, turn, knack; predisposition, disposition, inclination *ant* antipathy

proper **1** *syn* FIT, meet, appropriate, fitting, apt, happy, felicitous, suitable *rel* congruous, congenial, compatible, consonant; correct, nice, right; due, rightful, condign *ant* improper **2** *syn* DECOROUS, seemly, decent, nice *rel* formal, conventional, ceremonious, ceremonial

property *syn* QUALITY, character, attribute, accident *rel* peculiarity, individuality, characteristic

prophecy *syn* REVELATION, vision, apocalypse *rel* communication, impartation; inspiration

prophesy *syn* FORETELL, predict, forecast, prognosticate, augur, presage, portend, forebode *rel* foresee, foreknow, divine, apprehend, anticipate

propinquity *syn* PROXIMITY *rel* closeness, nearness; relatedness, relationship, kindredness, kindred

propitiate *syn* PACIFY, appease, placate, mollify, conciliate *rel* reconcile, conform, adjust, adapt; satisfy, content; intercede, mediate, interpose

propitious *syn* FAVORABLE, auspicious, benign *rel* benignant, kind, kindly; fortunate, lucky, providential, happy *ant* unpropitious; adverse

proportion *syn* SYMMETRY, balance, harmony

proportional • corresponding in size, degree, or intensity *syn* proportionate, commensurate, commensurable *rel* corresponding, correlative, reciprocal; relative, contingent, dependent

proportionate *syn* PROPORTIONAL, commensurate, commensurable *rel* corresponding, correlative, reciprocal *ant* disproportionate

proposal • something put forward, offered, or otherwise stated for consideration *syn* proposition

propose 1 *syn* INTEND, purpose, mean, design *rel* aim, aspire; plan, plot, scheme, project **2** • to set before the mind for consideration *syn* propound, pose *rel* state; offer, tender, present

proposition *syn* PROPOSAL

propound *syn* PROPOSE, pose *rel* ask, question, query; state

propriety *syn* DECORUM, decency, etiquette, dignity *rel* grace, elegance; form, usage, convention, convenance

prorate *syn* APPORTION, portion, parcel, ration

prosaic • having a plain, practical, everyday character or quality *syn* prosy, matter-of-fact *rel* practical, practicable; boring, tedious, irksome

proscribe *syn* SENTENCE, condemn, damn, doom

proselyte *syn* CONVERT

prospect • an advance realization of something to come *syn* outlook, anticipation, foretaste *rel* hope, expectation; foreseeing, foresight, foreknowing, foreknowledge, divining, divination

prosper *syn* SUCCEED, thrive, flourish *rel* increase, augment, multiply; bear, yield, produce, turn out

prostrate *syn* PRONE, supine, recumbent, couchant, dormant *rel* flat, level; abject, mean

prosy *syn* PROSAIC, matter-of-fact *rel* insipid, jejune, banal, inane; irksome, boring, tedious

protean *syn* CHANGEABLE, changeful, variable, mutable

protect *syn* DEFEND, shield, guard, safeguard *rel* save, preserve, conserve; ensure, insure, assure; shelter, harbor

protest 1 *syn* ASSERT, avouch, avow, profess, affirm, aver, declare, predicate, warrant **2** *syn* OBJECT, remonstrate, expostulate, kick *rel* oppose, resist, combat, fight; demur, scruple, balk *ant* agree

protract *syn* EXTEND, prolong, lengthen, elongate *rel* delay, retard, slow, slacken; defer, suspend, stay, postpone *ant* curtail

protrude *syn* BULGE, jut, stick out, project, overhang, beetle *rel* obtrude, intrude; extend, prolong; swell, distend, expand

protrusion *syn* PROJECTION, protuberance, bulge

protuberance *syn* PROJECTION, protrusion, bulge

protuberate *syn* BULGE, jut, stick out, protrude, project, overhang, beetle *rel* swell, distend, expand

proud 1 • showing scorn for inferiors *syn* arrogant, haughty, lordly, insolent, overbearing, supercilious, disdainful *rel* contemptuous, scornful; pretentious, ostentatious, showy; imperious, domineering, masterful *ant* humble; ashamed **2** • having or exhibiting undue or excessive pride esp. in one's appearance or achievements *syn* vain, vainglorious *rel* exalted, magnified, aggrandized; self-satisfied, complacent, smug; contented, satisfied *ant* ashamed; humble

prove 1 • to establish a point by appropriate objective means *syn* try, test, demonstrate *rel* corroborate, verify, substantiate, confirm; justify, warrant *ant* disprove **2** *syn* INDICATE, betoken, attest, bespeak, argue *rel* evidence, manifest, evince, show, demonstrate

provenance, provenience *syn* ORIGIN, source, inception, root, prime mover *rel* beginning, commencement, starting

provender *syn* FOOD, fodder, forage, feed, victuals, viands, provisions, comestibles

proverb *syn* SAYING, maxim, adage, motto, saw, epigram, aphorism, apothegm

provide • to give or acquire and make available something wanted or needed *syn* supply, furnish *rel* prepare, fit, ready; equip, outfit, arm, furnish; purvey, cater

providence *syn* PRUDENCE, foresight, forethought, discretion *rel* care, solicitude, concern; thoughtfulness, consideration; frugality, thriftiness, economy *ant* improvidence

provident *syn* PRUDENT, foresighted, forethoughtful, discreet *rel* careful, solicitous, concerned; thoughtful, considerate; sparing, economical, frugal, thrifty *ant* improvident

providential *syn* LUCKY, fortunate, happy *rel* benign, auspicious, propitious, favorable; benignant, kindly, kind

providing *syn* IF

province **1** *syn* FIELD, domain, sphere, territory, bailiwick *rel* limit, confine, bound, end **2** *syn* FUNCTION, office, duty *rel* work, calling, pursuit, business; task, job

provincial *syn* INSULAR, parochial, local, small-town *rel* circumscribed, confined, limited, restricted; narrow, narrow-minded, illiberal, intolerant, hidebound, bigoted *ant* catholic

provision **1** *syn* CONDITION, stipulation, terms, proviso, reservation, strings *rel* clause, article, paragraph; prerequisite, requisite, requirement **2** *pl* **provisions** *syn* FOOD, feed, victuals, viands, comestibles, provender, fodder, forage

provisional **1** • not final or definitive *syn* tentative *rel* temporary; conditional, dependent, contingent *ant* definitive **2** *syn* TEMPORARY, ad interim, acting

proviso *syn* CONDITION, stipulation, terms, provision, reservation, strings *rel* clause, article, paragraph; limitation, restriction; contingency, exigency

provoke **1** • to arouse as if pricking *syn* excite, stimulate, pique, quicken, galvanize *rel* arouse, rouse, stir; thrill, electrify, enthuse; incite, instigate, foment **2** *syn* IRRITATE, exasperate, nettle, aggravate, rile, peeve *rel* affront, offend, insult, outrage; anger, incense, madden; agitate, upset, perturb, discompose *ant* gratify

prowess *syn* HEROISM, valor, gallantry *rel* bravery, boldness, audacity, intrepidity; courage, mettle, spirit; strength, might, puissance, power

prowl *syn* WANDER, stray, roam, ramble, rove, range, gad, gallivant, traipse, meander

proximity • the quality or state of being near *syn* propinquity *rel* nearness, closeness; adjacency, contiguousness, juxtaposition *ant* distance

proxy *syn* AGENT, deputy, attorney, factor

prudence • good sense or shrewdness in the management of affairs *syn* providence, foresight, forethought, discretion *rel* caution, circumspection, calculation; expediency, advisableness; frugality, thriftiness, thrift

prudent **1** *syn* WISE, judicious, sensible, sane, sage, sapient *rel* intelligent, brilliant, bright, smart, alert; shrewd, perspicacious, sagacious, astute; disciplined, schooled **2** • making provision for the future *syn* provident, foresighted, forethoughtful, discreet *rel* cautious, circumspect, calculating, wary; politic, expedient, advisable; economical, frugal, thrifty, sparing

prudish *syn* PRIM, priggish, prissy, puritanical, straitlaced, stuffy *rel* rigid, strict; stern, severe, austere; formal, conventional, solemn, ceremonial

prune *syn* SHEAR, trim, lop, poll, clip, snip, crop *rel* enhance, heighten, intensify; eliminate, exclude

prying *syn* CURIOUS, inquisitive, snoopy, nosy *rel* meddlesome, officious, impertinent, intrusive, obtrusive

pseudo *syn* COUNTERFEIT, spurious, bogus, fake, sham, pinchbeck, phony *rel* false, wrong; misleading, deceptive, delusive, delusory

pseudonym • a fictitious or assumed name *syn* alias, nom de guerre, pen name, nom de plume, incognito

psyche *syn* MIND, intellect, soul, brain, intelligence, wit

psychic *syn* MENTAL, intellectual, intelligent, cerebral

psychosis *syn* INSANITY, lunacy, mania, dementia

puberty, pubescence *syn* YOUTH, adolescence

public *syn* FOLLOWING, clientele, audience

publication *syn* DECLARATION, announcement, advertisement, proclamation, promulgation, broadcasting

publicity • an act or device designed to attract public interest and to mold public opinion *syn* ballyhoo, promotion, propaganda *rel* advertisement, publication, announcement, promulgation, broadcasting

publish *syn* DECLARE, announce, advertise, proclaim, promulgate, broadcast *rel* divulge, disclose, reveal, discover; communicate, impart; vent, ventilate, utter, broach, express

puerile *syn* YOUTHFUL, juvenile, boyish, virgin, virginal, maiden *rel* immature, unmatured, unripe; raw, callow, green, rude *ant* adult

puff *syn* CRITICISM, critique, review, blurb

pugnacious *syn* BELLIGERENT, combative, bellicose, quarrelsome, contentious *rel* aggressive, militant, assertive, self-assertive, pushing, pushy *ant* pacific

puissance *syn* POWER, might, strength, force, energy

puissant *syn* POWERFUL, potent, forceful, forcible *ant* impuissant

pulchritudinous *syn* BEAUTIFUL, beauteous, good-looking, comely, bonny, pretty, handsome, fair, lovely

pull • to cause to move toward or after an applied force *syn* draw, drag, haul, hale, tug, tow

pulsate • to course or move with or as if with rhythmic strokes *syn* pulse, beat, throb, palpitate *rel* vibrate, fluctuate, waver, oscillate, swing; quiver, shudder, quaver, tremble, shake

pulsation • a rhythmical movement or one single step in recurring rhythmic steps *syn* pulse, beat, throb, palpitation

pulse *n, syn* PULSATION, beat, throb, palpitation *rel* rhythm, cadence, meter; vibration, fluctuation

pulse *vb, syn* PULSATE, beat, throb, palpitate *rel* move, drive, impel; vibrate, fluctuate, oscillate, swing

pummel *syn* BEAT, pound, buffet, baste, belabor, thrash *rel* strike, hit, smite, slug, punch

punch *vb* **1** *syn* STRIKE, hit, smite, slug, slog, swat, clout, slap, box, cuff *rel* beat, pound, pummel, baste, belabor **2** *syn* PERFORATE, puncture, prick, bore, drill *rel* pierce, penetrate, probe, enter

punch *n, syn* VIGOR, vim, spirit, dash, esprit, verve, élan, drive

punctilious *syn* CAREFUL, punctual, meticulous, scrupulous *rel* particular, fussy, squeamish, fastidious, nice; formal, conventional, ceremonious, ceremonial

punctual *syn* CAREFUL, punctilious, meticulous, scrupulous *rel* quick, prompt, ready; precise, correct, nice, right

puncture *syn* PERFORATE, punch, prick, bore, drill *rel* pierce, penetrate, enter; deflate, shrink, contract

pungent • sharp and stimulating to the mind or the senses *syn* piquant, poignant, racy, spicy, snappy *rel* incisive, trenchant, biting, cutting; penetrating, piercing, probing; exciting, stimulating, provoking, provocative *ant* bland

punish • to inflict a penalty on in requital for wrongdoing *syn* chastise, castigate, chasten, discipline, correct *rel* penalize, fine, amerce, mulct; imprison, incarcerate, immure; avenge, revenge *ant* excuse; pardon

puny *syn* PETTY, trivial, trifling, paltry, measly, picayunish, picayune *rel* feeble, weak, frail, infirm; small, little, diminutive; slight, tenuous, thin

purblind *syn* BLIND, sightless

purchase *syn* BUY *rel* gain, win, get, obtain, procure, secure

pure **1** • containing nothing that does not properly belong *syn* absolute, simple, sheer *rel* elemental, elementary; clear, transparent, lucid, limpid; genuine, authentic *ant* contaminated, polluted; adulterated applied (*of science*) **2** *syn* CHASTE, modest, decent *rel* clean, cleanly; virtuous, moral, ethical *ant* impure; immoral

purge *syn* RID, clear, unburden, disabuse *rel* cleanse, clean; eliminate, exclude, debar, shut out, rule out; eject, oust, dismiss, expel; expunge, erase, efface, delete

puritanical *syn* PRIM, priggish, prissy, prudish, straitlaced, stuffy *rel* rigid, rigorous, strict; plain, simple, homely, unpretentious; illiberal, narrow, narrow-minded, hidebound, intolerant, bigoted

purloin *syn* STEAL, pilfer, filch, lift, pinch, snitch, swipe, cop *rel* abstract, detach; rob, plunder, rifle, loot, burglarize

purport *syn* SUBSTANCE, gist, burden, core, pith *rel* significance, import, meaning, signification; tenor, tendency, drift, trend

purported *syn* SUPPOSED, supposititious, suppositious, reputed, putative, conjectural, hypothetical

purpose *n, syn* INTENTION, intent, design, aim, end, object, objective, goal *rel* ambition, aspiration; proposition, proposal; plan, project, scheme

purpose *vb, syn* INTEND, propose, design, mean *rel* meditate, ponder; weigh, consider, contemplate; plan, plot, scheme, project; determine, decide

pursue *syn* FOLLOW, chase, trail, tag, tail *rel* persevere, persist; practice, exercise; persecute, oppress; hound, ride, bait, badger

pursuit *syn* WORK, calling, occupation, employment, business

purvey *syn* CATER, pander *rel* furnish, equip, outfit

purview *syn* RANGE, gamut, reach, radius, compass, sweep, scope, orbit, horizon, ken

push • to press against with force so as to cause to move ahead or aside *syn* shove, thrust, propel *rel* move, drive, impel; force, compel, constrain, oblige

pushing, pushy *syn* AGGRESSIVE, militant, assertive, self-assertive *rel* vigorous, energetic, strenuous; officious, intrusive, obtrusive, impertinent; self-confident, confident, self-assured, assured

puss *syn* FACE, countenance, visage, physiognomy, mug

pustule *syn* ABSCESS, boil, furuncle, carbuncle, pimple

putative *syn* SUPPOSED, supposititious, suppositious, reputed, purported, conjectural, hypothetical *rel* alleged, advanced; assumed, pretended, simulated

putrefy *syn* DECAY, rot, decompose, spoil, disintegrate, crumble *rel* corrupt, vitiate, deprave, debase; deliquesce

putrid *syn* MALODOROUS, fetid, noisome, stinking, rank, rancid, fusty, musty *rel* decomposed, decayed, rotten, putrefied; corrupted, vitiated

putsch *syn* REBELLION, revolution, uprising, revolt, insurrection, mutiny, coup

put up *syn* RESIDE, live, dwell, sojourn, lodge, stay, stop

puzzle *vb* • to baffle and disturb mentally *syn* perplex, mystify, bewilder, distract, nonplus, confound, dumbfound *rel* amaze, astound, flabbergast, surprise; confuse, muddle, addle; embarrass, disconcert, discomfit

puzzle *n, syn* MYSTERY, problem, enigma, riddle, conundrum

pygmy *syn* DWARF, midget, manikin, homunculus, runt

Q

quack *syn* IMPOSTOR, faker, mountebank, charlatan *rel* pretender, simulator, counterfeiter, shammer; deceit, duplicity, dissimulation, cunning, guile

quail *syn* RECOIL, shrink, flinch, wince, blench *rel* cower, cringe, fawn; falter, waver, vacillate, hesitate; quake, quaver, tremble, shudder, shake

quaint *syn* STRANGE, odd, queer, outlandish, curious, peculiar, eccentric, erratic, singular, unique *rel* fantastic, bizarre, grotesque; droll, funny, laughable; archaic, antiquated, antique, old

quake *syn* SHAKE, tremble, totter, quiver, shiver, shudder, quaver, wobble, teeter, shimmy, dither *rel* quail, shrink, recoil; vibrate, fluctuate, waver, swing; falter, vacillate, hesitate

qualified *syn* ABLE, competent, capable *rel* trained, instructed, disciplined; examined, quizzed, catechized; tested, tried, proved *ant* unqualified

qualify **1** *syn* MODERATE, temper *rel* modify, vary, alter, change; adapt, adjust, conform, accommodate, reconcile **2** *syn* CHARACTERIZE, distinguish, mark *rel* ascribe, impute, attribute, assign; predicate, assert **3** *syn* PREPARE, fit, condition, ready *rel* empower, enable; endow, endue, dower; train, instruct, teach

quality **1** • an intelligible feature by which a thing may be identified *syn* property, character, attribute, accident *rel* predication, affirmation; peculiarity, individuality, characteristic **2** • a usu. high level of merit or superiority *syn* stature, caliber *rel* excellence, virtue; value, worth

qualm • a misgiving about what one is doing or is going to do *syn* scruple, compunction, demur *rel* misgiving, apprehension, foreboding, presentiment; doubt, mistrust, suspicion, uncertainty

quandary *syn* PREDICAMENT, dilemma, plight, scrape, fix, jam, pickle *rel* juncture, pass, exigency, emergency, contingency, crisis; difficulty, hardship, vicissitude; puzzling, puzzle, mystification, perplexity, bewilderment

quantity *syn* SUM, amount, aggregate, total, whole, number

quarrel *n* • a usu. verbal dispute marked by anger or discord *syn* wrangle, altercation, squabble, bickering, spat, tiff *rel* brawl, broil, fracas, melee, row, rumpus, scrap; contention, dissension, conflict, difference, variance, strife, discord

quarrel *vb, syn* wrangle, altercate, squabble, bicker, spat, tiff *rel* contend, fight, battle, war; dispute, agitate, argue, discuss

quarrelsome *syn* BELLIGERENT, pugnacious, combative, bellicose, contentious *rel* antagonistic, adverse, counter; hostile, inimical, antipathetic, rancorous

quarry *syn* VICTIM, prey

quash **1** *syn* ANNUL, abrogate, void, vacate **2** *syn* CRUSH, quell, extinguish, suppress, quench *rel* destroy; ruin, wreck; repress

quaver *syn* SHAKE, tremble, shudder, quake, totter, quiver, shiver, wobble, teeter, shimmy, dither *rel* falter, waver, vacillate, hesitate; vibrate, fluctuate, sway, swing

quay *syn* WHARF, dock, pier, slip, berth, jetty, levee

queenly *syn* KINGLY, regal, royal, imperial, princely

queer *syn* STRANGE, odd, erratic, eccentric, peculiar, quaint, outlandish, curious *rel* dubious, doubtful, questionable; droll, funny, laughable; bizarre, grotesque, fantastic

quell *syn* CRUSH, extinguish, suppress, quench, quash *rel* destroy; wreck, ruin; subdue, subjugate, overcome, vanquish, conquer *ant* foment

quench *syn* CRUSH, quell, extinguish, suppress, quash *rel* repress, suppress; end, terminate

querulous *syn* IRRITABLE, fretful, petulant, pettish, huffy, peevish, fractious, snappish, waspish *rel* crying, weeping, wailing, whimpering, blubbering; touchy, cranky, cross, irascible; lamenting, deploring, bemoaning

query *syn* ASK, question, interrogate, inquire, examine, quiz, catechize

quest *syn* ADVENTURE, enterprise *rel* exploit, feat, achievement

question *syn* ASK, interrogate, query, inquire, examine, quiz, catechize *ant* answer

questionable *syn* DOUBTFUL, dubious, problematic *rel* uncertain, suspicious; obscure, vague, equivocal *ant* authoritative; unquestioned

quick **1** *syn* FAST, fleet, swift, rapid, speedy, expeditious, hasty *rel* brisk, nimble, agile; abrupt, impetuous, precipitate, headlong **2** • able to respond without delay or hesitation or indicative of such ability *syn* prompt, ready, apt *rel* intelligent, clever, smart, quick-witted; deft, adroit, dexterous; sharp, acute, keen *ant* sluggish

quicken **1** • to make alive or lively *syn* animate, enliven, vivify *rel* activate, vitalize, energize; rouse, arouse, stir *ant* deaden **2** *syn* PROVOKE, excite, stimulate, pique, galvanize *rel* activate, actuate, motivate; spur, goad, induce; incite, foment *ant* arrest **3** *syn* SPEED, hasten, hurry, accelerate, precipitate *ant* slacken

quick-witted *syn* INTELLIGENT, clever, bright, smart, alert, knowing, brilliant *rel* ready, prompt, quick, apt; sharp, keen, acute; witty, humorous, facetious

quiescent *syn* LATENT, dormant, potential, abeyant *rel* quiet, still, silent; inert, inactive, passive, supine

quiet *adj, syn* STILL, silent, noiseless, stilly *rel* calm, serene, placid, tranquil, peaceful *ant* unquiet

quiet, quieten *vb, syn* CALM, compose, still, lull, soothe, settle, tranquilize *rel* allay, alleviate, assuage, relieve; abate, lessen, decrease *ant* disquiet; arouse, rouse

quip *syn* JOKE, jest, jape, witticism, wisecrack, crack, gag

quit 1 *syn* BEHAVE, acquit, comport, deport, demean, conduct *rel* see ACQUIT **2** *syn* GO, leave, depart, withdraw, retire *rel* forsake, desert, abandon; relinquish, surrender, resign; escape, flee, fly, abscond **3** *syn* STOP, cease, discontinue, desist

quiver *syn* SHAKE, shiver, shudder, quaver, totter, tremble, quake, wobble, teeter, shimmy, dither *rel* pulsate, pulse, beat, throb, palpitate; flutter, flicker, flitter, flit

quixotic *syn* IMAGINARY, chimerical, fantastic, visionary, fanciful *rel* sentimental, romantic; utopian, ambitious; ideal, transcendental, abstract

quiz *syn* ASK, question, interrogate, examine, catechize, query, inquire

quote • to speak or write again something already said or written by another *syn* cite, repeat *rel* adduce, allege, advance

quotidian *syn* DAILY, diurnal, circadian

R

rabid *syn* FURIOUS, frantic, frenzied, wild, frenetic, delirious *rel* maddened, enraged, infuriated, incensed, angered; violent, compulsive; insane, crazed, crazy, demented, deranged

race *syn* VARIETY, subspecies, breed, cultivar, strain, clone, stock

rack *syn* AFFLICT, torment, torture, try *rel* persecute, oppress, wrong; harry, harass, worry, annoy

racket *syn* DIN, uproar, pandemonium, hullabaloo, babel, hubbub, clamor

racking *syn* EXCRUCIATING, agonizing *rel* torturing, tormenting; intense, vehement, fierce, exquisite, violent; fierce, ferocious, barbarous, savage, cruel, inhuman

racy *syn* PUNGENT, piquant, poignant, spicy, snappy *rel* exciting, stimulating, quickening, provoking, provocative; spirited, mettlesome, fiery, gingery, peppery

radiant *syn* BRIGHT, brilliant, luminous, lustrous, effulgent, refulgent, beaming, lambent, lucent, incandescent *rel* splendid, resplendent, glorious, sublime; sparkling, glittering, gleaming, flashing, scintillating

radiate *syn* SPREAD, circulate, disseminate, diffuse, propagate *rel* distribute, dispense; disperse, scatter, dissipate; diverge

radical 1 *syn* FUNDAMENTAL, basic, basal, underlying *rel* cardinal, essential, vital; inherent, intrinsic, constitutional *ant* superficial **2** *syn* LIBERAL, advanced, progressive

radius *syn* RANGE, gamut, reach, compass, sweep, scope, orbit, horizon, ken, purview

rag *syn* BANTER, chaff, kid, rib, josh, jolly

rage 1 *syn* ANGER, ire, fury, indignation, wrath *rel* acrimony, asperity, acerbity; frenzy, mania, hysteria; agitation, upset, perturbation **2** *syn* FASHION, style, mode, vogue, craze, cry, dernier cri, fad *rel* caprice, freak, conceit, vagary, crotchet, whim, fancy

raid *syn* INVASION, incursion, inroad *rel* attack, assault, onslaught, onset

rail *syn* SCOLD, revile, vituperate, rate, berate, upbraid, tongue-lash, jaw, bawl, chew out, wig *rel* censure, denounce, condemn, reprobate, reprehend, criticize; reprimand, rebuke, reprove, reproach

raillery *syn* BADINAGE, persiflage *rel* bantering, banter, chaffing, chaff; sport, fun, game, jest, play; satire, sarcasm, irony, wit

raiment *syn* CLOTHES, apparel, attire, clothing, dress

raise 1 *syn* LIFT, elevate, hoist, heave, rear, boost *rel* rise, ascend, mount, soar; exalt, magnify, aggrandize; advance, promote, forward, further **2** *syn* BUILD, construct, erect, frame, rear *ant* raze

rally *vb, syn* STIR, rouse, arouse, awaken, waken *rel* excite, stimulate, quicken, provoke; fire, light; renew, restore, refresh

rally *vb, syn* RIDICULE, deride, mock, taunt, twit *rel* scoff, jeer, gibe, flout; tease, tantalize, worry, harass, harry

ram *syn* PACK, crowd, cram, stuff, tamp *rel* press, squeeze, jam; compact, concentrate, consolidate; compress

ramble *syn* WANDER, stray, roam, rove, range, prowl, gad, gallivant, traipse, meander

rampant *syn* RANK *rel* luxuriant, lush, exuberant, profuse, lavish; immoderate, excessive, inordinate

rampart *syn* BULWARK, breastwork, parapet, bastion

rancid *syn* MALODOROUS, stinking, fetid, rank, noisome, putrid, fusty, musty *rel* decomposed, decayed, spoiled; offensive, loathsome, repulsive

rancor *syn* ENMITY, antagonism, animosity, animus, antipathy, hostility *rel* hate, hatred, detestation, abhorrence, abomination; spite, malice, malevolence, malignity, malignancy, spleen, grudge

random • determined by accident rather than by design *syn* haphazard, chance, chancy, casual, desultory, hit-or-miss, happy-go-lucky *rel* fortuitous, accidental, casual; vagrant, vagabond, truant

range *n* **1** *syn* HABITAT, biotope, station **2** • the extent that lies within the powers of something to cover or control *syn* gamut, reach, radius, compass, sweep, scope, orbit, horizon, ken, purview *rel* extent, area; field, domain, province, sphere, territory; spread, stretch, expanse, amplitude

range *vb* **1** *syn* LINE, line up, align, array *rel* arrange, order, marshal; assort, sort, classify; incline, dispose, predispose, bias **2** *syn* WANDER, rove, ramble, roam, stray, prowl, gad, gallivant, traipse, meander

rank *adj* **1** • growing or increasing at an immoderate rate *syn* rampant *rel* coarse, gross, vulgar; exuberant, profuse, lavish, luxuriant **2** *syn* MALODOROUS, fusty, musty, rancid, stinking, fetid, noisome, putrid *rel* dank, humid, wet; offensive, loathsome, repulsive; decomposed, decayed, spoiled *ant* balmy **3** *syn* FLAGRANT, glaring, gross *rel* conspicuous, outstanding, noticeable; foul, filthy, squalid, nasty, dirty; outrageous, heinous, atrocious, monstrous

rank *n, syn* LINE, row, file, echelon, tier

rank *vb, syn* CLASS, grade, rate, graduate, gradate *rel* order, arrange; classify, assort, sort; divide, separate

ransack *syn* SEEK, search, hunt, rummage, scour, comb, ferret out *rel* investigate; penetrate, pierce, probe; examine, inspect, scrutinize

ransom *syn* RESCUE, deliver, redeem, reclaim, save *rel* free, release, liberate, emancipate, manumit; expiate, atone

rant *syn* BOMBAST, fustian, rodomontade, rhapsody *rel* inflatedness, inflation, turgidity, tumidity, flatulence

rap *n, syn* TAP, knock, thump, thud *rel* beating, pummeling, pounding

rap *vb, syn* TAP, knock, thump, thud *rel* smite, strike; pummel, beat

rapacious *syn* VORACIOUS, ravening, ravenous, gluttonous *rel* ferocious, fierce; greedy, grasping, covetous

rapacity *syn* CUPIDITY, greed, avarice *rel* covetousness, avariciousness, greediness, graspingness; exaction, demanding, demand, claiming, claim

rapid *syn* FAST, swift, fleet, quick, speedy, hasty, expeditious *rel* brisk, nimble, agile; hurried, quickened *ant* deliberate; leisurely

rapscallion *syn* VILLAIN, scoundrel, blackguard, knave, rascal, rogue, scamp, miscreant *rel* vagabond, vagrant, tramp, hobo, bum

rapt *syn* INTENT, absorbed, engrossed *rel* ecstatic, transported, rapturous; enchanted, captivated, fascinated

rapture *syn* ECSTASY, transport *rel* bliss, beatitude, blessedness, felicity, happiness

rare **1** *syn* THIN, tenuous, slight, slender, slim **2** *syn* CHOICE, delicate, dainty, exquisite, elegant, recherché *rel* excelling, excellent, transcending, transcendent, surpassing; superlative, supreme, incomparable **3** *syn* INFREQUENT, scarce, uncommon, occasional, sporadic *rel* exceptional; singular, unique, curious, strange

rarefy *syn* THIN, attenuate, extenuate, dilute *rel* diminish, reduce, lessen, decrease; expand, distend, inflate

rascal *syn* VILLAIN, scoundrel, blackguard, knave, rogue, scamp, rapscallion, miscreant

rash *syn* ADVENTUROUS, daring, daredevil, reckless, foolhardy, venturesome *rel* precipitate, abrupt, impetuous, sudden, hasty; desperate, forlorn, despondent *ant* calculating

rasp *syn* SCRAPE, scratch, grate, grind *rel* abrade , excoriate, chafe, fret; irritate, exasperate, aggravate; annoy, vex, irk, bother

rate *vb, syn* SCOLD, berate, upbraid, tongue-lash, jaw, bawl, chew out, wig, rail, revile, vituperate *rel* reprove, reproach, rebuke, reprimand, admonish, chide; censure, condemn, denounce, reprehend, reprobate, criticize

rate *vb* **1** *syn* ESTIMATE, value, evaluate, appraise, assess, assay *rel* calculate, compute, reckon; decide, determine, settle **2** *syn* CLASS, grade, rank, graduate, gradate *rel* order, arrange, systematize, methodize; assort, sort, classify

ratify • to make something legally valid or operative usu. by formal approval or sanctioning *syn* confirm *rel* authorize, accredit, license, commission; sanction, approve, endorse; validate, authenticate, confirm

ratiocination *syn* INFERENCE *ant* intuition

ratiocinative *syn* INFERENTIAL *ant* intuitive

ration *n* • an amount allotted or made available esp. from a limited supply *syn* allowance, dole, pittance *rel* apportionment, portioning, portion; sharing, share, participation, partaking

ration *vb, syn* APPORTION, portion, prorate, parcel *rel* divide, distribute, dispense, deal, dole; share, partake, participate

rational • relating to, based on, or agreeable to reason *syn* reasonable *ant* irrational; animal (*of nature*); demented (*of state of mind*); absurd (*of actions, behavior*)

rationalize *syn* EXPLAIN, account, justify

rattle *syn* EMBARRASS, faze, discomfit, disconcert, abash *rel* confuse, muddle, addle; agitate, upset, perturb, disturb, fluster, flurry, discompose; bewilder, distract, perplex, puzzle

raucous *syn* LOUD, stentorian, earsplitting, hoarse, strident, stertorous *rel* rough, harsh; gruff, brusque, bluff

ravage • to lay waste by plundering or destroying *syn* devastate, waste, sack, pillage, despoil, spoliate *rel* destroy, demolish, raze; plunder, loot, rob; ruin, wreck; invade, trespass, encroach

ravening *syn* VORACIOUS, rapacious, ravenous, gluttonous *rel* greedy, acquisitive, grasping, covetous

ravenous *syn* VORACIOUS, ravening, rapacious, gluttonous *rel* grasping, greedy, acquisitive, covetous; fierce, ferocious

ravish *syn* TRANSPORT, enrapture, entrance *rel* rejoice, delight, regale, please

raw *syn* RUDE, crude, callow, green, rough, uncouth *rel* elementary, elemental; ignorant, untaught, untutored; immature, unmatured, unripe

rawboned *syn* LEAN, gaunt, angular, lank, lanky, spare, scrawny, skinny

ray • a shaft of light *syn* beam

raze *syn* DESTROY, demolish *rel* efface, obliterate, erase; eradicate, extirpate, exterminate; ruin, wreck; abolish, extinguish, annihilate

reach *vb* • to arrive at a point by effort or work *syn* gain, compass, achieve, attain *rel* effect, fulfill, execute, accomplish, perform; get, obtain, procure, secure

reach *n, syn* RANGE, gamut, radius, compass, sweep, scope, orbit, horizon, ken, purview *rel* extent, area, magnitude, size; spread, stretch, expanse; capacity, capability, ability

react *syn* ACT, operate, work, function, behave

readiness • the power of doing something without evidence of effort *syn* ease, facility, dexterity *rel* quickness, promptness, aptness; alacrity, celerity, legerity; fluency, eloquence, volubility

ready *adj, syn* QUICK, prompt, apt *rel* expert, adept, skilled, skillful, proficient, masterly; active, live, dynamic

ready *vb, syn* PREPARE, fit, qualify, condition

real • corresponding to known facts *syn* actual, true *rel* being, existing, existent, subsisting, subsistent; certain, necessary, inevitable *ant* unreal; apparent; imaginary

realize **1** • to bring into concrete existence something that has existed as an abstraction or a conception or a possibility *syn* actualize, embody, incarnate, materialize, externalize, objectify, hypostatize, reify *rel* effect, fulfill, execute, accomplish, achieve, perform **2** *syn* THINK, conceive, imagine, fancy, envisage, envision *rel* understand, comprehend, appreciate

reap • to do the work of collecting ripened crops *syn* glean, gather, garner, harvest *rel* collect, assemble

rear *vb* **1** *syn* BUILD, construct, erect, frame, raise **2** *syn* LIFT, raise, elevate, hoist, heave, boost *rel* rise, ascend, mount, soar; nurse, nurture, foster; breed, propagate

rear *adj, syn* POSTERIOR, after, back, hind, hinder *ant* front

reason *n* **1** • a point or points that support something open to question *syn* ground, argument, proof *rel* explanation, justification, rationalization **2** *syn* CAUSE, determinant, antecedent, occasion *rel* motive, incentive, inducement, impulse; basis, foundation, ground **3** • the power of the mind by which man attains truth or knowledge *syn* understanding, intuition *rel* mind, intellect, intelligence, brain; ratiocination, inference

reason *vb, syn* THINK, reflect, deliberate, speculate, cogitate *rel* infer, deduce, conclude, judge, gather

reasonable *syn* RATIONAL *rel* sensible, sane, prudent, judicious, wise; fair, equitable, just *ant* unreasonable

rebate *syn* DEDUCTION, abatement, discount

rebel • one who rises up against constituted authority or the established order *syn* insurgent, iconoclast *rel* opponent, antagonist, adversary; assailant, attacker

rebellion • an outbreak against authority *syn* revolution, uprising, revolt, insurrection, mutiny, putsch, coup *rel* sedition, treason; resistance, opposition, combating, withstanding

rebellious *syn* INSUBORDINATE, mutinous, seditious, factious, contumacious *rel* recalcitrant, refractory, intractable, unruly, ungovernable; estranged, alienated, disaffected *ant* acquiescent, resigned; submissive

rebound • to spring back to an original position or shape *syn* reverberate, recoil, resile, repercuss *rel* bound, skip, ricochet

rebuild *syn* MEND, repair, patch *rel* renew, restore, renovate, refresh

rebuke *syn* REPROVE, reprimand, admonish, reproach, chide *rel* rate, upbraid, scold, berate; criticize, reprehend, reprobate

rebut *syn* DISPROVE, refute, confute, controvert

recalcitrant *syn* UNRULY, refractory, intractable, headstrong, willful, ungovernable *rel* rebellious, insubordinate, factious, contumacious; obstinate, stubborn; resisting, opposing, withstanding *ant* amenable

recall **1** *syn* REMEMBER, recollect, remind, reminisce, bethink, mind *rel* evoke, elicit, extract, educe; stir, rouse, arouse, waken, awaken **2** *syn* REVOKE, reverse, repeal, rescind *rel* annul, abrogate, void; retract, abjure, recant

recant *syn* ABJURE, retract, renounce, forswear *rel* withdraw, remove

recede • to move backward *syn* retreat, retrograde, retract, back *rel* withdraw, retire, depart; rebound, recoil *ant* proceed; advance

receipt • a formula or set of directions for the compounding of ingredients esp. in cookery and medicine *syn* recipe, prescription

receive • to bring and accept into one's possession, one's presence, a group, or the mind *syn* accept, admit, take *rel* enter, penetrate; seize, grasp

recent *syn* MODERN, late *rel* fresh, new, new-fashioned

recess *syn* PAUSE, respite, lull, intermission *rel* withdrawal, retirement; break, interruption, interval, gap; relaxation, leisure, rest

recherché *syn* CHOICE, elegant, exquisite, delicate, dainty, rare *rel* fresh, original, new, novel; select, exclusive, picked *ant* banal

recipe *syn* RECEIPT, prescription

reciprocal **1** • shared, felt, or shown by both sides concerned *syn* mutual, common *rel* shared, participated, partaken; interchanged, exchanged; balancing, compensating, counterpoising **2** • like, equivalent, or similarly related to each other (as in kind, quality, or value) *syn* corresponding, correlative, complementary, complemental, convertible *rel* equivalent, identical, same; related, associated, linked, united

reciprocate • to give back usu. in kind or in quantity *syn* retaliate, requite, return *rel* interchange, exchange; repay, compensate, recompense

recite *syn* RELATE, rehearse, recount, narrate, describe, state, report *rel* enumerate, tell, count, number; detail, itemize, particularize

reckless *syn* ADVENTUROUS, daring, daredevil, rash, foolhardy, venturesome *rel* precipitate, sudden, hasty, headlong, impetuous, abrupt; desperate, hopeless, despondent *ant* calculating

reckon **1** *syn* CALCULATE, compute, estimate *rel* enumerate, count, number; figure, total, add, sum, cast, foot **2** *syn* CONSIDER, regard, account, deem *rel* think, conceive, imagine, envision; conjecture, surmise, guess **3** *syn* RELY, count, bank, trust, depend

reclaim *syn* RESCUE, save, ransom, redeem, deliver *rel* renew, restore, renovate; reform, rectify, remedy, correct, amend *ant* abandon

recluse • a person who leads a secluded or

solitary life *syn* hermit, eremite, anchorite, cenobite

recognition • a learning process that relates a perception of something new to knowledge already possessed *syn* identification, assimilation, apperception

recognize *syn* ACKNOWLEDGE *rel* accept, admit, receive; notice, note, observe, remark, see

recoil **1** • to draw back in fear or distaste *syn* shrink, flinch, wince, blench, quail *rel* waver, falter, hesitate; shy, balk, stick, stickle, demur *ant* confront; defy **2** *syn* REBOUND, reverberate, resile, repercuss *rel* retreat, recede, back, retract; return, revert

recollect *syn* REMEMBER, recall, remind, reminisce, bethink, mind *rel* stir, rouse, arouse, rally, waken, awaken

recollection *syn* MEMORY, remembrance, reminiscence, mind, souvenir

recommend *syn* COMMEND, compliment, applaud *rel* approve, endorse, sanction; praise, extol, acclaim

recommendation *syn* CREDENTIAL, testimonial, character, reference *rel* approval, endorsement; commendation

recompense *syn* PAY, reimburse, indemnify, repay, satisfy, remunerate, compensate *rel* award, accord, vouchsafe, grant; balance, offset

reconcile *syn* ADAPT, conform, accommodate, adjust *rel* harmonize, accord, square, agree; correct, rectify, amend, revise

recondite • beyond the reach of the average intelligence *syn* abstruse, occult, esoteric *rel* scholarly, erudite, learned; pedantic, scholastic, academic

record *vb* • to set down in writing usu. for the purpose of written evidence or official record of *syn* register, list, enroll, catalog *rel* enter, admit, introduce

record *n, syn* DOCUMENT, monument, archive

recount *syn* RELATE, recite, rehearse, narrate, describe, state, report *rel* enumerate, count, number, tell; detail, itemize, particularize

recoup *syn* RECOVER, recruit, retrieve, regain *rel* compensate, balance, offset, counterpoise

recover **1** • to get back again *syn* regain, retrieve, recoup, recruit *rel* redeem, reclaim, rescue; compensate, offset, balance **2** *syn* IMPROVE, recuperate, convalesce, gain *rel* restore, refresh, rejuvenate, renew; revive, resuscitate, revivify

recreant *syn* RENEGADE, apostate, turncoat, backslider *rel* treacherousness, treachery, perfidiousness, perfidy, traitorousness

recreate *syn* AMUSE, divert, entertain *rel* renew, restore, refresh, rejuvenate; enliven, quicken, animate

recreation *syn* AMUSEMENT, diversion, entertainment *rel* relaxation, repose, ease, rest; play, sport, frolic, rollick; mirth, jollity, hilarity

recrudesce *syn* RETURN, revert, recur *rel* renew, renovate, refurbish

recrudescence *syn* RETURN, reversion, recurrence *rel* renewal, restoration, refreshment, renovation

recruit *syn* RECOVER, regain, retrieve, recoup *rel* renew, restore, renovate, refresh; repair, mend, rebuild

rectify *syn* CORRECT, emend, amend, reform, revise, remedy, redress *rel* improve, better, help, ameliorate; mend, repair, rebuild; adjust, regulate, fix

rectitude *syn* GOODNESS, virtue, morality *rel* integrity, probity, honesty, honor; righteousness, nobility; uprightness, justness, conscientiousness, scrupulousness

recumbent *syn* PRONE, supine, prostrate, couchant, dormant *ant* upright, erect

recuperate *syn* IMPROVE, recover, convalesce, gain *rel* invigorate, strengthen, fortify, energize

recur *syn* RETURN, revert, recrudesce *rel* repeat, iterate, reiterate

recurrence *syn* RETURN, reversion, recrudescence *rel* relapse; repeating, repetition, iteration

recurrent *syn* INTERMITTENT, periodic, alternate *rel* rhythmic, metrical; returning, reverting, recrudescing; fitful, spasmodic

redact *syn* EDIT, compile, revise, rewrite, adapt

redeem *syn* RESCUE, deliver, ransom, save, reclaim *rel* free, liberate, release, emancipate, manumit; restore, renew, renovate; recover, regain

redolence *syn* FRAGRANCE, perfume, incense, bouquet *rel* odor, aroma, smell; balminess, aromaticness, aromaticity

redolent *syn* ODOROUS, aromatic, balmy, fragrant *rel* pungent, poignant, piquant, racy, spicy; penetrating, piercing

redress *vb, syn* CORRECT, emend, remedy,

amend, rectify, reform, revise *rel* relieve, lighten, alleviate, assuage, mitigate, allay; repair, mend

redress *n, syn* REPARATION, amends, restitution, indemnity *rel* compensation, offsetting, balancing; retaliation, reprisal, vengeance, retribution

reduce **1** *syn* DECREASE, lessen, diminish, abate, dwindle *rel* shorten, abridge, abbreviate, curtail, retrench; contract, shrink, condense **2** *syn* CONQUER, vanquish, defeat, subjugate, beat, overcome, lick, subdue, surmount, overthrow, rout *rel* weaken, cripple, disable, undermine, enfeeble; humble, humiliate, degrade, debase, abase **3** *syn* DEGRADE, demote, declass, disrate *rel* humble, humiliate, debase, abase

redundancy *syn* VERBIAGE, tautology, pleonasm, circumlocution, periphrasis *rel* wordiness, verbosity, prolixity, diffuseness; inflatedness, inflation, turgidity, tumidity, flatulence; bombast, rant, fustian

redundant *syn* WORDY, verbose, prolix, diffuse *rel* superfluous, surplus, supernumerary, extra, spare; repeating, repetitious, iterating, reiterating *ant* concise

reef *syn* SHOAL, bank, bar

reel • to move uncertainly or uncontrollably or unsteadily (as from weakness or intoxication) *syn* whirl, stagger, totter *rel* turn, spin, revolve, rotate; sway, waver, swing; wobble, teeter, quiver, shake

refer **1** *syn* ASCRIBE, assign, credit, accredit, attribute, impute, charge *rel* associate, relate, connect, join; direct, aim, point, lay **2** *syn* RESORT, apply, go, turn *rel* consult, confer, commune, advise; address, direct **3** • to call or direct attention to something *syn* allude, advert *rel* introduce, insert, interpolate; quote, cite

referee *syn* JUDGE, umpire, arbiter, arbitrator

reference *syn* CREDENTIAL, testimonial, recommendation, character

referendum *syn* MANDATE, initiative, plebiscite

refinement *syn* CULTURE, cultivation, breeding *rel* suavity, urbanity; courtesy, politeness, civility; elegance, grace, dignity *ant* vulgarity

reflect *syn* THINK, cogitate, reason, speculate, deliberate *rel* consider, contemplate, study, weigh; ponder, muse, meditate, ruminate

reflection *syn* ANIMADVERSION, stricture, aspersion *rel* imputing, imputation, ascribing, ascription; criticizing, criticism, reprehending, reprehension, blaming, blame; attack, assault, onslaught, onset; disparagement, derogation, depreciation

reflective *syn* THOUGHTFUL, contemplative, meditative, pensive, speculative *rel* thinking, reasoning, deliberating, cogitating; analytical, logical, subtle

reform *syn* CORRECT, rectify, emend, amend, remedy, redress, revise *rel* mend, repair, rebuild; better, improve, help, ameliorate

refractory *syn* UNRULY, recalcitrant, intractable, ungovernable, headstrong, willful *rel* contrary, perverse, froward, wayward; insubordinate, rebellious, contumacious *ant* malleable; amenable

refrain • to hold oneself back from doing or indulging in *syn* abstain, forbear *rel* check, arrest, interrupt; restrain, curb, inhibit

refresh *syn* RENEW, restore, rejuvenate, renovate, refurbish *rel* enliven, quicken, animate, vivify; recruit, recover, regain; recreate, amuse, divert *ant* jade, addle

refuge *syn* SHELTER, asylum, sanctuary, cover, retreat *rel* safety, security; stronghold, citadel, fort, fortress; harbor, haven, port

refulgent *syn* BRIGHT, effulgent, luminous, radiant, lustrous, brilliant, beaming, lambent, lucent, incandescent

refurbish *syn* RENEW, renovate, refresh, restore, rejuvenate

refuse *vb, syn* DECLINE, reject, repudiate, spurn *rel* deny, gainsay; balk, baffle, frustrate, thwart, foil; debar, exclude, shut out

refuse *n* • matter that is regarded as worthless and fit only for throwing away *syn* waste, rubbish, trash, debris, garbage, offal

refute *syn* DISPROVE, confute, rebut, controvert *rel* contradict, impugn, traverse, negative, contravene, deny

regain *syn* RECOVER, recruit, recoup, retrieve *rel* gain, reach, compass, attain, achieve; redeem, reclaim, save, rescue; restore, renew

regal *syn* KINGLY, royal, queenly, imperial, princely *rel* majestic, imposing, stately, magnificent, august, grand; splendid, resplendent, glorious, sublime

regale *syn* PLEASE, tickle, gratify, delight, rejoice, gladden *ant* vex

regard *n* • a feeling of deferential approval and liking *syn* respect, esteem, admiration *rel* deference, honor, homage, reverence; appreciation, cherishing, prizing, valuing *ant* despite

regard *vb* **1** • to recognize the worth of a person or thing *syn* respect, esteem, admire *rel* appreciate, cherish, value, prize, treasure *ant* despise **2** *syn* CONSIDER, account, reckon, deem *rel* rate, estimate, value, assess, assay

regarding *syn* ABOUT, concerning, respecting

region *syn* AREA, tract, zone, belt *rel* locality, vicinity, district, neighborhood; section, sector, division, part; field, territory, province

register *n, syn* LIST, table, catalog, schedule, roll, roster, inventory

register *vb, syn* RECORD, list, enroll, catalog *rel* enter, admit; insert, introduce; fix, establish, set; preserve, conserve, save

regressive *syn* BACKWARD, retrogressive, retrograde *ant* progressive

regret *syn* SORROW, grief, heartache, heartbreak, anguish, woe *rel* compunction, remorse, penitence, repentance, contrition; qualm, scruple, demur

regular **1** • being of the sort or kind that is expected as usual, ordinary, or average *syn* normal, typical, natural *rel* usual, habitual, customary; common, ordinary, familiar *ant* irregular **2** *syn* ORDERLY, methodical, systematic, regular *rel* fixed, set, settled; constant, even, equable, steady, uniform *ant* irregular

regulate *syn* ADJUST, fix *rel* order, arrange, organize, systematize, methodize; temper, moderate; correct, rectify

regulation *syn* LAW, rule, precept, statute, ordinance, canon *rel* instruction, direction, bidding; deciding, decision, determination, ruling

regurgitate *syn* BELCH, burp, vomit, disgorge, spew, throw up

rehearse *syn* RELATE, narrate, describe, recite, recount, state, report *rel* repeat, iterate, reiterate; detail, itemize, particularize

reify *syn* REALIZE, actualize, embody, incarnate, materialize, externalize, objectify, hypostatize

reimburse *syn* PAY, indemnify, repay, recompense, compensate, remunerate, satisfy *rel* recoup, recover; balance, offset

reinforce *syn* STRENGTHEN, invigorate, fortify, energize *rel* increase, augment, multiply, enlarge; support, sustain, prop, bolster, buttress

reissue *syn* EDITION, impression, reprinting, printing

reiterate *syn* REPEAT, iterate, ingeminate

reject *syn* DECLINE, repudiate, spurn, refuse *rel* discard, cast, shed; oust, expel, dismiss, eject; exclude, debar, shut out, eliminate *ant* accept; choose, select

rejoice *syn* PLEASE, delight, gladden, gratify, tickle, regale *ant* grieve; aggrieve; bewail

rejoin *syn* ANSWER, respond, reply, retort

rejoinder *syn* ANSWER, response, reply, retort *rel* returning, return, reverting, reversion; retaliation, reprisal

rejuvenate *syn* RENEW, restore, refresh, renovate, refurbish

relapse *n, syn* LAPSE, backsliding *rel* reversion, atavism, throwback; degeneration, decline, declension, decadence, deterioration

relapse *vb, syn* LAPSE, backslide *rel* revert, return; degenerate, decline, deteriorate

relate **1** • to tell orally or in writing the details or circumstances of a situation *syn* rehearse, recite, recount, narrate, describe, state, report *rel* tell, reveal, disclose, divulge; detail, itemize, particularize **2** *syn* JOIN, associate, link, connect, conjoin, combine, unite *rel* attach, fasten, fix; refer, assign, credit, impute, ascribe **3** *syn* BEAR, pertain, appertain, belong, apply

related • connected by or as if by family ties *syn* cognate, kindred, allied, affiliated *rel* associated, connected; reciprocal, corresponding, correlative, convertible, complementary; akin, identical, alike, analogous, like; relevant, germane, pertinent

relative *syn* DEPENDENT, contingent, conditional *ant* absolute

relaxation *syn* REST, repose, leisure, ease, comfort *rel* amusement, diversion, recreation; relieving, relief, assuagement, alleviation, mitigation

relaxed *syn* LOOSE, slack, lax *rel* mitigated, lightened, alleviated, assuaged, relieved;

flexuous, sinuous; soft, mild, gentle, lenient *ant* stiff

release *syn* FREE, liberate, emancipate, manumit, discharge, *rel* detach, disengage; exculpate, exonerate, acquit; surrender, resign, yield, relinquish; deliver, enfrancise *ant* detain; check; oblige

relegate *syn* COMMIT, entrust, confide, consign *rel* refer, assign, credit, accredit, charge, ascribe

relent *syn* YIELD, submit, capitulate, succumb, defer, bow, cave *rel* comply, acquiesce; forbear, refrain, abstain; abate, subside, wane, ebb

relentless *syn* GRIM, unrelenting, merciless, implacable *rel* inexorable, obdurate, adamant, inflexible; strict, stringent, rigid, rigorous; fierce, ferocious, cruel, inhuman

relevant • relating to or bearing upon the matter in hand *syn* germane, material, pertinent, apposite, applicable, apropos *rel* related, cognate, allied; fitting, appropriate, proper; important, significant, weighty *ant* extraneous

reliable • having qualities that merit confidence or trust *syn* dependable, trustworthy, trusty, tried *rel* safe, secure; infallible, inerrable, inerrant, unerring; cogent, valid, sound, convincing, compelling, telling *ant* dubious

reliance *syn* TRUST, confidence, dependence, faith *rel* credence, credit, belief, faith; assurance, conviction, certitude, certainty

relieve • to make something more tolerable or less grievous *syn* alleviate, lighten, assuage, mitigate, allay *rel* comfort, console, solace; moderate, qualify, temper; diminish, reduce, lessen, decrease *ant* intensify; embarrass; alarm

religion • a system of religious belief or the body of persons who accept such a system *syn* denomination, sect, cult, communion, faith, creed, persuasion, church

religious *adj* **1** *syn* DEVOUT, pious, pietistic, sanctimonious *rel* faithful, staunch, steadfast, true; virtuous, righteous, noble, moral, ethical; upright, just, honorable, honest *ant* irreligious **2** *syn* HOLY, spiritual, sacred, divine, blessed *ant* secular; profane

religious *n* • a member of a religious order usu. bound by monastic vows of poverty, chastity, and obedience *syn* monk, friar, nun

relinquish • to give up completely *syn* yield, leave, resign, surrender, cede, abandon, waive *rel* abdicate, renounce; desert, forsake; forgo, forbear, abnegate, sacrifice; discard, shed, cast *ant* keep

relish *n* **1** *syn* TASTE, savor, tang, flavor, smack **2** *syn* TASTE, palate, gusto, zest *rel* liking, loving, enjoying, relishing; predilection, partiality, prepossession, prejudice, bias; propensity, leaning, flair, penchant

relish *vb, syn* LIKE, fancy, dote, enjoy, love *rel* appreciate, understand, comprehend; approve, endorse, sanction

relishing *syn* PALATABLE, appetizing, savory, sapid, tasty, toothsome, flavorsome *rel* pleasing, gratifying, delighting, rejoicing, tickling, regaling

reluctant *syn* DISINCLINED, indisposed, hesitant, loath, averse *rel* cautious, circumspect, chary, wary, calculating; antipathetic, unsympathetic

rely on, rely upon • to have or place full confidence *syn* trust, depend, count, reckon, bank *rel* confide, entrust, commit; hope, expect, look, await

remain *syn* STAY, wait, abide, tarry, linger *ant* depart

remainder • a remaining or left-over group, part, or trace *syn* residue, residuum, remains, leavings, rest, balance, remnant

remains *syn* REMAINDER, leavings, residue, residuum, rest, balance, remnant

remark *vb* **1** *syn* SEE, notice, note, observe, perceive, discern, behold, descry, espy, view, survey, contemplate **2** • to make observations and pass judgment thereon *syn* comment, commentate, animadvert

remark *n* • an expression of opinion or judgment *syn* observation, comment, commentary, note, obiter dictum

remarkable *syn* NOTICEABLE, prominent, outstanding, conspicuous, salient, signal, striking, arresting *rel* exceptional; important, significant, weighty, momentous; singular, unique, peculiar, strange

remedial *syn* CURATIVE, restorative, sanative, corrective *rel* healing, curing

remedy *n* • something prescribed or used for the treatment of disease *syn* cure, medicine, medicament, medication, specific, physic

remedy *vb* **1** *syn* CURE, heal **2** *syn* CORRECT, rectify, emend, amend, redress, reform, revise *rel* relieve, assuage, alleviate, lighten, mitigate; restore, renew, refresh

remember • to bring an image or idea from the past into the mind *syn* recollect, recall, remind, reminisce, bethink, mind *ant* forget

remembrance **1** *syn* MEMORY, recollection, reminiscence, mind, souvenir *ant* forgetfulness **2** • something that serves to keep a person or thing in mind *syn* remembrancer, reminder, memorial, memento, token, keepsake, souvenir *rel* gift, present, favor

remembrancer *syn* REMEMBRANCE, reminder, memorial, memento, token, keepsake, souvenir

remind *syn* REMEMBER, recollect, recall, reminisce, bethink, mind *rel* suggest, intimate, hint, imply

reminder *syn* REMEMBRANCE, remembrancer, memorial, memento, token, keepsake, souvenir *rel* memorandum; intimation, hint, suggestion

reminisce *syn* REMEMBER, recollect, recall, remind, bethink, mind

reminiscence *syn* MEMORY, remembrance, recollection, mind, souvenir

remiss *syn* NEGLIGENT, lax, slack, neglectful *rel* careless, heedless, thoughtless; forgetful, oblivious, unmindful; indolent, slothful, faineant, lazy *ant* scrupulous

remit **1** *syn* EXCUSE, pardon, forgive, condone *rel* exculpate, exonerate, acquit, vindicate, absolve **2** *syn* SEND, forward, transmit, route, ship, dispatch

remnant *syn* REMAINDER, residue, residuum, remains, leavings, rest, balance *rel* part, piece, fragment, segment, section; vestige, trace

remonstrate *syn* OBJECT, expostulate, protest, kick *rel* oppose, combat, resist, withstand, fight; criticize, denounce, reprobate

remorse *syn* PENITENCE, repentance, contrition, attrition, compunction *rel* regret, sorrow, grief; qualm, scruple, demur

remote *syn* DISTANT, far, faraway, far-off, removed *ant* close

remove *syn* MOVE, shift, transfer *rel* convey, carry, bear, transport, transmit; eradicate, extirpate, uproot, exterminate

removed *syn* DISTANT, remote, far-off, faraway, far

remunerate *syn* PAY, compensate, satisfy, reimburse, indemnify, repay, recompense *rel* award, accord, vouchsafe, grant

remunerative *syn* PAYING, gainful, lucrative, profitable *rel* handsome, bountiful, munificent, liberal; lavish, prodigal, profuse

rend *syn* TEAR, split, cleave, rive, rip *rel* separate, divide, sever, sunder

rendezvous *syn* ENGAGEMENT, tryst, appointment, assignation, date

renegade • a person who forsakes his or her faith, party, cause, or allegiance and aligns with another *syn* apostate, turncoat, recreant, backslider *rel* rebel, insurgent, iconoclast; deserter, forsaker, abandoner; heretic, schismatic *ant* adherent

renew • to make like new *syn* restore, refresh, renovate, refurbish, rejuvenate *rel* mend, repair, rebuild; reform, revise, rectify, correct

renounce **1** *syn* ABDICATE, resign *rel* sacrifice, abnegate, forgo, forbear, eschew *ant* arrogate; covet **2** *syn* ABJURE, forswear, recant, retract *rel* reject, repudiate, spurn; forgo, forbear, eschew *ant* confess; claim

renovate *syn* RENEW, refurbish, rejuvenate, restore, refresh *rel* mend, repair, patch; clean, cleanse

renown *syn* FAME, honor, glory, celebrity, reputation, repute, notoriety, éclat *rel* prestige, authority, influence, weight, credit

renowned *syn* FAMOUS, famed, celebrated, eminent, illustrious *rel* praised, acclaimed, lauded, extolled; outstanding, signal, prominent

rent *vb, syn* HIRE, let, lease, charter

rent *n, syn* BREACH, break, split, schism, rupture, rift *rel* separation, severance, division; tearing, tear, cleaving, cleavage; interruption, gap, hiatus

renunciation • voluntary surrender or putting aside of something desired or desirable *syn* abnegation, self-abnegation, self-denial *rel* sacrificing, sacrifice, forgoing, forbearing, eschewing

repair *syn* MEND, patch, rebuild *rel* remedy, redress, amend, emend, rectify, correct; renew, renovate, refurbish, restore

reparation • a return for something lost or

suffered, usu. through the fault of another *syn* redress, amends, restitution, indemnity *rel* expiation, atonement; compensation, remuneration, recompensing, recompense

repartee *syn* WIT, humor, irony, sarcasm, satire *rel* retort, rejoinder, response; badinage, persiflage, raillery

repay *syn* PAY, compensate, remunerate, recompense, satisfy, reimburse, indemnify *rel* balance, offset; accord, award

repeal *syn* REVOKE, reverse, rescind, recall *rel* abrogate, annul, void; cancel, expunge, erase

repeat **1** • to say or do again *syn* iterate, reiterate, ingeminate *rel* return, recur, revert, recrudesce; rehearse, recite, recount, relate **2** *syn* QUOTE, cite

repellent *syn* REPUGNANT, abhorrent, distasteful, obnoxious, invidious *rel* offensive, loathsome, repulsive, revolting *ant* attractive; pleasing

repentance *syn* PENITENCE, contrition, attrition, remorse, compunction *rel* regret, sorrow, grief

repercuss *syn* REBOUND, reverberate, recoil, resile

replace • to put out of a usual or proper place or into the place of another *syn* displace, supplant, supersede *rel* restore, renew; change, alter; recover, regain, recoup, retrieve

replete *syn* FULL, complete, plenary *rel* abundant, plentiful; sated, satiated, surfeited

replica *syn* REPRODUCTION, facsimile, duplicate, copy, carbon copy, transcript

reply *vb, syn* ANSWER, respond, rejoin, retort

reply *n, syn* ANSWER, response, rejoinder, retort *rel* acknowledgment, recognition

report *n* **1** • common talk or an instance of it that spreads rapidly *syn* rumor, gossip, hearsay *rel* talking, talk, conversing, conversation, speaking, speech; chatting, chattering, chatter, prating; news, tidings, intelligence, advice **2** *syn* ACCOUNT, story, chronicle, version **3** *syn* LETTER, dispatch, message, note, epistle, missive, memorandum

report *vb, syn* RELATE, narrate, describe, state, recite, recount, rehearse *rel* communicate, impart; reveal, disclose, discover, tell, divulge

repose *syn* REST, relaxation, leisure, ease, comfort *rel* calmness, tranquillity, serenity, placidity, peacefulness; refreshment, restoration, renewal

reprehend *syn* CRITICIZE, censure, reprobate, condemn, denounce, blame *rel* reprove, rebuke, reprimand, admonish, reproach, chide; scold, upbraid, berate, rate

represent • to present an image or lifelike imitation of (as in art) *syn* depict, portray, delineate, picture, limn *rel* exhibit, display, show; suggest, hint; sketch, outline, draft; describe, narrate, relate

representative *syn* DELEGATE, deputy

repress *syn* SUPPRESS *rel* restrain, curb, check, inhibit; subdue, overcome, conquer

reprimand *syn* REPROVE, rebuke, reproach, admonish, chide *rel* upbraid, rate, berate, scold; censure, denounce, blame, reprehend, reprobate, criticize

reprinting *syn* EDITION, impression, printing, reissue

reprisal *syn* RETALIATION, retribution, revenge, vengeance

reproach *syn* REPROVE, chide, admonish, rebuke, reprimand *rel* criticize, reprehend, censure, reprobate; warn, forewarn, caution; counsel, advise

reprobate *vb, syn* CRITICIZE, censure, reprehend, blame, condemn, denounce *rel* decry, derogate, detract, depreciate, disparage; reject, repudiate, spurn; reprimand, rebuke, reprove

reprobate *adj, syn* ABANDONED, profligate, dissolute *rel* vicious, iniquitous, corrupt, degenerate; blameworthy, guilty, culpable *ant* elect (*in theology*)

reprobate *n, syn* OUTCAST, castaway, derelict, pariah, untouchable *rel* sinner, offender; transgressor, trespasser; villain, scoundrel, blackguard

reproduce *syn* GENERATE, propagate, engender, breed, beget, get, sire, procreate *rel* produce, bear, yield; multiply, increase

reproduction • a thing made to closely resemble another *syn* duplicate, copy, carbon copy, facsimile, replica, transcript

reprove • to criticize adversely *syn* rebuke, reprimand, admonish, reproach, chide *rel* criticize, reprehend, censure, reprobate; chasten, correct, discipline, punish

repudiate **1** *syn* DECLINE, spurn, reject, refuse *rel* renounce, abjure; forgo, forbear, eschew, sacrifice *ant* adopt **2** *syn* DISCLAIM, disavow, disown, disallow *rel* abandon, desert, forsake; discard, cast *ant* own

repugnant **1** • so alien or unlikable as to arouse antagonism and aversion *syn* repellent, abhorrent, distasteful, obnoxious, invidious *rel* foreign, alien, extraneous, extrinsic; uncongenial, incompatible, incongruous, inconsonant; antipathetic, averse, unsympathetic *ant* congenial **2** *syn* OFFENSIVE, repulsive, revolting, loathsome *rel* odious, hateful, abominable, detestable; foul, nasty, dirty; vile, base, low

repulsive *syn* OFFENSIVE, repugnant, revolting, loathsome *rel* repellent, repugnant, abhorrent, obnoxious *ant* alluring, captivating

reputation *syn* FAME, repute, renown, honor, glory, celebrity, éclat, notoriety *rel* credit, weight, influence, authority, prestige

repute *syn* FAME, reputation, renown, celebrity, notoriety, éclat, honor, glory *ant* disrepute

reputed *syn* SUPPOSED, supposititious, suppositious, putative, purported, conjectural, hypothetical *rel* assumed, presumed

request *syn* ASK, solicit *rel* beg, entreat, beseech, implore, supplicate, importune; appeal, petition, sue, pray

require **1** *syn* DEMAND, exact, claim *rel* prescribe, assign, define; warrant, justify **2** *syn* LACK, want, need

requirement • something essential to the existence or occurrence of something else *syn* requisite, prerequisite

requisite *adj, syn* NEEDFUL, necessary, indispensable, essential *rel* compelled, compulsory, constrained, obliged, obligatory; fundamental, cardinal, vital

requisite *n, syn* REQUIREMENT, prerequisite

requite *syn* RECIPROCATE, retaliate, return *rel* repay, recompense, compensate, pay; satisfy, content; revenge, avenge

rescind *syn* REVOKE, reverse, repeal, recall *rel* cancel, expunge, erase; abrogate, annul, void

rescue • to set free from confinement or danger *syn* deliver, redeem, ransom, reclaim, save *rel* free, release, liberate, emancipate, manumit; preserve, conserve, save; extricate, disentangle, disembarrass

research *syn* INQUIRY, investigation, inquisition, inquest, probe

resemblance *syn* LIKENESS, similarity, similitude, analogy, affinity *rel* correspondence, agreement, harmonizing, harmony, conformity; comparison, parallel *ant* difference; distinction

resentment *syn* OFFENSE, umbrage, pique, dudgeon, huff *rel* rancor, animus, animosity, antipathy, antagonism, enmity; ill will, spite, malice, malignity, malignancy

reservation *syn* CONDITION, stipulation, terms, provision, proviso, strings *rel* limitation, restriction, circumscription; exception

reserve *syn* KEEP, keep back, keep out, hold, hold back, retain, withhold, detain *rel* save, preserve, conserve; appropriate, preempt, confiscate, arrogate

reserved *syn* SILENT, reticent, uncommunicative, taciturn, secretive, close, close-lipped, close-mouthed, tight-lipped *rel* aloof, detached, uninterested, disinterested, indifferent; shy, diffident, modest, bashful; formal, ceremonious, conventional, ceremonial *ant* affable; expansive; blatant

reside • to have as one's habitation or domicile *syn* live, dwell, sojourn, lodge, stay, put up, stop *rel* remain, abide; continue, endure

residence *syn* HABITATION, dwelling, abode, domicile, home, house

resident *syn* INHABITANT, denizen, citizen

residue, residuum *syn* REMAINDER, remains, leavings, rest, balance, remnant

resign **1** *syn* RELINQUISH, yield, surrender, leave, abandon, cede, waive *rel* forgo, eschew, sacrifice, forbear, abnegate; abjure, renounce, forswear **2** *syn* ABDICATE, renounce

resignation **1** *syn* COMPLIANCE, acquiescence *rel* submitting, submission, yielding, deferring, deference; meekness, modesty, humbleness, humility, lowliness **2** *syn* PATIENCE, long-suffering, longanimity, forbearance *rel* endurance, toleration, suffering, sufferance; fortitude, backbone, pluck

resigned *syn* COMPLIANT, acquiescent *rel* submissive, subdued, tame; reconciled, adjusted, adapted, accommodated, conformed *ant* rebellious

resile *syn* REBOUND, recoil, reverberate, repercuss

resilient **1** *syn* ELASTIC, springy, flexible, supple *rel* recoiling, resiling, rebounding; recovering, regaining, retrieving **2** *syn* ELASTIC, expansive, buoyant, volatile, effervescent *rel* responsive, sympathetic; spirited, high-spirited, mettlesome *ant* flaccid

resist • to stand firm against a person or influence *syn* withstand, contest, oppose, fight, combat, conflict, antagonize *rel* assail, attack, assault; impugn, gainsay, contravene; thwart, baffle, balk, foil, frustrate *ant* submit; abide

resolute *syn* FAITHFUL, steadfast, staunch, true, loyal *rel* determined, decided, resolved; intrepid, valiant, brave, courageous; stubborn, obstinate, pertinacious

resolution **1** *syn* ANALYSIS, dissection, breakdown *rel* separation, division; elucidation, interpretation, expounding, exposition, explaining, explanation **2** *syn* COURAGE, mettle, spirit, tenacity *rel* pluck, grit, fortitude, backbone, guts

resolve **1** *syn* ANALYZE, dissect, break down *rel* separate, part, divide; reduce, diminish, decrease; melt, fuse *ant* blend **2** *syn* DECIDE, determine, settle, rule *rel* purpose, propose, design, intend, mean; plan, scheme, project **3** *syn* SOLVE, unfold, unravel, decipher *rel* dispel, dissipate, disperse; clear, rid, purge, disabuse

resolved *syn* decided, decisive, determined

resonant • marked by conspicuously full and rich sounds or tones (as of speech or music) *syn* sonorous, ringing, resounding, vibrant, orotund *rel* full, replete; rich, opulent; intensified, enhanced, heightened

resort *n, syn* RESOURCE, expedient, shift, makeshift, stopgap, substitute, surrogate *rel* see RESOURCE 2

resort *vb* • to betake oneself or to have recourse when in need of help or relief *syn* refer, apply, go, turn *rel* direct, address, devote; use, employ, utilize

resounding *syn* RESONANT, sonorous, ringing, vibrant, orotund *rel* loud, stentorian, earsplitting; intensified, heightened

resource **1** *pl* **resources** *syn* POSSESSIONS, assets, belongings, effects, means **2** • something one turns to in the absence of the usual means or source of supply *syn* resort, expedient, shift, makeshift, stopgap, substitute, surrogate *rel* device, contrivance, contraption; invention, creation; method, manner, way, fashion, mode, system

respect *n, syn* REGARD, esteem, admiration *rel* reverence, awe, fear; honor, homage, deference; veneration, worship, adoration *ant* contempt

respect *vb, syn* REGARD, esteem, admire *rel* reverence, revere, venerate; value, prize, cherish, appreciate *ant* abuse; misuse

respecting *syn* ABOUT, concerning, regarding

respectively *syn* EACH, apiece, severally, individually

respite *syn* PAUSE, recess, lull, intermission *rel* leisure, ease, rest; interruption, interval, break

resplendent *syn* SPLENDID, gorgeous, glorious, sublime, superb *rel* effulgent, refulgent, radiant, brilliant, bright; blazing, glowing, flaming

respond *syn* ANSWER, reply, rejoin, retort *rel* react, behave, act

response *syn* ANSWER, reply, rejoinder, retort

responsible • subject to being held to account *syn* answerable, accountable, amenable, liable *rel* subject, open, exposed; reliable, dependable, trustworthy

responsive **1** *syn* SENTIENT, sensitive, impressible, impressionable, susceptible *rel* answering, responding, replying; reacting, acting, behaving *ant* impassive **2** *syn* TENDER, sympathetic, warm, warmhearted, compassionate *rel* gentle, mild, lenient, soft; sensible, conscious, alive, awake, aware; sensitive, susceptible, prone, liable

rest *n* • freedom from toil or strain *syn* repose, relaxation, leisure, ease, comfort *rel* intermitting, intermission, suspending, suspension, deferring; stillness, quietness, quiet, silentness, silence; calmness, calm, tranquillity, serenity

rest *vb, syn* BASE, found, ground, bottom, stay *rel* depend, hang, hinge; rely, count

rest *n, syn* REMAINDER, residue, residuum, remains, leavings, balance, remnant *rel* excess, superfluity, surplus, surplusage, overplus

restful *syn* COMFORTABLE, cozy, snug, easy *rel* soft, gentle, mild, lenient; still, quiet, silent; placid, peaceful, calm, serene, tranquil

restitution *syn* REPARATION, amends, redress, indemnity *rel* repayment, recompense, reimbursement

restive **1** *syn* CONTRARY, perverse, balky, froward, wayward *rel* intractable, unruly, ungovernable, refractory; obstinate, stubborn, mulish, stiff-necked, pigheaded **2** *syn* IMPATIENT, restless, nervous, unquiet, uneasy, fidgety, jumpy, jittery *rel* see RESTLESS

restless *syn* IMPATIENT, restive, nervous, unquiet, uneasy, fidgety, jumpy, jittery *rel* fitful, spasmodic; inconstant, capricious, unstable, fickle; agitated, disquieted, perturbed, discomposed

restorative *syn* CURATIVE, remedial, corrective, sanative *rel* stimulating, quickening

restore **1** *syn* RENEW, refresh, rejuvenate, renovate, refurbish *rel* save, reclaim, redeem, rescue; reform, revise, amend, correct; recover, regain, retrieve, recoup, recruit **2** • to help or cause to regain signs of life and vigor *syn* revive, revivify, resuscitate *rel* cure, heal, remedy; arouse, rouse, rally, stir

restrain • to hold back from or control in doing something *syn* curb, check, bridle, inhibit *rel* arrest, interrupt; abstain, refrain, forbear; hinder, impede, obstruct, block *ant* impel; incite; activate; abandon (*oneself*)

restraint *syn* FORCE, constraint, compulsion, coercion, duress, violence *rel* curbing, checking, inhibiting; hindering, impeding, obstructing, blocking *ant* incitement; liberty

restrict *syn* LIMIT, circumscribe, confine *rel* bind, tie; contract, shrink; restrain, curb, check

result *syn* EFFECT, consequence, upshot, aftereffect, aftermath, sequel, issue, outcome, event *rel* concluding, conclusion, ending, end, closing, close, termination; product, production

resuscitate *syn* RESTORE, revive, revivify *rel* reanimate; rekindle

retain *syn* KEEP, keep back, keep out, detain, withhold, reserve, hold, hold back *rel* have, own, possess, enjoy; save, preserve, conserve

retaliate *syn* RECIPROCATE, requite, return *rel* revenge, avenge; repay, recompense, compensate, pay

retaliation • the act of inflicting or the intent to inflict injury in return for injury *syn* reprisal, revenge, vengeance, retribution *rel* punishment, disciplining, discipline, correcting, correction; recompensing, recompense, indemnification, repayment

retard *syn* DELAY, slow, slacken, detain *rel* reduce, lessen, decrease; arrest, check, interrupt; clog, fetter, hamper; balk, baffle, frustrate *ant* accelerate; advance, further

reticent *syn* SILENT, reserved, uncommunicative, taciturn, secretive, close, close-lipped, closemouthed, tight-lipped *rel* restrained, inhibited, curbed, checked; discreet, prudent *ant* frank

retire *syn* GO, withdraw, leave, depart, quit *rel* recede, retreat; recoil, rebound, resile; relinquish, yield, surrender, abandon

retort *vb, syn* ANSWER, rejoin, reply, respond

retort *n, syn* ANSWER, rejoinder, reply, response *rel* retaliation, reprisal, revenge; repartee

retract **1** *syn* RECEDE, retrograde, back, retreat *ant* protract **2** *syn* ABJURE, recant, renounce, forswear *rel* eliminate, exclude, suspend, rule out

retreat *n, syn* SHELTER, cover, refuge, asylum, sanctuary *rel* harbor, haven, port; safety, security; seclusion, solitude

retreat *vb, syn* RECEDE, retrograde, back, retract *rel* withdraw, retire, depart, go; recoil, shrink, quail

retrench *syn* SHORTEN, curtail, abridge, abbreviate *rel* decrease, lessen, reduce, diminish

retribution *syn* RETALIATION, reprisal, vengeance, revenge *rel* reparation, redress, amends, restitution; visitation, tribulation, trial, affliction

retrieve *syn* RECOVER, regain, recoup, recruit *rel* amend, remedy, redress, reform, correct; repair, mend, rebuild *ant* lose

retrograde *adj, syn* BACKWARD, retrogressive, regressive *rel* reversed, inverted; relapsing, lapsing, backsliding

retrograde *vb, syn* RECEDE, retreat, back, retract *rel* return, revert; reverse, invert; relapse, lapse, backslide

retrogressive *syn* BACKWARD, regressive, retrograde *rel* reversing, inverting; receding, retreating, retrograding *ant* progressive

return *vb* **1** • to go or come back (as to a person, place, or condition) *syn* revert, recur, recrudesce *rel* advert; turn, rotate, revolve; restore, renew; recover, regain; reverberate, repercuss, rebound **2** *syn* RECIPROCATE, retaliate, requite *rel* repay, recompense, compensate; give, bestow

return *n* • the act of coming back to or from a place or condition *syn* reversion, recurrence, recrudescence

reveal • to make known what has been or should be concealed *syn* discover, disclose, divulge, tell, betray *rel* impart, communicate; suggest, adumbrate, shadow; declare, announce, publish *ant* conceal

revelation • disclosure or something disclosed by or as if by divine or preternatural means *syn* vision, apocalypse, prophecy *ant* adumbration

revenant *syn* APPARITION, phantasm, phantom, wraith, ghost, spirit, specter, shade

revenge *vb, syn* AVENGE *rel* recompense, repay, pay; vindicate, defend, justify

revenge *n, syn* RETALIATION, vengeance, retribution, reprisal *rel* reparation, redress, amends; recompensing, recompense, repayment

revengeful *syn* VINDICTIVE, vengeful *rel* implacable, relentless, unrelenting, merciless, grim; inexorable, obdurate, adamant, inflexible

reverberate *syn* REBOUND, repercuss, recoil, resile *rel* return, revert, recur

revere • to honor and admire profoundly and respectfully *syn* reverence, venerate, worship, adore *rel* esteem, respect, regard, admire; cherish, prize, value, treasure, appreciate *ant* flout

reverence *n* **1** *syn* HONOR, homage, deference, obeisance *rel* piety, devotion, fealty, loyalty, fidelity; esteem, respect, regard, admiration **2** • a feeling of worshipful respect *syn* veneration, worship, adoration *rel* fervor, ardor, zeal, passion; devoutness, piousness, religiousness **3** • the emotion inspired by what arouses one's deep respect or veneration *syn* awe, fear

reverence *vb, syn* REVERE, venerate, worship, adore *rel* love, enjoy, like; esteem, respect, regard, admire

reverse *vb* **1** • to change to the opposite position *syn* transpose, invert *rel* overturn, upset, capsize **2** *syn* REVOKE, repeal, rescind, recall *rel* upset, overturn; retract, recant, abjure, forswear; abrogate, annul

reverse *n, syn* OPPOSITE, contradictory, contrary, antithesis, antipode, antonym, converse, counter

reversion **1** *syn* RETURN, recurrence, recrudescence **2** • a return to an ancestral type or condition or an instance of such return *syn* atavism, throwback *rel* relapse, lapse, backsliding

reversionary • relating to a return to an ancestral type *syn* atavistic

revert *syn* RETURN, recur, recrudesce *rel* recede, retreat, retrograde, back; lapse, relapse, backslide

review **1** *syn* CRITICISM, critique, blurb, puff **2** *syn* JOURNAL, periodical, magazine, organ, newspaper

revile *syn* SCOLD, vituperate, rail, berate, rate, upbraid, tongue-lash, jaw, bawl, chew out, wig *rel* vilify, calumniate, malign, traduce, defame, asperse, slander, libel; execrate, objurgate, curse *ant* laud

revise **1** *syn* CORRECT, rectify, emend, remedy, redress, amend, reform *rel* improve, better, ameliorate; change, alter, modify **2** *syn* EDIT, compile, redact, rewrite, adapt *rel* amend, emend, correct, rectify; improve, better

revive *syn* RESTORE, revivify, resuscitate *rel* recover, recruit, regain; recuperate, improve, gain; refresh, rejuvenate, renew

revivify *syn* RESTORE, revive, resuscitate *rel* reanimate; vitalize, activate, energize; galvanize, quicken, stimulate, provoke

revoke • to annul by recalling or taking back *syn* reverse, repeal, rescind, recall *rel* annul, abrogate, void; cancel, expunge, erase; invalidate, nullify

revolt *syn* REBELLION, revolution, uprising, insurrection, mutiny, putsch, coup *rel* insubordination, seditiousness, sedition, factiousness, contumaciousness, contumacy

revolting *syn* OFFENSIVE, loathsome, repulsive, repugnant *rel* horrible, horrid,horrific; repellent, distasteful, obnoxious, abhorrent; odious, hateful, abominable

revolution *syn* REBELLION, uprising, revolt, insurrection, mutiny, putsch, coup *rel* overthrowing, overthrow, subverting, subversion, upsetting, upset, overturning, overturn; change, modification, alteration

revolve *syn* TURN, rotate, gyrate, circle, spin, twirl, whirl, wheel, eddy, swirl, pirouette *rel* swing, sway, oscillate, vibrate

reward *syn* PREMIUM, prize, award, meed, guerdon, bounty, bonus

rewrite *syn* EDIT, compile, revise, redact, adapt

rhapsody *syn* BOMBAST, rant, fustian, rodomontade

rhetorical • emphasizing style often at the expense of thought *syn* grandiloquent, magniloquent, aureate, flowery, euphuistic, bombastic *rel* eloquent, articulate, vocal, fluent, voluble, glib; florid, ornate, flamboyant; inflated, turgid, tumid, flatulent

rhymer, rhymester *syn* POET, versifier, poetaster, bard, minstrel, troubadour

rhythm • the regular rise and fall in intensity of sounds that is associated chiefly with poetry and music *syn* meter, cadence

rib *syn* BANTER, chaff, kid, rag, josh, jolly

ribald *syn* COARSE, obscene, gross, vulgar *rel* offensive, loathsome; indecent, indelicate, indecorous; lewd, lascivious, wanton, licentious; scurrilous, opprobrious

ribbon *syn* STRIP, fillet, band, stripe

rich • having goods, property, and money in abundance *syn* wealthy, affluent, opulent *ant* poor

ricochet *syn* SKIP, bound, hop, curvet, lope, lollop

rid • to set a person or thing free of something that encumbers *syn* clear, unburden, disabuse, purge *rel* free, release, liberate; exterminate, extirpate, eradicate, uproot; abolish, extinguish

riddle *syn* MYSTERY, puzzle, conundrum, enigma, problem

ride *vb* **1** • to travel by automobile or other conveyance *syn* drive **2** *syn* BAIT, badger, heckle, hector, chivy, hound *rel* worry, annoy, harass, harry; persecute, oppress; torment, torture, afflict

ride *n* • a usu. short trip in a vehicle or by other conveyance *syn* drive *rel* journey, tour, trip, excursion, expedition

ridicule • to make an object of laughter of *syn* deride, mock, taunt, twit, rally *rel* scoff, flout, jeer, gibe; caricature, burlesque, travesty

ridiculous *syn* LAUGHABLE, risible, ludicrous, droll, funny, comic, comical, farcical *rel* absurd, preposterous, foolish, silly; amusing, diverting, entertaining; fantastic, grotesque, bizarre, antic

rife *syn* PREVAILING, prevalent, current *rel* abundant, plentiful, copious, ample; common, ordinary, familiar

rifle *syn* ROB, plunder, loot, burglarize *rel* despoil, spoilate, ravage, pillage, sack, devastate; steal, pilfer, purloin, filch

rift *syn* BREACH, break, split, schism, rent, rupture *rel* crack, cleft, fissure; gap, interval, hiatus, interruption; separation, division

right *adj* **1** *syn* GOOD *ant* wrong **2** *syn* CORRECT, accurate, exact, precise, nice *rel* fitting, proper, meet, fit; decorous, decent, seemly *ant* wrong

right *n* • something to which one has a just claim *syn* prerogative, privilege, perquisite, appanage, birthright *rel* claim, title; freedom, license, liberty

righteous *syn* MORAL, virtuous, noble, ethical *rel* upright, honest, just, honorable *ant* iniquitous

rightful *syn* DUE, condign *rel* fair, equitable, just, impartial; lawful, legal, legitimate

rigid **1** *syn* STIFF, inflexible, tense, stark, wooden *rel* firm, hard, solid; compact, close; tough, tenacious, strong *ant* elastic **2** • extremely severe or stern *syn* rigorous, strict, stringent *rel* inflexible, inexorable, obdurate, adamant, adamantine; stern, severe, austere *ant* lax

rigor *syn* DIFFICULTY, hardship, vicissitude *rel* austerity, severity, sternness; harshness, roughness; trial, tribulation, visitation, affliction *ant* amenity

rigorous *syn* RIGID, strict, stringent *rel* stiff, inflexible; stern, austere, ascetic, severe; exacting, onerous, burdensome, oppressive

rile *syn* IRRITATE, exasperate, nettle, provoke, aggravate, peeve

rim *syn* BORDER, brim, brink, margin, verge, edge

rind *syn* SKIN, bark, peel, hide, pelt

ring *n, syn* COMBINATION, combine, party, bloc, faction

ring *vb, syn* SURROUND, environ, encircle, circle, encompass, compass, hem, gird, girdle *rel* confine, circumscribe, limit, restrict; enclose, corral, wall

ringing *syn* RESONANT, sonorous, resounding, vibrant, orotund

rip *syn* TEAR, rend, split, cleave, rive

ripe *syn* MATURE, matured, mellow, adult, grown-up *rel* seasonable, timely, well-timed; consummate, finished, accomplished *ant* green; unripe

ripen *syn* MATURE, develop, age *rel* improve, better; enhance, heighten, intensify; season

rise *vb* **1** *syn* SPRING, arise, originate, derive, flow, issue, emanate, proceed, stem *rel* appear, emerge, loom *ant* abate **2** • to move or come up from a lower to a higher level *syn* arise, ascend, mount, soar, tower, rocket, levitate, surge *rel* climb, ascend, scale; increase, enlarge, augment; lift, raise, elevate *ant* decline; set (*as the sun*)

rise *n, syn* BEGINNING, genesis, initiation *rel* origin, source, inception, root, provenance, provenience; derivation, origination *ant* fall

risible *syn* LAUGHABLE, droll, funny, ludicrous, ridiculous, comic, comical, farcical *rel* amusing, diverting, entertaining

risk *n, syn* DANGER, hazard, peril, jeopardy *rel* chance, fortune, luck, accident; exposedness, exposure, liableness, liability, openness

risk *vb, syn* VENTURE, hazard, chance, jeopardize, endanger, imperil *rel* dare, brave, beard, face, defy; confront, encounter, meet

risky *syn* DANGEROUS, precarious, hazardous, perilous *rel* adventurous, venturesome; chancy, random, haphazard, hit-or-miss, happy-go-lucky

rite, ritual *syn* FORM, liturgy, ceremonial, ceremony, formality

rival **1** • to strive to equal or surpass *syn* compete, vie, emulate *rel* strive, struggle, try, attempt; contend, fight **2** *syn* MATCH, equal, approach, touch

rive *syn* TEAR, cleave, split, rend, rip *rel* sever, sunder, divide, separate; cut, hew, chop

rivet *syn* SECURE, anchor, moor *rel* fasten, attach, affix, fix; join, unite, connect, link

roam *syn* WANDER, stray, ramble, rove, range, prowl, gad, gallivant, traipse, meander

roar *vb* • to make a very loud and often a continuous or protracted noise *syn* bellow, bluster, bawl, vociferate, clamor, howl, ululate *rel* reverberate, repercuss, rebound; yell, shout; bay, bark, growl, yelp

roar *n* • a very loud and often a continuous noise *syn* bellow, bluster, bawl, vociferation, ululation

rob • to take possessions unlawfully *syn* plunder, rifle, loot, burglarize *rel* steal, pilfer, purloin, filch, lift; defraud, swindle, cheat; despoil, pillage, sack, ravage

robber *syn* THIEF, burglar, larcener, larcenist

robbery *syn* THEFT, larceny, burglary

robe *syn* CLOTHE, attire, dress, apparel, array

robust *syn* HEALTHY, sound, wholesome, hale, well *rel* strong, sturdy, stout, stalwart; athletic, husky, muscular, sinewy; vigorous, energetic, lusty *ant* frail, feeble

rock *syn* SHAKE, agitate, convulse *rel* swing, sway, undulate, oscillate; totter, quake, tremble

rocket *syn* RISE, arise, ascend, mount, soar, tower, levitate, surge

rococo *syn* ORNATE, baroque, flamboyant, florid

rodomontade *syn* BOMBAST, rhapsody, rant, fustian *rel* boasting, bragging, vaunting; vainglory, vanity, pride; magniloquence, grandiloquence

rogue *syn* VILLAIN, scoundrel, blackguard, knave, rascal, scamp, rapscallion, miscreant *rel* vagabond, vagrant, tramp, hobo, bum; malefactor, culprit, delinquent, criminal

roguish *syn* PLAYFUL, frolicsome, sportive, waggish, impish, mischievous

roily *syn* TURBID, muddy

roll *syn* LIST, table, catalog, schedule, register, roster, inventory

rollick *vb, syn* PLAY, frolic, disport, sport, romp, gambol

rollick *n, syn* PLAY, frolic, disport, sport, romp, gambol

romantic *syn* SENTIMENTAL, mawkish, maudlin, soppy, mushy, slushy *rel* fanciful, imaginary, quixotic, fantastic, visionary; invented, created; picturesque, pictorial, vivid, graphic

romp *n, syn* PLAY, frolic, rollick, gambol, disport, sport

romp *vb, syn* PLAY, frolic, rollick, gambol, disport, sport

room **1** • space in a building enclosed or set apart by a partition *syn* chamber, apartment **2** • enough space or range for free movement *syn* berth, play, elbowroom, leeway, margin, clearance

roost *syn* ALIGHT, perch, light, land

root *n, syn* ORIGIN, source, inception, provenance, provenience, prime mover *rel* beginning, commencing, commencement, starting, start; foundation, basis, ground, base

root *vb, syn* APPLAUD, cheer

roseate *syn* HOPEFUL, optimistic, rose-colored

rose-colored *syn* HOPEFUL, optimistic, roseate

roster *syn* LIST, table, catalog, schedule, register, roll, inventory

rot *vb, syn* DECAY, decompose, putrefy, spoil, disintegrate, crumble *rel* corrupt, vitiate, debase; taint, contaminate, pollute, defile

rot *n, syn* NONSENSE, twaddle, drivel, bunk, balderdash, poppycock, gobbledygook, trash, bull

rotate **1** *syn* TURN, revolve, gyrate, circle, spin, twirl, whirl, wheel, eddy, swirl, pirouette **2** • to succeed or cause to succeed each other in turn *syn* alternate *rel* interchange, exchange, bandy; succeed, follow, ensue

rotter *syn* CAD, bounder

rotund *syn* FLESHY, plump, chubby, portly, stout, fat, corpulent, obese *ant* angular

rough **1** • not smooth or even *syn* harsh, uneven, rugged, scabrous *rel* hard, solid, firm; coarse, gross; rank, rampant *ant* smooth **2** *syn* RUDE, crude, uncouth, raw, callow, green *rel* brusque, crusty, gruff, curt, blunt, bluff; ungracious, uncivil, discourteous, impolite, rude; indecorous, unseemly, indecent, indelicate *ant* gentle

roundabout *syn* INDIRECT, circuitous *rel* sinuous, winding, tortuous, flexuous

rouse *syn* STIR, arouse, awaken, rally, waken *rel* enliven, quicken, animate, vivify; stimulate, excite, provoke; incite, foment, instigate

roustabout *syn* WORKER, workman, workingman, laborer, mechanic, artisan, operative, hand, craftsman, handicraftsman

rout *n, syn* CROWD, throng, press, crush, mob, horde

rout *vb, syn* CONQUER, vanquish, defeat, subdue, subjugate, reduce, overcome, surmount, overthrow, beat, lick

route *n, syn* WAY, course, passage, pass, artery

route *vb, syn* SEND, forward, transmit, remit, ship, dispatch

rove *syn* WANDER, stray, roam, ramble, range, prowl, gad, gallivant, traipse, meander

row *n, syn* LINE, rank, file, echelon, tier *rel* series, sequence, succession, train

row *n, syn* BRAWL, broil, fracas, melee, rumpus, scrap *rel* fight, affray, fray, combat, conflict, contest; altercation, wrangle, quarrel, squabble

royal *syn* KINGLY, regal, queenly, imperial, princely *rel* splendid, resplendent, glorious, superb; august, majestic, stately, imposing, grand

rubbish *syn* REFUSE, waste, trash, debris, garbage, offal

rube *syn* BOOR, bumpkin, hick, yokel, clodhopper, clown, lout, churl

rude **1** • lacking in social refinement *syn* rough, crude, raw, callow, green, uncouth *rel* boorish, churlish, clownish, loutish; rustic, rural, bucolic; barbarous, savage, barbarian; primitive, primary, primeval **2** • offensive in manner or action *syn* ill-mannered, impolite, discourteous, uncivil, ungracious *rel* brusque, curt, gruff, crusty, bluff; impertinent, intrusive, meddlesome; surly, crabbed, sullen *ant* civil; urbane

rudimentary *syn* ELEMENTARY, basal, beginning, elemental

rueful *syn* MELANCHOLY, dolorous, doleful, lugubrious, plaintive *rel* depressed, weighed down, oppressed; piteous, pitiful; despairing, despondent, hopeless

rugged *syn* ROUGH, scabrous, harsh, uneven *rel* robust, healthy; burly, brawny, husky, muscular; rank, rampant; arduous, hard, difficult *ant* fragile

ruin *n* • the bringing about of or the results of disaster *syn* havoc, devastation, destruction *rel* disintegration, crumbling

ruin *vb* • to subject to forces that are destructive of soundness, worth, or usefulness *syn* wreck, dilapidate *rel* destroy, demolish, raze; deface, disfigure; maim, mutilate, mangle

rule *n, syn* LAW, regulation, precept, statute, ordinance, canon *rel* order, mandate, dic-

tate, command; principle, axiom, fundamental; etiquette, decorum, propriety
rule *vb* **1** *syn* GOVERN *rel* guide, lead; manage, direct, control, conduct **2** *syn* DECIDE, determine, settle, resolve *rel* conclude, judge, gather, deduce, infer
rule out *syn* EXCLUDE, eliminate, debar, shut out, suspend, disbar, blackball *rel* bar, block, hinder; prevent, preclude, obviate
ruminate *syn* PONDER, muse, meditate *rel* consider, weigh, excogitate; reflect, deliberate, speculate, cogitate, think
rummage *syn* SEEK, comb, ransack, search, hunt, scour, ferret out *rel* examine, inspect, scrutinize
rumor *syn* REPORT, gossip, hearsay
rumpus *syn* BRAWL, broil, fracas, melee, row, scrap
runt *syn* DWARF, pygmy, midget, manikin, homunculus
rupture *syn* BREACH, break, split, schism, rent, rift *rel* separation, division, parting, severance, divorce; estrangement, alienation
rural • relating to or characteristic of the country *syn* rustic, pastoral, bucolic
ruse *syn* TRICK, stratagem, maneuver, gambit, ploy, artifice, wile, feint *rel* chicane, trickery, deception; expedient, shift, makeshift, resource, resort
rush • to move or cause to move quickly, impetuously, and often heedlessly *syn* dash, tear, shoot, charge *rel* speed, hurry, hasten; dart, fly, scud
rustic *syn* RURAL, pastoral, bucolic
ruth *syn* SYMPATHY, commiseration, compassion, pity, condolence, empathy *rel* mercy, grace, charity, clemency, lenity; forbearance, tolerance, indulgence

S

sack *n, syn* BAG, pouch
sack *vb, syn* DISMISS, discharge, cashier, drop, fire, bounce
sack *vb, syn* RAVAGE, pillage, despoil, spoliate, devastate, waste *rel* plunder, rob, loot, rifle; destroy, demolish, raze; strip, bare, denude
sacred **1** *syn* HOLY, divine, blessed, spiritual, religious *rel* dedicated, consecrated, hallowed; cherished, treasured, valued *ant* profane **2** • protected (as by law, custom, or human respect) against abuse *syn* sacrosanct, inviolate, inviolable *rel* protected, shielded, defended, guarded; revered, reverenced, venerated
sacrifice *syn* FORGO, abnegate, forbear, eschew *rel* renounce, abdicate; surrender, yield, resign, relinquish
sacrilege *syn* PROFANATION, desecration, blasphemy *rel* defilement, pollution; violation, transgression, trespass, breach; sin, crime, scandal, offense
sacrilegious *syn* IMPIOUS, blasphemous, profane *rel* polluting, defiling; profaning, desecrating
sacrosanct *syn* SACRED, inviolate, inviolable *rel* respected, regarded, esteemed; revered, venerated, reverenced
saddle *syn* BURDEN, encumber, cumber, weigh, weight, load, lade, tax, charge
sadness • the quality, state, or instance of being unhappy or low in spirits *syn* depression, melancholy, melancholia, dejection, gloom, blues, dumps *rel* sorrow, grief, anguish, woe; despondency, despair, hopelessness, forlornness *ant* gladness
safe • affording security from threat of danger, harm, or loss *syn* secure *rel* protected, guarded, shielded; reliable, dependable, tried *ant* dangerous
safeguard *syn* DEFEND, guard, shield, protect *rel* conserve, preserve, save; secure, insure, ensure, assure
sag *syn* DROOP, wilt, flag *rel* sink, slump, subside, fall, drop; hang, dangle, suspend
saga *syn* MYTH, legend
sagacious *syn* SHREWD, perspicacious, astute *rel* sharp, keen, acute; penetrating, piercing, probing; wise, judicious, sage, sapient
sage *syn* WISE, sapient, judicious, prudent, sensible, sane *rel* intelligent, knowing, brilliant; learned, erudite; sagacious, perspicacious, shrewd
sail *syn* FLY, float, skim, scud, shoot, dart

sailor *syn* MARINER, seaman, tar, gob, bluejacket

salary *syn* WAGE, wages, stipend, pay, hire, emolument, fee

salient *syn* NOTICEABLE, conspicuous, outstanding, signal, striking, arresting, prominent, remarkable *rel* significant, important, weighty; impressive, moving; obtrusive, intrusive

salubrious *syn* HEALTHFUL, healthy, wholesome, salutary, hygienic, sanitary *rel* beneficial, advantageous; benign, favorable

salutary *syn* HEALTHFUL, wholesome, healthy, salubrious, hygienic, sanitary *rel* beneficial, advantageous, profitable *ant* deleterious; evil

salutation *syn* GREETING, salute

salute *vb, syn* ADDRESS, greet, hail, accost

salute *n, syn* GREETING, salutation

same • not different or not differing from one another *syn* selfsame, very, identical, identic, equivalent, equal, tantamount *rel* alike, like, akin, parallel, uniform *ant* different

sample *syn* INSTANCE, specimen, example, case, illustration *rel* piece, part, portion, segment, fragment

sanative *syn* CURATIVE, remedial, restorative, corrective *rel* salutary, hygienic, sanitary, healthful; healing, curing, remedying

sanctimonious **1** *syn* DEVOUT, pietistic, religious, pious *rel* see SANCTIMONIOUS 2 **2** *syn* HYPOCRITICAL, pharisaical, canting *rel* affected, feigned, simulated, counterfeited, assumed, pretended; perfervid, fervid, ardent, fervent, impassioned

sanctimony *syn* HYPOCRISY, pharisaism, cant *rel* pretending, pretense, simulation, feigning, counterfeiting, affecting, affectation; enthusiasm, zealotry, fanaticism

sanction *syn* APPROVE, endorse, accredit, certify *rel* authorize, license, commission; confirm, ratify; enforce, implement *ant* interdict

sanctity *syn* HOLINESS

sanctuary *syn* SHELTER, refuge, asylum, cover, retreat *rel* safety, security; protection, shielding, shield, guarding, guard

sand *syn* FORTITUDE, grit, backbone, pluck, guts *rel* courage, mettle, spirit, resolution, tenacity

sane *syn* WISE, judicious, prudent, sensible, sage, sapient *rel* rational, reasonable; right, good; sound, cogent, convincing, compelling *ant* insane

sangfroid *syn* EQUANIMITY, phlegm, composure *rel* indifference, unconcernedness, unconcern, aloofness, detachment; self-possession, aplomb, self-assurance, assurance, self-confidence, confidence

sanguinary *syn* BLOODY, sanguine, sanguineous, gory

sanguine **1** *also* **sanguineous** *syn* BLOODY, sanguinary, gory *ant* bloodless **2** *syn* CONFIDENT, assured, sure, presumptuous *rel* hopeful, optimistic; positive, certain *ant* afraid

sanitary *syn* HEALTHFUL, hygienic, salutary, salubrious, healthy, wholesome *rel* curing, curative, healing, remedying; effective, efficacious, effectual *ant* noxious

sanitize *syn* STERILIZE, disinfect, fumigate

sap *syn* WEAKEN, undermine, enfeeble, debilitate, cripple, disable *rel* drain, deplete, exhaust, impoverish; ruin, wreck; destroy

sapid *syn* PALATABLE, appetizing, savory, tasty, toothsome, flavorsome, relishing *ant* insipid

sapient *syn* WISE, sage, judicious, prudent, sensible, sane *rel* learned, erudite, scholarly; sagacious, perspicacious, shrewd

sarcasm *syn* WIT, satire, irony, humor, repartee *rel* incisiveness, trenchancy, bitingness, cuttingness; mockery, taunting, derision

sarcastic • marked by bitterness and a power or will to cut or sting *syn* satiric, ironic, sardonic *rel* biting, cutting, trenchant, incisive; caustic, scathing, mordant

sardonic *syn* SARCASTIC, ironic, satiric *rel* bitter, acrid; deriding, derisive, mocking, taunting, ridiculing; sinister, malign

sate *syn* SATIATE, surfeit, cloy, pall, glut, gorge *rel* satisfy, content; indulge, pamper, humor; gratify, regale, please

satellite *syn* FOLLOWER, adherent, henchman, partisan, disciple, sectary *rel* sycophant, parasite, favorite, toady, lickspittle, bootlicker, hanger-on; devotee, votary, addict

satiate • to fill to repletion *syn* sate, surfeit, cloy, pall, glut, gorge *rel* satisfy, content; pamper, humor, indulge; gratify, regale, please

satiny *syn* SLEEK, silky, silken, velvety, glossy, slick

satire *syn* WIT, irony, humor, sarcasm, repartee *rel* raillery, persiflage, badinage; lampoon, pasquinade, libel, skit; ridiculing, ridicule, deriding, derision, taunting

satiric *syn* SARCASTIC, ironic, sardonic *rel* pungent, piquant, poignant; ridiculing, deriding, derisive, taunting, mocking; mordant, caustic, scathing

satisfied • showing or expressing satisfaction from the fulfillment of one's desires *syn* content, contented *rel* gratified, gladdened, pleased; appeased, pacified

satisfy **1** • to appease desires or longings *syn* content *rel* gratify, gladden, please; appease, pacify; satiate, sate *ant* tantalize **2** *syn* PAY, recompense, compensate, remunerate, repay, reimburse, indemnify *rel* balance, offset **3** • to measure up to a set of criteria or requirements *syn* fulfill, meet, answer *rel* prove, test, try, demonstrate; verify, substantiate, corroborate, confirm; match, equal, rival, approach, touch

saturate **1** *syn* SOAK, steep, impregnate, drench, sop, waterlog *rel* dip, immerse, submerge; absorb, imbibe, assimilate **2** *syn* PERMEATE, impregnate, impenetrate, interpenetrate, penetrate, pervade *rel* infuse, imbue, ingrain, inoculate; pierce, probe, enter

saturnine *syn* SULLEN, dour, gloomy, glum, morose, surly, sulky, crabbed *rel* grave, serious, solemn, somber, staid; taciturn, reserved, uncommunicative, silent *ant* genial; mercurial

saucy • flippant and bold in manner or attitude *syn* pert, arch *rel* flippant, frivolous, volatile, light-minded; intrusive, obtrusive, meddlesome, impertinent; brash, impudent, shameless; piquant, snappy

saunter • to walk slowly in an idle or aimless manner *syn* stroll, amble

savage **1** *syn* FIERCE, ferocious, barbarous, inhuman, cruel, fell, truculent *rel* implacable, relentless, unrelenting, merciless, grim; rapacious, voracious, ravenous **2** *syn* BARBARIAN, barbaric, barbarous *rel* primitive, primeval; rough, harsh; untaught, untutored, ignorant

save **1** *syn* RESCUE, deliver, redeem, ransom, reclaim *rel* free, release, liberate, emancipate; defend, protect, shield, guard, safeguard; recover, retrieve, recoup, recruit *ant* lose; waste; damn (*in theology*) **2** • to keep secure or maintain intact from injury, decay, or loss *syn* preserve, conserve *rel* have, hold, own, possess, enjoy; keep, retain, reserve *ant* spend; consume

savoir faire *syn* TACT, poise, address *rel* grace, dignity, elegance; ease, readiness, dexterity, facility; self-possession, self-assurance, aplomb, confidence

savor *syn* TASTE, flavor, tang, relish, smack *rel* quality, property, character, attribute; peculiarity, individuality, characteristic, distinctiveness; impression, impress, print, stamp

savory *syn* PALATABLE, appetizing, sapid, tasty, toothsome, flavorsome, relishing *ant* bland; acrid

saw *syn* SAYING, adage, proverb, maxim, motto, epigram, aphorism, apothegm

say • to express in words *syn* utter, tell, state *rel* pronounce, articulate, enunciate; express, voice, broach; speak, talk; declare, announce, proclaim; note, observe; comment, animadvert, remark; explain, expound; cite, quote, repeat; assert, affirm, aver, avow, protest

saying • an often repeated statement that usu. is brief and expresses a common observation or general truth *syn* saw, adage, proverb, maxim, motto, epigram, aphorism, apothegm

scabrous *syn* ROUGH, harsh, uneven, rugged *ant* glabrous; smooth

scale *syn* ASCEND, climb, mount

scamp *syn* VILLAIN, scoundrel, blackguard, knave, rascal, rogue, rapscallion, miscreant *rel* malefactor, culprit, delinquent, criminal

scamper *syn* SCUTTLE, scurry, skedaddle, sprint *rel* speed, hurry, hasten; rush, dash, shoot

scan *syn* SCRUTINIZE, examine, inspect, audit *rel* consider, study, contemplate; observe, survey, remark, notice, see

scandal **1** *syn* OFFENSE, sin, vice, crime *rel* indignity, insult, affront; offending, outraging, outrage; wrong, grievance, injury, injustice **2** *syn* DETRACTION, calumny, slander, backbiting *rel* gossiping, gossip, tattling; maligning, defaming, defamation, traducing

scanning *syn* SCRUTINY, examination, inspection, audit *rel* study, application, attention, concentration; oversight, supervision, surveillance; analysis, dissection

scant, scanty *syn* MEAGER, skimpy,

scrimpy, exiguous, spare, sparse *rel* deficient, defective; scarce, rare, infrequent *ant* plentiful; profuse

scarce *syn* INFREQUENT, rare, uncommon, occasional, sporadic *rel* deficient; curtailed, abridged, shortened *ant* abundant

scare *syn* FRIGHTEN, alarm, fright, terrify, terrorize, startle, affray, affright *rel* daunt, appall, dismay; intimidate, cow, browbeat; astound, amaze, flabbergast, astonish, surprise *ant* entice

scathing *syn* CAUSTIC, mordant, acrid *ant* scorching, searing, burning; fierce, ferocious, truculent, savage; incisive, biting, cutting, trenchant

scatter 1 • to cause to separate or break up *syn* disperse, dissipate, dispel *rel* throw, cast, fling, toss; distribute, dispense, divide; discard, shed **2** *syn* STREW, straw, broadcast, sow *rel* spread, disseminate; sprinkle, besprinkle

scent *syn* SMELL, odor, aroma *rel* emanation, issuing, issue

schedule 1 *syn* LIST, table, catalog, register, roll, roster, inventory **2** *syn* PROGRAM, timetable, agenda

scheme *n* **1** *syn* PLAN, design, plot, project *rel* proposal, proposition; arrangement, ordering; device, contrivance; expedient, shift, makeshift **2** *syn* SYSTEM, network, complex, organism *rel* organization, arrangement, ordering; whole, total, sum

scheme *vb, syn* PLAN, design, plot, project *rel* propose, purpose, intend; aim, aspire; manipulate, handle, swing, wield

schism *syn* BREACH, split, rupture, break, rent, rift *rel* division, separation, severance; estrangement, alienation; discord, dissension

schismatic *syn* HERETIC, sectarian, dissenter, nonconformist

scholarly *syn* LEARNED, erudite *rel* academic, scholastic, pedantic; abstruse, recondite; accurate, exact, precise, correct

scholarship *syn* KNOWLEDGE, learning, erudition, science, information, lore

scholastic *syn* PEDANTIC, academic, bookish *rel* conversant, versed; dry, arid; formal, conventional, ceremonial

school *syn* TEACH, discipline, train, instruct, educate *rel* practice, exercise, drill; guide, lead; conduct, control, direct, manage

science *syn* KNOWLEDGE, learning, erudition, scholarship, information, lore

scintillate *syn* FLASH, gleam, glance, glint, sparkle, glitter, glisten, coruscate, twinkle

scoff • to show one's contempt in derision or mockery *syn* jeer, gibe, fleer, gird, sneer, flout *rel* ridicule, deride, mock, taunt; scorn, disdain, scout, contemn, despise

scold *n, syn* VIRAGO, shrew, vixen, termagant, amazon

scold *vb* to reproach angrily and abusively *syn* upbraid, rate, berate, tongue-lash, jaw, bawl, chew out, wig, rail, revile, vituperate *rel* reprehend, reprobate, censure, blame, criticize; reproach, reprimand, reprove, rebuke, admonish, chide; execrate, objurgate

scoop *syn* DIP, bail, ladle, spoon, dish

scope *syn* RANGE, gamut, reach, radius, compass, sweep, orbit, horizon, ken, purview *rel* expanse, amplitude, spread, stretch; field, domain, sphere, territory, province; extent, area, size

scorch *syn* BURN, char, sear, singe *rel* wither, shrivel

scorn *n, syn* DISDAIN, contempt, despite *rel* superciliousness, insolence, disdainfulness; scoffing, flouting, jeering, gibing; deriding, derision, ridiculing, ridicule, taunting, mocking, mockery

scorn *vb, syn* DESPISE, disdain, scout, contemn *rel* repudiate, spurn, reject, decline; flout, scoff, jeer, gibe; deride, mock, taunt, ridicule

scoundrel *syn* VILLAIN, blackguard, knave, rascal, rogue, scamp, rapscallion, miscreant *rel* criminal, felon, malefactor, culprit

scour *syn* SEEK, search, hunt, ransack, rummage, comb, ferret out *rel* investigate; scrutinize, inspect, examine; range, roam, rove, wander

scout *syn* DESPISE, scorn, contemn, disdain *rel* flout, scoff, sneer, jeer; deride, taunt, mock, ridicule

scowl *syn* FROWN, glower, lower, gloom *rel* glare, stare, gaze

scrap *vb, syn* DISCARD, junk, cast, shed, molt, slough

scrap *n, syn* BRAWL, broil, fracas, melee, row, rumpus *rel* quarrel, altercation, squabble, wrangle; fight, affray, fray, combat, contest

scrape *vb* • to rub or slide against something that is harsh, rough, or sharp *syn* scratch, grate, rasp, grind *rel* erase, efface, delete; remove; rid, clear; abrade, chafe, excoriate

scrape *n, syn* PREDICAMENT, dilemma, quandary, plight, fix, jam, pickle *rel* difficulty, vicissitude; perplexity, bewilderment, distraction; embarrassment, discomfiture

scratch *syn* SCRAPE, grate, rasp, grind *rel* tear, rend; injure, damage, mar, impair, hurt; deface, disfigure

scrawny *syn* LEAN, skinny, lank, lanky, spare, gaunt, rawboned, angular *rel* thin, slim, slender; meager, exiguous *ant* brawny; fleshy; obese

scream *vb, syn* SHOUT, shriek, screech, yell, squeal, holler, whoop *rel* pierce, penetrate; vent, utter, voice, express, air

scream *n, syn* SHOUT, shriek, screech, yell, squeal, holler, whoop

screech *vb, syn* SHOUT, scream, shriek, yell, squeal, holler, whoop

screech *n, syn* SHOUT, scream, shriek, yell, squeal, holler, whoop

screen *syn* HIDE, conceal, secrete, cache, bury, ensconce *rel* defend, protect, shield, guard, safeguard; disguise, dissemble, cloak, mask, camouflage

scrimpy *syn* MEAGER, scanty, scant, skimpy, exiguous, spare, sparse *rel* thin, slight, slender, slim; niggardly, stingy, penurious, parsimonious

scruple *n, syn* QUALM, demur, compunction *rel* hesitation, hesitancy; doubt, uncertainty, suspicion, mistrust; misgiving, apprehension

scruple *vb, syn* DEMUR, balk, jib, shy, boggle, stickle, stick, strain *rel* hesitate, waver, falter, vacillate; object, protest

scrupulous **1** *syn* CAREFUL, meticulous, punctilious, punctual *rel* fastidious, particular, finicky, fussy; exact, accurate, precise, correct *ant* remiss **2** *syn* UPRIGHT, conscientious, honest, just, honorable *rel* moral, ethical, righteous, virtuous, noble; rigid, rigorous, strict *ant* unscrupulous

scrutinize • to look at or over *syn* scan, inspect, examine, audit *rel* consider, study, contemplate, weigh; analyze, resolve, dissect; penetrate, pierce, probe

scrutiny • a close study, inquiry, or visual inspection *syn* examination, scanning, inspection, audit *rel* investigation, research, probe, inquiry, inquisition; surveying, survey, observing, observation, viewing, view

scud *syn* FLY, skim, shoot, sail, dart, float

scuffle *syn* WRESTLE, tussle, grapple *rel* fight, contend; clash, conflict, collide, bump

sculpture, sculpt,, sculp *syn* CARVE, chisel, engrave, incise, etch *rel* shape, fashion, form, make; depict, portray, represent

scum *syn* FOAM, froth, spume, lather, suds, yeast

scurrility *syn* ABUSE, billingsgate, invective, vituperation, obloquy *rel* vilifying, vilification, maligning, traducing, calumniation; reviling, berating, upbraiding, rating, scolding

scurrilous *syn* ABUSIVE, opprobrious, vituperative, contumelious *rel* ribald, obscene, gross, coarse, vulgar; insulting, outraging, offending, offensive; foul, filthy, dirty

scurry *syn* SCUTTLE, scamper, skedaddle, sprint *rel* rush, dash, shoot, tear, charge; dart, fly, scud; hurry, speed, hasten

scurvy *syn* CONTEMPTIBLE, despicable, pitiable, sorry, cheap, beggarly, shabby *rel* base, low, vile; mean, abject

scuttle • to move with or as if with short brisk steps *syn* scurry, scamper, skedaddle, sprint *rel* shoot, tear, dash, rush, charge; fly, scud; hurry, speed, hasten

seaman *syn* MARINER, sailor, tar, gob, bluejacket

sear *syn* BURN, scorch, char, singe

search *syn* SEEK, scour, hunt, comb, ransack, rummage, ferret out *rel* investigate; inspect, examine, scrutinize; penetrate, pierce, probe

season *syn* HARDEN, acclimatize, acclimate *rel* habituate, accustom, inure; train, school, discipline, teach; practice, exercise, drill

seasonable • done or occurring at a good, suitable, or proper time *syn* timely, well-timed, opportune, pat *rel* apropos, apposite, pertinent, relevant; appropriate, happy, felicitous, apt, fit; welcome, grateful, gratifying, pleasant *ant* unseasonable

seclude *syn* ISOLATE, segregate, insulate, sequester *rel* enclose, envelop, fence, pen, cage, wall; confine, circumscribe, limit, restrict

seclusion *syn* SOLITUDE, isolation, alienation *rel* retirement, withdrawal; separation, parting, severing, severance

second *syn* INSTANT, moment, minute, flash, jiffy, twinkling, split second

secondary *syn* SUBORDINATE, dependent, subject, tributary, collateral *rel* auxiliary, accessory, subservient, subsidiary, contributory; incidental, accidental, adventitious *ant* primary

second-rate *syn* MEDIUM, mediocre, middling, moderate, average, fair, indifferent

secret • done without attracting observation *syn* covert, stealthy, furtive, clandestine, surreptitious, underhand, underhanded *rel* mysterious, inscrutable, arcane; puzzling, perplexing, mystifying; hidden, concealed, secreted, screened

secrete *syn* HIDE, conceal, screen, cache, bury, ensconce *rel* dissemble, cloak, mask, disguise, camouflage

secretive *syn* SILENT, close, close-lipped, closemouthed, tight-lipped, uncommunicative, taciturn, reticent, reserved *rel* cautious, circumspect, wary; restrained, inhibited

sect *syn* RELIGION, denomination, cult, communion, faith, creed, persuasion, church

sectary **1** *syn* FOLLOWER, adherent, disciple, partisan, henchman, satellite *rel* devotee, votary, addict **2** *also* **sectarian** *syn* HERETIC, schismatic, dissenter, nonconformist *rel* enthusiast, zealot, fanatic, bigot

section *syn* PART, sector, segment, division, portion, piece, detail, member, fraction, fragment, parcel *rel* district, locality, vicinity; region, tract, area, zone, belt; field, sphere, territory

sector *syn* PART, segment, section, division, portion, piece, detail, member, fraction, fragment, parcel

secular *syn* PROFANE, temporal, lay *rel* worldly, mundane, earthly, earthy, terrestrial *ant* religious; sacred; regular

secure *adj, syn* SAFE *rel* firm, solid; protected, shielded, guarded, safeguarded, defended; certain, positive, sure; impregnable, unassailable, invulnerable, invincible *ant* precarious, dangerous

secure *vb* **1** • to fasten or fix firmly *syn* anchor, moor, rivet *rel* establish, set, settle, fix; fasten, attach, affix **2** *syn* ENSURE, insure, assure *rel* protect, defend, safeguard, guard, shield; preserve, conserve, save; guarantee, guaranty; warrant, justify **3** *syn* GET, procure, obtain, acquire, gain, win *rel* seize, take, grasp; reach, attain, achieve; have, hold, own, possess

security *syn* GUARANTEE, surety, guaranty, bond, bail *rel* pledge, earnest, token

sedate *syn* SERIOUS, grave, staid, earnest, sober, solemn, somber *rel* placid, calm, serene, tranquil; collected, composed, imperturbable, cool; decorous, seemly, proper *ant* flighty

sediment *syn* DEPOSIT, precipitate, dregs, lees, grounds

sedition • an offense against a ruling authority to which one owes allegiance *syn* treason *rel* rebellion, revolt, revolution, uprising, insurrection, mutiny, putsch, coup; disaffection, alienation, estrangement

seditious *syn* INSUBORDINATE, mutinous, rebellious, factious, contumacious *rel* traitorous, treacherous, perfidious, disloyal, faithless; disaffected, alienated

seduce *syn* LURE, tempt, entice, inveigle, decoy *rel* mislead, beguile, delude, deceive; corrupt, debauch, deprave, pervert, debase; bewitch, captivate, allure, attract

sedulous *syn* BUSY, assiduous, diligent, industrious *rel* persevering, persistent; untiring, unwearied, indefatigable, tireless

see **1** • to take cognizance of by physical or mental vision *syn* behold, descry, espy, view, survey, contemplate, observe, notice, remark, note, perceive, discern *rel* scrutinize, scan, examine, inspect; pierce, penetrate, probe; consider, study, contemplate **2** • to perceive something by means of the eyes *syn* look, watch *rel* gaze, gape, stare, glare

seedy *syn* SHABBY, dilapidated, dingy, faded, threadbare *rel* drooping, flagging, sagging, wilting; sickly, unwholesome, morbid; worn, haggard

seek • to look for *syn* search, scour, hunt, comb, ferret out, ransack, rummage *rel* inquire, question, ask, interrogate; pursue, chase, follow, trail

seem • to give the impression of being without necessarily being so in fact *syn* look, appear *rel* infer, gather, judge, deduce, conclude

seeming *syn* APPARENT, illusory, ostensible *rel* plausible, specious, credible; dissembling, disguising, masking, cloaking, camouflaging

seemly *syn* DECOROUS, proper, nice, decent *rel* fitting, suitable, appropriate, meet, fit; congruous, compatible, congenial, consistent, consonant *ant* unseemly

seethe *syn* BOIL, simmer, parboil, stew

segment *syn* PART, section, sector, division, portion, piece, detail, member, fraction, fragment, parcel

segregate *syn* ISOLATE, seclude, insulate, sequester *rel* separate, divide, part, sever; detach, disengage; choose, select, single

seize *syn* TAKE, grasp, clutch, snatch, grab *rel* catch, capture, snare, ensnare, trap, entrap; appropriate, confiscate, usurp, arrogate

select *adj* • chosen from a number or group by fitness, superiority, or preference *syn* elect, picked, exclusive *rel* choice, exquisite, rare, delicate, dainty, recherché; superlative, surpassing, peerless, supreme *ant* indiscriminate

select *vb, syn* CHOOSE, elect, prefer, opt, pick, cull, single *rel* assort, sort, classify; discriminate, discern *ant* reject

selection *syn* CHOICE, preference, election, option, alternative *rel* choosing, culling, picking; discrimination, discernment, insight, acumen *ant* rejection

self-abnegation *syn* RENUNCIATION, abnegation, self-denial *rel* sacrificing, sacrifice, forbearance, forgoing, eschewal; surrendering, surrender, resignation, abandonment, relinquishment

self-assertive *syn* AGGRESSIVE, assertive, pushing, pushy, militant *rel* obtrusive, intrusive, officious, meddlesome, impertinent; bold, audacious, brave; positive, certain, sure, cocksure

self-assurance *syn* CONFIDENCE, assurance, self-confidence, aplomb, self-possession *rel* coolness, collectedness, imperturbability; composure, sangfroid, equanimity

self-complacent *syn* COMPLACENT, self-satisfied, smug, priggish *rel* see COMPLACENT

self-confidence *syn* CONFIDENCE, assurance, self-assurance, self-possession, aplomb *rel* composure, equanimity; sureness, sanguineness

self-denial *syn* RENUNCIATION, self-abnegation, abnegation *rel* sacrificing, sacrifice, forbearance; abstaining, refraining; restraining, restraint, curbing, curb, checking, check

self-esteem *syn* CONCEIT, self-love, egotism, egoism, amour propre *rel* pride, vanity; self-respect, self-regard, self-admiration *ant* self-distrust

self-love *syn* CONCEIT, self-esteem, egotism, egoism, amour propre *rel* pride, vanity, vainglory; complacency, self-complacency, smugness, priggishness *ant* self-forgetfulness

self-possession *syn* CONFIDENCE, self-confidence, assurance, self-assurance, aplomb *rel* equanimity, composure; coolness, collectedness, imperturbability, nonchalance; poise, savoir faire, tact

selfsame *syn* SAME, very, identical, identic, equivalent, equal, tantamount *rel* alike, like, uniform *ant* diverse

self-satisfied *syn* COMPLACENT, self-complacent, smug, priggish *rel* satisfied, content; conceited, egoistic, egotistic

semblance *syn* APPEARANCE, look, aspect *rel* likeness, similitude, resemblance, analogy, affinity; pose, affectation, air; form, figure, shape

sempiternal *syn* INFINITE, eternal, boundless, illimitable, uncircumscribed *rel* everlasting, endless, interminable, unceasing; immortal, deathless, undying; lasting, perdurable

send • to cause to go or be taken from one place, person or condition to another *syn* dispatch, forward, transmit, remit, route, ship *rel* speed, quicken; direct, order, command; go, leave, depart

senescence *syn* AGE, senility, dotage *ant* adolescence

senility *syn* AGE, dotage, senescence *rel* infirmity, feebleness, weakness, decrepitude; childishness, childlikeness; decay, disintegration

sensation **1** • awareness (as of heat or pain) due to stimulation of a sense organ *syn* percept, sense-datum, sensum, image *rel* impression, impress, print, stamp; feeling, feel; consciousness, awareness **2** • the power to respond or an act of responding to stimuli *syn* sense, feeling, sensibility *rel* perceptibleness, perceptibility, tangibleness, tangibility, palpableness, palpability, ponderableness, ponderability; reaction, action, behavior; response, answer

sense 1 *syn* SENSATION, feeling, sensibility *rel* awareness, consciousness, cognizance; perception, discernment, discrimination, penetration 2 • the ability to reach intelligent conclusions *syn* common sense, good sense, horse sense, gumption, judgment, wisdom *rel* prudence, foresight, discretion; understanding, comprehension, appreciation; intelligence, brain, wit, mind 3 *syn* MEANING, acceptation, signification, significance, import *rel* denotation, connotation

sense-datum *syn* SENSATION, sensum, percept, image

sensibility *syn* SENSATION, feeling, sense *rel* perception, discernment, penetration, discrimination, insight; sensitiveness, susceptibility; emotion, affection

sensible 1 *syn* MATERIAL, physical, corporeal, phenomenal, objective *ant* intelligible 2 *syn* PERCEPTIBLE, palpable, tangible, appreciable, ponderable *rel* sensational, perceptual, imaginal; obvious, patent, manifest, evident; carnal, fleshly, sensual *ant* insensible 3 *syn* AWARE, conscious, cognizant, alive, awake *rel* perceiving, noting, remarking, observing, seeing; knowing, intelligent; understanding, comprehending, appreciating; sensitive, susceptible, liable *ant* insensible (of *or* to) 4 *syn* WISE, prudent, sane, judicious, sage, sapient *rel* sagacious, perspicacious, astute, shrewd; foresighted, discreet, provident; reasonable, rational *ant* absurd, foolish; fatuous, asinine

sensitive 1 *syn* LIABLE, susceptible, subject, exposed, open, prone *rel* impressed, influenced, affected; predisposed, disposed, inclined *ant* insensitive 2 *syn* SENTIENT, impressible, impressionable, responsive, susceptible *rel* alert, watchful, vigilant, wide-awake; sharp, keen, acute; aware, conscious, cognizant, sensible, alive

sensual 1 *syn* CARNAL, fleshly, animal *rel* bodily, physical, corporeal, somatic; coarse, gross, vulgar; lewd, lascivious, lustful, wanton, licentious 2 *syn* SENSUOUS, luxurious, voluptuous, sybaritic, epicurean *rel* see SENSUAL 1

sensum *syn* SENSATION, sense-datum, percept, image

sensuous • relating to or providing pleasure through gratification of the senses *syn* sensual, luxurious, voluptuous, sybaritic, epicurean *rel* sensational, imaginal; delicious, delectable, luscious, delightful; aesthetic, artistic

sentence • to decree the fate or punishment of one adjudged guilty, unworthy, or unfit *syn* condemn, damn, doom, proscribe *rel* judge, adjudge, adjudicate; denounce, blame, criticize; determine, settle, rule, decide

sententious *syn* EXPRESSIVE, pregnant, meaningful, significant, eloquent *rel* formal, conventional, ceremonious, ceremonial; showy, ostentatious; terse, pithy, compendious, concise

sentient • readily affected by external stimuli *syn* sensitive, impressible, impressionable, responsive, susceptible

sentiment 1 *syn* FEELING, emotion, affection, passion *rel* thought, impression, notion, idea; ideal, standard, exemplar 2 *syn* OPINION, view, belief, conviction, persuasion *rel* truth, verity; conclusion, judgment

sentimental • unduly or affectedly emotional *syn* romantic, mawkish, maudlin, soppy, mushy, slushy *rel* emotional, affectionate, feeling, passionate; affecting, moving, pathetic, touching; affected, pretended, counterfeited, feigned, simulated

separate *vb* • to become or cause to become disunited or disjoined *syn* part, divide, sever, sunder, divorce *rel* cleave, rend, split, rive, tear; estrange, alienate; disperse, dispel, scatter; detach, disengage *ant* combine

separate *adj* 1 *syn* DISTINCT, several, discrete *rel* diverse, disparate, different, divergent, various; free, independent 2 *syn* SINGLE, solitary, particular, unique, sole, lone *rel* special, especial, specific, individual; peculiar, distinctive, characteristic; detached, disengaged

sequel *syn* EFFECT, outcome, issue, result, consequence, upshot, aftereffect, aftermath, event *rel* termination, end, ending; conclusion, closing, finishing, finish

sequence *syn* SUCCESSION, series, progression, chain, train, string *rel* ordering, order, arrangement

sequent, sequential *syn* CONSECUTIVE, successive, serial

sequester *syn* ISOLATE, segregate, seclude, insulate *rel* separate, sever, sunder

serene *syn* CALM, tranquil, peaceful,

placid, halcyon *rel* still, stilly, silent, noiseless, quiet; cool, collected, composed; smooth, effortless, easy

serial *syn* CONSECUTIVE, successive, sequent, sequential *rel* following, ensuing, succeeding; continuous, continual

series *syn* SUCCESSION, progression, sequence, chain, train, string

serious • not light or frivolous (as in disposition, appearance, or manner) *syn* grave, solemn, somber, sedate, staid, sober, earnest *rel* austere, stern, severe, ascetic; thoughtful, reflective, contemplative, meditative; deep, profound *ant* light, flippant

sermon *syn* SPEECH, homily, address, oration, harangue, talk, lecture

serpentine *syn* WINDING, sinuous, tortuous, flexuous *rel* circuitous, roundabout, indirect; crooked, devious

service *syn* USE, advantage, profit, account, avail *rel* usefulness, utility; worth, value; helping, help, aiding, aid, assistance

servile *syn* SUBSERVIENT, menial, slavish, obsequious *rel* mean, abject, ignoble; fawning, cringing, truckling, cowering *ant* authoritative

servitude • the state of subjection to a master *syn* slavery, bondage

set *vb* **1** • to position (something) in a specified place *syn* settle, fix, establish *rel* implant; fasten, attach, affix; prescribe, assign, define **2** *syn* COAGULATE, congeal, curdle, clot, jelly, jell *rel* harden, solidify; compact, consolidate, concentrate

set *n* • a group of persons associated by common interest *syn* circle, coterie, clique

setting *syn* BACKGROUND, environment, milieu, mise-en-scène, backdrop

settle **1** *syn* SET, fix, establish *rel* secure, anchor, moor, rivet; order, arrange *ant* unsettle **2** *syn* CALM, compose, quiet, quieten, still, lull, soothe, tranquilize *rel* placate, appease, pacify, mollify, conciliate *ant* unsettle **3** *syn* DECIDE, determine, rule, resolve *rel* judge, adjudge, adjudicate; close, end, conclude, terminate

sever *syn* SEPARATE, sunder, part, divide, divorce *rel* rive, cleave, rend, split, tear; cut, hew, chop; detach, disengage

several **1** *syn* DISTINCT, separate, discrete *rel* individual, particular, special, especial **2** *syn* MANY, sundry, various, divers, numerous, multifarious *rel* single, separate, particular; detached, disengaged

severally *syn* EACH, individually, respectively, apiece

severe • given to or marked by strict discipline and firm restraint *syn* stern, austere, ascetic *rel* exacting, oppressive, onerous, burdensome; rigid, rigorous, strict, stringent; hard, difficult, arduous; harsh, rugged, uneven, rough *ant* tolerant; tender

shabby **1** • being ill-kept and showing signs of wear and tear *syn* dilapidated, dingy, faded, seedy, threadbare *rel* worn, haggard; dowdy, frowzy, slatternly; shopworn, trite; decrepit **2** *syn* CONTEMPTIBLE, despicable, pitiable, sorry, scurvy, cheap, beggarly *rel* mean, sordid, ignoble; base, low, vile

shackle *syn* HAMPER, fetter, clog, trammel, manacle, hog-tie *rel* restrain, curb, check, inhibit; hinder, impede, obstruct, block, bar; restrict, circumscribe, confine, limit

shade **1** • comparative darkness or obscurity due to interception of light rays *syn* shadow, umbrage, umbra, penumbra, adumbration *rel* darkness, dimness, obscurity; shelter, cover, retreat **2** *syn* APPARITION, ghost, spirit, specter, phantasm, phantom, wraith, revenant **3** *syn* BLIND, shutter **4** *syn* COLOR, tint, hue, tinge, tone **5** *syn* GRADATION, nuance *rel* distinction, difference, dissimilarity; touch, suggestion, suspicion, soupçon, dash, tinge **6** *syn* TOUCH, suggestion, suspicion, soupçon, tinge, smack, spice, dash, vein, strain, tincture, streak *rel* trace, vestige; tint

shadow *n, syn* SHADE, umbrage, umbra, penumbra, adumbration *rel* form, figure, shape, conformation, configuration; darkness, obscurity, dimness; silhouette, contour, outline

shadow *vb, syn* SUGGEST, adumbrate *rel* foretell, forecast, predict, prognosticate; foresee, foreknow, divine

shake **1** • to exhibit vibratory, wavering, or oscillating movement often as an evidence of instability *syn* tremble, quake, totter, quiver, shiver, shudder, quaver, wobble, teeter, shimmy, dither *rel* oscillate, fluctuate, vibrate, waver, swing, sway **2** • to move up and down or to and fro with some violence *syn* agitate, rock, convulse *rel* move, drive, impel; flourish, brandish, swing, wave; disturb, derange, unsettle, disorder **3** *syn* SWING, wave, flourish, brandish, thrash

shallow *syn* SUPERFICIAL, cursory, uncritical *rel* slim, slight, slender, thin; trivial, trifling, petty, paltry; empty, hollow, idle, vain

sham *n, syn* IMPOSTURE, cheat, fake, humbug, fraud, deceit, deception, counterfeit *rel* pretense, pretension, make-believe; trick, ruse, feint, wile, gambit, ploy

sham *vb, syn* ASSUME, feign, simulate, counterfeit, pretend, affect *rel* invent, create; ape, mock, mimic, imitate, copy

sham *n, syn* COUNTERFEIT, spurious, bogus, fake, pseudo, pinchbeck, phony *rel* feigned, assumed, affected; hoaxing, bamboozling, hoodwinking, duping; deceptive, delusive, delusory, misleading

shame *syn* DISGRACE, dishonor, disrepute, infamy, ignominy, opprobrium, obloquy, odium *rel* humiliation, degradation, abasement; mortification, chagrin *ant* glory; pride

shameless • characterized by or exhibiting boldness and a lack of shame *syn* brazen, barefaced, brash, impudent *rel* abandoned, profligate, dissolute; hardened, indurated, callous; vicious, villainous, iniquitous

shape *vb, syn* MAKE, form, fashion, fabricate, manufacture, forge

shape *n, syn* FORM, figure, conformation, configuration *rel* outline, contour, profile, silhouette; appearance, look, aspect, semblance

shapeless *syn* FORMLESS, unformed *rel* rude, rough, crude *ant* shapely

share • to have, get, or use in common with another or others *syn* participate, partake *rel* communicate, impart; divide, dispense, distribute

sharp • having or showing alert competence and clear understanding *syn* keen, acute *rel* incisive, trenchant, cutting, biting; mordant, caustic, scathing; piercing, penetrating, probing; tricky, cunning, artful, wily, guileful, sly *ant* dull; blunt

shatter *syn* BREAK, shiver, crack, burst, bust, snap *rel* demolish, destroy; ruin, wreck; rend, split, rive, tear

shave *syn* BRUSH, graze, glance, skim *rel* touch, contact; escape, avoid

shear • to cut or cut off with or as if with shears *syn* poll, clip, trim, prune, lop, snip, crop *rel* cut, slit, slash, hew; split, rive, cleave, tear

shed *syn* DISCARD, cast, molt, slough, scrap, junk *rel* remove, shift, transfer, move; reject, repudiate, spurn

sheen *syn* LUSTER, gloss, glaze *rel* gleaming, gleam, glittering, glitter, flashing, flash

sheer *adj* **1** *syn* PURE, simple, absolute *rel* outright, out-and-out, arrant, unmitigated **2** *syn* STEEP, precipitous, abrupt *rel* perpendicular, vertical

sheer *vb, syn* TURN, divert, deflect, avert

shelter *n* • something that covers or affords protection *syn* cover, retreat, refuge, asylum, sanctuary *rel* protection, safeguarding, safeguard; harbor, haven, port

shelter *vb, syn* HARBOR, lodge, house, entertain, board *rel* defend, protect, shield, guard, safeguard; receive, accept, admit

shibboleth *syn* CATCHWORD, byword, slogan

shield *syn* DEFEND, protect, guard, safeguard *rel* preserve, conserve, save; harbor, shelter, lodge, house

shift *vb, syn* MOVE, remove, transfer *rel* displace, replace; change, alter, vary; veer, swerve, deviate

shift *n* **1** *syn* RESOURCE, makeshift, expedient, resort, stopgap, substitute, surrogate *rel* device, contrivance, contraption; ruse, trick, stratagem, maneuver, gambit, ploy, wile, feint, artifice **2** *syn* SPELL, tour, trick, turn, stint, bout, go *rel* change, alternation; allotment, assignment

shimmy *syn* SHAKE, tremble, quake, totter, quiver, shiver, shudder, quaver, wobble, teeter, dither

ship *n, syn* BOAT, vessel, craft

ship *vb, syn* SEND, forward, transmit, remit, route, dispatch

shipshape *syn* NEAT, tidy, trim, trig, snug, spick-and-span

shirk *syn* DODGE, parry, sidestep, duck, fence, malinger *rel* evade, elude, avoid, escape; recoil, shrink, quail, flinch

shiver *vb, syn* BREAK, shatter, crack, burst, bust, snap

shiver *vb, syn* SHAKE, quiver, shudder, quaver, tremble, quake, totter, wobble, teeter, shimmy, dither

shoal • a shallow place in a body of water *syn* bank, reef, bar

shock *n, syn* HEAP, cock, stack, pile, mass, bank

shock *vb, syn* HEAP, cock, stack, pile, mass, bank

shock *n, syn* IMPACT, collision, clash, concussion, impingement, percussion, jar, jolt *rel* encounter, skirmish; attack, assault, onslaught, onset; shaking, rocking, agitation, convulsion

shocking *syn* FEARFUL, appalling, awful, dreadful, frightful, terrible, terrific, horrible, horrific *rel* ghastly, gruesome, lurid, macabre, grisly, grim; odious, abhorrent, abominable, hateful; repugnant, repellent, distasteful, obnoxious

shoot *vb* **1** *syn* FLY, dart, float, skim, scud, sail *rel* hasten, quicken **2** *syn* RUSH, dash, tear, charge *rel* speed, hasten, hurry

shoot *n* • a branch or a part of a plant that is an outgrowth from a main stem *syn* branch, bough, limb

shopworn *syn* TRITE, hackneyed, stereotyped, threadbare *rel* wasted, haggard; attenuated, diluted, thinned; antiquated, obsolete, archaic, old

shore • land bordering a usu. large body of water *syn* coast, beach, strand, bank, littoral, foreshore

short **1** *syn* BRIEF *rel* decreased, lessened, reduced, diminished; shortened, abridged, abbreviated, curtailed; concise, terse, laconic *ant* long **2** *syn* FRAGILE, crisp, brittle, friable, frangible

shortcoming *syn* IMPERFECTION, deficiency, fault *rel* defect, flaw, blemish; failing, frailty, foible

shorten • to reduce in extent *syn* curtail, abbreviate, abridge, retrench *rel* reduce, decrease, lessen, diminish; contract, shrink, condense *ant* lengthen, elongate; extend

short-lived *syn* TRANSIENT, transitory, passing, ephemeral, momentary, fugitive, fleeting, evanescent *ant* agelong

shortly *syn* PRESENTLY, soon, directly

shout *vb* • to utter a sudden loud cry (as to attract attention) *syn* yell, shriek, scream, screech, squeal, holler, whoop *rel* roar, bellow, bawl, howl

shout *n* • a sudden loud cry *syn* yell, shriek, scream, screech, squeal, holler, whoop *rel* bellow, vociferation, clamor, bawl, roar

shove *syn* PUSH, thrust, propel *rel* force, constrain, oblige, compel, coerce; impel, drive, move

show *vb* **1** • to reveal outwardly or make apparent *syn* manifest, evidence, evince, demonstrate *rel* reveal, disclose, discover; present, offer, proffer, tender **2** • to present so as to invite notice or attention *syn* exhibit, display, expose, parade, flaunt *rel* indicate, betoken, attest, bespeak, argue, prove; intimate, hint, suggest *ant* disguise

show *n, syn* EXHIBITION, exhibit, exposition, fair

showy • given to excess outward display *syn* pretentious, ostentatious *rel* gaudy, tawdry, garish, flashy, meretricious; resplendent, gorgeous, splendid; opulent, sumptuous, luxurious

shrew *syn* VIRAGO, scold, vixen, termagant, amazon

shrewd • acute in perception and sound in judgment *syn* sagacious, perspicacious, astute *rel* knowing, intelligent, smart, clever, quick-witted; politic, diplomatic, smooth, suave; wise, prudent, sensible, judicious; penetrating, piercing, probing; sharp, keen, acute

shriek *vb, syn* SHOUT, yell, scream, screech, squeal, holler, whoop *rel* vociferate, clamor, bellow, roar; vent, ventilate, air, voice, express

shriek *n, syn* SHOUT, yell, scream, screech, squeal, holler, whoop *rel* vociferation, clamor, bellow, roar

shrink **1** *syn* CONTRACT, constrict, compress, condense, deflate *rel* decrease, reduce, diminish, lessen; shorten, abridge, retrench, curtail *ant* swell **2** *syn* RECOIL, flinch, quail, blench, wince *rel* cringe, cower; retreat, recede; balk, shy, boggle, scruple, demur

shrivel *syn* WITHER, wizen *rel* parch, desiccate, dry; sear, scorch, burn

shroud *syn* COVER, overspread, envelop, wrap, veil *rel* hide, conceal, screen, bury; cloak, mask, camouflage, disguise

shudder *syn* SHAKE, shiver, quiver, quaver, tremble, quake, totter, wobble, teeter, shimmy, dither

shun *syn* ESCAPE, avoid, evade, elude, eschew *rel* decline, refuse, reject; balk, shy, scruple, demur, stick, stickle; scorn, disdain, despise *ant* habituate

shut *syn* CLOSE

shut out *syn* EXCLUDE, eliminate, debar, rule out, blackball, disbar *rel* prevent, preclude, obviate; hinder, obstruct, block, bar

shutter *syn* BLIND, shade

shy *adj* • not inclined to be forward *syn* bashful, diffident, modest, coy *rel* timid, timorous; wary, chary, cautious, circumspect *ant* obtrusive

shy *vb, syn* DEMUR, balk, boggle, scruple, jib, stickle, stick, strain *rel* recoil, shrink, quail, blench; hesitate, waver, falter, vacillate

sic *syn* URGE, egg, exhort, goad, spur, prod, prick *rel* incite, instigate, abet; encourage, countenance, favor

sicken *syn* DISGUST, nauseate *rel* revolt, offend, repulse

sickly *syn* UNWHOLESOME, morbid, diseased, pathological *rel* ailing; weak, feeble, frail, infirm; mawkish, mushy, maudlin *ant* robust

side *syn* PHASE, aspect, facet, angle

sidereal *syn* STARRY, stellar, astral

sidestep *syn* DODGE, parry, shirk, duck, fence, malinger *rel* avoid, evade, elude, shun, escape

siege *syn* BLOCKADE

sigh *vb* • to let out a deep audible breath (as in weariness or sorrow) *syn* sob, moan, groan *rel* lament, deplore, bemoan, bewail; long, yearn, pine, hunger, thirst

sigh *n* • a usu. inarticulate sound indicating mental or physical pain or distress *syn* groan, moan, sob *rel* regret, sorrow, grief

sight *syn* LOOK, view, glance, glimpse, peep, peek *rel* prospect, outlook; vision, revelation

sightless *syn* BLIND, purblind

sign **1** • a discernible indication of what is not itself directly perceptible *syn* mark, token, badge, note, symptom *rel* indication, betokening, attesting, attestation; manifestation, evidencing, evidence, demonstration, showing, show; intimation, suggestion **2** • a motion, action, gesture, or word by which a command, thought, or wish is expressed *syn* signal *rel* gesture, gesticulation; symbol, emblem **3** *syn* CHARACTER, symbol, mark *rel* device, contrivance

signal *n, syn* SIGN *rel* alarm, tocsin, alert; gesture, gesticulation; motion, movement; device, contrivance, contraption

signal *adj, syn* NOTICEABLE, salient, striking, arresting, outstanding, prominent, remarkable, conspicuous *rel* distinctive, individual, peculiar, characteristic; eminent, illustrious, famous, renowned

significance **1** *syn* MEANING, signification, import, sense, acceptation *rel* denotation, connotation; suggestion, implication, intimation **2** *syn* IMPORTANCE, import, consequence, moment, weight *rel* worth, value; influence, authority, credit, prestige; merit, excellence, virtue, perfection

significant *syn* EXPRESSIVE, meaningful, pregnant, eloquent, sententious *rel* cogent, telling, convincing, compelling, valid, sound; forcible, forceful, powerful; important, momentous, weighty

signification *syn* MEANING, significance, import, sense, acceptation *rel* signifying, meaning, denoting; denotation, connotation

signify *syn* MEAN, import, denote *rel* convey, carry, bear; connote; imply, suggest

silent **1** • showing restraint in speaking *syn* uncommunicative, taciturn, reticent, reserved, secretive, close, close-lipped, closemouthed, tight-lipped *rel* restrained, curbed, checked, inhibited; discreet, prudent *ant* talkative **2** *syn* STILL, stilly, quiet, noiseless *rel* calm, serene, tranquil, placid, peaceful

silhouette *syn* OUTLINE, contour, profile, skyline *rel* shadow, shade, adumbration

silken, silky *syn* SLEEK, slick, glossy, velvety, satiny *rel* lustrous, luminous, lambent, bright

silly **1** *syn* SIMPLE, foolish, fatuous, asinine *rel* irrational, unreasonable; stupid, slow, dull, dense, crass, dumb; vacuous, empty **2** *syn* FOOLISH, absurd, preposterous *rel* inane, wishy-washy, insipid; puerile, juvenile, youthful; ridiculous, ludicrous, laughable

similar *syn* LIKE, alike, analogous, comparable, akin, parallel, uniform, identical *rel* same, equivalent, equal; corresponding, correlative, complementary, reciprocal *ant* dissimilar

similarity *syn* LIKENESS, resemblance, similitude, analogy, affinity *rel* comparison, contrast, collation, parallel; agreement, accordance, harmonizing, harmony, correspondence *ant* dissimilarity

simile *syn* ANALOGY, metaphor

similitude *syn* LIKENESS, similarity, resemblance, analogy, affinity *ant* dissimilitude, dissimilarity

simmer *syn* BOIL, seethe, parboil, stew

simper *vb, syn* SMILE, smirk, grin

simper *n, syn* SMILE, smirk, grin

simple *adj* **1** *syn* PURE, absolute, sheer *rel* elemental, elementary; single, sole *ant* compound; complex **2** *syn* EASY, facile, light, effortless, smooth *rel* clear, plain, distinct, obvious, evident, manifest; lucid, perspicuous *ant* complicated; difficult **3** *syn* PLAIN, homely, unpretentious *rel* ordinary, common, familiar; lowly, humble; insignificant, unimportant **4** *syn* NATURAL, ingenuous, naïve, unsophisticated, artless *rel* sincere, unfeigned; childlike, childish; open, plain, frank, candid **5** • actually or apparently deficient in intelligence *syn* foolish, silly, fatuous, asinine *rel* childish, childlike; dull, dense, dumb, slow, stupid, crass; ignorant, illiterate, untaught *ant* wise

simple *n, syn* DRUG, medicinal, pharmaceutical, biologic

simpleton *syn* FOOL, moron, imbecile, idiot, natural

simulate *syn* ASSUME, feign, counterfeit, sham, pretend, affect *rel* dissemble, disguise, cloak, mask, camouflage; ape, mock, mimic, imitate, copy

simultaneous *syn* CONTEMPORARY, synchronous, coincident, contemporaneous, coeval, coetaneous, concomitant, concurrent *rel* concurring, coinciding, agreeing

sin *syn* OFFENSE, vice, crime, scandal *rel* transgression, trespass, breach, violation; error, lapse, slip; fault, failing, frailty

since *syn* BECAUSE, for, as, inasmuch as

sincere • genuine in feeling *syn* wholehearted, whole-souled, heartfelt, hearty, unfeigned *rel* candid, open, frank, plain; honest, honorable, conscientious, scrupulous, upright; straightforward, aboveboard, forthright *ant* insincere

sinewy *syn* MUSCULAR, athletic, husky, brawny, burly *rel* robust, healthy, sound; strong, tough, tenacious, sturdy; nervous, vigorous, energetic

sing • to produce musical tones by or as if by means of the voice *syn* troll, carol, descant, warble, trill, hymn, chant, intone

singe *syn* BURN, sear, scorch, char

single *adj* **1** *syn* UNMARRIED, celibate, virgin, maiden **2** • one as distinguished from two or more or all others *syn* sole, unique, lone, solitary, separate, particular *rel* individual, special, especial, specific *ant* accompanied; supported; conjugal

single *vb, syn* CHOOSE, prefer, select, elect, opt, pick, cull *rel* take, seize, grasp, grab; accept, receive, admit; decide, determine, settle

singular *syn* STRANGE, unique, peculiar, eccentric, erratic, odd, queer, quaint, outlandish, curious *rel* different, diverse, divergent, disparate; exceptional; abnormal, atypical, aberrant

sinister • seriously threatening evil or disaster *syn* baleful, malign, malefic, maleficent *rel* ominous, portentous, fateful, unpropitious, inauspicious; secret, covert, furtive, underhand, underhanded; malicious, malignant, malevolent, spiteful

sink *syn* FALL, drop, slump, subside *rel* droop, sag, flag, wilt; submerge, immerse, dip; ebb, abate, wane; disappear, vanish

sinuous *syn* WINDING, flexuous, serpentine, tortuous *rel* circuitous, roundabout, indirect; crooked, devious

sire *syn* GENERATE, beget, get, procreate, engender, breed, propagate, reproduce

site *syn* PLACE, position, location, situation, spot, station *rel* area, tract, region, zone; field, territory, province; section, sector, part; locality, district

situation **1** *syn* PLACE, position, location, site, spot, station *rel* area, region, tract, zone; section, sector, part; locality, district, vicinity, neighborhood **2** *syn* STATE, condition, mode, posture, status *rel* juncture, pass, crisis, exigency, emergency; predicament, plight, quandary, dilemma; case, instance

size • the amount of measurable space or area occupied by a thing *syn* dimensions, area, extent, magnitude, volume *rel* amplitude, expanse, spread, stretch; bulk, mass, volume

skedaddle *syn* SCUTTLE, scurry, scamper, sprint *rel* flee, fly, escape, decamp; retreat, recede; withdraw, retire, go

skeleton *syn* STRUCTURE, anatomy, framework

skepticism *syn* UNCERTAINTY, doubt, dubiety, mistrust

sketch *n* **1** • a rough drawing representing the chief features of an object or scene *syn* outline, diagram, delineation, draft, tracing, plot, blueprint *rel* design, plan, scheme, project; chart, map **2** *syn* COM-

PENDIUM, précis, aperçu, syllabus, digest, pandect, survey

sketch *vb* • to make a sketch, rough draft, or outline of *syn* outline, diagram, delineate, draft, trace, plot, blueprint *rel* design, plan, scheme, project; chart, map, graph

skewbald *syn* VARIEGATED, parti-colored, motley, checkered, checked, pied, piebald, dappled, freaked

skid *syn* SLIDE, slip, glide, glissade, slither, coast, toboggan

skill *syn* ART, cunning, craft, artifice *rel* proficiency, adeptness, expertness; efficiency, effectiveness; readiness, facility, dexterity, ease

skilled *syn* PROFICIENT, skillful, adept, expert, masterly *rel* apt, ready, quick, prompt; practiced, exercised, drilled; competent, qualified, able, capable *ant* unskilled

skillful *syn* PROFICIENT, adept, expert, skilled, masterly *rel* dexterous, adroit, deft; efficient, effective; conversant, versed *ant* unskillful

skim **1** *syn* FLY, float, dart, scud, shoot, sail **2** *syn* BRUSH, graze, glance, shave *rel* slide, glide, slip, slither; flit, hover

skimpy *syn* MEAGER, scrimpy, exiguous, scanty, scant, spare, sparse

skin *n* • an outer or surface layer esp. the outer limiting layer of an animal body *syn* hide, pelt, rind, bark, peel

skin *vb* • to remove the surface, skin, or thin outer covering of *syn* decorticate, peel, pare, flay

skinny *syn* LEAN, scrawny, rawboned, angular, gaunt, lank, lanky, spare *ant* fleshy

skip • to move or advance with successive springs or leaps *syn* bound, hop, curvet, lope, lollop, ricochet

skirmish *syn* ENCOUNTER, brush *rel* contest, conflict, combat, fight, affray, fray; engagement, action, battle

skit *syn* LIBEL, squib, lampoon, pasquinade

skulk *syn* LURK, couch, slink, sneak *rel* secrete, hide, conceal

skyline *syn* OUTLINE, profile, contour, silhouette

slack **1** *syn* NEGLIGENT, lax, remiss, neglectful *rel* lazy, indolent, slothful, faineant; indifferent, unconcerned, detached, aloof; sluggish, lethargic **2** *syn* LOOSE, relaxed, lax *rel* weak, feeble, infirm; inert, supine, passive, inactive; slow, leisurely, laggard

slacken *syn* DELAY, retard, slow, detain *rel* abate, reduce, lessen, decrease; restrain, curb, check, inhibit; moderate, temper, qualify *ant* quicken

slander *n, syn* DETRACTION, calumny, backbiting, scandal *rel* defamation, vilification, aspersion, traducing; abuse, vituperation, invective, obloquy, scurrility

slander *vb, syn* MALIGN, defame, libel, calumniate, traduce, asperse, vilify *rel* decry, depreciate, detract, derogate, disparage, belittle; injure, damage, hurt; attack, assail

slang *syn* DIALECT, vernacular, patois, lingo, jargon, cant, argot

slant *vb* • to set or be set at an angle *syn* slope, incline, lean *rel* veer, swerve, deviate, diverge

slant *n, syn* POINT OF VIEW, viewpoint, standpoint, angle *rel* attitude, position, stand; bias, prejudice, predilection

slap *syn* STRIKE, hit, smite, punch, slug, slog, swat, clout, cuff, box

slash *syn* CUT, slit, hew, chop, carve *rel* rive, rend, cleave, split, tear; penetrate, pierce, enter

slatternly • being habitually untidy and very dirty esp. in dress or appearance *syn* dowdy, frowzy, blowsy *rel* slovenly, unkempt, disheveled, sloppy, slipshod

slaughter *syn* MASSACRE, butchery, carnage, pogrom

slavery *syn* SERVITUDE, bondage

slavish *syn* SUBSERVIENT, servile, menial, obsequious *rel* mean, abject, ignoble, sordid; tame, subdued, submissive; miserable, wretched

slay *syn* KILL, murder, assassinate, dispatch, execute

sleazy *syn* LIMP, flimsy, floppy, flaccid, flabby *rel* thin, tenuous, slight; loose, slack

sleek • having a smooth bright surface or appearance *syn* slick, glossy, velvety, silken, silky, satiny *rel* bright, lustrous, brilliant; smooth, even, level

sleep • to take rest by a suspension of consciousness *syn* slumber, drowse, doze, nap, catnap, snooze *rel* rest, repose, relax

sleepy • affected by or inducing of a desire to sleep *syn* drowsy, somnolent, slumberous *rel* lethargic, sluggish, comatose

slender *syn* THIN, slim, slight, tenuous, rare *rel* lean, spare, lanky, skinny; flimsy, flaccid, flabby, limp; trivial, trifling, petty, paltry, puny

slick **1** *syn* SLEEK, glossy, velvety, silken, satiny, silky *rel* finished, consummate; flawless, impeccable, faultless; shallow, superficial **2** *syn* FULSOME, oily, unctuous, oleaginous, soapy *rel* bland, smooth, diplomatic, politic, suave, urbane; specious, plausible

slide • to go or progress with a smooth continuous motion *syn* slip, glide, skid, glissade, slither, coast, toboggan

slight *adj, syn* THIN, tenuous, rare, slender, slim *rel* imperceptible, imponderable, impalpable, intangible, insensible, inappreciable; trifling, trivial, puny, petty, paltry; minute, diminutive, wee, little, small

slight *vb, syn* NEGLECT, ignore, overlook, disregard, omit, forget *rel* scorn, disdain, contemn, despise; flout, scoff

slighting *syn* DEROGATORY, depreciatory, depreciative, disparaging, pejorative *rel* contemptuous, disdainful, scornful, despiteful

slim *syn* THIN, slender, slight, tenuous, rare *rel* lean, spare, skinny, scrawny; meager, exiguous, scant, scanty; lithe, lithesome, lissome *ant* chubby

sling *vb, syn* THROW, hurl, fling, pitch, toss, cast *rel* heave, hoist, lift, raise; impel, drive; propel, shove, thrust, push

sling *vb, syn* HANG, suspend, dangle

slink *syn* LURK, skulk, sneak

slip *vb, syn* SLIDE, glide, skid, glissade, slither, coast, toboggan

slip *n* **1** *syn* WHARF, dock, pier, quay, berth, jetty, levee **2** *syn* ERROR, lapse, mistake, blunder, faux pas, bull, howler, boner *rel* accident, chance; inadvertence, carelessness, heedlessness; fault, failing, foible, frailty, vice

slipshod • negligent of or marked by lack of neatness and order esp. in appearance or dress *syn* slovenly, unkempt, disheveled, sloppy *rel* negligent, neglectful, slack, lax, remiss; careless, heedless, inadvertent; indifferent, unconcerned; slatternly, dowdy, frowzy, blowsy

slit *syn* CUT, slash, hew, chop, carve

slither *syn* SLIDE, slip, glide, skid, glissade, coast, toboggan

slog *syn* STRIKE, hit, smite, punch, slug, swat, clout, slap, cuff, box

slogan *syn* CATCHWORD, byword, shibboleth *rel* phrase, expression, locution, idiom

slope *syn* SLANT, incline, lean *rel* deviate, diverge, veer, swerve

sloppy *syn* SLIPSHOD, slovenly, unkempt, disheveled *rel* negligent, neglectful, slack, remiss, lax; mawkish, maudlin, soppy, slushy, sentimental; slatternly, dowdy, frowzy, blowsy

slothful *syn* LAZY, indolent, faineant *rel* inactive, inert, supine, passive, idle; slack, remiss, lax, negligent, neglectful; slow, leisurely, deliberate, dilatory, laggard *ant* industrious

slough *syn* DISCARD, cast, shed, molt, scrap, junk

slovenly *syn* SLIPSHOD, unkempt, disheveled, sloppy *rel* slatternly, dowdy, frowzy, blowsy; indifferent, unconcerned; negligent, neglectful, slack, lax, remiss

slow *adj* **1** *syn* STUPID, dull, dense, crass, dumb **2** • moving, flowing, or proceeding at less than the usual, desirable, or required speed *syn* dilatory, laggard, deliberate, leisurely *ant* fast

slow *vb, syn* DELAY, slacken, retard, detain *rel* moderate, temper, qualify; reduce, abate, decrease, lessen *ant* speed

slug *syn* STRIKE, hit, smite, punch, slog, swat, clout, slap, cuff, box

sluggish *syn* LETHARGIC, torpid, comatose *rel* inert, inactive; indolent, slothful, lazy; listless, languishing, languid *ant* brisk; expeditious; quick

sluice *syn* POUR, stream, gush *rel* flood, inundate, deluge; drench, soak

slumber *syn* SLEEP, drowse, doze, nap, catnap, snooze *rel* relax, rest, repose

slumberous *syn* SLEEPY, drowsy, somnolent

slump *syn* FALL, drop, sink, subside *rel* plunge, dive, pitch; sag, flag, droop

slushy *syn* SENTIMENTAL, mushy, romantic, mawkish, maudlin, soppy

sly • attaining or seeking to attain one's ends by devious means *syn* cunning, crafty, tricky, foxy, insidious, wily, guileful, artful *rel* furtive, clandestine, stealthy, covert, secret; devious, oblique, crooked; astute, shrewd

smack **1** *syn* TASTE, flavor, savor, tang, relish **2** *syn* TOUCH, suggestion, suspicion, soupçon, tincture, tinge, shade, spice, dash, vein, strain, streak

small • noticeably below average in size *syn* little, diminutive, petite, wee, tiny, teeny, weeny, minute, microscopic, miniature *rel* petty, puny, paltry, trifling, trivial *ant* large

small-town *syn* INSULAR, provincial, parochial, local *rel* narrow, narrow-minded, illiberal, intolerant, hidebound, bigoted; circumscribed, limited, confined, restricted *ant* cosmopolitan

smart **1** *syn* INTELLIGENT, bright, knowing, quick-witted, clever, alert *rel* sharp, keen, acute; quick, ready, prompt, apt; shrewd, astute, perspicacious *ant* dull (*of mind*) **2** *syn* STYLISH, modish, fashionable, chic, dashing *rel* elegant, exquisite, choice; finished, consummate *ant* dowdy, frowzy, blowsy

smash *syn* CRUSH, mash, bruise, squash, macerate *rel* shatter, burst, crack, break; press, squeeze, crowd, jam

smell • the quality that makes a thing perceptible to the olfactory sense *syn* scent, odor, aroma *rel* fragrance, redolence, perfume, bouquet, incense; savor, flavor, taste

smidgen *syn* PARTICLE, bit, mite, whit, atom, iota, jot, tittle

smile *vb* • to have, produce, or exhibit a smile *syn* grin, simper, smirk *ant* frown

smile *n* • a facial expression in which the lips curve slightly upward esp. in expression of pleasure or amusement *syn* simper, smirk, grin *ant* frown

smirch *syn* SOIL, dirty, sully, tarnish, foul, befoul, besmirch, grime, begrime

smirk *vb, syn* SMILE, simper, grin

smirk *n, syn* SMILE, simper, grin

smite *syn* STRIKE, hit, punch, slug, slog, swat, clout, slap, cuff, box *rel* beat, pummel, buffet; punish, discipline, correct

smog *syn* HAZE, fog, mist

smooth **1** *syn* LEVEL, even, plane, plain, flat, flush *rel* sleek, slick, glossy *ant* rough **2** *syn* EASY, effortless, light, simple, facile *rel* agreeable, pleasant, pleasing, gratifying, grateful; serene, tranquil, calm, placid, peaceful *ant* labored **3** *syn* SUAVE, bland, diplomatic, politic, urbane *rel* polite, courteous, courtly, civil; oily, unctuous, slick, fulsome *ant* bluff **4** *syn* SOFT, bland, mild, gentle, lenient, balmy

smother *syn* SUFFOCATE, asphyxiate, stifle, choke, strangle, throttle

smug *syn* COMPLACENT, self-complacent, self-satisfied, priggish *rel* self-respecting, self-esteeming, self-admiring; pharisaical, sanctimonious, hypocritical

smuggled • imported or exported secretly and in violation of the law *syn* bootleg, contraband

snag *syn* OBSTACLE, obstruction, impediment, bar *rel* projection, protuberance; difficulty, hardship, vicissitude; barring, blocking, block, hindering, hindrance

snap **1** *syn* JERK, twitch, yank *rel* seize, snatch, clutch, grasp, take **2** *syn* BREAK, crack, burst, bust, shatter, shiver *rel* part, separate, sever, sunder

snappish *syn* IRRITABLE, fractious, peevish, waspish, petulant, pettish, huffy, fretful, querulous *rel* testy, touchy, cranky, irascible; surly, crabbed, morose, sullen

snappy *syn* PUNGENT, piquant, poignant, racy, spicy *rel* sharp, keen, acute; vivacious, lively, animated; quick, prompt, ready; smart, dashing, chic, modish, stylish

snare *n, syn* LURE, trap, bait, decoy *rel* trickery, deception, chicanery, chicane

snare *vb, syn* CATCH, ensnare, trap, entrap, bag, capture *rel* lure, entice, inveigle, tempt, seduce, decoy

snarl *n, syn* CONFUSION, disorder, chaos, disarray, jumble, clutter, muddle *rel* complexity, complication, intricateness, intricacy; difficulty, hardship

snarl *vb, syn* BARK, bay, howl, growl, yelp, yap

snatch *syn* TAKE, grasp, grab, clutch, seize *rel* catch, capture; pull, drag, draw

sneak *syn* LURK, slink, skulk

sneer *syn* SCOFF, jeer, gird, flout, gibe, fleer *rel* deride, taunt, mock, ridicule; scout, despise, scorn, disdain

snip *syn* SHEAR, poll, clip, trim, prune, lop, crop *rel* cut, slit, slash, chop; bite

snitch *syn* STEAL, pilfer, filch, purloin, lift, pinch, swipe, cop

snoopy *syn* CURIOUS, inquisitive, prying, nosy *rel* meddlesome, officious, intrusive, impertinent, obtrusive; interfering, interposing

snooze *syn* SLEEP, slumber, drowse, doze, nap, catnap

snug **1** *syn* NEAT, trim, trig, shipshape, tidy, spick-and-span *rel* compact, close; orderly, methodical, systematic **2** *syn* COMFORTABLE, cozy, easy, restful *rel* safe, secure; familiar, intimate, close; sheltered, harbored

so *syn* THEREFORE, hence, consequently, then, accordingly

soak *vb* • to permeate or be permeated with a liquid *syn* saturate, drench, steep, impregnate, sop, waterlog *rel* dip, immerse, submerge; permeate, pervade, penetrate

soak *n, syn* DRUNKARD, inebriate, alcoholic, dipsomaniac, sot, toper, tosspot, tippler

soapy *syn* FULSOME, slick, oily, unctuous, oleaginous

soar *syn* RISE, arise, ascend, mount, tower, rocket, levitate, surge *rel* fly, dart, shoot; aspire, aim

sob *vb, syn* SIGH, moan, groan *rel* weep, wail, cry, blubber

sob *n, syn* SIGH, moan, groan *rel* weeping, wailing, crying, blubbering

sober **1** • having or exhibiting self-control and avoiding extremes of behavior *syn* temperate, continent, unimpassioned *rel* abstaining, refraining, forbearing; forgoing, eschewing, abnegating; cool, collected, composed; reasonable, rational *ant* drunk; excited **2** *syn* SERIOUS, grave, sedate, staid, solemn, somber, earnest *rel* decorous, decent, proper; calm, placid, tranquil, serene; dispassionate, impartial, fair, equitable *ant* gay

sobriety *syn* TEMPERANCE, abstinence, abstemiousness, continence *rel* moderateness, temperateness; quietness, stillness; seriousness, gravity, somberness, sedateness *ant* drunkenness; excitement

sociable *syn* GRACIOUS, cordial, affable, genial *rel* social, companionable, convivial, gregarious; intimate, familiar, close; amiable, obliging, complaisant, good-natured *ant* unsociable

social • inclined to seek or enjoy the company of others *syn* gregarious, cooperative, convivial, companionable, hospitable *rel* gracious, cordial, sociable, genial, affable; amicable, neighborly, friendly *ant* unsocial, antisocial, asocial

society **1** *syn* ARISTOCRACY, elite, nobility, gentry, county **2** *syn* ASSOCIATION, order, club

soft • free from all harshness, roughness, or intensity *syn* bland, mild, gentle, smooth, lenient, balmy *rel* moderated, tempered; smooth, effortless, easy; velvety, silken, sleek, slick; serene, tranquil, calm, placid, peaceful *ant* hard; stern

soil • to make or become unclean *syn* dirty, sully, tarnish, foul, befoul, smirch, besmirch, grime, begrime

sojourn *syn* RESIDE, lodge, stay, put up, stop, live, dwell

solace *syn* COMFORT, console *rel* relieve, assuage, mitigate, allay, alleviate, lighten; gladden, rejoice, delight, please, gratify

sole *syn* SINGLE, unique, solitary, lone, separate, particular *rel* alone, only; exclusive, picked, select

solecism *syn* BARBARISM, corruption, impropriety, vulgarism, vernacular

solemn **1** *syn* CEREMONIAL, ceremonious, formal, conventional *rel* liturgical, ritualistic; full, complete, plenary; imposing, august, majestic, magnificent, grand **2** *syn* SERIOUS, grave, somber, sedate, earnest, staid, sober *rel* impressive, moving; sublime, superb, splendid; ostentatious, showy

solemnize *syn* KEEP, celebrate, observe, commemorate

solicit **1** *syn* ASK, request *rel* resort, refer, apply, go, turn; beg, entreat, beseech, implore, supplicate **2** *syn* INVITE, bid, court, woo *rel* importune, adjure, beg; demand, claim, exact; evoke, elicit, extract, extort, educe

solicitor *syn* LAWYER, attorney, counselor, barrister, counsel, advocate

solicitous *syn* WORRIED, concerned, anxious *rel* apprehensive, fearful, afraid; agitated, disturbed, disquieted, upset; uneasy, fidgety, jittery, impatient *ant* unmindful; negligent

solicitude *syn* CARE, concern, anxiety, worry *rel* misgiving, apprehension, foreboding, presentiment; compunction, qualm, scruple; fear, alarm, consternation, dismay *ant* negligence; unmindfulness

solid *syn* FIRM, hard *rel* compact, close, dense; consolidated, concentrated, compacted *ant* fluid, liquid

solidarity *syn* UNITY, union, integrity *rel* consolidation, concentration, unification; cooperation, concurrence, combination

solidify *syn* HARDEN, indurate, petrify, cake *rel* compact, consolidate, concentrate; condense, contract, compress; congeal, coagulate, set, clot, jelly, jell

solitary **1** *syn* ALONE, lonely, lonesome, lone, forlorn, lorn, desolate *rel* isolated, secluded; retired, withdrawn; forsaken, deserted, abandoned **2** *syn* SINGLE, sole, unique, lone, separate, particular *rel* alone, only

solitude • the state of one who is alone *syn* isolation, alienation, seclusion *rel* retreat, refuge, asylum, shelter; retirement, withdrawal

solve • to find an explanation or solution for something obscure, mysterious, or incomprehensible *syn* resolve, unfold, unravel, decipher *rel* decide, determine, settle; illuminate, enlighten; interpret, elucidate, explain

somatic *syn* BODILY, physical, corporeal, corporal

somber *syn* SERIOUS, grave, solemn, sedate, staid, sober, earnest *rel* gloomy, dark, murky; dismal, bleak, cheerless; melancholy, melancholic *ant* garish

somnolent *syn* SLEEPY, drowsy, slumberous *rel* sluggish, comatose, lethargic; inert, inactive, passive, supine

sonorous *syn* RESONANT, ringing, resounding, vibrant, orotund *rel* deep, profound; rich, opulent; loud, stentorian

soon **1** *syn* PRESENTLY, shortly, directly **2** *syn* EARLY, beforehand, betimes

soothe *syn* CALM, compose, quiet, quieten, still, lull, settle, tranquilize *rel* mollify, appease, placate, pacify, propitiate, conciliate; allay, alleviate, assuage, mitigate, relieve *ant* annoy; excite

sop *syn* SOAK, saturate, drench, steep, impregnate, waterlog

sophism *syn* FALLACY, sophistry, casuistry

sophistical *syn* FALLACIOUS, casuistical *ant* valid

sophisticate *syn* ADULTERATE, load, weight, doctor

sophisticated • experienced in the ways of the world *syn* worldly-wise, worldly, blasé, disillusioned *rel* cultivated, cultured; intellectualized; knowing, brilliant, intelligent, clever, alert *ant* unsophisticated

sophistry *syn* FALLACY, sophism, casuistry *rel* plausibility, speciousness; equivocation, ambiguity, tergiversation; evading, evasion, avoiding, avoidance

soppy *syn* SENTIMENTAL, romantic, mawkish, maudlin, mushy, slushy

sorcery *syn* MAGIC, witchcraft, witchery, wizardry, alchemy, thaumaturgy

sordid *syn* MEAN, ignoble, abject *rel* mercenary, venal; squalid, foul, filthy, nasty, dirty; contemptible, despicable, sorry, scurvy, cheap, beggarly, shabby

sorrow *n* • distress of mind *syn* grief, heartache, heartbreak, anguish, woe, regret *rel* mourning, grieving; distress, suffering, misery, agony; melancholy, dejection, sadness, depression *ant* joy

sorrow *vb, syn* GRIEVE, mourn *rel* cry, weep, wail, keen; sob, moan, groan, sigh

sorry *syn* CONTEMPTIBLE, pitiable, despicable, scurvy, cheap, beggarly, shabby *rel* mean, ignoble, sordid, abject; miserable, wretched; paltry, petty, trifling, trivial

sort *n, syn* TYPE, kind, stripe, kidney, ilk, description, nature, character

sort *vb, syn* ASSORT, classify, pigeonhole *rel* arrange, methodize, systematize, order; cull, pick, choose, select

sot *syn* DRUNKARD, inebriate, alcoholic, dipsomaniac, soak, toper, tosspot, tippler

soul **1** *syn* MIND, intellect, psyche, brain, intelligence, wit *rel* powers, faculties, functions **2** • the immortal part of a human being believed to have permanent individual existence *syn* spirit *ant* body

sound *adj* **1** *syn* HEALTHY, wholesome, robust, hale, well *rel* vigorous, lusty, nervous, energetic, strenuous; strong, sturdy, stalwart, stout; intact, whole, entire, perfect **2** *syn* VALID, cogent, convincing, compelling, telling *rel* impeccable, flawless, faultless, errorless; correct, exact, precise, accurate; rational, reasonable *ant* fallacious

sound *n* • a sensation or effect produced by stimulation of the auditory receptors *syn* noise *ant* silence

sound *n, syn* STRAIT, channel, passage, narrows

sound *vb, syn* FATHOM, plumb

soupçon *syn* TOUCH, suspicion, suggestion, tincture, tinge, shade, smack, spice, dash, vein, strain, streak

sour • having a taste devoid of sweetness *syn* acid, acidulous, tart, dry *rel* bitter, acrid; sharp, keen; morose, sullen, glum, crabbed, saturnine, dour

source *syn* ORIGIN, root, inception, provenance, provenience, prime mover *rel* beginning, commencement, starting, start; cause, determinant, antecedent *ant* termination; outcome

souse *syn* DIP, immerse, submerge, duck, dunk *rel* soak, steep, saturate, impregnate

souvenir 1 *syn* REMEMBRANCE, remembrancer, reminder, memorial, memento, token, keepsake 2 *syn* MEMORY, remembrance, recollection, reminiscence, mind

sovereign 1 *syn* DOMINANT, predominant, paramount, preponderant, preponderating *rel* supreme, transcendent, surpassing; absolute, ultimate 2 *syn* FREE, independent, autonomous, autarchic, autarkic *rel* highest, loftiest; chief, principal, foremost; governing, ruling; commanding, directing

sovereignty *syn* FREEDOM, independence, autonomy, autarky, autarchy *rel* supremacy, ascendancy; command, sway, control, dominion, power, authority

sow *syn* STREW, straw, scatter, broadcast

spacious • larger in extent or capacity than the average *syn* commodious, capacious, ample *rel* vast, immense, enormous, huge; broad, wide, deep; extended, extensive

spade *syn* DIG, delve, grub, excavate

spangle *syn* SPOT, spatter, sprinkle, mottle, fleck, stipple, marble, speckle, bespangle

spangled *syn* SPOTTED, spattered, sprinkled, mottled, flecked, stippled, marbled, speckled, bespangled

spare 1 *syn* SUPERFLUOUS, extra, surplus, supernumerary *rel* excessive, immoderate, exorbitant, inordinate 2 *syn* LEAN, lank, lanky, skinny, scrawny, gaunt, rawboned, angular *rel* thin, slender, slim, slight; sinewy, athletic, muscular *ant* corpulent 3 *syn* MEAGER, exiguous, sparse, scanty, scant, skimpy, scrimpy *rel* economical, sparing, frugal, thrifty *ant* profuse

sparing • careful in the use of one's money or resources *syn* frugal, thrifty, economical *rel* meager, exiguous, spare; stingy, niggardly, parsimonious, penurious; moderate, temperate *ant* lavish

sparkle *syn* FLASH, gleam, glance, glint, glitter, glisten, scintillate, coruscate, twinkle

sparse *syn* MEAGER, spare, exiguous, scanty, scant, skimpy, scrimpy *rel* scattered, dispersed; sporadic, occasional, infrequent, uncommon; thin, slim, slender *ant* dense

spasm *syn* FIT, paroxysm, convulsion, attack, access, accession

spasmodic *syn* FITFUL, convulsive *rel* intermittent, alternate, recurrent, periodic; irregular, unnatural; abnormal, aberrant, atypical

spat *n, syn* QUARREL, bickering, squabble, wrangle, altercation, tiff *rel* dispute, controversy, argument; contention, difference, variance, discord

spat *vb, syn* QUARREL, bicker, squabble, wrangle, altercate, tiff *rel* dispute, argue, agitate, debate, discuss; differ, disagree

spate *syn* FLOOD, deluge, inundation, torrent, cataract *rel* flow, stream, current, tide; succession, progression, series

spatter *syn* SPOT, sprinkle, mottle, fleck, stipple, marble, speckle, spangle, bespangle *rel* bespatter, asperse, splash

spattered *syn* SPOTTED, sprinkled, mottled, flecked, stippled, marbled, speckled, spangled, bespangled

spay *syn* STERILIZE, castrate, emasculate, alter, mutilate, geld

speak • to articulate words so as to express thoughts *syn* talk, converse *rel* pronounce, articulate, enunciate; stammer, stutter; discourse, expatiate, dilate, descant

special • of or relating to one thing or class *syn* especial, specific, particular, individual *rel* distinctive, peculiar, characteristic; exceptional; uncommon, occasional, rare, infrequent

specie *syn* MONEY, cash, currency, legal tender, coin, coinage

specific *adj* 1 *syn* SPECIAL, especial, particular, individual *ant* generic 2 *syn* EXPLICIT, definite, express, categorical *rel* designating, naming; clear, lucid, perspicuous; precise, exact *ant* vague

specific *n, syn* REMEDY, cure, medicine, medicament, medication, physic

specify *syn* MENTION, name, instance *rel* cite, quote; stipulate

specimen *syn* INSTANCE, example, sample, illustration, case

specious *syn* PLAUSIBLE, believable, colorable, credible *rel* vain, nugatory, empty, hollow, idle; delusory, delusive, misleading, deceptive; deceitful, dishonest, untruthful, mendacious, lying

speckle *syn* SPOT, spatter, sprinkle, mottle, fleck, stipple, marble, spangle, bespangle

speckled *syn* SPOTTED, spattered, sprinkled, mottled, flecked, stippled, marbled, spangled, bespangled

spectator • one who looks on or watches *syn* observer, beholder, looker-on, onlooker, witness, eyewitness, bystander, kibitzer

specter *syn* APPARITION, spirit, ghost, phantasm, phantom, wraith, shade, revenant

speculate *syn* THINK, reason, reflect, cogitate, deliberate *rel* ponder, meditate, muse, ruminate; consider, weigh, study, contemplate, excogitate

speculative **1** *syn* THOUGHTFUL, contemplative, meditative, reflective, pensive *rel* conjecturing, conjectural, surmising, guessing; pondering, musing, ruminating **2** *syn* THEORETICAL, academic

speech **1** *syn* LANGUAGE, tongue, dialect, idiom **2** • a usu. formal discourse delivered to an audience *syn* address, oration, harangue, lecture, talk, sermon, homily

speechless *syn* DUMB, mute, inarticulate

speed *n* **1** *syn* HASTE, hurry, expedition, dispatch *rel* celerity, legerity, alacrity; fleetness, rapidity, swiftness, quickness; velocity, pace, headway **2** • rate of motion, performance, or action *syn* velocity, momentum, impetus, pace, headway

speed *vb* • to go or make go fast or faster *syn* accelerate, quicken, hasten, hurry, precipitate *rel* advance, forward, further, promote; adjust, regulate, fix

speedy *syn* FAST, expeditious, quick, swift, fleet, rapid, hasty *rel* brisk, nimble, agile; prompt, quick, ready *ant* dilatory

spell • a limited period or amount of activity *syn* shift, tour, trick, turn, stint, bout, go *rel* period; allotment, assignment, apportionment

spend • to use up or pay out *syn* expend, disburse *rel* distribute, dispense, divide, deal, dole; allot, assign, allocate, apportion; scatter, disperse, dissipate; pay, compensate, remunerate *ant* save

spendthrift • a person who spends foolishly and wastefully *syn* prodigal, profligate, waster, wastrel

spew *syn* BELCH, burp, vomit, disgorge, regurgitate, throw up

sphere *syn* FIELD, domain, province, territory, bailiwick *rel* dominion, sway, jurisdiction, control, power; range, reach, scope, compass; function, office, duty

spice *syn* TOUCH, suggestion, suspicion, soupçon, tincture, tinge, shade, smack, dash, vein, strain, streak

spick-and-span *syn* NEAT, tidy, trim, trig, snug, shipshape *rel* clean, cleanly; fresh, new *ant* filthy

spicy *syn* PUNGENT, piquant, poignant, racy, snappy *rel* spirited, high-spirited, gingery, fiery, peppery; aromatic, redolent, balmy, odorous

spin *syn* TURN, revolve, rotate, gyrate, circle, twirl, whirl, wheel, eddy, swirl, pirouette *rel* swing, sway, oscillate, vibrate

spine • the articulated column of bones that is the central and axial feature of a vertebrate skeleton *syn* backbone, back, vertebrae, chine

spirit **1** *syn* SOUL *rel* mind, intellect, psyche **2** *syn* APPARITION, ghost, phantasm, phantom, wraith, specter, shade, revenant **3** *syn* COURAGE, mettle, resolution, tenacity *rel* fortitude, pluck, grit, backbone, sand, guts; zeal, fervor, ardor, passion, enthusiasm; energy, strength, might, power, force **4** *syn* VIGOR, vim, dash, esprit, verve, punch, élan, drive *rel* vitality, animation, aliveness; vivacity, liveliness, gaiety, sprightliness

spirited • full of energy, animation, or courage *syn* high-spirited, mettlesome, spunky, fiery, peppery, gingery *rel* courageous, intrepid, bold, audacious, valiant, brave; impetuous, precipitate; eager, avid, keen; passionate, enthusiastic, zealous, fervent, ardent *ant* spiritless

spiritless *syn* LANGUID, languishing, languorous, listless, enervated, lackadaisical *rel* lethargic, sluggish, comatose; dull, slow, stupid, dense, crass; tame, subdued, submissive *ant* spirited

spiritual **1** *syn* IMMATERIAL, incorporeal *ant* physical **2** *syn* HOLY, sacred, divine, religious, blessed *rel* supernatural, supranatural; celestial, heavenly *ant* physical; carnal; material; temporal

spite *syn* MALICE, despite, malignity, malignancy, spleen, grudge, ill will, malevolence *rel* rancor, animus, antipathy, enmity; vindictiveness, revengefulness, revenge, vengefulness, vengeance

spiteful *syn* MALICIOUS, malignant, malevolent, malign *rel* rancorous, antipathetic, antagonistic, hostile; vindictive, revengeful, vengeful

spleen *syn* MALICE, malignity, malignancy,

grudge, spite, despite, malevolence, ill will *rel* animosity, antipathy, animus, rancor, antagonism, enmity; venom, poison; vindictiveness, revengefulness

splendid • extraordinarily or transcendently impressive *syn* resplendent, gorgeous, glorious, sublime, superb *rel* radiant, effulgent, luminous, brilliant, bright; illustrious, eminent, famous; excelling, excellent, surpassing, transcending, transcendent

splenetic *syn* IRASCIBLE, choleric, testy, touchy, cranky, cross *rel* morose, sullen, glum, gloomy; irritable, querulous, peevish, snappish; captious, carping, caviling, critical

split *vb, syn* TEAR, rend, cleave, rive, rip *rel* separate, part, divide, sever; cut, chop, hew

split *n, syn* BREACH, break, schism, rent, rupture, rift *rel* crack, cleft, fissure; estrangement, alienation; schism, heresy

split second *syn* INSTANT, moment, second, minute, flash, jiffy, twinkling

spoil *n* • something taken from another by force or craft *syn* plunder, booty, prize, loot, swag *rel* theft, robbery, larceny, burglary; acquisitions, acquirements

spoil *vb* **1** *syn* INJURE, harm, hurt, damage, impair, mar *rel* ruin, wreck; destroy, demolish **2** *syn* INDULGE, pamper, humor, baby, mollycoddle *rel* favor, accommodate, oblige; debase, deprave, vitiate, debauch **3** *syn* DECAY, decompose, rot, putrefy, disintegrate, crumble *rel* corrupt, vitiate, debase; ruin, wreck; impair, harm, injure

spoliate *syn* RAVAGE, despoil, devastate, waste, sack, pillage *rel* rob, plunder, rifle, loot; defraud, swindle, cheat

sponge, sponger *syn* PARASITE, sycophant, favorite, toady, lickspittle, bootlicker, hanger-on, leech

sponsor • one who assumes responsibility for some other person or thing *syn* patron, surety, guarantor, backer, angel *rel* supporter, support, upholder, champion, advocator, advocate; promoter, furtherer

spontaneity *syn* UNCONSTRAINT, abandon *rel* spontaneousness, instinctiveness, impulsiveness; extemporaneousness, offhandedness, unpremeditatedness; naturalness, simplicity, unsophistication, naïveté, ingenuousness

spontaneous • acting or activated without deliberation *syn* impulsive, instinctive, automatic, mechanical *rel* extemporaneous, extempore, impromptu, improvised, offhand, unpremeditated; natural, simple, ingenuous, unsophisticated

spoon *syn* DIP, ladle, dish, bail, scoop

sporadic *syn* INFREQUENT, occasional, rare, scarce, uncommon *rel* scattered, dispersed; sparse, exiguous, meager

sport *vb, syn* PLAY, disport, frolic, rollick, romp, gambol *rel* divert, amuse, recreate, entertain; skip, bound, hop

sport *n* **1** *syn* PLAY, disport, frolic, rollick, romp, gambol *rel* amusement, diversion, recreation, entertainment; merriment, jollity **2** *syn* FUN, jest, game, play *rel* mirth, glee, hilarity, jollity **3** *pl* **sports** *syn* ATHLETICS, games

sportive *syn* PLAYFUL, frolicsome, roguish, waggish, impish, mischievous *rel* blithe, merry, jocund, jovial, jolly; mirthful, gleeful, hilarious

spot *n, syn* PLACE, position, location, situation, site, station *rel* locality, district, neighborhood, vicinity; region, area, tract, belt, zone; section, sector, part

spot *vb* • to mark or become marked with or as if with spots or sometimes streaks *syn* spatter, sprinkle, mottle, fleck, stipple, marble, speckle, spangle, bespangle *rel* splash, bespatter, besprinkle, asperse; soil, sully, dirty, smirch, besmirch; variegate, checker, dapple, freak

spotted • marked with spots or streaks *syn* spattered, sprinkled, mottled, flecked, stippled, marbled, speckled, spangled, bespangled

sprain *n, syn* STRAIN

sprain *vb, syn* STRAIN

spread *vb* • to extend or cause to extend over an area or space *syn* circulate, disseminate, diffuse, propagate, radiate *rel* distribute, dispense, deal; scatter, dissipate

spread *n, syn* EXPANSE, amplitude, stretch *rel* extent, area, magnitude, size; range, reach, scope, compass

sprightly *syn* LIVELY, animated, vivacious, gay *rel* active, live, dynamic; agile, nimble, brisk, spry; merry, blithe, jocund

spring *vb* **1** • to come up or out of something into existence *syn* arise, rise, originate, derive, flow, issue, emanate, proceed, stem *rel* emerge, loom, appear; come, arrive; begin, commence, start **2** *syn* JUMP, leap, bound, vault *rel* frolic, rollick, gambol, disport, play

spring *n* **1** *syn* MOTIVE, impulse, incentive, inducement, spur, goad *rel* origin, source, root, inception; cause, determinant, antecedent; stimulus, stimulant, excitant, incitement, impetus **2** *syn* JUMP, leap, bound, vault

springy *syn* ELASTIC, resilient, flexible, supple *rel* yielding, submitting; recoiling, rebounding

sprinkle *syn* SPOT, spatter, mottle, fleck, stipple, marble, speckle, spangle, bespangle

sprinkled *syn* SPOTTED, spattered, mottled, flecked, stippled, marbled, speckled, spangled, bespangled

sprint *syn* SCUTTLE, scurry, scamper, skedaddle *rel* rush, dash, charge, shoot, tear; speed, hurry, hasten; dart, fly, scud

spry *syn* AGILE, brisk, nimble *rel* quick, ready, prompt; vigorous, energetic, strenuous; hale, healthy, sound, robust *ant* doddering

spume *syn* FOAM, froth, scum, lather, suds, yeast

spunky *syn* SPIRITED, high-spirited, mettlesome, fiery, peppery, gingery *rel* dauntless, undaunted, bold, brave; daring, venturesome, adventurous; restive, restless, impatient

spur *n, syn* MOTIVE, goad, spring, impulse, incentive, inducement *rel* stimulus, stimulant, excitant, incitement, impetus; activation, actuation, motivation; cause, determinant; provoking, provocation, exciting, excitement

spur *vb, syn* URGE, egg, exhort, goad, prod, prick, sic *rel* rouse, arouse, stir, awaken, rally; incite, instigate; excite, provoke, stimulate; encourage, countenance, favor *ant* curb

spurious *syn* COUNTERFEIT, bogus, fake, sham, pseudo, pinchbeck, phony *rel* false; simulated, feigned, shammed; supposititious, reputed, putative, supposed *ant* genuine

spurn *syn* DECLINE, reject, repudiate, refuse *rel* disdain, scorn, scout, despise, contemn; flout, scoff, sneer *ant* crave; embrace

squabble *n, syn* QUARREL, wrangle, altercation, bickering, spat, tiff *rel* dispute, controversy, argument; row, rumpus, scrap, brawl, broil

squabble *vb, syn* QUARREL, wrangle, altercate, bicker, spat, tiff *rel* contend, fight, battle, war; struggle, strive; dispute, agitate, argue, discuss

squalid *syn* DIRTY, nasty, filthy, foul *rel* slovenly, unkempt, disheveled, sloppy, slipshod; sordid, abject, mean; slatternly, frowzy

squander *syn* WASTE, dissipate, fritter, consume *rel* scatter, disperse, dissipate, dispel; spend, expend, disburse

square *syn* AGREE, conform, accord, harmonize, correspond, tally, jibe *rel* equal, match, approach, touch, rival; balance, offset, compensate; concur, coincide

squash *syn* CRUSH, mash, smash, bruise, macerate *rel* press, squeeze, jam, crowd; compact, concentrate, consolidate

squat *syn* STOCKY, thickset, thick, chunky, stubby, dumpy *ant* lanky

squeal *vb, syn* SHOUT, yell, shriek, scream, screech, holler, whoop *rel* cry, wail

squeal *n, syn* SHOUT, yell, shriek, scream, screech, holler, whoop

squeamish *syn* NICE, finicky, finicking, finical, particular, fussy, persnickety, pernickety, fastidious, dainty *rel* exacting, demanding, requiring; hypercritical, critical, faultfinding, caviling, captious, carping

squeeze *syn* PRESS, bear, bear down, crowd, jam *rel* compress, contract; extract, elicit, educe, extort; force, compel, constrain, coerce

squib *syn* LIBEL, skit, lampoon, pasquinade

squirm *syn* WRITHE, agonize *rel* twist, bend, curve; wince, flinch, blench, shrink, recoil

stabilize • to make or become stable, steadfast, or firm *syn* steady, poise, balance, ballast, trim *rel* regulate, adjust, fix; set, settle, establish

stable *syn* LASTING, durable, perdurable, permanent, perpetual *rel* enduring, persisting, abiding; secure, safe; steady, constant; staunch, steadfast, resolute *ant* unstable; changeable

stack *n, syn* HEAP, pile, mass, bank, shock, cock

stack *vb, syn* HEAP, pile, mass, bank, shock,

cock *rel* collect, gather, assemble; amass, accumulate, hoard

stagger *syn* REEL, whirl, totter *rel* sway, waver, fluctuate, swing; stumble, lurch, blunder, flounder

staid *syn* SERIOUS, sedate, grave, somber, sober, earnest *rel* decorous, decent, seemly; cool, collected, composed; smug, priggish, self-complacent, complacent *ant* jaunty

stain *syn* STIGMA, blot, brand *rel* blemish, defect, flaw; mark, sign, token; disgrace, dishonor

stake *syn* BET, wager, pot, ante

stalemate *syn* DRAW, tie, deadlock, standoff

stalwart *syn* STRONG, stout, sturdy, tough, tenacious *rel* husky, brawny, muscular, sinewy, athletic; lusty, nervous, vigorous; robust, sound, healthy

stammer • to make involuntary stops and repetitions in speaking *syn* stutter

stamp *vb, syn* MARK, brand, label, tag, ticket *rel* impress, imprint, print; authenticate, validate, confirm; avouch, warrant, assert

stamp *n* **1** *syn* IMPRESSION, impress, imprint, print **2** *syn* MARK, brand, label, tag, ticket

stand *vb, syn* BEAR, tolerate, brook, suffer, endure, abide

stand *n, syn* POSITION, attitude *rel* point of view, standpoint, viewpoint, slant, angle

standard **1** *syn* FLAG, ensign, banner, color, streamer, pennant, pendant, pennon, jack **2** • a means of determining what a thing should be *syn* criterion, gauge, yardstick, touchstone *rel* norm, median, par, mean, average; rule, law; principle, fundamental, axiom **3** *syn* MODEL, ideal, beau ideal, pattern, exemplar, example, mirror *rel* see STANDARD 2

stand-in *syn* SUBSTITUTE, supply, understudy, double, locum tenens, alternate, pinch hitter

standoff *syn* DRAW, tie, stalemate, deadlock

standpoint *syn* POINT OF VIEW, viewpoint, angle, slant *rel* stand, position, attitude

stare *syn* GAZE, gape, glare, peer, gloat *rel* look, watch, see; glower, lower, scowl, frown

stark *syn* STIFF, rigid, inflexible, tense, wooden *rel* settled, established, fixed, set

starry • of, relating to, or suggestive of a star or group of stars *syn* stellar, astral, sidereal

start *syn* BEGIN, commence, initiate, inaugurate *rel* institute, found, establish, organize; enter, penetrate; originate, proceed, spring

startle *syn* FRIGHTEN, scare, alarm, terrify, terrorize, fright, affray, affright *rel* surprise, astonish, astound; rouse, arouse, stir; electrify, thrill

state *n* • the way in which one manifests existence or the circumstances under which one exists or by which one is given distinctive character *syn* condition, mode, situation, posture, status *rel* phase, aspect; plight, predicament, quandary, dilemma; pass, juncture, exigency, emergency, crisis

state *vb* **1** *syn* SAY, utter, tell **2** *syn* RELATE, report, rehearse, recite, recount, narrate, describe *rel* expound, explain, elucidate, interpret; assert, affirm, declare, profess

stately *syn* GRAND, magnificent, imposing, majestic, august, noble, grandiose *rel* princely, regal, royal, kingly, imperial; splendid, glorious, superb, sublime; sumptuous, opulent, luxurious

statesman *syn* POLITICIAN, politico

station **1** *syn* PLACE, position, location, situation, site, spot *rel* locality, district, vicinity, neighborhood; region, area, zone, belt, tract **2** *syn* HABITAT, biotope, range

stature *syn* QUALITY, caliber *rel* capacity, ability; competence, qualification

status *syn* STATE, situation, posture, condition, mode

statute *syn* LAW, ordinance, regulation, rule, precept, canon

staunch *syn* FAITHFUL, loyal, true, constant, steadfast, resolute *rel* trusty, trustworthy, reliable, dependable, tried; stout, strong, tough, tenacious, sturdy, stalwart

stay *vb* **1** • to continue to be in one place for a noticeable time *syn* remain, wait, abide, tarry, linger *rel* delay, procrastinate, lag, loiter; arrest, check, interrupt; continue, persist **2** *syn* RESIDE, sojourn, lodge, put up, stop, live, dwell **3** *syn* DEFER, postpone, suspend, intermit *rel* delay, retard, slow, slacken, detain; restrain, check, curb; hinder, obstruct, impede

stay *vb, syn* BASE, found, ground, bottom, rest

steadfast *syn* FAITHFUL, staunch, resolute, constant, true, loyal *rel* settled, established, set, fixed; steady; stable, durable, perdurable, lasting; enduring, persisting, abiding *ant* capricious

steady *adj* • not varying throughout a course or extent *syn* uniform, even, equable, constant *rel* stable, durable, perdurable, perpetual, lasting; enduring, persisting, continuing; staunch, steadfast, resolute, faithful; persevering, persisting *ant* unsteady; nervous, jumpy

steady *vb, syn* STABILIZE, poise, balance, ballast, trim

steal • to take from another without right or without detection *syn* pilfer, filch, purloin, lift, pinch, snitch, swipe, cop *rel* rob, plunder, rifle, loot, burglarize

stealthy *syn* SECRET, covert, furtive, clandestine, surreptitious, underhand, underhanded *rel* sly, cunning, crafty, artful, tricky, wily; sneaking, slinking, skulking

steel *syn* ENCOURAGE, inspirit, hearten, embolden, cheer, nerve *rel* fortify, reinforce, invigorate, strengthen; determine, resolve, decide

steep *adj* • having an incline approaching the perpendicular *syn* abrupt, precipitous, sheer *rel* elevated, lifted, raised; lofty, high

steep *vb, syn* SOAK, saturate, impregnate, drench, sop, waterlog *rel* infuse, imbue, ingrain; penetrate, pierce, probe

steer *syn* GUIDE, lead, pilot, engineer *rel* conduct, direct, manage, control; govern, rule

stellar *syn* STARRY, sidereal, astral

stem *syn* SPRING, proceed, issue, emanate, derive, flow, originate, arise, rise

stentorian *syn* LOUD, earsplitting, hoarse, raucous, strident, stertorous *rel* resounding, orotund, resonant; vociferous, clamorous, blatant; harsh, rough

stereotyped *syn* TRITE, hackneyed, threadbare, shopworn *rel* conventional, formal, ceremonial; obsolete, archaic, antiquated, old; used, employed, utilized, applied *ant* changeful

sterile • not able to bear fruit, crops, or offspring *syn* barren, impotent, unfruitful, infertile *rel* bare, bald, naked; arid, dry; meager, exiguous; empty, hollow, nugatory, vain *ant* fertile; exuberant

sterilize **1** • to make incapable of producing offspring *syn* castrate, spay, emasculate, alter, mutilate, geld *ant* fertilize **2** • to free from living microorganisms *syn* disinfect, sanitize, fumigate

stern *syn* SEVERE, austere, ascetic *rel* strict, rigid, rigorous, stringent; grim, implacable, unrelenting; inflexible, inexorable; disciplined, trained, schooled *ant* soft; lenient

stertorous *syn* LOUD, stentorian, earsplitting, hoarse, raucous, strident *rel* harsh, rough

stew *syn* BOIL, seethe, simmer, parboil

stick **1** • to become or cause to become closely and firmly attached *syn* adhere, cohere, cling, cleave *rel* tie, bind; attach, fasten, affix, fix; implant **2** *syn* DEMUR, stickle, balk, shy, boggle, scruple, jib, strain

stickle *syn* DEMUR, balk, shy, boggle, jib, scruple, stick, strain *rel* hesitate, vacillate, falter, waver; object, kick, protest

stick out *syn* BULGE, jut, protrude, project, overhang, beetle *rel* extend, prolong, elongate, lengthen; expand, swell, distend; obtrude

stiff • difficult to bend *syn* rigid, inflexible, tense, stark, wooden *rel* tough, tenacious, strong, stout; firm, hard, solid; formal, conventional, ceremonious, ceremonial; frigid, cold, cool; difficult, hard, arduous *ant* relaxed; supple

stiff-necked *syn* OBSTINATE, stubborn, mulish, dogged, pertinacious, pigheaded, bullheaded

stifle *syn* SUFFOCATE, asphyxiate, smother, choke, strangle, throttle

stigma • a mark of shame or discredit *syn* brand, blot, stain *rel* disgrace, dishonor, opprobrium, odium, shame; contamination, tainting, taint, defilement, pollution

still *adj* • making no stir or noise *syn* stilly, quiet, silent, noiseless *rel* calm, tranquil, serene, placid, peaceful; restful, comfortable *ant* stirring; noisy

still *vb, syn* CALM, compose, quiet, quieten, lull, soothe, settle, tranquilize *rel* allay, assuage, alleviate, relieve; pacify, placate, mollify, appease; silence *ant* agitate

stilly *syn* STILL, quiet, silent, noiseless *rel* soft, gentle, mild, bland; placid, peaceful, calm, tranquil, serene

stimulant *syn* STIMULUS, excitant, incitement, impetus *rel* provocation, excitement, stimulation, quickening, galvanizing; incentive, spur, goad, motive *ant* anesthetic; anodyne

stimulate *syn* PROVOKE, excite, quicken, pique, galvanize *rel* animate, enliven, vivify; activate, energize, vitalize; rouse, arouse, stir, rally, waken, awaken *ant* unnerve; deaden

stimulus • something that rouses or incites to activity *syn* stimulant, excitant, incitement, impetus *rel* spur, goad, incentive, motive, inducement; excitement, piquing, provocation; irritation, nettling

stingy • being unwilling or showing unwillingness to share with others *syn* close, closefisted, tight, tightfisted, niggardly, parsimonious, penurious, miserly, cheeseparing, penny-pinching *rel* mean, sordid, ignoble; scrimpy, skimpy, meager; greedy, acquisitive, avaricious, covetous, grasping; sparing, economical, frugal, thrifty *ant* generous

stinking *syn* MALODOROUS, fetid, noisome, putrid, rank, rancid, fusty, musty *rel* foul, filthy, nasty, dirty; offensive, repulsive, revolting

stint **1** *syn* TASK, duty, assignment, job, chore *rel* quantity, amount, sum; allotment, apportionment; prescribing, prescription, assigning; sharing, share, participation **2** *syn* SPELL, bout, shift, tour, trick, turn, go

stipend *syn* WAGE, wages, salary, fee, emolument, pay, hire *rel* remuneration, compensation, recompensing, recompense

stipple *syn* SPOT, spatter, sprinkle, mottle, fleck, marble, speckle, spangle, bespangle

stippled *syn* SPOTTED, spattered, sprinkled, mottled, flecked, marbled, speckled, spangled, bespangled

stipulation *syn* CONDITION, terms, provision, proviso, reservation, strings *rel* specification; restriction, circumscription

stir *vb* • to cause to shift from quiescence or torpor into activity *syn* rouse, arouse, awaken, waken, rally *rel* excite, provoke, stimulate, quicken, galvanize; incite, foment, instigate; activate, energize, vitalize; move, drive, impel, actuate

stir *n* **1** *syn* MOTION, movement, move, locomotion *rel* acting, activity, working, work, behaving, behavior, reaction; change, alteration, variation, modification **2** • signs of excited activity, hurry, or commotion *syn* bustle, flurry, pother, fuss, ado *rel* agitation, disturbance, disquieting, disquiet; excitement, stimulation; din, uproar, hubbub, pandemonium *ant* tranquillity

stitch *syn* PAIN, twinge, ache, pang, throe

stock *syn* VARIETY, subspecies, race, breed, cultivar, strain, clone

stocky • compact, sturdy, and relatively thick in build *syn* thickset, thick, chunky, stubby, squat, dumpy

stodgy *syn* DULL, humdrum, dreary, monotonous, pedestrian *rel* heavy, weighty, ponderous; irksome, tedious, wearisome, tiresome, boring; stuffy, straitlaced, prudish, prim

stoic *syn* IMPASSIVE, phlegmatic, apathetic, stolid *rel* detached, aloof, indifferent, unconcerned; imperturbable, composed, collected, cool; unassailable, indomitable, invincible; patient, long-suffering, resigned

stoicism *syn* IMPASSIVITY, impassiveness, phlegm, apathy, stolidity *rel* fortitude, grit, backbone, pluck, guts, sand; detachment, aloofness, indifference, unconcernedness, unconcern

stolid *syn* IMPASSIVE, phlegmatic, apathetic *rel* dull, blunt, obtuse; stupid, slow, dense, crass, dumb; heavy, ponderous; passive, supine, inert, inactive *ant* adroit

stolidity *syn* IMPASSIVITY, impassiveness, phlegm, apathy, stoicism

stomach *syn* ABDOMEN, belly, paunch, gut

stoop • to descend from one's real or pretended level of dignity *syn* condescend, deign *rel* abase, demean, humble; vouchsafe, accord, grant, concede; favor, accommodate, oblige

stop **1** • to suspend or cause to suspend activity *syn* cease, quit, discontinue, desist *rel* arrest, check, interrupt; intermit, suspend, stay, defer, postpone; frustrate, thwart, foil, balk, circumvent **2** *syn* RESIDE, stay, put up, lodge, sojourn, live, dwell

stopgap *syn* RESOURCE, makeshift, shift, expedient, resort, substitute, surrogate

storm *syn* ATTACK, bombard, assault, assail

story **1** *syn* ACCOUNT, report, chronicle, version *rel* history, annals; relation, rehearsing, recital, recounting **2** • a recital of happenings less elaborate than a novel *syn* narrative, tale, anecdote, yarn *rel* narration, description; fiction, fable, fabrication **3** *syn* LIE, falsehood, untruth, fib, misrepresentation

stout **1** *syn* STRONG, sturdy, stalwart, tough, tenacious *rel* brave, bold, intrepid, valiant, valorous; indomitable, invincible; resolute, staunch, steadfast, faithful; vigorous, energetic, lusty **2** *syn* FLESHY, fat, portly, corpulent, obese, plump, rotund, chubby *rel* thick, thickset, stocky; burly, brawny, husky, muscular *ant* cadaverous

straightforward • free from all that is dishonest or secretive *syn* forthright, aboveboard *rel* honest, upright, honorable, just; fair, equitable, impartial; candid, frank, open, plain *ant* devious; indirect

strain *n* **1** *syn* VARIETY, subspecies, race, breed, cultivar, clone, stock **2** *syn* TOUCH, streak, vein, suggestion, suspicion, soupçon, tincture, tinge, shade, smack, spice, dash

strain *vb* **1** • to injure (as a body part) by overuse or misuse *syn* sprain **2** *syn* DEMUR, scruple, balk, jib, shy, boggle, stickle, stick

strain *n* **1** *syn* STRESS, pressure, tension **2** • an injury to a part of the body from undue stretching *syn* sprain

strained *syn* FORCED, labored, farfetched *rel* tense, taut, tight; artificial, factitious; unnatural, irregular; stiff, rigid, inflexible, wooden

strait **1** • a comparatively narrow stretch of water connecting two larger bodies of water *syn* sound, channel, passage, narrows **2** *syn* JUNCTURE, pass, exigency, pinch, emergency, contingency, crisis *rel* difficulty, hardship, vicissitude, rigor; perplexity, bewilderment, mystification; plight, predicament, fix, quandary

straitlaced *syn* PRIM, priggish, prissy, prudish, puritanical, stuffy *rel* narrow, narrow-minded, hidebound, intolerant, illiberal; rigid, rigorous, strict *ant* libertine

strand *syn* SHORE, coast, beach, bank, littoral, foreshore

strange • departing from what is ordinary, usual, and to be expected *syn* singular, unique, peculiar, eccentric, erratic, odd, queer, quaint, outlandish, curious *rel* abnormal, atypical, aberrant; fantastic, bizarre, grotesque; surprising, astonishing, amazing, flabbergasting *ant* familiar

stranger • a nonresident or an unknown person in a community *syn* foreigner, alien, outlander, outsider, immigrant, émigré

strangle *syn* SUFFOCATE, asphyxiate, stifle, smother, choke, throttle

stratagem *syn* TRICK, ruse, maneuver, gambit, ploy, artifice, wile, feint *rel* device, contrivance, contraption; expedient, shift, resource, resort; machination, intrigue, conspiracy, plot

strategic • of, relating to, or marked by strategy *syn* tactical, logistic

strategy • the art of devising or employing plans toward a usu. military goal *syn* tactics, logistics

straw *syn* STREW, scatter, sow, broadcast

stray *syn* WANDER, roam, ramble, rove, range, prowl, gad, gallivant, traipse, meander

streak *syn* TOUCH, strain, vein, suggestion, suspicion, soupçon, tincture, tinge, shade, smack, spice, dash

stream *n, syn* FLOW, current, flood, tide, flux

stream *vb, syn* POUR, gush, sluice *rel* flow, issue, emanate, proceed, spring; flood, deluge, inundate

streamer *syn* FLAG, pennant, pendant, pennon, banner, ensign, standard, color

strength *syn* POWER, force, might, energy, puissance *rel* stoutness, sturdiness, toughness, tenaciousness; soundness, healthiness; possessions, means, resources, assets

strengthen • to make strong or stronger *syn* invigorate, fortify, energize, reinforce *rel* embolden, steel, nerve, encourage, inspirit, hearten, cheer; vitalize, activate; galvanize, quicken, stimulate, provoke; intensify, heighten, aggravate *ant* weaken

strenuous *syn* VIGOROUS, energetic, lusty, nervous *rel* virile, manful, manly; dynamic, live, active, operative; spirited, high-spirited, mettlesome; vehement, intense, fierce, violent

stress **1** • the action or effect of force exerted within or upon a thing *syn* strain, pressure, tension **2** *syn* EMPHASIS, accent, accentuation

stretch *syn* EXPANSE, amplitude, spread *rel* area, tract, region; extent, magnitude, size

strew • to throw loosely or at intervals *syn*

straw, scatter, sow, broadcast *rel* spread, disseminate; disperse, dissipate, scatter

strict *syn* RIGID, stringent, rigorous *rel* stern, severe, austere, ascetic; inflexible, inexorable; exacting, oppressive, onerous, burdensome *ant* lax; loose; lenient, indulgent

stricture *syn* ANIMADVERSION, aspersion, reflection *rel* criticism, censuring, censure, condemnation, denouncing, denunciation *ant* commendation

strident **1** *syn* LOUD, stentorian, earsplitting, hoarse, raucous, stertorous *rel* harsh, rough; resounding, resonant **2** *syn* VOCIFEROUS, blatant, clamorous, boisterous, obstreperous *rel* harsh, uneven, rough

strife *syn* DISCORD, conflict, contention, dissension, difference, variance *rel* combat, conflict, fight, affray, fray, contest; dispute, controversy, argument; brawl, broil, fracas; altercation, wrangle, quarrel, squabble *ant* peace; accord

strike **1** • to deliver (a blow) in a strong, vigorous manner *syn* hit, smite, punch, slug, slog, swat, clout, slap, cuff, box *rel* beat, pummel, buffet, pound, baste, belabor, thrash **2** *syn* AFFECT, impress, touch, influence, sway

striking *syn* NOTICEABLE, arresting, signal, salient, conspicuous, outstanding, remarkable, prominent *rel* effective, effectual, efficacious; telling, convincing, compelling, cogent, valid; forcible, forceful, powerful; impressive, moving

string **1** *syn* SUCCESSION, progression, series, sequence, chain, train **2** *pl* **strings** *syn* CONDITION, stipulation, terms, provision, proviso, reservation

stringent *syn* RIGID, strict, rigorous *rel* severe, austere, stern; limiting, restricting, circumscribing, confining; restraining, curbing; exacting, oppressive, onerous

strip *vb* • to remove what clothes, furnishes, or invests a person or thing *syn* divest, denude, bare, dismantle *rel* despoil, spoliate, devastate, waste, ravage; rifle, loot, plunder, rob *ant* furnish; invest

strip *n* • long narrow piece or area *syn* stripe, band, ribbon, fillet

stripe **1** *syn* STRIP, band, ribbon, fillet **2** *syn* TYPE, character, description, nature, kind, sort, kidney, ilk

strive *syn* ATTEMPT, struggle, endeavor, essay, try *rel* work, labor, toil, travail; contend, fight

striving *syn* ATTEMPT, struggle, endeavor, essay, try *rel* work, labor, toil, travail; contending; contest, conflict, combat, fight

stroll *syn* SAUNTER, amble

strong • showing power to resist or to endure *syn* stout, sturdy, stalwart, tough, tenacious *rel* vigorous, energetic, lusty; powerful, potent, forcible, forceful; robust, sound, healthy; vehement, intense, fierce, exquisite, violent *ant* weak

stronghold *syn* FORT, citadel, fortress, fastness

structure **1** *syn* BUILDING, edifice, pile **2** • something made up of interdependent parts in a definite pattern of organization *syn* anatomy, framework, skeleton *rel* integration, articulation, concatenation; organization, arrangement; system, organism, scheme, complex

struggle *vb, syn* ATTEMPT, strive, endeavor, essay, try *rel* contend, fight; compete, vie, rival, emulate; toil, labor, work, travail

struggle *n, syn* ATTEMPT, striving, endeavor, essay, try *rel* toil, labor, work, travail; contest, conflict, fight, affray, fray; contending

strut • to walk with an air of pomposity or affected dignity *syn* swagger, bristle, bridle *rel* expose, exhibit, flaunt, parade, show

stubborn *syn* OBSTINATE, dogged, pertinacious, mulish, stiff-necked, pigheaded, bullheaded *rel* rebellious, contumacious, insubordinate; intractable, recalcitrant, refractory; obdurate, adamant, inexorable, inflexible

stubby *syn* STOCKY, thickset, thick, chunky, squat, dumpy

studied *syn* DELIBERATE, considered, advised, premeditated, designed *rel* thoughtful, considerate, attentive; intentional, voluntary, willing, willful

study *n, syn* ATTENTION, concentration, application *rel* consideration, contemplation, weighing; reflection, thought, speculation; pondering, musing, meditation, rumination

study *vb, syn* CONSIDER, contemplate, weigh, excogitate *rel* scrutinize, examine, inspect; ponder, muse, meditate; think, reflect, reason, speculate

stuff *n, syn* MATTER, substance, material *rel* constituent, ingredient, component, element; item, detail, particular

stuff *vb, syn* PACK, crowd, cram, ram, tamp *rel* distend, expand, swell; squeeze, jam, press; gorge, glut, surfeit, sate, satiate

stuffy *syn* PRIM, priggish, prissy, prudish, puritanical, straitlaced *rel* stodgy, dull, humdrum; irksome, tedious; narrow, narrow-minded, illiberal, hidebound

stumble • to move so clumsily or unsteadily as to fall or nearly fall *syn* trip, blunder, lurch, flounder, lumber, galumph, lollop, bumble *rel* stagger, totter, reel; plunge, pitch, dive; falter, hesitate, waver, vacillate; chance, venture; encounter, meet, confront

stun *syn* DAZE, bemuse, stupefy, benumb, paralyze, petrify *rel* astound, amaze, flabbergast, surprise; bewilder, dumbfound, nonplus, confound

stupefy *syn* DAZE, stun, bemuse, benumb, paralyze, petrify *rel* confuse, muddle, addle, fuddle, befuddle; faze, rattle; dumbfound, nonplus, bewilder, mystify, puzzle

stupendous *syn* MONSTROUS, tremendous, prodigious, monumental *rel* enormous, immense, huge, vast, colossal, gigantic; astounding, amazing, astonishing

stupid • lacking in power to absorb ideas or impressions *syn* slow, dull, dense, crass, dumb *rel* foolish, silly, simple, fatuous, asinine; sluggish, comatose, lethargic; inert, idle, supine, inactive; phlegmatic, stolid, impassive *ant* intelligent

stupor *syn* LETHARGY, torpor, torpidity, lassitude, languor *rel* phlegm, impassivity, stolidity; inertness, inertia, passivity, supineness, inactivity, idleness; insensibility, anesthesia

sturdy *syn* STRONG, stout, stalwart, tough, tenacious *rel* sound, robust, healthy; vigorous, energetic, lusty; dogged, pertinacious, obstinate *ant* decrepit

stutter *syn* STAMMER

stygian *syn* INFERNAL, chthonic, chthonian, Hadean, Tartarean, hellish

style **1** *syn* LANGUAGE, diction, phraseology, phrasing, vocabulary *rel* taste, zest, gusto, relish; form, convention, usage, convenance **2** *syn* FASHION, mode, vogue, fad, rage, craze, dernier cri, cry *rel* modishness, smartness, chicness, stylishness, fashionableness **3** *syn* NAME, designation, title, denomination, appellation

stylish • conforming to current fashion *syn* fashionable, modish, smart, chic, dashing *rel* new, novel, new-fashioned, newfangled, modernistic; showy, ostentatious, pretentious

suave • pleasantly tactful and well-mannered *syn* urbane, diplomatic, bland, smooth, politic *rel* gracious, cordial, affable, genial, sociable; courteous, courtly, polite, civil; fulsome, unctuous, slick *ant* bluff

subdue *syn* CONQUER, subjugate, reduce, overcome, surmount, overthrow, rout, vanquish, defeat, beat, lick *rel* control, manage, direct; discipline, punish, correct; foil, thwart, circumvent, frustrate; suppress, repress *ant* awaken, waken

subdued *syn* TAME, submissive *rel* meek, humble, modest, lowly; timid, timorous; docile, tractable, amenable, obedient *ant* intense; barbaric (*of taste*); bizarre (*of effects*); effervescent (*of character and temperament*)

subject *n* **1** *syn* CITIZEN, national *ant* sovereign **2** • the basic idea or the principal object of attention in a discourse or artistic composition *syn* matter, subject matter, argument, topic, text, theme, motive, motif, leitmotiv

subject *adj* **1** *syn* SUBORDINATE, dependent, secondary, tributary, collateral *rel* subservient, servile, slavish; conditional, contingent, dependent, relative *ant* sovereign, dominant **2** *syn* LIABLE, open, exposed, prone, susceptible, sensitive *rel* apt, likely *ant* exempt

subject matter *syn* SUBJECT, matter, argument, topic, text, theme, motive, motif, leitmotiv

subjoin *syn* ADD, append, annex, superadd *rel* attach, affix, fasten; unite, conjoin, combine

subjugate *syn* CONQUER, subdue, reduce, overcome, surmount, overthrow, rout, vanquish, defeat, beat, lick *rel* circumvent, outwit, foil, thwart, frustrate; compel, coerce, force

sublime *syn* SPLENDID, glorious, superb, resplendent, gorgeous *rel* transcendent, transcendental, ideal, abstract; divine, spiritual, sacred, holy; majestic, august, noble, stately, grand

sublunary *syn* EARTHLY, terrestrial, earthy, mundane, worldly

submerge *syn* DIP, immerse, duck, souse, dunk *rel* soak, saturate, drench, impregnate

submission *syn* SURRENDER, capitulation *rel* yielding, submitting, succumbing, bowing, caving in; compliance, acquiescence, resignation *ant* resistance

submissive *syn* TAME, subdued *rel* docile, tractable, amenable, biddable, obedient; meek, lowly, humble; subservient, servile, slavish, menial *ant* rebellious

submit *syn* YIELD, capitulate, succumb, relent, defer, bow, cave *rel* surrender, abandon, resign, relinquish; abide, endure, suffer, bear *ant* resist, withstand

subordinate *adj* • placed in or occupying a lower class, rank, or status *syn* secondary, dependent, subject, tributary, collateral *rel* auxiliary, subsidiary, subservient, contributory, adjuvant; accidental, incidental, fortuitous *ant* chief, leading; dominant

subordinate *n, syn* INFERIOR, underling *ant* chief

subscribe *syn* ASSENT, agree, acquiesce, consent, accede *rel* concur, coincide; approve, endorse, sanction; promise, pledge, covenant *ant* boggle

subservient **1** *syn* AUXILIARY, subsidiary, contributory, ancillary, adjuvant, accessory *rel* subordinate, secondary, dependent, subject **2** • showing or characterized by extreme compliance or abject obedience *syn* servile, slavish, menial, obsequious *rel* fawning, cringing, truckling, cowering; compliant, acquiescent, resigned; mean, ignoble, abject *ant* domineering; overbearing

subside **1** *syn* FALL, drop, sink, slump *rel* sag, flag, droop, wilt; shrink, contract, constrict **2** *syn* ABATE, wane, ebb *rel* dwindle, diminish, decrease

subsidiary *syn* AUXILIARY, contributory, subservient, ancillary, adjuvant, accessory

subsidy *syn* APPROPRIATION, grant, subvention

subsist *syn* BE, exist, live

subsistence *syn* LIVING, livelihood, sustenance, maintenance, support, keep, bread, bread and butter

subspecies *syn* VARIETY, race, breed, cultivar, strain, clone, stock

substance **1** • the inner significance or central meaning of something written or said *syn* purport, gist, burden, core, pith *rel* center, nucleus, heart, focus; principle, fundamental; foundation, base, groundwork **2** *syn* MATTER, material, stuff

substantial *syn* MASSIVE, massy, bulky, monumental *ant* airy, ethereal

substantiate *syn* CONFIRM, verify, corroborate, authenticate, validate *rel* prove, demonstrate, try, test

substitute **1** *syn* RESOURCE, surrogate, resort, expedient, shift, makeshift, stopgap *rel* device, contrivance, contraption; duplicate, copy, reproduction **2** • a person who takes the place of or acts instead of another *syn* supply, locum tenens, alternate, understudy, double, stand-in, pinch hitter

subsume *syn* INCLUDE, comprehend, embrace, involve, imply

subtle *syn* LOGICAL, analytical *rel* penetrating, piercing, probing; deep, profound; abstruse, recondite *ant* dense; blunt

subtract *syn* DEDUCT *ant* add

subvention *syn* APPROPRIATION, grant, subsidy

subvert *syn* OVERTURN, overthrow, capsize, upset *rel* ruin, wreck; destroy, demolish; corrupt, pervert, deprave, debase *ant* uphold, sustain

succeed **1** *syn* FOLLOW, ensue, supervene *rel* displace, supplant, replace, supersede *ant* precede **2** • to attain or be attaining a desired end *syn* prosper, thrive, flourish *rel* attain, achieve, gain, compass, reach; effect, fulfill, perform *ant* fail; attempt

succession • a number of things that follow each other in some order *syn* progression, series, sequence, chain, train, string *rel* consecutiveness, successiveness; articulation, concatenation, integration

successive *syn* CONSECUTIVE, sequent, sequential, serial *rel* continuous, continual, constant, incessant; rotating, alternating

succinct *syn* CONCISE, terse, laconic, summary, pithy, compendious *rel* brief, short; compressed, condensed, contracted; compact, close; curt, brusque, blunt, bluff *ant* discursive

succumb *syn* YIELD, submit, capitulate, relent, defer, bow, cave *rel* surrender, abandon, resign, relinquish

sudden *syn* PRECIPITATE, hasty, headlong, abrupt, impetuous *rel* quickened, hurried, speeded, accelerated; fast, rapid, swift, fleet, expeditious

suds *syn* FOAM, froth, spume, lather, scum, yeast

sue *syn* PRAY, plead, petition *rel* entreat, beseech, beg, importune, implore, supplicate; solicit, request, ask; demand, claim, exact, require

suffer **1** *syn* BEAR, endure, abide, tolerate, stand, brook *rel* accept, receive, admit; yield, submit, bow **2** *syn* EXPERIENCE, undergo, sustain *rel* submit, succumb, defer, yield **3** *syn* LET, permit, allow, leave

sufferance *syn* PERMISSION, leave *rel* toleration, endurance; acquiescence, resignation, compliance

suffering *syn* DISTRESS, misery, agony, dolor, passion *rel* affliction, tribulation, trial, visitation; adversity, misfortune; sorrow, grief, anguish, woe, heartache, heartbreak

sufficient • being what is necessary or desirable *syn* enough, adequate, competent

suffocate • to stop the respiration of *syn* asphyxiate, stifle, smother, choke, strangle, throttle

suffrage • the right, privilege, or power of expressing one's choice or wish (as in an election or in the determination of policy) *syn* franchise, vote, ballot

suffuse *syn* INFUSE, imbue, ingrain, inoculate, leaven *rel* introduce, interpose, interject; impregnate, penetrate, pervade, permeate

suggest **1** • to convey an idea indirectly *syn* imply, hint, intimate, insinuate *rel* present, offer; infuse, imbue, inoculate, leaven; advance, further; allude, refer, advert; connote, denote *ant* express **2** • to call to mind by thought, through close connection, or by association *syn* adumbrate, shadow *ant* manifest

suggestion *syn* TOUCH, suspicion, soupçon, tincture, tinge, shade, smack, spice, dash, vein, strain, streak

suit **1** *syn* PRAYER, plea, petition, appeal *rel* entreaty, importuning, importunity, imploring, supplication; asking, requesting, request, soliciting, solicitation **2** • a legal proceeding instituted for the sake of demanding justice or enforcing a right *syn* lawsuit, action, cause, case

suitable *syn* FIT, meet, proper, appropriate, fitting, apt, happy, felicitous *rel* decorous, decent, seemly, nice; advisable, expedient, politic; due, rightful, condign *ant* unsuitable; unbecoming

sulky *syn* SULLEN, surly, morose, glum, crabbed, saturnine, dour, gloomy *rel* cranky, cross, testy, touchy, irascible; peevish, petulant, fretful, querulous, irritable

sullen • showing a forbidding or disagreeable mood *syn* glum, morose, surly, sulky, crabbed, saturnine, dour, gloomy *rel* lowering, glowering, frowning, scowling; spiteful, malevolent, malicious, malign; cynical, pessimistic

sully *syn* SOIL, dirty, tarnish, foul, befoul, smirch, besmirch, grime, begrime *rel* spot, spatter, sprinkle; defile, pollute, taint, contaminate

sum *n* • the result of simple addition of all the numbers or particulars in a given group *syn* amount, number, aggregate, total, whole, quantity

sum *vb, syn* ADD, total, tot, cast, figure, foot *rel* compute, calculate, estimate, reckon; count, enumerate, number

summary *syn* CONCISE, pithy, compendious, terse, succinct, laconic *rel* brief, short; quick, prompt, ready, apt; compacted, compact, concentrated *ant* circumstantial

summative *syn* CUMULATIVE, accumulative, additive

summit • the highest point attained or attainable *syn* peak, pinnacle, climax, apex, acme, culmination, meridian, zenith, apogee

summon, summons • to demand or request the presence or service of *syn* call, cite, convoke, convene, muster *rel* command, order, bid, enjoin; evoke, elicit, educe

sumptuous *syn* LUXURIOUS, opulent *rel* magnificent, stately, majestic, grand; splendid, resplendent, gorgeous, superb; showy, ostentatious, pretentious; lavish, prodigal, profuse

sunder *syn* SEPARATE, sever, divide, part, divorce *rel* rend, rive, cleave, split, tear *ant* link

sundry *syn* MANY, several, various, divers, numerous, multifarious *rel* different, disparate, diverse, divergent; distinct, separate; individual, distinctive, peculiar

superadd *syn* ADD, annex, append, subjoin *rel* fasten, attach, affix

superannuated *syn* AGED, old, elderly

superb *syn* SPLENDID, resplendent, glorious, gorgeous, sublime *rel* superlative, transcendent, surpassing, supreme; sumptuous, luxurious, opulent; imposing, stately, majestic, magnificent, grand

supercilious *syn* PROUD, disdainful, overbearing, arrogant, haughty, lordly, insolent *rel* vain, vainglorious; contemptuous, scornful

supererogatory • given or done without compulsion, need, or warrant *syn* gratuitous, uncalled-for, wanton *rel* free, independent, autonomous; excessive, extreme, exorbitant; superfluous, supernumerary, extra, spare

superficial • lacking in depth or solidity *syn* shallow, cursory, uncritical *ant* radical

superfluity *syn* EXCESS, surplus, surplusage, overplus *rel* overflowing, overflow, teeming, swarming; exuberance, profusion, lavishness, prodigality

superfluous • exceeding what is needed or necessary *syn* surplus, supernumerary, extra, spare *rel* supererogatory, gratuitous, uncalled-for, wanton; profuse, lavish, prodigal, exuberant; excessive, inordinate, extravagant, extreme

superhuman *syn* SUPERNATURAL, preternatural, miraculous, supranatural *rel* potent, puissant, powerful, forcible, forceful; Herculean, cyclopean, titanic, gigantic

superimpose *syn* OVERLAY, superpose, appliqué

superior *syn* BETTER, preferable *ant* inferior

superlative *syn* SUPREME, transcendent, surpassing, peerless, incomparable, preeminent *rel* consummate, finished, accomplished; splendid, glorious, sublime, superb

supernatural • of or relating to an order of existence beyond the visible observable universe *syn* supranatural, preternatural, miraculous, superhuman *rel* divine, spiritual, sacred, holy, blessed; infinite, eternal, boundless, illimitable

supernumerary *syn* SUPERFLUOUS, surplus, extra, spare

superpose *syn* OVERLAY, superimpose, appliqué

supersede *syn* REPLACE, displace, supplant *rel* repudiate, spurn, reject; abandon, desert, forsake; stay, suspend, intermit, defer

supervene *syn* FOLLOW, succeed, ensue *rel* add, append, annex, subjoin, superadd; combine, unite, conjoin, cooperate

supervision *syn* OVERSIGHT, surveillance *rel* controlling, control, management, direction, conducting, conduct; leading, guiding

supine **1** *syn* PRONE, prostrate, recumbent, couchant, dormant **2** *syn* INACTIVE, inert, passive, idle *rel* slothful, lazy, indolent, faineant; lethargic, sluggish, torpid; apathetic, impassive, phlegmatic

supplant *syn* REPLACE, displace, supersede *rel* eject, oust, dismiss, expel; uproot, eradicate, extirpate, exterminate

supple **1** *syn* ELASTIC, flexible, resilient, springy *rel* pliable, pliant, plastic; soft, gentle, mild *ant* stiff **2** • able to bend or twist with ease and grace *syn* limber, lithe, lithesome, lissome *rel* graceful, elegant; easy, smooth, effortless, facile

supplement *n* **1** *syn* COMPLEMENT **2** *syn* APPENDIX, addendum, addenda

supplement *vb, syn* COMPLEMENT *rel* improve, better; heighten, enhance, aggravate, intensify

supplicate *syn* BEG, implore, beseech, entreat, importune, adjure *rel* pray, sue, plead, appeal, petition; ask, request, solicit

supply *vb, syn* PROVIDE, furnish *rel* replace, supplant, supersede; compensate, satisfy, recompense; fulfill, satisfy, answer; sustain, support, prop, bolster, buttress

supply *n, syn* SUBSTITUTE, locum tenens, alternate, understudy, pinch hitter, double, stand-in

supply *adj, syn* TEMPORARY, provisional, ad interim, acting

support *vb* **1** • to hold up in position by serving as a foundation or base for *syn* sustain, prop, bolster, buttress, brace *rel* carry, bear, convey; endure, suffer, stand; evidence, evince, show; indicate, attest, argue, betoken; uphold, advocate, back, champion **2** • to favor actively one that meets opposition *syn* uphold, advocate, back, champion *rel* approve, endorse, sanction; espouse, embrace, adopt; defend, protect, shield

support *n, syn* LIVING, maintenance, sustenance, livelihood, subsistence, keep, bread *ant* adversary, antagonist

supposed • accepted or advanced as true or real on the basis of less than conclusive evidence *syn* supposititious, suppositious, reputed, putative, purported, conjectural, hypothetical *rel* assumed, presumed, presupposed, postulated; tentative, provisional; doubtful, dubious, questionable; theoretical, speculative, academic; alleged *ant* certain

supposititious, suppositious *syn* SUPPOSED, reputed, putative, purported, conjectural, hypothetical *rel* pretended, simulated, feigned, shammed, counterfeited, counterfeit; questionable, dubious, doubtful; factitious, artificial

suppress **1** *syn* CRUSH, quell, extinguish, quench, quash *rel* subdue, overcome, surmount, conquer; abolish, annihilate; destroy; ruin, wreck **2** • to hold back more or less forcefully someone or something that seeks an outlet *syn* repress *rel* arrest, check, interrupt; extinguish, abolish, annihilate; forbid, prohibit, ban; subdue, overcome, surmount, conquer

supranatural *syn* SUPERNATURAL, miraculous, preternatural, superhuman

supremacy • the position of being first (as in rank, power, or influence) *syn* ascendancy *rel* preeminence, transcendence, superlativeness, peerlessness, incomparability; power, authority, dominion, control, sway

supreme • developed to the utmost and not exceeded by any other in degree, quality, or intensity *syn* superlative, transcendent, surpassing, preeminent, peerless, incomparable *rel* chief, foremost, leading, capital; predominant, dominant, paramount, sovereign

sure **1** *syn* CONFIDENT, assured, sanguine, presumptuous *rel* relying, trusting, depending, counting, banking; inerrant, unerring, infallible; safe, secure **2** • having no doubt or uncertainty *syn* certain, positive, cocksure *rel* decisive, decided; self-assured, assured, self-confident; dogmatic, doctrinaire, oracular, dictatorial *ant* unsure

surety **1** *syn* GUARANTEE, security, bond, guaranty, bail *rel* pledge, earnest, token, hostage, pawn **2** *syn* SPONSOR, guarantor, backer, patron, angel

surfeit *syn* SATIATE, sate, cloy, pall, glut, gorge *ant* whet

surge *syn* RISE, arise, ascend, mount, soar, tower, rocket, levitate

surly *syn* SULLEN, morose, glum, crabbed, sulky, saturnine, dour, gloomy *rel* rude, ungracious, ill-mannered, discourteous; boorish, churlish; snappish, waspish, fractious, irritable *ant* amiable

surmise *vb, syn* CONJECTURE, guess *rel* infer, gather, judge, deduce, conclude; think, conceive, fancy, imagine; consider, regard, deem

surmise *n, syn* CONJECTURE, guess *rel* inference, deduction, conclusion; hypothesis, theory

surmount *syn* CONQUER, overcome, overthrow, rout, vanquish, defeat, subdue, subjugate, reduce, beat, lick *rel* surpass, transcend, outdo, outstrip, excel, exceed

surpass *syn* EXCEED, transcend, excel, outdo, outstrip *rel* surmount, overcome, beat, conquer

surpassing *syn* SUPREME, transcendent, superlative, preeminent, peerless, incomparable *rel* excelling, outdoing, outstripping; consummate, finished, accomplished

surplus *n, syn* EXCESS, superfluity, surplusage, overplus *rel* remainder, residue, residuum *ant* deficiency

surplus *adj, syn* SUPERFLUOUS, supernumerary, extra, spare

surplusage *syn* EXCESS, surplus, superfluity, overplus *rel, ant* see SURPLUS *n*

surprise **1** • to attack unawares *syn* waylay, ambush *rel* catch, capture; take, seize, grasp, grab **2** • to impress forcibly through unexpectedness *syn* astonish, astound, amaze, flabbergast *rel* startle, alarm, scare, frighten; bewilder, nonplus, confound, dumbfound, puzzle; embarrass, disconcert, discomfit, rattle, faze

surrender *vb, syn* RELINQUISH, abandon, resign, yield, leave, cede, waive *rel* abdicate, renounce; forgo, forbear, sacrifice, eschew; submit, capitulate, succumb; commit, consign, confide, entrust

surrender *n* • the yielding of one's person, forces, or possessions to another *syn* submission, capitulation

surreptitious *syn* SECRET, underhand, underhanded, covert, stealthy, furtive, clandestine *rel* sneaking, slinking, skulking, lurking; hidden, concealed, screened

surrogate *syn* RESOURCE, substitute, shift, makeshift, expedient, resort, stopgap

surround • to close in or as if in a ring about something *syn* environ, encircle, circle, encompass, compass, hem, gird, girdle, ring *rel* enclose, envelop, wall, fence, cage, coop; circumscribe, confine, limit

surveillance *syn* OVERSIGHT, supervision *rel* inspection, scrutiny, examination

survey *vb, syn* SEE, view, espy, descry, behold, observe, notice, remark, note, perceive, discern *rel* scrutinize, scan, inspect, examine; look, watch

survey *n, syn* COMPENDIUM, syllabus, digest, pandect, sketch, précis, aperçu

survive *syn* OUTLIVE, outlast *rel* endure, continue, persist, last; withstand, resist, fight

susceptible **1** *syn* LIABLE, sensitive, subject, exposed, prone, open *rel* inclined, disposed, predisposed; alive, awake, sensible, conscious, aware *ant* immune **2** *syn* SENTIENT, sensitive, impressible, impressionable, responsive *rel* affected, impressed, touched, influenced, swayed; stirred, aroused, roused

suspect *syn* DISTRUST, mistrust, doubt, misdoubt

suspend **1** *syn* EXCLUDE, disbar, shut out, eliminate, debar, blackball, rule out *rel* eject, dismiss, oust; banish, exile, ostracize **2** *syn* DEFER, stay, intermit, postpone *rel* arrest, check, interrupt; stop, cease, discontinue; delay, detain, retard **3** *syn* HANG, sling, dangle *rel* poise, balance, steady, stabilize

suspended • hanging from or remaining in place as if hanging from a support *syn* pendent, pendulous

suspicion **1** *syn* UNCERTAINTY, mistrust, doubt, dubiety, dubiosity, skepticism *rel* misgiving, foreboding, presentiment, apprehension; distrust, mistrust **2** *syn* TOUCH, suggestion, soupçon, tincture, tinge, shade, smack, spice, dash, vein, strain, streak

sustain **1** *syn* SUPPORT, prop, bolster, buttress, brace *rel* continue, persist, endure, abide; uphold, back; prove, demonstrate *ant* subvert **2** *syn* EXPERIENCE, undergo, suffer *rel* receive, accept, take; endure, bear, stand, brook; meet, encounter, face, confront

sustenance **1** *syn* FOOD, nourishment, nutriment, aliment, pabulum, pap **2** *syn* LIVING, maintenance, support, livelihood, subsistence, keep, bread

suture *syn* JOINT, articulation

swag *syn* SPOIL, plunder, loot, booty, prize

swagger *syn* STRUT, bristle, bridle *rel* flourish, brandish, shake, swing, wave; brag, boast, vaunt, crow, gasconade

swallow *syn* EAT, ingest, devour, consume *rel* receive, accept, take; believe, credit; absorb, imbibe, assimilate

swarm *syn* TEEM, abound, overflow

swat *syn* STRIKE, hit, smite, punch, slug, slog, clout, slap, cuff, box *rel* beat, pound, pummel, baste, belabor

sway *vb* **1** *syn* SWING, oscillate, fluctuate, pendulate, vibrate, waver, undulate *rel* shake, rock, agitate, convulse **2** *syn* AFFECT, influence, impress, strike, touch *rel* control, direct, manage, conduct; rule, govern; bias, incline, dispose, predispose

sway *n, syn* POWER, dominion, control, command, authority *rel* supremacy, ascendancy; range, reach, scope, sweep; spread, stretch, amplitude, expanse

swearing *syn* BLASPHEMY, profanity, cursing

sweep *syn* RANGE, gamut, reach, radius, compass, scope, orbit, horizon, ken, purview *rel* expanse, amplitude, spread

sweeping *syn* INDISCRIMINATE, wholesale *rel* promiscuous, heterogeneous, motley, miscellaneous

sweet • distinctly pleasing or charming *syn* engaging, winning, winsome, dulcet *rel* pleasant, pleasing, agreeable, gratifying, grateful, welcome; delicious, delectable, luscious, delightful; lovely, fair, beautiful; ineffable, unutterable *ant* sour; bitter

swell *syn* EXPAND, amplify, distend, inflate, dilate *rel* extend, elongate, lengthen; intensify, heighten, enhance; increase, augment, enlarge *ant* shrink

swerve • to turn aside from a straight course *syn* veer, deviate, depart, digress, diverge *rel* turn, divert, deflect, sheer, avert; curve, bend

swift *syn* FAST, rapid, fleet, quick, speedy, hasty, expeditious *rel* easy, effortless, smooth, facile; headlong, precipitate, sudden

swimming *syn* GIDDY, dizzy, vertiginous, dazzled *rel* reeling, whirling, tottering; swaying, wavering, fluctuating

swindle *syn* CHEAT, overreach, cozen, defraud *rel* dupe, gull, bamboozle, hoodwink, trick; steal, pilfer, purloin, filch

swing 1 • to wield or cause to move to and fro or up and down *syn* wave, flourish, brandish, shake, thrash *rel* parade, flaunt, display, exhibit, show **2** • to move from one direction to its opposite *syn* sway, oscillate, vibrate, fluctuate, pendulate, waver, undulate *rel* turn, spin, whirl, wheel, revolve, rotate, gyrate; shake, tremble, quiver, quaver, quake **3** *syn* HANDLE, wield, manipulate, ply *rel* control, manage, direct, conduct

swipe *syn* STEAL, pilfer, filch, purloin, lift, pinch, snitch, cop

swirl *syn* TURN, circle, spin, twirl, whirl, wheel, eddy, revolve, rotate, gyrate, pirouette

sybaritic *syn* SENSUOUS, sensual, luxurious, voluptuous, epicurean

sycophant *syn* PARASITE, favorite, toady, lickspittle, bootlicker, hanger-on, leech, sponge, sponger *rel* blandisher, cajoler, wheedler; fawner, truckler

syllabus *syn* COMPENDIUM, digest, pandect, survey, sketch, précis, aperçu *rel* conspectus, synopsis, epitome, abridgment, brief, abstract

symbol 1 • something concrete that represents or suggests another thing that cannot in itself be pictured *syn* emblem, attribute, type *rel* sign, mark, token, badge; device, motif, design, figure, pattern **2** *syn* CHARACTER, sign, mark *rel* device, contrivance; diagram, delineation, outline, sketch

symbolism *syn* ALLEGORY

symmetry • beauty of form or arrangement arising from balanced proportions *syn* proportion, balance, harmony

sympathetic 1 *syn* CONSONANT, congenial, congruous, compatible, consistent *rel* agreeing, harmonizing, harmonious, accordant, correspondent **2** *syn* TENDER, compassionate, warm, warmhearted, responsive *rel* kindly, kind, benign, benignant; understanding, appreciating, comprehending *ant* unsympathetic

sympathy 1 *syn* ATTRACTION, affinity *rel* reciprocality, correspondence; harmony, consonance, accord, concord *ant* antipathy **2** • the act or capacity for sharing in the interests and esp. in the painful experiences of another *syn* pity, compassion, commiseration, condolence, ruth, empathy *rel* tenderness, warmheartedness, warmth, responsiveness; kindliness, kindness, benignness, benignancy

symptom *syn* SIGN, mark, token, badge

synchronous *syn* CONTEMPORARY, coeval, coetaneous, contemporaneous, simultaneous, coincident, concomitant, concurrent

syndicate *syn* MONOPOLY, corner, pool, trust, cartel

syndrome *syn* DISEASE, disorder, condition, affection, ailment, malady, complaint, distemper

synopsis *syn* ABRIDGMENT, brief, conspectus, epitome, abstract

synthetic *syn* ARTIFICIAL, ersatz, factitious

system 1 • an organized integrated whole made up of diverse but interrelated and interdependent parts *syn* scheme, network, complex, organism *ant* chaos **2** *syn* METHOD, mode, manner, way, fashion *rel* plan, project, scheme, design; procedure, process, proceeding

systematic *syn* ORDERLY, methodical, regular *rel* systematized, organized, ordered, arranged; logical, analytical

systematize *syn* ORDER, organize, methodize, arrange, marshal *rel* adjust, regulate, fix

T

table *syn* LIST, catalog, schedule, register, roll, roster, inventory

taciturn *syn* SILENT, uncommunicative, reserved, reticent, secretive, close, close-lipped, closemouthed, tight-lipped *rel* dumb, mute, inarticulate; restrained, inhibited, curbed, checked *ant* garrulous; clamorous (*esp. of crowds*); convivial

tackle *syn* EQUIPMENT, apparatus, machinery, paraphernalia, outfit, gear, matériel

tact • skill and grace in dealing with others *syn* address, poise, savoir faire *rel* diplomacy, policy, suavity, urbanity; courtesy, amenity, gallantry *ant* awkwardness

tactical *syn* STRATEGIC, logistic

tactics *syn* STRATEGY, logistics

tag *n, syn* MARK, brand, stamp, label, ticket

tag *vb* **1** *syn* MARK, brand, stamp, label, ticket **2** *syn* FOLLOW, pursue, chase, trail, tail

tail *syn* FOLLOW, pursue, chase, trail, tag

taint *syn* CONTAMINATE, pollute, defile *rel* debase, deprave, corrupt, vitiate; spoil, decompose, rot, putrefy, decay; imbue, inoculate, infuse

take **1** • to get hold of by or as if by catching up with the hand *syn* seize, grasp, clutch, snatch, grab *rel* have, hold, own, possess; catch, capture; confiscate, appropriate, preempt, arrogate **2** *syn* RECEIVE, accept, admit *rel* acquiesce, accede, assent, consent, subscribe **3** *syn* BRING, fetch *rel* carry, convey, bear

tale *syn* STORY, narrative, anecdote, yarn *rel* fiction, fable; myth, legend, saga

talent *syn* GIFT, genius, faculty, aptitude, knack, bent, turn *rel* capacity, ability, capability; art, skill, craft, cunning; endowment

talisman *syn* FETISH, charm, amulet

talk *vb, syn* SPEAK, converse *rel* discuss, dispute, argue; discourse, expatiate, dilate, descant; chat, chatter, prate

talk *n, syn* SPEECH, address, oration, harangue, lecture, sermon, homily

talkative • given to talk or talking *syn* loquacious, garrulous, voluble, glib *rel* vocal, fluent, articulate, eloquent; vociferous, clamorous *ant* silent

talkativeness • the inclination to talk or to talking *syn* loquacity, loquaciousness, garrulity, garrulousness, volubility, glibness *rel* fluency, articulateness, eloquence *ant* silence

tall *syn* HIGH, lofty *ant* short

tally *syn* AGREE, square, accord, harmonize, correspond, conform, jibe *rel* match, equal; coincide, concur

tame • made docile and tractable *syn* subdued, submissive *rel* tractable, amenable, docile, biddable, obedient; timid, timorous; pliant, pliable *ant* fierce

tamp *syn* PACK, crowd, cram, stuff, ram *rel* press, squeeze, jam; compact, consolidate, concentrate

tamper *syn* MEDDLE, interfere, intermeddle *rel* interpose, intervene; trouble, discommode, inconvenience

tang *syn* TASTE, flavor, savor, relish, smack *rel* pungency, piquancy, raciness

tangent *syn* ADJACENT, abutting, adjoining, contiguous, conterminous, juxtaposed

tangible *syn* PERCEPTIBLE, sensible, palpable, appreciable, ponderable *rel* material, physical, corporeal, objective; actual, real, true; obvious, evident, manifest *ant* intangible

tantalize *syn* WORRY, tease, harass, harry, annoy, plague, pester *rel* vex, irk, bother; torment, torture, try, afflict; bait, badger *ant* satisfy

tantamount *syn* SAME, selfsame, very, identical, identic, equivalent, equal *rel* like, alike, uniform, similar

tap *vb* • to strike or hit audibly *syn* knock, rap, thump, thud *rel* strike, smite; beat

tap *n* • a light usu. audible blow or the sound made by such a blow *syn* rap, knock, thump, thud

tar *syn* MARINER, sailor, seaman, gob, bluejacket

tardy • not arriving, occurring, or done at the set, due, or expected time *syn* late, behindhand, overdue *rel* dilatory, laggard, slow; delayed, detained, retarded *ant* prompt

tarnish *syn* SOIL, dirty, sully, foul, befoul, smirch, besmirch, grime, begrime *rel* darken, dim, bedim, obscure; defile, pollute, taint, contaminate *ant* polish

tarry *syn* STAY, remain, wait, abide, linger *rel* delay, procrastinate, lag, loiter, dawdle

tart *syn* SOUR, acid, acidulous, dry *rel* piquant, pungent; sharp, keen; curt, brusque, blunt, bluff; irritable, snappish, waspish

Tartarean *syn* INFERNAL, chthonian, chthonic, Hadean, stygian, hellish

task • a piece of work to be done *syn* duty, assignment, job, stint, chore *rel* function, office, province; work, labor, toil; employment, occupation, business

taste **1** • the property of a substance which makes it perceptible to the gustatory sense *syn* flavor, savor, tang, relish, smack **2** • a liking for or enjoyment of something because of the pleasure it gives *syn* palate, relish, gusto, zest *rel* predilection, prepossession, partiality; appreciation, understanding, comprehension; inclination, disposition, predisposition; discernment, discrimination, penetration, insight, acumen *ant* antipathy

tasty *syn* PALATABLE, savory, sapid, appetizing, toothsome, flavorsome, relishing *ant* bland

tat *syn* WEAVE, knit, crochet, braid, plait

tattle *syn* GOSSIP, blab *rel* divulge, disclose, betray, reveal

taunt *syn* RIDICULE, mock, deride, twit, rally *rel* scoff, jeer, gibe, flout; affront, insult, offend, outrage; scorn, disdain, scout, despise; chaff, banter

taut *syn* TIGHT, tense

tautology *syn* VERBIAGE, redundancy, pleonasm, circumlocution, periphrasis

tawdry *syn* GAUDY, garish, flashy, meretricious *rel* showy, pretentious; vulgar, gross, coarse; flamboyant, ornate, florid

tax *syn* BURDEN, encumber, cumber, weigh, weight, load, lade, charge, saddle

teach • to cause to acquire knowledge or skill *syn* instruct, educate, train, discipline, school *rel* impart, communicate; practice, drill, exercise; inculcate, instill, implant

tear • to separate forcibly *syn* rip, rend, split, cleave, rive *rel* slit, slash, cut; pull, drag; damage, injure, impair **2** *syn* RUSH, dash, shoot, charge *rel* speed, hasten, hurry; dart, fly, scud

tease *syn* WORRY, tantalize, pester, plague, harass, harry, annoy *rel* bait, badger, hector, chivy; importune, adjure, beg; fret, chafe, gall

tedious *syn* IRKSOME, tiresome, wearisome, boring *rel* burdensome, onerous, oppressive; fatiguing, exhausting, fagging, jading; slow, dilatory, deliberate *ant* exciting

tedium • a state of dissatisfaction and weariness *syn* boredom, ennui, doldrums *rel* irksomeness, tediousness, tiresomeness, wearisomeness; melancholy, dumps, blues, gloom, sadness

teem • to be present in large quantity *syn* abound, swarm, overflow *rel* bear, produce, yield, turn out; generate, engender, breed, propagate; multiply, augment, increase

teeny *syn* SMALL, tiny, little, diminutive, petite, wee, weeny, minute, microscopic, miniature

teeter *syn* SHAKE, tremble, quake, totter, quiver, shiver, shudder, quaver, wobble, shimmy, dither

tell 1 *syn* COUNT, enumerate, number **2** *syn* SAY, utter, state **3** *syn* REVEAL, divulge, discover, disclose, betray *rel* impart, communicate; relate, rehearse, recite, recount; inform, acquaint, apprise

telling *syn* VALID, compelling, convincing, cogent, sound *rel* forceful, forcible, powerful, potent; effective, effectual, efficacious; conclusive, decisive, determinative, definitive

temerity • conspicuous or flagrant boldness *syn* audacity, hardihood, effrontery, nerve, cheek, gall *rel* rashness, recklessness, foolhardiness, daring, venturesomeness; precipitateness, impetuosity, abruptness; impertinence, intrusiveness, officiousness *ant* caution

temper *vb, syn* MODERATE, qualify *rel* adjust, regulate, fix; mitigate, alleviate, lighten, assuage, allay, relieve; mollify, pacify, appease *ant* intensify

temper *n* **1** *syn* MOOD, humor, vein *rel* mettle, spirit, courage; emotion, feeling, affection, passion; attitude, position, stand **2** *syn* DISPOSITION, temperament, complexion, character, personality, individuality *rel* state, condition, posture, situation; quality, property, attribute

temperament *syn* DISPOSITION, temper, complexion, character, personality, individuality *rel* mind, soul; nature, kind, type

temperance • self-restraint in the gratification of appetites or passions *syn* sobriety, abstinence, abstemiousness, continence *rel* forgoing, forbearing, forbearance, sacrificing, sacrifice, eschewal; frugality, sparingness, thriftiness; restraining, curbing, checking

temperate 1 *syn* MODERATE *rel* mild, gentle, lenient, soft; steady, even, equable, constant; restrained, curbed, checked *ant* intemperate; inordinate **2** *syn* SOBER, continent, unimpassioned *rel* sparing, frugal, economical; abstaining, refraining, forbearing; dispassionate, just, equitable, fair

temporal *syn* PROFANE, secular, lay *rel* material, objective, physical, corporeal *ant* spiritual

temporary • lasting, continuing, or serving for a limited time *syn* provisional, ad interim, acting, *ant* permanent

tempt *syn* LURE, entice, inveigle, decoy, seduce *rel* allure, attract; invite, solicit, court, woo; induce, persuade, prevail, get

tenacious *syn* STRONG, tough, stout, sturdy, stalwart *rel* dogged, pertinacious, obstinate, stubborn; resolute, staunch, steadfast, true, faithful; persevering, persisting

tenacity *syn* COURAGE, resolution, spirit, mettle *rel* pluck, grit, guts, sand, fortitude, backbone; hardihood, audacity, nerve, temerity

tend • to supervise or take charge of *syn* attend, mind, watch *rel* defend, protect, shield, guard, safeguard; nurse, nurture, foster, cherish, cultivate

tendency • movement in a particular direction *syn* trend, drift, tenor *rel* leaning, propensity, penchant, proclivity; inclination, disposition, predisposition; bent, turn, genius, aptitude, gift

tender *adj* • showing or expressing interest in another *syn* compassionate, sympathetic, warm, warmhearted, responsive *rel* gentle, lenient, mild, soft; humane, benevolent, charitable, altruistic; pitiful, piteous *ant* callous; severe

tender *vb, syn* OFFER, proffer, present, prefer *rel* propose, purpose, design; suggest, intimate

tender *n, syn* OVERTURE, approach, advance, bid

tenet *syn* DOCTRINE, dogma *rel* belief, conviction, persuasion, view, opinion; principle, fundamental, axiom

tenor *syn* TENDENCY, drift, trend *rel* movement, motion, move; procedure, proceeding; meaning, significance, import

tense **1** *syn* TIGHT, taut *rel* strained; nervous, unquiet, uneasy, jittery, impatient *ant* slack **2** *syn* STIFF, rigid, inflexible, stark, wooden *rel* tough, tenacious, stout, strong; firm, hard *ant* expansive

tension **1** *syn* STRESS, strain, pressure **2** *syn* BALANCE, equilibrium, equipoise, poise

tentative *syn* PROVISIONAL *rel* temporary, ad interim, acting; testing, trying, demonstrating, proving *ant* definitive

tenuous *syn* THIN, rare, slender, slim, slight *rel* ethereal, aerial, airy *ant* dense

tergiversation *syn* AMBIGUITY, equivocation, double entendre

term **1** *syn* LIMIT, end, confine, bound **2** *syn* WORD, vocable **3** *pl* **terms** *syn* CONDITION, stipulation, provision, proviso, reservation, strings *rel* restriction, limit; requisite, prerequisite, requirement

termagant *syn* VIRAGO, scold, shrew, vixen, amazon

terminal *syn* LAST, final, concluding, latest, eventual, ultimate *rel* closing, ending, terminating, concluding *ant* initial

terminate *syn* CLOSE, end, conclude, finish, complete *rel* abolish, extinguish, abate; stop, cease, discontinue

termination *syn* END, ending, terminus *rel* result, issue, outcome; concluding, conclusion, completion, closing, close *ant* inception; source

terminus *syn* END, termination, ending *ant* starting point

terrestrial *syn* EARTHLY, earthy, mundane, worldly, sublunary *ant* celestial

terrible *syn* FEARFUL, terrific, frightful, dreadful, awful, horrible, horrific, shocking, appalling *rel* frightening, alarming, startling; agitating, upsetting, disturbing, perturbing

terrific *syn* FEARFUL, terrible, frightful, dreadful, horrible, horrific, awful, shocking, appalling *rel* frightening, alarming, terrorizing; agitating, upsetting, disquieting

terrify *syn* FRIGHTEN, fright, scare, alarm, terrorize, startle *rel* agitate, upset, perturb, disquiet, discompose; dismay, appall, horrify, daunt; cow, intimidate, browbeat, bulldoze

territory *syn* FIELD, domain, province, sphere, bailiwick *rel* region, tract, area, zone, belt; limits, confines, bounds

terror *syn* FEAR, panic, consternation, dread, fright, alarm, dismay, horror, trepidation *rel* apprehensiveness, fearfulness; agitation, disquiet, perturbation, upsetting, upset; appalling, daunting, dismaying

terrorize *syn* FRIGHTEN, terrify, fright, alarm, scare, startle, affray, affright *rel* intimidate, cow, bulldoze, browbeat; coerce, compel, force; drive, impel, move; agitate, upset, discompose

terse *syn* CONCISE, succinct, laconic, summary, pithy, compendious *rel* brief, short; compact, close; expressive, sententious, meaningful; incisive, crisp, clear-cut

test *n, syn* PROOF, trial, demonstration *rel* examination, inspection, scrutiny; verification, substantiation, corroboration, confirmation

test *vb, syn* PROVE, try, demonstrate *rel* essay, attempt; examine, inspect, scrutinize; verify, substantiate, confirm

testimonial *syn* CREDENTIAL, recommendation, character, reference *rel* commendation; approval, endorsement

testy *syn* IRASCIBLE, choleric, splenetic, touchy, cranky, cross *rel* irritable, peevish, snappish, waspish; hasty, sudden, impetuous; captious, carping, caviling, faultfinding, critical

text *syn* SUBJECT, topic, argument, theme, matter, subject matter, motive, motif, leitmotiv

thankful *syn* GRATEFUL *rel* appreciating, appreciative, valuing, prizing, cherishing, treasuring; satisfied, content *ant* thankless

thaumaturgy *syn* MAGIC, sorcery, witchcraft, witchery, wizardry, alchemy

thaw *syn* LIQUEFY, melt, deliquesce, fuse *ant* freeze

theatrical *syn* DRAMATIC, dramaturgic, melodramatic, histrionic *rel* artificial, factitious; formal, conventional, ceremonial, ceremonious; affecting, pretending, assuming, simulating, feigning; showy, pretentious, ostentatious

theft • an unlawful taking of property esp. personal property stolen from its rightful owner *syn* larceny, robbery, burglary

theme **1** *syn* SUBJECT, text, topic, argument, matter, subject matter, motive, motif, leitmotiv **2** *syn* ESSAY, composition, paper, article

then *syn* THEREFORE, hence, consequently, accordingly, so

theorem *syn* PRINCIPLE, axiom, fundamental, law

theoretical • concerned principally with abstractions and theories *syn* speculative, academic *rel* conjectural, hypothetical, supposed; postulated, premised, presupposed

therefore • for this or that reason *syn* hence, consequently, then, accordingly, so

thesis *syn* DISCOURSE, dissertation, treatise, monograph, disquisition *rel* exposition; argumentation, disputation; article, paper, essay

thespian *syn* ACTOR, player, impersonator, trouper, performer, mummer, mime, mimic

thick **1** *syn* STOCKY, thick, thickset, chunky, stubby, squat, dumpy *rel* broad, wide, deep *ant* thin **2** *syn* CLOSE, compact, dense *rel* condensed, compressed, contracted; concentrated, compacted **3** *syn* FAMILIAR, close, confidential, chummy, intimate

thickset *syn* STOCKY, thick, chunky, stubby, squat, dumpy *rel* bulky, massive, massy; fleshy, stout, portly, plump

thief • one that steals esp. stealthily or secretly *syn* robber, burglar, larcener, larcenist

thin *adj* • not thick, broad, abundant, or dense *syn* slender, slim, slight, tenuous, rare *rel* lean, spare, lank, lanky, gaunt; meager, exiguous, scanty; cadaverous, pinched, wasted, haggard; attenuated, extenuated, diluted *ant* thick

thin *vb* • to make thin or thinner or less dense *syn* attenuate, extenuate, dilute, rarefy *rel* reduce, lessen, diminish, decrease; liquefy, melt *ant* thicken

thing **1** *syn* AFFAIR, matter, concern, business **2** • whatever is apprehended as having actual, distinct, and demonstrable existence *syn* object, article *rel* item, detail, particular

think **1** • to form an idea of *syn* conceive, imagine, fancy, realize, envisage, envision *rel* consider, weigh, study, contemplate; understand, comprehend, appreciate; surmise, conjecture, guess **2** • to use one's powers of conception, judgment, or inference *syn* cogitate, reflect, reason, speculate, deliberate *rel* ponder, meditate, muse, ruminate; infer, deduce, conclude, judge

thirst *syn* LONG, hunger, pine, yearn, hanker *rel* covet, crave, desire, wish, want

though • in spite of the fact that *syn* although, albeit

thought *syn* IDEA, concept, conception, notion, impression *rel* opinion, view, sentiment, belief, conviction, persuasion

thoughtful **1** • characterized by or exhibiting the power to think *syn* reflective, speculative, contemplative, meditative, pensive *rel* serious, earnest, grave, sober; engrossed, absorbed, intent; abstracted, preoccupied **2** • mindful of others *syn* considerate, attentive *rel* solicitous, concerned, careful, anxious; courteous, polite, gallant, chivalrous, civil *ant* thoughtless

thoughtless *syn* CARELESS, heedless, inadvertent *rel* rash, reckless, foolhardy; indifferent, unconcerned, incurious, aloof; lax, remiss, negligent *ant* thoughtful

thrash **1** *syn* BEAT, pound, pummel, buffet, baste, belabor *rel* strike, smite, slug, slap **2** *syn* SWING, flourish, brandish, shake, wave *rel* wield, manipulate, ply, handle

threadbare **1** *syn* SHABBY, dilapidated, dingy, faded, seedy *rel* damaged, injured, impaired; worn, haggard **2** *syn* TRITE, shopworn, hackneyed, stereotyped *rel* antiquated, obsolete, archaic, old; exhausted, depleted, drained, impoverished

threaten • to announce or forecast impending danger or evil *syn* menace *rel* intimidate, bulldoze, cow, browbeat; forebode, portend, presage, augur, foretell; warn, forewarn, caution

thrifty *syn* SPARING, economical, frugal *rel* provident, prudent, foresighted; saving, preserving, conserving *ant* wasteful

thrill • to thrill with emotions that stir or excite or to be so excited *syn* electrify, enthuse *rel* excite, stimulate, galvanize, quicken, provoke; stir, arouse, rouse, rally; penetrate, pierce, probe, enter; quiver, tremble, shiver, shake

thrive *syn* SUCCEED, prosper, flourish *rel* increase, augment, multiply, enlarge *ant* languish

throb *vb, syn* PULSATE, beat, pulse, palpitate

throb *n, syn* PULSATION, beat, pulse, palpitation

throe *syn* PAIN, ache, pang, twinge, stitch

throng *syn* CROWD, press, crush, mob, rout, horde *rel* multitude, army, host, legion; assembly, congregation, gathering, collection

throttle *syn* SUFFOCATE, asphyxiate, stifle, smother, choke, strangle

through *syn* BY, with

throw • to cause to move swiftly through space by a propulsive movement or a propelling force *syn* cast, fling, hurl, pitch, toss, sling *rel* drive, impel; propel, thrust, shove, push; heave, raise, lift, boost

throwback *syn* REVERSION, atavism

throw up *syn* BELCH, burp, vomit, disgorge, regurgitate, spew

thrust *syn* PUSH, shove, propel *rel* throw, cast, fling; drive, impel, move; enter, penetrate, pierce

thud *vb, syn* TAP, thump, knock, rap *rel* hit, strike, smite; pound, beat

thud *n, syn* TAP, thump, knock, rap *rel* slumping, falling

thump *vb, syn* TAP, thud, knock, rap *rel* pound, beat, belabor; punch, smite, strike

thump *n, syn* TAP, thud, knock, rap *rel* pounding, beating, pummeling

thwart *syn* FRUSTRATE, foil, baffle, balk, circumvent, outwit *rel* hinder, impede, obstruct, block, bar; defeat, overcome, surmount, conquer; check, curb, restrain; prevent, forestall, anticipate

ticket *n, syn* MARK, brand, stamp, label, tag

ticket *vb, syn* MARK, brand, stamp, label, tag *rel* affix, attach, fasten; append, add

tickle *syn* PLEASE, regale, gratify, delight, rejoice, gladden *rel* divert, amuse, entertain; thrill, electrify

tide *syn* FLOW, flood, stream, current, flux

tidings *syn* NEWS, intelligence, advice

tidy *syn* NEAT, trim, trig, snug, shipshape, spick-and-span *rel* orderly, methodical, systematic *ant* untidy

tie *n* **1** *syn* BOND, band **2** *syn* DRAW, stalemate, deadlock, standoff *rel* equality, equivalence

tie *vb* • to make fast and secure *syn* bind *rel* fasten, attach; secure, rivet, anchor, moor; join, connect, link *ant* untie

tier *syn* LINE, row, rank, file, echelon

tiff *n, syn* QUARREL, bickering, spat, squabble, wrangle, altercation *rel* scrap, rumpus, row, brawl, broil; difference, variance, dissension, contention, discord

tiff *vb, syn* QUARREL, spat, bicker, squabble, wrangle, altercate *rel* dispute, argue; differ, disagree; contend, fight

tight **1** • fitting, drawn, or stretched so that there is no slackness or looseness *syn* taut, tense *rel* strict, stringent, rigid; close, compact; constricted, contracted, compressed, condensed, shrunken; snug, shipshape, neat *ant* loose **2** *also* **tightfisted** *syn* STINGY, close, closefisted, niggardly, parsimonious, penurious, miserly, cheeseparing, penny-pinching *rel* mean, ignoble, sordid, abject **3** *syn* DRUNK, tipsy, intoxicated, drunken, inebriated

tight-lipped *syn* SILENT, uncommunicative, taciturn, close, close-lipped, close-mouthed, reticent, reserved, secretive

time *syn* OPPORTUNITY, occasion, chance, break *rel* juncture, contingency, emergency, exigency

timely *syn* SEASONABLE, well-timed, opportune, pat *rel* appropriate, fitting, meet, proper, suitable, fit; fortunate, lucky, happy, providential *ant* untimely

timetable *syn* PROGRAM, schedule, agenda

timid • marked by or exhibiting a lack of boldness, courage, or determination *syn* timorous *rel* fearful, apprehensive, afraid; cautious, circumspect, calculating, wary, chary

timorous *syn* TIMID *rel* fearful, apprehensive, afraid; recoiling, shrinking, quailing, blenching; trembling, quivering, shivering, shuddering *ant* assured

tincture *syn* TOUCH, suggestion, tinge, suspicion, soupçon, shade, smack, spice, dash, vein, strain, streak

tinge **1** *syn* COLOR, tint, shade, hue, tone **2** *syn* TOUCH, tincture, suggestion, shade, suspicion, soupçon, smack, spice, dash, vein, strain, streak

tint *syn* COLOR, hue, shade, tinge, tone

tiny *syn* SMALL, minute, miniature, diminutive, wee, little, teeny, weeny

tippler *syn* DRUNKARD, inebriate, alcoholic, dipsomaniac, sot, soak, toper, tosspot

tipsy *syn* DRUNK, intoxicated, inebriated, drunken, tight

tirade • a violent, often long-winded, and usu. denunciatory speech or writing *syn* diatribe, jeremiad, philippic *rel* harangue, oration, speech; invective, vituperation, abuse; denunciation, censure, condemnation *ant* eulogy

tire • to make or become unable or unwilling to continue (as from a loss of physical strength or endurance) *syn* weary, fatigue, exhaust, jade, fag, tucker *rel* irk, vex, annoy, bother; deplete, drain, exhaust, impoverish, bankrupt

tireless *syn* INDEFATIGABLE, weariless, untiring, unwearying, unwearied, unflagging *rel* assiduous, sedulous, diligent, industrious, busy; energetic, strenuous, vigorous

tiresome *syn* IRKSOME, wearisome, tedious, boring *rel* oppressive, burdensome, onerous, exacting; fatiguing, exhausting, jading, fagging; arduous, hard, difficult

titanic *syn* HUGE, vast, immense, enormous, elephantine, mammoth, giant, gigantic, gigantean, colossal, gargantuan, Herculean, cyclopean, Brobdingnagian

title **1** *syn* CLAIM, pretension, pretense *rel* right, privilege, prerogative, birthright; reason, ground, argument, proof; due, desert, merit **2** *syn* NAME, designation, denomination, appellation, style

tittle *syn* PARTICLE, bit, mite, smidgen, whit, atom, iota, jot

toady *n, syn* PARASITE, sycophant, favorite, lickspittle, bootlicker, hanger-on, leech, sponge, sponger

toady *vb, syn* FAWN, truckle, cringe, cower *rel* follow, tag, trail, tail; blandish, cajole, wheedle, coax

toboggan *syn* SLIDE, coast, slip, glide, skid, glissade, slither

tocsin *syn* ALARM, alert *rel* signal, sign

toil *syn* WORK, labor, travail, drudgery, grind *rel* effort, exertion, pains, trouble; employment, occupation, calling, pursuit, business *ant* leisure

token **1** *syn* SIGN, mark, symptom, badge, note *rel* symbol, emblem, attribute; evidence, testimony; indication, proving, proof, betokening **2** *syn* PLEDGE, pawn, hostage *rel* guarantee, guaranty, security, surety **3** *syn* REMEMBRANCE, remembrancer, reminder, memorial, memento, keepsake, souvenir *rel* gift, present, favor

tolerance *syn* FORBEARANCE, leniency, indulgence, clemency, mercifulness *rel* mercy, charity, grace, lenity; patience, long-suffering, longanimity *ant* intolerance; loathing

tolerant *syn* FORBEARING, lenient, indulgent, clement, merciful *rel* charitable, benevolent, humane; forgiving, excusing, condoning *ant* intolerant; severe

tolerantly *syn* FORBEARINGLY, clemently, mercifully, leniently, indulgently

tolerate *syn* BEAR, endure, abide, suffer, stand, brook *rel* accept, receive; submit, yield, bow, succumb

tone *syn* COLOR, hue, shade, tint, tinge

tongue *syn* LANGUAGE, dialect, speech, idiom

tongue-lash *syn* SCOLD, upbraid, rate, berate, jaw, bawl, chew out, wig, rail, revile, vituperate

too *syn* ALSO, likewise, besides, moreover, furthermore

tool *syn* IMPLEMENT, instrument, appliance, utensil *rel* device, contrivance, contraption, gadget; machine, mechanism, apparatus; mean, instrument, instrumentality, agent, agency

toothsome *syn* PALATABLE, appetizing, savory, sapid, tasty, flavorsome, relishing

toper *syn* DRUNKARD, inebriate, alcoholic, dipsomaniac, sot, soak, tosspot, tippler

topic *syn* SUBJECT, matter, subject matter, argument, text, theme, motive, motif, leitmotiv

torment *syn* AFFLICT, torture, rack, try *rel* worry, annoy, harry, harass, plague, pester; distress, trouble; bait, badger, hector; agonize, writhe

tornado • a violent whirling wind accompanied by a funnel-shaped cloud *syn* cyclone, twister *rel* whirlwind, whirly; hurricane, tropical storm, typhoon

torpid *syn* LETHARGIC, sluggish, comatose *rel* inert, inactive, idle, passive; phlegmatic, impassive, stolid *ant* agile

torpidity *syn* LETHARGY, torpor, stupor, languor, lassitude *rel* inertness, inactivity, idleness, passiveness

torpor *syn* LETHARGY, torpidity, stupor, languor, lassitude *rel* apathy, phlegm, impassivity, stolidity; inertness, inertia, passiveness, inactivity *ant* animation

torrent *syn* FLOOD, deluge, inundation, spate, cataract

tortuous *syn* WINDING, sinuous, serpentine, flexuous *rel* crooked, devious; roundabout, circuitous, indirect

torture *syn* AFFLICT, rack, torment, try *rel* writhe, agonize; persecute, oppress, wrong; distress, trouble; worry, annoy, harry, harass; maim, mutilate, mangle

toss *syn* THROW, pitch, sling, cast, fling, hurl *rel* impel, drive; thrust, propel, push

tosspot *syn* DRUNKARD, inebriate, alcoholic, dipsomaniac, sot, soak, toper, tippler

tot *syn* ADD, total, sum, cast, figure, foot

total *adj, syn* WHOLE, entire, all, gross *rel* complete, full, plenary; including, inclusive, comprehending, comprehensive

total *n, syn* SUM, aggregate, whole, amount, number, quantity

total *vb, syn* ADD, tot, sum, figure, cast, foot

totter **1** *syn* SHAKE, tremble, quake, quaver, quiver, shiver, shudder, wobble, teeter, shimmy, dither *rel* rock, agitate, convulse; sway, swing, fluctuate, oscillate, waver **2** *syn* REEL, stagger, whirl *rel* stumble, lurch, blunder, flounder, trip

touch *vb* **1** • to probe with a sensitive part of the body (as a finger) so as to get or produce a sensation often in the course of examining or exploring *syn* feel, palpate, handle, paw *rel* examine, inspect, scrutinize; investigate **2** *syn* AFFECT, influence, impress, strike, sway *rel* arouse, stir; excite, stimulate, quicken, provoke; injure, harm, damage, hurt, impair **3** *syn* MATCH, approach, rival, equal

touch *n* **1** *syn* CONTACT *rel* feeling, sense, sensation, sensibility; tangibleness, palpableness; impact, impingement, shock, clash **2** • a very small amount or perceptible trace of something added *syn* suggestion, suspicion, soupçon, tincture, tinge, shade, smack, spice, dash, vein, strain, streak *rel* trace, vestige; contamination, pollution, defilement, tainting; impression, impress, imprint, stamp, print

touching *syn* MOVING, affecting, impressive, poignant, pathetic *rel* tender, responsive, sympathetic, compassionate; pitiful, piteous, pitiable

touchstone *syn* STANDARD, criterion, gauge, yardstick *rel* test, proof, trial, demonstration

touchy *syn* IRASCIBLE, choleric, splenetic, testy, cranky, cross *rel* irritable, fractious, snappish, waspish, peevish; captious, caviling, faultfinding, carping, critical *ant* imperturbable

tough *syn* STRONG, tenacious, stout, sturdy, stalwart *rel* resisting, resistant, withstanding, opposing; firm, hard; intractable, refractory, recalcitrant, headstrong; dogged, pertinacious, obstinate, stubborn *ant* fragile

tour **1** *syn* SPELL, shift, trick, turn, stint, bout, go **2** *syn* JOURNEY, voyage, trip, cruise, expedition, jaunt, excursion, pilgrimage

tow *syn* PULL, tug, haul, hale, draw, drag

tower *syn* RISE, mount, ascend, soar, rocket, arise, levitate, surge

toxic *syn* POISONOUS, venomous, virulent, mephitic, pestilent, pestilential, miasmic, miasmatic, miasmal

toxin *syn* POISON, venom, virus, bane

toy *syn* TRIFLE, dally, flirt, coquet *rel* play, sport, disport, frolic; fondle, caress, pet, cosset, cuddle, dandle

trace *n* • a perceptible sign made by something that has passed *syn* vestige, track *rel* sign, mark, token

trace *vb, syn* SKETCH, outline, diagram, delineate, draft, plot, blueprint *rel* copy, duplicate, reproduce; map, chart, graph

tracing *syn* SKETCH, outline, diagram, delineation, draft, plot, blueprint *rel* reproduction, copy, duplicate; plan, project, scheme, design

track *syn* TRACE, vestige *rel* print, stamp, imprint, impression; sign, mark, token

tract *syn* AREA, region, zone, belt *rel* expanse, stretch, spread, amplitude; locality, district, vicinity; section, sector, part, portion

tractable *syn* OBEDIENT, amenable, biddable, docile *rel* pliant, pliable, plastic; submissive, subdued, tame; compliant, acquiescent *ant* intractable; unruly

trade **1** • a pursuit followed as an occupation or means of livelihood and requiring technical knowledge and skill *syn* craft, handicraft, art, profession *rel* work, employment, occupation, pursuit **2** *syn* BUSINESS, commerce, industry, traffic

traduce *syn* MALIGN, asperse, vilify, calumniate, defame, slander, libel *rel* decry, detract, derogate, depreciate, disparage; revile, vituperate

traffic **1** *syn* BUSINESS, commerce, trade, industry *rel* transportation, conveyance, carrying **2** *syn* INTERCOURSE, commerce, dealings, communication, communion, conversation, converse, correspondence *rel* familiarity, intimacy, closeness

trail *syn* FOLLOW, pursue, chase, tag, tail

train *n, syn* SUCCESSION, progression, series, sequence, chain, string

train *vb* **1** *syn* TEACH, discipline, school, instruct, educate *rel* practice, exercise, drill; habituate, accustom; harden, season **2** *syn* DIRECT, aim, point, level, lay *rel* turn, divert, deflect

traipse *syn* WANDER, stray, roam, ramble, rove, range, prowl, gad, gallivant, meander

trait *syn* CHARACTERISTIC, feature *rel* quality, character, property, attribute

traitorous *syn* FAITHLESS, treacherous, perfidious, false, disloyal *rel* recreant, renegade, apostate; seditious, mutinous, rebellious, insubordinate; disaffected, estranged, alienated

trammel *syn* HAMPER, fetter, shackle, clog, manacle, hog-tie *rel* hinder, impede, obstruct, block, bar; restrain, curb, check, inhibit; limit, restrict, circumscribe, confine

tramp *syn* VAGABOND, vagrant, hobo, truant, bum

tranquil *syn* CALM, serene, placid, peaceful, halcyon *rel* quiet, still, silent, noiseless; soft, gentle, mild; restful, comfortable; cool, composed, collected *ant* troubled

tranquilize *syn* CALM, compose, quiet, quieten, still, lull, soothe, settle *rel* allay, assuage, alleviate, relieve; mollify, appease, pacify *ant* agitate

transcend *syn* EXCEED, surpass, excel, outdo, outstrip *rel* surmount, overcome, conquer

transcendent **1** *syn* SUPREME, surpassing, superlative, peerless, preeminent, incomparable *rel* consummate, finished, accomplished; perfect, entire, whole, intact **2** *syn* ABSTRACT, transcendental, ideal *rel* absolute, ultimate, categorical; infinite, boundless, eternal

transcendental *syn* ABSTRACT, transcendent, ideal *rel* supernatural, supranatural; categorical, ultimate

transcript *syn* REPRODUCTION, copy, carbon copy, duplicate, facsimile, replica

transfer **1** *syn* MOVE, remove, shift *rel* carry, convey, transport, transmit; commit, consign **2** • to shift title or possession from one owner to another *syn* convey, alienate, deed

transfiguration *syn* TRANSFORMATION, metamorphosis, transmutation, conversion, transmogrification *rel* exaltation, magnification; enhancing, heightening, intensifying

transfigure *syn* TRANSFORM, metamorphose, transmute, convert, transmogrify *rel* exalt, magnify; heighten, enhance, intensify

transform • to change a thing into a different thing *syn* metamorphose, transmute, convert, transmogrify, transfigure *rel* change, alter, modify, vary

transformation • change of one thing into another different thing *syn* metamorphosis, transmutation, conversion, transmogrification, transfiguration *rel* change, alteration, modification, variation; evolution, development

transgression *syn* BREACH, trespass, violation, infraction, infringement, contravention *rel* encroachment, invasion, entrenchment; slip, lapse, error; offense, sin, vice, crime

transient • lasting or staying only a short time *syn* transitory, passing, ephemeral, momentary, fugitive, fleeting, evanescent, short-lived *ant* perpetual

transitory *syn* TRANSIENT, passing, ephemeral, momentary, fugitive, fleeting, evanescent, short-lived *ant* everlasting; perpetual

translation • a restating often in a simpler language of something previously stated or written *syn* version, paraphrase, metaphrase

translucent *syn* CLEAR, lucid, pellucid, diaphanous, limpid, transparent *rel* luminous, radiant, brilliant, effulgent, bright; iridescent, opalescent, prismatic

transmit **1** *syn* SEND, forward, remit, route, ship, dispatch **2** *syn* CARRY, bear, convey, transport *rel* move, remove, shift, transfer; communicate, impart; propagate, breed, engender, generate

transmogrification *syn* TRANSFORMATION, metamorphosis, transmutation, conversion, transfiguration

transmogrify *syn* TRANSFORM, metamorphose, transmute, convert, transfigure

transmutation *syn* TRANSFORMATION, metamorphosis, conversion, transmogrification, transfiguration

transmute *syn* TRANSFORM, metamorphose, convert, transmogrify, transfigure

transparent *syn* CLEAR, lucid, pellucid, diaphanous, translucent, limpid *ant* opaque

transpire *syn* HAPPEN, occur, chance, befall, betide

transport *vb* **1** *syn* CARRY, bear, convey, transmit *rel* move, remove, shift, transfer; bring, fetch, take **2** • to carry away by strong and usu. pleasurable emotion *syn* ravish, enrapture, entrance *rel* quicken, stimulate, excite, provoke; agitate, upset, perturb, discompose; lift, elevate **3** *syn* BANISH, deport, exile, expatriate, ostracize, extradite *rel* expel, eject, oust

transport *n, syn* ECSTASY, rapture *rel* enthusiasm, passion, fervor, ardor; inspiration, fury, frenzy; bliss, beatitude, blessedness, felicity, happiness

transpose *syn* REVERSE, invert *rel* exchange, interchange; transfer, shift, move

trap *n, syn* LURE, bait, decoy, snare *rel* stratagem, ruse, trick, maneuver, gambit, ploy, artifice, wile, feint; ambush, ambuscade; intrigue, machination, plot, conspiracy

trap *vb, syn* CATCH, entrap, snare, ensnare, bag, capture *rel* seize, take, clutch, grasp; betray, beguile, delude, deceive

trash **1** *syn* REFUSE, waste, rubbish, debris, garbage, offal **2** *syn* NONSENSE, twaddle, drivel, bunk, balderdash, poppycock, gobbledygook, rot, bull

trauma, traumatism *syn* WOUND, lesion, bruise, contusion

travail *syn* WORK, labor, toil, drudgery, grind *rel* effort, exertion, pains, trouble

traverse *syn* DENY, gainsay, contradict, negative, impugn, contravene *rel* controvert, confute, refute, disprove, rebut *ant* allege

travesty *n, syn* CARICATURE, parody, burlesque

travesty *vb, syn* CARICATURE, parody, burlesque *rel* copy, mimic, ape, mock, imitate

treacherous *syn* FAITHLESS, perfidious, traitorous, false, disloyal *rel* betraying, deceiving, misleading, double-crossing; seditious, mutinous, rebellious, insubordinate; dangerous, perilous

treason *syn* SEDITION *rel* revolution, revolt, rebellion, uprising, insurrection; betrayal, deceiving, deception, double-crossing; overthrowing, overthrow, subverting, subversion *ant* allegiance

treasure *syn* APPRECIATE, prize, value, cherish *rel* esteem, respect, regard, admire; revere, reverence, venerate; save, preserve, conserve

treat **1** *syn* CONFER, parley, negotiate, commune, consult, advise *rel* discuss, dispute, argue, debate; consider, weigh, study; think, reason, deliberate **2** • to have to do with or behave toward (a person or thing) in a specified manner *syn* deal, handle *rel* conduct, manage; regard, respect; consider, account; estimate, appraise, evaluate, value, rate

treatise *syn* DISCOURSE, disquisition, dissertation, thesis, monograph *rel* article, paper, essay; exposition

treaty *syn* CONTRACT, bargain, compact, pact, entente, convention, cartel, concordat

tremble *syn* SHAKE, quake, quiver, shiver, shudder, quaver, totter, wobble, teeter, shimmy, dither *rel* thrill, electrify; falter, waver, hesitate; quail, shrink, wince, recoil

tremendous *syn* MONSTROUS, stupendous,

monumental, prodigious *rel* enormous, immense, huge, vast, gigantic, colossal; astounding, amazing, flabbergasting; terrifying, alarming, startling, frightening

trenchant *syn* INCISIVE, clear-cut, cutting, biting, crisp *rel* piercing, penetrating, probing; sharp, keen, acute; sarcastic, satiric, ironic, sardonic; caustic, mordant, acrid, scathing; poignant, pungent, piquant

trend *syn* TENDENCY, drift, tenor *rel* movement, motion, move; inclination, disposition, predisposition; progression, progress

trepidation *syn* FEAR, horror, terror, panic, consternation, dread, fright, alarm, dismay *rel* apprehensiveness, fearfulness; anxiety, worry, concern, solicitude, care; awe, reverence

trespass *n, syn* BREACH, transgression, violation, infraction, infringement, contravention *rel* invading, invasion, entrenchment, encroachment; intrusion, obtrusion; offense, sin, vice, crime

trespass *vb* • to make inroads upon the property, territory, or rights of another *syn* encroach, entrench, infringe, invade *rel* intrude, obtrude, interlope, butt in; interfere, intervene, interpose

trial **1** *syn* PROOF, test, demonstration *rel* inspection, examination, scanning, scrutiny; process, proceeding, procedure **2** • the state or fact of being tested (as by suffering) *syn* tribulation, affliction, visitation, cross *rel* distress, suffering, misery, agony; sorrow, grief, anguish, woe, heartbreak; misfortune, adversity; difficulty, hardship, vicissitude, rigor

tribulation *syn* TRIAL, affliction, visitation, cross *rel* oppression, persecution, wronging, wrong; sorrow, grief, anguish, woe; distress, suffering, misery, agony *ant* consolation

tributary *syn* SUBORDINATE, secondary, dependent, subject, collateral *rel* conquered, vanquished, subjugated, subdued; auxiliary, subsidiary, ancillary, adjuvant, contributory

tribute *syn* ENCOMIUM, eulogy, panegyric, citation

trick *n* **1** • an indirect means to gain an end *syn* ruse, stratagem, maneuver, gambit, ploy, artifice, wile, feint *rel* imposture, deceit, deception, counterfeit, humbug, fake, cheat, fraud; fun, jest, sport, game, play **2** *syn* SPELL, turn, tour, shift, stint, bout, go

trick *vb, syn* DUPE, gull, befool, hoax, hoodwink, bamboozle *rel* deceive, delude, beguile, mislead; outwit, circumvent; cajole, wheedle, blandish, coax

trickery *syn* DECEPTION, double-dealing, chicanery, chicane, fraud *rel* deceit, dissimulation, guile, cunning, duplicity; imposture, cheat, sham, fake, humbug, counterfeit

tricky *syn* SLY, crafty, foxy, insidious, cunning, wily, guileful, artful *rel* crooked, devious, oblique; deceptive, delusive, misleading, delusory; deceitful, dishonest

tried *syn* RELIABLE, dependable, trustworthy, trusty *rel* staunch, steadfast, constant, faithful; proved, demonstrated, tested

trifle • to deal with or act toward without serious purpose *syn* toy, dally, flirt, coquet *rel* palter, fib, equivocate, prevaricate, lie; waver, vacillate, falter, hesitate; dawdle

trifling *syn* PETTY, trivial, puny, paltry, measly, picayunish, picayune *rel* inane, wishy-washy, banal, jejune, vapid, insipid; vain, idle, otiose, nugatory, empty, hollow; venial, pardonable

trig *syn* NEAT, trim, tidy, spick-and-span, snug, shipshape *rel* orderly, methodical

trill *syn* SING, troll, carol, descant, warble, hymn, chant, intone

trim *vb* **1** *syn* SHEAR, poll, clip, prune, lop, snip, crop **2** *syn* STABILIZE, steady, poise, balance, ballast *rel* adjust, regulate, fix; counterbalance, counterpoise, offset, compensate

trim *adj, syn* NEAT, tidy, trig, snug, shipshape, spick-and-span *rel* clean, cleanly; compact, close *ant* frowzy

trip *vb, syn* STUMBLE, blunder, lurch, flounder, lumber, galumph, lollop, bumble *rel* totter, stagger, reel; fall, drop

trip *n, syn* JOURNEY, voyage, tour, excursion, cruise, expedition, jaunt, pilgrimage

trite • lacking the freshness that evokes attention or interest *syn* hackneyed, stereotyped, threadbare, shopworn *rel* old, antiquated, archaic, obsolete; banal, flat, jejune, insipid, vapid; depleted, exhausted, drained, impoverished *ant* original; fresh

triumph *syn* VICTORY, conquest *rel* vanquishing, subjugation, surmounting, overthrowing, routing

trivial *syn* PETTY, trifling, puny, paltry,

measly, picayunish, picayune *rel* small, little, diminutive; futile, vain, fruitless, bootless; slight, slim, slender, thin, tenuous *ant* weighty; momentous

troll *syn* SING, carol, descant, warble, trill, hymn, chant, intone

troop *syn* COMPANY, band, troupe, party *rel* crowd, throng, press; assembly, gathering, collection; legion, host, army, multitude

troubadour *syn* POET, versifier, rhymer, rhymester; poetaster, bard, minstrel

trouble *vb* **1** • to cause to be uneasy or upset *syn* distress, ail *rel* discompose, disquiet, disturb, perturb, upset, agitate; vex, irk, annoy, bother **2** *syn* INCONVENIENCE, incommode, discommode *rel* embarrass, discomfit, disconcert, abash; worry, annoy, plague, pester; perplex, puzzle, distract

trouble *n, syn* EFFORT, exertion, pains *rel* flurry, fuss, ado, stir, bustle, pother; labor, toil, work; difficulty, rigor, vicissitude, hardship

troupe *syn* COMPANY, troop, band, party

trouper *syn* ACTOR, player, performer, mummer, mime, mimic, thespian, impersonator

truant *syn* VAGABOND, vagrant, tramp, hobo, bum

truce • a suspension of or an agreement for suspending hostilities *syn* cease-fire, armistice, peace

truckle *syn* FAWN, toady, cringe, cower *rel* defer, succumb, bow, cave, yield, submit; follow, tag, trail, tail

truculent *syn* FIERCE, ferocious, barbarous, savage, inhuman, cruel, fell *rel* intimidating, cowing, bulldozing, browbeating, bullying; terrorizing, terrifying, frightening; threatening, menacing

true **1** *syn* FAITHFUL, loyal, constant, staunch, steadfast, resolute *rel* reliable, dependable, trustworthy, tried; persevering, persisting; sincere, wholehearted, whole-souled, unfeigned *ant* false; fickle **2** *syn* REAL, actual *rel* genuine, authentic, veritable, bona fide; exact, precise, correct, right; typical, natural, regular *ant* false

truism *syn* COMMONPLACE, platitude, bromide, cliche *rel* triteness, threadbareness; banality, jejuneness, inanity

trust *n* **1** • assured reliance on the character, ability, strength, or truth of someone or something *syn* confidence, reliance, dependence, faith *rel* assurance, conviction, certitude, certainty; belief, credence, credit *ant* mistrust **2** *syn* MONOPOLY, corner, pool, syndicate, cartel

trust *vb, syn* RELY, depend, count, reckon, bank *rel* confide, entrust, commit, consign; hope, expect, look

trustworthy *syn* RELIABLE, dependable, trusty, tried *rel* safe, secure; veracious, truthful; staunch, constant, steadfast, faithful; honest, upright, scrupulous *ant* deceitful; dubious

trusty *syn* RELIABLE, trustworthy, tried, dependable *rel* faithful, staunch, steadfast, constant

truth • the quality or state of keeping close to fact and avoiding distortion or misrepresentation *syn* veracity, verity, verisimilitude *rel* exactness, precision, correctness, rightness; authenticity, genuineness, veritableness *ant* untruth; lie, falsehood

try *vb* **1** *syn* PROVE, test, demonstrate *rel* judge, adjudge, adjudicate; inspect, examine, scrutinize **2** *syn* AFFLICT, torment, torture, rack *rel* worry, harass, harry, plague, pester; trouble, distress; irk, vex, bother, annoy **3** *syn* ATTEMPT, endeavor, essay, strive, struggle *rel* aim, aspire; intend, mean, propose, purpose, design

try *n, syn* ATTEMPT, endeavor, essay, striving, struggle *rel* effort, exertion, trouble, pains; test, trial, proof

tryst *syn* ENGAGEMENT, rendezvous, assignation, appointment, date

tucker *syn* TIRE, fatigue, exhaust, jade, fag, weary *rel* deplete, drain, exhaust, impoverish, bankrupt

tug *syn* PULL, tow, hale, haul, drag, draw

tumid *syn* INFLATED, flatulent, turgid *rel* expanded, distended, swollen, dilated; pretentious, showy, ostentatious; bombastic, grandiloquent, magniloquent, rhetorical

tumult *syn* COMMOTION, agitation, turmoil, turbulence, confusion, convulsion, upheaval *rel* agitation, perturbation, disturbance; uprising, insurrection, rebellion, revolt, mutiny; disorder, unsettlement; din, uproar, pandemonium

tune *n, syn* MELODY, air

tune *vb, syn* HARMONIZE, attune *rel* adjust, regulate, fix; adapt, accommodate, reconcile, conform

turbid • not clear or translucent but clouded with or as if with sediment *syn* muddy, roily *rel* obscure, dark, murky; dirty, foul, nasty *ant* clear; limpid

turbulence *syn* COMMOTION, agitation, tumult, turmoil, confusion, convulsion, upheaval *rel* din, uproar, babel, pandemonium; agitation, perturbation, disturbance

turgid *syn* INFLATED, tumid, flatulent *rel* expanded, distended, amplified, swollen; magniloquent, grandiloquent, rhetorical, bombastic

turmoil *syn* COMMOTION, agitation, tumult, turbulence, confusion, convulsion, upheaval *rel* agitation, disquiet, disturbance, perturbation; restlessness, nervousness, uneasiness, jitteriness

turn *vb* **1** • to move or cause to move in a curved or circular path on or as if on an axis *syn* revolve, rotate, gyrate, circle, spin, twirl, whirl, wheel, eddy, swirl, pirouette *rel* swing, oscillate, vibrate, fluctuate, pendulate, undulate **2** • to change or cause to change course or direction *syn* divert, deflect, avert, sheer *rel* swerve, veer, deviate, diverge, digress, depart; move, shift **3** *syn* RESORT, refer, apply, go **4** *syn* DEPEND, hinge, hang

turn *n* **1** *syn* SPELL, trick, tour, shift, stint, bout, go **2** *syn* GIFT, bent, faculty, aptitude, genius, talent, knack *rel* inclination, disposition, predisposition, bias; propensity, proclivity, penchant, leaning, flair

turncoat *syn* RENEGADE, apostate, recreant, backslider *rel* deserter, forsaker, abandoner

turn out *syn* BEAR, produce, yield *rel* make, form, fashion, shape, manufacture, fabricate; propagate, breed, generate, engender

tussle *syn* WRESTLE, grapple, scuffle *rel* contend, fight; resist, combat, withstand, oppose; compete, vie, rival

twaddle *syn* NONSENSE, drivel, bunk, balderdash, poppycock, gobbledygook, trash, rot, bull

tweet *n, syn* CHIRP, chirrup, cheep, peep, twitter, chitter

tweet *vb, syn* CHIRP, chirrup, cheep, peep, twitter, chitter

twine *syn* WIND, coil, curl, twist, wreathe, entwine *rel* curve, bend; interweave, interplait, weave; entangle, enmesh

twinge *syn* PAIN, ache, pang, throe, stitch

twinkle *syn* FLASH, gleam, glance, glint, sparkle, glitter, glisten, scintillate, coruscate

twinkling *syn* INSTANT, moment, minute, second, flash, jiffy, split second

twirl *syn* TURN, revolve, rotate, gyrate, circle, spin, whirl, wheel, eddy, swirl, pirouette

twist **1** *syn* WIND, coil, curl, twine, wreathe, entwine *rel* combine, unite, associate, join; plait, braid, knit, weave; encircle, surround **2** *syn* CURVE, bend *rel* spin, twirl, whirl, turn; contort, distort, deform

twister *syn* TORNADO, cyclone *rel* whirlwind, whirly; hurricane, tropical storm, typhoon

twit *syn* RIDICULE, deride, mock, taunt, rally *rel* reproach, chide, reprove; reprehend, blame, censure, criticize; scoff, jeer, gibe

twitch *syn* JERK, snap, yank *rel* pull, drag, tug; clutch, snatch, grasp

twitter *vb, syn* CHIRP, chirrup, cheep, peep, tweet, chitter

twitter *n, syn* CHIRP, chirrup, cheep, peep, tweet, chitter

type **1** *syn* SYMBOL, emblem, attribute *rel* sign, mark, token; intimation, suggestion; adumbration, shadowing *ant* antitype **2** • a number of individuals thought of as a group because of a common quality or qualities *syn* kind, sort, stripe, kidney, ilk, description, nature, character *rel* exemplar, example, model, pattern

typhoon *syn* HURRICANE, tropical storm *rel* whirlwind, whirly

typical *syn* REGULAR, natural, normal *rel* generic, general, universal, common; specific *ant* atypical; distinctive

tyrannical, tyrannous *syn* ABSOLUTE, despotic, arbitrary, autocratic *rel* dictatorial, authoritarian, magisterial; totalitarian; domineering, imperious, masterful

tyro *syn* AMATEUR, dilettante, dabbler *rel* novice, apprentice, probationer, neophyte

U

ubiquitous *syn* OMNIPRESENT

ugly • unpleasing to the sight *syn* hideous, ill-favored, unsightly *rel* plain, homely; grotesque, bizarre *ant* beautiful

ultimate **1** *syn* LAST, latest, final, terminal, concluding, eventual **2** • being so fundamental as to represent the extreme limit of actual or possible knowledge *syn* absolute, categorical

ululate *syn* ROAR, bellow, bluster, bawl, vociferate, clamor, howl *rel* wail, keen, weep, cry; bewail, lament

ululation *syn* ROAR, bellow, bluster, bawl, vociferation

umbra *syn* SHADE, penumbra, shadow, umbrage, adumbration

umbrage **1** *syn* SHADE, shadow, umbra, penumbra, adumbration **2** *syn* OFFENSE, resentment, pique, dudgeon, huff *rel* annoyance, vexation, irking; irritation, exasperation, provocation, nettling; indignation, rage, fury, wrath, anger, ire

umpire *syn* JUDGE, referee, arbiter, arbitrator

unacceptable *syn* OBJECTIONABLE, undesirable, unwanted, unwelcome

unaffected *syn* NATURAL, artless, simple, ingenuous, naïve, unsophisticated

unafraid *syn* BRAVE, fearless, dauntless, undaunted, bold, intrepid, audacious, courageous, valiant, valorous, doughty *rel* cool, composed, imperturbable; confident, assured, sure *ant* afraid

unassailable *syn* INVINCIBLE, impregnable, inexpugnable, invulnerable, unconquerable, indomitable *rel* stout, sturdy, tenacious, tough, strong, stalwart

unavoidable *syn* INEVITABLE, ineluctable, inescapable, unescapable *rel* certain, positive, sure

unbecoming *syn* INDECOROUS, improper, unseemly, indecent, indelicate *rel* unfitting, inappropriate, unsuitable, unfit; inept, awkward, maladroit, gauche, clumsy

unbelief • the attitude or state of mind of one who does not believe *syn* disbelief, incredulity *rel* uncertainty, doubt, dubiety, dubiosity, skepticism *ant* belief

unbeliever *syn* ATHEIST, freethinker, agnostic, infidel, deist

unbiased *syn* FAIR, impartial, dispassionate, just, equitable, uncolored, objective *rel* uninterested, disinterested, detached, aloof, indifferent *ant* biased

unburden *syn* RID, clear, disabuse, purge *rel* disencumber, unload, discharge; free, release, liberate *ant* burden

uncalled-for *syn* SUPEREROGATORY, gratuitous, wanton *rel* impertinent, intrusive, officious; foolish, silly, absurd, preposterous

uncanny *syn* WEIRD, eerie *rel* strange, singular, erratic, eccentric, odd, queer; mysterious, inscrutable

unceasing *syn* EVERLASTING, endless, interminable

uncertainty • lack of sureness about someone or something *syn* doubt, dubiety, dubiosity, skepticism, suspicion, mistrust *ant* certainty

uncircumscribed *syn* INFINITE, boundless, illimitable, sempiternal, eternal *ant* circumscribed

uncivil *syn* RUDE, ill-mannered, impolite, discourteous, ungracious *rel* boorish, loutish, churlish; brusque, blunt, gruff, crusty, bluff *ant* civil

uncolored **1** *syn* COLORLESS, achromatic **2** *syn* FAIR, dispassionate, impartial, objective, unbiased, just, equitable

uncommon *syn* INFREQUENT, scarce, rare, occasional, sporadic *rel* strange, singular, unique; exceptional; choice, exquisite *ant* common

uncommunicative *syn* SILENT, taciturn, reticent, reserved, secretive, close, close-lipped, closemouthed, tight-lipped *ant* communicative

unconcerned *syn* INDIFFERENT, incurious, aloof, detached, uninterested, disinterested *rel* cool, collected, composed, nonchalant; apathetic, impassive, stolid, phlegmatic *ant* concerned

uncongenial *syn* INCONSONANT, unsympathetic, incompatible, inconsistent, incongruous, discordant, discrepant *rel* antipathetic, unsympathetic, averse; repugnant, repellent, abhorrent, obnoxious *ant* congenial

unconquerable *syn* INVINCIBLE, indomitable, impregnable, inexpugnable, unassailable, invulnerable *ant* conquerable

unconstraint • freedom from constraint or pressure *syn* abandon, spontaneity *rel* spontaneousness, impulsiveness, instinctiveness; naturalness, simplicity, unsophistication, ingenuousness, naïveté

uncouth *syn* RUDE, rough, crude, raw, callow, green *rel* awkward, clumsy, gauche

uncritical *syn* SUPERFICIAL, shallow, cursory *ant* critical

unctuous *syn* FULSOME, oily, oleaginous, slick, soapy *rel* bland, politic, smooth, diplomatic, suave; obsequious, subservient *ant* brusque

undaunted *syn* BRAVE, courageous, unafraid, fearless, intrepid, valiant, valorous, dauntless, doughty, bold, audacious *rel* resolute, staunch, steadfast, faithful; confident, assured, sanguine, sure *ant* afraid

under *syn* BELOW, beneath, underneath

undergo *syn* EXPERIENCE, sustain, suffer *rel* bear, endure, abide, tolerate; accept, receive; submit, bow, yield, defer

underhand, underhanded *syn* SECRET, covert, stealthy, furtive, clandestine, surreptitious *rel* deceitful, dishonest; crooked, devious, oblique; sly, cunning, crafty, tricky, insidious, wily, guileful *ant* aboveboard

underling *syn* INFERIOR, subordinate *ant* leader, master

underlying **1** *syn* FUNDAMENTAL, basic, basal, radical *rel* essential, cardinal, vital; requisite, indispensable, necessary, needful **2** *syn* ELEMENTAL, basic, elementary, essential, fundamental, primitive

undermine *syn* WEAKEN, enfeeble, debilitate, sap, cripple, disable *rel* ruin, wreck; injure, damage, impair; thwart, foil, frustrate *ant* reinforce

underneath *syn* BELOW, under, beneath

understand • to have a clear or complete idea of *syn* comprehend, appreciate *rel* conceive, realize, envision, envisage, think; interpret, elucidate, construe, explain; penetrate, pierce, probe

understanding **1** *syn* REASON, intuition *rel* comprehension, apprehension; discernment, discrimination, insight, penetration **2** *syn* AGREEMENT, accord

understudy *syn* SUBSTITUTE, supply, locum tenens, alternate, pinch hitter, double, stand-in

undesirable *syn* OBJECTIONABLE, unacceptable, unwanted, unwelcome

undulate *syn* SWING, waver, sway, oscillate, vibrate, fluctuate, pendulate *rel* pulsate, pulse, beat, throb, palpitate

undying *syn* IMMORTAL, deathless, unfading *rel* everlasting, endless, unceasing, interminable

unearth *syn* DISCOVER, ascertain, determine, learn *rel* dig, delve; expose, exhibit, show; reveal, disclose, discover

uneasy *syn* IMPATIENT, nervous, unquiet, restless, restive, fidgety, jumpy, jittery *rel* anxious, worried, solicitous, concerned, careful; disturbed, perturbed, agitated, disquieted

uneducated *syn* IGNORANT, illiterate, unlettered, untaught, untutored, unlearned *rel* rude, crude, rough, raw, callow, green, uncouth *ant* educated

unerring *syn* INFALLIBLE, inerrable, inerrant *rel* reliable, dependable, trustworthy; exact, accurate, precise, correct

unescapable *syn* INEVITABLE, ineluctable, inescapable, unavoidable *rel, ant* see INESCAPABLE

uneven *syn* ROUGH, harsh, rugged, scabrous *ant* even

unfading *syn* IMMORTAL, deathless, undying *rel* everlasting, endless; lasting, perdurable, perpetual

unfeigned *syn* SINCERE, wholehearted, whole-souled, heartfelt, hearty *rel* genuine, veritable, bona fide, authentic; natural, simple, naïve; spontaneous, impulsive

unfit • not adapted or appropriate to a particular end or purpose *syn* unsuitable, improper, inappropriate, unfitting, inapt, unhappy, infelicitous *ant* fit

unfitting *syn* UNFIT, inappropriate, improper, unsuitable, inapt, unhappy, infelicitous *rel* unbecoming, unseemly, indecorous *ant* fitting

unflagging *syn* INDEFATIGABLE, unwearied, unwearying, tireless, untiring, weariless *rel* persevering, persisting, persistent; steady, constant

unflappable *syn* COOL, composed, collected, unruffled, imperturbable, nonchalant

unfold **1** • to disclose by degrees to the sight or understanding *syn* evolve, develop, elaborate, perfect *rel* show, manifest, evidence, evince, demonstrate; exhibit, display, expose **2** *syn* SOLVE, resolve, unravel, decipher

unformed *syn* FORMLESS, shapeless *ant* formed

unfortunate *syn* UNLUCKY, disastrous, ill-starred, ill-fated, calamitous, luckless, hapless *rel* baleful, malefic, sinister; miserable, wretched; unhappy, infelicitous *ant* fortunate

unfounded *syn* BASELESS, groundless, unwarranted *rel* false, wrong; misleading, deceptive; mendacious, dishonest, untruthful

unfruitful *syn* STERILE, barren, infertile, impotent *ant* fruitful, prolific

ungodly *syn* IRRELIGIOUS, godless, unreligious, nonreligious *rel* wicked, evil, ill, bad; reprobate, abandoned, profligate; impious, blasphemous, profane

ungovernable *syn* UNRULY, intractable, refractory, recalcitrant, willful, headstrong *rel* contrary, perverse, froward, wayward; contumacious, insubordinate, rebellious, factious *ant* governable; docile

ungracious *syn* RUDE, ill-mannered, impolite, discourteous, uncivil *rel* churlish, boorish; brusque, gruff, blunt, curt, bluff *ant* gracious

unhappy *syn* UNFIT, infelicitous, inapt, unsuitable, improper, inappropriate, unfitting *rel* inept, maladroit, gauche, awkward *ant* happy

uniform **1** *syn* LIKE, alike, similar, analogous, comparable, akin, parallel, identical *rel* same, equivalent, equal *ant* various **2** *syn* STEADY, constant, even, equable *rel* consistent, consonant, compatible; regular, orderly *ant* multiform

unify *syn* COMPACT, consolidate, concentrate *rel* integrate, articulate, concatenate; organize, systematize, order; unite, combine, conjoin

unimpassioned *syn* SOBER, temperate, continent *rel* cool, composed, collected, imperturbable; calm, serene, placid, tranquil; impassive, stolid, stoic, phlegmatic *ant* impassioned

uninterested *syn* INDIFFERENT, unconcerned, incurious, aloof, detached, disinterested

union *syn* UNITY, solidarity, integrity *rel* integration, articulation, concatenation; harmony, consonance, accord, concord

unique **1** *syn* SINGLE, sole, lone, solitary, separate, particular *rel* only, alone **2** *syn* STRANGE, singular, peculiar, eccentric, erratic, odd, queer, quaint, outlandish, curious *rel* exceptional; uncommon, rare, infrequent

unite **1** *syn* JOIN, conjoin, combine, connect, link, associate, relate *rel* mix, blend, merge, amalgamate; weave, knit; integrate, concatenate, articulate *ant* divide; alienate **2** • to join forces or act in concert *syn* combine, conjoin, cooperate, concur *rel* mingle, commingle, coalesce, fuse; adhere, cohere, stick, cling, cleave *ant* part

unity • the character of a thing that is a whole composed of many parts *syn* solidarity, integrity, union *rel* identification, incorporation, embodiment, assimilation; cooperation, concurrence, uniting, combining; integration, concatenation, articulation

universal **1** • present or significant throughout the world *syn* cosmic, ecumenical, catholic, cosmopolitan *rel* earthly, terrestrial, worldly, mundane; whole, entire, all, total **2** • of, belonging, or relating to all or the whole *syn* general, generic, common *ant* particular

unkempt *syn* SLIPSHOD, slovenly, sloppy, disheveled *rel* frowzy, slatternly, blowsy, dowdy; negligent, neglectful, lax, slack, remiss

unlawful • contrary to or prohibited by the law *syn* illegal, illegitimate, illicit *rel* iniquitous, nefarious, flagitious *ant* lawful

unlearned *syn* IGNORANT, illiterate, unlettered, uneducated, untaught, untutored *rel* crude, rude, rough, raw, callow, green, uncouth

unlettered *syn* IGNORANT, illiterate, uneducated, untaught, untutored, unlearned

unlikeness *syn* DISSIMILARITY, difference, divergence, divergency, distinction *rel* diversity, variety; disparity, variousness; discrepancy, discordance, incongruousness, incompatibility, inconsistency, inconsonance *ant* likeness

unlucky • involving or suffering misfortune that results from chance *syn* disastrous, ill-starred, ill-fated, unfortunate, calamitous, luckless, hapless *rel* inept, awkward; distressing, troubling; sinister, malign, baleful *ant* lucky

unman *syn* UNNERVE, emasculate, enervate *rel* sap, undermine, weaken, enfeeble, debilitate; abase, degrade; deplete, drain, exhaust, impoverish, bankrupt

unmarried • being without a spouse *syn* single, celibate, virgin, maiden

unmatured *syn* IMMATURE, unripe, unmellow *ant* matured

unmellow *syn* IMMATURE, unmatured, unripe *ant* mellow, mellowed

unmindful *syn* FORGETFUL, oblivious *rel* heedless, thoughtless, careless, inadvertent; negligent, neglectful, remiss *ant* mindful; solicitous

unmitigated *syn* OUTRIGHT, out-and-out, arrant

unnatural *syn* IRREGULAR, anomalous *rel* abnormal, aberrant, atypical; monstrous, prodigious; fantastic, grotesque, bizarre *ant* natural

unnerve • to deprive of strength or vigor and the capacity for effective action *syn* enervate, unman, emasculate *rel* upset, agitate, perturb, discompose; bewilder, distract, confound, puzzle; weaken, enfeeble, sap, undermine

unoffending *syn* HARMLESS, innocuous, innocent, inoffensive

unpremeditated *syn* EXTEMPORANEOUS, extempore, extemporary, improvised, impromptu, offhand *ant* premeditated

unpretentious *syn* PLAIN, homely, simple *rel* natural, unsophisticated, simple, ingenuous, unaffected; unassuming

unpropitious *syn* OMINOUS, portentous, fateful, inauspicious *rel* sinister, baleful, malign, malefic, maleficent; threatening, menacing; adverse, antagonistic, counter *ant* propitious

unqualified *syn* INCAPABLE, incompetent *rel* disabled, crippled, weakened, debilitated; unfit, unsuitable *ant* qualified

unquiet *syn* IMPATIENT, nervous, restless, restive, uneasy, fidgety, jumpy, jittery *rel* agitated, upset, perturbed, disquieted, disturbed; worried, anxious, solicitous, concerned, careful *ant* quiet

unravel *syn* SOLVE, resolve, unfold, decipher *rel* disentangle, untangle, extricate; elucidate, explicate, interpret, explain, expound

unreasonable *syn* IRRATIONAL *rel* absurd, preposterous, foolish, silly; simple, fatuous, asinine; excessive, immoderate, inordinate *ant* reasonable

unrelenting *syn* GRIM, implacable, relentless, merciless *rel* inexorable, obdurate, inflexible, adamant; stiff, rigid; severe, stern *ant* forbearing

unreligious *syn* IRRELIGIOUS, ungodly, godless, nonreligious

unremitting *syn* CONTINUAL, constant, incessant, continuous, perpetual, perennial *rel* unceasing, interminable, endless, everlasting; assiduous, sedulous, diligent; indefatigable, untiring

unripe *syn* IMMATURE, unmatured, unmellow *rel* crude, raw, green, callow, rude; premature, untimely, forward, precocious *ant* ripe

unruffled *syn* COOL, imperturbable, unflappable, nonchalant, composed, collected *rel* calm, placid, peaceful, serene, tranquil; poised, balanced *ant* ruffled; excited

unruly • not submissive to government or control *syn* ungovernable, intractable, refractory, recalcitrant, willful, headstrong *rel* insubordinate, rebellious, contumacious; obstreperous, boisterous, strident, vociferous; contrary, perverse, froward, wayward; fractious, irritable, snappish, waspish *ant* tractable, docile

unseemly *syn* INDECOROUS, improper, unbecoming, indecent, indelicate *rel* unfitting, unsuitable, inappropriate; incongruous, incompatible, inconsistent, inconsonant *ant* seemly

unsettle *syn* DISORDER, derange, disarrange, disorganize, disturb *rel* discommode, incommode, trouble, inconvenience; upset, agitate, perturb, discompose, disquiet *ant* settle

unsightly *syn* UGLY, hideous, ill-favored *rel* distasteful, obnoxious, repellent, repugnant; hateful, odious, detestable, abominable

unsocial • disliking or avoiding the company of others *syn* asocial, antisocial, nonsocial *ant* social

unsophisticated *syn* NATURAL, simple, ingenuous, naïve, artless *rel* candid, frank, open, plain; genuine, bona fide, authentic; crude, callow, green, uncouth, rude *ant* sophisticated

unspeakable *syn* UNUTTERABLE, inexpressible, ineffable, indescribable, indefinable *rel* offensive, loathsome, repulsive, revolting; repugnant, repellent, obnoxious, distasteful; abominable, odious, hateful, detestable

unstable *syn* INCONSTANT, fickle, capricious, mercurial *rel* changeable, variable, mutable, protean; volatile, effervescent, buoyant, resilient, elastic *ant* stable

unsuitable *syn* UNFIT, improper, inappropriate, unfitting, inapt, unhappy, infelicitous *rel* unbecoming, unseemly, indecorous, indecent; inept, maladroit, awkward, clumsy, gauche *ant* suitable

unsympathetic **1** *syn* INCONSONANT, uncongenial, discordant, incongruous, incompatible, inconsistent, discrepant *ant* sympathetic **2** *syn* ANTIPATHETIC *rel* indifferent, unconcerned, incurious, aloof; hardened, callous, indurated *ant* sympathetic

untangle *syn* EXTRICATE, disentangle, disencumber, disembarrass *rel* free, release, liberate

untaught *syn* IGNORANT, illiterate, unlettered, uneducated, untutored, unlearned *ant* taught

untimely *syn* PREMATURE, forward, advanced, precocious *rel* immature, unmatured, unripe, unmellow *ant* timely

untiring *syn* INDEFATIGABLE, tireless, weariless, unwearying, unwearied, unflagging *rel* unceasing, interminable, everlasting; assiduous, sedulous, diligent; persevering, persisting

untouchable *syn* OUTCAST, castaway, derelict, reprobate, pariah

untruth *syn* LIE, falsehood, fib, misrepresentation, story *rel* mendaciousness, mendacity, dishonesty, deceitfulness; equivocation, tergiversation, ambiguity *ant* truth

untruthful *syn* DISHONEST, lying, mendacious, deceitful *rel* false, wrong; misleading, deceptive, delusive, delusory *ant* truthful

untutored *syn* IGNORANT, illiterate, unlettered, uneducated, untaught, unlearned *ant* tutored

unusual *syn* exceptional, extraordinary, phenomenal unwonted

unutterable • not capable of being put into words *syn* inexpressible, unspeakable, ineffable, indescribable, indefinable

unwanted *syn* OBJECTIONABLE, unacceptable, undesirable, unwelcome

unwarranted *syn* BASELESS, groundless, unfounded *rel* unauthorized, unaccredited; unapproved, unsanctioned *ant* warranted

unwearied *syn* INDEFATIGABLE, tireless, weariless, untiring, unwearying, unflagging *rel* persevering, persisting, persistent; unceasing, interminable, everlasting; constant, steady

unwearying *syn* INDEFATIGABLE, tireless, weariless, untiring, unwearied, unflagging *rel* see UNTIRING

unwelcome *syn* OBJECTIONABLE, unacceptable, undesirable, unwanted

unwholesome • detrimental to physical, mental, or moral well-being *syn* morbid, sickly, diseased, pathological *rel* detrimental, deleterious, noxious, pernicious, baneful; toxic, poisonous; injurious, hurtful, harmful, mischievous *ant* wholesome

unwonted *syn* EXCEPTIONAL, extraordinary, phenomenal, unusual

upbraid *syn* SCOLD, rate, berate, tongue-lash, revile, vituperate, jaw, bawl, chew out, wig, rail *rel* reprehend, reprobate, blame, censure, denounce, criticize; reproach, reprimand, rebuke, reprove

upheaval *syn* COMMOTION, agitation, tumult, turmoil, turbulence, confusion, convulsion *rel* heaving, raising, lifting; alteration, change; cataclysm, catastrophe, disaster

uphold *syn* SUPPORT, advocate, back, champion *rel* help, aid, assist; defend, vindicate, justify, maintain; sanction, approve, endorse *ant* contravene; subvert

upright • having or showing a strict regard for what is morally right *syn* honest, just, conscientious, scrupulous, honorable *rel* moral, ethical, virtuous, righteous; fair, equitable, impartial; straightforward, aboveboard

uprising *syn* REBELLION, revolution, revolt, insurrection, mutiny, putsch, coup *rel* fight, combat, conflict, fray, contest; strife, contention, dissension, discord; aggression, attack

uproar *syn* DIN, pandemonium, hullabaloo, babel, hubbub, clamor, racket *rel* strife, contention, dissension, discord, conflict, variance; confusion, disorder, chaos; fracas, brawl, broil, melee

uproot *syn* EXTERMINATE, eradicate, deracinate, extirpate, wipe *rel* abolish, extinguish, annihilate, abate; supplant, displace, replace, supersede; subvert, overthrow, overturn; destroy, demolish *ant* establish; inseminate

upset 1 *syn* OVERTURN, capsize, overthrow, subvert *rel* invert, reverse; bend, curve **2** *syn* DISCOMPOSE, agitate, perturb, disturb, disquiet, fluster, flurry *rel* bewilder, distract, confound, puzzle; discomfit, rattle, faze, embarrass; unnerve, unman

upshot *syn* EFFECT, outcome, issue, result, consequence, aftereffect, aftermath, event, sequel *rel* end, termination, ending; climax, culmination; concluding, conclusion, finishing, finish, completion

urbane *syn* SUAVE, smooth, diplomatic, bland, politic *rel* courteous, polite, courtly, civil; poised, balanced; cultured, cultivated, refined *ant* rude; clownish, bucolic

urge *vb* • to press or impel to action, effort, or speed *syn* egg, exhort, goad, spur, prod, prick, sic *rel* impel, drive, actuate, move; stimulate, excite, quicken, provoke

urge *n, syn* DESIRE, lust, passion, appetite *rel* motive, spring, spur, goad, incentive; longing, yearning, pining; craving, coveting, desiring

urgent *syn* PRESSING, imperative, crying, importunate, insistent, exigent, instant *rel* impelling, driving; constraining, compelling, obliging

usage 1 *syn* HABIT, practice, custom, use, habitude, wont *rel* method, mode, manner, way, fashion; procedure, proceeding, process; guiding, guidance, leading, lead; choice, preference **2** *syn* FORM, convention, convenance *rel* formality, ceremony

use *n* **1** • a useful or valuable end, result, or purpose *syn* service, advantage, profit, account, avail *rel* benefit; value, worth; function, office, duty; purpose, intention, object **2** • a capacity for serving an end or purpose *syn* usefulness, utility *rel* applicability, relevance, pertinence; suitability, fitness, appropriateness **3** *syn* HABIT, wont, practice, usage, custom, habitude *rel* form, usage; rite, ceremony, formality

use *vb* • to put into service esp. to attain an end *syn* employ, utilize, apply, avail *rel* handle, manipulate, ply, wield; practice, exercise

usefulness *syn* USE, utility *rel* value, worth; excellence, merit

usual • familiar through frequent or regular repetition *syn* customary, habitual, wonted, accustomed *rel* regular, natural, normal, typical; common, ordinary, familiar; prevalent, prevailing, rife, current

usurp *syn* ARROGATE, preempt, appropriate, confiscate *rel* seize, take, grab, grasp *ant* abdicate

utensil *syn* IMPLEMENT, tool, instrument, appliance *rel* device, contrivance, contraption, gadget

utility *syn* USE, usefulness *rel* suitability, fitness, appropriateness; value, worth

utilize *syn* USE, employ, apply, avail *rel* benefit, profit; handle, manipulate, ply, wield; forward, further, promote, advance

utopian *syn* AMBITIOUS, pretentious *rel* impracticable, unfeasible, impossible; visionary, quixotic, chimerical, imaginary; ideal, transcendental, abstract

utter 1 *syn* SAY, tell, state *rel* enunciate, articulate, pronounce; speak, talk **2** *syn* EXPRESS, vent, voice, broach, air, ventilate *rel* reveal, disclose, discover, divulge; declare, announce, publish, advertise

V

vacant *syn* EMPTY, blank, vacuous *rel* bare, barren; destitute, void, devoid; idiotic, imbecilic, foolish

vacate *syn* ANNUL, abrogate, void, quash

vacillate *syn* HESITATE, waver, falter *rel* fluctuate, sway, oscillate, swing; demur, scruple, boggle

vacuous *syn* EMPTY, vacant, blank, void *rel* barren, bare; inane, wishy-washy, insipid

vacuum *syn* HOLE, void, cavity, hollow, pocket

vagabond • a person who wanders at will or as a habit *syn* vagrant, truant, tramp, bum, hobo *rel* wanderer, roamer, rover

vagary *syn* CAPRICE, freak, fancy, whim, whimsy, conceit, crotchet *rel* mood, humor, temper, vein; fancy, fantasy, dream, daydream; notion, idea

vagrant *n, syn* VAGABOND, truant, tramp, hobo, bum *rel* wanderer, roamer, rover

vagrant *adj, syn* ITINERANT, peripatetic, ambulatory, ambulant, nomadic *rel* moving, shifting; wandering, roaming, roving, rambling, straying, ranging; strolling, sauntering

vague *syn* OBSCURE, dark, enigmatic, cryptic, ambiguous, equivocal *rel* formless, unformed; doubtful, dubious; abstruse, recondite *ant* definite; specific; lucid

vain **1** • being without worth or significance *syn* nugatory, otiose, idle, empty, hollow **2** *syn* FUTILE, fruitless, bootless, abortive *rel* ineffective, ineffectual, inefficacious; trivial, trifling, puny, petty, paltry; delusive, delusory, misleading **3** *syn* PROUD, vainglorious *rel* self-satisfied, self-complacent, complacent, priggish, smug; conceited, egoistic, egotistic

vainglorious *syn* PROUD, vain *rel* arrogant, haughty, supercilious, disdainful, insolent; boasting, boastful, bragging, vaunting, gasconading

vainglory *syn* PRIDE, vanity *rel* pomp, display, parade; flaunting, parading, exhibition; rhapsody, rodomontade, rant, bombast

valiant *syn* BRAVE, courageous, unafraid, fearless, intrepid, valorous, dauntless, undaunted, doughty, bold, audacious *rel* stout, sturdy, tenacious, stalwart, strong; indomitable, unconquerable, invincible *ant* timid; dastardly

valid • having such force as to compel serious attention and usu. acceptance *syn* sound, cogent, convincing, compelling, telling *rel* conclusive, determinative, definitive, decisive; effective, effectual; legal, lawful, licit; logical, analytical, subtle *ant* fallacious, sophistical

validate *syn* CONFIRM, authenticate, substantiate, verify, corroborate *rel* certify, attest, witness, vouch *ant* invalidate

valor *syn* HEROISM, prowess, gallantry *rel* courage, mettle, tenacity, spirit, resolution; indomitableness, unconquerableness, invincibility; fortitude, guts, sand, backbone

valorous *syn* BRAVE, courageous, unafraid, fearless, intrepid, valiant, dauntless, undaunted, doughty, bold, audacious *rel* venturesome, daring, adventurous; stout, sturdy, tenacious, stalwart, tough, strong

valuable *syn* COSTLY, precious, invaluable, priceless, expensive, dear *rel* estimated, appraised, evaluated; valued, appreciated, prized, treasured; esteemed, admired, respected

value *n, syn* WORTH *rel* price, charge, cost, expense; importance, consequence, significance, weight; use, usefulness, utility

value *vb* **1** *syn* ESTIMATE, appraise, evaluate, rate, assess, assay *rel* calculate, compute, reckon; judge, adjudge, adjudicate **2** *syn* APPRECIATE, prize, treasure, cherish *rel* esteem, respect, admire; love, enjoy, like; revere, reverence, venerate

vanish • to pass from view or out of existence *syn* evanesce, evaporate, disappear, fade *rel* escape, flee, fly; dispel, disperse, dissipate, scatter *ant* appear; loom

vanity *syn* PRIDE, vainglory *rel* self-esteem, self-love, conceit, egotism, egoism, amour propre; complacency, self-complacency, self-satisfaction, smugness, priggishness; show, ostentation, pretense

vanquish *syn* CONQUER, defeat, beat, lick, subdue, subjugate, reduce, overcome, surmount, overthrow, rout *rel* frustrate, foil, outwit, circumvent; overturn, subvert

vanquisher *syn* VICTOR, conqueror, winner, champion

vapid *syn* INSIPID, flat, jejune, banal, wishy-washy, inane *rel* soft, bland, gentle, mild; tame, subdued, submissive; mawkish, maudlin, soppy, slushy, mushy, sentimental

variable *syn* CHANGEABLE, protean, changeful, mutable *rel* fitful, spasmodic; fickle, mercurial, unstable, inconstant, capricious; mobile, movable *ant* constant; equable

variance *syn* DISCORD, contention, dissension, difference, strife, conflict *rel* diversity, divergency, disparateness; separation, division, severing, sundering; incongruousness, uncongeniality, incompatibility, discordance, discrepancy

variation *syn* CHANGE, alteration, modification *rel* variety, diversity; difference, divergence, divergency, dissimilarity; deviation, deflection, aberration

variegated • having a pattern involving different colors or shades of color *syn* particolored, motley, checkered, checked, pied, piebald, skewbald, dappled, freaked *rel* flecked, stippled, marbled, mottled, spattered, spotted

variety **1** • the quality or state of being composed of different parts, elements, or individuals *syn* diversity *rel* dissimilarity, unlikeness, difference, divergence, divergency; multifariousness, variousness; miscellaneousness, miscellany, heterogeneousness, heterogeneity, assortedness, assortment **2** • a group of related plants or animals narrower in scope than a species *syn* subspecies, race, breed, cultivar, strain, clone, stock

various 1 *syn* DIFFERENT, diverse, divergent, disparate *rel* distinct, separate; distinctive, peculiar, individual; varying, changing *ant* uniform; cognate **2** *syn* MANY, several, sundry, divers, numerous, multifarious *rel* miscellaneous, heterogeneous, assorted

vary 1 *syn* CHANGE, alter, modify *rel* transform, metamorphose, convert **2** *syn* DIFFER, disagree, dissent *rel* deviate, diverge, digress, depart; separate, divide, part

vast *syn* HUGE, immense, enormous, elephantine, mammoth, giant, gigantic, gigantean, colossal, gargantuan, Herculean, cyclopean, titanic, Brobdingnagian *rel* stupendous, tremendous, prodigious, monstrous; large, big, great; spacious, capacious

vault *vb, syn* JUMP, leap, spring, bound *rel* surmount, conquer; mount, ascend, rise, soar

vault *n, syn* JUMP, leap, spring, bound *rel* surmounting; rising, mounting, ascending, soaring

vaunt *syn* BOAST, brag, crow, gasconade *rel* parade, flaunt, exhibit, display, show; magnify, aggrandize, exalt

veer *syn* SWERVE, deviate, depart, digress, diverge *rel* shift, transfer, move; turn, divert, deflect, sheer

vehement *syn* INTENSE, fierce, exquisite, violent *rel* forcible, forceful, powerful, potent; fervid, perfervid, impassioned, passionate, ardent; furious, frantic, wild, rabid, delirious

vehicle *syn* MEAN, instrument, instrumentality, agent, agency, medium, organ, channel

veil *syn* COVER, overspread, envelop, wrap, shroud *rel* mask, cloak, camouflage, disguise; conceal, hide, secrete, screen

vein 1 *syn* MOOD, humor, temper *rel* disposition, complexion, temperament **2** *syn* TOUCH, strain, streak, suggestion, suspicion, soupçon, tincture, tinge, shade, smack, spice, dash

velocity *syn* SPEED, momentum, impetus, pace, headway *rel* celerity, legerity, alacrity; haste, hurry, expedition, dispatch

velvety *syn* SLEEK, silken, silky, satiny, glossy, slick

venal *syn* MERCENARY, hireling, hack *rel* corrupt, nefarious, iniquitous, vicious, infamous, flagitious; sordid, ignoble, mean

venerable *syn* OLD, ancient, antique, antiquated, archaic, obsolete, antediluvian *rel* venerated, revered, reverenced; aged

venerate *syn* REVERE, reverence, worship, adore *rel* esteem, respect, admire, regard; cherish, prize, treasure, value, appreciate

veneration *syn* REVERENCE, worship, adoration *rel* deference, homage, obeisance, honor

vengeance *syn* RETALIATION, revenge, retribution, reprisal *rel* punishment, disciplining, discipline, castigation; avenging, revenging; recompensing, recompense, repayment

vengeful *syn* VINDICTIVE, revengeful *rel* rancorous, inimical, hostile, antagonistic; malevolent, spiteful, malicious, malignant

venial • not warranting punishment or the imposition of a penalty *syn* pardonable *ant* heinous; mortal

venom *syn* POISON, toxin, virus, bane

venomous *syn* POISONOUS, virulent, toxic, mephitic, pestilent, pestilential, miasmic, miasmatic, miasmal *rel* malignant, malign, malevolent, malicious; baleful, malefic, maleficent, sinister; pernicious, baneful, noxious, deleterious, detrimental

vent *syn* EXPRESS, utter, voice, broach, air, ventilate *rel* reveal, disclose, discover, divulge; assert, declare, aver, avow *ant* bridle

ventilate *syn* EXPRESS, vent, air, utter, voice, broach *rel* expose, exhibit, display, show; disclose, divulge, discover, reveal; publish, advertise, broadcast, declare

venture • to expose to risk or loss *syn* hazard, risk, chance, jeopardize, endanger, imperil

venturesome *syn* ADVENTUROUS, daring, daredevil, rash, reckless, foolhardy *rel* bold, audacious, intrepid, brave; stout, sturdy, stalwart, strong

veracity *syn* TRUTH, verity, verisimilitude *rel* integrity, probity, honesty, honor

verbiage • an excess of words usu. of little or obscure content *syn* redundancy, tautology, pleonasm, circumlocution, periphrasis *rel* wordiness, verboseness, prolixity, diffuseness

verbose *syn* WORDY, prolix, diffuse, redundant *rel* grandiloquent, magniloquent, flowery, bombastic; loquacious, voluble, glib, garrulous, talkative *ant* laconic

verge *syn* BORDER, edge, rim, brim, brink, margin *rel* bound, limit, end, confine; circumference, perimeter, compass

verify *syn* CONFIRM, corroborate, substantiate, authenticate, validate *rel* prove, test, try, demonstrate; certify, attest, witness, vouch; establish, settle

verisimilitude *syn* TRUTH, veracity, verity *rel* agreement, accordance, harmonizing, harmony, correspondence; likeness, similitude, resemblance

veritable *syn* AUTHENTIC, genuine, bona fide *rel* actual, real, true *ant* factitious

verity *syn* TRUTH, veracity, verisimilitude

vernacular **1** *syn* DIALECT, patois, lingo, jargon, cant, argot, slang **2** *syn* BARBARISM, corruption, impropriety, solecism, vulgarism

versatile • having a wide range of skills or abilities or many different uses *syn* many-sided, all-around *rel* gifted, talented; accomplished, finished, consummate; ready, apt, quick, prompt

verse *syn* PARAGRAPH, article, clause, plank, count

versed *syn* CONVERSANT *rel* learned, erudite; informed, acquainted; intimate, familiar

versifier *syn* POET, rhymer, rhymester, poetaster, bard, minstrel, troubadour

version **1** *syn* TRANSLATION, paraphrase, metaphrase **2** *syn* ACCOUNT, report, story, chronicle

vertebrae *syn* SPINE, backbone, back, chine

vertical • being at right angles to a base line *syn* perpendicular, plumb *ant* horizontal

vertiginous *syn* GIDDY, dizzy, swimming, dazzled *rel* reeling, whirling, staggering, tottering

verve *syn* VIGOR, vim, spirit, dash, esprit, punch, élan, drive *rel* vivacity, animation, liveliness; buoyancy, resiliency, elasticity

very **1** *syn* SAME, selfsame, identical, identic, equivalent, equal, tantamount **2** *syn* MERE, bare

vessel *syn* BOAT, ship, craft

vestige *syn* TRACE, track *rel* print, imprint, impression, stamp

vex *syn* ANNOY, irk, bother *rel* chafe, fret, gall, abrade; irritate, exasperate, nettle, provoke *ant* please, regale

viands *syn* FOOD, provisions, comestibles, feed, victuals, provender, fodder, forage

vibrant *syn* RESONANT, sonorous, ringing, resounding, orotund *rel* pulsating, pulsing, throbbing, beating; thrilling, electrifying

vibrate *syn* SWING, sway, oscillate, fluctuate, pendulate, waver, undulate *rel* pulsate, pulse, beat, throb, palpitate; quiver, quaver, tremble, shake

vice **1** *syn* FAULT, failing, frailty, foible *rel* defect, flaw, blemish; infirmity, weakness **2** *syn* OFFENSE, sin, crime, scandal *rel* transgression, trespass, violation, breach, infraction; immorality; evil, ill *ant* virtue

vicinity *syn* LOCALITY, neighborhood, district *rel* region, area; section, sector, part

vicious • highly reprehensible or offensive in character, nature, or conduct *syn* villainous, iniquitous, nefarious, flagitious, infamous, corrupt, degenerate *rel* debased, depraved, debauched, perverted; dissolute, profligate, abandoned, reprobate; lewd, lascivious, wanton, lecherous, libidinous, licentious *ant* virtuous

vicissitude **1** *syn* CHANGE, alteration, mutation, permutation *rel* turning, rotation, revolving, revolution; reversal, transposition; succession, progression, sequence, series; variety, diversity **2** *syn* DIFFICULTY, hardship, rigor *rel* misfortune, mischance, adversity; trial, tribulation, affliction

victim • one killed or injured for the ends of the one who kills or injures *syn* prey, quarry

victor • one that defeats an enemy or opponent *syn* winner, conqueror, champion, vanquisher

victory • a successful outcome in a contest or struggle *syn* conquest, triumph *rel* winning, gaining; ascendancy, supremacy; control, sway, dominion, command, power, authority *ant* defeat

victuals *syn* FOOD, feed, viands, provisions, comestibles, provender, fodder, forage

vie *syn* RIVAL, compete, emulate *rel* contend, fight; strive, struggle, essay, endeavor

view *n* **1** *syn* LOOK, sight, glance, glimpse, peep, peek *rel* scrutiny, scanning, inspection, examination **2** *syn* OPINION, belief, conviction, persuasion, sentiment *rel* idea, thought, concept, conception; inference, deduction, conclusion, judgment

view *vb, syn* SEE, survey, contemplate, observe, note, remark, notice, perceive, discern, behold, descry, espy *rel* scan, scrutinize, inspect, examine; consider, regard, account

viewpoint *syn* POINT OF VIEW, standpoint, angle, slant *rel* position, stand, attitude; ground, reason

vigilant *syn* WATCHFUL, alert, wide-awake *rel* anxious, agog, keen, avid, eager; circumspect, wary, chary, cautious; quick, ready, prompt; sharp, acute

vigor • a quality of force, forcefulness, or energy *syn* vim, spirit, dash, esprit, verve, punch, élan, drive *rel* strength, force, power, might, energy; soundness, healthiness; virility

vigorous • having or showing great vitality and force *syn* energetic, strenuous, lusty, nervous *rel* virile, manly, manful; muscular, athletic, sinewy, husky; stout, sturdy, stalwart, strong, tough *ant* languorous; lethargic

vile *syn* BASE, low *rel* depraved, corrupted, perverted, debased, debauched; coarse, vulgar, obscene, gross; foul, filthy, nasty, dirty; mean, abject, sordid; offensive, repulsive, revolting, loathsome

vilify *syn* MALIGN, traduce, asperse, calumniate, defame, slander, libel *rel* abuse, outrage, mistreat, misuse; assail, attack; revile, vituperate, berate *ant* eulogize

villain • a low, mean, reprehensible person utterly lacking in principles *syn* scoundrel, blackguard, knave, rascal, rogue, scamp, rapscallion, miscreant *rel* offender, sinner; criminal, malefactor

villainous *syn* VICIOUS, iniquitous, nefarious, flagitious, infamous, corrupt, degenerate *rel* debased, depraved, perverted; atrocious, outrageous, heinous; dissolute, profligate, abandoned

vim *syn* VIGOR, spirit, dash, esprit, verve, punch, élan, drive *rel* force, strength, power, energy

vindicate **1** *syn* MAINTAIN, justify, defend, assert *rel* support, uphold, advocate **2** *syn* EXCULPATE, exonerate, absolve, acquit *rel* disprove, refute, confute; defend, protect, shield, guard *ant* calumniate

vindictive • showing or motivated by a desire for vengeance *syn* revengeful, vengeful *rel* implacable, unrelenting, relentless, merciless, grim; spiteful, malicious, malignant, malign

violation *syn* BREACH, infraction, transgression, trespass, infringement, contravention *rel* offense, sin, vice, crime, scandal; desecration, profanation, sacrilege, blasphemy; invading, invasion, encroachment, entrenchment

violence *syn* FORCE, compulsion, coercion, duress, constraint, restraint *rel* vehemence, intensity, fierceness; effort, exertion, pains, trouble; attack, assault, onslaught, onset

violent *syn* INTENSE, vehement, fierce, exquisite *rel* powerful, potent, forceful, forcible; excessive, immoderate, inordinate, extreme, extravagant

virago • a loud, overbearing, ill-tempered woman *syn* amazon, termagant, scold, shrew, vixen

virgin *syn* UNMARRIED, single, celibate, maiden

virginal *syn* YOUTHFUL, maiden, boyish, juvenile, puerile *rel* chaste, pure, modest, decent; fresh, new

virile *syn* MALE, manful, manly, masculine, manlike, mannish *ant* effeminate; impotent[2]

virtual *syn* IMPLICIT, constructive *ant* actual

virtually • not absolutely or actually, yet so nearly so that the difference is negligible *syn* practically, morally

virtue **1** *syn* GOODNESS, morality, rectitude *rel* honor, honesty, integrity, probity; fidelity, piety, fealty, loyalty; righteousness, nobility, virtuousness *ant* vice **2** *syn* EXCELLENCE, merit, perfection *rel* worth, value; effectiveness, efficacy, effectualness; strength, might, power, force

virtuoso *syn* EXPERT, adept, artist, artiste, wizard

virtuous *syn* MORAL, ethical, righteous, noble *rel* pure, chaste, modest, decent; upright, just, honorable *ant* vicious

virulent *syn* POISONOUS, venomous, toxic, mephitic, pestilent, pestilential, miasmic, miasmatic, miasmal *rel* deadly, mortal, fatal, lethal; pernicious, noxious, baneful, deleterious; malignant, malign, malicious

visage *syn* FACE, countenance, physiognomy, mug, puss
vision **1** *syn* REVELATION, prophecy, apocalypse **2** *syn* FANCY, fantasy, phantasy, phantasm, dream, daydream, nightmare *rel* illusion, delusion, hallucination, mirage; imagination
visionary *syn* IMAGINARY, fanciful, fantastic, chimerical, quixotic *rel* romantic, sentimental, maudlin; utopian, ambitious, pretentious; ideal, transcendent, transcendental; illusory, seeming, apparent
visit • a usu. brief stay with another as an act of friendship or courtesy *syn* visitation, call
visitant *syn* VISITOR, guest, caller
visitation **1** *syn* VISIT, call **2** *syn* TRIAL, tribulation, affliction, cross *rel* misfortune, mischance, adversity; calamity, catastrophe, disaster; hardship, vicissitude, difficulty
visitor • one who visits another *syn* visitant, guest, caller
vital **1** *syn* LIVING, alive, animate, animated *rel* vigorous, energetic, lusty; active, live, dynamic **2** *syn* ESSENTIAL, fundamental, cardinal *rel* important, significant, consequential, weighty, momentous; indispensable, requisite, necessary, needful
vitalize • to arouse to activity, animation, or life *syn* energize, activate *rel* animate, quicken, enliven, vivify; stimulate, galvanize, excite, provoke *ant* atrophy
vitiate *syn* DEBASE, deprave, corrupt, pervert, debauch *rel* pollute, defile, taint, contaminate; degrade, demean, abase; impair, spoil, injure, damage; annul, invalidate, nullify
vitiated *syn* DEBASED, depraved, corrupted, debauched, perverted *rel* defiled, polluted, contaminated, tainted; impaired, spoiled, injured; invalidated, annulled
vituperate *syn* SCOLD, revile, berate, rate, upbraid, tongue-lash, jaw, bawl, chew out, wig, rail *rel* condemn, denounce, censure, blame, reprehend, reprobate, criticize; vilify, asperse, traduce, malign, calumniate; execrate, objurgate
vituperation *syn* ABUSE, invective, obloquy, scurrility, billingsgate *rel* animadversion, aspersion, stricture, reflection; attack, assault, onslaught, onset; condemnation, denunciation, censuring, censure; vilifying, vilification, maligning, calumniation *ant* acclaim, praise
vituperative *syn* ABUSIVE, opprobrious, contumelious, scurrilous *rel* coarse, vulgar, gross, obscene; insulting, offending, outraging; condemning, condemnatory, denouncing, denunciatory
vivacious *syn* LIVELY, animated, gay, sprightly *rel* buoyant, effervescent, volatile; merry, blithe, jocund; frolicsome, sportive, playful *ant* languid
vivid *syn* GRAPHIC, picturesque, pictorial *rel* sharp, keen, acute; dramatic, dramaturgic, theatrical; expressive, eloquent, meaningful; nervous, lusty, vigorous; clear, lucid, perspicuous
vivify *syn* QUICKEN, animate, enliven *rel* vitalize, energize, activate; renew, restore, re-fresh; stir, rouse, arouse; stimulate, galvanize, excite, provoke
vixen *syn* VIRAGO, shrew, scold, termagant, amazon
vocable *syn* WORD, term
vocabulary *syn* LANGUAGE, phraseology, diction, phrasing, style
vocal **1** • uttered by the voice or having to do with such utterance *syn* articulate, oral **2** • being able to express oneself clearly or easily *syn* articulate, fluent, eloquent, voluble, glib *rel* expressing, voicing, venting; expressive, sententious, eloquent
vociferate *syn* ROAR, bellow, bluster, bawl, clamor, howl, ululate *rel* shout, yell, shriek, scream, screech, holler
vociferation *syn* ROAR, bellow, bluster, bawl, ululation
vociferous • so loud or insistent as to compel attention *syn* clamorous, blatant, strident, boisterous, obstreperous *rel* noisy, sounding; bewildering, distracting
vogue *syn* FASHION, mode, style, fad, rage, craze, dernier cri, cry
voice *syn* EXPRESS, utter, vent, broach, air, ventilate *rel* reveal, disclose, tell, discover, divulge; communicate, impart; speak, talk
void *adj* **1** *syn* EMPTY, vacant, blank, vacuous *rel* exhausted, depleted, drained; bare, barren; hollow, empty, nugatory, vain **2** *syn* DEVOID, destitute
void *n, syn* HOLE, vacuum, hollow, cavity,

pocket *rel* emptiness, vacancy, vacuity; abyss, gulf, abysm

void *vb, syn* ANNUL, vacate, abrogate, quash

volatile *syn* ELASTIC, effervescent, buoyant, expansive, resilient *rel* unstable, mercurial, inconstant, fickle, capricious; light-minded, frivolous, flippant, flighty; variable, changeable, protean

volatility *syn* LIGHTNESS, light-mindedness, levity, frivolity, flippancy, flightiness *rel* vivaciousness, vivacity, gaiety, liveliness, animation, sprightliness; unstableness, instability, mercurialness, inconstancy; variability, changeableness

volcano *syn* MOUNTAIN, mount, peak, alp, mesa

volition *syn* WILL, conation *rel* choice, election, option

volubility *syn* TALKATIVENESS, glibness, garrulity, loquacity *rel* fluency, eloquence, articulateness

voluble **1** *syn* VOCAL, fluent, glib, eloquent, articulate *rel* copious, abundant, plentiful; easy, facile, effortless, smooth *ant* stuttering, stammering **2** *syn* TALKATIVE, glib, garrulous, loquacious *ant* curt

volume **1** *syn* SIZE, magnitude, extent, dimensions, area **2** *syn* BULK, mass

voluntary • done or brought about of one's own will *syn* intentional, deliberate, willful, willing *rel* chosen, elected, opted; free, independent, autonomous *ant* involuntary; instinctive

voluptuous *syn* SENSUOUS, luxurious, sybaritic, epicurean, sensual *rel* indulging, indulgent, pampering; luxurious, opulent, sumptuous *ant* ascetic

vomit *syn* BELCH, burp, disgorge, regurgitate, spew, throw up *rel* eject, expel, oust

voracious • excessively greedy *syn* gluttonous, ravenous, ravening, rapacious *rel* greedy, grasping, acquisitive, covetous; satiating, sating, surfeiting, gorging

vortex *syn* EDDY, whirlpool, maelstrom

votary *syn* ADDICT, devotee, habitué *rel* enthusiast, fanatic, zealot, bigot

vote *syn* SUFFRAGE, franchise, ballot

vouch *syn* CERTIFY, attest, witness *rel* support, uphold; confirm, substantiate, verify, corroborate

vouchsafe *syn* GRANT, accord, concede, award *rel* give, bestow, confer, present; condescend, deign, stoop; oblige, accommodate, favor

voyage *syn* JOURNEY, tour, trip, excursion, cruise, expedition, jaunt, pilgrimage

vulgar **1** *syn* COMMON, ordinary, familiar, popular *rel* universal, general; prevailing, prevalent, current, rife; usual, customary; crude, rude, rough, uncouth; sordid, ignoble, mean **2** *syn* COARSE, gross, obscene, ribald *rel* low, base, vile; offensive, loathsome, repulsive, revolting; indelicate, indecent, indecorous

vulgarism *syn* BARBARISM, corruption, impropriety, solecism, vernacular

W

wage, wages • the price paid a person for his or her labor or services *syn* salary, stipend, fee, pay, hire, emolument *rel* remuneration, recompensing, recompense

wager *syn* BET, stake, pot, ante

waggish *syn* PLAYFUL, sportive, frolicsome, impish, mischievous, roguish *rel* facetious, jocose, jocular, humorous, witty; jovial, jolly, merry; comic, comical, laughable, droll, ludicrous, funny

wail *syn* CRY, weep, whimper, blubber, keen *rel* mourn, grieve; lament, bewail, bemoan, deplore; moan, sob, sigh, groan

wait *syn* STAY, remain, abide, tarry, linger *rel* delay, loiter

waive *syn* RELINQUISH, cede, yield, resign, abandon, surrender, leave *rel* forgo, forbear, sacrifice; concede, grant, allow

waken *syn* STIR, awaken, arouse, rouse, rally *rel* excite, stimulate, quicken, galvanize, provoke; fire, kindle, light; impel, move, actuate, drive *ant* subdue

wall *syn* ENCLOSE, envelop, fence, pen, coop, corral, cage *rel* surround, environ, encircle, hem; confine, circumscribe, limit, restrict

wallow • to move clumsily and in a debased

or pitable condition *syn* welter, grovel *rel* crawl, creep; defile, pollute, contaminate, taint; debase, debauch, corrupt, deprave, pervert

wan *syn* PALE, pallid, ashen, ashy, livid *rel* blanched, whitened, decolorized; languid, languishing, languorous; haggard, cadaverous, worn

wander • to move about from place to place more or less aimlessly and without a plan *syn* stray, roam, ramble, rove, range, prowl, gad, gallivant, traipse, meander

wane *syn* ABATE, subside, ebb *rel* decrease, dwindle, lessen, diminish *ant* wax

want *vb* **1** *syn* LACK, need, require *rel* demand, claim, exact **2** *syn* DESIRE, wish, crave, covet *rel* long, yearn, hanker, pine, hunger, thirst; aspire, pant, aim

want *n* **1** *syn* LACK, dearth, absence, defect, privation *rel* need, necessity, exigency; deficiency **2** *syn* POVERTY, destitution, indigence, privation, penury *rel* pinch, strait, pass, exigency, juncture; meagerness, scantiness, exiguousness

wanton **1** *syn* LICENTIOUS, libertine, lewd, lustful, lascivious, libidinous, lecherous *rel* immoral, unmoral, amoral; abandoned, profligate, dissolute, reprobate *ant* chaste **2** *syn* SUPEREROGATORY, uncalled-for, gratuitous *rel* malicious, malevolent, spiteful; wayward, contrary, perverse

war *syn* CONTEND, battle, fight *rel* resist, withstand, combat, oppose; strive, struggle, endeavor, essay, attempt

warble *syn* SING, troll, carol, descant, trill, hymn, chant, intone

ward *syn* PREVENT, avert, preclude, obviate *rel* block, bar, obstruct, impede, hinder; forestall, anticipate, prevent; frustrate, balk, thwart, foil *ant* conduce to

wariness *syn* CAUTION, chariness, circumspection, calculation *rel* alertness, watchfulness; prudence, discretion, foresight, forethought, providence *ant* foolhardiness; brashness

warlike *syn* MARTIAL, military *rel* bellicose, belligerent, pugnacious, combative, contentious; fighting, warring, contending, battling

warm *syn* TENDER, warmhearted, sympathetic, compassionate, responsive *rel* loving, affectionate; cordial, gracious, affable; ardent, fervent, passionate; sincere, heartfelt, hearty, wholehearted *ant* cool; austere

warmhearted *syn* TENDER, warm, sympathetic, compassionate, responsive *rel* loving, affectionate; kind, kindly, benign, benignant; heartfelt, hearty, wholehearted, sincere *ant* coldhearted

warn • to let one know of approaching danger or risk *syn* forewarn, caution *rel* apprise, inform, advise, notify; admonish, reprove; counsel

warp *syn* DEFORM, distort, contort *rel* twist, bend, curve; injure, damage, impair, mar

warrant **1** *syn* ASSERT, declare, profess, affirm, aver, protest, avouch, avow, predicate *rel* state, relate; maintain, assert; assure, ensure, insure **2** *syn* JUSTIFY *rel* vindicate, maintain; sanction, approve, endorse; authorize

wary *syn* CAUTIOUS, chary, circumspect, calculating *rel* alert, watchful; prudent, discreet, foresighted, forethoughtful, provident *ant* foolhardy; brash

waspish *syn* IRRITABLE, snappish, fractious, peevish, petulant, pettish, huffy, fretful, querulous *rel* testy, touchy, cranky, cross, irascible; impatient; contrary, perverse; spiteful, malicious

waste *n* **1** • an area of the earth unsuitable for cultivation or general habitation *syn* desert, badlands, wilderness **2** *syn* REFUSE, rubbish, trash, debris, garbage, offal

waste *vb* **1** *syn* RAVAGE, devastate, sack, pillage, despoil, spoliate *rel* plunder, loot, rob, rifle; destroy, demolish; ruin, wreck *ant* conserve, save **2** • to spend or expend freely and usu. foolishly or futilely *syn* squander, dissipate, fritter, consume *rel* spend, expend, disburse; distribute, dispense; scatter, disperse, dispel; deplete, drain, exhaust, impoverish *ant* save; conserve

wasted *syn* HAGGARD, pinched, cadaverous, worn, careworn *rel* gaunt, scrawny, skinny, angular, rawboned, lean

waster *syn* SPENDTHRIFT, profligate, prodigal, wastrel *rel* idler, loafer, lounger; squanderer, dissipater, fritterer

wastrel *syn* SPENDTHRIFT, profligate, prodigal, waster *rel* reprobate, outcast; loafer, idler, lounger; scoundrel, rascal, rogue, scamp, villain

watch **1** *syn* TEND, mind, attend *rel* guard, protect, shield, safeguard, defend **2** *syn*

SEE, look *rel* gaze, gape, stare, glare; scrutinize, scan, inspect, examine

watchful • on the lookout esp. for danger or for opportunities *syn* vigilant, wide-awake, alert *rel* cautious, wary, chary, circumspect; quick, ready, prompt

waterlog *syn* SOAK, drench, saturate, steep, impregnate, sop

wave *syn* SWING, flourish, brandish, shake, thrash *rel* wield, swing, manipulate, handle, ply; undulate, sway, swing, fluctuate; shake, quiver, quaver

waver **1** *syn* SWING, fluctuate, oscillate, pendulate, vibrate, sway, undulate *rel* flicker, flutter, hover, flit, flitter; quiver, quaver, tremble, shake **2** *syn* HESITATE, falter, vacillate *rel* balk, boggle, stickle, scruple, demur, shy; fluctuate, oscillate, swing

way **1** • a track or path traversed in going from one place to another *syn* route, course, passage, pass, artery **2** *syn* METHOD, mode, manner, fashion, system *rel* procedure, process, proceeding; plan, design, scheme; practice, habit, habitude, custom, use, usage, wont

waylay *syn* SURPRISE, ambush *rel* attack, assault, assail; prevent, forestall

wayward *syn* CONTRARY, perverse, froward, restive, balky *rel* insubordinate, contumacious, rebellious; refractory, recalcitrant, intractable, headstrong, unruly; capricious, inconstant, fickle, unstable

weak • lacking physical, mental, or moral strength *syn* feeble, frail, fragile, infirm, decrepit *rel* debilitated, weakened, enfeebled; powerless, impotent *ant* strong

weaken • to lose or cause to lose strength, vigor, or energy *syn* enfeeble, debilitate, undermine, sap, cripple, disable *rel* enervate, emasculate, unnerve, unman; impair, injure, damage; dilute, thin, attenuate, extenuate *ant* strengthen

wealthy *syn* RICH, affluent, opulent *ant* indigent

wean *syn* ESTRANGE, alienate, disaffect *rel* separate, part, divide, sunder, sever, divorce *ant* addict

weariless *syn* INDEFATIGABLE, unwearying, unwearied, tireless, untiring, unflagging *rel* dogged, pertinacious, obstinate; assiduous, sedulous, diligent, busy

wearisome *syn* IRKSOME, tiresome, tedious, boring *rel* fatiguing, exhausting, fagging, tiring; dull, slow, stupid

weary *syn* TIRE, fatigue, exhaust, jade, fag, tucker *rel* debilitate, enfeeble, weaken; depress, oppress, weigh

weave • to make a textile or to form an article by interlacing threads or strands of material *syn* knit, crochet, braid, plait, tat

wedding *syn* MARRIAGE, matrimony, nuptial, espousal, wedlock

wedlock *syn* MARRIAGE, matrimony, nuptial, espousal, wedding

wee *syn* SMALL, diminutive, tiny, teeny, weeny, little, minute, microscopic, miniature, petite

weeny *syn* SMALL, tiny, teeny, wee, diminutive, minute, microscopic, miniature, little

weep *syn* CRY, wail, keen, whimper, blubber *rel* bewail, bemoan, lament, deplore; sob, moan, sigh, groan

weigh **1** *syn* CONSIDER, study, contemplate, excogitate *rel* ponder, meditate, ruminate, muse; think, reflect, cogitate, reason, speculate **2** *syn* BURDEN, encumber, cumber, weight, load, lade, tax, charge, saddle *rel* balance, ballast, trim, poise, stabilize; set, settle **3** *syn* DEPRESS, oppress *rel* worry, annoy, harass, harry; torment, torture, afflict, try, rack

weight *n* **1** *syn* IMPORTANCE, significance, moment, consequence, import *rel* worth, value; magnitude, size, extent; seriousness, gravity **2** *syn* INFLUENCE, authority, prestige, credit *rel* effectiveness, efficacy; emphasis, stress; powerfulness, potency, forcefulness, forcibleness

weight *vb* **1** *syn* ADULTERATE, load, sophisticate **2** *syn* BURDEN, encumber, cumber, weigh, load, lade, tax, charge, saddle *rel* see WEIGH 2

weighty *syn* HEAVY, ponderous, cumbrous, cumbersome, hefty *rel* onerous, burdensome, oppressive, exacting

weird • fearfully and mysteriously strange or fantastic *syn* eerie, uncanny *rel* mysterious, inscrutable; fearful, awful, dreadful, horrific; strange, odd, queer, curious, peculiar

welcome *syn* PLEASANT, pleasing, agreeable, grateful, gratifying *rel* satisfying, contenting; congenial, sympathetic, consonant *ant* unwelcome

well *syn* HEALTHY, sound, wholesome, robust, hale *ant* unwell, ill

well-nigh *syn* NEARLY, almost, approximately

well-timed *syn* SEASONABLE, timely, opportune, pat *rel* apt, happy, felicitous, appropriate, fitting, fit

welter *syn* WALLOW, grovel *rel* struggle, strive, attempt

wet • covered or more or less soaked with liquid *syn* damp, dank, moist, humid *rel* soaked, saturated, drenched, waterlogged *ant* dry

wharf • a structure used by boats and ships for taking on or landing cargo or passengers *syn* dock, pier, quay, slip, berth, jetty, levee

wheedle *syn* COAX, blandish, cajole *rel* entice, inveigle, lure, seduce, decoy

wheel *syn* TURN, revolve, rotate, gyrate, circle, spin, twirl, whirl, swirl, pirouette, eddy

while • to pass time, esp. leisure time, without boredom or in pleasant ways *syn* wile, beguile, fleet *rel* divert, amuse, entertain

whim *syn* CAPRICE, freak, fancy, whimsy, conceit, vagary, crotchet *rel* inclination, disposition; fancy, fantasy, vision, dream; notion, idea

whimper *syn* CRY, weep, blubber, wail, keen

whimsy *syn* CAPRICE, freak, fancy, whim, conceit, vagary, crotchet *rel* see WHIM

whirl **1** *syn* TURN, twirl, spin, wheel, swirl, revolve, rotate, gyrate, circle, pirouette, eddy **2** *syn* REEL, stagger, totter

whirlpool *syn* EDDY, maelstrom, vortex

whirlwind • a rotating windstorm of limited extent *syn* whirly *rel* cyclone, typhoon, hurricane, tornado, waterspout, twister

whirly *syn* WHIRLWIND

whit *syn* PARTICLE, mite, jot, iota, bit, smidgen, tittle, atom

whiten **1** • to change from an original color to white or almost to white *syn* blanch, bleach, decolorize, etiolate *ant* blacken **2** *syn* PALLIATE, whitewash, gloze, gloss, extenuate *rel* see WHITEWASH

whitewash *syn* PALLIATE, whiten, gloze, gloss, extenuate *rel* disguise, cloak, mask, dissemble, camouflage; condone, excuse

whole *adj* **1** *syn* PERFECT, entire, intact *rel* sound, well, healthy, robust, wholesome; complete, plenary, full **2** • having every constituent element or individual *syn* entire, total, all, gross *ant* partial

whole *n, syn* SUM, total, aggregate, amount, number, quantity *ant* part; constituent; particular

wholehearted *syn* SINCERE, whole-souled, heartfelt, hearty, unfeigned *rel* ardent, fervent, impassioned, passionate; genuine, bona fide, authentic; earnest, serious

wholesale *syn* INDISCRIMINATE, sweeping

wholesome **1** *syn* HEALTHFUL, healthy, salubrious, salutary, hygienic, sanitary *ant* noxious **2** *syn* HEALTHY, sound, robust, hale, well *rel* strong, sturdy, stalwart, stout

whole-souled *syn* SINCERE, wholehearted, heartfelt, hearty, unfeigned *rel* see WHOLEHEARTED

whoop *vb, syn* SHOUT, yell, shriek, scream, screech, squeal, holler

whoop *n, syn* SHOUT, yell, shriek, scream, screech, squeal, holler

wicked *syn* BAD, evil, ill, naughty *rel* immoral, unmoral, amoral; iniquitous, vicious, villainous; abandoned, reprobate, profligate, dissolute

wide *syn* BROAD, deep *rel* spacious, capacious, ample; extended, extensive *ant* strait

wide-awake *syn* WATCHFUL, vigilant, alert *rel* aware, alive, awake, conscious, sensible

wield *syn* HANDLE, swing, manipulate, ply *rel* flourish, brandish, shake, wave; control, direct, manage, conduct; exercise, drill, practice

wig *syn* SCOLD, tongue-lash, jaw, bawl, chew out, berate, upbraid, rate, rail, revile, vituperate *rel* reprimand, reproach, rebuke, reprove, chide

wild *syn* FURIOUS, frantic, frenzied, frenetic, delirious, rabid *rel* distracted, bewildered, perplexed, puzzled; confused, muddled, addled; agitated, upset, perturbed, discomposed; mad, crazy, demented, deranged, insane

wilderness *syn* WASTE, desert, badlands

wile *n, syn* TRICK, artifice, feint, ruse, maneuver, stratagem, gambit, ploy *rel* deception, fraud, trickery, chicanery, chicane; cunning, deceit, duplicity, dissimulation, guile

wile *vb, syn* WHILE, beguile, fleet *rel* see WHILE

will *n* • the power or act of making or effecting a choice or decision *syn* volition, conation *rel* intention, intent, purpose, design; choice, election, preference; character, disposition, temper, temperament

will *vb* • to give to another by will *syn* bequeath, devise, leave, legate

willful **1** *syn* VOLUNTARY, deliberate, intentional, willing *rel* determined, decided, resolved; intended, purposed; obstinate, stubborn, dogged, pertinacious **2** *syn* UNRULY, headstrong, intractable, refractory, recalcitrant, ungovernable *rel* rebellious, contumacious, factious, insubordinate; obstinate, mulish, bullheaded, pigheaded *ant* biddable

willing *syn* VOLUNTARY, intentional, deliberate, willful *rel* prone, open, liable; inclined, predisposed, disposed *ant* unwilling

wilt *syn* DROOP, flag, sag *rel* slump, sink, drop, fall; languish

wily *syn* SLY, cunning, crafty, tricky, foxy, insidious, guileful, artful *rel* astute, sagacious, shrewd; deceitful, cunning

win *syn* GET, gain, acquire, obtain, procure, secure *rel* achieve, accomplish, effect, perform; attain, reach, compass; induce, persuade, prevail *ant* lose

wince *syn* RECOIL, flinch, shrink, blench, quail *rel* cringe, cower, fawn; balk, shy, stick, stickle, demur; squirm, writhe

wind • to follow a circular, spiral, or writhing course *syn* coil, curl, twist, twine, wreathe, entwine *rel* bend, curve; surround, encircle, circle, gird, girdle; enclose, envelop

winding • curving repeatedly first one way and then another *syn* sinuous, serpentine, tortuous, flexuous *rel* curving, bending, twisting; circuitous, indirect, roundabout; crooked, devious; meandering, wandering *ant* straight

window • an opening in the wall of a building that is usu. covered with glass and serves to admit light and air *syn* casement, oriel

wing *syn* ANNEX, ell, extension

wink • to close and open one's eyelids quickly *syn* blink

winner *syn* VICTOR, conqueror, champion, vanquisher *ant* loser

winning *syn* SWEET, engaging, winsome, dulcet *rel* charming, alluring, captivating, enchanting, bewitching, attractive

winsome *syn* SWEET, engaging, winning, dulcet *rel* see WINNING

wipe *syn* EXTERMINATE, extirpate, eradicate, uproot, deracinate *rel* obliterate, erase, efface, expunge, blot out; abolish, extinguish, annihilate; destroy, demolish

wisdom *syn* SENSE, judgment, gumption *rel* discretion, prudence, foresight; judiciousness, sageness, saneness, sapience; sagacity, perspicacity, shrewdness *ant* folly; injudiciousness

wise • exercising or involving sound judgment *syn* sage, sapient, judicious, prudent, sensible, sane *rel* discreet, prudent, foresighted; cautious, circumspect, calculating; sagacious, perspicacious, shrewd, astute; knowing, intelligent, alert, bright, smart *ant* simple

wisecrack *syn* JOKE, crack, gag, jest, jape, quip, witticism

wish *syn* DESIRE, want, crave, covet *rel* long, yearn, hanker, pine, hunger, thirst; aspire, pant, aim; hope, expect

wishy-washy *syn* INSIPID, vapid, flat, jejune, banal, inane *rel* spiritless, enervated, languid, listless; weak, feeble; diluted, attenuated, thinned

wit **1** *syn* MIND, intelligence, brain, intellect, soul, psyche *rel* reason, understanding, intuition; comprehension, apprehension; sagaciousness, sagacity, perspicaciousness, perspicacity **2** • a mode of expression intended to arouse amusement *syn* humor, irony, sarcasm, satire, repartee *rel* quick-wittedness, alertness, brightness, brilliancy, cleverness, smartness, intelligence; raillery, badinage, persiflage; pungency, piquancy, poignancy

witchcraft *syn* MAGIC, wizardry, witchery, sorcery, alchemy, thaumaturgy

witchery *syn* MAGIC, sorcery, witchcraft, wizardry, alchemy, thaumaturgy

with *syn* BY, through

withdraw *syn* GO, leave, depart, quit, retire *rel* abscond, decamp, escape, flee, fly; retreat, recede

wither • to lose freshness and substance by or as if by loss of natural moisture *syn* shrivel, wizen *rel* dry, parch, desiccate; shrink, contract, constrict

withhold *syn* KEEP, detain, keep back, keep out, retain, hold, hold back, reserve *rel* restrain, curb, check, bridle, inhibit; refuse, decline

withstand *syn* RESIST, contest, oppose, fight, combat, conflict, antagonize *rel* bear, endure, stand, tolerate, suffer; thwart, baffle, balk, foil, frustrate; assail, attack, assault

witness *n, syn* SPECTATOR, observer, beholder, looker-on, onlooker, eyewitness, bystander, kibitzer

witness *vb, syn* CERTIFY, attest, vouch *rel* subscribe, assent

witticism *syn* JOKE, jest, jape, quip, wisecrack, crack, gag *rel* wit, humor, sarcasm, satire, irony, repartee

witty • provoking or intended to provoke laughter *syn* humorous, facetious, jocular, jocose *rel* amusing, diverting, entertaining; sparkling, scintillating; caustic, mordant, acrid, scathing; penetrating, piercing, probing

wizard *syn* EXPERT, adept, artist, artiste, virtuoso

wizardry *syn* MAGIC, witchcraft, witchery, sorcery, alchemy, thaumaturgy

wizen *syn* WITHER, shrivel *rel* shrink, contract; dwindle, diminish, reduce, decrease

wobble *syn* SHAKE, teeter, totter, shimmy, quiver, shiver, shudder, quaver, quake, tremble, dither

woe *syn* SORROW, grief, anguish, heartache, heartbreak, regret *rel* distress, suffering, misery, agony, dolor; lamenting, bewailing, bemoaning, deploring

woebegone *syn* DOWNCAST, disconsolate, dispirited, dejected, depressed *rel* melancholy, lugubrious, doleful; forlorn, despondent; spiritless, listless, languid

woman *syn* FEMALE, lady

womanish *syn* FEMALE, womanlike, womanly, ladylike, feminine *ant* mannish

womanlike *syn* FEMALE, womanly, womanish, ladylike, feminine

womanly *syn* FEMALE, womanlike, ladylike, womanish, feminine *rel* mature, matured, grown-up, adult *ant* unwomanly, manly

wonder 1 • something that causes astonishment or admiration *syn* marvel, prodigy, miracle, phenomenon **2** • the complex emotion aroused by the incomprehensible and esp. the awe-inspiring *syn* wonderment, amazement, admiration *rel* awe, reverence, fear; astonishment, amazement; perplexity, puzzlement, bewilderment

wonderment *syn* WONDER, amazement, admiration

wont *syn* HABIT, habitude, practice, usage, custom, use *rel* way, manner, fashion, method

wonted *syn* USUAL, accustomed, customary, habitual *rel* familiar, common, ordinary; natural, regular, normal, typical

woo *syn* INVITE, court, solicit, bid *rel* allure, attract; lure, entice, seduce; blandish, coax, cajole, wheedle; pursue, chase, follow, trail

wooden *syn* STIFF, rigid, inflexible, tense, stark *rel* firm, hard, solid; heavy, weighty, ponderous; clumsy, awkward

word • a pronounceable sound or combination of sounds that expresses and symbolizes an idea *syn* vocable, term *rel* expression, idiom, phrase, locution

wordy • using or marked by the use of more words than are necessary to express the thought *syn* verbose, prolix, diffuse, redundant *rel* inflated, turgid, tumid, flatulent; bombastic, rhetorical; loquacious, garrulous, voluble, glib, talkative

work *n* **1** • strenuous activity that involves difficulty and effort and usually affords no pleasure *syn* labor, travail, toil, drudgery, grind *rel* exertion, effort, pains, trouble; task, duty, job, chore *ant* play **2** • a sustained activity that affords one a livelihood *syn* employment, occupation, calling, pursuit, business *rel* trade, craft, handicraft, art, profession **3** • something brought into being by the exertion of effort and the exercise of skill *syn* product, production, opus, artifact *rel* article, object, thing; accomplishment, achievement, performance

work *vb, syn* ACT, operate, function, behave, react

worker • one who earns his living by labor, esp. by manual labor *syn* workman, workingman, laborer, craftsman, handicraftsman, mechanic, artisan, hand, operative, roustabout *ant* idler

workingman *syn* WORKER, workman, laborer, craftsman, handicraftsman, mechanic, artisan, operative, hand, roustabout

workman *syn* WORKER, workingman, laborer, craftsman, handicraftsman, mechanic, artisan, operative, hand, roustabout

world *syn* EARTH, globe, planet

worldly **1** *syn* EARTHLY, mundane, terrestrial, earthy, sublunary *rel* temporal, profane, secular; material, physical, corporeal; carnal, fleshly, sensual **2** *syn* SOPHISTICATED, worldly-wise, blasé, disillusioned

worldly-wise *syn* SOPHISTICATED, worldly, blasé, disillusioned

worn *syn* HAGGARD, careworn, pinched, wasted, cadaverous *rel* exhausted, tired, wearied, fatigued, fagged, jaded; gaunt, scrawny, skinny, lean

worried • distressed or troubled usu. about something anticipated *syn* anxious, concerned, careful, solicitous *rel* apprehensive, afraid, fearful; troubled, distressed; harassed, harried

worry *vb* • to disturb one or destroy one's peace of mind by repeated or persistent tormenting attacks *syn* annoy, harass, harry, plague, pester, tease, tantalize *rel* disquiet, disturb, discompose, perturb, agitate, upset; torment, try, torture, afflict; oppress, persecute, wrong, aggrieve

worry *n, syn* CARE, anxiety, concern, solicitude *rel* apprehension, foreboding, misgiving, presentiment; anguish, woe, heartache, sorrow; uncertainty, doubt, mistrust

worship *n, syn* REVERENCE, adoration, veneration *rel* honor, homage, obeisance; respect, regard, esteem, admiration

worship *vb* **1** *syn* REVERE, adore, venerate, reverence *rel* exalt, magnify; respect, esteem **2** *syn* ADORE, idolize *rel* love, dote, like; admire, regard

worth • equivalence in good qualities expressed or implied *syn* value *rel* excellence, merit, virtue, perfection; use, usefulness, utility

wound • an injury to the body *syn* trauma, traumatism, lesion, bruise, contusion *rel* injury, hurt; burning, burn

wraith *syn* APPARITION, phantasm, phantom, ghost, spirit, specter, shade, revenant

wrangle *vb, syn* QUARREL, altercate, squabble, bicker, spat, tiff *rel* argue, dispute, debate, discuss; fight, contend

wrangle *n, syn* QUARREL, altercation, squabble, bickering, spat, tiff *rel* argument, dispute, controversy; discord, contention, dissension, conflict

wrap *syn* COVER, overspread, envelop, shroud, veil *rel* enclose; surround, encompass, environ, gird, girdle; cloak, mask, camouflage, disguise

wrath *syn* ANGER, rage, indignation, ire, fury *rel* resentment, dudgeon, offense; acrimony, acerbity, asperity

wrathful *syn* ANGRY, irate, indignant, mad, wroth, acrimonious *rel* infuriated, incensed, enraged

wreathe *syn* WIND, coil, curl, twist, twine, entwine

wreck *syn* RUIN, dilapidate *rel* destroy, demolish, raze; injure, damage, impair

wrench • to turn or twist forcibly *syn* wrest, wring *rel* twist, bend, curve; force, compel, coerce, constrain; strain, sprain

wrest *syn* WRENCH, wring *rel* twist, bend, curve; usurp, arrogate, confiscate; extort, extract, elicit, educe; distort, contort, deform

wrestle • to struggle with an opponent at close quarters *syn* tussle, grapple, scuffle *rel* contend, fight, battle, war; resist, withstand, combat, oppose; strive, endeavor, essay, attempt; labor, toil, travail

wretched *syn* MISERABLE *rel* despondent, forlorn, hopeless, despairing; doleful, dolorous, melancholy; abject, sordid, mean; pitiable, piteous, pitiful

wring *syn* WRENCH, wrest *rel* press, squeeze; crush, mash, smash, bruise; extract, extort, elicit, educe; distort, contort, deform; twist, bend, curve

writhe • to twist or turn in physical or mental distress *syn* agonize, squirm *rel* twist, bend, curve; distort, contort, deform; wince, blench, flinch, recoil

wrong *n, syn* INJUSTICE, injury, grievance *rel* damage, injury, harm, mischief; violation, infraction, breach, trespass, transgression; hardship, difficulty

wrong *adj* **1** *syn* FALSE *rel* fallacious, sophistical; misleading, deceptive, delusive, delusory *ant* right **2** *syn* BAD, poor *rel* improper, unfit, inappropriate, unfitting, unsuitable, inapt, unhappy, infelicitous; awry, askew; amiss, astray

wrong *vb* • to inflict injury without just cause or in an outrageous manner *syn* oppress, persecute, aggrieve *rel* abuse, mistreat, maltreat, ill-treat, outrage; injure, harm, hurt

wroth *syn* ANGRY, irate, indignant, wrathful, acrimonious, mad

Y

yank *syn* JERK, snap, twitch *rel* pull, drag, tug; snatch, clutch, take; wrench, wrest

yap *syn* BARK, bay, howl, growl, snarl, yelp

yardstick *syn* STANDARD, criterion, gauge, touchstone

yarn *syn* STORY, tale, narrative, anecdote

yearn *syn* LONG, pine, hanker, hunger, thirst *rel* crave, desire, wish, want, covet; aspire, pant, aim

yeast *syn* FOAM, froth, spume, scum, lather, suds

yell *vb, syn* SHOUT, shriek, scream, screech, squeal, holler, whoop *rel* vociferate, roar, clamor, bellow, bawl

yell *n, syn* SHOUT, shriek, scream, screech, squeal, holler, whoop

yelp *syn* BARK, bay, howl, growl, snarl, yap

yield **1** *syn* BEAR, produce, turn out *rel* generate, engender, breed, propagate; create, invent; form, shape, make, fabricate, fashion **2** *syn* RELINQUISH, surrender, cede, abandon, leave, resign, waive *rel* forgo, forbear, abnegate, eschew, sacrifice; abdicate, renounce, resign **3** • to give way before a force that one cannot further resist *syn* submit, capitulate, succumb, relent, defer, bow, cave *rel* surrender, cede, waive, relinquish; concede, accord, award, grant

yoke *syn* COUPLE, pair, brace

yokel *syn* BOOR, bumpkin, hick, rube, clodhopper, clown, lout, churl

young *syn* OFFSPRING, progeny, issue, descendant, posterity

youth • the period in life when one passes from childhood to maturity *syn* adolescence, puberty, pubescence *ant* age

youthful • relating to or characteristic of one who is between childhood and adulthood *syn* juvenile, puerile, boyish, virgin, virginal, maiden *rel* immature, unmatured *ant* aged

Z

zeal *syn* PASSION, enthusiasm, fervor, ardor *rel* energy, force, power; zest, gusto, taste; earnestness, seriousness; intensity, vehemence, fierceness *ant* apathy

zealot *syn* ENTHUSIAST, fanatic, bigot *rel* partisan, sectary, adherent, disciple, follower; devotee, votary, addict

zenith *syn* SUMMIT, apogee, culmination, meridian, peak, pinnacle, climax, apex, acme *ant* nadir

zest *syn* TASTE, relish, gusto, palate *rel* enthusiasm, fervor, ardor, zeal, passion; spiritedness, spirit, high-spiritedness; enjoyment, delight, delectation, pleasure

zone *syn* AREA, belt, tract, region *rel* locality, district; section, sector, segment, part

Webster's Vocabulary Builder

Webster's Vocabulary Builder

Created in Cooperation with the Editors of
MERRIAM-WEBSTER

A Division of Merriam-Webster, Incorporated
Springfield, Massachusetts

This 2006 edition published by
Federal Street Press
A Division of Merriam-Webster, Incorporated
P.O. Box 281
Springfield, MA 01102

Federal Street Press books are available for bulk purchase for sales promotion and premium use.
For details write the manager of special sales,
Federal Street Press, P.O. Box 281, Springfield, MA 01102

ISBN 13 978-1-59695-009-2

Printed in the United States of America

08 09 10 5 4 3

Introduction

This book is designed to achieve two goals: to add a large number of words to your permanent working vocabulary, and to teach the most useful of the classical word-building roots to help you continue expanding your vocabulary in the future.

In order to achieve these goals, this volume employs an original approach that takes into account how people learn and remember. Many vocabulary builders simply present their words in alphabetical order, many provide little or no discussion of the words and how to use them, and a few even fail to show the kinds of sentences in which the words usually appear. But memorizing a series of random and unrelated things, especially for more than a few hours, can be difficult and time-consuming. The fact is that we tend to remember words easily and naturally when they appear in some meaningful text, when they have been shown to be useful and therefore worth remembering, and when they have been properly explained to us. Knowing precisely how to use a word is just as important as knowing what it means, and this book provides that needed additional information.

Greek and Latin have been the sources of most of the words in the English language. (The third principal source is the family of Germanic languages.) Almost all of these words were added to the language long after the fall of the Roman Empire, and they continue to be added to this day. New words are constantly being invented, and most of them, especially those in the sciences, are still making use of Greek and Latin roots. Many words contain more than one root, as you'll see in the following pages, and some mix Greek and Latin (and even Germanic) roots.

The roots in this book are only a fraction of those that exist, but they include the roots that have produced the largest number of common English words. These roots (sometimes called *stems*) all formed part of Greek and Latin words. Some are shown in more than one form (for example, FLECT/FLEX), which means that they changed form in the original language, just as *buy* and *bought* are forms of the same English word. A knowledge of Greek and Latin roots will help you remember the meanings of the words in this book, but it will also enable you to guess at the meanings of new words that you run into elsewhere. Remember what a root means and you will have at least a fighting chance of understanding a word in which it appears.

Each of the roots in this book is followed by four words based on the root. Each group of eight words (two roots) is followed by two quizzes. Every fifth group is a special eight-word section that may contain words based on classical mythology or history, words borrowed directly from Greek or Latin, or other special categories of terms. Each set of 40 words makes up a unit. In addition, the brief paragraphs discussing each word include in *italics* many words closely related to the main words, in order to at least suggest how those related words may be used as well. Mastering a single word—for example, *phenomenon*—can thus increase your vocabulary by several words—for example, *phenomenal, phenomenally,* and the plural form *phenomena.*

The words presented here are not all on the same level of difficulty—some are quite simple and some are truly challenging—but the great majority are words that could be encountered on the Scholastic Aptitude Test (SAT) and similar standardized tests. Most of them are in the vocabularies of well-educated Americans, including professionals such as scientists, lawyers, professors, doctors, and editors. Even those words you feel familiar with may only have a place in your *recognition* vocabulary—that is, the words that you recognize when you see or hear them but that you are not sure enough about to use in your own speech and writing.

Each main word is followed by its most common pronunciation. A few of the pronunciation symbols may be unfamiliar to you, but they can be learned very easily by referring to the pronunciation key on page ix.

The definition comes next. We have tried to provide only the most common senses or meanings of the word, in simple and straightforward language, and no more than two definitions of any word are given. A more complete range of definitions can be found in a college dictionary such as *Webster's New Explorer College Dictionary.*

An example sentence marked with a bullet (•) follows the definition. This sentence by itself can indicate a great deal about the word, including the kind of sentence in which it often appears. It can also serve as a memory aid, since when you meet the word in the future, you may recall the example sentence more easily than the definition.

An explanatory paragraph rounds out your introduction to each word. The paragraph may do a number of things. It may tell you what else you need to know in order to use the word intelligently and correctly, since the example sentence can't do this all by itself. It may tell you more about the word's roots and its history. It may discuss additional meanings. It will often give you additional example sentences that demonstrate various ways to use the word and to expect to see it used. It may demonstrate the use of closely related words. The paragraph may even offer an informative or entertaining glimpse into a subject not strictly related to the word. The intention is to make you as comfortable as possible with each word in turn and to enable you to start using it immediately, without fear of embarrassment.

The quizzes immediately following each eight-word group, along with the review quizzes at the end of each unit, will test your memory. Many of these quizzes are similar to those used on standardized tests such as the SAT. Some of them ask you to identify *synonyms,* words with the same or very similar meaning, or *antonyms,* words with the opposite meaning. Perhaps more difficult are the *analogies,* which ask that you choose the word that will make the relationship between the last two words the same as the relationship between the first two. Thus, you may be asked to complete the analogy "calculate : count :: expend :——" (which can be read as "*Calculate* is to *count* as *expend* is to——") by choosing one of four words: *stretch, speculate, pay,* and *explode.* Since *calculate* and *count* are nearly synonyms, you will choose a near synonym for *expend,* so the correct answer is *pay.*

Studies have shown that the only way a new word will remain alive in your vocabulary is if it is regularly reinforced through use and through reading. Learn the word here and look and listen for it elsewhere—you'll probably find yourself running into it frequently, just as when you have bought a new car you soon realize how many other people own the same model.

Start using the words immediately. As soon as you feel confident with a word, start trying to work it into your writing wherever appropriate—your papers and reports, your diary and your poetry. An old saying goes, "Use it three times and it's yours." That may be, but don't stop there. Make the words part of your *working* vocabulary, the words that you can not only recognize when you see or hear them, but that you can comfortably call on whenever you need them. Astonish your friends, amaze your relatives, astound *yourself*, and have fun.

Acknowledgments: This book has benefited from the contributions of numerous members of the Merriam-Webster staff. Michael G. Belanger, John M. Morse, Brett P. Palmer, Stephen J. Perrault, and Mark A. Stevens edited the manuscript. Brian M. Sietsema and Eileen M. Haraty entered the pronunciations. James G. Lowe prepared the answer key. Florence A. Fowler undertook the immense task of preparing the manuscript for typesetting. The text was proofread by Susan L. Brady, Rebecca R. Bryer, Paul F. Cappellano, Jennifer N. Cislo, Jill J. Cooney, Jennifer S. Goss, Donna L. Rickerby, Michael D. Roundy, Katherine C. Sietsema, Amy West, and Karen L. Wilkinson, under the direction of Maria A. Sansalone and Madeline L. Novak.

Pronunciation Symbols

ə ....abut, collect, suppose
ˈə, ˌə .humdrum
ər ....operation, further
a ....map, patch
ā ....day, fate
ä ....bother, cot, father
ȧ ....a sound between \a\ and \ä\ as in an Eastern New England pronunciation of aunt, ask
aů ...now, out
b ....baby, rib
ch ...chin, catch
d ....did, adder
e ....set, red
ē ....beat, easy
f .....fifty, cuff
g ....go, big
h ....hat, ahead
hw ...whale
i .....tip, banish
ī .....site, buy
j .....job, edge
k ....kin, cook
l .....lily, cool
m ....murmur, dim
n ....nine, own
ⁿ .....indicates that a preceding vowel is pronounced through both nose and mouth, as in French bon \bōⁿ\
ŋ ....sing, singer, finger, ink
ō ....bone, hollow
ȯ ....saw
ȯi ....toy
p ....pepper, lip
r .....rarity
s ....source, less
sh ...shy, mission
t .....tie, attack
th ....thin, ether
th ....then, either
ü ....boot, few \ˈfyü\
u̇ ....put, pure \ˈpyu̇r\
v ....vivid, give
w ....we, away
y ....yard, cue \ˈkyü\
z ....zone, raise
zh ...vision, pleasure
\ .....slant line used in pairs to mark the beginning and end of a transcription: \ˈpen\
ˈ .....mark at the beginning of a syllable that has primary (strongest) stress: \ˈshəf-əl-ˌbōrd\
ˌ .....mark at the beginning of a syllable that has secondary (next-strongest) stress: \ˈshəf-əl-ˌbōrd\
- .....mark of a syllable division in pronunciations

Unit 1

BELL comes from the Latin word meaning "war." *Bellona* was the little-known Roman goddess of war; her husband, Mars, was the god of war.

antebellum \ˌan-ti-ˈbe-ləm\ Existing before a war, especially before the American Civil War (1861–65).

• When World War I was over, the French nobility found it impossible to return to their extravagant antebellum way of life.

Often the word *antebellum* summons up images of ease, elegance, and entertainment on a grand scale that disappeared in the postwar years. That way of life in the American South depended on a social structure that collapsed after the war. The years after the Civil War—and many other wars—were colored for some people by nostalgia and bitterness (Margaret Mitchell's *Gone with the Wind* shows this through the eyes of the Southern gentry), and for others by relief and anticipation.

bellicose \ˈbe-li-ˌkōs\ Warlike, aggressive, quarrelsome.

• The country often elected the more bellicose party after a period of tension along the border, hoping that military action would result.

The international relations of a nation with a bellicose foreign policy tend to be stormy and difficult, since such a nation looks for opportunities to fight rather than to negotiate. Combative by nature, it is happiest when quarreling or, better yet, actively engaged in battle.

belligerence \bə-ˈli-jə-rəns\ Aggressiveness, combativeness.

• The belligerence in Turner's voice told them that the warning was a serious threat.

The belligerence of Marlon Brando's performance as the violent Stanley Kowalski in *A Streetcar Named Desire* electrified the country. *Belligerent* speeches by leaders of the Soviet Union and the United States throughout the Cold War kept the world on edge for years. Iraq's shocking belligerence toward Kuwait and its own Kurdish people resulted in hundreds of thousands of deaths.

rebellion \ri-'bel-yən\ Open defiance and opposition, sometimes armed, to a person or thing in authority.

• The substitute teacher attempted to end the student rebellion by insisting on absolute quiet.

These days, some degree of rebellion against parents and other authority figures is viewed as a normal part of growing up, as long as it is not destructive and does not go on too long. Rebellion, armed or otherwise, has often served to alert those in power to the discontent of those they control. The American War of Independence was first viewed by the British as a minor rebellion that would soon run its course.

PAC/PEAS is related to the Latin words for "agree" and "peace." The *Pacific Ocean*—that is, the "Peaceful Ocean"—was named by Magellan because it seemed so calm after the storms near Cape Horn. (He obviously never witnessed a Pacific hurricane.)

---

pacify \'pa-sə-ˌfī\ (1) To soothe anger or agitation. (2) To subdue by armed action.

• It took the police hours to pacify the angry demonstrators.

Unhappy babies are often given a rubber device for sucking called a *pacifier* to make them stop crying. In the same way, someone stirred up by anger or some other strong emotion can usually be pacified by resolving or removing its causes. In a usage that became popular during the Vietnam War, *pacification* of an area meant using armed force to neutralize the enemy there and to quiet the local people who may have been supporting them.

pacifist \'pa-sə-fist\ A person opposed to war or violence, especially someone who refuses to bear arms or to fight, on moral or religious grounds.

• Always a strong pacifist, in later life he took to promoting actively the cause of peace and nonviolence.

Pacifists have not always met with sympathy or understanding. Refusing to fight ever for any reason, or even just in a particular situation when the reasons for fighting seem clear to many others, calls for strong faith in one's own moral or religious convictions, since it has often resulted in persecution by those who disagree. The Quakers and the Jehovah's Witnesses are *pacifist* religious groups; Henry D. Thoreau and Martin Luther King are probably the most famous American pacifists.

pact \'pakt\ An agreement between two or more people or groups; a treaty or formal agreement between nations to deal with a problem or to resolve a dispute.

• The girls made a pact never to reveal what had happened on that terrifying night in the abandoned house.

Since a pact often ends a period of unfriendly relations, the word has "peace" at its root. *Pact* is generally used in the field of international relations, where we often speak of an "arms pact" or a "fishing-rights pact." But it may also be used for a solemn agreement or promise between two people.

appease \ə-'pēz\ To make peaceful and quiet; to calm, satisfy.

• The Aztecs offered mass human sacrifices—of 80,000 prisoners on one occasion!—in order to appease their gods.

When the European nations agreed to let Adolf Hitler take over part of Czechoslovakia in 1938, in a vain attempt to prevent a larger war, their opponents shouted that they were practicing a foolish *appeasement* that was doomed to fail. (They were right—within months Hitler had violated the *pact*.) A child's anger may be appeased with a little effort; an angry god or goddess may demand something extreme. We may speak of hunger being appeased by food. Appeasing usually involves giving something, whereas *pacifying* can refer to anything from stroking a baby to using armed force to stop an uprising.

Quizzes

A. Match the word on the left to the correct definition on the right:

1. antebellum — a. quarrelsome
2. appease — b. solemn agreement
3. rebellion — c. to make peaceful
4. pacify — d. before the war
5. pacifist — e. aggressiveness
6. belligerence — f. opposition to authority
7. pact — g. to calm by satisfying
8. bellicose — h. one who opposes war

B. Fill in each blank with the correct letter:

a. antebellum — e. rebellion
b. pacifist — f. bellicose
c. pact — g. pacify
d. appease — h. belligerence

1. The native ____ began at midnight, when a gang of youths massacred the Newton family and set the house afire.
2. The grand ____ mansion has hardly been altered since it was built in 1841.
3. The Senate Republicans, outraged by their treatment, were in a ____ mood.
4. To ____ the younger managers, the company will double their bonuses this year.
5. The cease-fire ____ that had been reached with such effort was shattered by the news of the slaughter.
6. Their relations during the divorce proceedings had been mostly friendly, so his ____ in the judge's chambers surprised her.
7. The world watched in amazement as the gentle ____ Gandhi won India its independence with almost no bloodshed.
8. Her soft lullabies could always ____ the unhappy infant.

HOSP/HOST comes from the Latin word *hospes* and its stem *hospit-* meaning both "host" and "guest." Many words based on it came to English through French, which often dropped the *-pi-*, leaving *host-*. *Hospitality* is what a good *host* or *hostess* offers to a guest. A *hospital* was once a house for religious pilgrims and other travelers, or a home for the aged.

hostage \'häs-tij\ A person given or held to ensure that an agreement, demand, or treaty is kept or fulfilled.

• The kidnappers released their hostage unharmed once all their demands were met.

Opponents in war sometimes exchange hostages to ensure that a truce or treaty remains unbroken. Hostages may also be taken by kidnappers or terrorists or rebels to use in bargaining for money or concessions. It may seem strange that the word *hostage* is connected with *host* and in fact with *guest* as well, since hostages are now unwilling guests, at the mercy of their *hostile* hosts.

hospice \'häs-pəs\ A place or program to help care for the terminally ill.

• Uncle Harold was moved to the hospice only after my aunt had almost collapsed with exhaustion while caring for him.

In the Middle Ages, hospices run by monks and nuns gave shelter and food to travelers and the poor. Now, hospices are institutions that take care of people who are too ill to be at home but whose lives cannot be saved by hospital care—often those with incurable cancer or AIDS, for example. More and more Americans are relying on "home hospice care"—care by visiting nurses and volunteers for terminally ill patients who have decided to live their last months at home.

hostel \'häs-təl\ An inexpensive, supervised place for young travelers to stay overnight.

• Generations of American college students have traveled through Europe cheaply by staying at hostels instead of hotels.

Throughout Europe and in some other parts of the world, a network of youth hostels provides cheap, safe (although not always quiet) overnight shelter for younger bicyclists, hikers, and canoeists. The United States has over 200 youth hostels, many of them in New England. Worldwide, there are more than 5,000.

inhospitable \ˌin-hä-ˈspi-tə-bəl\ (1) Not welcoming or generous; unfriendly. (2) Providing no shelter or food (such as a desert).

• Shot down by government agents, the smuggler struggled for survival on the rocky, inhospitable island.

An inhospitable host fails to make his guests comfortable, in order to show them they are unwelcome. An inhospitable territory, such as Death Valley or Antarctica, may be barren and harsh in its climate. In a similar way, a country may be called inhospitable to democracy, just as a company may be called inhospitable to new ideas.

AM/IM comes from the Latin word *amare,* "to love." *Amiable* means "friendly or good-natured," and *amigo* is Spanish for "friend."

---

amicable \ˈa-mi-kə-bəl\ Friendly, peaceful.

• Their relations with their in-laws were generally amicable, despite some bickering during the holidays.

Amicable often describes relations between two groups or especially two nations—for example, the United States and Canada, which are proud of sharing the longest unguarded border in the world. When *amicable* describes personal relations, it tends to indicate a rather formal friendliness.

enamored \i-ˈna-mərd\ Charmed or fascinated; inflamed with love.

• Rebecca quickly became enamored of the town's rustic surroundings, its slow pace, and its eccentric characters.

Computer hackers are always enamored of their new programs and games. Millions of readers have found themselves enamored with Jane Austen's novels. And Romeo and Juliet were utterly enamored of each other. (Note that both *of* and *with* are commonly used after *enamored.*)

inimical \i-ˈni-mi-kəl\ Hostile, unfriendly, or harmful.

• This latest report, like so many earlier ones, found that too great a concern with test scores was inimical to a broad education.

The *in-* with which *inimical* begins negates the meaning of the root. This word rarely describes a person; instead, it is generally used to describe forces, concepts, or situations. For example, high inflation may be called inimical to economic growth; tolerance of racist comments in an office may be seen as inimical to minorities; and rapid population growth may be inimical to a country's standard of living.

paramour \ˈpar-ə-ˌmu̇r\ A lover, often secret, not allowed by law or custom.

• He was her paramour for many years before she finally divorced her husband.

Paramour includes the prefix *par* -, "by or through." This implies a relationship based solely on love, often physical love, rather than on a social custom or ceremony. Today it usually refers to the lover of a married man or woman.

Quizzes

A. Choose the odd word:

1. hostel a. shelter b. hotel c. prison d. dormitory
2. inimical a. unfriendly b. sympathetic c. antagonistic d. harmful
3. hospice a. nursing b. travel c. hospital d. illness
4. amicable a. difficult b. friendly c. pleasant d. peaceful
5. enamored a. strengthened b. charmed c. fond d. fascinated
6. inhospitable a. inimical b. barren c. unfriendly d. inviting
7. paramour a. lover b. husband c. mistress d. significant other
8. hostage a. exchange b. guarantee c. pledge d. hotel

B. Complete the analogy:

1. charming : enchanting :: inimical : ____
   a. sublime b. harmful c. direct d. cautious

2. lush : barren :: inhospitable : ____
   a. deserted b. sunny c. rocky d. welcoming
3. house : mortgage :: hostage : ____
   a. treaty b. gunman c. terrorist d. prisoner
4. gentle : tender :: enamored : ____
   a. lively b. charmed c. cozy d. enraged
5. picnic : dinner :: hostel : ____
   a. restaurant b. supper c. bar d. inn
6. frozen : boiling :: amicable : ____
   a. calm b. comfortable c. shy d. unfriendly
7. auditorium : arena :: hospice : ____
   a. spa b. nursing home c. club d. motel
8. friend : companion :: paramour : ____
   a. lover b. theater c. mother d. wife

CRIM comes from the Latin for "fault or crime" or "accusation," and produces such English words as *crime* and *criminal*.

criminology \ˌkri-mə-ˈnä-lə-jē\ The study of crime, criminals, law enforcement, and punishment.

• His growing interest in criminology led him to become a probation officer.

Criminology includes the study of all aspects of crime and law enforcement—criminal psychology, the social setting of crime, prohibition and prevention, investigation and detection, apprehension and punishment. Thus, many of the people involved—legislators, social workers, probation officers, judges, etc.—could possibly be considered *criminologists*, though the word usually refers to scholars and researchers only.

decriminalize \dē-ˈkri-mə-nə-ˌlīz\ To remove or reduce the criminal status of.

• An angry debate over decriminalizing doctor-assisted suicide raged all day at the statehouse.

Decriminalization of various "victimless crimes"—crimes that do not directly harm others, such as private gambling and drug-taking—has been recommended by conservatives as well as liberals, who claim that it would ease the burden on the legal system and decrease the amount of money flowing to criminals. Decriminalization is sometimes distinguished from legalization, since it may still call for a small fine like a traffic ticket, or it may apply only to use or possession, leaving the actual sale of goods or services illegal.

incriminate \in-ˈkri-mə-ˌnāt\ To show evidence of involvement in a crime or a fault.

• The muddy tracks leading to and from the cookie jar were enough to incriminate them.

We often hear of *incriminating* evidence, the kind that strongly links a suspect to a crime. Verbal testimony may incriminate by placing the suspect at the scene of the crime or describe behavior that involves him or her in it. We can also say that a virus has been incriminated as the cause of a type of cancer, and that television has been incriminated in the decline in study skills among young people.

recrimination \rē-ˌkri-mə-ˈnā-shən\ An accusation in retaliation for an accusation made against oneself; the making of such an accusation.

• Their failure to find help led to endless and pointless recriminations over the responsibility for the accident.

Defending oneself from a verbal attack by means of a counterattack is almost as natural as physical self-defense. So a disaster often brings recriminations among those connected with it, and divorces and battles over child custody usually involve recriminations between husband and wife.

PROB/PROV comes from the Latin words for "prove or proof" and "honesty or integrity." To *prove* a statement is to "make it honest," and *probate* court is where the genuineness of the wills of deceased people must be *proved*.

---

approbation \ˌa-prə-ˈbā-shən\ A formal or official act of approving; praise, usually given with pleasure or enthusiasm.

• The senate signaled its approbation of the new plan by voting for it unanimously.

Approbation indicates both formal recognition of an accomplishment and happy acceptance of it. An official commendation for bravery is an example of approbation. Getting reelected to office usually indicates public approbation. The social approbation that comes from being a star quarterback in high school makes all the pain worthwhile.

disprove \dis-ˈprüv\ To show that something is not what it has been claimed to be; refute.

• A week before the election he was still struggling to disprove his opponent's lies about his connections to organized crime.

Disprove, which includes the negative prefix *dis-*, is clearly the opposite of *prove*. One may have to disprove something for which the evidence has already been accepted, so the *disprover* often encounters violent objections to the new evidence that weakens the old. Galileo was forced to deny the new findings with which he and Copernicus had disproved the old conception of the earth's being at the center of the planetary system.

probity \ˈprō-bə-tē\ Absolute honesty and uprightness.

• Her unquestioned probity helped win her the respect of her fellow judges.

Probity is a quality the American public generally hopes for in its elected officials but doesn't always get. Bankers, for example, have traditionally been careful to project an air of probity; the savings-and-loan scandal of the 1980s has made it even more necessary. An aura of probity surrounds such public figures as Walter Cronkite and Bill Moyers, men to whom many Americans would entrust their children and their finances.

reprobate \ˈre-prə-ˌbāt\ A person of thoroughly bad character.

• Finally, on the verge of physical and financial ruin, the reprobate dropped his lowlife friends, joined AA, and begged his wife to come back.

Reprobate (which includes the prefix *re-*, "back or backward") is often said in a tone of joshing affection. The related verb is *reprove* or "scold," since the reprobate deserves a constant scolding. Shakespeare's great character Falstaff—a lazy, lying, boastful, sponging drunkard—is the model of an old reprobate.

Quizzes

A. Indicate whether the following pairs of words have the same or different meanings:

1. decriminalize / tolerate — same __ / different __
2. probity / fraud — same __ / different __
3. criminology / murder — same __ / different __
4. incriminate / acquit — same __ / different __
5. disprove / distinguish — same __ / different __
6. recrimination / approbation — same __ / different __
7. reprobate / scoundrel — same __ / different __
8. approbation / criticism — same __ / different __

B. Match the definition on the left to the correct word on the right:

1.	utter honesty	a.	approbation
2.	approval	b.	reprobate
3.	rascal	c.	recrimination
4.	demonstrate as false	d.	criminology
5.	study of illegal behavior	e.	probity
6.	accuse	f.	disprove
7.	reduce penalty for	g.	decriminalize
8.	counterattack	h.	incriminate

GRAV comes from the Latin word meaning "heavy, weighty, serious." Thus, a *grave* matter is serious and important.

gravid \'gra-vəd\ Pregnant or enlarged with something.

• The gravid sow moved heavily from trough to tree, where she settled into the shaded dust and lay unmoving for the rest of the afternoon.

Gravid implies weight and bulk, but actually describes a pregnant female even at an early stage of her pregnancy. It has the related senses of inflation that results from any cause and that will lead to a change of some kind. Thus, a writer may be gravid with ideas as she sits down to write; a speaker may make a gravid pause before announcing his remarkable findings; and a cloud may be gravid with rain.

gravitas \'gra-və-ˌtäs\ Great or very dignified seriousness.

• The head of the committee never failed to carry herself with the gravitas she felt was appropriate to her office.

This word comes to us straight from Latin. Among the Romans, gravitas was thought to be essential to the character and functions of any adult (male) in authority. Even the head of a household or a low-level official would strive for this important quality. We use *gravitas* today to identify the same solemn dignity in men and women.

gravitate \'gra-və-ˌtāt\ To move or be drawn toward something, especially by natural tendency or as if by an invisible force.

• During hot weather, the town's social life gravitated toward the lake.

To gravitate implies a natural, perhaps irresistible, response to a force that works like *gravity*, drawing things steadily to it as if by their own weight. Thus, moths gravitate to a flame, children gravitate to an ice-cream truck, gawkers gravitate to an accident, and everyone at a party gravitates to the bar.

gravity \'gra-və-tē\ Weighty importance, seriousness, or dignity.

• Laughing and splashing each other, they failed to realize the gravity of their situation until the canoe was within twenty feet of the falls.

Although closely related to *gravitas*, *gravity* can apply to situations and problems as well as to people. Gravity in the physical sense is, of course, what gives us weight and holds us on the earth. But weight can also mean seriousness. Thus, gravity in the nonphysical sense can mean seriousness in a person's manner but also the seriousness or danger in a situation.

LEV comes from the Latin adjective *levis*, meaning "light," and the verb *levare*, meaning "to raise or lighten." *Levitation* is the magician's trick in which a body seems to rise into the air by itself. And a *lever* is a bar used to lift something by means of *leverage*.

alleviate \ə-'lē-vē-ˌāt\ To lighten, lessen, or relieve, especially physical or mental suffering.

• Cold compresses alleviated the pain of the physical injury, but only time could alleviate the effect of the insult.

Physical pain or emotional anguish, or a water shortage or traffic congestion, can all be alleviated by providing the appropriate remedy. However, some pain or anguish or shortage or congestion will remain: to alleviate is not to cure.

elevate \'e-lə-ˌvāt\ (1) To lift up or raise. (2) To raise in rank or status.

• Last year's juniors have been elevated to the privileged status of seniors.

An *elevator* lifts things up. You may elevate a sprained ankle to reduce the swelling. When a Boy Scout reaches the rank of Eagle Scout, his rank is as *elevated* as it can get. *Elevated* language is language that, as in many poems and speeches, sounds formal or intellectual or in some way "higher" than common speech.

leavening \'le-və-niŋ\ Something that lightens and raises; something that modifies, eases, or animates.

• The speech was on a dull subject—"Microeconomic Theory in the 1970s"—but its leavening of humor made the time pass quickly.

The word *leavening*, when used in the kitchen, usually refers to yeast or baking powder. (*Unleavened* bread is often hard and dense; when it is used in religious ceremonies, it may be intended as a reminder of past hardship.) Young children may provide the leavening at a family reunion, and a cheerful receptionist may be the leavening in an otherwise dull office.

levity \'le-və-tē\ Frivolity, lack of appropriate seriousness.

• The Puritan elders tried to ban levity of all sorts from the community's meetings.

Levity originally was thought to be a physical force exactly like gravity but pulling in the opposite direction. Even as late as the last century, scientists were arguing about its existence. But today *levity* refers to lightness in manner. This was once regarded as almost sinful, so the word has an old-fashioned ring to it and is usually used in a half-serious tone of disapproval.

Quizzes

A. Fill in each blank with the correct letter:

a. gravid
b. gravitate
c. gravitas
d. gravity
e. alleviate
f. leavening
g. levity
h. elevate

1. As the ____ of the situation slowly became apparent, the crowd's mood changed from anxiety to hysteria.
2. With no ____, the muffins came out dense, chewy, and inedible.
3. At their father's funeral they showed the same solemn ____ at which they had often laughed during his lifetime.
4. Uncomfortable with their mean jokes, he tried to ____ the tone of the conversation.
5. Attracted magically by the music, all animals and natural objects would ____ toward the sound of Orpheus's lyre.
6. The lightning hung in the air for a ____ moment before the explosion of thunder.
7. The neighboring nations organized an airlift of supplies to ____ the suffering caused by the drought.
8. The board meeting ended in an unusual mood of ____ when a man in a gorilla suit burst in.

B. Match the word on the left to the correct definition on the right:

1. levity
2. gravitas
3. gravid

a. solemn dignity
b. relieve
c. lift, raise

4.	alleviate	d.	something that lightens
5.	elevate	e.	move toward as if drawn
6.	gravity	f.	lack of seriousness
7.	leavening	g.	pregnant
8.	gravitate	h.	seriousness

Words from Mythology and History

cicerone \ˌsi-sə-ˈrō-nē\ A guide, especially one who takes tourists to museums, monuments, or architectural sites and explains what is being seen.

• While in Paris, they placed themselves in the care of a highly recommended cicerone to ensure that they saw and learned what was most noteworthy.

Cicerones (or *ciceroni*) take their name from the Roman statesman and orator Cicero, who was renowned for his long-windedness as well as for his elegant style, though they rarely match his scholarship or eloquence.

hector \ˈhek-tər\ To bully; to intimidate or harass by bluster or personal pressure.

• He would swagger around the apartment entrance with his friends and hector the terrified inhabitants going in and out.

In the *Iliad,* Hector was the leader of the Trojan forces, and the very model of nobility and honor. In the war against the Greeks he killed several great warriors before being slain by Achilles. His name began to take on its current meaning only after it was adopted by a crowd of bullying young rowdies in late-17th-century London.

hedonism \ˈhē-də-ˌni-zəm\ An attitude or way of life based on the idea that pleasure or happiness should be the chief goal.

• In her new spirit of hedonism she went for a massage, picked up champagne and chocolate truffles, and made a date with an old boyfriend for that evening.

Derived from the Greek word for "pleasure," hedonism over the ages has provided the basis for several philosophies. The ancient Epicureans and the more modern Utilitarians both taught and pursued *hedonistic* principles. Hedonism is often said to be more typical of those living in southern and tropical climates than of northerners, but it varies greatly from person to person everywhere.

nestor \'nes-ˌtȯr\ A senior figure or leader in one's field.

• After dinner the guest of honor, a nestor among journalists, shared some of his wisdom with the other guests.

Nestor was another character from the *Iliad,* the eldest of the Greek leaders at Troy. He was noted for his wisdom and his talkativeness, both of which increased as he aged. These days a nestor need not go on at such length; he may share his knowledge or give advice with few words.

spartan \'spär-tən\ Marked by simplicity and often strict self-discipline or self-denial.

• His spartan life bore no relation to the lush language of his poetry.

In ancient times, the Greek city of Sparta had a reputation for enforcing a highly disciplined, severe way of life among its citizens so as to keep them ready for war at any time. The city required physical training for men and women and maintained a common dining hall and communal child care, but provided few physical comforts. The term *spartan* today may sometimes suggest communal life (for example, in the army) but always signifies strictness and frugality.

stentorian \sten-'tȯr-ē-ən\ Extremely loud, often with especially deep richness of sound.

• Even without a microphone, his stentorian voice broadcast the message of peace to the farthest reaches of the auditorium.

Stentor, like Hector, was a warrior in the *Iliad,* but on the Greek side. His unusually powerful voice made him the natural choice for delivering announcements and proclamations to the assembled Greek army. One who speaks in a stentorian voice thus can be heard clearly at a considerable distance.

stoic \\'stō-ik\\ Seemingly indifferent to pleasure or pain.

• She bore the pain of her broken leg with stoic patience.

The *Stoics* were members of a philosophical movement that first appeared in ancient Greece and lasted through the Roman era. They taught that humans should seek to free themselves from joy, grief, and passions of all kinds in order to attain wisdom. They have given their name to a personal attitude that some cultures and individuals still proudly cultivate.

sybaritic \\ˌsi-bə-'ri-tik\\ Marked by a luxurious or sensual way of life.

• Eventually their sybaritic excesses consumed all their savings and forced them to lead a more restrained life.

The ancient city of Sybaris, founded by the Greeks in Italy, was famous for the wealth and hedonistic self-indulgence of its citizens, whose love of extravagance and sensuality made *sybaritic* a term for such leanings in any era.

Quiz

Choose the closest definition:

1. hedonism a. preference for males b. habit of gift-giving c. tendency to conceal feelings d. love of pleasure
2. hector a. encourage b. harass c. deceive d. swear
3. cicerone a. guide b. cartoon character c. orator d. lawyer
4. spartan a. cheap b. militaristic c. severe d. luxurious
5. nestor a. journalist b. long-winded elder c. domestic hen d. judge
6. stoic a. pleasure-seeking b. bullying c. repressed d. unaffected by pain
7. sybaritic a. pleasure-seeking b. free of luxury c. sisterly d. ice-cold
8. stentorian a. obnoxious b. muffled c. loud d. dictated

Review Quizzes

A. Fill in each blank with the correct letter:

a. belligerence
b. stentorian
c. appease
d. sybaritic
e. gravid
f. alleviate
g. inimical
h. inhospitable
i. incriminate
j. gravitate
k. hector
l. enamored
m. stoic
n. pacify

1. Councillor Hawkins had a folksy drawl, but his simplest statements were ____ with meaning.
2. The mood at the resort was ____, and the drinking and dancing continued long into the night.
3. To rattle the other team, they usually ____ them constantly.
4. The judge was known for issuing all his rulings in a ____ voice.
5. With its thin soil and long winters, the area is ____ to farming.
6. Thoroughly ____ of the splendid Victorian house, they began to plan their move.
7. She attempted to ____ his anxiety by convincing him he wasn't to blame.
8. Whenever she entered a bar alone, the lonely men would always ____ toward her.
9. Their refusal to cease work on nuclear weapons was seen as an ____ act by the neighboring countries.
10. There was nowhere for miles where he could ____ his intense nicotine craving.
11. Unable to calm the growing crowd, he finally ordered the police to ____ the area by force.
12. Whenever her boyfriend saw anyone looking at her, his ____ was alarming.
13. He bore all his financial losses with the same ____ calm.
14. Who would have guessed that it would take the killer's own daughter to ____ him.

B. Choose the closest definition:

1. hedonism a. fear of heights b. hatred of crowds c. liking for children d. love of pleasure
2. levity a. lightness b. policy c. leverage d. literacy
3. gravity a. disturbance b. danger c. engraving d. seriousness
4. reprobate a. researcher b. commissioner c. scoundrel d. reformer
5. bellicose a. fun-loving b. warlike c. impatient d. jolly
6. decriminalize a. discriminate b. legalize c. legislate d. decree
7. antebellum a. preventive b. unlikely c. impossible d. prewar
8. hostage a. prisoner b. hostess c. criminal d. hotel
9. pact a. bundle b. form c. agreement d. presentation
10. amicable a. technical b. sensitive c. friendly d. scenic
11. criminology a. crime history b. crime book c. crime study d. crime story
12. approbation a. approval b. resolution c. reputation d. substitution

C. Match the definition on the left to the correct word on the right:

1. secret lover	a. elevate
2. show as false	b. gravitas
3. accusation	c. disprove
4. integrity	d. probity
5. shelter	e. recrimination
6. nursing service	f. paramour
7. peace lover	g. hospice
8. raise	h. hostel
9. dignity	i. rebellion
10. revolt	j. pacifist

Unit 2

AG comes from the Latin word for "do, go, lead, drive." An *agenda* is a list of things to be done. An *agent* is usually someone who does things on behalf of another, just as an *agency* is an office that does business for others.

agitate \ˈa-jə-ˌtāt\ (1) To move something with an irregular, rapid, violent action. (2) To stir up or excite.

• Philip found Louisa highly agitated at the news of her son's disappearance.

Agitate can mean to shake or stir something physically, but more often its meaning is emotional or political. *Agitation* for a cause—a new union, civil rights, a change of government—involves talking it up, passing out information, and holding meetings, though sometimes as secretly as possible. An *agitated* person or animal usually feels severely anxious and upset, not pleasantly excited.

litigate \ˈli-tə-ˌgāt\ To carry on a lawsuit by judicial process.

• If the company chooses to litigate, it may give the protesters the chance to make their points even more effectively in the courts and newspapers.

Litigation has become almost a way of life in America, where there are many more lawyers than in any other country on earth. In this increasingly *litigious* society, the courts have been overwhelmed with petty disputes. Television has responded to the trend by producing heroes like Judge Wapner of *People's Court,* a man who can show *litigants* the absurdity of their case while rendering a just verdict. (The Latin *litigare* includes the root *lit,* "lawsuit," and thus means basically "to drive a lawsuit.")

prodigal \'prä-də-gəl\ Recklessly or wastefully extravagant; spendthrift.

• Rodney had been the most prodigal with his expected inheritance and had the most to gain from a redistribution of the estate.

The Latin *prodigere* means "to squander"—that is, to "drive away" money and goods. In the biblical story of the prodigal son, the father welcomes home the spendthrift and now-penniless young man, despite his *prodigality*, just as the Church stands ready to welcome back the repenting sinner. *Prodigal* can apply to more than money. Farmers may make prodigal use of their soil, or may give their animals prodigal amounts of antibiotics. Rich countries are almost always prodigal with their resources. In a bloody and pointless war, lives are lost on a prodigal scale.

synagogue \'si-nə-ˌgȯg\ The center of worship and communal life of a Jewish congregation; temple.

• Though the neighborhood was now dangerous at night, the older members refused to move and abandon the beloved synagogue they had attended since the 1940s.

Synagogue begins with the prefix *syn-*, "together," so the word refers basically to "coming together." Synagogues have existed for more than 2,500 years. The oldest synagogue in America, dating from 1763, was built in Rhode Island, the most religiously tolerant of the original thirteen colonies.

VEN/VENT comes from *venire,* the Latin verb meaning "come." To *intervene* in a case or an argument is to "come between" the two opponents. An *avenue* is a street, or originally an access road by which to "come toward" something. Groups "come together" at a *convention.*

---

advent \'ad-ˌvent\ A coming or arrival; a coming into use.

• The advent of spring was always marked by the blue crocuses pushing up through the snow.

Advent includes the prefix *ad-*, "to or toward," and thus means basically a "coming toward." The Advent season in the Christian religion consists of the weeks leading up to Christmas, when the coming of Christ is anticipated. The advent of mass printing with Gutenberg's printing press in the mid-15th century had an enormous effect on European society and politics; the advent of the computer in the mid-20th century has promised to change ours even more profoundly.

provenance \'präv-nəns\ Origin or source.

• The wedding guests wondered about the provenance of this mysterious woman, about whom Seth had never breathed a word.

Provenance refers to any source or origin in general, but is used particularly to refer to the history of ownership of a piece of art, which may be necessary to prove that a work is authentic. The provenance of Rubens's paintings is varied; some have been in a single family or in a single museum for centuries, while some have been lost without a trace, leaving their provenance a mystery. Tracing the provenance of an idea or invention such as television may be a complicated task.

venturesome \'ven-chər-ˌsəm\ Inclined to seek out risk or danger; bold, daring, adventurous.

• Kate, with her bungee jumping, free-falling, and rock climbing, had always been the most venturesome of the four.

America, perhaps with a touch of arrogance, likes to think of itself as a land of venturesome people who push fearlessly forward in all ages and in all fields, and it clearly took a venturesome spirit to mount the successful flight to the moon that ended in July 1969. In past centuries, however, the most venturesome explorers were to be found in Greece, Italy, Spain, Portugal, and Britain—that is, the rich countries on the sea or ocean.

venue \'ven-ˌyü\ (1) The place where a trial is held. (2) The locale of an event.

• To Dr. Slaughter the important thing was to get a change of venue; hoping to conceal his past, he wanted a judge who knew him neither by sight nor by reputation.

The importance of venue in jury makeup and the subsequent outcome of a trial was vividly shown in the famous Rodney King case.

A suburban jury acquitted the men accused of beating King; after a change of venue, an urban jury convicted two of the men. The venues of championship boxing matches, on the other hand, are chosen with maximum profits in mind.

Quizzes

A. Choose the correct synonym:

1. synagogue a. courthouse b. arena c. temple d. cinema
2. provenance a. part of France b. origin c. Italian cheese d. invitation
3. prodigal a. brilliant b. poor c. missing d. lavish
4. venturesome a. daring b. western c. forthright d. timid
5. agitate a. soothe b. vibrate c. consume d. shake up
6. advent a. propaganda b. arrival c. commerce d. departure
7. litigate a. select a jury b. judge c. argue in court d. negotiate
8. venue a. jury b. place c. menu d. decision

B. Complete the analogy:

1. venturesome : timid :: ____ : ____
   a. stiff : flexible b. antique : artificial c. attractive : shapely d. bellicose : belligerent
2. litigate : argue :: ____ : ____
   a. border : enclose b. negotiate : discuss c. demonstrate : describe d. scold : praise
3. synagogue : worship :: ____ : ____
   a. theater : ticket b. church : mosque c. stadium : match d. hymn : song
4. provenance : destination :: ____ : ____
   a. travel : itinerary b. menu : meal c. recording : transcript d. birthplace : hometown
5. agitate : placate :: ____ : ____
   a. alternate : switch b. hesitate : rush c. blame : scold d. modify : alter

6. venue : locale :: ____ : ____
   a. arrival : departure b. country : nation c. court : jury d. prosecutor : judge
7. advent : departure :: ____ : ____
   a. Christmas : New Year's b. poverty : wealth c. rainfall : precipitation d. journey : expedition
8. prodigal : spendthrift :: ____ : ____
   a. stingy : miserly b. cautious : reckless c. artificial : natural d. opposite : similar

CAP/CEP/CIP comes from *capere,* the Latin verb meaning "take, seize." *Capture,* which is what a *captor* does to a *captive,* has the same meaning. *Captivate* once meant literally "capture," but now means only to capture mentally through charm or appeal. In some other English words this root produces, its meaning is harder to find.

reception \ri-'sep-shən\ (1) The act of receiving. (2) A social gathering where guests are formally welcomed.

• Although the reception of her plan was enthusiastic, it was months before anything was done about it.

Reception is the noun form of *receive.* So at a formal reception guests are received or welcomed or "taken in." If your idea for a great practical joke gets a lukewarm reception, it has not been well-received or *accepted.* Bad TV reception means the signal isn't being received well. And when a new novel receives good reviews we say it has met with a good critical reception.

incipient \in-'si-pē-ənt\ Starting to come into being or to become evident.

• He felt the stirrings of incipient panic as he riffled through the file and realized that the letter had been removed.

An incipient career as an actor in New York tends to involve a lot of waiting on tables while waiting for auditions. Identifying a cancer at its incipient stage may allow its development to be slowed or reversed. An environmental pessimist may speak of the incipient extinction of whales or bald eagles.

perceptible \pər-'sep-tə-bəl\ Noticeable or able to be felt by the senses.

• Her change in attitude toward him was barely perceptible, and he couldn't be sure that he wasn't imagining it.

Perceptible includes the prefix *per-*, meaning "through," so the word refers to whatever can be taken in through the senses. A *perceptive* person picks up hints and shades of meaning that others can't *perceive*. Such people rely on their sharp *perceptions*, their observations of whatever kind. So very often what is perceptible to one person—a tiny sound, a slight change in the weather, a different tone of voice—will not be to another.

susceptible \sə-'sep-tə-bəl\ (1) Open to some influence; responsive. (2) Able to be submitted to an action or process.

• Impressed with her intelligence and self-confidence, he was highly susceptible to her influence.

With its prefix *sus-*, "up," *susceptible* refers to what "takes up" or absorbs like a sponge. When negotiating the settlement of World War II at Yalta with Churchill and Roosevelt, Stalin may have found the other two susceptible to his threats and bullying and thus managed to hold on to much of Eastern Europe. Students are usually susceptible to the teaching of a strong and imaginative professor. In a similar way, a sickly child will be susceptible to colds, and an unlucky adult will be susceptible to back problems.

FIN comes from the Latin word for "end" or "boundary." *Final* describes last things, and a *finale* or a *finish* is an ending. But its meaning is harder to trace in some of the other English words derived from it.

---

affinity \ə-'fi-nə-tē\ (1) Sympathy; attraction. (2) Relationship.

• He knew of Carl's affinity to both wine and violence, and intended to take advantage of them.

Affinity gives a sense of things touching along their boundaries and therefore being of interest to each other. Felix Mendelssohn showed an affinity for music at a very early age and composed several fully developed symphonies while still in his teens; Stevie Wonder revealed his own musical affinity long before he made his debut at the age of 10. A strong affinity for another person may deepen into love. A critic may notice affinities between the works of two writers. A naturalist may speak of the affinity between two bird species—that is, their close physical relation to each other.

definitive \di-'fi-nə-tiv\ (1) Authoritative and final. (2) Specifying perfectly or precisely.

• The team's brilliant research provided a definitive description of the virus and its strange mutation patterns.

Something definitive is complete and final. A definitive example is the perfect example. A definitive biography contains everything we'll ever need to know about someone. Ella Fitzgerald's 1950s recordings of American popular songs have even been called definitive, though no one has ever wanted them to be the last.

infinitesimal \ˌin-ˌfi-nə-'te-sə-məl\ Extremely or immeasurably small.

• Looking more closely at the research data, he now saw an odd pattern of changes so infinitesimal that they hadn't been noticed before.

Infinitesimal includes the negative prefix *in-*, "not"; the resulting word describes something endlessly small. When Antonie van Leeuwenhoek invented the microscope in the 17th century, he was able to see organisms that had been thought too *infinitesimally* small to exist. But today's electron microscope allows us to see infinitesimal aspects of matter even he could not have imagined.

finite \'fī-ˌnīt\ Having definite limits.

• Her ambitions were infinite, but her wealth was finite.

It came as a shock to America in the early 1970s to realize that world and national resources were finite rather than unlimited. The debate continues as to whether the universe is finite or *infinite* and, if it is finite, how to think about what lies beyond it. Religion has always concerned itself with the question of the finite (that is, human life on earth) versus the infinite (God, eternity, and infinity).

But *finite* is mostly used in scientific writing, often with the meaning "definitely measurable."

Quizzes

A. Fill in each blank with the correct letter:

a. affinity
b. susceptible
c. definitive
d. reception
e. finite
f. incipient
g. infinitesimal
h. perceptible

1. By the fall there had been a ___ change in the mood of the students.
2. An ___ speck of dust on the lens can keep a CD player from functioning.
3. They waited weeks to hear about the board's ___ of their proposal.
4. She feels an ___ to her imaginary friend that she has never felt to her parents.
5. Small children are often ___ to nightmares after hearing ghost stories in the dark.
6. When the power failed as the wind began to reach gale force, she sensed ___ disaster.
7. We have a ___ number of choices, in fact maybe only three or four.
8. This may be the best book on the subject so far, but I wouldn't call it ___.

B. Match the word on the left to the correct definition on the right:

1. affinity
2. susceptible
3. definitive
4. reception
5. finite
6. incipient
7. infinitesimal
8. perceptible

a. noticeable
b. ultimate
c. beginning
d. easily influenced
e. tiny
f. attraction
g. receiving
h. limited

JAC/JEC comes from *jacere,* the Latin verb meaning "throw" or "hurl." To *reject* something is to throw (or push) it back. To *eject* something is to throw (or drive) it out. To *object* is to throw something in the way of something else.

adjacent \ə-'jā-sənt\ (1) Near, neighboring. (2) Sharing a common boundary or border.

• The warehouse was adjacent to the junction of the two raging rivers, so the body could have been quickly disposed of.

Adjacent contains the prefix *ad-,* "near or toward," so what is adjacent lies near its neighbor. In the former Yugoslavia, the Serbs and Croats have seized adjacent land from the Bosnians. Anyone buying a house is naturally curious about who lives on the adjacent lots. In geometry we speak of adjacent sides and angles. Though in each of these cases *adjacent* means "touching," it may also mean simply "neighboring" or "nearby."

conjecture \kən-'jek-chər\ To guess.

• They could conjecture that he had met his end in the Andes at the hands of the guerrillas.

Formed with the prefix *con-, conjecture* means literally "to throw together"—that is, to produce a theory by putting together a number of facts. From his calculations, Columbus conjectured that he would reach Asia if he sailed westward. His later *conjecture* of a Northwest Passage from the Atlantic to the Pacific over the North American continent was eventually proved correct, but only after hundreds of years had passed.

dejected \di-'jek-təd\ Downcast, depressed.

• Despite the glorious weather, they walked home from the hospital dejected.

Dejected, which includes the prefix *de-,* meaning "down," literally means "thrown down" or "cast down." It usually refers to a temporary state of mind—for example, the mood of a losing football team or a *rejected* lover—rather than ongoing depression.

trajectory \trə-'jek-tə-rē\ The curved path that an object makes in space, or that a thrown object follows as it rises and falls to earth.

• Considering the likely range, trajectory, and accuracy of a bullet fired from a cheap handgun at 150 yards, the murder seemed incredible.

Formed with part of the prefix *trans-*, "across," *trajectory* means a "hurling across." By calculating the effect of gravitational and other forces, the trajectory of an object launched into space at a known speed can be computed precisely. Missiles stand a chance of hitting their target only if their trajectory has been plotted accurately. Though the word is most used in physics and engineering, we can also say, for example, that the trajectory of a whole life may be set in a person's youth, or that a historian has described the long trajectory of the French empire in a new book.

TRACT comes from *trahere*, the Latin verb meaning "drag or draw." Something *attractive* draws us toward it. A *tractor* drags other vehicles behind it, with the help of the *traction* of its wheels.

---

detract \di-'trakt\ To decrease the importance, value, or effectiveness of something.

• None of the gossip in the new biography detracts in the least from her greatness as a writer.

With the prefix *de-*, meaning "away," *detract* means "draw away from." A fact that doesn't match up with the rest of the prosecution's case detracts from it. Richard Nixon's involvement in the Watergate coverup was felt to detract so seriously from his ability to carry out his presidential duties that he had to resign, especially after his *detractors* had impeached him. (Don't confuse *detract* with *distract*, which means "take attention away from.")

protracted \prō-'trak-təd\ Drawn out, continued, or extended.

• No one was looking forward to a protracted struggle for custody of the baby.

Protracted usually applies to something drawn out in time. A protracted strike may cripple a company; a protracted rainy spell may rot the roots of vegetables. Before Jonas Salk and Albert Sabin discovered vaccines to prevent polio, the many victims of the disease had no choice but to suffer a protracted illness and its permanent aftereffects.

retraction \ri-'trak-shən\ A taking back or withdrawal; a denial of what one has previously said.

• The following week, the newspaper reluctantly printed a retraction of the errors in the article, but the damage had been done.

The prefix *re-* ("back") gives *retraction* the meaning of "drawing back." Someone who has been wrongly accused may demand a retraction from his accuser—though today it seems more likely that he'll just go ahead and sue. Thousands of citizens were forced to publicly *retract* their "wrong" ideas by the Soviet government in the 1930s and the Chinese government in the 1960s. Retractions tend to be rather formal and rarely private.

intractable \in-'trak-tə-bəl\ Not easily handled, led, taught, or controlled.

• The army's corruption was known to be the country's intractable problem, and all foreign aid ended up in the colonels' pockets.

Intractable simply means "untreatable," and even comes from the same root. It may describe both people and conditions. An intractable alcoholic goes back to the bottle immediately after "drying out." A cancer patient may suffer intractable pain that doctors are unable to treat. Homelessness is now regarded by many as an intractable problem—though it hardly existed twenty years ago.

Quizzes

A. Choose the odd word:

1. conjecture a. suppose b. conclude c. guess d. know
2. protracted a. lengthened b. continued c. circular d. extended
3. dejected a. excited b. downcast c. depressed d. forlorn
4. retraction a. withdrawal b. regret c. disavowal d. denial

5. trajectory a. curve b. path c. line d. target
6. detract a. decrease b. diminish c. defy d. minimize
7. adjacent a. near b. adjourned c. touching d. bordering
8. intractable a. impossible b. uncontrollable c. stubborn d. unteachable

B. Match each definition on the left to the correct word on the right:

1. denial	a. protracted
2. assume	b. adjacent
3. depressed	c. trajectory
4. difficult	d. retraction
5. take away	e. conjecture
6. drawn out	f. intractable
7. curved path	g. detract
8. nearby	h. dejected

DUC, from the Latin verb *ducere*, "to lead," shows up constantly in English. *Duke* means basically "leader." The Italian dictator Mussolini was known simply as "Il Duce." But such words as *produce* and *reduce* also contain the root, even though their meanings show it less clearly.

conducive \kən-ˈdü-siv\ Tending to promote, encourage, or assist; helpful.

• She found the atmosphere there conducive to study and even to creative thinking.

Something conducive "leads to" a desirable result. A cozy living room may be conducive to relaxed conversation, just as a boardroom may be conducive to more intense discussions. Particular tax policies are often conducive to savings and investment, whereas others are conducive to consumer spending. Notice that *conducive* is almost always followed by *to*.

deduction \dē-ˈdək-shən\ (1) Subtraction. (2) The reaching of a conclusion by reasoning.

• Foretelling the future by deduction based on a political or economic theory has proved to be extremely difficult.

A tax deduction is a subtraction from your gross income allowed by the government for certain expenses, which will result in your paying lower taxes. To *deduct* is simply to subtract. But *deduction* also means "reasoning," and particularly reasoning based on general principles to produce specific findings. Mathematical reasoning is almost always deduction, for instance, since it is based on general rules. But when Dr. Watson exclaims "Brilliant deduction, my dear Holmes!" he simply means "brilliant reasoning," since Sherlock Holmes's solutions are based on specific details he has noticed rather than on general principles.

induce \in-ˈdüs\ (1) Persuade, influence. (2) Bring about.

• To induce him to make the call we had to promise we wouldn't do it again.

Inducing often refers to gentle persuasion—inducing a friend to go to a concert, or inducing a child to stop crying, for instance. But an *inducement* may occasionally be a bit menacing, such as the Godfather's "Make him an offer he can't refuse." *Induce* also sometimes means "produce"; thus, doctors must at times induce labor in a pregnant woman. *Induction* often means the opposite of *deduction,* and is in fact closer to what Sherlock Holmes was actually doing.

seduction \si-ˈdək-shən\ (1) Temptation to wrong, especially temptation to sexual intercourse. (2) Attraction or charm.

• The company began its campaign of seduction of the smaller firm by inviting its top management to a series of weekends at expensive resorts.

Seduction, with its prefix *se-*, "aside," means basically "led aside or astray." In Nathaniel Hawthorne's novel *The Scarlet Letter,* Hester Prynne has to wear a scarlet A, for "adulteress," for all to see after it is revealed that she has been *seduced* by the Reverend Dimmesdale. Seduction also takes less physical forms. Advertisements constantly try to seduce us (often using sex as a temptation) into buying products we hadn't even known existed.

SEC/SEQU comes from the Latin verb *sequi,* meaning "to follow." A *sequel* follows the original novel, film, or television show. The *second* follows the first. But a *non sequitur* is a conclusion that does "not follow" from what was said before.

consequential \ˌkän-sə-ˈkwen-shəl\ (1) Resulting. (2) Important.

• None of our discussions thus far has been very consequential; next week's meeting will be the important one.

Something that is consequential follows or comes along with something else. The "resulting" meaning of *consequential* is usually seen in legal writing. For example, "consequential losses" are losses that are claimed to have resulted from some improper behavior, about which the lawyer's client is suing. But normally *consequential* means "significant" or "important," and is especially used for events that will produce large *consequences* or results.

execute \ˈek-si-ˌkyüt\ (1) To carry out or perform. (2) To put to death legally or formally.

• He was aware that he hadn't been hired to think independently but rather simply to execute the governor's policies.

Execute joins *ex-*, "out," and *sec* to produce the meaning "follow through" or "carry out." An artist executes (or produces) a painting or sculpture only after having planned it first. A policy or regulation must have been prepared before it can be executed (or put into practice). And a person may be executed (or put to death) by the state only after a death sentence has been issued.

obsequious \äb-ˈsē-kwē-əs\ Excessively submissive, obedient, or flattering.

• Since he loves flattery, he surrounds himself with obsequious people, none of whom he ever really trusts.

A man may be obsequious toward his overbearing wife, or vice versa. Obsequious assistants are often called "yes-men" or "toadies" or even less complimentary things behind their backs. (Uriah Heep, in *David Copperfield,* is probably the most famous example in literature.) *Obsequiousness* has never been admired, but it has often been adopted as a good strategy.

sequential \si-'kwen-chəl\ (1) Arranged in order or in a series. (2) Following in a series.

• In writing the history of the revolution, he found it hard to put some of the events in sequential order.

Things in *sequence*, or regular order, are arranged *sequentially*. Most novels and films move sequentially, but some use techniques such as flashbacks that interrupt the movement forward in time. Sequential courses in college must be taken in the proper order, just as sequential tasks or steps must be done in order.

Quizzes

A. Match the definition on the left to the correct word on the right:

1. flattering — a. deduction
2. persuade — b. obsequious
3. temptation — c. induce
4. subtraction — d. execute
5. helpful — e. seduction
6. ordered — f. consequential
7. produce — g. conducive
8. significant — h. sequential

B. Fill in each blank with the correct letter:

a. conducive — e. consequential
b. deduction — f. execute
c. induce — g. obsequious
d. seduction — h. sequential

1. The detectives insisted on a detailed and ____ account of the evening's events.
2. She fended off all his clumsy attempts at ____.
3. Conditions on the noisy hallway were not at all ____ to sleep.
4. She was barely able to ____ the task in the time allotted.
5. He sometimes thought that missing that plane had been the most ____ event of his life.
6. They arrived at the correct conclusion by simple ____.

7. The assistant's ____ manner drove the other employees wild.
8. He had tried to ____ sleep by all his usual methods, with no success.

Words from Mythology

apollonian \ˌa-pə-ˈlō-nē-ən\ Harmonious, ordered, rational, calm.

• After years of Romantic emotionality, many artists began to adopt a more apollonian style, producing carefully detailed patterns and avoiding extremes of all kinds.

The god Apollo governed the sun, light, and music. Due partly to the work of Nietzsche and other German scholars, we now associate Apollo with the forces of calm rationality and may call anything that has these qualities *apollonian*. This is not the whole story, however. Apollo was also the god of prophecy, so he was not entirely a force of reason; he had a terrible temper and an appetite for young girls as well.

bacchanalian \ˌba-kə-ˈnāl-yən\ Frenzied, orgiastic.

• The bacchanalian partying on graduation night resulted in three wrecked cars, two lawsuits by unamused parents, and more new experiences than most of the participants could remember the next day.

The Roman god of drama, wine, and ecstasy, Bacchus was the focus of a widespread celebration, the *Bacchanalia*, at which there was wine in abundance and celebrants were expected to cut loose from normal restraints and give in to all sorts of wild desires. The festivities got so out of hand that in 186 B.C. the Roman authorities had them banned. Much the same bacchanalian spirit fills New Orleans' Mardi Gras carnival each year.

delphic \ˈdel-fik\ Unclear, ambiguous, or confusing.

• All she could get from the old woman were a few delphic comments that left her more confused than ever about the missing documents.

Delphi in Greece was the site of a temple to Apollo at which there was an oracle, a woman through whom Apollo would speak, foretelling the future. The Greeks consulted the oracle frequently on matters both private and public. The prophecies were given in obscure poetry that had to be interpreted by priests, and even then was subject to disastrous misinterpretation. Modern-day descendants of the oracle include some political commentators, who continue to utter words of delphic complexity each week.

Dionysian \ˌdī-ə-ˈni-zhē-ən\ Frenzied, orgiastic.

• Only in the tropics did such festivals become truly Dionysian, he said, which was why he was booking his flight to Rio.

Dionysus was the Greek forerunner of Bacchus. He was the inventor of wine, the first intoxicant, which he gave to the human race. For that gift and for all the uninhibited behavior that it led to, Dionysus became immensely popular, and he appears in a great many myths. He is often shown with a wine goblet, his hair is full of vine leaves, and he is frequently attended by a band of goat-footed satyrs and wild female spirits called maenads. The Greek Dionysian worship began as solemn rituals but eventually became great celebrations with much drunken lewdness.

jovial \ˈjō-vē-əl\ Jolly, expansively good-natured.

• Their grandfather was as jovial as their grandmother was quiet and withdrawn.

Jove, or Jupiter, was the Romans' chief god. He was generally a cheerful, sociable, fatherly figure, although his anger could destroy offenders in a flash. Every department-store Santa Claus strives to attain this appearance of generous *joviality*.

mercurial \mər-ˈkyu̇r-ē-əl\ Having rapid and unpredictable changes of mood.

• His mother's always mercurial temper became even more unpredictable, to the point where the slightest thing would trigger a violent fit.

The god Mercury and the planet named for him were thought to govern eloquence and cleverness. As the gods' messenger, with his winged cap and sandals, he was the very symbol of speed. The planet Mercury was named for him because it is the fastest of the planets. His name was also given to the liquid silver metal that skitters out of one's hand so quickly it is almost impossible to hold. A mercurial person isn't necessarily physically quick, but changes moods with bewildering speed.

olympian \ō-'lim-pē-ən\ Lofty, superior, and detached.

• The mafia don's manner grew increasingly olympian as he aged, but the old-timers could still remember when he was a hotheaded young thug.

The Greek gods lived high atop Mount Olympus, which allowed them to watch what went on in the human realm below and intervene as they saw fit. But they tended not to worry much about the affairs of these weak and short-lived creatures, although they did insist on being properly worshiped by them. We American voters sometimes feel that Congress treats us in an olympian manner as it determines how our money will be spent.

venereal \və-'nir-ē-əl\ Having to do with sexual intercourse or diseases transmitted by it.

• In the 19th century syphilis especially was often fatal, and venereal diseases killed some of the greatest figures of the time.

Venus was the Roman goddess of love, the equivalent of the Greek Aphrodite. Since she governed all aspects of human sensuality and sexuality, she has given her name to the diseases acquired through sexual contact. Most of these venereal diseases have been around for centuries, but only in this century have doctors devised tests to identify them or medicines to cure them. Today the official term is *sexually transmitted disease*, or STD; but even this name turns out to be ambiguous, since some of these diseases can be contracted in other ways as well.

Quiz

Choose the correct synonym and the correct antonym:

1. Dionysian a. frenzied b. angry c. calm d. fatal
2. apollonian a. fruity b. irrational c. single d. harmonious

3. mercurial a. stable b. changeable c. sociable
   d. depressed
4. jovial a. youthful b. mean-spirited c. merry
   d. magical
5. olympian a. involved b. lame c. detached d. everyday
6. venereal a. sensual b. intellectual c. diseased
   d. arthritic
7. bacchanalian a. restrained b. dynamic c. orgiastic
   d. forthright
8. delphic a. clear b. dark c. stormy d. ambiguous

Review Quizzes

A. Choose the closest definition:

1. venue a. prosecution b. justice c. location d. street
2. incipient a. sensitive b. beginning c. visible d. final
3. affinity a. eternity b. attraction c. intensity
   d. retraction
4. deduction a. addition b. flirtation c. tax d. reasoning
5. execute a. dismiss b. carry out c. disturb d. announce
6. sequential a. important b. noticeable c. consecutive
   d. distant
7. obsequious a. powerful b. official c. notorious
   d. obedient
8. agitate a. excite b. amaze c. explain d. exclaim
9. prodigal a. poor b. departed c. wasteful d. returning
10. synagogue a. palace b. temple c. club d. society

B. Match the definition on the left to the correct word on the right:

1. guess	a. olympian
2. arrival	b. perceptible
3. lengthy	c. conjecture
4. godlike	d. venturesome
5. ordered	e. protracted
6. bold	f. advent
7. noticeable	g. susceptible

8. sensitive h. dejected
9. significant i. sequential
10. unhappy j. consequential

C. Fill in each blank with the correct letter:

a. mercurial f. litigate
b. obsequious g. bacchanalian
c. intractable h. detract
d. provenance i. retraction
e. adjacent j. trajectory

1. Before deciding to ____ the matter, they had tried to negotiate a solution out of court.
2. Nothing his enemies could say managed to ____ from his heroic public image.
3. The prison situation is ____, and likely to get worse.
4. The company issued a ____ the next day, apologizing to those who had been offended.
5. The new study of the painting's ____ proved it to be a genuine Monet.
6. Because they lived ____ to the paint factory, their garden suffered from the effects of pollution.
7. The disappointing ____ of his career often puzzled his friends.
8. The smilingly ____ sales clerk bustled off in search of more jackets.
9. By 2:00 a.m. the party was a scene of ____ frenzy.
10. Her only excuse for her behavior was her well-known ____ temper.

Unit 3

AMBI/AMPHI means "on both sides" or "around"; *ambi-* comes from Latin and *amphi-* from Greek. An *ambidextrous* person can use the right and the left hand equally well. An *amphibian*, such as a frog or salamander, is able to live and breathe both on land and in the water.

ambiguous \am-'bi-gyü-wəs\ (1) Doubtful or uncertain especially from being obscure or indistinct. (2) Unclear in meaning because of being understandable in more than one way.

• Successful politicians are good at giving ambiguous answers to questions on controversial issues.

Ambiguous comes from the Latin verb *ambigere*, "to be undecided," which in turn includes the verb *agere*, "to drive." Something that is ambiguous drives the observer in two directions. When we speak of eyes as being of an ambiguous color, we mean that we cannot decide which color they are—blue or green? The *ambiguity* of the smile of the Mona Lisa makes us wonder what she's thinking about. An ambiguous order is one that can be taken in at least two ways. An order to "shut up!," on the other hand, may be very rude, but at least it's *unambiguous*.

ambient \'am-bē-ənt\ Existing or present on all sides.

• The ambient lighting in the restaurant was low, but there was a bright candle at each table.

A scientist might measure how long it takes a heated substance to cool to the ambient temperature, the temperature of the surrounding air. Ambient light is the light that fills an area or surrounds something that is being viewed, like a television screen or a painting. A restaurant with low ambient light and candles at each table is probably trying for a romantic *ambience,* or atmosphere.

ambivalent \am-'bi-və-lənt\ (1) Holding opposite feelings and attitudes at the same time toward someone or something. (2) Continually wavering between opposites or alternate courses of action.

• He was extremely ambivalent about the trip: he badly wanted to travel but hated to miss the summer activities at home.

Ambivalent is a fairly new word, less than a hundred years old, but it is ultimately related to the Latin verb *valere,* which means "to be strong." An ambivalent person is someone who has strong feelings on more than one side of a question or issue. We might feel *ambivalence* about accepting a high-paying job that requires us to work long hours, or about lending money to someone we like but don't know well. Anyone who has ever been on a diet and been offered something like a Tutti-Frutti Chocolate Banana Sundae El Supremo probably knows what it's like to feel ambivalent.

amphitheater \'am-fə-ˌthē-ə-tər\ (1) An oval or circular building with an open area ringed by rising tiers of seats, used in ancient Rome for contests and spectacles. (2) A large modern theater or stadium.

• The Romans held popular contests between gladiators or between gladiators and wild beasts in their amphitheaters.

The basic design of an amphitheater reflects the forms of entertainment for which it was originally built: gladiatorial contests and other spectacles. The most famous of the ancient amphitheaters was Rome's Flavian Amphitheater, now more commonly known as the Colosseum. Built between 70 and 82 A.D., this structure could hold nearly 50,000 people. The ruins of more than 75 amphitheaters have been found in the ancient lands that were once part of the Roman Empire.

EP/EPI comes from Greek and means variously "upon," "besides," "attached to," "over," "outer," or "after." An *epiphenomenon* is a phenomenon that occurs as a result of the original phenomenon. An *epicenter* is the portion of the earth's surface directly over the focus of an earthquake. The *epidermis* is the outer layer of the skin, overlying the inner layer or "dermis."

---

ephemeral \i-'fe-mə-rəl\ (1) Lasting a day only. (2) Lasting a very short time.

• The benefits from the strategy will only be ephemeral, but we'll be paying for it for years to come.

Something that is literally ephemeral is "over" in a day, *hēmera* being the Greek word for "day." Ephemeral plants such as daylilies have blooms that last only a day. More often, though, *ephemeral* is not to be taken quite so literally. In the world of show business, for example, fame is apt to be breathtakingly ephemeral, a year in the limelight followed by total obscurity.

epiphyte \'e-pi-ˌfīt\ A plant that obtains its nutrients from the air and the rain and usually grows on another plant for support.

• The strangler fig begins life as an epiphyte on a tree branch, drops its tendrils to take root in the ground around the trunk, and slowly covers and strangles the tree to death.

Epiphytic plants are sometimes also known as "air plants" because they seemingly survive on thin air. They rely on their host plants merely for physical support, not nourishment. Tropical epiphytes include orchids, ferns, and members of the pineapple family. To a newcomer in the tropical rainforest, the sight of a great tree with large epiphytes hanging from every level can be eerie and astonishing. The less interesting epiphytes of the temperate zone include lichens, mosses, and algae.

epitaph \'e-pi-ˌtaf\ An inscription on a grave or tomb in memory of the one buried there.

• The great English architect Christopher Wren designed London's majestic St. Paul's Cathedral, the site of his tomb and epitaph: "Si monumentum requiris, circumspice" ("If you seek my monument, look around you").

Epitaph includes the root from the Greek word *taphos*, "tomb" or "funeral." Traditionally, *epitaph* refers to a tombstone inscription, but it can also refer to brief memorial statements that resemble such inscriptions. One of the most famous is Henry Lee's epitaph for George Washington: "First in war, first in peace, and first in the hearts of his countrymen."

epithet \'e-pi-ˌthet\ (1) A descriptive word or phrase occurring with or in place of the name of a person or thing. (2) An insulting or demeaning word or phrase.

• King Richard I was known by the epithet "Lionhearted."

Sometimes an epithet follows a given name, as in Erik the Red and Billy the Kid. Other times, the epithet precedes the personal name, as in Mahatma ("Great-souled") Gandhi. Still other times, the epithet is used in place of the actual name, as in the case of El Greco ("the Greek") and El Cid ("the Lord"). In its other commonly used sense, *epithet* refers to a name intended to insult or mock someone. When enemies are said to be "hurling epithets" at each other, it means they are exchanging angry insults.

Quizzes

A. Fill in each blank with the correct letter:

a. ambiguous
b. epiphyte
c. ambient
d. epitaph
e. epithet
f. ambivalent
g. ephemeral
h. amphitheater

1. An ____ seems to live on air and water alone.
2. When the ____ light is low, photographers use a flash.
3. She felt ____ about the invitation, and couldn't decide whether to accept or decline.
4. Is any ____ inscribed on Grant's Tomb?
5. Andrew Jackson's ____, describing his lean toughness, was "Old Hickory."
6. Lord Raglan's ____ order confused the commander of the Light Brigade and led to its disastrous charge.
7. Spring and all its blossoms are ____, here but a moment and then gone.
8. On New Year's Day, the ____ known as the Rose Bowl becomes the site of one of college football's great face-offs.

B. Match each word on the left with its correct definition on the right:

1. ambivalent
2. epithet

a. having more than one meaning

3.	amphitheater	b.	surrounding
4.	epiphyte	c.	wavering
5.	ambiguous	d.	grave inscription
6.	epitaph	e.	stage surrounded with tiered seats
7.	ambient	f.	descriptive nickname
8.	ephemeral	g.	short-lived
		h.	non-parasitic plant growing on another

HYPO/HYP as a prefix can mean variously "under," "beneath," "down," or "below normal." Many *hypo-* words are medical. A *hypodermic* needle injects medication under the skin. *Hypotension,* or low blood pressure, can be just as unhealthy as *hypertension,* and *hypoglycemia,* low blood sugar, just as unhealthy as diabetes.

hypochondriac \hī-pō-'kän-drē-ˌak\ A person unduly concerned with health and often suffering from delusions of physical disease.

• Hercule Poirot, the dapper hero of Agatha Christie's mysteries, is a notorious hypochondriac, always trying to protect himself from drafts.

One disease a hypochondriac really does suffer from is *hypochondria,* which is the mental depression that comes from worrying too much about health and is often accompanied by delusions of physical ailments. Somewhat surprisingly, *hypochondria* derives from *hypo-* and *chondros,* the Greek word for "cartilage." The cartilage in question is that of the sternum, or breastbone. From ancient times medical authorities had believed that certain internal organs or regions were the seat of various diseases, both physical and mental. The region beneath the centrally located breastbone was thought to be the seat of hypochondria.

hypocrisy \hi-'pä-krə-sē\ A pretending to be what one is not or to feel what one does not really feel.

• The protesters were objecting to the hypocrisy of doing business with a government whose racist policies were condemned by everyone.

Hypocrisy comes from a Greek word that means "the act of playing a part on a stage." A *hypocrite* is a person who says or does one thing while thinking or feeling something entirely different underneath. Most of us are good at detecting *hypocritical* behavior in others, but we don't always see it so easily in ourselves.

hypothermia \ˌhī-pō-ˈthər-mē-ə\ Subnormal temperature of the body.

• By the time rescuers were able to pull the skater from the pond's icy waters, hypothermia had reached a life-threatening stage.

Hypothermia may constitute a grave medical emergency. Typical causes include submersion in icy water and prolonged exposure to cold. Hypothermia begins to be a concern when body temperature dips below 95°F. Below 90°F, the point at which the normal reaction of shivering ceases, emergency treatment is called for.

hypothetical \ˌhī-pə-ˈthe-tə-kəl\ (1) Involving an assumption made for the sake of argument or for further study or investigation. (2) Imagined for purposes of example.

• The presidential candidate refused to say what she would do if faced with a hypothetical military crisis.

Hypothetical and its parent word *hypothesis* come from *hypo-* and the Greek verb *tithenai*, "to put." To *hypothesize* is to suppose, or to put (something) under consideration. *Hypothetical* applies to something that is assumed to be true so that it can serve as the basis for a line of reasoning. Thus, the theory that the dinosaurs became extinct because of a giant meteor striking the earth involves the hypothesis that such a collision would have certain effects on the earth's climate.

THERM/THERMO comes from the Greek word meaning "warm." A *thermometer* measures the amount of warmth in a body, the air, or an oven; a *thermostat* makes sure the temperature stays at the same level. In a *thermodynamic* process, heat affects the behavior of atoms, particles, or molecules. *Thermoelectricity* is produced by the direct action of heat on certain combinations of metals.

---

thermal \'thər-məl\ (1) Of, relating to, or caused by heat. (2) Designed to insulate in order to retain body heat.

• The glider circled slowly, seeking a thermal updraft from a plowed field that would take it spiraling upward.

Before polypropylene and thermal weave, union suits—that is, long thermal underwear that covered the entire body—were sometimes donned in October and not taken off until April. Worn by sodbusters, cowboys, and townsfolk alike, they kept America warm during its formative years. They undoubtedly also kept America itchy and a little on the smelly side through the cold months. But then, bathing even once a week was considered the height of cleanliness until very recently.

thermocline \'thər-mə-ˌklīn\ The region in a body of water that divides the warmer, oxygen-rich surface layer from the colder, oxygen-poor deep water.

• The warm water above the thermocline is relatively shallow: for most of the world's oceans the top layer is only about 150 to 300 feet deep.

The *-cline* of *thermocline* comes from a Greek word meaning "to slope" and refers to the gradual series of temperature changes that occur in this kind of zone. In a freshwater lake there is very little mixing between the layers of warm and cold water during the summer. During the autumn, however, a major turnover occurs. The oxygen-rich surface water cools and sinks to the bottom, and the nutrient-rich water near the bottom is displaced to the top. The cycle is reversed the following spring.

thermocouple \'thər-mō-ˌkə-pəl\ A device for measuring temperature that makes use of the way different metals respond to heat.

• Thermocouples can be used to measure temperatures as high as 2300°C or as low as -270°C, far beyond the range of ordinary thermometers.

Thermocouples use wires made of two different metals, such as copper and iron. The wires are joined at both ends; one end is placed against the object whose temperature is being measured, while the other end is kept at a known, constant temperature. The thermocouple generates a voltage that depends on the difference in temperature between the two joined ends of the wires and can be measured to obtain the temperature of the object.

thermonuclear \ˌthər-mō-ˈnü-klē-ər\ Of or relating to the changes in the nucleus of atoms with low atomic weight, such as hydrogen, that require a very high temperature to begin.

• During the 1950s and 1960s American families built thousands of home underground shelters to protect themselves from thermonuclear blasts.

The sun's light comes from a sustained thermonuclear reaction deep within it. On earth, such thermonuclear reactions have been used to develop the hydrogen bomb, a bomb based on a fusion reaction that must be triggered by a fission bomb that uses uranium or plutonium. "Little Boy" and "Fatman," the bombs dropped on Hiroshima and Nagasaki to end World War II, were fission bombs. The thermonuclear era began only in 1952, and has produced bombs hundreds of times more powerful.

Quizzes

A. Choose the closest definition:

1. hypothermia a. excitability b. subnormal temperature c. external temperature d. warmth
2. thermocline a. area of warm water b. area of cold water c. area between warm and cold water d. deep ocean water
3. hypocrisy a. dislike b. low energy c. insincerity d. nickname
4. thermal a. keeping out b. keeping warm c. keeping safe d. keeping cold
5. hypothetical a. typical b. substandard c. sympathetic d. assumed
6. hypochondriac a. person with imaginary visions b. person with heart congestion c. person with imaginary ailments d. person with imaginary relatives
7. thermocouple a. temperature gauge b. nuclear reaction trigger c. ocean current gauge d. altitude gauge

8. thermonuclear a. nuclear reaction requiring high heat b. chemical reaction requiring a vacuum c. biological reaction producing bright light d. nuclear reaction based on distance from the sun

B. Indicate whether the following pairs of words have the same or different meanings:

1. thermocouple / hot bodies same __ / different __
2. hypochondriac / invalid same __ / different __
3. thermal / insulating same __ / different __
4. thermonuclear / destructive same __ / different __
5. hypocrisy / truthfulness same __ / different __
6. hypothetical / supposed same __ / different __
7. thermocline / warm hillside same __ / different __
8. hypothermia / low blood sugar same __ / different __

POLY comes from *polys*, the Greek word for "many." *Polysyllabic* words, of which there are a few in this book, are words of many syllables. *Polygamy* is marriage in which one has many spouses, or at least more than the legal limit of one. A *polygraph* is an instrument for recording variations in many different bodily pulsations simultaneously to reveal whether someone is lying.

---

polychromatic \ˌpä-lē-krō-ˈma-tik\ Showing a variety or a change of colors; multicolored.

• *The Wizard of Oz* begins in black and white but suddenly becomes gloriously polychromatic once Dorothy and Toto land in Oz.

Male peacocks are almost miraculously polychromatic, with their feathers of gleaming blue, green, white, and brown. The polychromatic content of light becomes apparent when it passes through a prism like mist or a faceted piece of glass; the prism organizes it into its distinct wavelengths, each creating a band of color in the rainbow. *Polychromatic* takes its meaning straight from its roots: *poly-*, "many," and *chrom-*, "color."

polyglot \ˈpä-lē-ˌglät\ (1) One who can speak or write several languages. (2) Having or using several languages.

• As trade between countries increases, there is more need for polyglots who can act as negotiators.

Polyglot contains the root *glot,* meaning "language." It is used both as a noun and as an adjective. An international airport is bound to be polyglot, with people from all over the world speaking their native languages. One of history's more intriguing polyglots was the Holy Roman Emperor Charles V. He claimed that he addressed his horse only in German, he conversed with women in Italian and with men in French, but he reserved Spanish for his talks with God.

polymer \ˈpä-lə-mər\ A chemical compound formed by a reaction in which two or more molecules combine to form larger molecules with repeating structural units.

• Nylon, a polymer commercially introduced in 1938, can be spun and woven into fabrics or cast as tough, elastic blocks.

There are natural polymers, such as shellac and rubber, but synthetic polymers came into being in 1870 with Celluloid, which, although a synthetic compound, is made from natural cotton and camphor. After many decades of development, the *polymeric* compounds now include *polypropylene,* used in milk crates, luggage, and hinges; *polyurethane,* used in paints, adhesives, molded items, rubbers, and foams; and *polyvinyl chloride,* used to make pipes that won't rust.

polyphony \pə-ˈli-fə-nē\ Music consisting of two or more independent but harmonious melodies.

• At concerts she preferred Mahler and Beethoven, but when she was working she listened only to Renaissance polyphony.

Polyphony is usually avoided in American folk and popular music, which almost always employs a strong melody with a much less important accompaniment. But it is typical of Dixieland, bluegrass, and almost any kind of music where more than one musician improvises at once. *Polyphony* is used primarily for music of the Renaissance and Baroque eras from about 1400 to 1750; J. S. Bach is the most famous master of polyphony.

PRIM comes from *primus*, the Latin word for "first." Something that is *primary* is first in time, development, rank, or importance. A *primer* is a book of first instructions on a subject. A *primate* is a bishop or archbishop of the first rank—but also a monkey or ape. Something *primitive* is in its first stage of development. Something *primeval* had its origin in the first period of world or human history.

primal \'prī-məl\ (1) Original or primitive. (2) First in importance.

• She argued that to restore the economy, the primal necessity was to reform the health care system.

We might speak of the primal innocence of youth, or of the primal intensity of someone's devotion to a cause. Certain psychologists employ "primal scream" therapy, in which patients relive painful experiences from their past and express their frustration and anger through screaming and even violence.

primiparous \prī-'mi-pə-rəs\ (1) Bearing a first offspring. (2) Having borne only one previous offspring.

• The purpose of the study was to compare the average duration of labor for primiparous women with that of multiparous women.

Primiparous is used of animals as well as humans. It is typically used with *multiparous*, "having had one or more previous pregnancies." The terms are common in laboratory research, veterinary science, and human obstetrics. An individual who is a *primipara* may exhibit certain characteristics, or be subject to certain circumstances, that are peculiar to first pregnancies.

primogeniture \ˌprī-mō-'je-nə-ˌchu̇r\ An exclusive right of inheritance belonging to the eldest son of a single set of parents.

• Many of the world's monarchies descend by the principle of primogeniture.

Primogeniture arose in England following the Norman Conquest of 1066. The practice began as a means of ensuring that fiefs (that is, estates) would not be broken up among the sons of a vassal. Eventually the right of the eldest son to inherit all of his father's estate was written into law. Primogeniture was one of the English practices that Americans were eager to abolish once independence had been attained. Leading the campaign against it was Thomas Jefferson.

primordial \prī-ˈmȯr-dē-əl\ (1) First created or developed. (2) Existing in or from the very beginning.

• Many astronomers think the universe is continuing to evolve from a primordial cloud of gas.

Primordial can be traced back to the Latin word *primordium*, or "origin." It applies to something that is only the starting point in a course of development or progression. The substance out of which the earth was formed and all life on it evolved is commonly spoken of as "the primordial ooze." A primordial cell is the first formed and least specialized in a line of cells. A primordial landscape is one that bears no sign of human use.

Quizzes

A. Fill in each blank with the correct letter:

a. primiparous
b. polyglot
c. primogeniture
d. polyphony
e. polychromatic
f. primordial
g. polymer
h. primal

1. In the 1980s many women chose to remain ____, content with just one child.
2. Rubber is a natural ____ that remains the preferred material for many applications.
3. The asteroids in our solar system may be remnants of a ____ cloud of dust.
4. The Beatles occasionally experimented with ____, sometimes imitating the music of Bach.
5. Royal titles are still passed from one generation to the next on the basis of ____.
6. Having gone to school in four countries as a child, she was already a fluent ____.
7. They were charmed by the ____ innocence of the little village.
8. The house, once white, was now dazzlingly ____.

B. Indicate whether the following pairs of words have the same or different meanings:

1. polychromatic / overly dramatic same __ / different __
2. primogeniture / first generation same __ / different __
3. polymer / molecule with repeating units same __ / different __
4. primiparous / firstborn same __ / different __
5. polyglot / speaking many languages same __ / different __
6. primal / most important same __ / different __
7. polyphonic / many-colored same __ / different __
8. primordial / primitive same __ / different __

HOM/HOMO comes from *homos,* the Greek word for "same." In an English word it can mean "one and the same" or "similar" or "alike." A *homograph* is one of two or more words spelled alike but different in meaning or derivation or pronunciation. A *homosexual* is a person who exhibits sexual desire toward others of the same sex.

---

homonym \'hä-mə-ˌnim\ One of two or more words pronounced and/or spelled alike but different in meaning.

• The *pool* of "a pool of water" and the *pool* of "a game of pool" are homonyms.

Homonym is a troublesome word because it can refer to three distinct classes of words. Homonyms can be words that merely sound alike—such as *to, too,* and *two*—but are different in spelling and meaning. Homonyms can also be words that are spelled alike—such as *bow* (of a ship) and *bow* (and arrow)—but are different in pronunciation and meaning. Finally, homonyms can be words with identical spellings and pronunciations but different meanings—such as *quail* (the bird) and *quail* (to cringe). Some writers and speakers prefer to limit *homonym* to this last sense.

homogeneous \ˌhō-mə-'jē-nē-əs\ (1) Of the same or a similar kind. (2) Of uniform structure or composition throughout.

• Though she was raised in a small town, she liked living in the city because the population there wasn't so homogeneous.

A slab of rock is homogeneous if it consists of the same material throughout, like granite or marble. A neighborhood might be called homogeneous if all the people in it are similar, having pretty much the same background, education, and outlook. *Homogeneity* is fine in a rock, but some people find it a little boring in a neighborhood. Foods can be homogeneous too. Milk, for example, is *homogenized* so that its fatty part, the cream, is spread evenly throughout, giving the milk a consistent, homogeneous texture.

homologous \hō-ˈmä-lə-gəs\ Developing from the same or a similar part of a remote ancestor.

• Arms and wings are homologous structures that reveal our ancient relationship to the birds.

In his discussion of the panda's thumb, Stephen Jay Gould carefully explains how this thumb is not homologous to the human thumb. Although in function the two digits are similar, the panda's thumb developed from a bone in its wrist and is an addition to the five "fingers" of its paw. The panda's thumb is indispensable for stripping bamboo of its tasty leaves, the staple of the panda's diet; but it did not develop *homologously* with our thumb. The tiny stirrup and anvil bones of our inner ear, however, do seem to be homologous with the bones that allow a garter snake to swallow a frog whole.

homophone \ˈhä-mə-ˌfōn\ One of two or more words pronounced alike but different in meaning or derivation or spelling.

• The words *wood* and *would* are familiar homophones.

Since *phon-* means "sound," homophones basically sound the same. *Tide* and *tied, made* and *maid, horse* and *hoarse* are pronounced identically, but differ in meaning, derivation, and spelling. This occasionally leads to confusion. If Groucho Marx had said "I'm a little hoarse," we might well have expected him to give a little whinny. Puns depend on *homophonic* pairs for their effect; while many find that homophonic humor grates, others think it is just great.

DIS comes from Latin, where it means "apart." In English, its meanings have increased to include "do the opposite of" (as in *disestablish*), "deprive of" (as in *disfranchise*), "exclude or expel from" (*disbar*), "the opposite or absence of" (*disunion, disaffection*), "not" (*disagreeable*), and "completely" (*disannul*). The original meaning can still be seen in a word like *dissipate*, which means "to break up and scatter."

diffraction \di-'frak-shən\ (1) The bending or spreading of a beam of light especially when it passes through a narrow opening or is reflected from a ruled surface. (2) Similar changes in other waves, such as sound waves.

• Through the occurrence of diffraction, the thin bands of light passing through venetian blinds become a sea of soft light on the opposite wall.

Diffraction contains the root *fract-*, "broken" (*dis-* here has changed to *dif-*), so *diffracted* light is light that is broken up. Diffracted sound is also broken up. The diffraction of the sound waves bends them around the corner, so a conversation carried on in one room can be overheard in another.

dissension \di-'sen-shən\ Disagreement in opinion.

• There was so much dissension at the meeting that nothing got done, and everyone went home angry.

Dissension is a common feature of our political system. One party suggests a new law or policy, and then the other party often *dissents*, arguing that the new law or policy will have a terrible effect on the country, and proposing a different new law or policy of its own. This leads the first party to dissent in turn, and so on. Things usually get worked out in the end. Since *dissentious* behavior of this kind keeps everyone on their toes, most people feel that it's a good thing overall. But not everyone agrees.

disseminate \di-'se-mə-ˌnāt\ To spread widely as if by sowing seeds.

• Television and computer networks now make it possible to disseminate information throughout the world very quickly.

In *disseminate,* the prefix *dis-* keeps its original Latin sense "apart." This prefix was attached in Latin to the verb *seminare,* "to sow," which itself was derived from the noun *semen,* "seed." The image lying behind *disseminate* is that of a farmer sowing seeds over a wide area by throwing them with a sweep of the arm, the same image that has given us *broadcast* (which has the basic sense "to cast broadly"). It's appropriate, then, that one of the best ways to bring about the *dissemination* of news is by broadcasting it over television and radio.

dissipate \ˈdi-sə-ˌpāt\ (1)To cause to spread out to the point of vanishing; disperse. (2) To spend wastefully or foolishly; squander.

• The moderator's good humor slowly dissipated the tension that had filled the meeting room.

Dissipate suggests a gradual disintegration or vanishing, as if by crumbling, scattering, or evaporation. A police force dissipates an unruly mob. The sun dissipates the morning mist. In its second sense, *dissipate* implies frittering away something until it is exhausted. A foolish lottery winner might dissipate his or her money in extravagant spending sprees, buying 18 Ferraris, say, or a lifetime supply of expensive imported underwear.

Quizzes

A. Choose the closest definition:

1. dissipate a. drink slowly b. scatter c. make pale d. undo
2. homonym a. word meaning the same as another b. word spelled and sounded the same as another c. one with same name as another d. one who loves another of the same sex
3. disseminate a. spread widely b. plant in rows c. dissolve d. make longer
4. homogeneous a. self-loving b. unusually brilliant c. having many parts d. consistent throughout
5. diffraction a. breaking up of friendships b. breaking up of light waves c. breaking up of meetings d. breaking up of atoms

6. homologous a. of different length b. of similar size c. of different stages d. of similar origin
7. dissension a. confusion b. disagreement c. satisfaction d. curiosity
8. homophone a. word that sounds like another b. word that means the same thing as another c. word that looks like another d. word relating to sexual desire

B. Match the definition on the left to the correct word on the right:

1.	word spelled like another	a.	dissension
2.	spend foolishly	b.	homophone
3.	having a consistent texture	c.	diffraction
4.	conflict	d.	homonym
5.	evolutionarily related	e.	disseminate
6.	spread over a wide area	f.	homologous
7.	word sounding like another	g.	dissipate
8.	breaking up of light or sound waves	h.	homogeneous

Latin Borrowings

ad hoc \'ad-'häk\ Formed or used for a particular purpose or for immediate needs.

• The faculty formed an ad hoc committee to deal with the question of first-amendment rights on campus.

Ad hoc literally means "for this" in Latin, a meaning clearly reflected in its uses in English. An ad hoc investigating committee is authorized to look into a matter of limited scope and not to go on a fishing expedition for other wrongdoing. An ad hoc ruling by an athletic council is intended to settle a particular case, and is not meant to serve as a model for later rulings. Problems that come up in the course of a project often require immediate, ad hoc solutions.

ad hominem \'ad-'hä-mə-nem\ Marked by an attack on an opponent's character rather than by an answer to the arguments made or the issues raised.

• The presidential debates often consist of ad hominem attacks rather than serious discussion of important issues.

Ad hominem in Latin means "to the man." It comes from the field of rhetoric (that is, speaking and writing), where it was first used to describe arguments that appeal to the listener's emotions and not to the intellect. The easiest way to do this is to engage in personal attacks against one's opponent. When debaters cannot justify their own positions or prove their opponents wrong, they may resort to ad hominem charges. Ad hominem arguments require neither truth nor logic to be effective. Consequently, the popularity of such arguments has never waned.

alter ego \'ȯl-tər-'ē-gō\ (1) A trusted friend or personal representative. (2) The opposite side of a personality.

• The White House chief of staff is a political alter ego: he knows, or should know, who and what the President considers important.

In Latin, *alter ego* literally means "second I." An alter ego can be thought of as a person's clone or second self. A professional alter ego might be a trusted aide who knows exactly what the boss wants done. A personal alter ego might be a close friend who is almost like a twin. *Alter ego* can also refer to the second, hidden side of one's own self. In Robert Louis Stevenson's classic *The Strange Case of Doctor Jekyll and Mr. Hyde,* Dr. Jekyll is a good-hearted, honorable man. But after taking a potion, his alter ego, the loathsome and diabolical Mr. Hyde, takes control over his personality.

de facto \dē-'fak-tō\ Being such in practice or effect, although not formally recognized; actual.

• Although there was never a general declaration of war, the two countries were in a de facto state of war for almost a decade.

Literally meaning "from the fact," *de facto* in English is applied to whatever has the substance of something but not the formal name. A de facto government is one that operates with all of the power of a regular government, but without the official recognition. De facto segregation does not stem from any legislative order, but it is just as real and deep-rooted as segregation that has been authorized by law.

de jure \dē-'jür-ē\ By right of law.

• With the completion of the adoption proceedings, the Millers became the de jure as well as the de facto parents of the child.

Literally meaning "by right" in Latin, *de jure* is typically used in sentences where it is set in opposition to *de facto*. It is used with reference to things that have the force of law or operate under a right recognized by law. A de jure president is one duly elected under a nation's laws. A de facto ruler, on the other hand, may be exercising power that has been acquired through illegal means.

ex post facto \ˌeks-ˌpōst-'fak-tō\ Done, made, or formulated after the fact.

• Most of Carl's so-called reasons are merely ex post facto excuses for impulsive behavior.

Ex post facto is Latin for "from a thing done afterward." Approval for a project that is given ex post facto—after the project already has been begun or completed—is mainly given to save face. An ex post facto law is one that criminalizes an action after it was committed, even though the action was not a crime at the time that it was committed.

modus operandi \'mō-dəs-ˌä-pə-'ran-ˌdī\ A usual way of doing something.

• A criminal who commits repeated crimes can often be identified by his modus operandi.

Modus operandi is Latin for "method of operating." Although often associated with police work and a favorite word of mystery writers, *modus operandi* is used in other contexts as well. For example, a frequent gambler who likes to play the horses may have a particular modus operandi for picking winners. The modus operandi of a cutthroat retailer may be to undersell competitors, drive them out of business, and then raise prices afterwards.

modus vivendi \'mō-dəs-vi-'ven-dē\ (1) A practical compromise or arrangement that is acceptable to all concerned. (2) A way of life.

• During the budget crisis, the Democratic governor and the Republican legislature established a modus vivendi that let them put aside their differences and tackle the problem at hand.

Modus vivendi literally means "manner of living" in Latin, and it sometimes has that meaning in English as well. Usually, though, a modus vivendi is a working arrangement that disputing parties can live with, at least until a more permanent solution can be found. Typically, a modus vivendi is an arrangement that ignores differences and difficulties. Two people going through a bitter divorce may be able to arrive at a modus vivendi that allows them to at least maintain an appearance of civility and dignity.

Quiz

Choose the closest definition:

1. alter ego a. church structure b. bad conscience c. intimate friend d. self-love
2. modus vivendi a. pie with ice cream b. compromise c. stalemate d. immoral conduct
3. ad hoc a. for this purpose b. permanent c. long-range d. for many reasons
4. ex post facto a. in anticipation b. sooner or later c. coming after d. someday
5. ad hominem a. based on personalities b. based on logic c. based on issues d. based on sexual preference
6. modus operandi a. procedure b. way of moving c. crime d. arrest
7. de facto a. in transit b. in effect c. in debt d. in theory
8. de jure a. by might b. by claim c. by right d. by word

Review Quizzes

A. Complete the analogy:

1. monochromatic : dull :: polychromatic : ____ a. neutral b. bland c. sharp d. vivid
2. peace : tranquility :: dissension : ____ a. cooperation b. disagreement c. unity d. communication

3. brief : lengthy :: ex post facto : ____
   a. beforehand b. afterward c. during d. actually
4. local : here :: ambient : ____
   a. there b. somewhere c. nowhere d. everywhere
5. marriage : dowry :: primogeniture : ____
   a. favoritism b. flattery c. inheritance d. divorce
6. antonym : up / down :: homophone : ____
   a. pause / paws b. three / tree c. imagine / dream d. retreat / advance
7. seek : flee :: ad hominem : ____
   a. to the time b. to the issue c. to the end d. to the maximum
8. desirable : despised :: thermal : ____
   a. cool b. soft c. warm d. springy

B. Fill in each blank with the correct letter:

a. ad hoc
b. ambivalent
c. modus operandi
d. epithet
e. thermonuclear
f. de jure
g. polymer
h. homogeneous
i. diffraction
j. modus vivendi
k. primiparous
l. alter ego
m. polyglot
n. hypochondriac
o. amphitheater

1. A real ____, she could speak four languages and read three others.
2. The independent-minded teenager and her overprotective parents struggled to arrive at a ____ that both sides could accept.
3. The usual ____ for the songwriters was for one to write the lyrics first and then for the other to compose the music.
4. She is such a close friend that she seems like my ____.
5. The de facto segregation in the North closely resembled the ____ segregation of the South.
6. ____ explains why sound can be heard around a corner, even though no straight path between source and hearer exists.

7. Much thought has gone into the designing of ____ power plants that run on nuclear fusion.
8. The development of the first synthetic ____ for use as fabric revolutionized the garment industry.
9. "Gray-eyed" is the standard ____ used to describe the goddess Athena.
10. The ____ mothers were shown to have on average more complications during pregnancy.
11. Jessica was ____ about going to the party: it sounded exciting, but she wouldn't know any of the other guests.
12. In her middle age she became a thorough ____, always convinced she was suffering from some new disease.
13. You should blend all ingredients thoroughly to produce a ____ mixture.
14. An ____ committee should be named to come up with ideas for redecorating the waiting room.
15. The play was presented in the open-air ____ under the stars.

C. Indicate whether the following pairs have the same or different meanings:

1. de facto / actually — same __ / different __
2. hypothermia / heat prostration — same __ / different __
3. primordial / existing from the beginning — same __ / different __
4. thermocline / cold ocean depths — same __ / different __
5. polyphonic / religious — same __ / different __
6. primal / first — same __ / different __
7. ambiguous / unclear — same __ / different __
8. modus operandi / way of life — same __ / different __
9. homologous / blended — same __ / different __
10. disseminate / broadcast — same __ / different __
11. thermocouple / lovebirds — same __ / different __
12. epiphyte / parasite — same __ / different __
13. de jure / legally — same __ / different __
14. epitaph / grave inscription — same __ / different __
15. dissipate / dispel — same __ / different __

Unit 4

VOR, from the Latin verb *vorare,* means "to eat." The ending *-ivorous* shows up in words that refer to eaters of certain kinds of food. *Frugivorous* (for "fruit-eating"), *granivorous* (for "grain-eating"), and *graminivorous* (for "grass-eating") are somewhat common. Some *-ivorous* words such as *insectivorous* and *nectarivorous,* are easy to understand at a glance. Others can get pretty complex; insects that feed on the sap of plants, for instance, are *phytosuccivorous.*

carnivorous \kär-'ni-və-rəs\ Meat-eating or flesh-eating.

• The dragonfly lives up to its name by being a carnivorous terror that can pluck its prey out of midair at speeds up to 30 miles per hour.

Usually when we think of carnivorous beings we think of large animals such as lions, tigers, or cheetahs. However, many smaller animals, including some kinds of mice and the tiny creatures that make up coral reefs, are also *carnivores.* And there are even a few carnivorous plants, such as the Venus's-flytrap, the pitcher plant, and the sundew, all of which *devour* their insect prey after trapping them by ingenious means.

herbivorous \hər-'bi-və-rəs\ Plant-eating.

• In spite of their frightening appearance, marine iguanas are peaceable herbivorous animals that feed mostly on seaweed.

While many herbivorous animals (such as rabbits and cows) are noted for their passive ways, such behavior is not universal among *herbivores.* A rhinoceros is herbivorous but capable of inflicting serious damage if threatened. Among dinosaurs, the herbivorous

Diplodocus had a thick tail that could be used as a lethal weapon against attacking carnivorous enemies.

omnivorous \äm-ˈni-və-rəs\ (1) Feeding on both animals and plants. (2) Intensely interested in everything.

• Good writers are often also omnivorous readers who enjoy equally fiction and nonfiction, prose and poetry, philosophy and science.

We tend to think of human beings as omnivorous, but in fact there are many kinds of plants that we simply cannot digest. Bears are truer *omnivores*. Their diet can include bulbs, berries, nuts, young plant shoots, insects, grubs, and dead animals, including fish, deer, and beaver. Humans do seem to possess an omnivorous curiosity. And it probably took that kind of curiosity—plus a good deal of courage—to be the first human to eat an oyster.

voracious \və-ˈrā-shəs\ (1) Having a huge appetite. (2) Very eager.

• One of the hardest parts of dieting is watching skinny people with voracious appetites consume large amounts of food without gaining weight.

Voracious can be applied to both people and their appetites. Teenagers are voracious eaters because they have voracious appetites. Some vacationers become voracious readers; others are voracious for other kinds of pleasure. *Voracious* often suggests an appetite in excess of what is good for us. We are sometimes told that we are a nation of voracious borrowers because of our voracious demand for consumer goods and voracious government spending, and none of this is good news.

CARN comes from the Latin *carn-*, the stem of *caro,* "flesh," and words including this root usually refer to flesh in some form. The word *carnivore,* for example, which we met in the preceding section, means "an eater of meat."

---

carnage \ˈkär-nij\ Great destruction of life (as in a battle); slaughter.

• People from around the world made appeals to parties on all sides of the conflict to stop the carnage of the war in Bosnia.

Carnage does not refer only to slaughter on the battlefield. As long as tens of thousands of people die each year in automobile accidents, it is appropriate to speak of carnage on the nation's highways. And in some contexts *carnage* can simply mean violence or its results. Those concerned about the effect of all of the violence we are exposed to each day point in particular to the carnage on television and in the movies.

carnal \'kär-nəl\ Having to do with bodily pleasures.

• The news stories about students going on Spring Break focused as usual on the carnal pleasures associated with the annual ritual.

Carnal is sometimes used to mean "having to do with the human body," but more often it refers solely to the pleasures and appetites of the body. Most religions stress the superiority of spiritual enlightenment over carnal pleasures. Very frequently, *carnal* simply means "sexual," especially when the sexual activity is mostly physical in nature. Novels about Hollywood often rely heavily on detailed descriptions of the carnal adventures of their main characters.

carnival \'kär-nə-vəl\ (1) A season of merrymaking just before Lent; an occasion for festivities and excess. (2) A traveling group that presents a variety of amusements.

• Whether in Argentina, Brazil, or Trinidad, carnival is one of the most exciting events of the year, involving parades, parties, and dressing up in costume.

Just before Lent many cities hold a time of merrymaking called a carnival. The roots that apparently make up *carnival* mean "flesh" and "remove," and a common result of carnival was the eating up of meat that wouldn't keep through the 40-day season of Lent, a time of fasting and self-discipline when meat was indeed removed from the table. In the Americas, carnival is most famous in Rio de Janeiro and New Orleans (whose version of carnival is called Mardi Gras), but carnival takes place in most parts of the world where Lent is observed.

incarnation \ˌin-kär-ˈnā-shən\ (1) A particular physical form or version of something. (2) A person showing a trait to a marked degree.

• During the Gulf War, press reports depicted Saddam Hussein as the incarnation of evil.

Incarnation originally referred to gods and deities taking on fleshly form, but now it more commonly refers to anything in the physical world that clearly illustrates some principle. The crowded streets of Hong Kong are said to be the incarnation of business and commerce. Sometimes *incarnation* can simply mean "a version" or "a form or state." An old building, for instance, can pass through several incarnations—as first an inn, then a private home, and then a store—before being returned to its original purpose.

Quizzes

A. Indicate whether the following pairs have the same or different meanings:

1. carnage / slaughter same __ / different __
2. omnivorous / grazing same __ / different __
3. incarnation / burial same __ / different __
4. voracious / extremely hungry same __ / different __
5. carnal / spiritual same __ / different __
6. herbivorous / vegetarian same __ / different __
7. carnival / Lent same __ / different __
8. carnivorous / meat-eating same __ / different __

B. Fill in each blank with the correct letter:

a. incarnation
b. omnivorous
c. carnage
d. carnivorous
e. voracious
f. herbivorous
g. carnal
h. carnival

1. Sheep, cattle, and antelope are ____; unlike dogs and cats, they show no interest in meat.
2. The school tried to shield students from ____ temptations.
3. It took an hour and several full picnic baskets to satisfy the bear's ____ appetite.

4. My sister and I rode the Ferris wheel every night the ____ was in town.
5. From the variety of books on his shelves, we could tell he was an ____ reader.
6. Even the ambulance drivers were horrified by the ____ of the accident.
7. As a child she loved to watch them throw meat to the ____ ones, especially the lions and tigers.
8. In Greek mythology the ____ of Zeus could be in the form of a bull or a swan or golden rain as well as a human.

CRED comes from *credere,* the Latin verb meaning "to believe." If something is *credible* it is believable, and if it is *incredible* it is almost unbelievable. We have a good *credit* rating when institutions believe in our ability to repay a loan, and we carry *credentials* so that others will believe we are who we say we are.

---

credence \'krē-dəns\ Mental acceptance of something as true or real; belief.

• He scoffed and said that no one still gives any credence to the story of the Loch Ness monster.

Credence is close in meaning to *belief,* but there are differences. Unlike *belief, credence* is seldom used in connection with faith in a religion or philosophy. Instead *credence* is often used in reference to reports, rumors, and opinions. Claims that a political candidate can become the next President gain credence only after the candidate wins a few primaries. Stories about Elvis sightings persist, but they lack credence for most people.

creditable \'kre-di-tə-bəl\ Worthy of praise.

• Even though the young team did not win the tournament, they turned in a creditable performance in the playoffs.

A creditable performance is one that makes us believe in the worth or value of the performer. A creditable effort, a creditable first novel, or a creditable new restaurant are all worthy of praise. Don't let the similarity in spelling fool you: *creditable* does not mean the same thing as *credible*.

credulity \kri-'dü-lə-tē\ Readiness and willingness to believe on the basis of little evidence.

• Thrillers and action movies only succeed if they don't strain our credulity too much.

Credulity most often appears in the phrase "to strain credulity," but a particularly far-fetched story may also be said to stretch credulity or to put demands on or make claims on our credulity. Credulity is not always a bad thing. There is no limit to the credulity of Boston and Chicago baseball fans, for example, and that probably makes life bearable for them. The related adjective is *credulous*. F. Scott Fitzgerald once defined advertising as "making dubious promises to a credulous public"—that is, a naive or gullible public.

creed \'krēd\ (1) A statement of the basic beliefs of a religious faith. (2) A set of guiding principles or beliefs.

• She had made her money on Wall Street by following the simple creed: Buy low, sell high.

We get the word *creed* from the Latin *credo*, "I believe," which is the first word of many religious creeds, such as the Apostles' Creed and the Nicene Creed. *Creed* can refer both to the statement of beliefs of a religion and to the religion itself; hence our common phrase "regardless of race, creed, or color." It can also be applied to any guiding principles. Reducing the size of company workforces—making companies "lean and mean"—has become the central creed for many corporate executives.

FID comes from *fides*, the Latin word for faith. *Fidelity* is another word for "faithfulness." *Confidence* is having faith in someone or something. And an *infidel* is someone who lacks a particular kind of religious faith.

---

affidavit \ˌa-fə-'dā-vət\ A sworn statement made in writing.

• Each member of the family had signed an affidavit stating that he or she believed the will to be valid.

In Latin *affidavit* means "he or she has sworn an oath," and affidavits are always sworn written documents. During the McCarthy era in the 1950s, many people were forced to make affidavits in which they swore that they were not members of the Communist party. Affidavits are usually made without an opposing lawyer being present. When police officers file an affidavit to get a search warrant, they don't inform anyone except the judge of their intent. In this respect, affidavits are different from depositions, which are made with attorneys for both parties present and able to ask questions.

diffident \'di-fə-dənt\ (1) Lacking confidence; timid. (2) Cautious or unassertive.

• The teacher tried to encourage even the most diffident students to make a try at public speaking.

Diffident means lacking faith in oneself. It often refers to a distrust in one's abilities or opinions that leads to hesitation in acting or speaking. For example, many patients feel diffident around their doctors and don't dare ask them many questions. A helpful friend tries to instill confidence in place of *diffidence*.

fiduciary \fi-'dü-shē-ˌer-ē\ (1) Having to do with a confidence or trust. (2) Held in trust for another.

• Managers of pension funds have a fiduciary responsibility to invest funds for the sole and exclusive benefit of those who will receive the pensions.

A fiduciary relationship is one in which one person places faith in another. Stockbrokers and real-estate agents have fiduciary duties to their clients, which means that they must act in the clients' best financial interests. Similarly, members of a company's board of directors have a fiduciary responsibility to protect the financial interests of shareholders. There are legal requirements for those with fiduciary responsibility, and they can be sued for breach of fiduciary duty if they fail in their responsibilities.

perfidy \'pər-fə-dē\ Faithlessness, disloyalty, or treachery.

• While working for the CIA he became a double agent for another country, and it seems he paid a high price for his perfidy.

The Latin phrase *per fidem decipere,* meaning "to betray the trust of," may have been the original source of *perfidus,* from which *perfidy* comes. The most famously *perfidious* figure in U.S. history is probably Benedict Arnold, the American army officer in the Revolutionary War who plotted with the British to surrender West Point to them—an act that made his name an epithet for traitor.

Quizzes

A. Fill in each blank with the correct letter:

a. perfidy
b. creditable
c. diffident
d. credulity
e. creed
f. affidavit
g. fiduciary
h. credence

1. She gave little ____ to his story about his deranged girlfriend and the kitchen knife.
2. This is a ____ piece of work, one of the best reports I've received this year.
3. For her own best friend to take up with her former husband was ____ that could never be forgiven.
4. He's so ____ that you'd never believe he gives talks in front of international organizations.
5. The family trust had been so badly mismanaged that it appeared there had been a violation of ____ responsibility.
6. Their longtime ____ had been one of respect for the environment and all animal life.
7. The ____ stated that no oral agreement had ever been made.
8. Her ____ is enormous; no story in the supermarket tabloids is too far-fetched for her.

B. Match the definition on the left to the correct word on the right:

1. bad faith
2. timid
3. acceptance

a. perfidy
b. creditable
c. diffident

4.	trust-based	d.	credulity
5.	sworn document	e.	creed
6.	well-done	f.	affidavit
7.	principles	g.	fiduciary
8.	trustfulness	h.	credence

CURR/CURS comes from *currere,* the Latin verb meaning "to run." Although the sense of speed may be lacking from words based on this root, the sense of movement remains. *Current,* for instance, refers to running water in a stream or river. And an *excursion* is a trip from one place to another.

concurrent \kən-ˈkər-ənt\ Happening or operating at the same time.

• The convicted killer was sentenced to serve three concurrent life terms in prison.

Things that are concurrent usually not only happen at the same time but also are similar to each other. So, for example, multitasking computers are capable of performing concurrent tasks. When we take more than one medication at a time, we run the risks involved with concurrent drug use. And most movie theaters today run several movies concurrently.

cursory \ˈkər-sə-rē\ Hastily and often carelessly done.

• Having spent the weekend going to parties, she was only able to give the chapter a cursory reading before class on Monday.

Unlike the other words in this section, *cursory* always implies speed but also stresses a lack of attention to detail. When citizens complain about a cursory police investigation of a crime, they are distressed by its lack of thoroughness, not its speed. Cursory observations are made quickly, but more importantly they are probably shallow or superficial.

discursive \dis-ˈkər-siv\ Passing from one topic to another.

• Some days he allowed himself to write long discursive essays in his diary instead of his usual simple reporting of the day's events.

The Latin verb *discurrere* meant "to run about," and from this word we get our word *discursive,* which often means rambling about over a wide range of topics. A discursive writing style is generally not encouraged by writing teachers. But some of the great writers of the 19th century, such as Charles Lamb and Thomas de Quincey, have shown that the discursive essay, especially when gracefully written and somewhat personal in tone, can be a pleasure to read.

precursor \'prē-ˌkər-sər\ One that goes before and indicates the coming of another.

• Scientists are trying to identify special geological activity that may be a precursor to an earthquake, which will help them predict the quake's size, time, and location.

A precursor is literally a "forerunner," but the two words function a little differently. A forerunner may simply come before another thing, but a precursor generally paves the way for something. The Office of Strategic Services in World War II was the precursor of today's Central Intelligence Agency. The blues music of the 1930s and 1940s was a precursor to the rock and roll of today. The war in Bosnia could be a precursor to more armed conflict in Eastern Europe and the former Soviet Union.

PED comes from the Latin *ped-,* the stem of *pes,* meaning "foot," which is related to the Greek *pod-* and *pous,* with the same meaning. From *ped-* we get *pedicure,* "care of the feet, toes, and toenails." From *pod-* we get *podiatrist,* "a foot doctor."

---

expedient \ik-'spē-dē-ənt\ Suitable for bringing about a desired result, often without regard for what is fair or right.

• Reporters suggested that it would be politically expedient to nominate a vice-presidential candidate from a state with a large number of electoral votes.

Expedient comes from the Latin verb *expedire,* meaning "to prepare" or "to be useful"—perhaps because the best way to prepare for something is to get your feet moving. *Expedient* can simply mean "desirable" or "advantageous." For instance, it is often more expedient to take the train to New York than to drive and try to find a parking place. However, *expedient* often indicates placing self-interest ahead of moral concerns. As a company faces more and more lawsuits over its defective products, for example, it may realize that the expedient solution is to declare bankruptcy.

expedite \'ek-spə-ˌdīt\ To speed up the process or progress of.

• The sales department was looking for ways to expedite the shipping and billing of incoming orders.

Expedite comes from the same Latin verb as *expedient*, but *expedite* usually indicates only speed or efficiency and doesn't involve moral issues at all. Many people concerned about health-care issues, for example, have campaigned to get the FDA to expedite its approval of new drugs. And new kinds of educational software are expected to expedite the learning process.

impediment \im-'pe-də-mənt\ Something that interferes with movement or progress.

• Her poorly developed verbal ability was the most serious impediment to her advancement.

Impediment comes from a Latin verb that meant "to interfere with" or "to get in the way of progress"—perhaps by catching one's feet. In English, *impediment* still suggests an obstruction or obstacle along a path; for example, a lack of adequate roads and bridges is an impediment to economic development. Impediments usually get in the way of something we want. We speak of an impediment to communication, marriage, or progress, but something that slows the progress of aging, disease, or decay isn't usually called an impediment.

pedestrian \pə-'des-trē-ən\ Commonplace, ordinary, or unimaginative.

• While politicians endlessly discussed the great issues facing Russia, the Russians worried about such pedestrian concerns as finding enough food, shelter, and clothing.

A *pedestrian* is, of course, someone who travels on foot. But the sense of this word as defined above is actually its original meaning. To be pedestrian was to be drab or dull, as if plodding along on foot rather than speeding on horseback or by coach. *Pedestrian* is often used to describe a writing style that is colorless or lifeless, but it can also describe politicians, public tastes, and personal qualities and possessions. In comparison with the elaborate stage shows put on by today's rock artists, for instance, most of the stage antics of the rock stars of the 1960s seem pedestrian.

Quizzes

A. Fill in each blank with the correct letter:

a. concurrent
b. expedite
c. precursor
d. pedestrian
e. cursory
f. impediment
g. discursive
h. expedient

1. The warm days in March were a ____ to spring floods that were sure to come.
2. They hoped the new computer system would ____ the delivery of supplies.
3. After only a ____ look at the new car, he knew he had to have it.
4. The presence of her little sister was a definite ____ to her romantic plans for the evening.
5. She came to enjoy the ____ style of the older, rambling essays.
6. Putting the blame on others for her mistakes was the ____ solution, but it enraged her coworkers.
7. Convention-goers had to decide which of the ____ meetings to attend.
8. His sister's trips to Borneo made his vacations at the seashore seem ____.

B. Match the definition on the left to the correct word on the right:

1. simultaneous
2. obstacle
3. hasty
4. forerunner
5. convenient

a. impediment
b. precursor
c. expedient
d. discursive
e. pedestrian

6.	speed up	f.	expedite
7.	rambling	g.	cursory
8.	ordinary	h.	concurrent

FLECT/FLEX comes from *flectere,* the Latin verb meaning "to bend." Things that are *flexible* can be bent. When light is *reflected,* it is bent and bounces back to us.

deflect \di-ˈflekt\ To turn aside, especially from a straight or fixed course.

• The stealth technology used on some of our bombers and fighter planes works by deflecting radar energy.

The physical meaning of *deflect* is frequently used. Thus, residents along rivers will build levees to deflect flood waters away from their homes, and workers wear eye shields to deflect tiny particles flying out of machines. But the nonphysical meaning is also common. Politicians make highly publicized trips to deflect attention from scandals or a terrible economy. Celebrities make a show of giving to charity to deflect resentment over the amount of money they make. And we all have tried to change the subject to deflect questions we really didn't want to answer.

flexor \ˈflek-ˌsȯr\ A muscle that bends a part of the body, such as an arm or a leg.

• Her fitness instructor told her she could improve her posture by strengthening her hip flexors.

Flexors are any muscles that act to bend a part of the body, from neck to baby toe and all the *flexible* parts in between. Each flexor is paired with an *extensor* that acts to straighten the part after it is bent. Though you'll encounter *flexor* in reading about health and fitness, it is mostly a technical term. For instance, the names for the flexors that move the little toe (it takes three) are *flexor digiti minimi brevis, flexor digitorum brevis,* and *flexor digitorum longus.*

genuflect \ˈjen-yü-ˌflekt\ To kneel on one knee and then rise as an act of respect.

• Pilgrims in China not only genuflect before religious shrines but also may lay themselves flat on the ground and light incense as well.

Genuflection, which contains the root *genu-*, "knee," has long been a mark of respect and obedience. King Arthur's Knights of the Round Table genuflected not only when he knighted them but whenever they greeted him formally. This custom remains in countries today that are still ruled by royalty, and in some churches each worshiper is expected to genuflect whenever entering or leaving a pew on the central aisle. By genuflecting you show loyalty to a human or god and admit your duty to obey his or her orders.

inflection \in-ˈflek-shən\ A change in the pitch, tone, or loudness of the voice.

• She couldn't understand her grandfather's words, but she knew from his inflection that he was asking a question.

Changing the pitch, tone, or loudness of our words are ways we communicate meaning in speech, though not on the printed page. A rising inflection on the last syllable of a sentence generally indicates a question and a falling inflection indicates a statement, for example. Another way of *inflecting* words is by adding endings. We add *-s* to make nouns plural and *-ed* to put verbs in the past tense, and these changes are also referred to as inflections.

POST comes from a Latin word meaning "after" or "behind." A *postscript* is a note that comes after an otherwise completed letter, usually as an afterthought. *Postpartum* refers to the period following childbirth and all of its related events and complications. To *postdate* a check is to give it a date after the day when it was written.

---

posterior \pō-ˈstir-ē-ər\ Situated toward or on the back; rear.

• One of the goals of his fitness program was to reduce the dimensions of the posterior parts of his anatomy.

Posterior comes from the Latin word *posterus*, meaning "coming after." *Posterior* is often used as a technical term in biology and medicine to refer to the back side of things. It is the opposite of *anterior,* which refers to the front side. For example, as more people took up running as a sport, doctors began to see an increase in stress fractures along the posterior as well as the anterior surface of the lower leg bones. When used as a noun, *posterior* simply means "buttocks."

posthumous \'päs-chə-məs\ (1) Published after the death of the author. (2) Following or happening after one's death.

• Vincent Van Gogh's rise to posthumous fame as one of the world's great artists came despite the fact that he scarcely sold a single painting during his lifetime.

Posthumous fame is fame that comes a little late, since the meaning of *posthumous* in Latin is "late born." In fact, its original meaning in English is "born after the death of the father." Bill Clinton is the posthumous son of a father who died in an automobile accident. The word is now mostly used of artistic works that appear after the death of the artist. From the poetry of Emily Dickinson to the diary of Anne Frank, posthumous works have often become legendary.

postmodern \ˌpōst-'mä-dərn\ Having to do with a movement in art, architecture, or literature that is a reaction against modernism and that calls for the reintroduction of traditional elements and techniques as well as elements from popular culture.

• The postmodern AT&T building in New York, with its "Chippendale" top that makes it look a little like an antique dresser, aroused a storm of criticism.

Although *postmodern* literally translates as "after modern" and would therefore seem likely to mean "ultramodern," it usually really means "antimodern." In the 1970s architects began to be dissatisfied with the stark simplicity of most modern architecture and began to include in their designs traditional elements such as columns, arches, and keystones, and also startling color contrasts such as might have come from advertising and pop culture. Similar developments took place in literature, and there too the movement has been greeted with a mixture of approval, disapproval, and sometimes amusement.

postmortem \ˌpōst-'mȯr-təm\ (1) Occurring after death. (2) Following the event.

• In their postmortem discussion of the election, the reporters tried to explain how the polls and predictions could have been so completely wrong.

Post mortem is Latin for "after death." In English, *postmortem* refers to an examination, investigation, or process that takes place after death. Postmortem examinations of bodies are often needed to determine the time and cause of death; rigor mortis, the temporary stiffening of muscles after death, is one postmortem change that doctors look at to determine time of death. We have come to use *postmortem* to refer to any examination or discussion that takes place after an event.

Quizzes

A. Choose the closest definition:

1. posthumous a. before the event b. born prematurely c. occurring after death d. early in development
2. flexor a. radar detector b. muscle c. sunscreen d. bone
3. posterior a. on the front b. on the back c. underneath d. on top
4. deflect a. fold over b. kneel c. turn aside d. protect
5. postmodern a. ultramodern b. traditional c. contemporary d. using past styles
6. inflection a. style in art b. change in pitch c. muscle d. part to the rear
7. genuflect a. kneel b. flex a muscle c. fold back d. change one's tone of voice
8. postmortem a. after the event b. before the event c. caused by the event d. causing the event

B. Complete the analogy:

1. postscript : letter :: postmortem : ____ a. examination b. death c. body d. morgue
2. flexor : extensor :: bend : ____ a. fold b. twist c. straighten d. break
3. prenatal : before birth :: posthumous : ____ a. after birth b. before life c. after death d. famous
4. deflect : shield :: reflect : ____ a. shield b. laser c. metal d. mirror

5. inflection : tone of voice :: hue : ____
   a. cry b. color c. tone d. rainbow
6. genuflect : obedience :: wave : ____
   a. friendship b. respect c. awe d. power
7. inferior : better :: posterior : ____
   a. in front b. behind c. beside d. above
8. abstract : painting :: postmodern : ____
   a. tradition b. design c. style d. architecture

Words from Mythology

calypso \kə-'lip-sō\ A folk song or style of singing of West Indian origin that has a lively rhythm and words that are often made up by the singer.

• If you take a Caribbean vacation in December you end up listening to a lot of Christmas carols played to a calypso beat.

In Homer's *Odyssey,* the nymph Calypso detains Odysseus for seven years on his way home from the Trojan War. She uses all her wiles to hold him on her lush, hidden island, but he still longs for home. The calypso music of the West Indian islands has the same captivating, bewitching power as the nymph. The lyrics that are often improvised to the melodies, however, often make fun of local people and happenings. Calypso may not have been the original name for this music; it may instead have simply replaced a similar-sounding native Caribbean word.

odyssey \'ä-də-sē\ (1) A long, wandering journey full of trials and adventures. (2) A spiritual journey or quest.

• Their six-month camping trip around the country was an odyssey they would always remember.

Odysseus, the hero of Homer's *Odyssey,* spends 20 years traveling home from the Trojan War. He has astonishing adventures and learns a great deal about himself and the world; he even descends to the underworld to talk to the dead. Thus, an odyssey is any long, complicated journey, often a quest for a goal, and may be a spiritual or psychological journey as well as an actual voyage.

palladium \pə-'lā-dē-əm\ A precious, silver-white metal related to platinum that is used in electrical contacts and as an alloy with gold to form white gold.

• Most wedding rings today are simple bands of gold, platinum, or palladium.

Pallas Athena was one of the poetical names given to the Greek goddess Athena, although it is no longer clear what *Pallas* was supposed to mean. When an asteroid belt was discovered between Mars and Jupiter, most of the asteroids were named after figures in Greek mythology, and one of the first to be discovered was named Pallas, in 1803. In the same year, scientists first isolated the element palladium, and they named the new element in honor of the recently discovered asteroid.

Penelope \pə-ˈne-lə-pē\ A modest domestic wife.

• Critics of Hillary Rodham Clinton would perhaps have preferred her to be a Penelope, quietly keeping house and staying out of politics.

In the *Odyssey,* Penelope waits 20 long years for her husband Odysseus to return from Troy. During that time, she must raise their son and fend off the attentions of numerous rough suitors. She preserves herself for a long time by saying that she cannot remarry until she has finished weaving a funeral shroud for her aging father-in-law; however, what she weaves each day she secretly unravels each night. A Penelope, thus, appears to be the perfect, patient, faithful wife, and she uses her clever intelligence to keep herself that way.

procrustean \prō-ˈkrəs-tē-ən\ Ruthlessly disregarding individual differences or special circumstances.

• The school's procrustean approach to education seemed to assume that all children learned in the same way and at the same rate.

Procrustes was a bandit in the Greek tale of the hero Theseus. He ambushed travelers and, after robbing them, made them lie on an iron bed. He would make sure they fit this procrustean bed by cutting off the parts that hung off the ends or stretching those that were too short. Either way, they died. Something procrustean, therefore, takes no account of individual differences but cruelly and mercilessly makes everything the same.

protean \'prō-tē-ən\ (1) Displaying great versatility or variety. (2) Able to take on many different forms or natures.

• He was attempting to become the protean athlete, with contracts to play professional baseball, football, and basketball.

Proteus was the figure in the *Odyssey* who revealed to Menelaus how to get home to Sparta with the notorious Helen of Troy. Before he would give up the information, though, Menelaus had to capture him—no mean feat, since he had the ability to change into any natural shape he chose. The word *protean* came to describe this ability to change into many different shapes or to play many different roles in quick succession.

sibyl \'si-bəl\ A female prophet or fortune-teller.

• Her mother treated her as if she were the family sibyl, able to predict what fate was about to befall her sisters.

The sibyls were ancient prophetesses who lived in Babylonia, Greece, Italy, and Egypt. The most famous was the Sibyl of Cumae in Italy, a withered crone who lived in a cave. Her prophecies were collected into twelve books, three of which survived to be consulted by the Romans in times of national emergencies. Whether or not she was the first sibyl, her name or title became the term for all such prophets.

siren \'sī-rən\ A woman who tempts men with bewitching sweetness.

• Reporters treated her like a sex symbol, but she lacked the graceful presence and air of mystery of a real siren.

The sirens were a group of partly human female creatures in Greek mythology that lured sailors onto destructive rocks with their singing. Odysseus and his men encountered the sirens after leaving Troy. The only way to sail by them safely was to make oneself deaf to their enchanting song, so Odysseus packed the men's ears with wax. But he himself, ever curious, wanted to hear, so he had himself tied to the mast to keep from flinging himself into the water or steering his ship toward sure destruction. A siren today is almost always a woman, though she need not sing or cause shipwrecks. But a *siren song* may be any appeal that lures a person to act against his or her better judgment.

Quiz

Fill in each blank with the correct letter:

a. odyssey
b. calypso
c. Penelope
d. palladium
e. sibyl
f. procrustean
g. siren
h. protean

1. They danced and sang to the rhythm of the ____ music long into the night.
2. While he was away on maneuvers, his wife stayed loyally at home like a true ____.
3. He took a ____ attitude toward the needs of his employees, enforcing a single set of work rules for everyone.
4. On their four-month ____ they visited most of the major cities of Asia.
5. The wedding rings were white gold, a mixture of gold and ____.
6. She won her reputation as the office ____ after her third successful prediction of who would get married next.
7. Actors like Robin Williams seem ____ in their ability to assume different characters.
8. In her fatigued state, sleep's ____ song lured her from her duties.

Review Quizzes

A. Choose the closest definition:

1. carnival a. festival b. feast c. funeral d. frenzy
2. precursor a. shadow b. forerunner c. follower d. oath
3. diffident a. angry b. different c. aggressive d. shy
4. pedestrian a. useless b. footlike c. unusual d. boring
5. credence a. creation b. belief c. doubt d. destruction
6. creditable a. believable b. acceptable c. praiseworthy d. incredible
7. expedite a. speed up b. bounce off c. slow down d. absorb

8. impediment a. help b. obstacle c. footpath
   d. obligation
9. voracious a. vast b. hungry c. fierce
   d. unsatisfied
10. protean a. meaty b. powerful c. changeable
   d. professional

B. Indicate whether the following pairs of words have the same or different meanings:

1. procrustean / merciful same __ / different __
2. credulity / distrust same __ / different __
3. concurrent / simultaneous same __ / different __
4. flexor / straightener same __ / different __
5. odyssey / journey same __ / different __
6. deflect / absorb same __ / different __
7. perfidy / betrayal same __ / different __
8. posterior / front same __ / different __
9. siren / temptress same __ / different __
10. herbivorous / plant-eating same __ / different __

C. Complete the analogy:

1. fiduciary : trustworthy :: carnivorous : ____
   a. vegetarian b. meat-eating c. greedy d. hungry
2. cursory : brief :: carnal : ____
   a. musical b. festive c. deadly d. sexual
3. genuflect : kneel :: affidavit : ____
   a. financial affairs b. courtroom testimony c. legal advice d. sworn statement
4. sibyl : future :: creed : ____
   a. belief b. music c. attraction d. qualification
5. carnage : death :: Penelope : ____
   a. wife b. mother c. daughter d. siren
6. palladium : metal :: surgeon : ____
   a. farmer b. veterinarian c. doctor d. lawyer
7. expedient : effective :: discursive : ____
   a. fast b. slow-moving c. wide-ranging d. all-knowing
8. procrustean : inflexible :: inflection : ____
   a. way of life b. tone of voice c. financial affairs
   d. part of speech

Unit 5

MAL as a combining form means "bad." *Malpractice* is bad medical practice. A *malady* is a bad condition—a disease or illness—of the body or mind. *Malodorous* things smell bad. And a *malefactor* is someone guilty of bad deeds.

malevolent \mə-'le-və-lənt\ Having or showing intense ill will or hatred.

• Captain Ahab sees Moby Dick not simply as a whale but as a malevolent, evil foe.

Malevolence runs deep. Malevolent enemies have bitter and lasting feelings of ill will. Malevolent racism and bigotry can erupt in acts of violence against innocent people. Malevolence can also show itself in hurtful words, and sometimes it can be seen in something as small as an angry look or gesture.

malicious \mə-'li-shəs\ Desiring to cause pain, injury, or distress to another.

• The boys didn't take the apples with any malicious intent; they were just hungry and didn't know any better.

Malicious and *malevolent* are closely related. Both refer to ill will that shows itself in a desire to see someone else suffer. While *malevolent* suggests deep and lasting dislike, however, *malicious* usually means petty and spiteful. Malicious gossipers may be simply envious of their neighbor's good fortune. Vandals take malicious pleasure in destroying and defacing property.

malign \mə-'līn\ To make harsh and often false or misleading statements about.

• Captain Bligh of the *Bounty* may be one of the most unjustly maligned figures in British naval history.

Malign is related to words like *defame, slander,* and *libel.* It implies that the person or group being maligned is the victim of false or misleading statements, but not necessarily that the *maligner* is guilty of deliberate lying. Something that is frequently criticized is often said to be "much maligned," which suggests that the criticism is not entirely fair or deserved.

malnourished \ˌmal-ˈnər-isht\ Badly or poorly nourished.

• When they finally found the children in the locked cabin, they were pale and malnourished but unharmed.

Malnourished people can be found in all types of societies. Famine and poverty are only two of the common causes of *malnutrition.* In more affluent societies, it is often the result of poor eating habits. Any diet that fails to provide the nutrients needed for health and growth can lead to malnutrition, and some of the malnourished are actually fat.

CATA comes from the Greek *kata,* one of whose meanings was "down." A *catalogue* is a list of items put down on paper. A *catapult* is an ancient military weapon for hurling missiles down on one's enemies.

---

cataclysm \ˈka-tə-ˌkli-zəm\ (1) A violent and massive change of the earth's surface. (2) A momentous event that results in great upheaval and often destruction.

• World War I was a great cataclysm in modern history, marking the end of the old European social and political order.

A cataclysm causes great and lasting changes. An earthquake or other natural disaster that changes the landscape is one kind of cataclysm. We might also speak of the *cataclysmic* changes brought about by a political revolution. Even a new discovery or invention can be seen as cataclysmic if it brings great changes in how people think or work.

catacomb \'ka-tə-ˌkōm\ An underground cemetery of connecting passageways with recesses for tombs.

• The early Christian catacombs of Rome provide a striking glimpse into the ancient past for modern-day visitors.

About forty Christian catacombs have been found near the roads that once led into Rome. After the decline of the Roman empire these cemeteries were forgotten, not to be rediscovered until 1578. *Catacomb* has come to refer to different kinds of underground chambers and passageways. The catacombs of Paris are abandoned stone quarries that were not used for burials until 1787.

catalyst \'ka-tə-list\ (1) A substance that speeds up a chemical reaction or lets it take place under different conditions. (2) Someone or something that brings about or speeds significant change or action.

• The assassination of Archduke Ferdinand in Sarajevo in 1914 acted as the catalyst for World War I.

Although the Great Depression was a difficult and tragic period in this country, it served as the catalyst for many important social reforms. The Social Security Act of 1935 helped provide security for retired workers; it in turn became the catalyst for a number of laws concerning disabled and unemployed workers, health insurance, on-the-job safety, and dependents of deceased workers. The Depression was also the catalyst of many public-works projects, which were designed to put the unemployed back to work.

catatonic \ˌka-tə-'tä-nik\ (1) Relating to or suffering from a form of schizophrenia. (2) Showing an unusual lack of movement, activity, or expression.

• The audience sat in a catatonic stupor while the speaker droned on about the importance of a good vocabulary.

Catatonia is a form of the terrible mental disease known as schizophrenia. A common symptom is extreme muscular rigidity, so that catatonic patients may be "frozen" for hours or even days in a single position. In general use, *catatonic* most often describes people who are not ill but who likewise seem incapable of moving or of changing expression.

Quizzes

A. Choose the closest definition:

1. malevolent a. wishing evil b. wishing well c. blowing violently d. badly done
2. cataclysm a. loud applause b. feline behavior c. natural disaster d. inspiration
3. malign a. speak well of b. speak to c. speak ill of d. speak of repeatedly
4. catacomb a. underground road b. underground cemetery c. underground spring d. underground treasure
5. malicious a. vague b. explosive c. confusing d. mean
6. catatonic a. refreshing b. slow c. motionless d. boring
7. malnourished a. fed frequently b. fed poorly c. fed excessively d. fed occasionally
8. catalyst a. literary agent b. insurance agent c. cleaning agent d. agent of change

B. Indicate whether the following pairs of words have the same or different meanings:

1. catacomb / catastrophe same __ / different __
2. malnourished / overfed same __ / different __
3. cataclysm / disaster same __ / different __
4. malign / slander same __ / different __
5. catatonic / paralyzed same __ / different __
6. catalyst / cemetery same __ / different __
7. malicious / nasty same __ / different __
8. malevolent / pleasant same __ / different __

PROT/PROTO comes from Greek and has the basic meaning "first in time" or "first formed." *Protozoa* are one-celled animals, such as amoebas and paramecia, that are among the most basic members of the biological kingdom. A *proton* is an elementary particle that, along with neutrons, can be found in all atomic nuclei. A *protoplanet* is a whirling mass that is believed to give rise to a planet.

protagonist \prō-ˈta-gə-nist\ The main character in a literary work.

• Macbeth is the ruthlessly ambitious protagonist of Shakespeare's play, but it is his wife who pulls the strings.

Struggle, or conflict, is central to drama. The protagonist or hero of a play is involved in a struggle, either against someone or something else or even against his or her own emotions. So the hero is the "first struggler," which is the literal meaning of the Greek word *prōtagōnistēs*. A character who opposes the hero is the *antagonist,* from a Greek verb that means literally "to struggle against."

protocol \ˈprō-tə-ˌkȯl\ (1) An original copy or record of a document. (2) A code of diplomatic or military rules of behavior.

• The guests at the governor's dinner were introduced and seated according to the strict protocol governing such occasions.

Protocol comes from a Greek word that refers to the first sheet of a papyrus roll. As an English word, *protocol* originally meant "a first draft or record," after which it came to mean specifically the first draft of a diplomatic document, such as a treaty. The "diplomatic" connection led eventually to its current meaning of "rules of behavior." Someone wearing Bermuda shorts and sandals to a State dinner at the White House would not be acting "according to protocol." *Protocol* is also now used to refer to other kinds of rules, such as those for doing a scientific experiment or for handling computer data.

protoplasm \ˈprō-tō-ˌpla-zəm\ The substance that makes up the living parts of cells.

• Protoplasm is a mixture of organic and inorganic substances, such as protein and water, and is regarded as the physical basis of life.

The term *protoplasm* was first used with its present meaning in 1846 by Hugo von Mohl, a German professor of botany. After studying plant cells, he conceived the idea that the nucleus was surrounded by a jellylike material that formed the main substance of the cell. Von Mohl is also remembered for being the first to propose that new cells are formed by cell division.

prototype \'prō-tō-ˌtīp\ (1) An original model on which something is patterned. (2) A first, full-scale, usually working version of a new type or design.

• There was great excitement when, after years of top-secret development, the prototype of the new Stealth bomber first took to the skies.

A prototype is someone or something that serves as a model or inspiration. A successful fund-raising campaign can serve as a prototype for future campaigns. The legendary Robin Hood, the *prototypical* kindhearted, honorable outlaw, has been the inspiration for countless other romantic heroes. For over a century Vincent Van Gogh has been the prototype of the brilliant, tortured artist who is unappreciated in his own time.

ANTE is Latin for "before" or "in front of." *Antediluvian,* a word describing something very old or outdated, literally means "before the flood"—that is, the flood described in the Bible. *Antebellum* literally means "before the war," usually the American Civil War. *Antenatal* care is given during the period before birth.

---

antechamber \'an-ti-ˌchām-bər\ An outer room that leads to another and is often used as a waiting room.

• The antechamber to the lawyer's office was both elegant and comfortable, designed to inspire trust and confidence.

Antechamber suggests a room somewhat more formal than an *anteroom.* One expects to find an antechamber outside the private chambers of a Supreme Court Justice or leading into the great hall of a medieval castle. In the private end of the castle the lord's or lady's bedchamber would have its own antechamber, which served as a dressing room and sitting room, but could also house bodyguards if the castle came under siege.

antedate \'an-ti-ˌdāt\ (1) To date something (such as a check) with a date earlier than that of actual writing. (2) To precede in time.

• Nantucket Island has hundreds of beautifully preserved houses that antedate the Civil War.

Antedate is used when talking about things that can be given dates. Dinosaurs antedated the first human beings by about 65 million years, though this stubborn fact has never stopped cartoonists and moviemakers from having the two species inhabit the same story line. The oral use of a word often antedates its appearance in print by a number of years.

ante meridiem \ˌan-ti-mə-ˈri-dē-ˌem\ Before noon.

• On great ancient sundials the shadow crossed the central line at noon, dramatically marking the shift from ante meridiem to post meridiem.

Ante meridiem is almost always abbreviated as *a.m.* The term is spelled out only in the most formal contexts, such as laws and statutes. There is controversy about the use of *a.m.* and its counterpart *p.m.*, for *post meridiem,* when referring to twelve o'clock. Some people have argued that *12:00 a.m.* means midnight and *12:00 p.m.* means noon; others have insisted the opposite. There has never been any general agreement. If you want to avoid confusion, use *noon* or *midnight,* either alone or preceded by *12:00.*

anterior \an-ˈtir-ē-ər\ (1) Located before or toward the front or head. (2) Coming before in time or development.

• She joined the first-class passengers in the plane's anterior section and was delighted to recognize the governor in the next seat.

Anterior tends to appear in either technical or learned contexts. Anatomy books refer to the anterior lobe of the brain, the anterior cerebral artery, the anterior facial vein, etc. When used to refer to an earlier position in time or order, *anterior* is a somewhat formal word. Supporters of states' rights point out that the states enjoyed certain rights anterior to their joining the union. Prenuptial agreements are generally designed to protect the assets that one or both parties acquired anterior to the marriage.

Quizzes

A. Fill in each blank with the correct letter:

a. antedate
b. protoplasm
c. anterior
d. protagonist
e. prototype
f. ante meridiem
g. protocol
h. antechamber

1. The ____ of *The Wizard of Oz* is a Kansas farm girl named Dorothy.
2. According to official ____, the Ambassador from England precedes the Canadian Consul.
3. A butterfly's antennae are located on the most ____ part of its body.
4. There under the microscope we saw the cell's ____ in all its amazing complexity.
5. She was tempted to ____ the letter to make it seem that she had not forgotten to write it but only to mail it.
6. The engineers have promised to have the ____ of the new sedan finished by March.
7. Please step into the judge's ____; she'll be with you in a few minutes.
8. In Rome there were six "hours" ____ (that is, "before midday"), but the hours were shorter in winter than in summer.

B. Match the definition on the left to the correct word on the right:

1.	to date before	a.	protocol
2.	cell contents	b.	antechamber
3.	morning	c.	protagonist
4.	rules of behavior	d.	ante meridiem
5.	toward the front	e.	protoplasm
6.	model	f.	antedate
7.	waiting room	g.	prototype
8.	hero or heroine	h.	anterior

ORTH/ORTHO comes from *orthos,* the Greek word for "straight," "right," or "true." *Orthotics* is a branch of therapy that straightens out the stance or posture of the body by providing artificial support for weak joints or muscles. *Orthograde* animals, such as human beings, walk with their bodies in a "straight" or vertical position.

orthodontics \ˌȯr-thə-ˈdän-tiks\ A branch of dentistry that deals with the treatment and correction of crooked teeth and other irregularities.

• As much as she dreaded braces, Jennifer decided the time had come to consult a specialist in orthodontics.

Orthodontics of some kind has been practiced since ancient times, but the elaborate techniques and appliances familiar to us today were introduced only in the 20th century. Training to become an *orthodontist* usually consists of a two-year course following dental school. According to a 1939 text on dentistry, "Speech defects, psychiatric disturbances, personality changes, . . . all are correctable through *orthodontic* measures." Many adolescents, having endured the embarrassment of rubber bands breaking and even of entangling their braces while kissing, might disagree.

orthodox \ˈȯr-thə-ˌdäks\ (1) Holding established beliefs, especially in religion. (2) Conforming to established rules or traditions; conventional.

• The O'Briens remain orthodox Catholics, faithfully observing the time-honored rituals of their church.

An orthodox religious belief or interpretation is one handed down by the founders or leaders of a church. When capitalized, as in *Orthodox Judaism, Orthodox* refers to branches within larger religious organizations that claim to honor the religion's original or traditional beliefs. The steadfast holding of established beliefs that is seen in religious *orthodoxy* is apparent also in other kinds of orthodox behavior. Orthodox medical treatment, for example, follows the established practices of mainstream medicine.

orthopedics \ˌȯr-thə-ˈpē-diks\ The correction or prevention of deformities of the skeleton.

• The surgery to correct the child's spinal curvature was done by a leading specialist in orthopedics.

Just as an orthodontist corrects crookedness in the teeth, so does an *orthopedist* correct crookedness in the skeleton. The word *orthopedics* is formed in part from the Greek word for "child," and many *orthopedic* patients are in fact children. But adults also often have need for orthopedic therapy, as when suffering from a disease of the joints like arthritis or when recovering from a broken arm or leg.

orthography \or-'thä-grə-fē\ (1) The spelling of words according to standard usage. (2) The part of language study concerned with letters and spelling.

• George Washington and Thomas Jefferson—and at least one recent vice president—were deficient in the skill of orthography.

Even as recently as the 19th century, the orthography of the English language was still unsettled. Not until primers like "McGuffey's Readers" and dictionaries like Noah Webster's came along did uniform spelling become established. Before that, there was much *orthographic* variation, even among the more educated. Many people, of course, still have problems with spelling. They can take heart from the words of Mark Twain, who once remarked, "I don't give a damn for a man that can spell a word only one way."

RECT comes from the Latin word *rectus,* which means "straight" or "right." A *rectangle* is a four-sided figure whose parallel, straight sides meet at right angles. *Rectus,* short for Latin *rectus musculus,* may refer to any of several straight muscles, such as those of the abdomen. To *correct* something is to make it right.

---

rectitude \'rek-tə-ˌtüd\ (1) Moral integrity. (2) Correctness of procedure.

• The school superintendent wasn't popular, but no one could question her moral rectitude.

We associate straightness with honesty, so if we think someone is being misleading we might ask if they are being "straight" with us. A person whose rectitude is unquestionable is a person whose straightness, or honesty, is always apparent in his or her dealings with other people. Such a person might be called *rectitudinous,* although this uncommon adjective can also suggest an undesirable quality of self-righteousness.

rectify \'rek-tə-ˌfī\ (1) To set right; remedy. (2) To correct by removing errors; revise.

• You must try to rectify this unfortunate situation before anyone else gets hurt.

We rectify something by straightening it out or making it right. We might rectify an injustice by seeing to it that a wrongly accused person is cleared. An error in a financial record can be rectified by replacing an incorrect number with a correct one. If the error is in our tax return, the Internal Revenue Service will be happy to rectify it for us. We might then have to rectify the impression that we were trying to cheat on our taxes.

rectilinear \ˌrek-tə-ˈli-nē-ər\ (1) Moving in or forming a straight line. (2) Having many straight lines.

• After admiring Frank Lloyd Wright's highly rectilinear buildings for years, the public was astonished by the giant spiral of the Guggenheim Museum.

Rectilinear is a term used widely in physics. Rectilinear motion is motion in which the speed remains constant and the path is a straight line. Rectilinear rays, such as light rays, travel in a straight line. Rectilinear patterns or constructions are those in which straight lines are strikingly obvious. The trunks of trees in a forest form a strongly rectilinear pattern.

rector \ˈrek-tər\ (1) A clergyman in charge of a church or parish. (2) The head of a university or school.

• We asked the rector of our church to perform the marriage ceremony.

The fiery American preacher Jonathan Edwards began as rector of a church in Massachusetts. He was so convinced of his own ideas about *rectitude* and so harsh in condemning those who opposed him that he was eventually dismissed and turned out of the parish *rectory* where he lived. He spent his remaining years attempting to *rectify* the beliefs of Native Americans.

Quizzes

A. Choose the closest definition:

1. orthodox a. straight b. pier c. conventional d. waterfowl
2. rectify a. redo b. make right c. modify d. make longer
3. orthopedics a. foot surgery b. children's medicine c. medical dictionaries d. treatment of skeletal defects

4. rector a. warden b. headmaster c. direction d. effect
5. orthography a. correct color b. correct map c. correct direction d. correct spelling
6. rectitude a. roughness b. integrity c. certainty d. sameness
7. orthodontics a. dentistry for children b. dentistry for gums c. dentistry for crooked teeth d. dentistry for everyone
8. rectilinear a. moving in a straight line b. moving in a curved line c. moving at a 45° angle d. moving in a circle

B. Indicate whether the following pairs have the same or different meanings:

1. orthodox / crucial same __ / different __
2. rectitude / honesty same __ / different __
3. orthopedics / broken bones same __ / different __
4. rector / follower same __ / different __
5. orthography / architecture same __ / different __
6. rectilinear / straight same __ / different __
7. orthodontics / fixing of crooked teeth same __ / different __
8. rectify / damage same __ / different __

EU comes from the Greek word for "well"; in English words it can also mean "good" or "true." A person delivering a *eulogy* is full of good words, or praise, for the honoree. *Euthanasia* is regarded as a way of providing a hopelessly sick or injured person a "good" or easy death.

---

eugenic \yü-'je-nik\ (1) Relating to or fitted for the production of good offspring. (2) Relating to the science of improving the desirable traits of a race or breed through controlled breeding.

• Eugenic techniques have been part of cattle breeding for many years.

The word *eugenic* (like the name *Eugene*) was formed from the prefix *eu-* in combination with *-genes,* which in Greek means "born." Breeders of horses, cattle, and other animals hope that by using scientific, eugenic methods they can have better results, producing horses that run faster, for example, or cattle that provide more meat. Through *eugenics,* Guernsey cows have become one of the world's highest producers of milk. Earlier in this century there was much discussion of human eugenics, an idea that was taken up enthusiastically by the Nazis, with terrible consequences.

euphemism \'yü-fə-ˌmi-zəm\ (1) The use of an agreeable or inoffensive word or expression for one that may offend or disgust. (2) An expression used in this way.

• The Victorians, uncomfortable with the physical side of human existence, had euphemisms for most bodily functions.

Euphemism is an ancient part of the English language. While particular expressions come into and go out of vogue, the need for euphemism remains constant. *Golly* and *gosh* started out as euphemisms for *God,* and *darn* is a familiar euphemism for *damn. Shoot, shucks,* and *sugar* are all *euphemistic* substitutes for a well-known vulgar word. The standard household bathroom fixture has given rise to a host of euphemistic substitutes, including *convenience, head, john, potty, privy,* and *water closet.*

euphoria \yu̇-'fȯr-ē-ə\ A feeling of well-being or great elation.

• The whole city was swept up in the euphoria of a Super Bowl victory.

Euphoria describes a temporary, almost overpowering feeling of health or elation. In medical use, it normally refers to abnormal or inappropriate feelings, such as might be caused by a drug or by mental illness. But euphoria can also be natural and appropriate. When the home team wins the championship, or when we win enough money in the lottery to buy a fleet of yachts and several small Pacific islands, we have good reason to feel *euphoric.*

evangelism \i-'van-jə-ˌli-zəm\ (1) The enthusiastic preaching or proclamation of the Christian gospel. (2) Militant or crusading zeal.

• Their evangelism for the new program won many converts among those who had previously doubted its merits.

Evangelism comes from *euangelion,* the Greek word for "gospel" or "good news." The firm belief that they are bringing "good news" has traditionally filled Christian *evangelists* with fiery zeal. *Evangelism* can now refer to crusading zeal in behalf of any cause. The *evangelical* enthusiasm of some environmentalists has won over some segments of the general public while alienating others.

DYS comes from Greek, where it means "bad" or "difficult." As a prefix in English, it has the additional meanings "abnormal" and "impaired." *Dysphagia* is difficult or labored swallowing, and *dyspnea* is difficult or labored breathing. *Dysphasia,* which literally means "impaired speech," refers to a disorder in which the ability to use and understand language is seriously impaired as a result of injury to or disease of the brain.

---

dysfunctional \dis-ˈfəŋk-shə-nəl\ Operating or functioning in an impaired or abnormal way.

• His sisters constantly claimed that the family was dysfunctional, but he could never see it.

Neurologists speak of dysfunctional brain stems, and psychiatrists treat patients for dysfunctional sexual response. Political scientists wonder if the American two-party system has become dysfunctional, and sociologists point to the rising crime rate as evidence of a dysfunctional society. Nowadays *dysfunctional* more often describes families than anything else. In popular usage, any family with problems is likely to be characterized as dysfunctional.

dyslexia \dis-ˈlek-sē-ə\ A disturbance or interference with the ability to read or to use language.

• She managed to deal with her dyslexia through careful tutoring all throughout elementary school.

Dyslexia is a neurological disorder that usually affects people of average or superior intelligence. *Dyslexic* individuals have an impaired ability to recognize and process words and letters. Dyslexia usually shows itself in the tendency to read and write words and letters in reversed order. Sometimes similar reversals occur in the person's speech. Dyslexia has been shown to be treatable through lengthy instruction in proper reading techniques.

dyspeptic \dis-'pep-tik\ (1) Relating to or suffering from indigestion. (2) Having an irritable temperament; ill-humored.

• For decades the dyspeptic columnist served as the newspaper's—and the city's—resident grouch.

Dyspepsia comes from the Greek word for "bad digestion." Interestingly, the Greek verb *pessein* can mean either "to cook" or "to digest"; a lot of bad cooking has been responsible for a lot of dyspepsia. Dyspepsia can be caused by many diseases, but often dyspeptic individuals are the victims of their own habits and appetites. Worry, overeating, inadequate chewing, and excessive smoking and drinking can all bring on dyspepsia. Today we generally use *dyspeptic* to mean "irritable"—that is, in the kind of mood that could be produced by bad digestion.

dystrophy \'dis-trə-fē\ Any of several disorders involving nerves and muscles, especially a hereditary disease marked by a progressive wasting of muscles.

• In cases involving the most devastating type of muscular dystrophy, infections or respiratory failure can result in the victim's death before the age of 30.

Dystrophy in its original sense refers to a disorder brought about through faulty nutrition. (The *-trophy* element in *dystrophy* comes from the Greek word for "nutrition.") Today *dystrophy* most often refers to the progressive wasting away of the muscles that is known as *muscular dystrophy*. Actually, there are several types of muscular dystrophy, the most common of which is Duchenne's, which strikes males almost exclusively. Duchenne's muscular dystrophy occurs in about one out of 3,300 male births.

Quizzes

A. Fill in each blank with the correct letter:

a. euphemism
b. dystrophy
c. evangelism
d. dyspeptic
e. dyslexia
f. euphoria
g. dysfunctional
h. eugenic

1. There is many a ____ for the word *death*, and many more for the word *drunk*.

2. Some pop psychologists claim that every family is ____ and impaired in some way.
3. The organization campaigns against drunk driving with remarkable ____.
4. Because his ____ was discovered early, he was able to receive the special reading instruction he needed.
5. The end of the war was marked by widespread ____ and celebration.
6. Ebenezer Scrooge, in *A Christmas Carol,* is a thoroughly ____ character.
7. Though the dog is the product of generations of ____ breeding, she is high-strung and has terrible eyesight.
8. The symptoms of muscular ____ can be relieved through physical therapy, various supportive devices, or surgery.

B. Match the word on the left to the correct definition on the right:

1. dystrophy
2. euphemism
3. dyslexia
4. eugenic
5. dysfunctional
6. euphoria
7. dyspeptic
8. evangelism

a. impaired
b. beset by indigestion
c. muscular deterioration
d. crusading zeal
e. polite term
f. reading disorder
g. promoting superior offspring
h. great happiness

Latin Borrowings

a fortiori \ˌä-ˌfȯr-tē-ˈȯr-ē\ All the more certainly.

• If drug users are going to be subject to mandatory sentences, then a fortiori drug dealers should be subject to them also.

A fortiori in Latin literally means "from the stronger (argument)." It is used when drawing a conclusion that is even more obvious or convincing than the one just drawn. Thus, if teaching English grammar to native speakers is difficult, then, a fortiori, teaching English grammar to nonnative speakers is even more challenging.

a posteriori \ˌä-ˌpōs-tir-ē-'ȯr-ē\ Relating to or derived by reasoning from known or observed facts.

• The President had come to the a posteriori conclusion that the booming economy was entirely due to his economic policies.

A posteriori is a term from logic. It is Latin for "from the latter." *A posteriori* usually refers to reasoning that derives causes from effects. This kind of reasoning can sometimes lead to false conclusions. The rising of the sun following the crowing of a rooster, for example, does not mean that the rooster's crowing caused the sun to rise.

a priori \ˌä-prē-'ȯr-ē\ Relating to or derived by reasoning from self-evident propositions.

• Her colleagues rejected Professor Winslow's a priori argument because it rested on assumptions they felt were not necessarily true.

A priori is Latin for "from the former"; it is traditionally contrasted with *a posteriori*. It is usually applied to lines of reasoning or arguments that proceed from the general to the particular or from causes to effects. Whereas a posteriori knowledge is knowledge based solely on experience or personal observation, a priori knowledge is knowledge derived through the power of reasoning. An a priori argument is based on reasoning from what is self-evident; it does not rely on observed facts for its proof.

bona fide \'bō-nə-ˌfīd\ (1) Made in good faith, without deceit. (2) Authentic or genuine.

• They made a bona fide and sincere offer to buy the property at its fair market value.

Bona fide means "in good faith" in Latin. When applied to business deals and the like, it stresses the absence of fraud or deception. A bona fide sale of securities is an entirely aboveboard transaction. When used of matters outside of the legal or business worlds, *bona fide* implies sincerity and earnestness. A bona fide promise is one that the promisor has every intention of keeping. A bona fide proposal of marriage is one made by a suitor who isn't kidding around.

carpe diem \'kär-pā-'dē-ˌem\ Enjoy the pleasures or opportunities of the moment without concern about the future.

• He was convinced he would die young, so he told himself "carpe diem" and lived an adventurous life.

Carpe diem comes from Latin, where it literally means "Pluck the day," though it is usually translated as "Seize the day." A free translation might be "Enjoy yourself while you have the chance." Some people make *carpe diem* a kind of slogan for their lives, feeling that life is too short to spend it worrying about the future, and that we should grab the opportunities life gives us because they may not come again.

caveat emptor \'ka-vē-ˌät-'emp-tər\ Let the buyer beware.

• The best rule to keep in mind when buying anything from a pushcart is: "Caveat emptor."

"Without a warranty, the buyer must take the risk" is the basic meaning of the phrase *caveat emptor*. In olden days when buying and selling was carried on in the local marketplace, the rule was a practical one. Buyer and seller knew each other and were on equal footing. The nature of modern commerce and technology placed the buyer at a disadvantage, however, so a stack of regulations have been written by federal, state, and local agencies to protect the consumer against dangerous, defective, and ineffective products, fraudulent practices, and the like.

corpus delicti \'kȯr-pəs-di-'lik-ˌtī\ (1) The substantial and basic fact or facts necessary to prove that a crime has been committed. (2) The material substance, such as the murdered body, on which a crime has been committed.

• The police believed they had solved the crime, but they couldn't prove their case without the corpus delicti.

Corpus delicti literally means "body of the crime" in Latin. In its original sense the "body" in question refers not to a corpse but to the body of essential facts that taken together prove that a crime has been committed. In popular, nontechnical usage, *corpus delicti* also refers to the actual physical object upon which a crime has been committed. In a case of arson, it would be a ruined building.

In a murder case, as every fan of whodunits knows, it would be the victim's body.

curriculum vitae \kə-ˈri-kyu̇-ləm-ˈvē-ˌtī\ A short summary of one's career and qualifications, typically prepared by an applicant for an academic job; résumé.

• The job advertisement asked for an up-to-date curriculum vitae and three recommendations.

Curriculum vitae is a term usually used in academic circles where teaching positions are the issue. The phrase means "the course of one's life," and is often abbreviated *CV.* In other fields, *résumé* is more commonly used.

Quiz

Fill in each blank with the correct letter:

a. a priori
b. curriculum vitae
c. caveat emptor
d. a posteriori
e. carpe diem
f. a fortiori
g. corpus delicti
h. bona fide

1. To ensure that all reservations are ____, the cruise line requires a nonrefundable deposit.
2. If these two medium-sized cars won't hold all of us and our luggage, ____ those smaller cars won't even come close.
3. The philosopher published his own ____ proof of the existence of God.
4. When we're afraid to pursue our dreams, we sometimes have to tell ourselves, ____.
5. She sent out a ____ full of impressive educational and professional credentials.
6. All of the elements were available to establish the ____ of the defendant's crime.
7. This art critic takes the ____ position that if Pablo Picasso painted it, it's a masterpiece of modern art.
8. When you go out to buy a used car, the best advice, warranty or no warranty, is still ____.

Review Quizzes

A. Complete the analogy:

1. antagonist : villain :: protagonist : ____
   a. maiden b. wizard c. knight d. hero
2. radical : rebellious :: orthodox : ____
   a. routine b. conventional c. sane d. typical
3. fake : fraudulent :: bona fide : ____
   a. copied b. certain c. authentic d. desirable
4. slang : vulgar :: euphemism : ____
   a. habitual b. polite c. dirty d. dumb
5. identify : name :: rectify : ____
   a. make over b. make new c. make right d. make up
6. superior : inferior :: anterior : ____
   a. before b. beside c. above d. behind
7. warranty : guarantee :: caveat emptor : ____
   a. explanation b. warning c. endorsement d. contract
8. jovial : friendly :: dyspeptic : ____
   a. grumpy b. sleepy c. dopey d. happy
9. hot : cold :: catatonic : ____
   a. active b. petrified c. feline d. tired
10. benevolent : wicked :: malevolent : ____
    a. evil b. silly c. noisy d. kindly

B. Fill in each blank with the correct letter:

a. antechamber
b. a posteriori
c. euphoria
d. malign
e. a fortiori
f. orthography
g. prototype
h. rector
i. curriculum vitae
j. catacomb
k. dystrophy
l. eugenic
m. malnourished
n. protoplasm
o. orthodontics

1. Before car makers produce a new model, they always build and test a ____.
2. Please include a ____ so that we can evaluate your qualifications for this position.
3. They were shown into an elegant ____ where they awaited their audience with the king.

4. After graduation from dental school, Kyle took a postgraduate course in ____.
5. The philosopher's conclusion was based on ____ reasoning.
6. The jellylike substance in cells is called ____.
7. These abused and ____ childıen can't be expected to pay attention in class.
8. With some milder types of muscular ____, victims can function well into adulthood.
9. They felt such ____ that they almost wept with joy.
10. Since they earned high honors for achieving a 3.7 average, ____ we should do so for getting a 3.8.
11. Obsessed with ____, the teacher seemed to care not for what his students wrote, only for how it was spelled.
12. It is common for boxers to ____ each other in crude terms before a big match.
13. The ____ of their church gives excellent sermons full of sensible advice.
14. When they went to Rome, they made sure to visit at least one underground ____.
15. ____ experimentation has produced a new breed of sheep with thick, fast-growing wool.

C. Indicate whether the following pairs have the same or different meanings:

1. corpus delicti / basic evidence — same __ / different __
2. ante meridiem / after noon — same __ / different __
3. malicious / mean — same __ / different __
4. protocol / rules of behavior — same __ / different __
5. a priori / determined later — same __ / different __
6. dyslexia / speech patterns — same __ / different __
7. cataclysm / religious teachings — same __ / different __
8. antedate / occur before — same __ / different __
9. orthopedics / shoe repair — same __ / different __
10. rectilinear / curvy — same __ / different __
11. evangelism / crusading — same __ / different __
12. carpe diem / look ahead — same __ / different __
13. dysfunctional / damaged — same __ / different __
14. catalyst / distributor — same __ / different __
15. rectitude / stubbornness — same __ / different __

Unit 6

ROG comes from *rogare,* the Latin verb meaning "to ask." The ancient Romans also used this word to mean "to propose," thinking perhaps that when we propose an idea, we are actually asking someone to consider it. So *interrogate* means "to question systematically," and a *surrogate* (for example, a surrogate mother) is a substitute, someone who is proposed to stand in for another.

abrogate \'a-brə-ˌgāt\ (1) To abolish or annul. (2) To ignore or treat as if nonexistent.

• The proposed constitutional amendment would abrogate fundamental rights of citizens that had long been protected by the courts.

The Latin prefix *ab-* sometimes functions like the English prefix *un-,* so if the ancient Romans wanted to "un-propose" something—that is, propose that something no longer be done—the verb they used was *abrogare,* from which we get *abrogate.* Today, members of our Senate might consider abrogating a treaty if serious questions were raised about the way in which it was negotiated. Similarly, a manufacturer faced with large increases in the cost of materials may feel justified in abrogating contracts with its customers. And policies requiring doctors to give out information about their patients are said to abrogate the confidential patient-doctor relationship.

arrogate \'ar-ə-ˌgāt\ To claim or seize without justification.

• With this legislation, Governor Burns insisted, the federal government was trying to arrogate powers previously held by the states.

A project team will probably succeed best if individual members do not try to arrogate decision-making authority to themselves. And many of us are annoyed when television evangelists try to arrogate to themselves the right to decide what kind of faith is acceptable. (Because of their similarity, it is all too easy to confuse *arrogate* with *abrogate*—and with *arrogant*, for that matter. Study them carefully.)

derogatory \di-ˈrä-gə-ˌtȯr-ē\ Expressing a low or poor opinion of someone or something.

• The radio talk-show host tried to discredit the politician by making derogatory remarks about his appearance.

Derogatory also comes from the "propose" sense of *rogare*. When Romans wanted to propose that something be taken out of a law, the verb they used was *derogare,* and this word developed the general meaning of "take away from." A derogatory comment is one that takes away because it detracts from a person's reputation or lowers the person in the eyes of others. Derogatory remarks are a specialty of some comedians, though their meanness sometimes detracts from their humor.

prerogative \pri-ˈrä-gə-tiv\ A special or exclusive right, power, or privilege that sets one apart from others.

• It is the prerogative of governors and presidents to grant reprieves and pardons.

In some meetings in ancient Rome, the person asked to vote first on an issue was called the *praerogativus*. Voting first was considered a privilege, and so the Romans also had the word *praerogativa,* meaning "preference" or "privilege," from which we get our word *prerogative,* meaning a special right that one has because of one's office, rank, or character. So a company's president may have the prerogative to occupy the largest office with the best view. In a less official sense, a successful writer may claim the prerogative to invent new words. Speaking frankly is sometimes thought to be the prerogative of the senior citizen, but it is probably best exercised with caution.

QUIS is derived from the Latin verb *quaerere,* meaning "to seek or obtain." You can see it in our word *acquisitive,* which means "having a strong wish to possess things." The roots *quer, quir,* and *ques* are also derived from this word and give us words such as *inquiry,* "a search or request for information," and *question,* "something asked."

inquisition \ˌin-kwə-ˈzi-shən\ A questioning or examining that is often harsh or severe.

• The President's choice for the cabinet position turned down the appointment, fearing that the confirmation hearings would turn into an inquisition into her past.

While *inquiry* is a general term and can apply to almost any search for truth, *inquisition* suggests an ongoing search for hidden facts that is thorough and involves long and harsh questioning. Originally *inquisition* had about the same meaning as *inquiry,* but our current use is very much influenced by the Spanish Inquisition, an ongoing trial which began in the Middle Ages and was conducted by church-appointed *inquisitors* who sought out nonbelievers and Jews and sentenced thousands of them to torture and to burning at the stake. Because of this historical connection, the word today almost always means ruthless questioning conducted with complete disregard for human rights.

perquisite \ˈpər-kwə-zət\ (1) A privilege or profit that is provided in addition to one's base salary. (2) Something claimed as an exclusive possession or right.

• A new car, a big house, and yearly trips to Europe were among the perquisites that made the presidency of Wyndam College such an attractive position.

A perquisite, often referred to simply as a *perk,* is usually something of value to which the holder of a particular job or position is entitled. The President of the United States, for instance, enjoys the perquisites of the use of the White House, Camp David, and Air Force One. Perhaps because perquisites are usually available to only a small number of people, the word sometimes refers to non-job-related privileges that are claimed as exclusive rights. It often is very close in meaning to *prerogative* (see above).

acquisitive \ə-ˈkwi-zə-tiv\ Eager to acquire; greedy.

• With each year the couple became more madly acquisitive, buying jewelry, a huge yacht, and two country estates.

Many have observed that we live in an acquisitive society, a society devoted to getting and spending, unlike most tribal societies and some older nations. America often makes successfully acquisitive people into heroes; even Ebenezer Scrooge, that model of miserly greed and *acquisitiveness*, was once defended by the White House chief of staff. An acquisitive nation may seek to *acquire* other territories by force. But mental *acquisition* of specialized knowledge or skills—or new vocabulary!—doesn't deprive others of the same information.

requisition \ˌre-kwə-ˈzi-shən\ A demand or request (such as for supplies) made with proper authority.

• The teachers had grown impatient with having to submit a requisition for even routine classroom supplies.

Requisition is both a noun and a verb. We can speak of sending a requisition to the purchasing department, but we also refer to soldiers *requisitioning* food from civilians. The word has a bureaucratic flavor, but one of Hollywood's bittersweet love stories begins when Omar Sharif, playing a World War II freedom fighter, says to Ingrid Bergman, who is the owner of a stately old yellow Rolls Royce, "I've come to requisition your car."

Quizzes

A. Choose the word that does not belong:

1. derogatory a. critical b. unflattering c. admiring d. scornful
2. inquisition a. examination b. interrogation c. pardon d. inquiry
3. abrogate a. neglect b. abolish c. steal d. ignore
4. perquisite a. privilege b. bonus c. salary d. right
5. prerogative a. right b. persuasion c. power d. privilege
6. acquisitive a. grateful b. grasping c. grabby d. greedy

7. requisition a. purchase order b. receipt c. request d. demand
8. arrogate a. claim b. seize c. grab d. release

B. Fill in each blank with the correct letter:

a. prerogative
b. requisition
c. derogatory
d. perquisite
e. arrogate
f. acquisitive
g. abrogate
h. inquisition

1. She decided to ____ her family obligations for one day to go to the fair.
2. You couldn't even get a pencil unless you filled out a ____.
3. Rodney made ____ remarks about Philip's intelligence that insulted and angered him.
4. Jeannette discovered that a ____ to membership in Frank's family was the privilege of participating in all their quarrels.
5. The mayor tried to ____ to himself sole control of local political activity.
6. The whole family was ____ by nature, and there were bitter legal battles over the will.
7. His status as newcomer did carry the special ____ of being able to ask a lot of questions.
8. Louisa feared an ____ into her background and previous involvements.

PLE comes from a Latin word meaning "to fill." It can be seen in the word *complete,* meaning "possessing all necessary parts." The *ple* root has a Greek equivalent, *pleth,* seen in the word *plethora,* which means "multitude or abundance."

---

complement \'käm-plə-mənt\ (1) Something that fills up or makes perfect; the amount needed to make something complete. (2) A counterpart.

• In an inventive mind, imagination often serves as a necessary complement to reason.

A complement fills out or balances something. Salt is the complement of pepper, and the right necktie is a perfect complement to a good suit. *Complement* can also mean "the full quantity, number, or amount." A ship's complement of officers and crew is the whole force necessary for full operation. (Do not confuse with *compliment*, which means an expression of respect or affection.)

deplete \di-ˈplēt\ To reduce in amount by using up.

• Years of farming on the same small plot of land had left the soil depleted of minerals.

The *de-* prefix often means "do the opposite of," so *deplete* means the opposite of "fill." It can mean merely a lessening in amount; thus, food supplies can be rapidly depleted by hungry teenagers in the house. However, *deplete* usually suggests a reduction that endangers the ability to function. Desertions can deplete an army; layoffs can deplete an office staff; and too much exercise without rest can deplete a body's strength.

implement \ˈim-plə-ˌment\ To take steps to fulfill or put into practice.

• Senators and cabinet members were called in to discuss how to implement the President's new foreign policy.

Implement is usually used in connection with bills that have been passed, proposals that have been accepted, or policies that have been adopted. When companies develop new corporate strategies, they will often hire a new management team to implement the strategy; and when strategies succeed, credit should go to those responsible for both the original idea and its *implementation.*

replete \ri-ˈplēt\ Fully or abundantly filled or supplied.

• The retired professor's autobiography was a fascinating book, replete with details and anecdotes about academic life in the 1930s.

Replete implies that something is filled to capacity. Most people enjoy autumn weekends in New England, replete with colorful foliage, the smell of wood smoke, and a little chill in the air. Supermarket tabloids are usually replete with more details of stars' lives than anyone has any use for. After a big meal of lobster and all the trimmings, we feel replete and drowsy; better wait till later for any more volleyball.

METR comes to us from Greek by way of Latin; in both languages it refers to "measure." A *thermometer* measures heat; a *perimeter* is the measure around something; and things that are *isometric* are equal in measure.

metric \'me-trik\ (1) Relating to or based on the metric system. (2) Relating to or arranged in meter.

• Many Americans are beginning to become accustomed to metric units such as the liter, milligram, and kilometer.

The metric system, used in most of the world to measure distance, weight, and volume, is built in part on a unit length called the *meter*, from which it takes its name. Other metric units are the kilogram (the basic unit of weight) and the liter (the basic unit of volume). *Metric* can also refer to the meter, or rhythm, in songs and poetry, although the word *metrical* is used more often for this meaning. So while the scientists' measurements are usually metric, the poets' are usually metrical.

odometer \ō-'dä-mə-tər\ An instrument used to measure distance traveled.

• Jennifer watched the odometer to see how far she would have to drive to her new job.

Odometer includes the root from the Greek word *hodos,* meaning "road" or "trip." The odometer is what unscrupulous car salesmen illegally tamper with when they want to reduce the mileage a car registers as having traveled. One of life's little pleasures is watching the odometer when all of the numbers change at the same time.

symmetrical \sə-'me-tri-kəl\ (1) Having or exhibiting balanced proportions or the beauty that results from such balance. (2) Corresponding in size, shape, or other qualities on opposite sides of a dividing line or plane or around a center.

• Noting the dents in both front fenders, Robert comforted himself that at least his car was now symmetrical.

A key element in the appeal of most formal gardens is their symmetrical design, and *symmetry* plays a large part in the timeless beauty of Greek temples. Of course, the opposite can also be true. Cindy Crawford was not the first person to discover that a certain lack of symmetry can add interest to the human face.

tachometer \ta-'kä-mə-tər\ A device used to measure speed of rotation.

● Even though one purpose of having a tachometer is to help drivers keep their engine speeds down, most of us occasionally try to see how high we can make the needle go.

A tachometer is literally a "speed-measurer," since the Greek root *tach-* means "speed." This is clear in the name of the *tachyon,* a particle of matter that travels faster than the speed of light. If it exists, it is so fast that it is impossible to see. *Tachycardia* is a medical condition in which the heart races uncontrollably. Since the speed that a tachometer measures is speed of rotation, the numbers it reports are usually revolutions per minute, or rpm's.

Quizzes

A. Match the word on the left to the correct definition on the right:

1. symmetrical	a. drain
2. tachometer	b. put to use
3. metric	c. counterpart
4. replete	d. balanced
5. odometer	e. distance measurer
6. deplete	f. speed measurer
7. implement	g. full
8. complement	h. relating to a measuring system

B. Choose the closest definition:

1. deplete a. straighten out b. draw down c. fold d. abandon
2. replete a. refold b. repeat c. abundantly provided d. fully clothed
3. odometer a. intelligence measurer b. heart-rate measurer c. height measurer d. distance measurer

4. tachometer a. speed measurer b. sharpness measurer c. fatigue measurer d. size measurer
5. complement a. praise b. number required c. abundance d. usual dress
6. metric a. relating to poetic rhythm b. relating to ocean depth c. relating to books d. relating to particles of matter
7. implement a. put to death b. put to pasture c. put into practice d. put to sleep
8. symmetrical a. uncomplicated b. measured c. unattractive d. balanced

AUD, from the Latin verb *audire,* is the root that has to do with hearing. What is *audible* is hearable, and an *audience* is a group of people that listens, sometimes in an *auditorium.*

auditor \'ȯ-də-tər\ A person who formally examines and verifies financial accounts.

• It seems impossible that so many banks could have gotten themselves into so much trouble in the 1980s if their auditors had been doing their jobs.

We don't normally associate auditors with listening—looking and adding up numbers seems more their line of work. But auditors do have to listen to people's explanations, and perhaps that is the historical link. Both Latin and some old forms of French had words similar to our *auditor* which meant "hearer," "judge's assistant," and "one who examines accounts." So listening and judging have been intertwined with looking at the books for hundreds of years.

auditory \'ȯ-də-ˌtȯr-ē\ (1) Perceived or experienced through hearing. (2) Of or relating to the sense or organs of hearing.

• With the new sophisticated sound systems that are now available, going to a movie has become an auditory experience almost as much as a visual one.

Auditory is close in meaning to *acoustic* and *acoustical* as they all relate to the hearing of sounds. *Auditory,* however, usually refers more to hearing than to sound. For instance, many dogs have great auditory powers. The nerve that allows us to hear by connecting the inner ear to the brain is the auditory nerve. *Acoustic* and *acoustical* refer especially to instruments and to the conditions under which sound can be heard. So architects concern themselves with the acoustic (or acoustical) properties of an auditorium, and instrument makers with those of a clarinet or piano.

audition \ȯ-ˈdi-shən\ A trial performance to evaluate a performer's skills.

• Auditions for Broadway shows attract so many hopeful unknown performers that they are referred to as "cattle calls."

Most stars are discovered at auditions, where a number of candidates read the same part and the director chooses. Lana Turner, on the other hand, skipped the audition process altogether; once she was discovered sipping a soda at Schwab's, her future was secure. *Audition* can also be a verb. After Miss Turner won her stardom, the prize was the opportunity to audition to be her leading man.

inaudible \i-ˈnȯ-də-bəl\ Not heard or capable of being heard.

• The coach spoke to the young gymnast in a low voice that was inaudible to the rest of the team.

Inaudible adds the negative prefix *in-* to the adjective *audible* and turns it into its opposite. Modern spy technology (if movies like *Three Days of the Condor* or *Patriot Games* are accurate) can turn inaudible conversations into audible ones with the use of high-powered directional microphones. So if you think you're being spied on, make sure there's a lot of other noise around you.

SON is the Latin root meaning "sound," as in our word *sonata*, meaning a kind of music usually played by one or two instruments, and *sonorous*, usually meaning full, loud, or rich in sound.

---

dissonant \ˈdi-sə-nənt\ (1) Clashing or discordant, especially in music. (2) Incompatible or disagreeing.

• Critics of the health-care plan pointed to its two seemingly dissonant goals: cost containment, which would try to control spending, and universal coverage, which could increase spending.

Dissonant includes the negative prefix *dis-*. What is dissonant sounds or feels unresolved, unharmonic, and clashing. Twentieth-century composers such as Arnold Schoenberg and his students Alban Berg and Anton Webern developed the use of *dissonance* in music as a style in itself. To many, such visual and jarring sounds are still unbearable; most listeners prefer music based on traditional tonality.

resonance \'re-zə-nəns\ (1) A continuing or echoing of sound. (2) A richness and variety in the depth and quality of sound.

• Audiences for both *Star Wars* and CNN are drawn to the resonance in the voice of James Earl Jones.

Many of the finest musical instruments possess a high degree of resonance which, by producing additional vibrations and echoes of the original sound, enriches and amplifies it. Violins made by the masters Stradivari and Guarneri, for example, possess a quality of resonance that modern violinmakers have not been able to duplicate.

sonic \'sä-nik\ (1) Having to do with sound. (2) Having to do with the speed of sound in air (about 750 miles per hour).

• With a sonic depth finder, they determined the depth of the lake by bouncing a sound signal off the bottom.

In 1947 a plane burst the sound barrier and created a sonic boom for the first time. Now even commercial jetliners, including the Concorde, leave sonic booms in their wake as they exceed the speed of sound.

ultrasound \'əl-trə-ˌsau̇nd\ The use of sound vibrations above the limits of human hearing to produce images with which to diagnose internal bodily conditions.

• His doctor, who loved new technology, used CAT scans, MRI, and ultrasound to view his various organs.

The root *son-* came to be spelled *soun-* in medieval English, which led to *sound* and all the English words that now contain it. Ultrasound, or *ultrasonography,* works on the principle that sound is reflected at different speeds by tissues or substances of different densities. *Sonograms,* the pictures produced by ultrasound, can reveal heart defects, tumors, and gallstones, but are most often used to display fetuses during pregnancy in order to make sure they are healthy.

Quizzes

A. Indicate whether the following pairs of words have the same or different meanings:

1. dissonant / jarring — same __ / different __
2. inaudible / invisible — same __ / different __
3. resonance / richness — same __ / different __
4. audition / tryout — same __ / different __
5. ultrasound / harmony — same __ / different __
6. auditor / performer — same __ / different __
7. sonic / loud — same __ / different __
8. auditory / hearing — same __ / different __

B. Match the word on the left to the correct definition on the right:

1. inaudible	a. involving sound
2. auditory	b. impossible to hear
3. ultrasound	c. diagnostic technique
4. resonance	d. a critical hearing
5. auditor	e. relating to hearing
6. sonic	f. unharmonious
7. dissonant	g. financial examiner
8. audition	h. continuing or echoing sound

ERR, from the Latin verb *errare,* means "to wander" or "to stray." This root is easily seen in the word *error,* which means a wandering or straying from what is correct or true. We also use the word *erratum* to mean "a mistake" in a book or other printed material; its plural is *errata,* and the *errata* page is the book page that lists mistakes found too late to correct before publication.

aberrant \ə-'ber-ənt\ Straying or differing from the right, normal, or natural type.

• Richard's aberrant behavior began to make his colleagues fear that the stress of the project was getting to be too much for him.

Something that is aberrant has wandered away from the usual or normal path or form. Aberrant behavior is usually bad behavior and may be a symptom of other problems. However, in biology, the discovery of an aberrant variety of a species can be exciting news, and in medical research the discovery of an aberrant gene can lead the way to new cures for diseases.

errant \'er-ənt\ (1) Wandering or moving about aimlessly. (2) Straying outside proper bounds, or away from an accepted pattern or standard.

• Modern-day cowboys have been known to use helicopters to spot errant calves.

Errant means both "wandering" and "mistaken." A *knight-errant* was a wandering knight going about slaying dragons or rescuing damsels in distress. *Arrant* is a rarely used variant of *errant*, but we sometimes hear it in the phrase *arrant knave*, which comes from Shakespeare and refers to an extremely untrustworthy individual. More typical is the errant cloud or breeze that just happens along or the errant child that requires discipline.

erratic \i-'ra-tik\ (1) Having no fixed course. (2) Lacking in consistency.

• In the 1993 World Series, the Phillies weren't helped by the erratic performance of their ace relief pitcher, "Wild Thing."

Erratic can refer to literal "wandering." A missile that loses its guidance system may follow an erratic path, and a river with lots of twists and bends is said to have an erratic course. *Erratic* can also mean "inconsistent" or "irregular." So a stock market that often changes direction is said to be acting *erratically*. And Wild Thing's problem was erratic control: he could throw strikes but he also threw a lot of wild pitches.

erroneous \i-'rō-nē-əs\ Mistaken, incorrect.

• The chess wizard's parents formed an erroneous idea of his intelligence because he didn't talk until he was six.

Erroneous seems to be used most often with words that suggest mental activity. "Erroneous assumptions" and "erroneous ideas" are two very common phrases in English, perhaps because we suffer from so many of them. "Erroneous information" is also very common, and it leads to erroneous decisions, erroneous theories, and erroneous conclusions.

CED/CESS, from the Latin verb *cedere*, meaning "to go" or "to proceed," produces many English words, from *procession*, meaning something that goes forward, to *recession*, which is a moving back or away.

---

accede \ak-'sēd\ (1) To give in to a request or demand. (2) To give approval or consent.

• Voters tend to worry when Congress seems to be acceding to the demands of too many special-interest groups.

To accede usually means to yield, often under pressure, to the needs or requests of others. Sometimes this is a good thing, as when family members accede to the needs of others or we accede to our curiosity and take the peaceful back road to our destination. *Accede* often also implies reluctance. Patients may accede to surgery, and voters may accede to a tax increase, but eager shoppers do not accede to price reductions—they welcome them.

antecedent \ˌan-tə-'sē-dənt\ (1) A preceding event, state, or cause. (2) One's ancestor or parent.

• The harsh terms of the treaty that ended World War I are often said to have been antecedents of World War II.

Antecedents can be persons, conditions, or events that are responsible, if only in part, for a later person, condition, or event. So the rhythm-and-blues music of the 1940s and 1950s is an antecedent of today's rock and roll. And the breakup of the Soviet Union was surely an important antecedent of the war in Yugoslavia. Since our parents and ancestors are responsible for our existence, they are our own antecedents.

concession \kən-'se-shən\ (1) The yielding of a point or privilege, often unwillingly. (2) An acknowledgment or admission.

• When the company agreed to pay millions of dollars in damage claims, the payments were seen as a concession that somebody had done something wrong.

When the baseball strike of the 1980s was settled, both players and management had to make concessions. This meant that each side *conceded* (gave up or reduced) some of its demands until they reached agreement. *Concede* can also mean simply "admit." So your boss may concede that she is at fault for something, or you may have to concede that your opponent in an argument has some good points.

precedent \'pre-sə-dənt\ Something done or said that may be an example or rule to guide later acts of a similar kind.

• When Judy bought Christmas presents for all her relatives one year she claimed that it set no precedent, but it did.

The Supreme Court relies on precedents, earlier laws or decisions that provide some example or rule to guide them in the present case. Sometimes, as in the famous 1954 ruling that ordered public schools desegregated, the precedent lies in the Constitution and its Amendments.

Quizzes

A. Complete the analogy:

1. descending : ascending :: errant : ____
   a. moving b. wandering c. fixed d. straying
2. abundance : plenty :: antecedent : ____
   a. ancestor b. descendant c. relative d. protector
3. fruitful : barren :: erroneous : ____
   a. productive b. pleasant c. targeted d. correct
4. collision : hit :: concession : ____
   a. drive b. hover c. yielding d. refuse
5. stable : constant :: erratic : ____
   a. fast b. invisible c. mistaken d. unpredictable
6. swerve : veer :: accede : ____
   a. assent b. descent c. reject d. demand

7. typical : normal :: aberrant : ____
   a. burdened b. roving c. odd d. missing
8. etiquette : manners :: precedent : ____
   a. courtesy b. tradition c. rudeness d. behavior

B. Fill in each blank with the correct letter:

a. aberrant
b. errant
c. precedent
d. concession
e. erratic
f. erroneous
g. antecedent
h. accede

1. Her unfair opinion of him was based on several ____ assumptions.
2. They could find no ____ for this offense to guide them in deciding how to deal with it.
3. Doctors traced the ____ changes in his temperature to the attack of malaria.
4. Willy Loman lived the ____ life of the traveling salesman.
5. In agreeing to end the bombing, the rebels made only a single ____.
6. After repeated incidents of criminally ____ behavior, he finally got sent to jail.
7. After lengthy negotiations, the union will probably ____ to several of the company's terms.
8. She proudly claimed Booker T. Washington as her ____.

Words from Mythology and History

Augean stable \ȯ-ˈjē-ən-ˈstā-bəl\ A condition or place marked by great accumulation of filth or corruption.

• Leaders of many of the newly formed nations of Eastern Europe found that the old governments of their countries had become Augean stables that they must now clean out.

Augean stable most often appears in the phrase "clean the Augean stable," which usually means "clear away corruption" or "perform a large and unpleasant task that has long called for attention." Augeus, the mythical king of Elis, kept great stables that held 3,000 oxen and had not been cleaned for thirty years when Hercules was assigned the job. Thus, the word *Augean* by itself has come to mean "extremely difficult or distasteful," so we can also refer to Augean tasks or Augean labor, or even Augean clutter. By the way, Hercules cleaned the stables by causing two rivers to run through them.

Croesus \'krē-səs\ A very rich person.

• H. Ross Perot's many successful business ventures have made him an American Croesus.

Croesus most often appears in the phrase "rich as Croesus," which means "extremely rich." Bill Gates, founder of Microsoft, could fairly be called "rich as Croesus." Croesus himself was a sixth-century B.C. king of Lydia, an ancient kingdom in what is now Turkey. He conquered many surrounding regions, grew wealthy, and became the subject of many legends.

dragon's teeth \'dra-gənz-'tēth\ Seeds of conflict.

• We should realize that we sow dragon's teeth when we neglect the education of our children.

This term often appears in the phrase "sow dragon's teeth," which means to create the conditions for future trouble. In an ancient Greek legend, Cadmus killed a dragon and planted its teeth in the ground. Armed men immediately sprang up from where the teeth were sown and tried to kill him. The goddess Athena directed him to throw a precious stone into their midst and they proceeded to slaughter each other until only the five greatest warriors were left, and these became Cadmus's generals.

Hades \'hā-dēz\ The underground home of the dead in Greek mythology.

• Always careful not to offend, the angry Senator bellowed, "Who in Hades gave out this information about me?"

Hades is both the land of the dead and the god who rules there. Hades (Pluto) the god is the brother of Zeus (Jupiter) and Poseidon (Neptune), who rule the skies and the seas respectively. His own realm is Hades, the region under the earth, full of mineral wealth and fertility and home of the dead. There he rules with his wife Persephone (Proserpina). *Hades* has become a polite term for *Hell* and often appears in its place, as in the sentence "The restaurant became hotter than Hades after the air conditioner broke down."

lethargic \lə-'thär-jik\ (1) Lazily sluggish. (2) Indifferent or apathetic.

• Once again the long Sunday dinner had left most of the family feeling stuffed and lethargic.

The Greek philosopher Plato wrote that before a dead person could leave Hades to begin a new life, he or she had to drink from the River Lethe, whose name means "forgetfulness" in Greek. One would thereby forget all aspects of one's former life and the time spent in Hades (usually pretty awful, according to Plato). But our word *lethargic* and the related noun *lethargy* usually refer not to forgetting but rather to the weak, ghostly state of those who have drunk from Lethe as dead spirits—so weak that they may require a drink of blood before they can even speak.

Midas touch \'mī-dəs-'təch\ The talent for making money in every venture.

• For much of his career Donald Trump seemed to possess the Midas touch.

Midas was the legendary king of Phrygia who, when granted one wish by the god Dionysus, asked for the power to turn everything he touched into gold. When he found that even his food and drink turned to gold, he begged Dionysus to take back his gift. The moral of this tale of greed is usually ignored when the term is used today.

Pyrrhic victory \'pir-ik-'vik-tə-rē\ A victory won at excessive cost.

• The coach regarded their win as a Pyrrhic victory, as his best players sustained injuries that would sideline them for weeks.

Pyrrhic victories take their name from Pyrrhus, the king of Epirus, an ancient country in northwest Greece. Pyrrhus defeated the Romans at the Battle of Ausculum (279 B.C.) but lost all of his best officers and many men. He is said to have exclaimed after the battle, "One more such victory and we are lost."

stygian \'sti-jē-ən\ Extremely dark, dank, gloomy, and forbidding, like the River Styx.

• When the power went out in the building, the halls and stairwells were plunged in stygian darkness.

The word *stygian* comes from the name of the River Styx, which was the chief river of the Greek underground world of the dead and which had to be crossed in order to enter this world.

Quiz

Choose the word that does not belong:

1. lethargic a. lazy b. sluggish c. energetic d. indifferent
2. Croesus a. rich b. powerful c. impoverished d. successful
3. Midas touch a. talented b. unsuccessful c. rich d. prosperous
4. Pyrrhic victory a. unqualified b. costly c. dangerous d. destructive
5. Augean stable a. purity b. corruption c. filth d. Herculean
6. Hades a. underworld b. heaven c. dead d. eternity
7. dragon's teeth a. dangerous b. troublesome c. sensible d. conflict
8. stygian a. glamorous b. gloomy c. grim d. dank

Review Quizzes

A. Match each word on the left to its antonym on the right:

1. antecedent	a. true
2. erroneous	b. generous
3. dissonant	c. energetic
4. lethargic	d. fill
5. symmetrical	e. admiring
6. acquisitive	f. typical
7. deplete	g. descendant
8. derogatory	h. hearable
9. inaudible	i. unbalanced
10. aberrant	j. harmonious

B. Complete the analogies:

1. arrogate : ____ :: implement : ____
   a. question / serve b. surrogate / tool c. claim / accomplishment d. arrogant / rake
2. precedent : ____ :: prerogative : ____
   a. example / privilege b. sample / rule c. governor / request d. forerunner / introduction
3. odometer : ____:: Croesus : ____
   a. alphabet / dog b. intelligence / loyalty c. surprise / monster d. distance / wealth
4. audition : ____ :: inquisition : ____
   a. hearing / asking b. trying / cooking c. affecting / reflecting d. listening / seeing
5. ultrasound : ____ :: ultraviolet : ____
   a. loud / colorful b. inaudible / invisible c. medical / artistic d. excessive / exaggerated
6. concession : ____ :: perquisite : ____
   a. edible / necessary b. affordable / bearable c. reluctant / welcome d. appreciative / greedy
7. resonance : ____ :: replete : ____
   a. reworking / refilling b. echoing / full c. divided / united d. continuing / exhausted
8. stygian : ____ :: aberrant : ____
   a. muddy / angry b. dark / abnormal c. gloomy / bright d. light / simple
9. requisition : ____ :: errant : ____
   a. regular / stable b. demand / wandering c. refreshed / roving d. routine / usual
10. sonic : ____:: auditory : ____
    a. sound / hearing b. jet-propelled / taped c. tonic / radial d. audible / visual

C. Fill in each blank with the correct letter:

a.	abrogate	f.	erratic
b.	tachometer	g.	Midas touch
c.	dragon's teeth	h.	accede
d.	complement	i.	Pyrrhic victory
e.	Croesus	j.	metric

1. Through shrewd investing, she had become as rich as ____ .

2. The French use the ____ system to calculate volume.
3. If you want respect, you must never ____ your responsibilities.
4. The triumphant corporate takeover proved to be a ____, since the debt that resulted crippled the corporation for years.
5. The children made only ____ progress because they kept stopping to pick flowers.
6. At last the teachers decided to ____ to the students' request for less homework.
7. He knew that with her mean gossip in the office she was sowing ____, but he did nothing to stop her.
8. The ____ showed that the engine was racing much too fast.
9. Fresh, hot bread is the perfect ____ to any dinner.
10. He skipped his class reunion, preferring to avoid any successful former classmates who clearly had the ____.

Unit 7

VID/VIS comes from the Latin verb *videre,* and appears in words having to do with seeing and sight. A *videotape* is a collection of *visual* images—that is, images *visible* to our eyes. But this root does not always involve eyes. To *envision* something, for instance, is to see it with your imagination.

visage \ˈvi-zij\ The face or appearance of a person.

• A kindly man, he had a bright, cheerful visage that people found attractive.

Visage is one of several words for the human face. *Countenance* and *physiognomy* are two others. *Countenance* is usually used to refer to the face as it reveals mood or character, and *physiognomy* is used when referring to the shape or contour of the face. *Visage* is a more literary term and may refer either to the shape of the face or the impression it gives or the mood it reveals. FBI Most Wanted posters seem to emphasize the threatening visages of the suspects. Unlike *countenance* and *physiognomy,* the use of *visage* is not restricted to humans. We can speak, for instance, of the grimy visage of a mining town.

vis-à-vis \ˌvē-zä-ˈvē\ In relation to or compared with.

• Many financial reporters worry about the loss of U.S. economic strength vis-à-vis our principal trading partners.

Vis-à-vis comes from Latin by way of French. It means literally "face-to-face"; things that are face-to-face can easily be compared or contrasted. So, for example, the Red Sox have often fared badly vis-à-vis the Yankees, and a greyhound is very tall vis-à-vis a Scottie.

visionary \'vi-zhə-ˌner-ē\ (1) A person with foresight and imagination. (2) A dreamer whose ideas are often impractical.

• His followers regarded him as an inspired visionary; his opponents saw him as either a con man or a lunatic.

A visionary is someone who vividly imagines the future, whether accurately or not, with ideas that may either work brilliantly or fail miserably. Martin Luther King, Jr., was a visionary in his hopes and ideas for a just society; but this, like so many visions, has proved easier to *envision* than to achieve.

visitation \ˌvi-zə-'tā-shən\ (1) A visit or short stay, often for some definite, official purpose such as inspection. (2) A parent's privilege to have temporary access to or care of a child.

• The local ministers dreaded the annual visitation from the bishop's evaluation committee.

Visit and *visitation* share some meanings, since both refer to a fairly short call or stay. But *visit* is the more general word, while a visitation is normally a visit that is somehow out of the ordinary, such as by being formal or official. Faithful followers of religious leaders such as the Pope or the Dalai Lama look forward to visitations from these holy figures. Businesspeople, on the other hand, could probably do without annual visitations from the tax auditors.

SPIC/SPEC comes from the Latin verb *specere* or *spicere*, meaning "to look at or behold." Closely related is the root *specta-*, which comes from a slightly different verb and produces such words as *spectator*, *spectacles*, and *spectacular*.

---

auspicious \ó-'spi-shəs\ (1) Promising success; favorable. (2) Fortunate, prosperous.

• Martha was mildly superstitious, so breaking her mirror didn't seem an auspicious start to the day.

In ancient Rome there was an entire order of priests, the *auspices*, whose job it was to watch birds fly across the Roman sky. After noting what kinds of birds and how many had flown in which direction, they delivered prophecies according to what they had seen. For example, two eagles flying from east to west was usually considered auspicious, or favorable; two or more vultures flying west to east was *inauspicious,* unless the Romans were looking forward to a war. Thus, the auspices were birdwatchers, although not quite like birdwatchers today.

conspicuous \kən-ˈspi-kyü-wəs\ Obvious or noticeable; striking in a way that attracts attention.

• Soon after the shooting, "No Trespassing" signs appeared in conspicuous colors at conspicuous locations around the preserve.

Conspicuous usually refers to something so obvious that it cannot be missed by the eye or mind. We often speak, for instance, of conspicuous bravery or conspicuous generosity. It also frequently describes something that draws attention by being unpleasant or unusual. Businesspeople try to avoid making themselves conspicuous by their clothes or their personal habits. The phrase "conspicuous consumption" is often used to describe lavish spending intended to increase one's social prestige, a well-known aspect of American life.

introspection \ˌin-trō-ˈspek-shən\ A looking within oneself to examine one's own thoughts and feelings.

• The poet Sylvia Plath's journals are filled with the results of her constant introspection.

Introspection is a valuable resource of writers. In her autobiography, *The Road from Coorain,* Jill Ker Conway produces a fascinating, highly *introspective* portrayal of her life's journey from an Australian sheep farm to the president's office of a major American women's college, and beyond. We learn not only what her life was like but how she felt about it along the way and also in *retrospect*—that is, looking back.

perspicacious \ˌpər-spi-ˈkā-shəs\ Having acute or shrewd mental vision or judgment.

• Successful poker players are usually perspicacious judges of human character.

Perspicacious is derived from the Latin word *perspicere,* meaning "to look through" or "to see clearly," so *perspicacious,* usually means having unusual power to see through or understand. You tend to admire the *perspicacity* of the person who understands what a fine human being you are. (The confusingly similar word *perspicuous* comes from the same Latin word but means "plain to the understanding" or simply "clear." A writer will strive for a perspicuous style, for example, and a lawyer will try to present perspicuous arguments to a judge.)

Quizzes

A. Fill in each blank with the correct letter:

a. introspection	e. visitation
b. vis-à-vis	f. auspicious
c. perspicacious	g. visionary
d. conspicuous	h. visage

1. When she considered Cleveland ____ other cities where she might have to live, she always chose Cleveland.
2. The couple were ____ by their absence from the meeting.
3. His plans for the new city marked him as a true ____.
4. The beautiful sunrise provided an ____ start to their camping trip.
5. She was a ____ woman of rare judgment, who always seemed to know the right thing to say in even the most delicate situation.
6. The ____ of Marlene Dietrich gazed out from movie posters throughout Europe and America in the 1930s.
7. After the confrontation, both devoted themselves to long periods of ____ to try to understand their own feelings.
8. A visit from her mother-in-law always felt like a ____ of the plague.

B. Match the definition on the left to the correct word on the right:

1. compared to	a. introspection
2. shrewd	b. visitation
3. prophet	c. vis-à-vis
4. appearance	d. auspicious
5. self-examination	e. perspicacious

6.	noticeable	f.	visionary
7.	favorable	g.	conspicuous
8.	official call	h.	visage

VOC/VOK, from the Latin noun *vox* and the verb *vocare*, has to do with speaking and calling and the use of the voice. So a *vocation* is a special calling to a type of work; an *evocative* sight or smell calls forth memories and feelings; and a *vocal* ensemble is a singing group.

equivocate \i-ˈkwi-və-ˌkāt\ (1) To use ambiguous language, especially in order to deceive. (2) To avoid giving a direct answer.

• As the company directors continued to equivocate, the union prepared to return to the picket lines.

Equivocate contains the root *equi*, meaning "equal." It thus suggests that whatever is said has two equally possible meanings. The person who equivocates avoids giving a clear, *unequivocal* message. Politicians are often said to equivocate, but equivocating is also typical of used-car salesmen or nervous witnesses in a courtroom. Sometimes even husbands and wives will equivocate to avoid a quarrel.

irrevocable \i-ˈre-və-kə-bəl\ Impossible to call back or retract.

• By throwing her hat into the presidential race, the young governor made the irrevocable decision to put her family into the public eye.

The word *irrevocable* has a legal sound to it, and in fact is often used in legal contexts. Irrevocable trusts are trust funds that cannot be dissolved by the people who create them. An irrevocable credit is an absolute obligation from a bank to provide credit to a customer. Under U.S. tax law, irrevocable gifts are gifts that are given by one living person to another and that cannot be reclaimed by the giver. But we all have had to make irrevocable decisions, decisions that commit us absolutely to something.

provoke \prə-ˈvōk\ (1) To call forth or stimulate a feeling or action. (2) To anger.

• Before every boxing match, Cassius Clay (Muhammad Ali) would provoke his opponent with poetic taunts.

To provoke a response is to call for that response to happen. Funny stories should provoke laughter; angry comments can provoke a fight; and taking controversial stands may provoke opposition. Something is *provocative* if it has the power to produce a response. The provocative clothing and behavior of some rock-music performers seem designed to provoke criticism as much as admiring attention.

vociferous \vō-'si-fə-rəs\ Making noisy or emphatic outcries.

• Parents at soccer games are often known to make vociferous protests when they think the referee has made a bad call.

Someone who is vociferous shouts loudly and insistently. The group U2 draws vociferous crowds whose noisy din at times makes it hard to hear the music. And as at any rock concert, there are vociferous objections when the music ends.

PHON is a Greek root meaning "sound," "voice," or "speech." It is similar to the Latin *voc* in meaning but typically means only "sound" when used in such words as *telephone* ("far sound"), *microphone* ("small sound"), or *xylophone* ("wood sound").

---

cacophony \kə-'kä-fə-nē\ Harsh or unpleasant sound.

• To some people, much recent jazz sounds more like cacophony than like real music.

Cacophony employs the Greek prefix *caco-*, meaning "bad," but not everything we call *cacophonous* is necessarily bad. Open-air food markets may be marked by a cacophony of voices but also by wonderful sights and sounds. Heavy metal is probably the most cacophonous form of modern music but it is still very popular. On the other hand, few people can really enjoy, for more than a few minutes, the cacophony of jackhammers, car horns, and truck engines that assaults the city pedestrian on a hot day in August.

phonetic \fə-'ne-tik\ Relating to or representing the sounds of the spoken language.

• Some school systems teach first-graders to read by the phonetic method.

The English alphabet is phonetic; that is, the letters represent sounds. Certain other alphabets, such as Chinese, are not phonetic, since their symbols represent ideas rather than sounds. But even in English a letter does not always represent the same sound; the "a" in *cat, father,* and *mate,* for example, represents three different sounds. Because of this, books about words often use specially created phonetic alphabets in which each symbol stands for a single sound in order to represent pronunciations. So in this book, *cat, father,* and *mate* would be *phonetically* represented as \'kat\, \'fä- t͟hər\, and \'māt\.

polyphonic \ˌpä-lē-'fä-nik\ Referring to a style of music in which two or more melodies are sung or played against each other in harmony.

• The polyphonic chants of the monks punctuated the ceremony at important intervals.

Since *poly-* means "many," polyphonic music has "many voices." In *polyphony,* each part has its own melody. It reached its height during the 16th century with Italian madrigals and the sacred music of such composers as Palestrina, Tallis, and Byrd.

symphony \'sim-fə-nē\ A usually long and complex musical composition for orchestra.

• Beethoven, Bruckner, Mahler, and possibly Schubert completed nine symphonies each before their deaths.

Symphony includes the prefix *sym-* ("together") and thus means "a sounding together." The symphonies of Beethoven, most of which have four separate movements, are among the greatest ever composed. From the First, which is almost like the music of Mozart, to the magnificent choral Ninth, few other pieces of music compare to them in controlled intensity. "*Symphonic* poems" by such composers as Franz Liszt and Richard Strauss usually attempt to paint a picture or tell a dramatic story by means of music alone. Both require a symphony orchestra (sometimes called simply a "symphony" itself) made up of stringed, woodwind, brass, and percussion instruments.

Quizzes

A. Complete the analogy:

1. initial : beginning :: irrevocable : ____
   a. usual b. noisy c. final d. reversible
2. novel : literature :: symphony : ____
   a. dance b. poetry c. film d. music
3. soothe : quiet :: provoke : ____
   a. prevent b. project c. produce d. protect
4. multistoried : floor :: polyphonic : ____
   a. poetry b. melody c. story d. harmony
5. reject : accept :: equivocate : ____
   a. decide b. specify c. detect d. delay
6. melodic : notes :: phonetic : ____
   a. sounds b. signs c. ideas d. pages
7. monotonous : boring :: vociferous : ____
   a. vegetarian b. angry c. favorable d. noisy
8. stillness : quiet :: cacophony : ____
   a. melodious b. dissonant c. creative d. birdlike

B. Indicate whether the following pairs have the same or different meanings:

1. provoke / annoy — same __ / different __
2. phonetic / phonelike — same __ / different __
3. equivocate / refuse — same __ / different __
4. polyphonic / many-voiced — same __ / different __
5. irrevocable / unalterable — same __ / different __
6. cacophony / din — same __ / different __
7. vociferous / calm — same __ / different __
8. symphony / heavy metal — same __ / different __

CUR, from the Latin verb *curare,* means basically "care for." Our verb *cure* comes from this root, as do *manicure* ("care of the hands") and *pedicure* ("care of the feet").

curative \'kyůr-ə-tiv\ Having to do with curing diseases.

• As soon as the antibiotic entered his system, he imagined he could begin to feel its curative effects.

Medical researchers are finding curative substances in places that surprise them. Folklore has led to some "new" *cures* of old diseases, and natural substances never before tried have often proved effective. Taxol, a drug used in treating some cancers comes from the bark of a certain yew tree; the challenge now is to produce this *curative* synthetically, since natural supplies are limited.

curator \'kyůr-ˌā-tər\ Someone in charge of something where things are on exhibit, such as a collection, a museum, or a zoo.

• Curators of zoos continually try to make the animals' surroundings more and more like their natural homes.

A curator cares for some sort of collection, usually works of art or animals. Thomas Hoving, in his years as director of the Metropolitan Museum of Art, was responsible for supervising the curators of all the separate art collections and seeing that all *curatorial* duties were carried out: acquiring new artworks, caring for and repairing objects already owned, discovering frauds and counterfeits, returning some pieces to their country of origin, and mounting exhibitions of everything from Greek sculpture to 20th-century clothing.

procure \prō-'kyůr\ To get possession of; obtain.

• In an era of Defense Department cutbacks, military planners have had to look for more economical ways to procure the supplies they need.

While *procure* has the general meaning of "come into possession of," it usually implies that some effort is required. It may also suggest getting something through a formal set of procedures. In many business offices, there is a particular person responsible for procuring supplies, and many government agencies have formal *procurement* policies designed to prevent unauthorized spending. However, it sometimes seems that such policies cost more money to administer than they could possibly save.

sinecure \'si-nə-ˌkyůr\ A job or position requiring little work but usually providing some income.

• The job of Dean of Students at any college is no sinecure; the hours can be long and the work draining.

Sinecure contains the Latin word *sine,* "without," and thus means "without care." Many view the positions occupied by British royalty as sinecures, in which they earn enormous sums of money and inherit enormous amounts of property in return for nothing at all. But their many supporters defend them by pointing to the amount of public-service, charitable, and ceremonial work they perform, not to mention the effort they put into promoting Britain and all things British. Sinecure or not, many of us would probably like to try being king or queen for a day.

PERI usually means "going around something." With a *periscope,* you can see around corners. *Peristalsis* is the bodily function that moves food around the intestines; without it, digestion would grind to a halt. The moon's *perigee* is the point in its orbit where it is closest to the earth. The point in the earth's orbit around the sun that brings it closest to the sun is its *perihelion.*

perimeter \pə-'ri-mə-tər\ The boundary or distance around a body or figure.

• All along the city's perimeter the guerrillas kept up their attack night after night.

The perimeter of a prison is ringed with high walls and watchtowers, and the entire perimeter of Australia is bounded by water. To measure the perimeter of a square, multiply the length of one of its sides by four. Try not to confuse this word with *parameter,* which usually means a characteristic element or factor or a limit or boundary.

periodontal \ˌper-ē-ō-'dän-təl\ Surrounding the teeth; concerning or affecting the tissues around the teeth.

• Years of bad living had filled his teeth with cavities, but it was periodontal disease that finished them off.

There are dentists called *periodontists* who specialize in the treatment of periodontal problems. These specialists do their best to save a patient's teeth by making sure the periodontal tissues do not degenerate to the point where they can no longer hold the teeth in place. The *-odont-* root comes from the Greek word for "tooth," so the *endodontist,* unlike the periodontist, is concerned with problems inside the tooth.

peripatetic \ˌper-ə-pə-ˈte-tik\ (1) Having to do with walking. (2) Moving or traveling from place to place.

• She spent her early adult years as a peripatetic musician, traveling from one engagement to another.

Peripatetic was the name given to the philosopher Aristotle and his followers, since he used to teach them while walking up and down in a covered walkway called the *Peripatos.* The word kept this sense of traveling or moving about. Johnny Appleseed is a good example of a peripatetic soul, wandering far and wide while he planted his apple trees. Today peripatetic executives and salespeople move from one job to the next and stare into laptop computers while flying from city to city.

peripheral \pə-ˈri-fə-rəl\ (1) Having to do with the outer edges, especially of the field of vision. (2) Auxiliary or supplemental.

• The teacher seemed to have eyes in the back of her head, but what she really had was excellent peripheral vision and a thorough knowledge of how ten-year-olds behave.

Driving into or out of Chicago during rush hour requires excellent peripheral vision, especially when switching lanes. Peripheral vision relates to the outer area of the field of vision, where one can still detect movement and shape. Issues in a discussion may also be called peripheral—that is, not of primary importance. And *peripheral* now can act as a noun: computer peripherals are the added components that increase a computer's capacities.

Quizzes

A. Fill in each blank with the correct letter:

a. curative
b. sinecure
c. procure
d. curator
e. peripheral
f. perimeter
g. peripatetic
h. periodontal

1. The ____ benefits of antibiotics have saved many lives.
2. Testing ____ vision is part of most eye tests done in a doctor's office.

3. What he had hoped was an undemanding ____ turned out to be the hardest and most rewarding job of his career.
4. She knew she needed to put up a fence along the ____ of the garden.
5. We asked our purchasing manager to ____ new chairs for the office.
6. With tents and backpacks ready, the young couple were ready to become ____ vacationers.
7. At the museum we spoke to the ____ of African art.
8. Regular use of dental floss will prevent many kinds of ____ diseases.

B. Choose the closest definition:

1. sinecure a. hopeful sign b. fruitless search c. careless act d. easy job
2. curator a. doctor b. lawyer c. caretaker d. spectator
3. periodontal a. visual b. inside a tooth c. around a tooth d. wandering
4. peripatetic a. wandering b. unemployed c. surrounding d. old-fashioned
5. procure a. say b. obtain c. look after d. heal
6. curative a. purifying b. healing c. saving d. repairing
7. perimeter a. factor b. characteristic c. supplement d. boundary
8. peripheral a. supplementary b. around a tooth c. wandering d. dangerous

SENT/SENS, from the Latin verb *sentire*, meaning "to feel," or the noun *sensus*, meaning "feeling" or "sense," can signify different kinds of feeling. *Sentimental* has to do with emotions, whereas *sensual* relates more to physical *sensations*.

sensational \sen-'sā-shə-nəl\ (1) Exciting an intense but usually brief interest or emotional reaction. (2) Extremely or unexpectedly excellent.

• The sensational newspaper accounts of the marital problems of the royal couple fascinated many readers but made others a little uncomfortable.

The photos sent back from Jupiter by the Voyager satellite were sensational—both excellent and exciting. The murder of a pregnant woman by her husband was sensational also, although in a very different sense, since it was picked up by the tabloid press and *sensationalist* TV journalists, who thrive on such sordid tales and *sensationalize* every detail. Both stories, however, can be said to have created a *sensation*.

sentient \'sen-chənt\ Aware of and responsive to sense impressions.

• The planet Earth supports the only sentient beings that we yet know of in the universe.

Sentient describes beings that perceive and respond to sensations of whatever kind—sight, hearing, touch, taste, smell. The science of robotics is now capable of creating machines that *sense* things in much the way living beings do and respond in pretty much the same way as well; however, few of us are yet ready to refer to robots as sentient beings. Mary Shelley, in her novel *Frankenstein*, was among the first to suggest the possibility of creating sentient beings out of used parts.

sentiment \'sen-tə-mənt\ (1) A thought or attitude colored by feeling; opinion. (2) Tender feelings of affection.

• We don't care whose nephew he is; hiring decisions must be based on merit, not sentiment.

"My sentiments exactly!" expresses agreement to someone else's opinion. A sentiment is usually of gentle to moderate intensity. The refined women of Jane Austen's novels are full of sentiment that occasionally spills over into deep emotion but usually remains subdued and controlled. Similarly, a *sentimental* journey, as the old popular song suggests, satisfies feelings of longing and romantic homesickness rather than intense craving. *Sentiment* is used less today than it once was, and *sentimental* now usually means excessively emotional.

sensuous \'sen-shů-wəs\ (1) Highly pleasing to the senses. (2) Relating to the senses.

• A chef like Craig Claiborne takes sensuous pleasure in the smell and taste of well-prepared food.

Sensuous and *sensual* are closely related in meaning but not identical. *Sensuous* usually implies gratification of the senses for the sake of aesthetic pleasure; great music, for example, can be a source of sensuous delight. *Sensual,* on the other hand, usually describes gratification of the senses or physical appetites as an end in itself; thus we often think (perhaps unfairly) of wealthy Roman aristocrats leading lives devoted to sensual pleasure.

SOPH is a Greek root from the word meaning "wise" or "wisdom." In our language, the root often appears in words where the wisdom concerned is of the "wiseguy" variety. But in words such as *philosophy* we see a more respectful attitude toward wisdom.

---

sophistry \'sä-fə-strē\ Cleverly deceptive reasoning or argument.

• The defendant's claim that he wasn't guilty of the crime because he didn't actually pull the trigger was dismissed as pure sophistry.

Our words *sophist* and *sophistry* come from the name of a group of Greek teachers of rhetoric and philosophy who were famous during the 5th century B.C. Originally, the Sophists represented a respectable school of philosophy and were involved in serious educational efforts. But in time they fell into disrepute and gained a reputation for their abilities to persuade more by means of clever and often misleading arguments than by the merits of their positions. It is not difficult to see the Sophists as the natural ancestors of many of today's politicians.

sophisticated \sə-'fis-tə-ˌkā-təd\ (1) Having a thorough and refined knowledge of the ways of society. (2) Highly complex or developed.

• In *Woman of the Year* Katharine Hepburn plays a sophisticated newspaperwoman who can handle everything except Spencer Tracy.

A satellite is a sophisticated piece of technology, intricate and complex and designed to accomplish difficult tasks. A sophisticated argument is thorough and well-worked-out. A sophisticated person, such as Humphrey Bogart in *Casablanca,* knows how to get around in the world and is able to get pretty much what he or she wants; such *sophistication* can produce a bored, blasé attitude, as it does with Bogie until his long-lost love appears.

sophomoric \ˌsä-fə-ˈmȯr-ik\ Overly impressed with one's own knowledge, but in fact undereducated and immature.

• The kids at summer camp played the usual sophomoric pranks—short-sheeted beds, salt in the sugar bowl, shaving cream on the light switch, water bucket balanced on the door.

Sophomoric seems to include the roots *soph-*, "wise," and *moros,* "fool," so the contrast between wisdom and ignorance is built right into the word. A high-school or college *sophomore* has delusions of wisdom—but only the seniors are truly wise, as we all know. Sophomoric behavior and sophomoric jokes are typical of those who have gotten a small taste of experience but think they have experienced a lot.

theosophy \thē-ˈä-sə-fē\ A set of teachings about God and the world based on mystical insights into their nature and workings.

• She experimented with a number of beliefs, starting with theosophy and ending with a variety of Hinduism.

The best-known religious movement associated with theosophy began in the 19th century under the leadership of Helena Blavatsky. She combined elements of Platonic thought, Christian mysticism, and Hindu belief in a way she claimed had been divinely revealed to her. *Theosophical* beliefs include oneness with nature and reincarnation. The Theosophical Society, founded in 1875 to promote her beliefs, still exists, although scientific experiments had disproved many of her claims by the 20th century.

Quizzes

A. Indicate whether the following pairs of words have the same or different meanings:

1. sophisticated / worldly-wise same __ / different __
2. sensuous / sophisticated same __ / different __
3. theosophy / mythology same __ / different __

4. sentiment / feeling — same __ / different __
5. sophistry / wisdom — same __ / different __
6. sentient / romantic — same __ / different __
7. sophomoric / wise — same __ / different __
8. sensational / enormous — same __ / different __

B. Match the word on the left to the correct definition on the right:

1. theosophy	a. immaturely overconfident
2. sentiment	b. outstandingly excellent
3. sensuous	c. doctrine of God and the world
4. sophomoric	d. gratifying the senses
5. sophistry	e. false reasoning
6. sentient	f. opinion colored by emotion
7. sophisticated	g. receiving perceptions
8. sensational	h. highly complex

Words from Mythology and History

Achilles' heel \ə-'ki-lēz-'hēl\ A vulnerable point.

• Grafton had been an excellent manager in his first years there, but his Achilles' heel turned out to be his addiction to increasingly damaging drugs.

When the hero Achilles was an infant, his sea-nymph mother dipped him into the river Styx to make him immortal. But since she held him by one heel, this spot did not touch the water and so remained mortal and vulnerable. It was this heel where Achilles was eventually mortally wounded. Today, the tendon that stretches up the calf from each heel is called the *Achilles tendon*; however, the term *Achilles' heel* is only used figuratively; thus, it can refer to the weakest point in a country's military defenses, or a person's tendency to drink too much, for example.

arcadia \är-'kā-dēə\ A region or setting of rural pleasure and peacefulness.

• The Pocono Mountains of Pennsylvania are a vacationer's arcadia.

Arcadia, a beautiful rural area in Greece, became the favorite setting for poems about naive and ideal innocence unaffected by the passions of the larger world. There, shepherds play their pipes and sigh with longing for flirtatious nymphs; shepherdesses sing to their flocks, and goat-footed nature gods cavort in the fields and woods.

Cassandra \kə-'san-drə\ A person who predicts misfortune or disaster.

• The newspaper columnist was accused of being a Cassandra who always looked for the worst and predicted disaster, despite the fact that his predictions often came true.

Cassandra, the daughter of King Priam of Troy, was one of those beautiful young maidens with whom Apollo fell in love. He gave her the gift of prophecy in return for the promise of her sexual favors, but at the last minute she refused him. Though he could not take back his gift, he pronounced that no one would ever believe her predictions. Thus, her prophecy of the fall of Troy and the death of its heroes were laughed at by the Trojans. A modern-day Cassandra goes around predicting gloom and doom, like many current economists with their constant pessimistic forecasts.

cyclopean \ˌsī-klə-'pē-ən\ Huge or massive.

• The scale of the new ten-block high-rise medical center was cyclopean.

The Cyclops of Greek mythology were huge, crude giants, each with a single eye in the middle of his forehead. Odysseus had a terrible encounter with one of these creatures in his travels, and escaped being devoured only by blinding the monster with a burning stick. The great stone walls at such places as Troy, Tiryns, and Mycenae are called cyclopean because the stones are so massive and the construction so expert that it was assumed that only a superhuman race such as the Cyclops could have achieved such a feat.

draconian \drə-'kō-nē-ən\ Extremely severe or cruel.

• The new president thinks that only draconian spending limits and staff cutbacks can save the ailing company.

The word *draconian* comes from *Draco,* the name of a 7th-century B.C. Athenian legislator. Legends and stories about Draco hold that he created a very severe code of laws, which were sometimes said to have been written in blood rather than ink. Today, we use the word *draconian* in a wide variety of ways, sometimes even referring to something as minor as parking policies. (Because the word is derived from a person's name, *draconian* is often spelled with a capital *D.*)

myrmidon \'mər-mə-ˌdän\ A loyal follower, especially one who executes orders unquestioningly.

• Wherever the corporate tycoon went, he was surrounded by myrmidons all too eager to do his bidding.

Achilles' troops in the Trojan War, called Myrmidons, were created from ants. This insect origin explained their blind obedience to him, their willingness to carry out any order—such as refusing to fight even when it meant many lives would be lost. The Nazis expected all Germans in uniform to exhibit this same unquestioning loyalty and obedience; the postwar Nuremberg trials established the principle that the utter, unthinking obedience of a myrmidon does not excuse committing certain crimes against humanity in wartime.

nemesis \'ne-mə-səs\ A powerful, frightening opponent or rival who is usually victorious.

• During the 1970s and 1980s Japanese carmakers became the nemesis of the U.S. auto industry.

The Greek goddess Nemesis doled out rewards for noble acts and vengeance for evil ones. The Greeks believed that Nemesis did not always punish an offender right away, but might wait as much as five generations to avenge a crime. But whenever she worked, her cause was always just and her victory sure. Today, a nemesis may or may not be believed to be working justice. So most people agree that the weak economy was George Bush's nemesis in 1992, even if they voted for him.

Trojan horse \'trō-jən-'hȯrs\ Someone or something that works from within to defeat or undermine.

• Like a Trojan horse, she came back to school with a bad case of the flu that spread rapidly among the other students.

After besieging the walls of Troy for ten years, the Greeks built a huge, hollow wooden horse, secretly filled it with armed warriors, and presented it to the Trojans as a gift for the goddess Athena. The Trojans accepted the offering and took the horse inside the city's walls. That night, the armed Greeks swarmed out and captured and burned the city. A Trojan horse is thus anything that looks innocent but, once accepted, has power to harm or destroy—for example, a computer program that seems helpful but actually works to wipe out data and functions.

Quiz

Fill in each blank with the correct letter:

a. myrmidons
b. draconian
c. cyclopean
d. Trojan horse
e. Achilles' heel
f. nemesis
g. Cassandra
h. arcadia

1. The CEO expected immediate and absolute obedience from his ____, no matter what he asked.
2. Shortly after hiring him, they discovered that he was actually a ____, sent by a rival company to destroy the workers' faith in the company's plans.
3. The architect surrounded the pool and garden with a great stone wall modeled on the ____ walls of ancient Greece.
4. They considered their little corner of New Hampshire a true ____ in its freedom from the pressures of the modern world.
5. In eighth grade his ____ was a disagreeable girl named Rita who liked playing horrible little tricks.
6. In times of national crisis, each news commentator sounds more like a ____ than the next.
7. Historians point to the ____ treaty terms as one of the causes of the next war.
8. Believing the flattery of others and enjoying the trappings of power have often been the ____ of successful politicians.

Review Quizzes

A. Choose the correct synonym and the correct antonym:

1. auspicious a. bad b. birdlike c. good d. likely
2. sensational a. kindly b. exciting c. ordinary d. odoriferous
3. provoke a. soothe b. incite c. veto d. announce
4. curative a. drug b. poison c. recreation d. antidote
5. irrevocable a. final b. retractable c. unbelievable d. vocal
6. perimeter a. essence b. edge c. center d. spurt
7. nemesis a. ally b. no one c. enemy d. sibling
8. sophomoric a. silly b. sage c. cacophonous d. languid
9. Achilles' heel a. paradise b. heroism c. immortality d. vulnerability
10. peripatetic a. immobile b. exact c. wandering d. imprecise
11. conspicuous a. shrewd b. invisible c. noticeable d. promising
12. vociferous a. speechless b. steely c. pliant d. noisy
13. visionary a. idealist b. cinematographer c. conservative d. writer
14. sentient a. frantic b. unaware c. alert d. tranquil
15. sophisticated a. rejected b. advanced c. worldly wise d. naive

B. Choose the closest definition:

1. phonetic a. called b. twitched c. sounded d. remembered
2. sophistry a. deception b. musical composition c. sound reasoning d. pleasure
3. procure a. appoint b. obtain c. decide d. lose
4. visage a. imagination b. citation c. expression d. depression
5. symphony a. piano recital b. complex rhythm c. unison chant d. orchestral composition

6. vis-à-vis a. compared to b. allowed to c. rented to d. talked to
7. introspection a. critical judgment b. self-examination c. inquisition d. detention
8. peripheral a. auxiliary b. central c. relating to the sun d. philosophical
9. draconian a. rustic b. massive c. disastrous d. severe
10. polyphonic a. multi-melodic b. uniformly harmonic c. relatively boring d. intentionally imitative
11. cyclopean a. serpentine b. gigantic c. infinitesimal d. circular
12. visitation a. journey b. prayer c. official visit d. stimulation
13. periodontal a. relating to feet b. around the sun c. around the teeth d. around a corner
14. curator a. caretaker b. watcher c. doctor d. purchaser
15. Cassandra a. optimist b. economist c. pessimist d. oculist

C. Fill in each blank with the correct letter:

a. equivocate
b. sensuous
c. cacophony
d. sentiment
e. myrmidon
f. Trojan horse
g. arcadia
h. theosophy
i. sinecure
j. perspicacious

1. The job turned out to be a ____, and no one cared if he played golf twice a week.
2. The huge Senate bill was a ____, filled with items that almost none of the senators were aware of.
3. We opened the door onto a haze of cigarette smoke and a ____ of music and laughter.
4. In the old book on ____ she found a philosophy very similar to the one she and her friends were exploring.
5. One ____ after another scurried in and out of the boardroom on errands for the chairman.
6. It didn't require a ____ eye to see that their marriage was a difficult one.

7. The letter described their new Virginia farm as a kind of ____ of unspoiled nature.
8. Whenever they asked for a definite date, he would ____ and try to change the subject.
9. She lay in the bath with her eyes closed in a kind of ____ daydream.
10. He always tried to end his letters with an appropriate ____ and a warm closing.

Unit 8

TEND/TENT, from the Latin *tendere,* meaning "to stretch, extend, or spread," can be seen most simply in the English word *tent,* meaning a piece of material stretched or extended over a frame. It can also be seen in the word *extend,* which means "to stretch forth or stretch out," and in *tendon,* the word for a tough band of tissue that stretches from a muscle to a bone.

contentious \kən-'ten-chəs\ Having a tendency to pick fights; quarrelsome.

• The school board meeting lasted late into the night as contentious parents argued over every detail of the new bus routes.

Someone who is contentious seems to enjoy arguing and sometimes goes to great lengths to start a fight. Some legislative battles in Congress seem to be caused as much by contentious politicians as by the issues involved. The word *contentious* can also mean "likely to cause an argument." Reform of the health-care system, for instance, has been a very contentious issue.

distend \di-'stend\ To swell or become expanded.

• Television viewers were shocked to see the distended bellies of the young children, usually a sign of malnutrition and starvation.

Distend is generally used in medical or technical contexts, and it usually refers to swelling caused by pressure from within. A doctor examining a patient complaining of intestinal pain will look to see if the abdomen is distended. Hoses distend and straighten when water is pumped through them.

portend \pȯr-ˈtend\ (1) To give a sign or warning beforehand. (2) To indicate or signify.

• Although the warm spell in February was welcome, the huge puddles by the melting snowbanks portended the spring floods that were likely to follow.

Portend comes directly from the Latin verb *portendere,* meaning "to foretell or predict," both of which suggest a stretching out into the future. Predicting often involves interpreting signs and omens. When the Cubs lose on opening day at Wrigley Field it often portends another season of heartbreak for Chicago fans. *Portend* may be used for both favorable and unfavorable outcomes, but it usually indicates a threat of evil or disaster. Some foreign-policy experts saw that the breakup of the Soviet Union portended chaos and strife for many countries in Eastern Europe.

tendentious \ten-ˈden-shəs\ Leaning toward a particular point of view; biased.

• In his later years, the professor wrote a series of tendentious essays attacking many modern novelists and praising authors from earlier eras.

Political speeches can often be as tendentious as they are *contentious.* Politicians will adopt a particular philosophy, and from that day on they will tend to view matters from that point of view. Facts are replaced by tendentious claims, and debates become predictable and unproductive.

PEND/PENS, meaning "to hang, weigh, or cause to hang down," comes from the Latin verb *pendere.* We find it in English in words like *pensive,* meaning "thoughtful," and *appendix,* that useless and sometimes troublesome piece that hangs from the intestine.

---

appendage \ə-ˈpen-dij\ (1) Something joined on to a larger or more important body or thing. (2) A subordinate body part, such as an arm or a leg.

• Wives complain justifiably when they are treated by others as mere appendages of their husbands.

Appendage refers to an attachment that is less important than the thing to which it is attached. A controversial speaker, for instance, may add a few soothing remarks as an appendage to an otherwise fiery speech. Some appendages are important in their own right, but may not be viewed that way by some people. So residents of Staten Island don't like having their borough viewed as simply an appendage of New York City. And many Canadians fear that their U.S. neighbors view Canada, despite its size, as an appendage to the United States.

expend \ik-'spend\ (1) To pay out. (2) To use up.

• The company was taking steps to limit the funds it was expending on health-care costs and disability benefits.

Expend comes straight from the Latin word *expendere,* meaning "to weigh out" or "to spend." *Expend* is close in meaning to *spend,* but it is usually used more in reference to business, industry, finance, or government, and it therefore usually also implies larger sums of money. We have a deficit in this country because government expends more dollars than it collects. In its nonfinancial sense, *expend* suggests an unnecessary waste of something. The deficit may continue because more ink and paper are expended on stories of gossip and scandal than on the day-to-day operations of government.

propensity \prə-'pen-sə-tē\ An often intense natural inclination or preference.

• In-laws have a natural propensity to offer advice, especially when it hasn't been requested.

A propensity is a leaning toward something. We have a propensity for something when we have a natural tendency or are driven by a natural appetite. Good reporters have a propensity to ask questions; good politicians have a propensity for avoiding them. Small children have a propensity for getting sticky, and, for some reason, spilled food has a propensity for landing on new ties.

stipend \'stī-pənd\ A sum of money paid at regular intervals in return for services or to cover expenses.

• David's fellowship to graduate school included a stipend to cover his basic living expenses.

A stipend is a little like a salary, but there are differences. A stipend may be intended more to cover expenses than to pay for a service. A stipend may arrive weekly or annually, but the amount of money is usually small. Stipends are normally paid to people involved in noncommercial activities, such as scholars, artists, and amateur athletes. One very generous stipend is the one paid by the MacArthur Foundation, which often runs into the hundreds of thousands of dollars, with no strings attached. The only catch is that you need to be a genius to get one.

Quizzes

A. Complete the analogy:

1. calculate : count :: expend : ____
   a. stretch b. speculate c. pay d. explode
2. distort : warp :: distend : ____
   a. swell b. notice c. display d. shrink
3. abode : dwelling :: stipend : ____
   a. study b. salary c. mortgage d. advance
4. sensational : great :: tendentious : ____
   a. opinionated b. neutral c. important d. promotional
5. imaginary : unreal :: propensity : ____
   a. idea b. opinion c. inclination d. artistry
6. passionate : loving :: contentious : ____
   a. competitive b. continuous c. collected
   d. quarrelsome
7. laugh : giggle :: portend : ____
   a. bend b. indicate c. argue d. stretch
8. passage : opening :: appendage : ____
   a. hanger b. hangar c. limb d. branch

B. Fill in each blank with the correct letter:

a. contentious
b. distend
c. tendentious
d. portend
e. appendage
f. expend
g. propensity
h. stipend

1. These departments ____ the largest amount of money on new computers.
2. The bodies of snakes ____ as they eat their prey.

3. The eager assistant was willing to be seen as the necessary ____ to his boss.
4. Life with a disagreeable, ____ neighbor is not easy.
5. Her unusual talent and ____ for chess was obvious before she was five.
6. The senator made a highly ____ speech about U.S. involvement overseas.
7. As part of his scholarship, he received a small ____ to cover living expenses.
8. Those dark clouds rolling in ____ bad weather to come.

PAN comes from Greek with its spelling and meaning intact. It simply means "all" in Greek; as an English prefix it can also mean "completely," "whole," or "general." A *panoramic* view is a complete view in every direction. *Panchromatic* film is sensitive to the reflected light of all colors in the spectrum. *Pantheism* is the worship of all gods. A *pantheon* is a temple dedicated to all the gods of a particular religion. A *pandemic* outbreak of a disease may not literally affect the entire human population, but enough to create catastrophic problems.

---

panacea \ˌpa-nə-ˈsē-ə\ A remedy for all ills or difficulties; cure-all.

• Educational reform is sometimes viewed as the panacea for all of society's problems.

Panacea combines *pan-* and the Greek word *akos,* "remedy." A panacea is a magical medicine that can cure whatever ails you, or a magical solution that can solve a whole set of problems. But since no such medicine or solution exists, the word *panacea* almost always occurs in contexts where the writer is criticizing a single solution to an array of problems ("There is no panacea for the problems of the inner city"). *Panacea* is also applied to easy solutions to individual problems, although this use loses the original "cure-all" sense of the word. In the view of its opponents, for example, the proposed legalization of street drugs is a panacea doomed to create far more problems than it would solve.

pandemonium \ˌpan-də-ˈmō-nē-əm\ A wild uproar or commotion.

• Pandemonium erupted in the football stadium as the underdogs scored an upset victory in the final seconds.

In *Paradise Lost,* the fallen Satan has his heralds proclaim "A solemn Council forthwith to be held / At Pandaemonium, the high Capital / Of Satan and his Peers." John Milton got the name for his capital of hell from linking *pan* with the Latin word *daemonium,* "evil spirit," thus indicating the place where Satan gathered together all the demons. For later writers, *pandemonium* became a synonym for hell itself, since a traditional image of hell was of a place where noise and confusion abound. *Pandemonium* also came to be used of any wicked, lawless, or riotous place. But nowadays, it is used to refer to the uproar itself rather than the place where it occurs.

panegyric \ˌpa-nə-ˈjir-ik\ A formal speech or statement giving high praise to someone or something.

• Lincoln's "Gettysburg Address" is as much a panegyric celebrating American democratic ideals as it is a eulogy for the brave soldiers who died on the battlefield.

American presidents at their inaugurations typically deliver a panegyric in praise of their great nation and the people who have had the wisdom to elect them. Probably few of them have realized that in delivering their praise-filled speeches before a vast throng they have remained true to our cultural roots in ancient Greece. In Athens *panēgyris* was the name for a public assembly, the word coming from *pan-* plus *agyris,* "assembly." A chosen speaker would deliver a set oration in praise of those who had served the state. With time the Greek word *panēgyrikos* shifted from meaning "of or for a festival assembly" to "a praise-filled oration." Today a panegyric need not be a public speech—many panegyrics are private or written—but the word continues to suggest praise that is elaborate, highflown, and perhaps a bit excessive.

panoply \ˈpa-nə-plē\ (1) A magnificent or impressive array. (2) A display of all appropriate accessory items.

• The full panoply of a royal coronation was a thrilling sight for the throngs of sidewalk onlookers and the millions of television viewers.

Panoply originally referred to the full suit of armor donned by a soldier or knight in preparation for combat. In fact, *panoply* comes from a Greek word that includes the noun *hopla,* "arms or armor." *Panoply* may refer to full ceremonial dress of any kind or to something resembling a suit of armor in being protective. More commonly, *panoply* refers to striking spectacle: the breathtaking panoply of the autumn foliage, or the stirring panoply of a military parade, for example. Or it can mean an extensive array or succession of things, as in "The display windows of the electronics store feature the complete panoply of equipment that is now thought necessary for home entertainment."

EXTRA places words outside or beyond their usual or routine territory. *Extraterrestrial* and *extragalactic* affairs take place beyond the earth or the galaxy. Something *extravagant,* such as an *extravaganza,* goes beyond the limits of reason or necessity. And of course *extra* itself is a word, a shortening of *extraordinary,* "beyond the ordinary."

---

extramundane \ˌek-strə-ˌmən-ˈdān\ Situated in or relating to a region beyond the material world.

• Communism is atheistic, and admits no extramundane authority.

Extramundane uses an older meaning of *mundane,* "relating to this world" or "earthly." The events described in Dante's 14th-century *Divine Comedy,* where the author is taken on a tour through hell, purgatory, and heaven, are entirely extramundane. At the end of his journey, in the highest heaven, he has a vision of extramundane harmony and bliss, the reward of the blessed for their holy earthly lives. As you can see, when *extra-* is a prefix it never means "extremely" (as in "Go extra slow through here") but instead always means "outside or beyond."

extrapolate \ik-ˈstra-pə-ˌlāt\ To extend or project facts or data into an area not known in order to make assumptions or to predict facts or trends.

• Economists try to predict future buying trends by extrapolating from current economic data.

Scientists worry about the greenhouse effect because they have extrapolated the rate of carbon dioxide buildup and predicted that its effect on the atmosphere will become increasingly severe. On the basis of their *extrapolations,* they have urged governments and businesses to limit factory and automobile emissions, and have cautioned that the burning and clearing of the Amazon rain forest must stop. Other scientists, extrapolating from the same conditions, trends, and data, have concluded that the greenhouse effect is less dangerous than we have been led to believe. The problem is that by the time either extrapolation is proved to be true, we may be at a point where further damage cannot be prevented. Notice that it is acceptable to speak of extrapolating existing data (to produce new data), extrapolating *from* existing data (to produce new data), or extrapolating new data (from existing data)—in other words, it isn't easy to use this word wrong.

extrovert \'ek-strə-ˌvərt\ A person mainly concerned with things outside him- or herself; a sociable and outgoing person.

• A complete extrovert, she made friends easily and lived one day at a time.

Extrovert (sometimes spelled *extravert*) means basically "turned outward"—that is, toward things outside oneself. The opposite personality type is the *introvert,* which naturally means "turned inward." Some psychologists have said that the only personality traits that can be identified in newborn infants are shyness and lack of shyness, which are rather close to *introversion* and *extroversion.*

extraneous \ek-'strā-nē-əs\ (1) Existing or coming from the outside. (2) Not forming an essential part; irrelevant.

• Your essay should be well-focused and should not contain any extraneous material.

Homework is difficult enough with extraneous distractions: the television, the radio, phone calls, or a pesky brother or sister. The library may be a good place to study since librarians try to limit extraneous noise. But even under ideal conditions, you can still be diverted by extraneous thoughts: the weather conditions, what to have for dinner, or a really good joke you heard recently.

Quizzes

A. Fill in each blank with the correct letter:

a. extrapolate
b. panoply
c. extraneous
d. panacea
e. extramundane
f. panegyric
g. extrovert
h. pandemonium

1. From these figures, economists can ____ data that shows a steady increase in employment.
2. Being a natural ____, he took to his new career as a salesman easily.
3. The new voice-mail system, with its full ____ of options, impressed the whole staff.
4. ____ broke out at the news of the victory.
5. The pope's address stressed that concern with worldly things must not lead us to forget spiritual and ____ matters.
6. He locked himself in his studio to ensure that there would be no ____ distractions.
7. She had been thinking of vitamins as a ____, but they weren't able to fight off infections.
8. Then he launched into a ____ to his father, calling him brilliant, loving, and saintly.

B. Indicate whether the following pairs of terms have the same or different meanings:

1. panacea / antibiotic same __ / different __
2. pandemonium / chaos same __ / different __
3. panegyric / pep talk same __ / different __
4. panoply / display same __ / different __
5. extrapolate / project same __ / different __
6. extraneous / necessary same __ / different __
7. extramundane / very ordinary same __ / different __
8. extrovert / schizophrenic same __ / different __

PHOS/PHOT comes from the Greek word for "light." *Phos* can be seen in the word *phosphorus,* which refers generally to anything that glows in the dark and also to a particular glowing chemical element. *Phot,* the more familiar root, appears in words like *photography,* which is the use of light to create an image on film or paper.

---

phosphorescent \ˌfäs-fə-ˈre-sənt\ (1) Giving off a glow that continues after an energy source has stopped transmitting energy. (2) Giving off a glow over a period of time without producing noticeable heat.

• The boat's wake glittered in the night with phosphorescent sea creatures stirred up by its passing.

The waters of the Caribbean Sea are phosphorescent in some places and glow with beautiful glimmering twinkles at night. The effect is created by tiny marine organisms that give off light in the warm tropical seas. Some minerals are naturally phosphorescent as well, and new chemical combinations can produce long-lasting *phosphorescence* without heat. One popular use is in Halloween "torches" that can be carried safely by children in costume.

photogenic \ˌfō-tə-ˈje-nik\ Very suitable for being photographed.

• Visitors to New England are often disappointed to find that the photogenic small towns with white churches and tidy houses are actually few and far between.

Photogenic originally meant "produced by light" or "producing light" and was used mostly in scientific or technical contexts. During the 20th century *photogenic* developed its now most common sense, perhaps because the original technical meaning was simply ignored. So now we use *photogenic* to describe scenery, baby animals, and presidential candidates.

photon \ˈfō-ˌtän\ A tiny particle or bundle of radiant energy.

• The idea that light consists of photons is difficult until you begin to think of a ray of light as being caused by a stream of very small particles.

It was Albert Einstein who first theorized that the energy in a light beam exists in small bits or particles called photons, and scientists now realize that light sometimes behaves like a wave (somewhat like sound or water) and sometimes like a stream of particles. The amazing power of lasers is the result of a concentration of photons that have been made to travel together in order to hit their target at the same time.

photosynthesis \ˌfō-tō-ˈsin-thə-sis\ The process by which green plants use light to produce organic matter from carbon dioxide and water.

• Sagebrush survives in harsh climates because it is capable of carrying on photosynthesis at very low temperatures.

The Greek roots of *photosynthesis* combine to produce the basic meaning "to put together with the help of light." Sunlight splits the water molecules held in a plant's leaves and releases the oxygen in them into the air. (Photosynthesis is what first produced oxygen in the atmosphere billions of years ago, and it is still what keeps it there.) What is left over combines with carbon dioxide to produce carbohydrates, which the plant uses as food.

LUC comes from the Latin noun *lux,* "light," and the verb *lucere,* "to shine or glitter." *Lucid* prose is clear in meaning, as if light were shining through it. *Lucifer,* a name for the devil, means "Light-bearer," the name he had before he fell from heaven.

---

elucidate \i-ˈlü-sə-ˌdāt\ To clarify by explaining; explain.

• A good doctor should always be willing to elucidate any medical jargon he or she uses.

Elucidate means "to shed light on." When you elucidate, you make transparent or clear something that was formerly murky or confusing. Carl Sagan, the astrophysicist, has a gift for elucidating to a large audience information about the objects in the universe. Through his *lucid* explanations he has made clear how stars are born and die, how the universe may have begun, and much more.

lucent \ˈlü-sənt\ (1) Giving off light. (2) Easily seen through.

• Their romance began under a lucent moon on a Mediterranean island.

Lucent is most often used in poetry or literature, where its meaning is usually close to that of *luminous*. The lucent petals of buttercups are one of the joys of a bright summer's day. Brightly polished stones have a lucent appearance. And we may even admire the lucent performance of a gifted musician.

lucubration \ˌlü-kyü-ˈbrā-shən\ (1) Hard and difficult study. (2) The product of such study.

• By the end of the semester our professor admitted that he wasn't looking forward to reading through any more of our lucubrations on novels that no one enjoyed.

Lucubration came to mean "hard study" because it originally meant study done by lamplight, which in a world without electric lights was likely to be hard work. Abe Lincoln is known for having engaged in lucubration of this sort. The word has a literary feel to it and is often used with a touch of sarcasm.

translucent \tranz-ˈlü-sənt\ Partly transparent; allowing light to pass through but diffusing it so that objects beyond cannot be seen clearly.

• Architects have recently used industrial glass bricks in designing buildings because their translucent quality gives light but guards privacy.

Frosted glass is probably the most familiar translucent material. Stained glass is also translucent. Some red wines prove to be translucent when poured into a crystal goblet and held before a candle in a dark corner of a quiet restaurant.

Quizzes

A. Indicate whether the following pairs have the same or different meanings:

1. photogenic / glittering — same __ / different __
2. lucent / flashing — same __ / different __
3. photon / light particle — same __ / different __
4. translucent / beaming — same __ / different __

5. phosphorescent / pulsing same __ / different __
6. lucubration / vacation same __ / different __
7. photosynthesis / twinkling same __ / different __
8. elucidate / explain same __ / different __

B. Match the definition on the left to the correct word on the right:

1. glowing	a. lucubration
2. production of organic matter	b. phosphorescent
	c. translucent
3. clarify	d. elucidate
4. passing diffused light	e. photogenic
5. elemental particle	f. photosynthesis
6. brightly clear	g. photon
7. hard study	h. lucent
8. visually appealing	

MOR/MORT comes from the Latin *mori,* "to die," and *mort-*, the stem of *mors,* meaning "death." A *mortuary* is a place where dead bodies are kept until burial. A *postmortem* examination is one conducted on a recently dead body. And a *memento mori* (a Latin phrase meaning literally "Remember that you must die") is a reminder of death; the death's head carved onto an old gravestone is an example.

immortality \ˌi-ˌmȯr-ˈta-lə-tē\ (1) Deathless or unending existence. (2) Lasting fame.

• Michelangelo achieved immortality with his painting and sculpture, Beethoven with his music.

Most of the world's religions deal with the issue of immortality and give advice on how to achieve it. For Achilles and the Greek heroes, immortality and *mortality* existed side by side: the *mortal* bodies of heroes died, but their *immortal* fame lived on in song and story.

moribund \ˈmȯr-ə-bənd\ (1) In the process of dying or approaching death. (2) Inactive or becoming outmoded.

• Many economists believe that America must replace its moribund smokestack industries with businesses based on new technology.

Moribund can be used in its original literal sense of "approaching death." Doctors will speak of a moribund patient going into a coma or a deep stupor. But *moribund* is much more commonly used to refer to things. When the economy goes bad, we hear about moribund mills and factories and towns, and the economy itself may be called moribund. People who worry about culture will speak of the moribund state of poetry or the moribund film industry—which may just mean they haven't seen a good movie lately.

mortician \mȯr-'ti-shən\ A person who prepares the dead for burial or cremation and manages the funeral.

• Every town needs a mortician, but the job only seems popular at Halloween.

Modern morticians employ skills somewhat different from those of Egyptian times. In ancient Egypt, morticians removed the organs and placed them in ornamental jars, drained the blood, and set the dead body in a solution to dry it out. The body was then wrapped in linen and placed in a mummy case, which was in turn placed in a tomb. The Great Pyramids were the most magnificent of the Egyptian tombs.

mortify \'mȯr-tə-ˌfī\ (1) To subdue or deaden (the body) especially by self-discipline or self-inflicted pain. (2) To embarrass greatly; humiliate.

• Teenagers are often mortified by their parents' attempts to act youthful.

Mortify once meant "put to death," but no longer. The "subdue or deaden" sense of *mortify* is most familiar to us in the phrase "mortifying the flesh," which refers to an old custom once followed by devout Christians, who would starve themselves, deprive themselves of every comfort, and even whip themselves in order to subdue their bodily desires. But the most common use of *mortify* today is the "humiliate" sense, and its connection with death is still apparent when we speak of "dying of embarrassment."

NEC/NIC/NOX, from the Latin verb *necare* and the noun *noxa*, have to do with killing or slaying. These roots are related to the Greek *nekros*, "corpse," found in such words as *necrology*, "a list of the recently dead," and *necromancy*, "the art of conjuring up spirits of the dead."

internecine \ˌin-tər-ˈne-ˌsēn\ (1) Deadly; mutually destructive. (2) Involving conflict within a group.

• The downfall of the radical political group came as it succumbed to internecine struggles for power and influence.

The Latin word *internecinus* meant "to the death." An internecine battle, then, was simply a very bloody one. Over the years, the English word developed the sense of "mutually destructive." And during the 20th century the word developed its main meaning of "conflict within a group." So now internecine warfare seldom refers to bloody battles but instead to the internal bickering and fighting that go on within a political party, government, profession, or family.

necrosis \ne-ˈkrō-səs\ The usually localized death of living tissue.

• One danger for young athletes is that prolonged use of some pain medications can cause necrosis in the kidney.

Many kinds of injuries and ailments can cause the death of bodily tissue. A heart attack can cause necrosis of heart tissue, and one stage in appendicitis is necrosis of the appendix. Cirrhosis and hepatitis can cause the liver to become *necrotic*, and other kinds of diseases can cause necrotic gallbladders, corneas, or intestines. Infections resulting from injuries can create necrotic tissue that may have to be surgically removed in order for the injury to heal.

noxious \ˈnäk-shəs\ Harmful to or destructive of living things.

• The bombing of the World Trade Center caused noxious fumes and smoke to spread through the structure and cause injury to hundreds of people.

The Environmental Protection Agency regulates the disposal of noxious chemicals or wastes that would harm the environment or the creatures living in it. Such noxious residues of modern technological processes are proving harder and harder to get rid of safely. No one wants them nearby, and a way of making them disappear has simply not been found. The meaning of *noxious* is sometimes close to *obnoxious,* though it's not so often applied to people.

pernicious \pər-ˈni-shəs\ Extremely harmful or destructive.

• The debate goes on about whether censorship or pornography has the more pernicious effect on society.

Pernicious usually implies serious harm done by an evil or corrupting force. Violence on television may have a pernicious influence on children. Welfare is seen as a pernicious institution by those who believe it discourages individual initiative. And AIDS is rightly referred to as a pernicious disease.

Quizzes

A. Complete the analogy:

1. immortality : ____ :: heaven : hell
   a. eternity b. god c. death d. life
2. necrosis : ____ :: disease : sickness
   a. medicine b. cure c. damage d. prescription
3. mortician : ____ :: physician : doctor
   a. grave digger b. gardener c. underwear
   d. undertaker
4. internecine : ____ :: international : domestic
   a. external b. extracurricular c. extroverted
   d. extraordinary
5. mortify : ____ :: appeal : request
   a. paralyze b. humiliate c. embalm d. slay
6. noxious : ____ :: successful : failing
   a. noisy b. beautiful c. beneficial d. noticeable
7. moribund : ____ :: cautious : fearful
   a. concerned b. obstinate c. grim d. obsolete
8. pernicious : ____ :: fruitful : productive
   a. healthful b. particular c. deadly d. demanding

B. Fill in each blank with the correct letter:

a. pernicious
b. internecine
c. necrosis
d. noxious
e. moribund
f. mortify
g. immortality
h. mortician

1. As the textile industry moved south, mill towns in New England became ____.
2. When fire broke out in the hallway, ____ fumes from the burning carpet filled every room.
3. Achilles chose ____ in legend over a long, happy life.
4. The police turned the body over to a ____ when they had finished their examination.
5. The doctor said he had to stop drinking to avoid further ____ of the liver.
6. Some religious zealots still engage in acts designed to ____ the flesh.
7. The ____ effects of a teacher's constant criticism may show in her students' unwillingness to volunteer in class.
8. The wise leader guarded against ____ conflict by providing many opportunities for cooperation among his followers.

Words from Mythology and History

aeolian harp \ē-'ō-lē-ən-'härp\ A box with strings that produce musical sounds when wind blows on them.

• Poets have long been fascinated by the aeolian harp because it is an instrument that produces music without a human performer.

Aeolus was the king or guardian of the winds, according to the ancient Greeks. He lived in a cave with his many, many sons and daughters, and sent forth whatever wind Zeus asked for. When Odysseus stopped there on his way home from Troy, he received a bag of winds to fill his sails. His men, however, opened the bag and released them all while he was asleep, and the raging winds blew them all the way back to their starting point. An aeolian harp produces enchanting harmonies when the wind passes over it. According to Homer, it was the god Hermes who invented the harp, by having the wind blow over the dried sinews attached to a tortoise shell.

cynosure \'sī-nə-ˌshu̇r\ (1) A guide. (2) A center of attention.

• Whenever the latest hot young rock star enters the nightclub, he becomes the cynosure of the assembled crowd.

Cynosure means "dog's tail" in Greek and Latin. In those languages it was the name for the constellation Ursa Minor, or the Little Bear, whose tail is formed by the North Star. The North Star has always been a trusty guide for travelers, especially sailors, because unlike the other stars, it always remains in the same position in the northern sky. So cynosure came to mean both "guide" and "center of attention."

laconic \lə-'kä-nik\ Using extremely few words.

• Male movie stars usually don't have a lot of dialogue to learn because most scripts seem to call for laconic leading men who avoid conversation.

Ancient Sparta was located in the region known as Laconia. The disciplined and militaristic Spartans were known for using no more words than they had to. So this terse, abrupt way of speaking became known as *laconic* after them and their territory.

mnemonic \ni-'mä-nik\ Having to do with the memory; assisting the memory.

• Sales-training courses recommend mnemonic devices as a way of remembering peoples' names.

The Greek word for memory is *mnemosyne*; something that helps the memory is therefore a mnemonic aid. Such snappy mnemonic devices as KISS (Keep It Simple, Stupid) or Every Good Boy Does Fine (for the notes on the lines of a musical staff with a treble clef) help to recall simple rules or complicated series that might otherwise slip away.

platonic \plə-'tä-nik\ (1) Relating to the philosopher Plato or his teachings. (2) Involving a close relationship from which romance and sex are absent.

• The male and female leads in many situation comedies keep their relationship platonic for the first few seasons, but romance almost always wins out in the end.

The philosopher Plato taught that all objects here on earth are pale imitations of their ideal form, just as a shadow is a weak imitation of the real object or a painting fails to capture true reality. This true form has come to be called the "platonic form." Plato presented his theories in a series of dramatic conversations between the philosopher Socrates and other people, which became known as the "Platonic dialogues." Because these philosophers and their students were all male, and because Socrates in the dialogues sometimes goes to great lengths to avoid committing homosexual acts, despite his desires, close but nonsexual friendship between two people who might be thought to be romantically attracted to each other is today known as platonic love or friendship.

sapphic \'sa-fik\ (1) Lesbian. (2) Relating to a poetic verse pattern associated with Sappho.

• The Roman poets Catullus and Horace composed wonderful love poems in sapphic verse.

Sappho wrote poems of passion and self-reflection, some of them directed to the women attending the school she conducted on the Greek island of Lesbos around 600 B.C. The poems were written in an original rhythmical pattern, which has become known as sapphic verse. The island of Lesbos also gave its name to lesbianism, which is sometimes called sapphic love.

Socratic \sō-'kra-tik\ Having to do with the philosopher Socrates or with his teaching method, in which he systematically questioned the student in conversation in order to draw forth truths.

• The professor fascinated some students but annoyed others with her Socratic method of teaching, which required them to listen, think, and participate in class.

Socrates lived in Greece in the 5th century B.C. He left no writings behind, so all that we know of him is through the writings of his disciple Plato. Today he is most remembered for his method of teaching by asking questions. His name survives in terms such as *Socratic induction,* which is a method of gradually arriving at generalizations through a process of questions and answers, and *Socratic irony,* in which the teacher pretends ignorance, but questions his students skillfully to make them aware of their errors in understanding.

solecism \'sō-lə-ˌsi-zəm\ (1) A grammatical mistake in speaking or writing. (2) A blunder in etiquette or proper behavior.

• The poor boy committed his first solecism immediately on entering by tracking mud over the Persian rug in the dining room.

In ancient Asia Minor, there was a city called Soloi where the inhabitants spoke Greek that was full of grammatical errors. Any lapse in grammar or in formal social behavior has hence come to be known as a solecism. Such things as saying "ain't" or "they was" or using the hostess's best bath towel to dry off the dog are solecisms. The earth won't shatter from such acts, but sometimes a few nerves will.

Quiz

Fill in each blank with the correct letter:

a. solecism
b. sapphic
c. platonic
d. Socratic
e. cynosure
f. aeolian harp
g. mnemonic
h. laconic

1. The teacher quickly learned the students' names by using her own ____ devices.
2. We all were fascinated as breezes raised a tune from the ____.
3. New Yorkers tend to think of their city as the ____ of the nation.
4. The ____ method is inappropriate for normal courtroom interrogation.
5. After encountering the fifth ____ in the report, we began to lose faith in the writer.
6. Her father-in-law was ____ in her presence but extremely talkative around his son.
7. She knew he loved her when a love poem in ____ verse appeared on her desk.
8. The dinner was good, but saying that it approached the ____ ideal of a meal was probably too much.

Review Quizzes

A. Choose the correct antonym *and* the correct synonym

1. elucidate a. confuse b. count c. clarify d. describe
2. contentious a. continental b. quarrelsome c. conscious d. agreeable
3. solecism a. correctness b. love poem c. death wish d. error
4. noxious a. harmful b. beneficial c. intrusive d. annoying
5. pernicious a. dangerous b. large c. gentle d. impressive
6. laconic a. glad b. quiet c. beneficial d. talkative
7. moribund a. obsolete b. sashed c. delay d. healthy
8. distend a. shrink b. swell c. seek d. hold
9. immortality a. eternal damnation b. eternal flame c. eternal life d. eternal death
10. tendentious a. opinionated b. suitable c. common d. objective

B. Indicate whether the following pairs of words have the same or different meanings:

1. mnemonic / ideal same __ / different __
2. necrosis / infection same __ / different __
3. extrapolate / project same __ / different __
4. mortify / stiffen same __ / different __
5. appendage / attachment same __ / different __
6. cynosure / beacon same __ / different __
7. pernicious / destructive same __ / different __
8. propensity / projectile same __ / different __
9. mortician / philosopher same __ / different __
10. lucent / glittering same __ / different __
11. phosphorescent / sea green same __ / different __
12. translucent / cross-lighted same __ / different __
13. solecism / goof same __ / different __
14. elucidate / explain same __ / different __
15. distend / swell same __ / different __
16. lucubration / nightmare same __ / different __
17. photosynthesis / reproduction same __ / different __

18. panacea / remedy same __ / different __
19. photogenic / appealing same __ / different __
20. internecine / impassioned same __ / different __

C. Match the definition on the left to the correct word on the right:

1. question-and-answer	a. contentious
2. elementary particle of light	b. expend
3. allowance	c. sapphic
4. use up	d. portend
5. argumentative	e. translucent
6. nonsexual	f. platonic
7. foretell	g. photon
8. dying	h. Socratic
9. lesbian	i. stipend
10. light-diffusing	j. moribund

Unit 9

HER/HES, from the Latin verb *haerere,* means "to stick" or "to get stuck." This has produced words with two kinds of meaning. A word such as *adhesive* means basically "sticking," whereas a word such as *hesitate* means more or less "stuck in one place."

adherent \ad-'hir-ənt\ (1) Someone who follows a leader, a party, or a profession. (2) One who believes in a particular philosophy or religion.

• The general's adherents heavily outnumbered his opponents and managed to shout them down repeatedly.

A plan for cutting the deficit without raising taxes or reducing spending will usually attract adherents easily. In the 1992 presidential elections, Ross Perot inspired an army of enthusiastic adherents, more than any third-party candidate in U.S. history.

cohesion \kō-'hē-zhən\ The act or state of sticking together.

• Successful athletic teams usually achieve their victories through tight cohesion among the players.

Cohesion, which contains the prefix *co-,* "together," generally refers to similar things sticking together. *Adhesion,* on the other hand, usually means sticking to something of a different kind, in the way that *adhesive* tape or an *adherent* does. So a company may desire to create cohesion among its employees, and psychologists may seek to promote *cohesive* family units.

incoherent \ˌin-kō-'hir-ənt\ (1) Unclear or difficult to understand. (2) Loosely organized or inconsistent.

• She was tired of her boss's angry lectures, which usually turned into incoherent ranting and raving.

Incoherent is the opposite of *coherent*, and both commonly refer to words and thought. Just as *coherent* means well-ordered and clear, *incoherent* means disordered and hard to follow. *Incoherence* in speech may result from emotional stress, especially anxiety or anger. Incoherence in writing may simply result from poor planning; a twelve-page term paper that isn't written until the night before it is due will almost certainly suffer from incoherence.

inherent \in-'hir-ənt\ Part of something by nature or habit.

• A guiding belief behind our Constitution is that individuals have certain inherent rights that ought to be protected from governmental interference.

Inherent literally refers to something that "sticks in" or is "stuck in" something else. A plan may have an inherent flaw that will cause it to fail; a person may have inherent virtues that will bring him or her love and respect. Something inherent cannot be removed: the plan with inherent flaws may simply have to be thrown out, but the person with inherent virtues will never lose them.

FUG comes from the Latin verb *fugere*, meaning "to flee or escape." A *refugee* flees from some threat or danger to a *refuge*, which is a place that provides shelter and safety.

---

centrifugal \sen-'tri-fyù-gəl\ Moving outward from a center or central focus.

• Their favorite ride was the Round-up, in which centrifugal force flattened them against the outer wall of a rapidly spinning cage.

Part of an astronaut's training occurs in a *centrifuge*, a spinning machine that generates force equal to several times the force of gravity. The force sends the astronaut away from the machine's center; his or her sense of direction and balance as well as muscular strength thus become used to some of the centrifugal forces that will be at work during a real space mission.

fugitive \'fyü-jə-tiv\ A person who flees or tries to escape.

• The United States sometimes makes special allowances for refugees who are fugitives from persecution in their homelands.

The young outlaws Bonnie Parker and Clyde Barrow were high-spirited fugitives from justice for two years in the Depression era, fleeing and robbing banks across the Southwest, barely escaping the long arm of the law. Fugitives with Robin Hood-like style and glamour have always attracted interest and sympathy, especially from the poor.

fugue \'fyüg\ A musical form in which a theme is echoed and imitated by voices or instruments that enter one after another and interweave as the piece proceeds.

• For his debut on the new organ, the church organist chose a fugue by J. S. Bach.

Bach and Handel composed many fugues for harpsichord and organ in which the various parts (or voices) seem to flee from and chase each other in an intricate dance. Each part, after it has stated the theme or melody, apparently flees from the next part, which takes up the same theme and sets off in pursuit. Somewhat the same effect can be had by singing a round such as "Three Blind Mice" or "Row, Row, Row Your Boat."

subterfuge \'səb-tər-ˌfyüj\ (1) A trick designed to help conceal, escape, or evade. (2) A deceptive trick.

• The students employed every kind of subterfuge they knew to keep the substitute teacher from assigning homework.

Subterfuge contains the prefix *subter-* (related to *sub-*), meaning "under" or "secretly," so a subterfuge is something done secretly or "under the table." The spies depicted in John LeCarré's novels employ all kinds of subterfuge to accomplish their missions. The life of a spy sometimes seems appealing, but few of us have much experience with subterfuges more elaborate than claiming to have a previous engagement in order to avoid having dinner with our relatives.

Quizzes

A. Fill in each blank with the correct letter:

a. cohesion
b. fugitive
c. incoherent
d. fugue
e. centrifugal
f. adherent
g. subterfuge
h. inherent

1. The first-year students were sent off on a camping trip to create a greater sense of ____ within the class.
2. By ____ they had managed to infiltrate the enemy ranks and blow up the bridge.
3. The Christian Scientist philosophy of Mary Baker Eddy continued to attract many an ____.
4. Federal agents were pleased to have apprehended the ____.
5. By the time his fever reached 105°, the boy was mumbling ____ sentences.
6. A rock tied to a string and whirled about exerts ____ force on the string.
7. Mahatma Gandhi believed goodness was ____ in humans.
8. They chose a grand ____ by Bach as their wedding march.

B. Choose the closest definition:

1. inherent a. part of b. inherited c. confused d. loyal
2. fugue a. mathematical formula b. musical form c. marginal figure d. masonry foundation
3. adherent a. sticker b. stinker c. follower d. flower
4. centrifugal a. moving upward b. moving backward c. moving downward d. moving outward
5. cohesion a. unity b. thoughtfulness c. uniformity d. thoughtlessness
6. subterfuge a. overhead serve b. underhanded plot c. powerful force d. secret supporter
7. incoherent a. attached b. constant c. controlled d. confused
8. fugitive a. traveler b. sailor c. escapee d. drifter

COSM, from the Greek word meaning both "ornament" and "order," gives us two different groups of words. *Cosmetics* are the stuff we use to ornament our faces. The "order" meaning combines with the Greek belief that the universe was an orderly place, so words in this group relate to the universe and the worlds within it. *Cosmonaut*, for instance, is the word for a space traveler from the former Soviet Union.

cosmetic \käz-'me-tik\ Done or made for the sake of beauty or appearance.

• Renovating the house would involve more than just cosmetic changes such as fresh paint and new curtains.

Constant exposure to modern standards of beauty through advertisements prompts more and more people to make cosmetic changes in their appearance: a straightened nose, a lifted face, a tucked tummy. The cosmetic surgery that people undergo to achieve their new look does nothing to improve their underlying state of health. In fact, another meaning of *cosmetic* is "lacking substance, superficial." A company accused of corrupt practices may try to improve its image by making cosmetic changes, such as issuing idealistic policy statements or replacing a few guilty-looking executives.

cosmology \käz-'mä-lə-jē\ (1) A theory that describes the nature of the universe. (2) A branch of astronomy that deals with the origin and structure of the universe.

• Many New Age philosophies propose a cosmology that differs greatly from the traditional Jewish, Christian, or Islamic ways of viewing the universe.

Most religions and cultures include some kind of cosmology to explain the nature of the universe. In modern astronomy, the leading cosmology is still the Big Bang theory, which claims that the universe began with a huge explosion that sent matter and energy spreading out in all directions. One of the reasons fans watch "Star Trek" is for the various cosmologies depicted in the show, such as different conceptions of space, time, and the meaning of life.

cosmopolitan \ˌkäz-mə-ˈpä-lə-tən\ (1) Having international sophistication and experience. (2) Made up of persons, elements, or influences from many different parts of the world.

• New York, like most cosmopolitan cities, offers a wonderful array of restaurants featuring cooking styles from around the world.

Cosmopolitan includes the root *polit-*, meaning "citizen"; thus, someone who is cosmopolitan is a "citizen of the world." She may be able to read the morning paper in Rio de Janeiro and attend a lecture in Madrid with equal ease. And a city or a country that is cosmopolitan has aspects and elements that come from various countries.

cosmos \ˈkäz-ˌmōs\ (1) The universe, especially when it is viewed as orderly and systematic. (2) Any orderly system that is complete in itself.

• The biologist, the philosopher, and the astronomer all try in their own ways to understand the mysteries of the cosmos.

In some of its uses, *cosmos* simply means "universe." So we can say that the invention of the telescope helped us learn more about our cosmos. But usually *cosmos* is used to suggest an orderly or harmonious universe. Thus it may be the philosopher, or even the religious mystic, that helps put us in touch with the cosmos. In a similar way, *cosmic* rays come from outer space, but cosmic questions come from human attempts to find order in the universe.

SCI comes from the Latin verb *scire*, "to know" or "to understand." This root appears in the word *science*, which refers to factual knowledge, and in *conscience*, which refers to moral knowledge. And to be *conscious* is to be in a state where you are able to know or understand.

---

conscientious \ˌkän-chē-ˈen-chəs\ (1) Governed by morality; scrupulous. (2) Resulting from painstaking or exact attention.

• New employees should be especially conscientious about turning in all of their assignments on time.

Conscience and *conscientious* both come from a Latin verb meaning "to be aware of guilt." A conscientious person is one with a strong moral sense and one who has feelings of guilt when he or she violates it. *Conscientious* indicates extreme care, either in observing moral laws or in performing assigned duties. A conscientious public official has a moral code that is not easily broken. A conscientious worker has a sense of duty that forces him or her to do a careful job. A conscientious report shows painstaking work on the part of the writer.

omniscience \äm-'ni-shəns\ Infinite awareness, understanding, and insight.

• It was comforting to believe in the omniscience of a Supreme Being, and it kept him on his best behavior.

Omniscience includes another root, *omni-*, from a Latin word meaning "all," and literally means "knowing all." Omniscience is usually only possible for a god or supernatural being. However, the narrator in many novels is *omniscient*—able to see everything that is happening, no matter where or when, and able to know and understand everything going on in the minds of all the characters. For ordinary mortals such omniscience may sound attractive but would probably actually be quite a burden.

prescient \'pre-shənt\ Having or showing advance knowledge of what is going to happen.

• For years she had read *The Wall Street Journal* every morning in hopes of finding prescient warnings about future crashes, crises, and catastrophes.

Like being omniscient, being truly prescient would require supernatural powers. But well-informed people may have such good judgment as to appear prescient, and *prescient* is often used to mean "having good foresight." U.S. presidents hope to have prescient advisers or, at least once in a while, to receive a prescient analysis of world and domestic affairs. Some newspaper columnists appear to be prescient in their predictions, but we may suspect that leaks rather than *prescience* are the secret.

unconscionable \ən-'kän-chə-nə-bəl\ (1) Not guided by any moral sense; unscrupulous. (2) Shockingly excessive, unreasonable, or unfair.

• The used-car dealer was convicted of rolling back odometers and other unconscionable business practices.

The word *unconscionable* comes from *conscience*. An unconscionable person is one whose conduct is not guided by conscience. Unconscionable acts are immoral. Unconscionable things are those that cannot be tolerated in good conscience. The owner of a new house may not expect perfection, but if it has an unconscionable number of defects, it's a lemon.

Quizzes

A. Complete the analogy:

1. present : absent :: prescient : ____
   a. evil b. blind c. far-sighted d. painstaking
2. cosmic : universal :: cosmetic : ____
   a. decorative b. organized c. planetary d. starred
3. bold : shy :: cosmopolitan : ____
   a. planetary b. naive c. unique d. nearby
4. shining : glowing :: conscientious : ____
   a. careful b. all-seeing c. well-informed d. scientific
5. description : illustration :: cosmology : ____
   a. sophistication b. universe c. explanation
   d. appearance
6. truth : fiction :: omniscience : ____
   a. morality b. ignorance c. foresight d. worldliness
7. woods : forest :: cosmos : ____
   a. stars b. planets c. orbits d. universe
8. solid : liquid :: unconscionable : ____
   a. orderly b. attractive c. universal d. moral

B. Match the definition on the right to the correct word on the left:

1. cosmopolitan	a. having foresight
2. omniscience	b. universe
3. cosmetic	c. universal knowledge
4. conscientious	d. sophisticated
5. unconscionable	e. for the sake of appearance
6. cosmology	f. scrupulous
7. prescient	g. inexcusable
8. cosmos	h. description of the universe

JUNCT, from the Latin verb *jungere,* means "join." A *junction* is a place where things come together. A *conjunction* is a word (such as *and* or *or*) that joins two other words or groups of words: "this *and* that," "to be *or* not to be."

adjunct \'a-ˌjəŋkt\ Something joined or added to another thing of which it is not a part.

• The technical school promised formal classroom instruction that would be a valuable adjunct to the on-the-job training and experience.

The roots of *adjunct,* which includes the prefix *ad-*, meaning "to or toward," imply that one thing is "joined to" another. A car wash may be operated as an adjunct to a gas station. Teachers often take on advising students as an adjunct to their regular classroom duties. And anyone truly interested in expanding his or her vocabulary will find that daily reading of a newspaper or magazine is a valuable adjunct to studying this book.

disjunction \dis-'jəŋk-shən\ A break, separation, or sharp difference between two things.

• The best English teachers see no disjunction between theory and practice when it comes to good writing.

A disjunction is often simply a lack of connection between two things. For example, there is frequently a disjunction between what people expect from computers and what they actually know about them. Sometimes this takes the form of an abrupt break. In this sense, Ronald Reagan's policies seemed to represent a disjunction with the politics of the previous twenty years. And sometimes *disjunction* is used to suggest that two things are very different in some important way, and so we speak of a disjunction between science and morality, between doing and telling, or between knowing and explaining.

injunction \in-'jəŋk-shən\ (1) A warning, direction, or prohibition regarding an activity. (2) A court order commanding or forbidding the doing of some act.

• Her new fitness program included no injunctions against drinking beer and wine, she was glad to see.

Injunctions can either require or forbid something. "Eat your vegetables" and "Drive safely" are orders to do something. But injunctions are more frequently prohibitions. For instance, some English teachers uphold the injunction against beginning a sentence with "and." Similarly, legal injunctions can command or forbid; an injunction may require that a contract be honored, or may forbid a strike from taking place.

junta \'hůn-tə\ A committee that controls a government, especially after a revolution.

• Hopes for democratic reforms ended when the military junta took power and closed down the country's major newspaper.

The Latin root is a little hard to see in this word, because it comes into English through Spanish. Though we may think of a junta as a group that seizes power illegally, the word basically refers to the joining together of the group; in fact, the oldest meaning of *junta* is "a council or committee for political or governmental purposes." But today it generally means a close-knit group of people who dominate a government after seizing power in a revolution. Given the way juntas come to power, it should be no surprise that most are made up of military officers and few are overly concerned with protecting human rights.

PART, from the Latin word *pars*, meaning "part," comes into English most obviously in our word *part* but also in words like *apartment, compartment,* and *particle,* all of which are parts of a larger whole.

---

impart \im-'pärt\ (1) To give from one's store or abundance. (2) To make known; disclose.

• As a dedicated teacher, her primary goal was always to impart knowledge.

When we impart something, we give a piece of it, sometimes a big piece. The yellow corn in chicken feed imparts the yellow color to chickens that eat it. A speaker's manner of delivery can impart authority to what he or she says. To impart is also to say or communicate: "He finally decided to impart his plans to his family"; "She imparted her displeasure regarding absences to her staff in no uncertain terms."

impartial \im-'pär-shəl\ Fair and not biased; treating or affecting all equally.

• Representatives of labor and management agreed to have the matter decided by an impartial third party.

To be partial toward someone or something is to be somewhat biased or prejudiced, which means that a person who is partial really only sees part of the whole picture. To be impartial is the opposite of this. The United Nations sends impartial observers to monitor elections in troubled countries. We hope that juries will be impartial when they render verdicts. Grandparents, on the other hand, are not expected to be impartial when describing the good looks of a new grandchild.

participle \'pär-tə-ˌsi-pəl\ A word that is formed from a verb but used like an adjective.

• "Crying" in the phrase "the crying child" is a present participle; "guaranteed" in "satisfaction guaranteed" is a past participle.

English verbs can take several basic forms, which we call their principal parts: the infinitive ("to move," "to speak"), the past tense ("moved," "spoke"), the past participle ("moved," "spoken"), and the present participle ("moving," "speaking"). Past and present participles act like adjectives since they can modify nouns ("the spoken word," "a moving experience"). A grammatical error called a *dangling participle* occurs when a sentence begins with a participle that doesn't modify the subject. In the sentence "Climbing the mountain, the cabin came in view," "climbing" is a dangling participle since it doesn't modify "cabin."

partisan \'pär-tə-zən\ (1) A person who is strongly devoted to a particular cause or group. (2) A guerrilla fighter.

• The retiring Supreme Court justice was an unashamed partisan of the cause of free speech.

A partisan is one who supports one *part* or *party*. Sometimes the support takes the form of military action, as when guerrilla fighters engage in harassing government forces. *Partisan* can also be used as an adjective. In some families, the World Series can arouse partisan passions; most frequently, however, *partisan* refers to support of a political party, as in the phrase "partisan politics."

Quizzes

A. Choose the closest definition:

1. injunction a. order b. position c. fact d. connection
2. impartial a. fair b. biased c. accurate d. opinionated
3. adjunct a. warning b. addition c. disclosure d. difference
4. participle a. verb part b. warning c. supplement d. guerrilla fighter
5. junta a. dance b. point c. group d. symphony
6. impart a. separate b. support c. favor d. disclose
7. disjunction a. prohibition b. break c. requirement d. intersection
8. partisan a. judge b. teacher c. supporter d. leader

B. Indicate whether the following pairs of words have the same or different meanings:

1. impart / give same __ / different __
2. junta / guerrilla same __ / different __
3. participle / verb part same __ / different __
4. impartial / supportive same __ / different __
5. adjunct / supplement same __ / different __
6. injunction / warning same __ / different __
7. partisan / fighter same __ / different __
8. disjunction / connection same __ / different __

MIT/MIS, from the Latin verb *mittere*, "to send," appears in such English words as *missionary*, *missile*, and *emit*. A missionary is sent out to convert others to a new faith; a missile is sent to explode on some far spot; and to emit is to send something out.

emissary \ˈe-mə-ˌser-ē\ Someone sent out to represent another; an agent.

• The senior diplomat had served as a presidential emissary to many troubled regions of the world.

Like *missionaries,* emissaries are sent out on *missions.* However, emissaries are more likely to be representing governments, political leaders, or institutions other than churches. The mission of an emissary is usually to negotiate or to carry or collect information. Presidents send out emissaries to discuss peace terms. Politicians send out emissaries to lure major supporters. And advertising agencies find attractive models to act as emissaries for companies and products on television.

manumission \ˌman-yü-ˈmi-shən\ The act of freeing from slavery.

• Frederick Douglass, William Lloyd Garrison, and Harriet Tubman were major forces in the movement that led to the manumission of slaves in this country.

The verb *manumit* comes from a Latin verb made up of *manus,* meaning "hand," and *mittere,* which can mean both "let go" and "send." So *manumission,* like *emancipation,* suggests the "freeing of hands." *Emancipate* can mean to free from any kind of control or domination, but *manumit* and *manumission* always refer to liberation from slavery or servitude.

missive \ˈmi-siv\ A letter or written communication.

• We await further missives from your mother as to her health and sanity.

Missive simply means "letter," and its connection to the *mit-/mis-* root is that letters, after all, are meant to be sent. *Missive* is a rather formal word and is generally used humorously. A parent or grandparent teasing a college student for not writing home might say, "I've enjoyed your many missives," or might even begin a letter, "I hope this missive finds you in good health."

remittance \ri-ˈmi-təns\ (1) Money sent in payment. (2) The sending of money, especially to a distant place.

• The hardest part of April 15 is putting the remittance into the envelope with the 1040 form.

When we pay our bills and include a remittance, we are sending something back to pay for what we received. *Remittance* is a slightly formal word (in most cases, *payment* is just as good), but some bills do include the statement "Please remit" or "Please enclose remittance." Another common use of *remittance* is for payments that workers send back to their families when they are working outside of their home countries. The economies of many poor countries rely on such remittances from workers employed in more industrialized countries.

PEL/PULS comes from the Latin verb *pellere,* meaning "to move or drive." A *propeller* moves an airplane forward. When soldiers *repel* an enemy charge, they drive it back. And to *dispel* something is to drive it away.

compel \kəm-'pel\ To drive or urge with force.

• After learning more about the sufferings of the refugees, they felt compelled to make contributions to the relief agencies.

To compel is to drive powerfully. *Compulsion* is the noun form; in other words, a thing that compels. Most commonly a compulsion is a powerful inner urge—a *compelling* urge. You may feel compelled to speak to a friend about his drinking. But a compelling film is simply one that seems serious and important.

expel \ik-'spel\ (1) To drive or force out. (2) To force to leave, usually by official action.

• The doctor had him take a deep breath and then expel all the air from his lungs.

To expel is to drive out, and the noun associated with it is *expulsion*. *Expel* is similar in meaning to *eject,* except that *expel* suggests pushing out while *eject* suggests throwing out. Also, to expel usually means to force out permanently, whereas ejecting may only be temporary. The player ejected from the game may be back tomorrow; the student expelled from school is probably out forever.

impel \im-ˈpel\ To urge or drive forward by strong moral force.

• As the meeting wore on without any real progress being made, she felt impelled to stand and speak.

Impel is very similar in meaning to *compel* but suggests even more strongly an inner drive to do something, and often greater urgency in the desire to act. People who believe in civil disobedience feel impelled to resist unjust laws. True civil libertarians feel impelled to tolerate even what they intensely dislike.

repulsion \ri-ˈpəl-shən\ (1) The act of driving away or rejecting. (2) A feeling of great dislike; disgust.

• She overcame her feeling of repulsion long enough to notice the snake's beautiful diamond patterning.

Repulsion basically means "driving back" or the feeling that one wants to drive back something. So the goal of an armed attack is the repulsion of an enemy, and magnets exhibit both attraction and repulsion. But we generally use *repulsion* to mean strong dislike, which is also described by the adjectives *repellent* and *repulsive* (though *repellent* often appears in phrases like "water-repellent"). For example, "She considered most modern art to be meaningless and repellent," and "He said that the food at college was repulsive."

Quizzes

A. Fill in each blank with the correct letter:

a. manumission	e. expel
b. missive	f. impel
c. emissary	g. repulsion
d. remittance	h. compel

1. They knew that hunger would eventually ____ the grizzly to wake up.
2. An ____ was sent to the Duke with a new offer.
3. Children find the feeling of ____ caused by reptiles exciting.
4. Please enclose your ____ in the envelope provided.
5. Though the Senate can ____ a member for certain crimes, it has almost never been done.

6. His elegant Christmas ____ was always eagerly awaited.
7. Let your conscience ____ you to make the right choice.
8. Military victory of the Union forces was required to make ____ of the slaves a reality.

B. Match the definition on the left to the correct word on the right:

1.	force by moral pressure	a.	remittance
2.	letter	b.	compel
3.	drive irresistibly	c.	repulsion
4.	disgust	d.	manumission
5.	agent	e.	expel
6.	payment	f.	missive
7.	drive out	g.	impel
8.	emancipation	h.	emissary

Words from Mythology

arachnid \ə-'rak-ˌnid\ A member of the class Arachnida, which principally includes animals with four pairs of legs and no antennae, such as spiders, scorpions, mites, and ticks.

• My interest in arachnids began when I used to watch spiders build their gorgeous webs in the corners of the porch.

The Greek word for "spider" is *arachne*. According to Greek mythology, the original arachnid was a girl, Arachne. Like all good Greek girls, she spent much of her time weaving, but she made the mistake of claiming she was a better weaver than the goddess Athena. In a contest between the two, she angered the goddess by showing the gods at their worst in the pattern she wove. As punishment, Athena changed Arachne into a spider, fated to spend her life weaving.

calliope \kə-'lī-ə-pē\ A musical instrument similar to an organ in which whistles are sounded by steam or compressed air.

• The town's old calliope, with its unmistakable sound, summoned them to the fair every summer.

To the ancient Greeks, the muses were nine goddesses, each of whom was the spirit of one or more of the arts and sciences. Calliope was the muse of heroic or epic poetry and responsible for inspiring poets to write epics such as the *Iliad* and the *Odyssey*. Since these were generally sung and were usually very long, she was responsible for a great deal of musical reciting. When the hooting musical calliope was invented in America around 1855, her name seemed natural for it. Calliopes gave a festive air to river showboats; the loudest of them could supposedly be heard eight miles away. Today they are only heard on merry-go-rounds and at circuses.

dryad \'drī-əd\ A wood nymph.

• The Greeks' love of trees can be seen in their belief that every tree contained a dryad, which died when the tree was cut.

The term *dryad* comes from the Greek word for "oak tree." As the Greeks saw it, every tree (not only oaks) had a spirit. The myth of Daphne tells of a young woman who chose to become a dryad in order to escape an unwanted suitor, the god Apollo. Pursued by Apollo, she transformed herself into a laurel tree.

fauna \'fò-nə\ Animal life, especially the animals that live naturally in a given area or environment.

• In biology class they examined the fauna of the meadow next to the school.

Faunus and Fauna were the Roman nature god and goddess, part goat and part human, who were in charge of animals. Their helpers, who look just like them, are called *fauns*. Perhaps the most famous depiction of a faun is Debussy's orchestral work "Prelude to the Afternoon of a Faun," which was turned into a ballet by the great Russian dancer Nijinsky.

flora \'flòr-ə\ Plant life, especially the flowering plants that live naturally in a specific area or environment.

• Scientists are busily identifying the flora of the Amazon rain forest before the rapid expansion of the commercial interests consumes it.

The Roman Flora, which means "flower," was the goddess of spring and flowering plants, especially wildflowers and plants not raised for food. She was shown as a beautiful young woman in a long, flowing dress with flowers in her hair and cascading across her shoulders. English preserves her name in such words as *floral, floret,* and *flourish.*

herculean \ˌhər-kyü-ˈlē-ən\ (1) Extremely strong. (2) Extremely extensive, intense, or difficult.

• The whole family now faced the herculean task of cleaning out the attic.

The hero Hercules (in Greek, Heracles) had to perform twelve enormously difficult tasks, or "labors," to pacify the wrath of the god Apollo. Any job or task that is extremely difficult or calls for enormous strength, therefore, is called herculean.

Pandora's box \pan-ˈdȯr-əz-ˈbäks\ A source of many troubles.

• Raising the issue of a new tax opened a real Pandora's box of related economic problems.

The beautiful woman Pandora was created by the gods to punish the human race because Prometheus had stolen fire from heaven. As a gift, Zeus gave Pandora a box, but told her never to open it. However, as soon as he was out of sight she took off the lid, and out swarmed all the troubles of the world. Only Hope was left in the box, stuck under the lid. Anything that seems harmless but when opened or investigated brings forth problems is called a Pandora's box.

Scylla and Charybdis \ˈsi-lə-and-kə-ˈrib-dəs\ Two equally dangerous alternatives.

• As always, they feel caught between Scylla and Charybdis as they try to hold down costs while still investing for the future.

Scylla and Charybdis were two monsters in Greek mythology who endangered shipping in the Strait of Messina between Italy and Sicily. Scylla, a female monster with twelve feet and six heads, each with pointed teeth, barked like a dog from the rocks on the Italian side. Charybdis lived under a huge fig tree on the Sicilian side and caused a whirlpool by swallowing the waters of the sea. Being caught between Scylla and Charybdis is a lot like being between a rock and a hard place.

Quiz

Complete the analogy:

1. hobgoblin : ghost :: dryad : ____
   a. moth b. oak tree c. nymph d. dragonfly
2. difficult : simple :: herculean : ____
   a. intense b. easy c. mammoth d. strong
3. wrath : anger :: Scylla and Charybdis : ____
   a. rage b. peril c. ferocity d. whirlpool
4. piano : nightclub :: calliope : ____
   a. organ b. circus c. church d. steam
5. canine : dog :: flora : ____
   a. oak trees b. wood nymphs c. plants d. animals
6. reptile : snake :: arachnid : ____
   a. toad b. salamander c. bird d. scorpion
7. cabinet : china :: Pandora's box : ____
   a. pleasures b. troubles c. taxes d. music
8. cattle : livestock :: fauna : ____
   a. meadows b. flowers c. wildlife d. trees

Review Quizzes

A. Choose the correct antonym:

1. impartial a. fair b. biased c. cautious d. undecided
2. cosmopolitan a. bored b. intelligent
   c. inexperienced d. well-traveled
3. incoherent a. clear b. garbled c. confused d. unknown
4. manumission a. prohibition b. blockade
   c. liberation d. enslavement
5. compel a. drive b. prevent c. eject d. compare
6. inherent a. native b. inherited c. acquired d. internal
7. cosmos a. chaos b. order c. universe d. beauty
8. impart a. send b. stick c. combine d. withhold
9. adjunct a. added feature b. sharp break c. tight
   connection d. central core
10. repulsion a. disgust b. attraction c. offense d. battle

B. Match the definition on the right to the correct word on the left:

1.	emissary	a.	verb part
2.	junta	b.	cause to move
3.	participle	c.	equal perils
4.	impel	d.	agent
5.	dryad	e.	letter
6.	missive	f.	attachment
7.	Scylla and Charybdis	g.	ruling group
8.	cosmetic	h.	very difficult
9.	herculean	i.	beautifying
10.	adjunct	j.	tree spirit

C. Fill in each blank with the correct letter:

a.	adherent	f.	flora
b.	centrifugal	g.	cohesion
c.	conscientious	h.	prescient
d.	arachnid	i.	disjunction
e.	remittance	j.	subterfuge

1. The candidate's wife, his staunchest ____, was overjoyed by the victory.
2. The successful stockbroker won a reputation for being ____.
3. The philosopher saw no ____ between science and morality.
4. ____ force keeps the roller-coaster cars from crashing to the ground.
5. Please send your ____ immediately or we will be forced to take legal action.
6. The plateau is home to various members of the ____ family.
7. The ____ of the family was strengthened with each reunion.
8. She won praise for her ____ handling of details.
9. We managed to get hold of tickets for the Grateful Dead concert only by ____.
10. The ____ of the West Creek Valley includes at least a dozen rare species.

Unit 10

PUT, from the Latin verb *putare*, meaning "to think, consider, or believe," has come into English in a variety of forms. A *reputation*, for example, is what others think of you; a *deputy* is someone "considered as" the person who appointed him or her.

disputatious \ˌdis-pyu̇-ˈtā-shəs\ Inclined to argue or debate.

• Because both sides were so disputatious, it seemed as if a peace accord would never be reached.

A discussion may be called disputatious, and so may a subject about which people disagree, but normally we use the word to describe individuals. For example, Beethoven was the first composer of genius who dared to be disputatious with the European nobles who were the source of his income. Trial lawyers often cultivate a disputatious style, though at home they may argue no more than balloonists or lion tamers.

impute \im-ˈpyüt\ To attribute.

• The British imputed motives of piracy to American ships trying to prevent them from interfering with American trade during the War of 1812.

Imputing something to someone (or something) usually means observing something invisible in that person (or thing). We may impute meaning to a play or novel, or even to a casual remark by a friend, that was never intended. Imputing a particular character to a whole country—calling the Germans militaristic or the Italians amorous, for example—is very common but always risky. And many of us like to impute bad motives to others, while always regarding our own motives as pure.

putative \'pyü-tə-tiv\ Generally supposed; assumed to exist.

• To strengthen the case for the defense, a putative expert took the stand.

Putative is almost always used to express doubt or skepticism about a common belief. Thus, Tintagel Castle in Cornwall, a picturesque ruin, is the putative fortress of King Arthur. The residents of New York City are *putatively* rude, neurotic, chic, and dangerous. And in the era of Senator Joseph McCarthy, the State Department became the putative home of hundreds of Communists.

reputed \ri-'pyü-təd\ Believed to be a certain way by popular opinion.

• A 15th-century Romanian prince, Vlad the Impaler, is reputed to have been the inspiration for the character Dracula.

Reputed is used constantly today by reporters, almost always to describe suspected criminals—"a reputed mobster," "the reputed drug kingpin." But someone may equally well be reputed to have four dead husbands or a fortune in emeralds or an obsession with medieval catapults.

LOG, from the Greek word *logos,* meaning "word, speech, reason," is found particularly in English words that end in *-logy* and *-logue*. The ending *-logy* often means "the study of": *biology* is the study of life, and *anthropology* is the study of humans. The ending *-logue* usually indicates a type of discussion: *dialogue* is conversation between two people or groups, and an *epilogue* is an author's last words on a subject.

---

eulogy \'yü-lə-jē\ A speech in praise of someone, often someone who has died.

• At President Kennedy's funeral, Chief Justice Earl Warren delivered a moving eulogy.

Since the prefix *eu-* means "well or good," a eulogy speaks well of a person or thing. A speech at a funeral or memorial service is generally called a eulogy, but you may also *eulogize* a living person. At a party you may bore everyone with your eulogies to your hometown, your dog, or your favorite vitamin.

monologue \'mä-nə-ˌlȯg\ (1) A speech or dramatic scene spoken by one person or one actor. (2) Talk that dominates a conversation.

• Myra's loud and endless monologue about her travels was still ringing in our ears when we got home.

Dramatic monologues have often been used to let a character talk openly about himself or herself; the most famous of all is probably Hamlet's "To be or not to be." James Joyce and Virginia Woolf wrote long and memorable monologues for characters in their novels. Garrison Keillor, Lily Tomlin, and Bette Midler are present-day masters of the live comic monologue.

neologism \nē-'ä-lə-ˌji-zəm\ A new word, usage, or expression.

• Such neologisms as *cyberspace* and *virtual reality* come from computer technology.

Neologisms are appearing in English all the time, originating from a variety of sources. Though *-log-* means "word" (and *neo-* means "new"), a neologism doesn't have to be an entirely new word. *Rap,* a very old word, was first used in the 1920s to mean "talk," and in the 1970s to describe a new type of "talk music," and each new use was also a neologism in its time.

genealogy \ˌjē-nē-'a-lə-jē\ (1) The descent of a person or family from an ancestor, or a history of such descent. (2) The study of family history.

• In ancient Rome, prominent senators could trace their genealogies almost to the founding of the city.

In 1976, Alex Haley, Jr., published a partly fictional genealogy of his family in the form of a novel. *Roots* was not only a *genealogical* work but a history of the United States and colonial slavery told from an African-American standpoint. When its television version became the hugest success in the history of television, amateur genealogy became widely popular among both white and black Americans.

Quizzes

A. Indicate whether the following pairs of words have the same or different meanings:

1. putative / supposed — same __ / different __
2. neologism / terminology — same __ / different __
3. reputed / questioned — same __ / different __
4. genealogy / genetics — same __ / different __
5. disputatious / dysfunctional — same __ / different __
6. monologue / discussion — same __ / different __
7. impute / compute — same __ / different __
8. eulogy / praise — same __ / different __

B. Choose the closest definition:

1. monologue a. speech b. drama c. catalog d. boredom
2. impute a. imply b. revise c. attribute d. defy
3. reputed a. rethought b. accused c. determined d. believed
4. neologism a. new day b. new word c. new way d. new thought
5. putative a. assumed b. appointed c. solved d. ignored
6. genealogy a. generation b. inheritance c. family history d. height
7. disputatious a. courageous b. disproved c. unknown d. argumentative
8. eulogy a. high praise b. high flight c. high times d. high jump

---

TERR comes from the Latin *terra,* "earth." *Terra firma* is a Latin phrase that means "firm ground" as opposed to the swaying seas; a *terrace* is a leveled area along a sloping hill; the French call potatoes *pommes de terre,* literally "apples of the earth"; *territory* is a specific piece of land.

---

parterre \pär-'ter\ (1) A decorative garden with paths between the beds of plants. (2) The back area of the ground floor of a theater, often under the balcony.

• The city's park boasts a beautiful parterre with many varieties of roses.

Parterre comes to English by way of French, where it means "on the ground." In Shakespeare's day, the parterre of an English theater was filled with rowdy spectators whose response to the plays was noisy and often crude.

subterranean \ˌsəb-tə-ˈrā-nē-ən\ Underground.

• Carlsbad Caverns National Park has a subterranean chamber over half a mile long.

A subway is a subterranean railway; a tunnel can provide a subterranean pathway; the subterranean vaults at Fort Knox hold billions of dollars of gold reserves. Throughout New England are subterranean reservoirs, called *aquifers,* that are tapped for water. The pressure is great enough to push the subterranean water to the surface once a well provides an outlet; such wells are called *artesian.*

terrarium \tə-ˈrar-ē-əm\ An enclosure, usually transparent, with a layer of dirt in the bottom in which plants and sometimes small animals are kept indoors.

• When no one was watching, they dropped their snake in the fifth-grade terrarium, and then waited in the hall to hear the screams.

The turtle exhibit at a zoo is often in the form of a terrarium, as are some of the exhibits at a plant conservatory. Terrariums try to create conditions as close as possible to a natural habitat. A covered terrarium can often sustain itself for months on the moisture trapped inside.

terrestrial \tə-ˈres-trē-əl\ Having to do with the earth or its inhabitants.

• Although a largely terrestrial bird, the roadrunner can take to wing for short periods when necessary.

Everything on or having to do with the earth is terrestrial, although from the top of Mount Everest or K2 it may not seem that way, since the air is so thin that climbers need to carry extra oxygen to breathe. Something *extraterrestrial* comes from beyond the earth and its atmosphere; though the word is probably most familiar from science fiction, *extraterrestrial* can be used to describe anything " out of this world," from moon rocks to meteors. But Mercury, Venus, and Mars are often called the terrestrial planets, since they are rocky balls somewhat like Earth rather than great globes consisting largely of gas like most of the outer planets. In another usage of the word, animals may be divided into the terrestrial (land-living) and the aquatic (water-living).

MAR, from the Latin word *mare*, meaning "sea," brings its salty tang to English in words like *marine*, "having to do with the sea," and *submarine*, "under the sea."

---

aquamarine \ˌä-kwə-mə-ˈrēn\ (1) A pale blue or greenish blue that is the color of clear seawater in sunlight. (2) A transparent gem that is blue or blue-green.

• Many of the houses on the Italian Riviera are painted aquamarine to match the Mediterranean.

Aquamarine includes the root *aqua*, "water," and accurately describes limpid, clear seawater such as laps the shores of the islands of Greece or those of the Caribbean. The semiprecious gem called aquamarine, a form of beryl, is named for its color.

marina \mə-ˈrē-nə\ A dock or harbor where pleasure boats can be moored securely, often with facilities offering supplies or repairs.

• The coast of Florida has marinas all along it for the use of anything from enormous powerboats to the flimsiest sailboats.

The word *marina* comes straight from Latin, where it means "of the sea." At a marina sailors can acquire whatever they need for their next excursion, or they can tie up their boats until the next weekend comes along. John D. MacDonald's detective hero Travis McGee lives on his boat in Miami and rarely leaves the marina.

mariner \ˈmar-ə-nər\ A seaman or sailor.

• When he signed on as a mariner, the young Ishmael never suspected that the ship would be pursuing a great white whale.

In Coleridge's *Rime of the Ancient Mariner*, an old seaman tells the story of how he shot a friendly albatross and brought storms and disaster to his ship. As punishment, his shipmates hung the great seabird around the mariner's neck and made him wear it until it rotted.

maritime \'mar-ə-ˌtīm\ (1) Bordering on or having to do with the sea. (2) Having to do with navigation or commerce on the sea.

• Canada's Maritime Provinces—New Brunswick, Nova Scotia, and Prince Edward Island—have a late spring but a mild winter as a result of the ocean.

The maritime countries of Portugal and England produced many explorers during the 16th and 17th centuries, many of whom, like Ferdinand Magellan and Henry Hudson, sailed under the flags of other countries. Magellan sailed for Spain and captained the ship that was the first to circle the world, charting many new maritime routes as it went. Hudson, funded by the Dutch, sailed up what is now called the Hudson River in New York, claiming that maritime area for the Netherlands.

Quizzes

A. Complete the analogy:

1. crepe : pancake :: parterre : ____
   a. balcony b. planet c. garden d. parachute
2. motel : motorist :: marina : ____
   a. dock b. pier c. sailor d. boat
3. aquarium : water :: terrarium : ____
   a. plants b. turtles c. rocks d. earth
4. urban : city :: maritime : ____
   a. beach b. dock c. sea d. harbor
5. aquatic : water :: terrestrial : ____
   a. sea b. land c. forest d. mountain
6. pink : red :: aquamarine : ____
   a. blue b. watery c. turquoise d. yellow
7. submarine : wet :: subterranean : ____
   a. blue b. dark c. hollow d. full
8. logger : lumberjack :: mariner : ____
   a. doctor b. lawyer c. chief d. sailor

B. Match the definition on the left to the correct word on the right:

1.	theater area	a.	mariner
2.	blue-green gem	b.	terrestrial
3.	under the ground	c.	marina
4.	near the sea	d.	terrarium
5.	contained habitat	e.	maritime
6.	seaman	f.	parterre
7.	small harbor	g.	subterranean
8.	earthly	h.	aquamarine

PATH comes from the Greek word *pathos,* which means "suffering." A *pathetic* sight moves us to pity. *Pathos* itself is used in English to describe the intense emotions produced by tragedy.

apathetic \ˌa-pə-ˈthe-tik\ (1) Showing or feeling little or no emotion. (2) Having no interest.

• His apathetic response to the victory bewildered his friends.

Apathy, or lack of emotion, is central to Albert Camus's famous novel *The Stranger,* in which the main character's indifference toward almost everything, including his mother's death, results in his imprisonment. We feel little *sympathy* for him, and may even feel *antipathy,* or dislike. The American voter is often called apathetic; of all the industrial democracies, only in America does more than half the adult population fail to vote in major elections.

empathy \ˈem-pə-thē\ The feeling of, or the ability to feel, the emotions and sensations of another.

• Her maternal empathy was so strong that she often seemed to be living her son's life emotionally.

In the 19th century Charles Dickens counted on producing a strong *empathetic* response in his readers so that they would be involved enough to buy the next newspaper installment of each novel. Today, when reading a novel such as *A Tale of Two Cities,* only the hardest-hearted reader does not feel empathy for Sidney Carton as he approaches the guillotine. One who *empathizes* suffers along with the one who feels the sensations directly. Empathy is similar to *sympathy,* but empathy usually suggests stronger, more instinctive feeling. We may feel sympathy, or pity, for victims of a war in Asia, but we may feel empathy for a close friend going through a divorce, even though it is a much smaller disaster.

pathology \pa-'thä-lə-jē\ (1) The study of diseases. (2) The abnormalities that are characteristic of a disease.

• Scientists understood the pathology of smallpox long before they found a vaccine to prevent it.

Based on its roots, *pathology* would mean literally "the study of suffering," but it is actually used to describe the study of diseases. Scientists have found vaccines or cures for diseases from chicken pox to diphtheria by studying their pathology. In this role, the researchers are called *pathologists*. However, a psychiatrist might speak of pathologies of behavior, meaning only that the behavior in question is abnormal.

sociopath \'sō-shē-ō-ˌpath\ A mentally ill or unstable person who acts in a way that harms people and society; a psychopath.

• Controlling its sociopaths is a goal of every society.

One of the most famous sociopaths of history was Jack the Ripper, the mysterious serial killer who murdered at least seven London prostitutes in 1888. But a sociopath doesn't have to be a murderer; almost any person who is destructive or potentially dangerous can be described as a sociopath. Today psychiatrists use the bland term "antisocial personality" in place of *psychopath* or *sociopath.*

PEN/PUN comes from the Latin words *poena,* "penalty," and *punire,* "to punish." From them come such English words as *penalty* and *repentance*; when a penalty is given to someone, it is expected that he or she will be moved to repentance.

---

impunity \im-'pyü-nə-tē\ Freedom from punishment, harm, or loss.

• Under the flag of truce, the soldiers crossed the field with impunity.

Impunity is protection from punishment, just as immunity is protection from disease. Tom Sawyer, in Mark Twain's novel, broke his Aunt Polly's rules with near impunity because he could usually sweet-talk her into forgiving him; if that failed, he had enjoyed himself so much he didn't care what *punishment* she gave him.

penal \'pē-nəl\ Having to do with punishment or penalties, or institutions where punishment is given.

• The classic novels *Les Misérables* and *The Count of Monte Cristo* portray the terrible conditions in French penal institutions in the last century.

A state or country's *penal code* defines its crimes and describes its punishments. During the 18th and 19th centuries, many countries established penal colonies, where criminals were sent as punishment. Often these were unbearably severe; but it was to such colonies that some of Australia's and the United States' early white inhabitants came, and the convicts provided labor for the European settlement of these lands.

penance \'pe-nəns\ An act of self-punishment or religious devotion to show sorrow or regret for sin or wrongdoing.

• In the Middle Ages bands of pilgrims would trudge to distant holy sites as penance for their sins.

Penance as a form of apology for a mistake can be either voluntary or ordered by someone else. Many religions include penance among the ways in which believers can show *repentance* or regret for a misdeed. The Christian season of Lent, 40 days long, is traditionally a time for doing penance.

punitive \'pyü-nə-tiv\ Giving, involving, or aiming at punishment.

• The loser in a court case is often directed to pay punitive damages, money over and above the actual cost of the harm done to the other party.

Trade sanctions, which limit one country's trade with another, are a form of punitive action that may be taken against a government for its human-rights violations or for acts of war, among other reasons. On a smaller scale, a school principal may take punitive measures against a misbehaving football team.

Quizzes

A. Fill in each blank with the correct letter:

a. impunity
b. apathetic
c. punitive
d. sociopath
e. empathy
f. penal
g. pathology
h. penance

1. Speeders seem to feel they can break the speed limit with ____.
2. Louis Pasteur studied the ____ of rabies in order to produce a vaccine.
3. In some households, grounding is a severe form of ____ action.
4. The mildest of the federal ____ institutions are the so-called "country club" prisons.
5. The ____ crowd responded to the singer with weak applause.
6. As ____ the wrongdoers were made to wash all the windows, except the one their ball had shattered.
7. Almost everyone feels some ____ for a child's misery.
8. A brutal dictator is the most destructive kind of ____.

B. Complete the analogy:

1. passionate : emotional :: apathetic : ____
   a. caring b. unjust c. indifferent d. dominant
2. fine : speeding :: penance : ____
   a. misdeed b. credit card c. fee d. behavior
3. psychology : mind :: pathology : ____
   a. suffering b. maps c. life d. disease
4. immunity : sickness :: impunity : ____
   a. death b. flood c. harm d. sleep
5. station wagon : car :: empathy : ____
   a. bus b. emotion c. idea d. pity
6. social : studies :: penal : ____
   a. violence b. attitude c. colony d. dream

7. composer : music :: sociopath : ____
   a. crime b. illness c. harmony d. dread
8. constructive : idea :: punitive : ____
   a. place b. damages c. focus d. outlet

MATR/METR comes from the Greek and Latin words for "mother." A *matron* is a mature woman with children; *matrimony* is marriage itself, traditionally a first step toward motherhood; and a *matrix* is something in which something else is embedded or takes form, like a baby.

maternity \mə-'tər-nə-tē\ The state of being a mother; motherhood.

• Some think the Mona Lisa's smile is the result of her maternity.

Maternity is used as both a noun and an adjective. *Maternity benefits* are benefits specially provided by employers for women having babies, and usually include *maternity leave,* time off work. With maternity come *maternal* feelings. All species of warm-blooded animals show maternal instincts, as do a few reptiles such as crocodiles and alligators.

matriculate \mə-'tri-kyü-ˌlāt\ To enroll as a member of a group, especially a school or college.

• They matriculated together at both boarding school and college, but after college they disappeared entirely from each other's life.

Matriculate comes into English from *matrix,* which in Latin meant a female animal used for breeding purposes, or a plant that was used to produce other plants. It later acquired the meaning "list" or "register," for in ancient times a list might be thought of as the source or parent of the names appearing on it. A student who matriculates at a school basically signs up on a list of students. (And the school or college attended will become his or her *alma mater,* Latin for "fostering mother.")

matrilineal \ˌma-trə-'li-nē-əl\ Based on or tracing the family through the mother.

• Many of the peoples of Ghana in Africa trace their family through matrilineal connections.

Matrilineal means basically "through the mother's line"; *patrilineal* means "through the father's line." Most families that follow the European model take the father's name and are therefore patrilineal; many other peoples follow a matrilineal pattern. Under either system (but especially the latter) there can be *matriarchs*, mothers who rule (*arch*) or head their families or descendants.

metropolitan \ˌme-trə-ˈpä-lə-tən\ Having to do with a large, important city and sometimes also its surrounding suburbs.

• The Los Angeles metropolitan area is among the largest in the world and continues to grow.

Metropolis means basically "mother city," and in ancient Greece a metropolis was usually the original city of a colony—thus the mother from which the colony was born, so to speak. A modern *metropolitan area* can be immense, and in poor countries everywhere peasants are flooding into metropolitan centers in search of jobs, often simply exchanging one form of poverty for another even worse form.

MONI comes from the Latin verb *monere*, "to warn" or "to scold." Warning and scolding often are rather similar, since many warnings could be called "pre-scoldings."

---

admonish \ad-ˈmä-nish\ To warn or criticize mildly.

• The daydreaming student was admonished by the teacher, who told him to pay attention in the future.

The Senate may admonish, or "reprimand," a senator who has misbehaved, but this is far less serious than being "condemned" or actually expelled from the Senate. An *admonition* or *admonishment* usually is less severe than a scolding; it may simply caution against something, and it can even include encouragement.

monitory \ˈmä-nə-ˌtȯr-ē\ Giving warning; cautionary.

• Through the fog they could hear the mournful, monitory note of the foghorn.

A professor may start class with a monitory comment about final exams. A president may make a monitory speech addressed to a country that is ignoring its trade obligations. And a pope may issue a monitory message to the world on the subject of war or morality.

monitor \'mä-nə-tər\ To keep track of or watch, usually for a special reason.

• The North's armored ship the *Monitor* was designed to monitor the South's naval activities in the coastal waters.

Monitor can be both a verb and a noun. A heart monitor monitors a patient's heartbeat and warns of any problems. A hall monitor monitors students behavior in the hallways. Both machine and human monitors observe or supervise and give warnings if something goes wrong.

premonition \ˌpre-mə-'ni-shən\ (1) A previous warning or notice; forewarning. (2) A feeling about an event or situation before it happens.

• He now remembered how the birds had been restless and noisy, as though they had felt a premonition of the coming earthquake.

A premonition is literally a forewarning. A story about Abraham Lincoln holds that he had a premonition of his death in a dream shortly before he was assassinated, but the *premonitory* dream did not prevent him from going to Ford's Theatre on April 14, 1865. John Kennedy flew to Dallas in 1963 ignoring the dark premonition expressed by the statesman Adlai Stevenson. And Martin Luther King delivered a great speech containing premonitions of his death only days before he was murdered in 1968.

Quizzes

A. Choose the closest definition:

1. matriculate a. give birth b. enroll c. tickle d. adjust
2. premonition a. introduction b. scolding c. prematurity d. forewarning
3. matrilineal a. through the mother's family b. graduating c. adopted d. female
4. monitory a. monetary b. mean c. cautionary d. enthusiastic

5. metropolitan a. urban b. suburban c. rural d. oceanic
6. monitor a. think b. persuade c. avoid d. watch
7. maternity a. motherhood b. childhood c. Robin Hood d. sainthood
8. admonish a. praise b. arrest c. await d. scold

B. Match the definition on the left with the correct word on the right:

1. through the female line	a. monitor
2. warning	b. premonition
3. sign up at school	c. maternity
4. regulate	d. metropolitan
5. gently correct	e. matrilineal
6. early suspicion	f. matriculate
7. motherliness	g. admonish
8. city	h. monitory

Words from Mythology

cereal \'sir-ē-əl\ (1) A plant that produces grain that can be eaten as food, or the grain it produces. (2) The food made from grain.

• Rice is the main food cereal grown in Asia, whereas wheat is the main food cereal of the West.

The Roman goddess Ceres (the Greek Demeter) was a serene goddess who did not take part in the quarrels of the other gods. She was in charge of the food-giving plants, and the grains came to carry her name. Cereals of the Romans included wheat, barley, spelt, oats, and millet, but not corn (maize), which was a cereal of the Americas.

Junoesque \jü-nō-'esk\ Having mature, poised, and dignified beauty.

• In 1876, as a centennial gift, the French sent to America a massive statue of a robed Junoesque figure representing Liberty.

Juno was the wife of Jupiter, the chief of the Roman gods. She was a matron, mature and well filled out. Her presence was imposing; her authority as wife of Jupiter and her power in her own right gave her particular dignity. But the younger Diana, goddess of the hunt, perhaps came closer to today's ideals of slim and athletic female beauty.

martial \'mär-shəl\ Having to do with war and military life.

• The stirring, martial strains of "The British Grenadiers" echoed down the snowy street just as dawn was breaking.

Mars was the Roman god of war and one of the patron gods of Rome itself. He was in charge of everything military, from warriors to weapons to provisions to marching music. Thus, when *martial law* is proclaimed, a country's armed forces take over the functions of the police. *Martial arts* are skills of combat and self-defense also practiced as sport. And a *court-martial* is a military court or trial.

Promethean \prə-'mē-thē-ən\ New or creative in a daring way.

• At his best, Steven Spielberg has sometimes shown Promethean originality in the special effects of his movies.

Prometheus was a Titan, a generation older than Zeus. When Zeus overthrew his own father Cronus and seized power, Prometheus fought on the side of the gods and against his fellow Titans. But when Zeus later wanted to destroy the race of humans, Prometheus saved them by stealing fire for them from the gods. He also taught them how to write, farm, build houses, read the stars and weather, cure themselves when sick, and tame animals—in short, all the arts and skills that make humans unique. So inventive was he that anything that bears the stamp of creativity and originality can still be called Promethean. But for his disobedience Zeus had him chained to a rocky cliff, where for many long centuries an eagle daily tore at his liver. Thus, any suffering on a grand scale can also be called Promethean.

Sisyphean \ˌsi-sə-'fē-ən\ Endless and difficult.

• High-school dropouts usually find getting a good job to be a Sisyphean task.

Reputedly the cleverest man on earth, Sisyphus tricked the gods into bringing him back to life after he died. For this they punished him by sending him back to the underworld, where he must eternally roll a huge rock up a long, steep hill, only to watch it roll back to where he started. Something Sisyphean demands the same kind of unending, thankless, and ultimately unsuccessful efforts.

titanic \tī-'ta-nik\ Having great size, strength, or power; colossal.

• The titanic floods of 1993 destroyed whole towns on the Mississippi River.

The ocean liner *Titanic* was named for its unmatched size and strength and its assumed unsinkability. But a truly titanic iceberg ripped a fatal hole in the great ship on its maiden voyage in 1912, and more than 1,500 people perished in the icy waters off Newfoundland. In Greek mythology, the original Titans also came to a bad end. They belonged to the generation of giant creators that produced the younger, stronger, cleverer gods, who soon overpowered and replaced them (see *Promethean* above).

Triton \'trī-tən\ (1) A being with a human upper body and the lower body of a fish; a merman. (2) Any of various large mollusks with a heavy, conical shell.

• In one corner of the painting, a robust Triton emerges from the sea with his conch to announce the coming of the radiant queen.

Triton was originally the son of the sea god Poseidon/Neptune. A guardian of the fish and other creatures of the sea, he is usually shown as hearty, muscular, and cheerful. Like his father, he often carries a trident (a three-pronged fork) and sometimes rides in a chariot drawn by seahorses. Blowing on his conch shell, he creates the roar of the ocean. As a decorative image, Tritons are simply the male version of mermaids. The handsome seashells that bear his name are the very conchs on which he blows. Triton has also given his name to the planet Neptune's largest moon.

vulcanize \'vəl-kə-ˌnīz\ To treat crude or synthetic rubber or plastic so that it becomes elastic and strong and resists decay.

• The native islanders had even discovered how to vulcanize the rubber from the local trees in a primitive way.

The Roman god Vulcan (the Greek Hephaestus) was in charge of fire and the skills that use fire, especially blacksmithing. When Charles Goodyear accidentally discovered how to vulcanize rubber in 1839, he revolutionized the rubber industry. He called his process *vulcanization* because it used fire to heat the rubber (before the addition of sulfur and other ingredients). His discovery influenced the course of the Civil War, when balloons made of this new, stronger rubber carried Union spies over the Confederate armies.

Quiz

Fill in each blank with the correct letter:

a. Promethean
b. titanic
c. Triton
d. Junoesque
e. Sisyphean
f. vulcanize
g. cereal
h. martial

1. Doing the laundry and the ironing always seemed ____ in their endlessness and drudgery.
2. The bout between Muhammed Ali and George Foreman matched one ____ champion against another.
3. The aging jazz singer acquired a certain ____ quality in her mature years.
4. On each arm of the great candelabra was carved a ____ blowing on his conch.
5. Corn, unknown in ancient Europe, has become a staple ____ of the modern world.
6. When Goodyear discovered how to ____ rubber, he made Henry Ford's Model T possible.
7. Edison's mind may have been the most ____ since Leonardo da Vinci's.
8. The ____ arts of the Far East have become popular in the West as means of self-defense.

Review Quizzes

A. Indicate whether the following pairs of words have the same or different meanings:

1. aquamarine / navy blue — same __ / different __
2. subterranean / underground — same __ / different __

3. eulogy / poetry — same __ / different __
4. disputatious / passive — same __ / different __
5. empathy / sentimentality — same __ / different __
6. Junoesque / matriarchal — same __ / different __
7. Promethean / creative — same __ / different __
8. penance / regret — same __ / different __
9. matriculate / graduate — same __ / different __
10. monitory / warning — same __ / different __
11. titanic / powerful — same __ / different __
12. vulcanize / organize — same __ / different __
13. monitor / guard — same __ / different __
14. impunity / freedom from harm — same __ / different __
15. pathology / anger — same __ / different __
16. metropolitan / coastal — same __ / different __
17. marina / dock — same __ / different __
18. putative / natural — same __ / different __
19. terrarium / tank — same __ / different __
20. monologue / chorus — same __ / different __

B. Choose the word that does not belong:

1. Sisyphean a. difficult b.unending c. demanding d. rolling
2. maternity a. femininity b. parenthood c. motherliness d. motherhood
3. mariner a. sailor b. seaman c. crew member d. archer
4. cereal a. corn b. eggplant c. rice d. barley
5. reputed a. known b. reported c. believed d. thought
6. admonish a. warn b. scold c. ask d. correct
7. premonition a. sense b. proof c. omen d. forewarning
8. neologism a. new theory b. new word c. new usage d. new phrase
9. maritime a. coastal b. nautical c. oceangoing d. temperate
10. apathetic a. concerned b. unconcerned c. uncaring d. indifferent

C. Match the definition on the right to the correct word on the left:

1. punitive	a. fancy garden
2. martial	b. through the mother's line

3.	parterre	c.	relating to punishment
4.	sociopath	d.	antisocial person
5.	penal	e.	related to war
6.	matrilineal	f.	disciplinary
7.	terrestrial	g.	family history
8.	genealogy	h.	earthly

Unit 11

CANT, from the Latin verbs *canere* and *cantare,* meaning "sing," produces several words that come directly from Latin, and others that come by way of French and add an *h* to the root: for example, *chant* and *chantey.*

cantata \kən-'tä-tə\ A musical composition, particularly a religious work from the 17th or 18th century, for one or more voices accompanied by instruments.

• During the Baroque era, composers like Telemann composed sacred cantatas by the hundreds.

A cantata is sung, unlike a sonata, which is played on instruments only. Johann Sebastian Bach wrote the music for over 200 religious cantatas; he chose verses to set from hymns and new religious poems. His cantatas consisted of several different sections for different voices—solos, duets, and choruses. Some of his nonreligious cantatas have been performed like mini-operas.

incantation \ˌin-ˌkan-'tā-shən\ (1) A use of spells or verbal charms spoken or sung as part of a ritual of magic. (2) A formula of words used in, or as if in, such a ritual.

• He repeated the words like an incantation: "The only way! The only way! The only way!"

Magic and ritual have always been associated with chanting and music. *Incantation* comes directly from the Latin word *incantare,* "enchant," which itself has *cantare* as a root. Incantations are often in strange languages; "Abracadabra" is a not-so-serious version of an incantation.

cantor \'kan-tər\ An official of a Jewish synagogue who sings or chants the music of the services and leads the congregation in prayer.

• The congregation waited for the cantor to begin the prayers before joining in.

The cantor is, after the rabbi, the most important figure in a Jewish worship service. The cantor not only must possess an excellent singing voice but also must know by heart long passages of Hebrew. Basically, *cantor* simply means "singer." The comedian and singer Edward Israel Iskowitz renamed himself Eddie Cantor for his chosen profession and became enormously popular on stage, screen, radio, and television for over 40 years.

descant \'des-ˌkant\ An additional melody sung above the principal melody.

• The soprano added a soaring descant to the final chorus that held the listeners spellbound.

The prefix *des-*, "two" or "apart," indicates that the descant is a "second song" apart from the main melody. In popular songs a descant will often be sung at the very end to produce a thrilling climax.

LUD/LUS comes from the Latin verb *ludere*, "to play," and *ludum*, "play" or "game." An *interlude* thus is something "between games" (*inter-* meaning "between"). A *delusion* or an *illusion* plays tricks on a person.

---

allude \ə-'lüd\ To refer broadly or indirectly.

• She liked to allude constantly to her glamorous past without ever filling in the details.

Literature is full of *allusions* in which the author refers to other, earlier works. In his epic religious poem *Paradise Lost*, John Milton alludes constantly to Greek and Latin literature, but also to events of his own time such as the discoveries and new countries of the Americas. Modern authors continue to use allusions in their work, and there is a constant flow of new material available to which they can allude. Music and art are almost as full of allusions as literature is.

collusion \kə-'lü-zhən\ A secret agreement or conspiracy for an illegal or deceptive purpose.

• Cuban cigars have continued to be smoked in this country in spite of the embargo against them because of collusion between Cuban cigar makers and American smugglers.

Collusion and the verb *collude* contain the prefix *col-* (from *con-*), meaning "with"; thus, they contain the meaning "play along with." A common form of collusion involves businesses within the same industry. Rather than competing fairly, businesses will sometimes collude to keep prices artificially high. This type of *collusive* behavior has been found in businesses from oil companies to private universities to major-league baseball, whose owners were fined millions of dollars for collusion in the 1980s.

ludicrous \'lü-də-krəs\ Laughable because of clear absurdity, falseness, or foolishness.

• At the rodeo, the ludicrous antics of the clown distract the angry bull and entertain the crowd.

In Hans Christian Andersen's tale "The Ugly Duckling," the ducks find their bumbling, gawky baby's attempts to act like a duck ludicrous. When he grows into a swan, more graceful and elegant than they could ever hope to be, it is surprising that he himself doesn't find the waddling ducks ludicrous. Be careful when using the word: a comment like "What a ludicrous idea!" can be rather insulting.

prelude \'prāl-ˌyüd\ A performance, action, event, or piece of music that precedes and prepares for the more important thing that follows.

• The sound of a symphony orchestra tuning up is the *prelude* to a night of music.

A prelude (*pre-* meaning "before") goes before the main event, just as an *interlude* goes between sections of it. Dark clouds rolling in overhead can be the prelude to a storm. Graduation ceremonies are often called commencement ("beginning") because they are considered a prelude to a new life.

Quizzes

A. Choose the closest definition:

1. descant a. climb downward b. added melody c. supposed inability d. writing table
2. allude a. play b. detract c. avoid d. refer
3. incantation a. ritual chant b. ceremony c. solemn march d. recorded song
4. prelude a. aftermath b. conclusion c. introduction d. admission
5. cantata a. snack bar b. pasta dish c. sung composition d. farewell gesture
6. ludicrous a. tough b. laughable c. simple d. ugly
7. cantor a. singer b. refusal c. traitor d. gallop
8. collusion a. accidental crash b. illegal cooperation c. new material d. magic spell

B. Indicate whether the following pairs of words have the same or different meanings:

1. ludicrous / deceptive same __ / different __
2. incantation / sacred dance same __ / different __
3. prelude / introduction same __ / different __
4. descant / enchant same __ / different __
5. allude / begin same __ / different __
6. cantata / sonata same __ / different __
7. cantor / conductor same __ / different __
8. collusion / smuggling same __ / different __

PHAN/PHEN, from the Greek verbs that mean "to appear or seem" or "to present to the mind," has to do with the way things seem or appear rather than the way they really are. From these roots come words such as *fanciful* and *fantasy*, in which the imagination plays an important part.

phantasm \'fan-ˌta-zəm\ An illusion or a ghost produced by imagination or creative invention.

• When night fell, his imagination filled the old, dark house with phantasms.

In Edgar Allan Poe's poem "The Raven," a weary scholar who has fallen asleep at midnight while reading strange old books talks with a phantasm, a ghastly raven that has come to tell him that he will "nevermore" meet his dead love in a Christian afterlife, since there is none. In the words of the old saying, "The sleep of reason produces monsters"—that is, phantasms.

phantasmagoria \fan-ˌtaz-mə-ˈgȯr-ē-ə\ (1) A shifting succession of things seen or imagined. (2) A collection or combination of weird or imaginary things.

• Salvador Dalí's paintings offer a bizarre phantasmagoria of odd images.

To Western eyes an Arab souk, or market, can seem like a phantasmagoria of exotic items, but a Western supermarket can look equally *phantasmagorical* to a foreigner. A film or a novel can be *phantasmagoric*. The shifting content of a dream may seem like a phantasmagoria. To Sigmund Freud, these bizarre events and images had a deeper meaning: for Freud the key to a person's psychology lay in his or her *fantasies*.

phenomenon \fi-ˈnä-mə-ˌnän\ (1) A fact or event observed or known with the senses. (2) A rare, unusual, or important fact or event.

• To Noah and the others on his ark, the appearance of a rainbow was a joyous phenomenon.

Phenomena are "things" (though not generally "objects"), and sometimes "strange or unusual things." Something *phenomenal* is extraordinary, and *phenomenally* means "extremely" or "extraordinarily." Psychic phenomena, weather phenomena, social phenomena can all be either facts or events. A phenomenon is a single thing; the plural form is *phenomena*. Take care not to mix them up.

diaphanous \dī-ˈa-fə-nəs\ (1) Transparent. (2) Insubstantial or vague.

• The ballerinas of Tchaikovsky's *Swan Lake* wore diaphanous costumes that seemed to float.

Light mist is diaphanous, since things may be seen at least faintly through it. Gauzy fabric is diaphanous; another word for it is "sheer." A diaphanous princess might be a fantasy vision that is hardly real at all. And a diaphanous notion would be one without much real substance behind it.

VER comes from the Latin word for "truth." A *verdict* in a trial is "the truth spoken." But a just verdict may depend on the *veracity*, or "truthfulness," of the witnesses.

---

aver \ə-ˈvər\ To state positively as true; declare.

• The defendant averred that she was nowhere near the scene of the crime on the night in question.

You may aver anything that you're sure of. Since the word contains the "truth" root, it basically means "confirm as true." In legal situations it means to state or allege positively as a fact; thus, Perry Mason's clients aver that they are innocent, while the district attorney avers the opposite.

verify \ˈver-ə-ˌfī\ (1) To prove to be true or correct. (2) To check or test the accuracy of.

• It is the bank teller's job to verify the signature on a check.

During talks between the United States and the former Soviet Union on nuclear weapons reduction, one big problem was how to verify that weapons had been eliminated. Since neither side wanted the other to know its secrets, *verification* of the facts became a difficult issue. Because of the distrust on both sides, many thought that the real numbers would never be *verifiable*.

verisimilitude \ˌver-ə-sə-ˈmi-lə-ˌtüd\ (1) The appearance of being true or probable. (2) The depiction of realism in art or literature.

• By the beginning of the 20th century, the leading European painters were losing interest in verisimilitude and beginning to experiment with abstraction.

From its roots, *verisimilitude* means basically "like the truth." Most fiction writers and filmmakers aim at some kind of verisimilitude to give their stories an air of reality. This doesn't mean they need to show something actually true, or even very common—just simply possible and believable. A mass of good details in a play, novel, painting, or film may add verisimilitude. A spy novel without some verisimilitude won't interest many readers, but a fantastical novel may not even attempt to seem true to life.

verity \'ver-ə-tē\ A true fact or statement.

• Ben Franklin's statement that "in this world nothing can be said to be certain, except death and taxes" is held as a verity by many.

The phrase "eternal verity" is often used to mean an enduring truth or bit of wisdom. Some eternal verities are found in proverbs, such as "Haste makes waste." The statement in the Declaration of Independence that "all men are created equal" is now held by many Americans to be an eternal verity—but few earlier governments had ever been based on such a truth.

Quizzes

A. Fill in each blank with the correct letter:

a. phenomenon
b. aver
c. phantasmagoria
d. verify
e. diaphanous
f. verity
g. phantasm
h. verisimilitude

1. They had never before seen a natural ____ like the boiling lake.
2. A week after his mother's death, he saw her ____ beckoning to him from the dock at dusk.
3. The prosecutor expected the witness to ____ that the suspect was guilty.
4. Realists in art and literature work to achieve ____ as they sense it.
5. Each candle was surrounded by the ____ fluttering wings of moths.
6. The Mardi Gras parade was a ____ of bizarre images too numerous to even take in.
7. She was never able to ____ anything he had told her.

8. Sometimes what has always seemed a ____ suddenly is shown to be false.

B. Complete the analogy:

1. believe : doubt :: aver : ____
   a. state b. mean c. deny d. subtract
2. scent : smell :: phenomenon : ____
   a. odor b. sight c. event d. sensation
3. illusion : fantasy :: verisimilitude : ____
   a. appearance b. realism c. style d. truth
4. faint : dim :: diaphanous : ____
   a. filmy b. huge c. old-fashioned d. sensational
5. loyalty : treason :: verity : ____
   a. dishonor b. hatred c. honesty d. falsehood
6. ogre : monster :: phantasm : ____
   a. surprise b. raven c. ghost d. fanfare
7. praise : ridicule :: verify : ____
   a. testify b. contradict c. establish d. foretell
8. fantasy : illusion :: phantasmagoria : ____
   a. collection b. kaleidoscope c. sideshow d. visions

TURB comes from the Latin verb *turbare,* "to throw into confusion or upset," and the noun *turba,* "crowd" or "confusion." A *disturbance,* for example, confuses and upsets normal order or routine.

---

perturb \pər-ˈtərb\ To upset, confuse, or disarrange.

• News of the new peace accord was enough to perturb some radical opponents of any settlements.

If the root *-turb* means basically "upset," then *perturb* means "thoroughly upset." A person in a *perturbed* state of mind is more than merely bothered. On the other hand, someone *imperturbable* remains calm through the most trying experiences.

turbine \ˈtər-ˌbīn\ A rotary engine with blades made to turn and generate power by a current of water, steam, or air under pressure.

• The power plant used huge turbines powered by water going over the dam to generate electricity.

The oldest and simplest form of turbine is the waterwheel, which is made to rotate by water falling across its blades and into buckets suspended from them. Hero of Alexandria invented the first steam-driven turbine in the 1st century A.D.; but a commercially practical steam turbine was not developed until 1884. Steam-driven turbines are now the main elements of electric power stations. Jet engines are gas turbines. A *turbojet* engine uses a turbine to compress the incoming air that feeds the engine before being ejected to push the plane forward; a *turboprop* engine uses its exhaust to drive a turbine that spins a propeller.

turbulent \'tər-byů-lənt\ (1) Stirred up, agitated. (2) Stirring up unrest, violence, or disturbance.

• The huge ocean liner *Queen Elizabeth II* has never been much troubled by turbulent or stormy seas.

Often the captain of an airplane will warn passengers to fasten their seatbelts because of upper-air *turbulence,* which can make for a bumpy ride. El Niño, a seasonal current of warm water in the Pacific Ocean, may create turbulence in the winds across the United States, affecting patterns of rainfall and temperature as well. The late 1960s are remembered as turbulent years of social revolution in America and Europe. Some people lead turbulent lives, and some are constantly in the grip of turbulent emotions.

turbid \'tər-bid\ (1) Thick or murky, especially with churned-up sediment. (2) Unclear, confused, muddled.

• The crowd's mood was restless and turbid; any spark could have turned it into a mob.

The Colorado River in spring, swollen by melting snow from the high mountains, races through the Grand Canyon, turbid and churning. A chemical solution may be described as turbid rather than clear. And your emotions may be turbid as well, especially where love is involved: What did he mean by that glance? Why did she say it like that?

VOLU/VOLV comes from the Latin verb *volvere,* meaning "to roll, wind, turn around, or twist around." From this source come words like *volume,* which was originally the name of a scroll or roll of papyrus, and *revolve,* which simply means "turn in circles."

devolution \ˌde-və-ˈlü-shən\ (1) The transfer of rights, powers, property, or responsibility to others, especially from the central to local government. (2) Evolution toward an earlier or lower state.

• In the 1980s there was a devolution of responsibility for education from the federal government to state and local governments.

Devolution implies moving backward. Once powers have been centralized in a unified government, giving any powers back to smaller governmental units can seem to be reversing a natural development. But we may also speak of moral devolution, such as occurred in Germany in the 1930s, when a country with an extraordinarily high culture became a brutal, aggressive, murderous dictatorship. The verb form is *devolve*. Thus, a job that your boss doesn't want to do may devolve upon you.

evolution \ˌe-və-ˈlü-shən\ A process of change from a lower, simpler, or worse state to one that is higher, more complex, or better.

• Thomas Jefferson and the other Founding Fathers believed that political evolution reached its highest form in democracy.

Part of the humor of *The Flintstones* is that it contradicts what is known about evolution, since humans actually *evolved* long after dinosaurs were extinct. *Evolution* can also be used more broadly to refer to technology, society, and other human creations. For example, though many people don't believe that human beings truly become better with the passing centuries, many will argue that our societies tend to evolve, producing more goods and providing more protection for more people.

voluble \ˈväl-yü-bəl\ Speaking readily and rapidly; talkative.

• He proved to be a voluble informer who would tell stories of bookies, smugglers, and hit men to the detectives for hours.

A voluble person has words "rolling" off his or her tongue. In O. Henry's famous story "The Ransom of Red Chief" the kidnappers nab a boy who is so unbearably voluble that they can hardly wait to turn him loose again.

convoluted \ˈkän-və-ˌlü-təd\ (1) Having a pattern of curved windings. (2) Involved, intricate.

• After 15 minutes, Mr. Collins's strange story had become so convoluted that none of us could follow it.

Convolution originally meant a complex winding pattern such as those on the brain. So a convoluted argument or a convoluted explanation is one that winds this way and that. An official form may have to wind its way through a convoluted process and be stamped by eight people before being approved. Convoluted language makes many people suspicious; as a great philosopher once said, "Anything that can be said can be said clearly."

Quizzes

A. Choose the closest definition:

1. convoluted a. spinning b. babbling c. grinding d. winding
2. turbine a. whirlpool b. engine c. headdress d. carousel
3. evolution a. process of development b. process of democracy c. process of election d. process of elimination
4. perturb a. reset b. inset c. preset d. upset
5. voluble a. whirling b. unpleasant c. talkative d. garbled
6. turbulent a. churning b. turning c. yearning d. burning
7. turbid a. flat b. calm c. confused d. slow
8. devolution a. handing down b. handing in c. turning up d. turning around

B. Match the word on the left to the correct definition on the right:

1. voluble	a. murky
2. turbine	b. fluent
3. evolution	c. seething
4. turbid	d. complicated
5. devolution	e. turning engine
6. perturb	f. degeneration
7. convoluted	g. disturb
8. turbulent	h. progress

FAC/FEC/FIC comes from the Latin verb *facere,* meaning "to make or do." Thus, a *benefactor* is someone who does good. To *manufacture* is to make, usually in a *factory.*

confection \kən-'fek-shən\ (1) A sweet food or fancy dish prepared from a variety of ingredients. (2) A piece of fine craftsmanship.

• The children's eyes grew wide with delight at the sight of the confections in the baker's window.

A confection is *confected* from several different ingredients or elements. Among the tastiest confections are the marzipan (almond-paste) creations molded and painted to look like fruit. The word can also be used to refer to any finely worked piece of craftsmanship. So the lacy box containing chocolate confections can be called a confection itself.

facile \'fa-səl\ (1) Easily accomplished. (2) Shallow, superficial.

• The principal made a facile argument for the school's policy, but no one was convinced.

A facile writer seems to write too quickly and easily, and a careful reader discovers that the writer hasn't really said very much. A facile suggestion doesn't deal with the issue in any depth, and a facile solution may be only temporarily effective.

olfactory \ōl-'fak-tə-rē\ Having to do with the sense of smell.

• The olfactory sense of some dogs is so powerful that they can smell a human under 20 feet of snow.

Olfactory includes part of the Latin verb *olere,* meaning "to smell." The tasters of great wines depend more on their olfactory sense than they do on their taste buds. The olfactory nerve, which produces the sense of smell, is closely connected to the sense of taste. Since the *gustatory* (taste) nerves can only distinguish four different tastes (salt, sweet, sour, and bitter), the rest of our taste perception is actually olfactory.

proficient \prə-'fi-shənt\ Skilled in an art, occupation, or branch of knowledge.

• She's proficient at every aspect of the job; all she lacks is imagination.

Proficiency is achieved through hard work and maybe talent as well. You may be proficient at math or proficient in three languages, or you may be a proficient swimmer. A proficient pianist plays the piano with skill. But proficiency isn't genius, and even calling someone proficient may imply that the person isn't brilliantly gifted.

UT/US comes from the Latin verb *uti,* "to use, make use of, employ," and the related adjective *utilis,* "useful, fit." It is *used* in such words as *abuse,* "improper use," and *reuse,* "to use again."

---

usufruct \'yü-zə-ˌfrəkt\ (1) The right to use or enjoy something. (2) The legal right of using or enjoying the products or profits of something that belongs to someone else.

• When they sold the land, they retained the right by usufruct to pick the apples in the orchards they had planted.

Usufruct is a concept that has come down from ancient times. The original term in Latin was *usus et fructus,* meaning "use and enjoyment." It is an interesting concept: since the original owner can devolve the responsibility of upkeep and taxes onto someone else while keeping usufruct, he or she may get the best of the deal. Usufruct rights end at a certain point, often when the user dies, and do not permit changing or damaging the property. As Thomas Jefferson said (and many environmentalists have echoed), "The earth belongs in usufruct to the living." And as the Roman philosopher Lucretius said, life itself is given to us only in usufruct.

usury \'yü-zhə-rē\ The lending of money with a fee charged for its use, especially lending for an unusually high fee.

• He responded that demanding 25 percent interest on the loan was usury.

Shylock, in Shakespeare's *The Merchant of Venice,* is accused of usury, since he has bargained to take a pound of Antonio's flesh in place of the money Antonio owes him. Since this would result in Antonio's death, it seems like an excessive and *unusual* penalty for the failure to repay a debt. To the borrower, usury seems *abusive*; to the lender, it is a fair fee for use of the money. No wonder Polonius told Laertes in *Hamlet,* "Neither a borrower nor a lender be"; the borrower becomes careless about spending and ends up at the *usurer's* mercy, and the lender often becomes resented or even hated and may lose his or her money.

utilitarian \yü-ˌti-lə-ˈtar-ē-ən\ (1) Aiming at usefulness rather than beauty. (2) Useful for a specific purpose or end.

• Their view of life was strictly utilitarian; for them there was no room for art, pleasure, or relaxed conversation.

The Shakers, a religious group that dedicated itself to work and its work to God, had a utilitarian outlook on the design of furniture and household objects. Their finished pieces—whether tables, chairs, brooms, or baskets—are beautifully simple and very well fitted to their use. But *utilitarian* often means somewhat homely. Utilitarian architecture, such as many government housing projects, may be quite ugly, for example. If we say something has utilitarian value, however, we simply mean it is useful in some way.

utility \yü-ˈti-lə-tē\ (1) Usefulness. (2) A government-regulated business providing a public service; the service it provides.

• The book was an invention of such extraordinary utility that in 2,000 years no one has improved on it.

A dog bred for utility is one intended for a particular use such as hunting or herding. It may be called a *utility* dog, just as a Jeep may be called a utility vehicle. The local electric company is one kind of company often called a utility, and the electric, gas, and water service in your home are called utilities as well.

Quizzes

A. Fill in each blank with the correct letter:

a. usufruct	e. facile
b. utilitarian	f. confection
c. utility	g. olfactory
d. usury	h. proficient

1. They kept the right to use their neighbor's dock by ____.
2. The interest rate for the loan offered by the bank amounted to sheer ____.
3. She was quick-witted but often her reasoning was ____ and not deeply thoughtful.
4. She chose an inexpensive, ____ model with no radio and no power windows.
5. Mozart was ____ at the piano by the age of 5.
6. The ____ of his 1940s typewriter was such that he never felt the need for a word processor.
7. The gown in the window was a gorgeous ____ by the designer Ariane.
8. Commuting daily through the smog-filled air, she was grateful that her ____ sense was not very keen.

B. Indicate whether the following pairs of words have the same or different meanings:

1. proficient / skillful same __ / different __
2. usufruct / sweetness same __ / different __
3. confection / candy same __ / different __
4. utility / tool same __ / different __
5. olfactory / assembly same __ / different __
6. usury / customary same __ / different __
7. facile / slippery same __ / different __
8. utilitarian / useful same __ / different __

Words from Mythology and History

muse \'myüz\ A source of inspiration; a guiding spirit.

• At 8:00 each morning he sat down at his desk and summoned his muse, and she almost always responded.

The Muses were the nine Greek goddesses that presided over the arts (including *music*) and literature. Their temple was called in Latin the *Museum*. An artist or poet such as Homer, especially when about to begin work, would call on his particular Muse to inspire him. Today a muse may be one's special creative spirit, but some artists have also chosen living human beings to serve as their muses.

iridescent \ˌir-ə-ˈde-sənt\ Having a glowing, rainbowlike play of color that seems to change as the light shifts.

• The children shrieked with glee as they blew iridescent soap bubbles into the gentle breeze.

Iris, the Greek goddess of the rainbow, took messages from Mount Olympus to earth, and from gods to mortals or other gods, using the rainbow as her stairway. *Iridescence* is thus the glowing, shifting, colorful quality of a rainbow, also seen in an opal, a light oil slick, a butterfly wing, or the mother-of-pearl that lines an oyster shell.

mausoleum \ˌmȯ-zə-ˈlē-əm\ (1) A large tomb, especially one built aboveground with shelves for the dead. (2) A large, gloomy building or room.

• The family's grand mausoleum occupied a prominent spot in the cemetery, for all the good it did the silent dead within.

Mausolus was ruler of a kingdom in Asia Minor in the 4th century B.C. He beautified the capital, Halicarnassus, with all sorts of fine public buildings, but he is best known for the magnificent monument, the Mausoleum, that was built by his wife Artemisia after his death. The Mausoleum was one of the Seven Wonders of the Ancient World. Today any large tomb can be called a mausoleum, and so can any big, dark, echoing interior space.

mentor \ˈmen-ˌtȯr\ A trusted counselor, guide, tutor, or coach.

• This pleasant old gentleman had served as friend and mentor to a series of young lawyers in the firm.

Odysseus was away from home fighting and journeying for 20 years, according to Homer. During that time, the son he left as a babe in arms grew up under the supervision of Mentor, an old and trusted friend. When the goddess Athena decided it was time to complete young Telemachus's education by sending him off to learn about his father, she visited him disguised as Mentor and they set out together. From this, anyone such as a coach or tutor who gives another (usually younger) person help and advice on how to achieve success in the larger world is called a mentor.

narcissism \'när-si-ˌsi-zəm\ (1) Extreme self-centeredness or fascination with oneself. (2) Love or desire for one's own body.

• His girlfriend would complain about his narcissism, saying he spent more time looking in the mirror than looking at her.

Narcissus was a handsome youth in Greek mythology who inspired love in many who saw him. One was the nymph Echo, who could only repeat the last thing that anyone said. When Narcissus cruelly rejected her, she wasted away to nothing but her voice. Though he played with the affections of others, Narcissus became a victim of his own attractiveness. When he caught sight of his own reflection in a pool, he sat gazing at it in fascination, wasting away without food or drink, unable to touch or kiss the image he saw. When he finally died, the gods turned him into a flower, a narcissus, that stands with its head bent as though gazing at its own reflection. From this myth comes the name of a psychological disorder, narcissism, which is the excessive love of oneself, as well as a more common type of vanity and self-centeredness.

tantalize \'tan-tə-ˌlīz\ To tease or torment by offering something desirable but keeping it out of reach.

• The sight of a warm fire through the window tantalized the little match girl almost unbearably.

Tantalus, according to Greek mythology, killed his son Pelops and offered him to the gods in a stew for dinner. Almost all of the gods realized what was happening and refused the meal, but Demeter took a nibble out of Pelops's shoulder. The gods reconstructed Pelops, replacing the missing shoulder with a piece of ivory, and then punished Tantalus. In Hades he stands in water up to his neck under a tree laden with fruit. Each time he stoops to drink, the water moves out of reach; each time he reaches up to pick something, the branches move beyond his grasp. He is thus eternally tantalized by the water and fruit. Today anything or anyone that tempts but is unobtainable is tantalizing.

thespian \'thes-pē-ən\ (1) An actor. (2) Having to do with the drama; dramatic.

• In summer the towns of New England welcome troupes of thespians dedicated to presenting plays of all kinds.

Greek drama was originally entirely performed by choruses. Literary tradition says that Thespis, the Greek dramatist, was inventor of tragedy and the first to write roles for the individual actor as distinct from the chorus. Thespians fill all the roles in more modern plays. *Thespian* is also an adjective; thus, we can speak of "thespian ambitions" and "thespian traditions," for example.

zephyr \'ze-fər\ (1) A breeze from the west. (2) A gentle breeze.

• Columbus left Genoa sailing against the zephyrs that continually blow across the Mediterranean.

The ancient Greeks called the west wind Zephyrus and regarded him and his fellow winds as gods. A zephyr is a kind wind, bringer of clear skies and beautiful weather, though it may occasionally be more than a soft breeze.

Quiz

Fill in each blank with the correct letter:

a.	mausoleum	e.	muse
b.	thespian	f.	mentor
c.	iridescent	g.	zephyr
d.	tantalize	h.	narcissism

1. The couple felt timid and small inside the vast ____ where their lawyer asked them to come.
2. On fair days a gentle ____ would blow from morning until night.
3. The company president took the new recruit under her wing and acted as her ____ for the next several years.
4. He would often ____ her with talk of traveling to Brazil or India, but nothing ever came of it.
5. The puddle's surface was beautifully ____ in the slanting light.
6. After his last book of poetry was published, his ____ seemed to have abandoned him.
7. In everyone there is a bit of the ____ yearning for a stage.
8. By working as a model, she could satisfy her ____ while getting paid for it.

Review Quizzes

A. Choose the correct antonym and the correct synonym:

1. voluble a. argumentative b. mumbly c. speechless d. talkative
2. proficient a. lazy b. skilled c. inept d. professional
3. utilitarian a. useless b. useful c. usual d. unusual
4. zephyr a. stormy blast b. icy rain c. light shower d. gentle breeze
5. aver a. reject b. detract c. deny d. assert
6. diaphanous a. broken b. filmy c. muddy d. tattered
7. ludicrous a. serious b. ordinary c. laughable d. amazing
8. perturb a. soothe b. restore c. park d. upset
9. devolution a. decay b. turn c. suggestion d. improvement
10. usury a. sending b. lending c. giving d. mending
11. draconian a. precise b. gentle c. harsh d. inaccurate
12. turbulent a. churning b. official c. cloudy d. calm
13. tantalize a. visit b. satisfy c. tease d. watch
14. iridescent a. shimmering b. drab c. striped d. watery
15. mentor a. translator b. interpreter c. guide d. student
16. phantasm a. vision b. amazement c. actuality d. horror

B. Indicate whether the following pairs of terms have the same or different meanings:

1. thespian / teacher same __ / different __
2. facile / nasty same __ / different __
3. evolution / extinction same __ / different __
4. verify / prove same __ / different __
5. phenomenon / event same __ / different __
6. collusion / opposition same __ / different __
7. incantation / luxury same __ / different __
8. turbid / muddy same __ / different __
9. olfactory / smelling same __ / different __
10. usufruct / right of use same __ / different __

C. Fill in each blank with the correct letter:

a. prelude
b. narcissism
c. descant
d. verisimilitude
e. cantata
f. verity
g. confection
h. allude
i. cantor
j. phantasmagoria
k. turbine
l. mausoleum

1. It was accepted as a ____ in their household that the future would be better than the past.
2. They were a very attractive couple, but their ____ often annoyed other people.
3. The university chorus was going to perform a Bach ____ along with the Mozart *Requiem*.
4. The children were invited to choose one chocolate ____ apiece from the counter display.
5. He began his singing career as a ____ in Brooklyn and ended it as an international opera star.
6. She remembered Mardi Gras only as an endless ____ of swirling images.
7. One day in the cemetery the ____ door was open, and he peered in with horrified fascination.
8. She would try to ____ to the problem sometimes, but he never seemed to listen.
9. The cocktail party was only a ____ to the main event, the awards ceremony.
10. Her films showed her own reality, and she had no interest in ____.
11. The roar of the ____ was so loud they couldn't hear each other.
12. As part of their musical training, she always encouraged them to sing their own ____ over the main melody.

Unit 12

UMBR, from the Latin *umbra*, "shadow," is a shady customer. The familiar *umbrella*, with its ending meaning "little," casts a "little shadow" to keep off the sun or the rain.

adumbrate \'a-dəm-brāt\ (1) To give a sketchy outline or disclose in part. (2) To hint at or foretell.

• The Secretary of State would only adumbrate his ideas for bringing peace to Bosnia.

A synonym for *adumbrate* is *foreshadow*, which means to present a shadowy version of something before it becomes reality or is provided in full. Rats scurrying off a ship were believed to adumbrate a coming disaster at sea. A bad review by a critic may adumbrate the failure of a new film.

penumbra \pə-'nəm-brə\ (1) The partial shadow surrounding a complete shadow, as in an eclipse. (2) The fringe or surrounding area where something exists less fully.

• This area of the investigation was the penumbra where both the FBI and the CIA wanted to pursue their leads.

Every solar eclipse casts an *umbra*, the darker central area in which almost no light reaches the earth, and a penumbra, the area of partial shadow where part of the sun is still visible. *Penumbra* can thus be used to describe any "gray area" where things are not all black and white. For example, the right to privacy falls under the penumbra of the U.S. Constitution; though it is not specifically guaranteed there, the Supreme Court has held that it is implied, and thus that the government may not intrude into certain areas of a citizen's private life. Because its existence is still shadowy, however, the

Court is still determining how much of an individual's life is protected by the right to privacy.

umber \'əm-bər\ (1) A darkish brown mineral containing manganese and iron oxides used for coloring paint. (2) A color that is greenish brown to dark reddish brown.

• Van Dyke prized umber as a pigment and used it constantly in his oil paintings.

The mineral deposits of Italy provided sources of a number of natural pigments, among them umber. Since the late Renaissance, umber has been in great demand as a coloring agent. When crushed and mixed with paint it produces an olive, known as *raw umber*; when crushed and burnt it produces a darker tone, known as *burnt umber*.

umbrage \'əm-brij\ A feeling of resentment at some slight or insult, often one that is imagined rather than real.

• She often took umbrage at his treatment of her, without being able to pinpoint what was offensive about it.

An umbrage was originally a shadow, and soon also meant a shadowy suspicion. Then it came to mean displeasure as well—that is, a kind of shadow blocking the sunlight. *Umbrage* is now generally used in the phrase "take umbrage at." An overly sensitive person may take umbrage at something as small as having his or her name pronounced wrong.

VEST comes from the Latin verb *vestire*, "to clothe" or "to dress," and the related noun *vestis*, "clothing" or "garment." *Vest* is the shortest English word we have from this root, and is the name of a rather small piece of clothing.

---

divest \dī-'vest\ (1) To get rid of or free oneself of property, authority, or title. (2) To strip of clothing, ornaments, or equipment.

• In protest against apartheid, many universities in the 1980s divested themselves of all stock in South African companies.

When it turned out that the New York Marathon had been won by fraud, the "winner" was divested of her prize. When a church is officially abandoned, it is usually divested of its ornaments and furnishings. And if you decide to move or to enter a monastery, you may divest yourself of many of your possessions.

investiture \in-'ves-tə-ˌchu̇r\ The formal placing of someone in office.

• At an English monarch's investiture, he or she is presented with the crown, scepter, and sword, the symbols of power.

In its original meaning, *investiture* referred to clothing the new officeholder in the garments that symbolized power. The Middle Ages saw much debate over the investiture of bishops and abbots by kings and emperors. These rulers felt that high religious offices were theirs to give to whomever they chose as a reward for loyal service or as a guarantee of future support, but the popes saw these investitures as the buying and selling of church offices. The investiture struggle caused tension between popes and monarchs and even led to wars.

transvestite \tranz-'ves-ˌtīt\ A person, especially a male, who wears the clothing and adopts the mannerisms of the opposite sex.

• Gounod's opera *Romeo and Juliet* calls for a woman in the transvestite role of Romeo.

Transvestite includes the prefix *trans-*, "across," and thus means literally "cross-dresser." Today it is so acceptable for women to wear men's clothing that the word *transvestite* is generally applied only to men. In the theater, from ancient Greece to Elizabethan England, *transvestism* was common because all parts were played by men—even Juliet. Japanese Kabuki and No drama still employ transvestism of this sort.

travesty \'tra-vəs-tē\ (1) An inferior or distorted imitation. (2) A broadly comic imitation in drama, literature, or art that is usually grotesque and ridiculous.

• The senator shouted again that the new tax bill represented a travesty of tax reform.

The word *travesty* comes from the same prefix and root as *transvestite* and originally meant "to disguise." The "free elections" so often promised by military governments usually amount to a travesty of democracy—a disguise intended to fool the world. The variety show *Saturday Night Live* specializes in dramatic travesties mocking everything from political figures and issues to popular culture—"disguised" versions intended for entertainment. *Travesty* may also be a verb. Thus, Mel Brooks has travestied movies of all kinds—westerns, thrillers, and silent films, among others.

Quizzes

A. Fill in the blank with the correct letter:

a. penumbra
b. transvestite
c. investiture
d. travesty
e. divest
f. umber
g. umbrage
h. adumbrate

1. Titian employed assistants to mix the ____ and other pigments for his paintings.
2. The ____ of the prime minister was an occasion of pomp and ceremony.
3. Some people are quick to take ____ the moment they think they have been slighted.
4. Since all the judges were cronies of the dictator, the court proceedings were a ____ of justice.
5. The new director planned to ____ the museum of two of its Picassos.
6. The farther away a source of light is from the object casting a shadow, the wider will be that shadow's ____.
7. The young model became a notorious success when she was discovered to be a ____.
8. The increasing cloudiness and the damp wind seemed to ____ a stormy night.

B. Match the definition on the left to the correct word on the right:

1. resentment — a. penumbra
2. brownish color — b. travesty
3. installing in office — c. transvestite
4. cross-dresser — d. adumbrate
5. imitation — e. divest
6. get rid of — f. umbrage
7. near shadow — g. investiture
8. partially disclose — h. umber

THE/THEO comes from the Greek word meaning "god." *Theology* is the study of gods or religion. *Monotheism* is the worship of a single god; someone who is *polytheistic,* however, worships many gods.

apotheosis \ə-ˌpä-thē-ˈō-səs\ (1) Transformation into a god. (2) The perfect example.

• After his assassination Abraham Lincoln underwent an apotheosis that transformed the controversial politician into a saintly father of democracy.

The word *apotheosis* has the prefix *apo-,* "relating to"; thus, it suggests a human who has become godlike. In Greek mythology, very few humans were *apotheosized,* but Heracles (Hercules) was one who made the grade, and there are pictures painted on ancient vases showing the big party the rest of the gods held for him when he joined them after his apotheosis. Any great classic example of something can be called its apotheosis; a collector might state, for example, that the Duesenberg Phaeton was the apotheosis of the touring car.

atheistic \ˌā-thē-ˈis-tik\ Denying the existence of God or divine power.

• The atheistic Madalyn Murray O'Hair successfully sought the removal of prayer from American public schools in the 1960s.

In the Roman Empire, early Christians were said to be atheistic because they denied the existence of the gods of the pantheon. The Christian church, once established, in turn condemned the unconverted Romans as *atheists* because they did not believe in the Christian God. *Atheism* is different from *agnosticism,* which claims that the existence of any higher power is unknowable.

pantheistic \ˌpan-thē-ˈis-tik\ (1) Seeing the power of God in all the natural forces of the universe. (2) Worshiping all gods of all creeds and cults.

• Her personal religion was almost pantheistic; she saw the holy books of Hinduism and the rituals of Caribbean folk religion as expressions of the same essential truths.

Pan means "all"; thus, *pantheistic* refers to "all gods," or alternatively to "god in all things." Originally each Roman god and goddess had a temple where sacrifices were offered and sacred objects were stored. But there came a time when too many gods demanded attention, so only a big temple in honor of the entire group would do. Thus, the great temple known as the *Pantheon* was dedicated to all the gods. (These days, *pantheon* can also refer to a group of historical superstars in any one area—the pantheon of basketball or of literature, for example.)

theocracy \thē-'ä-krə-sē\ (1) Government by officials who are regarded as divinely inspired. (2) A state governed by a theocracy.

• The ancient Aztecs lived in a theocracy in which guidance came directly from the gods through the priests.

The ancient state of Israel and its related state of Judah were *monotheistic* (one-god) theocracies; the ancient state of the Aztecs in Mexico was a *polytheistic* (multi-god) theocracy, as was that of the ancient Sumerians. All four seem to have agreed that the power of the ruling god or gods was most forceful in high places. The Sumerians and Aztecs built enormous pyramidlike temples; the Jews sought divine guidance on mountaintops. Modern-day theocracies are rare; Iran has been the best-known recent *theocratic* government.

DE/DIV comes from two related Roman words, *deus,* "god," and *divus,* "divine." *Deism,* a philosophy that teaches natural religion, emphasizes morality, and denies that the creator god interferes with the laws of the universe, was the basic faith of many of America's Founding Fathers.

---

deity \'dē-ə-tē\ A god or goddess.

• The many-armed deity Kali, wife of Shiva, is the Hindu goddess of death.

The ancient Greek deities had special cities and places they protected in return for sacrifices and prayers and special celebrations in their honor. Athena was the deity in charge of Athens; Hera was responsible for Sparta and Argos, and Apollo for Delphi. Each deity also had responsibility for a specific function or area of life: Athena for weaving and other crafts, Hera for marriage, and Apollo for the lives of young men, music, and *divination* (foretelling the future).

deus ex machina \ˈdā-əs-ˌeks-ˈmä-ki-nə\ (1) In Greek and Roman drama, a god who enters above the stage by means of a crane and decides the play's outcome. (2) A person or thing that appears suddenly and solves an apparently unsolvable problem.

• Pinned down by enemy fire, the soldiers had nearly given up hope when a helicopter appeared like a deus ex machina.

Deus ex machina means literally "the god from the machine," referring to the crane that held the god over the stage. A character in a mystery who appears from out of nowhere with the solution near the end could be called a deus ex machina; however, dedicated mystery readers have contempt for such solutions.

divinatory \də-ˈvi-nə-ˌtȯr-ē\ Seeking to foresee or foretell the future, usually by interpreting signs or asking for supernatural help.

• Astrologers today claim to use divinatory methods handed down from the ancient Egyptians and Babylonians.

Throughout history, divinatory practices that seek to reveal the future have been popular. In Roman times, a *diviner* known as a "haruspex" would search the guts of sacrificed animals to foretell coming events. The flights of birds were interpreted by a type of *divination* known as "augury." Tarot cards, séances, Ouija boards, and palm readings continue to be used by people hoping to *divine* (predict) the future.

divinity \də-ˈvi-nə-tē\ (1) The state of being a god or goddess. (2) A god or goddess; a deity.

• Some early Christian sects, such as the Arians, questioned the actual divinity of Jesus Christ.

In the 5th century A.D., the Roman Empire was on the verge of collapse. Many Roman senators claimed that the divinities that had always protected the city had abandoned them because so many people worshiped a new divinity, the Christian God. In defense, St. Augustine wrote *The City of God,* arguing that all earthly cities must pass, and that only the one true Divinity is eternal.

Quizzes

A. Fill in each blank with the correct letter:

a. pantheistic
b. deus ex machina
c. atheistic
d. divinity
e. deity
f. apotheosis
g. divinatory
h. theocracy

1. There around the temple stood idols of all the gods of this ____ religion.
2. The psychic's ____ powers were regarded by her clients as astounding.
3. His well-known ____ beliefs meant the young politician could hope for only limited success.
4. There above the stage appeared Apollo, the ____, to solve the dilemma.
5. Being inducted into the Hall of Fame is as close as a modern ballplayer can come to ____.
6. She addressed her prayer to whatever ____ chose to listen.
7. When the young man's followers proclaimed his ____, the believing Christians were shocked.
8. The high priest in this medieval ____ was equivalent to a dictator.

B. Match the word on the left to its definition on the right:

1. deity
2. pantheistic
3. apotheosis
4. divinity
5. atheistic
6. divinatory
7. theocracy
8. deus ex machina

a. state ruled by religion
b. dramatic device
c. supreme being
d. nonbelieving
e. godliness
f. accepting all gods
g. prophetic
h. perfect example

DEMO comes from the Greek word meaning "people." A *demagogue* leads the people, usually into trouble, by lying and appealing to their prejudices.

demographic \ˌde-mə-ˈgra-fik\ Having to do with the study of human populations, especially their size, growth, density, and patterns of living.

• The government used the latest demographic figures to decide how much money to spend on education.

Demographic analysis, the statistical description of human populations, is a tool used by government agencies, political parties, and manufacturers of consumer goods. Polls conducted on every topic imaginable, from age to toothpaste preference, give the government and corporations an idea of who the public is and what it needs and wants. The government's census, which is conducted every ten years, is the largest demographic survey carried out in this country.

endemic \en-ˈde-mik\ (1) Found only in a given place or region. (2) Often found in a given occupation, area, or environment.

• Malaria is a disease that is endemic in tropical regions around the world.

Endemic means literally "in the population." Since the panda is found in the wild exclusively in central China and eastern Tibet, scientists say that it is "endemic to" those areas or that they are "endemic areas" for the panda. But the word can also mean simply "common" or "typical," so we can say that colds are "endemic in" nursery school and that love of Barbie dolls is "endemic among" young American girls.

pandemic \ˌpan-ˈde-mik\ Widespread and affecting a large portion of the people.

• The worldwide AIDS pandemic may eventually prove to be the most deadly such event in human history.

Pandemic is a stronger version of *epidemic*. In a pandemic outbreak, practically everyone may be affected. In 1348 a pandemic plague called the Black Death struck Western Europe and killed 25 million people. In 1918 a *pandemic* of influenza killed 20 million people around the world. Pandemic smallpox repeatedly swept through the world's populations until the 1970s, even though a vaccine had existed since 1798. When the Beatles first visited the United States in the early 1960s, they were greeted by pandemic "Beatlemania," a mild form of musical insanity.

demotic \di-ˈmä-tik\ Popular or common.

• Because of television, the demotic language and accents of the various regions of this country are becoming more and more similar.

Demotic describes what is done by ordinary people as a group. It often describes their speech—demotic Californian is different from demotic Texan, for example. The most demotic dress in America is probably blue jeans and sneakers, and those who wear them can be said to have demotic taste in fashion.

POPUL comes from the Latin word meaning "people," and in fact forms the basis of the word *people* itself. *Popular* means not only "liked by many people" but also "relating to the general public." *Popular culture* is thus the culture of the general public. And the *population* is the people of an area.

---

populist \ˈpä-pyə-list\ A believer in the rights, wisdom, or virtues of the common people.

• He decided that he would campaign as a populist in order to appeal to his working-class voters.

The word *populist* first appeared in the 1890s with the founding of the Populist Party, which stood primarily for the interests of the farmers against the big-money interests. In later years *populism* came to be associated with the white working class as well. Populism can swing from liberal to conservative. It sometimes has a religious tendency; it usually is not very interested in international affairs; it has sometimes been unfriendly to black interests; and it is often anti-intellectual. But the *populist* style always shows its concern with Americans with average incomes as opposed to the rich and powerful.

populace \ˈpä-pyů-ləs\ (1) The common people or masses. (2) Population.

• Perhaps Henry Ford's major achievement was to manufacture a car that the entire populace could afford—the Model T.

Franklin D. Roosevelt's famous radio "Fireside Chats" were designed to address the entire populace in a familiar way. He used the talks to *popularize* his economic programs and to give heart to the populace as they struggled through the Great Depression.

populous \'pä-pyů-ləs\ Numerous, densely settled, or having a large population.

• Though often ignored by Americans, Indonesia is the fourth most populous country in the world.

Modern Mexico City is the world's most populous city; its metropolitan area has about 25 million people. But even when Cortés came to the nearby Aztec city of Tenochtitlán in 1519, he found one of the largest cities in the world at that time. However, when he conquered the city in 1521 it wasn't nearly so populous, since European diseases had greatly reduced the population. (Avoid confusing *populous* and *populace*, which are pronounced exactly the same.)

vox populi \'väks-'pä-pyü-ˌlī\ Popular sentiment or opinion.

• Clever politicians always listen to the vox populi and adjust their opinions or language to get the voters on their side.

Vox populi is Latin for "the voice of the people." It comes from the old saying "Vox populi, vox Dei," or "The voice of the people is the voice of God"—in other words, the people are always right. In a democracy the vox populi is often regarded as almost sacred. We hear the vox populi loud and clear at every election, and by means of opinion polls we continue to hear it on every imaginable issue, from the President's personal affairs to U.S. military action overseas.

Quizzes

A. Choose the closest definition:

1. pandemic a. isolated b. widespread c. present d. absent
2. populace a. politics b. numerous c. masses d. popularity

3. endemic a. common b. absent c. infectious d. occasional
4. demotic a. devilish b. common c. cultural d. useful
5. populous a. well-liked b. foreign c. numerous d. obscure
6. demographic a. describing politics b. describing populations c. describing policies d. describing epidemics
7. populist a. communist b. campaigner c. socialist d. believer in the people
8. vox populi a. public policy b. public survey c. public opinion d. public outrage

B. Indicate whether the following pairs of words have the same or different meanings:

1. demotic / common — same __ / different __
2. populist / politician — same __ / different __
3. endemic / typical — same __ / different __
4. populace / popularity — same __ / different __
5. demographic / phonetic — same __ / different __
6. vox populi / mass sentiment — same __ / different __
7. pandemic / infectious — same __ / different __
8. populous / well-loved — same __ / different __

POLIS/POLIT comes from the Greek word for "city." "City-states" operated much like separate nations in ancient Greece, so all their *politics* was local, like all their public *policy*, and even all their *police*!

---

acropolis \ə-'krä-pə-ləs\ The high, fortified part of a city, especially an ancient Greek city.

• On the Athenian Acropolis, high above the rest of the city, stands the Parthenon, a temple to the goddess Athena.

Acropolis includes the root *acro-*, meaning "high." South American cities often contain a section on high ground that has been walled and built up so that the city can be defended. This fortified hill gives the defenders an automatic advantage over their attackers. In Europe, an acropolis often consisted of a walled castle inside which the population of the city and the surrounding area could retreat in case of attack. The Greeks and Romans included in their acropolises temples to the city's most important gods.

megalopolis \ˌme-gə-ˈlä-pə-ləs\ (1) A very large city. (2) A thickly populated area that includes one or more cities with the surrounding suburbs.

• With its rapid development, the southern coast of Florida around Miami quickly became a megalopolis.

A "large city" named Megalopolis was founded in ancient Greece to help defend Arcadia against Sparta. Today Megalopolis has only about 5,000 people. The megalopolis on the eastern U.S. seaboard that stretches from Boston to Washington, D.C., however, now is the home of almost 50 million people. The densely populated cities seem to flow into each other all along the coast. It is projected that this megalopolis will only grow as time goes on.

politic \ˈpä-lə-ˌtik\ (1) Cleverly tactful. (2) Wise in promoting a plan or plan of action.

• Anger is rarely a politic approach to seeking agreement, since it usually comes across as rude and self-righteous.

Once teenagers learn to drive, they quickly learn the politic way to ask for the car—that is, whatever gets the keys without upsetting the parents. It is never politic to ask for a raise when the boss is in a terrible mood. As these examples show, *politic* can be used for many such situations that have nothing to do with public *politics*.

politicize \pə-ˈli-tə-ˌsīz\ To give a political tone or character to.

• By 1968 the Vietnam War had deeply politicized most of the college campuses.

Sexual harassment was once seen as a private matter, but in recent years it has been thoroughly politicized. A number of the women who have politicized it may themselves have been politicized by it—that is, may have started to think in a *political* way because of it. Václav Havel was an *unpolitical* playwright who became politicized by events and ended up as president of the Czech Republic.

CIRCU/CIRCUM means "around" in Latin. So *circumnavigate* is "to navigate around," often describing a trip around the world, and *circumambulate* means "to walk around." A *circuit* can be a tour around an area or territory, or the complete path of an electric current.

circuitous \sər-'kyü-ə-təs\ (1) Having a circular or winding course. (2) Not forthright or direct in action.

• Some philosophers arrive at their conclusions by circuitous reasoning that most people can barely follow.

Circuitous is often the opposite of *direct.* A circuitous path is no shortcut: twisting and turning and cutting back on itself, it is the kind of route one would expect to find in the mountains. A lawyer may use circuitous arguments when defending an unsavory client. A clever businessman may use circuitous methods to raise the money for a real-estate deal. (Sometimes *circuitous* may even be a bit like *dishonest.*)

circumference \sər-'kəm-frəns\ (1) The perimeter or boundary of a circle. (2) The outer boundary or surface of a shape or object.

• To calculate the approximate circumference of a circle, multiply its diameter by 3.14.

Circumference means literally "carrying around"—that is, around the boundary of a circle or other geometric figure. Attempts have been made to measure the circumference of the earth since the time of Aristotle. Columbus believed one such calculation, and it led him to think he could reach China by sailing west more quickly than by sailing east. His measurement was wrong, calculating the Earth's circumference about a quarter too small, and many later attempts continued to produce different measurements for the earth's circumference.

circumspect \'sər-kəm-ˌspekt\ Careful to consider all circumstances and possible consequences; cautious.

• She never rushed into any decision but was instead always circumspect and thoughtful.

Since *-spect* comes from the Latin word for "look," *circumspect* basically means "looking around" yourself before you act. Being a doctor or a banker has traditionally called for a circumspect personality. In most dictatorships, authors must be circumspect in what they write, since any lack of *circumspection* could land them in prison, or worse.

circumvent \'sər-kəm-ˌvent\ (1) To make a circuit around. (2) To manage to get around, especially by clever means.

• We circumvented the traffic jam on the highway by using the back roads.

Achilles' mother, Thetis, hoped to circumvent the prophecy that Achilles would die in a war against Troy, so she disguised the boy as a woman among the women of his uncle's household. But clever Odysseus, recruiting for the Greek army, arrived disguised as a peddler, and among the jewelry pieces he displayed to the women he laid a sword. When Achilles ignored everything but the sword, he was found out and had to go to war. Though he was the best warrior on either side, Achilles could not circumvent his eventual fate, and was killed by Paris with a poison arrow to his heel.

Quizzes

A. Fill in each blank with the correct letter:

a. circumspect
b. megalopolis
c. circumference
d. politicize
e. acropolis
f. circumvent
g. politic
h. circuitous

1. She was ____ enough with the chairman to get the bill through the committee.
2. Only the Tokyo-Yokohama metropolitan area rivals the ____ of the East Coast.
3. The doctors were ____ about the prime minister's condition that morning.
4. Her clever attempts to ____ the official procedures failed miserably.
5. The entire ____ of the estate was lined with tall oaks.

6. The directions they were given were inaccurate, so their route turned out to be a ____ one.
7. In times of danger, the entire populace retreated to the ____.
8. They believed that if they could ____ the peasants they could force the government to resign.

B. Match the word on the left to the correct definition on the right:

1. politicize	a. high fortified area
2. megalopolis	b. make political
3. circumspect	c. avoid
4. circumvent	d. chain of cities
5. politic	e. outside
6. acropolis	f. cleverly tactful
7. circumference	g. careful
8. circuitous	h. roundabout

Animal Words

aquiline \'a-kwə-ˌlīn\ (1) Relating to eagles. (2) Curving like an eagle's beak.

• To judge from the surviving busts of noble Romans, many of the men had strong aquiline noses.

Aquiline, from the Latin word meaning "eagle," is most often used to describe a nose that has a broad curve and is slightly hooked, like a beak. The word for eagle itself, Aquila, has been given to a constellation in the northern hemisphere. The aquiline figure on the U.S. seal brandishes the arrows of war and the olive branch of peace.

asinine \'a-sə-ˌnīn\ Foolish, brainless.

• He's not so great when he's sober, but when he's drunk he gets truly asinine.

The donkey or *ass* has often been accused of stubborn, willful, and stupid behavior lacking in logic and common sense. Asinine behavior exhibits similar qualities. Idiotic or rude remarks, aggressive stupidity, and general immaturity can all earn someone (usually a man) this description. If you call him this to his face, however, he might behave even worse.

bovine \'bō-ˌvīn\ (1) Relating to cows and oxen. (2) Placid, dull, unemotional.

• The veterinarian specialized in bovine diseases.

Bovine comes from the Latin word for "cow." The goddess Hera, the wife of Zeus, is called "cow-eyed," and Zeus fairly melts when she turns those big bovine eyes on him. But *bovine* is normally used either technically, when discussing cows—"bovine diseases," "bovine anatomy," and so on—or to describe a human personality. However, it can be a rather unkind way to describe someone.

canine \'kā-ˌnīn\ Relating to dogs or the dog family; doglike.

• Throughout the election, her husband's almost canine devotion helped her survive the tough criticism of her opponents.

Dogs are not always given credit for their independence, but they are prized for their talents and their intelligence. And canine devotion and loyalty are legendary; in the old *Lassie* and *Rin-Tin-Tin* television series, there would be at least one heroic act of devotion per show.

feline \'fē-ˌlīn\ (1) Relating to cats or the cat family. (2) Like a cat in being sleek, graceful, sly, treacherous, or stealthy.

• The performers moved across the high wire with feline grace and agility.

Cats have always provoked a strong reaction from humans. The Egyptians worshiped them and left thousands of feline mummies and idols as evidence. In the Middle Ages, felines were feared as agents of the devil; they were thought to creep around silently at night doing evil and caring not at all for anything except themselves. (Notice that *feline* is also a noun.) Felines from lions and tigers down to domestic cats are smooth, silent, and often sleepy; feline independence, feline treachery, and feline slyness are other traits that some have seen in these mysterious creatures.

leonine \ˈlē-ə-ˌnīn\ Relating to lions; lionlike.

• As he conducted, Leonard Bernstein would fling his leonine mane wildly about.

The Latin word for "lion" is *leon,* so the names Leon, Leo, and Leona all mean "lion" as well. A leonine head usually has magnificent hair, like a male lion's mane, and someone may give an impression of leonine power or splendor. But the leonine character in *The Wizard of Oz* is notably lacking in the courage for which members of its family are famed.

porcine \ˈpȯr-ˌsīn\ Relating to pigs or swine; piglike.

• After a lifetime of overeating, his shape was porcine; unfortunately, his manners were also.

Whether deservedly or not, pigs don't enjoy a very flattering image, and they are rarely given credit for their high intelligence. While *porcine* is not as negative a term as *swinish,* it may describe things that are fat, greedy, pushy, or generally piggish—but primarily fat. Porky Pig and Miss Piggy are not porcine in their behavior, only in their appearance—that is, pink and pudgy.

vulpine \ˈvəl-ˌpīn\ (1) Relating to foxes; foxlike. (2) Sneaky, clever, or crafty; foxy.

• One glance at the vulpine faces of the two bond traders was enough to convince him of their true character.

Foxes may have beautiful coats and tails, but they are almost impossible to keep out of the henhouse. No matter how secure the place seems to be, their vulpine craftiness will find a way in. People who display the same kind of sneaky cleverness, especially in their faces, are also called vulpine.

Quiz

Fill in each blank with the correct letter:

a. leonine
b. aquiline
c. porcine
d. asinine
e. canine
f. feline
g. vulpine
h. bovine

1. Collies and chow chows often have splendid, ____ neck ruffs.
2. The dancer performed the piece with ____ grace.
3. Proud of the ____ curve of his nose, the silent-film star presented his profile to the camera at every opportunity.
4. The slick fellow offering his services as guide had a disturbingly ____ air about him.
5. Soldiers are expected to show ____ loyalty to their unit and commander.
6. The job applicant's ____ manner suggested a lack of ambition.
7. Jeff and his crowd were in the balcony, throwing down cans and being generally ____.
8. The ____ landlord climbed the stairs slowly, gasping for breath, with the eviction notice in his hand.

Review Quizzes

A. Choose the closest definition:

1. vulpine a. reddish b. sly c. trustworthy d. furry
2. circumspect a. boring b. long-winded c. roundabout d. cautious
3. politic a. governmental b. voting c. tactful d. clumsy
4. populous a. numerous b. populated c. popular d. common
5. atheistic a. without a clue b. faithful c. disbelieving d. without a doubt
6. endemic a. local b. neighborly c. sensational d. foreign
7. circuitous a. electrical b. mountainous c. indirect d. round
8. feline a. sleek b. clumsy c. crazy d. fancy
9. pantheistic a. of one god b. disbelieving c. nonreligious d. accepting all gods
10. deity a. discussion b. decision c. psychic d. god
11. pandemic a. widespread b. infectious c. hideous d. frightening
12. megalopolis a. monster b. dinosaur c. huge city d. huge mall

13. demotic a. reduced b. common c. upper-class
    d. demented
14. divinity a. prophecy b. mortality c. prayer
    d. godliness
15. circumvent a. surround b. circle c. get around
    d. discuss
16. divest a. add on b. take off c. take in d. add up

B. Fill in each blank with the correct letter:

a.	populist	f.	apotheosis
b.	demographic	g.	bovine
c.	theocracy	h.	populace
d.	investiture	i.	politicize
e.	aquiline	j.	circumference

1. The ____ of the great Albert Einstein seemed to occur while he was still living.
2. All the ____ surveys show that the U.S. population is growing older.
3. Nothing ever seemed to disturb her pleasant but ____ manner.
4. The younger ones stood around the ____ of the room while the older ones sat in the center.
5. The ____ of the society's new leader was a secret and solemn event.
6. With his ____ nose, he looked like a member of the ancient Roman senate.
7. By that fall they had managed to ____ the factory workers around the issue of medical benefits.
8. He was a ____ in his style, though he actually had a great deal of money.
9. The ____ of the country is mostly composed of three ethnic groups.
10. In a ____, the legal punishments are often those called for in the holy books.

C. Match the word on the left to the correct definition on the right:

1.	porcine	a.	half-shadow
2.	divinatory	b.	doglike

3.	asinine	c.	brownish coloring
4.	penumbra	d.	public opinion
5.	leonine	e.	cross-dresser
6.	umber	f.	unforeseen explanation
7.	vox populi	g.	uncouth
8.	deus ex machina	h.	plump
9.	transvestite	i.	like a lion
10.	canine	j.	prophetic

Unit 13

CORD, from the Latin word for "heart," turns up in many common English words. For example, the word *concord* (which includes the prefix *con-*, "with") means literally that one heart is *with* another heart, and thus that they are in agreement. So *discord* (with its prefix *dis-*, "apart") means "disagreement" or "conflict."

---

accord \ə-'kȯrd\ (1) To grant. (2) To be in harmony; agree.

• For the cast's brilliant performance of the play, the audience accorded them a standing ovation.

A new federal law may accord with—or be in *accordance* with—the guidelines that a company has already established. The rowdy behavior of the hero Beowulf accords with Norse ideals of the early Middle Ages, but would not be in accordance with the ideals of another young Danish lord of a later century, Shakespeare's Prince Hamlet.

concordance \kən-'kȯr-dəns\ An index of the important words in a book or in an author's works, with the passages in which they occur.

• A concordance to Shakespeare's plays makes it easy to find all the places he used the word *bodkin.*

A literary concordance lists all the places a given word appears in a work. *Concordance* resembles *concord,* but the "agreement" here is in the way that all the passages use the identical word. All concordances produced before the recent past had to be done by hand, and often were the work of several lifetimes. (Just imagine putting together a concordance for the Bible by hand.) Now, a computer with CD-ROM can search a book or an author's works in a flash, but concordances in book form are still valuable for many purposes.

cordial \'kȯr-jəl\ (1) Warm, friendly, gracious. (2) Something that warms and revives, especially a liqueur.

• After the meeting, the president extended a cordial invitation to everyone for coffee at her own house.

Anything that is cordial comes from the heart. A cordial greeting or cordial relations (for example, between two countries) are warm and honest without being passionate. A cordial or liqueur, such as crème de menthe or Drambuie, is alcoholic enough to warm the spirits and the heart.

discordant \dis-'kȯr-dənt\ Being at odds, conflicting, not in harmony.

• The one discordant note came from the only vegetarian present, who would not eat the main course, roast beef.

Drawing up a peace treaty may require that the parties to the treaty resolve their discordant aims. Even among allies, *discord* is not always absent. Stalin's goals after World War II did not at all *accord* with those of Russia's allies—England, America, and France; his discordant demands led to the division of Europe for almost half a century. The opinions of Supreme Court justices are frequently discordant. The discordant ethnic groups in the old Yugoslavia were controlled only by the iron hand of Marshal Tito.

CULP comes to English from the Latin word for "guilt." A *culprit* is someone who is guilty of a crime, though his or her *culpability*, or guilt, should not be assumed before it is proved.

---

culpable \'kəl-pə-bəl\ Deserving to be condemned or blamed.

• The company was found guilty of culpable negligence in allowing the chemical waste to leak into the groundwater.

A mother always thinks she knows which children are culpable when the cookie jar has been raided: their *culpability* is usually written all over their faces. *Culpable* is probably more commonly used in law than in everyday speech and writing.

exculpate \'ek-skəl-ˌpāt\ To clear from accusations of fault or guilt.

• The alleged mastermind of the plot managed to exculpate herself with an airtight alibi.

Exculpate comes to mean "to clear from guilt" through the prefix *ex-*, meaning "out of" or "away from." A suspected murderer may be exculpated by the confession of another person. The word has an extended meaning as well, referring to moral guilt or responsibility. In America a criminal is not exculpated because of a harsh childhood, but may be if found insane.

inculpate \in-'kəl-ˌpāt\ To accuse or incriminate; to show evidence of someone's involvement in a fault or crime.

• It was his own father who finally inculpated him, though without intending to.

Inculpate is the opposite of *exculpate*, but less often used. By inculpating someone else, an accused person may manage to exculpate himself. Through plea bargaining, the prosecution can often encourage a defendant to inculpate his friends in return for a lighter sentence.

mea culpa \ˌmā-ə-'ku̇l-pə\ An admission of personal fault or error.

• The principal said his mea culpa at the school board meeting, but not all the parents accepted it.

Mea culpa, "through my fault," comes from the prayer of confession in the Catholic Church. Said by itself today, it means "I apologize" or "It was my fault." But it is also a noun. A book may be a long mea culpa for the author's past treatment of women, or an oil company may issue a mea culpa after a tanker runs aground.

Quizzes

A. Choose the closest definition:

1. exculpate a. convict b. prove innocent c. suspect d. prove absent
2. discordant a. unpleasant b. relieved c. unlimited d. conflicting
3. culpable a. disposable b. refundable c. guilty d. harmless
4. cordial a. hateful b. friendly c. fiendish d. cool
5. inculpate a. incorporate b. resist c. incriminate d. offend
6. concordance a. index b. digit c. list d. disagreement
7. mea culpa a. rejection b. apology c. admission d. forgiveness
8. accord a. harmonize b. accept c. distress d. convince

B. Match the definition on the left to the correct word on the right:

1. accuse	a. accord
2. excuse	b. concordance
3. agreement	c. mea culpa
4. heartfelt	d. discordant
5. grant	e. culpable
6. blamable	f. cordial
7. disagreeing	g. inculpate
8. confession	h. exculpate

DIC, from *dicere*, the Latin word meaning "to speak," says a lot. A *contradiction* (with the prefix *contra-*, "against") speaks against or denies something. A *dictionary* is a treasury of words. And *diction* is another word for speech.

edict \'ē-ˌdikt\ (1) An official announcement that has the force of a law. (2) An order or command.

• In 1989 an edict by the leader of Iran pronouncing a death sentence on a British novelist stunned the world.

Edicts are few and far between in a democracy, since very few important laws can be made by a president or prime minister acting alone. But when a crisis arose in the Roman Republic, the senate would appoint a dictator to rule by edict. The dictator could make decisions quickly, and his edicts could be issued faster than the senate could act. When the crisis was over, the edicts were revoked and the dictator usually retired from public life.

interdiction \ˌin-tər-ˈdik-shən\ (1) An edict prohibiting something. (2) The destruction of or cutting off of an enemy's line of supply.

• U.S. forces repeatedly tried to halt the North Vietnamese by interdiction of their supplies.

An interdiction comes between and forbids or takes. From 1920 to 1933 the 18th Amendment attempted to *interdict* the production and drinking of alcohol. But such an interdiction proved useless; Americans of all social classes and every degree of respectability refused to give up their beloved beverages, and all attempts to interdict the supply by the "Untouchable" Eliot Ness and other government agents could not stop the flow of illegal moonshine and bathtub gin.

jurisdiction \ˌju̇r-is-ˈdik-shən\ (1) The power or right to control or exercise authority. (2) The territory where power may be exercised.

• Unluckily for the defendants, the case fell within the jurisdiction of the federal court rather than the more tolerant state court.

Gods and goddesses often intervened in the areas under their jurisdiction. Apollo, whose jurisdiction included archery, guided the arrow that killed Achilles in the Trojan War. Poseidon, angered at the blinding of his son the Cyclops, punished Odysseus with hard wanderings over the sea, where he had final jurisdiction. Today questions of jurisdiction are generally technical legal matters—questions about which law-enforcement agency can get involved, which court will hear the case, and so on—but matters that may be all-important in the final outcome of legal cases.

malediction \ˌma-lə-ˈdik-shən\ A curse.

• In the story of Sleeping Beauty, the evil fairy hurls a malediction at the infant princess, foretelling that she will prick her finger and die.

Maledictions, "evil sayings," are used less commonly in many cultures than they used to be. The Romans had a malediction for every purpose. They inscribed these curses on lead tablets and buried them in the ground. Archaeologists have found maledictions cursing the person who stole someone's lover, the person who stole prize apples, and the person who cursed the curser. Maledictions may call for every punishment imaginable, from sickness to injury and even death.

GNI/GNO comes from a Greek and Latin verb meaning "to know" (and led to the word *know* itself). In the group of words built from this root, you may *recognize* ("know again") some and be *ignorant* of ("not know") others. An *agnostic* is someone who claims that whatever is divine cannot be known. An *ignoramus* is a person who knows absolutely nothing.

---

cognitive \ˈkäg-nə-tiv\ (1) Having to do with the process of knowing, including awareness, judgment, and understanding. (2) Based on factual knowledge that has been or can be gained by experience.

• A child is not a computer; a third-grader's cognitive abilities are highly dependent on his or her upbringing and happiness.

Cognitive skills and knowledge involve the ability to acquire factual information, often the kind of knowledge that can easily be tested. *Cognition* is thus distinguished from social, emotional, and creative development and ability.

diagnosis \ˌdī-əg-ˈnō-səs\ (1) The identification of a disease by its symptoms. (2) An investigation of and conclusion about a situation or problem.

• However, according to Marianne's diagnosis the company's problem was its managers, not its workers.

A diagnosis identifies a disease or problem through its physical evidence. One of the most useful new *diagnostic* tools is MRI, or "magnetic resonance imaging," which allows doctors to see what is going on in the soft tissue, such as muscle, cartilage, and brain, that X rays see right through. With MRI, *diagnosticians* can be far more accurate in their diagnoses. (Notice how this plural is formed.)

incognito \ˌin-ˌkäg-ˈnē-tō\ In disguise or with one's identity concealed.

• Katherine Ann Power, an activist and bank robber, lived incognito for 23 years before giving herself up in 1993.

In the famous myth of Baucis and Philemon, Zeus and Hermes visit a village incognito to test the villagers. The seemingly poor travelers are turned away from every household except that of Baucis and Philemon. This elderly couple, though very poor themselves, provide the incognito gods with a feast. When the gods finally reveal themselves, the couple is rewarded for their hospitality, and the rest of the village is destroyed for their lack of it.

prognosis \präg-ˈnō-səs\ (1) The chance of recovery from a given disease or condition. (2) Forecast or prophecy.

• The prognosis for a patient with chicken pox is usually excellent; the prognosis for someone with liver cancer is terrible.

Prognosis contains the prefix *pro-*, meaning "before." It is thus "knowledge beforehand," based on the normal course of events in similar situations. Economists try to *prognosticate,* or predict, what the economy will do, based on the trends they see and their knowledge of where such trends tend to lead. A prognosis of recovery and growth is obviously much better than one of recession and stagnation.

Quizzes

A. Fill in each blank with the correct letter:

a. diagnosis
b. malediction
c. cognitive
d. jurisdiction
e. interdiction
f. incognito
g. edict
h. prognosis

1. Psychology is not entirely a ____ science, since it deals with behavior as well as the mind.
2. Belief in the power of a ____ to harm has faded with the advances of science and growing rejection of superstition.
3. Movie stars often go out in public ____, in faded sweatshirts, worn-out pants, and sunglasses.
4. When their dictatorial grandfather issued an ____, everyone obeyed it.
5. The electrician made a quick ____ and fixed the heater by replacing a faulty switch.
6. The ____ for the world's climate in the next century is uncertain.
7. An ____ of their supply lines by enemy mortars on the surrounding hills meant the loyalists would have to find new routes.
8. The judge refused to consider two elements in the case, saying that they lay outside his ____.

B. Indicate whether the following pairs of words have the same or different meanings:

1. diagnosis / analysis — same __ / different __
2. cognitive / digestive — same __ / different __
3. interdiction / prohibition — same __ / different __
4. malediction / curse — same __ / different __
5. incognito / hospitable — same __ / different __
6. jurisdiction / power — same __ / different __
7. prognosis / prophecy — same __ / different __
8. edict / order — same __ / different __

APT/EPT, from *aptare,* "to fit," and *aptus,* "fit," is endlessly *adaptable,* changing itself to fit many words and purposes. You are *apt,* or "likely," to come upon them when you least expect, so *adept* are they at fitting in.

---

adaptation \a-ˌdap-ˈtā-shən\ Adjustment to conditions of an environment, or to a new or different use.

• Humans have undergone many adaptations since the first hominids roamed the land.

Adaptation usually makes survival or success more likely. There are moths in England that were once light gray; on the bark of a tree they were practically invisible to birds looking for food. During the Industrial Revolution in England, when factory smoke turned the trees black with grime, the light-colored moths became clearly visible and were eaten. As the years passed, the moths went through a protective adaptation and became black or dark gray like the trees, and once again invisible to the birds.

aptitude \'ap-tə-ˌtüd\ (1) Natural tendency, talent, or ability. (2) Ability to learn.

• She longed to learn to play piano but feared she had no aptitude for music.

Most students applying for college take both aptitude tests and achievement tests. Aptitude tests claim to measure how much you are able to learn, and achievement tests how much you have already learned. That is, a math achievement test should require that you have memorized formulas and complex operations, whereas a math aptitude test should require only that you show you can work quickly and intelligently with basic operations. Many aptitudes, both physical and mental, show up clearly in children by the age of 3 or 4.

adept \ə-'dept\ Expert or highly skilled.

• The dollmaker was astonishingly adept at painting the features of famous dancers on her little porcelain heads.

Charlie Chaplin was adept at far more than acting, directing, and screenwriting; he was an acrobat of professional quality, and songs he wrote became popular hits. Most of us would settle for being adept in only a couple of areas.

inept \i-'nept\ Foolish, incompetent, bungling.

• The government's inept handling of the whole affair led to its defeat in the next election.

Inept is the opposite of *adept*. Inspector Clouseau has been the image of *ineptitude* for a generation of moviegoers, who may have caught a glimpse of themselves in his dignified but hopeless incompetence.

ART comes from the Latin word for "skill."Until a few centuries ago, almost no one made a strong distinction between skilled craftsmanship and what we would call "art." *Art* could also mean simply "cleverness." The result is that this root appears in some words where we might not expect it.

---

artful \'ärt-fəl\ (1) Skillful. (2) Wily, crafty, sly.

• It was an artful solution: each side was pleased with the agreement, but the lawyer himself stood to make the most money off of it.

A writer may produce an artful piece of prose, one that is clearly and elegantly written. The same writer, however, could also make an artful argument, one that leaves out certain details and plays up others so as to make a stronger case. In the first instance, the writer's work is well-crafted; in the second, he or she is instead crafty. (Try not to use *artful*, however, when you really mean "artistic.")

artifact \'är-ti-ˌfakt\ A usually simple object, such as a tool or ornament, made by human workmanship or modification.

• Archaeologists have found many artifacts that help us understand how the early Anasazi people of the Southwest lived.

One of the things that makes humans unique is their ability to make and use tools. These tools and the objects made with them are artifacts, a word that literally means "made with skill." Human cultures in all eras, from the Stone Age onward, have left behind artifacts from which we can learn about their lives.

artifice \'är-tə-fəs\ (1) Clever skill. (2) A clever trick.

• By his cunning and artifice, Iago convinces Othello that Desdemona has been unfaithful.

Artifice combines the same roots as *artifact*, but usually suggests something deceptive or tricky or at least highly *artificial*. Simplicity, honesty, and genuineness are the opposites of artifice, which is related to disguise, fantasy, and complexity. Starting with the Puritans, America has traditionally prided itself on its lack of artifice, seeing a character like Huckleberry Finn as an image of the essential American. But artifice is often in the eye of the beholder, and the book *Huckleberry Finn* is itself filled with literary artifice.

artisan \'är-tə-zən\ A skilled worker or craftsperson.

• At the fair, they saw examples of the best carving, pottery, and jewelry by local artisans.

In the Middle Ages artisans organized themselves into guilds. In every city each group of artisans, such as the weavers or carpenters, had its own guild. The guilds set wages and prices for the artisans' wares, and also protected them from competing artisans who did not belong. Guilds existed in some European countries until the 19th century. In America, however, most artisans have always been fiercely independent.

Quizzes

A. Complete the analogy:

1. sensation : feeling :: aptitude : ____
   a. amount b. emotion c. talent d. article
2. mournful : sad :: artful : ____
   a. clever b. doleful c. fake d. creative
3. strong : weak :: adept : ____
   a. skilled b. easy c. inept d. unjust
4. physician : doctor :: artisan : ____
   a. plumber b. nurse c. teacher d. craftsperson
5. life : death :: adaptation : ____
   a. sensation b. excitement c. stagnation d. rejection
6. labor : strength :: artifact : ____
   a. skill b. statuette c. remains d. trick
7. clumsy : grace :: inept : ____
   a. honesty b. competence c. stupidity d. ignorance
8. confession : true :: artifice : ____
   a. skill b. honest c. false d. ridiculous

B. Match the definition on the left to the correct word on the right:

1.	skilled craftsman	a.	artful
2.	natural talent	b.	artifice
3.	skillfully sly	c.	adaptation
4.	expert	d.	inept
5.	slyness	e.	artisan
6.	process of change	f.	aptitude
7.	man-made object	g.	adept
8.	awkward	h.	artifact

CAD/CID/CAS all comes from the same Latin verb, *cadere,* meaning "to fall, fall down, drop," or from the related noun *casus,* "fall or chance." An *accident* happens to you out of the blue. By *coincidence,* things fall together in a pattern. *Casual* dress is what you put on almost by chance. A *cascade* is a rushing down of something.

cadaver \kə-'da-vər\ A dead body, especially one that is to be dissected; a corpse.

• The cadaver she was given to work on was an unclaimed homeless woman and came from the Manhattan morgue.

The mystery writer P. D. James always produces a cadaver with a tale that must be unraveled by her sleuth, Adam Dalgliesh. And occasionally one of her living characters may have gaunt, *cadaverous* features, such as hollow cheeks and sunken eyes, which resemble the features of a corpse.

casualty \'ka-zhü-wəl-tē\ A person, especially a military person, or a thing that is injured, lost, or destroyed; a victim.

• When the platoon limped back to camp, they learned that Lieutenant Steiger had been a casualty of a land mine.

The casualty count in a war includes the dead, the wounded, and the seriously ill. In the American Civil War, for instance, deaths represented only about half of the total casualties—and most of the deaths resulted from infection and disease rather than from battle wounds alone. We may also use the term less literally. For example, if a woman's new husband doesn't get along with her best friend, the friendship may become a casualty of the marriage.

decadent \'de-kə-dənt\ (1) Self-indulgent. (2) Decaying or declining.

• The French Empire may have been at its most decadent just before the French Revolution.

Many of the rich people of ancient Rome lived decadent lives, full of every sort of excess imaginable, as their empire fell apart. No expense was spared to bring exotic delicacies to their tables, from African ostrich eggs to snow from the Alps—in the days before refrigeration! And Rome's emperors were often part of the problem. Commodus, the 18-year-old bodybuilder son of the emperor, was leading his troops against the barbarians on the frontier when he heard his father had died, and raced immediately back to Rome to take up a life of pleasure and *decadence*.

recidivism \ri-'si-də-ˌvi-zəm\ A tendency to fall back into earlier habits or modes of behaving, especially criminal habits.

• Recidivism among smokers who try to quit is very high.

Recidivism means literally "a falling back," and usually implies "into bad habits." Though the criminal justice system tries to reduce the rate of recidivism among criminals, most released prisoners return to a life of crime as *recidivists*.

CIS comes from the Latin verb meaning "to cut, cut down, or slay." An *incisor* is one of the big front biting teeth; beavers and woodchucks have especially large ones. A *decision* "cuts off" previous discussion and uncertainty.

---

concise \kən-'sīs\ Brief and condensed, especially in expression or statement.

• Professor Childs's exam asked for a concise, one-page summary of the causes of the American Revolution.

Most students, and many adults, think that adding unnecessary sentences with long words will make their writing more impressive. But in fact almost every reader values *concision*: concise writing is usually easier to read, better thought out, and better organized—that is, simply better writing.

excise \'ek-ˌsīz\ To cut out, especially surgically.

• The ancient Minoans from the island of Crete apparently excised the hearts of their human sacrifices.

Excise takes part of its meaning from the prefix *ex-*, "out." A writer may excise long passages of a novel to reduce it to a reasonable length, or merely excise sections that may give offense. A surgeon may excise a large cancerous tumor, or make a tiny *excision* to examine an organ's tissue.

incisive \in-'sī-siv\ Impressively direct and decisive.

• A few incisive questions were all that was needed to expose the weakness in the prosecutor's case.

To *incise* is to cut into; an incisive remark, then, "cuts into" the matter at hand. A good news analyst makes incisive comments about the story he or she is following, shedding light on the situation. A good movie critic *incisively* remarks on a film's strengths and weaknesses, helping us decide whether or not to see it.

precision \pri-'si-zhən\ (1) Exactness of definition or statement. (2) Accuracy of performance or measurement.

• Only slowly did he learn to speak with precision, to find the exact words for everything in place of the crude, awkward language of his friends.

The weather can never be predicted with absolute precision. Modern technology such as computer models and satellite photos help forecasters to be more *precise* than ever before, but there are so many factors involved in making the weather that any forecaster always runs the risk of being *imprecise*.

Quizzes

A. Fill in each blank with the correct letter:

a. casualty
b. decadent
c. cadaver
d. precision
e. concise
f. excise
g. incisive
h. recidivism

1. Ms. Raymond's report on her trip up the Amazon is ___ but fascinating.
2. They were a ___ crowd; rich and idle, they spent their days taking drugs and their nights hunting for pleasure in the clubs.
3. The medical students were assigned in threes to work on each ___.
4. The reporter was known for remarks that were so ___ that his interviewees were often embarrassed.
5. The first American ___ of the Revolutionary War may have been the black soldier Crispus Attucks.
6. ___ among chocolate lovers who try to limit their intake is appallingly high.
7. Before eating an apple, some people carefully ___ the brown spots.
8. What the tipsy darts players lacked in ___ they made up for in enthusiasm.

B. Choose the closest definition:

1. precision a. accuracy b. beauty c. conciseness d. dependence
2. decadent a. rotten b. generous c. self-indulgent d. ten years long
3. excise a. tax b. examine c. refuse d. cut out
4. recidivism a. backsliding b. backstabbing c. backscratching d. backslapping
5. incisive a. damaging b. direct c. dirty d. definite
6. casualty a. serious remark b. serious outlook c. serious condition d. serious injury
7. concise a. short b. sure c. shifting d. sharp
8. cadaver a. victim b. suspect c. corpse d. detective

Animal Words

apiary \'ā-pē-ˌer-ē\ A place where bees are kept for their honey.

• An apple orchard is an excellent site for an apiary, since the bees keep the apple trees productive by pollinating them.

The social life in an apiary is strange and marvelous. The queen bee, who will become the mother of an entire colony, is created by being fed "royal jelly" in her larval stage. The tens of thousands of worker bees are underdeveloped females; only a handful of the bees are male, and they do no work at all. The workers defend the hive by kamikaze means, stinging any intruder and dying as they do so.

caper \'kā-pər\ (1) A playful leap. (2) A prank or mischievous adventure.

• For their caper in the girls' bathroom, all three seniors were suspended for a week.

Caper in Latin means "a male goat." Anyone who has watched a young goat frolic in a field or clamber onto the roof of a car knows the kind of crazy fun the English word *caper* is referring to. A *capriole* is a backward kick done in midair by a trained horse. *Capricorn,* or "horned goat," is a constellation and one of the signs of the zodiac.

equestrian \i-'kwes-trē-ən\ Having to do with horseback riding.

• The equestrian acts, in which bareback riders performed daring acrobatic feats atop prancing horses, were her favorites.

The word *equestrian* comes from *equus,* Latin for "horse." War memorials often show great commanders in equestrian poses. In these sculptures the man always sits nobly upright, but the horse's stance varies. Depending on whether the rider was killed in battle or survived, was victorious or defeated, the horse stands with four, three, or two hooves on the ground. Equestrian statues have been popular through the centuries because until this century almost every commanding officer was trained in equestrian skills and combat.

lupine \'lü-ˌpīn\ Like a wolf; wolfish.

• They heard the resonant voices of a lupine chorus howling most of the night.

Lupine comes from *lupus,* the Latin word for "wolf," and the related adjective *lupinus,* "wolfish." Dogs often exhibit lupine behavior, since many of them are descended from wolves. Lupine groups have a highly organized social structure, in which leaders and followers are clearly distinguished, and dogs often show these lupine patterns when living in groups. *Lupine* is also a noun, the name of a well-known flower, which was once thought to drain, or "wolf," the soil of its nutrients.

lycanthropy \lī-'kan-thrə-pē\ The taking on of the form and behavior of a wolf by means of magic or witchcraft.

• The 1941 film *The Wolf Man* starred Lon Chaney, Jr., as a man cursed with lycanthropy.

For centuries a belief in lycanthropy has been part of the folk culture of lands where wolves exist. The word comes from the joining of two Greek roots—*lyc,* meaning "wolf," and *anthrop,* meaning "man." A victim of this enchantment is a *lycanthrope,* or werewolf. When the moon is full, the animal part of his nature takes over and he is transformed into a wolf, only much more bloodthirsty. The lycanthrope preys on humans, especially babies and buried corpses, and can even cause lycanthropy in others by biting them.

ornithologist \ˌȯr-nə-'thä-lə-jist\ A person who studies birds.

• John James Audubon, the great painter of the birds of early America, was also a writing ornithologist of great importance.

Ornithologist comes from two Greek roots, *ornith-,* meaning "bird," and *log-,* meaning "study." Roger Tory Peterson's numerous field guides have long been some of the amateur ornithologist's most useful tools.

serpentine \'sər-pən-ˌtīn\ Like a snake or serpent in shape or movement; winding.

• The Great Wall of China, the greatest construction of all time, wends its serpentine way for 1,200 miles.

A snake moves by curving and winding along the ground. Roads through the Pyrenees, the mountains that separate Spain from France, tend to be serpentine, curving back and forth upon themselves on the steep slopes. (*Serpentine* has many other meanings as well; it can describe human character or physique, for example, and it is also the name for a soft green mineral and for party streamers.)

simian \'si-mē-ən\ Having to do with monkeys or apes; monkeylike.

• In mid-afternoon the pale youth could be seen watching the simian antics in the Monkey House with strange intensity.

The Latin word for "ape" is *simia,* which itself comes from *simus,* "snub-nosed." Not only monkeys and apes can be simian. A human baby may cling to her mother in a simian way; a person may have a simian style of eating a banana; kids may display simian agility as they play on the jungle gym; and a grunt may be simian even when made by a human.

Quiz

Indicate whether the following pairs have the same or different meanings:

1. equestrian / horselike — same __ / different __
2. ornithologist / studier of birds — same __ / different __
3. lupine / apelike — same __ / different __
4. apiary / monkey colony — same __ / different __
5. lycanthropy / werewolfism — same __ / different __
6. caper / leap — same __ / different __
7. simian / clumsy — same __ / different __
8. serpentine / steep — same __ / different __

Review Quizzes

A. Fill in each blank with the correct letter:

a. artisan
b. edict
c. equestrian

k. recidivism
l. cadaver
m. inculpate

d. artifact
e. discordant
f. casualty
g. cognitive
h. apiary
i. exculpate
j. inept

n. serpentine
o. interdiction
p. precision
q. artifice
r. aptitude
s. prognosis
t. simian

1. The farmer tended his ____ lovingly and gathered delicious wildflower honey every year.
2. In trying to ____ herself, she only made herself look guiltier.
3. The enemy's ____ of supplies left the city helpless.
4. Though he showed astonishing mathematical ____ as a child, he spent his life as a salesman.
5. They arrived in time to see the top riders compete in the championship ____ event.
6. The doctor's ____ is guarded, but she is cautiously optimistic that recovery will be complete.
7. Fortunately, the accident caused only one minor ____.
8. We made our way slowly along the ____ course of the lazy river.
9. Each side's anger at the other has set a sadly ____ tone for the negotiations.
10. We set the clock with great ____ on the first day of every new year.
11. The thief tried hard to ____ as many of his friends in the crime as he could.
12. These beautiful handblown goblets were obviously made by a talented ____.
13. The final ____ from the presidential palace commanded every citizen to wear a baseball cap at all times.
14. The child scrambled over the wall with ____ agility.
15. As a baby, he was unusually quick to develop ____ skills.
16. She found a small clay ____ in the shape of a bear at the site of the ancient temple.
17. The local mechanics are ____ or dishonest or both, so I don't recommend them.
18. There bobbing by the wharf was a ____, the remains of a man in a white suit.

19. He used every ____ imaginable to hide his real age from the television cameras.
20. The rate of ____ for those imprisoned for felonies is alarmingly high.

B. Choose the correct synonym and the correct antonym:

1. accord a. give one's due b. give one's heart c. withhold what is earned d. withhold approval
2. malediction a. prayer b. benediction c. oath d. curse
3. artful a. lovely b. sly c. talented d. honest
4. decadent a. decaying b. ten-year c. twelfth d. growing
5. cordial a. amorous b. hostile c. terrific d. heartfelt
6. incognito a. indoors b. in disguise c. as oneself d. as you were
7. incisive a. toothed b. sharp c. toothless d. dull
8. concise a. lengthy b. wide c. dated d. brief
9. culpable a. doleful b. stentorian c. guilty d. innocent
10. adept a. changed b. skilled c. clumsy d. unwell

C. Choose the closest definition:

1. ornithologist a. student of fish b. student of words c. student of birds d. student of wolves
2. mea culpa a. through my eyes b. through my fault c. through my door d. through my work
3. lupine a. foxy b. horselike c. sheepish d. wolfish
4. adaptation a. process of going b. process of change c. process of mending d. process of canning
5. jurisdiction a. area of power b. area of coverage c. area of damage d. area of target
6. excise a. take out b. hold out c. cut out d. fold out
7. concordance a. index b. bible c. glossary d. contents
8. lycanthropy a. sorcery b. monstrosity c. vampirism d. werewolfism
9. diagnosis a. identification b. symptoms c. disease d. treatment
10. caper a. wolf b. goat c. dance d. prank

Unit 14

CRYPT/CRYPH comes from the Greek word for "hidden." To *encrypt* a message is to encode it—that is, to hide its meaning in code language. A medical term beginning with *crypto-* always means there is something hidden about the condition.

apocryphal \ə-ˈpä-krə-fəl\ Of doubtful genuineness or authenticity.

• Jason's story, they now realized, was completely apocryphal, though he himself may have believed it.

Both the Old and the New Testaments sometimes include books that have a doubtful status, since the leaders of the Jewish and Christian religions have determined that they aren't completely deserving of being included with the official scriptures. These documents are known as the *Apocrypha*; the root here suggests that the Apocrypha's origins are somewhat hidden and so not reliable. Today anything fake or counterfeit that is claimed to be genuine, such as the supposed diaries of Adolf Hitler in the 1980s, can be called apocryphal.

cryptic \ˈkrip-ˈtik\ (1) Mysterious; puzzlingly short. (2) Acting to hide or conceal.

• Louisa threw Philip a cryptic look whose meaning he couldn't be sure of.

Until the writing on the Rosetta Stone was finally translated in the early 19th century, Egyptian hieroglyphic writing was entirely cryptic, its meaning hidden from the modern world. In the same way, a cryptic comment or remark or look is one whose meaning is unclear and perhaps even mystifying. Cryptic coloring among plants and animals acts like camouflage; some moths, although very tasty to blue jays, are *cryptically* colored to look like bugs that the jays consider inedible.

cryptography \krip-'tä-grə-fē\ (1) Secret writing. (2) The encoding and decoding of messages.

• The instructions for the missile launch are translated into code by the cryptography team.

During World War II, cryptography became an extremely complex science for both the Allied and Axis powers. The Allies managed to get their hands on the Axis machine designed to produce unbreakable codes; the Axis *cryptographers,* on the other hand, never managed to crack the Americans' ultimate code—the Navajo language. In the age of computers, cryptography has become almost unbelievably complex; it is widely used in peacetime in such areas as banking telecommunications.

crypt \'kript\ A room completely or partly underground, especially under the main floor of a church; a room or area in a large aboveground tomb.

• His old nightmare was of being locked in a crypt with corpses as his only companions.

Hidden under the main floor of a great church is often a large room, the centerpiece of which may be a tomb. Many European churches were built over the tomb of a saint or other religious figure; the great St. Peter's Church in the Vatican is an example. A large mausoleum, or aboveground tomb, may contain crypts or small chambers for individual coffins.

AB/ABS comes to us from Latin, and means "from," "away," or "off." *Abuse* is the use of something in the wrong way. To *abduct* is to "lead away from" or kidnap. *Aberrant* behavior is behavior that "wanders away from" what is usually acceptable. But there are so many words that include these roots, it would be *absurd* to try to list them all here.

---

abscond \ab-'skänd\ To depart in secret and hide.

• We discovered the next morning that our guest had absconded with the family silver during the night.

In J.R.R. Tolkien's novel *The Hobbit,* Bilbo Baggins absconds from Gollum's caves with the ring he has found, the ring Gollum calls "my precious"; the results of his theft and absconding are detailed in the three-volume *Lord of the Rings.* Wagner's massive four-part opera *The Ring of the Nibelung* similarly begins with a dwarf absconding with gold which he turns into a magic ring. Absconding from a problem is often only a temporary relief from it; a young couple might abscond from their parents to get married, but sooner or later they must face those parents again.

abstemious \ab-'stē-mē-əs\ Restrained, especially in the consumption of food or alcohol.

• By living an abstemious life they managed to stay very healthy and to save enough money to take a trip every few years.

Many monks of the 14th century were held to the Rule of St. Benedict, which demand an abstemious life of obedience and poverty. But not all monks could maintain such abstemious habits. Chaucer's *Canterbury Tales* contains a portrait of a monk who is anything but abstemious: for instance, although monks were supposed to follow a vegetarian diet, he is an enthusiastic hunter who loves a fat swan best. He justifies breaking the Rule by saying that it is old, and he's just keeping up with modern times.

abstraction \ab-'strak-shən\ The consideration of a thing or idea without associating it with a particular example.

• All her ideas sounded like abstractions, since in fact she had no experience of actual nursing at all.

Abstract art is art that makes little attempt to show physical objects as they are usually seen. The roots of the word mean "to pull or draw away"; therefore, an abstract design distances itself from any particular object. Theories are often abstractions, especially when they "pull back" to take a broad view and try to apply to or explain everything of a certain kind—for example, all governments, all molecules, or all rock singers.

abstruse \ab-'strüs\ Hard to understand; deep or complex.

• The professor helpfully filled the blackboard with abstruse calculations, but they only served to confuse the class more.

Very often scientific writing is filled with an abstruse special vocabulary, or jargon, which is necessary for exact and precise descriptions. Unfortunately, the language of a science like quantum physics can make an already difficult subject even more abstruse to the average person. Luckily, there are books available that untangle the *abstrusities* in this and other sciences, and explain those difficult ideas in plain, everyday terms.

Quizzes

A. Match the definition on the left to the correct word on the right:

1. mysterious a. apocryphal
2. code writing b. abstraction
3. fake c. abscond
4. difficult d. cryptic
5. tomb e. abstruse
6. theory f. crypt
7. self-controlled g. cryptography
8. flee h. abstemious

B. Fill in each blank with the correct letter:

a. cryptic e. cryptography
b. abscond f. abstemious
c. abstraction g. apocryphal
d. crypt h. abstruse

1. Many an explorer believed the ____ stories of the City of Gold and died hunting for it.
2. His answer was so short and ____ that I have no idea what he meant.
3. The great, echoing ____ of St. Stephen's Cathedral could have held hundreds of people.
4. That is merely an ____; in the real world, things work very differently.

5. The ____ vocabulary of the literature professor led many students to drop her class.
6. He led an ____ life these days and rarely thought of his former high living.
7. Their ____ hadn't been revised in years, and there were worries about the security of their data.
8. The bride is so shy that her mother fears she'll ____ from the reception.

PED comes from the Greek word for "child" this time. See also its "foot" meaning in Unit 4. The two usually aren't hard to tell apart—but don't mistake a *pediatrician* for a *podiatrist.*

pedagogy \'pe-də-ˌgō-jē\ The art or profession of teaching; the study of teaching.

• His own pedagogy shows great style and imagination but received little recognition.

To the Greeks, a *pedagogue* was a slave who escorted boys to school and back, taught them manners, and offered extra help with their studies after school. In time the word came to mean simply "teacher." It has an antique ring to it, so it often means a stuffy, boring teacher. *Pedagogy* doesn't have much of that ring to it. It usually means "methods of teaching," while *pedagogic* training usually includes classroom practice.

encyclopedic \in-ˌsī-klə-'pē-dik\ (1) Of or relating to an encyclopedia. (2) Covering a wide range of subjects.

• The *Jeopardy* champion displayed her encyclopedic knowledge with great success.

In Greek, *paidaea* meant "child-rearing" or "education," and *kyklios* meant "circular" or "general"; thus, an encyclopedia is a work broad enough to provide a kind of general education. The *Encyclopaedia Britannica* is a huge work that covers nearly every field of human knowledge. Some dictionaries are also encyclopedic, since they give extended information about history, technology, science, and so on. But *encyclopedic* doesn't have to refer to books: a rock-and-roll radio station may have an encyclopedic collection of popular music, for example.

pediatrician \ˌpē-dē-ə-'tri-shən\ A doctor who specializes in the diseases, development, and care of children.

• A child usually sees a pediatrician until he or she turns 15.

Pediatrics is a fairly new medical specialty; up until about a hundred years ago children were considered small adults and given the same medical treatment, only milder. Benjamin Spock was America's most famous pediatrician through the middle of this century; his book *Baby and Child Care* changed the way people looked at raising children.

pedant \'pe-dənt\ (1) A formal, unimaginative teacher. (2) A person who shows off his or her learning.

• At one time or another, every student encounters a pedant who makes even the most interesting subject tedious.

It is not always easy to tell a *pedantic* teacher from one who is simply thorough. Half of *pedantry* is in the minds of the students. A pedant need not be a teacher; anyone who displays his or her knowledge in a boring manner can qualify.

NASC/NAT/NAI comes from the Latin verb *nasci*, meaning "to be born." Words that have come directly from Latin carry the root *nasc-* or *nat-*, but those that took a detour through French bear a telltale *nai-*—words like *renaissance*, "rebirth," or *naive*, "unsophisticated."

---

cognate \'käg-ˌnāt\ (1) Related or alike by nature. (2) Related because descended from the same language.

• The Italian word *ostinato* has its English cognate in *obstinate*; both come from the Latin word *obstinatus*.

The prefix *co-*, "with," gives *cognate* the meaning "born with" and therefore "related to." This relationship applies to people as well as to words. Your relatives on your mother's side are your cognate relatives; the ones on your father's side are called *agnate,* with a basic meaning of "born to."

innate \i-ˈnāt\ (1) Present from birth onward; inborn. (2) Part of the essential nature of something.

• The plan has innate problems that are going to make it unworkable.

What is innate in individuals, and in the human race in general, is a constant source of disagreement. No amount of education or experience alone could produce an Isaac Newton or a W.B. Yeats, and the athletic achievements of Michael Jordan or Chris Evert Lloyd required great innate ability. But even the most *natural* geniuses or athletes must work to develop their capacities, no matter how great their *native* talent may be.

nascent \ˈna-sənt\ Coming or having just come into being.

• The children excitedly watched the nascent butterfly emerge from its chrysalis and begin to stretch its crumpled wings.

With the breakup of the former Soviet Union, the many nascent independent governments in Eastern Europe have had to cope with *renascent* nationalism within their borders, with every ethnic group wanting its own nation. We actually speak of nascent ideas or thoughts or social creations more often than of nascent animals.

renaissance \ˌre-nə-ˈsäns\ (1) Rebirth or revival. (2) The period of European history between medieval and modern times, from about the 14th to the 17th century, which saw a revival of classical culture, a flowering of the arts and literature, and the beginnings of modern science.

• Rembrandt van Rijn, the Dutch painter, was one of the greatest artists produced by the European Renaissance.

The Renaissance is known chiefly for the discoveries of its explorers, the masterpieces its artists created, and its important scientific advances. Galileo made detailed observations of sunspots and the moons of Jupiter, and Copernicus identified the Earth as a planet revolving around the sun—ideas that were considered dangerous at the time. But we may also speak of a modern-day renaissance (uncapitalized)—for example, a renaissance of folk music or of weaving. The *cognate* word *renascence* is sometimes used as an alternative form.

Quizzes

A. Indicate whether the following pairs of words have the same or different meanings:

1. nascent / preexisting — same __ / different __
2. encyclopedic / narrow — same __ / different __
3. renaissance / rebirth — same __ / different __
4. cognate / related — same __ / different __
5. pediatrician / foot doctor — same __ / different __
6. innate / inborn — same __ / different __
7. pedagogy / teaching — same __ / different __
8. pedant / know-it-all — same __ / different __

B. Match the definition on the left to the correct word on the right:

1. thorough	a. renaissance
2. beginning	b. pediatrician
3. boring teacher	c. cognate
4. related	d. encyclopedic
5. present from birth	e. nascent
6. education	f. pedant
7. revival	g. innate
8. children's doctor	h. pedagogy

FER, from the Latin verb *ferre,* means "to carry." If you *refer* to an incident in your past, you "carry back" to that time. And *transfer* means "to carry across."

deferential \ˌde-fə-ˈren-chəl\ Showing respect or esteem.

• Wherever the chairman goes, he receives deferential treatment from his hosts.

As we all know, young people should always *defer* (that is, yield or submit) to their elders and betters, who deserve *deference* and appreciate manners that are properly deferential. Unfortunately, deference from young people isn't what it used to be. (We can also defer, or "put off," a decision until another time, but this meaning isn't found in *deferential*.)

fertile \'fər-təl\ (1) Bearing great quantities of fruit or imaginative ideas; productive or inventive. (2) Able to support abundant plant growth.

• Unfortunately, those with the most fertile minds often seem to have the most personal problems.

A fertile imagination and a fertile field are both very productive. The first might bring forth a whole new world, like J.R.R. Tolkien's Middle Earth; the second might bring forth enough corn for an entire town. But both have to be tended and nurtured in order to *confer* their benefits. *Fertile* and *infertile, fertility* and *infertility* often refer to the ability to bear children as well.

inference \'in-frəns\ (1) A conclusion arrived at from facts or statements taken as true. (2) A guess or assumption made on the basis of little or no evidence.

• Trial lawyers try to present evidence in such a way that the jury can draw from it only the inference that favors their client.

Inferences are risky. In the myth of Pyramus and Thisbe, an inference leads to disaster. When these two lovers are supposed to meet, Pyramus arrives late to find a lion and a bloodstained garment. From this he *infers* that Thisbe has been killed, and, unable to bear it, he kills himself. But Thisbe has only been hiding, and when she finds the dead Pyramus she kills herself in grief. (Shakespeare makes a humorous scene out of this story in *A Midsummer Night's Dream*. But his *Romeo and Juliet* tells the story of two lovers who die as the result of a very similar inference.)

proliferate \prə-'li-fə-ˌrāt\ To grow or increase by rapid production of new units; to multiply.

• Imitators of Ernest Hemingway began to proliferate as soon as he achieved success and popularity.

The literal meaning of *proliferate* is "to bear offspring," and all other usages begin with this. In "The Sorcerer's Apprentice" the apprentice learns how to order the first broom to multiply itself *prolifically*, but not how to command it to stop. Brooms proliferate wildly, each carrying buckets of water that soon flood the sorcerer's studio.

TRANS comes from Latin to indicate movement "through, across, or beyond" something. *Translation* carries the meaning from one language to another. A television signal is sent or *transmitted* through the air (or a cable) to your set. When making your way through a city on public *transportation*, you may have to *transfer* from one bus or subway across to another.

---

transfiguration \trans-ˌfi-gyə-ˈrā-shən\ A change in form or appearance; a glorifying spiritual change.

• Being in love caused a complete transfiguration of her personality.

The transfiguration of Christ from human to divine form, as his apostles watch, is related in the books of Matthew and Mark. From this Biblical origin, *transfiguration* and *transfigure* developed their general meaning, "a transformation" and "to transform." Ebenezer Scrooge undergoes a transfiguration from mean-spirited miser to loving benefactor by the end of *A Christmas Carol*. A face may be transfigured by joy, and an "ugly duckling" child may be slowly transfigured into a radiant beauty.

transfuse \trans-ˈfyüz\ (1) To spread into or throughout; to permeate. (2) To transfer into a vein of a person or animal.

• There was considerable excitement about the new president, who everyone expected to transfuse new life into the institution.

When blood *transfusions* were first attempted by Europeans in the early 1600s, they were met with skepticism. The established practice was to bleed patients, not transfuse them with blood. Some patients were transfused with animal blood, and so many died because of the procedure that it was outlawed in most of Europe by 1700. Not until 1900 were the major blood groups (A, B, AB, and O) recognized, making transfusions safer and more effective.

transient \'tran-chē-ənt\ (1) Not lasting long; short-lived. (2) Passing through a place and staying only briefly.

• They ran an inn in Vermont that was popular with the transient tourists who passed through the state to see the autumn foliage.

A summer job on a farm is transient work, lasting only as long as the growing season. A brief visit to a town on your way somewhere else is a transient visit. A transient mood is one that passes quickly. Doctors speak of transient episodes of dizziness or weakness, which vanish without a trace. *Transient* is also a noun, used for a person who passes through a place, staying only briefly. The hoboes and tramps of earlier years were some of our most colorful transients.

transcendent \tran-'sen-dənt\ (1) Exceeding or rising above usual limits; surpassing, supreme. (2) Beyond comprehension; beyond ordinary experience or material existence.

• Despite the chaos around her she remained calm, with a transcendent smile on her face.

In the Middle Ages the authority of the Pope was considered transcendent in Europe, above the power of kings and emperors, but in the 16th century the *transcendence* of the Papacy was challenged by Martin Luther and Henry VIII of England. A transcendent experience is one that takes you out of yourself and convinces you of a larger life or existence. In this sense, it means something close to "supernatural" or "spiritual."

Quizzes

A. Fill in each blank with the correct letter:

a. transfiguration	e. deferential
b. proliferate	f. transient
c. transfuse	g. inference
d. fertile	h. transcendent

1. Copies of American blue jeans seem to ____ in all parts of the world.
2. He lived a ____ existence, spending more nights in airport hotels than at home.
3. The private assumed her usual ____ attitude toward the lieutenant.

4. Waiting for the nurse to ____ her, she couldn't remember the accident clearly.
5. They had witnessed a complete ____, as a poor flower vendor became a lady of society.
6. The ____ Connecticut River valley is famous for its tobacco crops.
7. In search of a ____ experience, she had entered a monastery in Tibet.
8. Please don't draw the wrong ____ from what I've said about the building plans.

B. Match the word on the left to the correct definition on the right:

1.	fertile	a.	supreme
2.	transcendent	b.	implied conclusion
3.	deferential	c.	glorification
4.	transfiguration	d.	productive
5.	proliferate	e.	multiply
6.	transient	f.	yielding
7.	inference	g.	passing
8.	transfuse	h.	transfer

PON/POS, from the Latin verb *ponere*, means "put" or "place." You *expose* film by "placing it out" in the light. You *oppose* an *opponent* by "putting yourself against" him or her. You *postpone* a trip by "placing it after" its original date.

---

component \kəm-'pō-nənt\ A separate part of a whole; an ingredient or element.

• All the components of the agreement were in place, but the owner still hadn't given her final approval.

A component is what is "put together with" other parts to make a whole. A stereo system is made up of different components—tuner, cassette deck, CD player, phonograph, and speakers—each of which fills its own different function in the overall system. The components of a crime bill would include sections on sentencing and parole, prisons, the judicial system, and so on. But the pieces of a jigsaw puzzle may be too similar to be called components.

disposition \ˌdis-pə-ˈzi-shən\ (1) Tendency, inclination. (2) Basic outlook or attitude.

• It was his classmates' disposition to argue about everything that convinced him he didn't want to be a lawyer after all.

Animals and people may have sweet or sour dispositions, or personalities. Some of them also may share the tendency, or disposition, to eat greedily, to yawn loudly, or to dash about making odd noises. But many humans have a disposition to gossip, to tell stupid jokes, and to think gloomy thoughts about the future, which your dog may not have.

repository \ri-ˈpä-zə-ˌtȯr-ē\ A place or container where something is stored.

• The 98-year old Miss Sarah turned out to be a repository of lore about the glory days of Beale Street.

A vault or safe is the most secure repository for valuable possessions such as jewelry or money. A book may be a repository of wisdom. A mine is a repository of mineral resources like raw diamonds or gold ore. In all of these lie *deposits* that have been "replaced," and there they *repose* until disturbed.

superimpose \ˌsü-pər-im-ˈpōz\ To put or place one thing over something else.

• With the transparent sheet, the teacher superimposed national boundaries on an outline of the continent of Africa.

Using "mirror shots," with semitransparent mirrors set at 45° angles to the scene, filmmakers used to superimpose shadowy images of ghosts or scenes from a character's past onto scenes from the present. In a similar way, in your own papers you may try to superimpose your own obsession with cockroaches or Wallace Beery onto every historical or economic or literary subject, to the bafflement of your professors.

TEN/TIN/TAIN, from the Latin verb *tenere* and the related word *tenax,* basically means "hold" or "hold on to." A *tenant* is the "holder" of an apartment, house, or land, but not necessarily the owner. A *lieutenant* governor may "hold the position" or "serve in lieu" of the governor when necessary.

---

abstinence \'ab-stə-nəns\ Holding oneself back voluntarily from indulging an appetite or craving.

• Burned out by too many wild nights, she moved to the country and took up a life of abstinence.

Today we usually speak of abstinence from alcohol, rich foods, or sex. But religious beliefs lead many to *abstain* from much more, and abstinence can become a way of life. Certain religious sects may demand abstinence from such things as meat, dancing, and colorful clothing.

tenacious \tə-'nā-shəs\ Stubborn or persistent in clinging to a thing.

• He was known as a tenacious reporter who would stay with a story for months, sometimes risking his health and even his life.

Success requires a tenacious spirit and a drive to achieve. Nowhere is this more apparent than in the entertainment business. Thousands of actors and actresses work *tenaciously* to have a career in the movies. But without beauty or talent, *tenacity* isn't always rewarded, and only a few become stars.

tenable \'te-nə-bəl\ Capable of being held or defended; reasonable.

• She was depressed for weeks after her professor said that her theory wasn't tenable.

Tenable means "holdable." If you hold an opinion but good evidence appears that completely contradicts it, your opinion is no longer tenable. If your own evidence is shown to be false, it ceases to be tenable evidence. So the old ideas that cancer is infectious or that leeches can cure your whooping cough and criminal insanity are now probably *untenable*.

sustenance \'səs-tə-nəns\ (1) Something that gives support or strength. (2) Food, nourishment.

• Napoleon's invading army, forced to turn back from Moscow by the terrible Russian winter, ended up eating its horses when all other sustenance ran out.

Sustenance holds us up from underneath (the prefix *sus-* being a form of *sub-*, meaning "under"). Sustenance can be either physical or emotional. So a big Sunday dinner with your family can provide you with sustenance of both kinds.

Quizzes

A. Choose the closest definition:

1. disposition a. temperature b. personality c. anger d. riddance
2. tenacious a. sticking b. intelligent c. loving d. helping
3. superimpose a. surpass b. put into c. place over d. amaze
4. abstinence a. self-help b. self-will c. self-service d. self-restraint
5. repository a. tomb b. storage container c. office d. library
6. tenable a. decent b. tough c. reasonable d. controllable
7. component a. part b. whole c. some d. all
8. sustenance a. substance b. apartment c. clothing d. nourishment

B. Indicate whether the following pairs have the same or different meanings:

1. component / ingredient same __ / different __
2. sustenance / support same __ / different __
3. repository / return same __ / different __
4. abstinence / absence same __ / different __
5. superimpose / offend deeply same __ / different __
6. tenacious / sensible same __ / different __
7. disposition / nature same __ / different __
8. tenable / unlikely same __ / different __

Number Words

MONO is Greek for "one" or "only." So a *monorail* is a railroad that has only one rail, a *monotonous* voice seems to have only one tone, and a *monopoly* puts all ownership in the hands of a single company, eliminating any competition.

monogamous \mə-'nä-gə-məs\ Being married to one person or having one mate at a time.

• Geese, swans, and many other birds are monogamous and mate for life.

American marriage is by law monogamous; people are permitted to have only one spouse (husband or wife) at a time. There are cultures with laws that permit marriage to more than one person at a time, or *polygamy*. Some Islamic countries permit polygamy, as do some African tribes. In this country the Mormons were *polygamous* until 1890, when they were forced to practice *monogamy* by the unsympathetic federal government.

monograph \'mä-nə-ˌgraf\ A scholarly essay written on a single small topic and published separately.

• Her paper on the slang used by southern college students was printed as a monograph.

A monograph usually takes the form of a book, but a smallish book. The contents discuss a single area or subject. The subjects of monographs tend to be specialized—for example, *A Statistical Study of the Graphic System of Present-Day American English*.

monolithic \ˌmä-nə-'li-thik\ (1) Appearing to be a huge, featureless, often rigid whole. (2) Made up of material with no joints or seams.

• The sheer monolithic rock face of El Capitan looks impossible to climb, but its cracks and seams are enough for experienced rock climbers.

Monolithic combines *mono-* with *lith*, "stone," and *monolith* in its original sense means a huge stone like those at Stonehenge. Just as the face of a cliff can be monolithic, so can any huge or imposing institution. The former U.S.S.R. seemed monolithic and indestructible to the West, but the monolith crumbled with the breakup of the Soviet Union into independent republics. To a lone individual, a huge corporation or a government bureaucracy may seem equally monolithic.

monotheism \'mä-nō-thē-ˌi-zəm\ The worship of a single god.

• Christian monotheism finally triumphed in the Roman Empire in A.D. 392, when worship of all the pagan gods and goddesses was forbidden.

The monotheism of the ancient Hebrews had to combat the *polytheism* (worship of many gods) of the surrounding peoples from the earliest times. As the Bible relates, several times in their history the Hebrews turned away from their *monotheistic* religion and accepted foreign gods, such as those imported by King Solomon. Their own God would then punish them, and the people of Israel would return to monotheism.

UNI comes from the Latin word for "one." A *uniform* is a single design worn by everyone. A *united* group has one single opinion or forms a single *unit*. A *unitard* is a one-piece combination leotard and tights, very good for skating, skiing, dancing—or riding a one-wheeled *unicycle*.

---

unicameral \ˌyü-ni-'ka-mə-rəl\ Having only one lawmaking chamber.

• China has a unicameral system of government; a single group of legislators meets to make its laws.

Unicameral means "one-chambered," and the term is generally used only to describe a governing body. Our federal legislature, like those of most democracies, is *bicameral*, with two legislative (lawmaking) bodies—the Senate and the House of Representatives. Except for Nebraska, all the state legislatures are also bicameral. But nearly every city is governed by a unicameral council.

unilateral \ˌyü-ni-'la-tə-rəl\ (1) Done by one person or party; one-sided. (2) Affecting one side of the body.

• The Japanese Constitution of 1947 includes a unilateral rejection of warfare as an option for their country.

The United States announced a unilateral nuclear-arms reduction in the early 1990s. Such a reduction never occurred in the previous decades, when only *bilateral* ("two-sided") negotiations—that is, negotiations with the Soviet Union—ever resulted in reductions. *Multilateral* agreements, such as those reached at the great Earth Summit in Rio de Janeiro in 1992, may involve most of the world's nations.

unison \ˈyü-nə-sən\ (1) Perfect agreement. (2) Sameness of musical pitch.

• Unable to read music well enough to harmonize, the village choir sang only in unison.

This word usually appears in the phrase "in unison," which means "together, at the same time" or "at the same musical pitch." Music of the early Middle Ages was written to be sung in unison, which can sound strange to modern ears used to hearing rich rhythms and harmonies. An excited crowd responding to a speaker may shout in unison, and a group of demonstrators may chant in unison.

unitarian \ˌyü-nə-ˈter-ē-ən\ Relating or belonging to a religious group that believes that God exists only in one person and stresses individual freedom of belief.

• With his unitarian tendencies, he wasn't likely to get into fights over religious beliefs.

Unitarianism, originally a sect of Christianity believing in a single or *unitary* God, grew up in 18th-century England and developed in America in the early 19th century. By rejecting the idea of the three-part Trinity—God as father, son, and holy ghost—they denied that Christ was divine and thus cannot truly be considered Christian. In this century it joined with the *Universalist* Church, a movement founded on a belief in *universal* salvation—that is, the saving of every soul from damnation after death. Both have always been liberal and fairly small; today they count about half a million members.

Quiz

Fill in each blank with the correct letter:

a. monotheism
b. unilateral
c. monolithic
d. unison
e. unitarian
f. monograph
g. unicameral
h. monogamous

1. The President is allowed to make some ____ decisions without asking Congress's permission.
2. The relationship was unbalanced: she was perfectly ____, while he had two other women in his life.
3. In rejecting a ____ legislature, America seemed to follow Britain's lead.
4. The steep mountain face looked ____ and forbidding.
5. As a strict Catholic, she found ____ beliefs unacceptable.
6. Most religious groups in this country practice one or another form of ____.
7. She ordered a brief ____ on the subject of the origin of the thoroughbred.
8. The children recited the Halloween poems in ____.

Review Quizzes

A. Choose the correct synonym for the following:

1. fertile a. green b. productive c. barren d. bare
2. unilateral a. one-sided b. sideways c. complete d. multiple
3. abstinence a. self-love b. self-restraint c. self-criticism d. self-indulgence
4. innate a. natural b. acquired c. genuine d. official
5. repository a. bedroom b. storeroom c. bank window d. dispensary
6. cryptography a. gravestone writing b. physics writing c. code writing d. mathematical writing
7. sustenance a. subtraction b. nourishment c. poison d. addition
8. deferential a. respectful b. shy c. outgoing d. arrogant

9. monotheism a. nature worship b. worship of one god c. worship of pleasure d. sun worship
10. abscond a. steal b. discover c. retire d. flee
11. transcendent a. supreme b. beautiful c. heroic d. intelligent
12. inference a. conclusion b. claim c. concept d. refusal
13. transient a. flowing b. passing c. intense d. speeding
14. pedagogy a. study b. teaching c. research d. child abuse
15. nascent a. dying b. lasting c. eating d. beginning
16. unison a. solitude b. harmony c. collection d. agreement
17. proliferate a. survive b. prosper c. multiply d. die off
18. crypt a. code b. granite c. tomb d. church
19. superimpose a. increase b. lay over c. improve d. excel
20. monogamous a. with one spouse b. without a spouse c. with several spouses d. with someone else's spouse

B. Fill in each blank with the correct letter:

a. renaissance
b. pediatrician
c. monograph
d. unitarian
e. transfiguration
f. abstraction
g. tenacious
h. disposition
i. transfuse
j. abstruse

1. In the 1990s there has been a ____ of interest in goddess worship.
2. Tuesday the baby sees the ____ for its immunizations and checkups.
3. His ____ had gotten so bad that he found himself snapping angrily at his friends.
4. The anemia was serious enough that they had to ____ him with two pints of blood.
5. The notion of a savior was foreign to his ____ beliefs.
6. The ____ promised by their leader failed to occur on the predicted day.
7. The speech contained one ____ after another, but never a specific example.

8. She would occasionally publish a short ____ on the results of her recent research.
9. The sick child's ____ grip on life was their only hope now.
10. The researcher's writing was ____ but it was worth the effort to read it.

C. Indicate whether the following pairs of words have the same or different meanings:

1. component / part same __ / different __
2. pedant / pupil same __ / different __
3. cryptic / tomblike same __ / different __
4. monolithic / tedious same __ / different __
5. abstemious / self-controlled same __ / different __
6. cognate / related same __ / different __
7. apocryphal / sacred same __ / different __
8. tenable / reasonable same __ / different __
9. unicameral / one-chambered same __ / different __
10. abstruse / deep same __ / different __

Unit 15

TERM/TERMIN comes from the Latin verb *terminare,* "to limit, bound, or set limits to," or the related noun *terminus,* a "limit or boundary." In English, those boundaries or limits tend to be final: to *terminate* a sentence or a meeting or a ballgame means to end it, and a *term* goes on for a given amount of time and then ends.

indeterminate \ˌin-di-ˈtər-mə-nət\ Not precisely determined; vague.

• The law allowed for indeterminate sentences for certain unusual classes of offenders.

A mutt is usually the product of indeterminate breeding, since at least the father's identity is generally a mystery. An art object of indeterminate origins is normally less valued than one with a maker's name on it. If negotiations are left in an indeterminate state, nothing has been decided.

interminable \in-ˈtər-mə-nə-bəl\ Having or seeming to have no end; tiresomely drawn out.

• Their appeals to their audiences for money are so interminable that there's barely time for the sermons.

Nothing is literally endless except maybe the universe and time itself. So *interminable* as we use it is always an exaggeration. On an unlucky day you might sit through an interminable lecture, an interminable meeting, and an interminable film—all in less than 24 hours.

terminal \'tər-mə-nəl\ (1) Forming or relating to an end or limit. (2) Fatal.

• She knows these are the late stages of a terminal illness, and has already drawn up a will.

A terminal illness ends in death; with terminal boredom you are "bored to death." For some, a high-school diploma is their terminal degree; others finish college before *terminating* their education. A bus *terminal* should be the endpoint of a bus line; a computer terminal was originally the endpoint of a line connecting to a central computer. A terminal ornament may mark the end of a building, and terminal punctuation ends this sentence.

terminology \ˌtər-mə-'nä-lə-jē\ The words with specialized or precise meanings used in a field or subject.

• Civil engineers use a technical terminology that is like a foreign language to an outsider.

Terms—that is, specialized words or expressions—tend to have precise boundaries of meaning. Each field has its own terminology, or "jargon," which helps those who work in the field communicate with each other quickly and accurately. But the expert's workaday language is often the layperson's *terminological* hell.

VINC/VICT comes from the Latin verb *vincere,* which means "to conquer" or "to overcome." The *victor* defeats an enemy, whether on a battlefield or a football field. To *convince* someone that you're right is a *victory* of another kind.

---

evince \i-'vins\ To be outward evidence of; show or reveal.

• As a witness she evinced honesty and dignity, and the jury was favorably impressed.

A man may evince interest in a woman by casting glances, making small talk, and generally hanging around, or by even more obvious tactics. A novelist's writing may evince concern for refugees or the elderly. A country may evince a desire for closer relations by arranging a ping-pong competition, as China did with the United States in 1971.

invincible \in-'vin-sə-bəl\ Incapable of being conquered or overcome.

• The supposedly invincible Spanish Armada was defeated by a fleet of small English ships in 1588.

Antaeus, a giant and son of Poseidon, was invincible so long as he remained in contact with the ground. But his *invincibility* crumbled when he challenged Hercules to wrestle and Hercules held the giant over his head, thereby defeating his "invincible" foe.

provincial \prə-'vin-chəl\ (1) Having to do with a province. (2) Lacking polish, culture, and broad experience.

• They were both by now sick of Chicago and would gladly have exchanged the fast life for more provincial pleasures.

A *province* is an administrative section of a larger state or country. The word comes from Roman times. The Romans gained territory by conquest, and a conquered area might become a province. (There is still some question about how the word was actually formed.) The areas usually set up a local or provincial government. Life in these provinces was not as fancy as life at Rome, just as life in the rural, provincial parts of any country is not as polished or refined as life in its cities.

victimize \'vik-tə-ˌmīz\ To make a victim of; trick, deceive, or injure.

• Like most tourists there, we were victimized by the local merchants and guides.

A *victim* is the person who is victimized. Robin Hood and his band of merry men victimized the rich in order to give to the poor—but the rich noblemen and churchmen had gotten that way by victimizing the poor in the first place. Physical and emotional *victimization* by one's parents when young is a complaint heard often today from "adult children."

Quizzes

A. Choose the closest definition:

1. evince a. reveal b. throw out c. eject d. overcome
2. interminable a. remarkable b. unthinkable c. reliable d. eternal

3. terminology a. instruction b. design c. vocabulary d. technology
4. provincial a. professional b. global c. local d. national
5. invincible a. unsuitable b. impossible c. inflammable d. unconquerable
6. terminal a. fatal b. technical c. verbal d. similar
7. indeterminate a. lengthy b. uncertain c. unending d. likely
8. victimize a. conquer b. applaud c. deceive d. invite

B. Fill in each blank with the correct letter:

a. invincible
b. terminology
c. victimize
d. interminable
e. indeterminate
f. evince
g. terminal
h. provincial

1. Her manners were a bit rough and ____, but charming.
2. All day long, reports came in of people the con man had tried to ____.
3. We waited anxiously for the mare to ____ signs of giving birth.
4. The students generally find the ____ of psychology fairly easy to learn and use.
5. He was a man of ____ age, and mysterious in other ways as well.
6. Don't you ever have those great days when you feel absolutely ____?
7. He gave ____ lectures, and I usually dozed off in the middle.
8. Last week we assumed his condition was ____; today no one is making predictions.

SPHER comes from the Greek word for "ball," and it appears in words for things that have something round about them. A ball is itself a *sphere*. The *stratosphere* and the *ionosphere* are parts of the *atmosphere* that encircles the earth.

stratosphere \'stra-tə-ˌsfir\ (1) The part of the earth's atmosphere that extends from about seven to about 31 miles above the surface.

(2) A very high or the highest region.

• In the celebrity stratosphere she now occupied, a fee of two million dollars a film was a reasonable rate.

The stratosphere (*strato-* simply means "layer" or "level") lies above the earth's weather and mostly changes very little. About 20 miles above the earth's surface it contains the ozone layer, which shields us from the sun's ultraviolet radiation except where it has been harmed by manmade chemicals. The levels of the *atmosphere* are marked particularly by their temperatures; the *stratospheric* temperature hovers around 32°—very moderate considering that temperatures in the *troposphere* below may descend to about -70° and in the *ionosphere* above may rise to 1000°.

biosphere \'bī-ə-ˌsfir\ (1) The part of the world in which life can exist. (2) Living things and their environment.

• The moon has no biosphere, so an artificial one would have to be constructed for any long-term stay.

The *lithosphere* is the solid surface of the earth (*lith-* means "rock"); the *hydrosphere* is the earth's water (*hydro-* means "water"), including the clouds and water vapor in the air; the *atmosphere* is the earth's air (*atmos-* means "vapor"). The term *biosphere* can include all of these and the 10 million species of living things they contain. The biosphere recycles its air, water, organisms, and minerals constantly to maintain an amazingly balanced state; human beings should probably do their best to imitate it. Though the word has a new sound to it, it was first used a hundred years ago.

hemisphere \'he-mə-ˌsfir\ Half a sphere, especially half the global sphere as divided by the equator or a meridian.

• Sailors who cross the equator from the northern to the southern hemisphere for the first time are given a special initiation.

Hemisphere includes the prefix *hemi-*, meaning "half." The northern and southern hemispheres are divided by the equator. The eastern and western hemispheres aren't divided so exactly; usually the eastern hemisphere includes all of Europe, Africa, and Australia and almost all of Asia, and the western hemisphere contains North and South America and a great deal of ocean.

spherical \'sfir-ə-kəl\ Relating to a sphere; shaped like a sphere or one of its segments.

• The girls agreed that the spacecraft had been perfectly spherical and deep blue, and that its alien passengers had resembled large cockroaches.

Something spherical is like a *sphere* in being round, or more or less round, in three dimensions. Apples and oranges are both spherical, though never perfectly round. A *spheroid* has a roughly spherical shape; an asteroid is often a spheroid, fairly round but lumpy.

VERT/VERS, from the Latin verb *vertere*, means "to turn" or "to turn around." An *advertisement* turns your attention to a product or service. *Vertigo* is the dizziness that results from turning too rapidly or that makes you feel as if everything else is turning.

---

divert \dī-'vərt\ (1) To turn from one purpose or course to another. (2) To give pleasure to by distracting from burdens or distress.

• The farmers successfully diverted some of the river water to irrigate their crops during the drought.

The Roman circus was used to provide *diversion* for its citizens—and sometimes to divert their attention from the government's failings as well. The diversion was often in the form of a fight—men pitted against lions, bears, or each other—and the audience was sure to see blood and death. A *diverting* evening in the 1990s might instead include watching several murders on a movie screen.

perverse \pər-'vərs\ (1) Corrupt; improper; incorrect. (2) Stubbornly or obstinately wrong.

• The unsuspected murderer had apparently felt a perverse desire to chat with the police.

The 12th-century citizens of Paris thought keeping a cat or taking a bath without clothes on were perverse—that is, satanic or ungodly. But this is an older meaning; today *perverse* usually means somehow "contradictory" or "opposed to good sense." Someone who loves great art but collects cheap figurines may admit to having perverse tastes. To desire a stable life but still go out on drinking binges could be called acting *perversely* or even self-destructively. Don't confuse *perverse* with *perverted,* which today tends to mean "having strange sexual tastes." And likewise avoid confusing their noun forms, *perversity* and *perversion.*

avert \ə-ˈvərt\ (1) To turn away or aside (especially one's eyes). (2) To avoid or ward off; prevent.

• General Camacho's announcement of lower food prices averted an immediate worker's revolt.

Sensitive people avert their eyes from gory accidents and scenes of disaster. But we also speak of averting the disaster itself. Negotiators may avert, or avoid, a strike by all-night talks, and leaders may work to avert a war in the same way. In the Cuban missile crisis of 1962 it seemed that worldwide nuclear catastrophe was narrowly (or barely) averted. *Aversion* means "dislike or disgust"—that is, your feeling about something you don't want to look at.

versatile \ˈvər-sə-təl\ (1) Turning easily from one skill to another. (2) Having many uses.

• The versatile Gene Kelly acted, sang, and directed—and dazzled America with his dancing.

The horse was the most versatile and valuable asset of the armies of Attila the Hun. A Hun could stay in the saddle for weeks at a time, opening a vein in the horse's neck to suck the blood for food. The Huns made a kind of liquor from mare's milk. Extra horses were stampeded in battle to create *diversions*. Relying on this *versatility,* Attila and the Huns conquered much of eastern and central Europe in the 5th century.

Quizzes

A. Complete the analogy:

1. pint : quart :: hemisphere : ____
   a. ocean b. continent c. sphere d. globe
2. reasonable : sensible :: perverse : ____
   a. mistaken b. stupid c. contrary d. unlikely
3. forest : trees :: stratosphere : ____
   a. gases b. clouds c. planets d. altitude
4. accept : agree :: divert : ____
   a. distress b. amuse c. differ d. disturb

5. escape : flee :: avert : ____
   a. prevent b. throw c. entertain d. alarm
6. cube-shaped : square :: spherical : ____
   a. global b. oval c. curved d. circle
7. flexible : stretchable :: versatile : ____
   a. well-rounded b. similar c. skilled d. trained
8. atmosphere : stratosphere :: biosphere : ____
   a. recycling b. hydrosphere c. energy d. earth

B. Match the word on the left to the correct definition on the right:

1.	avert	a.	with many uses
2.	spherical	b.	upper atmosphere
3.	divert	c.	wrongheaded
4.	hemisphere	d.	avoid
5.	versatile	e.	half-sphere
6.	biosphere	f.	entertain
7.	stratosphere	g.	globelike
8.	perverse	h.	life zone

MORPH comes from the Greek word for "shape." *Morph* is itself an English word with a brand-new meaning; by morphing, filmmakers can now alter photographic images or shapes digitally, making them move or transform themselves in astonishing ways.

amorphous \ə-'mȯr-fəs\ Without a definite shape or form; shapeless.

• The sculptor took an amorphous lump of clay and molded it swiftly into a rough human shape.

A new word may appear to name a previously amorphous group of people, as the word *yuppie* did in 1983. An amorphous but terrifying thing may loom in a nightmare. In all the Greek myths of the creation the world begins in an amorphous state, just as at the beginning of the Bible "the earth was without form, and void."

anthropomorphic \ˌan-thrə-pə-'mȯr-fik\ (1) Having or described as having human form or traits. (2) Seeing human traits in nonhuman things.

• The old, diseased tree had always been like a companion to her, though she knew her anthropomorphic feelings about it were sentimental.

Anthropomorphic means a couple of different things. In its first sense, an anthropomorphic cup would be a cup in the shape of a human, and an anthropomorphic god would be one that looked and acted like a human. All the Greek and Roman gods are anthropomorphic, for example, even though Socrates and even earlier Greeks believed that their fellow Greeks had created their gods in their own image rather than the other way around. In its second sense, the animal characters in *Aesop's Fables* are anthropomorphic since they all have human feelings and motivations though they don't look like humans. When the fox calls the grapes sour simply because they are out of reach, it is a very human response. At least 3,000 years after Aesop, *anthropomorphism* is still alive and well, in the books of Beatrix Potter, George Orwell's *Animal Farm*, and hundreds of animated cartoons and comic strips.

metamorphosis \ˌme-tə-ˈmȯr-fə-səs\ (1) A physical change, especially one supernaturally caused. (2) A developmental change in an animal that occurs after birth or hatching.

• Day by day we watched the gradual metamorphosis of the tadpoles into frogs.

Many myths end in a metamorphosis. As Apollo is chasing the nymph Daphne, she calls on her river-god father for help and he turns her into a laurel tree to save her. Out of anger and jealousy, the goddess Athena turns the marvelous weaver Arachne into a spider that will spin only beautiful webs. But rocks may also *metamorphose,* or undergo metamorphosis; coal under great pressure over a long period of time will become diamonds. And the transformation of caterpillars into butterflies is the most famous of natural metamorphoses.

morphology \mȯr-ˈfä-lə-jē\ (1) The study of the structure and form of plants and animals. (2) The study of word formation.

• Her biology term paper discussed the morphology of three kinds of seaweed.

Morphology contains the root *log-*, "study." *Morphologists* study plants and animals and use the information to classify species. In language, morphology considers where words come from and why they look as they do.

FORM is the Latin root meaning "shape" or "form." Marching in *formation* is marching in ordered patterns. A *formula* is a standard form for expressing information, such as a recipe or a rule written in mathematical symbols.

---

conform \kən-'fȯrm\ (1) To be similar or identical; to be in agreement or harmony. (2) To follow ordinary standards or customs.

• Ignoring all pressure to conform, she would stride with her goats through the fields at sunset, her hair wild and her long skirts billowing.

Employees must usually conform with company procedures. A certain philosophy may be said to conform with American values. A Maine Coon cat or a Dandie Dinmont terrier must conform to its breed requirements in order to be registered for breeding purposes. A *nonconformist* ignores society's standards or deliberately violates them, and laughs at the whole idea of *conformity*. (Note that "conform to" and "conform with" are both correct, though "conform to" is more common.)

formality \fȯr-'ma-lə-tē\ (1) An established custom or way of behaving that is required or standard. (2) The following of formal or conventional rules.

• The bride and groom wanted a small, intimate wedding without all the usual formalities.

Formal behavior follows the proper *forms* or customs, and *informal* behavior ignores them. The formality of a dinner party is indicated by such formalities as invitations, required dress, and full table settings. Legal formalities may turn out to be all-important even if they seem minor. America requires fewer formalities than many other countries (in Germany you may know people for years before using their first names, for example), but even in relaxed situations Americans may be observing invisible formalities.

formative \'fȯr-mə-tiv\ (1) Giving or able to give form or shape; constructive. (2) Having to do with important growth or development.

• She lived in Venezuela during her formative years and grew up speaking both Spanish and English.

Whatever gives shape to something else may be called formative; thus, for example, the Grand Canyon was a product of the formative power of water. But it usually applies to nonphysical shaping. An ambitious plan goes through a formative stage of development. America's formative years included experimentation with various forms of government. And the automobile was a huge formative influence on the design of many of our cities.

format \'fȯr-ˌmat\ (1) The shape, size, and general makeup of something. (2) A general plan, arrangement, or choice of material.

• The new thesaurus would be published in three formats: as a large paperback, as a hardcover book, and as a CD-ROM.

TV news shows seem to change their formats, or general form, as often as their anchorpeople. The situation comedy is even called a format. The format of a book or newspaper page is its design or layout.

Quizzes

A. Indicate whether the following pairs of words have the same or different meanings:

1. formative / form-giving — same __ / different __
2. morphology / shapeliness — same __ / different __
3. conform / agree — same __ / different __
4. anthropomorphic / man-shaped — same __ / different __
5. format / arrangement — same __ / different __
6. amorphous / shapeless — same __ / different __
7. formality / convention — same __ / different __
8. metamorphosis / hibernation — same __ / different __

B. Fill in each blank with the correct letter:

a. morphology
b. formative
e. conform
f. amorphous

c. metamorphosis
d. format
g. formality
h. anthropomorphic

1. The newspaper's new ____ led the public to expect stories of glamour and scandal.
2. The job description seemed a bit ____, and she wondered what she would really be doing.
3. While on the base, you are expected to ____ with all official rules and regulations.
4. He sees many ____ traits in his dogs, but he thinks that one of them may be a space alien.
5. He seemed to undergo a complete ____ from child to young adult in just a few months.
6. The new couple found the ____ of the dinner a little overwhelming.
7. He had spent his life on the ____ of a single genus of dragonfly.
8. Among her ____ influences she included her favorite uncle, her ballet classes, and the Nancy Drew series.

DOC/DOCT comes from the Latin *docere,* which means "to teach." A *doctor* is a highly educated person capable of instructing others in the *doctrines,* or basic principles, of his or her field—which is not necessarily medicine.

doctrine \'däk-trən\ (1) Something that is taught. (2) An official principle, opinion, or belief.

• According to the 19th-century doctrine of papal infallibility, the pope's formal statements on matters of faith and morals must be regarded as the absolute truth.

The original doctrines were those of the Catholic Church, especially as taught by the so-called *doctors* (or religious scholars) of the Church. Other systems, organizations, and governments have taught their own doctrines. Traditional psychiatrists may still follow the doctrines of Sigmund Freud. Old and established legal principles are called legal doctrine. Communist doctrine was often the teachings of Lenin, which were regarded as almost sacred. In 1823 the Monroe Doctrine stated that the United States opposed European influence in the Americas, and in 1947 the Truman Doctrine held that America would support free countries against enemies outside and inside.

docile \'dä-səl\ Easily led, tamed, or taught; obedient.

• Training a dog is much easier if the animal has a docile temperament to start with.

A docile patient obeys all doctors and nurses, takes the prescribed medication, and doesn't nag anyone with questions. A docile labor force doesn't make demands or form unions. A docile population is easily led by even bad leaders. And a docile spouse does what he or she is told.

doctrinaire \ˌdäk-trə-'nar\ Tending to apply principles or theories without regard for practical difficulties or individual circumstance.

• She avoided taking a doctrinaire approach to teaching; education theories didn't always match the reality of instructing 25 lively students.

Someone doctrinaire sticks closely to official doctrines or principles. A doctrinaire judge will give identical sentences to everyone found guilty of a particular crime. A doctrinaire feminist will treat all men as if they were identical. A doctrinaire free-market economist will call for a single solution for the economic problems in all countries, regardless of their social and cultural history.

indoctrinate \in-'däk-trə-ˌnāt\ (1) To teach, especially basics or fundamentals. (2) To fill someone with a particular opinion or point of view.

• The sergeants had six months to indoctrinate the new recruits with army attitudes and discipline.

Indoctrinate simply means "brainwash" to many people. But its meaning isn't always so negative. Every society indoctrinates its young people with the values of their culture. In the United States we tend to be indoctrinated to love freedom, to be individuals, and to work hard for success, among many other things. A religious cult may indoctrinate its members to give up their freedom and individuality and to work hard only for its leader's goals. *Indoctrination* in these opposite values leads many to regard cults as dangerous.

TUT/TUI, from the Latin verb *tueri*, originally meant "to look at," but the English meaning of the root gradually came to be "to guide, guard, or teach." A *tutor* guides a student (or *tutee*) through a subject, saving the most careful tutoring for the most difficult areas.

intuition \ˌin-tü-ˈwi-shən\ (1) The power of knowing something immediately without mental effort; quick insight. (2) Something known in this way.

• She scoffed at the notion of "women's intuition," special powers of insight and understanding that only women are supposed to have.

Intuition is very close in meaning to *instinct*. The moment someone enters a room you may feel you know *intuitively* or instinctively everything about him or her. Highly rational people may try to ignore their intuition and insist on being able to explain everything they think. Artists and creative thinkers, on the other hand, tend to rely on their intuitive sense of things. Intuition can be closely related to their imagination, which seems to come from somewhere just as mysterious.

tuition \tü-ˈwi-shən\ (1) The act of teaching; instruction. (2) The cost of or payment for instruction.

• As Kara happily flipped through her college catalogs, her parents looked on in dismay, mentally calculating the total tuition costs.

The sense of *tuition* meaning "teaching" or "instruction" is mostly used in Britain today. In America *tuition* almost always means the costs charged by a school, college, or university. In the mid-1990s it was possible to receive an education through college for less than $20,000; but it was also possible to spend about $200,000 in tuition and fees for a boarding-school and college education.

tutelage \ˈtü-tə-lij\ Instruction or guidance of an individual; guardianship.

• Under the old man's expert tutelage, they learned how to carve and paint realistic decoys.

Tutelage usually implies specialized and individual guidance. Alexander the Great was under the tutelage of the philosopher Aristotle between the ages of 13 and 16, and his *tutor* inspired him with a love of philosophy, medicine, and science. At 16 he commanded his first army, and by his death 16 years later he had founded the greatest empire ever seen. But it's not so easy to trace the effects of the brilliant tutelage he had received in his youth.

tutorial \tü-ˈtȯr-ē-əl\ (1) A class for one student or a small group of students. (2) An instructional program that gives information about a specific subject.

• Students tend to learn more in a tutorial than they do in a large class.

Tutorials with live tutors are useful for both advanced students and struggling ones. Most computer programs include electronic tutorials to help the user get used to the program, leading him or her through the different operations to show what the program can do. But a difficult program might still require a real-life tutor to be fully understood.

Quizzes

A. Choose the closest definition:

1. docile a. tame b. learned c. taught d. beloved
2. tuition a. requirement b. instruction c. resolution d. housing
3. indoctrinate a. medicate thoroughly b. research thoroughly c. instruct thoroughly d. consider thoroughly
4. tutelage a. responsibility b. protection c. instruction d. safeguard
5. doctrine a. solution b. principle c. religion d. report
6. tutorial a. small class b. large class c. night class d. canceled class
7. doctrinaire a. by the way b. by the by c. by the rule d. by the glass
8. intuition a. ignorance b. quick understanding c. payment d. consideration

B. Match the word on the left to the correct definition on the right:

1. indoctrinate	a. instruction costs
2. tutelage	b. easily led
3. doctrine	c. fill with a point of view
4. tutorial	d. insight
5. doctrinaire	e. guardianship
6. intuition	f. teaching
7. docile	g. individual instruction
8. tuition	h. rigidly principled

Number Words

DI/DUO, the Greek and Latin prefixes meaning "two," show up in both technical and nontechnical terms. A *duel* is a battle between two people. A *duet* is music for a *duo*, or a pair of musicians. If you have *dual* citizenship, you belong to two countries at once. Most birds are *dimorphic*, with feathers of one color for males and another color for females.

dichotomy \dī-'kä-tə-mē\ (1) A division into two often contradictory groups. (2) Something with qualities that seem to contradict each other.

• With her first job she discovered the dichotomy between the theories she'd been taught and the realities of professional life.

In the modern United States there is a dichotomy between life in a big city and life in the country, big-city life being fast-paced and often dangerous, and country life being slow-moving and usually safe. But the dichotomy is nothing new: the Roman poet Horace was complaining about it in the 1st century B.C. Among other eternal dichotomies, there is the dichotomy between wealth and poverty, between the policies of the leading political parties, between a government's words and its actions—and between what would be most fun to do right this minute and what would be the mature and sensible and intelligent alternative.

diplomatic \ˌdi-plə-ˈma-tik\ (1) Relating to negotiations between nations. (2) Tactful.

• In his dealings with my cranky old Aunt Louisa, Alex was always diplomatic, and she was very fond of him.

The path from *di-*, "two," to *diplomatic* is a winding one. A Greek *diploma* was an official document folded in two and sealed, or a passport. So *diplomacy* came to mean the international carrying and exchanging of such documents for the purpose of negotiation. *Diplomats* are famous for their tact and sensitivity (and sometimes their insincerity), so it's natural that *diplomatic* should apply to social behavior as smooth and sensitive as an ambassador's.

duplex \ˈdü-ˌpleks\ (1) Having two principal elements; double. (2) Allowing electronic communication in two directions at the same time.

• Their splendid duplex apartment had a panoramic view or Paradise Park.

Duplex can describe a confusing variety of things, depending on the technical field. Most of us use it as a noun: a *duplex* generally is either a two-family house or a two-story apartment. In computer science and telecommunications, duplex (or *full-duplex*) communication can go in both directions at once, while *half-duplex* communication can go only one way at a time. In other areas, translate *duplex* as "double" and see if the sentence makes sense.

duplicity \du̇-ˈpli-sə-tē\ Deception by pretending to feel and act one way while acting in another.

• By the time Jackie's duplicity in the whole matter had come to light, she had moved leaving no forwarding address.

The Greek god Zeus often resorted to duplicity to get what he wanted, and most of the time what he wanted was some woman. His duplicity usually involved a disguise: he appeared to Leda as a swan, and to Europa as a bull. Sometimes he had to be *duplicitous* to get around his wife Hera. After he had had his way with Io and was about to get caught, he turned her into a cow to avoid Hera's wrath.

BI/BIN also means "two" or "double." A *bicycle* has two wheels; *binoculars* consist of two little telescopes; *bigamy* is marriage to two people at once. A road through the middle of a neighborhood *bisects* it into two pieces.

bipartisan \ˌbī-ˈpär-tə-zən\ Involving members of two political parties.

• The President named a bipartisan commission of four Republicans and three Democrats to look into the issue.

Since the United States has a two-party system of government, legislation often must have some bipartisan support in order to pass into law. Bipartisan committees review legislation, compromising on some points and removing or adding others in order to make the bill more agreeable to both parties and make bipartisan support more likely.

binary \ˈbī-nə-rē\ (1) Consisting of two things or parts; double. (2) Involving a choice between two alternatives.

• The Milky Way contains numerous binary stars, each consisting of two stars orbiting each other.

Binary has many uses, most of them in technical terms. Most computers, for example, are based on the binary number system, in which only two digits, 0 and 1, are used. (0 stands for a low-voltage impulse and 1 stands for a high-voltage impulse.) All their information is kept in this form. The word "HELLO," for example, looks like this: 1001000 1000101 1001100 1001100 1001111.

biennial \ˌbī-ˈe-nē-əl\ (1) Occurring every two years. (2) Continuing or lasting over two years.

• The great biennial show of new art usually either puzzled or angered the critics.

Biennial conventions, celebrations, competitions, and sports events come every two years. *Biennials* are plants that live two years, bearing flowers and fruit only in the second year. In contrast, *semiannual* means "twice a year." But no one can agree whether *biweekly* means "twice a week" or "every two weeks," and whether *bimonthly* means "twice a month" or "every two months.'' Maybe we should stop using both of them until we can decide.

bipolar \ˌbī-ˈpō-lər\ Having two opposed forces or views; having two poles or opposed points of attraction.

• Our bipolar earth spins on an axis that extends between the North and the South Pole.

Magnets are always bipolar: one pole attracts and the other repels or drives away. The Cold War arms race was bipolar, since it mainly involved the opposing powers of the United States and Russia. Evolutionism and creationism are bipolar views on the history of life, the two major opposing beliefs on the subject in America. And manic-depressive illness, in which the person swings between the two extremes of high excitation and deep depression, is now often called *bipolar disorder*.

Quiz

Fill in each blank with the correct letter:

a. bipolar
b. duplex
c. biennial
d. duplicity
e. diplomatic
f. binary
g. dichotomy
h. bipartisan

1. The new law was written in a thoroughly ____ way, and so passed through Congress easily.
2. In response to his angry questions she gave ____ but vague answers.
3. Powerful drugs like lithium are often prescribed for ____ depression.
4. A liar's ____ usually catches up with him sooner or later.
5. The ____ number system is at the heart of the modern technological revolution.
6. His father found there was a painful ____ between the tidy instructions and the messy assembly.
7. They shared the modest ____ with another family of four.
8. Every two years we get to hear Mildred McDermot sing ''Moonlight in Vermont'' at the ____ town picnic.

Review Quizzes

A. Fill in each blank with the correct letter:

a. anthropomorphic
b. doctrine
c. tuition
d. interminable
e. duplex
f. binary
g. formative
h. biennial
i. doctrinaire
j. spherical
k. provincial
l. versatile
m. conform
n. intuition
o. indeterminate
p. bipartisan
q. metamorphosis
r. diplomatic
s. tutelage
t. hemisphere

1. This marble was limestone before it underwent ____.
2. The computer works by making choices between ____ opposites.
3. The main piano competition is ____, but there are smaller ones on the off-years.
4. The number of places open is still ____, but probably about 20 or 30.
5. Your equipment doesn't ____ to our specifications, so we regret that we can't place an order.
6. My attitudes may be ____ but my ambitions are global.
7. I had an ____ wait in the doctor's office and didn't get home until 6:00.
8. The young woman's ____ told her this was a friendship she would treasure forever.
9. Hoping for a ____ career, she took three languages in college.
10. With her talent for singing, dancing, and playing piano, she was a ____ performer.
11. The governor named a ____ committee to keep the issue as nonpolitical as possible.
12. After this ____ payment there's only one more year before she graduates, thank God.
13. The ____ was roomy, but the other family made a great deal of noise.
14. Under the great man's ____, the young composer learned how to develop his ideas into full-fledged sonatas.

15. As a practicing Catholic, she thought frequently about the church ____ that life begins at conception.
16. Michelangelo's great painting shows an ____ God touching Adam's finger.
17. A ____ interpretation of these rules will leave no room for fun at all.
18. My trip to Australia was the first time I had left this ____.
19. I'd like you to write an essay about the person who had the greatest ____ influence on your thinking.
20. The inside of the ____ stone was a hollow lined entirely with purple cyrstals.

B. Choose the correct synonym and the correct antonym:

1. invincible a. vulnerable b. unbreakable c. inedible d. unconquerable
2. divert a. please b. entertain c. bore d. send
3. amorphous a. beginning b. shapeless c. shaping d. formed
4. terminal a. first b. final c. highest d. deathlike
5. duplicity a. desire b. two-facedness c. honesty d. complexity
6. formality a. convention b. black tie c. rationality d. casualness
7. evince a. hide b. reveal c. conquer d. defy
8. dichotomy a. operation b. negotiation c. contradiction d. agreement
9. docile a. rebellious b. angry c. passive d. soft
10. perverse a. brilliant b. reasonable c. amazing d. bizarre

C. Choose the closest definition:

1. format a. design b. formality c. formation d. concept
2. biosphere a. life cycle b. environment c. stratosphere d. evolution
3. morphology a. study of structure b. study of woods c. study of butterflies d. study of geometry
4. avert a. embrace b. prevent c. assert d. escape

5. bipolar a. depressed b. monopolistic c. opposing d. two-handed
6. indoctrinate a. teach b. demonstrate c. infiltrate d. consider
7. terminology a. study b. specialty c. jargon d. symbols
8. victimize a. suffer b. agonize c. harm d. complain
9. tutorial a. penalty b. teacher c. classroom d. lesson
10. stratosphere a. cloud level b. spherical body c. atmospheric layer d. ozone depletion

Answers

UNIT 1

p.4 A 1.d 2.g 3.f 4.c 5.h 6.e 7.b 8.a
B 1.e 2.a 3.f 4.d 5.c 6.h 7.b 8.g

p.7 A 1.c 2.b 3.b 4.a 5.a 6.d 7.b 8.d
B 1.b 2.d 3.a 4.b 5.d 6.d 7.b 8.a

p.11 A 1.S 2.D 3.D 4.D 5.D 6.D 7.S 8.D
B 1.e 2.a 3.b 4.f 5.d 6.h 7.g 8.c

p.14 A 1.d 2.f 3.c 4.h 5.b 6.a 7.e 8.g
B 1.f 2.a 3.g 4.b 5.c 6.h 7.d 8.e

p.17 1.d 2.b 3.a 4.c 5.b 6.d 7.a 8.c

p.18 A 1.e 2.d 3.k 4.b 5.h 6.l 7.f 8.j 9.g 10.c 11.n 12.a 13.m 14.i
B 1.d 2.a 3.d 4.c 5.b 6.b 7.d 8.a 9.c 10.c 11.c 12.a
C 1.f 2.c 3.e 4.d 5.h 6.g 7.j 8.a 9.b 10.i

UNIT 2

p.23 A 1.c 2.b 3.d 4.a 5.d 6.b 7.c 8.b
B 1.a 2.b 3.c 4.d 5.b 6.b 7.b 8.a

p.27 A 1.h 2.g 3.d 4.a 5.b 6.f 7.e 8.c
B 1.f 2.d 3.b 4.g 5.h 6.c 7.e 8.a

p.30 A 1.d 2.c 3.a 4.b 5.d 6.c 7.b 8.a
B 1.d 2.e 3.h 4.f 5.g 6.a 7.c 8.b

p.34 A 1.b 2.c 3.e 4.a 5.g 6.h 7.d 8.f
B 1.h 2.d 3.a 4.f 5.e 6.b 7.g 8.c

p.37 1.a,c 2.d,b 3.b,a 4.c,b 5.c,a 6.a,b 7.c,a 8.d,a

p.38 A 1.c 2.b 3.b 4.d 5.b 6.c 7.d 8.a 9.c 10.b
B 1.c 2.f 3.e 4.a 5.i 6.d 7.b 8.g 9.j 10.h
C 1.f 2.h 3.c 4.i 5.d 6.e 7.j 8.b 9.g 10.a

UNIT 3

p.43 A 1.b 2.c 3.f 4.d 5.e 6.a 7.g 8.h
B 1.c 2.f 3.e 4.h 5.a 6.d 7.b 8.g

p.47 A 1.b 2.c 3.c 4.b 5.d 6.c 7.a 8.a
B 1.D 2.D 3.S 4.D 5.D 6.S 7.D 8.D

p.51 A 1.a 2.g 3.f 4.d 5.c 6.b 7.h 8.e
B 1.D 2.D 3.S 4.D 5.S 6.S 7.D 8.D

p.55 A 1.b 2.b 3.a 4.d 5.b 6.d 7.b 8.a
B 1.d 2.g 3.h 4.a 5.f 6.e 7.b 8.c

p.59 1.c 2.b 3.a 4.c 5.a 6.a 7.b 8.c

p.59 A 1.d 2.b 3.a 4.d 5.c 6.a 7.b 8.a
B 1.m 2.j 3.c 4.l 5.f 6.i 7.e 8.g 9.d 10.k 11.b 12.n 13.h 14.a 15.o
C 1.S 2.D 3.S 4.D 5.D 6.S 7.S 8.D 9.D 10.S 11.D 12.D 13.S 14.S 15.S

UNIT 4

p.65 A 1.S 2.D 3.D 4.S 5.D 6.S 7.D 8.S
B 1.f 2.g 3.e 4.h 5.b 6.c 7.d 8.a

p.69 A 1.h 2.b 3.a 4.c 5.g 6.e 7.f 8.d
B 1.a 2.c 3.h 4.g 5.f 6.b 7.e 8.d

p.73 A 1.c 2.b 3.e 4.f 5.g 6.h 7.a 8.d
B 1.h 2.a 3.g 4.b 5.c 6.f 7.d 8.e

p.77	A	1.c 2.b 3.b 4.c 5.d 6.b 7.a 8.a
	B	1.b 2.c 3.c 4.d 5.b 6.a 7.a 8.d
p.81		1.b 2.c 3.f 4.a 5.d 6.e 7.h 8.g
p.81	A	1.a 2.b 3.d 4.d 5.b 6.c 7.a 8.b 9.b 10.c
	B	1.D 2.D 3.S 4.D 5.S 6.D 7.S 8.D 9.S 10.S
	C	1.b 2.d 3.d 4.a 5.a 6.c 7.c 8.b

UNIT 5

p.86	A	1.c 2.c 3.c 4.b 5.d 6.c 7.b 8.d
	B	1.D 2.D 3.S 4.S 5.S 6.D 7.S 8.D
p.89	A	1.d 2.g 3.c 4.b 5.a 6.e 7.h 8.f
	B	1.f 2.e 3.d 4.a 5.h 6.g 7.b 8.c
p.93	A	1.c 2.b 3.d 4.b 5.d 6.b 7.c 8.a
	B	1.D 2.S 3.D 4.D 5.D 6.S 7.S 8.D
p.97	A	1.a 2.g 3.c 4.e 5.f 6.d 7.h 8.b
	B	1.c 2.e 3.f 4.g 5.a 6.h 7.b 8.d
p.101		1.h 2.f 3.d 4.e 5.b 6.g 7.a 8.c
p.102	A	1.d 2.b 3.c 4.b 5.c 6.d 7.b 8.a 9.a 10.d
	B	1.g 2.i 3.a 4.o 5.b 6.n 7.m 8.k 9.c 10.e 11.f 12.d 13.h 14.j 15.l
	C	1.S 2.D 3.S 4.S 5.D 6.D 7.D 8.S 9.D 10.D 11.S 12.D 13.S 14.D 15.D

UNIT 6

p.107	A	1.c 2.c 3.c 4.c 5.b 6.a 7.b 8.d
	B	1.g 2.b 3.c 4.d 5.e 6.f 7.a 8.h
p.111	A	1.d 2.f 3.h 4.g 5.e 6.a 7.b 8.c
	B	1.b 2.c 3.d 4.a 5.b 6.a 7.c 8.d
p.115	A	1.S 2.D 3.S 4.S 5.D 6.D 7.D 8.S
	B	1.b 2.e 3.c 4.h 5.g 6.a 7.f 8.d

p.118 A 1.c 2.a 3.d 4.c 5.d 6.a 7.c 8.b
B 1.f 2.c 3.e 4.b 5.d 6.a 7.h 8.g

p.122 1.c 2.c 3.b 4.a 5.a 6.b 7.c 8.a

p.122 A 1.g 2.a 3.j 4.c 5.i 6.b 7.d 8.e 9.h 10.f
B 1.c 2.a 3.a 4.a 5.b 6.c 7.b 8.b 9.b 10.a
C 1.e 2.j 3.a 4.i 5.f 6.h 7.c 8.b 9.d 10.g

UNIT 7

p.128 A 1.b 2.d 3.g 4.f 5.a 6.h 7.a 8.e
B 1.c 2.e 3.f 4.h 5.a 6.g 7.d 8.b

p.132 A 1.c 2.d 3.c 4.b 5.b 6.a 7.d 8.b
B 1.S 2.D 3.D 4.S 5.S 6.S 7.D 8.D

p.135 A 1.a 2.e 3.b 4.f 5.c 6.g 7.d 8.h
B 1.d 2.c 3.c 4.a 5.b 6.b 7.d 8.a

p.139 A 1.S 2.D 3.D 4.S 5.D 6.D 7.D 8.D
B 1.c 2.f 3.d 4.a 5.e 6.g 7.h 8.b

p.143 1.a 2.d 3.c 4.h 5.f 6.g 7.b 8.e

p.144 A 1.c,a 2.b,c 3.b,a 4.d,b 5.a,b 6.b,c 7.c,a 8.a,b 9.d,c 10.c,a 11.c,b 12.d,a 13.a,c 14.c,b 15.c,d
B 1.c 2.a 3.b 4.c 5.d 6.a 7.b 8.a 9.d 10.a 11.b 12.c 13.c 14.a 15.c
C 1.i 2.f 3.c 4.h 5.e 6.j 7.g 8.a 9.b 10.d

UNIT 8

p.150 A 1.c 2.a 3.b 4.a 5.c 6.d 7.b 8.c
B 1.f 2.b 3.e 4.a 5.g 6.c 7.h 8.d

p.155 A 1.a 2.g 3.b 4.h 5.e 6.c 7.d 8.f
B 1.D 2.S 3.D 4.S 5.S 6.D 7.D 8.D

p.158 A 1.D 2.D 3.S 4.D 5.D 6.D 7.D 8.S
B 1.b 2.f 3.d 4.c 5.g 6.h 7.a 8.e

p.162 A 1.c 2.c 3.d 4.a 5.b 6.c 7.d 8.c
B 1.e 2.d 3.g 4.h 5.c 6.f 7.a 8.b

p.166 1.g 2.f 3.e 4.d 5.a 6.h 7.b 8.c

p.167 A 1.a,c 2.d,b 3.a,d 4.b,a 5.c,a 6.d,b 7.d,a 8.a,b 9.d,c 10.d,a
B 1.D 2.D 3.S 4.D 5.S 6.S 7.S 8.D 9.D 10.D 11.D 12.D 13.S 14.S 15.S 16.D 17.D 18.S 19.S 20.D
C 1.h 2.g 3.i 4.b 5.a 6.f 7.d 8.j 9.c 10.e

UNIT 9

p.172 A 1.a 2.g 3.f 4.b 5.c 6.e 7.h 8.d
B 1.a 2.b 3.c 4.d 5.a 6.b 7.d 8.c

p.176 A 1.b 2.a 3.b 4.a 5.b 6.b 7.d 8.d
B 1.d 2.c 3.e 4.f 5.g 6.h 7.a 8.b

p.180 A 1.a 2.a 3.b 4.a 5.c 6.d 7.b 8.c
B 1.S 2.D 3.S 4.D 5.S 6.S 7.D 8.D

p.183 A 1.h 2.c 3.g 4.d 5.e 6.b 7.f 8.a
B 1.g 2.f 3.b 4.c 5.h 6.a 7.e 8.d

p.187 1.c 2.b 3.b 4.b 5.c 6.d 7.b 8.c

p.187 A 1.b 2.c 3.a 4.d 5.b 6.c 7.a 8.d 9.d 10.b
B 1.d 2.g 3.a 4.b 5.j 6.e 7.c 8.i 9.h 10.f
C 1.a 2.h 3.i 4.b 5.e 6.d 7.g 8.c 9.j 10.f

UNIT 10

p.192 A 1.S 2.D 3.D 4.D 5.D 6.D 7.D 8.S
B 1.a 2.c 3.d 4.b 5.a 6.c 7.d 8.a

p.195 A 1.c 2.c 3.d 4.c 5.b 6.a 7.b 8.d
B 1.f 2.h 3.g 4.e 5.d 6.a 7.c 8.b

p.199 A 1.a 2.g 3.c 4.f 5.b 6.h 7.e 8.d
B 1.c 2.a 3.d 4.c 5.b 6.c 7.a 8.b

p.202 A 1.b 2.d 3.a 4.c 5.a 6.d 7.a 8.d
B 1.e 2.h 3.f 4.a 5.g 6.b 7.c 8.d

p.206 1.e 2.b 3.d 4.c 5.g 6.f 7.a 8.h

p.206 A 1.D 2.S 3.D 4.D 5.D 6.S 7.S 8.D 9.D 10.S 11.S 12.D 13.D 14.S 15.D 16.D 17.S 18.D 19.D 20.D
B 1.d 2.a 3.d 4.b 5.a 6.c 7.b 8.a 9.d 10.a
C 1.f 2.e 3.a 4.d 5.c 6.b 7.h 8.g

UNIT 11

p.212 A 1.b 2.d 3.a 4.c 5.c 6.b 7.a 8.b
B 1.D 2.D 3.S 4.D 5.D 6.D 7.D 8.D

p.215 A 1.a 2.g 3.b 4.h 5.e 6.c 7.d 8.f
B 1.c 2.c 3.b 4.a 5.d 6.c 7.b 8.b

p.219 A 1.d 2.b 3.a 4.d 5.c 6.a 7.c 8.a
B 1.b 2.e 3.h 4.a 5.f 6.g 7.d 8.c

p.222 A 1.a 2.d 3.e 4.b 5.h 6.c 7.f 8.g
B 1.S 2.D 3.S 4.D 5.D 6.D 7.D 8.S

p.226 1.a 2.g 3.f 4.d 5.c 6.e 7.b 8.h

p.227 A 1.c,d 2.c,b 3.a,b 4.a,d 5.c,d 6.c,b 7.a,c 8.a,d 9.d,a 10.c,b 11.b,c 12.d,a 13.b,c 14.b,a 15.d,c 16.c,a
B 1.D 2.D 3.D 4.S 5.S 6.D 7.D 8.S 9.S 10.S
C 1.f 2.b 3.e 4.g 5.i 6.j 7.l 8.h 9.a 10.d 11.k 12.c

UNIT 12

p.232 A 1.f 2.c 3.g 4.d 5.e 6.a 7.b 8.h
B 1.f 2.h 3.g 4.c 5.b 6.e 7.a 8.d

p.236 A 1.a 2.g 3.c 4.b 5.f 6.e 7.d 8.h
B 1.c 2.f 3.h 4.e 5.d 6.g 7.a 8.b

p.239 A 1.b 2.c 3.a 4.b 5.c 6.b 7.d 8.c
B 1.S 2.D 3.S 4.D 5.D 6.S 7.D 8.D

p.243 A 1.g 2.b 3.a 4.f 5.c 6.h 7.e 8.d
B 1.b 2.d 3.g 4.c 5.f 6.a 7.e 8.h

p.246 1.a 2.f 3.b 4.g 5.e 6.h 7.d 8.c

p.247 A 1.b 2.d 3.c 4.a 5.c 6.a 7.c 8.a 9.d 10.d 11.a 12.c 13.b 14.d 15.c 16.b
B 1.f 2.b 3.g 4.j 5.d 6.e 7.i 8.a 9.h 10.c
C 1.h 2.j 3.g 4.a 5.i 6.c 7.d 8.f 9.e 10.b

UNIT 13

p.253 A 1.b 2.d 3.c 4.b 5.c 6.a 7.b 8.a
B 1.g 2.h 3.b 4.f 5.a 6.e 7.d 8.c

p.256 A 1.c 2.b 3.f 4.g 5.a 6.h 7.e 8.d
B 1.S 2.D 3.S 4.S 5.D 6.S 7.S 8.S

p.260 A 1.c 2.a 3.c 4.d 5.d 6.a 7.b 8.c
B 1.e 2.f 3.a 4.g 5.b 6.c 7.h 8.d

p.264 A 1.e 2.b 3.c 4.g 5.a 6.h 7.f 8.d
B 1.a 2.c 3.d 4.a 5.b 6.d 7.a 8.c

p.267 1.D 2.S 3.D 4.D 5.S 6.S 7.D 8.D

p.267 A 1.h 2.i 3.o 4.r 5.c 6.s 7.f 8.n 9.e 10.p 11.m 12.a 13.b 14.t 15.g 16.d 17.j 18.l 19.q 20.k
B 1.b,d 2.d,b 3.b,d 4.a,d 5.d,b 6.b,c 7.b,d 8.d,a 9.c,d 10.b,c
C 1.c 2.b 3.d 4.b 5.a 6.c 7.a 8.d 9.a 10.d

UNIT 14

p.273 A 1.d 2.g 3.a 4.e 5.f 6.b 7.h 8.c
B 1.g 2.a 3.d 4.c 5.h 6.f 7.e 8.b

p.277 A 1.D 2.D 3.S 4.S 5.D 6.S 7.S 8.S
B 1.d 2.e 3.f 4.c 5.g 6.h 7.a 8.b

p.280 A 1.b 2.f 3.e 4.c 5.a 6.d 7.h 8.g
B 1.d 2.a 3.f 4.c 5.e 6.g 7.b 8.h

p.284 A 1.b 2.a 3.c 4.d 5.b 6.c 7.a 8.d
B 1.S 2.S 3.D 4.D 5.D 6.D 7.S 8.D

p.288 1.b 2.h 3.g 4.c 5.e 6.a 7.f 8.d

p.288 A 1.b 2.a 3.b 4.a 5.b 6.c 7.b 8.a 9.b 10.d 11.a 12.a 13.b 14.b 15.d 16.d 17.c 18.c 19.b 20.a
B 1.a 2.b 3.h 4.i 5.d 6.e 7.f 8.c 9.g 10.j
C 1.S 2.D 3.D 4.D 5.S 6.S 7.D 8.S 9.S 10.S

UNIT 15

p.293 A 1.a 2.d 3.c 4.c 5.d 6.a 7.b 8.c
B 1.h 2.c 3.f 4.b 5.e 6.a 7.d 8.g

p.297 A 1.c 2.c 3.a 4.b 5.a 6.d 7.a 8.d
B 1.d 2.g 3.f 4.e 5.a 6.h 7.b 8.c

p.301 A 1.S 2.D 3.S 4.S 5.S 6.S 7.S 8.D
B 1.d 2.f 3.e 4.h 5.c 6.g 7.a 8.b

p.305 A 1.a 2.b 3.c 4.c 5.b 6.a 7.c 8.b
B 1.c 2.e 3.f 4.g 5.h 6.d 7.b 8.a

p.309 1.h 2.e 3.a 4.d 5.f 6.g 7.b 8.c

p.310 A 1.q 2.f 3.h 4.o 5.m 6.k 7.d 8.n 9.r 10.l 11.p 12.c 13.e 14.s 15.b 16.a 17.i 18.t 19.g 20.j
B 1.d,a 2.b,c 3.b,d 4.b,a 5.b,c 6.a,d 7.b,a 8.c,d 9.c,a 10.d,b
C 1.a 2.b 3.a 4.b 5.c 6.a 7.c 8.c 9.d 10.c

Index

Webster's English Usage Guide

Webster's English Usage Guide

Created in Cooperation with the Editors of
MERRIAM-WEBSTER

A Division of Merriam-Webster, Incorporated
Springfield, Massachusetts

Federal Street Press is a trademark of
Federal Street Press, a division of Merriam-Webster, Incorporated.

This 2006 edition published by
Federal Street Press
A Division of Merriam-Webster, Incorporated
P.O. Box 281
Springfield, MA 01102

Federal Street Press books are available for bulk purchase
for sales promotion and premium use.
For details write the manager of special sales,
Federal Street Press, P.O. Box 281, Springfield, MA 01102

ISBN 13 978-1-59695-010-8

Printed in the United States of America

08 09 10 5 4 3

Contents

Preface

This book presents over 1,500 brief discussions of common problems in English usage. Its main strengths are its recognition of the historical background to questions of usage and the fact that it is based on a thorough examination of present-day usage. Merriam-Webster's extensive citation files of 15 million examples of English words used in context have been a valuable resource in developing this book.

While English, like some other languages, has long had its commentators who seek to proscribe certain usages and prescribe others, standard usage tends to evolve quite independently of such critics. This book sets out in concise form the standard uses to which common English words, phrases, and grammatical constructions are actually put, especially in writing.

Articles. Each article is introduced by one or more boldface words indicating the subject for discussion.

data

glance, glimpse

reason is because

In cases where it seemed helpful to do so, homographs are distinguished by italic labels indicating part of speech.

account, *noun*

account, *verb*

Otherwise such distinctions are made as part of the accompanying discussion.

An article that treats more than one aspect of its subject may be divided into sections, each section introduced by a boldface numeral. The topic of the section is occasionally indicated by an introductory word or phrase in italics.

> **allow 1.** *Allow, permit.* Usage commentators have long sought to distinguish between *allow* and *permit.* . . .
> **2.** *Allow of.* The intransitive *allow,* used with *of,* occurs primarily. . . .
> **3.** *Allow* in the sense "admit, concede". . . .

Verbal Illustrations. This book includes thousands of verbal illustrations offering examples primarily of standard, but also occasionally of nonstandard, usages. Standard usages are shown within angle brackets, with the particular word or words at issue in italics.

> When the verb *date* is used to point to a date of origin, it may be used with *from, back to,* or *to* <these vases *date from* the early Ming period> <the poem *dates back to* 1843> <the dispute *dates to* Japan's annexation of the islands>.

When two different but equally acceptable alternatives

are exemplified, the second appears in square brackets immediately after the first.

> *Farther and further* . . . continue to be used interchangeably when distance in space or time . . . is involved <traveled *further* [*farther*] today than yesterday> <taking the principle one step *farther* [*further*]>.

Nonstandard usages, as well as some that are standard but are associated with casual speech rather than with writing, are shown in quotation marks, usually inside parentheses.

> The conjunction *being* survives in various dialects (as in "*Being* you are family, I can tell you").

> *Off* in the sense of "from" (as in "we bought the tools *off* Joe" or "we recorded the show *off* the TV") . . . is found most often in speech and speechlike writing.

Cross-References. Directional cross-references to articles where relevant discussion may be found are shown in small capital letters. They may appear within or at the end of an article or section, or they may receive a separate entry.

> **gamut . . .** Some caution against confusing it with *run* the gauntlet (see GAUNTLET, GANTLET).
> . . .

> **different from, different than** Both of these phrases are standard. . . . See also THAN.
>
> **either . . . or** See EITHER 3, 5.

Cross-references to articles appearing in the Glossary, which begins on page 348, are identified as such.

> Because of the strength of NOTIONAL AGREEMENT (see Glossary), however, a plural verb is not uncommon. . . .

Pronunciation. The symbols used in most of the articles on pronunciation are explained in the table on page xi.

The text of this work was prepared by Michael Shally-Jensen. Jocelyn White Franklin helped compile the Glossary. Mark A. Stevens, E. Ward Gilman, and Frederick C. Mish reviewed the entire manuscript. Georgette B. Boucher assisted substantially in the keyboarding of the manuscript. Cross-referencing was done by Maria A. Sansalone and Adrienne M. Scholz, and proofreading was performed by Donna L. Rickerby and Adrienne M. Scholz under the direction of Madeline L. Novak.

Pronunciation Symbols

Slant lines (\ . . . \) used in pairs indicate the beginning and end of a pronunciation respelling. The symbol ˈ indicates primary (strongest) stress on the syllable that follows; the symbol ˌ indicates secondary (medium) stress. Parentheses surrounding an element indicate that it is optional.

ə	banana, collide
ˈə, ˌə	humdrum, abut
ər	further, merger, bird
a	mat, snap
ā	day, fade, aorta
ä	cart, cot, father
aü	now, loud
ch	chin, nature \ˈnā-chər\
ē	beat, nosebleed
e	bet, red, peck
i	tip, banish
ī	side, buy
ō	bone, know, beau
ȯ	saw, all, caught
ȯi	coin, destroy
ü	rule, youth
u̇	pull, wood, book, fury \ˈfyu̇r-ē\
y	yard, mute \ˈmyüt\

A

a, an In both speech and writing, *a* is used before a word beginning with a consonant <*a* door> <*a* symphony>. Before a word beginning with a vowel, *an* is usual <*an* icicle> <*an* operation>, but when the vowel is pronounced with an initial consonant sound, *a* is used <*a* one-time deal> <*a* union>. Before nouns beginning with *h, a* is used if the *h* is pronounced <*a* human> <*a* headache>; in a few cases where the first syllable is unaccented, either *a* or *an* can be used <*a(n)* historic event> <*a(n)* Hispanic applicant> <*a(n)* habitual liar>. *An* is used if the *h* is not pronounced <twice *an* hour>.

abhorrence *Abhorrence,* when followed by a preposition, takes of <an *abhorrence of* winter>. *To, for,* and *against* can also be found following *abhorrence* in older literature.

able to In sentences where *able* is followed by *to* and the infinitive, the infinitive is nearly always in the active voice <you used to be *able to* smoke in movie theaters>, whether the subject is human or nonhuman. The passive infinitive (as in "a simple test *able to* be performed at home") is generally thought to sound awkward and may usually be avoided easily <a test that can be performed at home>.

abound When something abounds—that is, is copiously supplied—it usually abounds *in* or *with* <the

house *abounded in* warmth and sunlight> <he *abounded with* good spirits>.

about See AT ABOUT.

above The use of *above* as both a noun <none of the *above*> and an adjective <please refer to the *above* table> has long been established as standard, even though some critics disapprove of it.

absent The use of *absent* as a preposition <*absent* any backing from the government, the project was forced to shut down> has been criticized, but it is currently in good use and is standard.

absolutely The use of *absolutely* as an intensifier may sometimes be judged overdramatic (as in "she was *absolutely* devastated when she wasn't invited"). In more measured uses, criticism of the word is not justified <no drug can be proved *absolutely* harmless>.

absolve When *absolve* is followed by a preposition, it is usually either *from* <*absolved from* their obligations> or *of* <cannot be *absolved of* blame>. Only rarely is *for* used <were *absolved for* the crimes they allegedly committed>.

abstain When *abstain* is followed by a preposition, it is normally *from* <decided to *abstain from* meat>. In reference to voting, *abstain* usually takes no preposition <20 delegates *abstained*>.

abstract When the verb *abstract* takes a preposition, it is generally *from* <*abstracted* the essential data *from* the report> but occasionally *by* <*abstracted by* a researcher>.

abut *On* is the preposition most frequently used with *abut* <land *abuts on* the road>. *Upon* and *into* are also occasionally used. The transitive *abut* is sometimes followed by a prepositional phrase <the horizontal piece *abuts* the vertical one at the base>.

accede *Accede* is normally followed by *to* <*acceding to* their demands>.

accept, except The verb *except* (meaning "omit") is sometimes mistakenly written in place of *accept* (meaning "receive willingly" or "agree to"). Be careful not to confuse the words because of their similarity in sound.

access When followed by a preposition, the noun access usually takes *to* <*access to* information>.

accidently, accidentally Though the spelling *accidently* has been used by some reputable writers, it is usually regarded as a misspelling.

accommodate When a preposition follows intransitive *accommodate,* it is usually *to* <she *accommodated* quickly *to* the changed circumstances>. *To* is also used with transitive *accommodate,* after a reflexive pronoun <he *accommodated* himself *to* these demands>; less frequently, *with* is used <*accommodate* you *with* a bowl of soup>. When the transitive *accommodate* is in the passive, it may take various other prepositions <we were *accommodated at* the station for the night>.

accompany *Accompanied by* is the usual form; *by* is always used with persons <children should be *accompanied by* an adult> and is usual with things as well <explosions *accompanied by* random gunfire>. *Accompanied with* is limited to things <has *accompanied* her drawings *with* some verse> and was used more in the past than it is now.

account, *noun* See ON ACCOUNT OF.

account, *verb* When *account* is used as an intransitive verb, it is normally followed by the preposition *for* <fails to *account for* the results>.

accountable One is accountable *to* someone who is due an explanation *for* something done or not done <elected officials are *accountable to* the people *for* their actions>.

accrue *Accrue* as an intransitive verb takes various prepositions, including *to* <*accrues to* her account>, *on* <interest *accrues on* a daily basis>, *with* <the wisdom that *accrues with* age>, *for* <whatever benefits *accrue for* their efforts>, *through* <market exposure *accruing through* the use of new business channels>, and *from* <have *accrued from* the current system>. It can be used without prepositions as well <no serious effects have *accrued*>. *Accrue* is also used as an transitive verb <*accruing* a mass of support>.

acknowledgment, acknowledgement *Acknowledgment* and *acknowledgement* are both acceptable spellings, but the first is much more prevalent in the U.S.

a couple of See COUPLE, *noun* 2.

acquaint *Acquaint* is most often followed by the preposition *with* <is *acquainted with* them>.

acquiesce *Acquiesce* is frequently followed by in <*acquiesced in* the decision>, less frequently by *to* <would *acquiesce to* those demands>.

acquit *Acquit* is often used in the construction *acquit* (a person) *of* (something charged). Far less frequently, *for* is used instead of *of* <should be *acquitted for* the crime>.

act, action Both *act* and *action* can be used to denote something done. When *act* is modified, it tends to be followed by *of* and a noun <an *act of* arson> <*acts of* kindness>. *Action* tends to be preceded by its modifier <a protest *action*> <unilateral *actions*>. *Action* is also used attributively <environmental *action* groups> <*action* photographs>, while *act* is not. In addition, both words appear in standard idioms <caught in the *act*> <a piece of the *action*>.

activate, actuate These two words are usually distinguished when applied to persons and things. *Activate* is more often used of things thought of as mechanical in their operation <*activate* the heat-exchange system>; when applied to people, it almost always indicates some external spur to action <he

lacked the charisma to *activate* voters>. *Actuate,* which has a long history of literary use, generally indicates internal motivation <people who are *actuated* by the hope of personal gain>.

actual, actually Both *actual* and *actually* are sometimes used in ways that do not add much meaning to a sentence (as in "made more in *actual* wages than in tips," or "I had been *actually* involved"). But they can sometimes improve the rhythm of a sentence or help to set off the more important words <whatever the *actual* human and physical cost> <but *actually* there is a pattern that underlies these facts>. In general, you should check to see whether they are actually necessary for meaning or style in your writing.

actuate See ACTIVATE, ACTUATE.

ad Although *ad* is considered by some to be an inappropriate shortening of *advertisement,* it is used widely in general and informal writing <found the *ad* too expensive to run>.

A.D., B.C. Do these abbreviations go before or after the year? Can they be used after the word *century? B.C.* almost always follows the year <sometime before 2000 *B.C.*> <from the fourth century *B.C.*>. *A.D.*, on the other hand, is usually, but not always, placed *before* the year <*A.D.* 22> <flourished 125–190 *A.D.*>. Both are standard when used after *century* <the third century *A.D.*>. Both are usually either capitalized or set in small capitals, and both generally use periods.

adapt, adopt These words may be distinguished as follows: *Adopt* suggests taking something over as it is <the committee voted to *adopt* a new set of rules>. *Adapt* suggests changing something to meet new needs <*adapt* a short story for television>.

adequate **1.** *Adequate* is most often used without a complement <an *adequate* sum>. When a complement is used, *adequate* is often followed by *to* and either a noun <a supply *adequate to* the demand> or an infinitive <more than *adequate to* cover the cost>. It is also frequently followed by *for* <seemed *adequate for* our needs>.

2. *Adequate* is considered by many to be an absolute adjective that doesn't lend itself to use with qualifiers like *more* or *less. More,* however, is sometimes used, usually with the meaning "more nearly" <were hoping for *more adequate* funding>.

adjacent *Adjacent* is often followed by *to* <the region *adjacent to* the Highlands>. The word can describe objects that touch each other <*adjacent* warm and cold masses of air> or do not touch <the *adjacent* islands of Nantucket and Martha's Vineyard>.

admission, admittance Both *admittance* and *admission* mean "permitted entrance." *Admittance* is usually applied to mere physical entrance to a locality or a building <members must show their cards upon *admittance*>, whereas *admission* applies to entrance or formal acceptance (as into a club) that carries with it rights, privileges, standing, or membership <two recommendations are required for *admission* to the club>. *Admission* is much more common for a fee to gain entrance <*admission* $5.00> <worth the price of *admission*>.

adopt See ADAPT, ADOPT.

adult The pronunciation with stress on the second syllable, \ə-ˈdəlt\, is the most common one in the U.S., although the alternative pronunciation, \ˈad-ˌəlt\, is also widely used (and is usual in Great Britain).

adverse, averse These words are similar in meaning, but *adverse* is the more generally useful word. It is commonly used to modify a following noun <*adverse* circumstances> <an *adverse* reaction>, whereas *averse* is not. *Adverse to* is used as a predicate adjective to describe things <testimony that was *adverse to* their cases>. For describing people, *averse to* is more common today and is especially frequent in negative constructions <is not *averse to* receiving praise>. See also AVERSE TO, AVERSE FROM.

advice, advise These two words are occasionally confused. Be careful not to mix up the noun *advice* <she offered good *advice*> with the verb *advise* <I must *advise* you>.

adviser, advisor Although both of these spellings are currently acceptable, *adviser* is the more frequently used.

advocate Though the verb *advocate* usually takes no preposition <*advocates* affirmative action>, it may be followed by a prepositional phrase introduced by *for, in, on,* or *by* <*advocates* affirmative action *for* economically disadvantaged groups>. The noun *advocate* usually takes *of* to introduce what is being advocated <an *advocate of* affirmative action>, although *for* is also sometimes used <is an *advocate for* the rights of minorities>.

affect, effect These words are commonly confused, but they are not synonyms. The verb *affect* means "to influence or act upon" <how the cutbacks will *affect* the company>, while the noun *effect* means "result" <the *effects* will be devastating>. Thus if you *affect* something, the result is an *effect. Effect* is also a verb meaning "to bring about" <a mandate to *effect* some serious changes>, and *affect* is a much rarer noun used by psychologists in describing emotional states.

affiliate As a verb (in participial form) *affiliate* is commonly used with the preposition *with* <he is *affiliated with* the University>. The noun *affiliate* is commonly followed by *of* <it is an *affiliate of* Encyclopaedia Britannica> or preceded by an attributive adjective <it is an Encyclopaedia Britannica *affiliate*>.

affinity *Affinity* is most often used with the prepositions *for* and *with* <have a real *affinity for* each other> <a language having some *affinity with* Norwegian>. Somewhat less often, it is used with *to* or *between*

<people with an *affinity to* darkness> <certain *affinities between* autism and genius>.

afflict See INFLICT, AFFLICT.

affluent The pronunciation in which the first syllable is accented is more standard than the one that puts the stress on the second syllable.

aforementioned This word is used in legal contexts but is generally avoided in ordinary writing, except when a humorous effect is intended <said the *aforementioned* spouse with a snarl>.

afraid *Afraid* can be followed by a *that* clause <is *afraid* that the request may be denied> or by an infinitive <is *afraid* to cross the street>. The usually preposition after *afraid* is *of,* which can be followed by a noun <*afraid of* machines> or a gerund <*afraid of* making waves>. *Afraid* is followed by *for* when the object is not the source of the threat but rather what is threatened <*afraid for* his job>.

African-American *African-American* (noun) is on its way to becoming the preferred term for an American of African descent, but *black* (sometimes capitalized) is still just about as frequent. *African-American* is used both in the singular and the plural, but *black* (which means "African-American") is almost always used in the plural <southern *blacks*>. As an adjective, *African-American* is applied to both people <an *African-American* author> and things <*African-Ameri-*

can music>, as is *black* <*black* voters> <*black* churches>. *Black*, however, seems to be used slightly more often of things than of people.

after *After* meaning "afterwards" can be found in the works of standard authors <we arrived shortly *after*> <returned 20 years *after*>, but it is not found in the most formal writing today.

afterward, afterwards *Afterward* is the more common form in the U.S., though both are quite common; *afterwards* is the form generally used in British English.

agenda Although it originated as the plural of the Latin *agendum, agenda* is standard in English as a singular noun <a political *agenda*>, with *agendas* as its plural <the *agendas* of the last three faculty meetings>.

aggravate, aggravation, aggravating *Aggravate* is used chiefly in two meanings, "to make worse" <*aggravated* her shoulder injury> <their financial position was *aggravated* by the market downturn> and to "irritate, annoy" <the President was *aggravated* by French intransigence>. The first sense is more common than the second in published prose. This is not true, however, of *aggravation,* which usually means "irritation" <an *aggravation* for him>, or *aggravating,* which almost always expresses annoyance <an *aggravating* situation>.

agree *To, on,* and *with* are the prepositions most frequently used with *agree* <the company *agreed to* mediation> <they *agreed on* a payment schedule> <she *agrees with* the experts>.

a half a(n) See HALF 2.

ahold See GET HOLD OF, GET AHOLD OF.

aim Some critics regard *aim to* as an outworn Americanism, but it is still widely used in both British and American English <a design *aimed to* give pleasure> <this provision *aims to* ensure stability>. *Aim at* is also very common <a story *aimed at* helping youths> <will *aim at* savings for homeowners>. *Aim for* may also be used <the thing to *aim for* in these negotiations>.

ain't Although widely disapproved, avoided in formal writing, and most common in the habitual speech of the less educated, *ain't* in the senses "am not, are not, is not" and "have not, has not" is flourishing in American English. It is used in both speech and writing to catch attention and emphasize. It is used especially in journalistic prose as part of a consistently informal style <things just *ain't* what they used to be>. This informal *ain't* is commonly distinguished from habitual *ain't* by its tendency to occur in fixed constructions and phrases <say it *ain't* so> <if it *ain't* broke, don't fix it>. In fiction *ain't* is used for purposes of characterization; in familiar correspondence it tends to be a mark of an easygoing friendship.

à la This imported (French) preposition is printed more often in English with its accent than without. Used in English since the end of the 16th century, it need not be italicized as a foreign term <chomping on a large cigar *à la* Groucho Marx>.

albeit Although some writers consider *albeit* old-fashioned, it is still very much in use <was treated as a partner, *albeit* a junior one>.

alien When *alien* is used with a preposition, the choice is most often *to* <a quality *alien to* the rest of his personality>.

all of The usage question here is whether *all* should be followed by *of* in expressions such as "all (of) the percussion instruments." While *all of* is required before personal pronouns <*all of* them>, *all* and *all of* are about equally common in most other cases <*all* the lawyers got together> <*all of* these rocks are striated>. See also BOTH 2.

allow **1.** *Allow, permit.* Usage commentators have long sought to distinguish between *allow* and *permit,* claiming that *permit* is for the giving of express consent or authorization <yes, you are *permitted* to go> and *allow* is for those instances in which no objection is attempted <employees are *allowed* 10 sick days>. Good writers, however, do as seems best to them: some observe the distinction, others do not.

2. *Allow of.* The intransitive *allow,* used with *of,* occurs primarily with impersonal subjects <problems that do not *allow of* easy solutions>.

3. *Allow* in the sense "admit, concede" <he *allows* that he might be wrong> is considered by some a regionalism, but it has a long tradition of mainstream use. Two senses of *allow* that *are* chiefly regional are those of "say" (as in "she *allowed* she saw you yesterday") and "suppose, think" (as in "we *allowed* you wasn't coming"). However, when these two senses combine to imply that someone both holds an opinion and expresses it <she *allows* that the subject is a timely one>, the usage is standard—particularly when followed by *that. Allow* with *as how* <the manager *allowed as how* he disliked making decisions> is sometimes used in journalism and other general writing, but is usually avoided in the most formal contexts. See also AS HOW.

all ready, already The distinction between *all ready* and *already* is one that some still get wrong. *All ready* as a fixed phrase <we are *all ready* to leave> means simply "ready" (*all* serves as an intensive). *Already* is an adverb; it is used in sentences like "They had *already* finished by the time we got there."

all right See ALRIGHT, ALL RIGHT.

all that Although this phrase is regarded by some as substandard in writing, it is commonly found in fiction, reportage, and occasionally more serious writing

<her upstate mansion was not *all that* impressive>. It is used for understatement, sometimes with ironic intent.

all the Commonly used as a simple intensifier of a comparative adverb <the crime was *all the* more heinous considering the victim's age>, *all the* is also used in many different regions of the country in spoken sentences like "That's *all the* higher I can jump." The conventional *as* . . . *as* construction <that's *as* high *as* I can jump> prevails in print.

all-time Though objected to by some as redundant or overused, *all-time* is often a useful intensifier <he holds the *all-time* record for runs batted in> <temperatures reached an *all-time* high>.

all together, altogether Occasionally the phrase *all together,* meaning "in a group" <taken *all together,* these developments indicate a positive trend>, is confused with the adverb *altogether,* meaning "completely" <she was *altogether* uninterested in the details>. You will want to take care in your choice of spelling.

allude **1.** Some insist that *allude* can mean only "to make indirect reference" and that use of the word to mean "refer" is a mistake. But in practice the word is frequently used in a way that makes it impossible to identify one meaning or the other <they did not *allude* to the subject at all> <the person whose work he was

alluding to was there>. *Allude* is also commonly used in the sense "to mention in passing" <the book *alludes* to her husband several times>. In short, the "indirect" sense often shades into the "direct" sense; you should not feel compelled to adhere to any strict distinction.

2. *Alude, elude.* Very occasionally these words are confused. Allude means "to refer" (see 1 above), elude "to evade" <*eluded* police>.

ally *Ally* is used with *to, with,* and *against* <*allied to* this concern was their fear of creating instability> <their efforts are *allied with* those of the Red Cross> <both provinces were *allied against* the central government>.

aloof The usual preposition with *aloof* is *from* <remains *aloof from* the family's financial affairs>. Occasionally *to* is used <*aloof to* the criticisms>. Other prepositions may be used to indicate somewhat different relationships <is *aloof with* strangers> <holds himself *aloof in* such matters>.

alot, a lot *A lot* is often written as one word, but two words is the accepted norm <*a lot* of junk in the attic>. See also LOTS, A LOT.

aloud See OUT LOUD.

already See ALL READY.

alright, all right *All right* is the commonly preferred form <it is *all right* to think that> <everyone is *all right*>. *Alright* is often found in journalistic and business publications <that's *alright* by his fans> and in transcribed speech <he said "*Alright* darling, I was wrong">.

also 1. Some critics dislike *also* used like *and* <found some old nails, *also* bits of pottery>. This use is common in wills but is not found very often elsewhere. *And also* is sometimes recommended as a replacement.

2. One of those traditional rules is that you should never begin a sentence with *also,* except when the sentence is inverted <*Also* discovered were three kittens>. Writers of high repute, however, have long used *also* as an opener <*Also,* he was in love>. You can ignore the old rule.

alternate, *verb* One person or one thing may alternate *with* another or others <able to *alternate* blue blocks *with* red ones>; one person or thing may alternate *between* two things <his views *alternate between* rigid orthodoxy and freewheeling independence>.

alternate, alternative, *adjectives* Traditionalists recommend using *alternate* to mean "occurring or succeeding by turns" <a day of *alternate* sunshine and rain>, and *alternative* to mean "offering or expressing a choice" <we had a set of *alternative* plans in case of rain>. The distinction is not always maintained in practice, however. In fact, *alternative* is becoming more and more a noun <the only *alternative* to intervention>, and the adjective is in the process of being replaced by *alternate* <they found an *alternate* source of merchandise> <they liked the *alternate* plans better>. The adjective *alternate* in its sense "by turns" is also undergoing change, giving way to the verb *alternate* and its participle *alternating* <strove to *alternate* men and women participants> <we'll see *alternating* sunshine and rain>. The antiestablishment use of the 1960s—"alternative journalism," "alternative schools," and the like—is expressed by both adjectives, with *alternative* somewhat more common.

alternative, *noun* Though some critics insist that alternatives come only in pairs, the evidence from usage indicates this is not true <we were given three *alternatives*>.

although, though These conjunctions have been essentially interchangeable for centuries, though people keep wondering whether one or the other is preferable. The difference is merely a matter of personal choice, but *though* is used more frequently than *although,* perhaps because it is shorter.

altogether See ALL TOGETHER, ALTOGETHER.

alumnus, alumna *Alumna* is the singular form of *alumnae, alumnus* the singular form of *alumni. Alumna* is used for female graduates and *alumnus* for males. *Alumni* is the form usually used for a mixed bag of graduates of both sexes. The clipped form *alum* is also used in less formal contexts.

amalgam *Amalgam* (in its nontechnical sense) takes *of* when it needs a preposition <an *amalgam of* fetishism, spiritism, and transcendentalism>.

amateur In recent years the adjective *amateur* has been used more frequently than the noun. Whereas in the past you might have been an *amateur of, in,* or *at* photography, for example, nowadays you are much more likely to be an *amateur photographer.*

ambiguous See AMBIVALENT, AMBIGUOUS; EQUIVOCAL, AMBIGUOUS.

ambition Both the prepositions *for* and *of* are used with *ambition* <an *ambition for* fame> <she harbors the *ambition of* becoming a broadcaster>. However, the infinitive follows even more commonly <her *ambition* to become a psychiatrist>.

ambivalent, ambiguous *Ambivalent* is used as a descriptive word for a state in which one experiences simultaneous contradictory feelings or in which one wavers between two polar opposites. *Ambiguous,* too, may connote duality, but it most often tends to stress uncertainty and is usually applied to external things <eyes of an *ambiguous* color> whereas *ambivalent* tends to stress duality and is usually applied to internal things <an *ambivalent* attitude toward his father>. *Ambivalent* may be followed by the prepositions *toward* and *about* <*ambivalent toward* her> <*ambiva-*

lent about taking the job>. See also EQUIVOCAL, AMBIGUOUS.

amenable *Amenable* is regularly followed by *to* <*amenable to* the idea>.

amend, emend *Amend,* the more common of these two words, means "to alter (in writing)" but is usually used figuratively <*amended* his ways>. *Emend* is much less often used and is usually applied to the correction of text <was *emended* in this edition>.

America, American People have long questioned the propriety or accuracy of using *America* to mean the United States only and *American* to mean an inhabitant or citizen of the United States. Despite the perceived difficulty with these uses, however, both are fully established. Other inhabitants of the Americas generally prefer using different terms for themselves.

American Indian See NATIVE AMERICAN.

amid, amidst **1.** Different writers have different preferences regarding use of these words. Some feel that neither should be used, while others feel that one or the other is somehow preferable. Actual usage indicates that both are standard; you can use whichever sounds better to you.

2. *Amid, amidst, among.* There exists a curious belief that *amid* and *amidst* should go with singular nouns and *among* with plural nouns. This distinction is not found in actual usage: *amid* and *amidst* are followed by both singular and plural nouns <*amid* a flood of gossip> <*amidst* charges of ethics violations>, and *among,* though commonly used with a plural noun, cannot always serve as a substitute for *amid* or *amidst.*

among **1.** For information about choosing between *among* and *between,* see BETWEEN, AMONG.

2. Some would restrict *among* to use with plural nouns <*among* the players>. While this use is common, an almost equally common use of *among* is with collective nouns <*among* a certain class of people> <*among* the evidence is a note>. Collective nouns are notionally plural, which is why they fit with *among* (see NOTIONAL AGREEMENT in Glossary).

3. *Among, amongst.* Our evidence shows amongst to be a bit less common in American than in British use.

amongst See AMONG 3.

amount **1.** *Amount, number. Amount* is most frequently used with singular mass nouns <a certain *amount* of trust> <the *amount* of money involved>; it is also used with plural nouns considered as an aggregate <requires a fixed *amount* of calories>. *Number* is regularly used with plural count nouns to indicate an indefinite number of individuals or items <a *number* of journalists> <a *number* of objections>.

2. The phrase *in the amount of* is sometimes considered wordy. One recommendation is to replace it with *for* or *of.* But the phrase is useful with large amounts of money <a trade balance favorable *in the amount of* $103,518,000>.

3. The verb *amount* is regularly followed by *to* <it *amounted to* a little more than $200>.

amuse The verb *amuse* (and its past participle *amused,* used as an adjective) is commonly followed by *at, by,* and *with; at* is somewhat less common than the others <we were *amused at* this observation> <he was *amused by* the childrens play> < busy *amusing* themselves *with* video games>. *Amuse* can also be followed by the infinitive <I was *amused* to find an article about it>.

an See A, AN.

analogous When it is followed by a prepositional phrase (as a complement), *analogous* almost always takes *to* <a situation *analogous to* that of Russia's following the collapse of Communism>.

analogy This noun is used with the prepositions *between* <an *analogy between* the Internet and the telephone system>, *among* <*analogies among* the classes of data>, *with* <on *analogy with* a library>, *of* <presents the *analogy of* a family>, and *to* <makes an *analogy to* rock climbing>.

anchorperson See PERSON 2.

and 1. It is all right to begin a sentence with *and,* though the practice is apparently still cautioned against by some schoolteachers.

2. For other usage problems involving *and,* see AND SO; AND WHICH, AND WHO; GOOD AND; TRY AND; ETC.; and in Glossary: AGREEMENT: SUBJECT-VERB; COMPOUND SUBJECT; PARALLELISM: FAULTY PARALLELISM.

and etc. See ETC.

and/or *And/or* has established itself as an acceptable term, but it should be used only between two alternatives, where the meaning will obviously be "A or B or both" <the student's test scores *and/or* general preparedness will help us determine eligibility>. If used in longer series, *and/or* is likely to be either vague or unnecessary.

and so *And so,* though disparaged by some, is in perfectly good use <*and so* they moved on>.

and which, and who The issue here, which involves faulty parallelism, is better exemplified than described: In the phrase "a lady very learned in stones, ferns, plants, and vermin, and who had written a book about petals" (Anthony Trollope, *Barchester Towers*), *and* joins a clause ("who had written a book . . . ") with an adjective phrase ("very learned in stones . . . ") that is not parallel to it. The usual correction would be to insert *who was* after *lady* and, optionally, omit the *who* after *and* <a lady who was very learned in stones . . . and had written a book>.

angle *Angle* in the sense "the viewpoint from which something is considered" is criticized in various handbooks, but is nevertheless standard; it is used frequently in reviews <the story describes the event from two different *angles*>.

Anglo *Anglo* is an ethnic term of relatively recent vintage (mid-1930s in the U.S., significantly earlier in Canada) used to distinguish those of English ethnic or English-speaking background from others. There are at present two chief uses. The first distinguishes a Canadian of English ethnic and language background from one whose background is French. The second generally distinguishes an American of English-speaking background from one of Spanish-speaking background. *Anglo* has occasionally been considered a derogatory term, but it seems not to be considered so by most people.

angry The chief prepositions used with *angry* are *with, at,* and *about. With* is the most frequently used when the object is a person <she was *angry with* me>, though *with* is also sometimes used with inanimate or abstract objects <*angry with* the decision>. *At* is used with objects that are persons, actions, or things <*angry at* her boss> <*angry at* the world>. *About* is likewise used of persons or actions or things <*angry about* her partner> <*angry about* it>.

annoy The prepositions that commonly go with *annoy* are *with* <I was *annoyed with* her>, *at* <she is *annoyed at* the gossip>, and *by* <he was *annoyed by* their lack of understanding>. Other constructions are also possible <it *annoyed* them to have to listen to it> <she was *annoyed* to see him there> <it's *annoying that* they're so careless>.

ante-, anti- *Ante-* means "earlier, before," and *anti-* "opposite, opposed, against." See a good dictionary for fuller definition.

anticipate Some criticize the use of *anticipate* to mean "expect" <we *anticipate* an early conclusion to the talks> <I *anticipate* that they will follow suit>. The criticism is ill-founded, however; use of the word in this sense is fully established.

antipathy *To* is the preposition most commonly used with *antipathy* <an *antipathy to* outdoor work>, though *for* and *toward* are also in regular use <an *antipathy for* the theater> <an *antipathy toward* intellectuals>. The use of *between,* while not common, is still current <the *antipathy between* Ms. Gross and Mr. Salinger> <an *antipathy between* development and conservation>.

anxious There are two issues here: whether *anxious* can be used to mean "eager" <she was *anxious* for another meeting>, and whether *anxious* can be followed by an infinitive <*anxious* to see the movie> <*anxious* to ease employees' fears>. Both uses are in fact standard and the latter use, especially when *anxious* means "worried," is in fact the most common. Other common uses of *anxious* (in the "worried" sense) are as an attributive adjective <an *anxious* demand> or a predicate adjective without any following prepositional phrase <left him feeling *anxious*>.

any 1. The pronoun *any* can be either singular <*is any* of these solutions the one for us?> or plural <*are any* of these solutions right for us?>.

2. Some maintain that *any* with a singular noun must be referred to by a singular pronoun <*any* participant who spots the difference can test *his or her* knowledge further>. But it is not at all uncommon to find singular *any* referred to by a plural pronoun <*any* driver here can have *their* privileges revoked>. See THEY, THEIR, THEM; AGREEMENT (in Glossary).

3. *Of any, than any* (illogical comparison). Constructions like "has written a better account *than any* before him" and "the finest *of any* I have seen" are sometimes objected to as illogical comparisons. (*Any* is said to logically *include* that which is being spoken of, making *any other* or *all* the better choice.) But such constructions have been around for centuries, even though in recent years they seem to be on the wane. You can revise *any* to *any other* or *all* if you want to, but you need not feel you must do so on logical grounds.

anybody, anyone 1. These indefinite pronouns take a singular verb <*is anybody* home?>, and either a singular or a plural pronoun <*anyone* requiring this service should contact *his or her* [*their*] physician>. The use of the plural pronoun—

they, their, them—has traditionally been disapproved by grammarians, but the use has long been established and is winning greater acceptance. See THEY, THEIR, THEM; and in Glossary: AGREEMENT: INDEFINITE PRONOUNS; NOTIONAL AGREEMENT.

2. *Anybody else's.* See ELSE.

anymore, any more **1.** Both *anymore* and *any more* are found in current written use <she scarcely knows him *anymore* [*any more*]>; the one-word styling is more common.

2. *Anymore* is regularly used in negative contexts <we don't go there *anymore*>. It is also widely used in positive contexts <all I do *anymore* is go to funerals>; this use continually surprises those unfamiliar with it, but it is widespread in most dialect areas except New England.

anyone See ANYBODY, ANYONE.

any other See ANY 3.

anyplace This adverb seems to be American in origin, having emerged in 1916 and later established itself as standard in American English <we could play *anyplace* but in the living room>. See also EVERYPLACE, SOMEPLACE.

anytime This adverb is generally spelled as one word (unless you mean to write "at any time"). It seems to be largely an Americanism <they were not leaving *anytime* soon>.

anyways None of the senses of *anyways* are standard contemporary English; they are limited to various American and English regional dialects.

anywheres *Anywheres* is a generally disparaged Americanism that seldom appears in print outside of dialogue in fiction. It is best avoided in other contexts.

apathy When *apathy* is used with a preposition, it is most frequently *toward* (or *towards*) <*apathy toward* her sister>. *About, to,* and *regarding* are also in use <*apathy about* the matter> <*apathy to* his cousin> <*apathy regarding* the election>.

apparently, evidently *Evidently* generally suggests that there is some overt reason for drawing an inference <*evidently* our team had won the game, because we could hear the cheering>. *Apparently* is used as a disclaimer, as if the author were telling us, "This is what it seems to be, but I wont vouch for it" <*apparently* his previous company let him go, but they wouldn't say so directly>. *Apparently* is used much more frequently than *evidently.*

append *Append* usually takes *to* <should *append* it *to* the file>.

appendix Both *appendixes* and *appendices* are standard and acceptable plurals for *appendix.*

apportion The verb *apportion* may take the prepositions *among, to,* and *between* when a prepositional phrase is required (as a complement) <to be *appor-*

tioned among the states> <*apportioned* duties *to* her subordinates> <*apportioned* responsibility *between* the higher and lower courts>.

apprehensive *Of* is the most frequently used preposition with *apprehensive* <*apprehensive of* so high a cost>, but *about* is also quite common <*apprehensive about* her situation> and *regarding* is sometimes chosen <*apprehensive regarding* his lack of stamina>.

appraise, apprise These words are sometimes confused, especially in speech. *Apprise,* which means "give notice to," usually occurs in the construction *apprise one of* <*apprised him of* her views>. *Appraise,* which means "evaluate," is used with inanimate or abstract objects <*appraised* the house> <*appraised* the situation> and sometimes people <*appraised* him>.

approve *Approve,* when used as an intransitive verb with the meaning "to take a favorable view," takes *of* <he generally *approves of* the effort>. When used as a transitive verb—usually in the sense "to sanction officially"—it can take *by* to indicate the agent of approval <the plan was *approved by* the board>. Some object to using the "favorable view" sense in such transitive constructions as "School officials could not *approve* such behavior on the part of students." This use, however, is standard.

approximately A common recommendation is that the adverb *approximately* should be replaced by the shorter *about* or *nearly* or *almost* when it can be.

However, in business and technical writing and in general prose of a serious cast, the word is standard. It is most commonly applied to numerical quantities <*approximately* 2 percent of the total> but also is used of other things <a boundary running *approximately* north and south>. In casual or informal contexts, you probably will have no need for it.

apropos, apropos of *Apropos of* has been functioning as a compound preposition in English since the middle of the 18th century <a story *apropos of* your interest in meeting him>. Early in the 20th century *apropos* began to be used without *of* as a preposition having the same meaning <I should mention, *apropos* our earlier discussion, that there is one condition>. Both are now standard.

apt See LIABLE, APT, LIKELY.

arguably Some feel that this word is overused and that *perhaps* or *probably* are preferable substitutes. But while *arguably* may be close in meaning to these other two words, it carries its own connotation. It functions as a hedge against too absolute a statement <*arguably* a plan that will satisfy everyone>, or as the qualifier of a superlative <*arguably* the fittest person for the job>. There seems to be no compelling reason to avoid using it.

around **1.** *Around, about.* The use of *around* in senses it share with *about,* especially the sense "approximately" or "near," has long been objected to

<*around* 30 percent> <*around* 4 oclock>. But this use of *around* is standard in American English. You can use it without apologizing.

2. *Around, round. Around* is more common in American English and *round* more common in British English. Both words are, however, in use on both sides of the Atlantic.

array The verb *array* is used with many prepositions. When used in the sense of "dress," it usually takes *in* <*arrayed in* finery>. If the sense is close to "equip," *in* or *with* may be used <towns in the war zone were *arrayed in* arms> <the boat was *arrayed with* sheet and sail>. When the meaning is "to get or place in order," many prepositions are possible <marchers *arrayed on* the parade grounds> <an orchestra *arrayed in front of* the stage> <Secret Service members *arrayed before* the podium> <lights *arrayed in* a Christmas-tree shape>. When there is a notion of drawing up forces, *against* is usual <officials *arrayed against* their opponents>.

arrive The question of what prepositions to use with *arrive* has been a matter of comment since 1770. Our evidence shows the following: When the place of arrival is the object, *in* and *at* are used <*arrived in* New York> <*arrive at* the courtroom>; *on* or *upon* may be used in some instances <will *arrive on* stage> <*arrived upon* the scene>. When things—material or immaterial—arrive, we find *in, at,* or *on* <word *arrived in* the classroom> <the letter *arrived at* her

desk> <the dinghy *arrived on* the beach>. If the object is the point of departure, *from* is the most common <*arrived from* Seattle>. When the object is the means of arrival, we find *by, on,* and occasionally *in* <*arriving by* limousine> <*arrive on* horseback> <*arrived in* a skiff>. In figurative use, the object is almost always the point of arrival and the preposition is at <*arrived at* his conclusion>.

as **1.** The use of *as* to mean "because" or "since" <I needed an answer on the spot, *as* my plane was about to depart> is sometimes said to be ambiguous. However, the surrounding context usually makes the meaning clear, and *as* used in this way is a standard and acceptable alternative to *because* and *since,* though less frequently used than either. See also SINCE.

2. The relative pronoun *as* may be preceded by *such* or *same* <*such* a racket *as* had never been heard before> <faced with much the *same* set of problems *as* confronted Europe in 1914>. The relative pronoun *as* without a preceding *such* or *same* (as in "took decisions *as* ought not to have been taken") is a dialectal form surviving from an older use.

3. The use of *as* as a conjunction where *that,* or sometimes *if* or *whether,* could be substituted (as in "I don't know *as* it matters") is primarily a speech form and is not found in ordinary written prose.

4. When *as* is used as a preposition in the same sense as *like* <he is not *as* other men>, it is standard. But care must be taken not to choose *as* simply to avoid *like* lest ambiguity with other senses of prepositional *as* result <the judge said they acted *as* buffoons>. See also LIKE.

as . . . as 1. *As . . . as, so . . . as.* *As . . . as* is used in positive statements <*as* good *as* it will ever be>, while either *as . . . as* or *so . . . as* may be used in negative statements <were not *as* accommodating *as* we had expected> <not *so* lucky *as* he used to be>.

2. If a pronoun follows an *as . . . as* comparison, is it to be in the nominative case <she is *as* tall as I> or the objective case <she is *as* tall as me>? Some object to the former as pretentious (though correct), while others object to the latter as ungrammatical (though common). The trend seems to be toward using the nominative case in rather formal contexts and the objective case in most others.

as bad or worse than See AS GOOD OR BETTER THAN.

as best In expressions like "We must carry on *as best* we can," *as best* is a perfectly respectable English idiom. *As best as,* as in "*As best as* I can recall," is disapproved by some critics and is mostly restricted to speech.

as far as, so far as The use of the phrase *as far as* (or *so far as*) without a following verb (such as *goes* or *is concerned* <there has been little improvement *as far as* eliminating street crime in the area> has been much objected to. Our evidence shows that this use is firmly established in speech but is not much used in writing.

as good as Complaints are sometimes heard about the use of *as good as* for *practically* <the plan is *as good as* dead> <she *as good as* told him to print the story>. But you can safely ignore the complaints, as this use is standard.

as good or better than This phrase—as in "Her work is *as good or better than* his"—and others of similar construction (e.g., *as good if not better than, as bad or worse than, as much or more than, as great or greater than*), have been the subject of corrective efforts since the 18th century. The usual suggestion is to supply the missing *as* ("*as* good *as* or better than"), but in a written sentence *or better than* should be set off with commas. Our evidence shows that *as good or better than* (like the others) is an old, well-established English idiom; it need not be routinely revised out unless you are striving for a more formal style.

as great or greater than See AS GOOD OR BETTER THAN.

as how *As how* has been aspersed as simply incorrect and as substandard for *that.* It is neither, however; it is simply dialectal. The expression, particularly in the combination *allow as how,* has current use in journalism, and especially political journalism <the group's spokesperson *allows as how* the decision could affect their most recent plans>. The combinations *being as how* and *seeing as how* are speech forms that do not often appear in print. See also ALLOW 3; BEING, BEING AS, BEING AS HOW, BEING THAT; SEEING AS, SEEING AS HOW, SEEING THAT.

Asian, Oriental *Asian* is now the preferred word, noun or adjective, especially for ethnic purposes <a number of *Asian* students>; *Oriental* is held to be mildly offensive.

aside from *Aside from* can mean either "besides" <*aside from* professional archaeologists, several amateurs have made discoveries> or "except for" <*aside from* this one accomplished piece, her contribution is negligible>. Because it can sometimes happen that you intend "besides" but your reader understands "except for," you must be sure to make your context clear.

as if, as though **1.** At one time the propriety of *as though* used for *as if* was considered dubious. Nowadays most observers find the two to be interchangeable <it's *as though* [*as if*] no one cared>.

2. In sentences like "She felt *as if* someone were [was] watching her," some critics insist on the subjunctive *were,* whereas others accept the indicative *was.* The evidence from usage shows both subjunctive and indicative in frequent respectable use. You may use whichever form you are most comfortable with.

3. See also LIKE 1.

ask *Ask* may be followed by an infinitive <was *asked* to return> or a clause <I *ask* that you not use it> <she *asked* how you were doing>.

When prepositions are used with *ask,* one convention is as follows: "Ask *of* a person *for* what is wanted, *after* one's health." *Of* may also be used with inanimate objects <*asks* too much *of* the program> and *for* with persons <*ask for* Ms. Smith>. *About* is often used when information is sought <*asking about* our plans>. When *ask* means "invite," it may be used with the adverb *out* or the preposition *to* <*asked* her *out* on a date> <was *asked to* the prom>.

as long as, so long as *As long as* and *so long as* are simply variants, being pretty much interchangeable in the sense "provided that" <*as long as* [*so long as*] you get it done in time> and in the more literal sense "for the period of time that" <*so long as* [*as long as*] I am in charge here>. *As long as* (but not *so long as*) is also used to mean "since" <*as long as* you're going out, could you return this video?>

as much or more than See AS GOOD OR BETTER THAN.

as of Although the use of *as of* has been disparaged, the phrase is in reputable American use, especially in business contexts <the figures are current *as of* June 30>. *As of* is also used with words relating to time other than dates. Combinations such *as of now, as of the moment, as of late* are primarily speech forms that are not often used in writing for publication.

as per *As per* is in use—perhaps overuse—in business correspondence and other types of more or less straightforward prose <*as per* the agreement> <*as per* our catalog description>. If you want to avoid it, you may try substituting *in accordance with* or using other constructions beginning with *as* <*as* described in our catalog>, or you may simply use *per* <*per* your memo>.

aspire *To* is the preposition most frequently used with *aspire* <*aspires to* a singing career>; *to* followed by the infinitive is also common <*aspired to* be the nation's best billiards player>. *Toward* (and *towards*) are also both found <*aspiring toward* full-scale arms-reduction talks>.

as regards See REGARD.

assent When the verb *assent* takes a preposition, it is *to* <*assented to* their demands>.

assimilate When the verb *assimilate* takes a preposition, it is most often *to* <*assimilate to* the conditions> and next most often *into* <*assimilated into* the platoon>. *By* indicates the agent <*assimilated by* her new country>.

assist **1.** The most common construction using *assist* appears in phrases like "*assist* patrons *in* using the library" (i.e., *assist* + object + *in* + gerund). Standard but somewhat less common are phrases like "*assisting* his parents *to* build a house" (*assist* + object + *to* + infinitive). Other constructions are found more rarely.

2. When *assist* clearly means "help," *in* or *with* are the usual prepositions <*assist in* finding the pet's owner> <*assisted with* clearing the table>. When *assist* means "be present," it regularly takes *at* <several ministers *assisted at* the signing>.

assume, presume These words are not synonymous, but they share the sense "suppose, expect, believe." *Presume* tends to convey more certainty than *assume* <he is *presumed* to be armed and dangerous> <she *assumed* that her friends would be there>. *Assume* has more meanings than *presume* and is the more common word.

assure **1.** For information about choosing among synonyms of *assure*, see ENSURE, INSURE, ASSURE.

2. *Assure* can take an ordinary noun object <to *assure* success> <we *assure* the quality of our workmanship>. The direct object may also be a clause <wanting to *assure* that their savings are safe>. But most often *assure*, much like *promise*, takes two objects—a direct and an indirect <thus *assuring* us another victory>. Usually the direct object is a clause, with or without *that* <*assured* them *that* they have nothing to worry about> <we were *assured* this wouldn't happen>. Sometimes the clause is replaced by a phrase with *of* <to assure them *of* a seat at the negotiating table>.

as though See AS IF, AS THOUGH.

as to **1.** *As to*, contrary to the opinion of some, is not legalese. Rather, it is a common compound preposition in wide use at every level of formality. It is used as an introducer <*As to* his suggestion about retiring, . . .> and to link a noun, an adjective, or a verb with the following matter <offered no opinion *as to* the likelihood of a settlement> <she was less sanguine *as to* the couple's long-term prospects> <slow to decide *as to* the best route to take>. You can use any of these constructions when they sound right to you.

2. Various commentators have complained about using *as to* in front of such conjunctions as *how, why,* and especially *whether* <questions were raised *as to how* to treat it> <no one can be certain *as to why* they left> <a disagreement *as to whether* she is capable of it>. There is, however, no solid basis to these complaints; use of *as to* in such constructions is standard.

astonished *Astonished* can be used with either *at* or *by,* though *at* is perhaps the more common <we were *astonished at* the force of the hurricane>. *By* is frequently followed by a gerund <he *astonished* the judging panel *by* withdrawing the piece>.

as well as *As well as,* besides being used in the literal, comparative way <she performed it *as well as* anyone could>, is used as a preposition and conjunction. As a preposition, it is usually followed by a gerund <*as well as* serving as chief counsel, Jim is the group's treasurer>. The most common use of the phrase, however, is as a conjunction. It joins nouns and noun phrases <two department stores *as well as*

a pharmacy>. It joins prepositional phrases <the room opens into the dining room *as well as* onto the deck>. It joins verbs <she drove *as well as* navigated> and verbal phrases <the firm was floundering financially *as well as* running into legal difficulties>. It joins adjectives <she seemed relaxed *as well as* confident>.

Sometimes *as well as* joins two words or phrases that are the subject of the same verb. Usually the first subject is plural, the verb is plural, and no commas are used <recent legislative actions *as well as* tighter enforcement make it unlikely>. Where the first subject is singular and the second plural, usage is somewhat mixed: the plural verb tends to be chosen when no commas are used <the harbor *as well as* the many inlets are quickly filling with sand>, and the singular is chosen when commas are used <the harbor, *as well as* the many inlets, is quickly filling with sand>. When both subjects are singular, commas and a singular verb are preferred <this statement, *as well as* the earlier one, is tantamount to libel>.

at See WHERE . . . AT.

at about Although various commentators have complained that *at about* is redundant <we left the arena *at about* two oclock> and have recommended eliminating one or the other of the two terms, our files show that *at about* is thoroughly reputable and firmly established.

at present, at the present time Though a few critics have discouraged the use of these phrases as merely wordy ways of saying *now,* it is difficult to see why. Both phrases can be useful in subtly emphasizing a contrast with time past or time future in a way that the less noticeable *now* cannot <his work is *at present* not widely supported within the scientific community>. You should feel free to use either phrase when it sounds right.

attain When used intransitively, *attain* is normally followed by *to* <he could only *attain to* a low-level job in the ministry>.

attempt **1.** The noun *attempt* frequently takes the preposition at <her first *attempt at* bareback riding>. *On* is the usual preposition when *attempt* means "an attempt to kill" <an *attempt on* the prime minister's life>; *against* and *upon* are also used <the failed *attempt against* Hitler> <*attempts upon* the crown>. And the infinitive is quite common <an *attempt* to escape>.

2. The idea that *try* should be substituted for *attempt* is occasionally put forward, but may be disregarded. Many good writers find *attempt* to be perfectly satisfactory <it is futile to *attempt* to eradicate a speech form by denouncing it in books on writing>.

at the present time See AT PRESENT, AT THE PRESENT TIME.

at this point in time See POINT IN TIME.

attitude *Attitude* is generally followed by the prepositions *toward, towards,* and *to. Toward* is the most frequent in American English <the assistants *attitude toward* the boss>. *Towards* is found chiefly in British English, and *to* is more common in British than American English <a critical *attitude to* her work>. *About* has some use, usually spoken, in American English <developed an *attitude about* it>.

augment *Augment,* often in the form of its past participle *augmented,* is used frequently with the preposition *by* <these resources were *augmented by* funds of her own>, and less frequently with *with* <ended up *augmenting* the divider *with* concrete barriers>.

auger, augur These two words are sometimes confused because of their similar spelling. *Auger* refers to tools for boring holes; *augur* (as in the phrase *augur well*) deals with foretelling future events from omens.

authority When *authority* refers to a person, it is most often followed by *on* <an *authority on* airplane disasters>, but a couple of other prepositions are possible <an *authority upon* virtually all subjects> <an *authority in* the field of high-density physics>. When *authority* refers to a cited source, *for* is usual <his *authority for* this observation is an 18th-century grammarian>. When it refers to a power or convincing force, *over* often follows *authority* <the state has no *authority over* federal wetlands> and *by* and *on* often precede it <*by* the *authority* invested in me> <*on* the *authority* of agency head Dixon>. *Authority* is also used with the infinitive <has *authority* to institute a manhunt if necessary>.

average According to some, *average* should not be used to mean "customary, ordinary, usual." But even though an occasional writer puts this sense in quotation marks <the "*average*" New Yorker> to indicate that the use is dubious, the issue is dead since this meaning has been completely standard for many years <the *average* Beltway politician> <the *average* dictionary user>.

averse to, averse from *Averse to* is the more common phrase in both British and American English <not *averse to* making money>, though *averse from* is still used in Britain.

aversion Of the prepositions that go with *aversion, to* is the most common <an *aversion to* being questioned>. *From* is the next most common <his *aversion from* sex>. The use of *for* goes back many years, but seems to be less common now than either *to* or *from* <a pronounced *aversion for* reading>.

awake, awaken *Awake* is a verb that, like WAKE (see entry), derives from a blend of two older verbs, one transitive (or causative) and the other intransitive. Because of this, it employs a mixture of regular and irregular principal parts. The past tense is either *awoke* or *awaked* <we *awoke* [*awaked*] from our reverie>, while the past participle is either *awoken* or *awaked* <they had *awoken* [*awaked*] to their own misery>.

The separate verb *awaken,* on the other hand, which has essentially the same meaning as *awake,* is perfectly regular, with *awakened* as its past <the experience *awakened* memories> and past participle <the company has *awakened* from its self-induced torpor>.

awesome The use of *awesome* as a generalized term of approval has been part of the standard hyperbole of sports broadcasting and writing for several years <an *awesome* fastball>. It has also been popular in speech, often attracting the intensifier *totally* <"the waves are *totally awesome,*" he reported>. In more formal contexts this "extraordinary" sense is probably best avoided.

The word also continues to carry its primary meaning of "inspiring awe" <an *awesome* show of force> <the *awesome* responsibility of becoming the child's permanent guardian>.

awful, awfully Any use of *awful* and *awfully* that doesn't convey the original sense of being "filled with awe" has traditionally been criticized. However, *awful* has long been acceptable in the meanings "extremely objectionable" <what an *awful* color> and "exceedingly great" <an *awful* lot of money> in speech and casual writing. Use of the adverbs *awful* and *awfully* as intensifiers <I'm *awful* tired> <he's *awfully* rich> is likewise common in informal prose. You probably will not want these where a formal tone is called for.

awhile, a while *Awhile,* like several other adverbs of time and place, is often used as the object of a preposition <after *awhile* I felt better> <for *awhile* she was silent>, though many consider this an error. If you want to play it safe, however, you should stick to the spelling *a while* <they had parted *a while* earlier>.

B

background Some have criticized the use of *background* in the senses "the sum of a person's experience or training" <the two boys' *backgrounds* are very different> and "the circumstances preceding a phenomenon or event" <gave us some *background* on the candidate's decision>. But the criticisms can be safely ignored; the use of *background* in these senses is standard.

back of, in back of Both *back of* and *in back of* are standard in American English <set up a dog kennel *in back of* [*back of*] the garage>.

bad, badly **1.** The standard use of the adverb *bad* is equivalent in meaning to *badly;* it often occurs with *off* <just how *bad off* were they?>. In speech and in some informal writing, *bad* is interchangeable with *badly* after *do, want,* and *need* <we didn't *do too bad,* considering the circumstances> <he says he *wants* justice *bad* enough to bring the case to trial>.

2. See FEEL BAD, FEEL BADLY.

bail, bale Watch your spelling here. *Bail* means "security given" <managed to post *bail*>, while *bale* means "a bundle of goods" <*bales* of hay>.

balance The extension of the meaning of this word to the remainder or rest of something other than money is a standard Americanism <the *balance* of the book's chapters>.

balding Though once criticized as nonexistent, *balding* has established itself as standard <a *balding* gentleman of middle years>.

bale See BAIL, BALE.

bare, bear Confusion or misspelling of these two words sometimes occurs. *Bare* as a verb means "to uncover" <*bared* his soul> and as an adjective "uncovered" <*bare*-headed>. The verb *bear* has a variety of meanings, among them "to carry" <*bears* the stamp of approval>, "to endure" <couldn't *bear* to watch>, "to press" <*bear* down hard>, and "to give birth to or produce" (see BORN, BORNE).

bargain The verb *bargain* takes *with* with a person or group of persons <the rules forbid *bargaining with* anyone>. *With* may also be used with something considered as a helpful tool <not much capital to *bargain with*>. You bargain *for* something <no one had *bargained for* these results>, and *about, over,* or *on* something or some subject <the right to *bargain about* [*over, on*] pensions>.

based *Based,* when used to mean "established, founded" and followed by a preposition, is most often used with on <*based on* the facts>. Less often, *based* is used with *upon* <*based upon* the sources>; and least often, it is used with *in* <*based in* a thorough modernism>. When used to mean "stationed or located at a base," *based* is most often followed by the prepositions *at* or *in* <a fleet *based at* Guantanamo> <she was *based in* California>.

based on, based upon When *based on* (or *based upon*) begins a sentence, it often ends up becoming a dangling modifier: "*Based on* this analysis, Porkco Inc. is running little risk." However, such sentences are usually perfectly understandable. When a *based on* phrase clearly modifies an element later in the sentence <*Based on* this analysis, the risk to Porkco Inc. is minimal>, it is not dangling and is fully acceptable.

basically Some object to what they consider the unnecessary use of *basically* as a sentence adverb: "*Basically,* they want to raze the neighborhood and build a highway." But *basically,* as used here, is one of those little space-makers carried over from speech to speechlike prose; it does not seem to be a serious fault in the kind of journalistic writing in which it usually appears. It should not be overdone, however.

basis **1.** *Basis* figures in two somewhat long-winded phrases that are often criticized—namely, *on the basis of* and *on a . . . basis.*

The first of these phrases is often considered a candidate for replacement by *on, by, after,* or *because of.* In the clause "not *on the basis of* the merits of that view but rather . . . ," for example, you could replace "on the basis of the merits of that view" with "on its own merits." Other cases are not so clear-cut, however; and sometimes the phrase is necessary <this cannot be proved *on the basis of* the postulates stated>. Conclusion: though mechanical substitution of another preposition or phrase will not necessarily make your text more readable, *on the basis of* can often be replaced by something shorter. Consider how the phrase fits the whole context of your piece and how it fits the rhythm and sense of the sentence.

The more challenging phrase is *on a . . . basis.* This phrase functions as an adverb <service *on a* pay-per-view *basis*>, and is found quite often in less-than-elegant writing. Its awkwardness seems to be its chief virtue, though, for it allows a writer to write what might otherwise not be easily expressible. Care and judgment are required in revising it out of your text; it may be better left alone than hastily revised.

2. When used with a preposition, *basis* usually takes *of* or *for* <the *basis of* the objection> <simple designs which became the *basis for* more elaborate ones>.

be *Be* continues to be used in its subjunctive function <any young man, *be* he rich or poor, . . .>, especially in a few fixed phrases <*be* that as it may> <so *be* it>. More frequently, however, *is* or *are* is used instead <if this *is* Tuesday, I must be in Moscow> <though they *are* down, they are not defeated>. *Be* is also used in various English dialects, such as Black English and

Irish English, to indicate habitual or continued action (as in "he *be* the one" and "sure the afternoon *be* a warm one"), but these usages are not yet part of ordinary standard English.

bear See BARE, BEAR; BORN, BORNE.

beat, beaten *Beaten* is by far the more common form of the past participle <he was *beaten* to a pulp>. *Beat* appears more often in older writing, but is still found in respectable circles <she had *beat* the odds>. *Beat* is common in sports writing after *get* <when they got *beat* in the finals>, and it is usual in the phrase *can't be beat* (where *beaten* is not used).

because **1.** The notion that *because* can be used only to introduce an adverbial clause and not a noun clause seems to be connected with opposition to the phrase *reason is because* (see REASON IS BECAUSE). Such sentences as "It is *because* he has never performed the stunt before a large crowd that he is so uneasy" (noun clause) and "*Because* he has never performed the stunt before a large crowd, he is uneasy" (adverbial clause) are, however, both entirely standard.

2. Some have criticized the practice of making a clause beginning with *because* or *just because* the subject of a sentence, as in "*Just because* I forgot to call doesn't mean I don't love you." This construction is more typical of speech than of highly serious writing. It is not wrong, but you probably will not want to use it in anything of a formal nature.

3. The rule that you can never begin a sentence with *because* is a myth. *Because* is frequently used to begin sentences, particularly in magazine and newspaper writing <*Because* no one returned her call, she took them to be less than enthusiastic about meeting with her>.

4. It is commonly observed that there can be ambiguity when *because* follows a negative verb in a sentence: "He didn't leave *because* he was afraid." The question here is, did he leave or did he stay? The usual advice is to solve the ambiguity with a comma: "He didn't leave, *because* he was afraid" means he stayed; "He didn't leave *because* he was afraid" means he left, but not because he was afraid. But sentences like this are better rewritten; professional writers seem to revise them, and you should too.

5. See AS 1; SINCE.

beg the question This phrase originated in a 16th-century translation of Aristotle, where the verb literally meant "beg" but was really closer in meaning to "assume." Thus the phrase was not clear to many readers and developed a second sense "to evade, sidestep." Both these uses are standard. More recently the phrase has been used in contexts in which *beg* is literal <the title "Improve Your Grammar" *begs the question:* Why?> This use seems to be on the way to establishing itself as standard.

behalf Some commentators have insisted on distinguishing between *in behalf of* (meaning "for the benefit of") and *on behalf of* (meaning "as the agent for"). But evidence from actual usage shows that there has never been a clear-cut distinction in meaning based on the choice of preposition. Both *in* and *on* are used interchangeably in American English in both the "benefit" sense and the "agent" sense, while modern British usage tends to favor *on* in all instances.

behest Sometimes criticized as old-fashioned or formal, *behest* is indeed an old word but it is still in current use in a variety of contexts. It suggests a stronger urging than *request* does <will investigate the matter at the *behest* of the Senate panel>.

behoove, behove *Behoove* is the usual spelling in the U.S. and *behove* the usual spelling in the U.K.

being, being as, being as how, being that The conjunction *being* survives in various dialects (as in "*Being as* you are family, I can tell you"). If any of these phrases are in your dialect and you use them in writing, it is likely to be noticed by those who do not have them in their dialect.

belabor, labor These two verbs are interchangeable in expressions such as "*belabor/labor* a point."

beside, besides *Beside* is used as a preposition <the table *beside* the couch>, and it also appears in two standard idioms: *beside oneself,* and *beside the point. Besides* is both an adverb <she was an experienced professional and a loving mother *besides*> and a preposition meaning "except, other than, together with" <she had nothing to worry about, *besides* the wedding>.

bestow In modern use, *upon* and *on* are the prepositions that usually go with *bestow* <*bestowed* good fortune *upon* them>.

be sure and See TRY AND.

bet The verb *bet* has two forms of the past tense and past participle: *bet* and *betted.* In the U.S., *bet* is usual <had not yet *bet* on the race>. In the U.K. both are used, but *bet* is more common.

better **1.** For the use of *better* in constructions like "a *better* kind of company," where no explicit comparison is made, see ABSOLUTE COMPARATIVE (in Glossary).

2. The use of *better* for *had better* is an acceptable idiom <you *better* not complain>, but it is not found in very formal surroundings.

3. The idiom *better than* used to mean "more than" (as in "*better than* two thirds were lawyers") is primarily a spoken idiom and is not generally found in formal writing.

between, among The notion that *between* can be used only of two items and that *among* must be used for more than two is persistent but unfounded. *Between* is especially appropriate to denote a one-to-one relationship, regardless of the number of items. It can be used when the number is unspecified <eco-

nomic cooperation *between* nations>, when more than two are mentioned <this is *between* you and me and the lamppost>, and even when only one item is noted but repetition is implied <paused *between* every sentence). *Among* is more appropriate when the emphasis is not strictly on individual relationships <discontent *among* the stockholders>. Automatically using *among* when more than two items are mentioned can result in awkwardness and may strain natural idiom.

between you and I Critical opinion holds that *between you and I* (or *between he and Jane*) should be *between you and me* (or *between him and Jane* or *between Jane and him*). The problem here is that *between* takes a compound object, which resists the government of the preposition. A few commentators think *between you and I* should be accepted as good English (it dates back as far as Shakespeare), but most resist it. You need not eliminate it from your speech, but you will probably want to avoid it in writing.

biannual, biennial These two words are usually differentiated, *biannual* meaning "occurring twice a year" and *biennial* usually meaning "occurring once in two years." See also BIMONTHLY, BIWEEKLY.

bid The verb *bid* has irregular inflected forms. When it means "to make a bid" it usually has the unchanged *bid* as both past tense and past participle <he *bid* on the piano> <we had *bid* for the job>. In other senses the most common past is *bade,* though *bid* is sometimes also found <she *bade* [*bid*] him farewell>. As past participle in those senses, *bid* and *bidden* are the most usual <we have *bid* adieu to the problem> <was *bidden* to speak>.

biennial See BIANNUAL, BIENNIAL.

bimonthly, biweekly Many people are puzzled about these two words, which are often ambiguous because the meaning of *bi-* in this context can be either "coming or occurring every two" (i.e., every other month, every other week) or "coming or occurring two times" (i.e., twice a month, twice a week). This ambiguity has existed for well over a century and seems unlikely to go away soon. The chief difficulty is that many users of these words, assuming that their readers know exactly what they mean, do not bother to make their context clear. So if you use *bimonthly* or *biweekly,* you should leave some clues to your meaning. See also BIANNUAL, BIENNIAL.

bite *Bitten* is the usual past participle <the shark has already *bitten* two bathers>. *Bit,* however, continues to be used in spoken dialect and now and then in various fixed phrases with *bite* <many such mining operations long ago *bit* the dust>.

biweekly See BIMONTHLY, BIWEEKLY.

black See AFRICAN-AMERICAN.

blame, *noun* The noun *blame* may be followed by the prepositions *for* or *on* <took all the *blame for* allowing it> <placed *blame* on the managers>.

blame on, blame for The real difference between "blame someone for" and "blame something on" is the direct object. In the first, the direct object is the cause of the problem <they *blamed* Kathy *for* the error> <the technicians were *blamed for* the outage>; in the second, the direct object is the problem <they *blamed* the error *on* Kathy> <the outage was *blamed on* the technicians>. The evidence shows *blame on* and *blame for* to be about equally frequent.

blend *Blend* is followed by *with* or *into* <*blending* these ideas *with* similar ones of his partner> <the structure *blends into* its surroundings>. Sometimes the phrase *blend in* is followed by *with* <we *blended* right *in with* the crowd>. In cookery, *blend* is regularly followed by *in* <*blend in* three eggs>.

bloc, block The spelling *bloc* is usual for the sense of a political combination <a *bloc* of voters>.

blow The usual inflected forms of *blow* are irregular: *blew* and *blown* <the wind *blew*> <our cover was *blown*>. *Blowed* is a speech form limited to some regional dialects.

boast **1.** Though questioned by some, the transitive sense of *boast,* "to possess and call attention to," has been in use since the late 17th century and is standard <the city *boasts* one of the largest convention centers in the nation>.

2. When *boast* is used as an intransitive with a preposition, *of* and *about* are usual <they would some-

times *boast of* their links to the underground> <she *boasts* too much *about* her experience and training>.

boost Occasionally someone complains about use of the noun *boost* to mean "increase, raise, rise." It is nevertheless standard <a *boost* in the prime lending rate> <a real *boost* to morale>.

border When *border* is used to mean "to approach the nature of a specific thing" and is followed by a preposition, *on* is the usual choice <a statement *bordering on* the ridiculous>. When the literal sense of *border* is used in the passive, the preposition most often used is *by; with* is less frequent <grounds *bordered by* [*with*] potted flowers>.

born, borne These two words, both past participles of the verb *bear,* are sometimes misused. *Born* should be used only in the passive of the literal or figurative act of birth <was *born* in 1989> or as an adjective <a *born* loser>. The active past participle for giving birth is *borne* <had *borne* three children>. *Borne* is used for all other senses <a pain that could hardly be *borne*> <not *borne* out by the facts>. See also BARE, BEAR.

borrow The usual preposition linking *borrow* to the person or source is *from* <she *borrowed* it *from* Sarah>. *Of* is used sometimes to link *borrow* with the object borrowed <he *borrowed* freely *of* Shakespeare's words in composing these lines>. *Against* and *on* tend to be used in more specialized contexts <*borrowed against* revenues> <he *borrows on* the philosophy of

Pragmatism>. The prepositions *off* and *off of* are limited to speech.

both **1.** *Both . . . and.* To achieve parallelism in your prose, it is best to place the same construction after both *both* and *and* <rights to *both* the cottage *and* the lakefront> <bowing *both* out of respect for her elders *and* out of fear in the presence of her mother-in-law>. In speech, this convention is not always adhered to.

2. *Both of. Both of* is just like ALL OF (see entry). The *of* after *both* can be omitted before a plural noun (although it need not be) <*both (of)* these rates are likely to increase>, but it must be kept before a pronoun in the objective case <we visited *both of* them>.

3. *The both. The both* is a fairly common spoken idiom (as in "To bed, *the both* of you!"), usually avoided in writing.

brand *Brand,* in the sense "a characteristic or distinctive kind" <a lively *brand* of theater>, is occasionally criticized. It is nevertheless standard.

bridegroom See GROOM.

break The past tense of *break* is *broke* <I *broke* the latch> and the standard past participle is *broken* <was *broken* in two>. *Broke* as a past participle was once standard but is now dialectal, except in the usage of those who train horses; they distinguish *broke* (desirable) from *broken* (undesirable).

bring, take The oft-stated and simple rule that *bring* implies movement toward the speaker and *take* implies movement away is reasonable as far as it goes, but it does not go far enough to account for actual use. The fact is that often direction or point of view is of little or no relevance to the reader (or hearer) <students must *bring* [*take*] report cards home to their parents> <"Be sure to *take* [*bring*] the umbrella," she told him>. In such instances, *bring* and *take* become virtually interchangeable. You should follow your natural inclination and not worry about what critics might prefer.

bring up See RAISE, REAR.

Brit, Briton, Britisher *Brit* is a relatively modern word (about a century old) that is a shortening of *Briton, Britisher,* or *British.* It is used to designate a native of England, and its use has been accelerating rapidly since the 1970s. Despite some British touchiness about it, *Brit* seems to be on its way to becoming a neutral, informal term on both sides of the Atlantic. *Briton* and *Britisher* also remain in reputable use.

broke **1.** Although *broke* in the sense "without funds, penniless" is maligned by some as slangy, it has been in good use for some three centuries.

2. See BREAK.

bulk of *The bulk of* is used with plural count nouns that may be thought of as a mass <*the bulk of* the voters> <*the bulk* of the books>. It is equally often used with mass nouns <*the bulk of* the evidence> <*the bulk of* the work>.

bunch *Bunch* is sometimes criticized as colloquial. Our evidence shows that it has long been in good use both as a generalized collective <a *bunch* of boys> <*bunches* of tourists> and as a word for a group of people <a literate *bunch*> <a tough-looking *bunch*>. It is also standard when used with mass nouns <a *bunch* of money> <a *bunch* of nonsense>. You can avoid it in formal contexts if you want, but there is no reason to do so other than your own preference.

burgeon It was decided in the 1960s that the use of *burgeon* to mean "bloom" or "flourish" <a *burgeoning* industry> was an error. It was not an error, having been in established use for well over a century. It is entirely standard.

burn Both the past tense and past participle of *burn* are spelled two different ways—*burned* and *burnt*. In American English *burned* is the more common form of the past tense <we were *burned* by the market> <the fire *burned* furiously>, while both *burnt* and *burned* are used as adjectives <a *burnt* almond flavor>. Intransitive *burned* and transitive *burnt* are preferred in British English.

bust The verb *bust,* though disparaged by some, has been gaining in respectability for a half century, and in some contexts is the right word to use <*busting* loose> <was *busted* for dealing drugs> <had to *bust* our butts

to get it done>. None of these suggest use in highly formal situations.

but **1.** Commentators agree that, contrary to what many people believe, it is okay to begin a sentence with *but.* The only caution they offer is that *but* is best not followed with a comma (as in "*But,* you won't know until you try it"), as this will weaken its force, unless the comma is one of a pair setting off a parenthetical clause <*But,* however you add it up, the fact remains . . .>.

2. *But* has functioned as both a conjunction and a preposition since Old English, and still does. As a conjunction, it is sometimes followed by a pronoun in the nominative case, particularly when it forms part of the subject <no one *but* I saw through the ruse>. When followed by a pronoun in the objective case that stands in a position normally calling for the objective, *but* can be interpreted either as a preposition or a conjunction <they questioned everyone *but* him>. Sometimes *but* is clearly a preposition and must be followed by the objective case of the pronoun <It seemed obvious to everyone in the group *but* her>. In such instances the style tends to be more conversational than when *but* is followed by a nominative pronoun. You may use *but* either way, depending on your audience and your preference.

3. *But for,* though used infrequently, functions as a compound preposition in exactly the same way that *except for* does <there *but for* the grace of God go I>.

4. When *but* (as an adverb) means "only," constructions such as "had he *but* informed the family of his wishes" are standard in written prose. An older, negative form (as in "We weren't *but* two months into the project when . . .") is now found chiefly in speech.

5. *But that,* as in "There is no question *but that* the game has changed" or "I don't doubt *but that* Congress will succeed," is a standard idiom, though in many contexts either word by itself will serve. *But what* (as in "I don't know *but what* you could find it there") is also a standard idiom, but one more likely to be found in speech and in the most informal kinds of writing.

buy **1.** *Noun. Buy* in the sense "bargain" has been in standard use since at least 1879 <many good *buys* at the flea market>.

2. *Verb.* The sense of the verb meaning "accept, believe" is no longer considered slang <few *buy* the idea that such increases are necessary>.

by means of Some assert that this "wordy" preposition should be replaced by *by, in,* or *with.* But *by means of* is often used precisely to avoid a simpler preposition when the simpler one might be ambiguous <learning about the past *by means of* artifacts discovered by archaeologists>. "Short and simple" may often be better, but longer is sometimes clearer.

C

callous, callus These two words are sometimes confused because of similar sound and spelling. *Callous* is generally limited to the sense "feeling no emotion or sympathy" <a *callous* person>. *Callus* is used to refer to a hard area on the skin.

can, may *Can* and *may* are frequently interchangeable in senses denoting possibility <do you think he *may* still be alive?> <those things *can* happen>. Because the possibility of one's doing something may depend on another's acquiescence, *can* and *may* have also become interchangeable in the sense denoting permission <you *can* [*may*] go now if you like>. The use of *can* to ask or grant permission has been common since the 19th century and is well established, though some language commentators feel that *may* is more appropriate in formal contexts. *May* is relatively rare in negative constructions; *cannot* and *can't* are more common in such constructions <the groom *cannot* see the bride until the ceremony begins>.

cannot, can not Both spellings are in use, but *cannot* is more frequent, especially in edited prose.

cannot but, cannot help, cannot help but These phrases all mean the same thing— "to be unable to do otherwise than"—and they are all standard <I *cannot but* recall that I too was once in that position> <I *can-*

not help thinking that their efforts are somehow misdirected> <one *cannot help but* admire his zeal>.

can't seem The expression *can't seem* <I *can't seem* to get any sleep lately> is an idiom that is mostly used in speech. It is an example of what linguists call "raising," the process by which a negative element like *can't* (or some other element) gets moved from a subordinate clause to the main clause. Another well-known example of raising is "I don't think it'll rain today" for "I think it won't rain today." Negative elements often tend to be raised in conjunction with *seem.* Thus, related expressions like *cannot seem, don't seem, did not seem,* etc., are all standard idioms and are not uncommon in print.

canvas, canvass *Canvas,* meaning "strong cloth" or "oil painting," is occasionally spelled *canvass,* but *canvas* remains more common. Similarly, *canvass,* meaning "to solicit votes or opinions," is sometimes spelled *canvas,* but the latter is only a secondary spelling variant.

capability *Capability* is commonly followed by *of* or *for* when it is used with a preposition <they are taught to trust in the *capabilities of* their superiors> <our *capability for* mutual destruction>. It is also commonly followed by *to* and an infinitive <the *capability to* produce mass quantities>.

capable When followed by a preposition, *capable* nearly always appears with *of* <*capable of* eliminating pests>. Use of *capable of* in passive constructions is also found <a substance *capable of* being altered by changes in temperature>, although some language arbiters would insist on converting these to active constructions.

capacity *Capacity,* when it refers to ability, potential, facility, or power, may be followed by *to* and the infinitive <a *capacity to* love>. It may also be followed by *for* and a noun <his *capacity for* mischief>, or *for* and a gerund phrase <a *capacity for* stirring controversy>. When *capacity* is used to designate volume, the preposition *of* follows it <a seating *capacity of* 500>. When denoting a position or role, *capacity* is used more often in the construction *in his* (*her, our,* etc.) *capacity as* than in the construction *in the* (*his, her,* etc.) *capacity of* <in her [the] *capacity* as [of] editor>.

capful See -FUL.

capital, capitol There are a number of things that the spelling *capital* is used for—letters, money, cities—but *capitol* always refers to a building (and is capitalized when denoting the federal Capitol).

care **1.** The verb *care* is often followed by *for* and *about* <the animal was being *cared for* by shelter volunteers> <I don't *care about* that>. *To* and the infinitive may also follow *care* <do you *care to* comment?>.

2. The noun *care* is commonly followed by *for* or *of* <specialized *care for* the aged> <in the *care of* his doctor>.

careen, career The verbs *careen* and *career* look a lot alike, sound a lot alike, and in fact are used a lot alike to refer to movement that is headlong, reckless, or uncontrolled. *Career* is used almost entirely in this sense; *careen* has other meanings as well. Consult a good dictionary for clarification.

careful, careless **1.** *Careful,* when used with a complement, is most often followed by the preposition *of* and a noun or a pronoun, or by *to* and an infinitive <be *careful of* your father-in-law> <had been *careful to* remove their belongings>. When *careful* is used to mean "exercising prudence," however, it may be followed by *about* or *with* <they are *careful about* such things> <be *careful with* the baby>.

2. *Careless* is most often used with *of* or *about* when it takes a complement <*careless of* time> <*careless about* dress>.

3. Both *careful* and *careless* are also used with *in* followed by a noun or gerund <*careful in* choosing a partner> <*careless in* style>.

catsup See CATSUP, KETCHUP, CATCHUP.

cater In current American usage, the usual preposition after *cater* is *to* <she *caters to* their every wish>. In British usage the usual preposition is *for.*

catsup, ketchup, catchup The spellings *catsup* and *ketchup* are used with about equal frequency; *catchup* is not as common as the other two, but it is used. All three spellings are standard.

cause The noun *cause* may be followed by the prepositions *of* and *for* <a *cause of* concern> <a *cause for* alarm>. Occasionally it is followed by the infinitive <she has no *cause* to interfere>.

Celtic As part of the name of a sports team, such as the Boston Celtics, this is pronounced \'sel-tik\. You will also hear this pronunciation in other contexts, and at times from very well-educated speakers. But the closer you get to circles concerned with Celtic lore and languages, the more likely you are to hear \'kel-tik\.

cement, concrete As a term for a mixture of ingredients that sets hard when combined with water, *concrete* is more frequently used—especially in technical writing—than *cement,* although *cement* is some 500 years older. Both words are common in figurative uses <is not a policy set in *concrete*> <it is the *cement* that holds the two parties together>.

center The intransitive verb *center* (meaning "to focus") is most commonly used with the prepositions *at, in, on,* and *around. At* is favored in mathematical contexts, while the others are found in a broad range of contexts. Some object to *center around* as illogical, though it is a standard idiom; if you want to avoid it, you can use *center on* (or *in*) or try *revolve around.*

certain The use of *certain* to mean "of a specific but unspecified character" <the house has a *certain* charm>, though criticized as ambiguous by some, continues to be widely used.

certainly Usage commentators have occasionally objected to the use of *certainly* as an intensifier <it is *certainly* true> <this is *certainly* something to consider>, but such use is perfectly standard in speech and is common enough in writing.

chair **1.** *Verb. Chair* is a verb formed from the noun. It has been in use since the 1920s and is standard <she *chairs* two different committees>.

2. *Noun. Chair* has been used in the sense "chairman, chairwoman" (see next entry) since the middle of the 17th century and is standard <it is for the *chair* to decide>.

chairman, chairwoman, chairperson *Chairman* is the oldest of these words and the most widely used. It has been and still is used of women. *Chairwoman* is an old and entirely respectable word but it seems not to have been used as often as it might, probably because it has long competed with *chairman* in application to women and has recently had competition from *chairperson. Chairperson* is a recent coinage as a gender-neutral term, and, in spite of the attacks of usage writers, has won fairly wide acceptance. All three of these words are in standard use. See also CHAIR 2.

chance **1.** *Noun.* The preposition used most frequently after *chance* is *of* <his *chances of* winning are good>. *Chance* is also used, in varying senses, with *at, for,* and *on* <she has a *chance at* taking the election>

<there is a *chance for* reaching an agreement> <took a *chance on* the lottery>. And it is used with the infinitive <a *chance* to go to Europe>.

2. *Verb*. The verb *chance* may be followed by the prepositions *on* or *upon* <we *chanced upon* him while crossing the fairgrounds>. It is also frequently followed by the infinitive <I *chanced* to pick up a copy>. Occasionally *into* and *by* are used <the celebrity couple *chanced into* a group of reporters> <I *chanced by* a phone booth>.

character *Character* is sometimes used unnecessarily as padding (as in "the furniture is rather rustic in *character*"). But the vagueness of the word can be useful <the negative *character* of these ads>, and it cannot always be easily replaced. You need not forgo use of the word entirely, but your use should have a purpose.

characteristic In general, when the adjective *characteristic* is followed by a preposition, the preposition is *of* <is *characteristic of* this administration>.

chary *Chary* is often followed by *of* and somewhat less often by *about* <a person very *chary of* compliments> <he remains a bit *chary about* giving advice>. Occasionally, *chary* may be found with *as to, in,* or *with* <*chary as to* their prospects> <*chary in* his expression of optimism> <*chary with* financial matters>.

chastened When *chastened* is used with a preposition, it is usually *by* <we left *chastened by* her neg-

ative comments>. *For* is often used to indicate the reason for the chastening <*chastened for* our lack of effort>.

chauvinism, chauvinist The use of *chauvinism* and *chauvinist* to mean "male chauvinism" and "male chauvinist" is often disapproved, since the words do have other meanings (including the original meaning, "excessive patriotism or nationalism"). It is generally advisable to be sure that either your context or your modifiers (e.g., *male chauvinism, female chauvinism, economic chauvinism, literary chauvinism, culinary chauvinism*) make your meaning plain.

cheap **1.** It is sometimes possible for the neutral sense of *cheap,* "inexpensive," to be taken as pejorative, particularly when used directly in front of the noun it modifies <a *cheap* sofa>. The likelihood of the pejorative connotation creeping in is greatest when the noun denotes a physical object—no one is confused about *cheap electric power* or *cheap travel rates.* If you mean to say that an object is not expensive by using *cheap,* you need to be sure your wording makes your meaning unmistakably clear.

2. *Cheap* is an adverb as well as *cheaply.* The adverb *cheap* is most frequently found in contexts of buying and selling, and it regularly follows the word it modifies <he got it *cheap*>. *Cheaply* is used in a wider range of meanings and may either precede or follow the word it modifies <*cheaply* produced movies> <it was all done rather *cheaply*>.

check *Check* as a verb is used with a number of common English particles. *Check into* means "investigate" <*check into* these rumors>. *Check out* is not reserved to a single meaning <*check out* the competition> <*check out* his story> <*check* it *out* with Barbara>. *Check on* is also common <*check on* the infant> <*check on* his progress>, as is *check up on* <*check up on* them for me>. (*Check up* followed by a clause is chiefly British.) And there are also *check over* <*check over* the invitation lists> and *check around* <*check around* to see where he might be>. These usages are all standard idioms.

Chicano *Chicano* first entered American English in the late 1940s, applied by some Mexican-Americans to themselves. It was first used by politically active groups and hence was a term considered offensive by those Mexican-Americans of different or opposed political views. But with wider application, especially since the 1960s, it has become a less politicized term, and objection to it has largely subsided. It is usually capitalized.

childish, childlike *Childish* usually implies a quality such as immaturity or lack of complexity. *Childlike* usually connotes some good quality such as innocence, trustfulness, or ingenuousness; it is also used in neutral description.

choice The notion that *choice* has but a single meaning—namely, "the act of choosing" <I have only one *choice*: A or B> as opposed to "a person or thing chosen" <I have two *choices,* either A or B> —is a false one. You can use the "thing chosen" sense if you need to; it is standard.

circle Some decry the use of the verb *circle* with *around* (or *round*) as redundant. But the historical evidence shows that these words, along with *about,* have been used with *circle* for several centuries <*circle around* the leader> <*circle about* the airport>. Note that *around* (or *round*) can suggest cautious avoidance of or failing to come to grips with something <*circled around* the problem rather than tackling it head-on>.

circumstances Is it better to use *under* or *in* as the preposition that goes with *circumstances* <*under* the *circumstances*> <*in* certain *circumstances*>? The historical evidence shows that both are in good repute and in standard use.

cite, site, sight These three verb homophones should not be confused. *Cite* means "to quote" or "to summon"; *site,* "to place in position"; and *sight,* "to get sight of." The last are also nouns.

civilian The use of *civilian* to distinguish a civilian from a member of a uniformed force (such as the military, the police, or the fire department) is standard. Some have objected to the use of *civilian* to distinguish ordinary people from members of any group, regardless of whether the group is uniformed or not <tax board officials say they have plans to make use of *civilian* volunteers next year>. Our files indicate that such usage is several decades old and is by now standard.

claim In spite of the disapproval of various usage commentators from the 19th century on, *claim* is regularly used to mean "assert, contend, maintain" <they *claim* their study was the first> and not just in the sense "to ask for as a right" <they *claim* the copyright>. The advantage *claim* can have over any of the oft-mentioned substitutes (*contend, assert, maintain,* etc.) is that it regularly introduces a connotation of doubt or skepticism.

clandestine *Clandestine* need not be limited in application to things that are illicit. It is indeed used of things kept secret because they are unlawful, but it is commonly used to suggest simple secrecy, often implying an underlying fear of discovery <a *clandestine* affair>.

classic, classical *Classic* is used in preference to *classical* in two recently established applications, namely, sports <a *classic* defense> and fashion <in *classic* colors>. *Classical* is used of science <*classical* physics> and is also usual in music <*classical* music>. In reference to the civilization of the ancient Greeks and Romans, *classical* is usual but *classic* is not unknown <*classical* [*classic*] Greek sculpture>. In the senses of "serving as a standard of excellence," "memorable," and "typical," *classic* is more common but *classical* is also used <a series of *classic* poems> <made a *classic* error> <in truly *classical* style>.

clean, cleanse Although *clean* is the more common verb, the older *cleanse* continues to be used. It is often used of the human body <*cleanse* the wound>; but mostly *cleanse* is used figuratively <*cleanse* them of their sins>.

clear, clearly Both *clear* and *clearly* are adverbs, but in recent use they do not overlap. *Clear* is most often used in the sense "all the way" <you could see *clear* across the bay>. *Clearly* is used in the sense "in a clear manner" <she writes very *clearly*>.

cliché *Cliché* is in origin a French word for a printing surface, but in English it came to mean "a trite phrase or expression." Since its introduction into English it has been extended from words to ideas to visual images to things of various kinds <his designs make deliberate use of architectural *clichés*>. The unaccented *cliche* is sometimes used, but the accented *cliché* is much more common.

client, customer One difference between these two words is that a customer buys goods whereas a client buys services from a professional (and perhaps especially from a lawyer). In recent use, however, *professional* tends to be construed broadly, so that the difference between goods and services is often blurred. The upshot is that you have some discretion in choosing *client* where in the past *customer* may have been preferred <the broker's *clients*> <the bookie's *clients*>.

climb 1. *Climb,* although originally an irregular verb of the same class as *sing* and *begin,* developed regular inflections, so that its principal parts are *climbed* (past) and *climbed* (past participle). Surviving forms of the old inflections, *clim, clomb,* and *clum,* are dialectal.

2. *Climb down, climb up.* Some usage commentators have attempted to do away with the particles *down* and *up* in combination with *climb,* claiming that *down* is wrong since *climb* means "to go up," and that *up* is simply redundant. Both *climb up* and *climb down,* however, are in perfectly good use as standard idioms.

cling *Cling* is an irregular verb that used to have a past tense and past participle similar to those of *ring*—namely, *clang* and *clung*. For the past two hundred years, however, both past and past participle have taken the form *clung*.

clique The anglicized pronunciation \'klik\ for this French loanword is firmly established but it is less frequent than \'klēk\.

close proximity See PROXIMITY.

coalesce When *coalesce* is used with a preposition, *into* is the one used most often, whatever the sense of the verb <the clouds *coalesced into* a threateningly dark mass>. Less frequently, *coalesce* may be followed by *with* or *in* <our plans *coalesced with* their ideals> <the separate decisions *coalesced in* one grand strategy>. When *coalesce* is used to mean "to unite for a common end," it may be also used with *around* <rep-

resentatives of those interests *coalesced around* the candidate>.

coed The noun *coed,* once an acceptable word for a female student at a coeducational institution, is now in disfavor and is rarely used. The adjective *coed* continues to be used, most often in the sense "open to or used by both men and women" <a *coed* dorm>.

cohort *Cohort* is in standard use to mean "companion, colleague, follower" <her *cohorts* came along to the game>, though some still claim it should only be used with its older meaning, "band or group" <a *cohort* of medieval enthusiasts>.

collaborate *Collaborate* is frequently used with *in, on,* and *with* <*collaborated in* its development> <*collaborating on* a book> <*collaborating with* the authorities>. *With* is often used with either *in* or *on* in the pattern "collaborate with someone in (or on) something" <she *collaborated with* her husband *on* the project>.

collectable, collectible *Collectible* is the more frequent spelling for both the noun and the adjective.

collide Some believe that *collide* can only be used when both objects in the encounter are moving, but there is little historical basis for this belief. Our evidence for the literal sense of *collide* shows that it is used standardly both when all bodies are in motion and when one object is stationary <the two planes

collided in midair> <the car *collided* with the railing>. *Collide* is most often used figuratively—in connection with ideologies, politicians, nations, and the like—and in these uses relative motion is not a consideration.

come and See TRY AND.

comic, comical *Comic* is a much more common word than *comical.* It can be used of anything that is funny <a *comic* character>, and in particular it may stress thoughtful amusement <his plays advance a *comic* perspective on the fate of the author>. *Comical* is not used in that way; it tends to stress spontaneous, unrestrained hilarity <you looked *comical* in that awful dress and silly hat>.

commence Some critics have complained that *commence* is too formal or affected a word and have recommended using *begin* or *start* instead. But *commence* has been in regular use since the 14th century, and has been used by writers of every stripe in all kinds of contexts. You need not routinely change it to *begin* or *start.*

commend When *commend* means "praise," it is usually used in the pattern "*commend* someone *for*" or "*commend* someone *on*" <they *commended* him *for* his effort> <we want to *commend* all of you *on* the diligence you have shown>. When it means "entrust" or "recommend," the pattern is usually "*commend* someone or something *to*" <she *commended* her beloved dog *to* her closest friend> <the group *commends* the book *to* all its members>.

commensurate *Commensurate,* when followed by a preposition, usually takes *with* <an objective *commensurate with* the candidate's own>. It is sometimes also used with *to* <proposed legislation *commensurate to* the expectations of the time>.

commiserate *Commiserate* used intransitively (a use more common now than the transitive use) is most often followed by *with* <sought to *commiserate with* her>. It is also used with *over* <*commiserated over* the bill's failure>, and sometimes both *with* and *over* phrases appear <*commiserated with* them *over* the loss of their house>.

commitment There is only one *t* in the middle of *commitment,* which contrasts with the spelling of *committed, committing, committal,* and *committee.* Take note.

commune The verb *commune,* in its modern usage, is almost always intransitive and followed by *with* <*commune with* nature>.

communicate *Communicate* is usually followed by *with* <she *communicated with* him>, but *to* is standard when there is a direct object <to *communicate to* him the wishes of her government>.

comparatively Some commentators have tried to argue that this adverb should not be used when no comparison is stated or implied. Judging from our evidence, the use is nevertheless standard <a *comparatively* wide outer margin allows for note taking>.

compare to, compare with The conventional rule is this: when you mean "to liken," use *compare to* <shall I *compare* thee *to* a summer's day?>; when you mean "to examine so as to discover the resemblances and differences," use *compare with* <these results *compare* favorably *with* those of 10 years ago>. The rule is usually followed when *compare* is used as an active verb (as it is in the examples above). There is still considerable variation, however, partly because in some contexts either sense of *compare* may apply <he *compares* them *to* [*with*] laws passed in the last century>. Thus, the rule is best regarded as a general guide. When *compared* is used as a detached participle, sometimes introduced by *as,* the prepositions *with* and *to* are equally common <*compared with* [*to*] last year's crop> <as *compared to* [*with*] someone who is self-employed>.

comparison 1. For a discussion of grammatical comparison (as distinct from the word *comparison,* which is treated below), see ABSOLUTE ADJECTIVE; DOUBLE COMPARISON (in Glossary).

2. The word *comparison* is frequently followed by *with* <hardly bears *comparison with* the riches of Holland> <meager findings in *comparison with* those revealed earlier>. It is less frequently followed by *to* <in *comparison to* other cities>. *Between* is used in sentences where both items being compared appear after *comparison* <a *comparison between* Freud's and Jung's versions of psychoanalysis>.

compatible When *compatible* is used with a preposition, it is usually *with* <a view *compatible with* reformist goals> <a device *compatible with* most existing systems>.

competence, competency *Competence* is more frequently used in general than *competency*; *competence* is used in a technical sense in linguistics; and *competency* (or *competencies*) is similarly used in the fields of education and law.

complacent When *complacent* is used with a preposition, the preposition is most likely to be *about* <rather *complacent about* the outcome>. Less frequently used are *with, of,* or *to* <*complacent with* the status quo> <*complacent of* his high standing>. Occasionally *complacent* is used in the sense "complaisant, disposed to please," in which case it may also be used with *to* <less *complacent to* the media than to her own fans>.

complement, compliment *Complement* ("something that completes") is sometimes misspelled as *compliment* ("flattering remark"). Watch that middle vowel. The same caution applies to the adjectives *complementary* and *complimentary*.

complete, completely *Complete* is one of those words some people think are absolute adjectives—adjectives that cannot be modified by *more, most,* or *less*. The word is, however, quite frequently so modified, and you need not worry about using it thus <the most *complete* record yet compiled>. The adverb *completely* is similarly modified, despite occasional objection.

complex Figurative use of this noun, derived from its psychological sense (as in *Oedipus complex*), has been criticized by some but nevertheless remains in frequent modern use <she developed a tennis prodigy *complex*>. It is not used very often in highly serious writing.

compliance The standard pattern in current English is *compliance with* (something) and *compliance of* (something) <in *compliance with* state statutes> <required the *compliance of* car manufacturers>.

compliment, complimentary See COMPLEMENT, COMPLIMENT.

comply The preposition most frequently used with *comply* is *with*, and *with* is always used when the agent is human <you must *comply with* the court order>. When the agent is mechanical, however, either *with* or *to* may be used <permits the bearing mounts to *comply to* the reduced shaft diameter>.

comprise The sense of *comprise* meaning "to compose or constitute" <the branches that *comprise* our government> rather than "to include or be made up of" <our government *comprises* various branches> has been attacked as wrong, for reasons that are unclear. Until recently, it was used chiefly in scientific and technical writing; today it has become the most widely used sense.

concensus See CONSENSUS 3.

concept Some commentators complain of a fad use of *concept* in a sense approximating *idea* <selling the *concept* to them> <a *concept* album>—a usage that has been around since the 16th century but which is prevalent nowadays mostly in the fields of business and entertainment, where it is standard. Our evidence suggests that *concept* is currently not in extensive literary use, but seemingly unfaddish general uses can be found <his *concept* of strategy was to wait and see what the other guy did>.

concern When the noun *concern* means "an uneasy state of interest or anxiety," it is used especially with the prepositions *over, for,* and *about* <*concern over* these issues> <*concern for* her safety> <*concern about* quality>. *With* is also used with this sense <a *concern with* city government>. When *concern* denotes marked interest or involvement, the usual preposition is *with* or *in* <his *concern with* achieving lasting peace> <her *concern in* the matter>.

concerned When the adjective *concerned* suggests worry or anxiety, it can be followed by any of several prepositions. The most frequent are *about* and *for* <*concerned about* public health> <*concerned for* the little tyke>. *Over, at,* and *by* are also used <*concerned over* their unwillingness> <*concerned at* the increasing pressures> <*concerned by* Mr. Roper's attitude>. When *concerned* conveys the notion of interested engagement, *with* is the most common preposition <*concerned with* winning approval>. *In* is also used; it tends to suggest involvement <has long been *concerned in* economic affairs> and is the preposition of choice when something criminal is suggested <he is suspected of being *concerned in* the Dutra murder>. When *concerned* suggests interest or care, it can also be followed by *to* and the infinitive (though this is more common in British English than in American) <is *concerned* not *to* appear weak>.

conciseness, concision *Concision* is currently used about as frequently as *conciseness* <has achieved greater *concision* [*conciseness*] in this rewriting>.

concrete See CEMENT, CONCRETE.

concur *Concur* may be used with various prepositions, primarily *with, in,* and *on* <we *concur with* his opinion> <they have *concurred in* finding him responsible for the mishap> <the two of them *concur on* this one point>. The infinitive can also follow *concur* to mean "to happen together, coincide" <this set of events *concurred* to produce the Industrial Revolution>.

condition Lamented by some as a euphemism (because of its time-honored application to pregnancy), *condition* is nevertheless standard in medical contexts where the precise ailment is unknown or not understood <a troublesome heart *condition*>.

conducive *Conducive* is almost always used with *to* <circumstances *conducive to* scholarly debate>.

confess The intransitive *confess* is often followed by the preposition *to* and either a gerund <*confesses to* having murdered her> or a noun <*confessed to* the crime>. The transitive *confess* is used with a direct (and possibly also an indirect) object <*confessed* his sins to the priest>.

confidant, confidante *Confidant* usually refers to a male, though it is also used of females <he [she] was my friend and *confidant*>. *Confidante* is usually applied to females, but it is also used of males <my wife [husband] and *confidante*>. (Though these gender endings seem to reflect French usage, the French words are actually spelled *confident* and *confidente*.)

confide *Confide* in its intransitive sense, is often used with *in* <they haven't *confided in* me>. *Confide* may also be followed by a dependent clause <she *confides* that no one has yet questioned her about it>. In its transitive sense *confide* may be followed by *to* and the indirect object, which may precede or follow the direct object <*confided to* her psychiatrist the nature of her anxiety> <*confided* his problem *to* his mother>.

confident When the adjective *confident* is followed by a preposition, *in* and *of* are the ones most likely to be used <*confident in* her ability> <*confident of* the ad's success>. Less frequently, *about, as to,* or *on* may be used <*confident about* the market> <*confident as to* the validity of her findings> <*confident on* the issue of wage increases>. Very often, of course, *confident* is followed by a dependent clause <we are *confident* that an agreement will be reached>.

conform When *conform* is followed by a preposition, it is most likely to be *to* <does not *conform to* the usual pattern>. *With* is also frequently used <this *conforms with* our understanding>.

conformity When followed by a preposition, *conformity* usually takes *to* or *with* <its *conformity to* standards of wear> <in *conformity with* international law>. When both related entities follow *conformity,* the first preposition may be *between* or *of* <*conformity between* past and present methods> <*conformity of* his principles with mine>.

congenial When *congenial* is used with a preposition, the preposition is usually *to* <a schedule *congenial to* her work habits>.

congruence For pronunciation, see INFLUENCE 2.

connect *Connect* is used with the prepositions *with* and *to*. Some commentators have tried to limit the use of *with* to figurative senses <he had been *connected with* a secret organization> and of *to* to concrete senses <the white wire *connects to* switch A>; this restriction is generally, but not always, followed in practice. Two things may also be connected *by* still another thing <these items are *connected by* their relation to a third>.

consensus **1.** *Consensus of opinion.* It is thought by some that the phrase *consensus of opinion* is redundant and that *of opinion* should be dropped. But since there are various other types of consensus (e.g., consensus of views, of experts, of values), *consensus of opinion* is really not a redundancy. You must decide whether you want to use *consensus of opinion,* and make your meaning perfectly clear while perhaps running the risk of being censured, or use *consensus* alone and perhaps risk less than full clarity. In any case, you are safe in using *consensus* alone when it is clear that you mean consensus of opinion, and most writers in fact do so.

2. *General consensus.* Whereas *consensus of opinion* is not necessarily a redundancy, *general consensus* in fact seems to be one, since generality is already part of the meaning of *consensus*. You can safely drop *general* and use *consensus* alone.

3. *Concensus.* This misspelling of *consensus* often turns up in publications where it should have been corrected. Resist the tempting influence of *census* when you spell the longer word; the two are not related.

consequent When *consequent* is used with a preposition, the preposition is usually *on* or *upon* <*consequent on* [*upon*] the cessation of hostilities>.

consequential Though *consequential* in the sense "important" is objected to by some, this use has a long history <the most *consequential* of her works>.

consider **1.** *Consider* in the sense "believe to be" can be used with several kinds of complements. It may be followed by a noun <he is *considered* a heavyweight>; an adjective <a river not *considered* dangerous>; an adjectival prepositional phrase <a poet once *considered* of some importance>; two nouns (or a pronoun and a noun), one the direct object and the other its complement <*considers* the effort puffery and no more> <*considers* it blasphemy>; a noun (or pronoun) and an adjective <*considered* the act irresponsible>; or a noun and a phrase introduced by an infinitive <they *consider* an early decision to be unlikely>.

Consider is also used in many of the same constructions with *as*: with a single noun <it had been *considered as* a means to an end>; with an adjective <ended up *considering* it *as* less than desirable>; or with two nouns, or a pronoun and a noun <*considers* liberty *as* a given> <has *considered* it *as* a liability>. It may also be followed by a participle <*considered as* stolen>. Our evidence suggests that the *as* constructions are perfectly idiomatic but are not as common as they once were.

Consider may also be followed by an infinitive phrase <is *considered* to appeal especially to elder voters>. And, finally, it may be followed by a *that* clause <they *considered* that little would come of the arrangement>.

2. In the sense "to think about with regard to taking action," *consider* can also be used with *for* <they *considered* her *for* the post>.

considerable **1.** The adjective *considerable* most commonly follows a determiner, a word like *a, the, his, one,* or *any* <the play was a *considerable* success> <her *considerable* fortune>. These uses are standard in both British and American English. When *considerable* modifies a mass noun, however, with no determiner, there is a slight difference between British and American usage. Both allow *considerable* to be used with nouns for immaterial things <offers the viewer *considerable* pleasure>. But the use of *considerable* with nouns for material things <found *considerable* dirt there> is American and tends to occur in works of a general but not a literary nature.

2. The adverb *considerable* is still alive in speech (as in "the circular saw speeded the work up *considerable*") but is seldom used in edited prose other than fiction. See also FLAT ADVERB (in Glossary).

consistent When *consistent* is used with a preposition, *with* is by far the most common <books *consistent with* the child's language abilities>. Other prepositions are used less often; the choice depends on the intended meaning <should be *consistent in* giving praise> <findings *consistent across* several disciplines> <remained *consistent throughout* this period> <*consistent as to* their purpose>.

consist in, consist of Many writers draw a distinction between *consist in,* "lie, reside (in)" <the painting's originality *consists in* its perspective>, and *consist of,* "to be composed or made up (of)" <the team *consists of* one senior and three junior debaters>. Although the distinction is generally observed, some variation occurs.

consonant When used with a preposition in contemporary English, the adjective *consonant* is followed by *with* <a practice *consonant with* our beliefs>.

constitute See COMPRISE.

contagious, infectious The standard medical distinction is this: Contagious diseases are spread by contact, and infectious diseases are spread by infectious agents. Thus, all contagious diseases are also infectious, but not all infectious diseases are contagious.

In figurative uses, there is no implied distinction between infection and contagion. But a difference in the use of *contagious* and *infectious* is observed: *Contagious* is used of both pleasant and unpleasant things <the idea that terrorism is *contagious*> <an enthusiasm that is *contagious*>, whereas *infectious* is almost always used of pleasant things <an *infectious* smile>.

contemporaneous See CONTEMPORARY.

contemporary *Contemporary* in the sense "present-day, modern," though objected to by some, has been fully established since the late 1940s <*contemporary* literature>. But because *contemporary* can also mean "existing at the same time," some commentators recommend the use of *contemporaneous* if the use of *contemporary* might cause confusion <Byron's *contemporaneous* critics>. *Contemporaneous* is in fact increasingly replacing *contemporary* in such contexts, while *contemporary* is being used chiefly in its "present-day" sense.

contemptible See CONTEMPTUOUS 1.

contemptuous 1. *Contemptible, contemptuous.* Though in earlier centuries these two words were used interchangeably, in current usage they are distinguished. *Contemptible* means "worthy of contempt" <a *contemptible* act>, while *contemptuous* means "showing contempt" <is *contemptuous* of the effort>.

2. When *contemptuous* is used in the predicate position and is followed by a prepositional phrase, the preposition is always *of* <have grown *contemptuous of* the public they are supposed to serve>.

contend The word *contend* is very commonly followed by a clause <she *contends* that she was out at the time>. *Contend* is also used with prepositions, usually *with* <had difficulty *contending with* the traffic>. Less frequently, *contend* is used with *against* <forces *against* which they could not successfully *contend*>. When the object of the preposition is the source of contention, *for* is the choice <*contended for* the Triple Crown in 1992>.

continual, continuous The conventional distinction between these two words is this: *continual* means "steadily recurring" <*continual* skirmishes>, and *continuous* means "continuing without interruption" <*continuous* driving>. The choice of word often seems to depend on whether a given writer perceives the activity as uninterrupted or not <*continual* [*continuous*] progress> <*continuous* [*continual*] crying>. You will have to rely on your own best judgment in the more problematic cases.

continually, continuously *Continually* is used where stress is laid on an uninterrupted flow that continues for an indefinite period of time <have the idea of freedom *continually* before you> <*continually* humid> <*continually* high spirits>. *Continually* is also the adverb of choice when repetition is emphasized <we *continually* reminded them>. *Continuously* is used where stress is laid on a prolonged succession of discrete time periods <the oldest *continuously* published newspaper in the United States> or ongoing recurrence <during that 18-month period, meetings were held *continuously* in the mayor's office>. The two words, however, are sometimes used as if they were interchangeable <*continually* beset by nightmares>; this is hardly surprising, since the standard distinction between the adverbs partially reverses the distinction between the adjectives *continual* and *continuous* (see entry above).

continue on Some dismiss *continue on* as a redundancy, the *on* supposedly being superfluous. Travel writers, on the other hand, find the phrase useful <we *continued on* to Tunis>. It is also used in other contexts <he *continued on* this way for many years>. There seems to be no good reason to avoid it.

continuous See CONTINUAL, CONTINUOUS.

continuously See CONTINUALLY, CONTINUOUSLY.

contrast **1.** As a noun, *contrast* is used with the prepositions *between, with,* and *to* <the *contrast between* old and new> <makes a *contrast with* her earlier style of writing> <offers a *contrast to* his own efforts>. When preceded by *in, contrast* may be followed by either *to* or with; *to* is somewhat more common in American English <in *contrast to* the relatively loose organization> <in *contrast with* other disciplines>.

2. As a verb, *contrast* is used with the prepositions *with* or *to*; *with* is used more frequently <*contrasted* her clean apartment *with* her boyfriend's messy digs> <*contrasting* their production methods *to* those of their rival>.

convenient As a predicate adjective, *convenient* can be followed by the infinitive <it is more *convenient to* order directly>. It can also be followed by prepositional phrases introduced by *for* or *to. For* is used mostly for persons or their activities <a *convenient* way *for* you to access it> <*convenient for* storing stationery>. *To* is used for persons <a decision *convenient to* them politically> but also for places <a location *convenient to* the mall>.

conversant *Conversant* usually takes the preposition *with* <is *conversant with* Sanskrit>. It also takes *in,* but less frequently <must be *conversant in* such matters>.

convict When the verb *convict* is followed by a preposition, the preposition is usually *of* <*convicted of* perjury>. Less frequently, *convict* is used with *on* <*convicted on* two counts of armed robbery>.

convince, persuade Earlier usage writers tried to maintain a rigid distinction between these two words, arguing that *convince* meant simply "bring about mental acceptance" and *persuade* meant "bring about mental acceptance followed by action." Such commentators thus rejected the use of *convince* followed by an infinitive <sought to *convince* them to halt the bombing>, claiming that only *persuade* could be used in such cases. For most people born after the 1920s, however, this use of *convince* sounds entirely standard. Also standard is the use of *convince* followed by a phrase beginning with *of* <*convinced of* the need> or a clause usually beginning with *that* <*convinced that* they can win>.

Persuade, for its part, has indeed long been used to imply action <was *persuaded* to bring her daughter home early>. But it also has been and is still used in the purely mental sense in which no action is implied <I wasn't *persuaded* of the innocence of it all>. In short, *convince* and *persuade* have moved into each other's sphere of influence over the years, and in many cases can be used more or less interchangeably.

cop The use of *cop* for "police officer" has gained respectability. *Cop* is used regularly in newspapers and magazines in the United States, Great Britain, and other countries using British English; it is common in novels and occasionally turns up in collections of essays, although it does not appear often in the most formal kinds of writing.

cope *Cope* in the sense "to deal with difficulties" has long been used with the preposition *with* <she was having trouble *coping with* her mother>. Around the middle of this century *cope* began to be used absolutely, with no preposition and no following object <he could no longer *cope*>. The latter usage, though objected to by some, is by now established as standard.

correct *Correct* is on some lists of ABSOLUTE ADJECTIVES (see Glossary). It has, however, been used in the comparative <his version seems more *correct* than hers> and superlative <recommends his own as most *correct*>.

correspond *Correspond,* in the senses meaning "to be in conformity or agreement" or "to compare closely, match," may be followed by either *to* or *with*; *to* seems to be more frequent <a reference that does not *correspond to* any published source>. When meaning "to write to someone," *correspond* is used with *with* exclusively <we *correspond with* them frequently>.

could care less, couldn't care less The negative *couldn't care less* is the older form of the expression. No one knows how the positive form developed. Some critics disparage it as illogical, but it is used nonetheless. Defenders of *could care less* point out that it is meant to be sarcastic. But it is easier to convey sarcasm by the spoken word than by the written word, so more writers choose the clearer *couldn't care less.*

could of See OF 2.

council, counsel These two words are sometimes confused, especially *council* for *counsel. Council* generally stands for some sort of deliberative or administrative body, while *counsel* is used for advice or for a lawyer and as a verb meaning "to advise" or "to consult."

counterproductive If *counterproductive* is a vogue word, as some critics have charged, its vogue has lasted for more than a quarter of a century and shows no sign of abating. You can use it if you need it.

couple, *noun* **1.** *Agreement. Couple* is a singular noun but it often takes a plural verb <the *couple* have been known to be extravagant>. Usually the plural verb appears when the sentence also has a pronoun referring to *couple* <the young *couple* were driving to their new home> since the pronoun will almost always be *they, their,* or *them.* The governing principle here is notional agreement: If the writer is thinking of two people as individuals, the verb is plural; if the writer is thinking of them as a unit, the verb is singular <the *couple* has two children> <the *couple* owns a house in Del Mar>. *They, their,* and *them* have been used to refer to nouns and pronouns that take singular verbs for centuries <the *couple* plans to relocate their business>, though many newspaper editors seem not to realize it. Use of the plural verb may work in some instances <the *couple* plan to relocate their business>, but in others you may have some complicated rewriting to do. British English generally prefers the plural verb.

2. *A couple of.* Some handbooks call *a couple of* colloquial or informal, but the phrase has been in use for 500 years <*a couple of* lost children>. Others have objected to the use of the phrase to mean "a small but indefinite number"<in just *a couple of* years>, but many notable writers have used it in that sense.

couple, *adjective* The adjective use of *a couple,* without *of,* has been called nonstandard, but it is not. In both British and American English it is standard before a word (such as *more*) indicating degree <a *couple* more tricks>. Its use before an ordinary plural noun is an Americanism, common in speech and in informal writing <they live a *couple* houses down the street> <their first *couple* recordings>. It is most frequently used with periods of time <a *couple* weeks> and numbers <a *couple* hundred> <a *couple* dozen>.

course *Course* as used in such phrases as *in the course of* or *during the course of,* is sometimes considered redundant for *during, while, at,* or other shorter alternatives. But phrases like these are often used for rhythm or space in a sentence—to keep other, important words from becoming too tightly packed to be immediately understood. In addition, these phrases can add emphasis to the notion of duration. Depending on their context, they can be either useful <when *in the course of* human events> or unnecessary (as in "were consolidated *during the course of* 1995"). You need not avoid them on principle, but you should weigh their use carefully.

craft Some usage commentators have turned thumbs down to *craft* used as a verb <her skill at *crafting* agreements>. But *craft* is well established in current American use both as a verb and as a participial adjective <finely *crafted* stories>. It is also sometimes used in British English.

credence, credibility The problem here involves the phrases *give credence to* and *lend credence to*. When the subject of the phrase is a person, the meaning of *credence* is the familiar one of "belief" <no one could *give* any *credence to* these ridiculous reports>; this sense is present even when the sentence is passive and the person understood <we question whether the stories should be *lent* any *credence*>. When the subject of these phrases is inanimate, we get a use closer in meaning to *credibility,* "trustworthiness" <a trend that *lends credence to* the view> <such findings *give credence to* earlier theories>. This use, which is sometimes criticized, is of 20th-century origin and seems to be increasing, especially in *lend credence to*. It is standard in both British and American English.

credibility See CREDENCE, CREDIBILITY; CREDULITY, CREDIBILITY.

credit **1.** A view is sometimes asserted that the verb *credit* should not be used to attribute something unfavorable or discreditable <insiders *credit* terrorists for the explosion>. This view overgeneralizes what is usually done into what must always be done. *Credit* is indeed usually used in a positive sense <have *credited* the show with creating the television news magazine format>, but not always. You may want to be credited with something I find reprehensible (as in the explosion example above). And *credit* is also used for things that fall between the laudable and the blameworthy <the difference was *credited* to timing> <the shortage of paper must be *credited* as a significant factor>.

2. *With* is the preposition most commonly linked with *credit*, but it is by no means the only one. The examples above also show *for, to,* and *as*.

credulity, credibility *Credulity* and *credibility* come close in meaning only when used with such verbs as *strain, tax,* or *stretch*. Even here, their use is quite straightforward in most instances. *Credulity* is used of the receiver <such lame dialogue taxes the audience's *credulity*>. *Credibility* is used of the sender <the

author's *credibility* as a journalist is stretched to the limit in this book>.

creep The predominant form of both the past tense and past participle is *crept* <the cat *crept* toward its victim> <a rate that has recently *crept* up>. But, like *leap, kneel,* and *dream, creep* has also developed the more regular past and past participle *creeped. Creeped* is generally heard in speech; in print, *crept* is still the usual form.

criterion, criteria The usual plural form of the singular *criterion* is *criteria* <the ability to communicate effectively was identified as the most important *criterion*> <several *criteria* were advanced>. *Criteria* is in fact more common than the singular *criterion,* and it is undoubtedly this frequency that has led to its perception by many as a singular. Although the singular *criteria* is found mostly in speech (as in "that's the main *criteria*"), it is not entirely absent from print, to the dismay of language commentators and editors. It has not yet reached the point of unquestioned acceptability, however. See also LATIN PLURALS.

criticize There is a neutral use of *criticize* that implies measured judgment or evaluation <the students' performance was favorably *criticized* by their professor>. But the most common use in recent years is the one implying censure <*criticized* the police for using violence>. It is probably the relatively high frequency of this "censure" sense that has caused the neutral sense to begin to carry connotations of disfavor and be increasingly replaced by *critique* as a verb (see CRITIQUE).

critique *Critique* has, despite grumbling from some critics, become firmly established as a verb. The negative overtones of *criticize* (see preceding entry) seem to have led to the revival of *critique* (which has been in intermittent use as a verb since 1751). In a headline like "Betty Friedan Critiques the Women's Movement" (*N.Y. Times*), you can see the usefulness of *critique*. *Criticize* would be interpreted as "censure," and *review* would suggest more of a historical overview than a critical examination.

culminate **1.** When *culminate* is used with a preposition, the choice is usually *in* <a depression that *culminated in* suicide>. *Culminate* is also occasionally followed by *with* <the celebration *culminates with* the sounding of the gong>.

2. The transitive use of *culminate* is no longer as rare as it once was <these summit talks *culminate* a long period of rapprochement>.

cum *Cum* was taken over into English from Latin in the 19th century. It is used in English primarily as a sort of combining word attached to the preceding and following nouns or adjectives by hyphens <her friend-*cum*-psychoanalyst Mary> <a tough-*cum*-innocent quality>. *Cum* is used mainly in writing and is standard in a considerable variety of contexts. It is fairly often italicized.

cupful The common plural is *cupfuls*; the variant *cupsful* is only occasionally found. See also -FUL.

cured When *cured* is followed by a preposition, it is usually *of* <he was *cured of* the habit>, though *from* was formerly also used in such cases.

curriculum *Curriculum* has two plurals: *curricula* and *curriculums*. *Curricula* is quite a bit more frequent, but both are standard. For other foreign plurals, see LATIN PLURALS.

customer See CLIENT, CUSTOMER.

cute *Cute* has been deplored by some commentators, who seem to find it too cute a word. It continues to be used, of course, but mostly in speech (real or fictional) and in informal writing.

D

dais The usual pronunciation is \ˈdā-əs\, rhyming with *pay us*. The second most common pronunciation is \ˈdī-əs\, as though the word were spelled (as it is, in fact, sometimes misspelled) *dias*.

dare *Dare* is both an ordinary verb and an auxiliary verb. As an auxiliary verb, *dare* is regularly followed by an infinitive phrase without *to* <no one *dared* say a word>. It has in its present tense the uninflected third-person singular *dare* <he *dare* not do anything upset-

ting now>. As a regular verb, *dare* has *dares* in the present third-person singular, and can be followed by an infinitive phrase with *to* <she *dares to* criticize me>. When preceded by other auxiliaries (such as *might, would,* and *do*), *dare* is followed by the infinitive without *to* <I wouldn't *dare* ask them> <do we *dare* call it quits?>.

daresay, dare say The one-word styling of this compound verb is slightly more common. It is used in the first-person singular of the present tense <I *daresay* your claim is a weak one>. In its transitive use (as in the example above), *daresay* is followed by a clause. Formerly the clause would never have been introduced by *that,* but in recent use *that* occurs <I *daresay that* your claim is a weak one>.

dastardly *Dastardly* is still alive and well in the language. Once meaning "cowardly," it has for the past hundred years or so been used to suggest underhandedness and treachery <a *dastardly* scheme to eliminate the opposition>. This use has spawned another heavily rhetorical use of *dastardly* that simply expresses disapproval, as of something considered villainous <a *dastardly* speech promoting white supremacy>.

data *Data* has become quite independent of *datum,* of which it was originally the plural. It occurs in two constructions: (1) as a plural noun (like *earnings*), taking a plural verb and plural modifiers (such as *these, many, a few*) but not cardinal numbers <these *data* show that

we're out of the recession>; and (2) as an abstract mass noun (like *information*), taking a singular verb and singular modifiers (such as *this, much,* or *little*) <much *data* on the subject is available>. Both constructions are standard. The plural construction is more common in print, evidently because the house editorial style of several publishers mandates it. See also LATIN PLURALS.

date When the verb *date* is used to point to a date of origin, it may be used with *from, back to,* or *to* <these vases *date from* the early Ming period> <the poem *dates back to* 1843> <the dispute *dates to* Japan's annexation of the islands>.

datum See DATA.

days See ADVERBIAL GENITIVE (in Glossary).

dead Sometimes considered to be an ABSOLUTE ADJECTIVE (see Glossary).

deal **1.** *Deal* belongs to a class of regular verbs including *feel, creep, kneel,* and *mean* in which the past tense and past participle have a short vowel (\e\) contrasting with the long vowel of the infinitive (\ē\). Some of these (see KNEEL; CREEP) have alternative forms, but *deal* has only *dealt* <*dealt* out two sandwiches apiece> <*dealt* him a blow>.

2. Use of the noun *deal* in the senses "transaction," "bargain," or "arrangement, agreement" has been thought slightly vulgar or infelicitous in the past, but these uses are now standard <a done *deal*> <what a

deal!> <the *deal* between the governor and the legislature>.

3. When the intransitive verb *deal* means "concern oneself" or "take action," its usual preposition is *with* <the book *deals with* education> <trying to *deal with* her son's death>.

When *deal* is used in relation to selling—literally or figuratively—the usual preposition is *in* <*deals in* insurance>.

dear, dearly The adverbs *dear* and *dearly* are interchangeable only in contexts dealing with cost <has cost us *dear* [*dearly*]>. *Dearly* is used in other contexts <loves him *dearly*>.

debacle This word was borrowed from French and is its second syllable is normally stressed as in that language: \di-ˈbä-kəl\ or, less often, \di-ˈbak-əl\.

debar When it is used with a preposition, *debar* most often appears with *from* <*debarred from* further negotiations>.

debut The verb *debut,* disapproved of by some, is standard in newspaper and magazine articles, since newsy writing often discusses first appearances of people, products, and the like. It seems to have almost no use in literature and other more formal writing. Intransitive uses <the show *debuted* in 1986> have been around since 1830, but transitive uses <*debuting* their fall line>, which have a more jargonish flavor, only since the 1950s.

decide Intransitive *decide* is used with several prepositions, of which *on, upon, for,* and *against* are the most common <*decided on* the latter> <*decide upon* it soon> <*decided for* the defendant> <*decided against* the proposition>. Sometimes a phrase may replace *for* <*decided* in favor of the defendant>. *Between* and *about* are also used <must *decide between* A and B> <still *deciding about* the house>.

deem A few commentators have labeled *deem* "pretentious." But the word is in wide literary and journalistic use and has been for generations <*deemed* it wise to go slow>. You may use it with impunity.

defect When *defect* is followed by a preposition, either *in* or *of* is chosen <the grave *defects in* [*of*] our foreign policy>.

defective, deficient The modern tendency is to use *defective* to emphasize a flaw <a *defective* pane of glass> <*defective* eyesight>, and *deficient* to emphasize a lack <*deficient* in judgment> <*deficient* strength>. See also DEFICIENT.

defend *Defend* may be followed by *against* or *from* <playing deep to *defend against* a pass> <*defended* herself *from* criticism>.

deficient When *deficient* is used with a preposition, the preposition is almost always *in* <a panel *deficient in* expertise>. See also DEFECTIVE, DEFICIENT.

defile When used with a prepositional phrase expressing means or agent, *defile* is followed by *by* or *with; by* occurs a little more frequently than *with* <the countryside *defiled by* billboards> <boots *defiled with* blood>.

definite **1.** This word is sometimes misspelled *definate.* Watch out for that second *i.*

2. *Definite, definitely.* Some commentators have objected to the use (or overuse) of these words as intensifiers <the quarterback was a *definite* hero today> <they were *definitely* ill at ease>. The use is established in general prose, but it seems to have made few inroads in literature and virtually none in any sort of formal writing.

degree The phrase *to a degree* originally meant (and still does in older literary English) "to the last degree" or "to a remarkable extent" <she is in most things sharp *to a degree,* but in others quite dull>. In current American usage, however, it means "in a moderate measure" or "in a small way" <*to a degree,* you are justified in complaining>. The newer sense has been objected to by some older critics, but it is established as standard. Standard, too, are phrases of the form *to a . . . degree,* <*to a* considerable *degree*> <*to an* extraordinary *degree*>.

déjà vu **1.** *Déjà vu* is a psychological term brought into English from French just after the turn of the century. It was used for an illusory feeling of having previously experienced something that was in fact happening for the first time. When it began to appear in popular writing it took on an additional meaning: "something overly or unpleasantly familiar" <I'm getting a strong sense of *déjà vu* from this movie>. And this popular use has produced an adjective <there was something *déjà vu* about the food there>. Both noun and adjective are now well established in professional writing.

2. The most common form of *déjà vu* has both accents and no hyphen. The word is still italicized about half the time.

delectable *Delectable* has been regarded variously as ironic, gushy, and arch by its critics, but you need not give a passing thought to the criticism. If the word fits, use it <a *delectable* dish> <*delectable* illustrations>.

delusion, illusion *Delusion* and *illusion* are often used in ways that overlap in meaning. *Delusion* is the stronger word; it denotes a longer lasting, more tenacious, and sometimes more harmful or dangerous notion <paranoid *delusions*> <*delusions* of grandeur>. *Illusion* seldom implies mental derangement, or even an inability to distinguish between the true and the false <artistic *illusion*> <a lover's *illusions*>. *Illusion* is the more common word in general contexts.

demand The noun *demand* is commonly used with the prepositions *for, on* or *upon,* and *of* <the *demand*

for lawyers> <*demands on* [*upon*] our time> <the *demands of* her career>.

demise Some feel that *demise* is a pretentious term for *death* or that it should not be used in a sense close to *decline*. Nevertheless, in current use (of a nonlegal sort) *demise* most often means "death" <met his *demise* on a cliff face>, or "a cessation of existence or activity" <bad business decisions caused the company's *demise*>. These uses are standard.

depart **1.** Quite a number of prepositions are used with *depart;* the choice is determined by the meaning and purpose of the prepositional phrase. The most common prepositions are *on, in,* or *at* for the time <*departed on* June 19> <*departed in* late December> <*departs at* 3:30>; *on* for the nature of the activity <*departing on* a visit home>; *for* for the destination <*departing for* Los Angeles>; and *from* for the point of departure, whether physical or nonphysical <*departed from* Denver> <*departs from* convention>.

2. Transitive use of *depart,* if once perhaps uncommon, is now standard <we *departed* San Francisco at noon> <he *departed* this life Saturday, Oct. 3>.

depend In most senses *depend* is followed by *on* or *upon* <life *depends on* [*upon*] food> <you can *depend on* [*upon*] me>. *Depend* is also used absolutely, though chiefly in conversation <Can I come? It *depends*>.

dependent **1.** *Adjective.* Like the verb *depend,* the adjective *dependent* is frequently used with *on* or *upon*

<the child is *dependent on* [*upon*] his parents>. The spelling *dependant*, once in use for the adjective, is no longer current.

2. *Noun.* The noun is usually spelled *dependant* in British English and *dependent* in American English.

deprive *Deprive* is usually used in the construction "*deprive* (someone or something) *of* (something)" <the painting deliberately *deprives* its subject *of* its individuality>.

de rigueur *De rigueur* is occasionally misspelled. There is a *u* both before and after the *e*.

derisive, derisory *Derisive* and *derisory* are sometimes used as synonyms in contemporary writing, but most often writers use *derisive* in its original sense, "causing or expressing derision" <*derisive* laughter>, and use *derisory* when they mean "worthy of ridicule" <a *derisory* sum>.

derive *Derive* is usually used with a prepositional phrase, which nearly always begins with *from* <a French loanword ultimately *derived from* Latin>.

derogate In its intransitive senses, *derogate* is used with *from* <some are trying to *derogate from* his reputation as a leader>.

derogation *Derogation,* when followed by a complement, usually takes *of* <a serious *derogation of* his influence and prestige>.

desert, deserts, dessert The problem here is one of spelling. There are two nouns spelled *desert.* The first of these is the barren *desert,* which, perhaps because of its distinct pronunciation, is infrequently mistaken for the others. The second *desert* is related to *deserve* and is pronounced like *dessert.* It is frequently used as a plural, especially in the phrase *just deserts.* The most common error is the substitution of *desert* for *dessert* ("sweet food"). Care, perhaps assisted by a dictionary, is all that is needed here.

design, intend Some maintain that *design* is overused and that *intend* is usually preferable. While there are indeed contexts in which the two words are nearly interchangeable <an event *designed* [*intended*] to show off the candidate's popularity> <moves *intended* [*designed*] to get his goat>, the automatic substitution of *intend* will not make you a better writer. Rather, stop and think (and consult your dictionary) when you go to write *design;* sometimes *intend* will be the better choice.

desirous While *desirous to* is sometimes still used <was *desirous to* gain her respect> *desirous of* is the more common modern construction <*desirous of* her respect>.

desist When *desist* takes a complement in the form of a prepositional phrase, the preposition is usually *from* <the city has been ordered to *desist from* further

levies>. Less frequently, *desist* is followed by *in* <has *desisted in* his effort to acquire the company>.

despair The verb *despair,* when used with a preposition, is usually used with *of* <*despaired of* winning>.

despoil When *despoil* is used with a preposition, it is *of* <*despoiled* the Aztecs *of* their wealth>.

dessert See DESERT, DESERTS, DESSERT.

destined *Destined* is almost always used with a preposition, either *to* or *for. Destined to* is most common when it is followed by an infinitive <a relationship *destined* to last>. When *destined* is used with *for,* it is followed by a noun or noun phrase <the younger son was *destined for* the priesthood>.

destruct, self-destruct *Destruct* is an old (17th-century) verb that reappeared as part of aerospace jargon in the 1950s <the missile will *destruct* upon impact>. It is seldom found outside technical contexts. *Self-destruct* was popularized by its use in the television series *Mission Impossible* <this tape will *self-destruct* in five seconds>. This verb rapidly established itself and is now standard. *Self-destruct* is also used as an adjective <a *self-destruct* mechanism>.

destructive When it is used with a preposition, *destructive* is most often used with *of* or *to,* with *of* occurring more frequently <*destructive of* firmly established ideas> <*destructive to* the animal's habitat>.

detract, distract The issue here is whether *detract* may replace *distract* in the phrase "*distract* (the) attention." The fact is that while "*distract* (the) attention" is far more common, "*detract* (the) attention" (which makes use of an older sense, "to divert") is also found in the works of standard authors <all the publicity *detracts* attention from the real accomplishment>.

When *detract* is used with a preposition, it is used with *from* <I didn't want to *detract from* your enjoyment>.

deviate When *deviate* is used with a preposition, it is most often used with *from* <she never *deviated from* her story>.

device, devise *Devise* is sometimes mistakenly used where *device* is expected. Mind your spelling.

devolve When used with a preposition, *devolve* usually appears with *on* or *upon* <his estate *devolved on* a distant cousin> <after the general fell, command *devolved upon* the colonel>. Less frequently, *devolve* is used with *to* or *into* <authority on this matter *devolves to* the states> <the peaceful protest *devolved into* skirmishes with police>. *Devolve* followed by *from*, at one time relatively rare, is becoming a little more frequent (perhaps influenced by *evolve*) <higher import taxes, which have *devolved from* years of trade imbalances>.

diagnose Complaints have been lodged against use of the verb *diagnose* with a person, rather than a condition or problem, as its object <*diagnosed* the patient>. But the usefulness of this sense of *diagnose* is obvious, and its use may well increase.

dialogue **1.** The spelling *dialogue* is much more commonly used than *dialog.*

2. Some commentators seem concerned about the sense of *dialogue* that means "an exchange of ideas and opinions" <the need now is for Palestinians and Israelis to hold a meaningful *dialogue*>. However, it is now standard.

3. The verb *dialogue* (which was formed from the noun as discussed above) is also standard <our attempt to *dialogue* with them proved a failure>, though deplored by many.

dice See DIE *noun,* DICE.

dichotomy *Dichotomy* is used in standard prose to mean "division" or "split" <a *dichotomy* between practice and theory> <a *dichotomy* between written and spoken evidence>. *Dichotomy* is also sometimes used to mean "paradox" or "problem," often in a rather vague way that suggests the writer is simply using a fancy, academic-sounding word for effect. If you want to use *dichotomy,* it would be best to stick to the "division" sense.

dictum While the plurals *dicta* and *dictums* are both in standard use, *dicta* is quite a bit more commonly used. See also LATIN PLURALS.

die, *verb* *Die* in various senses is used with a number of different prepositions. *Of* seems to be the most commonly used <*dying of* embarrassment>. *From* is also common <*dying from* fatigue>. *For* is frequently used <*dying for* a cigarette>. Other prepositions are also possible <the bill *died in* committee> <the secret *died with* him> <their anger *died at* these words>. *Die* is often used with the adverbs *away, down,* and *out* <criticism *died away*> <the storm *died down*> <the species *died out*>.

die *noun,* **dice** The use of the singular *dice,* rather than *die,* for one of the small cubes thrown in various games is objected to by some. Dice players use *dice* in speech, but in print the singular is usually *die.*

differ When *differ* means "to be unlike" and is followed by a preposition, it is followed by *from* <the laws of this state *differ from* those of neighboring states>. When *differ* means "to disagree," it is usually followed by *with* <*differs with* the Pentagon on the use of preemptive strikes>. *Among* is also found with the "disagree" sense <they *differ among* themselves>.

Several prepositions—*on, over, in, as to, about*—are used to indicate the subject of the difference <we *differ on* [*over, in*] religious matters> <they *differ as to* [*about*] the dating of the site>.

When *with* follows *differ* in its "be unlike" sense, *with* means something like "in the case of" <dietary preferences *differ with* each culture>.

different The use of *different* after a number <at least three *different* speakers>, is sometimes objected to on the ground that it is unnecessary. But this use of *different* is simply for emphasis. See also DIFFERENT FROM, DIFFERENT THAN.

different from, different than Both of these phrases are standard, in spite of some critics' disliking *different than.* Each form has its particular virtues. *Different from,* the more common, works best when followed by a noun or a pronoun <the new proposal is very *different from* the old one> <her view is so *different from* his>. *Different than* works best when a clause follows <expecting a *different* result *than* to be left penniless> <she looks little *different* now *than* we remember her from our school days>. *Different than* is also used in place of *different from* before the noun or pronoun <*different than* the old proposal> <*different than* mine>, though some editors may change it to *different from.* See also THAN.

British English allows *different to,* but the phrase is rare in American English.

differentiate When *differentiate* is used with a preposition, it is most often *from* <one of the things that *differentiated* a gentleman *from* a commoner>. Less frequently, *differentiate* is used with *between* <to *differentiate between* prose and poetry>.

dilemma Some insist that *dilemma* can only denote a choice between two or more unpleasant alternatives

<presents this *dilemma:* raise taxes or reduce services>. While this use is standard, *dilemma* is equally common in instances where no clear alternatives are expressed or implied <the traditional *dilemma* of how to secure campaign financing>. In this use the word becomes very close in meaning to *problem, difficulty, predicament.* Though objected to by some, the use is standard.

direct, directly These adverbs are sometimes interchangeable <flew *direct* [*directly*] to Chicago> <buy *direct* [*directly*] from the manufacturer>. *Directly* is used more often than *direct,* having uses and meanings that it does not share with *direct.* An important exclusive use of *directly* is to precede the word or phrase it modifies <*directly* relevant> <the road runs *directly* east and west>.

disagree When *disagree* is used with a preposition, the preposition is usually *with* <he *disagreed with* me on every point> <fried food *disagrees with* me>. Other prepositions are also used <they *disagreed about* [*over*] the exact nature of the conflict> <*disagreeing on* virtually every topic>.

disappointed When *disappointed* is used with a preposition in contemporary writing, it may take *about, at, by, over,* or *with* <*disappointed about* [*at, by, over, with*] the decision>. *Disappointed in* is also prevalent <*disappointed in* himself>.

disapprove When used with a preposition, *disapprove* is generally used with *of* <*disapproves of* the practice>. When the object of the preposition is the one disapproving, however, *by* is used <*disapproved by* the school board>.

disassociate See DISSOCIATE, DISASSOCIATE.

disburse, disperse Don't confuse *disburse,* "to pay out," with *disperse,* "to scatter."

discontent The noun *discontent* may be followed by *with* <workers' *discontent with* the new management>. Less frequently, *discontent* is used with *over* <expressed *discontent over* Congress's activities>.

discourage When *discourage* is used with a preposition, it is usually *from,* which in turn is often followed by a gerund phrase as its object <was *discouraged from* pursuing a literary career>. Occasionally *discourage from* is followed by a noun phrase <*discouraged from* the use of medications>.

discreet, discrete The history and spelling of *discreet* and *discrete* are closely intertwined, but in current usage they are distinguished. *Discreet* means "capable of keeping a secret" <very *discreet*> while *discrete* means "individually distinct" <*discrete* components>.

disinterest, disinterestedness *Disinterest* is used primarily to mean "absence of interest" <acknowledged voter *disinterest* in the issue>. It is also used, less frequently, as a synonym of *disinterestedness,* meaning "impartiality" <his methods reflect a studied *disinterest* in the outcome>. *Disinterestedness* is more common in this sense. See also DISINTERESTED, UNINTERESTED.

disinterested, uninterested In current use, *disinterested* has basically two meanings: "unbiased" <a *disinterested* decision> <*disinterested* intellectual curiosity>, and "not interested" <seemed *disinterested* in her work>, of which the latter is also the basic meaning of *uninterested.* Some critics object to the second use, but it is standard, and may even be chosen for purposes of emphasis or to suggest a loss of interest <became *disinterested* in the subject>.

disinterestedness See DISINTEREST, DISINTERESTEDNESS.

dislike 1. *Noun. Dislike* can take the prepositions *of* and *for* <a *dislike of* salty food> <expressed *dislike for* the new teacher>. The phrase *take a dislike* usually takes *to* as its preposition <*took a* strong *dislike to* the man>.

2. *Verb.* The verb *dislike* can take, besides a noun object <*dislikes* the ocean>, a participial phrase <*dislikes* having to take the subway> or, less commonly, an infinitive phrase <I *dislike* to disturb you at home>.

dismayed *By* is the usual preposition after *dismayed* <*dismayed by* his girlfriend's refusal>. *With* and *at* may also be used <*dismayed with* their negative attitude> <*dismayed at* the size of the job>. *Dismayed* can also be followed by the infinitive <*dismayed* to discover that she had lost>.

dispense *Dispense* is often used in the fixed expression *dispense with,* which means "to set aside, discard" <*dispensing with* the usual introduction> or "to do without" <could *dispense with* such a large staff>. When *dispense* is used in any of its senses involving portioning out or administering, and the phrase denotes the receiver, *dispense* is naturally used with *to* <*dispensing* medicines *to* the sick>.

disperse See DISBURSE, DISPERSE.

dispossess *Dispossess* is sometimes used with the preposition *of* <was *dispossessed of* his property>.

disqualify When used with a preposition, *disqualify* is used with either *from* or *for* <a conviction for perjury *disqualified* him *from* being a witness> <he was *disqualified for* cheating>.

disregard The noun *disregard* may be followed by *for* or *of* <a *disregard for* the safety of the passengers> <a *disregard of* legal restraints>. The phrases *with disregard for* and *with disregard of* are both quite common <*with disregard for* [*of*] the truth>; however, when *disregard* is preceded by *in,* it is followed by *of* <*in disregard of* the realities>.

dissatisfied, unsatisfied Though *dissatisfied* and *unsatisfied* appear to be synonyms, there are distinctions to be made. *Unsatisfied* is more frequently used to modify nonhuman terms (such as *ambition, debts, curiosity, demands, claims*) than human ones, and the meaning is generally "unfulfilled" or "unappeased" <their demand was left *unsatisfied*> <our curiosity went *unsatisfied*>. *Dissatisfied,* in contrast, is used primarily with respect to persons or groups in the sense of "not pleased or gratified" <these *dissatisfied* workers voted with their feet> <the tenants were *dissatisfied* with the repairs>.

While both *dissatisfied* and *unsatisfied,* when used with a preposition, are usually followed by *with,* both words may be followed by *by* <*dissatisfied with* the working conditions> <*unsatisfied by* the last-minute effort>.

dissent When *dissent,* as a noun or verb, is followed by a preposition, the preposition is usually *from* <*dissenting from* the prevailing opinion> <wrote in *dissent from* the majority opinion>.

dissimilar Some insist that *dissimilar* should be followed by *to* when it needs the complement or a prepositional phrase <were not *dissimilar to* those we identified previously>, but in actual usage *dissimilar* is just as likely to be followed by *from* <the defense's list was markedly *dissimilar from* the prosecution's>.

dissociate, disassociate *Dissociate* and *disassociate* share the sense "to separate from association or union with another," and both words, when used with a preposition, most often take *from* <*dissociated* [*disassociated*] himself *from* the business>. Both are in current good use, but *dissociate* is more common.

distaff *Distaff* has been disparaged as old-fashioned or mildly offensive to women (it originally denoted a staff for holding flax for spinning, and later came to mean "woman's work or domain"). But the adjective use of *distaff* shows no sign of waning. The word is used primarily as an alternative to *maternal* <the *distaff* side of the family> or *female* <*distaff* executives>. (It is also applied to horses with some frequency.)

distaste When used with a preposition, *distaste* overwhelmingly takes *for* <a *distaste for* opera>.

distill, distil *Distill* and *distil* are variant spellings, but *distill* is by far more common. *Distill* is used with a variety of prepositions, occuring most frequently with either *from* or *into* <a short volume *distilled from* a large mass of writings> <many years of thought *distilled into* a single powerful statement>. Other prepositions used with *distill* are *out of, through, to,* and *of* <*distilled out of* her experience in the foster care system> <*distilled through* the lens of a camera> <*distilled to* a single proposition> <*distilled of* a variety of red wines>.

distinguish When *distinguish* is used with a preposition, the preposition is most likely to be either *between* or *from* <to *distinguish between* truth and falsehood> <features which *distinguish* the language *from* Old Norse>. Less often, *distinguish* is used with *among* <*distinguishes among* several different shades>. In using *among*, writers seem to be influenced by the notion that *between* can be used only of two items and that *among* must be used for more than two. For a discussion of this issue see BETWEEN, AMONG.

distract See DETRACT, DISTRACT.

distrustful *Of* is the preposition used with *distrustful* <*distrustful of* their motives>.

dive, dived See DOVE.

divest When followed by a prepositional phrase, *divest* appears with *of* <the firm plans to *divest* itself *of* its foreign holdings>. *Divest* may also take as a direct object the thing that is given up <will *divest* several properties>.

divide **1.** The verb *divide* is used with a large number of prepositions, most frequently *into* and *in* <*divided into* equal portions> <*divided in* half>. *Divide* is also used with *between* and *among*, *between* occurring far more often <*divides* her time *between* home and the office> <to be *divided* equally *among* the partners>. (See also BETWEEN, AMONG.) The use of *divide* with *from* is also common, especially when both divisions are mentioned and one is the direct object <*divides* diehards *from* dilettantes>. In addition to the common mathematical use of *divide* with *by*, *divide by* is used in other contexts <the community was *divided by* the new freeway> <*divided by* several generations>. *Divide* may be used with *on* or *over* when the matter that causes the division is the object of the preposition <remain *divided on* [*over*] the issue>. *Divide with* occurs, but not very often <*divided* duties *with* her sister>. We also find occasional instances of *divide* being used with *as to, to, against,* and *toward.*

2. *Divide up.* This phrase is sometimes criticized as a redundancy, but it continues to be used by good writers <*divided up* the proceeds>.

divorce The verb *divorce* is almost always used with *from* when followed by a prepositional phrase <a solution *divorced from* any domestic considerations>.

dominate, domineer *Dominate* is used far more often than *domineer.* If either word is used intransitively with a complement, the preposition used is *over* <he *dominated* [*domineered*] *over* the proceedings>. When *dominate* is used in the passive voice, the agent is named in a phrase beginning with *by* <the debate was *dominated by* the Republicans>. *Domineer* occurs most frequently now as its present participle, *domineering,* which has taken on adjectival status <never imagined having such *domineering* in-laws>.

done *Done* in the sense "finished"—especially when used with a form of *be*—has been subject to a certain amount of criticism over the years, yet its use in this sense has long been standard <the job is finally *done*> <we're *done* with you now>.

don't seem See CAN'T SEEM.

don't think The placement of the negative in such sentences as "I don't think it will rain tonight" and "I don't think they have a chance" is a characteristic English idiom that is sometimes objected to on the grounds of logic. Such sentences exemplify a phenomenon known as "raising," the shifting of a negative (or other element) from a subordinate to the "higher" clause it is dependent on. See also CAN'T SEEM.

dote When *dote* is used with a preposition—and it almost always is—*on* is the usual choice <*doted on* her only grandchild>.

doubt, *verb* The transitive verb *doubt* may take a clause as its object. The clause may be a sort of CONTACT CLAUSE (see Glossary) without a conjunction, or a clause introduced by *that, whether,* or *if.* (In the past, *but* and *but that* were also used.) *That* is preferred when the main clause is negative <I wouldn't *doubt that* such a thing exists> <We never *doubted that* they would come>; *that* also tends to be used with a third-person subject <he *doubts that* the settlement will last>. When the subject is in the first person, which it very often is, most writers choose *if, that,* or *whether* by no other criterion than personal preference <I *doubt if* [*that, whether*] we'll ever know>. All are standard.

doubt, *noun* **1.** The noun *doubt,* when followed by a clause, may take a clause introduced by the conjunctions used for the verb (see DOUBT, *verb*), including the older *but* and *but that* <there is little *doubt that* [*but,*

but that] they will succeed> <the usual *doubt whether* the thing will succeed>.

2. *Doubt,* whether as a singular or a plural, is followed idiomatically by a number of prepositions <*doubt about* the outcome> <*doubt of* his authority> <*doubt over* the proposal> <*doubt as to* their motives>.

doubtful *Doubtful* is usually not followed by a clause, but when it is the clause can begin with *that, whether,* or *if* <It is *doubtful that* [*whether, if*] the deal will go through>. See also DUBIOUS, DOUBTFUL.

doubtless, no doubt, undoubtedly *Doubtless* and *no doubt* are often used to mean "probably" <seeing and *doubtless* believing it all> <dismayed, *no doubt,* by the recent announcement>; *undoubtedly* tends to carry more conviction <*undoubtedly* interested in retrieving her property>.

Ways of expressing greater certainty include the sometimes maligned *indubitably, without (a) doubt* and *beyond a doubt,* and even longer phrases such as *there can be no doubt* or *there is no doubt at all.*

dove The verb *dive* has the past tense *dived* or *dove.* Although *dived* is somewhat more common in writing in the U.S., and is usual in British English, *dove* is used in many regions of the U.S. and may even be spreading its range. You may use whichever is more natural to you.

dozen *Dozen* has two plurals: *dozen* (just like the singular) and *dozens*. When a number is put before the noun, *dozen* is used <three *dozen* lobsters>. When the number is not specified, *dozens* is usual <performed in *dozens* of off-Broadway plays>.

draft, draught In British English *draft* is used for a preliminary sketch and for the corresponding verb, and also for an order for payment (a bank draft); but *draught* is used for beer, horses, and a current of air. American English uses *draft* in all cases.

drank See DRINK.

drapes, draperies *Draperies* used to be preferred for the decorative fabric hung as curtains, and is still insisted upon by some, but *drapes* has established itself as a standard alternative.

draught See DRAFT, DRAUGHT.

dream 1. The verb *dream* has the past and past-participle forms *dreamt* and *dreamed*. Both forms are many centuries old and both are flourishing in current American use. You may use whichever one feels more natural to you.

2. *Dream* may take either *of* or *about* before a gerund or a noun object <*dreamt of* [*about*] riding an elevator> <*dreamed about* [*of*] the trip to her grandmother's>.

drench *Drench* is often used with a complement introduced by *in* or *with* <*drenched in* blood> <*drenched with* wealth>.

drink The usual past tense of this verb today is *drank* <we *drank* from the well>. The usual past participle is *drunk* <the guests had already *drunk* several bottles>. The past tense *drunk* was formerly common, but has mostly dropped from use. The past participle *drank* is still used in some Northern areas of the U.S. and in some areas of Canada, but chiefly in speech. It seldom appears in print.

drown It is a convention of newspaper writers and editors that *drowned* should be used for an accidental drowning, and *was drowned* for a murder or other intentional drowning. Unless you are reporting an intentional drowning, you probably don't need to use the passive.

drunk, drunken **1.** *Drunk* is normally used as a predicate adjective <he was *drunk* when he left the bar>, whereas *drunken* is usual when the adjective precedes the noun <stopped to pick up a *drunken* couple>. One key exception is that *drunk* is commonly used before the words *driver* and *driving* <a *drunk* driver>.

2. For use of *drunk* as an inflected form of *drink,* see DRINK.

dubious, doubtful Is it permissible to say that you are dubious about something? Some critics have tried to limit *dubious* to the person or thing that is the object of doubt, and *doubtful* to the person who questions. *Dubious* is indeed most frequently used in the sense of "giving rise to uncertainty" <felt that our plan was a little *dubious*>, but many good writers have used *dubious* to mean "doubting, unsettled in opinion, suspicious" <she was *dubious* about the truth of the claim>. Similarly, both *dubious* and *doubtful* are frequently used to refer to the object of doubt. *Doubtful* may imply a simple lack of conviction or certainty <the outcome of the election remains *doubtful*>, while *dubious* usually implies suspicion, mistrust, or hesitation. In many contexts, however, either word can be used.

due to When the *due* of *due to* is clearly an adjective <absences *due to* the flu> no one complains about the phrase. When *due to* is a preposition <*due to* the holiday, our offices will be closed>, some people object and call for *owing to* or *because of.* Both uses of *due to* are entirely standard, but in formal writing one of the alternatives for the prepositional use may be less likely to be criticized.

due to the fact that This phrase often can be replaced by the shorter *because* or *since,* but not always <the lower numbers are *due to the fact that* the test scores have been averaged>. Adding *the fact that* to *due to* allows a clause to be used as the object, which sometimes comes in handy.

during the course of See COURSE.

dwell **1.** Although there are two spellings—*dwelt* and *dwelled*—for the past tense of *dwell, dwelled* has steadily lost ground over the centuries, and *dwelt* is now found far more often <she *dwelt* on her plans for the future>.

2. *Live* is the more commonly used word for "reside," but *dwell* has by no means disappeared <*dwelt* beside the river>.

3. *Dwell* may take any number of prepositions. In addition to *behind, on, within, in,* and *at,* it is used with *among, beneath, outside, over, under, upon,* and *with.*

dying, dyeing You will want to take care not to use *dying,* the present participle of *die* <*dying* of cancer>, when you mean to use *dyeing,* the present participle of *dye* <*dyeing* it a shade of blue>.

E

each There are several problems about *each* and its agreement with either verb or pronoun. These problems are taken up separately below. See also AGREEMENT: INDEFINITE PRONOUNS (in Glossary).

1. When the pronoun *each* is the simple subject, the rule of thumb is that it takes a singular verb <*each is* ready to accept the terms> <*each holds* a secret for the discoverer>. Sometimes, NOTIONAL AGREEMENT (see Glossary) interferes with the singular construction when *each* has a plural antecedent <a number of

proposals; *each have* been reviewed>. Since this use may be criticized, it is safer to use the singular.

2. When the adjective *each* modifies a singular noun subject, the singular verb is normally used <*each* car *displays* the corporate logo> <*each* intern *is* trained in the technique>.

3. *Each of* is followed by a plural noun or pronoun and notional agreement is strong. Singular and plural verbs are about equally frequent <*each of* the animals *was* placed in a shelter> <*each of* his paintings *are* exercises in self-mockery>. Sticklers will insist on the singular.

4. When the adjective *each* follows a plural noun subject, the plural verb and the plural pronoun commonly follow <they *each have their* own constituencies> <we *each have our* stake in the outcome>.

5. *Each* shares with many indefinite pronouns the tendency to take a plural pronoun in reference <*each* of the waiting moviegoers pulled out *their* ticket>, even though this use is sometimes censured. And *each*, like other indefinite pronouns, often takes a singular verb but a plural pronoun <*each* branch library *strives* to provide superior service to *their* patrons>. The principle of notional agreement is strong in these instances.

each and every *Each and every* is an emphatic form of *each* or *every*. It is sometimes criticized as jargon or worse, but it remains in good use <*each and every* offer has been rebuffed>. You may use it if it seems to be called for, but be careful not to overdo it.

each of See EACH 3.

each other, one another **1.** A traditional rule calls for *each other* to be used in reference to two <the two girls looked at *each other* in surprise> and *one another* to be used in reference to three or more <there will be time for people to talk with *one another* after the meeting>. In fact, however, *each other* and *one another* are employed interchangeably.

2. The possessive is normally *each other's, one another's.* The following noun can be either singular or plural <invading *each other's* sphere of influence> <moving in *each other's* circles>.

eager When *eager* is used with a preposition, the preposition is usually *to* and it is followed by an infinitive <officials are *eager to* shut the operation down>. *Eager for* is also frequent in contemporary writing <they were *eager for* any news>.

early on *Early on,* having arisen in British English in the 1920s, came into frequent use in American English in the 1960s and is now well established on both sides of the Atlantic <*early on* in the process>. It cannot always be easily replaced by *early,* as some critics have claimed it can.

earth The names of planets other than our own are invariably capitalized, but *earth* is usually not. When the other planets are also being referred to, there is some tendency to capitalize *Earth* and to omit the article *the* which normally precedes it. Both treatments are perfectly acceptable. Choose whichever styling seems more natural to you in a particular context and use it consistently in similar contexts.

easy, easily *Easy* as an adverb has many uses, most of which have a somewhat informal quality <he was told to go *easy* on them> <his illness forced him to take it *easy*>. *Easily* is the more common adverb, and it has a wider range of applications <not *easily* fooled> <is *easily* the best place in town>. In situations where both adverbs are possible (such as "Laughs come *easy*" or "Laughs come *easily*"), you should choose whichever seems more natural and appropriate to the tone of your writing.

economic, economical *Economic* usually refers to economics or an economy, whereas *economical* usually means "thrifty" or "not wasteful." Some crossover does occur, however.

educationist In British English, *educationist* is an ordinary word synonymous with *educator.* But in American English, *educationist* most often serves as a term of disparagement for a stereotypically muddle-headed educational theorist.

educator *Educator* is more often used of administrators in education than of actual teachers. Its application to an actual teacher usually carries implications of responsibility or achievement outside the classroom.

effect See AFFECT, EFFECT.

e.g. See I.E., E.G.

either 1. *Either* as an adjective meaning "each" is still in common use, though it is not as common as *each* <a long straight path lined on *either* side by robust sycamores>.

2. *Either* is rarely used of more than two items when it is a pronoun <in *either* of the two buildings> or an adjective (see 1 above); but the conjunction *either* is commonly so used <it was sent by *either* Rachel, Lindsay, or Marisa>.

3. In *either . . . or* constructions, *either* should be placed where it will provide parallelism. Thus, the sentence "the sum will be donated *either* to the college, the public library, *or* the state education fund" should be altered to "the sum will be donated to *either* the college, the public library, *or* the state education fund" or "the sum will be donated *either* to the college, to the public library, *or* to the state education fund." Correction will result in greater elegance of expression, but the nonparallel sentence is just as easily understood. See also, in Glossary, AGREEMENT; PARALLELISM.

4. When the pronoun *either* is the subject of a clause, it takes a singular verb <Wilma and Betty are closer to each other than *either is* to Maud>. A plural verb is often used when *either* is followed by *of* and a plural noun or pronoun <*Are either of* you going?> <it would seem that *either of* them *are* acceptable>. This pattern of agreement seems to be more common in speech than writing.

5. In *either . . . or* constructions, if both subjects are singular the verb is traditionally singular <*either*

the cable *or* the connector *is* not functioning>. Because of the strength of NOTIONAL AGREEMENT (see Glossary), however, a plural verb is not uncommon <*either* the House committee *or* the Senate subcommittee *are* to review the matter>. When both subjects are plural, or the first is singular and the second plural, a plural verb is expected <*either* the rings *or* the satellites usually *obscure* the planet's surface> <*either* Maria *or* her cousins *are* bringing the salad>.

either . . . or See EITHER 3, 5.

elegy, eulogy An *elegy* (from the Greek *elegos,* "song of mourning") is a sorrowful or melancholy song or poem; a *eulogy* (from the Greek *eulogia,* "praise") is a formal statement or oration expressing praise. A funeral oration is called a *eulogy* because it praises the accomplishments and character of the person who has died. Sometimes *elegy* is mistakenly used to mean "a funeral oration, eulogy" because funerals are occasions for mourning. Use your dictionary if you are still in doubt.

elicit, illicit *Elicit,* "to draw forth," and *illicit,* "unlawful," are occasionally confused because of their similar pronunciations. Take care to use the right word.

eligible *Eligible* may be used with a prepositional phrase, and *for* or *to* are the prepositions used most often <she is *eligible for* tenure>. When *eligible* is used with *to,* an infinitive usually follows <he is *eligible to* retire>.

else In contemporary English, compound pronouns with *else*—such as *anybody else, somebody else,* and *who else*—take the *-'s* of the possessive on the *else* <nobody *else's* problem>.

elude See ALLUDE 2.

emanate *Emanate* is usually used with the preposition *from* <radio signals *emanating from* outer space>.

embark *Embark* may be used with a few different prepositions, but the usual choice is *on* (or *upon*) <*embarked on* a new career>. *For* is used when the object is a destination <*embarked for* Constantinople>. And *from* is occasionally used to indicate the point of departure <*embarked from* San Francisco harbor>.

embellish *Embellish* is most often used with *with* when it takes a complement <*embellished with* metalwork>. It is also used with *by* <*embellished by* many fine photographs>.

emend See AMEND, EMEND.

emerge When *emerge* is used with a preposition, the choice is most often *from* <they *emerged from* behind the curtain>. It is also very frequently used with *as* <*emerged as* the victor>. Other prepositions commonly used with *emerge* include *at, in, into, on, onto, out of, through, upon,* and *with. Emerge* is also sometimes followed by a *that* clause <it *emerged that* he had been receiving bribes>.

emigrate, immigrate *Emigrate* means "to leave a country," *immigrate* "to come into a place." Distinguishing between the two is easy if you remember that *emigrate* usually takes the preposition *from* <*emigrated from* Russia>, while *immigrate* usually takes *to* or *into* <*immigrated to* Canada>. Get the prepositions right, and you will be right.

eminent, imminent *Eminent* means "prominent" <an *eminent* author>; *imminent* means "soon to occur, impending" <in *imminent* danger>. Use of one word for the other does occur from time to time. Be careful.

emote The normal uses of *emote* are facetious <*emoting* all over the place>. Use of *emote* without humorous intent is generally only in reference to actors <learning how to *emote* before the camera>.

employ *Employ* and *use* are often interchangeable, but *employ* is most appropriate when the conscious application of something for a particular end is being stressed <the scene *employs* exotic costumes to good effect>.

emporium *Emporium* has two plurals, *emporiums* and *emporia,* both of which are in good use. *Emporiums* is the more common of the two.

enamor *Enamor* is used most often in the passive, and when used with a preposition usually takes *of* <we became *enamored of* the young boy>. Less frequently, it is followed by *with* <was *enamored with* foreign films>.

encroach When used with a preposition, *encroach* usually appears with *on* (or *upon*) <*encroaching upon* her territory>. Occasionally it is used with *into, onto,* and *to* <*encroaching into* domestic air space> <*encroaching onto* their neighbor's property> <*encroaching* ever closer *to* the city limits>.

end When *end* is used intransitively with a preposition, the preposition is often *by* <he *ended* the concert *by* playing Chopin>, or somewhat less frequently *as, at,* or *on* <the paper *ended as* a monthly with wide circulation> <the duty-free zone *ends at* the fence> <the session *ended on* a positive note>. See also END UP.

endeavor *Endeavor* is used as a somewhat formal synonym for *attempt* or *try.* It tends to connote a continuing and earnest effort, as in attempting to enact a long-range policy or to achieve a lasting result <the committee *endeavored* to settle all grievances>.

endemic *Endemic* can be followed by either *in* or *to* <a condition *endemic in* [*to*] the region>.

endow *Endow* is very often used with a preposition, and usually the preposition is *with* <*endowed with* political acumen>. *Endow* is used with *by* when the sense is "furnish with funds" <a hospital *endowed by* a local philanthropist>.

end result, end product Some people find *end* in these two phrases superfluous and advise that you should use only *result* or *product.* This is largely a matter of personal preference, though you probably will not want to overuse either phrase.

end up 1. Although *end up* is sometimes criticized as too informal and is occasionally changed to *end* by copy editors, it is useful when you want to emphasize the notion of everything that led up to a certain result <after all the wrangling, they still *ended up* producing nothing>. *End* is often not only an awkward synonym for *end up* but sometimes no synonym at all.

2. When *end up* is followed by a preposition, the preposition is usually *with, in, as, by,* or *at.*

enervate To *enervate* is "to lessen the vitality or strength of" or "to reduce the mental or moral vigor of" <completely *enervated* following a hectic weekend>. Some people use this word without really knowing what it means, or confuse it with *invigorate* or *energize.* Don't be misled by the superficial resemblance of *enervate* to these other words.

engage *Engage* may be used with several prepositions. It most often takes *in,* which is usually followed by a gerund or a noun <*engaged in* trade for a number of years>. Less frequently, it is used with *with* <*engaged with* his old publisher at the time> or, in British English, *on* or *upon* <*engaged on* a series of novels>. It may also be used with *by* <he was *engaged by* the local paper>, *for* <he *engages for* the honesty of his brother>, *as* <*engaged as* a manservant>, and *to* <*engaged to* be married>.

enormity *Enormity,* some people insist, is improperly used to merely denote large size. They insist on *enormousness* for this meaning, and would limit *enormity* to the meaning "great wickedness" <the *enormity* of his crimes>. In actual practice, however, it regularly denotes a considerable departure from the expected or normal <the *enormity* of their situation suddenly dawned on them>. When used to denote large size, either literal or figurative, it usually suggests something so large as to seem overwhelming <the *enormity* of the sea bottom> <the *enormity* of the task>. It can also emphasize momentousness <the *enormity* of the collapse of Communism>.

enquire See INQUIRE, ENQUIRE.

enquiry See INQUIRY, ENQUIRY.

en route This French phrase was first used in English in the 19th century. Its assimilation into our language was completed long ago, and there is no longer any need to underline or italicize it as a foreign term. It is used as both an adverb <he reads *en route*> and an adjective <arrived early despite *en route* delays> and is usually written as two words.

ensure, insure, assure *Ensure, insure,* and *assure* are interchangeable in many contexts where they indicate the making certain or inevitable of an outcome <will *ensure* [*insure, assure*] correct usage>, but *insure* sometimes stresses the taking of necessary measures beforehand <to *insure* safe passage> and *assure* distinctively implies the removal of doubt and suspense from a person's mind <*assures* them that the vehicle is perfect>.

enter *Enter* may be used with many prepositions, but most often it is used with *into* <*enter into* an agreement>. Less often, it is used with *upon* or *on* <*entering upon* a career>. It is also used with complements introduced by *in, for, as, at, by,* and *with* <ten were *entered in* the race> <*entered* purely *for* symbolic reasons> <she *entered as* a standby> <*entered* the building *at* 3 PM> <*entered by* another door> <*entering with* the rank of lieutenant>.

enthrall When *enthrall* is used with a preposition, it is usually used with *by* <*enthralled by* the mix of cultures>. Less frequently *enthrall* is followed by *with* <*enthralled with* the campaign>.

enthuse *Enthuse,* an apparent Americanism that has been disapproved since the late 1800s, is nonetheless flourishing on both sides of the Atlantic, especially in journalistic prose <*enthusing* over the food>.

entitle *Entitle* has two common meanings: "to give a title to, title" <a work *entitled* "Penance"> and "to give a right to" <this ticket *entitles* the bearer to free admission>. Both are standard.

envelope The two pronunciations \ˈen-və-ˌlōp\ and \ˈän-və-ˌlōp\ are used with about equal frequency and are both fully acceptable.

envisage, envision These two words are, in many respects, interchangeable. When, however, the thing envisaged or envisioned is an abstract concept rather than a mental image, *envisage* tends to be chosen <*envisages* an entirely new system of education>. When a specific picture is in mind, *envision* is more often chosen <*envisions* a career in the law>.

equal 1. When *equal* is used with a preposition, it is used most often with *to* <bored with work not *equal to* his abilities>. Occasionally it is used with *with* <a level more or less *equal with* that of the previous year>.

2. *Equal* is one of those adjectives that some insist are absolute and therefore incapable of comparison (as in "*more equal*"). (See ABSOLUTE ADJECTIVE in Glossary.) This opinion, however, fails to recognize the common use of *more* to mean "more nearly" <perhaps we are *more equal* now than were citizens of the antebellum period>. This use has been in existence at least since the 17th century and remains standard.

equally as This innocuous phrase has drawn criticism because of its supposed redundancy, in that either *equally* or *as* can usually stand alone in place of it. Indeed, "The old show was awful, and the new show is *equally as* bad" can be revised to ". . . the new show is *equally* bad" or ". . . the new show is *as* bad" with no change of meaning. What will change, though, is emphasis. The point of the *equally* in *equally as* is to make it clear that the comparison is unqualified.

Equally as, then, is an idiomatic phrase equivalent to *just as*. It occurs commonly in speech, but it has been criticized enough to make it relatively rare in edited prose, where *just as* is more common.

equivalent 1. When the adjective *equivalent* is used with a preposition, the choice is usually *to* <*equivalent to* one year's pay>.

2. When the noun *equivalent* is used with a preposition, it is usually used with *of* <the *equivalent of* religious heresy>.

equivocal, ambiguous These two words are essentially synonyms, but *equivocal* may suggest intent to deceive or evade <*equivocal* actions that no one knew how to interpret>. Often, though *equivocal* suggests no more than *ambiguous* <an *equivocal* translation of the original>. See also AMBIVALENT, AMBIGUOUS.

erotica *Erotica* has the form of a Greek plural, but it is now usually understood as a mass noun meaning "erotic material" and is treated as a singular <such *erotica* is now off-limits to Internet users>. Treatment of *erotica* as a plural still occurs, however, and is not incorrect <these *erotica* are quite revealing of the culture>. For other foreign plurals, see LATIN PLURALS.

err In current English, the standard pronunciation of this word is \'er\, rhyming with *air*. It was, however, traditionally pronounced \'ər\, rhyming with the last syllable of *prefer*, and some people still favor the latter pronunciation.

escape Does a prisoner escape jail or escape from jail? *Escape from* is the usual idiom, but *escape* is also occasionally used as a transitive verb in such a context, without *from* <we *escaped* the mortar attack only to run into snipers> <*escaped* the earth's gravitational field>.

espresso, expresso The strong brew made by forcing steam through finely ground coffee is known in Italian as *caffé espresso,* or just *espresso* for short. Contrary to a popular belief of English-speakers, *espresso* means not "fast" but "pressed out"—it refers to the process by which the coffee is made, not the speed of the process. The idea that *caffé espresso* means "fast coffee" may have contributed to the occurrence in English of the spelling *expresso,* which also more closely resembles a familiar English word than does *espresso.* In any case, *espresso* is the more common form, at least in writing.

Esquire (Esq.) *Esquire* (abbreviated *Esq.*), which in British English is used as a respectful title in addressing correspondence to a man, is in American English used mainly among attorneys, who likewise use it when referring to or addressing each other in writing. There is still some controversy about using *Esq.* after the name of a woman lawyer. Some lawyers are all in favor of such usage, while others are strongly opposed to it. Indications are that the pros are gradually winning out over the antis. Note that when *Esq.* is used as a title following a name, no other title or term of address is used before the name. You can write *Mr. John Smith* or *John Smith, Esq.*, but you should not write *Mr. John Smith, Esq.*

-ess Many so-called feminine nouns—*empress, duchess, princess, lioness, abbess, goddess,* and so forth—have never stirred up much controversy. But others—*authoress, poetess, sculptress*—have been decried in recent decades. You will have little need for them. And what about *waitress?* Is it really being displaced by the genderless *waitperson* or *waitron?* Perhaps not. As an informal verb, *waitress* has even become more common in print over the last 20 years or so. In British English, the word *manageress* continues in frequent use. Clearly this portion of our vocabulary is still evolving.

essential, *adjective* **1.** *Essential* is used most often with the preposition *to* when the phrase requires a preposition <*essential to* one's health>. Sometimes it is used with *in* <*essential in* hot climates>. Less often it is used with *as* <*essential as* a means of prevention>.

2. Some hold *essential* to be an absolute adjective that cannot be qualified by adverbs such as *more* or *most.* The use of such adverbs with *essential* is, however, common among writers. *Most essential* is used for emphasis <it is *most essential* that you attend>. So are *absolutely essential* and *so essential. More* and *most* are both used for comparison <observed that this action is *more essential* to

the peace process> <the *most essential* part of the book is the last one>.

essential, *noun* When the noun *essential* is used with a preposition, it is used most often with *of* <the *essentials of* astronomy>. Less frequently, it is used with *in, for,* or *to* <one of the *essentials in* this game> <an *essential for* visitors to Montreal> <an *essential to* the maintenance of proper form>.

estimate **1.** When the verb *estimate* is used with a preposition, it is usually *at* <*estimated* the crowd *at* two hundred>. There is also scattered use of *as, by, for,* and *from.*

2. The noun *estimate* is often used with *of* <an *estimate of* the firm's worth>.

estimation The use of *estimation* to mean "opinion, judgment" <in my *estimation,* it is sound> is entirely reputable, despite the disapproval of some critics. The use dates back to the 14th century and can be found in the works of many standard authors.

estrange When used with a preposition in contemporary English, *estrange* is used with *from* <*estranged from* her husband>.

et al. This Latin abbreviation means "and others" or "and the others." The most frequent use of it is in citing (as in a footnote or bibliography) a publication that has several or many authors <Ruth I. Anderson *et al., The Administrative Secretary*>. Some discourage the use of *et al.* in regular prose, but it is commonly so used <we have Shelley, Byron, Wordsworth, *et al.* to thank>. The period is generally retained after *al,* and regular roman type is normally used.

etc. **1.** This abbreviation of the Latin *et cetera* means literally "and others of the same kind." *Etc.* thus should not be preceded by *and* (as in ". . . *and etc.*") and it should not be used at the end of a list introduced by *for example* or *such as* (as in "*such* photographic material *as* lenses, filters, *etc.*"). *Etc.* now appears commonly in ordinary prose, though some critics feel it is inappropriate in formal writing. If you need an alternative, you can use *and so on, and so forth,* or *and the like.*

2. *Et cetera* is often mispronounced \ek-ˈset-ər-ə\, and *etc.* is often misspelled *ect.* Remembering that the phrase begins with the Latin *et,* "and," should prevent you from committing either the mispronunciation or the misspelling.

eulogy See ELEGY, EULOGY.

even *Even* is an adverb whose placement can affect its meaning. In speech, a natural place for *even* to fall is just before the verb <they *even* do windows>. In writing, where stress cannot be as clearly signaled and where complex sentences may more often occur, you should put the *even* directly in front of the word or phrase it qualifies <faithful *even* unto death>. See also ONLY.

event The phrase *in the event that* serves as a somewhat formal substitute for *if* <*in the event that* an actual emergency occurs>. The *that* is often omitted <*in the event* a parent or guardian cannot pick up the child>. Both versions are sometimes criticized for wordiness or pomposity, and there are certainly contexts in which neither would be appropriate ("*In the event that* I had a hammer, I'd hammer in the mornin'"). But their distinctive tone and rhythm make them useful in other contexts. In elevated writing, for instance, they are entirely at home.

eventuate *Eventuate,* meaning "to result, come about," is used primarily in scholarly writing, textbooks, and reference works. It has also had some use in popular magazines and newspapers, but it is not the best choice when you are aiming for simplicity, informality, or forcefulness in your style <*eventuating* in a kind of serendipitous euphony>.

every **1.** *Subject-verb agreement.* Since *every* normally modifies a singular noun, a singular verb usually follows <*every* page *contains* some new revelation>. When *every* modifies two or more nouns joined by *and,* the singular verb is common <*every* man, woman, and child *is* going to benefit>. But the plural verb is not rare <*every* plant, *every* rock, and *every* inhabitant of the garden *were* planned before we started>.

2. *Pronouns with every.* Since *every* modifies a singular noun, it would seem logical that it would be followed by singular pronouns. But it often is not; the effect of notional agreement and considerations of gender often result in plural pronouns. For instance, when there is no problem about males or females, the singular pronoun is usually used <*every* woman attorney knows *she* faces an uphill battle> <*every* man in the village can offer *his* opinion at the council meeting> <*every* knickknack was in *its* proper place>. But when inanimate objects are involved, notional agreement often causes a plural pronoun to be used <*every* doctor, *every* lawyer and *every* drugstore was on his route, and he visited *them* regularly>, though in edited prose the plural pronoun may often be changed to singular. Finally, when the reference is to both men and women or when the gender is unknown, the plural pronoun is almost always used <*every* man and woman of voting age should ask *themselves* that question> <*every* recipient was requested to write *their* answers on the back>.

everybody, everyone *Everyone* and *everybody* regularly take a singular verb but a plural pronoun—specifically, *they, their,* or *them* <*everyone* was on *their* best behavior> <*everybody* at the picnic had brought *their* assigned dishes>. You can use a singular pronoun if you want to (and you are more likely to use a singular with *everyone* than with *everybody*) <*everyone* had *his or her* ticket>, but the plural pronoun seems to sound more natural to most people. See THEY, THEIR, THEM; NOTIONAL AGREEMENT (in Glossary).

everyday, every day The single word *everyday* is an adjective <an *everyday* occurrence> <part of *everyday* life>; the two-word phrase *every day* functions either as a noun <*every day* is new> or as an adverb <I see her *every day*>. The adverbial phrase is increasingly written as a single word <*everyday* a new scandal is reported>, but the two-word styling is still more common.

everyone See EVERYBODY, EVERYONE.

everyplace *Everyplace* is a somewhat informal synonym of *everywhere* <we went here, there, and *everyplace* in between>. It is not highly regarded by some. See also ANYPLACE; SOMEPLACE.

everytime, every time *Every* and *time* form a common adverbial phrase that is normally written as two words <they'll do it *every time*> <*every time* it rains, the roof leaks>. There is, however, a persistent tendency to treat this two-word phrase as a single-word adverb, especially when it occurs at the beginning of a clause and means "whenever" <*everytime* a jet flies over, the house shakes>. Such usage seems to be slowly increasing, but the two-word styling is still more widely preferred.

every which way This expressive Americanism is perfectly standard <we chased him *every which way*>, despite the doubts of some critics.

evidence *Evidence* has been used as a transitive verb for many centuries <certificates *evidencing* stock ownership>. The word has, however, retained a formal quality. If the audience, tone, and subject of your writing make formality suitable, then *evidence* is as good a verb as any other.

evidently See APPARENTLY, EVIDENTLY.

evoke, invoke *Evoke* (from the Latin, *evocare,* "to call forth") is usually used to mean "to elicit," "to bring to mind," or "to recreate imaginatively" <a smell that *evokes* images of his childhood>. *Invoke* (from the Latin *invocare,* "to call upon, to appeal to") is usually used to mean "to appeal to or cite" or "to implement" <*invoke* the death penalty>. *Evoke* is sometimes used in place of *invoke* in the sense "to appeal to or cite" (as in "*evoked* the authority of the Bible"), but it is preferable to use *invoke* in such cases.

ex- The use of *ex-*, a hyphenated prefix meaning "former," to modify a noun phrase <*ex*-Chicago Bulls star> <*ex*-postal worker> is standard in general prose but is largely avoided in formal or literary writing.

exact same This phrase is sometimes criticized as faulty or redundant, but it is frequently used by educated speakers and writers <found in the *exact same* place>. Its use is especially common in speech. See also REDUNDANCY (in Glossary).

exception When *exception* takes a preposition, the preposition is usually *of* or *to* <with the *exception of* Randy> <she takes *exception to* Brand's characterization>.

exclude When *exclude* is used with a preposition, it is usually *from* <*excluded from* consideration>.

exclusive When *exclusive* is used with a preposition and the object is what is excluded, the preposition is *of* <all land *exclusive of* the state utility access road>. When *exclusive* means "limited," the preposition is *to* <a view *exclusive to* these houses>.

excuse When the verb *excuse* is used with a preposition, it ordinarily is used with *from* <*excused from* jury duty>, less often with *for* <*excused for* believing it>.

exhilarate, exhilaration Spell these words with caution, noting that each contains two *a*'s the first of which can easily turn into an *i* or an *e*. It may help to remember that they are related to *hilarious.*

exhorbitant See EXORBITANT.

exhuberance, exhuberant See EXUBERANCE, EXUBERANT.

existence, existent *Existence* is sometimes misspelled *existance,* and *existent* (perhaps because of confusion with the word *extant*) is sometimes misspelled *existant*. Be careful.

exonerate *Exonerate,* when used with a preposition, is usually used with *from* or *of, from* being more common <managed to *exonerate* himself *from* the charges> <was *exonerated of* all wrongdoing>.

exorbitant Note that there is no *h* following the *x* of *exorbitant.*

expatriate The misspelling *expatriot* occurs relatively frequently in print and should be guarded against.

expect **1.** Using *expect* to mean "suppose" or "think" in sentences such as "I *expect* you were sorry to hear that" is now far less controversial than it once was, although the use still has its detractors. *Expect* in this "suppose" sense is almost invariably used in the first person, and it therefore appears most often in speech and in the kinds of writing which make use of the first person—correspondence, dialogue, and informal prose. Whenever *I* is appropriate in a written context, the "suppose" sense of *expect* is likely to be appropriate also.

2. *Expect* is very often followed by the infinitive <researchers *expect* to find clues to the planet's origin>. Less often, but still very commonly, *expect* is used with *from* or *of* <what would you *expect from* the likes of Grady?> <little was *expected of* us>.

expel **1.** When *expel* is used with a preposition, the choice is almost always *from* <*expelled from* college>.

2. Do not misspell *expel* as *expell.*

experience When the verb *experience* is used with a preposition, the form is usually the past participle and the preposition is usually *in* <highly *experienced in*

foreign affairs>. Less frequently, *experience* is used with *as* <had *experienced* severe hardships *as* a child>.

expert **1.** When the adjective *expert* is used with a preposition, it is usually *in* <is *expert in* dealing with trauma> and sometimes *at* <quite *expert at* judging the stock market>.

2. The noun *expert,* when used with a preposition, is most often used with *on* <an *expert on* civil procedure>, sometimes with *in* <an *expert in* education>, and less frequently with *at* <an *expert at* juggling knives>.

exposé *Exposé* can be written with or without an acute accent. Both forms are widely used. The accented form is the more common, perhaps because it clearly indicates how the word is pronounced \ˌek-spō-'zā\.

expressive When it takes a complement in the form of a prepositional phrase, *expressive* is used with *of* <*expressive of* our inner longings>.

expresso See ESPRESSO, EXPRESSO.

exquisite Stressing the second syllable—\ek-'skwiz-ət\—is about as widespread as stressing the first syllable—\'ek-skwiz-ət\. Either way is correct.

extemporaneous, impromptu *Extemporaneous* in its oldest sense is synonymous with *impromptu,* and its use in describing off-the-cuff remarks is common and correct <some *extemporaneous* observations>. *Extemporaneous* is also, however, used to describe a prepared speech given without notes or text <the press secretary's somewhat *extemporaneous* summary>, while *impromptu* is almost always used in describing speech that is truly unprepared <these *impromptu* remarks came back to haunt him>.

extract When the verb *extract* is used with a preposition, the choice is almost always *from* <*extracted* a piece of shrapnel *from* his leg>.

exuberance, exuberant The same spelling error that occurs with *exorbitant* also occurs with *exuberance* and *exuberant*—an *h* slips in following the *x*. Watch out for it.

exude *Exude,* when used with a preposition, is usually used with *from* <pus *exuding from* the eye>.

F

faced When *faced* is used as an adjective with a preposition, the preposition is usually *with* <he was *faced with* ruin>. As a verb meaning "to cover a front or surface," *face* is used equally with *with* or *in* <*faced* the building *with* [*in*] marble>.

fact A few phrases built around *fact*—e.g., *the fact that, in point of fact,* and *the fact is*—are occasionally criticized as unnecessarily wordy, and they undoubtedly are in many cases. But such phrases can also help the writer get a sentence organized or make an awkward transition. You should not use these phrases in every other paragraph, but if you need them for emphasis or to make a smooth transition, you may use them. See also TRUE FACTS.

fact that See FACT.

factor It is all right to use *factor* when there is no need to be extremely precise, but it is used a great deal, and many critics think it overused. You do not want to depend on it too heavily.

fail When *fail* is used with a preposition, it is often *to* and the infinitive <*failed to* lock the door>. *Fail* is also sometimes used with *in* or *at* <*failed in* his duty> <*failed at* selling insurance> and occasionally with *as, by, for, from, on,* or *with.*

famed *Famed* is used today both as a predicate adjective, often with *for* <*famed for* great chili>, and as an attributive adjective <Johnson's *famed* companion, Boswell>. Both uses are perfectly standard, though *famous* is the word used more often.

familiar The usual prepositions used with *familiar,* when it is a predicate adjective, are *with* and *to* <*familiar with* the facts of the case> <her face looked *familiar to* him>.

farther, further *Farther* and *further* have long been used more or less interchangeably, but have for some time been diverging. As adverbs they continue still to be used interchangeably when distance in space or time (either figurative or literal) is involved <traveled *further* [*farther*] today than yesterday> <taking the principle one step *farther* [*further*]>. But where there is no notion of distance, *further* is used <our techniques can be *further* refined>. *Further* is also used as a sentence modifier <*Further*, the goals they established were unrealistic>, but *farther* is not. As adjectives they also appear to be diverging: *farther* is taking over the meaning of distance <the *farther* shore>, and *further* the meaning of addition <needed no *further* training>.

fascinated *Fascinated* is more often used with *by* than with any other preposition, and *by* can take either a human or nonhuman object <is *fascinated by* her> <was *fascinated by* carnivals>. *Fascinated with* takes only nonhuman objects <*fascinated with* power>.

fascination When used with a preposition, *fascination* is most often used with *for*, *of*, or *with* <a moth's *fascination for* the flame> <they experienced the *fascination of* the wild West> <a *fascination with* numbers>.

fatal, fateful There are a number of distinctions to be made between these two adjectives. *Fatal* has more meanings and is more common. It has long had the sense of "involving momentous consequences, portentous," though some critics prefer to restrict this meaning to *fateful* alone <that *fatal* day> <the *fatal* letter>. *Fateful* is also used in about the same way <a *fateful*

remark> <his *fateful* decision>, but it is sometimes has a more neutral (if not quite positive) tone. *Fatal* has some meanings not shared with *fateful*: it can mean "deadly," <a *fatal* accident>, "disastrous" <a *fatal* misstep>, or "powerful and dangerous" <*fatal* charms>.

favorable When *favorable* is followed by a preposition, the preposition is usually either *to* or *for*. When the meaning of *favorable* is "feeling or expressing support or approval," *to* is used <the committee was *favorable to* accepting such applications>. *For* is the usual choice when *favorable* means "suitable" <weather that was *favorable for* our yacht trip>. Both *to* and *for* are used when *favorable* means "advantageous," though *to* is more common <a provision *favorable to* homeowners>. An alternative preposition is *toward* <taking a *favorable* attitude *toward* our request>.

February Despite admonishments to pronounce this word as \ˈfeb-ru̇-ˌwer-ē\, the most widespread pronunciation among educated speakers is \ˈfeb-yə-ˌwer-ē\. A succession of *r* sounds within a single word presents a challenge to many speakers, and often one gets transformed or dropped. Thus *caterpillar* is often pronounced \ˈkat-ə-ˌpil-ər\, and the first *r* sound of *governor, surprise*, and *thermometer* is often dropped without bothering anyone. On the other hand, pronouncing *library* as \ˈlī-ˌber-ē\ is generally disapproved (except when it comes from the mouths of children).

feed *Feed,* when used with a preposition, is most often used with *on* <he *feeds on* newsmagazines and opinion columns>. It is also used with *upon* and *off* <such groups *feed upon* the unwary consumer> <she *feeds off* all the attention>. Less frequently, it is used with *into* and *from* <this line *feeds into* the main switch> <the holding tank is *fed from* the well>.

feel bad, feel badly The choice between *feel bad* and *feel badly* is related to the choice between *feel good* and *feel well* (see GOOD 1). Those who make a distinction use *feel well* for health and *feel good* for emotion; many make the same distinction with *bad* and *badly* <if you *feel bad* you should lie down> <we *felt badly* about forgetting to invite them>. Usage is divided, however. Some people do not observe these distinctions and use *bad* for the emotional state and (more rarely) *badly* for health.

feel good, feel well See GOOD 1.

feet See FOOT.

feisty A few critics call *feisty* slang or colloquial, but it is in standard use <the *feisty* new assistant D.A.>.

fell swoop Although this phrase has become a bit of a cliché, it has a fine pedigree. It was used by Shakespeare, for whom *fell* meant "cruel, savage, ruthless" (the image is of a hawk swooping down on defenseless prey). If you use the phrase, be sure to get it right and not write *fell stroke, full swoop, felt soup,* or some other approximation.

female The noun *female* used to be used widely in literature. It is from the French word *femelle,* and is unrelated to the word *male* except through a deliberate spelling change that made *male* and *female* rhyme. In the mid-19th century it began to be criticized as demeaning (since it classed people with nonhuman animals), and the criticism continued well into the 20th century. Various humorous and mildly negative uses persist, as does an indefinite or indeterminate use—describing a group or class of women or girls whose age is unknown or irrelevant <the term "police officer" includes *females* as well as males>. The latter usage is the most common, and is still common in literature.

female forms See -ESS; see also PERSON 2.

ferment, foment Among the figurative senses of *ferment* is "to work up" (as into a state of agitation) <discontent *fermented* by government inattention>. This sense comes close to *foment* when it means "to promote the growth and development of" <*fomenting* dissent>. One difference is that things that one fermented can be good or bad; things that are fomented are usually bad. *Foment* is, in any case, much more common in this context.

fewer See LESS, FEWER.

field The phrase *the field of,* as in "He is majoring in *the field of* physics," is often unnecessary and may be omitted—particularly before the name of a well-known field. It is sometimes useful, however, when the field of study is uncommon or is something not ordinarily thought of as a field <*the field of* credit-card fraud>.

figure *Figure* meaning "conclude, decide, think" is sometimes thought to be rural, slang, or unsophisticated. But it is in fact standard, though rarely used in formal writing <*figured* there was no use in pursuing the matter>.

final *Final* is sometimes used with words like *end, destination,* or *outcome* to emphasize the notion of finality <we reached our *final* destination>. Such use is entirely standard, though occasionally criticized.

finalize Though avoided by many writers, *finalize* is used frequently in business and government writing <the budget will be *finalized*>, where it is regarded as standard. It is usually not found in more literary writing.

fine **1.** The adjective *fine,* meaning "good" or "superior," is sometimes thought to be empty or overused, but it continues to be employed by experienced writers <a *fine* day> <a *fine* wine>.

2. The adverb *fine,* meaning "very well, excellently," is sometimes considered colloquial or overly casual, but it is common in published prose as well as in speech and friendly correspondence <she looked *fine*> <it seemed to suit them *fine*>.

finished In British English, sentences such as "He wasn't *finished* yet" (in which *finished* is an adjective) are often disapproved in favor of the form "He hadn't *finished* yet" (where *finished* is a participle). Both are common in British and American speech, but less common in standard prose. When *finished* has an impersonal subject <the work is *finished*>, its use with forms of *to be* is never criticized. See also DONE; THROUGH.

fire off *Fire off* has been disparaged as journalistic or worse, but it is in quite widespread use to denote the idea of sending in haste or anger. Memos are the thing most commonly fired off.

firm **1.** The noun *firm,* in the technical sense, means a partnership of two or more persons not recognized as a legal person distinct from its members. A firm thus contrasts with a corporation, which is a body with the legal rights and liabilities of a person, although constituted by one or more persons. *Firm* is nonetheless frequently used to mean simply any business unit or enterprise, especially when the precise legal basis on which the business is established is irrelevant to the reader. Such use is entirely standard.

2. The adverb *firm* is usually found in just a few fixed phrases, such as *hold firm* and *stand firm. Firmly* serves for other adverbial uses <she held the child *firmly* in her arms>.

first and foremost This phrase has become a cliché as an introduction to a speech (as in, "*First and foremost,* let me thank the good people of this fair city"). It is, however, still in good standing as an occasional alternative to *primarily* or *primary* <what he wanted *first and foremost* was a good assistant>.

firstly When *firstly* is used to begin an enumeration, it is commonly followed by *secondly, thirdly,* and so on. Most writers and editors, however, prefer *first, second, third,* etc. The principle of consistency is preached, whichever series you use. But history shows that many fine writers have been more interested in making their point than in being consistent with *first* or *firstly*. Consequently many mixed enumerations can be found. It is nice to be consistent, but good writers sometimes mix their enumerating words and even phrases (such as *first of all, in the second place,* etc.).

fit, fitted Both *fitted* and *fit* are used for both past and past participle in the United States <he was *fitted* [*fit*] for a new suit> <the theory *fit* [*fitted*] all the facts>; only *fitted* appears to be used in British English. *Fit* seems to be somewhat more common in speech, *fitted* more common in print.

fix 1. *Fix* in the senses "repair" and "prepare" is sometimes disapproved, but it is standard in less-than-formal prose <*fix* my watch> <*fix* some supper>.

2. The intransitive sense of *fix* meaning "to get set, be on the verge" (as in "we're *fixing* to leave soon") is used mostly in the South, though it occasionally finds its way into a national publication.

flack See FLAK, FLACK.

flair, flare Be careful with your spelling here. *Flair* is a noun meaning "talent" or "style," while *flare* is both a noun meaning "bright light" or "a spreading outward" and a verb meaning "to shine," "to break out," or "to spread outward."

flak, flack *Flak* was originally antiaircraft fire, and more recently hostile or unfriendly criticism. *Flack* was originally a press agent. Although *flack is* established as a variant spelling of *flak,* and *flak* is occasionally used for *flack,* we recommend that you use the original and still dominant spellings for each word.

flammable, inflammable These two words are synonyms. *Flammable* seems to be less common in British English than it is in American English. *Flammable* is always used literally <*flammable* liquid>; *inflammable* is occasionally used this way (to the chagrin of safety inspectors), but mostly it is used figuratively <his *inflammable* temper>.

flare See FLAIR, FLARE.

flaunt, flout *Flaunt* acquired its meaning "to treat with contempt" <*flaunting* the rules> from confusion with *flout,* which has always had this same meaning <*flouting* the rules>. If you use *flaunt* as a synonym of *flout,* you should be aware that many people will consider it a mistake. Conversely, *flout* is sometimes used to mean "to display ostentatiously" (as in "*flouted* their wealth"), but the standard term in such contexts is actually *flaunt*.

flautist, flutist Both *flautist* and *flutist* are used in American English for a musician who plays the flute, but *flutist* is by far the more common choice. British English favors *flautist*.

flounder, founder A person *flounders* by struggling to move or obtain footing <seemed to be *floundering* onstage), while a ship *founders* by filling with water and sinking <the ship *foundered* off the coast of Maine>. Extended senses are also in use <the firm had been *floundering* for some time> <it finally *foundered* in 1992>. Confusion of the two words sometimes occurs; be careful to keep them distinct.

flout See FLAUNT, FLOUT.

fluorine, fluorescent *Fluorine* and words derived from or related to it (like *fluorescent*) are often misspelled by transposing *uo* to *ou*. Watch out for this mistake.

flutist See FLAUTIST, FLUTIST.

folk, folks Either *folk* or *folks* can be used as an alternative to *people* in an appropriate context. *Folks* is used of people generally <but seriously, *folks*> and for one's family <her *folks* weren't home>. It is also used, although not as often as *folk*, for people of a particular class or kind <old *folks*>. *Folk* is somewhat more frequent in this sense <media *folk*> <country *folk*>. These uses are standard, although *folks* seems to be a tad breezier or more informal than *folk*.

following *Following* can be used as a preposition <*following* the lecture, tea was served>. Sometimes, however, it is used in such a way as to leave its meaning unclear: for example, "In March 1863, *following* the manifest intention of the British ministry to enforce the Foreign Enlistment Act more strictly, he went to Paris" (*Dict. of Am. Biog.*, 1929). If you use *following* as a preposition, make sure it cannot be misread as a participle.

foment See FERMENT, FOMENT.

fond *Fond,* when it is used with a preposition, is most often used with *of* followed by a noun phrase <*fond of* rice pudding> or a gerund <*fond of* traveling abroad>.

fondness *Fondness* is usually used with the preposition *for,* followed by a noun <had a *fondness for* argument> or a gerund <his *fondness for* carousing at night>.

foot *Foot* has two common plurals. The usual one is *feet,* the less usual is *foot.* The most common use of the plural *foot* is when it means a unit of measure; it normally occurs (where *feet* would not) joined to a number with a hyphen <an eight-*foot* ladder>. Both *feet* and *foot* occur between a number and an adjective; *feet* is more common in print <he was six *feet* nine inches tall>, *foot* occurring chiefly in speech (as in "a board about twelve *foot* long").

forbid When *forbid* is used with a preposition, *to* followed by the infinitive is the commonest choice <her mother *forbids* her *to* go>. *Forbid* is also used, although less often, with *from*, in which case it is followed by a gerund <the law *forbids* them *from* selling to minors>. *Forbid* is also occasionally used with a gerund not preceded by *from* <the rules *forbid* talking between partners>.

foreign plurals For a list of those most frequently disputed, see LATIN PLURALS.

foreword, forward Don't muddle these words. A *foreword* is a preface in a book; *forward* is a direction.

forget The past tense of *forget* is *forgot*; the past participle is *forgot* or *forgotten*. Both past participles are used in American English. *Forgotten* is more common, especially in print <we had *forgotten* the address>; *forgot* is somewhat more colloquial <he'd almost *forgot* how small the town was>. British English uses only *forgotten*.

formally, formerly There is no reason to confuse these words, although they are likely to sound pretty similar in dictated material. *Formally* means only "in a formal manner" <*formally* signed the bill into law>. *Formerly* means "at an earlier time" <*formerly* of this city>. If you are in doubt about meaning, check your dictionary.

former **1.** An old rule states that *former* refers to the first of two and *latter* to the second of two, and that neither should be used when three or more things are being discussed. In actual usage, however, we see a different pattern. *Former* and *latter* are certainly used when two items are being discussed, but they are also often used when three or more items are mentioned <delivered speeches in Denver, Fort Worth, and Memphis, accepting the nomination at the *latter* site>. The old rule is too restrictive. You may choose to use alternatives (such as *last* or *last-named* instead of *latter*) or repeat the word or phrase that *former* or *latter* might replace, and many writers do so. But as long as your meaning is clear and you do not interrupt the reader's train of thought, you should not feel compelled to substitute something else for *former* or *latter* just because more than two items are involved.

2. See EX-.

formerly See FORMALLY, FORMERLY.

formula The two plural forms, *formulas* and *formulae*, are both common and correct. You may use whichever one you prefer.

formulate *Formulate* is occasionally criticized as a pretentious substitute for *form* or *make*. It is, however, standard when the object is to imply greater complexity or more deliberate intent than *form* or *make* implies <*formulate* a policy>.

forte The noun *forte,* meaning "one's strong point," is commonly pronounced \ˈfȯr-tā\ or \ˈfȯr-tē\ (the last like *forty*), even though these pronunciations are considered by some less correct than \ˈfōrt\ or \ˈfȯrt\ (which are supposed to be closer to the French but are not). The adverb or adjective *forte,* meaning "loud," as used in music, is pronounced \ˈfȯr-tā\ or \ˈfȯr-tē\ and provokes no criticism.

fortuitous The sense of *fortuitous* meaning "lucky" <coming at a *fortuitous* time for us> is sometimes objected to but is nevertheless standard. A newer sense, "coming by a lucky chance" <our chances were improved by the *fortuitous* failure of our chief competitor>, is halfway between the "lucky" sense and the original "occurring by chance" sense. Only the original sense is likely to occur in a negative sentence <could not have been merely *fortuitous*>.

forward See FOREWORD, FORWARD.

founded *Founded,* when used with a preposition, is used most often with *on* <*founded on* high principles>. It is also used frequently with *in,* often to signify a date or place <*founded in* 1772>.

founder See FLOUNDER, FOUNDER.

freedom *Freedom* is used with a number of prepositions, but most often with *of* <*freedom of* choice>. Among the others are *for, from, in,* and *to* with the infinitive.

friend The preposition used with *friend* is most often *of* <a *friend of* mine>, less often *to* <a *friend to* young people>. *With* occurs in the phrases *be friends with* and *make friends with.*

friendly When *friendly* is used with a preposition, it is used most often with *to* <*friendly to* the administration>. Less frequently, it is followed by *with* <*friendly with* her> or *toward* <*friendly toward* Egypt>.

frightened The prepositions used after *frightened* are *of* and *by* <*frightened of* being left alone> <*frightened by* loud noises>, and less frequently *at* and *about* <*frightened at* the sound> <nothing to be *frightened about*>.

from whence *From whence* is a very old phrase (going back at least to 1388) that is still alive in both British and American English. Critics have argued that *from* is redundant, since the notion of *from* is already present in *whence* itself. The phrase is not as frequent as it was a century ago, but you can still use it if it sounds right <*from whence* they came>.

frown Of the prepositions used with *frown, upon* and *on* are the most frequent <critics *frowned upon* [*on*]

the idea>. Less often, *frown* is used with *at* <she *frowned at* her lover>.

fruitful When *fruitful* is used with a preposition, it is most often *of* <*fruitful of* meaningful debate>, less often by *in* <*fruitful in* that instance>, and occasionally *for* or *to* <*fruitful for* the novelist> <proved *fruitful to* pursue it>.

-ful Nouns ending in *-ful, such as cupful, spoonful,* and *capful,* normally form the plural by adding *-s* at the end: *cupfuls, spoonfuls, capfuls,* though variants such as *cupsful* and *teaspoonsful* are occasionally used.

full *Full* is very often followed by *of* <*full of* remorse>. The phrase *to have one's hands full,* however, is followed by *with* when it takes a preposition and is being used metaphorically <she *had her hands full with* her in-laws>.

fulsome The adjective *fulsome* can present a problem of ambiguity: two of its most frequently used senses mean very different things. In expressions such as "*fulsome* praise" or "a *fulsome* tribute," it can be hard to tell whether *fulsome* means "generous in amount, extent, or spirit" or "excessively complimentary or flattering." To avoid misinterpretation, be sure that the context in which you use the word makes the intended meaning clear or choose a different word.

further See FARTHER, FURTHER.

G

gage See GAUGE.

gainsay This synonym for *deny* is a somewhat literary word that usually occurs in negative contexts <his expertise cannot be *gainsaid*>.

gait, gate You should not misspell *gait,* "manner of walking," as *gate,* "door or opening in a wall or fence."

gambit A *gambit* is, in the original sense, a chess opening entailing the sacrifice of a minor piece. Although some insist on retaining this "sacrifice" aspect of its meaning even when the word is used outside of chess, *gambit* is most often used to mean "a calculated move" or "stratagem," with no implication of sacrifice <a legislative *gambit* to ensure the bill's passage>. The phrase *opening gambit,* felt by some to be redundant, is in frequent use and is standard.

gamble, gambol *Gamble,* "to play a game for money," and *gambol,* "to skip about," sound alike but are spelled differently.

gamut *Gamut,* meaning "an entire range or series," is often used in the phrase *run the gamut* <*ran the gamut* from praise to contempt>. Some caution against confusing it with *run the gauntlet* (see GAUNTLET, GANTLET), but such confusion does not appear to be widespread.

gantlet See GAUNTLET, GANTLET.

garb The noun *garb* in its literal sense most often denotes a highly distinctive outfit <in formal *garb*>. The verb *garb* occurs most often as a past participle <*garbed* in T-shirt and blue jeans>. Both uses are standard, despite the criticism that more straightforward words, such as *clothes* (noun) or *dress* (verb), are available.

gate See GAIT, GATE.

gauge Note the spelling of *gauge*. A common error puts the *u* before the *a*. The older spelling *gage* is now rarely used.

gauntlet, gantlet *Gauntlet* (from the French for "glove") is the usual spelling in the phrases *throw down the gauntlet* and *pick up the gauntlet*. Both *gauntlet* and *gantlet* (an early spelling variant), however, are used in the phrase *run the gauntlet* (*gantlet*), meaning "undergo a severe trial or ordeal" <*ran the gauntlet* of criticism and censure>. *Gauntlet* is more common in this usage, though purists claim—on mistaken etymological grounds—that *gantlet* is more correct. British English uses only *gauntlet* for all three phrases.

gay Ever since *gay* became the word of choice for homosexuals, many have bemoaned the loss of the traditional senses "merry," "bright," and "lively." The older senses, however, are still in regular use

<abandoned a sober traditional style for something more timely and *gay*> <*gay* sunny meadows>. Nevertheless, because of the more frequent use of *gay* in the "homosexual" sense, you may sometimes have to exercise care when using it in the traditional senses, and particularly when applying it to humans.

gender *Gender* meaning "sex" has become increasingly common in standard writing <has no relation to the writer's *gender*>. It is most frequently used as an attributive adjective where *sexual* might otherwise appear <*gender* identity> <*gender* roles>.

genealogy Most speakers pronounce *genealogy* \ˌjē-nē-ˈäl-ə-jē\, as though it were spelled *geneology*. Sometimes inattentive writers even spell it that way. Those whose pronunciation is more influenced by spelling (or who appreciate the word's Greek root *genea*) will tend to say \ˌjē-nē-ˈal-ə-jē\ (rhyming with *analogy*) or sometimes \ˌje-nē-ˈal-ə-jē\.

general consensus See CONSENSUS 2.

genuine The usual pronunciation of this word among educated speakers is \ˈjen-yə-wən\ or \ˈjen-yə-win\. But pronunciation with a long final vowel, \ˈjen-yə-ˌwīn\, is also found in most regions of the Unites States, especially in less educated speech.

get **1.** The past tense of *get* is *got* <she *got* a pencil from the desk>. The past participle is either *got* or *gotten* <they hadn't *got* the word> <he'd *gotten* up to leave>; you may pick whichever form seems more natural to you in a given context. The phrase *have gotten,* however, usually means that something has been obtained <the play has *gotten* good reviews>, while *have got* denotes simple possession <we haven't *got* the money>. See also HAVE GOT TO.

2. The pronunciation \ˈgit\ has been a part of some American (and British) dialects since at least the 16th century and remains in widespread use, especially when *get* helps form the passive <he should *get* married> or is an imperative <*get* up!>. Nevertheless, some disapprove of this pronunciation.

get hold of, get ahold of The usual written form is *get hold of* <*get hold of* the representative>. When the phrase is written with the article *a,* the article may be separate from *hold* <*get a hold of* him> or attached to it <*get ahold of* him>. *Get ahold of* is more conspicuous with *ahold* as one word; the phrase is widespread in dialect, and is more common in speech than in writing.

gibe See JIBE, GIBE.

gift Use of this verb in the sense of "present" <*gifted* her with a necklace> is detested by many commentators, perhaps because gossip columnists use it. It has been in use since the 17th century and is standard, but is not very commonly used.

give credence to See CREDENCE, CREDIBILITY.

glamour, glamor The spelling *glamour* is much more common than *glamor,* though the latter remains a respectable variant in the U.S.

glance, glimpse *Glance* is a noun meaning (among other things) "a quick look" <a mere *glance* at the manuscript>; it is also a verb meaning (among other things) "to give a quick look" <*glanced* at his watch>. *Gimpse* as a noun means "a fleeting view or look" <caught a *glimpse* of a boat in the fog>; as a verb it means "to get a brief look at" <*glimpsed* them in the shadows>. When in doubt, see your dictionary.

glow When the verb *glow* is used with a preposition, *with* is the most common choice <the children *glowed with* excitement>. *Glow* is less frequently used with *about, at, from, in, into, of, over,* and *to* in various senses and constructions.

go and *Go and* is often used to emphasize a following verb <why did you have to *go and* do that?> without implying any actual motion, or *going* anywhere. It can be used without *and* as well <*go* jump in a lake!>. It has the flavor of speech and is seldom used in standard writing. See also TRY AND.

goes without saying Some critics advise writers that if something truly goes without saying, there is no need to say or write it at all; and if you do need to say it, the phrase *goes without saying* is inaccurate. Nevertheless, the phrase (first recorded in the late

19th century) continues in common and reputable use. See also NEEDLESS TO SAY.

good **1.** *Feel good, feel well.* The phrase *feel good* <I *feel good*> can express good health alone, or it can suggest good spirits in addition to good health. *Feel well* <yes, she *feels well*> tends to express good health. Somewhat similarly, *look well* <they both *look well*> suggests good health; but *look good* <he *looks good*> <it *looks good* on paper> refers not to health but to appearance. See also FEEL BAD, FEEL BADLY.

2. Use of *good* as an adverb (as in "we got 'em *good*!" or "listen *good*!") has been criticized since the 19th century. It is primarily a spoken form; in writing it occurs only in dialogue or in very informal contexts. The adverb *well* is used much more frequently in standard writing <the orchestra played *well* this evening>.

3. *Good* used as an intensifier in phrases like "a *good* 20 years" or "a *good* many soldiers" is entirely standard, though it has been questioned by some.

4. See as GOOD AS.

good and *Good and* functions as an intensive adverb <when I'm *good and* ready> <I can see you've been *good and* busy>. It is not found in formal writing. See also NICE AND.

goodwill, good will *Goodwill* can be spelled either as one word or as two. *Goodwill* occurs more frequently, but *good will* is also common.

grateful *Grateful* in its sense "appreciative" may be used with the prepositions *for* or *to*. In general, *grateful for* is used with benefits received <*grateful for* the advice>, *grateful to* with people <*grateful to* her>.

gray, grey Both spellings are correct and common. In American English, the preference is for *gray,* but *grey* is also widely used. The British have a very definite preference for *grey.*

grill, grille The word for a cooking surface that resembles a grating is spelled *grill*; the word for a grating that forms a barrier or screen, such as on the front end of an automobile, is spelled either *grille* or *grill.*

grisly, grizzly The adjective that means "inspiring horror or disgust" is usually spelled *grisly* <a *grisly* scene>; the adjective that means "somewhat gray" is spelled *grizzly* <the *grizzly* old combat veteran>, though it is often supplanted by the past participle *grizzled* <a *grizzled* beard>.

groom A prejudice against the use of *groom* to mean "bridegroom" exists in some quarters, the apparent reason being that *groom* has associations with the stable. Nevertheless, the "bridegroom" sense of *groom* is recognized as standard by all dictionaries, and there is no sensible reason to avoid its use.

grope *Grope* is used most often with *for* <*groped for* the light switch>. Less frequently, it is used with *after* <*groping after* something>, *into* <*groped into* the matter>, *through* <*groped* our way *through* the dark>, *to* <*groped* closer *to* a solution>, and *toward* <*groping toward* an understanding>.

grow Some still occasionally object to the "become" sense of *grow,* especially in the phrase *grow smaller* <the town had *grown smaller*>. This usage is nevertheless completely standard. Standard too is the "cause to develop" sense of *grow* <*grow* wheat>, though when applied to nonliving things <*grow* the economy> it has the ring of jargon.

guarantee, guaranty Some writers and critics formerly preferred *guaranty* for the noun and *guarantee* for the verb, but *guarantee* is now the usual choice for both.

guerrilla, guerilla Both spellings of this word for a type of soldier are reputable, though *guerrilla* (the spelling of the original Spanish word) is the more common form.

guts The sense of *guts* meaning "courage" is over a hundred years old, but it still makes some people uneasy. If you want to use an alternative you might choose *courage, mettle, pluck, spirit,* or *resolution.*

guttural This word is frequently misspelled *gutteral.* If you use it, remember that there are two *u*'s and no relation to *gutter.*

guy *Guy* has gained respectability over the years and is currently in common use in standard journalism. It can mean “man, fellow” or, when used in the plural, “persons, members of a group” (regardless of sex) <saw her and the rest of the *guys*>.

gynecology The most widespread pronunciation of *gynecology* among both physicians and laypeople uses the hard *g*: \ˌgī-nə-ˈkäl-ə-jē\.

gyp *Gyp*, which means “to cheat or swindle,” is derived from a noun that is probably short for *Gypsy*. Its use may be offensive to some, though we have no evidence of ethnically derogatory use.

H

had better See BETTER 2.

had ought, hadn’t ought These two phrases are regionalisms and are largely confined to speech and fictional dialogue. See also OUGHT 1.

had rather *Had rather* is a perfectly respectable English idiom dating from the 15th century <I *had rather* you not call me at work>. You can use it or the alternative *would rather* as you like.

hail, hale The spelling *hale* is the choice for the verb meaning “to compel to go” <he was *haled* before the court>. *Hale* is also the spelling used for the adjective meaning “healthy” (see HALE AND HEARTY). The spelling *hail* is correctly used for the noun and verb relating to icy lumps of precipitation and for the verb meaning "greet or call for" <*hailed* a cab> or "acclaim" <was *hailed* for her efforts>. It also occurs in the idiom "hail from" <*hails from* Maine>.

hairbrained Most often this word is spelled *harebrained* (after the long-eared mammal), but since the 16th century *hairbrained* has remained a regular if less frequent variant.

hale See HAIL, HALE.

hale and hearty If you use this cliché, mind its spelling—the final word is not *hardy*. See also HAIL, HALE; HARDY, HEARTY.

half **1.** When *half,* either noun or adjective, is followed by a singular noun it takes a singular verb <*half* of the balcony was unfilled> <a *half* share is to be granted>. When followed by a plural noun, *half* takes a plural verb <*half* of their assets go to charity> <*half* smiles were visible on their faces>. The underlying principle here is NOTIONAL AGREEMENT (see Glossary).

2. The phrase *a half a(n)* is mostly a spoken one that occurs in fixed phrases like *a half an hour* or *a half a dollar*. In writing, the preferred forms are *half a(n)* <in *half an* hour> and *a half* <found *a half* dollar in change>.

handful *Handful* has two plurals, *handfuls* and *handsful*. The first is the more common and the one usually recommended.

hands-on *Hands-on* (first recorded in 1969) has become part of the standard vocabulary <*hands-on* experience>, though some still consider it jargon. Our only recommendation is that you avoid it in contexts where it may raise a smile by suggesting physical groping more than practical involvement (as in "a *hands-on* feel for the customer").

hanged, hung *Hanged* (as the past and past participle of *hang*) is usually preferred when the verb has the sense "to hang by the neck until dead," and *hung* is the correct choice for all other senses of the word. Nevertheless, *hung* for execution by hanging has been in use for a couple of centuries, even among highly educated speakers and writers.

hangar The name for a building in which aircraft are housed is *hangar*, not *hanger*.

hanker *Hanker,* when used with a preposition, is most frequently combined with *after* <*hankered after* recognition>. Nearly as often, it is used with *for* <*hankered for* some ice cream> or with the infinitive <is *hankering* to be released>.

harass *Harass* is sometimes misspelled with two *r*'s, probably because of its similarity to *embarrass*. It has been pronounced with stress on the second syllable (\hə-'ras\) for quite some time, despite some critics' preference for initial stress (\'har-əs\).

hardly Expressions such as *can't hardly* and *hasn't hardly* are primarily speech forms that should be avoided in writing other than fictional dialogue. (Such expressions are not double negatives, but are the same in meaning as the positive: "could *hardly* stop shaking" and "couldn't *hardly* stop shaking" are essentially synonymous.) The expression *without hardly* sometimes appears in newspaper reporting <*without hardly* a trace of evidence>. See also DOUBLE NEGATIVE (in Glossary).

hardy, hearty These two words sound much alike and are vaguely similar in meaning, but they are not interchangeable. You may refer to "a hardy crop" or "a hardy flower" as against "a hearty soup" or "a hearty endorsement." If in doubt, consult your dictionary. See also HALE AND HEARTY.

hark back, harken back, hearken back *Hark, harken,* and *hearken* all essentially mean "to listen, listen carefully." All three are today used primarily with the word *back* to mean "to turn back to an earlier topic or circumstance." *Harken* is simply the predominant American spelling of *hearken*. Thus, you may use *hark back, harken back,* or *hearken back* and be correct in each case. The use of *hark* by itself to mean "hark back" is becoming more common.

has got See HAVE GOT TO.

hassle Though neither the noun <faced *hassles* from regulators> nor the verb <feared being *hassled*> is used in literary or formal prose, *hassle* is quite frequent in general prose, such as journalism. You may use it, if you need it, in writing of that kind.

have got to This phrase is listed as incorrect by various handbooks, but it has been used by many literary figures, both English and American, and Presidents Truman, Eisenhower, and Carter, among others <I *have got to* lay off the caffeine>. There is no reason to avoid it.

havoc See WREAK, WRECK.

he, he or she Discussion of what third-person singular pronoun to use in referring to a neutral preceding noun <the researcher should take *his or her* time> dates back to the 18th century, and more recently feminists and others have rediscovered the topics. The usual recommendation on how to avoid using *he* to stand for *he or she* is to cast the sentence in the plural <researchers should take *their* time>, to address the reader directly in the second person <you should take *your* time>, or to remove the pronoun altogether <the researcher should take time>. The double pronoun *he or she* works well at times (see the first example above), but using it repeatedly can create awkward prose. See also THEY, THEIR, THEM; AGREEMENT (in Glossary).

headquarter The verb *headquarter* is a relatively recent word, first recorded in 1903. Some still consider it incorrect. But in its usual use as a past participle <is *headquartered* in New York>, *headquarter* is perfectly standard. The rarer intransitive use <will *headquarter* in New York> is more likely to raise your reader's or listeners' eyebrows.

head up A person can either *head* a committee or *head up* a committee. Both uses are standard.

healthy, healthful A conventional distinction between these two words is that *healthful* means "conducive to health" <a *healthful* diet> and *healthy* means "enjoying or evincing health" <a *healthy* complexion>. Since the 16th century, however, *healthy* has been in standard use in both senses <a *healthy* diet can produce a *healthy* complexion>, and *healthful*, the rarer of the two words, has occasionally been used to mean "healthy" <a *healthful* face>. So if you observe the conventional distinction (which was introduced only in the 1880s), you are correct but in the minority; if you ignore it, you are correct and in the majority. *Healthy* is also commonly used to mean "considerable" <a *healthy* respect for statistics>.

heap *Heap* has been used to mean "a great deal" since the 16th century; it usually occurs in writing that has a conversational tone <a *heap* of trouble> <flavored with *heaps* of sugar>. The adverbial phrase *a heap* (as in "thanks *a heap*") strikes most readers as rustic, and is found in writing only as part of fictional speech.

hearken back See HARK BACK, HARKEN BACK, HEARKEN BACK.

hearty See HARDY, HEARTY.

heave In standard English *heave* has two past-tense and past-participle forms, *heaved* and *hove*. In nautical contexts, *hove* is used <they *hove* up the anchor>. A second nautical sense, "to move in an indicated way" <the skiff *hove* into harm's way>, is sometimes used more generally <the diner *hove* into view as we turned the corner>. All other applications generally require *heaved* <*heaved* the dirt into the hole> <the wagon *heaved* back and forth> <we *heaved* at the rope>.

height Although \'hīt\ is the usual pronunciation, \'hītth\ is not all that uncommon and can be found in educated speech. It may have been influenced by the usual pronunciation of *eighth*. If \'hītth\ is your natural pronunciation, you can stick with it, but you may sometimes be corrected. The spellings *heighth* and *highth*, though older than *height*, are no longer used.

help See CANNOT BUT, CANNOT HELP, CANNOT HELP BUT.

hence See FROM WHENCE.

he or she See HE, HE OR SHE.

her See I, ME.

herb Americans usually do not pronounce the *h* in *herb* (\'ərb\), while Britishers normally do (\'hərb\), and Canadians are somewhat divided.

hers Although a few hundred years ago *hers* was frequently spelled with an apostrophe (as in "the book is *her's*"), in present-day use *her's* is considered a mistake.

herself See MYSELF.

hesitant *Hesitant* is often followed by *about* <*hesitant about* calling> or *to* and the infinitive <*hesitant to* get involved>. Less often, it is used with *in* <*hesitant in* asking customers if they need help>.

hiccup, hiccough *Hiccup* is the older and more common spelling, but *hiccough* (originating as a misunderstanding of *hiccup*) is in widespread and reputable use. Regardless of spelling, the word is pronounced so that it rhymes with *stickup*.

him See I, ME.

himself See MYSELF.

hinder When *hinder* is used with a preposition, the choice is usually *from* <wasn't *hindered from* publishing the attack>. Occasionally, *hinder* is used with *in* <was *hindered in* her work>. In the passive voice, *hinder* is often used with *by* <were *hindered by* high winds>.

hindrance 1. *Hindrance* is sometimes misspelled *hinderance*. Watch out for it.

2. When used with a preposition, *hindrance* is usually used with *to* <a real *hindrance to* them>. Less frequently but still commonly, it is used with *of* <a *hindrance of* market efficiency>.

hint When used with a preposition, *hint* is usually used with *at* <*hinted at* the possibility>. Less frequently, it is used with *of* <*hinted of* things to come>. Occasionally it is also used with *about, against,* or *for.*

his or her See HE, HE OR SHE.

historic, historical *Historic* and *historical* are simply variants of each other; but over the course of more than 200 years they have tended to diverge somewhat. *Historical* is the usual choice for the broad sense "of, relating to, or based on history" <a *historical* perspective> <*historical* preservation>. *Historic* most commonly means "famous, important in history" <*historic* battlefields> <an *historic* occasion>. Note, too, that both *a* and *an* are used before *historic* and *historical,* with *a* being slightly more common. See A, AN.

hitherto *Hitherto,* sometimes thought to be old-fashioned, is in frequent current use. It means "up to this or that time" or "previously" <a treasure of *hitherto* unheard-of proportions>.

hoard, horde A *hoard* is a hidden accumulation <a *hoard* of paper clips>. A *horde* is a throng or swarm <a

horde of holiday shoppers>. Be careful with the spelling of these words.

hold See GET HOLD OF, GET AHOLD OF.

home, house *Home* and *house* are used interchangeably by many reputable writers, despite the admonition of some to avoid using *home* to mean "a building (for human habitation)."

home in See HONE IN.

Hon. See HONORABLE.

hone in Many consider *hone in* a mistake for *home in*. The verb *home* was first used (of homing pigeons) in the sense "to fly back home" in the late 19th century. An extended use of this verb began to occur in the 1920s, and by the early 1950s the phrase *home in* (or *home in on*) was well established. *Hone in* began to appear only in the mid-1960s but is today quite common. If you nevertheless want to play it perfectly safe, use *home in* (or *zero in*) instead.

honor When used with a preposition, the verb *honor* may take *by* or *with* <*honored by* a special dinner> <*honored with* a commemorative plaque>. It is used less frequently with *for, at,* or *in* <*honored for* his contribution> <*honored at* town hall> <*honored in* grand style>.

Honorable *Honorable* is a title of respect in American use. It is usually capitalized, preceded by *the,* and followed by a given name, initials, or some other title <the *Honorable* James P. Scott>. It may be abbreviated to *Hon.* when this seems appropriate. As to the question of who is entitled to an *Honorable* and who is not, we suggest you consult a "Forms of Address" table or a book on etiquette.

hoof Both the plurals *hoofs* and *hooves* are in standard use. *Hooves* is more common, especially in livestock journals, but *hoofs* is not rare.

hope The noun *hope,* when used with a preposition, is usually followed by *of* <no *hope of* a cure> or, a little less frequently, by *for* <our only *hope for* a victory>. Occasionally it is used with *in, on, over,* or *to* and the infinitive <put his *hopes in* them> <shouldn't place your *hopes on* it> <some *hope over* the possibility of reaching an agreement> <their only *hope* was *to* head off a vote>. It may also be followed by a clause <expressed her *hope* that more would participate in the program>. And it is used idiomatically in the phrases *in the hope(s) of, in hope(s) of, in the hope(s) that, in hope(s) that, with the hope(s) of, and with the hope that.*

hopefully The use of *hopefully* as a sentence adverb to mean "I hope" <*hopefully,* they'll reach an accord soon> is often criticized, even though this sense has been in sporadic use since the 1930s (and frequent use since the 1960s) and even though other similar sentence adverbs (such as *frankly, clearly,* and *interest-*

ingly) are accepted by everyone. Despite the objections, this sense of *hopefully* is in standard use.

horde See HOARD, HORDE.

house See HOME, HOUSE.

hove See HEAVE.

how *How* as a conjunction in the sense of *that* <told them *how* he had a job> has a long history of literary use, but in the 20th century it seems to be mostly confined to speech. See also AS HOW.

how come *How come* is a familiar phrase of obscure origin that was first noticed as an Americanism in the mid-19th century. Since then it has been frequently criticized and defended. Writers seem to find it a sassier and more emphatic way of asking *why*? <*how come* no one reported it?>. It is completely standard, at least outside of the most formal prose, and occurs frequently in journalistic writing.

however The main issue with *however* is its placement in the sentence. When used to mean "on the other hand" some critics hold that *however* should not begin a sentence. However, evidence of actual usage puts that view in doubt. The only valid point that one can make about the placement of *however* is that there is no absolute rule; each writer must decide each instance on its own merits, and place the word where it best accomplishes its purpose.

human Even though this noun has been standard for some 450 years <transmitted the virus to *humans*>, many people still believe it is an incorrect or inappropriate shortening of *human being*. You have absolutely no reason to avoid it.

hung See HANGED, HUNG.

I

I, me In informal speech and writing, such phrases as "It's *me* (*him, her*)," "Susan is taller than *me* (*him, her*)," "He's as big as *me* (*him, her*)," "Who, *me*?" and "*Me,* too" are generally accepted. In formal writing, however, it is safer to use *I* (*he, she*) after forms of *be* <it was *I* (*he, she*) who discovered the mistake> and after *as* and *than* when the first term of the comparison is the subject of the sentence <Ms. Williams is more knowledgeable than *I* on the subject> <he is, if the truth be told, as responsible as *I*>. See also BETWEEN YOU AND I; MYSELF; PRONOUN (in Glossary).

idea The belief—expressed mostly in college English handbooks—that *idea* means "mental conception, notion" and that its use in other meanings is vague or imprecise, may be disregarded. *Idea* is a word of many standard meanings and uses. It may apply to a mental image or formulation of something seen or known or imagined <described his *idea* of a ski house> <my *idea* of paradise>, to a pure abstraction <the *idea* of

holiness>, or to something assumed or vaguely sensed <the child's *idea* of time> <innovative new *ideas*>.

identical *Identical* often takes a preposition, usually *with* or *to* <was *identical with* the one found earlier> <were not *identical to* those of their sister villages>. *Identical with* is the older form, dating back to the 17th century. *Identical to* is of this century. Both are used with about equal frequency.

identify When *identify* is used with a preposition, it is usually *with* <groups that are *identified with* conservation>. Formerly the reflexive pronoun was generally used <he *identifies himself* with the lead character>, but today the pronoun is optional <he *identifies* strongly with the lead character>.

idiosyncrasy, idiosyncracy *Idiosyncrasy* is by far the more common spelling, but *idiosyncracy* has been in use for so long (350 years) that it must be considered a legitimate variant.

i.e., e.g. These two abbreviations are sometimes confused with each other. The usual error is the use of *i.e.* in place of *e.g.* To avoid it, remember that *i.e.* (an abbreviation for the Latin *id est*) means "that is"; *e.g.* (an abbreviation of *exempli gratia*) means "for example." Like *that is, i.e.* typically introduces a rewording or clarification of a statement that has just been made or of a word that has just been used <services provided by the government—*i.e.*, the Food and Drug Administration>. Like *for example, e.g.* introduces one or more examples that illustrate something stated directly or shortly before it <services provided by the government, *e.g.*, food and drug testing>. Neither abbreviation is generally italicized today. Both are normally followed by a comma in American texts.

if 1. *If, whether.* Both *if* and *whether* are standardly used with such verbs as *doubt, see, ask, wonder, decide,* and *know* to introduce a noun clause <see *if* they will agree> <asked her *whether* she minded>. *Whether* tends to be used more often in formal contexts, perhaps because of the persistence of the notion that *if* is wrong. But there is nothing wrong with using *if;* its use after such verbs goes back to Shakespeare. Both *if* and *whether* are also sometimes used after an adjective <it is doubtful *whether* [*if*] it could succeed>.

2. *If* in the sense of "though" <an interesting *if* untenable argument> is sometimes questioned, but the usage is standard and in fact quite common.

3. *If* is often followed by a subjunctive verb, especially when the clause contains a condition that is clearly hypothetical or contrary to fact <*if* there were a simple rule to follow here, life would be easier>. The indicative is called for when the clause is clearly not hypothetical or identifies the truth <*if* there's one person who knows the answer, it's Packard>. The problem is that the dividing line between what is or could well be true and what is hypothetical or not true is not always clear—in fact it can often be an

entirely subjective judgment made by the writer <but *if* France was [were] threatened, the situation would be serious>. See also SUBJUNCTIVE (in Glossary).

if and when This phrase has some standing in the legal field, but outside of the law it is frequently attacked as wordy. It nevertheless remains in common and respectable use <*if and when* they decide>, and you may employ it where it seems useful. The construction with *to* and the infinitive (as in "must choose *if and when to* get married") can be criticized on grounds of faulty PARALLELISM (see Glossary); try replacing the *if* with *whether* instead <*whether* and when to get married>.

if worst comes to worst See WORST COMES TO WORST.

illegible, unreadable The distinction to be made between these words is that *illegible* usually means "impossible to read, indecipherable" while *unreadable* usually means "extremely dull or badly written."

illicit See ELICIT, ILLICIT.

illusion See DELUSION, ILLUSION.

illustrate When *illustrate* is used with a preposition, it may be used with *by, in,* or *with* <is *illustrated by* the plight of the refugees> <as *illustrated in* the exchange of letters> <banners *illustrated with* words and images>.

imaginary, imaginative In ordinary use, these words are not often confused. In the context of art and literature, however, the words can sometimes be close in meaning. In such use, *imaginative* is more common, and it stresses what is produced by the imagination <*imaginative* designs> as distinct from what merely exists in the imagination, for which *imaginary* is the usual word <*imaginary* landscapes>.

immigrate See EMIGRATE, IMMIGRATE.

imminent See EMINENT, IMMINENT.

immune When *immune* is used with a preposition, *from* or *to* is usual <are *immune from* arrest> <*immune to* all pleas>; *against* is sometimes used <*immune against* smallpox>.

immunity When *immunity* is used with a preposition, the latter is most commonly *from* <granted *immunity from* further prosecution>. Less frequently, it is used with *against* or *to* <*immunity against* outside attacks> <*immunity to* smallpox>. Occasionally it is found with *in* or *for* <*immunity in* newborns> <*immunity for* past offenses>.

immure **1.** Do not confuse *immure,* "to enclose within walls," with *inure,* "to accustom to something undesirable." See also INURE.

2. When *immure* is used with a preposition, it is usually *in* <*immured in* the recesses of the library>. Less frequently, it takes *behind* or *within* <*immured* *behind* stacks of new orders> <*immured within* those prison walls>.

impact *Impact* as a verb meaning "to have an impact" <how did the news *impact* on the panel?> or "to have an impact on" <the best way to *impact* that market> was already being used in the 1950s, but only came into widespread use in the 1980s. It has been roundly criticized. You need not use this verb if you find it unappealing; another verb such as *affect, influence, impinge,* or *hit,* can usually be substituted. But *impact* with these meanings has become established in journalism and official writing, though not in literary use.

impatient When used with a preposition, *impatient* is most often followed by *of* <*impatient of* delay>. Less frequently, it is used with *for, to,* or *with* <*impatient for* the results> <*impatient to* get home> <*impatient with* the children>.

impeach **1.** When used with a preposition, *impeach* usually takes *for* <*impeached for* malfeasance>. Occasionally it is used with *on* <*impeached on* several counts>.

2. When used in reference to political misconduct, *impeach* in edited prose usually means "to charge (an official) with misconduct" <the vote to *impeach* was the prelude to two months of hearings in which the governor struggled to retain his office>. But in popular—mostly spoken—usage, *impeach* means "to remove from office" <*Impeach* the bum!>. The popular meaning is partly kept alive by the fact that both meanings can be read into many of the contexts that appear in print.

implicit *Implicit* is often used with a preposition, which is usually *in* <it was *implicit in* their demands>. In other senses and contexts, *implicit* is also used with *from, with,* or *within* <*implicit from* the beginning> <always only *implicit with* them> <a criticism *implicit within* the report>.

imply See INFER, IMPLY.

important 1. *More important, more importantly.* Although opinion is divided as to which of these two phrases is preferable in sentences like "More *important(ly),* there is no time," the evidence from usage shows clearly that you can use either. Both are defensible grammatically and both are in respectable use; the choice is solely a matter of preference.

2. *Important* may be complemented by prepositional phrases beginning with *for, in,* or *to* <are *important for* us> <is *important in* such matters> <have been *important to* her>.

impose When used with a preposition, the transitive verb *impose* most often takes *on* (or *upon*) <*imposed* his views *on* the committee>. Much less frequently, *impose* is used with *against, around, as, between, from, in, into,* or *over.*

impossible This word is sometimes considered to be an ABSOLUTE ADJECTIVE (see Glossary).

impractical, impracticable *Impractical* is a 19th-century word that has, over the decades, outstripped the older (17th-century) *impracticable* in use, perhaps because it is easier to pronounce and spell. It may be applied to what has no practical value <an *impractical* device>. It is also used, as is *impracticable,* for what is not feasible <the logistics of the enterprise are completely *impractical* [*impracticable*]>.

impromptu See EXTEMPORANEOUS, IMPROMPTU.

improve When *improve* is used with a preposition, it is usually *on* or *upon* <it will be hard to *improve on* the first version>.

improvement The chief prepositions used with *improvement* are *on, in, of,* and *to* <an *improvement on* earlier efforts> <an *improvement in* her condition> <some *improvement of* their status> <*improvements to* the design>.

in, into The basic distinction between these two prepositions is simply stated: *into* is used with verbs of motion <moving *into* the light> <backed *into* a parked car>; *in* is used with verbs that show location <found the letter *in* the folder> <hid it *in* the closet>, but it is also used with some verbs of motion <spit *in* the ocean> <split *in* two>. Sometimes you can use either one <put the names *into* [*in*] a hat> <don't go *in* [*into*] the kitchen yet>, and in those instances remember that *into* gives more prominence to the idea of entrance.

in addition to Some disparage *in addition to* as a wordy alternative to *besides*, but *in addition to* is not always replaceable by *besides*. It may be usefully contrasted with another phrase <carried on *in addition to*, rather than as a substitute for, parental involvement> and it may be used to emphasize its literal sense <several new responsibilities, *in addition to* the basic ones>. It is most interchangeable with *besides* when it begins a sentence <*In addition to* relocating, she changed her name>.

in advance of *In advance of* can sometimes be replaced by the more concise *before*, but it can also be more specific then *before* and can carry more force <were urged to implement voting reforms *in advance of* the election>.

inasmuch as Some advise substituting the shorter *since*, *as*, or *because* for *inasmuch as*. But if you want a longer expression (writers do not always want to be brief), there is nothing wrong with *inasmuch as* <*inasmuch as* musical talent is part nature, part nurture>.

in back of See BACK OF, IN BACK OF.

in behalf of See BEHALF.

incentive When *incentive* is used with a preposition, it is usually *to* <as an *incentive to* finish it>; *for* is also common <the *incentive for* establishing the fund>. It is also occasionally used with *toward* <an *incentive toward* fostering economic cooperation>.

inchoate Some complain that the meaning of *inchoate* has expanded from "being only partly in existence or operation" to include "imperfectly formed or formulated, formless." This extended use is natural and probably inevitable, however: what is just begun is also unfinished, incomplete, and often also disorganized or incoherent.

incident *Incident* in the sense of "an action likely to lead to grave consequences" <a serious border *incident*> is regarded by some as an undesirable extension of the older meaning "a minor or unimportant occurrence." However, *incident* in the first sense has been in standard use since the early part of the 20th century.

incidental The usual preposition with *incidental* is *to* <problems *incidental to* a rapidly expanding economy>.

in . . . circumstances See CIRCUMSTANCES.

incite, insight Don't confuse or misuse these two words. *Incite* means "to urge on," while *insight* means "discernment" or "intuition."

include Contrary to the opinion of many language commentators, *include* may be and frequently is used when a complete list of items follows the verb <the book *includes* the usual preliminary matter, the text itself, and a bibliography and index>.

incongruous *Incongruous* may be used with the preposition *to* or *with* <must seem *incongruous to* his fans> <an attitude that was *incongruous with* what we knew of him>. Less frequently, it is used with *about, in,* or *on.*

in connection with The phrase *in connection with,* though sometimes disparaged as wordy, is in wide use <faced price increases *in connection with* the dollar's declining value>. The phrase can often be replaced by a shorter preposition such as *about, by, from, at, of, or concerning,* but not always.

incorporate When *incorporate* is used with a preposition, it is usually *in* or *into* <*incorporated* it *in* their motto> <*incorporate* the ideas *into* our system>.

incredulous, incredible *Incredible* means "impossible to believe" <an *incredible* story>; *incredulous* means "unwilling to believe, disbelieving" <an *incredulous* audience>. Although *incredulous* is sometimes used where *incredible* is expected, most writers restrict *incredulous* to its "disbelieving" sense, and we recommend that you do so as well.

inculcate When *inculcate* is used with a preposition, and the direct object denotes what is inculcated, the preposition is usually *in* or *into* <to subtly *inculcate in* the students the idea that learning can be fun> <had *inculcated* their values *into* us as children>. Occasionally *inculcate* is used with *with,* but then the sense of the verb is "to cause to be impressed" <tried to *incul-cate* the children *with* American ideals>.

incumbent When the adjective *incumbent* is used with a preposition, it is usually *upon* or *on* <is *incumbent upon* us to act responsibly> <*incumbent on* the company's officers>.

independence When used with a preposition, *independence* is used with either *from* or *of* <*independence from* the electorate> <an *independence of* mind>.

independent *Independent,* when used with a preposition, is usually used with *of* <*independent of* the changes at city hall>.

Indian See NATIVE AMERICAN.

indifferent The preposition used with *indifferent* is almost always *to* <*indifferent to* pleas on moral grounds>.

individual Use of the noun *individual* to mean simply "person," where there is no obvious contrast of the person with a larger unit (such as society) or no obvious stress on some special quality, is often discouraged. But the evidence from usage shows that *individual* (noun) is most often used in contexts that do imply such a contrast <are you the *individual* I spoke with on the telephone?> or special quality <an *individual* with a long criminal record>.

indulge When *indulge* (intransitive or transitive) is used with a preposition, it is usually *in* <*indulged in* games> <*indulging* his interest *in* butterflies>. Transitive *indulge* may also be used with *with* <*indulged* myself *with* food>.

indulgent When *indulgent* is used with a preposition, it may be *in, of, to,* or *with* <*indulgent in* its use of color> <*indulgent of* his shortcomings> <*indulgent to* their leaders> <*indulgent with* the child>.

inedible, uneatable *Inedible* is a considerably more common word than *uneatable*. Otherwise, these two words are more or less interchangeable except in scientific contexts, where *inedible* is standard.

infatuated *Infatuated* takes *with* when it uses a preposition <*infatuated with* Italy>.

infectious See CONTAGIOUS, INFECTIOUS.

infer, imply *Infer* is mostly used to mean "to draw a conclusion, conclude" and is commonly followed by *from* <I *infer from* your letter that everything was satisfactory>. *Imply* is used to mean "to suggest" <the letter *implies* that the service was not satisfactory>. The use of *infer* with a personal subject in the sense of *imply* (as in "Are you *inferring* that I made a mistake?") is widely criticized as a confusion, though in any given context, in fact, the meaning is never in doubt. Further, the use is mostly oral and has seldom been a problem in edited prose in recent years. Certainly the recommended distinction is easy enough to observe, and doing so will win you favor.

infested When *infested* is used with a preposition, it is most often *with* <*infested with* lice> and less frequently *by* <*infested by* a new virus>.

infiltrate When *infiltrate* is used with a preposition, *into* is by far the most common <had *infiltrated into* the Mafia>. When the object is the one doing the infiltrating, *with* or *by* is used <*infiltrating* the organization *with* undercover agents> <a language *infiltrated by* foreign loan words>.

infiltration When *infiltration* is used with a preposition, it is usually *of* <the *infiltration of* enemy lines>; *into* is used somewhat less frequently <the *infiltration into* the language of foreign expressions>.

inflammable See FLAMMABLE, INFLAMMABLE.

inflict, afflict If you need to distinguish between these two words, remember that something is usually inflicted *on* (or *upon*) somebody <*inflicted* ethics training *on* employees annually>, whereas someone is usually afflicted *with* or *by* something <grandfather was *afflicted with* [*by*] gout>.

influence **1.** When the noun *influence* is used with a preposition, *of* is the usual choice; it typically introduces the influence itself <a check against the *influence of* television>. When the one influenced is being introduced, *on* or *in* is used <Seneca's *influence on*

English literature> <the *influence* of the Protestant ethic *in* capitalist society>. *Influence* is also used with *over, upon, among, for, from,* and *with.*

2. Pronouncing *influence,* noun or verb, with stress on the second syllable—\in-ˈflü-əns\—is more common in the South than elsewhere. A similar variation is found in *congruence;* some stress the first syllable and some the second, but in this case the variation is not specific to a particular region.

informant, informer An *informer* is usually someone who informs against someone else underhandedly, such as a spy or a police informer who gets paid for information. An *informant* is usually someone who informs in a neutral way or provides cultural or linguistic information to a researcher.

infringe *Infringe* as an intransitive verb is often followed by *on* or *upon* <*infringing upon* our rights>.

infuse When *infuse* is used with a preposition, it is usually *with* <*infused with* her personal vision>. Less frequently, *infuse* is used with *by* <*infused by* the spirit of the times>. When it means "introduce, insinuate," *infuse* can appear with *into* <a new confidence was *infused into* the team>. *Infuse* is also sometimes used with *in* <*infused* new life *in* him>.

ingenious, ingenuous *Ingenious* means "very clever" <an *ingenious* plan>, whereas *ingenuous* means "innocent and candid" <an *ingenuous* rural

friendliness>. Although these words were once synonyms, they are seldom confused today.

in hope(s) of, in hope(s) that See HOPE.

in line See ON LINE.

inoculate *Inoculate* has only one *n* (unlike *innocuous,* which has two).

in order to Writers are often told to shorten *in order to* to simply *to*. But *in order to* has its place in contexts where reduction to *to* would be ambiguous <it may be necessary *in order to* preserve them in a pure state>. In many contexts ambiguity is not a problem <took on the job *in order to* prove his worth> and *in order* could justifiably be dropped. But *in order to* is one of those phrases that many writers find useful for reasons of rhythm and emphasis. It is not good practice to delete *in order* reflexively in every instance.

in point of fact See FACT.

input This fashionable word, which has spread into general use from the world of computers, is sometimes criticized as jargon or bureaucratese. Most of the objections are directed at the noun when used in the sense of "advice, opinion, comment" <she got *input* from her associates>. Despite the objections the word continues to be popular, largely because precise synonyms seem to be lacking (*advice, opinion,* and *comment* included) and a longer phrase may often be the only alternative. Whether you use the word or not may depend on whether its faddishness or its conciseness has more weight with you.

inquire, enquire **1.** *Inquire* occurs more often than *enquire* in American English; when *enquire* does appear, it is usually in bookish or formal contexts. In British English, *enquire* appears about as often as *inquire*.

2. When *inquire* (or *enquire*) is used with a preposition, it is most often *about* or *into* <*inquired about* the horses> <we are *inquiring into* the situation>. Less frequently, *after, for, as to,* or *concerning* is used <*inquired after* his friend's parents> <he continues to *inquire for* any news about her> <*inquired as to* the progress of the talks> <are *inquiring concerning* your health>. When the person asked for information is the object, *of* is the usual preposition <*inquired of* her>.

inquiry, enquiry **1.** Both *inquiry* and *enquiry* are used in American and British English, with the *i* spelling occurring more often.

2. When *inquiry* and *enquiry* are used with a preposition, *into* is most often the choice <an *inquiry into* the cause of the mishap>. Less frequently, they are used with *about, as to, in, of, on,* or *with* in various relations and senses.

in regard to See REGARD.

in respect to, with respect to Both of these phrases are in current good use, mostly in academic writing.

With respect to is the more common <*with respect to* your last letter>. *In respect to* is primarily American, whereas the British tend to prefer *in respect of.*

inroad 1. *Inroad* is generally used in the plural, but it also may appear in the singular <made little *inroad* into the market>.

2. When *inroad* is used with a preposition, it is most often *into* or *on* <serious *inroads into* Republican strongholds> <made deep *inroads on* cable TV's monopoly>. Less frequently, *inroad* is used with *in, upon, against, among,* or *with.*

insanitary See UNSANITARY, INSANITARY.

insensitive When *insensitive* is used with a preposition, it is generally *to* <*insensitive to* the demands of the public>.

inseparable When used with a preposition, *inseparable* takes *from* <a precept that is *inseparable from* the notion of freedom>.

inside of *Inside of,* most often used with expressions of time <*inside of* two hours>, is a somewhat informal but nevertheless standard preposition. *Inside* without *of* is more common in written English, however. See also OUTSIDE OF.

insight When *insight* is used with a preposition, the choice is usually *into* <*insight into* the matter>. Occasionally *insight* can be used with *about, as to, in, on, regarding,* or *to*. See also INCITE, INSIGHT.

insignia *Insignia* is used both as a plural and as a singular. Some insist on the Latin *insigne* for the singular, but this form is rarely used (and may seem pretentious). The plural *insignias* has also become common.

insist When *insist* is used with a preposition, it is usually *on* or (less often) *upon* <*insisted on* this point>. As a transitive verb, *insist* takes a clause as its object <Mr. Bergin *insists that* he has nothing to cover up>.

inspire When *inspire* is used with a preposition, it generally is used with *by* and the verb form is usually the past participle <was particularly *inspired by* the Romantics>. *Inspire* is also used, and not just as a past participle, with *in, to,* or (less frequently) *with* <to *inspire* confidence *in* him> <were *inspired to* fight it> <*inspiring* her *with* thoughts of becoming a veterinarian>.

instil, instill **1.** *Instill* is more common in American English, whereas British English favors the single *l* (although it is always doubled in the inflected forms *instilled* and *instilling*).

2. When instill (or *instil*) is used with a preposition, it is most often *in* <*instilled* the work ethic *in* him>. Less frequently *into* is used, and even less frequently *with, among, through,* or *without.*

instruct When *instruct* is used with a preposition, the one that occurs most frequently is *to* followed by an infinitive <was *instructed to* contact them>. *Instruct* is almost as frequently used with *in* <were *instructed in* the goldsmith's art>, occasionally with *as to* or *for*.

insure See ENSURE, INSURE, ASSURE.

intend *Intend* may be followed by an infinitive <never *intended* to upset them>. It may be followed by a direct object and an infinitive phrase <apparently *intended* the money to go to charity>. It may be followed by a gerund <the parents *intended* leaving the children with a relative>. It may be followed by a clause, with or without *that*; the verb in the clause will be a subjunctive or the equivalent of a subjunctive <events unfolded the way she *intended* they should>. Finally, *intend* may take a prepositional phrase introduced by *for* <not *intended for* consumer use>. In speech and speechlike writing, it is sometimes followed by *on* and a gerund (as in "I don't *intend on* answering her anytime soon"). See also DESIGN, INTEND.

intensive, intense These two words have evolved along different lines in this century. Today *intense* is generally limited to describing some inherent characteristic <*intense* pleasure> <*intense* heat>. *Intensive,* on the other hand, usually connotes something that is applied from the outside <*intensive* training> <*intensive* screening>.

intent, *noun* See INTENTION 1.

intent, *adjective* When the adjective *intent* is used with a preposition, it is usually *on* <*intent on* their work>. Less frequently, it is used with *upon* <*intent upon* finding them>, and even less frequently with *in* or *to* and the infinitive.

intention **1.** *Intention* and *intent* are often used very nearly interchangeably. But in general *intention* implies simply what one has in mind to do or bring about <announced his *intention* to marry>, while *intent* suggests clearer formulation or greater deliberateness <the clear *intent* of the statute>.

2. When *intention* is used with a preposition, it is most often *of,* which is followed by a gerund or a noun <with the *intention of* signing it later> <the *intentions of* the administration>. Almost as frequently, *intention* is used with *to* and the infinitive <the group's *intention to* halt the action>. *Intention* has also been used with *against, behind,* and *toward.*

in terms of *In terms of* is a compound preposition that emerged in the 1950s and has remained popular ever since <thinks of everything *in terms of* money>. Some say that it is imprecise or overused and that you should substitute a simple preposition for it, such as *by, with,* or *about.* If you seek to do so, however, you will likely find yourself making additional revisions, since a one-to-one exchange is not always available. *In terms of* seems to be one of those expressions whose imprecision is its greatest virtue—writers do not always want to be precise. There will be times when a reworking of your sentence will improve it, but there is no need to make a strict policy of avoiding *in terms of.*

interpretative, interpretive These words are synonyms. *Interpretative* is older by a century or so, but in recent use the shorter *interpretive* has become the more common of the two. Both forms are standard.

intervene *Intervene* is used with a variety of prepositions. It occurs most often with *in* <having authority to *intervene in* such disputes>. Less frequently, it is used with *between* or *with* <a lucidity that *intervenes between* episodes of derangement> <she *intervened with* the school principal to make an exception>. It has also been used with *after, against,* and *into.*

in the course of See COURSE.

in the event that See EVENT.

in the hope(s) of, in the hope(s) that See HOPE.

into **1.** For a discussion of distinguishing between *in* and *into,* see IN, INTO.

2. *Into, in to.* In a sentence such as "Turn this form *in to* your department head," the adverb *in* followed by the preposition *to* is not to be confused with or carelessly replaced by the preposition *into.*

introduce When *introduce* is used with a preposition, it is usually used with *to* or *into* <will serve to

introduce you *to* the subject> <after *introducing* the compound *into* the test material>. It has also been used with *among, at, between, for, in, round,* and *within.*

intrude When *intrude* is used with a preposition, the choice most often is *into* <*into* which *intrudes* a granite dome> or, slightly less frequently, *on* (or *upon*) <*intruding on* the rival gang's turf>. It is also occasionally used with *between* or *in.*

inundate When *inundate* is used with a preposition, *with* is usual <*inundated with* phone calls>. Less often, *inundate* is used with *by* <a scoop of vanilla *inundated by* cherries and sauce>.

inure *Inure,* when used with a preposition, almost always takes *to* <*inured to* pain>. See also IMMURE 1.

invite The noun *invite* has been in use for more than 300 years, but it is criticized by some as slang. It remains standard, though it does tend to have a light or humorous quality and is not used in formal prose <thanks for the *invite*>.

invoke See EVOKE, INVOKE.

involve When *involve* is used with a preposition, it is most often *in* <the right of Congress to *involve* the nation *in* war>. It is also used often with *with* <was *involved with* a married man>.

invulnerable This word is sometimes considered to be an ABSOLUTE ADJECTIVE (see Glossary).

iridescent This is sometimes misspelled *irridescent*. Like its close relative *iris*, the word should have only one *r*.

irregardless This adverb, apparently a blend of *irrespective* and *regardless*, originated in dialectal American speech in the early 20th century. It has continued in spoken use, and occasionally finds its way into edited prose. But *irregardless* is still a long way from winning general acceptance as a standard English word. Use *regardless* instead.

irrelevant This word is sometimes misspelled (and mispronounced) *irrevelant*, where the *l* and *v* are transposed.

is because See BECAUSE 1; REASON IS BECAUSE.

isolate When *isolate* is used with a preposition, the choice is usually *from* <*isolated from* her family>. Occasionally it is used with *in*, *by*, or *with*.

is when, is where See WHEN, WHERE.

it For *it* in reference to preceding ideas, topics, sentences, or paragraphs, see THIS.

iterate See REITERATE.

its, it's These two forms are sometimes mistakenly interchanged. *It's* is the contraction of *it is* and *it has* <*it's* not enough to simply apologize>. *Its* is a possessive pronoun <the earth and *its* atmosphere>.

it's me See I, ME.

-ize Almost any noun or adjective can be made into a verb by adding *-ize* (e.g., *hospitalize, familiarize, idolize*). Many technical terms are formed this way (*oxidize, crystallize*), as are verbs of ethnic derivation (*Americanize*) and verbs derived from proper names (*bowdlerize, mesmerize*). People have always complained about new words formed this way and they still do: *finalize* and *prioritize* are two fairly recent ones that have been criticized. Remember that some *-ize* words are special or technical terms regularly used in a particular field or profession. No matter how strange these may seem, they should not be avoided in materials intended for the specialists.

J

jealous When *jealous* is used with a preposition, it is usually used with *of* <is *jealous of* her friend's new relationship>.

jewelry This word is sometimes pronounced \ˈjü-lə-rē\ (a transposed form of \ˈjü-əl-rē\), but this is not yet a widely accepted pronunciation. See also REALTOR.

jibe, gibe The distinction between *jibe* and *gibe* is not as clear-cut as many seem to think. *Jibe* is the more common spelling. It is used primarily for the verb meaning "to be in accord, to agree" <their views

jibe with ours>. But it is also used as a variant of *gibe* for the verb meaning "to utter taunting words, to deride or tease" <*gibed* [*jibed*] at her about it> and for the noun meaning "a taunting remark, jeer" <a gentle *gibe* [*jibe*]>. Though *gibe* is occasionally used as a variant of *jibe* (as in "the two schedules *gibe*"), most still consider this use an error.

join 1. *Join* is used with any of several prepositions, most often *in, to,* or *with.* When *in* is used, it is followed by a noun <*joined in* marriage> or gerund <*joined in* singing>. *To* and *with* both occur in many situations <her grieving spirit, *joined to* her physical pain, caused her to do it> <a series of images *joined with* narrative captions>. When *join* is being used of persons, *with* is the more common preposition <we *joined with* another group>.

2. Some disapprove the phrase *join together,* considering it a redundancy. It is primarily a spoken rather than a written idiom, in which the purpose of *together* is to add emphasis <let us *join together* in honoring her memory>, but it is nevertheless standard.

judgment, judgement Both spellings have been in use for centuries. *Judgment* is currently more common in the U.S., *judgement* in Britain.

judicial, judicious *Judicial* has to do primarily with judges and the law <the *judicial* branch of the government>, while *judicious* relates to sound judgment of a general kind <a fair and *judicious* critic>. The use of *judicial* in the sense of "judicious," while standard, has been criticized as an error but is rare now.

juncture *Juncture* is used especially to denote an important or critical point brought about by a concurrence of circumstances or events <an important *juncture* in our country's history>, but also often simply to mean "a point in time" <at this *juncture*, the company's prospects look good>. Some criticize the latter use as pompous, suggesting that *point* or *time* would work as well, but the criticism seems to have had little effect on published prose.

junior, senior Unlike *major, minor, inferior,* and *superior,* the adjectives *junior* and *senior* are regularly preceded by *more* and *most* <the *most junior* member> <a *more senior* position>. They function in this capacity as IMPLICIT COMPARATIVES (see Glossary). See also MAJOR.

just As an adverb, *just* has many uses, almost all of which have a somewhat informal quality. It can mean "exactly" <*just* right>, "very recently" <someone *just* called>, "barely" <*just* in time>, "immediately" <*just* west of here>, "only" <*just* a reminder>, "very" <*just* wonderful>, and "possibly" <it *just* might work>. Handbooks on writing occasionally disparage one or more of these senses (the "very" sense, in particular, has often been criticized), but all of them occur commonly in writing that is not especially formal.

justify When *justify* is used with a preposition, it often occurs with *in* or *by*. When *by* is used, it is usually followed by a noun <an action *justified by* customer responses>, less often by a gerund <to *justify* himself *by* claiming ignorance>. Less frequently, *justify* is used with *as* or *to* <forced to *justify* it *as* a viable enterprise> <sought to *justify to* herself her decision>. *Justify* is also frequently followed by *on the ground(s)* <is *justified on the grounds* of states' rights>.

K

ketchup See CATSUP, KETCHUP, CATCHUP.

kick off *Kick off*, once considered slang, now occurs commonly in written English. Its most characteristic use is in describing the beginning—often ceremonial—of large-scale public events or activities <will *kick off* the campaign>. However, its tone is not solemn.

kid The "child" sense of *kid* <the *kid* on the pro golf tour> is sometimes criticized as unacceptable, even though it has been used in print for nearly 400 years. It has an informal quality, which means it is suited to most contexts.

kilometer In North American speech, *kilometer* is most often pronounced with primary stress on the second syllable. This pronunciation is also heard frequently in British speech. Those who object say that the first syllable should be stressed as it is in *centimeter, millimeter,* etc. However, second-syllable stress has a long history of use, and it shows no sign of receding.

kin The usual sense of *kin* is "relatives" <considered them close *kin*>. But it also is occasionally used to mean "kinsman" <he's no *kin* of mine>. The singular *kin* is not new (it was being used in the 13th century), but it is uncommon enough to draw attention to itself. See also KITH AND KIN.

kind **1.** *These* (or *those) kind* (or *sort) of.* Most of the standard handbooks and usage books state the following rule: Use *this* or *that* with singular *kind* or *sort* and follow *of* with a singular noun <*this kind of* argument>; use *these* or *those* with plural *kinds* or *sorts* and follow *of* with a plural noun <*these kinds of* warnings>. But this advice presents an unrealistically narrow set of options; real usage is more complex. Both *kind* and *sort* are often found in the singular preceded by a singular and followed by a plural <*the kind of* questions that must be asked> <*any sort of* contingencies>, and in the singular preceded by a plural and followed by a plural <*these sort of* people> <*those kind of* letters>. And *kinds* and *sorts* are followed not only by plurals but also by singulars <*several kinds of* decision making>. Despite these usages, the issue is a bugbear of American handbooks on writing, and you should be aware that any deviation from the common rule may be noticed with disfavor by some critic.

2. See KIND OF, SORT OF; KIND OF A, SORT OF A.

kindly *Kindly* is used both as an adjective <a *kindly* smile> and as an adverb <he smiled *kindly*>. It sometimes serves as a synonym of *please* <would you *kindly* refrain from doing that?>. The "please" sense is sometimes criticized as outmoded, but writers and speakers continue to find it useful and effective.

kind of, sort of *Kind of* and *sort of* appear in print mostly in fictional speech or in prose written in a light or familiar style <we just *kind of* took it on faith> <I always *sort of* liked him>.

kind of a, sort of a This English idiom has been around for a few hundred years but began to be criticized early in this century. Most modern critics advise omitting the *a,* and most writers do so. Still, there never has been a sound reason for questioning the less common idiom. If it is your idiom, there's no need to avoid it, especially in speech or in informal writing <some *kind of a* joke> <what *sort of a* person is she?>.

kith and kin This alliterative phrase—some would label it a cliché—is said by those who know its history to mean not "kinsfolk" but rather "countrymen and kinsfolk." However, the "kinsfolk" sense is now the more common.

kneel The past tense and past participle of *kneel* can be either *knelt* or *kneeled. Knelt* today occurs a little more frequently than *kneeled* <*knelt* [*kneeled*] before the altar>.

knit, knitted The past tense and past participle of *knit* can be either *knit* or *knitted* <a *knit* [*knitted*] shirt> <he *knitted* [*knit*] his brows in concentration>. *Knit* is definitely preferred, however, with such adverbs as *closely* and *tightly* <a closely *knit* family>.

kudo, kudos Some claim that since *kudos* is a singular word (derived from the Greek *kydos,* "fame, renown"), it cannot be used as a plural, and thus the word *kudo* is impossible. But *kudo* does exist, though it is far more often used in the plural than the singular <various *kudos* and other compliments>; it is simply one of the more recent words (*cherry* and *pea* are older examples) created by back-formation from another word misunderstood as a plural. While it is now standard, it has not yet penetrated the highest range of scholarly writing or literature.

L

labor See BELABOR, LABOR.

lack *In* and *for* are the prepositions used with the verb *lack* <*lacking in* decorum>; *for* usually appears in negative constructions <does not *lack for* supporters>. Both are often omitted <*lacking* decorum> <does not *lack* supporters>.

laden When *laden* is used with a preposition, the choice is almost always *with* <*laden with* goods>.

lady *Lady* is one of the fine old words of English. In the 19th century, after perhaps 1100 years of use, it began to be subject to criticism (as vulgar, affected, common, biased as to class, etc.). It has been long used as a polite way of referring to a woman <is the *lady* of the house in?> but many disapprove such use, finding it sexist or condescending. *Woman* is now the safest and usual choice, a notable exception being in the phrase *ladies and gentlemen,* which remains in very common use.

lament The verb *lament,* when used with a preposition, is used with *about, for,* or *over* <was *lamenting about* the situation with her daughter> <they *lamented for* her> <started to *lament over* the flood damage>. *About* and *over* can often be omitted <was *lamenting* the situation>.

last Some writers make the distinction that *last* means "final" and *latest* means "most recent." Others admit that both words can mean "most recent" <his *last* book> <his *latest* book> but insist that only *latest* conveys this meaning unambiguously. The context usually makes clear what sense of *last* is intended; if for some reason that clarity is missing from something you have written, you may want to substitute *latest* (or *final*).

late When should we stop referring to a dead person as *the late*? Ten years? Twenty years? Fifty years? The phrase is in fact generally applied to people whose lives were recent enough to exist within the living memory of the writer or speaker. Other than that, there is no hard-and-fast rule. See also WIDOW, WIDOWER.

Latin plurals The use of the plurals of foreign words—mostly, but not all, Latin—as singulars is a recurrent issue. For discussions of individual cases, see AGENDA; CRITERION, CRITERIA; CURRICULUM; DATA; DICTUM; EROTICA; MEDIA; MEMORANDUM; PHENOMENA; STRATA, STRATUM; TRIVIA.

latter See FORMER 1.

laudable, laudatory Very occasionally these words are confused, with *laudatory* used for *laudable*. *Laudable* means "deserving praise, praiseworthy" <*laudable* attempts to help the poor>, while *laudatory* means "giving praise, praiseful" <a *laudatory* book review>.

lay, lie *Lay* has been used as an intransitive verb meaning "lie" since the 14th century (as in "tried to make the book *lay* flat," or "*lay* down on the job"). By the last third of the 18th century, however, it was being regarded as a mistake. Since then schoolteachers and critics have succeeded in eliminating the use from most literary and learned writing, but it persists in familiar speech and in casual writing. Part of the problem lies in the confusing similarity of the inflected forms of the two words (*lay*'s past tense and past participle are both *laid; lie*'s are *lay* and *lain* respectively). Although many people will continue to use *lay* for *lie*, anyone who has invested effort in maintaining the distinction is likely to judge you unfavorably if you use it.

lead, led The past tense and past participle of the verb *lead* is spelled *led* <*led* his opponent in early returns> <were *led* to believe otherwise>. A common mistake is to spell it *lead*. See also MISLEAD, MISLED.

lean 1. In British English both *leant* and *leaned* are used for the past tense and past participle. In American English, *leaned* is used almost exclusively.

2. When *lean* is used with a preposition, the preposition is most often *on* <*leaned on* the counter>. *To, toward* (or *towards*), *upon, in, against, into, out of,* and *over* are also common.

leap *Leaped* and *leapt* are interchangeable both as the past tense <he *leaped* [*leapt*] over the ditch> and past participle <the song has *leapt* [*leaped*] to the top of the charts> in American English. In British English, *leapt* is the more common choice.

leary See LEERY, LEARY.

leave, let 1. Should you say "*leave* me alone" or "*let* me alone"? Our evidence shows that, despite some criticism, the phrases have long been used interchangeably.

2. *Leave* in the sense of "let" followed by a pronoun and an infinitive without *to* <*leave* it be> is a mostly spoken idiom used occasionally in writing for humorous effect. It is not often criticized in British English, but American commentators generally dislike it.

3. See LET.

led See LEAD, LED.

leery, leary 1. *Leery* and its less common variant *leary* have been in use for nearly 300 years. Perhaps because the word first appeared in thieves' cant, it was long regarded as slang. Today the word is quite common and is completely standard.

2. When *leery* (or *leary*) is used with a preposition, it is most likely to be *of* <*leery of* such pronouncements> or, less frequently, *about* <*leery about* discount offers>.

legitimate, legitimize Some have questioned the need for using *legitimize* (first recorded in 1848) when the older verb *legitimate* (first recorded in 1586) remains available. The use of *legitimize* (and the less common *legitimatize*) has certainly increased in the 20th century <the assault *legitimized* Republicans' call for an arms buildup>, but *legitimate* is still common <serves only to *legitimate* racial intolerance>.

lend See LOAN, LEND.

lend credence to See CREDENCE, CREDIBILITY.

less, fewer The traditional view is that *less* is used for matters of degree, value, or amount, and that it modifies nouns that refer to uncountable things <*less* hostility> <*less* clothing> while *fewer* modifies numbers and plural nouns <*fewer* students> <*fewer* than eight trees>. However, *less* has been used to modify plural nouns for centuries and today is actually more likely than *fewer* to be used of distances <*less* than 100 miles>, of sums of money <*less* than $2,000>, or in certain fixed phrases <in 25 words or *less*>. In other contexts, the traditional rule is a safe guide.

lesser **1.** The adjective *lesser,* sometimes thought to be a double comparative like *worser,* is in fact a standard comparative of *little.* It is used to indicate a difference in value or importance <a *lesser* woman would have caved in> <the *lesser* of the two piano works>. It is also sometimes used of numerical quantities where *smaller* or *lower* is more usual <took the *lesser* amount>. And it is used of size in the names of various plants and animals <*lesser* celandine> <*lesser* yellowlegs>.

2. The adverb *lesser* is today limited to modifying past participles—especially *known*—to which it may or may not be joined by a hyphen <one of the *lesser-known* authors>.

lest This conjunction is almost always followed by a verb in the subjunctive mood <hesitant to speak out *lest* he be fired>. It can also be followed by a *should* clause, though this was more common in the past than it is now <worried *lest* she should be late>. Occasionally a writer follows *lest* with a verb in the indicative mood (as in "*lest* the lesson is lost on us"), but this is liable to be regarded as a mistake.

let **1.** For a discussion of distinguishing between *let* and *leave*, see LEAVE, LET.

2. Is it preferable to say "*Let's* you and I get together" or "*Let's* you and me get together"? Both expressions are justifiable on historical grounds; however, you will probably not need either in anything you write that is more formal than casual speech.

3. The negative of *let's* is formed in three ways: *let's not,* which is widely used; *don't let's,* which is chiefly found in British English; and *let's don't,* which is used in speech and casual writing.

let's See LET 2, 3.

liable, apt, likely Both *liable* and *apt,* when followed by an infinitive, are used nearly interchangeably with *likely. Apt* and *likely,* however, are common in situations having a positive or neutral outcome <he's *likely* [*apt*] to be praised> or a negative outcome <is *apt* [*likely*] to falter>. *Liable,* on the other hand, is generally limited to situations having a negative outcome <is *liable* to get lost>.

liaison With its French origin and unusual sequence of vowels, *liaison* tends to be troublesome to pronounce. The two most common pronunciations are

\ˈlē-əˌzän\ and \lē-ˈā-ˌzän\. The variant \ˈlā-əˌzän\ is well entrenched in the military, but in other circles it is often regarded as an error.

The spelling of *liaison* also gives many people trouble, the tendency being to drop the second *i*. Watch out for it.

library For pronunciation, see FEBRUARY.

lie See LAY, LIE.

lighted, lit Both *lit* and *lighted* are acceptable and standard as the past tense and past participle of the verb *light*. Both forms have been used for centuries and currently appear with about equal frequency <rockets *lighted* [*lit*] up the sky> <a smile *lit* [*lighted*] up her face>.

lightning *Lightning* very often gets an extra *e* (*lightening*). Watch out for this mistake.

light-year Some have criticized the use of *light-year*—a unit of astronomical distance—to mean "a very long time" (as in "that was *light-years* ago"), since in figurative use *light-year* is generally restricted to the sense "a very great distance," with the distance referred to typically being more cultural than physical <we are *light-years* behind the Japanese>.

like **1.** *Like, as, as if.* *Like* has been used as a conjunction meaning "as" <it was well done, *like* you'd expect> and "as if" <looks *like* it will rain> for more than 600 years, though it was fairly rare until the 19th century, when an increase in use provoked critics to censure it. Though criticism persists even today, the usage has never been less than standard, even if more often spoken than written. Someone writing in a formal prose style may well prefer to use *as* or *as if* or to recast the sentence.

2. *Like, such as.* Should you write "cities *like* Chicago and Des Moines" or "cities *such as* Chicago and Des Moines"? You are in fact free to use either one or to change the latter to "*such* cities *as* Chicago and Des Moines."

liked to See LIKE TO, LIKED TO.

like for *Like for* is fairly common in spoken American English, especially as part of a request (as in "we'd *like for* you to come"), but you will not have much need for it in ordinary prose.

likely The use of *likely* as an adverb <he will *likely* be elected> without a qualifier such as *more, most, very,* or *quite* has been criticized as unidiomatic. But in fact the use is an old one, dating back to the 14th century, and is standard today. See also LIABLE, APT, LIKELY.

liken The verb *liken* takes the preposition *to* <*likened* it *to* putting a fox in charge of the henhouse>.

likes of The phrase *the likes of,* disparaged by many on uncertain grounds, goes back more than 200 years and is standard. It has two principal uses. In one, it takes a single object (often a pronoun) and carries overtones of disparagement <have no use for *the likes of* you>. In the other, it takes a multiple object (usually a list of names), means essentially "such people as" or "such things as," and carries no disparaging connotations <reads *the likes of* Jane Austen and Robert Browning>. *The like of* is also sometimes used, and it is probably a better choice when the reference is to a single object and no disparagement is intended <an achievement *the like of* which we have not often seen>.

like to, liked to Both of these phrases mean "came near (to), almost" (as in "I *liked to* die!"). Though they have had a long and distinguished literary career, since the first part of the 20th century they have been primarily used in speech rather than writing. In the United States in particular, they are associated with uneducated or old-fashioned speech, and you will not need them in ordinary prose.

lit See LIGHTED, LIT.

literally *Literally* means "in a literal sense or manner" <took the remark *literally*> or "actually" <was *literally* insane>. But it is also used as an intensifier to mean "in effect" or "virtually" <she *literally* flew up the stairs> <the performance *literally* brought the house down>. Though the latter use is often criticized as nonsensical, it is not supposed to make sense, but rather only to interject a bit of hyperbole. The word is often used (or overused) in contexts where no additional emphasis is necessary, however.

loan, lend The verb *loan* <*loaned* me the book> came to America with early settlers and continued in use here when it dropped out of use in Great Britain. Various 19th-century commentators decided that the use was improper, and a surprising number of critics still object to it. Nevertheless, *loan* is entirely standard as a verb. You should note that it is used only literally (as in the example above); *lend* is the verb used in figurative expressions, such as "*lend* a hand" or "*lending* a touch of class."

loath, loathe The spelling *loath* is used for the adjective <is *loath* to do it>, while *loathe* is used for the verb <she *loathes* him> and secondarily for the adjective. In pronouncing the adjective, some people rhyme it with the verb, voicing the *th*. This pronunciation causes many people to spell the adjective *loathe*. If you want to play it safe, use *loath* for the adjective and *loathe* for the verb. But if *loathe* represents your pronunciation of the adjective, you may use it.

loose, lose The issue here is faulty spelling. The verb *lose* rhymes with *choose*, and in casual writing it often gets an extra *o*. Be careful not to make this mistake.

lost This word is sometimes considered to be an ABSOLUTE ADJECTIVE (see Glossary).s

lots, a lot These expressions, though often labeled colloquial, have been used in serious but not highly formal writing for a long time <*a lot* of money> <*lots* of friends>. See also ALOT, A LOT.

loud, loudly *Loud* is most familiar as an adjective <a *loud* noise>. When used as an adverb, it always follows the verb that it modifies, and it occurs chiefly with only a few simple and familiar verbs, such as *talk, scream, shout,* or *cheer* <talks *loud*> <shouting as *loud* as she could>. In most other contexts, *loudly* is preferred <*loudly* proclaimed victory> <seagulls squawking *loudly* overhead>.

M

mad 1. The use of *mad* to mean "angry" (rather than "crazy, insane") has been criticized as slang or colloquial, but the usage is quite old (going back at least to Shakespeare) and remains in good standing <were particularly *mad* about the slow pace>. *Mad* in this sense is found today in fiction, general nonfiction, correspondence, and of course in speech.

2. *Mad* is followed by a number of different prepositions. People who are angry are *mad at* or less often, *mad with* people or things; they are also sometimes *mad about* things. People who are carried away by enthusiasm are *mad about, mad for,* or, if they are British, *mad on* something or someone. People who are frantic or wild are *mad with* something.

magnate, magnet These two words are occasionally confused. A *magnate* is a person of rank, influence, or distinction <publishing *magnate*>. A *magnet* is a body that attracts iron, or simply "something that attracts" <a *magnet* for fashion buyers>.

major **1.** Some complain that the word *major* is overused. It is true that it does appear frequently, and often in contexts where its meaning gets diluted (as in "a *major* motion picture," which is nothing more than a new movie). But you need not stop using a word simply because other people overuse it; just take care not to overuse it yourself.

2. Critics have claimed that *major* is a comparative, like *greater,* and so should not be used as a straight adjective <a *major* campaign speech>. They recommend substituting *important, principal,* or *big.* But *major* is perfectly standard in this use, and often preferable to any of the proposed substitutes. The same claim has been made with regard to *minor,* and the same conclusion applies.

majority **1.** *Majority* is used as a collective noun that takes either a singular or a plural verb, depending on whether the writer views the majority as a single unit or as a collection of individuals. When *majority* stands alone as the subject, it tends to be used with a singular verb <the *majority* has decided to support the mayor>. It also frequently takes a plural verb <the *majority* are unable to make new friends easily>. When *majority* is followed by *of* and a plural noun, a plural verb is usual <the *majority of* the bills have been paid>.

2. The use of *majority* with things that are not countable has been generally discouraged. While it is not as common as use with a plural, it is found in standard sources in scientific, legal, and general contexts <must contain a *majority* of dark matter> <the *majority* of the court> <the *majority* of the world's cocaine>.

male Although there has been controversy over the use of *female* (see entry), the parallel term *male* has escaped criticism. It is generally used as an adjective <a *male* collie>; when used as a noun, it is often paired with *female* <the gang included both *males* and females>.

man *Man* in the generic sense "a human being" <no *man* is an island> or "mankind" <*man*'s natural rights> has come under attack in recent years by people who feel, not unreasonably, that it slights women. *Human* and *human being* are sometimes used as replacements, though *man* is still used. See also MANKIND.

mankind *Mankind* has been open to some of the same objections as the generic use of *man* (see above). If *mankind* is offensive to you, you may substitute *humankind, human beings, humans,* or *people. Humankind,* like *mankind,* is a mass noun that is usually treated as singular <*humankind* worships many different gods>.

mantel, mantle *Mantel* refers to the shelf above a fireplace, *mantle* to a cloak or cover.

many a The phrase *many a* is followed by a singular noun and usually a singular verb <*many a* sprinter has tried>. When a pronoun is used as well, it may be either plural or singular <led *many a* good citizen to put *their* trust in him> <*many a* president has changed *his* mind>. (See NOTIONAL AGREEMENT in Glossary.)

mar When the verb *mar* takes a preposition, it is usually *by* <*marred by* a few gaffes>. Less frequently, *mar* takes *with* <*marred with* errors>.

marital, martial Note that a slip of the finger can easily transpose the *i* and the *t*, changing *marital* to *martial* or vice versa.

marshal, marshall The usual spelling of both the noun and verb is *marshal* <a federal *marshal*> <*marshaling* support>. The two-*l*'d *marshall*, however, is a variant that has been in use for centuries.

martial See MARITAL, MARTIAL.

martyr **1.** When the noun *martyr* is used with a preposition, it is usually *to* <a *martyr to* duty>. Occasionally *martyr* is followed by *for* or *of* <a *martyr for* academic freedom> <a *martyr of* love>.

2. When the verb *martyr* is used with a preposition, it is usually *for* <*martyring* herself *for* her family>.

masterful, masterly *Masterly* means "suitable to or resembling that of a master" <a *masterly* performance>. *Masterful* has several meanings, one of which is "masterly" <a *masterful* performance>. It has been argued that since *masterly* has only one meaning, it rather than *masterful* should be used whenever that meaning is intended. But *masterful* is in reputable use in this sense, so there is no need to prefer *masterly.* The distinction is easily observed, however, if you care to do so.

maximize Though *maximize* is sometimes regarded as jargon, perhaps because it occurs so commonly in business writing <*maximize* distribution>, it is in standard use today.

may See CAN, MAY.

may of See OF 2.

me See I, ME.

means **1.** *Means* in the sense of "something helpful in achieving a desired end" may be treated as either singular or plural <whether or not this is the proper *means*> <these *means* have been tried before>. *Means* in the sense of "material resources affording a secure life" is treated as plural when it takes a verb <the family's *means* were rather modest>.

2. When used with a preposition, *means* almost always takes *of* <a *means of* support>. Much less frequently, it takes *to* <a *means to* increase interest>, *toward* <the *means toward* an end>, or *for* <a *means for* solving these problems>.

3. See BY MEANS OF.

meddle When *meddle* is used with a preposition, the usual choice is *with* <*meddling with* others' work>. It is also used with *in* and *into* <had *meddled in* this matter> <to *meddle into* internal affairs>.

media *Media* is a plural of *medium*. For this reason many insist that it must be used with a plural verb. But a singular *media* (plural *medias*) has been in the advertising business for over half a century, and more recently a singular mass noun (with no plural) meaning "the news media" has become established. But this singular use is not yet as fully established as the mass-noun use of *data* (see entry). Usage in the media is mixed <the *media* have [has] exaggerated the issue> but the plural verb is still more frequent and is the safer choice <the *media* are not to be blamed>.

mediate *Mediate* is most often used with *between* when it takes a preposition <*mediating between* the two parties>. Occasionally it is used with *for* <*mediated for* the combatants>. As a transitive verb, it is also found with *through* <meanings that are *mediated through* the senses>.

mediocre This word is sometimes considered to be an ABSOLUTE ADJECTIVE (see Glossary).

medium See MEDIA.

meet, mete If you use the verb *mete* <to *mete* out punishment>, be sure not to misspell it *meet.*

memento See MOMENTO.

memorandum *Memorandum* is a singular noun with two acceptable plurals: *memorandums* and *memoranda. Memoranda* is sometimes mistakenly used as a singular (as in "wrote the *memoranda* and then quickly reviewed it"), and *memorandum* is sometimes mistakenly used as a plural (as in "circulated these *memorandum*"). Be careful.

mete See MEET, METE.

might could See DOUBLE MODAL in Glossary.

might of See OF 2.

mighty The use of *mighty* as an intensive usually conveys a folksy, down-home feeling <*mighty* satisfying>. It is used especially to create a chatty style or to stress a rural atmosphere. You will not need it in formal writing.

militate, mitigate *Militate* means "to have weight or effect" <conditions *militate* against expansion at this time>. *Mitigate,* which means "to make less severe" <circumstances which *mitigate* their involvement>, is sometimes mistakenly used (with *against*) in place of *militate.* You will want to avoid this use in your own writing.

millennium A common misspelling of this word drops one of the *n*'s. Remember that there are as many *n*'s as *l*'s.

mine See MY, MINE.

miniscule, minuscule This word is derived from the Latin *minusculus* and is related to the word *minus.* If you want to be consistent with etymology, spell it *minuscule,* as a majority of writers do. The spelling *miniscule* is also fairly common, especially for the meaning "very small." Even though some dictionaries recognize the *-i-* spelling, many consider it a misspelling.

minor See MAJOR 2.

minus Use of *minus* as a preposition meaning "without" <*minus* his hat> is sometimes objected to for sounding breezy and unserious. But the word has standard use in both humorous and serious, if not highly formal, writing.

minuscule See MINISCULE, MINUSCULE.

minutia The meaning of *minutia* is "a minute or minor detail." The word is almost always now used in its plural form *minutiae* <all the *minutiae* of daily living>. Using the singular *minutia* itself as a plural (as in "all the *minutia* of daily living") is considered an error.

mischievous The pronunciation \mis-ˈchē-vē-əs\ (rhyming with *devious*) and the consequent spelling *mischievious* are of long standing (going back to the 16th century), but both remain nonstandard.

mishap Some have argued that *mishap* applies only to minor accidents. The word is actually applied to both serious and inconsequential accidents <a mechanical *mishap* nearly caused the plant to shut down>, but it most often tends to downplay the seriousness of what happened.

mislead, misled The spelling error that occurs with the verb *lead* (see LEAD, LED) also occurs with *mislead*. The past tense and past participle, *misled*, is sometimes misspelled *mislead*. Remember: in the past tense or past participle, get the *-lead* out.

misspell *Misspell* is sometimes itself misspelled *mispell*, a mistake that has considerable potential to embarrass the misspeller.

mistrustful *Mistrustful* is usually used with *of* when it takes a preposition <*mistrustful of* them>. Sometimes *toward* is used instead <*mistrustful toward* her colleagues>.

mitigate See MILITATE, MITIGATE.

mix When *mix* takes a preposition, it is most often *with* <*mixes* business *with* pleasure>. Less often, *in* or *into* is used <decided not to *mix in* politics> <*mixing into* this ideological brew some rather silly notions>.

momentarily Despite the wish of some critics to limit the meaning of *momentarily* to "for a moment" <we were delayed *momentarily*>, an equally common meaning is "in a moment" <we'll be departing *momentarily*>. These two senses have coexisted in American English for many decades (in British English, the "in a moment" sense is rare), and both are standard, since the meaning is always made clear by the context.

momento The word *memento* ("souvenir") is spelled *momento* by enough people that the latter can be considered a variant form. If you want to stick to the original spelling, though, as most writers do, remember that *memento* is related to *memory* and *remember* and not to *moment*.

moneys, monies Though *money* has no plural in most of its uses, when the reference is to discrete sums of money obtained from various sources or distributed to various individuals or groups, the plural *moneys* or *monies* is often used <all *moneys* in the slush fund have been seized>. The plural *monies* has occasionally been criticized because it suggests a singular *mony* rather than *money*. It is, however, an old and perfectly respectable variant that is used almost as commonly as *moneys*.

monopoly *Monopoly* is used with several prepositions. Most often it is used with *on* <a *monopoly on* goodwill>. *Monopoly of* is also quite common <a

monopoly of technological know-how>. Less frequently, *monopoly* is used with *in* and *over* <a *monopoly in* that field> <a virtual *monopoly over* exports>.

moral, morale *Morale,* meaning "mental or emotional condition," is sometimes misspelled *moral,* which of course means "the practical meaning (as of a story)."

more important, more importantly See IMPORTANT 1.

more than one The idea of the phrase *more than one* is plural, but since it usually modifies a singular noun, it generally takes a singular verb <*more than one* fake is known to exist>. But sometimes a plural verb is used because the notion of plurality (see NOTIONAL AGREEMENT in Glossary) predominates <*more than one* deer are often spotted here by visitors> or because it is simply required by the context of the whole sentence <if there are *more than one,* they appear in alphabetical order>. When the phrase is followed by *of* and a plural noun, a plural verb is usual <where *more than one of* these problems are liable to turn up>.

Moslem, Muslim *Moslem* is the older spelling, but *Muslim* is more used today both because it is preferred by those of whom it is used and because it more closely represents the Arabic pronunciation.

most Although considered unacceptable by some, *most* in the sense "almost" <can be found *most* anywhere

today> is often used in spoken and, to a lesser extent, informal written English modifying such words as *all, everything, anyone,* and *always.*

mostly The propriety of using *mostly* (meaning "mainly") to modify a verb <they *mostly* just wanted to go home> has been questioned. Although this use may not be especially elegant, there is no question that it is standard and common. *Mostly* is also used at the beginning of a sentence <*Mostly,* the discussion focused on debt control>.

motive *Motive* is often followed by the preposition *for,* which is in turn often followed by a gerund <his *motives for* doing it>. *Motive* is also sometimes followed by *of* or *behind* <the *motive of* self-aggrandizement> <the *motives behind* their actions>, and sometimes by *to* and the infinitive <sufficient *motive to* carry it out>.

Ms. *Ms.*, a blend of *Miss* and *Mrs.*, has over the years become the standard form to use, especially in business correspondence, when addressing a woman whose marital status is unknown or irrelevant to matters at hand <Dear *Ms.* Smith>.

mucus, mucous The noun is spelled *mucus* <a buildup of *mucus*>, and the adjective is spelled *mucous* <*mucous* membrane>.

muse *Muse* is used about equally with *on, upon,* and *over* <started *musing on* [*upon, over*] it>. It also occurs, much less frequently, with *about* <mused *about* her role in the affair>.

Muslim See MOSLEM, MUSLIM.

must *Must* in the sense "something essential" used to require quotation marks around it, but now is so common that the quotes are generally omitted <experience using databases is a *must*>.

must of See OF 2.

my, mine *My* is sometimes combined, especially in speech, with another possessive pronoun to create an expression such as "*my* and her child both went." *Mine* is even occasionally used as well ("*mine* and her child both went"). This type of construction, while understandable in speech, should be recast in writing <*my* child and hers both went>.

myself *Myself* is often used in place of *I* or *me:* as subject <others and *myself* continued to press for the legislation>; after *as, than,* or *like* <paying such people as *myself* to tutor> <was enough to make a better man than *myself* quail> <old-timers like *myself*>; and as object <now here you see *myself* with the diver> <for my wife and *myself* it was a happy time>. Such uses often occur, as in some of the examples above, when the speaker or writer is referring to himself or herself as an object of discussion. (The other reflexive personal pronouns—*herself, himself, themselves*—are less frequently used in this way.) Critics have frowned on these uses since the start of the 20th century, but they serve a definite purpose and are standard.

N

naive, naïve, naïveté The adjective *naive* is spelled at least as often without the diaeresis over the *i* as with one. The noun *naïveté,* however, is most often spelled with both the diaeresis and an accent over the final *e.*

naked, nude *Naked* tends to suggest the absence of clothing in general contexts <*naked* above the waist>, while *nude* tends to refer to the unclothed human figure in the context of art <a *nude* model posing for art students>.

native Use of *native* for a nonwhite person indigenous to some place (as in "we conversed with the *natives* in French") is often considered offensive. In North America, however, especially in Alaska and Western Canada, *native* (usually capitalized) is frequently used nonpejoratively in the sense "Native American" <seminars on *Native* cultures>. It also continues to be used without offense of someone belonging to a particular place by birth <a *native* of Wisconsin>.

Native American *Native American* has become, for many, a term of choice to refer to a member of any of the aboriginal peoples of North America (except, usually, the Inuit, or Eskimo, peoples), but it has by no means displaced *American Indian* or *Indian.* All are in frequent use.

nature Phrases like *of this nature* or *of a . . . nature* (as in "The court does not normally hear cases *of a* probate *nature*") are often considered wordy. Though absolute concision is not necessary in every case, if wordiness or awkwardness is apparent the writer may consider revising (e.g., "The court does not normally hear probate cases").

nauseating, nauseous *Nauseous* is most frequently used to mean "physically affected with nausea" <the ride made me *nauseous*>, while *nauseating* is used to mean "causing nausea or disgust" <the *nauseating* violence on TV>.

naval, navel Watch your spelling here. *Naval* means "relating to a navy," while *navel* refers to the belly button.

near, nearly *Near* in the sense of "almost, nearly" <found *near* dead> <a *near*-perfect score>, though standard in speech and informal writing, may sound just a little old-fashioned to some. You can usually substitute *nearly*.

necessary *Necessary,* when used with a preposition, is most often used with *to* <the force *necessary to* apprehend the suspect>. It is less often used with *for* <is *necessary for* a lasting relationship>, and occasionally with *in* <*necessary in* the training of students>.

necessity When *necessity* is used with a preposition, it is usually either *of* or, less often, *for* <the *necessity of* choosing> <the *necessity for* greater clarity>.

née The literal meaning of this word in French is "born." Its usual function in English is to introduce a married woman's maiden name <Mrs. John Jones, *née* Smith>. Some literal-minded critics have warned against following it with a woman's given name <Peggy Lee, *née* Norma Egstrom>, because a person is born only with a last name—the given name comes later. But *née* in English is closer in meaning to "formerly or originally known as" than to "born," and its use before a woman's given name is standard.

need 1. *Noun.* The preposition that follows *need* is usually *for* <the *need for* regulations>, but *of* is also a common choice, especially in the phrase *in need of* <*in need of* repair> <the *needs of* the institution>. *Need* is also commonly followed by the infinitive <the *need* to begin a dialogue>.

2. *Verb. Need* as an auxiliary verb is followed by the bare infinitive without *to* <no one *need* know> <all she *need* do is apply>. As a regular verb it requires *to* <he *needed to* contact them>. It can also be followed by a gerund <it doesn't *need* repeating here>.

3. The verb *need* is sometimes followed directly by a past participle (as in "the car *needs* washed"). This is an American regional usage found in the Midland area and especially in Pennsylvania. It is primarily spoken but can be found in local newspapers.

needless to say This phrase is criticized on the same grounds as *goes without saying*. Yet it continues to be used standardly to emphasize that the writer or speaker regards the statement being made as in some way self-evident, and to provide a graceful transition between sentences or paragraphs. See also GOES WITHOUT SAYING.

neglectful *Neglectful* is used with *of* <*neglectful of* her chores>.

negligent When *negligent* is used with a preposition, the choice is usually *in* or *of* <*negligent* in settling the account> <*negligent of* the details>. *About* is also used <*negligent about* writing a note of thanks>.

neither **1.** The pronoun *neither* is traditionally used with a singular verb <*neither is* ideal>, especially in formal writing. However, when a prepositional phrase follows *neither*, a plural verb is common and acceptable <*neither* of those solutions *are* ideal>, especially in less formal contexts.

2. *Neither* as a conjunction is usually followed by *nor* <*neither* high winds *nor* freezing temperatures>, although use with *or* is found in casual writing <*neither* he *or* she knew the answer>.

3. The use of *neither* to refer to more than two nouns, though sometimes criticized, has been standard for centuries <*neither* the post office, the bank, nor City Hall is open today>.

4. *Neither . . . nor* with two (or more) singular subjects is governed by NOTIONAL AGREEMENT (see

Glossary) and may take either a singular or a plural verb <*neither* Johnson *nor* Ruskin *was* bothered by it> <*neither* the soloist *nor* the orchestra *were* in top form>. When the subjects are plural, or the last subject is plural, a plural verb is expected <*neither* local fishermen *nor* environmentalists *are* pleased with the decision> <*neither* you *nor* your associates *have* been forthcoming on the issue>. See also AGREEMENT (in Glossary).

never too See NOT TOO.

nice and Unlike the phrase *good and*, which may be followed by a variety of adjectives, *nice and* is generally restricted to a few approving phrases <*nice and* warm> <*nice and* easy>. Such phrases, though standard, are seldom employed in formal writing.

nickel, nickle *Nickel* is the original and generally accepted spelling. *Nickle* does appear in print, but many regard it as an error.

no See DOUBLE NEGATIVE in Glossary.

nobody, no one These indefinite pronouns for the most part follow the same pattern of notional agreement as the other indefinite pronouns: they regularly take a singular verb but may be referred to by either a singular or a plural pronoun <*nobody* wants to have *his* license revoked> <*no one* cares about how *their* lawn looks around here>. A singular pronoun is generally preferred in formal contexts <*no one* could convince top management of the merit of *his* idea>, but a plural pronoun, even though criticized, has the advantage of not forcing a choice between masculine and feminine singular forms <*no one* could convince top management of the merit of *their* idea>. See also THEY, THEIR, THEM; AGREEMENT: INDEFINITE PRONOUNS (in Glossary).

no doubt See DOUBTLESS, NO DOUBT, UNDOUBTEDLY.

noisome *Noisome* is almost always used to mean "noxious" or "disgusting" <the *noisome* exhaust from the truck ahead of us>. Occasionally someone spells it *noisesome* and uses it to mean "noisy" (as in "*noisesome* children running about"), but this is generally regarded as a mistake.

none *None* may take a singular verb <*none* of us is certain> but it may also take a plural verb <*none* of the questions were answered satisfactorily>; it has been used with both since Old English. Writers generally make it singular when they think of it as singular and plural when they think of it as plural (see NOTIONAL AGREEMENT in Glossary). Both uses are perfectly acceptable.

no one See NOBODY, NO ONE.

nor **1.** For the use of *nor* after *neither*, see NEITHER 2, 4.

2. *Nor* sometimes replaces *or* in negative statements <not done by you *nor* me *nor* anyone> to achieve a more emphatically negative effect than is possible with *or*.

no sooner This phrase is usually followed by *than* <had *no sooner* hung up *than* he realized his mistake>. In speech it is sometimes followed by *when,* but this is nonstandard in written English.

not all that See ALL THAT.

not as, not so See AS . . . AS 1.

not . . . but *Not . . . but* is a somewhat old-fashioned expression <did*n't* take *but* three minutes> found mostly in speech. Writers tend to avoid it in published prose <it took but three minutes> <it took barely three minutes>.

not hardly See HARDLY.

not only . . . but also **1.** The *also* in this set of conjunctions is optional and is frequently omitted, especially in shorter sentences <her approach was *not only* awkward *but* badly timed>.

2. As a general rule, identical constructions follow *not only* and *but (also)* <*not only* visited Great Britain *but also* traveled to India> in standard prose (see PARALLELISM in Glossary). However, nonparallel constructions are so common as to often go unnoticed <we were *not only* wined and dined there *but* found ourselves rather liking it>. For the related issue of the placement of *only* in a sentence, see ONLY 1.

not so See AS . . . AS 1.

not too The phrase *not too,* where *too* means "very," is most often used for mild understatement <such competency is *not too* difficult to achieve>. The *too* is also occasionally used with *never* <it was *never too* easy to gain his approval>. Some critics complain about these uses, but they are perfectly standard.

no way *No way,* an American expression that emerged in the 1960s, is now standard in speech and prose of a personal or casual nature <*no way* was I going to do that!>. You will not need it in formal writing.

nowhere near *Nowhere near* is a somewhat informal way of saying *not nearly,* but slightly more emphatic <has *nowhere near* the talent she has>. It is more common in speech than in writing.

nuclear The pronunciation \ˈnü-kyə-lər\ is used by many educated speakers. Many others, however, insist that the word's spelling dictates the pronunciation \ˈnü-klē-ər\.

nude See NAKED, NUDE.

number A rule of thumb is that *a number* takes a plural verb <*a* large *number* of inquiries were received> while *the number* takes a singular verb <*the number* of inquiries was high>. An adjective like *increasing* or *growing* used with *a number,* however, tends to emphasize that *number* is singular and may be followed by either a singular or a plural verb <an *increasing number* of workers are dissatisfied> <*a* continually *growing number* of cases is undermining the court's ability to function>. *The number,* on the other hand, is less subject to variation of this kind. See also AMOUNT 1; AGREEMENT (in Glossary).

O

obedient When *obedient* is used with a preposition, it is *to* <*obedient to* their masters>.

object When the verb *object* takes a preposition, it is usually *to.* What follows *to* may be a noun <didn't *object to* the proposal>, pronoun <has never *objected to* it>, or gerund <*objected to* going>. *Object* may also be followed by a clause <*objected* that the statement was misleading>.

objective Some critics prefer *object* or *aim* to *objective,* but *objective* is certainly in current good use. *Objective* tends to be found more often in serious prose <our *objectives* were fourfold> than in lighter writing.

obligated, obliged In the sense of being bound or constrained legally or morally, *obligated* and *obliged* are essentially interchangeable <felt *obligated* [*obliged*] to report the incident> <is not legally *obliged* [*obligated*] to respond>. When the constraint is applied by physical force or by circumstances, however, *obliged* rather than *obligated* is used <passengers were *obliged* to suffer a minor loss of cabin pressure>.

oblivious *Oblivious* is usually followed by the preposition *to* <*oblivious to* the complaints>, though *of* is not at all uncommon <*oblivious of* the noise>.

observance, observation The distinction between these two words is as follows: *Observance* is most often used in the sense "an act or instance of following a custom, rule, or law" <*observance* of the Sabbath>; *observation* is used in the sense "an act or instance of watching" <*observation* of a lunar eclipse>. However, *observance* is also sometimes used to mean "an act of watching" <in the *observance* of the child's behavior>.

observant *Observant,* when used with a preposition, takes *of* <always *observant of* social amenities>.

observation See OBSERVANCE, OBSERVATION.

obsessed When *obsessed* is used with a preposition, the choice is usually *with* <was *obsessed with* the idea>, though *by* is also common <*obsessed by* her own suspicions>.

obtuse *Obtuse* is well established in the meanings "not acute" <an *obtuse* angle> and "insensitive, stupid" <our hopelessly *obtuse* boss>. Recently, however, *obtuse* has begun to be used in the sense "difficult to comprehend, unclear" (as in "an *obtuse* explanation"), a usage probably based on confusion with *obscure* and *abstruse;* if you are chary of new uses, you may want to avoid it.

occasion **1.** *Occasion* is often followed by *for* or *of* <the *occasion for* the exercise> <the *occasion of* the discord>. It also is followed quite frequently by the infinitive, typically when *occasion* is the object of *have* <will *have occasion* to visit the site>.

2. A common error in spelling *occasion* is to use two *s*'s.

occupy When *occupy* is used with a preposition, *with* or *by* is the usual choice <was *occupied with* her extracurricular work> <seemed to be *occupied by* his thoughts>, but *in* is also used <*occupying* themselves *in* church work>.

occur See TAKE PLACE, OCCUR.

-odd When used to indicate a quantity somewhat greater than a given round number, *odd* is preceded by a hyphen <300-*odd* pages>. The redundant use of *some* with *-odd* (as in "*some* 60-*odd* people") occurs more frequently in speech than in writing.

of **1.** For use of *of* in certain compound prepositions, see INSIDE OF; OFF OF; OUTSIDE OF.

2. *Of* is occasionally mistakenly used as a spelling of the contraction *'ve* (for *have*) in sentences like "The time should *of* been listed as 8 p.m." because it sounds similar to *'ve* in such contexts *(could of, should of, would of, ought to of, might of, may of,* and *must of).*

Children and those who have not completed grammar school may have an excuse for making this mistake, but most others do not.

of a *Of a* in sentences like "He's not that good *of a* putter" is a spoken idiom that is not much used in writing except when *enough, more,* or *much* is used <is not *much of a* putter>. In writing *of* is not included <is not that good a putter>. See also KIND OF A, SORT OF A.

of a . . . nature See NATURE.

of any See ANY 3.

off *Off* in the sense of "from" (as in "we bought the tools *off* Joe," or "we recorded the show *off* the TV") has been objected to for about half a century (the use is over 400 years old), but no rational basis for the objection has ever been offered. It is found most often, however, in speech and speechlike writing. See also OFF OF.

offhand, offhanded *Offhand* has been in use as both an adjective <an *offhand* remark> and an adverb <cannot recall *offhand*> for about 300 years. The adjective *offhanded* is a more recent (19th-century) and somewhat uncommon synonym, but it is nevertheless standard and respectable <in an *offhanded* way>.

off of *Off of* is a compound preposition that is used in speech, in fictional dialogue, and in light and general writing <can't get the lid *off of* the jar> <traffic was routed *off of* the highway>. It is not found in highly formal writing.

oftener, oftenest These two inflected forms of *often* are in good use, but they occur only about half as much as *more often* and *most often.*

of this nature See NATURE.

O.K., OK, okay **1.** The spellings *O.K.*, *OK,* and *okay* are all in good use, with *okay* perhaps slightly more common than the other two.

2. *O.K.* (or *OK* or *okay*) is used as an adjective <an *OK* job>, adverb <she liked it *okay*), noun <gave it the *O.K.*>, and verb <was *okayed* by the FDA> in speech and in all except formal writing. Be advised, however, that the word is commonly condemned in college English handbooks, which seem in this instance to be out of step with contemporary usage.

on **1.** *On, upon.* Of these two prepositions, *on* is certainly the more common <places a burden *on* them>, though *upon* is far from rare <was agreed *upon* by all>. You may use whichever word you prefer.

2. See ONTO, ON TO.

on a . . . basis See BASIS 1.

on account of This phrase is commonly used as a preposition equivalent to *because of* <was denied the position *on account of* his medical condition>. Some occasionally object to it, but it has long been established as standard.

on behalf of See BEHALF.

one The use of *one* to indicate a generic individual <*one* never knows> lends formality to writing, since it suggests distance between the writer and the reader. Using *one* in place of *I* <*one* should like to be able to read more> or *me* <she gave *one* to believe that it had already been done>, though common in British English, may be thought odd or objectionably remote in American English. See also YOU 1, 2.

one another, one another's See EACH OTHER, ONE ANOTHER.

one in (out of) See AGREEMENT: SUBJECT FORMED BY *ONE IN (OUT OF)* in Glossary.

one of the . . . if not the Sentences like "It is *one of the* greatest, *if not the* greatest, mine disasters of this century" are occasionally objected to. The problem is that the part of the sentence outside the commas calls for the plural *disasters,* while the part inside the commas calls for the singular *disaster.* This construction is somewhat similar to *as good or better than* in that it contains a grammatical irregularity that normally does not bother ordinary readers but seems to trouble critics. If you feel the need to revise, you can shift the words around <*one of the* greatest mine disasters, *if not the* greatest, of this century>, but only if it feels natural to you. See also AS GOOD OR BETTER THAN.

one of those who The issue here is whether you should use a singular or a plural verb with the phrase *one of those who* <he is *one of those* people *who* rarely

takes [take] vacations>. Both have in fact been in standard use for centuries. The choice depends on whether the writer regards *one* or *those* as the word that controls the number of the verb (see NOTIONAL AGREEMENT in Glossary).

on line Do you stand *in* line or *on* line? Formerly *on line* was heard only in New York City and the Hudson Valley, but in recent decades the phrase has become known, if not actually used, nationally.

only The placement of *only* in a sentence has been a source of debate since the 18th century. After 200 years of discussion, usage remains varied. In standard spoken English, placement of *only* is not fixed; ambiguity is avoided through sentence stress <he'd *only* been there three weeks> <she *only* gave me $150> <we *only* knew enough to get by>. In casual prose that keeps close to the rhythms of speech, *only* is often placed where it would be in speech. In edited and more formal prose, *only* tends to be placed immediately before the word or words it modifies <he had been there *only* three weeks> <she gave me *only* $150> <we knew *only* enough to get by>.

on the basis of See BASIS 1.

on the part of This common idiomatic phrase <some unwillingness *on the part of* the Israelis> can often be replaced by a single preposition, such as *by* or *among*—and some critics think it always should be. Its use is easily avoided by anyone who finds it awkward or needlessly wordy, but many good writers apparently do not.

onto, on to Occasionally someone confuses the compound preposition *onto* with the adverb *on* followed by the preposition *to* (as in "traveled *onto* Seville"). This use is generally to be avoided; however, the phrase *hold onto* has become established <how long can the team *hold onto* first place?>. The preposition *onto* is, in American English, regularly closed up <opens *onto* the veranda>; in British English both *onto* and *on to* are used, though *onto* seems to be gaining ascendency.

onward, onwards *Onward* serves both as an adjective <an *onward* rush> and as an adverb <rushing *onward*>; *onwards* is an adverb only <from 1600 *onwards*>. *Onward* is the more common adverb in American English, *onwards* in British English.

opening gambit See GAMBIT.

opine This verb, used in English since the 15th century, is sometimes thought to be less than serious. It does turn up in humorous writing, but it also commonly serves to imply, seriously enough, some skepticism about the opinion being reported <she *opined* that the comet would strike the earth> or to emphasize that the opinion being reported is just that—an opinion <she *opined* that stock prices could soar>.

opportunity *Opportunity* is often used with *to* followed by an infinitive <an *opportunity to* get involved>.

Opportunity for frequently precedes a noun phrase <*opportunities for* discussions involving both parties> or a gerund <*opportunities for* investing abroad>. *Opportunity of,* once common in both American and British English, is now found chiefly in the latter.

opposite *Opposite* as an adjective or adverb is followed by either *to* or *from* <in a direction *opposite to* the one expected> <sat *opposite from* him>. As a noun, *opposite* is frequently followed by *of* <the *opposite of* what they wanted>. *To* is also sometimes used <the *opposite to* the plan announced earlier>.

opposition *Opposition,* when used with a preposition, usually takes *to* <in *opposition to* the regime>. *Opposition* is also used, in different constructions, with *between* and *of* <the natural *opposition between* imagination and reason> <the *opposition of* individual will and social norms>.

opt The verb *opt* (from French *opter,* "to choose") has a modern, clipped quality that may make it seem like a recent and perhaps illegitimate invention, but in fact it is more than a hundred years old and is established as standard <*opted* not to attend> <*opted* for short sleeves> <*opted* out of the competition>.

or See AND/OR; EITHER 3, 5; NEITHER 2; AGREEMENT: COMPOUND SUBJECTS JOINED BY *OR* (in Glossary).

oral See VERBAL, ORAL.

orchestrate Some charge that using *orchestrate* to mean "to arrange or combine for maximum effect" <*orchestrated* preparations for the banquet> is faddish or a cliché. This use, however, has been around since the late 1800s and continues to be employed by good writers.

order See IN ORDER TO.

ordinance, ordnance The more common of these two words, *ordinance* (meaning "municipal law"), is sometimes mistakenly used for the less common *ordnance* (meaning "military supplies").

Oriental See ASIAN, ORIENTAL.

originate *Originate,* when used with a preposition, is most often used with *in* <the idea *originated in* a meeting held in June>. A little less often, it is used with *from* <*originated from* outside the compound>. *Originate* is also used with *as, at, on, out of, outside of,* and *with.*

other Some critics claim that *other* can only be paired with *than* in constructions like "never looked on him in any *other* light *than* as my friend." However, use of *but* with *other* in such constructions <had no *other* choice *but* to sit and wait> is idiomatic and fully standard in American English.

ought *Ought* is a little awkward to put into the negative. In writing, *ought not* is the usual form, and it may be followed by the bare infinitive without *to* <one *ought not* complain about a tax benefit> or the infinitive with *to* <many *ought not to* be accepted as members>. Although *ought not* is used in speech, it can seem a bit stuffy for everyday use. *Oughtn't* is one spoken substitute; it is widespread but more common in the South. *Hadn't ought* is another; it too is widespread but is more common in the North. *Didn't ought* is mostly British.

ought to of The *of* here stands for *'ve* or *have.* See OF 2.

ours The possessive pronoun *ours,* like the possessive pronouns *its, theirs,* and *yours,* is properly spelled without an apostrophe.

out See OUT OF, OUT.

out loud *Out loud* was once widely decried as an error for *aloud,* and it is still sometimes described as too casual to be used in formal writing. Our evidence shows clearly that *out loud* is neither an error nor a casual spoken form, but it does appear less frequently than *aloud* in formal writing.

out of, out *Out of* and *out* are interchangeable only in a few restricted contexts. *Out* is used much more often as an adverb <turn *out* the light> than as a preposition. When used as a preposition, it seems most often to go with *door* or *window* <ran *out* the door> <looked *out* the window>. With *window, out of* is about equally common <leaned *out of* the window>. With nouns that designate places or things that can be thought of as containing or surrounding, *out of* is usual <walked *out of* the room> <step *out of* the car, please>.

outside of **1.** Some criticize using *outside of* as a synonym for *outside*. Our evidence suggests that competent writers and speakers retain the *of* when it sounds right to them for idiom and rhythm <he wasn't known *outside of* his own circle> and drop it when it does not <it falls *outside* the court's jurisdiction>. You have the same choice.

2. Some regard the use of *outside of* in the sense "except for" or "aside from" as improper. However, the usage is quite respectable in ordinary writing <*outside of* a few experts, no one was bothered by it>.

3. See INSIDE OF.

over Various reasons have been put forth as to why *over* in the sense of "more than" should be avoided, but none of these arguments holds water and they conflict with each other. *Over* has been used in this sense since the 14th century <in the business for *over* thirty years>, and there is no reason to avoid it.

overwhelmed Whether used as a passive form or as an adjective, *overwhelmed* is most often followed with *by* <the picnic area was *overwhelmed by* black flies> <a small building *overwhelmed by* its towering neighbors>, less frequently by *with* <she was suddenly *overwhelmed with* calls for interviews>.

owing to See DUE TO.

P

paid See PAY.

pair **1.** The usual plural of *pair* is *pairs*, when there is no preceding number or indicator of number (such as *several*) <*pairs* of stockings hung from various appurtenances>. When a number or indicator of number precedes *pair*, either *pair* or *pairs* may be used <five *pair* [*pairs*] of sox>.

2. *Pair* is one of those collective nouns that take a singular or plural verb according to notional agreement: If you are thinking of the individuals in the pair, you will use a plural verb <a *pair* of horses were grazing in the field>; if you are thinking of the pair as a unit, you will use the singular <a *pair* of eyes peeks out from behind the blinds>.

parallel **1.** *Parallel* is sometimes misspelled. Try thinking of the two *l*s in the middle as parallel lines cutting through the word.

2. The prepositions that occur after the adjective *parallel* are *to* and *with* <an opinion that runs *parallel to* her own> <an effort *parallel with* that of the group>. The noun *parallel* is followed by *to, with,* or *between* <looking for a *parallel to* the experience> <citing a *parallel with* Northern Ireland> <sees a *parallel between* the two methods>.

parameter This borrowing from mathematics and other technical writing has been much disparaged. Our evidence shows that it is not much used in general writing but is fairly common in technical and quasi-technical writing (such as about investment and consumer electronics).

paraphernalia Some regard *paraphernalia* (which was originally a Latin plural) as a plural noun <filled with those *paraphernalia* you see in such shops>, while others regard it as a singular <every kind of *paraphernalia* imaginable>. Both uses are proper.

part 1. *Part with* almost always means "give up" <hated to *part with* that money>. *Part from* generally means "leave" <he *parted from* the administration in May>.

2. See ON THE .ART OF.

partake As an intransitive verb, *partake* may be followed by *in* or *of*. *Partake in,* like *take part in,* implies active participation in something <*partaking in* the revelry>. *Partake of,* like *take part of,* usually means "share" or "possess" <the religion *partakes of* a certain mysticism>.

partial *Partial* is used with the preposition *to* when it means "markedly fond (of)" <*partial to* pizza>. Formerly this use was considered unacceptable by some, but nowadays it is accepted as standard.

partially, partly These two words have long been interchangeable in the sense "in some measure or degree" <her figure was *partly* enveloped in a shawl> <the hat-brim *partially* shaded his face>, though there is some tendency toward differentiation. *Partially* is used more often than *partly* to modify an adjective or past participle that names or suggests a process <the body was only *partially* concealed>. *Partly* is used more often before clauses and phrases offered by way of explanation <the work has not achieved canonical status, *partly* because of its density and length>. But there are plenty of exceptions to the general trend, and only time will tell whether the process of differentiation will continue.

participate *Participate* is most often used with *in* <always tried to *participate in* class discussions>.

partly See PARTIALLY, PARTLY.

party *Party* in the sense of "person" <didn't reach the *party* I sent it to> has been criticized from the days of Queen Victoria, apparently because it belonged to the language of the socially inferior. Criticism has continued through pure inertia, but this use is now standard.

pay *Paid* is the spelling for the past tense and past participle of *pay*. Only in the specialized nautical sense of *pay out* are they normally spelled *payed*.

peaceable, peaceful *Peaceable* means "disposed toward peace, preferring peace" <a *peaceable*

kingdom>, while *peaceful* means "characterized by peace" <a *peaceful* sleep>. However, *peaceable* and *peaceful* can also be properly used as synonyms, and they have been since the 14th century.

peak, peek, pique These soundalikes have a way of getting switched by inattentive writers. Most often, *peak* is substituted for one of the other two. Be sure to match your intended meaning to the correct spelling, using your dictionary for help as required. See also PIQUE.

pedal, peddle Once in a while the verb *peddle* is used where *pedal* is meant, as a result of carelessness.

peek See PEAK, PEEK, PIQUE.

people, persons Since the late 1800s critics have warned against using *people* to mean *persons,* especially when paired with modifiers such as *several, many,* or specific numbers like *a thousand* <several new *people* attended> <the facility can hold 22,500 *people*>. Despite the warnings, which were never based on very solid reasoning, *people* has continued to stand in for *persons* and is now recognized even by former critics as standard in such contexts. *Persons* continues to be used, often in the traditionally recommended way <eight *persons* were on board the small aircraft>, but also as an alternative where *people* has just been used <some 800 *people,* many of them older *persons*>.

per Though regarded by some as not quite an English word, *per* is completely standard when used with figures. It usually appears in the context of money <$100 *per* performance>, vehicles <65 miles *per* hour> <32 miles *per* gallon>, or sports <15 points *per* game>. It also appears regularly in business correspondence, where it means "according to" <*per* your instructions> and is standard (see also AS PER). Avoid inserting words like *a* or *each* between *per* and the word or words it modifies (as in "committed at least one typo *per* a paragraph").

percent, per cent You can use either the one-word or the two-word form, though the one-word form is more common in America. *Percent* can be followed by either a plural or singular verb; the number of the verb is usually dictated by the noun in the following *of* phrase <20 *percent* of families prefer product A> <over 75 *percent* of the population was in favor>. The percent sign (%) is generally avoided in discursive prose.

perfect The phrases *more perfect* and *most perfect* are considered by some as improper, since something is supposedly either perfect or not (see ABSOLUTE ADJECTIVE in Glossary). But *perfect* has been used in the comparative and superlative since the 14th century; and except in the minds of some critics, it has never been wrong to use the disputed phrases.

period of time This phrase, as many critics point out, can often be shortened to either *period* or *time* <during this *period* [*time*]>. However, when using the phrase improves the clarity of your sentence

<subjected to sensory deprivation for long *periods of time*>, you can safely choose the phrase.

permeate *Permeate* is used with *by* or *with* about equally. When used with *by*, the verb is almost always in the passive <was *permeated by* the stench>; when followed by *with*, the verb may appear in either the active <has *permeated* her work *with* her own sense of guilt> or the passive voice <a room *permeated with* tobacco smoke>.

permit See ALLOW 1.

permit of *Permit of*, like *admit of* and *allow of* (all of which mean "to make possible"), is almost always used with an impersonal subject <a situation that does not *permit of* a satisfying remedy>. See also ALLOW 2.

person **1.** For a discussion of choosing between *persons* and *people*, see PEOPLE, PERSONS.

2. In response to concern about sexism in language, recent decades have seen the coinage of compound terms in which the terminal element *-man* (as in *draftsman*), and sometimes *-woman* (as in *chairwoman*), is replaced by *-person*. Such terms as *chairperson, anchorperson,* and *spokesperson* are now well established. Bare designations such as *chair* and *anchor* are also common. Other terms (such as *waitperson*) have made inroads but still have a way to go before being fully accepted. Checking a recent dictionary or two should help you determine whether a given compound is established in current use.

persuade *Persuade* is most often used with *to* and an infinitive <*persuaded* us *to* drop the case>. It quite frequently introduces a clause <*persuading* them that they should go>. It is somewhat less often used with *of, by,* or *into* <to *persuade* her *of* his sincerity> <were *persuaded by* the weight of the facts> <*persuading* them *into* accepting his offer>, and occasionally with *as to, from, out of, with,* and *upon.* See also CONVINCE, PERSUADE.

pertinent *Pertinent* is usually used with *to* and a noun object <*pertinent to* the matter at hand>. Sometimes it is followed by the infinitive <it would be *pertinent* to discuss the issue at least>. It is also found with *as regards, for,* or *in.*

peruse *Peruse* has for a long time held two rather contradictory narrow meanings, namely, "to examine or consider with attention and in detail" and "to look over or through in a casual or cursory manner." In broader use it means simply "to read" and may suggest either an attentive or a quick reading. In our time it tends to have a literary flavor, whichever meaning is involved.

pervert The verb *pervert* is used with *into, to,* or *by* <*perverted* the trial *into* a media show> <*perverted* it *to* their own ends> <*perverting* the original play *by* introducing new scenes>. Somewhat less frequently, it is followed by *for, from,* or *with.*

phenomena *Phenomena* is the usual plural of *phenomenon* <scientists have yet to link these *phenomena* to a specific cause>. Use of *phenomena* as a singular (as in "St. Elmo's Fire is an eerie *phenomena*") is encountered in speech and now and then in writing, but it is nonstandard and it is safer to avoid it

phony *Phony* is an Americanism of obscure origin first attested in print in 1900. It was originally considered slang, but over the decades it has been used in contexts that are less and less slangy <used *phony* credentials to land the job>. By now it must be regarded as standard. The spellings *phony* and *phoney* are both found, but *phony* is the predominant form by a wide margin.

pianist Our evidence shows that the pronunciation \pē-ˈan-əst\ seems to prevail among classical musicians and radio announcers, \ˈpē-ə-nəst\ being less common.

pique When the verb *pique,* in the sense "to irritate," takes a preposition, it is either *at* or *by* <was *piqued at* them for discounting her claim> <was *piqued by* this reversal of fortune>. When *pique* means "to excite or arouse," the preposition of choice is *by* <was *piqued by* the unexpected news>.

place As in the case of *anyplace, everyplace,* and *someplace,* some critics worry that *place* itself in expressions like *going places, go any place,* or *going* *no place,* is substandard. Yet these uses are solidly established in American English, and there has never been any reason to avoid them in general writing.

plan **1.** Although some critics consider phrases like *plan ahead, plan in advance,* and *plan out* redundant, preferring *plan* by itself, such combinations serve the purpose of narrowing the focus of the verb, which has more than one sense. You may safely ignore the critics' complaints.

2. *Plan on, plan to. Plan on,* followed by a gerund <is *planning on* going>, is more often found in spoken than in written use. *Plan on* is also used with a noun object <*plan on* fewer guests than the number invited>. *Plan to* (followed by an infinitive) is more usual in general written use <had *planned to* complete the project by May>.

playwright, playwrite The *-wright* in *playwright* is from an obsolete sense of *wright* that meant "maker" (as in *wheelwright, shipwright,* and *wainwright*). The spelling *playwrite* for the noun is considered an error. However, the spellings *playwrighting* and *playwriting* are both common for the verbal noun <the art of *playwriting* [*playwrighting*]>.

plead *Plead* belongs to the same class of verbs as *bleed, lead, speed, read,* and *feed,* and like them it has a past tense and a past participle with a short vowel spelled *pled* or sometimes *plead.* However, the regular form *pleaded* has always competed with the short-vowel form. Both *pled* and *pleaded* are in good use in the United States today; only *pleaded* is standard in British English.

pleased *Pleased* is often followed by *to* and an infinitive <was *pleased to* arrange the meeting>. The passive *pleased* is often followed by prepositional phrases beginning with *with, about,* or *by* <is *pleased with* the results> <was *pleased about* the news> <were *pleased by* these signs of progress>.

pled See PLEAD.

plenty **1.** Many critics advise avoiding the adverb *plenty* in writing and replacing it with *very, quite,* or a more precise word. Actually, *plenty* is often more precise than its recommended replacements <it's already *plenty* hot in the kitchen> <the complaints were piling up *plenty* fast> <has *plenty more* to say>. However, it is not used in formal writing.

2. *Plenty* was once in literary use as a predicate adjective <whisky was *plenty*> but is not much used any more; as an attributive adjective (as in "there's *plenty* work to be done"), it is primarily found in spoken English.

plethora **1.** Some critics complain that *plethora* should not mean simply "a lot," as it often seems to in ordinary usage, but rather "an excessive amount." In actual practice, *plethora* may connote an undesirable excess, an undesirably large supply but not an excess, an excess that is not necessarily undesirable, or simply an abundant supply. All of these uses are well established and standard.

2. *Plethora* often occurs in the phrase *a plethora of* followed by a plural noun. When this unit governs the verb of a sentence, notional agreement prevails. Writers who view the plethora as a lump use a singular verb <*a plethora of* chorus-line dancers is used in the production>; those who view it as a collection of discrete items use a plural verb <*a plethora of* new films were on offer>.

plunge When *plunge* is used with a preposition, it is most often *into* <*plunged into* the river>. It is also frequently used with *in* <*plunged* right *in* the water>, somewhat less frequently with *through, to, beneath, down,* and *over* <*plunging through* the morass> <*plunged to* near zero> <*plunged beneath* the surface> <sales *plunge down* sharply at this point> <*plunging over* the goal line>, and additionally with *for, on,* and *toward* (or *towards*).

plus The preposition *plus* has long been used with a meaning equivalent to *and* <two *plus* two>; it is therefore not very surprising that in time it has come to be used as a conjunction <had a sandwich and juice *plus* dessert>. This use is now established in casual prose. The related sense "in addition" that is invoked when *plus* joins clauses <the apartment was small; *plus* it was unfurnished> is used chiefly in speech and in informal writing.

point in time This phrase is often criticized as a wordy locution for either *time* or *point* by itself. And yet a great many writers use it, including the critics themselves. If you need it for rhythm or another stylistic reason, you may use it; otherwise, one of the single words will be adequate.

point of view Constructions like "from a maintenance *point of view*" or "from the *point of view* of security" are sometimes thought to be awkward or wrong because a nonhuman subject cannot have a point of view. But it is hard to see anything seriously wrong with uses like these, since the human subject is always implicitly present, being (if no one else) the speaker or writer. What needs to be avoided is not so much the construction as overreliance on it.

politics *Politics* can take either a singular or a plural verb. When it means "a person's political opinions or sympathies," it is quite likely to be plural <his *politics* have caused him trouble>. Other senses may be either singular or plural <the *politics* of space exploration is [are] again in the news> <Russian *politics* are [is] unique>.

ponder The prepositions usually used with *ponder* are *on* and *over* <*pondered on* her fate> <*pondered over* these issues>, but *about* or *upon* are also found <*pondering about* welfare reform> <would *ponder upon* it>.

pore, pour These two verbs are occasionally switched by mistake. What usually happens is that *pour* is used when the less familiar *pore,* "to read or study attentively," is called for.

portentous *Portentous,* which has as its two earliest senses "relating to or being a portent or omen" <wondrous and *portentous* signs> and "eliciting amazement or wonder, prodigious" <the *portentous* size and strength of the gorilla>, more recently began to be used in a sense close to "pretentious" <a *portentous* air of military greatness>. Though the latter use is sometimes criticized, it is fully established.

possessed When *possessed* is used as a participle or adjective meaning "influenced or controlled," it takes *by* <*possessed by* personal demons> or, less frequently, *with* <*possessed with* the idea>. The phrase *to be possessed of* means "to be the owner of" <*is possessed of* a certain talent>.

possibility When some likelihood is being considered, we usually refer to the possibility *of* its occurrence or existence <the *possibility of* life on other planets>. When *possibility* is used in the plural with a meaning close to "opportunities," it can be followed by *for* <numerous *possibilities for* trade>.

possible **1.** *Possible* is sometimes considered to be an ABSOLUTE ADJECTIVE (see Glossary).

2. Critics occasionally quibble over the use of *may* with *possible* or *possibly,* thinking it redundant <*may* *possibly* upset the balance>. However, *possibly* actually serves to reinforce *may,* underlining its seriousness. There is nothing wrong with such use.

pour See PORE, POUR.

practicable, practical *Practicable* has two basic senses, "feasible" <the most *practicable* plan of the lot> and "usable" <a *practicable* route up the west face of the mountain>. *Practical* has a much wider range of meaning, but the sense closest to those of *practicable* is "capable of being put into use, useful" <a *practical* knowledge of French>. Our evidence suggests that writers generally successfully distinguish between these two words.

practically *Practically* has a sense meaning "almost, nearly, virtually" <*practically* everyone contributed> that some critics regard as a misuse. But this sense has been in everyday use for more than two centuries and continues to come naturally from the pens of reputable writers. It is entirely standard.

practice, practise The noun *practice* is almost always spelled with the second *c* in both Britain and American. The verb is normally spelled *practise* in Britain; in America it is spelled both *practice* and *practise.*

precede, proceed These two words are occasionally mixed up or misspelled (e.g., *preceed* for *precede, procede* for *proceed*). *Precede* means "to come before," *proceed* "to advance or continue."

precedence, precedents The substitution of *precedence* ("priority") for *precedents* ("earlier examples") occurs occasionally. Be sure to match your spelling to your meaning.

precedent 1. When the adjective *precedent* is used with a preposition, the preposition is usually *to* <a condition *precedent to* any early decision>, but occasionally *of* <a condition *precedent of* advancement>.

2. When the noun *precedent* takes a preposition, the preposition is most often *for* <cited two historical *precedents for* the situation>. It is somewhat less frequently used with *of* <setting a *precedent of* abusive rule> and occasionally with *against* or *to.*

3. See PRECEDENCE, PRECEDENTS.

precipitate, precipitous Many critics insist on keeping these adjectives distinct. *Precipitate,* they say, means "headlong," "abrupt," or "rash" <the army's *precipitate* withdrawal>; *precipitous* means only "steep" <a *precipitous* slope>. Actual usage, however, is somewhat more complicated. *Precipitous* and *precipitously* are commonly used figuratively to suggest abruptness, much as *precipitate* does <*precipitous* changes> <output dropped *precipitously*>. Overlap between the two words has existed for centuries, and almost all dictionaries show that *precipitous* has as one of its senses "precipitate." The use is standard.

predominate, predominately The adjective *predominate* (and its derivative *predominately*) is today what it has been since the 17th century: a less common alternative to *predominant* (and its derivative *predominantly*). It is not an error, as some critics charge, and not even particularly rare; but it is still distinctly a minority usage.

preface **1.** The noun *preface* is usually used with *to* <served as the young man's *preface to* politics>, but also sometimes with *for* <wrote the *preface for* the book>.

2. The verb *preface* may be used with *with* <*prefaced* his speech *with* a prayer> or, less often, with *by* <the race was *prefaced by* the traditional sounding of the horn>.

prefer When *prefer* is used to compare two things, the second, especially if it is a noun or pronoun, is usually introduced by *to* <*prefers* basketball *to* baseball>. *Over* is occasionally used, especially in advertising <most *prefer* it *over* the other brand>. *Rather than* is sometimes used—especially with two infinitives, the second often without *to* <*prefers* to rent the video *rather than* see the film in the theater>.

preferable *Preferable* is sometimes considered an ABSOLUTE ADJECTIVE (see Glossary) and the combination *more preferable* has been condemned. Almost no one uses *more preferable,* but *preferable* is used with many other modifiers, such as *much, greatly, far, slightly,* and *vastly.*

preference *Preference* is often followed by *for* <expressed a *preference for* shellfish>, but also often with *in, of,* and *regarding*. The phrase *in preference to* is also common <chose unemployment *in preference to* reduced pay>.

prejudice The most frequently used preposition with *prejudice,* noun and verb, is *against* <his *prejudice against* Asians> <*prejudiced against* women>. *In favor of* is used for the opposite meaning, though much less frequently <*prejudiced in favor of* high-income earners>.

preoccupied *Preoccupied* is almost always used with *with* <became *preoccupied with* his place in history>. It may also be followed by *about* or *by* <was *preoccupied about* increases in health-care costs> <were *preoccupied by* the children>.

preparatory When used with a preposition, *preparatory* takes *to* <a sketch *preparatory to* the actual painting>. Some critics consider *preparatory to* a pretentious or wordy substitute for *before,* but *before* does not always work in its place, and writers continue to find the phrase useful. See also PREVIOUS TO; PRIOR TO.

prerequisite **1.** The noun *prerequisite* is usually followed by *for* or *to* when it takes a preposition <one *prerequisite for* admission> <a *prerequisite to* the course>, and sometimes by *of* <the first *prerequisite of* newspaper reporting>.

2. The adjective *prerequisite* is usually followed by *to* when it takes a preposition <was *prerequisite to* gaining entry to the king's court>.

present The verb *present* is most commonly found with *to* or *with,* the former marking the receiver <was *presented to* them> and the latter the thing presented <were *presented with* an award>. *Present* is also used with *as* <*presented as* a gift>, *at* <*presented at* the ceremony>, or *for* <*presented for* valor in battle>.

presently The sense of *presently* meaning "at present" has been in more or less continuous standard use since the 15th century <are *presently* accepting recommendations>, though some critics, believing it should mean only "before long," continue to warn against its use.

preside When it takes a preposition, *preside* is most commonly found with *over* <*presiding over* the festivities>. Somewhat less frequently, it is used with *at* <*presiding at* the ceremony> and occasionally with *in* <*presides in* council meetings>.

presume See ASSUME, PRESUME.

pretense, pretence The usual spelling in America is *pretense;* the usual spelling in Britain is *pretence.*

pretty *Pretty* is used to tone down a statement <*pretty* cold weather> and is in wide use across the whole spectrum of English. It is common in informal speech and writing, but is neither rare nor wrong in more serious contexts <the reasons must be *pretty* cogent>.

prevail *Prevail* is most often used with *upon* when it means "to use persuasion successfully" <*prevailed* *upon* him to change his mind>, and less frequently with *on* <*prevailed on* her to meet him for dinner> or *with* <*prevailed with* the committee to introduce the bill>. When *prevail* means "to triumph," it is often used with *over* and *against* <the tenants *prevailed over* the landlord> <the status quo *prevailed against* change>.

prevent *Prevent* is used in a number of different standard constructions. There is *prevent* + a noun or pronoun + *from* + an *-ing* form of a verb <to *prevent* that from happening>. Then there is *prevent* + possessive pronoun or noun + *-ing* <to *prevent* their leaving>. And there is *prevent* + noun or objective pronoun + *-ing* <to *prevent* the car['s] rolling>. Finally, *prevent* + an *-ing* form with no noun or pronoun is sometimes used <to *prevent* being taken to the cleaners>.

preventative, preventive Both of these words have been around for over 300 years, and both have been frequently used by reputable writers. The only real difference is that *preventive* is much more common than *preventative*.

previous to This phrase has been widely condemned by many critics on a number of different grounds, none of them adding up to a serious argument against its use, though some commentators defend it. It is true that most writers find *before* (the critics' preferred substitute) more useful most of the time, but *previous to* and other compound prepositions like it (e.g., *preparatory* *to, prior to*) are available for variety when you want them. See also PREPARATORY; PRIOR TO.

principal, principle To rehearse what you must have learned in grammar school: Only *principal* is an adjective <the *principal* source used>, but it is also a noun, usually signifying either a person <the school *principal*> or money <still owed on the *principal*>. *Principle* is only a noun, usually designating a law or rule <the *principles* of good government>.

prioritize *Prioritize* remains a jargon word used in business and other specialized fields. Unless you are working in a field where the word is commonly used, you will probably not need it.

prior to Sometimes termed pompous or affected, *prior to* is a synonym of *before* that most often appears in rather formal contexts, such as the annual reports of corporations. It may occasionally emphasize the notion of anticipation <should be verified *prior to* proceeding>. It is also sometimes used in less formal contexts. See also PREPARATORY; PREVIOUS TO.

proceed See PRECEDE, PROCEED.

proficient *Proficient,* when used with a preposition, usually takes *in* or *at* <*proficient in* translating foreign languages> <*proficient at* chess>.

prohibit *Prohibit* is often followed by *from* and a gerund <were *prohibited from* selling the property>. *Prohibit from* can also be followed by a noun <was not

prohibited from use>. Without *from,* prohibit may be followed by a noun or gerund as direct object <*prohibit* the replacement of workers> <*prohibited* his going to school>.

prophecy, prophesy Mind your spelling here: *prophecy* is a noun <the ancient *prophecy*> and *prophesy* a verb <as he had *prophesied*>.

propitious *Propitious* is usually used with *for* or *to*. *For* is often followed by a gerund <the environment was *propitious for* starting a new business>; *to* is often followed by an infinitive <the moment was *propitious to* declare his love>.

prostrate, prostate These two words are sometimes switched by mistake. *Prostrate* refers to lying down or to being overwhelmed by something, *prostate* to a gland at the base of the male urethra.

protect *Protect* is frequently found with *from* and slightly less frequently with *against* <to *protect* the skin *from* exposure> <to *protect* yourself *against* criminals>. It is also often used with *by* and *with* to express a different relation <is *protected by* tenure from being removed> <*protected with* multiple layers>.

protest **1.** The noun *protest* is most often used with *against* <in *protest against* the regime>, less often with *at* <a storm of public *protest at* the removal>, and occasionally with *of* or *to* <in *protest of* [*to*] the decision>.

2. The verb *protest* appears with *about, at,* or *over* <*protesting about* the treatment of women> <*protested at* the incivility of it all> <*protested over* the denial of accreditation>.

proved, proven The past participle *proven* has gradually worked its way into standard English over the past 350 years. It is now about as frequent as *proved* in all contexts <demanded that it be *proved* [*proven*]>. As an attributive adjective <*proven* [*proved*] gas reserves>, *proven* is much more common than *proved.*

provide When *provide* is used intransitively, it is most often used with *for* <*provide for* the common defense>. When it is used transitively to mean "to supply or make available," a prepositional phrase beginning with *for* or *to* often follows <*provided* new uniforms *for* the band> <*provides* job-training opportunities *to* young people>. But when *provide* is used to mean "to make something available to," the prepositional phrase usually begins with *with* <*provided* the children *with* free balloons>. When used to mean "to stipulate," it is often followed by a clause <the contract *provides* that certain deadlines will be met>.

provided, providing Although occasionally still disapproved, *providing* is as well established as a conjunction as *provided* is <no reason not to use it, *provided* [*providing*] you use it sparingly>, though *provided* is more common.

proximity The phrase *close proximity* has been called redundant, but it is not necessarily so, as some things can be nearer than others. *Close* merely emphasizes the closeness. It is used in general writing <within *close proximity* of the park> and is quite common in technical contexts as well.

publically *Publically* is an infrequent variant spelling of *publicly.* Although it is not really a misspelling—it is recognized in a number of standard dictionaries—it will look unfamiliar to many who encounter it.

punish *Punish* is found most often with *for* and an object that names the offense <*punished for* stealing>. Less often it is used with *by* or *with* and an object that names the punishment <*punished* her *by* withdrawing his love> <*punished* him *with* a whipping>.

purposefully, purposely These two adverbs can be used in similar situations, but are usually distinguished by writers. *Purposely* is the simpler word, meaning merely "on purpose, not by accident" <she *purposely* spilled the milk to get attention>, while *purposefully* is intended to suggest that the person or persons written about did what they did for a purpose, perhaps even with determination <he strode *purposefully* to the front of the stage>.

Q

question **1.** When *question* is followed by a preposition, it is usually *of* <a *question of* propriety>. *Question* is also used, but much less frequently, with *about* and *as to* <*questions about* her past> <a *question as to* whether it was warranted>.

2. Preceded by a qualifier like *no* or *little, question* is often followed by a clause introduced by *but that, but what,* or simply *that* <no *question but that* they are sincere> <little *question that* it would take place>. *Question* may also be followed by a clause introduced by *whether* or *which* <the *question whether* the practice is fair> <the *question which* came first, the chicken or the egg>.

questionnaire This word is sometimes misspelled with only one *n*.

quick, quickly The adverb *quick* (as in "Come *quick!*"), though old, is now more likely to be encountered in speech than in writing, except when the writing is deliberately informal or includes dialogue. The usual choice in more formal prose is *quickly* <she moved *quickly*>.

quote **1.** The noun *quote,* short for *quotation,* was first recorded in the late 19th century and gradually made its way into standard if somewhat casual writing <plenty of *quotes* from Shakespeare>. But there will be contexts where *quotation* sounds better.

2. The noun *quote* is also used to mean "quotation mark." Like the "quotation" sense, this "mark" sense is about a hundred years old and is by now standard in informal writing.

R

rack, wrack The prescriptions of critics who seek sharp distinctions between these two words can be stated as follows: the verb *rack,* which is related to the noun designating an instrument of torture, means "strain" or "torment" and is the correct choice in *nerve-racking, rack one's brains,* and similar expressions. The verb *wrack* and noun *wrack,* on the other hand, are etymologically related to *wreck* and should be used when wreckage or destruction is being described, as in the phrases *storm-wracked* and *wrack and ruin.* Actual usage varies somewhat, however. *Wrack* is commonly used as a verb meaning "torment" <he *wracked* his brain> <it was nerve-*wracking*>, and the noun *rack* is sometimes used interchangeably with *wrack,* especially in *rack and ruin.* Many of these phrases are, in any case, clichés and perhaps best avoided on those grounds.

racket, racquet These spelling variants are both established in reputable use. *Racket* is the more common of the two.

raise, rear The notion that we *raise* plants and animals and *rear* children is often repeated by schoolteachers and language commentators, but the facts of actual usage differ somewhat. *Raise,* used of children, is perfectly respectable American English and is very common especially in the southern United States. *Rear* is still in common use too, and some writers use it interchangeably with *raise.* You may use either word.

rarely ever This phrase is an established spoken idiom <I *rarely ever* see them>. In writing, however, *rarely* is almost always used alone.

read where See WHERE 2.

real Most critics consider the adverb *real* (as in "a *real* hard time") to be informal and more suitable to speech than writing. Our evidence shows these observations to be true in the main, but *real* is becoming increasingly common in writing of an informal, conversational style ("it was *real* fun"). It is used as an intensifier only and is not interchangeable with *really* except in that use <*really* [*real*] fine work>.

Realtor This word is sometimes pronounce \ˈrē-lə-tər\, a switched-around form of \ˈrē-əl-tər\. While the latter pronunciation is standard, the former is not very well established.

rear See RAISE, REAR.

reason is because The locution *the reason is because* has been in use—including heavy literary use—for about 350 years, usually with words intervening between *reason* and *because* <*the reason* the practice continues *is because* no one has questioned it>. Nevertheless, many critics find fault with it—on grounds that are shaky both logically and grammatically. Though the phrase must be regarded as standard, disapproval of it will doubtless continue. But if you do use it, you will be in distinguished company that includes Francis Bacon, Jonathan Swift, W. B. Yeats, and Robert Frost.

reason why *Reason why* is denounced as redundant by many critics, who prefer that *why* be omitted. But it dates back to the 13th century and is well established as standard <there is no *reason why* anyone should be upset>.

reckon **1.** When used with a preposition, *reckon* is most often followed by *with,* a combination meaning "to take into consideration" <a force to be *reckoned with*>. Occasionally *reckon* is followed by *among, as, at, by, in,* or *on* (or *upon*).

2. *Reckon* in the sense "suppose, think" <party leaders *reckon* they have the votes> is common in British English and in some American dialects ("I *reckon* I'll be going"), but is generally avoided in standard American prose.

recollect, remember A distinction that can be made between these two words is that *recollect* implies a conscious effort to recall something to the mind <he tried to *recollect* the name of the street>, while *remember* more generally implies only having something available in one's memory <he always *remembered* what she had said>. But the distinction is not a very strong one, and for many writers the real distinguishing characteristic of *recollect* seems to be that it has a folksy quality suggestive of rustic speech. Thus, the use of *recollect* without connotations of conscious effort is not an error.

reconcile Two prepositions are commonly used after *reconcile—with* and *to* <couldn't *reconcile* his ideal *with* reality> <was *reconciled to* hardship>.

recur, recurrence, reoccur, reoccurrence Of these two pairs, *recur* and *recurrence* are by far the more common. Some criticize *reoccur* and *reoccurrence* as unnecessary, but the words are useful when you want to say simply that something happened a second time <a *reoccurrence* of this astronomical event is unlikely>. *Recur* and especially *recurrence,* in contrast, often suggest a periodic or frequent repetition <a *recurring* nightmare>.

refer This verb is often used with *back* <please *refer back* to the earlier passage>, a use that is sometimes criticized as redundant. But the "backward" connotations of *refer* are usually not strong, and *back* can be useful in reinforcing them.

referendums, referenda These two plurals are about equally common in current use. You may use whichever you prefer.

refute *Refute* has two senses, both of which are in common use but one of which is widely regarded as an error. The original and uncontroversial sense is "to prove wrong, show to be false or erroneous" <*refuted* the argument point by point>. The disputed sense is "to deny the truth or accuracy of" <*refuted* the allegations>. The latter sense originated in the 20th century, and, though fairly new, is thoroughly established as standard.

regard The expressions *in regard to, with regard to, as regards,* and *regarding* are sometimes criticized as wordy and jargonistic. The critics prefer such alternatives as *about, on,* and *concerning,* and you will often find these preferable. However, the issue of wordiness is generally secondary to the issue of how your sentence sounds; when longer phrases suit the rhythm of a sentence better than short ones, the longer ones are a better choice.

relate The intransitive sense of *relate* that means "to have or establish a relationship, interact" <can't *relate* to that kind of music> established itself in general use during the 1960s. Although it has been criticized, it is established in speech and in general (but not formal) writing. It is more likely to seem acceptable when followed by a *to* phrase (as above) than when alone (as in "she just can't *relate*").

relation **1.** *Relation, relative.* These two words are synonymous in the sense "a person to whom one is related," and they are frequently plural in that sense. Various critics prefer one or the other term, but they are both standard and common.

2. *Relation* is usually used with *of* in the sense of "relative" and sometimes in other senses <a distant *relation of* mine> <the *relation of* time and space>. But *to* is more common with most senses and with most of the idiomatic expressions <in *relation to*>. *With* and *between* (and occasionally *among*) are also used <her *relation with* her employees> <*relations between* the United States and Mexico>.

relative See RELATION 1.

relatively The use of *relatively* to modify an adjective when no comparison is stated or implied <looking *relatively* calm and composed> is sometimes criticized. However, this use is common and completely standard today. *Relatively* is also standard in explicit comparisons <compared with what happened later, the start of our acquaintance was *relatively* cordial>.

remedy When used with a preposition, *remedy* is often followed by *for* <a *remedy for* inaction>. Less frequently, it is used with *against* and *to* <a *remedy against* abuse of the system> <offers no *remedy to* the problem>.

remember See RECOLLECT, REMEMBER.

reoccur, reoccurrence See RECUR, RECURRENCE, REOCCUR, REOCCURRENCE.

reprisal The most common preposition following *reprisal* is *against* <*reprisals against* the government>. *On* (or *upon*) is also used <*reprisals on* enemy targets>, as is *for* <in *reprisal for* the attack>.

repugnance When *repugnance* is used with a preposition, it is usually *to* <a *repugnance to* pretense>. Other prepositions sometimes used with *repugnance* are *for* and *toward* (or *towards*) <a *repugnance for* the military solution> <a *repugnance toward* her department chair>.

resemblance When *resemblance* is followed by a preposition, the preposition is usually *to* <bears a *resemblance to* his cousin>, often *between* <a strong *resemblance between* the two>, and sometimes *among* <the *resemblance among* works in the series>.

resentment *Resentment* takes several different prepositions, most commonly *at* <her *resentment at* being treated that way>, *of* <his *resentment of* them>, and *against* <felt no *resentment against* the legal system>. Other possibilities are *toward* (or *towards*), *over,* and *for.*

respect See IN RESPECT TO, WITH RESPECT TO.

responsibility A person is usually said to have a responsibility *for* something and *to* someone <the *responsibility for* carrying out the project> <a *responsibility to* her students>. *Responsibility* is also frequently followed by *of,* with the same meaning as *for* <the *responsibility of* organizing the affair>. Other prepositions that sometimes occur with *responsibility* include *about, in,* and *toward* (or *towards*).

reticent *Reticent* has recently developed the new sense "hesitant" or "reluctant" <lawmakers have been *reticent* to take up the issue> that is sometimes criticized. The use, however, is well established. The older senses of *reticent,* "inclined to be silent" <an extremely *reticent* man> and "restrained in expression or appearance" <his poems have a certain *reticent* charm>, are not disputed. The noun *reticence* has similarly developed an extended meaning, "reluctance," which has likewise become well established.

revel *Revel* is most often used with the preposition *in* <*reveling in* their success>, but occasionally it occurs with *at, around, on,* or *with.*

revenge The noun *revenge* is often followed by *on, against,* or *for.* The first two of these prepositions mark the object of the revenge <taking *revenge on* innocent civilians> <wants *revenge against* his tormentor>, the last its motive <*revenge for* the slaying of his brother>.

revert Although *revert back* is frequently cited as a redundancy, its occurrence in edited writing is not rare <would *revert back* to an earlier phase>. But *revert* by itself occurs far more often.

reward One is usually rewarded *for* something done, *with* (or sometimes *by*) something desirable, and *by* someone or something that provides the reward.

rich When *rich* takes a preposition, it is usually *in* <a city *rich in* traditions>, though occasionally *with* is used <life seemed *rich with* promise>.

rid *Rid* is almost always used with *of* <to *rid* the dog *of* fleas>, though once in a while an older combination with *from* is used <*ridding* fleas *from* the dog>. *Rid* is also often used in the phrases "get rid of" and "be rid of."

right **1.** Various uses of the adverb *right* have been criticized on various grounds, but the disputed uses are standard in informal writing <you could see *right* through it> <should have left *right* away> <we came *right* at the end>. When used as an intensifier <was *right* proud of the child>, *right* is sometimes associated with the speech of Southern and nearby states, but this use is in fact fairly common in the informal writing of people from various parts of the country.

2. *Right, rightly.* See WRONG, WRONGLY.

rob When *rob* takes a preposition, it usually takes *of* <*robbed* them *of* their dignity>, though occasionally it takes *from* <*robs* some intensity *from* the performance>.

round See AROUND 2.

run the gauntlet [gantlet] See GAUNTLET, GANTLET.

S

said The use of *said* as an adjective meaning "aforementioned" <*said* agreement is effective immediately> is today found almost exclusively in legal and business contexts.

sake In the expressions *for goodness' sake* and *for conscience' sake,* where the possessive's \s\ sound is never articulated in speech, the apostrophe alone is generally used in writing. When the word is short, the -s is likely to be pronounced and *-'s* is likely to be written: *for peace's sake, for the human race's sake.*

same The use of *same* as a pronoun, often with *the* <have enclosed *same*> <more of *the same*> is often criticized as business jargon, but the word has been in continuous use in general contexts—including literary ones—since the 14th century. Especially without *the,* it can sound wooden in awkwardly written prose, but it is often simply a mark of an informal style <will be attending *same*>.

same as **1.** Critics sometimes warn against using *the same as* in place of *as* or *just as* <he acts *the same as* he used to> (instead of ". . . just as he used to"). It is true that *as* and *just as* are more common in writing than *the same as,* but *the same as* is by no means incorrect.

2. Another old controversy has to do with whether a clause following *same* should be introduced by *as* rather than *that.* Both are in fact in reputable use <the *same* amount of compensation *as* [*that*] the others got>.

sated, satiated Both *sated* and *satiated* are followed by *with* <readers were *sated with* sensationalistic stories> <the new parents were *satiated with* others' opinions on childrearing>.

saturate When *saturate* is followed by a preposition, the usual choice is *with* <the pack's contents were *saturated with* moisture>; *by* and *in* are also occasionally used <kids are being *saturated by* television advertising> <a room *saturated in* sunlight>. When the object of *saturate* is a reflexive pronoun, the preposition that follows is *in* <*saturated* himself *in* the literature of the era>.

scared 1. When used with a preposition, *scared* is most often followed by *of* <*scared of* snakes>. It is also used quite commonly with *about, at,* and *by* <*scared about* the change> <*scared at* the prospect> <*scared by* the news> and may be followed by *to* and the infinitive <*scared to* go out>.

2. The combination *scared of* <*scared of* snakes> has been criticized as a poor substitute for *afraid of.* But *scared of* is common—and standard—in speech and in casual and informal prose.

sceptic See SKEPTIC, SCEPTIC.

search When used with a preposition, the noun *search* is usually followed by *for* <a *search for* food>

except in the phrase *in search of* <had gone *in search of* help>.

Scotch, Scottish In Scotland, *Scottish* is the preferred adjective <*Scottish* tradition> <the *Scottish* philosopher>. *Scotch* is used chiefly in familiar compounds for well-known things like Scotch broth, Scotch whisky, the Scotch pine, and the Scotch terrier.

seasonable, seasonal Whereas *seasonable* means "suitable to the season" <*seasonable* temperatures>, *seasonal* means "of or relating to a season, occurring in a particular season" <*seasonal* migration>. They are sometimes confused.

secondly *Secondly* is used with some frequency in a series after *first* or *in the first place.* See FIRSTLY.

seeing as, seeing as how, seeing that The compounds *seeing as* and *seeing as how* (as in "*seeing as* the vote hasn't been taken" or "*seeing as how* the senator was the bill's original sponsor") are criticized by some as nonstandard, but rather they seem simply to be spoken forms. In writing, *seeing that* is the usual form <*seeing that* the climate has now changed>.

seek The verb *seek* is frequently used with *after* or *for. After* tends to occur most often with the past participle *sought* in a passive construction <the film star was much *sought after*>, but active use also occurs <we had better not *seek after* the cause>. *For* is common with all tenses and voices <*seeking for* clues>

<these results were not particularly *sought for*>. *Seek* is also commonly followed by *to* and an infinitive <*seeking to* place him at the scene>.

seem See CAN'T SEEM.

see where See WHERE 2.

seldom ever, seldom if ever These two idioms, and the related *seldom or ever* and *seldom or never,* are intensive forms of *seldom* that are sometimes criticized, rather inconsistently, as meaningless or redundant or self-contradictory. But *seldom if ever* is at least 100 years old, and the others are at least a few centuries old. There is no reason to avoid them, though only *seldom if ever* and *seldom or never* are common in 20th-century writing.

self-confessed *Self-confessed* has sometimes been regarded as a redundant substitute for *confessed.* But the meaning of *self-confessed* is typically closer to *admitted* or *avowed* than it is to *confessed* <a *self-confessed* eccentric>, and thus *confessed* will not always substitute for it comfortably.

self-destruct See DESTRUCT, SELF-DESTRUCT.

senior See JUNIOR, SENIOR.

senior citizen *Senior citizen,* though disliked by some as a vapid euphemism, is a well-established term. It is especially common in the plural.

sensitive When *sensitive* precedes a prepositional phrase, the preposition is often *to* <*sensitive to* cold>. The next most common preposition is *about* <somewhat *sensitive about* it>, followed by *of* and *on* <*sensitive of* the rights of minorities> <*sensitive on* most matters>. Very occasionally, *sensitive* has also been used with *as, to, for, in,* or *over.*

sensual, sensuous These two words are generally distinguished as follows: *sensuous* emphasizes aesthetic pleasure <the *sensuous* delights of great music> while *sensual* emphasizes gratification or indulgence of the physical appetites <a life devoted to *sensual* pleasures>. But both words have several meanings, and are close in some of them. If you are in doubt, check a good dictionary.

separate The common spelling *seperate* is considered a mistake. It may help to tell yourself that spelling this word right is *par* for the course.

service Many critics disparage the use of *service* as a verb in contexts where *serve* is also possible <we *service* the tristate area>. Nevertheless, the disapproved sense of *service* continues to be fairly common in general prose and is established as standard.

set, sit *Set* used in place of *sit* (as in "*set* next to me a spell") is primarily a spoken use, found most often in regional, uneducated, and rural speech, and is generally not used in writing except in dialogue. Some intransitive uses of *set* are standard: the sun sets, a hen sets, and so do jelly, plaster, and concrete. Intransitive *sit* <*sit* in a chair> <*sit* in Congress> is uncontroversial, and transitive *sit* is standard especially with *down* <*sit* yourself *down*> <she *sat* us *down*>.

shall, will *Shall* and *will* are generally interchangeable in present-day American English. In recent years, *shall* has been regarded as somewhat affected; *will* is much more common. However, *shall* is still common in questions expressing simple choice <*shall* we go now?>.

shame The noun *shame* can be followed by *at* or *for* or by both when you can feel shame for someone *at* something <her *shame at* the thought> <no *shame for* having done it> <*shame for* her father *at* his awkwardness>. *Over* and *about* may also follow *shame* <*shame over* her role in the affair> <no *shame about* who he is>.

share The newest sense of *share,* "tell, tell about" (as in "I'd like you to *share* what you're feeling"), is disliked by some critics. It is fairly well established in speech but is not much used in writing.

shined, shone *Shine* has had both *shined* and *shone* as its past tense and past participle since the 16th century. Today, we regularly use the transitive *shined* meaning "polished" <getting his shoes *shined*> and frequently use it for "directed the light of" <*shined* his flashlight on them>, though *shone* is also common here. The intransitive form tends to be *shone* <the sun *shone*>, though *shined* is also used in American English <the sun *shined* on the picnic>.

should of See OF 2.

showed, shown The usual past participle of *show* is *shown* <have *shown* their willingness to compromise>, though *showed* is also sometimes used <had *showed* some interest>.

show up *Show up* is sometimes considered colloquial or informal, but the phrase occurs widely in general prose, including formal prose <*showed up* my ignorance> <*showed up* late for the wedding>.

shrink *Shrank* is the usual written past tense of *shrink* <*shrank* from the challenge>, but in speech *shrunk* is also standard (as in "honey, I *shrunk* your sweater"). *Shrunk* and *shrunken* are both used as the past participle: *shrunk* is the usual choice when the participle is functioning as a verb <it seems to have *shrunk*>, *shrunken* when it is functioning as an adjective <a *shrunken* head>.

shy A person can be said to be shy *of* or *about* doing something. *Shy* can also be followed by *to* and the infinitive <*shy to* claim credit>. When *shy* means "showing a lack" or "short," it is followed by *of* <the stew is a little *shy of* seasoning> <just *shy of* six feet>.

sibling *Sibling* is to *brother* and *sister* more or less as *spouse* is to *husband* and *wife:* a formal word that is sometimes useful in contexts where either of the sexually specific words would be inappropriate. It most often occurs in scientific writing but sometimes shows up in general writing as well.

sight See CITE, SITE, SIGHT.

similar **1.** *Similar* is sometimes used as an adverb (as in "step 2 is completed *similar* to the way you completed step 1"). Such usage is regarded as an error but can easily be avoided, either by substituting *similarly* or by rearranging the parts of the sentence to make it read more smoothly: "Completing step 2 is *similar* to completing step 1."

2. One thing is said to be similar in some way *to* another, and two or more things are said to be similar *in* some respect.

simultaneous The use of *simultaneous* as an adverb in place of *simultaneously* (as in "*simultaneous* with this announcement, negotiations were taking place") is considered an error when it occurs in writing and seems to show up primarily in speech.

since Some critics warn that the conjunction *since,* when used to mean "because," can create ambiguity, particularly when both this "because" sense and the alternative "from the time when" sense are meaningful in the same context (as in "the President could have moved ahead, but *since* his opponents took the reins of Congress his efforts have been stymied"). But most writers recognize this ambiguity and try to avoid it. In most contexts there is no potential for ambiguity <*since* it was raining, she took an umbrella>. Though some critics prefer *because* as a causal conjunction in all cases, there is no need for you to adopt such a stringent policy.

sing *Sung* used as the past tense of *sing* is today not so much wrong as simply old-fashioned <*sung* out a round of praise>. *Sang* is the usual past tense, and *sung* is the past participle <they'd *sung* it every year>.

sink Both *sank* and *sunk* are used for the past tense of *sink* <*sank* [*sunk*] back into the chair>. *Sank* is used more often, but *sunk* is neither rare nor dialectal, though it occurs much more often as a past participle <had *sunk* like a stone>.

sit See SET, SIT.

site See CITE, SITE, SIGHT.

skeptic, sceptic *Skeptic* and related words (*skeptical, skepticism*) are usually spelled with a *k* in America and a *c* in Britain.

slow, slowly Some critics claim that careful writers avoid the adverb *slow,* even though it has been used for over four centuries. In actual practice, *slow* and *slowly* are not used in quite the same way. *Slow* is almost always used with verbs that denote movement or action, and it normally follows the verb it modifies <stew should be cooked long and *slow*>. *Slowly* can be used before the verb <outrage that *slowly* changed to

shame> and with participial adjectives <a *slowly* dawning awareness>; it is also used after verbs where *slow* could be used <burn *slowly* [*slow*]> as well as after verbs where *slow* would sound odd <he turned *slowly* toward the door>.

smell *Smell* is one of those verbs that are used with both adjectives and adverbs. When a writer is describing the quality of a smell, an adjective is usual <it *smells* good>. But *smell* can also be used with an adverb of manner, most often when *smell* means "stink" <began to *smell* badly>. *Smell* is also frequently followed by a prepositional phrase introduced by *of* <the place *smelled of* money and power>.

snuck From its earliest appearance in print in the late 19th century as a dialectal and probably uneducated form, the past tense and past participle *snuck* has risen to virtually equal status with *sneaked* <*snuck* down the fire escape> <had quietly *snuck* in>, and it is continuing to grow in frequency. It is most common in the United States and Canada, but has also been spotted in Australia.

so **1.** The use of the adverb *so* as an intensifier <the dialogue is *so* dull> <it is *so* unlike her to behave in that way> is widely condemned in college handbooks but is nonetheless standard in informal prose. *So* is also widely used in negative contexts <not *so* long ago> and when qualified by a dependent clause <was

so good at it that he began to consider it as a career>. These latter uses are never criticized.

2. The use of the conjunction *so* to introduce clauses of result <the acoustics are good, *so* every note is clear> and clauses of purpose <be quiet *so* he can sleep> is standard, though in clauses of purpose, *so that* is more common in formal writing than *so* alone <they want to raze the building *so that* new housing can be constructed>.

so . . . as See AS . . . AS 1.

so as to Because the *so as* of *so as to* can often be omitted <we left early [*so as*] *to* beat the traffic>, it has sometimes been called redundant. On the other hand, some critics suggest *so as to* plus an infinitive as a possible replacement for the conjunction *so* followed by a clause. Where the critics are at odds in this way, you must follow your ear. If a sentence sounds better without *so as,* omit it; if it sounds better with *so as,* keep it. And note that some contexts positively require *so as* or an equivalent like *in order* <they spoke in a whisper *so as* not *to* disturb the others>.

so-called Some critics find fault with using quotation marks to enclose a term or terms following *so-called* <you and your *so-called* "friends">. Their advice is to omit either the quotation marks <you and your *so-called* friends> or the *so-called* <you and your "friends">. In edited writing quotation marks are in fact usually omitted after *so-called,* but their use is not at all rare. Using them is not an error, but they are just as easily and sensibly omitted.

so far as See AS FAR AS, SO FAR AS.

so long as See AS LONG AS, SO LONG AS.

solution When used with a preposition, *solution* is usually followed by *of* or *to* <the *solution of* problems> <the *solution to* the puzzle>, and occasionally by *for* <a *solution for* their problems>.

some **1.** When *some* is used to modify a number, it is almost always a round number <a community of *some* 150,000 inhabitants>. But because some is slightly more emphatic than *about* or *approximately,* it is occasionally used with a more exact number <has *some* 125 tackles to his credit>.

2. When *some* is used without a number, most critics feel that *somewhat* is to be preferred. However, only when *some* modifies an adjective, usually a comparative, will *somewhat* always substitute smoothly <with *some* [*somewhat*] higher temperatures expected>. When *some* modifies a verb or adverb, and especially when it follows a verb, the substitution may prove awkward <forced me to grow up *some*> <I've been around *some* in my day>.

somebody, someone **1.** *Somebody* and *someone* are two of those curious indefinite pronouns that take a singular verb but are often referred to by the plural pronouns *they, their,* and *them* <if *someone* asks, tell *them* you're with me> <the minute *somebody* raises *their* hand>. Some critics are on record as insisting that singular pronouns be used. The governing principle in the choice of pronouns is notional agreement, and when the speaker or writer has more than one person in mind, or a very indefinite somebody, the plural pronoun tends to be used. When a singular pronoun is used to refer to *somebody* or *someone,* the speaker or writer often seems to have someone specific in mind <till *somebody* happened to note it as the second case *he* had heard of>.

2. *Somebody* used to be much more common than *someone;* today, however, *someone* is used more frequently than *somebody.* Both are equally standard; use whichever one you think sounds better in a given context.

somebody else's See ELSE.

some . . . -odd See -ODD.

someone See SOMEBODY, SOMEONE.

someplace *Someplace,* like *anyplace,* is an adverb that has become standard in American English during the 20th century <they were going *someplace* together>. A few critics continue to call it an informal word and to discourage its written use in favor of *somewhere,* but our evidence shows that *someplace* has been common even in academic writing since at least the 1940s. See also ANYPLACE; EVERYPLACE.

sometime The adverb *sometime* is written as a single word <he arrived *sometime* last night>. A phrase combining the adjective *some* and the noun *time* is written as two words <he needed *some time* to think> <we haven't seen them for *some time*>. An easy way to tell if *some* and *time* should be written as one word or two in most contexts is to insert *quite* before *some* and see if the passage still makes sense. If it does, *some* and *time* should be written separately <we haven't seen them for (quite) *some time*> <He arrived (quite) *some time* ago>. If it does not—as in "He arrived (quite) *sometime* last night"—*sometime* is the correct choice.

somewhat See SOME 2.

sooner See NO SOONER.

sort, sort of, sort of a See KIND 1; KIND OF, SORT OF; KIND OF A, SORT OF A.

so that See SO 2.

sparing *Sparing* is generally followed by *in* or *of* when it is complemented by a prepositional phrase <*sparing in* his praise> <*sparing of* their money>. Occasionally *sparing* is found with *with* <*sparing with* their money>.

spell Americans generally use *spelled* for the past tense and past participle of *spell*. British writers commonly use *spelt*.

spill In American English the usual past tense and past participle of *spill* is *spilled. Spilt* is common in British English. As an attributive adjective, *spilt* also occurs occasionally in American English <there's no use crying over *spilt* milk>.

spit The common verb *spit* has as its past tense and past participle either *spat* or *spit* <she *spat* [*spit*] out the words> <he actually *spit* [*spat*] on the ground>. The British prefer *spat.*

spoil In American English *spoiled* is usual for both the past tense and past participle of *spoil.* In British English both *spoiled* and *spoilt* are used.

spokesperson See PERSON 2.

spoonful See -FUL.

spring The past tense of the verb *spring* can be either *sprang* or *sprung. Sprang* is the more common form, but *sprung* is not at all rare. *Sprung* also serves as the past participle <the canoe had *sprung* a leak>.

staffer *Staffer* is a word that many people find handy and yet many others dislike. It has been around since the 1940s and has been a staple of journalism, though it is certainly not indispensable, even for journalists. Anyone determined to avoid it can easily replace it with such terms as *staff member, official,* or *employee.*

stanch, staunch These two spelling variants have been in reputable use for centuries, and they are standard for both the verb and the adjective, though *stanch* is much more common for the verb <used a tourniquet to *stanch* the flow> and *staunch* much more common for the adjective <a *staunch* ally>.

stationary, stationery The adjective that means "not moving" is *stationary* <a *stationary* object>; the noun that means "paper for writing letters" is *stationery* <purchased some *stationery* along with some pens and pencils>. The usual advice for remembering the distinction is to associate the *er* in *stationery* with the *er* in *letter* or *paper.*

staunch See STANCH, STAUNCH.

still and all This phrase is sometimes criticized, but it is clearly standard. Less formal than the starchy *nevertheless* and less abrupt than the simple *still,* it has a casual, conversational quality which is consistent with the informal tone of much modern prose <*still and all,* experimental economics is on the rise>.

stink Both *stank* and *stunk* are used as the past tense of *stink. Stank* is more common in edited prose, but both are standard. The past participle of *stink* is always *stunk* <the room has *stunk* of solvent ever since>.

straitened Though the adjective that means "distressed" or "deprived" <*straitened* circumstances> is actually the past participle of the verb *straiten* and has no relation to either *straight* or *straighten,* the spelling error *straightened* is still fairly easy to make in a moment of inattention.

strata, stratum The plural *strata* has occasionally been used as a singular (as in "one *strata* of society") since the 18th century and is sometimes given the plural *stratas* ("several *stratas* of bureaucracy"). However, these infrequent but persistent usages are generally considered nonstandard. See also LATIN PLURALS.

strike *Struck* is the past tense of *strike* <the clock *struck* twelve>, and usually also functions as its past participle <the tree was *struck* by lightning>. The alternative past participle *stricken* is used when *strike* has the sense "to afflict suddenly" <*stricken* with a heart attack>. It is also common for the sense "to cancel or delete" <*stricken* from the record>; and *stricken* has adjectival uses as well <*stricken* faces>.

strive *Strive* is most often followed by *to* and the infinitive <*striving to* keep a balance>. It is also frequently used with *for* <*strove for* reform>, and less frequently with *after, against, at, in, into, toward* (or *towards*), *with,* and *within.*

subject 1. *Noun.* When the noun *subject* is followed by a preposition, it is usually *of* <the *subject of* the book> and sometimes *for* <a *subject for* debate>.

2. *Adjective.* The adjective *subject* is usually used with *to* <was *subject to* asthma attacks>.

3. *Verb.* The verb *subject* is usually used with *to* <had never *subjected* himself *to* such a regimen>.

4. For a discussion of grammatical subject, see SUBJECT (in Glossary).

such Some critics disapprove of using *such* as a pronoun <*such* was the result> <tin and glass and *such*>, but dictionaries recognize it as standard.

such as See AS 2; LIKE 2.

suffer When followed by a preposition, *suffer* almost always takes *from* <*suffers from* rheumatism>. In speech, *with* is sometimes used (as in "*suffering with* this condition").

suitable The usual preposition after *suitable* is *for* <*suitable for* a wedding ceremony>. *To* is also used, but less commonly <was *suitable to* the couple>.

supersede, supercede *Supercede* has a long history as an occasional spelling variant of *supersede,* but most writers nowadays use *supersede.*

sure, surely Despite the suspicion of many writing handbooks, *sure* and *surely* are both standard adverbs. *Sure* is used much more in informal contexts than *surely,* which is the adverb of choice in a more elevated style. When they are used as intensifiers, *sure* is more emphatic and positive <he *sure* gets them to play hard>, while *surely* is less emphatic and more neutral and suggests that the writer or speaker is being hopeful or persuasive <*surely* such a book could be produced>.

sure and For constructions like *be sure and,* see TRY AND.

surprised The prepositions that occur after *surprised* are *at* and *by. By* is the choice when *surprised* means "taken unawares" <*surprised by* the force of the wind>. Both *at* and *by* are possible when *surprised* means "struck with wonder" or "taken aback" <*surprised at* [*by*] the announcement>.

swell This verb has two past participles, *swelled* and *swollen. Swollen* is the one used frequently as an attributive adjective <a *swollen* foot>; *swelled* is used in this way only in the idiom *swelled head.* Otherwise the two forms are more or less interchangeable, although *swollen* is more likely in describing a harmful or undesirable swelling <the door was *swollen* shut>, and *swelled* tends to be used in a neutral or positive way, especially in describing an increase in numbers <their ranks had *swelled* to 100,000>.

swim The standard past tense of *swim* is *swam* <Oliver and Katy *swam* by> and the standard past participle is *swum* <had *swum* the Channel>.

T

take, see BRING, TAKE.

take exception to See EXCEPTION.

take place, occur Some critics prefer to restrict *take place* to planned events and actions <the ceremony will *take place* on Friday afternoon> and *occur* to things that happen by chance <the accident *occurred* at a busy intersection>. While this tends to reflect actual usage, in much speech and writing planned events also "occur" and accidents also "take place." In short, *take place* and *occur* are synonyms, and there is no reason to adhere strictly to the critics' preference.

teaspoonful See -FUL.

tenant, tenet *Tenant,* meaning "occupant, landholder," is sometimes mistakenly used in place of *tenet,* meaning "principle, doctrine." To avoid this error, remember that *tenant* and *occupant* both end in *-ant.*

tendency A tendency may be either *to* or *toward* (or *towards*) something <a strong *tendency to* [*toward*] hyperbole>. In medical writing, *to* is preferred <a *tendency to* diabetes>.

tenet See TENANT, TENET.

terms See IN TERMS OF.

than *Than* followed by a third-person objective pronoun (as in "older *than* me," "stronger *than* him") is usually frowned upon when it occurs in edited prose. The construction is common in speech, however. In writing, *than* used as a conjunction is standard <older *than* I am> <easier said *than* done> <anywhere else *than* at home>.

than any See ANY 3.

thankfully The adverb *thankfully,* used as a sentence modifier <*thankfully,* it didn't rain>, is sometimes criticized, but the use is fairly common in general writing. See also HOPEFULLY.

thanks to *Thanks to* can be applied to negative causes <tripped over the last hurdle, *thanks to* a pulled ligament> as well as to positive or neutral ones <arrived early, *thanks to* good weather>. Both uses are standard, and in both informal and formal contexts.

that **1.** *That, which, who.* In current usage *that* refers to persons or things <the man *that* I love> <the book *that* she wrote>, *which* refers to things <a tree *which* bears apples>, and *who* refers to persons and sometimes to animals <the man *who* has everything> <buried my cat, *who* died yesterday>. The notion that *that* should not be used to refer to persons is without foundation; such use is entirely standard.

2. *That, which.* Although some critics say otherwise, *that* and *which* are both regularly used to introduce restrictive clauses—clauses essential to the description of the word they refer to <the book *that* [*which*] you ordered is in>. Only *which* is used to introduce nonrestrictive clauses—clauses that are not essential to the meaning of the preceding word <the door, *which* was painted pink, opened onto the garden>.

3. *That* is commonly used in negative statements as an intensifier <it's not *that* simple>. This use, though disliked by some, is standard. See also ALL THAT.

the both See BOTH 3.

the fact is, the fact that See FACT.

the late See LATE.

their **1.** *Their, there, they're.* It is not unusual to see these common words replace one another by mistake. Haste and inattention probably are more responsible than actual confusion about which word is which. However, for the record, *their* is a possessive pronoun <*their* house is down the street>; *there* has various uses as an adjective <that man *there*>, a noun <take it from *there*>, a pronoun <*there* shall come a time>, and, chiefly, an adverb <stop right *there*>; and *they're* is a contraction of *they are.* Remember that the spelling checker of a word processor will not identify a wrong use of one of these.

2. See THEY, THEIR, THEM.

theirs Like *its, ours,* and *yours, theirs* is spelled without an apostrophe in present-day English.

them See THEY, THEIR, THEM.

there See THEIR 1.

there is, there are When *there* is an anticipatory or "dummy" subject, the number of the verb is normally determined by the number of the true subject following: a singular verb precedes a singular noun <*there is* no more coffee>, and a plural verb precedes a plural noun <*there are* several rooms available>.

However, when a compound subject follows the verb and the first element is singular, the verb may be either singular or plural <*there is* a lake and several small streams> <*there are* a dog and a few cats in the house>, the singular construction being more common. Still, some writers insist on formal agreement and use a plural verb <*there were* an apartment house and a parking lot at the end of the block>.

When a collective noun (as subject) is followed by a prepositional phrase with a plural noun (as object) <*there is* a flock of geese overhead> <*there are* a passel of problems associated with it>, the verb is governed by notional agreement: When the speaker or writer has the collective in mind (e.g., *flock* in *flock of geese*), a singular verb is used; and when the plural noun is in mind (e.g., *problems* in *passel of problems*), a plural verb is used.

Some people prefer to say *there is* (or *there's*) in every case, even when the following subject is clearly plural (as in "a lottery where *there's* a hundred thousand losers to every winner"); such usage is generally avoided in writing.

the same as See SAME AS 1.

these kind of, these sort of See KIND 1.

they **1.** For *they* used to refer to a singular noun or pronoun, see THEY, THEIR, THEM.

2. *They* used as an indefinite subject <*they*'re tearing down the building next to my office> is sometimes objected to, primarily on the assumption that every pronoun should have an antecedent. But that assumption is without grammatical foundation; in this use *they* is an indefinite pronoun and indefinite pronouns do not require antecedents. The use is standard.

they, their, them English lacks a common-gender third-person singular pronoun that can be used to refer to indefinite pronouns such as *everyone, anyone,* or *someone*. Writers and speakers have for centuries supplied this lack by using the plural pronouns <everyone should try it once in *their* life> <anyone who knows *their* grammar knows this>. This use is well established in speech and writing, even in literary and formal contexts. You have the option of using the plural or singular pronouns according to which one you think sounds best in a given context <someone on my left kept bumping me with *his or her* [*their*] elbow>.

they're See THEIR 1.

thing *Thing* turns up frequently in speech and in writing that has something of the casual quality of speech <look at this *thing* another way> <the *thing* is to get well>. Some critics advise replacing *thing* with a more specific word or dropping it altogether (for example, "The first *thing* he told me was . . ." could be replaced by "First he told me . . ."). But should you? The answer really depends upon considerations of tone, rhythm, and idiom, and good writers are directed in such matters by their ear—their sense of what sounds right in a particular context.

this The use of *this* (and *that, which,* and *it* as well) as a pronoun to refer broadly to a preceding idea, topic, sentence, or paragraph <protest rallies were being mounted daily, but *this* only served to harden the regime's stance> used to be criticized but is now allowed to be respectable, as long as the reference is clear. See also WHICH 2.

those kind of, those sort of See KIND 1.

though See ALTHOUGH, THOUGH.

through The use of *through* to mean "finished" used to be criticized but is now considered standard. It usually describes either the completion of an activity <is *through* with the job> or a person who is washed-up <she was *through* as a box-office attraction>. See also DONE; FINISHED.

tight, tightly *Tight* is usually an adjective <security was *tight*>, but it is also commonly used as an adverb <the door was shut *tight*> <sleep *tight*>. Some of its adverbial uses overlap with those of *tightly,* but the two words are used mostly in distinct ways. *Tight* almost always follows the verb it modifies. It occurs especially in such idioms as "sit tight" and "sleep tight," as well as with such verbs as *hold, close, squeeze,* and *shut. Tightly* is a somewhat more common word that is used both before and after the verb or participle it modifies <*tightly* woven fabric> <clamped *tightly* in his hand>.

till, until The notion that *till* is a short form of *until* is erroneous; *till* is actually the older word, dating back to at least the 9th century. (*Until* is first recorded around 1200.) Today *until* is often considered somewhat more formal than *till,* and to be the better choice at the beginning of a sentence or clause. But *till,* although less common than *until,* shows up in highly serious writing and at the beginning of a sentence <*Till* his encounter with malaria, he had never known serious illness>.

times Critics sometimes complain about expressions such as "ten *times* less," "three *times* closer," and "five *times* more." Those who do not like the form with *less* insist that *times* invokes multiplication, and those who do not like the form with *more* say it creates mathematical uncertainty. These concerns are misplaced. Idiomatic expressions using *times* have been in use for over 300 years and there is no real reason to avoid them.

to, too, two These words are often inadvertently substituted for one another. Keep a sharp eye out for such errors when proofreading your writing.

to a degree See DEGREE.

to all intents and purposes This phrase has taken various forms throughout its history, including *to all intents, to all intent and purpose,* and *for all intents and purposes,* but *to all intents and purposes* has long been the most common. Critics sometimes call it wordy or hackneyed, but it is used by excellent writers and there is no compelling reason to avoid it. If you prefer a shorter alternative, the best one is usually *in effect.*

too See TO, TOO, TWO.

together with When *together with* serves to add a second noun to a singular noun that is the subject of a sentence <the singer, *together with* opening act Sir Prize, performs tonight>, the verb usually remains singular, especially when the segment introduced by *together with* is set off by commas, dashes, or parentheses. When it is not, the verb may be either singular or plural <the campaign leader *together with* selected staff members are [is] planning to review their strategy>. See also AGREEMENT (in Glossary).

total, totally The use of *total* and *totally* in such phrases as "total annihilation" and "totally destroyed" is occasionally criticized as redundant. *Total* and *totally* can usually be omitted from such phrases without a loss of meaning, but their omission will almost always result in a loss of emphasis, and the rhythm and idiom of the sentence should also be taken into account. If *total* or *totally* sounds right in its context, you may use it.

toward, towards Both *toward* and *towards* are commonly used in the United States, but *toward* is the usual choice. The British strongly favor *towards*. Otherwise, there is no difference between the two forms.

track, tract These words are sometimes confused in their outdoors senses. *Track* refers to a trail or course; *tract* refers to an area of land.

transpire Numerous critics have condemned the use of *transpire* to mean "to come to pass" or "occur" <the events that *transpired* last night> rather than "it was learned" or "it turned out" <it *transpired* that he had known all along>. However, the disputed use is firmly established in both informal and formal prose.

triple, treble Of these two forms, *triple* is the usual choice as either verb or adjective in American English, except that the verb *treble* is sometimes favored by business writers <profits have more than *trebled*>. In British usage, *treble* is the more common word.

triumphal, triumphant The distinction between these two words is basically this: *triumphal* is used with the meaning "ceremonially celebrating or commemorating a victory" <a *triumphal* procession>, and *triumphant* is used in most other cases, as with the meanings "having triumphed" <a *triumphant* army>, "rejoicing for victory" <a *triumphant* shout>, and "notably successful" <a *triumphant* performance>.

trivia *Trivia* is much like *data*—an English word that has the form of the original Latin plural but that is used as both a plural count noun <such *trivia* are his stock-in-trade> and a singular mass noun <a piece of *trivia*>. Some critics regard the singular use as unacceptable, but our evidence shows that it and the plural use are about equally common and are standard. See also LATIN PLURALS.

true When *true* means "faithful," it is often followed by *to* <*true to* her heart>. In other senses, *true* occurs commonly with *for* or *of* instead <the same is *true for* group B> <it is *true of* this particular case>.

trust The prepositions *in* and *to* both occur after the verb *trust* <*trust in* God> <*trust to* luck>. The noun *trust* is usually followed by *in* <placed her *trust in* him>.

try and The use of *try and* in sentences where *try to* would be possible <*try and* find it> <I'll *try and* write you soon> has long been criticized, but the use is an old one. It occurs mostly in speech and in casual writing, though it is not unknown in informal edited prose. A couple of other common verbs are used in similar constructions—namely, *go* <*go and* ask her> and *come* <*come and* see us>. *Be sure and* is also common <*be sure and* walk the dog today>. All these combinations are more characteristic of speech than of writing, but they are nonetheless standard. *Try and* is limited to one form; it cannot be inflected, as *try to* can <*tries to* help> <*tried to* do her best>.

two See TO, TOO, TWO.

type Objection is commonly made to the use of *type* in the sense "sort" to modify a preceding noun (as in "a sting *type* operation"). The standard way of getting around the criticism is to add *of* <a sting *type of* operation> or insert a hyphen before *type* <a sting-*type* operation> or simply drop *type* altogether <a sting operation>.

U

unaware, unawares *Unaware* is common as an adjective <seemed *unaware* of what was going on>. The usual adverb is *unawares* <was taken *unawares*>, but either is likely to occur following *catch* <caught him *unawares* [*unaware*]>.

unbeknown, unbeknownst Both *unbeknown* and *unbeknownst* are in standard use and have been for many years, but *unbeknownst* is the more common form <*unbeknownst* [*unbeknown*] to us>.

under . . . circumstances See CIRCUMSTANCES.

undoubtedly See DOUBTLESS, NO DOUBT, UNDOUBTEDLY.

undue, unduly *Undue* often means simply "not called for, not necessary or appropriate" <places *undue* hardships on the working poor>. More often, its meaning is closer to "inappropriately excessive or immoderate" <an *undue* hostility in those opposed to the accord>. And sometimes *undue* serves as a synonym of *excessive* or *great* <*undue* expansion of the state apparatus>. The same variation in meaning occurs in the adverb *unduly,* which is sometimes used to mean "excessively" or "extremely" <her *unduly* annoying voice>. Because of these variations in meaning, *undue* and *unduly* sometimes appear in contexts where they might seem to be redundant <no cause for *undue* alarm> <no reason to get *unduly* excited>. Many critics regard such usage as inelegant or simply wrong, but it is well established and perfectly standard.

uneatable See INEDIBLE, UNEATABLE.

unequal *Unequal* is often followed by *to* <was *unequal to* the task>.

unequivocally The adverb is *unequivocally* <is *unequivocally* opposed>. The nonstandard equivalent that sometimes shows up in print is *unequivocably.*

unexceptionable, unexceptional In current usage, *unexceptional* nearly always means "not out of the ordinary, not exceptional" <a standard restaurant with

an *unexceptional* menu>. *Unexceptionable,* the less common word, means "not open to objection or criticism" <a perfectly sound and *unexceptionable* argument>.

uninterested See DISINTERESTED, UNINTERESTED.

unique Critics have often claimed that *unique* is an absolute adjective and therefore cannot be modified by adverbs such as *more, most, somewhat,* and *very.* This claim is based on the mistaken assumption that *unique* can mean only "sole" or "unequaled." When *unique* is used in these senses, it is not qualified <his *unique* concern was to get everyone signed on before the project's May start date>. However, when *unique* is used with the more common meaning "unusual," words of comparison and qualification are widespread and standard <a rather *unique* program for the Senator to be sponsoring> <very *unique* diamond settings for this period>.

unlike The use of *unlike* as a conjunction <*unlike* with last year's model, there is no lack of engine power> is sometimes criticized, especially when the preposition following *unlike* is dropped ("*unlike* last year's model, . . ."), creating a false or incomplete comparison between two terms (*model* and *engine power,* rather than the engine power of last year's and this year's model). The construction with the preposition is established, whereas the one without it is not. See also LIKE, 1.

unreadable See ILLEGIBLE, UNREADABLE.

unsanitary, insanitary People sometimes express uncertainty about which of these words is the correct one. Our evidence shows that both are correct, common, and used in the same way.

unsatisfied See DISSATISFIED, UNSATISFIED.

unseasonable, unseasonal See SEASONABLE, SEASONAL.

until See TILL, UNTIL.

up, *adverb* **1.** *Up* is frequently used as a particle after a verb—for example, *burn up, end up, hurry up, climb up,* and *rise up.* Some critics have erroneously concluded that *up* is redundant or otherwise unnecessary in these combinations. But in fact these uses of *up* are a deeply rooted part of everyday conversational English and can often help a writer steer clear of awkward and stilted prose. We suggest that you let *up* fall where it naturally will and not become concerned with revising it out.

2. In two-word verbs like *hold up* or *stick up,* the particle *up* can either stay with the verb <the gunman *held up* the cashier> or follow the direct object <the gunman *held* the cashier *up*>. Some critics dislike the latter word order, but it is nevertheless established. Note that when the direct object is a pronoun, the particle almost always follows it <the gunman *held* her *up*>.

up, *verb* **1.** *Up* as a verb meaning "raise" or "increase" <*upped* the ante> is considered dubious by some. Our evidence shows that it is standard but is not used in formal writing.

2. Some critics view the phrase *up and* <expected them to *up and* walk out> with the same distaste they direct at *go and* and *try and* (see TRY AND). *Up and* is no rustic idiom, however; it is current on both sides of the Atlantic and is used in many general publications, though it is not formal.

upon See ON 1.

up until Since the meaning of *up until* is the same as that of *until* by itself, some critics recommend omitting the *up*. But *up until* is an idiomatic phrase that occurs naturally and appropriately in speech and in casual writing <*up until* the time of his enlistment>. Use your own judgment as to when the *up* sounds right and when it is not needed.

upward, upwards The adjective is *upward* <an *upward* spiral>. The adverb may be either *upward* or, less commonly, *upwards* <the kite rose *upward* [*upwards*]>. Both are standard. Both *upward* and *upwards* are used with *of* to mean "more than, in excess of"; *upwards of* is more common than *upward of* <they cost *upwards of* $25>.

us Like the other personal pronouns, *us* turns up in contexts where critics have long said it does not belong. It occurs after the verb *be* <it is *us*>. It is common in an emphatic position near the beginning of a statement <was *us* against them>. A little harder to explain is its appearance in the subject position <*us* conference attendees hadn't expected this>. These last two, particularly the latter, are more likely to be found in speech than in edited prose.

usage Critics have complained that the word *usage* should not be employed simply as a synonym of *use*. Almost any dictionary, however, defines *usage* to mean "act of use, use, employment" <a decrease in the *usage* of electricity> <their *usage* of migrant labor>. Though *use* is more common than *usage* in this sense, *usage* is not an error.

used to, use to The idiom *used to* meaning "to be accustomed or habituated" <we *used to* hike more than we do now> is extremely common in both speech and writing. Because the *d* is not pronounced, *used to* is indistinguishable in speech from *use to.* In writing, however, *use to* in place of *used to* is considered an error. When *did* is used with *used to,* we write "Did he *use to*?" rather than "Did he *used to*?" The usual negative form in American English is *didn't use to* <they *didn't use to* charge you for it>. See also SUPPOSED TO.

used to could Many writing handbooks attack *used to could* as nonstandard. It is not a complex verb form but a dialectal adverb, *used to,* tacked onto *could.* It is a speech form and is used in writing only for deliberate effect.

useful Something is said to be useful *to* somebody <should be *useful to* the beginner>. When the way in which something is useful is being described, either *in* or *for* may be used <is especially *useful in* [*for*] editing text>.

utilize Critics dislike *utilize* because they regard it as an inflated substitute for *use.* But *utilize* is actually used only when it has the meaning "to turn to practical use or account" <most homes do not *utilize* the entire array of channels available>, and it suggests, more than *use,* a deliberate decision or effort to employ something or someone for a practical purpose.

V

various *Various* is sometimes used as a pronoun, usually followed by *of* <*various of* them came up to us later>. This use was first recorded in British English in the middle of the 19th century and in American English a little later. It is fully established as standard in present-day American English and is fairly common in edited general prose <how the economy will behave if *various of* these factors change>. See also VARIOUS DIFFERENT.

various different This phrase has been criticized as redundant by those who do not recognize that its meaning is "a number of different," not "different different" <*various different* species could be seen>. Other critics have contended that it is incorrect to use *various* in this way to mean "of an indefinite number greater than one." Such use is actually well-established and is certainly standard <the *various* problems that he mentioned>. Even so, you may wish to steer clear of *various different* since it can give the appearance of redundancy. It seems not to occur often in edited prose.

vary One thing or group of things is said to vary *from* another <*vary from* the norm>. When a range of variation is being described, *vary* is followed by either *from* or *between* <the length *varies from* 20 to 25 inches> <the temperature *varies between* 38.6 and 45 degrees Fahrenheit>.

vast majority See MAJORITY.

've See OF 2.

vehicle The usual pronunciation of *vehicle* is without \h\. Pronunciation with \h\, however, is also widespread, especially in the South.

venal, venial *Venal,* which means "open to or characterized by corruption" <rooting out *venal* influences in the precinct> <a thoroughly *venal* man>, is sometimes confused with *venial,* which means "pardonable" <a *venial* fault>.

verbal, oral Some feel that *verbal* cannot be used to mean "spoken rather than written, oral" and views such use as a modern corruption. This is a popular myth; *verbal* is commonly used with such words as *agreement, commitment,* and *contract* in the disputed "oral" sense, and has been so used by major writers for centuries. There is no reason to avoid such use.

vest An abstract possession, such as a power or right, is vested *in* a person or institution <responsibilities *vested in* the federal government>, but a person or institution is vested *with* an abstract possession <*vested* the office *with* similar powers>. Both uses are common and correct.

via *Via* was taken into English directly from Latin in the late 18th century, with the meaning "by way of, by a route passing through" <traveled to Philadelphia *via* New York City>. Two centuries later it continues to be used in this sense—usually with no italics—as well as in the extended sense "through the medium or agency of" <went to Chicago *via* train> and in the sense "by way of" in contexts having nothing to do with travel <influence peddling *via* political action committees>. All of these uses are standard, though some critics dislike all but the original sense.

viable *Viable* is sometimes criticized as a fad word or cliché—especially in the phrase *viable alternative.* Although both the word and the phrase are perfectly standard, you may want to approach them with some caution.

vice, vise In American English, the "moral fault" is spelled *vice* while the "clamping tool" is spelled *vise.* In British English, *vice* is the preferred spelling for both.

vie *Vie* is typically used with the prepositions *with* and *for:* competitors vie *with* each other *for* something.

view The phrase *with a view* usually takes the preposition *to* or *toward* <*with a view to* [*toward*] establishing a consumer credit system>. When the phrase is *with the view, of* is almost invariably the preposition that follows <*with the view of* maintaining these ties>. See also POINT OF VIEW.

vigilant When *vigilant* is used with a preposition, the choice is most often *against, in,* or *to* <*vigilant against* attempts to impose such restraints> <*vigilant in* protecting these freedoms> <must be *vigilant to* prevent it>. Occasionally, *vigilant* may be followed by *about* or *for.*

vis-à-vis The literal meaning of *vis-à-vis* in French is "face to face," but in English *vis-à-vis* is used mostly in its two extended senses, "in relation to" <the role of the legislature *vis-à-vis* the judicial branch> and "in comparison with" <the new Russia *vis-à-vis* the old>. Both of these senses are standard (as they are in French), although a few critics insist on the literal sense only. *Vis-à-vis* has been in use in English since the 18th century and is usually not italicized as a foreign term.

vise See VICE, VISE.

W

wait on, wait for The use of *wait on* in contexts where some would prefer *wait for* or *await* <they no longer needed to *wait on* [*wait for, await*] Washington's approval> cannot be considered dialectal, colloquial, regional, or substandard. On the contrary, it is found in standard and widely circulated prose, even literary prose. If the use of *wait on,* or its occasional variant *wait upon,* is natural to you, there is no need to avoid it.

waitress See -ESS.

waive, wave The usual meaning of *waive* is "to relinquish" <*waived* his right> or "to refrain from enforcing" <*waiving* the rule>. When used where *wave* is expected (as in "to *waive* the whole matter aside"), it is widely regarded as an error and is undetectable by the spelling checker of a word processor.

wake *Wake* originated as two separate verbs that combined in the Middle Ages to produce our modern mixture of inflected forms (past tense: *woke* or *waked;* past participle: *woken, waked,* or occasionally *woke*). *Waked,* for the past tense, was more common formerly than it is now, but it has not disappeared from use <I *waked* just in time for breakfast>. *Woke* is at present the dominant form for the past tense <I *woke* before sunrise>. For the past participle, *woken* and *waked* are both used in American English <he had *woken*

[*waked*] the baby>, whereas British English prefers *woken*. *Woke* is also occasionally found as past participle <I must've *woke* him up>. To complicate matters, the separate but synonymous verb *waken* is regular (past and past participle: *wakened*).

wary *Wary* is often followed by *of* <is *wary of* phone solicitations>. Less commonly, *wary* is followed by *in*, usually when describing a cautious or hesitant approach toward *doing* something <leads us to be *wary in* believing such reports>. Occasionally *wary* is followed by *about* <*wary about* contacting them>.

wave See WAIVE, WAVE.

ways *Ways* has been used as a synonym of *way* in such expressions as "a long *ways* off" since the late 1500s, and is standard in American English. (In British English, it appears to have died out.) Its occurrence in writing is still frowned upon by some critics.

weave When *weave* is used in its literal senses, its usual past tense and past participle are *wove* and *woven* <they *wove* cloth> <a *woven* fabric>. The same forms are normally used in straightforward figurative examples of *weave* <*wove* together a number of different themes> <*woven* into the social fabric>. But when *weave* describes a winding course of movement, *weaved* usually serves as both its past tense and past participle <they *weaved* down the lane> <had already *weaved* past several obstacles>.

wed The past tense and past participle of *wed* is usually *wedded* <a poem in which he *wedded* everyday life and earthshaking events> <had long been *wedded* to the idea>, but the less common form *wed* is also used <they had been *wed* in the summer>.

well There are those who will criticize your "sing good" and your "feel badly," but you are safe no matter how you use *well. Well* has been both an adjective <I feel *well*> and an adverb <did *well* in math> for centuries, and you can use it safely either way. See also GOOD; FEEL BAD, FEEL BADLY.

well-nigh The adverb *well-nigh* has been called old-fashioned, but in fact it is a fairly common and perfectly good synonym for *nearly* <was *well-nigh* impossible>.

when, where Many critics balk at the use of *when* or *where,* preceded by *is,* in informal definitions such as "word processing *is where* you use a computer to type." These were used as standard defining patterns in reference works for many centuries, but in modern use they are mostly confined to informal defining, such as in glossaries published in newspapers, and to speech.

when and if See IF AND WHEN.

whence See FROM WHENCE.

where **1.** A number of critics worry about the use of *where* in the sense "that" after the verbs *see* and *read*

<I could see *where* he had a point> <you must have read *where* the President vetoed the bill>. This use appears to be more common in speech than in writing, but it is not rare in writing by any means. Similar uses are those in which *where* introduces a clause that modifies a noun, serving as an approximate equivalent to *in which* <an environment *where* people can thrive>, and in which it introduces a clause that is the object of a preposition <finally got him around to *where* he would listen to us>. All of these uses, though standard, are typically found in less formal writing.

2. For other senses and constructions, see WHEN, WHERE; WHERE . . . AT.

whereas See WHILE.

where . . . at The use of *at* following *where* <*where* is he *at*?> is routinely criticized, though it has been a part of American speech for well over 100 years. It was relatively rare in writing until the 1960s, when the phrases "where it's at" and "where you're [I'm, he's, etc.] at" came into widespread use. These phrases continue to be used today <that's *where* we're *at* now>, although they have some of the quality of dated slang. See also AT.

whether See IF 1.

whether or not Critics often point out that *or not* usually isn't necessary after *whether* <we don't know *whether (or not)* they'll come>. However, *or not* has gone with *whether* for more than 300 years and is good idiomatic English. In many instances the *or not* cannot be idiomatically omitted <*whether or not* you agree, this is what we're going to do>.

which **1.** For a discussion of *which* in restrictive and nonrestrictive clauses and of what it may refer to, see THAT 1, 2.

2. The use of *which* to refer to a whole sentence or clause <the language of the book is understood by only a few specialists, *which* prevents others from criticizing it> is often called a mistake by writing handbooks. The argument is that *which* should refer to a specific antecedent <this treatment, *which* has proven effective>. But the argument ignores the fact that the clause or sentence is clearly the antecedent. The handbooks also warn against the potential ambiguity of the use, but genuinely ambiguous examples are nearly impossible to find. This use is standard. See also THIS 1.

while The earliest meanings of *while* are related to time: "during the time that" <take a nap *while* I'm out> and "as long as" <*while* there's life there's hope>. But other senses, such as "whereas" <easy for an expert, *while* it is dangerous for a novice> and "although" <*while* respected, he is not liked>, have been established since Shakespeare's time. Despite misgivings among some critics, these uses do not inherently interfere with one another and are standard and common. There is no reason to avoid them, though you must be sure the context clearly indicates which meaning of *while* you intend.

who, whom **1.** *Whom* continues to flourish, though to many people it seems stilted or dated. It is used as the object of a verb <not sure *whom* he should hire> or a preceding preposition <for *whom* she has little regard>, and sometimes as the object of a preposition that follows it <the man *whom* you wrote to>. In speech and speechlike prose, *who* is commonly used in place of *whom* when the preposition or verb follows <*who* did you write to?> <*who* did you see?> <the man *who* you spoke to>. Uncertainty about whether to use *whom* or *who* has led to hypercorrect usage that is actually erroneous (as in "*whom* shall I say is calling?"). See also HYPERCORRECTION (in Glossary).

2. For a discussion of *who (whom), that,* and *which* in reference to persons or things, see THAT 1.

who else's See ELSE.

whoever, whomever These words are much less common than *who* and *whom,* but their usage problems are not substantially different. See WHO, WHOM 1.

whom See WHO, WHOM.

whomever See WHOEVER, WHOMEVER.

who's, whose See WHOSE 2.

whose **1.** *Whose, of which.* Traditional grammarians have long disapproved of the use of *whose* with inanimate things <a palace *whose* riches are magnificent>, preferring *of which* in such contexts <a palace the riches *of which* are magnificent>. The use, however, long predates any of its critics; it continues to flourish today and is appropriate in even the most formal writing.

2. *Whose, who's.* Because *whose* and *who's* are pronounced the same, people sometimes confuse them in their writing. *Whose* is a possessive pronoun <*whose* purse is this?>, while *who's* is a contraction of *who is* or *who has* <*who's* going to tell her?>.

widow, widower When a married man dies, is he survived by his widow or by his wife? A review of current practice in various newspapers shows that both *wife* and *widow* are used, but *wife* is more common. No such question is likely to arise when the person who has died is the wife rather than the husband; a woman is never said to be "survived by her widower." If the woman who has died was particularly noteworthy, her surviving husband may be identified as "widower of the late . . . ," but "husband of the late . . ." is more likely.

will See SHALL, WILL.

-wise The suffix *-wise* has been used for centuries to mean "in the manner of" (e.g., *crabwise, stepwise*) and "in the position or direction of" (e.g., *slantwise, clockwise*). Since at least the 1930s, it has also been used to mean "with regard to" <offers an advantage both price*wise* and convenience*wise*>. Critics continue to object to this use, but it is a common and handy way to create an adverb for the occasion <we are having

trouble temperature-*wise*>, and is sometimes used even in serious writing. Almost none of these coinages survive long enough to be recorded in dictionaries. Use of the hyphen before the suffix is optional.

wish *Wish* is commonly used as a transitive verb meaning "to want" or "to desire," often with an infinitive as its object <I *wished* to be gone.>. In another typical construction, the object is a proper name or personal pronoun followed by an infinitive <she *wished* John to call them>. These uses of *wish* are not controversial, although some people find them somewhat affected and prefer the use of *want* in such contexts. One point of dispute regarding *wish* is whether it should be used with a simple noun object <they *wished* a speedy resolution to the matter>. Although *wish* is certainly less common than *want* or *desire* in such constructions, it is nevertheless long-established and standard.

with a view, with the view See VIEW.

with disregard for, with disregard of See DISREGARD.

without hardly See HARDLY.

with regard to See REGARD.

with respect to See IN RESPECT TO, WITH RESPECT TO.

with the exception of See EXCEPTION.

with the hope(s) of, with the hope that See HOPE.

wont As an adjective, *wont* means "accustomed" or "inclined." It occurs only as a predicate adjective, almost always followed by an infinitive <got up early as she is *wont* to do>. As a noun meaning "habitual way of doing," *wont* occurs most often in phrases beginning with "as is" or "as was" <as was his *wont,* he slept until noon>.

won't *Won't* is one of the most irregular-looking of the negative contractions (others include *don't* and *shan't*), being a shortening of the earlier *wonnot,* which in turn was formed from *woll* (or *wol*), a variant form of *will,* and *not.* It is entirely acceptable in all varieties of writing <it *won't* be missed>.

worser See DOUBLE COMPARISON (in Glossary).

worst comes to worst This phrase has had several variants over its lifetime (it was first recorded in the late 16th century), but today the most common are *if worst comes to worst* and *if worse comes to worst.* There are those who regard the form having *worse* as incorrect, but its use is too widespread and well established for it to be regarded as anything other than standard.

would See SHALL, WILL.

would have The use of *would have* in place of *had* in the first part of a conditional sentence (as in "If they *would have* come earlier, we all could have left on time") has long been considered an error. It is characteristic of informal speech, but it is notorious in student writing. It occurs occasionally in the casual writing of others. In print it is mostly found in transcribed speech. The grammatical reasons for this use are not fully understood.

would of See OF 2.

would rather See HAD RATHER.

wrack See RACK, WRACK.

wreak, wreck Havoc is usually said to be wreaked <*wreak* havoc>, but occasionally the more familiar *wreck* is mistakenly substituted for *wreak*. Other verbs may also be used with *havoc,* including *create, play, raise,* and, occasionally, *work.* In the past tense, *work havoc* becomes either *worked havoc* or, more commonly, *wrought havoc.*

wrong, wrongly *Wrong* can be used as an adjective <took the *wrong* bus>, noun <two *wrongs* don't make a right>, or verb <a penal system that had *wronged* him>, and as an adverb. The adverbs *wrong* and *wrongly* are used differently, however. *Wrong* occurs most frequently with the verbs *do, get, have,* and especially *go* <how can you *go wrong*?>, but is also used with other verbs. It usually follows immediately after the verb, often at the end of a sentence or clause <she guessed *wrong*>. *Wrongly,* on the other hand, most often precedes the verb or participle being modified <was *wrongly* accused> <has

wrongly been criticized>, though it can also follow <applied the principle *wrongly*>. In general, the one that *sounds* correct *is* correct. If both sound right, either may be used. (This observation also holds true for the analogous adverbs *right* and *rightly*.)

X Y Z

Xmas *Xmas* has been used as a short form of *Christmas* since the 16th century. The *X* is derived from the Greek letter chi (X), which is the first letter in the Greek word for "Christ." *Xmas* is limited in current usage to advertisements, headlines, banners, and casual correspondence; in other contexts you will undoubtedly want to spell out *Christmas*.

yearn People who yearn usually yearn *for* something. Less commonly, the preposition following yearn may be *after, toward* (*or towards*), or *over*.

yet The use of *yet* with a verb in the plain past tense with *did* (as in "Did he leave *yet?*) is common and unobjectionable in ordinary speech, but in writing the present perfect is used <has he left *yet?*>.

you **1.** *You* is often used in addressing the reader directly <*you* should keep in mind the user's needs>. *One* may be used instead of *you* for a more formal, distant, and impersonal tone <*one* should be cautious in dealing with them>, but try not to mix the two. See also ONE.

2. *Indefinite* you. Related to the use of *you* to address the reader directly is the use of *you* to address no one in particular—in indefinite reference <*you* have to consider the long-term effects>. While some critics used to prefer the substitution of *one* <*one* has to consider the long-term effects>, or a passive construction <the long-term effects have to be considered>, most writers nowadays find indefinite *you* perfectly acceptable, if a bit informal.

your, you're 1. The possessive pronoun is *your* <*your* spelling is atrocious>. The contraction of *you are* is *you're* <*you're* an atrocious speller>.

2. *Your* is often used with an adjective such as *average, standard, ordinary, usual,* or *basic* <*your* average car salesman> in a sense more or less equivalent to *the.* This use is standard in casual prose.

yours Although the *-s* in *yours* marks the possessive <we'd like to have *yours* by March 28th>, and the possessive *-s* is normally preceded by an apostrophe, there is no apostrophe in *yours.*

zeal One may either have zeal *for doing* something or zeal *to do* something. Where the object is a noun rather than a gerund, *for* is the usual preposition after *zeal* <have shown tremendous *zeal for* the nationalist leader>.

Glossary

This glossary provides definitions, and sometimes discussions, of grammatical and other terms either used in the main A–Z section of the book or entered separately here to address additional problems of usage. Cross-references to entries in the main section are shown in SMALL CAPITALS; cross-references to entries within the glossary are shown in **boldface.**

abbreviation A shortened form of a written word or phrase used in place of the whole (such as *amt.* for *amount*, or *c/o* for *care of*).

Abbreviations can be used wherever they are customary, but note that what is customary in technical writing will be different from what is customary in journalism or other fields. If you are uncertain, consult a style manual. See also **acronym.**

absolute adjective An adjective that normally cannot be used comparatively <*ancillary* rights> <the *maximum* dose>.

Many absolute adjectives can be modified by adverbs such as *almost* or *near* <an *almost fatal* dose> <at *near maximum* capacity>. However, many adjectives considered to be absolute are in fact often preceded by comparative adverbs <a *more perfect* union> <a *less complete* account>. In such cases, *more* means "more nearly" and *less* "less nearly." Such use is long established in the language.

absolute comparative The comparative form of an adjective used where no comparison is implied or stated, although in some cases comparison may be inferred by the reader or hearer <*higher* education> <a *better* kind of company> <gives you a *brighter* smile> <an *older* woman>.

The absolute comparative is standard in general writing. See also **absolute adjective; comparison; double comparison; implicit comparative.**

acronym A word or abbreviation formed from the initial letter or letters of each of the major parts of a compound term, whether or not it is pronounceable as a word (such as *TQM* for *Total Quality Management,* or *UNPROFOR* for *United Nations Protection Force*); also called *initialism.*

active voice A verb form indicating that the subject of a sentence is performing the action <he *respects* the other scientists> <a bird *was singing*> <interest rates *rose*>; compare **passive voice.**

adjective A word that describes or modifies a noun <an *active* mind> <this is *serious*> <*full* and *careful* in its attention to detail>.

An adjective can follow a noun as a complement <the book made the bag *heavy*> and can sometimes modify larger units, like noun phrases <the *celebrated* "man in the street"> and noun clauses <it seemed *incomprehensible* that one senator could hold up the nomination>. See also **attributive; predicate adjective.**

adverb A word that modifies a verb, adjective, adverb, preposition, phrase, clause, or sentence.

Traditionally adverbs indicate time, place, or manner <do it *now*> <*there* they remained> <she went *willingly*>. They can connect statements <a small bomb had been found; *nevertheless,* they were continuing their search> and can tell the reader what the writer thinks about what is being said in the sentence <*luckily* I got there on time>. They can modify verbs <ran *fast*>, adjectives <an *awfully* long speech>, participles <a *well*-acted play>, adverbs <doing *fairly* well>, particles <woke *right* up>, indefinite pronouns <*almost* everyone>, cardinal numbers <*over* 200 guests>, prepositional phrases <*just* out of reach>, and more. Sometimes they modify a preceding noun <the great city *beyond*>, and some adverbs of place and time can serve as the objects of prepositions <since *when*> <before *long*>.

The notion that adverbs should not separate auxiliaries from their main verbs <you can *easily* see the river from here> <they should be *heartily* congratulated> is a false one, apparently based on fear of the split infinitive. See also **auxiliary verb; sentence adverb; split infinitive.**

adverbial genitive A form, or case, of some nouns used as adverbs of time, normally formed by adding *-s* <he worked *nights*> <the store is open *Sundays*>.

agreement A grammatical relationship that involves the correspondence in number either between the subject and verb of a sentence or between a pronoun and its antecedent; also called *concord.*

Subject-verb agreement for compound subjects joined by and When a subject is composed or two or more singular nouns joined by *and,* the plural verb is usually used <*the sentimentality and lack of originality* which *mark* his writing> <*the bitterness and heartache* that *fill* the world>. Occasionally when the nouns form a single conceptual unit, the singular verb can be used <*the report's depth and scope demonstrates*> <*her patience and calm was* remarkable>. *See also* **notional agreement.**

Compound subjects joined by or (or nor): When singular nouns are joined by *or,* the singular verb is usually used <*the average man or woman was* not interested>; when plural nouns are so joined, the plural verb is used <*wolves or coyotes have* depleted his stock>. When the negative *neither . . . nor* is used with singular nouns, it usually takes a singular verb <*neither she nor anyone else is* fond of the idea>; when used with plural nouns, it takes a plural verb <*neither the proponents nor their adversaries are* willing to accept>. But when *neither . . . nor* is used with nouns of differing number, the noun closest to the verb usually determines its number <*neither he nor his colleagues were* present> <*neither the teachers nor the principal was* interested>. Similar rules apply to *either . . . or.* See also EITHER 3.

Compound subjects joined by words or phrases like with or along with, or by punctuation: When a singular noun is joined to another by a word or phrase like *with, rather than,* or *as well as,* a singular verb is generally used <*that story, along with nine others, was* published> <*the battleship together with the destroyer was* positioned three miles offshore>. Parenthetical insertions set off by commas, dashes, or parentheses should not affect agreement <*this book, as well as various others, has* achieved notoriety> <*their management—and the company's balance sheets—has* suffered>.

Subject formed by a collective noun phrase: The usage question is this: In constructions like "a bunch of the boys were whooping it up" or "a fraction of the deposits are insured," which make use of a collective noun phrase (*a bunch of the boys, a fraction of the deposits*), should the verb be plural or singular? The answer is that since the sense of the phrase is normally plural, the verb should be as well. See also **collective noun.**

Subject expressing money, time, etc.: When an amount of money, a period of time, or some other plural noun phrase of quantity or measure forms the subject, a singular verb is used <*ten dollars is* all I have left> <*two miles is* as far as they can walk> <*two thirds of the area is* under water>.

Subject formed by one in (out of) . . . : Phrases such as "one in five" or "two out of three" may take either a singular or a plural verb <*one in four union members was* undecided> <*one out of ten soldiers were* unable to recognize the enemy>, though grammarians tend to favor the singular.

Pronoun-antecedent agreement for nouns joined by and, or: When antecedents are singular nouns joined by *and,* a plural pronoun is used <*the computer and the printer* were moved because *they* were in the way>. But singular nouns joined by *or* can use either a singular or a plural pronoun, whichever sounds best <either *Fred or Marianne* will give *their* presentation after lunch> <*each employee or supervisor* should give what *he or she* can afford>.

Agreement for indefinite pronouns: The indefinite pronouns *anybody, anyone, each, either, everybody, everyone, neither, nobody, none, no one, somebody,* and *someone,* though some of them are conceptually plural, are used with singular verbs <*everyone* in the company *was* pleased> <*nobody is* responsible>, but are commonly referred to by *they, their, them,* or *themselves* <*nobody* could get the crowd's attention when *they* spoke> <*everybody* there admits *they* saw it>. Writing handbooks prescribe *he, she,* or *he or she,* or some other construction instead of the plural pronouns (see ANYBODY; EACH; EVERYBODY, EVERYONE), but use of the plural *they, their,* or *them* has long been established and is standard. See also THEY, THEIR, THEM.

antecedent A word, phrase, or clause to which a subsequent pronoun refers <*Judy* wrote to say *she* is coming> <they saw *Bob* and called to *him*> <I hear *that he is ill* and *it* worries me>.

appositive A word, phrase, or clause that is equivalent to an adjacent noun <a biography of *the poet*

Robert Burns> <sales of *her famous novel,* Gone with the Wind, reached one million copies in six months > <*we grammarians* are never wrong>.

Restrictive and nonrestrictive appositives play different roles in a sentence and are traditionally distinguished by their punctuation. A nonrestrictive appositive <*his wife, Helen,* attended the ceremony> is generally set off with commas, while a restrictive appositive <he sent *his daughter Cicely* to college> uses no commas and indicates that one out of a group is being identified (in this case, one daughter from among two or more). Exceptions occur where no ambiguity would result <his wife Helen>. See also **nonrestrictive clause; restrictive clause.**

article One of three words (*a, an, the*) used with a noun to indicate definiteness <*the* blue car> or indefiniteness <*a* simple task> <*an* interesting explanation>.

attributive A modifier that immediately precedes the word it modifies <*black* tie, *U.S.* government, *kitchen* sink, *lobster* salad>.

Nouns have functioned like adjectives in this position for many centuries. In more recent years, some critics have objected to the proliferation of nouns used to modify other nouns: e.g., *language deterioration, health aspects, image enhancement.* While long or otherwise unexpected strings of this sort can occasionally be disorienting to the uninitiated (e.g., *management team strategy planning session*), the practice is flourishing and usually serves to compress information that the intended audience need not always have spelled out for it. Be sure, however, that the context and audience will allow for such compression.

A fairly recent trend toward using plural attributives has been attacked by some critics. There always had been a few plural attributives—*scissors grinder, physics laboratory, Civil Liberties Union, mathematics book*—but is it proper to use the more recent *weapons system, communications technology, operations program, systems analyst, earth-resources satellite, singles bar, enemies list?* The answer is that such plural attributives are standard. The plural form is chosen to stress plurality—more than one weapon, operation, enemy, etc.—or to otherwise distinguish its meaning from whatever the singular attributive might connote.

auxiliary verb A verb that accompanies another verb and typically expresses person, number, mood, or tense (such as *be, have, can, do*) <they *can* see the movie tomorrow> <she *has* left already>. See also **verb.**

cardinal number A number of the kind used in simple counting <*one, 1, thirty-five, 35*>; compare **ordinal number.**

case In English, a form of a noun or pronoun indicating its grammatical relation to other words in a sentence. See **nominative; objective; possessive.** See also **genitive.**

clause A group of words having its own subject and predicate but forming only part of a compound or complex sentence. A *main* or *independent clause* could stand alone as a sentence <*we will leave* as soon as the taxi arrives>; a *subordinate* or *dependent clause* requires a main clause <we will leave *as soon as the taxi arrives*>. See also **sentence; subordinate clause.**

collective noun A singular noun that stands for a number of persons or things considered as a group (such as *team, government, horde*).

Subject-verb agreement: Collective nouns have been used with both singular and plural verbs since Middle English. The principle involved is one of notional agreement. When the group is considered as a unit, the singular verb is used <the *government is* prepared for a showdown> <his *family is* from New England> <the *team has won* all of its home games>. When the group is thought of as a collection of individuals, the plural verb is sometimes used <her *family are* all staunch conservatives>. Singular verbs are more common in American English and plural verbs more common in British English, though usage remains divided in each case. See also **agreement; notional agreement.**

A collective noun followed by *of* and a plural noun follows the same rule as collective nouns in general. When the notion is that of plurality, the plural verb is normally used <an *assemblage of rocks were* laid out on the table> <a *group of jazz improvisers were* heard through the window>. When the idea of oneness or wholeness is stressed, the verb is generally singular <this *cluster of stars is* the largest yet identified>.

Pronoun agreement: The usual rule is that writers should take care to match their pronouns and verbs, singular with singular <the committee *is* hopeful that *it* will succeed>, plural with plural <the faculty *are* willing to drop *their* suit>. But in fact writers sometimes use a plural pronoun after a singular verb <the audience *was* on *their* way out>. (The reverse combination—plural verb with singular pronoun—is very rare.)

Organizations as collective nouns: The names of companies and other organizations are treated as either singular <*Harvard* may consider *itself* very fortunate> or, less commonly, plural <the *D.A.R. are* going to do another pageant>. Organizations also sometimes appear with a singular verb but a plural pronoun in reference <*M-G-M hopes* to sell *their* latest releases> <*Chrysler builds their* convertible in Kentucky>. This usage is standard, though informal.

colloquial An adjective describing usage that is characteristic of familiar and informal conversation.

While not intended to carry pejorative overtones, the label *colloquial* often implies that the usage is nonstandard. See also **dialect; nonstandard; standard English.**

comma fault (comma splice, comma error) The use of a comma instead of a semicolon to link two independent clauses (as in "I won't talk about myself, it's not a healthy topic"). Modern style calls for the semicolon, but comma splices are fairly common in casual and unedited prose.

comparison Modification of an adjective or adverb to show different levels of quality, quantity, or relation. The *comparative* form shows relation between two items, usually by adding *-er* or *more* or *less* to the adjective or adverb <he's short*er* than I am> <her second book sold *more* quickly>. The *superlative* form expresses an extreme among two or more items, usually by adding *-est* or *most* or *least* to the adjective or adverb <the cheetah is the fast*est* mammal> <that's the *least* compelling reason> <the *most* vexingly intractable issue>. See also **absolute adjective; absolute comparative; double comparison; implicit comparative.**

complement An added word or expression by which a predicate is made complete <they elected him *president*> <she thought it *beautiful*> <the critics called her *the best act of her kind since Carmen Miranda*>.

compound A combination of words or word elements that work together in various ways (*farmhouse; cost-effective; ex-husband; shoeless; figure out; in view of* that; *real estate* agent; *greenish white* powder; *carefully tended* garden; *great white shark*).

Compounds are written in one of three ways: solid <*workplace*>, hyphenated <*screenwriter-director*>, or open <*health care*>. Because of the variety of standard practice, the choice among these styles for a given compound represents one of the most common and bothersome of all style issues. A current desk dictionary will list many compounds, but those whose meanings are self-explanatory from the meanings of their component words will usually not appear. Most writers try to pattern any temporary compounds after similar permanent compounds such as are entered in dictionaries.

compound sentence See **sentence.**

compound subject Two or more nouns or pronouns usually joined by *and* that function as the subject of a clause or sentence <*doctors and lawyers* reported the highest incomes for that period> <*Peter, Karen, and I* left together>. See also **agreement; collective noun.**

concord See **agreement.**

conjunction A word or phrase that joins together words, phrases, clauses, or sentences. *Coordinating conjunctions* (such as *and, or, but*) join elements of a similar kind <they came early *and* stayed late>. *Correlative conjunctions* (such as *either . . . or, neither . . . nor*) are used in pairs and link alternatives <the proposal benefits *neither* residents *nor* visitors>. *Subordinating conjunctions* (such as *unless, whether*) join subordinate clauses to main clauses <don't call *unless* you're coming>.

conjunctive adverb A transitional adverb (such as *also, however, therefore*) that expresses the relationship between two independent clauses, sentences, or paragraphs <he enjoyed the movie; *however,* he had to leave before the end>.

contact clause A dependent clause attached to its antecedent without a relative pronoun such as *that, which,* or *who* <the key [that] *you lost*> <he is not the person [who] *we thought he was*>.

The construction has been in existence for several hundred years and is appropriate even in formal writing.

The predicate noun clause not introduced by the conjunction *that* <we believe [that] *the alliance is strong*> is as long and as well established in English as the contact clause. It is probably more common in casual and general prose than in formal prose. It is also more common after some verbs (such as *believe, hope, say, think*) than others (such as *assert, calculate, hold, intend*).

contraction A shortened form of a word or words in which an apostrophe usually replaces the omitted letter or letters (such as *dep't, don't, could've, o'clock, we'll*).

Contractions involving verbs used to be avoided more than they are today. In fact, many contemporary writing handbooks recommend using contractions to help you avoid sounding stilted. See WON'T.

count noun A noun that identifies things that can be counted <two *tickets*> <a *motive*> <many *people*>; compare **mass noun.**

dangling modifier A modifying phrase that lacks a normally expected grammatical relation to the rest of the sentence (as in "*Caught in the act,* his excuses were unconvincing").

The common construction called the *participial phrase* usually begins with a participle; in "*Chancing to meet them there,* I invited them to sit with us," the subject, "I," is left implicit in the preceding phrase, which modifies it. But a writer may inadvertently let a participial phrase modify a subject or some other noun in the sentence it was not intended to modify; the result is what grammarians call a *dangling participle.* Thus in "*Hoping to find him alone,* the presence of a stranger was irksome," it is the "presence" itself that may seem to be hoping.

Dangling participles can be found in the writing of many famous writers, and they are usually hardly noticeable except to someone looking for them. The important thing to avoid is creating an unintended humorous effect (as in "*Opening up the cupboard,* a cockroach ran for the corner").

dangling participle See **dangling modifier.**

dialect A variety of language distinguished by features of vocabulary, grammar, and pronunciation that is confined to a region or group. See also **nonstandard; standard English.**

direct object A word, phrase, or clause denoting the goal or result of the action of the verb <he closed the *valve*> <they'll do *whatever it takes*> <"*Do it now,*" he said>; compare **indirect object.**

direct question A question quoted exactly as spoken, written, or imagined <the only question is, *Will it work?*>; compare **indirect question.**

direct quotation Text quoted exactly as spoken or written <I heard her say, "*I'll be there at two o'clock*">; compare **indirect quotation.**

divided usage Widespread use of two or more forms for a single entity (such as *dived* and *dove* for the past tense of *dive*).

double comparison Use of the forms *more, most, less,* or *least* with an adjective already inflected for the comparative or superlative degree (such as *more wider, most widest*).

This construction results from using *more* and *most* as intensifiers <a *most* enjoyable meal>. In modern usage, double comparison has all but vanished from standard writing. See also **comparison; intensifier.**

Double comparison can also occur by inflection. Though forms such as *firstest, mostest,* and *bestest* are most typical of the speech of young children, the form *worser* (which has a long literary background) still persists in adult speech. You will want to avoid it in writing.

double genitive A construction in which possession is marked both by the preposition *of* and a noun or pronoun in the possessive case.

In expressions like "that song of Ella Fitzgerald's" or "a good friend of ours," the possessive relationship is indicated by both *of* and the genitive inflection (Fitzgerald*'s, ours*), even though only one or the other would seem to be strictly necessary. However, this construction, also known as the *double possessive,* is an idiomatic one of long standing and is standard in all kinds of writing. See also **genitive.**

double modal The use of two modal auxiliaries in succession, resulting in such expressions as *might can, might could,* and *might should.*

Today double modals tend to be found in Southern dialect and are unfamiliar to speakers from other parts of the country.

double negative A clause or sentence containing two negatives and having a negative meaning.

In modern usage, the double negative (as in "they did*n't* have *no* children" or "it would*n't* do *no* good") is widely perceived as a rustic or uneducated form, and is generally avoided in both writing and speech, other than the most informal.

A standard form of double negative is the rhetorical device known as *litotes,* which produces a weak affirmative meaning <a *not un*reasonable request>. It is used for understatement, but should not be overused.

double passive A construction that uses two verb forms in the passive voice, one being an infinitive (as in "the work of redesigning the office space *was requested to be done* by outside contractors").

The double passive is awkward and potentially ambiguous (did outside contractors ask for the work to be done, or were they asked to do the work?) and should be avoided.

double possessive See **double genitive.**

double superlative See **double comparison.**

false titles Appositive preceding a person's name with no preceding article or following comma, which thus resembles a title, though it is rarely capitalized <organized by *consumer advocate* Ralph Nader> <works of *1960s underground cartoonist* Robert Crumb>. The use of such titles is sometimes criticized, but it is standard in journalism.

faulty parallelism See **parallelism.**

flat adverb An adverb that has the same form as its related adjective, such as *sure* <you *sure* fooled me>, *bright* <the moon is shining *bright*>, and *flat* <she turned me down *flat*>.

Although such forms were once common, later grammarians saw them as faulty because they lacked the *-ly* ending. Today flat adverbs are few in number and some are widely regarded as incorrect. See BAD, BADLY; CHEAP 2; CONSIDERABLE 2; NEAR, NEARLY; QUICK, QUICKLY; SCARCELY 1; SLOW, SLOWLY; TIGHT, TIGHTLY.

formal agreement See **notional agreement.**

gender In English, a characteristic of certain nouns and pronouns that indicates sex (masculine, feminine, neuter) <*he, him, his, she, her, it, its; actor, actress; brother, sister; emperor, empress; heir, heiress; fiancé, fiancée; testator, testatrix*>.

genitive A form, or case, of a noun or pronoun that typically shows possession or source <the girl*'s* sweater> <nobody*'s* fool> <an uncle *of mine*> <some idea *of theirs*> <the company*'s* failure> <a year*'s* salary> <the nation*'s* capital> <a stone*'s* throw>.

The form is usually produced by adding -*'s* or a phrase beginning with *of.* While the possessive is the genitive's most common function, it has certain other functions as well; these include the *subjective* <Frost*'s* poetry>, *objective* <her son*'s* graduation>, *descriptive* <women*'s* colleges>, and *appositive* <the state *of Massachusetts*> <the office *of president*> genitives. See also **double genitive; possessive.**

gerund A verb form having the characteristics of both verb and noun and ending in *-ing* (also called a *verbal noun*) <the ice made *skiing* impossible>.

A gerund can be preceded by a possessive noun or pronoun <her husband's *snoring*> <their *filling* the position>. See also **possessive; possessive with gerund.**

hypercorrection The use of a nonstandard linguistic form or construction on the basis of a false analogy to a standard form or construction (as in "*whom* should I say is calling?"; "this is between you and *I*"; "no one but *he* would notice"; "open *widely*"). See also BETWEEN YOU AND I; WHO WHOM

idiom A common expression that is peculiar to itself grammatically <*it wasn't me*> or that cannot be understood from the meanings of its separate words <I told them to *step on it*> <the newspaper *had a field day*>.

imperative The form, or mood, of a verb that expresses a command or makes a request <*come* here> <please *don't*>; compare **indicative; subjunctive.**

implicit comparative One of a small group of adjectives (primarily *major, minor, inferior, superior*) whose meaning resembles a true comparative but which cannot be used with comparative forms (such as *more, most; less, least*) <a *major* contributor> <an *inferior* wine>.

However, two other implicit comparatives *junior* and *senior* can be used with comparative forms <a *more senior* diplomat> <the *least junior* of the new partners>. See also **comparison.**

indefinite pronoun A pronoun that designates an unidentified person or thing <*somebody* ate my dessert> <she saw *no one* she knew>.

Many indefinite pronouns are involved in usage questions of one kind or another. See ANYBODY, ANYONE; EACH; EITHER; EVERYBODY, EVERYONE; NEITHER; NOBODY, NO ONE; NONE; SOMEBODY, SOMEONE; THEY,

THEIR, THEM. See also **agreement; notional agreement.**

indicative The form, or mood, of a verb that states a fact or asks a question <the train *stopped*> <they*'ll be* along> <everyone *is* ravenous> <*has* the rain *begun*?> <who *knows*?>; compare **imperative; subjunctive.**

indirect object A grammatical object representing the secondary goal of the action of its verb <she gave *the dog* a bone>; compare **direct object.**

indirect question A statement of the substance of a question without using the speaker's exact words or word order <the officer asked *what the trouble was*> <they wondered *whether it would work*>; compare **direct question.**

indirect quotation A statement of the substance of a quotation without using the speaker's exact words <I heard her say *she'd be there at two o'clock*>; compare **direct quotation.**

infinitive A verb form having the characteristics of both verb and noun and usually used with *to* <we had *to stop*> <*to err* is human> <no one saw him *leave*>. See also **split infinitive.**

infinitive phrase A phrase that includes an infinitive and its modifiers and complements <we expect them *to arrive by five o'clock*> <he shouted *to be heard above the din*> <*to have earned a Ph.D. in four years* was impressive>.

inflection The change in form that words undergo to mark case, gender, number, tense, person, mood, voice, or comparison <*he, his, him*> <*waiter, waitress*> <rat, *rats*> <blame, *blames, blamed, blaming*> <who, *whom*> <she *is* careful, if she *were* careful, *be* careful> <like, *likes, is liked*> <wild, *wilder, wildest*>. See also **case; comparison; gender; mood; number; person; tense; voice.**

initialism See **acronym.**

intensifier A linguistic element used to give emphasis or additional strength to another word or statement <a *very* hot day> <it's a *complete* lie> <what *on earth* is he doing?> <she *herself* did it>. See AWFUL, AWFULLY; DEFINITE, DEFINITELY; REAL; RIGHT 1; SO 1; SURE, SURELY; THAT 3. See also **double comparison.**

interjection An exclamatory or interrupting word or phrase <*ouch!*> <*oh,* must you?> <she's *like* clueless>.

intransitive verb A verb not having a direct object <he *ran* away> <our cat *purrs* when I stroke her>; compare **transitive verb.**

linking verb A verb that links a subject with its predicate (such as *is, feel, look, become, seem*) <she is the new manager> <the future *looked* prosperous> <he *has become* disenchanted>.

main clause See *clause.*

mass noun A noun that denotes a thing or concept without subdivisions <some *money*> <great *courage*> <the study of *politics*>; compare **count noun.**

modifier A word or phrase that qualifies, limits, or restricts the meaning of another word or phrase. See **adjective; adverb.**

mood The form of a verb that shows whether the action or state it denotes is conceived as a fact or otherwise (e.g., a command, possibility, or wish). See **indicative; imperative; subjunctive.**

nominative A form, or case, of a noun or pronoun indicating its use as the subject of a verb <three *dogs* trotted by the open door> <later *we* ate dinner>; compare **objective; possessive.**

In English, nouns in the nominative case are unmarked except for number.

nonrestrictive clause A subordinate or dependent clause, set off by commas, that is not essential to the definiteness of the word it modifies and could be omitted without changing the meaning of the main clause (also called *nonessential clause*) <the author, *who turned out to be charming,* autographed my book>; compare **restrictive clause.**

nonstandard Not conforming to the usage generally characteristic of educated native speakers of a language; compare **standard English.** See also **dialect.**

notional agreement Agreement between a subject and a verb or between a pronoun and its antecedent that is determined by meaning rather than form; also called *notional concord.*

Notional agreement contrasts with *formal* or *grammatical agreement* (or *concord*), in which overt grammatical markers determine singular or plural agreement. Formally plural nouns such as *news, means,* and *politics* have long taken singular verbs; so when a plural noun considered a single entity takes a singular verb, notional agreement is at work and no one objects <the *United States is sending* its ambassador>. When a singular noun is used as a collective noun and takes a plural verb or a plural pronoun, we also have notional agreement <the *committee are* meeting on Tuesday> <the *group wants* to publicize *their* views>. Indefinite pronouns are heavily influenced by notional agreement and tend to take singular verbs but plural pronouns <*everyone is* required to show *their* identification>. See HE, HE OR SHE; THERE IS, THERE ARE; THEY, THEIR, THEM. See also **agreement; collective noun.**

notional concord See **notional agreement.**

noun A member of a class of words that can serve as the subject of a verb, can be singular or plural, can be replaced by a pronoun, and can refer to an entity, quality, state, action, or concept <*boy, Churchill, America, river, commotion, poetry, anguish, constitutionalism*>.

noun phrase A phrase formed by a noun and its modifiers <*portly pensioners* sat sunning themselves>

<they proclaimed *all the best features of the new financial offering*>.

number A characteristic of a noun, pronoun, or verb that signifies whether it is singular or plural. See **singular; plural.**

object A noun, noun phrase or clause, or pronoun that directly or indirectly receives the action of a verb or follows a preposition <she rocked *the baby*> <he saw *where they were going*> <I gave *him the news*> <over *the rainbow*> <after *a series of depressing roadhouse gigs*>. See **direct object; indirect object.**

objective A form, or case, of a pronoun indicating its use as the object of a verb or preposition <we spoke to *them* yesterday> <he's a man *whom* everyone should know>; compare **nominative; possessive.**

ordinal number A number designating the place occupied by an item in an ordered sequence <*first, 1st, second, 2nd*>; compare **cardinal number.**

parallelism Repeated syntactical similarities introduced in sentence construction, such as adjacent phrases and clauses that are equivalent, similar, or opposed in meaning and of identical construction <ecological problems of concern *to scientists, to businesspeople,* and *to all citizens*> <he was respected not only *for his intelligence* but also *for his integrity*> <*to err is human, to forgive, divine*>.

Parallelism is mainly used for rhetorical and clarifying effects, and its absence can sometimes create problems for the reader. *Faulty parallelism* is the name given to the use of different constructions within a sentence where you would ordinarily expect to find the same or similar constructions. Very often such faulty parallelism involves the conjunctions *and* and *or* or such other coordinators as *either* and *neither.* Consider the sentence "To allow kids to roam the streets at night and failing to give them constructive alternatives have been harmful." An infinitive phrase (*To allow kids to roam . . .*) and a participial phrase (*failing to give them . . .*) are treated as parallel when they are not. The meaning would be taken in more readily if both phrases were similar; replacing the infinitive with a participle achieves this parallelism (*Allowing kids to roam . . .* and *failing to give them . . .*). When such errors are obvious, they can be puzzling. Often, however, the problem is subtle and hardly noticeable, as in the sentence "Either I must send a fax or make a phone call." Here *or* is expected to precede the same parallel term as *either;* by repositioning *either,* you solve the problem <I must *either* send a fax *or* make a phone call>. Such examples of faulty parallelism are fairly common, but your writing will be more elegant if you avoid them. See also AND WHICH, AND WHO; EITHER 3.

parenthetical element An explanatory or modifying word, phrase, or sentence inserted in a passage, set off by parentheses, commas, or dashes <a ruling by the FCC (*Federal Communications Commission*)> <all of us, *to tell the truth,* were amazed> <the examiner chose—*goodness knows why*—to ignore it>.

participial phrase A participle with its complements and modifiers, functioning as an adjective <*hearing the bell ring,* he went to the door>.

participle A verb form having the characteristics of both verb <the noise has *stopped*> and adjective <a *broken* lawn mower>. The *present participle* ends in *-ing* <*fascinating*>; the *past participle* usually ends in *-ed* <*seasoned*>; the *perfect participle* combines *having* with the past participle <*having escaped*>. See also **auxiliary verb; dangling modifier; possessive.**

particle A short word (such as *by, to, in, up*) that expresses some general aspect of meaning or some connective or limiting relation <pay *up*> <heave *to*>.

parts of speech The classes into which words are grouped according to their function in a sentence. See **adjective; adverb; conjunction; interjection; noun; preposition; pronoun; verb.**

passive voice A verb form indicating that the subject of a sentence is being acted upon.

Though often considered a weaker form of expression than the active voice, the passive nevertheless has important uses—for example, when the receiver of the action is more important than the doer <*he is respected* by other scholars>, when the doer is unknown <*the lock had been picked* expertly> or is understood <*Jones was elected* on the third ballot>, or when discretion or tact require that the doer remain anonymous <mistakes *were made*>; compare **active voice.**

person A characteristic of a verb or pronoun that indicates whether a person is speaking (*first person*) <*I am, we are*>, is spoken to (*second person*) <*you are*>, or is spoken about (*third person*) <*he, she, it is; they are*>. See also **number.**

personal pronoun A pronoun that refers to beings and objects and reflects person, number, and often gender <*you* and *I* will attend> <*she* gave *him* the book> <*they*'re just old rags>. See also **pronoun.**

phrase A group of two or more words that does not contain both a subject and a verb and that functions as a noun, adjective, adverb, preposition, conjunction, or verb <*the old sinner*> <*stretching for miles*> <*without a limp*> <*in lieu of*> <*as far as*> <*break off*>. See also **noun phrase; participial phrase.**

plural A word form used to denote more than one <the *Browns*> <the *children*> <these *kinds*> <seven *deer*> <they *are* rich> <*we* do care>.

possessive A form, or case, of a noun or pronoun typically indicating ownership <the *president's* message> <*their* opinions> <*its* meter>; compare **nominative; objective.** See also **double genitive; genitive; possessive with gerund.**

possessive with gerund Use of a possessive form before a gerund.

In "the reason for everyone['s] wanting to join," either the possessive or the common form of *everyone* can be used. Writing handbooks recommend always using the possessive form, but the possessive is mandatory only when the *-ing* word is clearly a noun <*my being* here must embarrass you>. The possessive is quite common with proper nouns <the problem of *John's forgetting* the keys> but rare with plurals <learned of the *bills* [*bills'*] *being* paid>. In most other instances, either the possessive or common form can be used.

predicate The part of a sentence or clause that expresses what is said of the subject <Hargrove *threw a spitball*> <the teachers from the surrounding towns *are invited to the dinner*> <Jennifer *picked up her books and left to catch the bus*>.

predicate adjective An adjective that follows a linking verb (such as *be, become, feel, taste, smell, seem*) and modifies the subject <she is *happy* with the outcome> <the milk tastes *sour*> <he seemed *puzzled* by the answer>.

prefix An affix attached to the beginning of a word to change its meaning <*a*historical> <*pre*sorted> <*anti*-imperialist> <*post*hypnotic> <*over*extended>; compare **suffix.**

preposition A word or phrase that combines with a noun, pronoun, adverb, or prepositional phrase for use as a modifier or a predication <a book *on* the table> <you're *in* big trouble> <*outside* himself> <*because of* that> <came *from* behind> <peeking *from* behind the fence>.

Despite a widespread belief that a sentence cannot end with a preposition, there is no such grammatical rule. In fact, many sentences require the preposition at the end <what can she be thinking *of*?> <he got the answer he was looking *for*> <there are inconveniences that we must put up *with*> <they haven't been heard *from* yet> and many others are perfectly idiomatic in placing it there <you must know which shelf everything is *on*>.

prepositional phrase A group of words consisting of a preposition and its complement <*out of debt* is where we'd like to be!> <here is the desk *with the extra file drawer*> <he drove on *in a cold fury*>.

pronoun Any of a small set of words that are used as substitutes for nouns, phrases, or clauses and refer to someone or something named or understood in the context.

Many pronouns are involved in usage questions. See BETWEEN YOU AND I; BUT; I; IT'S ME; ME; MYSELF; ONE OF THOSE WHO; THAN; THAT; THEY, THEIR, THEM; WHO, WHOM; YOU. See also **agreement; indefinite pronoun.**

proper adjective An adjective that is derived from a proper noun and is usually capitalized <*Roman* sculpture> <*Jeffersonian* democracy> <*Middle Eastern* situation> <*french* fries>.

proper noun A noun that names a particular being or thing and is usually capitalized <*Susan, Haydn, New York, December, General Motors, Mormon,*

Library of Congress, Middle Ages, Spanish Civil War, Reaganomics>.

redundancy Repetition of information in a message.

Redundancy is an implicit part of the English language; it reinforces the message. In "Two birds were sitting on a branch," the idea of plurality is expressed three times: by the modifier *two*, by the *-s* on *bird*, and by the plural verb *were*. Many words can be accompanied by small words that given them extra emphasis <*final result*> <*past history*> <*climb up*> <*refer back*>. These are often attacked as needlessly wordy, but in most instances they are harmless, and sometimes they actually promote communication. The use and employment of many more words, phrases, and expressions than are strictly needed, necessary, wanted, or required should be avoided.

reflexive pronoun A pronoun that refers to the subject of the sentence, clause, or verbal phrase in which it stands, and is formed by compounding the personal pronouns *him, her, it, my, our, them,* and *your* with *-self* or *-selves* <she dressed *herself*> <the cook told us to help *ourselves* to seconds> <I *myself* am not concerned>. See also MYSELF; YOURSELF, YOURSELVES.

relative pronoun One of the pronouns (*that, which, who, whom,* and *whose*) that introduces a subordinate clause which qualifies an antecedent <a man *whom* we can trust> <her book, *which* sold well> <the light *that* failed>. See also THAT; WHICH; WHO, WHOM; WHOSE.

restrictive clause A subordinate clause not set off by commas that is essential to the definiteness of the word it modifies and cannot be omitted without changing the meaning of the main clause (also called *essential clause*) <textbooks *that are not current* should be returned>. See also **appositive; nonrestrictive clause.**

sentence A group of words usually containing a subject and a verb, and in writing ending with a period, question mark, or exclamation point. A *simple sentence* consists of one main or independent clause <*she read the announcement in yesterday's paper*>. A *compound sentence* consists of two or more main clauses <*he left at nine o'clock, and they planned to meet at noon*>. A *complex sentence* consists of a main clause and one or more subordinate clauses <*it began to snow before they reached the summit*>. A *compound-complex sentence* consists of two or more main clauses and one or more subordinate clauses <*Susan left for Masters Hall after the presentation; there she joined the new-product workshop, which was already in progress*>.See also **clause; subordinate clause.**

A *declarative sentence* makes a statement <*the cow jumped over the moon*>. An *exclamatory sentence* expresses strong feeling <*that's ridiculous!*>. An *interrogative sentence* asks a question <*who said that?*>. An *imperative sentence* expresses a command or request <*get in here now*>.

sentence adverb An adverb that modifies an entire sentence, rather than a specific word or phrase within the sentence <*fortunately* they had already placed their order>. See also HOPEFULLY; THANKFULLY.

sentence fragment A group of words punctuated like a sentence, but without a subject or a predicate or both <*So many men, so many opinions.*> <*Yeah, when you think about it.*>. See also **sentence; clause.**

singular A word form denoting one person, thing, or instance <*man*> <*tattoo*> <*eventuality*> <*she* left> <it *is* here>.

split infinitive An infinitive preceded by *to* and an adverb or adverbial phrase <*to ultimately avoid* trouble>.

Grammarians used to disapprove of the split infinitive, but most now admit that it is not a defect. It is useful when a writer wants to emphasize the adverb <were determined *to thoroughly enjoy* themselves>. See also **infinitive.**

standard English English that is substantially uniform, well-established in the speech and writing of educated people, and widely recognized as acceptable; compare **nonstandard.** See also *dialect.*

subject A word or group of words denoting the entity about which something is said <*he* stopped> <*it's* clouding up> <*all sixty members* voted> <*orthodoxy* *on every doctrinal issue* now reigned> <*what they want* is more opportunity> <*going to work* was what she hated most> <*to sing at the Met* had long been a dream of his>.

subject-verb agreement See **agreement.**

subjunctive The form, or mood, of a verb that expresses a condition contrary to fact or follows clauses of necessity, demand, or wishing <if he *were* here, he could answer that> <it's imperative that it *be* broadcast> <they asked that the meeting *proceed*> <I wish they *would come* soon>; compare **imperative; indicative.** See also IF 3.

subordinate clause A clause that functions as a noun, adjective, or adverb and is attached to a main clause <theirs is a cause *that will prevail*>. See also **clause; sentence.**

suffix An affix attached to the end of a word to modify its meaning <editor*s*> <county*wide*> <Hollywood*ish*> <umbrella*-like*>; compare **prefix.**

superlative See **comparison.**

tense The characteristic of a verb that expresses time present, past, or future <*see, saw, will see*>.

transitive verb A verb that acts upon a direct object <she *contributed* money> <he *runs* the store> <*express* your opinion>; compare **intransitive verb.**

verb A word or phrase that is the grammatical center of the predicate and is used to express action, occurrence, or state of being <*leap, carry out, feel, be*>. See also **auxiliary verb; linking verb; mood; voice.**

verbal One of a group of words derived from verbs. See **gerund; infinitive; participle.**

voice The property of a verb that indicates whether the subject acts or is acted upon. See **active voice; passive voice.**

Punctuation Guide

APOSTROPHE ’

1. **indicates the possessive case of nouns and indefinite pronouns** <the boy’s mother> <the boys’ mothers> <It’s anyone’s guess>.
2. **marks omissions in contracted words** <I’d> <didn’t> <o’clock>.
3. **often forms plurals of letters, figures, and words referred to as words** <You should dot your *i*’s and cross your *t*’s> <several 8’s> <She had trouble pronouncing her *the*’s>.

BRACKETS [ ]

1. **set off extraneous data such as editorial additions, especially within quoted material** <wrote that the author was “trying to dazzle his readers with phrases like *jeu de mots* [play on words]”>.
2. **function as parentheses within parentheses** <Bowman Act (22 Stat., ch. 4, § [or sec.] 4, p. 50)>.

COLON :

1. **introduces a word, clause, or phrase that explains, illustrates, amplifies, or restates what has gone before** <The sentence was poorly constructed: it lacked both unity and coherence>.
2. **introduces a series** <Three countries were represented: England, France, and Belgium>.
3. **introduces lengthy quoted material set off from the rest of a text by indentation but not by quotation marks** <I quote from the text of Chapter One:>.
4. **separates data in time-telling and data in bibliographic and biblical references** <8:30 a.m.> <New York: Random House, 1995> <John 4:10>.
5. **separates titles and subtitles (as of books)** *<The Tragic Dynasty: A History of the Romanovs>.*

6. **follows the salutation in formal correspondence** <Dear Sir or Madam:>.

COMMA ,

1. **separates main clauses joined by a coordinating conjunction (such as *and, but, or, nor,* or *for*) and very short clauses not so joined** <She knew very little about him, and he volunteered nothing> <I came, I saw, I conquered>.
2. **sets off an adverbial clause (or a long phrase) that precedes the main clause** <When she found that her friends had deserted her, she sat down and cried>.
3. **sets off from the rest of the sentence transitional words and expressions (such as *on the contrary, on the other hand*), conjunctive adverbs (such as *consequently, furthermore, however*), and expressions that introduce an illustration or example (such as *namely, for example*)** <Your second question, on the other hand, remains open> <The mystery, however, remains unsolved> <She expects to travel through two countries, namely, France and England>.
4. **separates words, phrases, or clauses in series and coordinate adjectives modifying a noun** <Men, women, and children crowded into the square> <A harsh, cold wind blew>.
5. **sets off parenthetic elements (such as nonrestrictive modifiers) from the rest of the sentence** <Our guide, who wore a blue beret, was an experienced traveler> <We visited Gettysburg, the site of a famous battle>.
6. **introduces a direct quotation, terminates a direct quotation that is neither a question nor an exclamation, and encloses split quotations** <John said, “I am leaving”> <“I am leaving,” John said> <“I am leaving,” John said, “even if you want me to stay”>.

7. **sets off words in direct address, absolute phrases, and mild interjections** <You may go, Mary, if you wish> <I fear the encounter, his temper being what it is> <Ah, that's my idea of an excellent dinner>.
8. **separates a question from the rest of the sentence which it ends** <It's a fine day, isn't it?>.
9. **indicates the omission of a word or words, and especially a word or words used earlier in the sentence** <Common stocks are preferred by some investors; bonds, by others>.
10. **is used to avoid ambiguity** <To Mary, Jane was someone special>.
11. **sets off geographical names (such as state or country), items in dates, and addresses from the rest of a text** <Shreveport, Louisiana, is the site of a large air base> <On Sunday, June 23, 1940, he was wounded> <Number 10 Downing Street, London, is a famous address>.
12. **follows the salutation in informal correspondence and follows the closing line of a formal or informal letter** <Dear Mary,> <Affectionately,> <Very truly yours,>.

DASH —

1. **usually marks an abrupt change or break in the continuity of a sentence** <When in 1960 the stockpile was sold off—indeed, dumped as surplus—natural-rubber sales were hard hit>.
2. **introduces a summary statement after a series** <Oil, steel, and wheat—these are the sinews of industrialization>.
3. **often precedes the attribution of a quotation** <My foot is on my native heath. . . . —Sir Walter Scott>.

ELLIPSIS . . . .

1. **indicates the omission of one or more words within a quoted passage** <The head is not more native to the heart

. . . than is the throne of Denmark to thy father—Shakespeare>; **four dots indicates the omission of one or more sentences within the passage or the omission of words at the end of a sentence** <Avoiding danger is no safer in the long run than outright exposure. . . . Life is either a daring adventure or nothing —Helen Keller>.

2. **indicates halting speech or an unfinished sentence in dialogue** <"I'd like to . . . that is . . . if you don't mind . . . ." He faltered and then stopped speaking>.

EXCLAMATION POINT !

1. **terminates an emphatic phrase or sentence** <Get out of here!>.
2. **terminates an emphatic interjection** <Encore!>.

HYPHEN -

1. **marks separation or division of a word at the end of a line.**
2. **is used between some prefix and word combinations, such as prefix + proper name** <pre-Renaissance>; **prefix ending with a vowel + a word beginning with a vowel, often the same vowel** <co-opted> <re-ink>; **or stressed prefix + word, especially when this combination is similar to a different one** <re-cover a sofa> *but* <recover from an illness>.
3. **is used in some compounds, especially those containing prepositions** <president-elect> <sister-in-law>.
4. **is often used between elements of a unit modifier in attributive position in order to avoid ambiguity** <He is a small-business man> <She has gray-green eyes>.
5. **suspends the first part of a hyphenated compound when used with another hyphenated compound** <a six- or eight-cylinder engine>.

6. **is used in writing out compound numbers between 21 and 99** <thirty-four> <one hundred twenty-eight>.
7. **is used between the numerator and the denominator in writing out fractions, especially when they are used as modifiers** <a two-thirds majority of the vote>.
8. **serves instead of the phrase "(up) to and including" between numbers and dates** <pages 40-98> <the decade 1990-99>.

PARENTHESES ( )

1. **set off supplementary, parenthetic, or explanatory material when the interruption is more marked than that usually indicated by commas** <Three old destroyers (all now out of commission) will be scrapped> <He is hoping (as we all are) that this time he will succeed>.
2. **enclose numerals which confirm a written number in a text** <Delivery will be made in thirty (30) days>.
3. **enclose numbers or letters in a series** <We must set forth (1) our long-term goals, (2) our immediate objectives, and (3) the means at our disposal>.

PERIOD .

1. **terminates sentences or sentence fragments that are neither interrogative nor exclamatory** <Obey the law.> <He obeyed the law.>.
2. **follows some abbreviations and contractions** <Dr.> <Jr.> <etc.> <cont.>.

QUESTION MARK ?

1. **terminates a direct question** <Who threw the bomb?> <"Who threw the bomb?" he asked> <To ask the question Who threw the bomb? is unnecessary>.
2. **indicates the writer's ignorance or uncertainty** <Omar Khayyám, Persian poet (1048?–1122)>.

QUOTATION MARKS, DOUBLE “ ”

1. **enclose direct quotations** <He said, “I am leaving”>.
2. **enclose words or phrases borrowed from others, words used in a special way, and often slang when it is introduced into formal writing** <He called himself “emperor,” but he was really just a dictator> <He was arrested for smuggling “smack”>.
3. **enclose titles of short poems, short stories, articles, lectures, chapters of books, songs, short musical compositions, and radio and TV programs** <Robert Frost’s “Dust of Snow”> <Pushkin’s “Queen of Spades”> <The third chapter of *Treasure Island* is entitled “The Black Spot”> <NBC’s “Today Show”> <Beethoven’s “Für Elise”>.
4. **are used with other punctuation marks in the following ways: the period and the comma fall *within* the quotation marks** <“I am leaving.”> <His camera was described as “waterproof,” but “moisture-resistant” would have been a better description>; **the semicolon falls *outside* the quotation marks** <He spoke of his “little cottage in the country”; he might better have called it a mansion>; **the dash, the question mark, and the exclamation point fall *within* the quotation marks when they refer to the quoted matter only, but *outside* when they refer to the whole sentence** <He asked, “When did you leave?”> <What is the meaning of “the open door”?> <The sergeant shouted “Halt!”> <Save us from his “mercy”!>.

QUOTATION MARKS, SINGLE ‘ ’

enclose a quotation within a quotation <The witness said, “I distinctly heard him say, ‘Don’t be late,’ and then I heard the door close”>.

SEMICOLON ;

1. **links main clauses not joined by coordinating conjunctions** <Some people have the ability to write well; others do not>.
2. **links main clauses joined by conjunctive adverbs (such as *consequently, furthermore, however*)** <Speeding is illegal; furthermore, it is very dangerous>.
3. **links clauses which themselves contain commas, even when such clauses are joined by coordinating conjunctions** <Mr. King, whom you met yesterday, will represent us on the committee; but you should follow the proceedings yourself, because they are vitally important to us>.

SLASH /

1. **separates alternatives** <designs intended for high-heat and/or high-speed applications>.
2. **separates the month, day, and year in dates** <8/14/97>.
3. **serves as a dividing line between run-in lines of poetry** <Say, sages, what's the charm on earth / Can turn death's dart aside? —Robert Burns>.
4. **often represents *per* in abbreviations** <9 ft/sec> <20 km/hr>.

This book belongs to:

____

Webster's Dictionary *for* Students

NEW EDITION

Created in Cooperation with the Editors of
MERRIAM-WEBSTER

A Division of Merriam-Webster, Incorporated
Springfield, Massachusetts

Federal Street Press is a trademark of Federal Street Press,
a division of Merriam-Webster, Incorporated.

This 2007 edition published by
Federal Street Press
A Division of Merriam-Webster, Incorporated
P.O. Box 281
Springfield, MA 01102

Federal Street Press books are available for bulk purchase for sales promotion and premium use. For details write the manager of special sales,
Federal Street Press, P.O. Box 281, Springfield, MA 01102

ISBN 13 978-1-59695-022-1

Printed in the United States of America

08 09 10 11 9 8 7 6

Contents

Preface

This volume, updated for 2007, defines over 32,000 words and phrases that reflect the vocabulary level, curriculum requirements, and personal interests of students. A special section on Confused, Misused, or Misspelled Words appears at the back of the book.

The features of this dictionary are similar to those of larger dictionaries. It is important to understand them to make best use of this valuable language tool.

The **bold** word that begins an entry is known as the main entry word. All of the material in the entry is related to the main entry word or to derived words or phrases that also appear in the entry.

> **as•pen** *n* : a poplar tree whose leaves move easily in the breeze

Centered dots in the bold forms show where the words may be hyphenated at the end of a line on a page and they serve as an aid in sounding out the words.

Other bold forms may appear in this entry, such as **variant spellings** and **inflected forms** of the main entry word. Inflected forms are the plurals of nouns, the principal parts of verbs, or the comparative and superlative forms of adjectives.

> [1]**cad•die** or **cad•dy** *n, pl* **cad•dies** : a person who carries a golfer's clubs
> [1]**free** *adj* **fre•er; freest 1** : having liberty : not being a slave . . .
> **pul•sate** *vb* **pul•sat•ed; pul•sat•ing** : to have or show a pulse or beats

Other bold items in the entry may be defined **run-on phrases** that have the main entry word in the phrase, and **run-in entries** that are being explained in the definition itself.

> [1]**stand** *vb* . . . — **stand by** : to be or remain loyal or true to — **stand for 1** : to be a symbol for . . . **2** : to put up with . . .
> **chest•nut** *n* **1** : a sweet edible nut that grows in burs on a tree (**chestnut tree**) related to the beech . . .

One of the more common bold forms appearing at an entry is the **undefined run-on entry**. This is a word at the end of an entry that is derived from the main entry by the addition of a common word ending (suffix).

> **har•mo•ni•ous . . .** — **har•mo•ni•ous•ly** *adv* — **har•mo•ni•ous•ness** *n*

Since you know the meaning of the main entry word and the meaning of the suffix, the meaning of the run-on entry is self-explanatory.

The way a word is used in a sentence, its *function*, sometimes called its *part of speech*, is indicated by any of several *italic* abbreviations: *n* for *noun* (**cat, dog, mother**), *vb* for *verb* (**run, jump, cry**), *adj* for *adjective* (**blue, tall, happy**), *adv* for *adverb* (**easily, fast, nearby**), *pron* for *pronoun* (**who, them, none**), *conj* for *conjunction* (**and, but, if**), *prep* for *preposition* (**about, for, to**), and *interj* for *interjection* (**hello, adios**). Others include *helping verb* (**may, can**), *prefix* (**anti-, bio-**), and *suffix* (**-age, -er, -graph**).

When there are two or more words that have the same spelling but are different in their meanings or how they function in a sentence, these are distinguished by a small superscript numeral in front of the spelling. The numeral is not part of the spelling; it is there in this dictionary to distinguish these identically spelled words (called **homographs**).

> [1]**seal** *n* **1** : a sea mammal . . .
> [2]**seal** *n* **1** : something (as a pledge) that makes safe or secure
> [3]**seal** *vb* **1** : to mark with a seal . . .

One very important way a dictionary saves space when two or more words have the same meaning is by putting the definition at the more common word and linking to that entry by means of a cross-reference in SMALL CAPITALS. Look at the following.

> **ductless gland** *n* : ENDOCRINE GLAND

The treatment here tells you to look at the entry **endocrine gland** for a definition of both *ductless gland* and *endocrine gland*. And this treatment tells you also that *ductless gland* and *endocrine gland* are **synonyms**.

Sometimes the synonym cross-reference is used in place of a definition and sometimes following a definition.

> **hare•brained** *adj* : FOOLISH
> **staunch** *adj* **1** : strongly built : SUBSTANTIAL

When the synonym cross-reference has a following sense number or has a superscript homograph number attached, it tells you which specific sense number and which homograph to look to for the shared meaning.

> [1]**dain•ty** *n, pl* **dain•ties** : DELICACY 1
> **mom** *n* : [1]MOTHER 1

Your dictionary also guides you in the way a particular word is used. **Usage notes** may follow a definition or be used in place of a definition.

> **air•wave** *n* : the radio waves used in radio and television transmission — usually used in *pl.*
> **rev•er•end** *adj* . . . **2** — used as a title for a member of the clergy

Guidance on capitalization for entries where the main entry word is not shown capitalized is usually shown by an italic note at the beginning of the definition.

> **brus•sels sprouts** *n pl, often cap B* : green heads like tiny cabbages . . .

As a special added feature, this dictionary has, ahead of the main A-Z section, a separate list of commonly used Abbreviations, and following the main A-Z section a special section of Confused, Misused, or Misspelled Words.

Abbreviations

Most of these abbreviations are shown in one form only. Variation in use of periods, in kind of type, and in capitalization is frequent and widespread (as mph, MPH, m.p.h., Mph)

abbr abbreviation
AD in the year of our Lord
adj adjective
adv adverb
AK Alaska
AL, Ala Alabama
alt alternate, altitude
a.m., A.M. before noon
Am, Amer America, American
amt amount
anon anonymous
ans answer
Apr April
AR Arkansas
Ariz Arizona
Ark Arkansas
assn association
asst assistant
atty attorney
Aug August
ave avenue
AZ Arizona

BC before Christ
bet between
bldg building
blvd boulevard
Br, Brit Britain, British
bro brother
bros brothers
bu bushel

c carat, cent, centimeter, century, chapter, cup
C Celsius, centigrade
CA, Cal, Calif California
Can, Canad Canada, Canadian
cap capital, capitalize, capitalized
Capt captain
ch chapter, church
cm centimeter
co company, county
CO Colorado
COD cash on delivery, collect on delivery
col column
Col colonel, Colorado
Colo Colorado
conj conjunction
Conn Connecticut
cpu central processing unit
ct cent, court
CT Connecticut
cu cubic
CZ Canal Zone

d penny
DC District of Columbia
DDS doctor of dental surgery
DE Delaware
Dec December
Del Delaware
dept department
DMD doctor of dental medicine
doz dozen
Dr doctor
DST daylight saving time

E east, eastern, excellent
ea each
e.g. for example
Eng England, English
esp especially
etc et cetera

f false, female, forte
F Fahrenheit
FBI Federal Bureau of Investigation
Feb February
fem feminine
FL, Fla Florida
fr father, from
Fri Friday
ft feet, foot, fort

g gram
G good
Ga, GA Georgia
gal gallon
GB gigabyte
gen general
geog geographic, geographical, geography
gm gram
gov governor
govt government
gt great
GU Guam

HI Hawaii
hr hour
HS high school
ht height
Ia, IA Iowa
ID Idaho
i.e. that is
IL, Ill Illinois
in inch
IN Indiana
inc incorporated
Ind Indian, Indiana
interj interjection
intrans intransitive

Jan January
jr, jun junior

Kan, Kans Kansas
KB kilobyte
kg kilogram
km kilometer
KS Kansas
Ky, KY Kentucky

l left, liter
La, LA Louisiana
lb pound
Lt lieutenant
ltd limited

m male, meter, mile
MA Massachusetts
Maj major
Mar March
masc masculine
Mass Massachusetts
MB megabyte
Md Maryland
MD doctor of medicine, Maryland
Me, ME Maine
Mex Mexican, Mexico
mg milligram
MI, Mich Michigan
min minute
Minn Minnesota
Miss Mississippi
ml milliliter
mm millimeter
MN Minnesota
mo month
Mo, MO Missouri
Mon Monday
Mont Montana
mpg miles per gallon
mph miles per hour

MS Mississippi
mt mount, mountain
MT Montana

n noun
N north, northern
NC North Carolina
ND, N Dak North Dakota
NE Nebraska, northeast
Neb, Nebr Nebraska
Nev Nevada
NH New Hampshire
NJ New Jersey
NM, N Mex New Mexico
no north, number
Nov November
NV Nevada
NW northwest
NY New York

O Ohio
obj object, objective
Oct October
off office
OH Ohio
OK, Okla Oklahoma
OR, Ore, Oreg Oregon
oz ounce, ounces

p page
Pa, PA Pennsylvania
part participle
pat patent
Penn, Penna Pennsylvania
pg page
pk park, peck
pkg package
pl plural
p.m., P.M. afternoon
PO post office
poss possessive
pp pages
pr pair
PR Puerto Rico
prep preposition
pres present, president
prof professor
pron pronoun
PS postscript, public school
pt pint, point
PTA Parent-Teacher Association
PTO Parent-Teacher Organization

qt quart

r right
rd road, rod
recd received
reg region, regular
res residence
Rev reverend
RFD rural free delivery
RI Rhode Island
rpm revolutions per minute
RR railroad
RSVP please reply
rt right
rte route

S south, southern
Sat Saturday
SC South Carolina
sci science
Scot Scotland, Scottish
SD, S Dak South Dakota
SE southeast
sec second
Sept September
SI International System of Units
sing singular
so south
sq square
sr senior
Sr sister
SS steamship
st state, street
St saint
Sun Sunday
SW southwest

t true
tbs, tbsp tablespoon
TD touchdown
Tenn Tennessee
Tex Texas
Thurs, Thu Thursday
TN Tennessee
trans transitive
tsp teaspoon
Tues, Tue Tuesday
TX Texas

UN United Nations
US United States
USA United States of America
USSR Union of Soviet Socialist Republics
usu usual, usually
UT Utah

v verb
Va, VA Virginia
var variant
vb verb
VG very good
vi verb intransitive
VI Virgin Islands
vol volume
VP vice president
vs versus
vt verb transitive
Vt, VT Vermont

W west, western
WA, Wash Washington
Wed Wednesday
WI, Wis, Wisc Wisconsin
wk week
wt weight
WV, W Va West Virginia
WWW World Wide Web
WY, Wyo Wyoming

yd yard
yr year

Webster's Dictionary *for* Students

NEW EDITION

A

¹a *n, pl* **a's** *or* **as** *often cap* **1 :** the first letter of the English alphabet **2 :** a grade that shows a student's work is excellent

²a *indefinite article* **1 :** some one not identified or known **2 :** the same **3 :** ¹ANY 1 **4 :** for or from each

a- *prefix* **1 :** on **:** in **:** at **2 :** in (such) a state, condition, or manner **3 :** in the act or process of

aard·vark *n* **:** an African animal with a long snout and a long sticky tongue that feeds mostly on ants and termites and is active at night

ab- *prefix* **:** from **:** differing from

aback *adv* **:** by surprise

aba·cus *n, pl* **aba·ci** *or* **aba·cus·es :** an instrument for doing arithmetic by sliding counters along rods or in grooves

abaft *adv* **:** toward or at the back part of a ship

ab·a·lo·ne *n* **:** a large sea snail that has a flattened shell with a pearly lining

¹aban·don *vb* **1 :** to give up completely **:** FORSAKE **2 :** to give (oneself) up to a feeling or emotion — **aban·don·ment** *n*

²abandon *n* **:** a complete yielding to feelings or wishes

aban·doned *adj* **:** given up **:** left empty or unused

abash *vb* **:** to destroy the self-confidence of

abate *vb* **abat·ed; abat·ing :** to make or become less

ab·bess *n* **:** the head of an abbey for women

ab·bey *n, pl* **abbeys 1 :** MONASTERY, CONVENT **2 :** a church that once belonged to an abbey

ab·bot *n* **:** the head of an abbey for men

ab·bre·vi·ate *vb* **ab·bre·vi·at·ed; ab·bre·vi·at·ing :** to make briefer **:** SHORTEN

ab·bre·vi·a·tion *n* **1 :** a making shorter **2 :** a shortened form of a word or phrase

ab·di·cate *vb* **ab·di·cat·ed; ab·di·cat·ing :** to give up a position of power or authority

ab·di·ca·tion *n* **:** the giving up of a position of power or authority

ab·do·men *n* **1 :** the part of the body between the chest and the hips including the cavity in which the chief digestive organs lie **2 :** the hind part of the body of an arthropod (as an insect)

ab·dom·i·nal *adj* **:** of, relating to, or located in the abdomen

ab·duct *vb* **:** to take a person away by force **:** KIDNAP

ab·duc·tion *n* **:** the act of abducting

abeam *adv or adj* **:** on a line at right angles to a ship's keel

abed *adv or adj* **:** in bed

ab·er·ra·tion *n* **:** a differing from what is normal or usual

ab·hor *vb* **ab·horred; ab·hor·ring :** to shrink from in disgust **:** LOATHE

ab·hor·rent *adj* **:** causing or deserving strong dislike

abide *vb* **abode** *or* **abid·ed; abid·ing 1 :** to bear patiently **:** TOLERATE **2 :** ENDURE 1 **3 :** to live in a place **:** DWELL — **abide by :** to accept the terms of **:** OBEY

abil·i·ty *n, pl* **abil·i·ties 1 :** power to do something **2 :** natural talent or acquired skill

-abil·i·ty *also* **-ibil·i·ty** *n suffix, pl* **-abil·i·ties** *also* **-ibil·i·ties :** ability, fitness, or likeliness to act or be acted upon in (such) a way

ab·ject *adj* **:** low in spirit or hope — **ab·ject·ly** *adv* — **ab·ject·ness** *n*

ablaze *adj* **1 :** being on fire **2 :** bright with light or color

able *adj* **abler; ablest 1 :** having enough power or skill to do something **2 :** having or showing much skill

-able *also* **-ible** *adj suffix* **1 :** capable of, fit for, or worthy of being **2 :** tending or likely to — **-ably** *also* **-ibly** *adv suffix*

ably *adv* **:** in an able way

ab·nor·mal *adj* **:** differing from the normal usually in a noticeable way — **ab·nor·mal·ly** *adv*

¹aboard *adv* **:** on, onto, or within a ship, train, bus, or airplane

²aboard *prep* **:** on or into especially for passage

¹abode *past of* ABIDE

²abode *n* **:** the place where one stays or lives

abol·ish *vb* **:** to do away with **:** put an end to

ab·o·li·tion *n* **:** a complete doing away with

A–bomb *n* **:** ATOMIC BOMB

abom·i·na·ble *adj* **1 :** deserving or causing disgust **2 :** very disagreeable or unpleasant — **abom·i·na·bly** *adv*

abominable snow·man *n, often cap A&S* **:** a mysterious creature with human or apelike characteristics reported to exist in the Himalayas

abom·i·na·tion *n* **:** something abominable

ab·orig·i·nal *adj* **1 :** being the first of its kind in a region **2:** of or relating to aborigines

ab·orig·i·ne *n, pl* **ab·orig·i·nes :** a member of the original race to live in a region **:** NATIVE

abound *vb* **1 :** to be plentiful **:** TEEM **2 :** to be fully supplied

¹about *adv* **1 :** ALMOST, NEARLY **2 :** on all sides **:** AROUND **3 :** in the opposite direction

²about *prep* **1 :** on every side of **:** AROUND **2 :** on the point of **3 :** having to do with
¹above *adv* **:** in or to a higher place
²above *prep* **1 :** higher than **:** OVER **2 :** too good for **3 :** more than
³above *adj* **:** said or written earlier
¹above·board *adv* **:** in an honest open way
²aboveboard *adj* **:** free from tricks and secrecy
ab·ra·ca·dab·ra *n* **:** a magical charm or word
abrade *vb* **abrad·ed; abrad·ing :** to wear away by rubbing
¹abra·sive *n* **:** a substance for grinding, smoothing, or polishing
²abrasive *adj* **:** having the effect of or like that of abrading
abreast *adv or adj* **1 :** side by side **2 :** up to a certain level of knowledge
abridge *vb* **abridged; abridg·ing :** to shorten by leaving out some parts
abridg·ment *or* **abridge·ment** *n* **:** a shortened form of a written work
abroad *adv or adj* **1 :** over a wide area **2 :** in the open **:** OUTDOORS **3 :** in or to a foreign country **4 :** known to many people
abrupt *adj* **1 :** happening without warning **:** SUDDEN **2 :** ¹STEEP 1 — **abrupt·ly** *adv* — **abrupt·ness** *n*
ab·scess *n* **:** a collection of pus with swollen and red tissue around it — **ab·scessed** *adj*
ab·sence *n* **1 :** a being away **2 :** ²LACK 1, WANT
¹ab·sent *adj* **1 :** not present **2 :** not existing **3 :** showing that one is not paying attention
²ab·sent *vb* **:** to keep (oneself) away
ab·sen·tee *n* **:** a person who is absent
ab·sent-mind·ed *adj* **:** not paying attention to what is going on or to what one is doing — **ab·sent-mind·ed·ly** *adv* — **ab·sent-mind·ed·ness** *n*
ab·so·lute *adj* **1 :** free from imperfection **:** PERFECT, COMPLETE **2 :** free from control or conditions **3 :** free from doubt **:** CERTAIN — **ab·so·lute·ly** *adv* — **ab·so·lute·ness** *n*
ab·so·lu·tion *n* **:** a forgiving of sins
ab·solve *vb* **ab·solved; ab·solv·ing :** to set free from a duty or from blame
ab·sorb *vb* **1 :** to take in or swallow up **2 :** to hold all of one's interest **3 :** to receive without giving back
ab·sor·ben·cy *n* **:** the quality or state of being absorbent
ab·sor·bent *adj* **:** able to absorb
ab·sorp·tion *n* **1 :** the process of absorbing or being absorbed **2 :** complete attention
ab·stain *vb* **:** to keep oneself from doing something — **ab·stain·er** *n*
ab·sti·nence *n* **:** an avoiding by choice especially of certain foods or of liquor
¹ab·stract *adj* **1 :** expressing a quality apart from an actual person or thing that posseses it **2 :** hard to understand — **ab·stract·ly** *adv* — **ab·stract·ness** *n*
²ab·stract *n* **:** ²SUMMARY
³ab·stract *vb* **1 :** to take away **:** SEPARATE **2 :** SUMMARIZE
ab·strac·tion *n* **1 :** the act of abstracting **:** the state of being abstracted **2 :** an abstract idea
ab·struse *adj* **:** hard to understand — **ab·struse·ly** *adv* — **ab·struse·ness** *n*
ab·surd *adj* **:** completely unreasonable or untrue **:** RIDICULOUS — **ab·surd·ly** *adv*
ab·sur·di·ty *n, pl* **ab·sur·di·ties 1 :** the fact of being absurd **2 :** something that is absurd
abun·dance *n* **:** a large quantity **:** PLENTY
abun·dant *adj* **:** more than enough **:** PLENTIFUL — **abun·dant·ly** *adv*
¹abuse *n* **1 :** a dishonest practice **2 :** wrong or unfair treatment or use **3 :** harsh insulting language
²abuse *vb* **abused; abus·ing 1 :** to blame or scold rudely **2 :** to use wrongly **:** MISUSE **3 :** to treat cruelly **:** MISTREAT
abu·sive *adj* **:** using or characterized by abuse — **abu·sive·ly** *adv* — **abu·sive·ness** *n*
abut *vb* **abut·ted; abut·ting :** to touch along a border or with a part that sticks out
abut·ment *n* **:** something against which another thing rests its weight or pushes with force
abyss *n* **:** a gulf so deep or space so great that it cannot be measured
ac·a·dem·ic *adj* **1 :** of or relating to schools or colleges **2 :** having no practical importance — **ac·a·dem·i·cal·ly** *adv*
acad·e·my *n, pl* **acad·e·mies 1 :** a private high school **2 :** a high school or college where special subjects are taught **3 :** a society of learned persons
ac·cede *vb* **ac·ced·ed; ac·ced·ing :** to agree to
ac·cel·er·ate *vb* **ac·cel·er·at·ed; ac·cel·er·at·ing 1 :** to bring about earlier **:** HASTEN **2 :** to move or cause to move faster
ac·cel·er·a·tion *n* **:** a speeding up
ac·cel·er·a·tor *n* **:** a pedal in an automobile for controlling the speed of the motor
¹ac·cent *vb* **1 :** to give a greater force or stress **2 :** to mark with a written or printed accent
²ac·cent *n* **1 :** a way of talking shared by a group (as the residents of a country) **2 :** greater stress or force given to a syllable of a word in speaking or to a beat in music **3 :** a mark (as ˈ or ˌ) used in writing or printing to show the place of greater stress on a syllable
ac·cen·tu·ate *vb* **ac·cen·tu·at·ed; ac·cen·tu·at·ing 1 :** ¹ACCENT **2 :** EMPHASIZE

ac·cept *vb* **1 :** to receive or take willingly **2 :** to agree to

ac·cept·able *adj* **1 :** worthy of being accepted **2 :** ADEQUATE — **ac·cept·able·ness** *n* — **ac·cept·ably** *adv*

ac·cep·tance *n* **1 :** the act of accepting **2 :** the quality or state of being accepted or acceptable

ac·cess *n* **1 :** the right or ability to approach, enter, or use **2 :** a way or means of approach

ac·ces·si·ble *adj* **1 :** capable of being reached **2 :** OBTAINABLE — **ac·ces·si·bly** *adv*

ac·ces·sion *n* **:** a coming to a position of power

[1]**ac·ces·so·ry** *n, pl* **ac·ces·so·ries** **1 :** a person who helps another in doing wrong **2 :** an object or device not necessary in itself but adding to the beauty or usefulness of something else

[2]**accessory** *adj* **:** adding to or helping in a secondary way **:** SUPPLEMENTARY

ac·ci·dent *n* **1 :** something that happens by chance or from unknown causes **:** MISHAP **2 :** lack of intention or necessity **:** CHANCE

ac·ci·den·tal *adj* **1 :** happening by chance or unexpectedly **2 :** not happening or done on purpose — **ac·ci·den·tal·ly** *adv*

[1]**ac·claim** *vb* **:** [1]PRAISE 1

[2]**acclaim** *n* **:** [2]PRAISE 1, APPLAUSE

ac·cli·mate *vb* **ac·cli·mat·ed; ac·cli·mat·ing** **:** to change to fit a new climate or new surroundings

ac·cli·ma·tize *vb* **ac·cli·ma·tized; ac·cli·ma·tiz·ing** **:** ACCLIMATE

ac·com·mo·date *vb* **ac·com·mo·dat·ed; ac·com·mo·dat·ing** **1 :** to provide with a place to stay or sleep **2 :** to provide with something needed **:** help out **3 :** to have room for

ac·com·mo·dat·ing *adj* **:** ready to help — **ac·com·mo·dat·ing·ly** *adv*

ac·com·mo·da·tion *n* **1 :** something supplied that is useful or handy **2 accommodations** *pl* **:** lodging and meals or traveling space and related services

ac·com·pa·ni·ment *n* **:** music played along with a solo part to enrich it

ac·com·pa·nist *n* **:** a musician who plays an accompaniment

ac·com·pa·ny *vb* **ac·com·pa·nied; ac·com·pa·ny·ing** **1 :** to go with as a companion **2 :** to play a musical accompaniment for **3 :** to happen at the same time as

ac·com·plice *n* **:** a partner in wrongdoing

ac·com·plish *vb* **:** to succeed in doing **:** manage to do

ac·com·plished *adj* **:** skilled through practice or training **:** EXPERT

ac·com·plish·ment *n* **1 :** the act of accomplishing **:** COMPLETION **2 :** something accomplished **3 :** an acquired excellence or skill

[1]**ac·cord** *vb* **1 :** [1]GIVE 6 **2 :** to be in harmony **:** AGREE

[2]**accord** *n* **1 :** AGREEMENT 1, HARMONY **2 :** willingness to act or to do something

ac·cor·dance *n* **:** AGREEMENT 1

ac·cord·ing·ly *adv* **1 :** in the necessary way **:** in the way called for **2 :** as a result **:** CONSEQUENTLY, SO

ac·cord·ing to *prep* **1 :** in agreement with **2 :** as stated by

[1]**ac·cor·di·on** *n* **:** a portable keyboard musical instrument played by forcing air from a bellows past metal reeds

[2]**accordion** *adj* **:** folding or creased or hinged to fold like an accordion

ac·cost *vb* **:** to approach and speak to often in a demanding or aggressive way

[1]**ac·count** *n* **1 :** a record of money received and money paid out **2 :** a statement of explanation or of reasons or causes **3 :** a statement of facts or events **:** REPORT **4 :** [2]WORTH 1, IMPORTANCE — **on account of :** for the sake of **:** BECAUSE OF — **on no account** **:** not ever or for any reason

[2]**account** *vb* **1 :** to think of as **:** CONSIDER **2 :** to give an explanation **3 :** to be the only or chief reason

ac·coun·tant *n* **:** a person whose job is accounting

ac·count·ing *n* **:** the work of keeping track of how much money is made and spent in a business

ac·cu·mu·late *vb* **ac·cu·mu·lat·ed; ac·cu·mu·lat·ing** **1 :** COLLECT 1, GATHER **2 :** to increase in quantity or number

ac·cu·mu·la·tion *n* **1 :** a collecting together **2 :** something accumulated **:** COLLECTION

ac·cu·ra·cy *n* **:** freedom from mistakes

ac·cu·rate *adj* **:** free from mistakes **:** RIGHT — **ac·cu·rate·ly** *adv* — **ac·cu·rate·ness** *n*

ac·cu·sa·tion *n* **:** a claim that someone has done something bad or illegal

ac·cuse *vb* **ac·cused; ac·cus·ing** **:** to blame a fault, wrong, or crime on (a person) — **ac·cus·er** *n*

ac·cus·tom *vb* **:** to cause (someone) to get used to something

ac·cus·tomed *adj* **1 :** CUSTOMARY 2, USUAL **2 :** familiar with **:** USED

[1]**ace** *n* **1 :** a playing card with one figure in its center **2 :** a person who is expert at something

[2]**ace** *adj* **:** of the very best kind

[1]**ache** *vb* **ached; ach·ing** **1 :** to suffer a dull continuous pain **2 :** YEARN

[2]**ache** *n* **:** a dull continuous pain

achieve *vb* **achieved; achiev·ing** **1 :** to

bring about : ACCOMPLISH **2 :** to get by means of one's own efforts : WIN

achieve·ment *n* **1 :** the act of achieving **2 :** something achieved especially by great effort

[1]**ac·id** *adj* **1 :** having a taste that is sour, bitter, or stinging **2 :** sour in temper : CROSS **3 :** of, relating to, or like an acid — **ac·id·ly** *adv*

[2]**acid** *n* **:** a chemical compound that tastes sour and forms a water solution which turns blue litmus paper red

acid·i·ty *n, pl* **acid·i·ties :** the quality, state, or degree of being acid

ac·knowl·edge *vb* **ac·knowl·edged; ac·knowl·edg·ing 1 :** to admit the truth or existence of **2 :** to recognize the rights or authority of **3 :** to make known that something has been received or noticed

ac·knowl·edged *adj* **:** generally accepted

ac·knowl·edg·ment *or* **ac·knowl·edge·ment** *n* **1 :** an act of acknowledging some deed or achievement **2 :** something done or given in return for something done or received

ac·ne *n* **:** a skin condition in which pimples and blackheads are present

acorn *n* **:** the nut of the oak tree

acous·tic *or* **acous·ti·cal** *adj* **1 :** of or relating to hearing or sound **2 :** deadening sound

acous·tics *n sing or pl* **1 :** a science dealing with sound **2 :** the qualities in a room or hall that affect how well a person in it can hear

ac·quaint *vb* **1 :** to cause to know personally **2 :** to make familiar

ac·quain·tance *n* **1 :** personal knowledge **2 :** a person one knows slightly

ac·qui·esce *vb* **ac·qui·esced; ac·qui·esc·ing :** to accept, agree, or give consent by keeping silent or by not making objections

ac·qui·es·cence *n* **:** the act of acquiescing

ac·quire *vb* **ac·quired; ac·quir·ing :** to get especially by one's own efforts : GAIN

ac·qui·si·tion *n* **1 :** the act of acquiring **2 :** something acquired

ac·quis·i·tive *adj* **:** GREEDY 2 — **ac·quis·i·tive·ly** *adv* — **ac·quis·i·tive·ness** *n*

ac·quit *vb* **ac·quit·ted; ac·quit·ting 1 :** to declare innocent of a crime or of wrongdoing **2 :** to conduct (oneself) in a certain way

ac·quit·tal *n* **:** the act of acquitting someone

acre *n* **:** a measure of land area equal to 43,560 square feet (about 4047 square meters)

acre·age *n* **:** area in acres

ac·rid *adj* **1 :** sharp or bitter in taste or odor **2 :** very harsh or unpleasant

ac·ro·bat *n* **:** a person (as a circus performer) who is very good at stunts like jumping, balancing, tumbling, and swinging from things

ac·ro·bat·ic *adj* **:** of or relating to acrobats or acrobatics

ac·ro·bat·ics *n sing or pl* **1 :** the art or performance of an acrobat **2 :** stunts of or like those of an acrobat

ac·ro·nym *n* **:** a word (as *radar*) formed from the first letter or letters of the words of a compound term

acrop·o·lis *n* **:** the upper fortified part of an ancient Greek city

[1]**across** *adv* **:** from one side to the other

[2]**across** *prep* **1 :** to or on the opposite side of **2 :** so as to pass, go over, or intersect at an angle

[1]**act** *n* **1 :** something that is done : DEED **2 :** a law made by a governing body **3 :** the doing of something **4 :** a main division of a play

[2]**act** *vb* **1 :** to perform (a part) on the stage **2 :** to behave oneself in a certain way **3 :** to do something : MOVE **4 :** to have a result : make something happen : WORK

act·ing *adj* **:** serving for a short time only or in place of another

ac·tion *n* **1 :** the working of one thing on another so as to produce a change **2 :** the doing of something **3 :** something done **4 :** the way something runs or works **5 :** combat in war

action figure *n* **:** a small figure often of a superhero used especially as a toy

ac·ti·vate *vb* **ac·ti·vat·ed; ac·ti·vat·ing :** to make active or more active

ac·tive *adj* **1 :** producing or involving action or movement **2 :** showing that the subject of a sentence is the doer of the action represented by the verb **3 :** quick in physical movement : LIVELY **4 :** taking part in an action or activity — **ac·tive·ly** *adv*

ac·tiv·i·ty *n, pl* **ac·tiv·i·ties 1 :** energetic action **2 :** something done especially for relaxation or fun

ac·tor *n* **:** a person who acts especially in a play or movie

ac·tress *n* **:** a woman or girl who acts especially in a play or movie

ac·tu·al *adj* **:** really existing or happening : not false

ac·tu·al·ly *adv* **:** in fact : REALLY

acute *adj* **acut·er; acut·est 1 :** measuring less than a right angle **2 :** mentally sharp **3 :** SEVERE **4 :** developing quickly and lasting only a short time **5 :** CRITICAL 4, URGENT — **acute·ly** *adv* — **acute·ness** *n*

ad *n* **:** ADVERTISEMENT

ad·age *n* **:** an old familiar saying : PROVERB

ad·a·mant *adj* **:** not giving in

Ad·am's apple *n* **:** the lump formed in the front of a person's neck by cartilage in the throat

adapt *vb* **:** to make or become suitable or able to function — **adapt·er** *n*
adapt·abil·i·ty *n* **:** the quality or state of being adaptable
adapt·able *adj* **:** capable of adapting or being adapted
ad·ap·ta·tion *n* **1 :** the act or process of adapting **2 :** something adapted or helping to adapt
add *vb* **1 :** to join or unite to something **2 :** to say something more **3 :** to combine numbers into a single sum
ad·dend *n* **:** a number that is to be added to another number
ad·den·dum *n, pl* **ad·den·da :** something added (as to a book)
ad·der *n* **1 :** any of several poisonous snakes of Europe or Africa **2 :** any of several harmless North American snakes (as the **puff adder**)
[1]**ad·dict** *vb* **:** to cause to have a need for something
[2]**ad·dict** *n* **:** a person who is addicted (as to a drug)
ad·dic·tion *n* **:** the state of being addicted (as to the use of harmful drugs)
ad·di·tion *n* **1 :** the adding of numbers to obtain their sum **2 :** something added — **in addition :** [2]BESIDES, ALSO — **in addition to :** over and above **:** [1]BESIDES
ad·di·tion·al *adj* **:** [1]EXTRA — **ad·di·tion·al·ly** *adv*
[1]**ad·di·tive** *adj* **:** relating to or produced by addition
[2]**additive** *n* **:** a substance added to another in small amounts
ad·dle *vb* **ad·dled; ad·dling :** to make confused
[1]**ad·dress** *vb* **1 :** to apply (oneself) to something **2 :** to speak or write to **3 :** to put directions for delivery on
[2]**ad·dress** *n* **1 :** a rehearsed speech **:** LECTURE **2 :** the place where a person can usually be reached **3 :** the directions for delivery placed on mail **4 :** the symbols (as numerals or letters) that identify the location where particular information (as a home page) is stored on a computer especially on the Internet
ad·dress·ee *n* **:** the person to whom something is addressed
ad·e·noids *n pl* **:** fleshy growths near the opening of the nose into the throat
ad·ept *adj* **:** very good at something — **adept·ly** *adv* — **adept·ness** *n*
ad·e·quate *adj* **1 :** [1]ENOUGH **2 :** good enough — **ad·e·quate·ly** *adv* — **ad·e·quate·ness** *n*
ad·here *vb* **ad·hered; ad·her·ing 1 :** to stay loyal (as to a promise) **2 :** to stick tight **:** CLING
ad·her·ence *n* **:** steady or faithful attachment
ad·her·ent *n* **:** a person who adheres to a belief, an organization, or a leader
ad·he·sion *n* **:** the act or state of adhering
[1]**ad·he·sive** *adj* **:** tending to stick **:** STICKY — **ad·he·sive·ly** *adv* — **ad·he·sive·ness** *n*
[2]**adhesive** *n* **:** an adhesive substance
adi·os *interj* — used instead of goodbye
ad·ja·cent *adj* **:** next to or near something — **ad·ja·cent·ly** *adv*
ad·jec·ti·val *adj* **:** of, relating to, or functioning as an adjective — **ad·jec·ti·val·ly** *adv*
ad·jec·tive *n* **:** a word that says something about a noun or pronoun
ad·join *vb* **:** to be next to or in contact with
ad·journ *vb* **:** to bring or come to a close for a period of time — **ad·journ·ment** *n*
ad·junct *n* **:** something joined or added to something else but not a necessary part of it
ad·just *vb* **1 :** to settle or fix by agreement **2 :** to move the parts of an instrument or a machine to make them work better **3 :** to become used to — **ad·just·er** *n*
ad·just·able *adj* **:** possible to adjust
ad·just·ment *n* **1 :** the act or process of adjusting **:** the state of being adjusted **2 :** a deciding about and paying of a claim or debt **3 :** something that is used to adjust one part to another
ad·ju·tant *n* **:** an officer who assists a commanding officer
ad–lib *vb* **ad–libbed; ad–lib·bing :** to improvise something and especially music or spoken lines
ad·min·is·ter *vb* **1 :** to be in charge of **:** MANAGE **2 :** to give out as deserved **3 :** to give or supply as treatment
ad·min·is·tra·tion *n* **1 :** the act or process of administering **2 :** the work involved in managing something **3 :** the persons who direct the business of something (as a city or school)
ad·min·is·tra·tive *adj* **:** of or relating to administration
ad·mi·ra·ble *adj* **:** deserving to be admired — **ad·mi·ra·bly** *adv*
ad·mi·ral *n* **:** a commissioned officer in the Navy or Coast Guard ranking above a vice admiral
ad·mi·ral·ty *adj* **:** of or relating to conduct on the sea
ad·mi·ra·tion *n* **:** great and delighted approval
ad·mire *vb* **ad·mired; ad·mir·ing :** to feel admiration for **:** think very highly of — **ad·mir·er** *n*
ad·mis·si·ble *adj* **:** deserving to be admitted or allowed **:** ALLOWABLE
ad·mis·sion *n* **1 :** an admitting of something that has not been proved **2 :** the act of admit-

ting **3 :** the right or permission to enter **4 :** the price of entrance

ad·mit *vb* **ad·mit·ted; ad·mit·ting 1 :** [1]PERMIT 2, ALLOW **2 :** to allow to enter : let in **3 :** to make known usually with some unwillingness

ad·mit·tance *n* **:** permission to enter

ad·mon·ish *vb* **1 :** to criticize or warn gently but seriously **2 :** to give friendly advice or encouragement

ad·mo·ni·tion *n* **:** a gentle or friendly criticism or warning

ado *n* **:** fussy excitement or hurrying about

ado·be *n* **1 :** brick made of earth or clay dried in the sun **2 :** a building made of adobe

ad·o·les·cence *n* **:** the period of life between childhood and adulthood

ad·o·les·cent *n* **:** a person who is no longer a child but not yet adult

adopt *vb* **1 :** to take (a child of other parents) as one's own **2 :** to take up and practice as one's own **3 :** to accept and put into action — **adopt·er** *n*

adop·tion *n* **:** the act of adopting : the state of being adopted

ador·able *adj* **:** CHARMING, LOVELY — **ador·able·ness** *n* — **ador·ably** *adv*

ad·o·ra·tion *n* **:** deep love

adore *vb* **adored; ador·ing 1 :** [2]WORSHIP 1 **2 :** to be very fond of — **ador·er** *n*

adorn *vb* **:** to try to make prettier by adding decorations

adorn·ment *n* **1 :** DECORATION 1 **2 :** [1]ORNAMENT 1

adren·a·line *n* **:** EPINEPHRINE

adrift *adv or adj* **:** in a drifting state

adroit *adj* **:** having or showing great skill or cleverness — **adroit·ly** *adv* — **adroit·ness** *n*

ad·u·la·tion *n* **:** very great admiration

[1]**adult** *adj* **:** fully developed and mature

[2]**adult** *n* **:** an adult person or thing

adul·ter·ate *vb* **adul·ter·at·ed; adul·ter·at·ing :** to make impure or weaker by adding something different or of poorer quality

adult·hood *n* **:** the period of being an adult

[1]**ad·vance** *vb* **ad·vanced; ad·vanc·ing 1 :** to help the progress of **2 :** to move forward **3 :** to raise to a higher rank **4 :** to give ahead of time **5 :** PROPOSE 1

[2]**advance** *n* **1 :** a forward movement **2 :** IMPROVEMENT 1 **3 :** a rise in price, value, or amount **4 :** a first step or approach **5 :** a giving (as of money) ahead of time — **in advance :** [1]BEFORE 1 — **in advance of :** ahead of

ad·vanced *adj* **1 :** being far along in years or progress **2 :** being beyond the elementary or introductory level

ad·vance·ment *n* **1 :** the action of advancing **:** the state of being advanced **2 :** a raising or being raised to a higher rank or position

ad·van·tage *n* **1 :** the fact of being in a better position or condition **2 :** personal benefit or gain **3 :** something that benefits the one it belongs to

ad·van·ta·geous *adj* **:** giving an advantage **:** HELPFUL — **ad·van·ta·geous·ly** *adv*

ad·vent *n* **:** the arrival or coming of something

[1]**ad·ven·ture** *n* **1 :** an action that involves unknown dangers and risks **2 :** an unusual experience

[2]**adventure** *vb* **ad·ven·tured; ad·ven·tur·ing :** to expose to or go on in spite of danger or risk — **ad·ven·tur·er** *n*

ad·ven·ture·some *adj* **:** likely to take risks **:** DARING

ad·ven·tur·ous *adj* **1 :** ready to take risks or to deal with new or unexpected problems **2 :** DANGEROUS 1, RISKY — **ad·ven·tur·ous·ly** *adv* — **ad·ven·tur·ous·ness** *n*

ad·verb *n* **:** a word used to modify a verb, an adjective, or another adverb and often used to show degree, manner, place, or time

ad·ver·bi·al *adj* **:** of, relating to, or used an an adverb — **ad·ver·bi·al·ly** *adv*

ad·ver·sary *n, pl* **ad·ver·sar·ies :** OPPONENT, ENEMY

ad·verse *adj* **1 :** acting against or in an opposite direction **2 :** not helping or favoring — **ad·verse·ly** *adv* — **ad·verse·ness** *n*

ad·ver·si·ty *n, pl* **ad·ver·si·ties :** hard times **:** MISFORTUNE

ad·ver·tise *vb* **ad·ver·tised; ad·ver·tis·ing 1 :** to announce publicly **2 :** to call to public attention to persuade to buy **3 :** to put out a public notice or request — **ad·ver·tis·er** *n*

ad·ver·tise·ment *n* **:** a notice or short film advertising something

ad·ver·tis·ing *n* **1 :** speech, writing, pictures, or films meant to persuade people to buy something **2 :** the business of preparing advertisements

ad·vice *n* **:** suggestions about a decision or action

ad·vis·able *adj* **:** reasonable or proper to do **:** DISCREET — **ad·vis·ably** *adv*

ad·vise *vb* **ad·vised; ad·vis·ing 1 :** to give advice to **:** COUNSEL **2 :** to give information about something — **ad·vis·er** *or* **ad·vi·sor** *n*

ad·vi·so·ry *adj* **1 :** having the power or right to advise **2 :** containing advice

[1]**ad·vo·cate** *n* **1 :** a person who argues for another in court **2 :** a person who argues for or supports an idea or plan

[2]**ad·vo·cate** *vb* **ad·vo·cat·ed; ad·vo·cat·ing :** to argue for

adz *or* **adze** *n* **:** a cutting tool that has a thin curved blade at right angles to the handle and is used for shaping wood

-aemia — see -EMIA

ae·on *or* **eon** *n* **:** a very long period of time **:** AGE

aer- *or* **aero-** *prefix* **:** air **:** atmosphere **:** gas

aer·ate *vb* **aer·at·ed; aer·at·ing 1 :** to supply (blood) with oxygen by breathing **2 :** to supply or cause to be filled with air **3 :** to combine or fill with gas — **aer·a·tor** *n*

aer·a·tion *n* **:** the process of aerating

[1]**ae·ri·al** *adj* **1 :** of, relating to, or occurring in the air **2 :** running on cables or rails that are raised above the ground **3 :** of or relating to aircraft **4 :** taken from or used in or against aircraft — **ae·ri·al·ly** *adv*

[2]**aer·i·al** *n* **:** ANTENNA 2

ae·rie *n* **:** the nest of a bird (as an eagle) high on a cliff or a mountaintop

aero·nau·ti·cal *or* **aero·nau·tic** *adj* **:** of or relating to aeronautics

aero·nau·tics *n* **:** a science dealing with the building and flying of aircraft

aero·sol *n* **1 :** a substance (as an insecticide) that is dispensed from a container as a spray of tiny solid or liquid particles in gas **2 :** a container that dispenses an aerosol

aero·space *n* **1 :** the earth's atmosphere and the space beyond **2 :** a science dealing with aerospace

aes·thet·ic *or* **es·thet·ic** *adj* **:** of or relating to beauty and what is beautiful — **aes·thet·i·cal·ly** *adv*

[1]**afar** *adv* **:** from, at, or to a great distance

[2]**afar** *n* **:** a long way off

af·fa·ble *adj* **:** polite and friendly in talking to others — **af·fa·bly** *adv*

af·fair *n* **1 affairs** *pl* **:** BUSINESS 1 **2 :** something that relates to or involves one **3 :** an action or occasion only partly specified

[1]**af·fect** *vb* **1 :** to be fond of using or wearing **2 :** ASSUME 3

[2]**affect** *vb* **1 :** to attack or act on as a disease does **2 :** to have an effect on

af·fect·ed *adj* **:** not natural or genuine — **af·fect·ed·ly** *adv*

af·fect·ing *adj* **:** causing pity or sadness

af·fec·tion *n* **:** a feeling of attachment **:** liking for someone

af·fec·tion·ate *adj* **:** feeling or showing a great liking for a person or thing **:** LOVING — **af·fec·tion·ate·ly** *adv*

af·fi·da·vit *n* **:** a sworn statement in writing

af·fil·i·ate *vb* **af·fil·i·at·ed; af·fil·i·at·ing :** to associate as a member or branch

af·fin·i·ty *n, pl* **af·fin·i·ties :** a strong liking for or attraction to someone or something

af·firm *vb* **1 :** to declare to be true **2 :** to say with confidence **:** ASSERT

af·fir·ma·tion *n* **:** an act of affirming

[1]**af·fir·ma·tive** *adj* **1 :** declaring that the fact is so **2 :** being positive or helpful

[2]**affirmative** *n* **1 :** an expression (as the word *yes*) of agreement **2 :** the affirmative side in a debate or vote

[1]**af·fix** *vb* **:** FASTEN 1, 2, ATTACH

[2]**af·fix** *n* **:** a letter or group of letters that comes at the beginning or end of a word and has a meaning of its own

af·flict *vb* **:** to cause pain or unhappiness to

af·flic·tion *n* **1 :** the state of being afflicted **2 :** something that causes pain or unhappiness

af·flu·ence *n* **:** the state of having much money or property

af·flu·ent *adj* **:** having plenty of money and things that money can buy

af·ford *vb* **1 :** to be able to do or bear without serious harm **2 :** to be able to pay for **3 :** to supply one with

[1]**af·front** *vb* **:** to insult openly

[2]**affront** *n* **:** [2]INSULT

afield *adv* **1 :** to, in, or into the countryside **2 :** away from home **3 :** outside of one's usual circle or way of doing **4 :** ASTRAY 2

afire *adj* **:** being on fire

aflame *adj* **:** burning with flames

afloat *adv or adj* **:** carried on or as if on water

aflut·ter *adj* **1 :** flapping quickly **2 :** very excited and nervous

afoot *adv or adj* **1 :** on foot **2 :** happening now **:** going on

afore·men·tioned *adj* **:** mentioned before

afore·said *adj* **:** named before

afraid *adj* **:** filled with fear

afresh *adv* **:** again from the beginning **:** from a new beginning

[1]**Af·ri·can** *n* **:** a person born or living in Africa

[2]**African** *adj* **:** of or relating to Africa or the Africans

African–American *n* **:** an American having African and especially black African ancestors — **African–American** *adj*

African violet *n* **:** a tropical African plant grown often for its showy white, pink, or purple flowers and its velvety leaves

Af·ro–Amer·i·can *n* **:** AFRICAN-AMERICAN — **Afro–American** *adj*

aft *adv* **:** toward or at the back part of a ship or the tail of an aircraft

[1]**af·ter** *adv* **:** following in time or place

[2]**after** *prep* **1 :** behind in time or place **2 :** for the reason of catching, seizing, or getting **3 :** with the name of

[3]**after** *conj* **:** following the time when

[4]**after** *adj* **1 :** later in time **2 :** located toward the back part of a ship or aircraft

af·ter·ef·fect *n* **:** an effect that follows its cause after some time has passed

af·ter·glow *n* **:** a glow remaining (as in the sky after sunset) where a light has disappeared

af·ter·life *n* : an existence after death
af·ter·math *n* : a usually bad result
af·ter·noon *n* : the part of the day between noon and evening
af·ter·thought *n* : a later thought about something one has done or said
af·ter·ward *or* **af·ter·wards** *adv* : at a later time
again *adv* **1** : once more : ANEW **2** : on the other hand **3** : in addition
against *prep* **1** : opposed to **2** : as protection from **3** : in or into contact with
agape *adj* : wide open
ag·ate *n* **1** : a mineral that is a quartz with colors arranged in stripes, cloudy masses, or mossy forms **2** : a child's marble of agate or of glass that looks like agate
aga·ve *n* : a plant that has sword-shaped leaves with spiny edges and is sometimes grown for its large stalks of flowers
[1]**age** *n* **1** : the time from birth to a specified date **2** : the time of life when a person receives full legal rights **3** : normal lifetime **4** : the later part of life **5** : a period of time associated with a special person or feature **6** : a long period of time
[2]**age** *vb* **aged; ag·ing** *or* **age·ing** **1** : to grow old or cause to grow old **2** : to remain or cause to remain undisturbed until fit for use : MATURE
-age *n suffix* **1** : collection **2** : action : process **3** : result of **4** : rate of **5** : house or place of **6** : state : rank **7** : fee : charge
aged *adj* **1** : very old **2** : of age
age·less *adj* : not growing old or showing the effects of age — **age·less·ly** *adv*
agen·cy *n, pl* **agen·cies** **1** : a person or thing through which power is used or something is achieved **2** : the office or function of an agent **3** : an establishment doing business for another **4** : a part of a government that runs projects in a certain area
agen·da *n* : a list of things to be done or talked about
agent *n* **1** : something that produces an effect **2** : a person who acts or does business for another
ag·gra·vate *vb* **ag·gra·vat·ed; ag·gra·vat·ing** **1** : to make worse or more serious **2** : to make angry by bothering again and again
ag·gra·va·tion *n* **1** : an act or the result of aggravating **2** : something that aggravates
[1]**ag·gre·gate** *adj* : formed by the collection of units or particles into one mass or sum
[2]**ag·gre·gate** *vb* **ag·gre·gat·ed; ag·gre·gat·ing** : to collect or gather into a mass or whole
[3]**ag·gre·gate** *n* **1** : a mass or body of units or parts **2** : the whole sum or amount
ag·gre·ga·tion *n* **1** : the collecting of units or parts into a mass or whole **2** : a group, body, or mass composed of many distinct parts
ag·gres·sion *n* : an attack made without reasonable cause
ag·gres·sive *adj* **1** : showing a readiness to attack others **2** : practicing aggression **3** : being forceful and sometimes pushy — **ag·gres·sive·ly** *adv* — **ag·gres·sive·ness** *n*
ag·gres·sor *n* : a person or a country that attacks without reasonable cause
ag·grieved *adj* **1** : having a troubled or unhappy mind **2** : having cause for complaint
aghast *adj* : struck with terror or amazement
ag·ile *adj* **1** : able to move quickly and easily **2** : having a quick mind — **ag·ile·ly** *adv*
agil·i·ty *n* : the ability to move quickly and easily
aging *present participle of* AGE
ag·i·tate *vb* **ag·i·tat·ed; ag·i·tat·ing** **1** : to move with an irregular rapid motion **2** : to stir up : EXCITE **3** : to try to stir up public feeling — **ag·i·ta·tor** *n*
ag·i·ta·tion *n* : the act of agitating : the state of being agitated
agleam *adj* : giving off gleams of light
aglow *adj* : glowing with light or color
ago *adv* : before this time
agog *adj* : full of excitement
ag·o·nize *vb* **ag·o·nized; ag·o·niz·ing** : to suffer greatly in body or mind
ag·o·ny *n, pl* **ag·o·nies** : great pain of body or mind
agree *vb* **agreed; agree·ing** **1** : to give one's approval or permission **2** : to have the same opinion **3** : ADMIT 3 **4** : to be alike **5** : to come to an understanding **6** : to be fitting or healthful
agree·able *adj* **1** : pleasing to the mind or senses **2** : willing to agree — **agree·able·ness** *n* — **agree·ably** *adv*
agree·ment *n* **1** : the act or fact of agreeing **2** : an arrangement made about action to be taken
ag·ri·cul·tur·al *adj* : of, relating to, or used in agriculture
ag·ri·cul·ture *n* : the cultivating of the soil, producing of crops, and raising of livestock
aground *adv or adj* : on or onto the shore or the bottom of a body of water
ah *interj* — used to express delight, relief, disappointment, or scorn
aha *interj* — used to express surprise, triumph, or scorn
ahead *adv or adj* **1** : in or toward the front **2** : into or for the future
ahead of *prep* **1** : in front of **2** : earlier than
ahoy *interj* — used in calling out to a passing ship or boat
[1]**aid** *vb* : [1]HELP 1, ASSIST
[2]**aid** *n* **1** : the act of helping **2** : help given **3**

: someone or something that is of help or assistance

aide *n* : a person who acts as an assistant

AIDS *n* : a serious disease of the human immune system in which large numbers of the cells that help the body fight infection are destroyed by the HIV virus carried in the blood and other fluids of the body

ail *vb* **1 :** to be wrong with **2 :** to suffer especially with ill health

ai·le·ron *n* : a movable part of an airplane wing that is used to steer it to one side or the other

ail·ment *n* : SICKNESS 2

[1]**aim** *vb* **1 :** to point a weapon toward an object **2 :** INTEND **3 :** to direct to or toward a specified object or goal

[2]**aim** *n* **1 :** the directing of a weapon or a missile at a mark **2 :** [1]PURPOSE

aim·less *adj* : lacking purpose — **aim·less·ly** *adv* — **aim·less·ness** *n*

[1]**air** *n* **1 :** the invisible mixture of odorless tasteless gases that surrounds the earth **2 :** air that is compressed **3 :** outward appearance **4 :** AIRCRAFT **5 :** AVIATION **6 :** a radio or television system **7 airs** *pl* : an artificial way of acting

[2]**air** *vb* **1 :** to place in the air for cooling, freshening, or cleaning **2 :** to make known in public

air bag *n* : an automobile safety device consisting of a bag that will inflate automatically in front of a rider to act as a cushion in an accident

air base *n* : a base of operations for military aircraft

air–con·di·tion *vb* : to equip with a device for cleaning air and controlling its humidity and temperature — **air con·di·tion·er** *n* — **air–con·di·tion·ing** *n*

air·craft *n, pl* **aircraft :** a vehicle (as a balloon, airplane, or helicopter) that can travel through the air and that is supported either by its own lightness or by the action of the air against its surfaces

air·drome *n* : AIRPORT

air·field *n* **1 :** the landing field of an airport **2 :** AIRPORT

air force *n* : the military organization of a nation for air warfare

air lane *n* : AIRWAY 2

air·lift *n* : a system of moving people or cargo by aircraft usually to or from an area that cannot be reached otherwise

air·line *n* : a system of transportation by aircraft including its routes, equipment, and workers

air·lin·er *n* : a large passenger airplane flown by an airline

[1]**air·mail** *n* **1 :** the system of carrying mail by airplanes **2 :** mail carried by airplanes

[2]**airmail** *vb* : to send by airmail

air·man *n, pl* **air·men 1 :** an enlisted person in the Air Force in one of the ranks below sergeant **2 :** AVIATOR

airman basic *n* : an enlisted person of the lowest rank in the Air Force

airman first class *n* : an enlisted person in the Air Force ranking above an airman second class

airman second class *n* : an enlisted person in the Air Force ranking above an airman basic

air·plane *n* : an aircraft with a fixed wing that is heavier than air, driven by a propeller or jet engine, and supported by the action of the air against its wings

air·port *n* : a place either on land or water that is kept for the landing and takeoff of aircraft and for receiving and sending off passengers and cargo

air·ship *n* : an aircraft lighter than air that is kept in the air by a container filled with gas and has an engine, propeller, and rudder

air·sick *adj* : sick to one's stomach while riding in an airplane because of its motion — **air·sick·ness** *n*

air·strip *n* : a runway without places (as hangars) for the repair of aircraft or shelter of passengers or cargo

air·tight *adj* : so tight that no air can get in or out — **air·tight·ness** *n*

air·wave *n* : the radio waves used in radio and television transmission — usually used in pl.

air·way *n* **1 :** a place for a current of air to pass through **2 :** a regular route for aircraft **3 :** AIRLINE

airy *adj* **air·i·er; air·i·est 1 :** of, relating to, or living in the air **2 :** open to the air : BREEZY **3 :** like air in lightness and delicacy

aisle *n* : a passage between sections of seats (as in a church or theater)

ajar *adv or adj* : slightly open

akim·bo *adv or adj* : with hands on hips

akin *adj* **1 :** related by blood **2 :** SIMILAR

[1]**-al** *adj suffix* : of, relating to, or showing

[2]**-al** *n suffix* : action : process

al·a·bas·ter *n* : a smooth usually white stone used for carving

à la carte *adv or adj* : with a separate price for each item on the menu

alac·ri·ty *n* : a cheerful readiness to do something

[1]**alarm** *n* **1 :** a warning of danger **2 :** a device (as a bell) that warns or signals people **3 :** the fear caused by sudden danger

[2]**alarm** *vb* : to cause a sense of danger in : FRIGHTEN

alarm clock *n* **:** a clock that can be set to sound an alarm at any desired time

alas *interj* — used to express unhappiness, pity, or worry

al·ba·tross *n* **:** a very large seabird with webbed feet

al·bi·no *n, pl* **al·bi·nos 1 :** a person or an animal that has little or no coloring matter in skin, hair, and eyes **2 :** a plant with little or no coloring matter

al·bum *n* **1 :** a book with blank pages in which to put a collection (as of photographs, stamps, or autographs) **2 :** one or more recordings (as on tape or disk) produced as one unit

al·bu·men *n* **1 :** the white of an egg **2 :** ALBUMIN

al·bu·min *n* **:** any of various proteins that are soluble in water and occur in plant and animal tissues

al·co·hol *n* **1 :** a colorless flammable liquid that in one form is the substance in fermented and distilled liquors (as beer, wine, or whiskey) that can make one drunk **2 :** a drink containing alcohol

¹al·co·hol·ic *adj* **1 :** of, relating to, or containing alcohol **2 :** affected with alcoholism

²alcoholic *n* **:** a person affected with alcoholism

al·co·hol·ism *n* **:** a sickness of body and mind caused by too much use of alcoholic drinks

al·cove *n* **:** a small part of a room set back from the rest of it

al·der *n* **:** a tree or shrub related to the birches that has toothed leaves and grows in moist soil

al·der·man *n* **:** a member of a lawmaking body in a city

ale *n* **:** an alcoholic drink made from malt and flavored with hops that is usually more bitter than beer

¹alert *adj* **1 :** watchful and ready to meet danger **2 :** quick to understand and act **3 :** ACTIVE 3, BRISK — **alert·ly** *adv* — **alert·ness** *n*

²alert *n* **1 :** a signal (as an alarm) of danger **2 :** the period during which an alert is in effect — **on the alert :** watchful against danger

³alert *vb* **:** to call to a state of readiness **:** WARN

al·fal·fa *n* **:** a plant with purple flowers that is related to the clovers and is grown as a food for horses and cattle

al·ga *n, pl* **al·gae :** any of a large group of simple plants and plant-like organisms that include the seaweeds and that include the seaweeds and that produce chlorophyll like plants but do not produce seeds and cannot be divided into roots, stems, and leaves

al·ge·bra *n* **:** a branch of mathematics in which symbols (as letters and numbers) are combined according to the rules of arithmetic

¹alias *adv* **:** otherwise known as

²alias *n* **:** a false name

¹al·i·bi *n, pl* **al·i·bis 1 :** the explanation given by a person accused of a crime that he or she was somewhere else when the crime was committed **2 :** ²EXCUSE 2

²alibi *vb* **al·i·bied; al·i·bi·ing 1 :** to offer an excuse **2 :** to make an excuse for

¹alien *adj* **:** FOREIGN 2

²alien *n* **:** a resident who was born elsewhere and is not a citizen of the country in which he or she now lives

alien·ate *vb* **alien·at·ed; alien·at·ing :** to cause (one who used to be friendly or loyal) to become unfriendly or disloyal

¹alight *vb* **alight·ed** *also* **alit; alight·ing 1 :** to get down **:** DISMOUNT **2 :** to come down from the air and settle

²alight *adj* **:** full of light **:** lighted up

align *vb* **:** to bring into line — **align·er** *n* — **align·ment** *n*

¹alike *adv* **:** in the same way

²alike *adj* **:** being like each other — **alike·ness** *n*

al·i·men·ta·ry *adj* **:** of or relating to food and nourishment

alimentary canal *n* **:** a long tube made up of the esophagus, stomach, and intestine into which food is taken and digested and from which wastes are passed out

al·i·mo·ny *n* **:** money for living expenses paid regularly by one spouse to another after their legal separation or divorce

alit *past of* ALIGHT

alive *adj* **1 :** having life **:** not dead **2 :** being in force, existence, or operation **3 :** aware of the existence of — **alive·ness** *n*

al·ka·li *n, pl* **al·ka·lies** *or* **al·ka·lis 1 :** any of numerous substances that have a bitter taste and react with an acid to form a salt **2 :** a salt or a mixture of salts sometimes found in large amounts in the soil of dry regions

al·ka·line *adj* **:** of or relating to an alkali

¹all *adj* **1 :** the whole of **2 :** the greatest possible **3 :** every one of

²all *adv* **1 :** COMPLETELY **2 :** so much **3 :** for each side

³all *pron* **1 :** the whole number or amount **2 :** EVERYTHING

Al·lah *n* **:** the Supreme Being of Muslims

all–around *adj* **1 :** having ability in many areas **2 :** useful in many ways

al·lay *vb* **1 :** to make less severe **2 :** to put to rest

al·lege *vb* **al·leged; al·leg·ing :** to state as fact but without proof

al·le·giance *n* **:** loyalty and service to a group, country, or idea

al·le·lu·ia *interj* : HALLELUJAH

al·ler·gen *n* : a substance that causes an allergic reaction

al·ler·gic *adj* : of, relating to, causing, or affected by allergy

al·ler·gist *n* : a medical doctor who specializes in treating allergies

al·ler·gy *n, pl* **al·ler·gies** : a condition in which a person is made sick by something that is harmless to most people

al·le·vi·ate *vb* **al·le·vi·at·ed; al·le·vi·at·ing** : to make easier to put up with

al·ley *n, pl* **al·leys** **1** : a narrow passageway between buildings **2** : a special narrow wooden floor on which balls are rolled in bowling

al·li·ance *n* **1** : connection between families, groups, or individuals **2** : an association formed by two or more nations for assistance and protection **3** : a treaty of alliance

al·lied *adj* **1** : being connected or related in some way **2** : joined in alliance

al·li·ga·tor *n* : a large four-footed water animal related to the snakes and lizards

all·o·sau·rus *n* : any of several very large meat-eating dinosaurs that were related to the tyrannosaur

al·lot *vb* **al·lot·ted; al·lot·ting** : to give out as a share or portion

al·lot·ment *n* **1** : the act of allotting **2** : something that is allotted

al·low *vb* **1** : to assign as a share or suitable amount (as of time or money) **2** : to take into account **3** : to accept as true : CONCEDE **4** : to give permission to **5** : to fail to prevent **6** : to make allowance

al·low·able *adj* : not forbidden

al·low·ance *n* **1** : a share given out **2** : a sum given as repayment or for expenses **3** : the taking into account of things that could affect a result

al·loy *n* : a substance made of two or more metals melted together

all right *adj or adv* **1** : satisfactory in quality or condition **2** : very well

all–round *adj* : ALL-AROUND

all–star *adj* : made up mainly or entirely of outstanding participants

al·lude *vb* **al·lud·ed; al·lud·ing** : to talk about or hint at without mentioning directly

al·lure *vb* **al·lured; al·lur·ing** : to try to influence by offering what seems to be a benefit or pleasure

al·lu·sion *n* : an act of alluding or of hinting at something

¹al·ly *vb* **al·lied; al·ly·ing** : to form a connection between : join in an alliance

²al·ly *n, pl* **allies** : one (as a person or a nation) associated or united with another in a common purpose

al·ma·nac *n* : a book containing a calendar of days, weeks, and months and usually facts about weather and astronomy and information of general interest

al·mighty *adj, often cap* : having absolute power over all

al·mond *n* : a nut that is the edible kernel of a small tree related to the peach

al·most *adv* : only a little less than : very nearly

alms *n, pl* **alms** : something and especially money given to help the poor : CHARITY

aloft *adv or adj* **1** : at or to a great height **2** : in the air and especially in flight **3** : at, on, or to the top of the mast or the higher rigging of a ship

¹alone *adj* **1** : separated from others **2** : not including anyone or anything else

²alone *adv* **1** : and nothing or no one else **2** : without company or help

¹along *prep* **1** : on or near in a lengthwise direction **2** : at a point on

²along *adv* **1** : farther forward or on **2** : as a companion or associate **3** : throughout the time

along·shore *adv or adj* : along the shore or coast

¹along·side *adv* : along or by the side

²alongside *prep* : parallel to

¹aloof *adv* : at a distance

²aloof *adj* : RESERVED 1 — **aloof·ly** *adv* — **aloof·ness** *n*

aloud *adv* : using the voice so as to be clearly heard

al·paca *n* : a South American animal related to the camel and llama that is raised for its long woolly hair which is woven into warm strong cloth

al·pha·bet *n* : the letters used in writing a language arranged in their regular order

al·pha·bet·i·cal *or* **al·pha·bet·ic** *adj* : arranged in the order of the letters of the alphabet — **al·pha·bet·i·cal·ly** *adv*

al·pha·bet·ize *vb* **al·pha·bet·ized; al·pha·bet·iz·ing** : to arrange in alphabetical order

al·ready *adv* : before a certain time : by this time

al·so *adv* : in addition : TOO

al·tar *n* **1** : a usually raised place on which sacrifices are offered **2** : a platform or table used as a center of worship

al·ter *vb* : to change partly but not completely

al·ter·ation *n* **1** : a making or becoming different in some respects **2** : the result of altering : MODIFICATION

¹al·ter·nate *adj* **1** : occurring or following by turns **2** : arranged one above, beside, or next to another **3** : every other : every second — **al·ter·nate·ly** *adv*

[2]**al·ter·nate** *vb* **al·ter·nat·ed; al·ter·nat·ing :** to take place or cause to take place by turns

[3]**al·ter·nate** *n* **:** a person named to take the place of another whenever necessary

alternating current *n* **:** an electric current that reverses its direction of flow regularly many times per second

al·ter·na·tion *n* **:** the act, process, or result of alternating

[1]**al·ter·na·tive** *adj* **:** offering or expressing a choice — **al·ter·na·tive·ly** *adv*

[2]**alternative** *n* **1 :** a chance to choose between two things **2 :** one of the things between which a choice is to be made

al·though *conj* **:** in spite of the fact that

al·ti·tude *n* **1 :** height above a certain level and especially above sea level **2 :** the perpendicular distance from the base of a geometric figure to the vertex or to the side parallel to the base

al·to *n, pl* **altos 1 :** the lowest female singing voice **2 :** the second highest part in four-part harmony **3 :** a singer or an instrument having an alto range or part

al·to·geth·er *adv* **1 :** COMPLETELY **2 :** on the whole

al·tru·ism *n* **:** unselfish interest in others

al·um *n* **:** either of two aluminum compounds that have a sweetish-sourish taste and puckering effect on the mouth and are used in medicine (as to stop bleeding)

alu·mi·num *n* **:** a silver-white light metallic chemical element that is easily worked, conducts electricity well, resists weathering, and is the most plentiful metal in the earth's crust

alum·na *n, pl* **alum·nae :** a girl or woman who has attended or has graduated from a school, college, or university

alum·nus *n, pl* **alum·ni :** one who has attended or has graduated from a school, college, or university

al·ways *adv* **1 :** at all times **2 :** throughout all time **:** FOREVER

am *present 1st sing of* BE

amal·gam·ation *n* **:** the combining of different elements into a single body

amass *vb* **:** to collect or gather together

[1]**am·a·teur** *n* **1 :** a person who takes part in sports or occupations for pleasure and not for pay **2 :** a person who takes part in something without having experience or skill in it — **am·a·teur·ish** *adj*

[2]**amateur** *adj* **:** of, relating to, or done by amateurs **:** not professional

amaze *vb* **amazed; amaz·ing :** to surprise or puzzle very much

amaze·ment *n* **:** great surprise

am·bas·sa·dor *n* **:** a person sent as the chief representative of his or her government in another country — **am·bas·sa·dor·ship** *n*

am·ber *n* **1 :** a hard yellowish to brownish clear substance that is a fossil resin from trees long dead, takes a polish, and is used for ornamental objects (as beads) **2 :** a dark orange yellow

ambi- *prefix* **:** both

am·bi·dex·trous *adj* **:** using both hands with equal ease — **am·bi·dex·trous·ly** *adv*

am·bi·gu·i·ty *n, pl* **am·bi·gu·i·ties :** the fact or state of being ambiguous

am·big·u·ous *adj* **:** able to be understood in more than one way — **am·big·u·ous·ly** *adv*

am·bi·tion *n* **1 :** a desire for success, honor, or power **2 :** the aim or object one tries for

am·bi·tious *adj* **1 :** possessing ambition **2 :** showing ambition — **am·bi·tious·ly** *adv*

[1]**am·ble** *vb* **am·bled; am·bling :** to go at an amble

[2]**amble** *n* **:** a slow easy way of walking

am·bu·lance *n* **:** a vehicle meant to carry sick or injured persons

[1]**am·bush** *vb* **:** to attack from an ambush

[2]**ambush** *n* **:** a hidden place from which a surprise attack can be made

amen *interj* — used to express agreement (as after a prayer or a statement of opinion)

ame·na·ble *adj* **:** readily giving in or agreeing

amend *vb* **1 :** to change for the better **:** IMPROVE **2 :** to change the wording or meaning of **:** ALTER

amend·ment *n* **:** a change in wording or meaning especially in a law, bill, or motion

amends *n sing or pl* **:** something done or given by a person to make up for a loss or injury he or she has caused

ame·ni·ty *n, pl* **ame·ni·ties 1 :** the quality of being pleasant or agreeable **2** *amenities pl* **:** something (as good manners or household appliances) that makes life easier or more pleasant

[1]**Amer·i·can** *n* **1 :** a person born or living in North or South America **2 :** a citizen of the United States

[2]**American** *adj* **1 :** of or relating to North or South America or their residents **2 :** of or relating to the United States or its citizens

American Indian *n* **:** a member of any of the first peoples to live in North and South America except usually the Eskimos

am·e·thyst *n* **:** a clear purple or bluish violet quartz used as a gem

ami·a·ble *adj* **:** having a friendly and pleasant manner — **ami·a·bly** *adv*

am·i·ca·ble *adj* **:** showing kindness or goodwill — **am·i·ca·bly** *adv*

amid *or* **amidst** *prep* **:** in or into the middle of

amid·ships *adv* **:** in or near the middle of a ship

ami·no acid *n* **:** any of numerous acids that contain carbon and nitrogen, include some which are the building blocks of protein, and are made by living plant or animal cells or obtained from the diet

[1]amiss *adv* **:** in the wrong way

[2]amiss *adj* **:** not right **:** WRONG

am·i·ty *n, pl* **am·i·ties :** FRIENDSHIP

am·me·ter *n* **:** an instrument for measuring electric current in amperes

am·mo·nia *n* **1 :** a colorless gas that is a compound of nitrogen and hydrogen, has a sharp smell and taste, can be easily made liquid by cold and pressure, and is used in making ice, fertilizers, and explosives **2 :** a solution of ammonia and water

am·mu·ni·tion *n* **1 :** objects fired from guns **2 :** explosive objects used in war

am·ne·sia *n* **:** an abnormal and usually complete loss of one's memory

amoe·ba *n, pl* **amoe·bas** *or* **amoe·bae :** a tiny water animal that is a single cell which flows about and takes in food

among *also* **amongst** *prep* **1 :** in or through the middle of **2 :** in the presence of **:** WITH **3 :** through all or most of **4 :** in shares to each of

[1]amount *vb* **1 :** to add up **2 :** to be the same in meaning or effect

[2]amount *n* **:** the total number or quantity

am·pere *n* **:** a unit for measuring the strength of an electric current

am·per·sand *n* **:** a character & standing for the word *and*

am·phet·amine *n* **:** a drug that makes the nervous system more active

am·phib·i·an *n* **1 :** any of a group of cold-blooded animals (as frogs and toads) that have gills and live in water as larvae but breathe air as adults **2 :** an airplane designed to take off from and land on either land or water

am·phib·i·ous *adj* **1 :** able to live both on land and in water **2 :** meant to be used on both land and water **3 :** made by land, sea, and air forces acting together — **am·phib·i·ous·ly** *adv* — **am·phib·i·ous·ness** *n*

am·phi·the·ater *n* **:** an arena with seats rising in curved rows around an open space

am·ple *adj* **:** more than enough in amount or size — **am·ply** *adv*

am·pli·fy *vb* **am·pli·fied; am·pli·fy·ing 1 :** to add to **2 :** to make louder or greater — **am·pli·fi·er** *n*

am·pu·tate *vb* **am·pu·tat·ed; am·pu·tat·ing :** to cut off

am·u·let *n* **:** a small object worn as a charm against evil

amuse *vb* **amused; amus·ing 1 :** to entertain with something pleasant **2 :** to please the sense of humor of

amuse·ment *n* **1 :** something that amuses or entertains **2 :** the condition of being amused

amusement park *n* **:** a park with many rides (as roller coasters) and games for entertainment

an *indefinite article* **:** [2]A — used before words beginning with a vowel sound

[1]-an *or* **-ian** *also* **-ean** *n suffix* **1 :** one that belongs to **2 :** one skilled in or specializing in

[2]-an *or* **-ian** *also* **-ean** *adj suffix* **1 :** of or relating to **2 :** like **:** resembling

an·a·bol·ic steroid *n* **:** a hormone that is used in medicine to help tissue grow and is sometimes abused by athletes to increase muscle size and strength even though it may have unwanted or harmful effects (as stunted growth in teenagers)

an·a·con·da *n* **:** a large South American snake of the boa family

anal·y·sis *n, pl* **anal·y·ses :** an examination of something to find out how it is made or works or what it is

an·a·lyst *n* **:** a person who analyzes or is skilled in analysis

an·a·lyt·ic *or* **an·a·lyt·i·cal** *adj* **:** of, relating to, or skilled in analysis — **an·a·lyt·i·cal·ly** *adv*

an·a·lyze *vb* **an·a·lyzed; an·a·lyz·ing :** to examine something to find out what it is or what makes it work

an·ar·chist *n* **:** a person who believes in or practices anarchy

an·ar·chy *n* **1 :** the condition of a country where there is no government or law and order **2 :** a state of confused disorder or lawlessness

an·a·tom·i·cal *or* **an·a·tom·ic** *adj* **:** of or relating to anatomy

anat·o·my *n, pl* **anat·o·mies 1 :** a science that has to do with the structure of the body **2 :** the structural makeup especially of a person or animal

-ance *n suffix* **1 :** action or process **2 :** quality or state **3 :** amount or degree

an·ces·tor *n* **:** one from whom an individual is descended

an·ces·tral *adj* **:** of, relating to, or coming from an ancestor

an·ces·try *n, pl* **an·ces·tries :** one's ancestors

[1]an·chor *n* **1 :** a heavy iron or steel device attached to a ship by a cable or chain and so made that when thrown overboard it digs into the bottom and holds the ship in place **2 :** something that keeps something else fastened or steady

[2]anchor *vb* **1 :** to hold or become held in place with an anchor **2 :** to fasten tightly

an·chor·age *n* **:** a place where boats can be anchored

[1]an·cient *adj* **1 :** very old **2 :** of or relating to a time long past or to those living in such a time

[2]ancient *n* **1 :** a very old person **2 ancients** *pl* **:** the civilized peoples of ancient times and especially of Greece and Rome

-an·cy *n suffix, pl* **-an·cies :** quality or state

and *conj* **1 :** added to **2 :** AS WELL AS, ALSO — **and so forth :** and others or more of the same kind — **and so on :** AND SO FORTH

and·iron *n* **:** one of a pair of metal supports for firewood in a fireplace

an·ec·dote *n* **:** a short story about something interesting or funny in a person's life

ane·mia *n* **:** a sickness in which there is too little blood or too few red blood cells or too little hemoglobin in the blood

an·e·mom·e·ter *n* **:** an instrument for measuring the speed of the wind

anem·o·ne *n* **:** a plant related to the buttercup that blooms in spring and is often grown for its large white or colored flowers

an·es·the·sia *n* **:** loss of feeling or consciousness

[1]an·es·thet·ic *adj* **:** of, relating to, or capable of producing anesthesia

[2]anesthetic *n* **:** something that produces anesthesia

anew *adv* **1 :** over again **2 :** in a new or different form

an·gel *n* **1 :** a spiritual being serving God especially as a messenger **2 :** a person thought to be like an angel (as in goodness or beauty)

[1]an·ger *vb* **:** to make strongly displeased

[2]anger *n* **:** a strong feeling of displeasure and often of active opposition to an insult, injury, or injustice

[1]an·gle *n* **1 :** a sharp corner **2 :** the figure formed by two lines meeting at a point **3 :** POINT OF VIEW

[2]angle *vb* **an·gled; an·gling :** to turn, move, or direct at an angle

[3]angle *vb* **an·gled; an·gling 1 :** to fish with hook and line **2 :** to try to get what one wants in a sly way

an·gler *n* **:** a person who fishes with hook and line especially for pleasure

an·gle·worm *n* **:** EARTHWORM

an·gling *n* **:** fishing with hook and line for pleasure

An·glo- *prefix* **1 :** English **2 :** English and

[1]An·glo–Sax·on *n* **1 :** a member of the German people who conquered England in the fifth century A.D. **2 :** a person whose ancestors were English

[2]Anglo–Saxon *adj* **:** relating to the Anglo-Saxons

an·go·ra *n* **:** cloth or yarn made from the soft silky hair of a special usually white domestic rabbit (**Angora rabbit**) or from the long shiny wool of a goat (**Angora goat**)

an·gry *adj* **an·gri·er; an·gri·est :** feeling or showing anger — **an·gri·ly** *adv*

an·guish *n* **:** great pain or trouble of body or mind

an·guished *adj* **:** full of anguish

an·gu·lar *adj* **1 :** having angles or sharp corners **2 :** being lean and bony

an·i·mal *n* **1 :** any of the great group of living beings (as jellyfishes, crabs, birds, and people) that differ from plants typically in being able to move about, in not having cell walls made of cellulose, and in depending on plants and other animals as sources of food **2 :** any of the animals lower than humans in the natural order **3 :** MAMMAL

animal kingdom *n* **:** a basic group of natural objects that includes all living and extinct animals

[1]an·i·mate *adj* **:** having life

[2]an·i·mate *vb* **an·i·mat·ed; an·i·mat·ing 1 :** to give life or energy to **:** make alive or lively **2 :** to make appear to move

an·i·mat·ed *adj* **1 :** full of life and energy **:** LIVELY **2 :** appearing to be alive or moving

an·i·mos·i·ty *n, pl* **an·i·mos·i·ties :** [1]DISLIKE, HATRED

an·kle *n* **1 :** the joint between the foot and the leg **2 :** the area containing the ankle joint

an·klet *n* **:** a sock reaching slightly above the ankle

an·ky·lo·saur *n* **:** any of several plant-eating dinosaurs with bony plates covering the back

an·nals *n pl* **1 :** a record of events arranged in yearly sequence **2 :** historical records **:** HISTORY

an·neal *vb* **:** to heat (as glass or steel) and then cool so as to toughen and make less brittle

[1]an·nex *vb* **:** to add (something) to something else usually so as to become a part of it

[2]an·nex *n* **:** something (as a wing of a building) added on

an·nex·ation *n* **:** an annexing especially of new territory

an·ni·hi·late *vb* **an·ni·hi·lat·ed; an·ni·hi·lat·ing :** to destroy entirely **:** put completely out of existence

an·ni·ver·sa·ry *n, pl* **an·ni·ver·sa·ries :** the return every year of the date when something special (as a wedding) happened

an·nounce *vb* **an·nounced; an·nounc·ing 1 :** to make known publicly **2 :** to give notice of the arrival, presence, or readiness of

an·nounce·ment *n* **1 :** the act of announcing **2 :** a public notice announcing something

an·nounc·er *n* **:** a person who introduces

radio or television programs, makes announcements, or gives station identification

an·noy *vb* **:** to disturb or irritate especially by repeated disagreeable acts

an·noy·ance *n* **1 :** the act of annoying **2 :** the feeling of being annoyed **3 :** a source or cause of being annoyed

an·noy·ing *adj* **:** causing annoyance — **an·noy·ing·ly** *adv*

[1]an·nu·al *adj* **1 :** coming, happening, done, made, or given once a year **2 :** completing the life cycle in one growing season — **an·nu·al·ly** *adv*

[2]annual *n* **:** an annual plant

annual ring *n* **:** the layer of wood produced by one year's growth of a woody plant (as in the trunk of a tree)

an·nu·ity *n, pl* **an·nu·ities :** a sum of money paid at regular intervals

an·nul *vb* **an·nulled; an·nul·ling :** to cancel by law **:** take away the legal force of — **an·nul·ment** *n*

an·ode *n* **1 :** the positive electrode of an electrolytic cell **2 :** the negative end of a battery that is delivering electric current **3 :** the electron-collecting electrode of an electron tube

anoint *vb* **1 :** to rub or cover with oil or grease **2 :** to put oil on as part of a religious ceremony

anon·y·mous *adj* **1 :** not named or identified **2 :** made or done by someone unknown — **anon·y·mous·ly** *adv*

[1]an·oth·er *adj* **1 :** some other **2 :** one more

[2]another *pron* **1 :** one more **2 :** someone or something different

[1]an·swer *n* **1 :** something said or written in reply (as to a question) **2 :** a solution of a problem

[2]answer *vb* **1 :** to speak or write in reply to **2 :** to take responsibility **3 :** [1]SERVE 5, DO

an·swer·able *adj* **1 :** RESPONSIBLE 1 **2 :** possible to answer

answering machine *n* **:** a machine that receives telephone calls by playing a recorded message and usually also recording messages from callers

ant *n* **:** a small insect related to the bees and wasps that lives in colonies and forms nests in the ground or in wood in which it stores food and raises its young

ant- *see* ANTI-

[1]-ant *n suffix* **1 :** one that does or causes a certain thing **2 :** thing that is acted upon in a certain way

[2]-ant *adj suffix* **1 :** doing a certain thing or being a certain way **2 :** causing a certain action

an·tag·o·nism *n* **:** a state of not liking and being against something

an·tag·o·nist *n* **:** a person who is against something or someone else **:** OPPONENT

an·tag·o·nis·tic *adj* **:** being against something or someone **:** HOSTILE, UNFRIENDLY — **an·tag·o·nis·ti·cal·ly** *adv*

an·tag·o·nize *vb* **an·tag·o·nized; an·tag·o·niz·ing :** to stir up dislike or anger in

ant·arc·tic *adj, often cap* **:** of or relating to the south pole or to the region around it

ante- *prefix* **1 :** before in time **:** earlier **2 :** in front of

ant·eat·er *n* **:** any of several animals that have long noses and long sticky tongues and feed chiefly on ants

an·te·cham·ber *n* **:** ANTEROOM

an·te·lope *n* **:** any of a group of cud-chewing animals that have horns that extend upward and backward

an·ten·na *n* **1** *pl* **an·ten·nae :** one of two or four threadlike movable feelers on the head of insects or crustaceans (as lobsters) **2** *pl* **an·ten·nas :** a metallic device (as a rod or wire) for sending or receiving radio waves

an·te·room *n* **:** a room used as an entrance to another

an·them *n* **1 :** a sacred song usually sung by a church choir **2 :** a patriotic song of praise and love for one's country

an·ther *n* **:** the enlargement at the tip of a flower's stamen that contains pollen

ant·hill *n* **:** a mound of dirt thrown up by ants in digging their nest

an·thol·o·gy *n, pl* **an·thol·o·gies :** a collection of writings (as stories and poems)

an·thra·cite *n* **:** a hard glossy coal that burns without much smoke

an·thrax *n* **:** a dangerous bacterial disease of warm-blooded animals that can affect humans

an·thro·poid *adj* **:** looking somewhat like humans

an·thro·pol·o·gy *n* **:** a science that studies people and especially their history, development, distribution and culture

anti- *or* **ant-** *prefix* **1 :** opposite in kind, position, or action **2 :** hostile toward

an·ti·bi·ot·ic *n* **:** a substance produced by living things and especially by bacteria and fungi that is used to kill or prevent the growth of harmful germs

an·ti·body *n, pl* **an·ti·bod·ies :** a substance produced by the body that counteracts the effects of a disease germ or its poisons

an·tic *n* **:** a wildly playful or funny act or action

an·tic·i·pate *vb* **an·tic·i·pat·ed; an·tic·i·pat·ing 1 :** to foresee and deal with or provide for beforehand **2 :** to look forward to

an·tic·i·pa·tion *n* **1 :** an action that takes into account and deals with or prevents a later

action **2 :** pleasurable expectation **3 :** a picturing beforehand of a future event or state
an·ti·cy·clone *n* **:** a system of winds that is like a cyclone but that rotates about a center of high atmospheric pressure in a clockwise direction north of the equator and a counterclockwise direction south of the equator
an·ti·dote *n* **:** something used to reverse or prevent the action of a poison
an·ti·freeze *n* **:** a substance added to the liquid in an automobile radiator to prevent its freezing
an·ti·mo·ny *n* **:** a silvery white metallic chemical element
an·tip·a·thy *n, pl* **an·tip·a·thies :** a strong feeling of dislike
an·ti·quat·ed *adj* **:** OLD-FASHIONED 1, OBSOLETE
[1]an·tique *n* **:** an object (as a piece of furniture) made at an earlier time
[2]antique *adj* **:** belonging to or like a former style or fashion
an·tiq·ui·ty *n* **1 :** ancient times **2 :** very great age
[1]an·ti·sep·tic *adj* **:** killing or making harmless the germs that cause decay or sickness
[2]antiseptic *n* **:** an antiseptic substance
an·ti·so·cial *adj* **1 :** being against or bad for society **2 :** UNFRIENDLY
an·tith·e·sis *n, pl* **an·tith·e·ses :** the exact opposite
an·ti·tox·in *n* **:** a substance that is formed in the blood of one exposed to a disease and that prevents or acts against that disease
ant·ler *n* **:** the entire horn or a branch of the horn of an animal of the deer family — **antlered** *adj*
ant lion *n* **:** an insect having a larva form with long jaws that digs a cone-shaped hole in which it waits for prey (as ants)
an·to·nym *n* **:** a word of opposite meaning
an·vil *n* **:** an iron block on which pieces of metal are hammered into shape
anx·i·ety *n, pl* **anx·i·eties :** fear or nervousness about what might happen
anx·ious *adj* **1 :** afraid or nervous about what may happen **2 :** wanting very much **:** EAGER — **anx·ious·ly** *adv*
[1]any *adj* **1 :** whatever kind of **2 :** of whatever number or amount
[2]any *pron* **1 :** any individuals **2 :** any amount
[3]any *adv* **:** to the least amount or degree
any·body *pron* **:** ANYONE
any·how *adv* **1 :** in any way, manner, or order **2 :** at any rate **:** in any case
any·more *adv* **:** NOWADAYS
any·one *pron* **:** any person
any·place *adv* **:** in any place
any·thing *pron* **:** a thing of any kind
any·way *adv* **:** ANYHOW
any·where *adv* **:** in, at, or to any place
any·wise *adv* **:** in any way whatever
A1 *adj* **:** of the very best kind
aor·ta *n* **:** the main artery that carries blood from the heart for distribution to all parts of the body
apace *adv* **:** at a quick pace **:** FAST
apart *adv* **1 :** away from each other **2 :** as something separated **:** SEPARATELY **3 :** into parts **:** to pieces **4 :** one from another
apart·ment *n* **1 :** a room or set of rooms used as a home **2 :** a building divided into individual apartments
ap·a·thet·ic *adj* **:** having or showing little or no feeling or interest — **ap·a·thet·i·cal·ly** *adv*
ap·a·thy *n* **:** lack of feeling or of interest **:** INDIFFERENCE
apato·sau·rus *n* **:** BRONTOSAURUS
[1]ape *n* **:** any of a group of tailless animals (as gorillas or chimpanzees) that are most closely related to humans — **ape·like** *adj*
[2]ape *vb* **aped; ap·ing :** to imitate (someone) awkwardly
ap·er·ture *n* **:** an opening or open space **:** HOLE
apex *n, pl* **apex·es** *or* **api·ces :** the highest point **:** PEAK
aphid *n* **:** any of various small insects that suck the juices of plants
apiece *adv* **:** for each one
aplomb *n* **:** complete freedom from nervousness or uncertainty
apol·o·get·ic *adj* **:** sorry for having done something wrong — **apol·o·get·i·cal·ly** *adv*
apol·o·gize *vb* **apol·o·gized; apol·o·giz·ing :** to make an apology
apol·o·gy *n, pl* **apol·o·gies :** an expression of regret (as for a mistake or a rude remark)
apos·tle *n* **1 :** one of the twelve close followers of Jesus sent out to teach the gospel **2 :** the first Christian missionary to a region **3 :** the person who first puts forward an important belief or starts a great reform — **apostle·ship** *n*
apos·tro·phe *n* **:** a mark ’ used to show that letters or figures are missing (as in “can’t” for “cannot” or “ ’76” for “1776”) or to show the possessive case (as in “James’s”) or the plural of letters or figures (as in “cross your t’s”)
apoth·e·cary *n, pl* **apoth·e·car·ies :** DRUGGIST
ap·pall *vb* **:** to shock or overcome with horror
ap·pall·ing *adj* **:** being shocking and terrible
ap·pa·ra·tus *n, pl* **apparatus** *or* **ap·pa·ra·tus·es :** the equipment or material for a particular use or job
ap·par·el *n* **:** things that are worn **:** WEAR 2
ap·par·ent *adj* **1 :** open to view **:** VISIBLE **2**

: clear to the understanding : EVIDENT **3** : appearing to be real or true — **ap·par·ent·ly** *adv* — **ap·par·ent·ness** *n*

ap·pa·ri·tion *n* **1 :** an unusual or unexpected sight **2 :** GHOST

[1]**ap·peal** *n* **1 :** a legal action by which a case is brought to a higher court for review **2 :** an asking for something badly needed or wanted : PLEA **3 :** the power to cause enjoyment : ATTRACTION

[2]**appeal** *vb* **1 :** to take action to have a case or decision reviewed by a higher court **2 :** to ask for something badly needed or wanted **3** : to be pleasing or attractive

ap·pear *vb* **1 :** to come into sight **2 :** to present oneself **3 :** SEEM 1 **4 :** to come before the public **5 :** to come into existence

ap·pear·ance *n* **1 :** the act or an instance of appearing **2 :** way of looking

ap·pease *vb* **ap·peased; ap·peas·ing 1 :** to make calm or quiet **2 :** to give in to — **ap·pease·ment** *n* — **ap·peas·er** *n*

ap·pend *vb* **:** to add as something extra

ap·pend·age *n* **:** something (as a leg) attached to a larger or more important thing

ap·pen·di·ci·tis *n* **:** inflammation of the intestinal appendix

ap·pen·dix *n, pl* **ap·pen·dix·es** *or* **ap·pen·di·ces 1 :** a part of a book giving added and helpful information (as notes or tables) **2 :** a small tubelike part growing out from the intestine

ap·pe·tite *n* **1 :** a natural desire especially for food **2 :** [2]TASTE 4

ap·pe·tiz·er *n* **:** a food or drink usually served before a meal to make one hungrier

ap·pe·tiz·ing *adj* **:** pleasing to the appetite

ap·plaud *vb* **1 :** [1]PRAISE 1 **2 :** to show approval especially by clapping the hands

ap·plause *n* **:** approval shown especially by clapping the hands

ap·ple *n* **:** the round or oval fruit with red, yellow, or green skin of a spreading tree (**apple tree**) that is related to the rose

ap·pli·ance *n* **1 :** a device designed for a certain use **2 :** a piece of household or office equipment that runs on gas or electricity

ap·pli·ca·ble *adj* **:** capable of being put to use or put into practice

ap·pli·cant *n* **:** a person who applies for something (as a job)

ap·pli·ca·tion *n* **1 :** the act or an instance of applying **2 :** something put or spread on a surface **3 :** [1]REQUEST 1 **4 :** ability to be put to practical use

ap·pli·ca·tor *n* **:** a device for applying a substance (as medicine or polish)

ap·ply *vb* **ap·plied; ap·ply·ing 1 :** to put to use **2 :** to lay or spread on **3 :** to place in contact **4 :** to give one's full attention **5 :** to have relation or a connection **6 :** to request especially in writing

ap·point *vb* **1 :** to decide on usually from a position of authority **2 :** to choose for some duty, job, or office

ap·poin·tee *n* **:** a person appointed to an office or position

ap·point·ment *n* **1 :** the act or an instance of appointing **2 :** a position or office to which a person is named **3 :** an agreement to meet at a fixed time **4 appointments** *pl* **:** FURNISHINGS

ap·po·si·tion *n* **:** a grammatical construction in which a noun is followed by another that explains it

ap·pos·i·tive *n* **:** the second of a pair of nouns in apposition

ap·prais·al *n* **:** an act or instance of appraising

ap·praise *vb* **ap·praised; ap·prais·ing :** to set a value on

ap·pre·cia·ble *adj* **:** large enough to be noticed or measured — **ap·pre·cia·bly** *adv*

ap·pre·ci·ate *vb* **ap·pre·ci·at·ed; ap·pre·ci·at·ing 1 :** to admire greatly and with understanding **2 :** to be fully aware of **3 :** to be grateful for **4 :** to increase in number or value

ap·pre·ci·a·tion *n* **1 :** the act of appreciating **2** : awareness or understanding of worth or value **3 :** a rise in value

ap·pre·cia·tive *adj* **:** having or showing appreciation — **ap·pre·cia·tive·ly** *adv*

ap·pre·hend *vb* **1 :** [1]ARREST 2 **2 :** to look forward to with fear and uncertainty **3 :** UNDERSTAND 1

ap·pre·hen·sion *n* **1 :** [2]ARREST **2 :** an understanding of something **3 :** fear of or uncertainty about what may be coming

ap·pre·hen·sive *adj* **:** fearful of what may be coming — **ap·pre·hen·sive·ly** *adv* — **ap·pre·hen·sive·ness** *n*

[1]**ap·pren·tice** *n* **:** a person who is learning a trade or art by experience under a skilled worker

[2]**apprentice** *vb* **ap·pren·ticed; ap·pren·tic·ing :** to set at work as an apprentice

ap·pren·tice·ship *n* **1 :** service as an apprentice **2 :** the period during which a person serves as an apprentice

[1]**ap·proach** *vb* **1 :** to come near or nearer : draw close **2 :** to begin to deal with

[2]**approach** *n* **1 :** an act or instance of approaching **2 :** a beginning step **3 :** a way (as a path or road) to get to some place

ap·proach·able *adj* **:** easy to meet or deal with

[1]**ap·pro·pri·ate** *vb* **ap·pro·pri·at·ed; ap·pro·pri·at·ing 1 :** to take possession of **2 :** to set apart for a certain purpose or use

[2]**ap·pro·pri·ate** *adj* **:** especially suitable — **ap·pro·pri·ate·ly** *adv* — **ap·pro·pri·ate·ness** *n*

ap·pro·pri·a·tion *n* **1 :** an act or instance of appropriating **2 :** a sum of money appropriated for a specific use

ap·prov·al *n* **:** an act or instance of approving

ap·prove *vb* **ap·proved; ap·prov·ing 1 :** to think well of **2 :** to accept as satisfactory

[1]**ap·prox·i·mate** *adj* **:** nearly correct or exact — **ap·prox·i·mate·ly** *adv*

[2]**ap·prox·i·mate** *vb* **ap·prox·i·mat·ed; ap·prox·i·mat·ing 1 :** to bring near or close **2 :** to come near **:** APPROACH

ap·prox·i·ma·tion *n* **1 :** a coming near or close (as in value) **2 :** an estimate or figure that is almost exact

apri·cot *n* **:** a small oval orange-colored fruit that looks like the related peach and plum

April *n* **:** the fourth month of the year

apron *n* **1 :** a piece of cloth worn on the front of the body to keep the clothing from getting dirty **2 :** a paved area for parking or handling airplanes

apt *adj* **1 :** just right **:** SUITABLE **2 :** having a tendency **:** LIKELY **3 :** quick to learn — **apt·ly** *adv* — **apt·ness** *n*

ap·ti·tude *n* **1 :** ability to learn **2 :** natural ability **:** TALENT

aqua *n* **:** a light greenish blue

aqua·ma·rine *n* **:** a transparent gem that is blue, blue-green, or green

aqua·naut *n* **:** a person who lives for a long while in an underwater shelter used as a base for research

aquar·i·um *n* **1 :** a container (as a tank or bowl) in which living water animals or water plants are kept **2 :** a building in which water animals or water plants are exhibited

Aquar·i·us *n* **1 :** a constellation between Capricorn and Pisces imagined as a man pouring water **2 :** the eleventh sign of the zodiac or a person born under this sign

aquat·ic *adj* **:** growing, living, or done in water

aq·ue·duct *n* **:** an artificial channel (as a structure that takes the water of a canal across a river or hollow) for carrying flowing water from one place to another

aque·ous *adj* **1 :** of, relating to, or like water **2 :** made of, by, or with water

-ar *adj suffix* **:** of or relating to

[1]**Ar·ab** *n* **1 :** a person born or living in the Arabian Peninsula **2 :** a member of a people that speaks Arabic

[2]**Arab** *adj* **:** of or relating to the Arabs **:** ARABIAN

[1]**Ara·bi·an** *n* **:** [1]ARAB 1

[2]**Arabian** *adj* **:** of or relating to the Arabian Peninsula or Arabs

[1]**Ar·a·bic** *n* **:** a language spoken in the Arabian Peninsula, Iraq, Jordan, Lebanon, Syria, Egypt, and parts of northern Africa

[2]**Arabic** *adj* **1 :** of or relating to Arabia, the Arabs, or Arabic **2 :** expressed in or making use of Arabic numerals

Arabic numeral *n* **:** one of the number symbols 1, 2, 3, 4, 5, 6, 7, 8, 9, and 0

ar·a·ble *adj* **:** fit for or cultivated by plowing **:** suitable for producing crops

Arap·a·ho *or* **Arap·a·hoe** *n, pl* **Arapaho** *or* **Arapahos** *or* **Arapahoe** *or* **Arapahoes :** a member of an Indian people of the plains region of the United States and Canada

ar·bi·ter *n* **1 :** ARBITRATOR **2 :** a person having the power to decide what is right or proper

ar·bi·trary *adj* **1 :** coming from or given to free exercise of the will without thought of fairness or right **2 :** seeming to have been chosen by chance — **ar·bi·trari·ly** *adv* — **ar·bi·trar·i·ness** *n*

ar·bi·trate *vb* **ar·bi·trat·ed; ar·bi·trat·ing 1 :** to settle a disagreement after hearing the arguments of both sides **2 :** to refer a dispute to others for settlement

ar·bi·tra·tion *n* **:** the settling of a disagreement in which both sides present their arguments to a third person or group for decision

ar·bi·tra·tor *n* **:** a person chosen to settle differences in a disagreement

ar·bor *n* **:** a shelter of vines or branches or of a frame covered with growing vines

ar·bo·re·al *adj* **1 :** of or relating to a tree **2 :** living in or often found in trees

ar·bo·re·tum *n, pl* **ar·bo·re·tums** *or* **ar·bo·re·ta :** a place where trees and plants are grown to be studied

ar·bor·vi·tae *n* **:** any of several evergreen trees with tiny scalelike leaves on flat branches shaped like fans

ar·bu·tus *n* **:** a plant that spreads along the ground and in the spring has bunches of small fragrant flowers with five white or pink petals

[1]**arc** *n* **1 :** a glowing light across a gap in an electric circuit or between electrodes **2 :** a part of a curved line between any two points on it

[2]**arc** *vb* **arced; arc·ing 1 :** to form an electric arc **2 :** to follow an arc-shaped course

ar·cade *n* **1 :** a row of arches with the columns that support them **2 :** an arched or covered passageway often between two rows of shops

[1]**arch** *n* **1 :** a usually curved part of a structure that is over an opening and serves as a support (as for the wall above the opening) **2 :** something suggesting an arch — **arched** *adj*

[2]**arch** *vb* **1 :** to cover with an arch **2 :** to form or shape into an arch

[3]**arch** *adj* **1 :** [2]CHIEF 1, PRINCIPAL **2 :** being

clever and mischievous — **arch·ly** *adv* — **arch·ness** *n*

ar·chae·ol·o·gy *or* **ar·che·ol·o·gy** *n* : a science that deals with past human life and activities as shown by fossils and the monuments and tools left by ancient peoples

ar·cha·ic *adj* **1 :** of or relating to an earlier time **2 :** surviving from an earlier period

arch·an·gel *n* : a chief angel

arch·bish·op *n* : the bishop of highest rank in a group of dioceses

ar·cher *n* : a person who shoots with a bow and arrow

ar·chery *n* : the sport or practice of shooting with bow and arrows

ar·chi·pel·a·go *n, pl* **ar·chi·pel·a·goes** *or* **ar·chi·pel·a·gos** **1 :** a body of water (as a sea) with many islands **2 :** a group of islands in an archipelago

ar·chi·tect *n* : a person who designs buildings

ar·chi·tec·tur·al *adj* : of or relating to architecture — **ar·chi·tec·tur·al·ly** *adv*

ar·chi·tec·ture *n* **1 :** the art of making plans for buildings **2 :** a style of building

ar·chive *n* : a place in which public records or historical papers are saved

arch·way *n* **1 :** a passage under an arch **2 :** an arch over a passage

-archy *n suffix, pl* **-archies** : rule : government

arc·tic *adj* **1** *often cap* : of or relating to the north pole or to the region around it **2 :** very cold

ar·dent *adj* : showing or having warmth of feeling : PASSIONATE — **ar·dent·ly** *adv*

ar·dor *n* **1 :** warmth of feeling **2 :** great eagerness : ZEAL

ar·du·ous *adj* : DIFFICULT 1 — **ar·du·ous·ly** *adv* — **ar·du·ous·ness** *n*

are *present 2d sing or present pl of* BE

area code *n* : a usually three-digit number that represents a telephone service area in a country

ar·ea *n* **1 :** a flat surface or space **2 :** the amount of surface included within limits **3 :** REGION 1 **4 :** a field of activity or study

are·na *n* **1 :** an enclosed area used for public entertainment **2 :** a building containing an arena **3 :** a field of activity

aren't : are not

ar·gue *vb* **ar·gued; ar·gu·ing** **1 :** to give reasons for or against something **2 :** to discuss some matter usually with different points of view **3 :** to persuade by giving reasons — **ar·gu·er** *n*

ar·gu·ment *n* **1 :** a reason for or against something **2 :** a discussion in which reasons for and against something are given **3 :** an angry disagreement : QUARREL

ar·id *adj* **1 :** not having enough rainfall to support agriculture **2 :** UNINTERESTING, DULL

Ar·ies *n* **1 :** a constellation between Pisces and Taurus imagined as a ram **2 :** the first sign of the zodiac or a person born under this sign

aright *adv* : in a correct way

arise *vb* **arose; aris·en; aris·ing** **1 :** to move upward **2 :** to get up from sleep or after lying down **3 :** to come into existence

ar·is·toc·ra·cy *n, pl* **ar·is·toc·ra·cies** **1 :** a government that is run by a small class of people **2 :** an upper class that is usually based on birth and is richer and more powerful than the rest of a society **3 :** persons thought of as being better than the rest of the community

aris·to·crat *n* : a member of an aristocracy

aris·to·crat·ic *adj* : of or relating to the aristocracy or aristocrats — **aris·to·crat·i·cal·ly** *adv*

[1]arith·me·tic *n* **1 :** a science that deals with the addition, subtraction, multiplication, and division of numbers **2 :** an act or method of adding, subtracting, multiplying, or dividing

[2]ar·ith·met·ic *or* **ar·ith·met·i·cal** *adj* : of or relating to arithmetic

ar·ith·met·ic mean *n* : a quantity formed by adding quantities together and dividing by their number

ark *n* **1 :** the ship in which an ancient Hebrew of the Bible named Noah and his family were saved from a great flood that God sent down on the world because of its wickedness **2 :** a sacred chest in which the ancient Hebrews kept the two tablets of the Law **3 :** a closet in a synagogue for the scrolls of the Law

[1]arm *n* **1 :** a human upper limb especially between the shoulder and wrist **2 :** something like an arm in shape or position **3 :** [1]POWER 1 **4 :** a foreleg of a four-footed animal — **armed** *adj*

[2]arm *vb* **1 :** to provide with weapons **2 :** to provide with a way of defense

[3]arm *n* **1 :** WEAPON, FIREARM **2 :** a branch of an army or of the military forces **3** **arms** *pl* : the designs on a shield or flag of a family or government **4** **arms** *pl* : actual fighting : WARFARE

ar·ma·da *n* **1 :** a large fleet of warships **2 :** a large number of moving things (as planes)

ar·ma·dil·lo *n, pl* **ar·ma·dil·los** : a small burrowing animal of Latin America and Texas whose head and body are protected by a hard bony armor

ar·ma·ment *n* **1 :** the military strength and equipment of a nation **2 :** the supply of materials for war **3 :** the process of preparing for war

ar·ma·ture *n* **:** the part of an electric motor or generator that turns in a magnetic field

arm·chair *n* **:** a chair with arms

arm·ful *n, pl* **arm·fuls** *or* **arms·ful :** as much as a person's arm can hold

ar·mi·stice *n* **:** a pause in fighting brought about by agreement between the two sides

ar·mor *n* **1 :** a covering (as of metal) to protect the body in battle **2 :** something that protects like metal armor **3 :** armored forces and vehicles (as tanks)

ar·mored *adj* **:** protected by or equipped with armor

ar·mory *n, pl* **ar·mor·ies 1 :** a supply of arms **2 :** a place where arms are kept and where soldiers are often trained **3 :** a place where arms are made

arm·pit *n* **:** the hollow under a person's arm where the arm joins the shoulder

arm·rest *n* **:** a support for the arm

ar·my *n, pl* **armies 1 :** a large body of men and women trained for land warfare **2** *often cap* **:** the complete military organization of a nation for land warfare **3 :** a great number of people or things **4 :** a body of persons organized to advance an idea

aro·ma *n* **:** a noticeable and pleasant smell

ar·o·mat·ic *adj* **:** of, relating to, or having an aroma

arose *past of* ARISE

[1]**around** *adv* **1 :** in circumference **2 :** in or along a curving course **3 :** on all sides **4 :** NEARBY **5 :** here and there in various places **6 :** to each in turn **7 :** in an opposite direction **8 :** in the neighborhood of **:** APPROXIMATELY

[2]**around** *prep* **1 :** in a curving path along the outside boundary of **2 :** on every side of **3 :** here and there in **4 :** near in number or amount

arouse *vb* **aroused; arous·ing 1 :** to awaken from sleep **2 :** to excite to action

ar·range *vb* **ar·ranged; ar·rang·ing 1 :** to put in order and especially a particular order **2 :** to make plans for **3 :** to come to an agreement about **:** SETTLE **4 :** to make a musical arrangement of — **ar·rang·er** *n*

ar·range·ment *n* **1 :** a putting in order **:** the order in which things are put **2 :** preparation or planning done in advance **3 :** something made by arranging **4 :** a changing of a piece of music to suit voices or instruments for which it was not first written

[1]**ar·ray** *vb* **1 :** to set in order **:** DRAW UP **2 :** to dress especially in fine or beautiful clothing

[2]**array** *n* **1 :** regular order or arrangement **2 :** a group of persons (as soldiers) drawn up in regular order **3 :** fine or beautiful clothing **4 :** an impressive group **5 :** a group of mathematical elements (as numbers or letters) arranged in rows and columns

ar·rears *n pl* **1 :** the state of being behind in paying debts **2 :** unpaid and overdue debts

[1]**ar·rest** *vb* **1 :** to stop the progress or movement of **:** CHECK **2 :** to take or keep in one's control by authority of law **3 :** to attract and hold the attention of

[2]**arrest** *n* **:** the act of taking or holding in one's control by authority of law

ar·riv·al *n* **1 :** the act of arriving **2 :** a person or thing that has arrived

ar·rive *vb* **ar·rived; ar·riv·ing 1 :** to reach the place one started out for **2 :** to gain a goal or object **3 :** COME 2 **4 :** to gain success

ar·ro·gance *n* **:** a sense of one's own importance that shows itself in a proud and insulting way

ar·ro·gant *adj* **:** overly proud of oneself or of one's own opinions — **ar·ro·gant·ly** *adv*

ar·row *n* **1 :** a weapon that is made to be shot from a bow and is usually a stick with a point at one end and feathers at the other **2 :** a mark to show direction

ar·row·head *n* **:** the pointed end of an arrow

ar·row·root *n* **:** a starch obtained from the roots of a tropical plant

ar·se·nal *n* **:** a place where military equipment is made and stored

ar·se·nic *n* **:** a solid poisonous chemical element that is usually steel gray and snaps easily

ar·son *n* **:** the illegal burning of a building or other property

art *n* **1 :** skill that comes through experience or study **2 :** an activity that requires skill **3 :** an activity (as painting, music, or writing) whose purpose is making things that are beautiful to look at, listen to, or read **4 :** works (as pictures, poems, or songs) made by artists

ar·tery *n, pl* **ar·ter·ies 1 :** one of the branching tubes that carry blood from the heart to all parts of the body **2 :** a main road or waterway

ar·te·sian well *n* **1 :** a bored well from which water flows up like a fountain **2 :** a deep bored well

art·ful *adj* **1 :** done with or showing art or skill **2 :** clever at taking advantage — **art·ful·ly** *adv* — **art·ful·ness** *n*

ar·thri·tis *n* **:** a condition in which the joints are painful and swollen

ar·thro·pod *n* **:** any of a large group of animals (as crabs, insects, and spiders) with jointed limbs and a body made up of segments

ar·ti·choke *n* **:** a tall plant of the aster family with a flower head cooked and eaten as a vegetable

ar·ti·cle *n* **1 :** a separate part of a document **2 :** a piece of writing other than fiction or poetry that forms a separate part of a publication (as a magazine) **3 :** a word (as *a, an,* or *the*) used with a noun to limit it or make it clearer **4 :** one of a class of things

[1]**ar·tic·u·late** *adj* **1 :** clearly understandable **2 :** able to express oneself clearly and well — **ar·tic·u·late·ly** *adv* — **ar·tic·u·late·ness** *n*

[2]**ar·tic·u·late** *vb* **ar·tic·u·lat·ed; ar·tic·u·lat·ing :** to speak clearly

ar·tic·u·la·tion *n* **:** the making of articulate sounds (as in speaking)

ar·ti·fice *n* **1 :** a clever trick or device **2 :** clever skill

ar·ti·fi·cial *adj* **1 :** made by humans **2 :** not natural in quality **3 :** made to look like something natural — **ar·ti·fi·cial·ly** *adv*

artificial respiration *n* **:** the forcing of air into and out of the lungs of a person whose breathing has stopped

ar·til·lery *n* **1 :** large firearms (as cannon or rockets) **2 :** a branch of an army armed with artillery

ar·ti·san *n* **:** a person (as a carpenter) who works at a trade requiring skill with the hands

art·ist *n* **1 :** a person skilled in one of the arts (as painting, music, or writing) **2 :** a person who is very good at a job requiring skill

ar·tis·tic *adj* **1 :** relating to art or artists **2 :** showing skill and imagination — **ar·tis·ti·cal·ly** *adv*

[1]**-ary** *n suffix, pl* **-ar·ies :** thing or person belonging to or connected with

[2]**-ary** *adj suffix* **:** of, relating to, or connected with

[1]**as** *adv* **1 :** to the same degree or amount **2 :** for example

[2]**as** *conj* **1 :** in equal amount or degree with **2 :** in the same way that **3 :** at the time that **4 :** BECAUSE, SINCE

[3]**as** *pron* **1 :** THAT, WHO, WHICH **2 :** a fact that

[4]**as** *prep* **1 :** [4]LIKE 1 **2 :** in the position or role of

as·bes·tos *n* **:** a grayish mineral that separates easily into long flexible fibers and is used in making fireproof materials

as·cend *vb* **:** to go up **:** RISE

as·cen·sion *n* **:** the act or process of ascending

as·cent *n* **1 :** the act of rising or climbing upward **2 :** an upward slope **:** RISE

as·cer·tain *vb* **:** to find out with certainty

as·cribe *vb* **as·cribed; as·crib·ing :** to think of as coming from a specified cause, source, or author

asex·u·al *adj* **:** of, relating to, or being a process of reproduction (as the dividing of one cell into two cells) that does not involve the combining of male and female germ cells — **asex·u·al·ly** *adv*

[1]**ash** *n* **:** a common shade tree or timber tree that has winged seeds and bark with grooves

[2]**ash** *n* **1 :** the solid matter left when something is completely burned **2 ashes** *pl* **:** the last remains of the dead human body

ashamed *adj* **1 :** feeling shame, guilt, or disgrace **2 :** kept back by fear of shame

ash·en *adj* **1 :** of the color of ashes **2 :** very pale

ashore *adv* **:** on or to the shore

ash·tray *n* **:** a container for tobacco ashes and cigarette and cigar butts

ashy *adj* **ash·i·er; ash·i·est 1 :** of or relating to ashes **2 :** very pale

[1]**Asian** *adj* **:** of or relating to Asia or the Asians

[2]**Asian** *n* **:** a person born or living in Asia

Asian–Amer·i·can *n* **:** an American who has Asian ancestors

aside *adv* **1 :** to or toward the side **2 :** out of the way **:** AWAY **3 :** away from one's thought

aside from *prep* **:** with the exception of

as if *conj* **1 :** the way it would be if **2 :** the way one would if **3 :** [2]THAT 1

ask *vb* **1 :** to seek information **2 :** to make a request **3 :** to set as a price **4 :** INVITE 2 **5 :** to behave as if looking

askance *adv* **1 :** with a side glance **2 :** with distrust or disapproval

askew *adv or adj* **:** out of line

aslant *adv or adj* **:** in a slanting direction

[1]**asleep** *adj* **1 :** being in a state of sleep **2 :** having no feeling

[2]**asleep** *adv* **:** into a state of sleep

as of *prep* **:** [1]ON 5, AT

as·par·a·gus *n* **:** a vegetable that is the thick young shoots of a garden plant that is related to the lilies and lives for many years

as·pect *n* **1 :** a position facing a certain direction **2 :** a certain way in which something appears or may be thought of **3 :** the appearance of an individual **:** LOOK

as·pen *n* **:** a poplar tree whose leaves move easily in the breeze

as·phalt *n* **1 :** a dark-colored substance obtained from natural beds or from petroleum **2 :** any of various materials made of asphalt that are used for pavements and as a waterproof cement

as·phyx·i·ate *vb* **as·phyx·i·at·ed; as·phyx·i·at·ing :** to cause (as a person) to become unconscious or die by cutting off the normal taking in of oxygen whether by blocking breathing or by replacing the oxygen of the air with another gas

as·pi·rant *n* **:** a person who aspires

as·pi·ra·tion *n* : a strong desire to achieve something high or great

as·pire *vb* **as·pired; as·pir·ing :** to very much want something and especially something high or fine

as·pi·rin *n* : a white drug used to relieve pain and fever

ass *n* **1 :** an animal that looks like but is smaller than the related horse and has shorter hair in mane and tail and longer ears : DONKEY **2 :** a dull stupid person

as·sail *vb* : to attack violently with blows or words

as·sail·ant *n* : a person who attacks

as·sas·sin *n* : one who kills another person either for pay or from loyalty to a cause

as·sas·si·nate *vb* **as·sas·si·nat·ed; as·sas·si·nat·ing :** to murder a usually important person by a surprise or secret attack

as·sas·si·na·tion *n* : the act of assassinating

[1]**as·sault** *n* **1 :** a violent or sudden attack **2 :** an unlawful attempt or threat to harm someone

[2]**assault** *vb* : to make an assault on

[1]**as·say** *n* : an analyzing (as of an ore or drug) to determine the presence, absence, or amount of one or more substances

[2]**as·say** *vb* : to analyze (as an ore) for one or more valuable substances

as·sem·blage *n* : a collection of persons or things

as·sem·ble *vb* **as·sem·bled; as·sem·bling 1 :** to collect in one place or group **2 :** to fit (parts) together **3 :** to meet together — **as·sem·bler** *n*

as·sem·bly *n, pl* **as·sem·blies 1 :** a gathering of persons : MEETING **2** *cap* **:** a lawmaking body **3 :** the act of assembling : the state of being assembled **4 :** a collection of parts that make up a complete unit

assembly line *n* : an arrangement for assembling a product mechanically in which work passes from one operation to the next in a direct line until the product is finished

[1]**as·sent** *vb* : to agree to something

[2]**assent** *n* : an act of assenting : AGREEMENT

as·sert *vb* **1 :** to state clearly and strongly **2 :** to show the existence of — **assert oneself :** to insist strongly that others respect one's rights

as·ser·tion *n* **1 :** the act of asserting **2 :** a positive statement

as·sess *vb* **1 :** to decide on the rate or amount of **2 :** to assign a value to for purposes of taxation **3 :** to put a charge or tax on — **as·ses·sor** *n*

as·set *n* **1 assets** *pl* **:** all the property belonging to a person or an organization **2 :** ADVANTAGE 3

as·sid·u·ous *adj* : DILIGENT — **as·sid·u·ous·ly** *adv* — **as·sid·u·ous·ness** *n*

as·sign *vb* **1 :** to appoint to a post or duty **2 :** to give out with authority **3 :** to decide on definitely

as·sign·ment *n* **1 :** the act of assigning **2 :** something assigned

as·sim·i·late *vb* **as·sim·i·lat·ed; as·sim·i·lat·ing :** to take something in and make it part of the thing it has joined

as·sim·i·la·tion *n* : the act or process of assimilating

[1]**as·sist** *vb* : to give aid : HELP

[2]**assist** *n* : an act of assisting

as·sis·tance *n* **1 :** the act of helping **2 :** the help given

[1]**as·sis·tant** *adj* : acting as a helper to another

[2]**assistant** *n* : a person who assists another

[1]**as·so·ci·ate** *vb* **as·so·ci·at·ed; as·so·ci·at·ing 1 :** to join or come together as partners, friends, or companions **2 :** to connect in thought

[2]**as·so·ciate** *adj* **1 :** closely joined with another (as in duties or responsibility) **2 :** having some but not all rights and privileges

[3]**as·so·ciate** *n* **1 :** a fellow worker : PARTNER **2 :** a person who is one's friend or companion

as·so·ci·a·tion *n* **1 :** the act of associating : the state of being associated **2 :** an organization of persons having a common interest **3 :** a feeling, memory, or thought connected with a person, place, or thing

as·so·cia·tive *adj* **1 :** serving to associate **2 :** being a property of a mathematical operation (as addition or multiplication) in which the result is independent of the original grouping of the elements

as·sort *vb* : to sort into groups

as·sort·ed *adj* **1 :** made up of various kinds **2 :** suited to one another

as·sort·ment *n* **1 :** the act of assorting : the state of being assorted **2 :** a collection of assorted things or persons

as·sume *vb* **as·sumed; as·sum·ing 1 :** to take upon oneself : UNDERTAKE **2 :** to take over usually by force **3 :** to pretend to have or be **4 :** to accept as true

as·sump·tion *n* **1 :** the act of assuming **2 :** something accepted as true

as·sur·ance *n* **1 :** the act of assuring **2 :** the state of being certain **3 :** a being sure and safe : SECURITY **4 :** confidence in one's own self

as·sure *vb* **as·sured; as·sur·ing 1 :** to make safe : INSURE **2 :** to give confidence to **3 :** to make sure or certain **4 :** to inform positively

as·sured *adj* **1 :** made sure or certain **2 :** very confident — **as·sured·ly** *adv* — **as·sured·ness** *n*

as·ter *n* : any of various herbs related to the

daisies that have leafy stems and white, pink, purple, or yellow flower heads which bloom in the fall

as·ter·isk *n* **:** a character * used in printing or in writing as a reference mark or to show that letters or words have been left out

astern *adv* **1 :** behind a ship or airplane **2 :** at or toward the stern **3 :** [1]BACKWARD 1

as·ter·oid *n* **:** one of thousands of small planets that move in orbits mostly between those of Mars and Jupiter and have diameters from a fraction of a kilometer to nearly 800 kilometers

asth·ma *n* **:** an ailment of which difficult breathing, wheezing, and coughing are symptoms

astir *adj* **1 :** showing activity **2 :** being out of bed **:** UP

as to *prep* **1 :** with respect to **:** ABOUT **2 :** ACCORDING TO 1

as·ton·ish *vb* **:** to strike with sudden wonder or surprise

as·ton·ish·ment *n* **:** great surprise **:** AMAZEMENT

as·tound *vb* **:** to fill with puzzled wonder

astray *adv or adj* **1 :** off the right path or route **2 :** in or into error

[1]**astride** *adv* **:** with one leg on each side

[2]**astride** *prep* **:** with one leg on each side of

as·trin·gent *adj* **:** able or tending to shrink body tissues — **as·trin·gent·ly** *adv*

astro- *prefix* **:** star **:** heavens **:** astronomical

as·trol·o·gy *n* **:** the study of the supposed influences of the stars and planets on human affairs by their positions in the sky in relation to each other

as·tro·naut *n* **:** a traveler in a spacecraft

as·tro·nau·tics *n* **:** the science of the construction and operation of spacecraft

as·tron·o·mer *n* **:** a person who is skilled in astronomy

as·tro·nom·i·cal *or* **as·tro·nom·ic** *adj* **1 :** of or relating to astronomy **2 :** extremely or unbelievably large — **as·tro·nom·i·cal·ly** *adv*

as·tron·o·my *n* **:** the science of celestial bodies and of their motions and makeup

as·tute *adj* **:** very alert and aware **:** CLEVER — **as·tute·ly** *adv* — **as·tute·ness** *n*

asun·der *adv or adj* **1 :** into parts **2 :** apart from each other in position

as well as *prep or conj* **:** in addition to **:** and also

asy·lum *n* **1 :** a place of protection and shelter **2 :** protection given especially to political refugees **3 :** a place for the care of the poor or sick and especially of the insane

at *prep* **1** — used to indicate a particular place or time **2** — used to indicate a goal **3** — used to indicate position or condition **4** — used to tell how or why something is done

ate *past of* EAT

[1]**-ate** *n suffix* **:** one acted upon in such a way

[2]**-ate** *n suffix* **:** office **:** rank **:** group of persons holding such an office or rank

[3]**-ate** *adj suffix* **:** marked by having

[4]**-ate** *vb suffix* **:** cause to be changed or influenced by **:** cause to become **:** furnish with

athe·ist *n* **:** a person who believes there is no God

ath·lete *n* **:** a person who is trained in or good at games and exercises that require physical skill, endurance, and strength

athlete's foot *n* **:** a fungus infection of the foot marked by blisters, itching, and cracks between and under the toes

ath·let·ic *adj* **1 :** of, relating to, or characteristic of athletes or athletics **2 :** vigorously active **3 :** STURDY 2

ath·let·ics *n sing or pl* **:** games, sports, and exercises requiring strength, endurance, and skill

-ation *n suffix* **:** action or process **:** something connected with an action or process

-ative *adj suffix* **1 :** of, relating to, or connected with **2 :** tending to

at·las *n* **:** a book of maps

ATM *n* **:** a computerized machine that performs basic banking functions (as cash withdrawals)

at·mo·sphere *n* **1 :** the gas surrounding a celestial body **:** AIR **2 :** the air in a particular place **3 :** a surrounding influence or set of conditions

at·mo·spher·ic *adj* **:** of or relating to the atmosphere

atoll *n* **:** a ring-shaped coral island consisting of a coral reef surrounding a lagoon

at·om *n* **1 :** a tiny particle **:** BIT **2 :** the smallest particle of an element that can exist alone or in combination

atom·ic *adj* **1 :** of or relating to atoms **2 :** NUCLEAR 3

atomic bomb *n* **:** a bomb whose great power is due to the sudden release of the energy in the nuclei of atoms

at·om·iz·er *n* **:** a device for spraying a liquid (as a perfume or disinfectant)

atone *vb* **atoned; aton·ing :** to do something to make up for a wrong

atone·ment *n* **:** a making up for an offense or injury

atop *prep* **:** on top of

atro·cious *adj* **1 :** savagely brutal, cruel, or wicked **2 :** very bad — **atro·cious·ly** *adv* — **atro·cious·ness** *n*

atroc·i·ty *n, pl* **atroc·i·ties :** an atrocious act, object, or situation

at sign *n* **:** the symbol @ used especially as part of an e-mail address

at·tach *vb* **1 :** to take (money or property) legally in order to obtain payment of a debt **2 :** to fasten one thing to another **3 :** to bind by feelings of affection **4 :** to assign by authority **5 :** to think of as belonging to something

at·tach·ment *n* **1 :** connection by feelings of affection or regard **2 :** a device that can be attached to a machine or tool **3 :** a connection by which one thing is joined to another

¹at·tack *vb* **1 :** to take strong action against **:** ASSAULT **2 :** to use unfriendly or bitter words against **3 :** to begin to affect or to act upon harmfully **4 :** to start to work on — **at·tack·er** *n*

²attack *n* **1 :** the act of attacking **2 :** beginning to work **3 :** a spell of sickness

at·tain *vb* **1 :** to reach as a desired goal **2 :** to come into possession of **3 :** to arrive at — **at·tain·able** *adj*

at·tain·ment *n* **1 :** the act of attaining **:** the state of being attained **2 :** ACCOMPLISHMENT 3

at·tar *n* **:** a sweet-smelling oil from flowers

¹at·tempt *vb* **1 :** to try to do or perform **2 :** to try to do something

²attempt *n* **:** the act or an instance of attempting

at·tend *vb* **1 :** to pay attention to **2 :** to go with especially as a servant or companion **3 :** to care for **4 :** to go to or be present at **5 :** to take charge

at·ten·dance *n* **1 :** the act of attending **2 :** the number of persons present

¹at·ten·dant *n* **:** a person who attends something or someone

²attendant *adj* **:** coming with or following closely as a result

at·ten·tion *n* **1 :** the act or the power of fixing one's mind on something **:** careful listening or watching **2 :** a state of being aware **3 :** careful thinking about something so as to be able to take action on it **4 :** an act of kindness or politeness **5 :** a military posture with body stiff and straight, heels together, and arms at the sides

attention deficit disorder *n* **:** a condition in which a person has trouble paying attention or is so active and impulsive that it is difficult to function in school or at work

at·ten·tive *adj* **1 :** paying attention **2 :** being thoughtful and polite — **at·ten·tive·ly** *adv* — **at·ten·tive·ness** *n*

at·test *vb* **:** to give proof of

at·tic *n* **:** a room or a space just under the roof of a building

¹at·tire *vb* **at·tired; at·tir·ing :** to put clothes and especially fine clothes on

²attire *n* **:** clothing meant for a particular occasion

at·ti·tude *n* **1 :** the position of the body, or of the parts of the body, or of an object **2 :** a feeling or opinion about a certain fact or situation

at·tor·ney *n, pl* **at·tor·neys :** a person who acts as agent for another in dealing with business or legal matters

at·tract *vb* **1 :** to draw to or toward oneself **2 :** to draw by appealing to interest or feeling

at·trac·tion *n* **1 :** the act or power of attracting **2 :** something that attracts or pleases

at·trac·tive *adj* **:** having the power or quality of attracting **:** PLEASING — **at·trac·tive·ly** *adv* — **at·trac·tive·ness** *n*

¹at·tri·bute *n* **1 :** a quality belonging to a particular person or thing **2 :** a word (as an adjective) indicating a quality

²at·trib·ute *vb* **at·trib·ut·ed; at·trib·ut·ing 1 :** to explain as the cause of **2 :** to think of as likely to be a quality of a person or thing

at·tri·bu·tion *n* **:** the act of attributing

at·tune *vb* **at·tuned; at·tun·ing :** to bring into harmony **:** TUNE

atyp·i·cal *adj* **:** not typical — **atyp·i·cal·ly** *adv*

au·burn *adj* **:** of a reddish brown color

¹auc·tion *n* **:** a public sale at which things are sold to those who offer to pay the most

²auction *vb* **:** to sell at auction

auc·tion·eer *n* **:** a person in charge of auctions

au·da·cious *adj* **1 :** very bold and daring **:** FEARLESS **2 :** very rude **:** INSOLENT — **au·da·cious·ly** *adv* — **au·da·cious·ness** *n*

au·dac·i·ty *n, pl* **au·dac·i·ties :** the fact or an instance of being audacious

au·di·ble *adj* **:** loud enough to be heard — **au·di·bly** *adv*

au·di·ence *n* **1 :** a group that listens or watches (as at a play or concert) **2 :** a chance to talk with a person of very high rank **3 :** those of the general public who give attention to something said, done, or written

¹au·dio *adj* **1 :** of or relating to sound or its reproduction **2 :** relating to or used in the transmitting or receiving of sound (as in radio or television)

²audio *n* **1 :** the transmitting, receiving, or reproducing of sound **2 :** the section of television equipment that deals with sound

au·dio·tape *n* **:** a tape recording of sound

au·dio·vi·su·al *adj* **:** of, relating to, or using both sound and sight

¹au·dit *n* **:** a thorough check of business accounts

²audit *vb* **:** to make an audit of

¹au·di·tion *n* **:** a short performance to test the talents of a singer, dancer, or actor

²audition *vb* **:** to test or try out in an audition

au·di·tor *n* **1 :** a person who listens especially as a member of a radio or TV audience **2 :** a person who audits business accounts
au·di·to·ri·um *n* **1 :** the part of a public building where an audience sits **2 :** a hall used for public gatherings
au·di·to·ry *adj* **:** of or relating to hearing
au·ger *n* **:** a tool used for boring holes
aught *n* **:** ZERO 1
aug·ment *vb* **:** to increase in size, amount, or degree
au·gust *adj* **:** being grand and noble **:** MAJESTIC — **au·gust·ly** *adv* — **au·gust·ness** *n*
Au·gust *n* **:** the eighth month of the year
auk *n* **:** a diving seabird of cold parts of the northern hemisphere with a heavy body and small wings
aunt *n* **1 :** a sister of one's parent **2 :** the wife of one's uncle
au·ra *n* **:** a feeling that seems to be given off by a person or thing
au·ral *adj* **:** of or relating to the ear or sense of hearing — **au·ral·ly** *adv*
au·ri·cle *n* **:** the part of the heart that receives blood from the veins
au·ro·ra bo·re·al·is *n* **:** broad bands of light that have a magnetic and electrical source and that appear in the sky at night especially in the arctic regions
aus·pic·es *n pl* **:** support and guidance of a sponsor
aus·pi·cious *adj* **1 :** promising success **2 :** PROSPEROUS 1 — **aus·pi·cious·ly** *adv*
aus·tere *adj* **1 :** seeming or acting harsh and stern **2 :** [1]PLAIN 1 — **aus·tere·ly** *adv*
aus·ter·i·ty *n, pl* **aus·ter·i·ties 1 :** an austere act or manner **2 :** lack of all luxury
[1]**Aus·tra·lian** *adj* **:** of or relating to Australia or the Australians
[2]**Australian** *n* **:** a person born or living in Australia
aut- *or* **au·to-** *prefix* **1 :** self **:** same one **2 :** automatic
au·then·tic *adj* **:** being really what it seems to be **:** GENUINE — **au·then·ti·cal·ly** *adv*
au·thor *n* **1 :** a person who writes something (as a novel) **2 :** one that starts or creates
au·thor·i·ta·tive *adj* **:** having or coming from authority — **au·thor·i·ta·tive·ly** *adv* — **au·thor·i·ta·tive·ness** *n*
au·thor·i·ty *n, pl* **au·thor·i·ties 1 :** a fact or statement used to support a position **2 :** a person looked to as an expert **3 :** power to influence the behavior of others **4 :** persons having powers of government
au·tho·rize *vb* **au·tho·rized; au·tho·riz·ing 1 :** to give authority to **:** EMPOWER **2 :** to give legal or official approval to
au·thor·ship *n* **:** the profession of writing
au·to *n, pl* **au·tos :** AUTOMOBILE
auto- — see AUT-
au·to·bi·og·ra·phy *n, pl* **au·to·bi·og·ra·phies :** the biography of a person written by that person
[1]**au·to·graph** *n* **:** a person's signature written by hand
[2]**autograph** *vb* **:** to write one's signature in or on (as a book)
au·to·mate *vb* **au·to·mat·ed; au·to·mat·ing :** to make automatic
[1]**au·to·mat·ic** *adj* **1 :** INVOLUNTARY **2 :** being a machine or device that acts by or regulates itself — **au·to·mat·i·cal·ly** *adv*
[2]**automatic** *n* **1 :** an automatic machine or device **2 :** an automatic firearm
au·to·ma·tion *n* **1 :** the method of making a machine, a process, or a system work automatically **2 :** automatic working of a machine, process, or system by mechanical or electronic devices that take the place of humans
[1]**au·to·mo·bile** *adj* **:** AUTOMOTIVE
[2]**automobile** *n* **:** a usually four-wheeled vehicle that runs on its own power and is designed to carry passengers
au·to·mo·tive *adj* **:** SELF-PROPELLED
au·tumn *n* **:** the season between summer and winter that in the northern hemisphere is usually the months of September, October, and November
au·tum·nal *adj* **:** of or relating to autumn
[1]**aux·il·ia·ry** *adj* **:** available to provide something extra
[2]**auxiliary** *n, pl* **aux·il·ia·ries 1 :** an auxiliary person, group, or device **2 :** HELPING VERB
[1]**avail** *vb* **:** to be of use or help
[2]**avail** *n* **:** help toward reaching a goal **:** USE
avail·able *adj* **1 :** SUITABLE, USABLE **2 :** possible to get **:** OBTAINABLE
av·a·lanche *n* **:** a large mass of snow and ice or of earth or rock sliding down a mountainside or over a cliff
av·a·rice *n* **:** strong desire for riches **:** GREED
av·a·ri·cious *adj* **:** greedy for riches — **av·a·ri·cious·ly** *adv* — **av·a·ri·cious·ness** *n*
avenge *vb* **avenged; aveng·ing :** to take revenge for — **aveng·er** *n*
av·e·nue *n* **1 :** a way of reaching a goal **2 :** a usually wide street
[1]**av·er·age** *n* **1 :** ARITHMETIC MEAN **2 :** something usual in a group, class, or series
[2]**average** *adj* **1 :** equaling or coming close to an average **2 :** being ordinary or usual
[3]**average** *vb* **av·er·aged; av·er·ag·ing 1 :** to amount to usually **2 :** to find the average of
averse *adj* **:** having a feeling of dislike
aver·sion *n* **1 :** a strong dislike **2 :** something strongly disliked
avert *vb* **1 :** to turn away **2 :** to keep from happening

avi·ary *n, pl* **avi·ar·ies :** a place (as a large cage) where birds are kept
avi·a·tion *n* **1 :** the flying of aircraft **2 :** the designing and making of aircraft
avi·a·tor *n* **:** the pilot of an aircraft
av·id *adj* **:** very eager — **av·id·ly** *adv*
av·o·ca·do *n, pl* **av·o·ca·dos :** a usually green fruit that is shaped like a pear or an egg, grows on a tropical American tree, and has a rich oily flesh
av·o·ca·tion *n* **:** an interest or activity that is not one's regular job **:** HOBBY
avoid *vb* **:** to keep away from
avoid·ance *n* **:** a keeping away from something
avow *vb* **:** to declare openly and frankly
avow·al *n* **:** an open declaration
await *vb* **1 :** to wait for **2 :** to be ready or waiting for
[1]**awake** *vb* **awoke; awo·ken** *or* **awaked; awak·ing 1 :** to arouse from sleep **:** wake up **2 :** to become conscious or aware of something
[2]**awake** *adj* **:** not asleep
awak·en *vb* **:** [1]AWAKE
[1]**award** *vb* **1 :** to give by judicial decision **2 :** to give or grant as deserved or needed
[2]**award** *n* **:** something (as a prize) that is awarded
aware *adj* **:** having or showing understanding or knowledge **:** CONSCIOUS — **aware·ness** *n*
awash *adv or adj* **1 :** washed by waves or tide **2 :** floating about **3 :** flooded or covered with water
[1]**away** *adv* **1 :** from this or that place **2 :** in another place or direction **3 :** out of existence **4 :** from one's possession **5 :** without stopping or slowing down **6 :** at or to a great distance in space or time **:** FAR
[2]**away** *adj* **1 :** [1]ABSENT 1 **2 :** DISTANT 1
[1]**awe** *n* **:** a feeling of mixed fear, respect, and wonder
[2]**awe** *vb* **awed; aw·ing :** to fill with awe
awe·some *adj* **:** causing a feeling of awe
aw·ful *adj* **1 :** causing fear or terror **2 :** very disagreeable or unpleasant **3 :** very great
aw·ful·ly *adv* **1 :** in a disagreeable or unpleasant manner **2 :** to a very great degree
awhile *adv* **:** for a while **:** for a short time
awk·ward *adj* **1 :** not graceful **:** CLUMSY **2 :** likely to embarrass **3 :** difficult to use or handle — **awk·ward·ly** *adv* — **awk·ward·ness** *n*
awl *n* **:** a pointed tool for making small holes (as in leather or wood)
aw·ning *n* **:** a cover (as of canvas) that shades or shelters like a roof
awoke *past of* AWAKE
awoken *past participle of* AWAKE
awry *adv or adj* **1 :** turned or twisted to one side **:** ASKEW **2 :** out of the right course **:** AMISS
ax *or* **axe** *n* **:** a tool that has a heavy head with a sharp edge fixed to a handle and is used for chopping and splitting wood
ax·i·om *n* **1 :** MAXIM **2 :** a statement thought to be clearly true
ax·is *n, pl* **ax·es :** a straight line about which a body or a geometric figure rotates or may be supposed to rotate
ax·le *n* **:** a pin or shaft on or with which a wheel or pair of wheels turns
ax·on *n* **:** a long fiber that carries impulses away from a nerve cell
[1]**aye** *adv* **:** [1]YES 1
[2]**aye** *n* **:** an affirmative vote or voter
aza·lea *n* **:** a usually small rhododendron that sheds its leaves in the fall and has flowers of many colors which are shaped like funnels
azure *n* **:** the blue color of the clear daytime sky

B

b *n pl* **b's** *or* **bs** *often cap* **1 :** the second letter of the English alphabet **2 :** a grade that shows a student's work is good
[1]**baa** *n* **:** the cry of a sheep
[2]**baa** *vb* **:** to make the cry of a sheep
[1]**bab·ble** *vb* **bab·bled; bab·bling 1 :** to make meaningless sounds **2 :** to talk foolishly **3 :** to make the sound of a brook — **bab·bler** *n*
[2]**babble** *n* **1 :** talk that is not clear **2 :** the sound of a brook
babe *n* **:** [1]BABY 1
ba·boon *n* **:** a large monkey of Africa and Asia with a doglike face
[1]**ba·by** *n pl* **babies 1 :** a very young child **2 :** the youngest of a group **3 :** a childish person
[2]**baby** *adj* **:** [1]YOUNG 1
[3]**baby** *vb* **ba·bied; ba·by·ing :** to treat as a baby
ba·by·hood *n* **1 :** the time in a person's life when he or she is a baby **2 :** the state of being a baby
ba·by·ish *adj* **:** like a baby
ba·by–sit *vb* **ba·by–sat; ba·by–sit·ting :** to care for children usually during a short absence of the parents
ba·by–sit·ter *n* **:** a person who baby-sits
baby tooth *n* **:** MILK TOOTH

bach·e·lor : a man who has not married

ba·cil·lus *n pl* **ba·cil·li** **1 :** a rod-shaped bacterium that forms internal spores **2 :** a bacterium that causes disease **:** GERM, MICROBE

[1]**back** *n* **1 :** the rear part of the human body from the neck to the end of the spine **:** the upper part of the body of an animal **2 :** the part of something that is opposite or away from the front part **3 :** a player in a team game who plays behind the forward line of players — **backed** *adj*

[2]**back** *adv* **1 :** to, toward, or at the rear **2 :** in or to a former time, state, or place **3 :** under control **4 :** in return or reply — **back and forth :** backward and forward **:** from one place to another

[3]**back** *adj* **1 :** located at the back **2 :** not yet paid **:** OVERDUE **3 :** no longer current

[4]**back** *vb* **1 :** to give support or help to **:** UPHOLD **2 :** to move back — **back·er** *n*

back·bone *n* **1 :** the column of bones in the back **:** SPINAL COLUMN **2 :** the strongest part of something **3 :** firmness of character

[1]**back·fire** *n* **1 :** a fire that is set to stop the spread of a forest fire or a grass fire by burning off a strip of land ahead of it **2 :** a loud engine noise caused by fuel igniting with a valve open

[2]**backfire** *vb* **back·fired; back·fir·ing** **1 :** to make a backfire **2 :** to have a result opposite to what was planned

back·ground *n* **1 :** the scenery or ground that is behind a main figure or object **2 :** a position that attracts little attention **3 :** the total of a person's experience, knowledge, and education

[1]**back·hand** *n* **1 :** a stroke made with the back of the hand turned in the direction in which the hand is moving **2 :** handwriting in which the letters slant to the left

[2]**backhand** *adv or adj* **:** with a backhand

back·hand·ed *adj* **1 :** [2]BACKHAND **2 :** not sincere

back of *prep* **:** [2]BEHIND 1

back·pack *n* **:** a carrying case strapped on the back **:** KNAPSACK

back·stage *adv or adj* **:** in or to the area behind the stage

back·track *vb* **:** to go back over a course or a path

[1]**back·ward** *or* **back·wards** *adv* **1 :** toward the back **2 :** with the back first **3 :** opposite to the usual way

[2]**backward** *adj* **1 :** turned toward the back **2 :** SHY **3 :** slow in learning or development

back·wa·ter *n* **1 :** water held or turned back from its course **2 :** a backward place or condition

back·woods *n pl* **1 :** wooded or partly cleared areas away from cities **2 :** a place that is backward in culture

back·yard *n* **:** an area in the back of a house

ba·con *n* **:** salted and smoked meat from the sides and the back of a pig

bac·te·ri·al *adj* **:** relating to or caused by bacteria

bac·te·ri·um *n pl* **bac·te·ria :** any of many single-celled microscopic organisms that are important to humans because of their chemical activities and as causes of disease

bad *adj* **worse; worst** **1 :** not good **:** POOR **2 :** not favorable **3 :** not fresh or sound **4 :** not good or right **:** EVIL **5 :** not enough **6 :** UNPLEASANT **7 :** HARMFUL **8 :** SEVERE 4 **9 :** not correct **10 :** [1]ILL 4, SICK **11 :** SORRY 1 — **bad·ness** *n*

bade *past of* BID

badge *n* **:** something worn to show that a person belongs to a certain group or rank

[1]**bad·ger** *n* **:** a furry burrowing animal with short thick legs and long claws on the front feet

[2]**badger** *vb* **:** to annoy again and again

bad·ly *adv* **worse; worst** **1 :** in a bad manner **2 :** very much

bad·min·ton *n* **:** a game in which a shuttlecock is hit back and forth over a net by players using light rackets

baf·fle *vb* **baf·fled; baf·fling :** to defeat or check by confusing

[1]**bag** *n* **1 :** a container made of flexible material (as paper or plastic) **2 :** [1]PURSE 1, HANDBAG **3 :** SUITCASE

[2]**bag** *vb* **bagged; bag·ging** **1 :** to swell out **2 :** to put into a bag **3 :** to kill or capture in hunting

ba·gel *n* **:** a roll shaped like a doughnut

bag·gage *n* **:** the trunks, suitcases, and personal belongings of travelers

bag·gy *adj* **bag·gi·er; bag·gi·est :** hanging loosely or puffed out like a bag

bag·pipe *n* **:** a musical instrument played especially in Scotland that consists of a tube, a bag for air, and pipes from which the sound comes

[1]**bail** *vb* **:** to dip and throw out water from a boat — usually used with *out*

[2]**bail** *n* **:** a promise or a deposit of money needed to free a prisoner until his or her trial

[3]**bail** *vb* **:** to get the release of (a prisoner) by giving bail

bail out *vb* **:** to jump out of an airplane with a parachute

[1]**bait** *vb* **1 :** to torment by mean or unjust attacks **2 :** to put bait on or in

[2]**bait** *n* **:** something used in luring especially to a hook or a trap

bake *vb* **baked; bak·ing** **1 :** to cook or become cooked in a dry heat especially in an oven **2 :** to dry or harden by heat

bak·er *n* **:** a person who bakes and sells bread, cakes, or pastry

baker's dozen *n* **:** THIRTEEN

bak·ery *n pl* **bak·er·ies :** a place where bread, cakes, and pastry are made or sold

baking powder *n* **:** a powder used to make the dough rise in making baked goods (as cakes)

baking soda *n* **:** SODIUM BICARBONATE

[1]**bal·ance** *n* **1 :** an instrument for weighing **2 :** a steady position or condition **3 :** equal total sums on the two sides of a bookkeeping account **4 :** something left over **:** REMAINDER **5 :** the amount by which one side of an account is greater than the other

[2]**balance** *vb* **bal·anced; bal·anc·ing 1 :** to make the two sides of (an account) add up to the same total **2 :** to make equal in weight or number **3 :** to weigh against one another **:** COMPARE **4 :** to put in or as if in balance

bal·co·ny *n pl* **bal·co·nies 1 :** a platform enclosed by a low wall or a railing built out from the side of a building **2 :** a platform inside a building extending out over part of a main floor (as of a theater)

bald *adj* **1 :** lacking a natural covering (as of hair) **2 :** [1]PLAIN 3 — **bald·ness** *n*

bald eagle *n* **:** a North American eagle that when full-grown has white head and neck feathers

[1]**bale** *n* **:** a large bundle of goods tightly tied for storing or shipping

[2]**bale** *vb* **baled; bal·ing :** to make up into a bale — **bal·er** *n*

ba·leen *n* **:** a tough material that hangs down from the upper jaw of whales without teeth and is used by the whale to filter small ocean animals out of seawater

[1]**balk** *n* **:** HINDRANCE

[2]**balk** *vb* **1 :** to keep from happening or succeeding **2 :** to stop short and refuse to go

balky *adj* **balk·i·er; balk·i·est :** likely to balk

[1]**ball** *n* **1 :** something round or roundish **2 :** a usually round object used in a game or sport **3 :** a game or sport (as baseball) played with a ball **4 :** a solid usually round shot for a gun **5 :** the rounded bulge at the base of the thumb or big toe **6 :** a pitched baseball that is not hit and is not a strike

[2]**ball** *vb* **:** to make or come together into a ball

[3]**ball** *n* **:** a large formal party for dancing

bal·lad *n* **1 :** a simple song **2 :** a short poem suitable for singing that tells a story in simple language

ball–and–socket joint *n* **:** a joint (as in the shoulder) in which a rounded part can move in many directions in a socket

bal·last *n* **1 :** heavy material used to make a ship steady or to control the rising of a balloon **2 :** gravel, cinders, or crushed stone used in making a roadbed

ball bearing *n* **1 :** a bearing in which the revolving part turns on metal balls that roll easily in a groove **2 :** one of the balls in a ball bearing

bal·le·ri·na *n* **:** a female ballet dancer

bal·let *n* **1 :** a stage dance that tells a story in movement and pantomime **2 :** a group that performs ballets

[1]**bal·loon** *n* **1 :** a bag that rises and floats above the ground when filled with heated air or with a gas that is lighter than air **2 :** a toy consisting of a rubber bag that can be blown up with air or gas **3 :** an outline containing words spoken or thought by a character (as in a cartoon)

[2]**balloon** *vb* **:** to swell or puff out like a balloon

[1]**bal·lot** *n* **1 :** an object and especially a printed sheet of paper used in voting **2 :** the action or a system of voting **3 :** the right to vote **4 :** the number of votes cast

[2]**ballot** *vb* **:** to vote or decide by ballot

ball·point *n* **:** a pen whose writing point is a small metal ball that inks itself from an inner supply

ball·room *n* **:** a large room for dances

balmy *adj* **balm·i·er; balm·i·est :** gently soothing

bal·sa *n* **:** the very light but strong wood of a tropical American tree

bal·sam *n* **1 :** a material with a strong pleasant smell that oozes from some plants **2 :** a plant (as the evergreen **balsam fir** often used as a Christmas tree) that yields balsam

bal·us·ter *n* **:** a short post that supports the upper part of a railing

bal·us·trade *n* **:** a row of balusters topped by a rail to serve as an open fence (as along the edge of a terrace or a balcony)

bam·boo *n* **:** a tall treelike tropical grass with a hard jointed stem that is used in making furniture and in building

[1]**ban** *vb* **banned; ban·ning :** to forbid especially by law or social pressure

[2]**ban** *n* **:** an official order forbidding something

ba·nana *n* **:** a yellow or red fruit that is shaped somewhat like a finger and grows in bunches on a large treelike tropical plant (**banana plant** or **banana tree**) with very large leaves

[1]**band** *n* **1 :** something that holds together or goes around something else **2 :** a strip of material around or across something **3 :** a range of frequencies (as of radio waves)

[2]**band** *vb* **1 :** to put a band on **:** tie together with a band **2 :** to unite in a group

[3]**band** *n* **1 :** a group of persons or animals **2 :** a group of musicians performing together

[1]**ban·dage** *n* **:** a strip of material used especially to dress and bind up wounds

[2]**bandage** *vb* **ban·daged; ban·dag·ing :** to bind or cover with a bandage

ban·dan·na *or* **ban·dana** *n* **:** a large handkerchief usually with a colorful design printed on it

ban·dit *n* **:** a lawless person **:** one who lives outside the law

band·stand *n* **:** an outdoor platform used for band concerts

band·wag·on *n* **1 :** a wagon carrying musicians in a parade **2 :** a candidate, side, or movement that attracts growing support

[1]**bang** *vb* **:** to beat, strike, or shut with a loud noise

[2]**bang** *n* **1 :** a violent blow **2 :** a sudden loud noise **3 :** [2]THRILL 1

[3]**bang** *n* **:** hair cut short across the forehead — usually used in pl.

[4]**bang** *vb* **:** to cut (hair) short and squarely across

ban·ish *vb* **1 :** to force to leave a country **2 :** to drive away **:** DISMISS

ban·ish·ment *n* **:** a banishing from a country

ban·is·ter *n* **1 :** one of the slender posts used to support the handrail of a staircase **2 :** a handrail and its supporting posts **3 :** the handrail of a staircase

ban·jo *n pl* **banjos :** a musical instrument with four or five strings and a fretted neck

[1]**bank** *n* **1 :** a mound or ridge especially of earth **2 :** something shaped like a mound **3 :** an undersea elevation **:** SHOAL **4 :** the rising ground at the edge of a river, lake, or sea

[2]**bank** *vb* **1 :** to raise a bank around **2 :** to heap up in a bank **3 :** to build (a curve) with the road or track sloping upward from the inside edge **4 :** to cover with fuel or ashes so as to reduce the speed of burning **5 :** to tilt an airplane to one side when turning

[3]**bank** *n* **1 :** a place of business that lends, exchanges, takes care of, or issues money **2 :** a small closed container in which money may be saved **3 :** a storage place for a reserve supply

[4]**bank** *vb* **1 :** to have an account in a bank **2 :** to deposit in a bank

[5]**bank** *n* **:** a group or series of objects arranged together in a row

bank·er *n* **:** a person who is engaged in the business of a bank

bank·ing *n* **:** the business of a bank or banker

[1]**bank·rupt** *n* **:** a person who becomes unable to pay his or her debts and whose property is by court order divided among the creditors

[2]**bankrupt** *adj* **:** unable to pay one's debts

[3]**bankrupt** *vb* **:** to make bankrupt

bank·rupt·cy *n pl* **bank·rupt·cies :** the state of being bankrupt

[1]**ban·ner** *n* **1 :** [1]FLAG **2 :** a piece of cloth with a design, a picture, or some writing on it

[2]**banner** *adj* **:** unusually good or satisfactory

ban·quet *n* **:** a formal dinner for many people often in honor of someone

ban·tam *n* **:** a miniature breed of domestic chicken often raised for exhibiting in shows

[1]**ban·ter** *vb* **:** to speak to in a friendly but teasing way

[2]**banter** *n* **:** good-natured teasing and joking

bap·tism *n* **:** the act or ceremony of baptizing

bap·tize *vb* **bap·tized; bap·tiz·ing 1 :** to dip in water or sprinkle water on as a part of the ceremony of receiving into the Christian church **2 :** to give a name to as in the ceremony of baptism **:** CHRISTEN

[1]**bar** *n* **1 :** a usually slender rigid piece (as of wood or metal) that has many uses (as for a lever or barrier) **2 :** a usually rectangular solid piece or block of something **3 :** something that blocks the way **4 :** a submerged or partly submerged bank along a shore or in a river **5 :** a court of law **6 :** the profession of law **7 :** a straight stripe, band, or line longer than it is wide **8 :** a counter on which liquor is served **9 :** a place of business for the sale of alcoholic drinks **10 :** a vertical line across a musical staff marking equal measures of time **11 :** [1]MEASURE 6

[2]**bar** *vb* **barred; bar·ring 1 :** to fasten with a bar **2 :** to block off **3 :** to shut out

[3]**bar** *prep* **:** with the exception of

barb *n* **:** a sharp point that sticks out and backward (as from the tip of an arrow or fishhook) — **barbed** *adj*

bar·bar·i·an *n* **:** an uncivilized person

bar·bar·ic *adj* **:** of, relating to, or characteristic of barbarians

bar·ba·rous *adj* **1 :** not civilized **2 :** CRUEL 2, HARSH — **bar·ba·rous·ly** *adv*

[1]**bar·be·cue** *vb* **bar·be·cued; bar·be·cu·ing 1 :** to cook over or before an open source of heat **2 :** to cook in a highly seasoned sauce

[2]**barbecue** *n* **1 :** a large animal roasted whole **2 :** an outdoor social gathering at which food is barbecued and eaten

bar·ber *n* **:** a person whose business is cutting and dressing hair and shaving beards

bard *n* **1 :** a person in ancient societies skilled at composing and singing songs about heroes **2 :** POET

[1]**bare** *adj* **bar·er; bar·est 1 :** having no covering **:** NAKED **2 :** [1]EMPTY 1 **3 :** having nothing left over or added **:** MERE **4 :** [1]PLAIN 3

[2]**bare** *vb* **bared; bar·ing :** UNCOVER 1, 2

bare·back *adv or adj* **:** on the bare back of a horse **:** without a saddle

bare·foot *adv or adj* **:** with the feet bare

bare·head·ed *adv or adj* : with the head bare : without a hat

bare·ly *adv* : with nothing to spare

[1]bar·gain *n* **1** : an agreement between persons settling what each is to give and receive in a business deal **2** : something bought or offered for sale at a desirable price

[2]bargain *vb* : to talk over the terms of a purchase or agreement

barge *n* : a broad boat with a flat bottom used chiefly in harbors and on rivers and canals

bar graph *n* : a chart that uses parallel bars whose lengths are in proportion to the numbers represented

bari·tone *n* **1** : a male singing voice between bass and tenor in range **2** : a singer having a baritone voice **3** : a horn used in bands that is lower than the trumpet but higher than the tuba

[1]bark *vb* **1** : to make the short loud cry of a dog **2** : to shout or speak sharply

[2]bark *n* : the sound made by a barking dog

[3]bark *n* : the outside covering of the trunk, branches, and roots of a tree

[4]bark *vb* : to rub or scrape the skin off

[5]bark *or* **barque** *n* **1** : a small sailing boat **2** : a three-masted ship with foremast and mainmast square-rigged

bark·er *n* : a person who stands at the entrance to a show and tries to attract people to it

bar·ley *n* : a cereal grass with flowers in dense heads that is grown for its grain which is used mostly to feed farm animals or make malt

bar mitz·vah *n, often cap B&M* **1** : a Jewish boy who at 13 years of age takes on religious responsibilities **2** : the ceremony recognizing a boy as a bar mitzvah

barn *n* : a building used for storing grain and hay and for housing farm animals

bar·na·cle *n* : a small saltwater shellfish that fastens itself on rocks or on wharves and the bottoms of ships

barn·yard *n* : a usually fenced area next to a barn

ba·rom·e·ter *n* : an instrument that measures air pressure and is used to forecast changes in the weather

bar·on *n* : a member of the lowest rank of the British nobility

bar·on·ess *n* **1** : the wife or widow of a baron **2** : a woman who holds the rank of a baron in her own right

bar·on·et *n* : the holder of a rank of honor below a baron but above a knight

ba·ro·ni·al *adj* : of, relating to, or suitable for a baron

barque *variant of* BARK

bar·racks *n sing or pl* : a building or group of buildings in which soldiers live

bar·rage *n* : a barrier formed by continuous artillery or machine-gun fire directed upon a narrow strip of ground

[1]bar·rel *n* **1** : a round bulging container that is longer than it is wide and has flat ends **2** : the amount contained in a full barrel **3** : something shaped like a cylinder

[2]barrel *vb* **bar·reled** *or* **bar·relled; bar·rel·ing** *or* **bar·rel·ling** : to move at a high speed

[1]bar·ren *adj* **1** : unable to produce seed, fruit, or young **2** : growing only poor or few plants

[2]barren *n* : an area of barren land

bar·rette *n* : a clasp or bar used to hold a girl's or woman's hair in place

[1]bar·ri·cade *vb* **bar·ri·cad·ed; bar·ri·cad·ing** : to block off with a barricade

[2]barricade *n* : a barrier made in a hurry for protection against attack or for blocking the way

bar·ri·er *n* **1** : something (as a fence) that blocks the way **2** : something that keeps apart or makes progress difficult

bar·ring *prep* : aside from the possibility of

[1]bar·row *n* : a castrated male hog

[2]barrow *n* **1** : WHEELBARROW **2** : PUSHCART

[1]bar·ter *vb* : to trade by exchanging one thing for another without the use of money

[2]barter *n* : the exchange of goods without the use of money

[1]base *n* **1** : a thing or a part on which something rests : BOTTOM, FOUNDATION **2** : a line or surface of a geometric figure upon which an altitude is or is thought to be constructed **3** : the main substance in a mixture **4** : a supporting or carrying substance (as in a medicine or paint) **5** : a place where a military force keeps its supplies or from which it starts its operations **6** : a number with reference to which a system of numbers is constructed **7** : a starting place or goal in various games **8** : any of the four stations a runner in baseball must touch in order to score **9** : a chemical substance (as lime or ammonia) that reacts with an acid to form a salt and turns red litmus paper blue

[2]base *vb* **based; bas·ing** : to provide with a base or basis

[3]base *adj* **bas·er; bas·est** **1** : of low value and not very good in some ways **2** : not honorable : MEAN — **base·ness** *n*

base·ball *n* **1** : a game played with a bat and ball by two teams of nine players on a field with four bases that mark the course a runner must take to score **2** : the ball used in baseball

base·board *n* : a line of boards or molding

extending around the walls of a room and touching the floor

base·ment *n* **:** the part of a building that is partly or entirely below ground level

bash *vb* **:** to hit very hard

bash·ful *adj* **:** uneasy in the presence of others

ba·sic *adj* **1 :** of, relating to, or forming the base of something **2 :** relating to or characteristic of a chemical base — **ba·si·cal·ly** *adv*

ba·sil *n* **:** a fragrant mint used in cooking

ba·sin *n* **1 :** a wide shallow usually round dish or bowl for holding liquids **2 :** the amount that a basin holds **3 :** a natural or artificial hollow or enclosure containing water **4 :** the land drained by a river and its branches

ba·sis *n pl* **ba·ses :** FOUNDATION 2, BASE

bask *vb* **:** to lie or relax in pleasantly warm surroundings

bas·ket *n* **1 :** a container made by weaving together materials (as reeds, straw, or strips of wood) **2 :** the contents of a basket **3 :** something that is like a basket in shape or use **4 :** a goal in basketball — **bas·ket·like** *adj*

bas·ket·ball *n* **1 :** a game in which each of two teams tries to throw a round inflated ball through a raised basketlike goal **2 :** the ball used in basketball

bas·ket·ry *n* **1 :** the making of objects (as baskets) by weaving or braiding long slender pieces (as of reed or wood) **2 :** objects made of interwoven twigs or reeds

bas-re·lief *n* **:** a sculpture in which the design is raised very slightly from the background

[1]**bass** *n pl* **bass** *or* **bass·es :** any of numerous freshwater and sea fishes that are caught for sport and food

[2]**bass** *n* **1 :** a tone of low pitch **2 :** the lowest part in harmony that has four parts **3 :** the lower half of the musical pitch range **4 :** the lowest male singing voice **5 :** a singer or an instrument having a bass range or part

bass drum *n* **:** a large drum with two heads that produces a low booming sound when played

bas·soon *n* **:** a double-reed woodwind instrument with a usual range two octaves lower than an oboe

bass viol *n* **:** DOUBLE BASS

bass·wood *n* **:** a pale wood with straight grain from the linden or a related tree

[1]**baste** *vb* **bast·ed; bast·ing :** to sew with long loose stitches so as to hold the work temporarily in place

[2]**baste** *vb* **bast·ed; bast·ing :** to moisten (as with melted fat or juices) while roasting

[1]**bat** *n* **1 :** a sharp blow or slap **2 :** an implement used for hitting the ball in various games **3 :** a turn at batting

[2]**bat** *vb* **bat·ted; bat·ting 1 :** to strike with or as if with a bat **2 :** to take one's turn at bat

[3]**bat** *n* **:** any of a group of mammals that fly by means of long front limbs modified into wings

batch *n* **1 :** a quantity of something baked at one time **2 :** a quantity of material for use at one time or produced at one operation **3 :** a group of persons or things

bath *n pl* **baths 1 :** a washing of the body **2 :** water for bathing **3 :** a place, room, or building where persons may bathe **4 :** BATHTUB **5 :** a liquid in which objects are placed so that it can act upon them

bathe *vb* **bathed; bath·ing 1 :** to take a bath **2 :** to go swimming **3 :** to give a bath to **4 :** to apply a liquid to **5 :** to cover with or as if with a liquid — **bath·er** *n*

bathing suit *n* **:** SWIMSUIT

bath·room *n* **:** a room containing a sink and toilet and often a bathtub or shower

bath·tub *n* **:** a tub in which to take a bath

bat mitz·vah *n, often cap B&M* **1 :** a Jewish girl who at 12 or 13 years of age takes on religious responsibilites **2 :** the ceremony recognizing a girl as a bat mitzvah

ba·ton *n* **1 :** a stick with which a leader directs an orchestra or band **2 :** a rod with a ball on one end carried by a drum major or drum majorette

bat·tal·ion *n* **1 :** a part of an army consisting of two or more companies **2 :** a large body of persons organized to act together

[1]**bat·ter** *vb* **1 :** to beat with repeated violent blows **2 :** to damage by blows or hard use

[2]**batter** *n* **:** a thin mixture made chiefly of flour and a liquid used in making cakes and biscuits

[3]**batter** *n* **:** the player whose turn it is to bat

bat·tered *adj* **:** worn down or injured by hard use

bat·ter·ing ram *n* **1 :** an ancient military machine that consisted of a heavy beam with an iron tip swung back and forth in order to batter down walls **2 :** a heavy metal bar with handles used (as by firefighters) to batter down doors or walls

bat·tery *n pl* **bat·ter·ies 1 :** two or more big military guns that are controlled as a unit **2 :** an electric cell for providing electric current or a group of such cells **3 :** a number of machines or devices grouped together

bat·ting *n* **:** cotton or wool in sheets used mostly for stuffing quilts or packaging goods

[1]**bat·tle** *n* **1 :** a fight between armies, warships, or airplanes **2 :** a fight between two

persons or animals **3 :** a long or hard struggle or contest **4 :** WARFARE

[2]**battle** *vb* **bat·tled; bat·tling :** to engage in battle

bat·tle–ax *or* **bat·tle–axe** *n* **:** an ax with a broad blade formerly used as a weapon

bat·tle·field *n* **:** a place where a battle is fought or was once fought

bat·tle·ground *n* **:** BATTLEFIELD

bat·tle·ment *n* **:** a low wall (as at the top of a castle) with openings to shoot through

bat·tle·ship *n* **:** a large warship with heavy armor and large guns

[1]**bawl** *vb* **1 :** to shout or cry loudly **2 :** to weep noisily

[2]**bawl** *n* **:** a loud cry

bawl out *vb* **:** to scold severely

[1]**bay** *n* **1 :** a reddish-brown horse **2 :** a reddish brown

[2]**bay** *vb* **:** to bark with long deep tones

[3]**bay** *n* **1 :** the baying of dogs **2 :** the position of an animal or a person forced to face pursuers when it is impossible to escape **3 :** the position of pursuers who are held off

[4]**bay** *n* **:** a part of a large body of water extending into the land

[5]**bay** *n* **:** the laurel or a related tree or shrub

bay·ber·ry *n pl* **bay·ber·ries :** a shrub with leathery leaves and small bluish white waxy berries used in making candles

[1]**bay·o·net** *n* **:** a weapon like a dagger made to fit on the end of a rifle

[2]**bayonet** *vb* **bay·o·net·ted; bay·o·net·ting :** to stab with a bayonet

bay·ou *n* **:** a creek that flows slowly through marshy land

bay window *n* **:** a window or a set of windows that sticks out from the wall of a building

ba·zaar *n* **1 :** a marketplace (as in southwestern Asia and northern Africa) containing rows of small shops **2 :** a large building where many kinds of goods are sold **3 :** a fair for the sale of goods especially for charity

ba·zoo·ka *n* **:** a portable shoulder gun consisting of a tube open at both ends that shoots an explosive rocket able to pierce armor

be *vb past 1st & 3d sing* **was;** *2d sing* **were;** *pl* **were;** *past subjunctive* **were;** *past participle* **been;** *present participle* **be·ing;** *present 1st sing* **am;** *2d sing* **are;** *3d sing* **is;** *pl* **are;** *present subjunctive* **be 1 :** to equal in meaning or identity **2 :** to have a specified character or quality **3 :** to belong to the class of **4 :** EXIST 1, LIVE **5** — used as a helping verb with other verbs

be- *prefix* **1 : on : around : over 2 : provide with or cover with : dress up with 3 : about : to : upon 4 : make : cause to be**

[1]**beach** *n* **:** a sandy or gravelly part of the shore of the sea or of a lake

[2]**beach** *vb* **:** to run or drive ashore

beach·head *n* **:** an area on an enemy shore held by an advance force of an invading army to protect the later landing of troops or supplies

bea·con *n* **1 :** a guiding or warning light or fire on a high place **2 :** a radio station that sends out signals to guide aircraft

[1]**bead** *n* **1 :** a small piece of solid material with a hole through it by which it can be strung on a thread **2 :** a small round mass **3 :** a small knob on a gun used in taking aim

[2]**bead** *vb* **1 :** to cover with beads **2 :** to string together like beads

beady *adj* **bead·i·er; bead·i·est :** like a bead especially in being small, round, and shiny

bea·gle *n* **:** a small hound with short legs and a smooth coat

beak *n* **1 :** the bill of a bird **2 :** a part shaped like a beak — **beaked** *adj*

bea·ker *n* **:** a deep cup or glass with a wide mouth and usually a lip for pouring

[1]**beam** *n* **1 :** a long heavy piece of timber or metal used as a main horizontal support of a building or a ship **2 :** a ray of light **3 :** a constant radio wave sent out from an airport to guide pilots along a course

[2]**beam** *vb* **1 :** to send out beams of light **2 :** to smile with joy **3 :** to aim a radio broadcast by use of a special antenna

bean *n* **1 :** the edible seed or pod of a bushy or climbing garden plant related to the peas and clovers **2 :** a seed or fruit like a bean

[1]**bear** *n pl* **bears 1** *or pl* **bear :** a large heavy mammal with long shaggy hair and a very short tail **2 :** a grumpy or glum person

[2]**bear** *vb* **bore; borne; bear·ing 1 :** [1]SUPPORT 4 **2 :** to have as a feature or characteristic **3 :** to bring forth **:** give birth to **4 :** to put up with **5 :** [2]PRESS 1 **6 :** to have a relation to the matter at hand

bear·able *adj* **:** possible to bear

beard *n* **1 :** the hair on the face of a man **2 :** a hairy growth or tuft

bear·er *n* **1 :** someone or something that bears, supports, or carries **2 :** a person holding a check or an order for payment

bear·ing *n* **1 :** the manner in which one carries or conducts oneself **2 :** a part of a machine in which another part turns **3 :** the position or direction of one point with respect to another or to the compass **4 bearings** *pl* **:** understanding of one's position or situation **5 :** CONNECTION 2

beast *n* **1 :** a mammal with four feet (as a bear, deer, or rabbit) **2 :** a farm animal especially when kept for work **3 :** a mean or horrid person

[1]**beat** *vb* **beat; beat·en** *or* **beat; beat·ing** **1** : to strike again and again **2** : [1]THROB 2, PULSATE **3** : to flap against **4** : to mix by stirring rapidly **5** : to win against **6** : to measure or mark off by strokes — **beat·er** *n*

[2]**beat** *n* **1** : a blow or a stroke made again and again **2** : a single pulse (as of the heart) **3** : a measurement of time or accent in music **4** : an area or place regularly visited or traveled through

[3]**beat** *adj* **1** : being very tired **2** : having lost one's morale

beat·en *adj* : worn smooth by passing feet

be·at·i·tude *n* : one of the statements made in the Sermon on the Mount (Matthew 5: 3-12) beginning "Blessed are"

beau *n pl* **beaux** *or* **beaus** : BOYFRIEND

beau·te·ous *adj* : BEAUTIFUL

beau·ti·cian *n* : a person who gives beauty treatments (as to skin and hair)

beau·ti·ful *adj* : having qualities of beauty : giving pleasure to the mind or senses — **beau·ti·ful·ly** *adv*

beau·ti·fy *vb* **beau·ti·fied; beau·ti·fy·ing** : to make beautiful

beau·ty *n pl* **beauties** **1** : the qualities of a person or a thing that give pleasure to the senses or to the mind **2** : a beautiful person or thing

beauty shop *n* : a place of business for the care of customers' hair, skin, and nails

bea·ver *n* : an animal related to the rats and mice that has webbed hind feet and a broad flat tail, builds dams and houses of sticks and mud in water, and is prized for its soft but strong fur

be·calm *vb* : to bring to a stop because of lack of wind

became *past of* BECOME

be·cause *conj* : for the reason that

because of *prep* : as a result of

beck *n* : a beckoning motion

beck·on *vb* : to call or signal by a motion (as a wave or nod)

be·come *vb* **be·came; become; be·com·ing** **1** : to come or grow to be **2** : to be suitable to : SUIT — **become of** : to happen to

be·com·ing *adj* : having a pleasing effect — **be·com·ing·ly** *adv*

[1]**bed** *n* **1** : a piece of furniture on which one may sleep or rest **2** : a place for sleeping or resting **3** : a level piece of ground prepared for growing plants **4** : the bottom of something **5** : LAYER 2

[2]**bed** *vb* **bed·ded; bed·ding** **1** : to put or go to bed **2** : to plant in beds

bed·bug *n* : a small wingless insect that sucks blood and is sometimes found in houses and especially in beds

bed·clothes *n pl* : coverings (as sheets and pillowcases) for a bed

bed·ding *n* **1** : BEDCLOTHES **2** : material for a bed

be·dev·il *vb* : to trouble or annoy again and again : PESTER, HARASS

bed·lam *n* : a place or scene of uproar and confusion

be·drag·gled *adj* **1** : limp and often wet as by exposure to rain **2** : soiled from or as if from being dragged in mud

bed·rid·den *adj* : forced to stay in bed by sickness or weakness

bed·rock *n* : the solid rock found under surface materials (as soil)

bed·room *n* : a room to sleep in

bed·side *n* : the place beside a bed

bed·spread *n* : a decorative top covering for a bed

bed·stead *n* : the framework of a bed

bed·time *n* : time to go to bed

bee *n* **1** : an insect with four wings that is related to the wasps, gathers pollen and nectar from flowers from which it makes beebread and honey for food, and usually lives in large colonies **2** : a gathering of people to do something together

bee·bread *n* : a bitter yellowish brown food material prepared by bees from pollen and stored in their honeycomb

beech *n* : a tree with smooth gray bark, deep green leaves, and small triangular nuts

beef *n pl* **beefs** *or* **beeves** **1** : the flesh of a steer, cow, or bull **2** : a steer, cow, or bull especially when fattened for food — **beef·like** *adj*

beef·steak *n* : a slice of beef suitable for broiling or frying

bee·hive *n* : HIVE 1

bee·line *n* : a straight direct course

been *past participle of* BE

beer *n* : an alcoholic drink made from malt and flavored with hops

bees·wax *n* : wax made by bees and used by them in building honeycomb

beet *n* : a leafy plant with a thick juicy root that is used as a vegetable or as a source of sugar

bee·tle *n* **1** : any of a group of insects with four wings the outer pair of which are stiff cases that cover the others when folded **2** : an insect (as a bug) that looks like a beetle

beeves *pl of* BEEF

be·fall *vb* **be·fell; be·fall·en; be·fall·ing** **1** : to take place : HAPPEN **2** : to happen to

be·fit *vb* **be·fit·ted; be·fit·ting** : to be suitable to or proper for

[1]**be·fore** *adv* **1** : in front : AHEAD **2** : in the past **3** : at an earlier time

²before *prep* **1 :** in front of **2 :** in the presence of **3 :** earlier than
³before *conj* **1 :** ahead of the time when **2 :** more willingly than
be·fore·hand *adv* **:** ¹BEFORE 1 **:** ahead of time
be·friend *vb* **:** to act as a friend to **:** help in a friendly way
beg *vb* **begged; beg·ging 1 :** to ask for money, food, or help as a charity **2 :** to ask as a favor in an earnest or polite way
beg·gar *n* **1 :** one who lives by begging **2 :** PAUPER
be·gin *vb* **be·gan; be·gun; be·gin·ning 1 :** to do the first part of an action **2 :** to come into existence
be·gin·ner *n* **:** a young or inexperienced person
be·gin·ning *n* **1 :** the point at which something begins **2 :** first part
be·gone *vb* **:** to go away **:** DEPART — used especially in the imperative mood
be·go·nia *n* **:** a plant with a juicy stem, ornamental leaves, and bright waxy flowers
be·grudge *vb* **be·grudged; be·grudg·ing :** to give or do reluctantly
begun *past of* BEGIN
be·half *n* **:** one's interest or support
be·have *vb* **be·haved; be·hav·ing 1 :** to conduct oneself **2 :** to conduct oneself properly **3 :** to act or function in a particular way
be·hav·ior *n* **1 :** the way in which one conducts oneself **2 :** the whole activity of something and especially a living being
be·head *vb* **:** to cut off the head of
¹be·hind *adv* **1 :** in a place that is being or has been departed from **2 :** at, to, or toward the back **3 :** not up to the general level
²behind *prep* **1 :** at or to the back of **2 :** not up to the level of
be·hold *vb* **be·held; be·hold·ing :** to look upon **:** SEE — **be·hold·er** *n*
beige *n* **:** a yellowish brown
be·ing *n* **1 :** the state of having life or existence **2 :** one that exists in fact or thought **3 :** a living thing
be·la·bor *vb* **:** to keep working on to excess
be·lat·ed *adj* **:** delayed beyond the usual or expected time
¹belch *vb* **1 :** to force out gas suddenly from the stomach through the mouth **2 :** to throw out or be thrown out violently
²belch *n* **:** a belching of gas
bel·fry *n pl* **belfries :** a tower or room in a tower for a bell or set of bells
¹Bel·gian *adj* **:** of or relating to Belgium or the Belgians
²Belgian *n* **:** a person born or living in Belgium
be·lief *n* **1 :** a feeling sure that a person or thing exists or is true or trustworthy **2 :** religious faith **:** CREED **3 :** something that one thinks is true
be·liev·able *adj* **:** possible to believe
be·lieve *vb* **be·lieved; be·liev·ing 1 :** to have faith or confidence in the existence or worth of **2 :** to accept as true **3 :** to accept the word of **4 :** THINK 2
be·liev·er *n* **:** one who has faith (as in a religion)
be·lit·tle *vb* **be·lit·tled; be·lit·tling :** to make (a person or a thing) seem small or unimportant
bell *n* **1 :** a hollow metallic device that is shaped somewhat like a cup and makes a ringing sound when struck **2 :** the stroke or sound of a bell that tells the hour **3 :** the time indicated by the stroke of a bell **4 :** a half-hour period of watch on shipboard **5 :** something shaped like a bell
bell·boy *n* **:** BELLHOP
bell·hop *n* **:** a hotel or club employee who answers calls for service by bell or telephone and assists guests with luggage
¹bel·lig·er·ent *adj* **1 :** carrying on war **2 :** eager to fight
²belligerent *n* **1 :** a nation at war **2 :** a person taking part in a fight
bell jar *n* **:** a usually glass vessel shaped like a bell and used to cover objects or to contain gases or a vacuum
¹bel·low *vb* **:** to give a loud deep roar like that of a bull
²bellow *n* **:** a loud deep roar
bel·lows *n sing or pl* **1 :** a device that produces a strong current of air when its sides are pressed together **2 :** the folding part of some cameras
¹bel·ly *n pl* **bellies 1 :** ABDOMEN 1 **2 :** the under part of an animal's body **3 :** STOMACH 1 **4 :** an internal cavity (as of the human body) **5 :** the thick part of a muscle
²belly *vb* **bel·lied; bel·ly·ing :** to swell out
belly button *n* **:** NAVEL
be·long *vb* **1 :** to be in a proper place **2 :** to be the property of a person or group of persons **3 :** to be a part of **:** be connected with **:** go with
be·long·ings *n pl* **:** the things that belong to a person
be·lov·ed *adj* **:** greatly loved **:** very dear
¹be·low *adv* **:** in or to a lower place
²below *prep* **:** lower than **:** BENEATH
¹belt *n* **1 :** a strip of flexible material (as leather or cloth) worn around a person's body for holding in or supporting clothing or weapons or for ornament **2 :** something like a belt **:** BAND, CIRCLE **3 :** a flexible endless band running around wheels or pulleys and used for moving or carrying something **4 :** a region suited to or producing something

or having some special feature — **belt·ed** *adj*

²belt *vb* **1 :** to put a belt on or around **2 :** to strike hard

be·moan *vb* **:** to express grief over

bench *n* **1 :** a long seat for two or more persons **2 :** a long table for holding work and tools **3 :** the position or rank of a judge

¹bend *vb* **bent; bend·ing 1 :** to make, be, or become curved or angular rather than straight or flat **2 :** to move out of a straight line or position **:** STOOP **3 :** to turn in a certain direction **:** DIRECT

²bend *n* **:** something that is bent **:** CURVE

¹be·neath *adv* **:** in a lower place

²beneath *prep* **1 :** lower than **:** UNDER **2 :** not worthy of

bene·dic·tion *n* **1 :** an expression of approval **2 :** a short blessing by a minister or priest at the end of a religious service

ben·e·fac·tor *n* **:** one who helps another especially by giving money

ben·e·fi·cial *adj* **:** producing good results **:** HELPFUL — **ben·e·fi·cial·ly** *adv*

ben·e·fi·cia·ry *n pl* **ben·e·fi·cia·ries :** a person who benefits or is expected to benefit from something

¹ben·e·fit *n* **1 :** something that does good to a person or thing **2 :** money paid in time of death, sickness, or unemployment or in old age (as by an insurance company)

²benefit *vb* **ben·e·fit·ed** *or* **ben·e·fit·ted; ben·e·fit·ing** *or* **ben·e·fit·ting 1 :** to be useful or profitable to **2 :** to receive benefit

be·nev·o·lence *n* **:** KINDNESS, GENEROSITY

be·nev·o·lent *adj* **:** having a desire to do good **:** KINDLY, CHARITABLE

be·nign *adj* **1 :** of a gentle disposition **2 :** likely to bring about a good outcome — **be·nign·ly** *adv*

¹bent *adj* **1 :** changed by bending **:** CROOKED **2 :** strongly favorable to **:** quite determined

²bent *n* **:** a strong or natural liking

be·queath *vb* **1 :** to give or leave by means of a will **2 :** to hand down

be·quest *n* **1 :** the act of bequeathing **2 :** something given or left by a will

¹be·reaved *adj* **:** suffering the death of a loved one

²bereaved *n pl* **bereaved :** a bereaved person

be·reft *adj* **1 :** not having something needed, wanted, or expected **2 :** ¹BEREAVED

be·ret *n* **:** a soft round flat cap without a visor

berg *n* **:** ICEBERG

beri·beri *n* **:** a disease caused by lack of a vitamin in which there is weakness, wasting, and damage to nerves

¹ber·ry *n pl* **berries 1 :** a small pulpy fruit (as a strawberry) **2 :** a simple fruit (as a grape or tomato) in which the ripened ovary wall is fleshy **3 :** a dry seed (as of the coffee tree)

²berry *vb* **ber·ried; ber·ry·ing :** to gather berries

berth *n* **1 :** a place where a ship lies at anchor or at a wharf **2 :** a bed on a ship, train, or airplane

be·seech *vb* **be·sought** *or* **be·seeched; be·seech·ing :** to ask earnestly

be·set *vb* **be·set; be·set·ting 1 :** to attack from all sides **2 :** SURROUND

be·side *prep* **1 :** by the side of **:** NEXT TO **2 :** compared with **3 :** ¹BESIDES **4 :** away from **:** wide of — **beside oneself :** very upset

¹be·sides *prep* **1 :** in addition to **2 :** other than

²besides *adv* **:** in addition **:** ALSO

be·siege *vb* **be·sieged; be·sieg·ing 1 :** to surround with armed forces for the purpose of capturing **2 :** to crowd around — **be·sieg·er** *n*

besought *past of* BESEECH

¹best *adj, superlative of* GOOD **:** good or useful in the highest degree **:** most excellent — **best part :** ³MOST

²best *adv, superlative of* WELL **1 :** in the best way **2 :** ²MOST 1

³best *n* **1 :** a person or thing or part of a thing that is best **2 :** one's greatest effort

⁴best *vb* **:** to get the better of

be·stir *vb* **be·stirred; be·stir·ring :** to stir up **:** rouse to action

be·stow *vb* **:** to present as a gift

¹bet *n* **1 :** an agreement requiring the person who guesses wrong about the result of a contest or the outcome of an event to give something to the person who guesses right **2 :** the money or thing risked in a bet

²bet *vb* **bet** *or* **bet·ted; bet·ting 1 :** to risk in a bet **2 :** to be sure enough to make a bet

be·tray *vb* **1 :** to give over to an enemy by treason or fraud **2 :** to be unfaithful to **3 :** REVEAL 2, SHOW

be·troth *vb* **:** to promise to marry or give in marriage

be·troth·al *n* **:** an engagement to be married

¹bet·ter *adj, comparative of* GOOD **1 :** more satisfactory than another thing **2 :** improved in health — **better part :** more than half

²better *vb* **:** to make or become better — **bet·ter·ment** *n*

³better *adv, comparative of* WELL **:** in a superior or more excellent way

⁴better *n* **1 :** a better person or thing **2 :** ADVANTAGE 1, VICTORY

bet·tor *or* **bet·ter** *n* **:** one that bets

¹be·tween *prep* **1 :** by the efforts of each of **2 :** in or into the interval separating **3 :** functioning to separate or tell apart **4 :** by comparing **5 :** shared by **6 :** in shares to each of

[2]**between** *adv* : in a position between others
[1]**bev·el** *n* : a slant or slope of one surface or line against another
[2]**bevel** *vb* **bev·eled** *or* **bev·elled; bev·el·ing** *or* **bev·el·ling** : to cut or shape (an edge or surface) so as to form a bevel
bev·er·age *n* : a liquid that is drunk for food or pleasure
be·ware *vb* : to be cautious or careful
be·whis·kered *adj* : having whiskers
be·wil·der *vb* : to fill with uncertainty : CONFUSE — **be·wil·der·ment** *n*
be·witch *vb* **1** : to gain an influence over by means of magic or witchcraft **2** : to attract or delight as if by magic — **be·witch·ment** *n*
[1]**be·yond** *adv* : on or to the farther side
[2]**beyond** *prep* **1** : on the other side of **2** : out of the reach or sphere of
bi- *prefix* **1** : two **2** : coming or occurring every two **3** : into two parts **4** : twice : doubly : on both sides
[1]**bi·as** *n* **1** : a seam, cut, or stitching running in a slant across cloth **2** : a favoring of one way of feeling or acting over another : PREJUDICE
[2]**bias** *vb* **bi·ased** *or* **bi·assed; bi·as·ing** *or* **bi·as·sing** : to give a bias to
bib *n* **1** : a cloth or plastic shield tied under a child's chin to protect the clothes **2** : the upper part of an apron or of overalls
Bi·ble *n* **1** : the book made up of the writings accepted by Christians as coming from God **2** : a book containing the sacred writings of a religion
bib·li·cal *adj* : relating to, taken from, or found in the Bible
bib·li·og·ra·phy *n pl* **bib·li·og·ra·phies** : a list of writings about an author or a subject
bi·car·bon·ate of soda : SODIUM BICARBONATE
bi·ceps *n pl* **biceps** *also* **bi·ceps·es** : a large muscle of the upper arm
bick·er *vb* : to quarrel in a cross or silly way
bi·cus·pid *n* : either of the two teeth with double points on each side of each jaw of a person
[1]**bi·cy·cle** *n* : a light vehicle having two wheels one behind the other, a saddle seat, and pedals by which it is made to move
[2]**bicycle** *vb* **bi·cy·cled; bi·cy·cling** : to ride a bicycle
bi·cy·clist *n* : a person who rides a bicycle
[1]**bid** *vb* **bade** *or* **bid; bid·den** *or* **bid; bid·ding** **1** : [1]ORDER 2, COMMAND **2** : to express to **3** : to make an offer for something (as at an auction) — **bid·der** *n*
[2]**bid** *n* **1** : an offer to pay a certain sum for something or to do certain work at a stated fee **2** : INVITATION 2
bide *vb* **bode** *or* **bid·ed; bid·ed; bid·ing** : to wait or wait for
[1]**bi·en·ni·al** *adj* **1** : occurring every two years **2** : growing stalks and leaves one year and flowers and fruit the next before dying — **bi·en·ni·al·ly** *adv*
[2]**biennial** *n* : a biennial plant
bier *n* : a stand on which a corpse or coffin is placed
big *adj* **big·ger; big·gest** **1** : large in size **2** : IMPORTANT 1 — **big·ness** *n*
Big Dipper *n* : a group of seven stars in the northern sky arranged in a form like a dipper with the two stars that form the side opposite the handle pointing to the North Star
big·horn *n* : a grayish brown wild sheep of mountainous western North America
big tree *n* : a very large California sequoia with light soft brittle wood
bike *n* **1** : BICYCLE **2** : MOTORCYCLE
bile *n* : a thick bitter yellow or greenish fluid supplied by the liver to aid in digestion
bi·lin·gual *adj* : of, expressed in, or using two languages
[1]**bill** *n* **1** : the jaws of a bird together with their horny covering **2** : a part of an animal (as a turtle) that suggests the bill of a bird — **billed** *adj*
[2]**bill** *n* **1** : a draft of a law presented to a legislature for consideration **2** : a record of goods sold, services performed, or work done with the cost involved **3** : a sign or poster advertising something **4** : a piece of paper money
[3]**bill** *vb* : to send a bill to
bill·board *n* : a flat surface on which outdoor advertisements are displayed
bill·fold *n* : a folding pocketbook especially for paper money : WALLET
bil·liards *n* : a game played by driving solid balls with a cue into each other or into pockets on a large rectangular table
bil·lion *n* **1** : a thousand millions **2** : a very large number
[1]**bil·lionth** *adj* : being last in a series of a billion
[2]**billionth** *n* : number 1,000,000,000 in a series
[1]**bil·low** *n* : a great wave
[2]**billow** *vb* **1** : to roll in great waves **2** : to swell out
bil·ly club *n* : a heavy club (as of wood) carried by a police officer
billy goat *n* : a male goat
bin *n* : a box or enclosed place used for storage
bi·na·ry *adj* : of, relating to, or being a number system with a base of 2
bind *vb* **bound; bind·ing** **1** : to fasten by tying **2** : to hold or restrict by force or obli-

gation **3 :** ²BANDAGE **4 :** to finish or decorate with a binding **5 :** to fasten together and enclose in a cover

bind·er *n* **1 :** a person who binds books **2 :** a cover for holding together loose sheets of paper **3 :** a machine that cuts grain and ties it into bundles

bind·ing *n* **1 :** the cover and the fastenings of a book **2 :** a narrow strip of fabric used along the edge of an article of clothing

bin·go *n* **:** a game of chance played by covering a numbered space on a card when the number is matched by one drawn at random and won by the first player to cover five spaces in a row

bin·oc·u·lar *adj* **:** of, using, or suited for the use of both eyes

bin·oc·u·lars *n pl* **:** a hand-held instrument for seeing at a distance that is made up of two telescopes usually having prisms

bio- *prefix* **:** living matter

bio·de·grad·able *adj* **:** possible to break down and make harmless by the action of living things (as bacteria)

bio·di·ver·si·ty *n* **:** biological variety in an environment as shown by numbers of different kinds of plants and animals

bio·graph·i·cal *adj* **:** of or relating to the history of people's lives

bi·og·ra·phy *n pl* **bi·og·ra·phies :** a written history of a person's life

bi·o·log·i·cal *adj* **:** of or relating to biology

bi·ol·o·gist *n* **:** a specialist in biology

bi·ol·o·gy *n* **:** a science that deals with living things and their relationships, distribution, and behavior

bio·re·gion *n* **:** a region whose limits are naturally defined by geographic and biological features (as mountains and ecosystems) — **bio·re·gion·al** *adj*

bio·tech·nol·o·gy *n* **:** the use of techniques from genetics to combine inherited characteristics selected from different kinds of organisms into one organism in order to produce useful products (as drugs)

bi·ped *n* **:** an animal (as a person) that has only two feet

bi·plane *n* **:** an airplane with two wings on each side of the body usually placed one above the other

birch *n* **:** a tree with hard wood and a smooth bark that can be peeled off in thin layers

bird *n* **:** an animal that lays eggs and has wings and a body covered with feathers

bird·bath *n* **:** a basin for birds to bathe in

bird dog *n* **:** a dog trained to hunt or bring in game birds

bird·house *n* **1 :** an artificial nesting place for birds **2 :** AVIARY

bird of prey : a bird (as an eagle or owl) that feeds almost entirely on meat taken by hunting

bird·seed *n* **:** a mixture of small seeds used chiefly for feeding wild or caged birds

bird's–eye *adj* **:** seen from above as if by a flying bird

birth *n* **1 :** the coming of a new individual from the body of its parent **2 :** the act of bringing into life **3 :** LINEAGE 1 **4 :** ORIGIN 2

birth·day *n* **1 :** the day on which a person is born **2 :** a day of beginning **3 :** the return each year of the date on which a person was born or something began

birth·mark *n* **:** an unusual mark or blemish on the skin at birth

birth·place *n* **:** the place where a person was born or where something began

birth·right *n* **:** a right belonging to a person because of his or her birth

bis·cuit *n* **1 :** CRACKER **2 :** a small cake of raised dough baked in an oven

bi·sect *vb* **1 :** to divide into two usually equal parts **2 :** INTERSECT

bish·op *n* **1 :** a member of the clergy of high rank **2 :** a piece in the game of chess

bis·muth *n* **:** a heavy grayish white metallic chemical element that is used in alloys and in medicine

bi·son *n pl* **bison :** a large animal with short horns and a shaggy mane that is related to the cows and oxen

¹bit *n* **1 :** a part of a bridle that is put in the horse's mouth **2 :** the cutting or boring edge or part of a tool

²bit *n* **1 :** a small piece or quantity **2 :** a short time **3 :** ¹SOMEWHAT

³bit *n* **:** a unit of computer information that represents the selection of one of two possible choices (as *on* or *off*)

bitch *n* **:** a female dog

¹bite *vb* **bit; bit·ten; bit·ing 1 :** to seize, grip, or cut into with or as if with teeth **2 :** to wound or sting usually with a stinger or fang **3 :** to cause to sting **4 :** to take a bait

²bite *n* **1 :** a seizing of something with the teeth or the mouth **2 :** a wound made by biting **:** STING **3 :** the amount of food taken at a bite **4 :** a sharp or biting sensation

bit·ing *adj* **:** producing bodily or mental distress **:** SHARP

bit·ter *adj* **1 :** sharp, biting, and unpleasant to the taste **2 :** hard to put up with **3 :** very harsh or sharp **:** BITING **4 :** caused by anger, distress, or sorrow — **bit·ter·ly** *adv* — **bit·ter·ness** *n*

bit·tern *n* **:** a brownish marsh bird which has a loud booming cry

¹bit·ter·sweet *n* **1 :** a poisonous vine with purple flowers and red berries **2 :** a North

American woody climbing plant with orange seedcases that open when ripe and show the red-coated seeds

[2]**bittersweet** *adj* **:** being partly bitter or sad and partly sweet or happy

bi·tu·mi·nous coal *n* **:** a soft coal that gives much smoke when burned

bi·zarre *adj* **:** very strange or odd

blab *vb* **blabbed; blab·bing :** to talk too much

[1]**black** *adj* **1 :** of the color black **2 :** very dark **3 :** of or relating to any peoples having dark skin and especially any of the original peoples of Africa south of the Sahara **4** *often cap* **:** of or relating to Americans having ancestors from Africa south of the Sahara **5 :** WICKED **6 :** very sad or gloomy **7 :** UNFRIENDLY — **black·ness** *n*

[2]**black** *n* **1 :** a black pigment or dye **2 :** the color of coal **:** the opposite of white **3 :** black clothing **4 :** a person belonging to a people having dark skin and especially a black African **5** *often cap* **:** an American having black African ancestors

[3]**black** *vb* **:** BLACKEN 1

black–and–blue *adj* **:** darkly discolored (as from a bruise)

black·ber·ry *n pl* **black·ber·ries :** the black or dark purple sweet juicy berry of a prickly plant related to the raspberry

black·bird *n* **:** any of several birds of which the males are mostly black

black·board *n* **:** a hard smooth usually dark surface used especially in a classroom for writing or drawing on with chalk

black·en *vb* **1 :** to make or become black **2 :** [2]SPOIL 2

black–eyed Su·san *n* **:** a daisy with yellow or orange petals and a dark center

black·head *n* **:** a dark plug of hardened oily material blocking the opening of a skin gland

black·ish *adj* **:** somewhat black

[1]**black·mail** *n* **1 :** the forcing of someone to pay money by threatening to reveal a secret that might bring disgrace on him or her **2 :** money paid under threat of blackmail

[2]**blackmail** *vb* **:** to threaten with the revealing of a secret unless money is paid — **black·mail·er** *n*

black·out *n* **1 :** a period of darkness enforced as a protection against air raids **2 :** a period of darkness caused by power failure **3 :** a temporary loss of vision or consciousness

black out *vb* **:** to lose consciousness or the ability to see for a short time

black·smith *n* **:** a person who makes things out of iron by heating and hammering it

black·snake *n* **:** either of two harmless snakes of the United States with blackish skins

black·top *n* **:** a black material used especially to pave roads

black widow *n* **:** a poisonous spider the female of which is black with a red mark shaped like an hourglass on the underside of the abdomen

blad·der *n* **1 :** a pouch into which urine passes from the kidneys **2 :** a container that can be filled with air or gas

blade *n* **1 :** a leaf of a plant and especially of a grass **2 :** the broad flat part of a leaf **3 :** something that widens out like the blade of a leaf **4 :** the cutting part of a tool or machine **5 :** SWORD **6 :** the runner of an ice skate — **blad·ed** *adj*

[1]**blame** *vb* **blamed; blam·ing 1 :** to find fault with **2 :** to hold responsible **3 :** to place responsibility for

[2]**blame** *n* **1 :** expression of disapproval **2 :** responsibility for something that fails — **blame·less** *adj*

blame·wor·thy *adj* **:** deserving blame

blanch *vb* **1 :** [1]BLEACH, WHITEN **2 :** to scald so as to remove the skin from **3 :** to turn pale

[1]**blank** *adj* **1 :** seeming to be confused **2 :** not having any writing or marks **3 :** having empty spaces to be filled in

[2]**blank** *n* **1 :** an empty space in a line of writing or printing **2 :** a paper with empty spaces to be filled in **3 :** a cartridge loaded with powder but no bullet

[1]**blan·ket** *n* **1 :** a heavy woven covering used for beds **2 :** a covering layer

[2]**blanket** *vb* **:** to cover with a blanket

[1]**blare** *vb* **blared; blar·ing 1 :** to sound loud and harsh **2 :** to present in a harsh noisy manner

[2]**blare** *n* **:** a harsh loud noise

[1]**blast** *n* **1 :** a strong gust of wind **2 :** a stream of air or gas forced through an opening **3 :** the sound made by a wind instrument **4 :** EXPLOSION 1

[2]**blast** *vb* **1 :** [2]BLIGHT **2 :** to break to pieces by an explosion **:** SHATTER

blast–off *n* **:** an instance of blasting off (as of a rocket)

blast off *vb* **:** to take off — used of vehicles using rockets for power

[1]**blaze** *n* **1 :** a bright hot flame **2 :** great brightness and heat **3 :** OUTBURST 1 **4 :** a bright display

[2]**blaze** *vb* **blazed; blaz·ing 1 :** to burn brightly **2 :** to shine as if on fire

[3]**blaze** *n* **:** a mark made on a tree by chipping off a piece of the bark

[4]**blaze** *vb* **blazed; blaz·ing 1 :** to make a blaze on **2 :** to mark by blazing trees

[1]**bleach** *vb* **:** to make white by removing the color or stains from

[2]**bleach** *n* **:** a preparation used for bleaching

bleach·er *n* **:** open seats for people to watch from (as at a game) usually arranged like steps — usually used in pl.

bleak *adj* **1 :** open to wind or weather **2 :** being cold and cutting **3 :** not hopeful or encouraging — **bleak·ly** *adv* — **bleak·ness** *n*

[1]**bleat** *vb* **:** to make the cry of a sheep, goat, or calf

[2]**bleat** *n* **:** the sound of bleating

bleed *vb* **bled; bleed·ing 1 :** to lose or shed blood **2 :** to feel pain or pity **3 :** to draw fluid from

[1]**blem·ish** *vb* **:** to spoil by or as if by an ugly mark

[2]**blemish** *n* **:** a mark that makes something imperfect **:** FLAW

[1]**blend** *vb* **1 :** to mix so completely that the separate things mixed cannot be told apart **2 :** to shade into each other **:** HARMONIZE

[2]**blend** *n* **1 :** a complete mixture **:** a product made by blending **2 :** a word formed by combining parts of two or more other words so that they overlap **3 :** a group of two or more consonants (as *gr-* in green) beginning a syllable without a vowel between

bless *vb* **blessed** *or* **blest; bless·ing 1 :** to make holy by a religious ceremony or words **2 :** to ask the favor or protection of God for **3 :** to praise or honor as holy **4 :** to give happiness or good fortune to

bless·ed *adj* **1 :** HOLY 1 **2 :** enjoying happiness — **bless·ed·ness** *n*

bless·ing *n* **1 :** the act of one who blesses **2 :** APPROVAL **3 :** something that makes one happy or content

blew *past of* BLOW

[1]**blight** *n* **1 :** a plant disease marked by drying up without rotting **2 :** an organism (as a germ or insect) that causes a plant blight

[2]**blight** *vb* **:** to injure or destroy by or as if by a blight

blimp *n* **:** an airship filled with gas like a balloon

[1]**blind** *adj* **1 :** unable or nearly unable to see **2 :** lacking in judgment or understanding **3 :** closed at one end **4 :** using only the instruments within an airplane and not landmarks as a guide — **blind·ly** *adv* — **blind·ness** *n*

[2]**blind** *vb* **1 :** to make blind **2 :** to make it impossible to see well **:** DAZZLE

[3]**blind** *n* **1 :** a device to reduce sight or keep out light **2 :** a place of hiding

[4]**blind** *adv* **:** with only instruments as guidance

[1]**blind·fold** *vb* **:** to shut light out of the eyes of with or as if with a bandage

[2]**blindfold** *n* **:** a covering over the eyes

blind·man's buff *n* **:** a game in which a blindfolded player tries to catch and identify one of the other players

blink *vb* **1 :** to look with partly shut eyes **2 :** to shut and open the eyes quickly **3 :** to shine with a light that goes or seems to go on and off

blink·er *n* **:** a light that blinks

bliss *n* **:** great happiness **:** JOY — **bliss·ful** *adj* — **bliss·ful·ly** *adv*

[1]**blis·ter** *n* **1 :** a small raised area of the skin filled with a watery liquid **2 :** a swelling (as in paint) that looks like a blister

[2]**blister** *vb* **1 :** to develop a blister or blisters **2 :** to cause blisters on

blithe *adj* **blith·er; blith·est :** free from worry **:** MERRY, CHEERFUL — **blithe·ly** *adv*

bliz·zard *n* **:** a long heavy snowstorm

bloat *vb* **:** to make swollen with or as if with fluid

blob *n* **:** a small lump or drop of something thick

[1]**block** *n* **1 :** a solid piece of some material (as stone or wood) usually with one or more flat sides **2 :** something that stops or makes passage or progress difficult **:** OBSTRUCTION **3 :** a case enclosing one or more pulleys **4 :** a number of things thought of as forming a group or unit **5 :** a large building divided into separate houses or shops **6 :** a space enclosed by streets **7 :** the length of one side of a block

[2]**block** *vb* **1 :** to stop or make passage through difficult **:** OBSTRUCT **2 :** to stop or make the passage of difficult **3 :** to make an opponent's movement (as in football) difficult **4 :** to mark the chief lines of

[1]**block·ade** *vb* **block·ad·ed; block·ad·ing :** to close off a place to prevent the coming in or going out of people or supplies

[2]**blockade** *n* **:** the closing off of a place (as by warships) to prevent the coming in or going out of persons or supplies

block and tackle *n* **:** an arrangement of pulleys in blocks with rope or cable for lifting or hauling

block·house *n* **:** a building (as of heavy timbers or of concrete) built with holes in its sides through which persons inside may fire out at an enemy

[1]**blond** *adj* **1 :** of a light color **2 :** having light hair and skin

[2]**blond** *or* **blonde** *n* **:** someone who is blond

blood *n* **1 :** the red fluid that circulates in the heart, arteries, capillaries, and veins of persons and animals **2 :** relationship through a common ancestor **:** KINSHIP — **blood·ed** *adj*

blood bank *n* **:** blood stored for emergency use in transfusion

blood·hound *n* : a large hound with long drooping ears, a wrinkled face, and a very good sense of smell

blood pressure *n* : pressure of the blood on the walls of blood vessels and especially arteries

blood·shed *n* : [1]MURDER, SLAUGHTER

blood·shot *adj* : being red and sore

blood·stream *n* : the circulating blood in the living body

blood·suck·er *n* : an animal that sucks blood — **blood·suck·ing** *adj*

blood·thirsty *adj* : eager to kill or hurt — **blood·thirst·i·ly** *adv* — **blood·thirst·i·ness** *n*

blood vessel *n* : an artery, vein, or capillary of the body

bloody *adj* **blood·i·er; blood·i·est** **1** : smeared or stained with blood **2** : causing or accompanied by bloodshed

[1]**bloom** *n* **1** : [1]FLOWER 1 **2** : the period or state of blooming **3** : a condition or time of beauty, freshness, and strength **4** : the rosy color of the cheek **5** : the delicate powdery coating on some fruits and leaves

[2]**bloom** *vb* **1** : to produce blooms : FLOWER **2** : to be in a state of youthful beauty and freshness

[1]**blos·som** *n* **1** : [1]FLOWER 1 **2** : [1]BLOOM 2

[2]**blossom** *vb* **1** : [2]BLOOM **2** : to unfold like a blossom

[1]**blot** *n* **1** : a spot or stain of dirt or ink **2** : STIGMA 1, REPROACH

[2]**blot** *vb* **blot·ted; blot·ting** **1** : [2]SPOT 1 **2** : to hide completely **3** : to dry with a blotter

blotch *n* **1** : a blemish on the skin **2** : a large irregular spot of color or ink — **blotched** *adj*

blot·ter *n* : a piece of blotting paper

blot·ting paper *n* : a soft spongy paper used to absorb wet ink

blouse *n* **1** : a loose outer garment like a smock **2** : the jacket of a uniform **3** : a loose garment for women and children covering the body from the neck to the waist

[1]**blow** *vb* **blew; blown; blow·ing** **1** : to move or be moved usually with speed and force **2** : to move in or with the wind **3** : to send forth a strong stream of air from the mouth or from a bellows **4** : to make a sound or cause to sound by blowing **5** : to clear by forcing air through **6** : to shape by forcing air into — **blow·er** *n*

[2]**blow** *n* : a blowing of wind : GALE

[3]**blow** *n* **1** : an act of hitting (as with the fist or a weapon) **2** : a sudden act **3** : a sudden happening that causes suffering or loss

blow·gun *n* : a tube from which a dart may be shot by the force of the breath

blow·out *n* : a bursting of a container (as an automobile tire) by pressure of the contents on a weak spot

blow·pipe *n* **1** : a small round tube for blowing air or gas into a flame so as to make it hotter **2** : BLOWGUN

blow·torch *n* : a small portable burner in which the flame is made hotter by a blast of air or oxygen

blow up *vb* **1** : EXPLODE 1 **2** : to fill with a gas (as air)

[1]**blub·ber** *vb* : to weep noisily

[2]**blubber** *n* : the fat of various sea mammals (as whales) from which oil can be obtained

[1]**blue** *adj* **blu·er; blu·est** **1** : of the color blue **2** : low in spirits : MELANCHOLY

[2]**blue** *n* **1** : the color in the rainbow between green and violet : the color of the clear daytime sky **2** : something blue in color — **out of the blue** : suddenly and unexpectedly

blue·bell *n* : a plant with blue flowers shaped like bells

blue·ber·ry *n pl* **blue·ber·ries** : a sweet blue berry that has small seeds and grows on a bush related to the huckleberry

blue·bird *n* : any of several small North American songbirds more or less blue above

blue·bot·tle *n* : a large blue hairy fly

blue cheese *n* : cheese ripened by and full of greenish blue mold

blue·fish *n* : a bluish saltwater food fish of the eastern coast of the United States

blue·grass *n* : a grass with bluish green stems

blueing *variant of* BLUING

blue jay *n* : any of several crested and mostly blue American birds related to the crows

blue jeans *n pl* : pants usually made of blue denim

[1]**blue·print** *n* **1** : a photographic print made with white lines on a blue background and used for copying maps and building plans **2** : a detailed plan of something to be done

[2]**blueprint** *vb* : to make a blueprint of

blues *n pl* **1** : low spirits **2** : a sad song in a style that was first used by American blacks

blue whale *n* : a very large whale that is probably the largest living animal

[1]**bluff** *adj* **1** : rising steeply with a broad front **2** : frank and outspoken in a rough but good-natured way — **bluff·ly** *adv* — **bluff·ness** *n*

[2]**bluff** *n* : a high steep bank : CLIFF

[3]**bluff** *vb* : to deceive or frighten by pretending to have more strength or confidence than one really has — **bluff·er** *n*

[4]**bluff** *n* **1** : an act or instance of bluffing **2** : a person who bluffs

blu·ing *or* **blue·ing** *n* : something made with blue or violet dyes that is added to the water when washing clothes to prevent yellowing of white fabrics

blu·ish *adj* : somewhat blue
[1]**blun·der** *vb* **1 :** to move in a clumsy way **2 :** to make a mistake — **blun·der·er** *n*
[2]**blunder** *n* : a bad or stupid mistake
blun·der·buss *n* : a short gun that has a barrel which is larger at the end and that was used long ago for shooting at close range without taking exact aim
[1]**blunt** *adj* **1 :** having a thick edge or point : DULL **2 :** speaking or spoken in plain language without thought for other people's feelings — **blunt·ly** *adv*
[2]**blunt** *vb* : to make or become blunt
[1]**blur** *n* : something that cannot be seen clearly
[2]**blur** *vb* **blurred; blur·ring 1 :** to make hard to see or read by smearing **2 :** to make or become smeared or confused
blurt *vb* : to say or tell suddenly and without thinking
[1]**blush** *n* **1 :** a reddening of the face from shame, confusion, or embarrassment **2 :** a rosy color
[2]**blush** *vb* **1 :** to become red in the face from shame, confusion, or embarrassment **2 :** to feel ashamed or embarrassed
[1]**blus·ter** *vb* **1 :** to blow hard and noisily **2 :** to talk or act in a noisy boastful way
[2]**bluster** *n* : noisy violent action or speech
boa *n* : a large snake (as a python) that coils around and crushes its prey
boar *n* **1 :** a male pig **2 :** a wild pig
[1]**board** *n* **1 :** a sawed piece of lumber that is much broader and longer than it is thick **2 :** a dining table **3 :** meals given at set times for a price **4 :** a number of persons having authority to manage or direct something **5 :** a usually rectangular piece of rigid material used for some special purpose **6 :** BLACKBOARD **7 boards** *pl* **:** the low wooden wall enclosing a hockey rink **8 :** a sheet of insulating material carrying electronic parts (as for a computer) — **on board** : ABOARD
[2]**board** *vb* **1 :** to go aboard **2 :** to cover with boards **3 :** to give or get meals at set times for a price
board·er *n* : a person who pays for meals or for meals and lodging at another's house
board·ing·house *n* : a house at which people are given meals and often lodging
boarding school *n* : a school at which most of the students live during the school year
board·walk *n* : a walk made of planks especially along a beach
[1]**boast** *n* **1 :** an act of boasting **2 :** a cause for boasting or pride
[2]**boast** *vb* **1 :** to praise what one has or has done **2 :** to have and be proud of having
boast·ful *adj* **1 :** having the habit of boasting **2 :** full of boasts — **boast·ful·ly** *adv* — **boast·ful·ness** *n*
[1]**boat** *n* **1 :** a small vessel driven on the water by oars, paddles, sails, or a motor **2 :** [1]SHIP 1
[2]**boat** *vb* : to use a boat — **boat·er** *n*
boat·house *n* : a house or shelter for boats
boat·man *n pl* **boat·men :** a person who works on or deals in boats
boat·swain *n* : a warrant officer on a warship or a petty officer on a commercial ship who has charge of the hull, anchors, boats, and rigging
[1]**bob** *vb* **bobbed; bob·bing 1 :** to move or cause to move with a short jerky motion **2 :** to appear suddenly **3 :** to try to seize something with the teeth
[2]**bob** *n* : a short jerky up-and-down motion
[3]**bob** *n* **1 :** a float used to buoy up the baited end of a fishing line **2 :** a woman's or child's short haircut
[4]**bob** *vb* **bobbed; bob·bing :** to cut in the style of a bob
bob·by pin *n* : a flat metal hairpin with the two ends pressed close together
bob·cat *n* : an American wildcat that is a small rusty brown variety of the lynx
bob·o·link *n* : an American songbird related to the blackbirds
bob·sled *n* : a racing sled made with two sets of runners, a hand brake, and often a steering wheel
bob·tail *n* **1 :** a short tail : a tail cut short **2 :** an animal with a short tail
bob·white *n* : an American quail with gray, white, and reddish coloring
bode *past of* BIDE
bod·ice *n* : the upper part of a dress
bodi·ly *adj* : of or relating to the body
body *n pl* **bod·ies 1 :** the material whole of a live or dead person or animal **2 :** the main part of a person, animal, or plant **3 :** the main or central part **4 :** a group of persons or things united for some purpose **5 :** a mass or portion of something distinct from other masses — **bod·ied** *adj*
body·guard *n* : a person or a group of persons whose duty it is to protect someone
[1]**bog** *n* : wet spongy ground that is usually acid and found next to a body of water (as a pond)
[2]**bog** *vb* **bogged; bog·ging :** to sink or stick fast in or as if in a bog
bo·gey *or* **bo·gy** *or* **bo·gie** *n pl* **bogeys** *or* **bogies 1 :** GHOST, GOBLIN **2 :** something one is afraid of without reason
[1]**boil** *n* : a hot red painful lump in the skin that contains pus and is caused by infection
[2]**boil** *vb* **1 :** to heat or become heated to the temperature (**boiling point**) at which bub-

bles rise and break at the surface **2 :** to cook or become cooked in boiling water **3 :** to become angry or upset

[3]**boil** *n* **:** the state of something that is boiling

boil·er *n* **1 :** a container in which something is boiled **2 :** a tank heating and holding water **3 :** a strong metal container used in making steam (as to heat buildings)

bois·ter·ous *adj* **:** being rough and noisy — **bois·ter·ous·ly** *adv* — **bois·ter·ous·ness** *n*

bold *adj* **1 :** willing to meet danger or take risks **:** DARING **2 :** not polite and modest **:** FRESH **3 :** showing or calling for courage or daring — **bold·ly** *adv* — **bold·ness** *n*

bold·face *n* **:** a heavy black type — **bold–faced** *adj*

bo·le·ro *n pl* **bo·le·ros 1 :** a Spanish dance or the music for it **2 :** a loose short jacket open at the front

boll *n* **:** the seedpod of a plant (as cotton)

boll weevil *n* **:** a grayish insect that lays its eggs in cotton bolls

bo·lo·gna *n* **:** a large smoked sausage usually made of beef, veal, and pork

[1]**bol·ster** *n* **:** a long pillow or cushion sometimes used to support bed pillows

[2]**bolster** *vb* **:** to support with or as if with a bolster

[1]**bolt** *n* **1 :** a stroke of lightning **:** THUNDERBOLT **2 :** a sliding bar used to fasten a door **3 :** the part of a lock worked by a key **4 :** a metal pin or rod usually with a head at one end and a screw thread at the other that is used to hold something in place **5 :** a roll of cloth or wallpaper

[2]**bolt** *vb* **1 :** to move suddenly and rapidly **2 :** to run away **3 :** to fasten with a bolt **4 :** to swallow hastily or without chewing

[1]**bomb** *n* **1 :** a hollow case or shell filled with explosive material and made to be dropped from an airplane, thrown by hand, or set off by a fuse **2 :** a container in which something (as an insecticide) is stored under pressure and from which it is released in a fine spray

[2]**bomb** *vb* **:** to attack with bombs

bom·bard *vb* **1 :** to attack with heavy fire from big guns **:** SHELL **2 :** to attack again and again

bomb·er *n* **:** an airplane specially made for dropping bombs

bon·bon *n* **:** a candy with a soft coating and a creamy center

[1]**bond** *n* **1 :** something that binds **2 :** a force or influence that brings or holds together **3 :** a legal agreement in which a person agrees to pay a sum of money if he or she fails to do a certain thing **4 :** a government or business certificate promising to pay a certain sum by a certain day

[2]**bond** *vb* **:** to stick or cause to stick together

bond·age *n* **:** SLAVERY

[1]**bone** *n* **1 :** the hard material of which the skeleton of most animals is formed **2 :** any of the pieces into which the bone of the skeleton is naturally divided — **bone·less** *adj*

[2]**bone** *vb* **boned; bon·ing :** to remove the bones from

bon·fire *n* **:** a large fire built outdoors

bong *n* **:** a deep sound like that of a large bell

bon·go *n pl* **bongos** *also* **bongoes :** either of a pair of small drums of different sizes fitted together and played with the fingers

bon·net *n* **:** a child's or woman's hat usually tied under the chin by ribbons or strings

bon·ny *or* **bon·nie** *adj* **bon·ni·er; bon·ni·est** *chiefly British* **:** HANDSOME 3, BEAUTIFUL

bo·nus *n* **:** something given to somebody (as a worker) in addition to what is usual or owed

bony *adj* **bon·i·er; bon·i·est 1 :** of or relating to bone **2 :** like bone especially in hardness **3 :** having bones and especially large or noticeable bones

[1]**boo** *interj* — used to express disapproval or to startle or frighten

[2]**boo** *n pl* **boos :** a cry expressing disapproval

[3]**boo** *vb* **:** to express disapproval of with boos

boo·by *n pl* **boobies :** an awkward foolish person

[1]**book** *n* **1 :** a set of sheets of paper bound together **2 :** a long written work **3 :** a large division of a written work **4 :** a pack of small items bound together

[2]**book** *vb* **:** to reserve for future use

book·case *n* **:** a set of shelves to hold books

book·end *n* **:** a support at the end of a row of books to keep them standing up

book·keep·er *n* **:** a person who keeps accounts for a business

book·keep·ing *n* **:** the work of keeping business accounts

book·let *n* **:** a little book usually having paper covers and few pages

book·mark *n* **:** something placed in a book to show the page one wants to return to later

book·mo·bile *n* **:** a truck with shelves of books that is a traveling library

[1]**boom** *vb* **1 :** to make a deep hollow rumbling sound **2 :** to increase or develop rapidly

[2]**boom** *n* **1 :** a booming sound **2 :** a rapid increase in activity or popularity

[3]**boom** *n* **1 :** a long pole used especially to stretch the bottom of a sail **2 :** a long beam sticking out from the mast of a derrick to support or guide something that is being lifted

boom box *n* **:** a large portable radio and often tape player with two attached speakers

boo·mer·ang *n* **:** a curved club that can be thrown so as to return to the thrower

boon *n* **1 :** something asked or granted as a favor **2 :** something pleasant or helpful that comes at just the right time

¹boost *vb* **1 :** to raise or push up from below **2 :** to make bigger or greater — **boost·er** *n*

²boost *n* **:** an act of boosting **:** a push up

¹boot *n* **:** a covering usually of leather or rubber for the foot and part of the leg

²boot *vb* **:** ¹KICK 1

boo·tee *or* **boo·tie** *n* **:** an infant's knitted sock

booth *n pl* **booths 1 :** a covered stall for selling or displaying goods (as at a fair or exhibition) **2 :** a small enclosure giving privacy for one person **3 :** a section of a restaurant consisting of a table between two backed benches

boo·ty *n* **:** goods seized from an enemy in war **:** PLUNDER

bo·rax *n* **:** a compound of boron used as a cleansing agent and water softener

¹bor·der *n* **1 :** the outer edge of something **2 :** a boundary especially of a country or state **3 :** an ornamental strip on or near the edge of a flat object

²border *vb* **1 :** to put a border on **2 :** to be close or next to

bor·der·line *adj* **:** not quite average, standard, or normal

¹bore *vb* **bored; bor·ing 1 :** to make a hole in especially with a drill **2 :** to make by piercing or drilling — **bor·er** *n*

²bore *n* **1 :** a hole made by boring **2 :** a cavity (as in a gun barrel) shaped like a cylinder **3 :** the diameter of a hole or cylinder

³bore *past of* BEAR

⁴bore *n* **:** an uninteresting person or thing

⁵bore *vb* **bored; bor·ing :** to make weary and restless by being uninteresting

bore·dom *n* **:** the state of being bored

bo·ric acid *n* **:** a weak acid containing boron used to kill germs

born *adj* **1 :** brought into life by birth **:** brought forth **2 :** having a certain characteristic from or as if from birth

borne *past participle of* BEAR

bo·ron *n* **:** a powdery or hard solid chemical element that melts at a very high temperature and is found in nature only in combination

bor·ough *n* **1 :** a self-governing town or village in some states **2 :** one of the five political divisions of New York City

bor·row *vb* **1 :** to take or receive something with the promise of returning it **2 :** to take for one's own use something begun or thought up by another **:** ADOPT — **bor·row·er** *n*

¹bos·om *n* **1 :** the front of the human chest **2 :** the breasts of a woman

²bosom *adj* **:** ³CLOSE 8, INTIMATE

¹boss *n* **1 :** the person (as an employer or foreman) who tells workers what to do **2 :** the head of a group (as a political organization)

²boss *vb* **1 :** to be in charge of **2 :** to give orders to

bossy *adj* **boss·i·er; boss·i·est :** liking to order people around

bo·tan·i·cal *adj* **:** of or relating to botany

bot·a·nist *n* **:** a specialist in botany

bot·a·ny *n* **:** a branch of biology dealing with plants

botch *vb* **:** to do clumsily and unskillfully **:** SPOIL, BUNGLE

¹both *pron* **:** the one and the other **:** the two

²both *conj* — used before two words or phrases connected with *and* to stress that each is included

³both *adj* **:** the two

¹both·er *vb* **1 :** to trouble (someone) in body or mind **:** DISTRACT, ANNOY **2 :** to cause to worry **3 :** to take the time or trouble

²bother *n* **1 :** someone or something that bothers in a small way **2 :** COMMOTION **3 :** the condition of being bothered

¹bot·tle *n* **1 :** a container (as of glass or plastic) usually having a narrow neck and mouth and no handle **2 :** the quantity held by a bottle

²bottle *vb* **bot·tled; bot·tling 1 :** to put into a bottle **2 :** to shut up as if in a bottle

bot·tle·neck *n* **:** a place or condition where improvement or movement is held up

bot·tom *n* **1 :** the under surface of something **2 :** a supporting surface or part **:** BASE **3 :** the bed of a body of water **4 :** the lowest part of something **5 :** low land along a river

bot·tom·less *adj* **1 :** having no bottom **2 :** very deep

bough *n* **:** a usually large or main branch of a tree

bought *past of* BUY

bouil·lon *n* **:** a clear soup made from meat (as beef or chicken)

boul·der *n* **:** a large detached and rounded or very worn mass of rock

bou·le·vard *n* **:** a wide avenue often having grass strips with trees along its center or sides

¹bounce *vb* **bounced; bounc·ing 1 :** to spring back or up after hitting a surface **2 :** to leap suddenly **3 :** to cause to bounce

²bounce *n* **1 :** a sudden leap **2 :** ²REBOUND 1

¹bound *adj* **:** going or intending to go

²bound *past of* BIND

³bound *vb* **:** to form the boundary of

⁴bound *adj* **1 :** tied or fastened with or as if

with bands **2 :** required by law or duty **3 :** covered with binding **4 :** firmly determined **5 :** very likely to do something : CERTAIN, SURE

⁵bound *n* **:** a fast easy leap

⁶bound *vb* **:** to make a bound or move in bounds

bound·ary *n pl* **bound·aries :** something that points out or shows a limit or end : a dividing line

bound·less *adj* **:** having no limits

bounds *n pl* **:** a point or a line beyond which a person or thing cannot go

boun·te·ous *adj* **1 :** LIBERAL 1 **2 :** ABUNDANT

boun·ti·ful *adj* **1 :** giving freely or generously **2 :** PLENTIFUL 2 — **boun·ti·ful·ly** *adv*

boun·ty *n pl* **boun·ties 1 :** GENEROSITY 1 **2 :** generous gifts **3 :** money given as a reward for killing certain harmful animals

bou·quet *n* **:** a bunch of flowers

bout *n* **1 :** a contest of skill or strength between two persons **2 :** ²ATTACK 3

bou·tique *n* **:** a small fashionable shop

¹bow *vb* **1 :** ¹YIELD 8 **2 :** to bend the head or body as an act of politeness or respect

²bow *n* **:** the act of bending the head or body to express politeness or respect

³bow *n* **1 :** a weapon used for shooting arrows and usually made of a strip of wood bent by a cord connecting the two ends **2 :** something shaped in a curve like a bow **3 :** a rod with horsehairs stretched from end to end used for playing a stringed instrument (as a violin) **4 :** a knot made with one or more loops

⁴bow *vb* **1 :** to bend into a bow **2 :** to play with a bow

⁵bow *n* **:** the forward part of a ship

bow·el *n* **1 :** INTESTINE — usually used in pl. **2 :** a part of the intestine

bow·er *n* **:** a shelter in a garden made of boughs of trees or vines

¹bowl *n* **1 :** a round hollow dish without handles **2 :** the contents of a bowl **3 :** something in the shape of a bowl (as part of a spoon or pipe)

²bowl *n* **:** a rolling of a ball in bowling

³bowl *vb* **1 :** to roll a ball in bowling **2 :** to move rapidly and smoothly as if rolling **3 :** ²SURPRISE 3 **4 :** IMPRESS 2

bow·legged *adj* **:** having the legs bowed outward

bow·line *n* **:** a knot used for making a loop that will not slip

bowl·ing *n* **:** a game in which balls are rolled so as to knock down pins

bow·man *n pl* **bow·men :** ARCHER

bow·sprit *n* **:** a large spar sticking out forward from the bow of a ship

bow·string *n* **:** the cord connecting the two ends of a bow

¹box *n* **:** an evergreen shrub or small tree used for hedges

²box *n* **1 :** a container usually having four sides, a bottom, and a cover **2 :** the contents of a box **3 :** an enclosed place for one or more persons

³box *vb* **:** to enclose in or as if in a box

⁴box *vb* **:** to engage in boxing

box·car *n* **:** a roofed freight car usually having sliding doors in the sides

box elder *n* **:** an American maple with leaves divided into several leaflets

¹box·er *n* **:** a person who boxes

²boxer *n* **:** a compact dog of German origin that is of medium size with a square build and has a short and often tan coat with a black mask

box·ing *n* **:** the sport of fighting with the fists

box office *n* **:** a place where tickets to public entertainments (as sports or theatrical events) are sold

boy *n* **1 :** a male child from birth to young manhood **2 :** a male servant

¹boy·cott *vb* **:** to join with others in refusing to deal with someone (as a person, organization, or country) usually to show disapproval or to force acceptance of terms

²boycott *n* **:** the process or an instance of boycotting

boy·friend *n* **:** a regular male companion of a girl or woman

boy·hood *n* **:** the time or condition of being a boy

boy·ish *adj* **:** of, relating to, or having qualities often felt to be typical of boys — **boy·ish·ly** *adv* — **boy·ish·ness** *n*

Boy Scout *n* **:** a member of a scouting program (as the Boy Scouts of America)

bra *n* **:** a woman's undergarment for breast support

¹brace *vb* **braced; brac·ing :** to make strong, firm, or steady

²brace *n* **1 :** two of a kind **2 :** a tool with a U-shaped bend that is used to turn wood-boring bits **3 :** something that braces **4 :** a usually wire device worn on the teeth for changing faulty position **5 :** a mark { or } used to connect words or items to be considered together

brace·let *n* **:** a decorative band or chain usually worn on the wrist or arm

brack·en *n* **:** a large coarse branching fern

¹brack·et *n* **1 :** a support for a weight (as a shelf) that is usually attached to a wall **2 :** one of a pair of marks [ ] (**square brackets**) used to enclose letters or numbers or in mathematics to enclose items to be treated together **3 :** one of a pair of marks ⟨ ⟩

(**angle brackets**) used to enclose letters or numbers

[2]**bracket** *vb* **1 :** to place within brackets **2 :** to put into the same class **:** GROUP

brack·ish *adj* **:** somewhat salty

brad *n* **:** a slender wire nail with a small longish but rounded head

brag *vb* **bragged; brag·ging :** [2]BOAST 1

brag·gart *n* **:** a person who brags a lot

[1]**braid** *vb* **:** to weave together into a braid

[2]**braid** *n* **:** a length of cord, ribbon, or hair formed of three or more strands woven together

braille *n, often cap* **:** a system of printing for the blind in which the letters are represented by raised dots

[1]**brain** *n* **1 :** the part of the nervous system that is inside the skull, consists of grayish nerve cells and whitish nerve fibers, and is the organ of thought and the central control point for the nervous system **2 brains** *pl* **:** a good mind **:** INTELLIGENCE **3 :** someone who is very smart

[2]**brain** *vb* **:** to hurt or kill by a blow on the head

brain·storm *n* **:** a sudden inspiration or idea

brainy *adj* **brain·i·er; brain·i·est :** very smart

[1]**brake** *n* **:** a thick growth of shrubs, small trees, or canes

[2]**brake** *n* **:** a device for slowing or stopping motion (as of a wheel) usually by friction

[3]**brake** *vb* **braked; brak·ing :** to slow or stop by using a brake

brake·man *n pl* **brake·men :** a crew member on a train whose duties include inspecting the train and helping the conductor

bram·ble *n* **:** any of a group of woody plants with prickly stems that include the raspberries and blackberries and are related to the roses

bran *n* **:** the broken coat of the seed of cereal grain separated (as by sifting) from the flour or meal

[1]**branch** *n* **1 :** a part of a tree that grows out from the trunk or from a large bough **2 :** something extending from a main line or body like a branch **3 :** a division or subordinate part of something — **branched** *adj*

[2]**branch** *vb* **:** to send out a branch **:** spread or divide into branches

[1]**brand** *n* **1 :** a mark of disgrace (as one formerly put on criminals with a hot iron) **2 :** a mark made by burning (as on cattle) or by stamping or printing (as on manufactured goods) to show ownership, maker, or quality **3 :** TRADEMARK **4 :** a class of goods identified by a name as the product of a certain maker

[2]**brand** *vb* **1 :** to mark with a brand **2 :** to show or claim (something) to be bad or wrong

bran·dish *vb* **:** to wave or shake in a threatening manner

brand–new *adj* **:** completely new and unused

bran·dy *n pl* **brandies :** an alcoholic liquor made from wine or fruit juice

brass *n* **1 :** an alloy made by combining copper and zinc **2 :** the musical instruments of an orchestra or band that are usually made of brass and include the cornets, trumpets, trombones, French horns, and tubas

brat *n* **:** a naughty annoying child

[1]**brave** *adj* **brav·er; brav·est :** feeling or showing no fear — **brave·ly** *adv*

[2]**brave** *vb* **braved; brav·ing :** to face or take bravely

[3]**brave** *n* **:** an American Indian warrior

brav·ery *n* **:** COURAGE

[1]**brawl** *vb* **:** to quarrel or fight noisily

[2]**brawl** *n* **:** a noisy quarrel or fight

brawn *n* **:** muscular strength

brawny *adj* **brawn·i·er; brawn·i·est :** having large strong muscles

[1]**bray** *vb* **:** to make the loud harsh cry of a donkey

[2]**bray** *n* **:** a sound of braying

bra·zen *adj* **1 :** made of brass **2 :** sounding harsh and loud **3 :** not ashamed of or embarrassed by one's bad behavior **:** IMPUDENT

Bra·zil nut *n* **:** a dark three-sided nut with a white kernel

[1]**breach** *n* **1 :** a breaking of a law **:** a failure to do what one should **2 :** an opening made by breaking

[2]**breach** *vb* **:** to make a break in

[1]**bread** *n* **1 :** a baked food made from flour or meal **2 :** FOOD 1

[2]**bread** *vb* **:** to cover with bread crumbs

breadth *n* **1 :** distance measured from side to side **2 :** SCOPE 2

[1]**break** *vb* **broke; bro·ken; break·ing 1 :** to separate into parts suddenly or forcibly **2 :** to fail to keep **3 :** to force a way **4 :** [2]TAME 1 **5 :** to reduce the force of **6 :** to do better than **7 :** to interrupt or put an end to **:** STOP **8 :** to develop or burst out suddenly **9 :** to make known **10 :** SOLVE **11 :** [1]CHANGE 4

[2]**break** *n* **1 :** an act of breaking **2 :** something produced by breaking **3 :** an accidental event

break·down *n* **:** bodily or mental collapse **:** FAILURE 6

brea·ker *n* **1 :** a person or thing that breaks something **2 :** a wave that breaks on shore

[1]**break·fast** *n* **:** the first meal of the day

[2]**breakfast** *vb* **:** to eat breakfast

break·neck *adj* **:** very fast or dangerous

break out *vb* **1 :** to develop a skin rash **2 :** to start up suddenly

break·through *n* **:** a sudden advance or successful development

break up *vb* **1 :** to separate into parts **2 :** to bring or come to an end **3 :** to end a romance **4 :** to go into a fit of laughter

break·wa·ter *n* **:** an offshore wall to protect a beach or a harbor from the sea

[1]**breast** *n* **1 :** a gland that produces milk **2 :** the front part of the body between the neck and the abdomen — **breast·ed** *adj*

[2]**breast** *vb* **:** to face or oppose bravely

breast·bone *n* **:** the bony plate at the front and center of the breast

breast–feed *vb* **breast–fed; breast–feed·ing :** to feed (a baby) from a mother's breast

breast·plate *n* **:** a piece of armor for covering the breast

breast·work *n* **:** a wall thrown together to serve as a defense in battle

breath *n* **1 :** a slight breeze **2 :** ability to breathe **:** ease of breathing **3 :** air taken in or sent out by the lungs — **out of breath :** breathing very rapidly as a result of hard exercise

breathe *vb* **breathed; breath·ing 1 :** to draw air into and expel it from the lungs **2 :** [1]LIVE 1 **3 :** [1]SAY 1, UTTER

breath·er *n* **:** a pause for rest

breath·less *adj* **1 :** panting from exertion **2 :** holding one's breath from excitement or fear — **breath·less·ly** *adv*

breath·tak·ing *adj* **:** very exciting

breech·es *n pl* **1 :** short pants fastening below the knee **2 :** PANTS

[1]**breed** *vb* **bred; breed·ing 1 :** to produce or increase (plants or animals) by sexual reproduction **2 :** to produce offspring by sexual reproduction **3 :** to bring up **:** TRAIN **4 :** to bring about **:** CAUSE — **breed·er** *n*

[2]**breed** *n* **1 :** a kind of plant or animal that is found only under human care and is different from related kinds **2 :** [1]CLASS 6, KIND

breed·ing *n* **:** training especially in manners **:** UPBRINGING

breeze *n* **:** a gentle wind

breezy *adj* **breez·i·er; breez·i·est 1 :** somewhat windy **2 :** lively and somewhat carefree — **breez·i·ly** *adv* — **breez·i·ness** *n*

breth·ren *pl of* BROTHER — used chiefly in some formal or solemn situations

breve *n* **:** a mark ˘ placed over a vowel to show that the vowel is short

brev·i·ty *n* **:** the condition of being short or brief

[1]**brew** *vb* **1 :** to make (beer) from water, malt, and hops **2 :** to prepare by soaking in hot water **3 :** [2]PLAN 2 **4 :** to start to form — **brew·er** *n*

[2]**brew** *n* **:** a brewed beverage

brew·ery *n pl* **brew·er·ies :** a place where malt liquors are brewed

bri·ar *variant of* BRIER

[1]**bribe** *n* **:** something given or promised to a person in order to influence a decision or action dishonestly

[2]**bribe** *vb* **bribed; brib·ing :** to influence or try to influence by a bribe

brib·ery *n pl* **brib·er·ies :** the act of giving or taking a bribe

[1]**brick** *n* **1 :** a building or paving material made from clay molded into blocks and baked **2 :** a block made of brick

[2]**brick** *vb* **:** to close, face, or pave with bricks

brick·lay·er *n* **:** a person who builds or paves with bricks

brid·al *adj* **:** of or relating to a bride or a wedding

bride *n* **:** a woman just married or about to be married

bride·groom *n* **:** a man just married or about to be married

brides·maid *n* **:** a woman who attends a bride at her wedding

[1]**bridge** *n* **1 :** a structure built over something (as water, a low place, or a railroad) so people can cross **2 :** a platform above and across the deck of a ship for the captain or officer in charge **3 :** something like a bridge

[2]**bridge** *vb* **bridged; bridg·ing :** to make a bridge over or across

[3]**bridge** *n* **:** a card game for four players in two teams

[1]**bri·dle** *n* **:** a device for controlling a horse made up of a set of straps enclosing the head, a bit, and a pair of reins

[2]**bridle** *vb* **bri·dled; bri·dling 1 :** to put a bridle on **2 :** RESTRAIN 2 **3 :** to hold the head high and draw in the chin as an expression of resentment

[1]**brief** *adj* **:** not very long **:** SHORT — **brief·ly** *adv*

[2]**brief** *vb* **:** to give information or instructions to

brief·case *n* **:** a flat case for carrying papers or books

briefs *n pl* **:** short snug underpants

bri·er *or* **bri·ar** *n* **:** a plant (as the rose or blackberry) with a thorny or prickly woody stem

brig *n* **:** a square-rigged sailing ship with two masts

bri·gade *n* **1 :** a body of soldiers consisting of two or more regiments **2 :** a group of persons organized for acting together

brig·a·dier general *n* **:** a commissioned officer in the Army, Air Force, or Marine Corps ranking above a colonel

bright *adj* **1 :** giving off or filled with much light **2 :** very clear or vivid in color **3 :** IN-

TELLIGENT, CLEVER **4 :** CHEERFUL — **bright·ly** *adv* — **bright·ness** *n*

bright·en *vb* **:** to make or become bright or brighter

bril·liance *n* **:** great brightness

bril·liant *adj* **1 :** flashing with light **:** very bright **2 :** very impressive **3 :** very smart or clever — **bril·liant·ly** *adv*

[1]brim *n* **1 :** the edge or rim of something hollow **2 :** the part of a hat that sticks out around the lower edge

[2]brim *vb* **brimmed; brim·ming :** to be or become full to overflowing

brin·dled *adj* **:** having dark streaks or spots on a gray or brownish background

brine *n* **1 :** water containing a great deal of salt **2 :** OCEAN

bring *vb* **brought; bring·ing 1 :** to cause to come with oneself by carrying or leading **:** take along **2 :** to cause to reach a certain state or take a certain action **3 :** to cause to arrive or exist **4 :** to sell for — **bring·er** *n*

bring about *vb* **:** to cause to happen **:** EFFECT

bring forth *vb* **:** to give birth to **:** PRODUCE

bring out *vb* **:** to produce and offer for sale

bring to *vb* **:** to bring back from unconsciousness **:** REVIVE

bring up *vb* **:** to bring to maturity through care and education

brink *n* **1 :** the edge at the top of a steep place **2 :** a point of beginning

briny *adj* **brin·i·er; brin·i·est :** of or like salt water **:** SALTY

brisk *adj* **1 :** very active **:** LIVELY **2 :** very refreshing — **brisk·ly** *adv* — **brisk·ness** *n*

[1]bris·tle *n* **1 :** a short stiff hair **2 :** a stiff hair or something like a hair fastened in a brush

[2]bristle *vb* **bris·tled; bris·tling 1 :** to rise up and stiffen like bristles **2 :** to show signs of anger

bris·tly *adj* **bris·tli·er; bris·tli·est :** of, like, or having many bristles

britch·es *n pl* **:** BREECHES

[1]Brit·ish *adj* **:** of or relating to Great Britain or the British

[2]British *n pl* **:** the people of Great Britain

brit·tle *adj* **brit·tler; brit·tlest :** hard but easily broken — **brit·tle·ness** *n*

broach *vb* **:** to bring up as a subject for discussion

broad *adj* **1 :** not narrow **:** WIDE **2 :** extending far and wide **:** SPACIOUS **3 :** [1]COMPLETE 1, FULL **4 :** not limited **5 :** not covering fine points **:** GENERAL — **broad·ly** *adv*

[1]broad·cast *adj* **1 :** scattered in all directions **2 :** made public by means of radio or television **3 :** of or relating to radio or television broadcasting

[2]broadcast *vb* **broadcast; broad·cast·ing 1 :** to scatter far and wide **2 :** to make widely known **3 :** to send out by radio or television from a transmitting station — **broad·cast·er** *n*

[3]broadcast *n* **1 :** an act of broadcasting **2 :** the material broadcast by radio or television **:** a radio or television program

broad·cloth *n* **:** a fine cloth with a firm smooth surface

broad·en *vb* **:** to make or become broad or broader **:** WIDEN

broad–mind·ed *adj* **:** willing to consider opinions, beliefs, and practices that are unusual or different from one's own — **broad–mind·ed·ly** *adv* — **broad–mind·ed·ness** *n*

[1]broad·side *n* **1 :** the part of a ship's side above the waterline **2 :** a firing of all of the guns that are on the same side of a ship

[2]broadside *adv* **1 :** with one side forward **2 :** from the side

broad·sword *n* **:** a sword having a broad blade

bro·cade *n* **:** a cloth with a raised design woven into it

broc·co·li *n* **:** an open branching form of cauliflower whose green stalks and clustered flower buds are used as a vegetable

broil *vb* **1 :** to cook or be cooked directly over or under a heat source (as a fire or flame) **2 :** to make or be extremely hot

broil·er *n* **:** a young chicken suitable for broiling

[1]broke *past of* BREAK

[2]broke *adj* **:** having no money

bro·ken *adj* **1 :** shattered into pieces **2 :** having gaps or breaks **3 :** not kept **4 :** imperfectly spoken

bro·ken·heart·ed *adj* **:** overwhelmed by grief **:** very sad

bro·ker *n* **:** a person who acts as an agent for others in the buying or selling of property

bro·mine *n* **:** a chemical element that is a deep red liquid giving off an irritating vapor of disagreeable odor

bron·chi·al *adj* **:** relating to the branches (**bronchial tubes**) of the windpipe

bron·chi·tis *n* **:** a sore raw state of the bronchial tubes

bron·co *n pl* **bron·cos :** MUSTANG

bron·to·sau·rus *n* **:** a huge plant-eating dinosaur with a long thin neck and tail and four thick legs

[1]bronze *vb* **bronzed; bronz·ing :** to give the appearance or color of bronze to

[2]bronze *n* **1 :** an alloy of copper and tin and sometimes other elements **2 :** a yellowish brown color

brooch *n* **:** an ornamental pin or clasp for the clothing

[1]brood *n* **1 :** the young of birds hatched at the

same time **2 :** a group of young children or animals having the same mother

²brood *vb* **1 :** to sit on eggs to hatch them **2 :** to think long and anxiously about something

brood·er *n* **1 :** one that broods **2 :** a building or a compartment that can be heated and is used for raising young fowl

brook *n* **:** a small stream — **brook·let** *n*

broom *n* **1 :** a woody plant of the pea family with long slender branches along which grow many drooping yellow flowers **2 :** a brush with a long handle used for sweeping

broom·stick *n* **:** the handle of a broom

broth *n* **:** the liquid in which a meat, fish, or vegetable has been boiled

broth·er *n pl* **brothers** *also* **breth·ren** **1 :** a boy or man related to another person by having the same parents **2 :** a fellow member of an organization

broth·er·hood *n* **1 :** the state of being a brother **2 :** an association of people for a particular purpose **3 :** those who are engaged in the same business or profession

broth·er–in–law *n pl* **broth·ers–in–law** **1 :** the brother of one's husband or wife **2 :** the husband of one's sister

broth·er·ly *adj* **1 :** of or relating to brothers **2 :** ¹KINDLY 2, AFFECTIONATE

brought *past of* BRING

brow *n* **1 :** EYEBROW **2 :** FOREHEAD **3 :** the upper edge of a steep slope

¹brown *adj* **1 :** of the color brown **2 :** having a dark or tanned complexion

²brown *n* **:** a color like that of coffee or chocolate

³brown *vb* **:** to make or become brown

brown·ie *n* **1 :** a cheerful elf believed to perform helpful services at night **2** *cap* **:** a member of a program of the Girl Scouts for girls in the first through third grades in school **3 :** a small rectangle of chewy chocolate cake

brown·ish *adj* **:** somewhat brown

browse *vb* **browsed; brows·ing** **1 :** to nibble young shoots and foliage **2 :** to read or look over something (as in a book or a store) in a light or careless way

brows·er *n* **1 :** one that browses **2 :** a computer program providing access to sites on the World Wide Web

bru·in *n* **:** ¹BEAR 1

¹bruise *vb* **bruised; bruis·ing :** to injure the flesh (as by a blow) without breaking the skin

²bruise *n* **:** a black-and-blue spot on the body or a dark spot on fruit caused by bruising (as from a blow)

¹bru·net *or* **bru·nette** *n* **:** someone who is brunet

²brunet *or* **brunette** *adj* **:** having dark brown or black hair and dark eyes

brunt *n* **:** the main force or stress (as of an attack)

¹brush *n* **:** BRUSHWOOD

²brush *n* **1 :** a tool made of bristles set in a handle and used for cleaning, smoothing, or painting **2 :** a bushy tail **3 :** an act of brushing **4 :** a light stroke

³brush *vb* **1 :** to scrub or smooth with a brush **2 :** to remove with or as if with a brush **3 :** to pass lightly across

⁴brush *n* **:** a brief fight or quarrel

brush·wood *n* **1 :** branches and twigs cut from trees **2 :** a heavy growth of small trees and bushes

brus·sels sprouts *n pl, often cap B* **:** green heads like tiny cabbages growing thickly on the stem of a plant of the cabbage family and used as a vegetable

bru·tal *adj* **:** being cruel and inhuman — **bru·tal·ly** *adv*

bru·tal·i·ty *n pl* **bru·tal·i·ties** **1 :** the quality of being brutal **2 :** a brutal act or course of action

¹brute *adj* **1 :** of or relating to beasts **2 :** typical of beasts **:** like that of a beast

²brute *n* **1 :** a four-footed animal especially when wild **2 :** a brutal person

brut·ish *adj* **:** being unfeeling and stupid

¹bub·ble *n* **1 :** a tiny round body of air or gas in a liquid **2 :** a round body of air within a solid **3 :** a thin film of liquid filled with air or gas

²bubble *vb* **bub·bled; bub·bling** **1 :** to form or produce bubbles **2 :** to flow with a gurgle

bu·bon·ic plague *n* **:** a dangerous disease which is spread by rats and in which fever, weakness, and swollen lymph glands are present

buc·ca·neer *n* **:** PIRATE

¹buck *n* **:** a male deer or antelope or a male goat, hare, rabbit, or rat

²buck *vb* **1 :** to spring or jump upward with head down and back arched **2 :** to charge or push against **3 :** to go against **:** OPPOSE

buck·board *n* **:** a lightweight carriage with four wheels that has a seat supported by a springy platform

buck·et *n* **1 :** a usually round container with a handle for holding or carrying liquids or solids **2 :** an object for collecting, scooping, or carrying something (as the scoop of an excavating machine) **3 :** BUCKETFUL

buck·et·ful *n pl* **buck·et·fuls** *or* **buck·ets·ful** **1 :** as much as a bucket will hold **2 :** a large quantity

buck·eye *n* **:** a horse chestnut or a closely related tree or shrub

¹buck·le *n* **:** a fastening device which is attached to one end of a belt or strap and through which the other end is passed and held

[2]**buckle** *vb* **buck·led; buck·ling** **1 :** to fasten with a buckle **2 :** to apply oneself earnestly **3 :** to bend, crumple, or give way

buck·shot *n* **:** coarse lead shot

buck·skin *n* **:** a soft flexible leather usually having a suede finish

buck·wheat *n* **:** a plant with pinkish white flowers that is grown for its dark triangular seeds which are used as a cereal grain

[1]**bud** *n* **1 :** a small growth at the tip or on the side of a stem that later develops into a flower or branch **2 :** a flower that has not fully opened **3 :** a part that grows out from the body of an organism and develops into a new organism **4 :** an early stage of development

[2]**bud** *vb* **bud·ded; bud·ding** **1 :** to form or put forth buds **2 :** to grow or reproduce by buds

Bud·dhism *n* **:** a religion of eastern and central Asia growing out of the teachings of Gautama Buddha

Bud·dhist *n* **:** a person whose religion is Buddhism

bud·dy *n pl* **buddies :** [1]CHUM

budge *vb* **budged; budg·ing :** to move or cause to move from one position to another

[1]**bud·get** *n* **1 :** a statement of estimated income and expenses for a period of time **2 :** a plan for using money

[2]**budget** *vb* **1 :** to include in a budget **2 :** to plan as in a budget

[1]**buff** *n* **1 :** an orange yellow **2 :** a stick or wheel with a soft surface for applying polish

[2]**buff** *vb* **:** to polish with or as if with a buff

buf·fa·lo *n pl* **buffalo** *or* **buf·fa·loes :** any of several wild oxen and especially the American bison

buffalo wing *n* **:** a deep-fried chicken wing coated with a spicy sauce and usually served with blue cheese dressing

[1]**buf·fet** *vb* **:** to pound repeatedly **:** BATTER

[2]**buf·fet** *n* **1 :** a cabinet or set of shelves for the display of dishes and silver **:** SIDEBOARD **2 :** a meal set out on a buffet or table from which people may serve themselves

bug *n* **1 :** an insect or other small creeping or crawling animal **2 :** any of a large group of insects that have four wings, suck liquid food (as plant juices or blood), and have young which resemble the adults but lack wings **3 :** FLAW **4 :** a person who is a fan of something

bug·a·boo *n pl* **bug·a·boos :** BUGBEAR

bug·bear *n* **1 :** an imaginary creature used to frighten children **2 :** something one is afraid of

bug·gy *n pl* **buggies :** a light carriage with a single seat that is usually drawn by one horse

bu·gle *n* **:** an instrument like a simple trumpet used chiefly for giving military signals

bu·gler *n* **:** a person who plays a bugle

[1]**build** *vb* **built; build·ing** **1 :** to make by putting together parts or materials **2 :** to produce or create gradually by effort **3 :** to move toward a peak

[2]**build** *n* **:** form or kind of structure **:** PHYSIQUE

build·er *n* **:** a person whose business is the construction of buildings

build·ing *n* **1 :** a permanent structure built as a dwelling, shelter, or place for human activities or for storage **2 :** the art, work, or business of assembling materials into a structure

built–in *adj* **:** forming a permanent part of a structure

bulb *n* **1 :** an underground resting form of a plant which consists of a short stem with one or more buds surrounded by thick leaves and from which a new plant can grow **2 :** a plant structure (as a tuber) that is somewhat like a bulb **3 :** a rounded object or part shaped more or less like a bulb

bul·bous *adj* **1 :** having a bulb **2 :** like a bulb in being round and swollen

[1]**bulge** *vb* **bulged; bulg·ing :** to swell or curve outward

[2]**bulge** *n* **:** a swelling part **:** a part that sticks out

bulk *n* **1 :** greatness of size or volume **2 :** the largest or chief part

bulk·head *n* **:** a wall separating sections in a ship

bulky *adj* **bulk·i·er; bulk·i·est** **1 :** having bulk **2 :** being large and awkward to handle

bull *n* **:** the male of an animal of the ox and cow family and of certain other large animals (as the elephant and the whale)

[1]**bull·dog** *n* **:** a dog of English origin with short hair and a stocky powerful build

[2]**bulldog** *vb* **bull·dogged; bull·dog·ging :** to throw by seizing the horns and twisting the neck

bull·doz·er *n* **:** a motor vehicle with beltlike tracks that has a broad blade for pushing (as in clearing land of trees)

bul·let *n* **:** a shaped piece of metal made to be shot from a firearm — **bul·let·proof** *adj*

bul·le·tin *n* **:** a short public notice usually coming from an informed or official source

bulletin board *n* **:** a board for posting bulletins and announcements

bull·fight *n* **:** a public entertainment in which people excite bulls, display daring in escaping their charges, and finally kill them — **bull·fight·er** *n*

bull·finch *n* : a European songbird that has a thick bill and a red breast and is often kept in a cage
bull·frog *n* : a large heavy frog that makes a booming or bellowing sound
bull·head *n* : any of various fishes with large heads
bul·lion *n* : gold or silver metal in bars or blocks
bull·ock *n* **1 :** a young bull **2 :** [1]STEER, OX
bull's–eye *n* **1 :** the center of a target **2 :** a shot that hits the center of a target
[1]**bul·ly** *n pl* **bul·lies :** a person who teases, hurts, or threatens smaller or weaker persons
[2]**bully** *vb* **bul·lied; bul·ly·ing :** to act like a bully toward
bul·rush *n* : any of several large rushes or sedges that grow in wet places
bul·wark *n* **1 :** a solid structure like a wall built for defense against an enemy **2 :** something that defends or protects
bum *n* **1 :** a person who avoids work and tries to live off others **2 :** [2]TRAMP 1, HOBO
bum·ble·bee *n* : a large hairy bee that makes a loud humming sound
[1]**bump** *n* **1 :** a sudden heavy blow or shock **2 :** a rounded swelling of flesh as from a blow **3 :** an unevenness in a road surface
[2]**bump** *vb* **1 :** to strike or knock against something **2 :** to move along unevenly **:** JOLT
[1]**bum·per** *adj* : larger or finer than usual
[2]**bump·er** *n* : a bar across the front or back of a motor vehicle intended to lessen the shock or damage from collision
bun *n* : a sweet or plain round roll
[1]**bunch** *n* **1 :** a number of things of the same kind growing together **2 :** [1]GROUP
[2]**bunch** *vb* : to gather in a bunch
[1]**bun·dle** *n* : a number of things fastened or wrapped together **:** PACKAGE
[2]**bundle** *vb* **bun·dled; bun·dling :** to make into a bundle **:** WRAP
bung *n* **1 :** the stopper in the bunghole of a barrel **2 :** BUNGHOLE
bun·ga·low *n* : a house with a single story
bung·hole *n* : a hole for emptying or filling a barrel
bun·gle *vb* **bun·gled; bun·gling :** to act, do, make, or work badly — **bun·gler** *n*
bun·ion *n* : a sore reddened swelling of the first joint of a big toe
[1]**bunk** *n* **1 :** a built-in bed **2 :** a sleeping place
[2]**bunk** *vb* : to share or sleep in a bunk
bunk bed *n* : one of two single beds usually placed one above the other
bun·ny *n pl* **bunnies :** RABBIT
[1]**bunt** *vb* : to strike or push with the horns or head **:** BUTT
[2]**bunt** *n* **:** [2]BUTT, PUSH
[1]**bun·ting** *n* : any of various birds that are similar to sparrows in size and habits but have stout bills
[2]**bunting** *n* **1 :** a thin cloth used chiefly for making flags and patriotic decorations **2 :** flags or decorations made of bunting
[1]**buoy** *n* **1 :** a floating object anchored in a body of water so as to mark a channel or to warn of danger **2 :** LIFE BUOY
[2]**buoy** *vb* **1 :** to keep from sinking **:** keep afloat **2 :** to brighten the mood of
buoy·an·cy *n* **1 :** the power of rising and floating (as on water or in air) **2 :** the power of a liquid to hold up a floating body
buoy·ant *adj* **1 :** able to rise and float in the air or on the top of a liquid **2 :** able to keep a body afloat **3 :** LIGHT-HEARTED, CHEERFUL
bur *or* **burr** *n* **1 :** a rough or prickly covering or shell of a seed or fruit **2 :** something that is like a bur (as in sticking)
[1]**bur·den** *n* **1 :** something carried **:** LOAD **2 :** something that is hard to take **3 :** the carrying of loads **4 :** the capacity of a ship for carrying cargo
[2]**burden** *vb* : to put a burden on
bur·den·some *adj* : so heavy or hard to take as to be a burden
bur·dock *n* : a tall coarse weed related to the thistles that has prickly purplish heads of flowers
bu·reau *n* **1 :** a low chest of drawers for use in a bedroom **2 :** a division of a government department **3 :** a business office that provides services
bur·glar *n* : a person who is guilty of burglary
bur·glary *n pl* **bur·glar·ies :** the act of breaking into a building to steal
buri·al *n* : the placing of a dead body in a grave or tomb
bur·lap *n* : a rough cloth made usually from jute or hemp and used mostly for bags and wrappings
bur·ly *adj* **bur·li·er; bur·li·est :** strongly and heavily built — **bur·li·ness** *n*
[1]**burn** *vb* **burned** *or* **burnt; burn·ing 1 :** to be on fire or to set on fire **2 :** to destroy or be destroyed by fire or heat **3 :** to make or produce by fire or heat **4 :** to give light **5 :** to injure or affect by or as if by fire or heat **6 :** to feel or cause to feel as if on fire
[2]**burn** *n* : an injury produced by burning
burn·er *n* : the part of a stove or furnace where the flame or heat is produced
bur·nish *vb* : to make shiny
burr *variant of* BUR
bur·ro *n pl* **burros :** a small donkey often used as a pack animal
[1]**bur·row** *n* : a hole in the ground made by an

animal (as a rabbit or fox) for shelter or protection

[2]**burrow** *vb* **1 :** to hide in or as if in a burrow **2 :** to make a burrow **3 :** to make one's way by or as if by digging

[1]**burst** *vb* **burst; burst·ing 1 :** to break open or in pieces (as by an explosion from within) **2 :** to suddenly show one's feelings **3 :** to come or go suddenly **4 :** to be filled to the breaking point

[2]**burst** *n* **:** a sudden release or effort

bury *vb* **bur·ied; bury·ing 1 :** to put (a dead body) in a grave or tomb **2 :** to place in the ground and cover over for concealment **3 :** to cover up **:** HIDE

bus *n pl* **bus·es** *or* **bus·ses :** a large motor vehicle for carrying passengers

bush *n* **1 :** a usually low shrub with many branches **2 :** a stretch of uncleared or lightly settled country

bush·el *n* **1 :** a unit of dry capacity equal to four pecks or thirty-two quarts (about thirty-five liters) **2 :** a container holding a bushel

bushy *adj* **bush·i·er; bush·i·est 1 :** overgrown with bushes **2 :** being thick and spreading

busi·ness *n* **1 :** the normal activity of a person or group **2 :** a commercial enterprise **3 :** the making, buying, and selling of goods or services **4 :** personal concerns

busi·ness·man *n pl* **busi·ness·men :** a man in business especially as an owner or a manager

busi·ness·wom·an *n pl* **busi·ness·wom·en :** a woman in business especially as an owner or a manager

[1]**bust** *n* **1 :** a piece of sculpture representing the upper part of the human figure including the head and neck **2 :** a woman's bosom

[2]**bust** *vb* **1 :** to hit with the fist **2 :** [1]BREAK 1

[1]**bus·tle** *vb* **bus·tled; bus·tling :** to move about in a fussy or noisy way

[2]**bustle** *n* **:** fussy or noisy activity

[1]**busy** *adj* **busi·er; busi·est 1 :** actively at work **2 :** being used **3 :** full of activity — **busi·ly** *adv*

[2]**busy** *vb* **bus·ied; busy·ing :** to make busy

busy·body *n pl* **busy·bod·ies :** a person who meddles in the affairs of others

[1]**but** *conj* **1 :** except that **:** UNLESS **2 :** while just the opposite **3 :** yet nevertheless

[2]**but** *prep* **:** other than **:** EXCEPT

[3]**but** *adv* **:** [2]ONLY 1

[1]**butch·er** *n* **1 :** one whose business is killing animals for sale as food **2 :** a dealer in meat **3 :** a person who kills in large numbers or in a brutal manner

[2]**butcher** *vb* **1 :** to kill and dress (an animal) for food **2 :** [2]MASSACRE **3 :** to make a mess of **:** BOTCH

but·ler *n* **:** the chief male servant of a household

[1]**butt** *vb* **:** to strike or thrust with the head or horns

[2]**butt** *n* **:** a blow or thrust with the head or horns

[3]**butt** *n* **:** a target of ridicule or hurtful jokes

[4]**butt** *n* **1 :** the thicker or bottom end of something **2 :** an unused remainder

butte *n* **:** an isolated hill with steep sides

[1]**but·ter** *n* **1 :** a solid yellowish fatty food obtained from cream or milk by churning **2 :** a substance that is like butter in texture and use

[2]**butter** *vb* **:** to spread with or as if with butter

but·ter·cup *n* **:** a common wildflower with bright yellow blossoms

but·ter·fat *n* **:** the natural fat of milk that is the chief ingredient of butter

but·ter·fly *n pl* **but·ter·flies :** an insect that has a slender body and large colored wings covered with tiny overlapping scales and that flies mostly in the daytime

but·ter·milk *n* **:** the liquid left after churning butter from milk or cream

but·ter·nut *n* **:** an eastern North American tree that has sweet egg-shaped nuts and is related to the walnuts

but·ter·scotch *n* **:** a candy made from sugar, corn syrup, and water

but·tock *n* **1 :** the back of the hip which forms one of the rounded parts on which a person sits **2 buttocks** *pl* **:** RUMP 1

[1]**but·ton** *n* **1 :** a small ball or disk used for holding parts of a garment together or as an ornament **2 :** something that suggests a button

[2]**button** *vb* **:** to close or fasten with buttons

but·ton·hole *n* **:** a slit or loop for fastening a button

but·ton·wood *n* **:** SYCAMORE 2

[1]**but·tress** *n* **1 :** a structure built against a wall or building to give support and strength **2 :** something that supports, props, or strengthens

[2]**buttress** *vb* **:** to support with or as if with a buttress

bux·om *adj* **:** having a healthy plump form

[1]**buy** *vb* **bought; buy·ing :** to get by paying for **:** PURCHASE — **buy·er** *n*

[2]**buy** *n* **:** [1]BARGAIN 2

[1]**buzz** *vb* **1 :** to make a low humming sound like that of bees **2 :** to be filled with a low hum or murmur **3 :** to fly an airplane low over

[2]**buzz** *n* **:** a sound of buzzing

buz·zard *n* **:** a usually large bird of prey that flies slowly

buzz·er *n* **:** an electric signaling device that makes a buzzing sound

[1]by *prep* **1 :** close to **:** NEAR **2 :** so as to go on **3 :** so as to go through **4 :** so as to pass **5 :** AT 1, DURING **6 :** no later than **7 :** with the use or help of **8 :** through the action of **9 :** ACCORDING TO **10 :** with respect to **11 :** to the amount of **12** — used to join two or more measurements or to join the numbers in a statement of multiplication or division

[2]by *adv* **1 :** near at hand **2 :** [4]PAST

by–and–by *n* **:** a future time

by and by *adv* **:** after a while

by·gone *adj* **:** gone by **:** PAST

by·gones *n pl* **:** events that are over and done with

[1]by·pass *n* **1 :** a way for passing to one side **2 :** a road serving as a substitute route around a crowded area

[2]bypass *vb* **:** to make a detour around

by–prod·uct *n* **:** something produced (as in manufacturing) in addition to the main product

by·stand·er *n* **:** a person present or standing near but taking no part in what is going on

byte *n* **:** a group of eight bits that a computer handles as a unit

by·way *n* **:** a less traveled road off a main highway

C

c *n, pl* **c's** *or* **cs** *often cap* **1 :** the third letter of the English alphabet **2 :** 100 in Roman numerals **3 :** a grade that shows a student's work is fair

cab *n* **1 :** a light closed carriage pulled by a horse **2 :** TAXICAB **3 :** the covered compartment for the engineer and the controls of a locomotive or for the operator of a truck, tractor, or crane

ca·bana *n* **:** a shelter usually with an open side facing the sea or a swimming pool

cab·bage *n* **:** a garden plant related to the turnips that has a firm head of leaves used as a vegetable

cab·in *n* **1 :** a private room on a ship **2 :** a place below deck on a small boat for passengers or crew **3 :** a part of an airplane for cargo, crew, or passengers **4 :** a small simple dwelling usually having only one story

cab·i·net *n* **1 :** a case or cupboard with shelves or drawers for keeping or displaying articles **2 :** a group of persons who act as advisers (as to the head of a country)

[1]ca·ble *n* **1 :** a very strong rope, wire, or chain **2 :** a bundle of wires to carry electric current **3 :** CABLEGRAM **4 :** CABLE TELEVISION

[2]cable *vb* **ca·bled; ca·bling :** to telegraph by underwater cable

ca·ble·gram *n* **:** a message sent by underwater cable

cable television *n* **:** a television system in which paying customers receive the television signals over electrical wires

ca·boose *n* **:** a car usually at the rear of a freight train for the use of the train crew

ca·cao *n, pl* **cacaos :** a South American tree with fleshy yellow pods that contain fatty seeds from which chocolate is made

[1]cache *n* **1 :** a place for hiding, storing, or preserving treasure or supplies **2 :** something hidden or stored in a cache

[2]cache *vb* **cached; cach·ing :** to place, hide, or store in a cache

[1]cack·le *vb* **cack·led; cack·ling 1 :** to make the noise or cry a hen makes especially after laying an egg **2 :** to laugh or chatter noisily

[2]cackle *n* **:** a cackling sound

cac·tus *n, pl* **cac·tus·es** *or* **cac·ti :** any of a large group of flowering plants of dry regions that have thick juicy stems and branches with scales or prickles

[1]cad·die *or* **cad·dy** *n, pl* **cad·dies :** a person who carries a golfer's clubs

[2]caddie *or* **caddy** *vb* **cad·died; cad·dy·ing :** to work as a caddie

cad·dis fly *n* **:** an insect that has four wings and a larva which lives in water in a silk case covered with bits of wood or gravel and is often used for fish bait

ca·dence *n* **:** the beat of rhythmic motion or sound (as of marching) **:** RHYTHM

ca·det *n* **:** a student in a military school or college

ca·fé *also* **ca·fe** *n* **1 :** [1]BAR 9 **2 :** RESTAURANT **3 :** NIGHTCLUB

caf·e·te·ria *n* **:** a restaurant where the customers serve themselves or are served at a counter but carry their own food to their tables

caf·feine *n* **:** a stimulating substance in coffee and tea

[1]cage *n* **1 :** a box or enclosure that has large openings covered usually with wire net or bars and is used to confine or carry birds or animals **2 :** an enclosure like a cage in shape or purpose

[2]cage *vb* **caged; cag·ing :** to put or keep in or as if in a cage

ca·gey *adj* **ca·gi·er; ca·gi·est :** hard to trap or trick

cais·son *n* **1 :** a chest for ammunition usually set on two wheels **2 :** a watertight box or chamber used for doing construction work under water or used as a foundation

ca·jole *vb* **ca·joled; ca·jol·ing :** to coax or persuade especially by flattery or false promises : WHEEDLE

[1]**cake** *n* **1 :** a small piece of food (as dough or batter, meat, or fish) that is baked or fried **2 :** a baked food made from a sweet batter or dough **3 :** a substance hardened or molded into a solid piece

[2]**cake** *vb* **caked; cak·ing 1 :** ENCRUST **2 :** to form or harden into a cake

ca·lam·i·ty *n, pl* **ca·lam·i·ties 1 :** great distress or misfortune **2 :** an event that causes great harm

cal·ci·um *n* **:** a silvery soft metallic chemical element that is an essential for most plants and animals

calcium carbonate *n* **:** a solid substance that is found as limestone and marble and in plant ashes, bones, and shells

cal·cu·late *vb* **cal·cu·lat·ed; cal·cu·lat·ing 1 :** to find by adding, subtracting, multiplying, or dividing : COMPUTE **2 :** [1]ESTIMATE 1 **3 :** to plan by careful thought

cal·cu·la·tion *n* **1 :** the process or an act of calculating **2 :** the result obtained by calculating

cal·cu·la·tor *n* **1 :** a person who calculates **2 :** a usually small electronic device for solving mathematical problems

cal·cu·lus *n* **:** TARTAR 2

caldron *variant of* CAULDRON

cal·en·dar *n* **1 :** a chart showing the days, weeks, and months of the year **2 :** a schedule of coming events

[1]**calf** *n, pl* **calves 1 :** the young of the cow **2 :** the young of various large animals (as the elephant, moose, or whale) **3** *pl* **calfs :** CALFSKIN

[2]**calf** *n, pl* **calves :** the muscular back part of the leg below the knee

calf·skin *n* **:** the skin of a calf or the leather made from it

cal·i·ber *or* **cal·i·bre** *n* **1 :** the diameter of a bullet **2 :** the diameter of the hole in the barrel of a gun

[1]**cal·i·co** *n, pl* **cal·i·coes** *or* **cal·i·cos :** cotton cloth especially with a colored pattern printed on one side

[2]**calico** *adj* **:** marked with blotches of color

cal·i·per *or* **cal·li·per** *n* **:** an instrument with two adjustable legs used to measure the thickness of objects or the distance between surfaces — usually used in pl.

ca·liph *or* **ca·lif** *n* **:** an important official in some Arab countries

cal·is·then·ics *n sing or pl* **:** exercise to develop strength and grace that is done without special equipment

[1]**call** *vb* **1 :** to speak in a loud clear voice so as to be heard at a distance : SHOUT **2 :** to say in a loud clear voice **3 :** to announce with authority : PROCLAIM **4 :** SUMMON 1, 2 **5 :** to bring into action or discussion **6 :** to make a request or demand **7 :** to get in touch with by telephone **8 :** to make a short visit **9 :** [2]NAME 1 **10 :** to estimate as — **call for :** to require as necessary or suitable

[2]**call** *n* **1 :** a loud shout or cry **2 :** a cry of an animal **3 :** a request or command to come or assemble **4 :** [1]DEMAND 1, CLAIM **5 :** [1]REQUEST 1 **6 :** a short visit **7 :** a name or thing called **8 :** the act of calling on the telephone

call down *vb* **:** [2]REPRIMAND

call·er *n* **:** one who calls

call·ing *n* **:** OCCUPATION 1, PROFESSION

cal·li·ope *n* **:** a keyboard musical instrument consisting of a set of steam whistles

cal·lous *adj* **1 :** having a callus **2 :** feeling no sympathy for others

cal·lus *n* **:** a hard thickened spot (as of skin)

[1]**calm** *n* **1 :** a period or condition of freedom from storm, wind, or rough water **2 :** a peaceful state : QUIET

[2]**calm** *vb* **:** to make or become calm

[3]**calm** *adj* **1 :** not stormy or windy : STILL **2 :** not excited or angry — **calm·ly** *adv* — **calm·ness** *n*

cal·o·rie *n* **1 :** a unit for measuring heat equal to the heat required to raise the temperature of one gram of water one degree Celsius **2 :** a unit equal to 1000 calories — used especially to indicate the value of foods for producing heat and energy in the human body

calve *vb* **calved; calv·ing :** to give birth to a calf

calves *pl of* CALF

ca·lyp·so *n, pl* **calypsos :** a folk song or style of singing of the West Indies

ca·lyx *n, pl* **ca·lyx·es** *or* **ca·ly·ces :** the outer usually green or leafy part of a flower

cam *n* **:** a device (as a tooth on a wheel) by which circular motion is changed to back-and-forth motion

cam·bi·um *n, pl* **cam·bi·ums** *or* **cam·bia :** soft tissue in woody plants from which new wood and bark grow

cam·cord·er *n* **:** a small portable device that is a combination of a camera and a videotape recording device

came *past of* COME

cam·el *n* **:** a large hoofed animal that chews the cud and is used in the deserts of Asia and Africa for carrying burdens and for riding

cam·era *n* **1 :** a box that has a lens on one side to let the light in and is used for taking pictures **2 :** the part of a television sending device in which the image to be sent out is formed

[1]**cam·ou·flage** *n* **1 :** the hiding or disguising of something by covering it up or changing

the way it looks **2 :** the material (as paint or branches) used for camouflage

²camouflage *vb* **cam·ou·flaged; cam·ou·flag·ing :** to hide or disguise by camouflage

¹camp *n* **1 :** a place where temporary shelters are erected **2 :** a place usually in the country for recreation or instruction during the summer **3 :** a group of people in a camp

²camp *vb* **1 :** to make or occupy a camp **2 :** to live in a camp or outdoors — **camp·er** *n*

¹cam·paign *n* **1 :** a series of military operations in a certain area or for a certain purpose **2 :** a series of activities meant to get a certain thing done

²campaign *vb* **:** to take part in a campaign — **campaign·er** *n*

Camp Fire Girl *n* **:** a member of a national organization for girls from seven to eighteen

cam·phor *n* **:** a white fragrant solid that comes from the wood and bark of a tall Asian tree (**camphor tree**) and is used mostly in medicine and in making plastics

cam·pus *n* **:** the grounds and buildings of a university, college, or school

¹can *helping verb, past* **could;** *present sing & pl* **can 1 :** know how to **2 :** be able to **3 :** be permitted by conscience to **4 :** have permission to **:** MAY

²can *n* **1 :** a usually cylindrical metal container **2 :** the contents of a can

³can *vb* **canned; can·ning :** to keep fit for later use by sealing (as in an airtight jar)

¹Ca·na·di·an *adj* **:** of or relating to Canada or the Canadians

²Canadian *n* **:** a person born or living in Canada

ca·nal *n* **1 :** an artificial waterway for boats or for irrigation of land **2 :** a tubelike passage in the body

ca·nary *n, pl* **ca·nar·ies :** a small usually yellow songbird often kept in a cage

can·cel *vb* **can·celed** *or* **can·celled; can·cel·ing** *or* **can·cel·ling 1 :** to cross out or strike out with a line **:** DELETE **2 :** to take back **:** WITHDRAW **3 :** to equal in force or effect **:** OFFSET **4 :** to remove (a common divisor) from numerator and denominator **:** remove (equivalents) on opposite sides of an equation or account **5 :** to mark (as a postage stamp) so as to make impossible to use again

can·cel·la·tion *n* **1 :** an act of canceling **2 :** a mark made to cancel something

can·cer *n* **1 :** a harmful growth on or in the body that may keep spreading and be fatal if not treated **2 :** a condition of the body characterized by a cancer or cancers

can·de·la·bra *n* **:** a candlestick or lamp that has several branches for lights

can·de·la·brum *n, pl* **can·de·la·bra** *also* **can·de·la·brums :** CANDELABRA

can·did *adj* **1 :** FRANK, STRAIGHTFORWARD **2 :** relating to photography of people acting naturally without being posed — **can·did·ly** *adv* — **can·did·ness** *n*

can·di·da·cy *n, pl* **can·di·da·cies :** the state of being a candidate

can·di·date *n* **:** a person who runs for or is nominated by others for an office or honor

can·died *adj* **:** preserved in or coated with sugar

¹can·dle *n* **:** a stick of tallow or wax containing a wick and burned to give light

²candle *vb* **can·dled; can·dling :** to examine (as eggs) by holding between the eye and a light — **can·dler** *n*

can·dle·light *n* **1 :** the light of a candle **2 :** a soft artificial light

can·dle·stick *n* **:** a holder for a candle

can·dor *n* **:** sincere and honest expression

¹can·dy *n, pl* **can·dies :** a sweet made of sugar often with flavoring and filling

²candy *vb* **can·died; can·dy·ing 1 :** to coat or become coated with sugar often by cooking **2 :** to crystallize into sugar

¹cane *n* **1 :** an often hollow, slender, and somewhat flexible plant stem **2 :** a tall woody grass or reed (as sugarcane) **3 :** WALKING STICK 1 **4 :** a rod for beating

²cane *vb* **caned; can·ing 1 :** to beat with a cane **2 :** to make or repair with cane

¹ca·nine *n* **1 :** a pointed tooth next to the incisors **2 :** a canine animal

²canine *adj* **1 :** of or relating to the dogs or to the group of animals (as wolves) to which the dog belongs **2 :** like or typical of a dog

can·is·ter *n* **:** a small box or can for holding a dry product

can·nery *n, pl* **can·ner·ies :** a factory where foods are canned

can·ni·bal *n* **1 :** a human being who eats human flesh **2 :** an animal that eats other animals of its own kind

can·non *n, pl* **cannon** *also* **cannons 1 :** a heavy gun mounted on a carriage **2 :** an automatic gun of heavy caliber on an airplane

can·non·ball *n* **:** a usually round solid missile for firing from a cannon

can·not : can not

can·ny *adj* **can·ni·er; can·ni·est :** watchful of one's own interest — **can·ni·ly** *adv*

¹ca·noe *n* **:** a long light narrow boat with sharp ends and curved sides usually driven by paddles

²canoe *vb* **ca·noed; ca·noe·ing :** to travel or carry in a canoe — **ca·noe·ist** *n*

can·on *n* **1 :** a rule or law of a church **2 :** an accepted rule

can·o·py *n, pl* **can·o·pies 1 :** a covering fixed over a bed or throne or carried on poles (as over a person of high rank) **2 :** something that hangs over and shades or shelters something else

can't : can not

can·ta·loupe *n* **:** a muskmelon usually with a hard ridged or rough skin and reddish orange flesh

can·tan·ker·ous *adj* **:** QUARRELSOME

can·ta·ta *n* **:** a poem or story set to music to be sung by a chorus and soloists

can·teen *n* **1 :** a store (as in a camp or factory) in which food, drinks, and small supplies are sold **2 :** a place of recreation for people in military service **3 :** a small container for carrying liquid (as drinking water)

can·ter *n* **:** a horse's gait like but slower than the gallop

can·ti·le·ver *n* **1 :** a beam or similar structure fastened (as by being built into a wall) only at one end **2 :** either of two structures that extend from piers toward each other and when joined form a span in a bridge (**cantilever bridge**)

can·to *n, pl* **can·tos :** one of the major divisions of a long poem

can·ton *n* **:** a division of a country (as Switzerland)

can·tor *n* **:** a synagogue official who sings religious music and leads the congregation in prayer

can·vas *n* **1 :** a strong cloth of hemp, flax, or cotton that is used sometimes for making tents and sails and as the material on which oil paintings are made **2 :** something made of canvas or on canvas

can·vas·back *n* **:** a North American wild duck with reddish head and grayish back

¹can·vass *vb* **:** to go through (a district) or go to (people) to ask for votes, contributions, or orders for goods or to determine public opinion — **can·vass·er** *n*

²canvass *n* **:** an act of canvassing

can·yon *n* **:** a deep valley with high steep slopes

¹cap *n* **1 :** a head covering that has a visor and no brim **2 :** something that serves as a cover or protection for something **3 :** a paper or metal container holding an explosive charge

²cap *vb* **capped; cap·ping 1 :** to cover or provide with a cap **2 :** to match with something equal or better

ca·pa·bil·i·ty *n, pl* **ca·pa·bil·i·ties :** the quality or state of being capable

ca·pa·ble *adj* **1 :** having the qualities (as ability, power, or strength) needed to do or accomplish something **2 :** able to do one's job well **:** EFFICIENT — **ca·pa·bly** *adv*

ca·pa·cious *adj* **:** able to hold a great deal

ca·pac·i·ty *n, pl* **ca·pac·i·ties 1 :** ability to contain or deal with something **2 :** mental or physical power **3 :** VOLUME 3 **4 :** ROLE 1, STATUS

¹cape *n* **:** a point of land that juts out into the sea or into a lake

²cape *n* **:** a sleeveless garment worn so as to hang over the shoulders, arms, and back

¹ca·per *vb* **:** to leap about in a lively way

²caper *n* **1 :** a gay bounding leap or spring **2 :** a playful or mischievous trick **3 :** an illegal or questionable act

¹cap·il·lary *adj* **1 :** having a long slender form and a small inner diameter **2 :** of or relating to capillary action or a capillary

²capillary *n, pl* **cap·il·lar·ies :** one of the slender hairlike tubes that are the smallest blood vessels and connect arteries with veins

capillary action *n* **:** the action by which the surface of a liquid where it is in contact with a solid (as in a capillary tube) is raised or lowered

¹cap·i·tal *n* **:** the top part of an architectural column

²capital *adj* **1 :** punishable by or resulting in death **2 :** being like the letters A, B, C, etc. rather than a, b, c, etc. **3 :** being the location of a government **4 :** of or relating to capital **5 :** EXCELLENT

³capital *n* **1 :** accumulated wealth especially as used to produce more wealth **2 :** persons holding capital **3 :** profitable use **4 :** a capital letter **5 :** a capital city

cap·i·tal·ism *n* **:** a system under which the ownership of land and wealth is for the most part in the hands of private individuals

¹cap·i·tal·ist *n* **1 :** a person who has capital and especially business capital **2 :** a person who favors capitalism

²capitalist *adj* **1 :** owning capital **2 :** CAPITALISTIC

cap·i·tal·is·tic *adj* **1 :** practicing or favoring capitalism **2 :** of or relating to capitalism or capitalists — **cap·i·tal·is·ti·cal·ly** *adv*

cap·i·tal·iza·tion *n* **1 :** the act or process of capitalizing **2 :** the amount of money used as capital in business

cap·i·tal·ize *vb* **cap·i·tal·ized; cap·i·tal·iz·ing 1 :** to write with a beginning capital letter or in capital letters **2 :** to use as capital (as in a business) **:** furnish capital for (a business) **3 :** to gain by turning something to advantage

cap·i·tol *n* **1 :** the building in which a state legislature meets **2** *cap* **:** the building in Washington in which the United States Congress meets

ca·po *n, pl* **capos :** a bar that can be fitted on the fingerboard especially of a guitar to raise the pitch of all the strings

ca·pon *n* **:** a castrated male chicken

ca·price *n* **:** a sudden change in feeling, opinion, or action **:** WHIM

ca·pri·cious *adj* : moved or controlled by caprice : likely to change suddenly — **ca·pri·cious·ly** *adv* — **ca·pri·cious·ness** *n*

cap·size *vb* **cap·sized; cap·siz·ing** : to turn over : UPSET

cap·stan *n* : a device that consists of a drum to which a rope is fastened and that is used especially on ships for moving or raising weights

cap·sule *n* **1** : a case enclosing the seeds or spores of a plant **2** : a small case of material that contains medicine to be swallowed **3** : a closed compartment for travel in space

¹cap·tain *n* **1** : a leader of a group : one in command **2** : a commissioned officer in the Navy or Coast Guard ranking above a commander **3** : a commissioned officer in the Army, Air Force, or Marine Corps ranking above a first lieutenant **4** : the commanding officer of a ship

²captain *vb* : to be captain of

cap·tion *n* **1** : the heading especially of an article or document **2** : a comment or title that goes with a picture (as in a book)

cap·ti·vate *vb* **cap·ti·vat·ed; cap·ti·vat·ing** : to fascinate by some special charm

¹cap·tive *adj* **1** : taken and held prisoner especially in war **2** : kept within bounds or under control **3** : of or relating to captivity

²captive *n* : one that is captive : PRISONER

cap·tiv·i·ty *n* : the state of being a captive

cap·tor *n* : one that has captured a person or thing

¹cap·ture *n* : the act of capturing

²capture *vb* **cap·tured; cap·tur·ing** **1** : to take and hold especially by force **2** : to put into a lasting form

car *n* **1** : a vehicle that moves on wheels **2** : the compartment of an elevator

ca·rafe *n* : a bottle that has a lip and is used to hold water or beverages

car·a·mel *n* **1** : burnt sugar used for coloring and flavoring **2** : a firm chewy candy

car·at *n* : a unit of weight for precious stones equal to 200 milligrams

car·a·van *n* **1** : a group (as of pilgrims) traveling together on a long journey through desert or in dangerous places **2** : a group of vehicles traveling together one behind the other

car·a·vel *n* : a small sailing ship of the fifteenth and sixteenth centuries with a broad bow and high stern and three or four masts

car·a·way *n* : an herb of the carrot family whose seeds are used in seasoning and medicine

car·bine *n* : a short light rifle

car·bo·hy·drate *n* : a nutrient that is rich in energy and is made up of carbon, hydrogen, and oxygen

car·bol·ic acid *n* : a poison present in coal tar and wood tar that is diluted and used as an antiseptic

car·bon *n* : a chemical element occurring as diamond and graphite, in coal and petroleum, and in plant and animal bodies

car·bon·ate *vb* **car·bon·at·ed; car·bon·at·ing** : to fill with carbon dioxide which escapes in the form of bubbles

carbon di·ox·ide *n* : a heavy colorless gas that is formed by burning fuels and by decay and that is the simple raw material from which plants build up compounds for their nourishment

carbon mon·ox·ide *n* : a colorless odorless very poisonous gas formed by incomplete burning of carbon

carbon tet·ra·chlo·ride *n* : a colorless poisonous liquid that does not burn and is used for dissolving grease

car·bu·re·tor *n* : the part of an engine in which liquid fuel (as gasoline) is mixed with air to make it burn easily

car·cass *n* : the body of an animal prepared for use as meat

¹card *vb* : to clean and untangle fibers and especially wool by combing with a card — **card·er** *n*

²card *n* : an instrument usually with bent wire teeth that is used to clean and untangle fibers (as wool)

³card *n* **1** : PLAYING CARD **2 cards** *pl* : a game played with playing cards **3** : a flat stiff piece of paper or thin pasteboard that can be written on or that contains printed information

card·board *n* : a stiff material made of wood pulp that has been pressed and dried

car·di·ac *adj* : of, relating to, or affecting the heart

¹car·di·nal *n* **1** : a high official of the Roman Catholic Church ranking next below the pope **2** : a bright red songbird with a crest and a whistling call

²cardinal *adj* : of first importance : MAIN, PRINCIPAL

cardinal flower *n* : the bright red flower of a North American plant that blooms in late summer

car·di·nal·i·ty *n, pl* **car·di·nal·i·ties** : the number of elements in a given mathematical set

cardinal number *n* : a number (as 1, 5, 22) that is used in simple counting and answers the question "how many?"

cardinal point *n* : one of the four chief points of the compass which are north, south, east, west

¹care *n* **1** : a heavy sense of responsibility **2** : serious attention **3** : PROTECTION 1, SUPERVISION **4** : an object of one's care

[2]**care** *vb* **cared; car·ing 1 :** to feel interest or concern **2 :** to give care **3 :** to have a liking or desire
ca·reer *n* **1 :** the course followed or progress made in one's job or life's work **2 :** a job followed as a life's work
care·free *adj* **:** free from care or worry
care·ful *adj* **1 :** using care **2 :** made, done, or said with care — **care·ful·ly** *adv* — **care·ful·ness** *n*
care·less *adj* **1 :** CAREFREE **2 :** not taking proper care **3 :** done, made, or said without being careful — **care·less·ly** *adv* — **care·less·ness** *n*
[1]**ca·ress** *n* **:** a tender or loving touch or hug
[2]**caress** *vb* **:** to touch in a tender or loving way
care·tak·er *n* **:** a person who takes care of property for another person
car·fare *n* **:** the fare charged for carrying a passenger (as on a bus)
car·go *n, pl* **cargoes** *or* **cargos :** the goods carried by a ship, airplane, or vehicle
car·i·bou *n* **:** a large deer of northern and arctic North America that is closely related to the Old World reindeer
car·ies *n, pl* **caries :** a decayed condition of a tooth or teeth
car·il·lon *n* **:** a set of bells sounded by hammers controlled by a keyboard
car·nage *n* **:** [1]SLAUGHTER 3
car·na·tion *n* **:** a fragrant usually white, pink, or red garden or greenhouse flower that is related to the pinks
car·ne·lian *n* **:** a hard reddish quartz used as a gem
car·ni·val *n* **1 :** a traveling group that puts on a variety of amusements **2 :** an organized program of entertainment or exhibition **:** FESTIVAL
car·ni·vore *n* **:** an animal that feeds on meat
car·niv·o·rous *adj* **1 :** feeding on animal flesh **2 :** of or relating to carnivores
[1]**car·ol** *n* **:** a usually religious song of joy
[2]**carol** *vb* **car·oled** *or* **car·olled; car·ol·ing** *or* **car·ol·ling 1 :** to sing in a joyful manner **2 :** to sing carols and especially Christmas carols — **car·ol·er** *or* **car·ol·ler** *n*
[1]**car·om** *n* **:** a bouncing back especially at an angle
[2]**carom** *vb* **:** to hit and bounce back at an angle
[1]**carp** *vb* **:** to find fault
[2]**carp** *n* **:** a freshwater fish that lives a long time and may weigh as much as eighteen kilograms
car·pel *n* **:** one of the ring of parts that form the ovary of a flower
car·pen·ter *n* **:** a worker who builds or repairs things made of wood
car·pen·try *n* **:** the work or trade of a carpenter
[1]**car·pet** *n* **1 :** a heavy woven fabric used especially as a floor covering **2 :** a covering like a carpet
[2]**carpet** *vb* **:** to cover with or as if with a carpet
car pool *n* **:** an arrangement by a group of automobile owners in which each takes turns driving his or her own car and giving the others a ride
car·riage *n* **1 :** the manner of holding the body **:** POSTURE **2 :** a vehicle with wheels used for carrying persons **3 :** a support with wheels used for carrying a load **4 :** a movable part of a machine that carries or supports some other moving part
car·ri·er *n* **1 :** a person or thing that carries **2 :** a person or business that transports passengers or goods **3 :** one that carries disease germs and passes them on to others
car·ri·on *n* **:** dead and decaying flesh
car·rot *n* **:** the long orange edible root of a garden plant (**carrot plant**)
car·ry *vb* **car·ried; car·ry·ing 1 :** to take or transfer from one place to another **2 :** [1]SUPPORT 4, BEAR **3 :** WIN 4 **4 :** to contain and direct the course of **5 :** to wear or have on one's person or have within one **6 :** to have as an element, quality, or part **7 :** to hold or bear the body or some part of it **8 :** to sing in correct pitch **9 :** to have for sale **10 :** PUBLISH 2 **11 :** to go over or travel a distance
car·ry·all *n* **:** a large carrying case
carry away *vb* **:** to cause strong feeling in
carry on *vb* **1 :** MANAGE 1 **2 :** to behave badly **3 :** to continue in spite of difficulties
carry out *vb* **:** to put into action or effect
car seat *n* **:** a seat for a small child that attaches to an automobile seat and holds the child safely
[1]**cart** *n* **1 :** a heavy vehicle with two wheels usually drawn by horses and used for hauling **2 :** a light vehicle pushed or pulled by hand
[2]**cart** *vb* **:** to carry in a cart — **cart·er** *n*
car·ti·lage *n* **:** an elastic tissue that makes up most of the skeleton of very young animals and is later mostly changed into bone
car·ti·lag·i·nous *adj* **:** of, relating to, or made of cartilage
car·ton *n* **:** a cardboard container
car·toon *n* **1 :** a drawing (as in a newspaper) making people or objects look funny or foolish **2 :** COMIC STRIP **3 :** a movie composed of cartoons
car·toon·ist *n* **:** a person who draws cartoons
car·tridge *n* **1 :** a case or shell containing gunpowder and shot or a bullet for use in a

firearm **2 :** a case containing an explosive for blasting **3 :** a container like a cartridge

cart·wheel *n* **:** a handspring made to the side with arms and legs sticking out

carve *vb* **carved; carv·ing 1 :** to cut with care **2 :** to make or get by cutting **3 :** to slice and serve (meat) — **carv·er** *n*

cas·cade *n* **:** a steep usually small waterfall

cas·cara *n* **:** the dried bark of a western North American shrub used as a laxative

[1]**case** *n* **1 :** a particular instance, situation, or example **2 :** a situation or an object that calls for investigation or action (as by the police) **3 :** a question to be settled in a court of law **4 :** a form of a noun, pronoun, or adjective showing its grammatical relation to other words **5 :** the actual situation **6 :** a convincing argument **7 :** an instance of disease or injury **8 :** [2]PATIENT

[2]**case** *n* **1 :** a container (as a box) for holding something **2 :** a box and its contents **3 :** an outer covering **4 :** the frame of a door or window

ca·sein *n* **:** a whitish to yellowish material made from milk especially by the action of acid and used in making paints and plastics

case·ment *n* **1 :** a window sash opening on hinges **2 :** a window with a casement

[1]**cash** *n* **1 :** money in the form of coins or bills **2 :** money or its equivalent (as a check) paid for goods at the time of purchase or delivery

[2]**cash** *vb* **:** to pay or obtain cash for

cash·ew *n* **:** an edible nut that is shaped like a kidney and comes from a tropical American tree

[1]**ca·shier** *vb* **:** to dismiss from service especially in disgrace

[2]**cash·ier** *n* **:** a person who is responsible for money (as in a bank or business)

cash·mere *n* **:** a soft yarn or fabric once made from the fine wool of an Indian goat but now often from sheep's wool

cas·ing *n* **:** something that covers or encloses

cask *n* **1 :** a container that is shaped like a barrel and is usually used for liquids **2 :** the amount contained in a cask

cas·ket *n* **1 :** a small box for storage or safekeeping (as for jewels) **2 :** COFFIN

cas·se·role *n* **1 :** a deep dish in which food can be baked and served **2 :** the food cooked and served in a casserole

cas·sette *n* **1 :** a container holding photographic film or plates that can be easily loaded into a camera **2 :** a container holding magnetic tape with the tape on one reel passing to the other

[1]**cast** *vb* **cast; cast·ing 1 :** [1]THROW 1 **2 :** to throw out, off, or away **:** SHED **3 :** to direct to or toward something or someone **4 :** to put on record **5 :** to assign a part or role to **6 :** to give shape to liquid material by pouring it into a mold and letting it harden **7 :** to make by looping or catching up — **cast lots :** to take or receive an object at random in order to decide something by chance

[2]**cast** *n* **1 :** an act of casting **:** THROW, FLING **2 :** the form in which a thing is made **3 :** the characters or the people acting in a play or story **4 :** the distance to which a thing can be thrown **5 :** something formed by casting in a mold or form **6 :** a stiff surgical dressing of plaster hardened around a part of the body **7 :** a hint of color **8 :** [2]SHAPE 1 **9 :** something (as the skin of an insect) thrown out or off

cas·ta·net *n* **:** a rhythm instrument that consists of two small ivory, wooden, or plastic shells fastened to the thumb and clicked by the fingers in time to dancing and music — usually used in pl.

[1]**cast·away** *adj* **1 :** thrown away **2 :** cast adrift or ashore

[2]**castaway** *n* **1 :** something that has been thrown away **2 :** a shipwrecked person

caste *n* **1 :** one of the classes into which the people of India were formerly divided **2 :** a division or class of society based on wealth, rank, or occupation **3 :** social rank **:** PRESTIGE

cast·er *n* **1 :** one that casts **2 :** a small container (as for salt or pepper) with holes in the top **3** *or* **cas·tor :** a small wheel that turns freely and is used for supporting furniture

cas·ti·gate *vb* **cas·ti·gat·ed; cas·ti·gat·ing :** to punish or correct with words or blows

cast·ing *n* **1 :** the act or action of one that casts **2 :** something that is cast in a mold **3 :** something (as skin or feathers) that is cast out or off

cast iron *n* **:** a hard and brittle alloy of iron, carbon, and silicon shaped by being poured into a mold while melted

cas·tle *n* **1 :** a large building or group of buildings usually having high walls with towers and a surrounding moat for protection **2 :** a large or impressive house

cast·off *n* **:** a cast-off person or thing

cast–off *adj* **:** thrown away or aside

cas·tor oil *n* **:** a thick yellowish liquid that comes from the seeds (**castor beans**) of a tropical herb and is used as a lubricant and as a strong laxative

cas·trate *vb* **cas·trat·ed; cas·trat·ing :** to remove the sex glands of

ca·su·al *adj* **1 :** happening unexpectedly or by chance **:** not planned or foreseen **2 :** occurring without regularity **:** OCCASIONAL **3 :** showing or feeling little concern **:** NONCHALANT **4 :** meant for informal use — **ca·su·al·ly** *adv*

ca·su·al·ty *n, pl* **ca·su·al·ties** **1 :** a serious or fatal accident **:** DISASTER **2 :** a military person lost (as by death) during warfare **3 :** a person or thing injured, lost, or destroyed

cat *n* **1 :** a common furry flesh-eating animal kept as a pet or for catching mice and rats **2 :** any of the group of mammals (as lions, tigers, and wildcats) to which the domestic cat belongs

[1]**cat·a·log** *or* **cat·a·logue** *n* **1 :** a list of names, titles, or articles arranged by some system **2 :** a book or file containing a catalog

[2]**catalog** *or* **catalogue** *vb* **cat·a·loged** *or* **cat·a·logued; cat·a·log·ing** *or* **cat·a·logu·ing** **1 :** to make a catalog of **2 :** to enter in a catalog — **cat·a·log·er** *or* **cat·a·logu·er** *n*

ca·tal·pa *n* **:** a tree of America and Asia with broad leaves, bright flowers, and long pods

[1]**cat·a·pult** *n* **1 :** an ancient military machine for hurling stones and arrows **2 :** a device for launching an airplane from the deck of a ship

[2]**catapult** *vb* **1 :** to throw or launch by or as if by a catapult **2 :** to become catapulted

ca·tarrh *n* **:** a red sore state of mucous membrane especially when chronic

ca·tas·tro·phe *n* **1 :** a sudden disaster **2 :** complete failure **:** FIASCO

cat·bird *n* **:** a dark gray songbird that has a call like a cat's mewing

cat·boat *n* **:** a sailboat with a single mast set far forward and a single large sail with a long boom

cat·call *n* **:** a sound like the cry of a cat or a noise expressing disapproval (as at a sports event)

[1]**catch** *vb* **caught; catch·ing** **1 :** to capture or seize something in flight or motion **2 :** to discover unexpectedly **3 :** to check suddenly **4 :** to take hold of **5 :** to get tangled **6 :** to hold firmly **:** FASTEN **7 :** to become affected by **8 :** to take or get briefly or quickly **9 :** to be in time for **10 :** to grasp by the senses or the mind **11 :** to play catcher on a baseball team

[2]**catch** *n* **1 :** something caught **:** the amount caught at one time **2 :** the act of catching **3 :** a pastime in which a ball is thrown and caught **4 :** something that checks, fastens, or holds immovable **5 :** a hidden difficulty

catch·er *n* **1 :** one that catches **2 :** a baseball player who plays behind home plate

catch·ing *adj* **1 :** INFECTIOUS 1, CONTAGIOUS **2 :** likely to spread as if infectious

catchy *adj* **catch·i·er; catch·i·est** **1 :** likely to attract **2 :** TRICKY 2

cat·e·chism *n* **1 :** a series of questions and answers used in giving instruction and especially religious instruction **2 :** a set of formal questions

cat·e·go·ry *n, pl* **cat·e·go·ries** **:** a basic division or grouping of things

ca·ter *vb* **1 :** to provide a supply of food **2 :** to supply what is needed or wanted — **ca·ter·er** *n*

cat·er·pil·lar *n* **:** a wormlike often hairy larva of an insect (as a moth or butterfly)

cat·fish *n* **:** any of a group of fishes with large heads and feelers about the mouth

cat·gut *n* **:** a tough cord made from intestines of animals (as sheep) and used for strings of musical instruments and rackets and for sewing in surgery

ca·the·dral *n* **:** the principal church of a district headed by a bishop

cath·o·lic *adj* **1 :** broad in range **2** *cap* **:** of or relating to the Roman Catholic Church

Catholic *n* **1 :** a member of a Christian church tracing its history back to the apostles **2 :** a member of the Roman Catholic Church

cat·kin *n* **:** a flower cluster (as of the willow and birch) in which the flowers grow in close circular rows along a slender stalk

cat·like *adj* **:** like a cat (as in grace or slyness)

cat·nap *n* **:** a very short light nap

cat·nip *n* **:** a plant of the mint family enjoyed by cats

cat–o'–nine–tails *n, pl* **cat–o'–nine–tails** **:** a whip made of nine knotted cords fastened to a handle

cat·sup *variant of* KETCHUP

cat·tail *n* **:** a tall plant with long flat leaves and tall furry stalks that grows in marshy areas

cat·tle *n, pl* **cattle** **:** domestic animals with four feet and especially cows, bulls, and calves

cat·walk *n* **:** a narrow walk or way (as along a bridge)

caught *past of* CATCH

caul·dron *or* **cal·dron** *n* **:** a large kettle or boiler

cau·li·flow·er *n* **:** a vegetable closely related to the cabbage that is grown for its white head of undeveloped flowers

[1]**caulk** *vb* **:** to fill up a crack, seam, or joint so as to make it watertight

[2]**caulk** *also* **caulk·ing** *n* **:** material used to caulk

[1]**cause** *n* **1 :** a person or thing that brings about a result **2 :** a good or good enough reason for something **3 :** something (as a question) to be decided **4 :** something supported or deserving support

[2]**cause** *vb* **caused; caus·ing** **:** to be the cause of

cause·way *n* **:** a raised road or way across wet ground or water

caus·tic *adj* **1 :** capable of eating away by

chemical action : CORROSIVE **2 :** [1]SHARP 8, BITING

[1]**cau·tion** *n* **1 :** ADMONITION **2 :** carefulness in regard to danger : PRECAUTION

[2]**caution** *vb* : to advise caution to : WARN

cau·tious *adj* : showing or using caution — **cau·tious·ly** *adv*

cav·al·cade *n* **1 :** a procession especially of riders or carriages **2 :** a dramatic series (as of related events)

[1]**cav·a·lier** *n* **1 :** a mounted soldier **2 :** a brave and courteous gentleman

[2]**cavalier** *adj* **1 :** easy and lighthearted in manner **2 :** tending to disregard the rights or feelings of others

cav·al·ry *n, pl* **cav·al·ries :** troops mounted on horseback or moving in motor vehicles

cav·al·ry·man *n, pl* **cav·al·ry·men :** a cavalry soldier

[1]**cave** *n* : a hollow underground place with an opening on the surface

[2]**cave** *vb* **caved; cav·ing :** to fall or cause to fall in or down : COLLAPSE

cave·man *n, pl* **cave·men :** a person living in a cave especially during the Stone Age

cav·ern *n* : a cave often of large or unknown size

cav·ern·ous *adj* **1 :** having caverns or hollow places **2 :** like a cavern because large and hollow

cav·i·ty *n, pl* **cav·i·ties :** a hollow place

ca·vort *vb* : to move or hop about in a lively way

[1]**caw** *vb* : to make a caw

[2]**caw** *n* : the cry of a crow or a raven

cay·enne pepper *n* : dried ripe hot peppers ground and used to add flavor to food

CD *n* : COMPACT DISC

CD–ROM *n* : a compact disc that contains computer data that cannot be changed

cease *vb* **ceased; ceas·ing :** to come or bring to an end : STOP

cease·less *adj* : CONSTANT 3

ce·cro·pia moth *n* : a silkworm moth that is the largest moth of the eastern United States

ce·dar *n* : any of a number of trees having cones and a strong wood with a pleasant smell

cede *vb* **ced·ed; ced·ing :** to give up especially by treaty

ceil·ing *n* **1 :** the overhead inside surface of a room **2 :** the greatest height at which an airplane can fly properly **3 :** the height above the ground of the bottom of the lowest layer of clouds **4 :** an upper limit

cel·e·brate *vb* **cel·e·brat·ed; cel·e·brat·ing 1 :** to perform publicly and according to certain rules **2 :** to observe in some special way (as by merrymaking or by staying away from business) **3 :** [1]PRAISE 1

cel·e·brat·ed *adj* : widely known and talked about

cel·e·bra·tion *n* **1 :** the act of celebrating **2 :** the activities or ceremonies for celebrating a special occasion

ce·leb·ri·ty *n, pl* **ce·leb·ri·ties 1 :** FAME **2 :** a celebrated person

cel·ery *n* : a plant related to the carrots whose crisp leafstalks are used for food

ce·les·tial *adj* **1 :** of, relating to, or suggesting heaven **2 :** of or relating to the sky

cell *n* **1 :** a very small room (as in a prison or a monastery) **2 :** a small enclosed part or division (as in a honeycomb) **3 :** a small mass of living matter that is made of protoplasm, includes a nucleus, is enclosed in a membrane, and is the basic unit of which all plants and animals are made up **4 :** a container with substances which can produce an electric current by chemical action **5:** a device that converts light (as sunlight) that falls on it into electrical energy that is used as a power source **6:** CELL PHONE — **celled** *adj*

cel·lar *n* : a room or set of rooms below the surface of the ground : BASEMENT

cel·lo *n, pl* **cel·los :** a large stringed instrument of the violin family that plays the bass part

cel·lo·phane *n* : a thin clear material made from cellulose and used as a wrapping

cell phone *n* : a portable telephone that connects to other telephones by radio through a system of transmitters each of which covers a limited geographical area

cel·lu·lar *adj* **1 :** of, relating to, or made up of cells **2 :** of, relating to, or being a cell phone

cel·lu·lose *n* : a substance that is the chief part of the cell walls of plants and is used in making various products (as paper and rayon)

cell wall *n* : the firm outer nonliving boundary of a plant cell

Cel·si·us *adj* : relating to or having a thermometer scale on which the interval between the freezing point and the boiling point of water is divided into 100 degrees with 0 representing the freezing point and 100 the boiling point

[1]**ce·ment** *n* **1 :** a powder that is made mainly from compounds of aluminum, calcium, silicon, and iron heated together and then ground, that combines with water and hardens into a mass, and that is used in mortar and concrete **2 :** [2]CONCRETE, MORTAR **3 :** a substance that by hardening sticks things together firmly

[2]**cement** *vb* **1 :** to join together with or as if with cement **2 :** to cover with concrete

ce·men·tum *n* **:** a thin bony layer covering the part of a tooth inside the gum

cem·e·tery *n, pl* **cem·e·ter·ies :** a place where dead people are buried **:** GRAVEYARD

Ce·no·zo·ic *n* **:** an era of geological history lasting from seventy million years ago to the present time in which there has been a rapid evolution of mammals and birds and of flowering plants

[1]**cen·sor** *n* **:** an official who checks writings or movies to take out things thought to be objectionable

[2]**censor** *vb* **:** to examine (as a book) to take out things thought to be objectionable

[1]**cen·sure** *n* **1 :** the act of finding fault with or blaming **2 :** an official criticism

[2]**censure** *vb* **cen·sured; cen·sur·ing :** to find fault with especially publicly

cen·sus *n* **:** a count of the number of people in a country, city, or town

cent *n* **1 :** a hundredth part of the unit of the money system in a number of different countries **2 :** a coin, token, or note representing one cent

cen·taur *n* **:** a creature in Greek mythology that is part man and part horse

cen·te·nar·i·an *n* **:** a person 100 or more years old

[1]**cen·ten·ni·al** *n* **:** a 100th anniversary or a celebration of this event

[2]**centennial** *adj* **:** relating to a period of 100 years

[1]**cen·ter** *n* **1 :** the middle point of a circle or a sphere equally distant from every point on the circumference or surface **2 :** one (as a person or area) that is very important to some activity or concern **3 :** the middle part of something **4 :** a player occupying a middle position on a team

[2]**center** *vb* **1 :** to place or fix at or around a center or central area **2 :** to collect at or around one point

center of gravity : the point at which the entire weight of a body may be thought of as centered so that if supported at this point the body would balance perfectly

cen·ter·piece *n* **:** a piece put in the center of something and especially a decoration (as flowers) for a table

centi- *prefix* **:** hundredth part — used in terms of the metric system

cen·ti·grade *adj* **:** CELSIUS

cen·ti·gram *n* **:** a unit of weight equal to 1/100 gram

cen·ti·li·ter *n* **:** a unit of liquid capacity equal to 1/100 liter

cen·ti·me·ter *n* **:** a unit of length equal to 1/100 meter

cen·ti·pede *n* **:** a small animal that has a long body and many legs and is related to the insects

cen·tral *adj* **1 :** containing or being the center **2 :** most important **:** CHIEF **3 :** placed at, in, or near the center — **cen·tral·ly** *adv*

[1]**Central American** *adj* **:** of or relating to Central America or the Central Americans

[2]**Central American** *n* **:** a person born or living in Central America

central angle *n* **:** an angle with its vertex at the center of a circle and with sides that are radii of the circle

cen·tral·ize *vb* **cen·tral·ized; cen·tral·iz·ing :** to bring to a central point or under a single control

central processing unit *n* **:** PROCESSOR 3

cen·trif·u·gal force *n* **:** the force that tends to cause a thing or parts of a thing to go outward from a center of rotation

cen·tu·ry *n, pl* **cen·tu·ries :** a period of 100 years

ce·ram·ic *n* **1 ceramics** *pl* **:** the art of making things (as pottery or tiles) of baked clay **2 :** a product made by ceramics

[1]**ce·re·al** *adj* **1 :** relating to grain or the plants that it comes from **2 :** made of grain

[2]**cereal** *n* **1 :** a plant (as a grass) that yields grain for food **2 :** a food prepared from grain

cer·e·bel·lum *n, pl* **cer·e·bel·lums** *or* **cer·e·bel·la :** a part of the brain concerned especially with the coordination of muscles and with keeping the body in proper balance

ce·re·bral *adj* **1 :** of or relating to the brain or mind **2 :** of, relating to, or affecting the cerebrum

ce·re·brum *n, pl* **ce·re·brums** *or* **ce·re·bra :** the enlarged front and upper part of the brain that is the center of thinking

[1]**cer·e·mo·ni·al** *adj* **:** of, relating to, or being a ceremony

[2]**ceremonial** *n* **:** a ceremonial act, action, or system

cer·e·mo·ni·ous *adj* **1 :** [1]CEREMONIAL **2 :** given to ceremony **:** FORMAL — **cer·e·mo·ni·ous·ly** *adv*

cer·e·mo·ny *n, pl* **cer·e·mo·nies 1 :** an act or series of acts performed in some regular way according to fixed rules **2 :** very polite behavior **:** FORMALITY

[1]**cer·tain** *adj* **1 :** being fixed or settled **2 :** known but not named **3 :** sure to have an effect **4 :** known to be true **5 :** bound by the way things are **6 :** assured in thought or action

[2]**certain** *pron* **:** certain ones

cer·tain·ly *adv* **1 :** with certainty **:** without fail **2 :** without doubt

cer·tain·ty *n, pl* **cer·tain·ties 1 :** something

that is certain **2 :** the quality or state of being certain

cer·tif·i·cate *n* **1 :** a written or printed statement that is proof of some fact **2 :** a paper showing that a person has met certain requirements **3 :** a paper showing ownership

cer·ti·fy *vb* **cer·ti·fied; cer·ti·fy·ing** **1 :** to show to be true or as claimed by a formal or official statement **2 :** to guarantee the quality, fitness, or value of officially **3 :** to show to have met certain requirements

ce·ru·le·an *adj* **:** somewhat like the blue of the sky

ces·sa·tion *n* **:** a coming to a stop

chafe *vb* **chafed; chaf·ing** **1 :** IRRITATE 1, VEX **2 :** to be bothered **:** FRET **3 :** to warm by rubbing **4 :** to rub so as to wear away or make sore

¹chaff *n* **1 :** the husks of grains and grasses separated from the seed in threshing **2 :** something worthless

²chaff *vb* **:** to tease in a friendly way

cha·grin *n* **:** a feeling of being annoyed by failure or disappointment

¹chain *n* **1 :** a series of links or rings usually of metal **2 :** something that restricts or binds **:** BOND **3 :** a series of things joined together as if by links

²chain *vb* **:** to fasten, bind, or connect with or as if with a chain

chain saw *n* **:** a portable saw that cuts using teeth that are linked together to form a continuous chain

chair *n* **1 :** a seat for one person usually having a back and either four legs or a swivel base **2 :** an official seat or a seat of authority or honor **3 :** an office or position of authority or honor **4 :** an official who conducts a meeting

chair·man *n, pl* **chair·men** **:** CHAIR 4 — **chair·man·ship** *n*

chair·per·son *n* **:** CHAIR 4

chair·wom·an *n, pl* **chair·wom·en** **:** a woman who conducts a meeting

chaise longue *n* **:** a long chair somewhat like a couch

chaise lounge *n* **:** CHAISE LONGUE

cha·let *n* **1 :** a herdsman's hut in the Alps away from a town or village **2 :** a Swiss dwelling with a roof that sticks far out past the walls **3 :** a cottage built to look like a chalet

chal·ice *n* **:** a drinking cup **:** GOBLET

¹chalk *n* **1 :** a soft white, gray, or buff limestone made up mainly of very small seashells **2 :** a material like chalk especially when used in the form of a crayon

²chalk *vb* **1 :** to rub, mark, write, or draw with chalk **2 :** to record or add up with or as if with chalk

chalk·board *n* **:** BLACKBOARD

chalky *adj* **chalk·i·er; chalk·i·est** **1 :** made of or like chalk **2 :** easily crumbled **3 :** very pale

¹chal·lenge *vb* **chal·lenged; chal·leng·ing** **1 :** to halt and demand a password from **2 :** to object to as bad or incorrect **:** DISPUTE **3 :** to demand proof that something is right or legal **4 :** to invite or dare to take part in a contest — **chal·leng·er** *n*

²challenge *n* **1 :** an objection to something as not being true, genuine, correct, or proper or to a person (as a juror) as not being qualified or approved **:** PROTEST **2 :** a demand that someone take part in a duel **3 :** a call or dare for someone to compete in a contest or sport

challenged *adj* **:** having a disability or deficiency

cham·ber *n* **1 :** a room in a house and especially a bedroom **2 :** an enclosed space, cavity, or compartment (as in a gun) **3 :** a meeting hall of a government body (as an assembly) **4 :** a room where a judge conducts business out of court **5 :** a group of people organized into a lawmaking body **6 :** a board or council of volunteers (as businessmen) — **cham·bered** *adj*

cham·ber·lain *n* **1 :** a chief officer in the household of a ruler or noble **2 :** TREASURER

cham·ber·maid *n* **:** a maid who takes care of bedrooms (as in a hotel)

chamber music *n* **:** instrumental music to be performed in a room or small hall

cha·me·leon *n* **:** a lizard that has the ability to change the color of its skin

cham·ois *n, pl* **cham·ois** **1 :** a small antelope living on the highest mountains of Europe and Asia **2 :** a soft yellowish leather made from the skin of the chamois or from sheepskin

¹champ *vb* **:** to bite and chew noisily

²champ *n* **:** ¹CHAMPION 2, 3

¹cham·pi·on *n* **1 :** a person who fights or speaks for another person or in favor of a cause **2 :** a person accepted as better than all others in a sport or in a game of skill **3 :** the winner of first place in a competition

²champion *vb* **:** to protect or fight for as a champion

cham·pi·on·ship *n* **1 :** the act of defending as a champion **2 :** the position or title of champion **3 :** a contest held to find a champion

¹chance *n* **1 :** the uncertain course of events **2 :** OPPORTUNITY 1 **3 :** ¹RISK, GAMBLE **4 :** PROBABILITY 1 **5 :** a ticket in a raffle

²chance *vb* **chanced; chanc·ing** **1 :** to take place by chance **2 :** to come unexpectedly **3 :** to leave to chance **:** RISK

³chance *adj* **:** happening by chance

chan·cel·lor *n* **1 :** a high state official (as in Germany) **2 :** a high officer of some universities **3 :** a chief judge in some courts — **chan·cel·lor·ship** *n*

chan·de·lier *n* **:** a lighting fixture with several branches that usually hangs from the ceiling

[1]**change** *vb* **changed; chang·ing 1 :** to make or become different **:** ALTER **2 :** to give a different position, course, or direction to **3 :** to put one thing in the place of another **:** SWITCH, EXCHANGE **4 :** to give or receive an equal amount of money in usually smaller units of value or in the money of another country **5 :** to put fresh clothes or covering on **6 :** to put on different clothes

[2]**change** *n* **1 :** the act, process, or result of changing **2 :** a fresh set of clothes **3 :** money in small units of value received in exchange for an equal amount in larger units **4 :** money returned when a payment is more than the amount due **5 :** money in coins

change·able *adj* **:** able or likely to change

[1]**chan·nel** *n* **1 :** the bed of a stream **2 :** the deeper part of a waterway (as a river or harbor) **3 :** a strait or a narrow sea **4 :** a closed course (as a tube) through which something flows **5 :** a long groove **6 :** a means by which something is passed or carried **7 :** a range of frequencies used by a single radio or television station in broadcasting

[2]**channel** *vb* **chan·neled** *or* **chan·nelled; chan·nel·ing** *or* **chan·nel·ling 1 :** to form a channel in **2 :** to direct into or through a channel

[1]**chant** *vb* **1 :** to sing especially in the way a chant is sung **2 :** to recite or speak with no change in tone

[2]**chant** *n* **1 :** a melody in which several words or syllables are sung on one tone **2 :** something spoken in the style of a chant

cha·os *n* **:** complete confusion and disorder

cha·ot·ic *adj* **:** being in a state of chaos

[1]**chap** *vb* **chapped; chap·ping :** to open in slits **:** CRACK

[2]**chap** *n* **:** [1]FELLOW 4

chap·el *n* **1 :** a building or a room or place for prayer or special religious services **2 :** a religious service or assembly held in a school or college

[1]**chap·er·on** *or* **chap·er·one** *n* **:** an older person who goes with and is responsible for a young woman or a group of young people (as at a dance)

[2]**chaperon** *or* **chaperone** *vb* **chap·er·oned; chap·er·on·ing :** to act as a chaperon

chap·lain *n* **1 :** a member of the clergy officially attached to a special group (as the army) **2 :** a person chosen to conduct religious services (as for a club)

chaps *n pl* **:** a set of leather coverings for the legs used especially by western ranch workers

chap·ter *n* **1 :** a main division of a book or story **2 :** a local branch of a club or organization

char *vb* **charred; char·ring 1 :** to change to charcoal by burning **2 :** to burn slightly **:** SCORCH

char·ac·ter *n* **1 :** a mark, sign, or symbol (as a letter or figure) used in writing or printing **2 :** [1]CHARACTERISTIC **3 :** the group of qualities that make a person, group, or thing different from others **4 :** a person who is unusual or peculiar **5 :** a person in a story or play **6 :** REPUTATION 1 **7 :** moral excellence

[1]**char·ac·ter·is·tic** *n* **:** a special quality or appearance that makes an individual or a group different from others

[2]**characteristic** *adj* **:** serving to stress some special quality of an individual or a group **:** TYPICAL

char·ac·ter·is·ti·cal·ly *adv* **:** in a characteristic way

char·ac·ter·ize *vb* **char·ac·ter·ized; char·ac·ter·iz·ing 1 :** to point out the character of an individual or a group **:** DESCRIBE **2 :** to be characteristic of

char·coal *n* **:** a black or dark absorbent carbon made by heating animal or vegetable material in the absence of air

[1]**charge** *n* **1 :** the amount (as of ammunition or fuel) needed to load or fill something **2 :** an amount of electricity available **3 :** a task, duty, or order given to a person **:** OBLIGATION **4 :** the work or duty of managing **5 :** a person or thing given to a person to look after **6 :** [2]COMMAND 2 **7 :** the price demanded especially for a service **8 :** an amount listed as a debt on an account **9 :** ACCUSATION **10 :** a rushing attack

[2]**charge** *vb* **charged; charg·ing 1 :** [1]FILL 1 **2 :** to give an electric charge to **3 :** to restore the active materials in a storage battery by passage of an electric current through it **4 :** to give a task, duty, or responsibility to **5 :** [1]COMMAND 1 **6 :** to accuse formally **7 :** to rush against **:** ASSAULT **8 :** to take payment from or make responsible for payment **9 :** to enter as a debt or responsibility on a record **10 :** to ask or set as a price

charg·er *n* **:** a cavalry horse

char·i·ot *n* **:** a vehicle of ancient times that had two wheels, was pulled by horses, and was used in war and in races and parades

char·i·ta·ble *adj* **1 :** freely giving money or help to needy persons **:** GENEROUS **2 :** given for the needy **:** of service to the needy **3 :** kindly in judging other people

char·i·ty *n, pl* **char·i·ties 1 :** love for others **2 :** kindliness in judging others **3 :** the giving of aid to the poor and suffering **4 :** public aid for the poor **5 :** an institution or fund for helping the needy

char·ley horse *n* **:** pain and stiffness in a muscle (as in a leg)

[1]**charm** *n* **1 :** a word, action, or thing believed to have magic powers **2 :** something worn or carried to keep away evil and bring good luck **3 :** a small decorative object worn on a chain or bracelet **4 :** a quality that attracts and pleases

[2]**charm** *vb* **1 :** to affect or influence by or as if by a magic spell **2 :** FASCINATE 2, DELIGHT **3 :** to protect by or as if by a charm **4 :** to attract by grace or beauty

charm·ing *adj* **:** very pleasing

[1]**chart** *n* **1 :** [1]MAP **2 :** a map showing coasts, reefs, currents, and depths of water **3 :** a sheet giving information in a table or lists or by means of diagrams

[2]**chart** *vb* **1 :** to make a map or chart of **2 :** to lay out a plan for

[1]**char·ter** *n* **1 :** an official document granting, guaranteeing, or showing the limits of the rights and duties of the group to which it is given **2 :** a contract by which the owners of a ship lease it to others

[2]**charter** *vb* **1 :** to grant a charter to **2 :** to hire (as a bus or an aircraft) for temporary use

charter school *n* **:** a school supported by taxes but run independently to achieve set goals under a charter between an official body (as a state government) and an outside group (as educators and businesses)

[1]**chase** *n* **1 :** the act of chasing **:** PURSUIT **2 :** the hunting of wild animals **3 :** something pursued

[2]**chase** *vb* **chased; chas·ing 1 :** to follow in order to catch up with or capture **2 :** [1]HUNT 1 **3 :** to drive away or out

chasm *n* **:** a deep split or gap in the earth

chas·sis *n, pl* **chas·sis :** a structure that supports the body (as of an automobile or airplane) or the parts (as of a television set)

chaste *adj* **chast·er; chast·est 1 :** pure in thought and act **:** MODEST **2 :** simple or plain in design

chas·ten *vb* **:** to correct by punishment or suffering **:** DISCIPLINE

chas·tise *vb* **chas·tised; chas·tis·ing :** to punish severely (as by whipping)

chas·ti·ty *n* **:** the quality or state of being chaste

[1]**chat** *vb* **chat·ted; chat·ting :** to talk in a friendly manner of things that are not serious

[2]**chat** *n* **:** a light friendly conversation

chat room *n* **:** an on-line computer site at which any visitor to the site can send messages that immediately appear on the screen for everyone to read

[1]**chat·ter** *vb* **1 :** to make quick sounds that suggest speech but lack meaning **2 :** to talk without thinking, without stopping, or fast **:** JABBER **3 :** to click again and again and without control — **chat·ter·er** *n*

[2]**chatter** *n* **:** the act or sound of chattering

chat·ter·box *n* **:** a person who talks all the time

chat·ty *adj* **chat·ti·er; chat·ti·est 1 :** TALKATIVE **2 :** having the style and manner of friendly conversation

chauf·feur *n* **:** a person hired to drive people around in a car

[1]**cheap** *adj* **1 :** not costing much **2 :** worth little **:** not very good **3 :** gained without much effort **4 :** lowered in one's own opinion **5 :** charging low prices — **cheap·ly** *adv*

[2]**cheap** *adv* **:** at low cost

cheap·en *vb* **:** to make or become cheap or cheaper

[1]**cheat** *vb* **1 :** to take something away from or keep from having something by dishonest tricks **:** DEFRAUD **2 :** to use unfair or dishonest methods to gain an advantage

[2]**cheat** *n* **1 :** an act of cheating **:** DECEPTION, FRAUD **2 :** a dishonest person

[1]**check** *n* **1 :** a sudden stopping of progress **:** PAUSE **2 :** something that delays, stops, or holds back **:** RESTRAINT **3 :** a standard or guide for testing and studying something **4 :** EXAMINATION 1, INVESTIGATION **5 :** a written order telling a bank to pay out money from a person's account to the one named on the order **6 :** a ticket or token showing a person's ownership, identity, or claim to something **7 :** a slip of paper showing the amount due **:** BILL **8 :** a pattern in squares **9 :** material with a design in squares **10 :** a mark typically ✓ placed beside a written or printed item to show that something has been specially noted

[2]**check** *vb* **1 :** to bring to a sudden stop **2 :** to keep from expressing **3 :** to make sure that something is correct or satisfactory **:** VERIFY **4 :** to mark with a check **5 :** to mark with squares **6 :** to leave or accept for safekeeping or for shipment **7 :** to be the same on every point **:** TALLY

check·er·board *n* **:** a board marked with sixty-four squares in two colors and used for games (as checkers)

check·ers *n* **:** a game played on a checkerboard by two players each having twelve pieces

check·up *n* **1 :** INSPECTION, EXAMINATION **2 :** a physical examination

cheek *n* **1 :** the side of the face below the eye

and above and beside the mouth **2 :** IMPUDENCE
[1]**cheep** *vb* **:** [1]PEEP, CHIRP
[2]**cheep** *n* **:** [1]CHIRP
[1]**cheer** *n* **1 :** state of mind or heart **:** SPIRIT **2 :** good spirits **3 :** something that gladdens **4 :** a shout of praise or encouragement
[2]**cheer** *vb* **1 :** to give hope to **:** make happier **:** COMFORT **2 :** to urge on especially with shouts or cheers **3 :** to shout with joy, approval, or enthusiasm **4 :** to grow or be cheerful — usually used with *up*
cheer·ful *adj* **:** full of good spirits **:** PLEASANT — **cheer·ful·ly** *adv* — **cheer·ful·ness** *n*
cheer·less *adj* **:** offering no cheer **:** GLOOMY
cheery *adj* **cheer·i·er; cheer·i·est :** merry and bright in manner or effect **:** CHEERFUL — **cheer·i·ly** *adv* — **cheer·i·ness** *n*
cheese *n* **:** the curd of milk pressed for use as food
cheese·cloth *n* **:** a thin loosely woven cotton cloth
cheesy *adj* **chees·i·er; chees·i·est :** like or suggesting cheese
chee·tah *n* **:** a long-legged spotted African and formerly Asian animal of the cat family that is the fastest animal on land
chef *n* **1 :** a chief cook **2 :** [1]COOK
[1]**chem·i·cal** *adj* **:** of or relating to chemistry or chemicals — **chem·i·cal·ly** *adv*
[2]**chemical** *n* **:** a substance (as an acid) that is formed when two or more other substances act upon one another or that is used to produce a change in another substance (as in making plastics)
chem·ist *n* **:** a person trained or engaged in chemistry
chem·is·try *n* **1 :** a science that deals with the composition and properties of substances and of the changes they undergo **2 :** chemical composition and properties
cher·ish *vb* **1 :** to hold dear **2 :** to keep deeply in mind **:** cling to
Cher·o·kee *n, pl* **Cherokee** *or* **Cherokees :** a member of an Indian people originally from the southern Appalachian Mountains
cher·ry *n, pl* **cherries 1 :** the round red or yellow fruit of a tree (**cherry tree**) that is related to the plum **2 :** a medium red
cher·ub *n* **1 :** a painting or drawing of a beautiful child usually with wings **2 :** a chubby rosy child
chess *n* **:** a game of capture played on a board by two players each using sixteen pieces that have set moves
chest *n* **1 :** a container (as a box or case) for storing, safekeeping, or shipping **2 :** a public fund **3 :** the part of the body enclosed by the ribs and breastbone — **chest·ed** *adj*
chest·nut *n* **1 :** a sweet edible nut that grows in burs on a tree (**chestnut tree**) related to the beech **2 :** a reddish brown
chev·ron *n* **:** a sleeve badge of one or more bars or stripes usually in the shape of an upside down V indicating the wearer's rank (as in the armed forces)
[1]**chew** *vb* **:** to crush or grind with the teeth
[2]**chew** *n* **1 :** the act of chewing **2 :** something for chewing
chew·ing gum *n* **:** gum usually of sweetened and flavored chicle prepared for chewing
chewy *adj* **chew·i·er; chew·i·est :** requiring chewing
[1]**chic** *n* **:** fashionable style
[2]**chic** *adj* **:** STYLISH, SMART
Chi·ca·na *n* **:** an American woman or girl of Mexican ancestry
[1]**Chi·ca·no** *n, pl* **Chicanos :** an American of Mexican ancestry
[2]**Chicano** *adj* **:** of or relating to Chicanos
chick *n* **1 :** a young chicken **2 :** CHILD 2
chick·a·dee *n* **:** a small bird with fluffy grayish feathers and usually a black cap
[1]**chick·en** *n* **1 :** the common domestic fowl especially when young **:** a young hen or rooster **2 :** the flesh of a chicken for use as food
[2]**chicken** *adj* **:** CHICKENHEARTED
chick·en·heart·ed *adj* **:** COWARDLY, TIMID
chicken pox *n* **:** a contagious disease especially of children in which there is fever and the skin breaks out in watery blisters
chick·weed *n* **:** a weedy plant related to the pinks that has small leaves and whitish flowers
chi·cle *n* **:** a gum obtained from the sap of a tropical American tree and used in making chewing gum
chide *vb* **chid** *or* **chid·ed; chid** *or* **chid·den** *or* **chided; chid·ing :** to find fault with **:** SCOLD
[1]**chief** *n* **:** the head of a group **:** LEADER — **in chief :** in the chief position or place
[2]**chief** *adj* **1 :** highest in rank or authority **2 :** most important **:** MAIN
chief·ly *adv* **1 :** above all **2 :** for the most part
chief master sergeant *n* **:** a noncommissioned officer in the Air Force ranking above a senior master sergeant
chief petty officer *n* **:** a petty officer in the Navy or Coast Guard ranking above a petty officer first class
chief·tain *n* **:** a chief especially of a band, tribe, or clan
chief warrant officer *n* **:** a warrant officer in any of the three top grades
chig·ger *n* **:** the larva of some mites that has six legs, clings to the skin, and causes itching
chil·blain *n* **:** a red swollen itchy condition

caused by cold that occurs especially on the hands or feet

child *n, pl* **chil·dren** **1 :** an unborn or recently born person **2 :** a young person of either sex between infancy and youth **3 :** one's son or daughter of any age

child·birth *n* **:** the act or process of giving birth to a child

child·hood *n* **:** the period of life between infancy and youth

child·ish *adj* **1 :** of, like, or thought to be suitable to children **2 :** showing the less pleasing qualities (as silliness) often thought to be those of children

child·like *adj* **1 :** of or relating to a child or childhood **2 :** showing the more pleasing qualities (as innocence and trustfulness) often thought to be those of children

child·proof*adj* **1:** made to prevent opening by children **2:** made safe for children

chili *or* **chile** *n, pl* **chil·ies** *or* **chil·es** **1 :** the small very sharply flavored fruit of a pepper plant **2 :** a spicy stew of ground beef and chilies usually with beans

[1]**chill** *n* **1 :** a feeling of coldness accompanied by shivering **2 :** unpleasant coldness

[2]**chill** *adj* **1 :** unpleasantly cold **:** RAW **2 :** not friendly

[3]**chill** *vb* **1 :** to make or become cold or chilly **2 :** to make cool especially without freezing **3 :** to harden the surface of (as metal) by sudden cooling

chilly *adj* **chill·i·er; chill·i·est :** noticeably cold — **chill·i·ness** *n*

[1]**chime** *vb* **chimed; chim·ing** **1 :** to make sounds like a bell **:** ring chimes **2 :** to call or indicate by chiming

[2]**chime** *n* **1 :** a set of bells tuned to play music **2 :** the music from a set of bells — usually used in pl. **3 :** a musical sound suggesting bells

chime in *vb* **:** to break into or join in a discussion

chim·ney *n, pl* **chimneys** **1 :** a passage for smoke especially in the form of a vertical structure of brick or stone that reaches above the roof of a building **2 :** a glass tube around a lamp flame

chimney sweep *n* **:** a person who cleans soot from chimneys

chimney swift *n* **:** a small dark gray bird with long narrow wings that often attaches its nest to chimneys

chimp *n* **:** CHIMPANZEE

chim·pan·zee *n* **:** an African ape that lives mostly in trees and is smaller than the related gorilla

[1]**chin** *n* **:** the part of the face below the mouth and including the point of the lower jaw

[2]**chin** *vb* **chinned; chin·ning :** to raise oneself while hanging by the hands until the chin is level with the support

chi·na *n* **1 :** porcelain ware **2 :** pottery (as dishes) for use in one's home

chin·chil·la *n* **:** a South American animal that is somewhat like a squirrel and is hunted or raised for its soft silvery gray fur

[1]**Chi·nese** *adj* **:** of or relating to China, the Chinese people, or Chinese

[2]**Chinese** *n, pl* **Chinese** **1 :** a person born or living in China **2 :** a group of related languages used in China

chink *n* **:** a narrow slit or crack (as in a wall)

[1]**chip** *n* **1 :** a small piece (as of wood, stone, or glass) cut or broken off **2 :** a thin crisp piece of food **3 :** POTATO CHIP **4 :** a flaw left after a small piece has been broken off **5 :** INTEGRATED CIRCUIT **6 :** a small slice of silicon containing electronic circuits (as for a computer)

[2]**chip** *vb* **chipped; chip·ping** **1 :** to cut or break chips from **2 :** to break off in small pieces

chip·munk *n* **:** a small striped animal related to the squirrels

chip·ping sparrow *n* **:** a small North American sparrow that often nests about houses and has a weak chirp as a call

[1]**chirp** *n* **:** the short sharp sound made by crickets and some small birds

[2]**chirp** *vb* **:** to make a chirp

[1]**chis·el** *n* **:** a metal tool with a sharp edge at the end of a usually flat piece used to chip away stone, wood, or metal

[2]**chisel** *vb* **chis·eled** *or* **chis·elled; chis·el·ing** *or* **chis·el·ling :** to cut or shape with a chisel

chiv·al·rous *adj* **1 :** of or relating to chivalry **2 :** having or showing honor, generosity, and courtesy **3 :** showing special courtesy and regard to women

chiv·al·ry *n* **1 :** a body of knights **2 :** the system, spirit, ways, or customs of knighthood **3 :** chivalrous conduct

chlo·rine *n* **:** a chemical element that is a greenish yellow irritating gas of strong odor used as a bleach and as a disinfectant to purify water

[1]**chlo·ro·form** *n* **:** a colorless heavy liquid used especially to dissolve fatty substances and in the past in medicine to deaden the pain of operations but now mostly replaced by less poisonous substances

[2]**chloroform** *vb* **:** to make unconscious or kill with chloroform

chlo·ro·phyll *n* **:** the green coloring matter by means of which green plants produce carbohydrates from carbon dioxide and water

chlo·ro·plast *n* **:** one of the tiny bodies in which chlorophyll is found

chock–full *or* **chuck–full** *adj* : full to the limit

choc·o·late *n* **1 :** a food prepared from ground roasted cacao beans **2 :** a beverage of chocolate in water or milk **3 :** a candy made or coated with chocolate

[1]**choice** *n* **1 :** the act of choosing : SELECTION **2 :** the power of choosing : OPTION **3 :** a person or thing chosen **4 :** the best part **5 :** a large enough number and variety to choose among

[2]**choice** *adj* **choic·er; choic·est :** of very good quality

choir *n* **1 :** an organized group of singers especially in a church **2 :** the part of a church set aside for the singers

[1]**choke** *vb* **choked; chok·ing 1 :** to keep from breathing in a normal way by cutting off the supply of air **2 :** to have the windpipe blocked entirely or partly **3 :** to slow or prevent the growth or action of **4 :** to block by clogging

[2]**choke** *n* **1 :** the act or sound of choking **2 :** something that chokes

choke·cher·ry *n, pl* **choke·cher·ries :** a wild cherry tree with long clusters of reddish black fruits that pucker the mouth

chol·era *n* : a dangerous infectious disease of Asian origin in which violent vomiting and dysentery are present

choose *vb* **chose; cho·sen; choos·ing 1 :** to select freely and after careful thought **2 :** DECIDE 3 **3 :** to see fit

choosy *adj* **choos·i·er; choos·i·est :** careful in making choices

[1]**chop** *vb* **chopped; chop·ping 1 :** to cut by striking especially over and over with something sharp **2 :** to cut into small pieces : MINCE **3 :** to strike quickly or again and again

[2]**chop** *n* **1 :** a sharp downward blow or stroke (as with an ax) **2 :** a small cut of meat often including a part of a rib **3 :** a short quick motion (as of a wave)

chop·per *n* **1 :** someone or something that chops **2 :** HELICOPTER

[1]**chop·py** *adj* **chop·pi·er; chop·pi·est :** frequently changing direction

[2]**choppy** *adj* **chop·pi·er; chop·pi·est 1 :** rough with small waves **2 :** JERKY

chops *n pl* : the fleshy covering of the jaws

chop·stick *n* : one of two thin sticks used chiefly in Asian countries to lift food to the mouth

cho·ral *adj* : of, relating to, or sung or recited by a chorus or choir or in chorus

cho·rale *n* **1 :** a hymn sung by the choir or congregation at a church service **2 :** CHORUS 1

[1]**chord** *n* **:** a group of tones sounded together to form harmony

[2]**chord** *n* **:** a straight line joining two points on a curve

chore *n* **1 chores** *pl* **:** the regular light work about a home or farm **2 :** an ordinary task **3 :** a dull, unpleasant, or difficult task

cho·re·og·ra·phy *n* **:** the art of dancing or of arranging dances and especially ballets — **cho·re·og·ra·pher** *n*

cho·ris·ter *n* : a singer in a choir

chor·tle *vb* **chor·tled; chor·tling :** to chuckle especially in satisfaction

[1]**cho·rus** *n* **1 :** a group of singers : CHOIR **2 :** a group of dancers and singers (as in a musical comedy) **3 :** a part of a song or hymn that is repeated every so often : REFRAIN **4 :** a song meant to be sung by a group : group singing **5 :** sounds uttered by a group of persons or animals together

[2]**chorus** *vb* **:** to speak, sing, or sound at the same time or together

chose *past of* CHOOSE

cho·sen *adj* **1 :** picked to be given favor or special privilege **2 :** picked by God for special protection

chow *n* **:** a muscular dog with a blue-black tongue, a short tail curled close to the back, straight legs, and a thick coat

chow·der *n* **:** a soup or stew made of fish, clams, or a vegetable usually simmered in milk

Christ *n* : JESUS

chris·ten *vb* **1 :** BAPTIZE 1 **2 :** to give a name to at baptism **3 :** to name or dedicate (as a ship) in a ceremony like that of baptism

Chris·ten·dom *n* **1 :** the entire body of Christians **2 :** the part of the world in which Christianity is most common

chris·ten·ing *n* : BAPTISM

[1]**Chris·tian** *n* **1 :** a person who believes in Jesus and follows his teachings **2 :** a member of a Christian church

[2]**Christian** *adj* **1 :** of or relating to Jesus or the religion based on his teachings **2 :** of or relating to Christians **3 :** being what a Christian should be or do

Chris·tian·i·ty *n* **1 :** CHRISTENDOM 1 **2 :** the religion of Christians

Christian name *n* : the personal name given to a person at birth or christening

Christ·mas *n* **:** December 25 celebrated in honor of the birth of Christ

Christ·mas·tide *n* **:** the season of Christmas

Christmas tree *n* **:** a usually evergreen tree decorated at Christmas

chro·mat·ic scale *n* **:** a musical scale that has all half steps

chrome *n* **1 :** CHROMIUM **2 :** something plated with an alloy of chromium

chro·mi·um *n* **:** a bluish white metallic chemical element used especially in alloys
chro·mo·some *n* **:** one of the rodlike bodies of a cell nucleus that contain genes and divide when the cell divides
chron·ic *adj* **1 :** continuing for a long time or returning often **2 :** HABITUAL 2 — **chron·i·cal·ly** *adv*
[1]chron·i·cle *n* **:** an account of events in the order of their happening **:** HISTORY
[2]chronicle *vb* **chron·i·cled; chron·i·cling :** to record in or as if in a chronicle
chron·o·log·i·cal *adj* **:** arranged in or according to the order of time — **chron·o·log·i·cal·ly** *adv*
chrys·a·lis *n* **:** a moth or butterfly pupa that is enclosed in a firm protective case
chry·san·the·mum *n* **:** a plant related to the daisies that has deeply notched leaves and brightly colored often double flower heads
chub·by *adj* **chub·bi·er; chub·bi·est :** [4]PLUMP
[1]chuck *vb* **1 :** to give a pat or tap to **2 :** [1]TOSS 2
[2]chuck *n* **1 :** a pat or nudge under the chin **2 :** [2]TOSS
chuck–full *variant of* CHOCK-FULL
[1]chuck·le *vb* **chuck·led; chuck·ling :** to laugh in a quiet way
[2]chuckle *n* **:** a low quiet laugh
chuck wagon *n* **:** a wagon carrying a stove and food for cooking
[1]chug *n* **:** a dull explosive sound
[2]chug *vb* **chugged; chug·ging :** to move with chugs
[1]chum *n* **:** a close friend **:** PAL
[2]chum *vb* **chummed; chum·ming :** to be chums
chum·my *adj* **chum·mi·er; chum·mi·est :** being on close friendly terms **:** SOCIABLE
chunk *n* **:** a short thick piece (as of ice)
chunky *adj* **chunk·i·er; chunk·i·est :** STOCKY
church *n* **1 :** a building for public worship and especially Christian worship **2 :** an organized body of religious believers **3 :** public worship
church·yard *n* **:** a yard that belongs to a church and is often used as a burial ground
[1]churn *n* **:** a container in which milk or cream is stirred or shaken in making butter
[2]churn *vb* **1 :** to stir or shake in a churn (as in making butter) **2 :** to stir or shake violently
chute *n* **1 :** a sloping plane, trough, or passage down or through which things are slid or dropped **2 :** [1]PARACHUTE
ci·ca·da *n* **:** an insect that has transparent wings and a stout body and is related to the true bugs
-cide *n suffix* **1 :** killer **2 :** killing
ci·der *n* **:** the juice pressed out of fruit (as apples) and used especially as a drink and in making vinegar
ci·gar *n* **:** a small roll of tobacco leaf for smoking
cig·a·rette *n* **:** a small roll of cut tobacco wrapped in paper for smoking
cil·i·um *n, pl* **cil·ia :** any of the structures on the surface of some cells that look like tiny flexible eyelashes
[1]cinch *n* **1 :** GIRTH 1 **2 :** a sure or an easy thing
[2]cinch *vb* **1 :** to fasten or tighten a girth on **2 :** to fasten with or as if with a girth
cin·cho·na *n* **:** a South American tree whose bark yields quinine
cin·der *n* **1 :** SLAG **2 :** a piece of partly burned coal or wood that is not burning **3 :** EMBER **4 cinders** *pl* **:** [2]ASH 1
cin·e·ma *n* **1 :** a movie theater **2 :** the movie industry
cin·na·mon *n* **:** a spice made from the fragrant bark of tropical trees related to the Old World laurel
[1]ci·pher *n* **1 :** ZERO 1 **2 :** an unimportant or worthless person **:** NONENTITY **3 :** a method of secret writing or the alphabet or letters and symbols used in such writing **4 :** a message in code
[2]cipher *vb* **:** to use figures in doing a problem in arithmetic **:** CALCULATE
[1]cir·cle *n* **1 :** a closed curve every point of which is equally distant from a central point within it **:** the space inside such a closed curve **2 :** something in the form of a circle or part of a circle **3 :** [1]CYCLE 2, ROUND **4 :** a group of people sharing a common interest
[2]circle *vb* **cir·cled; cir·cling 1 :** to enclose in or as if in a circle **2 :** to move or revolve around **3 :** to move in or as if in a circle
cir·cuit *n* **1 :** a boundary line around an area **2 :** an enclosed space **3 :** a moving around (as in a circle) **4 :** a traveling from place to place in an area (as by a judge) so as to stop in each place at a certain time **:** a course so traveled **5 :** the complete path of an electric current **6 :** a group of electronic parts
circuit breaker *n* **:** a switch that automatically stops the flow of electric current if a circuit becomes overloaded
cir·cu·i·tous *adj* **1 :** having a circular or winding course **2 :** not saying what one means in simple and sincere language
[1]cir·cu·lar *adj* **1 :** having the form of a circle **:** ROUND **2 :** passing or going around in a circle **3 :** CIRCUITOUS 2 **4 :** sent around to a number of persons
[2]circular *n* **:** a printed notice or advertisement given or sent to many people
cir·cu·late *vb* **cir·cu·lat·ed; cir·cu·lat·ing 1 :** to move around in a course **2 :** to pass or be

passed from place to place or from person to person

cir·cu·la·tion *n* **1 :** motion around in a course **2 :** passage from place to place or person to person **3 :** the average number of copies (as of a newspaper) sold in a given period

cir·cu·la·to·ry *adj* **:** of or relating to circulation (as of the blood)

circulatory system *n* **:** the system of the body that circulates blood and lymph and includes the heart and blood vessels

circum- *prefix* **:** around **:** about

cir·cum·fer·ence *n* **1 :** the line that goes around a circle **2 :** a boundary line or circuit enclosing an area **3 :** the distance around something

cir·cum·nav·i·gate *vb* **cir·cum·nav·i·gat·ed; cir·cum·nav·i·gat·ing :** to go completely around (as the earth) especially by water

cir·cum·po·lar *adj* **1 :** continually visible above the horizon **2 :** surrounding or found near a pole of the earth

cir·cum·stance *n* **1 :** a fact or event that must be considered along with another fact or event **2 circumstances** *pl* **:** conditions at a certain time or place **3 circumstances** *pl* **:** situation with regard to wealth **4 :** [1]CHANCE 1, FATE

cir·cum·vent *vb* **1 :** to go around **:** BYPASS **2 :** to get the better of or avoid the force or effect of by cleverness

cir·cus *n* **1 :** a show that usually travels from place to place and that has a variety of exhibitions including riding, acrobatic feats, wild animal displays, and the performances of jugglers and clowns **2 :** a circus performance **3 :** the performers and equipment of a circus

cir·rus *n, pl* **cir·ri :** a thin white cloud of tiny ice crystals that forms at a very high altitude

cis·tern *n* **:** an artificial reservoir or tank for storing water usually underground

cit·a·del *n* **1 :** a fortress that sits high above a city **2 :** a strong fortress

ci·ta·tion *n* **1 :** an act or instance of quoting **2 :** QUOTATION 1 **3 :** a formal statement of what a person did to be chosen to receive an award

cite *vb* **cit·ed; cit·ing 1 :** to quote as an example, authority, or proof **2 :** to refer to especially in praise

cit·i·zen *n* **1 :** a person who lives in a city or town **2 :** a person who owes loyalty to a government and is protected by it

cit·i·zen·ry *n* **:** all the citizens

cit·i·zen·ship *n* **:** the state of being a citizen

cit·ron *n* **1 :** a citrus fruit like the smaller lemon and having a thick rind that is preserved for use in cakes and puddings **2 :** a small hard watermelon used especially in pickles and preserves

cit·rus *adj* **:** of or relating to a group of trees and shrubs of warm regions whose fruits include the lemon, lime, orange, and grapefruit

city *n, pl* **cit·ies 1 :** a place in which people live that is larger or more important than a town **2 :** the people of a city

city hall *n* **:** the main administrative building of a city

civ·ic *adj* **:** of or relating to a citizen, a city, or citizenship

civ·ics *n* **:** a study of the rights and duties of citizens

civ·il *adj* **1 :** of or relating to citizens **2 :** of or relating to the state **3 :** of or relating to ordinary or government affairs rather than to those of the military or the church **4 :** polite without being friendly **5 :** relating to court action between individuals having to do with private rights rather than criminal action

[1]**ci·vil·ian** *n* **:** a person not on active duty in a military, police, or fire-fighting force

[2]**civilian** *adj* **:** of or relating to a civilian

ci·vil·i·ty *n, pl* **ci·vil·i·ties 1 :** civil behavior **2 :** COURTESY 1

civ·i·li·za·tion *n* **1 :** an advanced stage (as in art, science, and government) of social development **2 :** the way of life of a people

civ·i·lize *vb* **civ·i·lized; civ·i·liz·ing :** to cause to develop out of a primitive state

civil service *n* **:** the branch of a government that takes care of the business of running a state but that does not include the lawmaking branch, the military, or the court system

civil war *n* **:** a war between opposing groups of citizens of the same country

[1]**clack** *vb* **1 :** PRATTLE **2 :** to make or cause to make a clatter

[2]**clack** *n* **1 :** rapid continuous talk **:** CHATTER **2 :** a sound of clacking

clad *adj* **:** being covered **:** wearing clothes

[1]**claim** *vb* **1 :** to ask for as rightfully belonging to oneself **2 :** to call for **:** REQUIRE **3 :** to state as a fact **:** MAINTAIN **4 :** to make a claim

[2]**claim** *n* **1 :** a demand for something due or believed to be due **2 :** a right to something **3 :** a statement that may be doubted **4 :** something (as an area of land) claimed as one's own

[1]**clam** *n* **:** a shellfish with a soft body and a hinged double shell

[2]**clam** *vb* **clammed; clam·ming :** to dig or gather clams

clam·bake *n* **:** an outing where food is cooked usually on heated rocks covered by seaweed

clam·ber *vb* **:** to climb in an awkward way (as by scrambling)

clam·my *adj* **clam·mi·er; clam·mi·est :** unpleasantly damp, soft, sticky, and usually cool — **clam·mi·ly** *adv* — **clam·mi·ness** *n*

[1]**clam·or** *n* **1 :** a noisy shouting **2 :** a loud continous noise **3 :** strong and active protest or demand

[2]**clamor** *vb* **:** to make a clamor

clam·or·ous *adj* **:** full of clamor **:** very noisy

[1]**clamp** *n* **:** a device that holds or presses parts together firmly

[2]**clamp** *vb* **:** to fasten or to hold together with or as if with a clamp

clan *n* **1 :** a group (as in the Scottish Highlands) made up of households whose heads claim to have a common ancestor **2 :** a group of persons united by some common interest

[1]**clang** *vb* **:** to make or cause to make a loud ringing sound

[2]**clang** *n* **:** a loud ringing sound like that made by pieces of metal striking together

[1]**clank** *vb* **1 :** to make or cause to make a clank or series of clanks **2 :** to move with a clank

[2]**clank** *n* **:** a sharp short ringing sound

[1]**clap** *vb* **clapped; clap·ping 1 :** to strike noisily **:** SLAM, BANG **2 :** to strike (one's hands) together again and again in applause **3 :** to strike with the open hand **4 :** to put or place quickly or with force

[2]**clap** *n* **1 :** a loud noisy crash made by or as if by the striking together of two hard surfaces **2 :** a hard or a friendly slap

clap·board *n* **:** a narrow board thicker at one edge than at the other used as siding for a building

clap·per *n* **:** one (as the tongue of a bell) that makes a clapping sound

clar·i·fy *vb* **clar·i·fied; clar·i·fy·ing 1 :** to make or to become pure or clear **2 :** to make or become more easily understood

clar·i·net *n* **:** a woodwind instrument in the form of a tube with finger holes and keys

clar·i·on *adj* **:** being loud and clear

clar·i·ty *n* **:** clear quality or state

[1]**clash** *vb* **1 :** to make or cause to make a clash **2 :** to come into conflict **3 :** to not match well

[2]**clash** *n* **1 :** a loud sharp sound usually of metal striking metal **2 :** a struggle or strong disagreement

[1]**clasp** *n* **1 :** a device for holding together objects or parts of something **2 :** [2]GRASP 1, GRIP **3 :** [2]EMBRACE

[2]**clasp** *vb* **1 :** to fasten with or as if with a clasp **2 :** [1]EMBRACE 1 **3 :** [1]GRASP 1

[1]**class** *n* **1 :** a group of pupils meeting at set times for study or instruction **2 :** the period during which a study group meets **3 :** a course of instruction **4 :** a body of students who are to graduate at the same time **5 :** a group or rank of society **6 :** a group of plants or animals that ranks above the order and below the phylum or division in scientific classification **7 :** a grouping or standing (as of goods or services) based on quality

[2]**class** *vb* **:** CLASSIFY

[1]**clas·sic** *adj* **1 :** serving as a standard of excellence **2 :** fashionable year after year **3 :** of or relating to the ancient Greeks and Romans or their culture **4 :** being very good or typical of its kind

[2]**classic** *n* **1 :** a written work or author of ancient Greece or Rome **2 :** a great work of art **3 :** something regarded as outstanding of its kind

clas·si·cal *adj* **1 :** of or relating to the classics of literature or art and especially to the ancient Greek and Roman classics **2 :** of or relating to serious music in the European tradition **3 :** concerned with a general study of the arts and sciences

clas·si·fi·ca·tion *n* **1 :** the act of classifying or arranging in classes **2 :** an arrangement in classes

clas·si·fy *vb* **clas·si·fied; clas·si·fy·ing :** to group in classes

class·mate *n* **:** a member of the same class in a school or college

class·room *n* **:** a room in a school or college in which classes meet

[1]**clat·ter** *vb* **1 :** to make or cause to make a rattling sound **2 :** to move or go with a clatter

[2]**clatter** *n* **1 :** a rattling sound (as of hard objects striking together) **2 :** COMMOTION

clause *n* **1 :** a separate part of a document (as a will) **2 :** a group of words having its own subject and predicate but forming only part of a complete sentence

clav·i·cle *n* **:** COLLARBONE

[1]**claw** *n* **1 :** a sharp usually thin and curved nail on the finger or toe of an animal (as a cat or bird) **2 :** the end of a limb of a lower animal (as an insect, scorpion, or lobster) that is pointed or like pincers **3 :** something like a claw in shape or use

[2]**claw** *vb* **:** to scratch, seize, or dig with claws

clay *n* **1 :** an earthy material that is sticky and easily molded when wet and hard when baked **2 :** a plastic substance used like clay for modeling

[1]**clean** *adj* **1 :** free of dirt or evil **2 :** free of objectionable behavior or language **3 :** THOROUGH 1, COMPLETE **4 :** having a simple graceful form **:** TRIM **5 :** [1]SMOOTH 1

[2]**clean** *adv* **1 :** so as to clean **2 :** in a clean way **3 :** all the way

[3]**clean** *vb* **:** to make or become clean — **clean·er** *n*

clean·li·ness *n* **:** the condition of being clean **:** the habit of keeping clean

[1]**clean·ly** *adv* **:** in a clean way

[2]**clean·ly** *adj* **clean·li·er; clean·li·est 1 :** careful to keep clean **2 :** kept clean

cleanse *vb* **cleansed; cleans·ing :** to make clean

cleans·er *n* **:** a substance (as a scouring powder) used for cleaning

[1]**clear** *adj* **1 :** BRIGHT 1, LUMINOUS **2 :** free of clouds, haze, or mist **3 :** UNTROUBLED **4 :** free of blemishes **5 :** easily seen through **6 :** easily heard, seen, or understood **7 :** free from doubt **:** SURE **8 :** INNOCENT **9 :** not blocked or limited — **clear·ly** *adv* — **clear·ness** *n*

[2]**clear** *adv* **1 :** in a clear manner **2 :** all the way

[3]**clear** *vb* **1 :** to make or become clear **2 :** to go away **:** DISPERSE **3 :** to free from blame **4 :** to approve or be approved by **5 :** EXPLAIN 1 **6 :** to free of things blocking **7 :** to get rid of **:** REMOVE **8 :** [4]NET **9 :** to go over or by without touching

[4]**clear** *n* **:** a clear space or part — **in the clear :** free from guilt or suspicion

clear·ance *n* **1 :** the act or process of clearing **2 :** the distance by which one object avoids hitting or touching another

clear·ing *n* **:** an area of land from which trees and bushes have all been removed

cleat *n* **1 :** a wooden or metal device used to fasten a line or a rope **2 :** a strip or projection fastened on or across something to give strength or a place to hold or to prevent slipping

cleav·age *n* **1 :** the tendency of a rock or mineral to split readily in one or more directions **2 :** the action of cleaving **3 :** the state of being cleft

[1]**cleave** *vb* **cleaved** *or* **clove; cleav·ing :** to cling to a person or thing closely

[2]**cleave** *vb* **cleaved** *or* **cleft** *or* **clove; cleaved** *or* **cleft** *or* **clo·ven; cleav·ing :** to divide by or as if by a cutting blow **:** SPLIT

cleav·er *n* **:** a heavy knife used for cutting up meat

clef *n* **:** a sign placed on the staff in writing music to show what pitch is represented by each line and space

[1]**cleft** *n* **1 :** a space or opening made by splitting or cracking **:** CREVICE **2 :** [1]NOTCH 1

[2]**cleft** *adj* **:** partly split or divided

clem·en·cy *n, pl* **clemencies 1 :** MERCY 1 **2 :** an act of mercy

clench *vb* **1 :** to hold tightly **:** CLUTCH **2 :** to set or close tightly

cler·gy *n, pl* **clergies :** the group of religious officials (as priests, ministers, and rabbis) specially prepared and authorized to lead religious services

cler·gy·man *n, pl* **cler·gy·men :** a member of the clergy

cler·i·cal *adj* **1 :** of or relating to the clergy **2 :** of or relating to a clerk or office worker

[1]**clerk** *n* **1 :** a person whose job is to keep records or accounts **2 :** a salesperson in a store

[2]**clerk** *vb* **:** to act or work as a clerk

clev·er *adj* **1 :** showing skill especially in using one's hands **2 :** having a quick inventive mind **3 :** showing wit or imagination — **clev·er·ly** *adv* — **clev·er·ness** *n*

[1]**click** *vb* **1 :** to make or cause to make a click **2 :** to fit in or work together smoothly **3 :** to select or make a selection especially on a computer by pressing a button on a control device (as a mouse)

[2]**click** *n* **:** a slight sharp noise

click·er *n* **:** REMOTE CONTROL 2

cli·ent *n* **:** a person who uses the professional advice or services of another

cli·en·tele *n* **:** a group of clients

cliff *n* **:** a high steep surface of rock

cli·mate *n* **:** the average weather conditions of a place over a period of years

cli·max *n* **:** the time or part of something that is of greatest interest, excitement, or importance

[1]**climb** *vb* **1 :** to rise little by little to a higher point **2 :** to go up or down often with the help of the hands in holding or pulling **3 :** to go upward in growing (as by winding around something) — **climb·er** *n*

[2]**climb** *n* **1 :** a place where climbing is necessary **2 :** the act of climbing

clime *n* **:** CLIMATE

[1]**clinch** *vb* **1 :** to turn over or flatten the end of (as a nail sticking out of a board) **2 :** to fasten by clinching **3 :** to show to be certain or true

[2]**clinch** *n* **:** a fastening with a clinched nail, bolt, or rivet **:** the clinched part of a nail, bolt, or rivet

cling *vb* **clung; cling·ing 1 :** to hold fast or stick closely to a surface **2 :** to hold fast by grasping or winding around **3 :** to remain close

clin·ic *n* **1 :** a group meeting for teaching a certain skill and working on individual problems **2 :** a place where people can receive medical examinations and usually treatment for minor ailments

[1]**clink** *vb* **:** to make or cause to make a slight short sound like that of metal being struck

[2]**clink** *n* **:** a clinking sound

[1]**clip** *vb* **clipped; clip·ping :** to fasten with a clip

²clip *n* : a device that holds or hooks
³clip *vb* **clipped; clip·ping 1 :** to shorten or remove by cutting (as with shears or scissors) **2 :** to cut off or trim the hair or wool of
⁴clip *n* **1 :** an instrument with two blades for cutting the nails **2 :** a sharp blow **3 :** a rapid pace
clip art *n* : ready-made illustrations sold in books or as software from which they may be taken for use in a printed work
clip·board *n* **1:** a small board with a clip at the top for holding papers **2:** a part of computer memory that is used to store data (as items to be copied to another file) temporarily
clip·per *n* **1 :** a person who clips **2 clippers** *pl* : a device used for clipping especially hair or nails **3 :** a fast sailing ship with usually three tall masts and large square sails
clip·ping *n* : something cut out or off
clique *n* : a small group of people that keep out outsiders
¹cloak *n* **1 :** a long loose outer garment **2 :** something that hides or covers
²cloak *vb* : to cover or hide with a cloak
cloak·room *n* : a room (as in a school) in which coats and hats may be kept
¹clock *n* : a device for measuring or telling the time and especially one not meant to be worn or carried by a person
²clock *vb* **1 :** to time (as a person or a piece of work) by a timing device **2 :** to show (as time or speed) on a recording device
clock·wise *adv or adj* : in the direction in which the hands of a clock turn
clock·work *n* : machinery (as in mechanical toys) like that which makes clocks go
clod *n* **1 :** a lump or mass especially of earth or clay **2 :** a clumsy or stupid person
¹clog *n* **1 :** something that hinders or holds back **2 :** a shoe having a thick usually wooden sole
²clog *vb* **clogged; clog·ging :** to make passage through difficult or impossible : PLUG
¹clois·ter *n* **1 :** MONASTERY, CONVENT **2 :** a covered usually arched passage along or around the walls of a court
²cloister *vb* **1 :** to shut away from the world **2 :** to surround with a cloister
clop *n* : a sound like that of a hoof against pavement
¹close *vb* **closed; clos·ing 1 :** to stop up : prevent passage through **2 :** to fill or cause to fill an opening **3 :** to bring or come to an end **4 :** to end the operation of **5 :** to bring the parts or edges of together **6 :** ¹APPROACH 1
²close *n* : the point at which something ends
³close *adj* **clos·er; clos·est 1 :** having little space in which to move **2 :** SECRETIVE **3 :** lacking fresh or moving air **4 :** not generous **5 :** not far apart in space, time, degree, or effect **6 :** ¹SHORT 1 **7 :** very like **8 :** having a strong liking each one for the other **9 :** strict and careful in attention to details **10 :** decided by a narrow margin — **close·ly** *adv* — **close·ness** *n*
⁴close *adv* : ¹NEAR 1
close call *n* : a barely successful escape from a difficult or dangerous situation
closed *adj* **1 :** not open **2 :** having mathematical elements that when subjected to an operation produce only elements of the same set
¹clos·et *n* **1 :** a small room for privacy **2 :** a small room for clothing or for supplies for the house
²closet *vb* **1 :** to shut up in or as if in a closet **2 :** to take into a private room for an interview
close–up *n* : a photograph taken at close range
clo·sure *n* **1 :** an act of closing **2 :** the condition of being closed
¹clot *n* : a lump made by some substance getting thicker and sticking together
²clot *vb* **clot·ted; clot·ting :** to thicken into a clot
cloth *n, pl* **cloths 1 :** a woven or knitted material (as of cotton or nylon) **2 :** a piece of cloth for a certain use **3 :** TABLECLOTH
clothe *vb* **clothed** *or* **clad; cloth·ing 1 :** to cover with or as if with clothing : DRESS **2 :** to provide with clothes **3 :** to express in a certain way
clothes *n pl* : CLOTHING 1
clothes moth *n* : a small yellowish moth whose larvae feed on wool, fur, and feathers
clothes·pin *n* : a peg (as of wood) with the lower part slit or a clamp for holding clothes in place on a line
cloth·ing *n* **1 :** covering for the human body **2 :** COVERING
¹cloud *n* **1 :** a visible mass of tiny bits of water or ice hanging in the air usually high above the earth **2 :** a visible mass of small particles in the air **3 :** something thought to be like a cloud — **cloud·less** *adj*
²cloud *vb* **1 :** to make or become cloudy **2 :** to darken or hide as if by a cloud
cloud·burst *n* : a sudden heavy rainfall
cloudy *adj* **cloud·i·er; cloud·i·est 1 :** overspread with clouds **2 :** showing confusion **3 :** not clear — **cloud·i·ness** *n*
¹clout *n* : a blow especially with the hand
²clout *vb* : to hit hard
¹clove *n* : the dried flower bud of a tropical tree used as a spice
²clove *past of* CLEAVE
clo·ven *past participle of* ²CLEAVE

cloven hoof *n* : a hoof (as of a cow) with the front part divided into two sections

clo·ver *n* : any of various plants grown for hay and pasture that have leaves with three leaflets and usually roundish red, white, yellow, or purple flower heads

[1]**clown** *n* **1 :** a rude and often stupid person **2 :** a performer (as in a play or circus) who entertains by playing tricks and who usually wears comical clothes and makeup

[2]**clown** *vb* : to act like a clown : SHOW OFF

[1]**club** *n* **1 :** a heavy usually wooden stick used as a weapon **2 :** a stick or bat used to hit a ball in various games **3 :** a group of people associated because of a shared interest **4 :** the meeting place of a club

[2]**club** *vb* **clubbed; club·bing :** to beat or strike with or as if with a club

club·house *n* **1 :** a house used by a club **2 :** locker rooms used by an athletic team

club moss *n* : a low often trailing evergreen plant that forms spores instead of seeds

[1]**cluck** *vb* : to make or call with a cluck

[2]**cluck** *n* : the call of a hen especially to her chicks

clue *n* : something that helps a person to find something or to solve a mystery

[1]**clump** *n* **1 :** a group of things clustered together **2 :** a cluster or lump of something **3 :** a heavy tramping sound

[2]**clump** *vb* **1 :** to walk clumsily and noisily **2 :** to form or cause to form clumps

clum·sy *adj* **clum·si·er; clum·si·est 1 :** lacking skill or grace in movement **2 :** not knowing how to get along with others **3 :** badly or awkwardly made or done — **clum·si·ly** *adv* — **clum·si·ness** *n*

clung *past of* CLING

[1]**clus·ter** *n* : a number of similar things growing, collected, or grouped closely together : BUNCH

[2]**cluster** *vb* : to grow, collect, or assemble in a cluster

[1]**clutch** *vb* **1 :** to grasp or hold tightly with or as if with the hands or claws **2 :** to make a grab

[2]**clutch** *n* **1 :** the state of being clutched **2 :** a device for gripping an object **3 :** a coupling for connecting and disconnecting a driving and a driven part in machinery **4 :** a lever or pedal operating a clutch

[1]**clut·ter** *vb* : to throw into disorder : fill or cover with scattered things

[2]**clutter** *n* : a crowded or confused collection : DISORDER

co- *prefix* **1 :** with : together : joint : jointly **2 :** in or to the same degree **3 :** fellow : partner

[1]**coach** *n* **1 :** a large carriage that has four wheels and a raised seat outside in front for the driver and is drawn by horses **2 :** a railroad passenger car without berths **3 :** a class of passenger transportation in an airplane at a lower fare than first class **4 :** a person who teaches students individually **5 :** a person who instructs or trains a performer or team

[2]**coach** *vb* : to act as coach

coach·man *n, pl* **coach·men :** a person whose business is driving a coach or carriage

co·ag·u·late *vb* **co·ag·u·lat·ed; co·ag·u·lat·ing :** to gather into a thick compact mass : CLOT

coal *n* **1 :** a piece of glowing or charred wood : EMBER **2 :** a black solid mineral substance that is formed by the partial decay of vegetable matter under the influence of moisture and often increased pressure and temperature within the earth and is mined for use as a fuel

coarse *adj* **1 :** of poor or ordinary quality **2 :** made up of large particles **3 :** being harsh or rough **4 :** crude in taste, manners, or language — **coarse·ly** *adv* — **coarse·ness** *n*

coars·en *vb* : to make or become coarse

[1]**coast** *n* : the land near a shore

[2]**coast** *vb* **1 :** to slide downhill by the force of gravity over snow or ice **2 :** to move along (as on a bicycle when not pedaling) without applying power

coast·al *adj* : of, relating to, or located on, near, or along a coast

coast·er *n* **1 :** someone or something that coasts **2 :** a sled or small wagon used in coasting

coast guard *n* : a military force that guards a coast

[1]**coat** *n* **1 :** an outer garment that differs in length and style according to fashion or use **2 :** the outer covering (as fur or feathers) of an animal **3 :** a layer of material covering a surface — **coat·ed** *adj*

[2]**coat** *vb* : to cover with a coat or covering

coat·ing *n* : [1]COAT 3, COVERING

coat of arms : the heraldic arms belonging to a person, family, or group or a representation of these (as on a shield)

coat of mail : a garment of metal scales or rings worn long ago as armor

co·au·thor *n* : an author who works with another author

coax *vb* **1 :** to influence by gentle urging, special attention, or flattering **2 :** to get or win by means of gentle urging or flattery

cob *n* : CORNCOB

co·balt *n* : a tough shiny silvery white metallic chemical element found with iron and nickel

cob·bled *adj* : paved or covered with cobblestones

cob·bler *n* **1 :** a person who mends or makes

shoes **2 :** a fruit pie with a thick upper crust and no bottom crust that is baked in a deep dish

cob·ble·stone *n* **:** a naturally rounded stone larger than a pebble and smaller than a boulder once used in paving streets

co·bra *n* **:** a very poisonous snake of Asia and Africa that puffs out the skin around its neck into a hood when excited

cob·web *n* **1 :** the network spread by a spider **:** SPIDERWEB **2 :** tangles of threads of a cobweb

co·caine *n* **:** a habit-forming drug obtained from the leaves of a South American shrub and sometimes used as a medicine to deaden pain

coc·cus *n, pl* **coc·ci :** a bacterium shaped like a ball

[1]**cock** *n* **1 :** a male bird **:** ROOSTER **2 :** a faucet or valve for controlling the flow of a liquid or a gas **3 :** a cocked position of the hammer of a gun

[2]**cock** *vb* **1 :** to draw back the hammer of (a gun) in readiness for firing **2 :** to set or draw back in readiness for some action **3 :** to turn or tip upward or to one side

[3]**cock** *n* **:** the act of tipping at an angle **:** TILT

cock·a·too *n, pl* **cock·a·toos :** any of several large, noisy, and usually brightly colored crested parrots mostly of Australia

cock·eyed *adj* **1 :** tilted to one side **2 :** FOOLISH

cock·le *n* **:** an edible shellfish with a shell that has two parts and is shaped like a heart

cock·le·bur *n* **:** a plant with prickly fruit that is related to the thistles

cock·le·shell *n* **:** a shell of a cockle

cock·pit *n* **1 :** an open space in the deck from which a small boat (as a yacht) is steered **2 :** a space in an airplane for the pilot or pilot and passengers or pilot and crew

cock·roach *n* **:** a troublesome insect found in houses and ships and active chiefly at night

cocky *adj* **cock·i·er; cock·i·est :** very sure of oneself **:** boldly self-confident

co·coa *n* **1 :** chocolate ground to a powder after some of its fat is removed **2 :** a drink made from cocoa powder

co·co·nut *n* **:** a large nutlike fruit that has a thick husk and grows on a tall tropical palm (**coconut palm**)

co·coon *n* **:** the silky covering which caterpillars make around themselves and in which they are protected while changing into butterflies or moths

cod *n, pl* **cod :** a large food fish found in the deep colder parts of the northern Atlantic Ocean

cod·dle *vb* **cod·dled; cod·dling 1 :** to cook slowly in water below the boiling point **2 :** to treat with very much and usually too much care **:** PAMPER

[1]**code** *n* **1 :** a collection of laws arranged in some orderly way **2 :** a system of rules or principles **3 :** a system of signals or letters and symbols with special meanings used for sending messages **4 :** GENETIC CODE

[2]**code** *vb* **cod·ed; cod·ing :** to put in the form of a code

cod·fish *n, pl* **codfish** *or* **cod·fish·es :** COD

cod·ger *n* **:** an odd or cranky man

co·erce *vb* **co·erced; co·erc·ing :** [2]FORCE 1, COMPEL

cof·fee *n* **1 :** a drink made from the roasted and ground seeds of a tropical plant **2 :** the seeds of the coffee plant

cof·fee·pot *n* **:** a covered utensil for preparing or serving coffee

coffee table *n* **:** a low table usually placed in front of a sofa

cof·fer *n* **:** a box used especially for holding money and valuables

cof·fin *n* **:** a box or case to hold a dead body

cog *n* **:** a tooth on the rim of a wheel or gear

cog·i·tate *vb* **cog·i·tat·ed; cog·i·tat·ing :** to think over **:** PONDER

cog·i·ta·tion *n* **:** MEDITATION

cog·wheel *n* **:** a wheel with cogs on the rim

co·he·sion *n* **1 :** the action of sticking together **2 :** the force of attraction between the molecules in a mass

[1]**coil** *vb* **1 :** to wind into rings or a spiral **2 :** to form or lie in a coil

[2]**coil** *n* **1 :** a circle, a series of circles, or a spiral made by coiling **2 :** something coiled

[1]**coin** *n* **1 :** a piece of metal put out by government authority as money **2 :** metal money

[2]**coin** *vb* **1 :** to make coins especially by stamping pieces of metal **:** MINT **2 :** to make metal (as gold or silver) into coins **3 :** to make up (a new word or phrase)

coin·age *n* **1 :** the act or process of coining **2 :** something coined

co·in·cide *vb* **co·in·cid·ed; co·in·cid·ing 1 :** to occupy the same space **2 :** to happen at the same time **3 :** to agree exactly

co·in·ci·dence *n* **1 :** a coinciding in space or time **2 :** two things that happen at the same time by accident but seem to have some connection

coke *n* **:** gray lumps of fuel made by heating soft coal in a closed chamber until some of its gases have passed off

col- — see COM-

col·an·der *n* **:** a utensil with small holes for draining foods

[1]**cold** *adj* **1 :** having a low temperature or one much below normal **2 :** lacking warmth of feeling **:** UNFRIENDLY **3 :** suffering from

lack of warmth — **cold·ly** *adv* — **cold·ness** *n*

[2]**cold** *n* **1 :** a condition of low temperature **:** cold weather **2 :** the bodily feeling produced by lack of warmth **:** CHILL **3 :** COMMON COLD

cold–blood·ed *adj* **1 :** lacking or showing a lack of normal human feelings **2 :** having a body temperature that varies with the temperature of the environment **3 :** sensitive to cold

co·le·us *n* **:** a plant of the mint family grown for its many-colored leaves

col·ic *n* **:** sharp pain in the bowels — **col·icky** *adj*

col·i·se·um *n* **:** a large structure (as a stadium) for athletic contests or public entertainment

col·lab·o·rate *vb* **col·lab·o·rat·ed; col·lab·o·rat·ing** **1 :** to work with others (as in writing a book) **2 :** to cooperate with an enemy force that has taken over one's country

col·lage *n* **:** a work of art made by gluing pieces of different materials to a flat surface

[1]**col·lapse** *vb* **col·lapsed; col·laps·ing** **1 :** to break down completely **:** fall in **2 :** to shrink together suddenly **3 :** to suffer a physical or mental breakdown **4 :** to fold together

[2]**collapse** *n* **:** the act or an instance of collapsing **:** BREAKDOWN

col·laps·ible *adj* **:** capable of collapsing or possible to collapse

[1]**col·lar** *n* **1 :** a band, strap, or chain worn around the neck or the neckline of a garment **2 :** a part of the harness of draft animals fitted over the shoulders **3 :** something (as a ring to hold a pipe in place) that is like a collar — **col·lar·less** *adj*

[2]**collar** *vb* **1 :** to seize by or as if by the collar **:** CAPTURE, GRAB **2 :** to put a collar on

col·lar·bone *n* **:** a bone of the shoulder joined to the breastbone and the shoulder blade

col·league *n* **:** an associate in a profession **:** a fellow worker

col·lect *vb* **1 :** to bring or come together into one body or place **2 :** to gather from a number of sources **3 :** to gain or regain control of **4 :** to receive payment for

col·lect·ed *adj* **:** [3]CALM 2

col·lec·tion *n* **1 :** the act or process of gathering together **2 :** something collected and especially a group of objects gathered for study or exhibition **3 :** a gathering of money (as for charitable purposes)

col·lec·tive *adj* **1 :** having to do with a number of persons or things thought of as a whole **2 :** done or shared by a number of persons as a group — **col·lec·tive·ly** *adv*

col·lec·tor *n* **1 :** a person or thing that collects **2 :** a person whose business it is to collect money

col·lege *n* **:** a school higher than a high school

col·le·giate *adj* **1 :** having to do with a college **2 :** of, relating to, or characteristic of college students

col·lide *vb* **col·lid·ed; col·lid·ing** **1 :** to strike against each other **2 :** [1]CLASH 2

col·lie *n* **:** a large usually long-coated dog of a Scottish breed used to herd sheep

col·li·sion *n* **:** an act or instance of colliding

col·lo·qui·al *adj* **:** used in or suited to familiar and informal conversation

col·lo·qui·al·ism *n* **:** a colloquial word or expression

co·logne *n* **:** a perfumed liquid made up of alcohol and fragrant oils

[1]**co·lon** *n* **:** the main part of the large intestine

[2]**colon** *n* **:** a punctuation mark : used mostly to call attention to what follows (as a list, explanation, or quotation)

col·o·nel *n* **:** a commissioned officer in the Army, Air Force, or Marine Corps ranking above a lieutenant colonel

[1]**co·lo·nial** *adj* **1 :** of, relating to, or characteristic of a colony **2** *often cap* **:** of or relating to the original thirteen colonies that formed the United States

[2]**colonial** *n* **:** a member of or a person living in a colony

col·o·nist *n* **1 :** a person living in a colony **2 :** a person who helps to found a colony

col·o·nize *vb* **col·o·nized; col·o·niz·ing** **1 :** to establish a colony in or on **2 :** to settle in a colony

col·on·nade *n* **:** a row of columns usually supporting the base of a roof structure

col·o·ny *n, pl* **col·o·nies** **1 :** a group of people sent out by a state to a new territory **:** the territory in which these people settle **2 :** a distant territory belonging to or under the control of a nation **3 :** a group of living things of one kind living together **4 :** a group of people with common qualities or interests located in close association

[1]**col·or** *n* **1 :** the appearance of a thing apart from size and shape when light strikes it **2 :** a hue other than black, white, or gray **3 :** outward show **:** APPEARANCE **4 :** the normal rosy tint of skin **5 :** [1]BLUSH **6 colors** *pl* **:** an identifying flag **7 colors** *pl* **:** military service **8 :** [1]INTEREST 6

[2]**color** *vb* **1 :** to give color to **2 :** to change the color of **3 :** MISREPRESENT **4 :** to take on or change color **:** BLUSH

col·or·ation *n* **:** use or arrangement of colors or shades **:** COLORING

color–blind *adj* **:** unable to tell some colors apart

col·ored *adj* **:** having color

col·or·ful *adj* **1 :** having bright colors **2 :** full of variety or interest

col·or·ing *n* **1 :** the act of applying colors **2 :** something that produces color **3 :** the effect produced by the use of color **4 :** natural color **:** COMPLEXION

coloring book *n* **:** a book of drawings made in solid lines for coloring

col·or·less *adj* **1 :** having no color **2 :** WAN, PALE **3 :** [1]DULL 8

co·los·sal *adj* **:** very large **:** HUGE

colt *n* **1 :** FOAL **2 :** a young male horse

col·um·bine *n* **:** a plant related to the buttercups that has leaves with three parts and showy flowers usually with five petals ending in spurs

col·umn *n* **1 :** one of two or more vertical sections of a printed page **2 :** a special regular feature in a newspaper or magazine **3 :** a pillar supporting a roof or gallery **4 :** something like a column in shape, position, or use **5 :** a long straight row (as of soldiers)

col·um·nist *n* **:** a writer of a column in a newspaper or magazine

com- *or* **col-** *or* **con-** *prefix* **:** with **:** together **:** jointly — usually *com-* before *b, p,* or *m, col-* before *l* and *con-* before other sounds

co·ma *n* **:** a deep sleeplike state caused by sickness or injury

[1]**comb** *n* **1 :** a toothed implement used to smooth and arrange the hair or worn in the hair to hold it in place **2 :** a toothed instrument used for separating fibers (as of wool or flax) **3 :** a fleshy crest often with points suggesting teeth on the head of a fowl and some related birds **4 :** [1]HONEYCOMB 1

[2]**comb** *vb* **1 :** to smooth, arrange, or untangle with a comb **2 :** to search over or through carefully

[1]**com·bat** *n* **1 :** a fight or contest between individuals or groups **2 :** [1]CONFLICT 2 **3 :** active military fighting

[2]**com·bat** *vb* **com·bat·ed** *or* **com·bat·ted; com·bat·ing** *or* **com·bat·ting :** to fight with **:** fight against **:** OPPOSE

[1]**com·bat·ant** *n* **:** a person who takes part in a combat

[2]**combatant** *adj* **:** engaging in or ready to engage in combat

com·bi·na·tion *n* **1 :** a result or product of combining or being combined **2 :** a union of persons or groups for a purpose **3 :** a series of letters or numbers which when dialed by a disk on a lock will operate or open the lock **4 :** a union of different things

combination lock *n* **:** a lock with one or more dials or rings marked usually with numbers which are used to open the lock by moving them in a certain order to certain positions

[1]**com·bine** *vb* **com·bined; com·bin·ing :** to join together so as to make or to seem one thing **:** UNITE, MIX

[2]**com·bine** *n* **1 :** a union of persons or groups of persons especially for business or political benefits **2 :** a machine that harvests and threshes grain

com·bus·ti·ble *adj* **1 :** possible to burn **2 :** catching fire or burning easily

com·bus·tion *n* **:** the process of burning

come *vb* **came; come; com·ing 1 :** to move toward **:** APPROACH **2 :** to reach the point of being or becoming **3 :** to add up **:** AMOUNT **4 :** to take place **5 :** ORIGINATE 2, ARISE **6 :** to be available **7 :** [1]REACH 3

co·me·di·an *n* **1 :** an actor who plays comic roles **2 :** an amusing person

com·e·dy *n, pl* **com·e·dies 1 :** an amusing play that has a happy ending **2 :** an amusing and often ridiculous event

come·ly *adj* **come·li·er; come·li·est :** pleasing to the sight **:** good-looking

com·et *n* **:** a bright celestial body that develops a cloudy tail as it moves in an orbit around the sun

come to *vb* **:** to become conscious again

[1]**com·fort** *vb* **1 :** to give hope and strength to **:** CHEER **2 :** to ease the grief or trouble of

[2]**comfort** *n* **1 :** acts or words that comfort **2 :** the feeling of the one that is comforted **3 :** something that makes a person comfortable

com·fort·able *adj* **1 :** giving comfort and especially physical ease **2 :** more than what is needed **3 :** physically at ease — **com·fort·ably** *adj*

com·fort·er *n* **1 :** one that gives comfort **2 :** [1]QUILT

com·ic *adj* **1 :** of, relating to, or characteristic of comedy **2 :** FUNNY 1

com·i·cal *adj* **:** FUNNY 1, RIDICULOUS — **com·i·cal·ly** *adv*

comic book *n* **:** a magazine made up of a series of comic strips

comic strip *n* **:** a series of cartoons that tell a story or part of a story

com·ma *n* **:** a punctuation mark , used chiefly to show separation of words or word groups within a sentence

[1]**com·mand** *vb* **1 :** to order with authority **2 :** to have power or control over **:** be commander of **3 :** to have for one's use **4 :** to demand as right or due **:** EXACT **5 :** to survey from a good position

[2]**command** *n* **1 :** the act of commanding **2 :** an order given **3 :** the ability to control and use **:** MASTERY **4 :** the authority, right, or power to command **:** CONTROL **5 :** the people, area, or unit (as of soldiers and

weapons) under a commander **6 :** a position from which military operations are directed

com·man·dant *n* **:** a commanding officer

com·mand·er *n* **:** a commissioned officer in the Navy or Coast Guard ranking above a lieutenant commander

commander in chief : a person who holds supreme command of the armed forces of a nation

com·mand·ment *n* **:** something given as a command and especially one of the Ten Commandments in the Bible

com·man·do *n, pl* **com·man·dos** *or* **com·man·does 1 :** a band or unit of troops trained for making surprise raids into enemy territory **2 :** a member of a commando unit

command sergeant major *n* **:** a noncommissioned officer in the Army ranking above a first sergeant

com·mem·o·rate *vb* **com·mem·o·rat·ed; com·mem·o·rat·ing 1 :** to call or recall to mind **2 :** to observe with a ceremony **3 :** to serve as a memorial of

com·mem·o·ra·tion *n* **1 :** the act of commemorating **2 :** something (as a ceremony) that commemorates

com·mence *vb* **com·menced; com·menc·ing :** BEGIN, START

com·mence·ment *n* **1 :** the act or the time of commencing **:** BEGINNING **2 :** graduation exercises

com·mend *vb* **1 :** to give into another's care **:** ENTRUST **2 :** to speak of with approval **:** PRAISE

com·men·da·tion *n* **:** [2]PRAISE 1, APPROVAL

[1]**com·ment** *n* **1 :** an expression of opinion either in speech or writing **2 :** mention of something that deserves notice

[2]**comment** *vb* **:** to make a comment **:** REMARK

com·men·ta·tor *n* **1 :** a person who makes comments **2 :** a person who reports and discusses news events (as over radio)

com·merce *n* **:** the buying and selling of goods especially on a large scale and between different places **:** TRADE

[1]**com·mer·cial** *adj* **1 :** having to do with commerce **2 :** having financial profit as the chief goal — **com·mer·cial·ly** *adv*

[2]**commercial** *n* **:** an advertisement broadcast on radio or television

com·mer·cial·ize *vb* **com·mer·cial·ized; com·mer·cial·iz·ing :** to manage with the idea of making a profit

[1]**com·mis·sion** *n* **1 :** an order or instruction granting the power to perform various acts or duties **:** the right or duty in question **2 :** a certificate that gives military or naval rank and authority **:** the rank and authority given **3 :** authority to act as agent for another **:** a task or piece of business entrusted to an agent **4 :** a group of persons given orders and authority to perform specified duties **5 :** an act of doing something wrong **6 :** a fee paid to an agent for taking care of a piece of business

[2]**commission** *vb* **1 :** to give a commission to **2 :** to put (a ship) into service

commissioned officer *n* **:** an officer in the armed forces who ranks above the enlisted persons or warrant officers and who is appointed by a commission from the president

com·mis·sion·er *n* **1 :** a member of a commission **2 :** an official who is the head of a government department

com·mit *vb* **com·mit·ted; com·mit·ting 1 :** to make secure or put in safekeeping **:** ENTRUST **2 :** to place in or send to a prison or mental institution **3 :** to bring about **:** PERFORM **4 :** to pledge or assign to a certain course or use — **com·mit·ment** *n*

com·mit·tee *n* **:** a group of persons appointed or elected to consider some subject of interest or to perform some duty

com·mod·i·ty *n, pl* **com·mod·i·ties :** something produced by agriculture, mining, or manufacture

com·mo·dore *n* **1 :** a former wartime commissioned officer rank in the Navy and Coast Guard between the ranks of captain and rear admiral **2 :** the chief officer of a yacht club **3 :** the senior captain of a line of merchant ships

[1]**com·mon** *adj* **1 :** having to do with, belonging to, or used by everybody **:** PUBLIC **2 :** belonging to or shared by two or more individuals or by the members of a family or group **3 :** [1]GENERAL 1 **4 :** occurring or appearing frequently **5 :** not above the average in rank, excellence, or social position **6 :** falling below ordinary standards (as in quality or manners) **:** INFERIOR **7 :** COARSE 4, VULGAR

[2]**common** *n* **:** land (as a park) owned and used by a community — **in common :** shared together

common cold *n* **:** a contagious disease which causes the lining of the nose and throat to be sore, swollen, and red and in which there is usually much mucus and coughing and sneezing

common denominator *n* **:** a common multiple of the denominators of a number of fractions

com·mon·er *n* **:** one of the common people

common multiple *n* **:** a multiple of each of two or more numbers

common noun *n* **:** a noun that names a class of persons or things or any individual of a class and that may occur with a limiting modifier (as *a*, *the*, *some*, or *every*)

[1]**com·mon·place** *n* : something that is often seen or met with

[2]**commonplace** *adj* : often seen or met with : ORDINARY

common sense *n* : ordinary good sense and judgment

com·mon·wealth *n* **1** : a political unit (as a nation or state) **2** : a state of the United States and especially Kentucky, Massachusetts, Pennsylvania, or Virginia

com·mo·tion *n* : noisy excitement and confusion : TURMOIL

[1]**com·mune** *vb* **com·muned; com·mun·ing** : to be in close accord or communication with someone or something

[2]**com·mune** *n* : a community in which individuals have close personal ties to each other and share property and duties

com·mu·ni·ca·ble *adj* : possible to communicate

com·mu·ni·cate *vb* **com·mu·ni·cat·ed; com·mu·ni·cat·ing** **1** : to make known **2** : to pass (as a disease) from one to another : SPREAD **3** : to get in touch (as by telephone)

com·mu·ni·ca·tion *n* **1** : the exchange (as by speech or letter) of information between persons **2** : information communicated **3 communications** *pl* : a system of sending messages (as by telephone) **4 communications** *pl* : a system of routes for moving troops, supplies, and vehicles

com·mu·nion *n* **1** : an act or example of sharing **2** : a religious ceremony commemorating with bread and wine the last supper of Jesus **3** : the act of receiving the sacrament **4** : friendly communication **5** : a body of Christians having a common faith and discipline

com·mu·nism *n* **1** : a social system in which property and goods are held in common **2** : a theory that supports communism

com·mu·nist *n* **1** : a person who believes in communism **2** *cap* : a member or follower of a Communist party or plan for change

com·mu·ni·ty *n, pl* **com·mu·ni·ties** **1** : the people living in a certain place (as a village or city) : the area itself **2** : a natural group (as of kinds of plants and animals) living together and depending on one another for various necessities of life **3** : a group of people with common interests living together **4** : people in general : PUBLIC **5** : common ownership or participation

com·mu·ta·tive *adj* : being a property of a mathematical operation (as addition or multiplication) in which the result of combining elements is independent of the order in which they are taken

com·mute *vb* **com·mut·ed; com·mut·ing** **1** : to change (as a penalty) to something less severe **2** : to travel back and forth regularly — **com·mut·er** *n*

[1]**com·pact** *adj* **1** : closely united or packed **2** : arranged so as to save space **3** : not wordy : BRIEF — **com·pact·ly** *adv* — **com·pact·ness** *n*

[2]**com·pact** *n* **1** : a small case for cosmetics **2** : a somewhat small automobile

[3]**com·pact** *n* : AGREEMENT 2

compact disc *n* : a small plastic disc on which information (as music or computer data) is recorded

com·pan·ion *n* **1** : a person or thing that accompanies another **2** : one of a pair of matching things **3** : a person employed to live with and serve another

com·pan·ion·ship *n* : FELLOWSHIP 1, COMPANY

com·pan·ion·way *n* : a ship's stairway from one deck to another

com·pa·ny *n, pl* **com·pa·nies** **1** : FELLOWSHIP 1 **2** : a person's companions or associates **3** : guests or visitors especially at one's home **4** : a group of persons or things **5** : a body of soldiers and especially an infantry unit normally led by a captain **6** : a band of musical or dramatic performers **7** : the officers and crew of a ship **8** : an association of persons carrying on a business

com·pa·ra·ble *adj* : being similar or about the same

[1]**com·par·a·tive** *adj* **1** : of, relating to, or being the form of an adjective or adverb that shows a degree of comparison that is greater or less than its positive degree **2** : measured by comparisons : RELATIVE — **com·par·a·tive·ly** *adv*

[2]**comparative** *n* : the comparative degree or a comparative form in a language

com·pare *vb* **com·pared; com·par·ing** **1** : to point out as similar : LIKEN **2** : to examine for likenesses or differences **3** : to appear in comparison to others **4** : to state the positive, comparative, and superlative forms of an adjective or adverb

com·par·i·son *n* **1** : the act of comparing : the condition of being compared **2** : an examination of two or more objects to find the likenesses and differences between them **3** : change in the form and meaning of an adjective or an adverb (as by adding *-er* or *-est* to the word or by adding *more* or *most* before the word) to show different levels of quality, quantity, or relation

com·part·ment *n* **1** : one of the parts into which a closed space is divided **2** : a separate division or section

com·pass *n* **1** : BOUNDARY, CIRCUMFERENCE **2** : a closed-in space **3** : [1]RANGE 6, SCOPE **4** : a device having a magnetic needle that indicates direction on the earth's surface by pointing toward the north **5 :** a device that indicates direction by means other than a magnetic needle **6 :** an instrument for drawing circles or marking measurements consisting of two pointed legs joined at the top by a pivot — usually used in pl.

com·pas·sion *n* **:** pity for and a desire to help another

com·pas·sion·ate *adj* **:** having or showing compassion

com·pat·i·ble *adj* **:** capable of existing together in harmony

com·pa·tri·ot *n* **:** a person from one's own country

com·pel *vb* **com·pelled; com·pel·ling :** to make (as a person) do something by the use of physical, moral, or mental pressure **:** FORCE

com·pen·sate *vb* **com·pen·sat·ed; com·pen·sat·ing 1 :** to make up for **2 :** [1]RECOMPENSE, PAY

com·pen·sa·tion *n* **1 :** something that makes up for or is given to make up for something else **2 :** money paid regularly

com·pete *vb* **com·pet·ed; com·pet·ing :** to strive for something (as a prize or a reward) for which another is also striving

com·pe·tence *n* **:** the quality or state of being competent

com·pe·tent *adj* **:** CAPABLE 1, EFFICIENT

com·pe·ti·tion *n* **1 :** the act or process of competing **2 :** a contest in which all who take part compete for the same thing

com·pet·i·tive *adj* **:** relating to, characterized by, or based on competition

com·pet·i·tor *n* **:** someone or something that competes especially in the selling of goods or services **:** RIVAL

com·pile *vb* **com·piled; com·pil·ing 1 :** to collect into a volume or list **2 :** to collect information from books or documents and arrange it in a new form

com·pla·cence *n* **:** calm or satisfied feeling about one's self or one's position

com·pla·cen·cy *n* **:** COMPLACENCE

com·pla·cent *adj* **:** feeling or showing complacence

com·plain *vb* **1 :** to express grief, pain, or discontent **:** find fault **2 :** to accuse someone of wrongdoing — **com·plain·er** *n*

com·plaint *n* **1 :** expression of grief, pain, or discontent **2 :** a cause or reason for complaining **3 :** a sickness or disease of the body **4 :** a charge of wrongdoing against a person

[1]**com·ple·ment** *n* **:** something that completes or fills **:** the number required to complete or make perfect

[2]**com·ple·ment** *vb* **:** to form or serve as a complement to

com·ple·men·ta·ry *adj* **:** serving as a complement

[1]**com·plete** *adj* **1 :** having no part lacking **:** ENTIRE **2 :** brought to an end **3 :** THOROUGH 1 — **com·plete·ness** *n*

[2]**complete** *vb* **com·plet·ed; com·plet·ing 1 :** to bring to an end **:** FINISH **2 :** to make whole or perfect

com·plete·ly *adv* **:** as much as possible **:** in every way or detail

com·ple·tion *n* **:** the act or process of completing **:** the condition of being complete

com·plex *adj* **1 :** made up of two or more parts **2 :** not simple

complex fraction *n* **:** a fraction with a fraction or mixed number in the numerator or denominator or both

com·plex·ion *n* **1 :** the color or appearance of the skin and especially of the face **2 :** general appearance or impression

com·plex·i·ty *n, pl* **com·plex·i·ties 1 :** the quality or condition of being complex **2 :** something complex

com·pli·cate *vb* **com·pli·cat·ed; com·pli·cat·ing :** to make or become complex or difficult

com·pli·ca·tion *n* **1 :** a confused situation **2 :** something that makes a situation more difficult

[1]**com·pli·ment** *n* **1 :** an act or expression of praise, approval, respect, or admiration **2 compliments** *pl* **:** best wishes

[2]**com·pli·ment** *vb* **:** to pay a compliment to

com·pli·men·ta·ry *adj* **1 :** expressing or containing a compliment **2 :** given free as a courtesy or favor

com·ply *vb* **com·plied; com·ply·ing :** to act in agreement with another's wishes or in obedience to a rule

com·po·nent *n* **:** one of the parts or units of a combination, mixture, or system

com·pose *vb* **com·posed; com·pos·ing 1 :** to form by putting together **2 :** to be the parts or materials of **3 :** to put in order **:** SETTLE

com·posed *adj* **:** being calm and in control of oneself

com·pos·er *n* **1 :** a person who composes **2 :** a writer of music

com·pos·ite *adj* **:** made up of different parts or elements

composite number *n* **:** an integer that is a product of two or more whole numbers each greater than 1

com·po·si·tion *n* **1 :** the act of composing (as by writing) **2 :** the manner in which the parts of a thing are put together **3 :** MAKEUP 1, CONSTITUTION **4 :** a literary, musical, or

artistic production **5 :** a short piece of writing done as a school exercise
com·post *n* **:** decayed organic material used to improve soil for growing crops
com·po·sure *n* **:** calmness especially of mind, manner, or appearance
[1]**com·pound** *vb* **1 :** to mix or unite together into a whole **2 :** to form by combining separate things
[2]**com·pound** *adj* **:** made of or by the union of two or more parts
[3]**com·pound** *n* **1 :** a word made up of parts that are themselves words **2 :** something (as a chemical) that is formed by combining two or more parts or elements
[4]**com·pound** *n* **:** an enclosed area containing a group of buildings
compound fracture *n* **:** a breaking of a bone in which bone fragments stick out through the flesh
com·pre·hend *vb* **1 :** to understand fully **2 :** to take in **:** INCLUDE
com·pre·hen·sion *n* **:** ability to understand
com·pre·hen·sive *adj* **:** including much **:** INCLUSIVE — **com·pre·hen·sive·ness** *n*
[1]**com·press** *vb* **1 :** to press or squeeze together **2 :** to reduce the volume of by pressure
[2]**com·press** *n* **:** a pad (as of folded cloth) applied firmly to a part of the body (as to check bleeding)
com·pres·sion *n* **:** the process of compressing **:** the state of being compressed
com·pres·sor *n* **1 :** one that compresses **2 :** a machine for compressing something (as air)
com·prise *vb* **com·prised; com·pris·ing 1 :** to be made up of **:** consist of **2 :** [2]FORM 3
[1]**com·pro·mise** *n* **1 :** an agreement over a dispute reached by each side changing or giving up some demands **2 :** the thing agreed upon as a result of a compromise
[2]**compromise** *vb* **com·pro·mised; com·pro·mis·ing 1 :** to settle by compromise **2 :** to expose to risk, suspicion, or disgrace
com·pul·sion *n* **1 :** an act of compelling **:** the state of being compelled **2 :** a force that compels **3 :** a very strong urge to do something
com·pul·so·ry *adj* **1 :** required by or as if by law **2 :** having the power of forcing someone to do something
com·pu·ta·tion *n* **1 :** the act or action of computing **2 :** a result obtained by computing
com·pute *vb* **com·put·ed; com·put·ing :** to find out by using mathematics
com·put·er *n* **:** an automatic electronic machine that can store, recall, and process data
com·put·er·ize *vb* **com·put·er·ized; com·put·er·iz·ing 1 :** to carry out, control, or produce on a computer **2 :** to equip with computers **3 :** to put in a form that a computer can use
com·rade *n* **:** COMPANION 1
[1]**con** *adv* **:** on the negative side
[2]**con** *n* **:** an opposing argument, person, or position
con- — see COM-
con·cave *adj* **:** hollow or rounded inward like the inside of a bowl
con·ceal *vb* **1 :** to hide from sight **2 :** to keep secret
con·ceal·ment *n* **1 :** the act of hiding **:** the state of being hidden **2 :** a hiding place
con·cede *vb* **con·ced·ed; con·ced·ing 1 :** to grant as a right or privilege **2 :** to admit to be true
con·ceit *n* **:** too much pride in oneself or one's ability
con·ceit·ed *adj* **:** VAIN 2
con·ceiv·able *adj* **:** possible to conceive, imagine, or understand
con·ceive *vb* **con·ceived; con·ceiv·ing 1 :** to form an idea of **:** IMAGINE **2 :** THINK 2
con·cen·trate *vb* **con·cen·trat·ed; con·cen·trat·ing 1 :** to bring or come to or direct toward a common center **2 :** to make stronger or thicker by removing something (as water) **3 :** to fix one's powers, efforts, or attentions on one thing
con·cen·tra·tion *n* **1 :** the act or process of concentrating **:** the state of being concentrated **2 :** close mental attention to a subject
con·cept *n* **1 :** [2]THOUGHT 4 **2 :** a general idea
[1]**con·cern** *vb* **1 :** to relate to **:** be about **2 :** to be of interest or importance to **:** AFFECT **3 :** to be a care, trouble, or distress to **4 :** ENGAGE 3, OCCUPY
[2]**concern** *n* **1 :** something that relates to or involves a person **:** AFFAIR **2 :** a state of interest and uncertainty **3 :** a business organization
con·cerned *adj* **:** being worried and disturbed
con·cern·ing *prep* **:** relating to **:** ABOUT
con·cert *n* **1 :** AGREEMENT 1 **2 :** a musical performance by several voices or instruments or by both
con·cer·ti·na *n* **:** a small musical instrument like an accordion
con·cer·to *n, pl* **con·cer·tos :** a musical composition usually in three parts for orchestra with one or more principal instruments
con·ces·sion *n* **1 :** the act or an instance of granting something **2 :** something granted **3 :** a special right or privilege given by an authority
conch *n, pl* **conchs** *or* **conch·es :** a very large sea snail with a tall thick spiral shell
con·cil·i·ate *vb* **con·cil·i·at·ed; con·cil·i·at·ing**

1 : to bring into agreement : RECONCILE 2 : to gain or regain the goodwill or favor of

con·cise *adj* : expressing much in few words

con·clude *vb* **con·clud·ed; con·clud·ing** 1 : to bring or come to an end : FINISH 2 : to form an opinion 3 : to bring about as a result

con·clu·sion *n* 1 : final decision reached by reasoning 2 : the last part of something 3 : a final settlement

con·clu·sive *adj* : DECISIVE 1 — **con·clu·sive·ly** *adv*

con·coct *vb* 1 : to prepare (as food) by putting several different things together 2 : to make up : DEVISE

con·cord *n* : a state of agreement

con·course *n* 1 : a flocking, moving, or flowing together (as of persons or streams) : GATHERING 2 : a place where roads or paths meet 3 : an open space or hall (as in a mall or railroad terminal) where crowds gather

¹con·crete *adj* 1 : ¹MATERIAL 1, REAL 2 : made of or relating to concrete

²con·crete *n* : a hardened mixture of cement, sand, and water with gravel or broken stone used in construction (as of pavements and buildings)

con·cur *vb* **con·curred; con·cur·ring** 1 : to act or happen together 2 : to be in agreement (as in action or opinion) : ACCORD

con·cus·sion *n* 1 : a sharp hard blow or the effect of this 2 : injury to the brain by jarring (as from a blow)

con·demn *vb* 1 : to declare to be wrong 2 : to declare guilty 3 : ²SENTENCE 4 : to declare to be unfit for use

con·dem·na·tion *n* 1 : ¹CENSURE 1, BLAME 2 : the act of judicially condemning 3 : the state of being condemned

con·den·sa·tion *n* 1 : the act or process of condensing 2 : something that has been condensed

con·dense *vb* **con·densed; con·dens·ing** : to make or become more compact, more concise, closer, or denser : CONCENTRATE

con·de·scend *vb* 1 : to stoop to a level considered lower than one's own 2 : to grant favors with a show of being better than others

¹con·di·tion *n* 1 : something agreed upon or necessary if some other thing is to take place **2 conditions** *pl* : state of affairs 3 : state of being 4 : situation in life 5 : state of health or fitness

²condition *vb* 1 : to put into the proper or desired condition 2 : to change the habits of usually by training

con·di·tion·al *adj* : depending on a condition

con·dor *n* : a very large American vulture having a bare head and neck and a frill of white feathers on the neck

¹con·duct *n* 1 : the act or way of carrying something on 2 : personal behavior

²con·duct *vb* 1 : ²GUIDE 1 2 : to carry on or out from a position of command : LEAD 3 : BEHAVE 1 4 : to have the quality of transmitting light, heat, sound, or electricity

con·duc·tion *n* 1 : the act of transporting something 2 : transmission through a conductor

con·duc·tor *n* 1 : a person in charge of a public means of transportation (as a train) 2 : a person or thing that directs or leads 3 : a substance or body capable of transmitting light, electricity, heat, or sound

cone *n* 1 : the scaly fruit of certain trees (as the pine or fir) 2 : a solid body tapering evenly to a point from a circular base 3 : something resembling a cone in shape 4 : an ice-cream holder 5 : a cell of the retina of the eye that is sensitive to colored light

con·fec·tion *n* : a fancy dish or sweet : DELICACY, CANDY

con·fec·tion·er *n* : a maker of or dealer in confections (as candies)

con·fec·tion·ery *n, pl* **con·fec·tion·er·ies** 1 : sweet things to eat (as candy) 2 : a confectioner's business or place of business

con·fed·er·a·cy *n, pl* **con·fed·er·a·cies** 1 : a league of persons, parties, or states 2 *cap* : the eleven southern states that seceded from the United States in 1860 and 1861

¹con·fed·er·ate *adj* 1 : united in a league 2 *cap* : of or relating to the Confederacy

²confederate *n* 1 : a member of a confederacy 2 : ACCOMPLICE 3 *cap* : a soldier of or a person who sided with the Confederacy

³con·fed·er·ate *vb* **con·fed·er·at·ed; con·fed·er·at·ing** : to unite in an alliance or confederacy

con·fer *vb* **con·ferred; con·fer·ring** 1 : BESTOW, PRESENT 2 : to compare views especially in studying a problem

con·fer·ence *n* : a meeting for discussion or exchange of opinions

con·fess *vb* 1 : to tell of or make known (as something private or damaging to oneself) 2 : to make known one's sins to God or to a priest

con·fes·sion *n* 1 : an act of confessing 2 : an admission of guilt 3 : a formal statement of religious beliefs

con·fide *vb* **con·fid·ed; con·fid·ing** 1 : to have or show faith 2 : to show confidence by telling secrets 3 : to tell in confidence 4 : ENTRUST 2

con·fi·dence *n* 1 : a feeling of trust or belief 2 : SELF-CONFIDENCE 3 : reliance on another's secrecy or loyalty 4 : ²SECRET

con·fi·dent *adj* : having or showing confidence — **con·fi·dent·ly** *adv*

con·fi·den·tial *adj* **1 :** [1]SECRET 1 **2 :** [2]INTIMATE 2 **3 :** trusted with secret matters — **con·fi·den·tial·ly** *adv*

con·fine *vb* **con·fined; con·fin·ing** **1 :** to keep within limits **2 :** to shut up **:** IMPRISON **3 :** to keep indoors — **con·fine·ment** *n*

con·fines *n pl* **:** the boundary or limits of something

con·firm *vb* **1 :** to make firm or firmer (as in a habit, in faith, or in intention) **:** STRENGTHEN **2 :** APPROVE 2, ACCEPT **3 :** to administer the rite of confirmation to **4 :** to make sure of the truth of

con·fir·ma·tion *n* **1 :** an act of confirming **2 :** a religious ceremony admitting a person to full privileges in a church or synagogue **3 :** something that confirms

con·firmed *adj* **1 :** being firmly established **2 :** unlikely to change

con·fis·cate *vb* **con·fis·cat·ed; con·fis·cat·ing :** to seize by or as if by public authority

con·fla·gra·tion *n* **:** a large destructive fire

[1]**con·flict** *n* **1 :** an extended struggle **:** BATTLE **2 :** a clashing disagreement (as between ideas or interests)

[2]**con·flict** *vb* **:** to be in opposition

con·form *vb* **1 :** to make or be like **:** AGREE, ACCORD **2 :** COMPLY

con·for·mi·ty *n, pl* **con·for·mi·ties** **1 :** agreement in form, manner, or character **2 :** action in accordance with some standard or authority

con·found *vb* **:** to throw into disorder **:** mix up **:** CONFUSE

con·front *vb* **1 :** to face especially in challenge **:** OPPOSE **2 :** to cause to face or meet

con·fuse *vb* **con·fused; con·fus·ing** **1 :** to make mentally foggy or uncertain **:** PERPLEX **2 :** to make embarrassed **3 :** to fail to tell apart

con·fu·sion *n* **1 :** an act or instance of confusing **2 :** the state of being confused

con·geal *vb* **1 :** to change from a fluid to a solid state by or as if by cold **:** FREEZE **2 :** to make or become hard, stiff, or thick

con·ge·nial *adj* **1 :** alike or sympathetic in nature, disposition, or tastes **2 :** existing together in harmony **3 :** tending to please or satisfy

con·gest *vb* **:** to make too crowded or full **:** CLOG

[1]**con·glom·er·ate** *adj* **:** made up of parts from various sources or of various kinds

[2]**conglomerate** *n* **:** a mass (as a rock) formed of fragments from various sources

con·grat·u·late *vb* **con·grat·u·lat·ed; con·grat·u·lat·ing :** to express pleasure on account of success or good fortune

con·grat·u·la·tion *n* **1 :** the act of congratulating **2 :** an expression of joy or pleasure at another's success or good fortune — usually used in pl.

con·gre·gate *vb* **con·gre·gat·ed; con·gre·gat·ing :** to collect or gather into a crowd or group **:** ASSEMBLE

con·gre·ga·tion *n* **1 :** a gathering or collection of persons or things **2 :** an assembly of persons gathered especially for religious worship **3 :** the membership of a church or synagogue

con·gress *n* **1 :** a formal meeting of delegates for discussion and action **:** CONFERENCE **2 :** the chief lawmaking body of a nation and especially of a republic that in the United States is made up of separate houses of senators and representatives

con·gress·man *n, pl* **con·gress·men** **:** a member of a congress and especially of the United States House of Representatives

con·gress·wom·an *n, pl* **con·gress·wom·en** **:** a woman member of a congress and especially of the United States House of Representatives

con·gru·ent *adj* **:** having the same size and shape

con·ic *adj* **1 :** CONICAL **2 :** of or relating to a cone

con·i·cal *adj* **:** shaped like a cone

co·ni·fer *n* **:** any of a group of mostly evergreen trees and shrubs (as pines) that produce cones — **co·nif·er·ous** *adj*

[1]**con·jec·ture** *n* **:** [2]GUESS

[2]**conjecture** *vb* **con·jec·tured; con·jec·tur·ing :** [1]GUESS 1, SURMISE

con·junc·tion *n* **1 :** a joining together **:** UNION **2 :** a word or expression that joins together sentences, clauses, phrases, or words

con·jure *vb* **con·jured; con·jur·ing** **1 :** to beg earnestly or solemnly **:** BESEECH **2 :** to practice magical arts **3 :** IMAGINE 1

con·nect *vb* **1 :** to join or link together **2 :** to attach by close personal relationship **3 :** to bring together in thought — **con·nec·tor** *n*

con·nec·tion *n* **1 :** the act of connecting **2 :** the fact or condition of being connected **:** RELATIONSHIP **3 :** a thing that connects **:** BOND, LINK **4 :** a person connected with others (as by kinship) **5 :** a social, professional, or commercial relationship **6 :** the act or the means of continuing a journey by transferring (as to another train)

con·nois·seur *n* **:** a person qualified to act as a judge in matters involving taste and appreciation

con·quer *vb* **1 :** to get or gain by force **:** win by fighting **2 :** OVERCOME 1

con·quer·or *n* **:** one that conquers **:** VICTOR

con·quest *n* **1 :** the act or process of conquering : VICTORY **2 :** something that is conquered

con·quis·ta·dor *n, pl* **con·quis·ta·do·res** *or* **con·quis·ta·dors :** a leader in the Spanish conquest especially of Mexico and Peru in the sixteenth century

con·science *n* **:** knowledge of right and wrong and a feeling that one should do what is right

con·sci·en·tious *adj* **1 :** guided by or agreeing with one's conscience **2 :** using or done with careful attention

con·scious *adj* **1 :** aware of facts or feelings **2 :** known or felt by one's inner self **3 :** mentally awake or active **4 :** INTENTIONAL — **con·scious·ly** *adv*

con·scious·ness *n* **1 :** the condition of being conscious **2 :** the upper level of mental life involving conscious thought and the will

con·se·crate *vb* **con·se·crat·ed; con·se·crat·ing 1 :** to declare to be sacred or holy **:** set apart for the service of God **2 :** to dedicate to a particular purpose

con·sec·u·tive *adj* **:** following one another in order without gaps

[1]**con·sent** *vb* **:** to express willingness or approval **:** AGREE

[2]**consent** *n* **:** approval of or agreement with what is done or suggested by another person

con·se·quence *n* **1 :** something produced by a cause or following from a condition **2 :** real importance

con·se·quent *adj* **:** following as a result or effect

con·se·quent·ly *adv* **:** as a result

con·ser·va·tion *n* **1 :** PROTECTION 1, PRESERVATION **2 :** planned management of natural resources (as timber) to prevent waste, destruction, or neglect

[1]**con·ser·va·tive** *adj* **1 :** favoring a policy of keeping things as they are **:** opposed to change **2 :** favoring established styles and standards — **con·ser·va·tive·ly** *adv*

[2]**conservative** *n* **:** a person who holds conservative views **:** a cautious person

con·ser·va·to·ry *n, pl* **con·ser·va·to·ries 1 :** GREENHOUSE **2 :** a place of instruction in some special study (as music)

[1]**con·serve** *vb* **con·served; con·serv·ing :** to keep in a safe condition **:** SAVE

[2]**con·serve** *n* **1 :** a candied fruit **2 :** a rich fruit preserve

con·sid·er *vb* **1 :** to think over carefully **:** PONDER, REFLECT **2 :** to treat in a kind or thoughtful way **3 :** to think of in a certain way **:** BELIEVE

con·sid·er·able *adj* **:** rather large in extent, amount, or size — **con·sid·er·ably** *adv*

con·sid·er·ate *adj* **:** thoughtful of the rights and feelings of others

con·sid·er·ation *n* **1 :** careful thought **:** DELIBERATION **2 :** thoughtfulness for other people **3 :** something that needs to be considered before deciding or acting **4 :** a payment made in return for something

con·sign *vb* **1 :** ENTRUST 2 **2 :** to give, transfer, or deliver to another **3 :** to send (as goods) to an agent to be sold or cared for — **con·sign·ment** *n*

con·sist *vb* **:** to be made up or composed

con·sis·ten·cy *n, pl* **con·sis·ten·cies 1 :** degree of compactness, firmness, or stickiness **2 :** agreement or harmony between parts or elements **3 :** a sticking with one way of thinking or acting

con·sis·tent *adj* **:** showing consistency — **con·sis·tent·ly** *adv*

con·so·la·tion *n* **1 :** the act of consoling **:** the state of being consoled **2 :** something that lessens disappointment, misery, or grief

[1]**con·sole** *n* **1 :** the part of an organ at which the organist sits and which contains the keyboard and controls **2 :** a panel or cabinet on which are dials and switches for controlling an electronic or mechanical device **3 :** a radio, phonograph, or television cabinet that stands on the floor

[2]**con·sole** *vb* **con·soled; con·sol·ing :** to comfort in a time of grief or distress

con·sol·i·date *vb* **con·sol·i·dat·ed; con·sol·i·dat·ing 1 :** to join together into one whole **:** UNITE **2 :** STRENGTHEN

con·so·nant *n* **1 :** a speech sound (as \p\, \n\, or \s\) produced by narrowing or closing the breath channel at one or more points **2 :** a letter in the English alphabet other than *a, e, i, o,* or *u*

[1]**con·sort** *n* **:** a wife or husband especially of a king or queen

[2]**con·sort** *vb* **:** to go together as companions **:** ASSOCIATE

con·spic·u·ous *adj* **1 :** easily seen **2 :** attracting attention **:** PROMINENT

con·spir·a·cy *n, pl* **con·spir·a·cies 1 :** the act of conspiring or plotting **2 :** an agreement among conspirators **3 :** a group of conspirators

con·spir·a·tor *n* **:** a person who conspires

con·spire *vb* **con·spired; con·spir·ing 1 :** to make an agreement especially in secret to do an unlawful act **:** PLOT **2 :** to act together

con·sta·ble *n* **:** a police officer usually of a village or small town

con·stan·cy *n* **:** firmness and loyalty in one's beliefs or personal relationships

con·stant *adj* **1 :** always faithful and true **2 :** remaining steady and unchanged **3 :** occurring over and over again — **con·stant·ly** *adv*

con·stel·la·tion *n* **:** any of eighty-eight groups of stars forming patterns

con·ster·na·tion *n* **:** amazement, alarm, or disappointment that makes one feel helpless or confused

con·sti·pate *vb* **con·sti·pat·ed; con·sti·pat·ing :** to cause constipation in

con·sti·pa·tion *n* **:** difficult or infrequent passage of dry hard material from the bowels

[1]con·stit·u·ent *n* **1 :** one of the parts or materials of which something is made **:** ELEMENT, INGREDIENT **2 :** any of the voters who elect a person to represent them

[2]constituent *adj* **1 :** serving to form or make up a unit or whole **2 :** having power to elect or appoint or to make or change a constitution

con·sti·tute *vb* **con·sti·tut·ed; con·sti·tut·ing 1 :** to appoint to an office or duty **2 :** SET UP 2 **3 :** to make up **:** FORM

con·sti·tu·tion *n* **1 :** the bodily makeup of an individual **2 :** the basic structure of something **3 :** the basic beliefs and laws of a nation, state, or social group by which the powers and duties of the government are established and certain rights are guaranteed to the people

[1]con·sti·tu·tion·al *adj* **1 :** having to do with a person's bodily or mental makeup **2 :** of, relating to, or in agreement with a constitution (as of a nation)

[2]constitutional *n* **:** an exercise (as a walk) taken for one's health

con·strain *vb* **:** COMPEL, FORCE

con·straint *n* **1 :** COMPULSION 1, 2 **2 :** a keeping back of one's natural feelings

con·strict *vb* **:** to make narrower or smaller by drawing together **:** SQUEEZE

con·stric·tion *n* **:** an act or instance of constricting

con·stric·tor *n* **:** a snake (as a boa) that kills prey by crushing in its coils

con·struct *vb* **:** to make or form by combining parts

con·struc·tion *n* **1 :** the arrangement of words and the relationship between words in a sentence **2 :** the process, art, or manner of constructing **3 :** something built or put together **:** STRUCTURE **4 :** INTERPRETATION

construction paper *n* **:** a thick paper available in many colors for school art work

con·struc·tive *adj* **:** helping to develop or improve something

con·strue *vb* **con·strued; con·stru·ing :** to understand or explain the sense or intention of

con·sul *n* **:** an official appointed by a government to live in a foreign country in order to look after the commercial interests of citizens of the appointing country

con·sult *vb* **1 :** to seek the opinion or advice of **2 :** to seek information from **3 :** to talk something over

con·sul·ta·tion *n* **1 :** a discussion between doctors on a case or its treatment **2 :** the act of consulting

con·sume *vb* **con·sumed; con·sum·ing 1 :** to destroy by or as if by fire **2 :** to use up **:** SPEND **3 :** to eat or drink up **4 :** to take up the interest or attention of

con·sum·er *n* **1 :** one that consumes **2 :** a person who buys and uses up goods

con·sump·tion *n* **1 :** the act or process of consuming and especially of using up something (as food or coal) **2 :** a wasting away of the body especially from tuberculosis of the lungs

[1]con·tact *n* **1 :** a meeting or touching of persons or things **2 :** a person one knows who has influence especially in the business or political world

[2]contact *vb* **1 :** to come or bring into contact **2 :** to get in touch or communication with

[3]contact *adj* **:** involving or activated by contact

contact lens *n* **:** a thin lens used to correct bad eyesight and worn right over the cornea of the eye

con·ta·gion *n* **1 :** the passing of a disease from one individual to another as a result of some contact between them **2 :** a contagious disease

con·ta·gious *adj* **:** spreading by contagion

con·tain *vb* **1 :** to keep within limits **:** RESTRAIN, CHECK **2 :** to have within **:** HOLD **3 :** to consist of or include

con·tain·er *n* **:** something into which other things can be put (as for storage)

con·tam·i·nate *vb* **con·tam·i·nat·ed; con·tam·i·nat·ing 1 :** to soil, stain, or infect by contact or association **2 :** to make unfit for use by adding something harmful or unpleasant

con·tem·plate *vb* **con·tem·plat·ed; con·tem·plat·ing 1 :** to view with careful and thoughtful attention **2 :** to have in mind **:** plan on

con·tem·pla·tion *n* **1 :** the act of thinking about spiritual things **:** MEDITATION **2 :** the act of looking at or thinking about something for some time **3 :** a looking ahead to some future event

[1]con·tem·po·rary *adj* **1 :** living or occurring at the same period of time **2 :** MODERN 1

[2]contemporary *n, pl* **con·tem·po·rar·ies :** a person who lives at the same time or is of about the same age as another

con·tempt *n* **1 :** the act of despising **:** the state of mind of one who despises **2 :** the state of being despised

con·tempt·ible *adj* **:** deserving contempt

con·temp·tu·ous *adj* : feeling or showing contempt : SCORNFUL

con·tend *vb* **1 :** COMPETE **2 :** to try hard to deal with **3 :** to argue or state earnestly

[1]con·tent *adj* : pleased and satisfied with what one has or is

[2]content *vb* : to make content : SATISFY

[3]content *n* : freedom from care or discomfort

[4]con·tent *n* **1 :** something contained — usually used in pl. **2 :** the subject or topic treated (as in a book) — usually used in pl. **3 :** the important part or meaning (as of a book) **4 :** the amount contained or possible to contain

con·tent·ed *adj* : satisfied or showing satisfaction with one's possessions or one's situation in life

con·ten·tion *n* **1 :** an act or instance of contending **2 :** an idea or point for which a person argues (as in a debate or argument) **3 :** COMPETITION 2

con·tent·ment *n* : freedom from worry or restlessness : peaceful satisfaction

[1]con·test *vb* : to make (something) a cause of dispute or fighting

[2]con·test *n* : a struggle for victory : COMPETITION

con·tes·tant *n* : one who takes part in a contest

con·ti·nent *n* **1 :** one of the great divisions of land on the globe (as Africa, Antarctica, Asia, Australia, Europe, North America, or South America) **2** *cap* : the continent of Europe

con·ti·nen·tal *adj* : of or relating to a continent

con·tin·gent *adj* : depending on something else that may or may not exist or occur

con·tin·u·al *adj* **1 :** going on without stopping **2 :** occurring again and again at short intervals — **con·tin·u·al·ly** *adv*

con·tin·u·ance *n* **1 :** the act of continuing **2 :** the quality of being continual

con·tin·u·a·tion *n* **1 :** the making longer of a state or activity **2 :** a going on after stopping **3 :** a thing or part by which something is continued

con·tin·ue *vb* **con·tin·ued; con·tinu·ing 1 :** to do or cause to do the same thing without changing or stopping **2 :** to begin again after stopping

con·ti·nu·i·ty *n, pl* **con·ti·nu·i·ties :** the quality or state of being continuous

con·tin·u·ous *adj* : continuing without a stop — **con·tin·u·ous·ly** *adv*

con·tort *vb* : to give an unusual appearance or unnatural shape to by twisting

con·tor·tion *n* **1 :** a twisting or a being twisted out of shape **2 :** a contorted shape or thing

con·tour *n* **1 :** the outline of a figure, body, or surface **2 :** a line or a drawing showing an outline

contra- *prefix* **1 :** against : contrary : contrasting **2 :** pitched below normal bass

con·tra·band *n* **1 :** goods forbidden by law to be owned or to be brought into or out of a country **2 :** smuggled goods

[1]con·tract *n* **1 :** an agreement that the law can force one to keep **2 :** a writing made to show the terms and conditions of a contract

[2]con·tract *vb* **1 :** to agree by contract **2 :** to become sick with : CATCH **3 :** to draw together and make shorter and broader **4 :** to make or become smaller : SHRINK **5 :** to make (as a word) shorter by dropping sounds or letters

con·trac·tion *n* **1 :** the act or process of contracting : the state of being contracted **2 :** a shortening of a word or word group by leaving out a sound or letter **3 :** a form (as *don't* or *they've*) produced by contraction

con·tra·dict *vb* **1 :** to deny the truth of a statement : say the opposite of what someone else has said **2 :** to be opposed to

con·tra·dic·tion *n* : something (as a statement) that contradicts something else

con·tra·dic·to·ry *adj* : involving, causing, or being a contradiction

con·tral·to *n, pl* **con·tral·tos 1 :** the lowest female singing voice : ALTO **2 :** a singer with a contralto voice

con·trap·tion *n* : GADGET

[1]con·trary *n, pl* **con·trar·ies :** something opposite or contrary — **on the contrary :** just the opposite : NO

[2]con·trary *adj* **1 :** exactly opposite **2 :** being against what is usual or expected **3 :** not favorable **4 :** unwilling to accept control or advice

[1]con·trast *vb* **1 :** to show noticeable differences **2 :** to compare two persons or things so as to show the differences between them

[2]con·trast *n* **1 :** difference or the amount of difference (as in color or brightness) between adjacent parts **2 :** difference or amount of difference between related or similar things

con·trib·ute *vb* **con·trib·ut·ed; con·trib·ut·ing 1 :** to give along with others **2 :** to have a share in something **3 :** to supply (as an article) for publication especially in a magazine — **con·trib·u·tor** *n*

con·tri·bu·tion *n* **1 :** the act of contributing **2 :** the sum or thing contributed

con·trite *adj* : feeling or showing sorrow for some wrong that one has done : REPENTANT

con·triv·ance *n* : something (as a scheme or a mechanical device) produced with skill and cleverness

con·trive *vb* **con·trived; con·triv·ing** **1** : [2]PLAN 1, PLOT **2** : to form or make in some skillful or clever way **3** : to manage to bring about or do

[1]**con·trol** *vb* **con·trolled; con·trol·ling** **1** : to keep within bounds : RESTRAIN **2** : to have power over

[2]**control** *n* **1** : the power or authority to control or command **2** : ability to control **3** : SELF-RESTRAINT **4** : REGULATION **5** : a device used to start, stop, or change the operation of a machine or system **6** : something used in an experiment or study to provide a check on results

con·tro·ver·sial *adj* : relating to or causing controversy

con·tro·ver·sy *n, pl* **con·tro·ver·sies** **1** : an often long or heated discussion of something about which there is great difference of opinion **2** : [1]QUARREL 2

co·nun·drum *n* : [1]RIDDLE

con·va·lesce *vb* **con·va·lesced; con·va·lesc·ing** : to regain health and strength gradually after sickness or injury

con·va·les·cence *n* : the period or process of convalescing

[1]**con·va·les·cent** *adj* : passing through convalescence

[2]**convalescent** *n* : a person who is convalescent

con·vec·tion *n* : motion in a gas (as air) or a liquid in which the warmer portions rise and the colder portions sink

con·vene *vb* **con·vened; con·ven·ing** **1** : ASSEMBLE 3 **2** : to cause to assemble

con·ve·nience *n* **1** : the quality or state of being convenient **2** : personal comfort **3** : OPPORTUNITY 1 **4** : something that gives comfort or advantage

con·ve·nient *adj* **1** : suited to a person's comfort or ease **2** : suited to a certain use **3** : easy to get to — **con·ve·nient·ly** *adv*

con·vent *n* **1** : a group of nuns living together **2** : a house or a set of buildings occupied by a community of nuns

con·ven·tion *n* **1** : AGREEMENT 2 **2** : a custom or a way of acting and doing things that is widely accepted and followed **3** : a meeting of persons gathered together for a common purpose

con·ven·tion·al *adj* **1** : behaving according to convention **2** : used or accepted through convention

con·ver·sa·tion *n* : talking or a talk between two or more people

con·verse *vb* **con·versed; con·vers·ing** : to have a conversation

con·ver·sion *n* **1** : the act of converting : the state of being converted **2** : a change in the nature or form of a thing **3** : a change of religion

[1]**con·vert** *vb* **1** : to change from one belief, religion, view, or party to another **2** : to change from one form to another **3** : to exchange for an equivalent

[2]**con·vert** *n* : a person who has been converted

[1]**con·vert·ible** *adj* : possible to change in form or use

[2]**convertible** *n* **1** : something that is convertible **2** : an automobile with a top that can be raised, lowered, or removed

con·vex *adj* : rounded like the outside of a ball or circle

con·vey *vb* **con·veyed; con·vey·ing** **1** : to carry from one place to another : TRANSPORT **2** : to serve as a way of carrying **3** : IMPART 2, COMMUNICATE

con·vey·ance *n* **1** : the act of conveying **2** : something used to carry goods or passengers

[1]**con·vict** *vb* : to prove or find guilty

[2]**con·vict** *n* : a person serving a prison sentence usually for a long time

con·vic·tion *n* **1** : the act of convicting : the state of being convicted **2** : the state of mind of a person who is sure that what he or she believes or says is true **3** : a strong belief or opinion

con·vince *vb* **con·vinced; con·vinc·ing** : to argue so as to make a person agree or believe

con·vinc·ing *adj* : causing one to believe or agree : PERSUASIVE — **con·vinc·ing·ly** *adv*

con·vulse *vb* **con·vulsed; con·vuls·ing** : to shake violently or with jerky motions

con·vul·sion *n* **1** : an attack of violent involuntary muscular contractions : FIT **2** : a violent disturbance : UPHEAVAL

con·vul·sive *adj* : being or producing a convulsion — **con·vul·sive·ly** *adv*

[1]**coo** *vb* **cooed; coo·ing** **1** : to make the soft sound made by doves and pigeons or one like it **2** : to talk fondly or lovingly

[2]**coo** *n, pl* **coos** : the sound made in cooing

[1]**cook** *n* : a person who prepares food for eating

[2]**cook** *vb* **1** : to prepare food for eating by the use of heat **2** : to go through the process of being cooked

cook·book *n* : a book of cooking recipes and directions

cook·ie *or* **cooky** *n, pl* **cook·ies** : a small sweet cake

cook·out *n* : an outing at which a meal is cooked and served outdoors

cook up *vb* : to think up : DEVISE

[1]**cool** *adj* **1** : somewhat cold : not warm **2** : not letting or keeping in heat **3** : [3]CALM 2

4 : not friendly or interested : INDIFFERENT — **cool·ly** *adv*

[2]**cool** *vb* : to make or become cool

[3]**cool** *n* : a cool time or place

cool·er *n* : a container for keeping food or drink cool

coon *n* : RACCOON

[1]**coop** *n* : a building for housing poultry

[2]**coop** *vb* : to restrict to a small space

coo·per *n* : a worker who makes or repairs wooden casks, tubs, or barrels

co·op·er·ate *vb* **co·op·er·at·ed; co·op·er·at·ing** : to act or work together so as to get something done

co·op·er·a·tion *n* : the act or process of cooperating

[1]**co·op·er·a·tive** *adj* **1** : willing to cooperate or work with others **2** : of, relating to, or organized as a cooperative

[2]**cooperative** *n* : an association formed to enable its members to buy or sell to better advantage

[1]**co·or·di·nate** *adj* : equal in rank or importance

[2]**co·or·di·nate** *vb* **co·or·di·nat·ed; co·or·di·nat·ing** : to work or cause to work together smoothly

co·or·di·na·tion *n* : smooth working together (as of parts)

cop *n* : POLICE OFFICER

cope *vb* **coped; cop·ing** : to struggle or try to manage especially with some success

copi·er *n* **1** : a person who copies **2** : a machine for making copies (as of letters or drawings)

co·pi·lot *n* : an assistant airplane pilot

co·pi·ous *adj* : very plentiful : ABUNDANT — **co·pi·ous·ly** *adv*

cop·per *n* **1** : a tough reddish metallic chemical element that is one of the best conductors of heat and electricity **2** : a copper or bronze coin

cop·per·head *n* : a mottled reddish brown poisonous snake of the eastern United States

cop·pice *n* : a thicket, grove, or growth of small trees

co·pra *n* : dried coconut meat

copse *n* : COPPICE

[1]**copy** *n, pl* **cop·ies** **1** : something that is made to look exactly like something else : DUPLICATE **2** : one of the total number of books, magazines, or papers printed at one time **3** : written or printed material to be set in type

[2]**copy** *vb* **cop·ied; copy·ing** **1** : to make a copy of : DUPLICATE **2** : IMITATE 1, 3

[1]**copy·right** *n* : the legal right to be the only one to reproduce, publish, and sell the contents and form of a literary or artistic work

[2]**copyright** *vb* : to get a copyright on

[1]**cor·al** *n* **1** : a stony or horny material consisting of the skeletons of tiny colonial sea animals related to the jellyfishes and including one kind that is red and used in jewelry **2** : one or a colony of the animals that form coral **3** : a dark pink

[2]**coral** *adj* **1** : made of coral **2** : of the color of coral

coral snake *n* : a small poisonous American snake brightly ringed with red, black, and yellow or white

cord *n* **1** : material like a small thin rope that is used mostly for tying things **2** : something like a cord **3** : an amount of firewood equal to a pile of wood eight feet long, four feet high, and four feet wide or 128 cubic feet (about 3.6 cubic meters) **4** : a rib or ridge woven into cloth **5** : a ribbed fabric **6** : a small insulated cable used to connect an electrical appliance with an outlet

cord·ed *adj* : having or drawn into ridges or cords

cor·dial *adj* : being warm and friendly — **cor·dial·ly** *adv*

cor·dial·i·ty *n* : sincere affection and kindness

cor·du·roy *n* **1** : a heavy ribbed usually cotton cloth **2 corduroys** *pl* : trousers made of corduroy **3** : logs laid crosswise side by side to make a road surface

[1]**core** *n* **1** : the central part of some fruits (as pineapples or pears) **2** : the central part of a heavenly body (as the earth or sun) **3** : the basic or central part of something

[2]**core** *vb* **cored; cor·ing** : to remove the core from

[1]**cork** *n* **1** : the light but tough material that is the outer layer of bark of a tree (**cork oak**) and is used especially for stoppers and insulation **2** : a usually cork stopper for a bottle or jug

[2]**cork** *vb* : to stop with a cork

[1]**cork·screw** *n* : a pointed spiral piece of metal with a handle that is screwed into corks to draw them from bottles

[2]**corkscrew** *adj* : like a corkscrew

cor·mo·rant *n* : a large black seabird with a long neck and a slender hooked beak

[1]**corn** *n* **1** : the seeds or grain of a cereal plant (as wheat or oats) **2** : INDIAN CORN **3** : a plant whose seeds are corn

[2]**corn** *vb* : to preserve by packing with salt or by soaking in salty water

[3]**corn** *n* : a hardening and thickening of the skin (as on a person's toe)

corn·cob *n* : the woody core on which grains of Indian corn grow

cor·nea *n* : the transparent outer layer of the front of the eye covering the pupil and iris

[1]**cor·ner** *n* **1** : the point or place where edges or sides meet **2** : the place where two streets

or roads meet **3 :** a piece used to mark, form, or protect a corner (as of a book) **4 :** a place away from ordinary life or business **5 :** a position from which escape or retreat is difficult or impossible — **cor·nered** *adj*

²corner *adj* **1 :** located at a corner **2 :** used or usable in or on a corner

³corner *vb* **1 :** to drive into a corner **2 :** to put in a difficult position

cor·net *n* **:** a brass musical instrument similar to but shorter than a trumpet

corn·flow·er *n* **:** a European plant related to the daisies that is often grown for its bright heads of blue, pink, or white flowers

cor·nice *n* **1 :** an ornamental piece that forms the top edge of the front of a building or pillar **2 :** an ornamental molding placed where the walls meet the ceiling of a room

corn·meal *n* **:** meal ground from corn

corn·stalk *n* **:** a stalk of Indian corn

corn·starch *n* **:** a fine starch made from Indian corn and used as a thickening agent in cooking

corn syrup *n* **:** a syrup made from cornstarch and used chiefly in baked goods and candy

cor·nu·co·pia *n* **:** a container in the shape of a horn overflowing with fruits and flowers used as a symbol of plenty

corny *adj* **corn·i·er; corn·i·est :** so simple, sentimental, or old-fashioned as to be annoying

co·rol·la *n* **:** the part of a flower that is formed by the petals

cor·o·nary *adj* **:** of or relating to the heart or its blood vessels

cor·o·na·tion *n* **:** the act or ceremony of crowning a king or queen

cor·o·net *n* **1 :** a small crown worn by a person of noble but less than royal rank **2 :** an ornamental wreath or band worn around the head

¹cor·po·ral *adj* **:** of or relating to the body **:** BODILY

²corporal *n* **:** a noncommissioned officer ranking above a private in the Army or above a lance corporal in the Marine Corps

cor·po·ra·tion *n* **:** a group authorized by law to carry on an activity (as a business) with the rights and duties of a single person

cor·po·re·al *adj* **:** having, consisting of, or relating to a physical body

corps *n, pl* **corps 1 :** an organized branch of a country's military forces **2 :** a group of persons acting under one authority

corpse *n* **:** a dead body

cor·pu·lent *adj* **:** very stout and heavy **:** extremely fat

cor·pus·cle *n* **:** one of the very small cells that float freely in the blood

¹cor·ral *n* **:** an enclosure for keeping or capturing animals

²corral *vb* **cor·ralled; cor·ral·ling 1 :** to confine in or as if in a corral **2 :** to get hold of or control over

¹cor·rect *vb* **1 :** to make or set right **2 :** to change or adjust so as to bring to some standard or to a required condition **3 :** to punish in order to improve **4 :** to show how a thing can be improved or made right

²correct *adj* **1 :** meeting or agreeing with some standard **:** APPROPRIATE **2 :** free from mistakes **:** ACCURATE — **cor·rect·ly** *adv* — **cor·rect·ness** *n*

cor·rec·tion *n* **1 :** the act of correcting **2 :** a change that makes something right **3 :** PUNISHMENT 1

cor·re·spond *vb* **1 :** to be alike **:** AGREE **2 :** to be equivalent **3 :** to communicate with a person by exchange of letters

cor·re·spon·dence *n* **1 :** agreement between certain things **2 :** communication by means of letters **:** the letters exchanged

cor·re·spon·dent *n* **1 :** a person with whom another person communicates by letter **2 :** a person who sends news stories or comment to a newspaper, magazine, or broadcasting company especially from a distant place

cor·ri·dor *n* **:** a passage into which rooms open

cor·rode *vb* **cor·rod·ed; cor·rod·ing :** to wear away little by little (as by rust or acid)

cor·ro·sion *n* **:** the process or effect of corroding

cor·ro·sive *adj* **:** tending or able to corrode

cor·ru·gate *vb* **cor·ru·gat·ed; cor·ru·gat·ing :** to make wrinkles in or shape into wavy folds

¹cor·rupt *vb* **1 :** to change (as in morals, manners, or actions) from good to bad **2 :** to influence a public official in an improper way (as by a bribe)

²corrupt *adj* **1 :** morally bad **:** EVIL **2 :** behaving in a bad or improper way **:** doing wrong — **cor·rupt·ly** *adv* — **cor·rupt·ness** *n*

cor·rup·tion *n* **1 :** physical decay or rotting **2 :** lack of honesty **3 :** the causing of someone else to do something wrong **4 :** a being changed for the worse

cor·sage *n* **:** a bouquet of flowers usually worn on the shoulder

corse·let *or* **cors·let** *n* **:** the body armor worn by a knight especially on the upper part of the body

cor·set *n* **:** a tight undergarment worn to support or give shape to waist and hips

cos·met·ic *n* **:** material (as a cream, lotion, or powder) used to beautify especially the complexion

cos·mic *adj* **:** of or relating to the whole universe

cosmic ray *n* **:** a stream of very penetrating particles that enter the earth's atmosphere from outer space at high speed

cos·mo·naut *n* **:** a Soviet astronaut

cos·mos *n* **1 :** the orderly universe **2 :** a tall garden plant related to the daisies that has showy white, pink, or rose-colored flower heads

¹cost *n* **1 :** the amount paid or charged for something **:** PRICE **2 :** loss or penalty involved in gaining something

²cost *vb* **cost; cost·ing 1 :** to have a price of **2 :** to cause one to pay, spend, or lose

cost·ly *adj* **cost·li·er; cost·li·est 1 :** of great cost or value **:** EXPENSIVE, DEAR **2 :** made at great expense or sacrifice

¹cos·tume *n* **1 :** style of clothing, ornaments, and hair used especially during a certain period, in a certain region, or by a certain class or group **2 :** special or fancy dress (as for wear on the stage or at a masquerade) **3 :** a person's outer garments

²costume *vb* **cos·tumed; cos·tum·ing 1 :** to provide with a costume **2 :** to design costumes for

¹cot *n* **:** a small house **:** COTTAGE, HUT

²cot *n* **:** a narrow bed often made to fold up

cot·tage *n* **1 :** a small usually frame house for one family **2 :** a small house for vacation use

cottage cheese *n* **:** a very soft cheese made from soured skim milk

¹cot·ton *n* **1 :** a soft fluffy material made up of twisted hairs that surrounds the seeds of a tall plant (**cotton plant**) related to the mallows and that is spun into yarn **2 :** thread, yarn, or cloth made from cotton

²cotton *adj* **:** made of cotton

cotton gin *n* **:** a machine for removing seeds from cotton

cot·ton·mouth *n* **:** MOCCASIN 2

cot·ton·seed *n* **:** the seed of the cotton plant from which comes a meal rich in protein and an oil used especially in cooking

cot·ton·tail *n* **:** a small rabbit with a white tail

cot·ton·wood *n* **:** any of several poplar trees that have seeds with bunches of hairs suggesting cotton and that include some which grow rapidly

couch *n* **:** a piece of furniture (as a bed or sofa) that one can sit or lie on

cou·gar *n* **:** a large yellowish brown North American wild animal related to the domestic cat

¹cough *vb* **1 :** to force air from the lungs with a sharp short noise or series of noises **2 :** to get rid of by coughing

²cough *n* **1 :** a condition in which there is severe or frequent coughing **2 :** an act or sound of coughing

could *past of* CAN **1** — used as a helping verb in the past **2** — used as a polite form instead of *can*

couldn't : could not

coun·cil *n* **:** a group of persons appointed or elected to make laws or give advice

coun·cil·or *or* **coun·cil·lor** *n* **:** a member of a council

¹coun·sel *n* **1 :** advice given **2 :** the discussion of reasons for or against a thing **:** an exchange of opinions **3** *pl* **counsel :** a lawyer engaged in the trial and management of a case in court

²counsel *vb* **coun·seled** *or* **coun·selled; coun·sel·ing** *or* **coun·sel·ling 1 :** to give counsel **:** ADVISE **2 :** to seek counsel

coun·sel·or *or* **coun·sel·lor** *n* **1 :** a person who gives counsel **2 :** LAWYER **3 :** a supervisor of campers or activities at a summer camp

¹count *vb* **1 :** to add one by one in order to find the total number in a collection **2 :** to name the numerals in order up to a particular point **3 :** to name the numbers one by one or by groups **4 :** to include in counting or thinking about **5 :** to consider or judge to be **6 :** to include or leave out by or as if by counting **7 :** RELY, DEPEND **8 :** ²PLAN 1 **9 :** to have value, force, or importance

²count *n* **1 :** the act or process of counting **2 :** a total arrived at by counting **3 :** any one charge in a legal declaration or indictment

³count *n* **:** a European nobleman whose rank is like that of a British earl

count·down *n* **:** a counting off of the time remaining before an event (as the launching of a rocket)

¹coun·te·nance *n* **:** the human face or its expression

²countenance *vb* **coun·te·nanced; coun·te·nanc·ing :** to give approval or tolerance to

¹count·er *n* **1 :** a piece (as of plastic or ivory) used in counting or in games **2 :** a level surface usually higher than a table that is used for selling, serving food, displaying things, or working on

²count·er *n* **1 :** one that counts **2 :** a device for showing a number or amount

³coun·ter *vb* **1 :** to act in opposition to **:** OPPOSE **2 :** RETALIATE

⁴coun·ter *adv* **:** in another or opposite direction

⁵coun·ter *n* **:** an answering or opposing force or blow

⁶coun·ter *adj* **:** moving or acting in an opposite way **:** CONTRARY

coun·ter- *prefix* **1 :** opposite **2 :** opposing **3 :** like **:** matching **4 :** duplicate **:** substitute

coun·ter·act *vb* : to act against so as to prevent something from acting in its own way

coun·ter·clock·wise *adv or adj* : in a direction opposite to that in which the hands of a clock move

[1]**coun·ter·feit** *adj* **1 :** made in exact imitation of something genuine and meant to be taken as genuine **2 :** not sincere

[2]**counterfeit** *vb* **1 :** PRETEND 2 **2 :** to imitate or copy especially in order to deceive — **coun·ter·feit·er** *n*

[3]**counterfeit** *n* : something made to imitate another thing with the desire to deceive

coun·ter·part *n* : a person or thing that is very like or corresponds to another person or thing

coun·ter·point *n* : one or more independent melodies added above or below and in harmony with a given melody

coun·ter·sign *n* : a secret signal that must be given by a person wishing to pass a guard : PASSWORD

count·ess *n* **1 :** the wife or widow of a count or an earl **2 :** a woman who holds the rank of a count or an earl in her own right

counting number *n* : NATURAL NUMBER

count·less *adj* : too many to be counted

coun·try *n, pl* **coun·tries** **1 :** REGION 1, DISTRICT **2 :** a land lived in by a people with a common government **3 :** the people of a nation **4 :** open rural land away from big towns and cities

country and western *n* : music coming from or imitating the folk music of the southern United States or the Western cowboy

coun·try·man *n, pl* **coun·try·men** **1 :** a person born in the same country as another : a fellow citizen **2 :** a person living or raised in the country

coun·try·side *n* : a rural area or its people

coun·ty *n, pl* **coun·ties** : a division of a state or country for local government

cou·pé *or* **coupe** *n* **1 :** a carriage with four wheels and an enclosed body seating two persons and with an outside seat for the driver in front **2 :** an enclosed two-door automobile for usually two persons

[1]**cou·ple** *n* **1 :** two persons who are paired together or closely associated **2 :** two things of the same kind that are connected or that are thought of together

[2]**couple** *vb* **cou·pled; cou·pling** **1 :** to join or link together : CONNECT **2 :** to join in pairs

cou·plet *n* : two rhyming lines of verse one after another

cou·pling *n* **1 :** the act of bringing or coming together **2 :** something that joins or connects two parts or things

cou·pon *n* **1 :** a ticket or form that allows the holder to receive some service, payment, or discount **2 :** a part of an advertisement meant to be cut out for use as an order blank

cour·age *n* : the strength of mind that makes one able to meet danger and difficulties with firmness

cou·ra·geous *adj* : having or showing courage — **cou·ra·geous·ly** *adv*

[1]**course** *n* **1 :** motion from one point to another : progress in space or time **2 :** the path over which something moves **3 :** direction of motion **4 :** a natural channel for water **5 :** way of doing something **6 :** a series of acts or proceedings arranged in regular order **7 :** a series of studies leading to a diploma or a degree **8 :** a part of a meal served at one time **9 :** a continuous level range of brick or masonry throughout a wall — **of course :** as might be expected

[2]**course** *vb* **coursed; cours·ing** **1 :** to run through or over **2 :** to move rapidly : RACE

[1]**court** *n* **1 :** the home of a ruler **2 :** a ruler's assembly of advisers and officers as a governing power **3 :** the family and people who follow a ruler **4 :** an open space completely or partly surrounded by buildings **5 :** a short street **6 :** a space arranged for playing a certain game **7 :** an official meeting led by a judge for settling legal questions or the place where it is held **8 :** respect meant to win favor

[2]**court** *vb* **1 :** to try to gain or get the support of : SEEK **2 :** to seem to be asking for : TEMPT **3 :** to seek the liking of

cour·te·ous *adj* : showing respect and consideration for others : POLITE — **cour·te·ous·ly** *adv* — **cour·te·ous·ness** *n*

cour·te·sy *n, pl* **cour·te·sies** **1 :** the quality or state of being courteous **2 :** a courteous act or expression **3 :** something that is a favor and not a right

court·house *n* **1 :** a building in which courts of law are held **2 :** a building in which county offices are housed

court·i·er *n* : a member of a royal court

court·ly *adj* **court·li·er; court·li·est** : suitable to a royal court : ELEGANT, POLITE

court·ship *n* : the act or process of courting or seeking the liking of someone

court·yard *n* : [1]COURT 4

cous·in *n* : a child of one's uncle or aunt

cove *n* : a small sheltered inlet or bay

cov·e·nant *n* : a formal or solemn agreement

[1]**cov·er** *vb* **1 :** to provide protection to or against **2 :** to maintain a check on especially by patrolling **3 :** to hide from sight or knowledge **4 :** to place or spread something over **5 :** to dot thickly **6 :** to form a cover or covering over **7 :** to take into account **8 :** to have as one's field of activity or interest **9 :** to pass over or through

²cover *n* **1 :** something that protects, shelters, or hides **2 :** something that is placed over or about another thing **:** LID, TOP **3 :** a binding or a protecting case **4 :** a covering (as a blanket) used on a bed **5 :** an envelope or wrapper for mail

cov·er·age *n* **1 :** insurance against something **2 :** the value or amount of insurance

cov·er·all *n* **:** an outer garment that combines shirt and pants and is worn to protect one's regular clothes — usually used in pl.

covered wagon *n* **:** a large long wagon with a curving canvas top

cov·er·ing *n* **:** something (as a roof or an envelope) that covers or conceals

cov·er·let *n* **:** BEDSPREAD

¹co·vert *adj* **:** made or done secretly — **co·vert·ly** *adv* — **co·vert·ness** *n*

²covert *n* **1 :** a hiding place (as a thicket that gives shelter to game animals) **2 :** one of the small feathers around the bottom of the quills on the wings and tail of a bird

cov·et *vb* **:** to wish for greatly or with envy

cov·et·ous *adj* **:** having or showing too much desire for wealth or possessions or for something belonging to another person

cov·ey *n, pl* **coveys 1 :** a small flock (as of quail) **2 :** ¹GROUP

¹cow *n* **:** the adult female of cattle or of any of many large animals (as moose or seals)

²cow *vb* **:** to lower the spirits or courage of **:** make afraid

cow·ard *n* **:** a person who shows dishonorable fear

cow·ard·ice *n* **:** dishonorable fear

cow·ard·ly *adj* **:** being or behaving like a coward — **cow·ard·li·ness** *n*

cow·bell *n* **:** a bell hung around the neck of a cow to tell where it is

cow·bird *n* **:** a small American blackbird that lays its eggs in the nests of other birds

cow·boy *n* **:** a man or boy who works on a ranch or performs at a rodeo

cow·catch·er *n* **:** a strong frame on the front of a railroad engine for moving things blocking the track

cow·er *vb* **:** to shrink away or crouch down shivering (as from fear)

cow·girl *n* **:** a girl or woman who works on a ranch or performs at a rodeo

cow·hand *n* **:** a person who works on a cattle ranch

cow·herd *n* **:** a person who tends cows

cow·hide *n* **1 :** the hide of cattle or leather made from it **2 :** a whip of rawhide or braided leather

cowl *n* **:** a hood or long hooded cloak especially of a monk

cow·lick *n* **:** a small bunch of hair that sticks out and will not lie flat

cow·pox *n* **:** a disease of cattle that when given to humans (as by vaccination) protects from smallpox

cow·punch·er *n* **:** COWBOY

cow·slip *n* **1 :** a common Old World primrose with yellow or purple flowers **2 :** MARSH MARIGOLD

cox·swain *n* **:** the person who steers a boat

coy *adj* **:** falsely shy or modest

coy·ote *n* **:** a small wolf chiefly of western North America

¹co·zy *adj* **co·zi·er; co·zi·est :** enjoying or providing warmth and comfort — **co·zi·ly** *adv* — **co·zi·ness** *n*

²cozy *n, pl* **co·zies :** a padded covering for a container (as a teapot) to keep the contents hot

cpu *n, often cap C&P&U* **:** the part of a computer that does most of the processing of data

¹crab *n* **:** a sea animal related to the lobsters but having a flat shell and a small abdomen pressed against the underside of the body

²crab *vb* **crabbed; crab·bing :** COMPLAIN 1

³crab *n* **:** a person who is usually cross

crab apple *n* **1 :** a small wild sour apple **2 :** a cultivated apple with small usually brightly colored acid fruit

crab·bed *adj* **:** CRABBY

crab·by *adj* **crab·bi·er; crab·bi·est :** being cross and irritable

crab·grass *n* **:** a weedy grass with coarse stems that root at the joints

¹crack *vb* **1 :** to break or cause to break with a sudden sharp sound **2 :** to make or cause to make a sound of cracking as if breaking **3 :** to break often without completely separating into parts **4 :** to tell (a joke) especially in a clever way **5 :** to lose self-control **:** break down **6 :** to change in tone quality **7 :** to strike or receive a sharp blow

²crack *n* **1 :** a sudden sharp noise **2 :** a sharp clever remark **3 :** a narrow break or opening **4 :** a broken tone of the voice **5 :** the beginning moment **6 :** a sharp blow **7 :** ²ATTEMPT

³crack *adj* **:** of high quality or ability

crack·er *n* **:** a dry thin baked food made of flour and water

¹crack·le *vb* **crack·led; crack·ling 1 :** to make many small sharp noises **2 :** to form little cracks in a surface

²crackle *n* **:** the noise of repeated small cracks (as of burning wood)

crack–up *n* **1 :** BREAKDOWN **2 :** ²CRASH 3, WRECK

crack up *vb* **:** to cause or have a crack-up

¹cra·dle *n* **1 :** a baby's bed or cot usually on rockers **2 :** place of beginning **3 :** a framework or support resembling a baby's cradle in appearance or use **4 :** a rocking device used in panning gold **5 :** a support for a telephone receiver

[2]**cradle** *vb* **cra·dled; cra·dling 1 :** to hold or support in or as if in a cradle **2 :** to wash (as earth or sand) in a miner's cradle

craft *n* **1 :** skill in making things especially with the hands **2 :** an occupation or trade requiring skill with the hands or as an artist **3 :** skill in deceiving for a bad purpose : CUNNING **4 :** the members of a trade or a trade group **5** *pl usually* **craft :** a boat especially when of small size **6** *pl usually* **craft :** AIRCRAFT

crafts·man *n, pl* **crafts·men 1 :** a person who works at a trade or handicraft **2 :** a highly skilled worker in any field

crafty *adj* **craft·i·er; craft·i·est :** skillful at deceiving others : CUNNING — **craft·i·ly** *adv* — **craft·i·ness** *n*

crag *n* **:** a steep rock or cliff

crag·gy *adj* **crag·gi·er; crag·gi·est :** having many crags

cram *vb* **crammed; cram·ming 1 :** to stuff or pack tightly **2 :** to fill full **3 :** to study hard just before a test

[1]**cramp** *n* **1 :** a sudden painful involuntary tightening of a muscle **2 :** sharp pain in the abdomen — usually used in pl.

[2]**cramp** *vb* **1 :** to cause cramp in **2 :** to hold back from free action or expression : HAMPER

cran·ber·ry *n, pl* **cran·ber·ries :** a sour bright red berry that is eaten in sauces and jelly and is the fruit of an evergreen swamp plant related to the blueberries

[1]**crane** *n* **1 :** a tall wading bird that looks like a heron but is related to the rails **2 :** a machine with a swinging arm for lifting and carrying heavy weights **3 :** a mechanical arm that swings freely from a center and is used to support or carry a weight

[2]**crane** *vb* **craned; cran·ing :** to stretch one's neck to see better

cra·ni·al *adj* **:** of or relating to the cranium

cra·ni·um *n, pl* **cra·ni·ums** *or* **cra·nia 1 :** SKULL **2 :** the part of the skull enclosing the brain

[1]**crank** *n* **1 :** a bent armlike part with a handle that is turned to start or run machinery **2 :** a person with strange ideas **3 :** a cross or irritable person

[2]**crank** *vb* **:** to start or run by turning a crank

cranky *adj* **crank·i·er; crank·i·est :** easily angered or irritated — **crank·i·ness** *n*

cran·ny *n, pl* **cran·nies :** a small break or slit (as in a cliff)

crap·pie *n* **:** either of two sunfishes native to the Great Lakes and Mississippi valley of which the larger and darker one (**black crappie**) is an important sport fish and the other (**white crappie**) is used as a table fish

[1]**crash** *vb* **1 :** to break or go to pieces with or as if with violence and noise : SMASH **2 :** to fall or strike something with noise and damage **3 :** to hit or cause to hit something with force and noise **4 :** to make or cause to make a loud noise **5 :** to move or force a way roughly and noisily

[2]**crash** *n* **1 :** a loud sound (as of things smashing) **2 :** a breaking to pieces by or as if by hitting something : SMASH, COLLISION **3 :** the crashing of something **4 :** a sudden weakening or failure (as of a business or prices)

[1]**crate** *n* **:** a box or frame of wooden slats or boards for holding and protecting something in shipment

[2]**crate** *vb* **crat·ed; crat·ing :** to pack in a crate

cra·ter *n* **1 :** a hollow in the shape of a bowl around the opening of a volcano or geyser **2 :** a hole (as in the surface of the earth or moon) formed by an impact (as of a meteorite)

cra·vat *n* **:** NECKTIE

crave *vb* **craved; crav·ing 1 :** to ask for earnestly **2 :** to want greatly : long for

cra·ven *adj* **:** COWARDLY

crav·ing *n* **:** a great desire or longing

craw *n* **1 :** [1]CROP 2 **2 :** the stomach of an animal

craw·fish *n, pl* **crawfish :** CRAYFISH

[1]**crawl** *vb* **1 :** to move slowly with the body close to the ground : move on hands and knees **2 :** to go very slowly or carefully **3 :** to be covered with or have the feeling of being covered with creeping things

[2]**crawl** *n* **1 :** the act or motion of crawling **2 :** a swimming stroke that looks a little like crawling

cray·fish *n, pl* **crayfish 1 :** a freshwater shellfish that looks like the related lobster but is much smaller **2 :** a spiny saltwater shellfish that looks like the related lobster but lacks very large claws

[1]**cray·on** *n* **:** a stick of white or colored chalk or of colored wax used for writing or drawing

[2]**crayon** *vb* **:** to draw or color with a crayon

craze *n* **:** something that is very popular for a short while

cra·zy *adj* **cra·zi·er; cra·zi·est 1 :** having a diseased or abnormal mind : INSANE **2 :** not sensible or logical **3 :** very excited or pleased — **cra·zi·ly** *adv* — **cra·zi·ness** *n*

[1]**creak** *vb* **:** to make a long scraping or squeaking sound

[2]**creak** *n* **:** a long squeaking or scraping noise

creaky *adj* **creak·i·er; creak·i·est :** making or

likely to make a creaking sound — **creak·i·ly** *adv*

[1]cream *n* **1 :** the oily yellowish part of milk **2 :** a food prepared with cream **3 :** something having the smoothness and thickness of cream **4 :** the best part **5 :** a pale yellow

[2]cream *vb* **1 :** to furnish, prepare, or treat with cream **2 :** to rub or beat (as butter) until creamy

cream·ery *n, pl* **cream·er·ies :** DAIRY 1, 3

creamy *adj* **cream·i·er; cream·i·est 1 :** full of or containing cream **2 :** like cream in appearance, color, or taste — **cream·i·ness** *n*

[1]crease *n* **:** a line or mark usually made by folding or wrinkling

[2]crease *vb* **creased; creas·ing 1 :** to make a crease in or on **2 :** to become creased

cre·ate *vb* **cre·at·ed; cre·at·ing :** to cause to exist : bring into existence : PRODUCE

cre·a·tion *n* **1 :** the act of bringing the world into existence out of nothing **2 :** the act of making, inventing, or producing something **3 :** something created by human intelligence or imagination **4 :** the created world

cre·a·tive *adj* **:** able to create especially new and original things — **cre·a·tive·ly** *adv* — **cre·a·tive·ness** *n*

cre·a·tor *n* **1 :** one that creates or produces **2** *cap* **:** GOD 1

crea·ture *n* **1 :** a living being **2 :** a lower animal **3 :** PERSON 1

cred·i·ble *adj* **:** possible to believe : deserving belief — **cred·i·bly** *adv*

[1]cred·it *n* **1 :** the balance in an account in a person's favor **2 :** trust given to a customer for future payment for goods purchased **3 :** time given for payment **4 :** belief or trust in the truth of something **5 :** good reputation especially for honesty : high standing **6 :** a source of honor or pride **7 :** recognition or honor received for some quality or work **8 :** a unit of schoolwork

[2]credit *vb* **1 :** BELIEVE 2 **2 :** to place something in a person's favor on (a business account) **3 :** to give credit or honor to for something

cred·it·able *adj* **:** good enough to deserve praise

credit card *n* **:** a card with which a person can buy things on credit

cred·i·tor *n* **:** a person to whom a debt is owed

cred·u·lous *adj* **:** quick to believe especially without very good reasons

creed *n* **1 :** a statement of the basic beliefs of a religious faith **2 :** a set of guiding rules or beliefs

creek *n* **:** a stream of water usually larger than a brook and smaller than a river

creel *n* **:** a basket for holding a catch of fish

[1]creep *vb* **crept; creep·ing 1 :** to move along with the body close to the ground or floor : move slowly on hands and knees : CRAWL **2 :** to move or advance slowly, timidly, or quietly **3 :** to grow or spread along the ground or along a surface

[2]creep *n* **1 :** a creeping movement **2 :** a feeling as of insects crawling over one's skin : a feeling of horror — usually used in pl.

creep·er *n* **1 :** one that creeps **2 :** a small bird that creeps about trees and bushes in search of insects **3 :** a plant (as ivy) that grows by spreading over a surface

creepy *adj* **creep·i·er; creep·i·est 1 :** having or causing a feeling as of insects creeping on the skin **2 :** causing fear : SCARY — **creep·i·ness** *n*

cre·mate *vb* **cre·mat·ed; cre·mat·ing :** to burn (as a dead body) to ashes

cre·ma·tion *n* **:** the act or practice of cremating

crepe *n* **:** a thin crinkled fabric (as of silk or wool)

crepe paper *n* **:** paper with a crinkled or puckered look and feel

crept *past of* CREEP

cre·scen·do *n, pl* **cre·scen·dos** *or* **cre·scen·does :** a gradual increase in the loudness of music

[1]cres·cent *n* **1 :** the shape of the visible moon during about the first week after new moon or the last week before the next new moon **2 :** something shaped like a crescent moon

[2]crescent *adj* **:** shaped like the new moon

cress *n* **:** any of several salad plants of the mustard group

crest *n* **1 :** a showy growth (as of flesh or feathers) on the head of an animal **2 :** an emblem or design on a helmet (as of a knight) or over a coat of arms **3 :** something forming the top of something else — **crest·ed** *adj*

crest·fall·en *adj* **:** feeling disappointment and loss of pride

crev·ice *n* **:** a narrow opening (as in the earth) caused by cracking or splitting : FISSURE

crew *n* **1 :** a gathering of people **2 :** a group of people working together **3 :** the group of people who operate a ship, train, or airplane

crib *n* **1 :** a manger for feeding animals **2 :** a small bed frame with high sides for a child **3 :** a building or bin for storing

[1]crick·et *n* **:** a small leaping insect noted for the chirping notes of the males

[2]cricket *n* **:** a game played on a large field with bats, ball, and wickets by two teams of eleven players

cri·er *n* **:** one who calls out orders or announcements

crime *n* **1 :** the doing of an act forbidden by

law : the failure to do an act required by law **2 :** an act that is sinful, foolish, or disgraceful

¹crim·i·nal *adj* **1 :** being or guilty of crime **2 :** relating to crime or its punishment — **crim·i·nal·ly** *adv*

²criminal *n* **:** a person who has committed a crime

crim·son *n* **:** a deep purplish red

cringe *vb* **cringed; cring·ing 1 :** to shrink in fear : COWER **2 :** to behave in a very humble way : FAWN

crin·kle *vb* **crin·kled; crin·kling 1 :** to form or cause little waves or wrinkles on the surface : WRINKLE **2 :** ¹RUSTLE 1

crin·kly *adj* **crin·kli·er; crin·kli·est :** full of small wrinkles

¹crip·ple *n* **:** a lame or disabled person

²cripple *vb* **crip·pled; crip·pling 1 :** to cause to become a cripple **2 :** to make useless or imperfect

cri·sis *n, pl* **cri·ses 1 :** a turning point for better or worse in a disease **2 :** an unstable or critical time or state of affairs

¹crisp *adj* **1 :** being thin and hard and easily crumbled **2 :** pleasantly firm and fresh **3 :** having a sharp distinct outline **4 :** being clear and brief **5 :** pleasantly cool and invigorating : BRISK

²crisp *vb* **:** to make or become crisp

criss·cross *vb* **1 :** to mark with or make lines that cross one another **2 :** to go or pass back and forth

crit·ic *n* **1 :** a person who makes or gives a judgment of the value, worth, beauty, or quality of something **2 :** a person given to finding fault or complaining

crit·i·cal *adj* **1 :** inclined to criticize especially in an unfavorable way **2 :** consisting of or involving criticism or the judgment of critics **3 :** using or involving careful judgment **4 :** of, relating to, or being a turning point or crisis — **crit·i·cal·ly** *adv*

crit·i·cism *n* **1 :** the act of criticizing and especially of finding fault **2 :** a critical remark or comment **3 :** a careful judgment or review especially by a critic

crit·i·cize *vb* **crit·i·cized; crit·i·ciz·ing 1 :** to examine and judge as a critic **2 :** to find fault with

¹croak *vb* **1 :** to make a deep harsh sound **2 :** to speak in a hoarse throaty voice

²croak *n* **:** a hoarse harsh sound or cry

¹cro·chet *n* **:** work done or a fabric formed by crocheting

²crochet *vb* **:** to make (something) or create a fabric with a hooked needle by forming and interlacing loops in a thread

crock *n* **:** a thick pot or jar of baked clay

crock·ery *n* **:** EARTHENWARE

croc·o·dile *n* **:** a very large animal related to the alligator that crawls on short legs about tropical marshes and rivers

cro·cus *n* **:** a plant related to the irises that has grasslike leaves and is often planted for its white, yellow, or purple spring flowers

cro·ny *n, pl* **cro·nies :** a close companion : CHUM

¹crook *vb* **:** ²BEND 2, CURVE

²crook *n* **1 :** a shepherd's staff with one end curved into a hook **2 :** a dishonest person (as a thief or swindler) **3 :** a curved or hooked part of a thing : BEND

crook·ed *adj* **1 :** having bends and curves **2 :** not set or placed straight **3 :** DISHONEST — **crook·ed·ly** *adv* — **crook·ed·ness** *n*

croon *vb* **:** to hum or sing in a low soft voice

¹crop *n* **1 :** a short riding whip **2 :** an enlargement just above the stomach of a bird or insect in which food is stored for a while **3 :** the amount gathered or harvested : HARVEST **4 :** BATCH 3, LOT

²crop *vb* **cropped; crop·ping 1 :** to remove (as by cutting or biting) the upper or outer parts of : TRIM **2 :** to grow or yield a crop (as of grain) : cause (land) to bear a crop **3 :** to come or appear when not expected

cro·quet *n* **:** a game in which players drive wooden balls with mallets through a series of wickets set out on a lawn

cro·quette *n* **:** a roll or ball of hashed meat, fish, or vegetables fried in deep fat

¹cross *n* **1 :** a structure consisting of one bar crossing another at right angles **2** *often cap* **:** the structure on which Jesus was crucified used as a symbol of Christianity and of the Christian religion **3 :** sorrow or suffering as test of patience or virtue **4 :** an object or mark shaped like a cross **5 :** a mixing of breeds, races, or kinds : the product of such a mixing

²cross *vb* **1 :** to lie or be situated across **2 :** to divide by passing through or across (a line or area) : INTERSECT **3 :** to move, pass, or extend across or past **4 :** to make the sign of the cross upon or over (as in prayer) **5 :** to cancel by marking crosses on or by drawing a line through **6 :** to place one over the other **7 :** to act against : OPPOSE **8 :** to draw a line across **9 :** to cause (an animal or plant) to breed with one of another kind : produce hybrids **10 :** to pass going in opposite directions

³cross *adj* **1 :** lying, falling, or passing across **2 :** ²CONTRARY 1 **3 :** hard to get along with : IRRITABLE — **cross·ly** *adv* — **cross·ness** *n*

cross·bar *n* **:** a bar, piece, or stripe placed crosswise or across something

cross·bones *n pl* : two leg or arm bones placed or pictured as lying across each other

cross·bow *n* : a short bow mounted crosswise near the end of a wooden stock that shoots short arrows

cross–ex·am·ine *vb* **cross–ex·am·ined; cross–ex·am·in·ing** : to question (a person) in an effort to show that statements or answers given earlier were false — **cross–ex·am·in·er** *n*

cross–eyed *adj* : having one or both eyes turned toward the nose

cross·ing *n* **1** : a point where two lines, tracks, or streets cross each other **2** : a place provided for going across a street, railroad tracks, or a stream **3** : a voyage across a body of water

cross·piece *n* : something placed so as to cross something else

cross–ref·er·ence *n* : a reference made from one place to another (as in a dictionary)

cross·roads *n sing or pl* : a place where roads cross

cross section *n* **1** : a cutting made across something (as a log or an apple) **2** : a representation of a cross section **3** : a number of persons or things selected from a group to stand for the whole

cross·walk *n* : a specially paved or marked path for people walking across a street or road

cross·wise *adv* : so as to cross something : ACROSS

cross·word puzzle *n* : a puzzle in which words are filled into a pattern of numbered squares in answer to clues so that they read across and down

crotch *n* : an angle formed by the spreading apart of two legs or branches or of a limb from its trunk

[1]**crouch** *vb* : to stoop or bend low with the arms and legs close to the body

[2]**crouch** *n* : the position of crouching

croup *n* : a children's disease in which a hoarse cough and hard breathing are present

[1]**crow** *n* : a glossy black bird that has a harsh cry

[2]**crow** *vb* **1** : to make the loud shrill sound that a rooster makes **2** : to make sounds of delight **3** : [2]BOAST 1

[3]**crow** *n* **1** : the cry of a rooster **2** : a cry of triumph

crow·bar *n* : a metal bar used as a lever (as for prying things apart)

[1]**crowd** *vb* **1** : to press or push forward **2** : to press close **3** : to collect in numbers : THRONG **4** : to fill or pack by pressing together

[2]**crowd** *n* **1** : a large number of persons collected together : THRONG **2** : the population as a whole : ordinary people **3** : a group of people having a common interest

[1]**crown** *n* **1** : a wreath or band especially as a mark of victory or honor **2** : a royal headdress **3** : the highest part (as of a tree or mountain) **4** : the top of the head **5** : the top part of a hat **6** : the part of a tooth outside of the gum **7** : something suggesting a crown **8** *cap* : royal power or authority or one having such power **9** : any of various coins (as a British coin worth five shillings) — **crowned** *adj*

[2]**crown** *vb* **1** : to place a crown on : make sovereign **2** : to declare officially to be **3** : to give something as a mark of honor or reward **4** : [2]TOP 2 **5** : to bring to a successful conclusion : COMPLETE, PERFECT **6** : to put an artificial crown on a damaged tooth **7** : to hit on the head

crow's nest *n* : a partly enclosed place to stand high on the mast of a ship for use as a lookout

cru·cial *adj* **1** : being a final or very important test or decision : DECISIVE **2** : very important : SIGNIFICANT

cru·ci·ble *n* : a pot made of a substance not easily damaged by fire that is used for holding something to be treated under great heat

cru·ci·fix *n* : a cross with a figure of Christ crucified on it

cru·ci·fix·ion *n* **1** : an act of crucifying **2** *cap* : the crucifying of Christ on the cross

cru·ci·fy *vb* **cru·ci·fied; cru·ci·fy·ing** **1** : to put to death by nailing or binding the hands and feet to a cross **2** : to treat cruelly : TORTURE, PERSECUTE

crude *adj* **crud·er; crud·est** **1** : in a natural state and not changed by special treatment : RAW **2** : not having or showing good manners : VULGAR **3** : planned or done in a rough or unskilled way — **crude·ly** *adv* — **crude·ness** *n*

cru·el *adj* **cru·el·er** *or* **cru·el·ler; cru·el·est** *or* **cru·el·lest** **1** : ready to hurt others **2** : causing or helping to cause suffering — **cru·el·ly** *adv*

cru·el·ty *n, pl* **cru·el·ties** **1** : the quality or state of being cruel **2** : cruel treatment

cru·et *n* : a bottle for holding vinegar, oil, or sauce for table use

[1]**cruise** *vb* **cruised; cruis·ing** **1** : to travel by ship often stopping at a series of ports **2** : to travel for pleasure **3** : to travel at the best operating speed

[2]**cruise** *n* : an act or instance of cruising

cruis·er *n* **1** : a warship that is smaller than a battleship **2** : a police car used for patrolling streets and equipped with radio for communicating with headquarters **3** : a motorboat equipped for living aboard

crul·ler *n* : a small sweet cake made of egg batter usually cut in strips or twists and fried in deep fat

[1]**crumb** *n* **1** : a small piece especially of bread **2** : a little bit

[2]**crumb** *vb* : to break into crumbs : CRUMBLE

crum·ble *vb* **crum·bled; crum·bling** **1** : to break into small pieces **2** : to fall to pieces : fall into ruin

crum·bly *adj* **crum·bli·er; crum·bli·est** : easily crumbled

crum·ple *vb* **crum·pled; crum·pling** **1** : to press or crush out of shape : RUMPLE **2** : to become crumpled **3** : [1]COLLAPSE 1

[1]**crunch** *vb* **1** : to chew or grind with a crushing noise **2** : to make the sound of being crushed or squeezed

[2]**crunch** *n* : an act or sound of crunching

[1]**cru·sade** *n* **1** *cap* : one of the military expeditions made by Christian countries in the eleventh, twelfth, and thirteenth centuries to recover the Holy Land from the Muslims **2** : a campaign to get things changed for the better

[2]**crusade** *vb* **cru·sad·ed; cru·sad·ing** : to take part in a crusade

cru·sad·er *n* : a person who takes part in a crusade

[1]**crush** *vb* **1** : to squeeze together so as to change or destroy the natural shape or condition **2** : [1]HUG 1 **3** : to break into fine pieces by pressure **4** : OVERWHELM 2 **5** : OPPRESS 1

[2]**crush** *n* **1** : an act of crushing **2** : a tightly packed crowd **3** : a foolish or very strong liking : INFATUATION

crust *n* **1** : the hardened outside surface of bread **2** : a hard dry piece of bread **3** : the pastry cover of a pie **4** : a hard outer covering or surface layer **5** : the outer part of the earth

crus·ta·cean *n* : any of a large group of mostly water animals (as crabs, lobsters, and shrimps) with a body made of segments, a firm outer shell, two pairs of antennae, and limbs that are jointed

crusty *adj* **crust·i·er; crust·i·est** **1** : having or being a crust **2** : [3]CROSS 3

crutch *n* **1** : a support usually made with a piece at the top to fit under the armpit that is used by a lame person as an aid in walking **2** : something (as a prop or support) like a crutch in shape or use

[1]**cry** *vb* **cried; cry·ing** **1** : to make a loud call or cry : SHOUT, EXCLAIM **2** : to shed tears : WEEP **3** : to utter a special sound or call **4** : to make known to the public : call out

[2]**cry** *n, pl* **cries** **1** : a loud call or shout (as of pain, fear, or joy) **2** : [1]APPEAL 2 **3** : a fit of weeping **4** : the special sound made by an animal

cry·ba·by *n, pl* **cry·ba·bies** : a person who cries easily or who complains often

[1]**crys·tal** *n* **1** : quartz that is colorless and transparent or nearly so **2** : something transparent like crystal **3** : a body formed by a substance hardening so that it has flat surfaces in an even arrangement **4** : a clear colorless glass of very good quality **5** : the transparent cover over a clock or watch dial

[2]**crystal** *adj* : made of or being like crystal : CLEAR

crys·tal·line *adj* **1** : made of crystal or composed of crystals **2** : like crystal : TRANSPARENT

crys·tal·lize *vb* **crys·tal·lized; crys·tal·liz·ing** **1** : to form or cause to form crystals or grains **2** : to take or cause to take definite form

cub *n* **1** : the young of various animals (as the bear, fox, or lion) **2** : CUB SCOUT

cub·by·hole *n* : a snug place (as for storing things)

[1]**cube** *n* **1** : a solid body having six equal square sides **2** : the product obtained by multiplying the square of a number by the number itself

[2]**cube** *vb* **cubed; cub·ing** **1** : to take (a number) as a factor three times **2** : to form into a cube or divide into cubes

cu·bic *adj* : being the volume of a cube whose edge is a specified unit

cu·bi·cal *adj* **1** : having the form of a cube **2** : relating to volume

cu·bit *n* : a unit of length usually equal to about forty-six centimeters

Cub Scout *n* : a member of a program of the Boy Scouts for boys in the first through fifth grades in school

cuck·oo *n, pl* **cuckoos** **1** : any of several related birds (as a grayish brown European bird) that mostly lay their eggs in the nests of other birds for them to hatch **2** : the call of the European cuckoo

cu·cum·ber *n* : a long usually green-skinned vegetable that is used in salads and as pickles and is the fruit of a vine related to the melons and gourds

cud *n* : a portion of food brought up from the first stomach of some animals (as the cow and sheep) to be chewed again

cud·dle *vb* **cud·dled; cud·dling** **1** : to hold close for warmth or comfort or in affection **2** : to lie close : NESTLE, SNUGGLE

[1]**cud·gel** *n* : a short heavy club

[2]**cudgel** *vb* **cud·geled** *or* **cud·gelled; cud·gel·ing** *or* **cud·gel·ling** : to beat with or as if with a cudgel

[1]**cue** *n* **1** : a word, phrase, or action in a play

serving as a signal for the next actor to speak or to do something **2 :** something serving as a signal or suggestion **:** HINT

²cue *n* **:** a straight tapering stick used in playing billiards and pool

¹cuff *n* **1 :** a band or turned-over piece at the end of a sleeve **2 :** the turned-back hem of a trouser leg

²cuff *vb* **:** to strike especially with or as if with the palm of the hand **:** SLAP

³cuff *n* **:** ²SLAP 1

¹cull *vb* **1 :** to select from a group **2 :** to identify and remove the culls from

²cull *n* **:** something rejected from a group or lot as not as good as the rest

cul·mi·nate *vb* **cul·mi·nat·ed; cul·mi·nat·ing :** to reach the highest point

cul·pa·ble *adj* **:** deserving blame

cul·prit *n* **1 :** one accused of or charged with a crime or fault **2 :** one guilty of a crime or fault

cul·ti·vate *vb* **cul·ti·vat·ed; cul·ti·vat·ing 1 :** to prepare land for the raising of crops **2 :** to raise or assist the growth of crops by tilling or by labor and care **3 :** to improve or develop by careful attention, training, or study **:** devote time and thought to **4 :** to seek the company and friendship of

cul·ti·vat·ed *adj* **1 :** raised or produced under cultivation **2 :** having or showing good education and proper manners

cul·ti·va·tion *n* **1 :** the act or process of cultivating especially the soil **2 :** REFINEMENT 2

cul·ti·va·tor *n* **1 :** one (as a farmer) that cultivates something **2 :** a tool or machine for loosening the soil between rows of a crop

cul·tur·al *adj* **:** of or relating to culture — **cul·tur·al·ly** *adv*

cul·ture *n* **1 :** CULTIVATION 1 **2 :** the raising or development (as of a crop or product) by careful attention **3 :** the improvement of the mind, tastes, and manners through careful training **4 :** a certain stage, form, or kind of civilization

cul·tured *adj* **1 :** having or showing refinement in taste, speech, or manners **2 :** produced under artificial conditions

cul·vert *n* **:** a drain or waterway crossing under a road or railroad

cum·ber·some *adj* **:** hard to handle or manage because of size or weight

cu·mu·la·tive *adj* **:** increasing (as in force, strength, or amount) by one addition after another

cu·mu·lus *n, pl* **cu·mu·li :** a massive cloud form having a flat base and rounded outlines often piled up like a mountain

¹cu·ne·i·form *adj* **1 :** shaped like a wedge **2 :** made up of or written with marks or letters shaped like wedges

²cuneiform *n* **:** cuneiform writing

¹cun·ning *adj* **1 :** skillful and clever at using special knowledge or at getting something done **2 :** showing craftiness and trickery **3 :** CUTE, PRETTY

²cunning *n* **1 :** SKILL 1, DEXTERITY **2 :** cleverness in getting what one wants often by tricks or deceiving

¹cup *n* **1 :** something to drink out of in the shape of a small bowl usually with a handle **2 :** the contents of a cup **:** CUPFUL **3 :** a trophy in the shape of a cup with two handles **4 :** something like a cup in shape or use

²cup *vb* **cupped; cup·ping :** to curve into the shape of a cup

cup·board *n* **:** a closet usually with shelves for dishes or food

cup·cake *n* **:** a small cake baked in a mold shaped like a cup

cup·ful *n, pl* **cup·fuls** *or* **cups·ful 1 :** the amount held by a cup **2 :** a half pint **:** eight ounces (about 236 milliliters)

cu·pid *n* **:** a picture or statue of Cupid the Roman god of love often as a winged child with a bow and arrow

cu·pid·i·ty *n* **:** excessive desire for wealth **:** GREED

cu·po·la *n* **1 :** a rounded roof or ceiling **:** DOME **2 :** a small structure built on top of a roof

cur *n* **:** a worthless or mongrel dog

cur·able *adj* **:** possible to cure

cu·rate *n* **:** a member of the clergy who assists the rector or vicar of a church

¹curb *n* **1 :** a chain or strap on a horse's bit used to control the horse by pressing against the lower jaw **2 :** ¹CHECK 2 **3 :** an enclosing border (as of stone or concrete) often along the edge of a street

²curb *vb* **:** to control by or furnish with a curb

curb·ing *n* **1 :** material for making a curb **2 :** ¹CURB 3

curd *n* **:** the thickened or solid part of sour or partly digested milk

cur·dle *vb* **cur·dled; cur·dling :** to change into curd **:** COAGULATE

¹cure *n* **1 :** a method or period of medical treatment **2 :** recovery or relief from a disease **3 :** ¹REMEDY 1

²cure *vb* **cured; cur·ing 1 :** to make or become healthy or sound again **2 :** to prepare by a chemical or physical process for use or storage **3 :** to undergo a curing process

cur·few *n* **1 :** a rule requiring certain or all people to be off the streets or at home at a stated time **2 :** a signal (as the ringing of a bell) formerly given to announce the beginning of a curfew **3 :** the time when a curfew is sounded

cu·rio *n, pl* **cu·ri·os :** a rare or unusual article **:** CURIOSITY

cu·ri·os·i·ty *n, pl* **cu·ri·os·i·ties 1 :** an eager desire to learn and often to learn what does not concern one **2 :** something strange or unusual **3 :** an object or article valued because it is strange or rare

cu·ri·ous *adj* **1 :** eager to learn **:** INQUISITIVE **2 :** attracting attention by being strange or unusual **:** ODD — **cu·ri·ous·ly** *adv*

[1]**curl** *vb* **1 :** to twist or form into ringlets **2 :** to take or move in a curved form

[2]**curl** *n* **1 :** a lock of hair that coils **:** RINGLET **2 :** something having a spiral or winding form **:** COIL **3 :** the action of curling **:** the state of being curled

curly *adj* **curl·i·er; curl·i·est 1 :** tending to curl **2 :** having curls

cur·rant *n* **1 :** a small seedless raisin used in baking and cooking **2 :** a sour red or white edible berry produced by a low spreading shrub related to the gooseberry

cur·ren·cy *n, pl* **cur·ren·cies 1 :** common use or acceptance **2 :** money in circulation

[1]**cur·rent** *adj* **1 :** now passing **2 :** occurring in or belonging to the present time **3 :** generally and widely accepted, used, or practiced

[2]**current** *n* **1 :** a body of fluid moving in a specified direction **2 :** the swiftest part of a stream **3 :** the general course **:** TREND **4 :** a flow of charges of electricity

cur·ric·u·lum *n, pl* **cur·ric·u·la** *or* **cur·ric·u·lums :** all the courses of study offered by a school

cur·ry *vb* **cur·ried; cur·ry·ing :** to rub and clean the coat of

[1]**curse** *n* **1 :** a calling for harm or injury to come to someone **2 :** a word or an expression used in cursing or swearing **3 :** evil or misfortune that comes as if in answer to a curse **4 :** a cause of great harm or evil

[2]**curse** *vb* **cursed; curs·ing 1 :** to call upon divine power to send harm or evil upon **2 :** SWEAR 5 **3 :** to bring unhappiness or evil upon **:** AFFLICT

cur·sor *n* **:** a symbol (as an arrow or blinking line) on a computer screen that shows where the user is working

curt *adj* **:** rudely brief in language

cur·tail *vb* **:** to shorten or reduce by cutting off the end or a part of

[1]**cur·tain** *n* **1 :** a piece of material (as cloth) hung up to darken, hide, divide, or decorate **2 :** something that covers, hides, or separates like a curtain

[2]**curtain** *vb* **1 :** to furnish with curtains **2 :** to hide or shut off with a curtain

[1]**curt·sy** *or* **curt·sey** *vb* **curt·sied** *or* **curt·seyed; curt·sy·ing** *or* **curt·sey·ing :** to lower the body slightly by bending the knees as an act of politeness or respect

[2]**curtsy** *or* **curtsey** *n, pl* **curtsies** *or* **curtseys :** an act of politeness or respect made mainly by women and consisting of a slight lowering of the body by bending the knees

cur·va·ture *n* **1 :** a curving or bending **2 :** the state of being curved

[1]**curve** *vb* **curved; curv·ing 1 :** to turn or change from a straight line or course **2 :** to cause to curve

[2]**curve** *n* **1 :** a bending or turning without angles **:** BEND **2 :** something curved **3 :** a ball thrown so that it moves away from a straight course

[1]**cush·ion** *n* **1 :** a soft pillow or pad to rest on or against **2 :** something like a cushion in use, shape, or softness **3 :** something that serves to soften or lessen the effects of something bad or unpleasant

[2]**cushion** *vb* **1 :** to place on or as if on a cushion **2 :** to furnish with a cushion **3 :** to soften or lessen the force or shock of

cusp *n* **:** a point or pointed end (as on the crown of a tooth)

cus·pid *n* **:** [1]CANINE 1

cuss *vb* **:** SWEAR 5

cus·tard *n* **:** a sweetened mixture of milk and eggs baked, boiled, or frozen

cus·to·di·an *n* **:** one that guards and protects or takes care of

cus·to·dy *n* **1 :** direct responsibility for care and control **2 :** the state of being arrested or held by police

[1]**cus·tom** *n* **1 :** the usual way of doing things **:** the usual practice **2 customs** *pl* **:** duties or taxes paid on imports or exports **3 :** support given to a business by its customers

[2]**custom** *adj* **1 :** made or done to personal order **2 :** specializing in custom work

cus·tom·ary *adj* **1 :** based on or existing by custom **2 :** commonly done or observed

cus·tom·er *n* **:** a person who buys from or uses the services of a company especially regularly

[1]**cut** *vb* **cut; cut·ting 1 :** to penetrate or divide with or as if with an edged tool **:** CLEAVE **2 :** to undergo shaping or penetrating with an edged tool **3 :** to experience the growth of through the gum **4 :** to hurt someone's feelings **5 :** to strike sharply or at an angle **6 :** to make less **7 :** [2]CROSS 2, INTERSECT **8 :** to shape by carving or grinding **9 :** [1]SWERVE **10 :** to go by a short or direct path or course **11 :** to divide into two parts **12 :** to stop or cause to stop **13 :** [1]SNUB

[2]**cut** *n* **1 :** something cut or cut off **2 :** [1]SHARE 1 **3 :** something (as a gash or wound) produced by or as if by cutting **4 :** a passage made by digging or cutting **5 :** a pictorial il-

lustration (as in a book) **6 :** something done or said that hurts the feelings **7 :** a straight path or course **8 :** a cutting stroke or blow **9 :** the way in which a thing is cut, formed, or made **10 :** REDUCTION 1

cute *adj* **cut·er; cut·est 1 :** KEEN 4, SHREWD **2 :** attractive especially in looks or actions

cu·ti·cle *n* **1 :** an outer layer (as of skin or a leaf) often produced by the cells beneath **2 :** a dead or horny layer of skin especially around a fingernail

cut·lass *n* **:** a short heavy curved sword

cut·lery *n* **1 :** cutting tools (as knives and scissors) **2 :** utensils used in cutting, serving, and eating food

cut·let *n* **1 :** a small slice of meat cut for broiling or frying **2 :** a piece of food shaped like a cutlet

cut·out *n* **:** something cut out or intended to be cut out from something else

cut out *vb* **:** to form by cutting

cut·ter *n* **1 :** someone or something that cuts **2 :** a boat used by warships for carrying passengers and stores to and from the shore **3 :** a small sailing boat with one mast **4 :** a small armed boat used by the Coast Guard

cut·ting *n* **:** a part (as a shoot) of a plant able to grow into a whole new plant

cut·tle·fish *n* **:** a sea animal with ten arms that is related to the squid and octopus

cut·up *n* **:** a person who clowns or acts in a noisy manner

cut·worm *n* **:** a moth caterpillar that has a smooth body and feeds on the stems of plants at night

-cy *n suffix, pl* **-cies 1 :** action **:** practice **2 :** rank **:** office **3 :** body **:** class **4 :** state **:** quality

cy·a·nide *n* **:** any of several compounds containing carbon and nitrogen and including two very poisonous substances

cyber- *combining form* **:** relating to computers or computer networks

cy·ber·space *n* **:** the on-line world of computer networks

cy·cad *n* **:** a tropical tree like a palm but related to the conifers

[1]**cy·cle** *n* **1 :** a period of time taken up by a series of events or actions that repeat themselves again and again in the same order **2 :** a complete round or series **3 :** a long period of time **:** AGE **4 :** BICYCLE **5 :** TRICYCLE **6 :** MOTORCYCLE

[2]**cycle** *vb* **cy·cled; cy·cling :** to ride a cycle

cy·clist *n* **:** a person who rides a cycle and especially a bicycle

cy·clone *n* **1 :** a storm or system of winds that rotates about a center of low atmospheric pressure in a counterclockwise direction north of the equator and that moves forward at a speed of thirty to fifty kilometers per hour and often brings heavy rain **2 :** TORNADO

cyl·in·der *n* **:** a long round body whether hollow or solid

cy·lin·dri·cal *adj* **:** having the shape of a cylinder

cym·bal *n* **:** a brass plate that is struck with a drumstick or is used in pairs struck together to make a clashing sound

cy·press *n* **:** any of various evergreen trees and shrubs that are related to the pines and have overlapping leaves resembling scales

cyst *n* **1 :** an abnormal sac in a living body **2 :** a covering like a cyst or a body (as a spore) with such a covering

cy·to·plasm *n* **:** the protoplasm of a cell except for the nucleus

czar *n* **:** the ruler of Russia until the 1917 revolution

cza·ri·na *n* **1 :** the wife of a czar **2 :** a woman who has the rank of czar

D

d *n, pl* **d's** *or* **ds** *often cap* **1 :** the fourth letter of the English alphabet **2 :** 500 in Roman numerals **3 :** a grade that shows a student's work is poor

[1]**dab** *n* **1 :** a sudden poke **2 :** a small amount **3 :** a light quick touch

[2]**dab** *vb* **dabbed; dab·bing 1 :** to strike or touch lightly **2 :** to apply with light or uneven strokes — **dab·ber** *n*

dab·ble *vb* **dab·bled; dab·bling 1 :** to wet by splashing **:** SPATTER **2 :** to paddle in or as if in water **3 :** to work without real interest or effort — **dab·bler** *n*

dace *n, pl* **dace :** any of several small fishes related to the carps

dachs·hund *n* **:** a small hound with a long body, very short legs, and long drooping ears

dad *n* **:** [1]FATHER 1

dad·dy *n, pl* **daddies :** [1]FATHER 1

dad·dy long·legs *n, pl* **daddy longlegs 1 :** an insect like a spider but with a small rounded body and long slender legs **2 :** a slender two-winged fly with long legs

daf·fo·dil *n* **:** a plant that grows from a bulb and has long slender leaves and yellow, white, or pinkish flowers suggesting trumpets and having a scalloped edge and leaflike parts at the base

daft *adj* **:** FOOLISH, CRAZY — **daft·ly** *adv* — **daft·ness** *n*

dag·ger *n* : a short knife used for stabbing

dahl·ia *n* : a tall plant related to the daisies and widely grown for its bright flowers

[1]**dai·ly** *adj* **1 :** occurring, done, produced, or issued every day or every weekday **2 :** given or paid for one day

[2]**daily** *adv* : every day

[3]**daily** *n, pl* **dai·lies :** a newspaper published every weekday

[1]**dain·ty** *n, pl* **dain·ties :** DELICACY 1

[2]**dainty** *adj* **dain·ti·er; dain·ti·est 1 :** tasting good **2 :** pretty in a delicate way **3 :** having or showing delicate taste — **dain·ti·ly** *adv* — **dain·ti·ness** *n*

dairy *n, pl* **dair·ies 1 :** a place where milk is stored or is made into butter and cheese **2 :** a farm that produces milk **3 :** a company or a store that sells milk products

dairy·ing *n* : the business of producing milk or milk products

dairy·maid *n* : a woman or girl who works in a dairy

dairy·man *n, pl* **dairy·men :** a man who operates a dairy farm or works in a dairy

da·is *n* : a raised platform (as in a hall or large room)

dai·sy *n, pl* **daisies :** any of a large group of plants with flower heads consisting of one or more rows of white or colored flowers like petals around a central disk of tiny often yellow flowers closely packed together

dale *n* : VALLEY

dal·ly *vb* **dal·lied; dal·ly·ing 1 :** to act playfully **2 :** to waste time **3 :** LINGER, DAWDLE

dal·ma·tian *n, often cap* : a large dog having a short white coat with black or brown spots

[1]**dam** *n* : a female parent — used especially of a domestic animal

[2]**dam** *n* : a barrier (as across a stream) to hold back a flow of water

[3]**dam** *vb* **dammed; dam·ming :** to hold back or block with or as if with a dam

[1]**dam·age** *n* **1 :** loss or harm due to injury **2 damages** *pl* : money demanded or paid according to law for injury or damage

[2]**damage** *vb* **dam·aged; dam·ag·ing :** to cause damage to

dam·ask *n* : a fancy cloth used especially for household linen

dame *n* : a woman of high rank or social position

[1]**damn** *vb* **1 :** to condemn to everlasting punishment especially in hell **2 :** to declare to be bad or a failure **3 :** to swear at : CURSE

[2]**damn** *n* : the word *damn* used as a curse

dam·na·ble *adj* : very bad : OUTRAGEOUS — **dam·na·bly** *adv*

[1]**damned** *adj* **damned·er; damned·est 1 :** DAMNABLE **2 :** REMARKABLE

[2]**damned** *adv* : to a high degree : VERY

[1]**damp** *n* **1 :** a harmful gas found especially in coal mines **2 :** MOISTURE

[2]**damp** *vb* : DAMPEN

[3]**damp** *adj* : slightly wet : MOIST — **damp·ly** *adv* — **damp·ness** *n*

damp·en *vb* **1 :** to make dull or less active **2 :** to make or become damp — **damp·en·er** *n*

damp·er *n* **1 :** something that checks, discourages, or deadens **2 :** a valve or movable plate for controlling a flow of air

dam·sel *n* : GIRL 1, MAIDEN

[1]**dance** *vb* **danced; danc·ing 1 :** to glide, step, or move through a series of movements usually in time to music **2 :** to move about or up and down quickly and lightly **3 :** to perform or take part in as a dancer — **danc·er** *n*

[2]**dance** *n* **1 :** an act of dancing **2 :** a social gathering for dancing **3 :** a set of movements or steps for dancing usually in time to special music **4 :** the art of dancing

dan·de·li·on *n* : a weedy plant related to the daisies that has a ring of long deeply toothed leaves often eaten as cooked greens or in salad and bright yellow flowers with hollow stems

dan·druff *n* : thin dry whitish flakes that form on the scalp and come off freely

[1]**dan·dy** *n, pl* **dandies 1 :** a man who pays a great deal of attention to his clothes **2 :** an excellent or unusual example

[2]**dandy** *adj* **dan·di·er; dan·di·est :** very good

Dane *n* : a person born or living in Denmark

dan·ger *n* **1 :** the state of not being protected from harm or evil : PERIL **2 :** something that may cause injury or harm

dan·ger·ous *adj* **1 :** full of danger **2 :** able or likely to injure — **dan·ger·ous·ly** *adv*

dan·gle *vb* **dan·gled; dan·gling 1 :** to hang loosely especially with a swinging or jerking motion **2 :** to depend on something else **3 :** to cause to dangle

[1]**Dan·ish** *adj* : of or relating to Denmark, the Danes, or Danish

[2]**Danish** *n* **1 :** the language of the Danes **2 :** a piece of Danish pastry

Danish pastry *n* : a pastry made of rich raised dough

dank *adj* : unpleasantly wet or moist — **dank·ly** *adv* — **dank·ness** *n*

dap·per *adj* : neat and trim in dress or appearance

dap·ple *vb* **dap·pled; dap·pling :** to mark or become marked with rounded spots of color

[1]**dare** *vb* **dared; dar·ing 1 :** to have courage enough for some purpose : be bold enough — sometimes used as a helping verb **2 :** to challenge to do something especially as a proof of courage

²dare *n* : a demand that one do something difficult or dangerous as proof of courage

dare·dev·il *n* : a person so bold as to be reckless

¹dar·ing *adj* : ready to take risks : BOLD, VENTURESOME — **dar·ing·ly** *adv*

²daring *n* : bold fearlessness : readiness to take chances

¹dark *adj* **1** : being without light or without much light **2** : not light in color **3** : not bright and cheerful : GLOOMY **4** : being without knowledge and culture — **dark·ish** *adj* — **dark·ly** *adv* — **dark·ness** *n*

²dark *n* **1** : absence of light **2** : a place or time of little or no light

dark·en *vb* **1** : to make or grow dark or darker **2** : to make or become gloomy — **dark·en·er** *n*

dark·room *n* : a usually small lightproof room used in developing photographic plates and film

¹dar·ling *n* **1** : a dearly loved person **2** : ¹FAVORITE

²darling *adj* **1** : dearly loved **2** : very pleasing : CHARMING

¹darn *vb* : to mend by interlacing threads

²darn *n* : a place that has been darned

³darn *n* : ²DAMN

darning needle *n* : DRAGONFLY

¹dart *n* **1** : a small pointed object that is meant to be thrown **2 darts** *pl* : a game in which darts are thrown at a target **3** : a quick sudden movement **4** : a stitched fold in a garment

²dart *vb* : to move or shoot out suddenly and quickly

¹dash *vb* **1** : to knock, hurl, or shove violently **2** : ²SMASH 1 **3** : ¹SPLASH 2 **4** : DESTROY 1 **5** : to complete or do hastily **6** : to move with sudden speed

²dash *n* **1** : a sudden burst or splash **2** : a punctuation mark — that is used most often to show a break in the thought or structure of a sentence **3** : a small amount : TOUCH **4** : liveliness in style and action **5** : a sudden rush or attempt **6** : a short fast race **7** : a long click or buzz forming a letter or part of a letter (as in telegraphy) **8** : DASHBOARD

dash·board *n* : a panel across an automobile or aircraft below the windshield usually containing dials and controls

dash·ing *adj* : having clothes or manners that are very fancy and stylish

das·tard *n* : a mean and sneaky coward

das·tard·ly *adj* : of or like a dastard — **dastard·li·ness** *n*

da·ta *n sing or pl* **1** : facts about something that can be used in calculating, reasoning, or planning **2** : DATUM

da·ta·base *n* : a collection of data that is organized especially to be used by a computer

¹date *n* : the sweet brownish fruit of an Old World palm (**date palm**)

²date *n* **1** : the day, month, or year of a happening **2** : a statement of time on something (as a coin, letter, book, or building) **3** : APPOINTMENT 3 **4** : a person with whom one has a social engagement

³date *vb* **dat·ed; dat·ing** **1** : to find or show the date of **2** : to write the date on **3** : to make or have a date with **4** : to belong to or have survived from a time **5** : to show to be old-fashioned or belonging to a past time

da·tum *n, pl* **da·ta** *or* **datums** : a single piece of information : FACT

¹daub *vb* **1** : to cover with something soft and sticky **2** : to paint or color carelessly or badly — **daub·er** *n*

²daub *n* : something daubed on : SMEAR

daugh·ter *n* **1** : a female child or offspring **2** : a woman or girl associated with or thought of as a child of something (as a country, race, or religion) — **daugh·ter·ly** *adj*

daugh·ter–in–law *n, pl* **daugh·ters–in–law** : the wife of one's son

daunt *vb* : DISCOURAGE 1, INTIMIDATE

daunt·less *adj* : bravely determined — **daunt·less·ly** *adv* — **daunt·less·ness** *n*

dau·phin *n* : the oldest son of a king of France

dav·en·port *n* : a large sofa

da·vit *n* : one of a pair of posts fitted with ropes and pulleys and used for supporting and lowering a ship's boat

daw·dle *vb* **daw·dled; daw·dling** **1** : to spend time wastefully : DALLY **2** : to move slowly and without purpose — **daw·dler** *n*

¹dawn *vb* **1** : to begin to grow light as the sun rises **2** : to start becoming plain or clear

²dawn *n* **1** : the time when the sun comes up in the morning **2** : a first appearance : BEGINNING

day *n* **1** : the time between sunrise and sunset : DAYLIGHT **2** : the time the earth takes to make one turn on its axis **3** : a period of twenty-four hours beginning at midnight **4** : a specified day or date **5** : a specified period : AGE **6** : the time set apart by custom or law for work

day·bed *n* : a couch with low head and foot pieces

day·break *n* : ²DAWN 1

day care *n* **1:** care for children or disabled adults that is provided during the day by a person or organization **2:** a program or organization offering day care

¹day·dream *n* : a happy or pleasant imagining about oneself or one's future

²daydream *vb* : to have a daydream — **day·dream·er** *n*

day·light *n* **1** : the light of day **2** : DAYTIME **3** : ²DAWN 1 **4** *pl* : normal mental state

daylight saving time *n* : time usually one hour ahead of standard time

day·time *n* : the period of daylight

¹daze *vb* **dazed; daz·ing** : to stun especially by a blow

²daze *n* : a dazed state

daz·zle *vb* **daz·zled; daz·zling** **1** : to confuse or be confused by too much light or by moving lights **2** : to confuse, surprise, or delight by being or doing something special and unusual — **daz·zler** *n* — **daz·zling·ly** *adv*

DDT *n* : a chemical formerly used as an insecticide but found to damage the environment

de- *prefix* **1** : do the opposite of **2** : reverse of **3** : remove or remove from a specified thing **4** : reduce **5** : get off of

dea·con *n* **1** : an official in some Christian churches ranking just below a priest **2** : a church member who has special duties

¹dead *adj* **1** : no longer living **2** : having the look of death **3** : ¹NUMB 1 **4** : very tired **5** : never having lived : INANIMATE **6** : lacking motion, activity, energy, or power to function **7** : no longer in use : OBSOLETE **8** : lacking warmth or vigor **9** : ACCURATE, PRECISE **10** : being sudden and complete **11** : ¹COMPLETE 1, TOTAL

²dead *n, pl* **dead** **1** *dead pl* : those that are dead **2** : the time of greatest quiet

³dead *adv* **1** : in a whole or complete manner **2** : suddenly and completely **3** : ²STRAIGHT

dead·en *vb* : to take away some of the force of : make less

dead end *n* : an end (as of a street) with no way out

dead heat *n* : a contest that ends in a tie

dead letter *n* : a letter that cannot be delivered by the post office or returned to the sender

dead·line *n* : a date or time by which something must be done

¹dead·lock *n* : a stopping of action because both sides in a struggle are equally strong and neither will give in

²deadlock *vb* : to bring or come to a deadlock

¹dead·ly *adj* **dead·li·er; dead·li·est** **1** : causing or capable of causing death **2** : meaning or hoping to kill or destroy **3** : very accurate **4** : causing spiritual death **5** : suggestive of death **6** : ¹EXTREME 1 — **dead·li·ness** *n*

²deadly *adv* **1** : in a way suggestive of death **2** : to an extreme degree

deaf *adj* **1** : wholly or partly unable to hear **2** : unwilling to hear or listen — **deaf·ness** *n*

deaf·en *vb* **1** : to make deaf **2** : to stun with noise

deaf–mute *n* : a person who can neither hear nor speak

¹deal *n* **1** : an indefinite amount **2** : one's turn to deal the cards in a card game

²deal *vb* **dealt; deal·ing** **1** : to give out one or a few at a time **2** : ¹GIVE 5, ADMINISTER **3** : to have to do **4** : to take action **5** : to buy and sell regularly : TRADE — **deal·er** *n*

³deal *n* **1** : an agreement to do business **2** : treatment received **3** : a secret agreement **4** : ¹BARGAIN 2

deal·ing *n* **1** : ³DEAL 1 **2** : a way of acting or doing business

dean *n* **1** : a church official in charge of a cathedral **2** : the head of a section (as a college) of a university **3** : an official in charge of students or studies in a school or college — **dean·ship** *n*

¹dear *adj* **1** : greatly loved or cared about **2** — used as form of address especially in letters **3** : high-priced **4** : deeply felt : EARNEST — **dear·ly** *adv* — **dear·ness** *n*

²dear *adv* : at a high price

³dear *n* : a loved one : DARLING

dearth *n* : SCARCITY, LACK

death *n* **1** : the end or ending of life **2** : the cause of loss of life **3** : the state of being dead **4** : DESTRUCTION 2 — **death·less** *adj* — **death·like** *adj*

death·bed *n* **1** : the bed a person dies in **2** : the last hours of life

death·blow *n* : a fatal or crushing blow or event

¹death·ly *adj* : of, relating to, or suggesting death

²deathly *adv* : in a way suggesting death

de·bar *vb* **de·barred; de·bar·ring** : to keep from having or doing something

de·base *vb* **de·based; de·bas·ing** : to make less good or valuable than before — **de·base·ment** *n*

de·bat·able *adj* : possible to question or argue about

¹de·bate *n* **1** : a discussion or argument carried on between two teams **2** : DISCUSSION

²debate *vb* **de·bat·ed; de·bat·ing** **1** : to discuss a question by giving arguments on both sides : take part in a debate **2** : to consider reasons for and against — **de·bat·er** *n*

de·bil·i·tate *vb* **de·bil·i·tat·ed; de·bil·i·tat·ing** : to make feeble : WEAKEN

de·bil·i·ty *n, pl* **de·bil·i·ties** : a weakened state especially of health

¹deb·it *vb* : to record as a debit

²debit *n* : a business record showing money paid out or owed

deb·o·nair *adj* : gaily and gracefully charming — **deb·o·nair·ly** *adv* — **deb·o·nair·ness** *n*

de·bris *n, pl* **de·bris** : the junk or pieces left from something broken down or destroyed

debt *n* **1** : [1]SIN **2** : something owed to another **3** : the condition of owing money

debt·or *n* : a person who owes a debt

de·but *n* **1** : a first public appearance **2** : the formal entrance of a young woman into society

deb·u·tante *n* : a young woman making her debut

deca- *or* **dec-** *or* **deka-** *or* **dek-** *prefix* : ten

de·cade *n* : a period of ten years

deca·gon *n* : a closed figure having ten angles and ten sides

de·cal *n* : a design made to be transferred (as to glass) from specially prepared paper

deca·logue *n, often cap* : the ten commandments of God given to Moses on Mount Sinai

de·camp *vb* : to go away suddenly and usually secretly : run away

de·cant·er *n* : an ornamental glass bottle used especially for serving wine

de·cap·i·tate *vb* **de·cap·i·tat·ed; de·cap·i·tat·ing** : to cut off the head of : BEHEAD

[1]**de·cay** *vb* : to weaken in health or soundness (as by aging or rotting)

[2]**decay** *n* **1** : the state of something that is decayed or decaying : a spoiled or rotting condition **2** : a gradual getting worse or failing **3** : a natural change of a radioactive element into another form of the same element or into a different element

[1]**de·cease** *n* : DEATH 1

[2]**decease** *vb* **de·ceased; de·ceas·ing** : [1]DIE 1

de·ce·dent *n* : a dead person

de·ceit *n* **1** : the act or practice of deceiving : DECEPTION **2** : a statement or act that misleads a person or causes him or her to believe what is false : TRICK

de·ceit·ful *adj* : full of deceit : not honest — **de·ceit·ful·ly** *adv* — **de·ceit·ful·ness** *n*

de·ceive *vb* **de·ceived; de·ceiv·ing** **1** : to cause to believe what is not true : MISLEAD **2** : to be dishonest and misleading — **de·ceiv·er** *n*

de·cel·er·ate *vb* **de·cel·er·at·ed; de·cel·er·at·ing** : to slow down

De·cem·ber *n* : the twelfth month of the year

de·cen·cy *n, pl* **de·cen·cies** **1** : a way or habit of conducting oneself that is decent : modest or proper behavior **2** : something that is right and proper

de·cent *adj* **1** : meeting an accepted standard of good taste (as in speech, dress, or behavior) **2** : being moral and good : not dirty **3** : fairly good — **de·cent·ly** *adv*

de·cep·tion *n* **1** : the act of deceiving **2** : [1]TRICK 1

de·cep·tive *adj* : tending or able to deceive — **de·cep·tive·ly** *adv*

deci- *prefix* : tenth part

deci·bel *n* : a unit for measuring the relative loudness of sounds

de·cide *vb* **de·cid·ed; de·cid·ing** **1** : to make a judgment on **2** : to bring to an end **3** : to make or cause to make a choice

de·cid·ed *adj* **1** : UNMISTAKABLE **2** : free from doubt — **de·cid·ed·ly** *adv*

de·cid·u·ous *adj* : made up of or having a part that falls off at the end of a period of growth and use

[1]**dec·i·mal** *adj* **1** : based on the number 10 : numbered or counting by tens **2** : expressed in or including a decimal

[2]**decimal** *n* : a proper fraction in which the denominator is 10 or 10 multiplied one or more times by itself and is indicated by a point (**decimal point**) placed at the left of the numerator

deci·me·ter *n* : a unit of length equal to one tenth meter

de·ci·pher *vb* **1** : to translate from secret writing : DECODE **2** : to make out the meaning of something not clear

de·ci·sion *n* **1** : the act or result of deciding **2** : promptness and firmness in deciding

de·ci·sive *adj* **1** : deciding or able to decide a question or dispute **2** : RESOLUTE **3** : [1]CLEAR 7, UNMISTAKABLE — **de·ci·sive·ly** *adv* — **de·ci·sive·ness** *n*

[1]**deck** *n* **1** : a floor that goes from one side of a ship to the other **2** : something like the deck of a ship **3** : a pack of playing cards

[2]**deck** *vb* : to dress or decorate especially in a showy way

dec·la·ra·tion *n* **1** : an act of declaring **2** : something declared or a document containing such a declaration

de·clar·a·tive *adj* : making a statement

de·clare *vb* **de·clared; de·clar·ing** **1** : to make known in a clear or formal way **2** : to state as if certain

[1]**de·cline** *vb* **de·clined; de·clin·ing** **1** : to bend or slope downward **2** : to pass toward a lower, worse, or weaker state **3** : to refuse to accept, do, or agree

[2]**decline** *n* **1** : a gradual weakening in body or mind **2** : a change to a lower state or level **3** : the time when something is nearing its end

de·code *vb* **de·cod·ed; de·cod·ing** : to change a message in code into ordinary language

de·com·pose *vb* **de·com·posed; de·com·pos·ing** **1** : to separate a thing into its parts or into simpler compounds **2** : to break down in decaying — **de·com·pos·er** *n*

de·com·po·si·tion *n* **1** : the process of decomposing **2 :** the state of being decomposed

dec·o·rate *vb* **dec·o·rat·ed; dec·o·rat·ing** **1 :** to make more attractive by adding something nice looking **2 :** to award a decoration of honor to

dec·o·ra·tion *n* **1 :** the act of decorating **2 :** [1]ORNAMENT 1 **3 :** a badge of honor

dec·o·ra·tive *adj* **:** serving to decorate **:** ORNAMENTAL

dec·o·ra·tor *n* **:** a person who decorates especially the rooms of houses

de·co·rum *n* **:** proper behavior

[1]**de·coy** *n* **:** a person or thing (as an artificial bird) used to lead or lure into a trap or snare

[2]**decoy** *vb* **:** to lure by or as if by a decoy

[1]**de·crease** *vb* **de·creased; de·creas·ing :** to grow less or cause to grow less

[2]**de·crease** *n* **1 :** the process of decreasing **2 :** REDUCTION 2

[1]**de·cree** *n* **:** an order or decision given by a person or group in authority

[2]**decree** *vb* **de·creed; de·cree·ing :** to order by a decree

de·crep·it *adj* **:** worn out or weakened by age or use

de·cre·scen·do *n* **:** a gradual decrease in the loudness of music

ded·i·cate *vb* **ded·i·cat·ed; ded·i·cat·ing** **1 :** to set apart for some purpose and especially for a sacred or serious purpose **:** DEVOTE **2 :** to address or write something in (as a book) as a compliment to someone

ded·i·ca·tion *n* **1 :** an act of dedicating **2 :** something written in dedicating a book **3 :** devotion to the point of giving up what one needs or loves

de·duct *vb* **:** to take away an amount of something **:** SUBTRACT

de·duc·tion *n* **1 :** SUBTRACTION **2 :** an amount deducted

[1]**deed** *n* **1 :** a usually fine or brave act or action **:** FEAT **2 :** a legal document containing the record of an agreement or especially of a transfer of real estate

[2]**deed** *vb* **:** to transfer by a deed

deem *vb* **:** to hold as an opinion

[1]**deep** *adj* **1 :** reaching down far below the surface **2 :** reaching far back from the front or outer part **3 :** hard to understand **4 :** located well below the surface or well within the boundaries of **5 :** fully developed **:** PROFOUND **6 :** dark and rich in color **7 :** low in tone **8 :** completely busy — **deep·ly** *adv*

[2]**deep** *adv* **:** to a great depth **:** DEEPLY

[3]**deep** *n* **1 :** a very deep place or part **2 :** OCEAN 1

deep·en *vb* **:** to make or become deep or deeper

deep fat *n* **:** hot fat or oil deep enough in a cooking utensil to cover the food to be fried

deep–fry *vb* **:** to cook in deep fat

deer *n, pl* **deer :** any of a group of mammals that chew the cud and have cloven hoofs and in the male antlers which are often branched

deer·skin *n* **:** leather made from the skin of a deer or a garment made of such leather

de·face *vb* **de·faced; de·fac·ing :** to destroy or mar the face or surface of — **de·face·ment** *n* — **de·fac·er** *n*

[1]**de·fault** *n* **:** failure to do something required by law or duty

[2]**default** *vb* **:** to fail to do one's duty — **de·fault·er** *n*

[1]**de·feat** *vb* **1 :** to bring to nothing **2 :** to win victory over

[2]**defeat** *n* **:** loss of a contest or battle

de·fect *n* **:** a lack of something necessary for completeness or perfection

de·fec·tive *adj* **:** lacking something necessary **:** FAULTY

de·fend *vb* **1 :** to protect from danger or attack **2 :** to act or speak in favor of when others are opposed — **de·fend·er** *n*

de·fense *n* **1 :** the act of defending **2 :** something that defends or protects **3 :** a defensive team — **de·fense·less** *adj*

[1]**de·fen·sive** *adj* **1 :** serving or meant to defend or protect **2 :** of or relating to the attempt to keep an opponent from scoring (as in a game) — **de·fen·sive·ly** *adv*

[2]**defensive** *n* **:** a defensive position or attitude

[1]**de·fer** *vb* **de·ferred; de·fer·ring :** to put off to a future time — **de·fer·ment** *n*

[2]**defer** *vb* **de·ferred; de·fer·ring :** to yield to the opinion or wishes of another

def·er·ence *n* **:** respect and consideration for the wishes of another

de·fi·ance *n* **1 :** an act of defying **2 :** a willingness to resist

de·fi·ant *adj* **:** showing defiance — **de·fi·ant·ly** *adv*

de·fi·cien·cy *n, pl* **de·fi·cien·cies :** the state of being without something necessary and especially something required for health

de·fi·cient *adj* **:** lacking something necessary for completeness or health

def·i·cit *n* **:** a shortage especially in money needed

de·file *vb* **de·filed; de·fil·ing** **1 :** to make filthy **2 :** [1]CORRUPT 1 **3 :** [2]DISHONOR — **de·file·ment** *n*

de·fine *vb* **de·fined; de·fin·ing** **1 :** to set or mark the limits of **2 :** to make distinct in outline **3 :** to find out and explain the meaning of — **de·fin·er** *n*

def·i·nite *adj* **1 :** having certain or distinct limits **2 :** clear in meaning **3 :** UNQUESTION-

ABLE — **def·i·nite·ly** *adv* — **def·i·nite·ness** *n*
definite article *n* : the article *the* used to show that the following noun refers to one or more specific persons or things
def·i·ni·tion *n* **1 :** an act of defining **2 :** a statement of the meaning of a word or a word group **3 :** clearness of outline or detail
de·flate *vb* **de·flat·ed; de·flat·ing 1 :** to let the air or gas out of something that has been blown up **2 :** to reduce in size or importance
de·flect *vb* : to turn aside
de·for·est *vb* : to clear of forests
de·form *vb* : to spoil the form or the natural appearance of
de·for·mi·ty *n, pl* **de·for·mi·ties 1 :** the condition of being deformed **2 :** a flaw or blemish in something and especially in the body of a person or animal
de·frag·ment *vb* : to reorganize fragments of computer data into a continuous series
de·fraud *vb* : to take or keep something from by deceit : CHEAT
de·frost *vb* **1 :** to thaw out **2 :** to remove ice from — **de·frost·er** *n*
deft *adj* : quick and neat in action : SKILLFUL — **deft·ly** *adv* — **deft·ness** *n*
de·fy *vb* **de·fied; de·fy·ing 1 :** to challenge to do something thought to be impossible : DARE **2 :** to refuse boldly to obey or yield to **3 :** to resist the effects of or attempts at
deg·ra·da·tion *n* **1 :** an act of degrading **2 :** the state of being degraded
de·grade *vb* **de·grad·ed; de·grad·ing 1 :** to reduce from a higher to a lower rank or degree **2 :** to bring to a low state : DEBASE, CORRUPT
de·gree *n* **1 :** a step in a series **2 :** amount of something as measured by a series of steps **3 :** one of the three forms an adjective or adverb may have when it is compared **4 :** a title given (as to students) by a college or university **5 :** one of the divisions marked on a measuring instrument (as a thermometer) **6 :** a 360th part of the circumference of a circle **7 :** a line or space of the staff in music or the difference in pitch between two notes
de·hu·mid·i·fy *vb* **de·hu·mid·i·fied; de·hu·mid·i·fy·ing :** to take moisture from (as the air) — **de·hu·mid·i·fi·er** *n*
de·hy·drate *vb* **de·hy·drat·ed; de·hy·drat·ing 1 :** to take water from (as foods) **2 :** to lose water or body fluids
de·ice *vb* **de·iced; de·ic·ing :** to free or keep free of ice — **de·ic·er** *n*
de·i·fy *vb* **de·i·fied; de·i·fy·ing :** to make a god of
deign *vb* : CONDESCEND 1
de·i·ty *n, pl* **de·i·ties 1** *cap* : GOD 1 **2 :** GOD 2, GODDESS
de·ject·ed *adj* : low in spirits — **de·ject·ed·ly** *adv*
de·jec·tion *n* : a dejected state
deka- *or* **dek-** — see DECA-
[1]**de·lay** *n* **1 :** a putting off of something **2 :** the time during which something is delayed
[2]**delay** *vb* **1 :** to put off **2 :** to stop or prevent for a time **3 :** to move or act slowly
[1]**del·e·gate** *n* : a person sent with power to act for another or others
[2]**del·e·gate** *vb* **del·e·gat·ed; del·e·gat·ing 1 :** to entrust to another **2 :** to make responsible for getting something done
del·e·ga·tion *n* **1 :** the act of delegating **2 :** one or more persons chosen to represent others
de·lete *vb* **de·let·ed; de·let·ing :** to take out from something written especially by erasing, crossing out, or cutting
de·le·tion *n* **1 :** an act of deleting **2 :** something deleted
[1]**de·lib·er·ate** *vb* **de·lib·er·at·ed; de·lib·er·at·ing :** to think about carefully
[2]**de·lib·er·ate** *adj* **1 :** showing careful thought **2 :** done or said on purpose **3 :** slow in action : not hurried — **de·lib·er·ate·ly** *adv* — **de·lib·er·ate·ness** *n*
de·lib·er·a·tion *n* **1 :** careful thought : CONSIDERATION **2 :** the quality of being deliberate
del·i·ca·cy *n, pl* **del·i·ca·cies 1 :** something pleasing to eat that is rare or a luxury **2 :** fineness of structure **3 :** weakness of body : FRAILTY **4 :** a situation needing careful handling **5 :** consideration for the feelings of others
del·i·cate *adj* **1 :** pleasing because of fineness or mildness **2 :** able to sense very small differences **3 :** calling for skill and careful treatment **4 :** easily damaged **5 :** SICKLY 1 **6 :** requiring tact — **del·i·cate·ly** *adv*
del·i·ca·tes·sen *n* : a store where prepared foods (as salads and meats) are sold
de·li·cious *adj* : giving great pleasure especially to the taste or smell — **de·li·cious·ly** *adv* — **de·li·cious·ness** *n*
[1]**de·light** *n* **1 :** great pleasure or satisfaction : JOY **2 :** something that gives great pleasure
[2]**delight** *vb* **1 :** to take great pleasure **2 :** to give joy or satisfaction to
de·light·ed *adj* : very pleased
de·light·ful *adj* : giving delight : very pleasing — **de·light·ful·ly** *adv*
de·lir·i·ous *adj* **1 :** suffering delirium **2 :** wildly excited — **de·lir·i·ous·ly** *adv*
de·lir·i·um *n* **1 :** a condition of mind in which thought and speech are confused and which

often goes along with a high fever **2 :** wild excitement

de·liv·er *vb* **1 :** to set free : RESCUE **2 :** [1]TRANSFER 2 **3 :** to help in childbirth **4 :** [2]UTTER 2 **5 :** to send to an intended target — **de·liv·er·er** *n*

de·liv·er·ance *n* **:** an act of delivering or the state of being delivered : a setting free

de·liv·ery *n, pl* **de·liv·er·ies 1 :** a setting free (as from something that hampers or holds one back) **2 :** the transfer of something from one place or person to another **3 :** the act of giving birth **4 :** speaking or manner of speaking (as of a formal speech) **5 :** the act or way of throwing

dell *n* **:** a small valley usually covered with trees

del·phin·i·um *n* **:** a tall plant related to the buttercups and often grown for its large stalks of showy flowers

del·ta *n* **:** a piece of land in the shape of a triangle or fan made by deposits of mud and sand at the mouth of a river

de·lude *vb* **de·lud·ed; de·lud·ing :** DECEIVE, MISLEAD

[1]del·uge *n* **1 :** a flooding of land by water : FLOOD **2 :** a drenching rain **3 :** a sudden huge stream of something

[2]deluge *vb* **del·uged; del·ug·ing 1 :** [2]FLOOD 1 **2 :** to overwhelm as if with a deluge

de·lu·sion *n* **1 :** an act of deluding or the state of being deluded **2 :** a false belief that continues in spite of the facts

de·luxe *adj* **:** very fine or luxurious

delve *vb* **delved; delv·ing 1 :** DIG **2 :** to work hard looking for information in written records — **delv·er** *n*

[1]de·mand *n* **1 :** an act of demanding **2 :** an expressed desire to own or use something **3 :** a seeking or being sought after

[2]demand *vb* **1 :** to claim as one's right **2 :** to ask earnestly or in the manner of a command **3 :** to call for : REQUIRE — **de·mand·er** *n*

[1]de·mean *vb* **de·meaned; de·mean·ing :** to behave or conduct (oneself) usually in a proper way

[2]demean *vb* **:** to lower in character, status, or reputation

de·mean·or *n* **:** outward manner or behavior

de·ment·ed *adj* **:** INSANE 1, MAD — **de·ment·ed·ly** *adv*

de·mer·it *n* **:** a mark placed against a person's record for doing something wrong

demi- *prefix* **1 :** half **2 :** one that partly belongs to a specified type or class

demi·god *n* **:** one who is partly divine and partly human

de·mo·bi·lize *vb* **de·mo·bi·lized; de·mo·bi·liz·ing :** to let go from military service

de·moc·ra·cy *n, pl* **de·moc·ra·cies 1 :** government by the people : majority rule **2 :** government in which the highest power is held by the people and is usually used through representatives **3 :** a political unit (as a nation) governed by the people **4 :** belief in or practice of the idea that all people are socially equal

dem·o·crat *n* **:** one who believes in or practices democracy

dem·o·crat·ic *adj* **1 :** of, relating to, or favoring political democracy **2 :** believing in or practicing the idea that people are socially equal — **dem·o·crat·i·cal·ly** *adv*

de·mol·ish *vb* **1 :** to destroy by breaking apart **2 :** to ruin completely : SHATTER

de·mon *n* **1 :** an evil spirit : DEVIL **2 :** a person of great energy or skill

dem·on·strate *vb* **dem·on·strat·ed; dem·on·strat·ing 1 :** to show clearly **2 :** to prove or make clear by reasoning **3 :** to explain (as in teaching) by use of examples or experiments **4 :** to show to people the good qualities of an article or a product **5 :** to make a public display (as of feelings or military force)

dem·on·stra·tion *n* **1 :** an outward expression (as a show of feelings) **2 :** an act or a means of demonstrating **3 :** a showing or using of an article for sale to display its good points **4 :** a parade or a gathering to show public feeling

de·mon·stra·tive *adj* **1 :** pointing out the one referred to and showing that it differs from others **2 :** showing feeling freely

dem·on·stra·tor *n* **1 :** a person who makes or takes part in a demonstration **2 :** a manufactured article used for demonstration

de·mor·al·ize *vb* **de·mor·al·ized; de·mor·al·iz·ing :** to weaken the discipline or spirit of

de·mote *vb* **de·mot·ed; de·mot·ing :** to reduce to a lower grade or rank

de·mure *adj* **1 :** MODEST 3 **2 :** pretending to be modest : COY — **de·mure·ly** *adv* — **de·mure·ness** *n*

den *n* **1 :** the shelter or resting place of a wild animal **2 :** a quiet or private room in a home **3 :** a hiding place (as for thieves)

de·na·ture *vb* **de·na·tured; de·na·tur·ing :** to make alcohol unfit for humans to drink

den·drite *n* **:** any of the usually branched fibers that carry nerve impulses toward a nerve cell body

de·ni·al *n* **1 :** a refusal to give or agree to something asked for **2 :** a refusal to admit the truth of a statement **3 :** a refusal to accept or believe in someone or something **4 :** a cutting down or limiting

den·im *n* **1 :** a firm often coarse cotton cloth **2 denims** *pl* **:** overalls or pants of usually blue denim

de·nom·i·na·tion *n* **1 :** a name especially for a class of things **2 :** a religious body made up of a number of congregations having the same beliefs **3 :** a value in a series of values (as of money)

de·nom·i·na·tor *n* **:** the part of a fraction that is below the line

de·note *vb* **de·not·ed; de·not·ing 1 :** to serve as a mark or indication of **2 :** to have the meaning of **:** MEAN

de·nounce *vb* **de·nounced; de·nounc·ing 1 :** to point out as wrong or evil **:** CONDEMN **2 :** to inform against **:** ACCUSE — **de·nounce·ment** *n* — **de·nounc·er** *n*

dense *adj* **dens·er; dens·est 1 :** having its parts crowded together **:** THICK **2 :** STUPID 1 — **dense·ly** *adv* — **dense·ness** *n*

den·si·ty *n, pl* **den·si·ties 1 :** the state of being dense **2 :** the amount of something in a specified volume or area

[1]**dent** *vb* **1 :** to make a dent in or on **2 :** to become marked by a dent

[2]**dent** *n* **:** a notch or hollow made in a surface by a blow or by pressure

den·tal *adj* **:** of or relating to the teeth or dentistry — **den·tal·ly** *adv*

dental floss *n* **:** flat thread used for cleaning between teeth

den·ti·frice *n* **:** a powder, paste, or liquid used in cleaning the teeth

den·tin *or* **den·tine** *n* **:** a hard bony material that makes up the main part of a tooth

den·tist *n* **:** a person whose profession is the care, treatment, and repair of the teeth

den·tist·ry *n* **:** the profession or practice of a dentist

den·ture *n* **:** a set of false teeth

de·nude *vb* **de·nud·ed; de·nud·ing :** to strip of covering **:** make bare

de·ny *vb* **de·nied; de·ny·ing 1 :** to declare not to be true **2 :** to refuse to grant **3 :** DISOWN, REPUDIATE

de·odor·ant *n* **:** something used to remove or hide unpleasant odors

de·odor·ize *vb* **de·odor·ized; de·odor·iz·ing :** to remove odor and especially a bad smell from

de·part *vb* **1 :** to go away or go away from **:** LEAVE **2 :** [1]DIE 1 **3 :** to turn aside

de·part·ment *n* **:** a special part or division of an organization (as a government or college)

department store *n* **:** a store having individual departments for different kinds of goods

de·par·ture *n* **1 :** a going away **2 :** a setting out (as on a new course) **3 :** a turning away or aside (as from a way of doing things)

de·pend *vb* **1 :** to rely for support **2 :** to be determined by or based on some action or condition **3 :** [2]TRUST 1, RELY

de·pend·able *adj* **:** TRUSTWORTHY, RELIABLE — **de·pend·ably** *adv*

de·pen·dence *n* **1 :** a condition of being influenced and caused by something else **2 :** a state of being dependent on someone or something **3 :** [1]TRUST 1, RELIANCE

[1]**de·pen·dent** *adj* **1 :** CONTINGENT **2 :** relying on someone else for support **3 :** requiring something (as a drug) to feel or act normally

[2]**dependent** *n* **:** a person who depends upon another for support

de·pict *vb* **1 :** to represent by a picture **2 :** to describe in words

de·plete *vb* **de·plet·ed; de·plet·ing :** to reduce in amount by using up

de·plor·able *adj* **1 :** deserving to be deplored **:** REGRETTABLE **2 :** very bad **:** WRETCHED — **de·plor·ably** *adv*

de·plore *vb* **de·plored; de·plor·ing 1 :** to regret strongly **2 :** to consider deserving of disapproval

de·port *vb* **1 :** BEHAVE 1, CONDUCT **2 :** to force (a person who is not a citizen) to leave a country

de·port·ment *n* **:** BEHAVIOR 1

de·pose *vb* **de·posed; de·pos·ing :** to remove from a high office

[1]**de·pos·it** *vb* **1 :** to place for or as if for safekeeping **2 :** to put money in a bank **3 :** to give as a pledge that a purchase will be made or a service used **4 :** to lay down **:** PUT **5 :** to let fall or sink

[2]**deposit** *n* **1 :** the state of being deposited **2 :** money that is deposited in a bank **3 :** something given as a pledge or as part payment **4 :** something laid or thrown down **5 :** mineral matter built up in nature

de·pos·i·tor *n* **:** a person who makes a deposit especially of money in a bank

de·pot *n* **1 :** a place where military supplies are kept **2 :** STOREHOUSE 1 **3 :** a railroad or bus station

de·pre·ci·ate *vb* **de·pre·ci·at·ed; de·pre·ci·at·ing 1 :** to lower the price or value of **2 :** BELITTLE **3 :** to lose value

de·press *vb* **1 :** to press down **2 :** to lessen the activity or strength of **3 :** to lower the spirits of **:** make sad and dull

de·pres·sant *adj or n* **:** SEDATIVE

de·pres·sion *n* **1 :** an act of depressing **:** a state of being depressed **2 :** a hollow place or part **3 :** low spirits **4 :** a period of low activity in business with much unemployment

de·pri·va·tion *n* **1 :** an act or instance of depriving **2 :** the state of being deprived

de·prive *vb* **de·prived; de·priv·ing :** to take something away from or keep from having or doing something

depth *n* **1 :** a deep place in a body of water (as a sea or a lake) **2 :** measurement from top to bottom or from front to back **3 :** the innermost part of something : MIDDLE, MIDST **4 :** ABUNDANCE, COMPLETENESS **5 :** the quality of being deep

depth charge *n* **:** an explosive for use underwater especially against submarines

dep·u·tize *vb* **dep·u·tized; dep·u·tiz·ing :** to appoint as deputy

dep·u·ty *n, pl* **dep·u·ties :** a person appointed to act for or in place of another

de·rail *vb* **:** to cause to leave the rails — **de·rail·ment** *n*

de·range *vb* **de·ranged; de·rang·ing 1 :** to put out of order : DISARRANGE **2 :** to make insane — **de·range·ment** *n*

der·by *n, pl* **der·bies 1 :** a horse race for three-year-olds usually held every year **2 :** a stiff felt hat with a narrow brim and a rounded top

de·ride *vb* **de·rid·ed; de·rid·ing :** to laugh at in scorn : make fun of : RIDICULE

der·i·va·tion *n* **1 :** the formation of a word from an earlier word or root **2 :** ETYMOLOGY **3 :** ORIGIN 3, SOURCE **4 :** an act or process of deriving

[1]**de·riv·a·tive** *n* **1 :** a word formed by derivation **2 :** something derived

[2]**derivative** *adj* **:** derived from something else — **de·riv·a·tive·ly** *adv*

de·rive *vb* **de·rived; de·riv·ing 1 :** to receive or obtain from a source **2 :** to trace the derivation of **3 :** to come from a certain source

der·mal *adj* **:** of or relating to skin

der·mis *n* **:** the inner sensitive layer of the skin

de·rog·a·to·ry *adj* **:** intended to hurt the reputation of a person or thing

der·rick *n* **1 :** a machine for moving or lifting heavy weights by means of a long beam fitted with ropes and pulleys **2 :** a framework or tower over an oil well for supporting machinery

de·scend *vb* **1 :** to come or go down from a higher place or level to a lower one **2 :** to come down in sudden attack **3 :** to come down from an earlier time **4 :** to come down from a source : DERIVE **5 :** to be handed down to an heir **6 :** to sink in a social or moral scale : STOOP

de·scen·dant *n* **:** one that is descended from a particular ancestor or family

de·scent *n* **1 :** a coming or going down **2 :** one's line of ancestors **3 :** a downward slope **4 :** a sudden attack

de·scribe *vb* **de·scribed; de·scrib·ing 1 :** to write or tell about **2 :** to draw the outline of — **de·scrib·er** *n*

de·scrip·tion *n* **1 :** an account of something especially of a kind that presents a picture to a person who reads or hears it **2 :** [1]SORT 1, KIND

de·scrip·tive *adj* **:** serving to describe — **de·scrip·tive·ly** *adv*

des·e·crate *vb* **des·e·crat·ed; des·e·crat·ing :** to treat a sacred place or sacred object shamefully or with great disrespect

de·seg·re·gate *vb* **de·seg·re·gat·ed; de·seg·re·gat·ing :** to end segregation in : free of any law or practice setting apart members of a certain race

de·seg·re·ga·tion *n* **:** the act or process or an instance of desegregating

[1]**des·ert** *n* **:** a dry land with few plants and little rainfall

[2]**desert** *adj* **:** of, relating to, or being a desert

[3]**de·sert** *n* **1 :** worthiness of reward or punishment **2 :** a just reward or punishment

[4]**de·sert** *vb* **1 :** to leave usually without intending to return **2 :** to leave a person or a thing that one should stay with **3 :** to fail in time of need — **de·sert·er** *n*

de·serve *vb* **de·served; de·serv·ing :** to be worthy of : MERIT

de·served·ly *adv* **:** as one deserves

de·serv·ing *adj* **:** WORTHY

[1]**de·sign** *vb* **1 :** to think up and plan out in the mind **2 :** to set apart for or have as a special purpose : INTEND **3 :** to make a pattern or sketch of — **de·sign·er** *n*

[2]**design** *n* **1 :** [1]PLAN 2, SCHEME **2 :** a planned intention **3 :** a secret purpose : PLOT **4 :** a preliminary sketch, model, or plan **5 :** an arrangement of parts in a structure or a work of art **6 :** a decorative pattern

des·ig·nate *vb* **des·ig·nat·ed; des·ig·nat·ing 1 :** to mark or point out : INDICATE **2 :** to appoint or choose for a special purpose : NAME **3 :** to call by a name or title

des·ig·na·tion *n* **1 :** an act of designating **2 :** a name, sign, or title that identifies something

de·sign·ing *adj* **:** CRAFTY

de·sir·able *adj* **1 :** having pleasing qualities : ATTRACTIVE **2 :** worth having or seeking — **de·sir·ably** *adv*

[1]**de·sire** *vb* **de·sired; de·sir·ing 1 :** to long for : wish for in earnest **2 :** to express a wish for : REQUEST

[2]**desire** *n* **1 :** a strong wish : LONGING **2 :** a wish made known : REQUEST **3 :** something desired

de·sist *vb* **:** to stop doing something

desk *n* **:** a piece of furniture with a flat or sloping surface for use in writing or reading

desk·top *n* **1 :** the top of a desk **2 :** an area on a computer screen in which items are arranged as if they were objects on top of a desk **3 :** a computer that is used on a desk or table and is too big to be moved easily

[1]**des·o·late** *adj* **1 :** ABANDONED **2 :** having no comfort or companionship **:** LONELY **3 :** left neglected or in ruins **4 :** CHEERLESS, GLOOMY

[2]**des·o·late** *vb* **des·o·lat·ed; des·o·lat·ing :** to make or leave desolate

des·o·la·tion *n* **1 :** the state of being desolated **:** RUIN **2 :** sadness resulting from grief or loneliness

[1]**de·spair** *vb* **:** to give up or lose all hope or confidence

[2]**despair** *n* **1 :** loss of hope **:** a feeling of complete hopelessness **2 :** a cause of hopelessness

des·per·ate *adj* **1 :** being beyond or almost beyond hope **:** causing despair **2 :** reckless because of despair **:** RASH — **des·per·ate·ly** *adv* — **des·per·ate·ness** *n*

des·per·a·tion *n* **:** a state of hopeless despair leading to recklessness

de·spi·ca·ble *adj* **:** deserving to be despised — **de·spi·ca·bly** *adv*

de·spise *vb* **de·spised; de·spis·ing :** to consider as beneath one's notice or respect **:** feel scorn and dislike for

de·spite *prep* **:** in spite of

de·spoil *vb* **:** to rob of possessions or belongings **:** PLUNDER — **de·spoil·er** *n*

de·spon·den·cy *n* **:** MELANCHOLY, DEJECTION

de·spon·dent *adj* **:** feeling quite discouraged or depressed **:** being in very low spirits — **de·spon·dent·ly** *adv*

des·pot *n* **:** a ruler having absolute power and authority and especially one who rules cruelly

des·sert *n* **:** a course of sweet food, fruit, or cheese served at the end of a meal

des·ti·na·tion *n* **:** a place that one starts out for or that something is sent to

des·tine *vb* **des·tined; des·tin·ing 1 :** to decide in advance on the future condition, use, or action of **2 :** to set aside for a special purpose

des·ti·ny *n, pl* **des·ti·nies 1 :** the fate or lot to which a person or thing is destined **2 :** the course of events held to be arranged by a superhuman power

des·ti·tute *adj* **1 :** lacking something needed or desirable **2 :** very poor

de·stroy *vb* **1 :** to put an end to **:** do away with **2 :** [1]KILL 1

de·stroy·er *n* **1 :** one that destroys **2 :** a small fast warship armed with guns, depth charges, torpedoes, and sometimes missiles

de·struc·ti·ble *adj* **:** possible to destroy

de·struc·tion *n* **1 :** the act or process of destroying something **2 :** the state or fact of being destroyed **:** RUIN **3 :** something that destroys

de·struc·tive *adj* **1 :** causing destruction **2 :** not positive or helpful — **de·struc·tive·ly** *adv* — **de·struc·tive·ness** *n*

de·tach *vb* **:** to separate from something else or from others especially for a certain purpose — **de·tach·able** *adj*

de·tached *adj* **1 :** not joined or connected **:** SEPARATE **2 :** not taking sides or being influenced by others — **de·tached·ly** *adv*

de·tach·ment *n* **1 :** SEPARATION 1 **2 :** a body of troops or ships sent on special duty **3 :** a keeping apart **:** lack of interest in worldly concerns **4 :** IMPARTIALITY

[1]**de·tail** *n* **1 :** a dealing with something item by item **2 :** a small part **:** ITEM **3 :** a soldier or group of soldiers picked for special duty

[2]**detail** *vb* **1 :** to report in detail **:** give the details of **2 :** to select for some special duty

de·tailed *adj* **:** including many details

de·tain *vb* **1 :** to hold or keep in or as if in prison **2 :** to stop especially from going on **:** DELAY — **de·tain·ment** *n*

de·tect *vb* **:** to learn of the existence, presence, or fact of

de·tec·tion *n* **:** the act of detecting **:** the state or fact of being detected **:** DISCOVERY

[1]**de·tec·tive** *adj* **1 :** able to detect or used in detecting something **2 :** of or relating to detectives or their work

[2]**detective** *n* **:** a person (as a police officer) whose business is solving crimes and catching criminals or gathering information that is not easy to get

de·ten·tion *n* **1 :** the act of detaining **:** the state of being detained **:** CONFINEMENT **2 :** a forced delay

de·ter *vb* **de·terred; de·ter·ring :** to discourage or prevent from doing something

[1]**de·ter·gent** *adj* **:** able to clean **:** used in cleaning

[2]**detergent** *n* **:** a substance that is like soap in its ability to clean

de·te·ri·o·rate *vb* **de·te·ri·o·rat·ed; de·te·ri·o·rat·ing :** to make or become worse or of less value

de·ter·mi·na·tion *n* **1 :** a coming to a decision or the decision reached **2 :** a settling or making sure of the position, size, or nature of something **3 :** firm or fixed intention

de·ter·mine *vb* **de·ter·mined; de·ter·min·ing 1 :** to fix exactly and with certainty **2 :** to come to a decision **3 :** to learn or find out exactly **4 :** to be the cause of or reason for

de·ter·mined *adj* **1 :** free from doubt **2 :** not weak or uncertain **:** FIRM — **de·ter·mined·ly** *adv*

de·ter·min·er *n* **:** a word belonging to a group of noun modifiers that can occur before descriptive adjectives modifying the same noun

de·test *vb* : to dislike very much
de·test·able *adj* : causing or deserving strong dislike — **de·test·ably** *adv*
de·throne *vb* **de·throned; de·thron·ing** : to drive from a throne : DEPOSE — **de·throne·ment** *n*
[1]**de·tour** *n* : a roundabout way that temporarily replaces part of a regular route
[2]**detour** *vb* : to use or follow a detour
de·tract *vb* : to take away (as from value or importance)
det·ri·ment *n* : injury or damage or its cause : HARM
dev·as·tate *vb* **dev·as·tat·ed; dev·as·tat·ing** : to reduce to ruin : lay waste
dev·as·ta·tion *n* : the action of devastating : the state of being devastated
de·vel·op *vb* **1** : to make or become plain little by little : UNFOLD **2** : to apply chemicals to exposed photographic material (as a film) in order to bring out the picture **3** : to bring out the possibilities of : IMPROVE **4** : to make more available or usable **5** : to gain gradually **6** : to grow toward maturity — **de·vel·op·er** *n*
de·vel·oped *adj* : having many large industries and a complex economic system
de·vel·op·ment *n* **1** : the act or process of developing : a result of developing **2** : the state of being developed
de·vi·ate *vb* **de·vi·at·ed; de·vi·at·ing** : to turn aside from a course, principle, standard, or topic
de·vice *n* **1** : a scheme to deceive : TRICK **2** : a piece of equipment or mechanism for a special purpose **3** : [2]DESIRE 2, WILL
[1]**dev·il** *n* **1** *often cap* : the personal supreme spirit of evil **2** : an evil spirit : DEMON, FIEND **3** : a wicked or cruel person **4** : a reckless or dashing person **5** : a mischievous person **6** : a person to be pitied
[2]**devil** *vb* **dev·iled** *or* **dev·illed; dev·il·ing** *or* **dev·il·ling** **1** : to chop fine and season highly **2** : [1]TEASE, ANNOY
dev·il·ment *n* : reckless mischief
de·vise *vb* **de·vised; de·vis·ing** : to think up : PLAN, INVENT — **de·vis·er** *n*
de·void *adj* : entirely lacking
de·vote *vb* **de·vot·ed; de·vot·ing** **1** : to set apart for a special purpose **2** : to give up to entirely or in part
de·vot·ed *adj* **1** : completely loyal **2** : AFFECTIONATE, LOVING — **de·vot·ed·ly** *adv*
de·vo·tion *n* **1** : a religious exercise or practice (as prayers) especially for use in private worship **2** : an act of devoting : the quality of being devoted **3** : deep love or affection
de·vour *vb* **1** : to eat up greedily **2** : CONSUME 1 **3** : to take in eagerly by the senses or mind
de·vout *adj* **1** : devoted to religion **2** : warmly sincere and earnest — **de·vout·ly** *adv* — **de·vout·ness** *n*
dew *n* : moisture condensed on cool surfaces at night
dew·ber·ry *n, pl* **dew·ber·ries** : a sweet edible berry that grows on a prickly vine and is related to the blackberries
dew·lap *n* : a hanging fold of skin under the neck of some animals
dew point *n* : the temperature at which the moisture in the air begins to turn to dew
dewy *adj* **dew·i·er; dew·i·est** : moist with or as if with dew — **dew·i·ly** *adv* — **dew·i·ness** *n*
dex·ter·i·ty *n, pl* **dex·ter·i·ties** **1** : skill and ease in bodily activity **2** : mental skill or quickness
dex·ter·ous *or* **dex·trous** *adj* **1** : skillful with the hands **2** : mentally skillful and clever **3** : done with skill — **dex·ter·ous·ly** *adv* — **dex·ter·ous·ness** *n*
di·a·be·tes *n* : a disease in which too little insulin is produced and the body cannot use sugar and starch in the normal way
di·a·bet·ic *n* : a person with diabetes
di·a·crit·i·cal mark *n* : a mark used with a letter or group of letters to show a pronunciation different from that given a letter or group of letters not marked or marked in a different way
di·a·dem *n* : a band for the head worn especially by monarchs
di·ag·nose *vb* **di·ag·nosed; di·ag·nos·ing** : to recognize (as a disease) by signs and symptoms
di·ag·no·sis *n, pl* **di·ag·no·ses** : the art or act of recognizing a disease from its signs and symptoms
[1]**di·ag·o·nal** *adj* **1** : running from one corner to the opposite corner of a figure with four sides **2** : running in a slanting direction — **di·ag·o·nal·ly** *adv*
[2]**diagonal** *n* : a diagonal line, direction, or pattern
[1]**di·a·gram** *n* : a drawing, sketch, plan, or chart that makes something clearer or easier to understand
[2]**diagram** *vb* **di·a·gramed** *or* **di·a·grammed; di·a·gram·ing** *or* **di·a·gram·ming** : to put in the form of a diagram
[1]**di·al** *n* **1** : the face of a watch or clock **2** : SUNDIAL **3** : a face or series of marks on which some measurement or other number is shown usually by means of a pointer **4** : a disk usually with a knob or holes that may be turned to operate something (as a telephone)
[2]**dial** *vb* **di·aled** *or* **di·alled; di·al·ing** *or* **di·al·ling** : to use a dial to operate or select

di·a·lect *n* **1 :** a form of a language belonging to a certain region **2 :** a form of a language used by the members of a certain occupation or class

di·a·logue *or* **di·a·log** *n* **1 :** a conversation between two or more persons **2 :** conversation given in a written story or a play

di·am·e·ter *n* **1 :** a straight line that joins two points of a figure or body and passes through the center **2 :** the distance through the center of an object from one side to the other **:** THICKNESS

di·a·mond *n* **1 :** a very hard mineral that is a form of carbon, is usually nearly colorless, and is used especially in jewelry **2 :** a flat figure ♦ like one of the surfaces of certain cut diamonds **3 :** INFIELD 1

di·a·per *n* **:** a piece of absorbent material drawn up between the legs of a baby and fastened about the waist

di·a·phragm *n* **1 :** a muscular wall separating the chest from the abdomen **2 :** a thin circular plate (as in a microphone) that vibrates when sound strikes it

di·ar·rhea *n* **:** abnormally frequent and watery bowel movements

di·a·ry *n, pl* **di·a·ries 1 :** a daily record especially of personal experiences and thoughts **2 :** a book for keeping a diary

[1]**dice** *n, pl* **dice :** a small cube marked on each face with one to six spots and used usually in pairs in games

[2]**dice** *vb* **diced; dic·ing :** to cut into small cubes

dick·er *vb* **:** [2]BARGAIN, HAGGLE

[1]**dic·tate** *vb* **dic·tat·ed; dic·tat·ing 1 :** to speak or read for someone else to write down or for a machine to record **2 :** to say or state with authority **:** ORDER

[2]**dictate** *n* **:** a statement made or direction given with authority **:** COMMAND

dic·ta·tion *n* **1 :** the giving of orders often without thought of whether they are reasonable or fair **2 :** the dictating of words **3 :** something dictated or taken down from dictation

dic·ta·tor *n* **1 :** a person who rules with total authority and often in a cruel or brutal manner **2 :** a person who dictates — **dic·ta·tor·ship** *n*

dic·ta·to·ri·al *adj* **:** of, relating to, or like a dictator or a dictatorship

dic·tion *n* **1 :** choice of words especially with regard to correctness, clearness, and effectiveness **2 :** ENUNCIATION

dic·tio·nary *n, pl* **dic·tio·nar·ies 1 :** a book giving the meaning and usually the pronunciation of words listed in alphabetical order **2 :** an alphabetical reference book explaining words and phrases of a field of knowledge **3 :** a book listing words of one language in alphabetical order with definitions in another language

did *past of* DO

didn't : did not

[1]**die** *vb* **died; dy·ing 1 :** to stop living **2 :** to pass out of existence **3 :** to disappear little by little **4 :** to wish eagerly **5 :** [1]STOP 4

[2]**die** *n* **1** *pl* **dice :** [1]DICE **2** *pl* **dies :** a device for forming or cutting material by pressure

die·sel *n* **1 :** DIESEL ENGINE **2 :** a vehicle driven by a diesel engine

diesel engine *n* **:** an engine in which the mixture of air and fuel is compressed until enough heat is created to ignite the mixture

[1]**di·et** *n* **1 :** the food and drink that a person or animal usually takes **2 :** the kind and amount of food selected or allowed in certain circumstances (as ill health)

[2]**diet** *vb* **:** to eat or cause to eat less or according to certain rules — **di·et·er** *n*

[3]**diet** *adj* **:** reduced in calories

di·e·tary *adj* **:** of or relating to a diet or to rules of diet

di·e·ti·tian *or* **di·e·ti·cian** *n* **:** a person trained to apply the principles of nutrition to the planning of food and meals

dif·fer *vb* **1 :** to be not the same **:** be unlike **2 :** DISAGREE 2

dif·fer·ence *n* **1 :** what makes two or more persons or things different **2 :** a disagreement about something **3 :** REMAINDER 2

dif·fer·ent *adj* **1 :** not of the same kind **2 :** not the same — **dif·fer·ent·ly** *adv*

dif·fer·en·ti·ate *vb* **dif·fer·en·ti·at·ed; dif·fer·en·ti·at·ing 1 :** to make or become different **2 :** to recognize or state the difference between

dif·fer·en·ti·a·tion *n* **:** the process of change by which immature living structures develop to maturity

dif·fi·cult *adj* **1 :** hard to do or make **2 :** hard to deal with **3 :** hard to understand

dif·fi·cul·ty *n, pl* **dif·fi·cul·ties 1 :** the state of being difficult **2 :** great effort **3 :** OBSTACLE **4 :** a difficult situation

dif·fi·dent *adj* **1 :** lacking confidence **2 :** RESERVED 1 — **dif·fi·dent·ly** *adv*

dif·fuse *vb* **dif·fused; dif·fus·ing :** to undergo diffusion

dif·fu·sion *n* **:** the mixing of particles of liquids or gases so that they move from a region of high concentration to one of lower concentration

[1]**dig** *vb* **dug; dig·ging 1 :** to turn up, loosen, or remove the soil **2 :** to form by removing earth **3 :** to uncover or search by or as if by turning up earth **4 :** DISCOVER, UNCOVER **5 :** [1]PROD 1, POKE **6 :** to work hard — **dig·ger** *n*

²dig *n* **1 :** ²POKE, THRUST **2 :** a nasty remark
¹di·gest *n* **:** information in shortened form
²di·gest *vb* **1 :** to think over and get straight in the mind **2 :** to change (food) into simpler forms that can be taken in and used by the body **3 :** to become digested
di·gest·ible *adj* **:** possible to digest
di·ges·tion *n* **:** the process or power of digesting something (as food)
di·ges·tive *adj* **:** of, relating to, or functioning in digestion
dig·it *n* **1 :** any of the numerals 1 to 9 and the symbol 0 **2 :** ¹FINGER 1 ¹TOE 1
dig·i·tal *adj* **1 :** of, relating to, or done with a finger or toe **2 :** of, relating to, or using calculation directly with digits rather than through measurable physical quantities **3 :** of or relating to data in the form of numerical digits **4 :** providing displayed or recorded information in numerical digits from an automatic device — **dig·i·tal·ly** *adv*
digital camera *n* **:** a camera that records images as electronic data instead of on film
dig·ni·fied *adj* **:** having or showing dignity
dig·ni·fy *vb* **dig·ni·fied; dig·ni·fy·ing :** to give dignity or importance to
dig·ni·tary *n, pl* **dig·ni·tar·ies :** a person of high position or honor
dig·ni·ty *n, pl* **dig·ni·ties 1 :** the quality or state of being worthy of honor and respect **2 :** high rank or office **3 :** a dignified look or way of behaving
dike *n* **1:** a channel dig in the earth to carry water **2:** a bank of earth built to control water
di·lap·i·dat·ed *adj* **:** partly fallen apart or ruined from age or from lack of care
di·late *vb* **di·lat·ed; di·lat·ing :** to make or grow larger or wider
di·lem·ma *n* **:** a situation in which a person has to choose between things that are all bad or unsatisfactory
dil·i·gence *n* **:** careful and continued work
dil·i·gent *adj* **:** showing steady and earnest care and effort — **dil·i·gent·ly** *adv*
dill *n* **:** an herb related to the carrot with fragrant leaves and seeds used mostly in flavoring pickles
dil·ly·dal·ly *vb* **dil·ly·dal·lied; dil·ly·dal·ly·ing :** to waste time **:** DAWDLE
di·lute *vb* **di·lut·ed; di·lut·ing :** to make thinner or more liquid
di·lu·tion *n* **1 :** the act of diluting **:** the state of being diluted **2 :** something (as a solution) that is diluted
¹dim *adj* **dim·mer; dim·mest 1 :** not bright or distinct **:** FAINT **2 :** not seeing or understanding clearly — **dim·ly** *adv* — **dim·ness** *n*
²dim *vb* **dimmed; dim·ming 1 :** to make or become dim **2 :** to reduce the light from
dime *n* **:** a United States coin worth ten cents
di·men·sion *n* **:** the length, width, or height of something
di·men·sion·al *adj* **:** of or relating to dimensions
di·min·ish *vb* **1 :** to make less or cause to seem less **2 :** BELITTLE **3 :** DWINDLE — **di·min·ish·ment** *n*
di·min·u·en·do *n, pl* **di·min·u·en·dos** *or* **di·min·u·en·does :** DECRESCENDO
di·min·u·tive *adj* **:** very small **:** TINY
dim·mer *n* **:** a device for regulating the brightness of an electric lighting unit (as the lights of a room)
¹dim·ple *n* **:** a slight hollow spot especially in the cheek or chin
²dimple *vb* **dim·pled; dim·pling :** to mark with or form dimples
¹din *n* **:** loud confused noise
²din *vb* **dinned; din·ning 1 :** to make a din **2 :** to repeat again and again in order to impress on someone's mind
dine *vb* **dined; din·ing 1 :** to eat dinner **2 :** to give a dinner to
din·er *n* **1 :** a person eating dinner **2 :** a railroad dining car or a restaurant in the shape of one
di·nette *n* **:** a separate area or small room used for dining
ding·dong *n* **:** the sound of a bell ringing
din·ghy *n, pl* **dinghies 1 :** a small light rowboat **2 :** a rubber life raft
din·gle *n* **:** a small narrow wooded valley
din·gy *adj* **din·gi·er; din·gi·est :** rather dark and dirty — **din·gi·ness** *n*
din·ner *n* **1 :** the main meal of the day **2 :** BANQUET
di·no·saur *n* **:** any of a group of extinct mostly land-dwelling reptiles that lived millions of years ago
dint *n* **1 :** the force or power of something **2 :** ²DENT
di·o·cese *n* **:** the district over which a bishop has authority
¹dip *vb* **dipped; dip·ping 1 :** to sink or push briefly into a liquid **2 :** to take out with or as if with a ladle **3 :** to lower and quickly raise again **:** drop or sink and quickly rise again **4 :** to sink out of sight **5 :** to slope downward
²dip *n* **1 :** a plunge into water for fun or exercise **:** a short swim **2 :** a downward slope **3 :** something obtained by or used in dipping **4 :** a sauce into which solid food may be dipped
diph·the·ria *n* **:** a contagious disease in which the air passages become coated with a membrane that often makes breathing difficult

diph·thong *n* : two vowel sounds joined in one syllable to form one speech sound

di·plo·ma *n* : a certificate that shows a person has finished a course or graduated from a school

di·plo·ma·cy *n* **1** : the work of keeping up relations between the governments of different countries **2** : skill in dealing with others

dip·lo·mat *n* **1** : a person whose work is diplomacy **2** : a person who is good at not saying or doing things that hurt or make people angry

dip·lo·mat·ic *adj* **1** : of or relating to diplomats and their work **2** : TACTFUL — **dip·lo·mat·i·cal·ly** *adv*

dip·per *n* **1** : one that dips **2** : a ladle or scoop for dipping

dire *adj* **1** : causing horror or terror : DREADFUL **2** : very great — **dire·ly** *adv* — **dire·ness** *n*

¹di·rect *vb* **1** : to put an address on (as a letter) **2** : ¹AIM 3, TURN **3** : to show or tell the way **4** : to guide the production of **5** : ¹ORDER 2, COMMAND

²direct *adj* **1** : going from one point to another without turning or stopping : STRAIGHT **2** : going straight to the point **3** : being in an unbroken family line — **di·rect·ness** *n*

³direct *adv* : DIRECTLY 1

direct current *n* : an electric current flowing in one direction only

di·rec·tion *n* **1** : SUPERVISION, MANAGEMENT **2** : an order or instruction to be followed **3** : the path along which something moves, lies, or points

di·rect·ly *adv* **1** : in a direct course or way **2** : right away : IMMEDIATELY

direct object *n* : a word that represents the main goal or the result of the action of a verb

di·rec·tor *n* : a person who directs something

di·rec·to·ry *n, pl* **di·rec·to·ries** : a book containing an alphabetical list of names and addresses

dirge *n* : a song or hymn of grief

di·ri·gi·ble *n* : AIRSHIP

dirk *n* : a long dagger with a straight blade

dirt *n* **1** : a filthy or soiling substance (as mud or dust) **2** : ²SOIL

¹dirty *adj* **dirt·i·er; dirt·i·est** **1** : soiled or polluted by dirt or impurities **2** : UNFAIR, MEAN **3** : INDECENT, VULGAR **4** : not clear in color **5** : showing dislike or anger — **dirt·i·ness** *n*

²dirty *vb* **dirt·ied; dirty·ing** : to make or become dirty

dis- *prefix* **1** : do the opposite of **2** : deprive of **3** : expel from **4** : opposite or absence of **5** : not

dis·abil·i·ty *n, pl* **dis·abil·i·ties** **1** : the state of being disabled : lack of power to do something **2** : something that disables

dis·able *vb* **dis·abled; dis·abling** : to make unable or incapable — **dis·able·ment** *n*

disabled *adj* : not having the ability to do certain mental or physical tasks (as because of illness, injury, or a condition one is born with) that one would typically be expected to do

dis·ad·van·tage *n* : a state or condition that favors someone else

dis·ad·van·ta·geous *adj* : making it harder for a person to succeed or do something — **dis·ad·van·ta·geous·ly** *adv* — **dis·ad·van·ta·geous·ness** *n*

dis·agree *vb* **dis·agreed; dis·agree·ing** **1** : to be unlike each other : be different **2** : to have unlike ideas or opinions **3** : QUARREL **4** : to have an unpleasant effect

dis·agree·able *adj* **1** : UNPLEASANT **2** : having a bad disposition : PEEVISH — **dis·agree·ably** *adv*

dis·agree·ment *n* **1** : the act or fact of disagreeing **2** : the condition of being different **3** : a difference of opinion

dis·ap·pear *vb* **1** : to stop being visible : pass out of sight **2** : to stop existing

dis·ap·pear·ance *n* : the act or fact of disappearing

dis·ap·point *vb* : to fail to satisfy the hope or expectation of

dis·ap·point·ment *n* **1** : the act of disappointing **2** : the condition or feeling of being disappointed **3** : one that disappoints

dis·ap·prov·al *n* : the feeling of not liking or agreeing with something or someone

dis·ap·prove *vb* **dis·ap·proved; dis·ap·prov·ing** : to dislike or be against something

dis·arm *vb* **1** : to take weapons from **2** : to reduce the size and strength of the armed forces of a country **3** : to make harmless **4** : to remove any feelings of doubt, mistrust, or unfriendliness : win over — **dis·ar·ma·ment** *n*

dis·ar·range *vb* **dis·ar·ranged; dis·ar·rang·ing** : to make all mussed up or mixed up — **dis·ar·range·ment** *n*

di·sas·ter *n* : something (as a flood or a tornado) that happens suddenly and causes much suffering or loss : CALAMITY

di·sas·trous *adj* : being or resulting in a disaster — **di·sas·trous·ly** *adv*

dis·band *vb* : to break up and stop being a group — **dis·band·ment** *n*

dis·bar *vb* **dis·barred; dis·bar·ring** : to deprive (a lawyer) of the rights of membership in the legal profession — **dis·bar·ment** *n*

dis·be·lief *n* : refusal or inability to believe

dis·be·lieve *vb* **dis·be·lieved; dis·be·liev·ing**

: to think not to be true or real — **dis·be·liev·er** *n*

dis·burse *vb* **dis·bursed; dis·burs·ing** : to pay out — **dis·burse·ment** *n*

disc *variant of* DISK

[1]**dis·card** *vb* **1** : to throw down an unwanted playing card from one's hand **2** : to get rid of as useless or unwanted

[2]**dis·card** *n* **1** : the act of discarding **2** : something discarded

dis·cern *vb* : to see, recognize, or understand something

[1]**dis·charge** *vb* **dis·charged; dis·charg·ing** **1** : to relieve of a load or burden : UNLOAD **2** : SHOOT 1, 2, FIRE **3** : to set free **4** : to dismiss from service **5** : to let go or let off **6** : to give forth the contents (as a fluid) **7** : to get rid of by paying or doing

[2]**dis·charge** *n* **1** : the act of discharging, unloading, or releasing **2** : a certificate of release or payment **3** : a firing off **4** : a flowing out (as of blood or pus) **5** : a firing of a person from a job **6** : complete separation from military service

dis·ci·ple *n* **1** : a person who accepts and helps to spread the teachings of another **2** : APOSTLE 1

[1]**dis·ci·pline** *n* **1** : strict training that corrects or strengthens **2** : PUNISHMENT 1 **3** : habits and ways of acting that are gotten through practice **4** : a system of rules

[2]**discipline** *vb* **dis·ci·plined; dis·ci·plin·ing** **1** : to punish for the sake of discipline **2** : to train in self-control or obedience **3** : to bring under control

disc jockey *n* : a radio announcer who plays records

dis·claim *vb* : to deny being part of or responsible for

dis·close *vb* **dis·closed; dis·clos·ing** : to make known : REVEAL

dis·clo·sure *n* **1** : an act of disclosing **2** : something disclosed

dis·col·or *vb* : to change in color especially for the worse

dis·col·or·a·tion *n* **1** : change of color **2** : a discolored spot

dis·com·fort *n* : the condition of being uncomfortable

dis·con·cert *vb* : to make confused and a little upset

dis·con·nect *vb* : to undo the connection of

dis·con·nect·ed *adj* : INCOHERENT — **dis·con·nect·ed·ly** *adv*

dis·con·so·late *adj* : too sad to be cheered up — **dis·con·so·late·ly** *adv*

[1]**dis·con·tent** *vb* : to make dissatisfied

[2]**discontent** *n* : the condition of being dissatisfied

dis·con·tent·ed *adj* : not contented — **dis·con·tent·ed·ly** *adv*

dis·con·tin·ue *vb* **dis·con·tin·ued; dis·con·tinu·ing** : to bring to an end : STOP

dis·cord *n* : lack of agreement or harmony

dis·cor·dant *adj* : being in disagreement : not being in harmony

[1]**dis·count** *n* : an amount taken off a regular price

[2]**dis·count** *vb* **1** : to lower the amount of a bill, debt, or charge usually in return for cash or quick payment **2** : to believe only partly

dis·cour·age *vb* **dis·cour·aged; dis·cour·ag·ing** **1** : to make less determined, hopeful, or sure of oneself **2** : DETER **3** : to try to persuade not to do something — **dis·cour·age·ment** *n*

[1]**dis·course** *n* **1** : CONVERSATION **2** : a long talk or composition about a subject

[2]**dis·course** *vb* **dis·coursed; dis·cours·ing** : to talk especially for a long time

dis·cour·te·ous *adj* : not polite : RUDE — **dis·cour·te·ous·ly** *adv*

dis·cour·te·sy *n, pl* **dis·cour·te·sies** **1** : rude behavior **2** : a rude act

dis·cov·er *vb* : to find out, see, or learn of especially for the first time : FIND — **dis·cov·er·er** *n*

dis·cov·ery *n, pl* **dis·cov·er·ies** **1** : an act of discovering **2** : something discovered

[1]**dis·cred·it** *vb* **1** : to refuse to accept as true **2** : to cause to seem dishonest or untrue

[2]**discredit** *n* : loss of good name or respect

dis·creet *adj* : having or showing good judgment especially in conduct or speech — **dis·creet·ly** *adv*

dis·cre·tion *n* **1** : good sense in making decisions **2** : the power of deciding for oneself

dis·crim·i·nate *vb* **dis·crim·i·nat·ed; dis·crim·i·nat·ing** **1** : to be able to tell the difference between things **2** : to treat some people better than others without any fair reason

dis·crim·i·na·tion *n* **1** : the act of discriminating **2** : the ability to see differences **3** : the treating of some people better than others without any fair or proper reason

dis·crim·i·na·to·ry *adj* : showing discrimination : being unfair

dis·cus *n, pl* **dis·cus·es** : an object that is shaped like a disk and hurled for distance in a track-and-field event

dis·cuss *vb* **1** : to argue or consider fully and openly **2** : to talk about

dis·cus·sion *n* : conversation for the purpose of understanding a question or subject

[1]**dis·dain** *n* : a feeling of scorn for something considered beneath oneself — **dis·dain·ful** *adj* — **dis·dain·ful·ly** *adv*

[2]**disdain** *vb* **1** : to think oneself far too good

for something or someone **2 :** to refuse because of scorn

dis·ease *n* **1 :** a change in a living body (as of a person or plant) that interferes with its normal functioning **:** ILLNESS **2 :** an instance or a kind of disease — **dis·eased** *adj*

dis·em·bark *vb* **:** to go or put ashore from a ship

dis·en·fran·chise *vb* **dis·en·fran·chised; dis·en·fran·chis·ing :** to take away the right to vote

dis·en·tan·gle *vb* **dis·en·tan·gled; dis·en·tan·gling :** to straighten out **:** UNTANGLE — **dis·en·tan·gle·ment** *n*

dis·fa·vor *n* **1 :** DISAPPROVAL **2 :** the state of being disliked

dis·fig·ure *vb* **dis·fig·ured; dis·fig·ur·ing :** to spoil the looks of — **dis·fig·ure·ment** *n*

dis·fran·chise *vb* **dis·fran·chised; dis·fran·chis·ing :** DISENFRANCHISE — **dis·fran·chise·ment** *n*

[1]dis·grace *vb* **dis·graced; dis·grac·ing :** to bring shame to — **dis·grac·er** *n*

[2]disgrace *n* **1 :** the condition of being looked down on **:** loss of respect **2 :** [1]DISHONOR 1 **3 :** a cause of shame

dis·grace·ful *adj* **:** bringing or deserving disgrace — **dis·grace·ful·ly** *adv* — **dis·grace·ful·ness** *n*

dis·grun·tle *vb* **dis·grun·tled; dis·grun·tling :** to make grouchy or cross

[1]dis·guise *vb* **dis·guised; dis·guis·ing 1 :** to change the looks of so as to conceal identity **2 :** to keep from revealing

[2]disguise *n* **1 :** clothing put on to hide one's true identity or to imitate another's **2 :** an outward appearance that hides what something really is

[1]dis·gust *n* **:** the strong dislike one feels for something nasty and sickening

[2]disgust *vb* **:** to cause to feel disgust — **dis·gust·ed·ly** *adv*

dis·gust·ing *adj* **:** causing disgust — **dis·gust·ing·ly** *adv*

[1]dish *n* **1 :** a hollowed out vessel for serving food at table **2 :** the contents of a dish

[2]dish *vb* **:** to put into a dish **:** SERVE

dis·heart·en *vb* **:** DISCOURAGE 1 — **dis·heart·en·ing·ly** *adv*

di·shev·eled *or* **di·shev·elled** *adj* **:** mussed up **:** UNTIDY

dis·hon·est *adj* **:** not honest or trustworthy — **dis·hon·est·ly** *adv*

dis·hon·es·ty *n* **:** lack of honesty **:** the quality of being dishonest

[1]dis·hon·or *n* **1 :** loss of honor or good name **2 :** a cause of disgrace

[2]dishonor *vb* **:** to bring shame on **:** DISGRACE

dis·hon·or·able *adj* **:** not honorable **:** SHAMEFUL — **dis·hon·or·ably** *adv*

dis·il·lu·sion *vb* **:** to free from mistaken beliefs or foolish hopes — **dis·il·lu·sion·ment** *n*

dis·in·fect *vb* **:** to free from germs that might cause disease

[1]dis·in·fec·tant *n* **:** something that frees from germs

[2]disinfectant *adj* **:** serving to disinfect

dis·in·her·it *vb* **:** to deprive (an heir) of the right to inherit

dis·in·te·grate *vb* **dis·in·te·grat·ed; dis·in·te·grat·ing :** to separate or break up into small parts or pieces

dis·in·te·gra·tion *n* **:** the act or process of disintegrating **:** the state of being disintegrated

dis·in·ter·est·ed *adj* **1 :** not interested **2 :** free of selfish interest — **dis·in·ter·est·ed·ly** *adv* — **dis·in·ter·est·ed·ness** *n*

dis·joint·ed *adj* **:** not clear and orderly — **dis·joint·ed·ly** *adv*

disk *or* **disc** *n* **1 :** something that is or appears to be flat and round **2** *usually disc* **:** a phonograph record **3 :** a round flat plate coated with a magnetic substance on which data for a computer is stored — **disk·like** *adj*

disk drive*n* **:** a device for transferring computer data to and from a magnetic disk

disk·ette *n* **:** FLOPPY DISK

[1]dis·like *n* **:** a strong feeling of not liking or approving

[2]dislike *vb* **dis·liked; dis·lik·ing :** to feel dislike for

dis·lo·cate *vb* **dis·lo·cat·ed; dis·lo·cat·ing :** to displace a bone from its normal connections with another bone

dis·lo·ca·tion *n* **:** the state of being dislocated

dis·lodge *vb* **dis·lodged; dis·lodg·ing :** to force out of a place of resting, hiding, or defense

dis·loy·al *adj* **:** not loyal — **dis·loy·al·ly** *adv*

dis·loy·al·ty *n, pl* **dis·loy·al·ties 1 :** lack of loyalty **2 :** a disloyal act

dis·mal *adj* **:** very gloomy

dis·man·tle *vb* **dis·man·tled; dis·man·tling 1 :** to strip of furniture or equipment **2 :** to take completely apart (as for storing or repair) — **dis·man·tle·ment** *n*

[1]dis·may *vb* **:** to cause to be unable to act because of surprise, fear, or confusion

[2]dismay *n* **1 :** sudden loss of courage or determination because of fear **2 :** a feeling of fear or disappointment

dis·miss *vb* **1 :** to send away **2 :** to discharge from an office or job **3 :** to decide not to think about

dis·miss·al *n* **:** the act of dismissing **:** the state or fact of being dismissed

dis·mount *vb* **1 :** to get down from something (as a horse or bicycle) **2 :** to cause to

fall off or get off **3 :** to take (as a cannon) off a support **4 :** to take apart (as a machine)
dis·obe·di·ence *n* **:** an act or the fact of disobeying
dis·obe·di·ent *adj* **:** not obeying — **dis·obe·di·ent·ly** *adv*
dis·obey *vb* **dis·obeyed; dis·obey·ing :** to refuse, neglect, or fail to obey
[1]**dis·or·der** *vb* **1 :** to disturb the order of **2 :** to disturb the regular or normal functioning of
[2]**disorder** *n* **1 :** lack of order or of orderly arrangement **:** CONFUSION **2 :** an abnormal state of body or mind **:** SICKNESS
dis·or·der·ly *adj* **1 :** not behaving quietly or well **:** UNRULY **2 :** not neat or orderly — **dis·or·der·li·ness** *n*
dis·or·ga·nize *vb* **dis·or·ga·nized; dis·or·ga·niz·ing :** to break up the regular arrangement or system of
dis·own *vb* **:** to refuse to accept any longer as one's own
dis·par·age *vb* **dis·par·aged; dis·par·ag·ing :** to speak of as unimportant or not much good **:** BELITTLE — **dis·par·age·ment** *n*
dis·pas·sion·ate *adj* **:** not influenced by strong feeling **:** CALM, IMPARTIAL — **dis·pas·sion·ate·ly** *adv*
[1]**dis·patch** *vb* **1 :** to send away quickly to a certain place or for a certain reason **2 :** [1]KILL 1 — **dis·patch·er** *n*
[2]**dispatch** *n* **1 :** MESSAGE **2 :** a news story sent in to a newspaper **3 :** SPEED 1
dis·pel *vb* **dis·pelled; dis·pel·ling :** to drive away
dis·pense *vb* **dis·pensed; dis·pens·ing 1 :** to give out in shares **:** DISTRIBUTE **2 :** ADMINISTER 2 **3 :** to put up or prepare medicine in a form ready for use — **dispense with :** to do or get along without
dis·pens·er *n* **:** a container that gives out something one at a time or a little at a time
dis·perse *vb* **dis·persed; dis·pers·ing :** to break up and scatter
dispir·it *vb* **:** to take away the cheerfulness or enthusiasm of
dis·place *vb* **dis·placed; dis·plac·ing 1 :** to remove from the usual or proper place **2 :** to remove from office **:** DISCHARGE **3 :** to take the place of **:** REPLACE — **dis·place·ment** *n*
[1]**dis·play** *vb* **1 :** to put (something) in plain sight **2 :** to make clear the existence or presence of **:** show plainly
[2]**display** *n* **:** a showing of something
dis·please *vb* **dis·pleased; dis·pleas·ing :** to be or do something that makes (a person) cross or not pleased or satisfied
dis·plea·sure *n* **:** a feeling of dislike and irritation **:** DISSATISFACTION
dis·pos·able *adj* **:** made to be thrown away after use
dis·pos·al *n* **1 :** ARRANGEMENT 1 **2 :** a getting rid of **3 :** right or power to use **:** CONTROL
dis·pose *vb* **dis·posed; dis·pos·ing 1 :** to put in place **:** ARRANGE **2 :** to make ready and willing — **dis·pos·er** *n* — **dispose of 1 :** to finish with **2 :** to get rid of
dis·po·si·tion *n* **1 :** ARRANGEMENT 1 **2 :** one's usual attitude or mood **3 :** TENDENCY 2, LIKING
dis·pro·por·tion *n* **:** lack of normal or usual proportions
dis·prove *vb* **dis·proved; dis·prov·ing :** to show to be false
dis·put·able *adj* **:** not yet proved **:** DEBATABLE — **dis·put·ably** *adv*
[1]**dis·pute** *vb* **dis·put·ed; dis·put·ing 1 :** ARGUE 2 **2 :** to question or deny the truth or rightness of **3 :** to fight over — **dis·put·er** *n*
[2]**dispute** *n* **1 :** ARGUMENT 2, DEBATE **2 :** [1]QUARREL 2
dis·qual·i·fy *vb* **dis·qual·i·fied; dis·qual·i·fy·ing :** to make or declare unfit or not qualified
[1]**dis·qui·et** *vb* **:** to make uneasy or worried **:** DISTURB
[2]**disquiet** *n* **:** an uneasy feeling
dis·qui·et·ing *adj* **:** causing worry or uneasiness — **dis·qui·et·ing·ly** *adv*
[1]**dis·re·gard** *vb* **:** to pay no attention to
[2]**disregard** *n* **:** the act of disregarding **:** the state of being disregarded
dis·re·pair *n* **:** the condition of needing repair
dis·rep·u·ta·ble *adj* **:** not respectable — **dis·rep·u·ta·bly** *adv*
dis·re·spect *n* **:** lack of respect **:** DISCOURTESY — **dis·re·spect·ful** *adj* — **dis·re·spect·ful·ly** *adv*
dis·robe *vb* **dis·robed; dis·rob·ing :** UNDRESS
dis·rupt *vb* **:** to throw into disorder **:** BREAK UP
dis·sat·is·fac·tion *n* **:** a being dissatisfied
dis·sat·is·fy *vb* **dis·sat·is·fied; dis·sat·is·fy·ing :** to fail to satisfy **:** DISPLEASE
dis·sect *vb* **:** to cut or take apart especially for examination
dis·sen·sion *n* **:** disagreement in opinion **:** DISCORD
[1]**dis·sent** *vb* **:** DISAGREE 2 — **dis·sent·er** *n*
[2]**dissent** *n* **:** difference of opinion
dis·ser·vice *n* **:** a harmful, unfair, or unjust act
dis·sim·i·lar *adj* **:** not similar **:** DIFFERENT
dis·si·pate *vb* **dis·si·pat·ed; dis·si·pat·ing 1 :** to break up and drive off **:** DISPERSE **2 :** to scatter or waste foolishly **:** SQUANDER
dis·si·pat·ed *adj* **:** enjoying bad, foolish, or harmful activities
dis·si·pa·tion *n* **1 :** the act of dissipating or

the state of being dissipated **2 :** a dissipated way of life

dis·so·lute *adj* **:** having or showing bad morals or behavior — **dis·so·lute·ly** *adv* — **dis·so·lute·ness** *n*

dis·solve *vb* **dis·solved; dis·solv·ing 1 :** to mix or cause to mix with a liquid so that the result is a liquid that is the same throughout **2 :** to bring to an end **:** TERMINATE **3 :** to fade away as if by melting or breaking up

dis·so·nance *n* **:** an unpleasant combination of musical sounds

dis·suade *vb* **dis·suad·ed; dis·suad·ing :** to persuade or advise not to do something

dis·tance *n* **1 :** how far from each other two points or places are **2 :** the quality or state of not being friendly **:** RESERVE **3 :** a distant point or region

dis·tant *adj* **1 :** separated in space or time **2 :** REMOTE 1 **3 :** not closely related **4 :** [1]COLD 2, UNFRIENDLY — **dis·tant·ly** *adv*

dis·taste *n* **:** [1]DISLIKE

dis·taste·ful *adj* **:** UNPLEASANT

dis·tend *vb* **:** EXPAND 2, SWELL

dis·till *also* **dis·til** *vb* **dis·tilled; dis·till·ing :** to obtain or purify by distillation — **dis·till·er** *n*

dis·til·la·tion *n* **:** the process of heating a liquid or solid until it sends off a gas or vapor and then cooling the gas or vapor until it becomes liquid

dis·tinct *adj* **1 :** real and different from each other **2 :** easy to see, hear, or understand — **dis·tinct·ly** *adv* — **dis·tinct·ness** *n*

dis·tinc·tion *n* **1 :** the seeing or pointing out of a difference **2 :** DIFFERENCE 1 **3 :** great worth **:** EXCELLENCE **4 :** something that makes a person or thing special or different

dis·tinc·tive *adj* **1 :** clearly marking a person or a thing as different from others **2 :** having or giving a special look or way — **dis·tinc·tive·ly** *adv* — **dis·tinc·tive·ness** *n*

dis·tin·guish *vb* **1 :** to recognize by some mark or quality **2 :** to know the difference **3 :** to set apart as different or special

dis·tin·guish·able *adj* **:** possible to recognize or tell apart from others

dis·tin·guished *adj* **:** widely known and admired

dis·tort *vb* **1 :** to tell in a way that is misleading **:** MISREPRESENT **2 :** to twist out of shape — **dis·tort·er** *n*

dis·tor·tion *n* **:** the act of distorting **:** the state or fact of being distorted

dis·tract *vb* **1 :** to draw the mind or attention to something else **2 :** to upset or trouble in mind to the point of confusion

dis·trac·tion *n* **1 :** the act of distracting **:** the state of being distracted **2 :** complete confusion of mind **3 :** something that makes it hard to pay attention

[1]dis·tress *n* **1 :** suffering or pain of body or mind **2 :** DANGER 1 — **dis·tress·ful** *adj*

[2]distress *vb* **:** to cause distress to — **dis·tress·ing·ly** *adv*

dis·trib·ute *vb* **dis·trib·ut·ed; dis·trib·ut·ing 1 :** to divide among several or many **2 :** to spread out so as to cover something **3 :** to divide or separate especially into classes **:** SORT — **dis·trib·u·tor** *n*

dis·tri·bu·tion *n* **1 :** the act of distributing **2 :** the way things are distributed **3 :** something distributed

dis·trib·u·tive *adj* **1 :** of or relating to distribution **2 :** producing the same answer when operating on the sum of several numbers as when operating on each and collecting the results — **dis·trib·u·tive·ly** *adv*

dis·trict *n* **1 :** an area or section (as of a city or nation) set apart for some purpose **2 :** an area or region with some special feature

[1]dis·trust *n* **:** a lack of trust or confidence **:** SUSPICION — **dis·trust·ful** *adj* — **dis·trust·ful·ly** *adv*

[2]distrust *vb* **:** to have no trust or confidence in

dis·turb *vb* **1 :** to interfere with **:** INTERRUPT **2 :** to change the arrangements of **:** move from its place **3 :** to trouble the mind of **:** UPSET **4 :** to make confused or disordered

dis·tur·bance *n* **1 :** the act of disturbing **:** the state of being disturbed **2 :** [2]DISORDER 1, COMMOTION

dis·use *n* **:** lack of use

dis·used *adj* **:** not used any more

[1]ditch *n* **:** a long narrow channel or trench dug in the earth

[2]ditch *vb* **1 :** to dig a ditch in or around (as for drainage) **2 :** to get rid of **:** DISCARD **3 :** to make a forced landing in an airplane on water

dith·er *n* **:** a very nervous or excited state

dit·ty *n, pl* **ditties :** a short simple song

di·van *n* **:** a large couch often with no back or arms

[1]dive *vb* **dived** *or* **dove; div·ing 1 :** to plunge into water headfirst **2 :** SUBMERGE 1 **3 :** to fall fast **4 :** to descend in an airplane at a steep angle **5 :** to shove suddenly into or at something — **div·er** *n*

[2]dive *n* **1 :** an act of diving **2 :** a quick drop (as of prices)

di·verse *adj* **:** different from each other **:** UNLIKE — **di·verse·ly** *adv* — **di·verse·ness** *n*

di·ver·sion *n* **1 :** an act or instance of diverting or turning aside **2 :** something that relaxes, amuses, or entertains

di·ver·si·ty *n, pl* **di·ver·si·ties :** the condition or fact of being different

di·vert *vb* **1 :** to turn aside **:** turn from one course or use to another **2 :** to turn the attention away : DISTRACT **3 :** to give pleasure to : AMUSE

¹di·vide *vb* **di·vid·ed; di·vid·ing 1 :** to separate into two or more parts or pieces **2 :** to give out in shares **3 :** to be or make different in opinion or interest **4 :** to subject to mathematical division **5 :** to branch off : FORK — **di·vid·er** *n*

²divide *n* : WATERSHED 1

div·i·dend *n* **1 :** a sum to be divided and given out **2 :** a number to be divided by another number

¹di·vine *adj* **1 :** of or relating to God or a god **2 :** being in praise of God : RELIGIOUS, HOLY **3 :** GODLIKE — **di·vine·ly** *adv*

²divine *n* **:** a member of the clergy

di·vin·i·ty *n, pl* **di·vin·i·ties 1 :** the quality or state of being divine **2 :** DEITY **3 :** the study of religion

di·vis·i·ble *adj* **:** possible to divide or separate

di·vi·sion *n* **1 :** the act or process of dividing : the state of being divided **2 :** a part or portion of a whole **3 :** a large military unit **4** : something that divides, separates, or marks off **5 :** the finding out of how many times one number is contained in another **6 :** a group of plants that ranks above the class in scientific classification and is the highest group of the plant kingdom

di·vi·sor *n* **:** the number by which a dividend is divided

¹di·vorce *n* **1 :** a complete legal ending of a marriage **2 :** complete separation

²divorce *vb* **di·vorced; di·vorc·ing 1 :** to make or keep separate **2 :** to end one's marriage legally : get a divorce

di·vulge *vb* **di·vulged; di·vulg·ing :** to make public : REVEAL, DISCLOSE

dix·ie·land *n* **:** lively jazz music in a style developed in New Orleans

diz·zy *adj* **diz·zi·er; diz·zi·est 1 :** having the feeling of whirling **2 :** confused or unsteady in mind **3 :** causing a dizzy feeling — **diz·zi·ly** *adv* — **diz·zi·ness** *n*

DNA *n* **:** a complicated organic acid that carries genetic information in the chromosomes

¹do *vb* **did; done; do·ing; does 1 :** to cause (as an act or action) to happen : CARRY OUT, PERFORM **2 :** ²ACT 2, BEHAVE **3 :** to meet one's needs : SUCCEED **4 :** ¹FINISH 1 — used in the past participle **5 :** to put forth : EXERT **6 :** to work on, prepare, or put in order **7 :** to work at as a paying job **8 :** to serve the purpose : SUIT **9** — used as a helping verb (1) before the subject in a question , (2) in a negative statement , (3) for emphasis , and (4) as a substitute for a preceding predicate — **do away with 1 :** to get rid of **2** : ¹KILL 1

²do *n* **:** the first note of the musical scale

doc·ile *adj* **:** easily taught, led, or managed — **doc·ile·ly** *adv*

¹dock *vb* **1 :** to cut off the end of **2 :** to take away a part of

²dock *n* **1 :** an artificial basin for ships that has gates to keep the water in or out **2 :** a waterway usually between two piers to receive ships **3 :** a wharf or platform for loading or unloading materials

³dock *vb* **1 :** to haul or guide into a dock **2** : to come or go into a dock **3 :** to join (as two spacecraft) mechanically while in space

⁴dock *n* **:** the place in a court where a prisoner stands or sits during trial

¹doc·tor *n* **:** a person (as a physician or veterinarian) skilled and specializing in the art of healing

²doctor *vb* **1 :** to use remedies on or for **2 :** to practice medicine

doc·trine *n* **:** something (as a rule or principle) that is taught, believed in, or considered to be true

doc·u·ment *n* **1 :** a written or printed paper that gives information about or proof of something **2 :** a computer file (as a letter, essay, or chart) typed in by a user

¹dodge *n* **:** a sudden movement to one side

²dodge *vb* **dodged; dodg·ing 1 :** to move suddenly aside or to and fro **2 :** to avoid by moving quickly **3 :** EVADE — **dodg·er** *n*

dodge ball *n* **:** a game in which players stand in a circle and try to hit a player inside the circle by throwing a large inflated ball

do·do *n, pl* **dodoes** *or* **dodos :** a large heavy bird unable to fly that once lived on some of the islands of the Indian ocean

doe *n* **:** the female of an animal (as a deer) the male of which is called *buck*

do·er *n* **:** one that does

does *present third sing of* DO

doesn't : does not

doff *vb* **:** to take off (as one's hat as an act of politeness)

¹dog *n* **1 :** a domestic animal that eats meat and is related to the wolves and foxes **2 :** a device (as a metal bar with a hook at the end) for holding, gripping, or fastening something — **dog·like** *adj*

²dog *vb* **dogged; dog·ging :** to hunt, track, or follow like a hound

dog·cart *n* **1 :** a cart pulled by dogs **2 :** a light one-horse carriage with two seats back to back

dog·catch·er *n* **:** an official paid to catch and get rid of stray dogs

dog days *n pl* **:** the hot period between early July and early September

dog–eared *adj* **:** having a lot of pages with corners turned over

dog·fish *n* : any of several small sharks often seen near shore

dog·ged *adj* : stubbornly determined — **dog·ged·ly** *adv* — **dog·ged·ness** *n*

dog·gy *or* **dog·gie** *n, pl* **doggies** : a usually small or young dog

dog·house *n* : a shelter for a dog — **in the doghouse** : in trouble over some wrongdoing

dog·ma *n* **1** : something firmly believed **2** : a belief or set of beliefs taught by a church

dog·mat·ic *adj* **1** : of or relating to dogma **2** : seeming or sounding absolutely certain about something — **dog·mat·i·cal·ly** *adv*

[1]**dog·trot** *n* : a slow trot

[2]**dogtrot** *vb* **dog·trot·ted; dog·trot·ting** : to move at a dogtrot

dog·wood *n* : any of several shrubs and small trees with clusters of small flowers often surrounded by four showy leaves that look like petals

doi·ly *n, pl* **doilies** : a small often ornamental mat used on a table

do·ings *n pl* : things that are done or that go on

dol·drums *n pl* **1** : a spell of low spirits **2** : a part of the ocean near the equator known for its calms

[1]**dole** *n* **1** : a giving out especially of food, clothing, or money to the needy **2** : something given out as charity

[2]**dole** *vb* **doled; dol·ing** **1** : to give out as charity **2** : to give in small portions

dole·ful *adj* : full of grief : SAD — **dole·ful·ly** *adv* — **dole·ful·ness** *n*

doll *n* : a small figure of a human being used especially as a child's plaything

dol·lar *n* : any of various coins or pieces of paper money (as of the United States or Canada) equal to 100 cents

dolly *n, pl* **dollies** **1** : DOLL **2** : a platform on a roller or on wheels for moving heavy things

dol·phin *n* **1** : a small whale with teeth and a long nose **2** : either of two large food fishes of the sea

dolt *n* : a stupid person — **dolt·ish** *adj* — **dolt·ish·ly** *adv* — **dolt·ish·ness** *n*

-dom *n suffix* **1** : dignity : office **2** : realm : jurisdiction **3** : state or fact of being **4** : those having a certain office, occupation, interest, or character

do·main *n* **1** : land under the control of a ruler or a government **2** : a field of knowledge or activity **3:** a main subdivision of the Internet

dome *n* : a bulge or a rounded top or roof that looks like half of a ball — **domed** *adj*

[1]**do·mes·tic** *adj* **1** : of or relating to a household or a family **2** : of, relating to, made in, or done in one's own country **3** : living with or under the care of human beings : TAME — **do·mes·ti·cal·ly** *adv*

[2]**domestic** *n* : a household servant

do·mes·ti·cate *vb* **do·mes·ti·cat·ed; do·mes·ti·cat·ing** : to bring under the control of and make usable by humans

do·mi·cile *n* : a dwelling place

dom·i·nance *n* : the state or fact of being dominant

dom·i·nant *adj* : controlling or being over all others — **dom·i·nant·ly** *adv*

dom·i·nate *vb* **dom·i·nat·ed; dom·i·nat·ing** : to have a commanding position or controlling power over

dom·i·neer *vb* : to rule or behave in a bossy way

do·min·ion *n* **1** : ruling or controlling power : SOVEREIGNTY **2** : a territory under the control of a ruler : DOMAIN

dom·i·no *n, pl* **dom·i·noes** *or* **dom·i·nos** : one of a set of flat oblong dotted pieces used in playing a game (**dominoes**)

don *vb* **donned; don·ning** : to put on

do·nate *vb* **do·nat·ed; do·nat·ing** : to make a gift of : CONTRIBUTE — **do·na·tor** *n*

do·na·tion *n* : a giving of something without charge : the thing given (as to charity)

done *past participle of* DO

don·key *n, pl* **donkeys** **1** : an animal related to but smaller than the horse that has short hair in mane and tail and very large ears **2** : a silly or stupid person

do·nor *n* : one who gives, donates, or presents — **do·nor·ship** *n*

don't : do not

[1]**doo·dle** *vb* **doo·dled; doo·dling** : to make a doodle — **doo·dler** *n*

[2]**doodle** *n* : a scribble, design, or sketch done while thinking about something else

doo·dle·bug *n* : ANT LION

[1]**doom** *n* **1** : a decision made by a court : SENTENCE **2** : a usually unhappy end : FATE

[2]**doom** *vb* **1** : to give judgment against : CONDEMN **2** : to make sure that something bad will happen

dooms·day *n* : the day of final judgment : the end of the world

door *n* **1** : a usually swinging or sliding frame or barrier by which an entrance (as into a house) is closed and opened **2** : a part of a piece of furniture like a house's door **3** : DOORWAY

door·man *n, pl* **door·men** : a person who tends a door of a building

door·step *n* : a step or a series of steps before an outer door

door·way *n* : the opening or passage that a door closes

door·yard *n* **:** a yard outside the door of a house

dope *n* **1 :** a thick sticky material (as one used to make pipe joints tight) **2 :** a narcotic substance **3 :** a stupid person **4 :** INFORMATION 2

dop·ey *adj* **dop·i·er; dop·i·est 1 :** lacking alertness and activity **:** SLUGGISH **2 :** STUPID 2

dorm *n* **:** DORMITORY

dor·mant *adj* **:** being in an inactive state for the time being

dor·mer *n* **1 :** a window placed upright in a sloping roof **2 :** the structure containing a dormer window

dor·mi·to·ry *n, pl* **dor·mi·to·ries 1 :** a sleeping room especially for several people **2 :** a residence hall having many sleeping rooms

dor·mouse *n, pl* **dor·mice :** a small European animal that is like a squirrel, lives in trees, and feeds on nuts

dor·sal *adj* **:** of, relating to, or being on or near the surface of the body that in humans is the back but in most animals is the upper surface — **dor·sal·ly** *adv*

do·ry *n, pl* **dories :** a boat with a flat bottom, high sides that curve upward and outward, and a sharp bow

[1]**dose** *n* **:** a measured amount (as of a medicine) to be used at one time

[2]**dose** *vb* **dosed; dos·ing :** to give medicine to

[1]**dot** *n* **1 :** a small point, mark, or spot **2 :** a certain point in time **3 :** a short click forming a letter or part of a letter (as in telegraphy)

[2]**dot** *vb* **dot·ted; dot·ting :** to mark with or as if with dots

dote *vb* **dot·ed; dot·ing :** to be foolishly fond — **dot·er** *n* — **dot·ing·ly** *adv*

[1]**dou·ble** *adj* **1 :** having a twofold relation or character **:** DUAL **2 :** made up of two parts or members **3 :** being twice as great or as many **4 :** folded in two **5 :** having more than the usual number of petals

[2]**double** *vb* **dou·bled; dou·bling 1 :** to make or become twice as great or as many **:** multiply by two **2 :** to make of two thicknesses **3 :** CLENCH 2 **4 :** to become bent or folded usually in the middle **5 :** to take the place of another **6 :** to turn sharply and go back over the same course

[3]**double** *adv* **1 :** DOUBLY **2 :** two together

[4]**double** *n* **1 :** something that is twice another **2 :** a hit in baseball that enables the batter to reach second base **3 :** one that is very like another

double bass *n* **:** an instrument of the violin family that is the largest member and has the deepest tone

dou·ble–cross *vb* **:** BETRAY 2

dou·ble·head·er *n* **:** two games played one right after the other on the same day

dou·ble–joint·ed *adj* **:** having a joint that permits unusual freedom of movement of the parts that are joined

double play *n* **:** a play in baseball by which two base runners are put out

dou·blet *n* **:** a close-fitting jacket worn by men in Europe especially in the sixteenth century

dou·ble–talk *n* **:** language that seems to make sense but is actually a mixture of sense and nonsense

dou·bloon *n* **:** an old gold coin of Spain and Spanish America

dou·bly *adv* **:** to twice the amount or degree

[1]**doubt** *vb* **1 :** to be uncertain about **2 :** to lack confidence in **:** DISTRUST **3 :** to consider unlikely — **doubt·er** *n* — **doubt·ing·ly** *adv*

[2]**doubt** *n* **1 :** uncertainty of belief or opinion **2 :** the condition of being undecided **3 :** a lack of confidence **:** DISTRUST

doubt·ful *adj* **1 :** not clear or certain as to fact **2 :** of a questionable kind **3 :** undecided in opinion **4 :** not certain in outcome — **doubt·ful·ly** *adv*

doubt·less *adv* **1 :** without doubt **2 :** in all probability

dough *n* **1 :** a soft mass of moistened flour or meal thick enough to knead or roll **2 :** MONEY 1, 2

dough·nut *n* **:** a small ring of sweet dough fried in fat

dough·ty *adj* **dough·ti·er; dough·ti·est :** very strong and brave — **dough·ti·ly** *adv* — **dough·ti·ness** *n*

dour *adj* **:** looking or being stern or sullen — **dour·ly** *adv* — **dour·ness** *n*

douse *vb* **doused; dous·ing 1 :** to stick into water **2 :** to throw a liquid on **3 :** to put out **:** EXTINGUISH

[1]**dove** *n* **:** any of various mostly small pigeons

[2]**dove** *past of* DIVE

dowdy *adj* **dowd·i·er; dowd·i·est 1 :** not neatly or well dressed or cared for **2 :** not stylish — **dowd·i·ly** *adv* — **dowd·i·ness** *n*

dow·el *n* **:** a pin or peg used for fastening together two pieces of wood

[1]**down** *adv* **1 :** toward or in a lower position **2 :** to a lying or sitting position **3 :** toward or to the ground, floor, or bottom **4 :** in cash **5 :** in a direction opposite to up **6 :** to or in a lower or worse condition **7 :** from a past time **8 :** to or in a state of less activity

[2]**down** *prep* **:** down in **:** down along **:** down on **:** down through

[3]**down** *vb* **:** to go or cause to go or come down

[4]**down** *adj* **1 :** being in a low position **2 :** di-

rected or going downward **3 :** being at a lower level **4 :** low in spirits **:** DOWNCAST

⁵down *n* **:** a low or falling period

⁶down *n* **:** a rolling grassy upland — usually used in pl.

⁷down *n* **1 :** soft fluffy feathers (as of young birds) **2 :** something soft and fluffy like down — **down·like** *adj*

down·beat *n* **:** the first beat of a measure of music

down·cast *adj* **1 :** low in spirit **:** SAD **2 :** directed down

down·fall *n* **:** a sudden fall (as from power, happiness, or a high position) or the cause of such a fall — **down·fall·en** *adj*

¹down·grade *n* **:** a downward slope (as of a road)

²downgrade *vb* **down·grad·ed; down·grad·ing :** to lower in grade, rank, position, or standing

down·heart·ed *adj* **:** DOWNCAST 1 — **down·heart·ed·ly** *adv* — **down·heart·ed·ness** *n*

¹down·hill *adv* **:** ¹DOWNWARD 1

²down·hill *adj* **:** sloping downhill

down payment *n* **:** a part of a price paid when something is bought or delivered leaving a balance to be paid later

down·pour *n* **:** a heavy rain

¹down·right *adv* **:** REALLY, VERY

²downright *adj* **:** ²OUTRIGHT 1, ABSOLUTE

down·stage *adv or adj* **:** toward or at the front of a theatrical stage

¹down·stairs *adv* **:** down the stairs **:** on or to a lower floor

²down·stairs *adj* **:** situated on a lower floor or on the main or first floor

³down·stairs *n sing or pl* **:** the lower floor of a building

down·stream *adv* **:** in the direction a stream is flowing

down·town *adv or adj* **:** to, toward, or in the main business district

¹down·ward *or* **down·wards** *adv* **1 :** from a higher place or condition to a lower one **2 :** from an earlier time

²downward *adj* **:** going or moving down

down·wind *adv or adj* **:** in the direction the wind is blowing

downy *adj* **down·i·er; down·i·est 1 :** like down **2 :** covered with down

dow·ry *n, pl* **dowries :** the property that a woman brings to her husband in marriage

¹doze *vb* **dozed; doz·ing :** to sleep lightly — **doz·er** *n*

²doze *n* **:** a light sleep

doz·en *n, pl* **dozens** *or* **dozen :** a group of twelve

¹drab *n* **:** a light olive brown

²drab *adj* **drab·ber; drab·best 1 :** of the color drab **2 :** lacking change and interest **:** DULL — **drab·ly** *adv* — **drab·ness** *n*

¹draft *n* **1 :** the act of pulling or hauling **:** the thing or amount pulled **2 :** the act or an instance of drinking or inhaling **:** the portion drunk or inhaled at one time **3 :** a medicine prepared for drinking **4 :** something represented in words or lines **:** DESIGN, PLAN **5 :** a quick sketch or outline from which a final work is produced **6 :** the act of drawing out liquid (as from a cask) **:** a portion of liquid drawn out **7 :** the depth of water a ship needs in order to float **8 :** a picking of persons for required military service **9 :** an order made by one party to another to pay money to a third party **10 :** a current of air **11 :** a device to regulate an air supply (as in a stove)

²draft *adj* **1 :** used for pulling loads **2 :** TENTATIVE **3 :** ready to be drawn from a container

³draft *vb* **1 :** to pick especially for required military service **2 :** to make a draft of **:** OUTLINE **3 :** COMPOSE 1, PREPARE — **draft·er** *n*

drafts·man *n, pl* **drafts·men :** a person who draws plans (as for machinery) — **drafts·man·ship** *n*

drafty *adj* **draft·i·er; draft·i·est :** exposed to a draft or current of air — **draft·i·ness** *n*

¹drag *n* **1 :** something without wheels (as a sledge for carrying heavy loads) that is dragged, pulled, or drawn along or over a surface **2 :** something used for dragging (as a device used underwater to catch something) **3 :** something that stops or holds back progress **4 :** a dull event, person, or thing

²drag *vb* **dragged; drag·ging 1 :** to haul slowly or heavily **2 :** to move with distressing slowness or difficulty **3 :** to pass or cause to pass slowly **4 :** to hang or lag behind **5 :** to trail along on the ground **6 :** to search or fish with a drag

drag·gle *vb* **drag·gled; drag·gling 1 :** to make or become wet and dirty by dragging **2 :** to follow slowly **:** STRAGGLE

drag·net *n* **1 :** a net to be drawn along in order to catch something **2 :** a network of planned actions for going after and catching a criminal

drag·on *n* **:** an imaginary animal usually pictured as a huge serpent or lizard with wings and large claws

drag·on·fly *n, pl* **drag·on·flies :** a large insect with a long slender body and four wings

dra·goon *n* **:** a soldier on horseback

drag race *n* **:** a race for two vehicles at a time from a standstill to a point a quarter mile away

¹drain *vb* **1 :** to draw off or flow off gradually or completely **2 :** to make or become dry or

empty a little at a time **3 :** to let out surface or surplus water **4 :** [1]EXHAUST 3
[2]drain *n* **1 :** a means of draining (as a pipe, channel, or sewer) **2 :** the act of draining **3 :** a using up a little at a time
drain·age *n* **1 :** an act of draining **2 :** something that is drained off **3 :** a method of draining : system of drains
drain·pipe *n* **:** a pipe for drainage
drake *n* **:** a male duck
dra·ma *n* **1 :** a written work that tells a story through action and speech and is meant to be acted out on a stage **2 :** dramatic art, literature, or affairs
dra·mat·ic *adj* **1 :** of or relating to the drama **2 :** like that of the drama : VIVID — **dra·mat·i·cal·ly** *adv*
dra·ma·tist *n* **:** PLAYWRIGHT
dra·ma·tize *vb* **dram·a·tized; dram·a·tiz·ing** **1 :** to make into a drama **2 :** to present or represent in a dramatic manner — **dra·ma·ti·za·tion** *n*
drank *past of* DRINK
[1]drape *vb* **draped; drap·ing** **1 :** to decorate or cover with or as if with folds of cloth **2 :** to arrange or hang in flowing lines
[2]drape *n* **1 drapes** *pl* **:** DRAPERY 2 **2 :** arrangement in or of folds **3 :** the cut or hang of clothing
drap·ery *n, pl* **drap·er·ies** **1 :** a decorative fabric hung in loose folds **2 :** curtains of heavy fabric often used over thinner curtains
dras·tic *adj* **1 :** acting rapidly and strongly **2 :** severe in effect : HARSH — **dras·ti·cal·ly** *adv*
draught *chiefly Brit variant of* DRAFT
[1]draw *vb* **drew; drawn; draw·ing** **1 :** to cause to move by pulling : cause to follow **2 :** to move or go usually steadily or a little at a time **3 :** ATTRACT 1 **4 :** to call forth : PROVOKE **5 :** INHALE **6 :** to bring or pull out **7 :** to bring or get from a source **8 :** to need (a certain depth) to float in **9 :** to take or receive at random **10 :** to bend (a bow) by pulling back the string **11 :** to cause to shrink or pucker : WRINKLE **12 :** to leave (a contest) undecided : TIE **13 :** to produce a likeness of by making lines on a surface : SKETCH **14 :** to write out in proper form — often used with *up* **15 :** FORMULATE **16 :** to produce or make use of a current of air
[2]draw *n* **1 :** the act or the result of drawing **2 :** a tie game or contest **3 :** something that draws attention **4 :** a gully shallower than a ravine
draw·back *n* **:** [1]HANDICAP 3
draw·bridge *n* **:** a bridge made to be drawn up, down, or aside to permit or prevent passage
draw·er *n* **1 :** one that draws **2 :** a sliding boxlike compartment (as in a desk) **3 drawers** *pl* **:** an undergarment for the lower part of the body
draw·ing *n* **1 :** an act or instance of drawing lots **2 :** the act or art of making a figure, plan, or sketch by means of lines **3 :** a picture made by drawing
drawing room *n* **:** a formal room for entertaining company
[1]drawl *vb* **:** to speak slowly with vowel sounds drawn out beyond their usual length
drawl *n* **:** a drawling way of speaking
draw on *vb* **:** to come closer : APPROACH
draw out *vb* **:** to cause or encourage to speak freely
draw·string *n* **:** a string, cord, or tape used to close a bag, control fullness in clothes, or open or close curtains
draw up *vb* **1 :** to arrange (as a body of troops) in order **2 :** to straighten (oneself) to an erect posture **3 :** to bring or come to a stop
dray *n* **:** a strong low cart or wagon without sides for hauling heavy loads
[1]dread *vb* **1 :** to fear greatly **2 :** to be very unwilling to meet or face
[2]dread *n* **:** great fear especially of harm to come
[3]dread *adj* **:** causing great fear or anxiety
dread·ful *adj* **1 :** causing a feeling of dread **2 :** very disagreeable, unpleasant, or shocking — **dread·ful·ly** *adv* — **dread·ful·ness** *n*
dread·nought *n* **:** a very large battleship
[1]dream *n* **1 :** a series of thoughts, pictures, or feelings occurring during sleep **2 :** a dreamlike creation of the imagination : DAYDREAM **3 :** something notable for its pleasing quality **4 :** a goal that is longed for : IDEAL — **dream·like** *adj*
[2]dream *vb* **dreamed** *or* **dreamt; dream·ing** **1 :** to have a dream or dreams **2 :** to spend time having daydreams **3 :** to think of as happening or possible — **dream·er** *n*
dream·land *n* **:** an unreal delightful country existing only in imagination or in dreams
dream·less *adj* **:** having no dreams — **dream·less·ly** *adv* — **dream·less·ness** *n*
dreamy *adj* **dream·i·er; dream·i·est** **1 :** tending to spend time dreaming **2 :** having the quality of a dream **3 :** being quiet and soothing **4 :** SUPERB — **dream·i·ly** *adv* — **dream·i·ness** *n*
drea·ry *adj* **drea·ri·er; drea·ri·est** **:** DISMAL, GLOOMY — **drea·ri·ly** *adv* — **drea·ri·ness** *n*
[1]dredge *vb* **dredged; dredg·ing** **:** to dig or gather with or as if with a dredge — **dredg·er** *n*
[2]dredge *n* **1 :** a heavy iron frame with a net attached to be dragged (as for gathering oysters) over the sea bottom **2 :** a machine for

scooping up or removing earth usually by buckets on an endless chain or by a suction tube **3 :** a barge used in dredging

dregs *n pl* **1 :** solids that settle out of a liquid **2 :** the worst or most useless part

drench *vb* **:** to wet thoroughly

[1]**dress** *vb* **1 :** to make or set straight (as soldiers on parade) **2 :** to put clothes on **:** CLOTHE **3 :** to wear formal or fancy clothes **4 :** to trim or decorate for display **5 :** to treat with remedies and bandage **6 :** to arrange by combing, brushing, or curling **7 :** to prepare (a meat animal) for food **8 :** to apply fertilizer to

[2]**dress** *n* **1 :** CLOTHING 1, APPAREL **2 :** an outer garment with a skirt for a woman or child

[1]**dress·er** *n* **:** a piece of furniture (as a chest or a bureau) with a mirror

[2]**dresser** *n* **:** a person who dresses in a certain way

dress·ing *n* **1 :** the act or process of one who dresses **2 :** a sauce added to a food (as a salad) **3 :** a seasoned mixture used as a stuffing (as for a turkey) **4 :** material used to cover an injury **5 :** something used as a fertilizer

dress·mak·er *n* **:** a person who makes dresses

dress·mak·ing *n* **:** the process or occupation of making dresses

dress up *vb* **1 :** to put on one's best or formal clothes **2 :** to put on strange or fancy clothes

dressy *adj* **dress·i·er; dress·i·est 1 :** showy in dress **2 :** suitable for formal occasions

drew *past of* DRAW

[1]**drib·ble** *vb* **drib·bled; drib·bling 1 :** to fall or let fall in small drops **:** TRICKLE **2 :** [1]SLOBBER, DROOL **3 :** to move forward by bouncing, tapping, or kicking

[2]**dribble** *n* **1 :** a trickling flow **2 :** the act of dribbling a ball

drib·let *n* **1 :** a small amount **2 :** a falling drop

dri·er *or* **dry·er** *n* **1 :** something that removes or absorbs moisture **2 :** a substance that speeds up the drying of oils, paints, and inks **3** *usually dryer* **:** a device for drying

[1]**drift** *n* **1 :** the motion or course of something drifting **2 :** a mass of matter (as snow or sand) piled in a heap by the wind **3 :** a course something appears to be taking **4 :** the meaning of something said or implied

[2]**drift** *vb* **1 :** to float or to be driven along by winds, waves, or currents **2 :** to move along without effort or purpose **3 :** to pile up in drifts — **drift·er** *n*

drift·wood *n* **:** wood drifted or floated by water

[1]**drill** *vb* **1 :** to bore with a drill **2 :** to teach by means of repeated practice — **drill·er** *n*

[2]**drill** *n* **1 :** a tool for making holes in hard substances **2 :** the training of soldiers (as in marching) **3 :** regular strict training and instruction in a subject

[3]**drill** *n* **:** a farming implement for making holes or furrows and planting seeds in them

[4]**drill** *vb* **:** to sow seeds with or as if with a drill

drily *variant of* DRYLY

[1]**drink** *vb* **drank; drunk; drink·ing 1 :** to swallow liquid **2 :** to absorb a liquid **3 :** to take in through the senses **4 :** to drink alcoholic liquor — **drink·er** *n*

[2]**drink** *n* **1 :** BEVERAGE **2 :** alcoholic liquor

drink·able *adj* **:** suitable or safe for drinking

[1]**drip** *vb* **dripped; drip·ping 1 :** to fall or let fall in or as if in drops **2 :** to let fall drops of liquid

[2]**drip** *n* **1 :** a falling in drops **2 :** dripping liquid **3 :** the sound made by falling drops

[1]**drive** *vb* **drove; driv·en; driv·ing 1 :** to push or force onward **2 :** to direct the movement or course of **3 :** to go or carry in a vehicle under one's own control **4 :** to set or keep in motion or operation **5 :** to carry through **:** CONCLUDE **6 :** to force to work or to act **7 :** to bring into a specified condition — **driv·er** *n*

[2]**drive** *n* **1 :** a trip in a carriage or automobile **2 :** a collecting and driving together of animals **3 :** DRIVEWAY **4 :** an often scenic public road **5 :** an organized usually thorough effort to carry out a purpose **6 :** the means for giving motion to a machine or machine part **7 :** a device that transfers information to and from a storage material (as tape or disks)

drive–in *adj* **:** designed and equipped to serve customers while they remain in their automobiles

drive·way *n* **:** a private road leading from the street to a house or garage

[1]**driz·zle** *n* **:** a fine misty rain

[2]**drizzle** *vb* **driz·zled; driz·zling :** to rain in very small drops

droll *adj* **:** having an odd or amusing quality — **droll·ness** *n* — **drol·ly** *adv*

drom·e·dary *n, pl* **drom·e·dar·ies 1 :** a speedy camel trained for riding **2 :** the camel of western Asia and northern Africa that has only one hump

[1]**drone** *n* **1 :** a male bee **2 :** a lazy person **:** one who lives on the labor of others

[2]**drone** *vb* **droned; dron·ing :** to make or to speak with a low dull monotonous hum

[3]**drone** *n* **:** a droning sound

drool *vb* **:** to let liquid flow from the mouth **:** SLOBBER

[1]**droop** *vb* **1 :** to sink, bend, or hang down **2 :** to become sad or weak

[2]**droop** *n* **:** the condition or appearance of drooping

[1]**drop** *n* **1 :** the amount of liquid that falls naturally in one rounded mass **2 drops** *pl* **:** a dose of medicine measured by drops **3 :** something (as a small round candy) that is shaped like a liquid drop **4 :** an instance of dropping **5 :** the distance of a fall

[2]**drop** *vb* **dropped; drop·ping 1 :** to fall or let fall in drops **2 :** to let fall **3 :** to lower in pitch and volume **4 :** SEND 1 **5 :** to let go **:** DISMISS **6 :** to knock down **:** cause to fall **7 :** to go lower **8 :** to make a brief visit **9 :** to pass into a less active state **10 :** to withdraw from membership or from taking part **11 :** LOSE 4

drop·let *n* **:** a tiny drop

drop·out *n* **:** one that drops out especially from school or a training program

drop·per *n* **1 :** one that drops **2 :** a short glass tube with a rubber bulb used to measure out liquids by drops

drought *n* **1 :** lack of rain or water **2 :** a long period of dry weather

[1]**drove** *n* **1 :** a group of animals being driven or moving in a body **2 :** a crowd of people moving or acting together

[2]**drove** *past of* DRIVE

drov·er *n* **:** a worker who drives cattle or sheep

drown *vb* **1 :** to suffocate in a liquid and especially in water **2 :** to cover with water **:** FLOOD **3 :** to overpower especially with noise

[1]**drowse** *vb* **drowsed; drows·ing :** to be half asleep **:** sleep lightly

[2]**drowse** *n* **:** a light sleep **:** DOZE

drowsy *adj* **drows·i·er; drows·i·est 1 :** ready to fall asleep **2 :** making one sleepy — **drows·i·ly** *adv* — **drows·i·ness** *n*

drub *vb* **drubbed; drub·bing 1 :** to beat severely **2 :** to defeat completely

drudge *n* **:** a person who does hard or dull work

drudg·ery *n, pl* **drudg·er·ies :** hard or dull work

[1]**drug** *n* **1 :** a substance used as a medicine or in making medicines **2 :** medicine used to deaden pain or bring sleep **3 :** a substance that may harm or make an addict of a person who uses it

[2]**drug** *vb* **drugged; drug·ging 1 :** to poison with or as if with a drug **2 :** to dull a person's senses with drugs

drug·gist *n* **:** a seller of drugs and medicines **:** PHARMACIST

drug·store *n* **:** a retail store where medicines and often other things are sold **:** PHARMACY

[1]**drum** *n* **1 :** a percussion instrument usually consisting of a metal or wooden cylinder with flat ends covered by tightly stretched skin **2 :** a sound of or like a drum **3 :** an object shaped like a drum

[2]**drum** *vb* **drummed; drum·ming 1 :** to beat a drum **2 :** to beat or sound like a drum **3 :** to gather together by or as if by beating a drum **4 :** to drive or force by steady or repeated effort **5 :** to beat or tap in a rhythmic way

drum major *n* **:** the marching leader of a band or drum corps

drum ma·jor·ette *n* **:** a girl who is a drum major

drum·mer *n* **1 :** a person who plays a drum **2 :** a traveling salesman

drum·stick *n* **1 :** a stick for beating a drum **2 :** the lower section of the leg of a fowl

[1]**drunk** *past participle of* DRINK

[2]**drunk** *adj* **1 :** being so much under the influence of alcohol that normal thinking and acting become difficult or impossible **2 :** controlled by some feeling as if under the influence of alcohol

[3]**drunk** *n* **1 :** a period of drinking too much alcoholic liquor **2 :** a drunken person

drunk·ard *n* **:** a person who is often drunk

drunk·en *adj* **1 :** [2]DRUNK 1 **2 :** resulting from being drunk — **drunk·en·ly** *adv* — **drunk·en·ness** *n*

[1]**dry** *adj* **dri·er; dri·est 1 :** free or freed from water or liquid **:** not wet or moist **2 :** having little or no rain **3 :** lacking freshness **:** STALE **4 :** not being in or under water **5 :** THIRSTY 1, 2 **6 :** no longer liquid or sticky **7 :** containing no liquid **8 :** not giving milk **9 :** not producing phlegm **10 :** amusing in a sharp or acid way **11 :** UNINTERESTING **12 :** not sweet — **dry·ly** *adv* — **dry·ness** *n*

[2]**dry** *vb* **dried; dry·ing :** to make or become dry

dry cell *n* **:** a small cell producing electricity by means of chemicals in a sealed container

dry–clean *vb* **:** to clean (fabrics) with chemical solvents

dry cleaner *n* **:** one whose business is dry cleaning

dry cleaning *n* **1 :** the cleaning of fabrics with a substance other than water **2 :** something that is dry-cleaned

dryer *variant of* DRIER

dry goods *n pl* **:** cloth goods (as fabrics, lace, and ribbon)

dry ice *n* **:** solidified carbon dioxide used chiefly to keep something very cold

du·al *adj* **:** consisting of two parts **:** having two like parts **:** DOUBLE — **du·al·ly** *adv*

[1]**dub** *vb* **dubbed; dub·bing 1 :** to make a

knight of by a light tapping on the shoulder with a sword **2 :** [2]NAME 1, NICKNAME

[2]**dub** *vb* **dubbed; dub·bing :** to add (sound effects) to a film or broadcast

du·bi·ous *adj* **1 :** causing doubt **:** UNCERTAIN **2 :** feeling doubt **3 :** QUESTIONABLE 1 — **du·bi·ous·ly** *adv*

duch·ess *n* **1 :** the wife or widow of a duke **2 :** a woman who holds the rank of a duke in her own right

[1]**duck** *n* **:** any of a group of swimming birds that have broad flat bills and are smaller than the related geese and swans

[2]**duck** *vb* **1 :** to push or pull under water for a moment **2 :** to lower the head or body suddenly **3 :** [2]DODGE 1 **4 :** [2]DODGE 2 **5 :** to avoid a duty, question, or responsibility

[3]**duck** *n* **1 :** a coarse usually cotton fabric rather like canvas **2 ducks** *pl* **:** clothes (as trousers) made of duck

duck·bill *n* **:** PLATYPUS

duck·ling *n* **:** a young duck

duck·weed *n* **:** a very small stemless plant that floats in fresh water

duct *n* **:** a pipe, tube, or vessel that carries something (as a bodily secretion, water, or hot air) — **duct·less** *adj*

ductless gland *n* **:** ENDOCRINE GLAND

dud *n* **1 duds** *pl* **:** CLOTHING **2 :** a complete failure **3 :** a missile that fails to explode

dude *n* **:** a man who pays too much attention to his clothes

[1]**due** *adj* **1 :** owed or owing as a debt or a right **2 :** SUITABLE **3 :** being a result — used with *to* **4 :** required or expected to happen

[2]**due** *n* **1 :** something owed **:** DEBT **2 dues** *pl* **:** a regular or legal charge or fee

[3]**due** *adv* **:** DIRECTLY 1

[1]**du·el** *n* **1 :** a combat between two persons fought with deadly weapons by agreement and in the presence of witnesses **2 :** a contest between two opponents

[2]**duel** *vb* **du·eled** *or* **du·elled; du·el·ing** *or* **du·el·ling :** to fight in a duel — **du·el·ist** *n*

du·et *n* **1 :** a musical composition for two performers **2 :** two performers playing or singing together

due to *prep* **:** because of

dug *past of* DIG

dug·out *n* **1 :** a boat made by hollowing out a log **2 :** a shelter dug in a hillside or in the ground **3 :** a low shelter facing a baseball diamond and containing the players' bench

duke *n* **:** a member of the highest rank of the British nobility

[1]**dull** *adj* **1 :** mentally slow **:** STUPID **2 :** LISTLESS **3 :** slow in action **:** SLUGGISH **4 :** not sharp in edge or point **:** BLUNT **5 :** lacking brightness or luster **6 :** not clear and ringing **7 :** CLOUDY 1, OVERCAST **8 :** not interesting **:** TEDIOUS **9 :** slightly grayish — **dull·ness** *or* **dul·ness** *n* — **dul·ly** *adv*

[2]**dull** *vb* **:** to make or become dull

du·ly *adv* **:** in a due or suitable manner, time, or degree

dumb *adj* **1 :** lacking the normal power of speech **2 :** normally unable to speak **3 :** not willing to speak **:** SILENT **4 :** STUPID 1, FOOLISH — **dumb·ly** *adv* — **dumb·ness** *n*

dumb·bell *n* **1 :** a short bar with two weighted balls or disks at the ends usually used in pairs for strengthening the arms **2 :** a stupid person

dumb·found *or* **dum·found** *vb* **:** to cause to become speechless with astonishment

dumb·wait·er *n* **:** a small elevator for carrying food and dishes or other small items from one floor to another

dum·my *n, pl* **dummies 1 :** a person who does not have or seems not to have the power of speech **2 :** a stupid person **3 :** an imitation used as a substitute

[1]**dump** *vb* **:** to let fall in a heap **:** get rid of

[2]**dump** *n* **1 :** a place for dumping something (as trash) **2 :** a place for storage of military materials or the materials stored **3 :** a messy or shabby place

dump·ling *n* **:** a small mass of dough cooked by boiling or steaming

dumps *n pl* **:** low spirits

dumpy *adj* **dump·i·er; dump·i·est :** short and thick in build — **dump·i·ness** *n*

[1]**dun** *n* **:** a slightly brownish dark gray

[2]**dun** *vb* **dunned; dun·ning :** to make repeated demands upon for payment

dunce *n* **:** a stupid person

dune *n* **:** a hill or ridge of sand piled up by the wind

dung *n* **:** FECES

dun·ga·ree *n* **1 :** a heavy cotton cloth **2 dungarees** *pl* **:** clothes made of dungaree

dun·geon *n* **:** a dark usually underground prison

dung·hill *n* **:** a pile of manure

dunk *vb* **:** to dip (as a cookie) into liquid (as milk)

duo *n, pl* **du·os 1 :** a duet especially for two performers at two pianos **2 :** [1]PAIR 1

[1]**dupe** *n* **:** a person who has been or is easily deceived or cheated

[2]**dupe** *vb* **duped; dup·ing :** to make a dupe of **:** TRICK

du·plex *adj* **:** [1]DOUBLE 2

[1]**du·pli·cate** *adj* **1 :** having two parts exactly alike **2 :** being the same as another

[2]**du·pli·cate** *vb* **du·pli·cat·ed; du·pli·cat·ing 1 :** to make double **2 :** to make an exact copy of

[3]**du·pli·cate** *n* **:** a thing that is exactly like another

du·pli·ca·tion *n* **1 :** the act or process of duplicating **2 :** the state of being duplicated
du·ra·bil·i·ty *n* **:** ability to last or to stand hard or continued use
du·ra·ble *adj* **:** able to last a long time — **du·ra·ble·ness** *n* — **du·ra·bly** *adv*
du·ra·tion *n* **:** the time during which something exists or lasts
dur·ing *prep* **1 :** throughout the course of **2 :** at some point in the course of
dusk *n* **1 :** the darker part of twilight especially at night **2 :** partial darkness
dusky *adj* **dusk·i·er; dusk·i·est 1 :** somewhat dark in color **2 :** somewhat dark **:** DIM — **dusk·i·ness** *n*
[1]**dust** *n* **1 :** fine dry powdery particles (as of earth) **:** a fine powder **2 :** the powdery remains of bodies once alive **3 :** something worthless **4 :** the surface of the ground — **dust·less** *adj*
[2]**dust** *vb* **1 :** to make free of dust **:** brush or wipe away dust **2 :** to sprinkle with or as if with fine particles — **dust·er** *n*
dust·pan *n* **:** a pan shaped like a shovel and used for sweepings
dust storm *n* **:** a violent wind carrying dust across a dry region
dusty *adj* **dust·i·er; dust·i·est 1 :** filled or covered with dust **2 :** like dust
[1]**Dutch** *adj* **:** of or relating to the Netherlands, its people, or the Dutch language
[2]**Dutch** *n* **1 Dutch** *pl* **:** the people of the Netherlands **2 :** the language of the Dutch
Dutch door *n* **:** a door divided so that the lower part can be shut while the upper part remains open
Dutch treat *n* **:** a treat for which each person pays his or her own way
du·ti·ful *adj* **:** having or showing a sense of duty — **du·ti·ful·ly** *adv* — **du·ti·ful·ness** *n*
du·ty *n, pl* **duties 1 :** conduct owed to parents and those in authority **2 :** the action required by one's position or occupation **3 :** something a person feels he or she ought to do **4 :** a tax especially on imports into a country
DVD *n* **:** a plastic disk the same size as a compact disc but with a much higher storage capacity that is used to store information (as computer data or a movie) and is read using a laser
[1]**dwarf** *n, pl* **dwarfs** *also* **dwarves 1 :** a person, animal, or plant much below normal size **2 :** a small legendary being usually pictured as a deformed and ugly person
[2]**dwarf** *vb* **1 :** to prevent from growing to natural size **:** STUNT **2 :** to cause to appear smaller
[3]**dwarf** *adj* **:** of less than the usual size
dwell *vb* **dwelt** *or* **dwelled; dwell·ing 1 :** to stay for a while **2 :** to live in a place **:** RESIDE **3 :** to keep the attention directed — **dwell·er** *n*
dwell·ing *n* **:** RESIDENCE 2, 3
dwin·dle *vb* **dwin·dled; dwin·dling :** to make or become less
[1]**dye** *n* **:** a coloring matter
[2]**dye** *vb* **dyed; dye·ing :** to give a new color to
dye·stuff *n* **:** material used for dyeing
dying *present participle of* DIE
dy·nam·ic *adj* **:** full of energy **:** ACTIVE
[1]**dy·na·mite** *n* **:** an explosive used in blasting
[2]**dynamite** *vb* **dy·na·mit·ed; dy·na·mit·ing :** to blow up with dynamite — **dy·na·mit·er** *n*
dy·na·mo *n, pl* **dy·na·mos :** a machine for producing electric current
dy·nas·ty *n, pl* **dy·nas·ties :** a series of rulers of the same family
dys·en·tery *n* **:** a disease in which much watery material mixed with mucus and blood is passed from the bowels
dys·lex·ia *n* **:** a learning disability in which one usually has a problem in reading, spelling, and writing

E

e *n, pl* **e's** *or* **es** *often cap* **1 :** the fifth letter of the English alphabet **2 :** a grade that shows a student's work is failing
[1]**each** *adj* **:** being one of two or more individuals
[2]**each** *pron* **:** each one
[3]**each** *adv* **:** to or for each **:** APIECE
each other *pron* **:** each of two or more in a shared action or relationship
ea·ger *adj* **:** desiring very much **:** IMPATIENT — **ea·ger·ly** *adv* — **ea·ger·ness** *n*
ea·gle *n* **:** any of several large birds of prey noted for keen sight and powerful flight
ea·glet *n* **:** a young eagle
-ean — see -AN
[1]**ear** *n* **1 :** the organ of hearing **2 :** the sense of hearing **3 :** willing or sympathetic attention **4 :** something like an ear in shape or position — **eared** *adj*
[2]**ear** *n* **:** the seed-bearing head of a cereal grass
ear·ache *n* **:** an ache or pain in the ear
ear·drum *n* **:** the membrane that separates the outer and middle parts of the ear and vibrates when sound waves strike it
earl *n* **:** a member of the British nobility ranking below a marquess and above a viscount

[1]**ear·ly** *adv* **ear·li·er; ear·li·est** **1 :** at or near the beginning of a period of time or a series **2 :** before the usual time
[2]**early** *adj* **ear·li·er; ear·li·est :** occurring near the beginning or before the usual time
ear·muff *n* **:** one of a pair of coverings joined by a flexible band and worn to protect the ears from cold or noise
earn *vb* **1 :** to get for services given **2 :** to deserve especially as a reward or punishment
ear·nest *adj* **:** not light or playful — **ear·nest·ly** *adv* — **ear·nest·ness** *n*
earn·ings *n pl* **:** money received as wages or gained as profit
ear·phone *n* **:** a device that converts electrical energy into sound and is worn over the opening of the ear or inserted into it
ear·ring *n* **:** an ornament worn on the ear lobe
ear·shot *n* **:** the range within which an unaided human voice can be heard
earth *n* **1 :** [2]SOIL 1 **2 :** areas of land as distinguished from the sea and the air **3** *often cap* **:** the planet that we live on
earth·en *adj* **:** made of earth
earth·en·ware *n* **:** things (as dishes) made of baked clay
earth·ly *adj* **1 :** having to do with or belonging to the earth **:** not heavenly **2 :** IMAGINABLE, POSSIBLE
earth·quake *n* **:** a shaking or trembling of a portion of the earth
earth·worm *n* **:** a worm that has a long body made up of similar segments and lives in damp soil
earthy *adj* **earth·i·er; earth·i·est** **1 :** consisting of or like earth **2 :** PRACTICAL 4 **3 :** not polite **:** CRUDE
ear·wig *n* **:** an insect with long slender feelers and a large forcepslike organ at the end of its abdomen
[1]**ease** *n* **1 :** freedom from pain or trouble **:** comfort of body or mind **2 :** freedom from any feeling of difficulty or embarrassment
[2]**ease** *vb* **eased; eas·ing** **1 :** to free from discomfort or worry **:** RELIEVE **2 :** to make less tight **:** LOOSEN **3 :** to move very carefully
ea·sel *n* **:** a frame for holding a flat surface in an upright position
eas·i·ly *adv* **1 :** in an easy manner **:** without difficulty **2 :** without doubt or question
[1]**east** *adv* **:** to or toward the east
[2]**east** *adj* **:** placed toward, facing, or coming from the east
[3]**east** *n* **1 :** the direction of sunrise **:** the compass point opposite to west **2** *cap* **:** regions or countries east of a certain point
Eas·ter *n* **:** a Christian church festival observed in memory of the Resurrection
Easter lily *n* **:** a white garden lily that blooms in spring
east·er·ly *adj or adv* **1 :** toward the east **2 :** from the east
east·ern *adj* **1** *often cap* **:** of, relating to, or like that of the East **2 :** lying toward or coming from the east
east·ward *adv or adj* **:** toward the east
easy *adj* **eas·i·er; eas·i·est** **1 :** not hard to do or get **:** not difficult **2 :** not hard to please **3 :** free from pain, trouble, or worry **4 :** COMFORTABLE **5 :** showing ease **:** NATURAL
eat *vb* **ate; eat·en; eat·ing** **1 :** to chew and swallow food **2 :** to take a meal or meals **3 :** to destroy as if by eating **:** CORRODE — **eat·er** *n*
eat·able *adj* **:** fit to be eaten
eaves *n sing or pl* **:** the lower edge of a roof that sticks out past the wall
eaves·drop *vb* **eaves·dropped; eaves·drop·ping** **:** to listen secretly to private conversation
[1]**ebb** *n* **1 :** the flowing out of the tide **2 :** a passing from a high to a low point or the time of this
[2]**ebb** *vb* **1 :** to flow out or away **:** RECEDE **2 :** [1]DECLINE 2, WEAKEN
[1]**eb·o·ny** *n, pl* **eb·o·nies :** a hard heavy wood that wears well and comes from tropical trees related to the persimmon
[2]**ebony** *adj* **1 :** made of or like ebony **2 :** [1]BLACK 1
[1]**ec·cen·tric** *adj* **1 :** acting or thinking in a strange way **2 :** not of the usual or normal kind
[2]**eccentric** *n* **:** an eccentric person
ec·cle·si·as·ti·cal *adj* **:** of or relating to the church or its affairs
[1]**echo** *n, pl* **ech·oes :** the repeating of a sound caused by the reflection of sound waves
[2]**echo** *vb* **ech·oed; echo·ing** **1 :** to send back or repeat a sound **2 :** to say what someone else has already said
éclair *n* **:** an oblong pastry with whipped cream or custard filling
[1]**eclipse** *n* **1 :** a complete or partial hiding of the sun caused by the moon's passing between the sun and the earth **2 :** a darkening of the moon caused by the moon's entering the shadow of the earth **3 :** the hiding of any celestial body by another **4 :** a falling into disgrace or out of use or public favor
[2]**eclipse** *vb* **eclipsed; eclips·ing** **1 :** to cause an eclipse of **2 :** to be or do much better than **:** OUTSHINE
eco·log·i·cal *adj* **:** of or relating to the science of ecology or the ecology of a particular environment and the living things in it
ecol·o·gist *n* **:** a specialist in ecology
ecol·o·gy *n* **1 :** a branch of science dealing with the relation of living things to their en-

vironment **2 :** the pattern of relations between living things and their environment

eco·nom·ic *adj* **1 :** of or relating to economics **2 :** of, relating to, or based on the making, selling, and using of goods and services

eco·nom·i·cal *adj* **1 :** using what one has carefully and without waste : FRUGAL **2 :** operating with little waste or at a saving — **eco·nom·i·cal·ly** *adv*

eco·nom·ics *n* **:** the science that studies and explains facts about the making, selling, and using of goods and services

econ·o·mize *vb* **econ·o·mized; econ·o·miz·ing** **1 :** to practice economy : be thrifty **2 :** to reduce expenses : SAVE

econ·o·my *n, pl* **econ·o·mies** **1 :** the careful use of money and goods : THRIFT **2 :** the way an economic system (as of a country or a period in history) is organized

eco·sys·tem *n* **:** the whole group of living and nonliving things that make up an environment and affect each other

ec·sta·sy *n, pl* **ec·sta·sies :** very great happiness : extreme delight

ec·stat·ic *adj* **:** of, relating to, or showing ecstasy

ec·ze·ma *n* **:** a disease in which the skin is red, itchy, and marred by scaly or crusted spots

[1]**-ed** *vb suffix or adj suffix* **1** — used to form the past participle of verbs **2 :** having : showing **3 :** having the characteristics of

[2]**-ed** *vb suffix* — used to form the past tense of verbs

[1]**ed·dy** *n, pl* **eddies :** a current of air or water running against the main current or in a circle

[2]**eddy** *vb* **ed·died; ed·dy·ing :** to move in an eddy

[1]**edge** *n* **1 :** the cutting side of a blade **2 :** the line where a surface ends : MARGIN, BORDER — **edged** *adj* — **on edge** : NERVOUS 3, TENSE

[2]**edge** *vb* **edged; edg·ing** **1 :** to give an edge to **2 :** to move slowly and little by little

edge·ways *or* **edge·wise** *adv* **:** with the edge in front : SIDEWAYS

ed·i·ble *adj* **:** fit or safe to eat

edict *n* **:** a command or law given or made by an authority (as a ruler)

ed·i·fice *n* **:** a large or impressive building (as a church)

ed·it *vb* **1 :** to correct, revise, and get ready for publication : collect and arrange material to be printed **2 :** to be in charge of the publication of something (as an encyclopedia or a newspaper) that is the work of many writers

edi·tion *n* **1 :** the form in which a book is published **2 :** the whole number of copies of a book, magazine, or newspaper published at one time **3 :** one of several issues of a newspaper for a single day

ed·i·tor *n* **1 :** a person who edits **2 :** a person who writes editorials

[1]**ed·i·to·ri·al** *adj* **1 :** of or relating to an editor **2 :** being or like an editorial

[2]**editorial** *n* **:** a newspaper or magazine article that gives the opinions of its editors or publishers

ed·u·cate *vb* **ed·u·cat·ed; ed·u·cat·ing** **1 :** to provide schooling for **2 :** to develop the mind and morals of especially by formal instruction : TRAIN — **ed·u·ca·tor** *n*

ed·u·ca·tion *n* **1 :** the act or process of educating or of being educated **2 :** knowledge, skill, and development gained from study or training **3 :** the study or science of the methods and problems of teaching

ed·u·ca·tion·al *adj* **1 :** having to do with education **2 :** offering information or something of value in learning — **ed·u·ca·tion·al·ly** *adv*

[1]**-ee** *n suffix* **1 :** person who receives or benefits from a specified thing or action **2 :** person who does a specified thing

[2]**-ee** *n suffix* **1 :** a certain and especially a small kind of **2 :** one like or suggesting

eel *n* **:** a long snakelike fish with a smooth slimy skin

e'en *adv* **:** EVEN

-eer *n suffix* **:** person who is concerned with or conducts or produces as a profession

e'er *adv* **:** EVER

ee·rie *also* **ee·ry** *adj* **ee·ri·er; ee·ri·est :** causing fear and uneasiness : STRANGE

ef·face *vb* **ef·faced; ef·fac·ing :** to erase or blot out completely

[1]**ef·fect** *n* **1 :** an event, condition, or state of affairs that is produced by a cause **2 :** EXECUTION 1, OPERATION **3 :** REALITY 1, FACT **4 :** the act of making a certain impression **5 :** [1]INFLUENCE 1 **6 effects** *pl* **:** personal property or possessions

[2]**effect** *vb* **:** BRING ABOUT

ef·fec·tive *adj* **1 :** producing or able to produce a desired effect **2 :** IMPRESSIVE **3 :** being in actual operation — **ef·fec·tive·ly** *adv* — **ef·fec·tive·ness** *n*

ef·fec·tu·al *adj* **:** producing or able to produce a desired effect

ef·fi·ca·cy *n, pl* **ef·fi·ca·cies :** power to produce effects : efficient action

ef·fi·cien·cy *n, pl* **ef·fi·cien·cies :** the quality or degree of being efficient

ef·fi·cient *adj* **:** capable of bringing about a desired result with little waste (as of time or energy) — **ef·fi·cient·ly** *adv*

ef·fort *n* **1 :** hard work of mind or body : EXERTION **2 :** a serious attempt : TRY

ef·fort·less *adj* : showing or needing little or no effort — **ef·fort·less·ly** *adv*

[1]egg *vb* : INCITE, URGE

[2]egg *n* **1 :** a shelled oval or rounded body by which some animals (as birds or snakes) reproduce and from which the young hatches out **2 :** an egg cell usually together with its protective coverings

egg cell *n* : a cell produced by an ovary that when fertilized by a sperm cell can develop into an embryo and finally a new mature being

egg·nog *n* : a drink made of eggs beaten with sugar, milk or cream, and often alcoholic liquor

egg·plant *n* : an oval vegetable with a usually glossy purplish skin and white flesh that is the fruit of a plant related to the tomato

egg·shell *n* : the shell of an egg

egret *n* : any of various herons that have long plumes during the breeding season

[1]Egyp·tian *adj* : of or relating to Egypt or the Egyptians

[2]Egyptian *n* **1 :** a person who is born or lives in Egypt **2 :** the language of the ancient Egyptians

ei·der *n* : a large northern sea duck that is mostly white above and black below and has very soft down

ei·der·down *n* **1 :** the down of the eider used for filling quilts and pillows **2 :** a quilt filled with down

[1]eight *adj* : being one more than seven

[2]eight *n* : one more than seven : two times four : 8

[1]eigh·teen *adj* : being one more than seventeen

[2]eighteen *n* : one more than seventeen : three times six : 18

[1]eigh·teenth *adj* : coming right after seventeenth

[2]eighteenth *n* : number eighteen in a series

[1]eighth *adj* : coming right after seventh

[2]eighth *n* **1 :** number eight in a series **2 :** one of eight equal parts

[1]eight·i·eth *adj* : coming right after seventy-ninth

[2]eightieth *n* : number eighty in a series

[1]eighty *adj* : being eight times ten

[2]eighty *n* : eight times ten : 80

[1]ei·ther *adj* **1 :** [1]EACH **2 :** being one or the other

[2]either *pron* : the one or the other

[3]either *conj* — used before words or phrases the last of which follows "or" to show that they are choices or possibilities

ejac·u·late *vb* **ejac·u·lat·ed; ejac·u·lat·ing** : EXCLAIM

eject *vb* : to drive out or throw off or out

eke out *vb* **eked out; ek·ing out** **1 :** to add to bit by bit **2 :** to get with great effort

[1]elab·o·rate *adj* : worked out with great care or with much detail — **elab·o·rate·ly** *adv*

[2]elab·o·rate *vb* **elab·o·rat·ed; elab·o·rat·ing** : to work out in detail

elapse *vb* **elapsed; elaps·ing** : to slip past : go by

[1]elas·tic *adj* : capable of returning to original shape or size after being stretched, pressed, or squeezed together

[2]elastic *n* **1 :** an elastic fabric made of yarns containing rubber **2 :** a rubber band

elas·tic·i·ty *n* : the quality or state of being elastic

elate *vb* **elat·ed; elat·ing** : to fill with joy or pride

ela·tion *n* : the quality or state of being elated

[1]el·bow *n* **1 :** the joint of the arm or of the same part of an animal's forelimb **2 :** a part (as of a pipe) bent like an elbow

[2]elbow *vb* : to push or force a way through with the elbows

[1]el·der *n* : a shrub or small tree related to the honeysuckles that has flat clusters of white flowers followed by fruits like berries

[2]elder *adj* : being older than another person

[3]elder *n* **1 :** one who is older **2 :** a person having authority because of age and experience **3 :** an official in some churches

el·der·ber·ry *n, pl* **el·der·ber·ries** : the juicy black or red fruit of the elder

el·der·ly *adj* : somewhat old : past middle age

el·dest *adj* : being oldest of a group of people (as siblings)

[1]elect *adj* : chosen for office but not yet holding office

[2]elect *vb* **1 :** to select by vote **2 :** to make a choice

elec·tion *n* : an electing or being elected especially by vote

elec·tive *adj* : chosen or filled by election

elec·tor *n* : a person qualified or having the right to vote in an election

electr- *or* **electro-** *prefix* **1 :** electricity **2 :** electric **3 :** electric and **4 :** electrically

elec·tric *or* **elec·tri·cal** *adj* **1 :** of or relating to electricity or its use **2 :** heated, moved, made, or run by electricity **3 :** having a thrilling effect **4 :** giving off sounds through an electronic amplifier — **elec·tri·cal·ly** *adv*

electric eel : a large South American eel-shaped fish having organs that are able to give a severe electric shock

elec·tri·cian *n* : a person who installs, operates, or repairs electrical equipment

elec·tric·i·ty *n* **1 :** an important form of energy that is found in nature but that can be artificially produced by rubbing together two unlike things (as glass and silk), by the action of chemicals, or by means of a generator **2 :** electric current

elec·tri·fy *vb* **elec·tri·fied; elec·tri·fy·ing 1 :** to charge with electricity **2 :** to equip for use of electric power **3 :** to supply with electric power **4 :** to excite suddenly and sharply **:** THRILL

elec·tro·cute *vb* **elec·tro·cut·ed; elec·tro·cut·ing :** to kill by an electric shock

elec·trode *n* **:** a conductor (as a metal or carbon) used to make electrical contact with a part of an electrical circuit that is not metallic

elec·trol·y·sis *n* **:** the producing of chemical changes by passage of an electric current through a liquid

elec·tro·lyte *n* **:** a substance (as an acid or salt) that when dissolved (as in water) conducts an electric current

elec·tro·lyt·ic *adj* **:** of or relating to electrolysis or an electrolyte

elec·tro·mag·net *n* **:** a piece of iron encircled by a coil of wire through which an electric current is passed to magnetize the iron

elec·tro·mag·net·ic *adj* **:** of or relating to a magnetic field produced by an electric current

electromagnetic wave *n* **:** a wave (as a radio wave or wave of light) that travels at the speed of light and consists of a combined electric and magnetic effect

elec·tron *n* **:** a very small particle that has a negative charge of electricity and travels around the nucleus of an atom

elec·tron·ic *adj* **1 :** of, relating to, or using the principles of electronics **2 :** operating by means of or using an electronic device (as a computer) — **elec·tron·i·cal·ly** *adv*

electronic mail *n* **:** E-MAIL

elec·tron·ics *n* **:** a science that deals with the giving off, action, and effects of electrons in vacuums, gases, and semiconductors and with devices using such electrons

electron tube *n* **:** a device in which conduction of electricity by electrons takes place through a vacuum or a gas within a sealed container and which has various uses (as in radio and television)

elec·tro·scope *n* **:** an instrument for discovering the presence of an electric charge on a body and for finding out whether the charge is positive or negative

el·e·gance *n* **1 :** refined gracefulness **2 :** decoration that is rich but in good taste

el·e·gant *adj* **:** showing good taste (as in dress or manners) **:** having or showing beauty and refinement — **el·e·gant·ly** *adv*

el·e·gy *n, pl* **el·e·gies :** a sad or mournful poem usually expressing sorrow for one who is dead

el·e·ment *n* **1 :** one of the parts of which something is made up **2 :** something that must be learned before one can advance **3 :** a member of a mathematical set **4 :** any of more than 100 substances that cannot by ordinary chemical means be separated into different substances

el·e·men·ta·ry *adj* **:** of or relating to the beginnings or first principles of a subject

el·e·phant *n* **:** a huge thickset mammal with the nose drawn out into a long trunk and two large curved tusks

el·e·vate *vb* **el·e·vat·ed; el·e·vat·ing :** to lift up **:** RAISE

el·e·va·tion *n* **1 :** height especially above sea level **:** ALTITUDE **2 :** a raised place (as a hill) **3 :** the act of elevating **:** the condition of being elevated

el·e·va·tor *n* **1 :** a device (as an endless belt) for raising material **2 :** a floor or little room that can be raised or lowered for carrying persons or goods from one level to another **3 :** a building for storing grain **4 :** a winglike device on an airplane to produce motion up or down

[1]**elev·en** *adj* **:** being one more than ten

[2]**eleven** *n* **:** one more than ten **:** 11

[1]**elev·enth** *adj* **:** coming right after tenth

[2]**eleventh** *n* **:** number eleven in a series

elf *n, pl* **elves :** an often mischievous fairy

elf·in *adj* **1 :** of or relating to elves **2 :** having a strange beauty or charm

el·i·gi·ble *adj* **:** worthy or qualified to be chosen

elim·i·nate *vb* **elim·i·nat·ed; elim·i·nat·ing :** to get rid of **:** do away with

elim·i·na·tion *n* **:** a getting rid especially of waste from the body

elk *n* **1 :** the moose of Europe and Asia **2 :** a large North American deer with curved antlers having many branches

el·lipse *n* **:** a closed curve that looks like a circle pulled out on opposite sides

el·lip·ti·cal *or* **el·lip·tic** *adj* **:** of or like an ellipse

elm *n* **:** a tall shade tree with a broad rather flat top and spreading branches

el·o·cu·tion *n* **:** the art of reading or speaking well in public

elo·dea *n* **:** a common floating water plant with small green leaves

elon·gate *vb* **elon·gat·ed; elon·gat·ing :** to make or grow longer

elope *vb* **eloped; elop·ing :** to run away to be married — **elope·ment** *n*

el·o·quence *n* **1 :** speaking or writing that is forceful and able to persuade **2 :** the art or power of speaking or writing with force and in a way to persuade

el·o·quent *adj* **1 :** expressing oneself or expressed clearly and with force **2 :** clearly showing some feeling or meaning — **el·o·quent·ly** *adv*

[1]**else** *adv* **1 :** in a different way or place or at a different time **2 :** if the facts are or were different : if not

[2]**else** *adj* **1 :** being other and different **2 :** being in addition

else·where *adv* **:** in or to another place

elude *vb* **elud·ed; elud·ing :** to avoid or escape by being quick, skillful, or tricky

elu·sive *adj* **1 :** clever in eluding **2 :** hard to understand or define

elves *pl of* ELF

em- — see EN-

e –mail *n* **:** messages sent and received electronically (as between computer terminals)

e–mail *vb* **:** to send E-mail — **e–mailer** *n*

eman·ci·pate *vb* **eman·ci·pat·ed; eman·ci·pat·ing :** to set free from control or slavery : LIBERATE

eman·ci·pa·tion *n* **:** a setting free

em·balm *vb* **:** to treat a dead body so as to preserve it from decay — **em·balm·er** *n*

em·bank·ment *n* **:** a raised bank or wall to carry a roadway, prevent floods, or hold back water

em·bar·go *n, pl* **em·bar·goes :** an order of a government prohibiting commercial shipping from leaving its ports

em·bark *vb* **1 :** to go on or put on board a ship or an airplane **2 :** to begin some project or task

em·bar·rass *vb* **1 :** to involve in financial difficulties **2 :** to cause to feel confused and distressed **:** FLUSTER

em·bas·sy *n, pl* **em·bas·sies 1 :** an ambassador and his assistants **2 :** the residence or office of an ambassador

em·bed *or* **im·bed** *vb* **em·bed·ded** *or* **im·bed·ded; em·bed·ding** *or* **im·bed·ding :** to set solidly in or as if in a bed

em·bel·lish *vb* **:** to add ornamental details to — **em·bel·lish·ment** *n*

em·ber *n* **:** a glowing piece of coal or wood in the ashes from a fire

em·bez·zle *vb* **em·bez·zled; em·bez·zling :** to take (property entrusted to one's care) dishonestly for one's own use

em·bit·ter *vb* **:** to make bitter **:** stir bitter feeling in

em·blem *n* **:** an object or a likeness used to suggest a thing that cannot be pictured

em·body *vb* **em·bod·ied; em·body·ing 1 :** to give form to **2 :** to cause to become a body or system or part of a body or system **3 :** to represent in visible form

em·boss *vb* **:** to ornament with a raised pattern or design

[1]**em·brace** *vb* **em·braced; em·brac·ing 1 :** to clasp in the arms **2 :** to enclose on all sides **3 :** to take up readily or gladly **4 :** TAKE IN 5, INCLUDE

[2]**embrace** *n* **:** an encircling with the arms **:** HUG

em·broi·der *vb* **1 :** to make or fill in a design with needlework **2 :** to decorate with needlework **3 :** to add to the interest of (as a story) with details far beyond the truth

em·broi·dery *n, pl* **em·broi·der·ies 1 :** needlework done to decorate cloth **2 :** the act or art of embroidering

em·bryo *n, pl* **em·bry·os 1 :** an animal in the earliest stages of growth when its basic structures are being formed **2 :** a tiny young plant inside a seed

[1]**em·er·ald** *n* **:** a precious stone of a rich green color

[2]**emerald** *adj* **:** brightly or richly green

emerge *vb* **emerged; emerg·ing 1 :** to come out or into view (as from water or a hole) **2 :** to become known especially as a result of study or questioning

emer·gen·cy *n, pl* **emer·gen·cies :** an unexpected situation requiring prompt action

emergency room *n* **:** a room or place in a hospital with doctors, nurses, and medical equipment for treating people who need medical care immediately

em·ery *n, pl* **em·er·ies :** a mineral used in the form of powder or grains for polishing and grinding

-emia *or* **-ae·mia** *n suffix* **:** condition of having a specified disorder of the blood

em·i·grant *n* **:** a person who emigrates

em·i·grate *vb* **em·i·grat·ed; em·i·grat·ing :** to leave a country or region to settle somewhere else

em·i·gra·tion *n* **:** a going away from one region or country to live in another

em·i·nence *n* **1 :** the condition of being eminent **2 :** a piece of high ground **:** HILL

em·i·nent *adj* **:** standing above others in rank, merit, or worth

em·is·sary *n, pl* **em·is·sar·ies :** a person sent on a mission to represent another

emit *vb* **emit·ted; emit·ting :** to give out **:** send forth

emo·tion *n* **1 :** strong feeling **2 :** a mental and bodily reaction (as anger or fear) accompanied by strong feeling

emo·tion·al *adj* **1 :** of or relating to the emotions **2 :** likely to show or express emotion **3 :** expressing emotion — **emo·tion·al·ly** *adv*

em·per·or *n* **:** the supreme ruler of an empire

em·pha·sis *n, pl* **em·pha·ses 1 :** a forcefulness of expression that gives special importance to something **2 :** special force given to one or more words or syllables in speaking or reading **3 :** special importance given to something

em·pha·size *vb* **em·pha·sized; em·pha·siz·ing :** to give emphasis to

em·phat·ic *adj* **:** showing or spoken with emphasis

em·phy·se·ma *n* **:** a disease in which the lungs become stretched and inefficient

em·pire *n* **1 :** a group of territories or peoples under one ruler **2 :** a country whose ruler is called an emperor **3 :** the power or rule of an emperor

[1]**em·ploy** *vb* **1 :** to make use of **2 :** to use the services of **:** hire for wages or salary

[2]**employ** *n* **:** the state of being employed

em·ploy·ee *or* **em·ploye** *n* **:** a person who works for pay in the service of an employer

em·ploy·er *n* **:** one that employs others

em·ploy·ment *n* **1 :** OCCUPATION 1, ACTIVITY **2 :** the act of employing **:** the state of being employed

em·pow·er *vb* **:** to give authority or legal power to

em·press *n* **1 :** the wife of an emperor **2 :** a woman who is the ruler of an empire in her own right

[1]**emp·ty** *adj* **emp·ti·er; emp·ti·est 1 :** containing nothing **2 :** not occupied or lived in **:** VACANT — **emp·ti·ness** *n*

[2]**empty** *vb* **emp·tied; emp·ty·ing 1 :** to make empty **:** remove the contents of **2 :** to transfer by emptying a container **3 :** to become empty **4 :** [1]DISCHARGE 6

emp·ty–hand·ed *adj* **1 :** having nothing in the hands **2 :** having gotten or gained nothing

emp·ty–head·ed *adj* **:** having a merry silly nature

EMT *n* **:** a person that is trained to give medical care in an emergency to a patient before or during the trip to a hospital

emu *n* **:** a fast-running Australian bird that is like but smaller than the related ostrich

em·u·late *vb* **em·u·lat·ed; em·u·lat·ing :** to try hard to equal or do better than

em·u·la·tion *n* **:** ambition or effort to equal or do better than others

emul·si·fy *vb* **emul·si·fied; emul·si·fy·ing :** to make an emulsion of

emul·sion *n* **:** a material consisting of a mixture of liquids so that fine drops of one liquid are scattered throughout the other

en- *also* **em-** *prefix* **1 :** put into or onto **:** go into or onto **2 :** cause to be **3 :** provide with — in all senses usually *em-* before *b, m,* or *p*

[1]**-en** *also* **-n** *adj suffix* **:** made of **:** consisting of

[2]**-en** *vb suffix* **1 :** become or cause to be **2 :** cause or come to have

en·able *vb* **en·abled; en·abling :** to give strength, power, or ability to **:** make able

en·act *vb* **1 :** to make into law **2 :** to act the part of (as in a play) — **en·act·ment** *n*

[1]**enam·el** *vb* **enam·eled** *or* **enam·elled; enam·el·ing** *or* **enam·el·ling :** to cover with or as if with enamel

[2]**enamel** *n* **1 :** a glassy substance used for coating the surface of metal, glass, and pottery **2 :** the hard outer surface of the teeth **3 :** a paint that forms a hard glossy coat

en·camp *vb* **:** to set up and occupy a camp

en·camp·ment *n* **1 :** the act of making a camp **2 :** CAMP

en·case *vb* **en·cased; en·cas·ing :** to enclose in or as if in a case

-ence *n suffix* **:** action or process

en·chant *vb* **1 :** to put under a spell by or as if by charms or magic **2 :** to please greatly — **en·chant·er** *n* — **en·chant·ment** *n*

en·chant·ing *adj* **:** very attractive **:** CHARMING

en·chant·ress *n* **:** a woman who enchants **:** WITCH, SORCERESS

en·cir·cle *vb* **en·cir·cled; en·cir·cling 1 :** to form a circle around **:** SURROUND **2 :** to pass completely around

en·close *or* **in·close** *vb* **en·closed** *or* **in·closed; en·clos·ing** *or* **in·clos·ing 1 :** to close in all around **:** SURROUND **2 :** to put in the same parcel or envelope with something else

en·clo·sure *or* **in·clo·sure** *n* **1 :** the act of enclosing **2 :** an enclosed space **3 :** something (as a fence) that encloses **4 :** something enclosed (as in a letter)

en·com·pass *vb* **1 :** ENCIRCLE 1 **2 :** INCLUDE

[1]**en·core** *n* **1 :** a demand for the repeating of something on a program made by applause from an audience **2 :** a further appearance or performance given in response to applause

[2]**encore** *vb* **en·cored; en·cor·ing :** to call for an encore

[1]**en·coun·ter** *vb* **1 :** to meet as an enemy **:** FIGHT **2 :** to meet face-to-face or unexpectedly

[2]**encounter** *n* **1 :** a meeting with an enemy **:** COMBAT **2 :** a meeting face-to-face and often by chance

en·cour·age *vb* **en·cour·aged; en·cour·ag·ing 1 :** to give courage, spirit, or hope to **:** HEARTEN **2 :** to give help to **:** AID

en·cour·age·ment *n* **1 :** the act of encouraging **:** the state of being encouraged **2 :** something that encourages

en·croach *vb* **1 :** to take over the rights or possessions of another little by little or in secret **2 :** to go beyond the usual or proper limits

en·crust *also* **in·crust** *vb* **:** to cover with or as if with a crust

en·cum·ber *vb* **1 :** to weigh down **:** BURDEN **2 :** HINDER, HAMPER

-en·cy *n suffix, pl* **-en·cies :** quality or state

en·cy·clo·pe·dia *n* **:** a book or a set of books containing information on all branches of learning in articles arranged alphabetically by subject

[1]end *n* **1 :** the part near the boundary of an area **2 :** the point (as of time or space) where something ceases to exist **3 :** the first or last part of a thing **4 :** DEATH 1, DESTRUCTION **5 :** [1]PURPOSE, GOAL

[2]end *vb* **:** to bring or come to an end **:** STOP

en·dan·ger *vb* **:** [2]RISK 1

en·dear *vb* **:** to make dear or beloved

en·dear·ment *n* **:** a word or an act that shows love or affection

[1]en·deav·or *vb* **:** to make an effort **:** TRY

[2]endeavor *n* **:** a serious determined effort

end·ing *n* **:** the final part **:** END

en·dive *n* **:** either of two plants related to the daisies and often used in salads

end·less *adj* **1 :** having or seeming to have no end **2 :** joined at the ends — **end·less·ly** *adv* — **end·less·ness** *n*

en·do·crine gland *n* **:** any of several glands (as the thyroid or pituitary) that secrete hormones directly into the blood

en·dorse *also* **in·dorse** *vb* **en·dorsed** *also* **in·dorsed; en·dors·ing** *also* **in·dors·ing 1 :** to sign one's name on the back of (a check) to obtain payment **2 :** to give one's support to openly — **en·dorse·ment** *n*

en·dow *vb* **1 :** to provide with money for support **2 :** to provide with something freely or naturally

en·dow·ment *n* **:** the providing of a permanent fund for support or the fund provided

end·point *n* **:** either of two points that mark the ends of a line segment or a point that marks the end of a ray

en·dur·ance *n* **:** the ability to put up with strain, suffering, or hardship

en·dure *vb* **en·dured; en·dur·ing 1 :** to continue in existence **:** LAST **2 :** to put up with (as pain) patiently or firmly

end·ways *adv or adj* **1 :** on end **2 :** with the end forward **3 :** [1]LENGTHWISE

en·e·ma *n* **:** the injection of liquid into the bowel or the liquid injected

en·e·my *n, pl* **en·e·mies 1 :** one that hates another **:** one that attacks or tries to harm another **2 :** something that harms or threatens **3 :** a nation with which one's own country is at war or a person belonging to such a nation

en·er·get·ic *adj* **:** having or showing energy **:** ACTIVE, VIGOROUS — **en·er·get·i·cal·ly** *adv*

en·er·gize *vb* **en·er·gized; en·er·giz·ing :** to give energy to

en·er·gy *n, pl* **en·er·gies 1 :** ability to be active **:** strength of body or mind to do things or to work **2 :** usable power or the resources (as oil) for producing such power

en·fold *vb* **1 :** to wrap up **:** cover with or as if with folds **2 :** [1]EMBRACE 1

en·force *vb* **en·forced; en·forc·ing 1 :** to demand and see that one gets **2 :** to put into force — **en·force·ment** *n*

en·gage *vb* **en·gaged; en·gag·ing 1 :** to pledge (as oneself) to do something **:** PROMISE **2 :** to catch and hold fast (as the attention) **3 :** to take part in something **4 :** to enter into contest or battle with **5 :** to arrange for the services or use of **:** HIRE **6 :** to put or become in gear **:** MESH

en·gaged *adj* **1 :** busy with some activity **2 :** pledged to be married

en·gage·ment *n* **1 :** the act of engaging **:** the state of being engaged **2 :** EMPLOYMENT 2 **3 :** an appointment at a certain time and place **4 :** a fight between armed forces

en·gag·ing *adj* **:** ATTRACTIVE

en·gen·der *vb* **:** to cause to be or develop **:** PRODUCE

en·gine *n* **1 :** a mechanical tool or device **2 :** a machine for driving or operating something especially by using the energy of steam, gasoline, or oil **3 :** [1]LOCOMOTIVE

[1]en·gi·neer *n* **1 :** a member of a military group devoted to engineering work **2 :** a person who specializes in engineering **3 :** a person who runs or has charge of an engine or of machinery or technical equipment

[2]engineer *vb* **1 :** to plan, build, or manage as an engineer **2 :** to plan out **:** CONTRIVE

en·gi·neer·ing *n* **:** a science by which the properties of matter and the sources of energy in nature are made useful to man in structures (as roads and dams), machines (as automobiles and computers), and products (as plastics and radios)

[1]En·glish *adj* **:** of or relating to England, its people, or the English language

[2]English *n* **1 :** the language of England, the United States, and some other countries now or at one time under British rule **2 English** *pl* **:** the people of England

English horn *n* **:** a woodwind instrument that is similar to an oboe but is longer and has a deeper tone

en·grave *vb* **en·graved; en·grav·ing 1 :** to cut or carve (as letters or designs) on a hard surface **2 :** to cut lines, letters, figures, or designs on or into (a hard surface) often for use in printing **3 :** to print from a cut surface — **en·grav·er** *n*

en·grav·ing *n* **1 :** the art of cutting something especially into the surface of wood, stone, or metal **2 :** a print made from an engraved surface

en·gross *vb* : to take up the whole interest of

en·gulf *vb* : to flow over and swallow up

en·hance *vb* **en·hanced; en·hanc·ing** : to make greater or better

enig·ma *n* : something hard to understand

en·joy *vb* **1** : to take pleasure or satisfaction in **2** : to have for one's use or benefit

en·joy·able *adj* : being a source of pleasure

en·joy·ment *n* **1** : the action or condition of enjoying something **2** : something that gives pleasure

en·large *vb* **en·larged; en·larg·ing** : to make or grow larger : EXPAND

en·large·ment *n* **1** : an act of enlarging **2** : the state of being enlarged **3** : a photographic print made larger than the negative

en·light·en *vb* : to give knowledge to

en·list *vb* **1** : to join the armed forces as a volunteer **2** : to obtain the help of — **en·list·ment** *n*

en·list·ed man *n* : a man or woman serving in the armed forces who ranks below a commissioned officer or warrant officer

en·liv·en *vb* : to put life or spirit into : make active or cheerful

en·mi·ty *n, pl* **en·mi·ties** : hatred especially when shared : ILL WILL

enor·mous *adj* : unusually large : HUGE — **enor·mous·ly** *adv*

[1]**enough** *adj* : equal to the needs or demands

[2]**enough** *adv* : in sufficient amount or degree

[3]**enough** *pron* : a sufficient number or amount

en·rage *vb* **en·raged; en·rag·ing** : to fill with rage : ANGER

en·rich *vb* **1** : to make rich or richer **2** : to improve the quality of food by adding vitamins and minerals **3** : to make more fertile

en·roll *or* **en·rol** *vb* **en·rolled; en·roll·ing** : to include (as a name) on a roll or list

en·roll·ment *or* **en·rol·ment** *n* **1** : the act of enrolling or being enrolled **2** : the number of persons enrolled

en route *adv* : on or along the way

en·sem·ble *n* : a group of musicians or dancers performing together

en·shrine *vb* **en·shrined; en·shrin·ing** : to cherish as if sacred

en·sign *n* **1** : a flag flown as the symbol of nationality **2** : a commissioned officer of the lowest rank in the Navy or Coast Guard

en·slave *vb* **en·slaved; en·slav·ing** : to make a slave of

en·sue *vb* **en·sued; en·su·ing** : to come after in time or as a result : FOLLOW

en·sure *vb* **en·sured; en·sur·ing** : to make sure, certain, or safe : GUARANTEE

en·tan·gle *vb* **en·tan·gled; en·tan·gling** **1** : to make tangled or confused **2** : to catch in a tangle — **en·tan·gle·ment** *n*

en·ter *vb* **1** : to come or go in or into **2** : to put into a list : write down **3** : to become a member or a member of : JOIN **4** : to become a party to or take an interest in something **5** : PENETRATE 1, PIERCE **6** : to cause to be admitted (as to a school)

en·ter·prise *n* **1** : an undertaking requiring courage and energy **2** : willingness to engage in daring or difficult action **3** : a business organization or activity

en·ter·pris·ing *adj* : bold and energetic in trying or experimenting

en·ter·tain *vb* **1** : to greet in a friendly way and provide for especially in one's home : have as a guest **2** : to have in mind **3** : to provide amusement for

en·ter·tain·er *n* : a person who performs for public entertainment

en·ter·tain·ment *n* **1** : the act of entertaining or amusing **2** : something (as a show) that is a form of amusement or recreation

en·thrall *or* **en·thral** *vb* **en·thralled; en·thrall·ing** : to hold the attention of completely : CHARM

en·throne *vb* **en·throned; en·thron·ing** **1** : to seat on a throne **2** : to place in a high position

en·thu·si·asm *n* : strong feeling in favor of something

en·thu·si·ast *n* : a person filled with enthusiasm

en·thu·si·as·tic *adj* : full of enthusiasm : EAGER

en·thu·si·as·ti·cal·ly *adv* : with enthusiasm

en·tice *vb* **en·ticed; en·tic·ing** : to attract by raising hope or desire : TEMPT

en·tire *adj* : complete in all parts or respects — **en·tire·ly** *adv*

en·tire·ty *n, pl* **en·tire·ties** **1** : a state of completeness **2** : [2]WHOLE 2

en·ti·tle *vb* **en·ti·tled; en·ti·tling** **1** : to give a title to **2** : to give a right or claim to

en·trails *n pl* : the internal parts of an animal

[1]**en·trance** *n* **1** : the act of entering **2** : a door, gate, or way for entering **3** : permission to enter : ADMISSION

[2]**en·trance** *vb* **en·tranced; en·tranc·ing** **1** : to put into a trance **2** : to fill with delight and wonder

en·trap *vb* **en·trapped; en·trap·ping** : to catch in or as if in a trap

en·treat *vb* : to ask in an earnest way

en·treaty *n, pl* **en·treat·ies** : an act of entreating : PLEA

en·trust *or* **in·trust** *vb* **1** : to give care of something to as a trust **2** : to give to another with confidence

en·try *n, pl* **en·tries** **1** : the act of entering : ENTRANCE **2** : a place (as a hall or door) through which entrance is made **3** : the act of making (as in a book or a list) a written record of something **4 :** something entered in a list or a record **5 :** a person or thing entered in a contest

en·twine *vb* **en·twined; en·twin·ing :** to twist or twine together or around

enu·mer·ate *vb* **enu·mer·at·ed; enu·mer·at·ing 1 :** [1]COUNT 1 **2 :** to name one after another **:** LIST

enun·ci·ate *vb* **enun·ci·at·ed; enun·ci·at·ing 1 :** ANNOUNCE 1 **2 :** to pronounce words or parts of words

enun·ci·a·tion *n* **:** clearness of pronunciation

en·vel·op *vb* **:** to put a covering completely around **:** wrap up or in

en·ve·lope *n* **:** an enclosing cover or wrapper (as for a letter)

en·vi·ous *adj* **:** feeling or showing envy — **en·vi·ous·ly** *adv* — **en·vi·ous·ness** *n*

en·vi·ron·ment *n* **1 :** SURROUNDINGS **2 :** the surrounding conditions or forces (as soil, climate, and living things) that influence the form and ability to survive of a plant or animal or ecological community **3 :** the social and cultural conditions that influence the life of a person or human community

en·voy *n* **1 :** a representative sent by one government to another **2 :** MESSENGER

[1]**en·vy** *n, pl* **envies 1 :** a feeling of discontent at another's good fortune together with a desire to have the same good fortune oneself **2 :** a person or a thing that is envied

[2]**envy** *vb* **en·vied; en·vy·ing :** to feel envy toward or because of

en·zyme *n* **:** one of the substances produced by body cells that help bodily chemical activities (as digestion) to take place but are not destroyed in so doing

eon *variant of* AEON

[1]**ep·ic** *adj* **:** of, relating to, or characteristic of an epic

[2]**epic** *n* **:** a long poem that tells the story of a hero's deeds

[1]**ep·i·dem·ic** *adj* **:** spreading widely and affecting large numbers of people at the same time

[2]**epidemic** *n* **1 :** a rapidly spreading outbreak of disease **2 :** something that spreads or develops rapidly like an epidemic disease

epi·der·mis *n* **1 :** a thin outer layer of skin covering the dermis **2 :** any of various thin outer layers of plants or animals

ep·i·neph·rine *n* **:** a hormone that causes blood vessels to narrow and the blood pressure to increase

ep·i·sode *n* **:** an event or one of a series of events that stands out clearly in one's life, in history, or in a story

epis·tle *n* **:** [1]LETTER 2

ep·i·taph *n* **:** a brief statement on a tombstone in memory of a dead person

ep·och *n* **:** a period marked by unusual or important events

[1]**equal** *adj* **1 :** exactly the same in number, amount, degree, rank, or quality **2 :** evenly balanced **3 :** having enough strength, ability, or means — **equal·ly** *adv*

[2]**equal** *vb* **equaled** *or* **equalled; equal·ing** *or* **equal·ling :** to be equal to

[3]**equal** *n* **:** one that is equal to another

equal·i·ty *n, pl* **equal·i·ties :** the condition or state of being equal

equal·ize *vb* **equal·ized; equal·iz·ing :** to make equal or even

equa·tion *n* **1 :** a statement of the equality of two mathematical expressions **2 :** an expression representing a chemical reaction by means of chemical symbols

equa·tor *n* **:** an imaginary circle around the earth everywhere equally distant from the north pole and the south pole

equa·to·ri·al *adj* **1 :** of, relating to, or lying near the equator **2 :** of, coming from, or suggesting the region around the equator

eques·tri·an *adj* **:** of or relating to horses or to the riding or riders of horses

equi·lat·er·al *adj* **:** having all sides of equal length

equi·lib·ri·um *n* **1 :** a state of balance between opposing weights, forces, or influences **2 :** the normal bodily adjustment of a person or animal in relation to its environment

equi·nox *n* **:** either of the two times each year when the sun's center crosses the equator and day and night (as on March 21 and September 23) are everywhere of equal length

equip *vb* **equipped; equip·ping :** to make ready for a purpose by supplying what is necessary

equip·ment *n* **1 :** an act of equipping **2 :** supplies and tools needed for a special purpose

[1]**equiv·a·lent** *adj* **:** alike or equal in number, value, or meaning

[2]**equivalent** *n* **:** something equivalent

[1]**-er** *adj suffix or adv suffix* — used to form the comparative degree of adjectives and adverbs of one syllable and of some adjectives and adverbs of two or more syllables

[2]**-er** *also* **-ier** *or* **-yer** *n suffix* **1 :** a person whose work or business is connected with **2 :** a person or thing belonging to or associated with **3 :** a native of **:** resident of **4 :** one that has **5 :** one that produces **6 :** one that does or performs a specified action **7 :** one that is a suitable object of a specified action **8 :** one that is

era *n* **1 :** a period of time starting from some

special date or event **2 :** an important period of history

erad·i·cate *vb* **erad·i·cat·ed; erad·i·cat·ing :** to remove by or as if by tearing up by the roots : destroy completely

erase *vb* **erased; eras·ing 1 :** to cause to disappear by rubbing or scraping **2:** to remove recorded matter from

eras·er *n* **:** something for erasing marks

era·sure *n* **1 :** an act of erasing **2 :** something erased

¹ere *prep* **:** ²BEFORE 3

²ere *conj* **:** ³BEFORE 2

¹erect *adj* **:** being straight up and down — **erect·ly** *adv* — **erect·ness** *n*

²erect *vb* **1 :** to put up by fitting together materials or parts **2 :** to set straight up — **erec·tor** *n*

er·mine *n* **:** a weasel of northern regions that is valued for its winter coat of white fur with a tail tipped in black

erode *vb* **erod·ed; erod·ing :** to eat into : wear away : destroy by wearing away

ero·sion *n* **:** the act of eroding : the state of being eroded

err *vb* **1 :** to make a mistake **2 :** to do wrong : SIN

er·rand *n* **1 :** a short trip made to take care of some business **2 :** the business done on an errand

er·rant *adj* **1 :** wandering in search of adventure **2 :** straying from a proper course

er·rat·ic *adj* **:** not following the usual or expected course

er·ro·ne·ous *adj* **:** INCORRECT 1

er·ror *n* **:** a failure to be correct or accurate : MISTAKE

erupt *vb* **1 :** to burst forth or cause to burst forth **2 :** to break through a surface **3 :** to break out (as with a skin rash)

erup·tion *n* **1 :** a bursting forth **2 :** a breaking out (as of a skin rash) or the resulting rash

-ery *n suffix, pl* **-er·ies 1 :** qualities considered as a group : character : -NESS **2 :** art : practice **3 :** place of doing, keeping, producing, or selling **4 :** collection : aggregate **5 :** state or condition

¹-es *n pl suffix* **1** — used to form the plural of most nouns that end in *s, z, sh, ch,* or a final *y* that changes to *i* and of some nouns ending in *f* that changes to *v* **2 :** ¹-s 2

²-es *vb suffix* — used to form the third person singular present of most verbs that end in *s* , *z* , *sh* , *ch* , or a final *y* that changes to *i*

es·ca·la·tor *n* **:** a moving stairway arranged like an endless belt

es·ca·pade *n* **:** a daring or reckless adventure

¹es·cape *vb* **es·caped; es·cap·ing 1 :** to get away : get free or clear **2 :** to keep free of : AVOID **3 :** to fail to be noticed or remembered by **4 :** to leak out from some enclosed place

²escape *n* **1 :** the act of escaping **2 :** a way of escaping

¹es·cort *n* **1 :** one (as a person or group) that accompanies another to give protection or show courtesy **2 :** the man who goes on a date with a woman

²es·cort *vb* **:** to accompany as an escort

¹-ese *adj suffix* **:** of, relating to, or coming from a certain place or country

²-ese *n suffix, pl* **-ese 1 :** native or resident of a specified place or country **2 :** language of a particular place, country, or nationality **3 :** speech or literary style of a specified place, person, or group

Es·ki·mo *n, pl* **Es·ki·mos :** a member of a group of peoples of Alaska, northern Canada, Greenland, and northeastern Siberia

Eskimo dog *n* **:** a sled dog of northern North America

esoph·a·gus *n, pl* **esoph·a·gi :** the tube that leads from the mouth through the throat to the stomach

es·pe·cial *adj* **:** SPECIAL — **es·pe·cial·ly** *adv*

es·pi·o·nage *n* **:** the practice of spying : the use of spies

es·py *vb* **es·pied; es·py·ing :** to catch sight of

-ess *n suffix* **:** female

¹es·say *vb* **:** ¹TRY 6

²es·say *n* **1 :** ²ATTEMPT **2 :** a usually short piece of writing dealing with a subject from a personal point of view

es·say·ist *n* **:** a writer of essays

es·sence *n* **1 :** the basic part of something **2 :** a substance made from a plant or drug and having its special qualities **3 :** ¹PERFUME 2

¹es·sen·tial *adj* **1 :** forming or belonging to the basic part of something **2 :** important in the highest degree — **es·sen·tial·ly** *adv*

²essential *n* **:** something that is essential

-est *adj suffix or adv suffix* — used to form the superlative degree of adjectives and adverbs of one syllable and of some adjectives and adverbs of two or more syllables

es·tab·lish *vb* **1 :** to bring into being : FOUND **2 :** to put beyond doubt : PROVE

es·tab·lish·ment *n* **1 :** the act of establishing **2 :** a place for residence or for business

es·tate *n* **1 :** ¹STATE 1 **2 :** the property of all kinds that a person leaves at death **3 :** a fine country house on a large piece of land

¹es·teem *n* **:** high regard

²esteem *vb* **:** to think well or highly of

esthetic *variant of* AESTHETIC

¹es·ti·mate *vb* **es·ti·mat·ed; es·ti·mat·ing 1 :** to give or form a general idea of (as the value, size, or cost of something) **2 :** to form an opinion

²es·ti·mate *n* **1 :** an opinion or judgment especially of the value or quality of something **2 :** an approximation of the size or cost of something

es·ti·ma·tion *n* **1 :** the making of an estimate **:** JUDGMENT **2 :** an estimate formed **:** OPINION

es·tu·ary *n, pl* **es·tu·ar·ies :** an arm of the sea at the lower end of a river

et cet·era : and others of the same kind **:** and so forth **:** and so on

etch *vb* **:** to produce designs or figures on metal or glass by lines eaten into the substance by acid

etch·ing *n* **1 :** the art or process of producing drawings or pictures by printing from etched plates **2 :** a picture made from an etched plate

eter·nal *adj* **1 :** lasting forever **:** having no beginning and no end **2 :** continuing without interruption

eter·ni·ty *n, pl* **eter·ni·ties 1 :** time without end **2 :** the state after death **3 :** a period of time that seems to be endless

-eth — see -TH

ether *n* **1 :** the clear upper part of the sky **2 :** a light flammable liquid used to dissolve fats and as an anesthetic

ethe·re·al *adj* **1 :** HEAVENLY 1 **2 :** very delicate **:** AIRY

eth·i·cal *adj* **1 :** of or relating to ethics **2 :** following accepted rules of behavior

eth·ics *n sing or pl* **1 :** a branch of philosophy dealing with moral duty and with questions of what is good and bad **2 :** the rules of moral behavior governing an individual or a group

eth·nic *adj* **:** of or relating to groups of people with common characteristics and customs — **eth·ni·cal·ly** *adv*

et·i·quette *n* **:** the rules governing the proper way to behave or to do something

-ette *n suffix* **1 :** little one **2 :** female **3 :** imitation

et·y·mol·o·gy *n, pl* **et·y·mol·o·gies :** the history of a word shown by tracing it or its parts back to the earliest known forms and meanings both in its own language and any other language from which it may have been taken

eu·ca·lyp·tus *n, pl* **eu·ca·lyp·ti** *or* **eu·ca·lyp·tus·es :** a tree of a kind native mainly to western Australia and widely grown for shade, timber, gum, and oil

Eu·cha·rist *n* **:** COMMUNION 2

eu·gle·na *n* **:** any of numerous tiny single-celled organisms that contain chlorophyll, swim about by means of a flagellum, and are often classified in science as algae

eu·ro *n, pl* **euros :** a coin or bill used by countries of the European Union

¹Eu·ro·pe·an *adj* **:** of or relating to Europe or the Europeans

²European *n* **:** a native or resident of Europe

evac·u·ate *vb* **evac·u·at·ed; evac·u·at·ing 1 :** to make empty **:** empty out **2 :** to discharge waste matter from the body **3 :** to remove troops or people from a place of danger

evade *vb* **evad·ed; evad·ing :** to get away from or avoid meeting directly

eval·u·ate *vb* **eval·u·at·ed; eval·u·at·ing :** to find or estimate the value of

eval·u·a·tion *n* **:** the act or result of evaluating

evan·ge·list *n* **:** a Christian preacher who goes about from place to place trying to change or increase people's religious feelings

evap·o·rate *vb* **evap·o·rat·ed; evap·o·rat·ing 1 :** to change into vapor **2 :** to disappear without being seen to go **3 :** to remove some of the water from something (as by heating)

evap·o·ra·tion *n* **:** the process of evaporating

eve *n* **1 :** EVENING **2 :** the evening or day before a special day **3 :** the period just before an important event

¹even *adj* **1 :** being without breaks or bumps **2 :** staying the same over a period of time **3 :** being on the same line or level **4 :** equal in size, number, or amount **5 :** ¹EQUAL 2, FAIR **6 :** possible to divide by two — **even·ly** *adv* — **even·ness** *n*

²even *adv* **1 :** at the very time **:** JUST **2 :** INDEED **3** — used to stress an extreme or highly unlikely condition or instance **4 :** to a greater extent or degree **:** STILL **5 :** so much as

³even *vb* **:** to make or become even

eve·ning *n* **:** the final part of the day and early part of the night

evening star *n* **:** a bright planet (as Venus) seen in the western sky after sunset

event *n* **1 :** something usually of importance that happens **2 :** a social occasion (as a party) **3 :** the fact of happening **4 :** a contest in a program of sports

event·ful *adj* **1 :** filled with events **2 :** very important

even·tide *n* **:** EVENING

even·tu·al *adj* **:** coming at some later time — **even·tu·al·ly** *adv*

ev·er *adv* **1 :** at all times **:** ALWAYS **2 :** at any time **3 :** in any way

ev·er·glade *n* **:** a swampy grassland

¹ev·er·green *n* **1 :** an evergreen plant (as a pine or a laurel) **2 evergreens** *pl* **:** branches and leaves of evergreens used for decorations

²evergreen *adj* **:** having leaves that stay green through more than one growing season

ev·er·last·ing *adj* **1 :** lasting forever **:** ETER-

NAL **2 :** going on for a long time or for too long a time — **ev·er·last·ing·ly** *adv*

ev·er·more *adj* **:** FOREVER 1

ev·ery *adj* **:** being each of a group or series without leaving out any

ev·ery·body *pron* **:** every person

ev·ery·day *adj* **:** used or suitable for every day **:** ORDINARY

ev·ery·one *pron* **:** every person

ev·ery·thing *pron* **:** every thing **:** ALL

ev·ery·where *adv* **:** in or to every place or part

evict *vb* **:** to put out from property by legal action

ev·i·dence *n* **1 :** an outward sign **:** INDICATION **2 :** material presented to a court to help find the truth in a matter

ev·i·dent *adj* **:** clear to the sight or to the mind **:** PLAIN — **ev·i·dent·ly** *adv*

[1]**evil** *adj* **1 :** morally bad **:** WICKED **2 :** causing harm **:** tending to injure

[2]**evil** *n* **1 :** something that brings sorrow, trouble, or destruction **2 :** the fact of suffering or wrongdoing

evoke *vb* **evoked; evok·ing :** to call forth or up **:** SUMMON

evo·lu·tion *n* **1 :** the process of development of an animal or a plant **2 :** the theory that the various kinds of existing animals and plants have come from kinds that existed in the past

evolve *vb* **evolved; evolv·ing :** to grow or develop out of something

ewe *n* **:** a female sheep

ex- *prefix* **1 :** out of **:** outside **2 :** former

[1]**ex·act** *vb* **:** to demand and get by force or threat

[2]**exact** *adj* **:** showing close agreement with fact **:** ACCURATE — **ex·act·ly** *adv* — **ex·act·ness** *n*

ex·act·ing *adj* **:** making many or difficult demands upon a person **:** TRYING

ex·ag·ger·ate *vb* **ex·ag·ger·at·ed; ex·ag·ger·at·ing :** to enlarge a fact or statement beyond what is true

ex·ag·ger·a·tion *n* **1 :** the act of exaggerating **2 :** an exaggerated statement

ex·alt *vb* **1 :** to raise in rank or power **2 :** to praise highly

ex·am *n* **:** EXAMINATION

ex·am·i·na·tion *n* **1 :** the act of examining or state of being examined **2 :** a test given to determine progress, fitness, or knowledge

ex·am·ine *vb* **ex·am·ined; ex·am·in·ing 1 :** to look at or check carefully **2 :** to question closely

ex·am·ple *n* **1 :** a sample of something taken to show what the whole is like **:** INSTANCE **2 :** something to be imitated **:** MODEL **3 :** something that is a warning to others **4 :** a problem to be solved to show how a rule works

ex·as·per·ate *vb* **ex·as·per·at·ed; ex·as·per·at·ing :** to make angry

ex·as·per·a·tion *n* **:** extreme annoyance **:** ANGER

ex·ca·vate *vb* **ex·ca·vat·ed; ex·ca·vat·ing 1 :** to hollow out **:** form a hole in **2 :** to make by hollowing out **3 :** to dig out and remove **4 :** to expose to view by digging away a covering (as of earth)

ex·ca·va·tion *n* **1 :** the act of excavating **2 :** a hollow place formed by excavating

ex·ceed *vb* **1 :** to go or be beyond the limit of **2 :** to be greater than

ex·ceed·ing·ly *adv* **:** to a very great degree

ex·cel *vb* **ex·celled; ex·cel·ling :** to do better than others **:** SURPASS

ex·cel·lence *n* **1 :** high quality **2 :** an excellent quality **:** VIRTUE

ex·cel·lent *adj* **:** very good of its kind — **ex·cel·lent·ly** *adv*

[1]**ex·cept** *prep* **1 :** not including **2 :** other than **:** BUT

[2]**except** *vb* **:** to leave out from a number or a whole **:** EXCLUDE

[3]**except** *conj* **:** if it were not for the fact that **:** ONLY

ex·cep·tion *n* **1 :** the act of leaving out **2 :** a case to which a rule does not apply **3 :** an objection or a reason for objecting

ex·cep·tion·al *adj* **1 :** forming an exception **2 :** better than average **:** SUPERIOR — **ex·cep·tion·al·ly** *adv*

[1]**ex·cess** *n* **1 :** a state of being more than enough **2 :** the amount by which something is more than what is needed or allowed

[2]**excess** *adj* **:** more than is usual or acceptable

ex·ces·sive *adj* **:** showing excess — **ex·ces·sive·ly** *adv*

[1]**ex·change** *n* **1 :** a giving or taking of one thing in return for another **:** TRADE **2 :** the act of substituting one thing for another **3 :** the act of giving and receiving between two groups **4 :** a place where goods or services are exchanged

[2]**exchange** *vb* **ex·changed; ex·chang·ing :** to give in exchange **:** TRADE, SWAP

ex·cit·able *adj* **:** easily excited

ex·cite *vb* **ex·cit·ed; ex·cit·ing 1 :** to increase the activity of **2 :** to stir up feeling in **:** ROUSE

ex·cite·ment *n* **1 :** the state of being excited **:** AGITATION **2 :** something that excites or stirs up

ex·cit·ing *adj* **:** producing excitement

ex·claim *vb* **:** to cry out or speak out suddenly or with strong feeling

ex·cla·ma·tion *n* **1 :** a sharp or sudden cry of

strong feeling **2 :** strong expression of anger or complaint

exclamation point *n* **:** a punctuation mark ! used mostly to show a forceful way of speaking or strong feeling

ex·clam·a·to·ry *adj* **:** containing or using exclamation

ex·clude *vb* **ex·clud·ed; ex·clud·ing :** to shut out **:** keep out

ex·clu·sion *n* **:** the act of excluding **:** the state of being excluded

ex·clu·sive *adj* **1 :** excluding or trying to exclude others **2 :** [4]SOLE 2 **3 :** ENTIRE, COMPLETE **4 :** not including — **ex·clu·sive·ly** *adv*

ex·crete *vb* **ex·cret·ed; ex·cret·ing :** to separate and give off waste matter from the body usually as urine or sweat

ex·cre·tion *n* **1 :** the process of excreting **2 :** waste material excreted

ex·cre·to·ry *adj* **:** of or relating to excretion **:** used in excreting

ex·cur·sion *n* **1 :** a brief pleasure trip **2 :** a trip at special reduced rates

ex·cus·able *adj* **:** possible to excuse

[1]**ex·cuse** *vb* **ex·cused; ex·cus·ing 1 :** to make apology for **2 :** to overlook or pardon as of little importance **3 :** to let off from doing something **4 :** to be an acceptable reason for

[2]**ex·cuse** *n* **1 :** the act of excusing **2 :** something offered as a reason for being excused **3 :** something that excuses or is a reason for excusing

ex·e·cute *vb* **ex·e·cut·ed; ex·e·cut·ing 1 :** to put into effect **:** CARRY OUT, PERFORM **2 :** to put to death according to a legal order **3 :** to make according to a design

ex·e·cu·tion *n* **1 :** a carrying through of something to its finish **2 :** a putting to death as a legal penalty

[1]**ex·ec·u·tive** *adj* **1 :** fitted for or relating to the carrying of things to completion **2 :** concerned with or relating to the carrying out of the law and the conduct of public affairs

[2]**executive** *n* **1 :** the executive branch of a government **2 :** a person who manages or directs

ex·em·pli·fy *vb* **ex·em·pli·fied; ex·em·pli·fy·ing :** to show by example

[1]**ex·empt** *adj* **:** free or released from some condition or requirement that other persons must meet or deal with

[2]**exempt** *vb* **:** to make exempt

ex·emp·tion *n* **1 :** the act of exempting **:** the state of being exempt **2 :** something that is exempted

[1]**ex·er·cise** *n* **1 :** the act of putting into use, action, or practice **2 :** bodily activity for the sake of health **3 :** a school lesson or other task performed to develop skill **:** practice work **:** DRILL **4 exercises** *pl* **:** a program of songs, speeches, and announcing of awards and honors

[2]**exercise** *vb* **ex·er·cised; ex·er·cis·ing 1 :** to put into use **:** EXERT **2 :** to use again and again to train or develop **3 :** to take part in bodily activity for the sake of health or training

ex·ert *vb* **1 :** to put forth (as strength) **:** bring into play **2 :** to put (oneself) into action or to tiring effort

ex·er·tion *n* **1 :** the act of exerting **2 :** use of strength or ability

ex·hale *vb* **ex·haled; ex·hal·ing 1 :** to breathe out **2 :** to send forth **:** give off

[1]**ex·haust** *vb* **1 :** to draw out or let out completely **2 :** to use up completely **3 :** to tire out **:** FATIGUE

[2]**exhaust** *n* **1 :** the gas that escapes from an engine **2 :** a system of pipes through which exhaust escapes

ex·haus·tion *n* **1 :** the act of exhausting **2 :** the condition of being exhausted

[1]**ex·hib·it** *vb* **1 :** to show by outward signs **:** REVEAL **2 :** to put on display

[2]**exhibit** *n* **1 :** an article or collection shown in an exhibition **2 :** an article presented as evidence in a law court

ex·hi·bi·tion *n* **1 :** the act of exhibiting **2 :** a public showing (as of athletic skill or works of art)

ex·hil·a·rate *vb* **ex·hil·a·rat·ed; ex·hil·a·rat·ing :** to make cheerful or lively

ex·hort *vb* **:** to try to influence by words or advice **:** urge strongly

[1]**ex·ile** *n* **1 :** the sending or forcing of a person away from his or her own country or the situation of a person who is sent away **2 :** a person who is expelled from his or her own country

[2]**exile** *vb* **ex·iled; ex·il·ing :** to force to leave one's own country

ex·ist *vb* **1 :** to have actual being **:** be real **2 :** to continue to live **3 :** to be found **:** OCCUR

ex·is·tence *n* **1 :** the fact or the condition of being or of being real **2 :** the state of being alive **:** LIFE

[1]**ex·it** *n* **1 :** the act of going out of or away from a place **:** DEPARTURE **2 :** a way of getting out of a place

[2]**exit** *vb* **:** to go out **:** LEAVE, DEPART

ex·o·dus *n* **:** the going out or away of a large number of people

ex·or·bi·tant *adj* **:** going beyond the limits of what is fair, reasonable, or expected

exo·sphere *n* **:** the outer fringe region of the atmosphere

ex·ot·ic *adj* **:** introduced from a foreign country

ex·pand *vb* **1 :** to open wide **:** UNFOLD **2 :** to take up or cause to take up more space **3 :** to work out in greater detail
ex·panse *n* **:** a wide area or stretch
ex·pan·sion *n* **:** the act of expanding or the state of being expanded **:** ENLARGEMENT
ex·pect *vb* **1 :** to look for or look forward to something that ought to or probably will happen **2 :** to consider to be obliged
ex·pec·tant *adj* **:** looking forward to or waiting for something
ex·pec·ta·tion *n* **:** a looking forward to or waiting for something
ex·pe·di·ent *adj* **:** suitable for bringing about a desired result often without regard to what is fair or right — **ex·pe·di·ent·ly** *adv*
ex·pe·di·tion *n* **1 :** a journey for a particular purpose (as for exploring) **2 :** the people making an expedition
ex·pel *vb* **ex·pelled; ex·pel·ling 1 :** to force out **2 :** to drive away
ex·pend *vb* **1 :** to pay out **:** SPEND **2 :** to use up
ex·pen·di·ture *n* **1 :** the act of spending (as money, time, or energy) **2 :** something that is spent
ex·pense *n* **1 :** something spent or required to be spent **:** COST **2 :** a cause for spending
ex·pen·sive *adj* **:** COSTLY 1 — **ex·pen·sive·ly** *adv*
[1]**ex·pe·ri·ence** *n* **1 :** the actual living through an event or events **2 :** the skill or knowledge gained by actually doing a thing **3 :** something that one has actually done or lived through
[2]**experience** *vb* **ex·pe·ri·enced; ex·pe·ri·enc·ing :** to have experience of **:** UNDERGO
ex·pe·ri·enced *adj* **:** made skillful or wise through experience
[1]**ex·per·i·ment** *n* **:** a trial or test made to find out about something
[2]**ex·per·i·ment** *vb* **:** to make experiments
ex·per·i·men·tal *adj* **:** of, relating to, or based on experiment
[1]**ex·pert** *adj* **:** showing special skill or knowledge gained from experience or training — **ex·pert·ly** *adv* — **ex·pert·ness** *n*
[2]**ex·pert** *n* **:** a person with special skill or knowledge of a subject
ex·pi·ra·tion *n* **:** an act or instance of expiring
ex·pire *vb* **ex·pired; ex·pir·ing 1 :** [1]DIE 1 **2 :** to come to an end **3 :** to breathe out **:** EXHALE
ex·plain *vb* **1 :** to make clear **:** CLARIFY 2 **2 :** to give the reasons for or cause of — **explain·able** *adj*
ex·pla·na·tion *n* **1 :** the act or process of explaining **2 :** a statement that makes something clear
ex·plan·a·to·ry *adj* **:** giving explanation **:** helping to explain
ex·plic·it *adj* **:** so clear in statement that there is no doubt about the meaning
ex·plode *vb* **ex·plod·ed; ex·plod·ing 1 :** to burst or cause to burst with violence and noise **2 :** to burst forth
[1]**ex·ploit** *n* **:** a brave or daring act
[2]**ex·ploit** *vb* **1 :** to get the value or use out of **2 :** to make use of unfairly for one's own benefit
ex·plo·ra·tion *n* **:** the act or an instance of exploring
ex·plore *vb* **ex·plored; ex·plor·ing 1 :** to search through or into **:** examine closely **2 :** to go into or through for purposes of discovery
ex·plor·er *n* **:** a person (as a traveler seeking new geographical or scientific information) who explores something
ex·plo·sion *n* **1 :** the act of exploding **:** a sudden and noisy bursting (as of a bomb) **2 :** a sudden outburst of feeling
[1]**ex·plo·sive** *adj* **1 :** able to cause explosion **2 :** likely to explode — **ex·plo·sive·ly** *adv*
[2]**explosive** *n* **:** an explosive substance
ex·po·nent *n* **:** a numeral written above and to the right of a number to show how many times the number is to be used as a factor
[1]**ex·port** *vb* **:** to send or carry abroad especially for sale in foreign countries
[2]**ex·port** *n* **1 :** something that is exported **2 :** the act of exporting
ex·pose *vb* **ex·posed; ex·pos·ing 1 :** to leave without protection, shelter, or care **2 :** to let light strike the photographic film or plate in taking a picture **3 :** to put on exhibition **:** display for sale **4 :** to make known
ex·po·si·tion *n* **1 :** an explaining of something **2 :** a public exhibition
ex·po·sure *n* **1 :** an act of making something public **2 :** the condition of being exposed **3 :** the act of letting light strike a photographic film or the time during which a film is exposed **4 :** a section of a roll of film for one picture **5 :** position with respect to direction
ex·pound *vb* **1 :** EXPLAIN 1, INTERPRET **2 :** to talk especially for a long time
[1]**ex·press** *adj* **1 :** clearly stated **2 :** of a certain sort **3 :** sent or traveling at high speed
[2]**express** *n* **1 :** a system for the special transportation of goods **2 :** a vehicle (as a train or elevator) run at special speed with few or no stops
[3]**express** *vb* **1 :** to make known especially in words **2 :** to represent by a sign or symbol **3 :** to send by express
ex·pres·sion *n* **1 :** the act or process of expressing especially in words **2 :** a meaningful word or saying **3 :** a way of speaking,

singing, or playing that shows mood or feeling **4 :** the look on one's face — **ex·pres·sion·less** *adj*

ex·pres·sive *adj* **:** expressing something **:** full of expression — **ex·pres·sive·ly** *adv* — **ex·pres·sive·ness** *n*

ex·press·way *n* **:** a divided highway for rapid traffic

ex·pul·sion *n* **:** the act of expelling **:** the state of being expelled

ex·qui·site *adj* **1 :** finely made or done **2 :** very pleasing (as through beauty or fitness) **3 :** very severe **:** INTENSE

ex·tend *vb* **1 :** [1]STRETCH 2 **2 :** to hold out **3 :** to make longer **4 :** ENLARGE **5 :** to stretch out or across something

ex·ten·sion *n* **1 :** a stretching out **:** an increase in length or time **2 :** a part forming an addition or enlargement

ex·ten·sive *adj* **:** having wide extent **:** BROAD

ex·tent *n* **1 :** the distance or range over which something extends **2 :** the point, degree, or limit to which something extends

[1]**ex·te·ri·or** *adj* **:** EXTERNAL

[2]**exterior** *n* **:** an exterior part or surface

ex·ter·mi·nate *vb* **ex·ter·mi·nat·ed; ex·ter·mi·nat·ing :** to get rid of completely **:** wipe out

[1]**ex·ter·nal** *adj* **:** situated on or relating to the outside **:** OUTSIDE

[2]**external** *n* **:** something that is external

ex·tinct *adj* **1 :** no longer active **2 :** no longer existing

ex·tinc·tion *n* **1 :** an act of extinguishing or an instance of being extinguished **2 :** the state of being extinct

ex·tin·guish *vb* **1 :** to cause to stop burning **2 :** to cause to die out **:** DESTROY — **ex·tin·guish·er** *n*

ex·tol *vb* **ex·tolled; ex·tol·ling :** to praise highly **:** GLORIFY

[1]**ex·tra** *adj* **:** being more than what is usual, expected, or due

[2]**extra** *n* **1 :** something extra **2 :** an added charge **3 :** a special edition of a newspaper **4 :** a person hired for a group scene (as in a movie)

[3]**extra** *adv* **:** beyond the usual size, amount, or degree

extra- *prefix* **:** outside **:** beyond

[1]**ex·tract** *vb* **1 :** to remove by pulling **2 :** to get out by pressing, distilling, or by a chemical process **3 :** to choose and take out for separate use

[2]**ex·tract** *n* **1 :** a selection from a writing **2 :** a product obtained by extraction

ex·trac·tion *n* **1 :** an act of extracting **2 :** ORIGIN 1, DESCENT

ex·tra·cur·ric·u·lar *adj* **:** of or relating to those activities (as athletics) that are offered by a school but are not part of the course of study

ex·traor·di·nary *adj* **:** so unusual as to be remarkable — **ex·traor·di·nari·ly** *adv*

ex·trav·a·gance *n* **1 :** the wasteful or careless spending of money **2 :** something that is extravagant **3 :** the quality or fact of being extravagant

ex·trav·a·gant *adj* **1 :** going beyond what is reasonable or suitable **2 :** wasteful especially of money — **ex·trav·a·gant·ly** *adv*

[1]**ex·treme** *adj* **1 :** existing to a very great degree **2 :** farthest from a center — **ex·treme·ly** *adv*

[2]**extreme** *n* **1 :** something as far as possible from a center or from its opposite **2 :** the greatest possible degree **:** MAXIMUM

ex·trem·i·ty *n, pl* **ex·trem·i·ties 1 :** the farthest limit, point, or part **2 :** an end part of a limb of the body (as a foot) **3 :** an extreme degree (as of emotion or distress)

ex·tri·cate *vb* **ex·tri·cat·ed; ex·tri·cat·ing :** to free from entanglement or difficulty

ex·ult *vb* **:** to be in high spirits **:** REJOICE

ex·ul·tant *adj* **:** full of or expressing joy or triumph — **ex·ul·tant·ly** *adv*

-ey — see -Y

[1]**eye** *n* **1 :** the organ of seeing **2 :** the ability to see **3 :** the ability to recognize **4 :** GLANCE **5 :** close attention **:** WATCH **6 :** JUDGMENT 1 **7 :** something like or suggesting an eye **8 :** the center of something — **eyed** *adj* — **eye·less** *adj*

[2]**eye** *vb* **eyed; eye·ing** *or* **ey·ing :** to look at **:** watch closely

eye·ball *n* **:** the whole eye

eye·brow *n* **:** the arch or ridge over the eye **:** the hair on the ridge over the eye

eye·drop·per *n* **:** DROPPER 2

eye·glass *n* **1 :** a glass lens used to help one to see clearly **2 eyeglasses** *pl* **:** a pair of glass lenses set in a frame and used to help one to see clearly

eye·lash *n* **:** a single hair of the fringe on the eyelid

eye·let *n* **1 :** a small hole (as in cloth or leather) for a lace or rope **2 :** GROMMET

eye·lid *n* **:** the thin movable cover of an eye

eye·piece *n* **:** the lens or combination of lenses at the eye end of an optical instrument (as a microscope or telescope)

eye·sight *n* **:** [1]SIGHT 4, VISION

eye·sore *n* **:** something displeasing to the sight

eye·strain *n* **:** a tired or irritated state of the eyes (as from too much use)

eye·tooth *n, pl* **eye·teeth :** a canine tooth of the upper jaw

ey·rie *n* **:** AERIE

F

f *n, pl* **f's** *or* **fs** *often cap* **1 :** the sixth letter of the English alphabet **2 :** a grade that shows a student's work is failing

fa *n* **:** the fourth note of the musical scale

fa·ble *n* **1 :** a story that is not true **2 :** a story in which animals speak and act like people and which is usually meant to teach a lesson

fab·ric *n* **1 :** the basic structure **2 :** CLOTH 1 **3 :** a structural plan or material

fab·u·lous *adj* **1 :** like a fable especially in being marvelous or beyond belief **2 :** told in or based on fable

fa·cade *n* **:** the face or front of a building

[1]**face** *n* **1 :** the front part of the head **2 :** an expression of the face **3 :** outward appearance **4 :** GRIMACE **5 :** DIGNITY 1, PRESTIGE **6 :** a front, upper, or outer surface **7 :** one of the flat surfaces that bound a solid

[2]**face** *vb* **faced; fac·ing 1 :** to cover the front or surface of **2 :** to have the front or face toward **3 :** to oppose firmly

fac·et *n* **:** one of the small flat surfaces on a cut gem

fa·ce·tious *adj* **:** intended or trying to be funny

face–to–face *adv or adj* **:** in person

fa·cial *adj* **:** of or relating to the face — **fa·cial·ly** *adv*

fa·cil·i·tate *vb* **fa·cil·i·tat·ed; fa·cil·i·tat·ing :** to make easier

fa·cil·i·ty *n, pl* **fa·cil·i·ties 1 :** freedom from difficulty **2 :** ease in doing something **:** APTITUDE **3 :** something that makes an action, operation, or activity easier

fac·sim·i·le *n* **1 :** an exact copy **2 :** a system of transmitting and reproducing printed matter or pictures by means of signals sent over telephone lines

fact *n* **1 :** something (as an event or an act) that really exists or has occurred **2 :** physical reality or actual experience

[1]**fac·tor** *n* **1 :** something that helps produce a result **2 :** any of the numbers that when multiplied together form a product

[2]**factor** *vb* **:** to find the factors of a number

fac·to·ry *n, pl* **fac·to·ries :** a place where goods are manufactured

fac·tu·al *adj* **:** of, relating to, or based on facts — **fac·tu·al·ly** *adv*

fac·ul·ty *n, pl* **fac·ul·ties 1 :** ability to do something **:** TALENT **2 :** one of the powers of the mind or body **3 :** the teachers in a school or college

fad *n* **:** a way of doing or an interest widely followed for a time

fade *vb* **fad·ed; fad·ing 1 :** to dry up **:** WITHER **2 :** to lose or cause to lose brightness of color **3 :** to grow dim or faint

Fahr·en·heit *adj* **:** relating to or having a temperature scale on which the boiling point of water is at 212 degrees above the zero of the scale and the freezing point is at 32 degrees above zero

[1]**fail** *vb* **1 :** to lose strength **:** WEAKEN **2 :** to die away **3 :** to stop functioning **4 :** to fall short **5 :** to be or become absent or not enough **6 :** to be unsuccessful **7 :** to become bankrupt **8 :** DISAPPOINT, DESERT **9 :** [1]NEGLECT 2

[2]**fail** *n* **:** FAILURE 1

fail·ing *n* **:** a slight moral weakness or flaw

fail·ure *n* **1 :** a failing to do or perform **2 :** a state of being unable to work in a normal way **3 :** a lack of success **4 :** BANKRUPTCY **5 :** a falling short **6 :** a breaking down **7 :** a person or thing that has failed

[1]**faint** *adj* **1 :** lacking courage **:** COWARDLY **2 :** being weak or dizzy and likely to collapse **3 :** lacking strength **:** FEEBLE **4 :** not clear or plain **:** DIM — **faint·ly** *adv* — **faint·ness** *n*

[2]**faint** *vb* **:** to lose consciousness

[3]**faint** *n* **:** an act or condition of fainting

faint·heart·ed *adj* **:** TIMID

[1]**fair** *adj* **1 :** attractive in appearance **:** BEAUTIFUL **2 :** not stormy or cloudy **3 :** not favoring one over another **4 :** observing the rules **5 :** being within the foul lines **6 :** not dark **:** BLOND **7 :** neither good nor bad — **fair·ness** *n*

[2]**fair** *adv* **:** in a fair manner

[3]**fair** *n* **1 :** a gathering of buyers and sellers at a certain time and place for trade **2 :** an exhibition (as of livestock or farm products) usually along with entertainment and amusements **3 :** a sale of articles for a charitable purpose

fair·ground *n* **:** an area set aside for fairs, circuses, or exhibitions

fair·ly *adv* **1 :** in a manner of speaking **:** QUITE **2 :** in a fair manner **:** JUSTLY **3 :** for the most part **:** RATHER

[1]**fairy** *n, pl* **fair·ies :** an imaginary being who has the form of a very tiny human being and has magic powers

[2]**fairy** *adj* **:** of, relating to, or like a fairy

fairy·land *n* **1 :** the land of fairies **2 :** a place of delicate beauty or magical charm

fairy tale *n* **1 :** a story about fairies **2 :** a small lie **:** FIB

faith *n* **1 :** loyalty to duty or to a person **2 :** belief in God **3 :** firm belief even in the absence of proof **4 :** a system of religious beliefs **:** RELIGION

faith·ful *adj* **1 :** RELIABLE **2 :** firm in devotion or support **3 :** true to the facts **:** ACCURATE — **faith·ful·ly** *adv* — **faith·ful·ness** *n*

faith·less *adj* **:** not true to allegiance or duty — **faith·less·ly** *adv* — **faith·less·ness** *n*

[1]**fake** *adj* **:** [1]COUNTERFEIT

[2]**fake** *n* **:** a person or thing that is not really what is pretended

[3]**fake** *vb* **faked; fak·ing 1 :** to change or treat in a way that gives a false effect **2 :** [2]COUNTERFEIT 2 **3 :** PRETEND 1

fal·con *n* **1 :** a hawk trained for use in hunting small game **2 :** any of several small hawks with long wings and swift flight

fal·con·ry *n* **:** the art or sport of hunting with a falcon

[1]**fall** *vb* **fell; fall·en; fall·ing 1 :** to come or go down freely by the force of gravity **2 :** to come as if by falling **3 :** to become lower (as in degree or value) **4 :** to topple from an upright position **5 :** to collapse wounded or dead **6 :** to become captured **7 :** to occur at a certain time **8 :** to pass from one condition of body or mind to another — **fall short :** be lacking in something

[2]**fall** *n* **1 :** the act or an instance of falling **2 :** AUTUMN **3 :** a thing or quantity that falls **4 :** a loss of greatness **:** DOWNFALL **5 :** WATERFALL — usually used in pl. **6 :** a decrease in size, amount, or value **7 :** the distance something falls

fal·la·cy *n, pl* **fal·la·cies 1 :** a false or mistaken idea **2 :** false reasoning

fall back *vb* **:** [2]RETREAT

fall·out *n* **:** the usually radioactive particles falling through the atmosphere as a result of the explosion of an atomic bomb

fall out *vb* **:** [2]QUARREL 2

[1]**fal·low** *n* **:** land for crops that lies idle

[2]**fallow** *vb* **:** to till without planting a crop

[3]**fallow** *adj* **:** not tilled or planted

fallow deer *n* **:** a small European deer with broad antlers and a pale yellowish coat spotted with white in summer

[1]**false** *adj* **fals·er; fals·est 1 :** not true, genuine, or honest **2 :** not faithful or loyal **3 :** not based on facts or sound judgment — **false·ly** *adv* — **false·ness** *n*

[2]**false** *adv* **:** in a false or misleading manner

false·hood *n* **1 :** [3]LIE **2 :** the habit of lying

fal·si·fy *vb* **fal·si·fied; fal·si·fy·ing :** to make false

fal·si·ty *n, pl* **fal·si·ties 1 :** something false **2 :** the quality or state of being false

fal·ter *vb* **1 :** to move unsteadily **:** WAVER **2 :** to hesitate in speech **3 :** to hesitate in purpose or action

fame *n* **:** the fact or condition of being known to and usually thought well of by the public **:** RENOWN

famed *adj* **:** known widely and well **:** FAMOUS

fa·mil·ial *adj* **:** of, relating to, or typical of a family

fa·mil·iar *adj* **1 :** closely acquainted **:** INTIMATE **2 :** INFORMAL 1 **3 :** too friendly or bold **4 :** often seen or experienced **5 :** having a good knowledge of

fa·mil·iar·i·ty *n, pl* **fa·mil·iar·i·ties 1 :** close friendship **:** INTIMACY **2 :** good knowledge of something **3 :** INFORMALITY 1

fa·mil·iar·ize *vb* **fa·mil·iar·ized; fa·mil·iar·iz·ing :** to make familiar

fam·i·ly *n, pl* **fam·i·lies 1 :** a group of persons who come from the same ancestor **2 :** a group of persons living under one roof or one head **3 :** a group of things sharing certain characteristics **4 :** a social group made up of parents and their children **5 :** a group of related plants or animals that ranks above the genus and below the order in scientific classification

fam·ine *n* **1 :** a very great and general lack of food **2 :** a great shortage

fam·ish *vb* **:** to suffer from hunger **:** STARVE

fam·ished *adj* **:** very hungry

fa·mous *adj* **:** very well-known

fa·mous·ly *adv* **:** very well

[1]**fan** *n* **1 :** something (as a hand-waved semicircular device or a mechanism with rotating blades) for producing a current of air **2 :** something like a fan — **fan·like** *adj*

[2]**fan** *vb* **fanned; fan·ning 1 :** to move air with a fan **2 :** to direct a current of air upon with a fan

[3]**fan** *n* **:** an enthusiastic follower or admirer

[1]**fa·nat·ic** *adj* **:** too enthusiastic or devoted

[2]**fanatic** *n* **:** a fanatic person

fan·ci·ful *adj* **1 :** showing free use of the imagination **2 :** coming from fancy rather than reason — **fan·ci·ful·ly** *adv* — **fan·ci·ful·ness** *n*

[1]**fan·cy** *vb* **fan·cied; fan·cy·ing 1 :** [1]LIKE 1, ENJOY **2 :** IMAGINE 1

[2]**fancy** *n, pl* **fancies 1 :** the power of the mind to think of things that are not present or real **:** IMAGINATION **2 :** LIKING **3 :** IDEA 2, NOTION

[3]**fancy** *adj* **fan·ci·er; fan·ci·est 1 :** not plain or ordinary **2 :** being above the average (as in quality or price) **3 :** done with great skill and grace — **fan·ci·ly** *adv* — **fan·ci·ness** *n*

fang *n* **1 :** a long sharp tooth by which animals seize and hold their prey **2 :** one of the usually two long hollow or grooved teeth by which a poisonous snake injects its poison — **fanged** *adj*

fan·tas·tic *adj* **1 :** produced by or like something produced by the fancy **2 :** barely believable — **fan·tas·ti·cal·ly** *adv*

fan·ta·sy *or* **phan·ta·sy** *n, pl* **fan·ta·sies** *or* **phan·ta·sies 1 :** IMAGINATION 1 **2 :** something produced by the imagination

[1]**far** *adv* **far·ther** *or* **fur·ther; far·thest** *or* **fur·thest 1 :** at or to a great distance in space or time **2 :** to a great extent **:** MUCH **3 :** to or at a definite distance or point **4 :** to an advanced point

[2]**far** *adj* **far·ther** *or* **fur·ther; far·thest** *or* **fur·thest 1 :** very distant in space or time **2 :** LONG 3 **3 :** the more distant of two

far·away *adj* **1 :** REMOTE 1, DISTANT **2 :** PREOCCUPIED

[1]**fare** *vb* **fared; far·ing :** to get along **:** SUCCEED

[2]**fare** *n* **1 :** the money a person pays to travel (as on a bus) **2 :** a person paying a fare **3 :** FOOD 1

[1]**fare·well** *n* **:** an expression of good wishes at parting — often used as an interjection

[2]**fare·well** *adj* **:** of or relating to a time or act of leaving **:** FINAL

far·fetched *adj* **:** not likely to be true

[1]**farm** *n* **1 :** a piece of land used for raising crops or animals **2 :** an area of water where fish or shellfish are grown

[2]**farm** *vb* **:** to work on or run a farm — **farm·er** *n*

farm·hand *n* **:** a farm laborer

farm·house *n* **:** the dwelling house of a farm

farm·yard *n* **:** the yard around or enclosed by farm buildings

far–off *adj* **:** distant in time or space

far–reach·ing *adj* **:** EXTENSIVE

far·sight·ed *adj* **1 :** able to see distant things more clearly than near ones **2 :** able to judge how something will work out in the future — **far·sight·ed·ness** *n*

[1]**far·ther** *adv* **1 :** at or to a greater distance or more advanced point **2 :** [2]BESIDES

[2]**farther** *adj* **:** more distant

[1]**far·thest** *adj* **:** most distant

[2]**farthest** *adv* **1 :** to or at the greatest distance in space or time **2 :** to the most advanced point

fas·ci·nate *vb* **fas·ci·nat·ed; fas·ci·nat·ing 1 :** to seize and hold the attention of **2 :** to attract greatly

fas·ci·na·tion *n* **:** the state of being fascinated

fas·cism *n* **:** a political system headed by a dictator in which the government controls business and labor and opposition is not permitted

fas·cist *n, often cap* **:** one who approves of or practices fascism

[1]**fash·ion** *n* **1 :** the make or form of something **2 :** MANNER 2, WAY **3 :** the popular style of a thing at a certain time

[2]**fashion** *vb* **:** to give shape or form to **:** MOLD

fash·ion·able *adj* **:** following the fashion or established style — **fash·ion·ably** *adv*

[1]**fast** *adj* **1 :** firmly placed **2 :** totally loyal **3 :** moving, operating, or acting quickly **4 :** taking a short time **5 :** indicating ahead of the correct time **6 :** not likely to fade

[2]**fast** *adv* **1 :** in a fast or fixed way **2 :** to the full extent **:** SOUND **3 :** with great speed

[3]**fast** *vb* **1 :** to go without eating **2 :** to eat in small amounts or only certain foods

[4]**fast** *n* **1 :** the act of fasting **2 :** a period of fasting

fas·ten *vb* **1 :** to attach or join by or as if by pinning, tying, or nailing **2 :** to fix firmly **3 :** to become fixed or joined — **fas·ten·er** *n*

fas·ten·ing *n* **:** something that holds another thing shut or in the right position

fast–food *adj* **:** of, relating to, or specializing in food that can be prepared and served quickly — **fast–food** *n*

fas·tid·i·ous *adj* **:** hard to please **:** very particular

[1]**fat** *adj* **fat·ter; fat·test 1 :** having much body fat **2 :** [1]THICK 1 **3 :** richly rewarding or profitable **4 :** swollen up — **fat·ness** *n*

[2]**fat** *n* **1 :** animal or plant tissue containing much greasy or oily material **2 :** any of numerous compounds of carbon, hydrogen, and oxygen that make up most of animal or plant fat and that are important to nutrition as sources of energy **3 :** a solid fat as distinguished from an oil **4 :** the best or richest part

fa·tal *adj* **1 :** FATEFUL **2 :** causing death **:** MORTAL — **fa·tal·ly** *adv*

fa·tal·i·ty *n, pl* **fa·tal·i·ties :** a death resulting from a disaster or accident

fate *n* **1 :** a power beyond human control that is held to determine what happens **:** DESTINY **2 :** something that happens as though determined by fate **:** FORTUNE **3 :** final outcome

fate·ful *adj* **:** having serious results — **fate·ful·ly** *adv* — **fate·ful·ness** *n*

[1]**fa·ther** *n* **1 :** a male parent **2** *cap* **:** GOD 1 **3 :** ANCESTOR **4 :** one who cares for another as a father might **5 :** one deserving the respect and love given to a father **6 :** a person who invents or begins something **7 :** PRIEST — used especially as a title — **fa·ther·hood** *n* — **fa·ther·less** *adj*

[2]**father** *vb* **1 :** to become the father of **2 :** to care for as a father

fa·ther–in–law *n, pl* **fa·thers–in–law :** the father of one's husband or wife

fa·ther·land *n* **:** one's native land

fa·ther·ly *adj* **1 :** of or like a father **2 :** showing the affection or concern of a father

[1]**fath·om** *n* **:** a unit of length equal to six feet

(about 1.8 meters) used chiefly in measuring the depth of water

[2]**fathom** *vb* **1 :** to measure the depth of water by means of a special line **2 :** to see into and come to understand

[1]**fa·tigue** *n* **:** a state of being very tired

[2]**fatigue** *vb* **fa·tigued; fa·tigu·ing :** to tire by work or exertion

fat·ten *vb* **:** to make or become fat

fat·ty *adj* **fat·ti·er; fat·ti·est :** containing or like fat

fau·cet *n* **:** a fixture for controlling the flow of a liquid (as from a pipe or cask)

fault *n* **1 :** a weakness in character **:** FAILING **2 :** FLAW, IMPERFECTION **3 :** ERROR **4 :** responsibility for something wrong **5 :** a crack in the earth's crust along which movement occurs — **at fault :** BLAMEWORTHY

fault·less *adj* **:** free from fault **:** PERFECT — **fault·less·ly** *adv* — **fault·less·ness** *n*

faulty *adj* **fault·i·er; fault·i·est :** having a fault or blemish **:** IMPERFECT — **fault·i·ly** *adv* — **fault·i·ness** *n*

faun *n* **:** a Roman god of country life represented as part goat and part man

fau·na *n* **:** the animal life typical of a region, period, or special environment

[1]**fa·vor** *n* **1 :** APPROVAL, LIKING **2 :** a preferring of one side over another **:** PARTIALITY **3 :** an act of kindness **4 :** a small gift or decorative item

[2]**favor** *vb* **1 :** to regard with favor **2 :** OBLIGE 3 **3 :** to prefer especially unfairly **4 :** to make possible or easier **5 :** to look like

fa·vor·able *adj* **1 :** showing favor **2 :** PROMISING — **fa·vor·able·ness** *n* — **fa·vor·ably** *adv*

[1]**fa·vor·ite** *n* **:** a person or a thing that is favored above others

[2]**favorite** *adj* **:** being a favorite

[1]**fawn** *vb* **1 :** to show affection — used especially of a dog **2 :** to try to win favor by behavior that shows lack of self-respect

[2]**fawn** *n* **1 :** a young deer **2 :** a light grayish brown

[1]**fax** *n* **1 :** FACSIMILE 2 **2 :** a machine used to send or receive material by facsimile **3 :** something sent or received by facsimile

[2]**fax** *vb* **:** to send material by facsimile

faze *vb* **fazed; faz·ing :** DAUNT

[1]**fear** *vb* **:** to be afraid of **:** feel fear

[2]**fear** *n* **:** a strong unpleasant feeling caused by being aware of danger or expecting something bad to happen

fear·ful *adj* **1 :** causing fear **2 :** filled with fear **3 :** showing or caused by fear — **fear·ful·ly** *adv* — **fear·ful·ness** *n*

fear·less *adj* **:** free from fear **:** BRAVE — **fear·less·ly** *adv* — **fear·less·ness** *n*

fear·some *adj* **:** causing fear

fea·si·ble *adj* **:** possible to do or carry out

[1]**feast** *n* **1 :** a fancy meal **2 :** a religious festival

[2]**feast** *vb* **1 :** to eat well **2 :** [2]DELIGHT 1

feat *n* **:** an act showing courage, strength, or skill

[1]**feath·er** *n* **1 :** one of the light horny growths that make up the outer covering of a bird **2 :** VARIETY 3, SORT — **feath·ered** *adj* — **feath·er·less** *adj*

[2]**feather** *vb* **:** to grow or form feathers

feather bed *n* **1 :** a mattress filled with feathers **2 :** a bed with a feather mattress

feath·ery *adj* **1 :** like a feather or tuft of feathers **2 :** covered with feathers

[1]**fea·ture** *n* **1 :** a single part (as the nose or the mouth) of the face **2 :** something especially noticeable **3 :** a main attraction **4 :** a special story in a newspaper or magazine

[2]**feature** *vb* **fea·tured; fea·tur·ing :** to stand out or cause to stand out

Feb·ru·ary *n* **:** the second month of the year

fe·ces *n pl* **:** body waste that passes out from the intestine

fed·er·al *adj* **:** of or relating to a nation formed by the union of several states or nations

fee *n* **1 :** a fixed charge **2 :** a charge for services

fee·ble *adj* **fee·bler; fee·blest 1 :** lacking in strength or endurance **2 :** not loud — **fee·ble·ness** *n* — **fee·bly** *adv*

[1]**feed** *vb* **fed; feed·ing 1 :** to give food to or give as food **2 :** to take food into the body **:** EAT **3 :** to supply with something necessary (as to growth or operation) — **feed·er** *n*

[2]**feed** *n* **:** food especially for livestock

[1]**feel** *vb* **felt; feel·ing 1 :** to be aware of through physical contact **2 :** to examine or test by touching **3 :** to be conscious of **4 :** to seem especially to the touch **5 :** to sense oneself to be

[2]**feel** *n* **1 :** SENSATION 2, FEELING **2 :** the quality of something as learned through or as if through touch

feel·er *n* **1 :** a long flexible structure (as an insect's antenna) that is an organ of touch **2 :** a suggestion or remark made to find out the views of other people

feel·ing *n* **1 :** the sense by which a person knows whether things are hard or soft, hot or cold, heavy or light **2 :** a sensation of temperature or pressure **3 :** a state of mind **4 feelings** *pl* **:** the state of a person's emotions **5 :** the condition of being aware **6 :** IMPRESSION 4

feet *pl of* FOOT

feign *vb* **:** PRETEND 2

[1]**feint** *n* **:** a pretended blow or attack at one point or in one direction to take attention

away from the point or direction one really intends to attack

[2]**feint** *vb* **:** to make a feint

[1]**fe·line** *adj* **1 :** of or relating to cats or the cat family **2 :** like or like that of a cat

[2]**feline** *n* **:** a feline animal **:** CAT

[1]**fell** *vb* **:** to cut or knock down

[2]**fell** *past of* FALL

[1]**fel·low** *n* **1 :** COMPANION 1, COMRADE **2 :** an equal in rank, power, or character **3 :** one of a pair **:** MATE **4 :** a male person

[2]**fellow** *adj* **:** being a companion, mate, or equal

fel·low·man *n, pl* **fel·low·men :** a fellow human being

fel·low·ship *n* **1 :** friendly relationship existing among persons **2 :** a group with similar interests

fel·on *n* **:** [2]CRIMINAL

fel·o·ny *n, pl* **fel·o·nies :** a very serious crime

[1]**felt** *n* **:** a heavy material made by rolling and pressing fibers together

[2]**felt** *past of* FEEL

[1]**fe·male** *adj* **1 :** of, relating to, or being the sex that bears young or lays eggs **2 :** having a pistil but no stamens **3 :** of, relating to, or characteristic of females — **fe·male·ness** *n*

[2]**female** *n* **:** a female being

fem·i·nine *adj* **1 :** [1]FEMALE 1 **2 :** [1]FEMALE 3

fem·i·nism *n* **1 :** the theory that women and men should have equal rights and opportunities **2 :** organized activity on behalf of women's rights and interests — **fem·i·nist** *n or adj*

fen *n* **:** low land covered by water

[1]**fence** *n* **:** a barrier (as of wood or wire) to prevent escape or entry or to mark a boundary

[2]**fence** *vb* **fenced; fenc·ing 1 :** to enclose with a fence **2 :** to practice fencing — **fenc·er** *n*

fenc·ing *n* **:** the sport of having a pretended fight with blunted swords

fend *vb* **1 :** REPEL 1 **2 :** to try to get along without help

fend·er *n* **1 :** a frame on the lower front of a locomotive or streetcar to catch or throw off anything that is hit **2 :** a guard over an automobile or cycle wheel

[1]**fer·ment** *vb* **:** to undergo or cause to undergo fermentation

[2]**fer·ment** *n* **1 :** something (as yeast) that causes fermentation **2 :** a state of excitement

fer·men·ta·tion *n* **:** a chemical breaking down of an organic material that is controlled by an enzyme and usually does not require oxygen

fern *n* **:** a plant that produces spores instead of seeds and no flowers and whose leaves are usually divided into many parts — **fern·like** *adj*

fe·ro·cious *adj* **:** FIERCE 1, SAVAGE — **fe·ro·cious·ly** *adv* — **fe·ro·cious·ness** *n*

fe·roc·i·ty *n, pl* **fe·roc·i·ties :** the quality or state of being ferocious

[1]**fer·ret** *n* **:** a domesticated animal with usually white or light brown or gray fur that is descended from the European polecat

[2]**ferret** *vb* **1 :** to hunt with a ferret **2 :** to find by eager searching

Fer·ris wheel *n* **:** an amusement device consisting of a large vertical wheel that is driven by a motor and has seats around its rim

[1]**fer·ry** *vb* **fer·ried; fer·ry·ing 1 :** to carry by boat over a body of water **2 :** to cross by a ferry **3 :** to deliver an airplane under its own power **4 :** to transport in an airplane

[2]**ferry** *n, pl* **fer·ries 1 :** a place where persons or things are ferried **2 :** FERRYBOAT

fer·ry·boat *n* **:** a boat used to ferry passengers, vehicles, or goods

fer·tile *adj* **1 :** producing much vegetation or large crops **2 :** capable of developing and growing

fer·til·i·ty *n* **:** the condition of being fertile

fer·til·iza·tion *n* **1 :** an act or process of making fertile **2 :** the joining of an egg cell and a sperm cell to form the first stage of an embryo

fer·til·ize *vb* **fer·til·ized; fer·til·iz·ing :** to make fertile or more fertile

fer·til·iz·er *n* **:** material added to soil to make it more fertile

fer·vent *adj* **:** very warm in feeling **:** ARDENT — **fer·vent·ly** *adv*

fer·vor *n* **:** strong feeling or expression

fes·ter *vb* **:** to become painfully red and sore and usually full of pus

fes·ti·val *n* **1 :** a time of celebration **2 :** a program of cultural events or entertainment

fes·tive *adj* **1 :** having to do with a feast or festival **2 :** very merry and joyful

fes·tiv·i·ty *n, pl* **fes·tiv·i·ties 1 :** a festive state **2 :** festive activity **:** MERRYMAKING

[1]**fes·toon** *n* **:** an ornament (as a chain) hanging between two points

[2]**festoon** *vb* **:** to hang or form festoons on

fetch *vb* **1 :** to go after and bring back **2 :** to bring as a price **:** sell for

fetch·ing *adj* **:** very attractive — **fetch·ing·ly** *adv*

[1]**fet·ter** *n* **1 :** a shackle for the feet **2 :** something that holds back **:** RESTRAINT

[2]**fetter** *vb* **1 :** to put fetters on **2 :** to keep from moving or acting freely

fe·tus *n* **:** an animal not yet born or hatched but more developed than an embryo

[1]**feud** *n* **:** a long bitter quarrel carried on espe-

cially between families or clans and usually having acts of violence and revenge

²feud *vb* **:** to carry on a feud

feu·dal *adj* **:** of or relating to feudalism

feu·dal·ism *n* **:** a system of social organization existing in medieval Europe in which a vassal served a lord and received protection and land in return

fe·ver *n* **1 :** a rise of body temperature above normal **2 :** a disease in which fever is present

fe·ver·ish *adj* **1 :** having a fever **2 :** of, relating to, or being fever **3 :** showing great emotion or activity **:** HECTIC — **fe·ver·ish·ly** *adv* — **fe·ver·ish·ness** *n*

¹few *pron* **:** not many **:** a small number

²few *adj* **:** not many but some

³few *n* **:** a small number of individuals

fez *n, pl* **fez·zes :** a round red felt hat that usually has a tassel but no brim

fi·as·co *n, pl* **fi·as·coes :** a complete failure

¹fib *n* **:** an unimportant lie

²fib *vb* **fibbed; fib·bing :** to tell a fib — **fib·ber** *n*

fi·ber *or* **fi·bre** *n* **:** a long slender threadlike structure

fi·ber·glass *also* **fi·bre·glass** *n* **1 :** glass in the form of fibers used in various products (as filters and insulation) **2 :** a material of plastic and fiberglass

fiber op·tics *n pl* **:** thin transparent fibers of glass or plastic that transmit light throughout their length

fi·brous *adj* **:** containing, consisting of, or like fibers

-fi·ca·tion *n suffix* **:** the act or process of or the result of

fick·le *adj* **:** INCONSTANT — **fick·le·ness** *n*

fic·tion *n* **1 :** something told or written that is not fact **2 :** a made-up story

fic·tion·al *adj* **:** of, relating to, or suggesting fiction — **fic·tion·al·ly** *adv*

fic·ti·tious *adj* **:** not real

¹fid·dle *n* **:** VIOLIN

²fiddle *vb* **fid·dled; fid·dling 1 :** to play on a fiddle **2 :** to move the hands or fingers restlessly **3 :** to spend time in aimless activity **4 :** TAMPER — **fid·dler** *n*

fid·dle·sticks *n* **:** NONSENSE 1 — used as an interjection

fi·del·i·ty *n* **1 :** LOYALTY **2 :** ACCURACY

fidg·et *vb* **:** to move in a restless or nervous way

fidg·ets *n pl* **:** uneasy restlessness shown by nervous movements

fidg·ety *adj* **:** tending to fidget

fief *n* **:** an estate given to a vassal by a feudal lord

¹field *n* **1 :** a piece of open, cleared, or cultivated land **2 :** a piece of land put to a special use or giving a special product **3 :** an open space **4 :** an area of activity or influence **5 :** a background on which something is drawn, painted, or mounted

²field *adj* **:** of or relating to a field

³field *vb* **:** to catch or stop and throw a ball

field·er *n* **:** a baseball player other than the pitcher or catcher on the team that is not at bat

field glasses *n pl* **:** a hand-held instrument for seeing at a distance that is made up of two telescopes usually without prisms

field goal *n* **:** a score in football made by kicking the ball through the goal during ordinary play

fiend *n* **1 :** DEMON 1, DEVIL **2 :** a very wicked or cruel person — **fiend·ish** *adj*

fierce *adj* **fierc·er; fierc·est 1 :** likely to attack **2 :** having or showing very great energy or enthusiasm **3 :** wild or threatening in appearance — **fierce·ly** *adv* — **fierce·ness** *n*

fi·ery *adj* **fi·er·i·er; fi·er·i·est 1 :** being on fire **2 :** hot like a fire **3 :** full of spirit

fi·es·ta *n* **:** FESTIVAL 1, CELEBRATION

fife *n* **:** a small musical instrument like a flute that produces a shrill sound

¹fif·teen *adj* **:** being one more than fourteen

²fifteen *n* **:** one more than fourteen **:** three times five **:** 15

¹fif·teenth *adj* **:** coming right after fourteenth

²fifteenth *n* **:** number fifteen in a series

¹fifth *adj* **:** coming right after fourth

²fifth *n* **1 :** number five in a series **2 :** one of five equal parts

¹fif·ti·eth *adj* **:** coming right after forty-ninth

²fiftieth *n* **:** number fifty in a series

¹fif·ty *adj* **:** being five times ten

²fifty *n* **:** five times ten **:** 50

fig *n* **:** an edible fruit that is oblong or shaped like a pear and that grows on a tree related to the mulberry

¹fight *vb* **fought; fight·ing 1 :** to take part in a fight **:** COMBAT **2 :** to try hard **3 :** to struggle against — **fight·er** *n*

²fight *n* **1 :** a meeting in battle or in physical combat **2 :** ¹QUARREL 2 **3 :** strength or desire for fighting

¹fig·ure *n* **1 :** a symbol (as 1, 2, 3) that stands for a number **:** NUMERAL **2 figures** *pl* **:** ARITHMETIC 2 **3 :** value or price expressed in figures **4 :** the shape or outline of something **5 :** the shape of the body especially of a person **6 :** an illustration in a printed text **7 :** ¹PATTERN 3 **8 :** a series of movements in a dance **9 :** an outline traced by a series of movements (as by an ice skater) **10 :** a well-known or important person

²figure *vb* **fig·ured; fig·ur·ing 1 :** to decorate with a pattern **2 :** CALCULATE 1

fig·ure·head *n* **:** a figure, statue, or bust on the bow of a ship
figure of speech : an expression (as a simile or a metaphor) that uses words in other than a plain or literal way
figure out *vb* **:** to work out in the mind
fil·a·ment *n* **1 :** a fine thread **2 :** a fine wire (as in a light bulb) that is made to glow by the passage of an electric current **3 :** the stalk of a plant stamen that bears the anther — **fil·a·men·tous** *adj*
fil·bert *n* **:** the hazel or its nut
filch *vb* **:** PILFER
[1]**file** *n* **:** a steel tool with sharp ridges or teeth for smoothing or rubbing down hard substances
[2]**file** *vb* **filed; fil·ing :** to rub, smooth, or cut away with a file
[3]**file** *vb* **filed; fil·ing 1 :** to arrange in order **2 :** to enter or record officially
[4]**file** *n* **1 :** a device for keeping papers or records **2 :** a collection of papers or records kept in a file **3 :** a collection of data treated as a unit by a computer
[5]**file** *n* **:** a row of persons or things arranged one behind the other
[6]**file** *vb* **filed; fil·ing :** to move in a file
fil·ial *adj* **1 :** of, relating to, or suitable for a son or daughter **2 :** being or having the relation of offspring
[1]**fill** *vb* **1 :** to make or become full **2 :** to occupy fully **3 :** to spread through **4 :** to stop up **:** PLUG **5 :** to write information on or in **:** COMPLETE **6 :** to do the duties of **7 :** to supply according to directions
[2]**fill** *n* **1 :** an amount that satisfies **2 :** material for filling something
fill·er *n* **1 :** one that fills **2 :** a material used for filling
fil·let *n* **:** a piece of lean boneless meat or fish
fill·ing *n* **:** a substance used to fill something else
filling station *n* **:** SERVICE STATION
fil·ly *n, pl* **fillies :** a female foal **:** a young female horse
[1]**film** *n* **1 :** a thin coating or layer **2 :** a roll of material prepared for taking pictures **3 :** MOVIE
[2]**film** *vb* **1 :** to cover or become covered with film **2 :** to photograph on a film **3 :** to make a movie
film·strip *n* **:** a strip of film for projecting still pictures on a screen
filmy *adj* **film·i·er; film·i·est :** of, like, or made of film
[1]**fil·ter** *n* **1 :** a device or a mass of material (as sand) with tiny openings through which a gas or liquid is passed to separate out something which it contains **2 :** a transparent material that absorbs light of some colors and is used for changing light (as in photography)
[2]**filter** *vb* **1 :** to pass through a filter **2 :** to remove by means of a filter
filth *n* **:** disgusting dirt
filthy *adj* **filth·i·er; filth·i·est :** disgustingly dirty — **filth·i·ness** *n*
fil·tra·tion *n* **:** the process of filtering
fin *n* **1 :** any of the thin parts that stick out from the body of a water animal and especially a fish and are used in moving or guiding the body through the water **2 :** something shaped like a fin
[1]**fi·nal** *adj* **1 :** not to be changed **:** CONCLUSIVE **2 :** coming or happening at the end — **fi·nal·ly** *adv*
[2]**final** *n* **1 :** the last match or game of a tournament **2 :** a final examination in a course
fi·na·le *n* **:** the close or end of something (as a musical work)
fi·nal·i·ty *n* **:** the condition of being final
[1]**fi·nance** *n* **1 finances** *pl* **:** money available to a government, business, or individual **2 :** the system that includes the circulation of money, the providing of banks and credit, and the making of investments
[2]**finance** *vb* **fi·nanced; fi·nanc·ing :** to provide money for
fi·nan·cial *adj* **:** having to do with finance or with finances — **fi·nan·cial·ly** *adv*
fin·an·cier *n* **:** a specialist in finance and especially in the financing of businesses
finch *n* **:** a small songbird (as a sparrow, bunting, or canary) that eats seeds
[1]**find** *vb* **found; find·ing 1 :** to come upon by chance **2 :** to come upon by searching, study, or effort **3 :** to decide on **4 :** to know by experience **5 :** to gain or regain the use of — **find fault :** to criticize in an unfavorable way
[2]**find** *n* **:** something found
find·er *n* **1 :** one that finds **2 :** a device on a camera that shows the view being photographed
find out *vb* **:** to learn by studying or watching **:** DISCOVER
[1]**fine** *n* **:** a sum of money to be paid as a punishment
[2]**fine** *vb* **fined; fin·ing :** to punish by a fine
[3]**fine** *adj* **fin·er; fin·est 1 :** very small or thin **2 :** not coarse **3 :** very good in quality or appearance — **fine·ly** *adv* — **fine·ness** *n*
[4]**fine** *adv* **:** very well
fin·ery *n, pl* **fin·er·ies :** stylish or showy clothes and jewelry
[1]**fin·ger** *n* **1 :** one of the five divisions of the end of the hand including the thumb **2 :** something that is like or does the work of a finger **3 :** the part of a glove into which a finger goes — **fin·ger·like** *adj*

²finger *vb* **:** to touch with the fingers **:** HANDLE

fin·ger·board *n* **:** a strip on the neck of a stringed instrument (as a guitar) against which the fingers press the strings to change the pitch

finger hole *n* **:** any of a group of holes in a wind instrument that may be covered with a finger to change the pitch

fin·ger·ling *n* **:** a young fish

fin·ger·nail *n* **:** the hard covering at the end of a finger

¹fin·ger·print *n* **:** the pattern of marks made by pressing a finger on a surface especially when the pattern is made in ink in order to identify a person

²fingerprint *vb* **:** to take the fingerprints of

fin·icky *adj* **:** very hard to please **:** FUSSY — **fin·ick·i·ness** *n*

¹fin·ish *vb* **1 :** to bring or come to an end **:** COMPLETE **2 :** to put a final coat or surface on

²finish *n* **1 :** ¹END 2, CONCLUSION **2 :** the final treatment or coating of a surface or the appearance given by finishing

fi·nite *adj* **:** having certain limits

Finn *n* **:** a person born or living in Finland

finned *adj* **:** having fins

¹Finn·ish *adj* **:** of or relating to Finland, its people, or the Finnish language

²Finnish *n* **:** the language of the Finns

fiord *variant of* FJORD

fir *n* **:** a tall evergreen tree related to the pine that yields useful lumber

¹fire *n* **1 :** the light and heat and especially the flame produced by burning **2 :** fuel that is burning (as in a fireplace) **3 :** the destructive burning of something (as a building) **4 :** a being lively **:** ENTHUSIASM **5 :** the shooting of firearms — **on fire :** actively burning — **under fire 1 :** exposed to the firing of enemy guns **2 :** under attack

²fire *vb* **fired; fir·ing 1 :** to set on fire **2 :** EXCITE 2, STIR **3 :** to dismiss from employment **4 :** to set off **:** EXPLODE **5 :** ¹SHOOT 2 **6 :** to subject to great heat

fire alarm *n* **:** an alarm sounded to signal that a fire has broken out

fire·arm *n* **:** a small weapon from which shot or a bullet is driven by the explosion of gunpowder

fire·bug *n* **:** a person who sets destructive fires on purpose

fire·crack·er *n* **:** a paper tube containing an explosive to be set off for amusement

fire engine *n* **:** a truck equipped to fight fires

fire escape *n* **:** a stairway that provides a way of escape from a building in case of fire

fire extinguisher *n* **:** something (as a metal container filled with chemicals) that is used to put out a fire

fire·fight·er *n* **:** a person whose job is to put out fires

fire·fly *n, pl* **fire·flies :** a small beetle producing a soft light

fire·house *n* **:** FIRE STATION

fire·man *n, pl* **fire·men 1 :** FIREFIGHTER **2 :** a person who tends a fire (as in a large furnace)

fire·place *n* **:** a structure with a hearth on which an open fire can be built for heating or especially outdoors for cooking

fire·plug *n* **:** HYDRANT

fire·proof *adj* **:** not easily burned **:** made safe against fire

fire·side *n* **1 :** a place near the hearth **2 :** ¹HOME 1

fire station *n* **:** a building housing fire engines and usually firefighters

fire·wood *n* **:** wood cut for fuel

fire·work *n* **1 :** a device that makes a display of light or noise by the burning of explosive or flammable materials **2 fireworks** *pl* **:** a display of fireworks

¹firm *adj* **1 :** STRONG 1, VIGOROUS **2 :** having a solid compact texture **3 :** not likely to be changed **4 :** not easily moved or shaken **:** FAITHFUL **5 :** showing no weakness — **firm·ly** *adv* — **firm·ness** *n*

²firm *n* **:** BUSINESS 2

fir·ma·ment *n* **:** the arch of the sky

¹first *adj* **1 :** being number one **2 :** coming before all others

²first *adv* **1 :** before any other **2 :** for the first time

³first *n* **1 :** number one in a series **2 :** something or someone that is first

first aid *n* **:** care or treatment given to an ill or injured person before regular medical help can be gotten

first·hand *adj or adv* **:** coming right from the original source

first lieutenant *n* **:** a commissioned officer in the Army, Air Force, or Marine Corps ranking above a second lieutenant

first–rate *adj* **:** EXCELLENT

first sergeant *n* **1 :** a noncommissioned officer serving as the chief assistant to a military commander **2 :** a noncommissioned officer ranking above a sergeant first class in the Army or above a gunnery sergeant in the Marine Corps

firth *n* **:** a narrow arm of the sea

¹fish *n, pl* **fish** *or* **fish·es 1 :** an animal that lives in water — usually used in combination **2 :** any of a large group of vertebrate animals that live in water, breathe with gills, and usually have fins and scales — **fish·like** *adj*

²fish *vb* **1 :** to attempt to catch fish **2 :** to try to find or to find out something by groping

fish·er·man *n, pl* **fish·er·men :** a person who fishes

fish·ery *n, pl* **fish·er·ies 1 :** the business of catching fish **2 :** a place for catching fish

fish·hook *n* **:** a hook used for catching fish

fishy *adj* **fish·i·er; fish·i·est 1 :** of or like fish **2 :** QUESTIONABLE

fis·sion *n* **1 :** a splitting or breaking into parts **2 :** a method of reproduction in which a living cell or body divides into two or more parts each of which grows into a whole new individual **3 :** the splitting of an atomic nucleus with the release of large amounts of energy

fis·sure *n* **:** a narrow opening or crack

fist *n* **:** the hand with the fingers doubled tight into the palm

¹fit *adj* **fit·ter; fit·test 1 :** good enough **2 :** healthy in mind and body — **fit·ness** *n*

²fit *n* **:** a sudden attack or outburst

³fit *vb* **fit·ted; fit·ting 1 :** to be suitable for or to **2 :** to be the right shape or size **3 :** to bring to the right shape or size **4 :** EQUIP

⁴fit *n* **1 :** the way something fits **2 :** a piece of clothing that fits

fit·ful *adj* **:** IRREGULAR 4

¹fit·ting *adj* **:** ²APPROPRIATE, SUITABLE — **fit·ting·ly** *adv*

²fitting *n* **:** a small accessory part

¹five *adj* **:** being one more than four

²five *n* **1 :** one more than four **:** 5 **2 :** the fifth in a set or series

¹fix *vb* **1 :** to make firm or secure **2 :** to cause to combine chemically **3 :** to set definitely **:** ESTABLISH **4 :** to get ready **:** PREPARE **5 :** ¹REPAIR 1, MEND — **fix·er** *n*

²fix *n* **:** an unpleasant or difficult position

fixed *adj* **1 :** not changing **:** SET **2 :** not moving **:** INTENT — **fix·ed·ly** *adv*

fixed star *n* **:** a star so distant that its motion can be measured only by very careful observations over long periods

fix·ture *n* **:** something attached as a permanent part

¹fizz *vb* **:** to make a hissing or sputtering sound

²fizz *n* **1 :** a hissing or sputtering sound **2 :** a bubbling drink

¹fiz·zle *vb* **fiz·zled; fiz·zling :** to fail after a good start

²fizzle *n* **:** FAILURE 3

fjord *or* **fiord** *n* **:** a narrow inlet of the sea between cliffs or steep slopes

flab·by *adj* **flab·bi·er; flab·bi·est :** not hard and firm **:** SOFT — **flab·bi·ness** *n*

¹flag *n* **:** a piece of cloth with a special design or color that is used as a symbol (as of a nation) or as a signal

²flag *vb* **flagged; flag·ging :** to signal with or as if with a flag

³flag *vb* **flagged; flag·ging :** to become weak

fla·gel·lum *n, pl* **fla·gel·la :** a long whiplike structure by which some tiny plants and animals move

flag·man *n, pl* **flag·men :** a person who signals with a flag

flag·on *n* **:** a container for liquids usually having a handle, spout, and lid

flag·pole *n* **:** a pole from which a flag flies

fla·grant *adj* **:** so bad as to be impossible to overlook — **fla·grant·ly** *adv*

flag·ship *n* **:** the ship carrying the commander of a group of ships and flying a flag that tells the commander's rank

flag·staff *n, pl* **flag·staffs :** FLAGPOLE

flag·stone *n* **:** a piece of hard flat rock used for paving

¹flail *n* **:** a tool for threshing grain by hand

²flail *vb* **:** to hit with or as if with a flail

flair *n* **:** natural ability

¹flake *n* **:** a small thin flat piece

²flake *vb* **flaked; flak·ing :** to form or separate into flakes

flaky *adj* **flak·i·er; flak·i·est :** tending to flake — **flak·i·ness** *n*

flam·boy·ant *adj* **:** liking or making a dashing show — **flam·boy·ant·ly** *adv*

¹flame *n* **1 :** the glowing gas that makes up part of a fire **2 :** a condition or appearance suggesting a flame

²flame *vb* **flamed; flam·ing :** to burn with or as if with a flame

flame·throw·er *n* **:** a device that shoots a burning stream of fuel

fla·min·go *n, pl* **fla·min·gos** *or* **fla·min·goes :** a waterbird with very long neck and legs, scarlet wings, and a broad bill bent downward at the end

flam·ma·ble *adj* **:** capable of being easily set on fire and of burning quickly

¹flank *n* **1 :** the fleshy part of the side between the ribs and the hip **2 :** ¹SIDE 3 **3 :** the right or left side of a formation (as of soldiers)

²flank *vb* **1 :** to pass around the flank of **2 :** to be located at the side of **:** BORDER

flank·er *n* **:** a football player stationed wide of the formation

flan·nel *n* **:** a soft cloth made of wool or cotton

¹flap *n* **1 :** something broad and flat or limber that hangs loose **2 :** the motion made by something broad and limber (as a sail or wing) moving back and forth or the sound produced

²flap *vb* **flapped; flap·ping 1 :** to give a quick light blow **2 :** to move with a beating or fluttering motion

flap·jack *n* : PANCAKE

¹flare *vb* **flared; flar·ing 1 :** to burn with an unsteady flame **2 :** to shine with great or sudden light **3 :** to become angry **4 :** to spread outward

²flare *n* **1 :** a sudden blaze of light **2 :** a blaze of light used to signal, light up something, or attract attention **3 :** a device or material used to produce a flare **4 :** a sudden outburst (as of anger) **5 :** a spreading outward : a part that spreads outward

¹flash *vb* **1 :** to shine in or like a sudden flame **2 :** to send out in or as if in flashes **3 :** to come or pass very suddenly **4 :** to make a sudden display (as of feeling)

²flash *n* **1 :** a sudden burst of or as if of light **2 :** a very short time

³flash *adj* : beginning suddenly and lasting only a short time

flash·light *n* : a small portable electric light that runs on batteries

flashy *adj* **flash·i·er; flash·i·est :** GAUDY, SHOWY 2

flask *n* : a container like a bottle with a flat or rounded body

¹flat *adj* **flat·ter; flat·test 1 :** having a smooth level surface **2 :** spread out on or along a surface **3 :** having a broad smooth surface and little thickness **4 :** ²OUTRIGHT 1, POSITIVE **5 :** FIXED 1 **6 :** EXACT **7 :** INSIPID **8 :** having lost air pressure **9 :** lower than the true musical pitch **10 :** lower by a half step in music **11 :** free from gloss — **flat·ly** *adv* — **flat·ness** *n*

²flat *n* **1 :** a level place : PLAIN **2 :** a flat part or surface **3 :** a note or tone that is a half step lower than the note named **4 :** a sign ♭ meaning that the pitch of a musical note is to be lower by a half step **5 :** a deflated tire

³flat *adv* **1 :** on or against a flat surface **2 :** below the true musical pitch

⁴flat *n* : an apartment on one floor

flat·boat *n* : a large boat with a flat bottom and square ends

flat·car *n* : a railroad car without sides or a roof that is used to carry freight

flat·fish *n* : a fish (as the flounder) that swims on its side and has both eyes on the upper side

flat·iron *n* : ¹IRON

flat·ten *vb* : to make or become flat

flat·ter *vb* **1 :** to praise but not sincerely **2 :** to show too favorably — **flat·ter·er** *n* — **flat·ter·ing·ly** *adv*

flat·tery *n, pl* **flat·ter·ies :** praise that is not deserved or meant

flaunt *vb* **1 :** to wave or flutter in a showy way **2 :** to make too much show of : PARADE

¹fla·vor *n* **1 :** the quality of something that affects the sense of taste **2 :** a substance added to food to give it a desired taste — **fla·vored** *adj*

²flavor *vb* : to give or add a flavor to

fla·vor·ing *n* : ¹FLAVOR 2

flaw *n* : a small often hidden fault

flax *n* : a plant with blue flowers that is grown for its fiber from which linen is made and for its seed from which oil and livestock feed are obtained

flax·en *adj* **1 :** made of flax **2 :** having a light straw color

flax·seed *n* : the seed of flax from which linseed oil comes and which is used in medicine

flay *vb* **1 :** ²SKIN **2 :** to scold severely

flea *n* : a small bloodsucking insect that has no wings and a hard body

¹fleck *vb* : to mark with small streaks or spots

²fleck *n* **1 :** ¹SPOT 2, MARK **2 :** ¹FLAKE, PARTICLE

fledg·ling *n* : a young bird that has just grown the feathers needed to fly

flee *vb* **fled; flee·ing :** to run away or away from : FLY

¹fleece *n* : the woolly coat of an animal and especially a sheep

²fleece *vb* **fleeced; fleec·ing :** to take money or property from by trickery

fleecy *adj* **fleec·i·er; fleec·i·est :** covered with, made of, or like fleece

¹fleet *n* **1 :** a group of warships under one command **2 :** a country's navy **3 :** a group of ships or vehicles that move together or are under one management

²fleet *adj* : very swift — **fleet·ly** *adv* — **fleet·ness** *n*

Fleet Admiral *n* : the highest ranking commissioned officer in the Navy ranking above an admiral

flesh *n* **1 :** the soft and especially the edible muscular parts of an animal's body **2 :** a fleshy edible plant part (as the pulp of a fruit) — **fleshed** *adj*

fleshy *adj* **flesh·i·er; flesh·i·est 1 :** like or consisting of flesh **2 :** rather stout

flew *past of* FLY

flex *vb* : to bend often again and again

flex·i·bil·i·ty *n* : the quality or state of being flexible

flex·i·ble *adj* **1 :** possible to bend or flex **2 :** able or suitable to meet new situations — **flex·i·bly** *adv*

¹flick *n* : a light snapping stroke

²flick *vb* : to strike or move with a quick motion

¹flick·er *vb* : to burn unsteadily

²flicker *n* **1 :** a quick small movement **2 :** a flickering light

³flicker *n* : a large North American woodpecker

fli·er *or* **fly·er** *n* **1 :** one that flies **2 :** AVIATOR

[1]flight *n* **1 :** an act or instance of passing through the air by the use of wings **2 :** a passing through the air or space **3 :** the distance covered in a flight **4 :** a scheduled trip by an airplane **5 :** a group of similar things flying through the air together **6 :** a passing above or beyond ordinary limits **7 :** a continuous series of stairs

[2]flight *n* **:** the act of running away

flight·less *adj* **:** unable to fly

flighty *adj* **flight·i·er; flight·i·est 1 :** easily excited **:** SKITTISH **2 :** not wise or sober **:** FRIVOLOUS

flim·sy *adj* **flim·si·er; flim·si·est :** not strong or solid — **flim·si·ly** *adv* — **flim·si·ness** *n*

flinch *vb* **:** to draw back from or as if from pain

[1]fling *vb* **flung; fling·ing 1 :** to move suddenly **2 :** to throw hard or without care

[2]fling *n* **1 :** an act of flinging **2 :** a time of freedom for pleasure

flint *n* **:** a very hard stone that produces a spark when struck by steel

flint·lock *n* **:** an old-fashioned firearm using a flint for striking a spark to fire the charge

[1]flip *vb* **flipped; flip·ping :** to move or turn by or as if by tossing

[2]flip *n* **:** an act of flipping **:** TOSS

flip·pant *adj* **:** not respectful **:** SAUCY — **flip·pant·ly** *adv*

flip·per *n* **1 :** a broad flat limb (as of a seal) specialized for swimming **2 :** a flat rubber shoe with the front expanded into a paddle used in swimming

[1]flirt *vb* **:** to show a liking for someone of the opposite sex just for the fun of it

[2]flirt *n* **:** a person who flirts a lot

flit *vb* **flit·ted; flit·ting :** to move by darting about

[1]float *n* **1 :** something that floats in or on the surface of a liquid **2 :** a cork or bob that holds up the baited end of a fishing line **3 :** a floating platform anchored near a shore for the use of swimmers or boats **4 :** a hollow ball that controls the flow or level of the liquid it floats on (as in a tank) **5 :** a vehicle with a platform used to carry an exhibit in a parade

[2]float *vb* **1 :** to rest on the surface of a liquid **2 :** to drift on or through or as if on or through a fluid **3 :** to cause to float — **float·er** *n*

[1]flock *n* **1 :** a group of animals (as geese or sheep) living or kept together **2 :** a group someone (as a minister) watches over

[2]flock *vb* **:** to gather or move in a crowd

floe *n* **:** a sheet or mass of floating ice

flog *vb* **flogged; flog·ging :** to beat severely with a rod or whip

[1]flood *n* **1 :** a huge flow of water that rises and spreads over the land **2 :** the flowing in of the tide **3 :** a very large number or amount

[2]flood *vb* **1 :** to cover or become filled with water **2 :** to fill as if with a flood

flood·light *n* **:** a lamp that gives a bright broad beam of light

flood·plain *n* **:** low flat land along a stream that is flooded when the steam overflows

flood·wa·ter *n* **:** the water of a flood

[1]floor *n* **1 :** the part of a room on which one stands **2 :** the lower inside surface of a hollow structure **3 :** a ground surface **4 :** a story of a building

[2]floor *vb* **1 :** to cover or provide with a floor **2 :** to knock down

floor·ing *n* **1 :** [1]FLOOR 1 **2 :** material for floors

[1]flop *vb* **flopped; flop·ping 1 :** to flap about **2 :** to drop or fall limply **3 :** [1]FAIL 6

[2]flop *n* **1 :** the act or sound of flopping **2 :** FAILURE 3

[1]flop·py *adj* **flop·pi·er; flop·pi·est :** being soft and flexible

[2]floppy *n, pl* **floppies :** FLOPPY DISK

floppy disk *n* **:** a small flexible plastic disk with a magnetic coating on which computer data can be stored

flo·ra *n* **:** the plant life typical of a region, period, or special environment

flo·ral *adj* **:** of or relating to flowers

flo·ret *n* **:** a small flower

flo·rist *n* **:** a person who sells flowers and ornamental plants

[1]floss *n* **1 :** soft thread used in embroidery **2 :** fluffy material full of fibers

[2]floss *vb* **:** to use dental floss on (one's teeth)

flo·til·la *n* **:** a fleet of usually small ships

[1]flounce *vb* **flounced; flounc·ing :** to move with exaggerated jerky motions

[2]flounce *n* **:** a strip of fabric attached by its upper edge

[1]floun·der *n* **:** a flatfish used for food

[2]flounder *vb* **1 :** to struggle to move or get footing **2 :** to behave or do something in a clumsy way

flour *n* **:** the finely ground meal of a cereal grain and especially of wheat

[1]flour·ish *vb* **1 :** to grow well **:** THRIVE **2 :** to do well **:** PROSPER **3 :** to make sweeping movements with

[2]flourish *n* **1 :** a fancy bit of decoration added to something (as handwriting) **2 :** a sweeping motion

flout *vb* **:** to show lack of respect for **:** DISREGARD

[1]flow *vb* **1 :** to move in a stream **2 :** to glide along smoothly **3 :** to hang loose and waving

[2]**flow** *n* **1 :** an act of flowing **2 :** the rise of the tide **3 :** a smooth even movement **:** STREAM

[1]**flow·er** *n* **1 :** a plant part that produces seed **2 :** a plant grown chiefly for its showy flowers **3 :** the state of bearing flowers **4 :** the best part or example — **flow·ered** *adj* — **flow·er·less** *adj*

[2]**flower** *vb* **:** to produce flowers

flower head *n* **:** a tight cluster of small flowers that are arranged so that the whole looks like a single flower

flowering plant *n* **:** a seed plant whose seeds are produced in the ovary of a flower

flow·er·pot *n* **:** a pot in which to grow plants

flow·ery *adj* **1 :** having many flowers **2 :** full of fine words — **flow·er·i·ness** *n*

flown *past participle of* FLY

flu *n* **1 :** INFLUENZA **2 :** any of several virus diseases something like a cold

fluc·tu·ate *vb* **fluc·tu·at·ed; fluc·tu·at·ing :** to change continually and especially up and down

flue *n* **:** an enclosed passage (as in a chimney) for smoke or air

flu·en·cy *n* **:** the ability to speak easily and well

flu·ent *adj* **1 :** able to speak easily and well **2 :** that is smooth and correct **:** GOOD — **flu·ent·ly** *adv*

[1]**fluff** *n* **:** [7]DOWN, NAP

[2]**fluff** *vb* **:** to make or become fluffy

fluffy *adj* **fluff·i·er; fluff·i·est :** having, covered with, or like down

[1]**flu·id** *adj* **1 :** capable of flowing like a liquid or gas **2 :** being smooth and easy — **flu·id·ly** *adv*

[2]**fluid** *n* **:** something that tends to flow and take the shape of its container

flung *past of* FLING

flunk *vb* **:** [1]FAIL 6

fluo·res·cent *adj* **1 :** giving out visible light when exposed to external radiation **2 :** producing visible light by means of a fluorescent coating **3 :** extremely bright or glowing

fluo·ri·date *vb* **fluo·ri·dat·ed; fluo·ri·dat·ing :** to add a fluoride to (as drinking water) to reduce tooth decay

fluo·ri·da·tion *n* **:** the act of fluoridating

fluo·ride *n* **:** a compound of fluorine

fluo·rine *n* **:** a yellowish flammable irritating gaseous chemical element

[1]**flur·ry** *n, pl* **flurries 1 :** a gust of wind **2 :** a brief light snowfall **3 :** a brief outburst (as of activity)

[2]**flurry** *vb* **flur·ried; flur·ry·ing :** [1]FLUSTER, EXCITE

[1]**flush** *vb* **:** to begin or cause to begin flight suddenly

[2]**flush** *n* **1 :** an act of flushing **2 :** [1]BLUSH 1

[3]**flush** *vb* **1 :** [2]BLUSH **2 :** to pour water over or through

[4]**flush** *adj* **:** having one edge or surface even with the next

[5]**flush** *adv* **:** so as to be flush

[1]**flus·ter** *vb* **:** to make nervous and confused **:** UPSET

[2]**fluster** *n* **:** a state of nervous confusion

[1]**flute** *n* **:** a woodwind instrument in the form of a hollow slender tube open at only one end that is played by blowing across a hole near the closed end

[2]**flute** *vb* **flut·ed; flut·ing :** to make a sound like that of a flute

[1]**flut·ter** *vb* **1 :** to move the wings rapidly without flying or in making short flights **2 :** to move with a quick flapping motion **3 :** to move about busily without getting much done

[2]**flutter** *n* **:** an act of fluttering

[1]**fly** *vb* **flew; flown; fly·ing 1 :** to move in or pass through the air with wings **2 :** to move through the air or before the wind **3 :** to float or cause to float, wave, or soar in the wind **4 :** to run away **:** FLEE **5 :** to move or pass swiftly **6 :** to operate or travel in an aircraft

[2]**fly** *n, pl* **flies 1 :** a flap of material to cover a fastening in a garment **2 :** the outer canvas of a tent that has a double top **3 :** a baseball hit high in the air

[3]**fly** *n, pl* **flies 1 :** a winged insect **2 :** any of a large group of mostly stout-bodied two-winged insects (as the common housefly) **3 :** a fishhook made to look like an insect

fly·catch·er *n* **:** a small bird that eats flying insects

flyer *variant of* FLIER

fly·ing boat *n* **:** a seaplane with a hull designed to support it on the water

flying fish *n* **:** a fish with large fins that let it jump from the water and move for a distance through the air

fly·pa·per *n* **:** sticky paper to catch and kill flies

fly·speck *n* **:** a spot of feces left by a fly on a surface

fly·way *n* **:** a route regularly followed by migratory birds

[1]**foal** *n* **:** a young animal of the horse family especially while less than one year old

[2]**foal** *vb* **:** to give birth to a foal

[1]**foam** *n* **:** a mass of tiny bubbles that forms in or on the surface of liquids or in the mouths or on the skins of animals

[2]**foam** *vb* **:** to produce or form foam

foamy *adj* **foam·i·er; foam·i·est :** covered with or looking like foam — **foam·i·ness** *n*

fo·cal *adj* **:** of, relating to, or having a focus

[1]**fo·cus** *n, pl* **fo·cus·es** *or* **fo·ci 1 :** a point at which rays (as of light, heat, or sound) meet

after being reflected or bent : the point at which an image is formed **2 :** the distance from a lens or mirror to a focus **3 :** an adjustment (as of a person's eyes or glasses) that gives clear vision **4 :** a center of activity or interest

[2]**focus** *vb* **fo·cused** *or* **fo·cussed; fo·cus·ing** *or* **fo·cus·sing 1 :** to bring or come to a focus **2 :** to adjust the focus of

fod·der *n* **:** coarse dry food (as stalks of corn) for livestock

foe *n* **:** an enemy especially in war

[1]**fog** *n* **1 :** fine particles of water floating in the air at or near the ground **2 :** a confused state of mind

[2]**fog** *vb* **fogged; fog·ging :** to cover or become covered with fog

fog·gy *adj* **fog·gi·er; fog·gi·est 1 :** filled with fog **2 :** confused as if by fog — **fog·gi·ness** *n*

fog·horn *n* **:** a loud horn sounded in a fog to give warning

fo·gy *n, pl* **fogies :** a person with old-fashioned ideas

foi·ble *n* **:** an unimportant weakness or failing

[1]**foil** *vb* **:** to keep from succeeding or from reaching a goal

[2]**foil** *n* **1 :** a very thin sheet of metal **2 :** something that makes another thing more noticeable by being very different from it

[3]**foil** *n* **:** a fencing weapon having a light flexible blade with a blunt point

[1]**fold** *n* **:** an enclosure or shelter for sheep

[2]**fold** *vb* **:** to pen up (sheep) in a fold

[3]**fold** *vb* **1 :** to double something over itself **2 :** to clasp together **3 :** [1]EMBRACE 1

[4]**fold** *n* **1 :** a part doubled or laid over another part **:** PLEAT **2 :** a bend produced in a rock layer by pressure **3 :** a crease made by folding something (as a newspaper)

-fold *suffix* **1 :** multiplied by a specified number **:** times — in adjectives and adverbs **2 :** having so many parts

fold·er *n* **1 :** one that folds **2 :** a folded printed sheet **3 :** a folded cover or large envelope for loose papers

fo·li·age *n* **:** the leaves of a plant (as a tree) — **fo·li·aged** *adj*

[1]**folk** *or* **folks** *n pl* **1 :** persons of a certain class, kind, or group **2 folks** *pl* **:** people in general **3 folks** *pl* **:** the members of one's family **:** one's relatives

[2]**folk** *adj* **:** created by the common people

folk·lore *n* **:** customs, beliefs, stories, and sayings of a people handed down from generation to generation

folk·sing·er *n* **:** a person who sings songs (**folk songs**) created by and long sung among the common people

folk·tale *n* **:** a story made up and handed down by the common people

fol·low *vb* **1 :** to go or come after or behind **2 :** to be led or guided by **:** OBEY **3 :** to proceed along **4 :** to work in or at something as a way of life **5 :** to come after in time or place **6 :** to result from **7 :** to keep one's eyes or attention on — **fol·low·er** *n* — **follow suit 1 :** to play a card that belongs to the same group (as hearts or spades) as the one led **2 :** to do the same thing someone else has just done

[1]**fol·low·ing** *adj* **:** coming just after

[2]**following** *n* **:** a group of followers

follow through *vb* **:** to complete an action

follow up *vb* **:** to show continued interest in or take further action regarding

fol·ly *n, pl* **follies 1 :** lack of good sense **2 :** a foolish act or idea

fond *adj* **1 :** having a liking or love **2 :** AFFECTIONATE, LOVING — **fond·ly** *adv* — **fond·ness** *n*

fon·dle *vb* **fon·dled; fon·dling :** to touch or handle in a tender or loving manner

font *n* **:** a basin to hold water for baptism

food *n* **1 :** material containing carbohydrates, fats, proteins, and supplements (as minerals and vitamins) that is taken in by and used in the living body for growth and repair and as a source of energy for activities **2 :** inorganic substances taken in by green plants and used to build organic nutrients **3 :** organic materials formed by plants and used in their growth and activities **4 :** solid food as distinguished from drink

food chain *n* **:** a sequence of organisms in which each depends on the next and usually lower member as a source of food

food·stuff *n* **:** a substance with food value

[1]**fool** *n* **1 :** a person without good sense or judgment **2 :** JESTER 1

[2]**fool** *vb* **1 :** to spend time idly **2 :** to meddle or tamper with something **3 :** to speak or act in a playful way or in fun **:** JOKE **4 :** [2]TRICK

fool·har·dy *adj* **fool·har·di·er; fool·har·di·est :** foolishly adventurous or bold

fool·ish *adj* **:** showing or resulting from lack of good sense **:** SENSELESS — **fool·ish·ly** *adv* — **fool·ish·ness** *n*

fool·proof *adj* **:** done, made, or planned so well that nothing can go wrong

[1]**foot** *n, pl* **feet 1 :** the end part of the leg of an animal or person **:** the part of an animal on which it stands or moves **2 :** a unit of length equal to twelve inches (about .3 meter) **3 :** something like a foot in position or use — **on foot :** by walking

[2]**foot** *vb* **1 :** to go on foot **2 :** [1]PAY 2

foot·ball *n* **1 :** a game played with a blown up oval ball on a large field by two teams of eleven players that move the ball by kicking, passing, or running with it **2 :** the ball used in football

foot·ed *adj* **1 :** having a foot or feet **2 :** having such or so many feet

foot·fall *n* **:** the sound of a footstep

foot·hill *n* **:** a hill at the foot of higher hills

foot·hold *n* **:** a place where the foot may be put (as for climbing)

foot·ing *n* **1 :** a firm position or placing of the feet **2 :** FOOTHOLD **3 :** position in relation to others **4 :** social relationship

foot·lights *n pl* **:** a row of lights set across the front of a stage floor

foot·man *n, pl* **foot·men :** a male servant who lets visitors in and waits on table

foot·note *n* **:** a note at the bottom of a page

foot·path *n* **:** a path for walkers

foot·print *n* **:** a track left by a foot

foot·sore *adj* **:** having sore feet from walking a lot

foot·step *n* **1 :** a step of the foot **2 :** the distance covered by a step **3 :** FOOTPRINT

foot·stool *n* **:** a low stool to support the feet

foot·work *n* **:** the skill with which the feet are moved (as in boxing)

[1]**for** *prep* **1 :** by way of getting ready **2 :** toward the goal of **3 :** in order to reach **4 :** as being **5 :** because of **6** — used to show who or what is to receive something **7 :** in order to help or defend **8 :** directed at **:** AGAINST **9 :** in exchange as equal to **10 :** with regard to **:** CONCERNING **11 :** taking into account **12 :** through the period of

[2]**for** *conj* **:** BECAUSE

[1]**for·age** *n* **:** food (as pasture) for browsing or grazing animals

[2]**forage** *vb* **for·aged; for·ag·ing :** [1]SEARCH 1

for·ay *n* **:** [1]RAID

for·bear *vb* **for·bore; for·borne; for·bear·ing 1 :** to hold back **2 :** to control oneself when provoked

for·bid *vb* **for·bade** *or* **for·bad; for·bid·den; for·bid·ding :** to order not to do something

for·bid·ding *adj* **:** tending to frighten or discourage

[1]**force** *n* **1 :** POWER 4 **2 :** the state of existing and being enforced **:** EFFECT **3 :** a group of persons gathered together and trained for action **4 :** power or violence used on a person or thing **5 :** an influence (as a push or pull) that tends to produce a change in the speed or direction of motion of something

[2]**force** *vb* **forced; forc·ing 1 :** to make (as a person) do something **2 :** to get or make by using force **3 :** to break open by force **4 :** to speed up the development of

force·ful *adj* **:** having much force **:** VIGOROUS — **force·ful·ly** *adv* — **force·ful·ness** *n*

for·ceps *n, pl* **forceps :** an instrument for grasping, holding, or pulling on things especially in delicate operations (as by a jeweler or surgeon)

forc·ible *adj* **1 :** got, made, or done by force or violence **2 :** showing a lot of force or energy — **forc·ibly** *adv*

[1]**ford** *n* **:** a shallow place in a body of water where one can wade across

[2]**ford** *vb* **:** to cross by wading

[1]**fore** *adv* **:** in or toward the front

[2]**fore** *adj* **:** being or coming before in time, place, or order

[3]**fore** *n* **:** [1]FRONT 2

[4]**fore** *interj* — used by a golfer to warn someone within range of a hit ball

fore- *prefix* **1 :** earlier **:** beforehand **2 :** at the front **:** in front **3 :** front part of something specified

fore–and–aft *adj* **:** being in line with the length of a ship

fore·arm *n* **:** the part of the arm between the elbow and the wrist

fore·bear *n* **:** ANCESTOR

fore·bod·ing *n* **:** a feeling that something bad is going to happen

[1]**fore·cast** *vb* **forecast** *or* **fore·cast·ed; fore·cast·ing :** to predict often after thought and study of available evidence — **fore·cast·er** *n*

[2]**forecast** *n* **:** a prediction of something in the future

fore·cas·tle *n* **1 :** the forward part of the upper deck of a ship **2 :** quarters for the crew in the forward part of a ship

fore·fa·ther *n* **:** ANCESTOR

fore·fin·ger *n* **:** INDEX FINGER

fore·foot *n, pl* **fore·feet :** one of the front feet of an animal with four feet

fore·front *n* **:** the very front **:** VANGUARD

forego *variant of* FORGO

fore·go·ing *adj* **:** being before in time or place

fore·gone conclusion *n* **:** something felt to be sure to happen

fore·ground *n* **:** the part of a picture or scene that seems to be nearest to and in front of the person looking at it

fore·hand *n* **:** a stroke (as in tennis) made with the palm of the hand turned in the direction in which the hand is moving

fore·head *n* **:** the part of the face above the eyes

for·eign *adj* **1 :** located outside of a place or country and especially outside of one's country **2 :** belonging to a place or country other than the one under consideration **3 :** relating to or having to do with other nations **4 :** not normal or wanted

for·eign·er *n* **:** a person who is from a foreign country

fore·leg *n* **:** a front leg

fore·limb *n* : an arm, fin, wing, or leg that is or occupies the position of a foreleg

fore·man *n, pl* **fore·men** : the leader of a group of workers

fore·mast *n* : the mast nearest the bow of the ship

[1]fore·most *adj* : first in time, place, or order : most important

[2]foremost *adv* : in the first place

fore·noon *n* : MORNING

fore·quar·ter *n* : the front half of a side of the body or carcass of an animal with four feet

fore·run·ner *n* : one that comes before especially as a sign of the coming of another

fore·see *vb* **fore·saw; fore·seen; fore·see·ing** : to see or know about beforehand

fore·sight *n* **1** : the act or power of foreseeing **2** : care for the future : PRUDENCE

for·est *n* : a growth of trees and underbrush covering a large area — **for·est·ed** *adj*

fore·stall *vb* : to keep out, interfere with, or prevent by steps taken in advance

forest ranger *n* : a person in charge of the management and protection of a part of a public forest

for·est·ry *n* : the science and practice of caring for forests — **for·est·er** *n*

fore·tell *vb* **fore·told; fore·tell·ing** : to tell of a thing before it happens

fore·thought *n* : a thinking or planning for the future

for·ev·er *adv* **1** : for a limitless time **2** : at all times

for·ev·er·more *adv* : FOREVER 1

fore·word *n* : PREFACE

[1]for·feit *n* : something forfeited

[2]forfeit *vb* : to lose or lose the right to something through a fault, error, or crime

[1]forge *n* : a furnace or a place with a furnace where metal is shaped and worked by heating and hammering

[2]forge *vb* **forged; forg·ing** **1** : to shape and work metal by heating and hammering **2** : to produce something that is not genuine : COUNTERFEIT — **forg·er** *n*

[3]forge *vb* **forged; forg·ing** : to move forward slowly but steadily

forg·ery *n, pl* **forg·er·ies** **1** : the crime of falsely making or changing a written paper or signing someone else's name **2** : something that has been forged

for·get *vb* **for·got; for·got·ten** *or* **for·got; for·get·ting** **1** : to be unable to think of or recall **2** : to fail by accident to do (something) : OVERLOOK

for·get·ful *adj* : forgetting easily — **for·get·ful·ly** *adv* — **for·get·ful·ness** *n*

for·get–me–not *n* : a small low plant with bright blue flowers

for·give *vb* **for·gave; for·giv·en; for·giv·ing** : to stop feeling angry at or hurt by

for·give·ness *n* : the act of forgiving or the state of being forgiven

for·go *or* **fore·go** *vb* **for·went** *or* **fore·went; for·gone** *or* **fore·gone; for·go·ing** *or* **fore·go·ing** : to hold oneself back from : GIVE UP

[1]fork *n* **1** : an implement having a handle and two or more prongs for taking up (as in eating), pitching, or digging **2** : something like a fork in shape **3** : the place where something divides or branches **4** : one of the parts into which something divides or branches — **forked** *adj*

[2]fork *vb* **1** : to divide into branches **2** : to pitch or lift with a fork

for·lorn *adj* : sad from being left alone — **for·lorn·ly** *adv*

[1]form *n* **1** : the shape and structure of something **2** : an established way of doing something **3** : a printed sheet with blank spaces for information **4** : a mold in which concrete is placed to set **5** : [1]SORT 1, KIND **6** : a plan of arrangement or design (as for a work of art) **7** : one of the different pronunciations, spellings, or inflections a word may have

[2]form *vb* **1** : to give form or shape to **2** : DEVELOP 5 **3** : to come or bring together in making **4** : to take form : come into being

[1]for·mal *adj* : following established form, custom, or rule — **for·mal·ly** *adv*

[2]formal *n* : something (as a dress) formal in character

for·mal·i·ty *n, pl* **for·mal·i·ties** **1** : the quality or state of being formal **2** : an established way of doing something

for·ma·tion *n* **1** : a forming of something **2** : something that is formed **3** : an arrangement of something (as persons or ships)

for·mer *adj* : coming before in time

for·mer·ly *adv* : at an earlier time

for·mi·da·ble *adj* **1** : exciting fear or awe **2** : offering serious difficulties

form·less *adj* : having no regular form or shape — **form·less·ly** *adv* — **form·less·ness** *n*

for·mu·la *n* **1** : a direction giving amounts of the substances for the preparation of something (as a medicine) **2** : a milk mixture or substitute for feeding a baby **3** : a general fact or rule expressed in symbols **4** : an expression in symbols giving the makeup of a substance **5** : an established form or method

for·mu·late *vb* **for·mu·lat·ed; for·mu·lat·ing** : to state definitely and clearly

for·sake *vb* **for·sook; for·sak·en; for·sak·ing** : to give up or leave entirely

for·syth·ia *n* : a bush often grown for its bright yellow flowers that appear in early spring

fort *n* : a strong or fortified place

forth *adv* **1 :** onward in time, place, or order **2 :** out into view
forth·com·ing *adj* **1 :** being about to appear **2 :** ready or available when needed
forth·right *adj* **:** going straight to the point clearly and firmly — **forth·right·ly** *adv*
forth·with *adv* **:** without delay **:** IMMEDIATELY
[1]**for·ti·eth** *adj* **:** coming right after thirty-ninth
[2]**fortieth** *n* **:** number forty in a series
for·ti·fi·ca·tion *n* **1 :** the act of fortifying **2 :** something that strengthens or protects
for·ti·fy *vb* **for·ti·fied; for·ti·fy·ing 1 :** to make strong (as by building defenses) **2 :** ENRICH 2, 3
for·ti·tude *n* **:** strength of mind that lets a person meet and put up with trouble
fort·night *n* **:** two weeks
for·tress *n* **:** a fortified place
for·tu·nate *adj* **1 :** bringing some unexpected good **2 :** receiving some unexpected good **:** LUCKY — **for·tu·nate·ly** *adv*
for·tune *n* **1 :** favorable results that come partly by chance **2 :** what happens to a person **:** good or bad luck **3 :** what is to happen to one in the future **4 :** WEALTH
for·tune–tell·er *n* **:** a person who claims to foretell future events
[1]**for·ty** *adj* **:** being four times ten
[2]**forty** *n* **:** four times ten **:** 40
for·ty–nin·er *n* **:** a person in the California gold rush of 1849
fo·rum *n* **1 :** the marketplace or public place of an ancient Roman city serving as the center for public business **2 :** a program of open discussion
[1]**for·ward** *adj* **1 :** near, at, or belonging to the front part **2 :** lacking proper modesty or reserve **3 :** moving, tending, or leading to a position in front
[2]**forward** *adv* **:** to or toward what is in front
[3]**forward** *vb* **1 :** to help onward **:** ADVANCE **2 :** to send on or ahead
[4]**forward** *n* **:** a player at or near the front of his or her team or near the opponent's goal
for·wards *adv* **:** [2]FORWARD
fos·sil *n* **:** a trace or print or the remains of a plant or animal of a past age preserved in earth or rock
[1]**fos·ter** *adj* **:** giving, receiving, or sharing parental care even though not related by blood or legal ties
[2]**foster** *vb* **1 :** to give parental care to **2 :** to help the growth and development of
fought *past of* FIGHT
[1]**foul** *adj* **1 :** disgusting in looks, taste, or smell **2 :** full of or covered with dirt **3 :** being vulgar or insulting **4 :** being wet and stormy **5 :** very unfair **6 :** breaking a rule in a game or sport **7 :** being outside the foul lines — **foul·ly** *adv* — **foul·ness** *n*
[2]**foul** *n* **1 :** a breaking of the rules in a game or sport **2 :** a foul ball in baseball
[3]**foul** *vb* **1 :** to make or become foul or filthy **2 :** to make a foul **3 :** to become or cause to become entangled
foul line *n* **:** either of two straight lines running from the rear corner of home plate through first and third base to the boundary of a baseball field
foul play *n* **:** VIOLENCE 1
[1]**found** *past of* FIND
[2]**found** *vb* **:** ESTABLISH 1
foun·da·tion *n* **1 :** the act of founding **2 :** the support upon which something rests
[1]**found·er** *n* **:** a person who founds something
[2]**foun·der** *vb* **:** [1]SINK 1
found·ling *n* **:** an infant found after being abandoned by unknown parents
found·ry *n, pl* **foundries :** a building or factory where metals are cast
foun·tain *n* **1 :** a spring of water **2 :** SOURCE 1 **3 :** an artificial stream or spray of water (as for drinking or ornament) or the device from which it comes
fountain pen *n* **:** a pen with ink inside that is fed as needed to the writing point
[1]**four** *adj* **:** being one more than three
[2]**four** *n* **1 :** one more than three **:** two times two **:** 4 **2 :** the fourth in a set or series
four·fold *adj* **:** being four times as great or as many
four·score *adj* **:** [1]EIGHTY
four·some *adj* **:** a group of four persons or things
[1]**four·teen** *adj* **:** being one more than thirteen
[2]**fourteen** *n* **:** one more than thirteen **:** two times seven **:** 14
[1]**four·teenth** *adj* **:** coming right after thirteenth
[2]**fourteenth** *n* **:** number fourteen in a series
[1]**fourth** *adj* **:** coming right after third
[2]**fourth** *n* **1 :** number four in a series **2 :** one of four equal parts
Fourth of July *n* **:** INDEPENDENCE DAY
fowl *n, pl* **fowl** *or* **fowls 1 :** BIRD **2 :** a common domestic rooster or hen **3 :** the flesh of a mature domestic fowl for use as food
fox *n* **:** a wild animal closely related to the dog that has a sharp snout, pointed ears, and a long bushy tail
foxy *adj* **fox·i·er; fox·i·est :** cunning and careful in planning and action — **fox·i·ly** *adv* — **fox·i·ness** *n*
foy·er *n* **1 :** a lobby especially in a theater **2 :** an entrance hall
fra·cas *n* **:** a noisy quarrel **:** BRAWL
frac·tion *n* **1 :** a part of a whole **:** FRAGMENT **2 :** a number (as $\frac{1}{2}$, $\frac{2}{3}$, $\frac{17}{100}$) that indicates one or more equal parts of a whole or group and that may be considered as indicating also di-

vision of the number above the line by the number below the line

frac·tion·al *adj* **1 :** of, relating to, or being a fraction **2 :** fairly small

[1]**frac·ture** *n* **1 :** a breaking or being broken (as of a bone) **2 :** damage or an injury caused by breaking

[2]**fracture** *vb* **frac·tured; frac·tur·ing :** to cause a fracture in : BREAK

frag·ile *adj* : easily broken : DELICATE

frag·ment *n* : a part broken off or incomplete

frag·men·tary *adj* : made up of fragments : INCOMPLETE

fra·grance *n* : a sweet or pleasant smell

fra·grant *adj* : sweet or pleasant in smell — **fra·grant·ly** *adv*

frail *adj* : very delicate or weak in structure or being

frail·ty *n, pl* **frailties 1 :** the quality or state of being weak **2 :** a weakness of character

[1]**frame** *vb* **framed; fram·ing 1 :** [2]FORM 1, CONSTRUCT **2 :** to enclose in a frame

[2]**frame** *n* **1 :** the structure of an animal and especially a human body : PHYSIQUE **2 :** an arrangement of parts that give form or support to something **3 :** an open case or structure for holding or enclosing something **4 :** a particular state or mood

[3]**frame** *adj* : having a wooden frame

frame·work *n* : a basic supporting part or structure

franc *n* **1 :** a French coin or bill **2 :** any of various coins or bills used in countries where French is widely spoken

Fran·co- *prefix* **1 :** French and **2 :** French

frank *adj* : free in speaking one's feelings and opinions — **frank·ly** *adv* — **frank·ness** *n*

frank·furt·er *n* : a cooked sausage (as of beef or beef and pork)

frank·in·cense *n* : a fragrant gum that is burned for its sweet smell

fran·tic *adj* : wildly excited

fran·ti·cal·ly *adv* : in a frantic way

fra·ter·nal *adj* **1 :** having to do with brothers **2 :** made up of members banded together like brothers

fra·ter·ni·ty *n, pl* **fra·ter·ni·ties :** a society of boys or men (as in a college)

fraud *n* **1 :** TRICKERY, DECEIT **2 :** an act of deceiving : TRICK **3 :** a person who pretends to be what he or she is not

fraud·u·lent *adj* : based on or done by fraud — **fraud·u·lent·ly** *adv*

fraught *adj* : full of some quality

[1]**fray** *n* : [2]FIGHT 1, BRAWL

[2]**fray** *vb* : to wear into shreds

fraz·zle *n* : a tired or nervous condition

[1]**freak** *n* : a strange, abnormal, or unusual person, thing, or event

[2]**freak** *adj* : being or suggesting a freak : IMPROBABLE

[1]**freck·le** *n* : a small brownish spot on the skin

[2]**freckle** *vb* **freck·led; freck·ling :** to mark or become marked with freckles

[1]**free** *adj* **fre·er; fre·est 1 :** having liberty : not being a slave **2 :** not controlled by others **3 :** released or not suffering from something unpleasant or painful **4 :** given without charge **5 :** not held back by fear or distrust : OPEN **6 :** not blocked : CLEAR **7 :** not combined — **free·ly** *adv*

[2]**free** *vb* **freed; free·ing :** to make or set free

[3]**free** *adv* **1 :** in a free manner : FREELY **2 :** without charge

freed·man *n, pl* **freed·men :** a person freed from slavery

free·dom *n* **1 :** the condition of being free : LIBERTY, INDEPENDENCE **2 :** ability to move or act freely **3 :** the quality of being very frank : CANDOR **4 :** free and unlimited use

free·hand *adj or adv* : done without mechanical aids

free·man *n, pl* **free·men :** a free person : one who is not a slave

free·stand·ing *adj* : standing alone or on its own foundation free of attachment or support

free·way *n* : an expressway that can be used without paying tolls

[1]**freeze** *vb* **froze; fro·zen; freez·ing 1 :** to harden into or be hardened into a solid (as ice) by loss of heat **2 :** to be or become uncomfortably cold **3 :** to damage by cold **4 :** to clog or become clogged by ice **5 :** to become fixed or motionless

[2]**freeze** *n* **1 :** a period of freezing weather : cold weather **2 :** an act or instance of freezing **3 :** the state of being frozen

freez·er *n* : a compartment or room used to freeze food or keep it frozen

freezing point *n* : the temperature at which a liquid becomes solid

[1]**freight** *n* **1 :** the amount paid (as to a shipping company) for carrying goods **2 :** goods or cargo carried by a ship, train, truck, or airplane **3 :** the carrying (as by truck) of goods from one place to another **4 :** a train that carries freight

[2]**freight** *vb* : to send by freight

freight·er *n* : a ship or airplane used to carry freight

[1]**French** *adj* : of or relating to France, its people, or the French language

[2]**French** *n* **1 French** *pl* : the people of France **2 :** the language of the French

french fry *n, often cap 1st F* : a strip of potato fried in deep fat

French horn *n* : a circular brass musical instrument with a large opening at one end and a mouthpiece shaped like a small funnel

fren·zied *adj* : very excited and upset

fren·zy *n, pl* **frenzies** : great and often wild or disorderly activity

fre·quen·cy *n, pl* **fre·quen·cies** **1** : frequent repetition **2** : rate of repetition

[1]**fre·quent** *vb* : to visit often

[2]**fre·quent** *adj* : happening often — **fre·quent·ly** *adv*

fresh *adj* **1** : not salt **2** : PURE 1, BRISK **3** : not frozen, canned, or pickled **4** : not stale, sour, or spoiled **5** : not dirty or rumpled **6** : NEW 6 **7** : newly made or received **8** : IMPUDENT — **fresh·ly** *adv* — **fresh·ness** *n*

fresh·en *vb* : to make or become fresh

fresh·et *n* : a sudden overflowing of a stream

fresh·man *n, pl* **fresh·men** : a first year student (as in college)

fresh·wa·ter *adj* : of, relating to, or living in fresh water

[1]**fret** *vb* **fret·ted; fret·ting** : to make or become worried

[2]**fret** *n* : an irritated or worried state

[3]**fret** *n* : a design of short lines or bars

[4]**fret** *n* : one of a series of ridges fixed across the fingerboard of a stringed musical instrument — **fret·ted** *adj*

fret·ful *adj* : likely to fret : IRRITABLE — **fret·ful·ly** *adv* — **fret·ful·ness** *n*

fri·ar *n* : a member of a Roman Catholic religious order for men

fric·tion *n* **1** : the rubbing of one thing against another **2** : resistance to motion between bodies in contact **3** : disagreement among persons or groups

Fri·day *n* : the sixth day of the week

friend *n* **1** : a person who has a strong liking for and trust in another person **2** : a person who is not an enemy **3** : a person who aids or favors something — **friend·less** *adj*

friend·ly *adj* **friend·li·er; friend·li·est** **1** : showing friendship **2** : being other than an enemy — **friend·li·ness** *n*

friend·ship *n* : the state of being friends

frieze *n* : a band or stripe (as around a building) used as a decoration

frig·ate *n* **1** : a square-rigged warship **2** : a modern warship that is smaller than a destroyer

fright *n* **1** : sudden terror : great fear **2** : something that frightens or is ugly or shocking

fright·en *vb* : to make afraid : TERRIFY — **fright·en·ing·ly** *adv*

fright·ful *adj* **1** : causing fear or alarm **2** : SHOCKING, OUTRAGEOUS — **fright·ful·ly** *adv* — **fright·ful·ness** *n*

frig·id *adj* **1** : freezing cold **2** : not friendly — **frig·id·ly** *adv* — **frig·id·ness** *n*

frill *n* **1** : [2]RUFFLE **2** : something added mostly for show

frilly *adj* **frill·i·er; frill·i·est** : having frills

[1]**fringe** *n* **1** : a border or trimming made by or made to look like the loose ends of the cloth **2** : something suggesting a fringe

[2]**fringe** *vb* **fringed; fring·ing** **1** : to decorate with a fringe **2** : to serve as a fringe for

frisk *vb* : to move around in a lively or playful way

frisky *adj* **frisk·i·er; frisk·i·est** : tending to frisk : PLAYFUL, LIVELY

[1]**frit·ter** *n* : a small amount of fried batter often containing fruit or meat

[2]**fritter** *vb* : to waste on unimportant things

friv·o·lous *adj* **1** : of little importance : TRIVIAL **2** : lacking in seriousness : PLAYFUL

frizzy *adj* **frizz·i·er; frizz·i·est** : very curly

fro *adv* : in a direction away

frock *n* : a woman's or girl's dress

frog *n* **1** : a tailless animal with smooth skin and webbed feet that spends more of its time in water than the related toad **2** : an ornamental fastening for a garment — **frog in one's throat** : HOARSENESS

frog·man *n, pl* **frog·men** : a swimmer equipped to work underwater for long periods of time

[1]**frol·ic** *vb* **frol·icked; frol·ick·ing** : to play about happily : ROMP

[2]**frolic** *n* : FUN 1, GAIETY

frol·ic·some *adj* : given to frolic : PLAYFUL

from *prep* **1** — used to show a starting point **2** — used to show a point of separation **3** — used to show a material, source, or cause

frond *n* : a large leaf (as of a palm or fern) with many divisions or something like such a leaf

[1]**front** *n* **1** : a region in which active warfare is taking place **2** : the forward part or surface **3** : the boundary between bodies of air at different temperatures

[2]**front** *vb* : [2]FACE 2

[3]**front** *adj* : of, relating to, or situated at the front

fron·tal *adj* : of, relating to, or directed at the front

fron·tier *n* **1** : a border between two countries **2** : the edge of the settled part of a country

fron·tiers·man *n, pl* **fron·tiers·men** : a person living on the frontier

[1]**frost** *n* **1** : temperature cold enough to cause freezing **2** : a covering of tiny ice crystals on a cold surface formed from the water vapor in the air

[2]**frost** *vb* : to cover with frost or with something suggesting frost

frost·bite *n* : slight freezing of a part of the body or the effect of this

frost·ing *n* **1** : ICING **2** : a dull finish on glass

frosty *adj* **frost·i·er; frost·i·est** **1 :** cold enough to produce frost **2 :** covered with or appearing to be covered with frost — **frost·i·ly** *adv* — **frost·i·ness** *n*

[1]**froth** *n* **:** bubbles formed in or on liquids

[2]**froth** *vb* **:** to produce or form froth

frothy *adj* **froth·i·er; froth·i·est :** full of or made up of froth — **froth·i·ness** *n*

[1]**frown** *vb* **1 :** to wrinkle the forehead (as in anger or thought) **2 :** to look with disapproval

[2]**frown** *n* **:** a wrinkling of the brow

froze *past of* FREEZE

frozen *past participle of* FREEZE

fru·gal *adj* **:** careful in spending or using resources — **fru·gal·ly** *adv*

[1]**fruit** *n* **1 :** a pulpy or juicy plant part (as rhubarb or a strawberry) that is often eaten as a dessert and is distinguished from a vegetable **2 :** a reproductive body of a seed plant that consists of the ripened ovary of a flower with its included seeds **3 :** [2]RESULT 1, PRODUCT — **fruit·ed** *adj*

[2]**fruit** *vb* **:** to bear or cause to bear fruit

fruit·cake *n* **:** a rich cake containing nuts, dried or candied fruits, and spices

fruit·ful *adj* **1 :** very productive **2 :** bringing results — **fruit·ful·ly** *adv* — **fruit·ful·ness** *n*

fruit·less *adj* **1 :** not bearing fruit **2 :** UNSUCCESSFUL — **fruit·less·ly** *adv* — **fruit·less·ness** *n*

fruity *adj* **fruit·i·er; fruit·i·est :** relating to or suggesting fruit

frus·trate *vb* **frus·trat·ed; frus·trat·ing** **1 :** to prevent from carrying out a purpose **2 :** [1]DEFEAT 1 **3 :** DISCOURAGE 1

frus·tra·tion *n* **:** DISAPPOINTMENT 2, DEFEAT

[1]**fry** *vb* **fried; fry·ing :** to cook in fat

[2]**fry** *n, pl* **fry** **1 :** recently hatched or very young fishes **2 :** persons of a particular group

fudge *n* **:** a soft creamy candy often containing nuts

[1]**fu·el** *n* **:** a substance (as oil) that can be burned to produce heat or power

[2]**fuel** *vb* **fu·eled** *or* **fu·elled; fu·el·ing** *or* **fu·el·ling :** to supply with or take on fuel

[1]**fu·gi·tive** *adj* **:** running away or trying to escape

[2]**fugitive** *n* **:** a person who is running away

[1]**-ful** *adj suffix* **1 :** full of **2 :** characterized by **3 :** having the qualities of **4 :** -ABLE

[2]**-ful** *n suffix* **:** number or quantity that fills or would fill

ful·crum *n, pl* **fulcrums** *or* **ful·cra :** the support on which a lever turns in lifting something

ful·fill *or* **ful·fil** *vb* **ful·filled; ful·fill·ing** **1 :** ACCOMPLISH **2 :** SATISFY 1 — **ful·fill·ment** *n*

[1]**full** *adj* **1 :** containing as much as possible or normal **2 :** [1]COMPLETE 1 **3 :** plump and rounded in outline **4 :** having much material — **full·ness** *n*

[2]**full** *adv* **1 :** [2]VERY 1 **2 :** COMPLETELY

[3]**full** *n* **1 :** the highest state, extent, or degree **2 :** the complete amount

full moon *n* **:** the moon with its whole disk lighted

ful·ly *adv* **1 :** COMPLETELY **2 :** at least

[1]**fum·ble** *vb* **fum·bled; fum·bling :** to feel about for or handle something clumsily

[2]**fumble** *n* **:** an act of fumbling

[1]**fume** *n* **:** a disagreeable smoke, vapor, or gas — usually used in pl.

[2]**fume** *vb* **fumed; fum·ing** **1 :** to give off fumes **2 :** to show bad temper **:** be angry

fu·mi·gate *vb* **fu·mi·gat·ed; fu·mi·gat·ing :** to disinfect by exposing to smoke, vapor, or gas

fun *n* **1 :** someone or something that provides amusement or enjoyment **2 :** a good time **:** AMUSEMENT **3 :** words or actions to make someone or something an object of unkind laughter

[1]**func·tion** *n* **1 :** the action for which a person or thing is specially fitted or used **:** PURPOSE **2 :** a large important ceremony or social affair

[2]**function** *vb* **:** to serve a certain purpose **:** WORK

function key *n* **:** any of a set of keys on a computer keyboard that have or can be programmed to have special functions

fund *n* **1 :** [1]STOCK 4, SUPPLY **2 :** a sum of money for a special purpose **3 funds** *pl* **:** available money

[1]**fun·da·men·tal** *adj* **:** being or forming a foundation **:** BASIC, ESSENTIAL — **fun·da·men·tal·ly** *adv*

[2]**fundamental** *n* **:** a basic part

fu·ner·al *n* **:** the ceremonies held for a dead person (as before burial)

fun·gi·cide *n* **:** a substance used to kill fungi — **fun·gi·cid·al** *adj*

fun·gous *or* **fun·gal** *adj* **:** of, relating to, or caused by fungi

fun·gus *n, pl* **fun·gi** *also* **fun·gus·es :** any of a group of plantlike organisms (as mushrooms, molds, and rusts) that have no chlorophyll and must live on other plants or animals or on decaying material

fun·nel *n* **1 :** a utensil usually shaped like a hollow cone with a tube extending from the point and used to catch and direct a downward flow (as of liquid) **2 :** a large pipe for the escape of smoke or for ventilation (as on a ship)

fun·nies *n pl* **:** comic strips or a section containing comic strips (as in a newspaper)
fun·ny *adj* **fun·ni·er; fun·ni·est 1 :** causing laughter **2 :** STRANGE 3
fur *n* **1 :** a piece of the pelt of an animal **2 :** an article of clothing made with fur **3 :** the hairy coat of a mammal especially when fine, soft, and thick — **furred** *adj*
fu·ri·ous *adj* **1 :** very angry **2 :** very active **:** VIOLENT — **fu·ri·ous·ly** *adv*
furl *vb* **:** to wrap or roll close to or around something
fur·long *n* **:** a unit of length equal to 220 yards (about 201 meters)
fur·lough *n* **:** a leave of absence from duty
fur·nace *n* **:** an enclosed structure in which heat is produced (as for heating a house or for melting metals)
fur·nish *vb* **1 :** to provide with what is needed **2 :** to supply to someone or something
fur·nish·ings *n pl* **:** articles of furniture for a room or building
fur·ni·ture *n* **:** movable articles used to furnish a room
fur·ri·er *n* **:** a dealer in furs
¹fur·row *n* **1 :** a trench made by or as if by a plow **2 :** a narrow groove **:** WRINKLE
²furrow *vb* **:** to make furrows in
fur·ry *adj* **fur·ri·er; fur·ri·est 1 :** like fur **2 :** covered with fur
¹fur·ther *adv* **1 :** ¹FARTHER 1 **2 :** ²BESIDES, ALSO **3 :** to a greater degree or extent
²further *vb* **:** to help forward **:** PROMOTE
³further *adj* **1 :** ²FARTHER **2 :** going or extending beyond **:** ADDITIONAL
fur·ther·more *adv* **:** MOREOVER
fur·ther·most *adj* **:** most distant **:** FARTHEST
fur·thest *adv or adj* **:** FARTHEST
fur·tive *adj* **:** done in a sneaky or sly manner — **fur·tive·ly** *adv* — **fur·tive·ness** *n*
fu·ry *n, pl* **furies 1 :** violent anger **:** RAGE **2 :** wild and dangerous force
¹fuse *vb* **fused; fus·ing 1 :** to change into a liquid or to a plastic state by heat **2 :** to unite by or as if by melting together
²fuse *n* **:** a device having a metal wire or strip that melts and interrupts an electrical circuit when the current becomes too strong
³fuse *n* **1 :** a cord that is set afire to ignite an explosive by carrying fire to it **2** *usually* **fuze :** a device for setting off a bomb or torpedo
fu·se·lage *n* **:** the central body part of an airplane that holds the crew, passengers, and cargo
fu·sion *n* **1 :** a fusing or melting together **2 :** union by or as if by melting **3 :** union of atomic nuclei to form heavier nuclei resulting in the release of enormous quantities of energy
¹fuss *n* **1 :** unnecessary activity or excitement often over something unimportant **2 :** ¹PROTEST 2 **3 :** a great show of interest
²fuss *vb* **:** to make a fuss
fussy *adj* **fuss·i·er; fuss·i·est 1 :** inclined to complain or whine **2 :** needing much attention to details **3 :** hard to please
fu·tile *adj* **:** having no result or effect **:** USELESS — **fu·tile·ly** *adv* — **fu·tile·ness** *n*
fu·til·i·ty *n* **:** the quality or state of being futile
¹fu·ture *adj* **:** coming after the present
²future *n* **1 :** future time **2 :** the chance of future success
fuze *variant of* FUSE
fuzz *n* **:** fine light particles or fibers
fuzzy *adj* **fuzz·i·er; fuzz·i·est 1 :** covered with or looking like fuzz **2 :** not clear — **fuzz·i·ly** *adv* — **fuzz·i·ness** *n*
-fy *vb suffix* **-fied; -fy·ing 1 :** make **:** form into **2 :** make similar to

G

g *n, pl* **g's** *or* **gs** *often cap* **1 :** the seventh letter of the English alphabet **2 :** a unit of force equal to the weight of a body on which the force acts
¹gab *vb* **gabbed; gab·bing :** to talk in an idle way
²gab *n* **:** idle talk **:** CHATTER
gab·ar·dine *n* **:** a firm cloth with diagonal ribs and a hard smooth finish
¹gab·ble *vb* **gab·bled; gab·bling :** ¹CHATTER 2
²gabble *n* **:** loud or fast talk that has no meaning
gab·by *adj* **gab·bi·er; gab·bi·est :** given to talking a lot **:** TALKATIVE
ga·ble *n* **:** the triangular part of an outside wall of a building formed by the sides of the roof sloping down from the ridgepole to the eaves
gad *vb* **gad·ded; gad·ding :** to roam about **:** WANDER
gad·about *n* **:** a person who goes from place to place without much reason
gad·fly *n, pl* **gad·flies 1 :** a large biting fly **2 :** a person who is an annoying pest
gad·get *n* **:** an interesting, unfamiliar, or unusual device

gaff *n* **1 :** an iron hook with a handle **2 :** something hard to take

[1]**gag** *vb* **gagged; gag·ging 1 :** to keep from speaking or crying out by or as if by stopping up the mouth **2 :** to cause to feel like vomiting : RETCH

[2]**gag** *n* **1 :** something that gags **2 :** [1]JOKE 1, 2

gage *variant of* GAUGE

gai·ety *n, pl* **gai·eties 1 :** MERRYMAKING 1 **2 :** bright spirits or manner

gai·ly *adv* **1 :** in a merry or lively way **2 :** in a bright or showy way

[1]**gain** *n* **1 :** advantage gained or increased : PROFIT **2 :** an increase in amount, size, or degree

[2]**gain** *vb* **1 :** to get hold of often by effort or with difficulty : WIN **2 :** to get to : REACH **3 :** to get advantage : PROFIT — **gain·er** *n*

gain·ful *adj* : producing gain

gait *n* : way of walking or running

[1]**ga·la** *n* : a large showy entertainment celebrating a special occasion

[2]**gala** *adj* : of or being a gala

ga·lac·tic *adj* : of or relating to a galaxy

gal·axy *n, pl* **gal·ax·ies 1 :** MILKY WAY GALAXY **2 :** one of billions of collections of stars, gas, and dust that make up the universe

gale *n* **1 :** a strong wind **2 :** a wind of from about fourteen to twenty-four meters per second **3 :** OUTBURST 1

ga·le·na *n* : a bluish gray mineral that is the main ore of lead

[1]**gall** *n* **1 :** bile especially when obtained from an animal and used in the arts or medicine **2 :** rude boldness

[2]**gall** *n* : a sore spot (as on a horse's back) caused by rubbing

[3]**gall** *vb* **1 :** to make sore by rubbing **2 :** IRRITATE 1

[4]**gall** *n* : a swelling or growth on a twig or leaf

gal·lant *adj* **1 :** showing no fear : BRAVE **2 :** CHIVALROUS 2, NOBLE **3 :** very polite to women

gal·lant·ry *n* **1 :** polite attention shown to women **2 :** COURAGE, BRAVERY

gall·blad·der *n* : a small sac in which bile from the liver is stored

gal·le·on *n* : a large sailing ship of the time of Columbus and later

gal·lery *n, pl* **gal·ler·ies 1 :** a long narrow room or hall **2 :** an indoor structure (as in a theater or church) built out from one or more walls **3 :** a room or hall used for a special purpose (as showing art)

gal·ley *n, pl* **galleys 1 :** a large low ship of olden times moved by oars and sails **2 :** the kitchen of a ship

galley slave *n* : a person forced to row on a galley

gal·li·vant *vb* : GAD

gal·lon *n* : a unit of liquid capacity equal to four quarts (about 3.8 liters)

[1]**gal·lop** *vb* : to go or cause to go at a gallop

[2]**gallop** *n* **1 :** a fast springing way of running of an animal with four feet and especially a horse **2 :** a ride or run at a gallop

gal·lows *n, pl* **gallows** *or* **gal·lows·es :** a structure from which criminals are hanged

ga·lore *adj* : marked by large amounts — used after the word it modifies

ga·losh *n* : an overshoe worn in snow or wet weather

gal·va·nize *vb* **gal·va·nized; gal·va·niz·ing 1 :** to excite or stir by or as if by an electric shock **2 :** to coat with zinc for protection

[1]**gam·ble** *vb* **gam·bled; gam·bling 1 :** to play a game in which something (as money) is risked : BET **2 :** to take risks on the chance of gain : take a chance

[2]**gamble** *n* : something that is risky to do

gam·bler *n* : a person who gambles

gam·bol *vb* **gam·boled** *or* **gam·bolled; gam·bol·ing** *or* **gam·bol·ling :** to run or skip about playfully : FROLIC

[1]**game** *n* **1 :** AMUSEMENT, PLAY **2 :** a contest carried on according to rules with the players in direct opposition to each other **3 :** animals hunted for sport or for food **4 :** the meat from game animals

[2]**game** *adj* **gam·er; gam·est 1 :** full of spirit or eagerness **2 :** of or relating to animals that are hunted

game·cock *n* : a rooster trained for fighting

game·keep·er *n* : a person in charge of the breeding and protection of game animals or birds on private land

game·ly *adv* : with spirit and courage

game·ness *n* : the quality or state of being spirited and courageous

game show *n* : a television program on which contestants compete for prizes in a game (as a quiz)

game warden *n* : a person who sees that fishing and hunting laws are obeyed

gam·ing *n* : the practice of gambling

gam·ma rays *n pl* : very penetrating rays like X rays but of shorter wavelength

gamy *adj* **gam·i·er; gam·i·est :** having the flavor of wild game especially when slightly spoiled

gan·der *n* : a male goose

gang *n* **1 :** a group of persons working or going about together **2 :** a group of persons acting together to do something illegal

gan·gli·on *n, pl* **gan·glia :** a mass of nerve cells especially outside the brain or spinal cord

gang·plank *n* : a movable bridge from a ship to the shore

gan·grene *n* **:** death of body tissue when the blood supply is cut off
gang·ster *n* **:** a member of a gang of criminals
gang·way *n* **1 :** a way into, through, or out of an enclosed space **2 :** GANGPLANK
gan·net *n* **:** a large bird that eats fish and spends much time far from land
gan·try *n, pl* **gantries 1 :** a structure over railroad tracks for holding signals **2 :** a movable structure for preparing a rocket for launching
gap *n* **1 :** an opening made by a break or a coming apart **2 :** an opening between mountains **3 :** a hole or space where something is missing
[1]**gape** *vb* **gaped; gap·ing 1 :** to open the mouth wide **2 :** to stare with open mouth **3 :** to open or part widely
[2]**gape** *n* **:** an act or instance of gaping
[1]**ga·rage** *n* **:** a building where automobiles or trucks are repaired or kept when not in use
[2]**garage** *vb* **ga·raged; ga·rag·ing :** to keep or put in a garage
[1]**garb** *n* **:** style or kind of clothing
[2]**garb** *vb* **:** CLOTHE 1
gar·bage *n* **:** waste food especially from a kitchen
gar·ble *vb* **gar·bled; gar·bling :** to change or twist the meaning or sound of
[1]**gar·den** *n* **1 :** a piece of ground in which fruits, flowers, or vegetables are grown **2 :** an enclosure for the public showing of plants or animals
[2]**garden** *vb* **:** to make or work in a garden
gar·den·er *n* **:** a person who gardens especially for pay
gar·de·nia *n* **:** a large white or yellowish flower with a fragrant smell
[1]**gar·gle** *vb* **gar·gled; gar·gling :** to rinse the throat with a liquid kept in motion by air forced through it from the lungs
[2]**gargle** *n* **1 :** a liquid used in gargling **2 :** a gargling sound
gar·goyle *n* **:** a waterspout in the form of a strange or frightening human or animal figure sticking out at the roof or eaves of a building
gar·ish *adj* **:** too bright or showy **:** GAUDY
[1]**gar·land** *n* **:** a wreath or rope of leaves or flowers
[2]**garland** *vb* **:** to form into or decorate with a garland
gar·lic *n* **:** a plant related to the onion and grown for its bulbs that have a strong smell and taste and are used to flavor foods
gar·ment *n* **:** an article of clothing
gar·ner *vb* **:** to gather in and store
gar·net *n* **:** a deep red mineral used as a gem
[1]**gar·nish** *vb* **:** to add decorations or seasoning (as to food)
[2]**garnish** *n* **:** something used in garnishing
gar·ret *n* **:** a room or unfinished part of a house just under the roof
[1]**gar·ri·son** *n* **:** a place in which troops are regularly stationed
[2]**garrison** *vb* **1 :** to station troops in **2 :** to send (troops) to a garrison
gar·ter *n* **:** a band worn to hold up a stocking or sock
garter snake *n* **:** any of numerous harmless American snakes with stripes along the back
[1]**gas** *n, pl* **gas·es 1 :** a substance (as oxygen or hydrogen) having no fixed shape and tending to expand without limit **2 :** a gas or a mixture of gases used as a fuel or to make one unconscious (as for an operation) **3 :** a fluid that poisons the air or makes breathing difficult **4 :** GASOLINE
[2]**gas** *vb* **gassed; gas·sing; gas·ses 1 :** to treat with gas **2 :** to poison with gas **3 :** to supply with gas
gas·eous *adj* **:** of or relating to gas
[1]**gash** *n* **:** a long deep cut
[2]**gash** *vb* **:** to make a long deep cut in
gas mask *n* **:** a mask connected to a chemical air filter and used to protect the face and lungs from poisonous gases
gas·o·line *n* **:** a flammable liquid made especially from gas found in the earth and from petroleum and used mostly as an automobile fuel
[1]**gasp** *vb* **1 :** to breathe with difficulty **:** PANT **2 :** to utter with quick difficult breaths
[2]**gasp** *n* **1 :** the act of gasping **2 :** something gasped
gas station *n* **:** SERVICE STATION
gas·tric juice *n* **:** an acid liquid made by the stomach that helps to digest food
gate *n* **1 :** an opening in a wall or fence often with a movable frame or door for closing it **2 :** a part of a barrier (as a fence) that opens and closes like a door
[1]**gath·er** *vb* **1 :** to bring or come together **2 :** to pick out and collect **3 :** to gain little by little **4 :** to get an idea **:** CONCLUDE **5 :** to draw together in folds
[2]**gather** *n* **:** the result of gathering cloth **:** PUCKER
gath·er·ing *n* **:** a coming together of people **:** MEETING
gau·cho *n, pl* **gauchos :** a South American cowboy
gaudy *adj* **gaud·i·er; gaud·i·est :** too showy
[1]**gauge** *or* **gage** *n* **1 :** measurement according to a standard **2 :** SIZE 2 **3 :** an instrument for measuring, testing, or registering
[2]**gauge** *or* **gage** *vb* **gauged** *or* **gaged; gaug·ing** *or* **gag·ing 1 :** to measure exactly **2 :** to

find out the capacity or contents of **3 :** [1]ESTIMATE 1, JUDGE

gaunt *adj* **:** very thin and bony (as from illness or starvation)

[1]**gaunt·let** *n* **1 :** a glove made of small metal plates and worn with a suit of armor **2 :** a glove with a wide cuff that covers and protects the wrist and part of the arm

[2]**gauntlet** *n* **:** a double file of persons who beat someone forced to run between them

gauze *n* **:** a thin transparent fabric

gauzy *adj* **gauz·i·er; gauz·i·est :** thin and transparent like gauze

gave *past of* GIVE

gav·el *n* **:** a mallet with which the person in charge raps to call a meeting or court to order

gawk *vb* **:** to stare stupidly

gawky *adj* **gawk·i·er; gawk·i·est :** AWKWARD 1, CLUMSY — **gawk·i·ly** *adv* — **gawk·i·ness** *n*

gay *adj* **gay·er; gay·est 1 :** MERRY **2 :** brightly colored

[1]**gaze** *vb* **gazed; gaz·ing :** to fix the eyes in a long steady look

[2]**gaze** *n* **:** a long steady look

ga·zelle *n* **:** a swift graceful antelope with large bright eyes

ga·zette *n* **1 :** NEWSPAPER **2 :** a journal giving official information

gaz·et·teer *n* **:** a geographical dictionary

ga·zil·lion *n* **:** a large number — **gazillion** *adj*

[1]**gear** *n* **1 :** EQUIPMENT 2 **2 :** a group of parts that has a specific function in a machine **3 :** a toothed wheel **:** COGWHEEL **4 :** the position the gears of a machine are in when they are ready to work **5 :** one of the adjustments in a motor vehicle that determine the direction of travel and the relative speed between the engine and the motion of the vehicle

[2]**gear** *vb* **1 :** to make ready for operation **2 :** to make suitable

gear·shift *n* **:** a mechanism by which gears are connected and disconnected

gee *interj* — used to show surprise or enthusiasm

geese *pl of* GOOSE

Gei·ger counter *n* **:** an instrument for detecting the presence of cosmic rays or radioactive substances

gel·a·tin *n* **1 :** a protein obtained by boiling animal tissues and used especially as food **2 :** an edible jelly formed with gelatin

gem *n* **:** a usually valuable stone cut and polished for jewelry

Gem·i·ni *n* **1 :** a constellation between Taurus and Cancer imagined as twins **2 :** the third sign of the zodiac or a person born under this sign

gen·der *n* **:** SEX 1

gene *n* **:** a unit of DNA that controls the development of a single characteristic in an individual

ge·ne·al·o·gy *n, pl* **ge·ne·al·o·gies 1 :** a line of ancestors of a person or family or a history of such a line of ancestors **2:** the study of family lines of ancestors

genera *pl of* GENUS

[1]**gen·er·al** *adj* **1 :** having to do with the whole **2 :** not specific or detailed **3 :** not specialized

[2]**general** *n* **:** a military officer ranking above a lieutenant general

gen·er·al·iza·tion *n* **1 :** the act of generalizing **2 :** a general statement

gen·er·al·ize *vb* **gen·er·al·ized; gen·er·al·iz·ing :** to put in the form of a general rule **:** draw or state a general conclusion from a number of different items or instances

gen·er·al·ly *adv* **:** USUALLY

General of the Air Force : a general of the highest rank in the Air Force

General of the Army : a general of the highest rank in the Army

gen·er·ate *vb* **gen·er·at·ed; gen·er·at·ing :** to cause to come into being

gen·er·a·tion *n* **1 :** those being a step in a line from one ancestor **2 :** a group of individuals born about the same time **3 :** the act of generating something

gen·er·a·tor *n* **:** DYNAMO

gen·er·os·i·ty *n, pl* **gen·er·os·i·ties 1 :** willingness to give or to share **2 :** a generous act

gen·er·ous *adj* **1 :** free in giving or sharing **2 :** ABUNDANT — **gen·er·ous·ly** *adv*

gen·e·sis *n, pl* **gen·e·ses :** a coming into being

ge·net·ic *adj* **:** of or relating to genetics

genetic code *n* **:** the arrangement of chemical groups within the genes by which genetic information is passed on

ge·net·i·cist *n* **:** a specialist in genetics

ge·net·ics *n* **:** a branch of biology that deals with the heredity and variation of living things

ge·nial *adj* **:** pleasantly cheerful — **ge·nial·ly** *adv*

ge·nie *n* **:** a magic spirit believed to take human form and serve the person who calls it

gen·i·tal *adj* **:** of or relating to reproduction or sex

ge·nius *n* **1 :** great natural ability **2 :** a very gifted person

gen·teel *adj* **1 :** relating to the upper classes **2:** ELEGANT, GRACEFUL **3:** showing good manners or taste

gen·tian *n* **:** an herb with smooth opposite leaves and usually blue flowers

[1]**gen·tile** *n, often cap* : a person who is not Jewish
[2]**gentile** *adj, often cap* : of or relating to people not Jewish
gen·til·i·ty *n* **1 :** good birth and family **2 :** the qualities of a well-bred person **3 :** good manners
gen·tle *adj* **gen·tler; gen·tlest 1 :** easily handled : not wild **2 :** not harsh or stern : MILD **3 :** [1]MODERATE 1 — **gen·tle·ness** *n*
gen·tle·folk *n pl* : GENTRY 1
gen·tle·man *n, pl* **gen·tle·men 1 :** a man of good birth and position **2 :** a man of good education and social position **3 :** a man with very good manners **4 :** MAN — used in the plural when speaking to a group of men — **gen·tle·man·ly** *adj*
gen·tle·wom·an *n, pl* **gen·tle·wom·en 1 :** a woman of good birth and position **2 :** a woman with very good manners : LADY 2
gen·tly *adv* : in a gentle manner
gen·try *n* **1 :** people of good birth, breeding, and education **2 :** people of a certain class
gen·u·flect *vb* : to kneel on one knee and rise again as an act of deep respect
gen·u·ine *adj* **1 :** being just what it seems to be : REAL **2 :** HONEST 1, SINCERE — **gen·u·ine·ly** *adv* — **gen·u·ine·ness** *n*
ge·nus *n, pl* **gen·era :** a group of related plants or animals that ranks below the family in scientific classification and is made up of one or more species
geo- *prefix* **1 :** earth **2 :** geographical
geo·chem·is·try *n* : chemistry that deals with the earth's crust
geo·graph·ic *or* **geo·graph·i·cal** *adj* : of or relating to geography
ge·og·ra·phy *n* **1 :** a science that deals with the location of living and nonliving things on earth and the way they affect one another **2 :** the natural features of an area
geo·log·ic *or* **geo·log·i·cal** *adj* : of or relating to geology
ge·ol·o·gist *n* : a specialist in geology
ge·ol·o·gy *n* **1 :** a science that deals with the history of the earth and its life especially as recorded in rocks **2 :** the geologic features (as mountains or plains) of an area
geo·mag·net·ic *adj* : of or relating to the magnetism of the earth
geo·met·ric *adj* : of or relating to geometry
ge·om·e·try *n* : a branch of mathematics that deals with points, lines, angles, surfaces, and solids
ge·ra·ni·um *n* : an herb often grown for its bright flowers
ger·bil *n* : a small Old World leaping desert rodent
germ *n* **1 :** a bit of living matter capable of forming a new individual **2 :** a source from which something develops **3 :** a microbe that causes disease
[1]**Ger·man** *n* **1 :** a person born or living in Germany **2 :** the language spoken mainly in Germany, Austria, and parts of Switzerland
[2]**German** *adj* : of or relating to Germany, the Germans, or the German language
ger·ma·ni·um *n* : a white hard brittle element used as a semiconductor
germ cell *n* : a reproductive cell (as an egg or sperm cell)
ger·mi·cide *n* : a substance that destroys germs
ger·mi·nate *vb* **ger·mi·nat·ed; ger·mi·nat·ing** : [1]SPROUT
ger·mi·na·tion *n* : a beginning of development (as of a seed)
ges·tic·u·late *vb* **ges·tic·u·lat·ed; ges·tic·u·lat·ing** : to make gestures especially when speaking
[1]**ges·ture** *n* **1 :** a motion of the limbs or body that expresses an idea or a feeling **2 :** something said or done that shows one's feelings
[2]**gesture** *vb* **ges·tured; ges·tur·ing :** to make or direct with a gesture
get *vb* **got; got** *or* **got·ten; get·ting 1 :** to gain possession of (as by receiving, earning, buying, or winning) **2 :** ARRIVE 1 **3 :** GO 1, MOVE **4 :** BECOME 1 **5 :** [1]CATCH 7 **6 :** to cause to be **7 :** UNDERSTAND 1 **8 :** PERSUADE — **get ahead :** to achieve success (as in business) — **get around 1 :** to get the better of **2 :** EVADE — **get at 1 :** to reach with or as if with the hand **2 :** to turn one's attention to **3 :** to try to prove or make clear — **get away with :** to do (as something wrong) without being caught — **get back at :** to get even with — **get even :** to get revenge — **get even with :** to pay back for a real or imagined injury — **get one's goat :** to make one angry or annoyed — **get over :** to recover from — **get together 1 :** to bring or come together **2 :** to reach agreement — **get wind of :** to become aware of : hear about
get along *vb* **1 :** to approach old age **2 :** to meet one's needs **3 :** to stay friendly
get by *vb* **1 :** GET ALONG 2 **2 :** to succeed with the least possible effort or accomplishment
get off *vb* **1 :** START **2 :** to escape punishment or harm
get out *vb* **1 :** ESCAPE **2 :** to become known
get–to·geth·er *n* : an informal social gathering
get up *vb* **1 :** to arise from bed **2 :** to rise to one's feet **3 :** PREPARE, ORGANIZE **4 :** DRESS
gey·ser *n* : a spring that now and then shoots up hot water and steam
ghast·ly *adj* **ghast·li·er; ghast·li·est 1 :** HORRIBLE, SHOCKING **2 :** like a ghost : PALE

ghet·to *n, pl* **ghettos** *or* **ghettoes :** a part of a city in which members of a minority group live because of social, legal, or economic pressure

ghost *n* **:** the spirit of a dead person thought of as living in an unseen world or as appearing to living people

ghost·ly *adj* **ghost·li·er; ghost·li·est :** of, relating to, or like a ghost

ghost town *n* **:** a town deserted because some nearby natural resource has been used up

ghoul *n* **1 :** an evil being of legend that robs graves and feeds on corpses **2 :** someone whose activities suggest those of a ghoul

[1]**gi·ant** *n* **1 :** an imaginary person of great size and strength **2 :** a person or thing that is very large or powerful

[2]**giant** *adj* **:** much larger than ordinary **:** HUGE

giant panda *n* **:** a large black-and-white mammal of the bear family found mainly in central China

gib·ber·ish *n* **:** confused meaningless talk

gib·bon *n* **:** a small ape of southeastern Asia that has long arms and legs and lives mostly in trees

[1]**gibe** *or* **jibe** *vb* **gibed; gib·ing :** [1]JEER

[2]**gibe** *or* **jibe** *n* **:** [2]JEER

gib·let *n* **:** an edible inner organ (as the heart or liver) of a fowl

gid·dy *adj* **gid·di·er; gid·di·est 1 :** having a feeling of whirling or spinning about **:** DIZZY **2 :** causing dizziness **3 :** SILLY 3 — **gid·di·ness** *n*

gift *n* **1 :** a special ability **:** TALENT **2 :** something given **:** PRESENT

gift·ed *adj* **:** having great ability

gig *n* **1 :** a long light boat for a ship's captain **2 :** a light carriage having two wheels and pulled by a horse

giga·byte *n* **:** a unit of computer information storage capacity equal to 1,073,741,824 bytes

gi·gan·tic *adj* **:** like a giant (as in size, weight, or strength)

gig·gle *vb* **gig·gled; gig·gling :** to laugh with repeated short high sounds

Gi·la monster *n* **:** a large black and orange poisonous lizard of the southwestern United States

gild *vb* **gild·ed** *or* **gilt; gild·ing :** to cover with a thin coating of gold

[1]**gill** *n* **:** a unit of liquid capacity equal to a quarter of a pint (about 120 milliliters)

[2]**gill** *n* **:** an organ (as of a fish) for taking oxygen from water

[1]**gilt** *n* **:** gold or something like gold applied to a surface

[2]**gilt** *n* **:** a young female hog

gim·let *n* **:** a small tool for boring

[1]**gin** *n* **:** a machine to separate seeds from cotton

[2]**gin** *vb* **ginned; gin·ning :** to separate seeds from cotton in a gin

[3]**gin** *n* **:** a strong alcoholic liquor flavored with juniper berries

gin·ger *n* **:** a hot spice obtained from the root of a tropical plant and used to season foods (as cookies) or in medicine

ginger ale *n* **:** a soft drink flavored with ginger

gin·ger·bread *n* **:** a dark cake flavored with ginger and molasses

gin·ger·ly *adv* **:** with great caution or care

gin·ger·snap *n* **:** a thin brittle cookie flavored with ginger

ging·ham *n* **:** a cotton cloth in plain weave

gipsy *variant of* GYPSY

gi·raffe *n* **:** a spotted mammal of Africa that has a long neck and chews the cud

gird *vb* **gird·ed** *or* **girt; gird·ing :** to encircle or fasten with or as if with a belt or cord

gird·er *n* **:** a horizontal main supporting beam

[1]**gir·dle** *n* **1 :** something (as a belt or sash) that encircles or binds **2 :** a light corset worn below the waist

[2]**girdle** *vb* **gir·dled; gir·dling 1 :** to bind with or as if with a girdle, belt, or sash **:** ENCIRCLE **2 :** to strip a ring of bark from a tree trunk

girl *n* **1 :** a female child or young woman **2 :** a female servant **3 :** GIRLFRIEND

girl·friend *n* **1 :** a female friend **2 :** a regular female companion of a boy or man

girl·hood *n* **:** the state or time of being a girl

girl·ish *adj* **:** of, relating to, or having qualities often felt to be typical of a girl — **girl·ish·ly** *adv* — **girl·ish·ness** *n*

Girl Scout *n* **:** a member of the Girl Scouts of the United States of America

girth *n* **1 :** a band put around the body of an animal to hold something (as a saddle) on its back **2 :** the measure or distance around something

gist *n* **:** the main point of a matter

[1]**give** *vb* **gave; giv·en; giv·ing 1 :** to hand over to be kept **:** PRESENT **2 :** [1]PAY 1 **3 :** [2]UTTER **4 :** FURNISH, PROVIDE **5 :** to cause to have **6 :** to let someone or something have **7 :** to yield slightly **8 :** to yield as a product **:** PRODUCE — **give way 1 :** to yield oneself without control **2 :** to break down **:** COLLAPSE

[2]**give** *n* **:** the quality of being able to bend under pressure

give in *vb* **1 :** [1]OFFER 2 **2 :** [1]SURRENDER 1, YIELD

giv·en *adj* **1 :** being likely to have or do something **2 :** decided on beforehand

given name *n* **:** a first name (as *John* or *Susan*)

give up *vb* **1 :** to let go : ABANDON **2 :** to stop trying : QUIT
giz·zard *n* **:** a large muscular part of the digestive tube (as of a bird) in which food is churned and ground small
gla·cial *adj* **1 :** very cold **2 :** of or relating to glaciers
gla·cier *n* **:** a large body of ice moving slowly down a slope or over a wide area of land
glad *adj* **glad·der; glad·dest 1 :** being happy and joyful **2 :** bringing or causing joy **3 :** very willing — **glad·ly** *adv* — **glad·ness** *n*
glad·den *vb* **:** to make glad
glade *n* **:** a grassy open space in a forest
glad·i·a·tor *n* **:** a person taking part in a fight to the death as public entertainment for the ancient Romans
glad·i·o·lus *n, pl* **glad·i·o·li** *or* **gladiolus** *or* **glad·i·o·lus·es :** a plant with long stiff pointed leaves and stalks of brightly colored flowers
glad·some *adj* **:** giving or showing joy
glam·or·ous *adj* **:** full of glamour
glam·our *or* **glam·or** *n* **1 :** appeal or attractiveness especially when it is misleading **2 :** tempting or fascinating personal attraction
[1]**glance** *vb* **glanced; glanc·ing 1 :** to strike at an angle and fly off to one side **2 :** to give a quick look
[2]**glance** *n* **:** a quick look
gland *n* **:** an organ in the body that prepares a substance to be used by the body or given off from it
glan·du·lar *adj* **:** of or relating to glands
[1]**glare** *vb* **glared; glar·ing 1 :** to shine with a harsh bright light **2 :** to look fiercely or angrily
[2]**glare** *n* **1 :** a harsh bright light **2 :** a fierce or angry look
glar·ing *adj* **1 :** so bright as to be harsh **2 :** ANGRY, FIERCE **3 :** very noticeable
[1]**glass** *n* **1 :** a hard brittle usually transparent substance commonly made from sand heated with chemicals **2 :** something made of glass **3 glasses** *pl* **:** EYEGLASS 2 **4 :** the contents of a glass
[2]**glass** *vb* **:** to fit or protect with glass
glass·blow·ing *n* **:** the art of shaping a mass of melted glass by blowing air into it through a tube
glass·ful *n* **:** the amount a glass will hold
glass·ware *n* **:** articles of glass
glassy *adj* **glass·i·er; glass·i·est 1 :** like glass (as in smoothness) **2 :** not shiny or bright : DULL
[1]**glaze** *vb* **glazed; glaz·ing 1 :** to set glass in **2 :** to cover with a glassy surface **3 :** to become shiny or glassy
[2]**glaze** *n* **:** a glassy surface or coating
gla·zier *n* **:** a person who sets glass in window frames
[1]**gleam** *n* **1 :** a faint, soft, or reflected light **2 :** a small bright light **3 :** a short or slight appearance
[2]**gleam** *vb* **1 :** to shine with a soft light **2 :** to give out gleams of light
glean *vb* **1 :** to gather from a field what is left by the harvesters **2 :** to gather (as information) little by little with patient effort
glee *n* **:** great joy : DELIGHT
glee club *n* **:** a singing group organized especially as a social activity in a school or college
glee·ful *adj* **:** full of glee
glen *n* **:** a narrow hidden valley
glib *adj* **glib·ber; glib·best :** speaking or spoken with careless ease and often with little regard for the truth — **glib·ly** *adv* — **glib·ness** *n*
[1]**glide** *vb* **glid·ed; glid·ing :** to move with a smooth silent motion
[2]**glide** *n* **:** the act or action of gliding
glid·er *n* **1 :** an aircraft without an engine that glides on air currents **2 :** a porch seat hung from a frame (as by chains)
[1]**glim·mer** *vb* **:** to shine faintly and unsteadily
[2]**glimmer** *n* **:** a faint unsteady light
[1]**glimpse** *vb* **glimpsed; glimps·ing :** to catch a quick view of
[2]**glimpse** *n* **:** a short hurried look
[1]**glint** *vb* **:** to shine with tiny bright flashes
[2]**glint** *n* **:** a brief flash
glis·ten *vb* **:** to shine with a soft reflected light
glitch *n* **:** a usually minor problem
[1]**glit·ter** *vb* **1 :** to sparkle brightly **2 :** to sparkle with light that is harsh and cold **3 :** to be very bright and showy
[2]**glitter** *n* **:** sparkling brightness
gloat *vb* **:** to gaze at or think about something with great satisfaction and often with mean or selfish satisfaction
glob·al *adj* **1 :** shaped like a globe **2 :** having to do with the whole earth
global warming *n* **:** a warming of the earth's atmosphere and oceans as a result of air pollution
globe *n* **1 :** a round object : BALL, SPHERE **2 :** EARTH 3 **3 :** a round model of the earth or heavens
globe–trot·ter *n* **:** a person who travels widely
glob·u·lar *adj* **:** shaped like a globe : SPHERICAL
glob·ule *n* **:** a small round mass
glock·en·spiel *n* **:** a portable musical instrument consisting of a series of metal bars played with hammers

gloom *n* **1 :** partial or complete darkness **2 :** a sad mood

gloomy *adj* **gloom·i·er; gloom·i·est 1 :** partly or completely dark **2 :** SAD 1, BLUE **3 :** causing lowness of spirits **4 :** not hopeful **:** PESSIMISTIC

glo·ri·fi·ca·tion *n* **:** the act of glorifying **:** the state of being glorified

glo·ri·fy *vb* **glo·ri·fied; glo·ri·fy·ing 1 :** to honor or praise as divine **:** WORSHIP **2 :** to give honor and praise to **3 :** to show in a way that looks good

glo·ri·ous *adj* **1 :** having or deserving glory **2 :** having great beauty or splendor **3 :** DELIGHTFUL

[1]glo·ry *n, pl* **glories 1 :** praise, honor, and admiration given to a person by others **2 :** something that brings honor, praise, or fame **3 :** BRILLIANCE, SPLENDOR **4 :** HEAVEN 2

[2]glory *vb* **glo·ried; glo·ry·ing :** to rejoice proudly **:** be proud or boastful

[1]gloss *n* **1 :** brightness from a smooth surface **:** LUSTER, SHEEN **2 :** a falsely attractive surface appearance

[2]gloss *vb* **1 :** to give a gloss to **2 :** to smooth over **:** explain away

glos·sa·ry *n, pl* **glos·sa·ries :** a list of the hard or unusual words used in a book given with their meanings

glossy *adj* **gloss·i·er; gloss·i·est :** smooth and shining on the surface

glove *n* **:** a covering for the hand having a separate section for each finger

[1]glow *vb* **1 :** to shine with or as if with great heat **2 :** to show strong bright color **3 :** to be or to look warm and flushed (as with exercise)

[2]glow *n* **1 :** light such as comes from something that is very hot but not flaming **2 :** brightness or warmth of color **3 :** a feeling of physical warmth (as from exercise) **4 :** warmth of feeling

glow·er *vb* **:** to stare angrily **:** SCOWL

glow·worm *n* **:** an insect or insect larva that gives off light

glu·cose *n* **:** a sugar in plant saps and fruits that is the usual form in which carbohydrate is taken in by the animal body

[1]glue *n* **:** a substance used to stick things tightly together

[2]glue *vb* **glued; glu·ing :** to stick with or as if with glue

glu·ey *adj* **glu·i·er; glu·i·est 1 :** sticky like glue **2 :** covered with glue

glum *adj* **glum·mer; glum·mest 1 :** [1]SULKY **2 :** seeming gloomy and sad — **glum·ly** *adv* — **glum·ness** *n*

[1]glut *vb* **glut·ted; glut·ting 1 :** to make quite full **:** fill completely **2 :** to flood with goods so that supply is greater than demand

[2]glut *n* **:** too much of something

glu·ti·nous *adj* **:** like glue **:** STICKY — **glu·ti·nous·ly** *adv*

glut·ton *n* **:** a person or animal that overeats — **glut·ton·ous** *adj* — **glut·ton·ous·ly** *adv*

glut·tony *n, pl* **glut·ton·ies :** the act or habit of eating or drinking too much

glyc·er·in *or* **glyc·er·ine** *n* **:** a sweet thick liquid that is found in various oils and fats and is used to moisten or dissolve things

gly·co·gen *n* **:** a white tasteless starchy substance that is the chief stored carbohydrate of animals

G–man *n, pl* **G–men :** a special agent of the Federal Bureau of Investigation

gnarled *adj* **:** being full of knots, twisted, and rugged

gnash *vb* **:** to strike or grind (the teeth) together (as in anger)

gnat *n* **:** a very small two-winged fly

gnaw *vb* **gnawed; gnaw·ing :** to bite so as to wear away little by little **:** bite or chew upon

gnome *n* **:** one of an imaginary race of dwarfs believed to live inside the earth and guard treasure

gnu *n, pl* **gnu** *or* **gnus :** a large African antelope with a head like that of an ox, curving horns, a short mane, and a tail somewhat like that of a horse

go *vb* **went; gone; go·ing; goes 1 :** to pass from one place to or toward another **2 :** to move away **:** LEAVE **3 :** to become lost, used, or spent **4 :** to continue its course or action **:** RUN **5 :** to make its own special sound **6 :** to be suitable **:** MATCH **7 :** to reach some state

[1]goad *n* **1 :** a pointed rod used to keep an animal moving **2 :** something that stirs one to action

[2]goad *vb* **:** to drive or stir with a goad

goal *n* **1 :** the point at which a race or journey is to end **2 :** an area to be reached safely in certain games **3 :** [1]PURPOSE **4 :** an object into which a ball or puck must be driven in various games in order to score **5 :** a scoring of one or more points by driving a ball or puck into a goal

goal·ie *n* **:** GOALKEEPER

goal·keep·er *n* **:** a player who defends a goal

goal·post *n* **:** one of two usually upright posts often with a crossbar that serve as the goal in various games

goal·tend·er *n* **:** GOALKEEPER

goat *n* **:** a horned animal that chews the cud and is related to but more lively than the sheep — **goat·like** *adj*

goa·tee *n* **:** a small beard trimmed to a point

goat·herd *n* **:** a person who tends goats

goat·skin *n* : the skin of a goat or leather made from it

gob *n* : [1]LUMP

[1]**gob·ble** *vb* **gob·bled; gob·bling** : to eat fast or greedily

[2]**gobble** *vb* **gob·bled; gob·bling** : to make the call of a turkey or a similar sound

[3]**gobble** *n* : the loud harsh call of a turkey

go–be·tween *n* : a person who acts as a messenger or peacemaker

gob·let *n* : a drinking glass with a foot and stem

gob·lin *n* : an ugly imaginary creature with evil or sly ways

god *n* **1** *cap* : the Being considered the holy and ruling power who made and sustains all things of the universe **2** : a being believed to have more than human powers **3** : a natural or artificial object worshiped as divine **4** : something believed to be the most important thing in existence

god·child *n, pl* **god·chil·dren** : a person for whom another person is sponsor at baptism

god·dess *n* : a female god

god·fa·ther *n* : a boy or man who is sponsor for a child at its baptism

god·less *adj* **1** : not believing in God or a god **2** : WICKED 1, EVIL — **god·less·ness** *n*

god·like *adj* : like or suitable for God or a god

god·ly *adj* **god·li·er; god·li·est** : DEVOUT 1, PIOUS — **god·li·ness** *n*

god·moth·er *n* : a girl or woman who is sponsor for a child at its baptism

god·par·ent *n* : a sponsor at baptism

god·send *n* : some badly needed thing that comes unexpectedly

goes *present 3d sing of* GO

go–get·ter *n* : a very active and aggressive person

gog·gle *vb* **gog·gled; gog·gling** **1** : to roll the eyes **2** : to stare with bulging or rolling eyes

gog·gle–eyed *adj* : having bulging or rolling eyes

gog·gles *n pl* : eyeglasses worn to protect the eyes (as from dust, sun, or wind)

go·ings–on *n pl* : things that happen

goi·ter *n* : a swelling on the front of the neck caused by enlargement of the thyroid gland

gold *n* **1** : a soft yellow metallic chemical element used especially in coins and jewelry **2** : gold coins **3** : MONEY 3 **4** : a deep yellow

gold·en *adj* **1** : like, made of, or containing gold **2** : of the color of gold **3** : very good or desirable **4** : being prosperous and happy

gold·en·rod *n* : a plant with tall stiff stems topped with rows of tiny yellow flower heads on slender branches

golden rule *n* : a rule that one should treat others as one would want others to treat oneself

gold·finch *n* **1** : a European finch with a yellow patch on each wing **2** : an American finch that looks like the canary

gold·fish *n* : a small usually golden yellow or orange carp often kept in aquariums

gold·smith *n* : a person who makes or deals in articles of gold

golf *n* : a game played by driving a small ball (**golf ball**) with one of a set of clubs (**golf clubs**) around an outdoor course (**golf course**) and into various holes in as few strokes as possible

golf·er *n* : a person who plays golf

gol·ly *interj* — used to express surprise or annoyance

gon·do·la *n* **1** : a long narrow boat used in the canals of Venice, Italy **2** : a freight car with no top **3** : an enclosure that hangs from a balloon and carries passengers or instruments

gone *adj* **1** : ADVANCED 1 **2** : INFATUATED **3** : [1]DEAD 1 **4** : WEAK 1, LIMP

gon·er *n* : one whose case is hopeless

gong *n* : a metallic disk that produces a harsh ringing tone when struck

[1]**good** *adj* **bet·ter; best** **1** : suitable for a use : SATISFACTORY **2** : being at least the amount mentioned **3** : CONSIDERABLE **4** : DESIRABLE, ATTRACTIVE **5** : HELPFUL, KIND **6** : behaving well **7** : being honest and upright **8** : showing good sense or judgment **9** : better than average

[2]**good** *n* **1** : something good **2** : WELFARE 1, BENEFIT **3 goods** *pl* : WARE 2 **4 goods** *pl* : personal property **5 goods** *pl* : a length of cloth

[1]**good–bye** *or* **good–by** *interj* — used as a farewell remark

[2]**good–bye** *or* **good–by** *n* : a farewell remark

good–heart·ed *adj* : having a kindly generous disposition — **good–heart·ed·ly** *adv* — **good–heart·ed·ness** *n*

good–hu·mored *adj* : GOOD-NATURED — **good–hu·mored·ly** *adv* — **good–hu·mored·ness** *n*

good·ly *adj* **good·li·er; good·li·est** **1** : of pleasing appearance **2** : LARGE, CONSIDERABLE

good–na·tured *adj* : having or showing a pleasant disposition — **good–na·tured·ly** *adv*

good·ness *n* **1** : the quality or state of being good **2** : excellence of morals and behavior

good–tem·pered *adj* : not easily angered or upset

good·will *n* **1** : kindly feelings **2** : the value of the trade a business has built up

goody *n, pl* **good·ies :** something especially good to eat

[1]**goof** *n* **1 :** a stupid or silly person **2 :** [2]BLUNDER

[2]**goof** *vb* **:** to make a blunder

goofy *adj* **goof·i·er; goof·i·est :** SILLY 1

goose *n, pl* **geese 1 :** a waterbird with webbed feet that is related to the smaller duck and the larger swan **2 :** a female goose **3 :** the flesh of a goose used as food **4 :** a silly person

goose·ber·ry *n, pl* **goose·ber·ries :** the sour berry of a thorny bush related to the currant

goose bumps *n pl* **:** a roughness of the skin caused by cold, fear, or a sudden feeling of excitement

goose·flesh *n* **:** GOOSE BUMPS

goose pimples *n pl* **:** GOOSE BUMPS

go·pher *n* **1 :** a burrowing animal that is about the size of a rat and has strong claws on the forefeet and very large outside cheek pouches **2 :** a striped ground squirrel of the prairies **3 :** a burrowing American land tortoise

[1]**gore** *n* **:** shed or clotted blood

[2]**gore** *vb* **gored; gor·ing :** to pierce or wound with a horn or tusk

[1]**gorge** *n* **:** a narrow steep-walled canyon or part of a canyon

[2]**gorge** *vb* **gorged; gorg·ing :** to eat greedily

gor·geous *adj* **:** very beautiful — **gor·geous·ly** *adv* — **gor·geous·ness** *n*

go·ril·la *n* **:** a very large ape of the forests of central Africa that lives mostly on the ground

gory *adj* **gor·i·er; gor·i·est :** covered with gore

gos·ling *n* **:** a young goose

gos·pel *n* **1** *often cap* **:** the teachings of Christ and the apostles **2 :** something told or accepted as being absolutely true

gos·sa·mer *adj* **:** very light and flimsy

[1]**gos·sip** *n* **1 :** a person who repeats stories about other people **2 :** talk or rumors having no worth

[2]**gossip** *vb* **:** to spread gossip

got *past of* GET

gotten *past participle of* GET

[1]**gouge** *n* **1 :** a chisel with a curved blade for scooping or cutting holes **2 :** a hole or groove made with or as if with a gouge

[2]**gouge** *vb* **gouged; goug·ing :** to dig out with or as if with a gouge

gou·lash *n* **:** a beef stew made with vegetables and paprika

gourd *n* **:** the fruit of a vine (**gourd vine**) related to the pumpkin and melon

gour·met *n* **:** a person who appreciates fine food and drink

gov·ern *vb* **1 :** [2]RULE 2 **2 :** to influence the actions and conduct of **:** CONTROL

gov·ern·able *adj* **:** possible to govern

gov·ern·ess *n* **:** a woman who teaches and trains a child especially in a private home

gov·ern·ment *n* **1 :** control and direction of public business (as of a city or a nation) **2 :** a system of control **:** an established form of political rule **3 :** the persons making up a governing body

gov·ern·men·tal *adj* **:** of or relating to government or the government

gov·er·nor *n* **1 :** a person who governs and especially the elected head of a state of the United States **2 :** a device attached to an engine for controlling its speed

gov·er·nor·ship *n* **1 :** the office or position of governor **2 :** the term of office of a governor

gown *n* **1 :** a woman's dress **2 :** a loose robe

[1]**grab** *vb* **grabbed; grab·bing :** [1]SNATCH

[2]**grab** *n* **:** the act or an instance of grabbing

[1]**grace** *n* **1 :** GOODWILL 1, FAVOR **2 :** a short prayer at a meal **3 :** pleasing and attractive behavior or quality **4 :** the condition of being in favor **5 :** a sense of what is proper **6 :** beauty and ease of movement

[2]**grace** *vb* **graced; grac·ing 1 :** to do credit to **:** HONOR **2 :** to make more attractive **:** ADORN

grace·ful *adj* **:** showing grace or beauty in form or action — **grace·ful·ly** *adv* — **grace·ful·ness** *n*

grace·less *adj* **:** lacking grace — **grace·less·ly** *adv* — **grace·less·ness** *n*

gra·cious *adj* **1 :** being kind and courteous **2 :** GRACEFUL — **gra·cious·ly** *adv* — **gra·cious·ness** *n*

grack·le *n* **:** a large blackbird with shiny feathers that show changeable green, purple, and bronze colors

[1]**grade** *n* **1 :** a position in a scale of rank, quality, or order **2 :** a class of things that are of the same rank, quality, or order **3 :** a division of a school course representing a year's work **4 :** the group of pupils in a school grade **5 grades** *pl* **:** the elementary school system **6 :** a mark or rating especially in school **7 :** the degree of slope (as of a road or railroad track) **:** SLOPE

[2]**grade** *vb* **grad·ed; grad·ing 1 :** to arrange in grades **:** SORT **2 :** to make level or evenly sloping **3 :** to give a grade to **4 :** to assign to a grade

grade school *n* **:** a school including the first six or the first eight grades

grad·u·al *adj* **:** moving or happening by steps or degrees — **grad·u·al·ly** *adv*

[1]**grad·u·ate** *n* **:** a person who has completed the required course of study in a college or school

[2]**grad·u·ate** *vb* **grad·u·at·ed; grad·u·at·ing** : to become a graduate : finish a course of study

grad·u·a·tion *n* **1 :** the act or process of graduating **2 :** COMMENCEMENT 2

Graeco- — see GRECO-

graf·fi·ti *n* **:** writing or drawing made on a public structure without permission

[1]**graft** *n* **1 :** a grafted plant **2 :** the act of grafting **3 :** something (as skin or a bud) used in grafting **4 :** something (as money or advantage) gotten in a dishonest way and especially by betraying a public trust

[2]**graft** *vb* **1 :** to insert a twig or bud from one plant into another plant so they are joined and grow together **2 :** to join one thing to another as if by grafting **3 :** to gain money or advantage in a dishonest way — **graft·er** *n*

grain *n* **1 :** the edible seed or seedlike fruit of some grasses (as wheat or oats) or a few other plants (as buckwheat) **2 :** plants that produce grain **3 :** a small hard particle **4 :** a tiny amount **5 :** a unit of weight equal to 0.0648 gram **6 :** the arrangement of fibers in wood — **grained** *adj*

gram *n* **:** a unit of mass in the metric system equal to 1/1000 kilogram

-gram *n suffix* **:** drawing **:** writing **:** record

gram·mar *n* **1 :** the study of the classes of words and their uses and relations in sentences **2 :** the study of what is good and bad to use in speaking and writing **3 :** speech or writing judged according to the rules of grammar

gram·mat·i·cal *adj* **:** of, relating to, or following the rules of grammar — **gram·mat·i·cal·ly** *adv*

gra·na·ry *n, pl* **gra·na·ries :** a storehouse for grain

grand *adj* **1 :** higher in rank than others **:** FOREMOST **2 :** great in size **3 :** COMPREHENSIVE, INCLUSIVE **4 :** showing wealth or high social standing **5 :** IMPRESSIVE **6 :** very good — **grand·ly** *adv* — **grand·ness** *n*

grand·aunt *n* **:** GREAT-AUNT

grand·child *n, pl* **grand·chil·dren :** a child of one's son or daughter

grand·daugh·ter *n* **:** a daughter of one's son or daughter

gran·deur *n* **:** impressive greatness (as of power or nature)

grand·fa·ther *n* **1 :** the father of one's father or mother **2 :** ANCESTOR — **grand·fa·ther·ly** *adj*

grandfather clock *n* **:** a tall clock standing directly on the floor

grand·ma *n* **:** GRANDMOTHER 1

grand·moth·er *n* **1 :** the mother of one's father or mother **2 :** a female ancestor — **grand·moth·er·ly** *adj*

grand·neph·ew *n* **:** a grandson of one's brother or sister

grand·niece *n* **:** a granddaughter of one's brother or sister

grand·pa *n* **:** GRANDFATHER 1

grand·par·ent *n* **:** a parent of one's father or mother

grand·son *n* **:** a son of one's son or daughter

grand·stand *n* **:** the main stand (as on an athletic field) for spectators

grand·un·cle *n* **:** GREAT-UNCLE

gran·ite *n* **:** a very hard rock that is used for building and for monuments

gran·ny *n, pl* **gran·nies :** GRANDMOTHER 1

granny knot *n* **:** a knot that is not very firm and is often made accidentally instead of a square knot

gra·no·la *n* **:** a mixture of oats and other ingredients (as raisins, coconut, or nuts) that is eaten especially for breakfast or as a snack

[1]**grant** *vb* **1 :** to agree to **2 :** to give as a favor or right **3 :** to admit (something not yet proved) to be true

[2]**grant** *n* **1 :** the act of granting **2 :** GIFT 2

grape *n* **:** a juicy berry that has a smooth green or whitish to deep red, purple, or black skin and grows in clusters on a woody vine (**grapevine**)

grape·fruit *n* **:** a large fruit with a yellow skin that is related to the orange and lemon

graph *n* **:** a diagram that by means of dots and lines shows a system of relationships between things

-graph *n suffix* **1 :** something written **2 :** instrument for making or sending records

[1]**graph·ic** *adj* **1 :** being written, drawn, printed, or engraved **2 :** told or described in a clear vivid way **3 :** of or relating to the pictorial arts or to printing — **graph·i·cal·ly** *adv*

[2]**graphic** *n* **1 :** a picture, map, or graph used for illustration **2 graphics** *pl* **:** a display (as of pictures or graphs) generated by a computer on a screen or printer

graph·ite *n* **:** a soft black carbon used in making lead pencils and as a lubricant

-g·ra·phy *n suffix, pl* **-g·ra·phies :** writing or picturing in a special way, by a special means, or of a special thing

grap·nel *n* **:** a small anchor with several claws that can be used to anchor a boat or to take and keep a hold on an object (as another boat or something under water)

[1]**grap·ple** *n* **1 :** the act of grappling or seizing **2 :** a device for grappling

[2]**grapple** *vb* **grap·pled; grap·pling 1 :** to seize or hold with an instrument (as a hook) **2 :** to seize and struggle with another

[1]**grasp** *vb* **1 :** to seize and hold with or as if

with the hand : GRIP **2 :** to make the motion of seizing : CLUTCH **3 :** UNDERSTAND 1, COMPREHEND

[2]**grasp** *n* **1 :** the act of grasping : a grip of the hand **2 :** [2]CONTROL 1, HOLD **3 :** the power of seizing and holding : REACH **4 :** [1]UNDERSTANDING 1, COMPREHENSION

grasp·ing *adj* : GREEDY 2

grass *n* **1 :** plants suitable for or eaten by grazing animals **2 :** any of a large natural group of green plants with jointed stems, long slender leaves, and stalks of clustered flowers **3 :** GRASSLAND — **grass·like** *adj*

grass·hop·per *n* : a common leaping insect that feeds on plants

grass·land *n* : land covered with herbs (as grass and clover) rather than shrubs and trees

grassy *adj* **grass·i·er; grass·i·est :** of, like, or covered with grass

[1]**grate** *vb* **grat·ed; grat·ing 1 :** to break into small pieces by rubbing against something rough **2 :** to grind or rub against something with a scratching noise **3 :** to have a harsh effect

[2]**grate** *n* **1 :** a frame containing parallel or crossed bars (as in a window) **2 :** a frame of iron bars for holding burning fuel

grate·ful *adj* **1 :** feeling or showing thanks **2 :** providing pleasure or comfort — **grate·ful·ly** *adv* — **grate·ful·ness** *n*

grat·er *n* : a device with a rough surface for grating

grat·i·fi·ca·tion *n* **1 :** the act of gratifying : the state of being gratified **2 :** something that gratifies

grat·i·fy *vb* **grat·i·fied; grat·i·fy·ing :** to give pleasure or satisfaction to

grat·ing *n* : [2]GRATE 1

grat·i·tude *n* : the state of being grateful

[1]**grave** *n* : a hole in the ground for burying a dead body

[2]**grave** *adj* **grav·er; grav·est 1 :** deserving serious thought : IMPORTANT **2 :** having a serious look or way of acting — **grave·ly** *adv* — **grave·ness** *n*

grav·el *n* : small pieces of rock and pebbles larger than grains of sand

grav·el·ly *adj* **1 :** containing or made up of gravel **2 :** sounding harsh or scratchy

grave·stone *n* : a monument on a grave

grave·yard *n* : CEMETERY

grav·i·tate *vb* **grav·i·tat·ed; grav·i·tat·ing :** to move or be drawn toward something

grav·i·ta·tion *n* **1 :** a force of attraction that tends to draw particles or bodies together **2 :** the act or process of gravitating

grav·i·ty *n, pl* **grav·i·ties 1 :** the condition of being grave **2 :** the attraction of bodies by gravitation toward the center of the earth **3 :** GRAVITATION 1

gra·vy *n, pl* **gravies :** a sauce made from the juice of cooked meat

[1]**gray** *or* **grey** *adj* **1 :** of the color gray **2 :** having gray hair **3 :** lacking cheer or brightness — **gray·ness** *n*

[2]**gray** *or* **grey** *n* **1 :** something gray in color **2 :** a color that is a blend of black and white

[3]**gray** *or* **grey** *vb* : to make or become gray

gray·ish *adj* : somewhat gray

[1]**graze** *vb* **grazed; graz·ing 1 :** to eat grass **2 :** to supply with grass or pasture

[2]**graze** *vb* **grazed; graz·ing 1 :** to rub lightly in passing : barely touch **2 :** to scrape by rubbing against something

[3]**graze** *n* : a scrape or mark caused by grazing

[1]**grease** *n* **1 :** a more or less solid substance obtained from animal fat by melting **2 :** oily material **3 :** a thick lubricant

[2]**grease** *vb* **greased; greas·ing 1 :** to smear with grease **2 :** to lubricate with grease

grease·paint *n* : actors' makeup

greasy *adj* **greas·i·er; greas·i·est 1 :** smeared with grease **2 :** like or full of grease

great *adj* **1 :** very large in size : HUGE **2 :** large in number : NUMEROUS **3 :** long continued **4 :** much beyond the average or ordinary **5 :** IMPORTANT 1, DISTINGUISHED **6 :** remarkable in knowledge or skill **7 :** GRAND 6 — **great·ly** *adv*

great–aunt *n* : an aunt of one's father or mother

great–grand·child *n, pl* **great–grand·chil·dren :** a grandson (**great–grandson**) or granddaughter (**great–granddaughter**) of one's son or daughter

great–grand·par·ent *n* : a grandfather (**great–grandfather**) or grandmother (**great–grandmother**) of one's father or mother

great–un·cle *n* : an uncle of one's father or mother

grebe *n* : any of a group of swimming and diving birds related to the loons

Gre·cian *adj* : [2]GREEK

Gre·co- *or* **Grae·co-** *prefix* **1 :** Greece : Greeks **2 :** Greek and

greed *n* : greedy desire (as for money or food)

greedy *adj* **greed·i·er; greed·i·est 1 :** having a strong appetite for food or drink : very hungry **2 :** trying to grab more than one needs or more than one's share — **greed·i·ly** *adv* — **greed·i·ness** *n*

[1]**Greek** *n* **1 :** a person born or living in Greece **2 :** the language of the Greeks

[2]**Greek** *adj* : of or relating to Greece, its people, or the Greek language

[1]**green** *adj* **1 :** of the color green **2 :** covered with green vegetation **3 :** made of green plants or of the leafy parts of plants **4 :** not ripe **5 :** not fully processed, treated, or seasoned **6 :** lacking training or experience **7 :** supporting the preservation or improvement of the natural environment (as by controlling pollution) **8 :** helping to preserve the environment (as by being recyclable or not polluting) — **green·ly** *adv* — **green·ness** *n*

[2]**green** *n* **1 :** a color that ranges between blue and yellow **2 greens** *pl* **:** leafy parts of plants used for decoration or food **3 :** a grassy plain or plot

green·ery *n, pl* **green·er·ies :** green plants or foliage

green·horn *n* **:** a person who is new at something

green·house *n* **:** a building with glass walls and roof for growing plants

greenhouse effect *n* **:** warming of the lower atmosphere of the earth that occurs when radiation from the sun is absorbed by the earth and then given off again and absorbed by carbon dioxide and water vapor in the atmosphere

green·ish *adj* **:** somewhat green

green·ling *n* **:** any of a group of food and sport fishes of the Pacific coast

green manure *n* **:** a leafy crop (as of clover) plowed under to improve the soil

green thumb *n* **:** an unusual ability to make plants grow

green·wood *n* **:** a forest green with leaves

greet *vb* **1 :** to speak to in a friendly polite way upon arrival or meeting **2 :** to receive or react to in a certain way **3 :** to present itself to — **greet·er** *n*

greet·ing *n* **1 :** an expression of pleasure on meeting someone **2 :** SALUTATION 2 **3 :** an expression of good wishes

gre·gar·i·ous *adj* **:** tending to live together with or associate with others of one's own kind — **gre·gar·i·ous·ly** *adv* — **gre·gar·i·ous·ness** *n*

gre·nade *n* **:** a small bomb designed to be thrown by hand or fired (as by a rifle)

gren·a·dier *n* **:** a member of a European regiment formerly armed with grenades

grew *past of* GROW

grey *variant of* GRAY

grey·hound *n* **:** a tall swift dog with a smooth coat and good eyesight

grid *n* **1 :** a group of electrical conductors that form a network **2 :** a network of horizontal and perpendicular lines (as for locating places on a map)

grid·dle *n* **:** a flat surface or pan on which food is cooked

griddle cake *n* **:** PANCAKE

grid·iron *n* **1 :** a grate with parallel bars for broiling food **2 :** a football field

grief *n* **1 :** very deep sorrow **2 :** a cause of sorrow **3 :** MISHAP

griev·ance *n* **1 :** a cause of uneasiness or annoyance **2 :** a formal complaint

grieve *vb* **grieved; griev·ing 1 :** to cause grief to **2 :** to feel or show grief

griev·ous *adj* **1 :** causing suffering **2 :** SERIOUS 5, GRAVE

[1]**grill** *vb* **1 :** to broil on a grill **2 :** to distress with continued questioning

[2]**grill** *n* **1 :** a grate on which food is broiled **2 :** a dish of broiled food **3 :** a simple restaurant

grille *or* **grill** *n* **:** an often ornamental arrangement of bars (as of metal) forming a barrier or screen

grim *adj* **grim·mer; grim·mest 1 :** [1]SAVAGE 2, CRUEL **2 :** harsh in appearance **:** STERN **3 :** UNYIELDING 2 **4 :** FRIGHTFUL 1 — **grim·ly** *adv* — **grim·ness** *n*

[1]**gri·mace** *n* **:** a twisting of the face (as in disgust)

[2]**grim·ace** *vb* **grim·aced; grim·ac·ing :** to make a grimace

grime *n* **:** dirt rubbed into a surface

grimy *adj* **grim·i·er; grim·i·est :** full of grime **:** DIRTY

[1]**grin** *vb* **grinned; grin·ning :** to draw back the lips and show the teeth

[2]**grin** *n* **:** an act of grinning

[1]**grind** *vb* **ground; grind·ing 1 :** to make or be made into meal or powder by rubbing **2 :** to wear down, polish, or sharpen by friction **3 :** to rub together with a scraping noise **4 :** to operate or produce by or as if by turning a crank

[2]**grind** *n* **1 :** an act of grinding **2 :** steady hard work

grind·stone *n* **:** a flat round stone that turns on an axle and is used for sharpening tools and for shaping and smoothing

[1]**grip** *vb* **gripped; grip·ping 1 :** to grasp firmly **2 :** to hold the interest of

[2]**grip** *n* **1 :** a strong grasp **2 :** strength in holding **:** POWER **3 :** [1]HANDLE **4 :** a small suitcase

grippe *n* **:** a disease like or the same as influenza

gris·ly *adj* **gris·li·er; gris·li·est :** HORRIBLE, GHASTLY

grist *n* **:** grain to be ground or that is already ground

gris·tle *n* **:** CARTILAGE — **gris·tli·ness** *n* — **gris·tly** *adj*

grist·mill *n* **:** a mill for grinding grain

[1]**grit** *n* **1 :** rough hard bits especially of sand **2 :** strength of mind or spirit

[2]**grit** *vb* **grit·ted; grit·ting** : [1]GRIND 3, GRATE
grits *n pl* : coarsely ground hulled grain
grit·ty *adj* **grit·ti·er; grit·ti·est** **1** : containing or like grit **2** : bravely refusing to yield : PLUCKY — **grit·ti·ness** *n*
griz·zled *adj* : streaked or mixed with gray
griz·zly *adj* **griz·zli·er; griz·zli·est** : GRIZZLED, GRAYISH
grizzly bear *n* : a large powerful usually brownish yellow bear of western North America
[1]**groan** *vb* **1** : to make or express with a deep moaning sound **2** : to creak under a strain
[2]**groan** *n* : a low moaning sound
gro·cer *n* : a dealer in food
gro·cery *n, pl* **gro·cer·ies** **1** *groceries pl* : the goods sold by a grocer **2** : a grocer's store
grog·gy *adj* **grog·gi·er; grog·gi·est** : weak and confused and unsteady on one's feet — **grog·gi·ly** *adv* — **grog·gi·ness** *n*
groin *n* : the fold or area where the abdomen joins the thigh
grom·met *n* : an eyelet of firm material to strengthen or protect an opening
[1]**groom** *n* **1** : a servant especially in charge of horses **2** : BRIDEGROOM
[2]**groom** *vb* **1** : to make neat and attractive (as by cleaning and brushing) **2** : to make fit or ready
[1]**groove** *n* **1** : a narrow channel made in a surface (as by cutting) **2** : [1]ROUTINE
[2]**groove** *vb* **grooved; groov·ing** : to form a groove in
groovy *adj* **groov·i·er; groov·i·est** : very good : EXCELLENT
grope *vb* **groped; grop·ing** **1** : to feel one's way **2** : to seek by or as if by feeling around
gros·beak *n* : a finch with a strong conical bill
[1]**gross** *adj* **1** : GLARING 3 **2** : BIG 1 **3** : [1]THICK 3 **4** : consisting of a whole before anything is deducted **5** : COARSE 4, VULGAR
[2]**gross** *n* : the whole before anything is deducted
[3]**gross** *n, pl* **gross** : twelve dozen
gro·tesque *adj* : very strange and unexpected : FANTASTIC
grot·to *n, pl* **grottoes** **1** : [1]CAVE, CAVERN **2** : an artificial structure like a cave
[1]**grouch** *n* **1** : a fit of bad temper **2** : a person with a bad disposition
[2]**grouch** *vb* : [1]GRUMBLE 1, COMPLAIN
grouchy *adj* **grouch·i·er; grouch·i·est** : having a bad disposition : CANTANKEROUS — **grouch·i·ly** *adv* — **grouch·i·ness** *n*
[1]**ground** *n* **1** : the bottom of a body of water **2 grounds** *pl* : SEDIMENT 1 **3** : a reason for a belief, action, or argument **4** : the surface or material upon which something is made or displayed or against which it appears **5** : the surface of the earth : SOIL **6** : an area used for some purpose **7 grounds** *pl* : the land around and belonging to a building **8** : an area to be won or defended as if in a battle
[2]**ground** *vb* **1** : to instruct in basic knowledge or understanding **2** : to run or cause to run aground **3** : to connect electrically with the ground **4** : to prevent (a plane or pilot) from flying
[3]**ground** *past of* GRIND
ground crew *n* : the mechanics and technicians who take care of an airplane
ground·hog *n* : WOODCHUCK
ground·less *adj* : being without foundation or reason
ground swell *n* : a broad deep ocean swell caused by a distant storm or earthquake
ground·work *n* : FOUNDATION 2
[1]**group** *n* : a number of persons or things that form one whole
[2]**group** *vb* : to arrange in or put into a group
[1]**grouse** *n, pl* **grouse** : a game bird that is much like the domestic fowl
[2]**grouse** *vb* **groused; grous·ing** : [1]GRUMBLE 1, GROUCH
grove *n* : a small wood or a planting of trees
grov·el *vb* **grov·eled** *or* **grov·elled; grov·el·ing** *or* **grov·el·ling** **1** : to creep or lie face down on the ground (as in fear) **2** : CRINGE — **grov·el·er** *or* **grov·el·ler** *n*
grow *vb* **grew; grown; grow·ing** **1** : to spring up and develop to maturity **2** : to be able to live and develop **3** : to be related in some way by reason of growing **4** : [1]INCREASE, EXPAND **5** : BECOME 1 **6** : to cause to grow : RAISE — **grow·er** *n*
growing pains *n pl* : pains that occur in the legs of growing children but have not been proven to be caused by growth
[1]**growl** *vb* **1** : to make a rumbling noise **2** : to make a growl **3** : [1]GRUMBLE 1
[2]**growl** *n* **1** : a deep threatening sound (as of an animal) **2** : a grumbling or muttered complaint
grown *adj* : having reached full growth : MATURE
[1]**grown–up** *adj* : [1]ADULT
[2]**grown–up** *n* : an adult person
growth *n* **1** : a stage or condition in growing **2** : a process of growing **3** : a gradual increase **4** : something (as a covering of plants) produced by growing
grow up *vb* : to become adult
[1]**grub** *vb* **grubbed; grub·bing** **1** : to root out by digging **2** : to work hard

²grub *n* **1 :** a soft thick wormlike larva (as of a beetle) **2 :** FOOD 1

grub·by *adj* **grub·bi·er; grub·bi·est :** [1]DIRTY 1 — **grub·bi·ly** *adv* — **grub·bi·ness** *n*

¹grub·stake *n* **:** supplies or funds given to a prospector in return for a promise of a share in the finds

²grubstake *vb* **grub·staked; grub·stak·ing :** to provide with a grubstake

¹grudge *vb* **grudged; grudg·ing :** BEGRUDGE

²grudge *n* **:** a feeling of sullen dislike that lasts a long time

gru·el *n* **:** a thin porridge

gru·el·ing *or* **gru·el·ling** *adj* **:** calling for much effort

grue·some *adj* **:** HORRIBLE, GHASTLY — **grue·some·ly** *adv* — **grue·some·ness** *n*

gruff *adj* **:** rough in speech or manner **:** HARSH — **gruff·ly** *adv* — **gruff·ness** *n*

¹grum·ble *vb* **grum·bled; grum·bling 1 :** to complain or mutter in discontent **2 :** [1]RUMBLE

²grumble *n* **1 :** the act of grumbling **2 :** [2]RUMBLE

grumpy *adj* **grump·i·er; grump·i·est :** GROUCHY, CROSS — **grump·i·ly** *adv* — **grump·i·ness** *n*

¹grunt *vb* **:** to make a grunt — **grunt·er** *n*

²grunt *n* **:** a deep short sound (as of a hog)

¹guar·an·tee *n* **1 :** GUARANTOR **2 :** the act of guaranteeing **3 :** a promise that something will work the way it should **4 :** SECURITY 2

²guarantee *vb* **guar·an·teed; guar·an·tee·ing 1 :** to promise to answer for the debt or duty of another person **2 :** to give a guarantee on or about

guar·an·tor *n* **:** a person who gives a guarantee

¹guard *n* **1 :** the act or duty of keeping watch **2 :** a person or a body of persons that guards against injury or danger **3 :** a device giving protection

²guard *vb* **1 :** to protect from danger **:** DEFEND **2 :** to watch over so as to prevent escape **3 :** to keep careful watch

guard·ed *adj* **:** CAUTIOUS

guard·house *n* **1 :** a building used as a headquarters by soldiers on guard duty **2 :** a military jail

guard·ian *n* **1 :** a person who guards or looks after something **:** CUSTODIAN **2 :** a person who legally has the care of another person or of that person's property — **guard·ian·ship** *n*

guard·room *n* **:** a room used by a military guard while on duty

guards·man *n, pl* **guards·men :** a member of a military guard

gu·ber·na·to·ri·al *adj* **:** of or relating to a governor

guer·ril·la *or* **gue·ril·la** *n* **:** a member of a band of persons carrying on warfare but not part of a regular army

¹guess *vb* **1 :** to judge without sure knowledge **2 :** to solve correctly **3 :** THINK 2, BELIEVE — **guess·er** *n*

²guess *n* **:** an opinion formed by guessing

guess·work *n* **:** work done or results gotten by guessing

guest *n* **1 :** a person entertained in one's house or at one's table **2 :** a person using a hotel, motel, inn, or restaurant

¹guf·faw *n* **:** a burst of loud laughter

²guffaw *vb* **:** to laugh noisily

guid·ance *n* **:** the act or process of guiding or being guided **:** DIRECTION

¹guide *n* **:** someone or something (as a book) that leads, directs, or shows the right way

²guide *vb* **guid·ed; guid·ing 1 :** to show the way to **2 :** DIRECT, INSTRUCT

guide·book *n* **:** a book of information for travelers

guide dog *n* **:** a dog trained to lead a person who is blind

guide·post *n* **:** a post with signs giving directions for travelers

guide word *n* **:** either of the terms at the head of a page of an alphabetical reference work (as a dictionary) usually showing the first and last entries on the page

guild *n* **:** an association of persons with similar aims or common interests

guile *n* **:** sly trickery — **guile·ful** *adj* — **guile·ful·ly** *adv*

¹guil·lo·tine *n* **:** a machine for cutting off a person's head with a heavy blade that slides down two grooved posts

²guillotine *vb* **guil·lo·tined; guil·lo·tin·ing :** to cut off a person's head with a guillotine

guilt *n* **1 :** the fact of having done something wrong and especially something punishable by law **2 :** conduct that causes one to feel shame or regret or the feeling experienced — **guilt·less** *adj*

guilty *adj* **guilt·i·er; guilt·i·est 1 :** having done wrong **2 :** aware of, suffering from, or showing guilt — **guilt·i·ly** *adv* — **guilt·i·ness** *n*

guin·ea *n* **:** an old British gold coin

guinea fowl *n* **:** an African bird related to the pheasants that has a bare head and neck and usually dark gray feathers with white speckles and is sometimes raised for food

guinea pig *n* **:** a stocky rodent with short ears and a very short tail

guise *n* **1 :** a style of dress **2 :** outward appearance

gui·tar *n* **:** a musical instrument with six strings played by plucking or strumming

gulch *n* **:** RAVINE

gulf *n* **1 :** a part of an ocean or sea extending into the land **2 :** CHASM, ABYSS **3 :** a wide separation (as in age)

gull *n* **:** a waterbird with webbed feet that is usually blue-gray or whitish in color and has a thick strong bill

gul·let *n* **:** THROAT 2, ESOPHAGUS

gull·ible *adj* **:** easily tricked or misled

gul·ly *n, pl* **gullies :** a trench worn in the earth by running water

[1]**gulp** *vb* **1 :** to swallow eagerly or in large amounts at a time **2 :** to keep back as if by swallowing **3 :** to catch the breath as if after a long drink

[2]**gulp** *n* **1 :** the act of gulping **2 :** a large swallow

[1]**gum** *n* **:** the flesh along the jaws at the roots of the teeth

[2]**gum** *n* **1 :** a sticky substance obtained from plants that hardens on drying **2 :** a substance like a plant gum (as in stickiness) **3 :** CHEWING GUM

[3]**gum** *vb* **gummed; gum·ming :** to smear, stick together, or clog with or as if with gum

gum·bo *n, pl* **gumbos :** a rich soup thickened with okra pods

gum·drop *n* **:** a candy usually made from corn syrup and gelatin

gum·my *adj* **gum·mi·er; gum·mi·est 1 :** consisting of, containing, or covered with gum **2 :** GLUEY, STICKY

gump·tion *n* **:** [1]SPIRIT 5, COURAGE

[1]**gun** *n* **1 :** CANNON 1 **2 :** a portable firearm (as a rifle, shotgun, or pistol) **3 :** something like a gun in shape or function **4 :** a discharge of a gun (as in a salute)

[2]**gun** *vb* **gunned; gun·ning 1 :** to hunt with a gun **2 :** to open the throttle of quickly so as to increase speed

gun·boat *n* **:** a small armed ship for use in coastal waters

gun·fire *n* **:** the firing of guns

gun·man *n, pl* **gun·men :** a criminal armed with a gun

gun·ner *n* **:** a person who operates a gun

gun·nery *n* **:** the use of guns

gunnery sergeant *n* **:** a noncommissioned officer in the Marine Corps ranking above a staff sergeant

gun·ny *n, pl* **gun·nies 1 :** coarse jute sacking **2 :** BURLAP

gun·pow·der *n* **:** an explosive powder used in guns and blasting

gun·shot *n* **1 :** a shot from a gun **2 :** the effective range of a gun

gun·wale *n* **:** the upper edge of a ship's side

gup·py *n, pl* **guppies :** a small tropical minnow often kept as an aquarium fish

[1]**gur·gle** *vb* **gur·gled; gur·gling 1 :** to flow in a broken uneven noisy current **2 :** to sound like a liquid flowing with a gurgle

[2]**gurgle** *n* **:** a sound of or like gurgling liquid

[1]**gush** *vb* **1 :** [1]SPOUT 1, 3 **2 :** to be too affectionate or enthusiastic

[2]**gush** *n* **:** a sudden free pouring out

gush·er *n* **:** an oil well with a large natural flow

gust *n* **1 :** a sudden brief rush of wind **2 :** a sudden outburst (as of emotion)

gusty *adj* **gust·i·er; gust·i·est :** WINDY

[1]**gut** *n* **1 :** ENTRAILS — usually used in pl. **2 :** the digestive tube or a part of this **3 :** CATGUT **4 guts** *pl* **:** COURAGE

[2]**gut** *vb* **gut·ted; gut·ting 1 :** to remove the entrails from **2 :** to destroy the inside of

[1]**gut·ter** *n* **1 :** a trough along the eaves of a house to catch and carry off water **2 :** a low area (as at the side of a road) to carry off surface water

[2]**gutter** *vb* **1 :** to flow in small streams **2 :** to have wax flowing down the sides after melting through the rim

[1]**guy** *n* **:** a rope, chain, rod, or wire (**guy wire**) attached to something to steady it

[2]**guy** *n* **:** PERSON 1, FELLOW

gym *n* **:** GYMNASIUM

gym·na·si·um *n* **:** a room or building for sports events or gymnastics

gym·nast *n* **:** a person who is skilled in gymnastics

gym·nas·tic *adj* **:** of or relating to gymnastics

gym·nas·tics *n sing or pl* **:** physical exercises for developing skill, strength, and control in the use of the body or a sport in which such exercises are performed

Gyp·sy *or* **Gip·sy** *n, pl* **Gyp·sies** *or* **Gip·sies :** a member of a group of people coming from India to Europe long ago and living a wandering way of life

gypsy moth *n* **:** a moth whose caterpillar has a spotty grayish look and does great damage to trees by eating the leaves

gy·rate *vb* **gy·rat·ed; gy·rat·ing :** to move in a circle around a center **:** SPIN

gy·ro·scope *n* **:** a wheel mounted to spin rapidly so that its axis is free to turn in various directions

gy·ro·scop·ic *adj* **:** of or relating to a gyroscope

H

h *n, pl* **h's** *or* **hs** *often cap* **:** the eighth letter of the English alphabet

ha *interj* — used to show surprise or joy

hab·it *n* **1 :** clothing worn for a special purpose **2 :** usual way of behaving **3 :** a way of acting or doing that has become fixed by being repeated often **4 :** characteristic way of growing

hab·it·able *adj* **:** suitable or fit to live in

hab·i·tat *n* **:** the place where a plant or animal grows or lives in nature

hab·i·ta·tion *n* **1 :** the act of living in a place **2 :** a place to live

ha·bit·u·al *adj* **1 :** being or done by habit **2 :** doing or acting by force of habit **3 :** [1]REGULAR — **ha·bit·u·al·ly** *adv* — **ha·bit·u·al·ness** *n*

ha·ci·en·da *n* **1 :** a large estate especially in a Spanish-speaking country **2 :** the main house of a hacienda

[1]**hack** *vb* **1 :** to cut with repeated chopping blows **2 :** to cough in a short broken way **3 :** to write computer programs for enjoyment **4 :** to gain access to a computer illegally

[2]**hack** *n* **:** a short broken cough

[3]**hack** *n* **1 :** a horse let out for hire or used for varied work **2 :** a person who works for pay at a routine writing job **3 :** a writer who is not very good

hack·er *n* **1 :** one that hacks **2 :** a person who is unskilled at a particular activity **3 :** an expert at programming and solving problems with a computer **4 :** a person who illegally gains access to a computer system

hack·les *n pl* **:** hairs (as on the neck of a dog) that can be made to stand up

hack·ney *n, pl* **hack·neys :** a horse for ordinary riding or driving

hack·saw *n* **:** a saw used for cutting hard materials (as metal) that consists of a frame and a blade with small teeth

had *past of* HAVE

had·dock *n, pl* **haddock** *or* **haddocks :** a food fish related to but smaller than the cod

hadn't : had not

haf·ni·um *n* **:** a gray metallic chemical element

hag *n* **1 :** WITCH 1 **2 :** an ugly old woman

hag·gard *adj* **:** having a hungry, tired, or worried look

hag·gle *vb* **hag·gled; hag·gling :** to argue especially over a price — **hag·gler** *n*

ha–ha *interj* — used to show amusement or scorn

hai·ku *n, pl* **haiku 1 :** a Japanese verse form without rhyme having three lines with the first and last lines having five syllables and the middle having seven **2 :** a poem written in this form

[1]**hail** *n* **1 :** small lumps of ice and snow that fall from the clouds sometimes during thunderstorms **2 :** [1]VOLLEY 1

[2]**hail** *vb* **1 :** to fall as hail **2 :** to pour down like hail

[3]**hail** *interj* — used to show enthusiastic approval

[4]**hail** *vb* **1 :** GREET 1, WELCOME **2 :** to call out to — **hail from :** to come from

[5]**hail** *n* **:** an exclamation of greeting, approval, or praise

hail·stone *n* **:** a lump of hail

hail·storm *n* **:** a storm that brings hail

hair *n* **1 :** a threadlike growth from the skin of a person or lower animal **2 :** a covering or growth of hairs (as on one's head) **3 :** something (as a growth on a leaf) like an animal hair — **haired** *adj* — **hair·less** *adj* — **hair-like** *adj*

hair·brush *n* **:** a brush for the hair

hair·cut *n* **:** the act, process, or result of cutting the hair

hair·do *n, pl* **hairdos :** a way of arranging a person's hair

hair·dress·er *n* **:** one who dresses or cuts hair — **hair·dress·ing** *n*

hair·pin *n* **:** a pin in the shape of a U for holding the hair in place

hair–rais·ing *adj* **:** causing terror, excitement, or great surprise

hair·style *n* **:** HAIRDO

hairy *adj* **hair·i·er; hair·i·est :** covered with hair — **hair·i·ness** *n*

[1]**hale** *adj* **:** being strong and healthy

[2]**hale** *vb* **haled; hal·ing :** to force to go

[1]**half** *n, pl* **halves 1 :** one of two equal parts into which something can be divided **2 :** a part of something that is about equal to the remainder **3 :** one of a pair

[2]**half** *adj* **1 :** being one of two equal parts **2 :** amounting to about a half **:** PARTIAL

[3]**half** *adv* **1 :** to the extent of half **2 :** not completely

half brother *n* **:** a brother by one parent only

half·heart·ed *adj* **:** lacking spirit or interest — **half·heart·ed·ly** *adv* — **half·heart·ed·ness** *n*

half–knot *n* **:** a knot in which two rope ends are wrapped once around each other and which is used to start other knots

half–life *n, pl* **half–lives :** the time required for half of the atoms of a radioactive substance to change composition

half sister *n* **:** a sister by one parent only

¹half·way *adv* **:** at or to half the distance

²halfway *adj* **1 :** midway between two points **2 :** PARTIAL 3

half–wit *n* **:** a very stupid person — **half–wit·ted** *adj*

hal·i·but *n, pl* **halibut** *or* **halibuts :** a very large flatfish much used for food

hall *n* **1 :** a large building used for public purposes **2 :** a building (as of a college) set apart for a special purpose **3 :** an entrance room **4 :** CORRIDOR **5 :** AUDITORIUM

hal·le·lu·jah *interj* — used to express praise, joy, or thanks

hal·low *vb* **:** to set apart for holy purposes **:** treat as sacred

Hal·low·een *n* **:** October 31 observed with parties and with the playing of tricks by children during the evening

hal·lu·ci·na·tion *n* **:** the seeing of objects or the experiencing of feelings that are not real but are usually the result of mental disorder or the effect of a drug

hal·lu·ci·no·gen *n* **:** a drug that causes hallucinations — **hal·lu·ci·no·gen·ic** *adj*

hall·way *n* **:** CORRIDOR

ha·lo *n, pl* **halos** *or* **haloes 1 :** a circle of light around the sun or moon caused by tiny ice crystals in the air **2 :** a circle drawn or painted around the head of a person in a picture as a symbol of holiness

¹halt *vb* **:** HESITATE 1

²halt *n* **:** ¹END 2

³halt *vb* **1 :** to stop or cause to stop marching or traveling **2 :** ²END

hal·ter *n* **1 :** a rope or strap for leading or tying an animal **2 :** a headstall to which a halter may be attached **3 :** a brief blouse usually without a back and fastened by straps around the neck

halve *vb* **halved; halv·ing 1 :** to divide into halves **2 :** to reduce to one half

halves *pl of* HALF

hal·yard *n* **:** a rope for raising or lowering a sail

ham *n* **1 :** a buttock with the connected thigh **2 :** a cut of meat consisting of a thigh usually of pork **3 :** an operator of an amateur radio station

ham·burg·er *or* **ham·burg** *n* **1 :** ground beef **2 :** a sandwich made of a patty of ground beef in a split bun

ham·let *n* **:** a small village

¹ham·mer *n* **1 :** a tool consisting of a head fastened to a handle and used for pounding (as in driving nails) **2 :** something like a hammer in shape or action **3 :** a heavy metal ball with a flexible handle thrown for distance in a track-and-field contest (**hammer throw**)

²hammer *vb* **1 :** to strike with a hammer **2 :** to fasten (as by nailing) with a hammer **3 :** to produce by or as if by means of repeated blows

ham·mer·head *n* **:** any of various sharks having a wide flattened rectangular-shaped head with the eyes spaced widely apart

ham·mock *n* **:** a swinging cot usually made of canvas or netting

¹ham·per *vb* **:** to keep from moving or acting freely

²hamper *n* **:** a large basket usually with a cover

ham·ster *n* **:** a stocky rodent with a short tail and large cheek pouches

¹hand *n* **1 :** the part of the arm fitted (as in humans) for handling, grasping, and holding **2 :** a bodily structure (as the hind foot of an ape) like the human hand in function or form **3 :** something like a hand **4 :** ²CONTROL 1 **5 :** one side of a problem **6 :** a pledge especially of marriage **7 :** HANDWRITING **8 :** ABILITY 1 **9 :** a unit of measure equal to about ten centimeters **10 :** ²HELP 1, ASSISTANCE **11 :** a part or share in doing something **12 :** an outburst of applause **13 :** the cards held by a player in a card game **14 :** a hired worker **:** LABORER — **at hand :** near in time or place — **by hand :** with the hands — **in hand 1 :** in one's possession or control **2 :** in preparation — **off one's hands :** out of one's care — **on hand 1 :** in present possession **2 :** ³PRESENT 1 — **out of hand :** out of control

²hand *vb* **:** to give or pass with the hand

hand·bag *n* **:** a bag used for carrying money and small personal articles

hand·ball *n* **:** a game played by hitting a small ball against a wall or board with the hand

hand·bill *n* **:** a printed sheet (as of advertising) distributed by hand

hand·book *n* **:** a book of facts usually about one subject

hand·car *n* **:** a small railroad car that is made to move by hand or by a small motor

¹hand·cuff *n* **:** a metal fastening that can be locked around a person's wrist

²handcuff *vb* **:** to put handcuffs on

hand·ed *adj* **:** using a particular hand or number of hands

hand·ful *n, pl* **handfuls** *or* **hands·ful 1 :** as much or as many as the hand will grasp **2 :** a small amount or number

¹hand·i·cap *n* **1 :** a contest in which one more skilled is given a disadvantage and one less skilled is given an advantage **2 :** the disadvantage or advantage given in a contest **3 :** a disadvantage that makes progress or success difficult

²handicap *vb* **hand·i·capped; hand·i·cap-**

ping **1 :** to give a handicap to **2 :** to put at a disadvantage

hand·i·craft *n* **1 :** an occupation (as weaving or pottery making) that requires skill with the hands **2 :** articles made by one working at handicraft

hand·i·ly *adv* **:** in a handy manner **:** EASILY

hand·i·work *n* **:** work done by the hands

hand·ker·chief *n, pl* **hand·ker·chiefs :** a small usually square piece of cloth used for wiping the face, nose, or eyes

[1]**han·dle** *n* **:** the part by which something (as a dish or tool) is picked up or held — **han·dled** *adj*

[2]**handle** *vb* **han·dled; han·dling 1 :** to touch, feel, hold, or move with the hand **2 :** to manage with the hands **3 :** to deal with (as in writing or speaking) **4 :** MANAGE 1, DIRECT **5 :** to deal with or act on **6 :** to deal or trade in — **han·dler** *n*

han·dle·bars *n pl* **:** a bar (as on a bicycle) that has a handle at each end and is used for steering

hand·made *adj* **:** made by hand rather than by machine

hand–me–downs *n pl* **:** used clothes

hand organ *n* **:** a small musical instrument cranked by hand

hand·out *n* **:** something (as food) given to a beggar

hand·rail *n* **:** a rail to be grasped by the hand for support

hands down *adv* **:** without question **:** EASILY

hand·shake *n* **:** a clasping of hands by two people (as in greeting)

hand·some *adj* **hand·som·er; hand·som·est 1 :** CONSIDERABLE **2 :** more than enough **3 :** having a pleasing and impressive appearance

hand·spring *n* **:** a feat of tumbling in which the body turns forward or backward in a full circle from a standing position and lands first on the hands and then on the feet

hand·stand *n* **:** a stunt in which a person balances the body in the air upside down supported on the hands

hand–to–hand *adj* **:** involving bodily contact

hand·work *n* **:** work done by hand and not by machine

hand·writ·ing *n* **:** writing done by hand

handy *adj* **hand·i·er; hand·i·est 1 :** within easy reach **2 :** easy to use or manage **3 :** VERSATILE 2 **4 :** DEXTEROUS 1

[1]**hang** *vb* **hung** *also* **hanged; hang·ing 1 :** to fasten or be fastened to something without support from below **:** SUSPEND **2 :** to kill or be killed by suspending (as from a gallows) by a rope tied around the neck **3 :** to fasten so as to allow free motion forward and backward **4 :** to cause to droop — **hang on to :** to hold or keep with determination

[2]**hang** *n* **1 :** the way in which a thing hangs **2 :** MEANING 1 **3 :** KNACK 1

han·gar *n* **:** a shelter for housing and repairing aircraft

hang·er *n* **:** a device on which something hangs

hang·man *n, pl* **hang·men :** one who hangs criminals

hang·nail *n* **:** a bit of skin hanging loose about a fingernail

hang·out *n* **:** a place where a person spends much idle time or goes often

hang·over *n* **1 :** something (as a surviving custom) that remains from what is past **2 :** a sick uncomfortable state that comes from drinking too much liquor

han·ker *vb* **:** to have a great desire

han·som *n* **:** a light covered carriage that has two wheels and a driver's seat elevated at the rear

Ha·nuk·kah *n* **:** a Jewish holiday lasting eight days and celebrating the cleansing and second dedication of the Temple after the Syrians were driven out of Jerusalem in 165 B.C.

hap·haz·ard *adj* **:** marked by lack of plan, order, or direction — **hap·haz·ard·ly** *adv* — **hap·haz·ard·ness** *n*

hap·less *adj* **:** [1]UNFORTUNATE 1

hap·pen *vb* **1 :** to occur or come about by chance **2 :** to take place **3 :** to have opportunity **:** CHANCE **4 :** to come especially by way of injury or harm

hap·pen·ing *n* **:** something that happens

hap·py *adj* **hap·pi·er; hap·pi·est 1 :** FORTUNATE 1, LUCKY **2 :** being suitable for something **3 :** enjoying one's condition **:** CONTENT **4 :** JOYFUL **5 :** feeling or showing pleasure **:** GLAD — **hap·pi·ly** *adv* — **hap·pi·ness** *n*

hap·py–go–lucky *adj* **:** free from care

ha·rangue *n* **:** a scolding speech or writing

ha·rass *vb* **1 :** to worry and hinder by repeated attacks **2 :** to annoy again and again — **ha·rass·ment** *n*

[1]**har·bor** *n* **1 :** a place of safety and comfort **:** REFUGE **2 :** a part of a body of water (as a sea or lake) so protected as to be a place of safety for ships **:** PORT

[2]**harbor** *vb* **1 :** to give shelter to **2 :** to have or hold in the mind

[1]**hard** *adj* **1 :** not easily cut, pierced, or divided **:** not soft **2 :** high in alcoholic content **3 :** containing substances that prevent lathering with soap **4 :** difficult to put up with **:** SEVERE **5 :** UNFEELING 2 **6 :** carried on with steady and earnest effort **7 :** DILIGENT, ENERGETIC **8 :** sounding as in *cold* and *geese*

— used of *c* and *g* **9 :** difficult to do or to understand

²hard *adv* **1 :** with great effort or energy **2 :** in a violent way **3 :** with pain, bitterness, or resentment

hard copy *n* **:** a copy of information (as from computer storage) produced on paper in normal size

hard disk *n* **1 :** a rigid metal disk used to store computer data **2 :** HARD DRIVE

hard drive *n* **:** a computer-data storage device containing one or more hard disks

hard·en *vb* **1 :** to make or become hard or harder **2 :** to make or become hardy or strong **3 :** to make or become stubborn or unfeeling — **hard·en·er** *n*

hard·head·ed *adj* **1 :** STUBBORN 1 **2 :** using or showing good judgment — **hard·head·ed·ly** *adv* — **hard·head·ed·ness** *n*

hard·heart·ed *adj* **:** showing or feeling no pity **:** UNFEELING — **hard·heart·ed·ly** *adv* — **hard·heart·ed·ness** *n*

hard·ly *adv* **:** only just **:** BARELY

hard·ness *n* **:** the quality or state of being hard

hard palate *n* **:** the bony front part of the roof of the mouth

hard·ship *n* **:** something (as a loss or injury) that is hard to put up with

hard·tack *n* **:** a hard biscuit made of flour and water without salt

hard·ware *n* **1 :** things (as tools, cutlery, or parts of machines) made of metal **2 :** items of equipment or their parts used for a particular purpose

¹hard·wood *n* **:** the usually hard wood of a tree belonging to the group bearing broad leaves as distinguished from the wood of a tree (as a pine) with leaves that are needles

²hardwood *adj* **:** having or made of hardwood

har·dy *adj* **har·di·er; har·di·est 1 :** BOLD 1, BRAVE **2 :** able to stand weariness, hardship, or severe weather — **har·di·ness** *n*

hare *n* **:** a timid animal like the related rabbit but having young that are born with the eyes open and a furry coat

hare·brained *adj* **:** FOOLISH

hark *vb* **:** LISTEN

¹harm *n* **1 :** physical or mental damage **:** INJURY **2 :** MISCHIEF 1

²harm *vb* **:** to cause harm to **:** HURT

harm·ful *adj* **:** causing harm **:** INJURIOUS — **harm·ful·ly** *adv* — **harm·ful·ness** *n*

harm·less *adj* **:** not harmful — **harm·less·ly** *adv* — **harm·less·ness** *n*

har·mon·ic *adj* **:** of or relating to musical harmony rather than melody or rhythm — **har·mon·i·cal·ly** *adv*

har·mon·i·ca *n* **:** a small musical instrument held in the hand and played by the mouth **:** MOUTH ORGAN

har·mo·ni·ous *adj* **1 :** having a pleasant sound **:** MELODIOUS **2 :** combining so as to produce a pleasing result **3 :** showing harmony in action or feeling — **har·mo·ni·ous·ly** *adv* — **har·mo·ni·ous·ness** *n*

har·mo·nize *vb* **har·mo·nized; har·mo·niz·ing 1 :** to play or sing in harmony **2 :** to be in harmony — **har·mo·niz·er** *n*

har·mo·ny *n, pl* **har·mo·nies 1 :** the playing of musical tones together in chords **2 :** a pleasing arrangement of parts **3 :** AGREEMENT 1, ACCORD

¹har·ness *n* **:** an arrangement of straps and fastenings placed on an animal so as to control it or prepare it to pull a load

²harness *vb* **1 :** to put a harness on **2 :** to put to work **:** UTILIZE

¹harp *n* **:** a musical instrument consisting of a triangular frame set with strings that are plucked by the fingers

²harp *vb* **:** to call attention to something over and over again

¹har·poon *n* **:** a barbed spear used especially for hunting whales and large fish

²harpoon *vb* **:** to strike with a harpoon

harp·si·chord *n* **:** a keyboard instrument similar to a piano with strings that are plucked

¹har·row *n* **:** a heavy frame set with metal teeth or disks used in farming for breaking up and smoothing soil

²harrow *vb* **1 :** to drag a harrow over (plowed ground) **2 :** ²DISTRESS

har·ry *vb* **har·ried; har·ry·ing :** HARASS

harsh *adj* **1 :** having a coarse surface **:** rough to the touch **2 :** disagreeable to any of the senses **3 :** causing physical discomfort **4 :** SEVERE 1 — **harsh·ly** *adv* — **harsh·ness** *n*

¹har·vest *n* **1 :** the season when crops are gathered **2 :** the gathering of a crop **3 :** a ripe crop (as of grain)

²harvest *vb* **:** to gather in a crop

har·vest·er *n* **1 :** one that gathers by or as if by harvesting **2 :** a machine for harvesting field crops

has *present 3d sing of* HAVE

¹hash *vb* **:** to chop into small pieces

²hash *n* **1 :** cooked meat and vegetables chopped together and browned **2 :** ²JUMBLE

hash·ish *n* **:** a drug from the hemp plant that is used for its intoxicating effects

hash over *vb* **:** to talk about **:** DISCUSS

hasn't : has not

hasp *n* **:** a fastener (as for a door) consisting of a hinged metal strap that fits over a staple and is held by a pin or padlock

has·sle *n* **1 :** a loud angry argument **2 :** a brief fight **3 :** something that annoys or bothers

has·sock *n* : a firm stuffed cushion used as a seat or leg rest

haste *n* **1 :** quickness of motion or action : SPEED **2 :** hasty action

has·ten *vb* : to move or act fast : HURRY

hasty *adj* **hast·i·er; hast·i·est** **1 :** done or made in a hurry **2 :** made, done, or decided without proper care and thought — **hast·i·ly** *adv*

hat *n* : a covering for the head having a crown and usually a brim

¹hatch *n* **1 :** an opening in the deck of a ship or in the floor or roof of a building **2 :** a small door or opening (as in an airplane) **3 :** the cover for a hatch

²hatch *vb* **1 :** to produce from eggs **2 :** to come forth from an egg **3 :** to develop usually in secret

hatch·ery *n, pl* **hatch·er·ies** : a place for hatching eggs

hatch·et *n* : a small ax with a short handle

hatch·way *n* : a hatch usually having a ladder or stairs

¹hate *n* : deep and bitter dislike

²hate *vb* **hat·ed; hat·ing** : to feel great dislike toward

hate·ful *adj* **1 :** full of hate **2 :** causing or deserving hate — **hate·ful·ly** *adv* — **hate·ful·ness** *n*

ha·tred *n* : ¹HATE

hat·ter *n* : a person who makes, sells, or cleans and repairs hats

haugh·ty *adj* **haugh·ti·er; haugh·ti·est** : acting as if other people are not as good as oneself — **haugh·ti·ly** *adv* — **haugh·ti·ness** *n*

¹haul *vb* **1 :** to pull or drag with effort **2 :** to transport in a vehicle

²haul *n* **1 :** the act of hauling **2 :** an amount collected **3 :** the distance or route over which a load is moved

haunch *n* **1 :** HIP **2 :** HINDQUARTER

¹haunt *vb* **1 :** to visit often **2 :** to come to mind frequently **3 :** to visit or live in as a ghost

²haunt *n* : a place often visited

have *vb, past & past participle* **had;** *present participle* **hav·ing;** *present 3d sing* **has** **1 :** to hold for one's use or as property **2 :** to consist of **3 :** to be forced or feel obliged **4 :** to stand in some relationship to **5 :** OBTAIN, GAIN, GET **6 :** to possess as a characteristic **7 :** ²EXERCISE 1 **8 :** to be affected by **9 :** to be in : CARRY ON **10 :** to hold in the mind **11 :** to cause to be **12 :** to cause to **13 :** ¹PERMIT 1 **14 :** ²TRICK **15 :** to give birth to **16 :** to partake of **17** — used as a helping verb with the past participle of another verb

ha·ven *n* : a safe place

haven't : have not

hav·er·sack *n* : a bag worn over one shoulder for carrying supplies

hav·oc *n* **1 :** wide destruction **2 :** great confusion and lack of order

Ha·wai·ian *n* **1 :** a person born or living in Hawaii **2 :** the language of the Hawaiians

¹hawk *n* : a bird of prey that has a strong hooked bill and sharp curved claws and is smaller than most eagles

²hawk *vb* : to make a harsh coughing sound in clearing the throat

³hawk *vb* : to offer for sale by calling out in the street — **hawk·er** *n*

haw·ser *n* : a large rope for towing or tying up a ship

haw·thorn *n* : any of several thorny shrubs or small trees with shiny leaves, white, pink, or red flowers, and small red fruits

¹hay *n* : any of various herbs (as grasses) cut and dried for use as fodder

²hay *vb* : to cut plants for hay

hay fever *n* : a sickness like a cold usually affecting people sensitive to plant pollen

hay·loft *n* : a loft in a barn or stable for storing hay

hay·mow *n* : HAYLOFT

hay·stack *n* : a large pile of hay stored outdoors

hay·wire *adj* **1 :** working badly or in an odd way **2 :** CRAZY 1, WILD

¹haz·ard *n* : a source of danger

²hazard *vb* : to risk something : take a chance

haz·ard·ous *adj* : DANGEROUS — **haz·ard·ous·ly** *adv* — **haz·ard·ous·ness** *n*

¹haze *n* : fine dust, smoke, or fine particles of water in the air

²haze *vb* **hazed; haz·ing** : to make or become hazy or cloudy

ha·zel *n* **1 :** a shrub or small tree that bears an edible nut **2 :** a light brown

ha·zel·nut *n* : the nut of a hazel

hazy *adj* **haz·i·er; haz·i·est** **1 :** partly hidden by haze **2 :** not clear in thought or meaning : VAGUE — **haz·i·ly** *adv* — **haz·i·ness** *n*

H–bomb *n* : HYDROGEN BOMB

he *pron* **1 :** that male one **2 :** a or the person : ³ONE 2

¹head *n* **1 :** the part of the body containing the brain, eyes, ears, nose, and mouth **2 :** ¹MIND 2 **3 :** control of the mind or feelings **4 :** the side of a coin or medal usually thought of as the front **5 :** each person among a number **6** *pl* **head :** a unit of number **7 :** something like a head in position or use **8 :** the place a stream begins **9 :** a skin stretched across one or both ends of a drum **10 :** DIRECTOR, LEADER **11 :** a compact mass of plant parts (as leaves or flowers) **12 :** a part of a machine, tool, or weapon that performs the main work **13 :** a place of leadership or honor **14 :** CLIMAX, CRISIS — **out of one's head :** DELIRIOUS 1 — **over one's head :** beyond one's understanding

²head *adj* **1 :** ²CHIEF 1 **2 :** located at the head **3 :** coming from in front

³head *vb* **1 :** to provide with or form a head **2 :** to be or put oneself at the head of **3 :** to be or get in front of **4 :** to go or cause to go in a certain direction

head·ache *n* **1 :** pain in the head **2 :** something that annoys or confuses

head·band *n* **:** a band worn on or around the head

head·board *n* **:** a board forming the head (as of a bed)

head·dress *n* **:** a covering or ornament for the head

head·ed *adj* **:** having such a head or so many heads

head·first *adv* **:** with the head in front

head·gear *n* **:** something worn on the head

head·ing *n* **:** something (as a title or an address) at the top or beginning (as of a letter)

head·land *n* **:** a point of high land sticking out into the sea

head·light *n* **:** a light at the front of a vehicle

¹head·line *n* **:** a title of an article in a newspaper

²headline *vb* **head·lined; head·lin·ing :** to provide with a headline

¹head·long *adv* **1 :** HEADFIRST **2 :** without waiting to think things through

²headlong *adj* **1 :** ¹RASH, IMPULSIVE **2 :** plunging headfirst

head·mas·ter *n* **:** a man who heads the staff of a private school

head·mis·tress *n* **:** a woman who heads the staff of a private school

head–on *adv or adj* **:** with the front hitting or facing an object

head·phone *n* **:** an earphone held over the ear by a band worn on the head

head·quar·ters *n sing or pl* **:** a place where a leader gives out orders

head·stall *n* **:** an arrangement of straps or rope that fits around the head of an animal and forms part of a bridle or halter

head start *n* **:** an advantage given at the beginning (as to a school child or a runner)

head·stone *n* **:** a stone at the head of a grave

head·strong *adj* **:** always wanting one's own way

head·wait·er *n* **:** the head of the staff of a restaurant or of the dining room of a hotel

head·wa·ters *n pl* **:** the beginning and upper part of a stream

head·way *n* **1 :** movement in a forward direction (as of a ship) **2 :** ¹PROGRESS 2

heal *vb* **1 :** ²CURE 1 **2 :** to return to a sound or healthy condition — **heal·er** *n*

health *n* **1 :** the condition of being free from illness or disease **2 :** the overall condition of the body

health·ful *adj* **:** good for the health — **health·ful·ly** *adv* — **health·ful·ness** *n*

healthy *adj* **health·i·er; health·i·est 1 :** being sound and well **:** not sick **2 :** showing good health **3 :** aiding or building up health — **health·i·ly** *adv* — **health·i·ness** *n*

¹heap *n* **1 :** things or material piled together **2 :** a large number or amount

²heap *vb* **1 :** to throw or lay in a heap **:** make into a pile **2 :** to provide in large amounts **3 :** to fill to capacity

hear *vb* **heard; hear·ing 1 :** to take in through the ear **:** have the power of hearing **2 :** to gain knowledge of by hearing **3 :** to listen to with care and attention — **hear·er** *n*

hear·ing *n* **1 :** the act or power of taking in sound through the ear **:** the sense by which a person hears **2 :** EARSHOT **3 :** a chance to be heard or known

hearing aid *n* **:** an electronic device used by a partly deaf person to make sounds louder

hear·ken *vb* **:** LISTEN

hear·say *n* **:** something heard from another **:** RUMOR

hearse *n* **:** a vehicle for carrying the dead to the grave

heart *n* **1 :** a hollow organ of the body that expands and contracts to move blood through the arteries and veins **2 :** something shaped like a heart **3 :** the part nearest the center **4 :** the most essential part **5 :** human feelings **6 :** COURAGE — **by heart :** so as to be able to repeat from memory

heart·ache *n* **:** ¹SORROW 1, 2

heart·beat *n* **:** a single contracting and expanding of the heart

heart·break *n* **:** very great or deep grief

heart·break·ing *adj* **:** causing great sorrow

heart·bro·ken *adj* **:** overcome by sorrow

heart·en *vb* **:** to give new hope or courage to

heart·felt *adj* **:** deeply felt **:** SINCERE

hearth *n* **1 :** an area (as of brick) in front of a fireplace **2 :** the floor of a fireplace **3 :** ¹HOME 1

hearth·stone *n* **:** a stone forming a hearth

heart·i·ly *adv* **1 :** with sincerity or enthusiasm **2 :** COMPLETELY

heart·less *adj* **:** UNFEELING 2, CRUEL — **heart·less·ly** *adv* — **heart·less·ness** *n*

heart·sick *adj* **:** DESPONDENT

heart·wood *n* **:** the usually dark wood in the center of a tree

hearty *adj* **heart·i·er; heart·i·est 1 :** friendly and enthusiastic **2 :** strong, healthy, and active **3 :** having a good appetite **4 :** AMPLE — **heart·i·ness** *n*

¹heat *vb* **:** to make or become warm or hot

[2]**heat** *n* **1 :** a condition of being hot : WARMTH **2 :** high temperature **3 :** a form of energy that causes a body to rise in temperature **4 :** strength of feeling or force of action **5 :** a single race in a contest that includes two or more races

heat·ed *adj* **1 :** HOT 1 **2 :** ANGRY — **heat·ed·ly** *adv*

heat·er *n* **:** a device for heating

heath *n* **1 :** any of a group of low, woody, and often evergreen plants that grow on poor, sour, wet soil **2 :** a usually open level area of land on which heaths can grow

[1]**hea·then** *adj* **1 :** of or relating to the heathen **2 :** UNCIVILIZED 1

[2]**heathen** *n, pl* **heathens** *or* **heathen** **1 :** a person who does not know about and worship the God of the Bible : PAGAN **2 :** an uncivilized person

heath·er *n* **:** an evergreen heath of northern and mountainous areas with pink flowers and needlelike leaves

[1]**heave** *vb* **heaved** *or* **hove; heav·ing** **1 :** to raise with an effort **2 :** HURL, THROW **3 :** to utter with an effort **4 :** to rise and fall again and again **5 :** to be thrown or raised up

[2]**heave** *n* **1 :** an effort to lift or raise **2 :** a forceful throw **3 :** an upward motion (as of the chest in breathing)

heav·en *n* **1 :** SKY 1 — usually used in pl. **2** *often cap* **:** the dwelling place of God and of the blessed dead **3** *cap* **:** GOD 1 **4 :** a place or condition of complete happiness

heav·en·ly *adj* **1 :** of or relating to heaven or the heavens **2 :** of or relating to the Heaven of God and the blessed dead **3 :** entirely delightful

heav·i·ly *adv* **1 :** with or as if with weight **2 :** in a slow and difficult way **3 :** very much

heavy *adj* **heavi·er; heavi·est** **1 :** having great weight **2 :** hard to put up with **3 :** burdened by something important or troubling **4 :** having little strength or energy **5 :** unusually great in amount, force, or effect — **heav·i·ness** *n*

[1]**He·brew** *adj* **:** of or relating to the Hebrew peoples or Hebrew

[2]**Hebrew** *n* **1 :** a member of any of a group of peoples including the ancient Jews **2 :** JEW **3 :** the language of the Hebrews

hec·tic *adj* **:** filled with excitement, activity, or confusion

hecto- *prefix* **:** hundred

hec·to·me·ter *n* **:** a unit of length in the metric system equal to 100 meters

he'd : he had : he would

[1]**hedge** *n* **:** a fence or boundary made up of a thick growth of shrubs or low trees

[2]**hedge** *vb* **hedged; hedg·ing** **1 :** to surround or protect with a hedge **2 :** to avoid giving a direct or exact answer or promise

hedge·hog *n* **1 :** a European mammal that eats insects, has sharp spines mixed with the hair on its back, and is able to roll itself up into a ball **2 :** PORCUPINE

hedge·row *n* **:** a hedge of shrubs or trees around a field

[1]**heed** *vb* **:** to pay attention to : MIND

[2]**heed** *n* **:** ATTENTION 1 — **heed·ful** *adj* — **heed·ful·ly** *adv*

heed·less *adj* **:** not taking heed : CARELESS — **heed·less·ly** *adv* — **heed·less·ness** *n*

[1]**heel** *n* **1 :** the back part of the human foot behind the arch and below the ankle **2 :** the part of an animal's limb corresponding to a person's heel **3 :** one of the crusty ends of a loaf of bread **4 :** a part (as of a stocking) that covers the human heel **5 :** the solid part of a shoe that supports the heel **6 :** a rear, low, or bottom part **7 :** a mean selfish person — **heel·less** *adj*

[2]**heel** *vb* **:** to lean to one side

heft *vb* **:** to test the weight of by lifting

hefty *adj* **heft·i·er; heft·i·est :** HEAVY 1

heif·er *n* **:** a young cow

height *n* **1 :** the highest point or greatest degree **2 :** the distance from the bottom to the top of something standing upright **3 :** distance upward

height·en *vb* **1 :** to make greater : INCREASE **2 :** to make or become high or higher

Heim·lich maneuver *n* **:** the use of upward pressure upon the upper abdomen of a choking person to force out an object blocking the airway

heir *n* **1 :** a person who inherits or has the right to inherit property after the death of its owner **2 :** a person who has legal claim to a title or a throne when the person holding it dies

heir·ess *n* **:** a female heir

heir·loom *n* **:** a piece of personal property handed down in a family from one generation to another

held *past of* HOLD

he·li·cop·ter *n* **:** an aircraft supported in the air by horizontal propellers

he·li·port *n* **:** a place for a helicopter to land and take off

he·li·um *n* **:** a very light gaseous chemical element that is found in various natural gases, will not burn, and is used in balloons

hell *n* **1 :** a place where souls of the dead are believed to exist **2 :** a place or state of punishment for the wicked after death **3 :** a place or state of misery or wickedness — **hell·ish** *adj*

he'll : he shall : he will

hell·ben·der *n* : a large American salamander that lives in water

hel·lo *interj* — used as a greeting or to express surprise

helm *n* **1 :** a lever or wheel for steering a ship **2 :** a position of control

hel·met *n* : a protective covering for the head

[1]**help** *vb* **1 :** to provide with what is useful in achieving an end **2 :** to give relief from pain or disease **3 :** PREVENT 1 **4 :** [1]SERVE 9

[2]**help** *n* **1 :** an act or instance of helping **:** AID **2 :** the state of being helped **3 :** a person or a thing that helps **4 :** a body of hired helpers

help·er *n* **1 :** one that helps **2 :** a less skilled person who helps a skilled worker

help·ful *adj* : providing help — **help·ful·ly** *adv* — **help·ful·ness** *n*

help·ing *n* : a serving of food

helping verb *n* : a verb (as *am, may*, or *will*) that is used with another verb to express person, number, mood, or tense

help·less *adj* : not able to help or protect oneself — **help·less·ly** *adv* — **help·less·ness** *n*

hel·ter–skel·ter *adv* : in great disorder

[1]**hem** *n* : a border of a cloth article made by folding back an edge and sewing it down

[2]**hem** *vb* **hemmed; hem·ming 1 :** to finish with or make a hem **2 :** SURROUND

hemi- *prefix* : half

hemi·sphere *n* **1 :** one of the halves of the earth as divided by the equator into northern and southern parts (**northern hemisphere, southern hemisphere**) or by a meridian into two parts so that one half (**eastern hemisphere**) to the east of the Atlantic ocean includes Europe, Asia, and Africa and the half (**western hemisphere**) to the west includes North and South America and surrounding waters **2 :** a half of a sphere **3 :** either the left or the right half of the cerebrum

hemi·spher·ic *or* **hemi·spher·i·cal** *adj* : of or relating to a hemisphere

hem·lock *n* **1 :** a poisonous plant of the carrot family **2 :** an evergreen tree of the pine family

he·mo·glo·bin *n* : the coloring material of the red blood cells that carry oxygen from the lungs to the tissues

hem·or·rhage *n* : great loss of blood by bleeding

hemp *n* : a tall plant grown for its tough woody fiber that is used in making rope and for its flowers and leaves that yield drugs (as marijuana)

hen *n* **1 :** a female domestic fowl **2 :** a female bird

hence *adv* **1 :** from this place **2 :** from this time **3 :** as a result **:** THEREFORE

hence·forth *adv* : from this time on

hench·man *n, pl* **hench·men :** a trusted follower or supporter

hep·a·ti·tis *n* : a disease which is caused by a virus and in which the liver is damaged and there is yellowing of the skin and fever

hepta- *or* **hept-** *prefix* : seven

hep·ta·gon *n* : a closed figure having seven angles and seven sides

[1]**her** *adj* : of, relating, or belonging to her or herself

[2]**her** *pron, objective case of* SHE

[1]**her·ald** *n* **1 :** an official messenger **2 :** a person who brings news or announces something

[2]**herald** *vb* : to give notice of **:** ANNOUNCE

he·ral·dic *adj* : of or relating to heralds or heraldry

her·ald·ry *n* : the art or science of tracing a person's ancestors and determining what coat of arms his or her family has the right to

herb *n* **1 :** a plant with soft stems that die down at the end of the growing season **2 :** a plant or plant part used in medicine or in seasoning foods

her·biv·o·rous *adj* : eating or living on plants

[1]**herd** *n* : a number of animals of one kind kept or living together

[2]**herd** *vb* **1 :** to gather or join in a herd **2 :** to form into or move as a herd — **herd·er** *n*

herds·man *n, pl* **herds·men :** one who owns or tends a flock or herd

[1]**here** *adv* **1 :** in or at this place **2 :** [1]NOW 1 **3 :** to or into this place **:** HITHER

[2]**here** *n* : this place

here·abouts *or* **here·about** *adv* : near or around this place

[1]**here·af·ter** *adv* **1 :** after this **2 :** in some future time or state

[2]**hereafter** *n* **1 :** [2]FUTURE 1 **2 :** life after death

here·by *adv* : by means of this

he·red·i·tary *adj* **1 :** capable of being passed from parent to offspring **2 :** received or passing from an ancestor to an heir

he·red·i·ty *n, pl* **he·red·i·ties :** the passing on of characteristics (as looks or ability) from parents to offspring

here·in *adv* : in this

here·of *adv* : of this

here·on *adv* : on this

her·e·sy *n, pl* **her·e·sies 1 :** the holding of religious beliefs opposed to church doctrine **:** such a belief **2 :** an opinion opposed to a generally accepted belief

her·e·tic *n* : a person who believes or teaches something opposed to accepted beliefs (as of a church)

he·ret·i·cal *adj* : of, relating to, or being heresy

here·to·fore *adv* : HITHERTO

here·up·on *adv* : right after this

here·with *adv* : with this

her·i·tage *n* : something that comes to one from one's ancestors

her·mit *n* : one who lives apart from others especially for religious reasons

hermit crab *n* : any of various small crabs that live in the empty shells of mollusks (as snails)

he·ro *n, pl* **heroes** **1 :** a person admired for great deeds or fine qualities **2 :** one who shows great courage **3 :** the chief male character in a story, play, or poem

he·ro·ic *adj* **1 :** of, relating to, or like heroes **2 :** COURAGEOUS, DARING — **he·ro·ical·ly** *adv*

her·o·in *n* : a very harmful drug that comes from morphine

her·o·ine *n* **1 :** a woman admired for great deeds or fine qualities **2 :** the chief female character in a story, poem, or play

her·o·ism *n* **1 :** great courage especially for a noble purpose **2 :** the qualities of a hero

her·on *n* : a wading bird that has long legs, a long neck, a long thin bill, and large wings

her·ring *n* : a widely used food fish of the north Atlantic ocean

hers *pron* : that which belongs to her

her·self *pron* : her own self

he's : he is : he has

hes·i·tan·cy *n* : the quality or state of being hesitant

hes·i·tant *adj* : feeling or showing hesitation — **hes·i·tant·ly** *adv*

hes·i·tate *vb* **hes·i·tat·ed; hes·i·tat·ing** **1 :** to pause because of forgetfulness or uncertainty **2 :** to speak or say in a weak or broken way

hes·i·ta·tion *n* : an act or instance of hesitating

hew *vb* **hewed** *or* **hewn; hew·ing** **1 :** to chop down **2 :** to shape by cutting with an ax

hex *n* : a harmful spell : JINX

hexa- *or* **hex-** *prefix* : six

hexa·gon *n* : a closed figure having six angles and six sides

hex·ag·o·nal *adj* : having six sides — **hex·ag·o·nal·ly** *adv*

hey *interj* — used to call attention or to express surprise or joy

hey·day *n* : the time of greatest strength, energy, or success

hi *interj* — used especially as a greeting

hi·ber·nate *vb* **hi·ber·nat·ed; hi·ber·nat·ing** : to pass the winter in a resting state — **hi·ber·na·tor** *n*

hi·ber·na·tion *n* : the state of one that hibernates

[1]hic·cup *n* : a gulping sound caused by sudden movements of muscles active in breathing

[2]hiccup *vb* **hic·cuped** *also* **hic·cupped; hic·cup·ing** *also* **hic·cup·ping** : to make a hiccup

hick·o·ry *n, pl* **hick·o·ries** : a tall tree related to the walnuts that has strong tough elastic wood and bears an edible nut (**hickory nut**) in a hard shell

[1]hide *vb* **hid; hid·den** *or* **hid; hid·ing** **1 :** to put or stay out of sight **2 :** to keep secret **3 :** to screen from view

[2]hide *n* : the skin of an animal whether fresh or prepared for use

hide–and–go–seek *n* : HIDE-AND-SEEK

hide–and–seek *n* : a game in which one player covers his or her eyes and after giving the others time to hide goes looking for them

hide·away *n* : [1]RETREAT 3, HIDEOUT

hid·eous *adj* : very ugly or disgusting : FRIGHTFUL — **hid·eous·ly** *adv* — **hid·eous·ness** *n*

hide·out *n* : a secret place for hiding (as from the police)

hi·ero·glyph·ic *n* : any of the symbols in the picture writing of ancient Egypt

hi–fi *n* **1 :** HIGH FIDELITY **2 :** equipment for reproduction of sound with high fidelity

hig·gle·dy–pig·gle·dy *adv or adj* : in confusion : TOPSY-TURVY

[1]high *adj* **1 :** extending to a great distance above the ground **2 :** having a specified elevation : TALL **3 :** of greater degree, size, amount, or cost than average **4 :** of more than usual importance **5 :** having great force **6 :** pitched or sounding above some other sound

[2]high *adv* : at or to a high place or degree

[3]high *n* **1 :** the space overhead : SKY **2 :** a region of high barometric pressure **3 :** a high point or level **4 :** the arrangement of gears in an automobile giving the highest speed of travel

high·brow *n* : a person of great learning or culture

high fidelity *n* : the reproduction of sound with a high degree of accuracy

high·land *n* : high or hilly country

[1]high·light *n* : a very interesting event or detail

[2]highlight *vb* **high·light·ed; high·light·ing** **1 :** EMPHASIZE **2 :** to be a highlight of **3 :** to mark with a highlighter **4 :** to cause (something on a computer screen) to be displayed in a way that stands out

high·light·er *n* : a pen with a wide felt tip and brightly colored ink for marking text on a page

high·ly *adv* **1 :** to a high degree **:** very much **2 :** with much approval

high·ness *n* **1 :** the quality or state or being high **2** — used as a title for a person of very high rank

high school *n* **:** a school usually including the ninth to twelfth or tenth to twelfth grades

high seas *n pl* **:** the open part of a sea or ocean

high–spir·it·ed *adj* **:** LIVELY 1

high–strung *adj* **:** very sensitive or nervous

high tide *n* **:** the tide when the water is at its greatest height

high·way *n* **:** a main road

high·way·man *n, pl* **high·way·men :** a person who robs travelers on a road

hi·jack *also* **high·jack** *vb* **1 :** to stop and steal from a moving vehicle **2 :** to force a pilot to fly a plane where one wants — **high·jack·er** *n*

[1]**hike** *vb* **hiked; hik·ing :** to take a long walk — **hik·er** *n*

[2]**hike** *n* **:** a long walk especially for pleasure or exercise

hi·lar·i·ous *adj* **:** enjoying or causing hilarity **:** MERRY — **hi·lar·i·ous·ly** *adv* — **hi·lar·i·ous·ness** *n*

hi·lar·i·ty *n* **:** noisy fun

[1]**hill** *n* **1 :** a usually rounded elevation of land lower than a mountain **2 :** a little heap or mound of earth **3 :** several seeds or plants planted in a group rather than a row

[2]**hill** *vb* **1 :** to form into a heap **2 :** to draw earth around the roots or base of

hill·bil·ly *n, pl* **hill·bil·lies :** a person from a backwoods area

hill·ock *n* **:** a small hill

hill·side *n* **:** the part of a hill between the top and the foot

hill·top *n* **:** the highest part of a hill

hilly *adj* **hill·i·er; hill·i·est :** having many hills

hilt *n* **:** a handle especially of a sword or dagger

him *pron, objective case of* HE

him·self *pron* **:** his own self

hind *adj* **:** being at the end or back **:** REAR

hin·der *vb* **:** to make slow or difficult

hind·quar·ter *n* **:** the back half of a complete side of a four-footed animal or carcass

hin·drance *n* **:** something that hinders **:** OBSTACLE

hind·sight *n* **:** understanding of something only after it has happened

Hin·du·ism *n* **:** a set of cultural and religious beliefs and practices that originated in India

[1]**hinge** *n* **:** a jointed piece on which a door, gate, or lid turns or swings

[2]**hinge** *vb* **hinged; hing·ing 1 :** to attach by or provide with hinges **2 :** DEPEND 2

[1]**hint** *n* **1 :** information that helps one guess an answer or do something more easily **2 :** a small amount **:** TRACE

[2]**hint** *vb* **:** to suggest something without plainly asking or saying it

hin·ter·land *n* **:** a region far from cities

hip *n* **:** the part of the body that curves out below the waist on each side

hip·pie *or* **hip·py** *n, pl* **hippies :** a usually young person who typically has long hair, is against the values and practices of society, and often lives together with others

hip·po *n, pl* **hip·pos :** HIPPOPOTAMUS

hip·po·pot·a·mus *n, pl* **hip·po·pot·a·mus·es** *or* **hip·po·pot·a·mi :** a large hoglike animal with thick hairless skin that eats plants and lives in African rivers

hire *vb* **hired; hir·ing 1 :** [1]EMPLOY 2 **2 :** to get the temporary use of in return for pay **3 :** to take a job

[1]**his** *adj* **:** of or relating to him or himself

[2]**his** *pron* **:** that which belongs to him

[1]**His·pan·ic** *adj* **:** of or relating to people of Latin American origin

[2]**Hispanic** *n* **:** a person of Latin American origin

[1]**hiss** *vb* **1 :** to make a hiss **2 :** to show dislike by hissing

[2]**hiss** *n* **:** a sound like a long \s\ sometimes used as a sign of dislike

his·to·ri·an *n* **:** a person who studies or writes about history

his·tor·ic *adj* **:** famous in history

his·tor·i·cal *adj* **1 :** of, relating to, or based on history **2 :** known to be true — **his·tor·i·cal·ly** *adv*

his·to·ry *n, pl* **his·to·ries 1 :** a telling of events **:** STORY **2 :** a written report of past events **3 :** a branch of knowledge that records and explains past events

[1]**hit** *vb* **hit; hit·ting 1 :** to touch or cause to touch with force **2 :** to strike or cause to strike something aimed at **3 :** to affect as if by a blow **4 :** OCCUR 2 **5 :** to happen to get **:** come upon **6 :** to arrive at — **hit·ter** *n*

[2]**hit** *n* **1 :** a blow striking an object aimed at **2 :** COLLISION **3 :** something very successful **4 :** a batted baseball that enables the batter to reach base safely **5 :** a match in a computer search

hit–and–run *adj* **:** being or involving a driver who does not stop after being in an automobile accident

[1]**hitch** *vb* **1 :** to move by jerks **2 :** to fasten by or as if by a hook or knot **3 :** HITCHHIKE

[2]**hitch** *n* **1 :** a jerky movement or pull **2 :** an unexpected stop or obstacle **3 :** a knot used for a temporary fastening

hitch·hike *vb* **hitch·hiked; hitch·hik·ing :** to travel by getting free rides in passing vehicles — **hitch·hik·er** *n*

hith·er *adv* **:** to this place

hith·er·to *adv* **:** up to this time

HIV *n* **:** a virus that causes AIDS by destroying large numbers of cells that help the human body fight infection

hive *n* **1 :** a container for housing honeybees **2 :** the nest of bees **3 :** a colony of bees **4 :** a place swarming with busy people

hives *n pl* **:** an allergic condition in which the skin breaks out in large red itching patches

ho *interj* — used especially to attract attention

¹hoard *n* **:** a supply usually of something of value stored away or hidden

²hoard *vb* **:** to gather and store away — **hoard·er** *n*

hoar·frost *n* **:** ¹FROST 2

hoarse *adj* **hoars·er; hoars·est 1 :** harsh in sound **2 :** having a rough voice — **hoarse·ly** *adv* — **hoarse·ness** *n*

hoary *adj* **hoar·i·er; hoar·i·est :** gray or white with age

¹hoax *vb* **:** to trick into thinking something is true or real when it isn't

²hoax *n* **1 :** an act meant to fool or deceive **2 :** something false passed off as real

¹hob·ble *vb* **hob·bled; hob·bling 1 :** to walk with difficulty **:** LIMP **2 :** to tie the legs of to make movement difficult

²hobble *n* **1 :** a limping walk **2 :** something used to hobble an animal

hob·by *n, pl* **hobbies :** an interest or activity engaged in for pleasure

hob·by·horse *n* **1 :** a stick with a horse's head on which children pretend to ride **2 :** ROCKING HORSE

hob·gob·lin *n* **1 :** a mischievous elf **2 :** BOGEY 2

hob·nail *n* **:** a short nail with a large head driven into soles of heavy shoes to protect against wear — **hob·nailed** *adj*

ho·bo *n, pl* **hoboes :** ¹VAGRANT

hock·ey *n* **:** a game played on ice or in a field by two teams who try to drive a puck or ball through a goal by hitting it with a stick

hod *n* **1 :** a wooden tray or trough that has a long handle and is used to carry mortar or bricks **2 :** a bucket for holding or carrying coal

hodge·podge *n* **:** a disorderly mixture

¹hoe *n* **:** a tool with a long handle and a thin flat blade used for weeding and cultivating

²hoe *vb* **hoed; hoe·ing :** to weed or loosen the soil around plants with a hoe

¹hog *n* **1 :** an adult domestic swine **2 :** a greedy or dirty person

²hog *vb* **hogged; hog·ging :** to take more than one's share

ho·gan *n* **:** a Native American dwelling made of logs and mud with a door traditionally facing east

hog·gish *adj* **:** very selfish or greedy — **hog·gish·ly** *adv* — **hog·gish·ness** *n*

hogs·head *n* **1 :** a very large cask **2 :** a unit of liquid measure equal to sixty-three gallons (about 238 liters)

¹hoist *vb* **:** to lift up especially with a pulley

²hoist *n* **1 :** an act of hoisting **2 :** a device used for lifting heavy loads

¹hold *vb* **held; hold·ing 1 :** to have or keep in one's possession or under one's control **2 :** to limit the movement or activity of **:** RESTRAIN **3 :** to make accept a legal or moral duty **4 :** to have or keep in one's grasp **5 :** ¹SUPPORT 4 **6 :** to take in and have within **:** CONTAIN **7 :** to have in mind **8 :** CONSIDER 3, REGARD **9 :** to carry on by group action **10 :** to continue in the same way or state **:** LAST **11 :** to remain fast or fastened **12 :** to bear or carry oneself

²hold *n* **1 :** the act or way of holding **:** GRIP **2 :** ¹INFLUENCE 1 **3 :** a note or rest in music kept up longer than usual

³hold *n* **1 :** the part of a ship below the decks in which cargo is stored **2 :** the cargo compartment of an airplane

hold·er *n* **:** one that holds

hold out *vb* **:** to refuse to yield or agree

hold·up *n* **1 :** robbery by an armed robber **2 :** ¹DELAY

hold up *vb* **1 :** ²DELAY 2 **2 :** to rob while threatening with a weapon

hole *n* **1 :** an opening into or through something **2 :** CAVITY **3 :** DEN 1, BURROW

hol·i·day *n* **1 :** a day of freedom from work especially when celebrating some event **2 :** VACATION

ho·li·ness *n* **1 :** the quality or state of being holy **2** — used as a title for persons of high religious position

¹hol·ler *vb* **:** to cry out **:** SHOUT

²holler *n* **:** ²SHOUT, CRY

¹hol·low *n* **1 :** a low spot in a surface **2 :** VALLEY **3 :** CAVITY

²hollow *adj* **1 :** curved inward **:** SUNKEN **2 :** having a space inside **:** not solid **3 :** suggesting a sound made in an empty place **4 :** not sincere — **hol·low·ly** *adv* — **hol·low·ness** *n*

³hollow *vb* **:** to make or become hollow

hol·ly *n, pl* **hollies :** an evergreen tree or shrub that has shiny leaves with prickly edges and red berries much used for Christmas decorations

hol·ly·hock *n* **:** a plant with large rounded leaves and tall stalks of bright showy flowers

ho·lo·caust *n* **:** a complete destruction especially by fire

ho·lo·gram *n* **:** a three-dimensional picture made by laser light reflected onto a photographic substance without the use of a camera
hol·ster *n* **:** a usually leather case in which a pistol is carried or worn
ho·ly *adj* **ho·li·er; ho·li·est 1 :** set apart for the service of God or of a divine being **:** SACRED **2 :** having a right to expect complete devotion **3 :** pure in spirit
hom- *or* **homo-** *prefix* **:** one and the same **:** similar **:** alike
hom·age *n* **1 :** a feudal ceremony in which a person pledges loyalty to a lord and becomes a vassal **2 :** [1]RESPECT 2
[1]**home** *n* **1 :** the house in which one or one's family lives **2 :** the place where one was born or grew up **3 :** HABITAT **4 :** a place for the care of persons unable to care for themselves **5 :** the social unit formed by a family living together **6 :** [1]HOUSE 1 **7 :** the goal or point to be reached in some games — **home·less** *adj*
[2]**home** *adv* **1 :** to or at home **2 :** to the final place or limit
home·land *n* **:** native land
home·like *adj* **:** like a home (as in comfort and kindly warmth)
home·ly *adj* **home·li·er; home·li·est 1 :** suggesting home life **2 :** not handsome
home·made *adj* **:** made in the home
home·mak·er *n* **:** a person who manages a household especially as a wife and mother — **home·mak·ing** *n or adj*
home page *n* **:** the page of a World Wide Web site that is usually seen first and that usually contains links to the other pages of the site or to other sites
home plate *n* **:** the base that a baseball runner must touch to score
hom·er *n* **:** HOME RUN
home·room *n* **:** a schoolroom where pupils of the same class report at the start of each day
home run *n* **:** a hit in baseball that enables the batter to go around all the bases and score
home·school *vb* **:** to teach school subjects to one's children at home
home·school·er *n* **1 :** one that homeschools **2 :** a child who is homeschooled
home·sick *adj* **:** longing for home and family — **home·sick·ness** *n*
[1]**home·spun** *adj* **1 :** spun or made at home **2 :** made of homespun **3 :** not fancy **:** SIMPLE
[2]**homespun** *n* **:** a loosely woven usually woolen or linen fabric originally made from homespun yarn
[1]**home·stead** *n* **1 :** a home and the land around it **2 :** a piece of land gained from United States public lands by living on and farming it
[2]**homestead** *vb* **:** to acquire or settle on public land for use as a homestead — **home·stead·er** *n*
home·ward *or* **home·wards** *adv or adj* **:** toward home
home·work *n* **:** work (as school lessons) to be done at home
hom·ey *adj* **hom·i·er; hom·i·est :** HOMELIKE — **hom·ey·ness** *or* **hom·i·ness** *n*
ho·mi·cide *n* **:** a killing of one human being by another
hom·ing pigeon *n* **:** a racing pigeon trained to return home
hom·i·ny *n* **:** hulled corn with the germ removed
homo- — see HOM-
ho·mog·e·nize *vb* **ho·mog·e·nized; ho·mog·e·niz·ing :** to reduce the particles in (as milk or paint) to the same size and spread them evenly in the liquid
ho·mo·graph *n* **:** one of two or more words spelled alike but different in meaning or origin or pronunciation
hom·onym *n* **1 :** HOMOPHONE **2 :** HOMOGRAPH **3 :** one of two or more words spelled and pronounced alike but different in meaning
ho·mo·phone *n* **:** one of two or more words pronounced alike but different in meaning or origin or spelling
hone *vb* **honed; hon·ing :** to sharpen with or as if with a fine abrasive stone
hon·est *adj* **1 :** free from fraud or trickery **:** STRAIGHTFORWARD **2 :** not given to cheating, stealing, or lying **:** UPRIGHT, TRUSTWORTHY **3 :** being just what is indicated **:** REAL, GENUINE
hon·es·ty *n* **:** the quality or state of being honest
hon·ey *n* **1 :** a sweet sticky fluid made by bees from the liquid drawn from flowers **2 :** an outstanding example
hon·ey·bee *n* **:** a bee whose honey is used by people as food
[1]**hon·ey·comb** *n* **1 :** a mass of wax cells built by honeybees in their nest to contain young bees and stores of honey **2 :** something like a honeycomb in structure or appearance
[2]**honeycomb** *vb* **:** to make or become full of holes like a honeycomb
hon·ey·dew melon *n* **:** a pale muskmelon with greenish sweet flesh and smooth skin
[1]**hon·ey·moon** *n* **1 :** a holiday taken by a recently married couple **2 :** a period of harmony especially just after marriage
[2]**honeymoon** *vb* **:** to have a honeymoon — **hon·ey·moon·er** *n*
hon·ey·suck·le *n* **:** a climbing vine or a bush with fragrant white, yellow, or red flowers
[1]**honk** *vb* **:** to make a honk

²honk *n* **1 :** the cry of a goose **2 :** a sound like the cry of a goose

¹hon·or *n* **1 :** public admiration : REPUTATION **2 :** outward respect : RECOGNITION **3 :** PRIVILEGE **4** — used especially as a title for an official of high rank (as a judge) **5 :** a person whose worth brings respect or fame **6 :** evidence or a symbol of great respect **7 :** high moral standards of behavior

²honor *vb* **1 :** ²RESPECT **2 :** to give an honor to

hon·or·able *adj* **1 :** bringing about or deserving honor **2 :** observing ideas of honor or reputation **3 :** having high moral standards of behavior : ETHICAL, UPRIGHT

hon·or·ary *adj* **:** given or done as an honor

¹hood *n* **1 :** a covering for the head and neck and sometimes the face **2 :** something like a hood **3 :** the movable covering for an automobile engine — **hood·ed** *adj*

²hood *vb* **:** to cover with or as if with a hood

-hood *n suffix* **1 :** state : condition : quality : nature **2 :** instance of a specified state or quality **3 :** individuals sharing a specified state or character

hood·lum *n* **:** a brutal ruffian : THUG

hood·wink *vb* **:** to mislead by trickery

hoof *n, pl* **hooves** *or* **hoofs** **1 :** a covering of horn that protects the ends of the toes of some animals (as horses, oxen, or swine) **2 :** a hoofed foot (as of a horse) — **hoofed** *adj*

¹hook *n* **1 :** a curved device (as a piece of bent metal) for catching, holding, or pulling something **2 :** something curved or bent like a hook — **by hook or by crook :** in any way : fairly or unfairly

²hook *vb* **1 :** to bend in the shape of a hook **2 :** to catch or fasten with a hook

hook·worm *n* **:** a small worm that lives in the intestines and makes people sick by sucking their blood

hoop *n* **1 :** a circular band used for holding together the strips that make up the sides of a barrel or tub **2 :** a circular figure or object **3 :** a circle or series of circles of flexible material (as wire) used for holding a woman's skirt out from the body

hooray *variant of* HURRAH

¹hoot *vb* **1 :** to utter a loud shout usually to show disapproval **2 :** to make the noise of an owl or a similar cry **3 :** to express by hoots

²hoot *n* **1 :** a sound of hooting **2 :** the least bit

¹hop *vb* **hopped; hop·ping** **1 :** to move by short quick jumps **2 :** to jump on one foot **3 :** to jump over **4 :** to get aboard by or as if by hopping **5 :** to make a quick trip especially by air

²hop *n* **1 :** a short quick jump especially on one leg **2 :** ²DANCE 2 **3 :** a short trip especially by air

³hop *n* **1 :** a twining vine whose greenish flowers look like cones **2 hops** *pl* **:** the dried flowers of the hop plant used chiefly in making beer and ale and in medicine

¹hope *vb* **hoped; hop·ing :** to desire especially with expectation that the wish will be granted

²hope *n* **1 :** ¹TRUST 1 **2 :** desire together with the expectation of getting what is wanted **3 :** a cause for hope **4 :** something hoped for

hope·ful *adj* **1 :** full of hope **2 :** giving hope : PROMISING — **hope·ful·ly** *adv* — **hope·ful·ness** *n*

hope·less *adj* **1 :** having no hope **2 :** offering no hope — **hope·less·ly** *adv* — **hope·less·ness** *n*

hop·per *n* **1 :** one that hops **2 :** an insect that moves by leaping **3 :** a container usually shaped like a funnel for delivering material (as grain or coal) into a machine or a bin **4 :** a tank holding liquid and having a device for releasing its contents through a pipe

hop·scotch *n* **:** a game in which a player tosses a stone into sections of a figure drawn on the ground and hops through the figure and back to pick up the stone

horde *n* **:** MULTITUDE, SWARM

ho·ri·zon *n* **1 :** the line where the earth or sea seems to meet the sky **2 :** the limit of a person's outlook or experience

¹hor·i·zon·tal *adj* **:** level with the horizon — **hor·i·zon·tal·ly** *adv*

²horizontal *n* **:** something (as a line or plane) that is horizontal

hor·mone *n* **:** any of various chemical substances secreted by body cells especially into the blood and acting on cells or organs of the body usually at a distance from the place of origin

horn *n* **1 :** one of the hard bony growths on the head of many hoofed animals (as cattle, goats, or sheep) **2 :** the material of which horns are composed or a similar material **3 :** something made from a horn **4 :** something shaped like a horn **5 :** a musical or signaling instrument made from an animal's horn **6 :** a brass musical instrument (as a trumpet or French horn) **7 :** a usually electrical device that makes a noise like that of a horn — **horned** *adj* — **horn·less** *adj* — **horn·like** *adj*

horned toad *n* **:** a small harmless lizard with scales and hard pointed growths on the skin

hor·net *n* **:** a large wasp that can give a severe sting

horn of plenty : CORNUCOPIA

horny *adj* **horn·i·er; horn·i·est :** like or made of horn

hor·ri·ble *adj* **:** causing horror **:** TERRIBLE — **hor·ri·bly** *adv*

hor·rid *adj* **1 :** HORRIBLE **2 :** very unpleasant **:** DISGUSTING — **hor·rid·ly** *adv*

hor·ri·fy *vb* **hor·ri·fied; hor·ri·fy·ing :** to cause to feel horror

hor·ror *n* **1 :** great and painful fear, dread, or shock **2 :** great dislike **3 :** a quality or thing that causes horror

horse *n* **1 :** a large hoofed animal that feeds on grasses and is used as a work animal and for riding **2 :** a frame that supports something (as wood while being cut) **3 :** a piece of gymnasium equipment used for vaulting exercises — **horse·less** *adj* — **from the horse's mouth :** from the original source

[1]**horse·back** *n* **:** the back of a horse

[2]**horseback** *adv* **:** on horseback

horse·car *n* **1 :** a streetcar drawn by horses **2 :** a car for transporting horses

horse chestnut *n* **:** a shiny brown nut that is unfit to eat and is the fruit of a tall tree with leaves divided into fingerlike parts and large flower clusters shaped like cones

horse·fly *n, pl* **horse·flies :** a large swift two-winged fly the females of which suck blood from animals

horse·hair *n* **1 :** the hair of a horse especially from the mane or tail **2 :** cloth made from horsehair

horse latitudes *n pl* **:** either of two regions in the neighborhoods of 30° north and 30° south of the equator marked by calms and light changeable winds

horse·man *n, pl* **horse·men 1 :** a horseback rider **2 :** a person skilled in handling horses — **horse·man·ship** *n*

horse opera *n* **:** a movie or a radio or television play about cowboys

horse·play *n* **:** rough play

horse·pow·er *n* **:** a unit of power that equals the work done in raising 550 pounds one foot in one second

horse·rad·ish *n* **:** a hot relish made from the root of an herb of the mustard family

horse·shoe *n* **1 :** a protective iron plate that is nailed to the rim of a horse's hoof **2 :** something shaped like a horseshoe **3 horseshoes** *pl* **:** a game in which horseshoes are tossed at a stake in the ground

horse·tail *n* **:** any of a group of primitive plants that produce spores and have hollow stems with joints and leaves reduced to sheaths about the joints

horse·whip *vb* **horse·whipped; horse·whip·ping :** to beat severely with a whip made to be used on a horse

horse·wom·an *n, pl* **horse·wom·en :** a woman skilled in riding on horseback or in handling horses

hors·ey *or* **horsy** *adj* **hors·i·er; hors·i·est :** of or relating to horses or horsemen and horsewomen

ho·san·na *interj* — used as a cry of approval, praise, or love

[1]**hose** *n, pl* **hose** *or* **hos·es 1** *pl hose* **:** STOCKING, SOCK **2 :** a flexible tube for carrying fluid

[2]**hose** *vb* **hosed; hos·ing :** to spray, water, or wash with a hose

ho·siery *n* **:** stockings or socks in general

hos·pi·ta·ble *adj* **1 :** friendly and generous in entertaining guests **2 :** willing to deal with something new — **hos·pi·ta·bly** *adv*

hos·pi·tal *n* **:** a place where the sick and injured are cared for

hos·pi·tal·i·ty *n* **:** friendly and generous treatment of guests

hos·pi·tal·ize *vb* **hos·pi·tal·ized; hos·pi·tal·iz·ing :** to place in a hospital for care and treatment — **hos·pi·tal·iza·tion** *n*

[1]**host** *n* **1 :** ARMY 1 **2 :** MULTITUDE

[2]**host** *n* **:** one who receives or entertains guests

[3]**host** *vb* **:** to serve as host to or at

[4]**host** *n, often cap* **:** the bread used in Christian Communion

hos·tage *n* **:** a person given or held to make certain that promises will be kept

hos·tel *n* **:** a place providing inexpensive lodging for use by young travelers

host·ess *n* **:** a woman who receives or entertains guests

hos·tile *adj* **1 :** of or relating to an enemy **2 :** UNFRIENDLY

hos·til·i·ty *n, pl* **hos·til·i·ties 1 :** a hostile state, attitude, or action **2** *hostilities pl* **:** acts of warfare

hot *adj* **hot·ter; hot·test 1 :** having a high temperature **2 :** easily excited **3 :** having or causing the sensation of an uncomfortable degree of body heat **4 :** recently made or received **5 :** close to something sought **6 :** PUNGENT **7 :** RADIOACTIVE **8 :** recently stolen — **hot·ly** *adv* — **hot·ness** *n*

hot·bed *n* **:** a bed of heated earth covered by glass for growing tender plants early in the season

hot dog *n* **:** a frankfurter and especially a cooked one served in a long split roll

ho·tel *n* **:** a place that provides lodging and meals for the public **:** INN

hot·head *n* **:** a person who is easily excited or angered — **hot·head·ed** *adj*

hot·house *n* **:** a heated building enclosed by glass for growing plants

hot plate *n* **:** a small portable appliance for heating or cooking

hot rod *n* **:** an automobile rebuilt for high speed and fast acceleration

hot water *n* **:** a difficult or distressing situation

[1]**hound** *n* **:** a dog with drooping ears and deep bark that is used in hunting and follows game by the sense of smell

[2]**hound** *vb* **:** to hunt, chase, or annoy without ceasing

hour *n* **1 :** one of the twenty-four divisions of a day **:** sixty minutes **2 :** the time of day **3 :** a fixed or particular time **4 :** a measure of distance figured by the amount of time it takes to cover it

hour·glass *n* **:** a device for measuring time in which sand runs from the upper into the lower part of a glass in an hour

[1]**hour·ly** *adv* **:** at or during every hour

[2]**hourly** *adj* **1 :** occurring every hour **2 :** figured by the hour

[1]**house** *n, pl* **hous·es 1 :** a place built for people to live in **2 :** something (as a nest or den) used by an animal for shelter **3 :** a building in which something is kept **4 :** [1]HOUSEHOLD **5 :** FAMILY 1 **6 :** a body of persons assembled to make the laws for a country **7 :** a business firm **8 :** the audience in a theater or concert hall — **on the house :** free of charge

[2]**house** *vb* **1 :** to provide with living quarters or shelter **2 :** CONTAIN 3

house·boat *n* **:** a roomy pleasure boat fitted for use as a place to live

house·boy *n* **:** a boy or man hired to do housework

house·fly *n, pl* **house·flies :** a two-winged fly that is common about houses and often carries disease germs

[1]**house·hold** *n* **:** all the persons who live as a family in one house

[2]**household** *adj* **1 :** of or relating to a household **2 :** FAMILIAR

house·hold·er *n* **:** one who lives in a dwelling alone or as the head of a household

house·keep·er *n* **:** a person employed to take care of a house

house·keep·ing *n* **:** the care and management of a house

house·maid *n* **:** a woman or girl hired to do housework

house·moth·er *n* **:** a woman who acts as hostess, supervisor, and often housekeeper in a residence for young people

house·plant *n* **:** a plant grown or kept indoors

house·top *n* **:** [1]ROOF 1

house·warm·ing *n* **:** a party to celebrate moving into a new home

house·wife *n, pl* **house·wives :** a married woman in charge of a household

house·work *n* **:** the actual labor involved in housekeeping

hous·ing *n* **1 :** dwellings provided for a number of people **2 :** something that covers or protects

hove *past of* HEAVE

hov·el *n* **:** a small poorly built usually dirty house

hov·er *vb* **1 :** to hang fluttering in the air or on the wing **2 :** to move to and fro near a place

[1]**how** *adv* **1 :** in what way **:** by what means **2 :** for what reason **3 :** to what degree, number, or amount **4 :** in what state or condition — **how about :** what do you say to or think of — **how come :** [1]WHY — **how do you do :** HELLO

[2]**how** *conj* **:** in what manner or condition

how·ev·er *adv* **1 :** to whatever degree or extent **2 :** in whatever way **3 :** in spite of that

[1]**howl** *vb* **1 :** to make a loud long mournful sound like that of a dog **2 :** to cry out loudly (as with pain)

[2]**howl** *n* **1 :** a loud long mournful sound made by dogs **2 :** a long loud cry (as of distress, disappointment, or rage) **3 :** COMPLAINT 1 **4 :** something that causes laughter

HTML *n* **:** a computer language that is used to create pages on the World Wide Web that can include text, pictures, sound, video, and links to other Web pages

hub *n* **1 :** the center of a wheel, propeller, or fan **2 :** a center of activity

hub·bub *n* **:** UPROAR

huck·le·ber·ry *n, pl* **huck·le·ber·ries :** a dark edible berry with many hard seeds that grows on a bush related to the blueberry

huck·ster *n* **1 :** PEDDLER, HAWKER **2 :** a writer of advertising

[1]**hud·dle** *vb* **hud·dled; hud·dling 1 :** to crowd, push, or pile together **2 :** to get together to talk something over **3 :** to curl up

[2]**huddle** *n* **1 :** a closely packed group **2 :** a private meeting or conference

hue *n* **1 :** [1]COLOR 1 **2 :** a shade of a color

[1]**huff** *vb* **:** to give off puffs (as of air or steam)

[2]**huff** *n* **:** a fit of anger or temper

huffy *adj* **huff·i·er; huff·i·est 1 :** easily offended **:** PETULANT **2 :** [1]SULKY — **huff·i·ly** *adv* — **huff·i·ness** *n*

[1]**hug** *vb* **hugged; hug·ging 1 :** to clasp in the arms **:** EMBRACE **2 :** to keep close to

[2]**hug** *n* **:** [2]EMBRACE

huge *adj* **hug·er; hug·est :** very large **:** VAST

hulk *n* **1 :** a person or thing that is bulky or clumsy **2 :** the remains of an old or wrecked ship

hulk·ing *adj* **:** very large and strong **:** MASSIVE

[1]**hull** *n* **1 :** the outside covering of a fruit or seed **2 :** the frame or body of a ship, flying boat, or airship

[2]**hull** *vb* **:** to remove the hulls of — **hull·er** *n*

hul·la·ba·loo *n, pl* **hul·la·ba·loos :** a confused noise : HUBBUB, COMMOTION

[1]**hum** *vb* **hummed; hum·ming 1 :** to utter a sound like a long \m\ **2 :** to make the buzzing noise of a flying insect **3 :** to sing with closed lips **4 :** to give forth a low murmur of sounds **5 :** to be very busy or active

[2]**hum** *n* **:** the act or an instance of humming **:** the sound produced by humming

[1]**hu·man** *adj* **1 :** of, relating to, being, or characteristic of people as distinct from lower animals **2 :** having human form or characteristics

[2]**human** *n* **:** a human being — **hu·man·like** *adj*

hu·mane *adj* **:** having sympathy and consideration for others — **hu·mane·ly** *adv* — **hu·mane·ness** *n*

[1]**hu·man·i·tar·i·an** *n* **:** a person devoted to and working for the health and happiness of other people

[2]**humanitarian** *adj* **:** of, relating to, or characteristic of humanitarians

hu·man·i·ty *n, pl* **hu·man·i·ties 1 :** KINDNESS 2, SYMPATHY **2 :** the quality or state of being human **3** *humanities pl* **:** studies (as literature, history, and art) concerned primarily with human culture **4 :** the human race

hu·man·ly *adv* **:** within the range of human ability

[1]**hum·ble** *adj* **hum·bler; hum·blest 1 :** not bold or proud **:** MODEST **2 :** expressing a spirit of respect for the wishes of another **3 :** low in rank or condition — **hum·bly** *adv*

[2]**humble** *vb* **hum·bled; hum·bling 1 :** to make humble **2 :** to destroy the power of

[1]**hum·bug** *n* **1 :** FRAUD 3 **2 :** NONSENSE 1

[2]**humbug** *vb* **hum·bugged; hum·bug·ging :** DECEIVE 1

hum·ding·er *n* **:** something striking or extraordinary

hum·drum *adj* **:** MONOTONOUS

hu·mid *adj* **:** MOIST

hu·mid·i·fy *vb* **hu·mid·i·fied; hu·mid·i·fy·ing :** to make (as the air of a room) more moist — **hu·mid·i·fi·er** *n*

hu·mid·i·ty *n, pl* **hu·mid·i·ties :** the degree of wetness especially of the atmosphere **:** MOISTURE

hu·mil·i·ate *vb* **hu·mil·i·at·ed; hu·mil·i·at·ing :** to lower the pride or self-respect of

hu·mil·i·a·tion *n* **1 :** the state of being humiliated **2 :** an instance of being humiliated

hu·mil·i·ty *n* **:** the quality of being humble

hum·ming·bird *n* **:** a tiny brightly colored American bird whose wings make a humming sound in flight

hum·mock *n* **1 :** a rounded mound of earth **:** KNOLL **2 :** a ridge or pile of ice

[1]**hu·mor** *n* **1 :** state of mind **:** MOOD **2 :** the amusing quality of something **3 :** the ability to see or report the amusing quality of things

[2]**humor** *vb* **:** to give in to the wishes of

hu·mor·ist *n* **:** a person who writes or talks in a humorous way

hu·mor·ous *adj* **:** full of humor **:** FUNNY — **hu·mor·ous·ly** *adv*

hump *n* **1 :** a rounded bulge or lump (as on the back of a camel) **2 :** a difficult part (as of a task) — **humped** *adj*

hump·back *n* **1 :** a humped back **2 :** HUNCHBACK 2 — **hump·backed** *adj*

hu·mus *n* **:** the dark rich part of earth formed from decaying material

[1]**hunch** *vb* **1 :** to bend one's body into an arch or hump **2 :** to draw up close together or into an arch

[2]**hunch** *n* **1 :** HUMP 1 **2 :** a strong feeling about what will happen

hunch·back *n* **1 :** HUMPBACK 1 **2 :** a person with a humped or crooked back

[1]**hun·dred** *n* **1 :** ten times ten **:** 100 **2 :** a very large number

[2]**hundred** *adj* **:** being 100

[1]**hun·dredth** *adj* **:** coming right after ninety-ninth

[2]**hundredth** *n* **:** number 100 in a series

hung *past of* HANG

[1]**hun·ger** *n* **1 :** a desire or a need for food **2 :** a strong desire

[2]**hunger** *vb* **1 :** to feel hunger **2 :** to have a strong desire

hun·gry *adj* **hun·gri·er; hun·gri·est 1 :** feeling or showing hunger **2 :** having a strong desire — **hun·gri·ly** *adv*

hunk *n* **:** a large lump or piece

[1]**hunt** *vb* **1 :** to follow after in order to capture or kill **2 :** to try to find

[2]**hunt** *n* **:** an instance or the practice of hunting

hunt·er *n* **1 :** a person who hunts game **2 :** a dog or horse used or trained for hunting **3 :** a person who searches for something

hunts·man *n, pl* **hunts·men :** HUNTER 1

[1]**hur·dle** *n* **1 :** a barrier to be jumped in a race (**hur·dles**) **2 :** OBSTACLE

[2]**hurdle** *vb* **hur·dled; hur·dling 1 :** to leap over while running **2 :** OVERCOME

hur·dy–gur·dy *n, pl* **hur·dy–gur·dies :** HAND ORGAN

hurl *vb* **:** to throw with force

hur·rah *or* **hoo·ray** *also* **hur·ray** *interj* — used to express joy, approval, or encouragement

hur·ri·cane *n* **:** a tropical cyclone with winds of thirty-three meters per second or greater usually accompanied by rain, thunder, and lightning

hur·ried *adj* **1 :** going or working with speed **:** FAST **2 :** done in a hurry — **hur·ried·ly** *adv*

¹hur·ry *vb* **hur·ried; hur·ry·ing 1 :** to carry or cause to go with haste **2 :** to move or act with haste **3 :** to speed up

²hurry *n* **:** a state of eagerness or urgent need **:** extreme haste

¹hurt *vb* **hurt; hurt·ing 1 :** to feel or cause pain **2 :** to do harm to **:** DAMAGE **3 :** ²DISTRESS, OFFEND **4 :** to make poorer or more difficult

²hurt *n* **1 :** an injury or wound to the body **2 :** SUFFERING 1, ANGUISH **3 :** ¹WRONG

hurt·ful *adj* **:** causing injury or suffering

hur·tle *vb* **hur·tled; hur·tling 1 :** to rush suddenly or violently **2 :** to drive or throw violently

¹hus·band *n* **:** a married man

²husband *vb* **:** to manage with thrift **:** use carefully

hus·band·ry *n* **1 :** the management or wise use of resources **:** THRIFT **2 :** the business and activities of a farmer

¹hush *vb* **:** to make or become quiet, calm, or still **:** SOOTHE

²hush *n* **:** ¹QUIET

hush–hush *adj* **:** ¹SECRET 1, CONFIDENTIAL

¹husk *n* **:** the outer covering of a fruit or seed

²husk *vb* **:** to strip the husk from — **husk·er** *n*

¹hus·ky *adj* **hus·ki·er; hus·ki·est :** HOARSE — **hus·ki·ly** *adv* — **hus·ki·ness** *n*

²husky *n, pl* **huskies :** a strong dog with a thick coat used to pull sleds in the Arctic

³husky *n, pl* **huskies :** a husky person or thing

⁴husky *adj* **hus·ki·er; hus·ki·est :** STRONG 1, BURLY — **hus·ki·ness** *n*

¹hus·tle *vb* **hus·tled; hus·tling 1 :** to push, crowd, or force forward roughly **2 :** HURRY

²hustle *n* **:** energetic activity

hus·tler *n* **:** an energetic person who works fast

hut *n* **:** a small roughly made and often temporary dwelling

hutch *n* **1 :** a low cupboard usually having open shelves on top **2 :** a pen or coop for an animal

hy·a·cinth *n* **:** a plant of the lily family with stalks of fragrant flowers shaped like bells

¹hy·brid *n* **1 :** an animal or plant whose parents differ in some hereditary characteristic or belong to different groups (as breeds, races, or species) **2 :** something that is of mixed origin or composition

²hybrid *adj* **:** of or relating to a hybrid **:** of mixed origin

hydr- *or* **hydro-** *prefix* **1 :** water **2 :** hydrogen

hy·drant *n* **:** a pipe with a spout through which water may be drawn from the main pipes

hy·drau·lic *adj* **1 :** operated, moved, or brought about by means of water **2 :** operated by liquid forced through a small hole or through a tube — **hy·drau·li·cal·ly** *adv*

hy·dro·car·bon *n* **:** a substance containing only carbon and hydrogen

hy·dro·chlo·ric acid *n* **:** a strong acid formed by dissolving in water a gas made up of hydrogen and chlorine

hy·dro·elec·tric *adj* **:** relating to or used in the making of electricity by waterpower

hy·dro·gen *n* **:** a colorless, odorless, and tasteless flammable gas that is the lightest of the chemical elements

hydrogen bomb *n* **:** a bomb whose great power is due to the sudden release of energy when the central portions of hydrogen atoms unite

hydrogen peroxide *n* **:** a liquid chemical containing hydrogen and oxygen and used for bleaching and as an antiseptic

hy·dro·pho·bia *n* **:** RABIES

hy·dro·plane *n* **1 :** a speedboat whose hull is completely or partly raised as it glides over the water **2 :** SEAPLANE

hy·e·na *n* **:** a large mammal of Asia and Africa that lives on flesh

hy·giene *n* **1 :** a science that deals with the bringing about and keeping up of good health in the individual and the group **2 :** conditions or practices necessary for health

hy·gien·ic *adj* **:** of, relating to, or leading toward health or hygiene — **hy·gien·i·cal·ly** *adv*

hy·gien·ist *n* **:** a person skilled in hygiene and especially in a specified branch of hygiene

hy·grom·e·ter *n* **:** an instrument for measuring the humidity of the air

hymn *n* **:** a song of praise especially to God

hym·nal *n* **:** a book of hymns

hyper- *prefix* **:** excessively

hy·per·link *n* **:** an electronic link that allows a computer user to move directly from a marked place in a hypertext document to another in the same or a different document — **hyperlink** *vb*

hy·per·sen·si·tive *adj* **:** very sensitive

hy·per·text *n* **:** an arrangement of the information in a computer database that allows the user to get other information by clicking on text displayed on the screen

hy·pha *n, pl* **hy·phae :** one of the fine threads that make up the body of a fungus

¹hy·phen *n* **:** a mark - used to divide or to compound words or word elements

²hyphen *vb* **:** HYPHENATE

hy·phen·ate *vb* **hy·phen·at·ed; hy·phen·at·ing :** to connect or mark with a hyphen

hyp·no·sis *n* **:** a state which resembles sleep but is produced by a person who can then make suggestions to which the hypnotized person will respond

hyp·no·tism *n* **:** the study or act of producing a state like sleep in which the person in this state will respond to suggestions made by the hypnotist

hyp·no·tist *n* **:** a person who practices hypnotism

hyp·no·tize *vb* **hyp·no·tized; hyp·no·tiz·ing :** to affect by or as if by hypnotism

hy·poc·ri·sy *n, pl* **hy·poc·ri·sies :** a pretending to be what one is not or to believe or feel what one does not

hyp·o·crite *n* **:** a person who practices hypocrisy

hy·po·der·mic needle *n* **1 :** [1]NEEDLE 5 **2 :** a hypodermic syringe complete with needle

hypodermic syringe *n* **:** a small syringe used with a hollow needle to inject material (as a vaccine) into or beneath the skin

hy·pot·e·nuse *n* **:** the side of a right triangle that is opposite the right angle

hy·poth·e·sis *n, pl* **hy·poth·e·ses :** something not proved but assumed to be true for purposes of argument or further study or investigation

hy·po·thet·i·cal *adj* **1 :** involving or based on a hypothesis **2 :** being merely supposed — **hy·po·thet·i·cal·ly** *adv*

hys·te·ria *n* **1 :** a nervous disorder in which one loses control over the emotions **2 :** a wild uncontrolled outburst of emotion — **hys·ter·i·cal** *adj* — **hys·ter·i·cal·ly** *adv*

hys·ter·ics *n sing or pl* **:** a fit of uncontrollable laughing or crying **:** HYSTERIA

I

i *n, pl* **i's** *or* **is** *often cap* **1 :** the ninth letter of the English alphabet **2 :** one in Roman numerals

I *pron* **:** the person speaking or writing

-ial *adj suffix* **:** [1]-AL

-ian — see -AN

ibex *n, pl* **ibex** *or* **ibex·es :** a wild goat of the Old World with horns that curve backward

-ibility — see -ABILITY

ibis *n, pl* **ibis** *or* **ibis·es :** a bird related to the herons but having a slender bill that curves down

-ible — see -ABLE

-ic *adj suffix* **1 :** of, relating to, or having the form of **:** being **2 :** coming from, consisting of, or containing **3 :** in the manner of **4 :** associated or dealing with **:** using **5 :** characterized by **:** exhibiting **:** affected with

-ical *adj suffix* **:** -IC

[1]**ice** *n* **1 :** frozen water **2 :** a substance like ice **3 :** a frozen dessert usually made with sweetened fruit juice

[2]**ice** *vb* **iced; ic·ing 1 :** to coat or become coated with ice **2 :** to chill with ice **:** supply with ice **3 :** to cover with icing

ice age *n* **:** a period of time during which much of the earth is covered with glaciers

ice·berg *n* **:** a large floating mass of ice that has broken away from a glacier

ice·boat *n* **:** a boatlike frame driven by sails and gliding over ice on runners

ice·bound *adj* **:** surrounded or blocked by ice

ice·box *n* **:** REFRIGERATOR

ice·break·er *n* **:** a ship equipped to make and keep open a channel through ice

ice cap *n* **:** a large more or less level glacier flowing outward in all directions from its center

ice–cold *adj* **:** very cold

ice cream *n* **:** a frozen food containing sweetened and flavored cream or butterfat

ice–skate *vb* **:** to skate on ice — **ice skat·er** *n*

ici·cle *n* **:** a hanging mass of ice formed from dripping water

ic·ing *n* **:** a sweet coating for baked goods

icon *n* **1 :** a picture that represents something **2 :** a religious image usually painted on a small wooden panel **3 :** a small picture or symbol on a computer screen that suggests a function that the computer can perform

-ics *n sing or pl suffix* **1 :** study **:** knowledge **:** skill **:** practice **2 :** characteristic actions or qualities

icy *adj* **ic·i·er; ic·i·est 1 :** covered with, full of, or being ice **2 :** very cold **3 :** UNFRIENDLY — **ic·i·ly** *adv* — **ic·i·ness** *n*

I'd : I had **:** I should **:** I would

idea *n* **1 :** a plan of action **:** INTENTION **2 :** something imagined or pictured in the mind **:** NOTION **3 :** a central meaning or purpose

[1]**ide·al** *adj* **1 :** existing only in the mind **2 :** having no flaw **:** PERFECT — **ide·al·ly** *adv*

[2]**ideal** *n* **1 :** a standard of perfection, beauty, or excellence **2 :** a perfect type

iden·ti·cal *adj* **1 :** being one and the same **2 :** being exactly alike or equal

iden·ti·fi·ca·tion *n* **1 :** an act of identifying **:** the state of being identified **2 :** something that shows or proves identity

iden·ti·fy *vb* **iden·ti·fied; iden·ti·fy·ing 1 :** to think of as identical **2 :** [1]ASSOCIATE 2 **3 :** to find out or show the identity of

iden·ti·ty *n, pl* **iden·ti·ties 1 :** the fact or condition of being exactly alike **:** SAMENESS **2 :** INDIVIDUALITY 1 **3 :** the fact of being the same person or thing as claimed

id·i·o·cy *n, pl* **id·i·o·cies** **1 :** great lack of intelligence **2 :** something very stupid or foolish

id·i·om *n* **:** an expression that cannot be understood from the meanings of its separate words but must be learned as a whole

id·i·ot *n* **1 :** a person of very low intelligence **2 :** a silly or foolish person

id·i·ot·ic *adj* **:** showing idiocy **:** FOOLISH — **id·i·ot·i·cal·ly** *adv*

[1]**idle** *adj* **idler; idlest** **1 :** not based on facts **2 :** not working or in use **3 :** LAZY 1 — **idle·ness** *n* — **idly** *adv*

[2]**idle** *vb* **idled; idling** **1 :** to spend time doing nothing **2 :** to run without being connected for doing useful work — **idler** *n*

idol *n* **1 :** an image worshiped as a god **2 :** a much loved person or thing

idol·ize *vb* **idol·ized; idol·iz·ing :** to make an idol of **:** love or admire too much

-ie *also* **-y** *n suffix, pl* **-ies :** little one

-ier — see [2]-ER

if *conj* **1 :** in the event that **2 :** WHETHER 1

-ify *vb suffix* **-ified; -ify·ing :** -FY

ig·loo *n, pl* **igloos :** an Eskimo house often made of blocks of snow and shaped like a dome

ig·ne·ous *adj* **:** formed by hardening of melted mineral material

ig·nite *vb* **ig·nit·ed; ig·nit·ing** **1 :** to set on fire **:** LIGHT **2 :** to catch fire

ig·ni·tion *n* **1 :** the act or action of igniting **2 :** the process or means (as an electric spark) of igniting a fuel mixture

ig·no·ble *adj* **:** DISHONORABLE — **ig·no·bly** *adv*

ig·no·rance *n* **:** the state of being ignorant

ig·no·rant *adj* **1 :** having little or no knowledge **:** not educated **2 :** not knowing **:** UNAWARE **3 :** resulting from or showing lack of knowledge — **ig·no·rant·ly** *adv*

ig·nore *vb* **ig·nored; ig·nor·ing :** to pay no attention to

igua·na *n* **:** a very large tropical American lizard with a ridge of tall scales along its back

il- — see IN-

[1]**ill** *adj* **worse; worst** **1 :** [1]EVIL 2 **2 :** causing suffering or distress **3 :** not normal or sound **4 :** not in good health **5 :** [1]UNFORTUNATE 1, UNLUCKY **6 :** UNKIND, UNFRIENDLY **7 :** not right or proper

[2]**ill** *adv* **worse; worst** **1 :** with displeasure **2 :** in a harsh way **3 :** SCARCELY 1, HARDLY **4 :** in a faulty way

[3]**ill** *n* **1 :** the opposite of good **2 :** SICKNESS 2 **3 :** [2]TROUBLE 2

I'll : I shall **:** I will

il·le·gal *adj* **:** contrary to law **:** UNLAWFUL — **il·le·gal·ly** *adv*

il·leg·i·ble *adj* **:** impossible to read — **il·leg·i·bly** *adv*

il·le·git·i·mate *adj* **:** not legitimate — **il·le·git·i·mate·ly** *adv*

il·lic·it *adj* **:** not permitted **:** UNLAWFUL — **il·lic·it·ly** *adv*

il·lit·er·a·cy *n* **:** the quality or state of being illiterate

[1]**il·lit·er·ate** *adj* **1 :** unable to read or write **2 :** showing lack of education — **il·lit·er·ate·ly** *adv*

[2]**illiterate** *n* **:** an illiterate person

ill–man·nered *adj* **:** not polite

ill–na·tured *adj* **:** having a bad disposition — **ill–na·tured·ly** *adv*

ill·ness *n* **:** SICKNESS 1, 2

il·log·i·cal *adj* **:** not using or following good reasoning — **il·log·i·cal·ly** *adv*

ill–tem·pered *adj* **:** ILL-NATURED

ill–treat *vb* **:** to treat in a cruel or improper way — **ill–treat·ment** *n*

il·lu·mi·nate *vb* **il·lu·mi·nat·ed; il·lu·mi·nat·ing** **1 :** to supply with light **:** light up **2 :** to make clear **:** EXPLAIN

il·lu·mi·na·tion *n* **1 :** the action of illuminating **:** the state of being illuminated **2 :** the amount of light

ill–use *vb* **:** ILL-TREAT

il·lu·sion *n* **1 :** a misleading image presented to the eye **2 :** the state or fact of being led to accept as true something unreal or imagined **3 :** a mistaken idea

il·lu·sive *adj* **:** ILLUSORY

il·lu·so·ry *adj* **:** based on or producing illusion **:** DECEPTIVE

il·lus·trate *vb* **il·lus·trat·ed; il·lus·trat·ing** **1 :** to make clear by using examples **2 :** to supply with pictures or diagrams meant to explain or decorate **3 :** to serve as an example

il·lus·tra·tion *n* **1 :** the action of illustrating **:** the condition of being illustrated **2 :** an example or instance used to make something clear **3 :** a picture or diagram that explains or decorates

il·lus·tra·tive *adj* **:** serving or meant to illustrate

il·lus·tra·tor *n* **:** an artist who makes illustrations (as for books)

il·lus·tri·ous *adj* **:** EMINENT

ill will *n* **:** unfriendly feeling

im- — see IN-

I'm : I am

[1]**im·age** *n* **1 :** something (as a statue) made to look like a person or thing **2 :** a picture of a person or thing formed by a device (as a mirror or lens) **3 :** a person very much like another **4 :** a mental picture of something not present **:** IMPRESSION **5 :** a graphic representation

²image *vb* **im·aged; im·ag·ing 1 :** to describe in words or pictures **2 :** REFLECT 2

imag·in·able *adj* **:** possible to imagine

imag·i·nary *adj* **:** existing only in the imagination **:** not real

imag·i·na·tion *n* **1 :** the act, process, or power of forming a mental picture of something not present and especially of something one has not known or experienced **2 :** creative ability **3 :** a creation of the mind

imag·i·na·tive *adj* **1 :** of, relating to, or showing imagination **2 :** having a lively imagination — **imag·i·na·tive·ly** *adv*

imag·ine *vb* **imag·ined; imag·in·ing 1 :** to form a mental picture of **2 :** THINK 2

¹im·be·cile *n* **:** a person of such low intelligence as to need help in simple personal care

²imbecile *or* **im·be·cil·ic** *adj* **:** of very low intelligence **:** very stupid

im·be·cil·i·ty *n, pl* **im·be·cil·i·ties 1 :** the quality or state of being imbecile **2 :** something very foolish

imbed *variant of* EMBED

im·i·tate *vb* **im·i·tat·ed; im·i·tat·ing 1 :** to follow as a pattern, model, or example **2 :** to be or appear like **:** RESEMBLE **3 :** to copy exactly **:** MIMIC

¹im·i·ta·tion *n* **1 :** an act of imitating **2 :** ¹COPY 1

²imitation *adj* **:** like something else and especially something better

im·i·ta·tive *adj* **1 :** involving imitation **2 :** given to imitating

im·mac·u·late *adj* **1 :** having no stain or blemish **:** PURE **2 :** perfectly clean — **im·mac·u·late·ly** *adv*

im·ma·te·ri·al *adj* **:** not important **:** INSIGNIFICANT

im·ma·ture *adj* **:** not yet fully grown or ripe — **im·ma·ture·ly** *adv*

im·mea·sur·able *adj* **:** impossible to measure — **im·mea·sur·ably** *adv*

im·me·di·ate *adj* **1 :** acting or being without anything else between **2 :** being next in line or nearest in relationship **3 :** closest in importance **4 :** acting or being without any delay **5 :** not far away in time or space

im·me·di·ate·ly *adv* **1 :** with nothing between **2 :** right away

im·mense *adj* **:** very great in size or amount **:** HUGE — **im·mense·ly** *adv*

im·men·si·ty *n, pl* **im·men·si·ties :** the quality or state of being immense

im·merse *vb* **im·mersed; im·mers·ing 1 :** to plunge into something (as a fluid) that surrounds or covers **2 :** to become completely involved with

im·mi·grant *n* **:** a person who comes to a country to live there

im·mi·grate *vb* **im·mi·grat·ed; im·mi·grat·ing :** to come into a foreign country to live

im·mi·gra·tion *n* **:** an act or instance of immigrating

im·mi·nent *adj* **:** being about to happen — **im·mi·nent·ly** *adv*

im·mo·bile *adj* **:** unable to move or be moved

im·mo·bi·lize *vb* **im·mo·bi·lized; im·mo·bi·liz·ing :** to fix in place **:** make immovable

im·mod·est *adj* **:** not modest — **im·mod·est·ly** *adv*

im·mod·es·ty *n* **:** lack of modesty

im·mor·al *adj* **:** not moral **:** BAD 4 — **im·mor·al·ly** *adv*

im·mo·ral·i·ty *n, pl* **im·mo·ral·i·ties 1 :** the quality or state of being immoral **2 :** an immoral act or custom

¹im·mor·tal *adj* **:** living or lasting forever — **im·mor·tal·ly** *adv*

²immortal *n* **1 :** an immortal being **2 :** a person of lasting fame

im·mor·tal·i·ty *n* **1 :** the quality or state of being immortal **:** endless life **2 :** lasting fame or glory

im·mov·able *adj* **:** impossible to move **:** firmly fixed — **im·mov·ably** *adv*

im·mune *adj* **1 :** ¹EXEMPT **2 :** having a strong or special power to resist

immune system *n* **:** the system of the body that fights infection and disease and that includes especially the white blood cells and antibodies and the organs that produce them

im·mu·ni·ty *n, pl* **im·mu·ni·ties 1 :** EXEMPTION 1 **2 :** power to resist infection whether natural or acquired (as by vaccination)

im·mu·ni·za·tion *n* **:** treatment (as with a vaccine) to produce immunity to a disease

im·mu·nize *vb* **im·mu·nized; im·mu·niz·ing :** to make immune

imp *n* **1 :** a small demon **2 :** a mischievous child

im·pact *n* **1 :** a striking together of two bodies **2 :** a strong effect

im·pair *vb* **:** to make less (as in quantity, value, or strength) or worse **:** DAMAGE

im·pale *vb* **im·paled; im·pal·ing :** to pierce with something pointed

im·part *vb* **1 :** to give or grant from a supply **2 :** to make known

im·par·tial *adj* **:** not partial or biased **:** FAIR, JUST — **im·par·tial·ly** *adv*

im·par·tial·i·ty *n* **:** the quality or state of being impartial

im·pass·able *adj* **:** impossible to pass, cross, or travel

im·pas·sioned *adj* **:** showing very strong feeling

im·pas·sive *adj* **:** not feeling or showing emotion — **im·pas·sive·ly** *adv*

im·pa·tience *n* **1 :** lack of patience **2 :** restless or eager desire

im·pa·tient *adj* **1 :** not patient **2 :** showing or coming from impatience **3 :** restless and eager — **im·pa·tient·ly** *adv*

im·peach *vb* **:** to charge a public official formally with misconduct in office

im·pede *vb* **im·ped·ed; im·ped·ing :** to disturb the movement or progress of

im·ped·i·ment *n* **1 :** something that impedes **2 :** a defect in speech

im·pel *vb* **im·pelled; im·pel·ling :** to urge or drive forward or into action **:** FORCE

im·pend *vb* **:** to threaten to occur very soon

im·pen·e·tra·ble *adj* **1 :** impossible to penetrate **2 :** impossible to understand — **im·pen·e·tra·bly** *adv*

im·pen·i·tent *adj* **:** not penitent

im·per·a·tive *adj* **1 :** expressing a command, request, or strong encouragement **2 :** impossible to avoid or ignore **:** URGENT

im·per·cep·ti·ble *adj* **1 :** not perceptible by the senses or by the mind **2 :** very small or gradual — **im·per·cep·ti·bly** *adv*

im·per·fect *adj* **:** not perfect **:** FAULTY — **im·per·fect·ly** *adv*

im·per·fec·tion *n* **1 :** the quality or state of being imperfect **2 :** FLAW, FAULT

im·pe·ri·al *adj* **:** of or relating to an empire or its ruler — **im·pe·ri·al·ly** *adv*

im·per·il *vb* **im·per·iled** *or* **im·per·illed; im·per·il·ing** *or* **im·per·il·ling :** to place in great danger **:** ENDANGER

im·per·ish·able *adj* **:** INDESTRUCTIBLE — **im·per·ish·ably** *adv*

im·per·son·al *adj* **:** not referring or belonging to a specific person — **im·per·son·al·ly** *adv*

im·per·son·ate *vb* **im·per·son·at·ed; im·per·son·at·ing :** to pretend to be another person

im·per·son·a·tion *n* **:** the act of impersonating

im·per·ti·nence *n* **1 :** the quality or state of being impertinent **2 :** a rude act or remark

im·per·ti·nent *adj* **:** INSOLENT, RUDE — **im·per·ti·nent·ly** *adv*

im·per·turb·able *adj* **:** hard to disturb or upset — **im·per·turb·ably** *adv*

im·per·vi·ous *adj* **:** not letting something enter or pass through

im·pet·u·ous *adj* **:** IMPULSIVE, RASH — **im·pet·u·ous·ly** *adv*

im·pi·ous *adj* **:** not pious **:** IRREVERENT — **im·pi·ous·ly** *adv*

imp·ish *adj* **:** MISCHIEVOUS 3 — **imp·ish·ly** *adv*

im·pla·ca·ble *adj* **:** impossible to please, satisfy, or change — **im·pla·ca·bly** *adv*

im·plant *vb* **:** to fix or set securely or deeply

im·ple·ment *n* **:** an article (as a tool) intended for a certain use

im·pli·cate *vb* **im·pli·cat·ed; im·pli·cat·ing :** to show to be connected or involved

im·pli·ca·tion *n* **1 :** the act of implicating **:** the state of being implicated **2 :** the act of implying **3 :** something implied

im·plic·it *adj* **1 :** understood though not put clearly into words **2 :** ABSOLUTE 2 — **im·plic·it·ly** *adv*

im·plore *vb* **im·plored; im·plor·ing :** to call upon with a humble request **:** BESEECH

im·ply *vb* **im·plied; im·ply·ing :** to express indirectly **:** suggest rather than say plainly

im·po·lite *adj* **:** not polite — **im·po·lite·ly** *adv* — **im·po·lite·ness** *n*

¹im·port *vb* **1 :** ²MEAN 3 **2 :** to bring (as goods) into a country usually for selling

²im·port *n* **1 :** MEANING 1 **2 :** IMPORTANCE **3 :** something brought into a country

im·por·tance *n* **:** the quality or state of being important **:** SIGNIFICANCE

im·por·tant *adj* **1 :** SIGNIFICANT **2 :** having power or authority — **im·por·tant·ly** *adv*

im·por·ta·tion *n* **1 :** the act or practice of importing **2 :** something imported

im·por·tu·nate *adj* **:** making a nuisance of oneself with requests and demands — **im·por·tu·nate·ly** *adv*

im·por·tune *vb* **im·por·tuned; im·por·tun·ing :** to beg or urge so much as to be a nuisance

im·pose *vb* **im·posed; im·pos·ing 1 :** to establish or apply as a charge or penalty **2 :** to force someone to accept or put up with **3 :** to take unfair advantage

im·pos·ing *adj* **:** impressive because of size, dignity, or magnificence

im·pos·si·bil·i·ty *n, pl* **im·pos·si·bil·i·ties 1 :** the quality or state of being impossible **2 :** something impossible

im·pos·si·ble *adj* **1 :** incapable of being or of occurring **2 :** HOPELESS 2 **3 :** very bad or unpleasant — **im·pos·si·bly** *adv*

im·pos·tor *n* **:** a person who pretends to be someone else in order to deceive

im·pos·ture *n* **:** the act or conduct of an impostor

im·po·tence *n* **:** the quality or state of being impotent

im·po·tent *adj* **:** lacking in power or strength — **im·po·tent·ly** *adv*

im·pound *vb* **:** to shut up in or as if in an enclosed place

im·pov·er·ish *vb* **1 :** to make poor **2 :** to use up the strength or richness of

im·prac·ti·ca·ble *adj***:** difficult to put into practice or use

im·prac·ti·cal *adj* **:** not practical — **im·prac·ti·cal·ly** *adv*

im·pre·cise *adj* **:** not clear or exact — **im·pre·cise·ly** *adv*

im·preg·nate *vb* **im·preg·nat·ed; im·preg-**

nat·ing **1 :** to make pregnant **2 :** to cause (a material) to be filled with something

im·press *vb* **1 :** to fix in or on one's mind **2 :** to move or affect strongly

im·pres·sion *n* **1 :** the act or process of impressing **2 :** something (as a design) made by pressing or stamping **3 :** something that impresses or is impressed on one's mind **4 :** a memory or belief that is vague or uncertain

im·pres·sion·able *adj* **:** easy to impress or influence

im·pres·sive *adj* **:** having the power to impress the mind or feelings — **im·pres·sive·ly** *adv*

¹im·print *vb* **1 :** to mark by pressure **:** STAMP **2 :** to fix firmly

²im·print *n* **:** something imprinted or printed **:** IMPRESSION

im·pris·on *vb* **:** to put in prison

im·pris·on·ment *n* **:** the act of imprisoning **:** the state of being imprisoned

im·prob·a·bil·i·ty *n* **:** the quality or state of being improbable

im·prob·a·ble *adj* **:** not probable — **im·prob·a·bly** *adv*

im·prop·er *adj* **:** not proper, right, or suitable — **im·prop·er·ly** *adv*

improper fraction *n* **:** a fraction whose numerator is equal to or larger than the denominator

im·prove *vb* **im·proved; im·prov·ing :** to make or become better — **im·prov·er** *n*

im·prove·ment *n* **1 :** the act or process of improving **2 :** increased value or excellence **3 :** something that adds to the value or appearance (as of a house)

im·prov·i·sa·tion *n* **1 :** the act or art of improvising **2 :** something that is improvised

im·pro·vise *vb* **im·pro·vised; im·pro·vis·ing 1 :** to compose, recite, or sing without studying or practicing ahead of time **2 :** to make, invent, or arrange with whatever is at hand

im·pu·dence *n* **:** impudent behavior or speech **:** INSOLENCE, DISRESPECT

im·pu·dent *adj* **:** being bold and disrespectful **:** INSOLENT — **im·pu·dent·ly** *adv*

im·pulse *n* **1 :** a force that starts a body into motion **2 :** the motion produced by a starting force **3 :** a sudden stirring up of the mind and spirit to do something **4 :** the wave of change that passes along a stimulated nerve and carries information to the brain

im·pul·sive *adj* **1 :** acting or tending to act on impulse **2 :** resulting from a sudden impulse — **im·pul·sive·ly** *adv*

im·pure *adj* **1 :** not pure **:** UNCLEAN, DIRTY **2 :** mixed with something else that is usually not as good — **im·pure·ly** *adv*

im·pu·ri·ty *n, pl* **im·pu·ri·ties 1 :** the quality or state of being impure **2 :** something that is or makes impure

¹in *prep* **1 :** enclosed or surrounded by **:** WITHIN **2 :** INTO 1 **3 :** DURING **4 :** WITH 7 **5** — used to show a state or condition **6** — used to show manner or purpose **7 :** INTO 2

²in *adv* **1 :** to or toward the inside **2 :** to or toward some particular place **3 :** ¹NEAR 1 **4 :** into the midst of something **5 :** to or at its proper place **6 :** on the inner side **:** WITHIN **7 :** at hand or on hand

³in *adj* **1 :** being inside or within **2 :** headed or bound inward

¹in- *or* **il-** *or* **im-** *or* **ir-** *prefix* **:** not **:** NON-, UN- — usually *il-* before *l* and *im-* before *b, m,* or *p* and *ir-* before *r* and *in-* before other sounds

²in- *or* **il-** *or* **im-** *or* **ir-** *prefix* **1 :** in **:** within **:** into **:** toward **:** on — usually *il-* before *l, im-* before *b, m,* or *p, ir-* before *r,* and *in-* before other sounds **2 :** EN-

in·abil·i·ty *n* **:** the condition of being unable to do something **:** lack of ability

in·ac·ces·si·bil·i·ty *n* **:** the quality or state of being inaccessible

in·ac·ces·si·ble *adj* **:** hard or impossible to get to or at

in·ac·cu·ra·cy *n, pl* **in·ac·cu·ra·cies 1 :** lack of accuracy **2 :** ERROR, MISTAKE

in·ac·cu·rate *adj* **:** not right or correct **:** not exact — **in·ac·cu·rate·ly** *adv*

in·ac·tive *adj* **:** not active **:** IDLE

in·ac·tiv·i·ty *n* **:** the state of being inactive

in·ad·e·qua·cy *n, pl* **in·ad·e·qua·cies :** the condition of being not enough or not good enough

in·ad·e·quate *adj* **:** not enough or not good enough

in·ad·vis·able *adj* **:** not wise to do

in·alien·able *adj* **:** impossible to take away or give up

inane *adj* **:** silly and pointless — **inane·ly** *adv*

in·an·i·mate *adj* **:** not living

in·ap·pro·pri·ate *adj* **:** not appropriate — **in·ap·pro·pri·ate·ly** *adv*

in·as·much as *conj* **:** considering that **:** ²SINCE 2

in·at·ten·tion *n* **:** failure to pay attention

in·at·ten·tive *adj* **:** not paying attention — **in·at·ten·tive·ly** *adv*

in·au·di·ble *adj* **:** impossible to hear — **in·au·di·bly** *adv*

in·au·gu·ral *adj* **:** of or relating to an inauguration

in·au·gu·rate *vb* **in·au·gu·rat·ed; in·au·gu·rat·ing 1 :** to introduce into office with suitable ceremonies **:** INSTALL **2 :** to celebrate the opening of **3 :** to bring into being or action

in·au·gu·ra·tion *n* : an act or ceremony of inaugurating
in·born *adj* : INSTINCTIVE
in·breed *vb* **in·bred; in·breed·ing** : to breed with closely related individuals
in·can·des·cent *adj* : white or glowing with great heat
incandescent lamp *n* : a lamp whose light is produced by the glow of a wire heated by an electric current
in·ca·pa·ble *adj* : not able to do something
¹in·cense *n* **1** : material used to produce a perfume when burned **2** : the perfume given off by burning incense
²in·cense *vb* **in·censed; in·cens·ing** : to make very angry
in·cen·tive *n* : something that makes a person try or work hard or harder
in·ces·sant *adj* : going on and on : not stopping or letting up — **in·ces·sant·ly** *adv*
¹inch *n* : a unit of length equal to ¹⁄₃₆ yard or 2.54 centimeters
²inch *vb* : to move a little bit at a time
inch·worm *n* : any of numerous small caterpillars that are larvae of moths and move by bringing forward the hind part of the body and then extending forward the front part of the body
in·ci·dent *n* : an often unimportant happening that may form a part of a larger event
¹in·ci·den·tal *adj* **1** : happening by chance **2** : of minor importance
²incidental *n* : something incidental
in·ci·den·tal·ly *adv* : as a matter of less interest or importance
in·cin·er·ate *vb* **in·cin·er·at·ed; in·cin·er·at·ing** : to burn to ashes
in·cin·er·a·tor *n* : a furnace or a container for burning waste materials
in·cise *vb* **in·cised; in·cis·ing** : to cut into : CARVE, ENGRAVE
in·ci·sion *n* : a cutting into something or the cut or wound that results
in·ci·sor *n* : a tooth (as any of the four front teeth of the human upper or lower jaw) for cutting
in·cite *vb* **in·cit·ed; in·cit·ing** : to move to action : stir up : ROUSE
in·clem·ent *adj* : STORMY 1
in·cli·na·tion *n* **1** : an act or the action of bending or leaning **2** : a usually favorable feeling toward something **3** : ¹SLANT, TILT
¹in·cline *vb* **in·clined; in·clin·ing** **1** : to cause to bend or lean **2** : to be drawn to an opinion or course of action **3** : ¹SLOPE, LEAN
²in·cline *n* : ²SLOPE 2
in·clined *adj* **1** : having an inclination **2** : having a slope
inclose, inclosure *variant of* ENCLOSE, ENCLOSURE
in·clude *vb* **in·clud·ed; in·clud·ing** : to take in or have as part of a whole
in·clu·sion *n* **1** : an act of including : the state of being included **2** : something included
in·clu·sive *adj* **1** : covering everything or all important points **2** : including the stated limits and all in between
in·cog·ni·to *adv or adj* : with one's identity kept secret
in·co·her·ence *n* : the quality or state of being incoherent
in·co·her·ent *adj* : not connected in a clear or logical way — **in·co·her·ent·ly** *adv*
in·come *n* : a gain usually measured in money that comes in from labor, business, or property
income tax *n* : a tax on the income of a person or business
in·com·pa·ra·ble *adj* : MATCHLESS — **in·com·pa·ra·bly** *adv*
in·com·pat·i·ble *adj* : not able to live or work together in harmony — **in·com·pat·i·bly** *adv*
in·com·pe·tence *n* : the state or fact of being incompetent
in·com·pe·tent *adj* : not able to do a good job — **in·com·pe·tent·ly** *adv*
in·com·plete *adj* : not complete : not finished — **in·com·plete·ly** *adv*
in·com·pre·hen·si·ble *adj* : impossible to understand — **in·com·pre·hen·si·bly** *adv*
in·con·ceiv·able *adj* **1** : impossible to imagine or put up with **2** : hard to believe — **in·con·ceiv·ably** *adv*
in·con·gru·ous *adj* : not harmonious, suitable, or proper — **in·con·gru·ous·ly** *adv*
in·con·sid·er·ate *adj* : careless of the rights or feelings of others
in·con·sis·tent *adj* **1** : not being in agreement **2** : not keeping to the same thoughts or practices : CHANGEABLE
in·con·spic·u·ous *adj* : not easily seen or noticed — **in·con·spic·u·ous·ly** *adv*
¹in·con·ve·nience *n* **1** : the quality or state of being inconvenient **2** : something inconvenient
²inconvenience *vb* **in·con·ve·nienced; in·con·ve·nienc·ing** : to cause inconvenience to
in·con·ve·nient *adj* : not convenient — **in·con·ve·nient·ly** *adv*
in·cor·po·rate *vb* **in·cor·po·rat·ed; in·cor·po·rat·ing** **1** : to join or unite closely into a single mass or body **2** : to make a corporation of
in·cor·po·ra·tion *n* : an act of incorporating : the state of being incorporated
in·cor·rect *adj* **1** : not correct : not accurate or true : WRONG **2** : showing no care for duty or for moral or social standards — **in·cor·rect·ly** *adv* — **in·cor·rect·ness** *n*

[1]in·crease *vb* **in·creased; in·creas·ing** : to make or become greater (as in size)
[2]in·crease *n* **1** : the act of increasing **2** : something added (as by growth)
in·creas·ing·ly *adv* : more and more
in·cred·i·ble *adj* : too strange or unlikely to be believed — **in·cred·i·bly** *adv*
in·cre·du·li·ty *n* : the quality or state of being incredulous
in·cred·u·lous *adj* : feeling or showing disbelief : SKEPTICAL — **in·cred·u·lous·ly** *adv*
in·crim·i·nate *vb* **in·crim·i·nat·ed; in·crim·i·nat·ing** : to charge with or involve in a crime or fault : ACCUSE
incrust *variant of* ENCRUST
in·cu·bate *vb* **in·cu·bat·ed; in·cu·bat·ing** **1** : to sit upon eggs to hatch them by warmth **2** : to keep under conditions good for hatching or development
in·cu·ba·tion *n* **1** : an act of incubating : the state of being incubated **2** : the time between infection with germs and the appearance of disease symptoms
in·cu·ba·tor *n* **1** : an apparatus that provides enough heat to hatch eggs artificially **2** : an apparatus to help the growth of tiny newborn babies
in·cum·bent *n* : the holder of an office or position
in·cur *vb* **in·curred; in·cur·ring** : to bring upon oneself
in·cur·able *adj* : impossible to cure — **in·cur·ably** *adv*
in·debt·ed *adj* : being in debt : owing something — **in·debt·ed·ness** *n*
in·de·cen·cy *n, pl* **in·de·cen·cies** **1** : lack of decency **2** : an indecent act or word
in·de·cent *adj* : not decent : COARSE, VULGAR
in·de·ci·sion *n* : a swaying between two or more courses of action
in·de·ci·sive *adj* **1** : not decisive or final **2** : finding it hard to make decisions — **in·de·ci·sive·ly** *adv* — **in·de·ci·sive·ness** *n*
in·deed *adv* : in fact : TRULY
in·de·fen·si·ble *adj* : impossible to defend
in·def·i·nite *adj* **1** : not clear or fixed in meaning or details **2** : not limited (as in amount or length) — **in·def·i·nite·ly** *adv*
indefinite article *n* : either of the articles *a* or *an* used to show that the following noun refers to any person or thing of the kind named
in·del·i·ble *adj* **1** : impossible to erase, remove, or blot out **2** : making marks not easily removed — **in·del·i·bly** *adv*
in·del·i·cate *adj* : not polite or proper : COARSE — **in·del·i·cate·ly** *adv*
in·dent *vb* : to set (as the first line of a paragraph) in from the margin
in·den·ta·tion *n* **1** : a cut or dent in something **2** : the action of indenting or the state of being indented
in·de·pen·dence *n* : the quality or state of being independent
Independence Day *n* : July 4 observed as a legal holiday in honor of the adoption of the Declaration of Independence in 1776
[1]in·de·pen·dent *adj* **1** : not under the control or rule of another **2** : not connected with something else : SEPARATE **3** : not depending on anyone else for money to live on **4** : able to make up one's own mind — **in·de·pen·dent·ly** *adv*
[2]independent *n* : an independent person (as a voter who belongs to no political party)
in·de·scrib·able *adj* : impossible to describe — **in·de·scrib·ably** *adv*
in·de·struc·ti·ble *adj* : impossible to destroy — **in·de·struc·ti·bly** *adv*
[1]in·dex *n, pl* **in·dex·es** *or* **in·di·ces** **1** : a list of names or topics (as in a book) given in alphabetical order and showing where each is to be found **2** : POINTER 1 **3** : [1]SIGN 5, INDICATION
[2]index *vb* **1** : to provide with an index **2** : to list in an index
index finger *n* : the finger next to the thumb
[1]In·di·an *n* **1** : a person born or living in India **2** : AMERICAN INDIAN
[2]Indian *adj* **1** : of or relating to India or its peoples **2** : of or relating to the American Indians or their languages
Indian club *n* : a wooden club swung for exercise
Indian corn *n* : a tall American cereal grass widely grown for its large ears of grain which are used as food or for feeding livestock
Indian pipe *n* : a waxy white leafless woodland herb with nodding flowers
Indian summer *n* : a period of mild weather in late autumn or early winter
in·di·cate *vb* **in·di·cat·ed; in·di·cat·ing** **1** : to point out or point to **2** : to state or express briefly
in·di·ca·tion *n* **1** : the act of indicating **2** : something that indicates
in·dic·a·tive *adj* **1** : representing an act or state as a fact that can be known or proved **2** : pointing out
in·di·ca·tor *n* **1** : one that indicates **2** : a pointer on a dial or scale **3** : [1]DIAL 3, GAUGE 3
indices *pl of* INDEX
in·dict *vb* : to charge with an offense or crime : ACCUSE — **in·dict·ment** *n*
in·dif·fer·ence *n* **1** : the condition or fact of being indifferent **2** : lack of interest
in·dif·fer·ent *adj* **1** : having no choice : show-

ing neither interest nor dislike **2 :** neither good nor bad — **in·dif·fer·ent·ly** *adv*

in·di·gest·ible *adj* **:** not digestible **:** not easy to digest

in·di·ges·tion *n* **:** discomfort caused by slow or painful digestion

in·dig·nant *adj* **:** filled with or expressing indignation — **in·dig·nant·ly** *adv*

in·dig·na·tion *n* **:** anger caused by something unjust or unworthy

in·dig·ni·ty *n, pl* **in·dig·ni·ties 1 :** an act that injures one's dignity or self-respect **2 :** treatment that shows a lack of respect

in·di·go *n, pl* **in·di·gos** *or* **in·di·goes 1 :** a blue dye made artificially and formerly obtained from plants (**indigo plants**) **2 :** a dark grayish blue

in·di·rect *adj* **1 :** not straight or direct **2 :** not straightforward **3 :** not having a plainly seen connection — **in·di·rect·ly** *adv* — **in·di·rect·ness** *n*

indirect object *n* **:** an object that represents the secondary goal of the action of its verb

in·dis·creet *adj* **:** not discreet — **in·dis·creet·ly** *adv*

in·dis·cre·tion *n* **1 :** lack of discretion **2 :** an indiscreet act or remark

in·dis·crim·i·nate *adj* **:** showing lack of discrimination

in·dis·pens·able *adj* **:** [1]ESSENTIAL 2 — **in·dis·pens·ably** *adv*

in·dis·posed *adj* **1 :** somewhat unwell **2 :** not willing

in·dis·po·si·tion *n* **:** the condition of being indisposed **:** a slight illness

in·dis·put·able *adj* **:** not disputable **:** UNQUESTIONABLE — **in·dis·put·ably** *adv*

in·dis·tinct *adj* **:** not distinct — **in·dis·tinct·ly** *adv* — **in·dis·tinct·ness** *n*

in·dis·tin·guish·able *adj* **:** impossible to distinguish clearly — **in·dis·tin·guish·ably** *adv*

[1]**in·di·vid·u·al** *adj* **1 :** of or relating to an individual **2 :** intended for one person **3 :** [1]PARTICULAR 1, SEPARATE **4 :** having a special quality **:** DISTINCTIVE 1 — **in·di·vid·u·al·ly** *adv*

[2]**individual** *n* **1 :** a single member of a class **2 :** a single human being

in·di·vid·u·al·i·ty *n, pl* **in·di·vid·u·al·i·ties 1 :** the qualities that set one person or thing off from all others **2 :** the quality or state of being an individual

in·di·vis·i·ble *adj* **:** impossible to divide or separate — **in·di·vis·i·bly** *adv*

in·doc·tri·nate *vb* **in·doc·tri·nat·ed; in·doc·tri·nat·ing 1 :** INSTRUCT 1, TEACH **2 :** to teach the ideas, opinions, or beliefs of a certain group

in·doc·tri·na·tion *n* **:** the act or process of indoctrinating

in·do·lence *n* **:** LAZINESS

in·do·lent *adj* **:** LAZY, IDLE

in·dom·i·ta·ble *adj* **:** UNCONQUERABLE — **in·dom·i·ta·bly** *adv*

in·door *adj* **1 :** of or relating to the inside of a building **2 :** done, used, or belonging within a building

in·doors *adv* **:** in or into a building

indorse *variant of* ENDORSE

in·du·bi·ta·ble *adj* **:** being beyond question or doubt — **in·du·bi·ta·bly** *adv*

in·duce *vb* **in·duced; in·duc·ing 1 :** to lead on to do something **2 :** to bring about **:** CAUSE **3 :** to produce (as an electric current) by induction

in·duce·ment *n* **1 :** the act of inducing **2 :** something that induces

in·duct *vb* **1 :** to place in office **:** INSTALL **2 :** to take in as a member of a military service

in·duc·tion *n* **1 :** the act or process of inducting **2 :** the production of an electrical or magnetic effect through the influence of a nearby magnet, electrical current, or electrically charged body

in·dulge *vb* **in·dulged; in·dulg·ing 1 :** to give in to one's own or another's desires **:** HUMOR **2 :** to allow oneself the pleasure of having or doing something

in·dul·gence *n* **1 :** the act of indulging **:** the state of being indulgent **2 :** an indulgent act **3 :** something indulged in

in·dul·gent *adj* **:** characterized by indulgence **:** LENIENT — **in·dul·gent·ly** *adv*

in·dus·tri·al *adj* **1 :** of, relating to, or engaged in industry **2 :** having highly developed industries — **in·dus·tri·al·ly** *adv*

in·dus·tri·al·ist *n* **:** a person owning or engaged in the management of an industry

in·dus·tri·al·i·za·tion *n* **:** the process of industrializing **:** the state of being industrialized

in·dus·tri·al·ize *vb* **in·dus·tri·al·ized; in·dus·tri·al·iz·ing :** to make or become industrial

in·dus·tri·ous *adj* **:** working hard and steadily **:** DILIGENT — **in·dus·tri·ous·ly** *adv*

in·dus·try *n, pl* **in·dus·tries 1 :** the habit of working hard and steadily **2 :** businesses that provide a certain product or service **3 :** manufacturing activity

-ine *adj suffix* **:** of, relating to, or like

in·ed·i·ble *adj* **:** not fit for food

in·ef·fec·tive *adj* **:** not producing the desired effect — **in·ef·fec·tive·ly** *adv*

in·ef·fec·tu·al *adj* **:** not producing the proper or usual effect — **in·ef·fec·tu·al·ly** *adv*

in·ef·fi·cien·cy *n, pl* **in·ef·fi·cien·cies :** the state or an instance of being inefficient

in·ef·fi·cient *adj* **1 :** not effective **:** INEFFECTUAL **2 :** not able or willing to do something well — **in·ef·fi·cient·ly** *adv*

in·elas·tic *adj* **:** not elastic

in·el·i·gi·bil·i·ty *n* **:** the condition or fact of being ineligible
in·el·i·gi·ble *adj* **:** not eligible
in·ept *adj* **1 :** not suited to the occasion **2 :** lacking in skill or ability — **in·ept·ly** *adv* — **in·ept·ness** *n*
in·equal·i·ty *n, pl* **in·equal·i·ties 1 :** the quality of being unequal or uneven **2 :** an instance of being uneven
in·ert *adj* **:** unable or slow to move or react — **in·ert·ly** *adv* — **in·ert·ness** *n*
in·er·tia *n* **1 :** a property of matter by which it remains at rest or in motion in the same straight line unless acted upon by some external force **2 :** a tendency not to move or change
in·er·tial *adj* **:** of or relating to inertia
in·es·cap·able *adj* **:** INEVITABLE — **in·es·cap·ably** *adv*
in·ev·i·ta·bil·i·ty *n* **:** the quality or state of being inevitable
in·ev·i·ta·ble *adj* **:** sure to happen **:** CERTAIN — **in·ev·i·ta·bly** *adv*
in·ex·act *adj* **:** INACCURATE — **in·ex·act·ly** *adv* — **in·ex·act·ness** *n*
in·ex·cus·able *adj* **:** not to be excused — **in·ex·cus·ably** *adv*
in·ex·haust·ible *adj* **:** plentiful enough not to give out or be used up — **in·ex·haust·ibly** *adv*
in·ex·o·ra·ble *adj* **:** RELENTLESS — **in·ex·o·ra·bly** *adv*
in·ex·pe·di·ent *adj* **:** not suitable or advisable
in·ex·pen·sive *adj* **:** [1]CHEAP 1 — **in·ex·pen·sive·ly** *adv* — **in·ex·pen·sive·ness** *n*
in·ex·pe·ri·ence *n* **:** lack of experience
in·ex·pe·ri·enced *adj* **:** having little or no experience
in·ex·pli·ca·ble *adj* **:** impossible to explain or account for — **in·ex·pli·ca·bly** *adv*
in·ex·press·ible *adj* **:** being beyond one's power to express **:** INDESCRIBABLE — **in·ex·press·ibly** *adv*
in·fal·li·ble *adj* **1 :** not capable of being wrong **2 :** not likely to fail **:** SURE — **in·fal·li·bly** *adv*
in·fa·mous *adj* **1 :** having an evil reputation **2 :** DETESTABLE — **in·fa·mous·ly** *adv*
in·fa·my *n, pl* **in·fa·mies 1 :** an evil reputation **2 :** an infamous act
in·fan·cy *n, pl* **in·fan·cies 1 :** early childhood **2 :** a beginning or early period of existence
[1]**in·fant** *n* **1 :** a child in the first period of life **2 :** [2]MINOR
[2]**infant** *adj* **1 :** of or relating to infancy **2 :** intended for young children
in·fan·tile *adj* **:** CHILDISH
infantile paralysis *n* **:** POLIO
in·fan·try *n, pl* **in·fan·tries :** a branch of an army composed of soldiers trained to fight on foot
in·fat·u·at·ed *adj* **:** having a foolish or very strong love or admiration
in·fat·u·a·tion *n* **:** the state of being infatuated
in·fect *vb* **1 :** to cause disease germs to be present in or on **2 :** to pass on a germ or disease to **3 :** to enter and cause disease in **4 :** to cause to share one's feelings
in·fec·tion *n* **1 :** the act or process of infecting **:** the state of being infected **2 :** any disease caused by germs
in·fec·tious *adj* **1 :** passing from one to another in the form of a germ **2 :** capable of being easily spread
in·fer *vb* **in·ferred; in·fer·ring 1 :** to arrive at as a conclusion **2 :** [2]SURMISE **3 :** to point out **4 :** HINT, SUGGEST
in·fer·ence *n* **1 :** the act or process of inferring **2 :** something inferred
[1]**in·fe·ri·or** *adj* **1 :** situated lower down (as in place or importance) **2 :** of little or less importance, value, or merit
[2]**inferior** *n* **:** an inferior person or thing
in·fe·ri·or·i·ty *n* **1 :** the state of being inferior **2 :** a sense of being inferior
in·fer·nal *adj* **1 :** of or relating to hell **2 :** very bad or unpleasant **:** DAMNABLE — **in·fer·nal·ly** *adv*
in·fer·tile *adj* **:** not fertile
in·fest *vb* **:** to spread or swarm in or over in a troublesome manner
in·fi·del *n* **:** a person who does not believe in a certain religion
in·fi·del·i·ty *n, pl* **in·fi·del·i·ties 1 :** lack of belief in a certain religion **2 :** DISLOYALTY
in·field *n* **1 :** the diamond-shaped part of a baseball field inside the bases and home plate **2 :** the players in the infield
in·field·er *n* **:** a baseball player who plays in the infield
in·fi·nite *adj* **1 :** having no limits of any kind **2 :** seeming to be without limits — **in·fi·nite·ly** *adv*
in·fin·i·tive *n* **:** a verb form serving as a noun or as a modifier and at the same time taking objects and adverbial modifiers
in·fin·i·ty *n, pl* **in·fin·i·ties 1 :** the quality of being infinite **2 :** a space, quantity, or period of time that is without limit
in·firm *adj* **:** weak or frail in body (as from age or disease)
in·fir·ma·ry *n, pl* **in·fir·ma·ries :** a place for the care and housing of infirm or sick people
in·fir·mi·ty *n, pl* **in·fir·mi·ties :** the condition of being infirm
in·flame *vb* **in·flamed; in·flam·ing 1 :** to excite to too much action or feeling **2 :** to cause to redden or grow hot (as from anger) **3 :** to make or become sore, red, and swollen

in·flam·ma·ble *adj* **1 :** FLAMMABLE **2 :** easily inflamed **:** EXCITABLE
in·flam·ma·tion *n* **1 :** the act of inflaming **:** the state of being inflamed **2 :** a bodily response to injury in which heat, redness, and swelling are present
in·flam·ma·to·ry *adj* **1 :** tending to excite anger or disorder **2 :** causing or having inflammation
in·flat·able *adj* **:** possible to inflate
in·flate *vb* **in·flat·ed; in·flat·ing 1 :** to swell or fill with air or gas **2 :** to cause to increase beyond proper limits
in·fla·tion *n* **1 :** an act of inflating **:** the state of being inflated **2 :** a continual rise in the price of goods and services
in·flect *vb* **1 :** to change a word by inflection **2 :** to change the pitch of a person's voice
in·flec·tion *n* **1 :** a change in the pitch of a person's voice **2 :** a change in a word that shows a grammatical difference (as of number, person, or tense)
in·flec·tion·al *adj* **:** of or relating to inflection
in·flex·i·ble *adj* **1 :** not easily bent or twisted **:** RIGID **2 :** not easily influenced or persuaded **:** FIRM
in·flict *vb* **1 :** to give by or as if by striking **2 :** to cause to be put up with
in·flo·res·cence *n* **:** the arrangement of flowers on a stalk
[1]in·flu·ence *n* **1 :** the act or power of producing an effect without apparent force or direct authority **2 :** a person or thing that influences
[2]influence *vb* **in·flu·enced; in·flu·enc·ing :** to have an influence on
in·flu·en·tial *adj* **:** having influence
in·flu·en·za *n* **:** a very contagious virus disease like a severe cold with fever
in·fo·mer·cial *n* **:** a television program that is a long commercial often including a discussion or demonstration
in·form *vb* **1 :** to let a person know something **2 :** to give information so as to accuse or cause suspicion — **in·form·er** *n*
in·for·mal *adj* **1 :** not formal **2 :** suitable for ordinary or everyday use — **in·for·mal·ly** *adv*
in·for·mal·i·ty *n, pl* **in·for·mal·i·ties 1 :** the quality or state of being informal **2 :** an informal act
in·form·ant *n* **:** a person who informs
in·for·ma·tion *n* **1 :** the giving or getting of knowledge **2 :** knowledge obtained from investigation, study, or instruction **3 :** NEWS 3
information superhighway *n* **:** INTERNET
in·for·ma·tive *adj* **:** giving information **:** INSTRUCTIVE
in·frac·tion *n* **:** VIOLATION
in·fra·red *adj* **:** being, relating to, or producing rays like light but lying outside the visible spectrum at its red end
in·fre·quent *adj* **1 :** seldom happening **:** RARE **2 :** not placed, made, or done at frequent intervals — **in·fre·quent·ly** *adv*
in·fringe *vb* **in·fringed; in·fring·ing 1 :** to fail to obey or act in agreement with **:** VIOLATE **2 :** to go further than is right or fair to another **:** ENCROACH — **in·fringe·ment** *n*
in·fu·ri·ate *vb* **in·fu·ri·at·ed; in·fu·ri·at·ing :** to make furious **:** ENRAGE
in·fuse *vb* **in·fused; in·fus·ing 1 :** to put in as if by pouring **2 :** to steep without boiling — **in·fu·sion** *n*
[1]-ing *n suffix* **1 :** action or process **2 :** product or result of an action or process **3 :** something used in or connected with making or doing
[2]-ing *vb suffix or adj suffix* — used to form the present participle and sometimes to form adjectives that do not come from a verb
in·ge·nious *adj* **:** showing ingenuity **:** CLEVER — **in·ge·nious·ly** *adv*
in·ge·nu·ity *n, pl* **in·ge·nu·ities :** skill or cleverness in discovering, inventing, or planning
in·gen·u·ous *adj* **1 :** FRANK, STRAIGHTFORWARD **2 :** NAIVE 1 — **in·gen·u·ous·ly** *adv* — **in·gen·u·ous·ness** *n*
in·got *n* **:** a mass of metal cast into a shape that is easy to handle or store
in·gra·ti·ate *vb* **in·gra·ti·at·ed; in·gra·ti·at·ing :** to gain favor for by effort
in·gra·ti·at·ing *adj* **1 :** PLEASING **2 :** intended to gain someone's favor — **in·gra·ti·at·ing·ly** *adv*
in·grat·i·tude *n* **:** lack of gratitude
in·gre·di·ent *n* **:** one of the substances that make up a mixture
in·hab·it *vb* **:** to live or dwell in
in·hab·i·tant *n* **:** one who lives in a place permanently
in·ha·la·tion *n* **:** the act or an instance of inhaling
in·hale *vb* **in·haled; in·hal·ing 1 :** to draw in by breathing **2 :** to breathe in
in·hal·er *n* **:** a device used for inhaling medicine
in·her·ent *adj* **:** belonging to or being a part of the nature of a person or thing — **in·her·ent·ly** *adv*
in·her·it *vb* **1 :** to get by legal right from a person at his or her death **2 :** to get by heredity
in·her·i·tance *n* **1 :** the act of inheriting **2 :** something inherited
in·hib·it *vb* **:** to prevent or hold back from doing something
in·hos·pi·ta·ble *adj* **:** not friendly or generous **:** not showing hospitality — **in·hos·pi·ta·bly** *adv*

in·hu·man *adj* **1 :** lacking pity or kindness **2 :** unlike what might be expected by a human — **in·hu·man·ly** *adv*
in·hu·mane *adj* **:** not humane
in·hu·man·i·ty *n, pl* **in·hu·man·i·ties :** a cruel act or attitude
in·iq·ui·tous *adj* **:** WICKED 1
in·iq·ui·ty *n, pl* **in·iq·ui·ties :** [1]SIN 1
[1]**ini·tial** *adj* **1 :** of, relating to, or being a beginning **2 :** placed or standing at the beginning **:** FIRST
[2]**initial** *n* **1 :** the first letter of a name **2 :** a large letter beginning a text or a paragraph
[3]**initial** *vb* **ini·tialed** *or* **ini·tialled; ini·tial·ing** *or* **ini·tial·ling :** to mark with initials or an initial
ini·ti·ate *vb* **ini·ti·at·ed; ini·ti·at·ing 1 :** to set going **2 :** to admit into a club by special ceremonies
ini·ti·a·tion *n* **1 :** the act or an instance of initiating **:** the process of being initiated **2 :** the ceremonies with which one is initiated
ini·tia·tive *n* **1 :** a first step or movement **2 :** energy shown in initiating action
in·ject *vb* **1 :** to throw or drive into something **2 :** to force a fluid into (as a part of the body) for medical reasons
in·jec·tion *n* **1 :** an act or instance of injecting **2 :** something injected
in·junc·tion *n* **:** a court order commanding or forbidding the doing of some act
in·jure *vb* **in·jured; in·jur·ing 1 :** to do an injustice to **:** WRONG **2 :** to cause pain or harm to
in·ju·ri·ous *adj* **:** causing injury
in·ju·ry *n, pl* **in·ju·ries 1 :** an act that damages or hurts **2 :** hurt, damage, or loss suffered
in·jus·tice *n* **1 :** violation of a person's rights **2 :** an unjust act
[1]**ink** *n* **:** a usually liquid material for writing or printing
[2]**ink** *vb* **:** to put ink on
ink–jet *adj* **:** relating to or being a printer in which droplets of ink are sprayed onto the paper
in·kling *n* **:** a vague notion **:** HINT
ink·stand *n* **:** a small stand for holding ink and pens
ink·well *n* **:** a container for ink
inky *adj* **ink·i·er; ink·i·est 1 :** consisting of or like ink **2 :** soiled with or as if with ink
in·laid *adj* **1 :** set into a surface in a decorative design **2 :** decorated with a design or material set into a surface
[1]**in·land** *adj* **:** of or relating to the part of a country away from the coast
[2]**inland** *n* **:** the part of a country away from the coast or boundaries
[3]**inland** *adv* **:** into or toward the area away from a coast
in–law *n* **:** a relative by marriage
[1]**in·lay** *vb* **in·laid; in·lay·ing :** to set into a surface for decoration or strengthening
[2]**in·lay** *n* **:** inlaid work **:** material used in inlaying
in·let *n* **1 :** a small or narrow bay **2 :** an opening for intake
in–line skate *n* **:** a roller skate whose wheels are set in a line one behind the other
in·mate *n* **1 :** one of a group living in a single residence **2 :** a person confined in an institution (as a hospital or prison)
in·most *adj* **:** INNERMOST
inn *n* **:** a place that provides a place to sleep and food for travelers
in·ner *adj* **1 :** located farther in **2 :** of or relating to the mind or spirit
inner ear *n* **:** the inner hollow part of the ear that contains sense organs which perceive sound and help keep the body properly balanced
in·ner·most *adj* **:** farthest inward
in·ning *n* **:** a division of a baseball game that consists of a turn at bat for each team
inn·keep·er *n* **:** the person who runs an inn
in·no·cence *n* **:** the quality or state of being innocent
in·no·cent *adj* **1 :** free from sin **:** PURE **2 :** free from guilt or blame **3 :** free from evil influence or effect **:** HARMLESS — **in·no·cent·ly** *adv*
in·noc·u·ous *adj* **:** not harmful
in·no·va·tion *n* **1 :** the introduction of something new **2 :** a new idea, method, or device **:** NOVELTY
in·nu·mer·a·ble *adj* **:** too many to be counted
in·oc·u·late *vb* **in·oc·u·lat·ed; in·oc·u·lat·ing :** to inject a serum, vaccine, or weakened germ into to protect against or treat a disease
in·oc·u·la·tion *n* **1 :** the act or an instance of inoculating **2 :** material used in inoculating
in·of·fen·sive *adj* **1 :** not harmful **2 :** PEACEFUL 1 **3 :** not offensive
in·op·por·tune *adj* **:** INCONVENIENT
[1]**in·put** *n* **1 :** something (as power, a signal, or data) that is put into a machine or system **2 :** the point at which an input is made **3 :** the act of or process of putting in
[2]**input** *vb* **in·put·ted** *or* **input; in·put·ting :** to enter (as data) into a computer
in·quest *n* **:** an official investigation especially into the cause of a death
in·quire *vb* **in·quired; in·quir·ing 1 :** to ask about **2 :** to make an investigation **3 :** to ask a question — **in·quir·er** *n* — **in·quir·ing·ly** *adv*
in·qui·ry *n, pl* **in·qui·ries 1 :** the act of inquiring **2 :** a request for information **3 :** a thorough examination
in·quis·i·tive *adj* **1 :** given to seeking infor-

mation **2 :** tending to ask questions — **in·quis·i·tive·ly** *adv* — **in·quis·i·tive·ness** *n*

in·sane *adj* **1 :** not normal or healthy in mind **2 :** used by or for people who are insane — **in·sane·ly** *adv*

in·san·i·ty *n* **:** the condition of being insane : mental illness

in·sa·tia·ble *adj* **:** impossible to satisfy

in·scribe *vb* **in·scribed; in·scrib·ing 1 :** to write, engrave, or print as a lasting record **2 :** to write, engrave, or print something on or in

in·scrip·tion *n* **:** something that is inscribed

in·sect *n* **1 :** a small and often winged animal that has six jointed legs and a body formed of three parts **2 :** an animal (as a spider or a centipede) similar to the true insects

in·sec·ti·cide *n* **:** a chemical used to kill insects

in·se·cure *adj* **:** not safe or secure — **in·se·cure·ly** *adv*

in·se·cu·ri·ty *n* **:** the quality or state of being insecure

in·sen·si·ble *adj* **1 :** UNCONSCIOUS 2 **2 :** not able to feel **3 :** not aware of or caring about something

in·sen·si·tive *adj* **:** not sensitive : lacking feeling — **in·sen·si·tive·ly** *adv*

in·sen·si·tiv·i·ty *n* **:** lack of sensitivity

in·sep·a·ra·bil·i·ty *n* **:** the quality or state of being inseparable

in·sep·a·ra·ble *adj* **:** impossible to separate — **in·sep·a·ra·bly** *adv*

¹in·sert *vb* **1 :** to put in **2 :** to set in and make fast

²in·sert *n* **:** something that is or is meant to be inserted

in·ser·tion *n* **1 :** the act or process of inserting **2 :** ²INSERT

¹in·set *n* **:** ²INSERT

²inset *vb* **in·set** *or* **in·set·ted; in·set·ting :** ¹INSERT 2

¹in·side *n* **1 :** an inner side, surface, or space : INTERIOR **2 :** ENTRAILS — usually used in pl.

²inside *adv* **1 :** on the inner side **2 :** in or into the interior

³inside *adj* **1 :** of, relating to, or being on or near the inside **2 :** relating or known to a certain few people

⁴inside *prep* **1 :** to or on the inside of **2 :** before the end of : WITHIN

in·sid·er *n* **:** a person having information not generally available

in·sight *n* **:** the power or act of seeing what's really important about a situation

in·sig·nia *or* **in·sig·ne** *n, pl* **insignia** *or* **in·sig·ni·as :** an emblem of a certain office, authority, or honor

in·sig·nif·i·cance *n* **:** the quality or state of being insignificant

in·sig·nif·i·cant *adj* **:** not significant : UNIMPORTANT — **in·sig·nif·i·cant·ly** *adv*

in·sin·cere *adj* **:** not sincere — **in·sin·cere·ly** *adv*

in·sin·cer·i·ty *n* **:** lack of sincerity

in·sin·u·ate *vb* **in·sin·u·at·ed; in·sin·u·at·ing 1 :** to bring or get in little by little or in a secret way **2 :** ²HINT, IMPLY

in·sip·id *adj* **1 :** having little taste or flavor : TASTELESS **2 :** not interesting or challenging : DULL

in·sist *vb* **1 :** to place special stress or great importance **2 :** to make a demand

in·sis·tence *n* **:** the quality or state of being insistent

in·sis·tent *adj* **:** demanding attention : PERSISTENT — **in·sis·tent·ly** *adv*

in·so·lence *n* **:** lack of respect for rank or authority

in·so·lent *adj* **:** showing insolence — **in·so·lent·ly** *adv*

in·sol·u·bil·i·ty *n* **:** the quality or state of being insoluble

in·sol·u·ble *adj* **1 :** having no solution or explanation **2 :** difficult or impossible to dissolve — **in·sol·u·bly** *adv*

in·spect *vb* **1 :** to examine closely **2 :** to view and examine in an official way

in·spec·tion *n* **:** the act of inspecting

in·spec·tor *n* **:** a person who makes inspections

in·spi·ra·tion *n* **1 :** the act of breathing in **2 :** the act or power of arousing the mind or the emotions **3 :** the state of being inspired **4 :** something that is or seems inspired **5 :** an inspiring agent or influence

in·spire *vb* **in·spired; in·spir·ing 1 :** to move or guide by divine influence **2 :** to give inspiration to : ENCOURAGE **3 :** AROUSE 2 **4 :** to bring about : CAUSE **5 :** INHALE

in·sta·bil·i·ty *n* **:** the quality or state of being unstable

in·stall *vb* **1 :** to put in office with ceremony **2 :** to set up for use or service

in·stal·la·tion *n* **1 :** the act of installing : the state of being installed **2 :** something installed for use

¹in·stall·ment *or* **in·stal·ment** *n* **:** INSTALLATION 1

²installment *n* **:** one of the parts of a series

in·stance *n* **1 :** EXAMPLE 1 **2 :** a certain point in an action or process

¹in·stant *n* **:** MOMENT 1

²instant *adj* **1 :** happening or done at once **2 :** partially prepared by the manufacturer so that only final mixing is needed **3 :** made to dissolve quickly in a liquid

in·stan·ta·neous *adj* **1 :** happening in an instant **2 :** done without delay — **in·stan·ta·neous·ly** *adv*

in·stant·ly *adv* **:** IMMEDIATELY 2

in·stead *adv* **:** as a substitute

in·stead of *prep* **:** as a substitute for **:** rather than

in·step *n* **:** the arched middle part of the human foot in front of the ankle joint

in·sti·gate *vb* **in·sti·gat·ed; in·sti·gat·ing :** PROVOKE 2, INCITE

in·still *vb* **:** to put into the mind little by little

in·stinct *n* **1 :** a natural ability **2 :** an act or course of action in response to a stimulus that is automatic rather than learned **3 :** behavior based on automatic reactions

in·stinc·tive *adj* **:** of or relating to instinct **:** resulting from instinct — **in·stinc·tive·ly** *adv*

¹in·sti·tute *vb* **in·sti·tut·ed; in·sti·tut·ing 1 :** ESTABLISH 1 **2 :** to set going **:** INAUGURATE

²institute *n* **1 :** an organization for the promotion of a cause **2 :** a place for study usually in a special field

in·sti·tu·tion *n* **1 :** the act of instituting **:** ESTABLISHMENT **2 :** an established custom, practice, or law **3 :** an established organization

in·sti·tu·tion·al *adj* **:** of or relating to an institution

in·struct *vb* **1 :** to help to get knowledge to **:** TEACH **2 :** to give information to **3 :** to give commands to **:** DIRECT

in·struc·tion *n* **1 :** LESSON 3 **2 instructions** *pl* **:** DIRECTION 2, ORDER **3 instructions** *pl* **:** an outline of how something is to be done **4 :** the practice or method used by a teacher

in·struc·tive *adj* **:** helping to give knowledge — **in·struc·tive·ly** *adv*

in·struc·tor *n* **:** TEACHER

in·stru·ment *n* **1 :** a way of getting something done **2 :** a device for doing a particular kind of work **3 :** a device used to produce music **4 :** a legal document (as a deed) **5 :** a measuring device

in·stru·men·tal *adj* **1 :** acting to get something done **2 :** of or relating to an instrument **3 :** being music played on an instrument rather than sung — **in·stru·men·tal·ly** *adv*

in·sub·or·di·nate *adj* **:** unwilling to obey authority **:** DISOBEDIENT

in·sub·or·di·na·tion *n* **:** failure to obey authority

in·sub·stan·tial *adj* **1 :** not real **:** IMAGINARY **2 :** not firm or solid — **in·sub·stan·tial·ly** *adv*

in·suf·fer·able *adj* **:** impossible to endure **:** INTOLERABLE — **in·suf·fer·ably** *adv*

in·suf·fi·cien·cy *n, pl* **in·suf·fi·cien·cies 1 :** the quality or state of being insufficient **2 :** a shortage of something

in·suf·fi·cient *adj* **:** not sufficient **:** INADEQUATE — **in·suf·fi·cient·ly** *adv*

in·su·late *vb* **in·su·lat·ed; in·su·lat·ing 1 :** to separate from others **:** ISOLATE **2 :** to separate a conductor of electricity, heat, or sound from other conducting bodies by means of something that will not conduct electricity, heat, or sound

in·su·la·tion *n* **1 :** the act of insulating **:** the state of being insulated **2 :** material used in insulating

in·su·la·tor *n* **1 :** a material (as rubber or glass) that is a poor conductor of electricity or heat **2 :** a device made of an electrical insulating material and used for separating or supporting electrical conductors

in·su·lin *n* **:** a hormone from the pancreas that prevents or controls diabetes

¹in·sult *vb* **:** to treat with disrespect or scorn

²in·sult *n* **:** an act or expression showing disrespect or scorn

in·sur·ance *n* **1 :** the act of insuring **:** the state of being insured **2 :** the business of insuring persons or property **3 :** a contract by which someone guarantees for a fee to pay someone else for the value of property lost or damaged (as through theft or fire) or usually a specified amount for injury or death **4 :** the amount for which something is insured

in·sure *vb* **in·sured; in·sur·ing 1 :** to give or get insurance on or for **2 :** ENSURE — **in·sur·er** *n*

in·sured *n* **:** a person whose life or property is insured

¹in·sur·gent *n* **:** ²REBEL

²insurgent *adj* **:** REBELLIOUS 1

in·sur·rec·tion *n* **:** an act or instance of rebelling against a government

in·tact *adj* **:** not touched especially by anything that harms

in·take *n* **1 :** a place where liquid or air is taken into something (as a pump) **2 :** the act of taking in **3 :** something taken in

¹in·tan·gi·ble *adj* **1 :** not possible to touch **2 :** not possible to think of as matter or substance

²intangible *n* **:** something intangible

in·te·ger *n* **:** a number that is a natural number (as 1, 2, or 3), the negative of a natural number (as –1, –2, –3), or 0

in·te·gral *adj* **:** needed to make something complete

in·te·grate *vb* **in·te·grat·ed; in·te·grat·ing 1 :** to form into a whole **:** UNITE **2 :** to make a part of a larger unit **3 :** to make open to all races

integrated circuit *n* **:** a tiny group of electronic devices and their connections that is produced in or on a small slice of material (as silicon)

in·te·gra·tion *n* **:** an act, process, or instance of integrating

in·teg·ri·ty *n* **1 :** the condition of being free from damage or defect **2 :** total honesty and sincerity

in·tel·lect *n* **1 :** the power of knowing **2 :** the capacity for thought especially when highly developed **3 :** a person with great powers of thinking and reasoning

[1]**in·tel·lec·tu·al** *adj* **1 :** of or relating to the intellect or understanding **2 :** having or showing greater than usual intellect **3 :** requiring study and thought — **in·tel·lec·tu·al·ly** *adv*

[2]**intellectual** *n* **:** an intellectual person

in·tel·li·gence *n* **1 :** the ability to learn and understand **2 :** NEWS 3, INFORMATION **3 :** an agency that obtains information about an enemy or a possible enemy

in·tel·li·gent *adj* **:** having or showing intelligence or intellect — **in·tel·li·gent·ly** *adv*

in·tel·li·gi·ble *adj* **:** possible to understand — **in·tel·li·gi·bly** *adv*

in·tem·per·ance *n* **:** lack of self-control (as in satisfying an appetite)

in·tem·per·ate *adj* **1 :** not moderate or mild **2 :** lacking or showing a lack of self-control (as in the use of alcoholic drinks) — **in·tem·per·ate·ly** *adv*

in·tend *vb* **:** to have in mind as a purpose or aim **:** PLAN

in·tense *adj* **1 :** [1]EXTREME 1 **2 :** done with great energy, enthusiasm, or effort **3 :** having very strong feelings — **in·tense·ly** *adv*

in·ten·si·fi·ca·tion *n* **:** the act or process of intensifying

in·ten·si·fy *vb* **in·ten·si·fied; in·ten·si·fy·ing :** to make or become intense or more intensive **:** HEIGHTEN

in·ten·si·ty *n, pl* **in·ten·si·ties 1 :** extreme strength or force **2 :** the degree or amount of a quality or condition

[1]**in·ten·sive** *adj* **1 :** involving special effort or concentration **:** THOROUGH **2** — used to stress something

[2]**intensive** *n* **:** an intensive word

[1]**in·tent** *n* **1 :** [1]PURPOSE, INTENTION **2 :** MEANING 1

[2]**intent** *adj* **1 :** showing concentration or great attention **2 :** showing great determination — **in·tent·ly** *adv* — **in·tent·ness** *n*

in·ten·tion *n* **1 :** a determination to act in a particular way **2 :** [1]PURPOSE, AIM **3 :** MEANING 1, INTENT

in·ten·tion·al *adj* **:** done by intention **:** not accidental — **in·ten·tion·al·ly** *adv*

in·ter *vb* **in·terred; in·ter·ring :** BURY 1

inter- *prefix* **1 :** between **:** among **:** together **2 :** mutual **:** mutually **:** reciprocal **:** reciprocally **3 :** located, occurring, or carried on between

in·ter·act *vb* **:** to act upon one another

in·ter·ac·tion *n* **:** the action or influence of people, groups, or things on one another

in·ter·ac·tive *adj* **1 :** active between people, groups, or things **2 :** of, relating to, or allowing two-way electronic communications (as between a person and a computer) — **in·ter·ac·tive·ly** *adv*

in·ter·cede *vb* **in·ter·ced·ed; in·ter·ced·ing 1 :** to try to help settle differences between unfriendly individuals or groups **2 :** to plead for the needs of someone else

in·ter·cept *vb* **:** to take, seize, or stop before reaching an intended destination — **in·ter·cep·tor** *n*

in·ter·ces·sion *n* **:** the act of interceding

in·ter·ces·sor *n* **:** a person who intercedes

[1]**in·ter·change** *vb* **in·ter·changed; in·ter·chang·ing :** to put each in the place of the other **:** EXCHANGE

[2]**in·ter·change** *n* **1 :** an act or instance of interchanging **2 :** a joining of highways that permits moving from one to the other without crossing traffic lanes

in·ter·change·able *adj* **:** possible to interchange — **in·ter·change·ably** *adv*

in·ter·com *n* **:** a communication system with a microphone and loudspeaker at each end

in·ter·course *n* **:** dealings between persons or groups

in·ter·de·pen·dence *n* **:** the quality or state of being interdependent

in·ter·de·pen·dent *adj* **:** depending on one another — **in·ter·de·pen·dent·ly** *adv*

[1]**in·ter·est** *n* **1 :** a right, title, or legal share in something **2 :** WELFARE 1, BENEFIT **3 :** the money paid by a borrower for the use of borrowed money **4 interests** *pl* **:** a group financially interested in an industry or business **5 :** a feeling of concern, curiosity, or desire to be involved with something **6 :** the quality of attracting special attention or arousing curiosity **7 :** something in which one is interested

[2]**interest** *vb* **1 :** to persuade to become involved in **2 :** to arouse and hold the interest of

in·ter·est·ed *adj* **:** having or showing interest

in·ter·est·ing *adj* **:** holding the attention **:** arousing interest — **in·ter·est·ing·ly** *adv*

in·ter·fere *vb* **in·ter·fered; in·ter·fer·ing 1 :** to be in opposition **:** CLASH **2 :** to take a part in the concerns of others

in·ter·fer·ence *n* **1 :** the act or process of interfering **2 :** something that interferes

in·ter·im *n* **:** INTERVAL 1

[1]**in·te·ri·or** *adj* **1 :** being or occurring within the limits **:** INNER **2 :** far from the border or shore **:** INLAND

[2]**interior** *n* **:** the inner part of something

in·ter·ject *vb* **:** to put between or among other things

in·ter·jec·tion *n* **1 :** an interjecting of something **2 :** something interjected **3 :** a word or cry (as "ouch") expressing sudden or strong feeling

in·ter·lace *vb* **in·ter·laced; in·ter·lac·ing :** to unite by or as if by lacing together

in·ter·lock *vb* **:** to lock together

in·ter·lop·er *n* **:** INTRUDER

in·ter·lude *n* **1 :** an entertainment between the acts of a play **2 :** a period or event that comes between others **3 :** a musical composition between parts of a longer composition or of a drama

in·ter·mar·riage *n* **:** marriage between members of different groups

in·ter·mar·ry *vb* **in·ter·mar·ried; in·ter·mar·ry·ing :** to become connected by intermarriage

in·ter·me·di·ary *n, pl* **in·ter·me·di·ar·ies :** GO-BETWEEN

[1]**in·ter·me·di·ate** *adj* **:** being or occurring in the middle or between — **in·ter·me·di·ate·ly** *adv*

[2]**intermediate** *n* **:** someone or something that is intermediate

in·ter·ment *n* **:** BURIAL

in·ter·mi·na·ble *adj* **:** ENDLESS 1 — **in·ter·mi·na·bly** *adv*

in·ter·min·gle *vb* **in·ter·min·gled; in·ter·min·gling :** to mix together

in·ter·mis·sion *n* **1 :** [1]PAUSE 1, INTERRUPTION **2 :** a temporary halt (as between acts of a play)

in·ter·mit·tent *adj* **:** starting, stopping, and starting again — **in·ter·mit·tent·ly** *adv*

[1]**in·tern** *vb* **:** to force to stay within certain limits especially during a war — **in·tern·ment** *n*

[2]**in·tern** *or* **in·terne** *n* **:** a medical school graduate getting practical experience in a hospital — **in·tern·ship** *n*

[3]**in·tern** *vb* **:** to work as an intern

in·ter·nal *adj* **1 :** being within something **:** INTERIOR, INNER **2 :** having to do with the inside of the body **3 :** of or relating to the domestic affairs of a country — **in·ter·nal·ly** *adv*

in·ter·na·tion·al *adj* **:** of, relating to, or affecting two or more nations — **in·ter·na·tion·al·ly** *adv*

In·ter·net *n* **:** a communications system that connects groups of computers and databases all over the world

in·ter·plan·e·tary *adj* **:** existing, carried on, or operating between planets

in·ter·play *n* **:** INTERACTION

in·ter·pose *vb* **in·ter·posed; in·ter·pos·ing 1 :** to put between **2 :** to introduce between parts of a conversation **3 :** to be or come between

in·ter·po·si·tion *n* **1 :** the act of interposing **:** the state of being interposed **2 :** something that interposes or is interposed

in·ter·pret *vb* **1 :** to tell the meaning of **:** EXPLAIN, TRANSLATE **2 :** to understand according to one's own belief, judgment, or interest **3 :** to bring out the meaning of — **in·ter·pret·er** *n*

in·ter·pre·ta·tion *n* **:** the act or the result of interpreting

in·ter·pre·ta·tive *adj* **:** designed or serving to interpret

in·ter·pre·tive *adj* **:** INTERPRETATIVE

in·ter·ra·cial *adj* **:** of or involving members of different races

in·ter·re·late *vb* **in·ter·re·lat·ed; in·ter·re·lat·ing :** to bring into or have a relationship with each other

in·ter·re·la·tion *n* **:** relation with each other — **in·ter·re·la·tion·ship** *n*

in·ter·ro·gate *vb* **in·ter·ro·gat·ed; in·ter·ro·gat·ing :** to question thoroughly

in·ter·ro·ga·tion *n* **:** the act of interrogating

interrogation point *n* **:** QUESTION MARK

in·ter·rog·a·tive *adj* **:** asking a question

in·ter·rog·a·to·ry *adj* **:** containing or expressing a question

in·ter·rupt *vb* **1 :** to stop or hinder by breaking in **2 :** to put or bring a difference into

in·ter·rup·tion *n* **:** an act of interrupting **:** a state of being interrupted

in·ter·scho·las·tic *adj* **:** existing or carried on between schools

in·ter·sect *vb* **:** to cut or divide by passing through or across **:** CROSS

in·ter·sec·tion *n* **1 :** the act or process of intersecting **2 :** the place or point where two or more things (as streets) intersect **:** CROSSING **3 :** the set of mathematical elements common to two or more sets

in·ter·sperse *vb* **in·ter·spersed; in·ter·spers·ing 1 :** to insert here and there **2 :** to insert something at various places in or among

in·ter·state *adj* **:** existing between or including two or more states

in·ter·stel·lar *adj* **:** existing or taking place among the stars

in·ter·twine *vb* **in·ter·twined; in·ter·twin·ing :** to twine or cause to twine about one another

in·ter·val *n* **1 :** a space of time between events or states **2 :** a space between things **3 :** the difference in pitch between two tones

in·ter·vene *vb* **in·ter·vened; in·ter·ven·ing 1 :** to come between events, places, or points of time **2 :** to interfere with something so as to stop, settle, or change

in·ter·ven·tion *n* : the act or fact of intervening

¹in·ter·view *n* **1** : a meeting face to face to give or get information or advice **2** : a written report of an interview for publication

²interview *vb* : to meet and question in an interview — **in·ter·view·er** *n*

in·ter·weave *vb* **in·ter·wove; in·ter·wo·ven; in·ter·weav·ing 1** : to weave together **2** : INTERMINGLE

in·tes·ti·nal *adj* : of or relating to the intestine

in·tes·tine *n* : the lower narrower part of the digestive canal in which most of the digestion and absorption of food occurs and through which waste material passes to be discharged

in·ti·ma·cy *n, pl* **in·ti·ma·cies** : the state or an instance of being intimate

¹in·ti·mate *vb* **in·ti·mat·ed; in·ti·mat·ing** : to express (as an idea) indirectly : HINT

²in·ti·mate *adj* **1** : most private : PERSONAL **2** : marked by very close association **3** : suggesting comfortable warmth or privacy : COZY — **in·ti·mate·ly** *adv*

³in·ti·mate *n* : a very close friend

in·ti·ma·tion *n* **1** : the act of intimating **2** : ¹HINT 1

in·tim·i·date *vb* **in·tim·i·dat·ed; in·tim·i·dat·ing** : to frighten especially by threats

in·tim·i·da·tion *n* : the act of intimidating : the state of being intimidated

in·to *prep* **1** : to the inside of **2** : to the state, condition, or form of **3** : so as to hit : AGAINST

in·tol·er·a·ble *adj* : UNBEARABLE — **in·tol·er·a·bly** *adv*

in·tol·er·ance *n* : the quality or state of being intolerant

in·tol·er·ant *adj* : not tolerant — **in·tol·er·ant·ly** *adv*

in·to·na·tion *n* : the rise and fall in pitch of the voice in speech

in·tox·i·cate *vb* **in·tox·i·cat·ed; in·tox·i·cat·ing 1** : to make drunk **2** : to make wildly excited or enthusiastic

in·tox·i·ca·tion *n* **1** : an unhealthy state that is or is like a poisoning **2** : the state of one who has drunk too much liquor : DRUNKENNESS

in·tra·mu·ral *adj* : being or occurring within the limits usually of a school

in·tran·si·tive *adj* : not having or containing a direct object

in·trep·id *adj* : feeling no fear : BOLD — **in·trep·id·ly** *adv*

in·tri·ca·cy *n, pl* **in·tri·ca·cies 1** : the quality or state of being intricate **2** : something intricate

in·tri·cate *adj* **1** : having many closely combined parts or elements **2** : very difficult to follow or understand — **in·tri·cate·ly** *adv*

¹in·trigue *vb* **in·trigued; in·trigu·ing 1** : ²PLOT 2, SCHEME **2** : to arouse the interest or curiosity of

²in·trigue *n* : a secret or sly scheme often for selfish purposes

in·tro·duce *vb* **in·tro·duced; in·tro·duc·ing 1** : to bring into practice or use **2** : to lead or bring in especially for the first time **3** : to cause to be acquainted : make known **4** : to bring forward for discussion **5** : to put in : INSERT — **in·tro·duc·er** *n*

in·tro·duc·tion *n* **1** : the action of introducing **2** : something introduced **3** : the part of a book that leads up to and explains what will be found in the main part **4** : the act of making persons known to each other

in·tro·duc·to·ry *adj* : serving to introduce : PRELIMINARY

in·trude *vb* **in·trud·ed; in·trud·ing 1** : to force in, into, or on especially where not right or proper **2** : to come or go in without an invitation or right — **in·trud·er** *n*

in·tru·sion *n* : the act of intruding

intrust *variant of* ENTRUST

in·tu·i·tion *n* : a knowing or something known without mental effort

in·un·date *vb* **in·un·dat·ed; in·un·dat·ing** : to cover with a flood : OVERFLOW

in·un·da·tion *n* : ¹FLOOD 1

in·vade *vb* **in·vad·ed; in·vad·ing 1** : to enter by force to conquer or plunder **2** : to show lack of respect for — **in·vad·er** *n*

¹in·val·id *adj* : not valid

²in·va·lid *adj* **1** : SICKLY 1 **2** : of or relating to a sick person

³in·va·lid *n* : a sick or disabled person — **in·va·lid·ism** *n*

in·val·i·date *vb* **in·val·i·dat·ed; in·val·i·dat·ing** : to weaken or destroy the effect of

in·valu·able *adj* : having value too great to be estimated : PRICELESS

in·var·i·a·bil·i·ty *n* : the quality or state of being invariable

in·vari·able *adj* : not changing or capable of change — **in·vari·ably** *adv*

in·va·sion *n* : an act of invading

in·vei·gle *vb* **in·vei·gled; in·vei·gling** : to win over or obtain by flattery

in·vent *vb* **1** : to think up : make up **2** : to create or produce for the first time — **in·ven·tor** *n*

in·ven·tion *n* **1** : an original device or process **2** : ³LIE **3** : the act or process of inventing

in·ven·tive *adj* : CREATIVE

¹in·ven·to·ry *n, pl* **in·ven·to·ries 1** : a list of items (as goods on hand) **2** : the act or process of making an inventory

[2]**inventory** *vb* **in·ven·to·ried; in·ven·to·ry·ing** : to make an inventory of

[1]**in·verse** *adj* **1 :** opposite in order, nature, or effect **2 :** being a mathematical operation that is opposite in effect to another operation — **in·verse·ly** *adv*

[2]**inverse** *n* : something inverse

in·vert *vb* **1 :** to turn inside out or upside down **2 :** to reverse the order or position of

[1]**in·ver·te·brate** *adj* : having no backbone

[2]**invertebrate** *n* : an invertebrate animal

[1]**in·vest** *vb* **1 :** to give power or authority to **2 :** BESIEGE 1

[2]**invest** *vb* **1 :** to put out money in order to gain a financial return **2 :** to put out (as effort) in support of a usually worthy cause — **in·ves·tor** *n*

in·ves·ti·gate *vb* **in·ves·ti·gat·ed; in·ves·ti·gat·ing :** to study by close and careful observation — **in·ves·ti·ga·tor** *n*

in·ves·ti·ga·tion *n* **:** the act or process of investigating

in·ves·ti·ture *n* **:** the act of placing in office

in·vest·ment *n* **1 :** the investing of money **2 :** a sum of money invested **3 :** a property in which money is invested

in·vig·o·rate *vb* **in·vig·o·rat·ed; in·vig·o·rat·ing :** to give life and energy to

in·vin·ci·bil·i·ty *n* **:** the quality or state of being invincible

in·vin·ci·ble *adj* **:** impossible to defeat — **in·vin·ci·bly** *adv*

in·vi·o·la·ble *adj* **1 :** too sacred to be treated with disrespect **2 :** impossible to harm or destroy by violence

in·vi·o·late *adj* **:** not violated

in·vis·i·bil·i·ty *n* **:** the quality or state of being invisible

in·vis·i·ble *adj* **1 :** impossible to see **2 :** being out of sight **3 :** IMPERCEPTIBLE 1 — **in·vis·i·ble·ness** *n* — **in·vis·i·bly** *adv*

in·vi·ta·tion *n* **1 :** the act of inviting **2 :** the written or spoken expression by which a person is invited

in·vite *vb* **in·vit·ed; in·vit·ing 1 :** to tend to bring on **2 :** to request the presence or company of **3 :** [1]WELCOME 2

in·vit·ing *adj* **:** ATTRACTIVE — **in·vit·ing·ly** *adv*

in·vo·ca·tion *n* **:** a prayer for blessing or guidance (as at the beginning of a service)

[1]**in·voice** *n* **:** a list of goods shipped usually showing the price and the terms of sale

[2]**invoice** *vb* **in·voiced; in·voic·ing :** to make an invoice of

in·voke *vb* **in·voked; in·vok·ing 1 :** to call on for aid or protection (as in prayer) **2 :** to call forth by magic **3 :** to appeal to as an authority or for support

in·vol·un·tary *adj* **1 :** not made or done willingly or from choice **2 :** not under the control of the will — **in·vol·un·tari·ly** *adv*

in·volve *vb* **in·volved; in·volv·ing 1 :** to draw into a situation **:** ENGAGE **2 :** INCLUDE **3 :** to be sure to or need to be accompanied by — **in·volve·ment** *n*

in·volved *adj* **:** COMPLEX 2

in·vul·ner·a·bil·i·ty *n* **:** the quality or state of being invulnerable

in·vul·ner·a·ble *adj* **1 :** impossible to injure or damage **2 :** safe from attack — **in·vul·ner·a·bly** *adv*

[1]**in·ward** *adj* **1 :** situated on the inside **:** INNER **2 :** of or relating to the mind or spirit **3 :** directed toward the interior

[2]**inward** *or* **in·wards** *adv* **1 :** toward the inside or center **2 :** toward the mind or spirit

in·ward·ly *adv* **1 :** in the mind or spirit **2 :** beneath the surface **3 :** to oneself **:** PRIVATELY **4 :** toward the inside

io·dine *n* **1 :** a chemical element found in seawater and seaweeds and used especially in medicine and photography **2 :** a solution of iodine in alcohol used to kill germs

io·dize *vb* **io·dized; io·diz·ing :** to add iodine to

ion *n* **:** an atom or group of atoms that carries an electric charge

-ion *n suffix* **1 :** act or process **2 :** result of an act or process **3 :** state or condition

ion·ize *vb* **ion·ized; ion·iz·ing :** to change into ions

ion·o·sphere *n* **:** the part of the earth's atmosphere beginning at an altitude of about 30 miles (50 kilometers) and extending outward that contains electrically charged particles

io·ta *n* **:** a tiny amount **:** JOT

IOU *n* **:** a written promise to pay a debt

-ious *adj suffix* **:** -OUS

ir- — see IN-

[1]**Iraqi** *n, pl* **Iraqis :** a person born or living in Iraq

[2]**Iraqi** *adj* **:** of or relating to Iraq or its people

iras·ci·ble *adj* **:** easily angered

irate *adj* **:** ANGRY — **irate·ly** *adv* — **irate·ness** *n*

ire *n* **:** [2]ANGER, WRATH

ir·i·des·cence *n* **:** a shifting and constant change of colors producing rainbow effects

ir·i·des·cent *adj* **:** having iridescence — **ir·i·des·cent·ly** *adv*

irid·i·um *n* **:** a hard brittle heavy metallic chemical element

iris *n* **1 :** the colored part around the pupil of an eye **2 :** a plant with long pointed leaves and large usually brightly colored flowers

[1]**Irish** *adj* **:** of or relating to Ireland, its people, or the Irish language

²Irish *n* **1 Irish** *pl* **:** the people of Ireland **2 :** a language of Ireland

irk *vb* **:** to make weary, irritated, or bored

irk·some *adj* **:** causing boredom **:** TIRESOME — **irk·some·ness** *n*

¹iron *n* **1 :** a heavy silvery white metallic chemical element that rusts easily, is strongly attracted by magnets, occurs in meteorites and combined in minerals, and is necessary in biological processes **2 :** something made of iron **3 irons** *pl* **:** handcuffs or chains used to bind or to hinder movement **4 :** a device that is heated and used for pressing cloth

²iron *adj* **1 :** made of or relating to iron **2 :** like iron

³iron *vb* **:** to press with a heated iron — **iron·er** *n*

iron·ic *or* **iron·i·cal** *adj* **:** relating to, containing, or showing irony — **iron·i·cal·ly** *adv*

iron lung *n* **:** an apparatus in which a person whose breathing is damaged (as by polio) can be placed to help the breathing

iron·work *n* **1 :** work in iron **2 ironworks** *pl* **:** a mill where iron or steel is smelted or heavy iron or steel products are made

iro·ny *n, pl* **iro·nies 1 :** the use of words that mean the opposite of what one really intends **2 :** a result opposite to what was expected

ir·ra·di·ate *vb* **ir·ra·di·at·ed; ir·ra·di·at·ing 1 :** to cast rays of light on **2 :** to affect or treat with radiations (as X rays)

ir·ra·di·a·tion *n* **1 :** the giving off of radiant energy (as heat) **2 :** exposure to irradiation (as of X rays)

ir·ra·tio·nal *adj* **1 :** not able to reason **2 :** not based on reason — **ir·ra·tio·nal·ly** *adv*

ir·rec·on·cil·able *adj* **:** impossible to bring into harmony

ir·re·cov·er·able *adj* **:** impossible to recover or set right

ir·re·deem·able *adj* **:** impossible to redeem

ir·re·duc·ible *adj* **:** not possible to reduce

ir·re·fut·able *adj* **:** impossible to refute **:** INDISPUTABLE

ir·reg·u·lar *adj* **1 :** not following custom or rule **2 :** not following the usual manner of inflection **3 :** not even or having the same shape on both sides **4 :** not continuous or coming at set times — **ir·reg·u·lar·ly** *adv*

ir·reg·u·lar·i·ty *n, pl* **ir·reg·u·lar·i·ties 1 :** the quality or state of being irregular **2 :** something irregular

ir·rel·e·vance *n* **1 :** the quality or state of being irrelevant **2 :** something irrelevant

ir·rel·e·vant *adj* **:** not relevant — **ir·rel·e·vant·ly** *adv*

ir·re·li·gious *adj* **:** not having or acting as if one has religious emotions or beliefs

ir·rep·a·ra·ble *adj* **:** impossible to get back or to make right — **ir·rep·a·ra·bly** *adv*

ir·re·place·able *adj* **:** impossible to replace

ir·re·press·ible *adj* **:** impossible to repress or control

ir·re·proach·able *adj* **:** being beyond reproach

ir·re·sist·ible *adj* **:** impossible to resist — **ir·re·sist·ibly** *adv*

ir·res·o·lute *adj* **:** uncertain how to act or proceed — **ir·res·o·lute·ly** *adv*

ir·re·spec·tive of *prep* **:** without regard to

ir·re·spon·si·bil·i·ty *n* **:** the quality or state of being irresponsible

ir·re·spon·si·ble *adj* **:** having or showing little or no sense of responsibility — **ir·re·spon·si·bly** *adv*

ir·re·triev·able *adj* **:** impossible to get back — **ir·re·triev·ably** *adv*

ir·rev·er·ence *n* **1 :** lack of reverence **2 :** something said or done that is irreverent

ir·rev·er·ent *adj* **:** not reverent **:** DISRESPECTFUL — **ir·rev·er·ent·ly** *adv*

ir·re·vers·i·ble *adj* **:** impossible to reverse

ir·rev·o·ca·ble *adj* **:** impossible to take away or undo — **ir·rev·o·ca·bly** *adv*

ir·ri·gate *vb* **ir·ri·gat·ed; ir·ri·gat·ing 1 :** to supply (as land) with water by artificial means **2 :** to flush with a liquid

ir·ri·ga·tion *n* **:** an act or process of irrigating

ir·ri·ta·bil·i·ty *n* **:** the quality or state of being irritable

ir·ri·ta·ble *adj* **:** easily irritated — **ir·ri·ta·bly** *adv*

¹ir·ri·tant *adj* **:** tending to cause irritation

²irritant *n* **:** something that irritates

ir·ri·tate *vb* **ir·ri·tat·ed; ir·ri·tat·ing 1 :** to cause anger or impatience in **:** ANNOY **2 :** to make sensitive or sore

ir·ri·ta·tion *n* **1 :** the act of irritating **:** the state of being irritated **2 :** ²IRRITANT

is *present 3d sing of* BE

-ish *adj suffix* **1 :** of, relating to, or being **2 :** characteristic of **3 :** somewhat **4 :** about

isin·glass *n* **:** mica in thin sheets

Is·lam *n* **:** a religion based on belief in Allah as the only God, in Muhammad as his prophet, and in the Koran — **Is·lam·ic** *adj*

is·land *n* **1 :** an area of land surrounded by water and smaller than a continent **2 :** something suggesting an island in its isolation

is·land·er *n* **:** a person who lives on an island

isle *n* **:** a usually small island

is·let *n* **:** a small island

-ism *n suffix* **1 :** act **:** practice **:** process **2 :** manner of action or behavior like that of a specified person or thing **3 :** state **:** condition **4 :** teachings **:** theory **:** cult **:** system

isn't : is not

iso·bar *n* **:** a line on a map to indicate areas having the same atmospheric pressure

iso·late *vb* **iso·lat·ed; iso·lat·ing :** to place or keep apart from others

iso·la·tion *n* **:** the act of isolating **:** the condition of being isolated

isos·ce·les triangle *n* **:** a triangle having two sides of equal length

ISP *n* **:** a company that provides access to the Internet for a fee **:** Internet service provider

[1]**Is·rae·li** *adj* **:** of or relating to the Republic of Israel or the Israelis

[2]**Israeli** *n* **:** a person born or living in the Republic of Israel

Is·ra·el·ite *n* **:** a member of the Hebrew people having Jacob as an ancestor

is·su·ance *n* **:** the act of issuing

[1]**is·sue** *n* **1 :** the action of going, coming, or flowing out **2 :** OFFSPRING, PROGENY **3 :** what finally happens **:** RESULT **4 :** something that is disputed **5 :** a giving off (as of blood) from the body **6 :** the act of bringing out, offering, or making available **7 :** the thing or the whole quantity of things given out at one time

[2]**issue** *vb* **is·sued; is·su·ing 1 :** to go, come, or flow out **2 :** [1]RESULT 1 **3 :** to distribute officially **4 :** to send out for sale or circulation

-ist *n suffix* **1 :** performer of a specified action **:** maker **:** producer **2 :** one who plays a specified musical instrument or operates a specified mechanical device **3 :** one who specializes in a specified art or science or skill **4 :** one who follows or favors a specified teaching, practice, system, or code of behavior

isth·mus *n* **:** a neck of land separating two bodies of water and connecting two larger areas of land

[1]**it** *pron* **1 :** the thing, act, or matter about which these words are spoken or written **2 :** the whole situation **3** — used with little meaning of its own in certain kinds of sentences

[2]**it** *n* **:** the player who has to do something special in a children's game

[1]**Ital·ian** *n* **1 :** a person born or living in Italy **2 :** the language of the Italians

[2]**Italian** *adj* **:** of or relating to Italy, its people, or the Italian language

[1]**ital·ic** *adj* **:** of or relating to a type style with letters that slant to the right (as in *"these characters are italic"*)

[2]**italic** *n* **:** an italic letter or italic type

ital·i·cize *vb* **ital·i·cized; ital·i·ciz·ing 1 :** to print in italics **2 :** UNDERLINE 1

[1]**itch** *vb* **:** to have or cause an itch

[2]**itch** *n* **1 :** an uneasy irritating sensation in the skin **2 :** a skin disorder in which an itch is present **3 :** a restless usually constant desire

itchy *adj* **itch·i·er; itch·i·est :** that itches

it'd : it had **:** it would

-ite *n suffix* **1 :** native **:** resident **2 :** descendant **3 :** adherent **:** follower

item *n* **1 :** a single thing in a list, account, or series **2 :** a brief piece of news

item·ize *vb* **item·ized; item·iz·ing :** to set down one by one **:** LIST

[1]**itin·er·ant** *adj* **:** traveling from place to place

[2]**itinerant** *n* **:** a person who travels about

-itis *n suffix* **:** inflammation of

it'll : it shall **:** it will

its *adj* **:** of or relating to it or itself

it's 1 : it is **2 :** it has

it·self *pron* **:** its own self

-ity *n suffix, pl* **-ities :** quality **:** state **:** degree

I've : I have

-ive *adj suffix* **:** that does or tends to do a specified action

ivo·ry *n, pl* **ivo·ries 1 :** the hard creamy-white material of which the tusks of a tusked mammal (as an elephant) are made **2 :** a very pale yellow

ivy *n, pl* **ivies 1 :** a woody vine with evergreen leaves, small yellowish flowers, and black berries often found growing on buildings **2 :** a plant like ivy

-i·za·tion *n suffix* **:** action **:** process **:** state

-ize *vb suffix* **-ized; -iz·ing 1 :** cause to be or be like **:** form or cause to be formed into **2 :** cause to experience a specified action **3 :** saturate, treat, or combine with **4 :** treat like **5 :** engage in a specified activity

J

j *n, pl* **j's** *or* **js** *often cap* **:** the tenth letter of the English alphabet

[1]**jab** *vb* **jabbed; jab·bing :** to poke quickly or suddenly with or as if with something sharp

[2]**jab** *n* **:** a quick or sudden poke

[1]**jab·ber** *vb* **:** to talk too fast or not clearly enough to be understood

[2]**jabber** *n* **:** confused talk **:** GIBBERISH

[1]**jack** *n* **1 :** a playing card marked with the figure of a man **2 :** a device for lifting something heavy a short distance **3 :** JACKASS 1 **4 :** a small six-pointed usually metal object used in a children's game (**jacks**) **5 :** a small national flag flown by a ship **6 :** a socket used with a plug to connect one electric circuit with another

[2]**jack** *vb* **:** to move or lift by or as if by a jack

jack·al *n* **:** any of several Old World wild dogs like but smaller than wolves

jack·ass *n* **1 :** a male donkey **2 :** DONKEY 1 **3 :** a stupid person

jack·daw *n* **:** a European bird somewhat like a crow

jack·et *n* **1 :** a short coat or coatlike garment **2 :** an outer cover or casing

Jack Frost *n* **:** frost or frosty weather thought of as a person

jack–in–the–box *n, pl* **jack–in–the–box·es** *or* **jacks–in–the–box :** a small box out of which a comical toy figure springs when the lid is raised

jack–in–the–pul·pit *n, pl* **jack–in–the–pul·pits** *or* **jacks–in–the–pul·pit :** a plant that grows in moist shady woods and has a stalk of tiny yellowish flowers protected by a leaf bent over like a hood

[1]**jack·knife** *n, pl* **jack·knives :** a knife with folding blade or blades that can be carried in one's pocket

[2]**jackknife** *vb* **jack·knifed; jack·knif·ing :** to double up like a jackknife

jack–of–all–trades *n, pl* **jacks–of–all–trades :** a person who can do several kinds of work fairly well

jack–o'–lan·tern *n* **:** a lantern made of a pumpkin cut to look like a human face

jack·pot *n* **:** a large and often unexpected success or reward

jack·rab·bit *n* **:** a large North American hare with very long ears and long hind legs

jade *n* **:** a usually green mineral used for jewelry and carvings

jag·ged *adj* **:** having a sharply uneven edge or surface — **jag·ged·ly** *adv*

jag·uar *n* **:** a large yellowish brown black-spotted animal of the cat family found from Texas to Paraguay

[1]**jail** *n* **:** PRISON

[2]**jail** *vb* **:** to shut up in or as if in a prison

jail·bird *n* **:** a person who is or has been locked up in prison

jail·break *n* **:** escape from prison by the use of force

jail·er *or* **jail·or** *n* **:** a keeper of a prison

ja·lopy *n, pl* **ja·lop·ies :** a worn shabby old automobile or airplane

[1]**jam** *vb* **jammed; jam·ming 1 :** to crowd, squeeze, or wedge into a tight position **2 :** to put into action hard or suddenly **3 :** to hurt by pressure **4 :** to be or cause to be stuck or unable to work because a part is wedged tight **5 :** to cause interference in (radio or television signals)

[2]**jam** *n* **1 :** a crowded mass of people or things that blocks something **2 :** a difficult state of affairs

[3]**jam** *n* **:** a food made by boiling fruit with sugar until it is thick

jamb *n* **:** a vertical piece forming the side of an opening (as for a doorway)

jam·bo·ree *n* **1 :** a large jolly get-together **2 :** a national or international camping assembly of Boy Scouts

[1]**jan·gle** *vb* **jan·gled; jan·gling :** to make or cause to make a harsh sound

[2]**jangle** *n* **:** a harsh often ringing sound

jan·i·tor *n* **:** a person who takes care of a building (as a school)

Jan·u·ary *n* **:** the first month of the year

[1]**Jap·a·nese** *adj* **:** of or relating to Japan, its people, or the Japanese language

[2]**Japanese** *n, pl* **Japanese 1 :** a person born or living in Japan **2 :** the language of the Japanese

Japanese beetle *n* **:** a small glossy green or brown Asian beetle now found in the United States that as a grub feeds on roots and as an adult eats leaves and fruits

[1]**jar** *vb* **jarred; jar·ring 1 :** to make a harsh unpleasant sound **2 :** to have a disagreeable effect **3 :** to shake or cause to shake hard

[2]**jar** *n* **1 :** a harsh sound **2 :** [2]JOLT 1 **3 :** [2]SHOCK 3

[3]**jar** *n* **:** a usually glass or pottery container with a wide mouth

jar·gon *n* **1 :** the special vocabulary of an activity or group **2 :** language that is not clear and is full of long words

jas·mine *n* **:** any of various mostly climbing plants of warm regions with fragrant flowers

jas·per *n* **:** an opaque usually red, green, brown, or yellow stone used for making ornamental objects (as vases)

[1]**jaunt** *vb* **:** to make a short trip for pleasure

[2]**jaunt** *n* **:** a short pleasure trip

jaun·ty *adj* **jaun·ti·er; jaun·ti·est :** lively in manner or appearance — **jaun·ti·ly** *adv* — **jaun·ti·ness** *n*

Ja·va man *n* **:** a small-brained prehistoric human known from skulls found in Java

jav·e·lin *n* **1 :** a light spear **2 :** a slender rod thrown for distance in a track-and-field contest (**javelin throw**)

jaw *n* **1 :** either of the bony structures that support the soft parts of the mouth and usually bear teeth on their edge **2 :** a part of an invertebrate animal (as an insect) that resembles or does the work of a jaw **3 :** one of a pair of moving parts that open and close for holding or crushing something

jaw·bone *n* **:** JAW 1

jay *n* **:** a noisy bird related to the crow but with brighter colors

jay·walk *vb* **:** to cross a street in a place or in a way that is against traffic regulations — **jay·walk·er** *n*

jazz *n* **:** lively American music that developed from ragtime

jeal·ous *adj* **1 :** demanding complete faithfulness **2 :** feeling a mean resentment toward someone more successful than oneself **3 :** CAREFUL 1, WATCHFUL — **jeal·ous·ly** *adv*

jeal·ou·sy *n, pl* **jeal·ou·sies :** a jealous attitude or feeling

jeans *n pl* **:** pants made of a heavy cotton cloth

jeep *n* **:** a small motor vehicle used by the United States Army during World War II

[1]jeer *vb* **1 :** to speak or cry out in scorn **2 :** to scorn or mock with jeers

[2]jeer *n* **:** a scornful remark or sound **:** TAUNT

Je·ho·vah *n* **:** GOD 1

jell *vb* **1 :** to become as firm as jelly **:** SET **2 :** to take shape

[1]jel·ly *n, pl* **jellies :** a soft springy food made from fruit juice boiled with sugar, from meat juices, or from gelatin — **jel·ly·like** *adj*

[2]jelly *vb* **jel·lied; jel·ly·ing 1 :** JELL 1 **2 :** to make jelly

jelly bean *n* **:** a chewy bean-shaped candy

jel·ly·fish *n* **:** a free-swimming sea animal related to the corals that has a jellylike body shaped like a saucer

jen·net *n* **:** a female donkey

jeop·ar·dize *vb* **jeop·ar·dized; jeop·ar·diz·ing :** to expose to danger

jeop·ar·dy *n* **:** DANGER 1

[1]jerk *n* **1 :** a short quick pull or jolt **2 :** a foolish person

[2]jerk *vb* **1 :** to give a quick sharp pull or twist to **2 :** to move with jerks

jer·kin *n* **:** a close-fitting sleeveless jacket that extends to or just over the hips

jerky *adj* **jerk·i·er; jerk·i·est :** moving with sudden starts and stops — **jerk·i·ly** *adv* — **jerk·i·ness** *n*

jer·sey *n, pl* **jerseys 1 :** a knitted cloth (as of wool or cotton) used mostly for clothing **2 :** a close-fitting knitted garment (as a shirt)

[1]jest *n* **1 :** a comic act or remark **:** JOKE **2 :** a playful mood or manner

[2]jest *vb* **:** to make jests **:** JOKE

jest·er *n* **1 :** a person formerly kept in royal courts to amuse people **2 :** a person who often jests

Je·sus *n* **:** the founder of the Christian religion

[1]jet *n* **1 :** a black mineral that is often used for jewelry **2 :** a very dark black

[2]jet *vb* **jet·ted; jet·ting :** [1]SPURT 1

[3]jet *n* **1 :** a rush of liquid, gas, or vapor through a narrow opening or a nozzle **2 :** a nozzle for a jet of gas or liquid **3 :** JET ENGINE **4 :** JET AIRPLANE

jet airplane *n* **:** an airplane powered by a jet engine

jet engine *n* **:** an engine in which fuel burns to produce a jet of heated air and gases that shoot out from the rear and drive the engine forward

jet plane *n* **:** JET AIRPLANE

jet–pro·pelled *adj* **:** driven forward or onward by a jet engine

jet·sam *n* **:** goods thrown overboard to lighten a ship in danger of sinking

jet stream *n* **:** high-speed winds blowing from a westerly direction several kilometers above the earth's surface

jet·ti·son *vb* **:** to throw out especially from a ship or an airplane

jet·ty *n, pl* **jetties 1 :** a pier built to change the path of the current or tide or to protect a harbor **2 :** a landing wharf

Jew *n* **:** a person who is a descendant of the ancient Hebrews or whose religion is Judaism

jew·el *n* **1 :** an ornament of precious metal often set with precious stones and worn on the person **2 :** a person who is greatly admired **3 :** GEM **4 :** a bearing in a watch made of crystal or a precious stone

jew·el·er *or* **jew·el·ler** *n* **:** a person who makes or deals in jewelry and related articles (as silverware)

jew·el·ry *n* **:** ornamental pieces (as rings or necklaces) worn on the person

Jew·ish *adj* **:** of or relating to Jews or Judaism

Jew's harp *or* **Jews' harp** *n* **:** a small musical instrument that is held in the mouth and struck with the finger to give off a tone

jib *n* **:** a three-cornered sail extending forward from the foremast

[1]jibe *variant of* GIBE

[2]jibe *vb* **jibed; jib·ing 1 :** to shift suddenly from side to side **2 :** to change the course of a boat so that the sail jibes

[3]jibe *vb* **jibed; jib·ing :** to be in agreement

jif·fy *n, pl* **jiffies :** MOMENT 1

[1]jig *n* **:** a lively dance

[2]jig *vb* **jigged; jig·ging :** to dance a jig

[1]jig·gle *vb* **jig·gled; jig·gling :** to move or cause to move with quick little jerks

[2]jiggle *n* **:** a quick little jerk

jig·saw *n* **:** a machine saw used to cut curved and irregular lines or openwork patterns

jigsaw puzzle *n* **:** a puzzle made by cutting a picture into small pieces that must be fitted together again

jim·son·weed *n* **:** a coarse poisonous weedy plant related to the potato that is sometimes grown for its showy white or purple flowers

[1]jin·gle *vb* **jin·gled; jin·gling :** to make or cause to make a light clinking sound

[2]jingle *n* **1 :** a light clinking sound **2 :** a short verse or song that repeats bits in a catchy way — **jin·gly** *adj*

jinx *n* **:** a bringer of bad luck
jit·ters *n pl* **:** extreme nervousness
jit·tery *adj* **:** very nervous
job *n* **1 :** a piece of work usually done on order at an agreed rate **2 :** something produced by or as if by work **3 :** a regular paying employment **4 :** a special duty or function — **job·less** *adj*
jock·ey *n, pl* **jockeys 1 :** a professional rider in a horse race **2 :** OPERATOR 1
[1]**jog** *vb* **jogged; jog·ging 1 :** to give a slight shake or push to **:** NUDGE **2 :** to rouse to alertness **3 :** to move or cause to move at a jog **4 :** to run slowly (as for exercise) — **jog·ger** *n*
[2]**jog** *n* **1 :** a slight shake or push **2 :** a slow jolting gait (as of a horse) **3 :** a slow run
[3]**jog** *n* **:** a short change in direction
jog·gle *vb* **jog·gled; jog·gling :** to shake or cause to shake slightly
john·ny·cake *n* **:** a bread made of cornmeal, water or milk, and leavening with or without flour, shortening, and eggs
join *vb* **1 :** to come, bring, or fasten together **2 :** ADJOIN **3 :** to come or bring into close association **4 :** to come into the company of **5 :** to become a member of **6 :** to take part in a group activity **7 :** to combine the elements of
[1]**joint** *n* **1 :** a part of the skeleton where two pieces come together usually in a way that allows motion **2 :** a part of a plant stem where a leaf or branch develops **:** NODE **3 :** a place where two things or parts are joined — **joint·ed** *adj*
[2]**joint** *adj* **1 :** joined together **2 :** done by or shared by two or more — **joint·ly** *adv*
joist *n* **:** any of the small timbers or metal beams laid crosswise in a building to support a floor or ceiling
[1]**joke** *n* **1 :** something said or done to cause laughter or amusement **2 :** a very short story with a funny ending that is a surprise **3 :** something not worthy of being taken seriously
[2]**joke** *vb* **joked; jok·ing 1 :** to say or do something as a joke **2 :** to make jokes
jok·er *n* **1 :** a person who jokes **2 :** an extra card used in some card games
jok·ing·ly *adv* **:** in a joking manner
jol·li·ty *n* **:** the state of being jolly
[1]**jol·ly** *adj* **jol·li·er; jol·li·est :** full of fun or high spirits
[2]**jolly** *adv* **:** [2]VERY 1
[1]**jolt** *vb* **1 :** to move or cause to move with a sudden jerky motion **2 :** to cause to be upset
[2]**jolt** *n* **1 :** an abrupt jerky blow or movement **2 :** a sudden shock or disappointment
jon·quil *n* **:** a plant related to the daffodil but with fragrant yellow or white flowers with a short central tube
josh *vb* **1 :** [2]KID 1 **2 :** [2]JOKE
jos·tle *vb* **jos·tled; jos·tling :** to knock against so as to jar **:** push roughly
[1]**jot** *n* **:** the least bit
[2]**jot** *vb* **jot·ted; jot·ting :** to write briefly or in a hurry **:** make a note of
jounce *vb* **jounced; jounc·ing :** to move, fall, or bounce so as to shake
jour·nal *n* **1 :** a brief record (as in a diary) of daily happenings **2 :** a daily record (as of business dealings) **3 :** a daily newspaper **4 :** a magazine that reports on things of special interest to a particular group
jour·nal·ism *n* **1 :** the business of collecting and editing news (as for newspapers, radio, or television) **2 :** writing of general or popular interest
jour·nal·ist *n* **:** an editor or reporter of the news
[1]**jour·ney** *n, pl* **jour·neys :** a traveling from one place to another
[2]**journey** *vb* **jour·neyed; jour·ney·ing :** to go on a journey **:** TRAVEL — **jour·ney·er** *n*
jour·ney·man *n, pl* **jour·ney·men :** a worker who has learned a trade and usually works for another person by the day
[1]**joust** *vb* **:** to take part in a joust **:** TILT
[2]**joust** *n* **:** a combat on horseback between two knights with lances
jo·vial *adj* **:** [1]JOLLY — **jo·vial·ly** *adv*
[1]**jowl** *n* **:** loose flesh (as a double chin) hanging from the lower jaw and throat
[2]**jowl** *n* **1 :** an animal's jaw and especially the lower jaw **2 :** CHEEK 1
joy *n* **1 :** a feeling of pleasure or happiness that comes from success, good fortune, or a sense of well-being **2 :** something that gives pleasure or happiness
joy·ful *adj* **:** feeling, causing, or showing joy — **joy·ful·ly** *adv* — **joy·ful·ness** *n*
joy·ous *adj* **:** JOYFUL — **joy·ous·ly** *adv* — **joy·ous·ness** *n*
joy·stick *n* **:** a control lever (as for a computer display or an airplane) capable of motion in two or more directions
ju·bi·lant *adj* **:** expressing great joy especially with shouting **:** noisily happy
ju·bi·lee *n* **1 :** a fiftieth anniversary **2 :** time of celebration
Ju·da·ism *n* **:** a religion developed among the ancient Hebrews that stresses belief in one God and faithfulness to the moral laws of the Old Testament
[1]**judge** *vb* **judged; judg·ing 1 :** to form an opinion after careful consideration **2 :** to act as a judge (as in a trial) **3 :** THINK 2
[2]**judge** *n* **1 :** a public official whose duty is to decide questions brought before a court **2 :** a

person appointed to decide in a contest or competition **3 :** a person with the experience to give a meaningful opinion **:** CRITIC

judg·ment *or* **judge·ment** *n* **1 :** a decision or opinion (as of a court) given after judging **2 :** an opinion or estimate formed by examining and comparing **3 :** the ability for judging

ju·di·cial *adj* **:** of or relating to the providing of justice — **ju·di·cial·ly** *adv*

ju·di·cious *adj* **:** having, using, or showing good judgment **:** WISE — **ju·di·cious·ly** *adv* — **ju·di·cious·ness** *n*

ju·do *n* **:** a Japanese form of wrestling in which each person tries to throw or pin the opponent

jug *n* **:** a large deep usually earthenware or glass container with a narrow mouth and a handle

jug·gle *vb* **jug·gled; jug·gling 1 :** to keep several things moving in the air at the same time **2 :** to mix things up in order to deceive **3 :** to hold or balance insecurely — **jug·gler** *n*

juice *n* **1 :** the liquid part that can be squeezed out of vegetables and fruit **2 :** the fluid part of meat

juicy *adj* **juic·i·er; juic·i·est :** having much juice — **juic·i·ness** *n*

Ju·ly *n* **:** the seventh month of the year

¹jum·ble *vb* **jum·bled; jum·bling :** to mix in a confused mass

²jumble *n* **:** a disorderly mass or pile

jum·bo *n, pl* **jumbos :** something very large of its kind

¹jump *vb* **1 :** to spring into the air **:** LEAP **2 :** to make a sudden movement **:** START **3 :** to have or cause a sudden sharp increase **4 :** to make a hasty judgement **5 :** to make a sudden attack **6 :** to pass over or cause to pass over with or as if with a leap — **jump the gun 1 :** to start in a race before the starting signal **2 :** to do something before the proper time

²jump *n* **1 :** an act or instance of jumping **:** LEAP **2 :** a sudden involuntary movement **:** START **3 :** a sharp sudden increase **4 :** an initial advantage

jum·per *n* **1 :** a loose blouse or jacket often worn by workmen **2 :** a sleeveless dress worn usually with a blouse

jumpy *adj* **jump·i·er; jump·i·est :** NERVOUS 3

jun·co *n, pl* **juncos** *or* **juncoes :** a small mostly gray American finch usually having a pink bill

junc·tion *n* **1 :** an act of joining **2 :** a place or point of meeting

June *n* **:** the sixth month of the year

jun·gle *n* **1 :** a thick or tangled growth of plants **2 :** a large area of land usually in a tropical region covered with a thick tangled growth of plants

¹ju·nior *adj* **1 :** being younger — used to distinguish a son from a father with the same name **2 :** lower in rank **3 :** of or relating to juniors

²junior *n* **1 :** a person who is younger or lower in rank than another **2 :** a student in the next-to-last year (as at high school)

ju·ni·per *n* **:** any of various evergreen trees and shrubs related to the pines but having tiny berrylike cones

¹junk *n* **1 :** old iron, glass, paper, or waste **:** RUBBISH **2 :** a poorly made product

²junk *vb* **:** to get rid of as worthless **:** SCRAP

³junk *n* **:** a sailing ship of Chinese waters

junk food *n* **:** food that is high in calories but low in nutritional content

Ju·pi·ter *n* **:** the planet that is fifth in order of distance from the sun and is the largest of the planets with a diameter of about 140,000 kilometers

ju·ror *n* **:** a member of a jury

ju·ry *n, pl* **juries 1 :** a body of persons sworn to seek for and try to learn the truth about a matter put before them for decision **2 :** a committee that judges and awards prizes (as at an exhibition)

¹just *adj* **1 :** having a foundation in fact or reason **:** REASONABLE **2 :** agreeing with a standard of correctness **3 :** morally right or good **4 :** legally right — **just·ly** *adv*

²just *adv* **1 :** exactly as wanted **2 :** very recently **3 :** by a very small amount **4 :** by a very short distance **5 :** nothing more than **6 :** ²VERY 2

jus·tice *n* **1 :** just or right action or treatment **2 :** ²JUDGE 1 **3 :** the carrying out of law **4 :** the quality of being fair or just

jus·ti·fi·able *adj* **:** possible to justify — **jus·ti·fi·ably** *adv*

jus·ti·fi·ca·tion *n* **1 :** the act or an instance of justifying **2 :** something that justifies

jus·ti·fy *vb* **jus·ti·fied; jus·ti·fy·ing :** to prove or show to be just, right, or reasonable

jut *vb* **jut·ted; jut·ting :** to extend or cause to extend above or beyond a surrounding area

jute *n* **:** a strong glossy fiber from a tropical plant used chiefly for making sacks and twine

¹ju·ve·nile *adj* **1 :** incompletely developed **:** IMMATURE **2 :** of, relating to, or characteristic of children or young people

²juvenile *n* **:** a young person **:** YOUTH

K

k *n, pl* **k's** *or* **ks** *often cap* **1 :** the eleventh letter of the English alphabet **2 :** THOUSAND **3 :** KILOBYTE

kale *n* **:** a hardy cabbage with wrinkled leaves that do not form a head

ka·lei·do·scope *n* **1 :** a tube containing bits of colored glass or plastic and two mirrors at one end that shows many different patterns as it is turned **2 :** a changing pattern or scene

kan·ga·roo *n, pl* **kan·ga·roos :** any of numerous leaping mammals of Australia and nearby islands that feed on plants and have long powerful hind legs, a thick tail used as a support in standing or walking, and in the female a pouch on the abdomen in which the young are carried

ka·o·lin *n* **:** a very pure white clay used in making porcelain

kar·a·o·ke *n* **:** a device that plays music to which the user sings along and that records the user's singing with the music

kar·at *n* **:** a unit of fineness for gold

ka·ra·te *n* **:** an Oriental art of self-defense in which an attacker is defeated by kicks and punches

ka·ty·did *n* **:** any of several large green American grasshoppers with males that make shrill noises

kay·ak *n* **1 :** an Eskimo canoe made of a frame covered with skins except for a small opening in the center **2 :** a boat styled like an Eskimo kayak

ka·zoo *n, pl* **ka·zoos :** a toy musical instrument containing a membrane which produces a buzzing tone when one hums into the mouth hole

KB *n* **:** KILOBYTE

[1]**keel** *n* **:** a timber or plate running lengthwise along the center of the bottom of a ship and usually sticking out from the bottom

[2]**keel** *vb* **:** to turn over

keel over *vb* **:** to fall suddenly (as in a faint)

keen *adj* **1 :** having a fine edge or point **:** SHARP **2 :** seeming to cut or sting **3 :** full of enthusiasm **:** EAGER **4 :** having or showing mental sharpness **5 :** very sensitive (as in seeing or hearing) — **keen·ly** *adv* — **keen·ness** *n*

[1]**keep** *vb* **kept; keep·ing 1 :** to be faithful to **:** FULFILL **2 :** to act properly in relation to **3 :** PROTECT **4 :** to take care of **:** TEND **5 :** to continue doing something **6 :** to have in one's service or at one's disposal **7 :** to preserve a record in **8 :** to have on hand regularly for sale **9 :** to continue to have in one's possession or power **10 :** to prevent from leaving **:** DETAIN **11 :** to hold back **12 :** to remain or cause to remain in a given place, situation, or condition **13 :** to continue in an unspoiled condition **14 :** [1]REFRAIN

[2]**keep** *n* **1 :** the strongest part of a castle in the Middle Ages **2 :** the necessities of life — **for keeps 1 :** with the understanding that one may keep what is won **2 :** for a long time **:** PERMANENTLY

keep·er *n* **:** a person who watches, guards, or takes care of something

keep·ing *n* **1 :** watchful attention **:** CARE **2 :** a proper or fitting relationship **:** HARMONY

keep·sake *n* **:** something kept or given to be kept in memory of a person, place, or happening

keep up *vb* **1 :** MAINTAIN 1 **2 :** to stay well informed about something **3 :** to continue without interruption **4 :** to stay even with others (as in a race)

keg *n* **1 :** a small barrel holding about 114 liters **2 :** the contents of a keg

kelp *n* **:** a large coarse brown seaweed

ken *n* **1 :** range of vision **:** SIGHT **2 :** range of understanding

ken·nel *n* **1 :** a shelter for a dog **2 :** a place where dogs are bred or housed

kept *past of* KEEP

ker·chief *n, pl* **kerchiefs 1 :** a square of cloth worn as a head covering or as a scarf **2 :** HANDKERCHIEF

ker·nel *n* **1 :** the inner softer part of a seed, fruit stone, or nut **2 :** the whole grain or seed of a cereal

ker·o·sene *or* **ker·o·sine** *n* **:** a thin oil obtained from petroleum and used as a fuel and solvent

ketch *n* **:** a fore-and-aft rigged ship with two masts

ketch·up *n* **:** a thick seasoned sauce usually made from tomatoes

ket·tle *n* **1 :** a pot for boiling liquids **2 :** TEAKETTLE

ket·tle·drum *n* **:** a large brass or copper drum that has a rounded bottom and can be varied in pitch

[1]**key** *n* **1 :** an instrument by which the bolt of a lock (as on a door) is turned **2 :** a device having the form or function of a key **3 :** a means of gaining or preventing entrance, possession, or control **4 :** something (as a map legend) that gives an explanation **:** SOLUTION **5 :** one of the levers with a flat surface that is pressed with a finger to activate a mechanism of a machine or instrument **6 :** a system of seven musical tones arranged in

relation to a keynote from which the system is named **7 :** a characteristic way (as of thought) **8 :** a small switch for opening or closing an electric circuit

²key *vb* **keyed; key·ing 1 :** to regulate the musical pitch of **2 :** to bring into harmony

³key *adj* **:** of great importance **:** most important

⁴key *n* **:** a low island or reef

key·board *n* **1 :** a row of keys by which a musical instrument (as a piano) is played **2 :** a portable electronic musical instrument with a keyboard like that of a piano **3 :** the whole arrangement of keys (as on a typewriter or computer)

key·hole *n* **:** a hole for receiving a key

key·note *n* **1 :** the first and harmonically fundamental tone of a scale **2 :** the fundamental fact, idea, or mood

key·stone *n* **1 :** the wedge-shaped piece at the top of an arch that locks the other pieces in place **2 :** something on which other things depend for support

key up *vb* **:** to make nervous or tense

kha·ki *n* **1 :** a light yellowish brown **2 :** a light yellowish brown cloth used especially for military uniforms

khan *n* **1 :** a Mongolian leader **2 :** a local chieftain or man of rank in some countries of central Asia

ki·bitz·er *n* **:** a person who looks on and often offers unwanted advice

¹kick *vb* **1 :** to strike out or hit with the foot **2 :** to object strongly **:** PROTEST **3 :** to spring back when fired

²kick *n* **1 :** a blow with the foot **2 :** a sudden moving (as of a ball) with the foot **3 :** the sudden move backward of a gun when fired **4 :** a feeling of or cause for objection **5 :** a feeling or source of pleasure

kick·ball *n* **:** a form of baseball played with a large rubber ball that is kicked instead of hit with a bat

kick·off *n* **:** a kick that puts the ball into play (as in football or soccer)

kick off *vb* **1 :** to make a kickoff **2 :** BEGIN 1

kick·stand*n***:** a metal bar or rod attached to a two-wheeled vehicle (as a bicycle) and used to prop the vehicle up when it is not in use

¹kid *n* **1 :** the young of a goat or a related animal **2 :** the flesh, fur, or skin of a kid or something (as leather) made from one of these **3 :** CHILD — **kid·dish** *adj*

²kid *vb* **kid·ded; kid·ding 1 :** to deceive or trick as a joke **2 :** ¹TEASE — **kid·der** *n*

kid·nap *vb* **kid·napped** *or* **kid·naped; kid·nap·ping** *or* **kid·nap·ing :** to carry away a person by force or by fraud and against his or her will — **kid·nap·per** *or* **kid·nap·er** *n*

kid·ney *n, pl* **kid·neys :** either of a pair of organs near the backbone that give off waste from the body in the form of urine

kidney bean *n* **:** a common garden bean and especially one having large dark red seeds

¹kill *vb* **1 :** to end the life of **:** SLAY **2 :** to put an end to **3 :** to use up **4 :** ¹DEFEAT 1

²kill *n* **1 :** an act of killing **2 :** an animal killed

kill·deer *n* **:** a grayish brown North American plover that has a shrill mournful call

¹kill·er *n* **:** one that kills

²killer *adj* **1 :** very impressive or effective **2 :** very difficult **3 :** causing death or ruin

kill·joy *n* **:** a person who spoils the pleasure of others

kiln *n* **:** a furnace or oven in which something (as pottery) is hardened, burned, or dried

ki·lo *n, pl* **kilos :** KILOGRAM

kilo- *prefix* **:** thousand

ki·lo·byte *n* **:** a unit of computer information storage equal to 1024 bytes

ki·lo·gram *n* **:** a metric unit of weight equal to 1000 grams

ki·lo·me·ter *n* **:** a metric unit of length equal to 1000 meters

kilo·watt *n* **:** a unit of electrical power equal to 1000 watts

kilt *n* **:** a knee-length pleated skirt usually of tartan worn by men in Scotland

kil·ter *n* **:** proper condition

ki·mo·no *n, pl* **ki·mo·nos 1 :** a loose robe with wide sleeves that is traditionally worn with a broad sash as an outer garment by the Japanese **2 :** a loose dressing gown worn chiefly by women

kin *n* **1 :** a person's relatives **2 :** KINSMAN

-kin *also* **-kins** *n suffix* **:** little

¹kind *n* **:** a group of persons or things that can be recognized as belonging together or having something in common

²kind *adj* **1 :** wanting or liking to do good and to bring happiness to others **:** CONSIDERATE **2 :** showing or growing out of gentleness or goodness of heart

kin·der·gar·ten *n* **:** a school or a class for very young children

kind·heart·ed *adj* **:** having or showing a kind and sympathetic nature — **kind·heart·ed·ly** *adv* — **kind·heart·ed·ness** *n*

kin·dle *vb* **kin·dled; kin·dling 1 :** to set on fire **:** LIGHT **2 :** to stir up **:** EXCITE

kin·dling *n* **:** material that burns easily and is used for starting a fire

¹kind·ly *adj* **kind·li·er; kind·li·est 1 :** pleasant or wholesome in nature **2 :** sympathetic or generous in nature — **kind·li·ness** *n*

²kindly *adv* **1 :** in a willing manner **2 :** in a kind manner **3 :** in an appreciative manner **4 :** in an obliging manner

kind·ness *n* **1 :** a kind deed **:** FAVOR **2 :** the quality or state of being kind

kind of *adv* : to a moderate degree : SOMEWHAT

[1]**kin·dred** *n* **1 :** a group of related individuals **2 :** a person's relatives

[2]**kindred** *adj* **:** alike in nature or character

kin·folk *n* : [1]KINDRED 2

king *n* **1 :** a male ruler of a country who usually inherits his position and rules for life **2 :** a chief among competitors **3 :** the chief piece in the game of chess **4 :** a playing card bearing the figure of a king **5 :** a piece in checkers that has reached the opponent's back row — **king·ly** *adj*

king·dom *n* **1 :** a country whose ruler is a king or queen **2 :** one of the three basic divisions (**animal kingdom**, **plant kingdom**, **mineral kingdom**) into which natural objects are commonly grouped **3 :** a major category in scientific biological classification that ranks above the phylum and division and is the highest and broadest group

king·fish·er *n* **:** any of a group of usually crested birds with a short tail, long sharp bill, and bright feathers

king·let *n* **:** a small bird resembling a warbler

king–size *or* **king–sized** *adj* **:** unusually large

[1]**kink** *n* **1 :** a short tight twist or curl (as in a thread or rope) **2 :** [1]CRAMP 1 **3 :** an imperfection that makes something hard to use or work — **kinky** *adj*

[2]**kink** *vb* **:** to form or cause to form a kink in

-kins — see -KIN

kin·ship *n* **:** the quality or state of being kin

kins·man *n, pl* **kins·men :** a relative usually by birth

kins·wom·an *n, pl* **kins·wom·en :** a woman who is a relative usually by birth

[1]**kiss** *vb* **1 :** to touch with the lips as a mark of love or greeting **2 :** to touch gently or lightly

[2]**kiss** *n* **1 :** a loving touch with the lips **2 :** a gentle touch or contact **3 :** a bite-size candy often wrapped in paper or foil

kit *n* **1 :** a set of articles for personal use **2 :** a set of tools or supplies **3 :** a set of parts to be put together **4 :** a container (as a bag or case) for a kit

kitch·en *n* **:** a room in which cooking is done

kitch·en·ette *n* **:** a small kitchen

kitchen garden *n* **:** a piece of land where vegetables are grown for household use

kite *n* **1 :** a hawk with long narrow wings and deeply forked tail that feeds mostly on insects and small reptiles **2 :** a light covered frame for flying in the air at the end of a long string

kith *n* **:** familiar friends and neighbors or relatives

kit·ten *n* **:** a young cat — **kit·ten·ish** *adj*

kit·ty *n, pl* **kitties :** CAT, KITTEN

ki·wi *n* **1:** a grayish-brown bird of New Zealand that is unable to fly **2:** KIWIFRUIT

ki·wi·fruit *n* **:** the fruit of a Chinese vine having a fuzzy brown skin and slightly tart green flesh

klutz *n* **:** a clumsy person

knack *n* **1 :** a clever or skillful way of doing something **:** TRICK **2 :** a natural ability **:** TALENT

knap·sack *n* **:** a carrying case or pouch slung from the shoulders over the back

knave *n* **1 :** RASCAL 1 **2 :** [1]JACK 1

knead *vb* **1 :** to work and press into a mass with or as if with the hands **2 :** [2]MASSAGE — **knead·er** *n*

knee *n* **1 :** the joint or region in which the thigh and lower leg come together **2 :** something resembling a knee **3 :** the part of a garment covering the knee

knee·cap *n* **:** a thick flat movable bone forming the front part of the knee

kneel *vb* **knelt** *or* **kneeled; kneel·ing :** to bend the knee **:** support oneself on one's knees

[1]**knell** *vb* **1 :** to ring slowly and solemnly **:** TOLL **2 :** to summon, announce, or warn by a knell

[2]**knell** *n* **1 :** a stroke or sound of a bell especially when rung slowly for a death, funeral, or disaster **2 :** an indication (as a sound) of the end or failure of something

knew *past of* KNOW

knick·ers *n pl* **:** loose-fitting short pants gathered at the knee

knick·knack *n* **:** a small ornamental object

[1]**knife** *n, pl* **knives 1 :** a cutting instrument consisting of a sharp blade fastened to a handle **2 :** a cutting blade in a machine

[2]**knife** *vb* **knifed; knif·ing :** to stab, slash, or wound with a knife

[1]**knight** *n* **1 :** a warrior of olden times who fought on horseback, served a king, held a special military rank, and swore to behave in a noble way **2 :** a man honored by a sovereign for merit and in Great Britain ranking below a baronet **3 :** one of the pieces in the game of chess — **knight·ly** *adj*

[2]**knight** *vb* **:** to make a knight of

knight·hood *n* **1 :** the rank, dignity, or profession of a knight **2 :** the qualities a knight should have **3 :** knights as a class or body

knit *vb* **knit** *or* **knit·ted; knit·ting 1 :** to form a fabric or garment by interlacing yarn or thread in connected loops with needles (**knitting needles**) **2 :** to draw or come together closely as if knitted **:** unite firmly **3 :** [2]WRINKLE — **knit·ter** *n*

knob *n* **1 :** a rounded lump **2 :** a small rounded handle **3 :** a rounded hill

¹knock *vb* **1 :** to strike with a sharp blow **2 :** to bump against something **3 :** to make a pounding noise **4 :** to find fault with

²knock *n* **1 :** a sharp blow **2 :** a severe misfortune or hardship **3 :** a pounding noise

knock·er *n* **:** a device made like a hinge and fastened to a door for use in knocking

knock–kneed *adj* **:** having the legs bowed inward

knoll *n* **:** a small round hill

¹knot *n* **1 :** an interlacing (as of string or ribbon) that forms a lump or knob **2 :** PROBLEM 2 **3 :** a bond of union **4 :** the inner end of a branch enclosed in a plant stem or a section of this in sawed lumber **5 :** a cluster of persons or things **6 :** an ornamental bow of ribbon **7 :** one nautical mile per hour (about two kilometers per hour)

²knot *vb* **knot·ted; knot·ting 1 :** to tie in or with a knot **2 :** to unite closely

knot·hole *n* **:** a hole in wood where a knot has come out

knot·ty *adj* **knot·ti·er; knot·ti·est 1 :** full of knots **2 :** DIFFICULT 3

know *vb* **knew; known; know·ing 1 :** to have understanding of **2 :** to recognize the nature of **3 :** to recognize the identity of **4 :** to be acquainted or familiar with **5 :** to be aware of the truth of **6 :** to have a practical understanding of **7 :** to have information or knowledge **8 :** to be or become aware

know·ing *adj* **1 :** having or showing special knowledge, information, or intelligence **2 :** shrewdly and keenly alert **3 :** INTENTIONAL — **know·ing·ly** *adv*

know–it–all *n* **:** a person who always claims to know everything

knowl·edge *n* **1 :** understanding and skill gained by experience **2 :** the state of being aware of something or of having information **3 :** range of information or awareness **4 :** something learned and kept in the mind **:** LEARNING

knuck·le *n* **:** the rounded lump formed by the ends of two bones (as of a finger) where they come together in a joint

ko·ala *n* **:** a tailless Australian animal with thick fur and big hairy ears, sharp claws for climbing, and a pouch like the kangaroo's for carrying its young

kohl·ra·bi *n* **:** a cabbage that forms no head but has a fleshy edible stem

ko·mo·do dragon *n* **:** a lizard of Indonesia that is the largest of all known lizards

kook·a·bur·ra *n* **:** an Australian kingfisher that has a call resembling loud laughter

Ko·ran *n* **:** a book of sacred writings accepted by Muslims as revealed to Muhammad by Allah

¹Ko·re·an *n* **1 :** a person born or living in North Korea or South Korea **2 :** the language of the Koreans

²Korean *adj* **:** of or relating to North Korea or South Korea, the Korean people, or their language

ko·sher *adj* **1:** accepted by Jewish law **2 :** prepared as required by Jewish law

krill *n* **:** tiny floating sea creatures that are a chief food of whales

kud·zu *n* **:** an Asian vine of the pea family that is widely grown for hay and for use in erosion control and is often a serious weed in the southeastern United States

kum·quat *n* **:** a small citrus fruit with sweet rind and sour pulp that is used mostly in preserves

Kwan·zaa *n* **:** an African-American cultural festival held from December 26 to January 1

L

l *n, pl* **l's** *or* **ls** *often cap* **1 :** the twelfth letter of the English alphabet **2 :** fifty in Roman numerals

la *n* **:** the sixth note of the musical scale

lab *n* **:** LABORATORY

¹la·bel *n* **1 :** a slip attached to something to identify or describe it **2 :** a word or phrase that describes or names something

²label *vb* **la·beled** *or* **la·belled; la·bel·ing** *or* **la·bel·ling 1 :** to attach a label to **2 :** to name or describe with or as if with a label

la·bi·al *adj* **:** of or relating to the lips

¹la·bor *n* **1 :** effort that is hard and usually physical **2 :** the effort involved in giving birth **3 :** something that has to be done **:** TASK **4 :** workers as a body or class

²labor *vb* **1 :** to work hard **:** TOIL **2 :** to move slowly or heavily

lab·o·ra·to·ry *n, pl* **lab·o·ra·to·ries :** a room or building in which experiments and tests are done

Labor Day *n* **:** the first Monday in September observed as a legal holiday to honor the worker

la·bored *adj* **:** produced or done with effort or difficulty

la·bor·er *n* **:** a person who works on jobs that require strength rather than skill

la·bo·ri·ous *adj* **:** requiring much effort — **la·bo·ri·ous·ly** *adv*

labor union *n* **:** an organization of workers designed to help them get better pay and working conditions

[1]**lace** *vb* **laced; lac·ing :** to fasten with a lace
[2]**lace** *n* **1 :** a cord or string for pulling and holding together opposite edges (as of a shoe) **2 :** an ornamental net of thread or cord usually with a design
lac·er·ate *vb* **lac·er·at·ed; lac·er·at·ing :** to injure by tearing
lac·er·a·tion *n* **:** a lacerated place or wound
[1]**lack** *vb* **1 :** to be missing **2 :** to need or be without something
[2]**lack** *n* **1 :** the fact or state of being absent or needed **2 :** something that is absent or needed
[1]**lac·quer** *n* **:** a material like varnish that dries quickly into a shiny layer (as on wood or metal)
[2]**lacquer** *vb* **:** to coat with lacquer
la·crosse *n* **:** a ball game played outdoors using a long-handled stick with a shallow net for catching, throwing, and carrying the ball
lac·tose *n* **:** a sugar that is found in milk
lacy *adj* **lac·i·er; lac·i·est :** like or made of lace
lad *n* **:** BOY 1, YOUTH
lad·der *n* **:** a device used for climbing usually consisting of two long pieces of wood, rope, or metal joined at short distances by horizontal pieces
lad·die *n* **:** BOY 1, LAD
lad·en *adj* **:** heavily loaded
[1]**la·dle** *n* **:** a spoon with a long handle and a deep bowl that is used for dipping
[2]**ladle** *vb* **la·dled; la·dling :** to take up and carry in a ladle
la·dy *n, pl* **la·dies 1 :** a woman of high social position **2 :** a pleasant well-bred woman or girl **3 :** a woman of any kind or class — often used in speaking to a stranger **4 :** WIFE **5 :** a British noblewoman — used as a title
la·dy·bird *n* **:** LADYBUG
la·dy·bug *n* **:** a small rounded beetle that feeds mostly on plant lice
la·dy·like *adj* **:** WELL-BRED
la·dy·ship *n* **:** the rank of a lady — used as a title
lady's slipper *or* **lady slipper** *n* **:** any of several North American wild orchids whose flowers suggest a slipper in shape
[1]**lag** *n* **:** the act or the amount of lagging
[2]**lag** *vb* **lagged; lag·ging :** to move or advance slowly
[1]**lag·gard** *adj* **:** lagging behind **:** SLOW
[2]**laggard** *n* **:** a person who lags
la·goon *n* **:** a shallow channel or pond near or connected to a larger body of water
laid *past of* LAY
lain *past participle of* LIE
lair *n* **:** the den or resting place of a wild animal
lake *n* **:** a large inland body of still water
[1]**lamb** *n* **:** a young sheep usually less than one year old
[2]**lamb** *vb* **:** to give birth to a lamb
lamb·kin *n* **:** a young lamb
[1]**lame** *adj* **lam·er; lam·est 1 :** not able to get around without pain or difficulty **2 :** being stiff and sore **3 :** not very convincing **:** WEAK — **lame·ly** *adv* — **lame·ness** *n*
[2]**lame** *vb* **lamed; lam·ing :** to make or become lame
[1]**la·ment** *vb* **1 :** to mourn aloud **:** WAIL **2 :** to show sorrow for
[2]**lament** *n* **1 :** a crying out in sorrow **2 :** a sad song or poem
la·men·ta·ble *adj* **:** REGRETTABLE
lam·en·ta·tion *n* **:** the act of lamenting
lam·i·nat·ed *adj* **:** made of layers of material firmly joined together
lamp *n* **:** a device for producing light
lam·prey *n, pl* **lampreys :** a water animal that looks like an eel but has a sucking mouth with no jaws
[1]**lance** *n* **:** a weapon with a long handle and a sharp steel head used by knights on horseback
[2]**lance** *vb* **:** to cut open with a small sharp instrument
lance corporal *n* **:** an enlisted person in the Marine Corps ranking above a private first class
[1]**land** *n* **1 :** the solid part of the surface of the earth **2 :** a part of the earth's surface (as a country or a farm) marked off by boundaries **3 :** the people of a country — **land·less** *adj*
[2]**land** *vb* **1 :** to go ashore or cause to go ashore from a ship **2 :** to cause to reach or come to rest where planned **3 :** to catch and bring in **4 :** to get for oneself by trying **5 :** to come down or bring down and settle on a surface
land breeze *n* **:** a breeze blowing toward the sea
land·fill *n* **1:** a system of garbage and trash disposal in which trash and garbage are buried between layers of earth **2:** an area built up by such a landfill
land·hold·er *n* **:** an owner of land
land·ing *n* **1 :** the act of one that lands **2 :** a place for unloading or taking on passengers and cargo **3 :** the level part of a staircase (as between flights of stairs)
landing field *n* **:** a field where aircraft land and take off
landing strip *n* **:** AIRSTRIP
land·la·dy *n, pl* **land·la·dies 1 :** a woman who owns land or houses that she rents **2 :** a woman who runs an inn or rooming house
land·locked *adj* **1 :** shut in or nearly shut in

by land **2 :** kept from leaving fresh water by some barrier

land·lord *n* **1 :** a man who owns land or houses that he rents **2 :** a man who runs an inn or rooming house

land·lub·ber *n* **:** a person who lives on land and knows little or nothing about the sea

land·mark *n* **1 :** something (as a building, a large tree, or a statue) that is easy to see and can help a person find the way to a place near it **2 :** a very important event **3 :** a building of historical importance

land mine *n* **:** a mine placed just below the surface of the ground and designed to be exploded by the weight of vehicles or troops passing over it

land·own·er *n* **:** a person who owns land

[1]**land·scape** *n* **1 :** a picture of natural scenery **2 :** the land that can be seen in one glance

[2]**landscape** *vb* **land·scaped; land·scap·ing :** to improve the natural beauty of a piece of land

land·slide *n* **1 :** the slipping down of a mass of rocks or earth on a steep slope **2 :** the material that moves in a landslide **3 :** the winning of an election by a very large number of votes

lane *n* **1 :** a narrow path or road (as between fences or hedges) that is not used as a highway **2 :** a special route (as for ships) **3 :** a strip of road used for a single line of traffic

lan·guage *n* **1 :** the words and expressions used and understood by a large group of people **2 :** the speech of human beings **3 :** a means of expressing ideas or feelings **4 :** a formal system of signs and symbols that is used to carry information **5 :** the way in which words are used **6 :** the special words used by a certain group or in a certain field **7 :** the study of languages

lan·guid *adj* **:** having very little strength or energy — **lan·guid·ly** *adv* — **lan·guid·ness** *n*

lan·guish *vb* **:** to become weak especially from a lack of something needed or wanted — **lan·guish·er** *n* — **lan·guish·ing** *adj* — **lan·guish·ing·ly** *adv*

lan·guor *n* **1 :** weakness or weariness of body or mind **2 :** a state of dreamy idleness — **lan·guor·ous** *adj* — **lan·guor·ous·ly** *adv*

lank *adj* **1 :** not well filled out **:** THIN **2 :** hanging straight and limp without spring or curl — **lank·ly** *adv* — **lank·ness** *n*

lanky *adj* **lank·i·er; lank·i·est :** being very tall and thin — **lank·i·ly** *adv* — **lank·i·ness** *n*

lan·tern *n* **:** a usually portable lamp with a protective covering

lan·yard *n* **1 :** a short rope or cord used as a fastening on ships **2 :** a cord worn around the neck to hold a knife or whistle **3 :** a strong cord with a hook at one end used in firing cannon

[1]**lap** *n* **:** the front part of a person between the waist and the knees when seated

[2]**lap** *vb* **lapped; lap·ping :** OVERLAP

[3]**lap** *n* **1 :** a part of something that overlaps another part **2 :** one time around a racetrack **3 :** a stage in a trip

[4]**lap** *vb* **lapped; lap·ping 1 :** to scoop up food or drink with the tip of the tongue **2 :** to splash gently

[5]**lap** *n* **:** the act or sound of lapping

lap·dog *n* **:** a dog small enough to be held in the lap

la·pel *n* **:** the part of the front of a collar that is turned back

lap·ful *n, pl* **lap·fuls** *or* **laps·ful :** as much as the lap can hold

[1]**lapse** *n* **1 :** a slight error or slip **2 :** a gradual falling away from a higher to a lower condition **3 :** a gradual passing of time

[2]**lapse** *vb* **lapsed; laps·ing 1 :** to slip, pass, or fall gradually **2 :** to become little used **3 :** to come to an end — **laps·er** *n*

[1]**lap·top** *adj* **:** small enough to be used on one's lap — **laptop** *n*

[2]**laptop** *n* **:** a portable computer that is small enough to be used on one's lap, can run on battery power, and has the main parts (as keyboard and display screen) combined into a single unit

lar·board *n* **:** [3]PORT

lar·ce·ny *n, pl* **lar·ce·nies :** the unlawful taking of personal property without the owner's consent **:** THEFT

larch *n* **:** a tree related to the pine that sheds its needles each fall

[1]**lard** *vb* **:** to smear or soil with grease

[2]**lard** *n* **:** a white soft fat from fatty tissue of the hog

lar·der *n* **:** a place where food is kept

large *adj* **larg·er; larg·est :** more than most others of a similar kind in amount or size **:** BIG — **large·ness** *n* — **at large 1 :** not locked up **:** FREE **2 :** as a whole **3 :** representing a whole state or district

large-heart·ed *adj* **:** GENEROUS 1

large intestine *n* **:** the wide lower part of the intestine from which water is absorbed and in which feces are made ready for passage

large·ly *adv* **:** MOSTLY, CHIEFLY

lar·i·at *n* **:** a long light rope used to catch livestock or tie up grazing animals

[1]**lark** *n* **:** any of a group of mostly brownish songbirds of Europe and Asia

[2]**lark** *n* **:** something done for fun **:** PRANK

lark·spur *n* **:** a tall branching plant related to the buttercups that is often grown for its stalks of showy blue, purple, pink, or white flowers

lar·va *n, pl* **lar·vae** **1 :** a wingless form (as a grub or caterpillar) in which many insects hatch from the egg **2 :** an early form of any animal that at birth or hatching is very different from its parents

lar·yn·gi·tis *n* **:** inflammation of the larynx **:** a sore throat

lar·ynx *n, pl* **la·ryn·ges** *or* **lar·ynx·es :** the upper part of the windpipe that contains the vocal cords

la·ser *n* **:** a device that produces a very powerful beam of light

laser printer *n* **:** a printer for computer output that produces high-quality images formed by a laser

[1]**lash** *vb* **1 :** to move violently or suddenly **2 :** to hit with a whip — **lash·er** *n*

[2]**lash** *n* **1 :** a blow with a whip or switch **2 :** the flexible part of a whip **3 :** a sudden swinging blow **4 :** EYELASH

[3]**lash** *vb* **:** to tie down with a rope or chain

lash·ing *n* **:** something used for tying, wrapping, or fastening

lass *n* **:** GIRL 1

lass·ie *n* **:** GIRL 1, LASS

[1]**las·so** *vb* **:** to catch with a lasso

[2]**lasso** *n, pl* **lassos** *or* **lassoes :** a rope or long leather thong with a slipknot for catching animals

[1]**last** *vb* **1 :** to go on **2 :** to stay in good condition — **last·er** *n*

[2]**last** *adv* **1 :** at the end **2 :** most recently

[3]**last** *adj* **1 :** following all the rest **:** FINAL **2 :** most recent **3 :** lowest in rank or position **4 :** most unlikely

[5]**last** *n* **:** a person or thing that is last

last·ing *adj* **:** continuing for a long while — **last·ing·ly** *adv* — **last·ing·ness** *n*

last·ly *adv* **:** at or as the end

[1]**latch** *n* **:** a movable piece that holds a door or gate closed

[2]**latch** *vb* **:** to fasten with a latch

[1]**late** *adj* **lat·er; lat·est** **1 :** coming or remaining after the usual or proper time **2 :** coming toward the end (as of the day or night) **3 :** having died or recently left a certain position **4 :** RECENT 2 — **late·ness** *n*

[2]**late** *adv* **lat·er; lat·est** **1 :** after the usual or proper time **2 :** LATELY

late·com·er *n* **:** a person who arrives late

late·ly *adv* **:** not long ago **:** RECENTLY

la·tent *adj* **:** present but not visible or active — **la·tent·ly** *adv*

lat·er·al *adj* **:** being on or directed toward the side — **lat·er·al·ly** *adv*

la·tex *n* **1 :** a milky plant juice that is the source of rubber **2 :** a mixture of water and tiny particles of rubber or plastic used especially in paints

lath *n, pl* **laths :** a thin strip of wood used (as in a wall) as a base for plaster

lathe *n* **:** a machine in which a piece of material is held and turned while being shaped by a tool

[1]**lath·er** *n* **1 :** the foam made by stirring soap and water together **2 :** foam from sweating

[2]**lather** *vb* **1 :** to spread lather over **2 :** to form a lather

[1]**Lat·in** *adj* **1 :** of or relating to the language of the ancient Romans **2 :** of or relating to Latin America or the Latin Americans

[2]**Latin** *n* **1 :** the language of the ancient Romans **2 :** a member of a people whose language and customs have descended from the ancient Romans **3 :** a person born or living in Latin America

La·ti·na *n* **:** a woman or girl born or living in Latin America or of Latin-American origin living in the United States

Lat·in–Amer·i·can *adj* **:** of or relating to Latin America or its people

Latin American *n* **:** a person born or living in Latin America

La·ti·no *n, pl* **Latinos:** a person born or living in Latin America or of Latin-American origin living in the United States

lat·i·tude *n* **1 :** the distance north or south of the equator measured in degrees **2 :** REGION 3 **3 :** freedom to act or speak as one wishes

lat·ter *adj* **1 :** relating to or coming near the end **2 :** of, relating to, or being the second of two things referred to

lat·tice *n* **1 :** a structure made of thin strips of wood or metal that cross each other to form a network **2 :** a window or gate having a lattice

[1]**laud** *n* **:** [2]PRAISE 1, ACCLAIM

[2]**laud** *vb* **:** [1]PRAISE 1, ACCLAIM

[1]**laugh** *vb* **:** to show amusement, joy, or scorn by smiling and making sounds (as chuckling) in the throat

[2]**laugh** *n* **:** the act or sound of laughing

laugh·able *adj* **:** causing or likely to cause laughter — **laugh·able·ness** *n* — **laugh·ably** *adv*

laugh·ing·stock *n* **:** a person or thing that is made fun of

laugh·ter *n* **:** the action or sound of laughing

[1]**launch** *vb* **1 :** [1]THROW 1, 2, HURL **2 :** to set afloat **3 :** to send off especially with force **4 :** to give a start to

[2]**launch** *n* **:** an act of launching

[3]**launch** *n* **:** MOTORBOAT

launch·pad *n* **:** a nonflammable platform from which a rocket can be launched

laun·der *vb* **:** to wash or wash and iron clothes — **laun·der·er** *n*

laun·dress *n* **:** a woman whose work is washing clothes

laun·dry *n, pl* **laundries 1 :** clothes or linens that have been laundered or are to be laundered **2 :** a place where laundering is done

laun·dry·man *n, pl* **laun·dry·men :** a man who works in or for a laundry

lau·rel *n* **1 :** a small evergreen European tree with shiny pointed leaves used in ancient times to crown victors (as in sports) **2 :** any of various plants (as the American **mountain laurel**) that resemble the European laurel **3 :** a crown of laurel used as a mark of honor

la·va *n* **1 :** melted rock coming from a volcano **2 :** lava that has cooled and hardened

lav·a·to·ry *n, pl* **lav·a·to·ries 1 :** a small sink (as in a bathroom) **2 :** a room for washing that usually has a toilet **3 :** TOILET 3

lav·en·der *n* **1 :** a European mint with narrow leaves and stalks of small sweet-smelling pale violet flowers **2 :** a pale purple

[1]lav·ish *adj* **1 :** spending or giving more than is necessary **:** EXTRAVAGANT **2 :** spent, produced, or given freely — **lav·ish·ly** *adv* — **lav·ish·ness** *n*

[2]lavish *vb* **:** to spend, use, or give freely

law *n* **1 :** a rule of conduct or action that a nation or a group of people agrees to follow **2 :** a whole collection of established rules **3 :** a rule or principle that always works the same way under the same conditions **4 :** a bill passed by a legislative group **5 :** [2]POLICE **6** *cap* **:** the first part of the Jewish scriptures **7 :** trial in court **8 :** the profession of a lawyer

law–abid·ing *adj* **:** obeying the law

law·break·er *n* **:** a person who breaks the law

law·ful *adj* **1 :** permitted by law **2 :** approved by law — **law·ful·ly** *adv* — **law·ful·ness** *n*

law·less *adj* **1 :** having no laws **:** not based on or controlled by law **2 :** uncontrolled by law **:** UNRULY — **law·less·ly** *adv* — **law·less·ness** *n*

law·mak·er *n* **:** one who takes part in writing and passing laws **:** LEGISLATOR — **law·mak·ing** *adj or n*

lawn *n* **:** ground (as around a house) covered with grass that is kept mowed

lawn mower *n* **:** a machine used to mow the grass on lawns

lawn tennis *n* **:** TENNIS

law·suit *n* **:** a complaint brought before a court of law for decision

law·yer *n* **:** a person whose profession is to handle lawsuits for people or to give advice about legal rights and duties

lax *adj* **1 :** not firm or tight **:** LOOSE **2 :** not stern or strict — **lax·ly** *adv* — **lax·ness** *n*

[1]lax·a·tive *adj* **:** helpful against constipation

[2]laxative *n* **:** a laxative medicine that is nearly always mild

[1]lay *vb* **laid; lay·ing 1 :** to bring down (as with force) **2 :** to put down **3 :** to produce an egg **4 :** to cause to disappear **5 :** to spread over a surface **6 :** PREPARE 1, ARRANGE **7 :** to put to **:** APPLY

[2]lay *n* **:** the way a thing lies in relation to something else

[3]lay *past of* LIE

lay·away *n* **:** something held for a customer until the price is paid

lay away *vb* **:** to put aside for later use or delivery

lay·er *n* **1 :** one that lays something **2 :** one thickness of something laid over another

lay in *vb* **:** to store for later use

lay·man *n, pl* **lay·men 1 :** a person who is not a member of the clergy **2 :** a person who is not a member of a certain profession

lay off *vb* **1 :** to stop employing (a person) usually temporarily **2 :** to let alone

lay·out *n* **:** [1]PLAN 1, ARRANGEMENT

lay out *vb* **1 :** to plan in detail **2 :** ARRANGE 1, DESIGN

lay up *vb* **1 :** to store up **2 :** to be confined by illness or injury

la·zy *adj* **la·zi·er; la·zi·est 1 :** not willing to act or work **2 :** [1]SLOW 3, SLUGGISH — **la·zi·ly** *adv* — **la·zi·ness** *n*

leach *vb* **1 :** to treat (as earth) with a liquid (as water) to remove something soluble **2 :** to remove (as a soluble salt) by leaching

[1]lead *vb* **led; lead·ing 1 :** to guide on a way often by going ahead **2 :** to be at the head of **3 :** to go through **:** LIVE **4 :** to reach or go in a certain direction

[2]lead *n* **1 :** position at the front **2 :** the distance that a person or thing is ahead **3 :** the first part of a news story

[3]lead *n* **1 :** a heavy soft gray metallic element that is easily bent and shaped **2 :** AMMUNITION 1 **3 :** a long thin piece of graphite used in pencils

lead·en *adj* **1 :** made of lead **2 :** heavy as lead **3 :** dull gray — **lead·en·ly** *adv* — **lead·en·ness** *n*

lead·er *n* **:** one that leads or is able to lead — **lead·er·ship** *n*

[1]leaf *n, pl* **leaves 1 :** one of the usually flat green parts that grow from a plant stem and that together make up the foliage **2 :** FOLIAGE **3 :** a single sheet of a book making two pages **4 :** a movable part of a table top — **leaf·less** *adj* — **leaf·like** *adj*

[2]leaf *vb* **1 :** to grow leaves **2 :** to turn the leaves of a book

leaf·let *n* **1 :** a young or small leaf **2 :** a division of a compound leaf **3 :** PAMPHLET

leaf·stalk *n* **:** PETIOLE

leafy *adj* **leaf·i·er; leaf·i·est :** having, covered with, or like leaves

[1]league *n* **1 :** a group of nations working together for a common purpose **2 :** an association of persons or groups with common interests or goals **3 :** [1]CLASS 7

[2]**league** *vb* **leagued; leagu·ing :** to form a league

[1]**leak** *vb* **1 :** to enter or escape or let enter or escape usually by accident **2 :** to make or become known

[2]**leak** *n* **1 :** a crack or hole that accidentally lets fluid in or out **2 :** something that accidentally or secretly causes or permits loss **3 :** the act of leaking

leak·age *n* **1 :** the act or process of leaking **2 :** the thing or amount that leaks

leaky *adj* **leak·i·er; leak·i·est :** letting fluid leak in or out — **leak·i·ness** *n*

[1]**lean** *vb* **1 :** to bend or tilt from a straight position **2 :** to bend and rest one's weight on **3 :** DEPEND 1, RELY **4 :** to tend or move toward in opinion, taste, or desire

[2]**lean** *adj* **1 :** having too little flesh **:** SKINNY **2 :** containing very little fat **3 :** not large or plentiful — **lean·ness** *n*

lean–to *n, pl* **lean–tos 1 :** a building that has a roof with only one slope and is usually joined to another building **2 :** a rough shelter held up by posts, rocks, or trees

[1]**leap** *vb* **leaped** *or* **leapt; leap·ing 1 :** to jump or cause to jump from a surface **2 :** to move, act, or pass quickly — **leap·er** *n*

[2]**leap** *n* **1 :** an act of leaping **:** JUMP **2 :** a place leaped over **3 :** a distance leaped

leap·frog *n* **:** a game in which one player bends down and another leaps over

leap year *n* **:** a year of 366 days with February 29 as the extra day

learn *vb* **learned** *also* **learnt; learn·ing 1 :** to get knowledge of or skill in (by studying or practicing) **2 :** MEMORIZE **3 :** to become able through practice **4 :** to find out **5 :** to gain knowledge

learned *adj* **:** having or showing knowledge or learning

learn·ing *n* **1 :** the act of a person who learns **2 :** knowledge or skill gained from teaching or study

learning disability *n* **:** any of various conditions (as attention deficit disorder and dyslexia) that make learning difficult — **learning disabled** *adj*

[1]**lease** *n* **1 :** an agreement by which a person exchanges property (as real estate) for a period of time for rent or services **2 :** the period of time for which property is leased **3 :** a piece of property that is leased

[2]**lease** *vb* **leased; leas·ing :** to give or get the use of (property) in return for services or rent

[1]**leash** *n* **:** a line for leading or holding an animal

[2]**leash** *vb* **:** to put on a leash

[1]**least** *adj* **:** smallest in size or degree

[2]**least** *n* **:** the smallest or lowest amount or degree

[3]**least** *adv* **:** in or to the smallest degree

leath·er *n* **1 :** the tanned skin of an animal **2 :** something made of leather

leath·ery *adj* **:** like leather

[1]**leave** *vb* **left; leav·ing 1 :** to fail to include or take along **2 :** to have remaining **3 :** to give by will **4 :** to let stay without interference **5 :** to go away from **6 :** to give up **7 :** DELIVER 2

[2]**leave** *n* **1 :** PERMISSION **2 :** permitted absence from one's duty or work **3 :** the act of leaving and saying good-bye **4 :** a period of time during which a person is allowed to be absent from duties

leaved *adj* **:** having leaves

leaves *pl of* LEAF

leav·ings *n pl* **:** things remaining

[1]**lec·ture** *n* **1 :** a talk that teaches something **2 :** a severe scolding

[2]**lecture** *vb* **lec·tured; lec·tur·ing 1 :** to give a lecture **2 :** [2]SCOLD — **lec·tur·er** *n*

led *past of* LEAD

LED *n* **:** an electronic device that emits light when power is supplied to it

ledge *n* **1 :** a piece projecting from a top or an edge like a shelf **2 :** SHELF 2

[1]**lee** *n* **1 :** a protecting shelter **2 :** the side (as of a ship) sheltered from the wind

[2]**lee** *adj* **:** of or relating to the lee

leech *n* **1 :** a bloodsucking worm related to the earthworm **2 :** a person who clings like a leech to another person for what can be gained

leek *n* **:** a garden plant grown for its thick stems which taste like a mild onion

[1]**leer** *vb* **:** to look with a leer

[2]**leer** *n* **:** a mean or nasty glance

leery *adj* **:** SUSPICIOUS 2, WARY

[1]**lee·ward** *n* **:** the lee side

[2]**leeward** *adj* **:** located away from the wind

[1]**left** *adj* **1 :** on the same side of the body as the heart **2 :** located nearer to the left side of the body than to the right

[2]**left** *n* **:** the left side or the part on the left side

[3]**left** *past of* LEAVE

left–hand *adj* **1 :** located on the left **2 :** LEFT-HANDED

left–hand·ed *adj* **1 :** using the left hand better or more easily than the right **2 :** done or made with or for the left hand

left·over *n* **:** something left over

lefty *n, pl* **left·ies :** a left-handed person

leg *n* **1 :** one of the limbs of an animal or person that support the body and are used in walking and running **2 :** the part of the leg between the knee and the foot **3 :** something like a leg in shape or use **4 :** the part of a garment that covers the leg **5 :** a stage or part of a journey

leg·a·cy *n, pl* **leg·a·cies :** something left to a person by or as if by a will

le·gal *adj* **1 :** of or relating to law or lawyers **2 :** based on law **3 :** allowed by law or rules — **le·gal·ly** *adv*

le·gal·i·ty *n, pl* **le·gal·i·ties :** the quality or state of being legal

le·gal·ize *vb* **le·gal·ized; le·gal·iz·ing :** to make legal — **le·gal·iza·tion** *n*

leg·end *n* **1 :** an old story that is widely believed but cannot be proved to be true **2 :** writing or a title on an object **3 :** a list of symbols used (as on a map)

leg·end·ary *adj* **:** of, relating to, or like a legend

leg·ged *adj* **:** having legs

leg·ging *n* **:** an outer covering for the leg usually of cloth or leather

leg·i·ble *adj* **:** clear enough to be read — **leg·i·bly** *adv*

le·gion *n* **1 :** a group of from 3000 to 6000 soldiers that made up the chief army unit in ancient Rome **2 :** ARMY 1 **3 :** a very great number

leg·is·late *vb* **leg·is·lat·ed; leg·is·lat·ing :** to make laws — **leg·is·la·tor** *n*

leg·is·la·tion *n* **1 :** the action of making laws **2 :** the laws that are made

leg·is·la·tive *adj* **1 :** having the power or authority to make laws **2 :** of or relating to legislation — **leg·is·la·tive·ly** *adv*

leg·is·la·ture *n* **:** a body of persons having the power to make, change, or cancel laws

le·git·i·ma·cy *n* **:** the quality or state of being legitimate

le·git·i·mate *adj* **1 :** accepted by the law as rightful **:** LAWFUL **2 :** being right or acceptable — **le·git·i·mate·ly** *adv*

leg·less *adj* **:** having no legs

le·gume *n* **:** any of a large group of plants (as peas, beans, and clover) with fruits that are pods and root nodules containing bacteria that fix nitrogen

lei·sure *n* **1 :** freedom from work **2 :** time that is free for use as one wishes

lei·sure·ly *adj* **:** UNHURRIED

lem·on *n* **1 :** an oval yellow fruit with a sour juice that is related to the orange and grows on a small spiny tree **2 :** something unsatisfactory **:** DUD

lem·on·ade *n* **:** a drink made of lemon juice, sugar, and water

lend *vb* **lent; lend·ing 1 :** ²LOAN 1 **2 :** to give usually for a time **3 :** to make a loan or loans — **lend·er** *n*

length *n* **1 :** the measured distance from one end to the other of the longer or longest side of an object **2 :** a measured distance **3 :** amount of time something takes **4 :** the sound of a vowel or syllable as it is affected by the time needed to pronounce it **5 :** a piece of something that is long — **at length 1 :** very fully **2 :** at the end

length·en *vb* **:** to make or become longer

length·ways *adv* **:** LENGTHWISE

length·wise *adv or adj* **:** in the direction of the length

lengthy *adj* **length·i·er; length·i·est :** very long — **length·i·ly** *adv* — **length·i·ness** *n*

le·nient *adj* **:** being kind and patient — **le·nient·ly** *adv*

lens *n* **1 :** a clear curved piece of material (as glass) used to bend the rays of light to form an image **2 :** a part of the eye that focuses rays of light so as to form clear images

lent *past of* LEND

len·til *n* **:** the flattened round edible seed of a plant related to the pea

Leo *n* **1 :** a constellation between Cancer and Virgo imagined as a lion **2 :** the fifth sign of the zodiac or a person born under this sign

leop·ard *n* **:** a large cat of Asia and Africa that has a brownish buff coat with black spots

leop·ard·ess *n* **:** a female leopard

le·o·tard *n* **:** a tight one-piece garment worn by dancers or acrobats

le·sion *n* **:** an abnormal spot or area of the body caused by sickness or injury

¹less *adj* **1 :** being fewer **2 :** of lower rank, degree, or importance **3 :** not so much **:** a smaller amount of

²less *adv* **:** not so much or so well

³less *n* **1 :** a smaller number or amount **2 :** a thing that is poorer than another

⁴less *prep* **:** ¹MINUS 1

-less *adj suffix* **1 :** not having **2 :** not able to be acted on or to act in a specified way

less·en *vb* **:** to make or become less

¹less·er *adj* **:** of smaller size or importance

²lesser *adv* **:** ²LESS

les·son *n* **1 :** a part of the Scripture read in a church service **2 :** a reading or exercise assigned for study **3 :** something learned or taught

lest *conj* **:** for fear that

let *vb* **let; let·ting 1 :** to cause to **:** MAKE **2 :** to give use of in return for payment **3 :** to allow or permit to **4 :** to allow to go or pass

-let *n suffix* **1 :** small one **2 :** something worn on

let·down *n* **:** DISAPPOINTMENT 2

let down *vb* **1 :** DISAPPOINT **2 :** RELAX 3

let on *vb* **1 :** ADMIT 3 **2 :** PRETEND 1

let's : let us

¹let·ter *n* **1 :** one of the marks that are symbols for speech sounds in writing or print and that make up the alphabet **2 :** a written or printed communication (as one sent through the mail) **3 letters** *pl* **:** LITERATURE 2 **4 :** the strict or outward meaning **5 :** the initial of a school awarded to a student usually for athletic achievement

[2]**letter** *vb* **:** to mark with letters

letter carrier *n* **:** a person who delivers mail

let·ter·head *n* **1 :** stationery having a printed or engraved heading **2 :** the heading of a letterhead

let·ter·ing *n* **:** letters used in an inscription

let·tuce *n* **:** a garden plant related to the daisies that has large crisp leaves eaten in salad

let up *vb* **1 :** to slow down **2 :** [1]STOP 4, CEASE

leu·ke·mia *n* **:** a dangerous disease in which too many white blood cells are formed

le·vee *n* **1 :** a bank built along a river to prevent flooding **2 :** a landing place along a river

[1]**lev·el** *n* **1 :** a device used (as by a carpenter) to find a horizontal line or surface **2 :** a horizontal line or surface usually at a named height **3 :** a step or stage in height, position, or rank

[2]**level** *vb* **lev·eled** *or* **lev·elled ; lev·el·ing** *or* **lev·el·ling :** to make or become level, flat, or even — **lev·el·er** *or* **lev·el·ler** *n*

[3]**level** *adj* **1 :** having a flat even surface **2 :** HORIZONTAL **3 :** of the same height or rank **:** EVEN **4 :** steady and cool in judgment — **lev·el·ly** *adv* — **lev·el·ness** *n*

[1]**le·ver** *n* **1 :** a bar used to pry or move something **2 :** a stiff bar for lifting a weight at one point of its length by pressing or pulling at a second point while the bar turns on a support **3 :** a bar or rod used to run or adjust something

[2]**lever** *vb* **:** to raise or move with a lever

lev·i·tate *vb* **lev·i·tat·ed; lev·i·tat·ing:** to rise or make rise up in the air

[1]**levy** *n, pl* **lev·ies 1 :** a collection (as of taxes) by authority of the law **2 :** the calling of troops into service **3 :** something (as taxes) collected by authority of the law

[2]**levy** *vb* **lev·ied; levy·ing 1 :** to collect legally **2 :** to raise or collect troops for service

li·a·ble *adj* **1 :** forced by law or by what is right to make good **2 :** not sheltered or protected (as from danger or accident) **3 :** LIKELY 1

li·ar *n* **:** a person who tells lies

[1]**li·bel** *n* **:** something spoken or written that hurts a person's good name

[2]**libel** *vb* **li·beled** *or* **li·belled; li·bel·ing** *or* **li·bel·ling :** to hurt by a libel — **li·bel·er** *or* **li·bel·ler** *n*

lib·er·al *adj* **1 :** not stingy **:** GENEROUS **2 :** being more than enough **3 :** not strict **4 :** BROAD 4 — **lib·er·al·ly** *adv*

lib·er·ate *vb* **lib·er·at·ed; lib·er·at·ing :** to set free

lib·er·ty *n, pl* **lib·er·ties 1 :** the state of those who are free and independent **:** FREEDOM **2 :** freedom to do what one pleases **3 :** the state of not being busy **:** LEISURE **4 :** behavior or an act that is too free

Li·bra *n* **1 :** a constellation between Virgo and Scorpio imagined as a pair of scales **2 :** the seventh sign of the zodiac or a person born under this sign

li·brar·i·an *n* **:** a person in charge of a library

li·brary *n, pl* **li·brar·ies 1 :** a place where especially literary or reference materials (as books, manuscripts, recordings, or films) are kept for use but not for sale **2 :** a collection of such materials

lice *pl of* LOUSE

[1]**li·cense** *or* **li·cence** *n* **1 :** permission granted by qualified authority to do something **2 :** a paper showing legal permission **3 :** liberty of action that is carried too far

[2]**license** *or* **licence** *vb* **li·censed** *or* **li·cenced; li·cens·ing** *or* **li·cenc·ing :** to permit or authorize by license

li·chen *n* **:** a plant made up of an alga and a fungus growing together

[1]**lick** *vb* **1 :** to pass the tongue over **2 :** to touch or pass over like a tongue **3 :** to hit again and again **:** BEAT **4 :** to get the better of — **lick·ing** *n*

[2]**lick** *n* **1 :** the act of licking **2 :** a small amount **3 :** a place (**salt lick**) where salt is found on the top of the ground and animals come to lick it up

lick·e·ty–split *adv* **:** at top speed

lic·o·rice *n* **1 :** the dried root of a European plant related to the peas or a juice from it used in medicine and in candy **2 :** candy flavored with licorice

lid *n* **1 :** a movable cover **2 :** EYELID — **lid·ded** *adj* — **lid·less** *adj*

[1]**lie** *vb* **lay; lain; ly·ing 1 :** to stretch out or be stretched out (as on a bed or on the ground) **2 :** to be spread flat so as to cover **3 :** to be located or placed **4 :** to be or stay

[2]**lie** *vb* **lied; ly·ing :** to make a statement that one knows to be untrue

[3]**lie** *n* **:** something said or done in the hope of deceiving **:** an untrue statement

[1]**liege** *adj* **1 :** having the right to receive service and loyalty **2 :** owing or giving service to a lord

[2]**liege** *n* **1 :** VASSAL 1 **2 :** a feudal lord

lieu·ten·ant *n* **1 :** an official who acts for a higher official **2 :** a first lieutenant or second lieutenant (as in the Army) **3 :** a commissioned officer in the Navy or Coast Guard ranking above a lieutenant junior grade

lieutenant colonel *n* **:** a commissioned officer in the Army, Air Force, or Marine Corps ranking above a major

lieutenant commander *n* **:** a commissioned officer in the Navy or Coast Guard ranking above a lieutenant

lieutenant general *n* **:** a commissioned officer in the Army, Air Force, or Marine Corps ranking above a major general

lieutenant junior grade *n* **:** a commissioned officer in the Navy or Coast Guard ranking above an ensign

life *n, pl* **lives** **1 :** the quality that separates plants and animals from such things as water or rock **:** the quality that plants and animals lose when they die **2 :** all the experiences that make up the existence of a person **:** the course of existence **3 :** BIOGRAPHY **4 :** the period during which a person or thing is alive or exists **5 :** a way of living **6 :** a living being **7 :** [1]SPIRIT 5

life belt *n* **:** a life preserver worn like a belt

life·boat *n* **:** a sturdy boat (as one carried by a ship) for use in an emergency and especially in saving lives at sea

life buoy *n* **:** a life preserver in the shape of a ring

life·guard *n* **:** a guard employed at a beach or swimming pool to protect swimmers from drowning

life jacket *n* **:** a life preserver in the form of a vest

life·less *adj* **:** having no life

life·like *adj* **:** very like something that is alive

life·long *adj* **:** continuing through life

life preserver *n* **:** a device (as a life jacket or life buoy) designed to save a person from drowning by keeping the person afloat

life raft *n* **:** a raft usually made of wood or an inflatable material for use by people forced into the water

life·sav·er *n* **:** a person trained in lifesaving

life·sav·ing *n* **:** the methods that can be used to save lives especially of drowning persons

life–size *or* **life–sized** *adj* **:** of natural size **:** having the same size as the original

life·style *n* **:** the usual way of life of a person, group, or society **:** the way we live

life·time *n* **:** LIFE 4

life vest *n* **:** LIFE JACKET

[1]**lift** *vb* **1 :** to raise from a lower to a higher position, rate, or amount **2 :** to rise from the ground **3 :** to move upward and disappear or become scattered — **lift·er** *n*

[2]**lift** *n* **1 :** the amount that may be lifted at one time **:** LOAD **2 :** the action or an instance of lifting **3 :** help especially in the form of a ride **4** *chiefly British* **:** ELEVATOR 2 **5 :** an upward force (as on an airplane wing) that opposes the pull of gravity

lift·off *n* **:** a vertical takeoff (as by a rocket)

lig·a·ment *n* **:** a tough band of tissue or fibers that holds bones together or keeps an organ in place in the body

[1]**light** *n* **1 :** the bright form of energy given off by something (as the sun) that lets one see objects **2 :** a source (as a lamp) of light **3 :** DAYLIGHT 1 **4 :** public knowledge **5 :** something that helps one to know or understand

[2]**light** *adj* **1 :** having light **:** BRIGHT **2 :** not dark or deep in color

[3]**light** *vb* **light·ed** *or* **lit; light·ing** **1 :** to make or become bright **2 :** to burn or cause to burn **3 :** to lead with a light

[4]**light** *adj* **1 :** having little weight **:** not heavy **2 :** not strong or violent **3 :** not hard to bear, do, pay, or digest **4 :** active in motion **5 :** not severe **6 :** free from care **:** HAPPY **7 :** intended mainly to entertain — **light·ly** *adv* — **light·ness** *n*

[5]**light** *adv* **:** with little baggage

[6]**light** *vb* **light·ed** *or* **lit; light·ing** **1 :** [2]PERCH, SETTLE **2 :** to come by chance

light bulb *n* **:** INCANDESCENT LAMP

[1]**light·en** *vb* **1 :** to make or become light or lighter **:** BRIGHTEN **2 :** to grow bright with lightning — **light·en·er** *n*

[2]**lighten** *vb* **:** to make or become less heavy — **light·en·er** *n*

light·face *n* **:** a type having light thin lines — **light·faced** *adj*

light·heart·ed *adj* **:** free from worry — **light·heart·ed·ly** *adv* — **light·heart·ed·ness** *n*

light·house *n* **:** a tower with a powerful light at the top that is built on the shore to guide sailors at night

light·ing *n* **:** supply of light or of lights

light·ning *n* **:** the flashing of light caused by the passing of electricity from one cloud to another or between a cloud and the earth

lightning bug *n* **:** FIREFLY

light·proof *adj* **:** not letting in light

light·weight *adj* **:** having less than the usual or expected weight

light–year *n* **:** a unit of length in astronomy equal to the distance that light travels in one year or 9,458,000,000,000 kilometers

lik·able *or* **like·able** *adj* **:** easily liked — **lik·able·ness** *n*

[1]**like** *vb* **liked; lik·ing** **1 :** to have a liking for **:** ENJOY **2 :** to feel toward **:** REGARD **3 :** CHOOSE 3, PREFER

[2]**like** *n* **:** LIKING, PREFERENCE

[3]**like** *adj* **1 :** SIMILAR, ALIKE **2 :** similar to or to that of — used after the word modified

[4]**like** *prep* **1 :** similar or similarly to **2 :** typical of **3 :** likely to **4 :** such as

[5]like *n* : [3]EQUAL, COUNTERPART

[6]like *conj* **1 :** AS IF **2 :** in the same way that : [2]AS 2

like·li·hood *n* : PROBABILITY 1

[1]like·ly *adj* **1 :** very possibly going to happen **2 :** seeming to be the truth : BELIEVABLE **3 :** giving hope of turning out well : PROMISING — **like·li·ness** *n*

[2]likely *adv* : without great doubt

lik·en *vb* : COMPARE 1

like·ness *n* **1 :** the state of being like : RESEMBLANCE **2 :** a picture of a person : PORTRAIT

like·wise *adv* **1 :** in like manner **2 :** ALSO

lik·ing *n* : a being pleased with someone or something

li·lac *n* **1 :** a bush having clusters of fragrant grayish pink, purple, or white flowers **2 :** a medium purple

lilt *vb* : to sing or play in a lively cheerful manner — **lilt·ing·ly** *adv*

lily *n, pl* **lil·ies :** a plant (as the **Easter lily** or the **tiger lily**) that grows from a bulb and has a leafy stem and showy funnel-shaped flowers

lily of the valley : a low plant related to the lilies that has usually two leaves and a stalk of fragrant flowers shaped like bells

li·ma bean *n* : a bean with flat pale green or white seeds

limb *n* **1 :** any of the paired parts (as an arm, wing, or leg) of an animal that stick out from the body and are used mostly in moving or grasping **2 :** a large branch of a tree — **limbed** *adj* — **limb·less** *adj*

[1]lim·ber *adj* : bending easily — **lim·ber·ly** *adv* — **lim·ber·ness** *n*

[2]limber *vb* : to make or become limber

[1]lime *n* : a white substance made by heating limestone or shells that is used in making plaster and cement and in farming

[2]lime *vb* **limed; lim·ing :** to treat or cover with lime

[3]lime *n* : a small greenish yellow fruit that is related to the lemon and orange

lim·er·ick *n* : a humorous poem five lines long

lime·stone *n* : a rock formed chiefly from animal remains (as shells or coral) that is used in building and gives lime when burned

lime·wa·ter *n* : a colorless water solution that contains calcium and turns white when carbon dioxide is blown through it

[1]lim·it *n* **1 :** a boundary line **2 :** a point beyond which a person or thing cannot go

[2]limit *vb* : to set limits to

lim·i·ta·tion *n* **1 :** an act or instance of limiting **2 :** the quality or state of being limited

lim·it·less *adj* : having no limits

[1]limp *vb* : to walk lamely

[2]limp *n* : a limping movement or gait

[3]limp *adj* : not firm or stiff — **limp·ly** *adv* — **limp·ness** *n*

limy *adj* **lim·i·er; lim·i·est :** containing lime or limestone

lin·den *n* : a shade tree with heart-shaped toothed leaves, drooping clusters of yellowish white flowers, and hard fruits like peas

[1]line *n* **1 :** a long thin cord **2 :** a pipe carrying a fluid (as steam, water, or oil) **3 :** an outdoor wire carrying electricity for a telephone or power company **4 :** a row of letters or words across a page or column **5 lines** *pl* : the words of a part in a play **6 :** the direction followed by something in motion **7 :** the boundary or limit of a place or lot **8 :** the track of a railway **9 :** AGREEMENT 1, HARMONY **10 :** a course of behavior or thought **11 :** FAMILY 1 **12 :** a system of transportation **13 :** a long narrow mark (as one drawn by a pencil) **14 :** the football players whose positions are along the line of scrimmage **15 :** a geometric element produced by moving a point : a set of points **16 :** [1]OUTLINE 1, CONTOUR **17 :** a plan for making or doing something

[2]line *vb* **lined; lin·ing 1 :** to mark with a line or lines **2 :** to place or be placed in a line along **3 :** to form a line : form into lines

[3]line *vb* **lined; lin·ing :** to cover the inner surface of

lin·eage *n* **1 :** the ancestors from whom a person is descended **2 :** people descended from the same ancestor

lin·ear *adj* **1 :** of, relating to, or like a line : STRAIGHT **2 :** involving a single dimension

lin·en *n* **1 :** smooth strong cloth or yarn made from flax **2 :** household articles (as tablecloths or sheets) or clothing (as shirts or underwear) once often made of linen

line of scrimmage : an imaginary line in football parallel to the goal lines and running through the place where the ball is laid before each play begins

[1]lin·er *n* : a ship or airplane of a regular transportation line

[2]liner *n* : one that lines or is used to line something

line segment *n* : SEGMENT 3

line·up *n* **1 :** a line of persons arranged especially for police identification **2 :** a list of players taking part in a game (as baseball)

-ling *n suffix* **1 :** one associated with **2 :** young, small, or minor one

lin·ger *vb* : to be slow in leaving : DELAY

lin·guist *n* **1 :** a person skilled in languages **2 :** a person who specializes in linguistics

lin·guis·tics *n* : the study of human speech including the units, nature, structure, and development of language, languages, or a language

lin·i·ment *n* : a liquid medicine rubbed on the skin (as to ease pain)

lin·ing *n* : material that lines an inner surface

[1]**link** *n* **1** : a single ring of a chain **2** : something that connects **3** : HYPERLINK

[2]**link** *vb* : to join with or as if with links

linking verb *n* : an intransitive verb that links a subject with a word or words in the predicate

lin·net *n* : a common small European finch often kept as a cage bird

li·no·leum *n* : a floor covering with a canvas back and a surface of hardened linseed oil and usually cork dust

lin·seed *n* : FLAXSEED

linseed oil *n* : a yellowish oil obtained from flaxseed

lint *n* **1** : loose bits of thread **2** : [1]COTTON 1

lin·tel *n* : a horizontal piece or part across the top of an opening (as of a door) to carry the weight of the structure above it

li·on *n* : a large flesh-eating animal of the cat family that has a brownish buff coat, a tufted tail, and in the male a shaggy mane and that lives in Africa and southern Asia

li·on·ess *n* : a female lion

lip *n* **1** : either of the two folds of flesh that surround the mouth **2** : an edge (as of a flower or a wound) like or of flesh **3** : the edge of a hollow container especially where it is slightly spread out — **lip·less** *adj* — **lip·like** *adj* — **lipped** *adj*

lip·stick *n* : a waxy solid colored cosmetic for the lips usually in stick form

liq·ue·fy *vb* **liq·ue·fied; liq·ue·fy·ing** : to make or become liquid

[1]**liq·uid** *adj* **1** : flowing freely like water **2** : neither solid nor gaseous **3** : like liquid in clearness or smoothness **4** : made up of or easily changed into cash — **liq·uid·ly** *adv* — **liq·uid·ness** *n*

[2]**liquid** *n* : a liquid substance

liq·uor *n* **1** : a liquid substance or solution **2** : a strong alcoholic beverage (as whiskey)

[1]**lisp** *vb* : to pronounce the sounds \s\ and \z\ as \th\ and \th\

[2]**lisp** *n* : the act or habit of lisping

[1]**list** *n* : a leaning over to one side

[2]**list** *vb* : to lean to one side

[3]**list** *n* : a record or catalog of names or items

[4]**list** *vb* : to put into a list

lis·ten *vb* **1** : to pay attention in order to hear **2** : to give heed : follow advice — **lis·ten·er** *n*

list·less *adj* : too tired or too little interested to want to do things — **list·less·ly** *adv* — **list·less·ness** *n*

lit *past of* LIGHT

li·ter *n* : a metric unit of liquid capacity equal to 1.057 quarts

lit·er·al *adj* **1** : following the ordinary or usual meaning of the words **2** : true to fact — **lit·er·al·ly** *adv* — **lit·er·al·ness** *n*

lit·er·ary *adj* : of or relating to literature

lit·er·ate *adj* **1** : well educated : WELL-BRED **2** : able to read and write

lit·er·a·ture *n* **1** : written works having excellence of form or expression and ideas of lasting and widespread interest **2** : written material (as of a period or on a subject)

lithe *adj* : [1]LIMBER, SUPPLE — **lithe·ly** *adv* — **lithe·ness** *n*

lith·o·sphere *n* : the outer part of the solid earth

lit·mus paper *n* : paper treated with coloring matter that turns red in acid solutions and blue in alkaline solutions

[1]**lit·ter** *n* **1** : a covered and curtained couch having poles and used for carrying a single passenger **2** : a stretcher for carrying a sick or wounded person **3** : material spread out like a bed in places where farm animals (as cows or chickens) are kept to soak up their urine and feces **4** : the young born to an animal at a single time **5** : a messy collection of things scattered about : RUBBISH

[2]**litter** *vb* **1** : to cover with litter **2** : to scatter about in disorder

lit·ter·bug *n* : one that litters a public area

[1]**lit·tle** *adj* **lit·tler** *or* **less; lit·tlest** *or* **least** **1** : small in size **2** : small in quantity **3** : small in importance **4** : NARROW-MINDED, MEAN **5** : short in duration or extent — **lit·tle·ness** *n*

[2]**little** *adv* **less; least** : in a very small quantity or degree

[3]**little** *n* : a small amount or quantity

Little Dipper *n* : a group of seven stars in the northern sky arranged in a form like a dipper with the North Star forming the tip of the handle

li·tur·gi·cal *adj* : of, relating to, or like liturgy

lit·ur·gy *n, pl* **lit·ur·gies** : a religious rite or body of rites

[1]**live** *vb* **lived; liv·ing** **1** : to be alive **2** : to continue in life **3** : DWELL 2 **4** : to pass one's life — **live it up** : to live with great enthusiasm and excitement

[2]**live** *adj* **1** : not dead : ALIVE **2** : burning usually without flame **3** : not exploded **4** : of present and continuing interest **5** : charged with an electric current **6** : broadcast at the time of production

live·li·hood *n* : [2]LIVING 3

live·long *adj* : during all of

live·ly *adj* **live·li·er; live·li·est** **1** : full of life : ACTIVE **2** : KEEN 4 **3** : full of spirit or feeling : ANIMATED — **live·li·ness** *n*

liv·en *vb* : to make or become lively

live oak *n* **:** any of several American oaks that have evergreen leaves

liv·er *n* **:** a large gland of vertebrates (as fishes and humans) that has a rich blood supply, secretes bile, and helps in storing some nutrients and in forming some body wastes

liv·er·ied *adj* **:** wearing a livery

liv·er·wort *n* **:** any of a group of flowerless plants that are somewhat like mosses

liv·ery *n, pl* **liv·er·ies** **1 :** a special uniform worn by the servants of a wealthy household **2 :** the clothing worn to distinguish an association of persons **3 :** the care and stabling of horses for pay **4 :** the keeping of horses and vehicles for hire or a place (**livery stable**) engaged in this

lives *pl of* LIFE

live·stock *n* **:** animals kept or raised especially on a farm and for profit

live wire *n* **:** an alert active forceful person

liv·id *adj* **1 :** discolored by bruising **2 :** pale as ashes — **liv·id·ly** *adv* — **liv·id·ness** *n*

[1]liv·ing *adj* **1 :** not dead **:** ALIVE **2 :** ACTIVE 4 **3 :** true to life

[2]living *n* **1 :** the condition of being alive **2 :** conduct or manner of life **3 :** what one has to have to meet one's needs

living room *n* **:** a room in a house for general family use

liz·ard *n* **:** any of a group of reptiles having movable eyelids, ears that are outside the body, and usually four legs

lla·ma *n* **:** a South American hoofed animal that chews the cud

lo *interj* — used to call attention or to show wonder or surprise

[1]load *n* **1 :** something taken up and carried **:** BURDEN **2 :** a mass or weight supported by something **3 :** something that depresses the mind or spirits **4 :** a charge for a firearm **5 :** the quantity of material loaded into a device at one time

[2]load *vb* **1 :** to put a load in or on **2 :** to supply abundantly **3 :** to put a load into — **load·er** *n*

[1]loaf *n, pl* **loaves** **1 :** a usually oblong mass of bread **2 :** a dish (as of meat) baked in the form of a loaf

[2]loaf *vb* **:** to spend time idly or lazily — **loaf·er** *n*

loam *n* **:** a soil having the right amount of silt, clay, and sand for good plant growth

loamy *adj* **:** made up of or like loam

[1]loan *n* **1 :** money loaned at interest **2 :** something loaned for a time to a borrower **3 :** permission to use something for a time

[2]loan *vb* **1 :** to give to another for temporary use with the understanding that the same or a like thing will be returned **2 :** LEND 3

loath *or* **loth** *adj* **:** not willing

loathe *vb* **loathed; loath·ing** **:** to dislike greatly

loathing *n* **:** very great dislike

loath·some *adj* **:** very unpleasant **:** OFFENSIVE — **loath·some·ly** *adv* — **loath·some·ness** *n*

loaves *pl of* LOAF

[1]lob *vb* **lobbed; lob·bing :** to send (as a ball) in a high arc by hitting or throwing easily

[2]lob *n* **:** a lobbed throw or shot (as in tennis)

lob·by *n, pl* **lobbies** **:** a hall or entry especially when large enough to serve as a waiting room

lobe *n* **:** a rounded part — **lobed** *adj*

lob·ster *n* **:** a large edible sea crustacean with five pairs of legs of which the first pair usually has large claws

[1]lo·cal *adj* **1 :** of or relating to position in space **2 :** relating to a particular place — **lo·cal·ly** *adv*

[2]local *n* **1 :** a public vehicle (as a bus or train) that makes all or most stops on its run **2 :** a local branch (as of a lodge or labor union)

local area network *n* **:** a computer network that covers a small area (as an office building or a home)

lo·cal·i·ty *n, pl* **lo·cal·i·ties** **:** a place and its surroundings

lo·cal·ize *vb* **lo·cal·ized; lo·cal·iz·ing** **:** to make or become local

lo·cate *vb* **lo·cat·ed; lo·cat·ing** **1 :** to state and fix exactly the place or limits of **2 :** to settle or establish in a locality **3 :** to find the position of

lo·ca·tion *n* **1 :** the act or process of locating **2 :** a place fit for some use (as a building)

[1]lock *n* **:** a small bunch of hair or of fiber (as cotton or wool)

[2]lock *n* **1 :** a fastening (as for a door) in which a bolt is operated (as by a key) **2 :** the device for exploding the charge or cartridge of a firearm **3 :** an enclosure (as in a canal) with gates at each end used in raising or lowering boats as they pass from level to level

[3]lock *vb* **1 :** to fasten with or as if with a lock **2 :** to shut in or out by or as if by means of a lock **3 :** to make fast by the linking of parts together

lock·er *n* **:** a cabinet, compartment, or chest for personal use or for storing frozen food at a low temperature

lock·et *n* **:** a small ornamental case usually worn on a chain

lock·jaw *n* **:** TETANUS

lock·smith *n* **:** a worker who makes or repairs locks

lock·up *n* **:** PRISON

lo·co *adj* **:** not sane **:** CRAZY

lo·co·mo·tion *n* **:** the act or power of moving from place to place

lo·co·mo·tive *n* **:** a vehicle that moves under its own power and is used to haul cars on a railroad

lo·cust *n* **1 :** a grasshopper that moves in huge swarms and eats up the plants in its course **2 :** CICADA **3 :** a hardwood tree with feathery leaves and drooping flower clusters

lode·stone *n* **1 :** a rocky substance having magnetic properties **2 :** something that attracts strongly

¹lodge *vb* **lodged; lodg·ing 1 :** to provide temporary quarters for **2 :** to use a place for living or sleeping **3 :** to come to rest **4 :** ³FILE 2

²lodge *n* **1 :** a house set apart for residence in a special season or by an employee on an estate **2 :** the meeting place of a branch of a secret society

lodg·er *n* **:** a person who lives in a rented room in another's house

lodging *n* **1 :** a temporary living or sleeping place **2 lodgings** *pl* **:** a room or rooms in the house of another person rented as a place to live

loft *n* **1 :** an upper room or upper story of a building **2 :** a balcony in a church **3 :** an upper part of a barn

lofty *adj* **loft·i·er; loft·i·est 1 :** PROUD 1 **2 :** of high rank or fine quality **3 :** rising to a great height — **loft·i·ly** *adv* — **loft·i·ness** *n*

¹log *n* **1 :** a large piece of rough timber **:** a long piece of a tree trunk trimmed and ready for sawing **2 :** a device for measuring the speed of a ship **3 :** the daily record of a ship's speed and progress **4 :** the record of a ship's voyage or of an aircraft's flight **5 :** a record of how something (as a piece of equipment) works in actual use

²log *vb* **logged; log·ging 1 :** to engage in cutting trees for timber **2 :** to put details about in a log

log·ger·head *n* **:** a very large sea turtle found in the warmer parts of the Atlantic ocean

log·ic *n* **1 :** a science that deals with the rules and tests of sound thinking and reasoning **2 :** sound reasoning

log·i·cal *adj* **1 :** having to do with logic **2 :** according to the rules of logic **3 :** according to what is reasonably expected — **log·i·cal·ly** *adv* — **log·i·cal·ness** *n*

log in *vb* LOG ON — **log–in** *n*

log on *vb* **:** to establish a connection to and begin using a computer or network — **log–on** *n*

-logy *n suffix* **:** area of knowledge **:** science

loin *n* **1 :** the part of the body between the hip and the lower ribs **2 :** a piece of meat (as beef) from the loin of an animal

loi·ter *vb* **1 :** to linger on one's way **2 :** to hang around idly — **loi·ter·er** *n*

loll *vb* **1 :** to hang loosely **:** DANGLE **2 :** to lie around lazily

lol·li·pop *or* **lol·ly·pop** *n* **:** a lump of hard candy on the end of a stick

lone *adj* **1 :** having no companion **2 :** being by itself

lone·ly *adj* **lone·li·er; lone·li·est 1 :** LONE 1 **2 :** not often visited **3 :** longing for companions — **lone·li·ness** *n*

lone·some *adj* **1 :** saddened by a lack of companions **2 :** not often visited or traveled over — **lone·some·ly** *adv* — **lone·some·ness** *n*

¹long *adj* **lon·ger; lon·gest 1 :** of great length from end to end **:** not short **2 :** having a greater length than breadth **3 :** lasting for some time **:** not brief **4 :** having a stated length (as in distance or time) **5 :** of, relating to, or being one of the vowel sounds \ā, ȧ, ē, ī, ō, ü\ and sometimes \ä\ and \ȯ\

²long *adv* **1 :** for or during a long time **2 :** for the whole length of **3 :** at a distant point of time

³long *n* **:** a long time

⁴long *vb* **:** to wish for something very much — **long·ing·ly** *adv*

long·hand *n* **:** HANDWRITING

long·horn *n* **:** any of the half-wild cattle with very long horns that were once common in the southwestern United States

long–horned *adj* **:** having long horns or antennae

long·ing *n* **:** an eager desire

long·ish *adj* **:** somewhat long

lon·gi·tude *n* **:** distance measured in degrees east or west of a line drawn (as through Greenwich, England) between the north and south poles

lon·gi·tu·di·nal *adj* **:** placed or running lengthwise — **lon·gi·tu·di·nal·ly** *adv*

long–lived *adj* **:** living or lasting for a long time

long–range *adj* **1 :** capable of traveling or shooting great distances **2 :** lasting over or providing for a long period

long·sight·ed *adj* **:** FARSIGHTED — **long·sight·ed·ness** *n*

long–suf·fer·ing *adj* **:** very patient and forgiving

long–wind·ed *adj* **1 :** too long **2 :** given to talking too long

¹look *vb* **1 :** to use the power of vision **:** SEE **2 :** to appear suitable to **3 :** SEEM 1 **4 :** to turn one's attention or eyes **5 :** ²FACE 2 — **look after :** to take care of — **look down on :** to regard with contempt — **look up to :** RESPECT 1

²look *n* **1 :** an act of looking **2 :** the way one

appears to others **3 :** appearance that suggests what something is or means

looking glass *n* **:** [1]MIRROR 1

look·out *n* **1 :** a careful watch for something expected or feared **2 :** a high place from which a wide view is possible **3 :** a person who keeps watch

[1]**loom** *n* **:** a device for weaving cloth

[2]**loom** *vb* **:** to come into sight suddenly and often with a dim or strange appearance

loon *n* **:** a large diving bird that lives on fish and has webbed feet, a black head, and a black back spotted with white

[1]**loop** *n* **1 :** an almost oval form produced when something flexible and thin (as a wire or a rope) crosses itself **2 :** something (as a figure or bend) suggesting a flexible loop

[2]**loop** *vb* **:** to make a loop or loops in

loop·hole *n* **:** a way of escaping something

[1]**loose** *adj* **loos·er; loos·est 1 :** not tightly fixed or fastened **2 :** not pulled tight **3 :** not tied up or shut in **4 :** not brought together in a package or binding **5 :** not respectable **6 :** having parts that are not squeezed tightly together **7 :** not exact or careful — **loose·ly** *adv* — **loose·ness** *n*

[2]**loose** *vb* **loosed; loos·ing 1 :** to make loose **:** UNTIE **2 :** to set free

loose–leaf *adj* **:** arranged so that pages can be put in or taken out

loos·en *vb* **:** to make or become loose

[1]**loot** *n* **:** something stolen or taken by force

[2]**loot** *vb* **:** [1]PLUNDER — **loot·er** *n*

[1]**lope** *n* **:** a gait with long smooth steps

[2]**lope** *vb* **loped; lop·ing :** to go or ride at a lope

lop–eared *adj* **:** having ears that droop

lop·sid·ed *adj* **:** UNBALANCED 1 — **lop·sid·ed·ly** *adv* — **lop·sid·ed·ness** *n*

[1]**lord** *n* **1 :** a person having power and authority over others **2** *cap* **:** GOD 1 **3** *cap* **:** JESUS **4 :** a British nobleman or a bishop of the Church of England entitled to sit in the House of Lords — used as a title

[2]**lord** *vb* **:** to act in a proud or bossy way toward others

lord·ship *n* **:** the rank or dignity of a lord — used as a title

lore *n* **:** common knowledge or belief

lose *vb* **lost; los·ing 1 :** to be unable to find or have at hand **:** MISLAY **2 :** to be deprived of **3 :** [2]WASTE 2 **4 :** to be defeated in **5 :** to fail to keep — **los·er** *n* — **lose one's way :** to stray from the right path

loss *n* **1 :** the act or fact of losing something **2 :** harm or distress that comes from losing something **3 :** something that is lost **4 :** failure to win

[1]**lost** *past of* LOSE

[2]**lost** *adj* **1 :** not used, won, or claimed **2 :** unable to find the way **3 :** come or brought to a bad end **4 :** no longer possessed or known **5 :** fully occupied

lot *n* **1 :** an object used in deciding something by chance or the use of such an object to decide something **2 :** FATE 2 **3 :** a piece or plot of land **4 :** a large number or amount

loth *variant of* LOATH

lo·tion *n* **:** a liquid preparation used on the skin for healing or as a cosmetic

lot·tery *n, pl* **lot·ter·ies :** a way of raising money in which many tickets are sold and a few of these are drawn to win prizes

lo·tus *n* **:** any of various water lilies

[1]**loud** *adj* **1 :** not low, soft, or quiet in sound **:** NOISY **2 :** not quiet or calm in expression **3 :** too bright or showy to be pleasing — **loud·ly** *adv* — **loud·ness** *n*

[2]**loud** *adv* **:** in a loud manner

loud·speak·er *n* **:** an electronic device that makes sound louder

[1]**lounge** *vb* **lounged; loung·ing 1 :** to move or act in a slow, tired, or lazy way **2 :** to stand, sit, or lie in a relaxed manner

[2]**lounge** *n* **1 :** a comfortable room where one can relax or lounge **2 :** SOFA

louse *n, pl* **lice 1 :** a small, wingless, and usually flat insect that lives on the bodies of warm-blooded animals **2 :** PLANT LOUSE

lov·able *adj* **:** deserving to be loved or admired — **lov·able·ness** *n* — **lov·ably** *adv*

[1]**love** *n* **1 :** great and warm affection (as of a child for a parent) **2 :** a great liking **3 :** a beloved person

[2]**love** *vb* **loved; lov·ing 1 :** to feel warm affection for **2 :** to like very much — **lov·er** *n*

love·ly *adj* **love·li·er; love·li·est 1 :** very beautiful **2 :** very pleasing — **love·li·ness** *n*

lov·ing *adj* **:** feeling or showing love **:** AFFECTIONATE — **lov·ing·ly** *adv*

[1]**low** *vb* **:** to make the calling sound of a cow **:** MOO

[2]**low** *n* **:** the mooing of a cow **:** MOO

[3]**low** *adj* **1 :** not high **:** not tall **2 :** lying or going below the usual level **3 :** not loud **:** SOFT **4 :** deep in pitch **5 :** [1]PROSTRATE 3 **6 :** SAD 1 **7 :** less than usual (as in quantity or value) **8 :** COARSE 4, VULGAR **9 :** not favorable **:** POOR — **low·ness** *n*

[4]**low** *n* **1 :** something that is low **2 :** a region of low barometric pressure **3 :** the arrangement of gears in an automobile that gives the lowest speed of travel

[5]**low** *adv* **:** so as to be low

[1]**low·er** *adj* **1 :** being below the other of two similar persons or things **2 :** less advanced

[2]**lower** *vb* **1 :** to move to a lower level **:** SINK **2 :** to let or pull down **3 :** to make or become less (as in value or amount) **4 :** to make or become lower

low·land *n* : low flat country
[1]**low·ly** *adv* : in a humble way
[2]**lowly** *adj* **low·li·er; low·li·est** : of low rank or condition : HUMBLE — **low·li·ness** *n*
loy·al *adj* **1** : faithful to one's country **2** : faithful to a person or thing one likes or believes in — **loy·al·ly** *adv*
loy·al·ty *n, pl* **loy·al·ties** : the quality or state of being loyal
loz·enge *n* : a small candy often containing medicine
LSD *n* : a dangerous drug that causes hallucinations
lu·bri·cant *n* : something (as oil or grease) that makes a surface smooth or slippery
lu·bri·cate *vb* **lu·bri·cat·ed; lu·bri·cat·ing** **1** : to make smooth or slippery **2** : to apply oil or grease to
lu·bri·ca·tion *n* : the act or process of lubricating or the state of being lubricated
lu·cid *adj* **1** : showing a normal state of mind **2** : easily understood — **lu·cid·ly** *adv* — **lu·cid·ness** *n*
luck *n* **1** : something that happens to a person by or as if by chance **2** : the accidental way events occur **3** : good fortune
lucky *adj* **luck·i·er; luck·i·est** **1** : helped by luck : FORTUNATE **2** : happening because of good luck **3** : thought of as bringing good luck — **luck·i·ly** *adv*
lu·di·crous *adj* : funny because of being ridiculous : ABSURD — **lu·di·crous·ly** *adv* — **lu·di·crous·ness** *n*
lug *vb* **lugged; lug·ging** : to find hard to carry or haul
lug·gage *n* : BAGGAGE
luke·warm *adj* **1** : neither hot nor cold **2** : not very interested or eager
[1]**lull** *vb* : to make or become quiet or less watchful
[2]**lull** *n* : a period of calm (as in a storm)
lul·la·by *n, pl* **lul·la·bies** : a song for helping babies to sleep
[1]**lum·ber** *vb* : to move in an awkward way
[2]**lumber** *n* : timber especially when sawed into boards
[3]**lumber** *vb* : to cut logs : saw logs into lumber
lum·ber·jack *n* : a person who works at lumbering
lum·ber·man *n, pl* **lum·ber·men** : a person engaged in the lumber business
lum·ber·yard *n* : a place where a stock of lumber is kept for sale
lu·mi·nous *adj* : shining brightly — **lu·mi·nous·ly** *adv*
[1]**lump** *n* : a small uneven mass (as a chunk or a swelling)
[2]**lump** *vb* **1** : to form into a lump **2** : to group together
lu·nar *adj* **1** : of or relating to the moon **2** : measured by the revolutions of the moon
[1]**lu·na·tic** *adj* : INSANE 1, CRAZY
[2]**lunatic** *n* : an insane person
[1]**lunch** *n* **1** : a light meal especially when eaten in the middle of the day **2** : food prepared for lunch
[2]**lunch** *vb* : to eat lunch
lun·cheon *n* **1** : [1]LUNCH 1 **2** : a formal lunch
lung *n* : either of two organs in the chest that are like bags and are the main breathing structure in animals that breathe air
[1]**lunge** *n* : a sudden movement forward
[2]**lunge** *vb* **lunged; lung·ing** : to push or drive with force
lung·fish *n* : any of several fishes that breathe with structures like lungs as well as with gills
lu·pine *n* : a plant related to the clovers that has tall spikes of showy flowers like those of sweet peas
[1]**lurch** *n* **1** : a sudden roll of a ship to one side **2** : a swaying staggering movement or gait
[2]**lurch** *vb* : to move with a lurch
[1]**lure** *n* **1** : something that attracts or draws one on : TEMPTATION **2** : an artificial bait for catching fish
[2]**lure** *vb* **lured; lur·ing** : to tempt or lead away by offering some pleasure or advantage : ENTICE
lu·rid *adj* **1** : looking like glowing fire seen through smoke **2** : SENSATIONAL 2 — **lu·rid·ly** *adv* — **lu·rid·ness** *n*
lurk *vb* : to hide in or about a place
lus·cious *adj* **1** : very sweet and pleasing to taste and smell **2** : delightful to hear, see, or feel — **lus·cious·ly** *adv* — **lus·cious·ness** *n*
lush *adj* **1** : very juicy and fresh **2** : covered with a thick growth — **lush·ly** *adv* — **lush·ness** *n*
lus·ter *or* **lus·tre** *n* : a glow of reflected light : SHEEN
lus·trous *adj* : having luster
lute *n* : an old stringed instrument with a body shaped like a pear and usually paired strings played with the fingers
lux·u·ri·ant *adj* : growing freely and well — **lux·u·ri·ant·ly** *adv*
lux·u·ri·ous *adj* **1** : loving pleasure and luxury **2** : very fine and comfortable — **lux·u·ri·ous·ly** *adv* — **lux·u·ri·ous·ness** *n*
lux·u·ry *n, pl* **lux·u·ries** **1** : very rich, pleasant, and comfortable surroundings **2** : something desirable but expensive or hard to get **3** : something pleasant but not really needed for one's pleasure or comfort
[1]**-ly** *adj suffix* **1** : like : similar to **2** : happening in each specified period of time : every

[2]-ly *adv suffix* **1 :** in a specified manner **2 :** from a specified point of view
lye *n* **:** a dangerous compound containing sodium that dissolves in water and is used in cleaning
lying *present participle of* LIE
lymph *n* **:** a clear liquid like blood without the red cells that nourishes the tissues and carries off wastes
lym·phat·ic *adj* **:** of or relating to lymph
lym·pho·cyte *n* **:** any of the white blood cells of the immune system that play a role in recognizing and destroying foreign cells, particles, or substances that have invaded the body
lynx *n, pl* **lynx** *or* **lynx·es :** any of several wildcats with rather long legs, a short tail, and often ears with tufts of long hairs at the tip
lyre *n* **:** a stringed instrument like a harp used by the ancient Greeks
[1]lyr·ic *n* **1 :** a lyric poem **2 lyrics** *pl* **:** the words of a popular song
[2]lyric *adj* **1 :** suitable for singing **:** MUSICAL **2 :** expressing personal emotion
lyr·i·cal *adj* **:** [2]LYRIC

M

m *n, pl* **m's** *or* **ms** *often cap* **1 :** the thirteenth letter of the English alphabet **2 :** 1000 in Roman numerals
ma *n, often cap* **:** [1]MOTHER 1
ma'am *n* **:** MADAM
mac·ad·am *n* **:** a road surface made of small closely packed broken stone
ma·caque *n* **:** any of several mostly Asian monkeys with short tails
mac·a·ro·ni *n, pl* **macaronis** *or* **macaronies :** a food that is made of a mixture of flour and water formed into tubes and dried
mac·a·roon *n* **:** a cookie made of the white of eggs, sugar, and ground almonds or coconut
ma·caw *n* **:** a large parrot of Central and South America with a long tail, a harsh voice, and bright feathers
[1]mace *n* **:** a spice made from the dried outer covering of the nutmeg
[2]mace *n* **:** a fancy club carried before certain officials as a sign of authority
ma·chete *n* **:** a large heavy knife used for cutting sugarcane and underbrush and as a weapon
[1]ma·chine *n* **1 :** VEHICLE 2 **2 :** a device that combines forces, motion, and energy in a way that does some desired work
[2]machine *vb* **ma·chined; ma·chin·ing :** to shape or finish by tools run by machines
machine gun *n* **:** an automatic gun for continuous firing
ma·chin·ery *n* **1 :** a group of machines **2 :** the working parts of a machine **3 :** the people and equipment by which something is done
machine shop *n* **:** a workshop in which metal articles are machined and put together
ma·chin·ist *n* **:** a person who makes or works on machines
mack·er·el *n, pl* **mackerel** *or* **mackerels :** a food fish of the North Atlantic that is green with blue bars above and silvery below
mack·i·naw *n* **:** a short heavy woolen coat
ma·cron *n* **:** a mark {macr} placed over a vowel to show that the vowel is long
mad *adj* **mad·der; mad·dest 1 :** INSANE 1 **2 :** done or made without thinking **3 :** ANGRY **4 :** INFATUATED **5 :** having rabies **6 :** marked by intense and often disorganized activity — **mad·ly** *adv* — **mad·ness** *n*
mad·am *n, pl* **mes·dames** — used without a name as a form of polite address to a woman
[1]mad·cap *adj* **:** likely to do something mad or reckless **:** done for fun without thinking
[2]madcap *n* **:** a madcap person
mad·den *vb* **:** to make mad
made *past of* MAKE
made–up *adj* **:** showing more imagination than concern with fact
mad·house *n* **:** a place or scene of complete confusion
mag·a·zine *n* **1 :** a storehouse or warehouse for military supplies **2 :** a place for keeping explosives in a fort or ship **3 :** a container in a gun for holding cartridges **4 :** a publication issued at regular intervals (as weekly or monthly)
mag·got *n* **:** a legless grub that is the larva of a two-winged fly
[1]mag·ic *n* **1 :** the power to control natural forces possessed by certain persons (as wizards and witches) in folk tales and fiction **2 :** a power that seems mysterious **3 :** something that charms **4 :** the art or skill of performing tricks or illusions as if by magic for entertainment
[2]magic *adj* **1 :** of or relating to magic **2 :** having effects that seem to be caused by magic **3 :** giving a feeling of enchantment
mag·i·cal *adj* **:** [2]MAGIC
ma·gi·cian *n* **:** a person skilled in magic
magic lantern *n* **:** an early kind of slide projector
mag·is·trate *n* **1 :** a chief officer of government **2 :** a local official with some judicial power

mag·ma *n* : molten rock within the earth

mag·na·nim·i·ty *n* : the quality of being magnanimous

mag·nan·i·mous *adj* **1 :** having a noble and courageous spirit **2 :** being generous and forgiving — **mag·nan·i·mous·ly** *adv*

mag·ne·sium *n* **:** a silvery white metallic chemical element that is lighter than aluminum and is used in lightweight alloys

mag·net *n* **:** a piece of material (as of iron, steel, or alloy) that is able to attract iron

mag·net·ic *adj* **1 :** acting like a magnet **2 :** of or relating to the earth's magnetism **3 :** having a great power to attract people

magnetic field *n* **:** the portion of space near a magnetic body within which magnetic forces can be detected

magnetic needle *n* **:** a narrow strip of magnetized steel that is free to swing around to show the direction of the earth's magnetism

magnetic pole *n* **1 :** either of the poles of a magnet **2 :** either of two small regions of the earth which are located near the North and South Poles and toward which a compass needle points

magnetic tape *n* **:** a thin ribbon of plastic coated with a magnetic material on which information (as sound) may be stored

mag·ne·tism *n* **1 :** the power to attract that a magnet has **2 :** the power to attract others **:** personal charm

mag·ne·tize *vb* **mag·ne·tized; mag·ne·tiz·ing :** to cause to be magnetic

mag·ne·to *n, pl* **mag·ne·tos :** a small generator used especially to produce the spark in some gasoline engines

mag·nif·i·cent *adj* **:** having impressive beauty **:** very grand — **mag·nif·i·cent·ly** *adv*

mag·ni·fy *vb* **mag·ni·fied; mag·ni·fy·ing 1 :** to enlarge in fact or appearance **2 :** to cause to seem greater or more important **:** EXAGGERATE

magnifying glass *n* **:** a lens that magnifies something seen through it

mag·ni·tude *n* **:** greatness of size

mag·no·lia *n* **:** a tree or tall shrub having showy white, pink, yellow, or purple flowers that appear before or sometimes with the leaves

mag·pie *n* **:** a noisy black-and-white bird related to the jays

ma·hog·a·ny *n, pl* **ma·hog·a·nies :** a strong reddish brown wood that is used especially for furniture and is obtained from several tropical trees

maid *n* **1 :** an unmarried girl or woman **2 :** a female servant

¹maid·en *n* **:** an unmarried girl or woman

²maiden *adj* **1 :** UNMARRIED **2 :** ¹FIRST 2

maid·en·hair fern *n* **:** a fern with slender stems and delicate feathery leaves

maid·en·hood *n* **:** the state or time of being a maiden

maiden name *n* **:** a woman's family name before she is married

maid of honor : an unmarried woman who stands with the bride at a wedding

¹mail *n* **1 :** letters, parcels, and papers sent from one person to another through the post office **2 :** the whole system used in the public sending and delivering of mail **3 :** something that comes in the mail

²mail *vb* **:** to send by mail

³mail *n* **:** a fabric made of metal rings linked together and used as armor

mail·box *n* **1 :** a public box in which to place outgoing mail **2 :** a private box (as on a house) for the delivery of incoming mail

mail carrier *n* **:** LETTER CARRIER

mail·man *n, pl* **mail·men :** LETTER CARRIER

maim *vb* **:** to injure badly or cripple by violence

¹main *n* **1 :** physical strength **:** FORCE **2 :** HIGH SEAS **3 :** the chief part **:** essential point **4 :** a principal line, tube, or pipe of a utility system

²main *adj* **1 :** first in size, rank, or importance **:** CHIEF **2 :** PURE 3, SHEER — **main·ly** *adv*

main·land *n* **:** a continent or the main part of a continent as distinguished from an offshore island or sometimes from a cape or peninsula

main·mast *n* **:** the principal mast of a sailing ship

main·sail *n* **:** the principal sail on the mainmast

main·spring *n* **:** the principal spring in a mechanical device (as a watch or clock)

main·stay *n* **1 :** the large strong rope from the maintop of a ship usually to the foot of the foremast **2 :** a chief support

main·tain *vb* **1 :** to keep in a particular or desired state **2 :** to defend by argument **3 :** CARRY ON 3, CONTINUE **4 :** to provide for **:** SUPPORT **5 :** to insist to be true

main·te·nance *n* **1 :** the act of maintaining **:** the state of being maintained **2 :** UPKEEP

main·top *n* **:** a platform around the head of a mainmast

maize *n* **:** INDIAN CORN

ma·jes·tic *adj* **:** very impressive and dignified **:** NOBLE — **ma·jes·ti·cal·ly** *adv*

maj·es·ty *n, pl* **maj·es·ties 1 :** royal dignity or authority **2 :** the quality or state of being majestic **3** — used as a title for a king, queen, emperor, or empress

¹ma·jor *adj* **1 :** greater in number, quantity, rank, or importance **2 :** of or relating to a musical scale of eight notes with half steps between the third and fourth and between the seventh and eighth notes and with whole steps between all the others

[2]**major** *n* **:** a commissioned officer in the Army, Air Force, or Marine Corps ranking above a captain

major general *n* **:** a commissioned officer in the Army, Air Force, or Marine Corps ranking above a brigadier general

ma·jor·i·ty *n, pl* **ma·jor·i·ties 1 :** the age at which one is allowed to vote **2 :** a number greater than half of a total **3 :** the amount by which a majority is more than a minority **4 :** a group or party that makes up the greater part of a whole body of persons

[1]**make** *vb* **made; mak·ing 1 :** to cause to occur **2 :** to form or put together out of material or parts **3 :** to combine to produce **4 :** to set in order **:** PREPARE **5 :** to cause to be or become **6 :** [1]DO 1, PERFORM **7 :** to produce by action **8 :** COMPEL **9 :** GET 1, GAIN **10 :** to act so as to be — **make believe :** to act as if something known to be imaginary is real or true — **make good 1 :** FULFILL, COMPLETE **2 :** SUCCEED 3

[2]**make** *n* **1 :** the way in which a thing is made **:** STRUCTURE **2 :** [1]BRAND 4

[1]**make–be·lieve** *n* **:** a pretending to believe (as in children's play)

[2]**make–believe** *adj* **:** not real **:** IMAGINARY

make out *vb* **1 :** to write out **2 :** UNDERSTAND 1 **3 :** IDENTIFY 3 **4 :** [1]FARE

[1]**make·shift** *n* **:** a thing used as a temporary substitute for another

[2]**makeshift** *adj* **:** serving as a temporary substitute

make·up *n* **1 :** the way the parts or elements of something are put together or joined **2 :** materials used in changing one's appearance (as for a play or other entertainment) **3 :** any of various cosmetics (as lipstick or powder)

make up *vb* **1 :** to create from the imagination **2 :** [2]FORM 3, COMPOSE **3 :** [1]RECOMPENSE, ATONE **4 :** to become friendly again **5 :** to put on makeup — **make up one's mind :** to reach a decision

mal- *prefix* **1 :** bad **:** badly **2 :** abnormal **:** abnormally

mal·ad·just·ed *adj* **:** not properly adjusted

mal·a·dy *n, pl* **mal·a·dies :** a disease or ailment of body or mind

ma·lar·ia *n* **:** a serious disease with chills and fever that is spread by the bite of one kind of mosquito

[1]**male** *n* **:** an individual that produces germ cells (as sperm) that fertilize the eggs of a female

[2]**male** *adj* **1 :** of, relating to, or being the sex that fathers young **2 :** bearing stamens but no pistil **3 :** of, relating to, or like that of males — **male·ness** *n*

mal·for·ma·tion *n* **:** something that is badly or wrongly formed

mal·ice *n* **:** ILL WILL

ma·li·cious *adj* **1 :** doing mean things for pleasure **2 :** done just to be mean — **ma·li·cious·ly** *adv*

[1]**ma·lign** *adj* **:** MALIGNANT 1

[2]**malign** *vb* **:** to say evil things about **:** SLANDER

ma·lig·nant *adj* **1 :** evil in influence or result **:** INJURIOUS **2 :** MALICIOUS 1 **3 :** likely to cause death **:** DEADLY — **ma·lig·nant·ly** *adv*

mall *n* **1 :** a shaded walk **:** PROMENADE **2 :** a usually paved or grassy strip between two roadways **3 :** a shopping area in a community with a variety of shops around an often covered space for pedestrians

mal·lard *n* **:** a common wild duck of the northern hemisphere that is the ancestor of the domestic ducks

mal·lea·ble *adj* **:** capable of being beaten out, extended, or shaped by hammer blows

mal·let *n* **1 :** a hammer with a short handle and a barrel-shaped head of wood or soft material used for driving a tool (as a chisel) or for striking a surface without denting it **2 :** a club with a short thick rod for a head and a long thin rod for a handle

mal·low *n* **:** a tall plant related to the hollyhock that has usually lobed leaves and white, rose, or purplish flowers with five petals

mal·nu·tri·tion *n* **:** faulty nourishment

malt *n* **1 :** grain and especially barley soaked in water until it has sprouted **2 :** MALTED MILK

malt·ed milk *n* **:** a beverage made by dissolving a powder made from dried milk and cereals in a liquid (as milk)

mal·treat *vb* **:** to treat in a rough or unkind way **:** ABUSE

ma·ma *or* **mam·ma** *n* **:** [1]MOTHER 1

mam·mal *n* **:** a warm-blooded animal that feeds its young with milk and has a backbone, two pairs of limbs, and a more or less complete covering of hair

[1]**mam·moth** *n* **:** a very large hairy extinct elephant with tusks that curve upward

[2]**mammoth** *adj* **:** very large **:** HUGE

mam·my *n, pl* **mammies :** [1]MOTHER 1

[1]**man** *n, pl* **men 1 :** a human being **:** PERSON **2 :** an adult male human being **3 :** the human race **:** MANKIND **4 :** a member of the natural family to which human beings belong including both modern humans and extinct related forms **5 :** HUSBAND **6 :** an adult male servant or employee **7 :** one of the pieces

with which various games (as chess or checkers) are played

²**man** *vb* **manned; man·ning 1 :** to station crew members at **2 :** to do the work of operating

man·age *vb* **man·aged; man·ag·ing 1 :** to look after and make decisions about : be the boss of **2 :** to achieve what one wants to do

man·age·ment *n* **1 :** the managing of something **2 :** the people who manage

man·ag·er *n* : a person who manages — **man·ag·er·ship** *n*

man·a·tee *n* : a mainly tropical water-dwelling mammal that eats plants and has a broad rounded tail

man·da·rin *n* : a high public official of the Chinese Empire

man·date *n* **1 :** an order from a higher court to a lower court **2 :** a command or instruction from an authority **3:** the instruction given by voters to their elected representatives

man·da·tory *adj* : containing or being a command

man·di·ble *n* **1 :** a lower jaw often with its soft parts **2 :** either the upper or lower part of the bill of a bird **3 :** either of the first pair of mouth parts of some invertebrates (as an insect or crustacean) that often form biting organs

man·do·lin *n* : an instrument with four pairs of strings played by plucking

mane *n* : long heavy hair growing from the neck or shoulders of an animal (as a horse or lion) — **maned** *adj*

¹**ma·neu·ver** *n* **1 :** a planned movement of troops or ships **2 :** a training exercise by armed forces **3 :** skillful action or management

²**maneuver** *vb* **1 :** to move in a maneuver **2 :** to perform a maneuver **3 :** to guide skillfully — **ma·neu·ver·able** *adj*

ma·neu·ver·abil·i·ty *n* : the quality or state of being maneuverable

man·ga·nese *n* : a grayish white brittle metallic chemical element that resembles iron

mange *n* : a contagious skin disease usually of domestic animals in which there is itching and loss of hair

man·ger *n* : an open box in which food for farm animals is placed

man·gle *vb* **man·gled; man·gling 1 :** to cut or bruise with repeated blows **2 :** to spoil while making or performing

man·go *n, pl* **man·goes** *or* **man·gos :** a juicy yellowish red mildly tart tropical fruit that is borne by an evergreen tree related to the cashew

mangy *adj* **mang·i·er; mang·i·est 1 :** having mange or resulting from mange **2 :** SHABBY 2 **3 :** SEEDY 2

man·hole *n* : a covered hole (as in a street) large enough to let a person pass through

man·hood *n* **1 :** COURAGE **2 :** the state of being an adult human male **3 :** adult human males

ma·nia *n* **1 :** often violent or excited insanity **2 :** unreasonable enthusiasm

ma·ni·ac *n* : a violently insane person

¹**man·i·cure** *n* **1 :** MANICURIST **2 :** a treatment for the care of the hands and nails

²**manicure** *vb* **man·i·cured; man·i·cur·ing :** to give a manicure to

man·i·cur·ist *n* : a person who gives manicures

¹**man·i·fest** *adj* : clear to the senses or to the mind : easy to recognize : OBVIOUS

²**manifest** *vb* : to show plainly

man·i·fes·ta·tion *n* **1 :** the act of manifesting **2 :** something that makes clear : EVIDENCE

man·i·fold *adj* : of many and various kinds

ma·nip·u·late *vb* **ma·nip·u·lat·ed; ma·nip·u·lat·ing 1 :** to work with the hands or by mechanical means and especially with skill **2 :** to manage skillfully and especially with intent to deceive

man·kind *n* **1 :** human beings **2 :** men as distinguished from women

man·ly *adj* **man·li·er; man·li·est :** having qualities (as courage) often felt to be proper for a man — **man·li·ness** *n*

man–made *adj* : made by people rather than nature

man·na *n* : food supplied by a miracle to the Israelites in the wilderness

man·ne·quin *n* : a form representing the human figure used especially for displaying clothes

man·ner *n* **1 :** ¹SORT 1 **2 :** a way of acting **3 manners** *pl* : behavior toward or in the presence of other people

man·ner·ism *n* : a habit (as of looking or moving in a certain way) that one notices in a person's behavior

man·ner·ly *adj* : showing good manners : POLITE

man–of–war *n, pl* **men–of–war :** WARSHIP

man·or *n* : a large estate

man·sion *n* : a large fine house

man·slaugh·ter *n* : the unintentional but unlawful killing of a person

man·ta ray *n* : any of several very large rays of warm seas that have fins that resemble wings

man·tel *n* : a shelf above a fireplace

man·tel·piece *n* **1 :** a shelf above a fireplace along with side pieces **2 :** MANTEL

man·tis *n, pl* **man·tis·es** *or* **man·tes :** an insect related to the grasshoppers and roaches that feeds on other insects which are clasped in the raised front legs

man·tle *n* **1 :** a loose sleeveless outer garment **2 :** something that covers or wraps **3 :** a fold of the body wall of a mollusk that produces the shell material **4 :** the part of the earth's interior beneath the crust and above the central core

[1]**man·u·al** *adj* **1 :** of or relating to the hands **2 :** done or operated by the hands — **man·u·al·ly** *adv*

[2]**manual** *n* **:** HANDBOOK

manual training *n* **:** training in work done with the hands (as woodworking)

[1]**man·u·fac·ture** *n* **1 :** the making of products by hand or machinery **2 :** PRODUCTION 2

[2]**manufacture** *vb* **man·u·fac·tured; man·u·fac·tur·ing :** to make from raw materials by hand or machinery — **man·u·fac·tur·er** *n*

ma·nure *n* **:** material (as animal wastes) used to fertilize land

man·u·script *n* **1 :** a composition or document written by hand especially before the development of printing **2 :** a document submitted for publication **3 :** HANDWRITING

[1]**many** *adj* **more; most 1 :** amounting to a large number **2 :** being one of a large but not fixed number

[2]**many** *pron* **:** a large number

[3]**many** *n* **:** a large number

[1]**map** *n* **1 :** a picture or chart showing features of an area (as the surface of the earth or the moon) **2 :** a picture or chart of the sky showing the position of stars and planets

[2]**map** *vb* **mapped; map·ping 1 :** to make a map of **2 :** to plan in detail

ma·ple *n* **:** any of a group of trees having deeply notched leaves, fruits with two wings, and hard pale wood and including some whose sap is evaporated to a sweet syrup (**maple syrup**) and a brownish sugar (**maple sugar**)

mar *vb* **marred; mar·ring :** to make a blemish on **:** SPOIL

ma·ra·ca *n* **:** a musical rhythm instrument made of a dried gourd with seeds or pebbles inside that is usually played in pairs by shaking

mar·a·thon *n* **1 :** a long-distance running race **2 :** a long hard contest

[1]**mar·ble** *n* **1 :** limestone that is capable of taking a high polish and is used in architecture and sculpture **2 :** a little ball (as of glass) used in a children's game (**marbles**)

[2]**marble** *adj* **:** made of or like marble

[1]**march** *vb* **1 :** to move or cause to move along steadily usually with long even steps and in step with others **2 :** to make steady progress — **march·er** *n*

[2]**march** *n* **1 :** the action of marching **2 :** the distance covered in marching **3 :** a regular step used in marching **4 :** a musical piece in a lively rhythm with a strong beat that is suitable to march to

March *n* **:** the third month of the year

mar·chio·ness *n* **1 :** the wife or widow of a marquess **2 :** a woman who holds the rank of a marquess in her own right

mare *n* **:** an adult female of the horse or a related animal (as a zebra or donkey)

mar·ga·rine *n* **:** a food product made usually from vegetable oils and skim milk and used as a spread or for cooking

mar·gin *n* **1 :** the part of a page outside the main body of print or writing **2 :** [1]BORDER 1 **3 :** an extra amount (as of time or money) allowed for use if needed

mari·gold *n* **:** any of several plants related to the daisies that are grown for their yellow or brownish red and yellow flower heads

mar·i·jua·na *n* **:** dried leaves and flowers of the hemp plant smoked as a drug

ma·ri·na *n* **:** a dock or basin providing a place to anchor motorboats and yachts

[1]**ma·rine** *adj* **1 :** of or relating to the sea **2 :** of or relating to the navigation of the sea **:** NAUTICAL **3 :** of or relating to marines

[2]**marine** *n* **1 :** the ships of a country **2 :** one of a class of soldiers serving on board a ship or in close cooperation with a naval force

mar·i·ner *n* **:** SEAMAN 1, SAILOR

mar·i·o·nette *n* **:** a doll that can be made to move by means of strings **:** PUPPET

mar·i·tal *adj* **:** of or relating to marriage

mar·i·time *adj* **1 :** of or relating to ocean navigation or trade **2 :** bordering on or living near the sea

[1]**mark** *n* **1 :** something designed or serving to record position **2 :** something aimed at **:** TARGET **3 :** the starting line of a race **4 :** INDICATION 2 **5 :** a blemish (as a scratch or stain) made on a surface **6 :** a written or printed symbol **7 :** a grade or score showing the quality of work or conduct

[2]**mark** *vb* **1 :** to set apart by a line or boundary **2 :** to make a mark on **3 :** to decide and show the value or quality of by marks **:** GRADE **4 :** to be an important characteristic of **5 :** to take notice of — **mark·er** *n*

[3]**mark** *n* **:** a German coin or bill

marked *adj* **1 :** having a mark or marks **2 :** NOTICEABLE

[1]**mar·ket** *n* **1 :** a meeting of people at a fixed time and place to buy and sell things **2 :** a public place where a market is held **3 :** a store where foods are sold to the public **4 :** the region in which something can be sold

[2]**market** *vb* **:** to buy or sell in a market

mar·ket·place *n* **:** an open square or place in

a town where markets or public sales are held

mark·ing *n* **:** a mark made

marks·man *n, pl* **marks·men :** a person who shoots well — **marks·man·ship** *n*

mar·ma·lade *n* **:** a jam containing pieces of fruit and fruit rind

mar·mo·set *n* **:** a small monkey of South and Central America with soft fur and a bushy tail

mar·mot *n* **:** a stocky animal with short legs, coarse fur, and bushy tail that is related to the squirrels

¹ma·roon *vb* **:** to put ashore and abandon on a lonely island or coast

²maroon *n* **:** a dark red

mar·quess *n* **:** a British nobleman ranking below a duke and above an earl

mar·quis *n* **:** MARQUESS

mar·quise *n* **:** MARCHIONESS

mar·riage *n* **1 :** the legal relationship into which a man and a woman enter with the purpose of making a home and raising a family **2 :** the act of getting married

mar·row *n* **:** a soft tissue rich in fat and blood vessels that fills the cavities of most bones

mar·ry *vb* **mar·ried; mar·ry·ing 1 :** to join in marriage as husband and wife **2 :** to give (as one's child) in marriage **3 :** to take for husband or wife **4 :** to enter into a marriage relationship

Mars *n* **:** the planet that is fourth in order of distance from the sun, is known for its redness, and has a diameter of about 6800 kilometers

marsh *n* **:** an area of soft wet land usually overgrown with grasses and related plants

¹mar·shal *n* **1 :** a person who arranges and directs ceremonies **2 :** an officer of the highest rank in some military forces **3 :** a federal official having duties similar to those of a sheriff **4 :** the head of a division of a city government

²marshal *vb* **mar·shaled** *or* **mar·shalled; mar·shal·ing** *or* **mar·shal·ling :** to arrange in order

marsh·mal·low *n* **:** a soft spongy sweet made from corn syrup, sugar, and gelatin

marsh marigold *n* **:** a swamp plant with shiny leaves and bright yellow flowers like buttercups

marshy *adj* **marsh·i·er; marsh·i·est :** like or being a marsh

mar·su·pi·al *n* **:** any of a group of mammals (as kangaroos and opossums) that do not develop a true placenta and that usually have a pouch on the female's abdomen in which the young are carried

mart *n* **:** a trading place **:** MARKET

mar·ten *n* **:** a slender animal larger than the related weasels that eats flesh and is sought for its soft gray or brown fur

mar·tial *adj* **:** having to do with or suitable for war

martial art *n* **:** an art of combat and self-defense (as karate or judo) that is widely practiced as a sport

mar·tin *n* **1 :** a European swallow with a forked tail **2 :** any of several birds (as the American **purple martin**) resembling or related to the true martin

Mar·tin Lu·ther King Day *n* **:** the third Monday in January observed as a legal holiday in some states of the United States

¹mar·tyr *n* **:** a person who suffers greatly or dies rather than give up his or her religion or principles

²martyr *vb* **:** to put to death for refusing to give up a belief

¹mar·vel *n* **:** something that causes wonder or astonishment

²marvel *vb* **mar·veled** *or* **mar·velled; mar·vel·ing** *or* **mar·vel·ling :** to be struck with astonishment or wonder

mar·vel·ous *or* **mar·vel·lous** *adj* **1 :** causing wonder or astonishment **2 :** of the finest kind or quality — **mar·vel·ous·ly** *adv*

mas·cot *n* **:** a person, animal, or object adopted by a group and believed to bring good luck

mas·cu·line *adj* **1 :** of the male sex **2 :** ²MALE 3

¹mash *vb* **:** to make into a soft pulpy mass

²mash *n* **1 :** a mixture of ground feeds used for feeding livestock **2 :** a mass of something made soft and pulpy by beating or crushing

¹mask *n* **1 :** a cover for the face or part of the face used for disguise or protection **2 :** something that disguises or conceals **3 :** a copy of a face molded in wax or plaster

²mask *vb* **:** CONCEAL, DISGUISE

ma·son *n* **:** a person who builds or works with stone, brick, or cement

ma·son·ry *n, pl* **ma·son·ries 1 :** the art, trade, or occupation of a mason **2 :** the work done by a mason **3 :** something built of stone, brick, or concrete

masque *n* **1 :** ¹MASQUERADE 1 **2 :** an old form of dramatic entertainment in which the actors wore masks

¹mas·quer·ade *n* **1 :** a party (as a dance) at which people wear masks and costumes **2 :** a pretending to be something one is not

²masquerade *vb* **mas·quer·ad·ed; mas·quer·ad·ing 1 :** to disguise oneself **2 :** to pass oneself off as something one is not **:** POSE — **mas·quer·ad·er** *n*

¹mass *n* **1 :** an amount of something that holds or clings together **2 :** BULK 1, SIZE **3**

: the principal part : main body **4 :** a large quantity or number **5 masses** *pl* : the body of ordinary or common people

[2]**mass** *vb* : to collect into a mass

Mass *n* : a religious service in celebration of the Eucharist

[1]**mas·sa·cre** *n* : the violent and cruel killing of a large number of persons

[2]**massacre** *vb* **mas·sa·cred; mas·sa·cring** : to kill in a massacre : SLAUGHTER

[1]**mas·sage** *n* : treatment of the body by rubbing, kneading, and tapping

[2]**massage** *vb* **mas·saged; mas·sag·ing** : to give massage to

mas·sive *adj* : very large, heavy, and solid

mast *n* **1 :** a long pole that rises from the bottom of a ship and supports the sails and rigging **2 :** a vertical or nearly vertical tall pole — **mast·ed** *adj*

[1]**mas·ter** *n* **1 :** a male teacher **2 :** an artist or performer of great skill **3 :** one having authority over another person or thing **4 :** EMPLOYER **5** — used as a title for a young boy too young to be called *mister*

[2]**master** *vb* **1 :** to get control of **2 :** to become skillful at

master chief petty officer *n* : a petty officer in the Navy or Coast Guard ranking above a senior chief petty officer

mas·ter·ful *adj* **1 :** tending to take control : BOSSY **2 :** having or showing great skill

mas·ter·ly *adj* : showing the knowledge or skill of a master

mas·ter·piece *n* : a work done or made with supreme skill

master sergeant *n* : a noncommissioned officer in the Army ranking above a sergeant first class or in the Air Force ranking above a technical sergeant or in the Marine Corps ranking above a gunnery sergeant

mas·tery *n, pl* **mas·ter·ies 1 :** the position or authority of a master **2 :** VICTORY 1 **3 :** skill that makes one master of something

mast·head *n* : the top of a mast

mas·ti·cate *vb* **mas·ti·cat·ed; mas·ti·cat·ing** : [1]CHEW

mas·tiff *n* : a very large powerful dog with a smooth coat

[1]**mat** *n* **1 :** a piece of coarse woven or braided fabric used as a floor or seat covering **2 :** a piece of material in front of a door to wipe the shoes on **3 :** a piece of material (as cloth or woven straw) used under dishes or vases or as an ornament **4 :** a pad or cushion for gymnastics or wrestling **5 :** something made up of many tangled strands

[2]**mat** *vb* **mat·ted; mat·ting** : to form into a tangled mass

mat·a·dor *n* : a bullfighter who plays the chief human part in a bullfight

[1]**match** *n* **1 :** a person or thing that is equal to or as good as another **2 :** a thing that is exactly like another thing **3 :** two people or things that go well together **4 :** MARRIAGE 1 **5 :** a contest between two individuals or teams

[2]**match** *vb* **1 :** to place in competition **2 :** to choose something that is the same as another or goes with it **3 :** to be the same or suitable to one another

[3]**match** *n* **1 :** a wick or cord that is made to burn evenly and is used for lighting a charge of powder **2 :** a short slender piece of material tipped with a mixture that produces fire when scratched

match·book *n* : a small folder containing rows of paper matches

match·less *adj* : having no equal : better than any other of the same kind — **match·less·ly** *adv*

match·lock *n* : a musket with a hole at the rear of the barrel into which a slowly burning cord is lowered to ignite the charge

[1]**mate** *n* **1 :** COMPANION 1, COMRADE **2 :** an officer on a ship used to carry passengers or freight who ranks below the captain **3 :** either member of a married couple **4 :** either member of a breeding pair of animals **5 :** either of two matched objects

[2]**mate** *vb* **mat·ed; mat·ing** : to join as mates : MARRY

[1]**ma·te·ri·al** *adj* **1 :** of, relating to, or made of matter : PHYSICAL **2 :** of or relating to a person's bodily needs or wants **3 :** having real importance — **ma·teri·al·ly** *adv*

[2]**material** *n* **1 :** the elements, substance, or parts of which something is made or can be made **2 materials** *pl* : equipment needed for doing something

ma·te·ri·al·ize *vb* **ma·te·ri·al·ized; ma·te·ri·al·iz·ing 1 :** to cause to take on a physical form **2 :** to become actual fact

ma·ter·nal *adj* **1 :** of or relating to a mother **2** : related through one's mother — **ma·ter·nal·ly** *adv*

ma·ter·ni·ty *n* : the state of being a mother

math *n* : MATHEMATICS

math·e·mat·i·cal *adj* **1 :** of or relating to mathematics **2 :** [2]EXACT — **math·e·mat·i·cal·ly** *adv*

math·e·ma·ti·cian *n* : a specialist in mathematics

math·e·mat·ics *n* : the science that studies and explains numbers, quantities, measurements, and the relations between them

mat·i·nee *or* **mat·i·née** *n* : a musical or dramatic performance in the afternoon

ma·tri·arch *n* : a woman who is head of a family, group, or state

mat·ri·mo·ni·al *adj* : of or relating to marriage

mat·ri·mo·ny *n* : MARRIAGE 1
ma·tron *n* **1 :** a married woman **2 :** a woman who is in charge of the household affairs of an institution **3 :** a woman who looks after women prisoners in a police station or prison
[1]**mat·ter** *n* **1 :** something to be dealt with or considered **2 :** PROBLEM 2, DIFFICULTY **3 :** the substance things are made of : something that takes up space and has weight **4 :** material substance of a certain kind or function **5 :** PUS **6 :** a more or less definite quantity or amount **7 :** [1]MAIL 1 — **no matter :** it makes no difference
[2]**matter** *vb* : to be of importance
mat·ter–of–fact *adj* : sticking to or concerned with fact
mat·ting *n* : material for mats
mat·tress *n* **1 :** a springy pad for use as a resting place usually over springs on a bedstead **2 :** a sack that can be filled with air or water and used as a mattress
[1]**ma·ture** *adj* **1 :** fully grown or developed : ADULT, RIPE **2 :** like that of a mature person
[2]**mature** *vb* **ma·tured; ma·tur·ing :** to reach maturity
ma·tu·ri·ty *n* : the condition of being mature : full development
[1]**maul** *n* : a heavy hammer used especially for driving wedges or posts
[2]**maul** *vb* **1 :** to beat and bruise severely **2 :** to handle roughly
mauve *n* : a medium purple, violet, or lilac
maxi- *prefix* : very long or large
max·il·la *n, pl* **max·il·lae 1 :** an upper jaw especially of a mammal **2 :** either of the pair of mouth parts next behind the mandibles of an arthropod (as an insect or a crustacean)
max·im *n* : a short saying expressing a general truth or rule of conduct
[1]**max·i·mum** *n, pl* **maximums** *or* **max·i·ma** : the highest value : greatest amount
[2]**maximum** *adj* : as great as possible in amount or degree
may *helping verb, past* **might;** *present sing & pl* **may 1 :** have permission to **2 :** be in some degree likely to **3** — used to express a wish **4** — used to express purpose
May *n* : the fifth month of the year
may·be *adv* : possibly but not certainly
mayn't : may not
may·on·naise *n* : a creamy dressing usually made of egg yolk, oil, and vinegar or lemon juice
may·or *n* : an official elected to serve as head of a city or borough
maze *n* : a confusing arrangement of paths or passages
MB *n* : MEGABYTE

me *pron, objective case of* I
mead·ow *n* : usually moist and low grassland
mead·ow·lark *n* : a bird that has brownish upper parts and a yellow breast and is about as large as a robin
mea·ger *or* **mea·gre** *adj* **1 :** having little flesh : THIN **2 :** INSUFFICIENT
[1]**meal** *n* **1 :** the food eaten or prepared for eating at one time **2 :** the act or time of eating
[2]**meal** *n* **1 :** usually coarsely ground seeds of a cereal grass and especially of Indian corn **2 :** something like meal in texture
mealy *adj* **meal·i·er; meal·i·est :** like meal — **meal·i·ness** *n*
[1]**mean** *vb* **meant; mean·ing 1 :** to have in mind as a purpose : INTEND **2 :** to intend for a particular use **3 :** to have as a meaning : SIGNIFY
[2]**mean** *adj* **1 :** low in quality, worth, or dignity **2 :** lacking in honor or dignity **3 :** STINGY 1 **4 :** deliberately unkind **5 :** ASHAMED 1 — **mean·ly** *adv* — **mean·ness** *n*
[3]**mean** *adj* : occurring or being in a middle position : AVERAGE
[4]**mean** *n* **1 :** a middle point or something (as a place, time, number, or rate) that falls at or near a middle point : MODERATION **2 :** ARITHMETIC MEAN **3 means** *pl* : something that helps a person to get what he or she wants **4 means** *pl* : WEALTH 1 — **by all means :** CERTAINLY 1 — **by any means :** in any way — **by means of :** through the use of — **by no means :** certainly not
me·an·der *vb* **1 :** to follow a winding course **2 :** to wander without a goal or purpose
mean·ing *n* **1 :** the idea a person intends to express by something said or done **2 :** the quality of communicating something or of being important
mean·ing·ful *adj* : having a meaning or purpose — **mean·ing·ful·ly** *adv*
mean·ing·less *adj* : having no meaning or importance
[1]**mean·time** *n* : the time between two events
[2]**meantime** *adv* : in the meantime
[1]**mean·while** *n* : [1]MEANTIME
[2]**meanwhile** *adv* **1 :** [2]MEANTIME **2 :** at the same time
mea·sles *n sing or pl* **1 :** a contagious disease in which there are fever and red spots on the skin **2 :** any of several diseases (as **German measles**) resembling true measles
mea·sly *adj* **mea·sli·er; mea·sli·est :** so small or unimportant as to be rejected with scorn
mea·sur·able *adj* : capable of being measured
[1]**mea·sure** *n* **1 :** EXTENT 2, DEGREE, AMOUNT **2 :** the size, capacity, or quantity of some-

thing as fixed by measuring **3 :** something (as a yardstick or cup) used in measuring **4 :** a unit used in measuring **5 :** a system of measuring **6 :** the notes and rests between bar lines on a musical staff **7 :** a way of accomplishing something **8 :** a legislative bill or act

[2]**measure** *vb* **mea·sured; mea·sur·ing 1 :** to find out the size, extent, or amount of **2 :** [1]ESTIMATE 1 **3 :** to bring into comparison **4 :** to give a measure of **:** INDICATE **5 :** to have as its measurement

mea·sure·ment *n* **1 :** the act of measuring **2 :** the extent, size, capacity, or amount of something as fixed by measuring **3 :** a system of measures

measure up *vb* **:** to satisfy needs or requirements

meat *n* **1 :** solid food **2 :** the part of something that can be eaten **3 :** animal and especially mammal tissue for use as food **4 :** the most important part **:** SUBSTANCE — **meat·less** *adj*

meat·ball *n* **:** a small ball of chopped or ground meat

me·chan·ic *n* **:** a person who makes or repairs machines

me·chan·i·cal *adj* **1 :** of or relating to machinery **2 :** made or operated by a machine **3 :** done or produced as if by a machine — **me·chan·i·cal·ly** *adv*

me·chan·ics *n sing or pl* **1 :** a science dealing with the action of forces on bodies **2 :** the way something works or things are done

mech·a·nism *n* **1 :** a mechanical device **2 :** the parts by which a machine operates **3 :** the parts or steps that make up a process or activity

mech·a·nize *vb* **mech·a·nized; mech·a·niz·ing 1 :** to make mechanical or automatic **2 :** to equip with machinery

med·al *n* **:** a piece of metal often in the form of a coin with design and words in honor of a special event, a person, or an achievement

me·dal·lion *n* **1 :** a large medal **2 :** something like a large medal (as in shape)

med·dle *vb* **med·dled; med·dling :** to interest oneself in what is not one's concern

med·dle·some *adj* **:** given to meddling

media *pl of* MEDIUM

med·i·cal *adj* **:** of or relating to the science or practice of medicine or to the treatment of disease — **med·i·cal·ly** *adv*

med·i·cate *vb* **med·i·cat·ed; med·i·cat·ing 1 :** to use medicine on or for **2 :** to add medicinal material to

med·i·ca·tion *n* **1 :** the act or process of medicating **2 :** medicinal material

me·dic·i·nal *adj* **:** used or likely to relieve or cure disease — **me·dic·i·nal·ly** *adv*

med·i·cine *n* **1 :** something used to cure or relieve a disease **2 :** a science or art dealing with the prevention, cure, or relief of disease

medicine dropper *n* **:** DROPPER 2

medicine man *n* **:** a member of a primitive tribe believed to have magic powers and called on to cure illnesses and keep away evil spirits

me·di·eval *or* **me·di·ae·val** *adj* **:** of or relating to the Middle Ages

me·di·o·cre *adj* **:** neither good nor bad **:** ORDINARY

med·i·tate *vb* **med·i·tat·ed; med·i·tat·ing 1 :** to consider carefully **:** PLAN **2 :** to spend time in quiet thinking **:** REFLECT

med·i·ta·tion *n* **:** the act or an instance of meditating

Med·i·ter·ra·nean *adj* **:** of or relating to the Mediterranean sea or to the lands or peoples surrounding it

[1]**me·di·um** *n, pl* **me·di·ums** *or* **me·dia 1 :** something that is between or in the middle **2 :** the thing by which or through which something is done **3 :** the substance in which something lives or acts **4 :** a person through whom other persons try to communicate with the spirits of the dead

[2]**medium** *adj* **:** intermediate in amount, quality, position, or degree

med·ley *n, pl* **medleys 1 :** MIXTURE 2, JUMBLE **2 :** a musical selection made up of a series of different songs or parts of different compositions

me·dul·la ob·lon·ga·ta *n* **:** the last part of the brain that joins the spinal cord and is concerned especially with control of involuntary activities (as breathing and beating of the heart)

meed *n* **:** something deserved or earned **:** REWARD

meek *adj* **1 :** putting up with injury or abuse with patience **2 :** lacking spirit or self-confidence — **meek·ly** *adv* — **meek·ness** *n*

[1]**meet** *vb* **met; meet·ing 1 :** to come upon or across **2 :** to be at a place to greet or keep an appointment **3 :** to approach from the opposite direction **4 :** to come together **:** JOIN, MERGE **5 :** to be sensed by **6 :** to deal with **7 :** to fulfill the requirements of **:** SATISFY **8 :** to become acquainted **9 :** to hold a meeting

[2]**meet** *n* **:** a meeting for sports competition

meet·ing *n* **1 :** the act of persons or things that meet **2 :** ASSEMBLY 1

meet·ing·house *n* **:** a building used for public assembly and especially for Protestant worship

mega·byte *n* **:** a unit of computer information storage capacity equal to 1,048,576 bytes

mega·phone *n* : a device shaped like a cone that is used to direct the voice and increase its loudness

[1]mel·an·choly *n* : a sad or gloomy mood

[2]melancholy *adj* : SAD 1

[1]mel·low *adj* **1 :** tender and sweet because of ripeness **2 :** made mild by age **3 :** being clear, full, and pure : not coarse — **mel·low·ness** *n*

[2]mellow *vb* : to make or become mellow

me·lo·di·ous *adj* : agreeable to the ear because of its melody — **me·lo·di·ous·ly** *adv* — **me·lo·di·ous·ness** *n*

mel·o·dy *n, pl* **mel·o·dies** **1 :** pleasing arrangement of sounds **2 :** a series of musical notes or tones arranged in a definite pattern of pitch and rhythm **3 :** the leading part in a musical composition

mel·on *n* : a fruit (as a watermelon) having juicy and usually sweet flesh and growing on a vine related to the gourds

melt *vb* **1 :** to change from a solid to a liquid usually through the action of heat **2 :** to grow less : DISAPPEAR **3 :** to make or become gentle : SOFTEN **4 :** to lose clear outline

melting point *n* : the temperature at which a solid melts

mem·ber *n* **1 :** a part (as an arm, leg, leaf, or branch) of a person, animal, or plant **2 :** one of the individuals (as persons) or units (as species) making up a group **3 :** a part of a structure

mem·ber·ship *n* **1 :** the state or fact of being a member **2 :** the whole number of members

mem·brane *n* : a thin soft flexible layer especially of animal or plant tissue

mem·bra·nous *adj* : made of or like membrane

me·men·to *n, pl* **me·men·tos** *or* **me·men·toes** : something that serves as a reminder

mem·o·ra·ble *adj* : worth remembering : not easily forgotten — **mem·o·ra·bly** *adv*

mem·o·ran·dum *n, pl* **mem·o·ran·dums** *or* **mem·o·ran·da** **1 :** an informal record or message **2 :** a written reminder

[1]me·mo·ri·al *adj* : serving to preserve the memory of a person or event

[2]memorial *n* : something by which the memory of a person or an event is kept alive : MONUMENT

Memorial Day *n* **1 :** May 30 once observed as a legal holiday in remembrance of war dead **2 :** the last Monday in May observed as a legal holiday in most states of the United States

mem·o·rize *vb* **mem·o·rized; mem·o·riz·ing** : to learn by heart

mem·o·ry *n, pl* **mem·o·ries** **1 :** the power or process of remembering **2 :** the store of things learned and kept in the mind **3 :** the act of remembering and honoring **4 :** something remembered **5 :** the time within which past events are remembered **6 :** a device or part in a computer which can receive and store information for use when wanted **7** : capacity for storing information

men *pl of* MAN

[1]men·ace *n* **1 :** DANGER 2 **2 :** an annoying person

[2]menace *vb* **men·aced; men·ac·ing** : THREATEN 1

me·nag·er·ie *n* : a collection of confined wild animals

[1]mend *vb* **1 :** IMPROVE, CORRECT **2 :** to restore to a whole condition **3 :** to improve in health — **mend·er** *n*

[2]mend *n* **1 :** the process of improving **2 :** a mended place

men·folk *or* **men·folks** *n pl* : the men of a family or community

men·ha·den *n, pl* **menhaden** : a fish of the Atlantic coast of the United States that is related to the herrings and is a source of oil and fertilizer

[1]me·ni·al *n* : a household servant

[2]menial *adj* : of, relating to, or suitable for servants : not needing skill

men–of–war *pl of* MAN-OF-WAR

me·no·rah *n* : a holder for candles used in Jewish worship

men·stru·a·tion *n* : a periodic discharge of bloody fluid from the uterus

-ment *n suffix* **1 :** result, goal, or method of a specified action **2 :** action : process **3** : place of a specified action **4 :** state : condition

men·tal *adj* **1 :** of or relating to the mind **2** : done in the mind — **men·tal·ly** *adv*

men·tal·i·ty *n* : mental power : ability to learn

men·thol *n* : a white crystalline soothing substance from oils of mint

[1]men·tion *n* : a brief reference to something

[2]mention *vb* : to refer to : speak about briefly

menu *n* **1 :** a list of dishes served at or available for a meal **2 :** the dishes or kinds of food served at a meal **3 :** a list shown on a computer screen from which a user can select an operation for the computer to perform

[1]me·ow *n* : the cry of a cat

[2]meow *vb* : to utter a meow

mer·can·tile *adj* : of or relating to merchants or trade

[1]mer·ce·nary *n, pl* **mer·ce·nar·ies** : a soldier from a foreign country hired to fight in an army

[2]mercenary *adj* **1 :** doing something only for the pay or reward **2 :** greedy for money

mer·chan·dise *n* **:** goods that are bought and sold in trade

mer·chant *n* **1 :** a person who carries on trade especially on a large scale or with foreign countries **2 :** STOREKEEPER 2

mer·chant·man *n, pl* **mer·chant·men :** a ship used in trading

merchant marine *n* **1 :** the trading ships of a nation **2 :** the persons who work in a merchant marine

mer·ci·ful *adj* **:** having or showing mercy or compassion — **mer·ci·ful·ly** *adv*

mer·ci·less *adj* **:** having no mercy **:** PITILESS — **mer·ci·less·ly** *adv*

mer·cu·ric *adj* **:** of, relating to, or containing mercury

mer·cu·ry *n* **1 :** a heavy silvery white metallic chemical element that is liquid at ordinary temperatures **2 :** the column of mercury in a thermometer or barometer **3** *cap* **:** the planet that is nearest the sun and has a diameter of about 4700 kilometers

mer·cy *n, pl* **mer·cies 1 :** kind and gentle treatment of a wrongdoer, an opponent, or some unfortunate person **2 :** a kind sympathetic disposition **:** willingness to forgive, spare, or help **3 :** a blessing as an act of divine love **4 :** a fortunate happening

mere *adj, superlative* **mer·est :** nothing more than **:** SIMPLE

mere·ly *adv* **:** nothing else than **:** JUST

merge *vb* **merged; merg·ing :** to be or cause to be combined or blended into a single unit

merg·er *n* **:** a combination of two or more businesses into one

me·rid·i·an *n* **1 :** the highest point reached **2 :** any imaginary semicircle on the earth reaching from the north to the south pole **3 :** a representation of a meridian on a map or globe numbered according to degrees of longitude

me·ringue *n* **1 :** a mixture of beaten white of egg and sugar put on pies or cakes and browned **2 :** a shell made of baked meringue and filled with fruit or ice cream

me·ri·no *n, pl* **me·ri·nos 1 :** a sheep of a breed that produces a heavy fleece of white fine wool **2 :** a fine soft fabric like cashmere

[1]**mer·it** *n* **1 :** the condition or fact of deserving well or ill **2 :** [2]WORTH 1, VALUE **3 :** a quality worthy of praise **:** VIRTUE

[2]**merit** *vb* **:** to be worthy of or have a right to

mer·i·to·ri·ous *adj* **:** deserving reward or honor **:** PRAISEWORTHY — **mer·i·to·ri·ous·ly** *adv*

mer·maid *n* **:** an imaginary sea creature usually shown with a woman's body and a fish's tail

mer·man *n, pl* **mer·men :** an imaginary sea creature usually shown with a man's body and a fish's tail

mer·ri·ment *n* **:** GAIETY, MIRTH

mer·ry *adj* **mer·ri·er; mer·ri·est 1 :** full of good humor and good spirits **:** JOYOUS **2 :** full of gaiety or festivity — **mer·ri·ly** *adv*

mer·ry–go–round *n* **:** a circular revolving platform fitted with seats and figures of animals on which people sit for a ride

mer·ry·mak·er *n* **:** one taking part in merrymaking

mer·ry·mak·ing *n* **1 :** merry activity **2 :** a festive occasion **:** PARTY

me·sa *n* **:** a hill with a flat top and steep sides

mesdames *pl of* MADAM *or of* MRS.

[1]**mesh** *n* **1 :** one of the spaces enclosed by the threads of a net or the wires of a sieve or screen **2 :** NETWORK 1, 2 **3 :** the coming or fitting together of the teeth of two sets of gears

[2]**mesh** *vb* **:** to fit together **:** INTERLOCK

Mes·o·zo·ic *n* **:** an era of geological history which extends from the Paleozoic to the Cenozoic and in which dinosaurs are present and the first birds and mammals and flowering plants appear

mes·quite *n* **:** a spiny shrub or small tree of the southwestern United States and Mexico that is related to the clovers

[1]**mess** *n* **1 :** a group of people (as military personnel) who regularly eat together **2 :** the meal eaten by a mess **3 :** a state of confusion or disorder

[2]**mess** *vb* **1 :** to take meals with a mess **2 :** to make dirty or untidy **3 :** to mix up **:** BUNGLE **4 :** to work without serious goal **:** PUTTER **5 :** [2]FOOL 2, INTERFERE

mes·sage *n* **:** a communication in writing, in speech, or by signals

mes·sen·ger *n* **:** a person who carries a message or does an errand

Messrs. *pl of* MR.

messy *adj* **mess·i·er; mess·i·est :** UNTIDY — **mess·i·ly** *adv* — **mess·i·ness** *n*

met *past of* MEET

met·a·bol·ic *adj* **:** of or relating to metabolism — **met·a·bol·i·cal·ly** *adv*

me·tab·o·lism *n* **:** the processes by which a living being uses food to obtain energy and build tissue and disposes of waste material

[1]**met·al** *n* **1 :** a substance (as gold, tin, copper, or bronze) that has a more or less shiny appearance, is a good conductor of electricity and heat, and usually can be made into a wire or hammered into a thin sheet **2 :** METTLE

[2]**metal** *adj* **:** made of metal

me·tal·lic *adj* **1 :** of, relating to, or being a metal **2 :** containing or made of metal

met·al·lur·gi·cal *adj* : of or relating to metallurgy

met·al·lur·gy *n* : the science of obtaining metals from their ores and preparing them for use

meta·mor·phic *adj* : formed by the action of pressure, heat, and water that results in a more compact form

meta·mor·pho·sis *n, pl* **meta·mor·pho·ses** : a sudden and very great change especially in appearance or structure

met·a·phor *n* : a figure of speech comparing two unlike things without using *like* or *as*

mete *vb* **met·ed; met·ing** : ALLOT

me·te·or *n* : one of the small pieces of matter in the solar system that enter the earth's atmosphere where friction may cause them to glow and form a streak of light

me·te·or·ic *adj* **1** : of or relating to a meteor or group of meteors **2** : like a meteor in speed or in sudden and temporary brilliance

me·te·or·ite *n* : a meteor that reaches the surface of the earth

me·te·o·rol·o·gist *n* : a specialist in meteorology

me·te·o·rol·o·gy *n* : a science that deals with the atmosphere, weather, and weather forecasting

[1]me·ter *n* **1** : a planned rhythm in poetry that is usually repeated **2** : the repeated pattern of musical beats in a measure

[2]meter *n* : a measure of length on which the metric system is based and which is equal to about 39.37 inches

[3]meter *n* : an instrument for measuring and sometimes recording the amount of something

-meter *n suffix* : instrument for measuring

meth·od *n* **1** : a certain way of doing something **2** : careful arrangement : PLAN

me·thod·i·cal *adj* **1** : showing or done or arranged by method **2** : following a method out of habit : SYSTEMATIC — **me·thod·i·cal·ly** *adv*

me·tic·u·lous *adj* : extremely or overly careful in dealing with small details

met·ric *adj* **1** : of or relating to measurement **2** : of or relating to the metric system

met·ri·cal *adj* : of or relating to meter (as in poetry or music)

metric system *n* : a system of weights and measures in which the meter is the unit of length and the kilogram is the unit of weight

metric ton *n* : a unit of weight equal to 1000 kilograms

met·ro·nome *n* : a device for marking exact musical tempo by regularly repeated ticks

me·trop·o·lis *n* **1** : the chief or capital city of a country, state, or region **2** : a large or important city

met·ro·pol·i·tan *adj* : of, relating to, or like that of a metropolis

met·tle *n* : strength of spirit : COURAGE — **on one's mettle** : aroused to do one's best

[1]mew *vb* : to make a sound like a meow

[2]mew *n* : MEOW

[1]Mex·i·can *adj* : of or relating to Mexico or Mexicans

[2]Mexican *n* : a person born or living in Mexico

mi *n* : the third note of the musical scale

mi·ca *n* : a mineral that easily breaks into very thin transparent sheets

mice *pl of* MOUSE

micr- *or* **micro-** *prefix* **1** : small : tiny **2** : millionth

mi·crobe *n* : a very tiny and often harmful plant or animal : MICROORGANISM

mi·cro·com·put·er *n* : PERSONAL COMPUTER

mi·cro·film *n* : a film on which something (as printing or a drawing) is recorded in very much smaller size

mi·crom·e·ter *n* **1** : an instrument used with a telescope or microscope for measuring very small distances **2** : MICROMETER CALIPER

micrometer caliper *n* : an instrument having a rod moved by fine screw threads and used for making exact measurements

mi·cro·or·gan·ism *n* : an organism (as a bacterium) of microscopic or less than microscopic size

mi·cro·phone *n* : an instrument in which sound is changed into an electrical effect for transmitting or recording (as in radio or television)

mi·cro·pro·ces·sor *n* : a computer processor contained on an integrated-circuit chip

mi·cro·scope *n* : an instrument with one or more lenses used to help a person to see something very small by making it appear larger

mi·cro·scop·ic *adj* **1** : of, relating to, or conducted with the microscope **2** : so small as to be visible only through a microscope : very tiny — **mi·cro·scop·i·cal·ly** *adv*

[1]mi·cro·wave *n* **1** : a radio wave between one millimeter and one meter in wavelength **2** : MICROWAVE OVEN

[2]microwave *vb* : to cook or heat in a microwave oven

microwave oven *n* : an oven in which food is cooked by the heat produced as a result of penetration of the food by microwaves

[1]mid *adj* : being the part in the middle

[2]mid *prep* : AMID

mid·air *n* : a region in the air some distance above the ground

mid·day *n* : NOON

[1]mid·dle *adj* **1** : equally distant from the ends : CENTRAL **2** : being at neither extreme

[2]middle *n* **:** the middle part, point, or position **:** CENTER

middle age *n* **:** the period of life from about forty to about sixty years of age — **mid·dle–aged** *adj*

Middle Ages *n pl* **:** the period of European history from about A.D. 500 to about 1500

middle class *n* **:** a social class between that of the wealthy and the poor

middle school *n* **:** a school usually including grades 5 to 8 or 6 to 8

mid·dy *n, pl* **middies 1 :** MIDSHIPMAN **2 :** a loose blouse with a collar cut wide and square in the back

midge *n* **:** a very small fly or gnat

midg·et *n* **:** one (as a person) that is much smaller than usual or normal

mid·night *n* **:** twelve o'clock at night

mid·rib *n* **:** the central vein of a leaf

mid·riff *n* **1 :** the middle part of the surface of the human body **2 :** a part of a garment that covers the midriff

mid·ship·man *n, pl* **mid·ship·men :** a student naval officer

[1]midst *n* **1 :** the inside or central part **2 :** a position among the members of a group **3 :** the condition of being surrounded

[2]midst *prep* **:** in the midst of

mid·stream *n* **:** the part of a stream away from both sides

mid·sum·mer *n* **1 :** the middle of summer **2 :** the summer solstice

mid·way *adv or adj* **:** in the middle of the way or distance **:** HALFWAY

mid·win·ter *n* **1 :** the middle of winter **2 :** the winter solstice

mid·year *n* **:** the middle of a year

mien *n* **:** a person's appearance or way of acting that shows mood or personality

[1]might *past of* MAY — used as a helping verb to show that something is possible but not likely

[2]might *n* **:** power that can be used (as by a person or group)

mightn't : might not

[1]mighty *adj* **might·i·er; might·i·est 1 :** having great power or strength **2 :** done by might **:** showing great power **3 :** great in influence, size, or effect — **might·i·ly** *adv*

[2]mighty *adv* **:** [2]VERY 1

mi·grant *n* **:** one that migrates

mi·grate *vb* **mi·grat·ed; mi·grat·ing 1 :** to move from one country or region to another **2 :** to pass from one region to another on a regular schedule

mi·gra·tion *n* **1 :** the act or an instance of migrating **2 :** a group of individuals that are migrating

mi·gra·to·ry *adj* **1 :** having a way of life that includes making migrations **2 :** of or relating to migration

mike *n* **:** MICROPHONE

milch *adj* **:** giving milk **:** kept for milking

mild *adj* **1 :** gentle in personality or behavior **2 :** not strong or harsh in action or effect — **mild·ly** *adv* — **mild·ness** *n*

[1]mil·dew *n* **1 :** a thin whitish growth of fungus on decaying material or on living plants **2 :** a fungus that grows as a mildew

[2]mildew *vb* **:** to become affected with mildew

mile *n* **1 :** a measure of distance (**statute mile**) equal to 5280 feet (1609 meters) **2 :** a measure of distance (**geographical mile** or **nautical mile**) equal to about 6076 feet (1852 meters)

mile·age *n* **1 :** an amount of money given for traveling expenses at a certain rate per mile **2 :** distance or distance covered in miles **3 :** the number of miles that something (as a car or tire) will travel before wearing out **4 :** the average number of miles a car or truck will travel on a gallon of fuel

mile·stone *n* **1 :** a stone showing the distance in miles to a stated place **2 :** an important point in progress or development

[1]mil·i·tary *adj* **1 :** of or relating to soldiers, the army, or war **2 :** carried on by soldiers **:** supported by armed force

[2]military *n, pl* **military :** members of the armed forces

mi·li·tia *n* **:** a body of citizens having some military training but called into service only in emergencies

[1]milk *n* **1 :** a whitish liquid secreted by the breasts or udder of a female mammal as food for her young **2 :** a liquid (as a plant juice) like milk

[2]milk *vb* **:** to draw off the milk of (as by pressing or sucking)

milk·maid *n* **:** DAIRYMAID

milk·man *n, pl* **milk·men :** a person who sells or delivers milk

milk of mag·ne·sia : a white liquid containing an oxide of magnesium in water and used as a laxative

milk shake *n* **:** a drink made of milk, a flavoring syrup, and ice cream shaken or mixed thoroughly

milk tooth *n* **:** one of the first and temporary teeth that in humans number twenty

milk·weed *n* **:** any of a group of plants with milky juice and flowers in dense clusters

milky *adj* **milk·i·er; milk·i·est 1 :** like milk in color or thickness **2 :** full of or containing milk — **milk·i·ness** *n*

Milky Way *n* **1 :** a broad band of light that stretches across the sky and is caused by the light of a very great number of faint stars **2 :** MILKY WAY GALAXY

Milky Way galaxy *n* **:** the galaxy of which the sun and the solar system are a part and which contains the stars that make up the Milky Way

[1]**mill** *n* **1 :** a building in which grain is ground into flour **2 :** a machine used in processing (as by grinding, crushing, stamping, cutting, or finishing) raw material **3 :** a factory using machines

[2]**mill** *vb* **1 :** to grind into flour or powder **2 :** to shape or finish by means of a rotating cutter **3 :** to give a raised rim to (a coin) **4 :** to move about in a circle or in disorder

[3]**mill** *n* **:** one tenth of a cent

mil·len·ni·um *n, pl* **mil·len·nia** *or* **millenniums** **1 :** a period of 1000 years **2 :** a 1000th anniversary or its celebration — **mil·len·ni·al** *adj*

mill·er *n* **1 :** a person who works in or runs a flour mill **2 :** a moth whose wings seem to be covered with flour or dust

mil·let *n* **:** an annual grass with clusters of small usually white seeds that is grown as a cereal and for animals to graze

milli- *prefix* **:** thousandth

mil·li·gram *n* **:** a unit of weight equal to 1/1000 gram

mil·li·li·ter *n* **:** a unit of capacity equal to 1/1000 liter

mil·li·me·ter *n* **:** a unit of length equal to 1/1000 meter

mil·li·ner *n* **:** a person who makes, trims, or sells women's hats

[1]**mil·lion** *n* **1 :** one thousand thousands **:** 1,000,000 **2 :** a very large number

[2]**million** *adj* **:** being 1,000,000

mil·lion·aire *n* **:** a person having a million dollars or more

[1]**mil·lionth** *adj* **:** being last in a series of a million

[2]**millionth** *n* **:** number 1,000,000 in a series

mil·li·pede *n* **:** an animal that is an arthropod with a long body somewhat like that of a centipede but with two pairs of legs on most of its many body sections

mill·stone *n* **:** either of two circular stones used for grinding grain

mill wheel *n* **:** a waterwheel that drives a mill

mim·eo·graph *n* **:** a machine for making copies of typewritten, written, or drawn matter by means of stencils

[1]**mim·ic** *n* **:** one that mimics another

[2]**mimic** *vb* **mim·icked; mim·ick·ing** **1 :** to imitate very closely **2 :** to make fun of by imitating

min·a·ret *n* **:** a tall slender tower of a mosque with a balcony from which the people are called to prayer

mince *vb* **minced; minc·ing** **1 :** to cut or chop very fine **2 :** to act or speak in an unnaturally dainty way **3 :** to keep (what one says) within the bounds of politeness

mince·meat *n* **:** a mixture of finely chopped and cooked raisins, apples, suet, spices, and sometimes meat that is used chiefly as a filling for pie (**mince pie**)

[1]**mind** *n* **1 :** MEMORY 1 **2 :** the part of a person that feels, understands, thinks, wills, and especially reasons **3 :** INTENTION 1 **4 :** OPINION 1

[2]**mind** *vb* **1 :** to pay attention to **:** HEED **2 :** to pay careful attention to and obey **3 :** to be bothered about **4 :** to object to **:** DISLIKE **5 :** to take charge of

mind·ed *adj* **1 :** having a specified kind of mind **2 :** greatly interested in one thing

mind·ful *adj* **:** keeping in mind

[1]**mine** *pron* **:** that which belongs to me

[2]**mine** *n* **1 :** a pit or tunnel from which minerals (as coal, gold, or diamonds) are taken **2 :** an explosive buried in the ground and set to explode when disturbed (as by an enemy soldier or vehicle) **3 :** an explosive placed in a case and sunk in the water to sink enemy ships **4 :** a rich source of supply

[3]**mine** *vb* **mined; min·ing** **1 :** to dig a mine **2 :** to obtain from a mine **3 :** to work in a mine **4 :** to dig or form mines under a place **5 :** to lay military mines in or under — **min·er** *n*

[1]**min·er·al** *n* **1 :** a naturally occurring substance (as diamond or quartz) that results from processes other than those of plants and animals **2 :** a naturally occurring substance (as ore, coal, petroleum, natural gas, or water) obtained for humans to use usually from the ground

[2]**mineral** *adj* **1 :** of or relating to minerals **2 :** containing gases or mineral salts

mineral kingdom *n* **:** a basic group of natural objects that includes objects consisting of matter that does not come from plants and animals

min·gle *vb* **min·gled; min·gling** **1 :** to mix or be mixed so that the original parts can still be recognized **2 :** to move among others within a group

mini- *prefix* **:** very short or small

[1]**min·i·a·ture** *n* **1 :** a copy on a much reduced scale **2 :** a very small portrait especially on ivory or metal

[2]**miniature** *adj* **:** very small **:** represented on a small scale

min·i·mize *vb* **min·i·mized; min·i·miz·ing** **:** to make as small as possible

[1]**min·i·mum** *n, pl* **min·i·ma** *or* **min·i·mums** **:** the lowest amount

[2]**minimum** *adj* **:** being the least possible

min·ing *n* **:** the process or business of working mines

[1]**min·is·ter** *n* **1 :** a Protestant clergyman **2 :** a

government official at the head of a section of government activities **3 :** a person who represents his or her government in a foreign country

[2]**minister** *vb* **:** to give aid or service

min·is·try *n, pl* **min·is·tries** **1 :** the act of ministering **2 :** the office or duties of a minister **3 :** a body of ministers **4 :** a section of a government headed by a minister

mink *n* **1 :** an animal related to the weasel that has partly webbed feet and lives around water **2 :** the soft thick usually brown fur of a mink

min·now *n* **1 :** any of various small freshwater fishes (as a shiner) related to the carps **2 :** a fish that looks like a true minnow

[1]**mi·nor** *adj* **1 :** less in size, importance, or value **2 :** of or relating to a musical scale having the third tone lowered a half step

[2]**minor** *n* **:** a person too young to have full civil rights

mi·nor·i·ty *n, pl* **mi·nor·i·ties** **1 :** the state of being a minor **2 :** a number less than half of a total **3 :** a part of a population that is in some ways different from others and that is sometimes disliked or given unfair treatment

min·strel *n* **1 :** an entertainer in the Middle Ages who sang verses and played a harp **2 :** one of a group of entertainers with blackened faces who sing, dance, and tell jokes

[1]**mint** *n* **1 :** any of a group of fragrant herbs and shrubs (as catnip or peppermint) with square stems **2 :** a piece of candy flavored with mint

[2]**mint** *n* **1 :** a place where metals are made into coins **2 :** a great amount especially of money

[3]**mint** *vb* **1 :** [2]COIN 1 **2 :** to make into coin

min·u·end *n* **:** a number from which another number is to be subtracted

min·u·et *n* **:** a slow stately dance

[1]**mi·nus** *prep* **1 :** with the subtraction of **:** LESS **2 :** [1]WITHOUT 2

[2]**minus** *adj* **:** located in the lower part of a range

minus sign *n* **:** a sign – used especially in mathematics to indicate subtraction (as in 8–6=2) or a quantity less than zero (as in –10°)

[1]**min·ute** *n* **1 :** the sixtieth part of an hour or of a degree **:** sixty seconds **2 :** MOMENT 1 **3 minutes** *pl* **:** a brief record of what happened during a meeting

[2]**mi·nute** *adj* **mi·nut·er; mi·nut·est** **1 :** very small **:** TINY **2 :** paying attention to small details — **mi·nute·ly** *adv*

min·ute·man *n, pl* **min·ute·men** **:** a member of a group of armed men ready to fight at a minute's notice immediately before and during the American Revolution

mir·a·cle *n* **1 :** an extraordinary event taken as a sign of the power of God **2 :** something very rare, unusual, or wonderful

mi·rac·u·lous *adj* **:** being or being like a miracle — **mi·rac·u·lous·ly** *adv*

mi·rage *n* **:** an illusion sometimes seen at sea, in the desert, or over hot pavement that looks like a pool of water or a mirror in which distant objects are glimpsed

[1]**mire** *n* **:** heavy deep mud

[2]**mire** *vb* **mired; mir·ing** **:** to stick or cause to stick fast in mire

[1]**mir·ror** *n* **1 :** a glass coated on the back with a reflecting substance **2 :** something that gives a true likeness or description

[2]**mirror** *vb* **:** to reflect in or as if in a mirror

mirth *n* **:** the state of being happy or merry as shown by laughter

mirth·ful *adj* **:** full of or showing mirth — **mirth·ful·ly** *adv*

mis- *prefix* **1 :** in a way that is bad or wrong **2 :** bad **:** wrong **3 :** opposite or lack of

mis·ad·ven·ture *n* **:** an unfortunate or unpleasant event

mis·be·have *vb* **mis·be·haved; mis·be·hav·ing** **:** to behave badly

mis·car·ry *vb* **mis·car·ried; mis·car·ry·ing** **:** to go wrong **:** FAIL

mis·cel·la·neous *adj* **:** consisting of many things of different sorts

mis·chance *n* **1 :** bad luck **2 :** a piece of bad luck **:** MISHAP

mis·chief *n* **1 :** injury or damage caused by a person **2 :** conduct that annoys or bothers

mis·chie·vous *adj* **1 :** harming or intended to do harm **2 :** causing or likely to cause minor injury or harm **3 :** showing a spirit of irresponsible fun or playfulness — **mis·chie·vous·ly** *adv* — **mis·chie·vous·ness** *n*

[1]**mis·con·duct** *n* **:** wrong conduct **:** bad behavior

[2]**mis·con·duct** *vb* **:** to manage badly

mis·count *vb* **:** to count incorrectly

mis·cre·ant *n* **:** VILLAIN, RASCAL

mis·cue *n* **:** [2]MISTAKE 2

mis·deal *vb* **mis·dealt; mis·deal·ing** **:** to deal in an incorrect way

mis·deed *n* **:** a bad action

mis·di·rect *vb* **:** to direct incorrectly

mi·ser *n* **:** a stingy person who lives poorly in order to store away money

mis·er·a·ble *adj* **1 :** very unsatisfactory **2 :** causing great discomfort **3 :** very unhappy or distressed **:** WRETCHED — **mis·er·a·bly** *adv*

mi·ser·ly *adj* **:** of, relating to, or like a miser

mis·ery *n, pl* **mis·er·ies** **:** suffering or distress due to being poor, in pain, or unhappy

mis·fit *n* **1 :** something that fits badly **2 :** a person who cannot adjust to an environment
mis·for·tune *n* **1 :** bad luck **2 :** an unfortunate situation or event
mis·giv·ing *n* **:** a feeling of distrust or doubt especially about what is going to happen
mis·guid·ed *adj* **:** having mistaken ideas or rules of conduct
mis·hap *n* **:** an unfortunate accident
mis·judge *vb* **mis·judged; mis·judg·ing :** to judge incorrectly or unjustly
mis·lay *vb* **mis·laid; mis·lay·ing :** to put in a place later forgotten **:** LOSE
mis·lead *vb* **mis·led; mis·lead·ing :** to lead in a wrong direction or into error
mis·place *vb* **mis·placed; mis·plac·ing** **1 :** to put in a wrong place **2 :** MISLAY
mis·print *n* **:** a mistake in printing
mis·pro·nounce *vb* **mis·pro·nounced; mis·pro·nounc·ing :** to pronounce in a way considered incorrect
mis·pro·nun·ci·a·tion *n* **:** incorrect pronunciation
mis·read *vb* **mis·read; mis·read·ing** **1 :** to read incorrectly **2 :** MISUNDERSTAND 2
mis·rep·re·sent *vb* **:** to give a false or misleading idea of
[1]**miss** *vb* **1 :** to fail to hit, catch, reach, or get **2 :** [1]ESCAPE 2 **3 :** to fail to have or go to **4 :** to be aware of the absence of **:** want to be with
[2]**miss** *n* **:** failure to hit or catch
[3]**miss** *n* **1** — used as a title before the name of an unmarried woman **2 :** young lady — used without a name as a form of polite address to a girl or young woman
mis·shap·en *adj* **:** badly shaped
mis·sile *n* **:** an object (as a stone, arrow, bullet, or rocket) that is dropped, thrown, shot, or launched usually so as to strike something at a distance
miss·ing *adj* **1 :** [1]ABSENT 1 **2 :** [2]LOST 4
mis·sion *n* **1 :** a group of missionaries **2 :** a place where the work of missionaries is carried on **3 :** a group of persons sent by a government to represent it in a foreign country **4 :** a task that is assigned or begun
[1]**mis·sion·ary** *adj* **:** of or relating to religious missions
[2]**missionary** *n, pl* **mis·sion·ar·ies :** a person sent (as to a foreign country) to spread a religious faith
mis·sive *n* **:** [1]LETTER 2
mis·spell *vb* **:** to spell in an incorrect way
mis·spend *vb* **mis·spent; mis·spend·ing :** [2]WASTE 2
mis·step *n* **1 :** a wrong step **2 :** [2]MISTAKE 2, SLIP
[1]**mist** *n* **1 :** particles of water floating in the air or falling as fine rain **2 :** something that keeps one from seeing or understanding clearly
[2]**mist** *vb* **1 :** to be or become misty **2 :** to become or cause to become dim or blurred **3 :** to cover with mist
[1]**mis·take** *vb* **mis·took; mis·tak·en; mis·tak·ing** **1 :** MISUNDERSTAND 2 **2 :** to fail to recognize correctly
[2]**mistake** *n* **1 :** a wrong judgment **2 :** a wrong action or statement
mis·tak·en *adj* **1 :** being in error **:** judging wrongly **2 :** [2]WRONG 2, INCORRECT — **mis·tak·en·ly** *adv*
mis·ter *n* **1** *cap* — used sometimes in writing instead of the usual *Mr.* **2 :** SIR 2
mis·tle·toe *n* **:** a green plant with waxy white berries that grows on the branches and trunks of trees
mis·treat *vb* **:** to treat badly **:** ABUSE
mis·tress *n* **:** a woman who has control or authority
[1]**mis·trust** *n* **:** [1]DISTRUST
[2]**mistrust** *vb* **1 :** [2]DISTRUST, SUSPECT **2 :** to lack confidence in
misty *adj* **mist·i·er; mist·i·est** **1 :** full of mist **2 :** clouded by or as if by mist **3 :** VAGUE 3, INDISTINCT — **mist·i·ly** *adv* — **mist·i·ness** *n*
mis·un·der·stand *vb* **mis·un·der·stood; mis·un·der·stand·ing** **1 :** to fail to understand **2 :** to take in a wrong meaning or way
mis·un·der·stand·ing *n* **1 :** a failure to understand **2 :** DISAGREEMENT 3, QUARREL
[1]**mis·use** *vb* **mis·used; mis·us·ing** **1 :** to use in a wrong way **2 :** [2]ABUSE 3, MISTREAT
[2]**mis·use** *n* **:** incorrect or improper use
mite *n* **1 :** any of various tiny spiderlike animals often living on plants, animals, and stored foods **2 :** a very small coin or amount of money **3 :** a very small object or creature
mi·to·sis *n, pl* **mi·to·ses :** a process of cell division in which two new nuclei are formed each containing the original number of chromosomes
mitt *n* **1 :** MITTEN **2 :** a baseball catcher's or first baseman's glove
mit·ten *n* **:** a covering for the hand and wrist having a separate division for the thumb only
[1]**mix** *vb* **1 :** to make into one mass by stirring together **:** BLEND **2 :** to make by combining different things **3 :** to become one mass through blending **4 :** CONFUSE 1 — **mixer** *n*
[2]**mix** *n* **:** MIXTURE 2
mixed *adj* **1 :** made up of two or more kinds **2 :** made up of persons of both sexes
mixed number *or* **mixed numeral** *n* **:** a number (as $1\frac{2}{3}$) made up of a whole number and a fraction
mix·ture *n* **1 :** the act of mixing **2 :** something mixed or being mixed **3 :** two or more

substances mixed together in such a way that each remains unchanged

mix-up *n* : an instance of confusion

miz·zen *n* **1 :** a fore-and-aft sail set on the mizzenmast **2 :** MIZZENMAST

miz·zen·mast *n* : the mast behind or next behind the mainmast

¹moan *n* **1 :** a long low sound showing pain or grief **2 :** a mournful sound

²moan *vb* **1 :** COMPLAIN 1 **2 :** to utter a moan

moat *n* : a deep wide ditch around the walls of a castle or fort that is usually filled with water

¹mob *n* **1 :** the common masses of people **2 :** a rowdy excited crowd

²mob *vb* **mobbed; mob·bing :** to crowd about and attack or annoy

¹mo·bile *adj* **1 :** easily moved : MOVABLE **2 :** changing quickly in expression

²mo·bile *n* : an artistic structure whose parts can be moved especially by air currents

mo·bi·lize *vb* **mo·bi·lized; mo·bi·liz·ing :** to assemble (as military forces) and make ready for action

moc·ca·sin *n* **1 :** a soft shoe with no heel and the sole and sides made of one piece **2 :** a poisonous snake of the southern United States

moccasin flower *n* : LADY'S SLIPPER

¹mock *vb* **1 :** to treat with scorn : RIDICULE **2 :** ³MIMIC 2

²mock *adj* : not real : MAKE-BELIEVE

mock·ery *n, pl* **mock·er·ies 1 :** the act of mocking **2 :** a bad imitation : FAKE

mock·ing·bird *n* : a songbird of the southern United States noted for its sweet song and imitations of other birds

mock orange *n* : SYRINGA

¹mode *n* **1 :** a particular form or variety of something **2 :** a form or manner of expressing or acting : WAY

²mode *n* : a popular fashion or style

¹mod·el *n* **1 :** a small but exact copy of a thing **2 :** a pattern or figure of something to be made **3 :** a person who sets a good example **4 :** a person who poses for an artist or photographer **5 :** a person who wears and displays garments that are for sale **6 :** a special type of a product

²model *vb* **mod·eled** *or* **mod·elled; mod·el·ing** *or* **mod·el·ling 1 :** to plan or shape after a pattern **2 :** to make a model of **3 :** to act or serve as a model

³model *adj* **1 :** worthy of being imitated **2 :** being a miniature copy

mo·dem *n* : a device that changes electrical signals from one form to another and is used especially to send or receive computer data over a telephone line

¹mod·er·ate *adj* **1 :** neither too much nor too little **2 :** neither very good nor very bad **3 :** not expensive : REASONABLE — **mod·er·ate·ly** *adv*

²mod·er·ate *vb* **mod·er·at·ed; mod·er·at·ing :** to make or become less violent or severe

mod·er·a·tion *n* **1 :** the act of moderating **2 :** the condition of being moderate

mod·ern *adj* **1 :** of, relating to, or characteristic of the present time or times not long past **2 :** of the period from about 1500

mod·ern·ize *vb* **mod·ern·ized; mod·ern·iz·ing :** to make or become modern

mod·est *adj* **1 :** having a limited and not too high opinion of oneself and one's abilities : not boastful **2 :** limited in size or amount **3 :** clean and proper in thought, conduct, and dress — **mod·est·ly** *adv*

mod·es·ty *n* : the quality of being modest

mod·i·fi·ca·tion *n* **1 :** the act of modifying **2 :** the result of modifying : a slightly changed form

mod·i·fi·er *n* : a word (as an adjective or adverb) used with another word to limit its meaning

mod·i·fy *vb* **mod·i·fied; mod·i·fy·ing 1 :** to make changes in **2 :** to lower or reduce in amount or scale **3 :** to limit in meaning : QUALIFY

mod·u·late *vb* **mod·u·lat·ed; mod·u·lat·ing 1 :** to bring into proper proportion **2 :** to tone down : SOFTEN

mod·ule *n* : an independent unit of a spacecraft

mo·hair *n* : a fabric or yarn made from the long silky hair of an Asian goat

Mohammedan, Mohammedanism *variant of* MUHAMMADAN, MUHAMMADANISM

moist *adj* : slightly wet : DAMP — **moist·ness** *n*

moist·en *vb* : to make moist

mois·ture *n* : a small amount of liquid that causes moistness

mo·lar *n* : a tooth with a broad surface used for grinding : a back tooth

mo·las·ses *n* : a thick brown syrup that drains from sugar as it is being made

¹mold *or* **mould** *n* : light rich crumbly earth that contains decaying material

²mold *or* **mould** *n* **1 :** a hollow form in which something is shaped **2 :** something shaped in a mold

³mold *or* **mould** *vb* **1 :** to work and press into shape **2 :** to form in or as if in a mold

⁴mold *n* **1 :** an often woolly surface growth of fungus on damp or decaying material **2 :** a fungus that forms mold

⁵mold *vb* : to become moldy

mold·er *vb* : to crumble to bits by slow decay

mold·ing *n* **1 :** the act or work of a person who molds **2 :** a strip of material having a shaped surface and used as a decoration (as on a wall or the edge of a table)

moldy *adj* **mold·i·er; mold·i·est :** covered with or containing mold

[1]**mole** *n* **:** a small usually brown spot on the skin

[2]**mole** *n* **:** a small burrowing animal with very soft fur and very tiny eyes

mo·lec·u·lar *adj* **:** of or relating to a molecule

mol·e·cule *n* **1 :** the smallest portion of a substance having the properties of the substance **2 :** a very small particle

mole·hill *n* **:** a little ridge of earth pushed up by moles as they burrow underground

mo·lest *vb* **:** to disturb or injure by interfering

mol·li·fy *vb* **mol·li·fied; mol·li·fy·ing :** to soothe in temper or disposition

mol·lusk *n* **:** any of a large group of animals (as clams, snails, and octopuses) most of which live in water and have the body protected by a limy shell

molt *or* **moult** *vb* **:** to shed outer material (as hair, shell, or horns) that will be replaced by a new growth

mol·ten *adj* **:** melted especially by very great heat

mo·lyb·de·num *n* **:** a white metallic chemical element used in some steel to give greater strength and hardness

mom *n* **:** [1]MOTHER 1

mo·ment *n* **1 :** a very brief time **2 :** IMPORTANCE

mo·men·tary *adj* **:** lasting only a moment — **mo·men·tar·i·ly** *adv*

mo·men·tous *adj* **:** very important — **mo·men·tous·ness** *n*

mo·men·tum *n* **:** the force that a moving body has because of its weight and motion

mom·my *n, pl* **mom·mies :** [1]MOTHER 1

mon- *or* **mono-** *prefix* **:** one **:** single **:** alone

mon·arch *n* **1 :** a person who reigns over a kingdom or empire **2 :** a large orange and black American butterfly

mon·ar·chy *n, pl* **mon·ar·chies 1 :** a state or country having a monarch **2 :** the system of government by a monarch

mon·as·tery *n, pl* **mon·as·ter·ies :** a place where a community of monks live and work

mo·nas·tic *adj* **:** of or relating to monks or monasteries

Mon·day *n* **:** the second day of the week

mon·e·tary *adj* **:** of or relating to money

mon·ey *n, pl* **moneys** *or* **mon·ies 1 :** metal (as gold, silver, or copper) coined or stamped and issued for use in buying and selling **2 :** a printed or engraved certificate (**paper money**) legal for use in place of metal money **3 :** wealth figured in terms of money

money order *n* **:** a piece of paper like a check that can be bought (as at a post office) and that tells another office to pay the sum of money printed on it to the one named

[1]**Mon·go·lian** *adj* **:** of or relating to Mongolia or the Mongolians

[2]**Mongolian** *n* **:** a person born or living in Mongolia

mon·goose *n, pl* **mon·goos·es :** a long thin furry animal that eats snakes, eggs, and rodents

[1]**mon·grel** *n* **:** one (as a plant, person, or thing) of mixed or uncertain kind or origin

[2]**mongrel** *adj* **:** of mixed or uncertain kind or origin

[1]**mon·i·tor** *n* **1 :** a pupil in a school picked for a special duty (as keeping order) **2 :** a person or thing that watches or checks something **3 :** a video screen used for display (as of television pictures or computer information)

[2]**monitor** *vb* **:** to watch or check for a special reason

monk *n* **:** a member of a religious group of men who form a community and promise to stay poor, obey all the laws of their community, and not get married

[1]**mon·key** *n, pl* **monkeys 1 :** any of a group of mostly tropical furry animals that have a long tail and that along with the apes are most closely related to humans in the animal kingdom **2 :** a mischievous child

[2]**monkey** *vb* **mon·keyed; mon·key·ing 1 :** to act in a mischievous way **2 :** [2]TRIFLE 3, FOOL

mon·key·shine *n* **:** PRANK

monkey wrench *n* **:** a wrench with one fixed and one adjustable jaw

monks·hood *n* **:** a tall poisonous Old World plant related to the buttercups that is grown for its white or purplish flowers that are shaped like hoods or as a source of drugs

mono- — see MON-

mono·gram *n* **:** a design usually made by combining two or more of a person's initials

mono·plane *n* **:** an airplane with only one set of wings

mo·nop·o·lize *vb* **mo·nop·o·lized; mo·nop·o·liz·ing :** to get or have complete control over

mo·nop·o·ly *n, pl* **mo·nop·o·lies 1 :** complete control of the entire supply of goods or a service in a certain market **2 :** complete possession **3 :** a person or group having a monopoly

mono·syl·la·ble *n* **:** a word of one syllable

mo·not·o·nous *adj* **:** boring from being always the same — **mo·not·o·nous·ly** *adv*

mo·not·o·ny *n, pl* **mo·not·o·nies :** a boring lack of change

mon·soon *n* **1 :** a wind in the Indian ocean and southern Asia that blows from the southwest from April to October and from the northeast from October to April **2 :** the rainy season that comes with the southwest monsoon

mon·ster *n* **1 :** an animal or plant that is very unlike the usual type **2 :** a strange or horrible creature **3 :** something unusually large **4 :** an extremely wicked or cruel person

mon·strous *adj* **1 :** unusually large : ENORMOUS **2 :** very bad or wrong **3 :** very different from the usual form : ABNORMAL — **mon·strous·ly** *adv*

month *n* **:** one of the twelve parts into which the year is divided

[1]**month·ly** *adj* **1 :** happening, done, or published every month **2 :** figured in terms of one month **3 :** lasting a month

[2]**monthly** *n, pl* **monthlies :** a magazine published every month

mon·u·ment *n* **1 :** a structure (as a building, stone, or statue) made to keep alive the memory of a person or event **2 :** a work, saying, or deed that lasts or is worth keeping or remembering

[1]**moo** *vb* **mooed; moo·ing :** to make a moo : LOW

[2]**moo** *n, pl* **moos :** the low sound made by a cow

[1]**mood** *n* **:** a state or frame of mind : DISPOSITION

[2]**mood** *n* **:** a set of forms of a verb that show whether the action or state expressed is to be thought of as a fact, a command, or a wish or possibility

moody *adj* **mood·i·er; mood·i·est :** often feeling gloomy or in a bad mood — **mood·i·ly** *adv* — **mood·i·ness** *n*

[1]**moon** *n* **1 :** the natural celestial body that shines by reflecting light from the sun and revolves about the earth in about 29½ days **2 :** SATELLITE 1 **3 :** MONTH

[2]**moon** *vb* **:** to waste time by daydreaming

moon·beam *n* **:** a ray of light from the moon

moon·light *n* **:** the light of the moon

moon·stone *n* **:** a partly transparent shining stone used as a gem

[1]**moor** *n* **:** an area of open land that is too wet or too poor for farming

[2]**moor** *vb* **:** to fasten in place with cables, lines, or anchors

moor·ing *n* **1 :** a place where or an object to which a boat can be fastened **2 :** a chain or line by which an object is moored

moor·land *n* **:** land consisting of moors

moose *n* **:** a large deerlike animal with broad flattened antlers and humped shoulders that lives in forests of Canada, the northern United States, Europe, and Asia

[1]**mop** *n* **1 :** a tool for cleaning made of a bundle of cloth or yarn or a sponge fastened to a handle **2 :** something that looks like a cloth or yarn mop

[2]**mop** *vb* **mopped; mop·ping :** to wipe or clean with or as if with a mop

[1]**mope** *vb* **moped; mop·ing :** to be in a dull and sad state of mind

[2]**mope** *n* **:** a person without any energy or enthusiasm

mo·raine *n* **:** a pile of earth and stones left by a glacier

[1]**mor·al** *adj* **1 :** concerned with or relating to what is right and wrong in human behavior **2 :** able or fit to teach a lesson **3 :** [1]GOOD 7, VIRTUOUS **4 :** able to tell right from wrong — **mor·al·ly** *adv*

[2]**moral** *n* **1 :** the lesson to be learned from a story or experience **2 morals** *pl* **:** moral conduct **3 morals** *pl* **:** moral teachings or rules of behavior

mo·rale *n* **:** the condition of the mind or feelings (as in relation to enthusiasm, spirit, or hope) of an individual or group

mo·ral·i·ty *n, pl* **mo·ral·i·ties 1 :** moral quality : VIRTUE **2 :** moral conduct

mo·rass *n* **:** MARSH, SWAMP

mo·ray eel *n* **:** any of numerous often brightly colored eels of warm seas that have sharp teeth — called also *moray*

mor·bid *adj* **1:** not healthy **2:** HORRIBLE

[1]**more** *adj* **1 :** greater in amount, number, or size **2 :** [1]EXTRA, ADDITIONAL

[2]**more** *adv* **1 :** in addition **2 :** to a greater extent — often used with an adjective or adverb to form the comparative

[3]**more** *n* **1 :** a greater amount or number **2 :** an additional amount

more·over *adv* **:** in addition to what has been said : BESIDES

morn *n* **:** MORNING

morn·ing *n* **:** the early part of the day : the time from sunrise to noon

morning glory *n* **:** a vine that climbs by twisting around something and has large bright flowers that close in the sunshine

morning star *n* **:** any of the planets Venus, Jupiter, Mars, Mercury, or Saturn when rising before the sun

mo·ron *n* **:** a foolish person

mor·phine *n* **:** a habit-forming drug made from opium and used often to relieve pain

mor·row *n* **:** the next following day

mor·sel *n* **1 :** a small piece of food : BITE **2 :** a small amount : a little piece

[1]**mor·tal** *adj* **1 :** capable of causing death : FATAL **2 :** certain to die **3 :** very unfriendly **4 :** very great or overpowering **5 :** [1]HUMAN 1 — **mor·tal·ly** *adv*

[2]**mortal** *n* **:** a human being

[1]**mor·tar** *n* **1 :** a strong deep bowl in which substances are pounded or crushed with a

pestle **2 :** a short light cannon used to shoot shells high into the air

²mortar *n* **:** a building material made of lime and cement mixed with sand and water that is spread between bricks or stones so as to hold them together when it hardens

mor·ti·fy *vb* **mor·ti·fied; mor·ti·fy·ing :** to embarrass greatly **:** SHAME

mo·sa·ic *n* **:** a decoration on a surface made by setting small pieces of glass or stone of different colors into another material so as to make patterns or pictures

Moslem *variant of* MUSLIM

mosque *n* **:** a Muslim place of worship

mos·qui·to *n, pl* **mos·qui·toes :** a small two-winged fly the female of which punctures the skin of people and animals to suck their blood

moss *n* **1 :** any of a class of plants that have no flowers and grow as small leafy stems in cushion-like patches clinging to rocks, bark, or damp ground **2 :** any of various plants (as lichens) resembling moss

mossy *adj* **moss·i·er; moss·i·est :** like or covered with moss

¹most *adj* **1 :** the majority of **2 :** greatest in amount or extent

²most *adv* **1 :** to the greatest or highest level or extent — often used with an adjective or adverb to form the superlative **2 :** to a very great extent

³most *n* **:** the greatest amount, number, or part

most·ly *adv* **:** for the greatest part

mote *n* **:** a small particle **:** SPECK

mo·tel *n* **:** a building or group of buildings which provide lodgings and in which the rooms are usually reached directly from an outdoor parking area

moth *n, pl* **moths 1 :** CLOTHES MOTH **2 :** an insect that usually flies at night and has mostly feathery antennae and stouter body, duller coloring, and smaller wings than the related butterflies

¹moth·er *n* **1 :** a female parent **2 :** a nun in charge of a convent **3 :** ¹CAUSE 1, ORIGIN — **moth·er·hood** *n* — **moth·er·less** *adj*

²mother *adj* **1 :** of or having to do with a mother **2 :** being in the relation of a mother to others **3 :** gotten from or as if from one's mother

³mother *vb* **:** to be or act as a mother to

moth·er·board *n* **:** the main circuit board especially of a small computer

moth·er–in–law *n, pl* **mothers–in–law :** the mother of one's husband or wife

moth·er·ly *adj* **1 :** of, relating to, or characteristic of a mother **2 :** like a mother **:** MATERNAL

moth·er–of–pearl *n* **:** a hard pearly material that lines the shell of some mollusks (as mussels) and is often used for ornamental objects and buttons

¹mo·tion *n* **1 :** a formal plan or suggestion for action offered according to the rules of a meeting **2 :** the act or process of changing place or position **:** MOVEMENT — **mo·tion·less** *adj* — **mo·tion·less·ness** *n*

²motion *vb* **:** to direct or signal by a movement or sign

motion picture *n* **1 :** a series of pictures projected on a screen rapidly one after another so as to give the appearance of a continuous picture in which the objects move **2 :** MOVIE 1

mo·ti·vate *vb* **mo·ti·vat·ed; mo·ti·vat·ing :** to provide with a reason for doing something

¹mo·tive *n* **:** a reason for doing something

²motive *adj* **:** causing motion

mot·ley *adj* **1 :** having various colors **2 :** composed of various often unlike kinds or parts

¹mo·tor *n* **1 :** a machine that produces motion or power for doing work **2 :** ²AUTOMOBILE — **mo·tored** *adj*

²motor *adj* **1 :** causing or controlling activity (as motion) **2 :** equipped with or driven by a motor **3 :** of or relating to an automobile **4 :** designed for motor vehicles or motorists

³motor *vb* **:** ¹DRIVE 3

mo·tor·bike *n* **:** a light motorcycle

mo·tor·boat *n* **:** an often small boat driven by a motor

mo·tor·cade *n* **:** a line of motor vehicles traveling as a group

mo·tor·car *n* **:** ²AUTOMOBILE

mo·tor·cy·cle *n* **:** a motorized vehicle for one or two passengers that has two wheels

mo·tor·ist *n* **:** a person who travels by automobile

mo·tor·ize *vb* **mo·tor·ized; mo·tor·iz·ing :** to equip with a motor or with motor-driven vehicles

motor scooter *n* **:** a motorized vehicle having two or three wheels like a child's scooter but having a seat

motor vehicle *n* **:** a motorized vehicle (as an automobile or motorcycle) not operated on rails

mot·tled *adj* **:** having spots or blotches of different colors

mot·to *n, pl* **mottoes 1 :** a phrase or word inscribed on something (as a coin or public building) to suggest its use or nature **2 :** a short expression of a guiding rule of conduct

mould *variant of* MOLD

moult *variant of* MOLT

mound *n* **:** a small hill or heap of dirt

¹mount *n* **:** a high hill **:** MOUNTAIN — used especially before a proper name

[2]**mount** *vb* **1 :** ASCEND, CLIMB **2 :** to get up onto something **3 :** to increase rapidly in amount **4 :** to prepare for use or display by fastening in position on a support

[3]**mount** *n* **:** that on which a person or thing is or can be mounted

moun·tain *n* **1 :** an elevation higher than a hill **2 :** a great mass or huge number

moun·tain·eer *n* **1 :** a person who lives in the mountains **2 :** a mountain climber

mountain goat *n* **:** a goatlike animal of the mountains of western North America with thick white coat and slightly curved black horns

mountain lion *n* **:** COUGAR

moun·tain·ous *adj* **1 :** having many mountains **2 :** like a mountain in size **:** HUGE

moun·tain·side *n* **:** the side of a mountain

moun·tain·top *n* **:** the highest part of a mountain

mount·ing *n* **:** something that serves as a mount **:** SUPPORT

mourn *vb* **:** to feel or show grief or sorrow especially over someone's death — **mourn·er** *n*

mourn·ful *adj* **1 :** full of sorrow or sadness **2 :** causing sorrow — **mourn·ful·ly** *adv* — **mourn·ful·ness** *n*

mourn·ing *n* **1 :** the act of sorrowing **2 :** an outward sign (as black clothes or an arm band) of grief for a person's death

mourning dove *n* **:** a wild dove of the United States named from its mournful cry

mouse *n, pl* **mice 1 :** a furry gnawing animal like the larger related rats **2 :** a person without spirit or courage **3 :** a small movable device that is connected to a computer and used to move the cursor and select functions on the screen — **mouse·like** *adj*

mouse pad *n* **:** a thin flat pad (as of rubber) on which a computer mouse is used

mous·er *n* **:** a cat good at catching mice

moustache *variant of* MUSTACHE

[1]**mouth** *n, pl* **mouths 1 :** the opening through which food passes into the body **:** the space containing the tongue and teeth **2 :** an opening that is like a mouth **3 :** the place where a stream enters a larger body of water

[2]**mouth** *vb* **:** to repeat without being sincere or without understanding

mouth·ful *n* **1 :** as much as the mouth will hold **2 :** the amount put into the mouth at one time

mouth organ *n* **:** HARMONICA

mouth·piece *n* **:** the part put to, between, or near the lips

mov·able *or* **move·able** *adj* **1 :** possible to move **2 :** changing from one date to another

[1]**move** *vb* **moved; mov·ing 1 :** to go from one place to another **2 :** to change the place or position of **:** SHIFT **3 :** to set in motion **4 :** to cause to act **:** INFLUENCE **5 :** to stir the feelings of **6 :** to change position **7 :** to suggest according to the rules in a meeting **8 :** to change residence

[2]**move** *n* **1 :** the act of moving a piece in a game **2 :** the turn of a player to move **3 :** an action taken to accomplish something **:** MANEUVER **4 :** the action of moving **:** MOVEMENT

move·ment *n* **1 :** the act or process of moving **:** an instance of moving **2 :** a program or series of acts working toward a desired end **3 :** a mechanical arrangement (as of wheels) for causing a particular motion (as in a clock or watch) **4 :** RHYTHM 2, METER **5 :** a section of a longer piece of music **6 :** an emptying of the bowels **:** the material emptied from the bowels

mov·er *n* **:** a person or company that moves the belongings of others (as from one home to another)

mov·ie *n* **1 :** a story represented in motion pictures **2 :** a showing of a movie

mov·ing *adj* **1 :** changing place or position **2 :** having the power to stir the feelings or sympathies — **mov·ing·ly** *adv*

moving picture *n* **:** MOTION PICTURE 1

[1]**mow** *n* **:** the part of a barn where hay or straw is stored

[2]**mow** *vb* **mowed; mowed** *or* **mown; mow·ing 1 :** to cut down with a scythe or machine **2 :** to cut the standing plant cover from **3 :** to cause to fall in great numbers — **mow·er** *n*

Mr. *n, pl* **Messrs.** — used as a title before a man's name

Mrs. *n, pl* **mes·dames** — used as a title before a married woman's name

Ms. *n* — often used instead of *Miss* or *Mrs.*

[1]**much** *adj* **more; most :** great in amount or extent

[2]**much** *adv* **more; most 1 :** to a great or high level or extent **2 :** just about **:** NEARLY

[3]**much** *n* **:** a great amount or part

mu·ci·lage *n* **:** a water solution of a gum or similar substance used especially to stick things together

muck *n* **1 :** soft wet soil or barnyard manure **2 :** DIRT 1, FILTH

mu·cous *adj* **1 :** of, relating to, or like mucus **2 :** containing or producing mucus

mu·cus *n* **:** a slippery sticky substance produced especially by mucous membranes (as of the nose and throat) which it moistens and protects

mud *n* **:** soft wet earth or dirt

[1]**mud·dle** *vb* **mud·dled; mud·dling 1 :** to be or cause to be confused or bewildered **2 :** to

mix up in a confused manner **3 :** to make a mess of **:** BUNGLE

²muddle *n* **:** a state of confusion

¹mud·dy *adj* **mud·di·er; mud·di·est 1 :** filled or covered with mud **2 :** looking like mud **3 :** not clear or bright **:** DULL **4 :** being mixed up — **mud·di·ly** *adv* — **mud·di·ness** *n*

²muddy *vb* **mud·died; mud·dy·ing 1 :** to soil or stain with or as if with mud **2 :** to make cloudy or dull

¹muff *n* **:** a soft thick cover into which both hands can be shoved to protect them from cold

²muff *vb* **:** to handle awkwardly **:** BUNGLE

muf·fin *n* **:** a bread made of batter containing eggs and baked in a small cup-shaped container

muf·fle *vb* **muf·fled; muf·fling 1 :** to wrap up so as to hide or protect **2 :** to deaden the sound of

muf·fler *n* **1 :** a scarf for the neck **2 :** a device to deaden the noise of an engine (as of an automobile)

mug *n* **:** a large drinking cup

mug·gy *adj* **mug·gi·er; mug·gi·est :** being very warm and humid — **mug·gi·ness** *n*

Mu·ham·mad·an *or* **Mo·ham·med·an** *n* **:** MUSLIM

Mu·ham·mad·an·ism *or* **Mo·ham·med·an·ism** *n* **:** ISLAM

mul·ber·ry *n, pl* **mul·ber·ries :** a tree that bears edible usually purple fruit like berries and has leaves on which silkworms can be fed

¹mulch *n* **:** a material (as straw or sawdust) spread over the ground to protect the roots of plants from heat, cold, or drying of the soil or to keep fruit clean

²mulch *vb* **:** to cover with mulch

mule *n* **1 :** an animal that is an offspring of a donkey and a horse **2 :** a stubborn person

mule skinner *n* **:** a driver of mules

mu·le·teer *n* **:** a driver of mules

mul·ish *adj* **:** stubborn like a mule — **mul·ish·ly** *adv* — **mul·ish·ness** *n*

mul·let *n* **:** any of various freshwater or saltwater food fishes some mostly gray (**gray mullets**) and others red or golden (**red mullets**)

multi- *prefix* **1 :** many **:** much **2 :** more than two **3 :** many times over

mul·ti·cul·tur·al *adj* **:** of, relating to, or made up of several different cultures together

mul·ti·me·dia *adj* **:** using or composed of more than one form of communication or expression

¹mul·ti·ple *adj* **:** being more than one

²multiple *n* **:** the number found by multiplying one number by another

mul·ti·pli·cand *n* **:** a number that is to be multiplied by another number

mul·ti·pli·ca·tion *n* **:** a short way of finding out what would be the result of adding a figure the number of times indicated by another figure

mul·ti·pli·er *n* **:** a number by which another number is multiplied

mul·ti·ply *vb* **mul·ti·plied; mul·ti·ply·ing 1 :** to increase in number **:** make or become more numerous **2 :** to find the product of by means of multiplication

mul·ti·tude *n* **:** a great number of persons or things

mum *adj* **:** SILENT 1, 4

¹mum·ble *vb* **mum·bled; mum·bling :** to speak so that words are not clear

²mumble *n* **:** speech that is not clear enough to be understood

mum·my *n, pl* **mummies :** a dead body preserved in the manner of the ancient Egyptians

mumps *n sing or pl* **:** an infectious disease in which there is fever and swelling of glands and especially of those around the jaw

munch *vb* **:** to chew with a crunching sound

mu·nic·i·pal *adj* **:** having to do with the government of a town or city

mu·nic·i·pal·i·ty *n, pl* **mu·nic·i·pal·i·ties :** a town or city having its own local government

mu·ni·tions *n* **:** military equipment and supplies for fighting **:** AMMUNITION

¹mu·ral *adj* **:** having to do with a wall

²mural *n* **:** a painting on a wall

¹mur·der *n* **:** the intentional and unlawful killing of a human being

²murder *vb* **1 :** to commit murder **2 :** to spoil by performing or using badly — **mur·der·er** *n*

mur·der·ous *adj* **1 :** intending or capable of murder **:** DEADLY **2 :** very hard to bear or withstand — **mur·der·ous·ly** *adv*

murk *n* **:** GLOOM 1, DARKNESS

murky *adj* **murk·i·er; murk·i·est 1 :** very dark or gloomy **2 :** FOGGY 1 — **murk·i·ness** *n*

¹mur·mur *n* **:** a low faint sound

²murmur *vb* **1 :** to make a murmur **2 :** to say in a voice too low to be heard clearly

mus·ca·dine *n* **:** a grape of the southern United States

mus·cle *n* **1 :** an animal body tissue consisting of long cells that can contract and produce motion **2 :** a bodily organ that is a mass of muscle tissue attached at either end (as to bones) so that it can make a body part (as an arm) move **3 :** strength or development of the muscles

mus·cle–bound *adj* : having large muscles that do not move and stretch easily

mus·cu·lar *adj* **1** : of, relating to, or being muscle **2** : done by the muscles **3** : STRONG 1

muse *vb* **mused; mus·ing** : PONDER

mu·se·um *n* : a building in which are displayed objects of interest in one or more of the arts or sciences

[1]**mush** *n* : cornmeal boiled in water

[2]**mush** *vb* : to travel across snow with a sled drawn by dogs

[1]**mush·room** *n* **1** : a part of a fungus that bears spores, grows above ground, and suggests an umbrella in shape **2** : a fungus that produces mushrooms **3** : something shaped like a mushroom

[2]**mushroom** *vb* : to come into being suddenly or grow and develop rapidly

mushy *adj* **mush·i·er; mush·i·est** : soft like mush

mu·sic *n* **1** : the art of producing pleasing or expressive combinations of tones especially with melody, rhythm, and usually harmony **2** : compositions made according to the rules of music **3** : pleasing sounds **4** : a musical composition set down on paper

[1]**mu·si·cal** *adj* **1** : having to do with music or the writing or performing of music **2** : pleasing like music **3** : fond of or talented in music **4** : set to music — **mu·si·cal·ly** *adv*

[2]**musical** *n* : a movie or play that tells a story with both speaking and singing

music box *n* : a box that contains a mechanical device which uses gears like those of a clock to play a tune

mu·si·cian *n* : a person who writes, sings, or plays music with skill and especially as a profession

musk *n* **1** : a strong-smelling material from a gland of an Asian deer (**musk deer**) used in perfumes **2** : any of several plants with musky odors

mus·ket *n* : a firearm that is loaded through the muzzle and that was once used by infantry soldiers

mus·ke·teer *n* : a soldier armed with a musket

musk·mel·on *n* : a small round to oval melon with sweet usually green or orange flesh

musk–ox *n* : a shaggy animal like an ox found in Greenland and northern North America

musk·rat *n* : a North American water animal related to the rats that has webbed hind feet and a long scaly tail and is valued for its glossy usually dark brown fur

musky *adj* **musk·i·er; musk·i·est** : suggesting musk in odor — **musk·i·ness** *n*

Mus·lim *or* **Mos·lem** *n* : a person whose religion is Islam

mus·lin *n* : a cotton fabric of plain weave

[1]**muss** *n* : [2]DISORDER 1, CONFUSION

[2]**muss** *vb* : to make untidy

mus·sel *n* **1** : a sea mollusk that has a long dark shell in two parts and is sometimes used as food **2** : any of various American freshwater clams with shells from which mother-of-pearl is obtained

must *helping verb, present and past all persons* **must** **1** : to be required to **2** : to be very likely to

mus·tache *or* **mous·tache** *n* : the hair growing on the human upper lip

mus·tang *n* : a small hardy horse of western North America that is half wild

mus·tard *n* : a yellow powder that is prepared from the seeds of a plant related to the turnips, has a sharp taste, and is used in medicine and as a seasoning for foods

[1]**mus·ter** *n* **1** : a formal military inspection **2** : an assembled group : COLLECTION

[2]**muster** *vb* **1** : to call together (as troops) for roll call or inspection **2** : to bring into being or action

mustn't : must not

musty *adj* **must·i·er; must·i·est** : bad in odor or taste from the effects of dampness or mildew — **must·i·ness** *n*

[1]**mu·tant** *adj* : of, relating to, or resulting from mutation

[2]**mutant** *n* : a mutant individual

mu·tate *vb* **mu·tat·ed; mu·tat·ing** **1** : to undergo great changes **2** : to undergo mutation

mu·ta·tion *n* : a change in a gene or a resulting new trait inherited by an individual

[1]**mute** *adj* **mut·er; mut·est** **1** : unable to speak **2** : not speaking : SILENT

[2]**mute** *n* **1** : a person who cannot or does not speak **2** : a device on a musical instrument that deadens, softens, or muffles its tone

[3]**mute** *vb* **mut·ed; mut·ing** : to muffle or reduce the sound of

mu·ti·late *vb* **mu·ti·lat·ed; mu·ti·lat·ing** **1** : to cut off or destroy a necessary part (as a limb) : MAIM **2** : to make imperfect by cutting or changing

mu·ti·neer *n* : a person who is guilty of mutiny

mu·ti·nous *adj* : being inclined to or in a state of mutiny — **mu·ti·nous·ly** *adv*

[1]**mu·ti·ny** *n, pl* **mu·ti·nies** **1** : refusal to obey authority **2** : a turning of a group (as of sailors) against an officer in authority

[2]**mutiny** *vb* **mu·ti·nied; mu·ti·ny·ing** : to refuse to obey authority

mutt *n* : a mongrel dog

mut·ter *vb* **1** : to speak in a low voice with lips partly closed **2** : [1]GRUMBLE 1

mut·ton *n* : the flesh of a mature sheep

mu·tu·al *adj* **1 :** given and received in equal amount **2 :** having the same relation to one another **3 :** shared by two or more at the same time — **mu·tu·al·ly** *adv*

[1]**muz·zle** *n* **1 :** the nose and jaws of an animal **2 :** a fastening or covering for the mouth of an animal to prevent it from biting or eating **3 :** the open end of a gun from which the bullet comes out when the gun is fired

[2]**muzzle** *vb* **muz·zled; muz·zling 1 :** to put a muzzle on **2 :** to keep from free expression of ideas or opinions

my *adj* : of or relating to me or myself

my·nah *or* **my·na** *n* : an Asian starling that can be trained to pronounce words and is sometimes kept as a cage bird

[1]**myr·i·ad** *n* : a large but not specified or counted number

[2]**myriad** *adj* : extremely numerous

myrrh *n* : a brown slightly bitter fragrant material obtained from African and Arabian trees and used especially in perfumes or formerly in incense

myr·tle *n* **1 :** an evergreen shrub of southern Europe **2 :** [1]PERIWINKLE

my·self *pron* : my own self

mys·te·ri·ous *adj* : containing a mystery : hard to understand : SECRET — **mys·te·ri·ous·ly** *adv* — **mys·te·ri·ous·ness** *n*

mys·tery *n, pl* **mys·ter·ies 1 :** something that is beyond human power to understand **2 :** something that has not been explained **3 :** a piece of fiction about a mysterious crime

mys·ti·fy *vb* **mys·ti·fied; mys·ti·fy·ing :** CONFUSE 1

myth *n* **1 :** a legend that tells about a being with more than human powers or an event which cannot be explained or that explains a religious belief or practice **2 :** a person or thing existing only in the imagination

myth·i·cal *adj* **1 :** based on or told of in a myth **2 :** IMAGINARY

my·thol·o·gy *n, pl* **my·thol·o·gies :** a collection of myths

N

n *n, pl* **n's** *or* **ns** *often cap* : the fourteenth letter of the English alphabet

-n — see -EN

nab *vb* **nabbed; nab·bing :** [1]ARREST 2

na·cho *n, pl* **nachos :** a tortilla chip topped with melted cheese and often additional toppings

[1]**nag** *n* : a usually old or worn-out horse

[2]**nag** *vb* **nagged; nag·ging 1 :** to find fault continually : COMPLAIN **2 :** to annoy continually or again and again

na·iad *n, pl* **na·iads** *or* **na·ia·des 1 :** a nymph believed in ancient times to be living in lakes, rivers, and springs **2 :** the larva of an insect (as a dragonfly) that lives in water

[1]**nail** *n* **1 :** the horny scale at the end of each finger and toe **2 :** a slender pointed piece of metal driven into or through something for fastening

[2]**nail** *vb* : to fasten with or as if with a nail

nail·brush *n* : a brush for cleaning the hands and fingernails

na·ive *or* **na·ïve** *adj* **1 :** being simple and sincere **2 :** showing lack of experience or knowledge — **na·ive·ly** *adv*

na·ked *adj* **1 :** having no clothes on : NUDE **2 :** lacking a usual or natural covering **3 :** not in its case or covering **4 :** stripped of anything misleading : PLAIN **5 :** not aided by an artificial device — **na·ked·ly** *adv* — **na·ked·ness** *n*

[1]**name** *n* **1 :** a word or combination of words by which a person or thing is known **2 :** REPUTATION 2

[2]**name** *vb* **named; nam·ing 1 :** to give a name to : CALL **2 :** to refer to by name **3 :** to nominate for a job of authority : APPOINT **4 :** to decide on **5 :** [2]MENTION

[3]**name** *adj* **1 :** of, relating to, or having a name **2 :** well known because of wide distribution

name·less *adj* **1 :** having no name **2 :** not marked with a name **3 :** [1]UNKNOWN, ANONYMOUS **4 :** not to be described — **name·less·ness** *n*

name·ly *adv* : that is to say

name·sake *n* : a person who has the same name as another and especially one named for another

nan·ny *n, pl* **nannies :** a child's nurse

nanny goat *n* : a female domestic goat

[1]**nap** *vb* **napped; nap·ping 1 :** to sleep briefly especially during the day **2 :** to be unprepared

[2]**nap** *n* : a short sleep especially during the day

[3]**nap** *n* : a hairy or fluffy surface (as on cloth)

nape *n* : the back of the neck

naph·tha *n* : any of various usually flammable liquids prepared from coal or petroleum and used especially to dissolve substances

nap·kin *n* : a small square of cloth or paper used at table to wipe the lips or fingers and protect the clothes

nar·cis·sus *n, pl* **narcissus** *or* **nar·cis·sus·es** *or* **nar·cis·si** : a daffodil with flowers that have short tubes and that grow separately on the stalk

[1]**nar·cot·ic** *n* : a drug (as opium) that in small doses dulls the senses, relieves pain, and brings on sleep but in larger doses is a dangerous poison

[2]**narcotic** *adj* **1** : acting as or being the source of a narcotic **2** : of or relating to narcotics or their use or control

nar·rate *vb* **nar·rat·ed; nar·rat·ing** : to tell in full detail — **nar·ra·tor** *n*

nar·ra·tion *n* **1** : the act or process or an instance of narrating **2** : [1]NARRATIVE 1

[1]**nar·ra·tive** *n* **1** : something (as a story) that is narrated **2** : the art or practice of narrating

[2]**narrative** *adj* : of or relating to narration : having the form of a story

[1]**nar·row** *adj* **1** : of slender or less than usual width **2** : limited in size or extent **3** : not broad or open in mind or views **4** : barely successful : CLOSE — **nar·row·ly** *adv* — **nar·row·ness** *n*

[2]**narrow** *vb* : to make or become narrow

[3]**narrow** *n* : a narrow passage connecting two bodies of water — usually used in pl.

nar·row–mind·ed *adj* : [1]NARROW 3, INTOLERANT — **nar·row–mind·ed·ly** *adv* — **nar·row–mind·ed·ness** *n*

nar·whal *n* : an arctic marine animal that is related to the dolphin and in the male has a long twisted ivory tusk

[1]**na·sal** *n* : a nasal sound

[2]**nasal** *adj* **1** : of or relating to the nose **2** : uttered with the nose passage open — **na·sal·ly** *adv*

nas·tur·tium *n* : an herb with a juicy stem, roundish leaves, red, yellow, or white flowers, and seeds with a sharp taste

nas·ty *adj* **nas·ti·er; nas·ti·est** **1** : very dirty : FILTHY **2** : INDECENT **3** : [1]MEAN 4 **4** : HARMFUL, DANGEROUS **5** : very unpleasant — **nas·ti·ly** *adv* — **nas·ti·ness** *n*

na·tal *adj* : of, relating to, or associated with birth

na·tion *n* **1** : NATIONALITY 3 **2** : a community of people made up of one or more nationalities usually with its own territory and government **3** : COUNTRY

[1]**na·tion·al** *adj* : of or relating to a nation — **na·tion·al·ly** *adv*

[2]**national** *n* : a citizen of a nation

na·tion·al·ism *n* : devotion to the interests of a certain country

na·tion·al·ist *n* : a person who believes in nationalism

na·tion·al·is·tic *adj* **1** : of, relating to, or favoring nationalism **2** : [1]NATIONAL — **na·tion·al·is·ti·cal·ly** *adv*

na·tion·al·i·ty *n, pl* **na·tion·al·i·ties** **1** : the fact or state of belonging to a nation **2** : the state of being a separate nation **3** : a group of people having a common history, tradition, culture, or language

na·tion·al·ize *vb* **na·tion·al·ized; na·tion·al·iz·ing** : to place under government control

na·tion·wide *adj* : extending throughout a nation

[1]**na·tive** *adj* **1** : NATURAL 1 **2** : born in a certain place or country **3** : belonging to one because of one's place of birth **4** : grown, produced, or coming from a certain place

[2]**native** *n* : one that is native

Native American *n* : a member of any of the first peoples to live in North and South America and especially in the United States

na·tiv·i·ty *n, pl* **na·tiv·i·ties** **1** : BIRTH 1 **2** *cap* : the birth of Christ : CHRISTMAS

nat·ty *adj* **nat·ti·er; nat·ti·est** : very neat, trim, and stylish — **nat·ti·ly** *adv* — **nat·ti·ness** *n*

nat·u·ral *adj* **1** : born in or with one **2** : being such by nature : BORN **3** : found in or produced by nature **4** : of or relating to nature **5** : not made by humans **6** : being simple and sincere **7** : LIFELIKE **8** : being neither sharp nor flat : having neither sharps nor flats — **nat·u·ral·ly** *adv* — **nat·u·ral·ness** *n*

natural gas *n* : a flammable gas mixture from below earth's surface that is used especially as a fuel

nat·u·ral·ist *n* : a person who studies nature and especially plants and animals as they live in nature

nat·u·ral·i·za·tion *n* : the act or process of naturalizing : the state of being naturalized

nat·u·ral·ize *vb* **nat·u·ral·ized; nat·u·ral·iz·ing** **1** : to become or cause to become established as if native **2** : to admit to citizenship

natural number *n* : the number 1 or any number obtained by adding 1 to it one or more times

natural resource *n* : something (as a mineral, forest, or kind of animal) that is found in nature and is valuable to humans

na·ture *n* **1** : the basic character of a person or thing **2** : [1]SORT 1, VARIETY **3** : natural feelings : DISPOSITION, TEMPERAMENT **4** : the material universe **5** : the working of a living body **6** : natural scenery

[1]**naught** *or* **nought** *pron* : [1]NOTHING 1

[2]**naught** *or* **nought** *n* : ZERO 1, CIPHER

naugh·ty *adj* **naugh·ti·er; naugh·ti·est** : behaving in a bad or improper way — **naugh·ti·ly** *adv* — **naugh·ti·ness** *n*

nau·sea *n* **1** : a disturbed condition of the stomach in which one feels like vomiting **2** : deep disgust : LOATHING

nau·se·ate *vb* **nau·se·at·ed; nau·se·at·ing**

: to affect or become affected with nausea — **nau·se·at·ing** *adj* — **nau·se·at·ing·ly** *adv*

nau·seous *adj* **1 :** suffering from nausea **2 :** causing nausea

nau·ti·cal *adj* **:** of or relating to sailors, navigation, or ships — **nau·ti·cal·ly** *adv*

na·val *adj* **:** of or relating to a navy or warships

nave *n* **:** the long central main part of a church

na·vel *n* **:** a hollow in the middle of the abdomen that marks the place where the umbilical cord was attached

nav·i·ga·bil·i·ty *n* **:** the quality or state of being navigable

nav·i·ga·ble *adj* **1 :** deep enough and wide enough to permit passage of ships **2 :** possible to steer

nav·i·gate *vb* **nav·i·gat·ed; nav·i·gat·ing 1 :** to travel by water **2 :** to sail over, on, or through **3 :** to steer a course in a ship or aircraft **4 :** to steer or direct the course of (as a boat)

nav·i·ga·tion *n* **1 :** the act or practice of navigating **2 :** the science of figuring out the position and course of a ship or aircraft

nav·i·ga·tor *n* **:** an officer on a ship or aircraft responsible for its navigation

na·vy *n, pl* **navies 1 :** a nation's ships of war **2 :** the complete naval equipment and organization of a nation **3 :** a dark blue

[1]**nay** *adv* **:** [1]NO 2

[2]**nay** *n* **:** [3]NO 2

Na·zi *n* **:** a member of a political party controlling Germany from 1933 to 1945

Ne·an·der·thal man *n* **:** a long gone ancient human who made tools of stone and lived by hunting

[1]**near** *adv* **1 :** at, within, or to a short distance or time **2 :** ALMOST, NEARLY

[2]**near** *prep* **:** close to

[3]**near** *adj* **1 :** closely related or associated **2 :** not far away **3 :** coming close **:** NARROW **4 :** being the closer of two — **near·ly** *adv* — **near·ness** *n*

[4]**near** *vb* **:** to come near **:** APPROACH

near·by *adv or adj* **:** close at hand

near·sight·ed *adj* **:** able to see near things more clearly than distant ones — **near·sight·ed·ly** *adv* — **near·sight·ed·ness** *n*

neat *adj* **1 :** being simple and in good taste **2 :** SKILLFUL 2 **3 :** showing care and a concern for order — **neat·ly** *adv* — **neat·ness** *n*

neb·u·la *n, pl* **neb·u·las** *or* **neb·u·lae :** any of many clouds of gas or dust seen in the sky among the stars

neb·u·lous *adj* **:** not clear **:** VAGUE — **neb·u·lous·ly** *adv* — **neb·u·lous·ness** *n*

[1]**nec·es·sary** *adj* **:** needing to be had or done **:** ESSENTIAL — **nec·es·sar·i·ly** *adv*

[2]**necessary** *n, pl* **nec·es·sar·ies :** something that is needed

ne·ces·si·tate *vb* **ne·ces·si·tat·ed; ne·ces·si·tat·ing :** to make necessary **:** REQUIRE

ne·ces·si·ty *n, pl* **ne·ces·si·ties 1 :** the state of things that forces certain actions **2 :** very great need **3 :** the state of being without or unable to get necessary things **:** POVERTY **4 :** something that is badly needed

neck *n* **1 :** the part connecting the head and the main part of the body **2 :** the part of a garment covering or nearest to the neck **3 :** something like a neck in shape or position — **necked** *adj* — **neck and neck :** so nearly equal (as in a race) that one cannot be said to be ahead of the other

neck·er·chief *n, pl* **neck·er·chiefs :** a square of cloth worn folded around the neck like a scarf

neck·lace *n* **:** an ornament (as a string of beads) worn around the neck

neck·line *n* **:** the outline of the neck opening of a garment

neck·tie *n* **:** a narrow length of material worn around the neck and tied in front

nec·tar *n* **1 :** the drink of the Greek and Roman gods **2 :** a sweet liquid given off by plants and used by bees in making honey

nec·tar·ine *n* **:** a peach with a smooth skin

née *or* **nee** *adj* **:** BORN 1 — used to identify a woman by her maiden name

[1]**need** *n* **1 :** something that must be done **:** OBLIGATION **2 :** a lack of something necessary, useful, or desired **3 :** something necessary or desired

[2]**need** *vb* **1 :** to suffer from the lack of something important to life or health **2 :** to be necessary **3 :** to be without **:** REQUIRE

need·ful *adj* **:** [1]NECESSARY — **need·ful·ly** *adv* — **need·ful·ness** *n*

[1]**nee·dle** *n* **1 :** a slender pointed usually steel device used to make a hole and pull thread through in sewing **2 :** a slender pointed piece of metal or plastic (used for knitting) **3 :** a leaf (as of a pine) shaped like a needle **4 :** a pointer on a dial **5 :** a slender hollow instrument by which material is put into or taken from the body through the skin — **nee·dle·like** *adj*

[2]**needle** *vb* **nee·dled; nee·dling :** [1]TEASE, TAUNT

nee·dle·point *n* **:** embroidery done on canvas usually in simple even stitches across counted threads

need·less *adj* **:** UNNECESSARY — **need·less·ly** *adv* — **need·less·ness** *n*

nee·dle·work *n* **:** work (as sewing or embroidery) done with a needle

needn't : need not

needs *adv* **:** because of necessity

needy *adj* **need·i·er; need·i·est** : very poor — **need·i·ness** *n*

ne'er *adv* : NEVER

ne'er–do–well *n* : a worthless person who will not work

ne·gate *vb* **ne·gat·ed; ne·gat·ing** **1** : to deny the existence or truth of **2** : to cause to be ineffective

ne·ga·tion *n* : the action of negating : DENIAL

¹neg·a·tive *adj* **1** : making a denial **2** : not positive **3** : not helpful **4** : less than zero and shown by a minus sign **5** : of, being, or relating to electricity of which the electron is the unit and which is produced in a hard rubber rod that has been rubbed with wool **6** : having more electrons than protons **7** : being the part toward which the electric current flows from the outside circuit — **neg·a·tive·ly** *adv* — **neg·a·tiv·i·ty** *n*

²negative *n* **1** : something that is the opposite of something else **2** : a negative number **3** : an expression (as the word *no*) that denies or says the opposite **4** : the side that argues or votes against something **5** : a photographic image on film from which a final picture is made

¹ne·glect *vb* **1** : to fail to give the right amount of attention to **2** : to fail to do or look after especially because of carelessness

²neglect *n* **1** : an act or instance of neglecting something **2** : the state of being neglected

ne·glect·ful *adj* : tending to neglect : NEGLIGENT — **ne·glect·ful·ly** *adv* — **ne·glect·ful·ness** *n*

neg·li·gee *n* : a woman's loose robe worn especially while dressing or resting

neg·li·gence *n* **1** : the state of being negligent **2** : an act or instance of being negligent

neg·li·gent *adj* : likely to neglect things : CARELESS — **neg·li·gent·ly** *adv*

neg·li·gi·ble *adj* : so small or unimportant as to deserve little or no attention — **neg·li·gi·bly** *adv*

ne·go·tia·ble *adj* : possible to negotiate — **ne·go·tia·bil·i·ty** *n*

ne·go·ti·ate *vb* **ne·go·ti·at·ed; ne·go·ti·at·ing** **1** : to have a discussion with another in order to settle something **2** : to arrange for by discussing **3** : to give to someone in exchange for cash or something of equal value **4** : to be successful in getting around, through, or over — **ne·go·ti·a·tor** *n*

ne·go·ti·a·tion *n* : the act or process of negotiating or being negotiated

Ne·gro *n, pl* **Ne·groes** **1** : a member of any of the original peoples of Africa south of the Sahara **2** : a person with Negro ancestors — **Negro** *adj*

¹neigh *vb* : to make a neigh

²neigh *n* : the long loud cry of a horse

¹neigh·bor *n* **1** : a person living or a thing located near another **2** : a fellow human being

²neighbor *vb* : to be near or next to — **neigh·bor·ing** *adj*

neigh·bor·hood *n* **1** : a place or region near : VICINITY **2** : an amount, size, or range that is close to **3** : the people living near one another **4** : a section lived in by neighbors

neigh·bor·ly *adj* : of, relating to, or like neighbors : FRIENDLY — **neigh·bor·li·ness** *n*

¹nei·ther *conj* **1** : not either **2** : also not

²neither *pron* : not the one and not the other

³neither *adj* : not either

ne·on *n* **1** : a colorless gaseous chemical element found in very small amounts in the air and used in electric lamps **2** : a lamp in which the gas contains a large proportion of neon **3** : a sign made up of such lamps

neo·phyte *n* **1** : a new convert **2** : BEGINNER, NOVICE

neph·ew *n* : a son of one's brother or sister

Nep·tune *n* : the planet that is eighth in order of distance from the sun and has a diameter of about 49,000 kilometers

nep·tu·ni·um *n* : a radioactive chemical element similar to uranium

nerd *n* **1** : a person who is socially awkward, unattractive, or not fashionable **2** : a person who is extremely devoted to study and learning — **nerdy** *adj*

nerve *n* **1** : one of the bands of nerve fibers that join centers (as the brain) of the nervous system with other parts of the body and carry nerve impulses **2** : FORTITUDE, DARING **3** : IMPUDENCE **4 nerves** *pl* : JITTERS **5** : the sensitive soft inner part of a tooth — **nerve·less** *adj*

nerve cell *n* : a cell of the nervous system with fibers that conduct nerve impulses

nerve fiber *n* : any of the slender extensions of a nerve cell that carry nerve impulses

nerve impulse *n* : a progressive change of a nerve fiber by which information is brought to or orders sent from the central nervous system

ner·vous *adj* **1** : of or relating to nerve cells **2** : of, relating to, or made up of nerves or nervous tissue **3** : easily excited or upset **4** : TIMID — **ner·vous·ly** *adv* — **ner·vous·ness** *n*

nervous system *n* : a system of the body that in vertebrates includes the brain, spinal cord, nerves, and sense organs and receives, interprets, and responds to stimuli from inside and outside the body

nervy *adj* **nerv·i·er; nerv·i·est** **1** : showing calm courage : BOLD **2** : ¹FORWARD 2 **3** : NERVOUS 3 — **nerv·i·ness** *n*

-ness *n suffix* : state : condition

[1]**nest** *n* **1** : a shelter made by a bird for its eggs and young **2** : a place where the eggs of some animals other than birds are laid and hatched **3** : a cozy home : a snug shelter **4** : those living in a nest

[2]**nest** *vb* : to build or live in a nest

nes·tle *vb* **nes·tled; nes·tling** **1** : to lie close and snug : CUDDLE **2** : to settle as if in a nest

nest·ling *n* : a young bird not yet able to leave the nest

[1]**net** *n* **1** : a fabric made of threads, cords, ropes, or wires that weave in and out with much open space **2** : something made of net **3** : something that traps one as if in a net **4** : NETWORK 2 **5** *often cap* : INTERNET

[2]**net** *vb* **net·ted; net·ting** **1** : to cover with or as if with a net **2** : to catch in or as if in a net

[3]**net** *adj* : remaining after all charges or expenses have been subtracted

[4]**net** *vb* **net·ted; net·ting** : to gain or produce as profit : CLEAR

net·ting *n* : NETWORK 1, 2

net·tle *n* : a tall plant with stinging hairs on the leaves

net·work *n* **1** : a net fabric or structure **2** : an arrangement of lines or channels crossing as in a net **3** : a system of computers connected by communications lines **4** : a group of connected radio or television stations

neu·ron *n* : NERVE CELL

neu·ter *adj* : lacking sex organs : having sex organs that are not fully developed

[1]**neu·tral** *n* **1** : one that does not favor either side in a quarrel, contest, or war **2** : a grayish color **3** : a position of gears (as in the transmission of a motor vehicle) in which they are not in contact

[2]**neutral** *adj* **1** : not favoring either side in a quarrel, contest, or war **2** : of or relating to a neutral country **3** : being neither one thing nor the other **4** : having no color that stands out : GRAYISH **5** : neither acid nor basic **6** : not electrically charged

neu·tral·i·ty *n* : the quality or state of being neutral

neu·tral·ize *vb* **neu·tral·ized; neu·tral·iz·ing** **1** : to make chemically neutral **2** : to make ineffective — **neu·tral·i·za·tion** *n* — **neu·tral·iz·er** *n*

neu·tron *n* : a particle that has a mass nearly equal to that of the proton but no electrical charge and that is present in all atomic nuclei except those of hydrogen

nev·er *adv* **1** : not ever : at no time **2** : not to any extent or in any way

nev·er·more *adv* : never again

nev·er·the·less *adv* : even so : HOWEVER

[1]**new** *adj* **1** : not old : RECENT **2** : taking the place of one that came before **3** : recently discovered or learned about **4** : not known or experienced before **5** : not accustomed **6** : beginning as a repeating of a previous act or thing **7** : being in a position, place, or state the first time — **new·ness** *n*

[2]**new** *adv* : NEWLY, RECENTLY

new·born *adj* **1** : recently born **2** : made new or strong again

new·com·er *n* **1** : one recently arrived **2** : BEGINNER

new·el *n* : a post at the bottom or at a turn of a stairway

new·fan·gled *adj* : of the newest style : NOVEL

new·ly *adv* : not long ago : RECENTLY

new moon *n* **1** : the moon's phase when its dark side is toward the earth **2** : the thin curved outline of the moon seen shortly after sunset for a few days after the new moon

news *n* **1** : a report of recent events **2** : material reported in a newspaper or news magazine or on a newscast **3** : an event that is interesting enough to be reported

news·boy *n* : a person who delivers or sells newspapers

news·cast *n* : a radio or television broadcast of news

news·girl *n* : a girl who delivers or sells newspapers

news·man *n, pl* **news·men** : a person who gathers or reports news

news·pa·per *n* : a paper that is printed and sold usually every day or weekly and that contains news, articles of opinion, features, and advertising

news·pa·per·man *n, pl* **news·pa·per·men** : a man who owns or works on a newspaper

news·pa·per·wom·an *n, pl* **news·pa·per·wom·en** : a woman who owns or works on a newspaper

news·reel *n* : a short motion picture about current events

news·stand *n* : a place where newspapers and magazines are sold

news·wom·an *n, pl* **news·wom·en** : a woman who gathers or reports news

New World *n* : the lands in the western hemisphere and especially North and South America

newsy *adj* **news·i·er; news·i·est** : filled with news

newt *n* : a small salamander that lives mostly in water

New Year's Day *n* : January 1 observed as a legal holiday in many countries

[1]**next** *adj* : coming just before or after

[2]**next** *prep* : NEXT TO

[3]**next** *adv* **1** : in the nearest place, time, or order following **2** : at the first time after this

next–door *adj* : located in the next building, apartment, or room

[1]**next to** *prep* **1 :** BESIDE 1 **2 :** following right after

[2]**next to** *adv* : very nearly

nib *n* **1 :** a pointed object (as the bill of a bird) **2 :** the point of a pen

[1]**nib·ble** *vb* **nib·bled; nib·bling :** to bite or chew gently or bit by bit — **nib·bler** *n*

[2]**nibble** *n* **1 :** an act of nibbling **2 :** a very small amount

nice *adj* **nic·er; nic·est 1 :** very fussy (as about appearance, manners, or food) **2 :** able to recognize small differences between things **3 :** PLEASING, PLEASANT **4 :** well behaved — **nice·ly** *adv* — **nice·ness** *n*

ni·ce·ty *n, pl* **ni·ce·ties 1 :** something dainty, delicate, or especially nice **2 :** a fine detail

niche *n* **1 :** an open hollow in a wall (as for a statue) **2 :** a place, job, or use for which a person or a thing is best fitted

[1]**nick** *n* **1 :** a small cut or chip in a surface **2 :** the last moment

[2]**nick** *vb* : to make a nick in

[1]**nick·el** *n* **1 :** a hard silvery white metallic chemical element that can be highly polished, resists weathering, and is used in alloys **2 :** a United States coin worth five cents

[2]**nickel** *vb* **nick·eled** *or* **nick·elled; nick·el·ing** *or* **nick·el·ling :** to plate with nickel

[1]**nick·er** *vb* : [1]NEIGH, WHINNY

[2]**nicker** *n* : [2]NEIGH

[1]**nick·name** *n* **1 :** a usually descriptive name given in addition to the one belonging to an individual **2 :** a familiar form of a proper name

[2]**nickname** *vb* **nick·named; nick·nam·ing :** to give a nickname to

nic·o·tine *n* : a poisonous substance found in small amounts in tobacco and used especially to kill insects

niece *n* : a daughter of one's brother or sister

nig·gling *adj* : PETTY 1

[1]**nigh** *adv* **1 :** near in time or place **2 :** ALMOST, NEARLY

[2]**nigh** *adj* : [3]CLOSE 5, NEAR

night *n* **1 :** the time between dusk and dawn when there is no sunlight **2 :** NIGHTFALL **3 :** the darkness of night

night·club *n* : a place of entertainment open at night usually serving food and liquor and having music for dancing

night crawl·er *n* : EARTHWORM

night·fall *n* : the coming of night

night·gown *n* : a loose garment worn in bed

night·hawk *n* **1 :** a bird that is related to the whippoorwill, flies mostly at twilight, and eats insects **2 :** a person who stays up late at night

night·in·gale *n* : a reddish brown Old World thrush noted for the sweet song of the male

[1]**night·ly** *adj* **1 :** of or relating to the night or every night **2 :** happening or done at night or every night

[2]**nightly** *adv* **1 :** every night **2 :** at or by night

night·mare *n* **1 :** a frightening dream **2 :** a horrible experience — **night·mar·ish** *adj*

night·shirt *n* : a nightgown like a very long shirt

night·stick *n* : a police officer's club

night·time *n* : NIGHT 1

nil *n* : ZERO 4, NOTHING

nim·ble *adj* **nim·bler; nim·blest 1 :** quick and light in motion : AGILE **2 :** quick in understanding and learning : CLEVER — **nim·ble·ness** *n* — **nim·bly** *adv*

nim·bus *n, pl* **nim·bi** *or* **nim·bus·es :** a rain cloud that is evenly gray and that covers the whole sky

nin·com·poop *n* : [1]FOOL 1

[1]**nine** *adj* : being one more than eight

[2]**nine** *n* **1 :** one more than eight : three times three : 9 **2 :** the ninth in a set or series

[1]**nine·teen** *adj* : being one more than eighteen

[2]**nineteen** *n* : one more than eighteen : 19

[1]**nine·teenth** *adj* : coming right after eighteenth

[2]**nineteenth** *n* : number nineteen in a series

[1]**nine·ti·eth** *adj* : coming right after eighty-ninth

[2]**ninetieth** *n* : number ninety in a series

[1]**nine·ty** *adj* : being nine times ten

[2]**ninety** *n* : nine times ten : 90

nin·ja *n* : a person trained in ancient Japanese arts of fighting and defending oneself and employed especially for espionage and assassinations

nin·ny *n, pl* **ninnies :** [1]FOOL 1

[1]**ninth** *adj* : coming right after eighth

[2]**ninth** *n* **1 :** number nine in a series **2 :** one of nine equal parts

[1]**nip** *vb* **nipped; nip·ping 1 :** to catch hold of (as with teeth) and squeeze sharply though not very hard **2 :** to cut off by or as if by pinching sharply **3 :** to stop the growth or progress of **4 :** to injure or make numb with cold

[2]**nip** *n* **1 :** something that nips **2 :** the act of nipping **3 :** a small portion : BIT

[3]**nip** *n* : a small amount of liquor

nip and tuck *adj or adv* : so close that the lead shifts rapidly from one contestant to another

nip·ple *n* **1 :** the part of the breast from which a baby or young animal sucks milk **2 :** something (as the mouthpiece of a baby's bottle) like a nipple

nip·py *adj* **nip·pi·er; nip·pi·est :** CHILLY

nit *n* : the egg of a louse

ni·trate *n* : a substance that is made from or has a composition as if made from nitric acid

ni·tric acid *n* : a strong liquid acid that contains hydrogen, nitrogen, and oxygen and is used in making fertilizers, explosives, and dyes

ni·tro·gen *n* : a colorless odorless gaseous chemical element that makes up 78 percent of the atmosphere and forms a part of all living tissues

nitrogen cycle *n* : a continuous series of natural processes by which nitrogen passes from air to soil to organisms and back into the air

nitrogen fix·a·tion *n* : the changing of free nitrogen into combined forms especially by bacteria (**nitrogen-fixing bacteria**)

ni·tro·glyc·er·in *or* **ni·tro·glyc·er·ine** *n* : a heavy oily liquid explosive from which dynamite is made

nit·wit *n* : a very silly or stupid person

[1]**no** *adv* **1** : not at all : not any **2** : not so — used to express disagreement or refusal **3** — used to express surprise, doubt, or disbelief

[2]**no** *adj* **1** : not any **2** : hardly any : very little **3** : not a

[3]**no** *n, pl* **noes** *or* **nos** **1** : an act or instance of refusing or denying by the use of the word *no* : DENIAL **2** : a negative vote or decision **3** *noes or nos pl* : persons voting in the negative

no·bil·i·ty *n, pl* **no·bil·i·ties** **1** : the quality or state of being noble **2** : noble rank **3** : the class or a group of nobles

[1]**no·ble** *adj* **no·bler; no·blest** **1** : EMINENT, ILLUSTRIOUS **2** : of very high birth or rank **3** : having very fine qualities **4** : grand in appearance — **no·ble·ness** *n* — **no·bly** *adv*

[2]**noble** *n* : a person of noble birth or rank

no·ble·man *n, pl* **no·ble·men** : a man of noble rank

no·ble·wom·an *n, pl* **no·ble·wom·en** : a woman of noble rank

[1]**no·body** *pron* : no person : not anybody

[2]**nobody** *n, pl* **no·bod·ies** : a person of no importance

noc·tur·nal *adj* **1** : of, relating to, or happening at night : NIGHTLY **2** : active at night — **noc·tur·nal·ly** *adv*

[1]**nod** *vb* **nod·ded; nod·ding** **1** : to bend the head downward or forward (as in bowing, going to sleep, or indicating "yes") **2** : to move up and down **3** : to show by a nod of the head

[2]**nod** *n* : the action of bending the head downward and forward

node *n* : a thickened spot or part (as of a plant stem where a leaf develops)

nod·ule *n* : a small node (as of a clover root)

no·el *n* **1** : a Christmas carol **2** *cap* : the Christmas season

noes *pl of* NO

[1]**noise** *n* **1** : a loud unpleasant sound **2** : [3]SOUND 1 — **noise·less** *adj* — **noise·less·ly** *adv* — **noise·less·ness** *n*

[2]**noise** *vb* **noised; nois·ing** : to spread by rumor or report

noise·mak·er *n* : a device used to make noise especially at parties

noisy *adj* **nois·i·er; nois·i·est** **1** : making noise **2** : full of noise — **nois·i·ly** *adv* — **nois·i·ness** *n*

[1]**no·mad** *n* **1** : a member of a people having no fixed home but wandering from place to place **2** : WANDERER

[2]**nomad** *adj* : NOMADIC 2

no·mad·ic *adj* **1** : of or relating to nomads **2** : roaming about with no special end in mind

nom·i·nal *adj* **1** : being such in name only **2** : very small : TRIFLING — **nom·i·nal·ly** *adv*

nom·i·nate *vb* **nom·i·nat·ed; nom·i·nat·ing** : to choose as a candidate for election, appointment, or honor — **nom·i·na·tor** *n*

nom·i·na·tion *n* **1** : the act or an instance of nominating **2** : the state of being nominated

nom·i·na·tive *adj* : being or belonging to the case of a noun or pronoun that is usually the subject of a verb

nom·i·nee *n* : a person nominated for an office, duty, or position

non- *prefix* : not

non·al·co·hol·ic *adj* : containing no alcohol

non·cha·lance *n* : the state of being nonchalant

non·cha·lant *adj* : having a confident and easy manner — **non·cha·lant·ly** *adv*

non·com·bat·ant *n* **1** : a member (as a chaplain) of the armed forces whose duties do not include fighting **2** : [1]CIVILIAN

non·com·mis·sioned officer *n* : an officer in the Army, Air Force, or Marine Corps appointed from among the enlisted persons

non·com·mit·tal *adj* : not telling or showing what one thinks or has decided — **non·com·mit·tal·ly** *adv*

non·com·mu·ni·ca·ble *adj* : not spread from one individual to another

non·con·duc·tor *n* : a substance that conducts heat, electricity, or sound at a very low rate

non·con·form·ist *n* : a person who does not conform to generally accepted standards or customs

non·de·script *adj* : of no certain class or kind : not easily described

[1]**none** *pron* : not any : not one

[2]**none** *adv* **1** : not at all **2** : in no way

non·en·ti·ty *n, pl* **non·en·ti·ties** : someone or something of no importance
[1]**non·es·sen·tial** *adj* : not essential
[2]**nonessential** *n* : something that is not essential
none·the·less *adv* : NEVERTHELESS
non·fic·tion *n* : writings that are not fiction
non·flam·ma·ble *adj* : not flammable
non·green *adj* : having no chlorophyll
non·liv·ing *adj* : not living
non·par·ti·san *adj* : not partisan : not committed to one party or side
non·plus *vb* **non·plussed; non·plus·sing** : to cause to be at a loss as to what to say, think, or do : PERPLEX
non·poi·son·ous *adj* : not poisonous
non·prof·it *adj* : not existing or carried on to make a profit
[1]**non·res·i·dent** *adj* : not living in a certain place
[2]**nonresident** *n* : a nonresident person
non·sched·uled *adj* : licensed to carry pasengers or freight by air whenever demand requires
non·sec·tar·i·an *adj* : not limited to a particular religious group
non·sense *n* **1** : foolish or meaningless words or actions **2** : things of no importance or value
non·sen·si·cal *adj* : making no sense : ABSURD — **non·sen·si·cal·ly** *adv*
non·smok·er *n* : a person who does not smoke tobacco
non·smok·ing *adj* **1** : not in the habit of smoking tobacco **2** : reserved for the use of nonsmokers
non·stan·dard *adj* : not standard
non·stop *adv or adj* : without a stop
noo·dle *n* : a food like macaroni made with egg and shaped into flat strips — usually used in pl.
nook *n* **1** : an inner corner **2** : a sheltered or hidden place
noon *n* : the middle of the day : twelve o'clock in the daytime
noon·day *n* : NOON, MIDDAY
no one *pron* : [1]NOBODY
noon·tide *n* : NOON
noon·time *n* : NOON
noose *n* : a loop that passes through a knot at the end of a line so that it gets smaller when the other end of the line is pulled
nor *conj* : and not
norm *n* : [1]AVERAGE 2
[1]**nor·mal** *adj* **1** : of the regular or usual kind : REGULAR **2** : of average intelligence **3** : sound in body or mind — **nor·mal·ly** *adv*
[2]**normal** *n* **1** : one that is normal **2** : [1]AVERAGE 2
nor·mal·cy *n* : NORMALITY
nor·mal·i·ty *n* : the quality or state of being normal
Nor·man *n* **1** : one of the Scandinavians who conquered Normandy in the tenth century **2** : one of the people of mixed Norman and French blood who conquered England in 1066
Norse *n pl* **1** : people of Scandinavia **2** : people of Norway
[1]**north** *adv* : to or toward the north
[2]**north** *adj* : placed toward, facing, or coming from the north
[3]**north** *n* **1** : the direction to the left of one facing east : the compass point opposite to south **2** *cap* : regions or countries north of a point that is mentioned or understood
[1]**North American** *n* : a person born or living in North America
[2]**North American** *adj* : of or relating to North America or the North Americans
north·bound *adj* : going north
[1]**north·east** *adv* : to or toward the direction between north and east
[2]**northeast** *adj* : placed toward, facing, or coming from the northeast
[3]**northeast** *n* **1** : the direction between north and east **2** *cap* : regions or countries northeast of a point that is mentioned or understood
north·east·er·ly *adv or adj* **1** : from the northeast **2** : toward the northeast
north·east·ern *adj* **1** *often cap* : of, relating to, or like that of the Northeast **2** : lying toward or coming from the northeast
north·er·ly *adj or adv* **1** : toward the north **2** : from the north
north·ern *adj* **1** *often cap* : of, relating to, or like that of the North **2** : lying toward or coming from the north
northern lights *n pl* : AURORA BOREALIS
north·land *n, often cap* : land in the north : the north of a country or region
north pole *n* **1** *often cap N&P* : the most northern point of the earth : the northern end of the earth's axis **2** : the end of a magnet that points toward the north when the magnet is free to swing
North Star *n* : the star toward which the northern end of the earth's axis very nearly points
north·ward *adv or adj* : toward the north
[1]**north·west** *adv* : to or toward the direction between north and west
[2]**northwest** *adj* : placed toward, facing, or coming from the northwest
[3]**northwest** *n* **1** : the direction between north and west **2** *cap* : regions or countries northwest of a point that is mentioned or understood

north·west·er·ly *adv or adj* **1 :** from the northwest **2 :** toward the northwest

north·west·ern *adj* **1** *often cap* : of, relating to, or like that of the Northwest **2 :** lying toward or coming from the northwest

[1]**Nor·we·gian** *adj* : of or relating to Norway, its people, or the Norwegian language

[2]**Norwegian** *n* **1 :** a person who is born or lives in Norway **2 :** the language of the Norwegians

nos *pl of* NO

[1]**nose** *n* **1 :** the part of a person's face or an animal's head that contains the nostrils **2 :** the sense or organ of smell **3 :** something (as a point, edge, or the front of an object) that suggests a nose **4 :** an ability to discover — **nosed** *adj*

[2]**nose** *vb* **nosed; nos·ing 1 :** to detect by or as if by smell : SCENT **2 :** to touch or rub with the nose : NUZZLE **3 :** to search in a nosy way : PRY **4 :** to move ahead slowly or carefully

nose·bleed *n* : a bleeding at the nose

nose cone *n* : a protective cone forming the forward end of a rocket or missile

nose–dive *vb* **nose–dived; nose–div·ing** : to plunge suddenly or sharply

nose dive *n* **1 :** a downward plunge (as of an airplane) **2 :** a sudden sharp drop (as in prices)

nos·tal·gia *n* : a wishing for something past

nos·tril *n* : either of the outer openings of the nose through which one breathes

nos·trum *n* : a medicine of secret formula and doubtful worth : a questionable remedy

nosy *or* **nos·ey** *adj* **nos·i·er; nos·i·est :** tending to pry into someone else's business

not *adv* **1** — used to make a word or group of words negative **2** — used to stand for the negative of a group of words that comes before

[1]**no·ta·ble** *adj* **1 :** deserving special notice : REMARKABLE **2 :** DISTINGUISHED, PROMINENT — **no·ta·bly** *adv*

[2]**notable** *n* : a famous person

no·ta·rize *vb* **no·ta·rized; no·ta·riz·ing :** to sign as a notary public to show that a document is authentic

no·ta·ry public *n, pl* **notaries public** *or* **notary publics :** a public officer who witnesses the making of a document (as a deed) and signs it to show that it is authentic

no·ta·tion *n* **1 :** the act of noting **2 :** [2]NOTE 5 **3 :** a system of signs, marks, or figures used to give specified information

[1]**notch** *n* **1 :** a cut in the shape of a V in an edge or surface **2 :** a narrow pass between mountains **3 :** DEGREE 1, STEP

[2]**notch** *vb* : to cut or make notches in

[1]**note** *vb* **not·ed; not·ing 1 :** to notice or observe with care **2 :** to record in writing **3 :** to call attention to in speech or writing

[2]**note** *n* **1 :** a musical sound : TONE **2 :** a symbol in music that by its shape and position on the staff shows the pitch of a tone and the length of time it is to be held **3 :** the musical call or song of a bird **4 :** a quality that shows a feeling **5 :** something written down often to aid the memory **6 :** a printed comment in a book that helps explain part of the text **7 :** DISTINCTION 3 **8 :** a short written message or letter **9 :** careful notice **10 :** a promise to pay a debt **11 :** a piano key **12 :** frame of mind : MOOD

note·book *n* : a book of blank pages for writing in

not·ed *adj* : well-known and highly regarded

note·wor·thy *adj* : worthy of note : REMARKABLE — **note·wor·thi·ness** *n*

[1]**noth·ing** *pron* **1 :** not anything : no thing **2 :** one of no interest, value, or importance

[2]**nothing** *adv* : not at all : in no way

[3]**nothing** *n* **1 :** something that does not exist **2 :** ZERO 1, 4 **3 :** something of little or no worth or importance — **noth·ing·ness** *n*

[1]**no·tice** *n* **1 :** WARNING **2 :** an indication that an agreement will end at a specified time **3 :** ATTENTION 1, HEED **4 :** a written or printed announcement **5 :** a brief published criticism (as of a book or play)

[2]**notice** *vb* **no·ticed; no·tic·ing :** to take notice of : pay attention to

no·tice·able *adj* : deserving notice : likely to be noticed — **no·tice·ably** *adv*

no·ti·fi·ca·tion *n* **1 :** the act or an instance of notifying **2 :** something written or printed that gives notice

no·ti·fy *vb* **no·ti·fied; no·ti·fy·ing :** to give notice to : INFORM

no·tion *n* **1 :** IDEA 2 **2 :** WHIM **3 notions** *pl* : small useful articles (as buttons, needles, and thread)

no·to·ri·e·ty *n* : the state of being notorious

no·to·ri·ous *adj* : widely known for some bad characteristic — **no·to·ri·ous·ly** *adv*

[1]**not·with·stand·ing** *prep* : in spite of

[2]**notwithstanding** *adv* : NEVERTHELESS

nou·gat *n* : a candy consisting of a sugar paste with nuts or fruit pieces

nought *variant of* NAUGHT

noun *n* : a word or phrase that is the name of something (as a person, place, or thing) and that is used in a sentence especially as subject or object of a verb or as object of a preposition

nour·ish *vb* : to cause to grow or live in a healthy state especially by providing with enough good food — **nour·ish·ing** *adj*

nour·ish·ment *n* **1 :** something (as food) that

nourishes **2 :** the act of nourishing **:** the state of being nourished

[1]**nov·el** *adj* **1 :** new and different from what is already known **2 :** original or striking in design or appearance

[2]**novel** *n* **:** a long made-up story that usually fills a book

nov·el·ist *n* **:** a writer of novels

nov·el·ty *n, pl* **nov·el·ties 1 :** something new or unusual **2 :** the quality or state of being novel **3 :** a small article of unusual design intended mainly for decoration or adornment

No·vem·ber *n* **:** the eleventh month of the year

nov·ice *n* **1 :** a new member of a religious community who is preparing to take the vows of religion **2 :** a person who has no previous experience with something **:** BEGINNER

[1]**now** *adv* **1 :** at this time **2 :** immediately before the present time **3 :** in the time immediately to follow **4** — used to express command or introduce an important point **5 :** SOMETIMES **6 :** in the present state **7 :** at the time referred to

[2]**now** *conj* **:** in view of the fact that **:** [2]SINCE 2

[3]**now** *n* **:** the present time

now·a·days *adv* **:** at the present time

[1]**no·where** *adv* **1 :** not in or at any place **2 :** to no place

[2]**nowhere** *n* **:** a place that does not exist

nox·ious *adj* **:** causing harm

noz·zle *n* **:** a short tube with a taper or constriction often used on a hose or pipe to direct or speed up a flow of fluid

-n't *adv suffix* **:** not

nu·cle·ar *adj* **1 :** of, relating to, or being a nucleus (as of a cell) **2 :** of or relating to the nucleus of the atom **3 :** produced by a nuclear reaction **4 :** of, relating to, or being a weapon whose destructive power comes from an uncontrolled nuclear reaction **5 :** relating to or powered by nuclear energy

nu·cle·us *n, pl* **nu·clei 1 :** a central point, group, or mass **2 :** a part of cell protoplasm enclosed in a nuclear membrane, containing chromosomes and genes, and concerned especially with the control of vital functions and heredity **3 :** the central part of an atom that comprises nearly all of the atomic mass and that consists of protons and neutrons except in hydrogen in which it consists of one proton only

nude *adj* **nud·er; nud·est :** not wearing clothes **:** NAKED — **nude·ness** *n*

[1]**nudge** *vb* **nudged; nudg·ing :** to touch or push gently (as with the elbow) especially in order to attract attention

[2]**nudge** *n* **:** a slight push

nu·di·ty *n* **:** the quality or state of being nude

nug·get *n* **:** a solid lump especially of precious metal

nui·sance *n* **:** an annoying person or thing

null *adj* **:** having no legal force **:** not binding

null and void *adj* **:** NULL

[1]**numb** *adj* **1 :** lacking in sensation especially from cold **2 :** lacking feelings **:** INDIFFERENT — **numb·ly** *adv* — **numb·ness** *n*

[2]**numb** *vb* **:** to make or become numb

[1]**num·ber** *n* **1 :** the total of persons, things, or units taken together **:** AMOUNT **2 :** a total that is not specified **3 :** a quality of a word form that shows whether the word is singular or plural **4 :** NUMERAL **5 :** a certain numeral for telling one person or thing from another or from others **6 :** one of a series

[2]**number** *vb* **1 :** [1]COUNT 1 **2 :** INCLUDE **3 :** to limit to a certain number **4 :** to give a number to **5 :** to add up to or have a total of

num·ber·less *adj* **:** too many to count

number line *n* **:** a line in which points are matched to numbers

nu·mer·al *n* **:** a symbol or group of symbols representing a number

nu·mer·a·tion *n* **:** a system of counting

nu·mer·a·tor *n* **:** the part of a fraction that is above the line

nu·mer·i·cal *adj* **:** of or relating to number **:** stated in numbers — **nu·mer·i·cal·ly** *adv*

nu·mer·ous *adj* **:** consisting of a large number — **nu·mer·ous·ly** *adv*

num·skull *n* **:** a stupid person

nun *n* **:** a woman belonging to a religious community and living by vows

nun·cio *n, pl* **nun·ci·os :** the pope's representative to a civil government

nup·tial *adj* **:** of or relating to marriage or a wedding

nup·tials *n pl* **:** WEDDING

[1]**nurse** *n* **1 :** a woman employed for the care of a young child **2 :** a person skilled or trained in the care of the sick

[2]**nurse** *vb* **nursed; nurs·ing 1 :** to feed at the breast **2 :** to take care of (as a young child or a sick person) **3 :** to treat with special care

nurse·maid *n* **:** [1]NURSE 1

nurs·ery *n, pl* **nurs·er·ies 1 :** a place set aside for small children or for the care of small children **2 :** a place where young trees, vines, and plants are grown and usually sold

nurs·ery·man *n, pl* **nurs·ery·men :** a person whose occupation is the growing of trees, shrubs, and plants

nursery school *n* **:** a school for children usually under five years old

[1]**nur·ture** *n* **1 :** UPBRINGING **2 :** something (as food) that nourishes

[2]**nurture** *vb* **nur·tured; nur·tur·ing 1 :** to sup-

ply with food **2 :** EDUCATE 2 **3 :** to provide for growth of

¹nut *n* **1 :** a dry fruit or seed with a firm inner kernel and a hard shell **2 :** the often edible kernel of a nut **3 :** a piece of metal with a hole in it that is fastened to a bolt by means of a screw thread **4 :** a foolish or crazy person — **nut·like** *adj*

²nut *vb* **nut·ted; nut·ting :** to gather or seek nuts

nut·crack·er *n* **1 :** a device used for cracking the shells of nuts **2 :** a bird related to the crows that lives mostly on the seeds of pine trees

nut·hatch *n* **:** a small bird that creeps on tree trunks and branches and eats insects

nut·let *n* **1 :** a small nut **2 :** a small fruit like a nut

nut·meg *n* **:** a spice that is the ground seeds of a small evergreen tropical tree

nu·tri·ent *n* **:** a substance used in nutrition

nu·tri·ment *n* **:** something that nourishes

nu·tri·tion *n* **:** the act or process of nourishing or being nourished **:** the processes by which a living being takes in and uses nutrients

nu·tri·tion·al *adj* **:** of or relating to nutrition

nu·tri·tious *adj* **:** providing nutrients **:** NOURISHING

nu·tri·tive *adj* **1 :** NUTRITIONAL **2 :** NUTRITIOUS

nut·ty *adj* **nut·ti·er; nut·ti·est 1 :** not showing good sense **2 :** having a flavor like that of nuts

nuz·zle *vb* **nuz·zled; nuz·zling 1 :** to push or rub with the nose **2 :** to lie close **:** NESTLE

ny·lon *n* **:** a synthetic material used in the making of textiles and plastics

nymph *n* **1 :** one of many goddesses in old legends represented as beautiful young girls living in the mountains, forests, and waters **2 :** an immature insect that differs from the adult chiefly in the size and proportions of the body

O

o *n, pl* **o's** *or* **os** *often cap* **1 :** the fifteenth letter of the English alphabet **2 :** ZERO 1

O *variant of* OH

oaf *n* **:** a stupid or awkward person — **oaf·ish** *adj*

oak *n* **:** any of various trees and shrubs related to the beech and chestnut whose fruits are acorns and whose tough wood is much used for furniture and flooring

oak·en *adj* **:** made of or like oak

oar *n* **:** a long pole with a broad blade at one end used for rowing or steering a boat

oar·lock *n* **:** a usually U-shaped device for holding an oar in place

oars·man *n, pl* **oars·men :** a person who rows a boat

oa·sis *n, pl* **oa·ses :** a fertile or green spot in a desert

oat *n* **1 :** a cereal grass grown for its loose clusters of seeds that are used for human food and animal feed **2 oats** *pl* **:** a crop or the grain of the oat

oath *n, pl* **oaths 1 :** a solemn appeal to God or to some deeply respected person or thing to witness to the truth of one's word or the sacredness of a promise **2 :** a careless or improper use of a sacred name

oat·meal *n* **1 :** oats husked and ground into meal or flattened into flakes **2 :** a hot cereal made from meal or flakes of oats

obe·di·ence *n* **:** the act of obeying **:** willingness to obey

obe·di·ent *adj* **:** willing to obey **:** likely to mind — **obe·di·ent·ly** *adv*

obe·lisk *n* **:** a four-sided pillar that becomes narrower toward the top and ends in a pyramid

obese *adj* **:** very fat

obey *vb* **obeyed; obey·ing 1 :** to follow the commands or guidance of **2 :** to comply with **:** carry out

obit·u·ary *n, pl* **obit·u·ar·ies :** a notice of a person's death (as in a newspaper)

¹ob·ject *n* **1 :** something that may be seen or felt **2 :** something that arouses feelings in an observer **3 :** ¹PURPOSE, AIM **4 :** a noun or a term behaving like a noun that receives the action of a verb or completes the meaning of a preposition

²ob·ject *vb* **1 :** to offer or mention as an objection **2 :** to oppose something firmly and usually with words

ob·jec·tion *n* **1 :** an act of objecting **2 :** a reason for or a feeling of disapproval

ob·jec·tion·able *adj* **:** arousing objection **:** OFFENSIVE

¹ob·jec·tive *adj* **1 :** being outside of the mind and independent of it **2 :** being or belonging to the case of a noun or pronoun that is an object of a transitive verb or a preposition **3 :** dealing with facts without allowing one's feelings to confuse them — **ob·jec·tive·ly** *adv*

²objective *n* **:** ¹PURPOSE, GOAL

ob·jec·tiv·i·ty *n* **:** the quality or state of being objective

ob·li·gate *vb* **ob·li·gat·ed; ob·li·gat·ing 1 :** to make (someone) do something by law or because it is right **2 :** OBLIGE 2

ob·li·ga·tion *n* **1 :** an act of making oneself responsible for doing something **2 :** something (as the demands of a promise or contract) that requires one to do something **3 :** something one must do **:** DUTY **4 :** a feeling of being indebted for an act of kindness

oblige *vb* **obliged; oblig·ing 1 :** [2]FORCE 1, COMPEL **2 :** to earn the gratitude of **3 :** to do a favor for or do something as a favor

oblig·ing *adj* **:** willing to do favors — **oblig·ing·ly** *adv*

oblique *adj* **:** neither perpendicular nor parallel — **oblique·ly** *adv*

oblit·er·ate *vb* **oblit·er·at·ed; oblit·er·at·ing :** to remove or destroy completely

obliv·i·on *n* **1 :** the state of forgetting or having forgotten or of being unaware or unconscious **2 :** the state of being forgotten

obliv·i·ous *adj* **:** not being conscious or aware — **obliv·i·ous·ly** *adv* — **obliv·i·ous·ness** *n*

[1]**ob·long** *adj* **:** different from a square, circle, or sphere by being longer in one direction than the other

[2]**oblong** *n* **:** an oblong figure or object

ob·nox·ious *adj* **:** very disagreeable **:** HATEFUL — **ob·nox·ious·ly** *adv* — **ob·nox·ious·ness** *n*

oboe *n* **:** a woodwind instrument with two reeds that has a penetrating tone and a range of nearly three octaves

ob·scene *adj* **:** very shocking to one's sense of what is moral or decent

ob·scen·i·ty *n, pl* **ob·scen·i·ties 1 :** the quality or state of being obscene **2 :** something that is obscene

[1]**ob·scure** *adj* **1 :** [1]DARK 1, GLOOMY **2 :** SECLUDED **3 :** not easily understood or clearly expressed **4 :** not outstanding or famous

[2]**obscure** *vb* **ob·scured; ob·scur·ing :** to make obscure

ob·scu·ri·ty *n, pl* **ob·scu·ri·ties 1 :** the quality or state of being obscure **2 :** something that is obscure

ob·serv·able *adj* **:** NOTICEABLE — **ob·serv·ably** *adv*

ob·ser·vance *n* **1 :** an established practice or ceremony **2 :** an act of following a custom, rule, or law

ob·ser·vant *adj* **:** quick to take notice **:** WATCHFUL, ALERT — **ob·ser·vant·ly** *adv*

ob·ser·va·tion *n* **1 :** an act or the power of seeing or of fixing the mind upon something **2 :** the gathering of information by noting facts or occurrences **3 :** an opinion formed or expressed after observing **4 :** the fact of being observed

ob·ser·va·to·ry *n, pl* **ob·ser·va·to·ries :** a place that has instruments for making observations (as of the stars)

ob·serve *vb* **ob·served; ob·serv·ing 1 :** to act in agreement with **:** OBEY **2 :** CELEBRATE 2 **3 :** [1]WATCH 5 **4 :** [2]REMARK 2, SAY — **ob·serv·er** *n*

ob·sess *vb* **:** to occupy the mind of completely or abnormally

ob·ses·sion *n* **:** a disturbing and often unreasonable idea or feeling that cannot be put out of the mind

ob·sid·i·an *n* **:** a smooth dark rock formed by the cooling of lava

ob·so·lete *adj* **:** no longer in use **:** OUT-OF-DATE

ob·sta·cle *n* **:** something that stands in the way or opposes **:** HINDRANCE

ob·sti·na·cy *n* **:** the quality or state of being obstinate

ob·sti·nate *adj* **1 :** sticking stubbornly to an opinion or purpose **2 :** not easily overcome or removed — **ob·sti·nate·ly** *adv*

ob·struct *vb* **1 :** to stop up by an obstacle **:** BLOCK **2 :** to be or come in the way of **:** HINDER

ob·struc·tion *n* **1 :** an act of obstructing **:** the state of being obstructed **2 :** something that gets in the way **:** OBSTACLE

ob·tain *vb* **:** to gain or get hold of with effort

ob·tain·able *adj* **:** possible to obtain

ob·tuse *adj* **1 :** not pointed or sharp **:** BLUNT **2 :** measuring more than a right angle **3 :** not quick or keen of understanding or feeling

ob·vi·ous *adj* **:** easily found, seen, or understood — **ob·vi·ous·ly** *adv* — **ob·vi·ous·ness** *n*

oc·ca·sion *n* **1 :** a suitable opportunity **:** a good chance **2 :** the time of an event **3 :** a special event

oc·ca·sion·al *adj* **:** happening or met with now and then — **oc·ca·sion·al·ly** *adv*

oc·cu·pan·cy *n, pl* **oc·cu·pan·cies :** the act of occupying or taking possession

oc·cu·pant *n* **:** a person who occupies or takes possession

oc·cu·pa·tion *n* **1 :** one's business or profession **2 :** the taking possession and control of an area

oc·cu·pa·tion·al *adj* **:** of or relating to one's occupation — **oc·cu·pa·tion·al·ly** *adv*

oc·cu·py *vb* **oc·cu·pied; oc·cu·py·ing 1 :** to take up the attention or energies of **2 :** to fill up (an extent of time or space) **3 :** to take or hold possession of **4 :** to live in as an owner or tenant

oc·cur *vb* **oc·curred; oc·cur·ring 1 :** to be found or met with **:** APPEAR **2 :** to present itself **:** come by or as if by chance **3 :** to come into the mind

oc·cur·rence *n* **1 :** something that occurs **2 :** the action or process of occurring

ocean *n* **1 :** the whole body of salt water that covers nearly three fourths of the earth **2**

: one of the large bodies of water into which the great ocean is divided

oce·an·ic *adj* : of or relating to the ocean

ocean·og·ra·phy *n* : a science that deals with the ocean

oce·lot *n* : a medium-sized American wildcat that is tawny or grayish and blotched with black

o'·clock *adv* : according to the clock

octa- *or* **octo-** *also* **oct-** *prefix* : eight

oc·ta·gon *n* : a flat figure with eight angles and eight sides

oc·tag·o·nal *adj* : having eight sides

oc·tave *n* **1** : a space of eight steps between musical notes **2** : a tone or note that is eight steps above or below another note or tone

oc·tet *n* : a group or set of eight

Oc·to·ber *n* : the tenth month of the year

oc·to·pus *n, pl* **oc·to·pus·es** *or* **oc·to·pi** : a marine animal with no shell that has a rounded body with eight long flexible arms about its base which have sucking disks able to seize and hold things (as prey)

oc·u·lar *adj* : of or relating to the eye or eyesight

odd *adj* **1** : not one of a pair or a set **2** : not capable of being divided by two without leaving a remainder **3** : numbered with an odd number **4** : some more than the number mentioned **5** : not usual, expected, or planned **6** : not usual or traditional — **odd·ly** *adv* — **odd·ness** *n*

odd·ball *n* : a person who behaves strangely

odd·i·ty *n, pl* **odd·i·ties** **1** : something odd **2** : the quality or state of being odd

odds *n pl* **1** : a difference in favor of one thing over another **2** : DISAGREEMENT 1

odds and ends *n pl* : things left over : miscellaneous things

ode *n* : a lyric poem that expresses a noble feeling with dignity

odi·ous *adj* : causing hatred or strong dislike : worthy of hatred

odom·e·ter *n* : an instrument for measuring the distance traveled (as by a vehicle)

odor *n* **1** : a quality of something that one becomes aware of through the sense of smell **2** : a smell whether pleasant or unpleasant — **odored** *adj* — **odor·less** *adj*

odor·ous *adj* : having or giving off an odor

o'er *adv or prep* : OVER

of *prep* **1** : proceeding from : belonging to **2** : CONCERNING **3** — used to show what has been taken away or what one has been freed from **4** : on account of **5** : made from **6** — used to join an amount or a part with the whole which includes it **7** : that is **8** : that has : WITH 8

[1]**off** *adv* **1** : from a place or position **2** : from a course : ASIDE **3** : into sleep **4** : so as not to be supported, covering or enclosing, or attached **5** : so as to be discontinued or finished **6** : away from work

[2]**off** *prep* **1** : away from the surface or top of **2** : at the expense of **3** : released or freed from **4** : below the usual level of **5** : away from

[3]**off** *adj* **1** : more removed or distant **2** : started on the way **3** : not taking place **4** : not operating **5** : not correct : WRONG **6** : not entirely sane **7** : small in degree : SLIGHT **8** : provided for

of·fend *vb* **1** : to do wrong : SIN **2** : to hurt the feelings of : DISTRESS

of·fend·er *n* : a person who offends

of·fense *or* **of·fence** *n* **1** : an act of attacking : ASSAULT **2** : an offensive team **3** : the act of offending : the state of being offended **4** : WRONGDOING, SIN

[1]**of·fen·sive** *adj* **1** : relating to or made for or suited to attack **2** : of or relating to the attempt to score in a game or contest **3** : causing displeasure or resentment — **of·fen·sive·ly** *adv* — **of·fen·sive·ness** *n*

[2]**offensive** *n* **1** : the state or attitude of one who is making an attack **2** : [2]ATTACK 1

[1]**of·fer** *vb* **1** : to present as an act of worship : SACRIFICE **2** : to present (something) to be accepted or rejected **3** : to present for consideration : SUGGEST **4** : to declare one's willingness **5** : PUT UP 5

[2]**offer** *n* **1** : an act of offering **2** : a price suggested by one prepared to buy : BID

of·fer·ing *n* **1** : the act of one who offers **2** : something offered **3** : a sacrifice offered as part of worship **4** : a contribution to the support of a church

off·hand *adv or adj* : without previous thought or preparation

of·fice *n* **1** : a special duty or post and especially one of authority in government **2** : a place where business is done or a service is supplied

of·fice·hold·er *n* : a person who holds public office

of·fi·cer *n* **1** : a person given the responsibility of enforcing the law **2** : a person who holds an office **3** : a person who holds a commission in the armed forces

[1]**of·fi·cial** *n* : OFFICER 2

[2]**official** *adj* **1** : of or relating to an office **2** : having authority to perform a duty **3** : coming from or meeting the requirements of an authority **4** : proper for a person in office — **of·fi·cial·ly** *adv*

of·fi·ci·ate *vb* **of·fi·ci·at·ed; of·fi·ci·at·ing** **1** : to perform a ceremony or duty **2** : to act as an officer : PRESIDE

off·ing *n* : the near future or distance

off–line *adj or adv* **:** not connected to or directly controlled by a computer system

[1]**off·set** *n* **:** something that serves to make up for something else

[2]**offset** *vb* **offset; off·set·ting :** to make up for

off·shoot *n* **:** a branch of a main stem of a plant

[1]**off·shore** *adv* **:** from the shore **:** at a distance from the shore

[2]**off·shore** *adj* **1 :** coming or moving away from the shore **2 :** located off the shore

off·spring *n, pl* **offspring** *also* **off·springs :** the young of a person, animal, or plant

off·stage *adv or adj* **:** off or away from the stage

off–the–rec·ord *adj* **:** given or made in confidence and not for publication

oft *adv* **:** OFTEN

of·ten *adv* **:** many times

of·ten·times *adv* **:** OFTEN

ogle *vb* **ogled; ogling :** to look at (as a person) in a flirting way or with unusual attention or desire

ogre *n* **1 :** an ugly giant of fairy tales and folklore who eats people **2 :** a dreaded person or object

oh *or* **O** *interj* **1** — used to express an emotion (as surprise or pain) **2** — used in direct address

[1]**-oid** *n suffix* **:** something resembling a specified object or having a specified quality

[2]**-oid** *adj suffix* **:** resembling **:** having the form or appearance of

[1]**oil** *n* **1 :** any of numerous greasy usually liquid substances from plant, animal, or mineral sources that do not dissolve in water and are used especially as lubricants, fuels, and food **2 :** PETROLEUM **3 :** artists' paints made of pigments and oil **4 :** a painting in oils

[2]**oil** *vb* **:** to put oil on or in

oil·cloth *n* **:** cloth treated with oil or paint so as to be waterproof and used for shelf and table coverings

oily *adj* **oil·i·er; oil·i·est 1 :** of, relating to, or containing oil **2 :** covered or soaked with oil — **oil·i·ness** *n*

oint·ment *n* **:** a semisolid usually greasy medicine for use on the skin

[1]**OK** *or* **okay** *adv or adj* **:** all right

[2]**OK** *or* **okay** *n* **:** APPROVAL

[3]**OK** *or* **okay** *vb* **OK'd** *or* **okayed; OK'·ing** *or* **okay·ing :** APPROVE 2, AUTHORIZE

oka·pi *n* **:** an animal of the African forests related to the giraffe

okra *n* **:** a plant related to the hollyhocks and grown for its edible green pods which are used in soups and stews

[1]**old** *adj* **1 :** dating from the distant past **:** ANCIENT **2 :** having lasted or been such for a long time **3 :** having existed for a specified length of time **4 :** having lived a long time **5 :** FORMER **6 :** showing the effects of time or use

[2]**old** *n* **:** old or earlier time

old·en *adj* **:** of or relating to earlier days

Old English *n* **:** the language of the English people from the earliest documents in the seventh century to about 1100

old–fash·ioned *adj* **1 :** of, relating to, or like that of an earlier time **2 :** holding fast to old ways **:** CONSERVATIVE

Old French *n* **:** the French language from the ninth to the thirteenth century

Old Glory *n* **:** the flag of the United States

old maid *n* **1 :** an elderly unmarried woman **2 :** a very neat fussy person **3 :** a card game in which cards are matched in pairs and the player holding the extra queen at the end loses

old·ster *n* **:** an old person

old–time *adj* **:** [1]OLD 1

old–tim·er *n* **1 :** [1]VETERAN 1 **2 :** OLDSTER

old–world *adj* **:** having old-fashioned charm

Old World *n* **:** the lands in the eastern hemisphere and especially Europe but not including Australia

ol·fac·to·ry *adj* **:** of or relating to smelling or the sense of smell

ol·ive *n* **1 :** an oily fruit that is eaten both ripe and unripe, is the source of an edible oil (**olive oil**), and grows on an evergreen tree with hard smooth shining wood (**olive wood**) **2 :** a yellowish green

Olym·pic *adj* **:** of or relating to the Olympic Games

Olympic Games *n pl* **:** a series of international athletic contests held as separate winter and summer events in a different country every four years

om·e·lette *or* **om·e·let** *n* **:** eggs beaten with milk or water, cooked without stirring until firm, and folded in half often over a filling

omen *n* **:** a happening believed to be a sign or warning of a future event

om·i·nous *adj* **:** being a sign of evil or trouble to come — **om·i·nous·ly** *adv* — **om·i·nous·ness** *n*

omis·sion *n* **1 :** something omitted **2 :** the act of omitting **:** the state of being omitted

omit *vb* **omit·ted; omit·ting 1 :** to leave out **:** fail to include **2 :** to leave undone **:** NEGLECT

om·ni·bus *n* **:** BUS

om·nip·o·tent *adj* **:** having power or authority without limit **:** ALMIGHTY

[1]**on** *prep* **1 :** over and in contact with **2 :** AGAINST 3 **3 :** near or connected with **4 :** [1]TO 1 **5 :** sometime during **6 :** in the state or process of **7 :** [2]ABOUT 3 **8 :** by means of

²on *adv* **1 :** in or into contact with a surface **2 :** forward in time, space, or action **3 :** from one to another **4 :** into operation or a position allowing operation

³on *adj* **1 :** being in operation **2 :** placed so as to allow operation **3 :** taking place **4 :** having been planned

¹once *adv* **1 :** one time only **2 :** at any one time **:** EVER **3 :** at some time in the past **:** FORMERLY

²once *n* **:** one single time — **at once 1 :** at the same time **2 :** IMMEDIATELY 2

³once *conj* **:** as soon as **:** WHEN

once–over *n* **:** a quick glance or examination

on·com·ing *adj* **:** coming nearer

¹one *adj* **1 :** being a single unit or thing **2 :** being a certain unit or thing **3 :** being the same in kind or quality **4 :** not specified

²one *n* **1 :** the number denoting a single unit **:** 1 **2 :** the first in a set or series **3 :** a single person or thing

³one *pron* **1 :** a single member or individual **2 :** any person

one another *pron* **:** EACH OTHER

one·self *pron* **:** one's own self

one–sid·ed *adj* **1 :** having or happening on one side only **2 :** having one side more developed **3 :** favoring one side

one·time *adj* **:** FORMER

one–way *adj* **:** moving or allowing movement in one direction only

on·go·ing *adj* **:** being in progress or movement

on·ion *n* **:** the edible bulb of a plant related to the lilies that has a sharp odor and taste and is used as a vegetable and to season foods

on–line *adj or adv* **:** connected to, directly controlled by, or available through a computer system

on·look·er *n* **:** SPECTATOR

¹on·ly *adj* **1 :** best without doubt **2 :** alone in or of a class or kind **:** SOLE

²only *adv* **1 :** as a single fact or instance and nothing more or different **2 :** no one or nothing other than **3 :** in the end **4 :** as recently as

³only *conj* **:** except that

on·o·mato·poe·ia *n* **:** the forming of a word (as "buzz" or "hiss") in imitation of a natural sound

on·rush *n* **:** a rushing forward

on·set *n* **1 :** ²ATTACK 1 **2 :** BEGINNING

on·slaught *n* **:** a violent attack

on·to *prep* **:** to a position on or against

¹on·ward *adv* **:** toward or at a point lying ahead in space or time **:** FORWARD

²onward *adj* **:** directed or moving onward

oo·dles *n pl* **:** a great quantity

¹ooze *n* **:** soft mud **:** SLIME

²ooze *vb* **oozed; ooz·ing :** to flow or leak out slowly

opal *n* **:** a mineral with soft changeable colors that is used as a gem

opaque *adj* **1 :** not letting light through **:** not transparent **2 :** not reflecting light **:** DULL

¹open *adj* **1 :** not shut or blocked **:** not closed **2 :** not enclosed or covered **3 :** not secret **:** PUBLIC **4 :** to be used, entered, or taken part in by all **5 :** easy to enter, get through, or see **6 :** not drawn together **:** spread out **7 :** not decided or settled **8 :** ready to consider appeals or ideas — **open·ly** *adv* — **open·ness** *n*

²open *vb* **1 :** to change or move from a shut condition **2 :** to clear by or as if by removing something in the way **3 :** to make or become ready for use **4 :** to have an opening **5 :** BEGIN 1, START — **open·er** *n*

³open *n* **:** open space **:** OUTDOORS

open–air *adj* **:** OUTDOOR

open–and–shut *adj* **:** ¹PLAIN 3, OBVIOUS

open·heart·ed *adj* **1 :** FRANK **2 :** GENEROUS 1

open·ing *n* **1 :** an act of opening **2 :** an open place **:** CLEARING **3 :** BEGINNING **4 :** OCCASION 1 **5 :** a job opportunity

open letter *n* **:** a letter (as one addressed to an official) for the public to see and printed in a newspaper or magazine

open·work *n* **:** something made or work done so as to show openings through the fabric or material

op·era *n* **:** a play in which the entire text is sung with orchestral accompaniment

opera glasses *n* **:** small binoculars of low power for use in a theater

op·er·ate *vb* **op·er·at·ed; op·er·at·ing 1 :** to work or cause to work in a proper way **2 :** to take effect **3 :** MANAGE 1 **4 :** to perform surgery **:** do an operation on (as a person)

operating system *n* **:** a program or series of programs that controls the operation of a computer and directs the processing of the user's programs (as by assigning storage space and controlling input and output functions)

op·er·a·tion *n* **1 :** the act, process, method, or result of operating **2 :** the quality or state of being able to work **3 :** a certain piece or kind of surgery **4 :** a process (as addition or multiplication) of getting one mathematical expression from others according to a rule **5 :** the process of putting military or naval forces into action **6 :** a single step performed by a computer in carrying out a program

op·er·a·tion·al *adj* **1 :** of or relating to operation or an operation **2 :** ready for operation

op·er·a·tor *n* **1 :** a person who operates something (as a business) **2 :** a person in charge of a telephone switchboard

op·er·et·ta *n* **:** a light play set to music with speaking, singing, and dancing scenes

opin·ion *n* **1 :** a belief based on experience and on seeing certain facts but not amounting to sure knowledge **2 :** a judgment about a person or thing **3 :** a statement by an expert after careful study

opin·ion·at·ed *adj* **:** holding to one's opinions too strongly

opi·um *n* **:** a bitter brownish narcotic drug that is the dried juice of one kind of poppy

opos·sum *n* **:** a common American animal related to the kangaroos that lives mostly in trees and is active at night

op·po·nent *n* **:** a person or thing that opposes another

op·por·tu·ni·ty *n, pl* **op·por·tu·ni·ties 1 :** a favorable combination of circumstances, time, and place **2 :** a chance to better oneself

op·pose *vb* **op·posed; op·pos·ing 1 :** to be or place opposite to something **2 :** to offer resistance to **:** stand against **:** RESIST

[1]**op·po·site** *adj* **1 :** being at the other end, side, or corner **2 :** being in a position to oppose or cancel out **3 :** being as different as possible **:** CONTRARY

[2]**opposite** *n* **:** either of two persons or things that are as different as possible

[3]**opposite** *adv* **:** on the opposite side

[4]**opposite** *prep* **:** across from and usually facing or on the same level with

op·po·si·tion *n* **1 :** the state of being opposite **2 :** the action of resisting **3 :** a group of persons that oppose someone or something **4** *often cap* **:** a political party opposed to the party in power

op·press *vb* **1 :** to cause to feel burdened in spirit **2 :** to control or rule in a harsh or cruel way

op·pres·sion *n* **1 :** cruel or unjust use of power or authority **2 :** a feeling of low spirits

op·pres·sive *adj* **1 :** cruel or harsh without just cause **2 :** causing a feeling of oppression — **op·pres·sive·ly** *adv*

op·tic *adj* **:** of or relating to seeing or the eye

op·ti·cal *adj* **1 :** of or relating to the science of optics **2 :** of or relating to seeing **:** VISUAL **3 :** involving the use of devices that are sensitive to light to get information for a computer

optical fiber *n* **:** a single fiber used in fiber optics

optical illusion *n* **:** ILLUSION 1

op·ti·cian *n* **:** a person who prepares eyeglass lenses and sells glasses

op·tics *n* **:** a science that deals with the nature and properties of light and the changes that it undergoes and produces

op·ti·mism *n* **:** a habit of expecting things to turn out for the best

op·ti·mist *n* **:** an optimistic person

op·ti·mis·tic *adj* **:** showing optimism **:** expecting everything to come out all right **:** HOPEFUL

op·ti·mum *adj* **:** most desirable or satisfactory

op·tion *n* **1 :** the power or right to choose **2 :** a right to buy or sell something at a specified price during a specified period

op·tion·al *adj* **:** left to one's choice **:** not required

op·tom·e·trist *n* **:** a person who prescribes glasses or exercise to improve the eyesight

op·u·lent *adj* **:** having or showing much wealth

or *conj* — used between words or phrases that are choices

[1]**-or** *n suffix* **:** one that does a specified thing

[2]**-or** *n suffix* **:** condition **:** activity

or·a·cle *n* **1 :** a person (as a priestess in ancient Greece) through whom a god is believed to speak **2 :** the place where a god speaks through an oracle **3 :** an answer given by an oracle

orac·u·lar *adj* **:** of, relating to, or serving as an oracle

oral *adj* **1 :** [2]SPOKEN 1 **2 :** of, relating to, given by, or near the mouth — **oral·ly** *adv*

or·ange *n* **1 :** a sweet juicy fruit with a reddish yellow rind that grows on an evergreen citrus tree with shining leaves and fragrant white flowers **2 :** a color between red and yellow

or·ange·ade *n* **:** a drink made of orange juice, sugar, and water

orang·utan *or* **orang·ou·tan** *n* **:** a large ape of Borneo and Sumatra that eats plants, lives in trees, and has very long arms and hairless face, feet, and hands

ora·tion *n* **:** an important speech given on a special occasion

or·a·tor *n* **:** a public speaker noted for skill and power in speaking

or·a·tor·i·cal *adj* **:** of, relating to, or like an orator or oratory — **or·a·tor·i·cal·ly** *adv*

or·a·to·ry *n* **1 :** the art of an orator **2 :** the style of language used in an oration

orb *n* **:** something in the shape of a ball (as a planet or the eye)

[1]**or·bit** *n* **:** the path taken by one body circling around another body

[2]**orbit** *vb* **1 :** to move in an orbit around **:** CIRCLE **2 :** to send up so as to move in an orbit

or·chard *n* **1 :** a place where fruit trees are grown **2 :** the trees in an orchard

or·ches·tra *n* **1 :** a group of musicians who perform instrumental music using mostly stringed instruments **2 :** the front part of the main floor in a theater

or·ches·tral *adj* **:** of, relating to, or written for an orchestra

or·chid *n* **:** any of a large group of plants with usually showy flowers with three petals of which the middle petal is enlarged into a lip and differs from the others in shape and color

or·dain *vb* **1 :** to make a person a Christian minister or priest by a special ceremony **2 :** [2]DECREE **3 :** DESTINE 1, FATE

or·deal *n* **:** a severe test or experience

[1]**or·der** *vb* **1 :** to put into a particular grouping or sequence **:** ARRANGE **2 :** to give an order to or for

[2]**order** *n* **1 :** a group of people united (as by living under the same religious rules or by loyalty to common needs or duties) **2 orders** *pl* **:** the office of a person in the Christian ministry **3 :** a group of related plants or animals that ranks above the family and below the class in scientific classification **4 :** the arrangement of objects or events in space or time **5 :** the way something should be **6 :** the state of things when law or authority is obeyed **7 :** a certain rule or regulation **:** COMMAND **8 :** good working condition **9 :** a written direction to pay a sum of money **10 :** a statement of what one wants to buy **11 :** goods or items bought or sold — **in order to :** for the purpose of

[1]**or·der·ly** *adj* **1 :** being in good order **:** NEAT, TIDY **2 :** obeying orders or rules **:** well-behaved — **or·der·li·ness** *n*

[2]**orderly** *n, pl* **or·der·lies 1 :** a soldier who works for an officer especially to carry messages **2 :** a person who does cleaning and general work in a hospital

or·di·nal *n* **:** ORDINAL NUMBER

ordinal number *n* **:** a number that is used to show the place (as first, fifth, twenty-second) taken by an element in a series

or·di·nance *n* **:** a law or regulation especially of a city or town

or·di·nar·i·ly *adv* **:** in the usual course of events **:** USUALLY

[1]**or·di·nary** *n* **:** the conditions or events that are usual or normal

[2]**ordinary** *adj* **1 :** to be expected **:** NORMAL, USUAL **2 :** neither good nor bad **:** AVERAGE **3 :** not very good **:** MEDIOCRE — **or·di·nar·i·ness** *n*

ord·nance *n* **1 :** military supplies (as guns, ammunition, trucks, and tanks) **2 :** ARTILLERY 1

ore *n* **:** a mineral mined to obtain a substance (as gold) that it contains

or·gan *n* **1 :** a musical instrument played by means of one or more keyboards and having pipes sounded by compressed air **2 :** a part of a person, plant, or animal that is specialized to do a particular task **3 :** a way of getting something done

or·gan·ic *adj* **1 :** relating to an organ of the body **2 :** having parts that fit or work together **3 :** relating to or obtained from living things **4 :** relating to carbon compounds **:** containing carbon

or·gan·ism *n* **1 :** something having many related parts and functioning as a whole **2 :** a living being made up of organs and able to carry on the activities of life **:** a living person, animal, or plant

or·gan·ist *n* **:** a person who plays an organ

or·ga·ni·za·tion *n* **1 :** the act or process of organizing **2 :** the state or way of being organized **3 :** a group of persons united for a common purpose

or·ga·nize *vb* **or·ga·nized; or·ga·niz·ing 1 :** to make separate parts into one united whole **2 :** to put in a certain order **3:** to arrange by effort and planning — **or·ga·niz·er** *n*

ori·ent *vb* **1 :** to set or arrange in a position especially so as to be lined up with certain points of the compass **2 :** to acquaint with an existing situation or environment — **ori·en·ta·tion** *n*

Ori·en·tal *adj* **1 :** [1]ASIAN **2 :** of or relating to the region that includes the countries of eastern Asia (as China, Japan, Vietnam, and Korea)

ori·ga·mi *n* **:** the art of folding paper into three-dimensional figures or designs without cutting the paper or using glue

or·i·gin *n* **1 :** a person's ancestry **2 :** the rise, beginning, or coming from a source **3 :** basic source or cause

[1]**orig·i·nal** *n* **:** something from which a copy or translation can be made

[2]**original** *adj* **1 :** of or relating to the origin or beginning **:** FIRST **2 :** not copied from anything else **:** not translated **:** NEW **3 :** able to think up new things **:** INVENTIVE — **orig·i·nal·ly** *adv*

orig·i·nal·i·ty *n* **1 :** the quality or state of being original **2 :** the power or ability to think, act, or do something in ways that are new

orig·i·nate *vb* **orig·i·nat·ed; orig·i·nat·ing 1 :** to bring into being **:** cause to be **:** INVENT, INITIATE **2 :** to come into being — **orig·i·na·tor** *n*

ori·ole *n* **1 :** an Old World yellow and black bird related to the crow **2 :** an American songbird related to the blackbird and bobolink that has a bright orange and black male

[1]**or·na·ment** *n* **1 :** something that adds beauty **:** DECORATION **2 :** the act of beautifying
[2]**or·na·ment** *vb* **:** DECORATE 1
[1]**or·na·men·tal** *adj* **:** serving to ornament **:** DECORATIVE
[2]**ornamental** *n* **:** a plant grown for its beauty
or·na·men·ta·tion *n* **1 :** the act or process of ornamenting **:** the state of being ornamented **2 :** something that ornaments
or·nate *adj* **:** decorated in a fancy way — **or·nate·ly** *adv* — **or·nate·ness** *n*
or·nery *adj* **or·neri·er; or·neri·est :** having a bad disposition
[1]**or·phan** *n* **:** a child whose parents are dead
[2]**orphan** *vb* **:** to cause to become an orphan
or·phan·age *n* **:** an institution for the care of orphans
or·tho·don·tist *n* **:** a dentist who adjusts badly placed or irregular teeth
or·tho·dox *adj* **1 :** holding established beliefs especially in religion **2 :** approved as measuring up to some standard **:** CONVENTIONAL
[1]**-ory** *n suffix, pl* **-ories :** place of or for
[2]**-ory** *adj suffix* **:** of, relating to, or associated with
os·cil·late *vb* **os·cil·lat·ed; os·cil·lat·ing :** to swing back and forth like a pendulum
os·mo·sis *n* **:** a passing of material and especially water through a membrane (as of a living cell) that will not allow all kinds of molecules to pass
os·prey *n, pl* **ospreys :** a large hawk that feeds chiefly on fish
os·ten·si·ble *adj* **:** shown in an outward way **:** APPARENT — **os·ten·si·bly** *adv*
os·ten·ta·tious *adj* **:** having or fond of unnecessary show
os·tra·cize *vb* **os·tra·cized; os·tra·ciz·ing :** to shut out of a group by the agreement of all
os·trich *n* **:** a very large bird of Africa and the Arabian Peninsula that often weighs 300 pounds and runs very swiftly but cannot fly
[1]**oth·er** *adj* **1 :** being the one (as of two or more) left **2 :** [1]SECOND 1 **3 :** [1]EXTRA, ADDITIONAL
[2]**other** *n* **:** a remaining or different one
[3]**other** *pron* **:** another thing
oth·er·wise *adv* **1 :** in another way **2 :** in different circumstances **3 :** in other ways
ot·ter *n* **:** a web-footed animal related to the minks that feeds on fish
ouch *interj* — used especially to express sudden pain
ought *helping verb* **1** — used to show duty **2** — used to show what it would be wise to do **3** — used to show what is naturally expected **4** — used to show what is correct
oughtn't : ought not
ounce *n* **1 :** a unit of weight equal to $\frac{1}{16}$ pound (about 28 grams) **2 :** a unit of liquid capacity equal to $\frac{1}{16}$ pint (about 30 milliliters)
our *adj* **:** of or relating to us **:** done, given, or felt by us
ours *pron* **:** that which belongs to us
our·selves *pron* **:** our own selves
-ous *adj suffix* **:** full of **:** having **:** resembling
oust *vb* **:** to force or drive out (as from office or from possession of something)
oust·er *n* **:** the act or an instance of ousting or being ousted
[1]**out** *adv* **1 :** in a direction away from the inside, center, or surface **2 :** away from home, business, or the usual or proper place **3 :** beyond control or possession **4 :** so as to be used up, completed, or discontinued **5 :** in or into the open **6 :** ALOUD **7 :** so as to put out or be put out in baseball
[2]**out** *prep* **1 :** outward through **2 :** outward on or along
[3]**out** *adj* **1 :** located outside or at a distance **2 :** no longer in power or use **3 :** not confined **:** not concealed or covered **4 :** [1]ABSENT 1 **5 :** being no longer at bat and not successful in reaching base **6 :** no longer in fashion
[4]**out** *n* **:** PUTOUT
out- *prefix* **:** in a manner that goes beyond
out–and–out *adj* **:** THOROUGH 1
out·board motor *n* **:** a small gasoline engine with an attached propeller that can be fastened to the back end of a small boat
out·break *n* **:** something (as an epidemic of measles) that breaks out
out·build·ing *n* **:** a building (as a shed or stable) separate from a main building
out·burst *n* **1 :** a sudden violent expression of strong feeling **2 :** a sudden increase of activity or growth
[1]**out·cast** *adj* **:** rejected or cast out
[2]**outcast** *n* **:** a person who is cast out by society
out·class *vb* **:** EXCEL, SURPASS
out·come *n* **:** [2]RESULT 1
out·cry *n, pl* **out·cries 1 :** a loud and excited cry **2 :** a strong protest
out·dat·ed *adj* **:** OBSOLETE, OUTMODED
out·dis·tance *vb* **out·dis·tanced; out·dis·tanc·ing :** to go far ahead of (as in a race)
out·do *vb* **out·did; out·done; out·do·ing; out·does :** to do better than **:** SURPASS
out·door *adj* **1 :** of or relating to the outdoors **2 :** used, being, or done outdoors
[1]**out·doors** *adv* **:** outside a building **:** in or into the open air
[2]**outdoors** *n* **1 :** the open air **2 :** the world away from human dwellings
out·er *adj* **:** located on the outside or farther out
out·er·most *adj* **:** farthest out
outer space *n* **:** the region beyond earth's at-

mosphere and especially beyond the solar system

out·field *n* **:** the part of a baseball field beyond the infield and between the foul lines

out·field·er *n* **:** a baseball player who plays in the outfield

[1]**out·fit** *n* **1 :** the equipment or clothing for a special use **2 :** a group of persons working together or associated in the same activity

[2]**outfit** *vb* **out·fit·ted; out·fit·ting :** to supply with an outfit **:** EQUIP — **out·fit·ter** *n*

out·go *n, pl* **outgoes :** EXPENDITURE 2

out·go·ing *adj* **1 :** going out **2 :** retiring from a place or position **3 :** FRIENDLY 1

out·grow *vb* **out·grew; out·grown; out·grow·ing 1 :** to grow faster than **2 :** to grow too large for

out·growth *n* **:** something that grows out of or develops from something else

out·ing *n* **:** a brief usually outdoor trip for pleasure

out·land·ish *adj* **:** very strange or unusual **:** BIZARRE

out·last *vb* **:** to last longer than

[1]**out·law** *n* **:** a lawless person or one who is running away from the law

[2]**outlaw** *vb* **:** to make illegal

out·lay *n* **:** EXPENDITURE

out·let *n* **1 :** a place or opening for letting something out **2 :** a way of releasing or satisfying a feeling or impulse **3 :** a device (as in a wall) into which the prongs of an electrical plug are inserted for making connection with an electrical circuit

[1]**out·line** *n* **1 :** a line that traces or forms the outer limits of an object or figure and shows its shape **2 :** a drawing or picture giving only the outlines of a thing **:** this method of drawing **3 :** a short treatment of a subject **:** SUMMARY

[2]**outline** *vb* **out·lined; out·lin·ing :** to make or prepare an outline of

out·live *vb* **out·lived; out·liv·ing :** to live longer than **:** OUTLAST

out·look *n* **1 :** a view from a certain place **2 :** a way of thinking about or looking at things **3 :** conditions that seem to lie ahead

out·ly·ing *adj* **:** being far from a central point **:** REMOTE

out·mod·ed *adj* **:** no longer in style or in use

out·num·ber *vb* **:** to be more than in number

out of *prep* **1 :** from the inside to the outside of **:** not in **2 :** beyond the limits of **3 :** BECAUSE OF **4 :** in a group of **5 :** [1]WITHOUT 2 **6 :** FROM 3

out–of–bounds *adv or adj* **:** outside the limits of the playing field

out–of–date *adj* **:** OUTMODED

out–of–door *or* **out–of–doors** *adj* **:** OUTDOOR 2

out–of–doors *n* **:** [2]OUTDOORS

out·pa·tient *n* **:** a person who visits a hospital for examination or treatment but who does not stay overnight at the hospital

out·post *n* **1 :** a guard placed at a distance from a military force or camp **2 :** the position taken by an outpost **3 :** a settlement on a frontier or in a faraway place

[1]**out·put** *n* **1 :** something produced **2 :** the information produced by a computer

[2]**output** *vb* **out·put·ted** *or* **out·put; out·put·ting :** to produce as output

[1]**out·rage** *n* **1 :** an act of violence or cruelty **2 :** an act that hurts someone or shows disrespect for a person's feelings **3 :** angry feelings caused by injury or insult

[2]**outrage** *vb* **out·raged; out·rag·ing 1 :** to cause to suffer violent injury or great insult **2 :** to cause to feel anger or strong resentment

out·ra·geous *adj* **:** going far beyond what is right, decent, or just

[1]**out·right** *adv* **1 :** COMPLETELY **2 :** without holding back **3 :** on the spot **:** INSTANTLY

[2]**out·right** *adj* **1 :** being exactly what is said **2 :** given without restriction

out·run *vb* **out·ran; out·run; out·run·ning :** to run faster than

out·sell *vb* **out·sold; out·sell·ing :** to sell or be sold more than

out·set *n* **:** BEGINNING 1, START

out·shine *vb* **out·shone; out·shin·ing 1 :** to shine brighter than **2 :** OUTDO, SURPASS

[1]**out·side** *n* **1 :** a place or region beyond an enclosure or boundary **2 :** an outer side or surface **3 :** the greatest amount or limit **:** [3]MOST

[2]**outside** *adj* **1 :** of, relating to, or being on the outside **2 :** coming from outside **:** not belonging to a place or group

[3]**outside** *adv* **:** on or to the outside **:** OUTDOORS

[4]**outside** *prep* **:** on or to the outside of **:** beyond the limits of

out·sid·er *n* **:** a person who does not belong to a certain party or group

out·size *adj* **:** unusually large or heavy

out·skirts *n pl* **:** the area that lies away from the center of a place

out·smart *vb* **:** OUTWIT

out·spo·ken *adj* **:** direct or open in expression **:** BLUNT — **out·spo·ken·ly** *adv* — **out·spo·ken·ness** *n*

out·spread *adj* **:** spread out

out·stand·ing *adj* **1 :** UNPAID **2 :** standing out especially because of excellence — **out·stand·ing·ly** *adv*

out·stay *vb* **:** to stay beyond or longer than

out·stretched *adj* **:** stretched out

out·strip *vb* **out·stripped; out·strip·ping 1**

: to go faster or farther than **2 :** to do better than : EXCEL

[1]**out·ward** *adj* **1 :** moving or turned toward the outside or away from a center **2 :** showing on the outside

[2]**outward** *or* **out·wards** *adv* : toward the outside : away from a center

out·ward·ly *adv* : on the outside : in outward appearance

out·weigh *vb* : to be greater than in weight or importance

out·wit *vb* **out·wit·ted; out·wit·ting** : to get ahead of by cleverness : BEST

out·worn *adj* : no longer useful or accepted

[1]**oval** *n* : a figure or object having the shape of an egg or ellipse

[2]**oval** *adj* : having the shape of an oval : ELLIPTICAL

ova·ry *n, pl* **ova·ries** **1 :** an organ of the body in female animals in which eggs are produced **2 :** the larger lower part of the pistil of a flower in which the seeds are formed

ova·tion *n* : a making of a loud noise by many people (as by cheering or clapping) to show great liking or respect

ov·en *n* : a heated chamber (as in a stove) for baking, heating, or drying

[1]**over** *adv* **1 :** across a barrier or space **2 :** in a direction down or forward and down **3 :** across the brim **4 :** so as to bring the underside up **5 :** beyond a limit **6 :** more than needed **7 :** once more : AGAIN

[2]**over** *prep* **1 :** above in place : higher than **2 :** above in power or value **3 :** on or along the surface of **4 :** on or to the other side of : ACROSS **5 :** down from the top or edge of

[3]**over** *adj* **1 :** being more than needed : SURPLUS **2 :** brought or come to an end

[1]**over·all** *adv* : as a whole : in most ways

[2]**overall** *adj* : including everything

over·alls *n pl* : loose pants usually with shoulder straps and a piece in front to cover the chest

over·anx·ious *adj* : much too anxious

over·bear·ing *adj* : acting in a proud or bossy way toward other people

over·board *adv* **1 :** over the side of a ship into the water **2 :** to extremes of enthusiasm

over·bur·den *vb* : to burden too heavily

over·cast *adj* : clouded over

over·charge *vb* **over·charged; over·charg·ing** : to charge too much

over·coat *n* : a heavy coat worn over indoor clothing

over·come *vb* **over·came; overcome; over·com·ing** **1 :** to win a victory over : CONQUER **2 :** to make helpless

over·con·fi·dent *adj* : too sure of oneself

over·cooked *adj* : cooked too long

over·crowd *vb* : to cause to be too crowded

over·do *vb* **over·did; over·done; over·do·ing** **1 :** to do too much **2 :** EXAGGERATE **3 :** to cook too long

over·dose *n* : too large a dose (as of a drug)

over·dress *vb* : to dress too well for the occasion

over·due *adj* **1 :** not paid when due **2 :** delayed beyond an expected time

over·eat *vb* **over·ate; over·eat·en; over·eat·ing** : to eat too much

over·es·ti·mate *vb* **over·es·ti·mat·ed; over·es·ti·mat·ing** : to estimate too highly

over·flight *n* : a passage over an area in an airplane

[1]**over·flow** *vb* **1 :** to cover with or as if with water **2 :** to flow over the top of **3 :** to flow over bounds

[2]**over·flow** *n* **1 :** a flowing over : FLOOD **2 :** something that flows over : SURPLUS

over·grown *adj* : grown too big

[1]**over·hand** *adj* : made with a downward movement of the hand or arm

[2]**overhand** *adv* : with an overhand movement

overhand knot *n* : a simple knot often used to prevent the end of a cord from pulling apart

[1]**over·hang** *vb* **over·hung; over·hang·ing** : to stick out or hang over

[2]**overhang** *n* : a part that overhangs

[1]**over·haul** *vb* **1 :** to make a thorough examination of and make necessary repairs and adjustments on **2 :** to catch up with : OVERTAKE

[2]**over·haul** *n* : an instance of overhauling

[1]**over·head** *adv* **1 :** above one's head **2 :** in the sky

[2]**over·head** *adj* : placed or passing overhead

[3]**over·head** *n* : the general expenses (as for rent or heat) of a business

over·hear *vb* **over·heard; over·hear·ing** : to hear something said to someone else and not meant for one's own ears

over·heat *vb* : to heat too much : become too hot

over·joy *vb* : to make very joyful

[1]**over·land** *adv* : by land rather than by water

[2]**over·land** *adj* : going overland

over·lap *vb* **over·lapped; over·lap·ping** : to place or be placed so that a part of one covers a part of another

[1]**over·lay** *vb* **over·laid; over·lay·ing** : to lay or spread over or across

[2]**over·lay** *n* : something (as a veneer on wood) that is overlaid

over·load *vb* : to put too great a load on

over·look *vb* **1 :** to look over : INSPECT **2 :** to look down upon from a higher position **3 :** to fail to see : MISS **4 :** to pass over without notice or blame

over·lord *n* : a lord over other lords

over·ly *adv* : by too much

¹over·night *adv* **1** : during or through the night **2** : ²FAST 3, QUICKLY

²overnight *adj* **1** : done or lasting through the night **2** : staying for the night **3** : for use on short trips

over·pass *n* : a crossing (as of two highways or a highway and a railroad) at different levels usually by means of a bridge

over·pop·u·la·tion *n* : the condition of having too many people living in a certain area

over·pow·er *vb* **1** : to overcome by greater force : DEFEAT **2** : to affect by being too strong

over·rate *vb* **over·rat·ed; over·rat·ing** : to value or praise too highly

over·ride *vb* **over·rode; over·rid·den; over·rid·ing** : to push aside as less important

over·ripe *adj* : passed beyond ripeness toward decay

over·rule *vb* **over·ruled; over·rul·ing** **1** : to decide against **2** : to set aside a decision or ruling made by someone having less authority

over·run *vb* **over·ran; overrun; over·run·ning** **1** : to take over and occupy by force **2** : to run past **3** : to spread over so as to cover

¹over·seas *adv* : beyond or across the sea

²overseas *adj* : of, relating to, or intended for lands across the sea

over·see *vb* **over·saw; over·seen; over·see·ing** **1** : INSPECT 1, EXAMINE **2** : SUPERINTEND

over·seer *n* : a person whose business it is to oversee something

over·shad·ow *vb* **1** : to cast a shadow over : DARKEN **2** : to be more important than

over·shoe *n* : a shoe (as of rubber) worn over another for protection

over·shoot *vb* **over·shot; over·shoot·ing** : to miss by going beyond

over·sight *n* **1** : the act or duty of overseeing : watchful care **2** : an error or a leaving something out through carelessness or haste

over·sim·pli·fy *vb* **over·sim·pli·fied; over·sim·pli·fy·ing** : to make incorrect or misleading by simplifying too much

over·size *or* **over·sized** *adj* : larger than the usual or normal size

over·sleep *vb* **over·slept; over·sleep·ing** : to sleep beyond the usual time or beyond the time set for getting up

over·spread *vb* **overspread; over·spread·ing** : to spread over or above

over·state *vb* **over·stat·ed; over·stat·ing** : to put in too strong terms : EXAGGERATE

over·step *vb* **over·stepped; over·step·ping** : to step over or beyond : EXCEED

over·stuffed *adj* : covered completely and deeply with upholstery

over·sup·ply *n, pl* **over·sup·plies** : a supply that is too large

over·take *vb* **over·took; over·tak·en; over·tak·ing** **1** : to catch up with and often pass **2** : to come upon suddenly or without warning

¹over·throw *vb* **over·threw; over·thrown; over·throw·ing** **1** : OVERTURN 1 **2** : to cause the fall or end of : DEFEAT, DESTROY

²over·throw *n* : an act of overthrowing : the state of being overthrown : DEFEAT, RUIN

over·time *n* : time spent working that is more than one usually works in a day or a week

over·ture *n* **1** : something first offered or suggested with the hope of reaching an agreement **2** : a musical composition played by the orchestra at the beginning of an opera or musical play

over·turn *vb* **1** : to turn over : UPSET **2** : ¹OVERTHROW 2

¹over·weight *n* **1** : weight that is more than is required or allowed **2** : bodily weight that is greater than what is considered normal or healthy

²over·weight *adj* : weighing more than is right, necessary, or allowed

over·whelm *vb* **1** : to cover over completely : SUBMERGE **2** : to overcome completely

¹over·work *vb* **1** : to work or cause to work too much or too hard **2** : to make too much use of

²overwork *n* : too much work

ovip·a·rous *adj* : reproducing by eggs that hatch outside the parent's body

ovule *n* : any of the tiny egglike structures in a plant ovary that can develop into seeds

ovum *n, pl* **ova** : EGG CELL

owe *vb* **owed; ow·ing** **1** : to be obligated to pay, give, or return **2** : to be in debt to **3** : to have as a result

owing *adj* : due to be paid

owing to *prep* : BECAUSE OF

owl *n* : a bird with large head and eyes, hooked bill, and strong claws that is active at night and lives on rats and mice, insects, and small birds — **owl·ish** *adj*

owl·et *n* : a young or small owl

¹own *adj* : belonging to oneself or itself

²own *vb* **1** : to have or hold as property : POSSESS **2** : ADMIT 3, CONFESS 1

own·er *n* : a person who owns something

own·er·ship *n* : the state or fact of being an owner

ox *n, pl* **ox·en** *also* **ox** **1** : one of our common domestic cattle or a closely related animal **2** : an adult castrated male of domestic cattle used especially for meat or for hauling loads : STEER

ox·bow *n* : a bend in a river in the shape of a U

ox·cart *n* : a cart pulled by oxen

ox·ford *n* **:** a low shoe laced and tied over the instep
ox·i·da·tion *n* **:** the process of oxidizing
ox·ide *n* **:** a compound of oxygen with another element or with a group of elements
ox·i·dize *vb* **ox·i·dized; ox·i·diz·ing :** to combine with oxygen **:** add oxygen to
ox·y·gen *n* **:** a chemical element found in the air as a colorless odorless tasteless gas that is necessary for life
oys·ter *n* **:** a soft gray shellfish that lives on stony bottoms (**oyster beds**) in shallow seawater, has a shell made up of two hinged parts, and is used as food
ozone *n* **1 :** a faintly blue form of oxygen that is present in the air in small quantities **2 :** pure and refreshing air
ozone layer *n* **:** a layer of the upper atmosphere that is characterized by high ozone content which blocks most of the sun's radiation from entering the lower atmosphere

P

p *n, pl* **p's** *or* **ps** *often cap* **:** the sixteenth letter of the English alphabet
pa *n* **:** [1]FATHER 1
[1]**pace** *n* **1 :** rate of moving forward or ahead **2 :** a manner of walking **3 :** a horse's gait in which the legs on the same side move at the same time **4 :** a single step or its length
[2]**pace** *vb* **paced; pac·ing 1 :** to walk with slow steps **2 :** to move at a pace **3 :** to measure by steps **4 :** to walk back and forth across **5 :** to set or regulate the pace of
pa·cif·ic *adj* **1 :** making peace **:** PEACEABLE **2 :** [3]CALM, PEACEFUL **3** *cap* **:** relating to the Pacific ocean
pac·i·fy *vb* **pac·i·fied; pac·i·fy·ing :** to make peaceful or quiet **:** CALM, SOOTHE
[1]**pack** *n* **1 :** a bundle arranged for carrying especially on the back of a person or animal **2 :** a group of like persons or things **:** BAND, SET
[2]**pack** *vb* **1 :** to put into a container or bundle **2 :** to put things into **3 :** to crowd into so as to fill full **:** CRAM **4 :** to send away — **pack·er** *n*
pack·age *n* **1 :** a bundle made up for shipping **2 :** a box or case in which goods are shipped or delivered
pack·et *n* **:** a small package
pack·ing·house *n* **:** a building for preparing and packing food and especially meat
pact *n* **:** AGREEMENT 2, TREATY
[1]**pad** *vb* **pad·ded; pad·ding :** to walk or run with quiet steps
[2]**pad** *n* **1 :** something soft used for protection or comfort **:** CUSHION **2 :** a piece of material that holds ink used in inking rubber stamps **3 :** one of the cushioned parts of the underside of the foot of some animals (as a dog) **4 :** a floating leaf of a water plant **5 :** a tablet of writing or drawing paper
[3]**pad** *vb* **pad·ded; pad·ding 1 :** to stuff or cover with soft material **2 :** to make longer by adding words
pad·ding *n* **:** material used to pad something
[1]**pad·dle** *vb* **pad·dled; pad·dling :** to move or splash about in the water with the hands or feet **:** WADE
[2]**paddle** *n* **1 :** an instrument like an oar used in moving and steering a small boat (as a canoe) **2 :** one of the broad boards at the outer edge of a waterwheel or a paddle wheel **3 :** an instrument for beating, mixing, or hitting
[3]**paddle** *vb* **pad·dled; pad·dling 1 :** to move or drive forward with or as if with a paddle **2 :** to stir or mix with a paddle **3 :** to beat with or as if with a paddle
paddle wheel *n* **:** a wheel with paddles near its outer edge used to drive a boat
pad·dock *n* **1 :** an enclosed area where animals are put to eat grass or to exercise **2 :** an enclosed area where racehorses are saddled and paraded
pad·dy *n, pl* **paddies :** wet land in which rice is grown
[1]**pad·lock** *n* **:** a removable lock that has a curved piece that snaps into a catch
[2]**padlock** *vb* **:** to fasten with a padlock
[1]**pa·gan** *n* **:** [2]HEATHEN 1
[2]**pagan** *adj* **:** of or relating to pagans or their worship **:** HEATHEN
[1]**page** *n* **1 :** a boy being trained to be a knight in the Middle Ages **2 :** a person employed (as by a hotel or the United States congress) to carry messages or run errands
[2]**page** *vb* **paged; pag·ing :** to call out the name of (a person) in a public place
[3]**page** *n* **1 :** one side of a printed or written sheet of paper **2 :** a large section of computer memory **3 :** the block of information found at a single World Wide Web address
pag·eant *n* **1 :** a grand and fancy public ceremony and display **2 :** an entertainment made up of scenes based on history or legend
pa·go·da *n* **:** a tower of several stories built as a temple or memorial in the Far East
paid *past of* PAY
pail *n* **1 :** a usually round container with a handle **:** BUCKET **2 :** PAILFUL

pail·ful *n, pl* **pail·fuls** *or* **pails·ful** : the amount a pail holds

[1]**pain** *n* **1** : suffering that accompanies a bodily disorder (as a disease or an injury) **2** : a feeling (as a prick or an ache) that is caused by something harmful and usually makes one try to escape its source **3** : suffering of the mind or emotions : GRIEF **4 pains** *pl* : great care or effort — **pain·ful** *adj* — **pain·ful·ly** *adv* — **pain·less** *adj*

[2]**pain** *vb* **1** : to cause pain in or to **2** : to give or feel pain

pains·tak·ing *adj* : taking pains : showing care — **pains·tak·ing·ly** *adv*

[1]**paint** *vb* **1** : to cover a surface with or as if with paint **2** : to make a picture or design by using paints **3** : to describe clearly — **paint·er** *n*

[2]**paint** *n* : a mixture of coloring matter with a liquid that forms a dry coating when spread on a surface

paint·brush *n* : a brush for applying paint

paint·ing *n* **1** : a painted work of art **2** : the art or occupation of painting

[1]**pair** *n, pl* **pairs** *also* **pair** **1** : two things that match or are meant to be used together **2** : a thing having two similar parts that are connected **3** : a mated couple

[2]**pair** *vb* **1** : to arrange or join in pairs **2** : to form a pair : MATCH

pa·ja·mas *n pl* : loose clothes usually consisting of pants and top that match and that are worn for relaxing or sleeping

[1]**Pak·i·stani** *n* : a person born or living in Pakistan

[2]**Pakistani** *adj* : of or relating to Pakistan or the Pakistanis

pal *n* : a close friend

pal·ace *n* **1** : the home of a ruler **2** : a large or splendid house

pal·at·able *adj* : pleasant to the taste

pal·ate *n* **1** : the roof of the mouth made up of a bony front part (**hard palate**) and a soft flexible back part (**soft palate**) **2** : the sense of taste

[1]**pale** *adj* **pal·er; pal·est** **1** : not having the warm color of a healthy person **2** : not bright or brilliant **3** : light in color or shade — **pale·ness** *n*

[2]**pale** *vb* **paled; pal·ing** : to make or become pale

Pa·leo·zo·ic *n* : an era of geological history ending about 230,000,000 years ago which came before the Mesozoic and in which vertebrates and land plants first appeared

pal·ette *n* **1** : a thin board or tablet on which a painter puts and mixes colors **2** : the set of colors that a painter puts on a palette

pal·i·sade *n* **1** : a fence made of poles to protect against attack **2** : a line of steep cliffs

[1]**pall** *vb* : to become dull or uninteresting : lose the ability to give pleasure

[2]**pall** *n* **1** : a heavy cloth covering for a coffin, hearse, or tomb **2** : something that makes things dark and gloomy

pall·bear·er *n* : a person who helps to carry or follows a coffin at a funeral

pal·let *n* **1** : a mattress of straw **2** : a temporary bed on the floor

pal·lid *adj* : [1]PALE 1

pal·lor *n* : paleness of face

[1]**palm** *n* : any of a group of mostly tropical trees, shrubs, and vines with a simple but often tall stem topped with leaves that are shaped like feathers or fans

[2]**palm** *n* **1** : the under part of the hand between the fingers and the wrist **2** : a measure of length of about seven to ten centimeters

[3]**palm** *vb* : to hide in the hand

pal·met·to *n, pl* **pal·met·tos** *or* **pal·met·toes** : a low palm with leaves shaped like fans

palm off *vb* : to get rid of or pass on in a dishonest way

pal·o·mi·no *n, pl* **pal·o·mi·nos** : a small strong horse that is light tan or cream in color with a lighter mane and tail

pal·pi·tate *vb* **pal·pi·tat·ed; pal·pi·tat·ing** : [1]THROB 1

pal·sy *n* **1** : PARALYSIS **2** : an uncontrollable trembling of the body or a part of the body

pal·try *adj* **pal·tri·er; pal·tri·est** : of little importance : PETTY

pam·pas *n pl* : wide treeless plains of South America

pam·per *vb* : to give someone or someone's desires too much care and attention : INDULGE

pam·phlet *n* : a short publication without a binding : BOOKLET

[1]**pan** *n* **1** : a shallow open container used for cooking **2** : a container somewhat like a cooking pan

[2]**pan** *vb* **panned; pan·ning** : to wash earthy material so as to collect bits of metal (as gold)

pan·cake *n* : a flat cake made of thin batter and cooked on both sides on a griddle

pan·cre·as *n* : a large gland in the abdomen that produces insulin and a fluid (**pancreatic juice**) that aids digestion

pan·cre·at·ic *adj* : of or relating to the pancreas

pan·da *n* **1** : a long-tailed mainly plant-eating mammal that is related to and resembles the American raccoon, has long reddish fur, and is found from the Himalayas to China **2** : GIANT PANDA

pan·de·mo·ni·um *n* : wild uproar

pane *n* : a sheet of glass (as in a window)

[1]**pan·el** *n* **1 :** a group of persons appointed for some service **2 :** a group of persons taking part in a discussion or quiz program **3 :** a part of something (as a door or a wall) often sunk below the level of the frame **4 :** a piece of material (as plywood) made to form part of a surface (as of a wall) **5 :** a board into which instruments or controls are set

[2]**panel** *vb* **pan·eled** *or* **pan·elled; pan·el·ing** *or* **pan·el·ling :** to supply or decorate with panels

pan·el·ing *n* **:** panels joined in a continuous surface

pang *n* **:** a sudden sharp attack or feeling (as of hunger or regret)

[1]**pan·ic** *n* **:** a sudden overpowering fear especially without reasonable cause

[2]**panic** *vb* **pan·icked; pan·ick·ing :** to affect or be affected by panic

pan·icky *adj* **1 :** like or caused by panic **2 :** feeling or likely to feel panic

pan·o·rama *n* **:** a clear complete view in every direction

pan out *vb* **:** to give a good result **:** SUCCEED

pan·sy *n, pl* **pansies :** a garden plant related to the violets that has large velvety flowers with five petals usually in shades of yellow, purple, or brownish red

[1]**pant** *vb* **:** to breathe hard or quickly

[2]**pant** *n* **:** a panting breath

pan·ta·loons *n pl* **:** PANTS

pan·ther *n* **1 :** LEOPARD **2 :** COUGAR **3 :** JAGUAR

pant·ie *or* **panty** *n, pl* **pant·ies :** a woman's or child's undergarment with short legs or no legs

[1]**pan·to·mime** *n* **1 :** a show in which a story is told by using expressions on the face and movements of the body instead of words **2 :** a showing or explaining of something through movements of the body and face alone

[2]**pantomime** *vb* **pan·to·mimed; pan·to·mim·ing :** to tell through pantomime

pan·try *n, pl* **pan·tries :** a small room where food and dishes are kept

pants *n pl* **:** an outer garment reaching from the waist to the ankle or only to the knee and covering each leg separately

pa·pa *n* **:** [1]FATHER 1

pa·pal *adj* **:** of or relating to the pope

pa·paw *n* **1 :** PAPAYA **2 :** the greenish or yellow edible fruit of a North American tree with shiny leaves and purple flowers

pa·pa·ya *n* **:** a yellow edible fruit that looks like a melon and grows on a tropical American tree

[1]**pa·per** *n* **1 :** a material made in thin sheets from fibers (as of wood or cloth) **2 :** a sheet or piece of paper **3 :** a piece of paper having something written or printed on it **:** DOCUMENT **4 :** NEWSPAPER **5 :** WALLPAPER **6 :** a piece of written schoolwork

[2]**paper** *vb* **:** to cover or line with paper (as wallpaper)

[3]**paper** *adj* **1 :** made of paper **2 :** like paper in thinness or weakness

pa·per·back *n* **:** a book with a flexible paper binding

paper clip *n* **:** a clip of bent wire used to hold sheets of paper together

pa·pery *adj* **:** like paper

pa·poose *n* **:** a baby of North American Indian parents

pa·pri·ka *n* **:** a mild red spice made from the fruit of some sweet peppers

pa·py·rus *n, pl* **pa·py·rus·es** *or* **pa·py·ri 1 :** a tall African plant related to the grasses that grows especially in Egypt **2 :** a material like paper made from papyrus by ancient people and used by them to write on

par *n* **1 :** a fixed or stated value (as of money or a security) **2 :** an equal level **3 :** the score set for each hole of a golf course

par·a·ble *n* **:** a simple story that teaches a moral truth

[1]**para·chute** *n* **:** a folding device of light material shaped like an umbrella and used for making a safe jump from an airplane

[2]**parachute** *vb* **para·chut·ed; para·chut·ing :** to transport or come down by parachute

[1]**pa·rade** *n* **1 :** great show or display **2 :** the formation of troops before an officer for inspection **3 :** a public procession **4 :** a crowd of people walking at an easy pace

[2]**parade** *vb* **pa·rad·ed; pa·rad·ing 1 :** to march in an orderly group **2 :** SHOW OFF

par·a·dise *n* **1 :** the garden of Eden **2 :** HEAVEN 2 **3 :** a place or state of great happiness

par·a·dox *n* **:** a statement that seems to be the opposite of the truth or of common sense and yet is perhaps true

par·af·fin *n* **:** a white odorless tasteless substance obtained from wood, coal, or petroleum and used in coating and sealing and in candles

[1]**para·graph** *n* **:** a part of a piece of writing that is made up of one or more sentences and has to do with one topic or gives the words of one speaker

[2]**paragraph** *vb* **:** to divide into paragraphs

par·a·keet *or* **par·ra·keet** *n* **:** a small parrot with a long tail

[1]**par·al·lel** *adj* **:** lying or moving in the same direction but always the same distance apart

[2]**parallel** *n* **1 :** a parallel line or surface **2 :** one of the imaginary circles on the earth's surface parallel to the equator that mark lat-

itude **3 :** agreement in many or most details **4 :** COUNTERPART, EQUAL

[3]**parallel** *vb* **1 :** to be like or equal to **2 :** to move, run, or extend in a direction parallel with

par·al·lel·o·gram *n* **:** a plane figure with four sides whose opposite sides are parallel and equal

pa·ral·y·sis *n, pl* **pa·ral·y·ses :** partial or complete loss of one's ability to move or feel

par·a·lyze *vb* **par·a·lyzed; par·a·lyz·ing 1 :** to affect with paralysis **2 :** to destroy or decrease something's energy or ability to act

par·a·me·cium *n, pl* **par·a·me·cia** *also* **par·a·me·ciums :** a tiny water animal that is a single cell shaped like a slipper

para·med·ic *n* **:** a person specially trained to care for a patient before or during the trip to a hospital

par·a·mount *adj* **:** highest in importance or greatness

par·a·pet *n* **1 :** a wall of earth or stone to protect soldiers **2 :** a low wall or fence at the edge of a platform, roof, or bridge

[1]**para·phrase** *n* **:** a way of stating something again by giving the meaning in different words

[2]**paraphrase** *vb* **para·phrased; para·phras·ing :** to give the meaning of in different words

par·a·site *n* **1 :** a person who lives at the expense of another **2 :** a plant or animal that lives in or on some other living thing and gets food and sometimes shelter from it

par·a·sit·ic *adj* **:** of or relating to parasites or their way of life **:** being a parasite — **par·a·sit·i·cal·ly** *adv*

par·a·sol *n* **:** a light umbrella used as a protection against the sun

para·troop·er *n* **:** a soldier trained and equipped to parachute from an airplane

[1]**par·cel** *n* **1 :** a plot of land **2 :** PACKAGE 1

[2]**parcel** *vb* **par·celed** *or* **par·celled; par·cel·ing** *or* **par·cel·ling 1 :** to divide and give out by parts **2 :** to wrap up into a package

parcel post *n* **:** a mail service that handles packages

parch *vb* **:** to dry up from heat and lack of moisture

parch·ment *n* **1 :** the skin of a sheep or goat prepared so that it can be written on **2 :** a paper similar to parchment

[1]**par·don** *n* **1 :** forgiveness for wrong or rude behavior **2 :** a setting free from legal punishment

[2]**pardon** *vb* **1 :** to free from penalty for a fault or crime **2 :** to allow (a wrong act) to pass without punishment **:** FORGIVE

pare *vb* **pared; par·ing 1 :** to cut or shave off the outside or the ends of **2 :** to reduce as if by cutting

par·ent *n* **1 :** a father or mother of a child **2 :** an animal or plant that produces offspring

par·ent·age *n* **:** a line of ancestors

pa·ren·tal *adj* **:** of or relating to parents

pa·ren·the·sis *n, pl* **pa·ren·the·ses 1 :** a word, phrase, or sentence inserted in a passage to explain or comment on it **2 :** one of a pair of marks ( ) used to enclose a word or group of words or to group mathematical terms to be dealt with as a unit — **par·en·thet·ic** *or* **par·en·thet·i·cal** *adj*

par·fait *n* **:** a dessert made usually of layers of fruit, syrup, ice cream, and whipped cream

par·ish *n* **1 :** a section of a church district under the care of a priest or minister **2 :** the persons who live in a parish and attend the parish church **3 :** the members of a church **4 :** a division in the state of Louisiana that is similar to a county in other states

parish house *n* **:** a building for the educational and social activities of a church

pa·rish·io·ner *n* **:** a member or resident of a parish

[1]**park** *n* **1 :** an area of land set aside for recreation or for its beauty **2 :** an enclosed field for ball games

[2]**park** *vb* **:** to stop (as an auto or truck) and leave it for a while

par·ka *n* **:** a warm windproof jacket with a hood

park·way *n* **:** a broad landscaped highway

[1]**par·ley** *n, pl* **parleys :** a discussion with an enemy

[2]**parley** *vb* **par·leyed; par·ley·ing :** to hold a discussion of terms with an enemy

par·lia·ment *n* **:** an assembly that is the highest legislative body of a country (as the United Kingdom)

par·lor *n* **1 :** a room for receiving guests and for conversation **2 :** a usually small place of business

pa·ro·chi·al *adj* **:** of, relating to, or supported by a religious body (as a church)

pa·role *n* **:** an early release of a prisoner

parrakeet *variant of* PARAKEET

par·rot *n* **:** a brightly colored tropical bird that has a strong hooked bill and is sometimes trained to imitate human speech

[1]**par·ry** *vb* **par·ried; par·ry·ing 1 :** to turn aside an opponent's weapon or blow **2 :** to avoid by a skillful answer

[2]**parry** *n, pl* **par·ries :** an act or instance of parrying

pars·ley *n, pl* **pars·leys :** a garden plant related to the carrot that has finely divided leaves and is used to season or decorate various foods

pars·nip *n* : a vegetable that is the long white root of a plant related to the carrot
par·son *n* : [1]MINISTER 1
par·son·age *n* : a house provided by a church for its pastor to live in
[1]**part** *n* **1** : one of the sections into which something is divided : something less than a whole **2** : a voice or instrument **3** : the music for a voice or instrument **4** : a piece of a plant or animal body **5** : a piece of a machine **6** : a person's share or duty **7** : one of the sides in a disagreement **8** : the role of a character in a play **9** : a line along which the hair is divided
[2]**part** *vb* **1** : to leave someone : go away **2** : to divide into parts **3** : to hold apart **4** : to come apart
par·take *vb* **par·took; par·tak·en; par·tak·ing** : to take a share or part
part·ed *adj* : divided into parts
par·tial *adj* **1** : favoring one side of a question over another **2** : fond or too fond of someone or something **3** : of one part only **4** : not complete — **par·tial·ly** *adv*
par·ti·al·i·ty *n, pl* **par·ti·al·i·ties** : the quality or state of being partial
par·tic·i·pant *n* : a person who takes part in something
par·tic·i·pate *vb* **par·tic·i·pat·ed; par·tic·i·pat·ing** : to join with others in doing something
par·tic·i·pa·tion *n* : the act of participating
par·ti·ci·ple *n* : a word formed from a verb but often used like an adjective while keeping some verb characteristics (as tense and the ability to take an object)
par·ti·cle *n* : a very small bit of something
[1]**par·tic·u·lar** *adj* **1** : relating to one person or thing **2** : not usual : SPECIAL **3** : being one of several **4** : concerned about details — **par·tic·u·lar·ly** *adv*
[2]**particular** *n* : a single fact or detail
part·ing *n* : a place or point where a division or separation occurs
par·ti·san *n* **1** : a person who aids or approves something (as a party or a point of view) or someone **2** : a soldier who lives and fights behind enemy lines — **par·ti·san·ship** *n*
[1]**par·ti·tion** *n* **1** : an act of dividing into parts **2** : something that divides
[2]**partition** *vb* **1** : to divide into shares **2** : to divide into separate parts or areas
part·ly *adv* : somewhat but not completely
part·ner *n* **1** : a person who does or shares something with another **2** : either one of a married pair **3** : one who plays with another person on the same side in a game **4** : one of two or more persons who run a business together
part·ner·ship *n* **1** : the state of being a partner **2** : a group of people in business together
part of speech : a class of words (as adjectives, adverbs, conjunctions, interjections, nouns, prepositions, pronouns, or verbs) identified according to the kinds of ideas they express and the work they do in a sentence
partook *past of* PARTAKE
par·tridge *n, pl* **partridge** *or* **par·tridg·es** : any of several plump game birds related to the chicken
part-time *adj* : involving fewer than the usual hours
par·ty *n, pl* **par·ties** **1** . a group of persons who take one side of a question or share a set of beliefs **2** : a social gathering or the entertainment provided for it **3** : a person or group concerned in some action
[1]**pass** *vb* **1** : [1]MOVE 1, PROCEED **2** : to go away **3** : [1]DIE 1 **4** : to go by or move past **5** : to go or allow to go across, over, or through **6** : to move from one place or condition to another **7** : HAPPEN 2 **8** : to be or cause to be approved **9** : to go successfully through an examination or inspection **10** : to be or cause to be identified or recognized **11** : to transfer or throw to another person — **pass·er** *n*
[2]**pass** *n* **1** : an opening or way for passing along or through **2** : a gap in a mountain range
[3]**pass** *n* **1** : SITUATION 4 **2** : a written permit to go or come **3** : the act or an instance of passing (as a ball) in a game
pass·able *adj* **1** : fit to be traveled on **2** : barely good enough — **pass·ably** *adv*
pas·sage *n* **1** : the act or process of passing from one place or condition to another **2** : a means (as a hall) of passing or reaching **3** : the passing of a law **4** : a right or permission to go as a passenger **5** : a brief part of a speech or written work
pas·sage·way *n* : a road or way by which a person or thing may pass
pas·sen·ger *n* : someone riding on or in a vehicle
passenger pigeon *n* : a North American wild pigeon once common but now extinct
pass·er·by *n, pl* **pass·ers·by** : someone who passes by
[1]**pass·ing** *n* **1** : the act of passing **2** : DEATH 1
[2]**passing** *adj* **1** : going by or past **2** : lasting only for a short time **3** : showing haste or lack of attention **4** : used for passing **5** : showing satisfactory work in a test or course of study
pas·sion *n* **1** *cap* : the suffering of Christ between the night of the Last Supper and his

death **2 :** a strong feeling or emotion **3 :** strong liking or desire **:** LOVE **4 :** an object of one's love, liking, or desire

pas·sion·ate *adj* **1 :** easily angered **2 :** showing or affected by strong feeling — **pas·sion·ate·ly** *adv*

pas·sive *adj* **1 :** not acting but acted upon **2 :** showing that the person or thing represented by the subject is acted on by the verb **3 :** offering no resistance — **pas·sive·ly** *adv*

pass out *vb* **:** to become unconscious **:** FAINT

Pass·over *n* **:** a Jewish holiday celebrated in March or April in honor of the freeing of the Hebrews from slavery in Egypt

pass·port *n* **:** a government document that allows a citizen to leave his or her country

pass up *vb* **:** to let go by **:** REFUSE

pass·word *n* **:** a secret word or phrase that must be spoken by a person before being allowed to pass a guard

[1]past *adj* **1 :** of or relating to a time that has gone by **2 :** expressing a time gone by **3 :** no longer serving

[2]past *prep* **1 :** [2]BEYOND **2 :** going close to and then beyond

[3]past *n* **1 :** a former time **2 :** past life or history

[4]past *adv* **:** so as to pass by or beyond

pas·ta *n* **1 :** a dough of flour, eggs, and water made in different shapes and dried or used fresh **2 :** a dish of cooked pasta

[1]paste *n* **1 :** dough for pies or tarts **2 :** a soft smooth mixture **3 :** a mixture of flour or starch and water used for sticking things together

[2]paste *vb* **past·ed; past·ing :** to stick on or together with paste

paste·board *n* **:** a stiff material made of sheets of paper pasted together or of pulp pressed and dried

[1]pas·tel *n* **1 :** a crayon made by mixing ground coloring matter with a watery solution of a gum **2 :** a drawing made with pastel crayons **3 :** a soft pale color

[2]pastel *adj* **1 :** made with pastels **2 :** light and pale in color

pas·teur·i·za·tion *n* **:** the process or an instance of pasteurizing

pas·teur·ize *vb* **pas·teur·ized; pas·teur·iz·ing :** to keep a liquid (as milk) for a time at a temperature high enough to kill many harmful germs and then cool it rapidly — **pas·teur·iz·er** *n*

pas·time *n* **:** something (as a hobby) that helps to make time pass pleasantly

pas·tor *n* **:** a minister or priest in charge of a church

pas·to·ral *adj* **1 :** of or relating to shepherds or peaceful rural scenes **2 :** of or relating to the pastor of a church

pas·try *n, pl* **pas·tries 1 :** sweet baked goods (as pies) made mainly of flour and fat **2 :** a piece of pastry

[1]pas·ture *n* **1 :** plants (as grass) for feeding grazing animals **2 :** land on which animals graze

[2]pasture *vb* **pas·tured; pas·tur·ing 1 :** [1]GRAZE 1 **2 :** to supply (as cattle) with pasture

[1]pat *n* **1 :** a light tap with the open hand or a flat instrument **2 :** the sound of a pat or tap **3 :** a small flat piece (as of butter)

[2]pat *adj* **pat·ter; pat·test 1 :** exactly suitable **2 :** learned perfectly **3 :** not changing

[3]pat *vb* **pat·ted; pat·ting :** to tap or stroke gently with the open hand

[1]patch *n* **1 :** a piece of cloth used to mend or cover a torn or worn place **2 :** a small piece or area different from what is around it

[2]patch *vb* **:** to mend or cover with a patch

patch up *vb* **:** ADJUST 1

patch·work *n* **:** pieces of cloth of different colors and shapes sewed together

[1]pat·ent *adj* **1 :** protected by a patent **2 :** OBVIOUS, EVIDENT

[2]pat·ent *n* **:** a document that gives the inventor of something the only right to make, use, and sell the invention for a certain number of years

[3]pat·ent *vb* **:** to get a patent for

pa·ter·nal *adj* **1 :** of or relating to a father **:** FATHERLY **2 :** received or inherited from a father **3 :** related through the father

path *n, pl* **paths 1 :** a track made by traveling on foot **2 :** the way or track in which something moves **3 :** a way of life or thought — **path·less** *adj*

pa·thet·ic *adj* **:** making one feel pity, tenderness, or sorrow

path·way *n* **:** PATH 1

pa·tience *n* **:** the ability to be patient or the fact of being patient

[1]pa·tient *adj* **1 :** putting up with pain or troubles without complaint **2 :** showing or involving calm self-control — **pa·tient·ly** *adv*

[2]patient *n* **:** a person under medical care and treatment

pa·tio *n, pl* **pa·ti·os 1 :** an inner part of a house that is open to the sky **2 :** an open area next to a house that is usually paved

pa·tri·arch *n* **1 :** the father and ruler of a family or tribe **2 :** a respected old man

pa·tri·ot *n* **:** a person who loves his or her country and enthusiastically supports it

pa·tri·ot·ic *adj* **:** having or showing patriotism

pa·tri·ot·ism *n* **:** love of one's country

[1]pa·trol *n* **1 :** the action of going around an area for observation or guard **2 :** a person or group doing the act of patrolling **3 :** a part of a Boy Scout or Girl Scout troop

²patrol *vb* **pa·trolled; pa·trol·ling :** to go around an area for the purpose of watching or protecting

pa·trol·man *n, pl* **pa·trol·men :** a police officer who has a regular beat

pa·tron *n* **1 :** a person who gives generous support or approval **2 :** CUSTOMER **3 :** a saint to whom a church or society is dedicated

pa·tron·age *n* **1 :** the help or encouragement given by a patron **2 :** a group of patrons (as of a shop or theater) **3 :** the control by officials of giving out jobs, contracts, and favors

pa·tron·ize *vb* **pa·tron·ized; pa·tron·iz·ing 1 :** to act as a patron to or of **:** SUPPORT **2 :** to be a customer of **3 :** to treat (a person) as if one were better or more important

¹pat·ter *vb* **1 :** to strike again and again with light blows **2 :** to run with quick light steps

²patter *n* **:** a series of quick light sounds

¹pat·tern *n* **1 :** something worth copying **2 :** a model or guide for making something **3 :** a form or figure used in decoration **:** DESIGN — **pat·terned** *adj*

²pattern *vb* **:** to make or design by following a pattern

pat·ty *n, pl* **pat·ties :** a small flat cake of chopped food

pau·per *n* **:** a very poor person

¹pause *n* **1 :** a temporary stop **2 :** a sign â above a musical note or rest to show that the note or rest is to be held longer

²pause *vb* **paused; paus·ing :** to stop for a time **:** make a pause

pave *vb* **paved; pav·ing :** to make a hard surface on (as with concrete or asphalt)

pave·ment *n* **1 :** a paved surface (as of a street) **2 :** material used in paving

pa·vil·ion *n* **1 :** a very large tent **2 :** a building usually with open sides that is used as a place for entertainment or shelter in a park or garden

pav·ing *n* **:** PAVEMENT

¹paw *n* **:** the foot of a four-footed animal (as the lion, dog, or cat) that has claws

²paw *vb* **1 :** to touch in a clumsy or rude way **2 :** to touch or scrape with a paw **3 :** to beat or scrape with a hoof

¹pawn *n* **:** the piece of least value in the game of chess

²pawn *n* **1 :** something of value given as a guarantee (as of payment of a debt) **2 :** the condition of being given as a guarantee

³pawn *vb* **:** to leave as a guarantee for a loan **:** PLEDGE

pawn·bro·ker *n* **:** a person who makes a business of lending money and keeping personal property as a guarantee

pawn·shop *n* **:** a pawnbroker's shop

¹pay *vb* **paid; pay·ing 1 :** to give (as money) in return for services received or for something bought **2 :** to give what is owed **3 :** to get revenge on **4 :** to give or offer freely **5 :** to get a suitable return for cost or trouble **:** be worth the effort or pains required — **pay·er** *n*

²pay *n* **1 :** the act of paying **:** PAYMENT **2 :** the state of being paid or employed for money **3 :** SALARY

pay·able *adj* **:** that may, can, or must be paid

pay·check *n* **:** a check or money received as wages or salary

pay·ment *n* **1 :** the act of paying **2 :** money given to pay a debt

pay off *vb* **1 :** to pay in full **2 :** to have a good result

pay·roll *n* **1 :** a list of persons who receive pay **2 :** the amount of money necessary to pay the employees of a business

pay up *vb* **:** to pay in full especially debts that are overdue

PC *n, pl* **PCs** *or* **PC's :** PERSONAL COMPUTER

pea *n, pl* **peas** *also* **pease 1 :** a vegetable that is the round seed found in the pods of a garden plant (**pea vine**) related to the clovers **2 :** a plant (as the sweet pea) resembling or related to the garden pea

peace *n* **1 :** freedom from public disturbance or war **2 :** freedom from upsetting thoughts or feelings **3 :** agreement and harmony among persons **4 :** an agreement to end a war

peace·able *adj* **:** PEACEFUL 1, 3

peace·ful *adj* **1 :** liking peace **:** not easily moved to argue or fight **2 :** full of or enjoying peace, quiet, or calm **3 :** not involving fighting — **peace·ful·ly** *adv* — **peace·ful·ness** *n*

peace·mak·er *n* **:** a person who settles an argument or stops a fight

peace pipe *n* **:** a decorated pipe of the American Indians used for certain ceremonies

peach *n* **1 :** a fruit that is related to the plum and has a sweet juicy pulp, hairy skin, and a large rough stone **2 :** a pale yellowish pink color

pea·cock *n* **:** the male of a very large Asian pheasant with a very long brightly colored tail that can be spread or raised at will, a small crest, and in most forms brilliant blue or green feathers on the neck and shoulders

peak *n* **1 :** the part of a cap that sticks out in front **2 :** the pointed top of a hill or mountain **3 :** a mountain all by itself **4 :** the highest point of development

¹peal *n* **1 :** the sound of bells **2 :** a loud sound **:** a series of loud sounds

²peal *vb* **:** to give out peals

pea·nut *n* **:** a plant related to the peas that has yellow flowers and is grown for its underground pods of oily nutlike edible seeds which yield a valuable oil (**peanut oil**) or are crushed to form a spread (**peanut butter**)

pear *n* **:** the fleshy fruit that grows on a tree related to the apple and is commonly larger at the end opposite the stem

pearl *n* **1 :** a smooth body with a rich luster that is formed within the shell of some mollusks (as the **pearl oyster** of tropical seas) usually around something irritating (as a grain of sand) which has gotten into the shell **2 :** MOTHER-OF-PEARL **3 :** something like a pearl in shape, color, or value **4 :** a pale bluish gray color

pearly *adj* **pearl·i·er; pearl·i·est :** like a pearl especially in having a shining surface

peas·ant *n* **:** a farmer owning a small amount of land or a farm worker in European countries

pease *pl of* PEA

peat *n* **:** a blackish or dark brown material that is the remains of plants partly decayed in water and is dug and dried for use as fuel

peat moss *n* **:** a spongy brownish moss of wet areas that is often the chief plant making up peat

peb·ble *n* **:** a small rounded stone

pe·can *n* **:** an oval edible nut that usually has a thin shell and is the fruit of a tall tree of the central and southern United States related to the walnuts

pec·ca·ry *n, pl* **pec·ca·ries :** either of two mostly tropical American animals that gather in herds, are active at night, and look like but are much smaller than the related pigs

[1]**peck** *n* **1 :** a unit of capacity equal to one quarter of a bushel **2 :** a great deal **:** a large quantity

[2]**peck** *vb* **1 :** to strike or pick up with the bill **2 :** to strike with a sharp instrument (as a pick)

[3]**peck** *n* **1 :** the act of pecking **2 :** a mark made by pecking

pe·cu·liar *adj* **1 :** one's own **:** of or limited to some one person, thing, or place **2 :** different from the usual **:** ODD

pe·cu·li·ar·i·ty *n, pl* **pe·cu·li·ar·i·ties 1 :** the quality or state of being peculiar **2 :** something peculiar or individual

[1]**ped·al** *n* **:** a lever worked by the foot or feet

[2]**pedal** *vb* **ped·aled** *or* **ped·alled; ped·al·ing** *or* **ped·al·ling :** to use or work the pedals of something

ped·dle *vb* **ped·dled; ped·dling :** to go about especially from house to house with goods for sale

ped·dler *or* **ped·lar** *n* **:** someone who peddles

ped·es·tal *n* **1 :** a support or foot of an upright structure (as a column, statue, or lamp) **2 :** a position of high regard

pe·des·tri·an *n* **:** a person who is walking

pe·di·a·tri·cian *n* **:** a doctor who specializes in the care of babies and children

ped·i·gree *n* **1 :** a table or list showing the line of ancestors of a person or animal **2 :** a line of ancestors

pe·dom·e·ter *n* **:** an instrument that measures the distance one covers in walking

[1]**peek** *vb* **1 :** to look slyly or cautiously **2 :** to take a quick glance — **peek·er** *n*

[2]**peek** *n* **:** a short or sly look

[1]**peel** *vb* **1 :** to strip off the skin or bark of **2 :** to strip or tear off **3 :** to come off smoothly or in bits

[2]**peel** *n* **:** an outer covering and especially the skin of a fruit

[1]**peep** *vb* **:** to make a weak shrill sound such as a young bird makes — **peep·er** *n*

[2]**peep** *n* **:** a weak shrill sound

[3]**peep** *vb* **1 :** to look through or as if through a small hole or a crack **:** PEEK **2 :** to show slightly

[4]**peep** *n* **1 :** a brief or sly look **2 :** the first appearance

[1]**peer** *n* **1 :** a person of the same rank or kind **:** EQUAL **2 :** a member of one of the five ranks (duke, marquis, earl, viscount, and baron) of the British nobility

[2]**peer** *vb* **1 :** to look curiously or carefully **2 :** to come slightly into view **:** peep out

peer·less *adj* **:** having no equal

pee·vish *adj* **:** complaining a lot **:** IRRITABLE — **pee·vish·ly** *adv* — **pee·vish·ness** *n*

pee·wee *n* **:** one that is small

[1]**peg** *n* **1 :** a slender piece (as of wood or metal) used especially to fasten things together or to hang things on **2 :** a piece driven into the ground to mark a boundary or to hold something **3 :** a step or grade in approval or esteem

[2]**peg** *vb* **pegged; peg·ging 1 :** to mark or fasten with pegs **2 :** to work hard

pel·i·can *n* **:** a bird with a large bill, webbed feet, and a great pouch on the lower jaw that is used to scoop in fish for food

pel·la·gra *n* **:** a disease caused by a diet containing too little protein and too little of a necessary vitamin

pel·let *n* **1 :** a little ball (as of food or medicine) **2 :** a piece of small shot

pell–mell *adv* **1 :** in crowded confusion **2 :** in a big hurry

[1]**pelt** *n* **:** a skin of an animal especially with its fur or wool

[2]**pelt** *vb* **1 :** to strike with repeated blows **2 :** HURL, THROW **3 :** to beat or pound against something again and again

pel·vis *n* **:** the bowl-shaped part of the skeleton that supports the lower part of the abdomen and includes the hip bones and the lower bones of the backbone

[1]**pen** *vb* **penned; pen·ning :** to shut in a small enclosure

[2]**pen** *n* **:** a small enclosure especially for animals

[3]**pen** *n* **:** an instrument for writing with ink

[4]**pen** *vb* **penned; pen·ning :** to write with a pen

pe·nal *adj* **:** of or relating to punishment

pe·nal·ize *vb* **pe·nal·ized; pe·nal·iz·ing :** to give a penalty to

pen·al·ty *n, pl* **pen·al·ties 1 :** punishment for doing something wrong **2 :** a loss or handicap given for breaking a rule in a sport or game

pence *pl of* PENNY

[1]**pen·cil** *n* **:** a device for writing or drawing consisting of a stick of black or colored material enclosed in wood, plastic, or metal

[2]**pencil** *vb* **pen·ciled** *or* **pen·cilled; pen·cil·ing** *or* **pen·cil·ling :** to write, mark, or draw with a pencil

pen·dant *n* **:** an ornament (as on a necklace) allowed to hang free

[1]**pend·ing** *prep* **1 :** DURING 1 **2 :** while waiting for

[2]**pending** *adj* **:** not yet decided

pen·du·lum *n* **:** an object hung from a fixed point so as to swing freely back and forth under the action of gravity

pen·e·trate *vb* **pen·e·trat·ed; pen·e·trat·ing 1 :** to pass into or through **:** PIERCE **2 :** to see into or understand

pen·e·tra·tion *n* **1 :** the act or process of penetrating **2 :** keen understanding

pen·guin *n* **:** a seabird that cannot fly, has very short legs, and is found in the cold regions of the southern hemisphere

pen·i·cil·lin *n* **:** an antibiotic that is produced by a mold and is used especially against disease-causing round bacteria

pen·in·su·la *n* **:** a piece of land extending out into a body of water

pe·nis *n, pl* **pe·nes** *or* **pe·nis·es :** a male organ in mammals used for sexual intercourse and for urinating

pen·i·tence *n* **:** sorrow for one's sins or faults

[1]**pen·i·tent** *adj* **:** feeling or showing penitence

[2]**penitent** *n* **:** a penitent person

pen·i·ten·tia·ry *n, pl* **pen·i·ten·tia·ries :** a prison for criminals

pen·knife *n, pl* **pen·knives :** a small jackknife

pen·man *n, pl* **pen·men :** a person who uses a pen **:** WRITER

pen·man·ship *n* **:** writing with a pen **:** style or quality of handwriting

pen name *n* **:** a false name that an author uses on his or her work

pen·nant *n* **1 :** a narrow pointed flag used for identification, signaling, or decoration **2 :** a flag that serves as the emblem of a championship

pen·ni·less *adj* **:** very poor **:** having no money

pen·ny *n, pl* **pennies 1** *or pl* **pence :** a coin of the United Kingdom equal to $^1/_{100}$ pound **2 :** CENT

[1]**pen·sion** *n* **:** a sum paid regularly to a person who has retired from work

[2]**pension** *vb* **:** to grant or give a pension to

pen·sive *adj* **:** lost in sober or sad thought — **pen·sive·ly** *adv* — **pen·sive·ness** *n*

pent *adj* **:** penned up **:** shut up

penta- *or* **pent-** *prefix* **:** five

pen·ta·gon *n* **:** a flat figure having five angles and five sides

pen·tag·o·nal *adj* **:** having five sides

pen·tath·lon *n* **:** an athletic contest made up of five different events in which each person participates

pent·house *n* **:** an apartment built on the roof of a building

pe·on *n* **:** a member of the landless laboring class in Spanish America

pe·o·ny *n, pl* **pe·o·nies :** a plant related to the buttercup that lives for years and is widely grown for its very large usually double white, pink, or red flowers

[1]**peo·ple** *n, pl* **people** *or* **peoples 1 :** a body of persons making up a race, tribe, or nation **2 :** human beings — often used in compounds instead of *persons* **3 :** the persons of a certain group or place

[2]**people** *vb* **peo·pled; peo·pling 1 :** to supply or fill with people **2 :** to dwell on or in

[1]**pep** *n* **:** brisk energy or liveliness

[2]**pep** *vb* **pepped; pep·ping :** to put pep into

[1]**pep·per** *n* **1 :** a product from the fruit of an East Indian climbing shrub that is sharp in flavor, is used as a seasoning or in medicine, and consists of the whole ground dried berry (**black pepper**) or of the ground seeds alone (**white pepper**) **2 :** a plant related to the tomato that is grown for its fruits which may be very sharp in flavor (**hot peppers**) or mild and sweet (**sweet peppers** or **bell peppers**)

[2]**pepper** *vb* **1 :** to season with or as if with pepper **2 :** to hit with a shower of blows or objects

pep·per·mint *n* **:** a mint with stalks of small usually purple flowers that yields an oil (**peppermint oil**) which is sharp in flavor and is used especially to flavor candies

pep·py *adj* **pep·pi·er; pep·pi·est :** full of pep

pep·sin *n* **:** an enzyme that starts the digestion of proteins in the stomach

per *prep* **1 :** to or for each **2 :** ACCORDING TO 1

per an·num *adv* **:** by the year **:** in or for each year **:** ANNUALLY

per cap·i·ta *adv or adj* **:** by or for each person

per·ceive *vb* **per·ceived; per·ceiv·ing 1 :** to become aware of through the senses and especially through sight **2 :** UNDERSTAND 1

[1]**per·cent** *adv or adj* **:** out of every hundred **:** measured by the number of units as compared with one hundred

[2]**percent** *n, pl* **percent :** a part or fraction of a whole expressed in hundredths

per·cent·age *n* **1 :** a part of a whole expressed in hundredths **2 :** a share of profits

per·cep·ti·ble *adj* **:** possible to detect

per·cep·tion *n* **1 :** an act or the result of grasping with one's mind **2 :** the ability to grasp (as meanings and ideas) with one's mind **3 :** a judgment formed from information grasped

[1]**perch** *n* **1 :** a place where birds roost **2 :** a raised seat or position

[2]**perch** *vb* **:** to sit or rest on or as if on a perch

[3]**perch** *n, pl* **perch** *or* **perch·es 1 :** a European freshwater food fish that is mostly olive green and yellow **2 :** any of numerous fishes related to or resembling the European perch

per·chance *adv* **:** PERHAPS

per·co·late *vb* **per·co·lat·ed; per·co·lat·ing 1 :** to trickle or cause to trickle through something porous **:** OOZE **2 :** to prepare (coffee) by passing hot water through ground coffee beans again and again — **per·co·la·tor** *n*

per·co·la·tion *n* **:** the act or process of percolating

per·cus·sion *n* **1 :** a sharp tapping **2 :** the striking of an explosive cap to set off the charge in a gun **3 :** the musical instruments of a band or orchestra that are played by striking or shaking

percussion instrument *n* **:** a musical instrument (as a drum, cymbal, or maraca) sounded by striking or shaking

[1]**pe·ren·ni·al** *adj* **1 :** present all through the year **2 :** never ending **:** CONTINUOUS **3 :** living from year to year

[2]**perennial** *n* **:** a perennial plant

[1]**per·fect** *adj* **1 :** lacking nothing **:** COMPLETE **2 :** thoroughly skilled or trained **:** meeting the highest standards **3 :** having no mistake, error, or flaw — **per·fect·ly** *adv*

[2]**per·fect** *vb* **:** to make perfect

per·fec·tion *n* **1 :** completeness in all parts or details **2 :** the highest excellence or skill **3 :** a quality or thing that cannot be improved

per·fo·rate *vb* **per·fo·rat·ed; per·fo·rat·ing 1 :** to make a hole through **:** PIERCE **2 :** to make many small holes in

per·form *vb* **1 :** to carry out **:** ACCOMPLISH, DO **2 :** to do something needing special skill — **per·form·er** *n*

per·for·mance *n* **1 :** the carrying out of an action **2 :** a public entertainment

[1]**per·fume** *n* **1 :** a pleasant smell **:** FRAGRANCE **2 :** a liquid used to make things smell nice

[2]**per·fume** *vb* **per·fumed; per·fum·ing :** to make smell nice **:** add a pleasant scent to

per·haps *adv* **:** possibly but not certainly **:** MAYBE

per·il *n* **1 :** the state of being in great danger **2 :** a cause or source of danger

per·il·ous *adj* **:** DANGEROUS 1 — **per·il·ous·ly** *adv*

pe·rim·e·ter *n* **1 :** the whole outer boundary of a figure or area **2 :** the length of the boundary of a figure

pe·ri·od *n* **1 :** a punctuation mark . used chiefly to mark the end of a declarative sentence or an abbreviation **2 :** a portion of time set apart by some quality **3 :** a portion of time that forms a stage in the history of something **4 :** one of the divisions of a school day

pe·ri·od·ic *adj* **:** occurring at regular intervals

[1]**pe·ri·od·i·cal** *adj* **1 :** PERIODIC **2 :** published at regular intervals — **pe·ri·od·i·cal·ly** *adv*

[2]**periodical** *n* **:** a periodical publication (as a magazine)

peri·scope *n* **:** an instrument containing lenses and mirrors by which a person (as on a submarine) can get a view that would otherwise be blocked

per·ish *vb* **:** to become destroyed **:** DIE

per·ish·able *adj* **:** likely to spoil or decay

[1]**per·i·win·kle** *n* **:** an evergreen plant that spreads along the ground and has shining leaves and blue or white flowers

[2]**periwinkle** *n* **:** a small snail that lives along rocky seashores

perk *vb* **1 :** to lift in a quick, alert, or bold way **2 :** to make fresher in appearance **3 :** to become more lively or cheerful

perky *adj* **perk·i·er; perk·i·est :** being lively and cheerful

per·ma·nence *n* **:** the quality or state of being permanent

per·ma·nent *adj* **:** lasting or meant to last for a long time **:** not temporary — **per·ma·nent·ly** *adv*

per·me·able *adj* **:** having pores or openings that let liquids or gases pass through

per·me·ate *vb* **per·me·at·ed; per·me·at·ing 1 :** to pass through something that has pores or small openings or is in a loose form **2 :** to spread throughout

per·mis·sion *n* **:** the consent of a person in authority

[1]**per·mit** *vb* **per·mit·ted; per·mit·ting** **1 :** to give permission : ALLOW **2 :** to make possible : give an opportunity

[2]**per·mit** *n* **:** a statement of permission (as a license or pass)

per·ni·cious *adj* **:** causing great damage or harm

per·ox·ide *n* **:** an oxide containing much oxygen (as one of hydrogen used as an antiseptic)

[1]**per·pen·dic·u·lar** *adj* **1 :** exactly vertical **2 :** being at right angles to a line or surface — **per·pen·dic·u·lar·ly** *adv*

[2]**perpendicular** *n* **:** a perpendicular line, surface, or position

per·pe·trate *vb* **per·pe·trat·ed; per·pe·trat·ing :** to bring about or carry out : COMMIT — **per·pe·tra·tor** *n*

per·pet·u·al *adj* **1 :** lasting forever : ETERNAL **2 :** occurring continually : CONSTANT — **per·pet·u·al·ly** *adv*

per·pet·u·ate *vb* **per·pet·u·at·ed; per·pet·u·at·ing :** to cause to last a long time

per·plex *vb* **:** to confuse the mind of : BEWILDER

per·plex·i·ty *n, pl* **per·plex·i·ties** **1 :** a puzzled or anxious state of mind **2 :** something that perplexes

per·se·cute *vb* **per·se·cut·ed; per·se·cut·ing :** to treat continually in a way meant to be cruel and harmful

per·se·cu·tion *n* **1 :** the act of persecuting **2 :** the state of being persecuted

per·se·ver·ance *n* **:** the act or power of persevering

per·se·vere *vb* **per·se·vered; per·se·ver·ing :** to keep trying to do something in spite of difficulties

per·sim·mon *n* **:** a fruit of orange color that looks like a plum and grows on a tree related to the ebonies

per·sist *vb* **1 :** to keep on doing or saying something : continue stubbornly **2 :** to last on and on : continue to exist or occur

per·sist·ence *n* **1 :** the act or fact of persisting **2 :** the quality of being persistent : PERSEVERANCE

per·sist·ent *adj* **:** continuing to act or exist longer than usual — **per·sist·ent·ly** *adv*

per·son *n* **1 :** a human being — used in compounds especially by those who prefer to avoid *man* in words that apply to both sexes **2 :** the body of a human being **3 :** bodily presence **4 :** reference to the speaker, to the one spoken to, or to one spoken of as shown especially by means of certain pronouns

per·son·age *n* **:** an important or famous person

per·son·al *adj* **1 :** of, relating to, or belonging to a person : not public : not general **2 :** made or done in person **3 :** of the person or body **4 :** relating to a particular person or his or her qualities **5 :** intended for one particular person **6 :** relating to oneself — **per·son·al·ly** *adv*

personal computer *n* **:** a computer designed for an individual user

per·son·al·i·ty *n, pl* **per·son·al·i·ties** **1 :** the qualities (as moods or habits) that make one person different from others **2 :** a person's pleasing qualities **3 :** a person of importance or fame

personal pronoun *n* **:** a pronoun (as *I, you, it,* or *they*) used as a substitute for a noun that names a definite person or thing

per·son·i·fy *vb* **per·son·i·fied; per·son·i·fy·ing :** to think of or represent as a person

per·son·nel *n* **:** a group of people employed in a business or an organization

per·spec·tive *n* **1 :** the art of painting or drawing a scene so that objects in it seem to have their right shape and to be the right distance apart **2 :** the power to understand things in their true relationship to each other **3 :** the true relationship of objects or events to one another

per·spi·ra·tion *n* **1 :** the act or process of perspiring **2 :** salty liquid given off from skin glands

per·spire *vb* **per·spired; per·spir·ing :** to give off salty liquid through the skin

per·suade *vb* **per·suad·ed; per·suad·ing :** to win over to a belief or way of acting by argument or earnest request : CONVINCE

per·sua·sion *n* **1 :** the act of persuading **2 :** the power to persuade **3 :** a way of believing : BELIEF

per·sua·sive *adj* **:** able or likely to persuade — **per·sua·sive·ly** *adv* — **per·sua·sive·ness** *n*

pert *adj* **1 :** SAUCY 1 **2 :** PERKY

per·tain *vb* **1 :** to belong to as a part, quality, or function **2 :** to relate to a person or thing

per·ti·nent *adj* **:** relating to the subject that is being thought about or discussed : RELEVANT

per·turb *vb* **:** to disturb in mind : trouble greatly

pe·ruse *vb* **pe·rused; pe·rus·ing** **1 :** READ 1 **2 :** to read through carefully

per·vade *vb* **per·vad·ed; per·vad·ing :** to spread through all parts of : PERMEATE

per·verse *adj* **:** stubborn in being against what is right or sensible

pe·se·ta *n* **:** a Spanish coin or bill

pe·so *n, pl* **pesos** **1 :** an old silver coin of Spain and Spanish America **2 :** a coin of the Philippines or of any of various Latin American countries

pes·si·mist *n* **:** a pessimistic person

pes·si·mis·tic *adj* **1 :** having no hope that one's troubles will end or that success or happiness will come : GLOOMY **2 :** having the belief that evil is more common or powerful than good

pest *n* **1 :** PESTILENCE **2 :** a plant or animal that damages humans or their goods **3 :** NUISANCE

pes·ter *vb* **:** to bother again and again

pes·ti·cide *n* **:** a substance used to destroy pests

pes·ti·lence *n* **:** a contagious often fatal disease that spreads quickly

pes·tle *n* **:** a tool shaped like a small club for crushing substances in a mortar

[1]**pet** *n* **1 :** a tame animal kept for pleasure rather than for use **2 :** a person who is treated with special kindness or consideration

[2]**pet** *adj* **1 :** kept or treated as a pet **2 :** showing fondness **3 :** [2]FAVORITE

[3]**pet** *vb* **pet·ted; pet·ting 1 :** to stroke or pat gently or lovingly **2 :** to kiss and caress

pet·al *n* **:** one of the often brightly colored modified leaves that make up the corolla of a flower — **pet·aled** *or* **pet·alled** *adj* — **pet·al·less** *adj*

pet·i·ole *n* **:** the stalk of a leaf

pe·tite *adj* **:** having a small trim figure

[1]**pe·ti·tion** *n* **1 :** an earnest appeal **2 :** a document asking for something

[2]**petition** *vb* **:** to make a petition to or for — **pe·ti·tion·er** *n*

pe·trel *n* **:** a small seabird with long wings that flies far from land

pet·ri·fy *vb* **pet·ri·fied; pet·ri·fy·ing 1 :** to change plant or animal matter into stone or something like stone **2 :** to frighten very much

pe·tro·leum *n* **:** a raw oil that is obtained from wells drilled in the ground and that is the source of gasoline, kerosene, and fuel oils

pet·ti·coat *n* **:** a skirt worn under a dress or outer skirt

petting zoo *n* **:** a collection of farm animals or gentle exotic animals for children to pet and feed

pet·ty *adj* **pet·ti·er; pet·ti·est 1 :** small and of no importance **2 :** showing or having a mean narrow-minded attitude — **pet·ti·ly** *adv* — **pet·ti·ness** *n*

petty officer *n* **:** an officer in the Navy or Coast Guard appointed from among the enlisted people

petty officer first class *n* **:** a petty officer in the Navy or Coast Guard ranking above a petty officer second class

petty officer second class *n* **:** a petty officer in the Navy or Coast Guard ranking above a petty officer third class

petty officer third class *n* **:** a petty officer in the Navy or Coast Guard ranking above a seaman

pet·u·lant *adj* **:** easily put in a bad humor : CROSS

pe·tu·nia *n* **:** a plant related to the potato grown for its velvety brightly colored flowers that are shaped like funnels

pew *n* **:** one of the benches with backs and sometimes doors set in rows in a church

pe·wee *n* **:** a small grayish or greenish brown bird (as a phoebe) that eats flying insects

pew·ter *n* **1 :** a metallic substance made mostly of tin sometimes mixed with copper or antimony that is used in making utensils (as pitchers and bowls) **2 :** utensils made of pewter

phantasy *variant of* FANTASY

phan·tom *n* **:** an image or figure that can be sensed (as with the eyes or ears) but that is not real

pha·raoh *n* **:** a ruler of ancient Egypt

phar·ma·cist *n* **:** a person skilled or engaged in pharmacy

phar·ma·cy *n, pl* **phar·ma·cies 1 :** the art, practice, or profession of mixing and preparing medicines usually according to a doctor's prescription **2 :** the place of business of a pharmacist : DRUGSTORE

phar·ynx *n, pl* **pha·ryn·ges** *also* **phar·ynx·es :** the space behind the mouth into which the nostrils, gullet, and windpipe open — **pha·ryn·geal** *adj*

phase *n* **1 :** the way that the moon or a planet looks to the eye at any time in its series of changes with respect to how it shines **2 :** a step or part in a series of events or actions : STAGE **3 :** a particular part or feature : ASPECT

pheas·ant *n* **:** a large brightly colored game bird with a long tail that is related to the chicken

phe·nom·e·nal *adj* **:** very remarkable : EXTRAORDINARY

phe·nom·e·non *n, pl* **phe·nom·e·na** *or* **phe·nom·e·nons 1** *pl phenomena* **:** an observable fact or event **2 :** a rare or important fact or event **3** *pl phenomenons* **:** an extraordinary or exceptional person or thing

[1]**-phil** *or* **-phile** *n suffix* **:** lover : one having a strong attraction to

[2]**-phil** *or* **-phile** *adj suffix* **:** having a fondness for or strong attraction to

phil·an·throp·ic *adj* **:** of, relating to, or devoted to philanthropy : CHARITABLE — **phil·an·throp·i·cal·ly** *adv*

phi·lan·thro·pist *n* **:** a person who gives generously to help other people

phi·lan·thro·py *n, pl* **phi·lan·thro·pies 1 :** active effort to help other people **2 :** a philanthropic gift **3 :** an organization giving or supported by charitable gifts

phil·o·den·dron *n* **:** any of several plants that can stand shade and are often grown for their showy leaves

phi·los·o·pher *n* **1 :** a student of philosophy **2 :** a person who takes misfortunes with calmness and courage

phil·o·soph·i·cal *or* **phil·o·soph·ic** *adj* **1 :** of or relating to philosophy **2 :** showing the wisdom and calm of a philosopher — **phil·o·soph·i·cal·ly** *adv*

phi·los·o·phy *n, pl* **phi·los·o·phies 1 :** the study of the basic ideas about knowledge, right and wrong, reasoning, and the value of things **2 :** the philosophical teachings or principles of a person or a group **3 :** calmness of temper and judgment

phlox *n, pl* **phlox** *or* **phlox·es :** any of a group of plants grown for their showy clusters of usually white, pink, or purplish flowers

pho·bia *n* **:** an unreasonable, abnormal, and lasting fear of something

phoe·be *n* **:** a common American bird that is grayish brown above and yellowish white below and that eats flying insects

phon- *or* **phono-** *prefix* **:** sound **:** voice **:** speech

[1]**phone** *n* **:** [1]TELEPHONE

[2]**phone** *vb* **phoned; phon·ing :** [2]TELEPHONE

pho·neme *n* **:** one of the smallest units of speech that distinguish one utterance from another

pho·net·ic *adj* **:** of or relating to spoken language or speech sounds

pho·nics *n* **:** a method of teaching beginners to read and pronounce words by learning the usual sound of letters, letter groups, and syllables

pho·no·graph *n* **:** an instrument that reproduces sounds recorded on a grooved disk

pho·ny *adj* **:** not real or genuine

phos·pho·rus *n* **:** a white or yellowish waxlike chemical element that gives a faint glow in moist air and is necessary in some form to life

[1]**pho·to** *n, pl* **photos :** [1]PHOTOGRAPH

[2]**photo** *vb* **:** [2]PHOTOGRAPH

[1]**pho·to·copy** *n* **:** a copy of usually printed material made using a process in which an image is formed by the action of light on an electrically charged surface

[2]**photocopy** *vb* **:** to make a photocopy of — **pho·to·copi·er** *n*

[1]**pho·to·graph** *n* **:** a picture made by photography

[2]**photograph** *vb* **:** to take a picture of with a camera — **pho·tog·ra·pher** *n*

pho·to·graph·ic *adj* **:** obtained by or used in photography

pho·tog·ra·phy *n* **:** the making of pictures by means of a camera that directs the image of an object onto a film made sensitive to light

pho·to·syn·the·sis *n* **:** the process by which green plants form carbohydrates from carbon dioxide and water in the presence of light — **pho·to·syn·thet·ic** *adj*

[1]**phrase** *n* **1 :** a brief expression **2 :** a group of two or more words that express a single idea but do not form a complete sentence

[2]**phrase** *vb* **phrased; phras·ing :** to express in words

phy·lum *n, pl* **phy·la :** a group of animals that ranks above the class in scientific classification and is the highest group of the plant kingdom

phys ed *n* **:** PHYSICAL EDUCATION

phys·i·cal *adj* **1 :** of or relating to nature or the world as we see it **:** material and not mental, spiritual, or imaginary **2 :** of the body **:** BODILY **3 :** of or relating to physics — **phys·i·cal·ly** *adv*

physical education *n* **:** instruction in the care and development of the body

phy·si·cian *n* **:** a specialist in healing human disease **:** a doctor of medicine

phys·i·cist *n* **:** a specialist in physics

phys·ics *n* **:** a science that deals with the facts about matter and motion and includes the subjects of mechanics, heat, light, electricity, sound, and the atomic nucleus

phys·i·o·log·i·cal *or* **phys·i·o·log·ic** *adj* **:** of or relating to physiology

phys·i·ol·o·gist *n* **:** a specialist in physiology

phys·i·ol·o·gy *n* **1 :** a branch of biology that deals with the working of the living body and its parts (as organs and cells) **2 :** the processes and activities by which a living being or any of its parts functions

phy·sique *n* **:** the build of a person's body

pi *n, pl* **pis :** the symbol π representing the ratio of the circumference of a circle to its diameter or about 3.1416

pi·a·nist *n* **:** a person who plays the piano

pi·a·no *n, pl* **pianos :** a keyboard instrument having steel wire strings that sound when struck by hammers covered with felt

pi·az·za *n* **1 :** a large open square in an Italian town **2 :** PORCH, VERANDA

pic·co·lo *n, pl* **pic·co·los :** a small shrill flute

[1]**pick** *vb* **1 :** to strike or work on with a pointed tool **2 :** to remove bit by bit **3 :** to gather one by one **4 :** CHOOSE 1, SELECT **5 :** to eat sparingly or daintily **6 :** to steal from **7 :** to start (a fight) with someone else deliberately **8 :** to unlock without a key **9 :** to pluck with the fingers or with a pick — **pick·er** *n* — **pick on :** [1]TEASE

[2]pick *n* **1 :** PICKAX **2 :** a slender pointed instrument **3 :** a thin piece of metal or plastic used to pluck the strings of a musical instrument **4 :** the act or opportunity of choosing **5 :** the best ones

pick·ax *n* **:** a heavy tool with a wooden handle and a blade pointed at one or both ends for loosening or breaking up soil or rock

pick·er·el *n* **:** any of several fairly small fishes that look like the pike

[1]pick·et *n* **1 :** a pointed stake or slender post (as for making a fence) **2 :** a soldier or a group of soldiers assigned to stand guard **3 :** a person stationed before a place of work where there is a strike

[2]picket *vb* **1 :** [2]TETHER **2 :** to walk or stand in front of as a picket

[1]pick·le *n* **1 :** a mixture of salt and water or vinegar for keeping foods **:** BRINE **2 :** a difficult or very unpleasant condition **3 :** something (as a cucumber) that has been kept in a pickle of salty water or vinegar

[2]pickle *vb* **pick·led; pick·ling :** to soak or keep in a pickle

pick·pock·et *n* **:** a thief who steals from pockets and purses

pick·up *n* **:** a light truck with an open body and low sides

pick up *vb* **1 :** to take hold of and lift **2 :** to stop for and take along **3 :** to gain by study or experience **:** LEARN **4 :** to get by buying **:** BUY **5 :** to come to and follow **6 :** to bring within range of hearing **7 :** to get back speed or strength

[1]pic·nic *n* **1 :** an outdoor party with food taken along and eaten in the open **2 :** a nice experience

[2]picnic *vb* **pic·nicked; pic·nick·ing :** to go on a picnic

pic·to·graph *n* **:** a diagram showing information by means of pictures

pic·to·ri·al *adj* **1 :** of or relating to pictures **2 :** using pictures

[1]pic·ture *n* **1 :** an image of something formed on a surface (as by drawing, painting, printing, or photography) **2 :** a very clear description **3 :** an exact likeness **4 :** MOVIE **5 :** an image on the screen of a television set

[2]picture *vb* **pic·tured; pic·tur·ing 1 :** to draw or paint a picture of **2 :** to describe very clearly in words **3 :** to form a mental image of **:** IMAGINE

picture graph *n* **:** PICTOGRAPH

pic·tur·esque *adj* **:** like a picture **:** suggesting a painted scene

pie *n* **:** a food consisting of a crust and a filling (as of fruit or meat)

pie·bald *adj* **:** spotted or blotched with two colors and especially black and white

[1]piece *n* **1 :** a part cut, torn, or broken from a thing **2 :** one of a group, set, or mass of things **3 :** a portion marked off **4 :** a single item or example **5 :** a definite amount or size in which articles are made for sale or use **6 :** something made or written **7 :** [1]COIN 1

[2]piece *vb* **pieced; piec·ing 1 :** to repair or complete by adding a piece or pieces **2 :** to make out of pieces

piece·meal *adv* **:** one piece at a time **:** little by little

pied *adj* **:** having blotches of two or more colors

pier *n* **1 :** a support for a bridge **2 :** a structure built out into the water for use as a place to land or walk or to protect or form a harbor

pierce *vb* **pierced; pierc·ing 1 :** to run into or through **:** STAB **2 :** to make a hole in or through **3 :** to force into or through **4 :** to penetrate with the eye or mind **:** see through — **pierc·ing·ly** *adv*

pi·e·ty *n, pl* **pieties :** the state or fact of being pious **:** devotion to one's God

pig *n* **1 :** a swine especially when not yet mature **2 :** a person who lives or acts like a pig **3 :** a metal cast (as of iron) poured directly from the smelting furnace into a mold

pi·geon *n* **:** a bird with a stout body, short legs, and smooth feathers

pi·geon-toed *adj* **:** having the toes turned in

pig·gish *adj* **:** like a pig especially in greed or dirtiness

pig·gy·back *adv or adj* **:** on the back or shoulders

piggy bank *n* **:** a bank for coins often in the shape of a pig

pig·head·ed *adj* **:** STUBBORN 1, 2

pig·ment *n* **1 :** a substance that gives color to other substances **2 :** coloring matter in persons, animals, and plants

pigmy *variant of* PYGMY

pig·pen *n* **1 :** a place where pigs are kept **2 :** a dirty place

pig·sty *n* **:** PIGPEN

pig·tail *n* **:** a tight braid of hair

[1]pike *n, pl* **pike** *or* **pikes :** a long slender freshwater fish with a large mouth

[2]pike *n* **:** a long wooden pole with a steel point used long ago as a weapon by soldiers

[3]pike *n* **:** TURNPIKE, ROAD

[1]pile *n* **:** a large stake or pointed post driven into the ground to support a foundation

[2]pile *n* **1 :** a mass of things heaped together **:** HEAP **2 :** REACTOR 2

[3]pile *vb* **piled; pil·ing 1 :** to lay or place in a pile **:** STACK **2 :** to heap in large amounts **3 :** to move or push forward in a crowd or group

[4]pile *n* **:** a velvety surface of fine short raised fibers

pil·fer *vb* **:** to steal small amounts or articles of small value

pil·grim *n* **1 :** a person who travels to a holy place as an act of religious devotion **2** *cap* **:** one of the English colonists who founded the first permanent settlement in New England at Plymouth in 1620

pil·grim·age *n* **:** a journey made by a pilgrim

pil·ing *n* **:** a structure made of piles

pill *n* **:** medicine or a food supplement in the form of a small rounded mass to be swallowed whole

¹pil·lage *n* **:** the act of robbing by force especially in war

²pillage *vb* **pil·laged; pil·lag·ing :** to take goods and possessions by force

pil·lar *n* **1 :** a large post that supports something (as a roof) **2 :** a column standing alone (as for a monument) **3 :** something like a pillar **:** a main support

pil·lo·ry *n, pl* **pil·lo·ries :** a device once used for punishing someone in public consisting of a wooden frame with holes in which the head and hands can be locked

¹pil·low *n* **:** a bag filled with soft or springy material used as a cushion usually for the head of a person lying down

²pillow *vb* **1 :** to lay on or as if on a pillow **2 :** to serve as a pillow for

pil·low·case *n* **:** a removable covering for a pillow

¹pi·lot *n* **1 :** a person who steers a ship **2 :** a person especially qualified to guide ships into and out of a port or in dangerous waters **3 :** a person who flies or is qualified to fly an aircraft

²pilot *vb* **:** to act as pilot of

pi·mien·to *also* **pi·men·to** *n, pl* **pi·mien·tos** *also* **pi·men·tos :** a sweet pepper with a mild thick flesh

pim·ple *n* **:** a small swelling of the skin often containing pus — **pim·pled** *adj* — **pim·ply** *adj*

¹pin *n* **1 :** a slender pointed piece (as of wood or metal) usually having the shape of a cylinder used to fasten articles together or in place **2 :** a small pointed piece of wire with a head used for fastening cloth or paper **3 :** something (as an ornament or badge) fastened to the clothing by a pin **4 :** one of ten pieces set up as the target in bowling

²pin *vb* **pinned; pin·ning 1 :** to fasten or join with a pin **2 :** to hold as if with a pin

pin·a·fore *n* **:** a sleeveless garment with a low neck worn as an apron or a dress

pin·cer *n* **1 pincers** *pl* **:** an instrument with two handles and two jaws for gripping something **2 :** a claw (as of a lobster) like pincers

¹pinch *vb* **1 :** to squeeze between the finger and thumb or between the jaws of an instrument **2 :** to squeeze painfully **3 :** to cause to look thin or shrunken **4 :** to be thrifty or stingy

²pinch *n* **1 :** a time of emergency **2 :** a painful pressure or stress **3 :** an act of pinching **:** SQUEEZE **4 :** as much as may be picked up between the finger and the thumb

pinch hitter *n* **1 :** a baseball player who is sent in to bat for another **2 :** a person who does another's work in an emergency

pin·cush·ion *n* **:** a small cushion in which pins may be stuck when not in use

¹pine *n* **:** an evergreen tree that has narrow needles for leaves, cones, and a wood that ranges from very soft to hard

²pine *vb* **pined; pin·ing 1 :** to lose energy, health, or weight through sorrow or worry **2 :** to long for very much

pine·ap·ple *n* **:** a large juicy yellow fruit of a tropical plant that has long stiff leaves with spiny margins

pin·ey *also* **piny** *adj* **:** of, relating to, or like that of pine

pin·feath·er *n* **:** a new feather just breaking through the skin of a bird

pin·ion *n* **1 :** the wing or the end part of the wing of a bird **2 :** ¹FEATHER 1

¹pink *n* **1 :** any of a group of plants with thick stem joints and narrow leaves that are grown for their showy often fragrant flowers **2 :** the highest degree

²pink *n* **:** a pale red

³pink *adj* **:** of the color pink

⁴pink *vb* **:** to cut cloth, leather, or paper in an ornamental pattern or with an edge with notches

pink·eye *n* **:** a very contagious disease of the eyes in which the inner part of the eyelids becomes sore and red

pink·ish *adj* **:** somewhat pink

pin·na·cle *n* **1 :** a slender tower generally coming to a narrow point at the top **2 :** a high pointed peak **3 :** the highest point of development or achievement

pin·point *vb* **:** to locate or find out exactly

pint *n* **:** a unit of capacity equal to one half quart or sixteen ounces (about .47 liter)

pin·to *n, pl* **pintos :** a spotted horse or pony

pin·wheel *n* **:** a toy with fanlike blades at the end of a stick that spin in the wind

piny *variant of* PINEY

¹pi·o·neer *n* **1 :** a person who goes before and prepares the way for others to follow **2 :** an early settler

²pioneer *vb* **1 :** to explore or open up ways or regions for others to follow **2 :** to start up something new or take part in the early development of something

pi·ous *adj* **1 :** showing respect and honor toward God **2 :** making a show of being very good

pip *n* **:** a small fruit seed

[1]**pipe** *n* **1 :** a musical instrument or part of a musical instrument consisting of a tube (as of wood) played by blowing **2 :** one of the tubes in a pipe organ that makes sound when air passes through it **3 :** BAGPIPE — usually used in pl. **4 :** a long tube or hollow body for transporting a substance (as water, steam, or gas) **5 :** a tube with a small bowl at one end for smoking tobacco or for blowing bubbles

[2]**pipe** *vb* **piped; pip·ing 1 :** to play on a pipe **2 :** to have or utter in a shrill tone **3 :** to equip with pipes **4 :** to move by means of pipes — **pip·er** *n*

pipe·line *n* **:** a line of pipe with pumps and control devices (as for carrying liquids or gases)

pip·ing *n* **1 :** the music or sound of a person or thing that pipes **2 :** a quantity or system of pipes **3 :** a narrow fold of material used to decorate edges or seams

pi·ra·cy *n, pl* **pi·ra·cies 1 :** robbery on the high seas **2 :** the using of another's work or invention without permission

pi·ra·nha *n* **:** any of various usually small South American freshwater fishes that have very sharp teeth and that may attack human beings and animals in the water

pi·rate *n* **:** a robber on the high seas **:** a person who commits piracy

pis *pl of* PI

Pi·sces *n* **1 :** a constellation between Aquarius and Aries imagined as two fish **2 :** the twelfth sign of the zodiac or a person born under this sign

pis·ta·chio *n, pl* **pis·ta·chios :** the green edible seed of a small tree related to the sumacs

pis·til *n* **:** the central organ in a flower that contains the ovary and produces the seed

pis·tol *n* **:** a short gun made to be aimed and fired with one hand

pis·ton *n* **:** a disk or short cylinder that slides back and forth inside a larger cylinder and is moved by steam in steam engines and by the explosion of fuel in automobiles

[1]**pit** *n* **1 :** a cavity or hole in the ground **2 :** an area set off from and often sunken below neighboring areas **3 :** a hollow area usually of the surface of the body **4 :** an indented scar (as from a boil) — **pit·ted** *adj*

[2]**pit** *vb* **pit·ted; pit·ting 1 :** to make pits in or scar with pits **2 :** to set against another in a fight or contest

[3]**pit** *n* **:** a hard seed or stone (as of a cherry)

[4]**pit** *vb* **pit·ted; pit·ting :** to remove the pits from

[1]**pitch** *n* **1 :** a dark sticky substance left over from distilling tar and used in making roofing paper, in waterproofing seams, and in paving **2 :** resin from pine trees

[2]**pitch** *vb* **1 :** to set up and fix firmly in place **2 :** to throw (as hay) usually upward or away from oneself **3 :** to throw a baseball to a batter **4 :** to plunge or fall forward **5 :** [1]SLOPE **6 :** to fix or set at a certain pitch or level **7 :** to move in such a way that one end falls while the other end rises

[3]**pitch** *n* **1 :** the action or manner of pitching **2 :** highness or lowness of sound **3 :** amount of slope **4 :** the amount or level of something (as a feeling) — **pitched** *adj*

pitch·blende *n* **:** a dark mineral that is a source of radium and uranium

[1]**pitch·er** *n* **:** a container usually with a handle and a lip used for holding and pouring out liquids

[2]**pitcher** *n* **:** a baseball player who pitches

pitch·fork *n* **:** a fork with a long handle used in pitching hay or straw

pit·e·ous *adj* **:** seeking or deserving pity — **pit·e·ous·ly** *adv*

pit·fall *n* **1 :** a covered or camouflaged pit used to capture animals or people **:** TRAP **2 :** a danger or difficulty that is hidden or is not easily recognized

pith *n* **1 :** the loose spongy tissue forming the center of the stem in some plants **2 :** the important part

piti·able *adj* **:** PITIFUL

piti·ful *adj* **1 :** causing a feeling of pity or sympathy **2 :** deserving pitying scorn

piti·less *adj* **:** having no pity **:** MERCILESS

pi·tu·i·tary gland *n* **:** an endocrine organ at the base of the brain producing several hormones of which one affects growth

[1]**pity** *n* **1 :** a sympathetic feeling for the distress of others **2 :** a reason or cause of pity or regret

[2]**pity** *vb* **pit·ied; pity·ing :** to feel pity for

[1]**piv·ot** *n* **1 :** a point or a fixed pin on the end of which something turns **2 :** something on which something else turns or depends **:** a central member, part, or point

[2]**pivot** *vb* **1 :** to turn on or as if on a pivot **2 :** to provide with, mount on, or attach by a pivot

pix·el *n* **:** any of the small parts that make up an image (as on a computer or television screen)

pix·ie *or* **pixy** *n, pl* **pix·ies :** a mischievous elf or fairy

piz·za *n* **:** a dish made usually of flattened bread dough spread with a spiced mixture (as of tomatoes, cheese, and sausage) and baked

plac·ard *n* **:** a large card for announcing or advertising something **:** POSTER

pla·cate *vb* **pla·cat·ed; pla·cat·ing** : to calm the anger of : SOOTHE

[1]**place** *n* **1** : a short street **2** : an available space : ROOM **3** : a building or spot set apart for a special purpose **4** : a certain region or center of population **5** : a piece of land with a house on it **6** : position in a scale or series in comparison with another or others **7** : a space (as a seat in a theater) set aside for one's use **8** : usual space or use **9** : the position of a figure in a numeral **10** : a public square

[2]**place** *vb* **placed; plac·ing** **1** : to put or arrange in a certain place or position **2** : to appoint to a job or find a job for **3** : to identify by connecting with a certain time, place, or happening

place·hold·er *n* : a symbol (as *x*, Δ, *) used in mathematics in the place of a numeral

place·kick *n* : a kick in football made with the ball held in place on the ground

pla·cen·ta *n* : an organ that has a large blood supply and joins the fetus of a mammal to its mother's uterus

pla·gia·rism *n* : an act of stealing and passing off as one's own the ideas or words of another

[1]**plague** *n* **1** : something that causes much distress **2** : a cause of irritation : NUISANCE **3** : a destructive epidemic disease

[2]**plague** *vb* **plagued; plagu·ing** **1** : to strike or afflict with disease or distress **2** : [1]TEASE, TORMENT

plaid *n* **1** : TARTAN **2** : a pattern consisting of rectangles formed by crossed lines of various widths

[1]**plain** *adj* **1** : having no pattern or decoration **2** : open and clear to the sight **3** : clear to the mind **4** : FRANK **5** : of common or average accomplishments or position : ORDINARY **6** : not hard to do : not complicated **7** : not handsome or beautiful

[2]**plain** *n* : a large area of level or rolling treeless land

[3]**plain** *adv* : in a plain manner

plain·tive *adj* : showing or suggesting sorrow : MOURNFUL, SAD

[1]**plait** *n* **1** : a flat fold : PLEAT **2** : a flat braid (as of hair)

[2]**plait** *vb* **1** : [1]PLEAT **2** : [1]BRAID **3** : to make by braiding

[1]**plan** *n* **1** : a drawing or diagram showing the parts or outline of something **2** : a method or scheme of acting, doing, or arranging

[2]**plan** *vb* **planned; plan·ning** **1** : to form a plan of or for : arrange the parts of ahead of time **2** : to have in mind : INTEND

[1]**plane** *vb* **planed; plan·ing** **1** : to smooth or level off with a plane **2** : to remove with or as if with a plane

[2]**plane** *n* : a tool for smoothing wood

[3]**plane** *adj* : HORIZONTAL, FLAT

[4]**plane** *n* **1** : a surface any two points of which can be joined by a straight line lying wholly within it **2** : a level or flat surface **3** : a level of development **4** : AIRPLANE

plan·et *n* : a celestial body other than a comet or meteor that travels in orbit about the sun

plan·e·tar·i·um *n* : a building in which there is a device for projecting the images of celestial bodies on a ceiling shaped like a dome

plan·e·tary *adj* **1** : of or relating to a planet **2** : having a motion like that of a planet

plank *n* : a heavy thick board

plank·ton *n* : the tiny floating plants and animals of a body of water

[1]**plant** *vb* **1** : to place in the ground to grow **2** : to set firmly in or as if in the ground : FIX **3** : to introduce as a habit **4** : to cause to become established : SETTLE **5** : to stock with something

[2]**plant** *n* **1** : any member of the kingdom of living things (as mosses, ferns, grasses, and trees) that usually lack obvious nervous or sense organs and the ability to move about and that have cellulose cell walls **2** : the buildings and equipment of an industrial business or an institution — **plant·like** *adj*

[1]**plan·tain** *n* : any of several common weeds having little or no stem, leaves with parallel veins, and a long stalk of tiny greenish flowers

[2]**plantain** *n* : a banana plant having greenish fruit that is larger, less sweet, and more starchy than the ordinary banana

plan·ta·tion *n* **1** : a group of plants and especially trees planted and cared for **2** : a planted area (as an estate) cultivated by laborers **3** : COLONY 1

plant·er *n* **1** : one (as a farmer or a machine) that plants crops **2** : a person who owns or runs a plantation **3** : a container in which ornamental plants are grown

plant kingdom *n* : a basic group of natural objects that includes all living and extinct plants

plant louse *n* : APHID

plaque *n* **1** : a flat thin piece (as of metal) used for decoration or having writing cut in it **2** : a thin film containing bacteria and bits of food that forms on the teeth

plas·ma *n* : the watery part of blood, lymph, or milk

[1]**plas·ter** *n* : a paste (as of lime, sand, and water) that hardens when it dries and is used for coating walls and ceilings

[2]**plaster** *vb* **1** : to cover or smear with or as if with plaster **2** : to paste or fasten on especially so as to cover — **plas·ter·er** *n*

plaster of par·is *often cap 2d P* : a white

powder that mixes with water to form a paste that hardens quickly and is used for casts and molds

[1]**plas·tic** *adj* **1 :** capable of being molded or modeled **2 :** made of plastic

[2]**plastic** *n* **:** any of various manufactured materials that can be molded into objects or formed into films or fibers

[1]**plate** *n* **1 :** a thin flat piece of material **2 :** metal in sheets **3 :** a piece of metal on which something is engraved or molded **4 :** HOME PLATE **5 :** household utensils made of or plated with gold or silver **6 :** a shallow usually round dish **7 :** a main course of a meal **8 :** a sheet of glass coated with a chemical sensitive to light for use in a camera **9 :** an illustration often covering a full page of a book

[2]**plate** *vb* **plat·ed; plat·ing :** to cover with a thin layer of metal (as gold or silver)

pla·teau *n, pl* **plateaus** *or* **pla·teaux :** a broad flat area of high land

plat·form *n* **1 :** a statement of the beliefs and rules of conduct for which a group stands **2 :** a level usually raised surface (as in a railroad station) **3 :** a raised floor or stage for performers or speakers **4 :** an arrangement of computer components that uses a particular operating system

plat·i·num *n* **:** a heavy grayish white metallic chemical element

pla·toon *n* **:** a part of a military company usually made up of two or more squads

platoon sergeant *n* **:** a noncommissioned officer in the Army ranking above a staff sergeant

plat·ter *n* **:** a large plate especially for serving meat

platy·pus *n* **:** a small water-dwelling mammal of Australia that lays eggs and has webbed feet, dense fur, and a bill that resembles that of a duck

plau·si·ble *adj* **:** seeming to be reasonable — **plau·si·bly** *adv*

[1]**play** *n* **1 :** exercise or activity for amusement **2 :** the action of or a particular action in a game **3 :** one's turn to take part in a game **4 :** absence of any bad intention **5 :** quick or light movement **6 :** freedom of motion **7 :** a story presented on stage

[2]**play** *vb* **1 :** to produce music or sound **2 :** to take part in a game of **3 :** to take part in sport or recreation **:** amuse oneself **4 :** to handle something idly **:** TOY **5 :** to act on or as if on the stage **6 :** PRETEND 1 **7 :** to perform (as a trick) for fun **8 :** to play in a game against **9 :** [2]ACT 2, BEHAVE **10 :** to move swiftly or lightly **11 :** to put or keep in action — **play hooky :** to stay out of school without permission

play·act·ing *n* **:** an acting out of make-believe roles

play·er *n* **1 :** a person who plays a game **2 :** a person who plays a musical instrument **3 :** a device that reproduces sounds or video images that have been recorded (as on magnetic tape)

player piano *n* **:** a piano containing a mechanical device by which it may be played automatically

play·ful *adj* **1 :** full of play **:** MERRY **2 :** HUMOROUS — **play·ful·ly** *adv* — **play·ful·ness** *n*

play·ground *n* **:** an area used for games and playing

play·house *n* **1 :** THEATER 1 **2 :** a small house for children to play in

playing card *n* **:** any of a set of cards marked to show rank and suit (**spades**, **hearts**, **diamonds**, or **clubs**) and used in playing various games

play·mate *n* **:** a companion in play

play·pen *n* **:** a small enclosure in which a baby is placed to play

play·thing *n* **:** [1]TOY 2

play·wright *n* **:** a writer of plays

pla·za *n* **:** a public square in a city or town

plea *n* **1 :** an argument in defense **:** EXCUSE **2 :** an earnest appeal

plead *vb* **plead·ed** *or* **pled; plead·ing 1 :** to argue for or against **:** argue in court **2 :** to answer to a charge **3 :** to offer as a defense, an excuse, or an apology **4 :** to make an earnest appeal **:** BEG

pleas·ant *adj* **1 :** giving pleasure **:** AGREEABLE **2 :** having pleasing manners, behavior, or appearance — **pleas·ant·ly** *adv* — **pleas·ant·ness** *n*

[1]**please** *vb* **pleased; pleas·ing 1 :** to give pleasure or enjoyment to **2 :** to be willing **:** LIKE, CHOOSE

[2]**please** *adv* — used to show politeness in asking or accepting

pleas·ing *adj* **:** giving pleasure **:** AGREEABLE — **pleas·ing·ly** *adv*

plea·sur·able *adj* **:** PLEASANT 1

plea·sure *n* **1 :** a particular desire **2 :** a feeling of enjoyment or satisfaction **3 :** something that pleases or delights

[1]**pleat** *vb* **:** to arrange in folds made by doubling material over on itself

[2]**pleat** *n* **:** a fold (as in cloth) made by doubling material over on itself

pled *past of* PLEAD

[1]**pledge** *n* **1 :** something handed over to another to ensure that the giver will keep his or her promise or agreement **2 :** something that is a symbol of something else **3 :** a promise or agreement that must be kept

[2]**pledge** *vb* **pledged; pledg·ing 1 :** to give as a pledge **2 :** to hold by a pledge **:** PROMISE

plen·te·ous *adj* **:** PLENTIFUL 2

plen·ti·ful *adj* **1 :** giving or containing plenty **:** FRUITFUL **2 :** present in large numbers or amount **:** ABUNDANT — **plen·ti·ful·ly** *adv*

plen·ty *n* **:** a full supply **:** more than enough

pleu·ri·sy *n* **:** a sore swollen state of the membrane that lines the chest often with fever, painful breathing, and coughing

plex·us *n, pl* **plex·us·es** *or* **plex·us :** a network usually of nerves or blood vessels

pli·able *adj* **1 :** possible to bend without breaking **2 :** easily influenced

pli·ant *adj* **:** PLIABLE

pli·ers *n pl* **:** small pincers with long jaws used for bending or cutting wire or handling small things

plight *n* **:** a usually bad condition or state **:** PREDICAMENT

plod *vb* **plod·ded; plod·ding :** to move or travel slowly but steadily

[1]**plot** *n* **1 :** a small area of ground **2 :** the plan or main story of a play or novel **3 :** a secret usually evil scheme

[2]**plot** *vb* **plot·ted; plot·ting 1 :** to make a map or plan of **2 :** to plan or scheme secretly — **plot·ter** *n*

plo·ver *n* **:** any one of several shorebirds having shorter and stouter bills than the related sandpipers

[1]**plow** *or* **plough** *n* **1 :** a farm machine used to cut, lift, and turn over soil **2 :** a device (as a snowplow) used to spread or clear away matter on the ground

[2]**plow** *or* **plough** *vb* **1 :** to open, break up, or work with a plow **2 :** to move through or cut as a plow does

plow·share *n* **:** the part of a plow that cuts the earth

[1]**pluck** *vb* **1 :** to pull off **:** PICK **2 :** to remove something (as hairs) by or as if by plucking **3 :** to seize and remove quickly **:** SNATCH **4 :** to pull at (a string) and let go

[2]**pluck** *n* **1 :** a sharp pull **:** TUG, TWITCH **2 :** COURAGE, SPIRIT

plucky *adj* **pluck·i·er; pluck·i·est :** showing courage **:** BRAVE

[1]**plug** *n* **1 :** a piece (as of wood or metal) used to stop up or fill a hole **2 :** a device usually on a cord used to make an electrical connection by putting it into another part (as a socket)

[2]**plug** *vb* **plugged; plug·ging 1 :** to stop or make tight with a plug **2 :** to keep steadily at work or in action **3 :** to connect to an electric circuit

plum *n* **1 :** a roundish smooth-skinned edible fruit that has an oblong stone and grows on a tree related to the peaches and cherries **2 :** a dark reddish purple **3 :** a choice or desirable thing **:** PRIZE

plum·age *n* **:** the feathers of a bird

[1]**plumb** *n* **:** a small weight (as of lead) attached to a line and used to show depth or an exactly straight up-and-down line

[2]**plumb** *vb* **:** to measure or test with a plumb

plumb·er *n* **:** a person who puts in or repairs plumbing

plumb·ing *n* **1 :** a plumber's work **2 :** a system of pipes for supplying and carrying off water in a building

plume *n* **1 :** a large or showy feather of a bird **2 :** an ornamental feather or tuft of feathers (as on a hat) — **plumed** *adj*

plum·met *vb* **:** to fall straight down

[1]**plump** *vb* **1 :** to drop or fall heavily or suddenly **2 :** to come out in favor of something

[2]**plump** *adv* **1 :** with a sudden or heavy drop **2 :** DIRECTLY 1

[3]**plump** *vb* **:** to make or become rounded or filled out

[4]**plump** *adj* **:** having a pleasingly rounded form **:** well filled out — **plump·ness** *n*

[1]**plun·der** *vb* **:** to rob or steal especially openly and by force (as during war)

[2]**plunder** *n* **:** something taken by plundering **:** LOOT

[1]**plunge** *vb* **plunged; plung·ing 1 :** to thrust or force quickly **2 :** to leap or dive suddenly **3 :** to rush, move, or force with reckless haste **4 :** to dip or move suddenly downward or forward and downward

[2]**plunge** *n* **:** a sudden dive, rush, or leap

[1]**plu·ral** *adj* **:** of, relating to, or being a word form used to show more than one

[2]**plural** *n* **:** a form of a word used to show that more than one person or thing is meant

plu·ral·ize *vb* **plu·ral·ized; plu·ral·iz·ing :** to make plural or express in the plural form

[1]**plus** *adj* **:** falling high in a certain range

[2]**plus** *prep* **:** increased by **:** with the addition of

[1]**plush** *n* **:** a cloth like a very thick soft velvet

[2]**plush** *adj* **:** very rich and fine

plus sign *n* **:** a sign + used in mathematics to show addition (as in 8+6=14) or a quantity greater than zero (as in +10°)

Plu·to *n* **:** the planet that is farthest away from the sun and has a diameter of about 2300 kilometers

plu·to·ni·um *n* **:** a radioactive metallic chemical element formed from neptunium and used for releasing atomic energy

[1]**ply** *vb* **plied; ply·ing 1 :** to use something steadily or forcefully **2 :** to keep supplying **3 :** to work hard and steadily at

[2]**ply** *n, pl* **plies :** one of the folds, layers, or threads of which something (as yarn or plywood) is made up

ply·wood *n* **:** a strong board made by gluing together thin sheets of wood under heat and pressure

pneu·mat·ic *adj* **1 :** of, relating to, or using air, gas, or wind **2 :** moved or worked by the pressure of air **3 :** made to hold or be inflated with compressed air

pneu·mo·nia *n* **:** a serious disease in which the lungs are inflamed

[1]poach *vb* **:** to cook slowly in liquid

[2]poach *vb* **:** to hunt or fish unlawfully on private property

pock *n* **:** a small swelling like a pimple on the skin (as in smallpox) or the mark it leaves

[1]pock·et *n* **1 :** a small bag fastened into a garment for carrying small articles **2 :** a place or thing like a pocket **3 :** a condition of the air (as a down current) that causes an airplane to drop suddenly

[2]pocket *vb* **1 :** to put something in a pocket **2 :** to take for oneself especially dishonestly

[3]pocket *adj* **:** POCKET-SIZE

pock·et·book *n* **1 :** a case for carrying money or papers in the pocket **2 :** HANDBAG **3 :** amount of income

pock·et·knife *n, pl* **pock·et·knives :** a knife that has one or more blades that fold into the handle and that can be carried in the pocket

pock·et–size *adj* **:** small enough to fit in a pocket

pock·mark *n* **:** the mark left by a pock — **pock·marked** *adj*

pod *n* **:** a fruit (as of the pea or bean) that is dry when ripe and then splits open to free its seeds

po·di·um *n* **:** a raised platform especially for the conductor of an orchestra

po·em *n* **:** a piece of writing often having rhyme or rhythm which tells a story or describes a feeling

po·et *n* **:** a writer of poems

po·et·ic *or* **po·et·i·cal** *adj* **1 :** of, relating to, or like that of poets or poetry **2 :** written in verse

po·et·ry *n* **1 :** writing usually with a rhythm that repeats **:** VERSE **2 :** the writings of a poet

po·go stick *n* **:** a pole with a strong spring at the bottom and two rests for the feet on which a person stands and bounces along

poin·set·tia *n* **:** a tropical plant with showy usually red leaves that grow like petals around its small greenish flowers

[1]point *n* **1 :** a separate or particular detail **:** ITEM **2 :** an individual quality **3 :** the chief idea or meaning (as of a story or a speech) **4 :** [1]PURPOSE, AIM **5 :** a geometric element that has position but no dimensions and is pictured as a small dot **6 :** a particular place or position **7 :** a particular stage or moment **8 :** the sharp end (as of a sword, pin, or pencil) **9 :** a piece of land that sticks out **10 :** a dot in writing or printing **11 :** one of the thirty-two marks indicating direction on a compass **12 :** a unit of scoring in a game — **point·ed** *adj* — **point·less** *adj*

[2]point *vb* **1 :** to put a point on **2 :** to show the position or direction of something by the finger or by standing in a fixed position **3 :** to direct someone's attention to **4 :** [1]AIM 1, DIRECT

[1]point–blank *adj* **1 :** aimed at a target from a short distance away **2 :** [1]BLUNT 2

[2]point–blank *adv* **:** in a point-blank manner

point·er *n* **1 :** something that points or is used for pointing **2 :** a large hunting dog with long ears and short hair that is usually white with colored spots, hunts by scent, and points game **3 :** a helpful hint

point of view : a way of looking at or thinking about something

[1]poise *vb* **poised; pois·ing :** to hold or make steady by balancing

[2]poise *n* **1 :** the state of being balanced **2 :** a natural self-confident manner **3 :** BEARING 1

[1]poi·son *n* **:** a substance that by its chemical action can injure or kill a living thing

[2]poison *vb* **1 :** to injure or kill with poison **2 :** to put poison on or in

poison ivy *n* **:** a common woody plant related to the sumacs and having leaves with three leaflets that can cause an itchy rash when touched

poison oak *n* **:** a poison ivy that grows as a bush

poi·son·ous *adj* **:** containing poison **:** having or causing an effect of poison

poison sumac *n* **:** a poisonous American swamp shrub or small tree related to poison ivy

[1]poke *vb* **poked; pok·ing 1 :** JAB **2 :** to make by stabbing or piercing **3 :** to stick out, or cause to stick out **4 :** to search over or through usually without purpose **:** RUMMAGE **5 :** to move slowly or lazily

[2]poke *n* **:** a quick thrust **:** JAB

[1]pok·er *n* **:** a metal rod used for stirring a fire

[2]po·ker *n* **:** a card game in which each player bets on the value of his or her hand

poky *or* **pok·ey** *adj* **pok·i·er; pok·i·est 1 :** being small and cramped **2 :** so slow as to be annoying

po·lar *adj* **1 :** of or relating to a pole of the earth or the region around it **2 :** coming from or being like a polar region **3 :** of or relating to a pole of a magnet

polar bear *n* **:** a large creamy-white bear of arctic regions

Po·lar·is *n* **:** NORTH STAR

[1]pole *n* **:** a long slender piece (as of wood or metal)

[2]**pole** *vb* **poled; pol·ing :** to push or move with a pole

[3]**pole** *n* **1 :** either end of an axis and especially of the earth's axis **2 :** either of the two ends of a magnet **3 :** either of the terminals of an electric battery

Pole *n* **:** a person born or living in Poland

pole·cat *n* **1 :** a brown or black European animal related to the weasel **2 :** SKUNK

pole·star *n* **:** NORTH STAR

pole vault *n* **:** a track-and-field contest in which each athlete uses a pole to jump over a high bar

[1]**po·lice** *vb* **po·liced; po·lic·ing :** to keep order in or among

[2]**police** *n, pl* **police 1 :** the department of government that keeps order and enforces law, investigates crimes, and makes arrests **2** *police pl* **:** members of a police force

police dog *n* **:** a dog trained to help police

po·lice·man *n, pl* **po·lice·men :** a man who is a police officer

police officer *n* **:** a member of a police force

po·lice·wom·an *n, pl* **po·lice·wom·en :** a woman who is a police officer

[1]**pol·i·cy** *n, pl* **pol·i·cies :** a course of action chosen to guide people in making decisions

[2]**policy** *n, pl* **pol·i·cies :** a document that contains the agreement made by an insurance company with a person whose life or property is insured

po·lio *n* **:** a once common virus disease often affecting children and sometimes causing paralysis

po·lio·my·eli·tis *n* **:** POLIO

[1]**pol·ish** *vb* **1 :** to make smooth and glossy usually by rubbing **2 :** to smooth or improve in manners, condition, or style — **pol·ish·er** *n*

[2]**polish** *n* **1 :** a smooth glossy surface **2 :** good manners **:** REFINEMENT **3 :** a substance prepared for use in polishing

[1]**Pol·ish** *adj* **:** of or relating to Poland, the Poles, or Polish

[2]**Polish** *n* **:** the language of the Poles

po·lite *adj* **po·lit·er; po·lit·est :** showing courtesy or good manners — **po·lite·ly** *adv* — **po·lite·ness** *n*

po·lit·i·cal *adj* **:** of or relating to politics, government, or the way government is carried on — **po·lit·i·cal·ly** *adv*

pol·i·ti·cian *n* **:** a person who is actively taking part in party politics or in conducting government business

pol·i·tics *n sing or pl* **1 :** the science and art of government **:** the management of public affairs **2 :** activity in or management of the business of political parties

pol·ka *n* **:** a lively dance for couples or the music for it

pol·ka dot *n* **:** a dot in a pattern of evenly spaced dots

[1]**poll** *n* **1 :** the casting or recording of the votes or opinions of a number of persons **2 :** the place where votes are cast — usually used in pl.

[2]**poll** *vb* **1 :** to receive and record the votes of **2 :** to receive (votes) in an election **3 :** to cast a vote or ballot at a poll

pol·lack *or* **pol·lock** *n, pl* **pollack** *or* **pollock :** either of two food fishes of the northern Atlantic and the northern Pacific that are related to the cod

pol·len *n* **:** the fine usually yellow dust in the anthers of a flower that fertilizes the seeds

pol·li·nate *vb* **pol·li·nat·ed; pol·li·nat·ing :** to place pollen on the stigma of

pol·li·na·tion *n* **:** the act or process of pollinating

pol·li·wog *or* **pol·ly·wog** *n* **:** TADPOLE

pol·lut·ant *n* **:** something that causes pollution

pol·lute *vb* **pol·lut·ed; pol·lut·ing :** to make impure — **pol·lut·er** *n*

pol·lu·tion *n* **:** the action of polluting or the state of being polluted

po·lo *n* **:** a game played by teams of players on horseback who drive a wooden ball with long-handled mallets

poly- *prefix* **:** many **:** much **:** MULTI-

poly·es·ter *n* **:** a synthetic fiber used especially in clothing

poly·gon *n* **:** a plane figure having three or more straight sides

poly·mer *n* **:** a chemical compound or mixture of compounds that is formed by combination of smaller molecules and consists basically of repeating structural units

pol·yp *n* **:** a small sea animal (as a coral) having a tubelike body closed and attached to something (as a rock) at one end and opening at the other with a mouth surrounded by tentacles

pome·gran·ate *n* **:** a reddish fruit about the size of an orange that has a thick skin and many seeds in a pulp of tart flavor and grows on a tropical Old World tree

[1]**pom·mel** *n* **:** a rounded knob on the handle of a sword or at the front and top of a saddle

[2]**pommel** *vb* **pom·meled** *or* **pom·melled; pom·mel·ing** *or* **pom·mel·ling :** PUMMEL

pomp *n* **:** a show of wealth and splendor

pom-pom *or* **pom·pon** *n* **:** a fluffy ball used as trimming on clothing

pomp·ous *adj* **1 :** making an appearance of importance or dignity **2 :** SELF-IMPORTANT — **pomp·ous·ly** *adv* — **pomp·ous·ness** *n*

pon·cho *n, pl* **ponchos 1 :** a Spanish-American cloak like a blanket with a slit in the middle for the head **2 :** a waterproof garment like a poncho worn as a raincoat

pond *n* **:** a body of water usually smaller than a lake

pon·der *vb* **:** to think over carefully

pon·der·ous *adj* **1 :** very heavy **2 :** unpleasantly dull

pond scum *n* **:** a mass of algae in still water or an alga that grows in such masses

pon·toon *n* **1 :** a small boat with a flat bottom **2 :** a light watertight float used as one of the supports for a floating bridge **3 :** a float attached to the bottom of an airplane for landing on water

po·ny *n, pl* **ponies :** a small horse

pony express *n* **:** a rapid postal system that operated across the western United States in 1860–61 by changing horses and riders along the way

po·ny·tail *n* **:** a hairstyle in which the hair is pulled together and banded usually at the back of the head

poo·dle *n* **:** one of an old breed of active intelligent dogs with heavy coats of solid color

pooh *interj* — used to express contempt or disapproval

1pool *n* **1 :** a small deep body of usually fresh water **2 :** something like a pool **3 :** a small body of standing liquid **:** PUDDLE **4 :** SWIMMING POOL

2pool *n* **1 :** a game of billiards played on a table with six pockets **2 :** people, money, or things come together or put together for some purpose

3pool *vb* **:** to contribute to a common fund or effort

poor *adj* **1 :** not having riches or possessions **2 :** less than enough **3 :** worthy of pity **4 :** low in quality or value — **poor·ly** *adv* — **poor·ness** *n*

1pop *vb* **popped; pop·ping 1 :** to burst or cause to burst with a sharp sound **2 :** to move suddenly **3 :** to fire a gun **:** SHOOT **4 :** to stick out

2pop *n* **1 :** a short explosive sound **2 :** SODA POP

pop·corn *n* **1 :** corn whose kernels burst open when exposed to high heat to form a white or yellowish mass **2 :** the kernels after popping

pope *n, often cap* **:** the head of the Roman Catholic Church

pop·lar *n* **:** a tree that has rough bark, catkins for flowers, and a white cottonlike substance around its seeds

pop·py *n, pl* **poppies :** a plant with a hairy stem and showy usually red, yellow, or white flowers

pop·u·lace *n* **1 :** the common people **2 :** POPULATION 1

pop·u·lar *adj* **1 :** of, relating to, or coming from the whole body of people **2 :** enjoyed or approved by many people — **pop·u·lar·ly** *adv*

pop·u·lar·i·ty *n* **:** the quality or state of being popular

pop·u·late *vb* **pop·u·lat·ed; pop·u·lat·ing :** to provide with inhabitants

pop·u·la·tion *n* **1 :** the whole number of people in a country, city, or area **2 :** the people or things living in a certain place

pop·u·lous *adj* **:** having a large population

por·ce·lain *n* **:** a hard white ceramic ware used especially for dishes and chemical utensils

porch *n* **:** a covered entrance to a building usually with a separate roof

por·cu·pine *n* **:** a gnawing animal having stiff sharp quills among its hairs

1pore *vb* **pored; por·ing :** to read with great attention **:** STUDY

2pore *n* **:** a tiny opening (as in the skin or in the soil)

por·gy *n, pl* **porgies :** any of several food fishes of the Mediterranean sea and the Atlantic ocean

pork *n* **:** the fresh or salted flesh of a pig

po·rous *adj* **1 :** full of pores **2 :** capable of absorbing liquids

por·poise *n* **1 :** a sea animal somewhat like a small whale with a blunt rounded snout **2 :** DOLPHIN 1

por·ridge *n* **:** a food made by boiling meal of a grain or a vegetable (as peas) in water or milk until it thickens

1port *n* **1 :** a place where ships may ride safe from storms **2 :** a harbor where ships load or unload cargo **3 :** AIRPORT

2port *n* **1 :** an opening (as in machinery) for gas, steam, or water to go in or out **2 :** PORTHOLE

3port *n* **:** the left side of a ship or airplane looking forward

por·ta·ble *adj* **:** possible to carry or move about

por·tage *n* **:** the carrying of boats or goods overland from one body of water to another

por·tal *n* **:** a grand or fancy door or gate

port·cul·lis *n* **:** a heavy iron gate which can be let down to prevent entrance (as to a castle)

por·tend *vb* **:** to give a sign or warning of beforehand

por·tent *n* **:** a sign or warning that something is going to happen

por·ter *n* **1 :** a person who carries baggage (as at a terminal) **2 :** an attendant on a train

port·fo·lio *n, pl* **port·fo·li·os :** a flat case for carrying papers or drawings

port·hole *n* **:** a small window in the side of a ship or airplane

por·ti·co *n, pl* **por·ti·coes** *or* **por·ti·cos** : a row of columns supporting a roof around or at the entrance of a building

[1]**por·tion** *n* : a part or share of a whole

[2]**portion** *vb* : to divide into portions : DISTRIBUTE

por·trait *n* : a picture of a person usually showing the face

por·tray *vb* **1** : to make a portrait of **2** : to picture in words : DESCRIBE **3** : to play the role of

por·tray·al *n* : the act or result of portraying

[1]**Por·tu·guese** *adj* : of or relating to Portugal, its people, or the Portuguese language

[2]**Portuguese** *n, pl* **Portuguese** **1** : a person born or living in Portugal **2** : the language of Portugal and Brazil

[1]**pose** *vb* **posed; pos·ing** **1** : to hold or cause to hold a special position of the body **2** : to set forth **3** : to pretend to be what one is not

[2]**pose** *n* **1** : a position of the body held for a special purpose **2** : a pretended attitude

po·si·tion *n* **1** : the way in which something is placed or arranged **2** : a way of looking at or considering things **3** : the place where a person or thing is **4** : the rank a person has in an organization or in society **5** : JOB 3

[1]**pos·i·tive** *adj* **1** : definitely and clearly stated **2** : fully confident : CERTAIN **3** : of, relating to, or having the form of an adjective or adverb that shows no degree of comparison **4** : having a real position or effect **5** : having the light and shade the same as in the original subject **6** : being greater than zero and often shown by a plus sign **7** : of, being, or relating to electricity of a kind that is produced in a glass rod rubbed with silk **8** : having a deficiency of electrons **9** : being the part from which the electric current flows to the external circuit **10** : showing acceptance or approval **11** : showing the presence of what is looked for or suspected to be present — **pos·i·tive·ly** *adv*

[2]**positive** *n* : the positive degree or a positive form of an adjective or adverb

pos·sess *vb* **1** : to have and hold as property : OWN **2** : to enter into and control firmly — **pos·ses·sor** *n*

pos·ses·sion *n* **1** : the act of possessing or holding as one's own : OWNERSHIP **2** : something that is held as one's own property

[1]**pos·ses·sive** *adj* **1** : being or belonging to the case of a noun or pronoun that shows possession **2** : showing the desire to possess or control

[2]**possessive** *n* : a noun or pronoun in the possessive case

pos·si·bil·i·ty *n, pl* **pos·si·bil·i·ties** **1** : the state or fact of being possible **2** : something that may happen

pos·si·ble *adj* **1** : being within the limits of one's ability **2** : being something that may or may not happen **3** : able or fitted to be or to become

pos·si·bly *adv* **1** : by any possibility **2** : PERHAPS

pos·sum *n* : OPOSSUM

[1]**post** *n* : a piece of solid substance (as metal or timber) placed firmly in an upright position and used especially as a support

[2]**post** *vb* **1** : to fasten on a post, wall, or bulletin board **2** : to make known publicly as if by posting a notice **3** : to forbid persons from entering or using by putting up warning notices

[3]**post** *vb* **1** : to ride or travel with haste **2** : to send by mail : MAIL **3** : to make familiar with a subject

[4]**post** *n* **1** : the place at which a soldier or guard is stationed **2** : a place where a body of troops is stationed **3** : a place or office to which a person is appointed **4** : a trading settlement

[5]**post** *vb* : to station at a post

post- *prefix* : after : later : following : behind

post·age *n* : a fee for postal service

post·al *adj* : of or relating to the post office or the handling of mail

postal card *n* **1** : a blank card with a postage stamp printed on it **2** : POSTCARD 1

post·card *n* **1** : a card on which a message may be sent by mail without an envelope **2** : POSTAL CARD 1

post·er *n* : a usually large sheet with writing or pictures on it that is displayed as a notice, advertisement, or for decoration

pos·ter·i·ty *n* **1** : the line of individuals descended from one ancestor **2** : all future generations

post·man *n, pl* **post·men** : LETTER CARRIER

post·mark *n* : a mark put on a piece of mail especially for canceling the postage stamp

post·mas·ter *n* : a person in charge of a post office

post·mis·tress *n* : a woman in charge of a post office

post office *n* **1** : a government agency in charge of the mail **2** : a place where mail is received, handled, and sent out

post·paid *adv* : with postage paid by the sender

post·pone *vb* **post·poned; post·pon·ing** : to put off till some later time — **post·pone·ment** *n*

post·script *n* : a note added at the end of a finished letter or book

[1]**pos·ture** *n* : the position of one part of the

body with relation to other parts : the general way of holding the body

[2]**posture** *vb* **pos·tured; pos·tur·ing** : to take on a particular posture : POSE

po·sy *n, pl* **posies** **1** : [1]FLOWER 1, 2 **2** : BOUQUET

[1]**pot** *n* **1** : a deep rounded container for household purposes **2** : the amount a pot will hold

[2]**pot** *vb* **pot·ted; pot·ting** **1** : to put or pack in a pot **2** : to plant (as a flower) in a pot to grow — often used with *up*

pot·ash *n* : potassium or a compound of potassium

po·tas·si·um *n* : a silvery soft light metallic chemical element found especially in minerals

po·ta·to *n, pl* **po·ta·toes** : the thick edible underground tuber of a widely grown American plant related to the tomato

potato chip *n* : a very thin slice of potato fried crisp

po·tent *adj* **1** : having power or authority **2** : very effective : STRONG

po·ten·tial *adj* : existing as a possibility — **po·ten·tial·ly** *adv*

pot·hole *n* : a deep round hole (as in a stream bed or a road)

po·tion *n* : a drink especially of a medicine or of a poison

pot·luck *n* : a meal to which people bring food to share

pot·shot *n* : a shot taken in a casual manner or at an easy target

[1]**pot·ter** *n* : a person who makes pottery

[2]**potter** *vb* : PUTTER

pot·tery *n, pl* **pot·ter·ies** **1** : a place where clay articles (as pots, dishes, and vases) are made **2** : the art of making clay articles **3** : articles made from clay that is shaped while moist and hardened by heat

pouch *n* **1** : a small bag with a drawstring **2** : a bag often with a lock for carrying goods or valuables **3** : a bag of folded skin and flesh especially for carrying the young (as on the abdomen of a kangaroo) or for carrying food (as in the cheek of many animals of the rat family)

poul·tice *n* : a soft and heated mass usually containing medicine and spread on the body surface to relieve pain, inflammation, or congestion

poul·try *n* : birds (as chickens, turkeys, ducks, and geese) grown to furnish meat or eggs for human food

[1]**pounce** *vb* **pounced; pounc·ing** **1** : to swoop on and seize something with or as if with claws **2** : to leap or attack very quickly

[2]**pounce** *n* : an act of pouncing : a sudden swooping or springing on something

[1]**pound** *n* **1** : a measure of weight equal to sixteen ounces (about .45 kilogram) **2** : a unit of money used in several countries (as the United Kingdom and Egypt)

[2]**pound** *n* : a public enclosure where stray animals are kept

[3]**pound** *vb* **1** : to crush to a powder or pulp by beating **2** : to strike heavily again and again **3** : to move along heavily

pour *vb* **1** : to flow or cause to flow in a stream **2** : to let loose something without holding back **3** : to rain hard

[1]**pout** *vb* : to show displeasure by pushing out one's lips

[2]**pout** *n* : an act of pouting

pov·er·ty *n* **1** : the condition of being poor : lack of money or possessions **2** : a lack of something desirable

[1]**pow·der** *vb* **1** : to sprinkle with or as if with fine particles of something **2** : to reduce to powder **3** : to use face powder

[2]**powder** *n* **1** : the fine particles made (as by pounding or crushing) from a dry substance **2** : something (as a food, medicine, or cosmetic) made in or changed to the form of a powder **3** : an explosive used in shooting and in blasting

powder horn *n* : a cow or ox horn made into a flask for carrying gunpowder

pow·dery *adj* **1** : made of or like powder **2** : easily crumbled **3** : sprinkled with powder

[1]**pow·er** *n* **1** : possession of control, authority, or influence over others **2** : a nation that has influence among other nations **3** : the ability to act or to do **4** : physical might : STRENGTH **5** : the number of times as shown by an exponent a number is used as a factor to obtain a product **6** : force or energy used to do work **7** : the rate of speed at which work is done **8** : the number of times an optical instrument magnifies the apparent size of the object viewed — **pow·er·less** *adj*

[2]**power** *vb* : to supply with power

[3]**power** *adj* : relating to, supplying, or using mechanical or electrical power

pow·er·ful *adj* : full of or having power, strength, or influence — **pow·er·ful·ly** *adv*

pow·er·house *n* **1** : POWER PLANT **2** : a person or thing having unusual strength or energy

power plant *n* : a building in which electric power is generated

pow·wow *n* **1** : a North American Indian ceremony or conference **2** : a meeting for discussion

prac·ti·ca·ble *adj* : possible to do or put into practice

prac·ti·cal *adj* **1** : engaged in some work **2** : of or relating to action and practice rather than ideas or thought **3** : capable of being made use of **4 :** ready to do things rather than just plan or think about them

practical joke *n* **:** a joke made up of something done rather than said **:** a trick played on someone

prac·ti·cal·ly *adv* **1 :** ACTUALLY **2 :** ALMOST

[1]**prac·tice** *or* **prac·tise** *vb* **prac·ticed** *or* **prac·tised; prac·tic·ing** *or* **prac·tis·ing 1 :** to work at often so as to learn well **2 :** to engage in often or usually **3 :** to follow or work at as a profession

[2]**practice** *also* **practise** *n* **1 :** actual performance **:** USE **2 :** a usual way of doing **3 :** repeated action for gaining skill

prai·rie *n* **:** a large area of level or rolling grassland

prairie chicken *n* **:** a grouse of the Mississippi valley

prairie dog *n* **:** a burrowing animal related to the woodchuck but about the size of a large squirrel that lives in large colonies

prairie schooner *n* **:** a long covered wagon used by pioneers to cross the prairies

[1]**praise** *vb* **praised; prais·ing 1 :** to express approval of **2 :** to glorify God or a saint especially in song

[2]**praise** *n* **1 :** an expression of approval **2 :** [1]WORSHIP 1

praise·wor·thy *adj* **:** worthy of praise

prance *vb* **pranced; pranc·ing 1 :** to rise onto or move on the hind legs **2 :** to ride on a prancing horse **3 :** [1]STRUT

prank *n* **:** a mischievous act **:** PRACTICAL JOKE

prat·tle *vb* **prat·tled; prat·tling :** to talk a great deal without much meaning

prawn *n* **:** an edible shellfish that looks like a shrimp

pray *vb* **1 :** to ask earnestly **:** BEG **2 :** to address God with adoration, pleading, or thanksgiving

prayer *n* **1 :** a request addressed to God **2 :** the act of praying to God **3 :** a set form of words used in praying **4 :** a religious service that is mostly prayers

praying mantis *n* **:** MANTIS

pre- *prefix* **1 :** earlier than **:** before **2 :** beforehand **3 :** in front of **:** front

preach *vb* **1 :** to give a sermon **2 :** to urge publicly **:** ADVOCATE

preach·er *n* **1 :** a person who preaches **2 :** [1]MINISTER 1

pre·am·ble *n* **:** an introduction (as to a law) that often gives the reasons for what follows

pre·car·i·ous *adj* **1 :** depending on chance or unknown conditions **:** UNCERTAIN **2 :** lacking steadiness or security — **pre·car·i·ous·ly** *adv* — **pre·car·i·ous·ness** *n*

pre·cau·tion *n* **1 :** care taken beforehand **2 :** something done beforehand to prevent evil or bring about good results

pre·cede *vb* **pre·ced·ed; pre·ced·ing :** to be or go before in importance, position, or time

pre·ce·dent *n* **:** something that can be used as a rule or as a model to be followed in the future

pre·ced·ing *adj* **:** going before

pre·cinct *n* **1:** an administrative district especially of a town or city **2:** a surrounding or enclosed area

pre·cious *adj* **1 :** very valuable **2 :** greatly loved **:** DEAR

prec·i·pice *n* **:** a very steep and high face of rock or mountain **:** CLIFF

pre·cip·i·tate *vb* **pre·cip·i·tat·ed; pre·cip·i·tat·ing 1 :** to cause to happen suddenly or unexpectedly **2 :** to change from a vapor to a liquid or solid and fall as rain or snow **3 :** to separate from a solution

pre·cip·i·ta·tion *n* **1 :** unwise haste **2 :** water or the amount of water that falls to the earth as hail, mist, rain, sleet, or snow

pre·cise *adj* **1 :** exactly stated or explained **2 :** very clear **3 :** very exact **:** ACCURATE — **pre·cise·ly** *adv* — **pre·cise·ness** *n*

pre·ci·sion *n* **:** the quality or state of being precise

pre·co·cious *adj* **:** showing qualities or abilities of an adult at an unusually early age — **pre·co·cious·ly** *adv* — **pre·co·cious·ness** *n*

pre–Co·lum·bi·an *adj* **:** preceding or belonging to the time before the arrival of Columbus in America

pred·a·tor *n* **:** an animal that lives mostly by killing and eating other animals

pred·a·to·ry *adj* **:** living by preying upon other animals

pre·de·ces·sor *n* **:** a person who has held a position or office before another

pre·dic·a·ment *n* **:** a bad or difficult situation **:** FIX

pred·i·cate *n* **:** the part of a sentence or clause that tells what is said about the subject

predicate adjective *n* **:** an adjective that occurs in the predicate after a linking verb and describes the subject

predicate noun *n* **:** a noun that occurs in the predicate after a linking verb and refers to the same person or thing as the subject

pre·dict *vb* **:** to figure out and tell beforehand

pre·dic·tion *n* **1 :** an act of predicting **2 :** something that is predicted

pre·dom·i·nance *n* **:** the quality or state of being predominant

pre·dom·i·nant *adj* **:** greater than others in number, strength, influence, or authority

pre·dom·i·nate *vb* **pre·dom·i·nat·ed; pre·dom·i·nat·ing :** to be predominant

preen *vb* **1 :** to smooth with or as if with the bill **2 :** to make one's appearance neat and tidy

pre·fab·ri·cate *vb* **pre·fab·ri·cat·ed; pre·fab·ri·cat·ing :** to manufacture the parts of something beforehand so that it can be built by putting the parts together

pref·ace *n* **:** a section at the beginning that introduces a book or a speech

pre·fer *vb* **pre·ferred; pre·fer·ring :** to like better

pref·er·a·ble *adj* **:** deserving to be preferred — **pref·er·a·bly** *adv*

pref·er·ence *n* **1 :** a choosing of or special liking for one person or thing rather than another **2 :** the power or chance to choose **:** CHOICE **3 :** a person or thing that is preferred

¹pre·fix *vb* **:** to put or attach at the beginning of a word **:** add as a prefix

²prefix *n* **:** a letter or group of letters that comes at the beginning of a word and has its own meaning

preg·nan·cy *n, pl* **preg·nan·cies :** the state of being pregnant

preg·nant *adj* **1 :** carrying unborn offspring **2 :** full of meaning

pre·hen·sile *adj* **:** adapted for grasping by wrapping around

pre·his·tor·ic *adj* **:** of, relating to, or being in existence in the period before written history began

¹prej·u·dice *n* **1 :** injury or damage to a case at law or to one's rights **2 :** a liking or dislike for one rather than another without good reason

²prejudice *vb* **prej·u·diced; prej·u·dic·ing 1 :** to cause damage to (as a case at law) **2 :** to cause prejudice in

prel·ate *n* **:** a clergyman (as a bishop) of high rank

¹pre·lim·i·nary *n, pl* **pre·lim·i·nar·ies :** something that is preliminary

²preliminary *adj* **:** coming before the main part **:** INTRODUCTORY

pre·lude *n* **1 :** something that comes before and prepares for the main or more important parts **2 :** a short musical introduction (as for an opera) **3 :** a piece (as an organ solo) played at the beginning of a church service

pre·ma·ture *adj* **:** happening, coming, or done before the usual or proper time **:** too early — **pre·ma·ture·ly** *adv*

pre·med·i·tate *vb* **pre·med·i·tat·ed; pre·med·i·tat·ing :** to think about and plan beforehand

¹pre·mier *adj* **:** first in position or importance **:** CHIEF

²premier *n* **:** PRIME MINISTER

¹pre·miere *adj* **:** ²CHIEF 2

²premiere *n* **:** a first showing or performance

prem·ise *n* **1 :** a statement taken to be true and on which an argument or reasoning may be based **2 premises** *pl* **:** a piece of land with the buildings on it

pre·mi·um *n* **1 :** a prize to be gained by some special act **2 :** a sum over and above the stated value **3 :** the amount paid for a contract of insurance

pre·mo·lar *n* **:** any of the teeth that come between the canines and the molars and in humans are normally two in each side of each jaw

pre·mo·ni·tion *n* **:** a feeling that something is going to happen

pre·oc·cu·pied *adj* **:** lost in thought

prepaid *past of* PREPAY

prep·a·ra·tion *n* **1 :** the act of making ready beforehand for some special reason **2 :** something that prepares **3 :** something prepared for a particular purpose

pre·par·a·to·ry *adj* **:** preparing or serving to prepare for something

pre·pare *vb* **pre·pared; pre·par·ing 1 :** to make ready beforehand for some particular reason **2 :** to put together the elements of

pre·pay *vb* **pre·paid; pre·pay·ing :** to pay or pay for beforehand

prep·o·si·tion *n* **:** a word or group of words that combines with a noun or pronoun to form a phrase that usually acts as an adverb, adjective, or noun

prep·o·si·tion·al *adj* **:** of, relating to, or containing a preposition

pre·pos·ter·ous *adj* **:** making little or no sense **:** FOOLISH

pre·req·ui·site *n* **:** something that is needed beforehand or is necessary to prepare for something else

¹pre·school *adj* **:** of or relating to the time in a child's life that ordinarily comes before attendance at school

²preschool *n* **:** NURSERY SCHOOL

pre·school·er *n* **:** a child of preschool age

pre·scribe *vb* **pre·scribed; pre·scrib·ing 1 :** to lay down as a rule of action **:** ORDER **2 :** to order or direct the use of as a remedy

pre·scrip·tion *n* **1 :** a written direction or order for the preparing and use of a medicine **2 :** a medicine that is prescribed

pres·ence *n* **1 :** the fact or condition of being present **2 :** position close to a person **3 :** a person's appearance

presence of mind : ability to think clearly and act quickly in an emergency

¹pres·ent *n* **:** something presented or given **:** GIFT 2

²pre·sent *vb* **1 :** to introduce one person to another **2 :** to take (oneself) into another's presence **3 :** to bring before the public **4 :** to make a gift to **5 :** to give as a gift **6 :** to offer to view **:** SHOW, DISPLAY

³pres·ent *adj* **1 :** not past or future **:** now

going on **2 :** being before or near a person or in sight **:** being at a certain place and not elsewhere **3 :** pointing out or relating to time that is not past or future

[4]**pres·ent** *n* **:** the present time **:** right now

pre·sent·able *adj* **:** having a satisfactory or pleasing appearance

pre·sen·ta·tion *n* **1 :** an introduction of one person to another **2 :** an act of presenting **3 :** something offered or given

pres·ent·ly *adv* **1 :** before long **:** SOON **2 :** at the present time **:** NOW

pres·er·va·tion *n* **:** a keeping from injury, loss, or decay

pre·ser·va·tive *n* **:** something (as a substance added to food) that preserves

[1]**pre·serve** *vb* **pre·served; pre·serv·ing 1 :** to keep or save from injury or ruin **:** PROTECT **2 :** to prepare (as by canning or pickling) fruits or vegetables for keeping **3 :** MAINTAIN 1, CONTINUE — **pre·serv·er** *n*

[2]**preserve** *n* **1 :** fruit cooked in sugar or made into jam or jelly — often used in pl. **2 :** an area where animals are protected

pre·side *vb* **pre·sid·ed; pre·sid·ing 1 :** to act as chairperson of a meeting **2 :** to be in charge

pres·i·den·cy *n, pl* **pres·i·den·cies 1 :** the office of president **2 :** the term during which a president holds office

pres·i·dent *n* **1 :** a person who presides over a meeting **2 :** the chief officer of a company or society **3 :** the head of the government and chief executive officer of a modern republic

pres·i·den·tial *adj* **:** of or relating to a president or the presidency

[1]**press** *n* **1 :** [2]CROWD 1, THRONG **2 :** a machine that uses pressure to shape, flatten, squeeze, or stamp **3 :** a closet for clothing **4 :** the act of pressing **:** PRESSURE **5 :** a printing or publishing business **6 :** the newspapers and magazines of a country

[2]**press** *vb* **1 :** to bear down upon **:** push steadily against **2 :** to squeeze so as to force out the juice or contents **3 :** to flatten out or smooth by bearing down upon especially by ironing **4 :** to ask or urge strongly **5 :** to force or push one's way

press·ing *adj* **:** needing one's immediate attention

pres·sure *n* **1 :** the action of pressing or bearing down upon **2 :** a force or influence that cannot be avoided **3 :** the force with which one body presses against another **4 :** the need to get things done

pres·tige *n* **:** importance in the eyes of people **:** REPUTE

pres·to *adv or adj* **:** suddenly as if by magic

pre·sume *vb* **pre·sumed; pre·sum·ing 1 :** to undertake without permission or good reason **:** DARE **2 :** to suppose to be true without proof

pre·sump·tion *n* **1 :** presumptuous behavior or attitude **2 :** a strong reason for believing something to be so **3 :** something believed to be so but not proved

pre·sump·tu·ous *adj* **:** going beyond what is proper — **pre·sump·tu·ous·ly** *adv* — **pre·sump·tu·ous·ness** *n*

pre·tend *vb* **1 :** to make believe **:** SHAM **2 :** to put forward as true something that is not true — **pre·tend·er** *n*

pre·tense *or* **pre·tence** *n* **1 :** a claim usually not supported by facts **2 :** an effort to reach a certain condition or quality

pre·ten·tious *adj* **:** having or showing pretenses **:** SHOWY — **pre·ten·tious·ly** *adv* — **pre·ten·tious·ness** *n*

[1]**pret·ty** *adj* **pret·ti·er; pret·ti·est :** pleasing to the eye or ear especially because of being graceful or delicate — **pret·ti·ly** *adv* — **pret·ti·ness** *n*

[2]**pret·ty** *adv* **:** in some degree **:** FAIRLY

pret·zel *n* **:** a brown cracker that is salted and is usually hard and shaped like a loose knot

pre·vail *vb* **1 :** to win a victory **2 :** to succeed in convincing **3 :** to be or become usual, common, or widespread

prev·a·lence *n* **:** the state of being prevalent

prev·a·lent *adj* **:** accepted, practiced, or happening often or over a wide area

pre·vent *vb* **1 :** to keep from happening **2 :** to hold or keep back — **pre·vent·able** *adj*

pre·ven·tion *n* **:** the act or practice of preventing something

pre·ven·tive *adj* **:** used for prevention

pre·view *n* **:** a showing of something (as a movie) before regular showings

pre·vi·ous *adj* **:** going before in time or order **:** PRECEDING — **pre·vi·ous·ly** *adv*

[1]**prey** *n* **1 :** an animal hunted or killed by another animal for food **2 :** a person that is helpless and unable to escape attack **:** VICTIM **3 :** the act or habit of seizing or pouncing upon

[2]**prey** *vb* **1 :** to seize and eat something as prey **2 :** to have a harmful effect

[1]**price** *n* **1 :** the quantity of one thing given or asked for something else **:** the amount of money paid or to be paid **2 :** [2]REWARD **3 :** the cost at which something is gotten or done

[2]**price** *vb* **priced; pric·ing 1 :** to set a price on **2 :** to ask the price of

price·less *adj* **:** too valuable to have a price **:** not to be bought at any price

[1]**prick** *n* **1 :** a mark or small wound made by a pointed instrument **2 :** something sharp or pointed **3 :** a sensation of being pricked

[2]prick *vb* **1 :** to pierce slightly with a sharp point **2 :** to have or to cause a feeling of or as if of being pricked **3 :** to point upward

prick·er *n* **:** [1]PRICKLE 1

[1]prick·le *n* **1 :** a small sharp point (as a thorn) **2 :** a slight stinging pain

[2]prickle *vb* **prick·led; prick·ling :** [2]PRICK 2

prick·ly *adj* **prick·li·er; prick·li·est 1 :** having prickles **2 :** being or having a pricking

prickly pear *n* **:** a usually spiny cactus with flat branching joints and a sweet pulpy fruit shaped like a pear

[1]pride *n* **1 :** too high an opinion of one's own ability or worth **:** a feeling of being better than others **2 :** a reasonable and justifiable sense of one's own worth **:** SELF-RESPECT **3 :** a sense of pleasure that comes from some act or possession **4 :** something of which one is proud

[2]pride *vb* **prid·ed; prid·ing :** to think highly of (oneself)

priest *n* **:** a person who has the authority to lead or perform religious ceremonies

priest·ess *n* **:** a woman who is a priest

prim *adj* **prim·mer; prim·mest :** very fussy about one's appearance or behavior — **prim·ly** *adv*

pri·mar·i·ly *adv* **:** in the first place

[1]pri·ma·ry *adj* **1 :** first in time or development **2 :** most important **:** PRINCIPAL **3 :** not made or coming from something else **:** BASIC **4 :** of, relating to, or being the heaviest of three levels of stress in pronunciation

[2]primary *n, pl* **pri·ma·ries :** an election in which members of a political party nominate candidates for office

primary color *n* **:** any of a set of colors from which all other colors may be made with the colors for light being red, green, and blue and for pigments or paint being red, yellow, and blue

pri·mate *n* **:** any of a group of mammals that includes humans together with the apes and monkeys and a few related forms

[1]prime *n* **1 :** the first part **:** the earliest stage **2 :** the period in life when a person is best in health, looks, or strength **3 :** the best individual or part

[2]prime *adj* **1 :** first in time **:** ORIGINAL **2 :** having no factor except itself and one **3 :** first in importance, rank, or quality

[3]prime *vb* **primed; prim·ing 1 :** to put a first color or coating on (an unpainted surface) **2 :** to put into working order by filling **3 :** to tell what to say beforehand **:** COACH

prime minister *n* **:** the chief officer of the government in some countries

[1]prim·er *n* **1 :** a small book for teaching children to read **2 :** a book of first instructions on a subject

[2]prim·er *n* **1 :** a device (as a cap) for setting off an explosive **2 :** material used to prime a surface

pri·me·val *adj* **:** belonging to the earliest time **:** PRIMITIVE

prim·i·tive *adj* **1 :** of or belonging to very early times **2 :** of or belonging to an early stage of development

primp *vb* **:** to dress or arrange in a careful or fussy manner

prim·rose *n* **:** a low perennial plant with large leaves growing from the base of the stem and showy often yellow or pink flowers

prince *n* **1 :** MONARCH 1 **2 :** the son of a monarch **3 :** a nobleman of very high or the highest rank

prin·cess *n* **:** a daughter or granddaughter of a monarch **:** a female member of a royal family

[1]prin·ci·pal *adj* **:** highest in rank or importance **:** CHIEF — **prin·ci·pal·ly** *adv*

[2]principal *n* **1 :** a leading or most important person or thing **2 :** the head of a school **3 :** a sum of money that is placed to earn interest, is owed as a debt, or is used as a fund

prin·ci·pal·i·ty *n, pl* **prin·ci·pal·i·ties :** a small territory that is ruled by a prince

principal parts *n pl* **:** the infinitive, the past tense, and the past and present participles of an English verb

prin·ci·ple *n* **1 :** a general or basic truth on which other truths or theories can be based **2 :** a rule of conduct **3 :** a law or fact of nature which makes possible the working of a machine or device

[1]print *n* **1 :** a mark made by pressure **2 :** something which has been stamped with an impression or formed in a mold **3 :** printed matter **4 :** printed letters **5 :** a picture, copy, or design taken from an engraving or photographic negative **6 :** cloth upon which a design is stamped

[2]print *vb* **1 :** to put or stamp in or on **2 :** to make a copy of by pressing paper against an inked surface (as type or an engraving) **3 :** to stamp with a design by pressure **4 :** PUBLISH 2 **5 :** PRINT OUT **6 :** to write in separate letters like those made by a typewriter **7 :** to make a picture from a photographic negative

print·er *n* **1 :** a person whose business is printing **2 :** a machine that produces printouts

print·ing *n* **1 :** the process of putting something in printed form **2 :** the art, practice, or business of a printer

printing press *n* **:** a machine that makes printed copies

print·out *n* **:** a printed record produced by a computer

print out *vb* **:** to make a printout of

[1]pri·or *n* : a monk who is head of a priory
[2]prior *adj* **1 :** being or happening before something else **2 :** being more important than something else
pri·or·ess *n* : a nun who is head of a priory
pri·or·i·ty *n, pl* **pri·or·i·ties :** the quality or state of coming before another in time or importance
prior to *prep* : in advance of : BEFORE
pri·o·ry *n, pl* **pri·o·ries :** a religious house under a prior or prioress
prism *n* : a transparent object that usually has three sides and bends light so that it breaks up into rainbow colors
pris·on *n* : a place where criminals are locked up
pris·on·er *n* : a person who has been captured or locked up
pri·va·cy *n* **1 :** the state of being out of the sight and hearing of other people **2 :** SECRECY 2
[1]pri·vate *adj* **1 :** having to do with or for the use of a single person or group : not public **2 :** not holding any public office **3 :** [1]SECRET 1 — **pri·vate·ly** *adv* — **pri·vate·ness** *n*
[2]private *n* : an enlisted person of the lowest rank in the Marine Corps or of either of the two lowest ranks in the Army
pri·va·teer *n* **1 :** an armed private ship permitted by its government to make war on ships of an enemy country **2 :** a sailor on a privateer
private first class *n* : an enlisted person in the Army or Marine Corps ranking above a private
priv·et *n* : a shrub with white flowers that is related to the lilac and is often used for hedges
priv·i·lege *n* : a right or liberty granted as a favor or benefit especially to some and not others
priv·i·leged *adj* : having more things and a better chance in life than most people
[1]prize *n* **1 :** something won or to be won in a contest **2 :** something unusually valuable or eagerly sought
[2]prize *adj* **1 :** awarded a prize **2 :** awarded as a prize **3 :** outstanding of its kind
[3]prize *vb* **prized; priz·ing 1 :** to estimate the value of **2 :** to value highly : TREASURE
[4]prize *n* : something taken (as in war) by force especially at sea
prize·fight·er *n* : a professional boxer
[1]pro *n, pl* **pros :** an argument or evidence in favor of something
[2]pro *adv* : in favor of something
[3]pro *n or adj* : PROFESSIONAL
pro- *prefix* : approving : in favor of
prob·a·bil·i·ty *n, pl* **prob·a·bil·i·ties 1 :** the quality or state of being probable **2 :** something probable
prob·a·ble *adj* : reasonably sure but not certain of happening or being true : LIKELY
prob·a·bly *adv* : very likely
pro·ba·tion *n* : a period of trial for finding out or testing a person's fitness (as for a job)
[1]probe *n* **1 :** a slender instrument for examining a cavity (as a deep wound) **2 :** a careful investigation
[2]probe *vb* **probed; prob·ing 1 :** to examine with or as if with a probe **2 :** to investigate thoroughly
prob·lem *n* **1 :** something to be worked out or solved **2 :** a person or thing that is hard to understand or deal with
pro·bos·cis *n* : a long flexible hollow bodily structure (as the trunk of an elephant or the beak of a mosquito)
pro·ce·dure *n* **1 :** the manner or method in which a business or action is carried on **2 :** an action or series of actions
pro·ceed *vb* **1 :** to come from a source **2 :** to go or act by an orderly method **3 :** to go forward or onward : ADVANCE
pro·ceed·ing *n* **1 :** PROCEDURE 2 **2 proceedings** *pl* : things that happen
pro·ceeds *n pl* : the money or profit that comes from a business deal
[1]pro·cess *n* **1 :** [2]ADVANCE 1 **2 :** a series of actions, motions, or operations leading to some result **3 :** the carrying on of a legal action
[2]process *vb* **1 :** to change by a special treatment **2 :** to take care of according to a routine **3 :** to take in and organize for use in a variety of ways
pro·ces·sion *n* **1 :** continuous forward movement : PROGRESSION **2 :** a group of individuals moving along in an orderly often ceremonial way
pro·ces·sor *n* **1 :** a person or machine that processes **2 :** COMPUTER **3 :** the part of a computer that operates on data
pro·claim *vb* : to announce publicly : DECLARE
proc·la·ma·tion *n* **1 :** the act of proclaiming **2 :** something proclaimed
pro·cure *vb* **pro·cured; pro·cur·ing 1 :** OBTAIN **2 :** to bring about or cause to be done
[1]prod *vb* **prod·ded; prod·ding 1 :** to poke with something **2 :** to stir a person or animal to action
[2]prod *n* **1 :** something used for prodding **2 :** an act of prodding **3 :** a sharp urging or reminder
[1]prod·i·gal *adj* : carelessly wasteful
[2]prodigal *n* : somebody who wastes money carelessly
prod·i·gy *n, pl* **prod·i·gies 1 :** an amazing

event or action : WONDER **2** : an unusually talented child

[1]pro·duce *vb* **pro·duced; pro·duc·ing 1** : to bring to view : EXHIBIT **2** : to bring forth : YIELD **3** : to prepare (as a play) for public presentation **4** : MANUFACTURE — **pro·duc·er** *n*

[2]pro·duce *n* **1** : something produced **2** : fresh fruits and vegetables

prod·uct *n* **1** : the number resulting from the multiplication of two or more numbers **2** : something produced by manufacture, labor, thought, or growth

pro·duc·tion *n* **1** : something produced **2** : the act of producing **3** : the amount produced

pro·duc·tive *adj* **1** : having the power to produce plentifully **2** : producing something

[1]pro·fane *vb* **pro·faned; pro·fan·ing** : to treat with great disrespect — **pro·fan·er** *n*

[2]profane *adj* : showing no respect for God or holy things — **pro·fane·ly** *adv* — **pro·fane·ness** *n*

pro·fan·i·ty *n, pl* **pro·fan·i·ties** : profane language

pro·fess *vb* **1** : to declare openly **2** : PRETEND 2

pro·fes·sion *n* **1** : a public declaring or claiming **2** : an occupation (as medicine, law, or teaching) that is not mechanical or agricultural and that requires special education **3** : the people working in a profession

[1]pro·fes·sion·al *adj* **1** : of, relating to, or like that of a profession **2** : taking part in an activity (as a sport) that others do for pleasure in order to make money — **pro·fes·sion·al·ly** *adv*

[2]professional *n* : a person whose work is professional

pro·fes·sor *n* : a teacher especially of the highest rank at a college or university

prof·fer *vb* : [1]OFFER 2

pro·fi·cient *adj* : very good at doing something : EXPERT — **pro·fi·cient·ly** *adv*

pro·file *n* : something (as a head) seen or drawn from the side

[1]prof·it *n* **1** : the gain or benefit from something **2** : the gain after all the expenses are subtracted from the total amount received — **prof·it·less** *adj*

[2]profit *vb* **1** : to get some good out of something : GAIN **2** : to be of use to (someone)

prof·it·able *adj* : producing profit — **prof·it·ably** *adv*

pro·found *adj* **1** : having or showing great knowledge and understanding **2** : very deeply felt — **pro·found·ly** *adv* — **pro·found·ness** *n*

pro·fuse *adj* : very plentiful — **pro·fuse·ly** *adv* — **pro·fuse·ness** *n*

pro·fu·sion *n* : a plentiful supply : PLENTY

prog·e·ny *n, pl* **prog·e·nies** : human descendants or animal offspring

[1]pro·gram *n* **1** : a brief statement or written outline (as of a concert or play) **2** : PERFORMANCE 2 **3** : a plan of action **4** : a set of step-by-step instructions that tell a computer to do something with data

[2]program *vb* **pro·grammed; pro·gram·ming** : to provide with a program

pro·gram·mer *n* : a person who creates and tests programs for computers

[1]prog·ress *n* **1** : a moving toward a goal **2** : gradual improvement

[2]pro·gress *vb* **1** : to move forward : ADVANCE **2** : to move toward a higher, better, or more advanced stage

pro·gres·sion *n* **1** : the act of progressing or moving forward **2** : a continuous and connected series (as of acts, events, or steps)

pro·gres·sive *adj* **1** : of, relating to, or showing progress **2** : taking place gradually or step by step **3** : favoring or working for gradual political change and social improvement by action of the government — **pro·gres·sive·ly** *adv* — **pro·gres·sive·ness** *n*

pro·hib·it *vb* **1** : to forbid by authority **2** : to make impossible

pro·hi·bi·tion *n* **1** : the act of prohibiting something **2** : the forbidding by law of the sale or manufacture of alcoholic liquids for use as beverages

[1]proj·ect *n* **1** : a plan or scheme to do something **2** : a task or problem in school **3** : a group of houses or apartment buildings built according to a single plan

[2]pro·ject *vb* **1** : to stick out **2** : to cause to fall on a surface

pro·jec·tile *n* : something (as a bullet or rocket) that is thrown or driven forward especially from a weapon

pro·jec·tion *n* **1** : something that sticks out **2** : the act or process of projecting on a surface (as by means of motion pictures or slides)

pro·jec·tor *n* : a machine for projecting images on a screen

pro·lif·ic *adj* : producing young or fruit in large numbers

pro·long *vb* : to make longer than usual or expected

prom *n* : a usually formal dance given by a high school or college class

prom·e·nade *n* **1** : a walk or ride for pleasure or to be seen **2** : a place for walking

prom·i·nence *n* **1** : the quality, condition, or fact of being prominent : DISTINCTION **2** : something (as a mountain) that is prominent

prom·i·nent *adj* **1** : sticking out beyond the surface **2** : attracting attention (as by size or position) : CONSPICUOUS 3 : DISTINGUISHED, EMINENT — **prom·i·nent·ly** *adv*

¹prom·ise *n* **1 :** a statement by a person that he or she will do or not do something **2 :** a cause or ground for hope

²promise *vb* **prom·ised; prom·is·ing 1 :** to give a promise about one's own actions **2 :** to give reason to expect

prom·is·ing *adj* **:** likely to turn out well

prom·on·to·ry *n, pl* **prom·on·to·ries :** a high point of land sticking out into the sea

pro·mote *vb* **pro·mot·ed; pro·mot·ing 1 :** to move up in position or rank **2 :** to help (something) to grow or develop

pro·mo·tion *n* **1 :** a moving up in position or rank **2 :** the promoting of something (as growth of health)

¹prompt *vb* **1 :** to lead to do something **2 :** to remind of something forgotten or poorly learned **3 :** to be the cause of **:** INSPIRE — **prompt·er** *n*

²prompt *adj* **1 :** quick and ready to act **2 :** being on time **:** PUNCTUAL **3 :** done at once **:** given without delay — **prompt·ly** *adv* — **prompt·ness** *n*

prone *adj* **1 :** likely to be or act a certain way **2 :** having the front surface downward — **prone·ness** *n*

prong *n* **1 :** one of the sharp points of a fork **2 :** a slender part that sticks out (as a point of an antler)

prong·horn *n* **:** an animal like an antelope that lives in the treeless parts of the western United States and Mexico

pro·noun *n* **:** a word used as a substitute for a noun

pro·nounce *vb* **pro·nounced; pro·nounc·ing 1 :** to state in an official or solemn way **2 :** to use the voice to make the sounds of **3 :** to say correctly

pro·nounced *adj* **:** very noticeable

pro·nun·ci·a·tion *n* **:** the act or way of pronouncing a word or words

¹proof *n* **1 :** evidence of truth or correctness **2 :** ¹TEST 1 **3 :** a printing (as from type) prepared for study and correction **4 :** a test print made from a photographic negative

²proof *adj* **:** able to keep out something that could be harmful — usually used in compounds

proof·read *vb* **proof·read; proof·read·ing :** to read over and fix mistakes in (written or printed matter) — **proof·read·er** *n*

¹prop *n* **:** something that props or supports

²prop *vb* **propped; prop·ping 1 :** to keep from falling or slipping by providing a support under or against **2 :** to give help, encouragement, or support to

³prop *n* **:** PROPERTY 3

pro·pa·gan·da *n* **:** an organized spreading of certain ideas or the ideas spread in such a way

prop·a·gate *vb* **prop·a·gat·ed; prop·a·gat·ing 1 :** to have or cause to have offspring **2 :** to cause (as an idea or belief) to spread out and affect a greater number or wider area

prop·a·ga·tion *n* **:** an act or process of propagating

pro·pel *vb* **pro·pelled; pro·pel·ling :** to push or drive usually forward or onward

pro·pel·ler *n* **:** a device having a hub fitted with blades that is made to turn rapidly by an engine and that drives a ship, power boat, or airplane

prop·er *adj* **1 :** referring to one individual only **2 :** belonging naturally to a particular group or individual **:** CHARACTERISTIC **3 :** considered in its true or basic meaning **4 :** having or showing good manners **5 :** APPROPRIATE, SUITABLE

proper fraction *n* **:** a fraction in which the numerator is smaller than the denominator

prop·er·ly *adv* **1 :** in a fit or suitable way **2 :** according to fact

proper noun *n* **:** a noun that names a particular person, place, or thing

prop·er·ty *n, pl* **prop·er·ties 1 :** a special quality of a thing **2 :** something (as land or money) that is owned **3 :** something other than scenery or costumes that is used in a play or movie

proph·e·cy *n, pl* **proph·e·cies 1 :** the sayings of a prophet **2 :** something foretold **:** PREDICTION

proph·e·sy *vb* **proph·e·sied; proph·e·sy·ing 1 :** to speak or write as a prophet **2 :** FORETELL, PREDICT

proph·et *n* **1 :** one who declares publicly a message that one believes has come from God or a god **2 :** a person who predicts the future

pro·phet·ic *adj* **:** of or relating to a prophet or prophecy

¹pro·por·tion *n* **1 :** the size, number, or amount of one thing or group of things as compared to that of another thing or group of things **2 :** a balanced or pleasing arrangement **3 :** a statement of the equality of two ratios (as $\frac{4}{2} = \frac{10}{5}$) **4 :** a fair or just share **5 :** DIMENSION

²proportion *vb* **1 :** to adjust something to fit with something else **2 :** to make the parts of fit well with each other

pro·por·tion·al *adj* **:** being in proportion to something else — **pro·por·tion·al·ly** *adv*

pro·pos·al *n* **1 :** a stating or putting forward of something for consideration **2 :** something proposed **:** PLAN **3 :** an offer of marriage

pro·pose *vb* **pro·posed; pro·pos·ing 1 :** to

make a suggestion to be thought over and talked about : SUGGEST **2 :** to make plans : INTEND **3 :** to suggest for filling a place or office **4 :** to make an offer of marriage

prop·o·si·tion *n* **1 :** something proposed **2 :** a statement to be proved, explained, or discussed

pro·pri·e·tor *n* **:** a person who owns something : OWNER

pro·pri·ety *n, pl* **pro·pri·eties 1 :** the quality or state of being proper **2 :** correctness in manners or behavior **3** *proprieties pl* **:** the rules and customs of behavior followed by nice people

pro·pul·sion *n* **1 :** the act or process of propelling **2 :** something that propels

pros *pl of* PRO

prose *n* **1 :** the ordinary language that people use in speaking or writing **2 :** writing without the repeating rhythm that is used in verse

pros·e·cute *vb* **pros·e·cut·ed; pros·e·cut·ing 1 :** to follow up to the end : keep at **2 :** to carry on a legal action against an accused person to prove his or her guilt

pros·e·cu·tion *n* **1 :** the act of prosecuting especially a criminal case in court **2 :** the one bringing charges of crime against a person being tried **3 :** the state's lawyers in a criminal case

pros·e·cu·tor *n* **:** a person who prosecutes especially a criminal case as lawyer for the state

[1]**pros·pect** *n* **1 :** a wide view **2 :** an imagining of something to come **3 :** something that is waited for or expected : POSSIBILITY **4 :** a possible buyer or customer **5 :** a likely candidate

[2]**prospect** *vb* **:** to explore especially for mineral deposits

pro·spec·tive *adj* **1 :** likely to come about **2 :** likely to become — **pro·spec·tive·ly** *adv*

pros·pec·tor *n* **:** a person who explores a region in search of valuable minerals (as metals or oil)

pros·per *vb* **1 :** to succeed or make money in something one is doing **2 :** [1]FLOURISH 1, THRIVE

pros·per·i·ty *n* **:** the state of being prosperous or successful

pros·per·ous *adj* **1 :** having or showing success or financial good fortune **2 :** strong and healthy in growth — **pros·per·ous·ly** *adv*

[1]**pros·trate** *adj* **1 :** stretched out with face on the ground **2 :** spread out parallel to the ground **3 :** lacking strength or energy

[2]**prostrate** *vb* **pros·trat·ed; pros·trat·ing 1 :** to throw or put into a prostrate position **2 :** to bring to a weak and powerless condition

pro·tect *vb* **:** to cover or shield from something that would destroy or injure : GUARD

pro·tec·tion *n* **1 :** the act of protecting : the state of being protected **2 :** a protecting person or thing

pro·tec·tive *adj* **:** giving or meant to give protection — **pro·tec·tive·ly** *adv* — **pro·tec·tive·ness** *n*

pro·tec·tor *n* **:** a person or thing that protects or is intended to protect

pro·tein *n* **:** a nutrient containing nitrogen that is found in all living plant or animal cells, is a necessary part of the diet, and is supplied especially by such foods as meat, milk, and eggs

[1]**pro·test** *n* **1 :** the act of protesting **2 :** a complaint or objection against an idea, an act, or a way of doing things

[2]**pro·test** *vb* **1 :** to declare positively : ASSERT **2 :** to complain strongly about

[1]**Prot·es·tant** *n* **:** a member of a Christian church other than the Eastern Orthodox Church and the Roman Catholic Church

[2]**Protestant** *adj* **:** of or relating to Protestants

pro·ton *n* **:** a very small particle that occurs in the nucleus of every atom and has a positive charge of electricity

pro·to·plasm *n* **:** the usually colorless and jellylike living part of cells

pro·to·zo·an *n* **:** any of a large group of mostly microscopic animals whose body is a single cell

pro·tract *vb* **:** to make longer : draw out in time or space

pro·trac·tor *n* **:** an instrument used for drawing and measuring angles

pro·trude *vb* **pro·trud·ed; pro·trud·ing :** to stick out or cause to stick out

proud *adj* **1 :** having or showing a feeling that one is better than others : HAUGHTY **2 :** having a feeling of pleasure or satisfaction : very pleased **3 :** having proper self-respect — **proud·ly** *adv*

prove *vb* **proved; proved** *or* **prov·en; prov·ing 1 :** to test by experiment or by a standard **2 :** to convince others of the truth of something by showing the facts **3 :** to test the answer to and check the way of solving an arithmetic problem

prov·erb *n* **:** a short well-known saying containing a wise thought : MAXIM, ADAGE

pro·ver·bi·al *adj* **:** of, relating to, or being a proverb — **pro·ver·bi·al·ly** *adv*

pro·vide *vb* **pro·vid·ed; pro·vid·ing 1 :** to look out for or take care of beforehand **2 :** to make as a condition **3 :** to give something that is needed

pro·vid·ed *conj* **:** IF 1

pro·vid·er *n* **:** one that provides something

prov·i·dence *n* **1** *often cap* **:** help or care from God or heaven **2** *cap* **:** God as the guide and protector of all human beings **3** : PRUDENCE, THRIFT

prov·ince *n* **1** : a part of a country having a government of its own (as one of the divisions of the Dominion of Canada) **2** **provinces** *pl* : the part or parts of a country far from the capital or chief city **3** : an area of activity or authority

pro·vin·cial *adj* **1** : of, relating to, or coming from a province **2** : lacking the social graces and sophistication of the city

¹pro·vi·sion *n* **1** : the act of providing **2** : something done beforehand **3** : a stock or store of food — usually used in pl. **4** : ¹CONDITION 1

²provision *vb* : to supply with provisions

prov·o·ca·tion *n* **1** : the act of provoking **2** : something that provokes

pro·voc·a·tive *adj* : serving or likely to cause a reaction (as interest, curiosity, or anger) — **pro·voc·a·tive·ly** *adv*

pro·voke *vb* **pro·voked; pro·vok·ing** **1** : to cause to become angry **2** : to bring about

pro·vok·ing *adj* : causing mild anger — **pro·vok·ing·ly** *adv*

prow *n* : the bow of a ship

prow·ess *n* **1** : great bravery especially in battle **2** : very great ability

prowl *vb* : to move about quietly and secretly like a wild animal hunting prey — **prowl·er** *n*

proxy *n, pl* **prox·ies** **1** : authority to act for another or a paper giving such authority **2** : a person with authority to act for another

prude *n* : a person who cares too much about proper speech and conduct — **prud·ish** *adj*

pru·dence *n* : skill and good sense in taking care of oneself or of one's doings

pru·dent *adj* **1** : clever and careful in action or judgment **2** : careful in trying to avoid mistakes — **pru·dent·ly** *adv*

¹prune *n* : a dried plum

²prune *vb* **pruned; prun·ing** **1** : to cut off dead or unwanted parts of a bush or tree **2** : to cut out useless or unwanted parts (as unnecessary words or phrases in a composition)

¹pry *vb* **pried; pry·ing** : to be nosy about something

²pry *vb* **pried; pry·ing** **1** : to raise or open or try to do so with a lever **2** : to get at with great difficulty

pry·ing *adj* : rudely nosy

psalm *n* **1** : a sacred song or poem **2** *cap* : one of the hymns that make up the Old Testament Book of Psalms

psy·chi·a·trist *n* : a specialist in psychiatry

psy·chi·a·try *n* : a branch of medicine dealing with problems of the mind, emotions, or behavior

psy·cho·log·i·cal *adj* **1** : of or relating to psychology **2** : directed toward or meant to influence the mind

psy·chol·o·gist *n* : a specialist in psychology

psy·chol·o·gy *n* : the science that studies facts about the mind and its activities especially in human beings

pu·ber·ty *n* : the age at or period during which a person becomes able to reproduce sexually

¹pub·lic *adj* **1** : of or relating to the people as a whole **2** : of, relating to, or working for a government or community **3** : open to all **4** : known to many people : not kept secret **5** : WELL-KNOWN, PROMINENT — **pub·lic·ly** *adv*

²public *n* **1** : the people as a whole **2** : a group of people having common interests

pub·li·ca·tion *n* **1** : the act or process of publishing **2** : a printed work (as a book or magazine) made for sale or distribution

pub·lic·i·ty *n* **1** : public interest and approval **2** : something (as favorable news) used to attract public interest and approval

pub·li·cize *vb* **pub·li·cized; pub·li·ciz·ing** : to give publicity to

public school *n* : a free school paid for by taxes and run by a local government

pub·lish *vb* **1** : to make widely known **2** : to bring printed works (as books) before the public usually for sale — **pub·lish·er** *n*

puck *n* : a rubber disk used in hockey

¹puck·er *vb* : to draw or cause to draw up into folds or wrinkles

²pucker *n* : a fold or wrinkle in a normally even surface

pud·ding *n* : a soft spongy or creamy dessert

pud·dle *n* : a very small pool (as of dirty or muddy water)

pudgy *adj* **pudg·i·er; pudg·i·est** : being short and plump : CHUBBY

pueb·lo *n, pl* **pueb·los** : an Indian village of Arizona or New Mexico made up of groups of stone or adobe houses with flat roofs

¹Puer·to Ri·can *adj* : of or relating to Puerto Rico or the Puerto Ricans

²Puerto Rican *n* : a person born or living in Puerto Rico

¹puff *vb* **1** : to blow in short gusts **2** : to breathe hard : PANT **3** : to send out small whiffs or clouds (as of smoke) **4** : to swell up or become swollen with or as if with air

²puff *n* **1** : a quick short sending or letting out of air, smoke, or steam **2** : a slight swelling **3** : a soft pad for putting powder on the skin

puf·fin *n* : a seabird related to the auks that has a short thick neck and a deep grooved bill marked with several colors

puffy *adj* **puff·i·er; puff·i·est** **1** : blowing in puffs 2 : BREATHLESS 1 3 : somewhat swollen 4 : like a puff : FLUFFY

pug *n* 1 : a small dog having a thick body, a large round head, a square snout, a curled tail, and usually short hair 2 : a nose turning up at the tip and usually short and thick

[1]**pull** *vb* 1 : to separate from a firm or a natural attachment 2 : to use force on so as to cause or tend to cause movement toward the force 3 : to stretch repeatedly 4 : [1]MOVE 1 5 : to draw apart : TEAR, REND

[2]**pull** *n* 1 : the act or an instance of pulling 2 : the effort put forth in moving 3 : a device for pulling something 4 : a force that pulls

pull–down *adj* : appearing on a computer screen below a selected item

pul·let *n* : a young hen

pul·ley *n, pl* **pulleys** : a wheel that has a grooved rim in which a belt, rope, or chain runs and that is used to change the direction of a pulling force and in combination to increase the force applied for lifting

pull·over *n* : a garment (as a sweater) that is put on by being pulled over the head

pull through *vb* : to survive a very difficult or dangerous period

pul·mo·nary *adj* : of or relating to the lungs

[1]**pulp** *n* 1 : the soft juicy part of a fruit or vegetable 2 : a mass of vegetable matter from which the moisture has been squeezed 3 : the soft sensitive tissue inside a tooth 4 : a material prepared usually from wood or rags and used in making paper

[2]**pulp** *vb* : to make into a pulp

pul·pit *n* 1 : a raised place in which a clergyman stands while preaching or conducting a religious service 2 : preachers in general

pulp·wood *n* : wood (as of aspen or spruce) from which wood pulp is made

pulpy *adj* **pulp·i·er; pulp·i·est** : like or made of pulp

pul·sate *vb* **pul·sat·ed; pul·sat·ing** : to have or show a pulse or beats

pul·sa·tion *n* : pulsating movement or action

pulse *n* 1 : a regular beating or throbbing (as of the arteries) 2 : one complete beat of a pulse or the number of these in a given period (as a minute)

pul·ver·ize *vb* **pul·ver·ized; pul·ver·iz·ing** : to beat or grind into a powder or dust

pu·ma *n* : COUGAR

pum·ice *n* : a very light porous volcanic glass that is used in powder form for smoothing and polishing

pum·mel *vb* **pum·meled** *or* **pum·melled; pum·mel·ing** *or* **pum·mel·ling** : to strike again and again

[1]**pump** *n* : a device for raising, moving, or compressing fluids

[2]**pump** *vb* 1 : to raise, move, or compress by using a pump 2 : to free (as from water or air) by the use of a pump 3 : to fill by using a pump 4 : to draw, force, or drive onward in the manner of a pump 5 : to question again and again to find out something — **pump·er** *n*

pum·per·nick·el *n* : a dark rye bread

pump·kin *n* : a large round orange or yellow fruit of a vine related to the squash vine that is widely used as food

[1]**pun** *n* : a form of joking in which a person uses a word in two senses

[2]**pun** *vb* **punned; pun·ning** : to make a pun

[1]**punch** *vb* 1 : to care for (range cattle) 2 : to strike with the fist 3 : to press or strike by or as if by punching 4 : to pierce or stamp with a punch

[2]**punch** *n* : a blow with or as if with the fist

[3]**punch** *n* : a tool for piercing, stamping, or cutting

[4]**punch** *n* : a drink containing several things and often including wine or liquor

punc·tu·al *adj* : acting at the right time : not late

punc·tu·ate *vb* **punc·tu·at·ed; punc·tu·at·ing** : to mark or divide with punctuation marks

punc·tu·a·tion *n* 1 : the act of punctuating 2 : a system of using marks (**punctuation marks**) such as commas and periods to make clear the meaning of written matter

[1]**punc·ture** *n* 1 : an act of puncturing 2 : a hole or wound made by puncturing

[2]**puncture** *vb* **punc·tured; punc·tur·ing** 1 : to pierce with something pointed 2 : to make useless or destroy as if by a puncture

pun·gent *adj* : giving a sharp or biting sensation — **pun·gent·ly** *adv*

pun·ish *vb* 1 : to make suffer for a fault or crime 2 : to make someone suffer for (as a crime)

pun·ish·able *adj* : deserving to be punished

pun·ish·ment *n* 1 : the act of punishing : the state or fact of being punished 2 : the penalty for a fault or crime

[1]**punk** *n* : a petty gangster or hoodlum

[2]**punk** *adj* 1 : poor in quality 2 : UNWELL, SICK

[1]**punt** *vb* : to kick a ball dropped from the hands before it hits the ground — **punt·er** *n*

[2]**punt** *n* : an act or instance of punting a ball

pu·ny *adj* **pu·ni·er; pu·ni·est** : small and weak in size or power

pup *n* 1 : PUPPY 2 : one of the young of any of several animals (as a seal)

pu·pa *n, pl* **pu·pae** *or* **pupas** : an insect (as a bee, moth, or beetle) in an intermediate inactive stage of its growth in which it is enclosed in a cocoon or case

pu·pal *adj* : of, relating to, or being a pupa

[1]**pu·pil** *n* **:** a child in school or under the care of a teacher

[2]**pupil** *n* **:** the opening in the iris through which light enters the eye

pup·pet *n* **1 :** a doll moved by hand or by strings or wires **2 :** one (as a person or government) whose acts are controlled by another

pup·py *n, pl* **puppies :** a young dog

[1]**pur·chase** *vb* **pur·chased; pur·chas·ing :** to get by paying money

[2]**purchase** *n* **1 :** an act of purchasing **2 :** something purchased **3 :** a firm hold or grasp or a safe place to stand

pure *adj* **pur·er; pur·est 1 :** not mixed with anything else **:** free from everything that might injure or lower the quality **2 :** free from sin **:** INNOCENT, CHASTE **3 :** nothing other than **:** ABSOLUTE — **pure·ly** *adv* — **pure·ness** *n*

pure·bred *adj* **:** bred from ancestors of a single breed for many generations

[1]**purge** *vb* **purged; purg·ing 1 :** to make clean **2 :** to have or cause frequent bowel movements **3 :** to get rid of

[2]**purge** *n* **1 :** an act or instance of purging **2 :** the removal of members thought to be treacherous or disloyal

pu·ri·fi·ca·tion *n* **:** an act or instance of purifying or of being purified

pu·ri·fy *vb* **pu·ri·fied; pu·ri·fy·ing :** to make pure **:** free from impurities

pu·ri·tan *n* **1** *cap* **:** a member of a sixteenth and seventeenth century Protestant group in England and New England opposing formal customs of the Church of England **2 :** a person who practices or preaches or follows a stricter moral code than most people

pu·ri·ty *n* **1 :** freedom from dirt or impurities **2 :** freedom from sin or guilt

pur·ple *n* **:** a color between red and blue

pur·plish *adj* **:** somewhat purple

[1]**pur·pose** *n* **:** something set up as a goal to be achieved **:** INTENTION, AIM — **on purpose :** PURPOSELY

[2]**purpose** *vb* **pur·posed; pur·pos·ing :** to have as one's intention **:** INTEND

pur·pose·ful *adj* **:** having a clear purpose or aim — **pur·pose·ful·ly** *adv* — **pur·pose·ful·ness** *n*

pur·pose·ly *adv* **:** with a clear or known purpose

purr *vb* **:** to make the low murmuring sound of a contented cat or a similar sound

[1]**purse** *n* **1 :** a bag or pouch for money **2 :** HANDBAG **3 :** the contents of a purse **:** MONEY 1 **4 :** a sum of money offered as a prize or collected as a present

[2]**purse** *vb* **pursed; purs·ing :** to draw into folds

pur·sue *vb* **pur·sued; pur·su·ing 1 :** to follow after in order to catch or destroy **:** CHASE **2 :** to follow with an end in view **3 :** to go on with **:** FOLLOW — **pur·su·er** *n*

pur·suit *n* **1 :** the act of pursuing **2 :** ACTIVITY 2, OCCUPATION

pus *n* **:** thick yellowish matter (as in an abscess or a boil)

[1]**push** *vb* **1 :** to press against with force so as to drive or move away **2 :** to force forward, downward, or outward **3 :** to go or make go ahead

[2]**push** *n* **1 :** a sudden thrust **:** SHOVE **2 :** a steady applying of force in a direction away from the body from which it comes

push button *n* **:** a small button or knob that when pushed operates something usually by closing an electric circuit

push·cart *n* **:** a cart pushed by hand

push·over *n* **1 :** an opponent that is easy to defeat **2 :** something easily done

pushy *adj* **push·i·er; push·i·est :** too aggressive **:** FORWARD

puss *n* **:** CAT 1

pussy *n, pl* **puss·ies :** CAT 1

pussy willow *n* **:** a willow with large silky catkins

put *vb* **put; put·ting 1 :** to place in or move into a particular position **2 :** to bring into a specified state or condition **3 :** to cause to stand for or suffer something **4 :** to give expression to **5 :** to give up to or urge to an activity **6 :** to think something to have **:** ATTRIBUTE **7 :** to begin a voyage — **put forward :** PROPOSE 1

put away *vb* **1 :** to give up **:** DISCARD **2 :** to take in food and drink

put by *vb* **:** to lay aside **:** SAVE

put down *vb* **1 :** to bring to an end by force **2 :** to consider to belong to a particular class or to be due to a particular cause

put in *vb* **1 :** to ask for **2 :** to spend time in a place or activity

put off *vb* **:** DEFER

put on *vb* **1 :** to dress oneself in **2 :** PRETEND 2, SHAM **3 :** [1]PRODUCE 4

put down *vb* **1 :** to bring to an end by force **2 :** to consider to belong to a particular class or to be due to a particular cause

put in *vb* **1 :** to ask for **2 :** to spend time in a place or activity

put off *vb* **:** DEFER

put on *vb* **1 :** to dress oneself in **2 :** PRETEND 2, SHAM **3 :** [1]PRODUCE 4

put·out *n* **:** the causing of a batter or runner to be out in baseball

put out *vb* **1 :** to make use of **2 :** EXTINGUISH

1 **3 :** [1]MAKE 2 **4 :** IRRITATE 1, ANNOY **5 :** to cause to be out (as in baseball)

pu·trid *adj* **1 :** ROTTEN 1 **2 :** coming from or suggesting something rotten

put·ter *vb* **:** to act or work without much purpose

put through *vb* **:** to conclude with success

[1]**put·ty** *n, pl* **putties :** a soft cement (as for holding glass in a window frame)

[2]**putty** *vb* **put·tied; put·ty·ing :** to cement or seal up with putty

put up *vb* **1 :** to make (as food) ready or safe for later use **2 :** NOMINATE **3 :** to give or get shelter and often food **4 :** [1]BUILD 1 **5 :** to make by action or effort — **put up to :** to urge or cause to do something wrong or unexpected — **put up with :** to stand for **:** TOLERATE

[1]**puz·zle** *vb* **puz·zled; puz·zling 1 :** CONFUSE 1, PERPLEX **2 :** to solve by thought or by clever guessing

[2]**puzzle** *n* **1 :** something that puzzles **:** MYSTERY **2 :** a question, problem, or device intended to test one's skill or cleverness

[1]**pyg·my** *also* **pig·my** *n, pl* **pygmies** *also* **pigmies :** a person or thing very small for its kind **:** DWARF

[2]**pygmy** *adj* **:** very small

[1]**pyr·a·mid** *n* **1 :** a large structure built especially in ancient Egypt that usually has a square base and four triangular sides meeting at a point and that contains tombs **2 :** something that has the shape of a pyramid **3 :** a solid with a polygon for its base and three or more triangles for its sides which meet to form the top

[2]**pyramid** *vb* **:** to build up in the form of a pyramid

pyre *n* **:** a heap of wood for burning a dead body

py·thon *n* **:** any of various large nonpoisonous snakes of Africa, Asia, and Australia that squeeze and suffocate their prey

Q

q *n, pl* **q's** *or* **qs** *often cap* **:** the seventeenth letter of the English alphabet

[1]**quack** *vb* **:** to make the cry of a duck

[2]**quack** *n* **:** a cry made by or as if by quacking

[3]**quack** *n* **:** an ignorant person who pretends to have medical knowledge and skill

[4]**quack** *adj* **1 :** of, relating to, or like that of a quack **2 :** pretending to cure disease

quadri- *or* **quadr-** *or* **quadru-** *prefix* **1 :** four **2 :** fourth

quad·ri·lat·er·al *n* **:** a figure of four sides and four angles

quad·ru·ped *n* **:** an animal having four feet

qua·dru·plet *n* **1 :** one of four offspring born at one birth **2 :** a combination of four of a kind

quag·mire *n* **1 :** soft spongy wet ground that shakes or gives way under the foot **2:** a difficult situation from which it is hard to escape

[1]**quail** *n, pl* **quail** *or* **quails :** any of various mostly small plump game birds (as the bobwhite) that are related to the chicken

[2]**quail** *vb* **:** to lose courage **:** shrink in fear

quaint *adj* **1 :** being or looking unusual or different **2 :** pleasingly old-fashioned or unfamiliar — **quaint·ly** *adv* — **quaint·ness** *n*

[1]**quake** *vb* **quaked; quak·ing 1 :** to shake usually from shock or lack of stability **2 :** to tremble or shudder usually from cold or fear

[2]**quake** *n* **:** an instance (as an earthquake) of shaking or trembling

qual·i·fi·ca·tion *n* **1 :** the act or an instance of qualifying **2 :** the state of being qualified **3 :** a special skill, knowledge, or ability that fits a person for a particular work or position **4 :** LIMITATION 1

qual·i·fy *vb* **qual·i·fied; qual·i·fy·ing 1 :** to narrow down or make less general in meaning **2 :** to make less harsh or strict **:** SOFTEN **3 :** to fit by training, skill, or ability for a special purpose **4 :** to show the skill or ability needed to be on a team or take part in a contest

qual·i·ty *n, pl* **qual·i·ties 1 :** basic and individual nature **2 :** how good or bad something is **3 :** high social rank **4 :** what sets a person or thing apart **:** CHARACTERISTIC

qualm *n* **1 :** a sudden attack of illness, faintness, or nausea **2 :** a sudden fear **3 :** a feeling of doubt or uncertainty that one's behavior is honest or right — **qualm·ish** *adj*

quan·da·ry *n, pl* **quan·da·ries :** a state of doubt or puzzled confusion

quan·ti·ty *n, pl* **quan·ti·ties 1 :** [2]AMOUNT, NUMBER **2 :** a large number or amount

[1]**quar·an·tine** *n* **1 :** a halting or forbidding of the moving of people or things out of a certain area to prevent the spread of disease or pests **2 :** a period during which a person with a contagious disease is under quarantine **3 :** a place (as a hospital) where persons are kept in quarantine

[2]**quarantine** *vb* **quar·an·tined; quar·an·tin·ing :** to put or hold in quarantine

[1]**quar·rel** *n* **1 :** a cause of disagreement or complaint **2 :** an angry difference of opinion

[2]**quarrel** *vb* **quar·reled** *or* **quar·relled; quar-**

rel·ing *or* **quar·rel·ling 1 :** to find fault **2 :** to argue actively **:** SQUABBLE

quar·rel·some *adj* **:** usually ready to quarrel

[1]**quar·ry** *n, pl* **quar·ries :** an animal or bird hunted as game or prey

[2]**quarry** *n, pl* **quar·ries :** an open pit usually for obtaining building stone, slate, or limestone

[3]**quarry** *vb* **quar·ried; quar·ry·ing 1 :** to dig or take from or as if from a quarry **2 :** to make a quarry in — **quar·ri·er** *n*

quart *n* **:** a measure of capacity that equals two pints (about .95 liter)

[1]**quar·ter** *n* **1 :** one of four equal parts into which something can be divided **2 :** a United States coin worth twenty-five cents **3 :** someone or something (as a place, direction, or group) not clearly identified **4 :** a particular division or district of a city **5 quarters** *pl* **:** a dwelling place **6 :** MERCY 1

[2]**quarter** *vb* **1 :** to divide into four usually equal parts **2 :** to provide with lodgings or shelter

[3]**quarter** *adj* **:** consisting of or equal to a quarter

quar·ter·deck *n* **:** the part of the upper deck that is located toward the rear of a ship

quarter horse *n* **:** a stocky muscular saddle horse capable of high speed over short distances

[1]**quar·ter·ly** *adv* **:** four times a year

[2]**quarterly** *adj* **:** coming or happening every three months

[3]**quarterly** *n, pl* **quar·ter·lies :** a magazine published four times a year

quar·ter·mas·ter *n* **:** an army officer who provides clothing and supplies for troops

quar·tet *also* **quar·tette** *n* **:** a group or set of four

quartz *n* **:** a common mineral often found in the form of colorless transparent crystals but sometimes (as in amethysts, agates, and jaspers) brightly colored

qua·ver *vb* **1 :** [1]TREMBLE 1, SHAKE **2 :** to sound in shaky tones

quay *n* **:** a paved bank or a solid artificial landing for loading and unloading ships

quea·sy *adj* **quea·si·er; quea·si·est 1 :** somewhat nauseated **2 :** full of doubt

queen *n* **1 :** the wife or widow of a king **2 :** a woman who rules a kingdom in her own right **3 :** a woman of high rank, power, or attractiveness **4 :** the most powerful piece in the game of chess **5 :** a playing card bearing the figure of a queen **6 :** a fully developed adult female of social bees, ants, or termites — **queen·ly** *adj*

queer *adj* **:** oddly unlike the usual or normal — **queer·ly** *adv*

quell *vb* **1 :** to put down by force **2 :** [4]QUIET 1, CALM

quench *vb* **1 :** to put out (as a fire) **2 :** to end by satisfying

[1]**que·ry** *n, pl* **queries 1 :** [1]QUESTION 1 **2 :** a question in the mind **:** DOUBT

[2]**query** *vb* **que·ried; que·ry·ing 1 :** to put as a question **2 :** to ask questions about especially in order to clear up a doubt **3 :** to ask questions of especially to obtain official or expert information

[1]**quest** *n* **:** an act or instance of seeking **:** SEARCH

[2]**quest** *vb* **:** to search for

[1]**ques·tion** *n* **1 :** something asked **2 :** a topic discussed or argued about **3 :** a suggestion to be voted on **4 :** an act or instance of asking **5 :** OBJECTION 1, DISPUTE

[2]**question** *vb* **1 :** to ask questions of or about **2 :** to doubt the correctness of

ques·tion·able *adj* **1 :** not certain or exact **:** DOUBTFUL **2 :** not believed to be true, sound, or proper

question mark *n* **:** a punctuation mark ? used chiefly at the end of a sentence to indicate a direct question

ques·tion·naire *n* **:** a set of questions to be asked of a number of persons to collect facts about knowledge or opinions

[1]**queue** *n* **1 :** PIGTAIL **2 :** a waiting line

[2]**queue** *vb* **queued; queu·ing** *or* **queue·ing :** to form or line up in a queue

quib·ble *vb* **quib·bled; quib·bling 1 :** to talk about unimportant things rather than the main point **2 :** to find fault especially over unimportant points — **quib·bler** *n*

[1]**quick** *adj* **1 :** very swift **:** SPEEDY **2 :** mentally alert **3 :** easily stirred up — **quick·ly** *adv* — **quick·ness** *n*

[2]**quick** *n* **1 :** a very tender area of flesh (as under a fingernail) **2 :** one's innermost feelings

[3]**quick** *adv* **:** in a quick manner **:** FAST

quick·en *vb* **1 :** REVIVE 1 **2 :** AROUSE 2 **3 :** to make or become quicker **:** HASTEN **4 :** to begin or show active growth

quick·sand *n* **:** a deep mass of loose sand mixed with water into which heavy objects sink

quick·sil·ver *n* **:** MERCURY 1

quick–tem·pered *adj* **:** easily made angry

quick–wit·ted *adj* **:** mentally alert

[1]**qui·et** *n* **:** the quality or state of being quiet

[2]**quiet** *adj* **1 :** marked by little or no motion or activity **:** CALM **2 :** GENTLE 2, MILD **3 :** not disturbed **:** PEACEFUL **4 :** free from noise or uproar **:** STILL **5 :** not showy (as in color or style) **6 :** SECLUDED — **qui·et·ly** *adv* — **qui·et·ness** *n*

[3]**quiet** *adv* **:** in a quiet manner **:** QUIETLY

[4]**quiet** *vb* **1 :** to cause to be quiet **:** CALM **2 :** to become quiet
qui·etude *n* **:** the state of being quiet **:** REST
quill *n* **1 :** a large stiff feather **2 :** the hollow tubelike part of a feather **3 :** a spine of a hedgehog or porcupine **4 :** a pen made from a feather
[1]**quilt** *n* **:** a bed cover made of two pieces of cloth with a filling of wool, cotton, or down held together by patterned stitching
[2]**quilt** *vb* **:** to stitch or sew together as in making a quilt
quince *n* **:** a hard yellow fruit that grows on a shrubby tree related to the apple and is used especially in preserves
qui·nine *n* **:** a bitter drug obtained from cinchona bark and used to treat malaria
quin·tet *n* **:** a group or set of five
quin·tu·plet *n* **1 :** a combination of five of a kind **2 :** one of five offspring born at one birth
quirk *n* **:** a sudden turn, twist, or curve
quit *vb* **quit; quit·ting :** to finish doing, using, dealing with, working on, or handling **:** LEAVE
quite *adv* **1 :** beyond question or doubt **:** COMPLETELY **2 :** more or less **:** RATHER
quit·ter *n* **:** a person who gives up too easily
[1]**quiv·er** *n* **:** a case for carrying arrows
[2]**quiver** *vb* **:** to move with a slight trembling motion
[3]**quiver** *n* **:** the act or action of quivering
[1]**quiz** *n, pl* **quiz·zes :** a short oral or written test
[2]**quiz** *vb* **quizzed; quiz·zing :** to ask a lot of questions of
quoit *n* **:** a ring (as of rope) tossed at a peg in a game (**quoits**)
quo·rum *n* **:** the number of members of a group needed at a meeting in order for business to be legally carried on
quo·ta *n* **:** a share assigned to each member of a group
quo·ta·tion *n* **1 :** material (as a passage from a book) that is quoted **2 :** the act or process of quoting
quotation mark *n* **:** one of a pair of punctuation marks " " or ' ' used chiefly to indicate the beginning and end of a direct quotation
quote *vb* **quot·ed; quot·ing :** to repeat (someone else's words) exactly
quo·tient *n* **:** the number obtained by dividing one number by another

R

r *n, pl* **r's** *or* **rs** *often cap* **:** the eighteenth letter of the English alphabet
rab·bi *n, pl* **rab·bis 1 :** [1]MASTER 1, TEACHER — used as a term of address for Jewish religious leaders **2 :** a professionally trained leader of a Jewish congregation
rab·bit *n* **:** a long-eared short-tailed gnawing mammal that burrows
rab·ble *n* **1 :** a crowd that is noisy and hard to control **:** MOB **2 :** a group of people looked down upon as ignorant and hard to handle
ra·bid *adj* **1 :** very angry **:** FURIOUS **2 :** going to extreme lengths (as in interest or opinion) **3 :** affected with rabies — **ra·bid·ly** *adv* — **ra·bid·ness** *n*
ra·bies *n* **:** a deadly disease of the nervous system caused by a virus that is usually passed on through the bite of an infected animal
rac·coon *n* **:** a small North American animal that is mostly gray with a black mask, has a bushy ringed tail, is active mostly at night, and eats small animals, fruits, eggs, and insects
[1]**race** *n* **1 :** a strong or rapid current of water **2 :** a contest of speed **3 :** a contest involving progress toward a goal
[2]**race** *vb* **raced; rac·ing 1 :** to take part in a race **2 :** to go, move, or drive at top speed **3 :** to cause an engine of a motor vehicle in neutral to run fast
[3]**race** *n* **1 :** a group of individuals with the same ancestors **2 :** a category of humankind that shares distinctive physical traits **3:** a major group of living things
race·course *n* **:** a place for racing
race·horse *n* **:** a horse bred or kept for racing
rac·er *n* **1 :** one that races or is used for racing **2 :** any of several long slender active snakes (as a common American blacksnake)
race·track *n* **:** a usually oval course on which races are run
ra·cial *adj* **:** of, relating to, or based on race — **ra·cial·ly** *adv*
rac·ism *n* **1 :** belief that certain races of people are by birth and nature superior to others **2:** discrimination or hatred based on race
rac·ist *adj* **:** based on or showing racism — **racist** *n*
[1]**rack** *n* **1 :** an instrument of torture for stretching the body **2 :** a frame or stand for storing or displaying things
[2]**rack** *vb* **1 :** to cause to suffer torture, pain, or sorrow **2 :** to stretch or strain violently
[1]**rack·et** *n* **:** a light bat consisting of a handle and a frame with a netting stretched tight across it

[2]**racket** *n* **1 :** a loud confused noise **2 :** a dishonest scheme for obtaining money
rack·e·teer *n* **:** a person who gets money or advantages by using force or threats
racy *adj* **rac·i·er; rac·i·est :** full of energy or keen enjoyment
ra·dar *n* **:** a radio device for detecting the position of things in the distance and the direction of moving objects (as distant airplanes or ships)
ra·di·ance *n* **:** the quality or state of being radiant **:** SPLENDOR
ra·di·ant *adj* **1 :** giving out or reflecting rays of light **2 :** glowing with love, confidence, or joy **3 :** transmitted by radiation
radiant energy *n* **:** energy sent out in the form of electromagnetic waves
ra·di·ate *vb* **ra·di·at·ed; ra·di·at·ing 1 :** to send out rays **:** SHINE **2 :** to come forth in the form of rays **3 :** to spread around from or as if from a center
ra·di·a·tion *n* **1 :** the process of radiating and especially of giving off radiant energy in the form of waves or particles **2 :** something that is radiated
ra·di·a·tor *n* **:** a device to heat air (as in a room) or to cool an object (as an automobile engine)
[1]**rad·i·cal** *adj* **1 :** departing sharply from the usual or ordinary **:** EXTREME **2 :** of or relating to radicals in politics — **rad·i·cal·ly** *adv*
[2]**radical** *n* **:** a person who favors rapid and sweeping changes especially in laws and government
radii *pl of* RADIUS
[1]**ra·dio** *adj* **1 :** of or relating to radiant energy **2 :** of, relating to, or used in radio
[2]**radio** *n, pl* **ra·di·os 1 :** the sending or receiving of signals by means of electromagnetic waves without a connecting wire **2 :** a radio receiving set **3 :** a radio message **4 :** the radio broadcasting industry
[3]**radio** *vb* **:** to communicate or send a message to by radio
ra·dio·ac·tive *adj* **:** of, caused by, or exhibiting radioactivity
ra·dio·ac·tiv·i·ty *n* **:** the giving off of rays of energy or particles by the breaking apart of atoms of certain elements (as uranium)
radio wave *n* **:** an electromagnetic wave used in radio, television, or radar communication
rad·ish *n* **:** the fleshy edible root of a plant related to the mustards
ra·di·um *n* **:** a strongly radioactive element found in very small quantities in various minerals (as pitchblende) and used in the treatment of cancer
ra·di·us *n, pl* **ra·dii 1 :** the bone on the thumb side of the human forearm or a corresponding bone in lower forms **2 :** a straight line extending from the center of a circle to the circumference or from the center of a sphere to the surface **3 :** a nearly circular area defined by a radius
raf·fle *n* **:** the sale of chances for a prize whose winner is the one whose ticket is picked at a drawing
[1]**raft** *n* **:** a flat structure (as a group of logs fastened together) for support or transportation on water
[2]**raft** *n* **:** a large amount or number
raf·ter *n* **:** one of the usually sloping timbers that support a roof
rag *n* **1 :** a waste or worn piece of cloth **2 rags** *pl* **:** shabby or very worn clothing
rag·a·muf·fin *n* **:** a poorly clothed and often dirty child
[1]**rage** *n* **1 :** very strong and uncontrolled anger **:** FURY **2 :** violent action (as of wind or sea) **3 :** FAD
[2]**rage** *vb* **raged; rag·ing 1 :** to be in a rage **2 :** to continue out of control
rag·ged *adj* **1 :** having a rough or uneven edge or outline **2 :** very worn **:** TATTERED **3 :** wearing tattered clothes **4 :** done in an uneven way — **rag·ged·ly** *adv* — **rag·ged·ness** *n*
rag·gedy *adj* **:** RAGGED 2, 3
rag·tag *adj* **:** RAGGED 3
rag·time *n* **:** jazz music that has a lively melody and a steady rhythm like a march
rag·weed *n* **:** a common coarse weed with pollen that irritates the eyes and noses of some persons
[1]**raid** *n* **:** a sudden attack or invasion
[2]**raid** *vb* **:** to make a raid on — **raid·er** *n*
[1]**rail** *n* **1 :** a bar extending from one support to another and serving as a guard or barrier **2 :** a bar of steel forming a track for wheeled vehicles **3 :** RAILROAD
[2]**rail** *vb* **:** to provide with a railing
[3]**rail** *n* **:** any of a family of wading birds related to the cranes and hunted as game birds
[4]**rail** *vb* **:** to scold or complain in harsh or bitter language
rail·ing *n* **1 :** a barrier (as a fence) made up of rails and their supports **2 :** material for making rails
rail·lery *n, pl* **rail·ler·ies :** an act or instance of making fun of someone in a good-natured way
[1]**rail·road** *n* **1 :** a permanent road that has parallel steel rails that make a track for cars **2 :** a railroad together with the lands, buildings, locomotives, cars, and other equipment that belong to it
[2]**railroad** *vb* **:** to work on a railroad
rail·way *n* **:** [1]RAILROAD 1
rai·ment *n* **:** CLOTHING 1
[1]**rain** *n* **1 :** water falling in drops from the

clouds **2 :** a fall of rain **3 :** rainy weather **4 :** a heavy fall of objects

²rain *vb* **1 :** to fall as water in drops from the clouds **2 :** to send down rain **3 :** to fall like rain **4 :** to give in large amounts — **rain cats and dogs :** to rain very hard

rain·bow *n* **:** an arc of colors that appears in the sky opposite the sun and is caused by the sun shining through rain, mist, or spray

rain·coat *n* **:** a coat of waterproof or water-resistant material

rain·drop *n* **:** a drop of rain

rain·fall *n* **1 :** ¹RAIN 2 **2 :** amount of precipitation

rain forest *n* **:** a woodland with a high annual rainfall and very tall trees and that is often found in tropical regions

rain·proof *adj* **:** not letting in rain

rain·storm *n* **:** a storm of or with rain

rain·wa·ter *n* **:** water falling or fallen as rain

rainy *adj* **rain·i·er; rain·i·est :** having much rain

¹raise *vb* **raised; rais·ing 1 :** to cause to rise **:** LIFT **2 :** to give life to **:** AROUSE **3 :** to set upright by lifting or building **4 :** PROMOTE 1, ELEVATE **5 :** ²END **6 :** COLLECT 2 **7 :** to look after the growth and development of **:** GROW **8 :** to bring up a child **:** REAR **9 :** to give rise to **:** PROVOKE **10 :** to bring to notice **11 :** ¹INCREASE **12 :** to make light and airy **13 :** to cause to form on the skin — **rais·er** *n*

²raise *n* **:** an increase in amount (as of pay)

rai·sin *n* **:** a sweet grape dried for food

ra·ja *or* **ra·jah** *n* **:** an Indian prince

¹rake *n* **:** a garden tool with a long handle and a bar with teeth or prongs at the end

²rake *vb* **raked; rak·ing 1 :** to gather, loosen, or smooth with a rake **2 :** to search through **:** RANSACK **3 :** to sweep the length of with gunfire

³rake *n* **:** a person with bad morals and conduct

¹ral·ly *vb* **ral·lied; ral·ly·ing 1 :** to bring or come together for a common purpose **2 :** to bring back to order **3 :** to rouse from low spirits or weakness **4 :** ¹REBOUND 2

²rally *n, pl* **rallies 1 :** the act of rallying **2 :** a big meeting held to arouse enthusiasm

¹ram *n* **1 :** a male sheep **2 :** BATTERING RAM

²ram *vb* **rammed; ram·ming 1 :** to strike or strike against with violence **2 :** to force in, down, or together by driving or pressing **3 :** ²FORCE 2

RAM *n* **:** RANDOM-ACCESS MEMORY

Ram·a·dan *n* **:** the ninth month of the Islamic calendar observed as sacred with fasting practiced daily from dawn to sunset

¹ram·ble *vb* **ram·bled; ram·bling 1 :** to go aimlessly from place to place **:** WANDER **2 :** to talk or write without a clear purpose or point **3 :** to grow or extend irregularly

²ramble *n* **:** a long stroll with no particular destination

ram·bler *n* **:** a hardy climbing rose with large clusters of small flowers

ram·bunc·tious *adj* **:** UNRULY — **ram·bunc·tious·ly** *adv* — **ram·bunc·tious·ness** *n*

ram·i·fi·ca·tion *n* **1 :** a branching out **2 :** one thing that comes from another like a branch

ram·i·fy *vb* **ram·i·fied; ram·i·fy·ing :** to spread out or split up into branches or divisions

ramp *n* **:** a sloping passage or roadway connecting different levels

ram·page *n* **:** a course of violent or reckless action or behavior

ram·pant *adj* **:** not checked in growth or spread — **ram·pant·ly** *adv*

ram·part *n* **:** a broad bank or wall raised as a protective barrier

ram·rod *n* **:** a rod for ramming the charge down the barrel in a firearm that is loaded through the muzzle

ram·shack·le *adj* **:** ready to fall down

ran *past of* RUN

¹ranch *n* **1 :** a place for the raising of livestock (as cattle) on range **2 :** a farm devoted to a special crop

²ranch *vb* **:** to live or work on a ranch — **ranch·er** *n*

ran·cid *adj* **:** having the strong disagreeable smell or taste of stale oil or fat — **ran·cid·ness** *n*

ran·cor *n* **:** deep hatred

ran·cor·ous *adj* **:** showing rancor — **ran·cor·ous·ly** *adv*

ran·dom *adj* **:** lacking a clear plan, purpose, or pattern — **ran·dom·ly** *adv* — **ran·dom·ness** *n*

ran·dom–ac·cess *adj* **:** permitting access to stored data in any order the user desires

random–access memory *n* **:** a computer memory that provides the main storage available to the user for programs and data

rang *past of* RING

¹range *n* **1 :** a series of things in a line **2 :** a cooking stove **3 :** open land over which livestock may roam and feed **4 :** the distance a gun will shoot **5 :** a place where shooting is practiced **6 :** the distance or amount included or gone over **:** SCOPE **7 :** a variety of choices within a scale

²range *vb* **ranged; rang·ing 1 :** to set in a row or in proper order **2 :** to set in place among others of the same kind **3 :** to roam over or through **4 :** to come within an upper and a lower limit

rang·er *n* **1 :** FOREST RANGER **2 :** a member of a body of troops who range over a region

3 : a soldier specially trained in close-range fighting and in raiding tactics

rangy *adj* **rang·i·er; rang·i·est :** tall and slender in body build — **rang·i·ness** *n*

[1]**rank** *adj* **1 :** strong and active in growth **2 :** [1]EXTREME 1 **3 :** having an unpleasant smell — **rank·ly** *adv* — **rank·ness** *n*

[2]**rank** *n* **1 :** [3]ROW 1, SERIES **2 :** a line of soldiers standing side by side **3 ranks** *pl* **:** the body of enlisted persons in an army **4 :** position within a group **5 :** high social position **6 :** official grade or position

[3]**rank** *vb* **1 :** to arrange in lines or in a formation **2 :** to arrange in a classification **3 :** to take or have a certain position in a group

ran·kle *vb* **ran·kled; ran·kling :** to cause anger, irritation, or bitterness

ran·sack *vb* **1 :** to search thoroughly **2 :** to search through in order to rob

[1]**ran·som** *n* **1 :** something paid or demanded for the freedom of a captured person **2 :** the act of ransoming

[2]**ransom** *vb* **:** to free from captivity or punishment by paying a price — **ran·som·er** *n*

rant *vb* **:** to talk loudly and wildly — **rant·er** *n*

[1]**rap** *n* **:** a sharp blow or knock

[2]**rap** *vb* **rapped; rap·ping :** to give a quick sharp blow **:** [1]KNOCK 1

[3]**rap** *vb* **rapped; rap·ping 1 :** to talk freely and informally **2 :** to perform rap music

[4]**rap** *n* **1 :** an informal talk **:** CHAT **2 :** a rhythmic chanting often in unison of rhymed verses to a musical accompaniment

ra·pa·cious *adj* **1 :** very greedy **2 :** PREDATORY — **ra·pa·cious·ly** *adv* — **ra·pa·cious·ness** *n*

[1]**rape** *n* **:** a plant related to the mustards that is grown for animals to graze on and for its seeds used as birdseed and as a source of oil

[2]**rape** *vb* **raped; rap·ing :** to have sexual intercourse with by force

[3]**rape** *n* **:** an act of raping

rap·id *adj* **:** very fast — **rap·id·ly** *adv*

ra·pid·i·ty *n* **:** the quality or state of being rapid

rap·ids *n pl* **:** a part of a river where the current flows very fast usually over rocks

ra·pi·er *n* **:** a straight sword with a narrow blade having two sharp edges

rap·port : friendly relationship **:** ACCORD

rapt *adj* **:** showing complete delight or interest

rap·ture *n* **:** a strong feeling of joy, delight, or love

[1]**rare** *adj* **rar·er; rar·est 1 :** not thick or compact **:** THIN **2 :** very fine **:** EXCELLENT **3 :** very uncommon

[2]**rare** *adj* **rar·er; rar·est :** cooked so that the inside is still red

rar·e·fy *vb* **rar·e·fied; rar·e·fy·ing :** to make or become less dense or solid

rare·ly *adv* **:** not often **:** SELDOM

rar·i·ty *n, pl* **rar·i·ties 1 :** the quality, state, or fact of being rare **2 :** something that is uncommon

ras·cal *n* **1 :** a mean or dishonest person **2 :** a mischievous person

[1]**rash** *adj* **:** too hasty in decision, action, or speech — **rash·ly** *adv* — **rash·ness** *n*

[2]**rash** *n* **:** a breaking out of the skin with red spots (as in measles)

[1]**rasp** *vb* **1 :** to rub with or as if with a rough file **2 :** IRRITATE 1 **3 :** to make a harsh sound

[2]**rasp** *n* **1 :** a coarse file with cutting points instead of lines **2 :** a rasping sound or sensation

rasp·ber·ry *n, pl* **rasp·ber·ries :** a sweet edible red, black, or purple berry

[1]**rat** *n* **1 :** a gnawing animal with brown, black, white, or grayish fur that looks like but is larger than the mouse **2 :** a person who betrays friends

[2]**rat** *vb* **rat·ted; rat·ting 1 :** to betray one's friends **2 :** to hunt or catch rats

[1]**rate** *n* **1 :** a price or charge set according to a scale or standard **2 :** amount of something measured in units of something else — **at any rate :** in any case

[2]**rate** *vb* **rat·ed; rat·ing 1 :** CONSIDER 3, REGARD **2 :** to have a rating **:** RANK **3 :** to have a right to **:** DESERVE

rath·er *adv* **1 :** more willingly **2 :** more correctly or truly **3 :** INSTEAD **4 :** [2]SOMEWHAT

rat·i·fi·ca·tion *n* **:** the act or process of ratifying

rat·i·fy *vb* **rat·i·fied; rat·i·fy·ing :** to give legal approval to (as by a vote)

rat·ing *n* **:** a position within a grading system

ra·tio *n, pl* **ra·tios :** the relationship in number or quantity between two or more things

[1]**ra·tion** *n* **1 :** a food allowance for one day **2 rations** *pl* **:** [1]PROVISION 3 **3 :** the amount one is allowed by authority

[2]**ration** *vb* **1 :** to control the amount one can use **2 :** to use sparingly

ra·tio·nal *adj* **1 :** having the ability to reason **2 :** relating to, based on, or showing reason — **ra·tio·nal·ly** *adv*

ra·tio·nale *n* **:** a basic explanation or reason for something

ra·tio·nal·ize *vb* **ra·tio·nal·ized; ra·tio·nal·iz·ing :** to find believable but untrue reasons for (one's conduct)

rat·ter *n* **:** a dog or cat that catches rats

[1]**rat·tle** *vb* **rat·tled; rat·tling 1 :** to make or cause to make a rapid series of short sharp sounds **2 :** to move with a clatter **3 :** to say or do in a brisk lively way **4 :** to disturb the calmness of **:** UPSET

[2]rattle *n* **1 :** a series of short sharp sounds **2 :** a device (as a toy) for making a rattling sound **3 :** a rattling organ at the end of a rattlesnake's tail

rat·tler *n* **:** RATTLESNAKE

rat·tle·snake *n* **:** a poisonous American snake with a rattle at the end of its tail

rat·tle·trap *n* **:** something (as an old car) rickety and full of rattles

rau·cous *adj* **1 :** being harsh and unpleasant **2 :** behaving in a rough and noisy way — **rau·cous·ly** *adv* — **rau·cous·ness** *n*

[1]rav·age *n* **:** violently destructive action or effect

[2]ravage *vb* **rav·aged; rav·ag·ing :** to attack or act upon with great violence — **rav·ag·er** *n*

rave *vb* **raved; rav·ing 1 :** to talk wildly or as if crazy **2 :** to talk with great enthusiasm

rav·el *vb* **rav·eled** *or* **rav·elled; rav·el·ing** *or* **rav·el·ling :** UNRAVEL 1

[1]ra·ven *n* **:** a large shiny black bird like a crow that is found in northern regions

[2]raven *adj* **:** shiny and black like a raven's feathers

rav·en·ous *adj* **:** very hungry — **rav·en·ous·ly** *adv*

ra·vine *n* **:** a small narrow valley with steep sides that is larger than a gully and smaller than a canyon

rav·ish *vb* **1 :** to seize and take away by force **2 :** to overcome with a feeling and especially one of joy or delight

raw *adj* **1 :** not cooked **2 :** being in or nearly in the natural state **3 :** lacking a normal or usual finish **4 :** having the skin rubbed off **5 :** not trained or experienced **6 :** unpleasantly damp or cold — **raw·ly** *adv* — **raw·ness** *n*

raw·hide *n* **1 :** a whip of untanned hide **2 :** untanned cattle skin

[1]ray *n* **:** a flat broad fish related to the sharks that has its eyes on the top of its head

[2]ray *n* **1 :** one of the lines of light that appear to be given off by a bright object **2 :** a thin beam of radiant energy (as light) **3 :** light cast in rays **4 :** any of a group of lines that spread out from the same center **5 :** a straight line extending from a point in one direction only **6 :** a plant or animal structure like a ray **7 :** a tiny bit **:** PARTICLE

ray·on *n* **:** a cloth made from fibers produced chemically from cellulose

raze *vb* **razed; raz·ing :** to destroy completely by knocking down or breaking to pieces **:** DEMOLISH

ra·zor *n* **:** a sharp cutting instrument used to shave off hair

razz *vb* **:** to make fun of **:** TEASE

re *n* **:** the second note of the musical scale

re- *prefix* **1 :** again **2 :** back **:** backward

[1]reach *vb* **1 :** to stretch out **:** EXTEND **2 :** to touch or move to touch or take by sticking out a part of the body (as the hand) or something held in the hand **3 :** to extend or stretch to **4 :** to arrive at **:** COME **5 :** to communicate with

[2]reach *n* **1 :** an unbroken stretch (as of a river) **2 :** the act of reaching especially to take hold of something **3 :** ability to stretch (as an arm) so as to touch something

re·act *vb* **1 :** to act or behave in response (as to stimulation or an influence) **2 :** to oppose a force or influence — usually used with *against* **3 :** to go through a chemical reaction

re·ac·tion *n* **1 :** an instance of reacting **2 :** a response (as of body or mind) to a stimulus (as a treatment, situation, or stress) **3 :** a chemical change that is brought about by the action of one substance on another and results in a new substance being formed

re·ac·tion·ary *adj* **:** of, relating to, or favoring old-fashioned political or social ideas

re·ac·tor *n* **1 :** one that reacts **2 :** a device using atomic energy to produce heat

read *vb* **read; read·ing 1 :** to understand language through written symbols for speech sounds **2 :** to speak aloud written or printed words **3 :** to learn from what one has seen in writing or printing **4 :** to discover or figure out the meaning of **5 :** to give meaning to **6 :** to show by letters or numbers — **read between the lines :** to understand more than is directly stated

read·able *adj* **:** able to be read easily

read·er *n* **1 :** one that reads **2 :** a book for learning or practicing reading

read·ing *n* **1 :** something read or for reading **2 :** the form in which something is written **:** VERSION **3 :** the number or fact shown on an instrument

read–only memory *n* **:** a usually small computer memory that contains special-purpose information (as a program) which cannot be changed

read·out *n* **1 :** information from an automatic device (as a computer) that is recorded (as on a disk) or presented in a form that can be seen **2 :** an electronic device that presents information in a form that can be seen

[1]ready *adj* **read·i·er; read·i·est 1 :** prepared for use or action **2 :** likely to do something **3 :** WILLING 1 **4 :** showing ease and promptness **5 :** available right away **:** HANDY — **read·i·ly** *adv* — **read·i·ness** *n*

[2]ready *vb* **read·ied; ready·ing :** to make ready **:** PREPARE

ready–made *adj* **:** made beforehand in large numbers

re·al *adj* **1 :** of, relating to, or made up of land and buildings **2 :** not artificial **:** GENUINE **3 :** not imaginary **:** ACTUAL — **re·al·ness** *n*

real estate *n* : property consisting of buildings and land
re·al·ism *n* : willingness to face facts or to give in to what is necessary
re·al·is·tic *adj* **1** : true to life or nature **2** : ready to see things as they really are and to deal with them sensibly — **re·al·is·ti·cal·ly** *adv*
re·al·i·ty *n, pl* **re·al·i·ties** **1** : actual existence **2** : someone or something real or actual
re·al·iza·tion *n* : the action of realizing : the state of being realized
re·al·ize *vb* **re·al·ized; re·al·iz·ing** **1** : to bring into being : ACCOMPLISH **2** : to get as a result of effort : GAIN **3** : to be aware of : UNDERSTAND
re·al·ly *adv* **1** : in fact **2** : without question
realm *n* **1** : KINGDOM 1 **2** : field of activity or influence
real time *n* : the actual time during which something takes place — **real–time** *adj*
re·al·ty *n* : REAL ESTATE
[1]**ream** *n* **1** : a quantity of paper that may equal 480, 500, or 516 sheets **2 reams** *pl* : a great amount
[2]**ream** *vb* **1** : to shape or make larger with a reamer **2** : to clean or clear with a reamer
ream·er *n* : a tool with cutting edges for shaping or enlarging a hole
reap *vb* **1** : to cut (as grain) or clear (as a field) with a sickle, scythe, or machine **2** : HARVEST
reap·er *n* **1** : a worker who harvests crops **2** : a machine for reaping grain
re·ap·pear *vb* : to appear again
[1]**rear** *vb* **1** : to put up by building : CONSTRUCT **2** : to raise or set on end **3** : to take care of the breeding and raising of **4** : BRING UP **5** : to rise high **6** : to rise up on the hind legs
[2]**rear** *n* **1** : the part (as of an army) or area farthest from the enemy **2** : the space or position at the back
[3]**rear** *adj* : being at the back
rear admiral *n* : a commissioned officer in the Navy or Coast Guard ranking above a captain
re·ar·range *vb* **re·ar·ranged; re·ar·rang·ing** : to arrange again usually in a different way
[1]**rea·son** *n* **1** : a statement given to explain a belief or an act **2** : a good basis **3** : [1]CAUSE 1 **4** : the power to think **5** : a sound mind
[2]**reason** *vb* **1** : to talk with another so as to influence his or her actions or opinions **2** : to use the power of reason
rea·son·able *adj* **1** : not beyond what is usual or expected : MODERATE **2** : [1]CHEAP 1, INEXPENSIVE **3** : able to reason — **rea·son·able·ness** *n* — **rea·son·ably** *adv*
re·as·sure *vb* **re·as·sured; re·as·sur·ing** **1** : to assure again **2** : to give fresh confidence to : free from fear
[1]**re·bate** *vb* **re·bat·ed; re·bat·ing** : to make a rebate to or give as a rebate
[2]**rebate** *n* : a returning of part of a payment or of an amount owed
[1]**reb·el** *adj* **1** : being or fighting against one's government or ruler **2** : not obeying
[2]**rebel** *n* : a person who refuses to give in to authority
[3]**re·bel** *vb* **re·belled; re·bel·ling** **1** : to be or fight against authority and especially the authority of one's government **2** : to feel or show anger or strong dislike
re·bel·lion *n* **1** : open opposition to authority **2** : an open fight against one's government
re·bel·lious *adj* **1** : taking part in rebellion **2** : tending to fight against or disobey authority — **re·bel·lious·ly** *adv* — **re·bel·lious·ness** *n*
re·birth *n* **1** : a new or second birth **2** : a return to importance
re·born *adj* : born again
[1]**re·bound** *vb* **1** : to spring back on hitting something **2** : to get over a disappointment
[2]**re·bound** *n* **1** : the action of rebounding : RECOIL **2** : an immediate reaction to a disappointment
[1]**re·buff** *vb* : to refuse or criticize sharply
[2]**rebuff** *n* : a refusal to meet an advance or offer
re·build *vb* **re·built; re·build·ing** **1** : to make many or important repairs to or changes in **2** : to build again
[1]**re·buke** *vb* **re·buked; re·buk·ing** : to criticize severely
[2]**rebuke** *n* : an expression of strong disapproval
re·bus *n* : a riddle or puzzle made up of letters, pictures, and symbols whose names sound like the syllables and words of a phrase or sentence
re·but *vb* **re·but·ted; re·but·ting** : to prove to be wrong especially by argument or by proof that the opposite is right
[1]**re·call** *vb* **1** : to ask or order to come back **2** : to bring back to mind **3** : CANCEL 2, REVOKE
[2]**re·call** *n* **1** : a command to return **2** : remembrance of what has been learned or experienced
re·cap·ture *vb* **re·cap·tured; re·cap·tur·ing** **1** : to capture again **2** : to experience again
re·cede *vb* **re·ced·ed; re·ced·ing** **1** : to move back or away **2** : to slant backward
[1]**re·ceipt** *n* **1** : RECIPE **2** : the act of receiving **3 receipts** *pl* : something received **4** : a written statement saying that money or goods have been received

²receipt *vb* **1 :** to give a receipt for **2 :** to mark as paid

re·ceive *vb* **re·ceived; re·ceiv·ing 1 :** to take or get something that is given, paid, or sent **2 :** to let enter one's household or company **:** WELCOME **3 :** to be at home to visitors **4 :** ²EXPERIENCE **5 :** to change incoming radio waves into sounds or pictures

re·ceiv·er *n* **1 :** one that receives **2 :** a device for changing electricity or radio waves into light or sound

re·cent *adj* **1 :** of or relating to a time not long past **2 :** having lately appeared to come into being **:** NEW, FRESH — **re·cent·ly** *adv* — **re·cent·ness** *n*

re·cep·ta·cle *n* **:** something used to receive and contain smaller objects

re·cep·tion *n* **1 :** the act or manner of receiving **2 :** a social gathering at which someone is often formally introduced or welcomed **3 :** the receiving of a radio or television broadcast

re·cep·tion·ist *n* **:** an office employee who greets callers

re·cep·tive *adj* **:** able or willing to receive ideas — **re·cep·tive·ly** *adv* — **re·cep·tive·ness** *n*

re·cep·tor *n* **:** a cell or group of cells that receives stimuli **:** SENSE ORGAN

¹re·cess *n* **1 :** a secret or hidden place **2 :** a hollow cut or built into a surface (as a wall) **3 :** a brief period for relaxation between work periods

²recess *vb* **1 :** to put into a recess **2 :** to interrupt for or take a recess

re·ces·sion *n* **:** a period of reduced business activity

re·ces·sive *adj* **:** not dominant

rec·i·pe *n* **:** a set of instructions for making something (as a food dish) by combining various things

re·cip·i·ent *n* **:** one that receives

re·cip·ro·cal *n* **:** one of a pair of numbers (as 9 and $\frac{1}{9}$, $\frac{2}{3}$ and $\frac{3}{2}$) whose product is one

re·cit·al *n* **1 :** a reciting of something **2 :** a public performance given by one musician **3 :** a public performance by music or dance pupils

rec·i·ta·tion *n* **1 :** a complete telling or listing of something **2 :** the reciting before an audience of something memorized **3 :** a student's oral reply to questions

re·cite *vb* **re·cit·ed; re·cit·ing 1 :** to repeat from memory **2 :** to tell about in detail **3 :** to answer questions about a lesson

reck·less *adj* **:** being or given to wild careless behavior — **reck·less·ly** *adv* — **reck·less·ness** *n*

reck·on *vb* **1 :** ¹COUNT 1, COMPUTE **2 :** to regard or think of as **:** CONSIDER

re·claim *vb* **1 :** to make better in behavior or character **:** REFORM **2 :** to change to a desirable condition or state **3 :** to obtain from a waste product or by-product

rec·la·ma·tion *n* **:** the act or process of reclaiming **:** the state of being reclaimed

re·cline *vb* **re·clined; re·clin·ing 1 :** to lean backward **2 :** to lie down

rec·og·ni·tion *n* **1 :** the act of recognizing **2 :** special attention or notice

rec·og·nize *vb* **rec·og·nized; rec·og·niz·ing 1 :** to know and remember upon seeing **2 :** to be willing to acknowledge **3 :** to take approving notice of **4 :** to show one is acquainted with

¹re·coil *vb* **1 :** to draw back **2 :** to spring back to a former position

²recoil *n* **1 :** the act or action of recoiling **2 :** a springing back (as of a gun just fired) **3 :** the distance through which something (as a spring) recoils

rec·ol·lect *vb* **:** to call to mind **:** REMEMBER

rec·ol·lec·tion *n* **1 :** the act or power of recalling to mind **:** MEMORY **2 :** something remembered

rec·om·mend *vb* **1 :** to present or support as worthy or fit **2 :** to make acceptable **3 :** to make a suggestion **:** ADVISE

rec·om·men·da·tion *n* **1 :** the act of recommending **2 :** a thing or course of action recommended **3 :** something that recommends

¹rec·om·pense *vb* **rec·om·pensed; rec·om·pens·ing :** to pay for or pay back

²recompense *n* **:** a return for something done, suffered, or given **:** PAYMENT

rec·on·cile *vb* **rec·on·ciled; rec·on·cil·ing 1 :** to make friendly again **2 :** ¹SETTLE 7, ADJUST **3 :** to make agree **4 :** to cause to give in or accept

re·con·di·tion *vb* **:** to restore to good condition (as by repairing or replacing parts)

re·con·nais·sance *n* **:** a survey (as of enemy territory) to get information

re·con·noi·ter *vb* **:** to make a reconnaissance (as in preparation for military action)

re·con·sid·er *vb* **:** to consider again especially with a view to change

re·con·sid·er·a·tion *n* **:** the act of reconsidering **:** the state of being reconsidered

re·con·struct *vb* **:** to construct again **:** REBUILD, REMODEL

¹re·cord *vb* **1 :** to set down in writing **2 :** to register permanently **3 :** to change sound or visual images into a form (as on magnetic tape) that can be listened to or watched at a later time

²rec·ord *n* **1 :** the state or fact of being recorded **2 :** something written to preserve an account **3 :** the known or recorded facts about a person or thing **4 :** a recorded top performance **5 :** something on which sound or visual images have been recorded

[3]**rec·ord** *adj* **:** outstanding among other like things

re·cord·er *n* **1 :** a person or device that records **2 :** a musical instrument like a long hollow whistle with eight finger holes

re·cord·ing *n* **:** [2]RECORD 5

[1]**re·count** *vb* **:** to tell all about **:** NARRATE

[2]**re·count** *vb* **:** to count again

[3]**re·count** *n* **:** a counting again (as of election votes)

re·course *n* **1 :** a turning for help or protection **2 :** a source of help or strength

re·cov·er *vb* **1 :** to get back **:** REGAIN **2 :** to regain normal health, self-confidence, or position **3 :** to make up for **4 :** RECLAIM 2

re–cov·er *vb* **:** to cover again

re·cov·ery *n, pl* **re·cov·er·ies :** the act, process, or an instance of recovering

rec·re·a·tion *n* **1 :** a refreshing of mind or body after work or worry **2 :** a means of refreshing mind or body

[1]**re·cruit** *vb* **1 :** to form or strengthen with new members **2 :** to get the services of **3 :** to restore or increase the health or vigor of

[2]**recruit** *n* **:** a newcomer to a field of activity

rect·an·gle *n* **:** a four-sided figure with right angles and with opposite sides parallel

rect·an·gu·lar *adj* **:** shaped like a rectangle

rec·ti·fy *vb* **rec·ti·fied; rec·ti·fy·ing :** to set or make right

rec·tor *n* **:** PASTOR

rec·tum *n, pl* **rec·tums** *or* **rec·ta :** the last part of the large intestine

re·cu·per·ate *vb* **re·cu·per·at·ed; re·cu·per·at·ing :** to regain health or strength

re·cu·per·a·tion *n* **:** a getting back to health or strength

re·cur *vb* **re·curred; re·cur·ring :** to occur or appear again

re·cur·rence *n* **:** the state of occurring again and again

re·cy·cla·ble *adj* **:** that can be recycled

re·cy·cle *vb* **re·cy·cled; re·cy·cling :** to process (as paper, glass, or cans) in order to regain materials for human use

[1]**red** *adj* **red·der; red·dest 1 :** of the color red **2 :** of or relating to Communism or Communists — **red·ness** *n*

[2]**red** *n* **1 :** the color of fresh blood or of the ruby **2 :** something red in color **3 :** a person who seeks or favors revolution **4 :** COMMUNIST 2

red·bird *n* **:** any of several birds (as a cardinal) with mostly red feathers

red blood cell *n* **:** one of the tiny reddish cells of the blood that have no nuclei and carry oxygen from the lungs to the tissues

red·breast *n* **:** a bird (as a robin) with a reddish breast

red·cap *n* **:** PORTER 1

red cell *n* **:** RED BLOOD CELL

red·coat *n* **:** a British soldier especially during the Revolutionary War

red corpuscle *n* **:** RED BLOOD CELL

red·den *vb* **:** to make or become red

red·dish *adj* **:** somewhat red

re·deem *vb* **1 :** to buy back **2 :** to ransom, free, or rescue through payment or effort **3 :** to free from sin **4 :** to make good **:** FULFILL **5 :** to make up for — **re·deem·er** *n*

re·demp·tion *n* **:** the act or process or an instance of redeeming

red–hand·ed *adv or adj* **:** in the act of doing something wrong

red·head *n* **:** a person having reddish hair

red–hot *adj* **1 :** glowing red with heat **2 :** very active and emotional

re·di·rect *vb* **:** to change the course or direction of

re·dis·cov·er *vb* **:** to discover again

red–let·ter *adj* **:** of special importance **:** MEMORABLE

re·do *vb* **re·did; re·done; re·do·ing :** to do over or again

re·dress *vb* **:** to set right **:** REMEDY

red tape *n* **:** usually official rules and regulations that waste people's time

re·duce *vb* **re·duced; re·duc·ing 1 :** to make smaller or less **2 :** to force to surrender **3 :** to lower in grade or rank **4 :** to change from one form into another **5 :** to lose weight by dieting

re·duc·tion *n* **1 :** the act of reducing **:** the state of being reduced **2 :** something made by reducing **3 :** the amount by which something is reduced

red·wood *n* **:** a tall timber tree of California that bears cones and has a light long-lasting brownish red wood

reed *n* **1 :** a tall slender grass of wet areas that has stems with large joints **2 :** a stem or a growth or mass of reeds **3 :** a thin flexible piece of cane, plastic, or metal fastened to the mouthpiece or over an air opening in a musical instrument (as a clarinet or accordion) and set in vibration by an air current (as the breath)

reef *n* **:** a chain of rocks or ridge of sand at or near the surface of water

[1]**reek** *n* **:** a strong or unpleasant smell

[2]**reek** *vb* **:** to have a strong or unpleasant smell

[1]**reel** *n* **1 :** a device that can be turned round and round and on which something flexible may be wound **2 :** a quantity of something wound on a reel

[2]**reel** *vb* **1 :** to wind on a reel **2 :** to pull by the use of a reel

[3]**reel** *vb* **1 :** to whirl around **2 :** to be in a confused state **3 :** to fall back (as from a blow) **4 :** to walk or move unsteadily **:** STAGGER

[4]**reel** *n* **:** a reeling motion

[5]**reel** *n* **:** a lively folk dance

re·elect *vb* **:** to elect for another term

reel off *vb* **:** to tell or recite rapidly or easily

re·en·ter *vb* **:** to enter again

re·es·tab·lish *vb* **:** to establish again

re·fer *vb* **re·ferred; re·fer·ring 1 :** to send or direct to some person or place for treatment, aid, information, or decision **2 :** to call attention

[1]**ref·er·ee** *n* **1 :** a person to whom something that is to be investigated or decided is referred **2 :** a sports official with final authority for conducting a game or match

[2]**referee** *vb* **ref·er·eed; ref·er·ee·ing :** to act or be in charge of as referee

ref·er·ence *n* **1 :** the act of referring **2 :** a relation to or concern with something **3 :** something that refers a reader to another source of information **4 :** a person of whom questions can be asked about the honesty or ability of another person **5 :** a written statement about someone's honesty or ability **6 :** a work (as a dictionary) that contains useful information

ref·er·en·dum *n, pl* **ref·er·en·da** *or* **ref·er·en·dums :** the idea or practice of letting the voters approve or disapprove laws

[1]**re·fill** *vb* **:** to fill or become filled again

[2]**re·fill** *n* **:** a new or fresh supply of something

re·fine *vb* **re·fined; re·fin·ing 1 :** to bring to a pure state **2 :** to make better **:** IMPROVE

re·fined *adj* **1 :** having or showing good taste or training **2 :** freed from impurities **:** PURE

re·fine·ment *n* **1 :** the act or process of refining **2 :** excellence of manners, feelings, or tastes **3 :** something meant to improve something else

re·fin·ery *n, pl* **re·fin·er·ies :** a building and equipment for refining metals, oil, or sugar

re·fin·ish *vb* **:** to give (as furniture) a new surface

re·fit *vb* **re·fit·ted; re·fit·ting :** to get ready for use again

re·flect *vb* **1 :** to bend or throw back (waves of light, sound, or heat) **2 :** to give back an image or likeness of in the manner of a mirror **3 :** to bring as a result **4 :** to bring disapproval or blame **5 :** to think seriously

re·flec·tion *n* **1 :** the return of light or sound waves from a surface **2 :** an image produced by or as if by a mirror **3 :** something that brings blame or disgrace **4 :** an opinion formed or a remark made after careful thought **5 :** careful thought

re·flec·tor *n* **:** a shiny surface for reflecting light or heat

re·flex *n* **:** an action that occurs automatically when a sense organ is stimulated

reflex act *n* **:** REFLEX

re·for·est *vb* **:** to renew forest growth by planting seeds or young trees

re·for·es·ta·tion *n* **:** the act of reforesting

[1]**re·form** *vb* **1 :** to make better or improve by removal of faults **2 :** to correct or improve one's own behavior or habits

[2]**reform** *n* **1 :** improvement of what is bad **2 :** a removal or correction of a wrong or an error

ref·or·ma·tion *n* **:** the act of reforming **:** the state of being reformed

re·for·ma·to·ry *n, pl* **re·for·ma·to·ries :** an institution for reforming usually young or first offenders

re·form·er *n* **:** a person who works for reform

re·fract *vb* **:** to cause to go through refraction

re·frac·tion *n* **:** the bending of a ray when it passes at an angle from one medium into another in which its speed is different (as when light passes from air into water)

re·frac·to·ry *adj* **1 :** STUBBORN 3 **2 :** capable of enduring very high temperatures

[1]**re·frain** *vb* **:** to hold oneself back

[2]**refrain** *n* **:** a phrase or verse repeated regularly in a poem or song

re·fresh *vb* **:** to make fresh or fresher **:** REVIVE — **re·fresh·er** *n*

re·fresh·ment *n* **1 :** the act of refreshing **:** the state of being refreshed **2 :** something (as food or drink) that refreshes — often used in pl.

re·frig·er·ate *vb* **re·frig·er·at·ed; re·frig·er·at·ing :** to make or keep cold or cool

re·frig·er·a·tor *n* **:** a device or room for keeping articles (as food) cool

re·fu·el *vb* **:** to provide with or take on more fuel

ref·uge *n* **1 :** shelter or protection from danger or distress **2 :** a place that provides shelter or protection

ref·u·gee *n* **:** a person who flees for safety usually to a foreign country

[1]**re·fund** *vb* **:** to give back **:** REPAY

[2]**re·fund** *n* **:** a sum of money refunded

re·fus·al *n* **:** the act of refusing

[1]**re·fuse** *vb* **re·fused; re·fus·ing 1 :** to say one will not accept **2 :** to say one will not do, give, or allow something

[2]**ref·use** *n* **:** TRASH 1, RUBBISH

re·fute *vb* **re·fut·ed; re·fut·ing :** to prove wrong by argument or evidence — **re·fut·er** *n*

re·gain *vb* **1 :** to gain or get again **:** get back **2 :** to get back to **:** reach again

re·gal *adj* **:** of, relating to, or suitable for a monarch **:** ROYAL — **re·gal·ly** *adv*

re·gale *vb* **re·galed; re·gal·ing 1 :** to entertain richly **2 :** to give pleasure or amusement to

[1]**re·gard** *n* **1 :** [2]LOOK 1 **2 :** CONSIDERATION 2 **3 :** a feeling of respect **4 regards** *pl* **:** friendly greetings **5 :** a point to be considered

[2]**regard** *vb* **1 :** to pay attention to **2 :** to show respect or consideration for **3 :** to have a high opinion of **4 :** to look at **5 :** to think of **:** CONSIDER

re·gard·ing *prep* **:** relating to **:** ABOUT

re·gard·less *adv* **:** come what may

regardless of *prep* **:** in spite of

re·gat·ta *n* **:** a rowing, speedboat, or sailing race or a series of such races

re·gen·er·ate *vb* **re·gen·er·at·ed; re·gen·er·at·ing :** to form (as a lost part) once more

re·gent *n* **1 :** a person who governs a kingdom (as during the childhood of the monarch) **2 :** a member of a governing board (as of a state university)

re·gime *n* **:** a form or system of government or management

reg·i·men *n* **:** a systematic course of treatment

reg·i·ment *n* **:** a military unit made up usually of a number of battalions

re·gion *n* **1 :** an area having no definite boundaries **2 :** VICINITY 2 **3 :** a broad geographical area

re·gion·al *adj* **:** of, relating to, or characteristic of a certain region

[1]**reg·is·ter** *n* **1 :** a written record or list containing regular entries of items or details **2 :** a book or system of public records **3 :** a device for regulating ventilation or the flow of heated air from a furnace **4 :** a mechanical device (as a **cash register**) that records items

[2]**register** *vb* **1 :** to enter or enroll in a register (as a list of voters, students, or guests) **2 :** to record automatically **3 :** to get special protection for by paying extra postage **4 :** to show by expression and bodily movements

reg·is·tra·tion *n* **1 :** the act of registering **2 :** an entry in a register **3 :** the number of persons registered **4 :** a document showing that something is registered

reg·is·try *n, pl* **reg·is·tries :** a place where registration takes place

[1]**re·gret** *vb* **re·gret·ted; re·gret·ting 1 :** to mourn the loss or death of **2 :** to be sorry for

[2]**regret** *n* **1 :** sorrow aroused by events beyond one's control **2 :** an expression of sorrow **3 regrets** *pl* **:** a note politely refusing to accept an invitation

re·gret·ful *adj* **:** full of regret — **re·gret·ful·ly** *adv*

re·gret·ta·ble *adj* **:** deserving regret — **re·gret·ta·bly** *adv*

re·group *vb* **:** to form into a new grouping

reg·u·lar *adj* **1 :** formed, built, or arranged according to an established rule, law, principle, or type **2 :** even or balanced in form or structure **3 :** steady in practice or occurrence **4 :** following established usages or rules **5 :** [1]NORMAL 1 **6 :** of, relating to, or being a permanent army — **reg·u·lar·ly** *adv*

reg·u·lar·i·ty *n* **:** the quality or state of being regular

reg·u·late *vb* **reg·u·lat·ed; reg·u·lat·ing 1 :** to govern or direct by rule **2 :** to bring under the control of authority **3 :** to bring order or method to **4 :** to fix or adjust the time, amount, degree, or rate of — **reg·u·la·tor** *n*

reg·u·la·tion *n* **1 :** the act of regulating **:** the state of being regulated **2 :** a rule or order telling how something is to be done or having the force of law

re·hears·al *n* **:** a private performance or practice session in preparation for a public appearance

re·hearse *vb* **re·hearsed; re·hears·ing :** to practice in private in preparation for a public performance

[1]**reign** *n* **1 :** the authority or rule of a monarch **2 :** the time during which a monarch rules

[2]**reign** *vb* **1 :** to rule as a monarch **2 :** to be usual or widespread

re·im·burse *vb* **re·im·bursed; re·im·burs·ing :** to pay back **:** REPAY — **re·im·burse·ment** *n*

[1]**rein** *n* **1 :** a line or strap attached at either end of the bit of a bridle to control an animal — usually used in pl. **2 :** an influence that slows, limits, or holds back **3 :** controlling or guiding power

[2]**rein** *vb* **:** to check, control, or stop by or as if by reins

re·in·car·na·tion *n* **:** rebirth of the soul in a new body

rein·deer *n, pl* **reindeer :** a large deer that has antlers in both the male and the female and is found in northern regions

re·in·force *vb* **re·in·forced; re·in·forc·ing 1 :** to strengthen with extra troops or ships **2 :** to strengthen with new force, assistance, material, or support

re·in·force·ment *n* **1 :** the act of reinforcing **:** the state of being reinforced **2 :** something that reinforces

re·in·state *vb* **re·in·stat·ed; re·in·stat·ing :** to place again in a former position or condition — **re·in·state·ment** *n*

re·it·er·ate *vb* **re·it·er·at·ed; re·it·er·at·ing :** to say or do over again or repeatedly

[1]**re·ject** *vb* **1 :** to refuse to admit, believe, or

receive **2 :** to throw away as useless or unsatisfactory **3 :** to refuse to consider
[2]**re·ject** *n* **:** a rejected person or thing
re·jec·tion *n* **1 :** the act of rejecting **:** the state of being rejected **2 :** something rejected
re·joice *vb* **re·joiced; re·joic·ing 1 :** to give joy to **:** GLADDEN **2 :** to feel joy
re·join *vb* **1 :** to join again **:** return to **2 :** to reply sharply
re·join·der *n* **:** [2]REPLY
[1]**re·lapse** *n* **:** a fresh period of an illness after an improvement
[2]**re·lapse** *vb* **re·lapsed; re·laps·ing :** to slip or fall back into a former condition after a change for the better
re·late *vb* **re·lat·ed; re·lat·ing 1 :** to give an account of **:** NARRATE **2 :** to show or have a relationship to or between **:** CONNECT
re·lat·ed *adj* **:** connected by common ancestry or by marriage
re·la·tion *n* **1 :** the act of telling or describing **2 :** CONNECTION 2 **3 :** a related person **:** RELATIVE **4 :** RELATIONSHIP 2 **5 :** REFERENCE 2, RESPECT **6 relations** *pl* **:** business or public affairs
re·la·tion·ship *n* **1 :** the state of being related or connected **2 :** connection by blood or marriage
[1]**rel·a·tive** *n* **:** a person connected with another by blood or marriage
[2]**relative** *adj* **1 :** RELEVANT **2 :** existing in comparison to something else — **rel·a·tive·ly** *adv*
re·lax *vb* **1 :** to make or become loose or less tense **2 :** to make or become less severe or strict **3 :** to rest or enjoy oneself away from one's usual duties
re·lax·a·tion *n* **1 :** the act or fact of relaxing or of being relaxed **2 :** a relaxing activity or pastime
[1]**re·lay** *n* **1 :** a fresh supply (as of horses or people) arranged to relieve others **2 :** a race between teams in which each team member covers a certain part of the course
[2]**re·lay** *vb* **re·layed; re·lay·ing :** to pass along by stages
[1]**re·lease** *vb* **re·leased; re·leas·ing 1 :** to set free (as from prison) **2 :** to relieve from something that holds or burdens **3 :** to give up in favor of another **4 :** to permit to be published, sold, or shown — **re·leas·er** *n*
[2]**release** *n* **1 :** relief or rescue from sorrow, suffering, or trouble **2 :** a discharge from an obligation **3 :** a giving up of a right or claim **4 :** a setting free **:** the state of being freed **5 :** a device for holding or releasing a mechanism **6 :** the act of permitting publication or performance **7 :** matter released for publication or performance
re·lent *vb* **:** to become less severe, harsh, or strict
re·lent·less *adj* **:** very stern or harsh — **re·lent·less·ly** *adv* — **re·lent·less·ness** *n*
rel·e·vance *n* **:** relation to the matter at hand
rel·e·vant *adj* **:** having something to do with the matter at hand — **rel·e·vant·ly** *adv*
re·li·abil·i·ty *n* **:** the quality or state of being reliable
re·li·able *adj* **:** fit to be trusted **:** DEPENDABLE — **re·li·ably** *adv*
re·li·ance *n* **1 :** the act of relying **2 :** the condition or attitude of one who relies
rel·ic *n* **1 :** an object treated with great respect because of its connection with a saint or martyr **2 :** something left behind after decay or disappearance
re·lief *n* **1 :** removal or lightening of something painful or troubling **2 :** WELFARE 2 **3 :** military assistance in or rescue from a position of difficulty **4 :** release from a post or from performance of a duty **5 :** elevation of figures or designs from the background (as in sculpture) **6 :** elevations of a land surface
re·lieve *vb* **re·lieved; re·liev·ing 1 :** to free partly or wholly from a burden or from distress **2 :** to release from a post or duty **3 :** to break the sameness of — **re·liev·er** *n*
re·li·gion *n* **1 :** the service and worship of God or the supernatural **2 :** a system of religious beliefs and practices
re·li·gious *adj* **1 :** relating to or showing devotion to God or to the powers or forces believed to govern life **2 :** of or relating to religion **3 :** very devoted and faithful — **re·li·gious·ly** *adv* — **re·li·gious·ness** *n*
re·lin·quish *vb* **:** GIVE UP 1 **:** let go of
[1]**rel·ish** *n* **1 :** a pleasing taste **2 :** great enjoyment **3 :** a highly seasoned food eaten with other food to add flavor
[2]**relish** *vb* **1 :** to be pleased by **:** ENJOY **2 :** to like the taste of
re·live *vb* **re·lived; re·liv·ing :** to experience again (as in the imagination)
re·luc·tance *n* **:** the quality or state of being reluctant
re·luc·tant *adj* **:** showing doubt or unwillingness — **re·luc·tant·ly** *adv*
re·ly *vb* **re·lied; re·ly·ing :** to place faith or confidence **:** DEPEND
re·main *vb* **1 :** to be left after others have been removed, subtracted, or destroyed **2 :** to be something yet to be done or considered **3 :** to stay after others have gone **4 :** to continue unchanged
re·main·der *n* **1 :** a remaining group or part **2 :** the number left after a subtraction **3 :** the number left over from the dividend after division that is less than the divisor

re·mains *n pl* **1 :** whatever is left over or behind **2 :** a dead body
re·make *vb* **re·made; re·mak·ing :** to make again or in a different form
[1]**re·mark** *n* **1 :** a telling of something in speech or writing **2 :** a brief comment
[2]**remark** *vb* **1 :** to take note of **:** OBSERVE **2 :** to make a comment
re·mark·able *adj* **:** worth noticing **:** UNUSUAL — **re·mark·able·ness** *n* — **re·mark·ably** *adv*
re·match *n* **:** a second meeting between the same contestants
re·me·di·al *adj* **:** intended to make something better — **re·me·di·al·ly** *adv*
[1]**rem·e·dy** *n, pl* **rem·e·dies 1 :** a medicine or treatment that cures or relieves **2 :** something that corrects an evil
[2]**remedy** *vb* **rem·e·died; rem·e·dy·ing :** to provide or serve as a remedy for.
re·mem·ber *vb* **1 :** to bring to mind or think of again **2 :** to keep in mind **3 :** to pass along greetings from
re·mem·brance *n* **1 :** the act of remembering **2 :** something remembered **3 :** something (as a souvenir) that brings to mind a past experience
re·mind *vb* **:** to cause to remember — **re·mind·er** *n*
rem·i·nisce *vb* **rem·i·nisced; rem·i·nisc·ing :** to talk or think about things in the past
rem·i·nis·cence *n* **1 :** a recalling or telling of a past experience **2 reminiscences** *pl* **:** a story of one's memorable experiences
rem·i·nis·cent *adj* **1 :** of, relating to, or engaging in reminiscence **2 :** reminding one of something else
re·miss *adj* **:** careless in the performance of work or duty — **re·miss·ly** *adv* — **re·miss·ness** *n*
re·mit *vb* **re·mit·ted; re·mit·ting 1 :** [2]PARDON 2 **2 :** to send money (as in payment) — **re·mit·ter** *n*
re·mit·tance *n* **:** money sent in payment
rem·nant *n* **:** something that remains or is left over
re·mod·el *vb* **re·mod·eled** *or* **re·mod·elled; re·mod·el·ing** *or* **re·mod·el·ling :** to change the structure of
re·mon·strate *vb* **re·mon·strat·ed; re·mon·strat·ing :** [2]PROTEST 2
re·morse *n* **:** deep regret for one's sins or for acts that wrong others — **re·morse·ful** *adj* — **re·morse·less** *adj*
[1]**re·mote** *adj* **re·mot·er; re·mot·est 1 :** far off in place or time **2 :** SECLUDED **3 :** not closely connected or related **4 :** small in degree **5 :** distant in manner **:** ALOOF — **re·mote·ly** *adv* — **re·mote·ness** *n*
[2]**remote** *n* **:** REMOTE CONTROL
remote control *n* **1 :** control (as by a radio signal) of operation from a point some distance away **2 :** a device for controlling something from a distance
re·mov·able *adj* **:** possible to remove
re·mov·al *n* **:** the act of removing **:** the fact of being removed
re·move *vb* **re·moved; re·mov·ing 1 :** to move by lifting or taking off or away **2 :** to dismiss from office **3 :** to get rid of
re·mov·er *n* **:** something (as a chemical) used in removing a substance
Re·nais·sance *n* **1 :** the period of European history between the fourteenth and seventeenth centuries marked by a fresh interest in ancient art and literature and by the beginnings of modern science **2** *often not cap* **:** a movement or period of great activity in literature, science, and the arts
re·name *vb* **re·named; re·nam·ing :** to give a new name to
rend *vb* **rent; rend·ing :** to tear apart by force
ren·der *vb* **1 :** to obtain by heating **2 :** to furnish or give to another **3 :** to cause to be or become **4 :** PERFORM 2
ren·dez·vous *n, pl* **ren·dez·vous 1 :** a place agreed on for a meeting **2 :** a planned meeting
ren·di·tion *n* **:** an act or a result of rendering
ren·e·gade *n* **:** a person who deserts a faith, cause, or party
re·nege *vb* **re·neged; re·neg·ing :** to go back on a promise or agreement
re·new *vb* **1 :** to make or become new, fresh, or strong again **2 :** to make, do, or begin again **3 :** to put in a fresh supply of **4 :** to continue in force for a new period
re·new·al *n* **1 :** the act of renewing **:** the state of being renewed **2 :** something renewed
re·nounce *vb* **re·nounced; re·nounc·ing 1 :** to give up, abandon, or resign usually by a public declaration **2 :** REPUDIATE 1, DISCLAIM
ren·o·vate *vb* **ren·o·vat·ed; ren·o·vat·ing :** to put in good condition again — **ren·o·va·tor** *n*
re·nown *n* **:** the state of being widely and favorably known
re·nowned *adj* **:** having renown
[1]**rent** *n* **:** money paid for the use of another's property — **for rent :** available for use at a price
[2]**rent** *vb* **1 :** to take and hold property under an agreement to pay rent **2 :** to give the possession and use of in return for rent **3 :** to be for rent
[3]**rent** *past of* REND
[4]**rent** *n* **:** an opening (as in cloth) made by tearing

[1]**rent·al** *n* **:** an amount paid or collected as rent

[2]**rental** *adj* **:** of, relating to, or available for rent

rent·er *n* **:** a person who pays rent for something (as a place to live)

re·open *vb* **:** to open again

re·or·ga·nize *vb* **re·or·ga·nized; re·or·ga·niz·ing :** to organize again

[1]**re·pair** *vb* **1 :** to put back in good condition **2 :** to make up for

[2]**repair** *n* **1 :** the act or process of repairing **2 :** [1]CONDITION 3

rep·a·ra·tion *n* **1 :** the act of making up for a wrong **2 :** something paid by a country losing a war to the winner to make up for damages done in the war

re·past *n* **:** [1]MEAL

re·pay *vb* **re·paid; re·pay·ing 1 :** to pay back **2 :** to make a return payment to

re·pay·ment *n* **:** the act or an instance of paying back

re·peal *vb* **:** to do away with especially by legislative action

[1]**re·peat** *vb* **1 :** to state or tell again **2 :** to say from memory **:** RECITE **3 :** to make or do again — **re·peat·er** *n*

[2]**repeat** *n* **1 :** the act of repeating **2 :** something repeated

re·peat·ed *adj* **:** done or happening again and again — **re·peat·ed·ly** *adv*

re·pel *vb* **re·pelled; re·pel·ling 1 :** to drive back **2 :** to turn away **:** REJECT **3 :** to keep out **:** RESIST **4 :** [2]DISGUST

re·pel·lent *n* **:** a substance used to keep off pests (as insects)

re·pent *vb* **1 :** to feel sorrow for one's sin and make up one's mind to do what is right **2 :** to feel sorry for something done **:** REGRET

re·pen·tance *n* **:** the action or process of repenting

re·pen·tant *adj* **:** feeling or showing regret for something one has done — **re·pen·tant·ly** *adv*

re·per·cus·sion *n* **1 :** a return action or effect **2 :** a widespread, indirect, or unexpected effect of something said or done

rep·er·toire *n* **:** a list or supply of plays, operas, or pieces that a company or person is prepared to perform

rep·er·to·ry *n, pl* **rep·er·to·ries :** REPERTOIRE

rep·e·ti·tion *n* **1 :** the act or an instance of repeating **2 :** something repeated

re·place *vb* **re·placed; re·plac·ing 1 :** to put back in a former or proper place **2 :** to take the place of **3 :** to put something new in the place of

re·place·ment *n* **1 :** the act of replacing **:** the state of being replaced **2 :** [1]SUBSTITUTE

re·plen·ish *vb* **:** to make full or complete once more — **re·plen·ish·er** *n* — **re·plen·ish·ment** *n*

re·plete *adj* **:** well supplied — **re·plete·ness** *n*

rep·li·ca *n* **:** a very exact copy

[1]**re·ply** *vb* **re·plied; re·ply·ing :** to say or do in answer **:** RESPOND

[2]**reply** *n, pl* **re·plies :** something said, written, or done in answer

[1]**re·port** *n* **1 :** [1]RUMOR **2 :** REPUTATION 1 **3 :** a usually complete description or statement **4 :** an explosive noise

[2]**report** *vb* **1 :** to describe or tell something **2 :** to prepare or present an account of something (as for television or a newspaper) **3 :** to present oneself **4 :** to make known to the proper authorities **5 :** to make a charge of misconduct against — **re·port·er** *n*

report card *n* **:** a report on a student's grades that is regularly sent by a school to the student's parents or guardian

[1]**re·pose** *vb* **re·posed; re·pos·ing 1 :** to lay at rest **2 :** to lie at rest

[2]**repose** *n* **1 :** a state of resting and especially sleep after effort or strain **2 :** freedom from disturbance or excitement **:** CALM

rep·re·sent *vb* **1 :** to present a picture, image, or likeness of **:** PORTRAY **2 :** to be a sign or symbol of **3 :** to act for or in place of

rep·re·sen·ta·tion *n* **1 :** one (as a picture or symbol) that represents something else **2 :** the act of representing **:** the state of being represented (as in a legislative body)

[1]**rep·re·sen·ta·tive** *adj* **1 :** serving to represent **2 :** standing or acting for another **3 :** carried on by elected representatives **4 :** being a typical example of the thing mentioned

[2]**representative** *n* **1 :** a typical example (as of a group or class) **2 :** a person who represents another (as in a legislature)

re·press *vb* **:** to hold in check by or as if by pressure

[1]**re·prieve** *vb* **re·prieved; re·priev·ing :** to delay the punishment of (as a prisoner sentenced to die)

[2]**reprieve** *n* **1 :** a postponing of a prison or death sentence **2 :** a temporary relief

[1]**rep·ri·mand** *n* **:** a severe or formal criticism **:** CENSURE

[2]**reprimand** *vb* **:** to criticize (a person) severely or formally

re·pri·sal *n* **:** an act in return for harm done by another

[1]**re·proach** *n* **1 :** something that calls for blame or disgrace **2 :** an expression of disapproval

[2]**reproach** *vb* **:** to find fault with **:** BLAME

re·pro·duce *vb* **re·pro·duced; re·pro·duc·ing 1 :** to produce again **2 :** to produce another living thing of the same kind — **re·pro·duc·er** *n*

re·pro·duc·tion *n* **1 :** the act or process of reproducing **2 :** [1]COPY 1

re·pro·duc·tive *adj* **:** of, relating to, capable of, or concerned with reproduction

re·proof *n* **:** blame or criticism for a fault

re·prove *vb* **re·proved; re·prov·ing :** to express blame or disapproval of **:** SCOLD

rep·tile *n* **:** any of a group of vertebrates (as snakes, lizards, turtles, and alligators) that are cold-blooded, breathe air, and usually have the skin covered with scales or bony plates

re·pub·lic *n* **1 :** a government having a chief of state who is not a monarch and who is usually a president **2 :** a government in which supreme power lies in the citizens through their right to vote **3 :** a state or country having a republican government

[1]re·pub·li·can *n* **:** a person who favors a republican form of government

[2]republican *adj* **:** of, relating to, or like a republic

re·pu·di·ate *vb* **re·pu·di·at·ed; re·pu·di·at·ing 1 :** to refuse to have anything to do with **2 :** to refuse to accept, admit, or pay

[1]re·pulse *vb* **re·pulsed; re·puls·ing 1 :** to drive or beat back **:** REPEL **2 :** to treat with discourtesy **:** SNUB

[2]repulse *n* **1 :** [2]REBUFF, SNUB **2 :** the action of driving back an attacker

re·pul·sive *adj* **:** causing disgust — **re·pul·sive·ly** *adv* — **re·pul·sive·ness** *n*

rep·u·ta·ble *adj* **:** having a good reputation — **rep·u·ta·bly** *adv*

rep·u·ta·tion *n* **1 :** overall quality or character as seen or judged by people in general **2 :** notice by other people of some quality or ability

[1]re·pute *vb* **re·put·ed; re·put·ing :** CONSIDER 3

[2]repute *n* **1 :** REPUTATION 1 **2 :** good reputation **:** HONOR

[1]re·quest *n* **1 :** an asking for something **2 :** something asked for **3 :** the condition of being requested

[2]request *vb* **1 :** to make a request to or of **2 :** to ask for

re·qui·em *n* **1 :** a mass for a dead person **2 :** a musical service or hymn in honor of the dead

re·quire *vb* **re·quired; re·quir·ing 1 :** to have a need for **2 :** [1]ORDER 2, COMMAND

re·quire·ment *n* **:** something that is required or necessary

[1]req·ui·site *adj* **:** needed for reaching a goal or achieving a purpose

[2]requisite *n* **:** REQUIREMENT

re·read *vb* **re·read; re·read·ing :** to read again

[1]res·cue *vb* **res·cued; res·cu·ing :** to free from danger or evil **:** SAVE — **res·cu·er** *n*

[2]rescue *n* **:** an act of rescuing

re·search *n* **:** careful study and investigation for the purpose of discovering and explaining new knowledge — **re·search·er** *n*

re·sem·blance *n* **:** the quality or state of resembling something else

re·sem·ble *vb* **re·sem·bled; re·sem·bling :** to be like or similar to

re·sent *vb* **:** to feel annoyance or anger at

re·sent·ment *n* **:** a feeling of angry displeasure at a real or imagined wrong, insult, or injury

res·er·va·tion *n* **1 :** an act of reserving **2 :** an arrangement to have something (as a hotel room) held for one's use **3 :** something (as land) reserved for a special use **4 :** something that limits

[1]re·serve *vb* **re·served; re·serv·ing 1 :** to keep in store for future or special use **2 :** to hold over to a future time or place **3 :** to arrange to have set aside and held for one's use

[2]reserve *n* **1 :** something stored or available for future use **2 reserves** *pl* **:** military forces held back or available for later use **3 :** an area of land set apart **4 :** an act of reserving **5 :** caution in one's words and behavior

re·served *adj* **1 :** cautious in words and actions **2 :** kept or set apart for future or special use

res·er·voir *n* **:** a place where something (as water) is kept in store for future use

re·set *vb* **re·set; re·set·ting :** to set again

re·ship·ment *n* **:** an act of shipping again

re·side *vb* **re·sid·ed; re·sid·ing 1 :** to live permanently and continuously **:** DWELL **2 :** to have its place **:** EXIST

res·i·dence *n* **1 :** the act or fact of residing **2 :** the place where one actually lives **3 :** a building used for a home **4 :** the time during which a person lives in a place

[1]res·i·dent *adj* **1 :** living in a place for some length of time **2 :** serving in a full-time position

[2]resident *n* **:** a person who lives in a place

res·i·den·tial *adj* **1 :** used as a residence or by residents **2 :** suitable for or containing residences

res·i·due *n* **:** whatever remains after a part is taken, set apart, or lost

re·sign *vb* **1 :** to give up by a formal or official act **2 :** to prepare to accept something usually unpleasant

res·ig·na·tion *n* **1 :** an act of resigning **2 :** a letter or written statement that gives notice of resignation **3 :** the feeling of a person who is resigned

re·signed *adj* **:** giving in patiently (as to loss or sorrow) — **re·sign·ed·ly** *adv*

res·in *n* **1 :** a yellowish or brownish substance obtained from the gum or sap of some trees (as the pine) and used in varnishes and medicine **2 :** any of various manufactured products that are similar to natural resins in properties and are used especially as plastics

re·sist *vb* **1 :** to withstand the force or effect of **2 :** to fight against **:** OPPOSE

re·sis·tance *n* **1 :** an act or instance of resisting **2 :** the ability to resist **3 :** an opposing or slowing force **4 :** the opposition offered by a substance to the passage through it of an electric current

re·sis·tant *adj* **:** giving or capable of resistance

res·o·lute *adj* **:** firmly determined — **res·o·lute·ly** *adv* — **res·o·lute·ness** *n*

res·o·lu·tion *n* **1 :** the act of resolving **2 :** the act of solving **:** SOLUTION **3 :** something decided on **4 :** firmness of purpose **5 :** a statement expressing the feelings, wishes, or decisions of a group

[1]**re·solve** *vb* **re·solved; re·solv·ing 1 :** to find an answer to **:** SOLVE **2 :** to reach a firm decision about something **3 :** to declare or decide by a formal resolution and vote

[2]**resolve** *n* **1 :** something resolved **2 :** firmness of purpose

res·o·nance *n* **:** the quality or state of being resonant

res·o·nant *adj* **:** being or making sound with a rich vibrating quality — **res·o·nant·ly** *adv*

[1]**re·sort** *n* **1 :** one that is looked to for help **2 :** HANGOUT **3 :** a place where people go for pleasure, sport, or a change

[2]**resort** *vb* **1 :** to go often or again and again **2 :** to seek aid, relief, or advantage

re·sound *vb* **1 :** to become filled with sound **:** REVERBERATE **2 :** to sound loudly

re·source *n* **1 :** a new or a reserve source of supply or support **2 resources** *pl* **:** a usable stock or supply (as of money or products) **3 :** the ability to meet and deal with situations

re·source·ful *adj* **:** clever in dealing with problems — **re·source·ful·ly** *adv* — **re·source·ful·ness** *n*

[1]**re·spect** *n* **1 :** relation to or concern with something specified **2 :** high or special regard **:** ESTEEM **3 respects** *pl* **:** an expression of regard or courtesy **4 :** [1]DETAIL 2

[2]**respect** *vb* **1 :** to consider worthy of high regard **:** ESTEEM **2 :** to pay attention to — **re·spect·er** *n*

re·spect·able *adj* **1 :** deserving respect **2 :** decent or correct in conduct **:** PROPER **3 :** fair in size or quantity **4 :** fit to be seen **:** PRESENTABLE — **re·spect·ably** *adv*

re·spect·ful *adj* **:** showing respect — **re·spect·ful·ly** *adv* — **re·spect·ful·ness** *n*

re·spect·ing *prep* **:** CONCERNING

re·spec·tive *adj* **:** not the same or shared **:** SEPARATE — **re·spec·tive·ly** *adv*

re·spell *vb* **:** to spell again or in another way

res·pi·ra·tion *n* **1 :** the act or process of breathing **2 :** the physical and chemical processes (as breathing and oxidation) by which a living being gets the oxygen it needs to live

res·pi·ra·tor *n* **1 :** a device covering the mouth or nose especially to prevent the breathing in of something harmful **2 :** a device used for aiding one to breathe

res·pi·ra·to·ry *adj* **:** of, relating to, or concerned with respiration

respiratory system *n* **:** a system of the body used in breathing that in human beings consists of the nose, nasal passages, pharynx, larynx, trachea, bronchial tubes, and lungs

re·spire *vb* **re·spired; re·spir·ing :** BREATHE 1

res·pite *n* **1 :** a short delay **2 :** a period of rest or relief

re·splen·dent *adj* **:** shining brightly **:** SPLENDID — **re·splen·dent·ly** *adv*

re·spond *vb* **1 :** to say something in return **:** REPLY **2 :** to act in response **:** REACT

re·sponse *n* **1 :** an act or instance of replying **:** ANSWER **2 :** words said or sung by the people or choir in a religious service **3 :** a reaction of a living being (as to a drug)

re·spon·si·bil·i·ty *n, pl* **re·spon·si·bil·i·ties 1 :** the quality or state of being responsible **2 :** the quality of being dependable **3 :** something for which one is responsible

re·spon·si·ble *adj* **1 :** getting the credit or blame for one's acts or decisions **2 :** RELIABLE **3 :** needing a person to take charge of or be trusted with things of importance — **re·spon·si·bly** *adv*

re·spon·sive *adj* **1 :** giving response **2 :** quick to respond or react in a sympathetic way — **re·spon·sive·ly** *adv* — **re·spon·sive·ness** *n*

[1]**rest** *n* **1 :** [1]SLEEP 1 **2 :** freedom from activity or work **3 :** a state of not moving or not doing anything **4 :** a place for resting or stopping **5 :** a silence in music **6 :** a symbol in music that stands for a certain period of silence in a measure **7 :** something used for support

[2]**rest** *vb* **1 :** to get rest by lying down **:** SLEEP **2 :** to give rest to **3 :** to lie dead **4 :** to not take part in work or activity **5 :** to sit or lie fixed or supported **6 :** DEPEND 2 **7 :** to fix or be fixed in trust or confidence

[3]**rest** *n* : something that is left over : REMAINDER
re·state·ment *n* : a saying again or in another way
res·tau·rant *n* : a public eating place
rest·ful *adj* **1** : giving rest **2** : giving a feeling of rest : QUIET — **rest·ful·ly** *adv* — **rest·ful·ness** *n*
rest·ing *adj* : DORMANT
res·tive *adj* **1** : resisting control **2** : not being at ease — **res·tive·ly** *adv* — **res·tive·ness** *n*
rest·less *adj* **1** : having or giving no rest **2** : not quiet or calm — **rest·less·ly** *adv* — **rest·less·ness** *n*
res·to·ra·tion *n* **1** : an act of restoring : the condition of being restored **2** : something (as a building) that has been restored
re·store *vb* **re·stored; re·stor·ing** **1** : to give back : RETURN **2** : to put back into use or service **3** : to put or bring back to an earlier or original state
re·strain *vb* **1** : to keep from doing something **2** : to keep back : CURB — **re·strain·er** *n*
re·straint *n* **1** : the act of restraining : the state of being restrained **2** : a restraining force or influence **3** : control over one's thoughts or feelings
re·strict *vb* : to keep within bounds : set limits to
re·stric·tion *n* **1** : something (as a law or rule) that restricts **2** : an act of restricting : the condition of being restricted
re·stric·tive *adj* : serving or likely to restrict — **re·stric·tive·ly** *adv* — **re·stric·tive·ness** *n*
rest·room *n* : a room or set of rooms with sinks and toilets
[1]**re·sult** *vb* **1** : to come about as an effect **2** : to end as an effect
[2]**result** *n* **1** : something that comes about as an effect or end **2** : a good effect
re·sume *vb* **re·sumed; re·sum·ing** **1** : to take or occupy again **2** : to begin again
re·sump·tion *n* : the act of resuming
res·ur·rect *vb* **1** : to raise from the dead : bring back to life **2** : to bring to view or into use again
res·ur·rec·tion *n* **1** *cap* : the rising of Christ from the dead **2** *often cap* : the rising again to life of all human dead before the final judgment **3** : a coming back into use or importance
re·sus·ci·tate *vb* **re·sus·ci·tat·ed; re·sus·ci·tat·ing** : to bring back from apparent death or unconsciousness — **re·sus·ci·ta·tor** *n*
[1]**re·tail** *vb* : to sell in small amounts to people for their own use — **re·tail·er** *n*
[2]**retail** *n* : the sale of products or goods in small amounts to people for their own use
[3]**retail** *adj* : of, relating to, or engaged in selling by retail
re·tain *vb* **1** : to keep in one's possession or control **2** : to hold safe or unchanged
re·tal·i·ate *vb* **re·tal·i·at·ed; re·tal·i·at·ing** : to get revenge by returning like for like
re·tal·i·a·tion *n* : the act or an instance of retaliating
re·tard *vb* : to slow up : keep back : DELAY — **re·tard·er** *n*
retch *vb* : to vomit or try to vomit
re·ten·tion *n* **1** : the act of retaining : the state of being retained **2** : the power of retaining
ret·i·na *n, pl* **retinas** *or* **ret·i·nae** : the membrane that lines the back part of the eyeball and is the sensitive part for seeing
re·tire *vb* **re·tired; re·tir·ing** **1** : to get away from action or danger : RETREAT **2** : to go away especially to be alone **3** : to give up one's job permanently : quit working **4** : to go to bed **5** : to take out of circulation — **re·tire·ment** *n*
re·tired *adj* : not working at active duties or business
re·tir·ing *adj* : [1]SHY 2, RESERVED
[1]**re·tort** *vb* **1** : to answer back : reply angrily or sharply **2** : to reply with an argument against
[2]**retort** *n* : a quick, clever, or angry reply
re·trace *vb* **re·traced; re·trac·ing** : to go over once more
re·tract *vb* **1** : to pull back or in **2** : to take back (as an offer or statement) : WITHDRAW
[1]**re·tread** *vb* **re·tread·ed; re·tread·ing** : to put a new tread on the cord fabric of (a tire)
[2]**re·tread** *n* : a retreaded tire
[1]**re·treat** *n* **1** : an act of going away from something dangerous, difficult, or disagreeable **2** : a military signal for turning away from the enemy **3** : a place of privacy or safety : REFUGE **4** : a period in which a person goes away to pray, think quietly, and study
[2]**retreat** *vb* : to make a retreat
re·trieve *vb* **re·trieved; re·triev·ing** **1** : to find and bring in killed or wounded game **2** : to make good a loss or damage : RECOVER
re·triev·er *n* **1**: one that retrieves **2**: a dog that has a water-resistant coat and is skilled in retrieving game
ret·ro–rock·et *n* : a rocket (as on a space vehicle) used to slow forward motion
ret·ro·spect *n* : a looking back on things past
[1]**re·turn** *vb* **1** : to come or go back **2** : [2]ANSWER 1, REPLY **3** : to make an official report of **4** : to bring, carry, send, or put back : RESTORE **5** : [1]YIELD 4, PRODUCE **6** : REPAY 1
[2]**return** *n* **1** : the act of coming back to or from a place or condition **2** : RECURRENCE **3** : a report of the results of voting **4** : a

statement of income to be taxed **5 :** the profit from labor, investment, or business **6 :** the act of returning something (as to an earlier place or condition) **7 :** something given (as in payment)

[3]return *adj* **1 :** played or given in return **2 :** used for returning

re·union *n* **1 :** the act of reuniting **:** the state of being reunited **2 :** a reuniting of persons after being apart

re·unite *vb* **re·unit·ed; re·unit·ing :** to come or bring together again after being apart

rev *vb* **revved; rev·ving :** to increase the number of revolutions per minute of (a motor)

re·veal *vb* **1 :** to make known **2 :** to show clearly

rev·eil·le *n* **:** a signal sounded at about sunrise on a bugle to call soldiers or sailors to duty

[1]rev·el *vb* **rev·eled** *or* **rev·elled; rev·el·ing** *or* **rev·el·ling 1 :** to be social in a wild noisy way **2 :** to take great pleasure

[2]revel *n* **:** a noisy or merry celebration

rev·e·la·tion *n* **1 :** an act of revealing **2 :** something revealed

rev·el·ry *n, pl* **rev·el·ries :** rough and noisy merrymaking

[1]re·venge *vb* **re·venged; re·veng·ing :** to cause harm or injury in return for

[2]revenge *n* **1 :** an act or instance of revenging **2 :** a desire to repay injury for injury **3 :** a chance for getting satisfaction

re·venge·ful *adj* **:** given to or seeking revenge

rev·e·nue *n* **1 :** the income from an investment **2 :** money collected by a government (as through taxes)

re·ver·ber·ate *vb* **re·ver·ber·at·ed; re·ver·ber·at·ing :** to continue in or as if in a series of echoes

re·vere *vb* **re·vered; re·ver·ing :** to think of with reverence

[1]rev·er·ence *n* **:** honor and respect mixed with love and awe

[2]reverence *vb* **rev·er·enced; rev·er·enc·ing :** to show reverence to or toward

rev·er·end *adj* **1 :** worthy of honor and respect **2** — used as a title for a member of the clergy

rev·er·ent *adj* **:** very respectful — **rev·er·ent·ly** *adv*

rev·er·ie *also* **rev·ery** *n, pl* **rev·er·ies 1 :** [1]DAYDREAM **2 :** the condition of being lost in thought

re·ver·sal *n* **:** an act or the process of reversing

[1]re·verse *adj* **1 :** opposite to a previous or normal condition **2 :** acting or working in a manner opposite to the usual — **re·verse·ly** *adv*

[2]reverse *vb* **re·versed; re·vers·ing 1 :** to turn completely around or upside down or inside out **2 :** ANNUL **3 :** to go or cause to go in the opposite direction

[3]reverse *n* **1 :** something opposite to something else **:** CONTRARY **2 :** an act or instance of reversing **3 :** the back part of something **4 :** a gear that reverses something

re·vert *vb* **:** to come or go back

[1]re·view *n* **1 :** a military parade put on for high officers **2 :** a general survey **3 :** a piece of writing about the quality of a book, performance, or show **4 :** a fresh study of material studied before

[2]review *vb* **1 :** to look at a thing again **:** study or examine again **2 :** to make an inspection of (as troops) **3 :** to write a review about (as a book) **4 :** to look back on — **re·view·er** *n*

re·vile *vb* **re·viled; re·vil·ing :** to speak to or yell at in an insulting way — **re·vil·er** *n*

re·vise *vb* **re·vised; re·vis·ing 1 :** to look over again to correct or improve **2 :** to make a new version of

re·viv·al *n* **1 :** a reviving of interest (as in art) **2 :** a new presentation of a play or movie **3 :** a gaining back of strength or importance **4 :** a meeting or series of meetings led by a preacher to stir up religious feelings or to make converts

re·vive *vb* **re·vived; re·viv·ing 1 :** to bring back or come back to life, consciousness, freshness, or activity **2 :** to bring back into use

re·voke *vb* **re·voked; re·vok·ing :** to take away or cancel

[1]re·volt *vb* **1 :** to rebel against the authority of a ruler or government **2 :** to be or cause to be disgusted or shocked

[2]revolt *n* **:** REBELLION, INSURRECTION

rev·o·lu·tion *n* **1 :** the action by a celestial body of going round in a fixed course **2 :** completion of a course (as of years) **:** CYCLE **3 :** a turning round a center or axis **:** ROTATION **4 :** a single complete turn (as of a wheel) **5 :** a sudden, extreme, or complete change (as in manner of living or working) **6 :** the overthrow of one government and the substitution of another by the governed

rev·o·lu·tion·ary *adj* **1 :** of, relating to, or involving revolution **2 :** [1]RADICAL 2

rev·o·lu·tion·ist *n* **:** a person taking part in or supporting a revolution

rev·o·lu·tion·ize *vb* **rev·o·lu·tion·ized; rev·o·lu·tion·iz·ing :** to change greatly or completely

re·volve *vb* **re·volved; re·volv·ing 1 :** to think over carefully **2 :** to move in an orbit **3 :** ROTATE 1

re·volv·er *n* **:** a pistol having a revolving cylinder holding several bullets all of which may be shot without loading again

re·vue *n* **:** a theatrical entertainment consisting usually of short and often funny sketches and songs

[1]**re·ward** *vb* **:** to give a reward to or for

[2]**reward** *n* **:** something (as money) given or offered in return for a service (as the return of something lost)

re·wind *vb* **re·wound; re·wind·ing :** to reverse the winding of (as a videotape)

re·word *vb* **:** to state in different words

re·write *vb* **re·wrote; re·writ·ten; re·writ·ing :** to write over again especially in a different form

rhap·so·dy *n, pl* **rhap·so·dies :** a written or spoken expression of great emotion

rhea *n* **:** a tall flightless South American bird that has three toes on each foot and is like but smaller than the ostrich

rheu·mat·ic *adj* **:** of, relating to, or suffering from rheumatism — **rheu·mat·i·cal·ly** *adv*

rheu·ma·tism *n* **:** any of several disorders in which muscles or joints are red, hot, and painful

rhi·no *n, pl* **rhino** *or* **rhi·nos :** RHINOCEROS

rhi·noc·er·os *n, pl* **rhi·noc·er·os·es** *or* **rhinoceros :** a large mammal of Africa and Asia with a thick skin, three toes on each foot, and one or two heavy upright horns on the snout

rho·do·den·dron *n* **:** a shrub or tree with long usually shiny and evergreen leaves and showy clusters of white, pink, red, or purple flowers

rhom·bus *n* **:** a parallelogram whose sides are equal

rhu·barb *n* **:** a plant with broad green leaves and thick juicy pink or red stems that are used for food

[1]**rhyme** *or* **rime** *n* **1 :** close similarity in the final sounds of two or more words or lines of verse **2 :** a verse composition that rhymes

[2]**rhyme** *or* **rime** *vb* **rhymed** *or* **rimed; rhym·ing** *or* **rim·ing 1 :** to make rhymes **2 :** to end with the same sound **3 :** to cause lines or words to end with a similar sound

rhythm *n* **1 :** a flow of rising and falling sounds produced in poetry by a regular repeating of stressed and unstressed syllables **2 :** a flow of sound in music having regular accented beats **3 :** a movement or activity in which some action repeats regularly

rhyth·mic *or* **rhyth·mi·cal** *adj* **:** having rhythm — **rhyth·mi·cal·ly** *adv*

[1]**rib** *n* **1 :** one of the series of curved bones that are joined in pairs to the backbone of humans and other vertebrates and help to stiffen the body wall **2 :** something (as a piece of wire supporting the fabric of an umbrella) that is like a rib in shape or use **3 :** one of the parallel ridges in a knitted or woven fabric — **ribbed** *adj*

[2]**rib** *vb* **ribbed; rib·bing 1 :** to provide or enclose with ribs **2 :** to form ribs in (a fabric) in knitting or weaving

rib·bon *n* **1 :** a narrow strip of fabric (as silk) used for trimming or for tying or decorating packages **2 :** a long narrow strip like a ribbon **3 :** TATTER 1, SHRED

rice *n* **:** an annual cereal grass widely grown in warm wet regions for its grain that is a chief food in many parts of the world

rich *adj* **1 :** having great wealth **2 :** [1]VALUABLE 1, EXPENSIVE **3 :** containing much sugar, fat, or seasoning **4 :** high in fuel content **5 :** deep and pleasing in color or tone **6 :** ABUNDANT **7 :** FERTILE 1 — **rich·ly** *adv* — **rich·ness** *n*

rich·es *n pl* **:** things that make one rich **:** WEALTH

rick·ets *n* **:** a disease in which the bones are soft and deformed and which usually attacks the young and is caused by lack of the vitamin that controls the use of calcium and phosphorus

rick·ety *adj* **:** SHAKY, UNSOUND

rick·sha *or* **rick·shaw** *n* **:** a small hooded carriage with two wheels that is pulled by one person and was used originally in Japan

[1]**ric·o·chet** *n* **:** a bouncing off at an angle (as of a bullet off a wall)

[2]**ricochet** *vb* **ric·o·cheted; ric·o·chet·ing :** to bounce off at an angle

rid *vb* **rid** *also* **rid·ded; rid·ding :** to free from something **:** RELIEVE

rid·dance *n* **:** the act of ridding **:** the state of being rid of something

[1]**rid·dle** *n* **:** a puzzling question to be solved or answered by guessing

[2]**riddle** *vb* **rid·dled; rid·dling :** to pierce with many holes

[1]**ride** *vb* **rode; rid·den; rid·ing 1 :** to go on an animal's back or in a vehicle (as a car) **2 :** to sit on and control so as to be carried along **3 :** to float or move on water **4 :** to travel over a surface **5 :** CARRY 1 — **rid·er** *n*

[2]**ride** *n* **1 :** a trip on horseback or by vehicle **2 :** a mechanical device (as a merry-go-round) that one rides for fun **3 :** a means of transportation

ridge *n* **1 :** a range of hills or mountains **2 :** a raised strip **3 :** the line made where two sloping surfaces come together — **ridged** *adj*

ridge·pole *n* **:** the highest horizontal timber in a sloping roof to which the upper ends of the rafters are fastened

[1]**rid·i·cule** *n* **:** the act of making fun of someone

[2]**ridicule** *vb* **rid·i·culed; rid·i·cul·ing** : to make fun of : DERIDE

ri·dic·u·lous *adj* : causing or deserving ridicule : ABSURD — **ri·dic·u·lous·ly** *adv* — **ri·dic·u·lous·ness** *n*

riff·raff *n* : RABBLE 2

[1]**ri·fle** *vb* **ri·fled; ri·fling 1** : to search through fast and roughly especially in order to steal **2** : [1]STEAL 2

[2]**rifle** *n* : a gun having a long barrel with spiral grooves on its inside

rift *n* **1** : an opening made by splitting or separation : CLEFT **2** : a break in friendly relations

[1]**rig** *vb* **rigged; rig·ging 1** : to fit out (as a ship) with rigging **2** : CLOTHE 1, 2, DRESS **3** : EQUIP **4** : to set up usually for temporary use

[2]**rig** *n* **1** : the shape, number, and arrangement of sails on a ship of one class or type that sets it apart from ships of other classes or types **2** : apparatus for a certain purpose

rig·ging *n* : lines and chains used on a ship especially for moving the sails and supporting the masts and spars

[1]**right** *adj* **1** : being just or good : UPRIGHT **2** : ACCURATE, CORRECT **3** : SUITABLE, APPROPRIATE **4** : STRAIGHT 1 **5** : of, relating to, located on, or being the side of the body away from the heart **6** : located nearer to the right hand **7** : being or meant to be the side on top, in front, or on the outside **8** : healthy in mind or body — **right·ly** *adv* — **right·ness** *n*

[2]**right** *n* **1** : the ideal of what is right and good **2** : something to which one has a just claim **3** : the cause of truth or justice **4** : the right side or a part that is on or toward the right side

[3]**right** *adv* **1** : according to what is right **2** : in the exact location or position : PRECISELY **3** : in a direct line or course : STRAIGHT **4** : according to truth or fact **5** : in the right way : CORRECTLY **6** : all the way **7** : without delay : IMMEDIATELY **8** : on or to the right

[4]**right** *vb* **1** : to make right (something wrong or unjust) **2** : to adjust or restore to a proper state or condition **3** : to bring or bring back to a vertical position **4** : to become vertical

right angle *n* : an angle formed by two lines that are perpendicular to each other — **right–an·gled** *adj*

righ·teous *adj* : doing or being what is right — **righ·teous·ly** *adv* — **righ·teous·ness** *n*

right·ful *adj* : LAWFUL 2, PROPER — **right·ful·ly** *adv* — **right·ful·ness** *n*

right–hand *adj* **1** : located on the right **2** : RIGHT-HANDED **3** : relied on most of all

right–hand·ed *adj* **1** : using the right hand more easily than the left **2** : done or made with or for the right hand **3** : CLOCKWISE

right–of–way *n, pl* **rights–of–way 1** : the right to pass over someone else's land **2** : the right of some traffic to go before other traffic

right triangle *n* : a triangle having a right angle

rig·id *adj* **1** : not flexible : STIFF **2** : STRICT 1, SEVERE — **rig·id·ly** *adv* — **rig·id·ness** *n*

rig·ma·role *n* : NONSENSE 1

rig·or *n* : a harsh severe condition (as of discipline or weather)

rig·or·ous *adj* **1** : very strict **2** : hard to put up with : HARSH — **rig·or·ous·ly** *adv* — **rig·or·ous·ness** *n*

rill *n* : a very small brook

rim *n* **1** : an outer edge especially of something curved **2** : the outer part of a wheel — **rimmed** *adj*

[1]**rime** *n* : [1]FROST 2

[2]**rime** *variant of* RHYME

rind *n* : a usually hard or tough outer layer

[1]**ring** *n* **1** : a circular band worn as an ornament or used for holding or fastening **2** : something circular in shape **3** : a place for exhibitions (as at a circus) or contests (as in boxing) **4** : a group of persons who work together for selfish or dishonest purposes — **ringed** *adj* — **ring·like** *adj*

[2]**ring** *vb* **ringed; ring·ing 1** : to place or form a ring around : to throw a ring over (a peg or hook) in a game (as quoits)

[3]**ring** *vb* **rang; rung; ring·ing 1** : to make or cause to make a rich vibrating sound when struck **2** : to sound a bell **3** : to announce by or as if by striking a bell **4** : to sound loudly **5** : to be filled with talk or report **6** : to repeat loudly **7** : to seem to be a certain way **8** : to call on the telephone

[4]**ring** *n* **1** : a clear ringing sound made by vibrating metal **2** : a tone suggesting that of a bell **3** : a loud or continuing noise **4** : something that suggests a certain quality **5** : a telephone call

ring·lead·er *n* : a leader especially of a group of persons who cause trouble

ring·let *n* : a long curl

ring·worm *n* : a contagious skin disease with discolored rings on the skin

rink *n* : a place for skating

[1]**rinse** *vb* **rinsed; rins·ing 1** : to wash lightly with water **2** : to cleanse (as of soap) with clear water **3** : to treat (hair) with a rinse

[2]**rinse** *n* **1** : an act of rinsing **2** : a liquid used for rinsing **3** : a solution that temporarily tints hair

[1]**ri·ot** *n* **1** : public violence, disturbance, or disorder **2** : a colorful display

[2]**riot** *vb* : to create or take part in a riot

[1]**rip** *vb* **ripped; rip·ping :** to cut or tear open — **rip·per** *n*

[2]**rip** *n* **:** [3]TEAR 2

ripe *adj* **rip·er; rip·est 1 :** fully grown and developed **2 :** having mature knowledge, understanding, or judgment **3 :** [1]READY 1 — **ripe·ness** *n*

rip·en *vb* **:** to make or become ripe

[1]**rip·ple** *vb* **rip·pled; rip·pling 1 :** to become or cause to become covered with small waves **2 :** to make a sound like that of water flowing in small waves

[2]**ripple** *n* **1 :** the disturbing of the surface of water **2 :** a sound like that of rippling water

[1]**rise** *vb* **rose; ris·en; ris·ing 1 :** to get up from lying, kneeling, or sitting **2 :** to get up from sleep or from one's bed **3 :** to return from death **4 :** to take up arms **5 :** to appear above the horizon **6 :** to go up **:** ASCEND **7 :** to swell in size or volume **8 :** to become encouraged **9 :** to gain a higher rank or position **10 :** to increase in amount or number **11 :** ARISE 3 **12 :** to come into being **:** ORIGINATE **13 :** to show oneself equal to a demand or test — **ris·er** *n*

[2]**rise** *n* **1 :** an act of rising **:** a state of being risen **2 :** BEGINNING 1, ORIGIN **3 :** an increase in amount, number, or volume **4 :** an upward slope **5 :** a spot higher than surrounding ground **6 :** an angry reaction

[1]**risk** *n* **:** possibility of loss or injury

[2]**risk** *vb* **1 :** to expose to danger **2 :** to take the risk or danger of

risky *adj* **risk·i·er; risk·i·est :** DANGEROUS 1

rite *n* **1 :** a set form of conducting a ceremony **2 :** a ceremonial act or action

rit·u·al *n* **1 :** an established form for a ceremony **2 :** a system of rites

[1]**ri·val** *n* **:** one of two or more trying to get what only one can have

[2]**rival** *adj* **:** having the same worth

[3]**rival** *vb* **ri·valed** *or* **ri·valled; ri·val·ing** *or* **ri·val·ling 1 :** to be in competition with **2 :** [2]EQUAL

ri·val·ry *n, pl* **ri·val·ries :** the act of rivaling **:** the state of being a rival **:** COMPETITION

riv·er *n* **1 :** a natural stream of water larger than a brook or creek **2 :** a large stream

riv·et *n* **:** a bolt with a head at one end used for uniting two or more pieces by passing the shank through a hole in each piece and then beating or pressing down the plain end so as to make a second head

riv·u·let *n* **:** a small stream

roach *n* **:** COCKROACH

road *n* **1 :** an open way for vehicles, persons, and animals **2 :** PATH 3, ROUTE

road·bed *n* **1 :** the foundation of a road or railroad **2 :** the traveled surface of a road

road·side *n* **:** the strip of land along a road **:** the side of a road

road·way *n* **1 :** the strip of land over which a road passes **2 :** the part of the surface of a road traveled by vehicles

roam *vb* **:** to go from place to place with no fixed purpose or direction — **roam·er** *n*

[1]**roan** *adj* **:** of a dark color (as black or brown) sprinkled with white

[2]**roan** *n* **:** an animal (as a horse) with a roan coat

[1]**roar** *vb* **1 :** to utter a long full loud sound **2 :** to laugh loudly — **roar·er** *n*

[2]**roar** *n* **:** a long shout, bellow, or loud confused noise

[1]**roast** *vb* **1 :** to cook with dry heat (as in an oven) **2 :** to be or make very hot — **roast·er** *n*

[2]**roast** *n* **1 :** a piece of meat roasted or suitable for roasting **2 :** an outing at which food is roasted

[3]**roast** *adj* **:** cooked by roasting

rob *vb* **robbed; rob·bing 1 :** to take something away from a person or place in secrecy or by force, threat, or trickery **2 :** to keep from getting something due, expected, or desired — **rob·ber** *n*

rob·bery *n, pl* **rob·ber·ies :** the act or practice of robbing

[1]**robe** *n* **1 :** a long loose or flowing garment **2 :** a covering for the lower part of the body

[2]**robe** *vb* **robed; rob·ing 1 :** to put on a robe **2 :** [1]DRESS 2

rob·in *n* **1 :** a small European thrush with a yellowish red throat and breast **2 :** a large North American thrush with a grayish back and dull reddish breast

ro·bot *n* **1 :** a machine that looks and acts like a human being **2 :** a capable but unfeeling person

ro·bust *adj* **:** strong and vigorously healthy — **ro·bust·ly** *adv* — **ro·bust·ness** *n*

[1]**rock** *vb* **1 :** to move back and forth as in a cradle **2 :** to sway or cause to sway back and forth

[2]**rock** *n* **1 :** a rocking movement **2 :** popular music played on instruments that are amplified electronically

[3]**rock** *n* **1 :** a large mass of stone **2 :** solid mineral deposits **3 :** something like a rock in firmness

rock·er *n* **1 :** a curving piece of wood or metal on which an object (as a cradle) rocks **2 :** a structure or device that rocks on rockers **3 :** a mechanism that works with a rocking motion

[1]**rock·et** *n* **1 :** a firework that is driven through the air by the gases produced by a burning substance **2 :** a jet engine that operates like a firework rocket but carries the

oxygen needed for burning its fuel **3 :** a bomb, missile, or vehicle that is moved by a rocket

[2]**rocket** *vb* **1 :** to rise swiftly **2 :** to travel rapidly in or as if in a rocket

rock·ing chair *n* **:** a chair mounted on rockers

rocking horse *n* **:** a toy horse mounted on rockers

rock 'n' roll *or* **rock and roll** *n* **:** [2]ROCK 2

rock salt *n* **:** common salt in large crystals

rocky *adj* **rock·i·er; rock·i·est :** full of or consisting of rocks — **rock·i·ness** *n*

rod *n* **1 :** a straight slender stick or bar **2 :** a stick or bundle of twigs used in whipping a person **3 :** a measure of length equal to $16\frac{1}{2}$ feet (about 5 meters) **4 :** any of the sensory bodies shaped like rods in the retina that respond to faint light **5 :** a light flexible pole often with line and a reel attached used in fishing — **rod·like** *adj*

rode *past of* RIDE

ro·dent *n* **:** any of a group of mammals (as squirrels, rats, mice, and beavers) with sharp front teeth used in gnawing

ro·deo *n, pl* **ro·de·os 1 :** a roundup of cattle **2 :** an exhibition that features cowboy skills (as riding and roping)

roe *n* **:** the eggs of a fish especially while still held together in a membrane

roe deer *n* **:** a small deer of Europe and Asia with erect antlers forked at the tip

rogue *n* **1 :** a dishonest or wicked person **2 :** a pleasantly mischievous person

rogu·ish *adj* **:** being or like a rogue — **rogu·ish·ly** *adv* — **rogu·ish·ness** *n*

role *n* **1 :** a character assigned or taken on **2 :** a part played by an actor or singer **3 :** [1]FUNCTION 1

role model *n* **:** a person whose behavior in a certain role is imitated by others

[1]**roll** *n* **1 :** a writing that may be rolled up **:** SCROLL **2 :** an official list of names **3 :** something or a quantity of something that is rolled up or rounded as if rolled **4 :** a small piece of baked bread dough

[2]**roll** *vb* **1 :** to move by turning over and over on a surface without sliding **2 :** to shape or become shaped in rounded form **3 :** to make smooth, even, or firm with a roller **4 :** to move on rollers or wheels **5 :** to sound with a full echoing tone or with a continuous beating sound **6 :** to go by **:** PASS **7 :** to flow in a continuous stream **8 :** to move with a side-to-side sway

[3]**roll** *n* **1 :** a sound produced by rapid strokes on a drum **2 :** a heavy echoing sound **3 :** a rolling movement or action

roll·er *n* **1 :** a turning cylinder over or on which something is moved or which is used to press, shape, or smooth something **2 :** a rod on which something (as a map) is rolled up **3 :** a small wheel **4 :** a long heavy wave on the sea

roller coaster *n* **:** an elevated railway (as in an amusement park) with sharp curves and steep slopes on which cars roll

roller skate *n* **:** a skate that has wheels instead of a runner

roller–skate *vb* **:** to ride on roller skates

rolling pin *n* **:** a cylinder (as of wood) used to roll out dough

ROM *n* **:** READ-ONLY MEMORY

[1]**Ro·man** *n* **1 :** a person born or living in Rome **2 :** a citizen of an ancient empire centered on Rome **3** *not cap* **:** roman letters or type

[2]**Roman** *adj* **1 :** of or relating to Rome or the Romans **2** *not cap* **:** of or relating to a type style with upright characters (as in "these definitions")

[1]**ro·mance** *n* **1 :** an old tale of knights and noble ladies **2 :** an adventure story **3 :** a love story **4 :** a love affair **5 :** an attraction or appeal to one's feelings

[2]**romance** *vb* **ro·manced; ro·manc·ing :** to have romantic thoughts or ideas

Roman numeral *n* **:** a numeral in a system of figures based on the ancient Roman system

ro·man·tic *adj* **1 :** not founded on fact **:** IMAGINARY **2 :** IMPRACTICAL **3 :** stressing or appealing to the emotions or imagination **4 :** of, relating to, or associated with love — **ro·man·ti·cal·ly** *adv*

[1]**romp** *n* **:** rough and noisy play **:** FROLIC

[2]**romp** *vb* **:** to play in a rough and noisy way

romp·er *n* **:** a young child's one-piece garment having legs that can be unfastened around the inside — usually used in pl.

[1]**roof** *n, pl* **roofs 1 :** the upper covering part of a building **2 :** something like a roof in form, position, or purpose — **roofed** *adj*

[2]**roof** *vb* **:** to cover with a roof

roof·ing *n* **:** material for a roof

roof·tree *n* **:** RIDGEPOLE

[1]**rook** *n* **:** an Old World bird similar to the related crows

[2]**rook** *vb* **:** [1]CHEAT 1, SWINDLE

[3]**rook** *n* **:** one of the pieces in the game of chess

rook·ie *n* **:** BEGINNER, RECRUIT

[1]**room** *n* **1 :** available space **2 :** a divided part of the inside of a building **3 :** the people in a room **4 rooms** *pl* **:** LODGING 2 **5 :** a suitable opportunity

[2]**room** *vb* **:** to provide with or live in lodgings

room·er *n* **:** LODGER

rooming house *n* **:** a house for renting furnished rooms to lodgers

room·mate *n* **:** one of two or more persons sharing a room or dwelling

roomy *adj* **room·i·er; room·i·est :** SPACIOUS — **room·i·ness** *n*

[1]**roost** *n* **:** a support on which birds perch

[2]**roost** *vb* **:** to settle on a roost

roost·er *n* **:** an adult male chicken

[1]**root** *n* **1 :** a leafless underground part of a plant that stores food and holds the plant in place **2 :** the part of something by which it is attached **3 :** something like a root especially in being a source of support or growth **4 :** SOURCE 1 **5 :** [1]CORE 3 **6 :** a word or part of a word from which other words are obtained by adding a prefix or suffix — **root·ed** *adj*

[2]**root** *vb* **1 :** to form or cause to form roots **2 :** to attach by or as if by roots **3 :** UPROOT 1

[3]**root** *vb* **:** to turn up or dig with the snout

[4]**root** *vb* **:** [2]CHEER 2 — **root·er** *n*

root beer *n* **:** a sweet drink flavored with extracts of roots and herbs

[1]**rope** *n* **1 :** a large stout cord of strands (as of fiber or wire) twisted or braided together **2 :** a noose used for hanging **3 :** a row or string (as of beads) made by braiding, twining, or threading

[2]**rope** *vb* **roped; rop·ing 1 :** to bind, fasten, or tie with a rope **2 :** to set off or divide by a rope **3 :** [1]LASSO — **rop·er** *n*

ro·sa·ry *n, pl* **ro·sa·ries :** a string of beads used in counting prayers

[1]**rose** *past of* RISE

[2]**rose** *n* **1 :** a showy and often fragrant white, yellow, pink, or red flower that grows on a prickly shrub (**rose·bush**) with compound leaves **2 :** a moderate purplish red

rose·mary *n* **:** a fragrant mint that has branching woody stems and is used in cooking and in perfumes

ro·sette *n* **:** a badge or ornament of ribbon gathered in the shape of a rose

rose·wood *n* **:** a reddish or purplish wood streaked with black and that is valued for making furniture

Rosh Ha·sha·nah *n* **:** the Jewish New Year observed as a religious holiday in September or October

ros·in *n* **:** a hard brittle yellow to dark red substance obtained especially from pine trees and used in varnishes and on violin bows

ros·ter *n* **:** an orderly list usually of people belonging to some group

ros·trum *n, pl* **rostrums** *or* **ros·tra :** a stage or platform for public speaking

rosy *adj* **ros·i·er; ros·i·est 1 :** of the color rose **2 :** PROMISING, HOPEFUL

[1]**rot** *vb* **rot·ted; rot·ting 1 :** to undergo decay **:** SPOIL **2 :** to go to ruin

[2]**rot** *n* **1 :** the process of rotting **:** the state of being rotten **2 :** a disease of plants or of animals in which tissue decays

ro·ta·ry *adj* **1 :** turning on an axis like a wheel **2 :** having a rotating part

ro·tate *vb* **ro·tat·ed; ro·tat·ing 1 :** to turn about an axis or a center **2 :** to do or cause to do something in turn **3 :** to pass in a series

ro·ta·tion *n* **1 :** the act of rotating especially on an axis **2 :** the growing of different crops in the same field usually in a regular order

rote *n* **:** repeating from memory of forms or phrases with little or no attention to meaning

ro·tor *n* **1 :** the part of an electrical machine that turns **2 :** a system of spinning horizontal blades that support a helicopter in the air

rot·ten *adj* **1 :** having rotted **2 :** morally bad **3 :** very unpleasant or worthless — **rot·ten·ly** *adv* — **rot·ten·ness** *n*

ro·tund *adj* **1 :** somewhat round **2 :** [4]PLUMP — **ro·tund·ly** *adv* — **ro·tund·ness** *n*

rouge *n* **:** a cosmetic used to give a red color to cheeks or lips

[1]**rough** *adj* **1 :** uneven in surface **2 :** not calm **3 :** being harsh or violent **4 :** coarse or rugged in nature or look **5 :** not complete or exact — **rough·ly** *adv* — **rough·ness** *n*

[2]**rough** *n* **1 :** uneven ground covered with high grass, brush, and stones **2 :** something in a crude or unfinished state

[3]**rough** *vb* **1 :** ROUGHEN **2 :** to handle roughly **:** BEAT **3 :** to make or shape roughly — **rough it :** to live without ordinary comforts

rough·age *n* **:** coarse food (as bran) whose bulk increases the activity of the bowel

rough·en *vb* **:** to make or become rough

rough·neck *n* **:** a rough person **:** ROWDY

[1]**round** *adj* **1 :** having every part of the surface or circumference the same distance from the center **2 :** shaped like a cylinder **3 :** [4]PLUMP **4 :** [1]COMPLETE 1, FULL **5 :** nearly correct or exact **6 :** LARGE **7 :** moving in or forming a circle **8 :** having curves rather than angles — **round·ish** *adj* — **round·ly** *adv* — **round·ness** *n*

[2]**round** *adv* **:** [1]AROUND

[3]**round** *n* **1 :** something (as a circle or globe) that is round **2 :** a song in which three or four singers sing the same melody and words one after another at intervals **3 :** a round or curved part (as a rung of a ladder) **4 :** an indirect path **5 :** a regularly covered route **6 :** a series or cycle of repeated actions or events **7 :** one shot fired by a soldier or a gun **8 :** ammunition for one shot **9 :** a unit of play in a contest or game **10 :** a cut of beef especially between the rump and the lower leg

[4]**round** *vb* **1 :** to make or become round **2 :** to go or pass around **3 :** to bring to completion

4 : to express as a round number 5 : to follow a winding course

[5]**round** *prep* : [2]AROUND 1, 2, 3

round·about *adj* : not direct

round·house *n, pl* **round·hous·es** : a circular building where locomotives are kept or repaired

round trip *n* : a trip to a place and back usually over the same route

round·up *n* 1 : the gathering together of animals on the range by circling them in vehicles or on horseback and driving them in 2 : a gathering together of scattered persons or things 3 : [2]SUMMARY

round up *vb* 1 : to collect (as cattle) by circling in vehicles or on horseback and driving 2 : to gather in or bring together

round·worm *n* : any of a group of worms with long round bodies that are not segmented and that include serious parasites of people and animals

rouse *vb* **roused; rous·ing** 1 : [1]AWAKE 1 2 : to stir up : EXCITE

[1]**rout** *n* 1 : a state of wild confusion or disorderly retreat 2 : a disastrous defeat

[2]**rout** *vb* 1 : to put to flight 2 : to defeat completely

[1]**route** *n* : a regular, chosen, or assigned course of travel

[2]**route** *vb* **rout·ed; rout·ing** 1 : to send or transport by a selected route 2 : to arrange and direct the order of (as a series of factory operations)

[1]**rou·tine** *n* : a standard or usual way of doing

[2]**routine** *adj* 1 : [2]COMMONPLACE, ORDINARY 2 : done or happening in a standard or usual way — **rou·tine·ly** *adv*

rove *vb* **roved; rov·ing** : to wander without definite plan or direction — **rov·er** *n*

[1]**row** *vb* 1 : to move a boat by means of oars 2 : to travel or carry in a rowboat

[2]**row** *n* : an act or instance of rowing

[3]**row** *n* 1 : a series of persons or things in an orderly sequence 2 : [1]WAY 1, STREET

[4]**row** *n* : a noisy disturbance or quarrel

row·boat *n* : a boat made to be rowed

[1]**row·dy** *adj* **row·di·er; row·di·est** : coarse or rough in behavior — **row·di·ness** *n*

[2]**rowdy** *n, pl* **rowdies** : a rowdy person

roy·al *adj* 1 : of or relating to a sovereign : REGAL 2 : fit for a king or queen — **roy·al·ly** *adv*

roy·al·ty *n, pl* **roy·al·ties** 1 : royal status or power 2 : royal character or conduct 3 : members of a royal family 4 : a share of a product or profit (as of a mine) claimed by the owner for allowing another to use the property 5 : payment made to the owner of a patent or copyright for the use of it

[1]**rub** *vb* **rubbed; rub·bing** 1 : to move along the surface of a body with pressure 2 : to wear away or chafe with friction 3 : to cause discontent, irritation, or anger 4 : to scour, polish, erase, or smear by pressure and friction — **rub the wrong way** : to cause to be angry : IRRITATE

[2]**rub** *n* 1 : something that gets in the way : DIFFICULTY 2 : something that is annoying 3 : the act of rubbing

rub·ber *n* 1 : something used in rubbing 2 : an elastic substance obtained from the milky juice of some tropical plants 3 : a synthetic substance like rubber 4 : something (as an overshoe) made of rubber

rubber band *n* : a continuous band made of rubber for holding things together : ELASTIC

rubber stamp *n* : a stamp with a printing face of rubber

rub·bish *n* : TRASH

rub·ble *n* : a confused mass of broken or worthless things

ru·ble *n* : a Russian coin or bill

ru·by *n, pl* **rubies** 1 : a precious stone of a deep red color 2 : a deep purplish red

ruck·us *n* : [4]ROW

rud·der *n* : a movable flat piece attached at the rear of a ship or aircraft for steering

rud·dy *adj* **rud·di·er; rud·di·est** : having a healthy reddish color — **rud·di·ness** *n*

rude *adj* **rud·er; rud·est** 1 : roughly made 2 : not refined or cultured : UNCOUTH 3 : IMPOLITE — **rude·ly** *adv* — **rude·ness** *n*

ru·di·ment *n* : a basic principle

ru·di·men·ta·ry *adj* 1 : ELEMENTARY, SIMPLE 2 : not fully developed

rue *vb* **rued; ru·ing** : to feel sorrow or regret for

rue·ful *adj* 1 : exciting pity or sympathy 2 : MOURNFUL 1, REGRETFUL

ruff *n* 1 : a large round collar of pleated muslin or linen worn by men and women in the sixteenth and seventeenth centuries 2 : a fringe of long hair or feathers on the neck of an animal or bird

ruf·fi·an *n* : a brutal cruel person

[1]**ruf·fle** *vb* **ruf·fled; ruf·fling** 1 : to disturb the smoothness of 2 : [1]TROUBLE 1, VEX 3 : to erect (as feathers) in or like a ruff 4 : to make into or provide with a ruffle

[2]**ruffle** *n* : a strip of fabric gathered or pleated on one edge

rug *n* : a piece of thick heavy fabric usually with a nap or pile used especially as a floor covering

rug·ged *adj* 1 : having a rough uneven surface 2 : involving hardship 3 : STRONG 9, TOUGH — **rug·ged·ly** *adv* — **rug·ged·ness** *n*

[1]**ru·in** *n* 1 : complete collapse or destruction

2 ruins *pl* **:** the remains of something destroyed **3 :** a cause of destruction

²ruin *vb* **1 :** to reduce to ruins **2 :** to damage beyond repair **3 :** ³BANKRUPT

ru·in·ous *adj* **:** causing or likely to cause ruin **:** DESTRUCTIVE — **ru·in·ous·ly** *adv*

¹rule *n* **1 :** a guide or principle for conduct or action **2 :** an accepted method, custom, or habit **3 :** the exercise of authority or control **:** GOVERNMENT **4 :** the time of a particular sovereign's reign **5 :** RULER 2

²rule *vb* **ruled; rul·ing 1 :** ¹CONTROL 2, DIRECT **2 :** to exercise authority over **:** GOVERN **3 :** to be supreme or outstanding in **4 :** to give or state as a considered decision **5 :** to mark with lines drawn along the straight edge of a ruler

rul·er *n* **1 :** ¹SOVEREIGN 1 **2 :** a straight strip (as of wood or metal) with a smooth edge that is marked off in units and used for measuring or as a guide in drawing straight lines

rum *n* **:** an alcoholic liquor made from sugarcane or molasses

¹rum·ble *vb* **rum·bled; rum·bling :** to make or move with a low heavy rolling sound

²rumble *n* **:** a low heavy rolling sound

¹ru·mi·nant *n* **:** an animal (as a cow) that chews the cud

²ruminant *adj* **1 :** chewing the cud **2 :** of or relating to the group of hoofed mammals that chew the cud

ru·mi·nate *vb* **ru·mi·nat·ed; ru·mi·nat·ing 1 :** to engage in thought **:** MEDITATE **2 :** to bring up and chew again what has been previously swallowed

¹rum·mage *vb* **rum·maged; rum·mag·ing :** to make an active search especially by moving about, turning over, or looking through the contents of a place or container

²rummage *n* **:** a confused collection of different articles

rum·my *n* **:** a card game in which each player tries to lay down cards in groups of three or more

¹ru·mor *n* **1 :** widely held opinion having no known source **:** HEARSAY **2 :** a statement or story that is in circulation but has not been proven to be true

²rumor *vb* **:** to tell by rumor **:** spread a rumor

rump *n* **1 :** the back part of an animal's body where the hips and thighs join **2 :** a cut of beef between the loin and the round

rum·ple *vb* **rum·pled; rum·pling :** ²WRINKLE, MUSS

rum·pus *n* **:** ⁴ROW, FRACAS

¹run *vb* **ran; run; run·ning 1 :** to go at a pace faster than a walk **2 :** to take to flight **3 :** to move freely about as one wishes **4 :** to go rapidly or hurriedly **5 :** to do something by or as if by running **6 :** to take part in a race **7 :** to move on or as if on wheels **8 :** to go back and forth often according to a fixed schedule **9 :** to migrate or move in schools **10 :** ²FUNCTION, OPERATE **11 :** to continue in force **12 :** to pass into a specified condition **13 :** ¹FLOW 1 **14 :** DISSOLVE 1 **15 :** to give off liquid **16 :** to tend to develop a specified feature or quality **17 :** ¹STRETCH 2 **18 :** to be in circulation **19 :** ²TRACE 4 **20 :** to pass over, across, or through **21 :** to slip through or past **22 :** to cause to penetrate **23 :** to cause to go **24 :** INCUR — **run into :** to meet by chance

²run *n* **1 :** an act or the action of running **2 :** a continuous series especially of similar things **3 :** sudden heavy demands from depositors, creditors, or customers **4 :** the quantity of work turned out in a continuous operation **5 :** the usual or normal kind **6 :** the distance covered in a period of continuous traveling **7 :** a regular course or trip **8 :** freedom of movement **9 :** a way, track, or path frequented by animals **10 :** an enclosure for animals where they may feed and exercise **11 :** a score made in baseball by a base runner reaching home plate **12 :** ²SLOPE 1 **13 :** a ravel in a knitted fabric

¹run·away *n* **1 :** ²FUGITIVE **2 :** a horse that is running out of control

²runaway *adj* **:** running away **:** escaping from control

run–down *adj* **1 :** being in poor condition **2 :** being in poor health

¹rung *past participle of* RING

²rung *n* **1 :** a rounded part placed as a crosspiece between the legs of a chair **2 :** one of the crosspieces of a ladder

run–in *n* **:** an angry dispute **:** QUARREL

run·ner *n* **1 :** one that runs **2 :** MESSENGER **3 :** a thin piece or part on or in which something slides **4 :** a slender creeping branch of a plant that roots at the end or at the joints to form new plants **5 :** a plant that forms or spreads by runners **6 :** a long narrow carpet (as for a hall)

run·ner–up *n, pl* **run·ners–up :** the competitor in a contest who finishes next to the winner

run·ny *adj* **:** running or likely to run

run out *vb* **1 :** to come to an end **:** EXPIRE **2 :** to become exhausted or used up — **run out of :** to use up the available supply of

run over *vb* **:** ¹OVERFLOW 2

runt *n* **:** an unusually small person or animal

run·way *n* **1 :** a path beaten by animals in going to and from feeding grounds **2 :** a paved strip of ground on a landing field for the landing and takeoff of aircraft

ru·pee *n* **:** any of various coins (as of India or Pakistan)

[1]**rup·ture** *n* **1 :** a break in peaceful or friendly relations **2 :** a breaking or tearing apart (as of body tissue) **3 :** a condition in which a body part (as a loop of intestine) bulges through the weakened wall of the cavity that contains it

[2]**rupture** *vb* **rup·tured; rup·tur·ing 1 :** to part by violence **:** BREAK **2 :** to produce a rupture in **3 :** to have a rupture

ru·ral *adj* **:** of or relating to the country, country people or life, or agriculture

rural free delivery *n* **:** the free delivery of mail on routes in country districts

ruse *n* **:** [1]TRICK 4, ARTIFICE

[1]**rush** *n* **:** a grasslike marsh plant with hollow stems used in chair seats and mats

[2]**rush** *vb* **1 :** to move forward or act with great haste or eagerness **2 :** to perform in a short time or at high speed **3 :** [1]ATTACK 1, CHARGE — **rush·er** *n*

[3]**rush** *n* **1 :** a violent forward motion **2 :** a burst of activity or speed **3 :** an eager migration of people usually to a new place in search of wealth

[4]**rush** *adj* **:** demanding special speed

[1]**Rus·sian** *adj* **:** of or relating to Russia, its people, or the Russian language

[2]**Russian** *n* **1 :** a person born or living in Russia **2 :** a language of the Russians

[1]**rust** *n* **1 :** a reddish coating formed on metal (as iron) when it is exposed especially to moist air **2 :** a plant disease caused by fungi that makes spots on plants **3 :** a fungus that causes a rust — **rust·like** *adj*

[2]**rust** *vb* **:** to make or become rusty

[1]**rus·tic** *adj* **1 :** of, relating to, or suitable for the country **2 :** [1]PLAIN 5, SIMPLE

[2]**rustic** *n* **:** a person living or raised in the country

[1]**rus·tle** *vb* **rus·tled; rus·tling 1 :** to make or cause to make a rustle **2 :** to steal (as cattle) from the range — **rus·tler** *n*

[2]**rustle** *n* **:** a quick series of small sounds

rusty *adj* **rust·i·er; rust·i·est 1 :** affected by rust **2 :** less skilled and slow through lack of practice or old age — **rust·i·ness** *n*

[1]**rut** *n* **1 :** a track worn by a wheel or by habitual passage **2 :** [1]ROUTINE

[2]**rut** *vb* **rut·ted; rut·ting :** to make a rut in

ru·ta·ba·ga *n* **:** a turnip with a large yellow root

ruth·less *adj* **:** having no pity **:** CRUEL — **ruth·less·ly** *adv* — **ruth·less·ness** *n*

-ry *n suffix, pl* **-ries :** -ERY

rye *n* **:** a hardy cereal grass grown especially for its edible seeds that are used in flour and animal feeds and in making whiskey

S

s *n, pl* **s's** *or* **ss** *often cap* **1 :** the nineteenth letter of the English alphabet **2 :** a grade rating a student's work as satisfactory

[1]**-s** *n pl suffix* — used to form the plural of most nouns that do not end in *s, z, sh, ch,* or *y* following a consonant and with or without an apostrophe to form the plural of abbreviations, numbers, letters, and symbols used as nouns

[2]**-s** *adv suffix* — used to form adverbs showing usual or repeated action or state

[3]**-s** *vb suffix* — used to form the third person singular present of most verbs that do not end in *s, z, sh, ch,* or *y* following a consonant

-'s *n suffix or pron suffix* — used to form the possessive of singular nouns, of plural nouns not ending in *s*, and of some pronouns

Sab·bath *n* **1 :** the seventh day of the week in the Jewish calendar beginning at sundown on Friday and lasting until sundown on Saturday **2 :** the first day of the week (as Sunday) kept for rest and worship

sa·ber *or* **sa·bre** *n* **:** a cavalry sword with a curved blade

saber–toothed tiger *n* **:** a very large prehistoric cat with long sharp curved eyeteeth

Sa·bin vaccine *n* **:** a material that is taken by mouth to prevent polio

sa·ble *n* **1 :** the color black **2 :** a meat-eating animal of northern Europe and Asia that is related to the marten and prized for its soft rich brown fur

[1]**sab·o·tage** *n* **:** deliberate destruction of or damage to property or machinery (as by enemy agents) to block production or a nation's war effort

[2]**sabotage** *vb* **sab·o·taged; sab·o·tag·ing :** to damage or block by sabotage

sac *n* **:** a baglike part of a plant or animal often containing a liquid — **sac·like** *adj*

sa·chem *n* **:** a North American Indian chief

[1]**sack** *n* **1 :** [1]BAG 1 **2 :** a sack and its contents

[2]**sack** *vb* **:** to put into a sack

[3]**sack** *vb* **:** to loot after capture

[4]**sack** *n* **:** the looting of a city by its conquerors

sack·ing *n* **:** a strong rough cloth (as burlap) from which sacks are made

sac·ra·ment *n* **:** a religious act or ceremony that is considered especially sacred

sa·cred *adj* **1 :** HOLY 1 **2 :** RELIGIOUS 2 **3 :** deserving to be respected and honored — **sa·cred·ness** *n*

[1]**sac·ri·fice** *n* **1 :** the act or ceremony of making an offering to God or a god especially on an altar **2 :** something offered as a religious act **3 :** an unselfish giving **4 :** a loss of profit

[2]**sacrifice** *vb* **sac·ri·ficed; sac·ri·fic·ing 1 :** to offer or kill as a sacrifice **2 :** to give for the sake of something else **3 :** to sell at a loss

sad *adj* **sad·der; sad·dest 1 :** filled with sorrow or unhappiness **2 :** causing or showing sorrow or gloom — **sad·ly** *adv* — **sad·ness** *n*

sad·den *vb* **:** to make or become sad

[1]**sad·dle** *n* **1 :** a seat (as for a rider on horseback) that is padded and usually covered with leather **2 :** something like a saddle in shape, position, or use

[2]**saddle** *vb* **sad·dled; sad·dling 1 :** to put a saddle on **2 :** to put a load on **:** BURDEN

saddle horse *n* **:** a horse suited for or trained for riding

sa·fa·ri *n* **:** a hunting trip especially in Africa

[1]**safe** *adj* **saf·er; saf·est 1 :** free or secure from harm or danger **2 :** successful in reaching base in baseball **3 :** giving protection or security against danger **4 :** HARMLESS **5 :** unlikely to be wrong **:** SOUND **6 :** not likely to take risks **:** CAREFUL — **safe·ly** *adv* — **safe·ness** *n*

[2]**safe** *n* **:** a metal chest for keeping something (as money) safe

[1]**safe·guard** *n* **:** something that protects and gives safety

[2]**safeguard** *vb* **:** to keep safe

safe·keep·ing *n* **:** the act of keeping safe **:** protection from danger or loss

safe·ty *n* **:** freedom from danger **:** SECURITY

safety belt *n* **:** a belt for holding a person to something (as a car seat)

safety pin *n* **:** a pin that is bent back on itself to form a spring and has a guard that covers the point

saf·fron *n* **1 :** an orange powder used especially to color or flavor foods that consists of the dried stigmas of a crocus with purple flowers **2 :** an orange to orange yellow

[1]**sag** *vb* **sagged; sag·ging 1 :** to sink, settle, or hang below the natural or right level **2 :** to become less firm or strong

[2]**sag** *n* **:** a sagging part or area

sa·ga *n* **:** a story of heroic deeds

sa·ga·cious *adj* **:** quick and wise in understanding and judging — **sa·ga·cious·ly** *adv* — **sa·ga·cious·ness** *n*

[1]**sage** *adj* **:** [2]WISE 1 — **sage·ly** *adv*

[2]**sage** *n* **:** a very wise person

[3]**sage** *n* **1 :** a mint that grows as a low shrub and has grayish green leaves used to flavor foods **2 :** a mint grown for its showy usually scarlet flowers **3 :** SAGEBRUSH

sage·brush *n* **:** a western American plant related to the daisies that grows as a low shrub and has a bitter juice and sharp smell

Sag·it·tar·i·us *n* **1 :** a constellation between Scorpio and Capricorn imagined as a centaur **2 :** the ninth sign of the zodiac or a person born under this sign

sa·gua·ro *n, pl* **sa·gua·ros :** a giant cactus of the southwestern United States

said *past of* SAY

[1]**sail** *n* **1 :** a sheet of fabric (as canvas) used to catch enough wind to move boats through the water or over ice **2 :** the sails of a ship considered as a group **3 :** a trip in a sailing vessel

[2]**sail** *vb* **1 :** to travel on a boat moved by the wind **2 :** to travel by water **3 :** to move or pass over by ship **4 :** to manage or direct the motion of (a boat or ship moved by the wind) **5 :** to move or glide along

sail·boat *n* **:** a boat equipped with sails

sail·fish *n* **:** a fish related to the swordfish but with a large sail-like fin on its back

sail·or *n* **:** a person who sails

saint *n* **1 :** a good and holy person and especially one who is declared to be worthy of special honor **2 :** a person who is very good especially about helping others

Saint Ber·nard *n* **:** a very large powerful dog bred originally in the Swiss Alps

saint·ly *adj* **:** like a saint or like that of a saint — **saint·li·ness** *n*

sake *n* **1 :** [1]PURPOSE **2 :** WELFARE 1, BENEFIT

sal·able *or* **sale·able** *adj* **:** good enough to sell **:** likely to be bought

sal·ad *n* **1 :** a dish of raw usually mixed vegetables served with a dressing **2 :** a cold dish of meat, shellfish, fruit, or vegetables served with a dressing

sal·a·man·der *n* **:** any of a group of animals that are related to the frogs but look like lizards

sa·la·mi *n* **:** a highly seasoned sausage of pork and beef

sal·a·ry *n, pl* **sal·a·ries :** a fixed amount of money paid at regular times for work done

sale *n* **1 :** an exchange of goods or property for money **2 :** the state of being available for purchase **3 :** [1]AUCTION **4 :** a selling of goods at lowered prices

sales·clerk *n* **:** a person who sells in a store

sales·man *n, pl* **sales·men :** a person who sells either in a territory or in a store

sales·per·son *n* **:** one who sells especially in a store

sales tax *n* **:** a tax paid by the buyer on goods bought

sales·wom·an *n, pl* **sales·wom·en :** a woman who sells either in a territory or in a store

sa·li·va *n* **:** a watery fluid that contains enzymes which break down starch and is secreted into the mouth from glands in the neck

sal·i·vary *adj* : of, relating to, or producing saliva

Salk vaccine *n* : a material given by injection to prevent polio

sal·low *adj* : of a grayish greenish yellow color

[1]**sal·ly** *n, pl* **sallies 1 :** a rushing out to attack especially by besieged soldiers **2 :** a funny remark

[2]**sally** *vb* **sal·lied; sal·ly·ing :** to rush out

salm·on *n* **1 :** a large fish (**Atlantic salmon**) of the northern Atlantic Ocean valued for food and sport **2 :** any of several fishes (**Pacific salmon**) of the northern Pacific Ocean valued for food and sport

sa·loon *n* **1 :** a large public hall (as on a passenger ship) **2 :** a place where liquors are sold and drunk : BAR

sal·sa *n* **1 :** a spicy sauce of tomatoes, onions, and hot peppers **2 :** popular music of Latin American origin with characteristics of jazz and rock

[1]**salt** *n* **1 :** a colorless or white substance that consists of sodium and chlorine and is used in seasoning foods, preserving meats and fish, and in making soap and glass **2 :** a compound formed by replacement of hydrogen in an acid by a metal or group of elements that act like a metal

[2]**salt** *vb* : to add salt to

[3]**salt** *adj* : containing salt : SALTY

salt·wa·ter *adj* : of, relating to, or living in salt water

salty *adj* **salt·i·er; salt·i·est :** of, tasting of, or containing salt

sal·u·ta·tion *n* **1 :** an act or action of greeting **2 :** a word or phrase used as a greeting at the beginning of a letter

[1]**sa·lute** *vb* **sa·lut·ed; sa·lut·ing 1 :** to address with expressions of kind wishes, courtesy, or honor **2 :** to honor by a standard military ceremony **3 :** to give a sign of respect to (as a military officer) especially by a smart movement of the right hand to the forehead

[2]**salute** *n* **1 :** GREETING 1, SALUTATION **2 :** a military show of respect or honor **3 :** the position taken or the movement made to salute a military officer

[1]**sal·vage** *n* **1 :** money paid for saving a wrecked or endangered ship or its cargo or passengers **2 :** the act of saving a ship **3 :** the saving of possessions in danger of being lost **4 :** something that is saved (as from a wreck)

[2]**salvage** *vb* **sal·vaged; sal·vag·ing :** to recover (something usable) especially from wreckage

sal·va·tion *n* **1 :** the saving of a person from the power and the results of sin **2 :** something that saves

[1]**salve** *n* : a healing or soothing ointment

[2]**salve** *vb* **salved; salv·ing :** to quiet or soothe with or as if with a salve

[1]**same** *adj* **1 :** not another : IDENTICAL **2 :** UNCHANGED **3 :** very much alike

[2]**same** *pron* : something identical with or like another

same·ness *n* **1 :** the quality or state of being the same **2 :** MONOTONY

sam·pan *n* : a Chinese boat with a flat bottom that is usually moved with oars

[1]**sam·ple** *n* : a part or piece that shows the quality of the whole

[2]**sample** *vb* **sam·pled; sam·pling :** to judge the quality of by samples : TEST

sam·pler *n* : a piece of cloth with letters or verses embroidered on it

san·a·to·ri·um *n* : a place for the care and treatment usually of people recovering from illness or having a disease likely to last a long time

sanc·tion *n* **1 :** approval by someone in charge **2 :** an action short of war taken by several nations to make another nation behave

sanc·tu·ary *n, pl* **sanc·tu·ar·ies 1 :** a holy or sacred place **2 :** the most sacred part (as near the altar) of a place of worship **3 :** a building for worship **4 :** a place of safety **5 :** the state of being protected

[1]**sand** *n* **1 :** loose material in grains produced by the natural breaking up of rocks **2 :** a soil made up mostly of sand

[2]**sand** *vb* **1 :** to sprinkle with sand **2 :** to smooth or clean with sand or sandpaper — **sand·er** *n*

san·dal *n* : a shoe that is a sole held in place by straps

san·dal·wood *n* : the fragrant yellowish heartwood of an Asian tree

sand·bag *n* : a bag filled with sand and used as a weight (as on a balloon) or as part of a wall or dam

sand·bar *n* : a ridge of sand formed in water by tides or currents

sand·box *n* : a large box for holding sand especially for children to play in

sand dollar *n* : a flat round sea urchin

sand·man *n, pl* **sand·men :** a genie said to make children sleepy by sprinkling sand in their eyes

[1]**sand·pa·per** *n* : paper that has rough material (as sand) glued on one side and is used for smoothing and polishing

[2]**sandpaper** *vb* : to rub with sandpaper

sand·pip·er *n* : a small shorebird related to the plovers

sand·stone *n* **:** rock made of sand held together by a natural cement

sand·storm *n* **:** a storm of wind (as in a desert) that drives clouds of sand

[1]**sand·wich** *n* **:** two or more slices of bread or a split roll with a filling (as meat or cheese) between them

[2]**sandwich** *vb* **:** to fit in between things

sandy *adj* **sand·i·er; sand·i·est 1 :** full of or covered with sand **2 :** of a yellowish gray color

sane *adj* **san·er; san·est 1 :** having a healthy and sound mind **2 :** very sensible — **sane·ness** *n*

sang *past of* SING

san·i·tar·i·um *n* **:** SANATORIUM

san·i·tary *adj* **1 :** of or relating to health or hygiene **2 :** free from filth, infection, or other dangers to health

san·i·ta·tion *n* **1 :** the act or process of making sanitary **2 :** the act of keeping things sanitary

san·i·ty *n* **:** the state of being sane

sank *past of* SINK

San·ta Claus *n* **:** the spirit of Christmas as represented by a jolly old man in a red suit who gives toys to children

[1]**sap** *n* **:** a watery juice that circulates through a higher plant and carries food and nutrients

[2]**sap** *vb* **sapped; sap·ping :** to weaken or exhaust little by little

sap·ling *n* **:** a young tree

sap·phire *n* **:** a clear bright blue precious stone

sap·wood *n* **:** young wood found just beneath the bark of a tree and usually lighter in color than the heartwood

sar·casm *n* **:** the use of words that normally mean one thing to mean just the opposite usually to hurt someone's feelings or show scorn

sar·cas·tic *adj* **1 :** showing or related to sarcasm **2 :** having the habit of sarcasm — **sar·cas·ti·cal·ly** *adv*

sar·dine *n* **:** a young or very small fish often preserved in oil and used for food

sa·ri *n* **:** a piece of clothing worn mainly by women of southern Asia that is a long light cloth wrapped around the body

sar·sa·pa·ril·la *n* **:** the dried root of a tropical American plant used especially as a flavoring

[1]**sash** *n* **:** a broad band of cloth worn around the waist or over the shoulder

[2]**sash** *n* **1 :** a frame for a pane of glass in a door or window **2 :** the movable part of a window

[1]**sass** *n* **:** a rude fresh reply

[2]**sass** *vb* **:** to reply to in a rude fresh way

sas·sa·fras *n* **:** a tall tree of eastern North America whose dried root bark was formerly used in medicine or as a flavoring

sassy *adj* **sass·i·er; sass·i·est :** given to or made up of sass

sat *past of* SIT

Sa·tan *n* **:** [1]DEVIL 1

satch·el *n* **:** a small bag for carrying clothes or books

sat·el·lite *n* **1 :** a smaller body that revolves around a planet **2 :** a vehicle sent out from the earth to revolve around the earth, moon, sun, or a planet **3 :** a country controlled by another more powerful country

satellite dish *n* **:** a bowl-shaped antenna for receiving transmissions (as of television programs) from a satellite orbiting the earth

sat·in *n* **:** a cloth (as of silk) with a shiny surface

sat·ire *n* **:** writing or cartoons meant to make fun of and often show the weaknesses of someone or something

sa·tir·i·cal *adj* **:** of, relating to, or showing satire

sat·is·fac·tion *n* **1 :** the act of satisfying **:** the condition of being satisfied **2 :** something that satisfies

sat·is·fac·to·ry *adj* **:** causing satisfaction — **sat·is·fac·to·ri·ly** *adv* — **sat·is·fac·to·ri·ness** *n*

sat·is·fy *vb* **sat·is·fied; sat·is·fy·ing 1 :** to carry out the terms of (as a contract) **2 :** to make contented **3 :** to meet the needs of **4 :** CONVINCE

sat·u·rate *vb* **sat·u·rat·ed; sat·u·rat·ing :** to soak full or fill to the limit

Sat·ur·day *n* **:** the seventh day of the week

Sat·urn *n* **:** the planet that is sixth in distance from the sun and has a diameter of about 115,000 kilometers

sa·tyr *n* **:** a forest god of the ancient Greeks believed to have the ears and the tail of a horse or goat

sauce *n* **1 :** a tasty liquid poured over food **2 :** stewed fruit

sauce·pan *n* **:** a small deep cooking pan with a handle

sau·cer *n* **:** a small shallow dish often with a slightly lower center for holding a cup

saucy *adj* **sauc·i·er; sauc·i·est 1 :** being rude and disrespectful **2 :** [2]TRIM — **sauc·i·ly** *adv* — **sauc·i·ness** *n*

sau·er·kraut *n* **:** finely cut cabbage soaked in a salty mixture

saun·ter *vb* **:** to walk in a slow relaxed way **:** STROLL

sau·ro·pod *n* **:** any of a group of plant-eating dinosaurs (as a brontosaurus)

sau·sage *n* **1 :** spicy ground meat (as pork) usually stuffed in casings **2 :** a roll of sausage in a casing

[1]sav·age *adj* **1 :** not tamed **:** WILD **2 :** being cruel and brutal **:** FIERCE — **sav·age·ly** *adv* — **sav·age·ness** *n*

[2]savage *n* **1 :** a person belonging to a group with a low level of civilization **2 :** a cruel person

sav·age·ry *n, pl* **sav·age·ries** **1 :** an uncivilized condition **2 :** savage behavior

[1]save *vb* **saved; sav·ing** **1 :** to free from danger **2 :** to keep from being ruined **:** PRESERVE **3 :** to put aside for later use **4 :** to keep from being spent, wasted, or lost **5 :** to make unnecessary

[2]save *prep* **:** [1]EXCEPT

sav·ing *n* **1 :** the act of rescuing **2 :** something saved **3 savings** *pl* **:** money put aside (as in a bank)

sav·ior *or* **sav·iour** *n* **1 :** a person who saves from ruin or danger **2** *cap* **:** JESUS

sa·vo·ry *adj* **:** pleasing to the taste or smell

[1]saw *past of* SEE

[2]saw *n* **1 :** a tool with a tooth-edged blade for cutting hard material **2 :** a machine that operates a toothed blade

[3]saw *vb* **sawed; sawed** *or* **sawn; saw·ing** **:** to cut or shape with a saw

[4]saw *n* **:** a common saying **:** PROVERB

saw·dust *n* **:** tiny bits (as of wood) which fall from something being sawed

saw·horse *n* **:** a frame or rack on which wood is rested while being sawed

saw·mill *n* **:** a mill or factory having machinery for sawing logs

saw–toothed *adj* **:** having an edge or outline like the teeth of a saw

sax·o·phone *n* **:** a musical wind instrument with a reed mouthpiece and a bent tubelike metal body with keys

[1]say *vb* **said; say·ing** **1 :** to express in words **2 :** to give as one's opinion or decision **:** DECLARE **3 :** [1]REPEAT 2, RECITE

[2]say *n* **1 :** an expression of opinion **2 :** the power to decide or help decide

say·ing *n* **:** PROVERB

scab *n* **1 :** a crust that forms over and protects a sore or wound **2 :** a plant disease in which crusted spots form on stems or leaves

scab·bard *n* **:** a protective case or sheath for the blade of a sword or dagger

scab·by *adj* **scab·bi·er; scab·bi·est** **1 :** having scabs **2 :** diseased with scab

sca·bies *n, pl* **scabies** **:** an itch or mange caused by mites living as parasites in the skin

scaf·fold *n* **1 :** a raised platform built as a support for workers and their tools and materials **2 :** a platform on which a criminal is executed

[1]scald *vb* **1 :** to burn with or as if with hot liquid or steam **2 :** to pour very hot water over **3 :** to bring to a heat just below the boiling point

[2]scald *n* **:** an injury caused by scalding

[1]scale *n* **1 :** either pan of a balance or the balance itself **2 :** an instrument or machine for weighing

[2]scale *vb* **scaled; scal·ing** **1 :** to weigh on scales **2 :** to have a weight of

[3]scale *n* **1 :** one of the small stiff plates that cover much of the body of some animals (as fish and snakes) **2 :** a thin layer or part (as a special leaf that protects a plant bud) suggesting a fish scale — **scaled** *adj* — **scale·less** *adj* — **scale·like** *adj*

[4]scale *vb* **scaled; scal·ing** **1 :** to remove the scales of **2 :** [2]FLAKE

[5]scale *vb* **scaled; scal·ing** **1 :** to climb by or as if by a ladder **2 :** to regulate or set according to a standard — often used with *down* or *up*

[6]scale *n* **1 :** a series of tones going up or down in pitch in fixed steps **2 :** a series of spaces marked off by lines and used for measuring distances or amounts **3 :** a number of like things arranged in order from the highest to the lowest **4 :** the size of a picture, plan, or model of a thing compared to the size of the thing itself **5 :** a standard for measuring or judging

scale insect *n* **:** any of a group of insects that are related to the plant lice, suck the juices of plants, and have winged males and wingless females which look like scales attached to the plant

[1]scal·lop *n* **1 :** an edible shellfish that is a mollusk with a ribbed shell in two parts **2 :** any of a series of rounded half-circles that form a border on an edge (as of lace)

[2]scallop *vb* **1 :** to bake with crumbs, butter, and milk **2 :** to embroider, cut, or edge with scallops

[1]scalp *n* **:** the part of the skin and flesh of the head usually covered with hair

[2]scalp *vb* **:** to remove the scalp from

scaly *adj* **scal·i·er; scal·i·est** **:** covered with or like scales

scamp *n* **:** RASCAL

[1]scam·per *vb* **:** to run or move lightly

[2]scamper *n* **:** a playful scampering or scurrying

scan *vb* **scanned; scan·ning** **1 :** to read or mark verses so as to show stress and rhythm **2 :** to examine or look over **3 :** to examine with a sensing device (as a scanner) especially to obtain information

scan·dal *n* **1 :** something that causes a general feeling of shame **:** DISGRACE **2 :** talk that injures a person's good name

scan·dal·ous *adj* **1 :** being or containing scandal **2 :** very bad or objectionable

Scan·di·na·vian *n* **:** a person born or living in Scandinavia

scan·ner *n* **:** a device that converts a printed image (as text or a photograph) into a form a computer can use (as for displaying on the screen)

[1]**scant** *adj* **1 :** barely enough **2 :** not quite full **3 :** having only a small supply

[2]**scant** *vb* **:** to give or use less than needed **:** be stingy with

scanty *adj* **scant·i·er; scant·i·est :** barely enough

[1]**scar** *n* **1 :** a mark left after injured tissue has healed **2 :** an ugly mark (as on furniture) **3 :** the lasting effect of some unhappy experience

[2]**scar** *vb* **scarred; scar·ring :** to mark or become marked with a scar

scar·ab *n* **:** a large dark beetle used in ancient Egypt as a symbol of eternal life

scarce *adj* **scarc·er; scarc·est 1 :** not plentiful **2 :** hard to find **:** RARE — **scarce·ness** *n*

scarce·ly *adv* **1 :** only just **2 :** certainly not

scar·ci·ty *n, pl* **scar·ci·ties :** the condition of being scarce

[1]**scare** *vb* **scared; scar·ing :** to be or become frightened suddenly

[2]**scare** *n* **1 :** a sudden fright **2 :** a widespread state of alarm

scare·crow *n* **:** a crude human figure set up to scare away birds and animals from crops

scarf *n, pl* **scarves** *or* **scarfs 1 :** a piece of cloth worn loosely around the neck or on the head **2 :** a long narrow strip of cloth used as a cover (as on a bureau)

scar·la·ti·na *n* **:** a mild scarlet fever

[1]**scar·let** *n* **:** a bright red

[2]**scarlet** *adj* **:** of the color scarlet

scarlet fever *n* **:** a contagious disease in which there is a sore throat, a high fever, and a rash

scary *adj* **scar·i·er; scar·i·est :** causing fright

scat *vb* **scat·ted; scat·ting :** to go away quickly

scat·ter *vb* **1 :** to toss, sow, or place here and there **2 :** to separate and go in different ways

scat·ter·brain *n* **:** a flighty thoughtless person — **scat·ter·brained** *adj*

scav·en·ger *n* **1 :** a person who picks over junk or garbage for useful items **2 :** an animal that lives on decayed material

scene *n* **1 :** a division of an act in a play **2 :** a single interesting or important happening in a play or story **3 :** the place and time of the action in a play or story **4 :** the painted screens and slides used as backgrounds on the stage **:** SCENERY **5 :** something that attracts or holds one's gaze **:** VIEW **6 :** a display of anger or misconduct

scen·ery *n* **1 :** the painted scenes used on a stage and the furnishings that go with them **2 :** outdoor scenes or views

sce·nic *adj* **1 :** of or relating to stage scenery **2 :** giving views of natural scenery

[1]**scent** *n* **1 :** an odor left by some animal or person no longer in a place or given off (as by flowers) at a distance **2 :** a usual or particular and often agreeable odor **3 :** power or sense of smell **4 :** a course followed by someone in search or pursuit of something **5 :** [1]PERFUME 2

[2]**scent** *vb* **1 :** to become aware of or follow through the sense of smell **2 :** to get a hint of **3 :** to fill with an odor **:** PERFUME

scep·ter *or* **scep·tre** *n* **:** a rod carried by a ruler as a sign of authority

[1]**sched·ule** *n* **1 :** a written or printed list **2 :** a list of the times set for certain events **:** TIMETABLE **3 :** AGENDA, PROGRAM

[2]**schedule** *vb* **sched·uled; sched·ul·ing :** to form into or add to a schedule

[1]**scheme** *n* **1 :** a plan or program of something to be done **:** PROJECT **2 :** a secret plan **:** PLOT **3 :** an organized design

[2]**scheme** *vb* **schemed; schem·ing :** to form a scheme — **schem·er** *n*

Schick test *n* **:** a test to find out whether a person might easily catch diphtheria

schol·ar *n* **1 :** a student in a school **:** PUPIL **2 :** a person who knows a great deal about one or more subjects

schol·ar·ly *adj* **:** like that of or suitable to learned persons

schol·ar·ship *n* **1 :** the qualities of a scholar **:** LEARNING **2 :** money given a student to help pay for further education

scho·las·tic *adj* **:** of or relating to schools, pupils, or education

[1]**school** *n* **1 :** a place for teaching and learning **2 :** a session of school **3 :** SCHOOLHOUSE **4 :** the teachers and pupils of a school **5 :** a group of persons who share the same opinions and beliefs

[2]**school** *vb* **:** TEACH 2, TRAIN

[3]**school** *n* **:** a large number of one kind of fish or water animals swimming together

school·bag *n* **:** a bag for carrying schoolbooks

school·book *n* **:** a book used in schools

school·boy *n* **:** a boy who goes to school

school·girl *n* **:** a girl who goes to school

school·house *n, pl* **school·hous·es :** a building used as a place for teaching and learning

school·ing *n* **:** EDUCATION 1

school·mas·ter *n* **:** a man who has charge of a school or teaches in a school

school·mate *n* **:** a fellow pupil

school·mis·tress *n* : a woman who has charge of a school or teaches in a school
school·room *n* : CLASSROOM
school·teach·er *n* : a person who teaches in a school
school·work *n* : lessons done at school or assigned to be done at home
school·yard *n* : the playground of a school
schoo·ner *n* : a ship usually having two masts with the mainmast located toward the center and the shorter mast toward the front
schwa *n* **1** : an unstressed vowel that is the usual sound of the first and last vowels of the English word *America* **2** : the symbol ə commonly used for a schwa and sometimes also for a similarly pronounced stressed vowel (as in *cut*)
sci·ence *n* **1** : a branch of knowledge in which what is known is presented in an orderly way **2** : a branch of study that is concerned with collecting facts and forming laws to explain them
sci·en·tif·ic *adj* **1** : of or relating to science or scientists **2** : using or applying the methods of science — **sci·en·tif·i·cal·ly** *adv*
sci·en·tist *n* : a person who knows much about science or does scientific work
scis·sors *n sing or pl* : a cutting instrument with two blades fastened together so that the sharp edges slide against each other
scoff *vb* : to show great disrespect with mocking laughter or behavior
¹scold *n* : a person given to criticizing and blaming others
²scold *vb* : to find fault with or criticize in an angry way — **scold·ing** *n*
¹scoop *n* **1** : a large deep shovel for digging, dipping, or shoveling **2** : a shovellike tool or utensil for digging into a soft substance and lifting out some of it **3** : a motion made with or as if with a scoop **4** : the amount held by a scoop
²scoop *vb* **1** : to take out or up with or as if with a scoop **2** : to make by scooping
scoot *vb* : to go suddenly and fast
scoot·er *n* **1** : a vehicle consisting of a narrow base mounted between a front and a back wheel and guided by a handle attached to the front wheel **2** : MOTOR SCOOTER
scope *n* **1** : space or opportunity for action or thought **2** : the area or amount covered, reached, or viewed
scorch *vb* **1** : to burn on the surface **2** : to burn so as to brown or dry out
¹score *n* **1** : a group of twenty things : TWENTY **2** : a line (as a scratch) made with or as if with something sharp **3** : a record of points made or lost (as in a game) **4** : DEBT 2 **5** : a duty or an injury kept in mind for later action **6** : ¹GROUND 3, REASON **7** : the written or printed form of a musical composition — **score·less** *adj*
²score *vb* **scored; scor·ing** **1** : to set down in an account : RECORD **2** : to keep the score in a game **3** : to cut or mark with a line, scratch, or notch **4** : to make or cause to make a point in a game **5** : ACHIEVE 2, WIN **6** : ²GRADE 3, MARK
¹scorn *n* **1** : an emotion involving both anger and disgust **2** : a person or thing very much disliked
²scorn *vb* : to show scorn for
scorn·ful *adj* : feeling or showing scorn — **scorn·ful·ly** *adv*
Scor·pio *n* **1** : a constellation between Libra and Sagittarius imagined as a scorpion **2** : the eighth sign of the zodiac or a person born under this sign
scor·pi·on *n* : an animal related to the spiders that has a long jointed body ending in a slender tail with a poisonous stinger at the end
Scot *n* : a person born or living in Scotland
¹Scotch *adj* : ¹SCOTTISH
²Scotch *n pl* : ²SCOTTISH
scot–free *adj* : completely free from duty, harm, or punishment
¹Scot·tish *adj* : of or relating to Scotland or the Scottish
²Scottish *n pl* : the people of Scotland
scoun·drel *n* : a mean or wicked person : VILLAIN
¹scour *vb* **1** : to rub hard with a rough substance in order to clean **2** : to free or clear from impurities by or as if by rubbing
²scour *n* : an action or result of scouring
³scour *vb* : to go or move swiftly about, over, or through in search of something
¹scourge *n* **1** : ²WHIP 1 **2** : a cause of widespread or great suffering
²scourge *vb* **scourged; scourg·ing** **1** : to whip severely : FLOG **2** : to cause severe suffering to : AFFLICT
¹scout *vb* **1** : to go about in search of information **2** : to make a search
²scout *n* **1** : a person, group, boat, or plane that scouts **2** : the act of scouting **3** *often cap* : BOY SCOUT **4** *often cap* : GIRL SCOUT
scout·ing *n* **1** : the act of one that scouts **2** *often cap* : the general activities of Boy Scout and Girl Scout groups
scout·mas·ter *n* : the leader of a troop of Boy Scouts
scow *n* : a large boat with a flat bottom and square ends that is used chiefly for loading and unloading ships and for carrying rubbish
¹scowl *vb* : ¹FROWN 1
²scowl *n* : an angry look
scram *vb* **scrammed; scram·ming** : to go away at once

¹scram·ble *vb* **scram·bled; scram·bling 1** : to move or climb quickly on hands and knees **2** : to work hard to win or escape something **3** : to mix together in disorder **4** : to cook the mixed whites and yolks of eggs by stirring them while frying

²scramble *n* : the act or result of scrambling

¹scrap *n* **1 scraps** *pl* : pieces of leftover food **2** : a small bit **3** : waste material (as metal) that can be made fit to use again

²scrap *vb* **scrapped; scrap·ping 1** : to break up (as a ship) into scrap **2** : to throw away as worthless

³scrap *n* : ¹QUARREL 2, FIGHT

scrap·book *n* : a blank book in which clippings or pictures are kept

¹scrape *vb* **scraped; scrap·ing 1** : to remove by repeated strokes of a sharp or rough tool **2** : to clean or smooth by rubbing **3** : to rub or cause to rub so as to make a harsh noise : SCUFF **4** : to hurt or roughen by dragging against a rough surface **5** : to get with difficulty and a little at a time — **scrap·er** *n*

²scrape *n* **1** : the act of scraping **2** : a sound, mark, or injury made by scraping **3** : a disagreeable or trying situation

¹scratch *vb* **1** : to scrape or injure with claws, nails, or an instrument **2** : to make a scraping noise **3** : to erase by scraping

²scratch *n* : a mark or injury made by scratching

scratchy *adj* **scratch·i·er; scratch·i·est** : likely to scratch or make sore or raw

¹scrawl *vb* : to write quickly and carelessly : SCRIBBLE

²scrawl *n* : something written carelessly or without skill

scraw·ny *adj* **scraw·ni·er; scraw·ni·est** : poorly nourished : SKINNY

¹scream *vb* : to cry out (as in fright) with a loud and shrill sound

²scream *n* : a long cry that is loud and shrill

¹screech *n* : a shrill harsh cry usually expressing terror or pain

²screech *vb* : to cry out usually in terror or pain

¹screen *n* **1** : a curtain or wall used to hide or to protect **2** : a network of wire set in a frame for separating finer parts from coarser parts (as of sand) **3** : a frame that holds a usually wire netting and is used to keep out pests (as insects) **4** : the flat surface on which movies are projected **5** : the surface on which the image appears in an electronic display (as on a television set or computer terminal)

²screen *vb* **1** : to hide or protect with or as if with a screen **2** : to separate or sift with a screen

screen saver *n* : a computer program that usually displays images on the screen of a computer that is on but not in use so as to prevent damage to the screen

¹screw *n* **1** : a nail-shaped or rod-shaped piece of metal with a winding ridge around its length used for fastening and holding pieces together **2** : the act of screwing tight : TWIST **3** : PROPELLER

²screw *vb* **1** : to attach or fasten with a screw **2** : to operate, tighten, or adjust with a screw **3** : to turn or twist on a thread on or like that on a screw

screw·driv·er *n* : a tool for turning screws

¹scrib·ble *vb* **scrib·bled; scrib·bling** : to write quickly or carelessly — **scrib·bler** *n*

²scribble *n* : something scribbled

scribe *n* **1** : a teacher of Jewish law **2** : a person who copies writing (as in a book)

scrim·mage *n* **1** : a confused struggle **2** : the action between two football teams when one attempts to move the ball down the field

script *n* **1** : the written form of a play or movie or the lines to be said by a radio or television performer **2** : a type used in printing that resembles handwriting **3** : HANDWRITING

scrip·ture *n* **1** *cap* : BIBLE 1 **2** : writings sacred to a religious group

¹scroll *n* **1** : a roll of paper or parchment on which something is written or engraved **2** : an ornament resembling a length of paper usually rolled at both ends

²scroll *vb* : to move words or images up or down a display screen as if by unrolling a scroll

¹scrub *n* **1** : a thick growth of small or stunted shrubs or trees **2** : one of poor size or quality

²scrub *vb* **scrubbed; scrub·bing** : to rub hard in washing

³scrub *n* : the act or an instance or a period of scrubbing

scrub·by *adj* **scrub·bi·er; scrub·bi·est 1** : of poor size or quality **2** : covered with scrub

scruff *n* : the loose skin on the back of the neck

scruffy *adj* **scruff·i·er; scruff·i·est** : dirty or shabby in appearance

scru·ple *n* **1** : a sense of right and wrong that keeps one from doing as one pleases **2** : a feeling of guilt when one does wrong

scru·pu·lous *adj* : having or showing very careful and strict regard for what is right and proper — **scru·pu·lous·ly** *adv*

scuba *n* : equipment used for breathing while swimming underwater

scuba diver *n* : a person who swims underwater with scuba gear

scuff *vb* **1** : to scrape the feet while walking

2 : to become rough or scratched through wear

[1]**scuf·fle** *vb* **scuf·fled; scuf·fling 1 :** to struggle in a confused way at close quarters **2 :** to shuffle one's feet

[2]**scuffle** *n* **:** a rough confused struggle

scull *n* **1 :** an oar used at the rear of a boat to drive it forward **2 :** one of a pair of short oars **3 :** a boat driven by one or more pairs of sculls

sculp·tor *n* **:** one that sculptures

[1]**sculp·ture** *n* **1 :** the action or art of making statues by carving or chiseling (as in wood or stone), by modeling (as in clay), or by casting (as in melted metal) **2 :** work produced by sculpture

[2]**sculpture** *vb* **sculp·tured; sculp·tur·ing :** to make sculptures

scum *n* **1 :** a film of matter that rises to the top of a boiling or fermenting liquid **2 :** a coating on the surface of still water

scurf *n* **:** thin dry scales or a coating of these (as on a leaf or the skin)

[1]**scur·ry** *vb* **scur·ried; scur·ry·ing :** to move in a brisk way

[2]**scurry** *n, pl* **scur·ries :** the act of scurrying

[1]**scur·vy** *n* **:** a disease caused by lack of vitamin C in which the teeth loosen, the gums soften, and there is bleeding under the skin

[2]**scurvy** *adj* **scur·vi·er; scur·vi·est :** [1]MEAN 4, CONTEMPTIBLE

[1]**scut·tle** *n* **:** a pail or bucket for carrying coal

[2]**scuttle** *n* **:** a small opening with a lid or cover (as in the deck of a ship)

[3]**scuttle** *vb* **scut·tled; scut·tling :** to sink by cutting holes through the bottom or sides

[4]**scuttle** *vb* **scut·tled; scut·tling :** to run rapidly from view

scythe *n* **:** a tool with a curved blade on a long curved handle that is used to mow grass or grain by hand

sea *n* **1 :** a body of salt water not as large as an ocean and often nearly surrounded by land **2 :** OCEAN 1 **3 :** rough water **4 :** something suggesting a sea's great size or depth

sea anemone *n* **:** a hollow sea animal with a flowerlike cluster of tentacles about its mouth

sea·bird *n* **:** a bird (as a gull) that lives about the open ocean

sea·coast *n* **:** the shore of the sea

sea cucumber *n* **:** a sea animal related to the starfishes and sea urchins that has a long flexible muscular body shaped like a cucumber

sea dog *n* **:** an experienced sailor

sea·far·er *n* **:** a person who travels over the ocean **:** MARINER

[1]**sea·far·ing** *adj* **:** of, given to, or employed in seafaring

[2]**seafaring** *n* **:** a traveling over the sea as work or as recreation

sea·food *n* **:** edible saltwater fish and shellfish

sea·go·ing *adj* **:** suitable or used for sea travel

sea gull *n* **:** a gull that lives near the sea

sea horse *n* **:** a small fish with a head which looks like that of a horse

[1]**seal** *n* **1 :** a sea mammal that swims with flippers, lives mostly in cold regions, mates and bears young on land, eats flesh, and is hunted for fur, hides, or oil **2 :** the soft dense fur of a seal

[2]**seal** *n* **1 :** something (as a pledge) that makes safe or secure **2 :** a device with a cut or raised design or figure that can be stamped or pressed into wax or paper **3 :** a piece of wax stamped with a design and used to seal a letter or package **4 :** a stamp that may be used to close a letter or package **5 :** something that closes tightly **6 :** a closing that is tight and perfect

[3]**seal** *vb* **1 :** to mark with a seal **2 :** to close or make fast with or as if with a seal — **seal·er** *n*

sea level *n* **:** the surface of the sea midway between the average high and low tides

sea lion *n* **:** a very large seal of the Pacific Ocean

seal·skin *n* **:** [1]SEAL 2

[1]**seam** *n* **1 :** the fold, line, or groove made by sewing together or joining two edges or two pieces of material **2 :** a layer of a mineral or metal

[2]**seam** *vb* **1 :** to join with a seam **2 :** to mark with a line, scar, or wrinkle

sea·man *n, pl* **sea·men 1 :** a person who helps in the handling of a ship at sea **:** SAILOR **2 :** an enlisted person in the Navy or Coast Guard ranking above a seaman apprentice

seaman apprentice *n* **:** an enlisted person in the Navy or Coast Guard ranking above a seaman recruit

seaman recruit *n* **:** an enlisted person of the lowest rank in the Navy or Coast Guard

seam·stress *n* **:** a woman who sews especially for a living

sea·plane *n* **:** an airplane that can rise from and land on water

sea·port *n* **:** a port, harbor, or town within reach of seagoing ships

sear *vb* **1 :** to dry by or as if by heat **:** PARCH **2 :** to scorch or make brown on the surface by heat

[1]**search** *vb* **1 :** to go through carefully and thoroughly in an effort to find something **2 :** to look in the pockets or the clothing of for something hidden — **search·ing·ly** *adv*

[2]**search** *n* **:** an act or instance of searching

search engine *n* **:** computer software used to search data (as text or a database) for requested information
search·light *n* **:** a lamp for sending a beam of bright light
sea·shell *n* **:** the shell of a sea creature
sea·shore *n* **:** the shore of a sea
sea·sick *adj* **:** sick at the stomach from the pitching or rolling of a ship — **sea·sick·ness** *n*
sea·side *n* **:** SEACOAST
[1]**sea·son** *n* **1 :** one of the four quarters into which a year is commonly divided **2 :** a period of time associated with something special
[2]**season** *vb* **1 :** to make pleasant to the taste by use of seasoning **2 :** to make suitable for use (as by aging or drying)
sea·son·al *adj* **:** of, relating to, or coming only at a certain season
sea·son·ing *n* **:** something added to food to give it more flavor
[1]**seat** *n* **1 :** something (as a chair) used to sit in or on **2 :** the part of something on which one rests in sitting **3 :** the place on or at which a person sits **4 :** a place that serves as a capital or center — **seat·ed** *adj*
[2]**seat** *vb* **1 :** to place in or on a seat **2 :** to provide seats for
seat belt *n* **:** a strap (as in an automobile or airplane) designed to hold a person in a seat
sea urchin *n* **:** a rounded shellfish related to the starfishes that lives on or burrows in the sea bottom and is covered with spines
sea·wall *n* **:** a bank or a wall to prevent sea waves from cutting away the shore
sea·wa·ter *n* **:** water in or from the sea
sea·weed *n* **:** an alga (as a kelp) that grows in the sea
se·cede *vb* **:** to end one's association with an organization (as a country, church, or political party)
se·clud·ed *adj* **:** hidden from sight
se·clu·sion *n* **:** the condition of being secluded
[1]**sec·ond** *adj* **1 :** being next after the first **2 :** next lower in rank, value, or importance than the first
[2]**second** *adv* **:** in the second place or rank
[3]**second** *n* **:** one that is second
[4]**second** *n* **1 :** a sixtieth part of a minute of time or of a degree **2 :** MOMENT 1, INSTANT
[5]**second** *vb* **:** to support a motion or nomination so that it may be debated or voted on
sec·ond·ary *adj* **1 :** second in rank, value, or importance **2 :** of, relating to, or being the second of three levels of stress in pronunciation **3 :** derived from or coming after something original or primary
sec·ond·hand *adj* **1 :** not new **:** having had a previous owner **2 :** selling used goods
second lieutenant *n* **:** a commissioned officer of the lowest rank in the Army, Air Force, or Marine Corps
sec·ond·ly *adv* **:** in the second place
sec·ond–rate *adj* **:** of ordinary quality or value
se·cre·cy *n, pl* **se·cre·cies 1 :** the habit of keeping things secret **2 :** the quality or state of being secret or hidden
[1]**se·cret** *adj* **1 :** hidden from the knowledge of others **2 :** done or working in secrecy — **se·cret·ly** *adv*
[2]**secret** *n* **:** something kept or planned to be kept from others' knowledge
sec·re·tary *n, pl* **sec·re·tar·ies 1 :** a person who is employed to take care of records and letters for another person **2 :** an officer of a business corporation or society who has charge of the letters and records and who keeps minutes of meetings **3 :** a government official in charge of the affairs of a department **4 :** a writing desk with a top section for books
[1]**se·crete** *vb* **se·cret·ed; se·cret·ing :** to produce and give off as a secretion
[2]**secrete** *vb* **se·cret·ed; se·cret·ing :** to put in a hiding place
se·cre·tion *n* **1 :** the act or process of secreting some substance **2 :** a substance formed in and given off by a gland that usually performs a useful function in the body **3 :** a concealing or hiding of something
se·cre·tive *adj* **:** not open or frank
sect *n* **:** a group within a religion which has a special set of teachings or a special way of doing things
[1]**sec·tion** *n* **1 :** a part cut off or separated **2 :** a part of a written work **3 :** the appearance that a thing has or would have if cut straight through **4 :** a part of a country, group of people, or community
[2]**section** *vb* **:** to cut into sections
sec·tor *n* **:** a part of an area or of a sphere of activity
sec·u·lar *adj* **1 :** not concerned with religion or the church **2 :** not bound by a monk's vows **:** not belonging to a religious order
[1]**se·cure** *adj* **se·cur·er; se·cur·est 1 :** free from danger or risk **2 :** strong or firm enough to ensure safety **3 :** [1]SURE 5, ASSURED
[2]**secure** *vb* **se·cured; se·cur·ing 1 :** to make safe **2 :** to fasten tightly **3 :** to get hold of **:** ACQUIRE
se·cu·ri·ty *n, pl* **se·cu·ri·ties 1 :** the state of being secure **:** SAFETY **2 :** something given as a pledge of payment **3 :** something (as a

stock certificate) that is evidence of debt or ownership

se·dan *n* **1 :** SEDAN CHAIR **2 :** a closed automobile seating four or more persons that has two or four doors and a permanent top

sedan chair *n* **:** a portable and often covered chair made to hold one person and to be carried on two poles by two men

se·date *adj* **:** quiet and steady in manner or conduct — **se·date·ly** *adv* — **se·date·ness** *n*

[1]sed·a·tive *adj* **:** tending to calm or to relieve tension

[2]sedative *n* **:** a sedative medicine

sedge *n* **:** a plant that is like grass but has solid stems and grows in tufts in marshes

sed·i·ment *n* **1 :** the material from a liquid that settles to the bottom **2 :** material (as stones and sand) carried onto land or into water by water, wind, or a glacier

sed·i·men·ta·ry *adj* **:** of, relating to, or formed from sediment

se·duce *vb* **se·duced; se·duc·ing :** to persuade to do wrong

[1]see *vb* **saw; seen; see·ing 1 :** to have the power of sight **:** view with the eyes **2 :** to have experience of **3 :** to understand the meaning or importance of **4 :** to make sure **5 :** to attend to **6 :** to meet with **7 :** ACCOMPANY 1, ESCORT

[2]see *n* **1 :** the city in which a bishop's church is located **2 :** DIOCESE

[1]seed *n* **1 :** a tiny resting plant closed in a protective coat and able to develop under suitable conditions into a plant like the one that produced it **2 :** a small structure (as a spore or a tiny dry fruit) other than a true seed by which a plant reproduces itself **3 :** the descendants of one individual **4 :** a source of development or growth **:** GERM 2 — **seed·ed** *adj* — **seed·less** *adj*

[2]seed *vb* **1 :** [2]SOW 2, PLANT **2 :** to produce or shed seeds **3 :** to take the seeds out of

seed·case *n* **:** a dry hollow fruit (as a pod) that contains seeds

seed·ling *n* **1 :** a young plant grown from seed **2 :** a young tree before it becomes a sapling

seed plant *n* **:** a plant that reproduces by true seeds

seed·pod *n* **:** POD

seedy *adj* **seed·i·er; seed·i·est 1 :** having or full of seeds **2 :** poor in condition or quality

seek *vb* **sought; seek·ing 1 :** to try to find **2 :** to try to win or get **3 :** to make an attempt

seem *vb* **1 :** to give the impression of being **:** APPEAR **2 :** to suggest to one's own mind

seem·ing *adj* **:** APPARENT 3 — **seem·ing·ly** *adv*

seen *past participle of* SEE

seep *vb* **:** to flow slowly through small openings

seer *n* **:** a person who predicts events

[1]see·saw *n* **1 :** an up-and-down or backward-and-forward motion or movement **2 :** a children's game of riding on the ends of a plank balanced in the middle with one end going up while the other goes down **3 :** the plank used in seesaw

[2]seesaw *vb* **1 :** to ride on a seesaw **2 :** to move like a seesaw

seethe *vb* **seethed; seeth·ing 1 :** to move without order as if boiling **2 :** to be in a state of great excitement

seg·ment *n* **1 :** any of the parts into which a thing is divided or naturally separates **2 :** a part cut off from a figure (as a circle) by means of a line or plane **3 :** a part of a straight line included between two points — **seg·ment·ed** *adj*

seg·re·gate *vb* **seg·re·gat·ed; seg·re·gat·ing :** to set apart from others

seg·re·ga·tion *n* **1 :** an act, process, or instance of segregating **2 :** enforced separation of a race, class, or group from the rest of society

seis·mo·graph *n* **:** a device that measures and records vibrations of the earth — **seis·mo·graph·ic** *adj* — **seis·mog·ra·phy** *n*

seize *vb* **seized; seiz·ing 1 :** to take possession of by force **2 :** to take hold of suddenly or with force

sei·zure *n* **:** an act of seizing **:** the state of being seized

sel·dom *adv* **:** not often **:** RARELY

[1]se·lect *adj* **1 :** chosen to include the best or most suitable individuals **2 :** of special value or excellence

[2]select *vb* **:** to pick out from a number or group **:** CHOOSE

se·lec·tion *n* **1 :** the act or process of selecting **2 :** something that is chosen

se·lec·tive *adj* **:** involving or based on selection

se·le·ni·um *n* **:** a gray powdery chemical element used chiefly in electronic devices

self *n, pl* **selves 1 :** a person regarded as an individual apart from everyone else **2 :** a special side of a person's character

self- *prefix* **1 :** oneself or itself **2 :** of or by oneself or itself **3 :** to, with, for, or toward oneself or itself

self–ad·dressed *adj* **:** addressed for return to the sender

self–cen·tered *adj* **:** SELFISH

self–con·fi·dence *n* **:** confidence in oneself and one's abilities

self–con·scious *adj* **:** too much aware of one's feelings or appearance when in the presence of other people — **self–con·scious·ly** *adv* — **self–con·scious·ness** *n*

self–con·trol *n* **:** control over one's own impulses, emotions, or actions

self–de·fense *n* **:** the act of defending oneself or one's property

self–es·teem *n* **:** a satisfaction in oneself and one's own abilities

self–ev·i·dent *adj* **:** having no need of proof

self–gov·ern·ing *adj* **:** having self-government

self–gov·ern·ment *n* **:** government by action of the people making up a community **:** democratic government

self–im·por·tant *adj* **:** believing or acting as if one's importance is greater than it really is

self·ish *adj* **:** taking care of oneself without thought for others — **self·ish·ness** *n*

self·less *adj* **:** not selfish — **self·less·ly** *adv* — **self·less·ness** *n*

self–pro·pelled *adj* **:** containing within itself the means for its own movement

self–re·li·ance *n* **:** trust in one's own efforts and abilities

self–re·spect *n* **1 :** a proper regard for oneself as a human being **2 :** regard for one's standing or position

self–re·straint *n* **:** proper control over one's actions or emotions

self–righ·teous *adj* **:** strongly convinced of the rightness of one's actions or beliefs

self·same *adj* **:** exactly the same

self–ser·vice *n* **:** the serving of oneself with things to be paid for to a cashier usually upon leaving

self–worth *n* **:** SELF-ESTEEM

sell *vb* **sold; sell·ing 1 :** to betray a person or duty **2 :** to exchange in return for money or something else of value **3 :** to be sold or priced — **sell·er** *n*

selves *pl of* SELF

sem·a·phore *n* **1 :** a device for sending signals that can be seen by the receiver **2 :** a system of sending signals with two flags held one in each hand

sem·blance *n* **:** outward appearance

se·mes·ter *n* **:** either of two terms that make up a school year

semi- *prefix* **1 :** half **2 :** partly **:** not completely **3 :** partial

semi·cir·cle *n* **:** half of a circle

semi·cir·cu·lar *adj* **:** having the form of a semicircle

semi·co·lon *n* **:** a punctuation mark ; that can be used to separate parts of a sentence which need clearer separation than would be shown by a comma, to separate main clauses which have no conjunction between, and to separate phrases and clauses containing commas

semi·con·duc·tor *n* **:** a solid substance whose ability to conduct electricity is between that of a conductor and that of an insulator

[1]semi·fi·nal *adj* **:** coming before the final round in a tournament

[2]semi·fi·nal *n* **:** a semifinal match or game

sem·i·nary *n, pl* **sem·i·nar·ies 1 :** a private school at or above the high school level **2 :** a school for the training of priests, ministers, or rabbis

semi·sol·id *adj* **:** having the qualities of both a solid and a liquid

sen·ate *n* **1 :** the upper branch of a legislature in a country or state **2 :** a governing body

sen·a·tor *n* **:** a member of a senate

send *vb* **sent; send·ing 1 :** to cause to go **2 :** to set in motion by physical force **3 :** to cause to happen **4 :** to cause someone to pass a message on or do an errand **5 :** to give an order or request to come or go **6 :** to bring into a certain condition — **send·er** *n*

[1]se·nior *n* **1 :** a person older or higher in rank than someone else **2 :** a student in the final year of high school or college

[2]senior *adj* **1 :** being older — used to distinguish a father from a son with the same name **2 :** higher in rank or office **3 :** of or relating to seniors in a high school or college

senior airman *n* **:** an enlisted person in the Air Force who ranks above airman first class but who has not been made sergeant

senior chief petty officer *n* **:** a petty officer in the Navy or Coast Guard ranking above a chief petty officer

senior master sergeant *n* **:** a noncommissioned officer in the Air Force ranking above a master sergeant

sen·sa·tion *n* **1 :** awareness (as of noise or heat) or a mental process (as seeing or smelling) resulting from stimulation of a sense organ **2 :** an indefinite bodily feeling **3 :** a state of excited interest or feeling **4 :** a cause or object of excited interest

sen·sa·tion·al *adj* **:** causing or meant to cause great interest

[1]sense *n* **1 :** a meaning or one of a set of meanings a word, phrase, or story may have **2 :** a specialized function or mechanism (as sight, taste, or touch) of the body that involves the action and effect of a stimulus on a sense organ **3 :** a particular sensation or kind of sensation **4 :** awareness arrived at through or as if through the senses **5 :** an awareness or understanding of something **6 :** the ability to make wise decisions **7 :** good reason or excuse

[2]sense *vb* **sensed; sens·ing :** to be or become conscious of

sense·less *adj* **1 :** UNCONSCIOUS 2 **2 :** STU-

PID 2 — **sense·less·ly** *adv* — **sense·less·ness** *n*

sense organ *n* **:** a bodily structure (as the retina of the eye) that reacts to a stimulus (as light) and activates associated nerves so that they carry impulses to the brain

sen·si·bil·i·ty *n, pl* **sen·si·bil·i·ties 1 :** the ability to receive or feel sensations **2 :** the emotion or feeling of which a person is capable

sen·si·ble *adj* **1 :** possible to take in by the senses or mind **2 :** capable of feeling or perceiving **3 :** showing or containing good sense or reason — **sen·si·ble·ness** *n* — **sen·si·bly** *adv*

sen·si·tive *adj* **1 :** capable of responding to stimulation **2 :** easily or strongly affected, impressed, or hurt **3 :** readily changed or affected by the action of a certain thing — **sen·si·tive·ly** *adv* — **sen·si·tive·ness** *n*

sen·si·tiv·i·ty *n* **:** the quality or state of being sensitive

sen·so·ry *adj* **:** of or relating to sensation or the senses

sen·su·al *adj* **:** relating to the pleasing of the senses

sent *past of* SEND

[1]**sen·tence** *n* **1 :** JUDGMENT 1 **2 :** punishment set by a court **3 :** a group of words that makes a statement, asks a question, or expresses a command, wish, or exclamation **4 :** a mathematical statement (as an equation) in words or symbols

[2]**sentence** *vb* **sen·tenced; sen·tenc·ing :** to give a sentence to

sen·ti·ment *n* **1 :** a thought or attitude influenced by feeling **2 :** OPINION 1 **3 :** tender feelings of affection or yearning

sen·ti·men·tal *adj* **1 :** influenced strongly by sentiment **2 :** primarily affecting the emotions

sen·ti·nel *n* **:** SENTRY

sen·try *n, pl* **sentries :** a person (as a soldier) on duty as a guard

se·pal *n* **:** one of the specialized leaves that form the calyx of a flower

[1]**sep·a·rate** *vb* **sep·a·rat·ed; sep·a·rat·ing 1 :** to set or keep apart **2 :** to make a distinction between **3 :** to cease to be together **:** PART

[2]**sep·a·rate** *adj* **1 :** set or kept apart **2 :** divided from each other **3 :** not shared **:** INDIVIDUAL **4 :** having independent existence

sep·a·rate·ly *adv* **:** apart from others

sep·a·ra·tion *n* **1 :** the act of separating **:** the state of being separated **2 :** a point or line at which something is divided

sep·a·ra·tor *n* **:** a machine for separating cream from milk

Sep·tem·ber *n* **:** the ninth month of the year

sep·tet *n* **:** a group or set of seven

sep·ul·cher *or* **sep·ul·chre** *n* **:** [1]GRAVE, TOMB

se·quel *n* **1 :** an event that follows or comes afterward **:** RESULT **2 :** a book that continues a story begun in another

se·quence *n* **1 :** the condition or fact of following or coming after something else **2 :** [2]RESULT 1, SEQUEL **3 :** the order in which things are or should be connected, related, or dated

se·quin *n* **:** a bit of shiny metal or plastic used as an ornament usually on clothing

se·quoia *n* **1 :** a California tree that grows almost 100 meters tall and has needles as leaves and small egg-shaped cones **2 :** REDWOOD

se·ra·pe *n* **:** a colorful woolen shawl or blanket

ser·e·nade *n* **:** music sung or played at night under the window of a lady

se·rene *adj* **1 :** [1]CLEAR 2 **2 :** being calm and quiet — **se·rene·ly** *adv* — **se·rene·ness** *n*

se·ren·i·ty *n* **:** the quality or state of being serene

serf *n* **:** a servant or laborer of olden times who was treated as part of the land worked on and went along with the land if it was sold

serge *n* **:** a woolen cloth that wears well

ser·geant *n* **1 :** a noncommissioned officer in the Army or Marine Corps ranking above a corporal or in the Air Force ranking above an airman first class **2 :** an officer in a police force

sergeant first class *n* **:** a noncommissioned officer in the Army ranking above a staff sergeant

sergeant major *n* **1 :** the chief noncommissioned officer at a military headquarters **2 :** a noncommissioned officer in the Marine Corps ranking above a first sergeant **3 :** a staff sergeant major or command sergeant major in the Army

[1]**se·ri·al** *adj* **:** arranged in or appearing in parts or numbers that follow a regular order — **se·ri·al·ly** *adv*

[2]**serial** *n* **:** a story appearing (as in a magazine or on television) in parts at regular intervals

se·ries *n, pl* **series :** a number of things or events arranged in order and connected by being alike in some way

se·ri·ous *adj* **1 :** thoughtful or quiet in appearance or manner **2 :** requiring much thought or work **3 :** being in earnest **:** not light or casual **4 :** IMPORTANT 1 **5 :** being such as to cause distress or harm — **se·ri·ous·ly** *adv* — **se·ri·ous·ness** *n*

ser·mon *n* **1 :** a speech usually by a priest, minister, or rabbi for the purpose of giving religious instruction **2 :** a serious talk to a person about his or her conduct

ser·pent *n* **:** a usually large snake

se·rum *n* **:** the liquid part that can be separated from coagulated blood, contains antibodies, and is sometimes used to prevent or cure disease

ser·vant *n* **:** a person hired to perform household or personal services

[1]**serve** *vb* **served; serv·ing 1 :** to be a servant **2 :** to give the service and respect due **3 :** [2]WORSHIP 1 **4 :** to put in **:** SPEND **5 :** to be of use **:** answer some purpose **6 :** to provide helpful services **7 :** to be enough for **8 :** to hold an office **:** perform a duty **9 :** to help persons to food or set out helpings of food or drink **10 :** to furnish with something needed or desired **11 :** to make a serve (as in tennis)

[2]**serve** *n* **:** an act of putting the ball or shuttlecock in play (as in tennis or badminton)

[1]**ser·vice** *n* **1 :** the occupation or function of serving or working as a servant **2 :** the work or action of one that serves **3 :** [2]HELP 1, USE **4 :** a religious ceremony **5 :** a helpful or useful act **:** good turn **6 :** [2]SERVE **7 :** a set of dishes or silverware **8 :** a branch of public employment or the people working in it **9 :** a nation's armed forces **10 :** an organization for supplying some public demand or keeping up and repairing something

[2]**service** *vb* **ser·viced; ser·vic·ing :** to work at taking care of or repairing

ser·vice·able *adj* **1 :** fit for or suited to some use **2 :** lasting or wearing well in use — **ser·vice·able·ness** *n*

ser·vice·man *n, pl* **ser·vice·men :** a male member of the armed forces

service station *n* **:** a place for servicing motor vehicles especially with gasoline and oil

ser·vile *adj* **1 :** of or suitable to a slave **2 :** lacking spirit or independence

serv·ing *n* **:** a helping of food

ser·vi·tude *n* **:** the condition of a slave

ses·sion *n* **1 :** a single meeting (as of a court, lawmaking body, or school) **2 :** a whole series of meetings **3 :** the time during which a court, congress, or school meets

[1]**set** *vb* **set; set·ting 1 :** to cause to sit **2 :** to cover and warm eggs to hatch them **3 :** to put or fix in a place or condition **4 :** to arrange in a desired and especially a normal position **5 :** [1]START 5 **6 :** to cause to be, become, or do **7 :** to fix at a certain amount **:** SETTLE **8 :** to furnish as a model **9 :** to put in order for immediate use **10 :** to provide (as words or verses) with music **11 :** to fix firmly **12 :** to become or cause to become firm or solid **13 :** to form and bring to maturity **14 :** to pass below the horizon **:** go down — **set about :** to begin to do — **set forth :** to start out

[2]**set** *n* **1 :** the act or action of setting **:** the condition of being set **2 :** a number of persons or things of the same kind that belong or are used together **3 :** the form or movement of the body or of its parts **4 :** an artificial setting for a scene of a play or motion picture **5 :** a group of tennis games that make up a match **6 :** a collection of mathematical elements **7 :** an electronic apparatus

[3]**set** *adj* **1 :** fixed by authority **2 :** not very willing to change **3 :** [1]READY 1

set·back *n* **:** a slowing of progress **:** a temporary defeat

set down *vb* **1 :** to place at rest on a surface **2 :** to land an aircraft

set in *vb* **:** to make its appearance **:** BEGIN

set off *vb* **1 :** to cause to stand out **2 :** to set apart **3 :** to cause to start **4 :** EXPLODE 1 **5 :** to start a journey

set on *vb* **:** to urge to attack or chase

set out *vb* **1 :** UNDERTAKE 1 **2 :** to begin on a course or journey

set·tee *n* **:** a long seat with a back

set·ter *n* **1 :** one that sets **2 :** a large dog that has long hair and is used in hunting birds

set·ting *n* **1 :** the act of one that sets **2 :** that in which something is set or mounted **3 :** the background (as time and place) of the action of a story or play **4 :** a batch of eggs for hatching

[1]**set·tle** *vb* **set·tled; set·tling 1 :** to place so as to stay **2 :** to come to rest **3 :** to sink gradually to a lower level **4 :** to sink in a liquid **5 :** to make one's home **6 :** to apply oneself **7 :** to fix by agreement **8 :** to put in order **9 :** to make quiet **:** CALM **10 :** DECIDE 1 **11 :** to complete payment on **12 :** ADJUST 1

[2]**settle** *n* **:** a long wooden bench with arms and a high solid back

set·tle·ment *n* **1 :** the act of settling **:** the condition of being settled **2 :** final payment (as of a bill) **3 :** the act or fact of establishing colonies **4 :** a place or region newly settled **5 :** a small village **6 :** an institution that gives help to people in a crowded part of a city

set·tler *n* **:** a person who settles in a new region **:** COLONIST

set up *vb* **1 :** to place or secure in position **2 :** to put in operation **:** FOUND, ESTABLISH

[1]**sev·en** *adj* **:** being one more than six

[2]**seven** *n* **:** one more than six **:** 7

[1]**sev·en·teen** *adj* **:** being one more than sixteen

[2]**seventeen** *n* **:** one more than sixteen **:** 17

[1]**sev·en·teenth** *adj* **:** coming right after sixteenth

[2]**seventeenth** *n* : number seventeen in a series

[1]**sev·enth** *adj* : coming right after sixth

[2]**seventh** *n* **1** : number seven in a series **2** : one of seven equal parts

[1]**sev·en·ti·eth** *adj* : coming right after sixty-ninth

[2]**seventieth** *n* : number seventy in a series

[1]**sev·en·ty** *adj* : being seven times ten

[2]**seventy** *n* : seven times ten : 70

sev·er *vb* **1** : to put or keep apart : DIVIDE **2** : to come or break apart

[1]**sev·er·al** *adj* **1** : separate or distinct from others : DIFFERENT **2** : consisting of more than two but not very many

[2]**several** *pron* : a small number : more than two but not many

se·vere *adj* **se·ver·er; se·ver·est** **1** : very strict : HARSH **2** : serious in feeling or manner : GRAVE **3** : not using unnecessary ornament : PLAIN **4** : hard to bear or deal with — **se·vere·ly** *adv* — **se·vere·ness** *n*

se·ver·i·ty *n* : the quality or state of being severe

sew *vb* **sewed; sewn** *or* **sewed; sew·ing** **1** : to join or fasten by stitches **2** : to work with needle and thread

sew·age *n* : waste materials carried off by sewers

[1]**sew·er** *n* : one that sews

[2]**sew·er** *n* : a usually covered drain to carry off water and waste

sew·er·age *n* **1** : SEWAGE **2** : the removal and disposal of sewage by sewers **3** : a system of sewers

sew·ing *n* **1** : the act, method, or occupation of one that sews **2** : material being sewed or to be sewed

sex *n* **1** : either of two divisions of living things and especially humans, one made up of males, the other of females **2** : the things that make males and females different from each other **3** : sexual activity

sex·ism *n* : distinction and especially unjust distinction based on sex and made against one person or group (as women) in favor of another

sex·ist *adj* : based on or showing sexism — **sexist** *n*

sex·tet *n* : a group or set of six

sex·ton *n* : an official of a church who takes care of church buildings and property

sex·u·al *adj* **1** : of or relating to sex or the sexes **2** : of, relating to, or being the form of reproduction in which germ cells from two parents combine in fertilization to form a new individual — **sex·u·al·ly** *adv*

shab·by *adj* **shab·bi·er; shab·bi·est** **1** : dressed in worn clothes **2** : faded and worn from use or wear **3** : not fair or generous — **shab·bi·ly** *adv* — **shab·bi·ness** *n*

shack *n* : HUT, SHANTY

[1]**shack·le** *n* **1** : a ring or band that prevents free use of the legs or arms **2** : something that prevents free action **3** : a U-shaped metal device for joining or fastening something

[2]**shackle** *vb* **shack·led; shack·ling** **1** : to bind or fasten with a shackle **2** : HINDER

shad *n, pl* **shad** : any of several sea fishes related to the herrings that have deep bodies, swim up rivers to spawn, and are important food fish

[1]**shade** *n* **1** : partial darkness **2** : space sheltered from light or heat and especially from the sun **3** **shades** *pl* : the shadows that gather as darkness falls **4** : GHOST, SPIRIT **5** : something that blocks off or cuts down light **6** : the darkening of some objects in a painting or drawing to suggest that they are in shade **7** : the darkness or lightness of a color **8** : a very small difference or amount

[2]**shade** *vb* **shad·ed; shad·ing** **1** : to shelter from light or heat **2** : to mark with shades of light or color **3** : to show or begin to have slight differences of color, value, or meaning

[1]**shad·ow** *n* **1** : [1]SHADE 1 **2** : a reflected image **3** : shelter from danger or view **4** : the dark figure cast on a surface by a body that is between the surface and the light **5** : PHANTOM **6** **shadows** *pl* : darkness caused by the setting of the sun **7** : a very little bit : TRACE

[2]**shadow** *vb* **1** : to cast a shadow upon **2** : to cast gloom over **3** : to follow and watch closely especially in a secret way

shad·owy *adj* **1** : not realistic **2** : full of shadow

shady *adj* **shad·i·er; shad·i·est** **1** : sheltered from the sun's rays **2** : not right or honest — **shad·i·ness** *n*

shaft *n* **1** : the long handle of a weapon (as a spear) **2** : one of two poles between which a horse is hitched to pull a wagon or carriage **3** : an arrow or its narrow stem **4** : a narrow beam of light **5** : a long narrow part especially when round **6** : the handle of a tool or instrument **7** : a bar to support rotating pieces of machinery or to give them motion **8** : a tall monument (as a column) **9** : a mine opening made for finding or mining ore **10** : an opening or passage straight down through the floors of a building

shag·gy *adj* **shag·gi·er; shag·gi·est** **1** : covered with or made up of a long, coarse, and tangled growth (as of hair or vegetation) **2** : having a rough or hairy surface — **shag·gi·ly** *adv* — **shag·gi·ness** *n*

[1]**shake** *vb* **shook; shak·en; shak·ing 1 :** to tremble or make tremble : QUIVER **2 :** to make less firm : WEAKEN **3 :** to move back and forth or to and fro **4 :** to cause to be, become, go, or move by or as if by a shake

[2]**shake** *n* **:** the act or motion of shaking

shak·er *n* **:** one that shakes or is used in shaking

shaky *adj* **shak·i·er; shak·i·est :** easily shaken : UNSOUND — **shak·i·ly** *adv* — **shak·i·ness** *n*

shale *n* **:** a rock with a fine grain formed from clay, mud, or silt

shall *helping verb, past* **should;** *present sing & pl* **shall 1 :** am or are going to or expecting to : WILL **2 :** is or are forced to : MUST

[1]**shal·low** *adj* **1 :** not deep **2 :** showing little knowledge, thought, or feeling — **shal·low·ness** *n*

[2]**shallow** *n* **:** a shallow place in a body of water — usually used in pl.

[1]**sham** *n* **:** [3]COUNTERFEIT, IMITATION

[2]**sham** *adj* **:** not real : FALSE

[3]**sham** *vb* **shammed; sham·ming :** to act in a deceiving way

sham·ble *vb* **sham·bled; sham·bling :** to walk in an awkward unsteady way

sham·bles *n sing or pl* **:** a place or scene of disorder or destruction

[1]**shame** *n* **1 :** a painful emotion caused by having done something wrong or improper **2 :** ability to feel shame **3 :** [1]DISHONOR 1, DISGRACE **4 :** something that brings disgrace or causes shame or strong regret

[2]**shame** *vb* **shamed; sham·ing 1 :** to make ashamed **2 :** [2]DISHONOR **3 :** to force by causing to feel shame

shame·faced *adj* **:** seeming ashamed — **shame·faced·ly** *adv* — **shame·faced·ness** *n*

shame·ful *adj* **:** bringing shame : DISGRACEFUL — **shame·ful·ly** *adv* — **shame·ful·ness** *n*

shame·less *adj* **:** having no shame — **shame·less·ly** *adv* — **shame·less·ness** *n*

[1]**sham·poo** *vb* **:** to wash the hair and scalp

[2]**shampoo** *n, pl* **sham·poos 1 :** a washing of the hair **2 :** a cleaner made for washing the hair

sham·rock *n* **:** a plant (as some clovers) that has leaves with three leaflets and is used as an emblem by the Irish

shank *n* **1 :** the lower part of the human leg : the equivalent part of a lower animal **2 :** the part of a tool that connects the working part with a part by which it is held or moved

shan't : shall not

shan·ty *n, pl* **shanties :** a small roughly built shelter or dwelling

[1]**shape** *vb* **shaped; shap·ing 1 :** to give a certain form or shape to **2 :** DEVISE **3 :** to make fit especially for some purpose : ADAPT **4 :** to take on a definite form or quality : DEVELOP — **shap·er** *n*

[2]**shape** *n* **1 :** outward appearance : FORM **2 :** the outline of a body : FIGURE **3 :** definite arrangement and form **4 :** [1]CONDITION 3 — **shaped** *adj*

shape·less *adj* **1 :** having no fixed or regular shape **2 :** not shapely — **shape·less·ly** *adv* — **shape·less·ness** *n*

shape·ly *adj* **shape·li·er; shape·li·est :** having a pleasing shape — **shape·li·ness** *n*

[1]**share** *n* **1 :** a portion belonging to one person **2 :** the part given or belonging to one of a number of persons owning something together **3 :** any of the equal portions into which a property or corporation is divided

[2]**share** *vb* **shared; shar·ing 1 :** to divide and distribute in portions **2 :** to use, experience, or enjoy with others **3 :** to take a part

share·crop *vb* **share·cropped; share·cropping :** to farm another's land for a share of the crop or profit — **share·crop·per** *n*

[1]**shark** *n* **:** any of a group of mostly fierce sea fishes that are typically gray, have a skeleton of cartilage, and include some forms that may attack humans

[2]**shark** *n* **:** a sly greedy person who takes advantage of others

[1]**sharp** *adj* **1 :** having a thin edge or fine point **2 :** brisk and cold **3 :** QUICK-WITTED, SMART **4 :** ATTENTIVE 1 **5 :** having very good ability to see or hear **6 :** ENERGETIC, BRISK **7 :** SEVERE 1, ANGRY **8 :** very trying to the feelings : causing distress **9 :** strongly affecting the senses **10 :** ending in a point or edge **11 :** involving an abrupt change **12 :** DISTINCT 2 **13 :** raised in pitch by a half step **14 :** higher than true pitch — **sharp·ly** *adv* — **sharp·ness** *n*

[2]**sharp** *adv* **1 :** in a sharp manner **2 :** at an exact time

[3]**sharp** *n* **1 :** a note or tone that is a half step higher than the note named **2 :** a sign # that tells that a note is to be made higher by a half step

sharp·en *vb* **:** to make or become sharp or sharper — **sharp·en·er** *n*

shat·ter *vb* **1 :** to break or fall to pieces **2 :** to damage badly : RUIN, WRECK

[1]**shave** *vb* **shaved; shaved** *or* **shav·en; shav·ing 1 :** to cut or trim off with a sharp blade **2 :** to make bare or smooth by cutting the hair from **3 :** to trim closely

[2]**shave** *n* **1 :** an operation of shaving **2 :** a narrow escape

shav·ing *n* **:** a thin slice or strip sliced off with a cutting tool

shawl *n* **:** a square or oblong piece of cloth

used especially by women as a loose covering for the head or shoulders

she *pron* **:** that female one

sheaf *n, pl* **sheaves 1 :** a bundle of stalks and ears of grain **2 :** a group of things fastened together — **sheaf·like** *adj*

shear *vb* **sheared; sheared** *or* **shorn; shear·ing 1 :** to cut the hair or wool from **:** CLIP **2 :** to strip of as if by cutting **3 :** to cut or break sharply — **shear·er** *n*

shears *n pl* **:** a cutting tool like a pair of large scissors

sheath *n, pl* **sheaths 1 :** a case for a blade (as of a knife) **2 :** a covering (as the outer wings of a beetle) suggesting a sheath in form or use

sheathe *vb* **sheathed; sheath·ing 1 :** to put into a sheath **2 :** to cover with something that protects

sheath·ing *n* **:** the first covering of boards or of waterproof material on the outside wall of a frame house or on a timber roof

sheaves *pl of* SHEAF

[1]**shed** *vb* **shed; shed·ding 1 :** to give off in drops **2 :** to cause (blood) to flow from a cut or wound **3 :** to spread abroad **4 :** REPEL 3 **5 :** to cast (as a natural covering) aside

[2]**shed** *n* **:** a structure built for shelter or storage

she'd : she had **:** she would

sheen *n* **:** a bright or shining condition **:** LUSTER

sheep *n, pl* **sheep 1 :** an animal related to the goat that is raised for meat or for its wool and skin **2 :** a weak helpless person who is easily led

sheep·fold *n* **:** a pen or shelter for sheep

sheep·herd·er *n* **:** a worker in charge of a flock of sheep

sheep·ish *adj* **1 :** like a sheep **2 :** embarrassed especially over being found out in a fault — **sheep·ish·ly** *adv* — **sheep·ish·ness** *n*

sheep·skin *n* **:** the skin of a sheep or leather prepared from it

[1]**sheer** *adj* **1 :** very thin or transparent **2 :** THOROUGH 1, ABSOLUTE **3 :** very steep — **sheer·ly** *adv* — **sheer·ness** *n*

[2]**sheer** *adv* **1 :** COMPLETELY **2 :** straight up or down

[1]**sheet** *n* **1 :** a broad piece of cloth (as an article of bedding used next to the body) **2 :** a broad piece of paper (as for writing or printing) **3 :** a broad surface **4 :** something that is very thin as compared with its length and width — **sheet·like** *adj*

[2]**sheet** *n* **:** a rope or chain used to adjust the angle at which the sail of a boat is set to catch the wind

sheikh *or* **sheik** *n* **:** an Arab chief

shek·el *n* **1 :** any of various ancient units of weight (as of the Hebrews) **2 :** a coin weighing one shekel

shelf *n, pl* **shelves 1 :** a flat piece (as of board or metal) set above a floor (as on a wall or in a bookcase) to hold things **2 :** something (as a sandbar or ledge of rock) that suggests a shelf

[1]**shell** *n* **1 :** a stiff hard covering of an animal (as a turtle, oyster, or beetle) **2 :** the tough outer covering of an egg **3 :** the outer covering of a nut, fruit, or seed especially when hard or tough and fibrous **4 :** something like a shell (as in shape, function, or material) **5 :** a narrow light racing boat rowed by one or more persons **6 :** a metal or paper case holding the explosive charge and the shot or object to be fired from a gun or cannon — **shelled** *adj*

[2]**shell** *vb* **1 :** to take out of the shell or husk **2 :** to remove the kernels of grain from (as a cob of Indian corn) **3 :** to shoot shells at or upon

she'll : she shall **:** she will

[1]**shel·lac** *n* **:** a varnish made from a material given off by an Asian insect dissolved usually in alcohol

[2]**shellac** *vb* **shel·lacked; shel·lack·ing :** to coat with shellac

shell·fish *n, pl* **shellfish :** an invertebrate animal that lives in water and has a shell — used mostly of edible forms (as oysters or crabs)

[1]**shel·ter** *n* **1 :** something that covers or protects **2 :** the condition of being protected

[2]**shelter** *vb* **1 :** to be a shelter for **:** provide with shelter **2 :** to find and use a shelter

shelve *vb* **shelved; shelv·ing 1 :** to place or store on shelves **2 :** [1]DEFER

shelves *pl of* SHELF

[1]**shep·herd** *n* **:** a person who takes care of sheep

[2]**shepherd** *vb* **:** to care for as or as if a shepherd

shep·herd·ess *n* **:** a woman who takes care of sheep

sher·bet *n* **:** a frozen dessert of fruit juice to which milk, the white of egg, or gelatin is added before freezing

sher·iff *n* **:** the officer of a county who is in charge of enforcing the law

she's : she is **:** she has

Shet·land pony *n* **:** any of a breed of small stocky horses with shaggy coats

[1]**shield** *n* **1 :** a broad piece of armor carried on the arm to protect oneself in battle **2 :** something that serves as a defense or protection

[2]**shield** *vb* **:** to cover or screen with or as if with a shield

[1]**shift** *vb* **1 :** to exchange for another of the same kind **2 :** to change or remove from one person or place to another **3 :** to change the arrangement of gears transmitting power (as in an automobile) **4 :** to get along without help **:** FEND

[2]**shift** *n* **1 :** the act of shifting **:** TRANSFER **2 :** a group of workers who work together during a scheduled period of time **3 :** the period during which one group of workers is working **4 :** GEARSHIFT

shift·less *adj* **:** lacking in ambition and energy **:** LAZY — **shift·less·ly** *adv* — **shift·less·ness** *n*

shifty *adj* **shift·i·er; shift·i·est :** not worthy of trust **:** TRICKY — **shift·i·ly** *adv* — **shift·i·ness** *n*

shil·ling *n* **:** an old British coin equal to $\frac{1}{20}$ pound

shim·mer *vb* **:** to shine with a wavering light **:** GLIMMER

[1]**shin** *n* **:** the front part of the leg below the knee

[2]**shin** *vb* **shinned; shin·ning :** to climb (as a pole) by grasping with arms and legs and moving oneself upward by repeated jerks

[1]**shine** *vb* **shone** *or* **shined; shin·ing 1 :** to give light **2 :** to be glossy **:** GLEAM **3 :** to be outstanding **4 :** to make bright by polishing

[2]**shine** *n* **1 :** brightness from light given off or reflected **2 :** fair weather **:** SUNSHINE **3 :** [2]POLISH 1

shin·er *n* **1 :** a small silvery American freshwater fish related to the carp **2 :** an eye discolored by injury **:** a black eye

[1]**shin·gle** *n* **1 :** a small thin piece of building material (as wood or an asbestos composition) for laying in overlapping rows as a covering for the roof or sides of a building **2 :** a small sign

[2]**shingle** *vb* **shin·gled; shin·gling :** to cover with shingles

shin·ny *vb* **shin·nied; shin·ny·ing :** [2]SHIN

shiny *adj* **shin·i·er; shin·i·est :** bright in appearance

[1]**ship** *n* **1 :** a large seagoing boat **2 :** a ship's crew **3 :** AIRSHIP, AIRPLANE **4 :** a vehicle for traveling beyond the earth's atmosphere

[2]**ship** *vb* **shipped; ship·ping 1 :** to put or receive on board for transportation by water **2 :** to cause to be transported **3 :** to take into a ship or boat **4 :** to sign on as a crew member on a ship

-ship *n suffix* **1 :** state **:** condition **:** quality **2 :** office **:** rank **:** profession **3 :** skill **4 :** something showing a quality or state of being **5 :** one having a specified rank

ship·board *n* **1 :** a ship's side **2 :** [1]SHIP 1

ship·ment *n* **1 :** the act of shipping **2 :** the goods shipped

ship·ping *n* **1 :** the body of ships in one place or belonging to one port or country **2 :** the act or business of a person who ships goods

ship·shape *adj* **:** being neat and orderly **:** TIDY

[1]**ship·wreck** *n* **1 :** a wrecked ship **2 :** the loss or destruction of a ship

[2]**shipwreck** *vb* **1 :** to cause to experience shipwreck **2 :** to destroy (a ship) by driving ashore or sinking

ship·yard *n* **:** a place where ships are built or repaired

shirk *vb* **1 :** to get out of doing what one ought to do **2 :** AVOID

shirt *n* **1 :** a garment for the upper part of the body usually with a collar, sleeves, a front opening, and a tail long enough to be tucked inside pants or a skirt **2 :** UNDERSHIRT

[1]**shiv·er** *vb* **:** to be made to shake (as by cold or fear) **:** QUIVER

[2]**shiver** *n* **:** an instance of shivering

[1]**shoal** *adj* **:** [1]SHALLOW 1

[2]**shoal** *n* **1 :** a place where a sea, lake, or river is shallow **2 :** a bank or bar of sand just below the surface of the water

[3]**shoal** *n* **:** [3]SCHOOL

[1]**shock** *n* **:** a bunch of sheaves of grain or stalks of corn set on end in the field

[2]**shock** *n* **1 :** the sudden violent collision of bodies in a fight **2 :** a violent shake or jerk **3 :** a sudden and violent disturbance of mind or feelings **4 :** a state of bodily collapse that usually follows severe crushing injuries, burns, or hemorrhage **5 :** the effect of a charge of electricity passing through the body of a person or animal

[3]**shock** *vb* **1 :** to strike with surprise, horror, or disgust **2 :** to affect by electrical shock **3 :** to drive into or out of by or as if by a shock

[4]**shock** *n* **:** a thick bushy mass (as of hair)

shock·ing *adj* **:** causing horror or disgust — **shock·ing·ly** *adv*

shod·dy *adj* **shod·di·er; shod·di·est :** poorly done or made — **shod·di·ly** *adv* — **shod·di·ness** *n*

[1]**shoe** *n* **1 :** an outer covering for the human foot usually having a thick and somewhat stiff sole and heel and a lighter upper part **2 :** something (as a horseshoe) like a shoe in appearance or use

[2]**shoe** *vb* **shod** *also* **shoed; shoe·ing :** to put a shoe on **:** furnish with shoes

shoe·horn *n* **:** a curved piece (as of metal) to help in putting on a shoe

shoe·lace *n* **:** a lace or string for fastening a shoe

shoe·mak·er *n* **:** a person who makes or repairs shoes

shoe·string *n* **:** SHOELACE

shone *past of* SHINE

shoo *vb* : to wave, scare, or send away by or as if by crying *shoo*
shook *past of* SHAKE
[1]**shoot** *vb* **shot; shoot·ing** **1 :** to let fly or cause to be driven forward with force **2 :** to cause a missile to be driven out of **3 :** to cause a weapon to discharge a missile **4 :** to force (a marble) forward by snapping the thumb **5 :** to hit or throw (as a ball or puck) toward a goal **6 :** to score by shooting **7 :** [2]PLAY 2 **8 :** to strike with a missile from a bow or gun **9 :** to push or slide into or out of a fastening **10 :** to thrust forward swiftly **11 :** to grow rapidly **12 :** to go, move, or pass rapidly **13 :** to pass swiftly along or through **14 :** to stream out suddenly : SPURT — **shoot·er** *n*
[2]**shoot** *n* **1 :** the part of a plant that grows above ground or as much of this as comes from a single bud **2 :** a hunting party or trip
shooting star *n* : a meteor appearing as a temporary streak of light in the night sky
[1]**shop** *n* **1 :** a worker's place of business **2 :** a building or room where goods are sold at retail : STORE **3 :** a place in which workers are doing a particular kind of work
[2]**shop** *vb* **shopped; shop·ping :** to visit shops for the purpose of looking over and buying goods — **shop·per** *n*
shop·keep·er *n* : STOREKEEPER 2
shop·lift·er *n* : a person who steals merchandise on display in stores
[1]**shore** *n* : the land along the edge of a body of water (as the sea)
[2]**shore** *vb* **shored; shor·ing :** to support with one or more bracing timbers
shore·bird *n* : any of various birds (as the plovers) that frequent the seashore
shore·line *n* : the line where a body of water touches the shore
shorn *past participle of* SHEAR
[1]**short** *adj* **1 :** not long or tall **2 :** not great in distance **3 :** brief in time **4 :** cut down to a brief length **5 :** not coming up to the regular standard **6 :** less in amount than expected or called for **7 :** less than : not equal to **8 :** not having enough **9 :** FLAKY, CRUMBLY **10 :** of, relating to, or being one of the vowel sounds \ə, a, e, i, u̇\ and sometimes \ä\ and \ȯ\ — **short·ness** *n*
[2]**short** *adv* **1 :** with suddenness **2 :** so as not to reach as far as expected
[3]**short** *n* **1 :** something shorter than the usual or regular length **2 shorts** *pl* : pants that reach to or almost to the knees **3 shorts** *pl* : short underpants **4 :** SHORT CIRCUIT
short·age *n* : a lack in the amount needed : DEFICIT
short·cake *n* : a dessert made usually of rich biscuit dough baked and served with sweetened fruit
short circuit *n* : an electric connection made between points in an electric circuit between which current does not normally flow
short·com·ing *n* : FAULT 1
short·cut *n* : a shorter, quicker, or easier way
short·en *vb* : to make or become short or shorter
short·en·ing *n* : a fatty substance (as lard) used to make pastry flaky
short·hand *n* : a method of rapid writing by using symbols for sounds or words
short·horn *n* : any of a breed of beef cattle developed in England and including good producers of milk from which a separate dairy breed (**milking shorthorn**) has come
short–lived *adj* : living or lasting only a short time
short·ly *adv* **1 :** in a few words : BRIEFLY **2 :** in or within a short time : SOON
short–sight·ed *adj* : NEARSIGHTED
short·stop *n* : a baseball infielder whose position is between second and third base
[1]**shot** *n* **1 :** the act of shooting **2** *pl* **shot :** a bullet, ball, or pellet for a gun or cannon **3 :** something thrown, cast forth, or let fly with force **4 :** [2]ATTEMPT, TRY **5 :** the flight of a missile or the distance it travels : RANGE **6 :** a person who shoots **7 :** a heavy metal ball thrown for distance in a track-and-field contest (**shot put**) **8 :** a stroke or throw at a goal **9 :** an injection of something (as medicine) into the body
[2]**shot** *past of* SHOOT
shot·gun *n* : a gun with a long barrel used to fire shot at short range
should *past of* SHALL **1 :** ought to **2 :** happen to **3** — used as a politer or less assured form of *shall*
[1]**shoul·der** *n* **1 :** the part of the body of a person or animal where the arm or foreleg joins the body **2 :** the part of a garment at the wearer's shoulder **3 :** a part that resembles a person's shoulder **4 :** the edge of a road
[2]**shoulder** *vb* **1 :** to push with one's shoulder **2 :** to accept as one's burden or duty
shoulder blade *n* : the flat triangular bone in a person's or animal's shoulder
shouldn't : should not
[1]**shout** *vb* : to make a sudden loud cry (as of joy, pain, or sorrow)
[2]**shout** *n* : a sudden loud cry
[1]**shove** *vb* **shoved; shov·ing** **1 :** to push with steady force **2 :** to push along or away carelessly or rudely
[2]**shove** *n* : the act or an instance of shoving
[1]**shov·el** *n* **1 :** a broad scoop used to lift and throw loose material (as snow) **2 :** as much as a shovel will hold

[2]**shovel** *vb* **shov·eled** *or* **shov·elled; shov·el·ing** *or* **shov·el·ling** **1 :** to lift or throw with a shovel **2 :** to dig or clean out with a shovel **3 :** to throw or carry roughly or in a mass as if with a shovel

[1]**show** *vb* **showed; shown** *or* **showed; show·ing** **1 :** to place in sight : DISPLAY **2 :** REVEAL 2 **3 :** to give from or as if from a position of authority **4 :** TEACH 1, INSTRUCT **5 :** PROVE 2 **6 :** [1]DIRECT 3, USHER **7 :** to be noticeable

[2]**show** *n* **1 :** a display made for effect **2 :** an appearance meant to deceive : PRETENSE **3 :** an appearance or display that is basically true or real **4 :** an entertainment or exhibition especially by performers (as on TV or the stage)

show·boat *n* **:** a river steamboat used as a traveling theater

show·case *n* **:** a protective glass case in which things are displayed

[1]**show·er** *n* **1 :** a short fall of rain over a small area **2 :** something like a shower **3 :** a party where gifts are given especially to a bride or a pregnant woman **4 :** a bath in which water is showered on a person or a device for providing such a bath

[2]**shower** *vb* **1 :** to wet with fine spray or drops **2 :** to fall in or as if in a shower **3 :** to provide in great quantity **4 :** to bathe in a shower

show·man *n, pl* **show·men** **1 :** the producer of a theatrical show **2 :** a person having a special skill for presenting something in a dramatic way

shown *past participle of* SHOW

show off *vb* **:** to make an obvious display of one's abilities or possessions

show up *vb* **1 :** to reveal the true nature of : EXPOSE **2 :** APPEAR 2

showy *adj* **show·i·er; show·i·est** **1 :** attracting attention : STRIKING **2 :** given to or being too much outward display : GAUDY — **show·i·ly** *adv* — **show·i·ness** *n*

shrank *past of* SHRINK

shrap·nel *n* **1 :** a shell designed to burst and scatter the metal balls with which it is filled along with jagged fragments of the case **2 :** metal pieces from an exploded bomb, shell, or mine

[1]**shred** *n* **1 :** a long narrow piece torn or cut off : STRIP **2 :** [2]BIT 1, PARTICLE

[2]**shred** *vb* **shred·ded; shred·ding :** to cut or tear into shreds

shrew *n* **1 :** a small mouselike animal with a long pointed snout and tiny eyes that lives on insects and worms **2 :** an unpleasant quarrelsome woman

shrewd *adj* **:** showing quick practical cleverness : ASTUTE — **shrewd·ly** *adv* — **shrewd·ness** *n*

[1]**shriek** *vb* **:** to utter a sharp shrill cry

[2]**shriek** *n* **:** a sharp shrill cry

shrike *n* **:** a grayish or brownish bird with a hooked bill that feeds mostly on insects and often sticks them on thorns before eating them

[1]**shrill** *vb* **:** to make a high sharp piercing sound : SCREAM

[2]**shrill** *adj* **:** having a sharp high sound — **shrill·ness** *n* — **shril·ly** *adv*

shrimp *n* **1 :** a small shellfish related to the crabs and lobsters **2 :** a small or unimportant person or thing — **shrimp·like** *adj*

shrine *n* **1 :** a case or box for sacred relics (as the bones of saints) **2 :** the tomb of a holy person (as a saint) **3 :** a place that is considered sacred

shrink *vb* **shrank** *also* **shrunk; shrunk; shrink·ing** **1 :** to curl up or withdraw in or as if in fear or pain **2 :** to make or become smaller

shrink·age *n* **:** the amount by which something shrinks or becomes less

shriv·el *vb* **shriv·eled** *or* **shriv·elled; shriv·el·ing** *or* **shriv·el·ling :** to shrink and become dry and wrinkled

[1]**shroud** *n* **1 :** the cloth placed over or around a dead body **2 :** something that covers or shelters like a shroud **3 :** one of the ropes that go from the masthead of a boat to the sides to support the mast

[2]**shroud** *vb* **:** to cover with or as if with a shroud

shrub *n* **:** a woody plant having several stems and smaller than most trees

shrub·bery *n, pl* **shrub·ber·ies :** a group or planting of shrubs

shrug *vb* **shrugged; shrug·ging :** to draw or hunch up the shoulders usually to express doubt, uncertainty, or lack of interest

shrunk *past & past participle of* SHRINK

shrunk·en *adj* **:** made or grown smaller (as in size or value)

[1]**shuck** *n* **:** a covering shell or husk

[2]**shuck** *vb* **:** to free (as an ear of corn) from the shuck

[1]**shud·der** *vb* **:** to tremble with fear or horror or from cold

[2]**shudder** *n* **:** an act of shuddering : SHIVER

[1]**shuf·fle** *vb* **shuf·fled; shuf·fling** **1 :** to push out of sight or mix in a disorderly mass **2 :** to mix cards to change their order in the pack **3 :** to move from place to place **4 :** to move in a clumsy dragging way

[2]**shuffle** *n* **1 :** an act of shuffling **2 :** [2]JUMBLE **3 :** a clumsy dragging walk

shun *vb* **shunned; shun·ning :** to avoid purposely or by habit

shunt *vb* **1 :** to turn off to one side or out of the way **:** SHIFT **2 :** to switch (as a train) from one track to another

shut *vb* **shut; shut·ting 1 :** to close or become closed **2 :** to close so as to prevent entrance or leaving **:** BAR **3 :** to keep in a place by enclosing or by blocking the way out **:** IMPRISON **4 :** to close by bringing parts together

shut–in *n* **:** a sick person kept indoors

shut·out *n* **:** a game in which one side fails to score

shut·ter *n* **1 :** a movable cover for a window **2 :** a device in a camera that opens to let in light when a picture is taken

¹shut·tle *n* **1 :** an instrument used in weaving to carry the thread back and forth from side to side through the threads that run lengthwise **2 :** a vehicle (as a bus or train) that goes back and forth over a short route **3 :** SPACE SHUTTLE

²shuttle *vb* **shut·tled; shut·tling :** to move back and forth rapidly or often

shut·tle·cock *n* **:** a light object (as a piece of cork with feathers stuck in it) used in badminton

¹shy *adj* **shi·er** *or* **shy·er; shi·est** *or* **shy·est 1 :** easily frightened **:** TIMID **2 :** not feeling comfortable around people **:** not wanting or able to call attention to oneself **:** BASHFUL **3 :** having less than a full or an expected amount or number — **shy·ly** *adv* — **shy·ness** *n*

²shy *vb* **shied; shy·ing 1 :** to draw back in dislike or distaste **2 :** to move quickly to one side in fright

sick *adj* **1 :** affected with disease or ill health **:** not well **2 :** of, relating to, or intended for use in or during illness **3 :** affected with or accompanied by nausea **4 :** badly upset by strong emotion (as shame or fear) **5 :** tired of something from having too much of it **6 :** filled with disgust

sick·bed *n* **:** a bed on which a sick person lies

sick·en *vb* **:** to make or become sick

sick·en·ing *adj* **:** causing sickness or disgust — **sick·en·ing·ly** *adv*

sick·le *n* **:** a tool with a sharp curved metal blade and a short handle used to cut grass

sick·ly *adj* **sick·li·er; sick·li·est 1 :** somewhat sick **:** often ailing **2 :** caused by or associated with ill health **3 :** not growing well **:** SPINDLY

sick·ness *n* **1 :** ill health **:** ILLNESS **2 :** a specific disease **:** MALADY **3 :** NAUSEA 1

¹side *n* **1 :** the right or left part of the trunk of the body **2 :** a place, space, or direction away from or beyond a central point or line **3 :** a surface or line forming a border or face of an object **4 :** an outer part of a thing considered as facing in a certain direction **5 :** a position viewed as opposite to another **6 :** a body of contestants **7 :** a line of ancestors traced back from either parent

²side *adj* **1 :** of, relating to, or being on the side **2 :** aimed toward or from the side **3 :** related to something in a minor or unimportant way **4 :** being in addition to a main portion

³side *vb* **sid·ed; sid·ing :** to take the same side

side·arm *adv* **:** with the arm moving out to the side

side·board *n* **:** a piece of furniture for holding dishes, silverware, and table linen

side·burns *n pl***:** hair growing on the side of the face in front of the ears

sid·ed *adj* **:** having sides often of a stated number or kind

side·line *n* **1 :** a line marking the side of a playing field or court **2 :** a business or a job done in addition to one's regular occupation

¹side·long *adv* **:** out of the corner of one's eye

²sidelong *adj* **1 :** made to one side or out of the corner of one's eye **2 :** INDIRECT 2

side·show *n* **:** a small show off to the side of a main show or exhibition (as of a circus)

side·step *vb* **side·stepped; side·step·ping 1 :** to take a step to the side **2 :** to avoid by a step to the side **3 :** to avoid answering or dealing with

side·track *vb* **1 :** to transfer from a main railroad line to a side line **2 :** to turn aside from a main purpose or direction

side·walk *n* **:** a usually paved walk at the side of a street or road

side·ways *adv or adj* **1 :** from one side **2 :** with one side forward **3 :** to one side

side·wise *adv or adj* **:** SIDEWAYS

sid·ing *n* **1 :** a short railroad track connected with the main track **2 :** material (as boards or metal pieces) used to cover the outside walls of frame buildings

si·dle *vb* **si·dled; si·dling :** to go or move with one side forward

siege *n* **1 :** the moving of an army around a fortified place to capture it **2 :** a lasting attack (as of illness)

si·er·ra *n* **:** a range of mountains especially with jagged peaks

si·es·ta *n* **:** a nap or rest especially at midday

sieve *n* **:** a utensil with meshes or holes to separate finer particles from coarser ones or solids from liquids

sift *vb* **1 :** to pass or cause to pass through a sieve **2 :** to separate or separate out by or as if by passing through a sieve **3 :** to test or examine carefully — **sift·er** *n*

¹sigh *vb* **1 :** to take or let out a long loud

breath often as an expression of sadness or weariness **2 :** to make a sound like sighing **3 :** YEARN

[2]**sigh** *n* **:** the act or a sound of sighing

[1]**sight** *n* **1 :** something that is seen **:** SPECTACLE **2 :** something that is worth seeing **3 :** something that is peculiar, funny, or messy **4 :** the function, process, or power of seeing **:** the sense by which one becomes aware of the position, form, and color of objects **5 :** the act of seeing **6 :** the presence of an object within the field of vision **7 :** the distance a person can see **8 :** a device (as a small metal bead on a gun barrel) that aids the eye in aiming or in finding the direction of an object

[2]**sight** *vb* **1 :** to get sight of **:** SEE **2 :** to look at through or as if through a sight

sight·less *adj* **:** lacking sight **:** BLIND

sight·seer *n* **:** a person who goes about to see places and things of interest

[1]**sign** *n* **1 :** a motion, action, or movement of the hand that means something **2 :** one of the twelve parts of the zodiac **3 :** a symbol (as + or ÷) indicating a mathematical operation **4 :** a public notice that advertises something or gives information **5 :** something that indicates what is to come **6 :** [1]TRACE 2

[2]**sign** *vb* **1 :** to make or place a sign on **2 :** to represent or show by a sign or signs **3 :** to write one's name on to show that one accepts, agrees with, or will be responsible for **4 :** to communicate by using sign language

[1]**sig·nal** *n* **1 :** a sign, event, or word that serves to start some action **2 :** a sound, a movement of part of the body, or an object that gives warning or a command **3 :** a radio wave that transmits a message or effect (as in radio or television)

[2]**signal** *vb* **sig·naled** *or* **sig·nalled; sig·nal·ing** *or* **sig·nal·ling 1 :** to notify by a signal **2 :** to communicate by signals

[3]**signal** *adj* **1 :** unusually great **2 :** used for signaling

sig·na·ture *n* **1 :** the name of a person written by that person **2 :** a sign or group of signs placed at the beginning of a staff in music to show the key (**key signature**) or the meter (**time signature**)

sign·board *n* **:** a board with a sign or notice on it

sig·nif·i·cance *n* **1 :** MEANING 1 **2 :** IMPORTANCE

sig·nif·i·cant *adj* **1 :** having meaning and especially a special or hidden meaning **2 :** IMPORTANT 1

sig·ni·fy *vb* **sig·ni·fied; sig·ni·fy·ing 1 :** [2]MEAN 3, DENOTE **2 :** to show especially by a sign **:** make known **3 :** to have importance

sign language *n* **:** a system of hand movements used for communication (as by people who are deaf)

sign·post *n* **:** a post with a sign (as for directing travelers)

si·lage *n* **:** fodder fermented (as in a silo) to produce a good juicy feed for livestock

[1]**si·lence** *n* **1 :** the state of keeping or being silent **2 :** the state of there being no sound or noise **:** STILLNESS

[2]**silence** *vb* **si·lenced; si·lenc·ing 1 :** to stop the noise or speech of **:** cause to be silent **2 :** SUPPRESS 1

si·lent *adj* **1 :** not speaking **:** not talkative **2 :** free from noise or sound **:** STILL **3 :** done or felt without being spoken **4 :** making no mention **5 :** not active in running a business **6 :** not pronounced

[1]**sil·hou·ette** *n* **1 :** a drawing or picture of the outline of an object filled in with a solid usually black color **2 :** a profile portrait done in silhouette **3 :** [1]OUTLINE 1

[2]**silhouette** *vb* **sil·hou·ett·ed; sil·hou·ett·ing :** to represent by a silhouette **:** show against a light background

sil·i·con *n* **:** a chemical element that is found combined as the most common element next to oxygen in the earth's crust and is used especially in electronic devices

silk *n* **1 :** a fine fiber that is spun by many insect larvae usually to form their cocoon or by spiders to make their webs and that includes some kinds used for weaving cloth **2 :** thread, yarn, or fabric made from silk **3 :** something suggesting silk

silk·en *adj* **1 :** made of or with silk **2 :** like silk especially in its soft and smooth feel

silk·worm *n* **:** a yellowish hairless caterpillar that is the larva of an Asian moth (**silk moth** or **silkworm moth**), is raised in captivity on mulberry leaves, and produces a strong silk that is the silk most used for thread or cloth

silky *adj* **silk·i·er; silk·i·est :** soft and smooth as silk

sill *n* **1 :** a horizontal supporting piece at the base of a structure **2 :** a heavy horizontal piece (as of wood) that forms the bottom part of a window frame or a doorway

sil·ly *adj* **sil·li·er; sil·li·est 1 :** not very intelligent **2 :** showing a lack of common sense **3 :** not serious or important — **sil·li·ness** *n*

si·lo *n, pl* **silos :** a covered trench, pit, or especially a tall round building in which silage is made and stored

[1]**silt** *n* **1 :** particles of small size left as sediment from water **2 :** a soil made up mostly of silt and containing little clay

[2]**silt** *vb* **:** to choke, fill, cover, or block with silt

[1]**sil·ver** *n* **1 :** a soft white metallic chemical element that takes a high polish and is used

for money, jewelry and ornaments, and table utensils **2 :** coin made of silver **3 :** SILVERWARE **4 :** a medium gray

[2]**silver** *adj* **1 :** made of, coated with, or yielding silver **2 :** having the color of silver

[3]**silver** *vb* **:** to coat with or as if with silver

sil·ver·smith *n* **:** a person who makes objects of silver

sil·ver·ware *n* **:** things (as knives, forks, and spoons) made of silver, silver-plated metal, or stainless steel

sil·very *adj* **:** having a shine like silver

sim·i·lar *adj* **:** having qualities in common — **sim·i·lar·ly** *adv*

sim·i·lar·i·ty *n, pl* **sim·i·lar·i·ties :** the quality or state of being similar **:** RESEMBLANCE

sim·i·le *n* **:** a figure of speech comparing two unlike things using *like* or *as*

sim·mer *vb* **1 :** to cook gently at or just below the boiling point **2 :** to be on the point of bursting out with violence or anger

sim·ple *adj* **sim·pler; sim·plest 1 :** INNOCENT 1, MODEST **2 :** not rich or important **3 :** lacking in education, experience, or intelligence **4 :** not fancy **5 :** having few parts **:** not complicated **6 :** ABSOLUTE 2 **7 :** not hard to understand or solve **8 :** EASY 1, STRAIGHTFORWARD

sim·ple·ton *n* **:** a foolish or stupid person

sim·plic·i·ty *n, pl* **sim·plic·i·ties 1 :** the quality or state of being simple or plain and not complicated or difficult **2 :** SINCERITY **3 :** directness or clearness in speaking or writing

sim·pli·fy *vb* **sim·pli·fied; sim·pli·fy·ing :** to make simple or simpler **:** make easier

sim·ply *adv* **1 :** in a clear way **2 :** in a plain way **3 :** DIRECTLY 1, CANDIDLY **4 :** [2]ONLY 1, MERELY **5 :** in actual fact **:** REALLY, TRULY

si·mul·ta·neous *adj* **:** existing or taking place at the same time — **si·mul·ta·neous·ly** *adv*

[1]**sin** *n* **1 :** an action that breaks a religious law **2 :** an action that is or is felt to be bad

[2]**sin** *vb* **sinned; sin·ning :** to be guilty of a sin

[1]**since** *adv* **1 :** from a definite past time until now **2 :** before the present time **:** AGO **3 :** after a time in the past

[2]**since** *conj* **1 :** in the period after **2 :** BECAUSE

[3]**since** *prep* **1 :** in the period after **2 :** continuously from

sin·cere *adj* **1 :** HONEST 2, STRAIGHTFORWARD **2 :** being what it seems to be **:** GENUINE — **sin·cere·ly** *adv*

sin·cer·i·ty *n* **:** freedom from fraud or deception **:** HONESTY

sin·ew *n* **:** TENDON

sin·ewy *adj* **1 :** full of tendons **:** TOUGH, STRINGY **2 :** STRONG 1, POWERFUL

sin·ful *adj* **:** being or full of sin **:** WICKED

sing *vb* **sang** *or* **sung; sung; sing·ing 1 :** to produce musical sounds with the voice **2 :** to express in musical tones **3 :** [1]CHANT 2 **4 :** to make musical sounds **5 :** to make a small shrill sound **6 :** to speak with enthusiasm **7 :** to do something with song — **sing·er** *n*

[1]**singe** *vb* **singed; singe·ing 1 :** to burn lightly or on the surface **:** SCORCH **2 :** to remove the hair, down, or fuzz from by passing briefly over a flame

[2]**singe** *n* **:** a slight burn

[1]**sin·gle** *adj* **1 :** not married **2 :** being alone **:** being the only one **3 :** made up of or having only one **4 :** having but one row of petals or rays **5 :** being a separate whole **:** INDIVIDUAL **6 :** of, relating to, or involving only one person

[2]**single** *vb* **sin·gled; sin·gling :** to select or distinguish (as one person or thing) from a number or group

[3]**single** *n* **1 :** a separate individual person or thing **2 :** a hit in baseball that enables the batter to reach first base

sin·gle–hand·ed *adj* **1 :** done or managed by one person or with one hand **2 :** working alone **:** lacking help

sin·gly *adv* **:** one by one **:** INDIVIDUALLY

[1]**sin·gu·lar** *adj* **1 :** of, relating to, or being a word form used to show not more than one **2 :** [1]SUPERIOR 2, EXCEPTIONAL **3 :** of unusual quality **:** UNIQUE **4 :** STRANGE 3, ODD

[2]**singular** *n* **:** a form of a word used to show that only one person or thing is meant

sin·is·ter *adj* **1 :** [1]EVIL 1, CORRUPT **2 :** threatening evil, harm, or danger

[1]**sink** *vb* **sank** *or* **sunk; sunk; sink·ing 1 :** to move or cause to move downward so as to be swallowed up **2 :** to fall or drop to a lower level **3 :** to lessen in amount **4 :** to cause to penetrate **5 :** to go into or become absorbed **6 :** to form by digging or boring **7 :** to spend (money) unwisely

[2]**sink** *n* **:** a basin usually with water faucets and a drain fixed to a wall or floor

sin·ner *n* **:** a sinful person

si·nus *n* **:** any of several spaces in the skull mostly connected with the nostrils

[1]**sip** *vb* **sipped; sip·ping :** to take small drinks of

[2]**sip** *n* **1 :** the act of sipping **2 :** a small amount taken by sipping

[1]**si·phon** *n* **1 :** a bent pipe or tube through which a liquid can be drawn by air pressure up and over the edge of a container **2 :** a tubelike organ in an animal and especially a mollusk or arthropod used to draw in or squirt out a fluid

[2]**siphon** *vb* **:** to draw off by a siphon

sir *n* **1** *cap* — used as a title before the given name of a knight or a baronet **2** — used without a name as a form of polite address to a man

[1]**sire** *n* **1** *often cap* : [1]FATHER 1 **2** : ANCESTOR **3** : the male parent of an animal

[2]**sire** *vb* **sired; sir·ing** : to become the father of

si·ren *n* : a device that makes a loud shrill warning sound and is often operated by electricity

sir·loin *n* : a cut of beef taken from the part just in front of the rump

sirup *variant of* SYRUP

si·sal *n* **1** : a long strong white fiber used to make rope and twine **2** : a Mexican agave whose leaves yield sisal

sis·ter *n* **1** : a female person or animal related to another person or animal by having one or both parents in common **2** : a member of a religious society of women : NUN **3** : a woman related to another by a common tie or interest — **sis·ter·ly** *adj*

sis·ter·hood *n* **1** : the state of being a sister **2** : women joined in a group

sis·ter–in–law *n, pl* **sis·ters–in–law** **1** : the sister of one's husband or wife **2** : the wife of one's brother

sit *vb* **sat; sit·ting** **1** : to rest upon the part of the body where the hips and legs join **2** : to cause (as oneself) to be seated **3** : [2]PERCH **4** : to hold a place as a member of an official group **5** : to hold a session **6** : to pose for a portrait or photograph **7** : to be located **8** : to remain quiet or still

site *n* **1** : the space of ground a building rests upon **2** : the place where something (as a town or event) is found or took place **3** : WEB SITE

sit·ting *n* **1** : an act of one that sits : a single occasion of continuous sitting **2** : SESSION 1

sitting room *n* : LIVING ROOM

sit·u·at·ed *adj* **1** : having its place **2** : being in such financial circumstances

sit·u·a·tion *n* **1** : LOCATION 2, PLACE **2** : position or place of employment : JOB **3** : position in life : STATUS **4** : the combination of surrounding conditions

[1]**six** *adj* : being one more than five

[2]**six** *n* : one more than five : two times three : 6

six–gun *n* : a revolver having six chambers

six·pence *n* **1** : the sum of six pence **2** : an old British coin worth six pence

six–shoot·er *n* : SIX-GUN

[1]**six·teen** *adj* : being one more than fifteen

[2]**sixteen** *n* : one more than fifteen : four times four : 16

[1]**six·teenth** *adj* : coming right after fifteenth

[2]**sixteenth** *n* : number sixteen in a series

[1]**sixth** *adj* : coming right after fifth

[2]**sixth** *n* **1** : number six in a series **2** : one of six equal parts

[1]**six·ti·eth** *adj* : coming right after fifty-ninth

[2]**sixtieth** *n* : number sixty in a series

[1]**six·ty** *adj* : being six times ten

[2]**sixty** *n* : six times ten : 60

siz·able *or* **size·able** *adj* : fairly large

size *n* **1** : amount of space occupied : BULK **2** : the measurements of a thing **3** : one of a series of measures especially of manufactured articles (as clothing) — **sized** *adj*

siz·zle *vb* **siz·zled; siz·zling** : to make a hissing or sputtering noise in or as if in frying or burning

[1]**skate** *n* : a very flat fish related to the sharks that has large and nearly triangular fins

[2]**skate** *n* **1** : a metal runner fitting the sole of the shoe or a shoe with a permanently attached metal runner used for gliding on ice **2** : ROLLER SKATE

[3]**skate** *vb* **skat·ed; skat·ing** **1** : to glide along on skates **2** : to slide or move as if on skates — **skat·er** *n*

skate·board *n* : a short board mounted on small wheels that is used for coasting and often for performing athletic stunts — **skate·board·er** *n* — **skate·board·ing** *n*

skein *n* : a quantity of yarn or thread arranged in a loose coil

skel·e·tal *adj* : of, relating or attached to, forming, or like a skeleton

skel·e·ton *n* **1** : a firm supporting or protecting structure or framework of a living being : the usually bony framework of a vertebrate (as a fish, bird, or human) **2** : FRAMEWORK

skep·ti·cal *adj* : having or showing doubt

[1]**sketch** *n* **1** : a rough outline or drawing showing the main features of something to be written, painted, or built **2** : a short written composition (as a story or essay)

[2]**sketch** *vb* **1** : to make a sketch, rough draft, or outline of **2** : to draw or paint sketches

sketchy *adj* **sketch·i·er; sketch·i·est** **1** : like a sketch : roughly outlined **2** : lacking completeness or clearness

[1]**ski** *n, pl* **skis** : one of a pair of narrow wooden, metal, or plastic strips bound one on each foot and used in gliding over snow or water

[2]**ski** *vb* **skied; ski·ing** : to glide on skis — **ski·er** *n*

[1]**skid** *n* **1** : a support (as a plank) used to raise and hold an object **2** : one of the logs, planks, or rails along or on which something heavy is rolled or slid **3** : the act of skidding : SLIDE

[2]**skid** *vb* **skid·ded; skid·ding** **1** : to roll or slide on skids **2** : to slide sideways **3** : [1]SLIDE 1, SLIP

skiff *n* **1 :** a small light rowboat **2 :** a sailboat light enough to be rowed

ski·ing *n* **:** the art or sport of gliding and jumping on skis

skill *n* **1 :** ability that comes from training or practice **2 :** a developed or acquired ability

skilled *adj* **1 :** having skill **2 :** requiring skill and training

skil·let *n* **:** a frying pan

skill·ful *or* **skil·ful** *adj* **1 :** having or showing skill **:** EXPERT **2 :** done or made with skill — **skill·ful·ly** *adv*

skim *vb* **skimmed; skim·ming 1 :** to clean a liquid of scum or floating substance **:** remove (as cream or film) from the top part of a liquid **2 :** to read or examine quickly and not thoroughly **3 :** to throw so as to skip along the surface of water **4 :** to pass swiftly or lightly over

skim milk *n* **:** milk from which the cream has been taken

skimp *vb* **:** to give too little or just enough attention or effort to or funds for

skimpy *adj* **skimp·i·er; skimp·i·est :** not enough especially because of skimping **:** SCANTY

[1]**skin** *n* **1 :** the hide especially of a small animal or one that has fur **2 :** the outer limiting layer of an animal body that in vertebrate animals (as humans) is made up of two layers of cells forming an inner dermis and an outer epidermis **3 :** an outer or surface layer (as of a fruit) — **skin·less** *adj* — **skinned** *adj*

[2]**skin** *vb* **skinned; skin·ning 1 :** to strip, scrape, or rub off the skin of **2 :** to remove an outer layer from (as by peeling)

skin dive *vb* **:** to swim below the surface of water with a face mask and sometimes a portable breathing device — **skin diver** *n*

skin·ny *adj* **skin·ni·er; skin·ni·est :** very thin

[1]**skip** *vb* **skipped; skip·ping 1 :** to move lightly with leaps and bounds **2 :** to bound or cause to bound off one point after another **:** SKIM **3 :** to leap over lightly and nimbly **4 :** to pass over or omit an item, space, or step **5 :** to fail to attend

[2]**skip** *n* **1 :** a light bounding step **2 :** a way of moving by hops and steps

skip·per *n* **:** the master of a ship and especially of a fishing, trading, or pleasure boat

[1]**skir·mish** *n* **1 :** a minor fight in war **2 :** a minor dispute or contest

[2]**skirmish** *vb* **:** to take part in a skirmish

[1]**skirt** *n* **1 :** a woman's or girl's garment or part of a garment that hangs from the waist down **2 :** either of two flaps on a saddle covering the bars on which the stirrups are hung **3 :** a part or attachment serving as a rim, border, or edging

[2]**skirt** *vb* **1 :** [2]BORDER 2 **2 :** to go or pass around or about the outer edge of

skit *n* **:** a brief sketch in play form

skit·tish *adj* **:** easily frightened

skulk *vb* **:** to hide or move in a sly or sneaking way

skull *n* **:** the case of bone or cartilage that forms most of the skeleton of the head and face, encloses the brain, and supports the jaws

skunk *n* **1 :** a North American animal related to the weasels and minks that has coarse black and white fur and can squirt out a fluid with a very unpleasant smell **2 :** a mean person who deserves to be scorned

sky *n, pl* **skies 1 :** the upper air **:** the vast arch or dome that seems to spread over the earth **2 :** WEATHER, CLIMATE

sky·lark *n* **:** a European lark noted for its song

sky·light *n* **:** a window or group of windows in a roof or ceiling

sky·line *n* **1 :** the line where earth and sky seem to meet **:** HORIZON **2 :** an outline against the sky

sky·rock·et *n* **:** [1]ROCKET 1

sky·scrap·er *n* **:** a very tall building

sky·writ·ing *n* **:** writing formed in the sky by means of smoke or vapor released from an airplane

slab *n* **:** a flat thick piece or slice (as of stone, wood, or bread)

[1]**slack** *adj* **1 :** CARELESS 2, NEGLIGENT **2 :** not energetic **:** SLOW **3 :** not tight or firm **4 :** not busy or active

[2]**slack** *vb* **:** to make or become looser, slower, or less energetic **:** LOOSEN, SLACKEN

[3]**slack** *n* **1 :** a stopping of movement or flow **2 :** a part (as of a rope or sail) that hangs loose without strain **3 slacks** *pl* **:** pants especially for informal wear

slack·en *vb* **1 :** to make slower or less energetic **:** slow up **2 :** to make less tight or firm **:** LOOSEN

slag *n* **:** the waste left after the melting of ores and the separation of the metal from them

slain *past participle of* SLAY

slake *vb* **slaked; slak·ing 1 :** QUENCH 2 **2 :** to cause solid lime to heat and crumble by treating it with water

[1]**slam** *n* **1 :** a severe blow **2 :** a noisy violent closing **:** BANG

[2]**slam** *vb* **slammed; slam·ming 1 :** to strike or beat hard **2 :** to shut with noisy force **:** BANG **3 :** to put or place with force **4 :** to criticize harshly

[1]**slan·der** *vb* **:** to make a false and spiteful statement against **:** DEFAME

[2]**slander** *n* **:** a false and spiteful statement that damages another person's reputation

slang *n* **:** an informal nonstandard vocabulary composed mostly of invented words, changed words, and exaggerated or humorous figures of speech

[1]**slant** *n* **:** a direction, line, or surface that is neither level nor straight up and down **:** SLOPE

[2]**slant** *vb* **:** to turn or incline from a straight line or level **:** SLOPE

[3]**slant** *adj* **:** not level or straight up and down

slant·wise *adv or adj* **:** so as to slant **:** at a slant **:** in a slanting position

[1]**slap** *vb* **slapped; slap·ping 1 :** to strike with or as if with the open hand **2 :** to make a sound like that of slapping **3 :** to put, place, or throw with careless haste or force

[2]**slap** *n* **1 :** a quick sharp blow especially with the open hand **2 :** a noise like that of a slap

[1]**slash** *vb* **1 :** to cut by sweeping blows **:** GASH **2 :** to whip or strike with or as if with a cane **3 :** to reduce sharply

[2]**slash** *n* **1 :** an act of slashing **2 :** a long cut or slit made by slashing

slat *n* **:** a thin narrow strip of wood, plastic, or metal

slate *n* **1 :** a fine-grained usually bluish gray rock that splits into thin layers or plates and is used mostly for roofing and blackboards **2 :** a framed piece of slate used to write on

[1]**slaugh·ter** *n* **1 :** the act of killing **2 :** the killing and dressing of animals for food **3 :** destruction of many lives especially in battle

[2]**slaughter** *vb* **1 :** [2]BUTCHER 1 **2 :** [1]MASSACRE

slaugh·ter·house *n, pl* **slaugh·ter·hous·es :** an establishment where animals are killed and dressed for food

Slav *n* **:** a person speaking a Slavic language as a native tongue

[1]**slave** *n* **1 :** a person who is owned by another person and can be sold at the owner's will **2 :** one who is like a slave in not being his or her own master **3 :** DRUDGE

[2]**slave** *vb* **slaved; slav·ing :** to work like a slave

slave·hold·er *n* **:** an owner of slaves

slav·ery *n* **1 :** hard tiring labor **:** DRUDGERY **2 :** the state of being a slave **:** BONDAGE **3 :** the custom or practice of owning slaves

Slav·ic *adj* **:** of, relating to, or characteristic of the Slavs or their languages

slav·ish *adj* **1 :** of or characteristic of slaves **2 :** following or copying something or someone without questioning

slay *vb* **slew; slain; slay·ing :** [1]KILL 1 — **slay·er** *n*

[1]**sled** *n* **1 :** a vehicle on runners for carrying loads especially over snow **2 :** a small vehicle used mostly by children for sliding on snow and ice

[2]**sled** *vb* **sled·ded; sled·ding :** to ride or carry on a sled

[1]**sledge** *n* **:** SLEDGEHAMMER

[2]**sledge** *n* **:** a strong heavy sled

sledge·ham·mer *n* **:** a large heavy hammer usually used with both hands

[1]**sleek** *vb* **:** [1]SLICK

[2]**sleek** *adj* **1 :** smooth and glossy as if polished **2 :** having a healthy well-groomed look

[1]**sleep** *n* **1 :** a natural periodic loss of consciousness during which the body rests and refreshes itself **2 :** an inactive state (as hibernation or trance) like true sleep **3 :** DEATH — **sleep·less** *adj* — **sleep·less·ness** *n*

[2]**sleep** *vb* **slept; sleep·ing :** to take rest in sleep **:** be or lie asleep

sleep·er *n* **1 :** one that sleeps **2 :** a horizontal beam to support something on or near ground level **3 :** a railroad car with berths for sleeping

sleeping bag *n* **:** a large fabric bag that is warmly lined for sleeping outdoors or in a camp or tent

sleep·over *n* **:** an overnight stay at another's home

sleep·walk·er *n* **:** a person who walks about while asleep — **sleep·walk·ing** *n*

sleepy *adj* **sleep·i·er; sleep·i·est 1 :** ready to fall asleep **:** DROWSY **2 :** not active, noisy, or busy — **sleep·i·ness** *n*

[1]**sleet** *n* **:** frozen or partly frozen rain

[2]**sleet** *vb* **:** to shower sleet

sleeve *n* **1 :** the part of a garment covering the arm **2 :** a part that fits over or around something like a sleeve — **sleeved** *adj* — **sleeve·less** *adj*

[1]**sleigh** *n* **:** an open usually horse-drawn vehicle with runners for use on snow or ice

[2]**sleigh** *vb* **:** to drive or ride in a sleigh

sleight of hand : skill and quickness in the use of the hands especially in doing magic tricks

slen·der *adj* **1 :** gracefully thin **2 :** narrow for its height **3 :** very little

slept *past of* SLEEP

slew *past of* SLAY

[1]**slice** *vb* **sliced; slic·ing 1 :** to cut with or as if with a knife **2 :** to cut into thin flat pieces

[2]**slice** *n* **:** a thin flat piece cut from something

[1]**slick** *vb* **:** to make sleek or smooth

[2]**slick** *adj* **1 :** having a smooth surface **:** SLIPPERY **2 :** CRAFTY, CLEVER

slick·er *n* **:** a long loose raincoat

[1]**slide** *vb* **slid; slid·ing 1 :** to move or cause to move smoothly over a surface **:** GLIDE **2**

: to move or pass smoothly and without much effort

²slide *n* **1 :** the act or motion of sliding **2 :** a loosened mass that slides **:** AVALANCHE **3 :** a surface down which a person or thing slides **4 :** something that operates or adjusts by sliding **5 :** a transparent picture that can be projected on a screen **6 :** a glass plate for holding an object to be examined under a microscope

¹slight *adj* **1 :** not large or stout **2 :** FLIMSY, FRAIL **3 :** not important **:** TRIVIAL **4 :** small of its kind or in amount — **slight·ly** *adv*

²slight *vb* **:** to treat without proper care, respect, or courtesy

³slight *n* **1 :** an act or an instance of slighting **2 :** the state or an instance of being slighted

slight·ing *adj* **:** showing a lack of respect or caring

¹slim *adj* **slim·mer; slim·mest 1 :** SLENDER 1 **2 :** very small

²slim *vb* **slimmed; slim·ming :** to make or become slender

slime *n* **1 :** soft slippery mud **2 :** a soft slippery material (as on the skin of a slug or catfish)

slimy *adj* **slim·i·er; slim·i·est 1 :** having the feel or look of slime **2 :** covered with slime

¹sling *vb* **slung; sling·ing 1 :** to throw with a sudden sweeping motion **:** FLING **2 :** to hurl with a sling

²sling *n* **1 :** a device (as a short strap with a string attached at each end) for hurling stones **2 :** SLINGSHOT **3 :** a device (as a rope or chain) by which something is lifted or carried **4 :** a hanging bandage put around the neck to hold up the arm or hand

³sling *vb* **slung; sling·ing 1 :** to put in or move or support with a sling **2 :** to hang from two points

sling·shot *n* **:** a forked stick with an elastic band attached for shooting small stones

slink *vb* **slunk; slink·ing :** to move or go by or as if by creeping especially so as not to be noticed (as in fear or shame)

¹slip *vb* **slipped; slip·ping 1 :** to move easily and smoothly **2 :** to move quietly **:** STEAL **3 :** to pass or let pass or escape without being noted, used, or done **4 :** to get away from **5 :** to escape the attention of **6 :** to slide into or out of place or away from a support **7 :** to slide on a slippery surface so as to lose one's balance **8 :** to put on or take off a garment quickly and carelessly

²slip *n* **1 :** a ramp where ships can be landed or repaired **2 :** a place for a ship between two piers **3 :** a secret or quick departure or escape **4 :** a small mistake **:** BLUNDER **5 :** the act or an instance of slipping down or out of place **6 :** a sudden mishap **7 :** a fall from some level or standard **:** DECLINE **8 :** an undergarment made in dress length with straps over the shoulders **9 :** PILLOWCASE

³slip *n* **1 :** a piece of a plant cut for planting or grafting **2 :** a long narrow piece of material **3 :** a piece of paper used for some record **4 :** a young and slender person

⁴slip *vb* **slipped; slip·ping :** to take slips from (a plant)

slip·cov·er *n* **:** a cover (as for a sofa or chair) that may be slipped off and on

slip·knot *n* **:** a knot made by tying the end of a line around the line itself to form a loop so that the size of the loop may be changed by slipping the knot

slip·per *n* **:** a light low shoe that is easily slipped on the foot

slip·pery *adj* **slip·per·i·er; slip·per·i·est 1 :** having a surface smooth or wet enough to make something slide or make one lose one's footing or hold **2 :** not to be trusted **:** TRICKY

slip·shod *adj* **:** very careless **:** SLOVENLY

slip up *vb* **:** to make a mistake

¹slit *n* **:** a long narrow cut or opening

²slit *vb* **slit; slit·ting :** to make a long narrow cut in **:** SLASH

slith·er *vb* **:** ¹GLIDE

¹sliv·er *n* **:** a long slender piece cut or torn off **:** SPLINTER

²sliver *vb* **:** to cut or form into slivers

¹slob·ber *vb* **:** to let saliva or liquid dribble from the mouth

²slobber *n* **:** dripping saliva

slo·gan *n* **:** a word or phrase used by a party, a group, or a business to attract attention (as to its goal, worth, or beliefs)

sloop *n* **:** a sailing boat with one mast and a fore-and-aft mainsail and jib

¹slop *n* **1 :** thin tasteless drink or liquid food **2 :** liquid spilled or splashed **3 :** food waste or gruel fed to animals **4 :** body waste

²slop *vb* **slopped; slop·ping 1 :** to spill or spill something on or over **2 :** to feed slop to

¹slope *vb* **sloped; slop·ing :** to take a slanting direction

²slope *n* **1 :** a piece of slanting ground (as a hillside) **2 :** upward or downward slant

slop·py *adj* **slop·pi·er; slop·pi·est 1 :** wet enough to spatter easily **2 :** careless in work or in appearance

slosh *vb* **1 :** to walk with trouble through water, mud, or slush **2 :** ¹SPLASH 1, 2, 3

¹slot *n* **:** a narrow opening, groove, or passage

²slot *vb* **slot·ted; slot·ting :** to cut a slot in

sloth *n* **1 :** the state of being lazy **2 :** an animal of Central and South America that hangs back downward and moves slowly along the branches of trees on whose leaves, twigs, and fruits it feeds

¹slouch *n* **1 :** a lazy worthless person **2 :** a lazy drooping way of standing, sitting, or walking
²slouch *vb* **:** to walk, stand, or sit with a slouch
slough *n* **:** a wet marshy or muddy place
slov·en·ly *adj* **:** personally untidy
¹slow *adj* **1 :** not as smart or as quick to understand as most people **2 :** not easily aroused or excited **3 :** moving, flowing, or going at less than the usual speed **4 :** indicating less than is correct **5 :** not lively or active — **slow·ly** *adv* — **slow·ness** *n*
²slow *adv* **:** in a slow way
³slow *vb* **:** to make or go slow or slower
slow·poke *n* **:** a very slow person
sludge *n* **:** a soft muddy mass resulting from sewage treatment
¹slug *n* **:** a long wormlike land mollusk that is related to the snails but has an undeveloped shell or none at all
²slug *n* **1 :** a small piece of shaped metal **2 :** BULLET **3 :** a metal disk often used in place of a coin
³slug *n* **:** a hard blow especially with the fist
⁴slug *vb* **slugged; slug·ging :** to hit hard with the fist or with a bat
slug·gard *n* **:** a lazy person
slug·ger *n* **:** a boxer or baseball batter who hits hard
slug·gish *adj* **:** slow in movement or reaction — **slug·gish·ly** *adv* — **slug·gish·ness** *n*
¹sluice *n* **1 :** an artificial passage for water with a gate for controlling its flow or changing its direction **2 :** a device for controlling the flow of water **3 :** a sloping trough for washing ore or for floating logs
²sluice *vb* **sluiced; sluic·ing 1 :** to wash in a stream of water running through a sluice **2 :** ³FLUSH 2, DRENCH
slum *n* **:** a very poor crowded dirty section especially of a city
¹slum·ber *vb* **:** to be asleep
²slumber *n* **:** ¹SLEEP
¹slump *vb* **1 :** to drop or slide down suddenly **:** COLLAPSE **2 :** ²SLOUCH **3 :** to drop sharply
²slump *n* **:** a big or continued drop especially in prices, business, or performance
slung *past of* SLING
slunk *past of* SLINK
¹slur *n* **1 :** an insulting remark **2 :** STIGMA 1, STAIN
²slur *vb* **slurred; slur·ring 1 :** to pass over without proper mention or stress **2 :** to run one's speech together so that it is hard to understand
³slur *n* **:** a slurred way of talking
slush *n* **:** partly melted snow
sly *adj* **sli·er** *or* **sly·er; sli·est** *or* **sly·est 1 :** both clever and tricky **2 :** being sneaky and dishonest **3 :** MISCHIEVOUS 3 — **sly·ly** *adv* — **sly·ness** *n* — **on the sly :** so as not to be seen or caught **:** SECRETLY
¹smack *n* **:** a slight taste, trace, or touch of something
²smack *vb* **:** to have a flavor, trace, or suggestion
³smack *vb* **1 :** to close and open the lips noisily especially in eating **2 :** to kiss usually loudly or hard **3 :** to make or give a smack **:** SLAP
⁴smack *n* **1 :** a quick sharp noise made by the lips (as in enjoyment of some taste) **2 :** a loud kiss **3 :** a noisy slap or blow
¹small *adj* **1 :** little in size **2 :** few in numbers or members **3 :** little in amount **4 :** not very much **5 :** UNIMPORTANT **6 :** operating on a limited scale **7 :** lacking in strength **8 :** not generous **:** MEAN **9 :** made up of units of little worth **10 :** ¹HUMBLE 3, MODEST **11 :** lowered in pride **12 :** being letters that are not capitals — **small·ness** *n*
²small *n* **:** a part smaller and usually narrower than the rest
small intestine *n* **:** the long narrow upper part of the intestine in which food is mostly digested and from which digested food is absorbed into the body
small·pox *n* **:** an acute disease in which fever and skin eruptions occur and which is believed to be extinct due to vaccination against the virus causing it
¹smart *adj* **1 :** BRISK, SPIRITED **2 :** quick to learn or do **:** BRIGHT **3 :** SAUCY 1 **4 :** stylish in appearance — **smart·ly** *adv* — **smart·ness** *n*
²smart *vb* **1 :** to cause or feel a sharp stinging pain **2 :** to feel distress
³smart *n* **:** a stinging pain usually in one spot
smart al·eck *n* **:** a person who likes to show off
¹smash *n* **1 :** a violent blow or attack **2 :** the action or sound of smashing **3 :** a striking success
²smash *vb* **1 :** to break in pieces **:** SHATTER **2 :** to drive or move violently **3 :** to destroy completely **:** WRECK **4 :** to go to pieces **:** COLLAPSE
¹smear *n* **:** a spot or streak made by or as if by an oily or sticky substance **:** SMUDGE
²smear *vb* **1 :** to spread or soil with something oily or sticky **:** DAUB **2 :** to spread over a surface **3 :** to blacken the good name of
¹smell *vb* **smelled** *or* **smelt; smell·ing 1 :** to become aware of the odor of by means of sense organs located in the nose **2 :** to detect by means or use of the sense of smell **3 :** to have or give off an odor
²smell *n* **1 :** the sense by which a person or animal becomes aware of an odor **2 :** the

sensation one gets through the sense of smell : ODOR, SCENT

[1]**smelt** *n, pl* **smelts** *or* **smelt** : a small food fish that looks like the related trouts, lives in coastal sea waters, and swims up rivers to spawn

[2]**smelt** *vb* : to melt (as ore) in order to separate the metal : REFINE

smelt·er *n* **1** : a person whose work or business is smelting **2** : a place where ores or metals are smelted

[1]**smile** *vb* **smiled; smil·ing** **1** : to have, produce, or show a smile **2** : to look with amusement or scorn **3** : to express by a smile

[2]**smile** *n* : an expression on the face in which the lips curve upward especially to show amusement or pleasure

smite *vb* **smote; smit·ten; smit·ing** : to strike hard especially with the hand or a weapon

smith *n* **1** : a worker in metals **2** : BLACKSMITH

smithy *n, pl* **smith·ies** : the workshop of a smith and especially of a blacksmith

smock *n* : a loose outer garment worn especially for protection of clothing

smog *n* : a fog made heavier and thicker by the action of sunlight on air polluted by smoke and automobile fumes

[1]**smoke** *n* **1** : the gas of burning materials (as coal, wood, or tobacco) made visible by particles of carbon floating in it **2** : a mass or column of smoke : SMUDGE **3** : the act of smoking tobacco

[2]**smoke** *vb* **smoked; smok·ing** **1** : to give out smoke **2** : to draw in and breathe out the fumes of burning tobacco **3** : to drive (as mosquitoes) away by smoke **4** : to expose (as meat) to smoke to give flavor and keep from spoiling — **smok·er** *n*

smoke de·tec·tor *n* : a device that sounds an alarm automatically when it detects smoke

smoke·house *n, pl* **smoke·hous·es** : a building where meat or fish is cured with smoke

smoke·stack *n* : a large chimney or a pipe for carrying away smoke (as on a factory or ship)

smoky *adj* **smok·i·er; smok·i·est** **1** : giving off smoke especially in large amounts **2** : like that of smoke **3** : filled with or darkened by smoke

[1]**smol·der** *or* **smoul·der** *n* : a slow often smoky fire

[2]**smolder** *or* **smoulder** *vb* **1** : to burn slowly usually with smoke and without flame **2** : to burn inwardly

[1]**smooth** *adj* **1** : not rough or uneven in surface **2** : not hairy **3** : free from difficulties or things in the way **4** : moving or progressing without breaks, sudden changes, or shifts **5** : able to make things seem right or easy or good : GLIB — **smooth·ly** *adv* — **smooth·ness** *n*

[2]**smooth** *vb* **1** : to make smooth **2** : [1]POLISH 2, REFINE **3** : to free from trouble or difficulty

smote *past of* SMITE

smoth·er *vb* **1** : to overcome by depriving of air or exposing to smoke or fumes : SUFFOCATE **2** : to become suffocated **3** : to cover up : SUPPRESS **4** : to cover thickly

[1]**smudge** *vb* **smudged; smudg·ing** : to soil or blur by rubbing or smearing

[2]**smudge** *n* **1** : a blurred spot or streak : SMEAR **2** : a smoky fire (as to drive away mosquitoes or protect fruit from frost)

smug *adj* **smug·ger; smug·gest** : very satisfied with oneself — **smug·ly** *adv*

smug·gle *vb* **smug·gled; smug·gling** **1** : to export or import secretly and unlawfully especially to avoid paying taxes **2** : to take or bring secretly — **smug·gler** *n*

smut *n* **1** : something (as a particle of soot) that soils or blackens **2** : a destructive disease of plants (as cereal grasses) in which plant parts (as seeds) are replaced by masses of dark spores of the fungus that causes the disease **3** : a fungus that causes smut

snack *n* : a light meal : LUNCH

[1]**snag** *n* **1** : a stump or stub of a tree branch especially when hidden under water **2** : a rough or broken part sticking out from something **3** : an unexpected difficulty

[2]**snag** *vb* **snagged; snag·ging** : to catch or damage on or as if on a snag

snail *n* **1** : a small slow-moving mollusk with a spiral shell into which it can draw itself for safety **2** : a person who moves slowly

[1]**snake** *n* **1** : a limbless crawling reptile that has a long body and lives usually on large insects or small animals and birds **2** : a horrid or treacherous person

[2]**snake** *vb* **snaked; snak·ing** : to crawl, wind, or move like a snake

snaky *adj* **snak·i·er; snak·i·est** **1** : of or like a snake **2** : full of snakes

[1]**snap** *vb* **snapped; snap·ping** **1** : to grasp or grasp at something suddenly with the mouth or teeth **2** : to grasp at something eagerly **3** : to get, take, or buy at once **4** : to speak or utter sharply or irritably **5** : to break or break apart suddenly and often with a cracking noise **6** : to make or cause to make a sharp or crackling sound **7** : to close or fit in place with a quick movement **8** : to put into or remove from a position suddenly or with a snapping sound **9** : to close by

means of snaps or fasteners **10 :** to act or be acted on with snap **11 :** to take a snapshot of
[2]**snap** *n* **1 :** the act or sound of snapping **2 :** something that is easy and presents no problems **3 :** a small amount : BIT **4 :** a sudden spell of harsh weather **5 :** a catch or fastening that closes or locks with a click **6 :** a thin brittle cookie **7 :** SNAPSHOT **8 :** smartness of movement or speech : ENERGY
[3]**snap** *adj* **1 :** made suddenly or without careful thought **2 :** closing with a click or by means of a device that snaps **3 :** very easy
snap·drag·on *n* **:** a garden plant with stalks of mostly white, pink, crimson, or yellow flowers with two lips
snap·per *n* **1 :** one that snaps **2 :** SNAPPING TURTLE **3 :** an active sea fish important for sport and food
snap·ping tur·tle *n* **:** a large American turtle that catches its prey with a snap of the powerful jaws
snap·py *adj* **snap·pi·er; snap·pi·est 1 :** full of life : LIVELY **2 :** briskly cold : CHILLY **3 :** STYLISH, SMART
snap·shot *n* **:** a photograph taken usually with an inexpensive hand-held camera
[1]**snare** *n* **1 :** a trap (as a noose) for catching small animals and birds **2 :** something by which one is entangled, trapped, or deceived
[2]**snare** *vb* **snared; snar·ing :** to catch or entangle by or as if by use of a snare
snare drum *n* **:** a small drum with two heads that has strings stretched across its lower head to produce a rattling sound
[1]**snarl** *vb* **:** to get into a tangle
[2]**snarl** *n* **1 :** a tangle usually of hairs or thread : KNOT **2 :** a tangled situation
[3]**snarl** *vb* **1 :** to growl with a showing of teeth **2 :** to speak in an angry way **3 :** to utter with a growl
[4]**snarl** *n* **:** an angry growl
[1]**snatch** *vb* **:** to take hold of or try to take hold of something quickly or suddenly
[2]**snatch** *n* **1 :** an act of snatching **2 :** a brief period **3 :** something brief, hurried, or in small bits
[1]**sneak** *vb* **sneaked** *or* **snuck; sneak·ing :** to move, act, bring, or put in a sly or secret way
[2]**sneak** *n* **1 :** a person who acts in a sly or secret way **2 :** the act or an instance of sneaking
sneak·er *n* **:** a sports shoe with a rubber sole
sneaky *adj* **sneak·i·er; sneak·i·est :** behaving in a sly or secret way or showing that kind of behavior
[1]**sneer** *vb* **1 :** to smile or laugh while making a face that shows scorn **2 :** to speak or write in a scorning way
[2]**sneer** *n* **:** a sneering expression or remark
[1]**sneeze** *vb* **sneezed; sneez·ing :** to force out the breath in a sudden loud violent action
[2]**sneeze** *n* **:** an act or instance of sneezing
[1]**snick·er** *vb* **:** to give a small and often mean or sly laugh
[2]**snicker** *n* **:** an act or sound of snickering
[1]**sniff** *vb* **1 :** to draw air into the nose in short breaths loud enough to be heard **2 :** to show scorn **3 :** to smell by taking short breaths
[2]**sniff** *n* **1 :** the act or sound of sniffing **2 :** an odor or amount sniffed
snif·fle *vb* **snif·fled; snif·fling 1 :** to sniff repeatedly **2 :** to speak with sniffs
snif·fles *n pl* **:** a common cold in which the main symptom is a runny nose
[1]**snig·ger** *vb* **:** [1]SNICKER
[2]**snigger** *n* **:** [2]SNICKER
[1]**snip** *n* **1 :** a small piece that is snipped off **2 :** an act or sound of snipping
[2]**snip** *vb* **snipped; snip·ping :** to cut or cut off with or as if with shears or scissors
[1]**snipe** *n, pl* **snipes** *or* **snipe :** a game bird that lives in marshes and has a long straight bill
[2]**snipe** *vb* **sniped; snip·ing :** to shoot from a hiding place (as at individual enemy soldiers) — **snip·er** *n*
snob *n* **:** a person who imitates, admires, or wants to be friends with people of higher position and looks down on or avoids those felt to be less important
snob·bish *adj* **:** of, relating to, or being a snob
[1]**snoop** *vb* **:** to look or search especially in a sneaking or nosy way
[2]**snoop** *n* **:** SNOOPER
snoop·er *n* **:** a person who snoops
snoot *n* **:** [1]NOSE 1
[1]**snooze** *vb* **snoozed; snooz·ing :** to take a nap
[2]**snooze** *n* **:** a short sleep : NAP
[1]**snore** *vb* **snored; snor·ing :** to breathe with a rough hoarse noise while sleeping
[2]**snore** *n* **:** an act or sound of snoring
[1]**snor·kel** *n* **:** a tube used by swimmers for breathing with the head underwater
[2]**snorkel** *vb* **:** to swim underwater using a snorkel
[1]**snort** *vb* **:** to force air through the nose with a rough harsh sound
[2]**snort** *n* **:** an act or sound of snorting
snout *n* **1 :** a long projecting nose (as of a pig) **2 :** the front part of a head (as of a weevil) that sticks out like the snout of a pig **3 :** a usually large and ugly human nose
[1]**snow** *n* **1 :** small white crystals of ice formed directly from the water vapor of the air **2 :** a fall of snowflakes : a mass of snowflakes fallen to earth

²snow *vb* **1 :** to fall or cause to fall in or as snow **2 :** to cover or shut in with snow
snow·ball *n* **:** a round mass of snow pressed or rolled together
snow·bird *n* **:** a small bird (as a junco) seen mostly in winter
snow–blind *or* **snow–blind·ed** *adj* **:** having the eyes red and swollen and unable to see from the effect of glare reflected from snow — **snow blindness** *n*
snow·blow·er *n* **:** a machine in which rotating parts pick up snow and throw it aside
snow·board *n* **:** a board like a wide ski ridden in a surfing position over snow — **snow-board·er** *n* — **snowboarding** *n*
snow·bound *adj* **:** shut in or blocked by snow
snow·drift *n* **:** a bank of drifted snow
snow·fall *n* **1 :** a fall of snow **2 :** the amount of snow that falls in a single storm or in a certain period
snow·flake *n* **:** a snow crystal **:** a small mass of snow crystals
snow·man *n, pl* **snow·men :** snow shaped to look like a person
snow·mo·bile *n* **:** a motor vehicle designed for travel on snow
snow·plow *n* **:** any of various devices used for clearing away snow
¹snow·shoe *n* **:** a light frame of wood strung with a net (as of rawhide) and worn under one's shoe to prevent sinking into soft snow
²snowshoe *vb* **snow·shoed; snow·shoe·ing :** to go on snowshoes
snow·storm *n* **:** a storm of falling snow
snow thrower *n* **:** SNOWBLOWER
snowy *adj* **snow·i·er; snow·i·est 1 :** having or covered with snow **2 :** white like snow
¹snub *vb* **snubbed; snub·bing :** to ignore or treat rudely on purpose
²snub *n* **:** an act or an instance of snubbing
snub–nosed *adj* **:** having a stubby and usually slightly turned-up nose
snuck *past of* SNEAK
¹snuff *vb* **1 :** to cut or pinch off the burned end of the wick of a candle **2 :** EXTINGUISH 1
²snuff *vb* **:** to draw through or into the nose with force
³snuff *n* **:** powdered tobacco that is chewed, placed against the gums, or drawn in through the nostrils
¹snuf·fle *vb* **snuf·fled; snuf·fling :** to breathe noisily through a nose that is partly blocked
²snuffle *n* **:** the sound made in snuffling
snug *adj* **snug·ger; snug·gest 1 :** fitting closely and comfortably **2 :** COMFORTABLE 1, COZY **3 :** offering protection or a hiding place — **snug·ly** *adv*
snug·gle *vb* **snug·gled; snug·gling 1 :** to curl up comfortably or cozily **:** CUDDLE **2 :** to pull in close to one
¹so *adv* **1 :** in the way indicated **2 :** in the same way **:** ALSO **3 :** ¹THEN 2 **4 :** to an indicated extent or way **5 :** to a great degree **:** VERY, EXTREMELY **6 :** to a definite but not specified amount **7 :** most certainly **:** INDEED **8 :** THEREFORE
²so *conj* **1 :** in order that **2 :** and therefore
³so *pron* **1 :** the same **:** THAT **2 :** approximately that
¹soak *vb* **1 :** to lie covered with liquid **2 :** to place in a liquid to wet or as if to wet thoroughly **3 :** to enter or pass through something by or as if by tiny holes **:** PERMEATE **4 :** to draw out by or as if by soaking in a liquid **5 :** to draw in by or as if by absorption
²soak *n* **:** the act or process of soaking **:** the state of being soaked
¹soap *n* **:** a substance that is usually made by the action of alkali on fat, dissolves in water, and is used for washing
²soap *vb* **:** to rub soap over or into something
soap·stone *n* **:** a soft stone having a soapy or greasy feeling
soap·suds *n pl* **:** SUDS
soapy *adj* **soap·i·er; soap·i·est 1 :** smeared with or full of soap **2 :** containing or combined with soap **3 :** like soap
soar *vb* **:** to fly or sail through the air often at a great height
¹sob *vb* **sobbed; sob·bing 1 :** to cry or express with gasps and catching in the throat **2 :** to make a sobbing sound
²sob *n* **1 :** an act of sobbing **2 :** a sound of or like that of sobbing
¹so·ber *adj* **1 :** not drinking too much **:** TEMPERATE **2 :** not drunk **3 :** having a serious attitude **:** SOLEMN **4 :** having a quiet color **5 :** not fanciful or imagined
²sober *vb* **:** to make or become sober
so–called *adj* **:** usually but often wrongly so named
soc·cer *n* **:** a game played between two teams of eleven players in which a round inflated ball is moved toward a goal usually by kicking
so·cia·ble *adj* **1 :** liking to be around other people **:** FRIENDLY **2 :** involving pleasant social relations
¹so·cial *adj* **1 :** FRIENDLY 1, SOCIABLE **2 :** of or relating to human beings as a group **3 :** living or growing naturally in groups or communities **4 :** of, relating to, or based on rank in a particular society **5 :** of or relating to fashionable society — **so·cial·ly** *adv*
²social *n* **:** a friendly gathering usually for a special reason
so·cial·ism *n* **:** a theory or system of government based on public ownership and control

of the means of production and distribution of goods

so·cial·ist *n* **:** a person who believes in socialism

social studies *n pl* **:** the studies (as civics, history, and geography) that deal with human relationships and the way society works

so·ci·ety *n, pl* **so·ci·et·ies** **1 :** friendly association with others **2 :** human beings viewed as a system within which the individual lives **:** all of the people **3 :** a group of persons with a common interest or purpose **4 :** a part of a community thought of as different in some way **5 :** the group or set of fashionable persons

[1]**sock** *n, pl* **socks** *or* **sox :** a knitted or woven covering for the foot usually reaching past the ankle and sometimes to the knee

[2]**sock** *vb* **:** [1]HIT 1, PUNCH

[3]**sock** *n* **:** [2]PUNCH

sock·et *n* **:** a hollow thing or place that receives or holds something

sock·eye *n* **:** a small Pacific salmon that is the source of most of the salmon with red flesh that we eat

[1]**sod** *n* **:** the layer of the soil filled with roots (as of grass)

[2]**sod** *vb* **sod·ded; sod·ding :** to cover with sod

so·da *n* **1 :** a powdery substance like salt used in washing and in making glass or soap **2 :** SODIUM BICARBONATE **3 :** SODA WATER **4 :** SODA POP **5 :** a sweet drink made of soda water, flavoring, and ice cream

soda fountain *n* **:** a counter where soft drinks and ice cream are served

soda pop *n* **:** a flavored beverage containing carbon dioxide

soda water *n* **:** water with carbon dioxide added

sod·den *adj* **:** SOGGY

so·di·um *n* **:** a soft waxy silver-white chemical element occurring in nature in combined form (as in salt)

sodium bicarbonate *n* **:** a white powder used in cooking and medicine

sodium chlo·ride *n* **:** [1]SALT 1

so·fa *n* **:** a long upholstered seat usually with a back and arms

[1]**soft** *adj* **1 :** having a pleasing or comfortable effect **2 :** not bright or glaring **3 :** quiet in pitch or volume **4 :** smooth or delicate in appearance or feel **5 :** not violent **6 :** EASY 1 **7 :** sounding as in *ace* and *gem* — used of *c* and *g* **8 :** easily affected by emotions **9 :** lacking in strength **10 :** not hard, solid, or firm **11 :** free from substances that prevent lathering of soap **12 :** not containing alcohol — **soft·ness** *n*

[2]**soft** *adv* **:** SOFTLY

soft·ball *n* **1 :** a game like baseball played with a larger ball **2 :** the ball used in softball

soft·en *vb* **:** to make or become soft or softer — **soft·en·er** *n*

soft·ly *adv* **:** in a soft way **:** QUIETLY, GENTLY

soft·ware *n* **:** the programs and related information used by a computer

soft·wood *n* **:** the wood of a cone-bearing tree (as a pine or spruce)

sog·gy *adj* **sog·gi·er; sog·gi·est :** heavy with water or moisture

[1]**soil** *vb* **:** to make or become dirty

[2]**soil** *n* **1 :** the loose finely divided surface material of the earth in which plants have their roots **2 :** COUNTRY 2, LAND — **soil·less** *adj*

[1]**so·journ** *n* **:** a temporary stay

[2]**sojourn** *vb* **:** to stay as a temporary resident

sol *n* **:** the fifth note of the musical scale

so·lar *adj* **1 :** of or relating to the sun **2 :** measured by the earth's course around the sun **3 :** produced or made to work by the action of the sun's light or heat

solar system *n* **:** the sun and the planets, asteroids, comets, and meteors that revolve around it

sold *past of* SELL

[1]**sol·der** *n* **:** a metal or a mixture of metals used when melted to join or mend surfaces of metal

[2]**solder** *vb* **:** to join together or repair with solder

sol·dier *n* **:** a person in military service **:** an enlisted person who is not a commissioned officer

[1]**sole** *n* **:** a flatfish that has a small mouth and small eyes set close together and is a popular food fish

[2]**sole** *n* **1 :** the bottom of the foot **2 :** the bottom of a shoe, slipper, or boot

[3]**sole** *vb* **soled; sol·ing :** to furnish with a sole

[4]**sole** *adj* **1 :** [1]SINGLE 2, ONLY **2 :** limited or belonging only to the one mentioned

sole·ly *adv* **1 :** without another **:** ALONE **2 :** [2]ONLY 2

sol·emn *adj* **1 :** celebrated with religious ceremony **:** SACRED **2 :** [1]FORMAL **3 :** done or made seriously and thoughtfully **4 :** very serious **5 :** being dark and gloomy **:** SOMBER — **sol·emn·ly** *adv*

so·lem·ni·ty *n, pl* **so·lem·ni·ties** **1 :** a solemn ceremony, event, day, or speech **2 :** formal dignity

so·lic·it *vb* **1 :** to come to with a request or plea **2 :** to try to get

[1]**sol·id** *adj* **1 :** not hollow **2 :** not loose or spongy **:** COMPACT **3 :** neither liquid nor gaseous **4 :** made firmly and well **5 :** being

without a break, interruption, or change **6** : UNANIMOUS **7** : RELIABLE, DEPENDABLE **8** : of one material, kind, or color — **sol·id·ly** *adv* — **sol·id·ness** *n*

[2]**solid** *n* **1** : something that has length, width, and thickness **2** : a solid substance : a substance that keeps its size and shape

so·lid·i·fy *vb* **so·lid·i·fied; so·lid·i·fy·ing** : to make or become solid

so·lid·i·ty *n, pl* **so·lid·i·ties** : the quality or state of being solid

sol·i·taire *n* : a card game played by one person alone

sol·i·tary *adj* **1** : all alone **2** : seldom visited : LONELY **3** : growing or living alone : not one of a group or cluster

sol·i·tude *n* **1** : the quality or state of being alone or away from others : SECLUSION **2** : a lonely place

[1]**so·lo** *n, pl* **solos** **1** : music played or sung by one person either alone or with accompaniment **2** : an action (as in a dance) in which there is only one performer

[2]**solo** *adv or adj* : [2]ALONE 2

[3]**solo** *vb* : to fly solo in an airplane

so·lo·ist *n* : a person who performs a solo

sol·stice *n* : the time of the year when the sun is farthest north (**summer solstice**, about June 22) or south (**winter solstice**, about December 22) of the equator

sol·u·ble *adj* **1** : capable of being dissolved in liquid **2** : capable of being solved or explained

so·lu·tion *n* **1** : the act or process of solving **2** : the result of solving a problem **3** : the act or process by which a solid, liquid, or gas is dissolved in a liquid **4** : a liquid in which something has been dissolved

solve *vb* **solved; solv·ing** : to find the answer to or a solution for

sol·vent *n* : a usually liquid substance in which other substances can be dissolved or dispersed

som·ber *or* **som·bre** *adj* **1** : being dark and gloomy : DULL **2** : showing or causing low spirits

som·bre·ro *n, pl* **som·bre·ros** : a tall hat of felt or straw with a very wide brim worn especially in the Southwest and Mexico

[1]**some** *adj* **1** : being one unknown or not specified **2** : being one, a part, or an unspecified number of something **3** : being of an amount or number that is not mentioned **4** : being at least one and sometimes all of

[2]**some** *pron* : a certain number or amount

[1]**-some** *adj suffix* : distinguished by a specified thing, quality, state, or action

[2]**-some** *n suffix* : group of so many members

[1]**some·body** *pron* : some person

[2]**somebody** *n, pl* **some·bod·ies** : a person of importance

some·day *adv* : at some future time

some·how *adv* : in one way or another

some·one *pron* : some person

[1]**som·er·sault** *n* : a moving of the body through one complete turn in which the feet move up and over the head

[2]**somersault** *vb* : to turn a somersault

some·thing *pron* **1** : a thing that is not surely known or understood **2** : a thing or amount that is clearly known but not named **3** : SOMEWHAT

some·time *adv* **1** : at a future time **2** : at a time not known or not specified

some·times *adv* : now and then : OCCASIONALLY

some·way *adv* : SOMEHOW

[1]**some·what** *pron* : some amount or extent

[2]**somewhat** *adv* : to some extent

some·where *adv* **1** : in, at, or to a place not known or named **2** : at some time not specified

son *n* **1** : a male child or offspring **2** : a man or boy closely associated with or thought of as a child of something (as a country, race, or religion)

so·nar *n* : a device for detecting objects underwater using sound waves

so·na·ta *n* : a musical composition usually for a single instrument consisting of three or four separate sections in different forms and keys

song *n* **1** : vocal music **2** : poetic composition : POETRY **3** : a short musical composition of words and music **4** : a small amount

song·bird *n* : a bird that sings

song·ster *n* : a person or a bird that sings

son·ic *adj* : using, produced by, or relating to sound waves

sonic boom *n* : a sound like an explosion made by an aircraft traveling at supersonic speed

son–in–law *n, pl* **sons–in–law** : the husband of one's daughter

son·ny *n, pl* **son·nies** : a young boy — used mostly to address a stranger

so·no·rous *adj* **1** : producing sound (as when struck) **2** : loud, deep, or rich in sound : RESONANT

soon *adv* **1** : without delay : before long **2** : in a prompt way : QUICKLY **3** : [1]EARLY 2 **4** : by choice : WILLINGLY

soot *n* : a black powder formed when something is burned : the very fine powder that colors smoke

soothe *vb* **soothed; sooth·ing** **1** : to please by praise or attention **2** : RELIEVE 1 **3** : to calm down : COMFORT

sooth·say·er *n* : a person who claims to foretell events

sooty *adj* **soot·i·er; soot·i·est 1 :** soiled with soot **2 :** like soot especially in color

sop *vb* **sopped; sop·ping 1 :** to soak or dip in or as if in liquid **2 :** to mop up (as water)

soph·o·more *n* : a student in his or her second year at a high school or college

so·pra·no *n, pl* **so·pra·nos 1 :** the highest part in harmony having four parts **2 :** the highest singing voice of women or boys **3 :** a person having a soprano voice **4 :** an instrument having a soprano range or part

sor·cer·er *n* : a person who practices sorcery or witchcraft : WIZARD

sor·cer·ess *n* : a woman who practices sorcery or witchcraft : WITCH

sor·cery *n, pl* **sor·cer·ies :** the use of magic : WITCHCRAFT

sor·did *adj* **1 :** very dirty : FOUL **2 :** of low moral quality : VILE

[1]**sore** *adj* **sor·er; sor·est 1 :** causing distress **2 :** very painful or sensitive : TENDER **3 :** hurt or red and swollen so as to be or seem painful **4 :** ANGRY — **sore·ly** *adv* — **sore·ness** *n*

[2]**sore** *n* : a sore spot (as an ulcer) on the body usually with the skin broken or bruised and often with infection

sor·ghum *n* **1 :** a tall grass that looks like Indian corn and is used for forage and grain **2 :** syrup from the juice of a sorghum

so·ror·i·ty *n, pl* **so·ror·i·ties :** a club of girls or women especially at a college

[1]**sor·rel** *n* **1 :** an animal (as a horse) of a sorrel color **2 :** a brownish orange to light brown

[2]**sorrel** *n* : any of several plants with sour juice

[1]**sor·row** *n* **1 :** sadness or grief caused by loss (as of something loved) **2 :** a cause of grief or sadness **3 :** a feeling of regret

[2]**sorrow** *vb* : to feel or express sorrow : GRIEVE

sor·row·ful *adj* **1 :** full of or showing sorrow **2 :** causing sorrow

sor·ry *adj* **sor·ri·er; sor·ri·est 1 :** feeling sorrow or regret **2 :** causing sorrow, pity, or scorn : WRETCHED

[1]**sort** *n* **1 :** a group of persons or things that have something in common : KIND **2 :** PERSON 1, INDIVIDUAL **3 :** general disposition : NATURE — **out of sorts 1 :** not feeling well **2 :** easily angered : IRRITABLE

[2]**sort** *vb* : to separate and arrange according to kind or class : CLASSIFY

SOS *n* **1 :** an international radio code distress signal used especially by ships and airplanes calling for help **2 :** a call for help

[1]**so–so** *adv* : fairly well

[2]**so–so** *adj* : neither very good nor very bad

sought *past of* SEEK

soul *n* **1 :** the spiritual part of a person believed to give life to the body **2 :** the essential part of something **3 :** a person who leads or stirs others to action : LEADER **4 :** a person's moral and emotional nature **5 :** human being : PERSON

[1]**sound** *adj* **1 :** free from disease or weakness **2 :** free from flaw or decay **3 :** [1]SOLID 4, FIRM **4 :** free from error **5 :** based on the truth **6 :** THOROUGH 1 **7 :** [1]DEEP 5, UNDISTURBED **8 :** showing good sense : WISE — **sound·ly** *adv* — **sound·ness** *n*

[2]**sound** *adv* : to the full extent

[3]**sound** *n* **1 :** the sensation experienced through the sense of hearing : an instance or occurrence of this **2 :** one of the noises that together make up human speech **3 :** the suggestion carried or given by something heard or read **4 :** hearing distance : EARSHOT — **sound·less** *adj* — **sound·less·ly** *adv*

[4]**sound** *vb* **1 :** to make or cause to make a sound or noise **2 :** PRONOUNCE 2 **3 :** to make known : PROCLAIM **4 :** to order, signal, or indicate by a sound **5 :** to make or give an impression : SEEM

[5]**sound** *n* : a long stretch of water that is wider than a strait and often connects two larger bodies of water or forms a channel between the mainland and an island

[6]**sound** *vb* **1 :** to measure the depth of (as by a weighted line dropped down from the surface) **2 :** to find or try to find the thoughts or feelings of a person

sound·proof *adj* : capable of keeping sound from entering or escaping

sound wave *n* : a wave that is produced when a sound is made and is responsible for carrying the sound to the ear

soup *n* : a liquid food made from the liquid in which vegetables, meat, or fish have been cooked and often containing pieces of solid food

[1]**sour** *adj* **1 :** having an acid taste **2 :** having become acid through spoiling **3 :** suggesting decay **4 :** not pleasant or friendly **5 :** acid in reaction — **sour·ish** *adj* — **sour·ly** *adv* — **sour·ness** *n*

[2]**sour** *vb* : to make or become sour

source *n* **1 :** a cause or starting point **2 :** the beginning of a stream of water **3 :** one that supplies information

sou·sa·phone *n* : a large circular tuba designed to rest on the player's shoulder and used chiefly in marching bands

[1]**south** *adv* : to or toward the south

[2]**south** *adj* : placed toward, facing, or coming from the south

[3]**south** *n* **1 :** the direction to the right of one

facing east : the compass point opposite to north **2** *cap* : regions or countries south of a point that is mentioned or understood

[1]**South American** *adj* : of or relating to South America or the South Americans

[2]**South American** *n* : a person born or living in South America

south·bound *adj* : going south

[1]**south·east** *adv* : to or toward the southeast

[2]**southeast** *n* **1** : the direction between south and east **2** *cap* : regions or countries southeast of a point that is mentioned or understood

[3]**southeast** *adj* : placed toward, facing, or coming from the southeast

south·east·er·ly *adv or adj* **1** : from the southeast **2** : toward the southeast

south·east·ern *adj* **1** *often cap* : of, relating to, or like that of the Southeast **2** : lying toward or coming from the southeast

south·er·ly *adj or adv* **1** : toward the south **2** : from the south

south·ern *adj* **1** *often cap* : of, relating to, or like that of the South **2** : lying toward or coming from the south

South·ern·er *n* : a person who is born or lives in the South

south·paw *n* : a person (as a baseball pitcher) who is left-handed

south pole *n, often cap S&P* **1** : the most southern point of the earth : the southern end of the earth's axis **2** : the end of a magnet that points toward the south when the magnet is free to swing

south·ward *adv or adj* : toward the south

[1]**south·west** *adv* : to or toward the southwest

[2]**southwest** *n* **1** : the direction between south and west **2** *cap* : regions or countries southwest of a point that is mentioned or understood

[3]**southwest** *adj* : placed toward, facing, or coming from the southwest

south·west·er·ly *adv or adj* **1** : from the southwest **2** : toward the southwest

south·west·ern *adj* **1** : lying toward or coming from the southwest **2** *often cap* : of, relating to, or like that of the Southwest

sou·ve·nir *n* : something that serves as a reminder

sou'·west·er *n* : a waterproof hat with wide slanting brim longer in back than in front

[1]**sov·er·eign** *n* **1** : a person (as a king or queen) or body of persons having the highest power and authority in a state **2** : an old British gold coin

[2]**sovereign** *adj* **1** : highest in power or authority **2** : having independent authority

sov·er·eign·ty *n, pl* **sov·er·eign·ties** **1** : supreme power especially over a political unit **2** : freedom from outside control **3** : one (as a country) that is sovereign

[1]**sow** *n* : an adult female hog

[2]**sow** *vb* **sowed; sown** *or* **sowed; sow·ing** **1** : to plant or scatter (as seed) for growing **2** : to cover with or as if with scattered seed for growing **3** : to set in motion : cause to exist — **sow·er** *n*

sow bug *n* : WOOD LOUSE

sox *pl of* SOCK

soy·bean *n* : an annual Asian plant related to the clovers that is widely grown for its edible seeds which yield an oil rich in protein

soybean oil *n* : a pale yellow oil that is obtained from soybeans and is used chiefly as a food and in paints and soaps

soy sauce *n* : a brown sauce made from soybeans and used especially in Chinese and Japanese cooking

[1]**space** *n* **1** : a period of time **2** : a part of a distance, area, or volume that can be measured **3** : a certain place set apart or available **4** : the area without limits in which all things exist and move **5** : the region beyond the earth's atmosphere **6** : an empty place

[2]**space** *vb* **spaced; spac·ing** : to place with space between

space·craft *n, pl* **spacecraft** : a vehicle for travel beyond the earth's atmosphere

space·man *n, pl* **space·men** : a person who travels outside the earth's atmosphere

space·ship *n* : SPACECRAFT

space shuttle *n* : a spacecraft designed to transport people and cargo between earth and space that can be used repeatedly

space station *n* : an artificial satellite designed to stay in orbit permanently and to be occupied by humans for long periods

space suit *n* : a suit equipped to keep its wearer alive in space

spa·cious *adj* : having ample space

[1]**spade** *n* : a digging tool made to be pushed into the ground with the foot

[2]**spade** *vb* **spad·ed; spad·ing** : to dig with a spade

spa·ghet·ti *n* : pasta made in the form of strings

[1]**spam** *n* : e-mail sent to a large number of addresses and usually containing advertising

[2]**spam** *vb* : to send spam to — **spam·mer** *n*

[1]**span** *n* **1** : the distance from the end of the thumb to the end of the little finger when the hand is stretched wide open **2** : a limited portion of time **3** : the spread (as of an arch) from one support to another

[2]**span** *vb* **spanned; span·ning** **1** : to measure by or as if by the hand stretched wide open **2** : to reach or extend across **3** : to place or construct a span over

³span *n* **:** two animals (as mules) worked or driven as a pair

span·gle *n* **:** SEQUIN

Span·iard *n* **:** a person born or living in Spain

span·iel *n* **:** a small or medium-sized dog with a thick wavy coat, long drooping ears, and usually short legs

¹Span·ish *adj* **:** of or relating to Spain, its people, or the Spanish language

²Spanish *n* **1 :** the language of Spain and the countries colonized by Spaniards **2 Spanish** *pl* **:** the people of Spain

spank *vb* **:** to strike on the buttocks with the open hand

spank·ing *adj* **:** BRISK 1, LIVELY

¹spar *n* **:** a long rounded piece of wood or metal (as a mast) to which a sail is fastened

²spar *vb* **sparred; spar·ring 1 :** to box or make boxing movements with the fists for practice or in fun **2 :** ²SKIRMISH

¹spare *vb* **spared; spar·ing 1 :** to keep from being punished or harmed **:** show mercy to **2 :** to free of the need to do something **3 :** to keep from using or spending **4 :** to give up especially as not really needed **5 :** to have left over

²spare *adj* **spar·er; spar·est 1 :** held in reserve **2 :** being over what is needed **3 :** somewhat thin **4 :** SCANTY

³spare *n* **1 :** a spare or duplicate piece or part **2 :** the knocking down of all ten bowling pins with the first two balls

spare·ribs *n pl* **:** a cut of pork ribs separated from the bacon strips

spar·ing *adj* **:** careful in the use of money or supplies — **spar·ing·ly** *adv*

¹spark *n* **1 :** a small bit of burning material **2 :** a hot glowing bit struck from a mass (as by steel on flint) **3 :** a short bright flash of electricity between two points **4 :** ²SPARKLE 1 **5 :** ¹TRACE 2

²spark *vb* **1 :** to give off or cause to give off sparks **2 :** to set off

¹spar·kle *vb* **spar·kled; spar·kling 1 :** to throw off sparks **2 :** to give off small flashes of light **3 :** to be lively or active

²sparkle *n* **1 :** a little flash of light **2 :** the quality of sparkling

spar·kler *n* **:** a firework that throws off very bright sparks as it burns

spark plug *n* **:** a device used in an engine to produce a spark that ignites a fuel mixture

spar·row *n* **:** a small brownish bird related to the finches

sparrow hawk *n* **:** a small hawk or falcon

sparse *adj* **spars·er; spars·est :** not thickly grown or settled — **sparse·ly** *adv*

spasm *n* **1 :** a sudden involuntary and usually violent contracting of muscles **2 :** a sudden, violent, and temporary effort, emotion, or outburst

spas·mod·ic *adj* **:** relating to or affected by spasm **:** involving spasms — **spas·mod·i·cal·ly** *adv*

¹spat *past of* SPIT

²spat *n* **:** a cloth or leather covering for the instep and ankle

³spat *n* **:** a brief unimportant quarrel

spa·tial *adj* **:** of or relating to space

¹spat·ter *vb* **1 :** to splash with drops or small bits of something wet **2 :** to scatter by splashing

²spatter *n* **1 :** the act or sound of spattering **2 :** a drop or splash spattered on something **:** a spot or stain due to spattering

spat·u·la *n* **:** a knifelike instrument with a broad flexible blade that is used mostly for spreading or mixing soft substances or for lifting

¹spawn *vb* **:** to produce or deposit eggs or spawn

²spawn *n* **:** the eggs of a water animal (as an oyster or fish) that produces many small eggs

spay *vb* **:** to remove the ovaries of (a female animal)

speak *vb* **spoke; spo·ken; speak·ing 1 :** to utter words **:** TALK **2 :** to utter in words **3 :** to mention in speech or writing **4 :** to use or be able to use in talking

speak·er *n* **1 :** a person who speaks **2 :** a person who conducts a meeting **3 :** LOUDSPEAKER

¹spear *n* **1 :** a weapon with a long straight handle and sharp head or blade used for throwing or jabbing **2 :** an instrument with a sharp point and curved hooks used in spearing fish

²spear *vb* **:** to strike or pierce with or as if with a spear

³spear *n* **:** a usually young blade or sprout (as of grass)

¹spear·head *n* **1 :** the head or point of a spear **2 :** the person, thing, or group that is the leading force (as in a development or an attack)

²spearhead *vb* **:** to serve as leader of

spear·mint *n* **:** a common mint used for flavoring

spe·cial *adj* **1 :** UNUSUAL, EXTRAORDINARY **2 :** liked very well **3 :** UNIQUE 2 **4 :** ¹EXTRA **5 :** meant for a particular purpose or occasion — **spe·cial·ly** *adv*

spe·cial·ist *n* **1 :** a person who studies or works at a special occupation or branch of learning **2 :** a person working in a special skill in the Army in any of the four ranks equal to the ranks of corporal through sergeant first class

spe·cial·ize *vb* **spe·cial·ized; spe·cial·iz·ing** **1 :** to limit one's attention or energy to one business, subject, or study **2 :** to change and develop so as to be suited for some particular use or living conditions

spe·cial·ty *n, pl* **spe·cial·ties** **1 :** a product of a special kind or of special excellence **2 :** something a person specializes in

spe·cies *n, pl* **species** **1 :** a class of things of the same kind and with the same name **:** KIND, SORT **2 :** a category of plants or animals that ranks below a genus in scientific classification and that is made up of individuals able to produce young with one another

spe·cif·ic *adj* **1 :** being an actual example of a certain kind of thing **2 :** clearly and exactly presented or stated **3 :** of, relating to, or being a species

spec·i·fi·ca·tion *n* **1 :** the act or process of specifying **2 :** a single specified item **3 :** a description of work to be done or materials to be used — often used in pl.

spec·i·fy *vb* **spec·i·fied; spec·i·fy·ing** **1 :** to mention or name exactly and clearly **2 :** to include in a specification

spec·i·men *n* **:** a part or a single thing that shows what the whole thing or group is like **:** SAMPLE

speck *n* **1 :** a small spot or blemish **2 :** a very small amount **:** BIT

[1]**speck·le** *n* **:** a small mark (as of color)

[2]**speckle** *vb* **speck·led; speck·ling :** to mark with speckles

spec·ta·cle *n* **1 :** an unusual or impressive public display (as a big parade) **2 specta·cles** *pl* **:** a pair of glasses held in place by parts passing over the ears

spec·tac·u·lar *adj* **:** STRIKING, SHOWY

spec·ta·tor *n* **:** a person who looks on (as at a sports event)

spec·ter *or* **spec·tre** *n* **:** GHOST

spec·trum *n, pl* **spec·tra** *or* **spec·trums :** the group of different colors including red, orange, yellow, green, blue, indigo, and violet seen when light passes through a prism and falls on a surface or when sunlight is affected by drops of water (as in a rainbow)

spec·u·late *vb* **spec·u·lat·ed; spec·u·lat·ing** **1 :** MEDITATE 2 **2 :** to engage in a risky but possibly very profitable business deal

spec·u·la·tion *n* **1 :** [2]GUESS **2 :** the taking of a big risk in business in hopes of making a big profit

speech *n* **1 :** the communication or expression of thoughts in spoken words **2 :** something that is spoken **3 :** a public talk **4 :** a form of communication (as a language or dialect) used by a particular group **5 :** the power of expressing or communicating thoughts by speaking

speech·less *adj* **1 :** unable to speak **2 :** not speaking for a time **:** SILENT

[1]**speed** *n* **1 :** quickness in movement or action **2 :** rate of moving or doing

[2]**speed** *vb* **sped** *or* **speed·ed; speed·ing** **1 :** to move or cause to move fast **:** HURRY **2 :** to go or drive at too high a speed **3 :** to increase the speed of **:** ACCELERATE

speed·boat *n* **:** a fast motorboat

speed bump *n* **:** a low raised ridge across a roadway (as in a parking lot) to limit vehicle speed

speed·om·e·ter *n* **1 :** an instrument that measures speed **2 :** an instrument that measures speed and records distance traveled

speedy *adj* **speed·i·er; speed·i·est :** moving or taking place fast — **speed·i·ly** *adv*

[1]**spell** *vb* **1 :** to name, write, or print in order the letters of a word **2 :** to make up the letters of **3 :** to amount to **:** MEAN

[2]**spell** *n* **1 :** a spoken word or group of words believed to have magic power **:** CHARM **2 :** a very strong influence

[3]**spell** *n* **1 :** one's turn at work or duty **2 :** a period spent in a job or occupation **3 :** a short period of time **4 :** a stretch of a specified kind of weather **5 :** a period of bodily or mental distress or disorder

[4]**spell** *vb* **:** to take the place of for a time **:** RELIEVE

spell·bound *adj* **:** held by or as if by a spell

spell·er *n* **1 :** a person who spells words **2 :** a book with exercises for teaching spelling

spell·ing *n* **1 :** the forming of words from letters **2 :** the letters composing a word

spelling checker *also* **spell check** *or* **spell checker** *n* **:** a computer program that shows the user any words that might be incorrectly spelled

spend *vb* **spent; spend·ing** **1 :** to use up **:** pay out **2 :** to wear out **:** EXHAUST **3 :** to use wastefully **:** SQUANDER **4 :** to cause or allow (as time) to pass

spend·thrift *n* **:** one who spends wastefully

spent *adj* **1 :** used up **2 :** drained of energy

sperm *n* **:** SPERM CELL

sperm cell *n* **:** a male germ cell

sperm whale *n* **:** a huge whale with a large head having a closed cavity that contains a mixture of wax and oil

spew *vb* **:** to pour out

sphere *n* **1 :** a body (as the moon) shaped like a ball **2 :** a figure so shaped that every point on its surface is an equal distance from the center of the figure **3 :** a field of influence or activity

spher·i·cal *adj* **:** relating to or having the form of a sphere

sphinx *n* **:** an Egyptian figure having the

body of a lion and the head of a man, a ram, or a hawk

[1]**spice** *n* **1 :** a plant product (as pepper or nutmeg) that has a strong pleasant smell and is used to flavor food **2 :** something that adds interest

[2]**spice** *vb* **spiced; spic·ing :** to season with or as if with spices

spick–and–span *or* **spic–and–span** *adj* **1 :** quite new and unused **2 :** very clean and neat

spicy *adj* **spic·i·er; spic·i·est 1 :** flavored with or containing spice **2 :** somewhat shocking or indecent

spi·der *n* **1 :** a wingless animal somewhat like an insect but having eight legs instead of six and a body divided into two parts instead of three **2 :** a cast-iron frying pan

spi·der·web *n* **:** the silken web spun by most spiders and used as a resting place and a trap for prey

spig·ot *n* **1 :** a plug used to stop the vent in a barrel **2 :** FAUCET

[1]**spike** *n* **1 :** a very large nail **2 :** one of the metal objects attached to the heel and sole of a shoe (as a baseball shoe) to prevent slipping **3 :** something pointed like a spike

[2]**spike** *vb* **spiked; spik·ing 1 :** to fasten with spikes **2 :** to pierce or cut with or on a spike

[3]**spike** *n* **1 :** an ear of grain **2 :** a long usually rather narrow flower cluster in which the blossoms grow very close to a central stem

[1]**spill** *vb* **spilled** *also* **spilt; spill·ing 1 :** to cause (blood) to flow by wounding **:** [1]SHED 2 **2 :** to cause or allow to fall, flow, or run out so as to be wasted or scattered **3 :** to flow or run out, over, or off and become wasted or scattered **4 :** to make known

[2]**spill** *n* **1 :** an act of spilling **2 :** a fall especially from a horse or vehicle **3 :** something spilled

[1]**spin** *vb* **spun; spin·ning 1 :** to make yarn or thread from (fibers) **2 :** to make (yarn or thread) from fibers **3 :** to form threads or a web or cocoon by giving off a sticky fluid that quickly hardens into silk **4 :** to turn or cause to turn round and round rapidly **:** TWIRL **5 :** to feel as if in a whirl **6 :** to make up and tell using the imagination **7 :** to move swiftly on wheels or in a vehicle **8 :** to make, shape, or produce by or as if by whirling

[2]**spin** *n* **1 :** a rapid whirling motion **2 :** a short trip in or on a wheeled vehicle

spin·ach *n* **:** a leafy plant that is grown for use as food

spi·nal *adj* **:** of, relating to, or located near the backbone or the spinal cord — **spi·nal·ly** *adv*

spinal column *n* **:** BACKBONE 1

spinal cord *n* **:** the thick cord of nervous tissue that extends from the brain down the back, fills the cavity of the backbone, and is concerned especially with reflex action

spin·dle *n* **1 :** a slender round rod or stick with narrowed ends by which thread is twisted in spinning and on which it is wound **2 :** something (as an axle or shaft) which is shaped or turned like a spindle or on which something turns

spin·dly *adj* **spin·dli·er; spin·dli·est :** being thin and long or tall and usually feeble or weak

spine *n* **1 :** BACKBONE 1 **2 :** a stiff pointed part growing from the surface of a plant or animal

spine·less *adj* **1 :** lacking spines **2 :** having no backbone **3 :** lacking spirit, courage, or determination

spin·et *n* **1 :** an early harpsichord with one keyboard and only one string for each note **2 :** a small upright piano

spin·ning jen·ny *n, pl* **spin·ning jen·nies :** an early machine for spinning wool or cotton by means of many spindles

spinning wheel *n* **:** a small machine driven by the hand or foot that is used to spin yarn or thread

spin·ster *n* **:** an unmarried woman past the usual age for marrying

spiny *adj* **spin·i·er; spin·i·est :** covered with spines

spi·ra·cle *n* **:** an opening (as in the head of a whale or the abdomen of an insect) for breathing

[1]**spi·ral** *adj* **1 :** winding or circling around a center and gradually getting closer to or farther away from it **2 :** circling around a center like the thread of a screw — **spi·ral·ly** *adv*

[2]**spiral** *n* **1 :** a single turn or coil in a spiral object **2 :** something that has a spiral form

[3]**spiral** *vb* **spi·raled** *or* **spi·ralled; spi·ral·ing** *or* **spi·ral·ling :** to move in a spiral path

spire *n* **1 :** a pointed roof especially of a tower **2 :** STEEPLE

spi·rea *or* **spi·raea** *n* **:** a shrub related to the roses that bears clusters of small white or pink flowers

[1]**spir·it** *n* **1 :** a force within a human being thought to give the body life, energy, and power **:** SOUL **2** *cap* **:** the active presence of God in human life **:** the third person of the Trinity **3 :** a being (as a ghost) whose existence cannot be explained by the known laws of nature **4 :** [1]MOOD **5 :** a lively or brisk quality **6 :** an attitude governing one's actions **7 :** PERSON 1 **8 :** an alcoholic liquor — usually used in pl. **9 spirits** *pl* **:** a solution in

alcohol **10 :** real meaning or intention — **spir·it·less** *adj*

[2]**spirit** *vb* **:** to carry off secretly or mysteriously

spir·it·ed *adj* **:** full of courage or energy

[1]**spir·i·tu·al** *adj* **1 :** of, relating to, or consisting of spirit : not bodily or material **2 :** of or relating to sacred or religious matters — **spir·i·tu·al·ly** *adv*

[2]**spiritual** *n* **:** a religious folk song developed especially among Negroes of the southern United States

[1]**spit** *n* **1 :** a thin pointed rod for holding meat over a fire **2 :** a small point of land that runs out into a body of water

[2]**spit** *vb* **spit** *or* **spat; spit·ting 1 :** to cause (as saliva) to spurt from the mouth **2 :** to express by or as if by spitting **3 :** to give off usually briskly : EMIT **4 :** to rain lightly or snow in flurries

[3]**spit** *n* **1 :** SALIVA **2 :** the act of spitting **3 :** a foamy material given out by some insects **4 :** perfect likeness

[1]**spite** *n* **:** dislike or hatred for another person with a wish to torment, anger, or defeat — **in spite of :** without being prevented by

[2]**spite** *vb* **spit·ed; spit·ing :** ANNOY, ANGER

spite·ful *adj* **:** filled with or showing spite : MALICIOUS — **spite·ful·ly** *adv*

spit·tle *n* **1 :** SALIVA **2 :** [3]SPIT 3

[1]**splash** *vb* **1 :** to hit (something liquid or sloppy) and cause to move and scatter roughly **2 :** to wet or soil by spattering with water or mud **3 :** to move or strike with a splashing sound **4 :** to spread or scatter like a splashed liquid

[2]**splash** *n* **1 :** splashed material **2 :** a spot or smear from or as if from splashed liquid **3 :** the sound or action of splashing

[1]**splat·ter** *vb* **:** [1]SPLASH, SPATTER

[2]**splatter** *n* **:** [2]SPLASH

spleen *n* **:** an organ near the stomach that destroys worn-out red blood cells and produces some of the white blood cells

splen·did *adj* **1 :** having or showing splendor : BRILLIANT **2 :** impressive in beauty, excellence, or magnificence **3 :** GRAND 4 — **splen·did·ly** *adv*

splen·dor *n* **1 :** great brightness **2 :** POMP, GLORY

[1]**splice** *vb* **spliced; splic·ing 1 :** to unite (as two ropes) by weaving together **2 :** to unite (as rails or pieces of film) by connecting the ends together

[2]**splice** *n* **:** a joining or joint made by splicing

splint *n* **1 :** a thin flexible strip of wood woven together with others in making a chair seat or basket **2 :** a device for keeping a broken or displaced bone in place

[1]**splin·ter** *n* **:** a thin piece split or torn off lengthwise : SLIVER

[2]**splinter** *vb* **:** to break into splinters

[1]**split** *vb* **split; split·ting 1 :** to divide lengthwise or by layers **2 :** to separate the parts of by putting something between **3 :** to burst or break apart or in pieces **4 :** to divide into shares or sections

[2]**split** *n* **1 :** a product or result of splitting : CRACK **2 :** the act or process of splitting : DIVISION **3 :** the feat of lowering oneself to the floor or leaping into the air with the legs extended in a straight line and in opposite directions

[3]**split** *adj* **:** divided by or as if by splitting

[1]**spoil** *n* **:** stolen goods : PLUNDER

[2]**spoil** *vb* **spoiled** *or* **spoilt; spoil·ing 1 :** [1]PLUNDER, ROB **2 :** to damage badly : RUIN **3 :** to damage the quality or effect of **4 :** to decay or lose freshness, value, or usefulness by being kept too long **5 :** to damage the disposition of by letting get away with too much

spoil·age *n* **:** the action of spoiling or condition of being spoiled

[1]**spoke** *past of* SPEAK

[2]**spoke** *n* **:** one of the bars or rods extending from the hub of a wheel to the rim

[1]**spoken** *past participle of* SPEAK

[2]**spo·ken** *adj* **1 :** expressed in speech : ORAL **2 :** used in speaking **3 :** speaking in a specified manner

spokes·man *n, pl* **spokes·men :** SPOKESPERSON

spokes·per·son *n* **:** a person who speaks for another or for a group

spokes·wom·an *n, pl* **spokes·wom·en :** a woman who is a spokesperson

[1]**sponge** *n* **1 :** a springy mass of horny fibers that forms the skeleton of a group of sea animals, is able to absorb water freely, and is used for cleaning **2 :** any of a group of water animals that have the form of hollow cell colonies made up of two layers and that include those whose skeletons are sponges **3 :** a manufactured product (as of plastic) having the springy absorbent quality of natural sponge **4 :** a pad of folded gauze used in surgery and medicine — **sponge·like** *adj*

[2]**sponge** *vb* **sponged; spong·ing 1 :** to clean or wipe with a sponge **2 :** to absorb with or like a sponge **3 :** to get something or live at the expense of another

spongy *adj* **spong·i·er; spong·i·est :** like a sponge in appearance or in ability to absorb : soft and full of holes or moisture

[1]**spon·sor** *n* **1 :** a person who takes the responsibility for some other person or thing **2 :** GODPARENT **3 :** a person or an organization that pays for or plans and carries out a

project or activity **4 :** a person or an organization that pays the cost of a radio or television program — **spon·sor·ship** *n*

[2]**sponsor** *vb* **:** to act as sponsor for

spon·ta·ne·ous *adj* **1 :** done, said, or produced freely and naturally **2 :** acting or taking place without outside force or cause — **spon·ta·ne·ous·ly** *adv*

spontaneous combustion *n* **:** a bursting of material into flame from the heat produced within itself through chemical action

spook *n* **:** GHOST, SPECTER

spooky *adj* **spook·i·er; spook·i·est 1 :** like a ghost **2 :** suggesting the presence of ghosts

[1]**spool** *n* **:** a small cylinder which has a rim or ridge at each end and a hole from end to end for a pin or spindle and on which material (as thread, wire, or tape) is wound

[2]**spool** *vb* **:** to wind on a spool

[1]**spoon** *n* **:** an eating or cooking utensil consisting of a small shallow bowl with a handle

[2]**spoon** *vb* **:** to take up in or as if in a spoon

spoon·bill *n* **:** a wading bird related to the ibises and having a bill which widens and flattens at the tip

spoon·ful *n, pl* **spoon·fuls** *or* **spoons·ful :** as much as a spoon can hold

spore *n* **:** a reproductive body of various plants and some lower animals that consists of a single cell and is able to produce a new individual — **spored** *adj*

[1]**sport** *vb* **1 :** to amuse oneself **2 :** to speak or act in fun **3 :** SHOW OFF

[2]**sport** *n* **1 :** PASTIME, RECREATION **2 :** physical activity (as running or an athletic game) engaged in for pleasure **3 :** FUN 3 **4 :** a person thought of with respect to the ideals of sportsmanship

sports·man *n, pl* **sports·men :** a person who engages in or is interested in sports and especially outdoor sports (as hunting and fishing)

sports·man·ship *n* **:** fair play, respect for opponents, and gracious behavior in winning or losing

sports·wom·an *n, pl* **sports·wom·en :** a woman who engages in or is interested in sports and especially outdoor sports

[1]**spot** *n* **1 :** something bad that others know about one **:** FAULT **2 :** a small part that is different (as in color) from the main part **3 :** an area soiled or marked (as by dirt) **4 :** a particular place — **spot·ted** *adj* — **on the spot 1 :** right away **:** IMMEDIATELY **2 :** at the place of action **3 :** in difficulty or danger

[2]**spot** *vb* **spot·ted; spot·ting 1 :** to mark or be marked with spots **2 :** to single out **:** IDENTIFY

spot·less *adj* **:** free from spot or blemish **:** perfectly clean or pure — **spot·less·ly** *adv* — **spot·less·ness** *n*

[1]**spot·light** *n* **1 :** a spot of light used to show up a particular area, person, or thing (as on a stage) **2 :** public notice **3 :** a light to direct a narrow strong beam of light on a small area

[2]**spotlight** *vb* **spot·light·ed** *or* **spot·lit; spot·light·ing 1 :** to light up with a spotlight **2 :** to bring to public attention

spotted owl *n* **:** a rare brown owl with white spots and dark stripes that is found from British Columbia to southern California and central Mexico

spot·ty *adj* **spot·ti·er; spot·ti·est 1 :** having spots **2 :** not always the same especially in quality

spouse *n* **:** a married person **:** HUSBAND, WIFE

[1]**spout** *vb* **1 :** to shoot out (liquid) with force **2 :** to speak with a long and quick flow of words so as to sound important **3 :** to flow out with force **:** SPURT

[2]**spout** *n* **1 :** a tube, pipe, or hole through which something (as rainwater) spouts **2 :** a sudden strong stream of fluid

[1]**sprain** *n* **1 :** a sudden or severe twisting of a joint with stretching or tearing of ligaments **2 :** a sprained condition

[2]**sprain** *vb* **:** to injure by a sudden or severe twist

sprang *past of* SPRING

[1]**sprawl** *vb* **1 :** to lie or sit with arms and legs spread out **2 :** to spread out in an uneven or awkward way

[2]**sprawl** *n* **:** the act or posture of sprawling

[1]**spray** *n* **:** a green or flowering branch or a usually flat arrangement of these

[2]**spray** *n* **1 :** liquid flying in fine drops like water blown from a wave **2 :** a burst of fine mist (as from an atomizer) **3 :** a device (as an atomizer) for scattering a spray of liquid or mist

[3]**spray** *vb* **1 :** to scatter or let fall in a spray **2 :** to scatter spray on or into — **spray·er** *n*

spray gun *n* **:** a device for spraying paints, varnishes, or insect poisons

[1]**spread** *vb* **spread; spread·ing 1 :** to open over a larger area **2 :** to stretch out **:** EXTEND **3 :** SCATTER 1, STREW **4 :** to give out over a period of time or among a group **5 :** to put a layer of on a surface **6 :** to cover something with **7 :** to prepare for a meal **:** SET **8 :** to pass from person to person **9 :** to stretch or move apart

[2]**spread** *n* **1 :** the act or process of spreading **2 :** extent of spreading **3 :** a noticeable display in a magazine or newspaper **4 :** a food to be spread on bread or crackers **5 :** a very fine meal **:** FEAST **6 :** a cloth cover for a table or bed **7 :** distance between two points

spree *n* : an outburst of activity
sprig *n* : a small shoot or twig
spright·ly *adj* **spright·li·er; spright·li·est** : full of spirit : LIVELY
[1]**spring** *vb* **sprang** *or* **sprung; sprung; spring·ing** **1** : to appear or grow quickly **2** : to come from by birth or descent **3** : to come into being : ARISE **4** : to move suddenly upward or forward : LEAP **5** : to have (a leak) appear **6** : to move quickly by elastic force **7** : [2]WARP 1 **8** : to cause to operate suddenly
[2]**spring** *n* **1** : a source of supply (as of water coming up from the ground) **2** : the season between winter and summer including in the northern hemisphere usually the months of March, April, and May **3** : a time or season of growth or development **4** : an elastic body or device that recovers its original shape when it is released after being squeezed or stretched **5** : the act or an instance of leaping up or forward **6** : elastic power or force
spring·board *n* : a flexible board usually fastened at one end and used for jumping high in the air in gymnastics or diving
spring peep·er *n* : a small frog that lives in trees and makes a high peeping sound heard mostly in spring
spring·time *n* : the season of spring
springy *adj* **spring·i·er; spring·i·est** **1** : [1]ELASTIC **2** : having or showing a lively and energetic movement
[1]**sprin·kle** *vb* **sprin·kled; sprin·kling** **1** : to scatter in drops **2** : to scatter over or in or among **3** : to rain lightly — **sprin·kler** *n*
[2]**sprinkle** *n* **1** : a light rain **2** : SPRINKLING
sprin·kling *n* : a very small number or amount
[1]**sprint** *vb* : to run at top speed especially for a short distance — **sprint·er** *n*
[2]**sprint** *n* **1** : a short run at top speed **2** : a race over a short distance
sprite *n* : ELF, FAIRY
sprock·et *n* : one of many points that stick up on the rim of a wheel (**sprocket wheel**) shaped so as to fit into the links of a chain
[1]**sprout** *vb* : to produce or cause to produce fresh young growth
[2]**sprout** *n* : a young stem of a plant especially when coming directly from a seed or root
[1]**spruce** *vb* **spruced; spruc·ing** : to make something or oneself neat or stylish in appearance
[2]**spruce** *adj* **spruc·er; spruc·est** : neat or stylish in appearance
[3]**spruce** *n* : an evergreen tree shaped like a cone with a thick growth of short needles, drooping cones, and light soft wood
sprung *past of* SPRING
spry *adj* **spri·er** *or* **spry·er; spri·est** *or* **spry·est** : LIVELY 1, ACTIVE
spun *past of* SPIN
spunk *n* : COURAGE, SPIRIT
[1]**spur** *n* **1** : a pointed device fastened to the back of a rider's boot and used to urge a horse on **2** : something that makes one want to do something : INCENTIVE **3** : a stiff sharp point (as a horny spine on the leg of a rooster) **4** : a mass of jagged rock coming out from the side of a mountain **5** : a short section of railway track coming away from the main line — **spurred** *adj*
[2]**spur** *vb* **spurred; spur·ring** **1** : to urge a horse on with spurs **2** : INCITE
spurn *vb* : to reject with scorn
[1]**spurt** *vb* **1** : to pour out suddenly : SPOUT **2** : [1]SQUIRT
[2]**spurt** *n* : a sudden pouring out : JET
[3]**spurt** *n* : a brief burst of increased effort
[4]**spurt** *vb* : to make a spurt
[1]**sput·ter** *vb* **1** : to spit or squirt bits of food or saliva noisily from the mouth **2** : to speak in a hasty or explosive way in confusion or excitement **3** : to make explosive popping sounds
[2]**sputter** *n* : the act or sound of sputtering
[1]**spy** *vb* **spied; spy·ing** **1** : to watch secretly **2** : to catch sight of : SEE
[2]**spy** *n, pl* **spies** **1** : a person who watches the movement or actions of others especially in secret **2** : a person who tries secretly to get information especially about an unfriendly country or its plans and actions
spy·glass *n* : a small telescope
squab *n* : a young pigeon especially when about four weeks old and ready for use as food
[1]**squab·ble** *n* : a noisy quarrel usually over unimportant things
[2]**squabble** *vb* **squab·bled; squab·bling** : to quarrel noisily for little or no reason
squad *n* **1** : a small group of soldiers **2** : a small group working or playing together
squad car *n* : CRUISER 2
squad·ron *n* : a group especially of cavalry riders, military airplanes, or naval ships moving and working together
squal·id *adj* : filthy or degraded from a lack of care or money
[1]**squall** *vb* : to let out a harsh cry or scream
[2]**squall** *n* : a sudden strong gust of wind often with rain or snow
squal·or *n* : the quality or state of being squalid
squan·der *vb* : to spend foolishly : WASTE
[1]**square** *n* **1** : an instrument having at least one right angle and two or more straight edges used to mark or test right angles **2** : a flat figure that has four equal sides and four

right angles **3 :** something formed like a square **4 :** the product of a number or amount multiplied by itself **5 :** an open place or area where two or more streets meet **6 :** [1]BLOCK 6, 7

²square *adj* **squar·er; squar·est 1 :** having four equal sides and four right angles **2 :** forming a right angle **3 :** multiplied by itself **4 :** having outlines that suggest sharp corners rather than curves **5 :** being a unit of area consisting of a square whose sides have a given length **6 :** having a specified length in each of two equal dimensions **7 :** exactly adjusted **8 :** [1]JUST 3, FAIR **9 :** leaving no balance **:** EVEN **10 :** large enough to satisfy — **square·ly** *adv*

³square *vb* **squared; squar·ing 1 :** to make square **:** form with right angles, straight edges, and flat surfaces **2 :** to make straight **3 :** to multiply a number by itself **4 :** AGREE 4 **5 :** [2]BALANCE 1, SETTLE

square knot *n* **:** a knot made of two half-knots tied in opposite directions and typically used to join the ends of two cords

square–rigged *adj* **:** having the principal sails extended on yards fastened in a horizontal position to the masts at their center

square root *n* **:** a factor of a number that when multiplied by itself gives the number

¹squash *vb* **:** to beat or press into a soft or flat mass **:** CRUSH

²squash *n* **:** the fruit of any of several plants related to the gourds and usually eaten as a vegetable

¹squat *vb* **squat·ted; squat·ting 1 :** to crouch by bending the knees fully so as to sit on or close to the heels **2 :** to settle without any right on land that one does not own **3 :** to settle on government land in order to become its owner

²squat *adj* **squat·ter; squat·test 1 :** bent in a deep crouch **2 :** low to the ground **3 :** having a short thick body

³squat *n* **1 :** the act of squatting **2 :** a squatting posture

¹squawk *vb* **1 :** to make a harsh short scream **2 :** to complain or protest loudly or with strong feeling

²squawk *n* **1 :** a harsh short scream **2 :** a noisy complaint

¹squeak *vb* **1 :** to make a short shrill cry **2 :** to barely get, win, or pass

²squeak *n* **:** a sharp shrill cry or sound

squeaky *adj* **squeak·i·er; squeak·i·est :** likely to squeak

¹squeal *vb* **1 :** to make a sharp long shrill cry or noise **2 :** INFORM 2

²squeal *n* **:** a shrill sharp cry or noise

¹squeeze *vb* **squeezed; squeez·ing 1 :** to press together from the opposite sides or parts of **:** COMPRESS **2 :** to get by squeezing **3 :** to force or crowd in by compressing

²squeeze *n* **:** an act or instance of squeezing

squid *n* **:** a sea mollusk that is related to the octopus but has a long body and ten arms

¹squint *adj* **:** not able to look in the same direction — used of the two eyes

²squint *vb* **1 :** to have squint eyes **2 :** to look or peer with the eyes partly closed

³squint *n* **1 :** the condition of being cross-eyed **2 :** the action or an instance of squinting

¹squire *n* **1 :** a person who carries the shield or armor of a knight **2 :** [1]ESCORT 1 **3 :** an owner of a country estate

²squire *vb* **squired; squir·ing :** to act as a squire or escort for

squirm *vb* **1 :** to twist about like an eel or a worm **2 :** to feel very embarrassed

squir·rel *n* **:** a small gnawing animal (as the common American **red squirrel** and **gray squirrel**) usually with a bushy tail and soft fur and strong hind legs for leaping

¹squirt *vb* **:** to shoot out liquid in a thin stream **:** SPURT

²squirt *n* **1 :** an instrument for squirting liquid **2 :** a small powerful stream of liquid **:** JET **3 :** the action of squirting

¹stab *n* **1 :** a wound produced by or as if by a pointed weapon **2 :** [2]THRUST 1 **3 :** [3]TRY, EFFORT

²stab *vb* **stabbed; stab·bing 1 :** to wound or pierce with a stab **2 :** [1]DRIVE 2, THRUST

sta·bil·i·ty *n, pl* **sta·bil·i·ties :** the condition of being stable

sta·bi·lize *vb* **sta·bi·lized; sta·bi·liz·ing :** to make or become stable — **sta·bi·liz·er** *n*

¹sta·ble *n* **:** a building in which domestic animals are housed and cared for

²stable *vb* **sta·bled; sta·bling :** to put or keep in a stable

³stable *adj* **sta·bler; sta·blest 1 :** not easily changed or affected **2 :** not likely to change suddenly or greatly **3 :** LASTING **4 :** RELIABLE

stac·ca·to *adj* **1 :** cut short so as not to sound connected **2 :** played or sung with breaks between notes

¹stack *n* **1 :** a large pile (as of hay) usually shaped like a cone **2 :** a neat pile of objects usually one on top of the other **3 :** a large number or amount **4 :** CHIMNEY 1, SMOKESTACK **5 :** a structure with shelves for storing books

²stack *vb* **:** to arrange in or form a stack **:** PILE

sta·di·um *n, pl* **sta·di·ums** *or* **sta·dia :** a large outdoor structure with rows of seats for spectators at sports events

staff *n, pl* **staffs** *or* **staves 1 :** a pole, stick, rod, or bar used as a support or as a sign of authority **2 :** something that is a source of strength **3 :** the five parallel lines with their four spaces on which music is written **4** *pl staffs* **:** a group of persons serving as assistants to or employees under a chief **5** *pl staffs* **:** a group of military officers who plan and manage for a commanding officer

staff sergeant *n* **:** a noncommissioned officer in the Army, Air Force, or Marine Corps ranking above a sergeant

staff sergeant major *n* **:** a noncommissioned officer in the Army ranking above a master sergeant

[1]**stag** *n* **1 :** an adult male deer especially of the larger kind **2 :** a man who goes to a social gathering without escorting a woman

[2]**stag** *adj* **:** intended or thought suitable for men only

[1]**stage** *n* **1 :** a raised floor (as for speaking or giving plays) **2 :** a place where something important happens **3 :** the theatrical profession or art **4 :** a step forward in a journey, a task, a process, or a development **:** PHASE **5 :** STAGECOACH

[2]**stage** *vb* **staged; stag·ing :** to produce or show to the public on or as if on the stage

stage·coach *n* **:** a coach pulled by horses that runs on a schedule from place to place carrying passengers and mail

[1]**stag·ger** *vb* **1 :** to move unsteadily from side to side as if about to fall **:** REEL **2 :** to cause to move unsteadily **3 :** to cause great surprise or shock in **4 :** to place or arrange in a zigzag but balanced way

[2]**stagger** *n* **:** a reeling or unsteady walk

stag·nant *adj* **1 :** not flowing **2 :** not active or brisk **:** DULL

stag·nate *vb* **stag·nat·ed; stag·nat·ing :** to be or become stagnant

[1]**stain** *vb* **1 :** to soil or discolor especially in spots **2 :** [2]COLOR 2, TINGE **3 :** [1]CORRUPT 1 **4 :** [1]DISGRACE

[2]**stain** *n* **1 :** [1]SPOT 3, DISCOLORATION **2 :** a mark of guilt or disgrace **:** STIGMA **3 :** something (as a dye) used in staining — **stain·less** *adj*

stainless steel *n* **:** an alloy of steel and chromium that is resistant to stain, rust, and corrosion

stair *n* **1 :** a series of steps or flights of steps for going from one level to another — often used in pl. **2 :** one step of a stairway

stair·case *n* **:** a flight of stairs with their supporting structure and railings

stair·way *n* **:** one or more flights of stairs usually with connecting landings

[1]**stake** *n* **1 :** a pointed piece (as of wood) driven or to be driven into the ground as a marker or to support something **2 :** a post to which a person is tied to be put to death by burning **3 :** something that is put up to be won or lost in gambling **4 :** the prize in a contest **5 :** [1]SHARE 1, INTEREST — **at stake :** in a position to be lost if something goes wrong

[2]**stake** *vb* **staked; stak·ing 1 :** to mark the limits of by stakes **2 :** to fasten or support (as plants) with stakes **3 :** [2]BET 1 **4 :** to give money to to help (as with a project)

sta·lac·tite *n* **:** a deposit hanging from the roof or side of a cave in the shape of an icicle formed by the partial evaporating of dripping water containing lime

sta·lag·mite *n* **:** a deposit like an upside down stalactite formed by the dripping of water containing lime onto the floor of a cave

[1]**stale** *adj* **stal·er; stal·est 1 :** having lost a good taste or quality through age **2 :** used or heard so often as to be dull **3 :** not so strong, energetic, or effective as before — **stale·ly** *adv* — **stale·ness** *n*

[2]**stale** *vb* **staled; stal·ing :** to make or become stale

[1]**stalk** *n* **1 :** a plant stem especially when not woody **2 :** a slender supporting structure — **stalked** *adj* — **stalk·less** *adj*

[2]**stalk** *vb* **1 :** to hunt slowly and quietly **2 :** to walk in a stiff or proud manner **3 :** to move through or follow as if stalking prey — **stalk·er** *n*

[3]**stalk** *n* **1 :** the act of stalking **2 :** a stalking way of walking

[1]**stall** *n* **1 :** a compartment for one animal in a stable **2 :** a space set off (as for parking an automobile) **3 :** a seat in a church choir **:** a church pew **4 :** a booth, stand, or counter where business may be carried on or articles may be displayed for sale

[2]**stall** *vb* **1 :** to put or keep in a stall **2 :** to stop or cause to stop usually by accident

[3]**stall** *n* **:** a trick to deceive or delay

[4]**stall** *vb* **:** to distract attention or make excuses to gain time

stal·lion *n* **:** a male horse

stal·wart *adj* **:** STURDY, RESOLUTE

sta·men *n* **:** the male organ of a flower that produces pollen and that consists of an anther and a filament

stam·i·na *n* **:** VIGOR 1, ENDURANCE

[1]**stam·mer** *vb* **:** to speak with involuntary stops and much repeating — **stam·mer·er** *n*

[2]**stammer** *n* **:** an act or instance of stammering

[1]**stamp** *vb* **1 :** to bring the foot down hard and with noise **2 :** to put an end to by or as if by hitting with the bottom of the foot **3 :** to mark or cut out with a tool or device having a design **4 :** to attach a postage stamp to **5 :** CHARACTERIZE 1

[2]**stamp** *n* **1 :** a device or instrument for

stamping **2 :** the mark made by stamping **3 :** a sign of a special quality **4 :** the act of stamping **5 :** a small piece of paper or a mark attached to something to show that a tax or fee has been paid

¹stam·pede *n* **1 :** a wild dash or flight of frightened animals **2 :** a sudden foolish action or movement of a crowd of people

²stampede *vb* **stam·ped·ed; stam·ped·ing 1 :** to run or cause (as cattle) to run away in panic **2 :** to act or cause to act together suddenly and without thought

stance *n* **:** way of standing **:** POSTURE

stanch *vb* **:** to stop or check the flow of (as blood)

¹stand *vb* **stood; stand·ing 1 :** to be in or take a vertical position on one's feet **2 :** to take up or stay in a specified position or condition **3 :** to have an opinion **4 :** to rest, remain, or set in a usually vertical position **5 :** to be in a specified place **6 :** to stay in effect **7 :** to put up with **:** ENDURE **8 :** UNDERGO **9 :** to perform the duty of — **stand by :** to be or remain loyal or true to — **stand for 1 :** to be a symbol for **:** REPRESENT **2 :** to put up with **:** PERMIT

²stand *n* **1 :** an act of standing **2 :** a halt for defense or resistance **3 :** a place or post especially where one stands **:** STATION **4 :** a structure containing rows of seats for spectators of a sport or spectacle **5 :** a raised area (as for speakers or performers) **6 :** a stall or booth often outdoors for a small business **7 :** a small structure (as a rack or table) on or in which something may be placed **8 :** POSITION 2

¹stan·dard *n* **1 :** a figure used as a symbol by an organized body of people **2 :** the personal flag of the ruler of a state **3 :** something set up as a rule for measuring or as a model **4 :** an upright support

²standard *adj* **1 :** used as or matching a standard **2 :** regularly and widely used **3 :** widely known and accepted to be of good and permanent value

stan·dard·ize *vb* **stan·dard·ized; stan·dard·iz·ing :** to make standard or alike

standard time *n* **:** the time established by law or by common usage over a region or country

stand by *vb* **1 :** to be present **2 :** to be or get ready to act

¹stand·ing *adj* **1 :** ¹ERECT **2 :** not flowing **:** STAGNANT **3 :** remaining at the same level or amount until canceled **4 :** PERMANENT

²standing *n* **1 :** the action or position of one that stands **2 :** length of existence or service **3 :** POSITION 4, STATUS

stand out *vb* **:** to be easily seen or recognized

stand·point *n* **:** a way in which things are thought about **:** POINT OF VIEW

stand·still *n* **:** the condition of not being active or busy **:** STOP

stand up *vb* **1 :** to stay in good condition **2 :** to fail to keep an appointment with — **stand up for :** DEFEND 2 — **stand up to :** to face boldly

stank *past of* STINK

stan·za *n* **:** a group of lines forming a division of a poem

¹sta·ple *n* **1 :** a piece of metal shaped like a U with sharp points to be driven into a surface to hold something (as a hook, rope, or wire) **2 :** a short thin wire with bent ends that is driven through papers and clinched to hold them together or driven through thin material to fasten it to a surface

²staple *vb* **sta·pled; sta·pling :** to fasten with staples

³staple *n* **1 :** a chief product of business or farming of a place **2 :** something that is used widely and often **3 :** the chief part of something **4 :** fiber (as cotton or wool) suitable for spinning into yarn

⁴staple *adj* **1 :** much used, needed, or enjoyed usually by many people **2 :** ¹PRINCIPAL, CHIEF

sta·pler *n* **:** a device that staples

¹star *n* **1 :** any of those celestial bodies except planets which are visible at night and look like fixed points of light **2 :** a star or especially a planet that is believed in astrology to influence one's life **3 :** a figure or thing (as a medal) with five or more points that represents or suggests a star **4 :** the principal member of a theater or opera company **5 :** a very talented or popular performer

²star *vb* **starred; star·ring 1 :** to sprinkle or decorate with or as if with stars **2 :** to mark with a star as being special or very good **3 :** to mark with an asterisk **4 :** to present in the role of a star **5 :** to play the most important role **6 :** to perform in an outstanding manner

star·board *n* **:** the right side of a ship or airplane looking forward

¹starch *vb* **:** to stiffen with starch

²starch *n* **:** a white odorless tasteless substance that is the chief storage form of carbohydrates in plants, is an important food, and has also various household and business uses (as for stiffening clothes)

starchy *adj* **starch·i·er; starch·i·est :** like or containing starch

¹stare *vb* **stared; star·ing :** to look at hard and long often with wide-open eyes

²stare *n* **:** the act or an instance of staring

star·fish *n* **:** any of a group of sea animals mostly having five arms that spread out from a central disk and feeding mostly on mollusks

[1]**stark** *adj* **1 :** [1]BARREN 2, DESOLATE **2 :** [1]UTTER, ABSOLUTE

[2]**stark** *adv* **:** COMPLETELY

star·light *n* **:** the light given by the stars

star·ling *n* **:** a dark brown or in summer greenish black European bird about the size of a robin that is now common and often a pest in the United States

star·lit *adj* **:** lighted by the stars

star·ry *adj* **star·ri·er; star·ri·est :** full of stars **2 :** of, relating to, or consisting of stars **3 :** shining like stars

Stars and Stripes *n sing or pl* **:** the flag of the United States

[1]**start** *vb* **1 :** to move suddenly and quickly **:** give a sudden twitch or jerk (as in surprise) **2 :** to come or bring into being or action **3 :** to stick out or seem to stick out **4 :** SET OUT 2 **5 :** to set going

[2]**start** *n* **1 :** a sudden movement **2 :** a brief act, movement, or effort **3 :** a beginning of movement, action, or development **4 :** a place of beginning (as of a race)

start·er *n* **:** someone or something that starts something or causes something else to start

star·tle *vb* **star·tled; star·tling 1 :** to cause to move or jump (as in surprise or fear) **2 :** to frighten suddenly but slightly

star·tling *adj* **:** causing a moment of fright or surprise

star·va·tion *n* **:** the act or an instance of starving **:** the condition of being starved

starve *vb* **starved; starv·ing 1 :** to suffer or die or cause to suffer or die from lack of food **2 :** to suffer or cause to suffer from a lack of something other than food

[1]**state** *n* **1 :** manner or condition of being **2 :** a body of people living in a certain territory under one government **:** the government of such a body of people **3 :** one of the divisions of a nation having a federal government

[2]**state** *vb* **stat·ed; stat·ing 1 :** to set by rule, law, or authority **:** FIX **2 :** to express especially in words

state·house *n* **:** the building where the legislature of a state meets

state·ly *adj* **state·li·er; state·li·est 1 :** having great dignity **2 :** impressive especially in size **:** IMPOSING — **state·li·ness** *n*

state·ment *n* **1 :** something that is stated **:** REPORT, ACCOUNT **2 :** a brief record of a business account

state·room *n* **:** a private room on a ship or a train

states·man *n, pl* **states·men :** a person who is active in government and who gives wise leadership in making policies

[1]**stat·ic** *adj* **1 :** showing little change or action **2 :** of or relating to charges of electricity (as one produced by friction) that do not flow

[2]**static** *n* **:** noise produced in a radio or television receiver by atmospheric or electrical disturbances

[1]**sta·tion** *n* **1 :** the place or position where a person or thing stands or is assigned to stand or remain **2 :** a regular stopping place (as on a bus line) **:** DEPOT **3 :** a post or area of duty **4 :** POSITION 4, RANK **5 :** a place for specialized observation or for a public service **6 :** a collection of radio or television equipment for transmitting or receiving **7 :** the place where a radio or television station is

[2]**station** *vb* **:** to assign to or set in a station or position **:** POST

sta·tion·ary *adj* **1 :** having been set in a certain place or post **:** IMMOBILE **2 :** not changing **:** STABLE

sta·tion·ery *n* **:** writing paper and envelopes

station wagon *n* **:** an automobile that is longer on the inside than a sedan and has one or more folding or removable seats but no separate luggage compartment

stat·ue *n* **:** an image or likeness (as of a person or animal) sculptured, modeled, or cast in a solid substance (as marble or bronze)

stat·ure *n* **1 :** natural height (as of a person) **2 :** quality or fame one has gained (as by growth or development)

sta·tus *n* **1 :** position or rank of a person or thing **2 :** state of affairs **:** SITUATION

stat·ute *n* **:** LAW 4

staunch *adj* **1 :** strongly built **:** SUBSTANTIAL **2 :** LOYAL 2, STEADFAST — **staunch·ly** *adv*

[1]**stave** *n* **1 :** a wooden stick **:** STAFF **2 :** one of a number of narrow strips of wood or iron plates placed edge to edge to form the sides, covering, or lining of something (as a barrel or keg)

[2]**stave** *vb* **staved** *or* **stove; stav·ing 1 :** to break in the staves of **2 :** to smash a hole in **:** crush or break inward

stave off *vb* **:** to keep away **:** ward off

staves *pl of* STAFF

[1]**stay** *n* **:** a strong rope or wire used to steady or brace something (as a mast)

[2]**stay** *vb* **:** to fasten (as a smokestack) with stays

[3]**stay** *vb* **1 :** to stop going forward **:** PAUSE **2 :** [1]REMAIN 3, 4 **3 :** to stand firm **4 :** to live for a while **5 :** [2]CHECK 1, HALT

[4]**stay** *n* **1 :** the action of bringing to a stop **:** the state of being stopped **2 :** a period of living in a place

[5]**stay** *n* **1 :** [1]PROP, SUPPORT **2 :** a thin firm strip (as of steel or plastic) used to stiffen a

garment (as a corset) or part of a garment (as a shirt collar)

[6]**stay** *vb* **:** to hold up

stead *n* **1 :** [2]AVAIL — used mostly in the phrase *stand one in good stead* **2 :** the place usually taken or duty carried out by the one mentioned

stead·fast *adj* **1 :** not changing **:** RESOLUTE **2 :** LOYAL 2 — **stead·fast·ly** *adv* — **stead·fast·ness** *n*

[1]**steady** *adj* **steadi·er; steadi·est 1 :** firmly fixed in position **2 :** direct or sure in action **3 :** showing little change **4 :** not easily upset **5 :** RELIABLE — **stead·i·ly** *adv* — **stead·i·ness** *n*

[2]**steady** *vb* **stead·ied; steady·ing :** to make, keep, or become steady

steak *n* **1 :** a slice of meat and especially beef **2 :** a slice of a large fish (as salmon)

[1]**steal** *vb* **stole; sto·len; steal·ing 1 :** to come or go quietly or secretly **2 :** to take and carry away (something that belongs to another person) without right and with the intention of keeping **3 :** to get more than one's share of attention during **4 :** to take or get for oneself secretly or without permission

[2]**steal** *n* **1 :** the act or an instance of stealing **2 :** [1]BARGAIN 2

stealth *n* **:** sly or secret action

stealthy *adj* **stealth·i·er; stealth·i·est :** done in a sly or secret manner — **stealth·i·ly** *adv*

[1]**steam** *n* **1 :** the vapor into which water is changed when heated to the boiling point **2 :** steam when kept under pressure so that it supplies heat and power **3 :** the mist formed when water vapor cools **4 :** driving force **:** POWER

[2]**steam** *vb* **1 :** to rise or pass off as steam **2 :** to give off steam or vapor **3 :** to move or travel by or as if by the power of steam **4 :** to expose to steam (as for cooking)

steam·boat *n* **:** a boat driven by steam

steam engine *n* **:** an engine driven by steam

steam·er *n* **1 :** a container in which something is steamed **2 :** a ship driven by steam **3 :** an engine, machine, or vehicle run by steam

steam·roll·er *n* **:** a machine formerly driven by steam that has wide heavy rollers for pressing down and smoothing roads

steam·ship *n* **:** STEAMER 2

steam shovel *n* **:** a power machine for digging that was formerly operated by steam

steed *n* **:** a usually lively horse

[1]**steel** *n* **1 :** a hard and tough metal made by treating iron with great heat and mixing carbon with it **2 :** an article (as a sword) made of steel

[2]**steel** *vb* **:** to fill with courage or determination

[3]**steel** *adj* **:** made of or like steel

steely *adj* **steel·i·er; steel·i·est 1 :** made of steel **2 :** like steel (as in hardness or color)

[1]**steep** *adj* **1 :** having a very sharp slope **:** almost straight up and down **2 :** too great or high — **steep·ly** *adv* — **steep·ness** *n*

[2]**steep** *vb* **1 :** to soak in a liquid **2 :** to fill with or involve deeply

stee·ple *n* **1 :** a tall pointed structure usually built on top of a church tower **2 :** a church tower

stee·ple·chase *n* **1 :** a horse race across country **2 :** a race on a course that has hedges, walls, and ditches to be crossed

[1]**steer** *n* **:** a castrated bull usually raised for beef

[2]**steer** *vb* **1 :** to control a course or the course of **:** GUIDE **2 :** to follow a course of action **3 :** to be guided

steering wheel *n* **:** a wheel for steering something by hand

stego·sau·rus *n* **:** a large plant-eating dinosaur having bony plates along its back and tail with spikes at the end of the tail

[1]**stem** *n* **1 :** the main stalk of a plant that develops buds and sprouts and usually grows above ground **2 :** a plant part (as a leafstalk or flower stalk) that supports some other part **3 :** the bow of a ship **4 :** a line of ancestors **:** STOCK **5 :** the basic part of a word to which prefixes or suffixes may be added **6 :** something like a stalk or shaft — **stem·less** *adj*

[2]**stem** *vb* **stemmed; stem·ming 1 :** to make progress against **2 :** to check or hold back the progress of

[3]**stem** *vb* **stemmed; stem·ming 1 :** to come from a certain source **2 :** to remove the stem from

[4]**stem** *vb* **stemmed; stem·ming :** to stop or check by or as if by damming

stemmed *adj* **:** having a stem

[1]**sten·cil** *n* **1 :** a material (as a sheet of paper, thin wax, or woven fabric) with cut out lettering or a design through which ink, paint, or metallic powder is forced onto a surface to be printed **2 :** a pattern, design, or print produced with a stencil

[2]**stencil** *vb* **sten·ciled** *or* **sten·cilled; sten·cil·ing** *or* **sten·cil·ling 1 :** to mark or paint with a stencil **2 :** to produce with a stencil

ste·nog·ra·pher *n* **:** one employed chiefly to take and make a copy of dictation

[1]**step** *n* **1 :** a rest or place for the foot in going up or down **:** STAIR 2 **2 :** a movement made by raising one foot and putting it down in another spot **3 :** a combination of foot and body movements in a repeated pattern **4 :** manner of walking **5 :** FOOTPRINT **6 :** the sound of a footstep **7 :** the space passed over

in one step **8 :** a short distance **9 :** the height of one stair **10 steps** *pl* **:** [1]COURSE 3 **11 :** a level, grade, or rank in a scale or series **:** a stage in a process **12 :** [1]MEASURE 7 **13 :** a space in music between two notes of a scale or staff that may be a single degree of the scale (**half step**) or two degrees (**whole step**) — **in step :** with one's foot or feet moving in time with other feet or in time to music

[2]**step** *vb* **stepped; step·ping 1 :** to move by taking a step or steps **2 :** [1]DANCE 1 **3 :** to go on foot **:** WALK **4 :** to move at a good speed **5 :** to press down with the foot **6 :** to come as if at a single step **7 :** to measure by steps

step–by–step *adj or adv* **:** moving or happening by steps one after the other

step·fa·ther *n* **:** the husband of one's mother after the death or divorce of one's real father

step·lad·der *n* **:** a light portable set of steps with a hinged frame for steadying

step·moth·er *n* **:** the wife of one's father after the death or divorce of one's real mother

steppe *n* **:** land that is dry, usually rather level, and covered with grass in regions (as much of southeastern Europe and parts of Asia) of wide temperature range

step·ping–stone *n* **1 :** a stone on which to step (as in crossing a stream) **2 :** a means of progress or advancement

step up *vb* **:** to increase especially by a series of steps

-ster *n suffix* **1 :** one that does or handles or operates **2 :** one that makes or uses **3 :** one that is associated with or takes part in **4 :** one that is

ste·reo *n, pl* **ste·re·os 1 :** stereophonic reproduction **2 :** a stereophonic sound system

ste·reo·phon·ic *adj* **:** of or relating to sound reproduction designed to create the effect of listening to the original

ste·reo·scope *n* **:** an optical instrument that blends two pictures of one subject taken from slightly different points of view into one image that seems to be three-dimensional

[1]**ste·reo·type** *vb* **1 :** to make a printing plate by casting melted metal in a mold **2 :** to form a fixed mental picture of

[2]**stereotype** *n* **1 :** a printing plate of a complete page made by casting melted metal in a mold **2 :** a fixed idea that many people have about a thing or a group and that may often be untrue or only partly true

ste·reo·typed *adj* **:** following a pattern or stereotype **:** lacking individuality

ste·reo·typ·i·cal *also* **ste·reo·typ·ic** *adj* **:** based on or characteristic of a stereotype — **ste·reo·typ·i·cal·ly** *adv*

ster·ile *adj* **1 :** not able to produce fruit, crops, or offspring **:** not fertile **2 :** free from living germs

ster·il·ize *vb* **ster·il·ized; ster·il·iz·ing :** to make sterile and especially free from harmful germs

[1]**ster·ling** *n* **1 :** British money **2 :** sterling silver **:** articles made from sterling silver

[2]**sterling** *adj* **1 :** of or relating to British sterling **2 :** being or made of an alloy of 925 parts of silver with 75 parts of copper **3 :** EXCELLENT

[1]**stern** *adj* **1 :** hard and severe in nature or manner **2 :** firm and not changeable — **stern·ly** *adv* — **stern·ness** *n*

[2]**stern** *n* **:** the rear end of a boat

ster·num *n, pl* **ster·nums** *or* **ster·na :** BREASTBONE

ste·roid *n* **:** any one of a number of chemical compounds (as an anabolic steroid) including many hormones

stetho·scope *n* **:** an instrument used by doctors for listening to sounds produced in the body and especially in the chest

[1]**stew** *n* **1 :** food (as meat with vegetables) prepared by slow boiling **2 :** a state of excitement, worry, or confusion

[2]**stew** *vb* **1 :** to boil slowly **:** SIMMER **2 :** to become excited or worried

stew·ard *n* **1 :** a manager of a very large home, an estate, or an organization **2 :** a person employed to manage the supply and distribution of food (as on a ship) **3 :** a worker who serves and looks after the needs of passengers (as on an airplane or ship)

stew·ard·ess *n* **:** a woman who looks after passengers (as on an airplane or ship)

[1]**stick** *n* **1 :** a cut or broken branch or twig **2 :** a long thin piece of wood **3 :** WALKING STICK 1 **4 :** something like a stick in shape or use

[2]**stick** *vb* **stuck; stick·ing 1 :** to stab with something pointed **2 :** to cause to penetrate **3 :** to put in place by or as if by pushing **4 :** to push out, up, into, or under **5 :** to put in a specified place or position **6 :** to remain in a place, situation, or environment **7 :** to halt the movement or action of **8 :** BAFFLE **9 :** to burden with something unpleasant **10 :** to cling or cause to cling **11 :** to become blocked or jammed

stick·er *n* **:** something (as a slip of paper with glue on its back) that can be stuck to a surface

stick·le·back *n* **:** a small scaleless fish with sharp spines on its back

sticky *adj* **stick·i·er; stick·i·est 1 :** ADHESIVE 1 **2 :** coated with a sticky substance **3 :** MUGGY, HUMID **4 :** tending to stick — **stick·i·ness** *n*

stiff *adj* **1 :** not easily bent **2 :** not easily

moved **3 :** FIRM 5 **4 :** hard fought **:** STUBBORN **5 :** not easy or graceful in manner **:** FORMAL **6 :** POWERFUL, STRONG **7 :** not flowing easily **:** being thick and heavy **8 :** SEVERE 1 **9 :** DIFFICULT 1 — **stiff·ly** *adv* — **stiff·ness** *n*

stiff·en *vb* **:** to make or become stiff or stiffer — **stiff·en·er** *n*

sti·fle *vb* **sti·fled; sti·fling 1 :** to kill by depriving of or die from lack of oxygen or air **:** SMOTHER **2 :** to keep in check by deliberate effort

stig·ma *n, pl* **stig·ma·ta** *or* **stig·mas 1 :** a mark of disgrace or discredit **2 :** the upper part of the pistil of a flower which receives the pollen grains and on which they complete their development

stile *n* **1 :** a step or set of steps for crossing a fence or wall **2 :** TURNSTILE

sti·let·to *n, pl* **sti·let·tos** *or* **sti·let·toes :** a slender pointed dagger

[1]**still** *adj* **1 :** having no motion **2 :** making no sound **3 :** free from noise and confusion **:** QUIET — **still·ness** *n*

[2]**still** *vb* **:** to make or become still **:** QUIET

[3]**still** *adv* **1 :** without motion **2 :** up to this or that time **3 :** NEVERTHELESS **4 :** [2]EVEN 4

[4]**still** *n* **:** [1]QUIET, SILENCE

[5]**still** *n* **1 :** a place where alcoholic liquors are made **2 :** a device used in distillation

still·born *adj* **:** born dead

stilt *n* **1 :** one of a pair of tall poles each with a high step or loop for the support of a foot used to lift the person wearing them above the ground in walking **2 :** a stake or post used to support a structure above ground or water level

stilt·ed *adj* **:** not easy and natural

[1]**stim·u·lant** *n* **1 :** something (as a drug) that makes the body or one of its parts more active for a while **2 :** STIMULUS 1

[2]**stimulant** *adj* **:** stimulating or tending to stimulate

stim·u·late *vb* **stim·u·lat·ed; stim·u·lat·ing 1 :** to make active or more active **:** ANIMATE, AROUSE **2 :** to act toward as a bodily stimulus or stimulant

stim·u·la·tion *n* **:** an act or result of stimulating

stim·u·lus *n, pl* **stim·u·li 1 :** something that stirs or urges to action **2 :** an influence that acts usually from outside the body to partly change bodily activity (as by exciting a sense organ)

[1]**sting** *vb* **stung; sting·ing 1 :** to prick painfully usually with a sharp or poisonous stinger **2 :** to suffer or affect with sharp quick burning pain **3 :** to cause to suffer severely

[2]**sting** *n* **1 :** an act of stinging **2 :** a wound or pain caused by or as if by stinging **3 :** STINGER

sting·er *n* **:** a sharp organ by which an animal (as a wasp or scorpion) wounds and often poisons an enemy

sting·ray *n* **:** a very flat fish with a stinging spine on its whiplike tail

stin·gy *adj* **stin·gi·er; stin·gi·est 1 :** not generous **:** giving or spending as little as possible **2 :** very small in amount — **stin·gi·ly** *adv* — **stin·gi·ness** *n*

[1]**stink** *vb* **stank** *or* **stunk; stunk; stink·ing 1 :** to give off or cause to have a strong unpleasant smell **2 :** to be of very bad quality

[2]**stink** *n* **:** a strong unpleasant smell

stink·bug *n* **:** a bug that gives off a bad smell

stinky *adj* **:** having a strong unpleasant smell

[1]**stint** *vb* **:** to be stingy or saving

[2]**stint** *n* **:** an amount of work given to be done

[1]**stir** *vb* **stirred; stir·ring 1 :** to make or cause to make a usually slight movement or change of position **2 :** to make active (as by pushing, beating, or prodding) **3 :** to mix, dissolve, or make by a continued circular movement **4 :** AROUSE 2

[2]**stir** *n* **1 :** a state of upset or activity **2 :** a slight movement **3 :** the act of stirring

stir·ring *adj* **:** LIVELY 3, MOVING

stir·rup *n* **:** either of a pair of small light frames often of metal hung by straps from a saddle and used as a support for the foot of a horseback rider

[1]**stitch** *n* **1 :** a sudden sharp pain especially in the side **2 :** one in-and-out movement of a threaded needle in sewing **:** a portion of thread left in the material after one such movement **3 :** a single loop of thread or yarn around a tool (as a knitting needle or crochet hook) **4 :** a method of stitching

[2]**stitch** *vb* **1 :** to fasten or join with stitches **2 :** to make, mend, or decorate with or as if with stitches **3 :** SEW 2

[1]**stock** *n* **1 stocks** *pl* **:** a wooden frame with holes for the feet or the feet and hands once used to punish a wrongdoer publicly **2 :** the wooden part by which a rifle or shotgun is held during firing **3 :** an original (as a person, race, or language) from which others descend **4 :** the whole supply or amount on hand **5 :** farm animals **:** LIVESTOCK, CATTLE **6 :** the ownership element in a business which is divided into shares that can be traded independently **7 :** liquid in which meat, fish, or vegetables have been simmered — **in stock :** on hand **:** in the store and available for purchase

[2]**stock** *vb* **1 :** to provide with or get stock or a stock **2 :** to get or keep a stock of

[3]**stock** *adj* **1 :** kept regularly in stock **2 :** commonly used **:** STANDARD

stock·ade *n* **1 :** a line of strong posts set in the ground to form a defense **2 :** an enclosure formed by stakes driven into the ground

stock·bro·ker *n* **:** a person who handles orders to buy and sell stocks

stock·hold·er *n* **:** an owner of stock

stock·ing *n* **:** a close-fitting usually knit covering for the foot and leg

stock market *n* **:** a place where shares of stock are bought and sold

stocky *adj* **stock·i·er; stock·i·est :** compact, sturdy, and relatively thick in build **:** THICKSET

stock·yard *n* **:** a yard for stock and especially for keeping livestock about to be slaughtered or shipped

¹stole *past of* STEAL

²stole *n* **:** a long wide scarf worn about the shoulders

stolen *past participle of* STEAL

¹stom·ach *n* **1 :** the pouch into which food goes after it leaves the mouth and has passed down the throat **2 :** ABDOMEN 1 **3 :** ²DESIRE 1, LIKING

²stomach *vb* **:** to bear patiently **:** put up with

stomp *vb* **:** to walk heavily or noisily **:** STAMP

¹stone *n* **1 :** earth or mineral matter hardened in a mass **:** ROCK **2 :** a piece of rock coarser than gravel **3 :** GEM **4 :** a stony mass sometimes present in a diseased organ **5 :** the kernel of a fruit in its hard case **6** *pl usually* **stone :** an English measure of weight equaling fourteen pounds (about 6.5 kilograms)

²stone *vb* **stoned; ston·ing 1 :** to throw stones at **2 :** to remove the stones of

³stone *adj* **:** of, relating to, or made of stone

Stone Age *n* **:** the oldest period in which human beings are known to have existed **:** the age during which stone tools were used

stone–blind *adj* **:** completely blind

stone–deaf *adj* **:** completely deaf

stony *adj* **ston·i·er; ston·i·est 1 :** full of stones **2 :** insensitive as stone **:** UNFEELING **3 :** hard as stone

stood *past of* STAND

stool *n* **1 :** a seat without back or arms supported by three or four legs or by a central post **2 :** FOOTSTOOL **3 :** a mass of material discharged from the intestine

¹stoop *vb* **1 :** to bend down or over **2 :** to carry the head and shoulders or the upper part of the body bent forward **3 :** to do something that is beneath one

²stoop *n* **:** a forward bend of the head and shoulders

³stoop *n* **:** a porch, platform, or stairway at the entrance of a house or building

¹stop *vb* **stopped; stop·ping 1 :** to close an opening by filling or blocking it **:** PLUG **2 :** to hold back **:** RESTRAIN **3 :** to halt the movement or progress of **4 :** to come to an end **:** CEASE **5 :** to make a visit **:** STAY

²stop *n* **1 :** ¹END 2, FINISH **2 :** a set of organ pipes of one tone quality **:** a control knob for such a set **3 :** something that delays, blocks, or brings to a halt **4 :** STOPPER, PLUG **5 :** the act of stopping **:** the state of being stopped **6 :** a halt in a journey **:** STAY **7 :** a stopping place

stop·light *n* **1 :** a light on the rear of a motor vehicle that goes on when the driver presses the brake pedal **2 :** a signal light used in controlling traffic

stop·over *n* **:** a stop made during a journey

stop·page *n* **:** the act of stopping **:** the state of being stopped

stop·per *n* **:** something (as a cork or plug) used to stop openings

stop·watch *n* **:** a watch having a hand that can be started and stopped for exact timing (as of a race)

stor·age *n* **1 :** space or a place for storing **2 :** an amount stored **3 :** the act of storing **:** the state of being stored **4 :** the price charged for storing something

storage battery *n* **:** a battery that can be renewed by passing an electric current through it

¹store *vb* **stored; stor·ing 1 :** to provide with what is needed **:** SUPPLY **2 :** to place or leave something in a location (as a warehouse, library, or computer memory) to keep for later use or disposal **3 :** to put somewhere for safekeeping

²store *n* **1 stores** *pl* **:** something collected and kept for future use **2 :** a large quantity, supply, or number **3 :** a place where goods are sold **:** SHOP — **in store :** ¹READY 1

store·house *n, pl* **store·hous·es 1 :** a building for storing goods **2 :** a large supply or source

store·keep·er *n* **1 :** a person in charge of supplies (as in a factory) **2 :** an owner or manager of a store or shop

store·room *n* **:** a room for storing things not in use

stork *n* **:** a large Old World wading bird that looks like the related herons and includes one European form (the **white stork**) that often nests on roofs and chimneys

¹storm *n* **1 :** a heavy fall of rain, snow, or sleet often with strong wind **2 :** a violent outburst **3 :** a violent attack on a defended position

²storm *vb* **1 :** to blow hard and rain or snow heavily **2 :** to make a mass attack against **3 :** to be very angry **:** RAGE **4 :** to rush about violently

stormy *adj* **storm·i·er; storm·i·est 1 :** relating to or affected by a storm **2 :** displaying anger and excitement — **storm·i·ness** *n*

¹sto·ry *n, pl* **sto·ries** **1 :** a report about incidents or events : ACCOUNT **2 :** a short often amusing tale **3 :** a tale shorter than a novel **4 :** a widely told rumor **5 :** ³LIE, FALSEHOOD

²sto·ry *or* **sto·rey** *n, pl* **sto·ries** *or* **sto·reys** **:** a set of rooms or an area making up one floor level of a building

stout *adj* **1 :** of strong character : BRAVE, FIRM **2 :** of a strong or lasting sort : STURDY, TOUGH **3 :** bulky in body : FLESHY — **stout·ly** *adv* — **stout·ness** *n*

¹stove *n* **:** a structure usually of iron or steel that burns fuel or uses electricity to provide heat (as for cooking or heating)

²stove *past of* STAVE

stove·pipe *n* **:** a metal pipe to carry away smoke from a stove

stow *vb* **1 :** to put away : STORE **2 :** to arrange in an orderly way : PACK **3 :** ²LOAD 1

stow·away *n* **:** a person who hides (as in a ship or airplane) to travel free

strad·dle *vb* **strad·dled; strad·dling** **1 :** to stand, sit, or walk with the legs spread wide apart **2 :** to stand, sit, or ride with a leg on either side of **3 :** to favor or seem to favor two opposite sides of

strag·gle *vb* **strag·gled; strag·gling** **1 :** to wander from a straight course or way : STRAY **2 :** to trail off from others of its kind — **strag·gler** *n*

¹straight *adj* **1 :** following the same direction throughout its length : not having curves, bends, or angles **2 :** not straying from the main point or proper course **3 :** not straying from what is right or honest **4 :** correctly ordered or arranged — **straight·ness** *n*

²straight *adv* **:** in a straight manner, course, or line

straight·en *vb* **1 :** to make or become straight **2 :** to put in order

straight·for·ward *adj* **:** being plain and honest : FRANK — **straight·for·ward·ly** *adv* — **straight·for·ward·ness** *n*

straight·way *adv* **:** IMMEDIATELY 2

¹strain *n* **1 :** a line of ancestors to whom a person is related **2 :** a group of individuals that cannot be told from related kinds by appearance alone **3 :** a quality or disposition that runs through a family or race **4 :** a small amount : TRACE **5 :** MELODY 2, AIR

²strain *vb* **1 :** to stretch or be stretched, pulled, or used to the limit **2 :** to stretch beyond a proper limit **3 :** to try one's hardest **4 :** to injure or be injured by too much or too hard use or effort **5 :** to press or pass through a strainer : FILTER

³strain *n* **1 :** the act of straining **2 :** the state of being strained **3 :** ²OVERWORK, WORRY **4 :** bodily injury resulting from strain or from a wrench or twist that stretches muscles and ligaments

strained *adj* **1 :** not easy or natural **2 :** brought close to war

strain·er *n* **:** a device (as a screen, sieve, or filter) to hold back solid pieces while a liquid passes through

strait *n* **1 :** a narrow channel connecting two bodies of water **2 :** ¹DISTRESS 1, NEED — often used in pl.

¹strand *n* **:** the land bordering a body of water : SHORE, BEACH

²strand *vb* **1 :** to run, drive, or cause to drift onto a strand : run aground **2 :** to leave in a strange or unfavorable place especially without any chance to get away

³strand *n* **1 :** one of the fibers, threads, strings, or wires twisted or braided to make a cord, rope, or cable **2 :** something long or twisted like a rope

strange *adj* **strang·er; strang·est** **1 :** of or relating to some other person, place, or thing **2 :** UNFAMILIAR 1 **3 :** exciting curiosity, surprise, or wonder because of not being usual or ordinary **4 :** ill at ease : SHY — **strange·ly** *adv* — **strange·ness** *n*

strang·er *n* **1 :** one who is not in the place where one's home is : FOREIGNER **2 :** GUEST 1, VISITOR **3 :** a person whom one does not know or has not met

stran·gle *vb* **stran·gled; stran·gling** **1 :** to choke to death by squeezing the throat **2 :** to choke in any way — **stran·gler** *n*

¹strap *n* **:** a narrow strip of flexible material (as leather) used especially for fastening, binding, or wrapping

²strap *vb* **strapped; strap·ping** **1 :** to fasten with or attach by means of a strap **2 :** BIND 1, 2, CONSTRICT **3 :** to whip with a strap

strap·ping *adj* **:** LARGE, STRONG

strat·a·gem *n* **:** a trick in war to deceive or outwit the enemy

stra·te·gic *adj* **1 :** of, relating to, or showing the use of strategy **2 :** useful or important in strategy

strat·e·gy *n, pl* **strat·e·gies** **1 :** the skill of using military, naval, and air forces to win a war **2 :** a clever plan or method

strato·sphere *n* **:** an upper portion of the atmosphere more than eleven kilometers above the earth where temperature changes little and clouds rarely form

stra·tum *n, pl* **stra·ta** **:** LAYER 2

stra·tus *n, pl* **stra·ti** **:** a cloud extending over a large area at an altitude of from 600 to 2000 meters

straw *n* **1 :** stalks especially of grain after threshing **2 :** a single dry coarse plant stalk

: a piece of straw **3 :** a slender tube for sucking up a beverage

straw·ber·ry *n, pl* **straw·ber·ries :** the juicy edible usually red fruit of a low plant with white flowers and long slender runners

[1]**stray** *n* **:** a domestic animal that is wandering at large because it is lost or has been abandoned

[2]**stray** *vb* **1 :** to wander from a group or from the proper place **:** ROAM **2 :** to go off from a straight or the right course

[3]**stray** *adj* **1 :** having strayed or been lost **2 :** occurring here and there **:** RANDOM

[1]**streak** *n* **1 :** a line or mark of a different color or composition from its background **2 :** a narrow band of light **3 :** a small amount **:** TRACE, STRAIN **4 :** a short series of something — **streaked** *adj*

[2]**streak** *vb* **1 :** to make streaks in or on **2 :** to move swiftly **:** RUSH

[1]**stream** *n* **1 :** a body of water (as a brook or river) flowing on the earth **2 :** a flow of liquid **3 :** a steady series (as of words or events) following one another

[2]**stream** *vb* **1 :** to flow in or as if in a stream **2 :** to give out a bodily fluid in large amounts **3 :** to become wet with flowing liquid **4 :** to trail out at full length **5 :** to pour in large numbers

stream·er *n* **1 :** a flag that streams in the wind **:** PENNANT **2 :** a long narrow wavy strip (as of ribbon on a hat) suggesting a banner floating in the wind **3 streamers** *pl* **:** AURORA BOREALIS

stream·lined *adj* **1 :** designed or constructed to make motion through water or air easier or as if for this purpose **2 :** made shorter, simpler, or more efficient

street *n* **1 :** a public way especially in a city, town, or village **2 :** the people living along a street

street·car *n* **:** a passenger vehicle that runs on rails and operates mostly on city streets

strength *n* **1 :** the quality of being strong **2 :** power to resist force **3 :** power to resist attack **4 :** intensity of light, color, sound, or odor **5 :** force as measured in numbers

strength·en *vb* **:** to make, grow, or become stronger

stren·u·ous *adj* **1 :** very active **:** ENERGETIC **2 :** showing or requiring much energy — **stren·u·ous·ly** *adv*

strep·to·my·cin *n* **:** a substance produced by a soil bacterium and used especially in treating tuberculosis

[1]**stress** *n* **1 :** a force that tends to change the shape of a body **2 :** something that causes bodily or mental tension **:** a state of tension resulting from a stress **3 :** special importance given to something **4 :** relative prominence of sound **:** a syllable carrying this stress **:** ACCENT

[2]**stress** *vb* **1 :** to expose to stress **:** STRAIN **2 :** [1]ACCENT 1 **3 :** to give special importance to

stress mark *n* **:** a mark used with a written syllable in the respelling of a word to show that this syllable is to be stressed when spoken

[1]**stretch** *vb* **1 :** to reach out **:** EXTEND, SPREAD **2 :** to draw out in length or width or both **:** EXPAND, ENLARGE **3 :** to draw up from a cramped, stooping, or relaxed position **4 :** to pull tight **5 :** to cause to reach or continue **6 :** EXAGGERATE **7 :** to become extended without breaking

[2]**stretch** *n* **1 :** the act of extending or drawing out beyond ordinary or normal limits **2 :** the extent to which something may be stretched **3 :** the act or an instance of stretching the body or one of its parts **4 :** a continuous extent in length, area, or time

stretch·er *n* **1 :** one that stretches **2 :** a light bedlike device for carrying sick or injured persons

strew *vb* **strewed; strewed** *or* **strewn; strew·ing 1 :** to spread by scattering **2 :** to cover by or as if by scattering something

strick·en *adj* **1 :** hit or wounded by or as if by a missile **2 :** troubled with disease, misfortune, or sorrow

strict *adj* **1 :** permitting no avoidance or escape **2 :** kept with great care **:** ABSOLUTE **3 :** carefully observing something (as a rule or principle) **:** EXACT, PRECISE — **strict·ly** *adv* — **strict·ness** *n*

[1]**stride** *vb* **strode; strid·den; strid·ing 1 :** to walk or run with long even steps **2 :** to step over **:** STRADDLE

[2]**stride** *n* **1 :** a long step **:** the distance covered by such a step **2 :** a step forward **:** ADVANCE **3 :** a way of striding

strife *n* **1 :** bitter and sometimes violent disagreement **2 :** [2]STRUGGLE 1, CONTENTION

[1]**strike** *vb* **struck; struck** *or* **strick·en; strik·ing 1 :** GO 1, PROCEED **2 :** to touch or hit with force **3 :** to lower (as a flag or sail) usually in salute or surrender **4 :** to come into contact or collision with **5 :** to make a military attack **:** FIGHT **6 :** to remove or cancel with or as if with the stroke of a pen **7 :** to make known by sounding or cause to sound **8 :** to affect usually suddenly **9 :** to produce by stamping with a die or punch **10 :** to produce by or as if by a blow **11 :** to cause to ignite by scratching **12 :** to agree on the arrangements of **13 :** to make an impression on **14 :** to come upon **:** DISCOVER **15 :** to stop work in order to obtain a change in conditions of work

[2]**strike** *n* **1 :** an act or instance of striking **2**

: a stopping of work by workers to force an employer to agree to demands **3 :** a discovery of a valuable mineral deposit **4 :** a baseball pitch that is swung at or that passes through a certain area over home plate (**strike zone**) and that counts against the batter **5 :** DISADVANTAGE, HANDICAP **6 :** the knocking down of all ten bowling pins with the first ball **7 :** a military attack

strike·out *n* **:** an out in baseball that results from a batter's striking out

strike out *vb* **:** to be out in baseball by getting three strikes as a batter

strik·ing *adj* **:** attracting attention **:** REMARKABLE — **strik·ing·ly** *adv*

¹string *n* **1 :** a small cord used to bind, fasten, or tie **2 :** a thin tough plant structure (as the fiber connecting the halves of a bean pod) **3 :** the gut, wire, or plastic cord of a musical instrument that vibrates to produce a tone **4 strings** *pl* **:** the stringed instruments of an orchestra **5 :** a group, series, or line of objects threaded on a string or arranged as if strung together

²string *vb* **strung; string·ing 1 :** to provide with strings **2 :** to make tense **3 :** ²THREAD 4 **4 :** to tie, hang, or fasten with string **5 :** to remove the strings of **6 :** to set or stretch out in a line

string bass *n* **:** DOUBLE BASS

string bean *n* **:** a bean grown primarily for its pods which are eaten before the seeds are full grown

stringed instrument *n* **:** a musical instrument (as a violin, guitar, or banjo) sounded by plucking or striking or by drawing a bow across tight strings

string·er *n* **:** a long strong piece of wood or metal used for support or strengthening in building (as under a floor)

stringy *adj* **string·i·er; string·i·est :** containing, consisting of, or like string

¹strip *vb* **stripped; strip·ping 1 :** to remove clothes **:** UNDRESS **2 :** to remove a covering or surface layer from **3 :** to take away all duties, honors, or special rights **4 :** to remove furniture, equipment, or accessories from **5 :** to tear or damage the thread of a screw or bolt

²strip *n* **:** a long narrow piece or area

strip–crop·ping *n* **:** the growing of a food crop (as potatoes) in alternate strips with a crop (as grass) that forms sod and helps keep the soil from being worn away

¹stripe *vb* **striped; strip·ing :** to make stripes on

²stripe *n* **1 :** a line or long narrow division or section of something different in color or appearance from the background **2 :** a piece of material often with a special design worn (as on a sleeve) to show military rank or length of service

striped *adj* **:** having stripes

strive *vb* **strove; striv·en** *or* **strived; striv·ing 1 :** to carry on a conflict or effort **:** CONTEND **2 :** to try hard

strode *past of* STRIDE

¹stroke *vb* **stroked; strok·ing :** to rub gently in one direction

²stroke *n* **1 :** the act of striking **:** BLOW **2 :** a single unbroken movement especially in one direction **:** one of a series of repeated movements (as in swimming or rowing a boat) **3 :** the hitting of a ball in a game (as golf or tennis) **4 :** a sudden action or process that results in something being struck **5 :** a sudden or unexpected example **6 :** a sudden weakening or loss of consciousness and powers of voluntary movement that results from the breaking or blocking of an artery in the brain **7 :** effort by which something is done or the results of such effort **8 :** the sound of striking (as of a clock or bell) **9 :** a mark made by a single movement of a brush, pen, or tool

¹stroll *vb* **:** to walk in a leisurely manner **:** RAMBLE

²stroll *n* **:** a leisurely walk **:** RAMBLE

stroll·er *n* **:** a small carriage in which a baby can sit and be pushed around

strong *adj* **stron·ger; stron·gest 1 :** having great power in the muscles **2 :** HEALTHY 1, 2, ROBUST **3 :** having great resources **4 :** of a specified number **5 :** PERSUASIVE **6 :** having much of some quality **7 :** moving with speed and force **8 :** ENTHUSIASTIC, ZEALOUS **9 :** not easily injured or overcome **10 :** well established **:** FIRM — **strong·ly** *adv*

strong·hold *n* **:** FORTRESS

strove *past of* STRIVE

struck *past of* STRIKE

struc·tur·al *adj* **1 :** of, relating to, or affecting structure **2 :** used or formed for use in construction

struc·ture *n* **1 :** something built (as a house or dam) **2 :** the manner in which something is built **:** CONSTRUCTION **3 :** the arrangement or relationship of parts or organs

¹strug·gle *vb* **strug·gled; strug·gling 1 :** to make a great effort to overcome someone or something **:** STRIVE **2 :** to move with difficulty or with great effort

²struggle *n* **1 :** a violent effort **2 :** ²FIGHT 1, CONTEST

strum *vb* **strummed; strum·ming :** to play on a stringed instrument by brushing the strings with the fingers

strung *past of* STRING

¹strut *vb* **strut·ted; strut·ting :** to walk in a stiff proud way

[2]**strut** *n* **1 :** a bar or brace used to resist lengthwise pressure **2 :** a strutting step or walk

[1]**stub** *n* **1 :** a short part remaining after the rest has been removed or used up **2 :** a small part of a check kept as a record of what was on the detached check

[2]**stub** *vb* **stubbed; stub·bing :** to strike (as the toe) against an object

stub·ble *n* **1 :** the stem ends of herbs and especially cereal grasses left in the ground after harvest **2 :** a rough growth or surface like stubble in a field **:** a short growth of beard

stub·born *adj* **1 :** refusing to change an opinion or course of action in spite of difficulty or urging **2 :** PERSISTENT **3 :** difficult to handle, manage, or treat — **stub·born·ly** *adv* — **stub·born·ness** *n*

stub·by *adj* **stub·bi·er; stub·bi·est :** short and thick like a stub

stuc·co *n, pl* **stuc·cos** *or* **stuc·coes :** a plaster for coating walls

stuck *past of* STICK

stuck–up *adj* **:** VAIN 2, CONCEITED

[1]**stud** *n* **1 :** one of the smaller vertical braces of the walls of a building to which the wall materials are fastened **2 :** a removable device like a button used to fasten something or as an ornament **3 :** one of the metal cleats used on a snow tire to provide a better grip

[2]**stud** *vb* **stud·ded; stud·ding 1 :** to supply or cover with or as if with studs **2 :** to set thickly together

stu·dent *n* **:** a person who studies especially in school **:** PUPIL

stu·dio *n, pl* **stu·di·os 1 :** the place where an artist, sculptor, or photographer works **2 :** a place for the study of an art **3 :** a place where movies are made **4 :** a place from which radio or television programs are broadcast

stu·di·ous *adj* **:** devoted to and fond of study

[1]**study** *n, pl* **stud·ies 1 :** use of the mind to get knowledge **2 :** a careful investigation or examination of something **3 :** a room especially for study, reading, or writing

[2]**study** *vb* **stud·ied; study·ing 1 :** to use the mind to learn about something by reading, investigating, or memorizing **2 :** to give close attention to

[1]**stuff** *n* **1 :** materials, supplies, or equipment that people need or use **2 :** writing, speech, or ideas of little value **3 :** something mentioned or understood but not named **4 :** basic part of something **:** SUBSTANCE

[2]**stuff** *vb* **1 :** to fill by packing or crowding things in **:** CRAM **2 :** OVEREAT, GORGE **3 :** to fill with a stuffing **4 :** to stop up **:** CONGEST **5 :** to force into something **:** THRUST

stuff·ing *n* **1 :** material used in filling up or stuffing something **2 :** a mixture (as of bread crumbs and seasonings) used to stuff meat, vegetables, eggs, or poultry

stuffy *adj* **stuff·i·er; stuff·i·est 1 :** needing fresh air **2 :** stuffed or choked up **3 :** [1]DULL 8

[1]**stum·ble** *vb* **stum·bled; stum·bling 1 :** to trip in walking or running **2 :** to walk unsteadily **3 :** to speak or act in a clumsy manner **4 :** to come unexpectedly or accidentally

[2]**stumble** *n* **:** an act or instance of stumbling

[1]**stump** *n* **1 :** the part of something (as an arm, a tooth, or a pencil) that remains after the rest has been removed, lost, or worn away **:** STUB **2 :** the part of a tree that remains in the ground after the tree is cut down

[2]**stump** *vb* **1 :** PERPLEX, BAFFLE **2 :** to walk or walk over heavily, stiffly, or clumsily as if with a wooden leg **3 :** [2]STUB

stun *vb* **stunned; stun·ning 1 :** to make dizzy or senseless by or as if by a blow **2 :** to affect with shock or confusion **:** fill with disbelief

stung *past of* STING

stunk *past of* STINK

stun·ning *adj* **1 :** able or likely to make a person senseless or confused **2 :** unusually lovely or attractive **:** STRIKING

[1]**stunt** *vb* **:** to hold back the normal growth of

[2]**stunt** *n* **:** an unusual or difficult performance or act

stu·pe·fy *vb* **stu·pe·fied; stu·pe·fy·ing 1 :** to make stupid, groggy, or numb **2 :** ASTONISH, ASTOUND

stu·pen·dous *adj* **:** amazing especially because of great size or height

stu·pid *adj* **1 :** slow or dull of mind **2 :** showing or resulting from a dull mind or a lack of proper attention **3 :** not interesting or worthwhile — **stu·pid·ly** *adv*

stu·pid·i·ty *n, pl* **stu·pid·i·ties 1 :** the quality or state of being stupid **2 :** a stupid thought, action, or remark

stu·por *n* **:** a condition in which the senses or feelings become dull

stur·dy *adj* **stur·di·er; stur·di·est 1 :** firmly built or made **2 :** strong and healthy in body **:** ROBUST **3 :** RESOLUTE — **stur·di·ly** *adv* — **sturd·i·ness** *n*

stur·geon *n* **:** a large food fish with tough skin and rows of bony plates

[1]**stut·ter** *vb* **:** to speak or say in a jerky way with involuntary repeating or interruption of sounds

[2]**stutter** *n* **:** the act or an instance of stuttering

[1]**sty** *n, pl* **sties :** PIGPEN

[2]**sty** *or* **stye** *n, pl* **sties** *or* **styes :** a painful red swelling on the edge of an eyelid

[1]**style** *n* **1 :** the narrow middle part of the pistil of a flower **2 :** a way of speaking or writing **3 :** an individual way of doing something **4 :** a method or manner that is felt to be very respectable, fashionable, or proper **:** FASHION

[2]**style** *vb* **styled; styl·ing 1 :** to identify by some descriptive term **:** CALL **2 :** to design and make in agreement with an accepted or a new style

styl·ish *adj* **:** having style **:** FASHIONABLE — **styl·ish·ly** *adv* — **styl·ish·ness** *n*

sty·lus *n, pl* **sty·li** *or* **sty·lus·es :** a pointed instrument used in ancient times for writing on wax tablets

[1]**sub** *n* **:** [1]SUBSTITUTE

[2]**sub** *vb* **subbed; sub·bing :** to act as a substitute

[3]**sub** *n* **:** SUBMARINE

sub- *prefix* **1 :** under **:** beneath **:** below **2 :** lower in importance or rank **:** lesser **3 :** division or part of **4 :** so as to form, stress, or deal with lesser parts or relations

sub·di·vide *vb* **sub·di·vid·ed; sub·di·vid·ing 1 :** to divide the parts of into more parts **2 :** to divide into several parts

sub·di·vi·sion *n* **1 :** the act of subdividing **2 :** one of the parts into which something is subdivided

sub·due *vb* **sub·dued; sub·du·ing 1 :** to overcome in battle **2 :** to bring under control **3 :** to reduce the brightness or strength of **:** SOFTEN

sub·head *or* **sub·head·ing** *n* **:** a heading under which one of the divisions of a subject is listed

[1]**sub·ject** *n* **1 :** a person under the authority or control of another **2 :** a person who owes loyalty to a monarch or state **3 :** a course of study **4 :** an individual that is studied or experimented on **5 :** the person or thing discussed **:** TOPIC **6 :** the word or group of words about which the predicate makes a statement

[2]**subject** *adj* **1 :** owing obedience or loyalty to another **2 :** likely to be affected by **3 :** depending on

[3]**sub·ject** *vb* **1 :** to bring under control or rule **2 :** to cause to put up with

sub·lime *adj* **1 :** grand or noble in thought, expression, or manner **2 :** having beauty enough or being impressive enough to arouse a mixed feeling of admiration and wonder

submarine *n* **:** a naval ship designed to operate underwater

sub·merge *vb* **sub·merged; sub·merg·ing 1 :** to put under or plunge into water **2 :** to cover or become covered with or as if with water

sub·mis·sion *n* **1 :** the act of submitting something (as for consideration or comment) **2 :** the condition of being humble or obedient **3 :** the act of submitting to power or authority

sub·mis·sive *adj* **:** willing to submit to others

sub·mit *vb* **sub·mit·ted; sub·mit·ting 1 :** to leave to the judgment or approval of someone else **2 :** to put forward as an opinion, reason, or idea **3 :** to yield to the authority, control, or choice of another

[1]**sub·or·di·nate** *adj* **1 :** being in a lower class or rank **:** INFERIOR **2 :** yielding to or controlled by authority

[2]**subordinate** *n* **:** one that is subordinate

[3]**sub·or·di·nate** *vb* **sub·or·di·nat·ed; sub·or·di·nat·ing :** to make subordinate

sub·scribe *vb* **sub·scribed; sub·scrib·ing 1 :** to make known one's approval by or as if by signing **2 :** to agree to give or contribute by signing one's name with the amount promised **3 :** to place an order (as for a newspaper) with payment or a promise to pay — **sub·scrib·er** *n*

sub·scrip·tion *n* **1 :** an act or instance of subscribing **2 :** a thing or amount subscribed

sub·se·quent *adj* **:** following in time, order, or place — **sub·se·quent·ly** *adv*

sub·set *n* **:** a mathematical set each of whose members is also a member of a larger set

sub·side *vb* **sub·sid·ed; sub·sid·ing 1 :** to become lower **:** SINK **2 :** to become quiet or less

sub·sist *vb* **:** to continue living or being

sub·sis·tence *n* **:** the smallest amount (as of food and clothing) necessary to support life

sub·soil *n* **:** a layer of soil lying just under the topsoil

sub·stance *n* **1 :** ESSENCE 1 **2 :** the most important part **3 :** material of a certain kind **4 :** material belongings **:** WEALTH

sub·stan·dard *adj* **:** being below what is standard

sub·stan·tial *adj* **1 :** made up of or relating to substance **2 :** ABUNDANT **3 :** PROSPEROUS 1 **4 :** firmly constructed **5 :** large in amount

[1]**sub·sti·tute** *n* **:** a person or thing that takes the place of another

[2]**substitute** *vb* **sub·sti·tut·ed; sub·sti·tut·ing 1 :** to put in the place of another **2 :** to serve as a substitute

sub·sti·tu·tion *n* **:** the act or process of substituting

sub·tle *adj* **sub·tler; sub·tlest 1 :** DELICATE 1 **2 :** SHREWD, KEEN **3 :** CLEVER 2, SLY — **sub·tly** *adv*

sub·top·ic *n* **:** a topic (as in a composition) that is a division of a main topic

sub·tract *vb* **:** to take away (as one part or number from another) **:** DEDUCT

sub·trac·tion *n* **:** the subtracting of one number from another

sub·tra·hend *n* **:** a number that is to be subtracted from another number

sub·urb *n* **1 :** a part of a city or town near its outer edge **2 :** a smaller community close to a city **3 suburbs** *pl* **:** the area of homes close to or surrounding a city — **sub·ur·ban** *adj or n*

sub·way *n* **1 :** an underground tunnel **2 :** a usually electric underground railway

suc·ceed *vb* **1 :** to come after **:** FOLLOW **2 :** to take the place of a ruler or leader who has died, resigned, or been removed **3 :** to be successful

suc·cess *n* **1 :** satisfactory completion of something **2 :** the gaining of wealth, respect, or fame **3 :** a person or thing that succeeds

suc·cess·ful *adj* **1 :** resulting or ending well or in success **2 :** gaining or having gained success — **suc·cess·ful·ly** *adv*

suc·ces·sion *n* **1 :** the order, act, or right of succeeding to a throne, title, or property **2 :** a series of persons or things that follow one after another

suc·ces·sive *adj* **:** following in order and without interruption — **suc·ces·sive·ly** *adv*

suc·ces·sor *n* **:** a person who succeeds to a throne, title, property, or office

suc·cor *n* **:** [2]HELP 1, RELIEF

suc·cu·lent *adj* **:** JUICY

suc·cumb *vb* **1 :** to yield to force or pressure **2 :** [1]DIE 1

[1]**such** *adj* **1 :** of a kind just specified or to be specified **2 :** of the same class, type, or sort **:** SIMILAR **3 :** so great **:** so remarkable

[2]**such** *pron* **:** that sort of person, thing, or group

suck *vb* **1 :** to draw in liquid and especially mother's milk with the mouth **2 :** to draw liquid from by action of the mouth **3 :** to allow to dissolve gradually in the mouth **4 :** to put (as a thumb) into the mouth and draw on as if sucking **5 :** ABSORB 1

suck·er *n* **1 :** one that sucks **:** SUCKLING **2 :** a freshwater fish related to the carps that has thick soft lips for sucking in food **3 :** a new stem from the roots or lower part of a plant **4 :** LOLLIPOP **5 :** a person easily fooled or cheated

suck·le *vb* **suck·led; suck·ling :** to feed from the breast or udder

suck·ling *n* **:** a young mammal still sucking milk from its mother

suc·tion *n* **1 :** the act or process of sucking **2 :** the process of drawing something into a space (as in a pump) by removing air from the space **3 :** the force caused by suction

sud·den *adj* **1 :** happening or coming quickly and unexpectedly **2 :** met with unexpectedly **3 :** [1]STEEP 1 **4 :** HASTY 2 — **sud·den·ly** *adv* — **sud·den·ness** *n*

suds *n pl* **1 :** soapy water especially when foamy **2 :** the foam on soapy water

sue *vb* **sued; su·ing :** to seek justice or right by bringing legal action

suede *n* **:** leather tanned and rubbed so that it is soft and has a nap

su·et *n* **:** the hard fat about the kidneys in beef and mutton from which tallow is made

suf·fer *vb* **1 :** to feel pain **2 :** to experience something unpleasant **3 :** to bear loss or damage **4 :** [1]PERMIT — **suf·fer·er** *n*

suf·fer·ing *n* **1 :** the state or experience of one that suffers **2 :** a cause of distress **:** HARDSHIP

suf·fice *vb* **suf·ficed; suf·fic·ing 1 :** to satisfy a need **2 :** to be enough for

suf·fi·cient *adj* **:** enough to achieve a goal or fill a need — **suf·fi·cient·ly** *adv*

suf·fix *n* **:** a letter or group of letters that comes at the end of a word and has a meaning of its own

suf·fo·cate *vb* **suf·fo·cat·ed; suf·fo·cat·ing 1 :** to kill by stopping the breath or depriving of oxygen to breathe **2 :** to be or become choked or smothered **3 :** to have or cause to have a feeling of smothering

suf·fo·ca·tion *n* **:** the act of suffocating or state of being suffocated

suf·frage *n* **:** the right to vote

[1]**sug·ar** *n* **1 :** a sweet substance obtained from sugarcane, sugar beets, or maple syrup **2 :** any of numerous soluble and usually sweet carbohydrates

[2]**sugar** *vb* **1 :** to mix, cover, or sprinkle with sugar **2 :** to make something less hard to take or put up with **3 :** to change to crystals of sugar

sugar beet *n* **:** a large beet with white roots that is grown as a source of sugar

sug·ar·cane *n* **:** a tall strong grass with jointed stems widely raised in tropical regions for the sugar it yields

sugar maple *n* **:** an American maple tree with hard strong wood and a sweet sap that yields maple syrup and maple sugar

sug·gest *vb* **1 :** to put (as a thought or desire) into a person's mind **2 :** to offer as an idea **3 :** to bring into one's mind through close connection or association

sug·ges·tion *n* **1 :** the act or process of suggesting **2 :** a thought or plan that is suggested **3 :** [1]HINT 2

sug·ges·tive *adj* **1 :** giving a suggestion **2 :** full of suggestions **:** PROVOCATIVE **3 :** suggesting something improper or indecent

sui·cide *n* **1 :** the act of killing oneself purposely **2 :** a person who commits suicide

[1]**suit** *n* **1 :** an action in court for enforcing a

right or claim **2 :** an earnest request **3 :** COURTSHIP **4 :** a number of things used together **:** SET **5 :** all the playing cards of one kind (as spades) in a pack

²suit *vb* **1 :** to be suitable or satisfactory **2 :** to make suitable **:** ADAPT **3 :** to be proper for or pleasing with **4 :** to meet the needs or desires of

suit·abil·i·ty *n* **:** the quality or state of being suitable

suit·able *adj* **:** being fit or right for a use or group — **suit·ably** *adv*

suit·case *n* **:** a flat rectangular traveling bag

suite *n* **1 :** a number of connected rooms (as in a hotel) **2 :** a set of matched furniture for a room

suit·or *n* **:** a man who courts a woman

sul·fur *or* **sul·phur** *n* **:** a yellow chemical element that is found widely in nature and is used in making chemicals and paper

sul·fu·rous *or* **sul·phu·rous** *adj* **:** containing or suggesting sulfur

¹sulk *vb* **:** to be sullenly silent or irritable

²sulk *n* **1 :** the state of one sulking **2 :** a sulky mood or spell

¹sulky *adj* **sulk·i·er; sulk·i·est :** sulking or given to sulking

²sulky *n, pl* **sulk·ies :** a light vehicle with two wheels, a seat for the driver only, and usually no body

sul·len *adj* **1 :** not sociable **:** SULKY **2 :** GLOOMY 1, DREARY — **sul·len·ly** *adv*

sul·tan *n* **:** a ruler especially of a Muslim state

sul·ta·na *n* **:** the wife, mother, sister, or daughter of a sultan

sul·try *adj* **sul·tri·er; sul·tri·est :** very hot and humid

¹sum *n* **1 :** a quantity of money **2 :** the whole amount **3 :** the result obtained by adding numbers **4 :** a problem in arithmetic

²sum *vb* **summed; sum·ming :** to find the sum of by adding or counting

su·mac *or* **su·mach** *n* **:** any of a group of trees, shrubs, or woody vines having leaves with many leaflets and loose clusters of red or white berries

sum·ma·rize *vb* **sum·ma·rized; sum·ma·riz·ing :** to tell in or reduce to a summary

¹sum·ma·ry *adj* **1 :** expressing or covering the main points briefly **:** CONCISE **2 :** done without delay

²summary *n, pl* **sum·ma·ries :** a short statement of the main points (as in a book or report)

¹sum·mer *n* **1 :** the season between spring and autumn which is in the northern hemisphere usually the months of June, July, and August **2 :** YEAR 2

²summer *vb* **:** to pass the summer

sum·mer·time *n* **:** the summer season

sum·mery *adj* **:** of, relating to, or typical of summer

sum·mit *n* **:** the highest point (as of a mountain) **:** TOP

sum·mon *vb* **1 :** to call or send for **:** CONVENE **2 :** to order to appear before a court of law **3 :** to call into being **:** AROUSE — **sum·mon·er** *n*

sum·mons *n, pl* **sum·mons·es 1 :** the act of summoning **2 :** a call by authority to appear at a place named or to attend to some duty **3 :** a written order to appear in court

sump·tu·ous *adj* **:** very expensive or luxurious

sum up *vb* **:** SUMMARIZE

¹sun *n* **1 :** the celestial body whose light makes our day **:** the member of the solar system round which the planets revolve **2 :** a celestial body like our sun **3 :** SUNSHINE 1

²sun *vb* **sunned; sun·ning 1 :** to expose to or as if to the rays of the sun **2 :** to sun oneself

sun·bathe *vb* **sun·bathed; sun·bath·ing :** ²SUN 2

sun·beam *n* **:** a ray of sunlight

sun·block *n* **:** a strong sunscreen

sun·bon·net *n* **:** a bonnet with a wide curving brim that shades the face and usually a ruffle at the back that protects the neck from the sun

¹sun·burn *vb* **sun·burned** *or* **sun·burnt; sun·burn·ing :** to burn or discolor by the sun

²sunburn *n* **:** a sore red state of the skin caused by too much sunlight

sun·dae *n* **:** a serving of ice cream topped with fruit, syrup, or nuts

Sun·day *n* **:** the first day of the week **:** the Christian Sabbath

Sunday school *n* **:** a school held on Sunday in a church for religious education

sun·di·al *n* **:** a device to show the time of day by the position of the shadow cast onto a marked plate by an object with a straight edge

sun·down *n* **:** SUNSET

sun·dries *n pl* **:** various small articles or items

sun·dry *adj* **:** more than one or two **:** VARIOUS

sun·fish *n, pl* **sunfish** *or* **sun·fish·es :** any of numerous mostly small and brightly colored American freshwater fishes related to the perches

sun·flow·er *n* **:** a tall plant often grown for its large flower heads with brown center and yellow petals or for its edible oily seeds

sung *past of* SING

sun·glass·es *n pl* **:** glasses to protect the eyes from the sun

sunk *past of* SINK

sunk·en *adj* **1 :** lying at the bottom of a body

of water **2 :** fallen in : HOLLOW **3 :** built or settled below the surrounding or normal level

sun·less *adj* **:** being without sunlight : DARK

sun·light *n* **:** SUNSHINE

sun·lit *adj* **:** lighted by the sun

sun·ny *adj* **sun·ni·er; sun·ni·est 1 :** bright with sunshine **2 :** MERRY 1, CHEERFUL

sun·rise *n* **1 :** the apparent rise of the sun above the horizon : the light and color that go with this **2 :** the time at which the sun rises

sun·screen *n* **:** a substance used on the skin to help protect it from the sun's ultraviolet radiation

sun·set *n* **1 :** the apparent passing of the sun below the horizon : the light and color that go with this **2 :** the time at which the sun sets

sun·shade *n* **:** something (as a parasol) used to protect from the sun's rays

sun·shine *n* **1 :** the sun's light or direct rays : the warmth and light given by the sun's rays **2 :** something that spreads warmth or happiness

sun·stroke *n* **:** a disorder marked by high fever and collapse and caused by too much sun

sun·tan *n* **:** a browning of skin exposed to the sun

sun·up *n* **:** SUNRISE

sun·ward *adv or adj* **:** toward or facing the sun

su·per *adj* **1 :** very great **2 :** very good

super- *prefix* **1 :** more than **2 :** extremely : very

su·perb *adj* **:** outstandingly excellent, impressive, or beautiful

su·per·com·put·er *n* **:** a large very fast computer used especially for scientific computations

su·per·fi·cial *adj* **1 :** of or relating to the surface or appearance only **2 :** not thorough : SHALLOW — **su·per·fi·cial·ly** *adv*

su·per·flu·ous *adj* **:** going beyond what is enough or necessary : EXTRA

su·per·he·ro *n* **:** a fictional hero having extraordinary or superhuman powers

su·per·high·way *n* **:** an expressway for high-speed traffic

su·per·hu·man *adj* **:** going beyond normal human power, size, or ability

su·per·in·tend *vb* **:** to have or exercise the charge of

su·per·in·ten·dent *n* **:** a person who looks after or manages something (as schools or a building)

[1]**su·pe·ri·or** *adj* **1 :** situated higher up : higher in rank, importance, numbers, or quality **2 :** excellent of its kind : BETTER **3 :** feeling that one is better or more important than others : ARROGANT

[2]**superior** *n* **1 :** one that is higher than another in rank, importance, or quality **2 :** the head of a religious house or order

su·pe·ri·or·i·ty *n* **:** the state or fact of being superior

[1]**su·per·la·tive** *adj* **1 :** of, relating to, or being the form of an adjective or adverb that shows the highest or lowest degree of comparison **2 :** better than all others : SUPREME

[2]**superlative** *n* **:** the superlative degree or a superlative form in a language

su·per·mar·ket *n* **:** a self-service market selling foods and household items

su·per·nat·u·ral *adj* **:** of or relating to something beyond or outside of nature or the visible universe

su·per·sede *vb* **su·per·sed·ed; su·per·sed·ing :** to take the place or position of

su·per·son·ic *adj* **1 :** relating to or being vibrations too rapid to be heard **2 :** having a speed from one to five times that of sound

su·per·sti·tion *n* **:** beliefs or practices resulting from ignorance, fear of the unknown, or trust in magic or chance

su·per·sti·tious *adj* **:** of, relating to, showing, or influenced by superstition

su·per·vise *vb* **su·per·vised; su·per·vis·ing** : SUPERINTEND, OVERSEE

su·per·vi·sion *n* **:** the act of supervising : MANAGEMENT

su·per·vi·sor *n* **1 :** a person who supervises **2 :** an officer in charge of a unit or an operation of a business, government, or school

sup·per *n* **1 :** the evening meal especially when dinner is eaten at midday **2 :** refreshments served late in the evening especially at a social gathering

sup·plant *vb* **:** to take the place of another usually unfairly

sup·ple *adj* **sup·pler; sup·plest 1 :** ADAPTABLE **2 :** capable of bending or of being bent easily without stiffness, creases, or damage

[1]**sup·ple·ment** *n* **:** something that supplies what is needed or adds to something else

[2]**sup·ple·ment** *vb* **:** to add to : COMPLETE

sup·ple·men·ta·ry *adj* **:** added as a supplement : ADDITIONAL

sup·pli·cate *vb* **sup·pli·cat·ed; sup·pli·cat·ing :** to ask or beg in a humble way : BESEECH

sup·pli·ca·tion *n* **:** the act of supplicating

[1]**sup·ply** *vb* **sup·plied; sup·ply·ing 1 :** to provide for : SATISFY **2 :** to make available : FURNISH

[2]**supply** *n, pl* **sup·plies 1 :** the amount of something that is needed or can be gotten **2 :** [2]STORE 1 **3 :** the act or process of supplying something

¹sup·port *vb* **1 :** to take sides with **:** FAVOR **2 :** to provide evidence for **:** VERIFY **3 :** to pay the costs of **:** MAINTAIN **4 :** to hold up or in position **:** serve as a foundation or prop for **5 :** to keep going **:** SUSTAIN — **sup·port·er** *n*

²support *n* **1 :** the act of supporting **:** the condition of being supported **2 :** one that supports

sup·pose *vb* **sup·posed; sup·pos·ing 1 :** to think of as true or as a fact for the sake of argument **2 :** BELIEVE 2, THINK **3 :** ¹GUESS 1

sup·posed *adj* **1 :** believed to be true or real **2 :** forced or required to do something — **sup·pos·ed·ly** *adv*

sup·press *vb* **1 :** to put down (as by authority or force) **:** SUBDUE **2 :** to hold back **:** REPRESS

sup·pres·sion *n* **:** an act or instance of suppressing **:** the state of being suppressed

su·prem·a·cy *n, pl* **su·prem·a·cies :** the highest rank, power, or authority

su·preme *adj* **1 :** highest in rank, power, or authority **2 :** highest in degree or quality **:** UTMOST **3 :** ¹EXTREME 1, FINAL — **su·preme·ly** *adv*

Supreme Being *n* **:** GOD 1

Supreme Court *n* **:** the highest court of the United States consisting of a chief justice and eight associate justices

¹sure *adj* **sur·er; sur·est 1 :** firmly established **:** STEADFAST **2 :** RELIABLE, TRUSTWORTHY **3 :** having no doubt **:** CONFIDENT **4 :** not to be doubted **:** CERTAIN **5 :** bound to happen **6 :** bound as if by fate

²sure *adv* **:** SURELY 2, 3

sure·ly *adv* **1 :** with confidence **:** CONFIDENTLY **2 :** without doubt **3 :** beyond question **:** REALLY

¹surf *n* **1 :** the waves of the sea that splash on the shore **2 :** the sound, splash, and foam of breaking waves

²surf *vb* **1 :** to ride the surf (as on a surfboard) **2 :** to scan a wide range of offerings (as on television or the Internet) for something that is interesting or fills a need

¹sur·face *n* **1 :** the outside or any one side of an object **2 :** the outside appearance

²surface *adj* **1 :** of or relating to a surface **:** acting on a surface **2 :** not deep or real

³surface *vb* **sur·faced; sur·fac·ing 1 :** to give a surface to **:** make smooth (as by sanding or paving) **2 :** to come to the surface

surf·board *n* **:** a long narrow board that floats and is ridden in surfing

surf·ing *n* **:** the sport of riding waves in to shore usually while standing on a surfboard

¹surge *vb* **surged; surg·ing 1 :** to rise and fall with much action **2 :** to move in or as if in waves

²surge *n* **1 :** an onward rush like that of a wave **2 :** a large wave

sur·geon *n* **:** a doctor who specializes in surgery

sur·gery *n, pl* **sur·ger·ies 1 :** a branch of medicine concerned with the correction of defects, the repair and healing of injuries, and the treatment of diseased conditions by operation **2 :** the work done by a surgeon

sur·gi·cal *adj* **:** of, relating to, or associated with surgery or surgeons

sur·ly *adj* **sur·li·er; sur·li·est :** having a mean rude disposition **:** UNFRIENDLY

¹sur·mise *n* **:** a thought or idea based on very little evidence **:** ²GUESS

²surmise *vb* **sur·mised; sur·mis·ing :** to form an idea on very little evidence **:** ¹GUESS 1

sur·mount *vb* **1 :** OVERCOME 1 **2 :** to get to the top of **3 :** to be at the top of

sur·name *n* **:** a family name **:** a last name

sur·pass *vb* **1 :** to be greater, better, or stronger than **:** EXCEED **2 :** to go beyond the reach or powers of

¹sur·plus *n* **:** an amount left over **:** EXCESS

²surplus *adj* **:** left over **:** EXTRA

¹sur·prise *n* **1 :** an act or instance of coming upon without warning **2 :** something that surprises **3 :** ASTONISHMENT, AMAZEMENT

²surprise *vb* **sur·prised; sur·pris·ing 1 :** to attack without warning **:** capture by an unexpected attack **2 :** to come upon without warning **3 :** to cause to feel wonder or amazement because of being unexpected

sur·pris·ing *adj* **:** causing surprise **:** UNEXPECTED — **sur·pris·ing·ly** *adv*

¹sur·ren·der *vb* **1 :** to give oneself or something over to the power, control, or possession of another especially under force **:** YIELD **2 :** RELINQUISH

²surrender *n* **:** the act of giving up or yielding oneself or something into the possession or control of someone else

sur·rey *n, pl* **surreys :** a pleasure carriage that has two wide seats and four wheels and is drawn by horses

sur·round *vb* **:** to enclose on all sides **:** ENCIRCLE

sur·round·ings *n pl* **:** the circumstances, conditions, or things around an individual **:** ENVIRONMENT

¹sur·vey *vb* **sur·veyed; sur·vey·ing 1 :** to look over **:** EXAMINE **2 :** to find out the size, shape, or position of (as an area of land) **3 :** to gather information from **:** make a survey of

²sur·vey *n, pl* **surveys 1 :** the action or an instance of surveying **2 :** something that is surveyed **3 :** a careful examination to learn facts **4 :** a history or description that covers a large subject briefly

sur·vey·ing *n* **1 :** the act or occupation of a person who makes surveys **2 :** a branch of mathematics that teaches how to measure the earth's surface and record these measurements accurately

sur·vey·or *n* **:** a person who surveys or whose occupation is surveying

sur·viv·al *n* **1 :** a living or continuing longer than another person or thing **2 :** one that survives

sur·vive *vb* **sur·vived; sur·viv·ing 1 :** to remain alive : continue to exist **2 :** to live longer than or past the end of — **sur·vi·vor** *n*

sus·cep·ti·ble *adj* **1 :** of such a nature as to permit **2 :** having little resistance **3 :** easily affected or impressed by

[1]**sus·pect** *adj* **:** thought of with suspicion

[2]**sus·pect** *n* **:** a person who is suspected

[3]**sus·pect** *vb* **1 :** to have doubts of : DISTRUST **2 :** to imagine to be guilty without proof **3 :** to suppose to be true or likely

sus·pend *vb* **1 :** to force to give up some right or office for a time **2 :** to stop or do away with for a time **3 :** to stop operation or action for a time **4 :** to hang especially so as to be free except at one point

sus·pend·er *n* **:** one of a pair of supporting straps that fasten to trousers or a skirt and pass over the shoulders

sus·pense *n* **:** uncertainty or worry about the result of something

sus·pen·sion *n* **1 :** the act or an instance of suspending **2 :** the state of being suspended **3 :** the period during which someone or something is suspended

sus·pi·cion *n* **1 :** an act or instance of suspecting or the state of being suspected **2 :** a feeling that something is wrong : DOUBT

sus·pi·cious *adj* **1 :** likely to arouse suspicion **2 :** likely to suspect or distrust **3 :** showing distrust

sus·tain *vb* **1 :** to give support or relief to : HELP **2 :** to provide with what is needed **3 :** to keep up : PROLONG **4 :** to hold up the weight of : PROP **5 :** to keep up the spirits of **6 :** to put up with without giving in **7 :** [2]EXPERIENCE **8 :** to allow or uphold as true, legal, or fair **9 :** CONFIRM 1, PROVE

sus·te·nance *n* **1 :** [2]LIVING 3, SUBSISTENCE **2 :** the act of sustaining : the state of being sustained **3 :** [2]SUPPORT 2

SUV *n* **:** SPORT-UTILITY VEHICLE

[1]**swab** *n* **1 :** a yarn mop especially as used on a ship **2 :** a wad of absorbent material usually wound around the end of a small stick and used for applying or removing material (as medicine or makeup)

[2]**swab** *vb* **swabbed; swab·bing 1 :** to clean with or as if with a swab **2 :** to apply medication to with a swab

[1]**swag·ger** *vb* **:** to walk with a proud strut

[2]**swagger** *n* **:** an act or instance of swaggering

[1]**swal·low** *n* **:** any of a group of small migratory birds with long wings, forked tails, and a graceful flight

[2]**swallow** *vb* **1 :** to take into the stomach through the mouth and throat **2 :** to perform the actions used in swallowing something **3 :** to take in as if by swallowing : ENGULF **4 :** to accept or believe without question, protest, or anger **5 :** to keep from expressing or showing : REPRESS

[3]**swallow** *n* **1 :** an act of swallowing **2 :** an amount that can be swallowed at one time

swam *past of* SWIM

[1]**swamp** *n* **:** wet spongy land often partly covered with water

[2]**swamp** *vb* **1 :** to fill or cause to fill with water : sink after filling with water **2 :** OVERWHELM 2

swampy *adj* **swamp·i·er; swamp·i·est :** of, relating to, or like a swamp

swan *n* **:** a usually white waterbird with a long neck and a heavy body that is related to but larger than the geese

[1]**swap** *vb* **swapped; swap·ping :** to give in exchange : make an exchange : TRADE

[2]**swap** *n* **:** [1]EXCHANGE 1, TRADE

[1]**swarm** *n* **1 :** a large number of bees that leave a hive together to form a new colony elsewhere **2 :** a large moving crowd (as of people or insects)

[2]**swarm** *vb* **1 :** to form a swarm and leave the hive **2 :** to move or gather in a swarm or large crowd **3 :** to be filled with a great number : TEEM

swar·thy *adj* **swar·thi·er; swar·thi·est :** having a dark complexion

[1]**swat** *vb* **swat·ted; swat·ting :** to hit with a quick hard blow

[2]**swat** *n* **:** a hard blow

swath *or* **swathe** *n* **1 :** a sweep of a scythe or machine in mowing or the path cut in one course **2 :** a row of cut grass (as grain)

[1]**sway** *n* **1 :** a slow swinging back and forth or from side to side **2 :** a controlling influence or force : RULE

[2]**sway** *vb* **1 :** to swing slowly back and forth or from side to side **2 :** to change often between one point, position, or opinion and another **3 :** [2]INFLUENCE

swear *vb* **swore; sworn; swear·ing 1 :** to make a statement or promise under oath : VOW **2 :** to give an oath to **3 :** to bind by an oath **4 :** to take an oath **5 :** to use bad or vulgar language : CURSE

[1]**sweat** *vb* **sweat** *or* **sweat·ed; sweat·ing 1**

: to give off salty moisture through the pores of the skin : PERSPIRE **2 :** to collect moisture on the surface **3 :** to work hard enough to perspire

[2]**sweat** *n* **1 :** PERSPIRATION 2 **2 :** moisture coming from or collecting in drops on a surface **3 :** the condition of one sweating

sweat·er *n* : a knitted or crocheted jacket or pullover

sweat gland *n* : any of numerous small skin glands that give off perspiration

sweat·shirt *n* : a loose pullover or jacket without a collar and usually with long sleeves

Swede *n* : a person born or living in Sweden

[1]**Swed·ish** *adj* : of or relating to Sweden, the Swedes, or Swedish

[2]**Swedish** *n* : the language of the Swedes

[1]**sweep** *vb* **swept; sweep·ing 1 :** to remove with a broom or brush **2 :** to clean by removing loose dirt or small trash with a broom or brush **3 :** to move over or across swiftly with force or destruction **4 :** to move or gather as if with a broom or brush **5 :** to touch a surface as if with a brush **6 :** to drive along with steady force **7 :** to move the eyes or an instrument through a wide curve — **sweep·er** *n*

[2]**sweep** *n* **1 :** something that sweeps or works with a sweeping motion **2 :** an act or instance of sweeping **3 :** a complete or easy victory **4 :** a curving movement, course, or line **5 :** [1]RANGE 6, SCOPE **6 :** CHIMNEY SWEEP

[1]**sweep·ing** *n* **1 :** the act or action of one that sweeps **2 sweepings** *pl* : things collected by sweeping

[2]**sweeping** *adj* **1 :** moving or extending in a wide curve or over a wide area **2 :** EXTENSIVE

sweep·stakes *n, sing or pl* : a contest in which money or prizes are given to winners picked by chance (as by drawing names from a box)

[1]**sweet** *adj* **1 :** pleasing to the taste **2 :** containing or tasting of sugar **3 :** pleasing to the mind or feelings : AGREEABLE **4 :** [1]KINDLY 2, MILD **5 :** FRAGRANT **6 :** pleasing to the ear or eye **7 :** much loved : DEAR **8 :** not sour, stale, or spoiled **9 :** FRESH 1 — **sweet·ish** *adj* — **sweet·ly** *adv* — **sweet·ness** *n*

[2]**sweet** *n* **1 :** something (as candy) that is sweet to the taste **2 :** [1]DARLING 1, DEAR

sweet corn *n* : an Indian corn with kernels rich in sugar that is cooked as a vegetable while young

sweet·en *vb* : to make or become sweet or sweeter

sweet·en·ing *n* **1 :** the act or process of making sweet **2 :** something that sweetens

sweet·heart *n* : a person whom one loves

sweet·meat *n* : a food (as a piece of candy or candied fruit) rich in sugar

sweet pea *n* : a climbing plant related to the peas that is grown for its fragrant flowers of many colors

sweet potato *n* : the large sweet edible root of a tropical vine somewhat like a morning glory

sweet wil·liam *n, often cap W* : a European pink grown for its thick flat clusters of many-colored flowers

[1]**swell** *vb* **swelled; swelled** *or* **swol·len; swell·ing 1 :** to enlarge in an abnormal way usually by pressure from within or by growth **2 :** to grow or make bigger (as in size or value) **3 :** to stretch upward or outward : BULGE **4 :** to fill or become filled with emotion

[2]**swell** *n* **1 :** a becoming larger (as in size or value) **2 :** a long rolling wave or series of waves in the open sea **3 :** a very fashionably dressed person

[3]**swell** *adj* **1 :** STYLISH, FASHIONABLE **2 :** EXCELLENT, FIRST-RATE

swell·ing *n* : a swollen lump or part

swel·ter *vb* : to suffer, sweat, or be faint from heat

swept *past of* SWEEP

[1]**swerve** *vb* **swerved; swerv·ing :** to turn aside suddenly from a straight line or course

[2]**swerve** *n* : an act or instance of swerving

[1]**swift** *adj* **1 :** moving or capable of moving with great speed **2 :** occurring suddenly **3 :** [1]READY 3, ALERT — **swift·ly** *adv* — **swift·ness** *n*

[2]**swift** *adv* : SWIFTLY

[3]**swift** *n* : a small usually sooty black bird that is related to the hummingbirds but looks like a swallow

swig *n* : the amount drunk at one time : GULP

[1]**swill** *vb* : to eat or drink greedily

[2]**swill** *n* **1 :** [1]SLOP 3 **2 :** GARBAGE, REFUSE

[1]**swim** *vb* **swam; swum; swim·ming 1 :** to move through or in water by moving arms, legs, fins, or tail **2 :** to glide smoothly and quietly **3 :** to float on or in or be covered with or as if with a liquid **4 :** to be dizzy : move or seem to move dizzily **5 :** to cross by swimming — **swim·mer** *n*

[2]**swim** *n* **1 :** an act or period of swimming **2 :** the main current of activity

swimming *adj* **1 :** capable of swimming **2 :** used in or for swimming

swimming pool *n* : a tank (as of concrete or plastic) made for swimming

swim·suit *n* : a garment for swimming or bathing

[1]**swin·dle** *vb* **swin·dled; swin·dling :** to get money or property from by dishonest means : CHEAT

²swindle *n* **:** an act or instance of swindling
swin·dler *n* **:** a person who swindles
swine *n, pl* **swine :** a hoofed domestic animal that comes from the wild boar, has a long snout and bristly skin, and is widely raised for meat
swine·herd *n* **:** a person who tends swine
¹swing *vb* **swung; swing·ing 1 :** to move rapidly in a sweeping curve **2 :** to throw or toss in a circle or back and forth **3 :** to sway to and fro **4 :** to hang or be hung so as to move freely back and forth or in a curve **5 :** to turn on a hinge or pivot **6 :** to manage or handle successfully **7 :** to march or walk with free swaying movements
²swing *n* **1 :** an act of swinging **2 :** a swinging movement, blow, or rhythm **3 :** the distance through which something swings **4 :** a swinging seat usually hung by overhead ropes **5 :** a style of jazz marked by lively rhythm and played mostly for dancing
¹swipe *n* **:** a strong sweeping blow
²swipe *vb* **swiped; swip·ing :** ¹STEAL 2
¹swirl *vb* **:** to move with a whirling or twisting motion
²swirl *n* **1 :** a whirling mass or motion **:** EDDY **2 :** whirling confusion **3 :** a twisting shape or mark
¹swish *vb* **:** to make, move, or strike with a soft rubbing or hissing sound
²swish *n* **1 :** a hissing sound (as of a whip cutting the air) or a light sweeping or rubbing sound (as of a silk skirt) **2 :** a swishing movement
¹Swiss *n, pl* **Swiss :** a person born or living in Switzerland
²Swiss *adj* **:** of or relating to Switzerland or the Swiss
¹switch *n* **1 :** a narrow flexible whip, rod, or twig **2 :** an act of switching **3 :** a blow with a switch or whip **4 :** a change from one thing to another **5 :** a device for adjusting the rails of a track so that a train or streetcar may be turned from one track to another **6 :** SIDING 1 **7 :** a device for making, breaking, or changing the connections in an electrical circuit
²switch *vb* **1 :** to strike or whip with or as if with a switch **2 :** to lash from side to side **3 :** to turn, shift, or change by operating a switch **4 :** to make a shift or change
switch·board *n* **:** a panel for controlling the operation of a number of electric circuits used especially to make and break telephone connections
¹swiv·el *n* **:** a device joining two parts so that one or both can turn freely (as on a bolt or pin)
²swivel *vb* **swiv·eled** *or* **swiv·elled; swiv·el·ing** *or* **swiv·el·ling :** to turn on or as if on a swivel
swollen *past participle of* SWELL
¹swoon *vb* **:** ²FAINT
²swoon *n* **:** ³FAINT
¹swoop *vb* **:** to rush down or pounce suddenly like a hawk attacking its prey
²swoop *n* **:** an act or instance of swooping
sword *n* **:** a weapon having a long blade usually with a sharp point and edge
sword·fish *n, pl* **swordfish** *or* **sword·fish·es :** a very large ocean food fish having a long swordlike beak formed by the bones of the upper jaw
swords·man *n, pl* **swords·men :** a person who fights with a sword
swore *past of* SWEAR
sworn *past participle of* SWEAR
swum *past participle of* SWIM
swung *past of* SWING
syc·a·more *n* **1 :** the common fig tree of Egypt and Asia Minor **2 :** an American tree with round fruits and bark that forms flakes
syl·lab·ic *adj* **1 :** of, relating to, or being syllables **2 :** not accompanied by a vowel sound in the same syllable
syl·lab·i·cate *vb* **syl·lab·i·cat·ed; syl·lab·i·cat·ing :** SYLLABIFY
syl·lab·i·ca·tion *n* **:** the forming of syllables **:** the dividing of words into syllables
syl·lab·i·fi·ca·tion *n* **:** SYLLABICATION
syl·lab·i·fy *vb* **syl·lab·i·fied; syl·lab·i·fy·ing :** to form or divide into syllables
syl•la•ble *n* **1 :** a unit of spoken language that consists of one or more vowel sounds alone or of a syllabic consonant alone or of either of these preceded or followed by one or more consonant sounds **2 :** one or more letters (as syl, la, and ble) in a written word (as syl·la•ble) usually separated from the rest of the word by a centered dot or a hyphen and used as guides to the division of the word at the end of a line
sym·bol *n* **1 :** something that stands for something else **:** EMBLEM **2 :** a letter, character, or sign used instead of a word to represent a quantity, position, relationship, direction, or something to be done
sym·bol·ic *or* **sym·bol·i·cal** *adj* **:** of, relating to, or using symbols or symbolism
sym·bol·ize *vb* **sym·bol·ized; sym·bol·iz·ing :** to serve as a symbol of
sym·met·ri·cal *or* **sym·met·ric** *adj* **:** having or showing symmetry
sym·me·try *n, pl* **sym·me·tries :** close agreement in size, shape, and position of parts that are on opposite sides of a dividing line or center **:** an arrangement involving regular and balanced proportions
sym·pa·thet·ic *adj* **1 :** fitting one's mood or

disposition **2 :** feeling sympathy **3 :** feeling favorable — **sym·pa·thet·i·cal·ly** *adv*

sym·pa·thize *vb* **sym·pa·thized; sym·pa·thiz·ing 1 :** to feel or show sympathy **2 :** to be in favor of something

sym·pa·thy *n, pl* **sym·pa·thies 1 :** a relationship between persons or things in which whatever affects one similarly affects the other **2 :** readiness to think or feel alike **:** similarity of likes, interest, or aims that makes a bond of goodwill **3 :** readiness to favor or support **4 :** the act of or capacity for entering into the feelings or interests of another **5 :** sorrow or pity for another **6 :** a showing of sorrow for another's loss, grief, or misfortune

sym·phon·ic *adj* **:** of or relating to a symphony or symphony orchestra

sym·pho·ny *n, pl* **sym·pho·nies 1 :** harmonious arrangement (as of sound or color) **2 :** a usually long musical composition for a full orchestra **3 :** a large orchestra of wind, string, and percussion instruments

symp·tom *n* **1 :** a noticeable change in the body or its functions typical of a disease **2 :** INDICATION 2, SIGN

syn·a·gogue *or* **syn·a·gog** *n* **:** a Jewish house of worship

syn·apse *n* **:** the point at which a nerve impulse passes from one nerve cell to another

syn·co·pa·tion *n* **:** a temporary accenting of a normally weak beat in music to vary the rhythm

syn·o·nym *n* **:** a word having the same or almost the same meaning as another word in the same language

syn·on·y·mous *adj* **:** alike in meaning

syn·tax *n* **:** the way in which words are put together to form phrases, clauses, or sentences

syn·the·size *vb* **syn·the·sized; syn·the·siz·ing :** to build up from simpler materials

syn·thet·ic *adj* **:** produced artificially especially by chemical means **:** produced by human beings

sy·rin·ga *n* **:** a garden shrub with often fragrant flowers of a white or cream color

sy·ringe *n* **:** a device used to force fluid into or withdraw it from the body or its cavities

syr·up *or* **sir·up** *n* **1 :** a thick sticky solution of sugar and water often containing flavoring or a medicine **2 :** the juice of a fruit or plant with some of the water removed

sys·tem *n* **1 :** a group of parts combined to form a whole that works or moves as a unit **2 :** a body that functions as a whole **3 :** a group of bodily organs that together carry on some vital function **4 :** an orderly plan or method of governing or arranging **5 :** regular method or order **:** ORDERLINESS

sys·tem·at·ic *adj* **1 :** having, using, or acting on a system **2 :** carrying out a plan with thoroughness or regularity — **sys·tem·at·i·cal·ly** *adv*

sys·tem·ic *adj* **:** of or relating to the body as a whole

T

t *n, pl* **t's** *or* **ts** *often cap* **:** the twentieth letter of the English alphabet — **to a T :** just fine **:** EXACTLY

tab *n* **1 :** a short flap or tag attached to something for filing, pulling, or hanging **2 :** a careful watch

tab·by *n, pl* **tabbies 1 :** a domestic cat with a gray or tawny coat striped and spotted with black **2 :** a female domestic cat

tab·er·na·cle *n* **1** *often cap* **:** a structure of wood hung with curtains used in worship by the Israelites during their wanderings in the wilderness with Moses **2 :** a house of worship

[1]ta·ble *n* **1 :** a piece of furniture having a smooth flat top on legs **2 :** food to eat **3 :** the people around a table **4 :** short list **5 :** an arrangement in rows or columns for reference

[2]table *vb* **ta·bled; ta·bling 1 :** TABULATE **2 :** to put on a table

tab·leau *n, pl* **tableaus** *or* **tab·leaux :** a scene or event shown by a group of persons who remain still and silent

ta·ble·cloth *n* **:** a covering spread over a dining table before the places are set

ta·ble·land *n* **:** PLATEAU

ta·ble·spoon *n* **1 :** a large spoon used mostly for dishing up food **2 :** TABLESPOONFUL

ta·ble·spoon·ful *n, pl* **tablespoonfuls** *or* **ta·ble·spoons·ful 1 :** as much as a tablespoon will hold **2 :** a unit of measure used in cooking equal to three teaspoonfuls (about fifteen milliliters)

tab·let *n* **1 :** a thin flat slab used for writing, painting, or drawing **2 :** a number of sheets of writing paper glued together at one edge **3 :** a flat and usually round mass of material containing medicine

table tennis *n* **:** a game played on a table by two or four players who use paddles to hit a small hollow plastic ball back and forth over a net

ta·ble·ware *n* **:** utensils (as of china, glass, or silver) for use at the table

tab·u·late *vb* **tab·u·lat·ed; tab·u·lat·ing :** to put in the form of a table

tac·it *adj* **:** understood or made known without being put into words — **tac·it·ly** *adv*

[1]**tack** *n* **1 :** a small nail with a sharp point and usually a broad flat head for fastening a light object or material to a solid surface **2 :** the direction a ship is sailing as shown by the position the sails are set in or the movement of a ship with the sails set in a certain position **3 :** a change of course from one tack to another **4 :** a zigzag movement or course **5 :** a course of action **6 :** a temporary stitch used in sewing

[2]**tack** *vb* **1 :** to fasten with tacks **2 :** to attach or join loosely **3 :** to change from one course to another in sailing **4 :** to follow a zigzag course

[1]**tack·le** *n* **1 :** a set of special equipment **2 :** an arrangement of ropes and wheels for hoisting or pulling something heavy **3 :** an act of tackling

[2]**tackle** *vb* **tack·led; tack·ling 1 :** to seize and throw (a person) to the ground **2 :** to begin working on

ta·co *n, pl* **tacos :** a corn tortilla usually folded and fried and filled with a spicy mixture (as of ground meat and cheese)

tact *n* **:** a keen understanding of how to get along with other people

tact·ful *adj* **:** having or showing tact — **tact·ful·ly** *adv* — **tact·ful·ness** *n*

tac·tic *n* **:** a planned action for some purpose

tac·tics *n sing or pl* **1 :** the science and art of arranging and moving troops or warships for best use **2 :** a system or method for reaching a goal

tac·tile *adj* **:** of or relating to the sense of touch

tact·less *adj* **:** having or showing no tact — **tact·less·ly** *adv* — **tact·less·ness** *n*

tad·pole *n* **:** the larva of a frog or toad that has a long tail, breathes with gills, and lives in water

taf·fy *n, pl* **taffies :** a candy made usually of molasses or brown sugar boiled and pulled until soft

[1]**tag** *n* **:** a small flap or tab fixed or hanging on something **2 :** an often quoted saying

[2]**tag** *vb* **tagged; tag·ging 1 :** to put a tag on **2 :** to follow closely and continually

[3]**tag** *n* **:** a game in which one player who is it chases the others and tries to touch one of them to make that person it

[4]**tag** *vb* **tagged; tag·ging 1 :** to touch in or as if in a game of tag **2 :** to touch a runner in baseball with the ball and cause the runner to be out

[1]**tail** *n* **1 :** the rear part of an animal or a usually slender flexible extension of this part **2 :** something that in shape, appearance, or position is like an animal's tail **3 :** the back, last, or lower part of something **4 :** the side or end opposite the head — **tailed** *adj* — **tail·less** *adj* — **tail·like** *adj*

[2]**tail** *vb* **:** to follow closely to keep watch on

tail·gate *n* **:** a panel at the back end of a vehicle that can be let down for loading and unloading

tail·light *n* **:** a red warning light at the rear of a vehicle

[1]**tai·lor** *n* **:** a person whose business is making or making adjustments in men's or women's clothes

[2]**tailor** *vb* **1 :** to make or make adjustments in (clothes) **2 :** to change to fit a special need

tail·pipe *n* **:** the pipe carrying off the exhaust gases from the muffler of an engine in a car or truck

tail·spin *n* **:** a dive by an airplane turning in a circle

[1]**taint** *vb* **1 :** to affect slightly with something bad **2 :** to rot slightly

[2]**taint** *n* **:** a trace of decay

[1]**take** *vb* **took; tak·en; tak·ing 1 :** to get control of **:** CAPTURE **2 :** [1]GRASP 1 **3 :** to come upon **4 :** CAPTIVATE **5 :** to receive into the body **6 :** to get possession or use of **7 :** ASSUME 1 **8 :** to be formed or used with **9 :** to adopt as one's own or for oneself **10 :** WIN 3 **11 :** CHOOSE 1, SELECT **12 :** to sit in or on **13 :** to use as a way of going from one place to another **14 :** REQUIRE **15 :** to find out by special methods **16 :** to save in some permanent form **17 :** to put up with **:** ENDURE **18 :** BELIEVE 2, 3 **19 :** to be guided by **:** FOLLOW **20 :** to become affected suddenly **21 :** UNDERSTAND 4, INTERPRET **22 :** to react in a certain way **23 :** to carry or go with from one place to another **24 :** REMOVE 3, SUBTRACT **25 :** to do the action of **26 :** to have effect **:** be successful — **tak·er** *n* — **take advantage of 1 :** to make good use of **2 :** to treat (someone) unfairly — **take after :** RESEMBLE — **take care :** to be careful — **take care of :** to do what is needed **:** look after — **take effect 1 :** to go into effect **2 :** to have an intended or expected effect — **take hold :** to become attached or established — **take part :** to do or join in something together with others — **take place :** to come into being and last for a time — used of events or actions

[2]**take** *n* **1 :** the act of taking **2 :** something that is taken **3 :** a bodily reaction that shows a smallpox vaccination to be successful

take back *vb* **:** to try to cancel (as something said)

take in *vb* **1 :** to make smaller **2 :** to receive as a guest **3 :** to allow to join **4 :** to receive (work) to be done in one's home for pay **5 :** to have within its limits **6 :** to go to **7 :** to get the meaning of **8 :** [1]CHEAT 2

take·off *n* **1 :** an imitation especially to mock the original **2 :** an act or instance of taking off from the ground (as by an airplane) **3 :** a spot at which one takes off

take off *vb* **1 :** to take away (a covering) **:** REMOVE **2 :** DEDUCT **3 :** to leave a surface in beginning a flight or leap

take on *vb* **1 :** to begin (a task) or struggle against (an opponent) **2 :** to gain or show as or as if a part of oneself **3 :** [1]EMPLOY 2 **4 :** to make an unusual show of one's grief or anger

take over *vb* **:** to get control of

take up *vb* **1 :** to get together from many sources **2 :** to start something for the first time or after a pause **3 :** to change by making tighter or shorter

tak·ing *adj* **1 :** ATTRACTIVE **2 :** INFECTIOUS 1

talc *n* **:** a soft mineral that has a soapy feel and is used in making talcum powder and for coloring

tal·cum powder *n* **:** a usually perfumed powder for the body made of talc

tale *n* **1 :** something told **2 :** a story about an imaginary event **3 :** [3]LIE **4 :** a piece of harmful gossip

tal·ent *n* **1 :** unusual natural ability **2 :** a special often creative or artistic ability **3 :** persons having special ability — **tal·ent·ed** *adj*

tal·is·man *n, pl* **tal·is·mans :** a ring or stone carved with symbols and believed to have magical powers **:** CHARM

[1]**talk** *vb* **1 :** to express in speech **:** SPEAK **2 :** to speak about **:** DISCUSS **3 :** to cause or influence by talking **4 :** to use a certain language **5 :** to exchange ideas by means of spoken words **:** CONVERSE **6 :** to pass on information other than by speaking **7 :** [2]GOSSIP **8 :** to reveal secret information — **talk·er** *n*

[2]**talk** *n* **1 :** the act of talking **:** SPEECH **2 :** a way of speaking **:** LANGUAGE **3 :** CONFERENCE **4 :** [1]RUMOR 2, GOSSIP **5 :** the topic of comment or gossip **6 :** an informal address

talk·a·tive *adj* **:** fond of talking — **talk·a·tive·ness** *n*

talk·ing–to *n* **:** an often wordy scolding

[1]**tall** *adj* **1 :** having unusually great height **2 :** of a stated height **3 :** made up — **tall·ness** *n*

[2]**tall** *adv* **:** so as to be or look tall

tal·low *n* **:** a white solid fat obtained by heating fatty tissues of cattle and sheep

[1]**tal·ly** *n, pl* **tallies 1 :** a device for keeping a count **2 :** a recorded count **3 :** a score or point made (as in a game)

[2]**tally** *vb* **tal·lied; tal·ly·ing 1 :** to keep a count of **2 :** to make a tally **:** SCORE **3 :** CORRESPOND 1

tal·on *n* **:** the claw of a bird of prey — **tal·oned** *adj*

ta·ma·le *n* **:** seasoned ground meat rolled in cornmeal, wrapped in corn husks, and steamed

tam·bou·rine *n* **:** a small shallow drum with only one head and loose metal disks around the rim that is played by shaking or hitting with the hand

[1]**tame** *adj* **tam·er; tam·est 1 :** made useful and obedient to humans **:** DOMESTIC 3 **2 :** not afraid of people **3 :** not interesting **:** DULL — **tame·ly** *adv* — **tame·ness** *n*

[2]**tame** *vb* **tamed; tam·ing 1 :** to make or become gentle or obedient **2 :** [2]HUMBLE — **tam·able** *or* **tame·able** *adj* — **tam·er** *n*

tamp *vb* **:** to drive down or in with several light blows

tam·per *vb* **:** to interfere in a secret or incorrect way

[1]**tan** *vb* **tanned; tan·ning 1 :** to change hide into leather by soaking in a tannin solution **2 :** to make or become brown or tan in color **3 :** [1]BEAT 1, THRASH

[2]**tan** *adj* **tan·ner; tan·nest :** of a light yellowish brown color

[3]**tan** *n* **1 :** a brown color given to the skin by the sun or wind **2 :** a light yellowish brown color

tan·a·ger *n* **:** a very brightly colored bird related to the finches

[1]**tan·dem** *n* **1 :** a carriage pulled by horses hitched one behind the other **2 :** TANDEM BICYCLE

[2]**tandem** *adv* **:** one behind another

tandem bicycle *n* **:** a bicycle for two people sitting one behind the other

tang *n* **:** a sharp flavor or smell

tan·ger·ine *n* **:** a Chinese orange with a loose skin and sweet pulp

tan·gi·ble *adj* **1 :** possible to touch or handle **2 :** actually real **:** MATERIAL — **tan·gi·bly** *adv*

[1]**tan·gle** *vb* **tan·gled; tan·gling :** to twist or become twisted together into a mass hard to straighten out again

[2]**tangle** *n* **1 :** a tangled twisted mass (as of yarn) **2 :** a complicated or confused state

[1]**tank** *n* **1 :** an often large container for a liquid **2 :** an enclosed combat vehicle that has heavy armor and guns and a tread which is an endless belt

[2]**tank** *vb* **:** to put, keep, or treat in a tank

tan·kard *n* **:** a tall cup with one handle and often a lid

tank·er *n* **:** a vehicle or ship with tanks for carrying a liquid

tan·ner *n* **:** a person who tans hides into leather

tan·nery *n, pl* **tan·ner·ies :** a place where hides are tanned

tan·nin *n* **:** a substance often made from oak

bark or sumac and used in tanning, dyeing, and making ink

tan·ta·lize *vb* **tan·ta·lized; tan·ta·liz·ing :** to make miserable by or as if by showing something desirable but keeping it out of reach — **tan·ta·liz·er** *n*

tan·trum *n* **:** an outburst of bad temper

[1]**tap** *n* **:** FAUCET, SPIGOT — **on tap :** on hand **:** AVAILABLE

[2]**tap** *vb* **tapped; tap·ping 1 :** to let out or cause to flow by making a hole or by pulling out a plug **2 :** to make a hole in to draw off a liquid **3 :** to draw from or upon **4 :** to connect into (a telephone wire) to listen secretly — **tap·per** *n*

[3]**tap** *vb* **tapped; tap·ping 1 :** to hit lightly **2 :** to make by striking something lightly again and again — **tap·per** *n*

[4]**tap** *n* **:** a light blow or its sound

[1]**tape** *n* **1 :** a narrow band of cloth **2 :** a narrow strip or band of material (as paper, steel, or plastic) **3 :** MAGNETIC TAPE **4 :** TAPE RECORDING

[2]**tape** *vb* **taped; tap·ing 1 :** to fasten, cover, or hold up with tape **2 :** to make a record of on tape

tape deck *n* **:** a device used to play back and often to record on magnetic tapes

tape measure *n* **:** a tape marked off for measuring

[1]**ta·per** *n* **1 :** a slender candle **2 :** a gradual lessening in thickness or width in a long object

[2]**taper** *vb* **1 :** to make or become gradually smaller toward one end **2 :** to grow gradually less and less

tape recorder *n* **:** a device for recording on and playing back magnetic tapes

tape recording *n* **:** a recording made on magnetic tape

tap·es·try *n, pl* **tap·es·tries :** a heavy cloth that has designs or pictures woven into it and is used especially as a wall hanging — **tap·es·tried** *adj*

tape·worm *n* **:** a worm with a long flat body that lives in human or animal intestines

tap·i·o·ca *n* **:** small pieces of starch from roots of a tropical plant used especially in puddings

ta·pir *n* **:** a large hoofed mammal of tropical America, Malaya, and Sumatra that has thick legs, a short tail, and a long flexible snout

tap·root *n* **:** a main root of a plant that grows straight down and gives off smaller side roots

taps *n sing or pl* **:** the last bugle call at night blown as a signal to put out the lights

[1]**tar** *n* **:** a thick dark sticky liquid made from wood, coal, or peat

[2]**tar** *vb* **tarred; tar·ring :** to cover with or as if with tar

[3]**tar** *n* **:** SAILOR

ta·ran·tu·la *n* **1 :** a large European spider whose bite was once believed to cause a wild desire to dance **2 :** any of a group of large hairy spiders of warm regions of North and South America whose bite is sharp but not serious except for some South American species

tar·dy *adj* **tar·di·er; tar·di·est :** not on time **:** LATE — **tar·di·ly** *adv* — **tar·di·ness** *n*

tar·get *n* **1 :** a mark or object to shoot at **2 :** a person or thing that is talked about, criticized, or laughed at **3 :** a goal to be reached

tar·iff *n* **1 :** a list of taxes placed by a government on goods coming into a country **2 :** the tax or the rate of taxation set up in a tariff list

[1]**tar·nish** *vb* **:** to make or become dull, dim, or discolored

[2]**tarnish** *n* **:** a surface coating formed during tarnishing

tar·pau·lin *n* **:** a sheet of waterproof canvas

[1]**tar·ry** *vb* **tar·ried; tar·ry·ing 1 :** to be slow in coming or going **2 :** to stay in or at a place

[2]**tar·ry** *adj* **:** of, like, or covered with tar

[1]**tart** *adj* **1 :** pleasantly sharp to the taste **2 :** BITING — **tart·ly** *adv* — **tart·ness** *n*

[2]**tart** *n* **:** a small pie often with no top crust

tar·tan *n* **:** a woolen cloth with a plaid design first made in Scotland

tar·tar *n* **1 :** a substance found in the juices of grapes that forms a reddish crust on the inside of wine barrels **2 :** a crust that forms on the teeth made up of deposits of saliva, food, and calcium

task *n* **:** a piece of assigned work

tas·sel *n* **1 :** a hanging ornament made of a bunch of cords of the same length fastened at one end **2 :** something like a tassel

[1]**taste** *vb* **tast·ed; tast·ing 1 :** [2]EXPERIENCE **2 :** to find out the flavor of something by taking a little into the mouth **3 :** to eat or drink usually in small amounts **4 :** to recognize by the sense of taste **5 :** to have a certain flavor — **tast·er** *n*

[2]**taste** *n* **1 :** a small amount tasted **2 :** the one of the special senses that recognizes sweet, sour, bitter, or salty flavors and that acts through sense organs (**taste buds**) in the tongue **3 :** the quality of something recognized by the sense of taste or by this together with smell and touch **:** FLAVOR **4 :** a personal liking **5 :** the ability to choose and enjoy what is good or beautiful

taste·ful *adj* **:** having or showing good taste — **taste·ful·ly** *adv* — **taste·ful·ness** *n*

taste·less *adj* **1 :** having little flavor **2 :** not having or showing good taste — **taste·less·ly** *adv* — **taste·less·ness** *n*

tasty *adj* **tast·i·er; tast·i·est** : pleasing to the taste — **tast·i·ness** *n*

tat·ter *n* **1** : a part torn and left hanging : SHRED **2 tatters** *pl* : ragged clothing

tat·tered *adj* **1** : torn in or worn to shreds **2** : dressed in ragged clothes

tat·tle *vb* **tat·tled; tat·tling 1** : PRATTLE **2** : to give away secrets : tell on someone — **tat·tler** *n*

tat·tle·tale *n* : a person who tattles

[1]**tat·too** *vb* **tat·tooed; tat·too·ing** : to mark the body with a picture or pattern by using a needle to put color under the skin — **tat·too·er** *n*

[2]**tattoo** *n, pl* **tat·toos** : a picture or design made by tattooing

taught *past of* TEACH

[1]**taunt** *n* : a mean insulting remark

[2]**taunt** *vb* : to make fun of or say insulting things to

Tau·rus *n* **1** : a constellation between Aries and Gemini imagined as a bull **2** : the second sign of the zodiac or a person born under this sign

taut *adj* **1** : tightly stretched **2** : HIGH-STRUNG, TENSE **3** : kept in good order — **taut·ly** *adv* — **taut·ness** *n*

tav·ern *n* **1** : a place where beer and liquor are sold and drunk **2** : INN

taw·ny *adj* **taw·ni·er; taw·ni·est** : of a brownish orange color

[1]**tax** *vb* **1** : to require to pay a tax **2** : to accuse of something **3** : to cause a strain on — **tax·er** *n*

[2]**tax** *n* **1** : money collected by the government from people or businesses for public use **2** : a difficult task

tax·able *adj* : subject to tax

tax·a·tion *n* **1** : the action of taxing **2** : money gotten from taxes

[1]**taxi** *n, pl* **tax·is** : TAXICAB

[2]**taxi** *vb* **tax·ied; taxi·ing** *or* **taxy·ing 1** : to go by taxicab **2** : to run an airplane slowly along the ground under its own power

taxi·cab *n* : an automobile that carries passengers for a fare usually determined by the distance traveled

taxi·der·my *n* : the art of stuffing and mounting the skins of animals

tax·on·o·my *n* **1** : the study of classification **2** : a classification (as of animals) using a system that is usually based on relationship

tax·pay·er *n* : a person who pays or is responsible for paying a tax

TB *n* : TUBERCULOSIS

T–ball *n* : baseball for young children in which the ball is batted from a tee rather than being pitched

tea *n* **1** : the dried leaves and leaf buds of a shrub widely grown in eastern and southern Asia **2** : a drink made by soaking tea in boiling water **3** : a drink or medicine made by soaking plant parts (as dried roots) **4** : refreshments often including tea served in late afternoon **5** : a party at which tea is served

teach *vb* **taught; teach·ing 1** : to show how **2** : to guide the studies of **3** : to cause to know the unpleasant results of something **4** : to give lessons in

teach·er *n* : a person who teaches

teaching *n* **1** : the duties or profession of a teacher **2** : something taught

tea·cup *n* : a cup used with a saucer for hot drinks

teak *n* : the hard wood of a tall tree which grows in the East Indies and resists decay

tea·ket·tle *n* : a covered kettle that is used for boiling water and has a handle and spout

teal *n* : a small swift wild duck

[1]**team** *n* **1** : two or more animals used to pull the same vehicle or piece of machinery **2** : a group of persons who work or play together

[2]**team** *vb* **1** : to haul with or drive a team **2** : to form a team

team·mate *n* : a person who belongs to the same team as someone else

team·ster *n* : a worker who drives a team or a truck

team·work *n* : the work of a group of persons acting together

tea·pot *n* : a pot for making and serving tea

[1]**tear** *n* : a drop of the salty liquid that keeps the eyeballs and inside of the eyelids moist

[2]**tear** *vb* **tore; torn; tear·ing 1** : to pull into two or more pieces by force **2** : LACERATE **3** : to remove by force **4** : to move powerfully or swiftly

[3]**tear** *n* **1** : the act of tearing **2** : damage from being torn

tear·drop *n* : [1]TEAR

tear·ful *adj* : flowing with, accompanied by, or causing tears — **tear·ful·ly** *adv*

[1]**tease** *vb* **teased; teas·ing** : to annoy again and again — **teas·er** *n*

[2]**tease** *n* **1** : the act of teasing : the state of being teased **2** : a person who teases

tea·spoon *n* **1** : a small spoon used especially for stirring drinks **2** : TEASPOONFUL

tea·spoon·ful *n, pl* **teaspoonfuls** *or* **tea·spoons·ful 1** : as much as a teaspoon can hold **2** : a unit of measure used especially in cooking and pharmacy equal to about five milliliters

teat *n* : NIPPLE 1 — used mostly of domestic animals

tech·ni·cal *adj* **1** : having special knowledge especially of a mechanical or scientific subject **2** : of or relating to a single and especially a practical or scientific subject **3** : according to a strict explanation of the rules — **tech·ni·cal·ly** *adv*

tech·ni·cal·i·ty *n, pl* **tech·ni·cal·i·ties** : something having meaning only to a person with special training

technical sergeant *n* : a noncommissioned officer in the Air Force ranking above a staff sergeant

tech·ni·cian *n* : a person skilled in the details or techniques of a subject, art, or job

tech·nique *n* **1** : the manner in which technical details are used in reaching a goal **2** : technical methods

tech·no·log·i·cal *adj* : of or relating to technology

tech·nol·o·gist *n* : a specialist in technology

tech·nol·o·gy *n, pl* **tech·nol·o·gies** **1** : the use of science in solving problems (as in industry or engineering) **2** : a technical method of doing something

ted·dy bear *n* : a stuffed toy bear

te·dious *adj* : tiring because of length or dullness — **te·dious·ly** *adv* — **te·dious·ness** *n*

tee *n* : a device (as a post or peg) on which a ball is placed to be hit or kicked in various sports

teem *vb* : to be full of something

teen·age *or* **teen·aged** *adj* : of, being, or relating to teenagers

teen·ag·er *n* : a person in his or her teens

teens *n pl* : the years thirteen through nineteen in a person's life

tee·ny *adj* **tee·ni·er; tee·ni·est** : TINY

tee shirt *variant of* T-SHIRT

tee·ter *vb* **1** : to move unsteadily **2** : [2]SEESAW

tee·ter–tot·ter *n* : [1]SEESAW

teeth *pl of* TOOTH

teethe *vb* **teethed; teeth·ing** : to cut one's teeth : grow teeth

tele- *or* **tel-** *prefix* **1** : at a distance **2** : television

[1]**tele·cast** *n* : a program broadcast by television

[2]**telecast** *vb* **telecast** *also* **tele·cast·ed; tele·cast·ing** : to broadcast by television — **tele·cast·er** *n*

tele·gram *n* : a message sent by telegraph

[1]**tele·graph** *n* : an electric device or system for sending messages by a code over connecting wires

[2]**telegraph** *vb* **1** : to send by telegraph **2** : to send a telegram to

te·leg·ra·phy *n* : the use of a telegraph

tele·mar·ket·ing *n* : the selling of goods or services by telephone

te·lep·a·thy *n* : communication which appears to take place from one mind to another without speech or signs

[1]**tele·phone** *n* : an instrument for transmitting and receiving sounds over long distances by electricity

[2]**telephone** *vb* **tele·phoned; tele·phon·ing** : to speak to by telephone

[1]**tele·scope** *n* : an instrument shaped like a long tube that has lenses for viewing objects at a distance and especially for observing objects in outer space

[2]**telescope** *vb* **tele·scoped; tele·scop·ing** : to slide or force one part into another like the sections of a small telescope

tele·vise *vb* **tele·vised; tele·vis·ing** : to send (a program) by television

tele·vi·sion *n* **1** : an electronic system of sending images together with sound over a wire or through space by devices that change light and sound into electrical waves and then change these back into light and sound **2** : a television receiving set **3** : television as a way of communicating

tell *vb* **told; tell·ing** **1** : [1]COUNT 1 **2** : to describe item by item **3** : [1]SAY 1 **4** : to make known **5** : to let a person know something : to give information to **6** : [1]ORDER 2 **7** : to find out by observing **8** : to act as a tattletale **9** : to have a noticeable result **10** : to act as evidence

tell·er *n* **1** : NARRATOR **2** : a person who counts votes **3** : a bank employee who receives and pays out money

[1]**tem·per** *vb* **1** : SOFTEN **2** : to make a substance as thick, firm, or tough as is wanted **3** : to heat and cool a substance (as steel) until it is as hard, tough, or flexible as is wanted

[2]**temper** *n* **1** : the hardness or toughness of a substance (as metal) **2** : characteristic state of feeling **3** : calmness of mind **4** : an angry mood

tem·per·a·ment *n* : a person's attitude as it affects what he or she says or does

tem·per·a·men·tal *adj* : having or showing a nervous sensitive temperament — **tem·per·a·men·tal·ly** *adv*

tem·per·ance *n* **1** : control over one's actions, thoughts, or feelings **2** : the use of little or no alcoholic drink

tem·per·ate *adj* **1** : keeping or held within limits : MILD **2** : not drinking much liquor **3** : showing self-control **4** : not too hot or too cold

tem·per·a·ture *n* **1** : degree of hotness or coldness as shown by a thermometer **2** : level of heat above what is normal for the human body : FEVER

tem·pest *n* **1** : a strong wind often accompanied by rain, hail, or snow **2** : UPROAR

tem·pes·tu·ous *adj* : very stormy — **tem·pes·tu·ous·ly** *adv*

[1]**tem·ple** *n* : a building for worship

[2]**temple** *n* : the space between the eye and forehead and the upper part of the ear

tem·po *n, pl* **tem·pi** *or* **tempos** : the rate of speed at which a musical composition is played or sung

tem·po·ral *adj* : of, relating to, or limited by time

tem·po·rary *adj* : not permanent — **tem·po·rar·i·ly** *adv*

tempt *vb* **1** : to make someone think of doing wrong (as by promise of gain) **2** : to risk the dangers of — **tempt·er** *n*

temp·ta·tion *n* **1** : the act of tempting or the state of being tempted **2** : something that tempts

[1]**ten** *adj* : being one more than nine

[2]**ten** *n* : one more than nine : two times five : 10

te·na·cious *adj* **1** : not easily pulled apart **2** : PERSISTENT

te·nac·i·ty *n* : the quality or state of being tenacious

[1]**ten·ant** *n* **1** : a person who rents property (as a house) from the owner **2** : OCCUPANT, DWELLER

[2]**tenant** *vb* : to hold or live in as a tenant

[1]**tend** *vb* **1** : to pay attention **2** : to take care of **3** : to manage the operation of

[2]**tend** *vb* **1** : to move or turn in a certain direction : LEAD **2** : to be likely

ten·den·cy *n, pl* **ten·den·cies** **1** : the direction or course toward something **2** : a leaning toward a particular kind of thought or action

[1]**ten·der** *adj* **1** : not tough **2** : DELICATE 4 **3** : YOUTHFUL 1 **4** : feeling or showing love **5** : very easily hurt — **ten·der·ly** *adv* — **ten·der·ness** *n*

[2]**tender** *vb* **1** : to offer in payment **2** : to present for acceptance

[3]**tender** *n* **1** : [2]OFFER **2** : something (as money) that may be offered in payment

[4]**tend·er** *n* **1** : a ship used to attend other ships (as to supply food) **2** : a boat that carries passengers or freight to a larger ship **3** : a car attached to a locomotive for carrying fuel or water

ten·der·foot *n, pl* **ten·der·feet** *also* **ten·der·foots** : a person who is not used to a rough outdoor life

ten·der·heart·ed *adj* : easily affected with feelings of love, pity, or sorrow

ten·don *n* : a strip or band of tough white fiber connecting a muscle to another part (as a bone)

ten·dril *n* **1** : a slender leafless winding stem by which some climbing plants fasten themselves to a support **2** : something that winds like a plant's tendril

ten·e·ment *n* **1** : a house used as a dwelling **2** : APARTMENT 1 **3** : a building divided into separate apartments for rent

ten·nis *n* : a game played on a level court by two or four players who use rackets to hit a ball back and forth across a low net dividing the court

ten·or *n* **1** : the next to the lowest part in harmony having four parts **2** : the highest male singing voice **3** : a singer or an instrument having a tenor range or part

ten·pins *n* : a bowling game played with ten pins

[1]**tense** *n* : a form of a verb used to show the time of the action or state

[2]**tense** *adj* **tens·er; tens·est** **1** : stretched tight **2** : feeling or showing nervous tension **3** : marked by strain or uncertainty — **tense·ly** *adv* — **tense·ness** *n*

[3]**tense** *vb* **tensed; tens·ing** : to make or become tense

ten·sion *n* **1** : the act of straining or stretching : the condition of being strained or stretched **2** : a state of mental unrest **3** : a state of unfriendliness

[1]**tent** *n* : a portable shelter (as of canvas) stretched and supported by poles

[2]**tent** *vb* : to live in a tent — **ten·ter** *n*

ten·ta·cle *n* : one of the long thin flexible structures that stick out about the head or the mouth of an animal (as an insect or fish) and are used especially for feeling or grasping

ten·ta·tive *adj* : not final — **ten·ta·tive·ly** *adv*

tent caterpillar *n* : any of several caterpillars that spin tent-like webs in which they live in groups

[1]**tenth** *adj* : coming right after ninth

[2]**tenth** *n* **1** : number ten in a series **2** : one of ten equal parts

te·pee *n* : a tent shaped like a cone and used as a home by some American Indians

tep·id *adj* : LUKEWARM 1

[1]**term** *n* **1** : a period of time fixed especially by law or custom **2 terms** *pl* : conditions that limit the nature and scope of something (as a treaty or a will) **3** : a word or expression that has an exact meaning in some uses or is limited to a subject or field **4** : the numerator or denominator of a fraction **5** : any one of the numbers in a series **6 terms** *pl* : relationship between people

[2]**term** *vb* : to apply a term to

[1]**ter·mi·nal** *adj* : of, relating to, or forming an end

[2]**terminal** *n* **1** : a part that forms the end : EXTREMITY **2** : a device at the end of a wire or on a machine for making an electrical connection **3** : either end of a transportation line or a passenger or freight station located at it **4** : a device (as in a computer system) used to put in, receive, and display information

ter·mi·nate *vb* **ter·mi·nat·ed; ter·mi·nat·ing** : END, CLOSE

ter·mi·na·tion *n* **1 :** the end of something **2 :** the act of ending something

ter·mi·nus *n, pl* **ter·mi·ni** *or* **ter·mi·nus·es** **1 :** final goal : END **2 :** either end of a transportation line or travel route

ter·mite *n* : a chewing antlike insect of a light color that lives in large colonies and feeds on wood

tern *n* : any of numerous small slender sea gulls with black cap, white body, and narrow wings

¹ter·race *n* **1 :** a flat roof or open platform **2 :** a level area next to a building **3 :** a raised piece of land with the top leveled **4 :** a row of houses on raised ground or a slope

²terrace *vb* **ter·raced; ter·rac·ing :** to form into a terrace or supply with terraces

ter·rain *n* : the features of the surface of a piece of land

ter·ra·pin *n* : a North American turtle that eats flesh and lives in water

ter·rar·i·um *n, pl* **ter·rar·ia** *or* **ter·rar·i·ums :** a usually glass container used for keeping plants or small animals indoors

ter·res·tri·al *adj* **1 :** of or relating to the earth or its people **2 :** living or growing on land

ter·ri·ble *adj* **1 :** causing great fear **2 :** very great in degree : INTENSE **3 :** very bad — **ter·ri·bly** *adv*

ter·ri·er *n* : any of various usually small dogs originally used by hunters to drive animals from their holes

ter·rif·ic *adj* **1 :** causing terror : TERRIBLE **2 :** very unusual : EXTRAORDINARY **3 :** EXCELLENT — **ter·rif·i·cal·ly** *adv*

ter·ri·fy *vb* **ter·ri·fied; ter·ri·fy·ing :** to frighten greatly

ter·ri·to·ri·al *adj* : of or relating to a territory

ter·ri·to·ry *n, pl* **ter·ri·to·ries** **1 :** a geographical area belonging to or under the rule of a government **2 :** a part of the United States not included within any state but organized with a separate governing body **3 :** REGION 1, DISTRICT

ter·ror *n* **1 :** a state of great fear **2 :** a cause of great fear

ter·ror·ism *n* : the use of threat or violence especially as a means of forcing others to do what one wishes

ter·ror·ize *vb* **ter·ror·ized; ter·ror·iz·ing** **1 :** to fill with terror **2 :** to use terrorism against

terse *adj* **ters·er; ters·est :** being brief and to the point — **terse·ly** *adv* — **terse·ness** *n*

¹test *n* **1 :** a means of finding out the nature, quality, or value of something **2 :** a set of questions or problems by which a person's knowledge, intelligence, or skills are measured

²test *vb* : to put to a test : EXAMINE

tes·ta·ment *n* **1 :** either of two main parts (**Old Testament** and **New Testament**) of the Bible **2 :** ²WILL 3

tes·ti·fy *vb* **tes·ti·fied; tes·ti·fy·ing :** to make a formal statement of what one swears is true

tes·ti·mo·ny *n, pl* **tes·ti·mo·nies :** a statement made by a witness under oath especially in a court

tes·tis *n, pl* **tes·tes** : a male reproductive gland

test tube *n* : a plain tube of thin glass closed at one end and used especially in chemistry and biology

tet·a·nus *n* : a dangerous disease in which spasms of the muscles occur often with locking of the jaws and which is caused by poison from a germ that enters wounds

¹teth·er *n* : a line by which an animal is fastened so as to limit where it can go

²tether *vb* : to fasten by a tether

teth·er·ball *n* : a game played with a ball attached by a string to an upright pole in which the object is to wrap the string around the pole by hitting the ball in a direction opposite to that of the other player

text *n* **1 :** the actual words of an author's work **2 :** the main body of printed or written matter on a page **3 :** a passage from the Bible chosen as the subject of a sermon **4 :** TEXTBOOK

text·book *n* : a book that presents the important information about a subject and is used as a basis of instruction

tex·tile *n* : a woven or knit cloth

tex·ture *n* : the structure, feel, and appearance of something (as cloth)

-th *or* **-eth** *adj suffix* — used to form numbers that show the place of something in a series

than *conj* : when compared to the way in which, the extent to which, or the degree to which

thank *vb* **1 :** to express gratitude to **2 :** to hold responsible

thank·ful *adj* : feeling or showing thanks : GRATEFUL — **thank·ful·ly** *adv* — **thank·ful·ness** *n*

thank·less *adj* **1 :** UNGRATEFUL **2 :** not appreciated

thanks *n pl* **1 :** GRATITUDE **2 :** an expression of gratitude (as for something received) — **thanks to** **1 :** with the help of **2 :** BECAUSE OF

thanks·giv·ing *n* **1 :** the act of giving thanks **2 :** a prayer expressing gratitude **3** *cap* : THANKSGIVING DAY

Thanksgiving Day *n* : the fourth Thursday in November observed as a legal holiday for public thanksgiving to God

¹that *pron, pl* **those** **1 :** the one seen, men-

tioned, or understood **2 :** the one farther away **3 :** the one **:** the kind
[2]**that** *conj* **1 :** the following, namely **2 :** which is, namely **3 :** [2]SO 1 **4 :** as to result in the following, namely **5 :** BECAUSE
[3]**that** *adj, pl* **those** **1 :** being the one mentioned, indicated, or understood **2 :** being the one farther away
[4]**that** *pron* **1 :** WHO 3, WHOM [2]WHICH 2 **2 :** in, on, or at which
[5]**that** *adv* **:** to such an extent or degree
[1]**thatch** *vb* **:** to cover with thatch
[2]**thatch** *n* **:** a plant material (as straw) for use as roofing
[1]**thaw** *vb* **1 :** to melt or cause to melt **2 :** to grow less unfriendly or quiet in manner
[2]**thaw** *n* **1 :** the action, fact, or process of thawing **2 :** a period of weather warm enough to thaw ice and snow
[1]**the** *definite article* **1 :** that or those mentioned, seen, or clearly understood **2 :** that or those near in space, time, or thought **3 :** [1]EACH **4 :** that or those considered best, most typical, or most worth singling out **5 :** any one typical of or standing for the entire class named **6 :** all those that are
[2]**the** *adv* **1 :** than before **2 :** to what extent **3 :** to that extent
the·ater *or* **the·atre** *n* **1 :** a building in which plays or motion pictures are presented **2 :** a place like a theater in form or use **3 :** a place or area where some important action is carried on **4 :** plays or the performance of plays
the·at·ri·cal *adj* **:** of or relating to the theater or the presentation of plays
thee *pron, archaic objective case of* THOU
theft *n* **:** the act of stealing
their *adj* **:** of or relating to them or themselves especially as owners or as agents or objects of an action
theirs *pron* **:** that which belongs to them
them *pron, objective case of* THEY
theme *n* **1 :** a subject of a work of art, music, or literature **2 :** a specific quality, characteristic, or concern **3:** a written exercise
theme park *n* **:** an amusement park in which the rides and buildings are based on a central theme
them·selves *pron* **:** their own selves
[1]**then** *adv* **1 :** at that time **2 :** soon after that **:** NEXT **3 :** in addition **:** BESIDES **4 :** in that case **5 :** as an expected result
[2]**then** *n* **:** that time
[3]**then** *adj* **:** existing or acting at that time
thence *adv* **1 :** from that place **2 :** from that fact
thence·forth *adv* **:** from that time on
thence·for·ward *adv* **:** onward from that place or time
the·ol·o·gy *n, pl* **the·ol·o·gies :** the study and explanation of religious faith, practice, and experience
the·o·ry *n, pl* **the·o·ries** **1 :** the general rules followed in a science or an art **2 :** a general rule offered to explain experiences or facts **3 :** an idea used for discussion or as a starting point for an investigation
ther·a·peu·tic *adj* **:** MEDICINAL
ther·a·pist *n* **:** a specialist in therapy and especially in methods of treatment other than drugs and surgery
ther·a·py *n, pl* **ther·a·pies :** treatment of an abnormal state in the body or mind
[1]**there** *adv* **1 :** in or at that place **2 :** to or into that place **3 :** in that situation or way
[2]**there** *pron* — used to introduce a sentence in which the subject comes after the verb
[3]**there** *n* **:** that place
there·abouts *or* **there·about** *adv* **1 :** near that place or time **2 :** near that number, degree, or amount
there·af·ter *adv* **:** after that
there·at *adv* **1 :** at that place **2 :** because of that
there·by *adv* **1 :** by that **2 :** related to that
there·fore *adv* **:** for that reason
there·in *adv* **:** in or into that place, time, or thing
there·of *adv* **1 :** of that or it **2 :** from that cause
there·on *adv* **:** on that
there·to *adv* **:** to that
there·up·on *adv* **1 :** on that thing **2 :** for that reason **3 :** immediately after that **:** at once
there·with *adv* **:** with that
ther·mal *adj* **:** of, relating to, caused by, or saving heat
ther·mom·e·ter *n* **:** an instrument for measuring temperature usually in the form of a glass tube with mercury or alcohol sealed inside and with a scale marked in degrees on the outside
ther·mos *n* **:** a container (as a bottle or jar) that has a vacuum between an inner and an outer wall and is used to keep liquids hot or cold for several hours
ther·mo·stat *n* **:** a device that automatically controls temperature
the·sau·rus *n, pl* **the·sau·ri** *or* **the·sau·rus·es :** a book of words and their synonyms
these *pl of* THIS
the·sis *n, pl* **the·ses** **1 :** a statement that a person wants to discuss or prove **2 :** an essay presenting results of original research
they *pron* **:** those individuals **:** those ones
they'd : they had **:** they would
they'll : they shall **:** they will
they're : they are
they've : they have

thi·a·min *n* : a member of the vitamin B complex whose lack causes beriberi

[1]thick *adj* **1** : having great size from one surface to its opposite **2** : heavily built **3** : closely packed together **4** : occurring in large numbers : NUMEROUS **5** : not flowing easily **6** : having haze, fog, or mist **7** : measuring a certain amount in the smallest of three dimensions **8** : not clearly spoken **9** : STUPID 1 — **thick·ly** *adv*

[2]thick *n* **1** : the most crowded or active part **2** : the part of greatest thickness

thick·en *vb* : to make or become thick — **thick·en·er** *n*

thick·et *n* : a thick usually small patch of bushes or low trees

thick·ness *n* **1** : the quality or state of being thick **2** : the smallest of three dimensions

thick·set *adj* **1** : closely placed or planted **2** : STOCKY

thief *n, pl* **thieves** : a person who steals : ROBBER

thieve *vb* **thieved; thiev·ing** : [1]STEAL 2, ROB

thiev·ery *n, pl* **thiev·er·ies** : THEFT

thiev·ish *adj* **1** : likely to steal **2** : of, relating to, or like a thief

thigh *n* : the part of a leg between the knee and the main part of the body

thim·ble *n* : a cap or cover used in sewing to protect the finger that pushes the needle

[1]thin *adj* **thin·ner; thin·nest** **1** : having little size from one surface to its opposite : not thick **2** : having the parts not close together **3** : having little body fat **4** : having less than the usual number **5** : not very convincing **6** : somewhat weak or shrill — **thin·ly** *adv* — **thin·ness** *n*

[2]thin *vb* **thinned; thin·ning** : to make or become thin

thine *pron, singular, archaic* : YOURS

thing *n* **1** : AFFAIR 2, MATTER **2 things** *pl* : state of affairs **3** : EVENT 1 **4** : [1]DEED 1, ACHIEVEMENT **5** : something that exists and can be talked about **6 things** *pl* : personal possessions **7** : a piece of clothing **8** : [1]DETAIL 2 **9** : what is needed or wanted **10** : an action or interest that one very much enjoys

think *vb* **thought; think·ing** **1** : to form or have in the mind **2** : to have as an opinion or belief **3** : REMEMBER 1 **4** : to use the power of reason **5** : to invent something by thinking **6** : to hold a strong feeling **7** : to care about — **think·er** *n*

thin·ner *n* : a liquid used to thin paint

[1]third *adj* : coming right after second

[2]third *n* **1** : number three in a series **2** : one of three equal parts

[1]thirst *n* **1** : a feeling of dryness in the mouth and throat that accompanies a need for liquids **2** : the bodily condition that produces thirst **3** : a strong desire

[2]thirst *vb* **1** : to feel thirsty **2** : to have a strong desire

thirsty *adj* **thirst·i·er; thirst·i·est** **1** : feeling thirst **2** : needing moisture **3** : having a strong desire : EAGER — **thirst·i·ly** *adv*

[1]thir·teen *adj* : being one more than twelve

[2]thirteen *n* : one more than twelve : 13

[1]thir·teenth *adj* : coming right after twelfth

[2]thirteenth *n* : number thirteen in a series

[1]thir·ti·eth *adj* : coming right after twenty-ninth

[2]thirtieth *n* : number thirty in a series

[1]thir·ty *adj* : being three times ten

[2]thirty *n* : three times ten : 30

[1]this *pron, pl* **these** **1** : the one close or closest in time or space **2** : what is in the present or is being seen or talked about

[2]this *adj, pl* **these** **1** : being the one present, near, or just mentioned **2** : being the one nearer or last mentioned

[3]this *adv* : to the degree suggested by something in the present situation

this·tle *n* : a prickly plant related to the daisies that has usually purplish often showy heads of mostly tubular flowers

thith·er *adv* : to that place : THERE

thong *n* : a strip of leather used especially for fastening something

tho·rax *n, pl* **tho·rax·es** *or* **tho·ra·ces** **1** : the part of the body of a mammal that lies between the neck and the abdomen and contains the heart and lungs **2** : the middle of the three main divisions of the body of an insect

thorn *n* **1** : a woody plant (as hawthorn) with sharp briers, prickles, or spines **2** : a short hard sharp-pointed leafless branch on a woody plant

thorny *adj* **thorn·i·er; thorn·i·est** **1** : full of or covered with thorns **2** : full of difficulties

thor·ough *adj* **1** : being such to the fullest degree : COMPLETE **2** : careful about little things — **thor·ough·ly** *adv* — **thor·ough·ness** *n*

[1]thor·ough·bred *adj* **1** : bred from the best blood through a long line **2** *cap* : of, relating to, or being a member of the Thoroughbred breed of horses

[2]thoroughbred *n* **1** *cap* : any of an English breed of light speedy horses kept mainly for racing **2** : a purebred or pedigreed animal **3** : a very fine person

thor·ough·fare *n* **1** : a street or road open at both ends **2** : a main road

thor·ough·go·ing *adj* : THOROUGH 1

those *pl of* THAT

thou *pron, singular, archaic* : YOU

[1]though *conj* : ALTHOUGH

²though *adv* : HOWEVER 3, NEVERTHELESS

¹thought *past of* THINK

²thought *n* **1 :** the act or process of thinking and especially of trying to decide about something **2 :** power of reasoning and judging **3 :** power of imagining **4 :** something (as an idea or fancy) formed in the mind

thought·ful *adj* **1 :** deep in thought **2 :** showing careful thinking **3 :** considerate of others — **thought·ful·ly** *adv* — **thought·ful·ness** *n*

thought·less *adj* **1 :** not careful and alert **2 :** NEGLIGENT **3 :** not considerate of others — **thought·less·ly** *adv* — **thought·less·ness** *n*

¹thou·sand *n* **1 :** ten times one hundred : 1000 **2 :** a very large number

²thousand *adj* : being 1000

¹thou·sandth *adj* : coming right after 999th

²thousandth *n* : number 1000 in a series

thrash *vb* **1 :** THRESH 1 **2 :** to beat very hard **3 :** to move about violently

¹thrash·er *n* : one that thrashes

²thrasher *n* : an American bird (as the common reddish brown **brown thrasher**) related to the thrushes and noted for its song

¹thread *n* **1 :** a thin fine cord formed by spinning and twisting short fibers into a continuous strand **2 :** something suggesting a thread **3 :** the ridge or groove that winds around a screw **4 :** a line of reasoning or train of thought that connects the parts of an argument or story — **thread·like** *adj*

²thread *vb* **1 :** to put a thread in working position (as in a needle) **2 :** to pass through like a thread **3 :** to make one's way through or between **4 :** to put together on a thread : STRING

thread·bare *adj* **1 :** worn so much that the thread shows : SHABBY **2 :** TRITE

threat *n* **1 :** a showing of an intention to do harm **2 :** something that threatens

threat·en *vb* **1 :** to make threats against **2 :** to give warning of by a threat or sign — **threat·en·ing·ly** *adv*

¹three *adj* : being one more than two

²three *n* **1 :** one more than two : 3 **2 :** the third in a set or series

3–D *adj* : THREE-DIMENSIONAL 2

three–dimensional *adj* **1 :** of, relating to, or having the three dimensions of length, width, and height **2 :** giving the appearance of depth or varying distances

three·fold *adj* : being three times as great or as many

three·score *adj* : SIXTY

thresh *vb* **1 :** to separate (as grain from straw) by beating **2 :** THRASH 3

thresh·er *n* : THRESHING MACHINE

threshing machine *n* : a machine used in harvesting to separate grain from straw

thresh·old *n* **1 :** the sill of a door **2 :** a point or place of beginning or entering

threw *past of* THROW

thrice *adv* : three times

thrift *n* : careful management especially of money

thrifty *adj* **thrift·i·er; thrift·i·est 1 :** tending to save money **2 :** doing well in health and growth

¹thrill *vb* **1 :** to have or cause to have a sudden feeling of excitement or pleasure **2 :** ¹TREMBLE 2, VIBRATE — **thrill·er** *n*

²thrill *n* **1 :** a feeling of being thrilled **2 :** VIBRATION 3

thrive *vb* **throve** *or* **thrived; thriv·en** *also* **thrived; thriv·ing 1 :** to grow very well : FLOURISH **2 :** to gain in wealth or possessions

throat *n* **1 :** the part of the neck in front of the backbone **2 :** the passage from the mouth to the stomach and lungs **3 :** something like the throat especially in being an entrance or a narrowed part

¹throb *vb* **throbbed; throb·bing 1 :** to beat hard or fast **2 :** to beat or rotate in a normal way

²throb *n* : ²BEAT 2, PULSE

throne *n* **1 :** the chair of state especially of a monarch or bishop **2 :** royal power and dignity

¹throng *n* : a large group of assembled persons : CROWD

²throng *vb* : ¹CROWD 4

¹throt·tle *vb* **throt·tled; throt·tling 1 :** STRANGLE 1, CHOKE **2 :** to reduce the speed of (an engine) by closing the throttle

²throttle *n* **1 :** a valve for regulating the flow of steam or fuel in an engine **2 :** a lever that controls the throttle valve

¹through *prep* **1 :** into at one side and out at the other side of **2 :** by way of **3 :** AMONG 1 **4 :** by means of **5 :** over the whole of **6 :** during the whole of

²through *adv* **1 :** from one end or side to the other **2 :** from beginning to end **3 :** to completion **4 :** in or to every part **5 :** into the open

³through *adj* **1 :** allowing free or continuous passage : DIRECT **2 :** going from point of origin to destination without changes or transfers **3 :** coming from and going to points outside a local zone **4 :** having reached an end

¹through·out *adv* **1 :** EVERYWHERE **2 :** from beginning to end

²throughout *prep* **1 :** in or to every part of **2 :** during the whole period of

throughway *variant of* THRUWAY

throve *past of* THRIVE

¹throw *vb* **threw; thrown; throw·ing** **1 :** to send through the air with a quick forward motion of the arm **2 :** to send through the air in any way **3 :** to cause to fall **4 :** to put suddenly in a certain position or condition **5 :** to put on or take off in a hurry **6 :** to move quickly **7 :** to move (as a switch) to an open or closed position **8 :** to give by way of entertainment — **throw·er** *n*

²throw *n* **1 :** an act of throwing **2 :** the distance something is or may be thrown

throw up *vb* **:** ²VOMIT

thrum *vb* **thrummed; thrum·ming :** to play a stringed instrument idly **:** STRUM

thrush *n* **:** any of numerous songbirds that eat insects and are usually of a plain color but sometimes spotted below

¹thrust *vb* **thrust; thrust·ing** **1 :** to push or drive with force **:** SHOVE **2 :** PIERCE 1, STAB **3 :** to push forth **:** EXTEND **4 :** to press the acceptance of on someone

²thrust *n* **1 :** a lunge with a pointed weapon **2 :** a military attack **3 :** a forward or upward push

thru·way *or* **through·way** *n* **:** EXPRESSWAY

¹thud *n* **:** a dull sound **:** THUMP

²thud *vb* **thud·ded; thud·ding :** to move or strike so as to make a dull sound

thug *n* **:** RUFFIAN

¹thumb *n* **1 :** the short thick finger next to the forefinger **2 :** the part of a glove covering the thumb

²thumb *vb* **1 :** to turn the pages of quickly with the thumb **2 :** to seek or get (a ride) in a passing automobile by signaling with the thumb

thumb·tack *n* **:** a tack with a broad flat head for pressing into a board or wall with the thumb

¹thump *vb* **1 :** to strike or beat with something thick or heavy so as to cause a dull sound **2 :** ³POUND 2, KNOCK

²thump *n* **1 :** a blow with something blunt or heavy **2 :** the sound made by a thump

¹thun·der *n* **1 :** the loud sound that follows a flash of lightning **2 :** a noise like thunder

²thunder *vb* **1 :** to produce thunder **2 :** to make a sound like thunder **3 :** ¹ROAR 1, SHOUT

thun·der·bolt *n* **:** a flash of lightning and the thunder that follows it

thun·der·cloud *n* **:** a dark storm cloud that produces lightning and thunder

thun·der·head *n* **:** a rounded mass of dark cloud with white edges often appearing before a thunderstorm

thun·der·show·er *n* **:** a shower with thunder and lightning

thun·der·storm *n* **:** a storm with thunder and lightning

thun·der·struck *adj* **:** stunned as if struck by a thunderbolt

Thurs·day *n* **:** the fifth day of the week

thus *adv* **1 :** in this or that way **2 :** to this degree or extent **:** so **3 :** because of this or that **:** THEREFORE

thwart *vb* **:** to oppose successfully

thy *adj, singular, archaic* **:** YOUR

thyme *n* **:** a mint with tiny fragrant leaves used to season foods or formerly in medicine

thy·roid *n* **:** an endocrine gland at the base of the neck that produces a secretion which affects growth, development, and metabolism

thy·self *pron, archaic* **:** YOURSELF

ti *n* **:** the seventh note of the musical scale

¹tick *n* **1 :** an animal with eight legs that is related to the spiders and attaches itself to humans and animals from which it sucks blood **2 :** a wingless fly that sucks blood from sheep

²tick *n* **1 :** a light rhythmic tap or beat (as of a clock) **2 :** a small mark used chiefly to draw attention to something or to check an item on a list

³tick *vb* **1 :** to make a tick or a series of ticks **2 :** to mark, count, or announce by or as if by ticks **3 :** OPERATE 1, RUN **4 :** ²CHECK 4

¹tick·et *n* **1 :** a summons or warning issued to a person who breaks a traffic law **2 :** a document or token showing that a fare or an admission fee has been paid **3 :** a list of candidates for nomination or election **4 :** a slip or card recording a sale or giving information

²ticket *vb* **1 :** to attach a ticket to **:** LABEL **2 :** to give a traffic ticket to

ticket office *n* **:** an office (as of a transportation company or a theater) where tickets are sold and reservations made

¹tick·le *vb* **tick·led; tick·ling** **1 :** to have a tingling or prickling sensation **2 :** to excite or stir up agreeably **3 :** AMUSE 2 **4 :** to touch (a body part) lightly so as to excite the surface nerves and cause uneasiness, laughter, or jerky movements

²tickle *n* **:** a tickling sensation

tick·lish *adj* **1 :** sensitive to tickling **2 :** calling for careful handling

tid·al *adj* **:** of or relating to tides **:** flowing and ebbing like tides

tidal wave *n* **1 :** a great wave of the sea that sometimes follows an earthquake **2 :** an unusual rise of water along a shore due to strong winds

tid·bit *n* **1 :** a small tasty piece of food **2 :** a pleasing bit (as of news)

¹tide *n* **1 :** the rising and falling of the surface of the ocean caused twice daily by the attraction of the sun and the moon **2 :** something that rises and falls like the tides of the sea

[2]**tide** *vb* **tid·ed; tid·ing :** to help to overcome or put up with a difficulty

tide pool *n* **:** a pool of salt water left behind when the tide goes out

tid·ings *n pl* **:** NEWS 3

[1]**ti·dy** *adj* **ti·di·er; ti·di·est 1 :** well ordered and cared for **:** NEAT **2 :** LARGE, SUBSTANTIAL — **ti·di·ness** *n*

[2]**tidy** *vb* **ti·died; ti·dy·ing 1 :** to put in order **2 :** to make things tidy

[1]**tie** *n* **1 :** a line, ribbon, or cord used for fastening, joining, or closing **2 :** a part (as a beam or rod) holding two pieces together **3 :** one of the cross supports to which railroad rails are fastened **4 :** a connecting link **:** BOND **5 :** an equality in number (as of votes or scores) **6 :** a contest that ends with an equal score **7 :** NECKTIE

[2]**tie** *vb* **tied; ty·ing** *or* **tie·ing 1 :** to fasten, attach, or close by means of a tie **2 :** to form a knot or bow in **3 :** to bring together firmly **:** UNITE **4 :** to hold back from freedom of action **5 :** to make or have an equal score with in a contest

tier *n* **:** a row, rank, or layer usually arranged in a series one above the other

ti·ger *n* **:** a large Asian flesh-eating animal of the cat family that is light brown with black stripes

[1]**tight** *adj* **1 :** so close in structure as not to allow a liquid or gas to pass through **2 :** fixed or held very firmly in place **3 :** firmly stretched or drawn **:** TAUT **4 :** fitting too closely **5 :** difficult to get through or out of **6 :** firm in control **7 :** STINGY 1 **8 :** very closely packed or compressed **9 :** low in supply **:** SCARCE — **tight·ly** *adv* — **tight·ness** *n*

[2]**tight** *adv* **1 :** in a firm, secure, or close manner **2 :** in a deep and uninterrupted manner **:** SOUNDLY

tight·en *vb* **:** to make or become tight

tight·rope *n* **:** a rope or wire stretched tight on which an acrobat performs

tights *n pl* **:** a garment closely fitted to the body and covering it usually from the waist down

tight squeeze *n* **:** a difficult situation that one can barely get through

tight·wad *n* **:** a stingy person

ti·gress *n* **:** a female tiger

til·de *n* **:** a mark ˜ placed especially ver the letter *n* (as in Spanish *señor*) to indicate a sound that is approximately \nyə\

[1]**tile** *n* **1 :** a thin piece of material (as plastic, stone, concrete, or rubber) used especially for roofs, walls, floors, or drains **2 :** a pipe of earthenware used for a drain

[2]**tile** *vb* **tiled; til·ing :** to cover with tiles

[1]**till** *prep or conj* **:** UNTIL

[2]**till** *vb* **:** to work by plowing, sowing, and raising crops on

[3]**till** *n* **:** a drawer for money

till·age *n* **:** cultivated land

til·ler *n* **:** a lever used to turn the rudder of a boat from side to side

[1]**tilt** *n* **1 :** a contest on horseback in which two opponents charging with lances try to unhorse one another **:** [2]JOUST **2 :** [1]SPEED 2 **3 :** [1]SLANT

[2]**tilt** *vb* **1 :** to move or shift so as to slant or tip **2 :** to take part in a contest with lances **:** [1]JOUST

tim·ber *n* **1 :** wood suitable for building or for carpentry **2 :** a large squared piece of wood ready for use or forming part of a structure

tim·ber·land *n* **:** wooded land especially as a source of timber

tim·ber·line *n* **:** the upper limit beyond which trees do not grow (as on mountains)

[1]**time** *n* **1 :** a period during which an action, process, or condition exists or continues **2 :** part of the day when one is free to do as one pleases **3 :** a point or period when something occurs **:** OCCASION **4 :** a set or usual moment or hour for something to occur **5 :** an historical period **:** AGE **6 :** conditions of a period — usually used in pl. **7 :** rate of speed **:** TEMPO **8 :** RHYTHM 2 **9 :** a moment, hour, day, or year as shown by a clock or calendar **10 :** a system of determining time **11 :** one of a series of repeated instances or actions **12 times** *pl* **:** multiplied intances **13 :** a person's experience during a certain period — **at times :** SOMETIMES — **for the time being :** for the present — **from time to time :** once in a while — **in time 1 :** soon enough **2 :** as time goes by **3 :** at the correct speed in music — **time after time :** over and over again — **time and again :** over and over again

[2]**time** *vb* **timed; tim·ing 1 :** to arrange or set the time or rate at which something happens **2 :** to measure or record the time, length of time, or rate of — **tim·er** *n*

time capsule *n* **:** a container holding records or objects representative of a current culture that is put in a safe place for discovery in the future

time·keep·er *n* **1 :** a clerk who keeps records of the time worked by employees **2 :** an official who keeps track of the time in a sports contest

time·less *adj* **:** not restricted to a certain time or date

time·ly *adj* **time·li·er; time·li·est** **1 :** coming early or at the right time **2 :** especially suitable to the time
time·piece *n* **:** a device (as a clock or watch) to measure the passing of time
times *prep* **:** multiplied by
time·ta·ble *n* **:** a table telling when something (as a bus or train) leaves or arrives
time zone *n* **:** a geographic region within which the same standard time is used
tim·id *adj* **:** feeling or showing a lack of courage or self-confidence **:** SHY — **tim·id·ly** *adv* — **tim·id·ness** *n*
tim·o·rous *adj* **:** easily frightened **:** FEARFUL — **tim·o·rous·ly** *adv*
tin *n* **1 :** a soft bluish white metallic chemical element used chiefly in combination with other metals or as a coating to protect other metals **2 :** something (as a can or sheet) made from tinplate
tin·der *n* **:** material that burns easily and can be used as kindling
tin·foil *n* **:** a thin metal sheeting usually of aluminum or an alloy of tin and lead
[1]tin·gle *vb* **tin·gled; tin·gling :** to feel or cause a prickling or thrilling sensation
[2]tingle *n* **:** a tingling sensation or condition
tin·ker *vb* **:** to repair or adjust something in an unskilled or experimental manner
[1]tin·kle *vb* **tin·kled; tin·kling :** to make or cause to make short high ringing or clinking sounds
[2]tinkle *n* **:** a sound of tinkling
tin·plate *n* **:** thin steel sheets covered with tin
tin·sel *n* **1 :** a thread, strip, or sheet of metal, paper, or plastic used to produce a glittering effect **2 :** something that seems attractive but is of little worth
tin·smith *n* **:** a worker in tin or sometimes other metals
[1]tint *n* **1 :** a slight or pale coloring **2 :** a shade of a color
[2]tint *vb* **:** to give a tint to **:** COLOR
ti·ny *adj* **ti·ni·er; ti·ni·est :** very small
[1]tip *vb* **tipped; tip·ping 1 :** to turn over **2 :** to bend from a straight position **:** SLANT **3 :** to raise and tilt forward
[2]tip *vb* **tipped; tip·ping 1 :** to attach an end or point to **2 :** to cover or decorate the tip of
[3]tip *n* **1 :** the usually pointed end of something **2 :** a small piece or part serving as an end, cap, or point
[4]tip *n* **:** a piece of useful or secret information
[5]tip *vb* **tipped; tip·ping :** to give a small sum of money for a service
[6]tip *n* **:** a small sum of money given for a service
[1]tip·toe *n* **:** the position of being balanced on the balls of the feet and toes with the heels raised — usually used with *on*
[2]tiptoe *adv or adj* **:** on or as if on tiptoe
[3]tiptoe *vb* **tip·toed; tip·toe·ing :** to walk tiptoe
[1]tip·top *n* **:** the highest point
[2]tiptop *adj* **:** EXCELLENT, FIRST-RATE
[1]tire *vb* **tired; tir·ing 1 :** to make or become weary **2 :** to wear out the patience or attention of **:** BORE
[2]tire *n* **1 :** a metal band that forms the tread of a wheel **2 :** a rubber cushion that usually contains compressed air and fits around a wheel (as of an automobile)
tired *adj* **:** [1]WEARY 1
tire·less *adj* **:** able to work a long time without becoming tired — **tire·less·ly** *adv* — **tire·less·ness** *n*
tire·some *adj* **:** likely to tire one because of length or dullness **:** BORING — **tire·some·ly** *adv*
'tis : it is
tis·sue *n* **1 :** a fine lightweight fabric **2 :** a piece of soft absorbent paper **3 :** a mass or layer of cells usually of one kind that together with their supporting structures form a basic structural material of an animal or plant body
tit *n* **:** NIPPLE 1, TEAT
ti·tan·ic *adj* **:** enormous in size, force, or power **:** GIGANTIC
ti·tle *n* **1 :** a legal right to the ownership of property **2 :** the name given to something (as a book, song, or job) to identify or describe it **3 :** a word or group of words attached to a person's name to show an honor, rank, or office **4 :** CHAMPIONSHIP
tit·mouse *n, pl* **tit·mice :** any of several small birds that have long tails and are related to the nuthatches
TNT *n* **:** an explosive used in artillery shells and bombs and in blasting
[1]to *prep* **1 :** in the direction of **2 :** AGAINST 3, ON **3 :** as far as **4 :** so as to become or bring about **5 :** [2]BEFORE 3 **6 :** [1]UNTIL **7 :** fitting or being a part of **8 :** along with **9 :** in relation to or comparison with **10 :** in agreement with **11 :** within the limits of **12 :** contained, occurring, or included in **13 :** TOWARD 3 **14** — used to show the one or ones that an action is directed toward **15 :** for no one except **16 :** into the action of **17** — used to mark an infinitive
[2]to *adv* **1 :** in a direction toward **2 :** to a conscious state
toad *n* **:** a tailless leaping amphibian that has rough skin and usually lives on land
toad·stool *n* **:** a mushroom especially when poisonous or unfit for food
[1]toast *vb* **1 :** to make (as bread) crisp, hot, and brown by heat **2 :** to warm completely
[2]toast *n* **1 :** sliced toasted bread **2 :** a person

in whose honor other people drink **3 :** a highly admired person **4 :** an act of drinking in honor of a person

[3]**toast** *vb* **:** to suggest or drink to as a toast

toast·er *n* **:** an electrical appliance for toasting

to·bac·co *n, pl* **to·bac·cos :** a tall plant related to the potato that has pink or white flowers and broad sticky leaves which are prepared for use in smoking or chewing or as snuff

[1]**to·bog·gan** *n* **:** a long light sled made without runners and curved up at the front

[2]**toboggan** *vb* **:** to slide on a toboggan

[1]**to·day** *adv* **1 :** on or for this day **2 :** at the present time

[2]**today** *n* **:** the present day, time, or age

tod·dler *n* **:** a small child

[1]**toe** *n* **1 :** one of the separate parts of the front end of a foot **2 :** the front end or part of a foot or hoof — **toed** *adj*

[2]**toe** *vb* **toed; toe·ing :** to touch, reach, or kick with the toes

toe·nail *n* **:** the hard covering at the end of a toe

to·fu *n* **:** a soft food product prepared from soybeans

to·ga *n* **:** the loose outer garment worn in public by citizens of ancient Rome

to·geth·er *adv* **1 :** in or into one group, body, or place **2 :** in touch or in partnership with **3 :** at one time **4 :** one after the other **:** in order **5 :** in or by combined effort **6 :** in or into agreement **7 :** considered as a whole

[1]**toil** *n* **:** long hard labor

[2]**toil** *vb* **1 :** to work hard and long **2 :** to go on with effort

toi·let *n* **1 :** the act or process of dressing and making oneself neat **2 :** BATHROOM **3 :** a device for removing body wastes consisting essentially of a bowl that is flushed with water

to·ken *n* **1 :** an outer sign **:** PROOF **2 :** an object used to suggest something that cannot be pictured **3 :** SOUVENIR **4 :** INDICATION 2 **5 :** a piece like a coin that has a special use

told *past of* TELL

tol·er·a·ble *adj* **1 :** capable of being put up with **2 :** fairly good — **tol·er·a·bly** *adv*

tol·er·ance *n* **1 :** ability to put up with something harmful or bad **2 :** sympathy for or acceptance of feelings or habits which are different from one's own

tol·er·ant *adj* **:** showing tolerance — **tol·er·ant·ly** *adv*

tol·er·ate *vb* **tol·er·at·ed; tol·er·at·ing 1 :** to allow something to be or to be done without making a move to stop it **2 :** to stand the action of

[1]**toll** *n* **1 :** a tax paid for a privilege (as the use of a highway or bridge) **2 :** a charge paid for a service **3 :** the cost in life or health

[2]**toll** *vb* **1 :** to announce or call by the sounding of a bell **2 :** to sound with slow strokes

[3]**toll** *n* **:** the sound of a bell ringing slowly

[1]**tom·a·hawk** *n* **:** a light ax used as a weapon by North American Indians

[2]**tomahawk** *vb* **:** to cut, strike, or kill with a tomahawk

to·ma·to *n, pl* **to·ma·toes :** a red or yellow juicy fruit that is used as a vegetable or in salads and is produced by a hairy plant related to the potato

tomb *n* **1 :** [1]GRAVE **2 :** a house or burial chamber for dead people

tom·boy *n* **:** a girl who enjoys things that some people think are more suited to boys

tomb·stone *n* **:** GRAVESTONE

tom·cat *n* **:** a male cat

[1]**to·mor·row** *adv* **:** on or for the day after today

[2]**tomorrow** *n* **:** the day after today

tom–tom *n* **1 :** a drum (as a traditional Asian, African, or American Indian drum) that is beaten with the hands **2 :** a deep drum with a low hollow tone that is usually played with soft mallets or drumsticks and is often part of a drum set in a band

ton *n* **:** a measure of weight equal either to 2000 pounds (about 907 kilograms) (**short ton**) or 2240 pounds (about 1016 kilograms) (**long ton**) with the short ton being more frequently used in the United States and Canada

[1]**tone** *n* **1 :** quality of spoken or musical sound **2 :** a sound on one pitch **3 :** an individual way of speaking or writing **4 :** a shade of color **5 :** a color that changes another **6 :** a healthy state of the body or any of its parts **7 :** common character or quality

[2]**tone** *vb* **toned; ton·ing 1 :** to give tone to **:** STRENGTHEN **2 :** to soften or blend in color, appearance, or sound

tongs *n pl* **:** a device for taking hold of something that consists usually of two movable pieces joined at one end

tongue *n* **1 :** an organ of the mouth used in tasting, in taking and swallowing food, and by human beings in speaking **2 :** the power of communication **:** SPEECH **3 :** LANGUAGE 1 **4 :** something like an animal's tongue in being long and fastened at one end

tongue–tied *adj* **:** unable to speak clearly or freely (as from shyness)

[1]**ton·ic** *adj* **:** making (as the mind or body) stronger or healthier

[2]**tonic** *n* **1 :** a tonic medicine **2 :** the first note of a scale

[1]**to·night** *adv* **:** on this present night or the night following this present day

[2]tonight *n* **:** the present or the coming night
ton·nage *n* **1 :** a tax on ships based on tons carried **2 :** ships in terms of the total number of tons that are or can be carried **3 :** total weight in tons shipped, carried, or mined
ton·sil *n* **:** either of a pair of masses of spongy tissue at the back of the mouth
ton·sil·li·tis *n* **:** a sore reddened state of the tonsils
too *adv* **1 :** in addition **:** ALSO **2 :** to a greater than wanted or needed degree **3 :** [2]VERY 1
took *past of* TAKE
[1]tool *n* **1 :** an instrument (as a saw, file, knife, or wrench) used or worked by hand or machine **2 :** something that helps to gain an end **3 :** a person used by another **:** DUPE
[2]tool *vb* **1 :** to shape, form, or finish with a tool **2 :** to equip a plant or industry with machines and tools for production
tool·box *n* **:** a box for storing or carrying tools
tool·shed *n* **:** a small building for storing tools
[1]toot *vb* **1 :** to sound a short blast **2 :** to blow or sound an instrument (as a horn) especially in short blasts
[2]toot *n* **:** a short blast (as on a horn)
tooth *n, pl* **teeth 1 :** one of the hard bony structures set in sockets on the jaws of most vertebrates and used in taking hold of and chewing food and in fighting **2 :** something like or suggesting an animal's tooth in shape, arrangement, or action **3 :** one of the projections around the rim of a wheel that fit between the projections on another part causing the wheel or the other part to move along — **tooth·less** *adj*
tooth·ache *n* **:** pain in or near a tooth
tooth·brush *n* **:** a brush for cleaning the teeth — **tooth·brush·ing** *n*
toothed *adj* **1 :** having teeth or such or so many teeth **2 :** JAGGED
tooth·paste *n* **:** a paste for cleaning the teeth
tooth·pick *n* **:** a pointed instrument for removing substances caught between the teeth
[1]top *n* **1 :** the highest point, level, or part of something **2 :** the upper end, edge, or surface **3 :** the stalk and leaves of a plant and especially of one with roots that are used for food **4 :** an upper piece, lid, or covering **5 :** the highest position
[2]top *vb* **topped; top·ping 1 :** to remove or cut the top of **2 :** to cover with a top or on the top **3 :** to be better than **4 :** to go over the top of
[3]top *adj* **:** of, relating to, or at the top
[4]top *n* **:** a child's toy with a tapering point on which it can be made to spin
to·paz *n* **:** a mineral that when occurring as perfect yellow crystals is valued as a gem
top·coat *n* **:** a lightweight overcoat
top·ic *n* **1 :** a heading in an outline of a subject or explanation **2 :** the subject or a section of the subject of a speech or writing
topic sentence *n* **:** a sentence that states the main thought of a paragraph
top·knot *n* **:** a tuft of feathers or hair on the top of the head
top·mast *n* **:** the second mast above a ship's deck
top·most *adj* **:** highest of all
top·ple *vb* **top·pled; top·pling 1 :** to fall from being too heavy at the top **2 :** to push over
top·sail *n* **1 :** the sail next above the lowest sail on a mast in a square-rigged ship **2 :** the sail above the large sail on a mast in a ship with a fore-and-aft rig
top·soil *n* **:** the rich upper layer of soil in which plants have most of their roots
top·sy–tur·vy *adv or adj* **1 :** upside down **2 :** in complete disorder
torch *n* **1 :** a flaming light that is made of something which burns brightly and that is usually carried in the hand **2 :** something that guides or gives light or heat like a torch **3 :** a portable device for producing a hot flame
tore *past of* TEAR
[1]tor·ment *n* **1 :** extreme pain or distress of body or mind **2 :** a cause of suffering in mind or body
[2]tor·ment *vb* **1 :** to cause severe suffering of body or mind to **2 :** VEX 1, HARASS
torn *past participle of* TEAR
tor·na·do *n, pl* **tor·na·does** *or* **tor·na·dos :** a violent whirling wind accompanied by a cloud that is shaped like a funnel and moves overland in a narrow path
[1]tor·pe·do *n, pl* **tor·pe·does :** a self-propelled underwater weapon shaped like a cigar that is used for blowing up ships
[2]torpedo *vb* **tor·pe·doed; tor·pe·do·ing :** to hit with or destroy by a torpedo
tor·pid *adj* **1 :** having lost motion or the power of exertion or feeling **2 :** having too little energy or strength **:** DULL
tor·rent *n* **1 :** a rushing stream of liquid **2 :** [3]RUSH 1, 2
tor·rid *adj* **:** very hot and usually dry
tor·so *n* **:** the human body except for the head, arms, and legs
tor·ti·lla *n* **:** a round flat bread made of corn or wheat flour and usually rolled with a filling and eaten hot
tor·toise *n* **1 :** any of a family of turtles that live on land **2 :** TURTLE
tor·toise·shell *n* **1 :** the hornlike covering of the shell of a sea tortoise that is mottled brown and yellow and is used for ornamen-

tal objects **2 :** any of several brightly colored butterflies

tor·tu·ous *adj* **:** having many twists and turns

[1]**tor·ture** *n* **1 :** the causing of great pain especially to punish or to obtain a confession **2 :** distress of body or mind

[2]**torture** *vb* **tor·tured; tor·tur·ing 1 :** to punish or force someone to do or say something by causing great pain **2 :** to cause great suffering to — **tor·tur·er** *n*

[1]**toss** *vb* **1 :** to throw or swing to and fro or up and down **2 :** to throw with a quick light motion **3 :** to lift with a sudden motion **4 :** to be thrown about rapidly **5 :** to move about restlessly **6 :** to stir or mix lightly

[2]**toss** *n* **:** an act or instance of tossing

tot *n* **:** a young child

[1]**to·tal** *adj* **1 :** of or relating to the whole of something **2 :** making up the whole **3 :** being such to the fullest degree **4 :** making use of every means to do something — **to·tal·ly** *adv*

[2]**total** *n* **1 :** a result of addition **:** SUM **2 :** an entire amount

[3]**total** *vb* **to·taled** *or* **to·talled; to·tal·ing** *or* **to·tal·ling 1 :** to add up **2 :** to amount to **:** NUMBER

tote *vb* **tot·ed; tot·ing :** CARRY 1, HAUL

to·tem *n* **1 :** an object (as an animal or plant) serving as the emblem of a family or clan **2 :** a carving or picture representing such an object

totem pole *n* **:** a pole or pillar carved and painted with totems and placed before the houses of Indian tribes of the northwest coast of North America

tot·ter *vb* **1 :** to sway or rock as if about to fall **2 :** to move unsteadily **:** STAGGER

tou·can *n* **:** a brightly colored tropical bird that has a very large beak and feeds on fruit

[1]**touch** *vb* **1 :** to feel or handle (as with the fingers) especially so as to be aware of with the sense of touch **2 :** to be or cause to be in contact with something **3 :** to be or come next to **4 :** to hit lightly **5 :** [2]HARM **6 :** to make use of **7 :** to refer to in passing **8 :** to affect the interest of **9 :** to move emotionally

[2]**touch** *n* **1 :** a light stroke or tap **2 :** the act or fact of touching or being touched **3 :** the special sense by which one is aware of light pressure **4 :** an impression gotten through the sense of touch **5 :** a state of contact or communication **6 :** a small amount **:** TRACE

touch·down *n* **:** a score made in football by carrying or catching the ball over the opponent's goal line

touch·ing *adj* **:** causing a feeling of tenderness or pity

touch pad *n* **:** a flat surface on an electronic device (as a microwave oven) divided into several differently marked areas that are touched to make choices in controlling the device

touch screen *n* **:** a display screen (as for a computer) on which the user selects options by touching the screen

touch–tone *adj* **:** relating to or being a telephone with push buttons that produce tones corresponding to the numbers

touch up *vb* **:** to improve by or as if by small changes

touchy *adj* **touch·i·er; touch·i·est 1 :** easily hurt or insulted **2 :** calling for tact or careful handling

[1]**tough** *adj* **1 :** strong or firm but flexible and not brittle **2 :** not easily chewed **3 :** able to put up with strain or hardship **4 :** STUBBORN 1 **5 :** very difficult **6 :** LAWLESS 2 — **tough·ness** *n*

[2]**tough** *n* **:** [2]ROWDY, RUFFIAN

tough·en *vb* **:** to make or become tough

[1]**tour** *n* **1 :** a fixed period of duty **2 :** a trip usually ending at the point where it started

[2]**tour** *vb* **:** to make a tour of **:** travel as a tourist

tour·ist *n* **:** a person who travels for pleasure

tour·na·ment *n* **1 :** a contest of skill and courage between knights wearing armor and fighting with blunted lances or swords **2 :** a series of contests played for a championship

tour·ni·quet *n* **:** a device (as a bandage twisted tight) for stopping bleeding or blood flow

tou·sle *vb* **tou·sled; tou·sling :** to put into disorder by rough handling

[1]**tow** *vb* **:** to draw or pull along behind

[2]**tow** *n* **1 :** a rope or chain for towing **2 :** an act or instance of towing **:** the fact or state of being towed **3 :** something (as a barge) that is towed

[3]**tow** *n* **:** short broken fiber of flax, hemp, or jute used for yarn, twine, or stuffing

to·ward *or* **to·wards** *prep* **1 :** in the direction of **2 :** along a course leading to **3 :** in regard to **4 :** so as to face **5 :** [2]NEAR **6 :** as part of the payment for

tow·el *n* **:** a cloth or piece of absorbent paper for wiping or drying

[1]**tow·er** *n* **1 :** a building or structure that is higher than its length or width, is high with respect to its surroundings, and may stand by itself or be attached to a larger structure **2 :** CITADEL 1

[2]**tower** *vb* **:** to reach or rise to a great height

tow·er·ing *adj* **1 :** rising high **:** TALL **2 :** reaching a high point of strength or force **3 :** going beyond proper bounds

tow·head *n* **:** a person having soft whitish hair

town *n* **1 :** a compactly settled area that is

usually larger than a village but smaller than a city **2 :** CITY 1 **3 :** the people of a town

town·ship *n* **1 :** a unit of local government in some northeastern and north central states **2 :** a division of territory in surveys of United States public lands containing thirty-six square miles (about ninety-three square kilometers)

tox·ic *adj* **:** of, relating to, or caused by a poison

tox·in *n* **:** a poison produced by an animal, a plant, or germs

[1]**toy** *n* **1 :** something of little or no value **2 :** something for a child to play with **3 :** something small of its kind

[2]**toy** *vb* **:** to amuse oneself as if with a toy

[1]**trace** *n* **1 :** a mark left by something that has passed or is past **2 :** a very small amount

[2]**trace** *vb* **traced; trac·ing 1 :** [2]SKETCH 1 **2 :** to form (as letters) carefully **3 :** to copy (as a drawing) by following the lines as seen through a transparent sheet placed over the thing copied **4 :** to follow the footprints, track, or trail of **5 :** to study or follow the development of in detail — **trac·er** *n*

[3]**trace** *n* **:** either of the two straps, chains, or ropes of a harness that fasten a horse to a vehicle

trace·able *adj* **:** capable of being traced

tra·chea *n, pl* **tra·che·ae 1 :** WINDPIPE **2 :** a breathing tube of an insect

trac·ing *n* **1 :** the act of a person that traces **2 :** something that is traced

[1]**track** *n* **1 :** a mark left by something that has gone by **2 :** PATH 1, TRAIL **3 :** a course laid out for racing **4 :** the rails of a railroad **5 :** awareness of things or of the order in which things happen or ideas come **6 :** either of two endless metal belts on which a vehicle (as a tank) travels **7 :** track-and-field sports

[2]**track** *vb* **1 :** to follow the tracks or traces of **2 :** to make tracks on or with

track–and–field *adj* **:** relating to or being sports events (as racing, throwing, and jumping contests) held on a running track and on an enclosed field

[1]**tract** *n* **:** a pamphlet of political or religious ideas and beliefs

[2]**tract** *n* **1 :** an indefinite stretch of land **2 :** a defined area of land **3 :** a system of body parts or organs that serve some special purpose

trac·tor *n* **1 :** a vehicle that has large rear wheels or moves on endless belts and is used especially for pulling farm implements **2 :** a short truck for hauling a trailer

[1]**trade** *n* **1 :** the business or work in which a person takes part regularly **:** OCCUPATION **2 :** an occupation requiring manual or mechanical skill **:** CRAFT **3 :** the persons working in a business or industry **4 :** the business of buying and selling items **:** COMMERCE **5 :** an act of trading **:** TRANSACTION **6 :** a firm's customers

[2]**trade** *vb* **trad·ed; trad·ing 1 :** to give in exchange for something else **2 :** to take part in the exchange, purchase, or sale of goods **3 :** to deal regularly as a customer

trade·mark *n* **:** a device (as a word) that points clearly to the origin or ownership of merchandise to which it is applied and that is legally reserved for use only by the owner

trad·er *n* **1 :** a person who trades **2 :** a ship engaged in trade

trades·man *n, pl* **trades·men 1 :** a person who runs a retail store **2 :** CRAFTSMAN 1

trades·peo·ple *n pl* **:** people engaged in trade

trade wind *n* **:** a wind blowing steadily toward the equator from an easterly direction

trad·ing post *n* **:** a station or store of a trader or trading company set up in a thinly settled region

tra·di·tion *n* **1 :** the handing down of information, beliefs, or customs from one generation to another **2 :** a belief or custom handed down by tradition

tra·di·tion·al *adj* **1 :** handed down from age to age **2 :** based on custom **:** CONVENTIONAL — **tra·di·tion·al·ly** *adv*

[1]**traf·fic** *n* **1 :** the business of carrying passengers or goods **2 :** the business of buying and selling **:** COMMERCE **3 :** exchange of information **4 :** the persons or goods carried by train, boat, or airplane or passing along a road, river, or air route **5 :** the movement (as of vehicles) along a route

[2]**traffic** *vb* **traf·ficked; traf·fick·ing :** [2]TRADE 2

traffic light *n* **:** a visual signal (as a set of colored lights) for controlling the flow of traffic

trag·e·dy *n, pl* **trag·e·dies 1 :** a serious play that has a sorrowful or disastrous ending **2 :** a disastrous event

trag·ic *adj* **1 :** of or relating to tragedy **2 :** very unfortunate

[1]**trail** *vb* **1 :** to drag or draw along behind **2 :** to lag behind **3 :** to follow in the tracks of **:** PURSUE **4 :** to hang or let hang so as to touch the ground or float out behind **5 :** to become weak, soft, or less

[2]**trail** *n* **1 :** something that trails or is trailed **2 :** a trace or mark left by something that has passed or been drawn along **3 :** a beaten path **4 :** a path marked through a forest or mountainous region

trail·er *n* **1 :** a vehicle designed to be hauled **2 :** a vehicle designed to serve wherever parked as a dwelling or a place of business

[1]**train** *n* **1 :** a part of a gown that trails behind the wearer **2 :** the followers of an important

person **3 :** a moving line of persons, vehicles, or animals **4 :** a connected series **5 :** a connected series of railway cars usually hauled by a locomotive

²train *vb* **1 :** to direct the growth of (a plant) usually by bending, pruning, and tying **2 :** to give or receive instruction, discipline, or drill **3 :** to teach in an art, profession, or trade **4 :** to make ready (as by exercise) for a test of skill **5 :** to aim (as a gun) at a target — **train·er** *n*

train·ing *n* **1 :** the course followed by one who trains or is being trained **2 :** the condition of one who has trained for a test or contest

training wheels *n pl* **:** a pair of small wheels connected to the rear axle of a bicycle to help a beginning rider keep balance

trait *n* **:** a quality that sets one person or thing off from another

trai·tor *n* **1 :** a person who betrays another's trust or is false to a personal duty **2 :** a person who commits treason

trai·tor·ous *adj* **1 :** guilty or capable of treason **2 :** amounting to treason — **trai·tor·ous·ly** *adv*

¹tramp *vb* **1 :** to walk heavily **2 :** to tread on forcibly and repeatedly **3 :** to travel or wander through on foot

²tramp *n* **1 :** a person who wanders from place to place, has no home or job, and often lives by begging or stealing **2 :** ²HIKE **3 :** the sounds made by the beat of marching feet

tram·ple *vb* **tram·pled; tram·pling** **1 :** to tramp or tread heavily so as to bruise, crush, or injure something **2 :** to crush under the feet **3 :** to injure or harm by treating harshly and without mercy

tram·po·line *n* **:** a canvas sheet or web supported by springs in a metal frame used for springing and landing in acrobatic tumbling

trance *n* **1 :** STUPOR **2 :** a condition like sleep (as deep hypnosis) **3 :** a state of being so deeply absorbed in something as not to be aware of one's surroundings

tran·quil *adj* **:** very calm and quiet **:** PEACEFUL

tran·quil·iz·er *n* **:** a drug used to ease worry and nervous tension

tran·quil·li·ty *or* **tran·quil·i·ty** *n* **:** the state of being calm **:** QUIET

trans- *prefix* **1 :** on or to the other side of **:** across **:** beyond **2 :** so as to change or transfer

trans·act *vb* **:** to carry on **:** MANAGE, CONDUCT

trans·ac·tion *n* **1 :** a business deal **2 trans·actions** *pl* **:** the record of the meeting of a club or organization

trans·at·lan·tic *adj* **:** crossing or being beyond the Atlantic ocean

tran·scend *vb* **1 :** to rise above the limits of **2 :** to do better or more than

trans·con·ti·nen·tal *adj* **:** crossing, extending across, or being on the farther side of a continent

tran·scribe *vb* **tran·scribed; tran·scrib·ing** **:** to make a copy of

tran·script *n* **1 :** ¹COPY 1 **2 :** an official copy of a student's school record

¹trans·fer *vb* **trans·ferred; trans·fer·ring** **1 :** to pass or cause to pass from one person, place, or condition to another **2 :** to give over the possession or ownership of **3 :** to copy (as by printing) from one surface to another by contact **4 :** to move to a different place, region, or job **5 :** to change from one vehicle or transportation line to another

²trans·fer *n* **1 :** a giving over of right, title, or interest in property by one person to another **2 :** an act or process of transferring **3 :** someone or something that transfers or is transferred **4 :** a ticket allowing a passenger on a bus or train to continue the journey on another route without paying more fare

trans·fix *vb* **:** to pierce through with or as if with a pointed weapon

trans·form *vb* **:** to change completely — **trans·form·er** *n*

trans·for·ma·tion *n* **:** the act or process of transforming **:** a complete change

trans·fu·sion *n* **1 :** a passing of one thing into another **2 :** a transferring (as of blood or salt solution) into a vein of a person or animal

¹tran·sient *adj* **:** not lasting or staying long

²transient *n* **:** a person who is not staying long in a place

tran·sis·tor *n* **:** a small solid electronic device used especially in radios for controlling the flow of electricity

tran·sit *n* **1 :** a passing through or across **2 :** the act or method of carrying things from one place to another **3 :** local transportation of people in public vehicles **4 :** a surveyor's instrument for measuring angles

tran·si·tion *n* **:** a passing from one state, stage, place, or subject to another **:** CHANGE

tran·si·tive *adj* **:** having or containing a direct object

trans·late *vb* **trans·lat·ed; trans·lat·ing** **1 :** to change from one state or form to another **2 :** to turn from one language into another

trans·la·tion *n* **:** the act, process, or result of translating

trans·lu·cent *adj* **:** not transparent but clear enough to allow rays of light to pass through — **trans·lu·cent·ly** *adv*

trans·mis·sion *n* **1 :** an act or process of transmitting **2 :** the gears by which the power is transmitted from the engine to the axle that gives motion to a motor vehicle

trans·mit *vb* **trans·mit·ted; trans·mit·ting 1** : to transfer from one person or place to another **2 :** to pass on by or as if by inheritance **3 :** to pass or cause to pass through space or through a material **4 :** to send out by means of radio waves

trans·mit·ter *n* **1 :** one that transmits **2 :** the instrument in a telegraph system that sends out messages **3 :** the part of a telephone that includes the mouthpiece and a device that picks up sound waves and sends them over the wire **4 :** the device that sends out radio or television signals

tran·som *n* **1 :** a piece that lies crosswise in a structure (as in the frame of a window or of a door that has a window above it) **2 :** a window above a door or another window

trans·par·en·cy *n* **:** the quality or state of being transparent

trans·par·ent *adj* **1 :** clear enough or thin enough to be seen through **2 :** easily detected — **trans·par·ent·ly** *adv*

trans·pi·ra·tion *n* **:** an act or instance of transpiring

trans·pire *vb* **trans·pired; trans·pir·ing 1** : to give off or pass off in the form of a vapor usually through pores **2 :** to become known or apparent **3 :** to come to pass **:** HAPPEN

[1]**trans·plant** *vb* **1 :** to dig up and plant again in another soil or location **2 :** to remove from one place and settle or introduce elsewhere

[2]**trans·plant** *n* **1 :** something transplanted **2** : the process of transplanting

[1]**trans·port** *vb* **1 :** to carry from one place to another **2 :** to fill with delight

[2]**trans·port** *n* **1 :** the act of transporting **:** TRANSPORTATION **2 :** a state of great joy or pleasure **3 :** a ship for carrying soldiers or military equipment **4 :** a vehicle used to transport persons or goods

trans·por·ta·tion *n* **1 :** an act, instance, or means of transporting or being transported **2 :** public transporting of passengers or goods especially as a business

trans·pose *vb* **trans·posed; trans·pos·ing 1** : to change the position or order of **2 :** to write or perform in a different musical key

trans·verse *adj* **:** lying or being across **:** placed crosswise — **trans·verse·ly** *adv*

[1]**trap** *n* **1 :** a device for catching animals **2** : something by which one is caught or stopped unawares **3 :** a light one-horse carriage with springs **4 :** a device that allows something to pass through but keeps other things out

[2]**trap** *vb* **trapped; trap·ping 1 :** to catch in a trap **2 :** to provide (a place) with traps **3 :** to set traps for animals especially as a business — **trap·per** *n*

trap·door *n* **:** a lifting or sliding door covering an opening in a floor or roof

tra·peze *n* **:** a short horizontal bar hung from two parallel ropes and used by acrobats

trap·e·zoid *n* **:** a figure with four sides but with only two sides parallel

trap·pings *n pl* **1 :** ornamental covering especially for a horse **2 :** outward decoration or dress

trash *n* **1 :** something of little or no worth **2** : low worthless persons

[1]**trav·el** *vb* **trav·eled** *or* **trav·elled; trav·el·ing** *or* **trav·el·ling 1 :** to journey from place to place or to a distant place **2 :** to get around : pass from one place to another **3 :** to journey through or over — **trav·el·er** *or* **trav·el·ler** *n*

[2]**travel** *n* **1 :** the act or a means of traveling **2** : [1]JOURNEY, TRIP — often used in pl. **3 :** the number traveling **:** TRAFFIC

traveling bag *n* **:** a bag carried by hand and designed to hold a traveler's clothing and personal articles

tra·verse *vb* **tra·versed; tra·vers·ing :** to pass through, across, or over

[1]**trawl** *vb* **:** to fish or catch with a trawl

[2]**trawl** *n* **:** a large net in the shape of a cone dragged along the sea bottom in fishing

trawl·er *n* **:** a boat used for trawling

tray *n* **:** an open container with a flat bottom and low rim for holding, carrying, or showing articles

treach·er·ous *adj* **1 :** guilty of or likely to commit treachery **2 :** not to be trusted **3** : not safe because of hidden dangers — **treach·er·ous·ly** *adv*

treach·ery *n, pl* **treach·er·ies 1 :** a betraying of trust or faith **2 :** an act or instance of betraying trust

[1]**tread** *vb* **trod; trod·den** *or* **trod; tread·ing 1** : to step or walk on or over **2 :** to move on foot **:** WALK **3 :** to beat or press with the feet — **tread water :** to keep the body upright in the water and the head above water by a walking motion of the legs helped by moving the hands

[2]**tread** *n* **1 :** a mark made by or as if by treading **2 :** the action, manner, or sound of treading **3 :** the part of something (as a shoe or tire) that touches a surface **4 :** the horizontal part of a step

trea·dle *n* **:** a device worked by the foot to drive a machine

tread·mill *n* **1 :** a mill moved by persons treading on steps around the rim of a wheel or by animals walking on an endless belt **2** : a device having an endless belt on which an individual walks or runs in place for exercise **3 :** a tiresome routine

trea·son *n* **1 :** the betraying of a trust **2 :** the crime of trying or helping to overthrow the government of one's country or cause its defeat in war

[1]**trea·sure** *n* **1 :** wealth (as money or jewels) stored up or held in reserve **2 :** something of great value

[2]**treasure** *vb* **trea·sured; trea·sur·ing :** to treat as precious : CHERISH

trea·sur·er *n* **:** a person (as an officer of a club) who has charge of the money

trea·sury *n, pl* **trea·sur·ies 1 :** a place in which stores of wealth are kept **2 :** a place where money collected is kept and paid out **3** *cap* **:** a government department in charge of finances

[1]**treat** *vb* **1 :** to have as a subject especially in writing **2 :** to handle, use, or act toward in a usually stated way **3 :** to pay for the food or entertainment of **4 :** to give medical or surgical care to : to use a certain medical care on **5 :** to expose to some action (as of a chemical)

[2]**treat** *n* **1 :** an entertainment given without expense to those invited **2 :** an often unexpected or unusual source of pleasure or amusement

treat·ment *n* **1 :** the act or manner of treating someone or something **2 :** a substance or method used in treating

trea·ty *n, pl* **trea·ties :** an agreement between two or more states or sovereigns

[1]**tre·ble** *n* **1 :** the highest part in harmony having four parts : SOPRANO 1 **2 :** an instrument having the highest range or part **3 :** a voice or sound that has a high pitch **4 :** the upper half of the musical pitch range

[2]**treble** *adj* **1 :** being three times the number or amount **2 :** relating to or having the range of a musical treble

[3]**treble** *vb* **tre·bled; tre·bling :** to make or become three times as much

[1]**tree** *n* **1 :** a woody plant that lives for years and has a single usually tall main stem with few or no branches on its lower part **2 :** a plant of treelike form **3 :** something suggesting a tree — **tree·less** *adj* — **tree·like** *adj*

[2]**tree** *vb* **treed; tree·ing :** to drive to or up a tree

tree fern *n* **:** a tropical fern with a tall woody stalk and a crown of often feathery leaves

tree house *n* **:** a structure (as a playhouse) built among the branches of a tree

tre·foil *n* **1 :** a clover or related plant having leaves with three leaflets **2 :** a fancy design with three leaflike parts

[1]**trek** *vb* **trekked; trek·king :** to make one's way with difficulty

[2]**trek** *n* **:** a slow or difficult journey

trel·lis *n* **:** a frame of lattice used especially as a screen or a support for climbing plants

[1]**trem·ble** *vb* **trem·bled; trem·bling 1 :** to shake without control (as from fear or cold) : SHIVER **2 :** to move, sound, or happen as if shaken **3 :** to have strong fear or doubt

[2]**tremble** *n* **:** the act or a period of trembling

tre·men·dous *adj* **1 :** causing fear or terror : DREADFUL **2 :** astonishingly large, strong, or great — **tre·men·dous·ly** *adv*

trem·or *n* **1 :** a trembling or shaking especially from weakness or disease **2 :** a shaking motion of the earth (as during an earthquake)

trem·u·lous *adj* **1 :** marked by trembling or shaking **2 :** FEARFUL 2, TIMID

trench *n* **:** a long narrow ditch

[1]**trend** *vb* **:** to have or take a general direction

[2]**trend** *n* **:** general direction taken in movement or change

[1]**tres·pass** *n* **1 :** [1]SIN, OFFENSE **2 :** unlawful entry upon someone's land

[2]**trespass** *vb* **1 :** to do wrong : SIN **2 :** to enter upon someone's land unlawfully — **tres·pass·er** *n*

tress *n* **:** a long lock of hair

tres·tle *n* **1 :** a braced frame consisting usually of a horizontal piece with spreading legs at each end that supports something (as the top of a table) **2 :** a structure of timbers or steel for supporting a road or railroad over a low place

T. rex *n* **:** TYRANNOSAUR

tri- *prefix* **:** three

tri·ad *n* **:** a chord made up usually of the first, third, and fifth notes of a scale

tri·al *n* **1 :** the action or process of trying or testing **2 :** the hearing and judgment of something in court **3 :** a test of faith or of one's ability to continue or stick with something **4 :** an experiment to test quality, value, or usefulness **5 :** [2]ATTEMPT

tri·an·gle *n* **1 :** a figure that has three sides and three angles **2 :** an object that has three sides and three angles **3 :** a musical instrument made of a steel rod bent in the shape of a triangle with one open angle

tri·an·gu·lar *adj* **1 :** of, relating to, or having the form of a triangle **2 :** having three angles, sides, or corners **3 :** of, relating to, or involving three parts or persons

trib·al *adj* **:** of, relating to, or like that of a tribe

tribe *n* **1 :** a group of people including many families, clans, or generations **2 :** a group of people who are of the same kind or have the same occupation or interest **3 :** a group of related plants or animals

tribes·man *n, pl* **tribes·men :** a member of a tribe

trib·u·la·tion *n* **1 :** distress or suffering resulting from cruel and unjust rule of a leader, persecution, or misfortune **2 :** an experience that is hard to bear

tri·bu·nal *n* **:** a court of justice

[1]trib·u·tary *adj* **:** flowing into a larger stream or a lake

[2]tributary *n, pl* **trib·u·tar·ies :** a stream flowing into a larger stream or a lake

trib·ute *n* **1 :** a payment made by one ruler or state to another especially to gain peace **2 :** a tax put on the people to raise money for tribute **3 :** something given to show respect, gratitude, or affection

tri·cer·a·tops *n, pl* **triceratops :** a large plant-eating dinosaur with three horns, a large bony crest around the neck, and hoofed toes

tri·chi·na *n, pl* **tri·chi·nae :** a small roundworm which enters the body when infected meat is eaten and whose larvae form cysts in the muscles and cause a painful and dangerous disease (**trichinosis**)

[1]trick *n* **1 :** an action intended to deceive or cheat **2 :** a mischievous act **:** PRANK **3 :** an unwise or childish action **4 :** an action designed to puzzle or amuse **5 :** a quick or clever way of doing something **6 :** the cards played in one round of a game

[2]trick *vb* **:** to deceive with tricks **:** CHEAT

trick·ery *n, pl* **trick·er·ies :** the use of tricks to deceive or cheat

[1]trick·le *vb* **trick·led; trick·ling 1 :** to run or fall in drops **2 :** to flow in a thin slow stream

[2]trickle *n* **:** a thin slow stream

trick or treat *n* **:** a children's Halloween practice of asking for treats from door to door and threatening to play tricks on those who refuse

trick·ster *n* **:** a person who uses tricks

tricky *adj* **trick·i·er; trick·i·est 1 :** likely to use tricks **2 :** requiring special care and skill

tri·cy·cle *n* **:** a vehicle with three wheels that is moved usually by pedals

tri·dent *n* **:** a spear with three prongs

[1]tried *past of* TRY

[2]tried *adj* **:** found good or trustworthy through experience or testing

[1]tri·fle *n* **1 :** something of little importance **2 :** a small amount (as of money)

[2]trifle *vb* **tri·fled; tri·fling 1 :** to talk in a joking way **2 :** to act in a playful way **3 :** to handle something in an absentminded way **:** TOY

tri·fling *adj* **1 :** not serious **:** FRIVOLOUS **2 :** of little value

trig·ger *n* **:** the part of the lock of a gun that is pressed to release the hammer so that it will fire

[1]trill *n* **1 :** a quick movement back and forth between two musical tones one step apart **2 :** [1]WARBLE 1 **3 :** the rapid vibration of one speech organ against another

[2]trill *vb* **:** to utter as or with a trill

tril·lion *n* **:** a thousand billions

tril·li·um *n* **:** a plant related to the lilies that has three leaves and a single flower with three petals and that blooms in the spring

[1]trim *vb* **trimmed; trim·ming 1 :** to put ornaments on **:** ADORN **2 :** to make neat especially by cutting or clipping **3 :** to free of unnecessary matter **4 :** to cause (as a ship) to take the right position in the water by balancing the load carried **5 :** to adjust (as an airplane or submarine) for horizontal movement or for motion upward or downward **6 :** to adjust (as a sail) to a desired position — **trim·mer** *n*

[2]trim *adj* **trim·mer; trim·mest :** neat and compact in line or structure — **trim·ly** *adv*

[3]trim *n* **1 :** the state of a ship as being ready for sailing **2 :** good condition **:** FITNESS **3 :** material used for ornament or trimming **4 :** the woodwork in the finish of a building especially around doors and windows

trim·ming *n* **1 :** the action of one that trims **2 :** something that trims, ornaments, or completes **3 trimmings** *pl* **:** parts removed by trimming

trin·ket *n* **:** a small ornament (as a jewel)

trio *n, pl* **tri·os 1 :** a musical composition for three instruments or voices **2 :** a group or set of three

[1]trip *vb* **tripped; trip·ping 1 :** to move (as in dancing) with light quick steps **2 :** to catch the foot against something so as to stumble **:** cause to stumble **3 :** to make or cause to make a mistake **4 :** to release (as a spring) by moving a catch

[2]trip *n* **1 :** a traveling from one place to another **:** VOYAGE **2 :** a brief errand having a certain aim or being more or less regular **3 :** the action of releasing something mechanically **4 :** a device for releasing something by tripping a mechanism

tripe *n* **:** a part of the stomach of a cow used for food

[1]tri·ple *vb* **tri·pled; tri·pling :** to make or become three times as great or as many

[2]triple *n* **1 :** a sum, amount, or number that is three times as great **2 :** a combination, group, or series of three **3 :** a hit in baseball that lets the batter reach third base

[3]triple *adj* **1 :** having three units or parts **2 :** being three times as great or as many **3 :** repeated three times

trip·let *n* **1 :** a combination, set, or group of three **2 :** one of three offspring born at one birth

tri·pod *n* **1 :** something (as a container or

stool) resting on three legs **2 :** a stand (as for a camera) having three legs

trite *adj* **trit·er; trit·est :** so common that the newness and cleverness have worn off **:** STALE — **trite·ness** *n*

[1]**tri·umph** *n* **1 :** the joy of victory or success **2 :** an outstanding victory

[2]**triumph** *vb* **1 :** to celebrate victory or success in high spirits and often with boasting **2 :** to gain victory **:** WIN

tri·um·phal *adj* **:** of or relating to a triumph

tri·um·phant *adj* **1 :** VICTORIOUS, SUCCESSFUL **2 :** rejoicing for or celebrating victory — **tri·um·phant·ly** *adv*

triv·i·al *adj* **:** of little worth or importance

trod *past of* TREAD

trodden *past participle of* TREAD

[1]**troll** *vb* **1 :** to sing the parts of (a song) in succession **2 :** to fish with a hook and line drawn through the water

[2]**troll** *n* **:** a lure or a line with its lure and hook used in trolling

[3]**troll** *n* **:** a dwarf or giant of folklore living in caves or hills

trol·ley *n, pl* **trolleys** **1 :** a device (as a grooved wheel on the end of a pole) that carries current from a wire to an electrically driven vehicle **2 :** a passenger car that runs on tracks and gets its power through a trolley **3 :** a wheeled carriage running on an overhead track

trom·bone *n* **:** a brass musical instrument made of a long bent tube that has a wide opening at one end and one section that slides in and out to make different tones

[1]**troop** *n* **1 :** a cavalry unit **2 troops** *pl* **:** armed forces **:** MILITARY **3 :** a group of beings or things **4 :** a unit of boy or girl scouts under a leader

[2]**troop** *vb* **:** to move or gather in groups

troop·er *n* **1 :** a soldier in a cavalry unit **2 :** a mounted police officer **3 :** a state police officer

tro·phy *n, pl* **trophies** **1 :** something taken in battle or conquest especially as a memorial **2 :** something given to celebrate a victory or as an award for achievement

trop·ic *n* **1 :** either of two parallels of the earth's latitude of which one is about 23½ degrees north of the equator and the other about 23½ degrees south of the equator **2 tropics** *pl, often cap* **:** the region lying between the two tropics

trop·i·cal *adj* **:** of, relating to, or occurring in the tropics

tropical fish *n* **:** any of various small often brightly colored fishes kept in aquariums

[1]**trot** *n* **1 :** a moderately fast gait of an animal with four feet in which a front foot and the opposite hind foot move as a pair **2 :** a human jogging pace between a walk and a run

[2]**trot** *vb* **trot·ted; trot·ting** **1 :** to ride, drive, or go at a trot **2 :** to cause to go at a trot **3 :** to go along quickly **:** HURRY

[1]**trou·ble** *vb* **trou·bled; trou·bling** **1 :** to disturb or become disturbed mentally or spiritually **:** WORRY **2 :** to produce physical disorder in **:** AFFLICT **3 :** to put to inconvenience **4 :** to make an effort

[2]**trouble** *n* **1 :** the quality or state of being troubled **:** MISFORTUNE **2 :** an instance of distress or disturbance **3 :** a cause of disturbance or distress **4 :** extra work or effort **5 :** ill health **:** AILMENT **6 :** failure to work normally

trou·ble·some *adj* **1 :** giving trouble or anxiety **2 :** difficult to deal with — **trou·ble·some·ly** *adv* — **trou·ble·some·ness** *n*

trough *n* **1 :** a long shallow open container especially for water or feed for livestock **2 :** a channel for water **:** GUTTER **3 :** a long channel or hollow

trounce *vb* **trounced; trounc·ing** **1 :** to beat severely **:** FLOG **2 :** to defeat thoroughly

troupe *n* **:** a group especially of performers on the stage

trou·sers *n pl* **:** PANTS — used chiefly of such a garment for men and boys

trout *n, pl* **trout :** a freshwater fish related to the salmon and valued for food and sport

trow·el *n* **1 :** a small hand tool with a flat blade used for spreading and smoothing mortar or plaster **2 :** a small hand tool with a curved blade used by gardeners

tru·ant *n* **1 :** a person who neglects his or her duty **2 :** a student who stays out of school without permission

truce *n* **1 :** ARMISTICE **2 :** a short rest especially from something unpleasant

[1]**truck** *n* **1 :** [2]BARTER **2 :** goods for barter or for small trade **3 :** close association

[2]**truck** *n* **:** a vehicle (as a strong heavy wagon or motor vehicle) for carrying heavy articles or hauling a trailer

[3]**truck** *vb* **:** to transport on a truck

trudge *vb* **trudged; trudg·ing :** to walk or march steadily and usually with much effort

[1]**true** *adj* **tru·er; tru·est** **1 :** completely loyal **:** FAITHFUL **2 :** that can be relied on **:** CERTAIN **3 :** agreeing with the facts **:** ACCURATE **4 :** HONEST 1, SINCERE **5 :** properly so called **:** GENUINE **6 :** placed or formed accurately **:** EXACT **7 :** being or holding by right **:** LEGITIMATE

[2]**true** *adv* **1 :** in agreement with fact **:** TRUTHFULLY **2 :** in an accurate manner **:** ACCURATELY **3 :** without variation from type

[3]**true** *n* **:** the quality or state of being accurate (as in alignment)

[4]true *vb* **trued; true·ing** *also* **tru·ing :** to bring to exactly correct condition as to place, position, or shape

true–blue *adj* **:** very faithful

truf·fle *n* **:** the edible usually dark and wrinkled fruiting body of a European fungus that grows in the ground

tru·ly *adv* **:** in a true manner

[1]trum·pet *n* **1 :** a brass musical instrument that consists of a tube formed into a long loop with a wide opening at one end and that has valves by which different tones are produced **2 :** something that is shaped like a trumpet **3 :** a sound like that of a trumpet

[2]trumpet *vb* **1 :** to blow a trumpet **2 :** to make a sound like that of a trumpet — **trum·pet·er** *n*

trumpet creeper *n* **:** a North American woody vine having red flowers shaped like trumpets

trumpet vine *n* **:** TRUMPET CREEPER

[1]trun·dle *vb* **trun·dled; trun·dling :** to roll along **:** WHEEL

[2]trundle *n* **1 :** a small wheel or roller **2 :** a cart or truck with low wheels

trundle bed *n* **:** a low bed on small wheels that can be rolled under a higher bed

trunk *n* **1 :** the main stem of a tree apart from branches and roots **2 :** the body of a person or animal apart from the head, arms, and legs **3 :** a box or chest for holding clothes or other articles especially for traveling **4 :** the enclosed space usually in the rear of an automobile for carrying articles **5 :** the long round muscular nose of an elephant **6 trunks** *pl* **:** men's shorts worn chiefly for sports

[1]truss *vb* **1 :** to bind or tie firmly **2 :** to support, strengthen, or stiffen by a truss

[2]truss *n* **1 :** a framework of beams or bars used in building and engineering **2 :** a device worn to hold a ruptured body part in place

[1]trust *n* **1 :** firm belief in the character, strength, or truth of someone or something **2 :** a person or thing in which confidence is placed **3 :** confident hope **4 :** financial credit **5 :** a property interest held by one person or organization (as a bank) for the benefit of another **6 :** a combination of firms or corporations formed by a legal agreement and often held to reduce competition **7 :** something (as a public office) held or managed by someone for the benefit of another **8 :** responsibility for safety and well-being

[2]trust *vb* **1 :** to place confidence **:** DEPEND **2 :** to be confident **:** HOPE **3 :** to place in one's care or keeping **:** ENTRUST **4 :** to rely on or on the truth of **:** BELIEVE **5 :** to give financial credit to

trust·ee *n* **:** a person who has been given legal responsibility for someone else's property

trust·ful *adj* **:** full of trust — **trust·ful·ly** *adv* — **trust·ful·ness** *n*

trust·ing *adj* **:** having trust, faith, or confidence

trust·wor·thy *adj* **:** deserving trust and confidence — **trust·wor·thi·ness** *n*

[1]trusty *adj* **trust·i·er; trust·i·est :** TRUSTWORTHY, RELIABLE

[2]trusty *n, pl* **trust·ies :** a convict considered trustworthy and allowed special privileges

truth *n, pl* **truths 1 :** the quality or state of being true **2 :** the body of real events or facts **3 :** a true or accepted statement **4 :** agreement with fact or reality

truth·ful *adj* **:** telling or being in the habit of telling the truth — **truth·ful·ly** *adv* — **truth·ful·ness** *n*

[1]try *vb* **tried; try·ing 1 :** to examine or investigate in a court of law **2 :** to conduct the trial of **3 :** to put to a test **4 :** to test to the limit **5 :** to melt down (as tallow) and obtain in a pure state **6 :** to make an effort to do

[2]try *n, pl* **tries :** an effort to do something **:** ATTEMPT

try·ing *adj* **:** hard to bear or put up with

try on *vb* **:** to put on (a garment) to test the fit

try·out *n* **:** a test of the ability (as of an athlete or an actor) to fill a part or meet standards

T–shirt *also* **tee shirt** *n* **1 :** a cotton undershirt with short sleeves and no collar **2 :** a cotton or wool jersey outer shirt designed like a T-shirt

tsu·na·mi *n* **:** a large sea wave produced especially by an earthquake or volcanic eruption under the sea **:** TIDAL WAVE

[1]tub *n* **1 :** a wide low container **2 :** an old or slow boat **3 :** BATHTUB **4 :** BATH 1 **5 :** the amount that a tub will hold

[2]tub *vb* **tubbed; tub·bing :** to wash or bathe in a tub

tu·ba *n* **:** a brass musical instrument of lowest pitch with an oval shape and valves for producing different tones

tube *n* **1 :** a long hollow cylinder used especially to carry fluids **2 :** a slender channel within a plant or animal body **:** DUCT **3 :** a soft container shaped something like a tube whose contents (as toothpaste or glue) can be removed by squeezing **4 :** a hollow cylinder of rubber inside a tire to hold air **5 :** ELECTRONIC TUBE **6 :** TELEVISION — always used with *the* — **tubed** *adj* — **tube·less** *adj* — **tube·like** *adj*

tu·ber *n* **:** a short fleshy usually underground stem (as of a potato plant) bearing tiny leaves like scales each with a bud at its base

tu·ber·cu·lo·sis *n* **:** a disease (as of humans or cattle) which is caused by a bacillus and in which fever, wasting, and formation of cheesy nodules especially in the lungs occur

tu·ber·ous *adj* : of, relating to, or like a tuber

tu·bu·lar *adj* **1 :** having the form of or made up of a tube **2 :** made with tubes

[1]tuck *vb* **1 :** to pull up into a fold **2 :** to make stitched folds in **3 :** to put or fit into a snug or safe place **4 :** to push in the edges of **5 :** to cover by tucking in bedclothes

[2]tuck *n* : a fold stitched into cloth usually to alter it

Tues·day *n* : the third day of the week

[1]tuft *n* **1 :** a small bunch of long flexible things (as hairs) growing out **2 :** a bunch of soft fluffy threads used for ornament **3 :** [1]CLUMP 1

[2]tuft *vb* **1 :** to provide or decorate with a tuft **2 :** to grow in tufts **3 :** to make (as upholstery) firm by stitching through the stuffing here and there

[1]tug *vb* **tugged; tug·ging 1 :** to pull hard **2 :** to move by pulling hard : DRAG **3 :** to tow with a tugboat

[2]tug *n* **1 :** an act of tugging : PULL **2 :** a strong pulling force **3 :** a struggle between two people or forces **4 :** TUGBOAT

tug·boat *n* : a small powerful boat used for towing ships

tug–of–war *n, pl* **tugs–of–war 1 :** a struggle to win **2 :** a contest in which two teams pull against each other at opposite ends of a rope

tu·ition *n* : money paid for instruction (as at a college)

tu·lip *n* : a plant related to the lilies that grows from a bulb and has a large cup-shaped flower in early spring

[1]tum·ble *vb* **tum·bled; tum·bling 1 :** to perform gymnastic feats of rolling and turning **2 :** to fall suddenly and helplessly **3 :** to suffer a sudden downward turn or defeat **4 :** to move or go in a hurried or confused way **5 :** to come to understand **6 :** to toss together into a confused mass

[2]tumble *n* **1 :** a messy state or collection **2 :** an act or instance of tumbling and especially of falling down

tum·ble·down *adj* : DILAPIDATED

tum·bler *n* **1 :** a person (as an acrobat) who tumbles **2 :** a drinking glass **3 :** a movable part of a lock that must be adjusted (as by a key) before the lock will open

tum·ble·weed *n* : a plant that breaks away from its roots in autumn and is tumbled about by the wind

tum·my *n, pl* **tummies :** [1]STOMACH 1, 2

tu·mor *n* : an abnormal growth of body tissue

tu·mult *n* **1 :** UPROAR **2 :** great confusion of mind

tu·mul·tu·ous *adj* : being or suggesting tumult

tu·na *n, pl* **tuna** *or* **tunas :** a large sea fish valued for food and sport

tun·dra *n* : a treeless plain of arctic regions

[1]tune *n* **1 :** a series of pleasing musical tones : MELODY **2 :** the main melody of a song **3 :** correct musical pitch or key **4 :** AGREEMENT 1, HARMONY **5 :** general attitude — **tune·ful** *adj*

[2]tune *vb* **tuned; tun·ing 1 :** to adjust in musical pitch **2 :** to come or bring into harmony **3 :** to adjust a radio or television set so that it receives clearly — often used with *in* **4 :** to put (as an engine) in good working order — often used with *up* — **tun·er** *n*

tung·sten *n* : a grayish-white hard metallic chemical element used especially for electrical purposes (as for the fine wire in an electric light bulb) and to make alloys (as steel) harder

tu·nic *n* **1 :** a usually knee-length belted garment worn by ancient Greeks and Romans **2 :** a shirt or jacket reaching to or just below the hips

tuning fork *n* : a metal instrument that gives a fixed tone when struck and is useful for tuning musical instruments

[1]tun·nel *n* : a passage under the ground

[2]tunnel *vb* **tun·neled** *or* **tun·nelled; tun·nel·ing** *or* **tun·nel·ling :** to make a tunnel

tun·ny *n, pl* **tun·nies :** TUNA

tur·ban *n* **1 :** a head covering worn especially by Muslims and made of a long cloth wrapped around the head or around a cap **2 :** a woman's small soft hat with no brim

tur·bid *adj* : dark or discolored with sediment

tur·bine *n* : an engine whose central driving shaft is fitted with a series of winglike parts that are whirled around by the pressure of water, steam, or gas

tur·bot *n, pl* **turbot :** a large brownish flatfish

tur·bu·lent *adj* : causing or being in a state of unrest, violence, or disturbance

tu·reen *n* : a deep bowl from which food (as soup) is served

turf *n* : the upper layer of soil bound into a thick mat by roots of grass and other plants

Turk *n* : a person born or living in Turkey

tur·key *n, pl* **turkeys :** a large American bird related to the chicken and widely raised for food

[1]Turk·ish *adj* : of or relating to Turkey, the Turks, or Turkish

[2]Turkish *n* : the language of the Turks

tur·moil *n* : a very confused or disturbed state or condition

[1]turn *vb* **1 :** to move or cause to move around a center : ROTATE **2 :** to twist so as to bring about a desired end **3 :** [1]WRENCH 2 **4 :** to change in position usually by moving through an arc of a circle **5 :** to think over

: PONDER **6 :** to become dizzy : REEL **7** : [1]UPSET 3 **8 :** to set in another and especially an opposite direction **9 :** to change course or direction **10 :** to go around **11 :** to reach or pass beyond **12 :** to move or direct toward or away from something **13 :** to make an appeal **14 :** to become or make very unfriendly **15 :** to make or become spoiled **16 :** to cause to be or look a certain way **17 :** to pass from one state to another **18 :** [1]CHANGE 1, TRANSFORM **19 :** TRANSLATE 2 **20 :** to give a rounded form to (as on a lathe) — **turn a hair :** to be or become upset or frightened — **turn tail :** to turn so as to run away — **turn the trick :** to bring about the desired result — **turn turtle :** OVERTURN 1

²turn *n* **1 :** a turning about a center **2 :** a change or changing of direction, course, or position **3 :** a change or changing of the general state or condition **4 :** a place at which something turns **5 :** a short walk or ride **6 :** an act affecting another **7 :** proper place in a waiting line or time in a schedule **8 :** a period of action or activity : SPELL **9 :** a special purpose or need **10 :** special quality **11 :** the shape or form in which something is molded : CAST **12 :** a single circle or loop (as of rope passed around an object) **13 :** natural or special skill — **at every turn :** all the time : CONSTANTLY, CONTINUOUSLY — **to a turn :** precisely right

turn·about *n* **:** a change from one direction or one way of thinking or acting to the opposite

turn down *vb* **1 :** to fold back or down **2 :** to lower by using a control **3 :** [1]REFUSE 1, REJECT

tur·nip *n* **:** the thick white or yellow edible root of a plant related to the cabbage

turn off *vb* **1 :** to turn aside **2 :** to stop by using a control

turn on *vb* **:** to make work by using a control

turn·out *n* **:** a gathering of people for a special reason

turn out *vb* **1 :** TURN OFF 2 **2 :** to prove to be

turn·pike *n* **1 :** a road that one must pay to use **2 :** a main road

turn·stile *n* **:** a post having arms that turn around set in an entrance or exit so that persons can pass through only on foot one by one

turn·ta·ble *n* **:** a round flat plate that turns a phonograph record

tur·pen·tine *n* **1 :** a mixture of oil and resin obtained mostly from pine trees **2 :** an oil made from turpentine and used as a solvent and as a paint thinner

tur·quoise *n* **:** a blue to greenish gray mineral used in jewelry

tur·ret *n* **1 :** a little tower often at a corner of a building **2 :** a low usually rotating structure (as in a tank, warship, or airplane) in which guns are mounted

tur·tle *n* **:** any of a large group of reptiles living on land, in water, or both and having a toothless horny beak and a shell of bony plates which covers the body and into which the head, legs, and tail can usually be drawn

tur·tle·dove *n* **:** any of several small wild pigeons

tur·tle·neck *n* **:** a high turned-over collar (as of a sweater)

tusk *n* **:** a very long large tooth (as of an elephant) usually growing in pairs and used in digging and fighting — **tusked** *adj*

¹tus·sle *n* **1 :** a physical contest or struggle **2 :** a rough argument or a struggle against difficult odds

²tussle *vb* **tus·sled; tus·sling :** to struggle roughly : SCUFFLE

tus·sock *n* **:** a compact tuft or clump (as of grass)

¹tu·tor *n* **:** a person who has the responsibility of instructing and guiding another

²tutor *vb* **:** to teach usually individually

TV *n* **:** TELEVISION

twad·dle *n* **:** silly idle talk

twain *n* **:** [2]TWO 1

¹twang *n* **1 :** a harsh quick ringing sound **2 :** nasal speech

²twang *vb* **1 :** to sound or cause to sound with a twang **2 :** to speak with a nasal twang

'twas : it was

¹tweak *vb* **:** to pinch and pull with a sudden jerk and twist

²tweak *n* **:** an act of tweaking

tweed *n* **1 :** a rough woolen cloth **2 tweeds** *pl* **:** tweed clothing (as a suit)

¹tweet *n* **:** a chirping sound

²tweet *vb* **:** [2]CHIRP

tweez·ers *n pl* **:** a small instrument that is used like pincers in grasping or pulling something

¹twelfth *adj* **:** coming right after eleventh

²twelfth *n* **:** number twelve in a series

¹twelve *adj* **:** being one more than eleven

²twelve *n* **:** one more than eleven : three times four : 12

twelve·month *n* **:** YEAR

¹twen·ti·eth *adj* **:** coming right after nineteenth

²twentieth *n* **:** number twenty in a series

¹twen·ty *adj* **:** being one more than nineteen

²twenty *n* **:** one more than nineteen : four times five : 20

twen·ty–first *adj* **:** coming right after twentieth

¹twen·ty–one *adj* **:** being one more than twenty

²twenty–one *n* **:** one more than twenty : 21

twice *adv* **:** two times

twid·dle *vb* **twid·dled; twid·dling :** [1]TWIRL
twig *n* **:** a small shoot or branch
twi·light *n* **:** the period or the light from the sky between full night and sunrise or between sunset and full night
twill *n* **:** a way of weaving cloth that produces a pattern of diagonal lines
[1]**twin** *n* **1 :** either of two offspring produced at one birth **2 :** one of two persons or things closely related to or very like each other
[2]**twin** *adj* **1 :** born with one other or as a pair at one birth **2 :** made up of two similar, related, or connected members or parts **3 :** being one of a pair
[1]**twine** *n* **:** a strong string of two or more strands twisted together
[2]**twine** *vb* **twined; twin·ing 1 :** to twist together **2 :** to coil around a support
[1]**twinge** *vb* **twinged; twing·ing** *or* **twinge·ing :** to affect with or feel a sudden sharp pain
[2]**twinge** *n* **:** a sudden sharp stab (as of pain)
[1]**twin·kle** *vb* **twin·kled; twin·kling 1 :** to shine or cause to shine with a flickering or sparkling light **2 :** to appear bright with amusement **3 :** to move or flutter rapidly
[2]**twinkle** *n* **1 :** a very short time **2 :** [2]SPARKLE 1, FLICKER
twin·kling *n* **:** [2]TWINKLE 1
[1]**twirl** *vb* **:** to turn or cause to turn rapidly — **twirl·er** *n*
[2]**twirl** *n* **:** an act of twirling
[1]**twist** *vb* **1 :** to unite by winding one thread, strand, or wire around another **2 :** [2]TWINE 2 **3 :** to turn so as to sprain or hurt **4 :** to change the meaning of **5 :** to pull off, rotate, or break by a turning force **6 :** to follow a winding course
[2]**twist** *n* **1 :** something that is twisted **2 :** an act of twisting **:** the state of being twisted **3 :** a spiral turn or curve **4 :** a strong personal tendency **:** BENT **5 :** a changing of meaning **6 :** something (as a plan of action) that is both surprising and strange **7 :** a lively dance in which the hips are twisted
twist·er *n* **1 :** TORNADO **2 :** WATERSPOUT 2
[1]**twitch** *vb* **1 :** to move or pull with a sudden motion **:** JERK **2 :** [1]PLUCK 1 **3 :** [2]QUIVER
[2]**twitch** *n* **1 :** an act of twitching **2 :** a short sharp contracting of muscle fibers
[1]**twit·ter** *vb* **1 :** to make a series of chirping noises **2 :** to talk in a chattering fashion **3 :** to make or become very nervous and upset
[2]**twitter** *n* **1 :** a nervous upset state **2 :** the chirping of birds **3 :** a light chattering
[1]**two** *adj* **:** being one more than one
[2]**two** *n* **1 :** one more than one **:** 2 **2 :** the second in a set or series
two–dimensional *adj* **:** having the two dimensions of length and width
two·fold *adj* **:** being twice as great or as many
two–way *adj* **1 :** moving or acting or allowing movement or action in either direction **2 :** involving two persons or groups **3 :** made to send and receive messages
two–winged fly *n* **:** an insect belonging to the same group as the housefly
ty·coon *n* **:** a very powerful and wealthy business person
tying *present participle of* TIE
[1]**type** *n* **1 :** a set of letters or figures that are used for printing or the letters or figures printed by them **2 :** the special things by which members of a group are set apart from other groups **3 :** VARIETY 3
[2]**type** *vb* **typed; typ·ing 1 :** TYPEWRITE **2 :** to identify as belonging to a type
type·write *vb* **type·wrote; type·writ·ten; type·writ·ing :** to write with a typewriter
type·writ·er *n* **:** a machine that prints letters or figures when a person pushes its keys down
type·writ·ing *n* **1 :** the use of a typewriter **2 :** writing done with a typewriter
[1]**ty·phoid** *adj* **1 :** of, relating to, or like typhus **2 :** of, relating to, or being typhoid
[2]**typhoid** *n* **:** a disease in which a person has fever, diarrhea, an inflamed intestine, and great weakness and which is caused by a bacterium (**typhoid bacillus**) that passes from one person to another in dirty food or water
ty·phoon *n* **:** a tropical cyclone in the region of the Philippines or the China Sea
ty·phus *n* **:** a disease carried to people especially by body lice and marked by high fever, stupor and delirium, severe headache, and a dark red rash
typ·i·cal *adj* **:** combining or showing the special characteristics of a group or kind — **typ·i·cal·ly** *adv*
typ·i·fy *vb* **typ·i·fied; typ·i·fy·ing 1 :** REPRESENT 2 **2 :** to have or include the special or main characteristics of
typ·ist *n* **:** a person who uses a typewriter
ty·ran·ni·cal *adj* **:** of, relating to, or like that of tyranny or a tyrant
ty·ran·no·saur *n* **:** a huge North American meat-eating dinosaur that had small forelegs and walked on its hind legs
ty·ran·no·sau·rus *n* **:** TYRANNOSAUR
tyr·an·ny *n, pl* **tyr·an·nies 1 :** a government in which all power is in the hands of a single ruler **2 :** harsh, cruel, and severe government or conduct **3 :** a tyrannical act
ty·rant *n* **1 :** a ruler who has no legal limits on his or her power **2 :** a ruler who exercises total power harshly and cruelly **3 :** a person who uses authority or power harshly

U

u *n, pl* **u's** *or* **us** *often cap* **1 :** the twenty-first letter of the English alphabet **2 :** a grade rating a student's work as unsatisfactory

ud·der *n* **:** an organ (as of a cow) made up of two or more milk glands enclosed in a common pouch but opening by separate nipples

ugh *interj* — used to indicate the sound of a cough or to express disgust or horror

ug·ly *adj* **ug·li·er; ug·li·est 1 :** unpleasant to look at **:** not attractive **2 :** [1]OFFENSIVE 3 **3 :** not pleasant **:** TROUBLESOME **4 :** showing a mean or quarrelsome disposition — **ug·li·ness** *n*

uku·le·le *n* **:** a musical instrument like a small guitar with four strings

ul·cer *n* **:** an open sore in which tissue is eaten away and which may discharge pus

ul·cer·ate *vb* **ul·cer·at·ed; ul·cer·at·ing :** to cause or have an ulcer

ul·cer·ation *n* **1 :** the process of forming or state of having an ulcer **2 :** ULCER

ul·cer·ous *adj* **:** being or accompanied by ulceration

ul·na *n, pl* **ul·nas** *or* **ul·nae :** the bone on the side of the forearm opposite the thumb

ul·te·ri·or *adj* **:** not seen or made known

ul·ti·mate *adj* **1 :** last in a series **:** FINAL **2 :** [1]EXTREME 1 **3 :** FUNDAMENTAL, ABSOLUTE — **ul·ti·mate·ly** *adv*

ul·ti·ma·tum *n, pl* **ul·ti·ma·tums** *or* **ul·ti·ma·ta :** a final condition or demand that if rejected could end peaceful talks and lead to forceful action

ul·tra *adj* **:** [1]EXTREME 1, EXCESSIVE

ultra- *prefix* **1 :** beyond in space **:** on the other side **2 :** beyond the limits of **:** SUPER- **3 :** beyond what is ordinary or proper **:** too

ul·tra·vi·o·let *adj* **:** relating to or producing ultraviolet light

ultraviolet light *n* **:** waves that are like light but cannot be seen, that lie beyond the violet end of the spectrum, and that are found especially along with light from the sun

um·bil·i·cal cord *n* **:** a cord joining a fetus to its placenta

um·brel·la *n* **:** a fabric covering stretched over folding ribs attached to a rod or pole and used as a protection against rain or sun

umi·ak *n* **:** an open Eskimo boat made of a wooden frame covered with hide

um·pire *n* **:** a sports official who rules on plays

[1]**un-** *prefix* **:** not **:** IN-, NON-

[2]**un-** *prefix* **1 :** do the opposite of **:** DE- 1, DIS- 1 **2 :** deprive of, remove a specified thing from, or free or release from **3 :** completely

un·able *adj* **:** not able

un·ac·count·able *adj* **:** not accountable **:** not to be explained **:** STRANGE — **un·ac·count·ably** *adv*

un·ac·cus·tomed *adj* **:** not accustomed **:** not customary

un·af·fect·ed *adj* **1 :** not influenced or changed **2 :** free from false behavior intended to impress others **:** GENUINE — **un·af·fect·ed·ly** *adv*

un·afraid *adj* **:** not afraid

un·aid·ed *adj* **:** not aided

un·al·loyed *adj* **:** PURE 1, 3

unan·i·mous *adj* **1 :** having the same opinion **2 :** showing total agreement

un·armed *adj* **:** having no weapons or armor

un·asked *adj* **:** not asked or asked for

un·as·sum·ing *adj* **:** MODEST 1

un·at·trac·tive *adj* **:** not attractive **:** [1]PLAIN 7

un·avoid·able *adj* **:** INEVITABLE — **un·avoid·ably** *adv*

[1]**un·aware** *adv* **:** UNAWARES

[2]**unaware** *adj* **:** not aware **:** IGNORANT — **un·aware·ness** *n*

un·awares *adv* **1 :** without knowing **:** UNINTENTIONALLY **2 :** without warning **:** by surprise

un·bal·anced *adj* **1 :** not balanced **2 :** not completely sane

un·bear·able *adj* **:** seeming too great or too bad to put up with — **un·bear·ably** *adv*

un·be·com·ing *adj* **:** not becoming **:** not suitable or proper — **un·be·com·ing·ly** *adv*

un·be·lief *n* **:** lack of belief

un·be·liev·able *adj* **:** too unlikely to be believed — **un·be·liev·ably** *adv*

un·be·liev·er *n* **1 :** a person who doubts what is said **2 :** a person who has no religious beliefs

un·bend *vb* **un·bent; un·bend·ing :** RELAX 3

un·bend·ing *adj* **:** not relaxed and easy in manner

un·bi·ased *adj* **:** free from bias

un·bind *vb* **un·bound; un·bind·ing 1 :** to remove a band from **:** UNTIE **2 :** to set free

un·born *adj* **:** not yet born

un·bos·om *vb* **:** to tell someone one's own thoughts or feelings

un·bound·ed *adj* **:** having no limits

un·break·able *adj* **:** not easily broken

un·bro·ken *adj* **1 :** not damaged **:** WHOLE **2 :** not tamed for use **3 :** not interrupted

un·buck·le *vb* **un·buck·led; un·buck·ling :** to unfasten the buckle of (as a belt)

un·bur·den *vb* **1 :** to free from a burden **2 :** to free oneself from (as cares)

un·but·ton *vb* **:** to unfasten the buttons of (as a garment)

un·called–for *adj* **:** not needed or wanted **:** not proper

un·can·ny *adj* **1 :** MYSTERIOUS, EERIE **2 :** suggesting powers or abilities greater than normal for humans — **un·can·ni·ly** *adv*

un·ceas·ing *adj* **:** never stopping **:** CONTINUOUS — **un·ceas·ing·ly** *adv*

un·cer·tain *adj* **1 :** not exactly known or decided on **2 :** not known for sure **3 :** not sure **4 :** likely to change **:** not dependable — **un·cer·tain·ly** *adv*

un·cer·tain·ty *n, pl* **un·cer·tain·ties 1 :** lack of certainty **:** DOUBT **2 :** something uncertain

un·change·able *adj* **:** not changing or capable of being changed

un·changed *adj* **:** not changed

un·chang·ing *adj* **:** not changing or able to change

un·charged *adj* **:** having no electric charge

un·civ·il *adj* **:** IMPOLITE — **un·civ·il·ly** *adv*

un·civ·i·lized *adj* **1 :** not civilized **:** BARBAROUS **2 :** far away from civilization **:** WILD

un·cle *n* **1 :** the brother of one's father or mother **2 :** the husband of one's aunt

un·clean *adj* **1 :** not pure and innocent **:** WICKED **2 :** not allowed for use by religious law **3 :** DIRTY 1, FILTHY — **un·clean·ness** *n*

¹un·clean·ly *adj* **:** UNCLEAN 1, 3 — **un·clean·li·ness** *n*

²un·clean·ly *adv* **:** in an unclean manner

un·cleared *adj* **:** not cleared especially of trees or brush

Un·cle Sam *n* **:** the American government, nation, or people pictured or thought of as a person

un·clothed *adj* **:** NAKED 1, 2

un·com·fort·able *adj* **1 :** causing discomfort **2 :** feeling discomfort **:** UNEASY — **un·com·fort·ably** *adv*

un·com·mon *adj* **1 :** not often found or seen **:** UNUSUAL **2 :** not ordinary **:** REMARKABLE — **un·com·mon·ly** *adv* — **un·com·mon·ness** *n*

un·com·pro·mis·ing *adj* **:** not willing to give in even a little — **un·com·pro·mis·ing·ly** *adv*

un·con·cern *n* **:** lack of care or interest **:** INDIFFERENCE

un·con·cerned *adj* **1 :** not involved or interested **2 :** free of worry — **un·con·cern·ed·ly** *adv*

un·con·di·tion·al *adj* **:** without any special exceptions — **un·con·di·tion·al·ly** *adv*

un·con·quer·able *adj* **:** not capable of being beaten or overcome

un·con·scious *adj* **1 :** not aware **2 :** having lost consciousness **3 :** not intentional or planned — **un·con·scious·ly** *adv* — **un·con·scious·ness** *n*

un·con·sti·tu·tion·al *adj* **:** not according to the constitution (as of a government)

un·con·trol·la·ble *adj* **:** hard or impossible to control — **un·con·trol·la·bly** *adv*

un·con·trolled *adj* **:** not being controlled

un·couth *adj* **:** vulgar in conduct or speech **:** CRUDE — **un·couth·ly** *adv*

un·cov·er *vb* **1 :** to make known **2 :** to make visible by removing some covering

un·cul·ti·vat·ed *adj* **:** not cultivated

un·curl *vb* **:** to make or become straightened out from a curled position

un·cut *adj* **1 :** not cut down or cut into **2 :** not shaped by cutting

un·daunt·ed *adj* **:** not discouraged or frightened **:** FEARLESS

un·de·cid·ed *adj* **1 :** not settled **2 :** not having decided

un·de·clared *adj* **:** not announced or openly confessed

un·de·fined *adj* **:** not defined

un·de·ni·able *adj* **:** plainly true — **un·de·ni·ably** *adv*

¹un·der *adv* **1 :** in or into a position below or beneath something **2 :** below some quantity or level **3 :** so as to be covered or hidden

²under *prep* **1 :** lower than and topped or sheltered by **2 :** below the surface of **3 :** in or into such a position as to be covered or hidden by **4 :** commanded or guided by **5 :** controlled or limited by **6 :** affected or influenced by the action or effect of **7 :** within the division or grouping of **8 :** less or lower than (as in size, amount, or rank)

³under *adj* **1 :** lying or placed below or beneath **2 :** ¹SUBORDINATE 1

un·der·brush *n* **:** shrubs and small trees growing among large trees

un·der·clothes *n pl* **:** UNDERWEAR

un·der·cloth·ing *n* **:** UNDERWEAR

un·der·dog *n* **:** a person or team thought to have little chance of winning (as an election or a game)

un·der·foot *adv* **1 :** under the feet **2 :** close about one's feet **:** in one's way

un·der·gar·ment *n* **:** a garment to be worn under another

un·der·go *vb* **un·der·went; un·der·gone; un·der·go·ing :** to have (something) done or happen to oneself **:** EXPERIENCE

¹un·der·ground *adv* **1 :** beneath the surface of the earth **2 :** in or into hiding or secret operation

²un·der·ground *n* **1 :** SUBWAY 2 **2 :** a secret political movement or group

³un·der·ground *adj* **1 :** being or growing

under the surface of the ground **2 :** done or happening secretly

un·der·growth *n* **:** UNDERBRUSH

[1]**un·der·hand** *adv* **:** in a secret or dishonest manner

[2]**underhand** *adj* **1 :** done in secret or so as to deceive **2 :** made with an upward movement of the hand or arm

un·der·hand·ed *adj* **:** [2]UNDERHAND 1 — **un·der·hand·ed·ly** *adv* — **un·der·hand·ed·ness** *n*

un·der·lie *vb* **un·der·lay; un·der·lain; un·der·ly·ing 1 :** to be under **2 :** to form the foundation of **:** SUPPORT

un·der·line *vb* **un·der·lined; un·der·lin·ing 1 :** to draw a line under **2 :** EMPHASIZE

un·der·lip *n* **:** the lower lip

un·der·mine *vb* **un·der·mined; un·der·min·ing 1 :** to dig out or wear away the supporting earth beneath **2 :** to weaken secretly or little by little

[1]**un·der·neath** *prep* **:** directly under

[2]**underneath** *adv* **1 :** below a surface or object **:** BENEATH **2 :** on the lower side

un·der·nour·ished *adj* **:** given too little nourishment — **un·der·nour·ish·ment** *n*

un·der·pants *n pl* **:** pants worn under an outer garment

un·der·part *n* **:** a part lying on the lower side especially of a bird or mammal

un·der·pass *n* **:** a passage underneath something (as for a road passing under a railroad or another road)

un·der·priv·i·leged *adj* **:** having fewer advantages than others especially because of being poor

un·der·rate *vb* **un·der·rat·ed; un·der·rat·ing :** to rate too low **:** UNDERVALUE

un·der·score *vb* **un·der·scored; un·der·scor·ing :** UNDERLINE

[1]**un·der·sea** *adj* **1 :** being or done under the sea or under the surface of the sea **2 :** used under the surface of the sea

[2]**un·der·sea** *or* **un·der·seas** *adv* **:** under the surface of the sea

un·der·sell *vb* **un·der·sold; un·der·sell·ing :** to sell articles cheaper than

un·der·shirt *n* **:** a collarless garment with or without sleeves that is worn next to the body

un·der·side *n* **:** the side or surface lying underneath

un·der·skirt *n* **:** PETTICOAT

un·der·stand *vb* **un·der·stood; un·der·stand·ing 1 :** to get the meaning of **2 :** to know thoroughly **3 :** to have reason to believe **4 :** to take as meaning something not openly made known **5 :** to have a sympathetic attitude **6 :** to accept as settled

un·der·stand·able *adj* **:** possible or easy to understand — **un·der·stand·ably** *adv*

[1]**un·der·stand·ing** *n* **1 :** ability to get the meaning of and judge **2 :** AGREEMENT 2

[2]**understanding** *adj* **:** having or showing kind or favorable feelings toward others **:** SYMPATHETIC

un·der·study *n, pl* **un·der·stud·ies :** an actor who is prepared to take over another actor's part if necessary

un·der·take *vb* **un·der·took; un·der·tak·en; un·der·tak·ing 1 :** to plan or try to accomplish **2 :** to take on as a duty **:** AGREE

un·der·tak·er *n* **:** a person whose business is to prepare the dead for burial and to take charge of funerals

un·der·tak·ing *n* **1 :** the act of a person who undertakes something **2 :** the business of an undertaker **3 :** something undertaken

un·der·tone *n* **1 :** a low or quiet tone **2 :** a partly hidden feeling

un·der·tow *n* **:** a current beneath the surface of the water that moves away from or along the shore while the surface water above it moves toward the shore

un·der·val·ue *vb* **un·der·val·ued; un·der·valu·ing :** to value below the real worth

[1]**un·der·wa·ter** *adj* **:** lying, growing, worn, or operating below the surface of the water

[2]**un·der·wa·ter** *adv* **:** under the surface of the water

un·der·wear *n* **:** clothing worn next to the skin and under other clothing

un·der·weight *adj* **:** weighing less than what is normal, average, or necessary

underwent *past of* UNDERGO

un·der·world *n* **:** the world of organized crime

[1]**un·de·sir·able** *adj* **:** not desirable — **un·de·sir·ably** *adv*

[2]**undesirable** *n* **:** an undesirable person

un·de·vel·oped *adj* **:** not developed

un·di·gest·ed *adj* **:** not digested

un·dig·ni·fied *adj* **:** not dignified

un·dis·cov·ered *adj* **:** not discovered

un·dis·put·ed *adj* **:** not disputed **:** UNQUESTIONABLE

un·dis·turbed *adj* **:** not disturbed

un·do *vb* **un·did; un·done; un·do·ing; un·does 1 :** UNTIE, UNFASTEN **2 :** UNWRAP, OPEN **3 :** to destroy the effect of **4 :** to cause the ruin of

un·do·ing *n* **1 :** an act or instance of unfastening **2 :** a cause of ruin or destruction

un·done *adj* **:** not done or finished

un·doubt·ed *adj* **:** not doubted

un·doubt·ed·ly *adv* **:** without doubt **:** SURELY

un·dress *vb* **:** to remove the clothes or covering of

un·dy·ing *adj* **:** living or lasting forever **:** IMMORTAL

un·earth *vb* **1 :** to drive or draw from the earth : dig up **2 :** to bring to light : UNCOVER
un·easy *adj* **un·eas·i·er; un·eas·i·est 1 :** not easy in manner : AWKWARD **2 :** disturbed by pain or worry : RESTLESS — **un·eas·i·ly** *adv* — **un·eas·i·ness** *n*
un·ed·u·cat·ed *adj* : not educated
un·em·ployed *adj* : not employed : having no job
un·em·ploy·ment *n* : the state of being unemployed
un·end·ing *adj* : having no ending : ENDLESS — **un·end·ing·ly** *adv*
un·equal *adj* **1 :** not alike (as in size or value) **2 :** badly balanced or matched **3 :** not having the needed abilities — **un·equal·ly** *adv*
un·equaled *adj* : not equaled
un·even *adj* **1 :** ODD 2 **2 :** not level or smooth **3 :** IRREGULAR 3 **4 :** varying in quality **5 :** UNEQUAL 2 — **un·even·ly** *adv* — **un·even·ness** *n*
un·event·ful *adj* : not eventful : including no interesting or important happenings — **un·event·ful·ly** *adv*
un·ex·pect·ed *adj* : not expected — **un·ex·pect·ed·ly** *adv* — **un·ex·pect·ed·ness** *n*
un·fail·ing *adj* : not failing or likely to fail — **un·fail·ing·ly** *adv*
un·fair *adj* : not fair, honest, or just — **un·fair·ly** *adv* — **un·fair·ness** *n*
un·faith·ful *adj* : not faithful : DISLOYAL — **un·faith·ful·ly** *adv* — **un·faith·ful·ness** *n*
un·fa·mil·iar *adj* **1 :** not well known : STRANGE **2 :** not well acquainted
un·fa·mil·iar·i·ty *n* : the quality or state of being unfamiliar
un·fas·ten *vb* : to make or become loose : UNDO
un·fa·vor·able *adj* **1 :** not approving **2 :** likely to make difficult or unpleasant — **un·fa·vor·ably** *adv*
un·feel·ing *adj* **1 :** not able to feel **2 :** having no kindness or sympathy : CRUEL — **un·feel·ing·ly** *adv*
un·fin·ished *adj* : not finished
un·fit *adj* **1 :** not suitable **2 :** not qualified **3 :** UNSOUND 1, 2 — **un·fit·ness** *n*
un·fledged *adj* : not feathered or ready for flight
un·fold *vb* **1 :** to open the folds of : open up **2 :** to lay open to view : REVEAL **3 :** to develop gradually
un·fore·seen *adj* : not known beforehand
un·for·get·ta·ble *adj* : not likely to be forgotten — **un·for·get·ta·bly** *adv*
un·for·giv·able *adj* : not to be forgiven or pardoned — **un·for·giv·ably** *adv*
[1]**un·for·tu·nate** *adj* **1 :** not fortunate : UNLUCKY **2 :** not proper or suitable — **un·for·tu·nate·ly** *adv*
[2]**unfortunate** *n* : an unfortunate person
un·found·ed *adj* : being without a sound basis
un·friend·ly *adj* **un·friend·li·er; un·friend·li·est :** not friendly or favorable : HOSTILE — **un·friend·li·ness** *n*
un·fruit·ful *adj* **1 :** not bearing fruit or offspring **2 :** not producing a desired result
un·furl *vb* : to open out from a rolled or folded state
un·fur·nished *adj* : not supplied with furniture
un·gain·ly *adj* **un·gain·li·er; un·gain·li·est :** CLUMSY 1, AWKWARD — **un·gain·li·ness** *n*
un·god·ly *adj* **un·god·li·er; un·god·li·est 1 :** disobedient to or denying God : IMPIOUS **2 :** SINFUL, WICKED **3 :** not normal or bearable
un·gra·cious *adj* : not gracious or polite — **un·gra·cious·ly** *adv*
un·grate·ful *adj* : not grateful — **un·grate·ful·ly** *adv* — **un·grate·ful·ness** *n*
[1]**un·gu·late** *adj* : having hooves
[2]**ungulate** *n* : a hoofed animal
un·hand *vb* : to remove the hand from : let go
un·hap·py *adj* **un·hap·pi·er; un·hap·pi·est 1 :** not fortunate : UNLUCKY **2 :** not cheerful : SAD **3 :** not suitable — **un·hap·pi·ly** *adv* — **un·hap·pi·ness** *n*
un·health·ful *adj* : not healthful
un·healthy *adj* **un·health·i·er; un·health·i·est 1 :** not good for one's health **2 :** not in good health : SICKLY **3 :** HARMFUL, BAD — **un·health·i·ly** *adv*
un·heard *adj* : not heard
un·heard–of *adj* : not known before
un·hin·dered *adj* : not hindered : not kept back
un·hitch *vb* : to free from being hitched
un·ho·ly *adj* **un·ho·li·er; un·ho·li·est 1 :** not holy : WICKED **2 :** UNGODLY 3 — **un·ho·li·ness** *n*
un·hook *vb* **1 :** to remove from a hook **2 :** to unfasten the hooks of
un·horse *vb* **un·horsed; un·hors·ing :** to cause to fall from or as if from a horse
un·hur·ried *adj* : not hurried
uni- *prefix* : one : single
uni·corn *n* : an imaginary animal that looks like a horse with one horn in the middle of the forehead
un·iden·ti·fied *adj* : not identified
uni·fi·ca·tion *n* : the act, process, or result of unifying : the state of being unified
[1]**uni·form** *adj* **1 :** having always the same form, manner, or degree : not changing **2 :** of the same form with others — **uni·form·ly** *adv*
[2]**uniform** *n* : special clothing worn by members of a particular group (as an army)
uni·formed *adj* : dressed in uniform

uni·for·mi·ty *n, pl* **uni·for·mi·ties** : the quality or state or an instance of being uniform
uniform resource lo·ca·tor *n* : URL
uni·fy *vb* **uni·fied; uni·fy·ing** : to make into or become a unit : UNITE
un·im·por·tant *adj* : not important
un·in·hab·it·ed *adj* : not lived in or on
un·in·tel·li·gi·ble *adj* : impossible to understand
un·in·ten·tion·al *adj* : not intentional — **un·in·ten·tion·al·ly** *adv*
un·in·ter·est·ed *adj* : not interested
un·in·ter·est·ing *adj* : not attracting interest or attention
un·in·ter·rupt·ed *adj* : not interrupted : CONTINUOUS
union *n* **1** : an act or instance of uniting two or more things into one **2** : something (as a nation) formed by a combining of parts or members **3** : a device for connecting parts (as of a machine) **4** : LABOR UNION
Union *adj* : of or relating to the side favoring the federal union in the American Civil War
unique *adj* **1** : being the only one of its kind **2** : very unusual — **unique·ly** *adv* — **unique·ness** *n*
uni·son *n* **1** : sameness of musical pitch **2** : the state of being tuned or sounded at the same pitch or at an octave **3** : exact agreement
unit *n* **1** : the least whole number : ONE **2** : a fixed quantity (as of length, time, or value) used as a standard of measurement **3** : a single thing, person, or group forming part of a whole **4** : a part of a school course with a central theme
unite *vb* **unit·ed; unit·ing** **1** : to put or come together to form a single unit **2** : to bind by legal or moral ties **3** : to join in action
unit·ed *adj* **1** : made one **2** : being in agreement
uni·ty *n* **1** : the quality or state of being one **2** : the state of those who are in full agreement : HARMONY
uni·ver·sal *adj* **1** : including, covering, or taking in all or everything **2** : present or happening everywhere — **uni·ver·sal·ly** *adv*
universal resource lo·ca·tor *n* : URL
uni·verse *n* : all created things including the earth and celestial bodies viewed as making up one system
uni·ver·si·ty *n, pl* **uni·ver·si·ties** : an institution of higher learning that gives degrees in special fields (as law and medicine) as well as in the arts and sciences
un·just *adj* : not just : UNFAIR — **un·just·ly** *adv*
un·kempt *adj* **1** : not combed **2** : not neat and orderly : UNTIDY
un·kind *adj* : not kind or sympathetic — **un·kind·ly** *adv* — **un·kind·ness** *n*
[1]**un·known** *adj* : not known
[2]**unknown** *n* : one (as a quantity) that is unknown
un·lace *vb* **un·laced; un·lac·ing** : to untie the laces of
un·latch *vb* : to open by lifting a latch
un·law·ful *adj* : not lawful : ILLEGAL — **un·law·ful·ly** *adv*
un·learned *adj* **1** : not educated **2** : not based on experience : INSTINCTIVE
un·leash *vb* : to free from or as if from a leash
un·less *conj* : except on the condition that
[1]**un·like** *adj* : DIFFERENT, UNEQUAL — **un·like·ness** *n*
[2]**unlike** *prep* **1** : different from **2** : unusual for **3** : differently from
un·like·ly *adj* **un·like·li·er; un·like·li·est** **1** : not likely **2** : not promising — **un·like·li·ness** *n*
un·lim·it·ed *adj* **1** : having no restrictions or controls **2** : BOUNDLESS, INFINITE
un·load *vb* **1** : to take away or off : REMOVE **2** : to take a load from **3** : to get rid of or be freed from a load or burden
un·lock *vb* **1** : to unfasten the lock of **2** : to make known
un·looked–for *adj* : not expected
un·loose *vb* **un·loosed; un·loos·ing** **1** : to make looser : RELAX **2** : to set free
un·lucky *adj* **un·luck·i·er; un·luck·i·est** **1** : not fortunate **2** : likely to bring misfortune **3** : causing distress or regret — **un·luck·i·ly** *adv* — **un·luck·i·ness** *n*
un·man·age·able *adj* : hard or impossible to manage
un·man·ner·ly *adj* : not having or showing good manners
un·mar·ried *adj* : not married
un·mis·tak·able *adj* : impossible to mistake for anything else — **un·mis·tak·ably** *adv*
un·moved *adj* **1** : not moved by deep feelings or excitement : CALM **2** : staying in the same place or position
un·nat·u·ral *adj* **1** : not natural or normal **2** : ARTIFICIAL 3 — **un·nat·u·ral·ly** *adv* — **un·nat·u·ral·ness** *n*
un·nec·es·sary *adj* : not necessary — **un·nec·es·sar·i·ly** *adv*
un·nerve *vb* **un·nerved; un·nerv·ing** : to cause to lose confidence, courage, or self-control
un·no·tice·able *adj* : not easily noticed
un·num·bered *adj* **1** : not numbered **2** : INNUMERABLE
un·ob·served *adj* : not observed
un·oc·cu·pied *adj* **1** : not busy **2** : not occupied : EMPTY

un·of·fi·cial *adj* **:** not official — **un·of·fi·cial·ly** *adv*

un·pack *vb* **1 :** to separate and remove things that are packed **2 :** to open and remove the contents of

un·paid *adj* **:** not paid

un·paint·ed *adj* **:** not painted

un·par·al·leled *adj* **:** having no parallel or equal

un·pleas·ant *adj* **:** not pleasant — **un·pleas·ant·ly** *adv* — **un·pleas·ant·ness** *n*

un·pop·u·lar *adj* **:** not popular

un·pre·dict·able *adj* **:** impossible to predict

un·prej·u·diced *adj* **:** not prejudiced

un·pre·pared *adj* **:** not prepared

un·prin·ci·pled *adj* **:** not having or showing high moral principles

un·ques·tion·able *adj* **:** being beyond question or doubt — **un·ques·tion·ably** *adv*

un·rav·el *vb* **un·rav·eled** *or* **un·rav·elled; un·rav·el·ing** *or* **un·rav·el·ling 1 :** to separate the threads of **:** UNTANGLE **2 :** SOLVE

un·re·al *adj* **:** not real

un·rea·son·able *adj* **:** not reasonable — **un·rea·son·able·ness** *n* — **un·rea·son·ably** *adv*

un·re·lent·ing *adj* **1 :** not giving in or softening in determination **:** STERN **2 :** not letting up or weakening in energy or pace — **un·re·lent·ing·ly** *adv*

un·re·li·able *adj* **:** not reliable

un·rest *n* **:** a disturbed or uneasy state

un·righ·teous *adj* **:** not righteous — **un·righ·teous·ly** *adv* — **un·righ·teous·ness** *n*

un·ripe *adj* **:** not ripe or mature

un·ri·valed *or* **un·ri·valled** *adj* **:** having no rival

un·roll *vb* **1 :** to unwind a roll of **2 :** to become unrolled

un·ruf·fled *adj* **1 :** not upset or disturbed **2 :** [1]SMOOTH 4

un·ruly *adj* **un·rul·i·er; un·rul·i·est :** not yielding easily to rule or restriction — **un·rul·i·ness** *n*

un·safe *adj* **:** exposed or exposing to danger

un·san·i·tary *adj* **:** not sanitary

un·sat·is·fac·to·ry *adj* **:** not satisfactory — **un·sat·is·fac·to·ri·ly** *adv*

un·sat·is·fied *adj* **:** not satisfied

un·say *vb* **un·said; un·say·ing :** to take back (something said)

un·schooled *adj* **:** not trained or taught

un·sci·en·tif·ic *adj* **:** not scientific — **un·sci·en·tif·i·cal·ly** *adv*

un·scram·ble *vb* **un·scram·bled; un·scram·bling :** to make orderly or clear again

un·screw *vb* **1 :** to remove the screws from **2 :** to loosen or withdraw by turning

un·scru·pu·lous *adj* **:** not scrupulous — **un·scru·pu·lous·ly** *adv*

un·seal *vb* **:** to break or remove the seal of **:** OPEN

un·sea·son·able *adj* **:** happening or coming at the wrong time — **un·sea·son·ably** *adv*

un·sea·soned *adj* **:** not made ready or fit for use (as by the passage of time)

un·seat *vb* **1 :** to throw from one's seat **2 :** to remove from a position of authority

un·seem·ly *adj* **un·seem·li·er; un·seem·li·est :** not polite or proper

un·seen *adj* **:** not seen **:** INVISIBLE

un·self·ish *adj* **:** not selfish — **un·self·ish·ly** *adv* — **un·self·ish·ness** *n*

un·set·tle *vb* **un·set·tled; un·set·tling :** to disturb the quiet or order of **:** UPSET

un·set·tled *adj* **1 :** not staying the same **2 :** not calm **3 :** not able to make up one's mind **:** DOUBTFUL **4 :** not paid **5 :** not taken over and lived in by settlers

un·shaped *adj* **:** imperfect especially in form

un·sheathe *vb* **un·sheathed; un·sheath·ing :** to draw from or as if from a sheath

un·sight·ly *adj* **:** not pleasant to look at **:** UGLY — **un·sight·li·ness** *n*

un·skilled *adj* **1 :** not skilled **2 :** not needing skill

un·skill·ful *adj* **:** not skillful **:** not having skill — **un·skill·ful·ly** *adv*

un·sound *adj* **1 :** not healthy or in good condition **2 :** being or having a mind that is not normal **3 :** not firmly made or placed **4 :** not fitting or true — **un·sound·ly** *adv* — **un·sound·ness** *n*

un·speak·able *adj* **1 :** impossible to express in words **2 :** extremely bad — **un·speak·ably** *adv*

un·spec·i·fied *adj* **:** not specified

un·spoiled *adj* **:** not spoiled

un·sta·ble *adj* **:** not stable

un·steady *adj* **un·stead·i·er; un·stead·i·est :** not steady **:** UNSTABLE — **un·stead·i·ly** *adv*

un·stressed *adj* **:** not stressed

un·suc·cess·ful *adj* **:** not successful — **un·suc·cess·ful·ly** *adv*

un·sup·port·ed *adj* **1 :** not supported or proved **2 :** not held up

un·sur·passed *adj* **:** not surpassed (as in excellence)

un·sus·pect·ing *adj* **:** having no suspicion **:** TRUSTING

un·tan·gle *vb* **un·tan·gled; un·tan·gling 1 :** to remove a tangle from **2 :** to straighten out

un·tanned *adj* **:** not put through a tanning process

un·think·able *adj* **:** not to be thought of or considered as possible

un·think·ing *adj* **:** not taking thought **:** HEEDLESS

un·ti·dy *adj* **un·ti·di·er; un·ti·di·est** : not neat — **un·ti·di·ly** *adv* — **un·ti·di·ness** *n*
un·tie *vb* **un·tied; un·ty·ing** *or* **un·tie·ing** : to free from something that ties, fastens, or holds back
[1]**un·til** *prep* : up to the time of
[2]**until** *conj* : up to the time that
[1]**un·time·ly** *adv* : before a good or proper time
[2]**untimely** *adj* **1** : happening or done before the expected, natural, or proper time **2** : coming at the wrong time — **un·time·li·ness** *n*
un·tir·ing *adj* : not making or becoming tired : TIRELESS — **un·tir·ing·ly** *adv*
un·to *prep* : [1]TO
un·told *adj* **1** : not told or made public **2** : not counted : VAST
un·to·ward *adj* : causing trouble or unhappiness : UNLUCKY
un·trou·bled *adj* : not troubled : free from worry
un·true *adj* **1** : not faithful : DISLOYAL **2** : not correct : FALSE — **un·tru·ly** *adv*
un·truth *n* **1** : the state of being false **2** : [3]LIE
un·truth·ful *adj* : not containing or telling the truth : FALSE — **un·truth·ful·ly** *adv* — **un·truth·ful·ness** *n*
un·used *adj* **1** : not accustomed **2** : not having been used before **3** : not being used
un·usu·al *adj* : not usual — **un·usu·al·ly** *adv*
un·ut·ter·able *adj* : being beyond one's powers of description
un·veil *vb* : to show or make known to the public for the first time
un·voiced *adj* : VOICELESS
un·want·ed *adj* : not wanted
un·wary *adj* **un·war·i·er; un·war·i·est** : easily fooled or surprised — **un·war·i·ness** *n*
un·washed *adj* : not having been washed : DIRTY
un·wea·ried *adj* : not tired
un·well *adj* : being in poor health
un·whole·some *adj* : not good for bodily, mental, or moral health
un·wieldy *adj* : hard to handle or control because of size or weight — **un·wield·i·ness** *n*
un·will·ing *adj* : not willing — **un·will·ing·ly** *adv* — **un·will·ing·ness** *n*
un·wind *vb* **un·wound; un·wind·ing** **1** : UNROLL **2** : RELAX 3
un·wise *adj* : not wise : FOOLISH — **un·wise·ly** *adv*
un·wor·thy *adj* **un·wor·thi·er; un·wor·thi·est** : not worthy — **un·wor·thi·ly** *adv* — **un·wor·thi·ness** *n*
un·wrap *vb* **un·wrapped; un·wrap·ping** : to remove the wrapping from
un·writ·ten *adj* : not in writing : followed by custom
un·yield·ing *adj* **1** : not soft or flexible : HARD **2** : showing or having firmness or determination
[1]**up** *adv* **1** : in or to a higher position : away from the center of the earth **2** : from beneath a surface (as ground or water) **3** : from below the horizon **4** : in or into a vertical position **5** : out of bed **6** : with greater force **7** : in or into a better or more advanced state **8** : so as to make more active **9** : into being or knowledge **10** : for discussion **11** : into the hands of another **12** : COMPLETELY **13** — used to show completeness **14** : into storage **15** : so as to be closed **16** : so as to approach or arrive **17** : in or into pieces **18** : to a stop
[2]**up** *adj* **1** : risen above the horizon or ground **2** : being out of bed **3** : unusually high **4** : having been raised or built **5** : moving or going upward **6** : being on one's feet and busy **7** : well prepared **8** : going on **9** : at an end **10** : well informed
[3]**up** *prep* **1** : to, toward, or at a higher point of **2** : to or toward the beginning of **3** : [1]ALONG 1
[4]**up** *n* : a period or state of doing well
[5]**up** *vb* **upped; up·ping** **1** : to act suddenly or surprisingly **2** : to make or become higher
up·beat *n* : a beat in music that is not accented and especially one just before a downbeat
up·braid *vb* : to criticize or scold severely
up·bring·ing *n* : the process of raising and training
up·com·ing *adj* : coming soon
up·draft *n* : an upward movement of gas (as air)
up·end *vb* : to set, stand, or rise on end
up·grade *vb* **up·grad·ed; up·grad·ing** **1:** to raise to a higher grade or position **2:** to improve or replace old software or an old device for increased usefulness
up·heav·al *n* : a period of great change or violent disorder
[1]**up·hill** *adv* **1** : in an upward direction **2** : against difficulties
[2]**up·hill** *adj* **1** : going up **2** : DIFFICULT 1
up·hold *vb* **up·held; up·hold·ing** **1** : to give support to **2** : to lift up
up·hol·ster *vb* : to provide with or as if with upholstery — **up·hol·ster·er** *n*
up·hol·stery *n, pl* **up·hol·ster·ies** : materials used to make a soft covering for a seat
up·keep *n* : the act or cost of keeping something in good condition
up·land *n* : high land usually far from a coast or sea
[1]**up·lift** *vb* **1** : to lift up **2** : to improve the moral, mental, or bodily condition of
[2]**up·lift** *n* : an act, process, or result of uplifting

up·on *prep* : [1]ON 1, 2, 3, 4, 8
[1]**up·per** *adj* **1** : higher in position or rank **2** : farther inland
[2]**upper** *n* : something (as the parts of a shoe above the sole) that is upper
upper hand *n* : ADVANTAGE 1
up·per·most *adj* **1** : farthest up **2** : being in the most important position
up·raise *vb* **up·raised; up·rais·ing** : to raise or lift up
[1]**up·right** *adj* **1** : VERTICAL 2 **2** : straight in posture **3** : having or showing high moral standards — **up·right·ly** *adv* — **up·right·ness** *n*
[2]**upright** *n* **1** : the state of being upright **2** : something that is upright
up·rise *vb* **up·rose; up·ris·en; up·ris·ing** : [1]RISE 1, 2, 7
up·ris·ing *n* : REBELLION
up·roar *n* : a state of commotion, excitement, or violent disturbance
up·root *vb* **1** : to take out by or as if by pulling up by the roots **2** : to take, send, or force away from a country or a traditional home
[1]**up·set** *vb* **up·set; up·set·ting** **1** : to force or be forced out of the usual position : OVERTURN **2** : to worry or make unhappy **3** : to make somewhat ill **4** : to cause confusion in **5** : to defeat unexpectedly
[2]**up·set** *n* : an act or result of upsetting : a state of being upset
up·shot *n* : the final result
up·side *n* : the upper side or part
up·side down *adv* **1** : in such a way that the upper part is underneath and the lower part is on top **2** : in or into great confusion
upside–down *adj* **1** : having the upper part underneath and the lower part on top **2** : showing great confusion
[1]**up·stairs** *adv* : up the stairs : on or to an upper floor
[2]**up·stairs** *adj* : being on or relating to an upper floor
[3]**up·stairs** *n* : the part of a building above the ground floor
up·stand·ing *adj* : HONEST 2
up·start *n* : a person who gains quick or unexpected success and who makes a great show of pride in that success
up·stream *adv* : at or toward the beginning of a stream
up·swing *n* : a great increase or rise
up to *prep* **1** : as far as **2** : in accordance with **3** : to the limit of
up–to–date *adj* **1** : lasting up to the present time **2** : knowing, being, or making use of what is new or recent
up·town *adv* : to, toward, or in what is thought of as the upper part of a town or city
[1]**up·turn** *vb* : to turn upward or up or over
[2]**up·turn** *n* : an upward turning
[1]**up·ward** *or* **up·wards** *adv* **1** : in a direction from lower to higher **2** : toward a higher or better state **3** : toward a greater amount or a higher number or rate
[2]**upward** *adj* : turned toward or being in a higher place or level — **up·ward·ly** *adv*
up·wind *adv or adj* : in the direction from which the wind is blowing
ura·ni·um *n* : a radioactive metallic chemical element used as a source of atomic energy
Ura·nus *n* : the planet that is seventh in order of distance from the sun and has a diameter of about 47,000 kilometers
ur·ban *adj* : of, relating to, or being a city
ur·chin *n* **1** : a mischievous or disrespectful youngster **2** : SEA URCHIN
-ure *suffix* **1** : act : process **2** : office : duty **3** : body performing an office or duty
urea *n* : a compound of nitrogen that is the chief solid substance dissolved in the urine of a mammal and is formed by the breaking down of protein
[1]**urge** *vb* **urged; urg·ing** **1** : to try to get (something) accepted : argue in favor of **2** : to try to convince **3** : [2]FORCE 1, DRIVE
[2]**urge** *n* : a strong desire
ur·gen·cy *n* : the quality or state of being urgent
ur·gent *adj* **1** : calling for immediate action **2** : having or showing a sense of urgency — **ur·gent·ly** *adv*
uri·nal *n* **1** : a container for urine **2** : a place for urinating
uri·nary *adj* : of or relating to urine or the organs producing it
uri·nate *vb* **uri·nat·ed; uri·nat·ing** : to discharge urine
uri·na·tion *n* : the act of urinating
urine *n* : the yellowish liquid produced by the kidneys and given off from the body as waste
URL *n* : the address of a computer or a document on the Internet
urn *n* **1** : a container usually in the form of a vase resting on a stand **2** : a closed container with a faucet used for serving a hot beverage
us *pron, objective case of* WE
us·able *adj* : suitable or fit for use
us·age *n* **1** : usual way of doing things **2** : the way in which words and phrases are actually used **3** : the action of using : USE
[1]**use** *n* **1** : the act of using something **2** : the fact or state of being used **3** : way of using **4** : the ability or power to use something **5** : the quality or state of being useful **6** : a reason or need to use **7** : LIKING
[2]**use** *vb* **used; us·ing** **1** : to put into action or service : make use of **2** : to take into the

body **3 :** to do something by means of **4 :** to behave toward : TREAT **5** — used with *to* to show a former custom, fact, or state — **us·er** *n*

used *adj* **1 :** SECONDHAND 1 **2 :** having the habit of doing or putting up with something

use·ful *adj* : that can be put to use : USABLE — **use·ful·ly** *adv* — **use·ful·ness** *n*

use·less *adj* : being of or having no use — **use·less·ly** *adv* — **use·less·ness** *n*

us·er–friend·ly *adj* : easy to learn, use, understand, or deal with — **user–friendliness** *n*

[1]**ush·er** *n* : a person who shows people to seats (as in a theater)

[2]**usher** *vb* **1 :** to show to a place as an usher **2 :** to come before as if to lead in or announce

usu·al *adj* : done, found, used or existing most of the time — **usu·al·ly** *adv*

usurp *vb* : to take and hold unfairly or by force — **usurp·er** *n*

uten·sil *n* **1 :** a tool or container used in a home and especially a kitchen **2 :** a useful tool

uter·us *n, pl* **uteri** : the organ of a female mammal in which the young develop before birth

util·i·ty *n, pl* **util·i·ties** **1 :** the quality or state of being useful **2 :** a business that supplies a public service (as electricity or gas) under special regulation by the government

uti·li·za·tion *n* : the action of utilizing : the state of being utilized

uti·lize *vb* **uti·lized; uti·liz·ing** : to make use of especially for a certain job

[1]**ut·most** *adj* : of the greatest or highest degree or amount

[2]**utmost** *n* : the most possible

[1]**ut·ter** *adj* : in every way : TOTAL — **ut·ter·ly** *adv*

[2]**utter** *vb* **1 :** to send forth as a sound **2 :** to express in usually spoken words

ut·ter·ance *n* : something uttered

V

v *n, pl* **v's** *or* **vs** *often cap* **1 :** the twenty-second letter of the English alphabet **2 :** five in Roman numerals

va·can·cy *n, pl* **va·can·cies** **1 :** something (as an office or hotel room) that is vacant **2 :** empty space **3 :** the state of being vacant

va·cant *adj* **1 :** not filled, used, or lived in **2 :** free from duties or care **3 :** showing a lack of thought : FOOLISH

va·cate *vb* **va·cat·ed; va·cat·ing** : to leave vacant

[1]**va·ca·tion** *n* **1 :** a period during which activity (as of a school) is stopped for a time **2 :** a period spent away from home or business in travel or amusement

[2]**vacation** *vb* : to take or spend a vacation — **va·ca·tion·er** *n*

vac·ci·nate *vb* **vac·ci·nat·ed; vac·ci·nat·ing** : to inoculate with weak germs in order to protect against a disease

vac·ci·na·tion *n* **1 :** the act of vaccinating **2 :** the scar left by vaccinating

vac·cine *n* : a material (as one containing killed or weakened bacteria or virus) used in vaccinating

vac·il·late *vb* **vac·il·lat·ed; vac·il·lat·ing** : to hesitate between courses or opinions : be unable to choose

[1]**vac·u·um** *n, pl* **vac·u·ums** *or* **vac·ua** **1 :** a space completely empty of matter **2 :** a space from which most of the air has been removed (as by a pump) **3 :** VACUUM CLEANER

[2]**vacuum** *adj* : of, containing, producing, or using a partial vacuum

[3]**vacuum** *vb* : to use a vacuum cleaner on

vacuum bottle *n* : THERMOS

vacuum cleaner *n* : an electrical appliance for cleaning (as floors or rugs) by suction

vacuum tube *n* : an electron tube having a high vacuum

[1]**vag·a·bond** *adj* : moving from place to place without a fixed home

[2]**vagabond** *n* : a person who leads a vagabond life

va·gi·na *n* : a canal leading out from the uterus

[1]**va·grant** *n* : a person who has no steady job and wanders from place to place

[2]**vagrant** *adj* **1 :** wandering about from place to place **2 :** having no fixed course

vague *adj* **vagu·er; vagu·est** **1 :** not clearly expressed **2 :** not clearly understood **3 :** not clearly outlined : SHADOWY — **vague·ly** *adv* — **vague·ness** *n*

vain *adj* **1 :** having no success **2 :** proud of one's looks or abilities — **vain·ly** *adv* — **in vain** **1 :** without success **2 :** in an unholy way

vain·glo·ri·ous *adj* : being vain and boastful — **vain·glo·ri·ous·ly** *adv* — **vain·glo·ri·ous·ness** *n*

vain·glo·ry *n* : too much pride especially in what one has done

vale *n* : VALLEY

val·e·dic·to·ri·an *n* : a student usually of the highest standing in a class who gives the farewell speech at the graduation ceremonies

val·en·tine *n* **1 :** a sweetheart given something as a sign of affection on Saint Valentine's Day **2 :** a greeting card or gift sent or given on Saint Valentine's Day
va·let *n* **:** a male servant or hotel employee who takes care of a man's clothes and does personal services
val·iant *adj* **1 :** boldly brave **2 :** done with courage **:** HEROIC — **val·iant·ly** *adv*
val·id *adj* **1 :** legally binding **2 :** based on truth or fact — **val·id·ly** *adv*
val·i·date *vb* **val·i·dat·ed; val·i·dat·ing :** to make valid
va·lid·i·ty *n* **:** the quality or state of being valid
va·lise *n* **:** TRAVELING BAG
val·ley *n, pl* **valleys :** an area of lowland between ranges of hills or mountains
val·or *n* **:** COURAGE
val·or·ous *adj* **:** having or showing valor **:** BRAVE — **val·or·ous·ly** *adv*
¹valu·able *adj* **1 :** worth a large amount of money **2 :** of great use or service
²valuable *n* **:** a personal possession (as a jewel) of great value
¹val·ue *n* **1 :** a fair return in goods, services, or money for something exchanged **2 :** worth in money **3 :** worth, usefulness, or importance in comparison with something else **4 :** a principle or quality that is valuable or desirable — **val·ue·less** *adj*
²value *vb* **val·ued; val·u·ing 1 :** to estimate the worth of **2 :** to think highly of
valve *n* **1 :** a structure in a tube of the body (as a vein) that closes temporarily to prevent passage of material or allows movement of a fluid in one direction only **2 :** a mechanical device by which the flow of liquid, gas, or loose material may be controlled by a movable part **3 :** a device on a brass musical instrument that changes the pitch of the tone **4 :** one of the separate pieces that make up the shell of some animals (as clams) and are often hinged — **valve·less** *adj*
vam·pire *n* **:** the body of a dead person believed to come from the grave at night and suck the blood of sleeping persons
vampire bat *n* **:** a bat of tropical America that feeds on the blood of birds and mammals often including domestic animals
¹van *n* **:** VANGUARD
²van *n* **:** a usually closed wagon or truck for moving goods or animals
va·na·di·um *n* **:** a metallic chemical element used in making a strong alloy of steel
van·dal *n* **:** a person who destroys or damages property on purpose
van·dal·ism *n* **:** intentional destruction of or damage to property
van·dal·ize *vb* **van·dal·ized; van·dal·iz·ing:** to destroy or damage property on purpose
vane *n* **1 :** WEATHER VANE **2 :** a flat or curved surface that turns around a center when moved by wind or water
van·guard *n* **1 :** the troops moving at the front of an army **2 :** FOREFRONT
va·nil·la *n* **:** a substance extracted from vanilla beans and used as a flavoring for sweet foods and beverages
vanilla bean *n* **:** the long pod of a tropical American climbing orchid from which vanilla is extracted
van·ish *vb* **:** to pass from sight or existence **:** DISAPPEAR
van·i·ty *n, pl* **van·i·ties 1 :** something that is vain **2 :** the quality or fact of being vain **3 :** a small box for cosmetics
van·quish *vb* **:** OVERCOME 1
va·por *n* **1 :** fine bits (as of fog or smoke) floating in the air and clouding it **2 :** a substance in the form of a gas
va·por·ize *vb* **va·por·ized; va·por·iz·ing :** to turn from a liquid or solid into vapor — **va·por·iz·er** *n*
¹var·i·able *adj* **1 :** able to change **:** likely to be changed **:** CHANGEABLE **2 :** having differences **3 :** not true to type — **var·i·able·ness** *n* — **var·i·ably** *adv*
²variable *n* **1 :** something that is variable **2 :** PLACEHOLDER
var·i·ant *n* **1 :** an individual that shows variation from a type **2 :** one of two or more different spellings or pronunciations of a word
var·i·a·tion *n* **1 :** a change in form, position, or condition **2 :** amount of change or difference **3 :** departure from what is usual to a group
var·ied *adj* **1 :** having many forms or types **2 :** VARIEGATED 2
var·ie·gat·ed *adj* **1 :** having patches, stripes, or marks of different colors **2 :** full of variety
va·ri·ety *n, pl* **va·ri·et·ies 1 :** the quality or state of having different forms or types **2 :** a collection of different things **:** ASSORTMENT **3 :** something differing from others of the class to which it belongs **4 :** entertainment made up of performances (as dances and songs) that follow one another and are not related
var·i·ous *adj* **1 :** of different kinds **2 :** different one from another **:** UNLIKE **3 :** made up of an indefinite number greater than one
¹var·nish *n* **:** a liquid that is spread on a surface and dries into a hard coating
²varnish *vb* **:** to cover with or as if with varnish
var·si·ty *n, pl* **var·si·ties :** the main team that represents a school or club in contests
vary *vb* **var·ied; vary·ing 1 :** to make a partial change in **2 :** to make or be of different

kinds **3** : DEVIATE **4** : to differ from the usual members of a group

vas·cu·lar *adj* : of, relating to, containing, or being bodily vessels

vase *n* : an often round container of greater depth than width used chiefly for ornament or for flowers

vas·sal *n* : a person in the Middle Ages who received protection and land from a lord in return for loyalty and service

vast *adj* : very great in size or amount — **vast·ly** *adv* — **vast·ness** *n*

vat *n* : a large container (as a tub) especially for holding liquids in manufacturing processes

vaude·ville *n* : theatrical entertainment made up of songs, dances, and comic acts

[1]**vault** *n* **1** : an arched structure of stone or concrete forming a ceiling or roof **2** : an arch suggesting a vault **3** : a room or compartment for storage or safekeeping **4** : a burial chamber

[2]**vault** *vb* : to leap with the aid of the hands or a pole

[3]**vault** *n* : [2]LEAP

VCR *n* : a device for recording (as television programs) on videocassettes and playing them back

veal *n* : a young calf or its flesh for use as meat

vec·tor *n* : a creature (as a fly) that carries disease germs

vee·jay *n* : an announcer of a program (as on television) that features music videos

veer *vb* : to change direction or course

vee·ry *n, pl* **veeries** : a common brownish woodland thrush of the eastern United States

[1]**veg·e·ta·ble** *adj* **1** : of, relating to, or made up of plants **2** : gotten from plants

[2]**vegetable** *n* **1** : [2]PLANT 1 **2** : a plant or plant part grown for use as human food and usually eaten with the main part of a meal

veg·e·tar·i·an *n* : a person who lives on plants and their products

veg·e·ta·tion *n* : plant life or cover (as of an area)

veg·e·ta·tive *adj* **1** : of, relating to, or functioning in nutrition and growth rather than reproduction **2** : of, relating to, or involving reproduction by other than sexual means

ve·he·mence *n* : the quality or state of being vehement

ve·he·ment *adj* **1** : showing great force or energy **2** : highly emotional — **ve·he·ment·ly** *adv*

ve·hi·cle *n* **1** : a means by which something is expressed, achieved, or shown **2** : something used to transport persons or goods

[1]**veil** *n* **1** : a piece of cloth or net worn usually by women over the head and shoulders and sometimes over the face **2** : something that covers or hides like a veil

[2]**veil** *vb* : to cover or provide with a veil

vein *n* **1** : a long narrow opening in rock filled with mineral matter **2** : one of the blood vessels that carry the blood back to the heart **3** : one of the bundles of fine tubes that make up the framework of a leaf and carry food, water, and nutrients in the plant **4** : one of the thickened parts that support the wing of an insect **5** : a streak of different color or texture (as in marble) **6** : a style of expression — **veined** *adj*

veld *or* **veldt** *n* : an area of grassy land especially in southern Africa

ve·loc·i·ty *n, pl* **ve·loc·i·ties** : quickness of motion : SPEED

[1]**vel·vet** *n* : a fabric with short soft raised fibers

[2]**velvet** *adj* **1** : made of or covered with velvet **2** : VELVETY

vel·vety *adj* : soft and smooth like velvet

ve·na·tion *n* : an arrangement or system of veins

vend *vb* : to sell or offer for sale — **vend·er** *or* **ven·dor** *n*

vending machine *n* : a machine for selling merchandise operated by putting a coin or coins into a slot

[1]**ve·neer** *n* **1** : a thin layer of wood bonded to other wood usually to provide a finer surface or a stronger structure **2** : a protective or ornamental facing (as of brick)

[2]**veneer** *vb* : to cover with a veneer

ven·er·a·ble *adj* **1** : deserving to be venerated — often used as a religious title **2** : deserving honor or respect

ven·er·ate *vb* **ven·er·at·ed; ven·er·at·ing** : to show deep respect for

ven·er·a·tion *n* **1** : the act of venerating : the state of being venerated **2** : a feeling of deep respect

ve·ne·re·al *adj* : of or relating to sexual intercourse or to diseases that pass from person to person by it

ve·ne·tian blind *n* : a blind having thin horizontal slats that can be adjusted to keep out light or to let light come in between them

ven·geance *n* : punishment given in return for an injury or offense

ven·i·son *n* : the flesh of a deer used as food

ven·om *n* : poisonous matter produced by an animal (as a snake) and passed to a victim usually by a bite or sting

ven·om·ous *adj* : having or producing venom : POISONOUS

ve·nous *adj* : of, relating to, or full of veins

[1]**vent** *vb* **1** : to provide with an outlet **2** : to serve as an outlet for **3** : [3]EXPRESS 1

[2]**vent** *n* **1 :** OUTLET 1, 2 **2 :** an opening for the escape of a gas or liquid

ven·ti·late *vb* **ven·ti·lat·ed; ven·ti·lat·ing 1 :** to discuss freely and openly **2 :** to let in air and especially a current of fresh air **3 :** to provide with ventilation

ven·ti·la·tion *n* **1 :** the act or process of ventilating **2 :** a system or means of providing fresh air

ven·ti·la·tor *n* **:** a device for letting in fresh air or driving out bad or stale air

ven·tral *adj* **:** of, relating to, or being on or near the surface of the body that in man is the front but in most animals is the lower surface

ven·tri·cle *n* **:** the part of the heart from which blood passes into the arteries

ven·tril·o·quist *n* **:** a person skilled in speaking in such a way that the voice seems to come from a source other than the speaker

[1]**ven·ture** *vb* **ven·tured; ven·tur·ing 1 :** to expose to risk **2 :** to face the risks and dangers of **3 :** to offer at the risk of being criticized **4 :** to go ahead in spite of danger

[2]**venture** *n* **:** a task or an act involving chance, risk, or danger

ven·ture·some *adj* **1 :** tending to take risks **2 :** involving risk — **ven·ture·some·ly** *adv* — **ven·ture·some·ness** *n*

ven·tur·ous *adj* **:** VENTURESOME — **ven·tur·ous·ly** *adv* — **ven·tur·ous·ness** *n*

Ve·nus *n* **:** the planet that is second in order of distance from the sun and has a diameter of about 12,200 kilometers

ve·ran·da *or* **ve·ran·dah** *n* **:** a long porch extending along one or more sides of a building

verb *n* **:** a word that expresses an act, occurrence, or state of being

[1]**ver·bal** *adj* **1 :** of, relating to, or consisting of words **2 :** of, relating to, or formed from a verb **3 :** spoken rather than written — **ver·bal·ly** *adv*

[2]**verbal** *n* **:** a word that combines characteristics of a verb with those of a noun or adjective

ver·be·na *n* **:** a garden plant with fragrant leaves and heads of white, pink, red, blue, or purple flowers with five petals

ver·dant *adj* **:** green with growing plants — **ver·dant·ly** *adv*

ver·dict *n* **1 :** the decision reached by a jury **2 :** JUDGMENT 2, OPINION

ver·dure *n* **:** green vegetation

[1]**verge** *n* **1 :** something that borders, limits, or bounds **:** EDGE **2 :** THRESHOLD 2, BRINK

[2]**verge** *vb* **verged; verg·ing :** to come near to being

ver·i·fi·ca·tion *n* **:** the act or process of verifying **:** the state of being verified

ver·i·fy *vb* **ver·i·fied; ver·i·fy·ing 1 :** to prove to be true or correct **:** CONFIRM **2 :** to check or test the accuracy of

ver·mi·cel·li *n* **:** a food similar to but thinner than spaghetti

ver·min *n, pl* **vermin :** small common harmful or objectionable animals (as fleas or mice) that are difficult to get rid of

ver·sa·tile *adj* **1 :** able to do many different kinds of things **2 :** having many uses

ver·sa·til·i·ty *n* **:** the quality or state of being versatile

verse *n* **1 :** a line of writing in which words are arranged in a rhythmic pattern **2 :** writing in which words are arranged in a rhythmic pattern **3 :** STANZA **4 :** one of the short parts of a chapter in the Bible

versed *adj* **:** having knowledge or skill as a result of experience, study, or practice

ver·sion *n* **1 :** a translation especially of the Bible **2 :** an account or description from a certain point of view

ver·sus *prep* **:** AGAINST 1

ver·te·bra *n, pl* **ver·te·brae :** one of the bony sections making up the backbone

[1]**ver·te·brate** *adj* **1 :** having vertebrae or a backbone **2 :** of or relating to the vertebrates

[2]**vertebrate** *n* **:** any of a large group of animals that includes the fishes, amphibians, reptiles, birds, and mammals all of which have a backbone extending down the back of the body

ver·tex *n, pl* **ver·ti·ces** *or* **ver·tex·es 1 :** the point opposite to and farthest from the base of a geometrical figure **2 :** the common endpoint of the sides of an angle

[1]**ver·ti·cal** *adj* **1 :** directly overhead **2 :** rising straight up and down from a level surface — **ver·ti·cal·ly** *adv*

[2]**vertical** *n* **:** something (as a line or plane) that is vertical

ver·ti·go *n, pl* **ver·ti·goes** *or* **ver·ti·gos :** a dizzy state

[1]**very** *adj* **1 :** [2]EXACT, PRECISE **2 :** exactly suitable or necessary **3 :** MERE, BARE **4 :** exactly the same

[2]**very** *adv* **1 :** to a great degree **:** EXTREMELY **2 :** in actual fact **:** TRULY

ves·pers *n pl, often cap* **:** a late afternoon or evening church service

ves·sel *n* **1 :** a hollow utensil (as a cup or bowl) for holding something **2 :** a craft larger than a rowboat for navigation of the water **3 :** a tube (as an artery) in which a body fluid is contained and carried or circulated

[1]**vest** *vb* **1 :** to place or give into the possession or control of some person or authority **2 :** to clothe in vestments

²vest *n* **:** a sleeveless garment usually worn under a suit coat

ves·ti·bule *n* **:** a hall or room between the outer door and the inside part of a building

ves·tige *n* **:** a tiny amount or visible sign of something lost or vanished **:** TRACE

ves·ti·gial *adj* **:** of, relating to, or being a vestige

vest·ment *n* **:** an outer garment especially for wear during ceremonies or by an official

¹vet *n* **:** VETERINARIAN

²vet *n* **:** ¹VETERAN 2

¹vet·er·an *n* **1 :** a person who has had long experience **2 :** a former member of the armed forces especially in war

²veteran *adj* **:** having gained skill through experience

vet·er·i·nar·i·an *n* **:** a doctor who treats diseases and injuries of animals

¹vet·er·i·nary *adj* **:** of, relating to, or being the medical care of animals and especially domestic animals

²veterinary *n, pl* **vet·er·i·nar·ies :** VETERINARIAN

¹ve·to *n, pl* **vetoes 1 :** a forbidding of something by a person in authority **2 :** the power of a president, governor, or mayor to prevent something from becoming law

²veto *vb* **1 :** FORBID, PROHIBIT **2 :** to prevent from becoming law by use of a veto

vex *vb* **1 :** to bring trouble, distress, or worry to **2 :** to annoy by small irritations

vex·a·tion *n* **1 :** the quality or state of being vexed **2 :** the act of vexing **3 :** a cause of trouble or worry

via *prep* **:** by way of

vi·a·ble *adj* **1 :** capable of living or growing **2 :** possible to use or apply

via·duct *n* **:** a bridge for carrying a road or railroad over something (as a gorge or highway)

vi·al *n* **:** a small container (as for medicines) that is usually made of glass or plastic

vi·brant *adj* **:** having or giving the sense of life, vigor, or action — **vi·brant·ly** *adv*

vi·brate *vb* **vi·brat·ed; vi·brat·ing :** to swing or cause to swing back and forth

vi·bra·tion *n* **1 :** a rapid motion (as of a stretched cord) back and forth **2 :** the action of vibrating **:** the state of being vibrated **3 :** a trembling motion

vi·bur·num *n* **:** any of a group of shrubs often grown for their broad clusters of usually white flowers

vic·ar *n* **1 :** a minister in charge of a church who serves under the authority of another minister **2 :** a church official who takes the place of or represents a higher official

vi·car·i·ous *adj* **:** experienced or understood as if happening to oneself — **vi·car·i·ous·ly** *adv* — **vi·car·i·ous·ness** *n*

vice *n* **1 :** evil conduct or habits **2 :** a moral fault or weakness

vice- *prefix* **:** one that takes the place of

vice admiral *n* **:** a commissioned officer in the Navy or Coast Guard ranking above a rear admiral

vice pres·i·dent *n* **:** an official (as of a government) whose rank is next below that of the president and who takes the place of the president when necessary

vice ver·sa *adv* **:** with the order turned around

vi·cin·i·ty *n, pl* **vi·cin·i·ties 1 :** the state of being close **2 :** a surrounding area **:** NEIGHBORHOOD

vi·cious *adj* **1 :** doing evil things **:** WICKED **2 :** very dangerous **3 :** filled with or showing unkind feelings — **vi·cious·ly** *adv* — **vi·cious·ness** *n*

vic·tim *n* **1 :** a living being offered as a religious sacrifice **2 :** an individual injured or killed (as by disease) **3 :** a person who is cheated, fooled, or hurt by another

vic·tim·ize *vb* **vic·tim·ized; vic·tim·iz·ing :** to make a victim of

vic·tor *n* **:** WINNER, CONQUEROR

vic·to·ri·ous *adj* **:** having won a victory — **vic·to·ri·ous·ly** *adv*

vic·to·ry *n, pl* **vic·to·ries 1 :** the defeating of an enemy or opponent **2 :** success in a struggle against difficulties

vict·ual *n* **1 :** food fit for humans **2 victuals** *pl* **:** supplies of food

vi·cu·ña *or* **vi·cu·na** *n* **:** a wild animal of the Andes that is related to the llama and produces a fine wool

¹vid·eo *n* **1 :** TELEVISION **2 :** the visual part of television **3 :** ¹VIDEOTAPE 1 **4 :** a videotaped performance of a song

²video *adj* **1 :** relating to or used in the sending or receiving of television images **2 :** being, relating to, or involving images on a television screen or computer display

video camera *n* **:** a camera (as a camcorder) that records video and usually also audio

vid·eo·cas·sette *n* **1 :** a case containing videotape for use with a VCR **2 :** a recording (as of a movie) on a videocassette

videocassette recorder *n* **:** VCR

video game *n* **:** a game played with images on a video screen

¹vid·eo·tape *n* **1 :** a recording of visual images and sound (as of a television production) made on magnetic tape **2 :** the magnetic tape used for such a recording

²videotape *vb* **:** to make a videotape of

videotape recorder *n* **:** a device for recording on videotape

vie *vb* **vied; vy·ing** : COMPETE

[1]Viet·nam·ese *n* **1:** a person born or living in Vietnam **2:** the language of the Vietnamese

[2]Vietnamese *adj* : of or relating to Vietnam, the Vietnamese people, or their language

[1]view *n* **1** : the act of seeing or examining **2** : an opinion or judgment influenced by personal feeling **3** : all that can be seen from a certain place : SCENE **4** : range of vision **5** : [1]PURPOSE **6** : a picture that represents something that can be seen

[2]view *vb* **1** : to look at carefully **2** : [1]SEE 1 — **view·er** *n*

view·point *n* : the angle from which something is considered

vig·il *n* **1** : the day before a religious feast **2** : a keeping watch especially when sleep is usual

vig·i·lance *n* : a staying alert especially to possible danger

vig·i·lant *adj* : alert especially to avoid danger — **vig·i·lant·ly** *adv*

vig·i·lan·te *n* : a member of a group of volunteers who decide on their own to stop crime and punish criminals

vig·or *n* **1** : strength or energy of body or mind **2** : active strength or force

vig·or·ous *adj* **1** : having vigor **2** : done with vigor — **vig·or·ous·ly** *adv*

Vi·king *n* : a member of the Scandinavian invaders of the coasts of Europe in the eighth to tenth centuries

vile *adj* **vil·er; vil·est** **1** : of little worth **2** : WICKED 1 **3** : very objectionable — **vile·ly** *adv* — **vile·ness** *n*

vil·i·fy *vb* **vil·i·fied; vil·i·fy·ing** : to speak of as worthless or wicked

vil·la *n* **1** : an estate in the country **2** : a large expensive home in the country or suburbs

vil·lage *n* : a place where people live that is usually smaller than a town

vil·lag·er *n* : a person who lives in a village

vil·lain *n* : a wicked person

vil·lain·ous *adj* : WICKED

vil·lainy *n, pl* **vil·lain·ies** : conduct or actions of or like those of a villain

vil·lus *n, pl* **vil·li** : one of the tiny extensions shaped like fingers that line the small intestine and are active in absorbing nutrients

vim *n* : ENERGY 1, VIGOR

vin·di·cate *vb* **vin·di·cat·ed; vin·di·cat·ing** **1** : to free from blame or guilt **2** : to show to be true or correct : JUSTIFY

vin·dic·tive *adj* : likely to seek revenge : meant to be harmful

vine *n* : a plant whose stem requires support and which climbs by tendrils or twining or creeps along the ground — **vine·like** *adj*

vin·e·gar *n* : a sour liquid made from cider, wine, or malt and used to flavor or preserve foods

vin·e·gary *adj* : like vinegar

vine·yard *n* : a field of grapevines

vin·tage *n* **1** : the grapes grown or wine made during one season **2** : a usually excellent wine of a certain type, region, and year **3** : the time when something started or was made

vi·nyl *n* : a plastic substance or product (as a fiber) made from a synthetic polymer

[1]vi·o·la *n* : a hybrid garden flower that looks like but is smaller than a pansy

[2]vi·o·la *n* : an instrument of the violin family slightly larger and having a lower pitch than a violin

vi·o·late *vb* **vi·o·lat·ed; vi·o·lat·ing** **1** : to fail to keep : BREAK **2** : to do harm or damage to **3** : to treat in a very disrespectful way **4** : DISTURB 1 — **vi·o·la·tor** *n*

vi·o·la·tion *n* : an act or instance of violating : the state of being violated

vi·o·lence *n* **1** : the use of force to harm a person or damage property **2** : great force or strength

vi·o·lent *adj* **1** : showing very strong force **2** : [1]EXTREME 1, INTENSE **3** : caused by force — **vi·o·lent·ly** *adv*

vi·o·let *n* **1** : a wild or garden plant related to the pansies that has small often fragrant white, blue, purple, or yellow flowers **2** : a reddish blue

vi·o·lin *n* : a stringed musical instrument with four strings that is usually held against the shoulder under the chin and played with a bow

vi·o·lon·cel·lo *n, pl* **vi·o·lon·cel·los** : CELLO

vi·per *n* : a snake that is or is believed to be poisonous

vir·eo *n, pl* **vir·e·os** : a small songbird that eats insects and is olive-green or grayish in color

[1]vir·gin *n* **1** : an unmarried woman devoted to religion **2** : a person who has not had sexual intercourse

[2]virgin *adj* **1** : not soiled **2** : being a virgin **3** : not changed by human actions

Vir·go *n* **1** : a constellation between Leo and Libra imagined as a woman **2** : the sixth sign of the zodiac or a person born under this sign

vir·ile *adj* **1** : having qualities generally associated with a man **2** : ENERGETIC, VIGOROUS

vir·tu·al *adj* : being almost but not quite complete — **vir·tu·al·ly** *adv*

virtual reality *n* : an artificial environment which is experienced through sights and sounds provided by a computer and in which one's actions partly decide what happens in the environment

vir·tue *n* **1 :** moral excellence **:** knowing what is right and acting in a right way **2 :** a desirable quality

vir·tu·o·so *n, pl* **vir·tu·o·sos** *or* **vir·tu·o·si :** a person who is an outstanding performer especially in music

vir·tu·ous *adj* **:** having or showing virtue — **vir·tu·ous·ly** *adv*

vir·u·lent *adj* **:** very infectious or poisonous **:** DEADLY

vi·rus *n* **1 :** an agent too tiny to be seen by the ordinary microscope that causes disease and that may be a living organism or may be a very special kind of protein molecule **2 :** a disease caused by a virus **3 :** a usually hidden computer program that causes harm by making copies of itself and inserting them into other programs

vis·count *n* **:** a British nobleman ranking below an earl and above a baron

vis·count·ess *n* **1 :** the wife or widow of a viscount **2 :** a woman who holds the rank of a viscount in her own right

vise *n* **:** a device with two jaws that works by a screw or lever for holding or clamping work

vis·i·bil·i·ty *n* **1 :** the quality or state of being visible **2 :** the degree of clearness of the atmosphere

vis·i·ble *adj* **1 :** capable of being seen **2 :** easily seen or understood **:** OBVIOUS — **vis·i·bly** *adv*

vi·sion *n* **1 :** something seen in the mind (as in a dream) **2 :** a vivid picture created by the imagination **3 :** the act or power of imagination **4 :** unusual ability to think or plan ahead **5 :** the act or power of seeing **:** SIGHT **6 :** the special sense by which the qualities of an object (as color) that make up its appearance are perceived

vi·sion·ary *n, pl* **vi·sion·ar·ies :** a person whose ideas or plans are impractical

[1]**vis·it** *vb* **1 :** to go to see in order to comfort or help **2 :** to call on as an act of friendship or courtesy or as or for a professional service **3 :** to stay with for a time as a guest **4 :** to go to for pleasure **5 :** to come to or upon

[2]**visit** *n* **1 :** a brief stay **:** CALL **2 :** a stay as a guest **3 :** a professional call

vis·i·tor *n* **:** a person who visits

vi·sor *n* **1 :** the movable front upper piece of a helmet **2 :** a part that sticks out to protect or shade the eyes

vis·ta *n* **:** a distant view through an opening or along an avenue

vi·su·al *adj* **1 :** of, relating to, or used in vision **2 :** obtained by the use of sight **3 :** appealing to the sense of sight — **vi·su·al·ly** *adv*

vi·su·al·ize *vb* **vi·su·al·ized; vi·su·al·iz·ing :** to see or form a mental image

vi·tal *adj* **1 :** of or relating to life **2 :** concerned with or necessary to the continuation of life **3 :** full of life and energy **4 :** very important — **vi·tal·ly** *adv*

vi·tal·i·ty *n, pl* **vi·tal·i·ties 1 :** capacity to live and develop **2 :** ENERGY 1

vi·tals *n pl* **:** the vital organs (as heart, lungs, and liver) of the body

vi·ta·min *n* **:** any of a group of organic substances that are found in natural foods, are necessary in small quantities to health, and include one (**vitamin A**) found mostly in animal products and needed for good vision, several (**vitamin B complex**) found in many foods and needed especially for growth, one (**vitamin C**) found in fruits and leafy vegetables and used as an enzyme and to prevent scurvy, and another (**vitamin D**) found in fish-liver oils, eggs, and milk and needed for healthy bone development

vi·va·cious *adj* **:** full of life **:** LIVELY — **vi·va·cious·ly** *adv*

vi·vac·i·ty *n* **:** the quality or state of being vivacious

vi·var·i·um *n, pl* **vi·var·ia** *or* **vi·var·i·ums :** an enclosure for keeping or studying plants or animals indoors

viv·id *adj* **1 :** seeming full of life and freshness **2 :** very strong or bright **3 :** producing strong mental images **4 :** acting clearly and powerfully — **viv·id·ly** *adv* — **viv·id·ness** *n*

vi·vip·a·rous *adj* **:** giving birth to living young rather than laying eggs

viv·i·sec·tion *n* **:** the operating or experimenting on a living animal usually for scientific study

vix·en *n* **:** a female fox

vo·cab·u·lary *n, pl* **vo·cab·u·lar·ies 1 :** a list or collection of words defined or explained **2 :** a stock of words used in a language, by a group or individual, or in relation to a subject

vo·cal *adj* **1 :** uttered by the voice **:** ORAL **2 :** composed or arranged for or sung by the human voice **3 :** of, relating to, or having the power of producing voice — **vo·cal·ly** *adv*

vocal cords *n pl* **:** membranes at the top of the windpipe that produce vocal sounds when drawn tight and vibrated by the outgoing breath

vo·cal·ist *n* **:** SINGER

vo·ca·tion *n* **1 :** a strong desire for a certain career or course of action **2 :** the work in which a person is regularly employed **:** OCCUPATION

vo·ca·tion·al *adj* **1 :** of, relating to, or concerned with a vocation **2 :** concerned with choice of or training in a vocation — **vo·ca·tion·al·ly** *adv*

vod·ka *n* **:** a colorless alcoholic liquor

vogue *n* **1 :** the quality or state of being popular at a certain time **2 :** a period in which something is in fashion **3 :** something that is in fashion at a certain time

¹voice *n* **1 :** sound produced through the mouth by vertebrates and especially by human beings in speaking or shouting **2 :** musical sound produced by the vocal cords **3 :** SPEECH 5 **4 :** a sound similar to vocal sound **5 :** a means of expression **6 :** the right to express a wish, choice, or opinion

²voice *vb* **voiced; voic·ing :** to express in words

voice box *n* **:** LARYNX

voiced *adj* **:** spoken with vibration of the vocal cords

voice·less *adj* **:** spoken without vibration of the vocal cords

voice mail *n* **:** an electronic communication system in which spoken messages are recorded to be played back later

¹void *adj* **:** containing nothing **:** EMPTY

²void *n* **:** empty space

vol·a·tile *adj* **1 :** easily becoming a vapor at a fairly low temperature **2 :** likely to change suddenly

vol·ca·nic *adj* **1 :** of or relating to a volcano **2 :** likely to explode

vol·ca·no *n, pl* **vol·ca·noes** *or* **vol·ca·nos 1 :** an opening in the earth's crust from which hot or melted rock and steam come **2 :** a hill or mountain composed of material thrown out in a volcanic eruption

vole *n* **:** any of various small rodents that look like fat mice or rats with short tails and are sometimes harmful to crops

vo·li·tion *n* **:** the act or power of making one's own choices or decisions **:** WILL

¹vol·ley *n, pl* **volleys 1 :** a group of missiles (as arrows or bullets) passing through the air **2 :** a firing of a number of weapons (as rifles) at the same time **3 :** a bursting forth of many things at once **4 :** the act of volleying

²volley *vb* **vol·leyed; vol·ley·ing 1 :** to shoot in a volley **2 :** to hit an object (as a ball) while it is in the air before it touches the ground

vol·ley·ball *n* **:** a game played by volleying a large ball filled with air across a net

volt *n* **:** a unit for measuring the force that moves an electric current

volt·age *n* **:** electric force measured in volts

vol·u·ble *adj* **:** having a smooth and fast flow of words in speaking — **vol·u·bly** *adv*

vol·ume *n* **1 :** ¹BOOK 1 **2 :** any one of a series of books that together form a complete work or collection **3 :** space included within limits as measured in cubic units **4 :** ²AMOUNT **5 :** the degree of loudness of a sound

vo·lu·mi·nous *adj* **1 :** of great volume or bulk **2 :** filling or capable of filling a large volume or several volumes

vol·un·tary *adj* **1 :** done, given, or made of one's own free will or choice **2 :** not accidental **:** INTENTIONAL **3 :** of, relating to, or controlled by the will — **vol·un·tar·i·ly** *adv*

¹vol·un·teer *n* **1 :** a person who volunteers for a service **2 :** a plant growing without direct human care especially from seeds lost from a previous crop

²volunteer *adj* **:** of, relating to, or done by volunteers

³volunteer *vb* **1 :** to offer or give without being asked **2 :** to offer oneself for a service of one's own free will

¹vom·it *n* **:** material from the stomach gotten rid of through the mouth

²vomit *vb* **:** to rid oneself of the contents of the stomach through the mouth

vo·ra·cious *adj* **1 :** greedy in eating **2 :** very eager — **vo·ra·cious·ly** *adv*

¹vote *n* **1 :** a formal expression of opinion or will (as by ballot) **2 :** the decision reached by voting **3 :** the right to vote **4 :** the act or process of voting **5 :** a group of voters with some common interest or quality

²vote *vb* **vot·ed; vot·ing 1 :** to express one's wish or choice by or as if by a vote **2 :** to elect, decide, pass, defeat, grant, or make legal by a vote **3 :** to declare by general agreement

vot·er *n* **:** a person who votes or who has the legal right to vote

vouch *vb* **:** to give a guarantee

vouch·safe *vb* **vouch·safed; vouch·saf·ing :** to grant as a special favor

¹vow *n* **:** a solemn promise or statement

²vow *vb* **:** to make a vow **:** SWEAR

vow·el *n* **1 :** a speech sound (as \ə\, \ā\, or \ȯ\) produced without obstruction or audible friction in the mouth **2 :** a letter (as *a, e, i, o, u*) representing a vowel

¹voy·age *n* **:** a journey especially by water from one place or country to another

²voyage *vb* **voy·aged; voy·ag·ing :** to take a trip — **voy·ag·er** *n*

vul·ca·nize *vb* **vul·ca·nized; vul·ca·niz·ing :** to treat rubber with chemicals in order to give it useful properties (as strength)

vul·gar *adj* **1 :** of or relating to the common people **2 :** having poor taste or manners **:** COARSE **3 :** offensive in language

vul·gar·i·ty *n, pl* **vul·gar·i·ties 1 :** the quality or state of being vulgar **2 :** a vulgar expression or action

vul·ner·a·ble *adj* **1 :** possible to wound or hurt **2 :** open to attack or damage — **vul·ner·a·bly** *adv*

vul·ture *n* **:** a large bird related to the hawks and eagles that has a naked head and feeds mostly on animals found dead

vying *present participle of* VIE

W

w *n, pl* **w's** *or* **ws** *often cap* **:** the twenty-third letter of the English alphabet

wacky *or* **whacky** *adj* **wack·i·er** *or* **whack·i·er; wack·i·est** *or* **whack·i·est :** CRAZY 2, INSANE

[1]wad *n* **1 :** a small mass or lump **2 :** a soft plug or stopper to hold a charge of powder (as in cartridges) **3 :** a soft mass of cotton, cloth, or fibers used as a plug or pad

[2]wad *vb* **wad·ded; wad·ding :** to form into a wad

[1]wad·dle *vb* **wad·dled; wad·dling :** to walk with short steps swaying like a duck

[2]waddle *n* **:** a waddling walk

wade *vb* **wad·ed; wad·ing 1 :** to walk through something (as water or snow) that makes it hard to move **2 :** to proceed with difficulty **3 :** to pass or cross by stepping through water

wading bird *n* **:** a shorebird or waterbird with long legs that wades in water in search of food

wa·fer *n* **:** a thin crisp cake or cracker

waf·fle *n* **:** a crisp cake of batter baked in a waffle iron

waffle iron *n* **:** a cooking utensil with two hinged metal parts that come together for making waffles

waft *vb* **:** to move or be moved lightly by or as if by the action of waves or wind

[1]wag *vb* **wagged; wag·ging :** to swing to and fro or from side to side

[2]wag *n* **1 :** a wagging movement **2 :** a person full of jokes and humor

[1]wage *n* **1 :** payment for work done especially when figured by the hour or day **2 wages** *sing or pl* **:** REWARD

[2]wage *vb* **waged; wag·ing :** to engage in **:** CARRY ON

[1]wa·ger *n* **1 :** [1]BET 1 **2 :** the act of betting

[2]wager *vb* **:** to bet on the result of a contest or question — **wa·ger·er** *n*

wag·gish *adj* **:** showing or done in a spirit of harmless mischief

wag·gle *vb* **wag·gled; wag·gling :** to move backward and forward or from side to side

wag·on *n* **:** a vehicle having four wheels and used for carrying goods

waif *n* **:** a stray person or animal

[1]wail *vb* **:** to utter a mournful cry

[2]wail *n* **:** a long cry of grief or pain

wain·scot *n* **:** the bottom part of an inside wall especially when made of material different from the rest

wain·scot·ing *or* **wain·scot·ting** *n* **:** WAINSCOT

waist *n* **1 :** the part of the body between the chest and the hips **2 :** the central part of a thing when it is narrower or thinner than the rest **3 :** a garment or part of a garment covering the body from the neck to the waist

[1]wait *vb* **1 :** to stay in a place looking forward to something that is expected to happen **2 :** to serve food as a waiter or waitress **3 :** [2]DELAY 1

[2]wait *n* **1 :** [2]AMBUSH — used chiefly in the expression *lie in wait* **2 :** an act or period of waiting

wait·er *n* **:** a man who serves food to people at tables (as in a restaurant)

waiting room *n* **:** a room for the use of persons waiting (as for a train)

wait·ress *n* **:** a girl or woman who serves food to people at tables

waive *vb* **waived; waiv·ing :** to give up claim to

[1]wake *vb* **waked** *or* **woke; waked** *or* **woken; wak·ing 1 :** to be or stay awake **2 :** to stay awake on watch especially over a corpse **3 :** [1]AWAKE 1

[2]wake *n* **:** a watch held over the body of a dead person before burial

[3]wake *n* **:** a track or mark left by something moving especially in the water

wake·ful *adj* **1 :** VIGILANT **2 :** not sleeping or able to sleep — **wake·ful·ness** *n*

wak·en *vb* **:** [1]AWAKE 1

[1]walk *vb* **1 :** to move or cause to move along on foot at a natural slow pace **2 :** to cover or pass over at a walk **3 :** to go or cause to go to first base after four balls in baseball — **walk·er** *n*

[2]walk *n* **1 :** a going on foot **2 :** a place or path for walking **3 :** distance to be walked often measured in time required by a walker to cover **4 :** position in life or the community **5 :** way of walking **6 :** an advance to first base after four balls in baseball

walk·ie–talk·ie *n* **:** a small portable radio set for receiving and sending messages

walking stick *n* **1 :** a stick used in walking **2 :** a sticklike insect with a long round body and long thin legs

walk·out *n* **1 :** a labor strike **2 :** the leaving of a meeting or organization as a way of showing disapproval

walk·over *n* **:** an easy victory

[1]wall *n* **1 :** a solid structure (as of stone) built to enclose or shut off a space **2 :** something like a wall that separates one thing from another **3 :** a layer of material enclosing space — **walled** *adj*

[2]**wall** *vb* **:** to build a wall in or around

wall·board *n* **:** a building material (as of wood pulp) made in large stiff sheets and used especially for inside walls and ceilings

wal·let *n* **:** a small flat case for carrying paper money and personal papers

wall·eye *n* **:** a large strong American freshwater sport and food fish that is related to the perches but looks like a pike

[1]**wal·lop** *vb* **:** to hit hard

[2]**wallop** *n* **:** a hard blow

[1]**wal·low** *vb* **1 :** to roll about in or as if in deep mud **2 :** to be too much interested or concerned with

[2]**wallow** *n* **:** a muddy or dust-filled hollow where animals wallow

wall·pa·per *n* **:** decorative paper for covering the walls of a room

wal·nut *n* **:** the edible nut (as the American **black walnut** with a rough shell or the Old World **English walnut** with a smoother shell) that comes from trees related to the hickories and including some valued also for their wood

wal·rus *n* **:** a large animal of northern seas related to the seals and hunted for its hide, for the ivory tusks of the males, and for oil

[1]**waltz** *n* **:** a dance in which couples glide to music having three beats to a measure

[2]**waltz** *vb* **:** to dance a waltz — **waltz·er** *n*

wam·pum *n* **:** beads made of shells and once used for money or ornament by North American Indians

wan *adj* **wan·ner; wan·nest :** having a pale or sickly color — **wan·ly** *adv* — **wan·ness** *n*

wand *n* **:** a slender rod (as one carried by a fairy or one used by a magician in doing tricks)

wan·der *vb* **1 :** to move about without a goal or purpose **:** RAMBLE **2 :** to follow a winding course **3 :** to get off the right path **:** STRAY — **wan·der·er** *n*

wan·der·lust *n* **:** a strong wish or urge to travel

wane *vb* **waned; wan·ing 1 :** to grow smaller or less **2 :** to lose power or importance **:** DECLINE

[1]**want** *vb* **1 :** to be without **:** LACK **2 :** to feel or suffer the need of something **3 :** to desire, wish, or long for something

[2]**want** *n* **1 :** [2]LACK 2, SHORTAGE **2 :** the state of being very poor **3 :** a wish for something **:** DESIRE

want·ing *adj* **:** falling below a standard, hope, or need

wan·ton *adj* **1 :** PLAYFUL 1 **2 :** not modest or proper **:** INDECENT **3 :** showing no thought or care for the rights, feelings, or safety of others — **wan·ton·ly** *adv* — **wan·ton·ness** *n*

[1]**war** *n* **1 :** a state or period of fighting between states or nations **2 :** the art or science of warfare **3 :** a struggle between opposing forces

[2]**war** *vb* **warred; war·ring :** to make war **:** FIGHT

[1]**war·ble** *n* **1 :** low pleasing sounds that form a melody (as of a bird) **2 :** the action of warbling

[2]**warble** *vb* **war·bled; war·bling :** to sing with a warble

war·bler *n* **1 :** any of a group of Old World birds related to the thrushes and noted for their musical song **2 :** any of a group of brightly colored American migratory songbirds that eat insects and have a weak call

[1]**ward** *n* **1 :** a part of a hospital **2 :** one of the parts into which a town or city is divided for management **3 :** a person under the protection of a guardian

[2]**ward** *vb* **1 :** to keep watch over **:** GUARD **2 :** to turn aside

[1]**-ward** *also* **-wards** *adj suffix* **1 :** that moves, faces, or is pointed toward **2 :** that is found in the direction of

[2]**-ward** *or* **-wards** *adv suffix* **1 :** in a specified direction **2 :** toward a specified place

war·den *n* **1 :** a person who sees that certain laws are followed **2 :** the chief official of a prison

ward·robe *n* **1 :** a room or closet where clothes are kept **2 :** the clothes a person owns

ware *n* **1 :** manufactured articles or products of art or craft **2 :** items (as dishes) of baked clay **:** POTTERY

ware·house *n, pl* **ware·hous·es :** a building for storing goods and merchandise

war·fare *n* **1 :** military fighting between enemies **2 :** strong continued effort **:** STRUGGLE

war·like *adj* **1 :** fond of war **2 :** of or relating to war **3 :** threatening war

[1]**warm** *adj* **1 :** somewhat hot **2 :** giving off heat **3 :** making a person feel heat or experience no loss of bodily heat **4 :** having a feeling of warmth **5 :** showing strong feeling **6 :** newly made **:** FRESH **7 :** near the object sought **8 :** of a color in the range yellow through orange to red — **warm·ly** *adv*

[2]**warm** *vb* **1 :** to make or become warm **2 :** to give a feeling of warmth **3 :** to become more interested than at first

warm–blood·ed *adj* **1 :** able to keep up a body temperature that is independent of that of the surroundings **2 :** warm in feeling — **warm–blood·ed·ness** *n*

warmth *n* **1 :** gentle heat **2 :** strong feeling

warm–up *n* **:** the act or an instance of warming up

warm up *vb* **1 :** to exercise or practice lightly in preparation for more strenuous activity or a performance **2 :** to run (as a motor) at slow speed before using

warn *vb* **1 :** to put on guard : CAUTION **2 :** to notify especially in advance

warn·ing *n* **:** something that warns

[1]warp *n* **1 :** the threads that go lengthwise in a loom and are crossed by the woof **2 :** a twist or curve that has developed in something once flat or straight

[2]warp *vb* **1 :** to curve or twist out of shape **2 :** to cause to judge, choose, or act wrongly

war·path *n* **:** the route taken by a group of American Indians going off to fight — **on the warpath :** ready to fight or argue

war·plane *n* **:** a military or naval airplane

[1]war·rant *n* **1 :** a reason or cause for an opinion or action **2 :** a document giving legal power

[2]warrant *vb* **1 :** to be sure of or that **2 :** [2]GUARANTEE 2 **3 :** to call for : JUSTIFY

warrant officer *n* **1 :** an officer in the armed forces in one of the grades between commissioned officers and enlisted persons **2 :** a warrant officer of the lowest rank

war·ren *n* **:** a place for keeping or raising small game (as rabbits)

war·rior *n* **:** a person who is or has been in warfare

war·ship *n* **:** a ship armed for combat

wart *n* **:** a small hard lump of thickened skin

warty *adj* **wart·i·er; wart·i·est 1 :** covered with or as if with warts **2 :** like a wart

wary *adj* **war·i·er; war·i·est :** very cautious — **war·i·ly** *adv* — **war·i·ness** *n*

was *past 1st & 3d sing of* BE

[1]wash *vb* **1 :** to cleanse with water and usually a cleaning agent (as soap) **2 :** to wet completely with liquid **3 :** to flow along or overflow against **4 :** to remove by the action of water **5 :** to stand washing without injury

[2]wash *n* **1 :** articles (as of clothing) in the laundry **2 :** the flow, sound, or action of water **3 :** a backward flow of water (as made by the motion of a boat) **4 :** material carried or set down by water

wash·able *adj* **:** capable of being washed without damage

wash·board *n* **:** a grooved board to scrub clothes on

wash·bowl *n* **:** a large bowl for water to wash one's hands and face

wash·er *n* **1 :** WASHING MACHINE **2 :** a ring (as of metal) used to make something fit tightly or to prevent rubbing

wash·ing *n* **:** [2]WASH 1

washing machine *n* **:** a machine used especially for washing clothes and household linen

wash·out *n* **1 :** the washing away of earth (as from a road) **2 :** a place where earth is washed away **3 :** a complete failure

wash·tub *n* **:** a tub for washing clothes or for soaking them before washing

wasn't : was not

wasp *n* **:** a winged insect related to the bees and ants that has a slender body with the abdomen attached by a narrow stalk and that in females and workers is capable of giving a very painful sting

wasp·ish *adj* **:** [3]CROSS 3, IRRITABLE — **waspish·ly** *adv* — **wasp·ish·ness** *n*

[1]waste *n* **1 :** [1]DESERT, WILDERNESS **2 :** WASTELAND **3 :** the action of wasting : the state of being wasted **4 :** material left over or thrown away **5 :** material produced in and of no further use to the living body

[2]waste *vb* **wast·ed; wast·ing 1 :** to bring to ruin **2 :** to spend or use carelessly or uselessly **3 :** to lose or cause to lose weight, strength, or energy

[3]waste *adj* **1 :** being wild and not lived in or planted to crops : BARREN **2 :** of no further use

waste·bas·ket *n* **:** an open container for odds and ends to be thrown away

waste·ful *adj* **1 :** wasting or causing waste **2 :** spending or using in a careless or foolish way — **waste·ful·ly** *adv* — **waste·ful·ness** *n*

waste·land *n* **:** land that is barren or not fit for crops

[1]watch *vb* **1 :** to stay awake **2 :** to be on one's guard **3 :** to take care of : TEND **4 :** to be on the lookout **5 :** to keep one's eyes on — **watch·er** *n*

[2]watch *n* **1 :** an act of keeping awake to guard or protect **2 :** close observation **3 :** [1]GUARD 2 **4 :** the time during which one is on duty to watch **5 :** a small timepiece to be worn or carried

watch·dog *n* **:** a dog kept to watch and guard property

watch·ful *adj* **:** ATTENTIVE 1, VIGILANT — **watch·ful·ly** *adv* — **watch·ful·ness** *n*

watch·man *n, pl* **watch·men :** a person whose job is to watch and guard property at night or when the owners are away

watch·tow·er *n* **:** a tower on which a guard or watchman is placed

watch·word *n* **:** PASSWORD

[1]wa·ter *n* **1 :** the liquid that comes from the clouds as rain and forms streams, lakes, and seas **2 :** a liquid that contains or is like water **3 :** a body of water or a part of a body of water

[2]water *vb* **1 :** to wet or supply with water **2 :** to add water to **3 :** to fill with liquid (as tears)

wa·ter·bird *n* **:** a swimming or wading bird

water buffalo *n* : a buffalo of Asia with large curving horns often used as a work animal
water clock *n* : a device or machine for measuring time by the fall or flow of water
wa·ter·col·or *n* **1** : a paint whose liquid part is water **2** : a picture painted with watercolor **3** : the art of painting with watercolor
wa·ter·course *n* **1** : a channel in which water flows **2** : a stream of water (as a river or brook)
wa·ter·cress *n* : a plant related to the mustards that grows in cold flowing waters and is used especially in salads
wa·ter·fall *n* : a fall of water from a height
water flea *n* : a small active often brightly colored freshwater animal related to the crabs and lobsters
wa·ter·fowl *n* **1** : a bird that is found in or near water **2 waterfowl** *pl* : swimming birds (as wild ducks and geese) hunted as game
wa·ter·front *n* : land or a section of a town that borders on a body of water
water hyacinth *n* : a floating water plant that often blocks streams in the southern United States
water lily *n* : any of a group of water plants with rounded floating leaves and showy often fragrant flowers with many petals
wa·ter·line *n* : any of several lines marked on the outside of a ship that match the surface of the water when the ship floats evenly
wa·ter·logged *adj* : so filled or soaked with water as to be heavy or hard to manage
wa·ter·mark *n* **1** : a mark that shows a level to which water has risen **2** : a mark made in paper during manufacture and visible when the paper is held up to the light
wa·ter·mel·on *n* : a large edible fruit with a hard rind and a sweet red juicy pulp
water moccasin *n* : MOCCASIN 2
water park *n* : an amusement park with pools and wetted slides
water polo *n* : a ball game played in water by teams of swimmers
wa·ter·pow·er *n* : the power of moving water used to run machinery
¹wa·ter·proof *adj* : not letting water through
²waterproof *vb* : to make waterproof
wa·ter·shed *n* **1** : a dividing ridge (as a mountain range) separating one drainage area from others **2** : the whole area that drains into a lake or river
wa·ter·spout *n* **1** : a pipe for carrying off water from a roof **2** : a slender cloud that is shaped like a funnel and extends down to a cloud of spray torn up from the surface of a body of water by a whirlwind
water strid·er *n* : a bug with long legs that skims over the surface of water
wa·ter·tight *adj* : so tight as to be waterproof
wa·ter·way *n* : a channel or a body of water by which ships can travel
wa·ter·wheel *n* : a wheel turned by a flow of water against it
wa·ter·works *n pl* : a system of dams, reservoirs, pumps, and pipes for supplying water (as to a city)
wa·tery *adj* **1** : of or relating to water **2** : full of or giving out liquid **3** : being like water **4** : being soft and soggy
watt *n* : a unit for measuring electric power
wat·tle *n* : a fleshy flap of skin that hangs from the throat (as of a bird)
¹wave *vb* **waved; wav·ing** **1** : to move like a wave **2** : to move (as one's hand) to and fro as a signal or in greeting **3** : to curve like a wave or series of waves
²wave *n* **1** : a moving ridge on the surface of water **2** : a shape like a wave or series of waves **3** : something that swells and dies away **4** : a waving motion **5** : a rolling movement passing along a surface or through the air **6** : a motion that is somewhat like a wave in water and transfers energy from point to point
wave·length *n* : the distance in the line of advance of a wave from any one point to the next similar point
wave·let *n* : a little wave
wa·ver *vb* **1** : to sway one way and the other **2** : to be uncertain in opinion **3** : to move unsteadily
wavy *adj* **wav·i·er; wav·i·est** : like, having, or moving in waves — **wav·i·ness** *n*
¹wax *n* **1** : a dull yellow sticky substance made by bees and used in building honeycomb : BEESWAX **2** : a substance like beeswax
²wax *vb* : to treat with wax
³wax *vb* **1** : to grow larger or stronger **2** : BECOME 1, GROW
wax bean *n* : a string bean with yellow waxy pods
wax·en *adj* : of or like wax
wax myrtle *n* : the bayberry shrub
wax·wing *n* : a crested mostly brown bird having smooth feathers (as the American **cedar waxwing** with yellowish belly)
waxy *adj* **wax·i·er; wax·i·est** **1** : being like wax **2** : made of or covered with wax
¹way *n* **1** : a track for travel : PATH, STREET **2** : the course traveled from one place to another : ROUTE **3** : a course of action **4** : personal choice as to situation or behavior : WISH **5** : the manner in which something is done or happens **6** : a noticeable point **7** : ¹STATE 1 **8** : ¹DISTANCE 1 **9** : progress along a course **10** : a special or personal manner of behaving **11** : NEIGHBORHOOD 1,

DISTRICT **12 :** room to advance or pass **13 :** CATEGORY, KIND
[2]**way** *adv* **:** [1]FAR 1
way·far·er *n* **:** a traveler especially on foot
way·lay *vb* **way·laid; way·lay·ing :** to attack from hiding
-ways *adv suffix* **:** in such a way, direction, or manner
way·side *n* **:** the edge of a road
way·ward *adj* **1 :** DISOBEDIENT **2 :** opposite to what is wished or hoped for
we *pron* **:** I and at least one other
weak *adj* **1 :** lacking strength of body, mind, or spirit **2 :** not able to stand much strain or force **3 :** easily overcome **4 :** not able to function well **5 :** not rich in some usual or important element **6 :** lacking experience or skill **7 :** of, relating to, or being the lightest of three levels of stress in pronunciation
weak·en *vb* **:** to make or become weak or weaker
weak·fish *n* **:** any of several sea fishes related to the perches (as a common sport and market fish of the eastern coast of the United States)
weak·ling *n* **:** a person or animal that is weak
[1]**weak·ly** *adv* **:** in a weak manner
[2]**weakly** *adj* **weak·li·er; weak·li·est :** not strong or healthy
weak·ness *n* **1 :** lack of strength **2 :** a weak point **:** FLAW
wealth *n* **1 :** a large amount of money or possessions **2 :** a great amount or number
wealthy *adj* **wealth·i·er; wealth·i·est :** having wealth **:** RICH
wean *vb* **1 :** to get a child or young animal used to food other than its mother's milk **2 :** to turn one away from desiring a thing one has been fond of
weap·on *n* **:** something (as a gun, knife, or club) to fight with
[1]**wear** *vb* **wore; worn; wear·ing 1 :** to use as an article of clothing or decoration **2 :** to carry on the body **3 :** [1]SHOW 1 **4 :** to damage, waste, or make less by use or by scraping or rubbing **5 :** to make tired **6 :** to cause or make by rubbing **7 :** to last through long use — **wear·er** *n*
[2]**wear** *n* **1 :** the act of wearing **:** the state of being worn **2 :** things worn or meant to be worn **3 :** the result of wearing or use
wea·ri·some *adj* **:** TEDIOUS, DULL
wear out *vb* **1 :** to make useless by long or hard use **2 :** [1]TIRE 1
[1]**wea·ry** *adj* **wea·ri·er; wea·ri·est 1 :** made tired usually from work **2 :** having one's patience, pleasure, or interest worn out **3 :** causing a loss of strength or interest — **wea·ri·ly** *adv* — **wea·ri·ness** *n*
[2]**weary** *vb* **wea·ried; wea·ry·ing :** to make or become weary
wea·sel *n* **:** a small slender active animal related to the minks that feeds on small birds and animals (as mice)
[1]**weath·er** *n* **:** the state of the air and atmosphere in regard to how warm or cold, wet or dry, or clear or stormy it is
[2]**weather** *vb* **1 :** to expose to the weather **2 :** to change (as in color or structure) by the action of the weather **3 :** to be able to last or come safely through
[3]**weather** *adj* **:** [1]WINDWARD
weath·er·cock *n* **:** a weather vane shaped like a rooster
weath·er·man *n, pl* **weath·er·men :** a person who reports and forecasts the weather
weath·er·per·son *n* **:** WEATHERMAN
weather vane *n* **:** a movable device attached to something high (as a roof or spire) to show which way the wind is blowing
[1]**weave** *vb* **wove; wo·ven; weav·ing 1 :** to form (as cloth) by lacing together strands of material **2 :** [1]SPIN 3 **3 :** to make by or as if by lacing parts together **4 :** to move back and forth, up and down, or in and out — **weav·er** *n*
[2]**weave** *n* **:** a method or pattern of weaving
[1]**web** *n* **1 :** a woven fabric on a loom or coming from a loom **2 :** COBWEB 1 **3 :** something like a cobweb **4 :** a membrane especially when joining toes (as of a duck) **5** *cap* **:** WORLD WIDE WEB
[2]**web** *vb* **webbed; web·bing :** to join or surround with a web
web·foot *n, pl* **web·feet :** a foot (as of a duck) having the toes joined by webs — **web–foot·ed** *adj*
Web site *n* **:** a group of World Wide Web pages usually containing links to each other and made available on-line by an individual, company, or organization
wed *vb* **wed·ded** *also* **wed; wed·ding 1 :** MARRY **2 :** to attach firmly
we'd : we had **:** we should **:** we would
wed·ding *n* **:** a marriage ceremony
[1]**wedge** *n* **1 :** a piece of wood or metal that tapers to a thin edge and is used for splitting (as logs) or for raising something heavy **2 :** something (as a piece of cake) with a triangular shape
[2]**wedge** *vb* **wedged; wedg·ing 1 :** to fasten or tighten with a wedge **2 :** to crowd or squeeze in
wed·lock *n* **:** MARRIAGE 1
Wednes·day *n* **:** the fourth day of the week
wee *adj* **:** very small **:** TINY
[1]**weed** *n* **:** a plant that tends to grow where not wanted and to choke out more desirable plants

²weed *vb* **1 :** to remove weeds from **2 :** to get rid of what is not wanted

weedy *adj* **weed·i·er; weed·i·est 1 :** full of or consisting of weeds **2 :** like a weed especially in coarse strong rapid growth **3 :** very skinny

week *n* **1 :** seven days in a row especially beginning with Sunday and ending with Saturday **2 :** the working or school days that come between Sunday and Saturday

week·day *n* **:** a day of the week except Sunday or sometimes except Saturday and Sunday

week·end *n* **:** the period between the close of one work or school week and the beginning of the next

¹week·ly *adj* **1 :** happening, done, produced, or published every week **2 :** figured by the week

²weekly *n, pl* **weeklies :** a newspaper or magazine published every week

weep *vb* **wept; weep·ing :** to shed tears **:** CRY

weep·ing *adj* **:** having slender drooping branches

weep·ing willow *n* **:** a willow originally from Asia that has slender drooping branches

wee·vil *n* **:** any of various small beetles with a hard shell and a long snout many of which are harmful to fruits, nuts, grain, or trees

weigh *vb* **1 :** to find the weight of **2 :** to think about as if weighing **3 :** to measure out on or as if on scales **4 :** to lift an anchor before sailing **5 :** to have weight or a specified weight

weigh down *vb* **:** to cause to bend down

¹weight *n* **1 :** the amount that something weighs **2 :** the force with which a body is pulled toward the earth **3 :** a unit (as a kilogram) for measuring weight **4 :** an object (as a piece of metal) of known weight for balancing a scale in weighing other objects **5 :** a heavy object used to hold or press down something **6 :** ¹BURDEN 2 **7 :** strong influence **:** IMPORTANCE

²weight *vb* **1 :** to load or make heavy with a weight **2 :** to trouble with a burden

weighty *adj* **weight·i·er; weight·i·est 1 :** having much weight **:** HEAVY **2 :** very important

weird *adj* **1 :** of or relating to witchcraft or magic **2 :** very unusual **:** STRANGE, FANTASTIC

weirdo *n, pl* **weird·os :** a very strange person

¹wel·come *vb* **wel·comed; wel·com·ing 1 :** to greet with friendship or courtesy **2 :** to receive or accept with pleasure

²welcome *adj* **1 :** greeted or received gladly **2 :** giving pleasure **:** PLEASING **3 :** willingly permitted to do, have, or enjoy something **4** — used in the phrase "You're welcome" as a reply to an expression of thanks

³welcome *n* **:** a friendly greeting

¹weld *vb* **1 :** to join two pieces of metal or plastic by heating and allowing the edges to flow together **2 :** to join closely **3 :** to become or be capable of being welded — **weld·er** *n*

²weld *n* **:** a welded joint

wel·fare *n* **1 :** the state of being or doing well **2 :** aid in the form of money or necessities for people who are poor, aged, or disabled

¹well *n* **1 :** a source of supply **2 :** a hole made in the earth to reach a natural deposit (as of water, oil, or gas) **3 :** something suggesting a well

²well *vb* **:** to rise to the surface and flow out

³well *adv* **bet·ter; best 1 :** so as to be right **:** in a satisfactory way **2 :** in a good-hearted or generous way **3 :** in a skillful or expert manner **4 :** by as much as possible **:** COMPLETELY **5 :** with reason or courtesy **6 :** in such a way as to be pleasing **:** as one would wish **7 :** without trouble **8 :** in a thorough manner **9 :** in a familiar manner **10 :** by quite a lot

⁴well *interj* **1** — used to express surprise or doubt **2** — used to begin a conversation or to continue one that was interrupted

⁵well *adj* **1 :** being in a satisfactory or good state **2 :** free or recovered from ill health **:** HEALTHY **3 :** FORTUNATE 1

we'll : we shall **:** we will

well–be·ing *n* **:** WELFARE 1

well–bred *adj* **:** having or showing good manners **:** POLITE

well–known *adj* **:** known by many people

well–nigh *adv* **:** ALMOST

well–to–do *adj* **:** having plenty of money and possessions

¹Welsh *adj* **:** of or relating to Wales or the people of Wales

²Welsh *n* **:** the people of Wales

welt *n* **:** a ridge raised on the skin by a blow

¹wel·ter *vb* **1 :** to twist or roll one's body about **2 :** to rise and fall or toss about in or with waves

²welter *n* **:** a confused jumble

wend *vb* **:** to go one's way **:** PROCEED

went *past of* GO

wept *past of* WEEP

were *past 2d sing, past pl, or past subjunctive of* BE

we're : we are

weren't : were not

were·wolf *n, pl* **were·wolves :** a person in folklore who is changed or is able to change into a wolf

¹west *adv* **:** to or toward the west

²west *adj* **:** placed toward, facing, or coming from the west

³west *n* **1 :** the direction of sunset **:** the compass point opposite to east **2** *cap* **:** regions or countries west of a point that is mentioned or understood

west·bound *adj* **:** going west

west·er·ly *adj or adv* **1 :** toward the west **2 :** from the west

¹west·ern *adj* **1** *often cap* **:** of, relating to, or like that of the West **2 :** lying toward or coming from the west

²western *n, often cap* **:** a story, film, or radio or television show about life in the western United States especially in the last part of the nineteenth century

west·ward *adv or adj* **:** toward the west

¹wet *adj* **wet·ter; wet·test 1 :** containing, covered with, or soaked with liquid (as water) **2 :** RAINY **3 :** not yet dry — **wet·ness** *n*

²wet *n* **1 :** ¹WATER **2 :** MOISTURE **3 :** rainy weather **:** RAIN

³wet *vb* **wet** *or* **wet·ted; wet·ting :** to make wet

we've : we have

¹whack *vb* **:** to hit with a hard noisy blow

²whack *n* **1 :** a hard noisy blow **2 :** the sound of a whack

whacky *variant of* WACKY

¹whale *n* **:** a warm-blooded sea animal that looks like a huge fish but breathes air and feeds its young with its milk

²whale *vb* **whaled; whal·ing :** to hunt whales

whale·boat *n* **:** a long rowboat once used by whalers

whale·bone *n* **:** a substance like horn from the upper jaw of some whales

whal·er *n* **:** a person or ship that hunts whales

wharf *n, pl* **wharves** *or* **wharfs :** a structure built on the shore for loading and unloading ships

¹what *pron* **1 :** which thing or things **2 :** which sort of thing or person **3 :** that which — **what for :** ¹WHY — **what if 1 :** what would happen if **2 :** what does it matter if

²what *adv* **1 :** in what way **:** HOW **2** — used before one or more phrases that tell a cause

³what *adj* **1** — used to ask about the identity of a person, object, or matter **2 :** how remarkable or surprising **3 :** ²WHATEVER 1

¹what·ev·er *pron* **1 :** anything that **2 :** no matter what **3 :** what in the world

²whatever *adj* **1 :** any and all **:** any . . . that **2 :** of any kind at all

wheat *n* **:** a cereal grain that grows in tight clusters on the tall stalks of a widely cultivated grass, yields a fine white flour, is the chief source of bread in temperate regions, and is also important in animal feeds

wheat·en *adj* **:** containing or made from wheat

whee·dle *vb* **whee·dled; whee·dling 1 :** to get (someone) to think or act a certain way by flattering **:** COAX **2 :** to gain or get by coaxing or flattering

¹wheel *n* **1 :** a disk or circular frame that can turn on a central point **2 :** something like a wheel (as in being round or in turning) **3 :** something having a wheel as its main part **4 wheels** *pl* **:** moving power **:** necessary parts — **wheeled** *adj*

²wheel *vb* **1 :** to carry or move on wheels or in a vehicle with wheels **2 :** ROTATE 1 **3 :** to change direction as if turning on a central point

wheel·bar·row *n* **:** a small vehicle with two handles and usually one wheel for carrying small loads

wheel·chair *n* **:** a chair with wheels in which a disabled or sick person can get about

wheel·house *n, pl* **wheel·hous·es :** a small house containing a ship's steering wheel that is built on or above the top deck

¹wheeze *vb* **wheezed; wheez·ing 1 :** to breathe with difficulty and usually with a whistling sound **2 :** to make a sound like wheezing

²wheeze *n* **:** a wheezing sound

whelk *n* **:** a large sea snail that has a spiral shell and is used in Europe for food

¹whelp *n* **:** one of the young of an animal that eats flesh and especially of a dog

²whelp *vb* **:** to give birth to whelps

¹when *adv* **1 :** at what time **2 :** the time at which **3 :** at, in, or during which

²when *conj* **1 :** at, during, or just after the time that **2 :** in the event that **:** IF **3 :** ALTHOUGH

³when *pron* **:** what or which time

whence *adv* **1 :** from what place, source, or cause **2 :** from or out of which

when·ev·er *conj or adv* **:** at whatever time

¹where *adv* **1 :** at, in, or to what place **2 :** at or in what way or direction

²where *conj* **1 :** at, in, or to the place indicated **2 :** every place that

³where *n* **:** what place, source, or cause

¹where·abouts *adv* **:** near what place

²whereabouts *n sing or pl* **:** the place where someone or something is

where·as *conj* **1 :** since it is true that **2 :** while just the opposite

where·by *adv* **:** by or through which

where·fore *adv* **:** ¹WHY

where·in *adv* **1 :** in what way **2 :** in which

where·of *conj* **:** of what **:** that of which

where·on *adv* **:** on which

where·up·on *conj* **:** and then **:** at which time

¹wher·ev·er *adv* **:** where in the world

[2]wherever *conj* **1 :** at, in, or to whatever place **2 :** in any situation in which : at any time that

whet *vb* **whet·ted; whet·ting 1 :** to sharpen the edge of by rubbing on or with a stone **2 :** to make (as the appetite) stronger

wheth·er *conj* **1 :** if it is or was true that **2 :** if it is or was better **3** — used to introduce two or more situations of which only one can occur

whet·stone *n* **:** a stone on which blades are sharpened

whew *n* **:** a sound almost like a whistle made as an exclamation chiefly to show amazement, discomfort, or relief

whey *n* **:** the watery part of milk that separates after the milk sours and thickens

[1]which *adj* **:** what certain one or ones

[2]which *pron* **1 :** which one or ones **2** — used in place of the name of something other than people at the beginning of a clause

[1]which·ev·er *adj* **:** being whatever one or ones : no matter which

[2]whichever *pron* **:** whatever one or ones

[1]whiff *n* **1 :** a small gust **2 :** a small amount (as of a scent or a gas) that is breathed in **3 :** a very small amount : HINT

[2]whiff *vb* **:** to puff, blow out, or blow away in very small amounts

[1]while *n* **1 :** a period of time **2 :** time and effort used in doing something

[2]while *conj* **1 :** during the time that **2 :** ALTHOUGH

[3]while *vb* **whiled; whil·ing :** to cause to pass especially in a pleasant way

whim *n* **:** a sudden wish or desire : a sudden change of mind

[1]whim·per *vb* **:** to cry in low broken sounds : WHINE

[2]whimper *n* **:** a whining cry

whim·si·cal *adj* **1 :** full of whims **2 :** DROLL

[1]whine *vb* **whined; whin·ing 1 :** to make a shrill troubled cry or a similar sound **2 :** to complain by or as if by whining

[2]whine *n* **:** a whining cry or sound

[1]whin·ny *vb* **whin·nied; whin·ny·ing :** to neigh usually in a low gentle way

[2]whinny *n, pl* **whinnies :** a low gentle neigh

[1]whip *vb* **whipped; whip·ping 1 :** to move, snatch, or jerk quickly or with force **2 :** to hit with something slender and flexible : LASH **3 :** to punish with blows **4 :** to beat into foam **5 :** to move back and forth in a lively way

[2]whip *n* **1 :** something used in whipping **2 :** a light dessert made with whipped cream or whipped whites of eggs

whip·pet *n* **:** a small swift dog that is like a greyhound and is often used for racing

whip·poor·will *n* **:** a bird of eastern North America that flies at night and eats insects and is named from its peculiar call

[1]whir *vb* **whirred; whir·ring :** to fly, move, or turn rapidly with a buzzing sound

[2]whir *n* **:** a whirring sound

[1]whirl *vb* **1 :** to turn or move in circles rapidly **2 :** to feel dizzy **3 :** to move or carry around or about very rapidly

[2]whirl *n* **1 :** a whirling movement **2 :** something that is or seems to be whirling **3 :** a state of busy movement : BUSTLE

whirl·pool *n* **:** a rapid swirl of water with a low place in the center into which floating objects are drawn

whirl·wind *n* **:** a small windstorm in which the air turns rapidly in circles

[1]whisk *n* **1 :** a quick sweeping or brushing motion **2 :** a kitchen utensil of wire used for whipping eggs or cream

[2]whisk *vb* **1 :** to move suddenly and quickly **2 :** to beat into foam **3 :** to brush with or as if with a whisk broom

whisk broom *n* **:** a small broom with a short handle used especially as a clothes brush

whis·ker *n* **1 whiskers** *pl* **:** the part of the beard that grows on the sides of the face and on the chin **2 :** one hair of the beard **3 :** a long bristle or hair growing near the mouth of an animal

whis·key *or* **whis·ky** *n, pl* **whis·keys** *or* **whis·kies :** a strong drink containing alcohol and usually made from grain

[1]whis·per *vb* **1 :** to speak very low **2 :** to tell by whispering **3 :** to make a low rustling sound

[2]whisper *n* **1 :** a low soft way of speaking that can be heard only by persons who are near **2 :** the act of whispering **3 :** something said in a whisper **4 :** [1]HINT 1

[1]whis·tle *n* **1 :** a device by which a shrill sound is produced **2 :** a shrill sound of or like whistling

[2]whistle *vb* **whis·tled; whis·tling 1 :** to make a shrill sound by forcing the breath through the teeth or lips **2 :** to move, pass, or go with a shrill sound **3 :** to sound a whistle **4 :** to express by whistling

whit *n* **:** a very small amount

[1]white *adj* **whit·er; whit·est 1 :** of the color white **2 :** light or pale in color **3 :** pale gray : SILVERY **4 :** having a light skin **5 :** [1]BLANK 2 **6 :** not intended to cause harm **7 :** SNOWY 1 — **white·ness** *n*

[2]white *n* **1 :** the color of fresh snow : the opposite of black **2 :** the white part of something (as an egg) **3 :** white clothing **4 :** a person belonging to a white race

white blood cell *n* **:** one of the tiny whitish cells of the blood that help fight infection

white·cap *n* : the top of a wave breaking into foam
white cell *n* : WHITE BLOOD CELL
white·fish *n* : a freshwater fish related to the trouts that is greenish above and silvery below and is used for food
white flag *n* : a flag of plain white raised in asking for a truce or as a sign of surrender
whit·en *vb* : to make or become white : BLEACH
white oak *n* : a large oak tree known for its hard strong wood that lasts well and is not easily rotted by water
white–tailed deer *n* : the common deer of eastern North America with the underside of the tail white
[1]**white·wash** *vb* **1 :** to cover with whitewash **2 :** to try to hide the wrongdoing of
[2]**whitewash** *n* : a mixture (as of lime and water) for making a surface (as a wall) white
whith·er *adv* **1 :** to what place **2 :** to which place
whit·ish *adj* : somewhat white
whit·tle *vb* **whit·tled; whit·tling 1 :** to cut or shave off chips from wood : shape by such cutting or shaving **2 :** to reduce little by little
[1]**whiz** *or* **whizz** *vb* **whizzed; whiz·zing :** to move, pass, or fly rapidly with a buzzing sound
[2]**whiz** *n* : a buzzing sound
who *pron* **1 :** what person or people **2 :** the person or people that **3** — used to stand for a person or people at the beginning of a clause
whoa *vb* — used as a command to an animal pulling a load to stop
who·ev·er *pron* : whatever person
[1]**whole** *adj* **1 :** completely healthy or sound in condition **2 :** not cut up or ground **3 :** keeping all its necessary elements in being made ready for the market **4 :** made up of all its parts : TOTAL **5 :** not scattered or divided **6 :** each one of the — **whole·ness** *n*
[2]**whole** *n* **1 :** something that is whole **2 :** a sum of all the parts and elements — **on the whole 1 :** all things considered **2 :** in most cases
whole·heart·ed *adj* : not holding back
whole number *n* : a number that is zero or any of the natural numbers
[1]**whole·sale** *n* : the sale of goods in large quantities to dealers
[2]**wholesale** *adj* **1 :** of, relating to, or working at wholesaling **2 :** done on a large scale
[3]**wholesale** *vb* **whole·saled; whole·sal·ing :** to sell to dealers usually in large lots — **whole·sal·er** *n*
whole·some *adj* **1 :** helping to improve or keep the body, mind, or spirit in good condition **2 :** sound in body, mind, or morals — **whole·some·ness** *n*
whol·ly *adv* : to the limit : COMPLETELY
whom *pron, objective case of* WHO
whom·ev·er *pron, objective case of* WHOEVER
[1]**whoop** *vb* **1 :** to shout or cheer loudly and strongly **2 :** to make the shrill gasping sound that follows a coughing attack in whooping cough
[2]**whoop** *n* : a whooping sound
whooping cough *n* : a bacterial disease especially of children in which severe attacks of coughing are often followed by a shrill gasping intake of breath
whooping crane *n* : a large white nearly extinct North American crane that has a loud whooping call
whop·per 1 : something huge of its kind **2 :** a monstrous lie
whorl *n* **1 :** a row of parts (as leaves or petals) encircling a stem **2 :** something that whirls or winds
[1]**whose** *adj* : of or relating to whom or which
[2]**whose** *pron* : whose one : whose ones
[1]**why** *adv* : for what cause or reason
[2]**why** *conj* **1 :** the cause or reason for which **2 :** for which
[3]**why** *n, pl* **whys :** the cause of or reason for something
[4]**why** *interj* — used to express surprise, uncertainty, approval, disapproval, or impatience
wick *n* : a cord, strip, or ring of loosely woven material through which a liquid (as oil) is drawn to the top in a candle, lamp, or oil stove for burning
wick·ed *adj* **1 :** bad in behavior, moral state, or effect : EVIL **2 :** DANGEROUS 2 — **wick·ed·ly** *adv* — **wick·ed·ness** *n*
[1]**wick·er** *n* **1 :** a flexible twig (as of willow) used in basketry **2 :** WICKERWORK
[2]**wicker** *adj* : made of wicker
wick·er·work *n* : basketry made of wicker
wick·et *n* **1 :** a small gate or door in or near a larger gate or door **2 :** a small window (as in a bank or ticket office) through which business is conducted **3 :** either of the two sets of three rods topped by two crosspieces at which the ball is bowled in cricket **4 :** an arch (as of wire) through which the ball is hit in the game of croquet
[1]**wide** *adj* **wid·er; wid·est 1 :** covering a very large area **2 :** measured across or at right angles to length **3 :** having a large measure across : BROAD **4 :** opened as far as possible **5 :** not limited **6 :** far from the goal or truth — **wide·ly** *adv* — **wide·ness** *n*
[2]**wide** *adv* **wid·er; wid·est 1 :** over a wide area **2 :** to the limit : COMPLETELY

wide–awake *adj* : not sleepy, dull, or without energy : ALERT

wid·en *vb* : to make or become wide or wider

wide·spread *adj* **1 :** widely stretched out **2 :** widely scattered

[1]**wid·ow** *n* : a woman who has lost her husband by death

[2]**widow** *vb* : to make a widow or widower of

wid·ow·er *n* : a man who has lost his wife by death

width *n* **1 :** the shortest or shorter side of an object **2 :** BREADTH 1

wield *vb* **1 :** to use (as a tool) in an effective way **2 :** [2]EXERCISE 1

wie·ner *n* : FRANKFURTER

wife *n, pl* **wives :** a married woman — **wife·ly** *adj*

wig *n* : a manufactured covering of natural or artificial hair for the head

[1]**wig·gle** *vb* **wig·gled; wig·gling 1 :** to move to and fro in a jerky way **2 :** to proceed with twisting and turning movements

[2]**wiggle** *n* : a wiggling motion

wig·gler *n* : WRIGGLER

wig·gly *adj* **wig·gli·er; wig·gli·est 1 :** given to wiggling **2 :** WAVY

wig·wag *vb* **wig·wagged; wig·wag·ging :** to signal by movement of a flag or light

wig·wam *n* : an Indian hut made of poles spread over with bark, rush mats, or hides

[1]**wild** *adj* **1 :** living in a state of nature and not under human control and care : not tame **2 :** growing or produced in nature : not cultivated by people **3 :** not civilized : SAVAGE **4 :** not kept under control **5 :** wide of the intended goal or course — **wild·ly** *adv* — **wild·ness** *n*

[2]**wild** *n* : WILDERNESS

wild boar *n* : an Old World wild hog from which most domestic swine derive

wild·cat *n* : any of various cats (as an ocelot or bobcat) of small or medium size

wil·der·ness *n* : a wild region which is not used for farming and in which few people live

wild·fire *n* : a fire that destroys a wide area

wild·flower *n* : the flower of a wild plant or the plant bearing it

wild·fowl *n, pl* **wildfowl :** a bird and especially a waterfowl hunted as game

wild·life *n* : creatures that are neither human nor domesticated : the wild animals of field and forest

[1]**wile** *n* : a trick meant to trap or deceive

[2]**wile** *vb* **wiled; wil·ing :** [2]LURE

[1]**will** *helping verb, past* **would;** *present sing & pl* **will 1 :** wish to **2 :** am, is, or are willing to **3 :** am, is, or are determined to **4 :** am, is, or are going to **5 :** is or are commanded to

[2]**will** *n* **1 :** a firm wish or desire **2 :** the power to decide or control what one will do or how one will act **3 :** a legal paper in which a person states to whom the things which he or she owns are to be given after death

[3]**will** *vb* **1 :** [1]ORDER 2, DECREE **2 :** to bring to a certain condition by the power of the will **3 :** to leave by will

will·ful *or* **wil·ful** *adj* **1 :** STUBBORN 1 **2 :** INTENTIONAL — **will·ful·ly** *adv* — **will·ful·ness** *n*

will·ing *adj* **1 :** feeling no objection **2 :** not slow or lazy **3 :** made, done, or given of one's own choice : VOLUNTARY — **will·ing·ly** *adv* — **will·ing·ness** *n*

wil·low *n* **1 :** a tree or bush with narrow leaves, catkins for flowers, and tough flexible stems used in making baskets **2 :** the wood of the willow tree

[1]**wilt** *vb* **1 :** to lose freshness and become limp **2 :** to lose strength

[2]**wilt** *n* : a plant disease (as of tomatoes) in which wilting and browning of leaves leads to death of the plant

wily *adj* **wil·i·er; wil·i·est :** full of tricks : CRAFTY

win *vb* **won; win·ning 1 :** to achieve the victory in a contest **2 :** to get by effort or skill : GAIN **3 :** to obtain by victory **4 :** to be the victor in **5 :** to ask and get the favor of

wince *vb* **winced; winc·ing :** to draw back (as from pain)

winch *n* : a machine that has a roller on which rope is wound for pulling or lifting

[1]**wind** *n* **1 :** a movement of the air : BREEZE **2 :** power to breathe **3 :** air carrying a scent (as of game) **4 :** limited knowledge especially about something secret : HINT **5 winds** *pl* : wind instruments of a band or orchestra

[2]**wind** *vb* **1 :** to get a scent of **2 :** to cause to be out of breath

[3]**wind** *vb* **wound; wind·ing :** to sound by blowing

[4]**wind** *vb* **wound; wind·ing 1 :** to twist around **2 :** to cover with something twisted around : WRAP **3 :** to make the spring of tight **4 :** to move in a series of twists and turns

[5]**wind** *n* : [2]BEND

wind·break *n* : something (as a growth of trees and shrubs) that breaks the force of the wind

wind·fall *n* **1 :** something (as fruit from a tree) blown down by the wind **2 :** an unexpected gift or gain

wind instrument *n* : a musical instrument (as a clarinet, harmonica, or trumpet) sounded by the vibration of a stream of air and especially by the player's breath

wind·lass *n* **:** a winch used especially on ships for pulling and lifting

wind·mill *n* **:** a mill or a machine (as for pumping water) worked by the wind turning sails or vanes at the top of a tower

win·dow *n* **1 :** an opening in a wall to admit light and air **2 :** the glass and frame that fill a window opening **3 :** any of the areas into which a computer display may be divided and on which different types of information may be shown

window box *n* **:** a box for growing plants in or by a window

win·dow·pane *n* **:** a pane in a window

wind·pipe *n* **:** a tube with a firm wall that connects the pharynx with the lungs and is used in breathing

wind·proof *adj* **:** protecting from the wind

wind·shield *n* **:** a clear screen (as of glass) attached to the body of a vehicle (as a car) in front of the riders to protect them from the wind

wind·storm *n* **:** a storm with strong wind and little or no rain

wind·up *n* **1 :** the last part of something **:** FINISH **2 :** a swing of a baseball pitcher's arm before the pitch is thrown

wind up *vb* **1 :** to bring to an end **:** CONCLUDE **2 :** to swing the arm before pitching a baseball

[1]**wind·ward** *adj* **:** moving or placed toward the direction from which the wind is blowing

[2]**windward** *n* **:** the side or direction from which the wind is blowing

windy *adj* **wind·i·er; wind·i·est :** having much wind

wine *n* **1 :** fermented grape juice containing various amounts of alcohol **2 :** the usually fermented juice of a plant product (as a fruit) used as a drink

win·ery *n, pl* **win·er·ies :** a place where wine is made

[1]**wing** *n* **1 :** one of the paired limbs or limblike parts with which a bird, bat, or insect flies **2 :** something like a wing in appearance, use, or motion **3 :** a part (as of a building) that sticks out from the main part **4 :** a division of an organization **5 wings** *pl* **:** an area just off the stage of a theater — **wing·like** *adj* — **on the wing :** in flight

[2]**wing** *vb* **:** to go with wings **:** FLY

winged *adj* **:** having wings or winglike parts

wing·less *adj* **:** having no wings

wing·spread *n* **:** the distance between the tips of the spread wings

[1]**wink** *vb* **1 :** to close and open the eyelids quickly **2 :** to close and open one eye quickly as a signal or hint

[2]**wink** *n* **1 :** a brief period of sleep **2 :** a hint or sign given by winking **3 :** an act of winking **4 :** a very short time

win·ner *n* **:** one that wins

[1]**win·ning** *n* **1 :** the act of one that wins **2 :** something won especially in gambling — often used in pl.

[2]**winning** *adj* **1 :** being one that wins **2 :** tending to please or delight

win·now *vb* **:** to remove (as waste from grain) by a current of air

win·some *adj* **:** [2]WINNING 2

[1]**win·ter** *n* **1 :** the season between autumn and spring (as the months of December, January, and February in the northern half of the earth) **2 :** YEAR 2

[2]**winter** *vb* **1 :** to pass the winter **2 :** to keep, feed, or manage during the winter

win·ter·green *n* **:** a low evergreen plant with white flowers that look like little bells and are followed by red berries which produce an oil (**oil of wintergreen**) used in medicine and flavoring

win·ter·time *n* **:** the winter season

win·try *adj* **win·tri·er; win·tri·est 1 :** of, relating to, or characteristic of winter **2 :** not friendly **:** COLD

[1]**wipe** *vb* **wiped; wip·ing 1 :** to clean or dry by rubbing **2 :** to remove by or as if by rubbing — **wip·er** *n*

[2]**wipe** *n* **:** an act of wiping **:** RUB

wipe out *vb* **:** to destroy completely

[1]**wire** *n* **1 :** metal in the form of a thread or slender rod **2 :** a telephone or telegraph wire or system **3 :** TELEGRAM, CABLEGRAM

[2]**wire** *vb* **wired; wir·ing 1 :** to provide or equip with wire **2 :** to bind, string, or mount with wire **3 :** to send or send word to by telegraph

[1]**wire·less** *adj* **1 :** having no wire **2 :** relating to communication by electric waves but without connecting wires **:** RADIO 2

[2]**wireless** *n* **1 :** wireless telegraphy **2 :** [2]RADIO

wiry *adj* **wir·i·er; wir·i·est 1 :** of or like wire **2 :** being slender yet strong and active

wis·dom *n* **:** knowledge and the ability to use it to help oneself or others

wisdom tooth *n* **:** the last tooth of the full set on each half of each jaw of an adult

[1]**wise** *n* **:** MANNER 2, WAY — used in such phrases as *in any wise, in no wise, in this wise*

[2]**wise** *adj* **wis·er; wis·est 1 :** having or showing good sense or good judgment **:** SENSIBLE **2 :** having knowledge or information — **wise·ly** *adv*

-wise *adv suffix* **1 :** in the manner of **2 :** in the position or direction of **3 :** with regard to

wise·crack *n* **:** a clever and often insulting statement usually made in joking

[1]wish *vb* **1 :** to have a desire for : WANT **2 :** to form or express a desire concerning
[2]wish *n* **1 :** an act or instance of wishing **2 :** something wished **3 :** a desire for happiness or good fortune
wish·bone *n* **:** a bone in front of a bird's breastbone that is shaped like a V
wish·ful *adj* **:** having, showing, or based on a wish
wishy–washy *adj* **:** lacking spirit, courage, or determination : WEAK
wisp *n* **1 :** a small bunch of hay or straw **2 :** a thin piece or strand **3 :** a thin streak
wispy *adj* **wisp·i·er; wisp·i·est :** being thin and flimsy
wis·tar·ia *n* **:** WISTERIA
wis·te·ria *n* **:** a woody vine related to the beans that is grown for its long clusters of violet, white, or pink flowers
wist·ful *adj* **:** feeling or showing a timid longing — **wist·ful·ly** *adv* — **wist·ful·ness** *n*
wit *n* **1 :** power to think, reason, or decide **2 :** normal mental state — usually used in pl. **3 :** cleverness in making sharp and usually amusing comments **4 :** witty comments, expressions, or talk **5 :** a witty person
witch *n* **1 :** a woman believed to have magic powers **2 :** an ugly or mean old woman
witch·craft *n* **:** the power or doings of a witch
witch doctor *n* **:** a person who uses magic to cure illness and fight off evil spirits
witch·ery *n, pl* **witch·er·ies 1 :** WITCHCRAFT **2 :** power to charm or fascinate
witch ha·zel *n* **1 :** a shrub with small yellow flowers in late fall or very early spring **2 :** a soothing alcoholic lotion made from witch hazel bark
with *prep* **1 :** AGAINST 2 **2 :** in shared relation to **3 :** having in or as part of it **4 :** in regard to **5 :** compared to **6 :** in the opinion or judgment of **7 :** by the use of **8 :** so as to show **9 :** in the company of **10 :** in possession of **11 :** as well as **12 :** FROM 2 **13 :** BECAUSE OF **14 :** DESPITE **15 :** if given **16 :** at the time of or shortly after **17 :** in support of **18 :** in the direction of
with·draw *vb* **with·drew; with·drawn; with·draw·ing 1 :** to draw back : take away **2 :** to take back (as something said or suggested) **3 :** to go away especially for privacy or safety
with·draw·al *n* **:** an act or instance of withdrawing
with·er *vb* **:** to shrink up from or as if from loss of natural body moisture : WILT
with·ers *n pl* **:** the ridge between the shoulder bones of a horse
with·hold *vb* **with·held; with·hold·ing :** to refuse to give, grant, or allow
[1]with·in *adv* **:** [2]INSIDE
[2]within *prep* **1 :** [4]INSIDE 1 **2 :** not beyond the limits of
[1]with·out *prep* **1 :** [4]OUTSIDE **2 :** completely lacking **3 :** not accompanied by or showing
[2]without *adv* **:** [3]OUTSIDE
with·stand *vb* **with·stood; with·stand·ing 1 :** to hold out against **2 :** to oppose (as an attack) successfully
wit·less *adj* **:** lacking in wit or intelligence : FOOLISH
[1]wit·ness *n* **1 :** TESTIMONY **2 :** a person who sees or otherwise has personal knowledge of something **3 :** a person who gives testimony in court **4 :** a person who is present at an action (as the signing of a will) so as to be able to say who did it
[2]witness *vb* **1 :** to be a witness to **2 :** to give testimony to : testify as a witness **3 :** to be or give proof of
wit·ted *adj* **:** having wit or understanding — used in combination
wit·ty *adj* **wit·ti·er; wit·ti·est :** having or showing wit
wives *pl of* WIFE
wiz·ard *n* **1 :** SORCERER, MAGICIAN **2 :** a very clever or skillful person
[1]wob·ble *vb* **wob·bled; wob·bling :** to move from side to side in a shaky manner — **wob·bly** *adj*
[2]wobble *n* **:** a rocking motion from side to side
woe *n* **:** great sorrow, grief, or misfortune : TROUBLE
woe·ful *adj* **1 :** full of grief or misery **2 :** bringing woe or misery
woke *past of* WAKE
woken *past participle of* WAKE
[1]wolf *n, pl* **wolves 1 :** a large intelligent doglike wild animal that eats flesh and has ears which stand up and a bushy tail **2 :** a person felt to resemble a wolf (as in craftiness or fierceness) — **wolf·ish** *adj*
[2]wolf *vb* **:** to eat greedily
wolf dog *n* **1 :** WOLFHOUND **2 :** the hybrid offspring of a wolf and a domestic dog **3 :** a dog that looks like a wolf
wolf·hound *n* **:** any of several large dogs used in hunting large animals
wol·fram *n* **:** TUNGSTEN
wol·ver·ine *n* **:** a blackish wild animal with shaggy fur that is related to the martens and sables, eats flesh, and is found chiefly in the northern parts of North America
wolves *pl of* WOLF
wom·an *n, pl* **wom·en 1 :** an adult female person **2 :** women considered as a group
wom·an·hood *n* **1 :** the state of being a woman **2 :** womanly characteristics **3 :** WOMAN 2
wom·an·kind *n* **:** WOMAN 2

wom·an·ly *adj* : having the characteristics of a woman

womb *n* : UTERUS

wom·en·folk *or* **wom·en·folks** *n pl* : women especially of one family or group

won *past of* WIN

[1]**won·der** *n* **1** : something extraordinary : MARVEL **2** : a feeling (as of astonishment) caused by something extraordinary

[2]**wonder** *vb* **1** : to feel surprise or amazement **2** : to be curious or have doubt

won·der·ful *adj* **1** : causing wonder : MARVELOUS **2** : very good or fine — **won·der·ful·ly** *adv*

won·der·ing·ly *adv* : in or as if in wonder

won·der·land *n* : a place of wonders or surprises

won·der·ment *n* : AMAZEMENT

won·drous *adj* : WONDERFUL 1

[1]**wont** *adj* : being in the habit of doing

[2]**wont** *n* : usual custom : HABIT

won't : will not

woo *vb* **wooed; woo·ing** **1** : to try to gain the love of **2** : to try to gain

[1]**wood** *n* **1** : a thick growth of trees : a small forest — often used in pl. **2** : a hard fibrous material that makes up most of the substance of a tree or shrub within the bark and is often used as a building material or fuel

[2]**wood** *adj* **1** : WOODEN 1 **2** : used for or on wood **3** *or* **woods** : living or growing in woodland

wood·bine *n* : any of several climbing vines of Europe and America (as honeysuckle)

wood·carv·er *n* : a person who carves useful or ornamental things from wood

wood·chuck *n* : a reddish brown rodent that hibernates : GROUNDHOG

wood·cock *n* : a brown game bird that has a long bill and is related to the snipe

wood·craft *n* : knowledge about the woods and how to take care of oneself in them

wood·cut·ter *n* : a person who cuts wood especially as an occupation

wood·ed *adj* : covered with trees

wood·en *adj* **1** : made of wood **2** : stiff like wood : AWKWARD **3** : lacking spirit, ease, or charm

wood·land *n* : land covered with trees and shrubs : FOREST

wood·lot *n* : a small wooded section (as of a farm) kept to meet fuel and timber needs

wood louse *n* : a small flat gray crustacean that lives usually under stones or bark

wood·peck·er *n* : a bird that climbs trees and drills holes in them with its bill in search of insects

wood·pile *n* : a pile of wood especially for use as fuel

wood·shed *n* : a shed for storing wood and especially firewood

woods·man *n, pl* **woods·men** **1** : a person who cuts down trees as an occupation **2** : a person skilled in woodcraft

woodsy *adj* : of, relating to, or suggestive of woodland

wood thrush *n* : a large thrush of eastern North America noted for its loud clear song

wood·wind *n* : one of the group of wind instruments consisting of the flutes, oboes, clarinets, bassoons, and sometimes saxophones

wood·work *n* : work (as the edge around doorways) made of wood

wood·work·ing *n* : the art or process of shaping or working with wood

woody *adj* **wood·i·er; wood·i·est** **1** : being mostly woods **2** : of or containing wood or wood fibers **3** : very much like wood

woof *n* **1** : the threads that cross the warp in weaving a fabric **2** : a woven fabric or its texture

wool *n* **1** : soft heavy wavy or curly hair especially of the sheep **2** : a substance that looks like a mass of wool **3** : a material (as yarn) made from wool

wool·en *or* **wool·len** *adj* **1** : made of wool **2** : of or relating to wool or cloth made of wool

wool·ly *adj* **wool·li·er; wool·li·est** : made of or like wool

[1]**word** *n* **1** : a sound or combination of sounds that has meaning and is spoken by a human being **2** : a written or printed letter or letters standing for a spoken word **3** : a brief remark or conversation **4** : [2]COMMAND 2, ORDER **5** : NEWS **6** : [1]PROMISE 1 **7 words** *pl* : remarks said in anger or in a quarrel

[2]**word** *vb* : to express in words : PHRASE

word·ing *n* : the way something is put into words

word processing *n* : the production of typewritten documents (as business letters) with automated and usually computerized equipment

word processor *n* **1** : a terminal operated by a keyboard for use in word processing usually having a video display and a magnetic storage device **2** : software (as for a computer) to perform word processing

wordy *adj* **word·i·er; word·i·est** : using or containing many words or more words than are needed — **word·i·ness** *n*

wore *past of* WEAR

[1]**work** *n* **1** : the use of a person's strength or ability in order to get something done or get some desired result : LABOR **2** : OCCUPATION 1, EMPLOYMENT **3** : something that needs to be done : TASK, JOB **4** : DEED 1, ACHIEVEMENT **5** : something produced by effort or

hard work **6 works** *pl* : a place where industrial labor is done : PLANT, FACTORY **7 works** *pl* : the working or moving parts of a mechanical device **8** : the way one works : WORKMANSHIP

²work *vb* **worked** *or* **wrought; work·ing 1** : to do work especially for money or because of a need instead of for pleasure : labor or cause to labor **2** : to perform or act or to cause to act as planned : OPERATE **3** : to move or cause to move slowly or with effort **4** : to cause to happen **5** : ¹MAKE 2, SHAPE **6** : to carry on one's occupation in, through, or along **7** : EXCITE 2, PROVOKE

work·able *adj* : capable of being worked or done

work·bench *n* : a bench on which work is done (as by mechanics)

work·book *n* : a book made up of a series of problems or practice examples for a student to use as part of a course of study

work·er *n* **1** : a person who works **2** : one of the members of a colony of bees, ants, wasps, or termites that are only partially developed sexually and that do most of the labor and protective work of the colony

work·ing *adj* **1** : doing work especially for a living **2** : relating to work **3** : good enough to allow work or further work to be done

work·ing·man *n, pl* **work·ing·men** : a person who works for wages usually at manual labor

work·man *n, pl* **work·men 1** : WORKINGMAN **2** : a skilled worker (as a carpenter)

work·man·ship *n* **1** : the art or skill of a workman **2** : the quality of a piece of work

work·out *n* : an exercise or practice to test or increase ability or performance

work out *vb* : to invent or solve by effort

work·shop *n* : a shop where work and especially skilled work is carried on

work·sta·tion *n* **1** : an area with equipment for the performance of a particular task usually by one person **2** : a computer usually connected to a computer network

world *n* **1** : EARTH 3 **2** : people in general : HUMANITY **3** : a state of existence **4** : a great number or amount **5** : a part or section of the earth and the people living there

world·ly *adj* **world·li·er; world·li·est** : of or relating to this world

¹world·wide *adj* : extending or involving the entire world

²worldwide *adv* throughout the world

World Wide Web *n* : a part of the Internet designed to allow easier navigation of the network through the use of text and graphics that link to other documents

¹worm *n* **1** : any of various long creeping or crawling animals that usually have soft bodies **2** : a person hated or pitied **3 worms** *pl* : the presence of or disease caused by worms living in the body

²worm *vb* **1** : to move slowly by creeping or wriggling **2** : to get hold of or escape from by trickery **3** : to free from worms

wormy *adj* **worm·i·er; worm·i·est** : containing worms

worn *past participle of* WEAR

worn–out *adj* **1** : useless from long or hard wear **2** : very weary

wor·ri·some *adj* **1** : given to worrying **2** : causing worry

¹wor·ry *vb* **wor·ried; wor·ry·ing 1** : to shake and tear or mangle with the teeth **2** : to make anxious or upset : DISTURB **3** : to feel or express great concern

²worry *n, pl* **worries 1** : ANXIETY **2** : a cause of great concern

¹worse *adj, comparative of* BAD *or of* ILL **1** : more bad or evil : poorer in quality or worth **2** : being in poorer health

²worse *n* : something worse

³worse *adv, comparative of* BADLY *or of* ILL : not as well : in a worse way

wors·en *vb* : to get worse

¹wor·ship *n* **1** : deep respect toward God, a god, or a sacred object **2** : too much respect or admiration

²worship *vb* **wor·shiped** *or* **wor·shipped; wor·ship·ing** *or* **wor·ship·ping 1** : to honor or respect as a divine being **2** : to regard with respect, honor, or devotion **3** : to take part in worship or an act of worship — **wor·ship·er** *or* **wor·ship·per** *n*

¹worst *adj, superlative of* BAD *or of* ILL : most bad, ill or evil

²worst *adv, superlative of* ILL *or of* BADLY : in the worst way possible

³worst *n* : a person or thing that is worst

⁴worst *vb* : to get the better of : DEFEAT

wor·sted *n* **1** : a smooth yarn spun from pure wool **2** : a fabric woven from a worsted yarn

¹worth *n* **1** : the quality or qualities of a thing making it valuable or useful **2** : value as expressed in money **3** : EXCELLENCE 1

²worth *prep* **1** : equal in value to **2** : having possessions or income equal to **3** : deserving of **4** : capable of

worth·less *adj* **1** : lacking worth **2** : USELESS

worth·while *adj* : being worth the time spent or effort used

wor·thy *adj* **wor·thi·er; wor·thi·est 1** : having worth or excellence **2** : having enough value or excellence — **wor·thi·ness** *n*

would *past of* WILL **1** : strongly desire : WISH **2** — used as a helping verb to show that something might be likely or meant to happen under certain conditions **3** : prefers or prefer to **4** : was or were going to **5** : is or are able to : COULD **6** — used as a politer form of *will*

wouldn't : would not

[1]**wound** *n* **1** : an injury that involves cutting or breaking of bodily tissue (as by violence, accident, or surgery) **2** : an injury or hurt to a person's feelings or reputation

[2]**wound** *vb* **1** : to hurt by cutting or breaking tissue **2** : to hurt the feelings or pride of

[3]**wound** *past of* WIND

wove *past of* WEAVE

woven *past participle of* WEAVE

[1]**wran·gle** *vb* **wran·gled; wran·gling** **1** : to have an angry quarrel : BICKER **2** : ARGUE 2, DEBATE

[2]**wrangle** *n* : [1]QUARREL 2

wran·gler *n* **1** : a person who wrangles **2** : a worker on a ranch who tends the saddle horses

[1]**wrap** *vb* **wrapped; wrap·ping** **1** : to cover by winding or folding **2** : to enclose in a package **3** : to wind or roll together : FOLD **4** : to involve completely

[2]**wrap** *n* : a warm loose outer garment (as a shawl, cape, or coat)

wrap·per *n* **1** : what something is wrapped in **2** : a person who wraps merchandise **3** : a garment that is worn wrapped about the body

wrap·ping *n* : something used to wrap something else : WRAPPER

wrap up *vb* **1** : to bring to an end **2** : to put on warm clothing

wrath *n* : violent anger : RAGE

wrath·ful *adj* **1** : full of wrath **2** : showing wrath

wreak *vb* : to bring down as or as if punishment

wreath *n, pl* **wreaths** : something twisted or woven into a circular shape

wreathe *vb* **wreathed; wreath·ing** **1** : to form into wreaths **2** : to crown, decorate, or cover with or as if with a wreath

[1]**wreck** *n* **1** : the remains (as of a ship or vehicle) after heavy damage usually by storm, collision, or fire **2** : a person or animal in poor health or without strength **3** : the action of breaking up or destroying something

[2]**wreck** *vb* **1** : [2]SHIPWRECK 2 **2** : to damage or destroy by breaking up **3** : to bring to ruin or an end

wreck·age *n* **1** : a wrecking or being wrecked **2** : the remains of a wreck

wreck·er *n* **1** : a person who wrecks something or deals in wreckage **2** : a ship used in salvaging wrecks **3** : a truck for removing wrecked or broken-down cars

wren *n* : any of a group of small brown songbirds (as the **house wren**) with short rounded wings and short erect tail

[1]**wrench** *vb* **1** : to pull or twist with sudden sharp force **2** : to injure or cripple by a sudden sharp twisting or straining

[2]**wrench** *n* **1** : a violent twist to one side or out of shape **2** : an injury caused by twisting or straining : SPRAIN **3** : a tool used in turning nuts or bolts

wrest *vb* **1** : to pull away by twisting or wringing **2** : to obtain only by great and steady effort

[1]**wres·tle** *vb* **wres·tled; wres·tling** **1** : to grasp and attempt to turn, trip, or throw down an opponent or to prevent the opponent from being able to move **2** : to struggle to deal with

[2]**wrestle** *n* : [2]STRUGGLE 1

wres·tling *n* : a sport in which two opponents wrestle each other

wretch *n* **1** : a miserable unhappy person **2** : a very bad person : WRONGDOER

wretch·ed *adj* **1** : very unhappy or unfortunate : suffering greatly **2** : causing misery or distress **3** : of very poor quality : INFERIOR

wrig·gle *vb* **wrig·gled; wrig·gling** **1** : to twist or move like a worm : SQUIRM, WIGGLE **2** : to advance by twisting and turning

wrig·gler *n* **1** : one that wriggles **2** : a mosquito larva or pupa

wring *vb* **wrung; wring·ing** **1** : to twist or press so as to squeeze out moisture **2** : to get by or as if by twisting or pressing **3** : to twist so as to strangle **4** : to affect as if by wringing

wring·er *n* : a machine or device for squeezing liquid out of something (as laundry)

[1]**wrin·kle** *n* **1** : a crease or small fold (as in the skin or in cloth) **2** : a clever notion or trick

[2]**wrinkle** *vb* **wrin·kled; wrin·kling** : to mark or become marked with wrinkles

wrist *n* : the joint or the region of the joint between the hand and arm

wrist·band *n* **1** : the part of a sleeve that goes around the wrist **2** : a band that goes around the wrist (as for support or warmth)

wrist·watch *n* : a watch attached to a bracelet or strap and worn on the wrist

writ *n* : an order in writing signed by an officer of a court ordering someone to do or not to do something

write *vb* **wrote; writ·ten; writ·ing** **1** : to form letters or words with pen or pencil **2** : to form the letters or the words of (as on paper) **3** : to put down on paper **4** : to make up and set down for others to read **5** : to write a letter to

writ·er *n* : a person who writes especially as a business or occupation

writhe *vb* **writhed; writh·ing** **1** : to twist and

turn this way and that **2 :** to suffer from shame or confusion : SQUIRM

writ·ing *n* **1 :** the act of a person who writes **2 :** HANDWRITING **3 :** something (as a letter or book) that is written

[1]wrong *n* **:** something (as an idea, rule, or action) that is wrong

[2]wrong *adj* **1 :** not right : SINFUL, EVIL **2 :** not correct or true : FALSE **3 :** not the one wanted or intended **4 :** not suitable **5 :** made so as to be placed down or under and not to be seen **6 :** not proper — **wrong·ly** *adv* — **wrong·ness** *n*

[3]wrong *adv* **:** in the wrong direction, manner, or way

[4]wrong *vb* **:** to do wrong to

wrong·do·er *n* **:** a person who does wrong and especially a moral wrong

wrong·do·ing *n* **:** bad behavior or action

wrong·ful *adj* **1 :** [2]WRONG 1, UNJUST **2 :** UNLAWFUL

wrote *past of* WRITE

[1]wrought *past of* WORK

[2]wrought *adj* **1 :** beaten into shape by tools **2 :** much too excited

wrung *past of* WRING

wry *adj* **wry·er; wry·est** **1 :** turned abnormally to one side **2 :** made by twisting the features

x *n, pl* **x's** *or* **xs** *often cap* **1 :** the twenty-fourth letter of the English alphabet **2 :** ten in Roman numerals **3 :** an unknown quantity

Xmas *n* **:** CHRISTMAS

x–ray *vb, often cap X* **:** to examine, treat, or photograph with X rays

X ray *n* **1 :** a powerful invisible ray made up of very short waves that is somewhat similar to light and that is able to pass through various thicknesses of solids and act on photographic film like light **2 :** a photograph taken by the use of X rays

xy·lo·phone *n* **:** a musical instrument consisting of a series of wooden bars of different lengths made to sound the musical scale and played with two wooden hammers

y *n, pl* **y's** *or* **ys** *often cap* **:** the twenty-fifth letter of the English alphabet

[1]-y *also* **-ey** *adj suffix* **-i·er; -i·est** **1 :** showing, full of, or made of **2 :** like **3 :** devoted to : enthusiastic about **4 :** tending to **5 :** somewhat : rather

[2]-y *n suffix, pl* **-ies** **1 :** state : condition : quality **2 :** occupation, place of business, or goods dealt with **3 :** whole body or group

[3]-y *n suffix, pl* **-ies** **:** occasion or example of a specified action

[4]-y — see -IE

[1]yacht *n* **:** a small ship used for pleasure cruising or racing

[2]yacht *vb* **:** to race or cruise in a yacht

yacht·ing *n* **:** the action, fact, or recreation of racing or cruising in a yacht

yachts·man *n, pl* **yachts·men** **:** a person who owns or sails a yacht

yak *n* **:** a wild or domestic ox of the uplands of Asia that has very long hair

yam *n* **1 :** the starchy root of a plant related to the lilies that is an important food in much of the tropics **2 :** a sweet potato with a moist and usually orange flesh

[1]yank *n* **:** a strong sudden pull : JERK

[2]yank *vb* **:** [2]JERK 1

Yan·kee *n* **1 :** a person born or living in New England **2 :** a person born or living in the northern United States **3 :** a person born or living in the United States

[1]yap *vb* **yapped; yap·ping** **1 :** to bark in yaps **2 :** [2]SCOLD, CHATTER

[2]yap *n* **:** a quick shrill bark

[1]yard *n* **1 :** a small and often fenced area open to the sky and next to a building **2 :** the grounds of a building **3 :** a fenced area for livestock **4 :** an area set aside for a business or activity **5 :** a system of railroad tracks especially for keeping and repairing cars

[2]yard *n* **1 :** a measure of length equal to three feet or thirty-six inches (about .91 meter) **2 :** a long pole pointed toward the ends that holds up and spreads the top of a sail

yard·age *n* **1 :** a total number of yards **2 :** the length or size of something measured in yards

yard·arm *n* **:** either end of the yard of a square-rigged ship

yard·mas·ter *n* **:** the person in charge of operations in a railroad yard

yard·stick *n* **1 :** a measuring stick a yard long **2 :** a rule or standard by which something is measured or judged

[1]yarn *n* **1 :** natural or manufactured fiber (as cotton, wool, or rayon) formed as a continuous thread for use in knitting or weaving **2 :** an interesting or exciting story
[2]yarn *vb* **:** to tell a yarn
yawl *n* **:** a sailboat having two masts with the shorter one behind the point where the stern enters the water
[1]yawn *vb* **1 :** to open wide **2 :** to open the mouth wide usually as a reaction to being tired or bored
[2]yawn *n* **:** a deep drawing in of breath through the wide-open mouth
ye *pron, archaic* **:** YOU 1
[1]yea *adv* **:** [1]YES 1 — used in spoken voting
[2]yea *n* **1 :** a vote in favor of something **2 :** a person casting a yea vote
year *n* **1 :** the period of about 365¼ days required for the earth to make one complete trip around the sun **2 :** a period of 365 days or in leap year 366 days beginning January 1 **3 :** a fixed period of time
year·book *n* **1 :** a book published yearly especially as a report **2 :** a school publication recording the history and activities of a graduating class
year·ling *n* **:** a person or animal that is or is treated as if a year old
year·ly *adj* **:** [1]ANNUAL 1
yearn *vb* **:** to feel an eager desire
yearn·ing *n* **:** an eager desire
year–round *adj* **:** being in operation for the full year
yeast *n* **1 :** material that may be found on the surface or at the bottom of sweet liquids, is made up mostly of the cells of a tiny fungus, and causes a reaction in which alcohol is produced **2 :** a commercial product containing living yeast plants and used especially to make bread dough rise **3 :** any of the group of tiny fungi that form alcohol or raise bread dough
[1]yell *vb* **:** to cry or scream loudly
[2]yell *n* **1 :** [2]SCREAM, SHOUT **2 :** a cheer used especially in schools to encourage athletic teams
[1]yel·low *adj* **1 :** of the color yellow **2 :** COWARDLY
[2]yellow *n* **1 :** the color in the rainbow between green and orange **2 :** something yellow in color
[3]yellow *vb* **:** to turn yellow
yellow fever *n* **:** a disease carried by mosquitoes in hot countries
yel·low·ish *adj* **:** somewhat yellow
yellow jacket *n* **:** a small wasp with yellow markings that usually nests in colonies in the ground
[1]yelp *n* **:** a quick shrill bark or cry
[2]yelp *vb* **:** to make a quick shrill bark or cry
yen *n* **:** a strong desire **:** LONGING
yeo·man *n, pl* **yeo·men 1 :** a naval petty officer who works as a clerk **2 :** a small farmer who cultivates his or her own land
-yer — see [2]-ER
[1]yes *adv* **1** — used to express agreement **2** — used to introduce a phrase with greater emphasis or clearness **3** — used to show interest or attention
[2]yes *n* **:** a positive reply
[1]yes·ter·day *adv* **:** on the day next before today
[2]yesterday *n* **1 :** the day next before this day **2 :** time not long past
yes·ter·year *n* **:** the recent past
[1]yet *adv* **1 :** [2]BESIDES **2 :** [2]EVEN 4 **3 :** up to now **:** so far **4 :** at this or that time **5 :** up to the present **6 :** at some later time **7 :** NEVERTHELESS
[2]yet *conj* **:** but nevertheless
yew *n* **:** a tree or shrub with stiff poisonous evergreen leaves, a fleshy fruit, and tough wood used especially for bows and small articles
Yid·dish *n* **:** a language that comes from German and is used by some Jews
[1]yield *vb* **1 :** to give up possession of on claim or demand **2 :** to give (oneself) up to a liking, temptation, or habit **3 :** to bear as a natural product **4 :** to return as income or profit **5 :** to be productive **:** bring good results **6 :** to stop opposing or objecting to something **7 :** to give way under physical force so as to bend, stretch, or break **8 :** to admit that someone else is better
[2]yield *n* **:** the amount produced or returned
[1]yip *vb* **yipped; yip·ping :** [2]YELP — used chiefly of a dog
[2]yip *n* **:** a noise made by or as if by yelping
[1]yo·del *vb* **yo·deled** *or* **yo·delled; yo·del·ing** *or* **yo·del·ling 1 :** to sing with frequent sudden changes from the natural voice range to a higher range and back **2 :** to call or shout in the manner of yodeling — **yo·del·er** *n*
[2]yodel *n* **:** a yodeled shout
yo·gurt *n* **:** a soft food that is made of milk soured by the addition of bacteria and that is often flavored and sweetened
[1]yoke *n* **1 :** a wooden bar or frame by which two work animals (as oxen) are harnessed at the heads or necks for drawing a plow or load **2 :** a frame fitted to a person's shoulders to carry a load in two equal parts **3 :** a clamp that joins two parts to hold or connect them in position **4** *pl usually* **yoke :** two animals yoked together **5 :** something that brings to a state of hardship, humiliation, or slavery **6 :** SLAVERY 2 **7 :** [1]TIE 4, BOND **8 :** a fitted or shaped piece at the shoulder of a garment or at the top of a skirt

²yoke *vb* **yoked; yok·ing 1 :** to put a yoke on **2 :** to attach a work animal to

yo·kel *n* **:** a country person with little education or experience

yolk *n* **:** the yellow inner part of the egg of a bird or reptile containing stored food material for the developing young — **yolked** *adj*

Yom Kip·pur *n* **:** a Jewish holiday observed in September or October with fasting and prayer

¹yon *adj* **:** ²YONDER 2

²yon *adv* **1 :** ¹YONDER **2 :** THITHER

¹yon·der *adv* **:** at or in that place

²yonder *adj* **1 :** more distant **2 :** being at a distance within view

yore *n* **:** time long past

you *pron* **1 :** the one or ones these words are spoken or written to **2 :** ³ONE 2

you'd : you had **:** you would

you'll : you shall **:** you will

¹young *adj* **youn·ger; youn·gest 1 :** being in the first or an early stage of life or growth **2 :** INEXPERIENCED **3 :** recently come into being **:** NEW **4 :** YOUTHFUL 1

²young *n, pl* **young 1 young** *pl* **:** young persons **2 young** *pl* **:** immature offspring **3 :** a single recently born or hatched animal

youn·gest *n, pl* **youngest :** one that is the least old especially of a family

young·ster *n* **1 :** a young person **:** YOUTH **2 :** CHILD

your *adj* **1 :** of or belonging to you **2 :** by or from you **3 :** affecting you **4 :** of or relating to one **5** — used before a title of honor in addressing a person

you're : you are

yours *pron* **:** that which belongs to you

your·self *pron, pl* **your·selves :** your own self

youth *n, pl* **youths 1 :** the period of life between being a child and an adult **2 :** a young man **3 :** young people **4 :** the quality or state of being young

youth·ful *adj* **1 :** of or relating to youth **2 :** being young and not yet fully grown **3 :** having the freshness of youth — **youth·ful·ly** *adv* — **youth·ful·ness** *n*

you've : you have

¹yowl *vb* **:** ¹WAIL

²yowl *n* **:** a loud long moaning cry (as of a cat)

yo–yo *n, pl* **yo–yos** *also* **yo–yoes :** a thick divided disk that is made to fall and rise to the hand by unwinding and winding again on a string

yuc·ca *n* **:** a plant related to the lilies that grows in dry regions and has stiff pointed leaves at the base of a tall stiff stalk of usually whitish flowers

yule *n, often cap* **:** CHRISTMAS

yule log *n, often cap Y* **:** a large log once put in the fireplace on Christmas Eve as the foundation of the fire

yule·tide *n, often cap* **:** the Christmas season

Z

z *n, pl* **z's** *or* **zs** *often cap* **:** the twenty-sixth letter of the English alphabet

¹za·ny *n, pl* **zanies 1 :** ¹CLOWN 2 **2 :** a silly or foolish person

²zany *adj* **za·ni·er; za·ni·est 1 :** being or like a zany **2 :** FOOLISH, SILLY

zeal *n* **:** eager desire to get something done or see something succeed

zeal·ous *adj* **:** filled with or showing zeal — **zeal·ous·ly** *adv* — **zeal·ous·ness** *n*

ze·bra *n* **:** an African wild animal related to the horses that has a hide striped in black and white or black and buff

ze·bu *n* **:** an Asian domestic ox that differs from the related European cattle in having a large hump over the shoulders and a loose skin with hanging folds

ze·nith *n* **1 :** the point in the heavens directly overhead **2 :** the highest point

zeph·yr *n* **1 :** a breeze from the west **2 :** a gentle breeze

zep·pe·lin *n* **:** a huge long balloon that has a metal frame and is driven through the air by engines carried on its underside

ze·ro *n, pl* **zeros** *or* **zeroes 1 :** the numerical symbol 0 meaning the absence of all size or quantity **2 :** the point on a scale (as on a thermometer) from which measurements are made **3 :** the temperature shown by the zero mark on a thermometer **4 :** a total lack of anything **:** NOTHING **5 :** the lowest point

zest *n* **1 :** an enjoyable or exciting quality **2 :** keen enjoyment — **zest·ful** *adj* — **zest·ful·ly** *adv* — **zest·ful·ness** *n*

¹zig·zag *n* **1 :** one of a series of short sharp turns or angles in a course **2 :** a line, path, or pattern that bends sharply this way and that

²zigzag *adv* **:** in or by a zigzag path or course

³zigzag *adj* **:** having short sharp turns or angles

⁴zigzag *vb* **zig·zagged; zig·zag·ging :** to form into or move along a zigzag

zinc *n* **:** a bluish white metal that tarnishes only slightly in moist air and is used mostly to make alloys and to give iron a protective coating

zing *n* **1 :** a shrill humming sound **2 :** a lively or energetic quality

zin·nia *n* **:** a tropical American herb related to the daisies that is widely grown for its bright flower heads that last a long time

¹zip *vb* **zipped; zip·ping 1 :** to move or act with speed and force **2 :** to move or pass with a shrill hissing or humming sound

²zip *n* **1 :** a sudden shrill hissing sound **2 :** ENERGY 1

³zip *vb* **zipped; zip·ping :** to close or open with a zipper

zip code *or* **ZIP Code** *n* **:** a number consisting of five digits that identifies each postal area in the United States

zip·per *n* **:** a fastener (as for a jacket) consisting of two rows of metal or plastic teeth on strips of tape and a sliding piece that closes an opening by drawing the teeth together — **zip·pered** *adj*

zip·py *adj* **zip·pi·er; zip·pi·est :** full of energy **:** LIVELY

zith·er *n* **:** a stringed instrument with usually thirty to forty strings that are plucked with the fingers or with a pick

zo·di·ac *n* **:** an imaginary belt in the heavens that includes the paths of most of the planets and is divided into twelve constellations or signs

zom·bie *or* **zom·bi** *n* **:** a person who is believed to have died and been brought back to life

¹zone *n* **1 :** any of the five great parts that the earth's surface is divided into according to latitude and temperature **2 :** a band or belt that surrounds **3 :** a section set off or marked as different in some way

²zone *vb* **zoned; zon·ing :** to divide into zones for different uses

zoo *n, pl* **zoos :** a collection of living animals for display

zoo·log·i·cal *adj* **:** of or relating to zoology

zoological garden *n* **:** a garden or park where wild animals are kept for exhibition

zo·ol·o·gist *n* **:** a specialist in zoology

zo·ol·o·gy *n* **1 :** a branch of biology dealing with animals and animal life **2 :** animal life (as of a region)

¹zoom *vb* **1 :** to speed along with a loud hum or buzz **2 :** to move upward quickly at a sharp angle

²zoom *n* **1 :** an act or process of zooming **2 :** a zooming sound

zuc·chi·ni *n* **:** a smooth cylinder-shaped green-skinned vegetable that is a type of squash

zwie·back *n* **:** a usually sweetened bread made with eggs that is baked and then sliced and toasted until dry and crisp

zy·gote *n* **:** the new cell produced when a sperm cell joins with an egg

Confused, Misused, or Misspelled Words

a/an 'A' is used before a word beginning with a consonant or consonant sound ("a door," "a one-time deal"). 'An' is usually used before a word beginning with a vowel or vowel sound ("an operation"). 'A' is used before *h* when the *h* is pronounced ("a headache"); 'an' is used if the *h* is not pronounced ("an honor").

accept/except The verb 'accept' means "to agree to, receive" ("accept a gift"). 'Except' most often means "not including" ("will visit all national parks except the Grand Canyon").

adapt/adopt The verb 'adapt' means "to change or modify" ("adapt to the warmer climate"); the verb 'adopt' means "to take as one's own" ("adopt a child").

affect/effect The verb 'affect' means to "cause a change in something" ("rain affects plant growth"); the noun 'effect' means "the result" ("the effect of rain on plant growth").

ain't 'Ain't' is used by some people in informal speech to mean "are not," "is not," or "am not," among other things. Because "ain't" is considered very informal, it is not generally used in schoolwork or in formal speech and writing.

aisle/isle 'Aisle' means "a walkway between seats"; 'isle' is a poetic word meaning "island."

a lot, allot 'A lot', meaning "a great number," is spelled as two words; it is sometimes written incorrectly as 'alot'. 'Allot' is a verb meaning "to set aside or give out in portions" ("alloted one hour for homework").

an See *a/an*.

apt See *liable/likely/apt*.

as. . . as Is it more correct to say "she is as smart as I" or "she is as smart as me"? Actually, both forms are commonly used. In comparisons with "as . . . as," it is okay to use either subject pronouns (like "I', "you," "he," "she," "it," "we," and "they") or object pronouns (like "me," "you," "him," "her," "it," "us," and "them") after the second 'as'. However, subject pronouns sound more formal and are frequently used with a form of the verb "be" ("she is as smart as I [am]"). So you may want to use subject pronouns in your comparisons when you are doing schoolwork or anytime you are writing or speaking formally.

as/like Sometimes 'as' is used with the same meaning as 'like' ("do as I do", "do like I do"). At other times, 'as' means "in the role of" ("worked as a substitute teacher").

as well as When 'as well as' is used in a comparison, the pronoun following the second 'as' is usually in the subject form ("she can spell as well as I [can]," not "she can spell as well as me"). (For a list of subject pronouns, see *as . . . as*.)

aural/oral 'Aural' and 'oral' are sometimes pronounced the same, but they have different meanings. 'Aural' means "of or relating to the ear or sense of hearing." It comes from the Latin word for "ear." 'Oral' means "of, relating to, given by, or near the mouth," and comes from a Latin word for "mouth." (See also 'verbal/oral'.)

bare/bear 'Bare' means "without clothes or a covering" ("bare feet"); 'bear' means "to carry."

bazaar/bizarre 'Bazaar' is a fair; 'bizarre' means "weird."

beside/besides 'Beside' generally means "next to or at the side" of something; 'besides' means "in addition to."

born/borne 'Born' is having come into life; 'borne' means "carried."

bring/take 'Bring' usually means "to carry to a closer place"; 'take', "to carry to a farther place."

can/may 'Can' usually means "to be able to or know how to" ("they can read and write"); 'may' means "to have permission to" ("may I go?"). In casual conversation, 'can' is often used to mean "to have permission to" ("can I go?"), but 'may' is used instead in more formal speech or in writing.

canvas/canvass 'Canvas' is a cloth; 'canvass' means to ask people's opinions.

capital/capitol 'Capital' is the place or city of government; 'capitol' is the building of government.

cereal/serial 'Cereal' is a breakfast food; 'serial' is a story presented in parts.

colonel/kernal These two words are pronounced the same but have different meanings. 'Colonel' is a military rank; 'kernel' is a part of a seed.

compliment/complement A 'compliment' is a nice thing to say; a 'complement' is something that completes.

council/counsel A 'council' is a group of people meeting; 'counsel' is advice or one who gives advice.

country/county 'Country' is a nation; 'county' is a small, local government area.

data This was originally a plural form, but today it is used as both a singular and a plural noun.

desert/dessert 'Desert' (with one *s*) is a dry, barren place; 'dessert' (with two *s*'s) is a sweet eaten after a meal.

die/dye To 'die' is to cease to live; to 'dye' is to change the color of something.

dived/dove Both spellings are common as a past tense of the verb 'dive' ("she dived into the pool," "she dove into the pool").

effect See *affect/effect.*

except See *accept/except.*

farther/further 'Farther' usually refers to distance ("he ran farther than I did"). 'Further' refers to degree or extent ("she explained the situation further").

flammable/inflammable Both words mean "capable of catching fire," but 'inflammable' is also sometimes used to mean "excitable."

forth/fourth 'Forth' means "forward" ("they went forth to seek their fortune"); 'fourth' means "number four in a sequence."

further See *farther/further.*

good/well 'To feel good' generally means "to be in good health and good spirits." 'To feel well' usually means "to be healthy."

half/half a/a half a The 'l' in 'half' is silent; it is used in writing, but it is not pronounced. 'Half' is often used with the word 'a', which can either come before 'half' or after it ("ate a half sandwich," "ate half a sandwich"). In casual speech, 'a half a' is sometimes used ("ate a half a sandwich"), but it is avoided in more formal speech and in writing.

hanged/hung Both 'hanged' and 'hung' are used as the past tense of the verb 'to hang'. 'Hanged' is used when referring to execution by hanging; 'hung' is used in all other senses.

hardy/hearty 'Hardy' (suggestive of 'hard') means "strong"; 'hearty' (suggestive of 'heart') means "friendly, enthusiastic."

isle See *aisle/isle.*

its/it's 'Its' means "of or relating to it or itself" ("the dog wagged its tail"). 'It's' is a contraction of 'it is' ("it's polite to say 'thank you' ").

kernel See *colonel/kernel.*

later/latter 'Later' is the comparative form of 'late'; it means "after a given time" ("they started later than they had intended"). 'Latter' is an adjective that refers to the second of two things mentioned, or the last one of a sequence ("of the two choices, the latter is preferred").

lead/led These two words are pronounced the same but have different meanings. 'Lead' is a metal; 'led' is the past tense of the verb 'to lead'.

less/fewer 'Less' is usually used with things that cannot be counted ("there is less sunshine today"), and 'fewer' is used with things that can be counted ("there are fewer people here today").

liable/likely/apt All three words mean the same thing, but 'likely' and 'apt' are more often used in situations that could have a positive or neutral outcome ("she's apt to burst out laughing," "they'll likely visit today"). 'Liable' is usually used where there is a possibility of a negative outcome ("you're liable to get hurt").

lie See *lay/lie.*

like See *as/like.*

liter/litter A 'liter' is a unit of measurement; 'litter' is a messy collection of things.

loose/lose 'Loose' means "not tight"; 'lose' means "to misplace or fail to win."

marital/martial 'Marital' has to do with marriage; 'martial' has to do with the military.

may See *can/may.*

moral/morale 'Moral' has to do with high ideals or ethical behavior; 'morale' is the state of feelings of a person or group ("after the victory, morale was high").

naval/navel 'Naval' has to do with the Navy; a 'navel' is a belly button.

no way 'No way' is an expression meaning "no" or "not at all." It is used in everyday speech, but is usually considered too casual for formal speech and writing.

oral See *verbal/oral* and 'aural/oral'.

peace See *piece/peace.*

pedal/peddle 'Pedal' as a verb means "to use or work the pedals of something" ("pedal a bicycle"). 'Peddle' means "to sell from house to house."

piece/peace A 'piece' is a portion of something ("a piece of cake"); 'peace' is the freedom from stress or from war or fighting.

precede/proceed 'Precede' means "to go ahead of or come before"; 'proceed' means "to start or move forward."

principal/principle A 'principal' is the head of a school; a 'principle' is a rule or guiding truth. It may help you to remember that 'principal' ends with the word 'pal', and that 'principle' and 'rule' end with the same two letters.

serial See *cereal/serial*.

set/sit The verb 'set' means "to place (something) down or to arrange or make settled" ("set the date"); 'sit' means "to rest on the part of the body where the hips and legs join."

stationary/stationery Something that is stationary stands still; 'stationery' is paper that is used for writing letters. It's easy to tell these two words apart if you remember that 'stationery' and 'letter' both contain *er*.

take See *bring/take*.

than/then 'Than' is used to indicate a comparison ("better than that"); 'then' means "at that time" ("then we went home").

there/their 'There' points to a place ("there it is"); 'their' refers to "what belongs to them" ("that is their house").

to/too/two 'To' implies a direction ("went to the store"). 'Too' means "also," "very," or "excessively" ("brought a pen and pencil too," "not too difficult," "too much"). 'Two' is the number 2.

used to/use to The phrases 'used to' and 'use to' are often confused since they have the same pronunciation. 'Used to' is correct in most instances ("we used to go to the lake every summer," "I used to know that"). But when it follows 'did' or 'didn't', the correct spelling is 'use to' ("that didn't use to be a problem").

verbal/oral Both 'verbal' and 'oral' are sometimes used to mean "spoken rather than written" ("a verbal agreement," "an oral agreement"). 'Verbal' can also mean "of, relating to, or formed by a verb," or "of, relating to, or consisting of words." (For more about 'oral', see *aural/oral*.)

want See *won't/want*.

were/we're 'Were' is a past tense verb form of 'be' ("they were very young"); 'we're' is a contraction of 'we are' ("we're glad to see you").

who's/whose The word 'who's' is a contraction of 'who is' ("who's there?"); 'whose' is an adjective indicating ownership or quality ("whose book is this?")

who/whom 'Who' is used as the subject of a clause (where one would use 'he', 'she', or 'they'). 'Whom' is used as the object of a clause (where one would use 'him', 'her', or 'them'), and often follows prepositions like 'to', 'for', 'from', or 'with'. Subject: "Who is coming to the party?" "He is coming to the party." Object: "John is coming with whom?" "John is coming with them."

won't/want 'Won't is a contraction of 'will not' ("I won't go"); 'want' is a verb meaning "to need or desire" ("do you want some milk?").

Xmas 'Xmas' is a shortened form of the word 'Christmas'; the 'X' comes a Greek letter which is the first letter of the Greek word for 'Christ'. 'Xmas' is used in very casual writing but is inappropriate for formal writing or schoolwork.

your/you're 'Your' is an adjective meaning "that which belongs to you" ("is that your sister?"). 'You're' is a contraction of 'you are' ("you're going, aren't you?").

Frequently Misspelled Words

about
accept
accidental
accidentally
accommodate
ache
acquire
across
adapt
address
adopt
affect
afternoon
again
aisle
all right
along
already
always
among
answer
antarctic
anything
anyway
apparent
appear
appearance
April
apt
arctic
attendance
aunt
awhile
balloon
bare
bargain
bazaar
bear
because
before
beginning
believable
believe
beside
besides
between
bicycle
birthday
bizarre
born
borne
bought
boys
bring
brother
brought
build
built
bureau
business
busy
buy
calendar
can
cannot
can't
canvas
canvass
capital
capitol
ceiling
cellar
cemetery
cereal
changeable
chief
children
choose
chose
close
cocoa
colonel
column
coming
commit
commitment
committee
complement
compliment
concede
conceive
conscience
conscious
cough
could
couldn't
council
counsel
country
county
cousin
cylinder
data
debt
definite
dependent
describe
description
desert
dessert
develop
diction
dictionary
didn't
die
different
dived
divine
doctor
does
done
don't
dove
down
dye
early
easily
easy
effect
eight
eighth
eligible
embarrass
encyclopedia
enough
envelop (verb)
envelope (noun)
environment
every
everybody
everything
exceed
except
existence
familiar
farther
father
February
fewer
fine
first
flammable
foreign
forth
forty
fourth
freight
Friday
friend
fulfill
further
getting
goes
going
good-by
good-bye
government
grammar
guess
half
handkerchiefs
hanged
hardy
haven't
having
hear
heard
hearty
height
hello
hoarse
hospital
hour
house
how's
hung
hygiene
illegal
imagine
independence
inflammable
instead
isle
isn't
its
January
judgment
kernal
knew
know
knowledge
laboratory
laid
later
latter
laugh
lay
lead
league
led
leisure
less
letter
liable
library
license
lie
like
likely
liter
litter
little
loose
lose
lovely
loving
lying
maintenance

management
manual
marital
marshal
martial
mathematics
may
maybe
meant
minute
mischief
misspell
moral
morale
morning
mosquito
mosquitoes
mother
movable
naval
navel
neighbor
nice
nickel
niece
ninety
ninth
none
noticeable
nowadays
occur
occurrence
o'clock
offense
often
once
oral
ought
parallel
parliament
peace
pedal
peddle
people
piece
please
pneumonia
prairie
precede
principal
principle
probably
proceed
quiet
quit
quite
raise
raspberry
ready
receipt
receive
recommend
remember
rhyme
rhythm
right
said
sandwich
satellite
Saturday
says
schedule
school
scissors
secretary
separate
serial
set
sheriff
sincerely
sit
somebody
something
sometime
speech
squirrel
stationary
stationery
straight
strength
studying
succeed
sugar
superintendent
supersede
suppose
sure
surely
surprise
synagogue
take
tear
than
their
them
then
there
though
thought
thoughtful
through
Thursday
to
together
tomorrow
tonight
too
trouble
truly
Tuesday
two
tying
unique
until
usable
used to
use to
usual
usually
vacation
vacuum
vegetable
verbal
villain
visible
volume
want
weak
wear
weather
Wednesday
week
weird
were
when
whether
which
who
whole
wholly
whom
who's
whose
witch
women
won't
would
wouldn't
write
writing
wrote
Xmas
X-ray
yacht
yeast
yield
your
you're
youthful
zenith
zodiac

Ten General Spelling Rules

1) In general, 'i' comes before 'e' except after 'c' or in words like 'neighbor' and 'weigh'.
2) Words that end in a /seed/ sound: 'supersede' is the only word ending in 'sede'; 'exceed', 'proceed' and 'succeed' are the only three words ending in 'ceed'; all others end in 'cede'.
3) Words ending in a hard 'c' sound usually change to 'ck' before adding 'e', 'i', or 'y': picnic (r) picnicked, picnicking but picnics.
4) Words ending in a stressed single vowel + single consonant usually double the consonant before a suffix: abet (r) abetted, abetting; begin (r) beginner.
5) Words ending in silent 'e' usually drop the 'e' before a suffix that begins with a vowel but not before a suffix beginning with a consonant: bone (r) boned, boning but boneless.
6) Words ending in stressed 'ie' usually change to 'y' before a suffixal 'i': die (r) dying.
7) Words ending in a double vowel usually remain unchanged before a suffix: agree (r) agreeable; blue (r) blueness; coo (r) cooing.
8) Words ending in a consonant plus 'y' usually change the 'y' to 'i' before a suffix: beauty (r) beautiful; happy (r) happiness.
9) Words ending in a vowel plus 'y' usually do not change before a suffix: boy (r) boys; enjoy (r) enjoying.
10) Words ending in 'll' usually drop one 'l' when adding another word to form a compound: all + ready (r) already; full + fill (r) fulfill; hate + full (r) hateful.

Ten Rules for Forming Plurals

1) Most nouns form the plural by adding 's': bag (r) bags.
2) Words that end in silent 'e' usually just add 's': college (r) colleges.
3) Nouns ending in 'x', 'z', 'ch', 'sh', and 'ss' usually add 'es': fox (r) foxes; buzz (r) buzzes; church (r) churches; bush (r) bushes; boss (r) bosses.
4) Words ending in a consonant + 'y' usually change the 'y' to 'i' and add 'es': army (r) armies; sky (r) skies.
5) Words ending in a vowel + 'y' usually add 's' with no change: day (r) days; boy (r) boys; key (r) keys.
6) Words ending in a vowel + 'o' usually add 's' with no change: duo (r) duos; studio (r) studios.
7) Words ending in a consonant + 'o': some add 's' and some add 'es': ego (r) egos; piano (r) pianos; echo (r) echoes; tomato (r) tomatoes.
8) Words ending in 'f' usually change the 'f' to 'v' and add 'es': leaf (r) leaves; self (r) selves; thief (r) thieves; but chief (r) chiefs.
9) Words ending in 'fe' usually change the 'fe' to 'v' and add 'es': knife (r) knives; life (r) lives.
10) Words that are the names of fishes, birds, and mammals usually have an unchanging form for the plural or have the unchanging form and an 's' plural, depending on meaning.

Webster's Punctuation Guide

Created in Cooperation with the Editors of
MERRIAM-WEBSTER

A Division of Merriam-Webster, Incorporated
Springfield, Massachusetts

This 2006 edition published by
Federal Street Press
A Division of Merriam-Webster, Incorporated
P.O. Box 281
Springfield, MA 01102

Federal Street Press books are available for bulk purchase
for sales promotion and premium use.
For details write the manager of special sales,
Federal Street Press, P.O. Box 281, Springfield, MA 01102

ISBN 13 978-1-59695-008-5

Printed in the United States of America

08 09 10 5 4 3

Contents

Preface

This volume is designed to be a concise handbook on the conventions of contemporary American English—in particular, the conventions of punctuation, capitalization, italicization, abbreviation, quotation, and documentation of sources.

Just as the Merriam-Webster dictionaries strive to mirror the language as it is actually used, this book strives to reflect the practices actually employed in published writing. It is based on a continuous study of the ways Americans use their language, and it draws on Merriam-Webster's extensive citation files of 15 million examples of English words used in context, gathered from a broad selection of books, newspapers, magazines, and other publications.

Firmly based on real-life source material, this book attempts to reflect both the consensus and the variety evident in mainstream American published writing. When a statement about style must be qualified, the word *usually, generally,* or *normally* indicates that a significant minority of writers and editors follow another practice. *Sometimes* is used when describing an alternative, minority practice. *Often* or *frequently* indicates that a convention is commonly but not universally followed; it does not necessarily identify a majority practice.

Whenever a practice raises questions that require an explanation, a brief note is provided. Conventions restricted to journalism or specialized fields are labeled as such.

1 Punctuation

Punctuation marks are used to help clarify the structure and meaning of sentences. They separate groups of words for meaning and emphasis; they convey an idea of the variations in pitch, volume, pauses, and intonation of the spoken language; and they help avoid ambiguity. The choice of what punctuation to use, if any, will often be clear and unambiguous. In other cases, a sentence may allow for several punctuation patterns. In cases like these, varying notions of correctness have developed, and two writers might, with equal correctness, punctuate the same sentence quite differently, relying on their individual judgment and taste.

Apostrophe

The apostrophe is used to form most possessives and contractions as well as some plurals and inflections.

1. The apostrophe is used to indicate the possessive of nouns and indefinite pronouns. (For details, see the section beginning on page 124.)

   the girl's shoe
   the boys' fathers
   Simmons's role
   children's laughter
   anyone's guess
   the Browns' house
   Arkansas's capital

2. Apostrophes are sometimes used to form plurals of letters, numerals, abbreviations, symbols, and words referred to as words. (For details, see the section beginning on page 114.)

   cross your *t*'s
   three 8's *or* three 8s

two L.H.D.'s *or* two L.H.D.s
used &'s instead of *and*'s

3. Apostrophes mark omissions in contractions made of two or more words and in contractions of single words.

   wasn't
   they're
   she'd rather not
   Jake's had it
   ass'n
   dep't

4. The apostrophe is used to indicate that letters have been intentionally omitted from a word in order to imitate informal speech.

   "Singin' in the Rain," the popular song and movie
   "Snap 'em up" was his response.

   Sometimes such words are so consistently spelled with an apostrophe that the spelling becomes an accepted variant.

   rock 'n' roll [*for* rock and roll]
   ma'am [*for* madam]
   sou'wester [*for* southwester]

5. Apostrophes mark the omission of digits in numerals.

   class of '98
   fashion in the '90s

If the apostrophe is used when writing the plurals of numerals, either the apostrophe that stands for the missing figures is omitted or the word is spelled out.

90's *or* nineties *but not* '90's

6. In informal writing, apostrophes are used to produce forms of verbs that are made of individually pronounced letters. An apostrophe or a hyphen is also sometimes used to add an -er ending to an abbreviation; if no confusion would result, the apostrophe is usually omitted.

   OK'd the budget
   X'ing out the mistakes
   4-H'er
   49er

Brackets

Outside of mathematics and chemistry texts, brackets are primarily used for insertions into carefully handled quoted matter. They are rarely seen in general writing but are common in historical and scholarly contexts.

1. Brackets enclose editorial comments, corrections, and clarifications inserted into quoted matter.

   Surely that should have peaked [sic] the curiosity of a serious researcher.

> Here they much favour the tiorba [theorbo], the arclute [archlute], and the cittarone [chitarrone], while we at home must content ourselves with the lute alone.

> In Blaine's words, "All the vocal aristocracy showed up—Nat [Cole], Billy [Eckstine], Ella [Fitzgerald], Mabel Mercer—'cause nobody wanted to miss that date."

2. Brackets enclose insertions that take the place of words or phrases.

> And on the next page: "Their assumption is plainly that [Durocher] would be the agent in any such negotiation."

3. Brackets enclose insertions that supply missing letters.

> A postscript to a December 17 letter to Waugh notes, "If D[eutsch] won't take the manuscript, perhaps someone at Faber will."

4. Brackets enclose insertions that alter the form of a word used in an original text.

> He dryly observes (p. 78) that the Gravely investors had bought stocks because "they want[ed] to see themselves getting richer."

5. Brackets are used to indicate that capitalization has been altered. This is generally optional; it is standard practice only where meticulous handling of original source material is crucial (particularly legal and scholarly contexts).

As Chief Justice Warren held for the Court, "[T]he Attorney General may bring an injunctive action . . ."

or in general contexts

"The Attorney General may bring . . ."

Brackets also enclose editorial notes when text has been italicized for emphasis.

But tucked away on page 11 we find this fascinating note: "In addition, we anticipate that *siting these new plants in marginal neighborhoods will decrease the risk of organized community opposition*" [italics added].

6. Brackets function as parentheses within parentheses, especially where two sets of parentheses could be confusing.

Posner's recent essays (including the earlier *Law and Literature* [1988]) bear this out.

7. In mathematical copy, brackets are used with parentheses to indicate units contained within larger units. They are also used with various meanings in chemical names and formulas.

$x + 5[(x + y)(2x - y)]$

$Ag[Pt(NO_2)_4]$

With Other Punctuation

8. Punctuation that marks the end of a phrase, clause, item in a series, or sentence follows any bracketed material appended to that passage.

The report stated, "if we fail to find additional sources of supply [of oil and gas], our long-term growth will be limited."

When brackets enclose a complete sentence, closing punctuation is placed within the brackets.

[Since this article was written, new archival evidence of document falsification has come to light.]

Colon

The colon is usually a mark of introduction, indicating that what follows it—generally a clause, a phrase, or a list—has been pointed to or described in what precedes it. (For the use of capitals following a colon, see paragraphs 7–8 on page 74.)

With Phrases and Clauses

1. A colon introduces a clause or phrase that explains, illustrates, amplifies, or restates what has gone before.

   An umbrella is a foolish extravagance: if you don't leave it in the first restaurant, a gust of wind will destroy it on the way home.

   Dawn was breaking: the distant peaks were already glowing with the sun's first rays.

2. A colon introduces an amplifying word, phrase, or clause that acts as an apposi-

tive. (For details on appositives, see the section on pages 17–18.)

> That year Handley's old obsession was replaced with a new one: jazz.
>
> The issue comes down to this: Will we offer a reduced curriculum, or will we simply cancel the program?

3. A colon introduces a list or series, often following a phrase such as *the following* or *as follows.*

> She has trial experience on three judicial levels: county, state, and federal.
>
> Anyone planning to participate should be prepared to do the following: hike five miles with a backpack, sleep on the ground without a tent, and paddle a canoe through rough water.

It is occasionally used like a dash to introduce a summary statement following a series.

> Baseball, soccer, skiing, track: he excelled in every sport he took up.

4. Although the colon usually follows a full independent clause, it also often interrupts a sentence before the clause is complete.

> The nine proposed program topics are: offshore supply, vessel traffic, ferry services, ship repair, . . .
>
> Information on each participant includes: name, date of birth, mailing address, . . .

For example: 58 percent of union members voted, but only 44 percent of blue-collar workers as a whole.

The association will:

Act with trust, integrity, and professionalism.

Operate in an open and effective manner.

Take the initiative in seeking diversity.

With Quotations

5. A colon usually introduces lengthy quoted material that is set off from the rest of a text by indentation but not by quotation marks.

The *Rumpole* series has been nicely encapsulated as follows:

> Rumpled, disreputable, curmudgeonly barrister Horace Rumpole often wins cases despite the disdain of his more aristocratic colleagues. Fond of cheap wine ("Château Thames Embankment") and Keats's poetry, he refers to his wife as "She Who Must Be Obeyed" (an allusion to the title character of H. Rider Haggard's *She*).

6. A colon is often used before a quotation in running text, especially when (1) the quotation is lengthy, (2) the quotation is a formal statement or is being given special emphasis, or (3) a full independent clause precedes the colon.

Said Murdoch: "The key to the success of this project is good planning. We need to know precisely what steps we will need to take, what kind of staff we will require, what the project will cost, and when we can expect completion."

The inscription reads: "Here lies one whose name was writ in water."

This was his verbatim response: "At this time Mr. Wilentz is still in the company's employ, and no change in his status is anticipated imminently."

Other Uses

7. A colon separates elements in bibliographic publication data and page references, in biblical citations, and in formulas used to express time and ratios. No space precedes or follows a colon between numerals.

   Stendhal, *Love* (New York: Penguin, 1975)
   Paleobiology 3:121
   John 4:10
   8:30 a.m.
   a winning time of 3:43:02
   a ratio of 3:5

8. A colon separates titles and subtitles.

   Southwest Stories: Tales from the Desert

9. A colon follows the salutation in formal correspondence.

   Dear Judge Wright:
   Dear Laurence:
   Dear Product Manager:
   Ladies and Gentlemen:

10. A colon follows headings in memorandums, government correspondence, and general business letters.

    TO:
    SUBJECT:
    VIA:
    REFERENCE:

11. An unspaced colon separates the writer's and typist's initials in the identification lines of business letters.

    WAL:jml

    A colon also separates copy abbreviations from the initials of copy recipients. (The abbreviation *cc* stands for *carbon* or *courtesy copy; bcc* stands for *blind carbon* or *courtesy copy.*) A space follows a colon used with the fuller name of a recipient.

    cc:RSP
      JES
    bcc:MWK
    bcc: Mr. Jones

With Other Punctuation

12. A colon is placed outside quotation marks and parentheses that punctuate the larger sentence.

    The problem becomes most acute in "Black Rose and Destroying Angel": plot simply ceases to exist.

    Wilson and Hölldobler remark on the same phenomenon in *The Ants* (1990):

Comma

The comma is the most frequently used punctuation mark in English and the one that provides the most difficulties to writers. Its most common uses are to separate items in a series and to set off or distinguish grammatical elements within sentences.

Between Main Clauses

1. A comma separates main clauses joined by a coordinating conjunction, such as *and, but, or, nor,* or *so.*

   She knew very little about the new system, and he volunteered nothing.

   The trial lasted for nine months, but the jury took only four hours to reach its verdict.

   We will not respond to any more questions on that topic this afternoon, nor will we respond to similar questions in the future.

   All the first-floor windows were barred, so he had clambered up onto the fire escape.

2. When one or both of the clauses are short or closely related in meaning, the comma is often omitted.

   They said good-bye and everyone hugged.

   If commas set off another phrase that modifies the whole sentence, the comma between main clauses is often omitted.

Six thousand years ago, the top of the volcano blew off in a series of powerful eruptions and the sides collapsed into the middle.

3. Commas are sometimes used to separate short and obviously parallel main clauses that are not joined by conjunctions.

   One day you're a successful corporate lawyer, the next day you're out of work.

   Use of a comma to join clauses that are neither short nor obviously parallel, called *comma fault* or *comma splice,* is avoided. Clauses not joined by conjunctions are normally separated by semicolons. For details, see paragraph 1 on page 65.

4. If a sentence is composed of three or more clauses that are short and free of commas, the clauses are occasionally all separated by commas even if the last two are not joined by a conjunction. If the clauses are long or punctuated, they are separated with semicolons; the last two clauses are sometimes separated by a comma if they are joined by a conjunction. (For more details, see paragraph 5 on pages 66–67.)

   Small fish fed among the marsh weed, ducks paddled along the surface, an occasional muskrat ate greens along the bank.

The kids were tired and whiny; Napoleon, usually so calm, was edgy; Tabitha seemed to be going into heat, and even the guinea pigs were agitated.

With Compound Predicates

5. Commas are not normally used to separate the parts of a compound predicate.

The firefighter tried to enter the burning building but was turned back by the thick smoke.

However, they are often used if the predicate is long and complicated, if one part is being stressed, or if the absence of a comma could cause a momentary misreading.

The board helps to develop the financing and marketing strategies for new corporate divisions, and issues periodic reports on expenditures, revenues, and personnel appointments.

This is an unworkable plan, and has been from the start.

I try to explain to him what I want him to do, and get nowhere.

With Subordinate Clauses and Phrases

6. Adverbial clauses and phrases that begin a sentence are usually set off with commas.

Having made that decision, we turned our attention to other matters.

In order to receive a high school diploma, a student must earn 16 credits from public or private secondary schools.

In addition, staff members respond to queries, take new orders, and initiate billing.

If the sentence can be easily read without a comma, the comma may be omitted. The phrase will usually be short—four words or less—but even after a longer phrase the comma is often omitted.

As cars age, they depreciate.
or As cars age they depreciate.

In January the firm will introduce a new line of investigative services.

On the map the town appeared as a small dot in the midst of vast emptiness.

If nobody comes forward by Friday I will have to take further steps.

7. Adverbial clauses and phrases that introduce a main clause other than the first main clause are usually set off with commas. If the clause or phrase follows a conjunction, one comma often precedes the conjunction and one follows the clause or phrase. Alternatively, one comma precedes the conjunction and two more enclose the clause or phrase, or a single comma precedes the conjunction. Short

phrases, and phrases in short sentences, tend not to be enclosed in commas.

> They have redecorated the entire store, but[,] to the delight of their customers, it retains much of its original flavor.
>
> We haven't left Springfield yet, but when we get to Boston we'll call you.

8. A comma is not used after an introductory phrase if the phrase immediately precedes the main verb.

> From the next room came a loud expletive.

9. A subordinate clause or phrase that modifies a noun is not set off by commas if it is *restrictive* (or *essential*)—that is, if its removal would alter the noun's meaning.

> The man who wrote this obviously had no firsthand knowledge of the situation.
>
> They entered through the first door that wasn't locked.

If the meaning would not be altered by its removal, the clause or phrase is considered *nonrestrictive* (or *nonessential*) and usually is set off by commas.

> The new approach, which was based on team teaching, was well received.
>
> Wechsler, who has done solid reporting from other battlefronts, is simply out of his depth here.
>
> They tried the first door, which led nowhere.

10. Commas set off an adverbial clause or phrase that falls between the subject and the verb.

    The Clapsaddle sisters, to keep up appearances, rode to the park every Sunday in their rented carriage.

11. Commas set off modifying phrases that do not immediately precede the word or phrase they modify.

    Scarbo, intent as usual on his next meal, was snuffling around the butcher's bins.

    The negotiators, tired and discouraged, headed back to the hotel.

    We could see the importance, both long-term and short-term, of her proposal.

12. An absolute phrase (a participial phrase with its own subject that is grammatically independent of the rest of the sentence) is set off with commas.

    Our business being concluded, we adjourned for refreshments.

    We headed southward, the wind freshening behind us, to meet the rest of the fleet in the morning.

    I'm afraid of his reaction, his temper being what it is.

With Appositives

13. Commas set off a word, phrase, or clause that is in apposition to (that is, equivalent

to) a preceding or following noun and that is nonrestrictive.

It sat nursing its front paw, the injured one.

Aleister Crowley, Britain's most infamous satanist, is the subject of a remarkable new biography.

A cherished landmark in the city, the Hotel Sandburg has managed once again to escape the wrecking ball.

The committee cochairs were a lawyer, John Larson, and an educator, Mary Conway.

14. Restrictive appositives are not set off by commas.

He next had a walk-on role in the movie *The Firm.*

Longfellow's poem *Evangeline* was a favorite of my grandmother's.

The committee cochairs were the lawyer John Larson and the educator Mary Conway.

Lord Castlereagh was that strange anomaly[,] a Labor-voting peer.

With Introductory and Interrupting Elements

15. Commas set off transitional words and phrases.

Indeed, close coordination will be essential.

Defeat may be inevitable; however, disgrace is not.

The second report, on the other hand, shows a strong bias.

When such words and phrases fall in the middle of a clause, commas are sometimes unnecessary.

They thus have no chips left to bargain with.

The materials had indeed arrived.

She would in fact see them that afternoon.

16. Commas set off parenthetical elements, such as authorial asides.

All of us, to tell the truth, were completely amazed.

It was, I should add, not the first time I'd seen him in this condition.

17. Commas are often used to set off words or phrases that introduce examples or explanations, such as *namely, for example,* and *that is.*

He expects to visit three countries, namely, France, Spain, and Germany.

I would like to develop a good, workable plan, that is, one that would outline our goals and set a timetable for accomplishing them.

Such introductory words and phrases may also often be preceded by a dash, parenthesis, or semicolon. Regardless of the punctuation that precedes the word or phrase, a comma usually follows it.

Sports develop two valuable traits—namely, self-control and the ability to make quick decisions.

In writing to the manufacturer, be as specific as possible (i.e., list the missing or defective parts, describe the malfunction, and identify the store where the unit was purchased).

Most had traveled great distances to participate; for example, three had come from Australia, one from Japan, and two from China.

18. Commas set off words in direct address.

This is our third and final notice, Mr. Sutton.

The facts, my fellow Americans, are very different.

19. Commas set off mild interjections or exclamations.

Ah, the mosaics in Ravenna are matchless.

Uh-oh, His Eminence seems to be on the warpath this morning.

With Contrasting Expressions

20. A comma is sometimes used to set off contrasting expressions within a sentence.

This project will take six months, not six weeks.

21. When two or more contrasting modifiers or prepositions, one of which is introduced by a conjunction or adverb, apply to a noun that follows immediately, the second is set off by two commas or a single comma, or not set off at all.

A solid, if overly wordy, assessment
or a solid, if overly wordy assessment
or a solid if overly wordy assessment

This street takes you away from, not toward, the capitol.
or This street takes you away from, not toward the capitol.

grounds for a civil, and maybe a criminal, case
or grounds for a civil, and maybe a criminal case
or grounds for a civil and maybe a criminal case

Dashes or parentheses are often used instead of commas in such sentences.

grounds for a civil (and maybe a criminal) case

22. A comma does not usually separate elements that are contrasted through the use of a pair of correlative conjunctions such as *either . . . or, neither . . . nor,* and *not only . . . but also.*

Neither my brother nor I noticed the error.

He was given the post not only because of his diplomatic connections but also because of his great tact and charm.

When correlative conjunctions join main clauses, a comma usually separates the clauses unless they are short.

Not only did she have to see three salesmen and a visiting reporter, but she also had to prepare for next day's meeting.

•

Either you do it my way or we don't do it at all.

23. Long parallel contrasting and comparing clauses are separated by commas; short parallel phrases are not.

 The more that comes to light about him, the less savory he seems.

 The less said the better.

With Items in a Series

24. Words, phrases, and clauses joined in a series are separated by commas.

 Men, women, and children crowded aboard the train.

 Her job required her to pack quickly, to travel often, and to have no personal life.

 He responded patiently while reporters shouted questions, flashbulbs popped, and the crowd pushed closer.

When the last two items in a series are joined by a conjunction, the final comma is often omitted, especially where this would not result in ambiguity. In individual publications, the final comma is usually consistently used, consistently omitted, or used only where a given sentence would otherwise be ambiguous or hard to read. It is consistently used in most nonfiction books; elsewhere it tends to be used or generally omitted equally often.

We are looking for a house with a big yard, a view of the harbor[,] and beach and docking privileges.

25. A comma is not generally used to separate items in a series all of which are joined with conjunctions.

I don't understand what this policy covers or doesn't cover or only partially covers.

They left behind the fogs and the wood storks and the lonesome soughing of the wind.

26. When the elements in a series are long or complex or consist of clauses that themselves contain commas, the elements are usually separated by semicolons, not commas. See paragraph 7 on pages 67–68.

With Coordinate Modifiers

27. A comma is generally used to separate two or more adjectives, adverbs, or phrases that modify the same word or phrase.

She spoke in a calm, reflective manner.

They set to their work again grimly, intently.

The comma is often omitted when the adjectives are short.

one long thin strand

a small white stone

little nervous giggles

skinny young waiters
in this harsh new light

The comma is generally omitted where it is ambiguous whether the last modifier and the noun—or two of the modifiers—constitute a unit.

the story's stark dramatic power
a pink stucco nightclub

In some writing, especially works of fiction, commas may be omitted from most series of coordinate modifiers as a matter of style.

28. A comma is not used between two adjectives when the first modifies the combination of the second plus the noun it modifies.

the last good man
a good used car
his protruding lower lip
the only fresh water
the only freshwater lake
their black pickup truck

A comma is also not used to separate an adverb from the adjective or adverb that it modifies.

this formidably difficult task

In Quotations

29. A comma usually separates a direct quotation from a phrase identifying its source

or speaker. If the quotation is a question or an exclamation and the identifying phrase follows the quotation, the comma is replaced by a question mark or an exclamation point.

> She answered, "I'm afraid it's all we've got."
>
> "The comedy is over," he muttered.
>
> "How about another round?" Elaine piped up.
>
> "I suspect," said Mrs. Horowitz, "we haven't seen the last of her."
>
> "You can sink the lousy thing for all I care!" Trumbull shouted back.
>
> "And yet . . . [,]" she mused.
>
> "We can't get the door op—" Captain Hunt is heard shouting before the tape goes dead.

In some cases, a colon can replace a comma preceding a quotation; see paragraph 6 on pages 9–10.

30. When short or fragmentary quotations are used in a sentence that is not primarily dialogue, they are usually not set off by commas.

> He glad-handed his way through the small crowd with a "Looking good, Joe" or "How's the wife" for every beaming face.
>
> Just because he said he was "about to leave this minute" doesn't mean he actually left.

Sentences that fall within sentences and do not constitute actual dialogue are not usually set off with commas. These may be mottoes or maxims, unspoken or imaginary dialogue, or sentences referred to as sentences; and they may or may not be enclosed in quotation marks. Where quotation marks are not used, a comma is often inserted to mark the beginning of the shorter sentence clearly. (For the use of quotation marks with such sentences, see paragraph 6 on pages 58–59.)

> "The computer is down" was the response she dreaded.
>
> He spoke with a candor that seemed to insist, This actually happened to me and in just this way.
>
> The first rule is, When in doubt, spell it out.

When the shorter sentence functions as an appositive (the equivalent to an adjacent noun), it is set off with commas when nonrestrictive and not when restrictive.

> We had the association's motto, "We make waves," printed on our T-shirts.
>
> He was fond of the slogan "Every man a king, but no man wears a crown."

31. A comma introduces a directly stated question, regardless of whether it is enclosed in quotation marks or if its first word is capitalized. It also introduces a tag question.

> I wondered, what is going on here?
>
> The question is, How do we get out of this situation?
>
> That's obvious, isn't it?

A comma is not used to set off indirect discourse or indirect questions introduced by a conjunction (such as *that* or *what*).

Margot replied quietly that she'd never been happier.

I wondered what was going on here.

The question is how do we get out of this situation.

32. The comma is usually omitted before quotations that are very short exclamations or representations of sounds.

He jumped up suddenly and cried "I've got it!"

Replacing Omitted Words

33. A comma may indicate the omission of a word or phrase in parallel constructions where the omitted word or phrase appears earlier in the sentence. In short sentences, the comma is usually omitted.

The larger towns were peopled primarily by shopkeepers, artisans, and traders; the small villages, by peasant farmers.

Seven voted for the proposal, three against.

He critiqued my presentation and I his.

34. A comma sometimes replaces the conjunction *that*.

The smoke was so thick, they were forced to crawl.

Chances are, there are still some tickets left.

With Addresses, Dates, and Numbers

35. Commas set off the elements of an address except for zip codes.

    Write to Bureau of the Census, Washington, DC 20233.

    In Needles, California, their luck ran out.

    When a city name and state (province, country, etc.) name are used together to modify a noun that follows, the second comma may be omitted but is more often retained.

    We visited their Enid, Oklahoma plant.

    but more commonly

    We visited their Enid, Oklahoma, plant.

36. Commas set off the year in a full date.

    On July 26, 1992, the court issued its opinion.

    Construction for the project began on April 30, 1995.

    When only the month and year are given, the first comma is usually omitted.

    In December 1903, the Wright brothers finally succeeded in keeping an airplane aloft for a few seconds.

    October 1929 brought an end to all that.

37. A comma groups numerals into units of three to separate thousands, millions, and so on.

2,000 case histories
15,000 units
a population of 3,450,000
a fee of $12,500

Certain types of numbers do not contain commas, including decimal fractions, street addresses, and page numbers. (For more on the use of the comma with numbers, see paragraphs 1–3 on page 181.)

2.5544
12537 Wilshire Blvd.
page 1415

With Names, Degrees, and Titles

38. A comma separates a surname from a following professional, academic, honorary, or religious degree or title, or an abbreviation for a branch of the armed forces.

Amelia P. Artandi, M.D.
Robert Hynes Menard, Ph.D., L.H.D.
John L. Farber, Esq.
Sister Mary Catherine, S.C.
Admiral Herman Washington, USN

39. A comma is often used between a surname and the abbreviations *Jr.* and *Sr.*

Douglas Fairbanks, Sr.
or Douglas Fairbanks Sr.
Dr. Martin Luther King, Jr.
or Dr. Martin Luther King Jr.

40. A comma is often used to set off corporate identifiers such as *Incorporated, Inc., Ltd., P.C.,* and *L.P.* However, many company names omit this comma.

StarStage Productions, Incorporated
Hart International Inc.
Walsh, Brandon & Kaiser, P.C.
The sales manager from Doyle Southern, Inc., spoke at Tuesday's meeting.

Other Uses

41. A comma follows the salutation in informal correspondence and usually follows the complimentary close in both informal and formal correspondence.

Dear Rachel,
Affectionately,
Very truly yours,

42. The comma is used to avoid ambiguity when the juxtaposition of two words or expressions could cause confusion.

Under Mr. Thomas, Jefferson High School has flourished.
He scanned the landscape that opened out before him, and guided the horse gently down.

43. When normal sentence order is inverted, a comma often precedes the subject and verb. If the structure is clear without it, it is often omitted.

That we would succeed, no one doubted.
And a splendid occasion it was.

With Other Punctuation

44. Commas are used next to brackets, ellipsis points, parentheses, and quotation marks. Commas are not used next to colons, dashes, exclamation points, question marks, or semicolons. If one of the latter falls at the same point where a comma would fall, the comma is dropped. (For more on the use of commas with other punctuation, see the sections for each individual mark.)

"If they find new sources [of oil and gas], their earnings will obviously rebound. . . ."

"This book takes its place among the most serious, . . . comprehensive, and enlightened treatments of its great subject."

There are only six small files (at least in this format), which take up very little disk space.

According to Hartmann, the people are "savage," their dwellings are "squalid," and the landscape is "a pestilential swamp."

Dash

The dash can function like a comma, a colon, or a parenthesis. Like commas and parentheses, dashes set off parenthetical material such as examples, supplemental facts, and explanatory or descriptive phrases. Like a colon, a dash introduces clauses that explain or expand upon something that precedes them. Though sometimes considered a less formal equivalent of the colon and parenthesis, the dash may be found in all kinds of writing, including the most formal, and the choice of which mark to use is often a matter of personal preference.

The common dash (also called the *em dash,* since it is approximately the width of a capital M in typeset material) is usually represented by two hyphens in typed and keyboarded material. (Word-processing programs make it available as a special character.)

Spacing around the dash varies. Most newspapers insert a space before and after the dash; many popular magazines do the same; but most books and journals omit spacing.

The *en dash* and the *two-* and *three-em dashes* have more limited uses, which are explained in paragraphs 13–15 on pages 37–38.

Abrupt Change or Suspension

1. The dash marks an abrupt change or break in the structure of a sentence.

   > The stude ts seemed happy enough with the new plan, but the alumni—there was the problem.

2. A dash is used to indicate interrupted speech or a speaker's confusion or hesitation.

"The next point I'd like to bring up—" the speaker started to say.

"Yes," he went on, "yes—that is—I guess I agree."

Parenthetical and Amplifying Elements

3. Dashes are used in place of commas or parentheses to emphasize or draw attention to parenthetical or amplifying material.

With three expert witnesses in agreement, the defense can be expected to modify its strategy—somewhat.

This amendment will finally prevent corporations—large and small—from buying influence through exorbitant campaign contributions.

When dashes are used to set off parenthetical elements, they often indicate that the material is more digressive than elements set off with commas but less digressive than elements set off by parentheses. For examples, see paragraph 16 on page 19 and paragraph 1 on pages 46–47.

4. Dashes set off or introduce defining phrases and lists.

The fund sought to acquire controlling positions—a minimum of 25% of outstanding voting securities—in other companies.

Davis was a leading innovator in at least three styles—bebop, cool jazz, and jazz-rock fusion.

5. A dash is often used in place of a colon or semicolon to link clauses, especially when the clause that follows the dash explains, summarizes, or expands upon the preceding clause in a somewhat dramatic way.

   The results were in—it had been a triumphant success.

6. A dash or a pair of dashes often sets off illustrative or amplifying material introduced by such phrases as *for example, namely,* and *that is,* when the break in continuity is greater than that shown by a comma, or when the dash would clarify the sentence structure better than a comma. (For more details, see paragraph 17 on page 19.)

   After some discussion the motion was tabled—that is, it was removed indefinitely from the board's consideration.

   Lawyers should generally—in pleadings, for example—attempt to be as specific as possible.

7. A dash may introduce a summary statement that follows a series of words or phrases.

Crafts, food booths, children's activities, cider-making demonstrations—there was something for everyone.

Once into bankruptcy, the company would have to pay cash for its supplies, defer maintenance, and lay off workers—moves that could threaten its future.

8. A dash often precedes the name of an author or source at the end of a quoted passage—such as an epigraph, extract, or book or film blurb—that is not part of the main text. The attribution may appear immediately after the quotation or on the next line.

"I return to her stories with more pleasure, and await them with more anticipation, than those of any of her contemporaries."—William Logan, *Chicago Tribune*

Only the sign is for sale.

—Søren Kierkegaard

With Other Punctuation

9. If a dash appears at a point where a comma could also appear, the comma is omitted.

Our lawyer has read the transcript—all 1,200 pages of it—and he has decided that an appeal would not be useful.

If we don't succeed—and the critics say we won't—then the whole project is in jeopardy.

In a series, dashes that would force a comma to be dropped are often replaced by parentheses.

> The holiday movie crowds were being entertained by street performers: break dancers, a juggler (who doubled as a sword swallower), a steel-drummer, even a three-card-monte dealer.

10. If the second of a pair of dashes would fall where a period should also appear, the dash is omitted.

> Instead, he hired his mother—an odd choice by any standard.

Much less frequently, the second dash will be dropped in favor of a colon or semicolon.

> Valley Health announced general improvements to its practice—two to start this week: evening office hours and a voice-mail message system.

> His conduct has always been exemplary—near-perfect attendance, excellent productivity, a good attitude; nevertheless, his termination cannot be avoided.

11. When a pair of dashes sets off material ending with an exclamation point or a question mark, the mark is placed inside the dashes.

> His hobby was getting on people's nerves—especially mine!—and he was extremely good at it.

There would be a "distinguished guest speaker"—was there ever any other kind?—and plenty of wine afterwards.

12. Dashes are used inside parentheses, and vice versa, to indicate parenthetical material within parenthetical material. The second dash is omitted if it would immediately precede the closing parenthesis; a closing parenthesis is never omitted.

We were looking for a narrator (or narrators—sometimes a script calls for more than one) who could handle a variety of assignments.

The wall of the Old City contains several gates—particularly Herod's Gate, the Golden Gate, and Zion Gate (or "David's Gate")—with rich histories.

En Dash and Long Dashes

13. The *en dash* generally appears only in typeset material; in typed or keyboarded material the simple hyphen is usually used instead. (Word-processing programs provide the en dash as a special character.) Newspapers similarly use the hyphen in place of the en dash. The en dash is shorter than the em dash but longer than the hyphen. It is most frequently used between numbers, dates, or other notations to signify "(up) to and including."

pages 128–34
1995–97

September 24–October 5
8:30 a.m.–4:30 p.m.

The en dash replaces a hyphen in compound adjectives when at least one of the elements is a two-word compound. It replaces the word *to* between capitalized names, and is used to indicate linkages such as boundaries, treaties, and oppositions.

post–Cold War era
Boston–Washington train
New Jersey–Pennsylvania border
male–female differences
or male-female differences

14. A *two-em dash* is used to indicate missing letters in a word and, less frequently, to indicate a missing word.

    The nearly illegible letter is addressed to a Mr. P—— of Baltimore.

15. A *three-em dash* indicates that a word has been left out or that an unknown word or figure is to be supplied.

    The study was carried out in ———, a fast-growing Sunbelt city.

Ellipsis Points

Ellipsis points (also known as *ellipses, points of ellipsis,* and *suspension points*) are periods, usually in groups of three, that signal an omission from quoted material or indicate a pause or trailing off of speech. A space usually precedes and follows each ellipsis point. (In newspaper style, spaces are usually omitted.)

1. Ellipsis points indicate the omission of one or more words within a quoted sentence.

    We the People of the United States . . . do ordain and establish this Constitution for the United States of America.

2. Ellipsis points are usually not used to indicate the omission of words that precede the quoted portion. However, in some formal contexts, especially when the quotation is introduced by a colon, ellipsis points are used.

    He ends with a stirring call for national resolve that "government of the people, by the people, for the people shall not perish from the earth."

    Its final words define the war's purpose in democratic terms: ". . . that government of the people, by the people, for the people shall not perish from the earth."

    Ellipsis points following quoted material are omitted when it forms an integral part of a larger sentence.

    She maintained that it was inconsistent with "government of the people, by the people, for the people."

3. Punctuation used in the original that falls on either side of the ellipsis points is often omitted; however, it may be retained, especially if this helps clarify the sentence structure.

   Now we are engaged in a great civil war, testing whether that nation . . . can long endure.

   We the People of the United States, in Order to . . . establish Justice, . . . and secure the Blessings of Liberty . . . , do ordain and establish this Constitution for the United States of America.

   For details on punctuating omissions within block quotations, see Chapter 6, "Quotations."

4. If the last words of a quoted sentence are omitted and the original sentence ends with punctuation other than a period, the end punctuation often follows the ellipsis points, especially if it helps clarify the quotation.

   He always ends his harangues with some variation on the question, "What could you have been thinking when you . . . ?"

5. When ellipsis points are used to indicate that a quotation has been intentionally left unfinished, the terminal period is omitted. No space separates the last ellipsis point and the quotation mark.

The paragraph beginning "Recent developments suggest . . ." should be deleted.

6. A line of ellipsis points indicates that one or more lines have been omitted from a poem. Its length usually matches the length of the line above. (For more details on quoting verse, see the section beginning on page 223.)

   When I heard the learned astronomer,
   . . . .
   How soon unaccountable I became tired and sick,
   Til rising and gliding out I wandered off by myself,
   In the mystical moist night-air, and from time to time,
   Looked up in perfect silence at the stars.

7. Ellipsis points are used to indicate faltering speech, especially if the faltering involves a long pause or a sentence that trails off or is intentionally left unfinished. Generally no other terminal punctuation is used.

   The speaker seemed uncertain. "Well, that's true . . . but even so . . . I think we can do better."

   "Despite these uncertainties, we believe we can do it, but . . ."

   "I mean . . ." he said, "like . . . How?"

8. Ellipsis points are sometimes used informally as a stylistic device to catch a

reader's attention, often replacing a dash or colon.

They think that nothing can go wrong . . . but it does.

9. In newspaper and magazine columns consisting of social notes, local events listings, or short items of celebrity news, ellipsis points often take the place of paragraphing to separate the items. (Ellipsis points are also often used in informal personal correspondence in place of periods or paragraphing.)

   Congratulations to Debra Morricone, our up-and-coming singing star, for her full scholarship to the Juilliard School this fall! . . . And kudos to Paul Chartier for his winning All-State trumpet performance last Friday in Baltimore! . . . Look for wit and sparkling melody when the Lions mount their annual Gilbert & Sullivan show at Syms Auditorium. This year it's . . .

Exclamation Point

The exclamation point is used to mark a forceful comment or exclamation.

1. An exclamation point can punctuate a sentence, phrase, or interjection.

   There is no alternative!
   Without a trace!
   My God! It's monstrous!

2. The exclamation point may replace the question mark when an ironic, angry, or emphatic tone is more important than the actual question.

   Aren't you finished yet!
   Do you realize what you've done!
   Why me!

   Occasionally it is used *with* the question mark to indicate a very forceful question.

   How much did you say?!
   You did what!?

3. The exclamation point falls within brackets, dashes, parentheses, and quotation marks when it punctuates only the enclosed material. It is placed outside them when it punctuates the entire sentence.

   All of this proves—at long last!—that we were right from the start.
   Somehow the dog got the gate open (for the third time!) and ran into the street.
   He sprang to his feet and shouted "Point of order!"
   At this rate the national anthem will soon be replaced by "You Are My Sunshine"!

4. If an exclamation point falls where a comma could also go, the comma is dropped.

   "Absolutely not!" he snapped.
   They wouldn't dare! she told herself over and over.

If the exclamation point is part of a title, it may be followed by a comma. If the title falls at the end of a sentence, no period follows it.

Hello Dolly!, which opened in 1964, would become one of the ten longest-running shows in Broadway history.

His favorite management book is still *Up the Organization!*

Hyphen

Hyphens have a variety of uses, the most significant of which is to join the elements of compound nouns and modifiers.

1. Hyphens are used to link elements in compound words. (For more on compound words, see the section beginning on page 129.)

   secretary-treasurer
   cost-effective
   fund-raiser
   spin-off

2. In some words, a hyphen separates a prefix, suffix, or medial element from the rest of the word. Consult a dictionary in doubtful cases. (For details on using a hyphen with a prefix or a suffix, see the section beginning on page 146.)

anti-inflation
umbrella-like
jack-o'-lantern

3. In typed and keyboarded material, a hyphen is generally used between numbers and dates with the meaning "(up) to and including." In typeset material it is replaced by an en dash. (For details on the en dash, see paragraph 13 on page 37.)

   pages 128–34
   the years 1995–97

4. A hyphen marks an end-of-line division of a word.

   In 1975 smallpox, formerly a great scourge, was declared totally eradicated by the World Health Organization.

5. A hyphen divides letters or syllables to give the effect of stuttering, sobbing, or halting speech.

   "S-s-sammy, it's my t-toy!"

6. Hyphens indicate a word spelled out letter by letter.

   l-i-a-i-s-o-n

7. Hyphens are sometimes used to produce inflected forms of verbs made of individually pronounced letters or to add an *-er* ending to an abbreviation. However, apostrophes are more commonly used for

these purposes. (For details on these uses of the apostrophe, see paragraph 6 on page 4.)

DH-ing for the White Sox
or DH'ing for the White Sox
a dedicated UFO-er
or a dedicated UFO'er

Parentheses

Parentheses generally enclose material that is inserted into a main statement but is not intended to be an essential part of it. For some of the cases described below, commas or dashes are frequently used instead. (For examples, see paragraph 16 on page 19 and paragraph 3 on page 33.) Parentheses are particularly used when the inserted material is only incidental. Unlike commas and dashes, an opening parenthesis is always followed by a closing one. Because parentheses are almost always used in pairs, and their shapes indicate their relative functions, they often clarify a sentence's structure better than commas or dashes.

Parenthetical Elements

1. Parentheses enclose phrases and clauses that provide examples, explanations, or supplementary facts or numerical data.

Nominations for principal officers (president, vice president, treasurer, and secretary) were heard and approved.

Four computers (all outdated models) will be replaced.

Although we liked the restaurant (their Italian food was the best), we seldom had time for the long trip into the city.

First-quarter sales figures were good (up 8%), but total revenues showed a slight decline (down 1%).

2. Parentheses sometimes enclose phrases and clauses introduced by expressions such as *namely, that is, e.g.,* and *i.e.,* particularly where parentheses would clarify the sentence's structure better than commas. (For more details, see paragraph 17 on page 19.)

In writing to the manufacturer, be as specific as possible (i.e., list the defective parts, describe the malfunction, and identify the store where the unit was purchased), but also as concise.

3. Parentheses enclose definitions or translations in the main part of a sentence.

The company announced plans to sell off its housewares (small-appliances) business.

The *grand monde* (literally, "great world") of prewar Parisian society consisted largely of titled aristocracy.

4. Parentheses enclose abbreviations that follow their spelled-out forms, or spelled-out forms that follow abbreviations.

   She cited a study by the Food and Drug Administration (FDA).

   They attended last year's convention of the ABA (American Booksellers Association).

5. Parentheses often enclose cross-references and bibliographic references.

   Specialized services are also available (see list of stores at end of brochure).

   The diagram (Fig. 3) illustrates the action of the pump.

   Subsequent studies (Braxton 1990; Roh and Weinglass 1993) have confirmed these findings.

6. Parentheses enclose numerals that confirm a spelled-out number in a business or legal context.

   Delivery will be made in thirty (30) days.

   The fee is Four Thousand Dollars ($4,000), payable to UNCO, Inc.

7. Parentheses enclose the name of a state that is inserted into a proper name for identification.

   the Kalispell (Mont.) Regional Hospital

   the *Sacramento* (Calif.) *Bee*

8. Parentheses may be used to enclose personal asides.

   Claims were made of its proven efficacy (some of us were skeptical).

   or

   Claims were made of its proven efficacy. (Some of us were skeptical.)

9. Parentheses are used to enclose quotations that illustrate or support a statement made in the main text.

   After he had a few brushes with the police, his stepfather had him sent to jail as an incorrigible ("It will do him good").

Other Uses

10. Parentheses enclose unpunctuated numbers or letters indicating individual elements or items in a series within a sentence.

    Sentences can be classified as (1) simple, (2) multiple or compound, and (3) complex.

11. Parentheses indicate alternative terms.

    Please sign and return the enclosed form(s).

12. Parentheses may be used to indicate losses in accounting.

Operating Profits (in millions)	
Cosmetics	26.2
Food products	47.7
Food services	54.3
Transportation	(17.7)
Sporting goods	(11.2)
Total	99.3

With Other Punctuation

13. When an independent sentence is enclosed in parentheses, its first word is capitalized and a period (or other closing punctuation) is placed inside the parentheses.

    The discussion was held in the boardroom. (The results are still confidential.)

    A parenthetical expression that occurs within a sentence—even if it could stand alone as a separate sentence—does not end with a period but may end with an exclamation point, a question mark, or quotation marks.

    Although several trade organizations opposed the legislation (there were at least three paid lobbyists working on Capitol Hill), the bill passed easily.

    The conference was held in Portland (Me., not Ore.).

    After waiting in line for an hour (why do we do these things?), we finally left.

A parenthetical expression within a sentence does not require capitalization unless it is a quoted sentence.

> He was totally confused ("What can we do?") and refused to see anyone.

14. If a parenthetical expression within a sentence is composed of two independent clauses, a semicolon rather than a period usually separates them. Independent sentences enclosed together in parentheses employ normal sentence capitalization and punctuation.

> We visited several showrooms, looked at the prices (it wasn't a pleasant experience; prices in this area have not gone down), and asked all the questions we could think of.

> We visited several showrooms and looked at the prices. (It wasn't a pleasant experience. Prices in this area have not gone down.)

Entire paragraphs are rarely enclosed in parentheses; instead, paragraphs of incidental material often appear as footnotes or endnotes.

15. No punctuation (other than a period after an abbreviation) is placed immediately before an opening parenthesis within a sentence; if punctuation is required, it follows the final parenthesis.

> I'll get back to you tomorrow (Friday), when I have more details.

Tickets cost $14 in advance ($12 for seniors); the price at the door is $18.

The relevant figures are shown below (in millions of dollars):

16. Parentheses sometimes appear within parentheses when no confusion would result; alternatively, the inner parentheses are replaced with brackets.

Checks must be drawn in U.S. dollars. (*Please note:* We cannot accept checks drawn on Canadian banks for amounts less than four U.S. dollars ($4.00). The same regulation applies to Canadian money orders.)

17. Dashes and parentheses may be used together to set off parenthetical material. (For details, see paragraph 12 on page 37.)

The orchestra is spirited, and the cast—an expert and enthusiastic crew of Savoyards (some of them British imports)—comes through famously.

Period

Periods almost always serve to mark the end of a sentence or abbreviation.

1. A period ends a sentence or a sentence fragment that is neither a question nor an exclamation.

From the Format menu, choose Style.

Robert decided to bring champagne.
Unlikely. In fact, inconceivable.

Only one period ends a sentence.

The jellied gasoline was traced to the Trenton-based Quality Products, Inc.

Miss Toklas states categorically that "This is the best way to cook frogs' legs."

2. A period punctuates some abbreviations. No space follows an internal period within an abbreviation. (For details on punctuating abbreviations, see the section beginning on page 153.)

Assn.	e.g.
Dr.	Ph.D.
etc.	p.m.

3. Periods are used with a person's initials, each followed by a space. (Newspaper style omits the space.) If the initials replace the name, they are unspaced and may also be written without periods.

J. B. S. Haldane
L.B.J. *or* LBJ

4. A period follows numerals and letters when they are used without parentheses in outlines and vertical lists.

I. Objectives
  A. Economy
    1. Low initial cost
    2. Low maintenance cost
  B. Ease of operation

Required skills are:
1. Shorthand
2. Typing
3. Transcription

5. A period is placed within quotation marks, even when it did not punctuate the original quoted material. (In British practice, the period goes outside the quotation marks whenever it does not belong to the original quoted material.)

The founder was known to his employees as "the old man."

"I said I wanted to fire him," Henry went on, "but she said, 'I don't think you have the contractual privilege to do that.'"

6. When brackets or parentheses enclose an independent sentence, the period is placed inside them. When brackets or parentheses enclose a sentence that is part of a larger sentence, the period for the enclosed sentence is omitted.

Arturo finally arrived on the 23rd with the terrible news that Katrina had been detained by the police. [This later proved to be false; see letter 255.]

I took a good look at her (she was standing quite close to me).

Question Mark

The question mark always indicates a question or doubt.

1. A question mark ends a direct question.

   What went wrong?
   "When do they arrive?" she asked.

   A question mark follows a period only when the period punctuates an abbreviation. No period follows a question mark.

   Is he even an M.D.?
   "Will you arrive by 10 p.m.?"
   A local professor would be giving a paper with the title "Economic Stagnation or Equilibrium?"

2. Polite requests that are worded as questions usually take periods, because they are not really questions. Conversely, a sentence that is intended as a question but whose word order is that of a statement is punctuated with a question mark.

   Could you please send the necessary forms.
   They flew in yesterday?

3. The question mark ends a question that forms part of a sentence. An indirect question is not followed by a question mark.

   What was her motive? you may be asking.
   I naturally wondered, Will it really work?
   I naturally wondered whether it would really work.
   He asked when the report was due.

4. The question mark punctuates each element of a series of questions that share a

single beginning and are neither numbered nor lettered. When the series is numbered or lettered, only one question mark is generally used.

> Can you give us a reasonable forecast? Back up your predictions? Compare them with last year's earnings?
>
> Can you (1) give us a reasonable forecast, (2) back up your predictions, and (3) compare them with last year's earnings?

5. The question mark indicates uncertainty about a fact or the accuracy of a transcription.

> Homer, Greek epic poet (9th–8th? cent. B.C.)
>
> He would have it that Farjeon[?] is the onlie man for us.

6. The question mark is placed inside brackets, dashes, parentheses, or quotation marks when it punctuates only the material enclosed by them and not the sentence as a whole. It is placed outside them when it punctuates the entire sentence.

> I took a vacation in 1992 (was it really that long ago?), but I haven't had time for one since.
>
> What did Andrew mean when he called the project "a fiasco from the start"?
>
> Williams then asks, "Do you realize the extent of the problem [the housing shortage]?"

Quotation Marks

The following paragraphs describe the use of quotation marks to enclose quoted matter in regular text, and for other, less frequent uses. For the use of quotation marks to enclose titles, see paragraph 70 on page 104.

Basic Uses

1. Quotation marks enclose direct quotations but not indirect quotations or paraphrases.

   Dr. Mee added, "We'd be grateful for anything you could do."

   "We just got the lab results," he crowed, "and the blood types match!"

   "I'm leaving," she whispered. "This meeting could go on forever."

   "Mom, we *tried* that already!" they whined in unison.

   "Ssshh!" she hissed.

   She said she was leaving.

   Algren once said something like, Don't ever play poker with anyone named Doc, and never eat at a diner called Mom's.

2. Quotation marks enclose fragments of quoted matter.

   The agreement makes it clear that he "will be paid only upon receipt of an acceptable manuscript."

   As late as 1754, documents refer to him as "yeoman" and "husbandman."

3. Quotation marks enclose words or phrases borrowed from others, and words of obvious informality introduced into formal writing. Words introduced as specialized terminology are sometimes enclosed in quotation marks but more often italicized.

   Be sure to send a copy of your résumé—or as some folks would say, your "biodata summary."

   They were afraid the patient had "stroked out"—had had a cerebrovascular accident.

   New Hampshire's only "green" B&B

   referred to as "closed" or "privately held" corporations

   but more frequently

   referred to as *closed* or *privately held* corporations

4. Quotation marks are sometimes used to enclose words referred to as words. Italics are also frequently used for this purpose.

   changed every "he" to "she"

   or

   changed every *he* to *she*

5. Quotation marks may enclose representations of sounds, though these are also frequently italicized.

   If it sounds like "quank, quank" [*or* like *quank, quank*], it may be the green treefrog.

6. Quotation marks often enclose short sentences that fall within longer sentences,

especially when the shorter sentence is meant to suggest spoken dialogue. Mottoes and maxims, unspoken or imaginary dialogue, and sentences referred to as sentences may all be treated in this way.

On the gate was the inscription "Arbeit macht frei" [or *Arbeit macht frei*]—"Work will make you free."

The fact was, the poor kid didn't know "C'mere" from "Sic 'em."

In effect, the voters were saying "You blew it, and you don't get another chance."

Their reaction could only be described as "Kill the messenger."

She never got used to their "That's the way it goes" attitude.

or

She never got used to their that's-the-way-it-goes attitude.

Quotation marks are often omitted in sentences of this kind when the structure is clear without them. (For the use of commas in such sentences, see paragraphs 29–30 on pages 24–26.)

The first rule is, When in doubt, spell it out.

7. Direct questions are enclosed in quotation marks when they represent quoted dialogue, but usually not otherwise.

She asked, "What went wrong?"

The question is, What went wrong?

We couldn't help wondering, Where's the plan?

or

We couldn't help wondering, "Where's the plan?"

8. Quotation marks enclose translations of foreign or borrowed terms.

This is followed by the Dies Irae ("Day of Wrath"), a climactic movement in many settings of the Requiem.

The term comes from the Latin *sesquipedalis,* meaning "a foot and a half long."

They also frequently enclose definitions.

Concupiscent simply means "lustful."

or

Concupiscent simply means lustful.

9. Quotation marks sometimes enclose letters referred to as letters.

The letter "m" is wider than the letter "i."

Put an "x" in the right spot.

However, such letters are more frequently italicized (or underlined), or left undifferentiated from the surrounding text where no confusion would result.

How many *e*'s are in her name?

a V-shaped blade

He was happy to get a B in the course.

With Longer Quotations

10. Quotation marks are not used with longer passages of prose or poetry that are

indented as separate paragraphs, called *block quotations* or *extracts.* For a thorough discussion of quotations, see Chapter 6.

11. Quotation marks enclose lines of poetry run in with the text. A spaced slash separates the lines. (For details on poetry set as an extract, see the section beginning on page 223.)

    When Gerard Manley Hopkins wrote that "Nothing is so beautiful as spring— / When weeds, in wheels, shoot long and lovely and lush," he probably had my yard in mind.

12. Quotation marks are not used with epigraphs. However, they are generally used with advertising blurbs. (For details on epigraphs and blurbs, see the section beginning on page 219.)

    The whole of science is nothing more than a refinement of everyday thinking.

    —Albert Einstein

    "A brutal irony, a slam-bang humor and a style of writing as balefully direct as a death sentence."—*Time*

With Other Punctuation

13. When a period or comma follows text enclosed in quotation marks, it is placed within the quotation marks, even if the original language quoted was not followed by a period or comma.

He smiled and said, "I'm happy for you."

But perhaps Pound's most perfect poem was "The Return."

The cameras were described as "waterproof," but "moisture-resistant" would have been a better description.

In British usage, the period or comma goes outside the quoted matter whenever the original text did not include the punctuation.

14. When a colon or semicolon follows text enclosed in quotation marks, the colon or semicolon is placed outside the quotation marks.

But they all chimed in on "O Sole Mio": raw adolescents, stately matrons, decrepit old pensioners, their voices soaring in passion together.

She spoke of her "little cottage in the country"; she might better have called it a mansion.

15. The dash, question mark, and exclamation point are placed inside quotation marks when they punctuate the quoted matter only, but outside the quotation marks when they punctuate the whole sentence.

"I can't see how—" he started to say.

He thought he knew where he was going—he remembered her saying, "Take two lefts, then stay to the right"—but the streets didn't look familiar.

He asked, "When did they leave?"

What is the meaning of "the open door"?

She collapsed in her seat with a stunned "Good God!"

Save us from his "mercy"!

Single Quotation Marks

16. Single quotation marks replace double quotation marks when the quoted material occurs within quoted material.

The witness said, "I distinctly heard him say, 'Don't be late,' and then I heard the door close."

"We'd like to close tonight with that great Harold Arlen wee-hours standard, 'One for My Baby.'"

This analysis is indebted to Del Banco's "Elizabeth Bishop's 'Insomnia': An Inverted View."

When both single and double quotation marks occur at the end of a sentence, the period falls within both sets of marks.

The witness said, "I distinctly heard him say, 'Don't be late.'"

British usage often reverses American usage, enclosing quoted material in single quotation marks, and enclosing quotations within quotations in double quotation marks. In British usage, commas and periods following quoted material go inside only those quotation marks that enclose material that originally included the period or comma.

17. A quotation within a quotation within a quotation is usually enclosed in double quotation marks. (Such constructions are usually avoided by rewriting.)

As the *Post* reported it, "Van Houten's voice can be clearly heard saying, 'She said "You wouldn't dare" and I said "I just did."' "

or

The *Post* reported that Van Houten's voice was clearly heard saying, "She said 'You wouldn't dare' and I said 'I just did.'"

Semicolon

The semicolon may be used much like the comma, period, or colon, depending on the context. Like a comma, it may separate elements in a series. Like a period or colon, it frequently marks the end of a complete clause, and like a colon it signals that the remainder of the sentence is closely related to the first part. However, in each case the semicolon is normally used in a distinctive way. It serves as a higher-level comma; it connects clauses, as a period does not; and it does not imply any following exemplification, amplification, or description, as a colon generally does.

Between Clauses

1. A semicolon separates related independent clauses joined without a coordinating conjunction.

   Cream the shortening and sugar; add the eggs and beat well.

   The river rose and overflowed its banks; roads became flooded and impassable; freshly plowed fields disappeared from sight.

2. A semicolon often replaces a comma between two clauses joined by a coordinating conjunction if the sentence might otherwise be confusing—for example, because of particularly long clauses or the presence of other commas.

   In a society that seeks to promote social goals, government will play a powerful role; and taxation, once simply a means of raising money, becomes, in addition, a way of furthering those goals.

3. A semicolon joins two clauses when the second includes a conjunctive adverb such as *accordingly, however, indeed,* or *thus,* or a phrase that acts like a conjunctive adverb such as *in that case, as a result,* or *on the other hand.*

   Most people are covered by insurance of some kind; indeed, many don't even see their medical bills.

It won't be easy to sort out the facts; a decision must be made, however.

The case could take years to work its way through the courts; as a result, many plaintiffs will accept settlements.

When *so* and *yet* are treated as conjunctive adverbs, they are often preceded by a semicolon and followed by a comma. When treated as coordinating conjunctions, as they usually are, they are generally only preceded by a comma.

The new recruits were bright, diligent, and even enthusiastic; yet[,] the same problems persisted.

His grades improved sharply, yet the high honor roll still eluded him.

4. A semicolon may join two statements when the second clause is elliptical, omitting essential words that are supplied by the first. In short sentences, a comma often replaces the semicolon.

The conference sessions, designed to allow for full discussions, were much too long; the breaks between them, much too short.

The aged Scotch was haunting, the Asiago piquant.

5. When a series of clauses are separated by semicolons and a coordinating conjunction precedes the final clause, the final semicolon is sometimes replaced with a comma.

The bars had all closed hours ago; a couple of coffee shops were open but deserted[; *or* ,] and only a few lighted upper-story windows gave evidence of other victims of insomnia.

6. A semicolon is often used before introductory expressions such as *for example, that is,* and *namely,* in place of a colon, comma, dash, or parenthesis. (For more details, see paragraph 17 on page 19.)

   On one point only did everyone agree; namely, too much money had been spent already.

   We were fairly successful on that project; that is, we made our deadlines and met our budget.

In a Series

7. A semicolon is used in place of a comma to separate phrases or items in a series when the phrases or items themselves contain commas. A comma may replace the semicolon before a conjunction that precedes the last item in a series.

   The assets in question include $22 million in land, buildings, and equipment; $34 million in cash, investments, and accounts receivable; and $8 million in inventory.

   The votes against were: Precinct 1, 418; Precinct 2, 332; Precinct 3, 256.

   The debate about the nature of syntactic variation continues to this day (Labov 1991; Dines 1991, 1993; Romaine 1995).

The Pissarro exhibition will travel to Washington, D.C.; Manchester, N.H.; Portland, Ore., and Oakland, Calif.

When the items in a series are long or are sentences themselves, they are usually separated by semicolons even if they lack internal commas.

Among the committee's recommendations were the following: more hospital beds in urban areas where there are waiting lines for elective surgery; smaller staff size in half-empty rural hospitals; and review procedures for all major purchases.

With Other Punctuation

8. A semicolon that punctuates the larger sentence is placed outside quotation marks and parentheses.

I heard the senator on yesterday's "All Things Considered"; his views on Medicare are encouraging.

She found him urbane and entertaining (if somewhat overbearing); he found her charmingly ingenuous.

Slash

The slash (also known as the *virgule, diagonal, solidus, oblique,* and *slant*) is most commonly used in place of a short word or a hyphen or en dash, or to separate numbers or text elements. There is generally no space on either side of the slash.

1. A slash represents the words *per* or *to* when used between units of measure or the terms of a ratio.

   40,000 tons/year
   29 mi/gal
   price/earnings ratio
     or price–earnings ratio
   cost/benefit analysis
     or cost–benefit analysis
   a 50/50 split *or* a 50-50 split
   20/20 vision

2. A slash separates alternatives, usually representing the words *or* or *and/or.*

   alumni/ae
   his/her
   the *affect/effect* problem
     or the *affect-effect* problem

3. A slash replaces the word *and* in some compound terms.

   air/sea cruise *or* air-sea cruise
   the May/June issue *or* the May-June issue
   1996/97 *or* 1996–97
   travel/study trip *or* travel-study trip

4. A slash is sometimes used to replace certain prepositions such as *at, versus,* and *for.*

U.C./Berkeley *or* U.C.–Berkeley
parent/child issues *or* parent–child issues
Vice President/Editorial
or Vice President, Editorial

5. A slash punctuates a few abbreviations.

w/o [*for* without]
c/o [*for* care of]
I/O [*for* input/output]
d/b/a [*for* doing business as]
w/w [*for* wall-to-wall]
o/a [*for* on or about]

6. The slash separates the elements in a numerical date, and numerators and denominators in fractions.

11/29/95
2 3/16 inches wide *or* $2\frac{3}{16}$ inches wide
a 7/8-mile course *or* a $\frac{7}{8}$-mile course

7. The slash separates lines of poetry that are run in with the text around them. A space is usually inserted before and after the slash.

Alexander Pope once observed: "'Tis with our judgments as our watches, none / Go just alike, yet each believes his own."

2 Capitals and Italics

Words and phrases are capitalized or italicized (underlining takes the place of italics in typed or handwritten text) to indicate that they have a special significance in particular contexts. (Quotation marks sometimes perform the same functions; see paragraphs 69–71 on pages 103–5 and the section on quotation marks beginning on page 57.)

Beginnings

1. The first word of a sentence or sentence fragment is capitalized.

   They make a desert and call it peace.
   So many men, so many opinions.
   O times! O customs!

2. The first word of a sentence contained within parentheses is capitalized. How-

ever, a parenthetical sentence occurring inside another sentence is not capitalized unless it is a complete quoted sentence.

> No one answered the telephone. (They were probably on vacation.)
>
> The road remains almost impassable (the locals don't seem to care), and the journey is only for the intrepid.
>
> After waiting in line for an hour (what else could we do?), we finally left.
>
> In the primary election Evans placed third ("My campaign started late").

3. The first word of a direct quotation is capitalized. However, if the quotation is interrupted in mid-sentence, the second part does not begin with a capital.

> The department manager explained, "We have no budget for new computers."
>
> "We have no budget for new computers," explained the department manager, "but we may next year."

4. When a quotation, whether a sentence fragment or a complete sentence, is syntactically dependent on the sentence in which it occurs, the quotation does not begin with a capital.

> The brochure promised a tour of "the most exotic ancient sites."
>
> His first response was that "there is absolutely no truth to the reports."

5. The first word of a sentence within a sentence that is not a direct quotation is usually capitalized. Examples include mottoes and rules, unspoken or imaginary dialogue, sentences referred to as sentences, and direct questions. (For the use of commas and quotation marks with such sentences, see paragraphs 30–31 on pages 25–27 and paragraphs 6–7 on pages 58–60.)

   You know the saying "Fools rush in where angels fear to tread."

   The first rule is, When in doubt, spell it out.

   One ballot proposition sought to enforce the sentencing rule of "Three strikes and you're out."

   My question is, When can we go?

6. The first word of a line of poetry is traditionally capitalized. However, in the poetry of this century line beginnings are often lowercased. The poem's original capitalization is always reproduced.

   Death is the mother of beauty, mystical,
   Within whose burning bosom we devise
   Our earthly mothers waiting, sleeplessly.
   —Wallace Stevens

   If tributes cannot
   be implicit,
   give me diatribes and the fragrance of iodine,
   the cork oak acorn grown in Spain . . .
   —Marianne Moore

7. The first word following a colon is lowercased when it begins a list and usually lowercased when it begins a complete sentence. However, when the sentence introduced is lengthy and distinctly separate from the preceding clause, it is often capitalized.

   In the early morning they broadcast an urgent call for three necessities: bandages, antibiotics, and blood.

   The advantage of this system is clear: it's inexpensive.

   The situation is critical: This company cannot hope to recoup the fourth-quarter losses that were sustained in five operating divisions.

8. If a colon introduces a series of sentences, the first word of each sentence is capitalized.

   Consider the steps we have taken: A subcommittee has been formed to evaluate past performance. New sources of revenue are being explored. Several candidates have been interviewed for the new post of executive director.

9. The first words of items that form complete sentences in run-in lists are usually capitalized, as are the first words of items in vertical lists. However, numbered phrases within a sentence are lowercased.

For details, see the section beginning on page 194.

10. The first word in an outline heading is capitalized.

    I. Editorial tasks
    II. Production responsibilities
        A. Cost estimates
        B. Bids

11. In minutes and legislation, the introductory words *Whereas* and *Resolved* are capitalized (and *Resolved* is also italicized). The word immediately following is also capitalized.

    Whereas, Substantial benefits . . .
    Resolved, That . . .

12. The first word and certain other words of the salutation of a letter and the first word of a complimentary close are capitalized.

    Dear Sir or Madam:
    Ladies and Gentlemen:
    To whom it may concern:
    Sincerely yours,
    Very truly yours,

13. The first word and each subsequent major word following a SUBJECT or TO heading in a memorandum are capitalized.

SUBJECT: Pension Plans
TO: All Department Heads and Editors

Proper Nouns and Adjectives

The following paragraphs describe the ways in which a broad range of proper nouns and adjectives are styled. Capitals are always employed, sometimes in conjunction with italics or quotation marks.

Abbreviations

1. Abbreviated forms of proper nouns and adjectives are capitalized, just as the spelled-out forms would be. (For details on capitalizing abbreviations, see the section beginning on page 155.)

   Jan. [*for* January]
   NATO [*for* North Atlantic Treaty Organization]

Abstractions and Personifications

2. Abstract concepts and qualities are sometimes capitalized when the concept or quality is being personified. If the term is simply used in conjunction with other words that allude to human characteristics or qualities, it is not capitalized.

as Autumn paints each leaf in fiery colors
the statue of Justice with her scales
hoping that fate would lend a hand

Academic Degrees

3. The names of academic degrees are capitalized when they follow a person's name. The names of specific degrees used without a person's name are usually lowercased. More general names for degrees are lowercased.

Lawton I. Byrne, Doctor of Laws
earned his associate in science degree
or earned his Associate in Science degree
completed course work for his doctorate
working for a master's degree

Abbreviations for academic degrees are always capitalized. (For details, see paragraphs 11–12 on pages 163–64.)

Susan L. Wycliff, M.S.W.
received her Ph.D. in clinical psychology

Animals and Plants

4. The common names of animals and plants are not capitalized unless they contain a proper noun, in which case the proper noun is usually capitalized and any name element preceding (but not following) it is often capitalized. When in doubt, consult a dictionary. (For scientific names, see the section on pages 99–100.)

the springer spaniel	Queen Anne's lace
Holstein cows	black-eyed Susan
California condor	mayflower
a Great Dane	jack-in-the-pulpit

Awards and Prizes

5. Names of awards and prizes are capitalized. Words and phrases that are not actually part of the award's name are lowercased.

   Academy Award
   Emmy
   Rhodes Scholarship
   Rhodes scholar
   Pulitzer Prize–winning novelist
   Nobel Prize winner
   Nobel Prize in medicine
   but
   Nobel Peace Prize

Derivatives of Proper Names

6. Derivatives of proper names are capitalized when used in their primary sense. If the derived term has taken on a specialized meaning, it is often lowercased. Consult a dictionary when in doubt.

   Roman sculpture
   Viennese culture
   Victorian prudery
   a Britishism
   Hodgkin's disease

chinaware
pasteurized milk
french fries
but
American cheese
Dutch door

Geographical and Topographical References

7. Terms that identify divisions of the earth's surface and distinct areas, regions, places, or districts are capitalized, as are derivative nouns and adjectives.

the Pacific Rim	Burgundy
the Great Lakes	Burgundians
Arnhem Land	the Highlands
the Golan Heights	Highland attitudes

8. Popular names of localities are capitalized.

Little Italy	the Sunbelt
the Left Bank	the Big Easy

9. Compass points are capitalized when they refer to a geographical region or form part of a place-name or street name. They are lowercased when they refer to a simple direction.

the Southwest	North Pole
West Coast	north of the Rio Grande

North Atlantic	born in the East
East Pleasant Street	driving east on I-90

10. Nouns and adjectives that are derived from compass points and that designate or refer to a specific geographical region are usually capitalized.

    Southern hospitality
    Easterners
    Southwestern recipes
    Northern Europeans

11. Words designating global, national, regional, and local political divisions are capitalized when they are essential elements of specific names. They are usually lowercased when they precede a proper name or are not part of a specific name.

    the Roman Empire
    British Commonwealth nations
    New York State
    the state of New York
    the Third Precinct
    voters in three precincts

    In legal documents, such words are often capitalized regardless of position.

    the State of New York

12. Generic geographical terms (such as *lake, mountain, river,* or *valley*) are capitalized if they are part of a proper name.

Lake Tanganyika	Cape of Good Hope
Great Salt Lake	Massachusetts Bay
Atlas Mountains	Cayman Islands
Mount Everest	Yosemite Valley

When a place-name is subsequently referred to by its generic term, the term is lowercased.

They went water-skiing on Lake Michigan that afternoon; the lake was calm and the weather beautiful.

When *the* precedes the generic term, the term is lowercased.

the river Nile

13. Generic geographical terms preceding two or more names are usually capitalized.

Lakes Huron and Erie
Mounts McKinley, Whitney, and Shasta

14. Generic geographical terms that are not used as part of a single proper name are not capitalized. These include plural terms that follow two or more proper names, and terms that are used descriptively or alone.

the Indian and South Pacific oceans
the Mississippi and Missouri rivers
the Pacific coast of Mexico
Caribbean islands
the river delta

15. The names of streets, monuments, parks, landmarks, well-known buildings, and other public places are capitalized. However, common terms that are part of these names (such as *street, park,* or *bridge*) are lowercased when they occur after multiple names or are used alone.

State Street
the Lincoln Memorial
Statue of Liberty
the Pyramids
Grant Park
Golden Gate Bridge
Empire State Building
Beverly Hills Hotel
back to the hotel
Main and Oak streets

Well-known shortened forms of placenames are capitalized.

the Hill [*for* Capitol Hill]
the Channel [*for* English Channel]
the Street [*for* Wall Street]

Governmental, Judicial, and Political Bodies

16. Full names of legislative, deliberative, executive, and administrative bodies are capitalized, as are easily recognizable short forms of these names. However, nonspecific noun and adjective references to them are usually lowercased.

United States Congress
Congress
the House

the Fed
congressional hearings
a federal agency

When words such as *department, committee,* or *agency* are used in place of a full name, they are most often capitalized when the department or agency is referring to itself, but otherwise usually lowercased.

This Department welcomes constructive criticism . . .
The department claimed to welcome such criticism . . .

When such a word is used in the plural to describe more than one specific body, it is usually capitalized when it precedes the names and lowercased when it follows them.

involving the Departments of State and Justice
a briefing from the State and Justice departments

17. Full names of high courts are capitalized. Short forms of such names are often capitalized in legal documents but lowercased otherwise.

. . . in the U.S. Court of Appeals for the Ninth Circuit
International Court of Justice
The court of appeals [*or* Court of Appeals] held . . .

the Virginia Supreme Court
a federal district court
the state supreme court

However, both the full and short names of the U.S. Supreme Court are capitalized.

the Supreme Court of the United States
the Supreme Court
the Court

18. Names of city and county courts are usually lowercased.

the Springfield municipal court
small-claims court
the county court
juvenile court

19. The noun *court,* when it applies to a specific judge or presiding officer, is capitalized in legal documents.

It is the opinion of this Court that . . .
The Court found that . . .

20. The terms *federal* and *national* are capitalized only when they are essential elements of a name or title. (*Federal* is also capitalized when it refers to a historical architectural style, to members of the original Federalist party, or to adherents of the Union in the Civil War.)

Federal Election Commission
a federal commission

Federalist principles
National Security Council
national security

21. The word *administration* is sometimes capitalized when it refers to the administration of a specific U.S. president, but is more commonly lowercased. Otherwise, it is lowercased except when it is a part of the official name of a government agency.

the Reagan administration
or the Reagan Administration
the administration *or* the Administration
from one administration to the next
the Social Security Administration

22. Names of political organizations and their adherents are capitalized, but the word *party* is often lowercased.

the Democratic National Committee
the Republican platform
the Christian Coalition
most Republicans
the Democratic party
or the Democratic Party
party politics

Names of less-distinct political groupings are usually lowercased, as are their derivative forms.

the right wing
the liberals

the conservative agenda
but often
the Left
the Right

23. Terms describing political and economic philosophies are usually lowercased; if derived from proper names, they are usually capitalized. Consult a dictionary for doubtful cases.

authoritarianism	nationalism
democracy	social Darwinist
fascism *or* Fascism	Marxist

Historical Periods and Events

24. The names of some historical and cultural periods and movements are capitalized. When in doubt, consult a dictionary or encyclopedia.

Bronze Age	Third Reich
Middle Ages	the atomic age
Prohibition	Victorian era
the Renaissance	age of Pericles
New Deal	the baby boom
Fifth Republic	

25. Century and decade designations are normally lowercased.

the nineteenth century
the twenties
the turn of the century
a 12th-century manuscript

but
Gay Nineties
Roaring Twenties

26. The names of conferences, councils, expositions, and specific sporting, cultural, and historical events are capitalized.

Fourth World Conference on Women
Council of Trent
New York World's Fair
Super Bowl
Cannes Film Festival
Miss America Contest
San Francisco Earthquake
Johnstown Flood

27. Full names of specific treaties, laws, and acts are capitalized.

Treaty of Versailles
the Nineteenth Amendment
the Bill of Rights
Clean Air Act of 1990
but
gun-control laws
an equal-rights amendment

28. The words *war, revolution,* and *battle* are capitalized when they are part of a full name. Official names of actions are capitalized. Descriptive terms such as *assault* and *siege* are usually lowercased even

when used in conjunction with a place-name.

War of the Roses
World War II
the French Revolution
Battle of Gettysburg
Operation Desert Storm
between the two world wars
the American and French revolutions
the siege of Leningrad
Washington's winter campaign

Hyphenated Compounds

29. The second (third, etc.) element of a hyphenated compound is generally capitalized only if it is itself a proper noun or adjective. (For hyphenated titles, see paragraph 65 on pages 102–3.)

Arab-Israeli negotiations
or Arab–Israeli negotiations
East-West trade agreements
or East–West trade agreements
French-speaking peoples
Forty-second street
twentieth-century architecture

30. When joined to a proper noun or adjective, common prefixes (such as *pre-* or *anti-*) are usually lowercased, but geographical and ethnic combining forms (such as *Anglo-* or *Sino-*) are capitalized.

(For details, see paragraphs 45 and 52 on pages 147 and 149.)

anti-Soviet forces
Sino-Japanese relations

Legal Material

31. The names of the plaintiff and defendant in legal case titles are italicized. The *v.* (for *versus*) may be roman or italic. Cases that do not involve two opposing parties are also italicized. When the party involved rather than the case itself is being discussed, the reference is not italicized. In running text, a case name involving two opposing parties may be shortened.

Jones v. *Massachusetts*
Smith et al. v. Jones
In re Jones
She covered the Jones trial for the newspaper.
The judge based his ruling on a precedent set in the *Jones* decision.

Medical Terms

32. Proper names that are elements in terms designating diseases, symptoms, syndromes, and tests are capitalized. Common nouns are lowercased; however, abbreviations of such nouns are all-capitalized.

Alzheimer's disease	black lung disease
Tourette's syndrome	mumps
Schick test	AIDS

33. Scientific names of disease-causing organisms follow the rules discussed in paragraph 58 on page 99. The names of diseases or conditions derived from scientific names of organisms are lowercased and not italicized.

a neurotoxin produced by *Clostridium botulinum*
nearly died of botulism

34. Generic names of drugs are lowercased; trade names should be capitalized.

retinoic acid
Retin-A

Military Terms

35. The full titles of branches of the U.S. armed forces are capitalized, as are standard short forms.

U.S. Marine Corps	the Marines
the Marine Corps	the Corps

Those of other countries are capitalized when the precise title is used; otherwise they are usually lowercased. The plurals of *army, navy, air force,* and *coast guard* are lowercased.

Royal Air Force
the Guatemalan army
the tiny armies of both countries

The modifiers *army, navy, marine, coast guard,* and *air force* are usually lowercased; *naval* is lowercased unless it is part of an official name. The noun *marine* is usually lowercased.

an army helicopter
the first naval engagement
a career navy man
the Naval Reserves
the marine barracks
a former marine

Full or shortened names of specific units of a branch are usually capitalized.

U.S. Army Corps of Engineers
the Third Army
the Eighty-second [*or* 82nd] Airborne
the U.S. Special Forces, or Green Berets
. . . of the First Battalion. The battalion commander . . .

36. Military ranks are capitalized when they precede the names of their holders, or replace the name in direct address. Otherwise they are lowercased.

Major General Smedley Butler
Please be seated, Admiral.
The major arrived precisely on time.

37. The names of decorations, citations, and medals are capitalized.

    Medal of Honor
    Purple Heart

Numerical Designations

38. A noun introducing a reference number is usually capitalized. The abbreviation *No.* is usually omitted.

Order 704	Form 2E
Flight 409	Policy 118-4-Y

39. Nouns used with numbers or letters to refer to major reference entities or actual captions in books or periodicals are usually capitalized. Nouns that designate minor reference entities and do not appear in captions are lowercased.

Book II	Figure D.4
Volume 5	page 101
Chapter 2	line 8
Table 3	paragraph 6.1
Example 16.2	question 21

Organizations

40. Names of organizations, corporations, and institutions, and terms derived from those names to designate their members, are capitalized.

    the League of Women Voters
    General Motors Corporation

the Smithsonian Institution
the University of the South
the Rotary Club
all Rotarians

Common nouns used descriptively or occurring after the names of two or more organizations are lowercased.

enrolled at the university
Yale and Harvard universities
but
the Universities of Utah and Nevada

41. Words such as *agency, department, division, group,* or *office* that designate corporate and organizational units are capitalized only when used as part of a specific proper name. (For governmental units, see paragraph 16 on pages 82–83.)

head of the Sales Division of K2 Outfitters
a memo to the sales divisions of both companies

42. Nicknames for organizations are capitalized.

the Big Six accounting firms
referred to IBM as Big Blue
trading on the Big Board

People

43. The names and initials of persons are capitalized. If a name is hyphenated, both

elements are capitalized. Particles forming the initial elements of surnames (such as *de, della, der, du, l', la, le, ten, ter, van,* and *von*) may or may not be capitalized, depending on the practice of the family or individual. However, the particle is always capitalized at the beginning of a sentence. The prefixes *Mac, Mc,* and *O'* are always capitalized.

Cecil Day-Lewis
Agnes de Mille
Cecil B. DeMille
Walter de la Mare
Mark deW. Howe
Martin Van Buren
. . . of van Gogh's life. Van Gogh's technique is . . .

44. A nickname or epithet that either is added to or replaces the name of a person or thing is capitalized.

Babe Ruth	the Sun King
Stonewall Jackson	Deep Throat
Billy the Kid	Big Mama Thornton

A nickname or epithet placed between a person's first and last name is enclosed in quotation marks or parentheses or both. If it precedes the first name, it is sometimes enclosed in quotation marks but more often not.

Charlie "Bird" [*or* ("Bird") *or* (Bird)] Parker
Mother Maybelle Carter

45. Words of family relationship preceding or used in place of a person's name are capitalized; otherwise, they are lowercased.

Uncle Fred	her uncle's book
Mother's birthday	my mother's legacy

46. Words designating languages, nationalities, peoples, races, religious groups, and tribes are capitalized. Designations based on color are usually lowercased.

Spanish
Muslims
Spaniards
Assiniboin
Chinese
both blacks and whites
Asians
white, black, and Hispanic jurors

47. Corporate, professional, and governmental titles are capitalized when they immediately precede a person's name, unless the name is being used as an appositive.

President John Tyler
Professor Wendy Doniger of the University of Chicago
Senator William Fulbright of Arkansas
Arkansas's late former senator, William Fulbright

48. When corporate or governmental titles are used as part of a descriptive phrase to

identify a person rather than as part of the name itself, the title is lowercased.

> Marcia Ramirez, president of Logex Corp.
>
> the president of Logex Corp., Marcia Ramirez
>
> *but*
>
> Logex Corp.'s prospects for the coming year were outlined by President Marcia Ramirez.

49. High governmental titles may be capitalized when used in place of individuals' names. In minutes and official records of proceedings, corporate or organizational titles are capitalized when used in place of individuals' names.

> The Secretary of State objected.
>
> The Judge will respond to questions in her chambers.
>
> The Treasurer then stated his misgivings about the project.
>
> *but*
>
> The report reached the senator's desk yesterday.
>
> The judge's rulings were widely criticized.
>
> The co-op's treasurer, it turned out, had twice been convicted of embezzlement.

50. The word *president* may be capitalized whenever it refers to the U.S. presidency, but more commonly is capitalized only when it refers to a specific U.S. president.

> It is the duty of the president [*or* President] to submit a budget to Congress.

The President's budget, due out on Wednesday, is being eagerly awaited.

51. Titles are capitalized when they are used in direct address.

Is it very contagious, Doctor?
You may call your next witness, Counselor.

Religious Terms

52. Words designating the supreme being are capitalized. Plural forms such as *gods, goddesses,* and *deities* are not.

Allah	the Almighty
Brahma	the Trinity
Jehovah	in the eyes of God
Yahweh	the angry gods

53. Personal pronouns referring to the supreme being are often capitalized, especially in religious writing. Relative pronouns (such as *who, whom,* and *whose*) usually are not.

God gave His [*or* his] Son
Allah, whose Prophet, Muhammad . . .

54. Traditional designations of apostles, prophets, and saints are capitalized.

the Madonna
the Twelve
the Prophet
St. John of the Cross

Moses the Lawgiver
John the Baptist

55. Names of religions, denominations, creeds and confessions, and religious orders are capitalized, as are adjectives and nouns derived from these names.

Judaism	Eastern Orthodox
Church of England	Islamic
Apostles' Creed	Jesuit teachers
Society of Jesus	a Buddhist

Full names of specific places of worship are capitalized, but terms such as *church, synagogue,* and *mosque* are lowercased when used alone. The word *church* is sometimes capitalized when it refers to the worldwide Catholic Church.

Hunt Memorial Church
the local Baptist church
Beth Israel Synagogue
services at the synagogue

56. Names of the Bible and other sacred works, their books and parts, and versions or editions of them are capitalized but not italicized. Adjectives derived from the names of sacred books are capitalized, except for the words *biblical* and *scriptural.*

Bible
biblical
the Scriptures

Talmud
Revised Standard Version
Talmudic
Old Testament
Koran *or* Qur'an
Book of Revelation
Koranic *or* Qur'anic

57. The names of prayers and well-known passages of the Bible are capitalized.

the Ave Maria
Ten Commandments
Lord's Prayer
Sermon on the Mount
the Our Father
the Beatitudes

Scientific Terms

58. Genus names in biological binomial nomenclature are capitalized; species names are lowercased, even when derived from a proper name. Both names are italicized.

Both the wolf and the domestic dog are included in the genus *Canis.*

The California condor *(Gymnogyps californianus)* is facing extinction.

The names of races, varieties, or subspecies are lowercased and italicized.

Hyla versicolor chrysoscelis
Otis asio naevius

59. The New Latin names of classes, families, and all groups above the genus level in zoology and botany are capitalized but not italicized. Their derivative nouns and adjectives are lowercased.

Gastropoda	gastropod
Thallophyta	thallophytic

60. The names, both scientific and informal, of planets and their satellites, stars, constellations, and other specific celestial objects are capitalized. However, except in technical writing, the words *sun, earth,* and *moon* are usually lowercased unless they occur with other astronomical names. A generic term that follows the name of a celestial object is usually lowercased.

Jupiter
Mars, Venus, and Earth
the North Star
life on earth
Andromeda
a voyage to the moon
Ursa Major
Halley's comet
the Little Dipper

Names of meteorological phenomena are lowercased.

aurora australis
northern lights
parhelic circle

61. Terms that identify geological eons, eras, periods, systems, epochs, and strata are capitalized. The generic terms that follow them are lowercased.

Mesozoic era
Upper Cretaceous epoch
Quaternary period
in the Middle Ordovician
the Age of Reptiles

62. Proper names that are elements of the names of scientific laws, theorems, and principles are capitalized, but the common nouns *law, theorem, theory,* and the like are lowercased. In the names of popular or fanciful theories or observations, such words are usually capitalized as well.

Mendel's law
the Pythagorean theorem
Occam's razor
Einstein's theory of relativity
Murphy's Law
the Peter Principle

63. The names of computer services and databases are capitalized. Some names of computer languages are written with an initial capital letter, some with all letters capitalized, and some commonly both ways. When in doubt, consult a dictionary.

America Online
World Wide Web

CompuServe
Microsoft Word
Pascal *or* PASCAL
BASIC
Internet *or* internet

Time Periods and Dates

64. The names of the days of the week, months of the year, and holidays and holy days are capitalized. Names of the seasons are lowercased.

Tuesday	Ramadan
June	Holy Week
Yom Kippur	last winter's storm
Veterans Day	

Titles of Works

65. Words in titles of books, magazines, newspapers, plays, movies, long poems, and works of art such as paintings and sculpture are capitalized except for internal articles, coordinating conjunctions, prepositions, and the *to* of infinitives. Prepositions of four or more letters are often capitalized. The entire title is italicized. For sacred works, see paragraph 56 on pages 98–99.

Far from [or *From*] *the Madding Crowd*
Wolfe's *Of Time and the River*
Publishers Weekly
USA Today
the original play *A Streetcar Named Desire*

All about [or *About*] *Eve*, with Bette Davis
Monet's *Water-Lily Pool*, in the Louvre
Rodin's *Thinker*

The elements of hyphenated compounds in titles are usually capitalized, but articles, coordinating conjunctions, and prepositions are lowercased.

Knock-offs and Ready-to-Wear: The Low End of Fashion
Politics in Early Seventeenth-Century England

66. The first word following a colon in a title is capitalized.

Jane Austen: A Literary Life

67. An initial article that is part of a title is capitalized and italicized. It is often omitted if it would be awkward in context.

The Oxford English Dictionary
the 20-volume *Oxford English Dictionary*

68. In the titles of newspapers, the city or local name is usually italicized, but the preceding *the* is usually not italicized or capitalized. (In newspaper writing, any *the* is generally capitalized, see example in paragraph 69 below.)

reported in the *New York Times*
last Thursday's *Atlanta Constitution*

69. Many periodicals, especially newspapers, do not use italics for titles, but instead

either simply capitalize the important words of the title or, more commonly, capitalize the words and enclose the title in quotation marks.

the NB. column in The Times Literary Supplement

The Nobel committee singled out Walcott's book-length epic "Omeros."

70. The titles of articles in periodicals, short poems, short stories, essays, lectures, dissertations, chapters of books, episodes of radio and television programs, and novellas published in a collection are capitalized and enclosed in quotation marks. The capitalization of articles, conjunctions, and prepositions follows the rules explained in paragraph 65 above.

an article on Rwanda, "After the Genocide," in the *New Yorker*

Robert Frost's "Death of the Hired Man"

O'Connor's story "Good Country People"

"The Literature of Exhaustion," John Barth's seminal essay

last Friday's lecture, "Labor's Task: A View for the Nineties"

The Jungle Book's ninth chapter is the well-known "Rikki-tikki-tavi."

*M*A*S*H*'s final episode, "Goodbye, Farewell and Amen"

71. The titles of long musical compositions are generally capitalized and italicized; the titles of songs and other short com-

positions are capitalized and enclosed in quotation marks, as are the popular names of longer works. The titles of compositions identified primarily by their musical forms (such as *quartet, sonata,* or *mass*) are capitalized only, as are movements identified by their tempo markings.

Mozart's *The Magic Flute*
Frank Loesser's *Guys and Dolls*
"The Lady Is a Tramp"
Beethoven's "Für Elise"
the Piano Sonata in C-sharp minor, Op. 27, No. 2, or "Moonlight" Sonata
Symphony No. 104 in D major
Brahms's Violin Concerto in D
the Adagietto movement from Mahler's Fifth Symphony

72. Common titles of book sections (such as *preface, introduction,* or *index*) are usually capitalized when they refer to a section of the same book in which the reference is made. Otherwise, they are usually lowercased. (For numbered sections of books, see paragraph 39 on page 92.)

See the Appendix for further information.
In the introduction to her book, the author explains her goals.

Trademarks

73. Registered trademarks, service marks, collective marks, and brand names are capitalized. They do not normally require any

further acknowledgment of their special status.

Frisbee	Jacuzzi
Levi's	Coke
Kleenex	Vaseline
College Board	Velcro
Dumpster	Realtor
Xerox	Scotch tape
Walkman	Band-Aid
Teflon	

Transportation

74. The names of individual ships, submarines, airplanes, satellites, and space vehicles are capitalized and italicized. The designations *U.S.S.*, *S.S.*, *M.V.*, and *H.M.S.* are not italicized.

    Challenger
    Enola Gay
    H.M.S. *Bounty*

    The names of train lines, types of aircraft, and space programs are not italicized.

    Metroliner
    Boeing 727
    Pathfinder Program

Other Styling Conventions

1. Foreign words and phrases that have not been fully adopted into English are itali-

cized. In general, any word that appears in the main section of *Merriam-Webster's Collegiate Dictionary* does not need to be italicized.

These accomplishments will serve as a monument, *aere perennius,* to the group's skill and dedication.

"The cooking here is *wunderbar*!"

The prix fixe lunch was $20.

The committee meets on an ad hoc basis.

A complete foreign-language sentence (such as a motto) can also be italicized. However, long sentences are usually treated as quotations; that is, they are set in roman type and enclosed in quotation marks. (For details, see paragraph 6 on pages 58–59.)

The inscription *Honi soit qui mal y pense* encircles the seal.

2. In nonfiction writing, unfamiliar words or words that have a specialized meaning are set in italics on their first appearance, especially when accompanied by a short definition. Once these words have been introduced and defined, they are not italicized in subsequent references.

Vitiligo is a condition in which skin pigment cells stop making pigment. Vitiligo usually affects . . .

Another method is the *direct-to-consumer* transaction, in which the publisher markets directly to the individual by mail or door-to-door.

3. Italics are often used to indicate words referred to as words. However, if the word was actually spoken, it is usually enclosed in quotation marks instead.

   Purists still insist that *data* is a plural noun.

   Only can also be an adverb, as in "I *only* tried to help."

   We heard his warning, but we weren't sure what "repercussions" meant in that context.

4. Italics are often used for letters referred to as letters, particularly when they are shown in lowercase.

   You should dot your *i*'s and cross your *t*'s.

   If the letter is being used to refer to its sound and not its printed form, slashes or brackets are used instead of italics in technical contexts.

   The pure /p/ sound is rarely heard in the mountain dialect.

   A letter used to indicate a shape is capitalized but not italicized. Such letters are often set in sans-serif type.

   an A-frame house
   the I beam
   Churchill's famous V sign
   forming a giant X

5. Italics are often used to show numerals referred to as numerals. However, if there is no chance of confusion, they are usually not italicized.

   The first *2* and the last *1* are barely legible.

   Anyone whose ticket number ends in 4 or 6 will win a door prize.

6. Italics are used to emphasize or draw attention to words in a sentence.

   Students must notify the dean's office *in writing* of any added or dropped courses.

   It was not *the* model for the project, but merely *a* model.

7. Italics are used to indicate a word created to suggest a sound.

   Its call is a harsh, drawn-out *kreee-awww.*

8. Individual letters are sometimes italicized when used for lists within sentences or for identifying elements in an illustration.

   providing information about *(a)* typing, *(b)* transcribing, *(c)* formatting, and *(d)* graphics located at point *A* on the diagram

9. Commas, colons, and semicolons that follow italicized words are usually italicized.

   the Rabbit tetralogy *(Rabbit Run, Rabbit Redux, Rabbit Is Rich,* and *Rabbit at Rest); Bech: A Book; S;* and others

However, question marks, exclamation points, quotation marks, and apostrophes are not italicized unless they are part of an italicized title.

Did you see the latest issue of *Newsweek*?

Despite the greater success of *Oklahoma!* and *South Pacific*, Rodgers was fondest of *Carousel.*

"Over Christmas vacation he finished *War and Peace.*"

Students always mistake the old script *s*'s for *f*'s.

Parentheses and brackets may be italicized if most of the words they enclose are also italicized, or if both the first and last words are italicized.

(see also Limited Partnership)

[German, *Dasein*]

(and is replaced throughout by *&)*

10. Full capitalization is occasionally used for emphasis or to indicate that a speaker is talking very loudly. It is avoided in formal writing, where italics are far more often used for emphasis.

Term papers received after Friday, May 18, WILL BE RETURNED UNREAD.

Scalpers mingled in the noisy crowd yelling "SIXTY DOLLARS!"

11. The text of signs, labels, and inscriptions may be reproduced in various ways.

a poster reading SPECIAL THRILLS COMING SOON

a gate bearing the infamous motto "Arbeit macht frei"

a Do Not Disturb sign

a barn with an old CHEW MAIL POUCH ad on the side

the stop sign

12. *Small capitals*, identical to large capitals but usually about the height of a lowercase *x*, are commonly used for era designations and computer commands. They may also be used for cross-references, for headings in constitutions and bylaws, and for speakers in a dramatic dialogue.

    The dwellings date from A.D. 200 or earlier.

    Press ALT+CTRL+PLUS SIGN on the numeric keyboard.

    (See LETTERS AS LETTERS, page 162.)

    SECTION IV. The authority for parliamentary procedure in meetings of the Board . . .

    LADY WISHFORT. O dear, has my Nephew made his Addresses to Millamant? I order'd him.

    FOIBLE. Sir Wilfull is set in to drinking, Madam, in the Parlour.

13. *Underlining* indicates italics in typed material. It is almost never seen in typeset text.

14. *Boldface* type has traditionally been used primarily for headings and captions. It is

sometimes also used in place of italics for terminology introduced in the text, especially for terms that are accompanied by definitions; for cross-references; for headwords in listings such as glossaries, gazetteers, and bibliographies; and for page references in indexes that locate a specific kind of material, such as illustrations, tables, or the main discussions of a given topic. (In mathematical texts, arrays, tensors, vectors, and matrix notation are standardly set bold as well.)

> **Application Forms and Tests** Many offices require applicants to fill out an employment form. Bring a copy . . .
>
> **Figure 4.2: The Electromagnetic Spectrum**
>
> The two axes intersect at a point called the **origin**.
>
> See **Medical Records**, page 123.
>
> **antecedent:** the noun to which a pronoun refers
>
> **appositive:** a word, phrase, or clause that is equivalent to a preceding noun
>
> Records, medical, **123–37**, 178, 243
> Referrals, **38–40**, 139

Punctuation that follows boldface type is set bold when it is part of a heading or heading-like text; otherwise it is generally set roman.

> **Table 9:** Metric Conversion

Warning: This and similar medications . . .

Excellent fourth-quarter earnings were reported by the pharmaceutical giants **Abbott Laboratories, Glaxo Wellcome**, and **Merck**.

3 Plurals, Possessives, and Compounds

This chapter describes the ways in which plurals, possessives, and compounds are most commonly formed.

In regard to plurals and compounds, consulting a dictionary will solve many of the problems discussed in this chapter. A good college dictionary, such as *Merriam-Webster's Collegiate Dictionary,* will provide plural forms for any common word, as well as a large number of permanent compounds. Any dictionary much smaller than the *Collegiate* will often be more frustrating in what it fails to show than helpful in what it shows.

Plurals

The basic rules for writing plurals of English words, stated in paragraph 1, apply in the vast majority of cases. The succeeding paragraphs treat the categories of words whose plurals are most apt to raise questions.

Most good dictionaries give thorough coverage to irregular and variant plurals, and many of the rules provided here are reflected in the dictionary entries.

The symbol → is used here to link the singular and plural forms.

1. The plurals of most English words are formed by adding *-s* to the singular. If the noun ends in *-s, -x, -z, -ch,* or *-sh,* so that an extra syllable must be added in order to pronounce the plural, *-es* is added. If the noun ends in a *-y* preceded by a consonant, the *-y* is changed to *-i* and *-es* is added.

   voter → voters
   anticlimax → anticlimaxes
   blitz → blitzes
   blowtorch → blowtorches
   calabash → calabashes
   allegory → allegories

Abbreviations

2. The plurals of abbreviations are commonly formed by adding *-s* or *-'s;* however, there are some significant exceptions. (For details, see paragraphs 1–5 on pages 157–58.)

   yr. → yrs. M.B.A. → M.B.A.'s
   TV → TVs p. → pp.

Animals

3. The names of many fishes, birds, and mammals have both a plural formed with a suffix and one that is identical with the singular. Some have only one or the other.

   bass → bass *or* basses
   partridge → partridge *or* partridges
   sable → sables *or* sable
   lion → lions
   sheep → sheep

   Many of the animals that have both plural forms are ones that are hunted, fished, or trapped; those who hunt, fish for, and trap them are most likely to use the unchanged form. The *-s* form is often used to emphasize diversity of kinds.

   caught three bass
   but
   basses of the Atlantic Ocean
   a place where antelope feed
   but
   antelopes of Africa and southwest Asia

Compounds and Phrases

4. Most compounds made up of two nouns—whether they appear as one word, two words, or a hyphenated word—form their plurals by pluralizing the final element only.

   courthouse → courthouses

judge advocate → judge advocates
player-manager → player-managers

5. The plural form of a compound consisting of an *-er* noun and an adverb is made by pluralizing the noun element only.

runner-up → runners-up
onlooker → onlookers
diner-out → diners-out
passerby → passersby

6. Nouns made up of words that are not nouns form their plurals on the last element.

show-off → show-offs
pushover → pushovers
tie-in → tie-ins
lineup → lineups

7. Plurals of compounds that consist of two nouns separated by a preposition are normally formed by pluralizing the first noun.

sister-in-law → sisters-in-law
attorney-at-law → attorneys-at-law
power of attorney → powers of attorney
chief of staff → chiefs of staff
grant-in-aid → grants-in-aid

8. Compounds that consist of two nouns separated by a preposition and a modifier form their plurals in various ways.

snake in the grass → snakes in the grass
justice of the peace → justices of the peace
jack-in-the-box → jack-in-the-boxes
or jacks-in-the-box
will-o'-the wisp → will-o'-the-wisps

9. Compounds consisting of a noun followed by an adjective are usually pluralized by adding -s to the noun. If the adjective tends to be understood as a noun, the compound may have more than one plural form.

attorney general → attorneys general
or attorney generals
sergeant major → sergeants major
or sergeant majors
poet laureate → poets laureate
or poet laureates
heir apparent → heirs apparent
knight-errant → knights-errant

Foreign Words and Phrases

10. Many nouns of foreign origin retain the foreign plural. However, most also have a regular English plural.

alumnus → alumni
genus → genera
crisis → crises
criterion → criteria
appendix → appendixes *or* appendices

concerto → concerti *or* concertos
symposium → symposia *or* symposiums

11. Phrases of foreign origin may have a foreign plural, an English plural, or both.

pièce de résistance → pièces de résistance
hors d'oeuvre → hors d'oeuvres
beau monde → beau mondes
or beaux mondes

Irregular Plurals

12. A few English nouns form their plurals by changing one or more of their vowels, or by adding *-en* or *-ren.*

foot → feet	woman → women
goose → geese	tooth → teeth
louse → lice	ox → oxen
man → men	child → children
mouse → mice	

13. Some nouns do not change form in the plural. (See also paragraph 3 above.)

series → series	corps → corps
politics → politics	species → species

14. Some nouns ending in *-f, -fe,* and *-ff* have plurals that end in *-ves.* Some of these also have regularly formed plurals.

elf → elves
loaf → loaves

scarf → scarves *or* scarfs
wife → wives
staff → staffs *or* staves

Italic Elements

15. Italicized words, phrases, abbreviations, and letters are usually pluralized by adding *-s* or *-'s* in roman type. (See also paragraphs 16, 21, and 26 below.)

three *Fortunes* missing from the stack
a couple of *Gravity's Rainbows* in stock
used too many *etc.*'s in the report
a row of *x*'s

Letters

16. The plurals of letters are usually formed by adding *-'s*, although capital letters are often pluralized by adding *-s* alone.

p's and q's
V's of migrating geese
or Vs of migrating geese
dot your *i*'s
straight As *or* straight A's

Numbers

17. Numerals are pluralized by adding *-s* or, less commonly, *-'s*.

two par 5s *or* two par 5's
1990s *or* 1990's
in the 80s *or* in the 80's *or* in the '80s
the mid-$20,000s *or* the mid-$20,000's

18. Written-out numbers are pluralized by adding -s.

    all the fours and eights
    scored three tens

Proper Nouns

19. The plurals of proper nouns are usually formed with *-s* or *-es.*

    Clarence → Clarences
    Jones → Joneses
    Fernandez → Fernandezes

20. Plurals of proper nouns ending in *-y* usually retain the *-y* and add *-s.*

    Sunday → Sundays
    Timothy → Timothys
    Camry → Camrys

    Words ending in *-y* that were originally proper nouns are usually pluralized by changing *-y* to *-i* and adding *-es,* but a few retain the *-y.*

    bobby → bobbies
    johnny → johnnies
    Tommy → Tommies
    Bloody Mary → Bloody Marys

Quoted Elements

21. The plural of words in quotation marks are formed by adding *-s* or *-'s* within the quotation marks, or *-s* outside the quo-

tation marks. (See also paragraph 26 below.)

too many "probably's" [*or* "probablys"] in the statement
one "you" among millions of "you"s
a record number of "I can't recall"s

Symbols

22. When symbols are referred to as physical characters, the plural is formed by adding either *-s* or *-'s*.

printed three *s
used &'s instead of *and*'s
his π's are hard to read

Words Ending in -ay, -ey, and -oy

23. Words that end in *-ay, -ey,* or *-oy,* unlike other words ending in *-y,* are pluralized by simply adding *-s.*

castaways
donkeys
envoys

Words Ending in *-ful*

24. Any noun ending in *-ful* can be pluralized by adding *-s,* but most also have an alternative plural with *-s* preceding the suffix.

handful → handfuls
teaspoonful → teaspoonfuls
armful → armfuls *or* armsful
bucketful → bucketfuls *or* bucketsful

Words Ending in -o

25. Most words ending in *-o* are normally pluralized by adding *-s*. However, some words ending in *-o* preceded by a consonant take *-es* plurals.

    solo → solos
    photo → photos
    tomato → tomatoes
    potato → potatoes
    hobo → hoboes
    hero → heroes
    cargo → cargoes *or* cargos
    proviso → provisos *or* provisoes
    halo → haloes *or* halos
    echo → echoes
    motto → mottoes

Words Used as Words

26. Words referred to as words and italicized usually form their plurals by adding *-'s* in roman type. (See also paragraph 21 above.)

    five *and*'s in one sentence
    all those *wherefore*'s and *howsoever*'s

    When a word referred to as a word has become part of a fixed phrase, the plural is usually formed by adding *-s* without the apostrophe.

    oohs and aahs
    dos and don'ts *or* do's and don'ts

Possessives

Common Nouns

1. The possessive of singular and plural common nouns that do not end in an *s* or *z* sound is formed by adding *-'s* to the end of the word.

    the child's skates
    women's voices
    the cat's dish
    this patois's range
    people's opinions
    the criteria's common theme

2. The possessive of singular nouns ending in an *s* or *z* sound is usually formed by adding *-'s*. A less common alternative is to add *-'s* only when it is easily pronounced; if it would create a word that is difficult to pronounce, only an apostrophe is added.

    the witness's testimony
    the disease's course
    the race's sponsors
    the prize's recipient
    rickets's symptoms *or* rickets' symptoms

    A multisyllabic singular noun that ends in an *s* or *z* sound drops the *-s* if it is followed by a word beginning with an *s* or *z* sound.

    for appearance' sake
    for goodness' sake

3. The possessive of plural nouns ending in an *s* or *z* sound is formed by adding only an apostrophe. However, the possessive of one-syllable irregular plurals is usually formed by adding *-'s*.

dogs' leashes	buyers' guarantees
birds' migrations	lice's lifespans

Proper Names

4. The possessives of proper names are generally formed in the same way as those of common nouns. The possessive of singular proper names is formed by adding *-'s*.

   Jane's rules of behavior
   three books of Carla's
   Tom White's presentation
   Paris's cafes

   The possessive of plural proper names, and of some singular proper names ending in an *s* or *z* sound, is made by adding just an apostrophe.

   the Stevenses' reception
   the Browns' driveway
   Massachusetts' capital
   New Orleans' annual festival
   the United States' trade deficit
   Protosystems' president

5. The possessive of singular proper names ending in an *s* or *z* sound may be formed by adding either *-'s* or just an apostrophe.

Adding *-'s* to all such names, without regard for the pronunciation of the resulting word, is more common than adding just the apostrophe. (For exceptions see paragraph 6 below.)

Jones's car *or* Jones' car
Bliss's statue *or* Bliss' statue
Dickens's novels *or* Dickens' novels

6. The possessive form of classical and biblical names of two or more syllables ending in *-s* or *-es* is usually made by adding just an apostrophe. If the name has only one syllable, the possessive form is made by adding *-'s*.

Socrates' students	Elias' prophecy
Claudius' reign	Zeus's warnings
Ramses' kingdom	Cis's sons

The possessives of the names *Jesus* and *Moses* are always formed with just an apostrophe.

Jesus' disciples
Moses' law

7. The possessive of names ending in a silent *-s*, *-z*, or *-x* are usually formed with *-'s*.

Des Moines's recreation department
Josquin des Prez's music
Delacroix's painting

8. When the possessive ending is added to an italicized name, it is not italicized.

East of Eden's main characters
the *Spirit of St. Louis*'s historic flight
Brief Encounter's memorable ending

Pronouns

9. The possessive of indefinite pronouns is formed by adding *-'s*.

anyone's rights
everybody's money
someone's coat
somebody's wedding
one's own
either's preference

Some indefinite pronouns usually require an *of* phrase to indicate possession.

the rights of each
the inclination of many
the satisfaction of all

10. Possessive pronouns do not include apostrophes.

mine	hers
ours	his
yours	theirs
its	

Miscellaneous Styling Conventions

11. No apostrophe is generally used today with plural nouns that are more descriptive than possessive.

weapons systems
managers meeting
singles bar
steelworkers union
awards banquet

12. The possessive form of a phrase is made by adding an apostrophe or *-'s* to the last word in the phrase.

    his father-in-law's assistance
    board of directors' meeting
    from the student of politics' point of view
    after a moment or so's thought

    Constructions such as these are often rephrased.

    from the point of view of the student of politics
    after thinking for a moment or so

13. The possessive form of words in quotation marks can be formed in two ways, with *-'s* placed either inside the quotation marks or outside them.

    the "Marseillaise"'s [*or* "Marseillaise's"] stirring melody

    Since both arrangements look awkward, this construction is usually avoided.

    the stirring melody of the "Marseillaise"

14. Possessives of abbreviations are formed like those of nouns that are spelled out. The singular possessive is formed by

adding *-'s;* the plural possessive, by adding an apostrophe only.

the IRS's ruling
AT&T's long-distance service
IBM Corp.'s annual report
Eli Lilly & Co.'s chairman
the HMOs' lobbyists

15. The possessive of nouns composed of numerals is formed in the same way as for other nouns. The possessive of singular nouns is formed by adding *-'s;* the possessive of plural nouns is formed by adding an apostrophe only.

1996's commencement speaker
the 1920s' greatest jazz musicians

16. Individual possession is indicated by adding *-'s* to each noun in a sequence. Joint possession may be indicated in the same way, but is most commonly indicated by adding an apostrophe or *-'s* to the last noun in the sequence.

Joan's and Emily's friends
Jim's, Ed's, and Susan's reports
her mother and father's anniversary
Peter and Jan's trip *or* Peter's and Jan's trip

Compounds

A compound is a word or word group that consists of two or more parts that work together as a unit to express a specific concept. Compounds can be formed by combining two or more words (as in *double-check, cost-effective, farmhouse, graphic equalizer, park bench, around-the-clock,* or *son of a gun*), by combining prefixes or suffixes with words (as in *ex-president, shoeless, presorted,* or *uninterruptedly*), or by combining two or more word elements (as in *macrophage* or *photochromism*). Compounds are written in one of three ways: solid (as in cottonmouth), hyphenated (*screenwriter-director*), or open (*health care*). Because of the variety of standard practice, the choice among these styles for a given compound represents one of the most common and vexing of all style issues that writers encounter.

A good dictionary will list many *permanent compounds,* compounds so commonly used that they have become permanent parts of the language. It will not list *temporary compounds,* those created to meet a writer's need at a particular moment. Most compounds whose meanings are self-evident from the meanings of their component words will not be listed, even if they are permanent and quite widely used. Writers thus cannot rely wholly on dictionaries to guide them in writing compounds.

One approach is to hyphenate all compounds not in the dictionary, since hyphenation immediately identifies them as compounds. But hyphenating all such compounds runs counter to some well-established American practice and can therefore call too much attention to the compound and momentarily distract the reader. Another approach (which applies only to compounds whose elements are complete words) is to leave open any compound not in the dictionary. Though this is widely done, it can result in the reader's failing to recognize a compound for what it is. A third approach is to pattern the compound after other similar ones. Though this approach is likely to be more complicated, it can make the compound look more familiar and thus less distracting or confusing. The paragraphs that follow are intended to help you use this approach.

As a general rule, writing meant for readers in specialized fields usually does not hyphenate compounds, especially technical terminology.

Compound Nouns

Compound nouns are combinations of words that function in a sentence as nouns. They may consist of two or more nouns, a noun and a modifier, or two or more elements that are not nouns.

Short compounds consisting of two nouns often begin as open compounds but tend to close up as they become familiar.

1. **noun + noun** Compounds composed of two nouns that are short and commonly used, of which the first is accented, are usually written solid.

farmhouse	paycheck
hairbrush	football
lifeboat	workplace

2. When a noun + noun compound is short and common but pronounced with nearly equal stress on both nouns, it is more likely to be open.

fuel oil	health care
park bench	desk lamp

3. Noun + noun compounds that consist of longer nouns and are self-evident or temporary are usually written open.

   costume designer
   computer terminal
   billiard table

4. When a noun + noun compound describes a double title or double function, the compound is hyphenated.

   hunter-gatherer
   secretary-treasurer
   bar-restaurant

   Sometimes a slash is used in place of the hyphen.

   bar/restaurant

5. Compounds formed from a noun or adjective followed by *man, woman, person,* or *people* and denoting an occupation are normally solid.

anchorman	spokesperson
congresswoman	salespeople

6. Compounds that are units of measurement are hyphenated.

foot-pound	column-inch
kilowatt-hour	light-year

7. **adjective + noun** Most adjective + noun compounds are written open.

municipal court	minor league
genetic code	nuclear medicine
hazardous waste	basic training

8. Adjective + noun compounds consisting of two short words are often written solid when the first word is accented. However, some are usually written open, and a few are hyphenated.

notebook	dry cleaner
bluebird	steel mill
shortcut	two-step

9. **participle + noun** Most participle + noun compounds are written open.

landing craft	barbed wire
frying pan	preferred stock
sounding board	informed consent

10. **noun's + noun** Compounds consisting of a possessive noun followed by another noun are usually written open; a few are hyphenated. Compounds of this type that have become solid have lost the apostrophe.

fool's gold	cat's-paw
hornet's nest	bull's-eye
seller's market	foolscap
Queen Anne's lace	menswear

11. **noun + verb + *-er* or *-ing*** Compounds in which the first noun is the object of the verb are most often written open but sometimes hyphenated. Permanent compounds like these are sometimes written solid.

problem solver	fund-raiser
deal making	gene-splicing
air conditioner	lifesaving

12. **object + verb** Noun compounds consisting of a verb preceded by a noun that is its object are written in various ways.

fish fry	bodyguard
eye-opener	roadblock

13. **verb + object** A few, mostly older compounds are formed from a verb followed by a noun that is its object; they are written solid.

cutthroat	carryall
breakwater	pickpocket

14. **noun + adjective** Compounds composed of a noun followed by an adjective are written open or hyphenated.

sum total	president-elect
consul general	secretary-general

15. **particle + noun** Compounds consisting of a particle (usually a preposition or adverb) and a noun are usually written solid, especially when they are short and the first syllable is accented.

downturn	undertone
outfield	upswing
input	afterthought
outpatient	onrush

A few particle + noun compounds, especially when composed of longer elements or having equal stress on both elements, are hyphenated or open.

on-ramp	off year
cross-reference	cross fire

16. **verb + particle; verb + adverb** These compounds may be hyphenated or solid. Compounds with particles such as *to, in,* and *on* are often hyphenated. Compounds with particles such as *up, off,* and *out* are hyphenated or solid with about

equal frequency. Those with longer particles or adverbs are usually solid.

lean-to	spin-off
trade-in	payoff
add-on	time-out
start-up	turnout
backup	hideaway

17. **verb + *-er* + particle; verb + *-ing* + particle** Except for *passerby,* these compounds are hyphenated.

runner-up	carrying-on
diners-out	talking-to
listener-in	falling-out

18. **letter + noun** Compounds formed from a single letter (or sometimes a combination of them) followed by a noun are either open or hyphenated.

T square	T-shirt
B vitamin	f-stop
V neck	H-bomb
Rh factor	A-frame
D major	E-mail *or* e-mail

19. **Compounds of three or four elements** Compounds of three or four words may be either hyphenated or open. Those incorporating prepositional phrases are more often open; others are usually hyphenated.

editor in chief	right-of-way
power of attorney	jack-of-all-trades
flash in the pan	give-and-take
base on balls	rough-and-tumble

20. **Reduplication compounds** Compound words that are formed by reduplication and so consist of two similar-sounding elements are hyphenated if each element has more than one syllable. If each element has only one syllable, the compound is often written solid. Very short words and newly coined words are more often hyphenated.

namby-pamby	singsong
razzle-dazzle	sci-fi
crisscross	hip-hop

Compound Adjectives

Compound adjectives are combinations of words that work together to modify a noun—that is, they work as *unit modifiers*. As unit modifiers they can be distinguished from other strings of adjectives that may also precede a noun.

For instance, in "a low, level tract of land" the two adjectives each modify the noun separately; the tract is both low and level. These are *coordinate* (i.e., equal) *modifiers*. In "a low monthly fee" the first adjective modifies the noun plus the second adjective; the phrase denotes a monthly fee that is low. It could not be revised to "a monthly and low fee" without altering or confusing its meaning. Thus, these are *noncoordinate modifiers.* However, "low-level radiation" does not mean radiation that is low and level or level radiation that is low, but rather radiation that is at a low level. Both words work as a unit to modify the noun.

Unit modifiers are usually hyphenated, in order to help readers grasp the relationship of the words and to avoid confusion. The hyphen in "a call for more-specialized controls" removes any ambiguity as to which word *more* modifies. By contrast, the lack of a hyphen in a phrase like "graphic arts exhibition" may give it an undesirable ambiguity.

21. **Before the noun (attributive position)** Most two-word compound adjectives are hyphenated when placed before the noun.

    the fresh-cut grass
    its longer-lasting effects
    her lace-trimmed dress
    a made-up excuse
    his best-selling novel
    projected health-care costs

22. Compounds whose first word is an adverb ending in -ly are usually left open.

    a privately chartered boat
    politically correct opinions
    its weirdly skewed perspective
    a tumultuously cascading torrent

23. Compounds formed of an adverb not ending in *-ly* followed by a participle (or sometimes an adjective) are usually hyphenated when placed before a noun.

 the well-worded statement
 more-stringent measures
 his less-exciting prospects
 their still-awaited assignments
 her once-famous uncle

24. The combination of *very* + adjective is not a unit modifier. (See also paragraph 33 below.)

 a very happy baby

25. When a compound adjective is formed by using a compound noun to modify another noun, it is usually hyphenated.

 a hazardous-waste site
 the basic-training period
 a minor-league pitcher
 a roll-call vote
 their problem-solving abilities

 Some familiar open compound nouns are frequently left open when used as adjectives.

 a high school diploma
 or a high-school diploma
 a real estate license
 or a real-estate license
 an income tax refund
 or an income-tax refund

26. A proper name used as a modifier is not hyphenated. A word that modifies the proper name is attached by a hyphen (or an en dash in typeset material).

the Civil War era
a New England tradition
a *New York Times* article
the Supreme Court decision
the splendid *Gone with the Wind* premiere
a Los Angeles-based company
a Pulitzer Prize–winning author
pre–Bull Run skirmishes

27. Compound adjectives composed of foreign words are not hyphenated when placed before a noun unless they are hyphenated in the foreign language itself.

per diem expenses
an ad hoc committee
her *faux-naïf* style
a comme il faut arrangement
the a cappella chorus
a ci-devant professor

28. Compounds that are quoted, capitalized, or italicized are not hyphenated.

a "Springtime in Paris" theme
the book's "I'm OK, you're OK" tone
his AMERICA FIRST sign
the *No smoking* notice

29. Chemical names and most medical names used as modifiers are not hyphenated.

a sodium hypochlorite bleach
the amino acid sequence
a new Parkinson's disease medication

30. Compound adjectives of three or more words are hyphenated when they precede the noun.

step-by-step instructions
state-of-the-art equipment
a wait-and-see attitude
a longer-than-expected list
turn-of-the-century medicine

31. **Following the noun** When a compound adjective follows the noun it modifies, it usually ceases to be a unit modifier and is therefore no longer hyphenated.

instructions that guide you step by step
a list that was longer than expected

However, a compound that follows the noun it modifies often keeps its hyphen if it continues to function as a unit modifier, especially if its first element is a noun.

hikers who were ill-advised to cross the glacier
an actor too high-strung to relax
industries that could be called low-tech
metals that are corrosion-resistant
tends to be accident-prone

32. Permanent compound adjectives are usually written as they appear in the dictio-

nary even when they follow the noun they modify.

for reasons that are well-known
a plan we regarded as half-baked
The problems are mind-boggling.

However, compound adjectives of three or more words are normally not hyphenated when they follow the noun they modify, since they usually cease to function as adjectives.

These remarks are off the record.
medical practice of the turn of the century

When compounds of three or more words appear as hyphenated adjectives in dictionaries, the hyphens are retained as long as the phrase is being used as a unit modifier.

The candidate's position was middle-of-the-road.

33. When an adverb modifies another adverb that is the first element of a compound modifier, the compound may lose its hyphen. If the first adverb modifies the whole compound, however, the hyphen is retained.

a very well developed idea
but
a delightfully well-written book
a most ill-timed event

34. Adjective compounds that are color names in which each element can function as a noun are almost always hyphenated.

    red-orange fabric
    The fabric was red-orange.

    Color names in which the first element can only be an adjective are often unhyphenated before a noun and usually unhyphenated after.

    a bright red tie
    the pale yellow-green chair
    reddish orange fabric
    or reddish-orange fabric
    The fabric was reddish orange.

35. Compound modifiers that include a number followed by a noun (except for the noun *percent*) are hyphenated when they precede the noun they modify, but usually not when they follow it. (For details on measurement, see paragraph 42 on pages 203–4.)

    the four-color press
    a 12-foot-high fence
    a fence 12 feet high
    a 300-square-mile area
    an area of 300 square miles
    but
    a 10 percent raise

    If a currency symbol precedes the number, the hyphen is omitted.

    an $8.5 million deficit

36. An adjective composed of a number followed by a noun in the possessive is not hyphenated.

a nine days' wonder
a two weeks' wait
but
a two-week wait

Compound Adverbs

37. Adverb compounds consisting of preposition + noun are almost always written solid. However, there are a few important exceptions.

downstairs
uphill
offshore
overnight
but
in-house
off-key
on-line

38. Compound adverbs of more than two words are usually written open, and they usually follow the words they modify.

here and there
more or less
head and shoulders
hand in hand
every which way
once and for all
but
a more-or-less certain result

A few three-word adverbs are usually hyphenated, but many are written open even if the corresponding adjective is hyphenated.

placed back-to-back
met face-to-face
but
a word-for-word quotation
quoted word for word
software bought off the shelf

Compound Verbs

39. Two-word verbs consisting of a verb followed by an adverb or a preposition are written open.

follow up	take on
roll back	run across
strike out	set back

40. A compound composed of a particle followed by a verb is written solid.

overlook	undercut
outfit	download

41. A verb derived from an open or hyphenated compound noun is hyphenated.

double-space	water-ski
rubber-stamp	field-test

42. A verb derived from a solid noun is written solid.

mastermind	brainstorm
highlight	sideline

Compounds Formed with Word Elements

Many new and temporary compounds are formed by adding word elements to existing words or by combining word elements. There are three basic kinds of word elements: prefixes (such as *anti-*, *non-*, *pre-*, *post-*, *re-*, *super-*), suffixes (such as *-er*, *-fold*, *-ism*, *-ist*, *-less*, *-ness*), and combining forms (such as *mini-*, *macro-*, *pseudo-*, *-graphy*, *-logy*). Prefixes and suffixes are usually attached to existing words; combining forms are usually combined to form new words.

43. **prefix + word** Except as specified in the paragraphs below, compounds formed from a prefix and a word are usually written solid.

anticrime	subzero
nonaligned	superheroine
premedical	transnational
reorchestration	postdoctoral

44. If the prefix ends with a vowel and the word it is attached to begins with the same vowel, the compound is usually hyphenated.

anti-incumbent	semi-independent
de-escalate	intra-arterial
co-organizer	pre-engineered

However, there are many exceptions.

reelect
preestablished
cooperate

45. If the base word or compound to which a prefix is added is capitalized, the resulting compound is almost always hyphenated.

pre-Victorian
anti-Western
post-Darwinian
non-English-speaking
but
transatlantic
transalpine

If the prefix and the base word together form a new proper name, the compound may be solid with the prefix capitalized.

Postimpressionists
Precambrian
but
Pre-Raphaelite

46. Compounds made with *ex-*, in its "former" sense, and *self-* are hyphenated.

ex-mayor	self-control
ex-husband	self-sustaining

Compounds formed from *vice-* are usually hyphenated. Some permanent compounds are open.

vice-chair	vice president
vice-consul	vice admiral

A temporary compound with *quasi(-)* or *pseudo(-)* may be written open (if *quasi* or *pseudo* is being treated as a modifier) or hyphenated (if it is being treated as a combining form).

quasi intellectual
  or quasi-intellectual
pseudo liberal
  or pseudo-liberal

47. If a prefix is added to a hyphenated compound, it may be either followed by a hyphen or closed up solid to the next element. Permanent compounds of this kind should be checked in a dictionary.

unair-conditioned
ultra-up-to-date
non-self-governing
unself-confident

48. If a prefix is added to an open compound, the hyphen is often replaced by an en dash in typeset material.

ex–campaign treasurer
post–World War I era

49. A compound that would be identical with another word if written solid is usually hyphenated to prevent misreading.

a re-creation of the setting
shopped at the co-op
multi-ply fabric

50. Compounds that might otherwise be solid are often hyphenated in order to clarify their formation, meaning, or pronunciation.

tri-city	non-news
de-iced	anti-fur
re-oil	pro-choice

51. When prefixes are attached to numerals, the compounds are hyphenated.

pre-1995 models
post-1945 economy
non-19th-century architecture

52. Compounds created from proper ethnic or national combining forms are hyphenated when the second element is an independent word, but solid when it is a combining form.

Anglo-Saxon	Anglophile
Judeo-Christian	Francophone
Sino-Japanese	Sinophobe

53. Prefixes that are repeated in the same compound are separated by a hyphen.

re-refried
post-postmodern

54. Compounds consisting of different prefixes or adjectives with the same base word which are joined by *and* or *or* are

shortened by pruning the first compound back to a hyphenated prefix.

pre- and postoperative care
anti- or pro-Revolutionary sympathies
over- and underachievers
early- and mid-20th-century painters
4-, 6-, and 8-foot lengths

55. **word + suffix** Except as noted in the paragraphs below, compounds formed by adding a suffix to a word are written solid.

Fourierism	characterless
benightedness	custodianship
yellowish	easternmost

56. Compounds made with a suffix or a terminal combining form are often hyphenated if the base word is more than two syllables long, if it ends with the same letter the suffix begins with, or if it is a proper name.

industry-wide	jewel-like
recession-proof	Hollywood-ish
American-ness	Europe-wide

57. Compounds made from a number + *-odd* are hyphenated. A number + *-fold* is written solid if the number is spelled out but hyphenated if it is in numerals.

fifty-odd	tenfold
50-odd	10-fold

58. Most compounds formed from an open or hyphenated compound + a suffix do not separate the suffix with a hyphen. But combining forms that also exist as independent words, such as *-like, -wide, -worthy,* and *-proof,* are attached by a hyphen.

self-righteousness
middle-of-the-roadism
bobby-soxer
a Red Cross-like approach
a New York-wide policy

Open compounds often become hyphenated when a suffix is added unless they are proper nouns.

flat-taxer
Ivy Leaguer
World Federalist

59. **combining forms** New terms in technical fields created with one or more combining forms are normally written solid.

cyberworld
macrographic

4 Abbreviations

Abbreviations may be used to save space and time, to avoid repetition of long words and phrases, or simply to conform to conventional usage.

The contemporary styling of abbreviations is inconsistent and arbitrary, and no set of rules can hope to cover all the possible variations, exceptions, and peculiarities encountered in print. The form abbreviations take—capitalized vs. lowercased, punctuated vs. unpunctuated—often depends on a writer's preference or a publisher's or organization's policy. However, the following paragraphs provide a number of useful guidelines to contemporary practice. In doubtful cases, a good general dictionary or a dictionary of abbreviations will usually show standard forms for common abbreviations.

The present discussion deals largely with general, nontechnical writing. In scientific writing, abbreviations are almost never punctuated.

An abbreviation is not divided at the end of a line.

Abbreviations are almost never italicized. An abbreviation consisting of single initial letters, whether punctuated or not, never standardly has spacing between the letters. (Initials of personal names, however, normally are separated by spaces.)

The first reference to any frequently abbreviated term or name that could be confusing or unfamiliar is commonly spelled out, often followed immediately by its abbreviation in parentheses. Later references employ the abbreviation alone.

Punctuation

1. A period follows most abbreviations that are formed by omitting all but the first few letters of a word.

    cont. [*for* continued]
    enc. [*for* enclosure]
    Oct. [*for* October]
    univ. [*for* university]

    Former abbreviations that are now considered words do not need a period.

lab	photo
gym	ad

2. A period follows most abbreviations that are formed by omitting letters from the middle of a word.

govt. [*for* government]
atty. [*for* attorney]
bros. [*for* brothers]
Dr. [*for* Doctor]

Some abbreviations, usually called *contractions,* replace the omitted letters with an apostrophe. Such contractions do not end with a period. (In American usage, very few contractions other than two-word contractions involving verbs are in standard use.)

ass'n *or* assn. [*for* association]
dep't *or* dept. [*for* department]
nat'l *or* natl. [*for* national]
can't [*for* cannot]

3. Periods are usually omitted from abbreviations made up of single initial letters. However, for some of these abbreviations, especially uncapitalized ones, the periods are usually retained. No space follows an internal period.

GOP [*for* Grand Old Party]
PR [*for* public relations]
CEO *or* C.E.O. [*for* chief executive officer]
a.m. [*for* ante meridiem]

4. A few abbreviations are punctuated with one or more slashes in place of periods. (For details on the slash, see the section beginning on page 68.)

c/o [*for* care of]
d/b/a *or* d.b.a. [*for* doing business as]

w/o [*for* without]
w/w [*for* wall-to-wall]

5. Terms in which a suffix is added to a numeral are not genuine abbreviations and do not require a period. (For details on ordinal numbers, see the section on page 178.)

1st	3d
2nd	8vo

6. Isolated letters of the alphabet used to designate a shape or position in a sequence are not abbreviations and are not punctuated.

T square
A1
F minor

7. When a punctuated abbreviation ends a sentence, its period becomes the terminal period.

For years she claimed she was "the oldest living fossil at Briggs & Co."

Capitalization

1. Abbreviations are capitalized if the words they represent are proper nouns or adjectives.

F [*for* Fahrenheit]
IMF [*for* International Monetary Fund]

Jan. [*for* January]
Amer. [*for* American]
LWV [*for* League of Women Voters]

2. Abbreviations are usually all-capitalized when they represent initial letters of lowercased words. However, some common abbreviations formed in this way are often lowercased.

   IQ [*for* intelligence quotient]
   U.S. [*for* United States]
   COLA [*for* cost-of-living allowance]
   FYI [*for* for your information]
   f.o.b. *or* FOB [*for* free on board]
   c/o [*for* care of]

3. Most abbreviations formed from single initial letters that are pronounced as words, rather than as a series of letters, are capitalized. Those that are not proper nouns and have been assimilated into the language as words in their own right are most often lowercased.

   OSHA snafu
   NATO laser
   CARE sonar
   NAFTA scuba

4. Abbreviations that are ordinarily capitalized are commonly used to begin sentences, but abbreviations that are ordinarily uncapitalized are not.

Dr. Smith strongly disagrees.

OSHA regulations require these new measures.

Page 22 [*not* P. 22] was missing.

Plurals, Possessives, and Compounds

1. Punctuated abbreviations of single words are pluralized by adding *-s* before the period.

   yrs. [*for* years]
   hwys. [*for* highways]
   figs. [*for* figures]

2. Punctuated abbreviations that stand for phrases or compounds are usually pluralized by adding *-'s* after the last period.

   M.D.'s *or* M.D.s
   Ph.D.'s *or* Ph.D.s
   LL.B.'s *or* LL.B.s
   v.p.'s

3. All-capitalized, unpunctuated abbreviations are usually pluralized by adding a lowercase *-s.*

   IRAs CPAs
   PCs SATs

4. The plural form of a few lowercase one-letter abbreviations is made by repeating the letter.

ll. [*for* lines]
pp. [*for* pages]
nn. [*for* notes]
vv. [*for* verses]
ff. *or* ff [*for* and the following ones *or* folios]

5. The plural form of abbreviations of units of measurement (including one-letter abbreviations) is the same as the singular form. (For more on units of measurement, see the section on pages 203–5.)

   10 cc *or* cc. [*for* cubic centimeters]
   30 m *or* m. [*for* meters]
   15 mm *or* mm. [*for* millimeters]
   24 h. [*for* hours]
   10 min. [*for* minutes]
   45 mi. [*for* miles]

   However, in informal nontechnical text several such abbreviations are pluralized like other single-word abbreviations.

   lbs. qts.
   gals. hrs.

6. Possessives of abbreviations are formed like those of spelled-out nouns: the singular possessive is formed by adding *-'s*, the plural possessive simply by adding an apostrophe.

   the CEO's speech
   Apex Co.'s profits
   the PACs' influence
   Brown Bros.' ads

7. Compounds that consist of an abbreviation added to another word are formed in the same way as compounds that consist of spelled-out nouns.

   an FDA-approved drug
   an R&D-driven company
   the Eau Claire, Wisc.–based publisher

   Compounds formed by adding a prefix or suffix to an abbreviation are usually hyphenated.

   pre-CD recordings
   non-IRA deductions
   a CIA-like operation
   a PCB-free product

Specific Styling Conventions

A and *An*

1. The choice of the article *a* or *an* before abbreviations depends on the sound, rather than the actual letter, with which the abbreviation begins. If it begins with a consonant sound, *a* is normally used; if with a vowel sound, *an* is used.

   a CD-ROM version
   a YAF member
   a U.S. Senator
   an FDA-approved drug
   an M.D. degree
   an ABA convention

A.D. and B.C.

2. The abbreviations A.D. and B.C. and other abbreviated era designations usually appear in books and journals as small capitals; in newspapers and in typed or keyboarded material, they usually appear as full capitals. The abbreviation B.C. follows the date; A.D. usually precedes the date, though in many publications A.D. follows the date as well. In references to whole centuries, A.D. follows the century. (For more on era designations, see paragraph 12 on pages 190–91.)

   A.D. 185 *but also* 185 A.D.
   41 B.C.
   the fourth century A.D.

Agencies, Associations, Organizations, and Companies

3. The names of agencies, associations, and organizations are usually abbreviated after being spelled out on their first occurrence in a text. If a company is easily recognizable from its initials, the abbreviation is likewise usually employed after the first mention. The abbreviations are usually all-capitalized and unpunctuated. (In contexts where the abbreviation will be recognized, it often replaces the full name throughout.)

Next, the president of the Pioneer Valley Transit Authority presented the annual PVTA award.

. . . at the American Bar Association (ABA) meeting in June. The ABA's new officers . . .

International Business Machines released its first-quarter earnings figures today. An IBM spokesperson . . .

4. The words *Company, Corporation, Incorporated,* and *Limited* in company names are commonly abbreviated even at their first appearance, except in quite formal writing.

   Procter & Gamble Company
   or Procter & Gamble Co.
   Brandywine Corporation
   or Brandywine Corp.

Ampersand

5. The ampersand (&), representing the word *and,* is often used in the names of companies.

   H&R Block
   Standard & Poor's
   Ogilvy & Mather

   It is not used in the names of federal agencies.

   U.S. Fish and Wildlife Service
   Office of Management and Budget

Even when a spelled-out *and* appears in a company's official name, it is often replaced by an ampersand in writing referring to the company, whether for the sake of consistency or because of the writer's inability to verify the official styling.

6. When an ampersand is used in an abbreviation, there is usually no space on either side of the ampersand.

   The Barkers welcome all guests to their B&B at 54 West Street.

   The S&P 500 showed gains in technology stocks.

   The Texas A&M Aggies prevailed again on Sunday.

7. When an ampersand is used between the last two elements in a series, the comma is omitted.

   Jones, Kuhn & Malloy, Attorneys at Law

Books of the Bible

8. Books of the Bible are spelled out in running text but generally abbreviated in references to chapter and verse.

   The minister based his first Advent sermon on Matthew.

   Ye cannot serve God and mammon.—Matt. 6:24

Compass Points

9. Compass points are normally abbreviated when they follow street names; these abbreviations may be punctuated and are usually preceded by a comma.

   1600 Pennsylvania Avenue[,] NW [N.W.]

   When a compass point precedes the word *Street, Avenue,* etc., or when it follows the word but forms an integral part of the street name, it is usually spelled out.

   230 West 43rd Street
   50 Park Avenue South

Dates

10. The names of days and months are spelled out in running text.

    at the Monday editorial meeting
    the December issue of *Scientific American*
    a meeting held on August 1, 1998

    The names of months usually are not abbreviated in datelines of business letters, but they are often abbreviated in government and military correspondence.

    business dateline: November 1, 1999
    military dateline: 1 Nov 99

Degrees and Professional Ratings

11. Abbreviations of academic degrees are usually punctuated; abbreviations of pro-

fessional ratings are slightly more commonly unpunctuated.

Ph.D.
B.Sc.
M.B.A.
PLS
or P.L.S. [*for* Professional Legal Secretary]
CMA
or C.M.A. [*for* Certified Medical Assistant]
FACP
or F.A.C.P. [*for* Fellow of the American College of Physicians]

12. Only the first letter of each element in abbreviations of degrees and professional ratings is generally capitalized.

D.Ch.E. [*for* Doctor of Chemical Engineering]
Litt.D. [*for* Doctor of Letters]
D.Th. [*for* Doctor of Theology]
but
LL.B. [*for* Bachelor of Laws]
LL.M. [*for* Master of Laws]
LL.D. [*for* Doctor of Laws]

Geographical Names

13. When abbreviations of state names are used in running text immediately following the name of a city or county, the traditional state abbreviations are often used.

Ellen White of 49 Lyman St., Saginaw, Mich., has been chosen . . .

the Dade County, Fla., public schools
but
Grand Rapids, in western Michigan, . . .

Official postal service abbreviations for states are used in mailing addresses.

6 Bay Rd.
Gibson Island, MD 21056

14. Terms such as *Street, Road,* and *Boulevard* are often written as punctuated abbreviations in running text when they form part of a proper name.

an accident on Windward Road [*or* Rd.]
our office at 1234 Cross Blvd. [*or* Boulevard]

15. Names of countries are usually spelled in full in running text.

South Africa's president urged the United States to impose meaningful sanctions.

Abbreviations for country names (in tables, for example), are usually punctuated. When formed from the single initial letters of two or more individual words, they are sometimes unpunctuated.

Mex.	Scot.
Can.	U.K. *or* UK
Ger.	U.S. *or* US

16. *United States* is normally abbreviated when used as an adjective or attributive. When used as a noun, it is generally spelled out.

the U.S. Department of Justice
U.S. foreign policy
The United States has declined to participate.

17. *Saint* is usually abbreviated when it is part of a geographical or topographical name. *Mount, Point,* and *Fort* may be either spelled out or abbreviated. (For the abbreviation of *Saint* with personal names, see paragraph 25 below.)

St. Paul, Minnesota
or Saint Paul, Minnesota
St. Thomas, U.S.V.I. *or* Saint Thomas
Mount Vernon *or* Mt. Vernon
Point Reyes *or* Pt. Reyes
Fort Worth *or* Ft. Worth
Mt. Kilimanjaro *or* Mount Kilimanjaro

Latin Words and Phrases

18. Several Latin words and phrases are almost always abbreviated. They are punctuated, lowercased, and usually not italicized.

etc.	ibid.
i.e.	op. cit.
e.g.	q.v.
cf.	c. *or* ca.
viz.	fl.
et al.	et seq.

Versus is usually abbreviated *v.* in legal writing, *vs.* otherwise.

Da Costa v. *United States*
good vs. evil
or good versus evil

Latitude and *Longitude*

19. The words *latitude* and *longitude* are abbreviated in tables and in technical contexts but often written out in running text.

in a table: lat. 10°20′N *or* lat. 10-20N
in text: from 10°20′ north latitude to 10°30′ south latitude
or from lat. 10°20′N to lat. 10°30′S

Military Ranks and Units

20. Official abbreviations for military ranks follow specific unpunctuated styles for each branch of the armed forces. Nonmilitary writing usually employs a punctuated and less concise style.

in the military:
BG Carter R. Stokes, USA
LCDR Dawn Wills-Craig, USN
Col S. J. Smith, USMC
LTJG Carlos Ramos, USCG
Sgt Bernard P. Brodkey, USAF

outside the military:
Brig. Gen. Carter R. Stokes
Lt. Comdr. Dawn Wills-Craig
Col. S. J. Smith
Lt. (j.g.) Carlos Ramos
Sgt. Bernard P. Brodkey

21. Outside the military, military ranks are usually given in full when used with a surname only but abbreviated when used with a full name.

    Major Mosby
    Maj. John S. Mosby

Number

22. The word *number,* when followed by a numeral, is usually abbreviated to *No.* or *no.*

    The No. 1 priority is to promote profitability.
    We recommend no. 6 thread.
    Policy No. 123-5-X
    Publ. Nos. 12 and 13

Personal Names

23. When initials are used with a surname, they are spaced and punctuated. Unspaced initials of a few famous persons, which may or may not be punctuated, are sometimes used in place of their full names.

    E. M. Forster
    C. P. E. Bach
    JFK *or* J.F.K.

24. The abbreviations *Jr.* and *Sr.* may or may not be preceded by a comma.

    Martin Luther King Jr.
    or Martin Luther King, Jr.

Saint

25. The word *Saint* is often abbreviated when used before the name of a saint. When it forms part of a surname or an institution's name, it follows the style used by the person or institution. (For the styling of *Saint* in geographical names, see paragraph 17 on page 166.)

    St. [*or* Saint] Teresa of Avila
    Augustus Saint-Gaudens
    Ruth St. Denis
    St. Martin's Press
    St. John's College

Scientific Terms

26. In binomial nomenclature, a genus name may be abbreviated to its initial letter after the first reference. The abbreviation is always capitalized, punctuated, and italicized.

    . . . its better-known relative *Atropa belladonna* (deadly nightshade).
    Only *A. belladonna* is commonly found in . . .

27. Abbreviations for the names of chemical compounds and the symbols for chemical elements and formulas are unpunctuated.

MSG	O
PCB	NaCl
Pb	FeS

28. Abbreviations in computer terms are usually unpunctuated.

PC	Esc
RAM	Alt
CD-ROM	Ctrl
I/O	ASCII
DOS	EBCDIC

Time

29. When time is expressed in figures, the abbreviations *a.m.* *(ante meridiem)* and *p.m.* *(post meridiem)* are most often written as punctuated lowercase letters, sometimes as punctuated small capital letters. In newspapers, they usually appear in full-size capitals. (For more on *a.m.* and *p.m.*, see paragraph 39 on pages 202–3.)

    8:30 a.m. *or* 8:30 A.M. *or* 8:30 A.M.
    10:00 p.m. *or* 10:00 P.M. *or* 10:00 P.M.

    Time-zone designations are usually capitalized and unpunctuated.

    9:22 a.m. EST [*for* eastern standard time]
    4:45 p.m. CDT [*for* central daylight time]

Titles and Degrees

30. The courtesy titles *Mr., Ms., Mrs.,* and *Messrs.* occur only as abbreviations today. The professional titles *Doctor, Professor, Representative,* and *Senator* are often abbreviated.

Ms. Lee A. Downs
Messrs. Lake, Mason, and Nambeth
Doctor Howe *or* Dr. Howe

31. Despite some traditional objections, the honorific titles *Honorable* and *Reverend* are often abbreviated, with and without *the* preceding the titles.

the Honorable Samuel I. O'Leary
or [the] Hon. Samuel I. O'Leary
the Reverend Samuel I. O'Leary
or [the] Rev. Samuel I. O'Leary

32. When an abbreviation for an academic degree, professional certification, or association membership follows a name, no courtesy or professional title precedes it.

Dr. Jesse Smith *or* Jesse Smith, M.D.
but not Dr. Jesse Smith, M.D.
Katherine Fox Derwinski, CLU
Carol W. Manning, M.D., FACPS
Michael B. Jones II, J.D.
Peter D. Cohn, Jr., CPA

33. The abbreviation *Esq.* (for *Esquire*) often follows attorneys' names in correspondence and in formal listings, and less often follows the names of certain other professionals, including architects, consuls, clerks of court, and justices of the peace. It is not used if a degree or professional rating follows the name, or if a

courtesy title or honorific (*Mr., Ms., Hon., Dr.,* etc.) precedes the name.

Carolyn B. West, Esq.
not Ms. Carolyn B. West, Esq.
and not Carolyn B. West, J.D., Esq.

Units of Measurement

34. A unit of measurement that follows a figure is often abbreviated, especially in technical writing. The figure and abbreviation are separated by a space. If the numeral is written out, the unit should also be written out.

15 cu. ft. *but* fifteen cubic feet
What is its capacity in cubic feet?

35. Abbreviations for metric units are usually unpunctuated; those for traditional units are usually punctuated in nonscientific writing. (For more on units of measurement, see the section on pages 203–5.)

14 ml	8 ft.
12 km	4 sec.
50 m	20 min.

5 Numbers

The treatment of numbers presents special difficulties because there are so many conventions to follow, some of which may conflict in a particular passage. The major issue is whether to spell out numbers or to express them in figures, and usage varies considerably on this point.

Numbers as Words or Figures

At one style extreme—usually limited to proclamations, legal documents, and some other types of very formal writing—all numbers (sometimes even including dates) are written out. At the other extreme, some types of technical writing may contain no written-out numbers. Figures are generally easier to read than spelled-out numbers; however, the spelled-out forms are helpful in certain circumstances, and are often felt to be less jarring than figures in nontechnical writing.

Basic Conventions

1. Two alternative basic conventions are in common use. The first and more widely used system requires that numbers up through nine be spelled out, and that figures be used for exact numbers greater than nine. (In a variation of this system, the number ten is spelled out.) Round numbers that consist of a whole number between one and nine followed by *hundred, thousand, million,* etc., may either be spelled out or expressed in figures.

   The museum includes four rooms of early American tools and implements, 345 pieces in all.

   He spoke for almost three hours, inspiring his audience of 19,000 devoted followers.

   They sold more than 700 [*or* seven hundred] TVs during the 10-day sale.

   She'd told him so a thousand times.

2. The second system requires that numbers from one through ninety-nine be spelled out, and that figures be used for all exact numbers above ninety-nine. (In a variation of this system, the number one hundred is spelled out.) Numbers that consist of a whole number between one and ninety-nine followed by *hundred, thousand, million,* etc., are also spelled out.

   Audubon's engraver spent nearly twelve years completing these four volumes, which comprise 435 hand-colored plates.

In the course of four hours, she signed twenty-five hundred copies of her book.

3. Written-out numbers only use hyphens following words ending in *-ty*. The word *and* before such words is usually omitted.

twenty-two
five hundred ninety-seven
two thousand one hundred forty-nine

Sentence Beginnings

4. Numbers that begin a sentence are written out. An exception is occasionally made for dates. Spelled-out numbers that are lengthy and awkward are usually avoided by restructuring the sentence.

Sixty-two new bills will be brought before the committee.
or There will be 62 new bills brought before the committee.

Nineteen ninety-five was our best earnings year so far.
or occasionally 1995 was our best earnings year so far.

One hundred fifty-seven illustrations, including 86 color plates, are contained in the book.
or The book contains 157 illustrations, including 86 color plates.

Adjacent Numbers and Numbers in Series

5. Two separate figures are generally not written adjacent to one another in run-

ning text unless they form a series. Instead, either the sentence is rephrased or one of the figures is spelled out—usually the figure with the shorter written form.

> sixteen ½-inch dowels
> worked five 9-hour days in a row
> won twenty 100-point games
> lost 15 fifty-point matches
> By 1997, thirty schools . . .

6. Numbers paired at the beginning of a sentence are usually written alike. If the first word of the sentence is a spelled-out number, the second number is also spelled out. However, each number may instead be styled independently, even if that results in an inconsistent pairing.

> Sixty to seventy-five copies will be required.
> *or* Sixty to 75 copies will be required.

7. Numbers that form a pair or a series within a sentence or a paragraph are often treated identically even when they would otherwise be styled differently. The style of the largest number usually determines that of the others. If one number is a mixed or simple fraction, figures are used for all the numbers in the series.

> She wrote one composition for English and translated twelve [*or* 12] pages for French that night.

His total record sales came to a meager 8 [*or* eight] million; Bing Crosby's, he mused, may have surpassed 250 million.

The three jobs took 5, 12, and 4½ hours, respectively.

Round Numbers

8. Approximate or round numbers, particularly those that can be expressed in one or two words, are often spelled out in general writing. In technical and scientific writing, they are expressed as numerals.

seven hundred people *or* 700 people
five thousand years *or* 5,000 years
four hundred thousand volumes
or 400,000 volumes
but not 400 thousand volumes

but in technical writing
200 species of fish
50,000 people per year
300,000 years

9. Round (and round-appearing) numbers of one million and above are often expressed as figures followed by the word *million, billion,* and so forth. The figure may include a one- or two-digit decimal fraction; more exact numbers are written entirely in figures.

the last 600 million years
about 4.6 billion years old
1.2 million metric tons of grain

$7.25 million
$3,456,000,000

Ordinal Numbers

10. Ordinal numbers generally follow the styling rules for cardinal numbers. In technical writing, ordinal numbers are usually written as figure-plus-suffix combinations. Certain ordinal numbers—for example, those for percentiles and latitudes—are usually set as figures even in nontechnical contexts.

    entered the seventh grade
    wrote the 9th [*or* ninth] and 12th [*or* twelfth] chapters
    in the 21st [*or* twenty-first] century
    the 7th percentile
    the 38th parallel

11. In figure-plus-suffix combinations where the figure ends in 2 or 3, either a one- or a two-letter suffix may be used. A period does not follow the suffix.

    2d *or* 2nd
    33d *or* 33rd
    102d *or* 102nd

Roman Numerals

12. Roman numerals are traditionally used to differentiate rulers and popes with identical names.

King George III
Henri IV
Innocent X

13. When Roman numerals are used to differentiate related males with the same name, they are used only with the full name. Ordinals are sometimes used instead of Roman numerals. The possessive is formed in the usual way. (For the use of *Jr.* and *Sr.*, see paragraph 24 on page 168.)

James R. Watson II
James R. Watson 2nd *or* 2d
James R. Watson II's [*or* 2nd's *or* 2d's] alumni gift

14. Lowercase Roman numerals are generally used to number book pages that precede the regular Arabic sequence (often including a table of contents, acknowledgments, foreword, or other material).

on page iv of the preface
See Introduction, pp. ix–xiii.

15. Roman numerals are used in outlines; see paragraph 23 on page 197.

16. Roman numerals are found as part of a few established scientific and technical terms. Chords in the study of music harmony are designated by capital and lowercase Roman numerals (often followed

by small Arabic numbers). Most technical terms that include numbers, however, express them in Arabic form.

blood-clotting factor VII
cranial nerves II and IX
cancer stage III
Population II stars
type I error
vii_6 chord

but

adenosine 3′,5′-monophosphate
cesium 137
HIV-2

17. Miscellaneous uses of Roman numerals include the Articles, and often the Amendments, of the Constitution. Roman numerals are still sometimes used for references to the acts and scenes of plays and occasionally for volume numbers in bibliographic references.

Article IX
Act III, Scene ii *or* Act 3, Scene 2
(III, ii) *or* (3, 2)
Vol. XXIII, No. 4 *but usually* Vol. 23, No. 4

Punctuation

These paragraphs provide general rules for the use of commas, hyphens, and en dashes with compound and large numbers. For specific categories of numbers, such as dates, money, and decimal fractions, see Specific Styling Conventions, beginning on page 186.

Commas in Large Numbers

1. In general writing, figures of four digits may be written with or without a comma; including the comma is more common. If the numerals form part of a tabulation, commas are necessary so that four-digit numerals can align with numerals of five or more digits.

   2,000 cases *or less commonly* 2000 cases

2. Whole numbers of five digits or more (but not decimal fractions) use a comma to separate three-digit groups, counting from the right.

   a fee of $12,500
   15,000 units
   a population of 1,500,000

3. Certain types of numbers of four digits or more do not contain commas. These include decimal fractions and the numbers of policies and contracts, checks, street addresses, rooms and suites, telephones, pages, military hours, and years.

2.5544	Room 1206
Policy 33442	page 145
check 34567	1650 hours
12537 Wilshire Blvd.	in 1929

4. In technical writing, the comma is frequently replaced by a thin space in numerals of five or more digits. Digits to the right of the decimal point are also separated in this way, counting from the decimal point.

   28 666 203
   209.775 42

Hyphens

5. Hyphens are used with written-out numbers between 21 and 99.

   forty-one years old
   his forty-first birthday
   Four hundred twenty-two visitors were counted.

6. A hyphen is used in a written-out fraction employed as a modifier. A nonmodifying fraction consisting of two words only is usually left open, although it may also be hyphenated. (For details on fractions, see the section beginning on page 192.)

   a one-half share
   three fifths of her paycheck
   or three-fifths of her paycheck
   but
   four five-hundredths

7. Numbers that form the first part of a modifier expressing measurement are followed by a hyphen. (For units of meas-

urement, see the section beginning on page 203.)

a 5-foot board
a 28-mile trip
an eight-pound baby
but
a $6 million profit

8. Serial numbers, Social Security numbers, telephone numbers, and extended zip codes often contain hyphens that make lengthy numerals more readable or separate coded information.

020-42-1691
413-734-3134 *or* (413) 734-3134
01102-2812

9. Numbers are almost never divided at the end of a line. If division is unavoidable, the break occurs only after a comma.

Inclusive Numbers

10. Inclusive numbers—those that express a range—are usually separated either by the word *to* or by a hyphen or en dash, meaning "(up) to and including."

spanning the years 1915 to 1941
the fiscal year 1994–95
the decade 1920–1929
pages 40 to 98
pp. 40–98

Inclusive numbers separated by a hyphen or en dash are not used after the words *from* or *between.*

from page 385 to page 419
not from page 385–419
from 9:30 to 5:30 *not* from 9:30–5:30
between 1997 and 2000
not between 1997–2000
between 80 and 90 percent
not between 80–90 percent

11. Inclusive page numbers and dates may be either written in full or elided (i.e., shortened) to save space or for ease of reading.

pages 523–526 *or* pages 523–26
1955–1969 *or* 1955–69

However, inclusive dates that appear in titles and other headings are almost never elided. Dates that appear with era designations are also not elided.

England and the French Revolution 1789–1797
1900–1901 *not* 1900–01 *and not* 1900–1
872–863 B.C. *not* 872–63 B.C.

12. The most common style for the elision of inclusive numbers is based on the following rules: Never elide inclusive numbers that have only two digits.

24–28 *not* 24–8
86–87 *not* 86–7

Never elide inclusive numbers when the first number ends in 00.

100–103 *not* 100–03 *and not* 100–3
300–329 *not* 300–29

In other numbers, do not omit the tens digit from the higher number. *Exception:* Where the tens digit of both numbers is zero, write only one digit for the higher number.

234–37 *not* 234–7
3,824–29 *not* 3,824–9
605–7 *not* 605–07

13. Units of measurement expressed in words or abbreviations are usually used only after the second element of an inclusive number. Symbols, however, are repeated.

ten to fifteen dollars
30 to 35 degrees Celsius
an increase in dosage from 200 to 500 mg
but
45° to 48° F
\$50–\$60 million
or \$50 million to \$60 million

14. Numbers that are part of an inclusive set or range are usually styled alike: figures with figures, spelled-out words with other spelled-out words.

from 8 to 108 absences
five to twenty guests

300,000,000 to 305,000,000
not 300 million to 305,000,000

Specific Styling Conventions

The following paragraphs, arranged alphabetically, describe styling practices commonly followed for specific situations involving numbers.

Addresses

1. Numerals are used for all building, house, apartment, room, and suite numbers except for *one,* which is usually written out.

6 Lincoln Road	Room 982
1436 Fremont Street	Suite 2000
Apartment 609	One Bayside Drive

   When the address of a building is used as its name, the number in the address is often written out.

   the sophisticated elegance of Ten Park Avenue

2. Numbered streets have their numbers written as ordinals. Street names from First through Tenth are usually written out, and numerals are used for all higher-numbered streets. Less commonly, all numbered street names up to and including One Hundredth are spelled out.

167 Second Avenue
19 South 22nd Street
or less commonly
19 South Twenty-second Street
145 East 145th Street
in the 60s
or in the Sixties [streets from 60th to 69th]
in the 120s [streets from 120th to 129th]

When a house or building number immediately precedes the number of a street, a spaced hyphen may be inserted between the two numbers, or the street number may be written out, for the sake of clarity.

2018 - 14th Street
2018 Fourteenth Street

3. Arabic numerals are used to designate highways and, in some states, county roads.

Interstate 90 *or* I-90
U.S. Route 1 *or* U.S. 1
Texas 23
County 213

Dates

4. Year numbers are written as figures. If a year number begins a sentence, it may be left as a figure but more often is spelled out; the sentence may also be rewritten to avoid beginning it with a figure.

Nineteen thirty-seven marked the opening of the Golden Gate Bridge.

or The year 1937 marked the opening of the Golden Gate Bridge.
or The Golden Gate Bridge opened in 1937.
the 1997 edition

5. A year number may be abbreviated to its last two digits when an event is so well known that it needs no century designation. In these cases an apostrophe precedes the numerals.

the blizzard of '88
class of '91 *or* class of 1991
the Spirit of '76

6. Full dates are traditionally written in the sequence month-day-year, with the year set off by commas that precede and follow it. An alternative style, used in the military and in U.S. government publications, is the inverted sequence day-month-year, which does not require commas.

traditional: July 8, 1976, was a warm, sunny day in Philadelphia.
the explosion on July 16, 1945, at Alamogordo
military: the explosion on 16 July 1945 at Alamogordo
the amendment ratified on 18 August 1920

7. Ordinal numbers are not used in full dates. Ordinals are sometimes used, how-

ever, for a date without an accompanying year, and they are always used when preceded in a date by the word *the.*

December 4, 1829
on December 4th
or on December 4
on the 4th of December

8. All-figure dating, such as 6-8-95 or 6/8/95, is usually avoided in formal writing. For some readers, such dates are ambiguous; the examples above generally mean June 8, 1995, in the United States, but in almost all other countries mean August 6, 1995.

9. Commas are usually omitted from dates that include the month and year but not the day. The word *of* is sometimes inserted between the month and year.

in October 1997
back in January of 1981

10. References to specific centuries may be either written out or expressed in figures.

in the nineteenth century
or in the 19th century
a sixteenth-century painting
or a 16th-century painting

11. The name of a specific decade often takes a short form, usually with no apostrophe

and uncapitalized. When the short form is part of a set phrase, it is capitalized.

a song from the sixties
occasionally a song from the 'sixties
or a song from the Sixties
tunes of the Gay Nineties

The name of a decade is often expressed in numerals, in plural form. The figure may be shortened, with an apostrophe to indicate the missing numerals; however, apostrophes enclosing the figure are generally avoided. Any sequence of such numbers is generally styled consistently.

the 1950s and 1960s
or the '50s and '60s
but not
the '50's and '60's
the 1950s and '60s
the 1950s and sixties

12. Era designations precede or follow words that specify centuries or numerals that specify years. Era designations are unspaced abbreviations, punctuated with periods. They are usually typed or keyboarded as regular capitals, and typeset in books as small capitals and in newspapers as full-size capitals. The abbreviation B.C. (before Christ) is placed after the date, while A.D. (*anno Domini*, "in the year of our Lord") is usually placed before the

date but after a century designation. Any date given without an era designation or context is understood to mean A.D.

1792–1750 B.C.
between 600 and 400 B.C.
from the fifth or fourth millennium to c. 250 B.C.
between 7 B.C. and A.D. 22
c. A.D. 100 to 300
the second century A.D.
the 17th century

13. Less common era designations include A.H. (*anno Hegirae,* "in the year of [Muhammad's] Hegira," or *anno Hebraico,* "in the Hebrew year"); B.C.E. (before the common era; a synonym for B.C.); C.E. (of the common era; a synonym for A.D.); and B.P. (before the present; often used by geologists and archaeologists, with or without the word *year*). The abbreviation A.H. is usually placed before a specific date but after a century designation, while B.C.E., C.E., and B.P. are placed after both a date and a century.

the tenth of Muharram, A.H. 61 (October 10, A.D. 680)
the first century A.H.
from the 1st century B.C.E. to the 4th century C.E.
63 B.C.E.
the year 200 C.E.

5,000 years B.P.
two million years B.P.

Degrees of Temperature and Arc

14. In technical writing, a quantity expressed in degrees is generally written as a numeral followed by the degree symbol (°). In the Kelvin scale, neither the word *degree* nor the symbol is used with the figure.

 a 45° angle
 6°40′10″N
 32° F
 0° C
 Absolute zero is zero kelvins or 0 K.

15. In general writing, the quantity expressed in degrees may or may not be written out. A figure may be followed by either the degree symbol or the word *degree;* a spelled-out number is always followed by the word *degree.*

 latitude 43°19″N
 latitude 43 degrees N
 a difference of 43 degrees latitude
 The temperature has risen about thirty degrees.

Fractions and Decimal Fractions

16. In nontechnical prose, fractions standing alone are usually written out. Common

fractions used as nouns are usually unhyphenated, although the hyphenated form is also common. When fractions are used as modifiers, they are hyphenated.

lost three quarters of its value
or lost three-quarters of its value
had a two-thirds chance of winning

Multiword numerators and denominators are usually hyphenated, or written as figures.

one one-hundredth of an inch
or 1/100 of an inch

17. Mixed fractions (fractions with a whole number, such as 3½) and fractions that form part of a modifier are usually expressed in figures in running text.

waiting 2½ hours
a ⅞-mile course
2½-pound weights

Fractions that are not on the keyboard or available as special characters on a computer may be typed in full-sized digits; in mixed fractions, a space is left between the whole number and the fraction.

a 7/8-mile course
waiting 2 3/4 hours

18. Fractions used with units of measurement are usually expressed in figures, but common short words are often written out.

1/10 km	half a mile
1/3 oz.	a half-mile walk
7/8 inch	a sixteenth-inch gap

19. Decimal fractions are always set as figures. In technical writing, a zero is placed to the left of the decimal point when the fraction is less than a whole number; in general writing, the zero is usually omitted. Commas are not used in numbers following a decimal point.

    An example of a pure decimal fraction is 0.375, while 1.402 is classified as a mixed decimal fraction.
    a .22-caliber rifle
    0.142857

20. Fractions and decimal fractions are usually not mixed in a text.

    weights of 5½ lbs., 3¼ lbs., and ½ oz.
    or weights of 5.5 lbs., 3.25 lbs., and .5 oz.
    not weights of 5.5 lbs., 3¼ lbs., and ½ oz.

Lists and Outlines

21. Both run-in and vertical lists are often numbered. In run-in numbered lists—that is, numbered lists that form part of a normal-looking sentence—each item is preceded by a number (or, less often, an italicized letter) enclosed in parentheses. The items are separated by commas if they are brief and unpunctuated; if they

are complex or punctuated, they are separated by semicolons. The entire list is introduced by a colon if it is preceded by a full clause, and often when it is not.

> Among the fastest animals with measured maximum speeds are (1) the cheetah, clocked at 70 mph; (2) the pronghorn antelope, at 61 mph; (3) the lion, at 50 mph; (4) the quarter horse, at 47 mph; and (5) the elk, at 45 mph.
>
> The new medical dictionary has several special features: *(a)* common variant spellings; (*b*) examples of words used in context; *(c)* abbreviations, combining forms, prefixes, and suffixes; and *(d)* brand names for drugs and their generic equivalents.

22. In vertical lists, each number is followed by a period; the periods align vertically. Runover lines usually align under the item's first word. Each item may be capitalized, especially if the items are syntactically independent of the words that introduce them.

> The English peerage consists of five ranks, listed here in descending order:
>
> 1. Duke (duchess)
> 2. Marquess (marchioness)
> 3. Earl (countess)
> 4. Viscount (viscountess)
> 5. Baron (baroness)

The listed items end with periods (or question marks) when they are complete sentences, and also often when they are not.

> We require answers to the following questions:
>
> 1. Does the club intend to engage heavy-metal bands to perform in the future?
> 2. Will any such bands be permitted to play past midnight on weekends?
> 3. Are there plans to install proper acoustic insulation?

Items that are syntactically dependent on the words that introduce them often begin with a lowercase letter and end with a comma or semicolon just as in a run-in series in an ordinary sentence.

> Among the courts that are limited to special kinds of cases are
>
> 1. probate courts, for the estates of deceased persons;
> 2. commercial courts, for business cases;
> 3. juvenile courts, for cases involving children under 18; and
> 4. traffic courts, for minor cases involving highway and motor vehicle violations.

A vertical list may also be unnumbered, or may use bullets (•) in place of numerals, especially where the order of the items is not important.

> Chief among the advances in communication were these 19th-century inventions:
>
> Morse's telegraph

Daguerre's camera
Bell's telephone
Edison's phonograph

This book covers in detail:

- Punctuation
- Capitalization and italicization
- Numbers
- Abbreviations
- Grammar and composition
- Word usage

23. Outlines standardly use Roman numerals, capitalized letters, Arabic numerals, and lowercase letters, in that order. Each numeral or letter is followed by a period, and each item is capitalized.

III. The United States from 1816 to 1850
  A. Era of mixed feelings
    1. Effects of the War of 1812
    2. National disunity
  B. The economy
    1. Transportation revolution
      a. Waterways
      b. Railroads
    2. Beginnings of industrialization
IV. The Civil War and Reconstruction, 1850–77

Money

24. A sum of money that can be expressed in one or two words is usually written out in running text, as is the unit of currency.

But if several sums are mentioned in the sentence or paragraph, all are usually expressed as figures and are used with the unspaced currency symbol.

The scalpers were asking eighty dollars.

Grandfather remembered the days of the five-cent cigar.

The shoes on sale are priced at $69 and $89.

Jill wanted to sell the lemonade for 25¢, 35¢, and 45¢.

25. Monetary units of mixed dollars-and-cents amounts are expressed in figures.

$16.75
$307.02

26. Even-dollar amounts are often expressed in figures without a decimal point and zeros. But when even-dollar amounts appear near amounts that include cents, the decimal point and zeros are usually added for consistency. The dollar sign is repeated before each amount in a series or inclusive range.

They paid $500 for the watercolor.

The price had risen from $8.00 to $9.95.

bids of $80, $90, and $100

in the $80–$100 range

27. Sums of money in the millions or above rounded to no more than one decimal

place are usually expressed in a combination of figures and words.

a $10-million building program
$4.5 billion

28. In legal documents a sum of money is usually written out fully, often capitalized, with the corresponding figures in parentheses immediately following.

Twenty-five Thousand Dollars ($25,000)

Organizations and Governmental Entities

29. Ordinal numbers in the names of religious organizations and churches are usually written out.

Seventh-Day Adventists
Third Congregational Church

30. Local branches of labor unions and fraternal organizations are generally identified by a numeral, usually placed after the name.

Motion Picture Studio Mechanics Local 476
Loyal Order of Moose No. 220
Local 4277 Communications Workers of America

31. In names of governmental bodies and electoral, judicial, and military units, ordi-

nal numbers of one hundred or below are usually written out but often not.

Second Continental Congress
Fifth Republic
First Congressional District
Court of Appeals for the Third Circuit
U.S. Eighth Army
Twelfth Precinct *or* 12th Precinct
Ninety-eighth Congress *or* 98th Congress

Percentages

32. In technical writing, and often in business and financial writing, percentages are written as a figure followed by an unspaced % symbol. In general writing, the word *percent* normally replaces the symbol, and the number may either be written out (if it does not include a decimal) or expressed as a figure.

technical: 15%
13.5%

general: 15 percent
87.2 percent
Fifteen percent of the applicants were accepted.
a four percent increase
or a 4% increase

33. In a series or range, the percent sign is usually included with all numbers, even if one of the numbers is zero.

rates of 8.3%, 8.8%, and 9.1%
a variation of 0% to 10%
or a 0%–10% variation

Plurals

34. The plurals of written-out numbers, including fractions, are formed by adding *-s* or *-es.*

at sixes and sevens
divided into eighths
ever since the thirties
still in her thirties

35. The plurals of figures are formed by adding *-s* or less commonly *-'s,* especially where the apostrophe can prevent a confusing typographic appearance.

in the '80s
since the 1980s [*or less commonly* 1980's]
temperatures in the 80s and 90s [*or* 80's and 90's]
the *1*'s looked like *l*'s

Ratios

36. Ratios are generally expressed in figures, usually with the word *to;* in technical writing the figures may be joined by a colon or a slash instead. Ratios expressed in words use a hyphen (or en dash) or the word *to.*

odds of 10 to 1
a proportion of 1 to 4
a 3:1 ratio
29 mi/gal
a fifty-fifty chance
a ratio of ten to four

Time of Day

37. In running text, the time of day is usually spelled out when expressed in even, half, or quarter hours or when it is followed by *o'clock*.

    around four-thirty
    arriving by ten
    planned to leave at half past five
    now almost a quarter to two
    arrived at nine o'clock

38. Figures are generally used when specifying a precise time.

    an appointment at 9:30 tomorrow morning
    buses at 8:42, 9:12, and 10:03 a.m.

39. Figures are also used when the time of day is followed by *a.m.* and *p.m.* These are usually written as punctuated lowercase letters, sometimes as small capital letters. They are not used with *o'clock* or with other words that specify the time of day.

    8:30 a.m. *or* 8:30 A.M.
    10:30 p.m. *or* 10:30 P.M.

8 a.m. *or* 8 A.M.
home by nine o'clock
9:15 in the morning
eleven in the evening

With *twelve o'clock* or 12:00, it is helpful to specify *midnight* or *noon* rather than the ambiguous *a.m.* or *p.m.*

The third shift begins at 12:00 (midnight).

40. Even-hour times are generally written with a colon and two zeros when used in a series or pairing with any times not ending in two zeros.

started at 9:15 a.m. and finished at 2:00 p.m.
worked from 8:30 to 5:00

41. The 24-hour clock system—also called *military time*—uses no punctuation and omits *o'clock, a.m., p.m.,* or any other additional indication of the time of day. The word *hours* sometimes replaces them.

from 0930 to 1100
at 1600 hours

Units of Measurement

42. In technical writing, all numbers used with units of measurement are written as numerals. In nontechnical writing, such numbers often simply follow the basic conventions explained on pages 174–75;

alternatively, even in nontechnical contexts all such numbers often appear as numerals.

In the control group, only 8 of the 90 plants were affected.
picked nine quarts of berries
chugging along at 9 [*or* nine] miles an hour
a pumpkin 5 [*or* five] feet in diameter
weighing 7 pounds 9 ounces
a journey of 3 hours and 45 minutes

The singular form of units of measurement is used in a modifier before a noun, the plural form in a modifier that follows a noun.

a 2- by 9-inch board
or a two-inch by nine-inch board
or a two- by nine-inch board
measured 2 inches by 9 inches
or measured two inches by nine inches
a 6-foot 2-inch man
is 6 feet 2 inches tall
or is six feet two inches tall
is six feet two *or* is 6 feet 2

43. When units of measurement are written as abbreviations or symbols, the adjacent numbers are always figures. (For abbreviations with numerals, see the section on page 172.)

6 cm	67.6 fl. oz.
1 mm	4′
$4.25	98.6°

44. When two or more quantities are expressed, as in ranges or dimensions or series, an accompanying symbol is usually repeated with each figure.

> 4″ × 6″ cards
> temperatures of 30°, 55°, 43°, and 58°
> $450–$500 suits

Other Uses

45. Figures are generally used for precise ages in newspapers and magazines, and often in books as well.

> Taking the helm is Colin Corman, 51, a risk-taking high roller.
> At 9 [*or* nine] she mastered the Mendelssohn Violin Concerto.
> the champion 3[*or* three]-year-old filly
> for anyone aged 62 and over

46. Figures are used to refer to parts of a book, such as volume, chapter, illustration, and table numbers.

> vol. 5, p. 202
> Chapter 8 *or* Chapter Eight
> Fig. 4

47. Serial, policy, and contract numbers use figures. (For punctuation of these numbers, see paragraph 3 on page 181.)

> Serial No. 5274
> Permit No. 63709

48. Figures are used to express stock-market quotations, mathematical calculations, scores, and tabulations.

Industrials were up 4.23.
3 × 15 = 45
a score of 8 to 2 *or* a score of 8–2
the tally: 322 ayes, 80 nays

6 Quotations

Writers and editors rely on two common conventions to indicate that a passage of prose or poetry is quoted directly from another source. Short quotations are usually run in with the rest of the text and enclosed by quotation marks. Longer passages are usually set off distinctively as separate paragraphs; these paragraphs, called *block quotations* or *extracts,* are the main subject of this chapter. For the treatment of short run-in quotations, see the sections beginning on page 57 (for punctuation) and page 71 (for capitalization).

For prose quotations, length is generally assessed in terms of either the number of words or the number of lines. Quoted text is usually set as a block when it runs longer than about 50 words or three lines. However, individual requirements of consistency, clarity, or emphasis may alter these limits. A uniform policy should generally be observed throughout a given work.

Running in longer quotations can make

a passage read more smoothly; alternatively, setting even short quotations as extracts can make them easier for the reader to locate.

For quotations of poetry, different criteria are used. Even a single line of poetry is usually set as an extract, although it is also common to run one or two lines into the text.

Attribution of quotations to their author and source (other than epigraphs and blurbs) is dealt with in Chapter 7, "Notes and Bibliographies." (The unattributed borrowed quotations in this chapter are from William Shakespeare, the *Congressional Record,* Abraham Lincoln, the U.S. Constitution, Martin Lister, the Song of Songs, William Wordsworth, John Keats, T. S. Eliot, Walt Whitman, Ezra Pound, and Matthew Arnold.)

Styling Block Quotations

Block quotations are generally set off from the text that precedes and follows them by adding extra space above and below the quotation, indenting the quoted matter on the left and often on the right as well, and setting the quotation in smaller type with less leading.

Introductory Punctuation, Capitalization, and Indention

Block quotations are usually preceded by a sentence ending with a colon or a period, and they usually begin with a capitalized first word.

> Fielding hides his own opinions on the matter deep in *Tom Jones:*
>
> > Now, in reality, the world have paid too great a compliment to critics, and have imagined them men of much greater profundity than they really are. From this complaisance the critics have been emboldened to assume a dictatorial power, and have so far succeeded that they are now become the masters, and have the assurance to give laws to those authors from whose predecessors they originally received them.

If the quoted passage continues an obviously incomplete (unquoted) sentence that precedes it, a comma may be used instead, or no punctuation at all, depending on the sentence's syntax, and the following extract will usually begin with a lowercase letter.

> According to Fielding,
>
> > the critics have been emboldened to assume a dictatorial power, and have so far succeeded that they are now become the masters, and have the assurance to give laws to those authors from whose predecessors they originally received them.

When the beginning of a block quotation is also the beginning of a paragraph in the original, the first line of the quotation is normally indented like a paragraph, and any subsequent paragraph openings in an extract are similarly indented.

> Expanding on his theme, his tone veers toward the contemptuous:
>
> > The critic, rightly considered, is no more than the clerk, whose office it is to transcribe the rules and laws laid down by those great judges whose vast strength of genius hath placed them in the light of legislators, in the several sciences over which they presided. This office was all which the critics of old aspired to; nor did they ever dare to advance a sentence without supporting it by the authority of the judge from whence it was borrowed.
> >
> > But in process of time, and in ages of ignorance, the clerk began to invade the power and assume the dignity of his master. The laws of writing were no longer founded on the practice of the author, but on the dictates of the critic. The clerk became the legislator, and those very peremptorily gave laws whose business it was, at first, only to transcribe them.

Quotations within an Extract

If a block quotation itself contains quoted material, double quotation marks enclose that material. (In a run-in quotation, these would be set as single quotation marks.)

> Davenport reports what may have been the last words Pound ever spoke in public:
>
> > "Tempus loquendi," the frail voice said with its typical rising quaver, "tem-

> pus tacendi," quoting Ecclesiastes, Malatesta, and Thomas Jefferson simultaneously, and explaining, in this way, that he had said quite enough.

Dialogue in a block quotation is enclosed in quotation marks, and the beginning of each speech is marked by paragraph indention, just as in the original.

> Next O'Connor's hapless protagonist is collared and grilled by the retired schoolteacher in the second-floor apartment:
>
> > "Florida is not a noble state," Mr. Jerger said, "but it is an important one."
> >
> > "It's important alrighto," Ruby said.
> >
> > "Do you know who Ponce de Leon was?"
> >
> > "He was the founder of Florida," Ruby said brightly.
> >
> > "He was a Spaniard," Mr. Jerger said. "Do you know what he was looking for?"
> >
> > "Florida," Rudy said.
> >
> > "Ponce de Leon was looking for the fountain of youth," Mr. Jerger said, closing his eyes.
> >
> > "Oh," Ruby muttered.

If a speech runs to more than one paragraph, open quotation marks appear at the beginning of each paragraph of the extract; closing quotation marks appear only at the end of the final paragraph.

For dialogue from a play or meeting minutes, the speakers' names are set on a small indention, in italics or small capitals, followed by a period or colon. Runover lines generally indent about an em space further.

> This vein of rustic drollery resurfaces in the scene where the transformed Bottom meets the fairies (act 2, scene 1):
>
> *Bottom.* I cry your worship's mercy, heartily: I beseech your worship's name.
> *Cobweb.* Cobweb.
> *Bottom.* I shall desire you of more acquaintance, good Master Cobweb: if I cut my finger, I shall make bold with you. Your name, honest gentleman?
> *Peaseblossom.* Peaseblossom.
> *Bottom.* I pray you, commend me to Mistress Squash, your mother, and to Master Peascod, your father.

> SEN. BAUCUS: Mr. President, I suggest the absence of a quorum.
> THE PRESIDING OFFICER: The clerk will call the roll.
> The legislative clerk proceeded to call the roll.
> SEN. WARNER: Madam President, I ask unanimous consent that the order for the quorum call be rescinded.
> THE PRESIDING OFFICER: Without objection, it is so ordered.

Alterations and Omissions

Although absolute accuracy is always of first importance when quoting from another source, there are certain kinds of alterations and omissions that authors and editors are traditionally allowed to make. (The conventions described in this section are illustrated with block quotations; however, the conventions are equally applicable to run-in quotations.)

Obviously, the author must always be careful not to change the essential meaning of a quotation by making deletions or alterations or by putting quotations in contexts that may tend to mislead the reader.

Changing Capital and Lowercase Letters

If the opening words of a quotation act as a sentence within the quotation, the first word is capitalized, even if that word did not begin a sentence in the original version.

> Henry Fielding was already expressing identical sentiments in 1749:
>
> > The critics have been emboldened to assume a dictatorial power, and have so far succeeded that they are now become the masters. . . .

In situations in which meticulous handling of original source material is crucial (particularly in legal and scholarly writing), the capital letter would be placed in brackets to indicate that it was not capitalized in the original source.

> [T]he critics have been emboldened to assume a dictatorial power, and have so far succeeded that they are now become the masters. . . .

Even if the quotation's first word was capitalized in the original, it is generally not capitalized when the quoted passage is joined syntactically to the sentence that precedes it.

> Fielding asserts boldly that
>
> > the critic, rightly considered, is no more than the clerk, whose office it is to transcribe the rules and laws laid down by those great judges whose vast strength of genius hath placed them in the light of legislators, in the several sciences over which they presided.

Omissions at the Beginning or End of a Quotation

Since it is understood that most quotations are extracted from a larger work, ellipsis points at the beginning and end of the quotation are usually unnecessary. If a quotation ends in the middle of a sentence, however, the period following the omission is closed up to the last word and followed by three ellipsis points. Any punctuation that immediately follows the last quoted word in the original is generally dropped.

> We are met on a great battlefield of that war. We have come to dedicate a portion

> of that field, as a final resting place for those who here gave their lives. . . .

If the omission in the quoted passage ends with a question mark or an exclamation point, such punctuation follows the three ellipsis points. (Some style guides ask that these marks precede the ellipsis points.)

Omissions within Quotations

Omissions from quoted material that fall within a sentence are indicated by three ellipsis points.

> The Place where it is kept . . . is a very Pit or Hole, in the middle of the Fauxbourg, and belongs to the Great Abbey of that Name.

Punctuation used in the original that falls on either side of the ellipsis points is often omitted; however, it may be retained, especially to help clarify the meaning or structure of the sentence.

> We the People of the United States, in Order to . . . establish Justice, . . . provide for the common defence, . . . and secure the Blessings of Liberty . . . , do ordain and establish this Constitution for the United States of America.

If an omission includes one or more entire sentences, or the beginning or end of a sentence, within a paragraph, the end punctuation preceding or following the omission is retained and followed by three ellipsis points.

> We can not dedicate—we can not consecrate—we can not hallow—this ground. The brave men, living and dead, who struggled here, have consecrated it, far above our poor power to add or detract. . . . It is for us the living, rather, to be dedicated here to the unfinished work which they who fought here have thus far so nobly advanced.

If a full paragraph or more is omitted, the omission is indicated by ellipsis points at the end of the paragraph that precedes the omission.

> The words were written in 1915 by Hans Leip (1893–1983), a German soldier on his way to the Russian front parting from his sweetheart. His "Lili Marleen" was really a combination of two girls, his own, Lili, and his buddy's, Marleen. The poem was published in 1937 in a book of Leip's poems entitled *Die kleine Hafenorgel* ("The Little Harbor Organ"). Norbert Schultze (1911–), who would become the prominent composer of such propaganda titles as "The Panzers Are Rolling in Africa," set "Lili Marleen" the next year. . . .
>
> It was Lale Andersen, a singer in literary cabarets in Munich and Berlin, whose

> record of the song was released in late 1939. It was not initially a success, but on August 18, 1941, a German shortwave radio station in Belgrade broadcast the song to Rommel's troops in North Africa.

If text is omitted from the beginning of any paragraph other than the first, three indented ellipsis points mark the omission. Note that they do not stand in for any omitted text preceding the paragraph.

> We were in Paris at the time of the Fair of St. Germain. It lasts six weeks at least: The Place where it is kept, well bespeaks its Antiquity; for it is a very Pit or Hole, in the middle of the Fauxbourg, and belongs to the Great Abbey of that Name. . . .
>
> . . . Knavery here is in perfection as with us; as dextrous Cut-Purses and Pick-Pockets. A Pick-Pocket came into the Fair at Night, extreamly well Clad, with four Lacqueys with good Liveries attending him: He was caught in the Fact, and more Swords were drawn in his Defence than against him; but yet he was taken, and delivered into the Hands of Justice, which is here sudden and no jest.

Other Minor Alterations

Archaic spellings and styles of type, punctuation, and capitalization should be preserved in direct quotations if they do not interfere with a reader's comprehension.

> Also he shewed us the *Mummy of a Woman* intire. The scent of the Hand was to me not unpleasant; but I could not liken it to any Perfume now in use with us.

If such archaisms occur frequently, the author may wish to modernize them, adding an explanation to this effect in a note or in the preface. (Several passages quoted in this chapter have been tacitly modernized.) Obvious typographical errors in modern works may be corrected without comment. Inserting *sic* in brackets after a misspelling in the original version is not necessary unless there is a specific reason for calling attention to the variant. The same holds for using *sic* for other small apparent errors of fact, grammar, punctuation, or word choice or omission.

Sometimes an author wishes to insert a brief explanation, clarification, summary of omitted material, or correction. These insertions, or *interpolations,* are enclosed in brackets. (For more on this use of brackets, see the section beginning on page 4.)

> For, lo, the winter is past, the rain is over and gone;
> The flowers appear on the earth; the time of the singing of birds is come, and the voice of the turtle [i.e., turtle-dove] is heard in our land.

Words that were not originally italicized may be italicized in the quoted passage for the sake of emphasis, as long as the author adds a bracketed notation such as "Italics mine," "Italics added," or "Emphasis added" immediately following the italicized portion or (more often) at the end of the passage.

> Both Russell and Ochs had noted the same reference: "Portions of the Feingold collection found their way into the hands of Goering and Hess; others would later surface in Romania, Argentina and Paraguay; and *the still unaccounted-for pieces were rumored to be part of a prominent Alsatian estate,* but no systematic effort was made to recover them." [Italics mine.]

Any footnote or endnote numbers or parenthetical references in the original version are usually omitted from short quotations; in their place authors often insert their own references.

Epigraphs and Blurbs

Thorough documentation is normally required only in scholarly writing, and even in scholarly contexts certain kinds of set-off quotations need not be exhaustively documented. These include quotations from classic sources—which will have been published in a number of different editions, and therefore have various possible publishing data—

and casual allusions that are not essential to the author's central argument.

Such quotations may particularly be employed as *epigraphs*—short quotations from another source placed at the beginning of an article, chapter (where they may be placed above the title), or book. Other instances would include examples illustrating grammatical elements or word usage, and dictionaries of quotations.

For such quotations, the attribution is generally set by itself on the line below the quotation. Alternatively (and especially if space is a concern), it is run in on the last line of the quotation. When set on its own line, it is generally preceded by an em dash; somewhat less frequently, it is set without an em dash, often enclosed in parentheses. Whatever its punctuation, it is normally set flush right. When run in with the quotation, it usually follows the latter immediately with no intervening space, separated only by either an em dash or parentheses.

The name of the quotation's author is normally set roman, and the name of the publication in which it originally appeared is normally set italic. Either may instead be set in small caps. If all the attributions consist only of authors' names, they may be set in italics.

> I went to the woods because I wished to live deliberately, to front only the essential fact of life, and see if I could not learn

> what it had to teach, and not, when I came to die, discover that I had not lived.
> —Henry David Thoreau, *Walden*
> *or*
> (Henry David Thoreau)

Epigraph attributions are often very brief; this one, for example, could have read "H. D. Thoreau," "Thoreau, *Walden*," or simply "Thoreau."

Advertising *blurbs*—favorable quotations from reviewers or customers that appear on book jackets or advertising materials—are standardly enclosed in quotation marks, and the attribution is never enclosed in parentheses. But the latter's placement may vary, subject to the overall design of the jacket or advertisement. The attribution may appear on its own line or be run in with the blurb; it may be preceded by an em dash or unpunctuated; it may be set flush with the right margin of the quotation, run in with the quotation with no intervening space, centered on its own line, or aligned on a set indention.

> "Ms. Kingston finds the necessary, delicate links between two cultures, two centuries, two sexes. Seldom has the imagination performed a more beautiful feat."—*Washington Post*

When an attribution line follows a passage of poetry, the line may be set flush right, centered on the longest line in the quotation, or indented a standard distance from the right margin.

> Bring me my Bow of burning gold,
> Bring me my Arrows of desire,
> Bring me my Spear; O clouds unfold!
> Bring me my Chariot of fire!
>
> —William Blake, *Milton*

An attribution line following quoted lines from a play or the Bible may include the act and scene or the book and verse.

> All the world's a stage
> And all the men and women merely
>   players;
> They have their exits and their
>   entrances;
> And one man in his time plays many
>   parts,
> His acts being seven ages.
>
> (*As You Like It*, 2.7)

> A feast is made for laughter, and wine
>   maketh merry:
> but money answereth all things.
>
> (Ecclesiastes, 10:19)

(For details on documenting other sources of quotations, see Chapter 7, "Notes and Bibliographies," and the section beginning on page 229.)

Quoting Verse

The major difference between quotations of prose and poetry is that lines of poetry always keep their identity as separate lines. When run in with the text, the poetic lines are separated by a spaced slash.

> Was it Whistler, Wilde, or Swinburne that Gilbert was mocking in the lines "Though the Philistines may jostle, you will rank as an apostle in the high aesthetic band, / If you walk down Piccadilly with a poppy or a lily in your medieval hand"?

When poetic lines are set as extracts, the lines are divided exactly as in the original.

> Dickinson describes this post-traumatic numbness as death in life:
>
> This is the Hour of Lead—
> Remembered, if outlived,
> As Freezing persons, recollect the
> Snow—
> First—Chill—then Stupor—then the
> letting go—

Up to three or four short lines of poetry are occasionally run in if they are closely integrated with the text.

> In the thoroughly miscellaneous stanza that follows—"He has many friends, lay men and clerical, / Old Foss is the name of his cat; / His body is perfectly spherical, / He weareth a runcible hat"—Lear seems to

> bestow new meaning on his older coinage *runcible.*

However, quotations of as few as one or two lines are usually set off from the text as extracts.

> He experienced the heady exaltation of Revolutionary idealism:
>
> > Bliss was it in that dawn to be alive,
> > But to be young was very Heaven!

The horizontal placement of a poetry excerpt is normally determined by its longest line, which is centered horizontally, all the other lines aligning accordingly.

The relative indentions of an excerpt's lines should always be preserved.

> The famous first stanza may have given the English-speaking world its lasting image of the Romantic poet:
>
> > My heart aches, and a drowsy numbness pains
> >   My sense, as though of hemlock I had drunk,
> > Or emptied some dull opiate to the drains
> >   One minute past, and Lethe-wards had sunk:
> > 'Tis not through envy of thy happy lot,
> >   But being too happy in thine happiness,—
> >   That thou, light winged Dryad of the trees,
> >   In some melodious plot

Of beechen green, and shadows numberless,
Singest of summer in full-throated ease.

If the quotation does not start at the beginning of a line, it should be indented accordingly.

I do not find
The Hanged Man. Fear death by water.

If the lines of a poem are too long to center, the quotation may be set using a standard indention, with runover lines indented further.

As it nears its end, the poem's language becomes increasingly evocative:

The last scud of day holds back for me,
It flings my likeness after the rest and true as any on the shadowed wilds,
It coaxes me to vapor and the dusk.

In a speech that extends over several lines, quotation marks are placed at the beginning and end of the speech. If a speech extends beyond one stanza or section, quotation marks are placed at the beginning of each stanza or section within the speech.

In the cream gilded cabin of his steam yacht
Mr. Nixon advised me kindly, to advance with fewer
Dangers of delay. "Consider
Carefully the reviewer.

> "I was as poor as you are;
> When I began I got, of course,
> Advance on royalties, fifty at first," said
> Mr. Nixon,

It was formerly common to begin every line within a speech with quotation marks, but these added quotation marks are now standardly removed without comment by modern editors.

When a full line or several consecutive lines of poetry are omitted from an extract, the omission is indicated by a line of ellipsis points extending the length of either the preceding line or the missing line.

> Ah, love, let us be true
> To one another! for the world, which
> seems
> To lie before us like a land of dreams,
>
> . . . .
>
> Hath really neither joy, nor love, nor
> light,

Poetry extracts that do not end in a period or other terminal punctuation may be followed by ellipsis points; alternatively, the original punctuation (or lack of it) may be left by itself.

> This royal throne of kings, this scepter'd
> isle,
> This earth of majesty, this seat of Mars,
> This other Eden, demi-paradise, [. . .]

7 Notes and Bibliographies

Writers and editors use various methods to indicate the source of a quotation or piece of information borrowed from another work.

In high-school papers and in popular writing, sources are usually identified only by casual mentions within the text itself.

In college term papers, in serious nonfiction books published for the general public, and traditionally in scholarly books and articles in the humanities, footnotes or endnotes are preferred. In this system, sequential numbers within the text refer the reader to notes at the bottom of the page or at the end of the article, chapter, or book; these notes contain full bibliographic information on the works cited.

In scholarly works in the natural sciences and social sciences, and increasingly in the humanities as well, parenthetical references within the text refer the reader to an alphabetically arranged list of references at the end of the article, chapter, or book.

The system of footnotes or endnotes is the more flexible, since it allows for commentary on the work or subject and can also be used for brief discussions not tied to any specific work. However, style manuals tend to encourage the use of parenthetical references in addition to or instead of footnotes or endnotes, since for most kinds of material they are efficient and convenient for both writer and reader.

In a carefully documented work, an alphabetically ordered bibliography or list of references normally follows the entire text (including any endnotes), regardless of which system is used.

Though different publishers and journals have adopted slightly varying styles, the following examples illustrate standard styles for footnotes and endnotes, parenthetical references, and bibliographic entries. For more extensive treatment than can be provided here, consult *Merriam-Webster's Manual for Writers and Editors* (2nd ed., Merriam-Webster, 1995); *The Chicago Manual of Style* (14th ed., Univ. of Chicago Press, 1993); *MLA Handbook for Writers of Research Papers* (5th ed., Modern Language Assn. of America, 1999); or *Scientific Style and Format* (6th ed., Cambridge Univ. Press, 1994).

Footnotes and Endnotes

Footnotes and endnotes are usually indicated by superscript numbers placed immediately after the material to be documented, whether it is an actual quotation or a paraphrase of the language used in the source. The number is placed at the end of a paragraph, sentence or clause, or at some other natural break in the sentence; it follows all marks of punctuation except the dash.

> As one observer noted, "There was, moreover, a degree of logic in the new LDP-SDPJ axis, in that the inner cores of both parties felt threatened by the recent electoral reform legislation,"[7] and . . .

The numbering is consecutive throughout a paper, article, or monograph; in a book, it usually starts over with each new chapter.

The note itself begins with the corresponding number. Footnotes appear at the bottom of the page; endnotes, which take exactly the same form as footnotes, are gathered at the end of the article, chapter, or book.

Endnotes are generally preferred over footnotes by writers and publishers because they are easier to handle when preparing both manuscript and printed pages, though they can be less convenient for the reader.

Both footnotes and endnotes provide full bibliographic information for a source the first time it is cited. In subsequent references, this information is shortened to the author's last name and the page number. If more than one book by an author is cited, a shortened form of the title is also included. The Latin abbreviation *ibid.* is sometimes used to refer to the book cited in the immediately preceding note.

The following examples describe specific elements of first references and reflect humanities citation style; notes 12–14 show examples of subsequent references. All of the cited works appear again in the Bibliographies and Reference Lists section beginning on page 235.

Books

The basic elements for book citations are (1) the author's name; (2) the book's title (in italics); (3) the place of publication, publisher, and date of publication (in parentheses); and (4) the page(s) where the information appears.

One author: 1. Elizabeth Bishop, *The Complete Poems: 1927–1979* (New York: Farrar, Straus & Giroux, 1983), 46.

Two or three authors: 2. Bert Hölldobler and Edward O. Wilson, *The Ants* (Cambridge, Mass.: Belknap–Harvard Univ. Press, 1990), 119.

3. Gerald J. Alred, Charles T. Brusaw, and Walter E. Oliu, *The Business*

Writer's Handbook, 6th ed. (New York: St. Martin's, 2000), 182–84.

Four or more authors: 4. Randolph Quirk et al., *A Comprehensive Grammar of the English Language* (London: Longman, 1985), 135.

Corporate author: 5. Commission on the Humanities, *The Humanities in American Life* (Berkeley: Univ. of California Press, 1980), 58.

No author: 6. *The World Almanac and Book of Facts 2000* (Mahwah, N.J.: World Almanac Books, 1999), 763.

Editor and/or translator: 7. Arthur S. Banks and Thomas C. Muller, eds., *Political Handbook of the World, 1999* (Binghamton, N.Y.: CSA Publications, 1999), 293–95.

8. Simone de Beauvoir, *The Second Sex,* trans. and ed. H. M. Parshley (New York: Knopf, 1953; Vintage, 1989), 446.

Part of a book: 9. G. Ledyard Stebbins, "Botany and the Synthetic Theory of Evolution," *The Evolutionary Synthesis: Perspectives on the Unification of Biology,* ed. Ernst Mayr and William B. Provine (1980; reprint, Cambridge, Mass.: Harvard Univ. Press, 1998), 382–89.

Second or later edition: 10. Albert C. Baugh and Thomas Cable, *A History of the English Language,* 4th ed. (Englewood Cliffs, N.J.: Prentice Hall, 1992), 14.

Two or more volumes: 11. Ronald M. Nowak, *Walker's Mammals of the World,* 6th ed., 2 vols. (Baltimore: Johns Hopkins Univ. Press, 1999), 2: 461.

In subsequent references: 12. Nowak, 462.

13. Baugh and Cable, *History,* 18–19.

14. Ibid., 23.

Articles

The basic elements for citations of articles are (1) the author's name, (2) the article's title (in quotation marks), (3) the name of the periodical (in italics), with information identifying the issue (following the form the periodical itself uses), and (4) the page(s) referred to.

Weekly magazine: 15. Richard Preston, "A Reporter at Large: Crisis in the Hot Zone," *New Yorker,* Oct. 26, 1992: 58.

Monthly magazine: 16. John Lukacs, "The End of the Twentieth Century," *Harper's,* Jan. 1993: 40.

Journal paginated by issue: 17. Roseann Duenas Gonzalez, "Teaching Mexican American Students to Write: Capitalizing on the Culture," *English Journal* 71, no. 7 (Nov. 1982): 22–24.

Journal paginated by volume: 18. Stephen Jay Gould and Niles Eldredge, "Punctuated Equilibria: The Tempo and Mode of Evolution Reconsidered," *Paleobiology* 3 (1977): 121.

Newspaper: 19. William J. Broad, "Big Science Squeezes Small-Scale Researchers," *New York Times*, Dec. 29, 1992: C1.

Signed review: 20. Gordon Craig, review of *The Wages of Guilt: Memories of War in Germany and Japan*, by Ian Buruma, *New York Review of Books*, July 14, 1994: 43–45.

In subsequent reference: 21. Gonzalez, 23.

Parenthetical References

Parenthetical references are highly abbreviated bibliographic citations that appear within the text itself, enclosed in parentheses. These direct the reader to a detailed bibliography or reference list at the end of the work, often removing the need for footnotes or endnotes.

A parenthetical reference, like a footnote or endnote number, is placed immediately after the quotation or piece of information whose source it refers to; punctuation not associated with a quotation follows the reference.

> As one observer noted, "There was, moreover, a degree of logic in the new LDP-SDPJ axis, in that the inner cores of both parties felt threatened by the recent electoral reform legislation" (Banks, 448), and . . .

Any element of a reference that is clear from the context of the running text may be omitted.

> As noted in Banks, "There was, moreover, a degree of logic in the new LDP-SDPJ axis, in that the inner cores of both parties felt threatened by the recent electoral reform legislation" (448), and . . .

Parenthetical references in the humanities usually include only the author's (or editor's) last name and a page reference (see extract above). This style is known as the *author-page system.*

In the sciences, the year of publication is included after the author's name with no intervening punctuation, and the page number is usually omitted. This scientific style is commonly called the *author-date system.*

> As some researchers noted, "New morphological, biochemical, and karyological studies suggest that *P. boylii* actually comprises several distinct species" (Nowak 1999), and . . .

To distinguish among cited works by the same author, the author's name may be followed by the specific work's title, which is usually shortened. (If the author-date system is being used, a lowercase letter can be added after the year—e.g., 1999a, 1999b—to distinguish between works published in the same year.)

Each of the following references is keyed to an entry in the bibliographic listings in the following section.

Humanities style:	(Banks, 448)
	(Quirk et al., 135)
	(Baugh and Cable, *History*, 14)
	(Comm. on the Humanities, 58)
Sciences style:	(Gould and Eldredge 1977)
	(Nowak 1999a)

Bibliographies and Reference Lists

A *bibliography* lists all of the works that a writer has found relevant in writing the text. A *reference list* includes only works specifically mentioned in the text or from which a particular quotation or piece of information was taken. In all other respects, the two listings are identical.

Bibliographies and reference lists both differ from bibliographic endnotes in that their entries are unnumbered, are arranged in alphabetical order by author, and use different patterns of indention and punctuation. The basic elements are (1) the author's name (inverted for the first author); (2) the book's title (in italics); (3) the place of publication, publisher, and date of publication; and (4) for periodical articles only, the page(s) where the information appears. The following lists illustrate standard styles employed in, respectively, the humanities and social sciences and the natural sciences.

The principal differences between the two styles are these: In the sciences, (1) an initial is generally used instead of the author's first name, (2) the date is placed directly after the author's name, (3) all words in titles are lowercased except the first word, the first word of any subtitle, and proper nouns and adjectives, and (4) article titles are not enclosed in quotation marks. Increasingly in scientific publications, (5) the author's first and middle initials are closed up without any punctuation, and (6) book and journal titles are not italicized. The following bibliographic lists include both books and periodical articles.

Humanities style

Alred, Gerald J., Charles T. Brusaw, and Walter E. Oliu. *The Business Writer's Handbook.* 6th ed. New York: St. Martin's, 2000.

Banks, Arthur S., and Thomas C. Muller, eds. *Political Handbook of the World, 1999.* Binghamton, N.Y.: CSA Publications, 1999.

Baugh, Albert C., and Thomas Cable. *A History of the English Language.* 4th ed. Englewood Cliffs, N.J.: Prentice Hall, 1992.

Beauvoir, Simone de. *The Second Sex.* Trans. and ed. H. M. Parshley. New York: Alfred A. Knopf, 1953; Vintage, 1989.

Bishop, Elizabeth. *The Complete Poems: 1927–1979.* New York: Farrar, Straus & Giroux, 1983.

Commission on the Humanities. *The Humanities in American Life.* Berkeley: University of California Press, 1980.

Craig, Gordon. Review of *The Wages of Guilt: Memories of War in Germany and Japan,* by Ian Buruma. *New York Review of Books,* July 14, 1994: 43–45.

Gonzalez, Roseann Duenas. "Teaching Mexican American Students to Write: Capitalizing on the Culture." *English Journal* 71, no. 7 (November 1982): 22–24.

Lukacs, John. "The End of the Twentieth Century." *Harper's,* January 1993: 39–58.

Quirk, Randolph, Sidney Greenbaum, Geoffrey Leech, and Jan Svartvik. *A Comprehensive Grammar of the English Language.* London: Longman, 1985.

The World Almanac and Book of Facts 2000. Mahwah, N.J.: World Almanac Books, 1999.

Sciences style

Broad, W.J. 1992. Big science squeezes small-scale researchers. *New York Times*, 29 Dec.:C1.

Gould, S.J., and N. Eldredge. 1977. Punctuated equilibria: The tempo and mode of evolution reconsidered. *Paleobiology* 3:115–51.

Hölldobler, B., and E.O. Wilson. 1990. *The ants*. Cambridge, Mass.: Belknap–Harvard Univ. Press.

Nowak, R.M. 1999. *Walker's mammals of the world*. 6th ed. 2 vols. Baltimore: Johns Hopkins Univ. Press.

Preston, R. 1992. A reporter at large: Crisis in the hot zone. *New Yorker*, 26 Oct.:58–81.

Stebbins, G.L. Botany and the synthetic theory of evolution. 1980. *The evolutionary synthesis: Perspectives on the unification of biology*. Ed. E. Mayr and W.B. Provine. Reprint, Cambridge, Mass.: Harvard Univ. Press, 1998.

Special Cases

Reference lists frequently contain items that do not fit neatly into any of the categories described above. Some are printed items such as government publications, others are nonprint items. These special references are styled in formats similar to those used for books and articles.

Television and radio programs

"Goodbye, Farewell, and Amen." *M*A*S*H.* CBS. WFSB-TV, Hartford, Conn. 28 Feb. 1983.

Burns, Ken. *Baseball.* PBS. WGBY-TV, Springfield, Mass. 28 Sept. 1994.

Computer software

Import/Export USA. CD-ROM. Detroit: Gale Research, 1998. Windows.

On-line sources

Kinsley, Michael. "Totally Disingenuous." *Slate,* 11 Sept. 2000. http://slate.msn.com/Readme/00-09-11/Readme.asp [13 Sept. 2000].

"French Truckers Create Blockades." *AP Online.* 4 Sept. 2000. Lexis-Nexis [14 Sept. 2000].

Microform

"Marine Mammals; Permit Modification: Naval Facilities Engineering Commission (P8D)." *Federal Register* 55.1:90. Washington: CIS, 1990. Microfiche.

Government publications

U.S. Department of Labor. *Occupational Outlook Handbook, 2000-1.* Washington, D.C.: GPO, 2000.

U.S. Congress. Senate. Subcommittee on Administrative Law and Government Relations of the Committee on the Judiciary. *Hearings on Post-Employment Restrictions for Federal Officers and Employees.* 101st Cong., 1st sess. 27 Apr. 1989. H.R. 2267.

Cong. Rec. [*Congressional Record*]. 29 June 1993: S8269–70.

Personal interview

Norris, Nancy Preston. Conversation with author. Wilkes-Barre, Pa., 10 October 1995.

Christian, Dr. Lionel. Telephone conversation with author, 2 January 1996.

Appendix A

Word Usage

Problems in Word Usage

The following list discusses words that present a variety of problems to writers. Review it from time to time to keep yourself alert to potential usage issues in your own writing. (See also the next section, which provides a list of easily confused words and clichés.)

aggravate *Aggravate* is used chiefly in two meanings: "to make worse" ("aggravated her shoulder injury," "their financial position was aggravated by the downturn") and "to irritate, annoy" ("The President was aggravated by the French intransigence"). The latter is not often seen in writing. However, *aggravation* usually means "irritation," and *aggravating* almost always expresses annoyance.

almost, most *Most* is often used like *almost* in speech ("Most everyone was there"), but it is rarely seen in writing.

alot, a lot *Alot* hardly ever appears in print and is usually regarded as an error.

alright Though the business community has been using the one-word *alright* since the 1920s, it is only gradually gaining acceptance and is still often regarded as an error. It is rarely seen in published works outside of newspaper writing.

amount, number *Number* is normally used with nouns that can form a plural and can be used with a numeral ("a large number of orders," "any number of times"). *Amount* is mainly used with nouns that denote a substance or concept that can't be divided and counted up ("the annual amount of rainfall," "a large amount of money"). The use of *amount* with count nouns, usually when the number of things can be thought of as a mass or collection ("a substantial amount of job offers"), is often criticized; and many people will regard it as an error.

apt, liable Both *liable* and *apt,* when followed by an infinitive, are used nearly interchangeably with *likely* ("more liable to get tired easily," "roads are apt to be slippery"). This use of *apt* is widely accepted, but some people think *liable* should be limited to situations risking an undesirable outcome ("If you speed, you're liable to be caught") and it is generally used this way in writing.

as, as if, like *Like* used as a conjunction in the sense of *as* ("just like I used to do") or *as if* ("It looks like it will rain") has been frequently criticized, especially since its use in a widely publicized cigarette commercial slogan. Though *like* has been used in these ways for nearly 600 years, it is safer to use *as* or *as if* instead.

as far as "As far as clothes, young people always know best" is an example of *as far as* used as a preposition. This use developed from the more common conjunction use ("As far as clothes are concerned . . .") by omitting the following verb or verb phrase; it is very widely used in speech but is often regarded as an error in print.

awful It has been traditional to criticize any use of *awful* and *awfully* that doesn't convey the original sense of being filled with awe. However, *awful* has long been acceptable in the meanings "extremely objectionable" ("What an awful color") and "exceedingly great" ("an awful lot of money") in speech and casual writing. Use of *awful* and *awfully* as intensifiers ("I'm awful tired," "he's awfully rich") is likewise common in informal prose, but it is safer to avoid them in formal writing.

between, among It is often said that *between* can only be used when dealing with two items ("between a rock and a hard place"), and that *among* must be used for three or more items ("strife among Croats, Serbs, and Muslims"). However, *between* is actually quite acceptable in these latter cases, especially when specifying one-to-one relationships, regardless of the number of items ("between you and me and the lamppost").

can, may Both *can* and *may* are used to refer to possibility ("Can the deal still go through?" "It may still happen"). Since the possibility of someone's doing something may depend on someone else's agreeing to it, the two words have become interchangeable when they refer to permission ("You can [may] go now if you like"). Though the use of *can* to ask or grant permission has been common since the last century, *may* is more appropriate in formal correspondence. However, this meaning of *may* is relatively rare in negative constructions, where *cannot* and *can't* are more usual ("They can't [may not] use it without paying").

comprise The sense of *comprise* meaning "to compose or constitute" ("the branches that comprise our government") rather than "to include or be made up of" ("Our government comprises various branches") has been attacked as wrong, for reasons that are unclear. Until recently, it was used chiefly in scientific and technical writing; today it has become the most widely used sense. But it still may be safer to use *compose* or *make up* instead.

contact Though some regard *contact* as only a noun and an adjective, its use as a verb, especially to mean "get in touch with"

("Contact your local dealer"), has long been widely accepted.

data *Data* has firmly established itself with a meaning independent of its use as the plural form of *datum.* It is used in one of two ways: as a plural noun (like *earnings*), taking a plural verb and plural modifiers (such as *these* or *many*) but not cardinal numbers ("These data show that we're out of the recession"); or as an abstract mass noun (like *information*), taking a singular verb and singular modifiers (such as *this, much,* or *little*) ("The data on the subject is plentiful"). Both constructions are standard, but many people are convinced that only the plural form is correct, and thus the plural form is somewhat more common in print. What you want to avoid is mixing in signs of the singular (like *this* or *much*) when you use a plural verb.

different from, different than Both of these phrases are standard; however, some people dislike the latter and will insist that, for example, "different than the old proposal" be changed to "different from the old proposal." *Different from* works best when you can take advantage of the *from* ("The new proposal is very different from the old one"). *Different than* works best when a clause follows ("very different in size than it was two years ago").

disinterested, uninterested *Disinterested* has basically two meanings: "unbiased" ("a disinterested decision," "disinterested intellectual curiosity"), and "not interested," which is also the basic meaning of *uninterested.* Though this second use of *disinterested* is widespread, some people object to it and it may be safer to avoid it.

due to When the *due* of *due to* is clearly an adjective ("absences due to the flu") no one complains about the phrase. When *due to* is a preposition ("Due to the holiday, our office will be closed"), some people object and call for *owing to* or *because of.* Both uses of *due to* are entirely standard, but in formal writing one of the alternatives for the prepositional use may be safer.

each other, one another The traditional rules call for *each other* to be used in reference to two ("The two girls looked at each other in surprise") and *one another* to be used in reference to three or more ("There will be time for people to talk with one another after the meeting"). In fact, however, they are employed interchangeably.

finalize Though avoided by many writers, *finalize* occurs frequently in business and government contexts ("The budget will be finalized," "finalizing the deal"), where it is regarded as entirely standard.

good, well Both *good* and *well* are acceptable when used to express good health ("I feel good," "I feel well"), and *good* may also connote good spirits. However, the adverb *good* has been much criticized, with people insisting that *well* be used instead ("The orchestra played well this evening"), and this adverbial use should be avoided in writing.

hardly *Hardly* meaning "certainly not" is sometimes used with *not* for added emphasis ("Just another day at the office? Not hardly"). *Hardly* is also used like *barely* or *scarcely* to emphasize a minimal amount ("I hardly knew her," "Almost new—hardly a scratch on it"). When *hardly* is used with a negative verb (such as *can't, couldn't, didn't*) it is often called a double negative, though it is really a weaker negative. *Hardly* with a negative is a spoken form, and should be avoided in writing (except when quoting someone directly).

hopefully When used to mean "I hope" or "We hope" ("Hopefully, they'll reach an agreement"), as opposed to "full of hope" ("We continued our work hopefully and cheerfully"), *hopefully* is often criticized, even though other similar sentence adverbs (such as *frankly, clearly,* and *interestingly*) are accepted by everyone. Despite the objections, this sense of *hopefully* is now in standard use.

I, me In informal speech and writing, such phrases as "It's me," "Susan is taller than me," "He's as big as me," "Who, me?" and "Me too" are generally accepted. In formal writing, however, it is safer to use *I* after *be* ("It was I who discovered the mistake") and after *as* and *than* when the first term of the comparison is the sentence's subject ("Susan is taller than I," "He is as big as I").

imply, infer *Infer* is mostly used to mean "to draw a conclusion, to conclude" and is commonly followed by *from* ("I infer from your comments that . . . "). *Imply* is used to mean "to suggest" ("The letter implies that our service was not satisfactory"). The use of *infer,* with a personal subject, as a synonym of *imply* ("Are you inferring that I made a mistake?") is not widely accepted in print and is best avoided.

irregardless *Irregardless,* though a real word (and not uncommon in speech), is still a long way from general acceptance; use *regardless* (or *irrespective*) instead.

lay, lie Though *lay* has long been used as an intransitive verb meaning "lie" ("tried to make the book lay flat," "lay down on the job"), it is generally condemned. In writing it is safer to keep the two words distinct, and to keep their various easily confused forms *(lie, lying, lay, lain; lay, laying, laid)* distinct as well.

lend, loan Some people still object to the use of *loan* as a verb ("loaned me the book") and insist on *lend*. Nevertheless, *loan* is in standard use. *Loan* is used only literally ("loans large sums of money"), however, while *lend* can be used both literally ("lends large sums of money") and figuratively ("Would you please lend me a hand?").

less, fewer The traditional view is that *less* is used for matters of degree, value, or amount, and that it modifies nouns that refer to uncountable things ("less hostility," "less clothing") while *fewer* modifies numbers and plural nouns ("fewer students," "fewer than eight trees"). However, *less* has been used to modify plural nouns for centuries. Today *less* is actually more likely than *fewer* to modify plural nouns when distances, sums of money, and certain common phrases are involved ("less than 100 miles," "less than $2000," "in 25 words or less") and just as likely to modify periods of time ("in less [fewer] than four hours"). But phrases such as "less bills," "less vacation days," and "less computers" should be avoided.

like, such as Should you write "cities like Chicago and Des Moines" or "cities such as Chicago and Des Moines"? You are in fact free to use either one, or change the latter to "such cities as Chicago and Des Moines."

media Media is the plural of *medium.* With all the references to the mass media today, *media* is often used as a singular mass noun ("The media always wants a story"). But this singular use is not as well established as the similar use of *data,* and, except in the world of advertising, you will probably want to keep *media* plural in most writing.

memorandum *Memorandum* is a singular noun with two acceptable plurals: *memorandums* and *memoranda. Memoranda* is not yet established as a singular form.

neither The use of *neither* to refer to more than two nouns, though sometimes criticized, has been standard for centuries ("Neither the post office, the bank, nor City Hall is open today"). Traditionally, the pronoun *neither* is used with a singular verb ("Neither is ideal"). However, when a prepositional phrase follows *neither,* a plural verb is common and acceptable ("Neither of those solutions are ideal").

one The use of *one* to indicate a generic individual lends formality to writing, since it suggests distance between the writer and the reader ("One never knows" is more formal than "You never know"). Using *one* in place of *I* or *me* ("I'd like to read more, but one doesn't have the time") is common in British English but may be thought odd or objectionable in American English.

people, persons *People* is used to designate an unspecified number of persons ("People everywhere are talking about the new show"), and *persons* is commonly used when a definite number is specified ("Occupancy by more than 86 persons is prohibited"). However, the use of *people* where numbers are mentioned is also acceptable nowadays ("Ten people were questioned").

per *Per,* meaning "for each," is most commonly used with figures, usually in relation to price ("$150 per performance"), vehicles ("25 miles per gallon," "55 miles per hour"), or sports ("15 points per game"). Avoid inserting words like *a* or *each* between *per* and the word or words it modifies ("could type 70 words per each minute").

phenomena *Phenomena* is the usual plural of *phenomenon.* Use of *phenomena* as a singular ("St. Elmo's Fire is an eerie phenomena") is encountered in speech and now and then in writing, but it is nonstandard and it is safer to avoid it.

plus The use of *plus* to mean "and" ("a hamburger plus french fries for lunch") or "besides which" ("We would have been on time, but we lost the car keys. Plus, we forgot the map") is quite informal and is avoided in writing.

presently The use of *presently* to mean "at the present time" ("I am presently working up a report") rather than "soon" ("He'll be with you presently"), while often criticized, is standard and acceptable.

pretty *Pretty,* when used as an adverb to tone down or moderate a statement ("pretty cold weather"), is avoided in formal writing, so using it in correspondence will lend an informal tone.

prior to *Prior to,* a synonym of *before,* most often appears in fairly formal contexts. It is especially useful in suggesting anticipation ("If all specifications are finalized prior to system design, cost overruns will be avoided").

proved, proven Both *proved* and *proven* are past participles of *prove.* Earlier in this century, *proved* was more common than *proven,* but today they are about equally common. As a past participle, either is acceptable ("has been proved [proven] effective"), but *proven* is more frequent as an adjective ("proven gas reserves").

providing, provided Although *providing* in the sense of "if" or "on condition that" has occasionally been disapproved ("providing he finds a buyer"), both *providing* and*provided* are well established, and either may be used. *Provided* is somewhat more common.

real The adverb *real* is used interchangeably with *really* only as an intensifier ("a real tough assignment"). This use is very common in speech and casual writing, but you should not use it in anything more formal.

set, sit *Set* generally takes an object ("Set the lamp over there") and *sit* does not ("sat for an hour in the doctor's office"). There are exceptions when *set* is used intransitively ("The sun will set soon," "The hen was setting") and *sit* takes an object ("I sat her down by her grandfather"). When used of people, however, intransitive *set* is a spoken use that should be avoided in writing.

shall, will *Shall* and *will* are generally interchangeable in present-day American English. In recent years, *shall* has been regarded as somewhat affected; *will* is much more common. However, *shall* is more appropriate in questions to express simple choice ("Shall we go now?") because *will* in such a context suggests prediction ("Will the prototype be ready next week?").

slow, slowly *Slow* used as an adverb (meaning "slowly") has often been called an error. *Slow* is almost always used with verbs indicating motion or action, and it typically follows the verb it modifies ("a stew cooked long and slow"). *Slowly* can be used in the same way ("drove slowly"), but it also is used before the verb ("The winds slowly subsided"), with adjectives formed from verbs ("the slowly sinking sun"), and in places where *slow* would sound inappropriate ("turned slowly around").

so The use of the adverb *so* to mean "very" or "extremely" is widely disapproved of in formal writing, except in negative contexts ("not so long ago") or when followed by an explaining clause ("cocoa so hot that I burned my tongue"). The use of the conjunction *so* to introduce clauses of result ("The acoustics are good, so every note is clear") and purpose ("Be quiet so I can sleep") is sometimes criticized, but these uses are standard. In the latter case (when used to mean "in order that"), *so that* is more common in formal writing ("to cut spending so that the deficit will be reduced").

such Some people disapprove of using *such* as a pronoun ("such was the result," "sorting out glass and newspapers and such"), but dictionaries recognize it as standard.

Frequently Confused Words

Misusing one word for another in one's writing is a common source of confusion, embarrassment, and unintentional humor. Computer spell checkers will not identify a word that is being wrongly used in place of the proper word. Try to review the following list periodically in order to avert word confusions you may be overlooking.

abjure to reject solemnly
adjure to command

abrogate to nullify
arrogate to claim

abstruse hard to understand
obtuse dull, slow

accede to agree
exceed to go beyond

accent to emphasize
ascent climb
assent to agree to something

access right or ability to enter
excess intemperance

ad advertisement
add to join to something; to find a sum

adapt to adjust to something
adept highly skilled
adopt to take as one's child; to take up

addenda additional items
agenda list of things to be done

addition part added
edition publication

adjoin to be next to
adjourn to suspend a session
adjure to command

adverse unfavorable
averse disinclined

advert to refer
avert to avoid
overt unconcealed

advice counsel or information
advise to give advice

affect to act upon or influence
effect result; to bring about

agenda *see* ADDENDA

alimentary relating to nourishment
elementary simple or basic

allude to refer indirectly
elude to evade

allusion indirect reference
illusion misleading image

amenable accountable, agreeable
amendable modifiable

amend to alter in writing
emend to correct

ante- prior to or earlier than
anti- opposite or against

anymore any longer, now
any more more

appraise to set a value on
apprise to give notice of
apprize to appreciate or value

arraign to bring before a court
arrange to come to an agreement

arrogate *see* ABROGATE

ascent *see* ACCENT

assay to test for valuable content
essay to try tentatively

assent *see* ACCENT

assure to give confidence to
ensure to make certain
insure to guarantee against loss

aural relating to the ear or hearing
oral relating to the mouth, spoken

averse *see* ADVERSE

avert *see* ADVERT

bail security given
bale bundle of goods

base bottom
bass fish; deep voice

biannual usually twice a year; sometimes every two years
biennial every two years

bloc group working together
block tract of land

born produced by birth
borne carried

breadth width
breath breathed air
breathe to draw in air

callous hardened
callus hard area on skin

canvas strong cloth; oil painting
canvass to solicit votes or opinions

capital city that is the seat of government
capitol state legislature building
Capitol U.S. Congress building

casual not planned
causal relating to or being a cause

casually by chance or accident
casualty one injured or killed

censor to examine for improper content
censure to express disapproval of

cession a yielding
session meeting

cite to summon; to quote
sight payable on presentation
site piece of land

collaborate to work or act jointly
corroborate to confirm

collision act of colliding
collusion secret cooperation for deceit

complacent self-satisfied
complaisant amiable

complement remainder
compliment admiring remark

concert to act in harmony or conjunction
consort to keep company

consul diplomatic official
council administrative body
counsel legal representative; to give advice

corespondent joint respondent
correspondent one who communicates

corroborate *see* COLLABORATE

council *see* CONSUL

councilor member of a council
counselor lawyer

counsel *see* CONSUL

credible worthy of being believed
creditable worthy of praise
credulous gullible

currant raisinlike fruit
current stream; belonging to the present

cynosure one that attracts
sinecure easy job

decent good or satisfactory
descent downward movement
dissent difference of opinion

decree official order
degree extent or scope

defuse to make less harmful
diffuse to pour out or spread widely

deluded misled or confused
diluted weakened in consistency

demur to protest
demure shy

deposition testimony
disposition personality; outcome

depraved corrupted
deprived divested or stripped

deprecate to disapprove of
depreciate to lower the worth of

descent *see* DECENT

desperate having lost hope
disparate distinct

detract to disparage or reduce
distract to draw attention away

device piece of equipment or tool
devise to invent, to plot

diffuse *see* DEFUSE

diluted *see* DELUDED

disassemble to take apart
dissemble to disguise feelings or intentions

disburse to pay out
disperse to scatter

discreet capable of keeping a secret
discrete individually distinct

disparate *see* DESPERATE

disperse *see* DISBURSE

disposition *see* DEPOSITION

dissemble *see* DISASSEMBLE

dissent *see* DECENT

distract *see* DETRACT

edition *see* ADDITION

effect *see* AFFECT

e.g. for example
i.e. that is

elementary *see* ALIMENTARY

elicit to draw or bring out
illicit not lawful

eligible qualified to have
illegible not readable

elude *see* ALUDE

emanate to come out from a source
eminent standing above others
immanent inherent
imminent ready to take place

emend *see* AMEND

emigrate to leave a country
immigrate to come into a place

eminence prominence or superiority
immanence restriction to one domain
imminence state of being imminent

ensure *see* ASSURE

envelop to surround
envelope letter container

equable free from unpleasant extremes
equitable fair

erasable removable by erasing
irascible hot-tempered

essay *see* ASSAY

every day each day
everyday ordinary

exceed *see* ACCEDE

excess *see* ACCESS

extant currently existing
extent size, degree, or measure

flaunt to display ostentatiously
flout to scorn

flounder to struggle
founder to sink

forego to precede
forgo to give up

formally in a formal manner
formerly at an earlier time

forth forward, out of
fourth 4th

gage security deposit
gauge to measure

gait manner of walking
gate opening in a wall or fence

generic general
genetic relating to the genes

gibe to tease or mock
jibe to agree
jive foollish talk

guarantee to promise to be responsible for
guaranty something given as a security

hail to greet
hale to compel to go; healthy

hearsay rumor
heresy dissent from a dominant theory

i.e. *see* E.G.

illegible *see* ELIGIBLE

illicit *see* ELICIT

illusion *see* ALLUSION

immanence *see* EMINENCE

immanent *see* EMANATE

immigrate *see* EMIGRATE

imminence *see* EMINENCE

imminent *see* EMANATE

imply hint, indicate
infer conclude, deduce

impracticable not feasible
impractical not practical

inapt not suitable
inept unfit or foolish

incite to urge on
insight discernment

incredible unbelievable
incredulous disbelieving, astonished

incurable not curable
incurrable capable of being incurred

inept *see* INAPT

inequity lack of equity
iniquity wickedness

infer *see* IMPLY

ingenious very clever
ingenuous innocent and candid

inherent intrinsic
inherit to receive from an ancestor

iniquity *see* INEQUITY

insight *see* INCITE

install to set up for use
instill to impart gradually

insure *see* ASSURE

interment burial
internment confinement or impounding

interstate involving more than one state
intestate leaving no valid will
intrastate existing within a state

irascible *see* ERASABLE

it's it is
its belonging to it

jibe *see* GIBE

jive *see* GIBE

lead to guide; heavy metal
led guided

lean to rely on for support
lien legal claim on property

lesser smaller
lessor grantor of a lease

levee embankment to prevent flooding
levy imposition or collection of a tax

liable obligated by law
libel to make libelous statements; false publication

lien *see* LEAN

material having relevance or importance; matter
matériel equipment and supplies

median middle value in a range
medium intermediate; means of communication

meet to come into contact with
mete to allot

meretricious falsely attractive
meritorious deserving reward or honor
meticulous extremely careful about details

militate to have effect
mitigate to make less severe

miner mine worker
minor one of less than legal age; not important or serious

moot having no practical significance
mute a person unable to speak; to tone down or muffle

naval relating to a navy
navel belly button

obtuse *see* ABSTRUSE

oral *see* AURAL

ordinance law, rule, or decree
ordnance military supplies
ordonnance compilation of laws

overt *see* ADVERT

parlay to bet again a stake and its winnings
parley discussion of disputed points

peer one of equal standing
pier bridge support

peremptory ending a right of action, debate or delay
preemptory preemptive

perpetrate to be guilty of
perpetuate to make perpetual

perquisite a right or privilege
prerequisite a necessary preliminary

persecute to harass injuriously
prosecute to proceed against at law

personal relating to a particular person
personnel body of employees

perspective view of things
prospective relating to the future
prospectus introductory description of an enterprise

perspicacious very discerning
perspicuous easily understood

pier *see* PEER

plain ordinary
plane airplane; surface

plaintiff complaining party in litigation
plaintive sorrowful

plat plan of a piece of land
plot small piece of land

pole long slender piece of wood or metal
poll sampling of opinion

pore to read attentively
pour to dispense from a container

practicable feasible
practical capable of being put to use

precede to go or come before
proceed to go to law

precedence priority
precedents previous examples to follow

preemptory *see* PEREMPTORY

preposition part of speech
proposition proposal

prerequisite *see* PERQUISITE

prescribe to direct to use; to assert a prescriptive right
proscribe to forbid

preview advance view
purview part or scope of a statute

principal main body of an estate; chief person or matter
principle basic rule or assumption

proceed *see* PRECEDE

proposition *see* PREPOSITION

proscribe *see* PRESCRIBE

prosecute *see* PERSECUTE

prospective *see* PERSPECTIVE

prostate gland
prostrate prone; to reduce to helplessness

purview *see* PREVIEW

raise to lift, to increase
raze to destroy or tear down

reality the quality or state of being real
realty real property

rebound to spring back or recover
redound to have an effect

recession ceding back
recision cancellation
rescission act of rescinding or abrogating

respectfully with respect
respectively in order

resume to take up again
résumé summary

role part, function
roll turn

session *see* CESSION

shear to cut off
sheer very thin or transparent

sight *see* CITE

sinecure *see* CYNOSURE

site *see* CITE

stationary still
stationery writing material

statue piece of sculpture
stature natural height or achieved status
statute law enacted by a legislature

tack course of action
tact sense of propriety

tenant one who occupies a rental dwelling
tenet principle

therefor for that
therefore thus

tortuous lacking in straightforwardness
torturous very painful or distressing

track path or course
tract stretch of land; system of body organs

trustee one entrusted with something
trusty convict allowed special privileges

venal open to bribery
venial excusable

waive to give up voluntarily
wave to motion with the hands

waiver act of waiving a right
waver to be irresolute

who's who is
whose of whom

your belonging to you
you're you are

Appendix B

Grammar Glossary

This glossary provides definitions, and sometimes discussions, of grammatical and grammar-related terms, many of which appear in the text. Examples are enclosed in angle brackets. Cross-references to other glossary entries are shown in boldface.

abbreviation A shortened form of a written word or phrase used in place of the whole (such as *amt.* for *amount,* or *c/o* for *care of*).

Abbreviations can be used wherever they are customary, but note that what is customary in technical writing will be different from what is customary in journalism or other fields. See also **acronym**.

absolute adjective An adjective that normally cannot be used comparatively <*ancillary* rights> <the *maximum* dose>.

Many absolute adjectives can be modified by adverbs such as *almost* or *near* <an *almost fatal* dose> <at *near maximum* capacity>. However, many adjectives considered to be absolute are in fact often preceded by comparative adverbs <a *more perfect* union> <a *less complete* account>. In such cases, *more* means "more nearly" and *less* "less nearly."

absolute comparative The comparative form of an adjective used where no comparison is implied or stated, although in some cases comparison may be inferred by the reader or hearer <*higher* education> <a *better* kind of company> <gives you a *brighter* smile> <an *older* woman>. See also **absolute adjective**; **comparison**; **double comparison**; **implicit comparative**.

acronym A word or abbreviation formed from the initial letter or letters of each of the major parts of a compound term, whether or not it is pronounceable as a word (such as *TQM* for *Total Quality Management*, or *UNPROFOR* for *United Nations Protection Force*); also called *initialism*.

active voice A verb form indicating that the subject of a sentence is performing the action <he *respects* the other scientists> <a bird *was singing*> <interest rates *rose*>; compare **passive voice**.

adjective A word that describes or modifies a noun <an *active* mind> <this is *serious*> <*full* and *careful* in its attention to detail>.

An adjective can follow a noun as a complement <the book made the bag *heavy*> and can sometimes modify larger units, like noun phrases <the *celebrated* "man in the street"> and noun clauses <it seemed *incomprehensible* that one senator could hold up the nomination>.

Adjectives can be described as *coordinate adjectives* when they share equal relationships to the nouns they modify <a *concise, coherent* essay> <a *soft, flickering, bluish* light>, and as *noncoordinate adjectives* when the first of two adjectives modifies the second adjective and the noun together <a *low monthly* fee> <the *first warm* day>.

An *indefinite adjective* designates unidentified or not immediately identifiable persons or things <*some* children> <*other* hotels>.

An *interrogative adjective* is used in asking questions <*whose* book is this?> <*which* color looks best?>.

A *possessive adjective* is the possessive form of a personal pronoun <*her* idea> <*its* second floor>.

A *relative adjective (which, that, who, whom, whose, where)* introduces an adjectival clause or a clause that functions as a noun <at the April conference, by *which* time the report should be finished> <not knowing *whose* lead she should follow>. See also **absolute adjective**; **attributive**; **demonstrative adjective**; **predicate adjective**.

adverb A word that modifies a verb, adjective, adverb, preposition, phrase, clause, or sentence.

Traditionally adverbs indicate time, place, or manner <do it *now*> <*there* they remained> <she went *willingly*>. They can connect statements <a small bomb had been found; *nevertheless,* they were continuing their search> and can tell the reader what the writer thinks about what is being said in the sentence <*luckily* I got there on time>. They can modify verbs <ran *fast*>, adjectives <an *awfully* long speech>, participles <a *well*-acted play>, adverbs <doing *fairly* well>, particles <woke *right* up>, indefinite pronouns <*almost* everyone>, cardinal numbers <*over* 200 guests>, prepositional phrases <*just* out of reach>, and more. Sometimes they modify a preceding noun <the great city *beyond*>, and some adverbs of place and time can serve as the objects of prepositions <since *when*> <before *long*>.

The notion that adverbs should not separate auxiliaries from their main verbs <you can *easily* see the river from here> <they should be *heartily* congratulated> is a false one, apparently based on fear of the split infinitive. See also **auxiliary verb**; **sentence adverb**; **split infinitive**.

adverbial genitive A form, or case, of some nouns used as adverbs of time, normally formed by adding *-s* <he worked *nights*> <the store is open *Sundays*>.

agreement A grammatical relationship that involves the correspondence in number either between the subject and verb of a sentence or between a pronoun and its antecedent; also called *concord.*

Subject-verb agreement for compound subjects joined by and: When a subject is composed of two or more singular nouns joined by *and,* the plural verb is usually used <*the sentimentality and lack of originality* which *mark* his writing> <*the bitterness and heartache* that *fill* the world>. Occasionally when the nouns form a single conceptual unit, the singular verb can be used <*the report's depth and scope demonstrates*> <*her patience and calm was* remarkable>. See also **notional agreement**.

Compound subjects joined by or (or nor): When singular nouns are joined by *or,* the singular verb is usually used <*the average man or woman was* not interested>; when plural nouns are so joined, the plural verb is used <*wolves or coyotes have* depleted his stock>. When the negative *neither . . . nor* is used with singular nouns, it usually takes a singular verb <*neither she nor anyone else is* fond of the idea>; when used with plural nouns, it takes a plural verb <*neither the proponents nor their adversaries are* willing to accept>. But when *neither . . . nor* is used with nouns of differing number, the noun closest to the verb usually determines its number <*neither he nor his colleagues were* present> <*neither the teachers nor the principal was* interested>. Similar rules apply to *either . . . or.*

Compound subjects joined by words or phrases like with or along with, or by punctuation: When a singular noun is joined to another by a word or phrase like *with, rather than,* or *as well as,* a singular verb is generally used <*that story, along with nine others, was* published> <*the battleship together with the destroyer was* positioned three miles offshore>. Parenthetical insertions set off by commas, dashes, or parentheses should not affect agreement <*this book, as well as various others, has* achieved notoriety> <*their management—and the company's balance sheets—has* suffered>.

Subject formed by a collective noun phrase: In constructions like "a bunch of the boys were whooping it up" or "a fraction of the deposits are insured," which make use of a collective noun phrase (*a bunch of the boys, a fraction of the deposits*), the verb is usually plural, since the sense of the phrase is normally plural. See also **collective noun**.

Subject expressing money, time, etc.: When an amount of money, a period of time, or some other plural noun phrase of quantity or measure forms the subject, a singular verb is used <*ten dollars is* all I have left> <*two miles is* as far as they can walk> <*two thirds of the area is* under water>.

Subject formed by one in (out of) . . . : Phrases such as "one in five" or "two out of three" may take either a singular or a plural verb <*one in four union members was* undecided>

<*one out of ten soldiers were* unable to recognize the enemy>, though grammarians tend to favor the singular.

Pronoun-antecedent agreement for nouns joined by *and, or:* When antecedents are singular nouns joined by *and,* a plural pronoun is used <*the computer and the printer* were moved because *they* were in the way>. But singular nouns joined by *or* can use either a singular or a plural pronoun, whichever sounds best <either *Fred or Marianne* will give *their* presentation after lunch> <*each employee or supervisor* should give what *he or she* can afford>.

Agreement for indefinite pronouns: The indefinite pronouns *anybody, anyone, each, either, everybody, everyone, neither, nobody, none, no one, somebody,* and *someone,* though some of them are conceptually plural, are used with singular verbs <*everyone* in the company *was* pleased> <*nobody is* responsible>, but are commonly referred to by *they, their, them,* or *themselves* <*nobody* could get the crowd's attention when *they* spoke> <*everybody* there admits *they* saw it>. Writing handbooks prescribe *he, she,* or *he or she,* or some other construction instead of the plural pronouns, but use of the plural *they, their,* or *them* has long been established and is standard.

antecedent A word, phrase, or clause to which a subsequent pronoun refers <*Judy* wrote to say *she* is coming> <they saw *Bob*

and called to *him*> <I hear *that he is ill* and *it* worries me>.

appositive A word, phrase, or clause that is equivalent to an adjacent noun <a biography of *the poet Robert Burns*> <sales of *her famous novel, Gone with the Wind,* reached one million copies in six months > <*we grammarians* are never wrong>.

Restrictive and nonrestrictive appositives play different roles in a sentence and are traditionally distinguished by their punctuation. A nonrestrictive appositive <*his wife, Helen,* attended the ceremony> is generally set off with commas, while a restrictive appositive <he sent *his daughter Cicely* to college> uses no commas and indicates that one out of a group is being identified (in this case, one daughter from among two or more). Exceptions occur where no ambiguity would result <his wife Helen>. See also **nonrestrictive clause**; **restrictive clause**.

article One of three words *(a, an, the)* used with a noun to indicate definiteness <*the* blue car> or indefiniteness <*a* simple task> <*an* interesting explanation>.

attributive A modifier that immediately precedes the word it modifies <*black* tie, *U.S.* government, *kitchen* sink, *lobster* salad>.

Nouns have functioned like adjectives in this position for many centuries. In more recent years, some critics have objected to the proliferation of nouns used to modify other nouns: e.g., *language deterioration, health aspects, image enhancement.* While long or otherwise unexpected strings of this sort can occasionally be disorienting to the uninitiated (e.g., *management team strategy planning session*), the practice is flourishing and usually serves to compress information that the intended audience need not always have spelled out for it. Be sure, however, that the context and audience will allow for such compression.

A fairly recent trend toward using plural attributives has been attacked by some critics. There always had been a few plural attributives—*scissors grinder, physics laboratory, Civil Liberties Union, mathematics book*—but is it proper to use the more recent *weapons system, communications technology, operations program, systems analyst, earth-resources satellite, singles bar, enemies list?* The answer is that such plural attributives are standard. The plural form is chosen to stress plurality—more than one weapon, operation, enemy, etc.—or to otherwise distinguish its meaning from whatever the singular attributive might connote.

auxiliary verb A verb that accompanies another verb and typically expresses person, number, mood, or tense (such as *be, have, can, do*) <they *can* see the movie tomorrow> <she *has* left already>. See also **verb**.

cardinal number A number of the kind used in simple counting <*one, 1, thirty-five, 35*>; compare **ordinal number**.

case In English, a form of a noun or pronoun indicating its grammatical relation to other words in a sentence. See **nominative**; **objective**; **possessive**. See also **genitive**.

clause A group of words having its own subject and predicate but forming only part of a compound or complex sentence. A *main* or *independent clause* could stand alone as a sentence <*we will leave* as soon as the taxi arrives>; a *subordinate* or *dependent clause* requires a main clause <we will leave *as soon as the taxi arrives*>.

There are three basic types of clauses—all subordinate clauses—that have part-of-speech functions. An *adjective clause* modifies a noun or pronoun <the clown, *who was also a horse trainer*> <I can't see the reason *why you're upset*>. An *adverb clause* modifies a verb, adjective, or another adverb <*when it rains,* it pours> <I'm certain *that he is guilty*> <we accomplished less *than we did before*>. A *noun clause* fills a noun slot in a sentence and thus can be a subject, object, or complement <*whoever is qualified* should apply> <I don't know *what his problem is*> <the trouble is *that she has no alternative*>. See also **sentence**; **subordinate clause**.

collective noun A singular noun that stands for a number of persons or things considered as a group (such as *team, government, horde*).

Subject-verb agreement: Collective nouns have been used with both singular and plural verbs since Middle English. The principle involved is one of notional agreement. When the group is considered as a unit, the singular verb is used <the *government is* prepared for a showdown> <his *family is* from New England> <the *team has won* all of its home games>. When the group is thought of as a collection of individuals, the plural verb is sometimes used <her *family are* all staunch conservatives>. Singular verbs are more common in American English and plural verbs more common in British English, though usage remains divided in each case. See also **agreement**; **notional agreement**.

A collective noun followed by *of* and a plural noun follows the same rule as collective nouns in general. When the notion is that of plurality, the plural verb is normally used <an *assemblage of rocks were* laid out on the table> <a *group of jazz improvisers were* heard through the window>. When the idea of oneness or wholeness is stressed, the verb is generally singular <this *cluster of stars is* the largest yet identified>.

Pronoun agreement: The usual rule is that writers should take care to match their pronouns and verbs, singular with singular <the

committee *is* hopeful that *it* will succeed>, plural with plural <the faculty *are* willing to drop *their* suit>. But in fact writers sometimes use a plural pronoun after a singular verb <the audience *was* on *their* way out>. (The reverse combination—plural verb with singular pronoun—is very rare.)

Organizations as collective nouns: The names of companies and other organizations are treated as either singular <*Harvard* may consider *itself* very fortunate> or, less commonly, plural <the *D.A.R. are* going to do another pageant>. Organizations also sometimes appear with a singular verb but a plural pronoun in reference <*M-G-M hopes* to sell *their* latest releases> <*Chrysler builds their* convertible in Kentucky>. This usage is standard, though informal.

colloquial An adjective describing usage that is characteristic of familiar and informal conversation.

While not intended to carry pejorative overtones, the label *colloquial* often implies that the usage is nonstandard. See also **dialect**; **nonstandard**; **standard English**.

comma fault (comma splice, comma error) The use of a comma instead of a semicolon to link two independent clauses (as in "I won't talk about myself, it's not a healthy topic"). Modern style calls for the semicolon, but comma splices are fairly common in casual and unedited prose.

comparison Modification of an adjective or adverb to show different levels of quality, quantity, or relation. The *comparative* form shows relation between two items, usually by adding *-er* or *more* or *less* to the adjective or adverb <he's short*er* than I am> <her second book sold *more* quickly>. The *superlative* form expresses an extreme among two or more items, usually by adding *-est* or *most* or *least* to the adjective or adverb <the cheetah is the fast*est* mammal> <that's the *least* compelling reason> <the *most* vexingly intractable issue>. See also **absolute adjective**; **absolute comparative**; **double comparison**; **implicit comparative**.

complement An added word or expression by which a predicate is made complete <they elected him *president*> <she thought it *beautiful*> <the critics called her *the best act of her kind since Carmen Miranda*>.

compound A combination of words or word elements that work together in various ways (*farmhouse; cost-effective; ex-husband; shoeless; figure out; in view of* that; *real estate* agent; *greenish white* powder; *carefully tended* garden; *great white shark*).

Compounds are written in one of three ways: solid <*workplace*>, hyphenated

<*screenwriter-director*>, or open <*health care*>. Because of the variety of standard practice, the choice among these styles for a given compound represents one of the most common and bothersome of all style issues. A current desk dictionary will list many compounds, but those whose meanings are self-explanatory from the meanings of their component words will usually not appear. Most writers try to pattern any temporary compounds after similar permanent compounds such as are entered in dictionaries.

compound subject Two or more nouns or pronouns usually joined by *and* that function as the subject of a clause or sentence <*doctors and lawyers* reported the highest incomes for that period> <*Peter, Karen, and I* left together>. See also **agreement**; **collective noun**.

concord See **agreement**.

conjunction A word or phrase that joins together words, phrases, clauses, or sentences.

Coordinating conjunctions (such as *and, because, but, or, nor, since, so*) join elements of equal weight, to show similarity <they came early *and* stayed late>, to exclude or contrast <he is a brilliant *but* arrogant man>, to offer alternatives <she can wait here *or* return later>, to propose reasons or grounds <the timetable is useless, *because* it is out-of-date>, or to specify a result <his diction is excellent, *so* every word is clear>.

Correlative conjunctions (such as *either . . . or, neither . . . nor*) are used in pairs and link alternatives or equal elements <*either* you go *or* you stay> <the proposal benefits *neither* residents *nor* visitors> <she showed *not only* perceptive understanding *but also* mature judgment>.

Subordinating conjunctions (such as *unless, whether*) join subordinate clauses to main clauses and are used to express cause <*because* she learns quickly, she is an eager student>, condition <don't call *unless* you're coming>, manner <it looks *as though* it's clearing>, purpose <he gets up early *so that* he can exercise before work>, time <she kept a diary *when* she was a teenager>, place <I don't know *where* he went>, or possibility <they were undecided *whether* to go or stay>.

conjunctive adverb A transitional adverb (such as *also, however, therefore*) that expresses the relationship between two independent clauses, sentences, or paragraphs.

Conjunctive adverbs are used to express addition <he enjoyed the movie; *however,* he had to leave before the end>, emphasis <he is brilliant; *indeed,* he is a genius>, contrast <that was unfortunate; *nevertheless,* they should have known the danger>, elaboration <on one point only did everyone agree: *namely,* too much money had been spent already>, conclusion <the case could take

years to work its way through the courts; *as a result,* many plaintiffs will accept settlements>, or priority <*first* cream the shortening and sugar, *then* add the eggs and beat well>.

contact clause A dependent clause attached to its antecedent without a relative pronoun such as *that, which,* or *who* <the key [that] *you lost*> <he is not the person [who] *we thought he was*>.

The predicate noun clause not introduced by the conjunction *that* <we believe [that] *the alliance is strong*> is as long and as well established in English as the contact clause. It is probably more common in casual and general prose than in formal prose. It is also more common after some verbs (such as *believe, hope, say, think*) than others (such as *assert, calculate, hold, intend*).

contraction A shortened form of a word or words in which an apostrophe usually replaces the omitted letter or letters (such as *dep't, don't, could've, o'clock, we'll*).

Contractions involving verbs used to be avoided more than they are today. In fact, many contemporary writing handbooks recommend using contractions to help you avoid sounding stilted.

count noun A noun that identifies things that can be counted <two *tickets*> <a *motive*> <many *people*>; compare **mass noun**.

dangling modifier A modifying phrase that lacks a normally expected grammatical relation to the rest of the sentence (as in "*Caught in the act,* his excuses were unconvincing").

The common construction called the *participial phrase* usually begins with a participle; in "*Chancing to meet them there,* I invited them to sit with us," the subject, "I," is left implicit in the preceding phrase, which modifies it. But a writer may inadvertently let a participial phrase modify a subject or some other noun in the sentence it was not intended to modify; the result is what grammarians call a *dangling participle.* Thus in "*Hoping to find him alone,* the presence of a stranger was irksome," it is the "presence" itself that may seem to be hoping.

Dangling participles can be found in the writing of many famous writers, and they are usually hardly noticeable except to someone looking for them. The important thing to avoid is creating an unintended humorous effect (as in "*Opening up the cupboard,* a cockroach ran for the corner").

dangling participle See **dangling modifier**.

demonstrative adjective One of four adjectives—*this, that, these,* and *those*—that points to what it modifies in order to distinguish it from others. The number (singular or plural) of the adjective should agree with the noun it modifies <*this* type of person> <*that* shelf of books> <*these* sorts of jobs> <*those* varieties of apples>.

demonstrative pronoun One of the words *this, that, these,* and *those* classified as pronouns when they function as nouns <*this* is my desk; *that* is yours> <*these* are the best popovers in town> <*those* are strong words>.

dialect A variety of language distinguished by features of vocabulary, grammar, and pronunciation that is confined to a region or group. See also **nonstandard**; **standard English**.

direct object A word, phrase, or clause denoting the goal or result of the action of the verb <he closed the *valve*> <they'll do *whatever it takes*> <"*Do it now,*" he said>; compare **indirect object**.

direct question A question quoted exactly as spoken, written, or imagined <the only question is, *Will it work?*>; compare **indirect question**.

direct quotation Text quoted exactly as spoken or written <I heard her say, "*I'll be there at two o'clock*">; compare **indirect quotation**.

divided usage Widespread use of two or more forms for a single entity (such as *dived* and *dove* for the past tense of *dive*).

double comparison Use of the forms *more, most, less,* or *least* with an adjective already inflected for the comparative or superlative degree (such as *more wider, most widest*).

This construction results from using *more* and *most* as intensifiers <a *most* enjoyable meal>. In modern usage, double comparison has all but vanished from standard writing. See also **comparison**; **intensifier**.

Double comparison can also occur by inflection. Though forms such as *firstest, mostest,* and *bestest* are most typical of the speech of young children, the form *worser* (which has a long literary background) still persists in adult speech. You will want to avoid it in writing.

double genitive A construction in which possession is marked both by the preposition *of* and a noun or pronoun in the possessive case.

In expressions like "that song of Ella Fitzgerald's" or "a good friend of ours," the possessive relationship is indicated by both *of* and the genitive inflection (*Fitzgerald's, ours*), even though only one or the other would seem to be strictly necessary. However, this construction, also known as the *double possessive,* is an idiomatic one of long standing and is standard in all kinds of writing. See also **genitive**.

double modal The use of two modal auxiliaries in succession, resulting in such expressions as *might can, might could,* and *might should.*

Today double modals tend to be found in Southern dialect and are unfamiliar to speakers from other parts of the country.

double negative A clause or sentence containing two negatives and having a negative meaning.

In modern usage, the double negative (as in "they did*n't* have *no* children" or "it would*n't* do *no* good") is widely perceived as a rustic or uneducated form, and is generally avoided in both writing and speech, other than the most informal.

A standard form of double negative is the rhetorical device known as *litotes,* which produces a weak affirmative meaning <a *not un*reasonable request>. It is used for understatement, but should not be overused.

double passive A construction that uses two verb forms in the passive voice, one being an infinitive (as in "the work of redesigning the office space *was requested to be done* by outside contractors").

The double passive is awkward and potentially ambiguous (did outside contractors ask for the work to be done, or were they asked to do the work?) and should be avoided.

double possessive See **double genitive.**

double superlative See **double comparison.**

false titles Appositive preceding a person's name with no preceding article or following comma, which thus resembles a title, though it is rarely capitalized <organized by *consumer advocate* Ralph Nader> <works of *1960s underground cartoonist* Robert Crumb>. The use of such titles is sometimes criticized, but it is standard in journalism.

faulty parallelism See **parallelism**.

flat adverb An adverb that has the same form as its related adjective, such as *sure* <you *sure* fooled me>, *bright* <the moon is shining *bright*>, and *flat* <she turned me down *flat*>.

Although such forms were once common, later grammarians saw them as faulty because they lacked the *-ly* ending. Today flat adverbs are few in number and some are widely regarded as incorrect.

formal agreement See **notional agreement**.

gender In English, a characteristic of certain nouns and pronouns that indicates sex (masculine, feminine, neuter) <*he, him, his, she, her, it, its; actor, actress; brother, sister; emperor, empress; heir, heiress; fiancé, fiancée; testator, testatrix*>.

genitive A form, or case, of a noun or pronoun that typically shows possession or source <the girl*'s* sweater> <nobody*'s* fool>

<an uncle *of mine*> <some idea *of theirs*> <the company*'s* failure> <a year*'s* salary> <the nation*'s* capital> <a stone*'s* throw>.

The form is usually produced by adding *-'s* or a phrase beginning with *of.* While the possessive is the genitive's most common function, it has certain other functions as well; these include the *subjective* <Frost*'s* poetry>, *objective* <her son*'s* graduation>, *descriptive* <women*'s* colleges>, and *appositive* <the state *of Massachusetts*> <the office *of president*> genitives. See also **double genitive; possessive**.

gerund A verb form having the characteristics of both verb and noun and ending in *-ing* (also called a *verbal noun*) <the ice made *skiing* impossible>.

A gerund can be preceded by a possessive noun or pronoun <her husband's *snoring*> <their *filling* the position>. See also **possessive; possessive with gerund**.

hypercorrection The use of a nonstandard linguistic form or construction on the basis of a false analogy to a standard form or construction (as in "*whom* should I say is calling?"; "this is between you and *I*"; "no one but *he* would notice"; "open *widely*").

idiom A common expression that is peculiar to itself grammatically <*it wasn't me*> or that cannot be understood from the meanings of its separate words <I told them to *step on it*> <the newspaper *had a field day*>.

imperative The form, or mood, of a verb that expresses a command or makes a request <*come* here> <please *don't*>; compare **indicative**; **subjunctive**.

implicit comparative One of a small group of adjectives (primarily *major, minor, inferior, superior*) whose meaning resembles a true comparative but which cannot be used with comparative forms (such as *more, most; less, least*) <a *major* contributor> <an *inferior* wine>.

However, two other implicit comparatives *junior* and *senior* can be used with comparative forms <a *more senior* diplomat> <the *least junior* of the new partners>. See also **comparison**.

indefinite pronoun A pronoun that designates an unidentified person or thing <*somebody* ate my dessert> <she saw *no one* she knew>.

Many indefinite pronouns should agree in number with their verbs. See **agreement**. See also **notional agreement**; **pronoun**.

indicative The form, or mood, of a verb that states a fact or asks a question <the train *stopped*> <they*'ll be* along> <everyone *is* ravenous> <*has* the rain *begun*?> <who *knows*?>; compare **imperative**; **subjunctive**.

indirect object A grammatical object representing the secondary goal of the action of its verb <she gave *the dog* a bone>; compare **direct object**.

indirect question A statement of the substance of a question without using the speaker's exact words or word order <the officer asked *what the trouble was*> <they wondered *whether it would work*>; compare **direct question**.

indirect quotation A statement of the substance of a quotation without using the speaker's exact words <I heard her say *she'd be there at two o'clock*>; compare **direct quotation**.

infinitive A verb form having the characteristics of both verb and noun and usually used with *to* <we had *to stop*> <*to err* is human> <no one saw him *leave*>. See also **split infinitive**.

infinitive phrase A phrase that includes an infinitive and its modifiers and complements <we expect them *to arrive by five o'clock*> <he shouted *to be heard above the din*> <*to have earned a Ph.D. in four years* was impressive>.

inflection The change in form that words undergo to mark case, gender, number, tense, person, mood, voice, or comparison

<*he, his, him*> <*waiter, waitress*> <rat, *rats*> <blame, *blames, blamed, blaming*> <who, *whom*> <she *is* careful, if she *were* careful, *be* careful> <like, *likes, is liked*> <wild, *wilder, wildest*>. See also **case**; **comparison**; **gender**; **mood**; **number**; **person**; **tense**; **voice**.

initialism See **acronym**.

intensifier A linguistic element used to give emphasis or additional strength to another word or statement <a *very* hot day> <it's a *complete* lie> <what *on earth* is he doing?> <she *herself* did it>. See also **double comparison.**

interjection An exclamatory or interrupting word or phrase <*ouch!*> <*oh no,* not that again>.

interrogative pronoun One of the pronouns *what, which, who, whom,* and *whose,* as well as combinations of these words with the suffix *-ever,* used to introduce direct and indirect questions <*who* is she?> <he asked me *who* she was> <*which* did they choose?> <I wondered *which* they chose>.

Who is frequently substituted for *whom* to introduce a question even when it is the object of a preposition <*who* are you going to listen to?> <*who* do you work for?>.

intransitive verb A verb not having a direct object <he *ran* away> <our cat *purrs* when I stroke her>; compare **transitive verb**.

linking verb A verb that links a subject with its predicate (such as *is, feel, look, become, seem*) <she *is* the new manager> <the future *looked* prosperous> <he *has become* disenchanted>.

Linking verbs such as the so-called "sense" verbs *feel, look, taste,* and *smell* often cause confusion, since writers sometimes mistakenly follow these words with adverbs <this scent *smells nicely*> instead of adjectives <this scent *smells nice*>.

main clause See **clause**.

mass noun A noun that denotes a thing or concept without subdivisions <some *money*> <great *courage*> <the study of *politics*>; compare **count noun**.

modifier A word or phrase that qualifies, limits, or restricts the meaning of another word or phrase. See **adjective**; **adverb**.

mood The form of a verb that shows whether the action or state it denotes is conceived as a fact or otherwise (e.g., a command, possibility, or wish). See **indicative**; **imperative**; **subjunctive**.

nominal A word or group of words that functions as a noun, which may be an adjective <the *good* die young>, a gerund <*seeing* is *believing*>, or an infinitive <*to see* is *to believe*>.

nominative A form, or case, of a noun or pronoun indicating its use as the subject of a verb <three *dogs* trotted by the open door> <later *we* ate dinner>; compare **objective**; **possessive**.

nonrestrictive clause A subordinate or dependent clause, set off by commas, that is not essential to the definiteness of the word it modifies and could be omitted without changing the meaning of the main clause (also called *nonessential clause*) <the author, *who turned out to be charming*, autographed my book>; compare **restrictive clause**. See also **appositive**.

nonstandard Not conforming to the usage generally characteristic of educated native speakers of a language; compare **standard English**. See also **dialect**.

notional agreement Agreement between a subject and a verb or between a pronoun and its antecedent that is determined by meaning rather than form; also called *notional concord*.

Notional agreement contrasts with *formal* or *grammatical agreement* (or *concord*), in which overt grammatical markers determine singular or plural agreement. Formally plural nouns such as *news, means,* and *politics* have long taken singular verbs; so when a plural noun considered a single entity takes a singular verb, notional agreement is at work and no one objects <the *United States is sending* its ambassador>. When a singular noun is used as a collective noun and takes a plural verb or a plural pronoun, we also have notional agreement <the *committee are* meeting on Tuesday> <the *group* wants to publicize *their* views>. Indefinite pronouns are heavily influenced by notional agreement and tend to take singular verbs but plural pronouns <*everyone is* required to show *their* identification>. See also **agreement**; **collective noun**.

notional concord See **notional agreement**.

noun A member of a class of words that can serve as the subject of a verb, can be singular or plural, can be replaced by a pronoun, and can refer to an entity, quality, state, action, or concept <*boy, Churchill, America, river, commotion, poetry, anguish, constitutionalism*>.

Nouns are used as subjects <the *artist* painted still lifes>, direct objects <critics praised the *artist*>, objects of prepositions <a painting signed by the *artist*>, indirect objects <the council gave the *artist* an award>, retained objects <an artist was given the *award*>, predicate nouns <Petra Smith is this year's *award winner*>, objective complements <they announced Petra Smith as this year's *award winner*>, and appositives <Petra Smith, this year's *award winner*>. See also **collective noun**; **count noun**; **mass noun**; **nominal**; **proper noun**.

noun phrase A phrase formed by a noun and its modifiers <*portly pensioners* sat sunning themselves> <they proclaimed *all the best features of the new financial offering*>.

number A characteristic of a noun, pronoun, or verb that signifies whether it is singular or plural. See **singular**; **plural**.

object A noun, noun phrase or clause, or pronoun that directly or indirectly receives the action of a verb or follows a preposition <she rocked *the baby*> <he saw *where they were going*> <I gave *him the news*> <over *the rainbow*> <after *a series of depressing roadhouse gigs*>. See **direct object**; **indirect object**.

objective A form, or case, of a pronoun indicating its use as the object of a verb or preposition <we spoke to *them* yesterday> <he's a man *whom* everyone should know>; compare **nominative**; **possessive**.

ordinal number A number designating the place occupied by an item in an ordered sequence <*first, 1st, second, 2nd*>; compare **cardinal number**.

parallelism Repeated syntactical similarities introduced in sentence construction, such as adjacent phrases and clauses that are equivalent, similar, or opposed in meaning and of identical construction <ecological

problems of concern *to scientists, to businesspeople,* and *to all citizens*> <he was respected not only *for his intelligence* but also *for his integrity*> <*to err is human, to forgive, divine*>.

Parallelism is mainly used for rhetorical and clarifying effects, and its absence can sometimes create problems for the reader. *Faulty parallelism* is the name given to the use of different constructions within a sentence where you would ordinarily expect to find the same or similar constructions. Very often such faulty parallelism involves the conjunctions *and* and *or* or such other coordinators as *either* and *neither.* Consider the sentence "To allow kids to roam the streets at night and failing to give them constructive alternatives have been harmful." An infinitive phrase (*To allow kids to roam . . .*) and a participial phrase (*failing to give them . . .*) are treated as parallel when they are not. The meaning would be taken in more readily if both phrases were similar; replacing the infinitive with a participle achieves this parallelism (*Allowing kids to roam . . .* and *failing to give them . . .*). When such errors are obvious, they can be puzzling. Often, however, the problem is subtle and hardly noticeable, as in the sentence "Either I must send a fax or make a phone call." Here *or* is expected to precede the same parallel term as *either;* by repositioning *either,* you solve the problem <I must *either*

send a fax *or* make a phone call>. Such examples of faulty parallelism are fairly common, but your writing will be more elegant if you avoid them.

parenthetical element An explanatory or modifying word, phrase, or sentence inserted in a passage, set off by parentheses, commas, or dashes <a ruling by the FCC (*Federal Communications Commission*)> <all of us, *to tell the truth*, were amazed> <the examiner chose—*goodness knows why*—to ignore it>.

participial phrase A participle with its complements and modifiers, functioning as an adjective <*hearing the bell ring*, he went to the door>.

participle A verb form having the characteristics of both verb <the noise has *stopped*> and adjective <a *broken* lawn mower>. The *present participle* ends in *-ing* <*fascinating*>; the *past participle* usually ends in *-ed* <*seasoned*>; the *perfect participle* combines *having* with the past participle <*having escaped*>. See also **auxiliary verb**; **dangling modifier**; **possessive**.

particle A short word (such as *by*, *to*, *in*, *up*) that expresses some general aspect of meaning or some connective or limiting relation <pay *up*> <heave *to*>.

parts of speech The classes into which words are grouped according to their function in a sentence. See **adjective**; **adverb**; **conjunction**; **interjection**; **noun**; **preposition**; **pronoun**; **verb**.

passive voice A verb form indicating that the subject of a sentence is being acted upon.

Though often considered a weaker form of expression than the active voice, the passive nevertheless has important uses—for example, when the receiver of the action is more important than the doer <*he is respected* by other scholars>, when the doer is unknown <*the lock had been picked* expertly> or is understood <*Jones was elected* on the third ballot>, or when discretion or tact require that the doer remain anonymous <mistakes *were made*>; compare **active voice**.

person A characteristic of a verb or pronoun that indicates whether a person is speaking (*first person*) <*I am, we are*>, is spoken to (*second person*) <*you are*>, or is spoken about (*third person*) <*he, she, it is; they are*>. See also **number**.

personal pronoun A pronoun that refers to beings and objects and reflects person, number, and often gender.

A personal pronoun's function within a sentence determines its case. The *nominative* case (*I, we, you, he, she, it, they*) is used for pronouns that act as subjects of sentences or as predicate nouns <*he* and *I* will attend> <our new candidate will be *you*>.

The *possessive* case (*my, mine, our, ours, your, yours, his, her, hers, its, their, theirs*) is used for pronouns that express possession or a similar relationship <*our* own offices> <*its* beak>.

The *objective* case (*me, us, you, him, her, it, them*) is used for pronouns that are direct objects, indirect objects, retained objects, or objects of prepositions <he told *me* about the new contract> <she gave *him* the manuscripts> <he was given *them* yesterday> <this is between *you* and *her*>. See also **indefinite pronoun**; **pronoun**.

phrase A group of two or more words that does not contain both a subject and a verb and that functions as a noun, adjective, adverb, preposition, conjunction, or verb <*the old sinner*> <*stretching for miles*> <*without a limp*> <*in lieu of*> <*as far as*> <*break off*>.

There are seven basic types of phrases. An *absolute phrase* consists of a noun followed by a modifier (such as a participial phrase) and acts independently within a sentence without modifying a particular element of the sentence <he stalked out, *his eyes staring straight ahead*>.

A *gerund phrase* includes a gerund and its modifiers, and it functions as a noun <*eating two doughnuts* is Mike's idea of breakfast>.

An *infinitive phrase* includes an infinitive and may function as a noun, adjective, or adverb <*to do that* would be stupid> <this was

an occasion *to remember*> <they struggled *to get free*>.

A *participial phrase* includes a participle and functions as an adjective <*hearing the bell ring,* he went to the door>.

A *verb phrase* consists of a verb and any other terms that either modify it or complete its meaning <he *comes once a month*> <she *will have arrived too late*>. See also **noun phrase**; **participial phrase**.

plural A word form used to denote more than one <the *Browns*> <the *children*> <these *kinds*> <seven *deer*> <they *are* rich> <*we* do care>.

possessive A form, or case, of a noun or pronoun typically indicating ownership <the *president's* message> <*their* opinions> <*its* meter>; compare **nominative**; **objective**. See also **double genitive**; **genitive**; **possessive with gerund**.

possessive with gerund Use of a possessive form before a gerund.

In "the reason for everyone['s] wanting to join," either the possessive or the common form of *everyone* can be used. Writing handbooks recommend always using the possessive form, but the possessive is mandatory only when the *-ing* word is clearly a noun <*my being* here must embarrass you>. The possessive is quite common with proper nouns <the problem of *John's forgetting* the

keys> but rare with plurals <learned of the *bills* [*bills'*] *being* paid>. In most other instances, either the **possessive** or common form can be used.

predicate The part of a sentence or clause that expresses what is said of the subject <Hargrove *threw a spitball*> <the teachers from the surrounding towns *are invited to the dinner*> <Jennifer *picked up her books and left to catch the bus*>.

predicate adjective An adjective that follows a linking verb (such as *be, become, feel, taste, smell, seem*) and modifies the subject <she is *happy* with the outcome> <the milk tastes *sour*> <he seemed *puzzled* by the answer>.

prefix An affix attached to the beginning of a word to change its meaning <*a*historical> <*pre*sorted> <*anti*-imperialist> <*post*hypnotic> <*over*extended>; compare **suffix**.

preposition A word or phrase that combines with a noun, pronoun, adverb, or prepositional phrase for use as a modifier or a predication <a book *on* the table> <you're *in* big trouble> <*outside* himself> <*because of* that> <came *from* behind> <peeking *from* behind the fence>.

Despite a widespread belief that a sentence cannot end with a preposition, there is no such grammatical rule. In fact, many sentences require the preposition at the end <what can she be thinking *of*?> <he got the

answer he was looking *for*> <there are inconveniences that we must put up *with*> <they haven't been heard *from* yet> and many others are perfectly idiomatic in placing it there <you must know which shelf everything is *on*>.

prepositional phrase A group of words consisting of a preposition and its complement <*out of debt* is where we'd like to be!> <here is the desk *with the extra file drawer*> <he drove on *in a cold fury*>.

pronoun Any of a small set of words that are used as substitutes for nouns, phrases, or clauses and refer to someone or something named or understood in the context.

Pronouns can be divided into seven major categories, each with its own function. See **demonstrative pronoun**; **indefinite pronoun**; **interrogative pronoun**; **personal pronoun**; **reciprocal pronoun**; **reflexive pronoun**; **relative pronoun**. See also **agreement**.

proper adjective An adjective that is derived from a proper noun and is usually capitalized <*Roman* sculpture> <*Jeffersonian* democracy> <*Middle Eastern* situation> <*french* fries>.

proper noun A noun that names a particular being or thing and is usually capitalized <*Susan, Haydn, New York, December, General Motors, Mormon, Library of Congress, Middle Ages, Spanish Civil War, Reaganomics*>.

reciprocal pronoun One of the pronouns *each other* and *one another* used in the object position to indicate a mutual action or cross-relationship <chased *each other* around the yard> <fighting with *one another*>.

Reciprocal pronouns may also be used in the possessive <they depend on *each other's* ideas> <borrowed *one another's* sweaters>.

redundancy Repetition of information in a message.

Redundancy is an implicit part of the English language; it reinforces the message. In "Two birds were sitting on a branch," the idea of plurality is expressed three times: by the modifier *two,* by the *-s* on *bird,* and by the plural verb *were.* Many words can be accompanied by small words that give them extra emphasis <*final result*> <*past history*> <*climb up*> <*refer back*>. These are often attacked as needlessly wordy, but in most instances they are harmless, and sometimes they actually promote communication. The use and employment of many more words, phrases, and expressions than are strictly needed, necessary, wanted, or required should be avoided.

reflexive pronoun A pronoun that refers to the subject of the sentence, clause, or verbal phrase in which it stands, and is formed by compounding the personal pronouns *him, her, it, my, our, them,* and *your* with *-self* or

-selves <she dressed *herself*> <the cook told us to help *ourselves* to seconds> <I *myself* am not concerned>.

relative pronoun One of the pronouns (*that, which, who, whom,* and *whose*) that introduces a subordinate clause which qualifies an antecedent <a man *whom* we can trust> <her book, *which* sold well> <the light *that* failed>.

The relative pronoun *who* typically refers to persons and some animals <a man *who* sought success> <a person *whom* we can trust> <Seattle Slew, *who* won horse racing's Triple Crown>; *which* refers to things and animals <a book *which* sold well> <a dog *which* barked loudly>; and *that* refers to persons, animals, and things <a man *that* sought success> <a dog *that* barked loudly> <a book *that* sold well>.

Whom is commonly used as the object of a preposition in a clause that it introduces <she is someone *for whom* I would gladly work>. However, *who* is commonly used to introduce a question even when it is the object of a preposition <*who* are you going to listen to?> <*who* do you work for?>.

restrictive clause A subordinate clause not set off by commas that is essential to the definiteness of the word it modifies and cannot be omitted without changing the meaning of the main clause (also called *essential* *clause*) <textbooks *that are not current* should be returned>. See also **appositive**; **nonrestrictive clause**.

sentence A group of words usually containing a subject and a verb, and in writing ending with a period, question mark, or exclamation point. A *simple sentence* consists of one main or independent clause <*she read the announcement in yesterday's paper*>. A *compound sentence* consists of two or more main clauses <*he left at nine o'clock, and they planned to meet at noon*>. A *complex sentence* consists of a main clause and one or more subordinate clauses <*it began to snow before they reached the summit*>. A *compound-complex sentence* consists of two or more main clauses and one or more subordinate clauses <*Susan left for Masters Hall after the presentation; there she joined the new-product workshop, which was already in progress*>. See also **clause**; **subordinate clause**.

A *declarative sentence* makes a statement <*the cow jumped over the moon*>. An *exclamatory sentence* expresses strong feeling <*that's ridiculous!*>. An *interrogative sentence* asks a question <*who said that?*>. An *imperative sentence* expresses a command or request <*get in here now*>.

A *cumulative sentence* is structured so that its main point appears first and is followed by other phrases or clauses expanding on or supporting it. A *periodic sentence* is structured so that its main idea or thrust is suspended until the end, thereby drawing the reader's attention to an emphatic conclusion. A *topic sentence* is a key sentence to which the other sentences in a paragraph are related; it may be placed either at the beginning (as a *lead-in* topic sentence) or the end of a paragraph (as a *terminal* topic sentence).

sentence adverb An adverb that modifies an entire sentence, rather than a specific word or phrase within the sentence <*fortunately* they had already placed their order>.

sentence fragment A group of words punctuated like a sentence, but without a subject or a predicate or both <*So many men, so many opinions.*> <*Yeah, when you think about it.*>. See also **sentence**; **clause**.

singular A word form denoting one person, thing, or instance <*man*> <*tattoo*> <*eventuality*> <*she* left> <it *is* here>.

split infinitive An infinitive preceded by *to* and an adverb or adverbial phrase <*to ultimately avoid* trouble>.

Grammarians used to disapprove of the split infinitive, but most now admit that it is not a defect. It is useful when a writer wants to emphasize the adverb <were determined *to thoroughly enjoy* themselves>. See also **infinitive**.

standard English English that is substantially uniform, well-established in the speech and writing of educated people, and widely recognized as acceptable; compare **nonstandard**. See also **dialect**.

subject A word or group of words denoting the entity about which something is said <*he* stopped> <*it*'s clouding up> <*all sixty members* voted> <*orthodoxy on every doctrinal issue* now reigned> <*what they want* is more opportunity> <*going to work* was what she hated most> <*to sing at the Met* had long been a dream of his>.

subject-verb agreement See **agreement**.

subjunctive The form, or mood, of a verb that expresses a condition contrary to fact or follows clauses of necessity, demand, or wishing <if he *were* here, he could answer that> <it's imperative that it *be* broadcast> <they asked that the meeting *proceed*> <I wish they *would come* soon>; compare **imperative**; **indicative**.

subordinate clause A clause that functions as a noun, adjective, or adverb and is attached to a main clause <theirs is a cause *that will prevail*>. See also **clause**; **sentence**.

suffix An affix attached to the end of a word to modify its meaning <editor*s*> <county*wide*> <Hollywood-*ish*> <umbrella-*like*>; compare **prefix**.

superlative See **comparison**.

tense The characteristic of a verb that expresses time present <*see*>, past <*saw*>, or future <*will see*>.

Aspect involves the use of auxiliary verbs to indicate time relations other than the simple present, past, or future tenses. The *progressive* tenses express action either in progress <*is seeing*>, in the past <*was seeing*>, or in the future <*will be seeing*>. The *perfect* tenses may express action that began in the past and continues in the present <*has seen*>, that was completed before another past action <*had seen*>, or that will be completed before some future action <*will have seen*>.

transitive verb A verb that acts upon a direct object <she *contributed* money> <he *runs* the store> <*express* your opinion>; compare **intransitive verb**.

verb A word or phrase that is the grammatical center of the predicate and is used to express action, occurrence, or state of being <*leap, carry out, feel, be*>. See also **auxiliary verb**; **linking verb**; **mood**; **voice**.

verbal One of a group of words derived from verbs. See **gerund**; **infinitive**; **participle**.

voice The property of a verb that indicates whether the subject acts or is acted upon. See **active voice**; **passive voice**.

Index